WOMEN'S HEALTH

Principles and
Clinical Practice

 Iris Cantor–UCLA
Women's Health
Center
_____
Education
and
Resource Center

WOMEN'S HEALTH

Principles and Clinical Practice

JANET P. PREGLER, MD

ALAN H. DeCHERNEY, MD

2002

B.C. Decker Inc

Hamilton • London

BC Decker Inc
20 Hughson Street South
P.O. Box 620, LCD 1
Hamilton, Ontario L8N 3K7
Tel: 905-522-7017; 1-800-568-7281
Fax: 905-522-7839; 1-888-311-4987
E-mail: info@bcdecker.com
Website: www.bcdecker.com

02 03 04 05 / UTP / 9 8 7 6 5 4 3 2 1

ISBN 1-55009-170-0
Printed in Canada

Sales and Distribution

United States
BC Decker Inc.
P.O. Box 785
Lewiston, NY 14092-0785
Tel: 905-522-7017; 800-568-7281
Fax: 905-522-7839
E-mail: info@bcdecker.com
Web site: www.bcdecker.com

Canada
BC Decker Inc.
20 Hughson Street South
P.O. Box 620, LCD 1
Hamilton, ON L8N 3K7
Tel: 905-522-7017; 800-568-7281
Fax: 905-522-7839
E-mail: info@bcdecker.com
Web site: www.bcdecker.com

Foreign Rights
John Scott & Company
International Publishers' Agency
P.O. Box 878
Kimberton, PA 19442
Tel: 610-827-1640
Fax: 610-827-1671
E-mail: jsco@voicenet.com

Japan
Igaku-Shoin Ltd.
Foreign Publications Department
3-24-17 Hongo
Bunkyo-ku, Tokyo, Japan 113-8719
Tel: 3 3817 5680
Fax: 3 3815 6776
E-mail: fd@igaku-shoin.co.jp

UK, Europe, Scandinavia, Middle East
Elsevier Science
Customer Service Department
Foots Cray High Street
Sidcup, Kent
DA14 5HP, UK
Tel: 44 (0) 208 308 5760
Fax: 44 (0) 181 308 5702
E-mail: cservice@harcourt.com

Singapore, Malaysia, Thailand, Philippines, Indonesia, Vietnam, Pacific Rim, Korea
Elsevier Science Asia
583 Orchard Road
#09/01, Forum
Singapore 238884
Tel: 65-737-3593
Fax: 65-753-2145

Australia, New Zealand
Elsevier Science Australia
Customer Service Department
STM Division
Locked Bag 16
St. Peters, New South Wales, 2044
Australia
Tel: 61 02 9517-8999
Fax: 61 02 9517-2249
E-mail: stmp@harcourt.com.au
Web site: www.harcourt.com.au

Notice: The authors and publisher have made every effort to ensure that the patient care recommended herein, including choice of drugs and drug dosages, is in accord with the accepted standard and practice at the time of publication. However, since research and regulation constantly change clinical standards, the reader is urged to check the product information sheet included in the package of each drug, which includes recommended doses, warnings, and contraindications. This is particularly important with new or infrequently used drugs. Any treatment regimen, particularly one involving medication, involves inherent risk that must be weighed on a case-by-case basis against the benefits anticipated. The reader is cautioned that the purpose of this book is to inform and enlighten; the information contained herein is not intended as, and should not be employed as, a substitute for individual diagnosis and treatment.

CONTRIBUTORS

David Ahdoot, MD, FACOG
Department of Obstetrics and Gynecology
Northridge Hospital Family Practice
Northridge, California

Gayane Ambartsumyan, MD
Department of Obstetrics and Gynecology
University of California
Los Angeles, California

Martin Anderson, MD, FACOG
Department of Pediatrics
University of California
Los Angeles, California

Benjamin J. Ansell, MD
Department of Medicine
University of California
Los Angeles, California

Carol Archie, MD
Department of Obstetrics and Gynecology
University of California
Los Angeles, California

Fikret Atamdede, MD
Department of Obstetrics and Gynecology
University of California
Los Angeles, California

Robert W. Baloh, MD
Department of Neurology
University of California
Los Angeles, California

Kathleen Behr, MD
Department of Medicine
University of California
Los Angeles, California

Leslie Born, MSc
Institute of Medical Science
University of Toronto
Toronto, Ontario

Michael Broder, MD, MSHS
Department of Obstetrics and Gynecology
University of California
Los Angeles, California

Michael P. Brousseau, MD
Department of Internal Medicine
University of California
Los Angeles, California

Vivien Burt, MD, PhD
Department of Psychiatry and Behavioral Sciences
University of California
Los Angeles, California

Belinda J. Chan, MD
Internal Medicine of Clinton
Clinton, Connecticut

Lin Chang, MD
Division of Digestive Disease
University of California
Los Angeles, California

Linnea I. Chap, MD
Department of Medicine
University of California
Los Angeles, California

Karen Cheng, MD
Department of Medicine
University of California
Los Angeles, California

Annapoorna Chirra, MD
Department of Medicine
University of California
Los Angeles, California

Inder J. Chopra, MD
Department of Medicine
University of California
Los Angeles, California

Jenell S. Coleman, MD
Department of Obstetrics and Gynecology
University of California
Los Angeles, California

Andrew Concoff, MD
Departments of Internal Medicine and
   Rheumetology Orthopedics
University of Texas, Houston School of Medicine
Houston, Texas

Christopher Cooper, MD
Department of Medicine
University of California
Los Angeles, California

Carolyn Crandall, MD, FACP
Department of Internal Medicine
University of California
Los Angeles, California

Jeffrey L. Cummings, MD
Department of Neurology
University of California
Los Angeles, California

Christine Darwin, MD
Department of Medicine
University of California
Los Angeles, California

Ann Davis, MD
Department of Obstetrics and Gynecology
Harvard University
Boston, Massachusetts

Camelia Davtyan, MD
Department of Internal Medicine
University of California
Los Angeles, California

Alan H. DeCherney, MD
Department of Obstetrics and Gynecology
University of California
Los Angeles, California

Dawn E. DeWitt, MD, MSc
Department of Medicine
University of Washington
Seattle, Washington

Richard A. Deyo, MD, MPH
Department of Medicine
University of Washington
Seattle, Washington

Allison L. Diamant, MD, MSHS
Department of Medicine
University of California
Los Angeles, California

Britta Dickhaus, MD
Department of Neuroeutemic Disease
University of California
Los Angeles, California

Natalie Driessen, BSc
Department of Biochemistry
University of California
Riverside, California

David Eschenback, MD
Department of Obstetrics and Gynecology
University of Washington
Seattle, Washington

Michelle Eslami, MD
Department of Medicine
University of California
Los Angeles, California

Zenaida Feliciano, MD
Department of Medicine
University of California
Los Angeles, California

Karen A. Filkins, MD
Department of Obstetrics and Gynecology
University of California
Los Angeles, California

Edith Flores, MD
Department of Internal Medicine
University of California
Los Angeles, California

Jodi Friedman, MD
Department of Internal Medicine
University of California
Los Angeles, California

Joseph C. Gambone, DO, MPH
Department of Obstetrics and Gynecology
University of California
Los Angeles, California

Patricia A. Ganz, MD
Department of Health Services
UCLA School of Medicine and Public Health
Los Angeles, California

Rosa Elena Garcia, MPH
Sleep Disorders Center
UCLA/Santa Monica Hospital
Los Angeles, California

Sherry Goldman, RN, NP
Department of Breast Cancer
University of California
Los Angeles, California

Jeffrey Goldsmith, MD
Department of Medicine
University of California
Los Angeles, California

Alan H. Gorn, MD
Department of Medicine
University of California
Los Angeles, California

Gail A. Greendale, MD
Division of Geriatrics
University of California
Los Angeles, California

Jennifer M. Grossman, MD
Department of Medicine
University of California
Los Angeles, California

Marsha K. Guess, MD
Department of Obstetrics and Gynecology
University of California
Los Angeles, California

Parul Gupta, MD
Department of Obstetrics and Gynecology
Kern Medical Center
Bakersfield, California

Jesse Hade, MD
Department of Obstetrics and Gynecology
University of California
Los Angeles, California

Michele A. Hamilton, MD, FACC
Department of Medicine
University of California
Los Angeles, California

Mary Lu Hickman, MD
Department of Developmental Services
Prevention and Child Services Branch
Sacramento, California

Christine H. Holschneider, MD
Department of Obstetrics and Gynecology
University of California
Los Angeles, California

Willa A. Hsueh, MD
Department of Medicine
University of California
Los Angeles, California

Andrew Ippoliti, MD
Department of Medicine
University of California
Los Angeles, California

Lawrence Kagan, BS
Department of Biochemistry
University of California
Los Angeles, California

Anupama Kalsi, MD
Psychiatry and Bio-behavioral Sciences
University of California
Los Angeles, California

Kenneth Kalunian, MD
Department of Medicine
University of California
Los Angeles, California

Anh Kieu, MD
Department of Internal Medicine
University of California
Los Angeles, California

Karen Kish, MD
Department of Obstetrics and Gynecology
UCLA Medical Center
Los Angeles, California

David J. Klashman, MD
Department of Medicine
University of California
Los Angeles, California

Eric Kleerup, MD
Department of Medicine
University of California
Los Angeles, California

Brian Koos, MD
Department of Obstetrics and Gynecology
University of California
Los Angeles, California

Mitzi Krockover, MD
Sokolov, Sokolov, Burgess
Louisville, Kentucky

Donelle Laughlin, MD
Mission Medical Group
Templeton, California

Mary Ann Lewis, DrPH, RN, FAAN
Department of Nursing
University of California
Los Angeles, California

Andrew John Li, MD
Department of Obstetrics and Gynecology
University of California
Los Angeles, California

Jessica S. Lu, MPH
Department of Community Health Sciences
University of California
Los Angeles, California

Michael C. Lu, MD, MPH
Obstetrics and Gynecology
    Community Health Services
UCLA School of Medicine and Public Health
Los Angeles, California

Michael Malamed, MD
Department of Medicine
Tel Aviv University School of Medicine
Tel Aviv, Israel

Farhad Melamed, MD
Department of Medicine
University of California
Los Angeles, California

Mary B. Migeon, MD
Department of Medicine
University of Washington
Seattle, Washington

Judith A. Mikacich, MD
Department of Obstetrics and Gynecology
University of California
Los Angeles, California

Karen Miotto, MD
Department of Psychiatry
University of California
Los Angeles, California

Ardis Moe, MD
Department of Medicine
University of California
Los Angeles, California

Cindy S. Moskovic, MSW
Department of Medicine
Iris Cantor – UCLA Women's Health Education
  and Resources Center
Los Angeles, California

Vidya Nagaraj-Palta, MD
Department of Obstetrics and Gynecology
University of California
Los Angeles, California

Giselle Cabello Namazie, MD
Department of Medicine
University of California
Los Angeles, California

Barbara Natterson, MD
Department of Medicine
University of California
Los Angeles, California

Claire Panosian, MD
Department of Medicine
University of California
Los Angeles, California

Teresa Pham, MD
Onlok Senior Health Services
San Francisco, California

Hyunah Poa, MD
Department of Internal Medicine
University of California
Los Angeles, California

Verna R. Porter, MD
Department of Neurology
University of California
Los Angeles, California

Janet P. Pregler, MD
Department of Medicine
University of California
Los Angeles, California

Jeanie Rahimian, MD
Department of Obstetrics and Gynecology
University of California
Los Angeles, California

Andrea J. Rapkin, MD
Department of Obstetrics and Gynecology
University of California
Los Angeles, California

Natalia Rasgon, MD, PhD
Department of Psychiatry
University of California
Los Angeles, California

Bennett E. Roth, MD
Department of Medicine
University of California
Los Angeles, California

Joseph Russo, MD
Department of Obstetrics and Gynecology
University of California
Los Angeles, California

Carolyn Sachs, MD, MPH
Department of Medicine
University of California
Los Angeles, California

Ernestina Saxton, MD
Department of Neurology
UCLA School of Medicine and Public Health
Los Angeles, California

Gary J. Schiller, MD
Department of Medicine
University of California
Los Angeles, California

Max J. Schmulson, MD
Department of Gastroenterology
Universidad Panamericana
Mexico City, Mexico

Joyce L. Seldon, MS, CGC
Jonsson Comprehensive Cancer Center
University of California
Los Angeles, California

Jeffrey K. Shimoyama, MD
Department of Internal Medicine
Kaiser Permanente Hospital
Los Angeles, California

Robert Shpiner, MD
Department of Medicine
University of California
Los Angeles, California

Samuel A. Skootsky, MD
Department of Medicine
University of California
Los Angeles, California

Sheldon Spector, MD
Department of Medicine
UCLA Medical Center
Los Angeles, California

Thomas O. Staiger, MD
Department of Medicine
University of Washington School of Medicine
Seattle, Washington

Meir Steiner, MD, PhD, FRCPC
Departments of Psychiatry and Behavioral
    Neuroscience and Obstetrics and Gynecology
McMaster University
Hamilton, Ontario

Eric Strom, MD
Department of Medicine
UCLA Medical Center
Los Angeles, California

Elizabeth Suti, MFT
Department of Adult Psychiatry
University of California Neuropsychiatric Hospital
Los Angeles, California

Ricardo A. Tan, MD
California Allergy and Asthma
Medical Group, Inc.
Los Angeles, California

Cynthia Thaik, MD, FACC
Department of Medicine
University of California
Los Angeles, California

Jan H. Tillisch, MD
Department of Medicine
University of California
Los Angeles, California

Thuy T. Tran, MD
Department of General Internal Medicine
University of California
Los Angeles, California

Co. T. Truong, BS
Psychiatry and Bio-behavioral Sciences
University of California
Los Angeles, California

Andre J. Van Herle, MD
Department of Medicine
University of California
Los Angeles, California

Katja Van Herle, MD
Department of Medicine
University of California
Los Angeles, California

Marilene B. Wang, MD
Department of Surgery
University of California
Los Angeles, California

Michael S. Wilkes, MD, PhD
Department of Medicine
University of California
Davis, California

Emily Wong, MD
Department of Medicine
University of Washington
Seattle, Washington

T. C. Jackson Wu, MD, PhD
Department of Obstetrics and Gynecology
University of California
Los Angeles, California

Joel Yager, MD
Department of Psychiatry
University of New Mexico
Alburquerque, New Mexico

Frisca Yan-Go, MD
Department of Neurology
University of California
Los Angeles, California

To Johnathan, Kate, and Claire
—Janet P. Pregler, MD

To Deedee, Peter, Emily and Alec
—Alan H. DeCherney, MD

PREFACE

This book is written as a practical guide and reference text for clinicians who provide comprehensive care to women as part of their practices. As we planned this book, one of the most difficult decisions we faced was the choice of topics to include. As the readers of this text well know, a complete summary of all medical knowledge potentially applicable to women would fill a library. Expanding this to include potentially relevant psychosocial information and commentary would fill several.

Given our goal of a text of manageable length, we chose to include the most frequently encountered topics in women's health clinical practice. We made choices based on our experience of providing comprehensive care to women patients and of working together to train current and future obstetrician-gynecologists, internists, family physicians, and other women's health clinicians. To validate our own impressions, we reviewed national data on the most common conditions encountered when treating female patients.

In our experience, residents and practicing physicians often express the need to know more about common conditions that traditionally have not been addressed in their own specialty training. For that reason, we have attempted to present topics in sufficient breadth, depth, and detail for clinicians to use this text to develop and expand expertise in treating common conditions. Women's health clinicians often also have primary expertise treating women in one part of the life cycle and wish to expand their knowledge of younger or older women. For that reason, we included chapters on the approach to women at varying stages of life. We also included chapters on the care of women who have traditionally been invisible or ignored in clinical training, including lesbians and women with developmental disabilities. Finally, we chose a strong emphasis on preventive health, including an approach to newer areas, such as the care of women at genetic risk for cancer.

Clinicians who expand their practice expertise need to keep current. For this reason, we have included, wherever possible, a list of organizations (and Web sites) that provide up-to-date, evidence-based information on the topics we present in this text. We have also included such resources for patients. We are aware of the perils of publishing Web addresses, which often change frequently. For this reason, we have included addresses and telephone numbers for the organizations whose Web sites we recommend.

We would like to thank Iris Cantor, a tireless supporter of a comprehensive approach to women's health care, without whose support our collaboration and this text would not have happened. We would also like to thank Julie Eisenberg Levis, who was an invaluable assistant in manuscript preparation, Joseph Martin, Josephine Herrera, Danielle Bereskin, Mary Chen, Linda Kwon, Carol Mendoza, Janet Mendoza, Ryan Nguyen, Emma Rao, Julie Shih, Thomas Yan, and Simon Yao. Finally, thank you to TP Graphix for numerous illustrations.

Janet P. Pregler, MD
Alan H. DeCherney, MD

CONTENTS

OBSTETRICS

DISORDERS OF THE BREAST

ALLERGIC, UPPER RESPIRATORY, PULMONARY AND CARDIOVASCULAR DISORDERS

DISORDERS OF BONES, MUSCLES, AND JOINTS

DISORDERS OF THE SKIN

ENDOCRINE DISORDERS

NEUROLOGICAL AND PSYCHIATRIC DISORDERS

BLOOD DISORDERS

INFECTIOUS DISEASES

GENITOURINARY DISORDERS

SPECIAL TOPICS

1

WHAT IS WOMEN'S HEALTH?

Janet P. Pregler, MD, and Alan H. DeCherney, MD

Women are different. This simple statement, self-evident to humanity since the dawn of time, has generated profound dialogue and debate within the medical community over the past 30 years. As a growing body of scientific literature has supported sex and gender differences between men and women affecting all specialties of medicine, the term "women's health," understood previously to be synonymous with women's reproductive health, has been redefined.

For a period of over 100 years, starting in the mid-nineteenth century, modern Western medicine, and later the specialty of obstetrics and gynecology, focused on reproductive health as the principal means of improving the health of women. Preventive health care measures including widespread use of contraception and the implementation of cytologic screening for cervical cancer, as well as improvements in obstetric care, were successful in extending women's life spans. In 1900 the average woman in the United States had a life expectancy of 48 years, and childbirth was rivaled only by tuberculosis as the leading cause of death for women. Because of deaths from childbirth, elderly men outnumbered elderly women in the United States. By 1991 the life expectancy for women was nearly 79 years, and chronic illnesses of aging and cancer, rather than reproductive issues, were the leading causes of death for women. In the United States, the majority of elderly persons are now women. By 2020 it is estimated that 60% of persons over age 65 years in the United States will be women.[1]

The modern women's health movement has its roots in populist activism. In the 1960s and 1970s, a grassroots women's health movement focused on empowering women to take control of their own health. Activists stressed the importance of lay health education, of dialogue and discussion with physicians and other health care clinicians, and of psycho-social factors, such as violence, racism, and sexism, in determining women's well-being. The bible of this movement was the book *Our Bodies, Ourselves.* Authored by a group of women participating in a course on health, sexuality, and childbearing, from a biomedical standpoint, its focus was primarily on reproductive health issues.[2]

This early women's health movement operated outside of the mainstream of traditional medicine. In particular, women's health advocates at this time were not necessarily advocates for women's health research. In the 1950s in Europe, in spite of data suggesting that it might cause adverse affects, thalidomide was prescribed to thousands of pregnant women to combat nausea. Babies born to these women were at high risk for severe limb deformities and other birth defects. Diethylstilbestrol (DES) was prescribed to women in the United States to prevent miscarriage, even after research studies had shown it to be ineffective. In the 1970s it was recognized that the daughters born to women given DES were at high risk for genital abnormalities, infertility, and a rare type of vaginal cancer. The intrauterine contraceptive device marketed under the name "Dalkon Shield" was withdrawn after 4 years because of high uterine infection rates; congressional hearings found that poor research methodology had failed to identify its risks prior to its widespread use. Mindful of these events, women's health advocates in the early women's health movement focused on encouraging women to avoid possibly exploitive and coercive aspects of research. The women's health movement of the time did not oppose new federal policies in the 1970s that classified pregnant women, like children, prisoners, and mentally disabled persons, as especially protected (and therefore often excluded) from medical research.[3] During this period many large clinical trials addressing issues common to both men and women (such as heart disease) excluded women entirely.

By the 1980s activists began to focus on the biologic aspects of sex, leading to strong support and interest in defining differences in diseases that affect both women and men. It was during the 1980s that the definition of women's health came to include sex and gender differences apart from reproductive health and psychosocial issues. Rather than seeking to avoid medical research on women, the women's health movement now sought government support to mandate it. The reasons for this change are complex but probably included the growing number of women living beyond their reproductive years and experiencing chronic illness and the growing number of women reaching positions of influence in the medical and research establishments. In 1993 a law was passed requiring the National Institutes of Health to ensure the inclusion of women in most clinical trials.[3]

BIOLOGY OF SEX AND GENDER DIFFERENCES

Medical research in women's health has traditionally focused on understanding the female reproductive system. Paralleling the women's health movement, research first moved beyond the female reproductive system into understanding societal influences on women's health. More recently, clinical researchers began to study differences at the level of the whole organism between men and women in organ systems beyond the reproductive system. In the past several years, the research community has begun to systematically study sex differences at the basic molecular and cellular levels.

In 2001 the Institute of Medicine of the National Academy of Sciences published a report on the status of understanding sex differences and their effects on health and illness. This report concluded that compelling reasons exist to study sex differences at a biologic level, including differences in human disease between the sexes that remain unexplained. Examples of unexplained differences in human disease include the marked predominance of female patients among persons with some types of autoimmune diseases, including Hashimoto's thyroiditis, systemic lupus erythematosus, and multiple sclerosis, and the marked predominance of men

among persons with other types of autoimmune diseases, such as amyotrophic lateral sclerosis and Goodpasture's nephritis/pneumonitis. It is not known why women develop heart disease later than do men, why women have more "silent" myocardial infarctions, or why women with myocardial infarctions are more likely to have courses complicated by heart failure and stroke. It is not understood why men are more likely to die of melanoma than are women. Understanding why sex matters will likely lead to better preventive and treatment strategies for both men and women.[4]

Current evidence supports the hypothesis that although, in many cases, sex differences can be explained by direct or indirect effects of reproductive hormones, not all differences can be explained hormonally. Most of what is currently known about sex differences has been a by-product of other areas of research, rather than information that was specifically sought to define and explain sex differences. Much work remains to be done[4] (Table 1–1).

PSYCHOSOCIAL ISSUES AND WOMEN'S HEALTH

Some have suggested that the term "women's health" be replaced by the term "gender-based medicine." Those who advocate the use of the term "gender-based medicine" point out that research on the effects of sex and gender on health benefits both men and women. However, the field of women's health is inclusive not only of biologic differences between the sexes but also psychosocial issues that uniquely or disproportionately affect the physical and mental well-being of women. Women are more likely than are men to be poor, to be raising children alone, and to be victims of sexual and/or domestic violence.[1] All of these factors have a profound impact on the health of women. Therefore, women's health must be studied in a context that includes these gender-specific psychosocial factors.

Health insurance is less likely to pay for health-related costs incurred by women in the United States. Differences in employment patterns result in fewer working women being medically insured than men, strongly affecting access to health care and health status.[1] Research published in the early 1990s demonstrated that federally sponsored health insurance for the elderly in the United States (Medicare) covers less overall health care costs for men than

TABLE 1–1. Recommendations of the Institute of Medicine Committee on Understanding the Biology of Sex and Gender Differences

Promote research on sex at the cellular level
- Determine the functions and effects of X- and Y-chromosome-linked genes in somatic and germline cells
- Determine how genetic sex differences influence cells, organs, organ systems, and organisms
- Determine how genetic sex differences influence susceptibility to disease
- Develop systems that can identify and distinguish between the effects of genes and the effects of hormones

Study sex differences across the life span
- Include sex as a variable in basic research designs
- Expand studies to reveal the mechanisms of intrauterine effects
- Encourage studies at different stages of life to determine how sex differences influence health, illness, and longevity

Develop appropriate animal models that mirror human sex differences; search for unexpected phenotypic sex differences in genetically modified animals

Investigate natural variation, including genetic variability, disorders of sex differentiation, reproductive status, and environmental influences to better understand human health

Expand research on sex differences in brain organization and function

Monitor sex differences and similarities for all human diseases that affect both sexes
- Consider sex as a biologic variable in all biomedical and health-related research
- Design studies that will control for exposure, susceptibility, metabolism, physiology, and immune-response variables
- Design studies that will determine how ethical concerns (eg, risk of fetal injury) constrain study designs and affect outcomes
- Design studies that will detect sex differences across the life span

Clarify the use of the terms *sex* and *gender*
- In the study of human subjects, the term *sex* should be used as a classification, generally as male or female, according to the reproductive organs and functions that derive from the chromosomal complement
- In the study of human subjects, the term *gender* should be used to refer to a person's self-representation as male or female or how that person is responded to by social institutions on the basis of the individual's gender presentation
- In most studies of nonhuman animals, the term *sex* should be used

Support and conduct additional research on sex differences

Make sex-specific data more readily available

Determine and disclose the sex of origin of biologic research materials

Conduct longitudinal studies that are constructed so that results can be analyzed by sex

Identify the endocrine status of research subjects (eg, pre- or postmenopausal)

Encourage and support interdisciplinary research on sex differences

Reduce the potential for discrimination based on identified sex differences

Adapted from Haseltine FP, Greenberg Jacobson B. Women's health research: a medical and policy primer. Washington (DC): Health Press International; 1997.

women. This is because women are more likely than are men to require ongoing, rather than episodic, treatment for their health conditions, and treatments such as oral medications and long-term nursing home care are not covered under the current Medicare system.[5] Private insurance for women of reproductive age often does not cover the costs of contraceptives. Federally sponsored insurance for the poor in the United States (Medicaid) does not pay for abortion services; in 2001 only 16 of 50 states chose to use other funding to provide abortions to women with Medicaid.[6] Medicaid coverage

TABLE 1–2. Most Frequent Reasons for Office Visits by Women, in Order of Frequency, United States, 1997–1998*

All Ages	Age 15–44 Yr	Age 45–64 Yr	Age 65+ Yr
1. General medical examination	1. Prenatal care	1. General medical examination	1. General medical examination
2. Prenatal care	2. General medical examination	2. Abdominal discomfort	2. Vision problems
3. Abdominal pain, cramps, and spasm	3. Abdominal pain, cramps, and spasm	3. Cough	3. Cough
4. Cough	4. Throat problems	4. Hypertension	4. Hypertension
5. Vision problems	5. Headache	5. Depression	5. Chest pain and related symptoms
6. Headache	6. Cough	6. Back symptoms	6. Blood pressure check
7. Throat symptoms	7. Depression	7. Knee symptoms	7. Abdominal pain, cramps, and spasm
8. Back symptoms	8. Back symptoms	8. Chest pain and related symptoms	8. Knee symptoms

*Excludes postoperative visits and routine follow-up visits for which the reason was not specified.
Adapted from Brett KM, Burt CW. Utilization of ambulatory Medicare by women: United States, 1997–98. Vital Health Stat 13 2001;149:1–43.

is not available to all poor women, and millions lack any type of health insurance coverage.[1]

Minority women face exceptional barriers to receiving appropriate health care. Latinas have lower rates of screening preventive examinations than have Caucasian or African American women. African American women have especially low rates of mammography screening.[1] These gaps may be partially explained by socioeconomic factors. However, studies have also suggested that minority women, even more than minority men, are less likely to be offered appropriate medical interventions than are Caucasians. In one study internists and family physicians were given medical information and shown videotapes of individuals with identical medical histories and physical examination and laboratory findings. The cases differed only by the age, gender, and race of the actor in the videotape. The information presented was deemed by experts to represent a situation in which the patient should receive referral for cardiac angiography. The physicians studied, all attendees at national meetings of a prestigious medical organization, were significantly less likely to suggest further evaluation for an African American woman than for either a Caucasian or African American man or a Caucasian woman.[7]

A CLINICAL DEFINITION OF WOMEN'S HEALTH

In 1994 the National Academy on Women's Health Education adopted the following definition:

Women's health is devoted to facilitating the preservation of wellness and prevention of illness in women and includes screening, diagnosis, and management of conditions which are unique to women, are more common or more serious in women, or have manifestations, risk factors, or interventions which are different in women.[1]

Over the past decade, there has been increasing interest in training clinicians able to provide comprehensive care for women, including preventive, reproductive, and nonreproductive care for most common clinical conditions. This has included an expectation that women's health clinicians will be sensitive to psychosocial issues and be able to care for groups of women who have been previously marginalized by the health care system, including lesbians, minority women, and women with disabilities.

With rare exception, all physicians and other clinicians include some aspect of women's health in their practice. Commonly encountered clinical

---

TABLE 1–3. Association of Professors of Gynecology and Obstetrics (APGO) Women's Health Education Retreat 2000: Women's Health Core Competencies for Medical Students

---

Graduates of medical schools will be able to:

Explain sex and gender differences in normal development and pathophysiology as they apply to prevention and management of diseases
- Compare differences in biologic functions, development, and pharmacologic response in males and females
- Discuss the pathophysiology, etiology, differential diagnosis, and treatment options for conditions and functions that are specific to women
- Discuss the pathophysiology, etiology, differential diagnosis, and treatment options for conditions that are more common, are more serious, or have interventions that are different in women

Effectively communicate with patients, demonstrating awareness of gender and cultural differences
- Demonstrate interviewing and communication skills that are sensitive to individual abilities and perspectives
- Perform a comprehensive women's health history

Perform a sex-, gender-, and age-appropriate physical examination

Discuss the impact of gender-based societal and cultural roles and contexts on health care and on women

Identify and assist victims of physical, emotional, and sexual violence and abuse

Assess and counsel women for sex- and gender-appropriate reduction of risk, including lifestyle changes and genetic testing
- Describe current recommendations for preventive screening and routine health maintenance throughout the life cycle
- Assess risk and counsel for prevention of specific conditions

Access and critically evaluate new information and adopt best practices that incorporate knowledge of sex and gender differences in health and disease

Discuss the impact of health care delivery systems on populations and individuals receiving health care

---

diagnoses for primary care physicians are displayed in Table 1–2. Recent recommendations for competencies for all physicians are summarized in Table 1–3.

SUMMARY

Thirty years ago the medical community understood women to be different from men mainly in terms of issues related to reproduction. Today the term "women's health" describes a field that strives to understand women as whole organisms from a biological, clinical, and psychosocial perspective. From the standpoint of biological and clinical issues not related to reproduction, research in women's health is still in its infancy; many fundamental genetic and endocrinologic questions remain to be answered.

REFERENCES

1. Council on Graduate Medical Education. Fifth report: women & medicine. Dept. of Health and Human Services (US). Publication No: HRSA-P-DM-95-1.

2. The Boston Women's Health Collective. Our bodies, ourselves. New York: Touchstone; 1998.

3. Haseltine FP, Greenberg Jacobson B. Women's health research: a medical and policy primer. Washington (DC): Health Press International; 1997.

4. Institute of Medicine (US). Exploring the biological contributions to human health: does sex matter? Washington (DC): National Academy Press; 2001.

5. Clancy CM, Massion CT. American women's health care. JAMA 1992;269:1918–20.

6. Gold RB, Richards CL. Medicaid support for family planning in the managed care era. New York: The Alan Guttmacher Institute; 2001.

7. Brett KM, Burt CW. Utilization Ambulatory Medicare by women: United States, 1997–98. Vital Health Statistics Senses 13, Number 149, July 2001:1–43.

8. Schulman KA, Berlin JA, Harless H, et al. The effect of race and sex on physicians' recommendations for cardiac catheterization. N Engl J Med 1999;340:618–26.

2

COMMUNICATION BETWEEN CLINICIAN AND PATIENT: SPECIAL ISSUES IN THE CARE OF WOMEN

Joseph C. Gambone, DO, MPH, and Cindy S. Moskovic, MSW

PHYSICIAN-PATIENT COMMUNICATION AND COLLABORATION

The noted medical educator Eric Cassel has stated that "All medical care flows from the relationship between caregiver and patient. The spoken word is the most important tool in health care."[1] Health services research clearly shows that the majority of patients want to communicate effectively with their physicians and other health care professionals in a way that enables them to participate constructively in their care.[1] This desire for more effective communication and participation is particularly true in women's health care.

In the past, medical care has been structured in a way that fosters patient dependency and helplessness. Traditionally, defining the health problem, setting treatment goals, and choosing among alternatives has been done by the physician alone. This type of approach, however, often can lead to poor patient adherence and low satisfaction.[2] Consumers now are more knowledgeable about their health care than they were in the past. Most patients, therefore, want to participate in a meaningful way in the health care decision-making process.

Experts now agree that many malpractice claims would not be pursued if the patient or the patient's family were not angry about a lack of communication with their health care clinician. This lack of communication may decrease dramatically the quality of the relationship. Patients seek the advice and services of health care professionals to protect or improve their health status. Effective communication between clinicians and patients is essential, so that the need for a recommended procedure or plan is understood, and so that adherence is improved.

Communication involves both developing rapport with patients and giving them information that they need. These two aspects of the personal physician-patient relationship are central to educating patients and securing adherence to therapeutic recommendations.

There has been considerable research supporting the importance of effective physician-patient communication and collaboration. The message from this research is that patients benefit greatly from taking an active role in their medical care. Figure 2–1 shows a model for health care collaboration modified from Ballard-Reisch[3] that suggests that both total patient control on the one hand and complete clinician control with patient abdication on the other hand are less acceptable than is a collaborative effort between clinician and patient. Current research also suggests that collaboration is particularly important in women's health care because of important gender differences.

Health Care Decision-Making

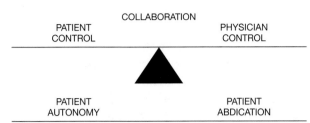

FIGURE 2–1. A health care decision-making continuum. Actual clinical practice tends to be weighted toward physician control and patient abdication. Adapted from Ballard-Reisch DS. Health care providers and consumers: making decisions together. In: Thornton BC, Krebs GL, editors. Health communication. 2nd ed. New York: Waveland Press; 1993.p. 70.

GENDER DIFFERENCES IN HEALTH CARE COMMUNICATION

Because men and women differ in other ways, it should not be surprising that there may be communication problems when the genders of physician and patient differ. These problems involve not only the way that clinician-patient communication occurs, but also the emphasis and priority that is placed on factors within this relationship. Whereas men generally problem solve in a "fix-it" mode, "additionally building a relationship" appears to be a meaningful factor for women. For women the ability to establish a relationship, build rapport, and have two-way communication are all important aspects of the clinician-patient relationship. Women build relationships and a context for understanding their health status through comparison of experiences and by discovering similarities.[4] Differences also occur between the genders in the way symptoms are described. Women tend to relay their symptoms in a longer and more personal conversational manner, whereas men tend to use a shorter more reserved factual approach.[5]

These gender-based communication differences can lead to misinterpretation and potential conflict between clinicians and patients when they are of different genders. Further, as health care consumers, many women are no longer willing to accept difficulties in communication with their physicians. In a national study of women from all socioeconomic backgrounds, one-third of the women who reported changing physicians cited communication problems as the reason.[6]

Gender differences in communication techniques also exist between female and male physicians. Positive talk, relationship building, smiling and nodding, conducting longer office visits, and asking of questions generally are displayed more frequently by female physicians.[7,8] Hodne and Reiter[9] suggest that these communication styles used by female physicians are more conducive to patient-centered models of decision making.

Awareness of gender differences in communication is the first step in building a positive clinician-patient relationship. Further enhancement of the relationship requires deliberate modifications in the manner in which clinicians conduct their interactions with patients to support these preferred communication styles.

DIVERSITY AND PATIENT COMMUNICATION

Diversity in patient populations is now a common reality for many clinicians. The clinician who understands how age, culture, ethnicity, and sexual orientation impact the patient's health care choices and decisions likely experiences an improved dialogue. Both written and oral communications, should be personally relevant to a patient's unique needs and condition.

Indeed, *perceptions* of problems can be shaped significantly by cultural or ethnic issues. As stated by Devore and Schlesinger[10] "each individual has an ethnic history with roots in the past. Traditions, customs, rituals, and behavioral expectations all interface with life in America. These aspects of the past have the potential of affecting perceptions of problems in the present." This concept can be extended further to include the viewing of health, illness, and their interactions within women's social context—those factors at the individual level, such as physical and psychological state, and social, cultural, and economic position; and those factors at the collective/group level, such as environment, power, and inequality.[5] The appreciation of a woman's social context can be crucial to building the framework for effective communication. The patient's social context also can influence her expectations. Social environment and existing circumstances are significant factors in the female patient's process of constructing meaning from her illness.[11]

The issues of diversity and patient communication are complicated. How women prefer to refer to themselves can be quite complex, yet it can rest at the heart of establishing the understanding needed for the physician-patient relationship. Delgado[12] addressed the issue of identification among Hispanic women: "We have much in common with each other. At the same time we are different from one another. Some of us prefer to be referred to as Hispanic women, Latinas, Chicanas, Boricuas, Cubanas. Each one of us identifies with one or more of our ancestral roots: Spanish, Latin, American, Native American, European, African, or Asian. . . ." Thus, to communicate well, it is important that the physician attempts to understand the patient's own unique view of herself.

Lesbian women often encounter a health care system that not only lacks relevance but also may be filled with misconceptions, wrongful assumptions, and bias.[6,13] Studies have shown that some lesbian women believe their primary care clinicians are homophobic, and that many physicians and counselors feel uncomfortable treating lesbian, gay, bisexual, and transgender individuals.[14,15] This blending of perception and reality can have a deleterious effect on communication between physician and patient. Misconceptions to be avoided include assumptions that all women who seek gynecologic care are heterosexual, that all women need contraception, that lesbian women are not interested in reproductive health issues such as contraception or childbearing, and that self-identified lesbians are not at risk for developing sexually transmitted diseases. Physicians should be sensitive and ask the appropriate questions to facilitate a discussion before making recommendations and interventions.[13]

Cultural differences can result in differing expectations, setting the stage for conflict. Communication difficulties due to differences in language and context of illness can add the additional obstacles of misunderstanding and strain to the physician-patient relationship. Clinicians need to examine further their own values, beliefs, and attitudes if health care delivery is to be improved in our multicultural society.[9] Clinicians must be able to understand and be responsive to the needs of diverse populations. Failure to do so diminishes the establishment of a genuine therapeutic relationship. The differences women of varied cultures bring to the medical setting can and should be viewed in the context of a challenging yet positive and enlightening aspect of a medical practice.

Communication deals not just with the spoken word but with obvious environmental factors that can either provide a welcoming message or make a patient feel alone or alienated. While Keeling[13] detailed some of the following recommendations for providing university-based health care services to lesbian, gay, transgender, and bisexual individuals, these recommendations can be modified to be appropriate in creating an atmosphere where women of many diverse backgrounds will feel comfortable:

- Every office or practice form completed should be inclusive of all women, and clinical record forms used in medical clinics or counseling services should not assume heterosexual orientation
- A selection of periodicals that appeal to women of diverse backgrounds should be placed in the waiting room
- Illustrations on brochures should be inclusive of all women, depicting women of different ages, cultures, ethnicity, and sexual orientation
- Office, examination room, and waiting area decorations should be inclusive of all women, and artwork and posters should depict a variety of issues that may be particularly pertinent to diverse groups

Women's health education should be oriented to all physical, psychological, and social health issues and not limited to reproductive concerns. Women, especially those in their forties and fifties, may not be content with basic knowledge about a particular health issue of concern to them but, rather, may want detailed coverage of the subject. A patient should be asked how much material she wants on a topic, so as not to overwhelm her or underestimate her needs. Brochures and pamphlets should be varied not only in topic but also in level of comprehension, amount of detail covered, and languages appropriate for the setting.

IMPACT OF MANAGED CARE ON HEALTH CARE COMMUNICATION

Managed care, which has been defined as the application of evidence-based guidelines to the practice of medicine, tends to emphasize the need for greater efficiencies in health services to reduce health care expenditures. Physicians and other health care clinicians are finding themselves in practice settings

---

HELPFUL HINTS FOR PATIENTS

We encourage you to communicate with your doctor
- You are the best guide to your body and health. Speak openly and candidly about your health, lifestyle, or any other factors that will help your doctor arrive at an appropriate diagnosis and treatment plan.
- Ask questions that will assist you in clarifying the problem, diagnosis, or treatment.
- Do not wait until the problem is severe before scheduling an appointment.

Make a detailed personalized list that includes
- Your health concern(s)—remember that you may not be able to discuss all of your issues in one appointment
- All medications you are taking including prescription and over-the-counter medications, vitamins, and herbal supplements; bring the bottles with you when possible
- Notes on family history, dates and types of surgeries, and lifestyles
- Symptoms you are experiencing, when they started, their frequency and intensity, what makes them better or worse, and other symptoms or events associated with them
- Names of health care clinicians previously seen and their phone numbers

Timing is everything, please
- Try to arrive 5 to 10 minutes early for front office check-in procedures.
- If laboratory work (blood or urine tests) is needed, it will require extra time in your schedule.
- We value your time. However, try to be understanding about delays. Someday it could be you in the examination room who needs additional time with the physician.
- Check your menstrual calendar prior to scheduling the time for an annual pelvic examination and pap smear, so that the appointment does not occur during the menstrual period.

What to bring
- Insurance card-to every appointment
- Previous test results if they are from another doctor or facility
- Medications
- Paper to take notes

What to ask prior to the appointment
- Will I need to fast before any laboratory work (blood or urine tests)?
- What means of payment does the office accept (eg, check, credit card)?
- Should I call the day of my appointment to ask if the doctor is on schedule?

What you should know after the visit
- Details of any diagnosis and treatment plan
- What medications you are taking, why you are taking them, and how you should be taking them
- Any additional tests the doctor has recommended and why
- If there should be a follow-up appointment and when

FIGURE 2–2. Information for patients to assist in communication and decision making. These can be sent to patients in a newsletter or presented in a waiting-room pamphlet.

where less time is available for patient visits. At the same time, consumers of health care services are demanding a higher quality of communication with their health care clinicians. Reaching this seemingly impossible goal is a great challenge. Fortunately, research shows that communication techniques can be modified and improved to maintain or even decrease office visit times while increasing patient satisfaction with respect to the quality of communi-

cation. The quality of time, particularly in terms of the patient's perception of an interested and caring attitude of the clinician, is more important than the actual duration of the visit.[16,17]

One strategy that has been used by a number of managed care organizations to improve communication has been referred to as "demand management." Members of the health care organization are provided access to information about health and health care interventions before and after visits to health care clinicians. Some of these organizations provide toll-free phone numbers, and members can access a library of audiotapes or even talk to a nurse on a "call line" to request more specific information about their health care needs and health status. In addition to improving satisfaction levels and meeting the expectations of plan members for communication and information, these programs have been shown to significantly reduce health care use. One study documented a 40% decrease in expensive emergency department visits after an easy-access toll-free helpline was initiated.[18] Individual physicians and smaller physician practices can institute their own communication-enhancing educational programs for their patients. Suggestions for implementation are presented below.

INFORMING AND COLLABORATING WITH PATIENTS IN HEALTH CARE DECISION MAKING

Informed consent is a legal process based upon the ethical principles of autonomy and beneficence. Individuals are to be informed so that they can actively agree to health care interventions that are usually in their own self-interest (autonomy). At the same time, physicians and other health care clinicians are expected to act in the best interest of their patients (beneficence). These two principles can only be fulfilled when physicians adequately and selflessly assist patients to make informed choices about their care.

Unfortunately, studies indicate that the goal of informed consent appears to be met less than half the time.[19] Recently, health care consumers, especially women, have become more active in the pursuit of information about their health care. In particular, they express a desire for more information, collaboration, and communication, during health care decision making. One useful tool that can be used to improve communication during health care decision making and informed consent[20] is shown in Figure 2–2.

The communication process is facilitated by following a checklist that ensures that the *procedure* or *plan* is discussed, the *reason* for the procedure or plan is explained, the *expectations* of benefit or possible failure are discussed, and that consideration is given to the *preferences* of the patient, for example,

to avoid surgery if possible or to have the treatment that takes the least time. All reasonable *alternative* treatment options for the condition or problem that is being treated should be discussed, along with the *risks* involved. Finally the *expenses* that pertain to each option are discussed. After this communication process occurs, an informed collaborative decision can be reached.

SUMMARY

Effective physician-patient communication is an essential component of modern health care delivery. Women have unique needs, and most prefer a style of communication that consists of meaningful dialogue and active participation in health care decision making. Gender differences in health care communication should be recognized, and physicians and other health care professionals should make efforts to accommodate individual patient preferences. Diverse populations of women present for medical and surgical care. Their differences should be recognized and respected, and a safe context for effective communication should be provided.

Managed care presents new challenges for health care clinicians, since time constraints and use issues can decrease the quality of the clinician-patient relationship. Newer tools such as decision-support checklists, telephone helplines, and Internet information resources are becoming increasingly available to enhance communication efforts.

At the University of California, Los Angeles (UCLA) Iris Cantor–UCLA Women's Health Education and Resource Center, a "Prescription for Patient Education" is given to each patient (Figure 2–3). The prescription was developed to enhance the integration of patient education and clinical services. Rationale for development of the prescription was based on three primary factors. First, the time physicians can spend with patients is increasingly limited by managed care and financial realities. Use of the prescription allows the physician to spend more time on diagnostic and treatment issues and less time doing preliminary education. Second, it has been our observation that when the physician "prescribes" this education, the patient is more apt to consider the importance of receiving the information than if the information is given in another way. Finally, and most importantly, the prescription allows the patient to receive education on issues specific to her health and to

Iris Cantor-UCLA Women's Health Education & Resource Center
UCLA National Center of Excellence in Women's Health

Prescription for Patient Education

Patient Name: _____   Age: _____   Physician's Signature: _____

☐ AIDS/STDs (specify)_____
☐ Aerobic Exercise
☐ Alzheimer's Disease/Dementia
☐ Arthritis
☐ Asthma
☐ Back Health
☐ Breast Health
☐ Cancer (specify)_____
☐ Cardiovascular Disease
☐ Cholesterol
☐ Birth Control (specify)_____
☐ Depression
☐ Diabetes
☐ Drugs/Alcohol (specify)_____
☐ Endometriosis
☐ GI Problems (specify)_____

☐ Headache
☐ High Blood Pressure
☐ HRT
☐ Menopause
☐ Musculoskeletal (specify)_____
☐ Nutrition (specify)_____
☐ Osteoporosis
☐ Prenatal Health
☐ Sinusitis/Nasal Allergies
☐ Skin Diseases (specify)_____
☐ Stress Management
☐ Thyroid
☐ Urinary Incontinence
☐ Urinary Tract Infections
☐ Vaginitis
☐ Other (specify)_____

We would like to share all our resources in person. If you prefer the information be mailed, please call 310/794-9039.

FIGURE 2–3. The Iris Cantor–UCLA Women's Health Education and Resource Center, UCLA National Center of Excellence in Women's Health Prescription for Patient Education.

become a more informed and empowered health care consumer.

All printed materials and Web sites used for the prescriptions are evaluated by the Iris Cantor-UCLA Women's Health Center, UCLA National Center of Excellence in Women's Health faculty for validity, content, and appropriateness for the patient population. *We feel that it is vital that there is a mechanism for physician evaluation of educational materials used in any practice setting.*

RESOURCES

The National Women's Health Information Center
US Department of Health & Human Services
200 Independence Avenue SW, Room 730F
Washington, DC 20201
Telephone: 1-800-994-WOMAN (1-800-994-9662)
Web site: www.4woman.org

The US Public Health Service, Office on Women's Health, offers a toll-free number and Web site for health information on a variety of topics of interest to women. The Web site includes a section on frequently asked health questions, the ability to search for information based on health topic, information in Spanish, and news updates on health topics.

Health Topics/American Medical Women's Association
801 North Fairfax Street, Suite 400
Alexandria, Virginia 22314
Telephone: (703) 838-0500
Web site: www.amwa-doc.org/healthtopics/healthlist.html

The American Medical Women's Association site for patients contains patient information on a variety of topics. It is particularly strong in the area of prevention.

RESOURCES (continued)

Informacion sobre la salud/ National Institutes of Health
Institutos Nacionales de la Salud
Bethesda, Maryland 20892
Telephone: (301) 496-4000
Web site: www.nih.gov/welcome/hispanic/salud

This Spanish language site includes information on a variety of health topics as well as clinical trials supported by the NIH. Health topic information includes written materials in Spanish, as well as information about Spanish language "hot lines."

REFERENCES

1. DiMatteo MR. The physician-patient relationship: effects on the quality of health care. Clin Obstet Gynecol 1994;37:149–61.

2. Gambone JC, Reiter RC, DiMatteo MR. The PRE-PARED provider: a guide for improved patient care. Beaverton (OR): Mosby/Great Performance; 1994. p. 1–16.

3. Ballard-Reisch DS. A model of participative decision-making for physician-patient interaction. Health Commun 1990;2:91–6.

4. Allen D, Gilchrist V, Levinson W, Roter D. Caring for women: is it different? Patient Care 1993;Nov. 15:183–99.

5. Gijsbers Van Wijk CMT, Van Vliet KP, Kolk AM. Gender perspectives and quality of care: towards appropriate and adequate health care for women. Soc Sci Med 1996;43:707–20.

6. US Department of Health and Human Services. Fifth report of Council on Graduate Medical Education. Health Resources and Services Administration: HRSA-P-DM-95-1 1995;15:26–7.

7. Roter D, Lipkin M, Korsgaard A. Sex differences in patients' and physicians' communication during primary care medical visits. Med Care 1991;29:1083–93.

8. Hall JA, Irish JT, Roter DL, et al. Gender in medical encounters: an analysis of physician and patient communication in a primary care setting. Health Psychol 1994;13:384–92.

9. Hodne CJ, Reiter RC. Decision-making in women's health care. Clin Obstet Gynecol 1994;37:162–79.

10. Devore W, Schlesinger EG. Ethnic-sensitive social work practice. Columbus: Charles E. Merrill Publishing Company; 1986. p. 139.

11. Hunt LM, Jordan B, Irwin S. Views of what's wrong: diagnosis and patients' concepts of illness. Soc Sci Med 1989;28:945–56.

12. Delgado JL. Salud! New York: Harper Collins; 1997. p. 4–5.

13. Keeling R. Effective and human campus health and counseling services. In: Sanlo R, editor. Working with lesbian, gay, bisexual, and transgender college students: a handbook for faculty and administrators. Connecticut: Greenwood Press; 1998. p. 147–57.

14. Hayes JA, Gelso CJ. Male counselors' discomfort with gay and HIV-infected clients. J Counsel Psychol 1993;40:86–93.

15. Rudolph J. Counselors' attitudes toward homosexuality: some tentative findings. Psychol Rep 1990; 66:1352–4.

16. Bertakis KD, Azari R, Callahan EJ, et al. Comparison of primary care resident physicians' practice styles during initial and return patient visits. J Gen Intern Med 1999;14:495–8.

17. Pitts JS, Thompson SC, Gambone JC, et al. The influence of involvement in treatment decisions on patient satisfaction. Presented at the Annual Meeting of the Society for Medical Decision Making; 1998 Sept; Toronto, Canada.

18. Jeffrey NA. Health care: who's crowding ER's now? Wall Street Journal 1999 July 20; Sect B:1.

19. Wu WC, Pearlman RA. Consent in medical decision-making: the role of communication. J Gen Intern Med 1988;3:9–19.

20. Reiter RC, Lench JB, Gambone JC. Consumer advocacy, elective surgery, and the "golden era of medicine." Obstet Gynecol 1989;74:815–7.

3

APPROACH TO THE
ADOLESCENT PATIENT

Michael S. Wilkes, MD, PhD, and Martin Anderson, MD, FACOG

Traditionally, little attention in the training of physicians has focused on the health needs of adolescents. While this group generally has little contact with the medical profession, when contact is made there are great opportunities that exist to enhance not only the immediate health of the adolescent, but also her health as she moves toward adulthood. The goal of this chapter is to provide an integrated approach to caring for the adolescent, including risk assessment, counseling strategies, and ethical issues involving both the adolescent and the family unit.

INITIAL APPROACH

As in most doctor-patient encounters, issues of trust are of paramount importance in assuming effective two-way communication with the adolescent. In caring for adolescents, it is important that the clinician is committed to being an advocate for the patient. Issues of confidentiality, and the limits of confidentiality, need to be discussed early and honestly in the interaction.[1,2]

One approach is to meet initially with both the adolescent and parent(s). During this initial encounter it is important to take a clear focused history of past medical problems and family history. It is often difficult to obtain detailed facts from the adolescent on such items as past immunizations, surgeries, and prior illnesses. Similarly, the adolescent may not be clear on the details of close family members with medical problems, particularly mental health problems, such as depression, suicide, anxiety, and eating disorders. It is quite often useful to elicit a parent's perspective on the chief medical problems, even though it may not

be as accurate as is a private discussion with the adolescent.

Next, parents should be asked to wait in the waiting room so that the clinician can begin to establish a relationship with the adolescent on their own. On occasion, parents may express some resistance at leaving their child alone. At this juncture, the goal is to explain to the parent the importance of the adolescent being able to confide in her physician and discuss difficult issues that may arise in the future. Parents should be reassured that, at the end of the encounter, they will be invited back into the room to discuss any remaining issues. Substantial resistance is rarely encountered to such a suggestion. When resistance is encountered, particular attention should be paid to the exploring the parent-child relationship and the possibility of a "family secret," such as domestic violence or substance abuse.

In certain circumstances, parents like to meet alone with the clinician. This can be comfortably provided either while the adolescent is changing in preparation for the physical examination or prior to beginning the initial discussion with the adolescent. On the other hand, prior to calling the parents back into the consultation room at the end of the visit, it is useful to set an agenda with the adolescent for the discussion with the parents including topics to be discussed and likely responses the clinician will make. In this way the teen will help plan what is to be discussed and what will remain confidential. The parents should be offered a chance to ask about issues of interest to them.

Once alone with the adolescent , it is important to explain that the clinician's role is to act as an

TABLE 3–1. **Important Aspects of Communication with Adolescent Patients**

Premise	Description
Facts	Establish that the patient understands the facts of her illness. Remember, however, in some situations denial can be healthy, if it allows the patient to function better.
Fears	Try to address any fears that the patient may have about the illness or treatment.
Fables	Clear up any misunderstandings, misconceptions, or myths. Dispel any *incorrect* assumptions that she somehow deserved the illness.
Family	How is the family affected? Can they help? Answer their questions.
Future	Tell the patient what to expect and when and under what circumstances to contact you or to follow up. Outline the plan.

advocate and that conversations are confidential, to the extent allowed by law. Out of respect for patient autonomy, teens should be informed of the specific limitations of confidentiality, which vary according to state law, even though this may serve as a barrier to open discussion of some topics.[1,2]

It often is useful to begin discussions with the teen with several minutes of nonthreatening discussion on topics that may be of interest to her, such as exploring her extracurricular activities or favorite music. It is important that the clinician not come across as authoritarian but, rather, as authoritative. Similarly, it is important to be nonjudgmental and also to avoid acting or speaking like an adolescent. A useful technique is echoing—repeating back a few words from what the teen has just said. For example, "I see, so you and your mother quarrel often."

During the discussion with the adolescent, it is important to listen carefully both to what is said and to what is not said, paying attention to nonverbal cues. An important goal of interactions with the adolescent should be to instill responsibility, empowering the adolescent to identify risky behaviors so that the clinician can suggest interventions that may decrease risk.[3] However, whereas an important goal may be getting to know the adolescent and discovering a bit about her health risks, the primary goal should be to discuss the adolescent's agenda.

There are five premises (the five "Fs") that are important in caring for the adolescent (Table 3–1). The adolescent needs to leave the office with a clear understanding of the *facts* of her illness or concern including implications for others such as her family, sexual partners, and classmates. *Fears*, (real or perceived) that the adolescent may have concerning her illness or life situation need to be addressed. She may also be worried about body image, identity, or peers or other interpersonal relationships. It is important to clarify any *fables*, including misunderstandings and misconceptions she may have about her illness or about adolescence relating to such topics as sexuality, pregnancy, drug use, and masturbation. It is important to explore the adolescent's relationship with her *family*. What are communication and trust like within the family unit? How does the teen settle conflicts that arise at home? Last, it is important to understand how the adolescent views the *future*. In addition, it should be clear that the clinician is accessible. A contact number should be provided, and the teen should be instructed to call should the need arise.

In offices where there are a variety of patients of different ages, it may be helpful to schedule teens at specific designated times. In so doing, their comfort level can be increased by having other teens in the waiting area. This also provides an opportunity to play educational videotapes, have different devices or materials out for display, or provide educational brochures that may not be appropriate for other age groups.

HISTORY

A systematic approach to history taking is particularly important in assessing adolescents. Adolescents see physicians infrequently, and well over 75% of physician visits in the United States last less than 15 minutes.[4] For doctor-patient communication to be practical, clinicians must be able to integrate into their routine evaluation of adolescents the particular risk factors to which adolescents are most often exposed. Further, while a focused physician examination may be helpful, the history is where the bulk of diagnoses are made.

The HEADSSS psychosocial assessment tool (HEADSSS—*h*ome, *e*ducation, *a*ctivities, *d*rugs, *s*exuality, *s*uicide/depression, *s*afety) provides an entree to discuss the major psychosocial issues of adolescents (Table 3–2).[5,6] The HEADSSS assessment should be completed after the clinician and adolescent have met and the parent(s) have left the room. It is important that a discussion of confidentiality and its limits occurs prior to beginning the HEADSSS assessment. Some physicians prefer to have teens complete a written questionnaire while in the waiting room.[1] The problem with this approach is that such questionnaires are often completed in the parents' presence. Additionally, there is information to be obtained from verbal responses and nonverbal behaviors.

There are other issues of prevention that need to be discussed, including issues related to diet, physical appearance, exercise, and anticipatory counseling. It is most useful for an adolescent to hear her clinician review some of the changes (both physical and mental) that she can anticipate experiencing in the next several years.

PHYSICAL EXAMINATION

To allow more time for taking the psychosocial history, the physical examination during the first visit often can be abbreviated. Far more information can be obtained from a careful history and attention to developing an effective therapeutic relationship than from a screening physical examination in an otherwise healthy teenager.

One important point that needs to be considered is whether the patient needs a pelvic examination. Performing a gynecologic examination can often be an important part of providing health care to adolescent teen.[7,8] There are several indications for a pelvic examination, including (1) the patient's request, (2) the patient is sexually active, (3) the patient is without periods and is greater than 14 years old, or (4) the patient has other specific symptoms. Simply being an adolescent female in and of itself does not mandate a pelvic examination. Fears about a first pelvic examination lead many teens to avoid getting the care they need. Despite this, with proper attitude, time, and bedside manner, the pelvic examination need not lead to apprehension.

Obtaining the initial history with the patient clothed, rather than gowned, may allay some nervousness and embarrassment. Teens may be concerned about a variety of issues related to the pelvic examination, including fears of pain, being judged, being diagnosed with an illness, or being violated. It often is helpful to directly ask the adolescent about her concerns prior to the examination. The first pelvic examination may, in most cases, be equally diagnostic and educational. Charts, diagrams, and a teaching hand-held mirror are helpful adjuncts. The patient should be told clearly that she is in control and may request that the examination be stopped at any time. Each part of the examination should be explained. Finally, the rectal examination should be performed only if actually indicated for symptoms, as there is no data that it is useful as a screening examination.

CONCLUSION OF THE INTERVIEW AND FOLLOW-UP

After the initial history and physical examination of the adolescent have been completed, there are several issues that need to be discussed prior to closing the interview. The first and foremost concern is to leave open the option for the adolescent to return or call when further issues arise. Second, it is important to specifically address the topic of adherence. Tools that can be used to enhance adherence are reviewed in Table 3–3.

It is important to remember that the teen is the patient, not the parent. Occasionally, the clinician may be unable to separate duty to the teen from duty to the parent. In these cases, the teen should be referred to another clinician. It is also important to realize that often the care of the adolescent is best accomplished with an interdisciplinary approach; a nurse, social worker, or other practitioner may best develop a relationship with the patient. These relationships can be used to deliver optimal health care to the teen.

TABLE 3–2. Psychosocial Assessment of Adolescent Patients

Issue	Questions	Issue	Questions
Home	Where do you live? Who do you live with? Do you share a bedroom? With whom? How do you get along with the people you live with? How much time do you spend at home? What do you and your family argue about? Can you go to your parents with problems? Have you ever run away from home?	**S**exual activity/ sexual identity	Have you ever had sex with men? Women? Both? Have you ever had sex unwillingly? How many sexual partners have you had? How old were you when you first had sex? Have you ever been pregnant? Have you ever had an infection as the result of sex? Do you use condoms and/or another form of contraception/STD prevention? (Use specific names for STDs). Have you ever traded sex for money, drugs, clothes, or a place to stay? Have you ever been tested for HIV? Do you think it would be a good idea to be tested?
Education	What grade are you in? What grades are you earning? Have they changed? What are you best/worst classes? Why? Do you need extra help in school? Do you work after school or on weekends? Have you ever failed any classes or a grade? Do you ever cut classes?		
Activities	What do you do for fun? What activities are you involved in during and after school? Are you active in sports? Do you exercise? Who do you do fun things with? Do you have a best friend? Who do you hang out with? Who are your friends? Who do you go to with problems? What do you do on weekends? Evenings?	**S**uicide/ depression	How do you feel today on a scale of 0 to 10 (0=very sad, 10=very happy)? Have you ever felt less than 5? What made you feel that way? Did you ever think about hurting yourself, that life wasn't worth living, or hope that when you went to sleep you wouldn't wake up again?
Drugs	Do you drink coffee or tea? Do you smoke cigarettes? Have you ever smoked one? Have you ever tasted alcohol? When? What kind and how often? Do any of your friends drink or use drugs? What drugs have you tried? Have you ever injected drugs or steroids? When? How often do you use them? How did you pay for the drugs?	**S**afety	Do you regularly wear seatbelts when riding in a car? Do you skateboard, or roller-blade, and, if so, do you wear protective gear? Does anyone at home own a gun? If so, where is it kept? Does it have a safety latch on it? Has anyone ever hurt you or intentionally destroyed something you value? Do you ever feel unsafe at home, school, or at work/play? How do you and your parents resolve conflicts? Have you ever been hit, pushed, or shoved? Has anyone ever touched you in a private place against your will?

STD = sexually transmitted disease; HIV = human immunodeficiency virus.
Adapted from Goldenring JM, Cohen E. Getting into adolescent heads. Contemp Pediatr, 1998;5:75.

TABLE 3–3. Techniques to Improve Adherence

Simplify the regimen and tailor it to the adolescent's lifestyle as much as possible.

Provide written instructions. Outline clearly how a dose should be increased if the medicine is given with instructions to gradually increase the dose.

Discuss potential side effects of the medication and encourage the patient to ask questions before stopping the medication. Educate the patient as to the purpose and consequences of complying or not complying with the treatment regimen.

Do not assume that an intelligent, well-educated patient will comply, nor that a poorly educated patient will not comply.

Enlist the adolescent's cooperation in the treatment plan. Work with her on ways to remember to take the medicine (ie, alarms; associating the medication with daily activities such as brushing teeth, taking a shower or eating dinner). A pillbox with spaces for each day's medication can assist a patient in remembering to take the medication correctly.

Avoid instilling in a patient fear of long-term consequences of noncompliance, since it is rarely successful. Fear is a poor long-term motivating factor.

Make the patient responsible for the treatment as much as possible. Self-management techniques such as a medication log or a symptom diary can assist with promoting the patient's feeling of self-efficacy.

Share with the patient that you are aware that it is difficult to comply with a medication regimen. Assure her that you will not be angry with her if she admits to difficulties adhering to the treatment plan. Encourage discussion of difficulties so that, together, you can try to make taking the medicine less difficult.

If you need to involve the parents in the supervision of treatment, do this in cooperation with the teen and emphasize how they can work together. Discourage parents from taking complete control, yet keep safety in mind with medications that have an abuse potential (eg, Ritalin) or a narrow safety margin (eg, tricyclic antidepressants or lithium).

The longer the treatment regimen, the more often you need to reinforce the importance of the medication. Use praise liberally when the patient complies. Use every opportunity to bolster the patient's self-esteem and sense of self-efficacy. Avoid criticism or arguments/confrontations over noncompliance. Showing empathy for the patient's difficulty in compliance will ultimately be more effective than trying to "force compliance."

Be aware that there may be cultural, religious, or financial reasons for noncompliance. A parent or patient may be embarrassed to admit that he or she can not afford a medication or a patient visit.

RESOURCES

American Academy of Pediatrics
141 Northwest Point Boulevard
Elk Grove Village, Illinois 60007-1098
Telephone: (847) 434-4000
Web site: www.AAP.org

The AAP has 55,000 physician members from throughout North and South America. Its goal is to promote the health, safety, and well-being of infants and youth, including adolescents and young adults. The AAP Web site contains clinical guidelines and positions on a variety of topics pertinent to the care of adolescents. It also contains patient-oriented health information appropriate for adolescents and their families.

REFERENCES

1. Ginsberg K, Menapace A, Slap G. Factors affecting the decision to seek health care: the voice of adolescents. Pediatrics 1997;100:922–30.

2. Ford CA, Millstein SG, Halpern Fisher BL, Charles IE. Influence to physician confidentiality assurances on adolescents' willingness to disclose information and seek future health care. JAMA 1997;278:1029–34.

3. Goldenring JM, Cohen E. Getting into adolescent heads. Contemp Pediatr 1988;5:75.

4. Ziv A, Boulet JR, Slap GB. Utilization of physician offices by adolescents in the United States. Pediatrics 1999;104:35–42.

5. Malus M, Chance PA, Larry L. Priorities in adolescent health care: the teenager's viewpoint. J Fam Pract 1987;25:159.

6. Gruber E, Machamer AM. Risk of school failure as a clear indicator of other health risk behavior in American high school students. Health Risk Soc 2(1):200.

7. Kahm J, Emans SJ. Pap smears in adolescents: to screen or not to screen? Pediatrics 1999;103:673–4.

8. American Academy of Pediatrics. Recommendations for preventative pediatric health care. Pediatrics 1995;96:712.

4

APPROACH TO
THE MENOPAUSAL PATIENT

Gail A. Greendale, MD

Menopause is the permanent cessation of menstruation that results from loss of ovarian follicular function. By definition menopause has occurred after the passage of 12 months of amenorrhea. Therefore, the timing of menopause (ie, the final menstrual period) can only be known in retrospect. The average age at which menopause occurs is between 48 and 52 years.[1]

Menopause (the termination of ovulation) does not happen abruptly. Rather, current theory holds that the menopause transition, also called perimenopause, begins between 2 and 8 years before the final menses. In general, this transition is characterized by changes in ovarian follicular function and associated hormonal feedback loops. At present our knowledge of the hormonal and clinical details of perimenopause is rudimentary. A three-staged theoretic model is reviewed briefly here; ongoing studies will elucidate this process more clearly.

In *early perimenopause* menstrual cycle lengths appear normal or can be abbreviated due to a shortened follicular phase. Follicle stimulating hormone (FSH) levels are higher than are those of younger women,[2,3] perhaps due to the presence of fewer follicles or decreased secretion of inhibin.[4,5] *Middle perimenopause* is characterized by a less predictable menstrual cycle pattern.[6] One such pattern is marked by short cycles interspersed with long amenorrheic intervals. Some perimenopausal cycles are ovulatory, whereas others are anovulatory (estrogen levels rise and fall without progesterone secretion).[7] In middle perimenopause FSH values can be markedly higher than are those of younger cycling women (ie, in what is commonly thought of

as the "postmenopausal range"). Therefore menopause is not diagnosed by a high FSH value in a woman who is still menstruating. Women may experience hot flashes, breast tenderness, and menorrhagia during middle perimenopause.[8] The year after the final menstrual period is designated *late perimenopause.*

There are probably many patterns of menopause transitions. The percentage of women who manifest changes in cycle length, perimenopausal symptoms and the relation between symptoms, menstrual cycle characteristics, and hormonal correlates are presently unknown but are areas of intensive investigation.

SYMPTOMS AND TREATMENTS

The hot flash is a definite symptom of perimenopause and postmenopause. Hot flashes range from a sense of warmth to drenching sweats. Skin flushing, heart pounding or palpitations, and a sense of fullness in the head are common accompanying features of the hot flash. A chill may follow, if core temperature drops after the sweating phase. Flashes may last seconds to hours and may be innocuous or extremely disruptive of daily function or sleep. In the majority of women, hot flashes begin in the few years prior to the final period, and they abate in a similar amount of time after menopause;[6] however, the persistence of hot flashes varies greatly. Ethnic variation in hot flash experience is also large, with up to 80% of women from Western countries but as few as 10% of women from Eastern countries reporting them.[9,10]

Hot flashes respond to estrogen therapy in a dose-dependent manner. Using standard dosages (see "Postmenopausal Hormone Therapy", page 21), hot flashes are reduced by about 70 to 80% within 6 weeks of initiating treatment. Women with a sub-optimal response to standard doses may benefit from a higher dose (eg, 1.25 mg of conjugated equine estrogens instead of 0.625 mg). Downward titration should be attempted within 1 to 2 years, however, to reduce the risk of long-term exposure to high estrogen doses. Methyldopa, clonidine, medroxyprogesterone acetate (MPA), and megestrol acetate are nonestrogen treatments for hot flashes.[11,12] Of these, megestrol acetate is most effective, resulting in a 70% decrease in hot flashes.

Vaginal atrophy is a well-known clinical correlate of the postmenopause, but careful epidemiologic studies of this syndrome are lacking. Women who experience vaginal dryness, itching, irritation, and dyspareunia may have accompanying vaginal examination findings of atrophy such as epithelial pallor, friability, and diminished rugae. However, women may also have vaginal symptoms without these physical findings, and they may have atrophic examination findings without any symptoms.[13] Unlike hot flashes, vaginal atrophy tends to become more pronounced with increasing time after menopause.

Usual systemic doses of estrogen are generally effective for the treatment of vaginal atrophic symptoms; however, it is sometimes necessary to add additional local therapy in those women who do not obtain adequate symptom relief. Options include local topical estrogen or vaginal moisturizers (such as Astroglide, Moist Again, Replens (polycarbophil), and Gyne-Moistrin).

The relation between menopause and urinary tract pathology remains uncertain, but several anatomic and physiologic alterations in the urinary tract that accompany menopause suggest a plausible association.[14] After menopause, several changes occur in the urinary tract that may lead to incontinence or irritative voiding symptoms (frequency and urgency). These include atrophy of the bladder trigone, thinning of the urethral mucosa, and diminished sensitivity of the bladder neck and urethral sphincter α-adrenergic receptors. In addition, menopause may be a risk factor for urinary tract infection due to the presence of a higher vaginal pH and to vaginal colonization with gram-negative organisms.

Studies using estrogen to treat urinary incontinence have had positive and negative results.[15–17] However, most studies have been done in small samples, types of incontinence have been heterogeneous, and forms and doses of estrogen have varied. Thus, many clinicians offer a trial of estrogen treatment (systemic or topical) for irritative voiding symptoms, stress incontinence, and urge incontinence. Although based on limited data, evidence for a beneficial effect of estrogen on recurrent urinary tract infection is striking. One randomized trial reported almost complete prevention of recurrences in women treated with vaginal estriol compared with recurrences in those women given placebo.[18] A recent randomized trial of a low-dose estradiol vaginal ring among women with recurrent urinary tract infections found that the likelihood of remaining infection free was 45% in the treated women compared with 20% in women randomized to placebo.[19]

Whether menopause-related changes affect sexual function remains unclear. In cross-sectional studies, women report diminishing desire and intercourse frequency with increasing chronologic age, but the role of menopause per se as well as the impact of other important factors such as partner's sexual capability and relationship quality as etiologies of sexual dysfunction are poorly understood.[20,21]

Despite the absence of formal studies, few would argue that dyspareunia is unlikely to benefit from systemic or vaginal estrogen therapy. Less certain is whether sexual desire, orgasm, or arousal will improve similarly with estrogen treatment, although an estrogen trial for these conditions is reasonable. Controversy surrounds the use of testosterone to enhance sexual desire in postmenopausal women. In randomized placebo-controlled studies, women who have undergone oophorectomy and treatment with high doses of testosterone report increased desire,[22] whether these results can be generalized to naturally menopausal women and whether the high-dose testosterone used is safe are debated.[23] A recent randomized trial of low-dose transdermal testosterone patches (150 or 300 μg) among women with bilateral oophorectomy reported significant increases in reported frequency of sexual activity, pleasure, and orgasm. At the higher dose, women reported better mood and well-being.[24] Although there are minimal supporting data,[25] a trial of low-dose oral methyltestosterone (1.25 to 2.50 mg daily) may be considered for women whose major complaint is decreased desire. Although even low doses of oral methyltestosterone can lead to acne, hirsutism, or virilization, it is relatively safe, especially if used for less than 2 years.[26]

Several population-based longitudinal studies find no relation between menopause and depression.[27] However, one subgroup of women appears more vulnerable to affective disorders during the transition to menopause: cohort studies show that women with a prior history of depressive illness are at risk for a recurrence of depression during the perimenopause.[28,29] However, the prevalence of clinical depression in women presenting for medical care around the time of the menopause is quite high—45% of the women attending one menopause clinic.[30] The striking contrast between the results of population-based research (concluding no association between menopause and depression) compared with rate of depression in clinical samples seeking menopause care suggests a high degree of self-selection on the part of women with depressive symptoms.

Estrogen should not be used as monotherapy for peri- and postmenopausal women with clinical depression. However, a secondary analysis of a large clinical trial suggested that estrogen augments responsiveness to fluoxetine;[31] results of ongoing studies attempting to replicate this finding are awaited.

CHRONIC DISEASES

The occurrence of several major chronic diseases may have a temporal relation to menopause (Table 4–1). Rates of cardiovascular disease and osteoporosis increase. There are proposed relations between numerous other illnesses and menopause, including osteoarthritis, cataracts, periodontal disease and tooth loss, colon cancer, and dementia. An extensive review of the data supporting these associations is beyond the scope of this chapter. The reader is referred to recent reviews and manuscripts for further information.[32–39]

POSTMENOPAUSAL HORMONE THERAPY

In formulating a treatment plan for menopause, it is critical to establish each patient's objectives. If hormone therapy is directed primarily at symptom relief, it can usually be given for a relatively short time or as local treatment, therefore obviating potential concerns about long-term risks. In contrast estrogen for chronic disease prevention or treatment generally is ongoing, thus requiring detailed consideration of long-term benefits and risks of treatment. Postmenopausal hormones have been prescribed for primary prevention of cardiovascular disease and osteoporosis.[40] This is described further in Chapter 34, "Coronary Artery Disease," and Chapter 47, "Osteoporosis." However, results of randomized controlled trials with clinical heart disease and fracture outcomes are not yet available.

A second overall consideration is that doses and routes of hormone treatment for the menopause vary according to indication. For example, perimenopausal hot flashes may temporarily need high systemic doses of estrogen, whereas vaginal atrophy may respond to very-low-dose local treatment.

Examples of commonly used systemic estrogen and progestin doses and regimens are summarized

TABLE 4–1. Symptoms and Syndromes that May Be Associated with Menopause and Postmenopause*

Perimenopause and Early Postmenopause[†]	*Mid-postmenopause*[‡]	*Later Menopause*[§]
Irregular menses	Stress incontinence	Cardiovascular disease
Hot flashes	Sensory-urge incontinence	Osteoporotic fractures
Dysphoric mood	Urinary urgency	Cognitive impairment
Interrupted sleep	Dysuria	Cataracts
Self-reported memory problems	Dyspareunia	Tooth loss
	Atrophic vaginitis	

* Associations between menopause and many of these symptoms and diseases are not definitive. Please see text and references.
† 5 years before to 5 years after onset of menopause.
‡ 5 to 10 years after onset of menopause.
§ 10 or more years after onset of menopause.

TABLE 4–2. Systemic Estrogen and Progestogen Doses and Regimens Used for Postmenopausal Hormone Therapy

Generic Name	Dose and Route	Regimen
Estrogens		
Conjugated equine estrogens	0.625 mg, PO	Daily
Estropipate	0.625 mg, PO	Daily
17-ß estradiol valerate	2.0 mg, PO	Daily
17-ß estradiol patch	0.5 mg, topical	Change 2 times/wk
17-ß estradiol gel	1.0 mg, topical	Daily
Progestogens		
Medroxyprogesterone acetate	5–10 mg, PO	Calendar days 1–12
	2.5–5.0 mg, PO	Daily
Micronized progesterone	200 mg, PO	Calendar days 1–12
Norethisterone	0.7–2.0 mg, PO	Calendar days 1–12
	0.35–0.5 mg, PO	Daily

PO = per os (by mouth).

in Table 4–2. These are considered standard, as the estrogen doses are those shown to preserve bone density in clinical trials, and the progestin doses and regimens are those that prevent endometrial hyperplasia (evidenced by endometrial biopsy). Randomized controlled trials show that unopposed estrogen causes endometrial hyperplasia,[41] a precursor to cancer. Observational studies demonstrate a link between unopposed estrogen and endometrial cancer,[42] and also find that this risk is obviated by proper use of progestins.[43]

Continuous (daily) administration of estrogen is recommended because daily use is easy to remember and avoids symptom breakthrough. Monthly cyclic (progestogen used on calendar days 1 to 12 monthly) or daily continuous progestogen schedules are recommended. These facilitate adherence and also make it easy to characterize onset and duration of vaginal bleeding related to cyclical progestogen use. A quarterly progestogen regimen (progestogen given four times per year) is not recommended, as this schedule has been associated with an unacceptably high incidence of hyperplasia.[44]

Each of the progestogen dose-duration regimens shown in Table 4–2 has undergone testing in clinical trials that used biopsy-based assessments of the endometrium. However, the sample sizes and lengths of studies have varied. For example, the safety of the cyclic 5-mg dose of MPA was tested in a 1-year study,[45] whereas that of the 10-mg dose has

been tested for up to 3 years.[41] A continuous daily regimen of 2.5 mg of MPA has been studied for 3 years.[41] Because daily use of 5.0 mg of MPA militates against estrogen's beneficial lipid effects more than does 2.5 mg of MPA, the lower daily MPA dose is preferred. However, women who are experiencing a lot of spotting and bleeding during the first months of continuous estrogen and progestin use benefit from the higher (5.0 mg) MPA dose, as it promotes endometrial atrophy more quickly than does the lower dose. Cyclically prescribed micronized progesterone, 200 mg for 12 days per month, when used for up to 3 years, does not cause hyperplasia.[41] Daily use of 100 mg of micronized progesterone has been studied in only small numbers of women and for short periods of time (maximum 6 months); thus it is not recommended at this time.[46,47]

Systemic Estrogens

Estrogen can be given orally, transdermally (by patch or cream), intradermally (by implantable pellet), and intramuscularly (by injection) (see Table 4–2). The intradermal and intramuscular modes of administration are not used commonly in the United States and are not discussed further here.

All transdermal estrogen patches contain 17-ß estradiol. There are reservoir systems, which are alcohol based (eg, Estraderm) and matrix systems (eg, Climara, Vivelle), in which the estrogen is in the adhesive. Patches vary in the amount of 17-ß estradiol

TABLE 4–3. Vaginal Estrogen Preparations and Regimens

Generic Name	Dose and Formulation	Regimen
Estradiol ring	Elastomer ring releases 7.5 µg estradiol/d	Replace every 90 days
Estriol cream	0.5-mg cream	0.5 mg 2 times/wk[*]
Estradiol tablet	25-µg tablet	1 tablet 2 times/wk

[*]Other vaginal estrogen creams not extensively studied to demonstrate lack of systemic effect.

released, ranging from 0.035 to 1.0 mg per 24 hours. Non-oral estrogen administration circumvents first-pass liver metabolism and is therefore particularly appropriate for women with high serum triglycerides, with liver function abnormalities, or who are at high risk for cholelithiasis. Skin rash occurs in 10% of reservoir-based and 5% of matrix-based patch users; these reactions occur more often in tropical climates, likely due to high humidity.[48]

Cutaneous 17-ß estradiol cream is available in Europe; its main shortcoming has been difficulty standardizing the amount applied. New metered-dose measurement systems circumvent this problem; we may therefore see approval of this form of administration in the United States. Creams may be of use in those women who desire non-oral administration but prefer not to wear a patch or who are intolerant to it.

Vaginal Estrogens

Vaginal estrogens are intended to have a local effect on vaginal epithelial tissues without stimulation of other estrogen-responsive tissues (eg, the endometrium or the liver) or production of measurable increases in estradiol or estrone levels as a result of treatment. In recent years new methods of vaginal delivery of estrogens have undergone careful testing and appear to achieve some or all of these safety goals; examples are listed in Table 4–3.

Because patients and physicians often raise questions about the whether vaginal estrogen administration is truly local treatment, some topical vaginal estrogen studies are detailed. A 1-year trial of low-dose (25 µg) 17-ß estradiol vaginal tablets resulted in no biopsy-assessed endometrial hyperplasia in 43 treated women,[49] although 3 women developed weakly proliferative endometrial histology. Estradiol, FSH, and luteinizing hormone were unchanged. A 22-week intervention in 20 women using 25-µg 17-ß estradiol tablets similarly found no endometrial hyperplasia.[50] Pooled data from

12 studies of low-dose estriol vaginal cream (0.5 mg daily for 2 to 3 weeks followed by 0.5 mg twice weekly) did not demonstrate any endometrial proliferation in 61 biopsies taken after 6 months or in 58 additional biopsies performed after 12 months.[51] Serum estriol levels did rise, however, with low-dose estriol vaginal cream.[52] Open-label nonplacebo controlled studies of Estring, a vaginal ring that releases 17-ß estradiol, 7.5 µg per 24 hours, used a progestin challenge test (PCT) at 13 weeks to evaluate endometrial safety (bleeding after administration of progestin indicates endometrial stimulation).[53] In one study 5 of 122 participants had positive PCTs, and in another trial 2 of 58 challenges were positive. Endometrial biopsies performed on 4 of the 7 women with positive PCTs were negative for hyperplasia. Two other studies raised some concerns about a possible systemic effect of the vaginal estrogen ring. Estrone levels increased to 950 pmol/L after 48 weeks of ring use (within the "postmenopausal range" but higher than baseline);[54] surprisingly, another small trial found that the vaginal estradiol ring preserved bone density.[55] Two older vaginal preparations, conjugated equine estrogens cream and 17-ß estradiol vaginal cream are not discussed here as there are no comprehensive data available for low-dose vaginal application of these products.

Overall, low-dose estriol vaginal cream, the 17-ß estradiol vaginal tablet, and the vaginal estrogen ring appear safe with respect to the endometrium, causing weakly proliferative endometrial tissue, at most. However, mildly increased serum estrogen levels and estrogen effects on other tissues such as bone have not been ruled out. Therefore, in women in whom no systemic exogenous estrogen exposure is desired, vaginal estrogens should be used with caution.

Vaginal atrophy also can be managed with moisturizers, such as Astroglide, Gyne-Moistrin, Moist Again, and Replens. Replens decreases vaginal pH and thus may offer some protection against recurrent urinary tract infections, but it has not been studied for this indication.[56]

Progestogens

Progestogens, when used in appropriate doses and for adequate duration, prevent endometrial hyperplasia; postmenopausal women without a uterus do not require a progestogen as part of their hormone therapy. Progestogens can be classifed as the C-21 derivatives of progesterone (eg, MPA and dydrogesterone), C-19 derivatives of nortestosterone (eg, norethisterone), and natural progesterone. Although each of these subgroups differs with respect to effects on intermediate end points, such as the impact on serum lipid profiles,[57,58] cohort studies have not corroborated a meaningful difference in clinical outcomes[59] or risk factor profiles resulting from use of differing classes of progestins.[60]

Bleeding Patterns

The clinician must know the expected bleeding patterns for each type of postmenopausal hormone regimen, as aberrant bleeding signals the need for investigation. When a monthly cyclic progestogen is used, most women (estimates vary between 70 to 90%) have regular bleeding, commencing after the ninth day of taking the progestogen. If vaginal bleeding starts earlier than day 9, or if it is more intense or longer in duration than the individual's usual pattern, endometrial biopsy is advised.

Continuous combined estrogen-progestogen regimens cause erratic spotting and bleeding for up to 12 months after initiation. The higher (5 mg) dose of daily MPA causes more rapid cessation of bleeding than does the 2.5-mg MPA daily dose.[61] Continuous combined regimens induce endometrial atrophy, which is the reason that bleeding ceases within the first year of using this regimen. Because endometrial atrophy is likely to be present already in older women who have not used hormones since menopause, they tend to have little or no bleeding with continuous combined estrogen-progestin. Although few studies of bleeding patterns in older women have been done, one study of women aged 65 years and over when continuous combined therapy was begun reported that only 30% experienced any vaginal bleeding during the first year.[62] When continuous estrogen-progestin is prescribed, endometrial assessment is recommended during the first year only if vaginal bleeding is heavy or extended;

this is a rather subjective judgment. If bleeding continues beyond 12 months, endometrial assessment is recommended.

Rarely, a woman with an intact uterus (eg, someone who has been intolerant to any progestogen regimen) will want to use unopposed estrogen. In the longest trial of unopposed estrogen use (with 0.625 mg of conjugated equine estrogens), 62% of women randomized to this treatment developed endometrial hyperplasia over the 3 years of the study; roughly half of the cases of hyperplasia were complex or atypical.[41] Baseline and annual endometrial biopsies are necessary when using unopposed estrogen, and any vaginal bleeding requires endometrial biopsy assessment.

Endometrial Monitoring

Endometrial biopsy is necessary for surveillance of endometrial safety during the use of unopposed estrogen. Vaginal ultrasound is not helpful, as virtually all women taking unopposed estrogen develop a double-layer endometrial thickness greater than 5 mm.[63] Thus, the specificity of vaginal ultrasound to diagnose endometrial hyperplasia (using a 5-mm cut point) is only 10%; this increases slightly, to 12%, if simple hyperplasia is excluded from consideration. Relaxing the abnormal criterion to a 9-mm double-layer ultrasound thickness increases the positive predictive value to only 15%. Conversely, the negative predictive value of a vaginal ultrasound thickness of less than 5 mm used is 99%. However, because most women using unopposed estrogen have a measurement of greater than 5 mm, testing women with ultrasound prior to performing a biopsy would seldom prevent the performance of biopsies.

When cyclic or continuous combined estrogen and progestogen regimens are used, baseline or routine follow-up assessments of the endometrium are unnecessary. However, evaluation is recommended if bleeding does not cease after approximately 12 months of continuous combined hormone use, if vaginal bleeding occurs prior to day 9 of cyclic progestogen use, and if the patient's bleeding pattern changes markedly with either regimen. In the case of continuous or cyclic combined hormone use, the negative predictive value of a vaginal ultrasound thickness of less than 5 mm is 99% for any degree of endometrial hyperplasia.[63] At first it may seem that vaginal ultrasound testing would be a good first test to evaluate unscheduled or uncharacteristic bleeding; however, approximately half of women taking either cyclic or continuous combination therapy develop an endometrial thickness of greater than 5 mm; thus, this strategy is not an efficient one.

Contraindications and Complications

Undiagnosed vaginal bleeding, current breast or endometrial cancer, and active deep vein thrombosis are absolute contraindications to estrogen use. Other medical conditions that require special consideration with respect to safety, but do not exclude hormone use, include cured stage 1 endometrial cancer, melanoma, and breast cancer. Use of estrogen after low-grade stage 1 endometrial cancer has not been associated with adverse effects, and most experts find it acceptable to prescribe hormone replacement

in such cases.[64] Although the data for an association between melanoma and estrogen treatment are not strong, the use of estrogen in this instance remains controversial.[65] Recent years have witnessed continued debate over the use of postmenopausal hormones by breast cancer survivors;[66] definitive evidence for toxicity or safety does not exist. Oral estrogens may pose risks to women with hepatobiliary disease and hypertriglyceridemia. Transdermal estrogen may be a safer choice, as it avoids first-pass hepatic metabolism. Observational studies and a large clinical trial have found that estrogens, both oral and transdermal, increase the risk of deep vein thrombosis (DVT) by approximately two- to threefold.[67–69] Estrogens should therefore be used with caution in women who are at high risk for DVT. Oral estrogens increase the risk of cholelithiasis.[69]

RESOURCE

The North American Menopause Society
5900 Landerbrook Drive, Suite 195
Mayfield Heights, Ohio 44124
Telephone: (440) 442-7550
Web site: www.menopause.org

The *North American Menopause Society provides information about menopause for clinicians and patients including updates on traditional treatments, complimentary approaches, and research advances.*

REFERENCES

1. Greendale GA, Sowers MF. The menopause transition. Endocrinol Metab Clin North Am 1997;26:261–77.
2. Lee SJ, Lenton EA, Sexton L, Cooke ID. The effect of age on the cyclical patterns of plasma LH, FSH, oestradiol and progesterone in women with regular menstrual cycles. Hum Reprod 1988;3:851–55.
3. MacNaughton J, Bangah M, McCloud P, et al. Age related changes in follicle stimulating hormone, luteinizing hormone, oestradiol and immunoreactive inhibin in women of reproductive age. Clin Endocrinol 1992;36:339–45.
4. Metcalf MG, Livesey JG. Gonadotrophin excretion in fertile women: effect of age and the onset of the menopausal transition. J Endocrinol 1985;104:357–62.
5. Burger HG, Dudley EC, Hopper JL, et al. The endocrinology of the menopausal transition: a cross-sectional study of a population-based sample. J Clin Endocrinol Metab 1995;80:3537–45.
6. McKinlay SM, Brambilla PJ, Posner JG. The normal menopause transition. Maturitas 1992;14:103–15.
7. Sherman BM, West JM, Korenman SC. The menopausal transition: analysis of LH, FSH, estradiol and progesterone concentrations during menstrual cycles of older women. J Clin Endocrinol Metab 1976;42:629–36.
8. Vagenakis AG. Endocrine aspects of menopause. Clin Rheumatol 1989;8:48–51.
9. Thompson B, Hart SA, Durno D. Menopausal age and symptomatology in a general practice. J Biosoc Sci 1973;5:71–82.
10. Beyene Y. Cultural significance and physiological manifestations of menopause: a biocultural analysis. Cult Med Psychiatry 1986;10:47–71.

11. Ginsberg ES. Hot flashes-physiology, hormonal therapy, and alternative therapies. Obstet Gynecol Clin North Am 1994;21:381–90.

12. Loprinzi CL, Michalak JC, Quella SK, et al. Megestrol acetate for the prevention of hot flashes. N Engl J Med 1994;331:347–52.

13. Greendale GA, Zibecchi L, Petersen L, et al. Development and validation of a physical examination scale to assess vaginal atrophy and inflammation. Climacteric 1999;2:197–204.

14. Griebling TL, Nygaard IE. The role of estrogen replacement therapy in the management of urinary incontinence and urinary tract infection in postmenopausal women. Endocrinol Metab Clin North Am 1997;26:347–60.

15. Walter S, Wolf H, Barlebo H. Urinary incontinence in postmenopausal women treated with estrogens. Urol Int 1978;33:135–43.

16. Fantl JA, Bump RC, Robinson D, et al. Efficacy of estrogen supplementation in the treatment of urinary incontinence. Obstet Gynecol 1996;88:745–9.

17. Fantl JA, Cardozo L, McClish DK, Estrogen therapy in the management of urinary incontinence in postmenopausal women: a meta-analysis. Obstet Gynecol 1994:83:12–8.

18. Raz R, Stamm WE. A controlled trial of intravaginal estriol in postmenopausal women with recurrent urinary tract infections. N Engl J Med 1993;329:753–60.

19. Eriksen BC. A randomized, open, parallel-group study on the preventive effect of an estradiol-releasing vaginal ring (Estring) on recurrent urinary tract infections in postmenopausal women. Am J Obstet Gynecol 1999;180:1072–9.

20. Diokno AC, Brown MB, Herzog AR. Sexual function in the elderly. Arch Intern Med 1990;150:197–200.

21. Lindgren R, Berg G, Hammar M, Zuccon E. Hormonal replacement therapy and sexuality in a population of Swedish postmenopausal women. Acta Obstet Gynecol Scand 1993;72:292–7.

22. Sherwin BB, Gelfand MM, Brender W. Androgen enhances sexual motivation in females: a prospective, crossover study of sex steroid administration in the surgical menopause. Psychosom Med 1985;47:339–51.

23. Casson PR, Carson SA. Androgen replacement therapy in women: myths and realities. Int J Fertil 1996;41:412–22.

24. Shifren JL, Braunstein GD, Simon JA, et al. Transdermal testosterone treatment in women with impaired sexual function after oophorectomy. N Engl J Med 2000;343:682–8.

25. Myers LS, Dixen J, Morrissette D, et al. Effects of estrogen, androgen and progestin on sexual psychophysiology and behavior in postmenopausal women. J Clin Endocrinol Metab 1990;70:1124–31.

26. Gelfand MM, Wittu B. Androgen and estrogen-androgen hormone replacement therapy: a review of the safety literature, 1941–1996. Clin Ther 1997;19:383–404.

27. Pearlstein T, Rosen K, Stone AB. Mood disorders and menopause. Endocrinol Metab Clin North Am 1997;26:279–94.

28. Avis NE, Brambilla D, McKinlay SM, Vass K. A longitudinal analysis of the association between menopause and depression. Results from the Massachusetts Women's Health Study. Ann Epidemiol 1994;4:214–20.

29. Hunter MS. Psychological and somatic experience of the menopause: a prospective study. Psychosom Med 1990;52:357–67.

30. Hay AG, Bancroft J, Johnstone EC. Affective symptoms in women attending a menopause clinic. Br J Psychiatry 1994;164:513–6.

31. Schneider LS, Small GW, Hamilton SH, et al. Estrogen replacement and response to fluoxetine in a multicenter geriatric depression trial. Am J Geriatr Psychiatry 1997;5:97–106.

32. Greendale GA, Lee NP, Arriola ER. The menopause. Lancet 1999;353:571–80

33. Steinberg KK, Thaker, SB, Smith J, et al. Meta-analysis of the effect of estrogen replacement therapy on the risk of breast cancer. JAMA 1991;265:1985–90.

34. Chai CU, Redker PM, Manson JE. Postmenopausal hormone replacement and cardiovascular disease. Thromb Haemost 1997;78:70–80.

35. Cumming RG, Mitchell P. Hormone replacement therapy, reproductive factors, and cataract. Am J Epidemiol 1997;145:242–9.

36. Yaffee K, Sawaya G, Lieberburg I, Grady D. Estrogen therapy in postmenopausal women: effects on cognitive function and dementia. JAMA 1998;279:688–95.

37. Krall EA, Dawson-Hughes B, Hannan MT, et al. Postmenopausal estrogen replacement and tooth retention. Am J Med 1997;102:536–42.

38. Potter JD. Hormones and colon cancer. J Natl Cancer Inst 1995;87:1039–40.

39. Sowers MFR, La Pietra MT. Menopause: its epidemiology and association with chronic diseases. Epidemiol Rev 1995;17:287–302.

40. Grady D, Rubin SM, Petitti DB, et al. Hormone therapy to prevent disease and prolong life in post-

menopausal women. Ann Intern Med 1992; 117:1016–37.

41. The Writing Group for the PEPI Trial. Effects of hormone therapy on endometrial histology in postmenopausal women: the Postmenopausal Estrogen/ Progestin Interventions (PEPI) trial. JAMA 1996; 275:370–5.

42. Mack TM, Pike MC, Henderson BE, et al. Estrogens and endometrial cancer in a retirement community. N Engl J Med 1976;294:1262–7.

43. Grady D, Ernster VL. Hormone replacement therapy and endometrial cancer: are current regimens safe [Editorial]? J Natl Cancer Inst 1997;89:1088–9.

44. Cerin A, Heldaas K, Moeller B. Adverse endometrial effects of long-cycle estrogen and progestogen replacement therapy [letter]. N Engl J Med 1996; 334:668–9.

45. Woodruff JD, Pickar JH. Incidence of endometrial hyperplasia in postmenopausal women taking conjugated estrogens (Premarin) with medroxyprogesterone acetate or conjugated estrogens alone. Am J Obstet Gynecol 1994;170:1213–23.

46. Bolaji II, Grimes H, Mortimer G, et al. Low-dose progesterone therapy in oestrogenised postmenopausal women: effects on plasma lipids, lipoproteins and liver function parameters. Eur J Obstet Gynecol Reprod Biol 1993;48:61–8.

47. Gillet JY, Andre G, Faguer B, et al. Induction of amenorrhea during hormone replacement therapy: optimal micronized progesterone dose: a multicenter study. Maturitas 1994;19:103–15.

48. The Transdermal HRT Investigators Group. A randomized study to compare the effectiveness, tolerability, and acceptability of two different transdermal estradiol replacement therapies. Int J Fertil 1993;38:5–11.

49. Mettler L, Olsen PG. Long-term treatment of atrophic vaginitis with low-dose oestradiol vaginal tablets. Maturitas 1991;14:12–31.

50. Mattson LA, Cullberg G, Eriksson O, Knutsson F. Vaginal administration of low-dose oestradiol-effects on the endometrium and vaginal cytology. Maturitas 1989;11:217–222.

51. Vooijs GP, Geurts TBP. Review of the endometrial safety during intravaginal treatment with estriol. Eur J Obstet Gynecol Reprod Biol 1995;62:101–06.

52. Kicovic PM, Cortes-Prieto J, Milojevic S., et al. The treatment of postmenopausal vaginal atrophy with ovestin vaginal cream or suppositories: clinical, endocrinological and safety aspects. Maturitas 1992;2:275–82.

53. Nachtigall LE. Clinical trial of the estradiol vaginal ring in the U.S. Maturitas 1995;22:S43–7.

54. Smith P, Heimer G, Lindskog M, Ulmsten U. Oestradiol-releasing vaginal ring for treatment of postmenopausal urogenital atrophy. Maturitas 1995;16:145–54.

55. Naessen T, Bergund L, Ulmsten U. Bone loss in elderly women prevented by ultralow doses of parenteral 17beta-estradiol. Am J Obstet Gynecol 1997;177:115–19.

56. Nachtigall LE. Replens versus local estrogen in menopausal women. Fertil Steril 1994;61:178–80.

57. The Writing Group for the PEPI Trial. Effects of estrogen or estrogen/progestin regimens on heart disease risk factors in postmenopausal women. JAMA 1995;273:199–208.

58. Jensen J. The effects of sex steroids on serum lipids and lipoproteins. Baillieres Clin Obstet Gynaecol 1991;5:867–87.

59. Grodstein F, Stampfer MJ, Manson JE, et al. Postmenopausal estrogen and progestin use and the risk of cardiovascular disease. N Engl J Med 1996; 335:453–61.

60. Nabulsi AA, Folsom AR, White A, et al. Association of hormone-replacement therapy with various cardiovascular risk factors in postmenopausal therapy with various cardiovascular risk factors in postmenopausal women. N Engl J Med 1993;328:1069–75.

61. Archer DF, Pickar JH, Bottoglioni F, for the Menopause Study Group. Bleeding patterns in postmenopausal women taking continuous combined or sequential regimens of medroxyprogesterone acetate. Obstet Gynecol 1994;83:686–92.

62. Christiansen C, Riis BJ. 17ß-estradiol and continuous norethisterone: a unique treatment for established osteoporosis in elderly women. J Clin Endocrinol Metab 1990;71:836–41.

63. Langer RD, Pierce JJ, O'Hanlan KA, et al. Transvaginal ultrasonography compared with endometrial biopsy for the detection of endometrial disease. N Engl J Med 1997;337:1792–8.

64. ACOG committee opinion: Committee on Gynecologic Practice. Estrogen replacement therapy and endometrial cancer. J Gynecol Obstet 1993;43:89.

65. Francheschi S, Baron AE, La Vecchia C. The influence of female hormones on malignant melanoma. Tumori 1990;76:439–49.

66. Cobleigh MA, Berris RF, Bush T, et al. Estrogen replacement in breast cancer survivors. A time for change. JAMA 1994;272:540–5.

67. Perez Gutthan S, Garcia Rodriguez LA, Castellsague J, Duque Oliart A. Hormone replacement therapy and risk of venous thromboembolism: population based case-control study. BMJ 1997;314:796–800.

68. Douketis JD, Ginsbert JS, Holbrook A, et al. A re-evaluation of the risk for venous thromboembolism with the use of oral contraceptives and hormone replacement therapy. Arch Intern Med 1997;157: 1522–30.

69. Hulley S, Grady D, Bush T, et al. Randomized trial of estrogen plus progestin for secondary prevention of coronary heart disease in postmenopausal women. Heart and Estrogen/Progestin Replacement Study (HERS) research group. JAMA 1998;280:605–13.

5

APPROACH TO THE

GERIATRIC PATIENT

Teresa Pham, MD

The geriatric population is widely heterogeneous, ranging from the active person who is fully independent to the frail elderly person with multiple chronic medical conditions and functional disabilities. As the prevalence of chronic diseases increases with age, clinicians face the challenge of shifting from the paradigm of curing a disease to one of identifying and treating modifiable factors with the goal of optimizing functional status and preserving social independence. A comprehensive approach that goes beyond the medical evaluation and incorporates cognitive, psychological, environmental, and socioeconomic factors is essential in accomplishing this goal. This chapter focuses on the approach to the geriatric patient in the ambulatory care setting.

MEDICAL ASSESSMENT

Several features distinguish the medical assessment of the elderly from that of the younger patient. Many elderly tend to under-report their illness symptoms.[1] This may be a reflection of cultural or educational biases or the belief that illness is a normal part of the aging process and that nothing can be done about it.[2] In addition, the fear of disability and loss of independence can contribute to the denial process. This can lead to a delay in diagnosis and treatment, with increased morbidity and functional losses. The presentation of diseases in the elderly can be nonspecific or atypical due to altered age-related physiologic responses.[3] For example, a myocardial infarction or perforated ulcer can be painless. A patient with pneumonia may present without fever or chills and minimal cough. Thyro-

toxicosis may present as severe apathy associated with weight loss, mimicking depression.[4] An acute decline in functional status (eg, worsening confusion, increased falls, new-onset incontinence) may be the primary presentation of an illness. In addition to obtaining the standard medical history, clinicians should screen for common geriatric conditions, including visual and hearing impairments, impaired mobility, malnutrition, urinary incontinence, and polypharmacy.

Sensory Impairment

Visual and hearing impairments are common in the elderly and can significantly impact function, safety, and quality of life. The leading causes of visual impairment in elderly people are presbyopia, cataracts, age-related macular degeneration, glaucoma, and diabetic retinopathy.[5] Visual impairment is often under-reported in the elderly population. A standard screen of visual acuity is the Snellen eye chart. Patients fail the screen if they are unable to read the letters on the 20/40 line from 20 feet away with their corrective lenses on (when applicable). Visual function also can be assessed by having patient read a headline and sentence from a newspaper. Patients with visual-related complaints or with functionally significant visual loss should be referred for further evaluation. However, tests of visual acuity alone may not detect early signs of age-related macular degeneration, glaucoma, or diabetic retinopathy. The US Preventive Services Task Force (USPSTF)[6] and Canadian Task Force[5] recommend that diabetics and older persons at higher risk for glaucoma (ie, with a positive family history, diabetic, with severe myopia, or African American over age 40 years) be referred for periodic complete opthalmologic examination.

Hearing impairment affects at least one-third of those over 65 years and three-fourths of those over 80 years.[7] The most common cause is presbycusis, with bilateral loss of high frequencies. Many older patients may not complain of, or even recognize, that they have a problem with their hearing. However, as hearing loss can negatively impact social, emotional, and cognitive function, older patients or their families should be asked periodically about problems with their hearing. Screening in the office can be performed using an audioscope. Further audiologic testing is indicated if a patient is unable to hear either 1,000- or 2,000-Hz frequency in both ears or both 1,000- and 2,000-Hz frequencies in one ear. An alternative test is the "whisper test."[8] Three to six random words are whispered behind the patient's ear, with the opposite ear covered. Failure to repeat half of the words correctly indicates a need for further testing. Cerumen impaction can contribute to hearing impairment; therefore cerumen should be removed prior to audiologic testing. Useful techniques to optimize communication include speaking to the patient in a low-pitched voice, elimination of background noise, and directly facing the patient.

Malnutrition and Weight Loss

The prevalence of malnutrition in the elderly population was found to be about 3% in a population of ambulatory care patients.[9] The prevalence is higher in hospitalized and institutionalized patients, approaching 50 to 60%. Physicians often underdiagnose malnutrition.[10] A history of weight loss of more than 5% of total body weight in 1 month or 10% in 6 months is clinically significant and warrants further evaluation. Serum albumin level is an indicator of chronic protein status and has been used as a marker of malnutrition. However, it is also a negative acute-phase reactant and can decrease in acute illness in the absence of protein deprivation. Hypocholesterolemia has been associated with increased mortality in the elderly and may be another marker of malnutrition.

In addition to acute illness and recent surgery, multiple other factors may contribute to weight loss in the elderly. Of particular note, low income and functional disabilities may be barriers to access to food. Xerostomia may occur from medication use or radiotherapy. Prior stroke and/or dementia may

TABLE 5–1. Risk Factors for Weight Loss and Malnutrition

Barriers to access to food
Functional impairment
Poverty
Impaired taste sensation
Xerostomia
Sjögren's syndrome
Dental problems
Loose fitting dentures
Oral lesions
Dementia
Depression
Hyperthyroidism
Chronic pain
Dysphagia
Parkinson's disease
Malabsorption
Alcoholism
Malignancy
Hyperthyroidism

contribute to dysphagia. Dental problems such as loose-fitting dentures and oral lesions are common reasons for weight loss and malnutrition. These and other causes of weight loss and malnutrition are summarized in Table 5–1.

Gait and Balance Impairment

Accidents are the fifth leading cause of death in the elderly, with two-thirds of accidents being related to falls. Falls occur in about one-third of community-dwelling elderly above the age of 65 years, and about half of those who fall do so repeatedly.[11] Falls are a significant source of morbidity in the elderly, with about 15% of falls resulting in physical injury requiring medical attention, and 5% of falls resulting in fractures.[12] In addition to the physical consequences, a psychological fear of falling may develop, which often leads to a limitation of activities. Falls are a significant contributing factor in admissions to nursing homes.

The causes of falls are usually multifactorial. Chronic medical conditions that impair sensory, neurologic, and musculoskeletal functioning can predispose to instability of gait and balance. Acute medical illnesses such as pneumonia, urosepsis, and

---

TABLE 5–2. Risk Factors for Falls

Acute illness (pneumonia, urosepsis, CHF)

Sensory deficits (vision, hearing, vestibular, proprioception)

Cardiovascular (cardiac arrhythmias, aortic stenosis, syncope, carotid sinus hypersensitivity)

Neurologic (stroke, dementia, Parkinson's disease, seizure disorder, cervical/lumbar myelopathy, radiculopathy, cerebellar disease, normal pressure hydrocephalus, CNS lesions, vestibular disease, peripheral neuropathy)

Musculoskeletal (foot deformities, callouses, bunions, arthritis)

Drug-related causes (sedatives, antipsychotics, alcohol, antihypertensives, diuretics, oral hypoglycemics)

Orthostatic hypotension (drug-induced, autonomic dysfunction, deconditioning, postprandial)

Environmental hazards (poor lighting, slippery surfaces, loose rugs, ill-fitting shoes)

CHF = congestive heart failure, CNS = central nervous system.

congestive heart failure can precipitate falls. Other risk factors for falls include postural hypotension, use of sedatives, and polypharmacy.[13] Environmental hazards also contribute to a large number of falls. An assessment of the intrinsic and extrinsic risk factors (Table 5–2), along with a targeted physical examination and a gait-and-balance evaluation are key components to formulating interventions to decrease the risk of falls and resultant morbidity.

The "Get Up and Go" test,[14] which can be done quickly in the office, is a useful tool for assessing functional mobility. The patient is asked to rise from an arm chair, walk 3 m, turn, walk back, and sit down again. Observation of sitting and standing balance, ability to transfer, pace, and stability with walking and turning can provide useful insight into the level of intervention needed. Any difficulties warrant further evaluation, particularly focusing on the cardiovascular, neurologic, and musculoskeletal examination. Modification of risk factors has been shown to decrease the risk of falling among community-dwelling elderly.[15] In addition to medical or surgical interventions directed at the underlying problems, some patients also may benefit from physical therapy aimed at gait, balance training, and strengthening exercises. Environmental modifications including a home safety evaluation and assess-

ment for appropriate use of assistive devices are also essential components of intervention. A home safety checklist (Figure 5–1) can be distributed to patients and their families.

Urinary Incontinence

The prevalence of urinary incontinence in community-dwelling adults is estimated to be about 15 to 30%,[16] affecting twice as many women as men. It is commonly under-reported, either because of embarrassment or because of misconception that the condition is untreatable or is a normal part of aging. As urinary incontinence can be a social and psychological burden for the patient, treatment can significantly improve quality of life. Furthermore, most initial treatment options are nonsurgical (Kegel exercises, medications, management of fluid intake, biofeedback, timed voiding). Incontinence can be screened for by asking patients, "In the last year, have you ever lost your urine or gotten wet?" For further details on urinary incontinence, refer to Chapter 86.

Polypharmacy

Most elderly persons take at least one medication and many take more than one due to multiple chronic medical conditions. They are at higher risk for adverse reactions and drug interactions.[17] All medications taken by the patient, including over-the-counter drugs, should be reviewed at every visit. In prescribing medications, physicians should keep in mind factors that may limit patient compliance, including cost, frequency of dosing, and side effect profile.

COGNITIVE ASSESSMENT

The prevalence of dementia increases with age, affecting 5 to 15% of those older than 65 years and 20 to 50% of those greater than 85 years. Patients with dementia have a higher mortality rate and greater use of health care services.[18] The early diagnosis of dementia is important, as there is evidence supporting the use of cholinesterase inhibitors and antioxidants to improve function in mild to moderate stages of Alzheimer's dementia.[19,20] Cognitive impairment affects all aspects of functioning, and in the advanced stages it can pose a significant psychological and financial burden for the caregiver. With early diagnosis families can be provided with

	YES	NO
Housekeeping		
Do you clean up spills as soon as they occur?	☐	☐
Do you keep floors and stairways free of clutter?	☐	☐
Do you put away personal items as soon as you are through with them?	☐	☐
Floors		
Do you stay off newly washed floors till they dry?	☐	☐
If you wax floors, do you apply thin coats and buff thoroughly or use self-polishing nonskid wax?	☐	☐
Do all small rugs have nonskid backings?	☐	☐
Have you eliminated small rugs at the head and foot of each stairway?	☐	☐
Are rugs and carpets free of tears and other defects?	☐	☐
Do you have carpeting with short dense pile?	☐	☐
Bathroom		
Have you installed rubber mats or nonslip decals in tubs or showers?	☐	☐
Do you have grab bars in tubs and showers?	☐	☐
Do you have a nonskid rug on the bathroom floor?	☐	☐
Do you keep soap in an easy-to-reach receptacle?	☐	☐
Traffic Lane		
Can you walk through rooms without detouring the furniture?	☐	☐
Are paths from bedrooms to bathrooms obstacle free?	☐	☐
Are telephone and appliance cords kept off floors where people walk?	☐	☐
Lighting		
Do you have a light switch near every doorway?	☐	☐
Does your lighting eliminate shadowy areas?	☐	☐
Is a lamp or light switch within reach of your bed?	☐	☐
Are there night-lights in bathrooms and hallways?	☐	☐
Are all stairways well lighted?	☐	☐
Stairways		
Do handrails extend the full length of the stairs?	☐	☐
Can you get a good grip on handrails?	☐	☐
Are stairways free of broken or sagging steps?	☐	☐
Are all stairway carpets and molding edges securely fastened and in good condition?	☐	☐
Have you replaced single steps with ramps or made sure such steps are well lighted?	☐	☐

	YES	NO
Ladders and Step Stools		
Do you have a step stool to reach high shelves?	☐	☐
Are ladders and step stools in good condition?	☐	☐
Do you always set up a ladder or step stool on firm level base, free of clutter?	☐	☐
Are items on shelves within easy reach?	☐	☐
Before you climb a stepladder, do you make sure it is fully open and the spreaders are locked?	☐	☐
When you use a ladder, do you face the steps and keep your body between the side rails?	☐	☐
Do you avoid standing on the top step of a stepladder?	☐	☐
Outdoor Areas		
Are outside walks and driveways free of breaks?	☐	☐
Do you put away garden tools and hoses after use?	☐	☐
Are outdoor areas kept free of tripping hazards?	☐	☐
Do you keep outdoor, walkways, steps and porches free of wet leaves and snow?	☐	☐
Do you have doormats at doorways?	☐	☐
Footwear		
Do your shoes provide good traction?	☐	☐
Do you wear house slippers that fit snuggly?	☐	☐
Do you avoid walking in stocking feet?	☐	☐
Do you wear oxfords, loafers, or sneakers when you work in the house or yard?	☐	☐
Personal Precautions		
Are you always alert for unexpected hazards?	☐	☐
If children visit, do you watch for them playing on the floor or for toys left in your path?	☐	☐
If you have pets, do you watch for them when they get underfoot?	☐	☐
Do you make sure that bulky packages you carry do not obstruct your vision?	☐	☐
Do you carry small loads instead of big ones?	☐	☐
When you reach or bend, do you hold onto a support and refrain from turning too far?	☐	☐
Do you avoid rushing to answer the phone or front door?	☐	☐
Do you pause to get your balance when you sit up or stand up?	☐	☐
Is your eyeglass prescription up-to-date?	☐	☐
If you live alone, do you have daily contact with a relative, friend or neighbor?	☐	☐

FIGURE 5–1. Home safety checklist. Reproduced with permission from The National Safety Council. Falling—an unexpected trip: a safety program for older adults. Program Leader's Guide. Chicago: National Safety Council; 1982.

prognostic information and assistance in planning for future health care and psychosocial needs. The most commonly used screening instrument in the United States is the Mini-Mental State Examination (Figure 5–2), which tests for orientation, attention, short-term memory, language, calculation, and construction abilities. A score of less than 24 is suggestive of a moderately severe cognitive impairment; however, this must be interpreted within context of the patient's educational and cultural background. Superimposed depression also may impair cognitive performance, contributing to a "pseudodementia" syndrome. Documentation of mental status is useful to establish a baseline for patients with cognitive impairments, as they are at increased risk for delerium, particularly in the setting of a superimposed acute illness. Chapter 65, "Dementia," contains detailed information on currently available treatments.

AFFECTIVE ASSESSMENT

The prevalence of major depression among community-dwelling older persons is estimated to be up to about 5%,[21] similar to that of general population. Depressive symptoms, however, are much more common in the elderly. Depression is often under-recognized by both patients and physicians because many somatic symptoms of depression (eg, fatigue, poor appetite, insomnia) also accompany many of the medical illnesses common to the elderly. Depression in the elderly also can manifest with symptoms of dementia such as memory loss, poor concentration, and disorientation. Patients can be screened with the question, "Do you often feel sad or depressed?"[22] or with Yesavage's Geriatric Depression Scale (Figure 5–3).

FUNCTIONAL ASSESSMENT

The measurement of functional status is a key component in the evaluation of the geriatric patient. It is a measure of the patient's capacity to perform functional tasks necessary for daily living within the context of her medical conditions and social support system. The basic activities of daily living are basic self-care tasks (bathing, dressing, toileting, feeding, and transferring). The instrumental or intermediate activities of daily living assesses for ability to perform skills necessary to live independently in the community (shopping, housework, food preparation, transportation, using the telephone, taking medications, handling finances). Identification of impairments should trigger inquiry into the causes and potential for intervention. For example, an abrupt functional decline may be due to a potentially reversible acute illness. Functional status provides prognostic information and can be an essential factor in guiding and planning for future care.

SOCIAL ASSESSMENT

An essential part of the social history is identification of caregivers and social support network (eg, spouse, family, friends, neighbors). The extent of social support available can be the key determinant in the elderly person's ability to remain living in the community. Economic factors also impact on the patient's ability to obtain food and medications. The health care clinician can facilitate referrals to social work for assistance in determining eligibility for benefits as well as making provisions for long-term care. The frail older patient also may benefit from referrals to community resources such as adult day care, home health care services, and meal delivery programs.

Caring for an elderly family member with physical and cognitive impairments can be physically and psychologically stressful. The current trend suggests that increasingly adults are becoming caregivers to their elderly parents, spouses, or relatives. Almost three-fourths of all caregivers are women, with one-fourth being over 65 years themselves.[23] Health care clinicians should not overlook an assessment of caregiver burden and, when appropriate, make referrals for home care services, respite care, or support groups.

ADVANCE DIRECTIVES

A discussion of the patient's goals and treatment preferences should be a part of the comprehensive assessment. Documentation of an advance directive is useful for guiding therapy, particularly when the patient is no longer able to speak for herself. In the durable power of attorney for health care, the patient designates a surrogate to make medical decisions in the event that the patient is incapable of doing so. Particularly in the patient with early dementia, these issues should be addressed while the patient is capable cognitively.

MiniMental LLC

NAME OF SUBJECT _____ Age _____

NAME OF EXAMINER _____ Years of School Completed _____

Approach the patient with respect and encouragement. Date of Examination _____

Ask: Do you have any trouble with your memory? ☐ Yes ☐ No

May I ask you some questions about your memory? ☐ Yes ☐ No

SCORE ITEM

5 ( ) **TIME ORIENTATION**
Ask:
What is the year _____ (1), season _____ (1),
month of the year _____ (1), date _____ (1),
day of the week _____ (1)?

5 ( ) **PLACE ORIENTATION**
Ask:
Where are we now? What is the state _____ (1), city_____ (1),
part of the city _____ (1), building _____ (1),
floor of the building _____ (1)?

3 ( ) **REGISTRATION OF THREE WORDS**
Say: Listen carefully. I am going to say three words. You say them back after I stop.
Ready? Here they are—PONY (wait 1 second), QUARTER (wait 1 second), ORANGE (wait one second).
What were those words?
_____ (1)
_____ (1)
_____ (1)
Give 1 point for each correct answer, then repeat them until the patient learns all three.

5 ( ) **SERIAL 7s AS A TEST OF ATTENTION AND CALCULATION**
Ask: Subtract 7 from 100 and continue to subtract 7 from each subsequent remainder until I tell you to stop. What is 100 take away 7 ? _____ (1)
Say:
Keep going. _____ (1), _____ (1),
_____ (1), _____ (1).

3 ( ) **RECALL OF THREE WORDS**
Ask:
What were those three words I asked you to remember?
Give one point for each correct answer. _____ (1),
_____ (1), _____ (1).

2 ( ) **NAMING**
Ask:
What is this? (show pencil) _____ (1). What is this? (show watch) _____ (1)

1 ( ) **REPETITION**
Say:
Now I am going to ask you to repeat what I say. Ready? No ifs, ands, or buts.
Now you say that. _____ (1)

3 ( ) **COMPREHENSION**
Say:
Listen carefully because I am going to ask you to do something:
Take this paper in your left hand (1), fold it in half (1), and put it on the floor. (1)

1 ( ) **READING**
Say:
Please read the following and do what it says, but do not say it aloud. (1)

Close your eyes

1 ( ) **WRITING**
Say:
Please write a sentence. If patient does not respond, say: Write about the weather. (1)
_____
_____

1 ( ) **DRAWING**
Say: Please copy this design.

[DoM1]

| | TOTAL SCORE | Assess level of consciousness along a continuum | | | | FUNCTION BY PROXY |

Alert Drowsy Stupor Coma

	YES	NO		YES	NO	
Cooperative:	☐	☐	Deterioration from			Please record date when patient was last able to perform the following tasks. Ask caregiver if patient independently handles:
Depressed:	☐	☐	previous level of functioning:	☐	☐	
Anxious:	☐	☐	Family History of Dementia:	☐	☐	
Poor Vision:	☐	☐	Head Trauma:	☐	☐	
Poor Hearing:	☐	☐	Stroke:	☐	☐	
Native Language:	☐	☐	Alcohol Abuse:	☐	☐	
			Thyroid Disease:	☐	☐	

FUNCTION BY PROXY

	YES	NO	DATE
Money/Bills:	☐	☐	_____
Medication:	☐	☐	_____
Transportation:	☐	☐	_____
Telephone:	☐	☐	_____

FIGURE 5–2. The Annotated Mini Mental State Examination. Reproduced with permission from "Mini-Mental State." A practical method for grading the cognitive state of patients for the clinician. J Psychiatr Res 1975;12(3):189–98. © 1975, 1998 MiniMental LLC.

Choose the best answer to describe how you have felt over the past week:

1. Are you basically satisfied with your life? . . . . YES / **NO**
2. Have you dropped many of your activities and interests? . . . . **YES** / NO
3. Do you feel that your life is empty?. . . . . **YES** / NO
4. Do you often get bored?. . . . . **YES** / NO
5. Are you in good spirits most of the time?. . . . . YES / **NO**
6. Are you afraid that something bad is going to happen to you? . . . . **YES** / NO
7. Do you feel happy most of the time?. . . . . YES / **NO**
8. Do you often feel helpless?. . . . . **YES** / NO
9. Do you prefer to stay at home, rather than going out and doing new things?. . . . . **YES** / NO
10. Do you feel you have more problems with memory than most? . . . . **YES** / NO
11. Do you think it is wonderful to be alive now?. . . . . YES / **NO**
12. Do you feel pretty worthless the way you are now? . . . . **YES** / NO
13. Do you feel full of energy?. . . . . YES / **NO**
14. Do you feel that your situation is hopeless? . . . . **YES** / NO
15. Do you think that most people are better off than you are?. . . . . **YES** / NO

Answers indicating depression appear in bold type. Each of these answers counts 1 point; a score between 5 and 9 indicates a strong probability of depression, and a score of 10 is almost always indicative of depression.

FIGURE 5–3. Scoring key and geriatric depression scale (short form). Reproduced with permission from Yesavage JA. Depression in the elderly. How to recognize masked symptoms and choose appropriate therapy. Postgrad Med,1992; 91:255–8. © The McGraw-Hill Companies.

PREVENTIVE HEALTH

The goals of preventive health in the elderly include reduction of morbidity and mortality as well as maximizing functional status and quality of life. There is often insufficient data or conflicting recommendations with regard to primary prevention in the elderly, particularly regarding the upper age limits for screening. The heterogeneity of the older population frequently calls for an individualized approach. The life expectancy of a healthy 65 year old is 15 to 20 years, whereas that of an 85 year old is about 5 to 7 years.[24] Some have proposed age 85 years as a point for cessation of screening, particularly in the cases of screening for early malignancies or asymptomatic disease that may take several years to manifest clinically. The potential benefits of screening must be considered within the context of the patient's remaining quality and quantity of life and the potential burden of diagnoses and treatment.

Cardiovascular Disease

Cardiovascular disease is the leading cause of mortality in women in the United States, accounting for more than one-third of deaths, with the incidence increasing with age. Modifiable risks for athero-sclerosis include hypertension, hyperlipidemia, diabetes, and cigarette smoking. The diagnosis and treatment of hypertension, including isolated systolic hypertension, have been shown to decrease the incidence and morbidity of cerebrovascular and cardiac events in the elderly.[25] Tobacco cessation reduces cardiovascular and pulmonary complications in all patients, including the elderly and women.[26] The treatment of hyperlipidemia in individuals with coronary heart disease (including the elderly) has been shown to decrease cardiovascular morbidity and mortality.[27,28] However, there is, insufficient data currently to support cholesterol screening in asymptomatic elderly patients over 75 years of age.[6]

Studies support the use of aspirin in patients with ischemic cardiovascular disease.[29] Low-dose aspirin (80 to 325 mg) is recommended for the prevention of cardiovascular and cerebrovascular events in men with risk factors for coronary heart disease and with no contraindication to aspirin use. To date there is inconclusive evidence in support of recommendations for aspirin use in women for primary prevention.

Cancer

Fifty percent of all cancers occur in older adults, with breast cancer being the most common cancer in women. The American Cancer Society[30] recommends annual mammograms for those over 40 years, with no upper age limit. The American Geriatrics Society[31] supports mammography every 2 to 3 years until at least age 85 years. The Forum for Breast Cancer Screening in Older Women recommends clinical breast examination yearly and biannual mammograms in women over 75 years in generally good health and with good life expectancy.[32]

Colorectal cancer is the second most common cancer, with the peak incidence occurring in the 70 to 80-year-old group. The American Cancer Society[6] recommends screening with annual fecal occult blood test after the age of 50 years and flexible sigmoidoscopy every 3 to 5 years. The USPSTF also supports checking fecal occult blood testing and/or flexible sigmoidoscopy, with unspecified frequency and no upper age limit.[6] However, as with screening for other cancers, the potential benefit of detection must be weighed with the overall health status and active life expectancy.

The USPSTF[6] and American College of Physicians[66] recommend that Papanicolaou (Pap) smear screening can cease after age 65 years if the patient has had regular prior normal screening Pap smears. The ACP recommends PAP screening every 3 years for those between 66 and 75 years of age who were not adequately screened previously, assuming that overall health and life expectancy warrant screening and treatment if indicated.

Immunizations

The pneumococcal polysaccharide vaccine and yearly influenza vaccine are generally recommended for all older persons without known contraindications.[66] The American College of Physicians recommends revaccination with the pneumoccal vaccine if the initial vaccine was given more than 6 years prior to age 65 years.[24] Tetanus is an uncommon disease; however 60% of the cases that occur are in those over 60 years.[33] The tetanus-diptheria booster is recommended every 10 years. Those who did not receive the primary series should receive three toxoid doses over 6 to 12 months.[6]

Osteoporosis

Osteoporotic fractures, particularly of the hip, are associated with decline in functional status and quality of life. About 25% of women over age 60 years have spinal compression fractures, and 15% sustain a hip fracture in their lifetime.[34] Risk factors for osteoporosis include female gender, low dietary intake of calcium, age, early menopause, low body weight, excessive alcohol intake, and sedentary lifestyle. Current use of estrogen is associated with a decreased risk for fractures, particularly when initiated within 5 years of menopause.[35] There is some evidence that initiation of estrogen in those well past menopause and into their seventies also decreases bone loss. The potential benefits of estrogen replacement therapy, must be weighed against the increased risk for endometrial and breast cancer with long-term use. Calcium (1200 mg/d) and vitamin D supplementation (800 IU/d) has been shown to reduce the risk of hip and other nonvertebral fractures.[36] Patients should be counseled regarding smoking cessation and regular weight-bearing exercises, which have been shown to improve bone mass. Alendronate, an oral bisphosphonate that inhibits bone resorption, also is approved for the prevention and treatment of osteoporosis.[37] It has been shown to increase bone mineral density and decrease risk of vertebral fracture. Other treatments for osteoporosis include risedronate, another biphosphonate raloxifene and calcitonin. This is discussed further in Chapter 47, "Osteoporosis." In the frail elderly patient with established osteoporosis and bone mass density below the fracture threshold, treatment of osteoporosis must be combined with measures to reduce risk for falls.

Thyroid disease

Screening for thyroid dysfunction in the asymptomatic general population is not warranted. However, as the prevalence of abnormal thyroid function is higher in older women, the American College of Physicians recommends screening women older than 50 years for unsuspected but symptomatic thyroid disease with a sensitive thyroid-stimulating hormone test.[38]

DRIVING SAFETY

Studies have shown higher rates of motor vehicle accidents in drivers with dementia.[39] Functional declines in vision, hearing, and motor skills, which are more prevalent with aging, also can impair driving safety. The state of California requires reporting of individuals with dementia by physicians to licensing agencies, although other states do not. Although a physician may advise a demented patient not to drive, actual compliance often requires reinforce-ment from family and friends. The American Association of Retired Persons offers driver re-education and testing programs for older drivers.

RESOURCES

American Association of Retired Persons
601 E Street, Northwest
Washington, DC 20049
Telephone: 1-800-424-3410
Web site: www.aarp.org

The American Association of Retired Persons (AARP) is a nonprofit, nonpartisan membership organization for people age 50 years and over. The AARP Web site offers health information, including information about community resources for the elderly and extensive information for caregivers.

American Geriatrics Society
The Empire State Building
350 Fifth Avenue, Suite 801
New York, New York 10118
Telephone: (212) 308-1414
Web site: www.americangeriatrics.org

The American Geriatrics Society is a professional society of over 6,000 physicians and other health care providers. Its Web site contains clinical practice guidelines and other information useful for the care of older women.

REFERENCES

1. Leventhal EA, Prohaska TR. Age, symptom interpretation, and health behavior. J Am Geriatr Soc 1986; 34:185–91.
2. Levkoff SE, Cleary PD, Wetle T, et al. Illness behavior in the aged. J Am Geriatr Soc. 1988;36:622–9.
3. Hodkinson HM. Non-specific presentation of illness. Br Med J 1973;4:96–8.
4. Thomas FB, Mazzaferri U, Skillman TG. Apathetic thyrotoxicosis: a distinctive clinical and laboratory entity. Ann Intern Med 1970;72:679–85.
5. Canadian Task Force on the Periodic Health Examination. Periodic health examination, 1995 update: 3. Screening for visual problems among elderly patients. Can Med Assoc J 1995;152:1211–22.
6. US Preventive Services Task Force. Guide to clinical and preventive services, 2nd ed. Baltimore: Williams & Wilkins; 1996.
7. Wilson PS, Fleming DM, Donaldson I. Prevalence of hearing loss among people aged 65 years and over; screening and hearing aid provision. Bri J Gen Pract 1993;43:406–9.
8. Macfee GJ, Crowther JA, McAlpine CH. A simple screening test for hearing impairment in elderly patients. Age Ageing 1988;17:347–51.
9. Manson A, Shea S. Malnutrition in elderly ambulatory medical patients. Am J Public Health 1991;81:1195–7.
10. Morley JE. Why do physicians fail to recognize and treat malnutrition in older persons. J Am Geriatr Soc 1991;39:1139–40.
11. Campbell AJ, Reinken J, Allen B, Martinez GS. Falls in old age: a study of frequency and related clinical factors. Age Ageing 1981;10:264–70.
12. Tinneti ME, Speechley M. Prevention of falls among the elderly. N Engl J Med 1989;320:1055–9.
13. Tinneti ME, Speechley M, Ginter SF. Risk factors for falls among elderly persons living in the community. N Engl J Med 1988;319:1701–7.
14. Mathias S, Nayak US, Isaacs B. Balance in elderly patients: the "Get Up and Go" test. Arch Phys Med Rehabil 1986;67:387–9.
15. Tinetti ME, Baker DI, McAvay G, et al. A multifunctional intervention to reduce the risk of falling among

elderly people living in the community. N Engl J Med 1994;331:821–7.

16. Diokno AC, Grock BM, Brown MB, et al. Prevalence of urinary incontinence and other urological symptoms in the noninstitutionalized elderly. J Urol 1986; 136:1022–5.

17. Montamat SC, Cusack KF, Vestal RE. Management of drug therapy in the elderly. N Engl J Med 1989; 321:303–9.

18. Callahan CM, Hendric HC, Tierney WM. Documentation and evaluation of cognitive impairment in elderly primary care patients. Ann Intern Med 1995;122:422–9.

19. Rogers SL, Farlow MR, Doody RS, et al. A 24-week, double-blind, placebo-controlled trial of donepezil in patients with Alzheimer's disease. Neurology 1998;50:136–45.

20. Sano M, Ernesto C, Thomas RG, et al. A controlled trial of selegiline, alpha-tocopherol, or both as treatment for Alzheimer's disease. N Engl J Med 1997; 336:1216–22.

21. Blazer D, Hughes DC, Tierney WN. The epidemiology of depression in an elderly community population. Gerontologist 1987;27:281–7.

22. Mahoney A, Drinkin JK, Abler R, et al. Screening for depression: single question vs. GDS. American Geriatrics Society. J Am Geriatr Soc 1994;42:1006–8.

23. Stone R, Caffereata GL, Sangl J. Caregivers of the frail elderly: a national profile. Gerontologist 1987;27: 616–26.

24. Goldberg TH, Chavin SI. Preventive medicine and screening in older adults. J Am Geriatr Soc. 1997; 45:344–54.

25. SHEP Cooperative Research Group. Prevention of stroke by antihypertensive drug treatment in older persons with isolated systolic hypertension: final results of the Systolic Hypertension in the Elderly Program (SHEP). JAMA 1991;265:3255–64.

26. Jajich C, Ostfeld A, Freeman D. Smoking and coronary heart disease mortality in the elderly. JAMA 1984;252:2831–4.

27. Scandinavian Simvastatin Survival Study Group. Randomized trial of cholesterol lowering in 4444 patients with coronary heart disease: the Scandinavian Simvastatin Survival Study (4S). Lancet 1994;344:1383–9.

28. Pederson TR, Kjekshus J, Pyorala K, et al. Effect of simvastatin on survival and coronary morbidity in coronary heart disease patients 65 or older. Circulation 1995;92:2419–25.

29. Krumholz HM, Radford MJ, Ellerbeck EF, et al. Aspirin for secondary prevention after acute myocardial infarction in the elderly: prescribed use and outcomes. Ann Intern Med 1996;124:292–8.

30. Smith RA, Mettlin CJ, Davis KJ, et al. American Cancer Society guidelines for the early detection of cancer. CA Cancer J Clin 2000;50:34–49.

31. Clinical Practice Committee, American Geriatrics Society. Screening for breast cancer in elderly women. J Am Geriatr Soc 1989;37:833–4.

32. Costanza ME. Breast cancer screening in older women: synopsis of a forum. Cancer 1992;69:1925–31.

33. Richardson JP, Knight AL. The prevention of tetanus in the elderly. Arch Intern Med 1991;151:1712–7.

34. Cummings SR, Kelsey JL, Nevitt MC, et al. Epidemiology of osteoporosis and osteoporotic fractures. Epidemiol Rev 1985;7:178–208.

35. Cauley JA. Seely DG, Ensrud K, et al. Estrogen replacement therapy and fractures in older women. Ann Intern Med 1995;122:9–16.

36. Chapuy MC, Arlot ME, Duboeuf F, et al. Vitamin D and calcium to prevent hip fractures in elderly women. N Engl J Med 1992;327:1637–42.

37. McClung M, Clemmesen B, Daifotis A, et al. Alendronate prevents postmenopausal bone loss in women without osteoporosis. Ann Intern Med 1998; 128:253–61.

38. American College of Physicians. Clinical guideline part 1. Screening for thyroid disease. Ann Intern Med 1998;129:141–3.

39. Friedland RP, Koss E, Kumar A, et al. Motor behicle crashes in dementia of the Alzheimer type. Ann Neurol 1988;24:782–6.

6

APPROACH TO THE PATIENT WITH DEVELOPMENTAL DISABILITIES

Mary Ann Lewis, DrPH, RN, FAAN, and Mary Lu Hickman, MD

Concepts of women's health are changing to include more wellness-oriented and holistic approaches that view women in the context of their lives. Nowhere is this more relevant than when it pertains to the health of women with developmental disabilities. Women with disabilities have not been viewed as being capable of making choices about a healthy lifestyle and being independent. On the contrary, women with disabilities have been perceived as being dependent, passive, and asexual beings incapable of human reproduction. They have been victimized and subject to physical, emotional, and sexual abuse.[1] One must be aware that individuals with developmental disabilities have the same capacity for emotional involvement, relationships, and depth of character as do all human beings. However, their disabilities make it difficult to develop the skills necessary to convey thoughts that reveal these capacities.

The purpose of this chapter is to increase health care clinicians' knowledge and understanding of the special health care needs of this unique population and to enhance expertise for delivering services in empowering ways that better assist women with developmental disabilities to attain balanced and healthy lifestyles.

The chapter briefly reviews the leading causes of developmental disabilities and the impact that level of cognition or the diagnosed condition exerts on prevalence of the most common health problems across the life span. Tips for managing the disability and, of equal importance, preventing secondary conditions that may lead to further limitations also are presented. This is followed by an exploration of issues pertinent to women with disabilities, including identification and management of problems of

depression, sexuality, and reproductive health, and counseling for avoidance of violence and abuse. We focus on assisting health professionals to develop attitudes that can enhance the quality of the patient-clinician interaction and increase the likelihood of optimal patient outcomes.

DEFINITION AND ETIOLOGY

During the late 1960s the term "developmental disabilities" was introduced to define clinical disorders and diseases that began early in life and required interdisciplinary and other support services.[2] The definition included a range of mild to serious impairments, including mental retardation, cerebral palsy, epilepsy, genetic disorders, and other childhood chronic diseases associated with developmental delay. Subsequent legislation in the United States [3,4] narrowed the definition to the onset of severe and chronic conditions, prior to 22 years of age, that are due to a mental or physical impairment and require interdisciplinary care. The impairments prevent an individual from performing the basic activities of daily living (bathing, dressing, toileting [continence bladder/bowel], walking, eating, and grooming) and intermediate activities of daily living (using the telephone, shopping, preparing meals, housekeeping, doing laundry, using public transportation, taking medications, and handling finances).

Currently, developmental disabilities affect approximately 4% of the U.S. population.[5] Prevalence data vary from state to state due to differing definitions. Therefore, accurate information is difficult to obtain. The diseases and clinical disorders associated

TABLE 6–1. Category of Origin, Associated Cause/Pathology, and Examples* of Developmental Disabilities

Category of Origin	Cause/Pathology	Examples† (prevalence per 1,000)
Hereditary	Metabolic disorders	Tay-Sachs disease (>0.01)[a]
		Phenylketonuria (0.08)[b]
		Maternal phenylketonuria (0.08)[c]
		Congenital hypothyroidism (0.33)[a]
		Hurler's syndrome (0.01)[b]
	Other single-gene abnormalities	Neurofibromatosis (0.02)[b]
		Tuberous sclerosis (0.6)[d]
		Muscular dystrophy (0.02–0.10)[d]
	Chromosomal abnormalities	Fragile X syndrome (0.7)[d]
Early alterations of embryonic development	Chromosomal changes	Down syndrome (1.0)[a]
	Intrauterine toxicity	Fetal alcohol syndrome (1.4)[a]
		Lead exposure toxicity
	Intrauterine infection	Congenital rubella syndrome (<0.1)[b]
		Congenital cytomegalovirus infections (3.0)[b]
		Congenital syphilis (0.2)[b]
	Structural malformations	Absence of or shortened limbs (0.5)[a]
		Hydrocephalus (1.8)[a]
		Microcephalus (0.5)[a]
		Spina bifida (0.4)[a]
Late pregnancy or perinatal conditions	Premature birth	Very low birth weight: <1500 g (12)[a]
		Central nervous system hemorrhage (6)[e]
		Retrolental fibroplasia (0.07)[b]
	Perinatal hypoxia	5-minute Apgar score <4 (6)[a]
Infection	Infection	Perinatally acquired human immunodeficiency virus infection (0.4)[b]
Acquired childhood conditions	Postnatal infection	Bacterial meningitis (0.8)[b]
		Measles encephalopathy (<0.1)[d]
	Childhood injury	Spinal cord injury (0.04)[f], (0.4)[g]
		Traumatic brain injury (2.2)[d]
		Near drowning (1.0)[d]
	Environmental toxicity	Lead encephalopathy (>0.1)[d]
		Low-lead toxicity (not available)[d]
	Psychosocial disadvantage	Mental retardation of deprivational causes (3–5)[d]
Unknown	Unknown	Autism (0.4)[d]
		Cerebral palsy (2–4)[d]
		Epilepsy (3.5)[d]
		Mental retardation of unknown cause (3–5)[d]
		Learning disorders (50–100)[d]

*With prevalence estimates.
†Superscript letters indicate the age group used in determining the prevalence estimates, as follows: [a] = at birth; [b] = early childhood; [c] = of all births; [d] = childhood; [e] = newborn period; [f] = age 10 years; and [g] = age 20 years.
Reproduced with permission from Institute of Medicine. Disability in America: toward a national agenda for prevention. Washington (DC): National Academy Press; 1991.

with developmental disabilities categorized by time of onset are presented in Table 6–1.[5]

The five categories include hereditary disorders, early alterations of embryonic development, late pregnancy or perinatal conditions, acquired childhood conditions, and conditions without a known etiology. The following conditions represent a few of the more common disabilities encountered in general practice.

Hereditary Disorders

FRAGILE X SYNDROME

Fragile X syndrome accounts for approximately one-half of X-linked mental retardation and is the second most common chromosomal cause of mental impairment, after Down syndrome. Resulting from an abnormal gene caused by a mutation involving the repetition of a trinucleotide sequence, the phenotype includes mild to severe mental retardation, macro-orchidism in males, large ears, prominent jaw, and high-pitched jocular speech. Fragile X syndrome occurs in 1 in 1,500 males and 1 in 2,500 females.[6]

In medical management of women with fragile X syndrome, one must assess for occurrence of seizure disorders and anxiety and affective disorders, as well as an increase in mitral valve prolapse, dislocated hips, and serous otitis. As all mothers of fragile X males are carriers of some form of the deletion, thus justifying genetic counseling and appropriate laboratory tests in patients whose family members have this syndrome.[7–10]

NEUROFIBROMATOSIS TYPE I

Neurofibromatosis type I is a progressive multisystem disorder in which persons develop both benign and malignant tumors. It is transmitted by an autosomal dominant mode of inheritance, due to a new mutation on chromosome 17 in approximately half of the patients. This condition occurs in 1 of 3,000 individuals and usually includes at least two or more of the following characteristics:[11]

- Six or more café-au-lait maculae
- Two or more neurofibromata or one plexiform neurofibroma
- Freckling in the axillary or inguinal region
- Optic glioma
- Two or more iris hamartomas

- An osseous lesion such as sphenoid dysplasia or cortical thinning of long bones
- A parent, sibling, or child with neurofibromatosis type I

Expressions of this condition vary widely. Symptoms are dependent on the location of the brain and nerve tumors, and the presence of associated seizures, gastrointestinal bleeding, hypertension, kyphosis and/or scoliosis, and mental retardation. Management includes referral for annual opthalmologic examinations, neurologic evaluation, and surgical consultations as appropriate, and discussion of genetics and inheritance of the condition with its implications for childbearing.

Early Alterations of Embryonic Development

DOWN SYNDROME

Down syndrome is the most common and readily identifiable chromosomal condition associated with mental retardation.[12,13] It usually is caused by an abnormality of cell division known as nondisjunction, which affects the 21st chromosome and results in trisomy 21 (in 93 to 96% of occurrences). Other causes of Down syndrome include translocation (in 3 to 4%) and trisomy 21 mosaicism (in 1 to 2%). Down syndrome occurs in 1 in 1,000 live births[14] and increases with advancing maternal age to more than 10 in 1,000 women over 40 years.[15]

Characteristic features in addition to mental retardation include hypotonia; a small brachycephalic head; a flattened midface; a small mouth with a protuberant tongue; excess folds of skin on the back of the neck; and shortened limbs, hands, and fingers. More serious associations include hearing deficiency (in 75%), eye disease (strabismus, cataracts, nystagmus, severe refractive errors; in 60%), thyroid disease (in 15%), and congenital heart disease (in 50%), the latter of which is a major cause of death.[16] Adults with Down syndrome who were unaffected as children are also at risk for developing conditions such as hypothyroidism[17] and hearing loss.[18] Acquired cervical spine problems also occur due to increased mobility at the first and second vertebrae (atlantoaxial instability). As a result of this instability, spinal cord compression can result. Symptoms can include neck pain, unusual posturing of the head and neck (torticollis), gait changes, loss of upper body strength, abnormal neurologic reflexes, and changes in bowel/bladder functioning.[19]

As people with Down syndrome age, they become at risk for developing Alzheimer's disease.[20] Symptoms of dementia among individuals with Down syndrome include loss of function and memory, ataxia, seizures, and incontinence of stool and urine.[14] Depression also occurs with increased frequency in adults with Down syndrome, and it should be considered if caregivers note a decline in activity, and a loss of ability to perform basic and intermediate activities of daily living. Treatment with antidepressants, in particular selective serotonin-reuptake inhibitors, often can reverse these behavioral trends with demonstrable improvement in function and quality of life.

FETAL ALCOHOL SYNDROME

Fetal alcohol syndrome (FAS), the most common *preventable* cause of mental retardation, is a constellation of physical and mental birth defects that occur as a direct result of prenatal alcohol exposure. Three criteria are necessary for diagnosis: abnormalities in growth, central nervous system dysfunction, and characteristic facial features.[21] Fetal alcohol effect (FAE) is a less severe condition with similar symptoms.

Occurrence is difficult to ascertain, as FAS is thought to be widely underdiagnosed. Experts estimate the prevalence of FAS to be 2 to 3 per 1,000 live births[22] and of FAE to be 1 per 300 live births.[22]

Characteristic features of FAS include low birth weight (in 80% of occurrences), microcephaly (in 80%), prenatal and postnatal growth deficiency (in 80%), small head size, narrow eye slits, flat midface, low nasal ridge, and serious central nervous system dysfunction (in 80%).[23] In adolescence and adulthood, practitioners must continue to monitor for cardiac, visual, and hearing difficulties; assist with dental care; and refer for stress and behavioral management when necessary. It is also particularly important to assess for alcohol and drug abuse, referring for treatment when indicated.

Conditions of Unknown Origin

CEREBRAL PALSY

Cerebral palsy (CP) is an "umbrella" term for a group of nonprogressive, but often changing, motor impairment syndromes occurring as a result of lesions or anomalies of the brain arising in early stages of its development.[24] Cerebral palsy may be *congenital* (in 90% of occurrences), caused by difficulties during pregnancy or birth, or *acquired*, caused by head trauma, infections, or severe malnutrition, for example, in the first few months after birth. The incidence of congenital CP is estimated to be 1.5 to 2.5 per 1,000 live births.[25] Ultimately, 2 to 4 children out of a 1,000 are afflicted with CP. Common associations include mental retardation, which occurs in almost half of persons with CP.[25]

There are four types of CP:[26]

1. Spastic CP (50% of cases). Spastic cerebral palsy is characterized by loss of movement of the extremites, including diplegia, quadriplegia, and hemiplegia. Persons with diplegia are usually of normal intelligence but experience difficulty drawing, writing, and crossing their legs. Persons with quadriplegia often have mild mental retardation and seizures. Persons with hemiplegia are usually of normal intelligence.

2. Athetoid CP (20% of cases). All extremities are involved in persons with athetoid CP. Athetotic and hypotonic neurologic dysfunction results in abnormal, involuntary, and uncontrollable movements (eg, twitching, twisting, and writhing). There may be hearing and speech deficiencies, and unsteady balance and gait. Normal intelligence is usually present. One should note that new cases of athetoid CP are now markedly reduced due to the identification and treatment of neonatal hyperbilirubinemia, which was the primary cause of this disability.

3. Ataxic CP (10% of cases). Persons with ataxic CP may have atonic diplegia or congenital cerebellar ataxis, usually associated with hypotonia. With ataxia only, there may be mild mental retardation accompanied by disturbed balance and depth perception, difficulty with rapid or fine movements, tremors, unsteadiness, and choreic movements.

4. Mixed CP (20% of cases). The diagnosis of mixed CP is used for persons who exhibit characteristics of more than one of the other types of CP.

Approximately one-third of persons with CP have seizures of all types.[26] Other associated problems include visual disorders (eg, strabismus or visual field defects), which occur in more than 50% of persons.[27] Hearing impairment occurs in 5 to

15% of individuals with CP. Other common problems include communication and adjustment disorders, and urinary tract infections.[28]

Medical management must address primary and associated conditions, in addition to the secondary conditions, such as contractures, skin breakdown, joint or muscle pain, and osteoporosis that often result as a result of the immobility. Gastrointestinal problems, such as oral motor dysfunction, gastroesophageal reflux, esophagitis, gastritis, and constipation, occur frequently and should always be addressed as early as possible to avoid serious morbidity and mortality. Respiratory complications are also common, because of scoliosis and swallowing dysfunction. Clinicians should watch closely for signs of aspiration and pneumonia.

EPILEPSY

Among persons with mental retardation, seizure disorders are more common than in the general population; approximately 1 in 5 has such a disorder.[29-34] Among those with mental retardation and CP, the risk is increased to 1 in 2. Despite the frequency of seizures in this population, other conditions are sometimes confused with seizures by care clinicians and others. Conditions confused with seizures include syncope, migraines, breath holding spells, hypoglycemia, hypocalcemia, and night terrors. The goals for seizure treatment are the same as for those without developmental disabilities, that is, to eliminate seizures, avoid side effects of medications, and promote involvement in rehabilitation and psychosocial adjustment. Clinicians in licensed community care facilities also should be instructed regarding procedures for managing status epilepticus and guidelines for calling paramedics through 911.

During her reproductive years, the woman with epilepsy must have special reproductive counseling to be aware of the potential risks for birth defects resulting from the use of such medications as phenytoin, valproic acid, and carbamazepine. The risk of using these medications for seizure control must be weighed against the risk to the fetus.

AUTISM

Autism is a behavioral syndrome that involves neurologic dysfunction, impaired social interaction, and impaired verbal and nonverbal communication.[35] At least two of the impaired social interactions include lack of awareness of feelings of others, failure to seek comfort when distressed, inability to imitate, abnormal social play, and impaired ability to initiate peer friendships. At least two of the impaired communication and imaginative activities include absent communication, abnormal nonverbal communication, abnormal speech production or speech content, and inability to initiate or sustain conversation. At least one of the restricted repertoire of activities and interests includes stereotyped body movements, preoccupation with objects, distress with environmental change, insistence on following routines, and a restricted range of interests. Many developmental syndromes such as fragile X, Prader-Willi, and Angelman's syndromes, and other deletional or unbalanced chromosome translocation disorders include autistic-like features.

MENTAL RETARDATION

Cognition, the process related to learning, perceiving, and making judgments, is determined by the level of intelligence quotient (IQ).[28] Cognition is a primary determinant of a woman's functional status, that is, the ability to participate in basic and intermediate activities of daily living that are critical to understanding how to prevent complications and comply with treatment instructions.

The ability of women with developmental disabilities to provide a health history and describe the chief complaint depends on her level of cognition that is, the ability to learn, understand concepts and issues, and remember past events. Cognition is a major factor in the patients' ability to provide an accurate health information for the history of the present illness, and prior medical history, and to assist in the development of a diagnosis and a therapeutic plan of care. It is also critical to the evaluation of the effectiveness of the treatment, including any side effects, and to the counseling of the patient regarding health promotion and disease prevention activities.

Mental retardation is defined as a substantial limitation in function with subaverage intellectual function that is at least two standard deviations from the mean.[36] It includes additional limitation in two or more adaptive skill areas: communication, self-care, self-direction, home living, social skill, use of community resources, health and safety, academic functions, leisure, and work. The four categories of mental retardation appear in Table 6–2.

TABLE 6–2. The Four Categories of Mental
Retardation

IQ	Level of MR	Grade Equivalent
70–55	Mild	3–5
54–40	Moderate	1–2
39–25	Severe	< 1
< 25	Profound	Total dependence

IQ = intelligence quotient; MR = mental retardation.

APPROACH TO THE PATIENT

Self-Appraisal

The first step to providing services for a patient
with developmental disabilities is to identify one's
own feelings about a person who is mentally
retarded or has physical impairments. Do you make
preliminary judgments and "categorizations" on
seeing a woman who looks different and who may
be drooling, stuttering, and unable to talk clearly,
and/or walking with arms and legs flailing? Are you
repulsed? Is there an assumption made that the person is severely mentally retarded and will be unable
to discuss her health problems? How should you
interact and talk with her? Should you ever use a
parental, condescending, or disrespectful tone of
voice? To understand how the patient might feel,
visualize being the patient and imagine her feelings
related to the problems at hand. How then would
you want to be treated?

Clearly, to provide optimal services for this
population, the health care professional must learn
to be comfortable with feelings about those individuals who are physically unattractive and who may
or may not be mentally retarded. In a society that
values physical beauty, high intelligence, and
achievement, many clinicians are uncomfortable
caring for women who lack these characteristics.

Arranging the Office Visit

For many women with developmental disabilities, a
visit to the health care clinician may be associated
with prior unpleasant experiences. To overcome
fears of a potentially frightening experience, it can
be helpful to arrange for the patient and caregiver,
if applicable, to visit the office once or twice prior
to the initial health evaluation. Some experts advise
premedication with a benzodiazepine (eg, lorazepam 0.5 mg orally) 1 hour prior to the office visit if

immunizations, blood tests, or a gynecologic examination are to be performed.[37] Also, the patient or
caregiver should be advised to bring a list of current
medications, a copy of any previous medical
records or a summary of the patient's medical and
developmental histories, and immunization record
including past tuberculin testing and hepatitis B
antigen or vaccination status, if she lives in a group
setting or has close proximity with others in sheltered work environments.

Ascertaining the Patient's Cognitive Level and Ability to Cooperate

At the initial visit, the clinician should determine
the woman's ability to understand and participate in
a partnership of care. This involves either having
information about cognitive status or level of mental retardation or making that assessment. If there is
no impairment or mild retardation, the clinician
should talk directly with the patient to assess the
chief complaint or reason for the visit. Information
about past medical history may be obtained from
the patient and/or previous medical records. If the
patient has a moderate, severe, or profound level of
mental retardation, the current health history
should be obtained from the caregiver who accompanies the patient and from the medical records. In
this case, the clinician should talk directly with both
the patient and the caregiver, knowing that the latter
will provide the information.

The Health Examination

Women with physical disabilities may need assistance with preparing for the physical examination,
with both removing clothing and putting on examination attire, and sitting on the examination table.
Procedures should be altered to accommodate
patients with orthopedic deformities or spasticity of
extremities. In patients with cognitive deficiencies, it
is essential to develop early rapport, explaining in
simple terms the purpose of the visit: for example, if
the patient is ill, explain that the goal is to make her
"feel better;" or if the visit is routine, explain that
body parts will "be checked to make sure they are all
right." Explain each step in a calm and reassuring
manner; follow this with praise, since it is important
for good compliance.

If touch is not permitted by the patient, or if
anxiety precludes examination, referral for desensitization or relaxation techniques should be considered

TABLE 6–3. Examples of Possible Secondary Conditions in Persons with Cerebral Palsy and Down Syndrome

Circumstance	Cerebral Palsy	Down Syndrome
Complication	Decubitus ulcer	Subluxation of cervical spine
Contingency	Pulmonary fibrosis	Conductive hearing loss
Unexpected progression	Loss of ambulation	Acquired hypothyroidism
Comorbidity	Development of seizures	Effects of preterm birth
Other health concerns	Breast cancer	Cancer of the bowel
Effects of aging	Memory loss	Arthritis

to allay fear and promote cooperation for doctor visits. If the patient resists necessary medical intervention, the use of psychopharmacologic agents such as neuroleptics or sedative-hypnotics should be considered, as mentioned above. The use of general anesthesia should be considered if the above recommendations are unsuccessful, coordinating, when possible, multiple examinations/procedures into one visit or hospital admission. In some cases, the risks of anesthesia/sedation in patients with compromised cardiac or pulmonary function must be weighed against the benefits of routine preventive examinations.

HEALTH PROMOTION AND DISEASE PREVENTION

The quality of life for a person who has a disability depends on the degree to which complications or secondary handicapping conditions can be prevented by good medical case management. As aptly summarized by Crocker, there are at least six circumstances that should be considered in understanding sources of secondary conditions.[27]

- A complication—an untoward occurrence originating in direct features of the disability
- A contingency—an event in another system, but ultimately deriving from conditions of the disability
- An unexpected progression—a troubling extension of the potential natural history of the disability
- Co-morbidity—another disability deriving from the same background as the first one
- Other health concerns—ill health from another origin, masked or confounded by the disability
- Effects of aging—dysfunctions of advancing years may be additive to the disability

Examples of secondary conditions in women with CP and Down syndrome are summarized in Table 6–3.

Health care service protocols should encompass "disease or disability management" that will limit secondary conditions rather than embrace a management style that responds only to symptoms or complaints when they occur. Such a program of prevention is outlined in Table 6–4.

Immunizations

The guidelines for immunization of women with developmental disabilities are the same as for the general population.[38] These are reviewed in Chapter 8 on preventive health. Special consideration should be given to evaluating the need for influenza and hepatitis B vaccines for those living in group facilities and/or working in sheltered work environments.

Vision and Hearing

Vision and hearing testing should be done at more frequent intervals than in the general population, due to a higher risk of loss of function in these areas.

TABLE 6–4. Elements of Programming for the Prevention of Secondary Conditions

Organization and delivery of services—involves planning and coordination

Use of appropriate assistive technologies to enhance capacity, strength, and protection

Adoption of health-promoting behavior: promote good nutrition and exercise, and prescribe minimal medications

Education and information—these should be available for the public and providers

Consideration of environment such as patient's friends, community, residence and work

Dental Care

Preventive dental care is important and may require additional orientation to the dental office. As stated earlier, individuals with Down syndrome and other disorders are at high risk for valvular disease; prophylatic antibiotic therapy may be required prior to a visit to the dentist.

Exercise

The guidelines for exercise are the same as are those for the general population. However, in the large population of women with congenital abnormalities of the spine such as atlantoaxial subluxation, it may be necessary to limit activities that are likely to involve trauma to the spine, or to obtain radiographs and/or orthopedic consultation to determine safe activities.

IMPORTANT CONSIDERATIONS

Since individuals with chronic conditions are more likely to suffer from depression,[39,40] a thorough psychiatric history and symptom review should be elicited. Depressive symptoms also may be related to the taking of multiple drugs;[41,42] therefore, a thorough review of medications should be included in the evaluation.

Sexuality and reproductive health issues are as important to discuss with women who have disabilities as with women in general. Discussion may be particularly important in the prevention of sexually transmitted diseases, since women with disabilities are likely to have received less information during adolescence on the topic of sexuality than are other women.[43]

Women with developmental disabilities are not only at higher risk for emotional, physical, and sexual abuse, but the duration of the abuse is often longer than that for women without physical disabilities.[1] Patients should be screened to determine if they have experienced any of these types of abuse, to ascertain the need for referral and subsequent intervention. This topic is discussed further in Chapter 88, "Domestic Violence."

Finally, women who are nonverbal may present with a variety of behaviors that may signal acute or chronic medical issues. The "whole person" should be evaluated by relying on information from the care clinician regarding clues of medical distress, in addition to obtaining good accounts of the type and frequency of unusual behavior. As an example, in the chronically "fussy" or disturbed nonverbal adult, one should consider reflux esophagitis, dental disease, or bone injury (eg, fracture with osteoporosis, dislocated hip, or bone infection) as potential causes. Chronic chewing of the hand or fingers also may signal gastroesophageal reflux, dental disease, or sinus and middle ear problems. Other nonverbal silent clues to medical distress may include uneven sitting positions (these may indicate hip pain, genital discomfort, or rectal pain); unusual or recurrent masturbation (which may signal urinary tract infection, candidal vaginitis, or pinworms); head banging (which may occur with increased intracranial pressure [as with a shunt for hydrocephalus], migraine, dental pain, otitis, mastoiditis, or sinusitis); and general scratching (which may suggest eczema, drug effects, liver/renal disorder, or scabies).

Even during a serious illness, symptomatology may be quite vague, with the nonverbal woman showing apparent discomfort, often associated with altered vital signs such as changes in blood pressure or pulse. The care giver may describe the person as "not herself."

SUMMARY

The woman with a developmental disability should receive the same good basic medical care as anyone else, with a goal of sustaining her best level of functioning. Routine health screening, consideration of hormonal replacement in menopause, dental care, and appropriate vaccines should be provided. Additionally, monitoring for chronic and often preventable secondary conditions that may occur in those with a disability is of paramount importance. Finally, remembering that the person with a disability is both unique and special, communicating with her in the mode she best understands, and conveying a sense of caring and respect will do much to ensure the well-being of both clinician and patient.

REFERENCES

1. Young ME, Nosek MA, Howland C, et al. Prevalence of abuse of women with physical disabilities. Arch Phys Med Rehab 1997:98 Suppl 5:S34–8.
2. Luckasson R, Coulter DL, Polloway EA, et al. editors. Mental retardation: definition, classification and systems of supports. 9th ed. Washington (DC): American Association on Mental Retardation; 1992.

3. Public Law 91–517, The Development Disabilities Services and Facilities Construction Act. October 30, 1970.

4. Public Law 98–527, The Developmental Disabilities Act of 1984. October 19, 1984.

5. Institute of Medicine. Disability in America: toward a national agenda for prevention. Washington (DC): National Academy Press; 1991.

6. Capute AJ, Pasquale JA. Developmental disabilities in infancy and childhood. Vol. 1: Neurodevelopment diagnosis and treatment. Baltimore: Paul H. Brookes Publishing Co., Inc.; 1996.

7. Blomquist HK, Gustavson KH, Holmgren G, et al. Fragile X syndrome in mildly retarded children in a northern Swedish country: a prevalence study. Clin Genet 1983;24:393–8.

8. Froster-Iskenius U, Felsch G, Shirren C, Schwinger E. Screening for fragile X q in population of mentally retarded males. Hum Genet 1983;63:153–7.

9. Herbst DS, Miller JR. Nonspecific X-linked mental retardation. II: The frequency in British Columbia. Am J Med Genet 1980;7:461–9.

10. Sutherland GR. Heritable fragile sites on the human chromosomes. 8. Preliminary population cytogenetic data on the folic-acid-sensitive fragile sites. Am J Hum Genet 1982;34:452–8.

11. Guttman DH, Aylsworth A, Carey JC, et al. The diagnostic evaluation and multidisciplinary management of neurofibromatosis 1 and neurofibromatosis 2. J Am Med Assoc 1997;278:51–7.

12. Cicchetti D, Sroufe L. The relationship between affective and cognitive development in Down's syndrome infants. Child Dev 1976;47:920–9.

13. Dahle AJ, McCollister FP. Hearing and otologic disorders in children with Down syndrome. Am J Ment Defic 1986;90:636–42.

14. Cohen WI. Health care guidelines for individuals with Downs syndrome. Downs Syndr Q 1996;1(2):1–10.

15. Hook EB, Lindsjo A. Down syndrome in live births by single year maternal age interval in a Swedish study: comparative results from a New York study. Am J Hum Genet 1978;30:19–27.

16. Masoki M, Higurashi M, Iijima K, et al. Mortality and survival for Down syndrome in Japan. Am J Hum Genet 1981;33:629–39.

17. Cutler AT, Benezra-Obeiter R, Brink SJ. Thyroid functions in young children with Down syndrome. Am J Dis Child 1986;140:479–83.

18. Balkany TJ, Downs MP, Jafek BW, et al. Hearing loss in Down's syndrome. Clin Pediatr 1979;18:116–8.

19. Van Dyke DC, Gahagan CA. Down syndrome. Cervical spine abnormalities problems. Clin Pediatr 1988;27:415–8

20. Miniszek NA. Development of Alzheimer disease in Down syndrome individuals. Am J Ment Defic 1983;87:377–85.

21. Rosett HL, Weiner L, Zuckerman B, et al. Reduction of alcohol consumption during pregnancy with benefits to the newborn. Alcohol Clin Exp Res 1980; 4(2):178–84.

22. Aase JM. Clinical recognition of FAS: difficulties of detection and diagnosis. Alcohol Health Res World 1994;18:5–9.

23. Streissguth AP. Fetal alcohol syndrome and fetal alcohol effects. A clinical perspective of later developmental consequences. In Zagon IS, Slotkin TA, editors. Maternal substance abuse and the developing nervous system. San Diego: Academic Press; 1992. p. 5–25.

24. Kuban KC, Leviton A. Cerebral palsy. N Engl J Med 1994;330:188–95.

25. Bhushan V, Paneth N, Kiely JL. Impact of improved survival of very low birth weight infants on recent secular trends in the prevalence of cerebral palsy. Pediatrics 1993;91:1091–100.

26. Wilson JM. Cerebral palsy. In: Campbell SK, editor. Pediatric neurologic physical therapy. 2nd ed. New York: Churchill Livingston; 1991. p. 301–60.

27. Lollar D. Preventing secondary conditions associated with spina bifida or cerebral palsy: proceedings and recommendations of a symposium. Washington (DC): Spina Bifida Association of America; 1994.

28. Crocker AC. The causes of mental retardation. Pediatr Ann 1989;18:623–36.

29. Richardson SA, Katz M, Koller H, et al. Some characteristics of a population of mentally retarded young adults in a British city. J Ment Defic Res 1979; 23:275–87.

30. Corbett JA. Epilepsy and mental retardation. In: Reynolds EH, Trimble MR, editors. Epilepsy and psychiatry. Edinburgh: Churchill Livingston; 1981. p. 138–46.

31. Bicknell DJ. Epilepsy and mental handicap. Royal Society of Medicine Round Table Series No. 2. London: Royal Society of Medicine; 1985.

32. Shepard C, Hosking G. Epilepsy in school children with intellectual impairments in Sheffield: the size and nature of the problem and the implications for service provision. J Ment Defic Res 1989;33:511–4.

33. Coulter DL. Epilepsy and mental retardation: an overview. Am J Ment Retard 1993;98:SI–II.

34. Kerr M, Fraser W, Felce D. Primary heath care for people with a learning disability; a keynote review. Br J Learn Disabil 1996;24:2–8.

35. Wing L. The diagnosis of autism. In: Gill C, editors. Diagnosis and treatment of autism. Plenum Press: New York; 1989. p. 5–22.

36. American Psychiatric Association. Diagnostic and statistical manual of mental disorders. 4th ed. Washington (DC): American Psychiatric Association; 1994;27:886.

37. Messinger BJ, Rapport DJ. Primary care for the developmentally disabled adult. J Gen Intern Med 1997;12:629–36.

38. Centers for Disease Control and Prevention. Recommendations of the Advisory Committee on Immunization Practices, the American Academy of Pediatrics, and the American Academy of Family Physicians: use of reminder and recall by vaccination providers to increase vaccination rates. JAMA 1998;280:1043.

39. Lamberg L. Treating depression in medical conditions may improve quality of life. JAMA 1996;276:857–8.

40. Spitzer RL, Kroenke K, Linzer M, et al. 1995 Health-related quality of life in primary care patients with mental disorders: results from the PRIME-MD 1000 study. JAMA 1995;274:1511–7.

41. Tabrizi K, Littman A, Williams RB, Scheidt S. Psychopharmacology and cardiac disease. In: Robert AL, Scheidt SS, et al, editors. Heart and mind: the practice of cardia psychology. Washington (DC): American Psychological Association; 1996. p. 397–419.

42. Zelnik T. Depressive effects of drugs. In: Oliver G, Cameron, editors. Presentations of depression: depressive symptoms in medical and other psychiatric disorders. Oxford, England: John Wiley & Sons; 1987. p. 355–99.

43. Becker H, Stuifbergen A, Tinkle M. Reproductive health care experiences of women with physical disabilities: a qualitative study. Arch Phys Med Rehabil 1997;78(12 Suppl 5):526–33.

7

LESBIAN HEALTH

Allison L. Diamant, MD, MSHS

One of the most significant aspects of lesbian health is that so little is known, and what is known comes mostly from nonpopulation-based samples. The effects of health-related risk factors on lesbian health, as well as the existence of risk factors that may be unique to lesbians, have been largely unexplored. Although there appears to be an increasing awareness among health care clinicians and patients of the need to study and understand this aspect of women's health, there has been limited interest from the medical and research communities, including a lack of available funding. Because of the paucity of available information about lesbian health, and the lack of a cohesive research agenda, the Institute of Medicine Committee on Lesbian Health Research Priorities was convened in 1997. The committee was invested with a threefold purpose: to evaluate the available scientific evidence describing the health of lesbians (physical and mental), to identify the methodologic challenges involved in the study of lesbian health, and to suggest specific areas for research.[1]

The World Health Organization has described health as physical, emotional, and social well-being and not merely the absence of disease.[2] Relative to this definition the health of individual lesbians and communities can be studied at the interface of three domains: society as a whole, the health care system, and within the context of women's health. This chapter reviews what is currently known about lesbian health, including health behaviors, risk for common medical conditions, and access to and use of health care services, as they impact on the clinical care of lesbians.

RESEARCH

In the 1950s Kinsey et al reported that an estimated 5 to 10% of US adults were homosexual;[3] and in 1994

Laumann et al reported that less than 10% of women who participated in a national survey reported ever having had a same-sex partner since puberty.[4] Although lesbians appear to comprise a minority population of women, interested health care professionals have identified several important rationale for studying lesbian health. These rationale include (1) obtaining information that is useful for improving the medical care and health status of lesbians, (2) confirming beliefs and countering misconceptions that exist about the health risks for lesbians, and (3) identifying medical conditions for which lesbians may be at an increased risk.[1] However, there may be hidden assumptions in the generally accepted health model (ie, health versus disease) that make it inaccurate when applied to women's sexuality. These assumptions may include normalcy and deviance (ie, sexuality can be described as either healthy or unhealthy), universality (ie, it assumes that health is based on pancultural standards of biologic function and malfunction), individualism (ie, it focuses on women's sexuality as individual capacity and may ignore the larger political/ideologic framework), and biologic (ie, research focusing on biology predominates and is considered more central and definitive than is research that focuses on sociocultural "influences").[5-7]

The majority of available research on lesbian health has provided important descriptive data, but this information has not necessarily been representative of or generalizable to all lesbians. The lack of representative and generalizable data is due to three major methodologic constraints: sampling, definition of the term "lesbian," and comparability (ie, to heterosexual women).

Sampling

Lesbians do not constitute an easily identifiable or homogeneous population of women. Most studies from the late 1970s to the present have relied on nonprobability samples because of the difficulty in identifying lesbians.[1,8–41] Identification of the population to be studied has been limited severely by the societal lack of acceptance for same-gender relationships. Age, education, income, occupation, and geographic area of residence do not determine whether a woman is lesbian, although the decision to disclose one's sexual orientation may be affected significantly by these individual and environmental characteristics. For example, many women have moved to cities and geographic areas where they feel safe and comfortable, able to be open about their sexual orientation if they so choose; this is why some particular cities or states have a higher percentage of lesbians. The recent inclusion of sexual orientation as a risk factor for health disparities in Healthy People 2010 may result in an increase in the number of studies looking at lesbian health issues.[42]

Definition

It is important for health care clinicians to understand that there are differences between sexual identity, attraction, and behavior. Health care clinicians should realize that individual women characterize their sexual orientation based on one, two, or all three of these domains.[17,26,43–45] Therefore, the common perception of a lesbian as someone who sees herself as physically and emotionally attracted to other women and has only same-sex relationships, may not describe all women who self-identify as lesbian. In many of the available studies the operational definition of a lesbian has varied or has not been well described.[1] In addition, views of sexual identity and behavior may vary across cultures, and self-reported rates of sexual orientation may be affected significantly by cultural and social perceptions, acceptability, and norms. For example, it appears that homosexuality may be reported more commonly by certain racial and ethnic groups (eg, Caucasians and African Americans/Blacks) and less so by others (eg, Latinas/Hispanics, Asians/Pacific Islanders).[46–50]

Comparability

Most studies on lesbian health have not been population based and have included only lesbians and bisexual women from nonprobability samples, thus limiting comparability with similar heterosexual women. However, limited data from recent population-based samples are becoming available.[43,51] In addition, the lack of standard measures and a paucity of longitudinal data have further limited comparison to heterosexual women and women in general.[52,53]

LESBIAN HEALTH AND THE ENVIRONMENT

One factor that may have a significant effect on lesbian health is stress. Research has revealed that racial discrimination is a potent etiology of stress and that it may have negative health effects.[54] Stress is characterized by the exposure to events that require one to adapt to situations (good or bad), especially if one perceives that the demands exceed their capabilities to cope.[55] The associated physiologic responses to stress can have a wide range of negative impacts on short- and long-term health.[56,57]

Consideration of stress and its affects is an important aspect of health, as many lesbians are likely to experience stress as a result of living in a heterosexist society where homophobia is encountered not infrequently.[58] Homophobia is the fear of homosexuality and may be characterized by a range of feelings and behaviors from mild distaste and disregard to overt hostility and violence. Women who are the focus of these negative societal influences may suffer stresses that have an adverse impact on their physical, psychological, and emotional well-being.[59–61]

Stress in lesbians may be initiated and exacerbated by a perceived need to keep their lesbian identity a secret (eg, from family, friends, or co-workers), a concern about negative attitudes and experiences within the health care system (eg, being excluded by physicians from making health care decisions for an ill lesbian partner), and a fear of being the target of physical violence or other hate crimes.[59–62] Stress effects may be greatest for lesbians who are members of under-represented groups on the basis of age, race/ethnicity, or religion, and who therefore are subject to multiple forms of discrimination.[48] The results of a national study indicated that African American lesbians and bisexual women exhibit higher levels of stress and distress than do gay men.[60]

However, research also has indicated that exposure to stress may be protective in stimulating the search for individual forms of support (eg, family, schools, religious institutions, or community/social groups) and the formation of well-developed social systems.[63] Although studies specific to lesbians are limited, information is available that suggest factors that may be protective of lesbian health (eg, strong family support and involvement in the lesbian community).[64–66]

LESBIAN HEALTH AND THE HEALTH CARE SYSTEM

The provision of health care is characterized by the physician-patient relationship, and the quality of health care depends in part on the clinician's ability to meet the patient's needs. Care that is provided in a sensitive and nonjudgmental fashion can foster a helpful and healthful relationship, whereas care that is characterized by negative attitudes is of diminished quality.[67–69] The quality of care provided to lesbians may be affected by a lack of knowledge and awareness by both the patient and clinician of lesbians' unique health care needs.[70] Lesbians have been described as being invisible in society, especially with regard to their health care needs, and older lesbians and lesbians of color may be at an even greater risk for marginalization.[71,72] The lack of acknowledgment of lesbians in female populations has resulted in limited knowledge of their health and health care needs.

Studies have demonstrated that lesbians' health risks and health-seeking behaviors are associated with ease of access to care and their ability to communicate with their primary care clinician.[18,28,43,73] Despite the prevalence of homosexuality, many clinicians believe that they do not care for lesbian patients, and that they can identify their patients' sexual orientation without taking a complete sexual history.[71] Asking all patients about their sexual behavior history is an essential component of good medical care.[74] However, many physicians feel uncomfortable asking the items that comprise detailed sexual histories, including asking about same-sex behavior.[74–77] This hesitancy may arise from limited training and experience in taking a sexual history.

The invisibility of lesbians is perpetuated by limited inclusion of curricula in medical training that describe the health care issues of lesbians.[78,79] Although there has been an increased focus on lesbian health, the values of a dominant heterosexual culture have influenced academic research and have contributed to lesbian invisibility. Multiple studies have documented homophobia among health care clinicians, including physicians, nurses, psychologists, social workers, and medical students.[80–84]

For health care professionals to provide good quality medical care and to accurately assess their patients' risk factors for poor health, it is important that they know their patients' sexual orientation and health behaviors.[17,85–87] Several studies have noted that most of the lesbians sampled do not disclose their sexual orientation when they seek medical care, for fear of embarrassment and potential compromise including discrimination and the receipt of poor quality care.[28,47,85,86] Specific examples of negative experiences have included reluctance or refusal on the part of health care professionals to provide medical care, perjorative comments from the clinician during treatment, and unnecessary discomfort for the patient during the physical examination.[88] Lesbians report not infrequently that these negative experiences have led them to avoid seeking further needed health care.[9,11,47,89,90] However, findings from a large national study indicated that lesbians with a regular source of care who had disclosed their sexual orientation were more likely to have had appropriate cervical cancer screening.[18]

Lesbians may experience other barriers to health care that do not appear to be directly related to the doctor-patient relationship. In a population-based study of women in Los Angeles County, lesbians were more likely than heterosexual women to have lacked health insurance during the preceding year, and were more likely to report having gone without needed medical care during that time for financial reasons.[43] Lesbians also have reported not knowing where to go to for their health care, as they have perceived obstetrician/gynecologists and women's clinics as being focused on the reproductive needs of women.[11]

LESBIAN HEALTH AND WOMEN'S HEALTH

Lesbian health should be viewed within the overall context of women's health, including the presence or absence of risk factors for health problems such as heart disease, cancer, osteoporosis, and other conditions. However, one should consider that primary care for women still tends to be organized around reproductive health needs, with the majority of public funding focused on family planning and pre-natal care.[28,89,91] A key question is whether lesbians have the same level of risk for medical conditions, or a risk that is increased or decreased compared to heterosexual women. Potential health concerns specific to lesbians are discussed here because (1) there is some evidence to support the belief that lesbians are at increased risk for certain medical conditions, (2) there are widely held assumptions among lesbian patients and their clinicians of greater or lesser risk that may not be evidence based, and (3) the existence of misconceptions about lesbians' health risks may have important implications for their health, the receipt of health care services, and health-seeking behavior.

It is important to note that variation in health risk among women may be due to a wide range of factors, including differences in health behaviors (eg, cigarette smoking, alcohol use), the stresses to which they are exposed (eg, homophobia), and the way they interact with the health care system (eg, access to health care including health insurance and other financial barriers, positive and negative inter-actions with individual clinicians, and access to systems of care that are sensitive to sexual orientation).

Disclosure of Sexual Orientation

Many of the developmental issues that lesbians face are the same as those encountered by other females: sexist/gender-based attitudes, entrance into the workforce, the development of support systems including the identification of mentors and friends, finding a loving partner and developing a satisfying sexual life, the decision of whether to have children, and negotiation of the aging process.[92] However, lit-tle information is available regarding the unique challenges that lesbians face throughout their life-times. One process presumably unique to lesbians is the awareness of a sexual orientation (ie, "coming out") that is not considered the norm by society.

Coming out is the process of acknowledging one's sexual orientation to oneself and to others including family, friends, and colleagues; however, lesbians do not experience this process in identical ways.[48,93,94] For some, coming out may be more or less stressful and can affect short- and long-term health. Importantly, coming out to oneself has been shown to be associated with good mental health for lesbians, such as increased self-esteem, better psy-chological adjustment, greater personal satisfaction, and less depression and stress compared with les-bians and gay men who are at conflict with their identity.[95] The presence of a health care clinician who is sensitive to the varying aspects of the com-ing out process and lesbian patients' needs can pro-vide a healthful environment.

Health Behaviors

SMOKING

Studies have reported higher rates of cigarette use for lesbians than for women of similar ages in the general population.[18,39,43,96] More recent data from the Women's Health Initiative (WHI) indicate sig-nificant differences in cigarette smoking depending on sexual orientation, with lesbians significantly more likely than heterosexual women to be heavy smokers and less likely to be lifetime nonsmokers.[1] Although the WHI is not a probability sample and is limited to women ≥ 50 years, these findings are supported by results from a population-based sam-ple of women in Los Angeles County where 32% of lesbians compared with 14% of heterosexual women reported current use of tobacco, and 38% versus 63% had never smoked.[43]

ALCOHOL

From the data available approximately 30 to 35% of lesbians may have alcohol problems.[19,43,96–105] Risk factors for alcohol abuse include stress, anxiety, depression, genetic predisposition, and histories of childhood sexual abuse or violence.[106] However, it is important to note that although lesbians have the same risk factors for alcohol abuse as do other women, some of these factors may be closely tied to the limited support systems available to them (eg, bars being the only place to meet and socialize with other lesbians).[92]

Although many of the often cited studies have significant methodologic limitations including interviewing lesbians at or in the near proximity of bars, or at social events, and a lack of comparable samples, recent studies may support these results.[19,59,107–110] Findings from a recent population-based study indicate that lesbians were significantly more likely than were heterosexual women to report consuming any quantity of alcohol, and they were more likely to drink alcohol in larger quanti-ties and with greater frequency.[43]

WEIGHT CONTROL

Research findings appear to indicate that lesbians have a higher body mass index (BMI) than do age-matched heterosexual women.[24,111] Findings from the WHI indicated that lesbians ≥50 years were more likely than were heterosexual women to be overweight; note, however, that the majority of women in the sample are Caucasian.[1] In a recent population-based sample of ethnically diverse women, lesbians were more likely than were heterosexual women to be obese.[112]

History of Pregnancy

As for many other important aspects of lesbian health, reliable estimates are lacking for the proportion of lesbians who have had a biologic child, as well as for those who have adopted children. In the WHI sample, lesbians were much less likely to have ever been pregnant than were heterosexual women of similar ages.[1] In the National Lesbian Health Care Survey, 29% (n = 556) of lesbians reported having been pregnant, of which 22% had not carried the infant to term;[11] in another national study of lesbians, 12% (n = 853) reported having delivered a child.[18] Unfortunately, this information does not give us an accurate sense of how likely lesbians are to have biologic children (although we are aware of significant differences by age); as alternative forms of conception become increasingly available, more lesbians may choose to have biologic children.[22]

Use of Oral Contraceptives

In a national sample 37% of lesbians reported having used oral contraceptives (OCPs) for at least 6 months, with an increasing likelihood of use among older lesbians.[18] In the WHI sample, oral contraceptive use was measured for women between the ages of 25 and 35 years, and mature lesbians were most likely to have used OCPs (42.4%), followed by heterosexual women (32.0%), and lifetime lesbians (ie, those having had no male sexual partners) (16.7%).[1]

Physical Health

Little data are available currently that indicate whether lesbians are at higher or lower risk for certain health problems relative to heterosexual women or women in general. For example, little is known about the prevalence of medical conditions (eg, cancer, hypertension, diabetes, mental health, sexually transmitted diseases [STDs], and human immunodeficiency virus [HIV]) among lesbians compared with heterosexual women.[113] The data describing disease prevalence among lesbians is limited, and when information is available it focuses almost exclusively on samples of white middle-class lesbians (because of the methodologic limitations discussed previously). Research that has focused on racial and ethnic minority women in general has rarely collected information on sexual orientation. A population-based study of women found not dissimilar rates for many medical conditions, including arthritis, diabetes, heart disease, cancer, kidney disease, and lung disease between lesbians and heterosexual women, and a comparable self-reported health status. However, in this study, lesbians appeared to have slightly higher rates of hypertension[43] (Table 7–1). In the National Lesbian Health Care Survey the rates of past and current medical conditions were reported, as well as the proportion of lesbians with each medical condition who were receiving care (although without comparison).[11] A history of gynecologic conditions and STDs in lesbians is reported from a larger national sample (Table 7–2).[17]

CANCER

Factors have been identified that put women at increased or decreased risk for particular cancers. Excluding skin cancers, breast cancer is the most common cancer among women.[114] The risk for most cancers increases with age as well as with a positive family history for a particular type of cancer. However, for some malignancies, there are behavioral factors such as smoking, consumption of alcohol, or sexual history that can increase the risk of cancer.

Assessment of lesbians' risk for malignancy has focused primarily on breast cancer with some mention of ovarian and cervical cancer. The assumption that lesbians are at a higher risk than are heterosexual women for breast cancer is based primarily on data from studies that suggest that certain risk factors for cancer occur with greater frequency and degree of severity in lesbians.[64] These risk factors include a higher prevalence of smoking, greater alcohol use, poor diet, increased BMI, and lower rates of child-bearing. However, there are no epidemiologic studies to support the conclusion that lesbians are at an increased risk for breast cancer or other malignancies. Even though there is no direct evidence that lesbians have a higher prevalence of breast cancer than do heterosexual women, there is a common

TABLE 7–1. Health and Health Status of Women by Sexual Orientation

Medical Problem	Heterosexual Women (n = 4,610) Unadjusted %	Lesbians (n = 51) Unadjusted %	p Value
Arthritis	21	31	*
Diabetes	6	2	**
Heart disease	5	4	NS
Cancer	1	0	NS
Kidney disease	1	2	NS
Lung disease	1	2	NS
HIV/AIDS	<1	2	**
Hypertension	17	8	***

*p < 0.1; **p < 0.05; ***p < 0.01.
NS = not significant; HIV = human immunodeficiency virus; AIDS = acquired immunodeficiency syndrome.
Adapted from Diamant AL, Wold C, Spritzer K, Gelberg L. Health behaviors, health status, and access to and use of health care: a population-based study of lesbian, bisexual and heterosexual women. Arch Fam Med 2000;9:1043–51.

perception in the lesbian community that lesbians are at an increased risk for a breast malignancy.[1] However, the results of a recent meta-analysis do not support the hypothesis that lesbians carry an increased risk for breast cancer.[39] In a controlled trial of breast cancer risk for lesbians and women in the general population, women in the general sample were found to have a 13% mean risk of breast cancer by age 80 years, whereas women in the lesbian sample were found to have an 11% mean risk.[115] However, women in both groups perceived their lifetime risk for breast cancer to be much higher (lesbians: 36% mean lifetime risk; women in the general population: 50% mean lifetime risk).[115]

Cervical cancer has the ninth highest cancer mortality rate among US women and accounts for 6% of all cancers in women.[116] Among women in general the risk for cervical cancer is highly associated with a number of factors including sexual behavior (eg, the number of lifetime male sexual partners, early age at first intercourse, unprotected sex), infection with certain genotypes of human papillomavirus-[HPV], infection with HIV, and cigarette smoking.[117]

The well-documented association between the risk for cervical cancer and sexual activity with men might appear to imply that lesbians are not at risk for cervical cancer. However, a majority of the lesbians included in the available studies on lesbian health report having had heterosexual intercourse in their lifetime.[11,15,17,45,118–120] Therefore, lesbians remain at risk for cervical cancer—not because of their sexual orientation or identity, but because of their sexual behavior. Of note, recent information appears to indicate that HPV may be transmitted between female sexual partners.[24,41] Cervical neoplasia associated with HPV infection was detected among lesbians who had sex with men, as well as among those who did not report a history of male sexual partners.[13,24,121]

It is important to note that screening for cervical cancer is associated with effective and significant

TABLE 7–2. Prevalence of Gynecologic Conditions among Lesbians (N = 6,935)

Gynecologic Condition	Percentage
Lumps/fibroids on breast biopsy	12
Breast cancer	0.6
Irregular Papanicolaou's smear	0.7
Cervical cancer	0.9
Ovarian cancer	0.3
Endometriosis	7
Gonorrhea	2
Chlamydia	5
Trichomoniasis	6
Pelvic inflammatory disease	2
Syphilis	0.3
Genital or anal herpes	3
Genital or anal warts	5
Any sexually transmitted disease	17

Adapted from Diamant AL, Schuster MA, McGuigan K, Lever J. Lesbians' sexual history with men: implications for taking a sexual history. Arch Intern Med 1999;159:2730–6.

reductions in related morbidity and mortality. A complete understanding of lesbians' receipt of Pap smears does not exist because of the methodologic limitations of most studies and the variation in the findings. Evidence is mixed about whether significant differences are present between lesbians and heterosexual women with regard to the rates for receipt of Pap smears, as well as the need for cervical cancer screening. Information from a number of studies,[11,18,22,45] including findings from a recent population-based sample of women,[43] suggest that lesbians do not receive Pap tests according to national guidelines and that they receive this screening test less frequently than do heterosexual women. However, some studies[1,117] have found no significant differences between heterosexual women and lesbians in Pap test screening rates and behavior. Therefore, further study of Pap test screening of lesbians should be performed including an assessment of screening rates among lesbians who have never had sex with men, and identification of factors that may contribute to less frequent Pap test screening (eg, perception of low risk for cervical cancer, and barriers to health care).

Even less information is available about the prevalence of other cancers and the existence of unique risk factors for these malignancies among lesbians. However, if (as data appear to indicate) lesbians have higher rates of smoking than do heterosexual women, their risk for lung cancer is increased. In addition, as discussed previously, there is some evidence that lesbians tend to have a higher BMI[24,111,112] and to consume a high-fat diet.[1] If this information is accurate, lesbians may be at greater risk for colorectal, ovarian, and endometrial cancers.[122–126] Other risk factors for ovarian cancer include nulliparity, early age at menarche, and late age at menopause. Of note, the use of OCPs has been shown to be protective for ovarian cancer.[127,128] Based on the data currently available, lesbians may be at a relatively higher risk for ovarian and endometrial cancers than are women in the general population because lesbians appear to be less likely to conceive and bear children, and to use OCPs.[1,11,18] However, because the necessary epidemiologic data on health risk factors among lesbians are not available at this time, it is not possible to determine whether lesbians are at increased risk for these malignancies compared with similar heterosexual women.

CARDIOVASCULAR DISEASES

Heart disease, stroke, and atherosclerosis are the leading causes of death for women.[114] Known risk factors for heart disease include hypertension, high cholesterol, excessive weight, cigarette smoking, and physical inactivity.[129] Whether lesbians are at an increased risk for cardiovascular disease, or have protective factors against it, is not known due to the limited population-based data on cardiovascular disease among lesbians. Findings from a population-based study that included a relatively small proportion of lesbians indicate a slightly increased risk for hypertension among lesbians compared with that of heterosexual women.[30] In addition, lesbians may have an increased risk for cardiovascular disease due to their health behaviors as previously discussed (eg, greater prevalence of tobacco use and higher BMI).

Other than data from nonprobability samples, little is known about the prevalence of other medical conditions among lesbians such as diabetes and arthritis (see Tables 7–1 and 7–2).[11,43]

SEXUALLY TRANSMITTED DISEASES

The risk of infection from STDs depends on several factors, including type of sexual contact, use of protective barriers, single versus repeated exposures, number of sexual partners, and concomitant medical conditions including other STDs.[130] Heterosexual vaginal and rectal intercourse without the use of a protective barrier are known to carry a high risk of infection for women, because the amount of bacteria or virus that is transmitted with penile insertion and ejaculation is much higher than in other kinds of sexual activity.[131] However, the use of condoms has been proven to reduce the transmission of STDs between males and females.[132,133] In addition, research has shown that many STDs are transmitted more readily from men to women than from women to men.[134]

Lesbians are often perceived to be at a minimal risk for STDs for a number of reasons: reports of low STD prevalence among women who have sex with women;[11,13,17] the presumption that lesbian sex does not involve contact between mucous membranes—such as during vaginal-penile sex—implying a low risk for infection; and the assumption that lesbian patients do not have male sexual partners. However, there are no epidemiologic studies to assess the prevalence of STDs among lesbians, and there is little information about the level of risk for transmission of STDs associated with the sexual activities in which lesbians engage.[135] Several studies have examined genital infection with HPV and bacterial vaginosis (BV) among women who have sex with women and have found higher rates of these organisms among the female partners of infected women than among heterosexual women.[14,24,39,136] It is known that some STDs (eg, herpesvirus) can be transmitted through skin contact and others (eg, trichomoniasis) through exposure to mucous secretions on hands or sex toys which could potentially introduce pathogens into the vagina.[137] It is important to note that a majority of lesbians have had male sexual partners and that an estimated 21% to 30% continue to have male sexual partners.[17,25,119,121] However, data from prospective population-based studies that assess sexual behavior (ie, gender of sexual partners and specific sexual activities and exposures) and rates of STDs are not available.

Human immunodeficiency virus. Although lesbians may be represented in some of the same HIV exposure categories as women in general, (injection drug use, heterosexual contact, history of blood transfusions, and "no identified risk"), an accurate estimate of HIV rates for lesbians in each category is unknown.[20,138] Research on HIV has not targeted this population, even though women comprise the population with the fastest-growing rates of HIV.[20,139] This lack of important information is due in part to the absence of a mechanism to report same-sex contact among women on AIDS case report forms.[138] The few studies of women who have sex with women (WSW) that assessed HIV seroprevalence provide varying estimates of HIV infection rates, probably due to the variation in the characteristics of the populations sampled. Some studies have reported higher HIV seroprevalence among WSW compared with exclusively heterosexual women;[15,140–143] however, the prevalence of known HIV risk factors has differed significantly. For example, WSW who had high rates of injection drug use and sexual contact with male partners were at high risk for HIV[15,16] versus women who self-identified as being lesbian in population-based and national samples.[11,17,43] Of particular concern regarding HIV transmission was the finding across several studies that a significant percentage of women (16 to 34%) reported having had sex with men who have had sex

with men.[1,12,16,26,144,145] One study found that sexually active female adolescents who had same-gender sexual partners were more likely than were heterosexually active female adolescents to engage in unprotected sex with male and female partners.[146]

Prospective studies of HIV transmission between WSW are limited to only one study that followed eighteen female couples, of which one woman was HIV positive (from sex with HIV-positive male partners or injection drug use) for 6 months.[147,148] Seroconversion did not occur among any of the HIV-negative partners.[147]

Although the validity of these findings has been questioned due to the small sample size and limited follow-up, they are consistent with the small number of cases of female-to-female transmission reported in the literature.[149–153] Of note, more systematic attempts to identify cases of female-to-female transmission of HIV are currently underway by the Centers for Disease Control and Prevention.[154]

Mental Health

The most common mental disorders experienced by women in general are anxiety disorders (30.5% lifetime occurrence; 22.6% within the past year), followed by affective disorders (23.9% lifetime occurrence; 14.1% within the past year), of which depression is the most commonly reported (21.3% lifetime occurrence; 12.9% within the past year).[155] However, little is known about lesbians' mental health including the prevalence and incidence of depression, anxiety disorders, psychotic disorders, dissociative disorders, and personality disorders.[11,58,62,156]

Early studies of lesbians' mental health relied on samples of women who were receiving mental health services, and were therefore biased to overreport the burden of mental illness among lesbians. However, among nonclinical samples of lesbians, studies have not found differences in the psychological adjustment between lesbians and other women,[156] and the reported rates of depression appear to be somewhat similar. Information about access to and use of mental health care services by lesbians is limited, as is variation among lesbian subgroups. Research also is needed to examine the experiences that lesbians have in mental health care settings and the effectiveness of various therapeutic approaches for lesbians.

Domestic Violence

Although there appears to be an increasing awareness of the issue of domestic violence by the lesbian community, there remains an unwillingness to recognize that it exists with the same violence, fear, and secrecy as in abusive heterosexual relationships.[157–163] Lesbian relationships may be susceptible to unique stressors due to the ongoing and cumulative effects of living in a homophobic society. These stressors may have a negative effect on the process of developing healthy relationships with others, and may be related to the presence of domestic violence in the lesbian community.[158–160] In addition, lesbian domestic violence may be perceived erroneously as "mutual" aggression, and therefore it may be taken less seriously than if the perpetrator were a man.

The societal perception of lesbian invisibility and the further aversion to address the issue of domestic violence results in minimal support, both within and outside lesbian communities, for lesbian victims of domestic violence. Not dissimilar to the heterosexual situation, lesbian victims of domestic violence frequently blame themselves for the abuse they sustain[141–143] and batterers often reinforce this belief to avoid accountability and to maintain control over the victim. A study of lesbians living in a large urban area found that emotional and physical abuse was reported in approximately 1 of 3 and 1 of 6 relationships, respectively. The greater rate of emotional abuse is consistent with the existent literature.[157,164]

SUMMARY

Due to the limited epidemiologic data currently available, understanding the health care problems of lesbians remains incomplete. It appears that lesbians are at an increased risk for not receiving adequate and appropriate health care, which may have a negative impact on short- and long-term health. Increased use of alcohol and tobacco may put lesbians at risk for heart disease, cancer, and other medical conditions to the same degree as heterosexual women who use these substances. Further study of lesbian health that relies on sound epidemiologic data is needed.

REFERENCES

1. Solarz AL. Lesbian health: current assessment and directions for the future. Institute of Medicine. Washington (DC): National Academy Press; 1999.
2. World Health Organization. Constitution of the World Health Organization. New York: International Health Conference; 1946.
3. Kinsey AC, Pomeroy W, Martin CE, Gebbard PE. Sexual behavior in the human female. New York: W.B. Saunders; 1953.
4. Laumann EO, Gagnon JH, Michael RT, Michaels S. The social organization of sexuality: sexual practices in the United States. Chicago: University of Chicago Press; 1994.
5. Tiefer, L. Social constructionism and the study of human sexuality. In: Shaver P, Hendrick C, editors. Sex and gender. Newbury Park (CA): Sage Publications, Inc.; 1987. p. 70–94.
6. Tiefer L, Kring B. Gender and the organization of sexual behavior. Psychiatr Clin North Am 1995;18: 25–37.
7. Tiefer L. The medicalization of sexuality: conceptual, normative, and professional issues. Ann Rev Sex Res 1996;7:252–82.
8. Johnson SR, Guenther SM, Laube D, et al. Factors influencing lesbian gynecologic care: a preliminary study. Am J Obstet Gynecol 1981;140:20–8.
9. Johnson SR, Smith EM, Guenther SM. Comparison of gynecologic health care problems between lesbians and bisexual women; a survey of 2,345 women. J Reprod Med 1987;32:805–11.
10. Smith EM, Johnson SR, Guenther SM. Health care attitudes and experiences during gynecologic care among lesbians and bisexuals. Am J Public Health 1985;5:1805–7.
11. Bradford J, Ryan C. The National Lesbian Health Care Survey: final report. Washington (DC): National Lesbian and Gay Health Foundation; 1987.
12. Cochran SD, Bybee D, Gage S, Mays VM. Prevalence of HIV-related self-reported sexual behaviors, sexually transmitted diseases, and problems with drugs and alcohol in 3 large surveys of lesbian and bisexual women: a look into a segment of the community. Women's Health Res Gender Behav Policy 1996; 2(1–2):11–33.
13. Robertson P, Schachter J. Failure to identify venereal disease in a lesbian population. Sex Transm Dis 1981; 8(2):75–6.
14. Berger BJ, Kolton S, Zenilman JM, et al. Bacterial vaginosis in lesbians: a sexually transmitted disease. Clin Infect Dis 1995;21:1402–5.
15. Bevier PJ, Chaisson MA, Heffernan RT, Castro KG. Women at a sexually transmitted disease clinic who reported same-sex contact: their HIV seroprevalence

and risk behaviors. Am J Public Health 1995;85: 1366–71.

16. Lemp GF, Jones M, Kellogg TA, et al. HIV seroprevalence and risk behaviors among lesbians and bisexual women in San Francisco and Berkeley, California. Am J Public Health 1995;85:1549–52.

17. Diamant AL, Schuster MA, McGuigan K, Lever J. Lesbians' sexual history with men: implications for taking a sexual history. Arch Intern Med 1999;159: 2730–6.

18. Diamant AL, Schuster M, Lever J. Receipt of preventive health services by lesbians. Am J Prev Med 2000; 19:141–8.

19. Skinner WF, Otis MD. Drug and alcohol use among lesbian and gay people in a southern US sample: epidemiological, comparative, and methodological findings from the Trilogy Project. J Homosex 1996;30(3):59–92.

20. Kennedy MB, Scarlett MI, Duerr AC, Chu SY. Assessing HIV risk among women who have sex with women: scientific and communication issues. J Am Med Womens Assoc 1995;50(3–4):103–7.

21. Bybee D. The Michigan Lesbian Health Survey. Detroit (MI): Michigan Department of Public Health; 1990.

22. Rankow EJ. Breast and cervical cancer among lesbians. Womens Health Issues 1995;5(3):123–9.

23. Warshafsky L. Lesbian health needs assessment. Los Angeles (CA): Los Angeles Gay and Lesbian Community Center; 1990.

24. Marrazzo JM, Koutsky LA, Stine K, et al. Genital human papillomavirus infection in women who have sex with women. J Infect Dis 1998;8:1604–9.

25. Einhorn L, Polgar M. HIV-risk behavior among lesbians and bisexual women. AIDS Educ Prev 1994; 6:514–23.

26. Gomez CA, Garcia DR, Kegebein VJ, et al. Sexual identity versus sexual behavior: implications for HIV prevention strategies for women who have sex with women. Women's Health Res Gender Behav Policy 1996;2(1–2):91–109.

27. Gage S. Preliminary findings: The National Lesbian and Bisexual Women's Health Survey. Lesbian Health Project of Los Angeles. New York: National Lesbian and Gay Health Conference; 1994.

28. White JC, Dull VT. Health risk factors and health-seeking behavior in lesbians. J Womens Health 1997; 6(1):103–12.

29. Zeidenstein L. Gynecological and childbearing needs of lesbians. J Nurse Midwifery 1990;35(1):10–8.

30. Fobair P, O'Hanlan K, Koopman C, et al. Comparison of lesbian and heterosexual women's response to newly diagnosed breast cancer. Psychooncology 2001;10(1):40–51.

31. Clark ME, Landers S, Linde R, Sperber J. The GLBT Health Access Project: a state-funded effort to improve access to care. Am J Public Health 2001;91: 895–6.

32. Mayer K, Appelbaum J, Rogers T, et al. The evolution of the Fenway Community Health model. Am J Public Health 2001;91(6):892–4.

33. Bailey JV, Kavanagh J, Owen C, et al. Lesbians and cervical screening. Br J Gen Prac, 2000;50:481–2.

34. Diamant AL, Schuster MA, Lever J. Receipt of preventive health care services by lesbians. Am J Prev Med, 2000;19:141–8.

35. Diamant AL, Schuster MA, McGuigan K, Lever J. Lesbians' sexual history with men: implications for taking a sexual history. Arch Intern Med, 1999; 159:2730–6.

36. Koh AS. Use of preventive health behaviors by lesbian, bisexual, and heterosexual women: questionnaire survey. West J Med, 2000;172:379–84.

37. Rothblum ED. Factor R. Lesbians and their sisters as a control group: demographic and mental health factors. Psychol Sci 2001;12(1):63–9.

38. Matthews AK, Hughes TL. Mental health service use by African American women: exploration of subpopulation differences. Cultur Divers Ethni Minor Psychol 2001;7(1):75–87.

39. Cochran S, Mays VM, Bowen D, et al. Cancer-related risk indicators and preventive screening behaviors among lesbians and bisexual women. Am J Public Health 2001;91:591–7.

40. Marrazzo JM, Koutsky LA, Stine KL, et al. Genital human papillomavirus infection in women who have sex with women. J Infect Dis 1998;8:1604–9.

41. Marrazzo JM, Koutsky LA, Kiviat NB, et al. Papanicolaou test screening and prevalence of genital human papillomavirus among women who have sex with women. Am J Public Health, 2001;91:947–52.

42. Sell RL, Becker JB. Sexual orientation data collection and progress toward Healthy People 2010. Am J Public Health 2001;91:876–82.

43. Diamant AL, Wold C, Spritzer K, Gelberg L. Health behaviors, health status, and access to and use of health care; a population-based study of lesbian, bisexual, and heterosexual women. Arch Fam Med, 2000;9:1043–51.

44. Rankow E. Sexual identity vs. sexual behavior. Am J Public Health 1996;86:1822–3.

45. White JC. HIV risk assessment and prevention among lesbians and women who have sex with women: Practical information for clinicians. Health Care Women Int 1997;18(2):127–38.

46. Chan CS. Issues of sexual identity in an ethnic minority: the case of Chinese American lesbians, gay men, and bisexual people. In: D'Augelli AR, Patterson CJ, editors. Lesbian, gay, and bisexual identities over the lifespan: psychological perspectives. New York: Oxford University Press; 1995. p. 87–101.

47. Cochran SD, Mays VM. Disclosure of sexual preference to physicians by black lesbian and bisexual women. Western J Med 1988;149:616–9.

48. Greene B. Lesbian women of color: triple jeopardy. In: Comas-Diaz L, Greene B, editors. Women of color: integrating ethnic and gender identities in psychotherapy. New York: Guilford Press; 1994. p. 389–427.

49. Nakajima GA, Chan YH, Lee K. Mental health issues for gay and lesbian Asian Americans. In: Cabaj RP, Stein TS, editors. Textbook of homosexuality and mental health. Washington (DC): American Psychiatric Press; 1996. p. 563–81.

50. Whitam FL, Daskalos C, Sobolewski CG, Padilla P. The emergence of lesbian sexuality and identity cross-culturally: Brazil, Peru, the Philipines, and the United States. Arch Sexual Behav 1998;27(1):31–56.

51. Cochran SD, Mays VM. Relation between psychiatric syndromes and behaviorally defined sexual orientation in a sample of the US population. Am J Epidemiol, 2000;151:516–23.

52. Peters DK, Cantrell PJ. Factors distinguishing samples of lesbians and heterosexual women. J Homosex 1991;21:1–15.

53. Brogan D, Frank E, Elon L, O'Hanlan KA. Methodologic concerns in defining lesbian for health research. Epidemiology 2001;12:109–13.

54. Krieger N, Sidney S. Prevalence and health implications of anti-gay discrimination: a study of black and white women and men in the CARDIA cohort. Int J Health Serv 1997;27(1):157–76.

55. Adler NE, Boyce T, Chesney MA, et al. Socioeconomic status and health: the challenge of the gradient. Am Psychol 1994;49(1):15–24.

56. McEwen BS. Protective and damaging effects of stress mediators. Semin Med Beth Israel Deaconess Medical Center 1998;338(3):171–9.

57. Gillow KE, Davis LL. Lesbian stress and coping methods. J Psychosoc Nurs 1987;25:28–32.

58. Bradford J, Ryan C, Rothblum ED. National Lesbian Health Care Survey: implications for mental health care. J Consult Clin Psychol 1994;62:228–42

59. O'Hanlan KA. Lesbian health and homophobia: perspectives for the treating obstetrician/gynecologist. Curr Probl Obstet Gynecol Fertility 1995;18(4): 93–136.

60. Cochran SD, Mays VM. Depressive distress among homosexually active African-American men and women. Am J Psychiatry 1994;151:524–9.

61. Seeman TE, McEwen B. Impact of social environment characteristics on neuroendocrine regulation. Psychosom Med 1996;58:459–71.

62. Trippet SE. Lesbians' mental health concerns. Health Care Women Int 1994;15:317–23.

63. Institute of Medicine. Reducing risks for mental disorders: frontiers for preventive intervention research. Washington (DC): National Academy Press; 1994.

64. White J, Levinson W. Primary care of lesbian patients. J Gen Intern Med 1993;8(1):41–7.

65. American Psychological Association, 1997. http://www.apa.org.

66. Laird J, Green RJ, editors. Lesbians and gays in couples and families: a handbook for therapists. San Francisco (CA): Jossey-Bass; 1996. p. 153–82.

67. Reagan P. The interaction of health professionals and their lesbian clients. Patient Counsel Health Educ 1981;3:21–5.

68. Stevens PE, Hall JM. Stigma, health beliefs, and experiences with health care in lesbian women. Image J Nurs Sch 1988;20:69–73.

69. Stevens PE. Lesbians and HIV: clinical, research, and policy issues. Am J Orthopsychiatry 1993;63: 289–94.

70. Moran N. Lesbian health care needs. Can Fam Physician 1996;42:879–84.

71. Trippet SE, Bain J. Reasons American lesbians fail to seek traditional health care. Health Care Women Int 1990;13:145–53.

72. Deevey S. Older lesbian women: an invisible minority. J Gerontol Nurs 1990;16:35–9.

73. Dardick L, Grady KE. Openness between gay persons and health professionals. Ann Intern Med 1980; 93:115–9.

74. Kripke CC, Vaias L, Elliott A. The importance of taking a sensitive sexual history. Tarna 1994;271:713.

75. Merrill JM, Laux LF, Thornby JI. Why doctors have difficulty with sex histories. South Med J 1990; 83:613–7.

76. Temple-Smith M, Hammond J, Pyett P, Preswell N. Barriers to sexual history taking in general practice. Aust Fam Phys 1996;25 (9 Suppl 2):673–9.

77. Vollmer SA, Wells KB. The preparedness of freshman medical students for taking sexual histories. Arch Sex Behav 1989,18:167–77.

78. Tesar CM, Rovi SLD. Survey of curriculum on homosexuality/bisexuality in departments of family medicine. Fam Med 1998;30:283–7.

79. Townsend MH, Wallick MM. "Gay, lesbian, and bisexual issues in medical schools. In: Cabaj RP, Stein TS, editors. Textbook of homosexuality and mental health. Washington (DC): American Psychiatric Press, Inc.; 1996. p. 633–655.

80. Stevens PE. Lesbian health care research: a review of the literature from 1970 to 1990. Health Care Women Int 1992;13(2):91–120.

81. Chaimowitz GA. Homophobia among psychiatric residents, family practice residents and psychiatric faculty. Canadian J of Psychiatry 1991;36(5):353–356.

82. Kelly CE. Bringing homophobia out of the closet: antigay bias within the patient-physician relationship. Pharos 1992;Winter:2–8.

83. Ramos MM, Tellez CM, Palley TB, et al. Attitudes of physicians practicing in New Mexico toward gay men and lesbians in the profession. Acad Med 1998; 73:436–8.

84. Matthews WC, Booth MW, Turner JD, Kessler L. Physician's attitudes toward homosexuality: survey of a California county medical society. West J Med 1986;144:106–10.

85. Geddes VA. Lesbian expectations and experiences with family doctors. How much does the physician's sex matter to lesbians? Can Fam Phys 1994;40: 908–20.

86. White JC, Levinson W. Lesbian health care. What a primary care physician needs to know. West J Med 1995;162:463–6.

87. Rankow EJ. Lesbian health issues for the primary care provider [comment and discussion J Fam Pract 1995;41:224, 227]. J Fam Pract 1995;40:486–96.

88. Smith EM, Johnson SR, Guenther SM. Health care attitudes and experiences gynecologic care among lesbians and bisexuals. Am J Public Health 1985; 75:1086–7.

89. Denenberg R. Report on lesbian health. Womens Health Issues 1995;5(2):81–91.

90. Roberts SJ, Sorensen L. Lesbian health care: a review and recommendations for health promotion in primary care settings. Nurse Pract 1995;20(6):42–7.

91. Stevens PE. Structural and interpersonal impact of heterosexual assumptions on lesbian health care clients. Nurs Res 1995;44(1):25–30.

92. D'Augelli AR, Garnets LD. Lesbian, gay, and bisexual communities. In: D'Augelli AR, Patterson CJ, editors. Lesbian, gay, and bisexual identities over the lifespan: psychological perspectives. New York: Oxford University Press; 1995. p. 293–320.

93. Hollander J, Haber L. Ecological transition: using Bronfenbrenner's model to study sexual identity change. In: Stern P, editor. Lesbian health: what are the issues? Washington (DC): Taylor and Frances; 1993. p. 31–9.

94. Morrow DF. Coming out issues for adult lesbians: a group intervention. Soc Work 1996;41:647–56.

95. Savin-Williams RC, Rodriguez RG. A developmental, clinical perspective on lesbian, gay male, and bisexual youths. In: Gullotta TP, Adams GR, Montemayor R, editors. Adolescent sexuality. Advances in adolescent development. Newbury Park (CA): Sage Publications; 1993. p. 77–101.

96. Cabaj RP. Substance abuse in the gay and lesbian community. In: Lowenson J, Ruiz P, Millman R, eds. Substance Abuse: A Comprehensive Textbook. Baltimore, MD: Williams and Wilkins, 1992:852–860.

97. Cabaj RP. Substance abuse in gay men, lesbians, and bisexuals. In: Cabaj RP, Stein TS, editors. Textbook of homosexuality and mental health. Washington (DC): American Psychiatric Press, Inc.; 1996. p. 783–799.

98. Finnegan DG, McNally EB. Lesbian women. In: Engs RC, editor. Women: alcohol and other drugs. Dubuque (IA): Kendall/Hunt Publishing Company; 1990. p. 149–56.

99. Glaus KO. Alcoholism. Chemical dependency and the lesbian client. Women Ther 1989;8(2):131–44.

100. Hall JM. Lesbians and alcohol: patterns and paradoxes in medical notions and lesbians' beliefs. J Psychoactive Drugs 1993;25(2):109–19.

101. National Gay and Lesbian Task Force. Lesbian health issues and recommendations. Washington (DC): National Gay and Lesbian Task Force; 1993.

102. Skinner WF. The prevalence and demographic predictors of illicit and licit drug use among lesbians and gay men. Am J Public Health 1994;84: 1307–10.

103. Bloomfield K. A comparison of alcohol consumption between lesbians and heterosexual women in

an urban population. Drug Alcohol Depend 1993; 33:257–69.

104. Hall JM. Lesbians recovering from alcohol problems: an ethnographic study of health care experiences. Nurs Res 1994;43:238–44.

105. Turner CF, Ku L, Rogers SM, et al. Adolescent sexual behavior, drug use, and violence: increased reporting with computer survey technology. Science 1998;280:867–73.

106. Neisen JH, Sandall H. Alcohol and other drug abuse in gay/lesbian populations: related to victimization? J Psychol Human Sex 1990;3(1):151–68.

107. Cassidy MA, Hughes TL. Lesbian health: barriers to care. In: McElmurry BJ, Parker RS, editors. Annual review of women's health. Vol. 3. New York: National League for Nursing Press; 1997. p. 67–87.

108. Hughes TL, Wilsnack SC. Use of alcohol among lesbians: research and clinical implications. Am J Orthopsychiatry 1997;67(1):20–36.

109. Eliason MJ. Caring for the lesbian, gay, or bisexual patient: issues for critical care nurses. Crit Care Nurs Q 1996;19(1):65–72.

110. Haas AP. Lesbian health issues: an overview. In: Dan AJ, editor. Reframing women's health: multidisciplinary research and practice. Thousand Oaks (CA): Sage Publications; 1994. p. 339–56.

111. Carroll N, Goldstein RS, Lo W, Mayer KH. Gynecological infections and sexual practices of Massachusetts lesbian and bisexual women. J Gay Lesbian Med Assoc 1997;1(1):15–23.

112. Diamant AL, Wold C. Variation in physical and mental health and functioning among women: studying the association with sexual orientation. National Lesbian Health Conference 2001, San Francisco, CA, June 2001.

113. Valanis BG, Bowen DJ, Bassford T, et al. Sexual orientation and health: comparisons in the women's health initiative sample. Arch Fam Med, 2000;9: 843–53.

114. Pamuk E, Makuc D, Heck K, et al. Socioeconomic status and health chartbook. Health, United States, 1998. Hyattsville (MD): National Center for Health Statistics; 1998.

115. Bowen D, Hickman KM, Powers D. Importance of psychological variables in understanding risk perceptions and breast cancer screening of African-American women. Womens Health 1997; 3:227–42.

116. American Cancer Society. Cancer facts and figures 1997. http://www.cancer.org.

117. Price JH, Easton AN, Telljohann SK, Wallace PB. Perceptions of cervical cancer and Pap smear screening behavior by women's sexual orientation. J Community Health 1996;21(2):89–105.

118. Bybee D, Roeder V. Michigan Lesbian Health Survey: results relevant to AIDS. A report to the Michigan Organization for Human Rights and the Michigan Department of Public Health. Lansing (MI): Department of Health and Human Services; 1990.

119. Ferris DG, Batish S, Wright TC, et al. A neglected lesbian health concern: cervical neoplasia. J Fam Pract 1996;43:581–4.

120. Skinner CJ, Stokes J, Kirlew Y, et al. A case-controlled study of the sexual health needs of lesbians. Genitourin Med 1996;72:277–80.

121. O'Hanlan KA, Crum CP. Human papillomavirus-associated cervical intraepithelial neoplasia following lesbian sex. Obstet Gynecol 1996;4(Pt 2):702–3.

122. Dashwood RH. Early detection and prevention of colorectal cancer [review]. Oncol Rep 1999;6: 277–81.

123. Krebs-Smith SM. Progress in improving diet to reduce cancer risk [comments]. Cancer 1998;83: 1425–32.

124. Mink PJ, Folsom AR, Sellers TA, Kushi LH. Physical activity, waist-to-hip ration, and other risk factors for ovarian cancer; a follow-up study of older women. Epidemiology 1996;7(1):38–45.

125. Pukkala E, Weiderpass E. Time trends in socio-economic differences in incidence rates of cancers of the breast and female genital organs (Finland, 1971–1995). Int J Cancer 1999;81(1):56–61.

126. Greven KM, Corn BW. Endometrial cancer. Curr Probl Cancer 1997;21(2):65–127.

127. La Vecchia C, Franceschi S. Oral contraceptives and ovarian cancer. Eur J Cancer Prev 1999;8:297–304.

128. Sulak PJ. Oral contraceptives: therapeutic uses and quality-of-life benefits-case presentations. Contraception 1999;599(1 Suppl):35–8S.

129. National Heart Lung and Blood Institute. Facts about heart disease and women: are you at risk? 1997.

130. Kost K, Forrest JD. American women's sexual behavior and exposure to risk of sexually transmitted diseases. Fam Plann Perspect 1992;24:244–54.

131. Lazzarin A, Saracco A, Musiccom, et al. Man-to-woman sexual transmission of the human immunodeficiency virus. Arch Intern Med 1991;151: 2411–6.

132. CDC-MMWR-1993 Centers for Disease Control and Prevention. Sexually transmitted disease

surveillance, 1995. Atlanta (GA): Centers for Disease Control and Prevention, Division of STD Prevention; 1996.

133. Cates W Jr, Stone KM. Family planning, sexually transmitted diseases and contraceptive choice: a literature update—Part II. Fam Plann Perspect 1992; 24(3):122–8.

134. Institute of Medicine. The hidden epidemic: confronting sexually transmitted diseases. Washington (DC): National Academy Press; 1997.

135. Diamant AL, Lever J. Sexual activities and risk reduction for sexually transmitted diseases among lesbians. J Gay Lesbian Med Assoc 2000;4(2):41–8.

136. Edwards A, Thin RN. Sexually transmitted diseases in lesbians. Int J STD AIDS 1990;1:178–81.

137. Eschenbach DA. Bacterial vaginosis and anaerobes in obstetric-gynecologic infection. Clin Infect Dis 1993;16:S282–7.

138. Chu SY, Buehler JW, Fleming PL, Berkelman RL. Epidemiology of reported cases of AIDS in lesbians, United States 1980–89. Am J Public Health 1990; 80:1380–1.

139. Solomon L, Moore J, Gleghorn A, et al. HIV testing behaviors in a population of inner-city women at high risk for HIV infection. J Acquir Immune Defic Syndr Hum Retrovirol 1996;13:267–72.

140. Cohen H, Marmor M, Wolfe H, Ribble D. Risk assessment of HIV transmission among lesbians [letter]. J Acquir Immune Defic Syndr 1993;6: 1173–4.

141. Mays VM. Are lesbians at risk for HIV infection? Womens Health Res Gender Behav Policy 1996;2 (1–2):1–9.

142. Mays VM, Cochran SD, Pies C, et al. The risk of HIV infection for lesbians and other women who have sex with women: implications for HIV research, prevention, policy, and services. Womens Health Res Gender Behav Policy 1996;2(1–2):119–39.

143. Young RM, Weissman G, Cohen JB. Assessing the risk in the absence of information: HIV risk among women injection drug users who have sex with women. AIDS Public Policy J 1992;7:175–83.

144. Reinisch JM, Ziemba-Davis M, Sanders SA. Sexual behavior and AIDS: lessons from art and sex research. In: Voeller B, Reinisch JM, Gottlieb M, editors. AIDS and sex: an integrated biomedical and biobehavioral approach. New York: Oxford University Press; 1990. p. 37–80.

145. Ziemba-Davis M, Sanders SA, Reinisch JM. Lesbians' sexual interactions with men: behavioral

bisexuality and risk for sexually transmitted disease (STD) and human immunodeficiency virus (HIV). Women's Health: Research on Gender Behavior and Policy 1996;2(1–2):61–74.

146. Hunter J, Rosario M. Rotheram-Borus MJ. Sexual and substance abuse acts that place adolescent lesbians at risk for HIV. In: IXth International Conference on AIDS and the IVth STD World Congress. Berlin: IXth International Conference on AIDS; 1993.

147. Raiteri R, Fora R, Gioannini P, et al. Seroprevalence, risk factors and attitude to HIV-1 in a representative sample of lesbians in Turin. Genitourin Med 1994; 70:200–5.

148. Raiteri R, Fora R, Sinicco A. No HIV-1 transmission through lesbian sex. Lancet 1994;344:270.

149. Marmor M, Weiss LR, Lyden M, et al. Ann Intern Med 1986;105:969.

150. Monzon OT, Capellan JM. Female-to-female transmission of HIV. Lancet 1987;2(8549):40–1.

151. Perry S, Jacobsberg L, Fogel K. Orogenital transmission of human immunodeficiency virus. Ann Intern Med 1989;111:951–2.

152. Chu SY, Hammett TA, Buehler JW. Update: epidemiology of reported cases of AIDS in women who report sex only with other women, United States, 1980–1991 [letter]. AIDS 1992;6:518–9.

153. Reynolds G. HIV and lesbian sex. Lancet 1994;344): 544–5.

154. Centers for Disease Control. HIV/AIDS surveillance report, 1996. Vol. 8. Atlanta (GA): Centers for Disease Prevention; 1997.

155. Kessler RC, McGonagle KA, Zhao S, et al. Lifetime and 12-month prevalence of DSM-III-R psychiatric disorders in the United States: results from the National Comorbidity Survey. Arch Gen Psychiatry 1994;51:8–19.

156. Rothblum ED. Depression among lesbian: an invisible and unresearched phenomenon. J Gay Lesbian Psychother 1990;1(3):67–87.

157. Brand PA, Kidd AH. Frequency of physical aggression in heterosexual and female homosexual dyads. Psychol Rep 1986;59:1307–13.

158. Hammond N. Lesbian victims of relationship violence. Women Ther 1988;8(1–2):89–105.

159. Hart B. Safe space for battered lesbians. In: Lobel K, editor. Naming the violence: speaking out about lesbian battering. Seattle: Seal Press; 1986. p. 95–7.

160. Hart B. Lesbian battering: an examination. In: Lobel K, editor. Naming the violence: speaking out

about lesbian battering. Seattle: Seal Press; 1986. p. 173–200.

161. Kanuha V. Compounding the triple jeopardy: battering in lesbian of color relationships. Women Ther 1990;9(1–2):169–84

162. Kelly EE, Warshafsky L. Partner abuse in gay male and lesbian couples. Paper presented at the Third National Conference for Family Violence Researchers. Durham (NH): 1987.

163. Leeder E. Enmeshed in pain: counseling the lesbian battering couple. Women Ther 1988;7(1):81–99.

164. Renzetti, CM. Building a second closet: third party responses to victims of lesbian partner abuse. Fam Relations 1988;38:157–63.

8

THE PERIODIC SCREENING EXAMINATION AND CURRENT PREVENTIVE HEALTH RECOMMENDATIONS

Jodi Friedman, MD

Preventive medicine may be defined as the practice of protecting and promoting health in a prospective manner. Over the last century, dramatic improvements in health and life expectancy in the United States have occurred as a result of public health and preventive medicine practices; however, the vast majority of premature death and disability continues to be attributable to preventable causes.[1] The purpose of this chapter is to review basic principles of prevention and to provide the clinician with a practical and comprehensive guide to recommended preventive services for the nonpregnant adult woman. Unfortunately, however, preventive services recommendations often differ between major organizations because of different interpretations of the literature or, more commonly, because there is little or no data available to support the intervention. For this reason, it is essential that the practicing clinician understand the fundamental principles of prevention to develop his or her own prevention strategy with each patient.

PRINCIPLES OF PREVENTIVE MEDICINE

Preventive interventions may be broken down into four general categories: screening tests, counseling interventions, immunizations, and chemoprophylactic regimens. **Primary prevention** measures refer to those interventions that result in preventing a target condition from ever developing (eg, tetanus immunization or smoking cessation). When possible, primary prevention is the preferred prevention strategy for a given target condition. **Secondary prevention** is aimed at detecting a disease in an early and presymptomatic stage and making an intervention that prevents the disease from further development. Screening practices are, for the most part, examples of secondary prevention; that is, they are used to find existent asymptomatic diseases. An important exception to this, however, is a screening test used to identify risk factors for another disease. Screening for hypercholesterolemia, for example, is a form of primary prevention for the development of coronary artery disease (CAD); that is, we are identifying a risk factor and then making an intervention in hopes of preventing CAD from ever developing. **Tertiary prevention** measures are actually forms of treatment of clinical disease, such as insulin therapy to prevent the complications of diabetes mellitus, and are beyond the scope of this chapter.

When practicing any form of preventive medicine it is essential to remember a fundamental principle in the practice of medicine: primum non nocere ("first do no harm"). By definition, preventive medicine deals with asymptomatic (and predominantly healthy) people, so it is imperative that clinicians pay close attention to risk-to-benefit ratios before recommending an intervention. Accordingly, the practice of evidence-based medicine is probably more important in guiding preventive services than in any other area of medicine.

For a preventive service to be effective, several criteria must be met. Screening tests must have adequate accuracy in detecting presymptomatic disease, and treatment at a presymptomatic stage must yield therapeutic results superior to treating patients when they present with signs or symptoms of the disease. Similarly, counseling interventions should be based on changing behaviors that have been shown to effectively reduce the risk for a given target condition, and there should be some evidence that the counseling may actually be effective in changing behavior. Offering immunizations and chemoprophylaxis should likewise be based on evidence of efficacy of these interventions in preventing disease.

The potential adverse effects of preventive measures are considerable and should not be underestimated. In addition to direct physical complications of the intervention (such as a colonic perforation during endoscopy or an immunization reaction), one must consider the potential adverse outcomes associated with a positive screening test (remembering that a substantial proportion of positive results will be false-positives.) Positive test results may lead to marked anxiety, possible complications of the ensuing work-up, and labeling and insurability problems. Of course there are also important economic implications to consider, as preventive services are applied to large populations.

SOURCES OF PREVENTIVE SERVICES RECOMMENDATIONS

Preventive services recommendations come from a variety of sources, and, as stated, there is often discordance among these various sources. Expert panels have extensively evaluated a wide variety of preventive services and have developed guidelines based on rigorous literature review. Two of the most commonly cited are the United States Preventive Services Task Force (USPSTF) and the Canadian Task Force on the Periodic Health Exam (CTF), which has been renamed the Canadian Task Force on Preventive Health Care. In general, these organizations tend to recommend relatively fewer interventions than the various subspecialty societies (such as the American Cancer Society) because of their more rigorous

TABLE 8–1. Quality of Evidence

Level Description

I	Evidence obtained from at least one properly randomized controlled trial
II–1	Evidence obtained from well-designed controlled trials without randomization
II–2	Evidence obtained from well-designed cohort or case-control analytic studies, preferably from more than one center or research group
II–3	Evidence obtained from multiple time series with or without the intervention; Dramatic results in uncontrolled experiments (eg, the results of the introduction of penicllin treatment in the 1940s) could also be regarded as this type of evidence
III	Opinions of respected authorities, based on clinical experience; descriptive studies and case reports; or reports of expert committees

From US Preventive Services Task Force. Guide to clinical preventive services. 2nd ed. Baltimore: Williams and Wilkins; 1996.

requirements of proof of efficacy for any given intervention that they recommend.

The USPSTF and the CTF have devised a *quality-of-evidence* rating system that is applied to each preventive service intervention they review.[2] The highest rating is given to those interventions that are supported by at least one properly randomized controlled trial. Well-designed cohort or case-controlled studies receive the next highest quality rating, whereas opinions of well-respected authorities and expert committees receive the lowest quality-of-evidence scores (Table 8–1). Recommendations from USPSTF and CTF are then graded on a five-point scale (A to E) that takes into account the quality of evidence in support of the given intervention (Table 8–2). Interventions that have proved effective in well-designed studies (or have shown consistent benefit in many weaker-designed studies) receive A or B recommendations. Interventions that have proved to be ineffective or harmful (in this same manner) are given D or E recommendations. For many preventive services, however, there is insufficient evidence available to recommend either for or against its use—these measures are given a C recommendation.

The lack of evidence for the effectiveness of these interventions with a C rating does not mean they are necessarily ineffective; what it does mean is

TABLE 8–2. Strength of Recommendations

Scale	Description
A	There is good evidence to support the recommendation that the condition be specifically considered in a periodic health examination.
B	There is fair evidence to support the recommendation that the condition be specifically considered in a periodic health examination.
C	There is insufficient evidence to recommend for or against the inclusion of the condition in a periodic health examination, but recommendation may be made on other grounds.
D	There is fair evidence to support the recommendation that the condition be excluded from consideration in a periodic health examination.
E	There is good evidence to support the recommendation that the condition be excluded from consideration in a periodic health examination.

From US Preventive Services Task Force. Guide to Clinical preventive services. 2nd ed. Baltimore: Williams and Wilkins; 1996.

that the clinician must make the decision of whether or not to make these interventions without the benefit of convincing evidence. For some interventions, where the burden of suffering from the target condition is high and the risks of the intervention are low, it may be prudent to perform the intervention despite the lack of available evidence. Counseling patients to avoid driving while under the influence of alcohol or drugs would be an example of this type of intervention. In contrast, there are other services with a C recommendation where the potential risks of the intervention are great, such as in routinely prescribing aspirin as a prophylaxis for myocardial infarction in women without CAD. Here, one would want a reasonably strong evidence of efficacy to justify making this potentially higher-risk intervention.

Recommended services are usually tailored to the age, sex, and particular risk factors of individual patients. By doing so, emphasis is placed on the periodic health visit, in contrast to the older concept of the annual comprehensive physical examination. Instead of performing a complete physical examination and a battery of tests on all patients indiscriminately, the periodic health visit is a time when the clinician can review lifestyle and behaviors, and update family history to reassess a patient's risk factors for various conditions. Preventive services can then be offered based on the updated assessment of this particular patient's risk profile for target conditions.

SCREENING

Screening is defined as the application of a test to detect a disease or condition in a person who has no known signs or symptoms of that disease or condition. The appropriateness of a given screening test depends on characteristics of the target disease, the test, and the population being screened. The disease should have a significant burden of suffering, have effective and available treatment, and be detectable during an early stage when treatment is more effective than in later stages. The test should have low morbidity, appropriate levels of sensitivity and specificity, and be acceptable to the patient in terms of cost and discomfort. The population should have a sufficiently high prevalence of the disease, access to the test, and access to further work-up and treatment if the test results are positive.

The **sensitivity** of a test is the percentage of individuals with the condition that test positive. If the sensitivity of a screening test is too low, an unacceptable rate of false-negatives will result; this may lead to false reassurance that can delay the ultimate diagnosis of the disease. An individual with a false sense of security might delay seeking medical attention when warning symptoms of the disease develop, or exhibit decreased compliance with risk-reducing behaviors. The **specificity** of a test is the percentage of individuals without the disease that test negative. If the specificity of a screening test is too low, there will be an unacceptable number of healthy persons who test positive for the disease. The potential harms of false-positive results include physical complications of the ensuing work-up, psychological distress, difficulties with future insurability, and significant financial costs. Given the fact that no screening test is 100% sensitive and 100% specific, the clinician needs to make a determination of the likelihood that the patient with a positive test result actually has the condition. This determination is referred to as the **positive predictive value (PPV)** of a test: the proportion of positive test results that are correct (true-positives). For any given sensitivity and specificity of a test, the PPV increases and decreases with the prevalence of the disease in the population being screened. Because of this relationship between PPV and prevalence, screening tests

TABLE 8–3. Screening Recommendations

Target Condition	Screening Test	Ages	Time Interval	Source of Recommendation
Breast cancer	BSE	Adult women	Monthly self-examination	ACS, ACOG
	CBE	40 or 50–70 yr	Annually	Most groups
	Mammography	40 or 50–69 yr (or beyond if reasonable life expectancy)	Every 1–2 yr	All groups (ACS, ACOG—begin at 40 yr)
Cervical cancer	Pap smear	18 yr (or first sexual activity) to 65 yr (or longer if screening not up to date)	Every 1–3 yr	All groups
Colorectal cancer	DRE	50+ yr	With pelvic examination	ACS and ACOG only
	FOBT	50+ yr	Annually	Most groups
	Sigmoidoscopy	50+ yr	Every 3–5 yr	Most groups
Ovarian cancer	Bimanual pelvic examination	Adult women	At time of Pap smear	ACS and ACOG only
Skin cancer	Total skin examination	20–39 yr	Every 3 yr	ACS only
		40+ yr	Yearly	ACS only
High blood pressure	Blood pressure	All adults	Every 2 yr	All groups
High cholesterol	Lipoprotein profile	All adults	Every 5 yr	NCEP
		45–65 yr	Periodically	USPSTF, ACP, AAFP
STDs	Cervical samples for chlamydia and gonorrhea Serologic tests for syphilis HIV test	High-risk women	Discretionary	All groups (see text)
TB	PPD	High-risk women	Discretionary	All groups
Diabetes mellitus	Fasting plasma glucose	45+ yr	Every 3 yr	American Diabetes Association (other groups suggest to screen high-risk women only)
Thyroid disease	TSH	65+ yr	Every 3–5 yr	ACOG only (USPSTF, ACP, and CTF recommend against routine screening)
Obesity	Height and weight	All women	At routine office visits	All groups

AAFP = American Academy of Family Physicians; ACOG = American College of Obstetricians and Gynecologists; ACP = American College of Physicians; ACS = American Cancer Society; BSE = breast self-examination; CBE = clinical breast examination; CTF = Canadian Task Force on Preventive Health Care; DRE = digital rectal examination; FOBT = fecal occult blood test; HDL = high-density lipoproteins; HIV = human immunodeficiency virus; NCEP = National Cholesterol Education Panel; Pap = Papanicolaou's; PPD = purified protein derivative of tuberculin; STD = sexually transmitted disease; TB = tuberculosis; TSH = thyroid-stimulating hormone; USPSTF = US Preventive Services Task Force.

perform the best when we can identify sufficiently high-risk populations in which the prevalence of the disease is higher, and then selectively screen these individuals.

Finally, when evaluating the effectiveness of screening strategies, one should keep in mind that there are potential biases that may exaggerate the perceived benefits of screening. **Lead-time bias** refers to the observation that survival is lengthened in a screened individual when, in truth, all that has been done is that the time of diagnosis has occurred earlier; that is, the period of time between diagnosis and death has been lengthened without any true prolongation of life, as the natural history of the disease has not been changed.

Length bias refers to the tendency of screening to detect a disproportionate number of less aggressive cases of a disease, because there is a longer period of time when the individual is alive with the disease (as compared with individuals with rapidly progressing forms of the disease), and therefore a greater chance that these less aggressive cases will be detected at any given point in time. In this way, aggressive cases of the disease are under-represented in the cases detected by screening, and therefore survival rates for screened individuals are favorable when compared with unscreened cases, even if the screening itself does not improve outcome.

Screening Recommendations

In this section, recommendations for a variety of screening tests are reviewed, with specific emphasis placed on recommendations from major organizations. These include screening for neoplastic, cardiovascular, infectious, and metabolic diseases. See Table 8–3 for a quick reference guide to these recommended screening interventions. Screening for specific geriatric syndromes is covered in Chapter 85.

Neoplastic Diseases
Breast cancer is the most common type of nonskin cancer in women, and it is the second leading cause of cancer mortality in women in the United States, following lung cancer.[1] A woman's lifetime risk of developing breast cancer is about 12%, and she has a 3.6% lifetime chance of dying from breast cancer.[3] The three screening modalities employed for early detection of breast cancer are breast self-examination (BSE), clinical breast examination (CBE), and mammography.

Data regarding the accuracy and efficacy of BSE are extremely limited and somewhat conflicting. The American Academy of Family Physicians (AAFP), American College of Obstetricians and Gynecologists (ACOG), and American Cancer Society (ACS) recommend routine teaching of BSE to all adult women. Because of the limited and conflicting available evidence, USPSTF, CTF, and American College of Physicians (ACP) do not include BSE in their recommendations for breast cancer screening.[1]

Although there is no direct evidence assessing the effectiveness of CBE alone, multiple studies have shown that CBE in conjunction with mammography is effective in reducing breast cancer mortality in women aged 50 to 70 years.[4-6] The ACOG and ACS recommend CBE during the periodic health examination and then annually beginning at age 40 years. The ACP recommends CBE annually beginning at age 40 years, and CTF and AAFP recommend CBE annually from ages 50 to 69 years. The USPSTF states there is insufficient evidence to recommend for or against CBE alone.[2]

Mammography is the most effective screening modality for the early detection of breast cancer, yet there exists considerable controversy over the appropriate age range for screening. Seven randomized controlled trials evaluating annual or biennial screening mammography have consistently shown reductions in breast cancer mortality by 25 to 30% in women aged 50 to 69 years.[7]

Subgroup analyses of those studies that included women in their forties have yielded conflicting results, with only one study showing statistically significant improvements in mortality for women beginning screening between ages 40 and 49 years.[2,8] None of these studies (except the Canadian NCSS 1 Trial), however, was designed to have the power to test the effectiveness of screening in this age group alone. The Canadian NBSS 1 Trial was a randomized controlled trial specifically designed to test the effectiveness of screening mammography for women in their forties. The results showed *no* risk reduction in breast cancer mortality at 7 years; unfortunately, this study has been widely criticized for methodologic problems with the randomization process as well as poor mammogram quality.[6,7] A meta-analysis of all the randomized controlled trials that have included screening women in their forties reveals a *nonsignificant* trend of a 15 to 17% reduction in breast cancer mortality. However, if the Canadian study is taken out of the meta-analysis, then the 15% breast cancer mortality reduction does reach statistical significance.[7]

There is also limited and conflicting evidence regarding screening of women aged 70 to 74 years,[2] and there are no clinical trials evaluating screening mammography in women over age 74 years. Because the incidence of breast cancer and the sensitivity of mammography both increase with age, the positive predictive value of mammography increases in older women, and therefore one would expect that mammography would only become increasingly effective as a screening tool for breast cancer in women as they age. It must be remembered, however, that as women get older and develop an increasing number of medical illnesses, any single screening intervention will have less of an effect on total mortality because of competing comorbidities contributing to mortality rates.

For women of average risk, USPSTF and AAFP recommend screening mammography every 1 to 2 years for women aged 50 to 69 years, and consideration of screening beyond this if the woman has a reasonable life expectancy. The CTF recommends annual screening mammography for all women aged 50 to 69 years, whereas the ACP recommends screening women aged 50 to 74 years every 1 to 2 years. The ACOG and ACS both recommend beginning regular screening at age 40 years, without commenting on an upper age limit. The American Geriatrics Society recommends that women over 65 years should be screened every 2 to 3 years until age 85 years. For high-risk women (defined as having a first-degree relative with premenopausal breast cancer or a personal history of endometrial or ovarian cancer), CTF and ACOG recommend beginning screening mammography at age 35 years. The USPSTF states that although there is no direct evidence evaluating the effectiveness of screening mammography in high-risk women under 50 years of age, recommendations for screening such women can be made on other grounds. The ACP states that high-risk women should receive the same screening as average-risk women, unless a woman is extremely anxious and desires more intensive screening.[1,2]

Cervical cancer mortality has decreased by anywhere from 20 to 60%, and the incidence of invasive cervical cancer has decreased by approximately 70% since the introduction of the Papanicolaou (Pap) smear. All organizations agree that adult women who are sexually active should undergo routine Pap smear testing, although there remains disagreement over when to start, how often to do it, and when to stop. Many groups (eg, ACOG, ACS, AAFP, and ACP) recommend starting at 18 to 20 years of age or when a woman becomes sexually active, whichever comes first; however, there is substantial evidence that women who have never engaged in sexual intercourse are not at risk for cervical cancer and therefore do not require screening.[2] The USPSTF and CTF therefore recommend that Pap smears only be performed on women who have been sexually active, but they point out that if the sexual history is thought to be unreliable, then screening should begin at 18 years of age.[1,2] All groups agree that Pap smears should be performed at least every 3 years, and the general consensus is that a woman should first receive three annual examinations that are normal before the screening interval is increased (although this is not specified by USPSTF or ACP). If a woman has risk factors for cervical cancer such as early age of first intercourse, multiple sexual partners, a history of abnormal Pap smears, or evidence of human papillomavirus (HPV), she should receive more frequent screening. Additionally, women infected with human immunodeficiency virus (HIV) should be screened every 6 months.[9] Women who do not have a cervix do not require Pap smears unless they have a history of cervical cancer or cervical carcinoma in situ.[2] The USPSTF and ACP recommend that screening may be discontinued after age 65 years if the woman has had regular and normal screening over the previous 10 years. If not, screening should be performed every 3 years until age 75 years. The CTF recommends that screening be discontinued after age 69 years; whereas ACOG, ACS, and AAFP do not comment on an upper age limit for Pap smears.[1,2]

Colorectal cancer is the third leading cause of cancer mortality for both women and men in the United States, and a woman's lifetime risk for developing colorectal cancer is approximately 5%.[1,10] Persons at highest risk of colorectal cancer are those with familial syndromes (ie, hereditary polyposis and hereditary nonpolyposis syndromes) and those with a history of long-standing ulcerative colitis. Other risk factors include a history of colorectal cancer or adenomatous polyps in a first-degree relative, a personal history of adenomatous polyps, or a personal history of colorectal, breast, endometrial, or ovarian cancer.[2,10] Screening tests to consider for colorectal cancer include the digital rectal examination (DRE), fecal occult blood testing (FOBT), and sigmoidoscopy. Colonoscopy and air-contrast barium enema are advocated primarily as screening for high-risk individuals.

The DRE is of limited value as a screening test, as less than 10% of colorectal cancers can be palpated.[11] Nevertheless, ACS and ACOG recommend regular DRE in women aged 50 years and over. Several observational studies have demonstrated the effectiveness of FOBT in reducing mortality from colorectal cancer, but the most compelling evidence comes from a large randomized controlled trial of over 46,000 subjects over the age of 50 years. In this study, persons who were screened with annual FOBT had a 33% reduction in colorectal cancer mortality at 13 years of follow-up.[12] Additionally, two randomized controlled trials out of Europe evaluated biennial FOBT in patients aged 45 to 74 years and found a 15% and 18% reduction in mortality.[13,14] Essentially all major organizations recommend annual FOBT in average-risk women, beginning at age 50 years.

Sigmoidoscopy is most effective when it is performed with a 60-cm endoscope, which can reach the splenic flexure and identify approximately 60% of colonic lesions. Two large case-control studies have demonstrated significant decreases in colorectal cancer mortality (59 to 79%) among patients screened with sigmoidoscopy compared with those not screened.[15,16] The ACS, ACOG, and American Gastroenterological Association (AGA) all recommend screening sigmoidoscopy every 5 years in average-risk women beginning at age 50 years. The USPSTF also supports screening sigmoidoscopy every 3 to 5 years; however, it states that there is insufficient evidence to determine if performing both FOBT and sigmoidoscopy together produces a greater benefit than does either method alone. The ACP recommends screening sigmoidoscopy every 10 years, but states that in some settings performing colonoscopy or air-contrast barium enema instead of sigmoidoscopy may be acceptable.[1,2] The AGA also states that colonoscopy or double contrast barium enema every 10 years are acceptable alternative methods of screening average-risk women aged 50 years and older.[11]

Recently there has been much attention focused on the role of colonoscopy in screening aver-

age risk persons for colorectal cancer. Two recent studies have demonstrated that approximately 50% of proximal lesions have no accompanying distal lesions—that is, they would not be detected by conventional screening with sigmoidoscopy alone. However, the overall percentage of patients screened who had these proximal lesions in the absence of distal lesions was only 1.5% (of 1,564 patients) and 2.7% (of 3,121 patients)[17,18] To date, there is still no direct evidence regarding screening colonoscopy and colorectal cancer mortality. The potential risks of colonoscopy must be weighed against the potential lives saved before this can be endorsed as the preferred method of screening for average risk patients.

Women with a first-degree relative with colorectal cancer have a two- to threefold increased risk of colorectal cancer, and they develop it at an earlier age. Most groups agree that these individuals should receive more intensive screening, although the exact nature and frequency of recommended screening varies. The AGA recommends that women with one first-degree relative with colorectal cancer begin standard screening at age 40 years. If the relative was diagnosed before 55 years of age, or if the first-degree relative had an adenomatous polyp before 60 years of age, "special efforts should be made to assure that screening takes place." Furthermore, they state that for people whose first-degree relative developed colorectal cancer or an adenoma at a relatively early age, periodic complete evaluation of the colon may be preferable, although there are no studies that have addressed the effectiveness of this approach directly.[11]

Lung cancer is the leading cause of death from cancer in both women and men in the United States, and tobacco is associated with 87% of all cases of cancer of the lung, trachea, and bronchus. Although screening may increase detection of early resectable cancers, controlled trials have not demonstrated that screening reduces lung cancer mortality.[2] Therefore, no organization currently recommends routine screening of either the general population or of smokers for lung cancer.

Ovarian cancer has the highest mortality rate of any of the gynecologic cancers, and it is the fifth leading cause of cancer deaths among women. Screening tests that have been considered for ovarian cancer include pelvic examination, the CA 125 tumor marker, and pelvic ultrasonography. One of the major obstacles to effective and safe screening for this disease, however, is the fact that the large majority of women with abnormal tests will not have cancer, yet will require invasive procedures such as laparoscopy to rule out cancer.[2]

Although ovarian cancers detected by pelvic examination are usually advanced and have a poor prognosis, ACOG recommends that women undergo routine pelvic examinations as a screening test for ovarian cancer at the time they are receiving a Pap smear. The ACS also recommends pelvic examinations as a screening test for ovarian cancer, and they specifically state that although Pap smears may be performed less frequently, the pelvic examination should be performed every 1 to 3 years in women aged 18 to 39 years, and then annually for women 40 years of age and older.[1] The USPSTF, ACP, and CTF do not recommend the pelvic examination be done as a screening test for ovarian cancer in average-risk women, although CTF does state that it is reasonable to perform a pelvic examination at the time a Pap smear is being obtained.[1] Because of relatively poor positive predictive values (coupled with the high morbidity associated with evaluating positive tests), no organizations recommend CA 125 or pelvic ultrasound as a screening test for ovarian cancer in average risk women, and USPSTF, ACP, and CTF specifically recommend against it.[2] A woman from a family with the hereditary ovarian cancer syndrome (less than 1% of women with ovarian cancer) probably should be referred to a gynecologic oncologist to discuss prevention strategies, as her lifetime risk for developing ovarian cancer is at least 50%.

Skin cancer is the most common type of cancer in the United States.[1] Over 95% of skin cancers are basal cell and squamous cell carcinomas, which rarely metastasize but may cause significant disfigurement and functional impairment if not treated early. Risk factors for these cancers include older age; fair skin, eyes, and hair; poor ability to tan; and a history of prolonged sun exposure. Malignant melanoma is far less common but is considerably more deadly. Significant risk factors for melanoma include white race, atypical moles, increased numbers of common moles, immunosuppression, and a personal history of skin cancer.[2] While USPSTF and CTF state that there is insufficient evidence to recommend for or against screening for skin cancer with periodic total skin examination, they do state that clinicians should stay alert for skin lesions with malignant features while examining patients for

other reasons,[2] especially patients with risk factors. Malignant features of a lesion include asymmetry, border irregularity, color variation, diameter > 6 mm, or rapidly changing lesions. ACOG recommends that skin examination be performed for individuals with a family or personal history of skin cancer, increased exposure to sunlight, or clinical evidence of precursor lesions, although they do not specify the frequency of these examinations. ACS recommends that patients undergo a total skin examination every 3 years between the ages of 20 to 39 years, and yearly after 40 years of age.[1]

CARDIOVASCULAR DISEASES

Cardiovascular disease is the leading cause of death for women in the United States. Recommendations for screening for cardiovascular disease are aimed at screening for important risk factors such as hypertension and elevated blood cholesterol levels, and not at screening for asymptomatic CAD. The only interventions proven to reduce coronary events and death in asymptomatic persons are modifications of risk factors such as high blood pressure, elevated cholesterol, and smoking; more invasive treatments of CAD have not been proven to improve outcomes in asymptomatic individuals.[2] All organizations recommend that blood pressure should be measured on some regular basis in adults. In general, blood pressure should be checked every 2 years and at all office visits if possible. Additionally, the National High Blood Pressure Education Program of the National Heart, Lung, and Blood Institute recommend that blood pressure be measured annually in patients whose diastolic pressure is between 85 and 89 mm Hg.[19]

Screening for high cholesterol is somewhat more controversial. While aggressive cholesterol lowering is clearly associated with decreased cardiovascular events and total mortality in both women and men with known CAD, the benefits are not so clear in persons with no known CAD (primary prevention data). Many primary prevention trials have demonstrated a reduction in coronary events with cholesterol lowering in these asymptomatic populations; however, a reduction in overall mortality has only been shown in one trial, and that study included only men aged 45 to 65 years.[20] The benefits of cholesterol lowering in asymptomatic patients over 65 years of age have not been specifically studied, and cholesterol levels in general are not a reliable predictor of cardiovascular risk in asymptomatic persons over 75 years of age. The National Cholesterol Education Panel recommends that asymptomatic adults should have a fasting lipid profile (total cholesterol high-density lipoprotein, low-density lipoprotein, and triglycerides) measured every 5 years, and ACOG recommends testing cholesterol every 3 to 5 years in women aged 19 to 64 years of age. The USPSTF, ACP and AAFP recommend total cholesterol measurements periodically for women ages 45 to 65 years of age. Testing before or after this age range may be indicated for patients with other risk factors.

INFECTIOUS DISEASES

Sexually transmitted diseases (STDs) are common and may lead to significant morbidity in women, ranging from infertility to death. Because the majority of women with STDs are asymptomatic in early stages of infection and treatment of early disease is highly effective, screening plays an important role in decreasing the overall morbidity and mortality from STDs. Most organizations agree that screening for chlamydia and gonorrhea should be performed with routine pelvic examination in the following women: those with a history of a prior STD, those with new or multiple sexual partners in the past year, those under age 20 to 25 years who are sexually active, those who use barrier contraception inconsistently, sex workers, and those with recent sexual partners who have had a documented STD. It also is recommended that women attending clinics with a known high prevalence of chlamydia or gonorrhea (such as STD, family planning, or adolescent health clinics) should be screened. In addition, clinicians should remain alert for findings suggestive of chlamydia infection such as mucopurulent discharge, cervical erythema, or cervical friability during pelvic examination, and such individuals should be screened.[2] Routine serologic screening for syphilis is recommended for all women at increased risk for infection, including sex workers, women who exchange sex for drugs, women with other STDs, and women who have sexual contact with persons with active syphilis. Human immunodeficiency virus screening should be offered to the following women: those with a history of another STD, past or present injection-drug users, those with a history of prostitution or multiple sexual partners, and patients with a history of a blood transfusion between 1978 and 1985.[1] Some groups also recommend routine screening for individuals in high-risk communities, although the definition of a "high-risk community" is imprecise. It may be reasonable to offer testing to prisoners, runaway youths, and homeless persons.[2]

Screening high-risk individuals for **tuberculosis** (TB) and providing chemoprophylaxis with isoniazid plays a central role in controlling TB infection in the United States. Screening for TB infection by tuberculin skin testing is recommended for all persons at increased risk of developing the disease. Persons at increased risk include those infected with HIV, close contacts of persons with known or suspected TB (including health care workers), those with medical risk factors associated with TB, immigrants from countries with a high TB prevalence (eg, Africa, Asia, and Latin America), medically underserved low-income populations, alcoholics, injection-drug users, and residents of long-term care facilities (eg, prisons, mental institutions, or nursing homes).

METABOLIC DISEASES

Screening for **diabetes mellitus** (DM) in the asymptomatic nonpregnant woman can be performed by measuring a fasting plasma glucose level. Although evidence of benefit of early detection is not available for any given group of individuals, most organizations agree that women with an increased risk for developing DM may benefit from periodic screening. This includes women who are obese and are over 40 years of age, those who have a strong family history of DM, and those who are of high-risk ethnicity (eg, American Indian, Hispanic, or African American). Additionally, ACOG recommends that women with a history of glucose intolerance, hypertension, hyperlipidemia, or gestational diabetes or macrosomia also be screened periodically.[1] The American Diabetes Association recently revised their screening recommendations, and they now recommend that all adults aged 45 years and over should be screened for DM every 3 years. Testing should begin at a younger age and more frequently in persons with any of the risk factors already mentioned above.[1]

The USPSTF, CTF, and ACP recommend against routine screening for **thyroid disease** in asymptomatic adults, but caution clinicians to maintain a high index of suspicion and a low threshold for diagnostic evaluation, even in the presence of vague complaints. The ACOG recommends that thyroid stimulating hormone levels be measured every 3 to 5 years in all women aged 65 years and older.[1]

TABLE 8–4. Topics of Counseling Interventions

Substance use
  Tobacco avoidance/cessation
  Avoidance of alcohol/drug use eg, while driving, swimming, boating

Diet and exercise
  Limit of fat and cholesterol intake; maintenance of caloric balance; intake of grains, fruits, vegetables
  Adequate calcium intake
  Regular physical activity

Injury and violence prevention
  Seat belt use
  Motorcycle and bicycle helmet use
  Smoke detector installation
  Safe storage or removal of firearms
  Domestic/family violence (a form of screening)
  Fall prevention (for women 65 + yr)
  Setting of hot water heater to < 120–130°F (for women 65 + yr)
  CPR training for household members (for women 65 + yr)

Sexual behavior
  STD prevention; avoidance of high-risk behavior; use of barriers with spermicide
  Contraception use

Dental health
  Regular visits to dental care clinician
  Proper dental hygiene including flossing and brushing with fluoride toothpaste daily

---

STD = sexually transmitted disease.
Adapted from US Preventive Services Task Force. Guide to clinical preventive services. 2nd ed. Baltimore: Williams and Wilkins; 1996.

Routine screening for **anemia** in nonpregnant adults is not recommended by any group except ACOG, who recommends that hemoglobin levels be measured as part of routine preventive care for women with a history of heavy menstrual flow.[1]

The USPSTF, CTF, and ACP do not recommend routine bone densitometry screening for **osteoporosis**, but state that bone-density measurements may be useful to guide treatment in selected postmenopausal women considering hormone replacement therapy.[1] The National Osteoporosis Foundation recommends bone mineral density testing for women with risk factors for osteoporosis who are deciding on treatment. This is discussed in more detail in Chapter 47.

All organizations agree that women should be screened periodically for **obesity** by measuring their height and weight routinely at office visits.

COUNSELING

Counseling and patient education play a pivotal role in preventive health care. As a primary prevention strategy, counseling is aimed at influencing health-related behaviors that will result in preventing the target disease from ever developing. For some of these behaviors, such as smoking and problem drinking, there is good evidence that counseling by a clinician can change patient behavior;[2] whereas, for many behaviors, the effectiveness of clinician counseling has not been studied in appropriately designed studies. Given the safety and relatively low cost of counseling interventions, it is reasonable to routinely address major health-related behaviors that are associated with common target conditions, even in the absence of evidence of efficacy. See Table 8–4 for topics of counseling interventions that may be incorporated into the periodic health visit.

IMMUNIZATIONS

Like counseling interventions, immunizations are a form of primary prevention and are aimed at preventing a target disease from ever developing. In fact, immunizations are among the most effective interventions available in preventive medicine. Unfortunately, surveys have shown that adult immunizations are significantly underused as a tool in disease prevention, despite strong evidence of efficacy and safety.[21] The periodic health visit is a time when a patient's immunization status should be reviewed and updated as necessary. Recommendations on the administration of adult vaccines are issued regularly by the Advisory Committee on Immunization Practices of the Centers for Disease Control (ACIP), and these are the recommendations that are outlined below (see Table 8–5 for a quick reference).[22]

Tetanus-diphtheria. Tetanus occurs almost exclusively in nonimmunized or incompletely immunized persons. The majority of these cases are in elderly patients who either did not complete a primary tetanus-diphtheria (Td) series of three shots or did not receive boosters. All adults should receive a Td booster vaccination every 10 years. If a patient presents with a serious or dirty wound, she should receive a booster if more than 5 years have passed since her last one. If she has not completed a primary series, or her immune status is unknown, then she should also receive passive immunity with the administration of tetanus immune globulin.[17]

Adverse reactions to Td are usually minor local reactions consisting of erythema, induration, and tenderness at the site of injection. Fever and other systemic reactions such as malaise and headache are rare. A history of neurologic or anaphylactic sensitivity to a previous dose of Td toxoid is the only contraindication to the vaccine. Pregnant or breast-feeding women can be given the vaccine safely.

Rubella. Although the incidence of rubella has decreased markedly since the introduction of the rubella vaccine in 1969, it continues to be a concern for nonimmunized women of childbearing age. If contracted during early pregnancy, rubella can result in miscarriage, stillbirth, or the development of congenital rubella syndrome. All women of childbearing age who lack documentation of immunity or prior immunization (two separate doses of vaccine, the first given on or after their first birthday) should be immunized. The vaccine is given as the live MMR (measles, mumps, rubella) vaccine.[23]

Approximately 25% of adults receiving the MMR develop arthralgias, usually beginning 1 to 3 weeks after vaccination and persisting for 1 day to 3 weeks. Paresthesias and pain in the arms and legs also may develop rarely and seem to follow the same time-course as described for arthralgias. Rubella vaccine is contraindicated for all pregnant women, and women who receive the vaccine should be counseled not to become pregnant for 3 months.

Measles. Adult cases of measles occur primarily in persons who have not been naturally infected or appropriately vaccinated in the past, as well as those who were vaccinated before 12 months. Persons born before 1957 are likely to have been naturally infected and are not considered susceptible.[2] Persons born after 1956 who are attending college, who are newly employed in situations that put them at high-risk for measles transmission (eg, health care facilities), or who are traveling to areas endemic for measles should have documentation of having received two doses of live MMR on or after their first birthday or have other evidence of immunity. It is not harmful to revaccinate a person who already has immunity to measles, mumps, or rubella.

Influenza. Anywhere from 20,000 to 40,000 deaths occur in the United States each year due to influenza epidemics. Approximately 90% of these mortalities occur in people age 65 years and older. Adults with chronic pulmonary or cardiovascular disease, diabetes mellitus, renal disease, hemoglobinopathies, or immunosupression are also at increased risk for influenza-related complications. The influenza vaccine is trivalent, containing virus particles from two type A and one type B influenza viruses, and it is updated annually according to antigenic changes in the viruses causing infection. All adults age 50 years and older should receive annual vaccination, ideally between October and November. Any person at increased risk for influenza-related complications (as described above) as well as healthy pregnant women who will be in their second or third trimesters during the influenza season also should be vaccinated. Additionally, any person who can transmit influenza to those at high risk (eg, all

TABLE 8–5. Adult Immunizations

Vaccine (Route)	Indications	Schedule	Contraindications/Precautions
Tetanus, diphtheria (IM)	All adolescents and adults	Booster every 10 yr after primary series of 3 doses	Previous anaphylactic or neurologic reaction to this vaccine Moderate or severe acute illness
Measles, mumps, rubella (SQ)	Persons born after 1956 need 1 dose on or after first birthday High-risk groups* and childbearing-age women without proof of immunity should receive 2nd dose	1 or 2 doses 2nd dose at least 4 wk after 1st dose	Previous anaphylactic reaction Pregnancy or possibility of pregnancy within 3 mo Immunocompromised persons Moderate or severe acute illness
Influenza (IM)	Adults 50+ yr High-risk persons* Pregnant women who will be in their 2nd or 3rd trimesters during influenza season	Given every year October through November is optimal time	Previous anaphylactic reaction to this vaccine or to eggs Moderate or severe acute illness
Pneumococcal (IM or SQ)	Adults 65+ yr High-risk persons*	1 dose Revaccinate highest-risk-persons (asplenic renal failure, nephrotic syndrome) every 5 yr	Previous anaphylactic reaction Moderate or severe acute illness
Hepatitis B (IM)	All adolescents High-risk adults* Health care workers or other workers with occupational risks	3 doses on a 0-, 1-, 6-mo schedule	Previous anaphylactic reactions Moderate or severe acute illness
Hepatitis A (IM)	Travel to developing countries High-risk adults*	2 doses 2nd dose 6–12 mo after 1st dose	Previous anaphylactic reaction Moderate or severe acute illness Safety not determined during pregnancy
Varicella (SQ)	All susceptible adults and adolescents who have contact with high risk persons* Nonpregnant women of childbearing age	2 doses 2nd dose 4–8 wk after 1st dose	Previous anaphylactic reaction Moderate or severe acute illness Pregnancy or possibility of pregnancy within 1 month Immunocompromised persons If blood products or immune globulin have been administered within 5 months, consult ACIP recommendations

*See text for details.
IM = intramuscular; SQ = subcutaneous; ACIP = Advisory Committee on Immunization Practices.

health care workers, employees of nursing homes and chronic care facilities, and caregivers and household members of persons in high-risk groups) should be vaccinated regularly.[24]

Soreness at the site of injection persisting up to 2 days is the most common side effect of the vaccine; fever, malaise, and myalgia occur infrequently. Because the vaccine contains only noninfectious viruses, it cannot cause influenza. Since the vaccine is made from highly purified egg-grown viruses, it may contain residual egg proteins, and, therefore, should not be given to any person with a true egg allergy. Influenza vaccine is safe to administer to breast-feeding mothers.

Pneumococcus. As with influenza, mortality from pneumococcal disease occurs predominantly in persons aged 65 years and over and in those with chronic disease. In addition, persons who are either anatomically or functionally asplenic, have chronic liver disease, are alcoholics, or are infected with HIV are all at increased risk of significant morbidity and mortality from pneumococcal disease. The pneumococcal vaccine is now a 23-valent vaccine that replaced the 14-valent vaccine in 1983. The 23 serotypes included in this vaccine are responsible for approximately 85 to 90% of the serotypes of *Streptococcus pneumoniae*–causing bacteremia in the United States.[1] All adults ages 65 years and older should receive one dose of the pneumococcal vaccine. Immunization also is indicated for persons younger than age 65 years who have medical conditions that put them at an increased risk for invasive disease, as described above. Routine revaccination generally is not necessary, but it should be considered every 5 years for individuals who are at risk for waning antibody levels, such as persons with chronic renal failure or nephrotic syndrome, or those at highest risk for invasive disease (asplenic individuals). Revaccination also should be considered for anyone who received their vaccine before 1983, when only the 14-valent vaccine was available, as well as for adults over age 75 years who have significant chronic disease.[2]

Adverse reactions to the vaccination are generally mild. Erythema and pain at the injection site occur in approximately 50% of patients. Fever, myalgia, and severe local reactions are reported in fewer than 1% of persons vaccinated. High-risk women may be safely immunized during pregnancy or breast-feeding.

Hepatitis B. Women at increased risk for developing hepatitis B include intravenous drug users, women with more than one sex partner in the previous 6 months, household contacts and sex partners of persons with chronic hepatitis B, hemodialysis patients, hemophiliacs, inmates of long-term correctional institutions, and health care workers or others with increased occupational risks. In addition to immunizing women in these high-risk groups, some authorities now recommend vaccinating all adolescents and young adults up to age 24 years.[1] It is also recommended that all women with chronic hepatitis C infection receive hepatitis B vaccination. The vaccine consists of a three-dose series, with the second and third doses given at 1 and 6 months following the first dose. The available vaccines in the United States are both recombinant derived; therefore, they pose no risk of infection. Side effects of the vaccine tend to be relatively minor including pain at the injection site and temperature over 37.7°C in a minority of patients.

In addition, any nonimmunized woman who has been acutely exposed to hepatitis B within the previous 14 days should receive a prophylactic dose of HBIG (hepatitis B immune globulin). The first dose of the hepatitis B vaccine series may be given concurrently with HBIG.

Definitive safety of the hepatitis B vaccine during pregnancy and lactation have not yet been established. However, according to the Centers for Disease Control (CDC), there is no apparent risk to the developing fetus based on unpublished data. Further, hepatitis B can be transmitted vertically from mother to newborn. Because maternal hepatitis B infection represents a significant health risk to both the mother and newborn, the CDC recommends that pregnant women at high risk for hepatitis B be vaccinated.[25]

Hepatitis A. Hepatitis A vaccine is recommended for women in high-risk groups; this includes persons traveling to developing countries, intravenous drug users, persons with clotting-factor disorders, persons with chronic liver disease (including chronic hepatitis B or C infections), and military personnel. People traveling to Canada, Western Europe, Japan, Australia, or New Zealand do not need to be vaccinated. The hepatitis A vaccine consists of inactivated virus and therefore cannot cause infection. Two doses of the vaccine should be given, the second one between 6 and 12 months after the first. If immediate protection is necessary, immune globulin may need to be administered with the first vaccine dose, as it takes at least 2 weeks to achieve 90% efficacy of the vaccine,[2,26] Safety of vaccination during pregnancy has not yet been determined.

Varicella. Varicella vaccine should be administered to all susceptible women who have close contact with persons who are at high risk for serious complications (eg, health care workers and family contacts of immunocompromised persons). In addition, the vaccine should be considered for susceptible women in the following high-risk groups: (1) persons who live or work in environments where transmission of varicella is likely (eg, teachers of young children, day care employees, staff and residents in institutional settings, military personnel, and college students); (2) nonpregnant women of childbearing age; (3) adolescents and adults living in households with children; and (4) international travelers. The vaccine available in the United States is a live cell-free preparation, and, therefore, immunocompromised individuals (including those taking chronic steroids) should not receive the vaccination because of the potential of active infection due to the vaccine. Likewise, pregnant women should not be vaccinated, and all women should be counseled on avoiding pregnancy for 1 month following vaccination.

The vaccine is given in two doses, separated by 4 to 8 weeks. It is usually well tolerated, with approximately 25% of recipients developing a mild local reaction at the injection site. Fewer than 10% of recipients develop a maculopapular or varicelliform rash, but, if this does occur, these individuals need to avoid contact with immunocompromised or pregnant susceptible persons, because there is a small chance of transmission of the vaccine virus.[1,27]

CHEMOPROPHYLAXIS

Chemoprophylaxis is a form of primary prevention that refers to the use of drugs taken by asymptomatic persons in an effort to reduce the risk of developing a target condition. Examples of chemoprophylaxis in the nonpregnant woman include the use of hormone replacement therapy in postmenopausal women, the use of calcium and other prescription medications to prevent osteoporosis, and the use of lipid-lowering therapy to prevent CAD. These topics are discussed elsewhere in this book.

Although there has been much interest recently in the use of antioxidant therapy in the prevention of a variety of diseases, trials including women have yielded conflicting results, and, thus, firm recommendations are lacking. Aspirin also has been studied as a possible primary preventive intervention in the development of cardiovascular disease, although most trials have included men only. The Nurses Health Study, however, was a prospective cohort trial including over 80,000 women, and it showed that low-dose aspirin use is associated with a decrease in the incidence of first myocardial infarction in middle-aged women. However, there was no statistically significant decrease in total cardiovascular mortality observed.[1,2] There have been no randomized controlled trials studying aspirin use as a form of primary prevention in women.

RESOURCES

Canadian Task Force on Preventive Health Care
St. Joseph's Health Centre-Parkwood Suite
801 Commissioners Road East
London, Ontario, Canada N6C 5J1
Telephone: (519) 685-4292
Web site: www.ctfphc.org

The web site of the Canadian Task Force on Preventive Health Care (formerly the Canadian Task Force on the Periodic Health Exam) contains full text of systematic reviews of various health topics of interest to clinicians.

RESOURCES (continued)

Centers for Disease Control and Prevention
1600 Clifton Road
Atlanta, Georgia 30333
Telephone: 1-800-311-3435
Web site: www.cdc.gov

The Centers for Disease Control and Prevention (CDC) provide comprehensive information on vaccines and vaccination strategies, which are available in full text at their web site. The site also contains information on CDC publications, including patient education materials on issues related to preventive health.

Publications
US Public Health Service. The clinician's handbook of preventive services. 2nd ed. McLean (VA): International Medical Publishing, Inc.; 1997.

REFERENCES

1. Expert Panel on Detection, Evaluation and Treatment of High Blood Cholesterol in Adults. Executive summary of the third report of the National Cholesterol Education Program (NCEP) Expert Panel on Detection, Evaluation and Treatment of High Blood Cholesterol in Adults (Adult Treatment Panel III). JAMA 2001; 285:2486–97.

2. US Preventive Services Task Force. Guide to clinical preventive services. 2nd ed. Baltimore: Williams and Wilkins; 1996.

3. Ries LAG, Miller BA, Hawkey BF, et al. SEER cancer statistics review, 1973–1991: tables and graphs. Bethesda: National Cancer Institute; 1994.

4. Shapiro S, Venet W, Strax P, Venet L. Periodic screening for breast cancer: the health insurance plan project and its sequence, 1963–1986. Baltimore: Johns Hopkins University Press; 1988.

5. Alexander FE, Anderson TJ, Brown HK, et al. The Edinburgh randomized trial of breast cancer screening: results after 10 years of follow-up. Br J Cancer 1994;70:542–8.

6. Miller AB, Baives CJ, To T, Wall C. Canadian National Breast Screening Study: 1. Can Med Assoc J 1992; 147:1459–76.

7. Antman K, Shea S. Screening mammograph under age 50. JAMA 1999;281:1470–82.

8. Bjurgstom N, Bjornfeld L, Duffy SW, et al. The Gothenburg screening trial: first results on mortality, incidence and mode of detection for women ages 39–49 years at randomization. Cancer 1997;80:2091–9.

9. El-Sadr W, Olseki JM, Agins BD, et al. Evaluation and management of early HIV infection. Clinical practice guideline no. 7. Rockville (MD): Agency for Health Care Policy and Research; 1994. p. 60–5.

10. Weinberg DS, Newschaffer CJ, Topham A. Colorectal cancer after gynecologic cancer. Ann Intern Med 1999;131:189–93.

11. Mandel JS, Bond JH, Church TR, et al. Reducing mortality from colorectal cancer by screening for fecal occult blood. N Engl J Med 1993;328:1365–71.

12. Selby JV, Friedman GD, Queensberg CD, Weiss NS. A case control study of screening sigmoidoscopy and mortality from colorectal cancer. N Engl J Med 1992;326:653–7.

13. Hardcastle JD, Chamberlain JO, Robinson MHE, et al. Randomised controlled trial of faecal occult blood screening for colorectal cancer. Lancet 1996;348:1472–7.

14. Kronberg O, Fenger C, Olsen J, et al. Randomised study of screening for colorectal cancer with faecal occult blood test. Lancet 1996;348:1467–71.

15. Newcomb PA, Norfleet RG, Storer D, et al. Screening sigmoidoscopy and colorectal cancer mortality. J Natl Cancer Inst 1992;84:1572–5.

16. Winawer SJ, Fletcher RH, Miller L, et al. Colorectal cancer screening: clinical guidelines and rationale. Gastroenterology 1997;112:594–642.

17. Lieberman DA, Weiss DG, Bone JH, et al. Use of colonoscopy to screen asymptomatic adults for colorectal cancer. N Engl J Med 2000;343:162–8.

18. Imperiale TF, Wagner DR, Lin CY, et al. Risk of advanced proximal neoplasms in asymptomatic adults according to the distal colorectal findings. N Engl J Med 2000;343:169–74.

19. Joint National Committee on Detection, Evaluation and Treatment of High Blood Pressure. The sixth report of the Joint National Committee on Detection, Evaluation and Treatment of High Blood Pressure (JNCVI). Arch Intern Med 1997;157:2413–46.

20. Shepherd J, Cobbe SM, Ford I, et al. Prevention of coronary breast disease with pravastatin in men with hypercholesterolemia. N Engl J Med 1995;333: 1301–7.

21. Reid KC, Grizzard TA, Poland GA. Adult immunizations: recommendations for practice. Mayo Clin Proc 1999;74:377–84.

22. Centers for Disease Control. Diphtheria, tetanus, and pertussis: recommendations of the Advisory Committee on Immunization Practices (ACIP). MMWR 1991;40:1–28.

23. Centers for Disease Control. Rubella prevention: recommendations of the Advisory Committee on Immunization Practices (ACIP). MMWR 1990;39:1–13.

24. Centers for Disease Control. Prevention and control of influenza: recommendations of the Advisory Committee on Immunization Practices (ACIP). MMWR 2000;49(RR-3):1–27.

25. Centers for Disease Control. Hepatitis B virus: a comprehensive strategy for elimination of transmission in the United States through universal childhood vaccination. Recommendations of the immunizing practices advisory committee. MMWR 1991;40:1–19.

26. Centers for Disease Control. Prevention of hepatitis A through active or passive immunization: recommendations of the Advisory Committee on Immunization Practices (ACIP). MMWR 1999;48:1–37.

27. Centers for Disease Control. Prevention of varicella. Updated recommendations of the Advisory Committee on Immunization Practices (ACIP). MMWR 1999;48:1–5.

9

CONTRACEPTION

Camelia Davtyan, MD

The desire for fertility control has been prominent in all human societies for millennia, despite the natural reproductive restraints of female fertility being limited to a few days each cycle between menarche and menopause, inhibited by breast-feeding, and naturally absent in a minority of women. Before the twentieth century, fertility control was attempted using methods such as abortion, infanticide, plant and animal-derived pessaries and douches, coitus interruptus, condoms, the diaphragm, basal body temperature monitoring, and periodic abstinence.

The world population was 1.6 billion people in the year 1900. Even with the advent of modern contraception, the global population of the year 2000 was 6 billion people, and will rise to the 10 billion mark by the year 2100, with most of the growth happening in the developing countries. The second millennium population was determined by mortality, whereas the third millennium population will largely be determined by fertility. As a result, voluntary prevention of unwanted pregnancy will continue to play an important role in shaping the future of humanity.

In the United States, there are 63 million women between the childbearing ages of 13 and 44 years. Over half of them need contraceptive services (ie, they are sexually active, not pregnant or seeking pregnancy, not postpartum, and not sterilized), of whom 15% are teenagers and 15% have incomes below the federal poverty level. About 5% of the women in need of contraception are not using any method of pregnancy prevention. There are more than 3 million unwanted pregnancies in the United States annually, of which 53% happen in women who use a contraceptive method in an inconsistent or incorrect way, or due to the inherent failure rate of a certain method.[1,2] The chance of pregnancy at 1 year of unprotected intercourse is 85%. There are

multiple fertility control methods available, that can decrease the 1-year pregnancy rate to as low as 0.05%.[3] These are summarized in Table 9–1.

In the United States sterilization is the most popular contraceptive method, followed by oral hormonal contraception, the male condom, vasectomy, coitus interruptus, injectable progestin (medroxyprogesterone acetate), periodic abstinence, the diaphragm, subcutaneous progestin implants (levonorgestrel), and the intrauterine contraceptive device (IUD).[4]

ABSTINENCE

Abstinence as a contraceptive method can be defined as refraining from vaginal intercourse. It can be primary, when the subject has never engaged in vaginal intercourse or secondary, when a sexually experienced subject avoids vaginal intercourse. It is not uncommon among adolescents and has gained even more popularity since the risk of infection with human immunodeficiency virus (HIV) was recognized in the early 1980s.

In a survey of women aged 15 to 44 years, 17% of them had not had intercourse in the 3 months prior to the interview, and, of the abstainers, 11% had never had intercourse.[1] About half of all teenagers aged 15 to 19 years reported primary abstinence; by ages 20 to 24 years, about 12% continue to abstain.[5]

Abstinence can be continuous or limited to the fertile period of a woman's menstrual cycle (periodic abstinence).

Periodic Abstinence and Fertility Awareness Methods

Using periodic abstinence for fertility control requires accurate identification of the potentially

TABLE 9–1. Currently Available Methods of Contraception

Abstinence
    Continuous
    Periodic/fertility awareness methods
        Calendar
        Cervical mucus
        Basal body temperature
        Symptothermal
        Ovulation prediction kit
        Electronic fertility monitor

Coitus interruptus (withdrawal)

Breast-feeding

Barrier methods
    Female
        Condom
        Diaphragm
        Cervical cap
    Male
        Condom

Spermicides (foam, film, jelly, suppositories)

Hormonal
    Oral hormonal contraceptives
        Estrogen and progestin combination
        Progestin alone
    Injectable estrogen-progestin combination (Lunelle)
    Injectable progestin medroxyprogesterone acetate
    Subcutaneous progestin implants (Norplant)

Intrauterine contraceptive devices

Sterilization
    Female
        Surgical
        Chemical
    Male
        Surgical

Emergency contraception
    Hormonal
        Estrogen and progestin combination
        Progestin alone
        Danazol
        Mifepristone (RU 486)
    Intrauterine contraceptive devices

fertile days, when the couple can either abstain (natural family planning) or use another contraceptive method, such as barrier methods or withdrawal (fertility awareness-combined methods).

The fertile time each cycle is about 6 days long and represents the combined life spans of sperm (5 days) and egg (1 day);[6] therefore, a couple is fertile 5 days before ovulation and on the day of ovulation.

Natural family planning is likely to be acceptable to women of various cultural and religious backgrounds, whereas barrier, chemical, and hormonal contraceptions are unacceptable to certain women. Natural family planning requires a high degree of partner cooperation, which might be difficult for some women to obtain.

CALENDAR METHOD

This method is based on the assumption that ovulation occurs on day 14 ± 2 before the onset of next menses. The woman measures the length of 6 to 12 cycles and subtracts 18 to 22 days (14 ± 2 plus the 6-day life span of gametes) from the shortest length cycle to mark the beginning of the fertile period, and 9 to 11 days (the number of days after the egg's life span ended until next menses) from the longest length cycle to mark the end of the fertile period. Perfect use of this method is associated with a 9% pregnancy rate with 1 year of use. Typical use results in a pregnancy rate of 26% at 1 year.[3,7,8]

CERVICAL MUCUS METHOD

To use the cervical mucus method, the woman must observe her cervical mucus and appreciate that, as ovulation approaches, the mucus is more abundant, clear, slippery, and stretchable; the last day of clear stretchable mucus is assumed to be the day of ovulation. The rest of the time, the mucus is scant or absent, thick, cloudy, and sticky. The fertile period begins when cervical secretions are first felt until 4 days past the last day of clear copious mucus. Perfect use of this method is associated with a 3% pregnancy rate after 1 year of use. Typical use results in a pregnancy rate of 20% at 1 year.[3]

BASAL BODY TEMPERATURE METHOD

Basal body temperature (BBT) is the temperature on awakening measured orally, vaginally, or rectally. It rises about 0.4°F around the time of ovulation, until the onset of the next menses. The fertile period is considered to start after menses and end after 3 consecutive days of higher BBT. Perfect use of this method is associated with a 3% pregnancy rate at 1 year of use.[7]

SYMPTOTHERMAL METHOD

The symptothermal method is a combination of cervical secretion and BBT monitoring, as well as observing symptoms such as mittelschmerz (ovulatory pain) or breast tenderness to calculate the fertile period. Because of the increase in variables being monitored, the combined method is likely to be more effective than is each individual modality alone. The pregnancy rate at 1 year of perfect use is 2%.[9]

OVULATION PREDICTION KIT

The ovulation prediction kit was developed initially for women with fertility problems but it can also be used to calculate the fertile period of each cycle. It is based on detecting luteinizing hormone (LH), which can be detected 1 day before or on the day of ovulation. The couple should abstain for 5 days before the test is positive and for 2 days after. There is no published data on efficacy, but it is presumed to be similar or better than the calendar method.

ELECTRONIC FERTILITY MONITOR

A palm-sized electronic urine-testing system (ClearPlan Easy Fertility Monitor) is available for purchase over the counter in the United States. It tests urinary metabolites of estrogen (eg, estrone-3 glucuronide [E3G]) to indicate the start of the fertile phase and LH to indicate the end of fertility. The test converts E3G and LH into colored signals, which can be read by the monitor. These identify three levels of fertility: low, high (4 to 5 days before the LH reading), and peak (after LH reading, for 24 to 36 hours). The cost is $180 for the monitor and $45 for a pack of 30 test strips. There is no data on efficacy, but is presumed to be similar or better than the calendar method.

ULTRASOUND MONITORING

An area of future development in the use of fertility awareness methods is ultrasound monitoring of the dominant follicle during the periovulatory period.

COITUS INTERRUPTUS

According to Population Action International's estimate, about 13% of all users of temporary contraceptive methods rely on coitus interruptus (withdrawal) for pregnancy prevention, two-thirds of whom live in developing countries.[10] This method requires withdrawal of the penis from the vagina prior to ejaculation. It appears to be more acceptable to couples in long-term monogamous than in other relationships. Religion, cultural acceptability, perceptions about effectiveness, and the impact on sexual satisfaction are factors that influence the use of this method for pregnancy prevention.

Withdrawal requires self-control on the part of the male partner; health care clinicians rarely offer it as an option, due to the belief that the sperm present in the pre-ejaculate makes the method ineffective. This opinion has not been substantiated by studies of pre-ejaculatory fluid.[11,12] The rate of pregnancy at 1 year is 4% for perfect use and 19% for typical use.[3,13]

Other previously reported possible problems such as prostate disease and psychological problems in both men and women using coitus interruptus for contraception date back to Freud's time (the late 1800s), but they have not been validated scientifically.[13]

BREAST-FEEDING

Full lactation in a woman who has not experienced postpartum menses provides more than 98% contraception in the first 6 months following childbirth.[14] In the developing world, lactational amenorrhea is an important factor in fertility control. In the United States, where only half of all new mothers attempt to breast-feed and most of them breast-feed partially and for short durations, the impact of lactational amenorrhea on pregnancy prevention is minimal.

BARRIER METHODS

An advantage of barrier methods is that they provide protection against sexually transmitted diseases (STDs). They do not interfere with the menstrual cycle, are effective immediately, have no systemic effects, and can be used to increase the efficacy of other contraceptive methods. If barrier methods fail, there is no effect on a resulting pregnancy.

Problems associated with these methods are their high failure rate; discomfort for the woman or her partner; difficulty with correct placement and removal of certain devices; possibility of dislodgment, allergic reactions, toxic shock syndrome;

and the fact that they can interfere with the act of intercourse.

Male Condoms

Male condoms can be made of latex or polyurethane. Plastic materials also are being studied for condom manufacture; the Tactylon condom made of a material used in nonallergenic examination gloves has been available since 1999. The 1-year pregnancy rate varies depending on the study population. It is about 3% with perfect use and 14% with typical use.[3]

Some of the failures are due to condom breakage and slippage, as well as factors such as the use of oil-based lubricants, which weaken latex.[15] Condom use reduces the risk of transmission of gonorrhea, HIV, herpes simplex virus (HSV), chlamydia, and hepatitis viruses, as well as the risk of pelvic inflammatory disease. Among barrier methods, the condom provides the best protection against STDs.[16,17]

Male condoms can be used alone or to enhance other methods (only female condoms cannot be used at the same time), while providing protection from STDs. Spermicidal condoms are lubricated with 1 to 12% nonoxynol-9. Using a separate vaginal spermicide adds to its efficacy.[18]

Condoms are widely available at a low cost without a prescription. They provide contraceptive control to the male partner. They also protect against STDs and indirectly against infertility and ectopic pregnancy. These aspects make them popular despite their fairly high failure rate.

Female Barrier Methods

Vaginal barrier methods protect against STDs to a lesser degree than do male condoms. They also reduce the risk of cervical dysplasia and cancer. These methods should not be used in women with a history of toxic shock syndrome or latex allergy (except for female condoms, which are made of polyurethane). Good candidates for these methods are women at low risk for STDs who are able and willing to use the method correctly, or women who want to use a vaginal barrier in combination with male condoms. These methods can be used while another method (eg, oral contraceptives [OCPs]) is being initiated or if OCPs have been missed.

FEMALE CONDOM

The female condom is made of polyurethane. Its users experience a pregnancy rate of 5% at 1 year of perfect use and of 21% with typical use.[3,19] It should not be used with a male condom because they can adhere to each other. It is available over the counter.

DIAPHRAGM

The diaphragm is a dome-shaped rubber device available in different styles and sizes. It is inserted into the vagina with spermicide before intercourse to cover the cervix. It needs to be left in place for 6 hours after intercourse but no longer than 24 hours because of the risk of toxic shock syndrome. After 6 hours, additional spermicide has to be added for repeated intercourse. The 1-year pregnancy rate is 6% with perfect use and 20% with typical use.[3,20] To fit a diaphragm, the index and middle finger of the examiner's hand are inserted into the patient's vagina until the middle finger reaches the posterior wall of the vagina. With the tip of the examiner's thumb, the point at which the index finger touches the pubic bone is marked. The examining fingers are then removed from the vagina, and the diaphragm rim is placed on the tip of the middle finger. If the diaphragm size is appropriate, the opposite rim should be just in front of the examiner's thumb. Then, a sterilized selected sample diaphragm is inserted in the vagina. Its rim should be in contact with the lateral walls and posterior fornix without tension against the walls. There should be enough space to insert a fingertip between the pubic bone and the anterior edge of the diaphragm rim. The largest comfortable rim size should be used, since the vaginal depth increases during sexual arousal.

The diaphragm needs to be refitted after weight gain or loss of over 5 kg, and after abortion, childbirth, or pelvic surgery.

Some women experience more frequent urinary tract infections, vaginal irritation, yeast vaginitis, or bacterial vaginosis when using the diaphragm. This may indicate the need for refitting with a smaller size or different style diaphragm or a cervical cap, or changing to a nonspermicidal contraceptive method.

CERVICAL CAP

The cervical cap is a rubber device shaped like a cup with a firm round rim. Spermicide is added before insertion. It covers the cervix and can be left in place for 48 hours without adding spermicide for repeated intercourse. The 1-year pregnancy rate in parous women is 40% for typical users and 26%

with perfect use.[3] In nulliparous women, the 1-year pregnancy rate is 20% for typical users and 9% with perfect use.[3,20]

Future Barrier Devices

In the near future, new cervical caps made of different materials will be available, as will disposable diaphragms that release spermicides. The bikini condom is a female condom attached to a G-string that makes it easier to wear. Lea's Shield is a device with a silicone valve that permits one way drainage of cervical secretions but blocks penetration of sperm. It comes in one size, fits over the cervix and can be left in place for 48 hours with or without spermicide.[21]

SPERMICIDES

The active chemical ingredients available in spermicides are nonoxynol-9 (most commonly used), octoxynol, and benzalkonium chloride. All are surfactants that destroy the sperm membrane.

Spermicides are available over the counter to use alone or to enhance another contraceptive method, are easy to insert, and are effective immediately. They do not seem to have systemic side effects or to influence pregnancies that result from contraceptive failure.[22–24] They do not interfere with the menstrual cycle, and may offer some protection from STDs and cervical cancer.[25] Nonoxynol-9 is a microbicide in vitro. However, human studies have shown variable results regarding its in vivo activity.[26–28] The local irritation caused by repeated spermicide use could theoretically increase STD transmission.[29,30]

There are various spermicidal formulations available: film, suppository, gel, aerosol foam, cream, and spermicidal condoms. The spermicidal sponge, currently unavailable in the United States, may soon be re-introduced. Future sponges will incorporate several spermicides, one of them being benzalkonium chloride, which has antiviral properties. Efficacy varies widely among typical users, with a reported pregnancy rate at 1 year of use of 5 to 50%.[3] Spermicides frequently are used in combination with barrier methods, increasing their contraceptive efficacy.

Some women experience local irritation or more frequent yeast vaginitis, bacterial vaginosis, or urinary tract infections because of selective colonization with species resistant to nonoxynol-9.[31,32]

Recently, there has been a growing interest in developing new spermicides, some of them plant derived (eg, Praneem, derived from the dried seed of *Azadiarachta indica* and the fruit of *Sapindus* species[33,34]) and others that are nondetergent and microbicidal.[35,36]

HORMONAL CONTRACEPTION

Combination Oral Hormonal Contraceptives

Combination oral contraceptives prevent pregnancy by systemic administration of estrogen and progesterone. Contraception is achieved by inhibition of follicle-stimulating hormone (FSH) and LH secretion in the pituitary gland, thickening of the cervical mucus, and inhibition of capacitation of the sperm and egg implantation in an altered endometrial structure.[3] The basis for the development of hormonal contraception was laid in 1940, when Sturgis and Albright described the effect of estrogen on ovulation inhibition in humans.[37]

The estrogenic component of combination oral contraceptives consists of either ethinyl estradiol or mestranol, which is converted to ethinyl estradiol in the liver. The progestin component consists of either norethindrone, norethindrone acetate, norgestrel, levonorgestrel, ethynodiol diacetate, or the "new" (third-generation) progestins: desogestrel, norgestimate, and gestodene. For the content of specific OCP formulations, see Table 9–2.

For perfect users, the failure rate of OCPs is 0.1% at 1 year of use.[3] Pill-taking mistakes in typical users are associated with a failure rate of 5% at 1 year of use.[3] Overall, 16% of pill users are inconsistent in their pill taking.[38,39]

The OCPs in common use today contain no more than 35 µg of ethinyl estradiol. Under special circumstances a 50-µg estrogen-containing OCP can be used to manage spotting or absence of withdrawal bleeding on a lower-dose pill, or to treat acne, dysfunctional bleeding, ovarian cysts, or endometriosis. Fifty-microgram OCPs also may be indicated for women who became pregnant while correctly using a lower-dose OCP or for those taking hepatic enzyme-inducing medications such as rifampin or phenytoin.

The multiple effects of OCPs have been studied widely. They are safe to use throughout reproductive years in most women. In some countries, they are available over the counter.[40] Use of OCPs

TABLE 9–2. Content of Oral Contraceptives

OCP	Estrogen	Progestin	Androgenic Activity
Orthocyclen	EE 35 μg	Norgestimate	Low
Orthotricyclen	EE triphasic	Norgestimate	Low
Cyclessa	EE 25 μg	Desogestrel 0.15 mg	Low
Desogen	EE 30 μg	Desogestrel 0.15 mg	Low
Ortho-Cept	EE 30 μg	Desogestrel 0.15 mg	Low
Mircette	EE 20 μg d 1–21 EE 10 μg d 24–28	Desogestrel 0.15 mg	Low
Ovcon 35	EE 35 μg	Norethindrone 0.4 mg	Low
Modicon, Brevicon, Genora 0.5/35, Nelova 0.5/35, NEE 0.5/35	EE 35 μg	Norethindrone 0.5 mg	Low
Norinyl 1/80, Ortho–Novom 1/80	80 μg	Norethindrone 1 mg	Medium
Ovcon–Novom 50, Demulen 1/50, Ovral	EE 50 μg	Norethindrone 1 mg	Medium
Ortho 1/50, Norinyl 1/50	M 50 μg	Norethindrone 1 mg	Medium
Genora 1/35, Nelova 1/35E, Norcept 1/35E, Norethin 1/35E, Nee 1/35, Ortho-Novum 1/35, Norinyl 1/35,	EE 35 μg	Norethindrone 1 mg	Medium
Tri-Norinyl, Ortho Novum 7/7/7, Estrostep	EE triphasic	Norethindrone	Medium
Norlestrin 1/50	EE 50 μg	Norethindrone acetate 1 mg	Medium
Lo Estrin 1/20	EE 20 μg	Norethindrone acetate 1 mg	Medium
Ovulen	M 100 μg	Ethynodiol diacetate 1 mg	Medium
Demulen 1/50	EE 50 μg	Ethynodiol diacetate 1 mg	Medium
Demulen 1/35	EE 35 μg	Ethynodiol diacetate 1 mg	Medium
Alesse	EE 20 μg	Levo-norgestrel 0.1 mg	Medium
Triphasil, Tri-Levlen	EE triphasic	Levo-norgestrel triphasic	Medium
Lo/Ovral	EE 30 μg	Norgestrel 0.3 mg	High
Ovral	EE 50 μg	Norgestrel 0.5 mg	High
Lo Estrin 1.5/30	EE 30 μg	Norethindrone acetate 1.5 mg	High
Norlestrin 2.5/50	EE 50 μg	Norethindrone acetate 2.5 mg	High
Norinyl 2, Ortho 2	M 100 μg	Norethindrone 2 mg	High
Enovid E	M 100 μg	Norethindrone 2.5 mg	High
Nordette, Levlen, Levora	EE 30 μg	Levo-norgestrel 0.15 mg	High

*Most of the 80 to 100 μg estrogen-containing combination oral contraceptives (OCPs) have been removed from the US market. EE = ethinyl estradiol; M = mestranol.

does not alter fertility, although pregnancy might be delayed several months after discontinuing this method.[41,42]

Selection of an OCP can be a difficult task, especially for women with concurrent medical conditions. Noncontraceptive benefits of OCPs are summarized in Table 9–3.[43–60] Risks and side effects are summarized in Table 9–4.[60–67] An OCP containing a progestin with low to medium androgenic activity is preferred for women with acne, obesity, and controlled hypertension. In patients with hyperlipidemia, if triglycerides are mildly elevated,

TABLE 9–3. Noncontraceptive Benefits of Oral Contraceptive Use

Menstrual
    Less bleeding and pain
    Less PMS[43]
    Predictable menses
Cancer prevention[44–48]
    Ovarian cancer
        30% less if OCPs used for ≤ 4 yr
        60% less if OCPs used for 5–11 yr
        80% less if OCPs used for ≥ 12 or more yr
    Uterine cancer
        40% less if OCPs used for ≥ 2 yr
        60% less if OCPs used for ≥ 4 yr
Prevention of ovarian cysts[49,50]
Decreased risk of benign breast disease
Decrease risk of ectopic pregnancy[51,52]
Improvement in acne[53]
Improvement in hirsutism[54]
Improvement in endometriosis[56]
Improvement in lipid profile[59]
    Decreased LDLs
Improvement in libido (less concern with risk of pregnancy)[60]
Improvement in depressive symptoms
Increased bone density[55]
Improvement in symptoms of rheumatoid arthritis[57,58]

PMS = premenstrual syndrome; OCP = combination oral contraceptive; LDL = low-density lipoprotein; HDL = high-density lipoprotein.

TABLE 9–4. Disadvantages and Side Effects of Oral Contraceptive Use

No protection against STDs
Need for daily compliance with pill taking
Irregular menstrual pattern
    Missed menses
    Scanty bleeding
    Spotting
    Breakthrough bleeding
New onset or worsening of previous headaches
New onset or worsening of depression[*]
Loss of libido[60*]
Cervical ectopy[61]
Chlamydia cervicitis[62]
Breast tenderness
Nausea and vomiting
Gallbladder disease progression in susceptible women[63]
Hypertension[64,65]
Hepatocellular adenoma[66†]
Growth of leiomyomas[‡]
Leukorrhea
Skin changes (eg, chloasma, telangiectasias) and hair loss
Acne/oily skin[*]
Lipid abnormalities[*]
    Decreased HDLs
    Increased triglycerides
Fatigue[*]
Increased appetite and weight gain[*]
Increased insulin resistance[*]
Decreased glucose tolerence[*]

[*]Androgenic properties of progesterone component.
[†]Less with low-dose OCPs.[67]
[‡]Generally not clinically significant.
STD = sexually transmitted disease; HDL = high-density lipoprotein.

norgestimate-containing OCPs are preferred. An OCP with low to medium androgenic progestins generally are also safe in patients with sickle cell anemia, prosthetic heart valves, mitral valve prolapse, migraine without aura, depression, benign breast disease, or uncomplicated diabetes, as well as smokers under 35 years of age; women with a family history of coronary disease, breast cancer, or ovarian cancer; and anticoagulant users. For patients with seizure disorder, an OCP containing 50 μg estrogen might be preferable, since anticonvulsants induce the hepatic microsomal enzyme system.

    Combination oral contraceptives can be used for therapeutic reasons in women with ovulatory dysfunctional uterine bleeding, dysmenorrhea (preferably use an OCP with the least androgenic progestin possible), persistent anovulation, premature ovarian failure, and mittelschmerz (use of an OCP with a progestin with low to medium androgenic activity is preferred). For functional ovarian cysts, a monophasic OCP containing a progestin with high androgenic activity can be useful. For women with disabling pain from endometriosis or heavy bleeding due to blood dyscrasias, continuous administration of a monophasic OCP with a progestin of medium to high androgenic activity is indicated.

SPECIAL CONSIDERATIONS

Cardiovascular disease and thromboembolic risk. The small increase in risk of cardiovascular events from OCPs[68,69] is thought to be mediated through estrogenic hypercoagulable effects, an increase in blood pressure, and altered lipid profile (including a decrease in HDLs and an increase in triglycerides), which are mostly related to the androgenic properties of progestins.

Out of 100,000 women taking OCPs, 1 will have a myocardial infarction, 3 will have a stroke, and 11 will have a thromboembolic event. These complications are more likely to occur in older women, smokers, hypertensives, diabetics, or women with hyperlipidemia.[68,69] Low-dose estrogen pills containing a progestin with low androgenic activity have a more favorable effect on cardiovascular risk.[69]

Recently, there has been a debate over the third-generation progestins and their associated increased risk of venous thromboembolic events compared with the first- second-generation progestins. Overall, studies do not indicate a consistent statistically significant difference in thromboembolic risk among users of combined OCPs containing different progestins. Given the low incidence of these complications, a case fatality rate of less than 2% and low residual morbidity, the small differences in odds ratios cannot be regarded as being clinically significant.[70-73] There is an increased risk of venous thrombembolism in factor V Leiden mutation carriers who are on OCPs. Routine screening for factor V Leiden is not recommended because of the limited benefit of preventing deep venous thromboses, unless the patient has a family history of unexplained thromboembolic events.[74]

Cancer. There is an increased risk of breast cancer in current users of OCPs,[75] as well as a slightly increased risk of cervical cancer.[76] A meta-analysis of the data available on cancer risk in women using OCPs showed that long-term use (more than 8 years) is associated with an excess of 151 in 100,000 cases of breast cancer, 125 in 100,000 cases of cervical cancer, and 41 in 100,000 cases of liver cancer, and with a decrease of 197 of 100,000 less cases of endometrial cancer and of 193 of 100,000

less cases of ovarian cancer.[45] From a population perspective, the net risk is not significant.

A 1996 analysis of more than 50 studies showed current OCP users at a 24% increased risk of having breast cancer diagnosed. The risk decreases after the OCP is stopped, with no difference at 10 years after stopping OCPs.[75]

GUIDELINES FOR USE

Combination oral contraceptives should generally not be used in women with a history of thromboembolic events, cerebrovascular accidents, coronary artery disease, structural heart disease complicated by atrial fibrillation or pulmonary hypertension, diabetes with complications (eg, retinopathy, neuropathy, nephropathy, or vascular complications), breast cancer, liver adenomas, liver cancer or significant liver disease, uncontrolled hypertension, or vascular disease. They should also be avoided in women undergoing major surgery with prolonged immobilization and women over 35 years of age who smoke more than 15 cigarettes per day.[77] They should not be given to pregnant women, and OCP use should be deferred for lactating women less than 6 weeks postpartum, as it may diminish milk production.

Physicians should be cautious in prescribing OCPs to women less than 3 weeks postpartum (hypercoagulable state), lactating women 6 weeks to 6 months postpartum, women with undiagnosed abnormal genital bleeding, smokers over 35 years of age (less than 15 cigarettes per day), patients with a past history of breast cancer but free of disease for more than 5 years, women who take medications that affect liver enzymes (eg, rifampin, phenytoin, barbiturates), and women with gallbladder disease.

Advantages are considered to outweigh the risks in headache (including migraine sufferers); women with uncomplicated diabetes; patients undergoing major surgery without prolonged immobilization; women with sickle cell anemia, controlled hypertension, undiagnosed breast mass, cervical intraepithelial neoplasia, or cancer awaiting treatment; women over 50 years; women with a family history of hyperlipidemia or premature coronary artery disease (CAD);and women with conditions that impair compliance with daily pill taking (eg, mental retardation, psychiatric disease, or substance abuse).

Use of OCPs should not be restricted for women more than 3 weeks postpartum; women who have just had an abortion; women with history of gestational diabetes, obesity, thyroid disease, varicose veins, headaches, irregular menses, past, recent, or current pelvic inflammatory disease (PID) or STD, vaginitis without purulent cervicitis, cervical ectropion, HIV, acquired immunodeficiency syndrome (AIDS) or risk of HIV infection, benign breast disease, early-stage endometrial cancer or ovarian cancer, viral hepatitis carrier state, leiomyomas, ectopic pregnancy, pelvic surgery, or gestational trophoblastic disease; women with a family history of breast cancer; women who are anemic, have epilepsy, endometriosis, severe dysmenorrhea, infections such as tuberculosis or malaria, or benign ovarian tumors; or women who use antibiotics.

PROBLEMS ASSOCIATED WITH USE

Lack of withdrawal bleeding. Pregnancy should be ruled out in cases of lack of withdrawal bleeding. Patients may be induced to withdrawal bleed by switching to the use of a different OCP preparation, such as one containing a new progestin (eg, Desogen or Ortho-Cept) or a triphasic OCP (eg, Orthotricyclen or Triphasil). If this is ineffective, a 50-μg estrogen pill might be considered if the side effects are acceptable to the patient and if there are no contraindications to the higher-dose pill.[3] Alternatively, a 20-μg ethinyl estradiol pill can be added to the patient's OCP. In the absence of pregnancy, lack of withdrawal bleeding does not represent a contraindication to OCP use.

Androgenic effects. Oily skin, acne, and hirsutism while on OCPs can be due to high endogenous androgenic production or to a progestin with high androgenic activity in the OCP. If other causes have been ruled out, the OCP can be changed to a combination of a higher estrogen dose and a less androgenic progestin (eg, Ovcon-35, Brevicon, Modicon, or an OCP containing a new progestin).[53,54] All OCPs can have a beneficial effect on acne, but the only one approved by the US Food and Drug Administration (FDA) for treatment of acne is Orthotricyclen.

Breakthrough spotting or bleeding. Such problems are more common with lower-dose pills. Breakthrough bleeding usually decreases over the first four cycles of pill use. Causes such as forgetting to take pills, impaired absorption due to concurrent medications,

ectopic pregnancy, genital infections, endometriosis, and endometrial or cervical abnormalities (eg, polyps, myomas, cancer) have to be ruled out before deciding to change the pill preparation.[3]

To minimize the problem of breakthrough bleeding, more progestin can be used, or the estrogenic potency can be increased. Estrostep is a triphasic OCP with increasing amounts of ethinyl estradiol (20, 30, and 35 μg) as the cycle progresses, which should minimize spotting. Other alternatives include Desogen, Ortho-Cept, Orthotriyclen, Levlen and a 50-μg estrogen OCP. The same effect can be achieved by adding 20 μg ethinyl estradiol to the daily OCP.

Lactation problems. The estrogen in combined OCPs can diminish milk production.[78] Combined OCPs should be avoided for the first 6 weeks and preferably for the first 6 months of lactation. Progestin-based methods are better alternatives for lactating women.[79]

Mastalgia. Breast tenderness improves in most cases after a few cycles of pill use. Lowering the estrogen dose can decrease the symptoms, as can avoidance of dietary methylxanthines. Vitamin E 400 IU twice daily may be helpful.[3]

Skin conditions. Chloasma, telangiectasias, erythema multiforme, eczema, photosensitivity, and hair loss can be associated with OCP use.[3] Use of sunscreen can minimize OCP-related skin problems worsened by sun exposure. Sometimes OCPs have to be replaced with a progestin-based or other contraceptive method.

Mood changes. Although OCPs can improve depression, they can also worsen it-mostly because of progestogenic effects. A deficiency in vitamin B_6 also may be associated with mood changes in OCP users.[80] Depending on the severity of symptoms, changing to an OCP with a lower hormonal content, or stopping the OCPs and monitoring for resolution of mood changes can be tried. If OCPs are continued, vitamin B_6 supplements may be helpful.[81]

If mood changes are related to the pill-free interval, taking the active pills continuously for three cycles may be an alternative strategy.

Galactorrhea. Combination oral contraceptives suppress the prolactin-inhibiting factor and potentially can cause galactorrhea, but other causes should be ruled out (eg, pituitary adenoma, drugs). If the OCP is the cause and is stopped, galactorrhea disappears in 3 to 6 months. This side effect does not represent a contraindication to OCP use.

Headaches. Serious causes of headaches should be ruled out. Lowering the estrogen and progestin dose can be tried. If the headache occurs in the pill-free interval, taking the pill continuously for three cycles and eliminating the inactive pills or trying Mircette (which has a shorter pill-free interval) can be considered.

Decreased libido. Decreased libido while taking OCPs can be caused by decreased endogenous androgen production. Decreased vaginal lubrication also can be a contributing factor. If bothersome, a more androgenic progestin can be tried or another method of contraception considered.

Nausea and vomiting. Gastrointestinal side effects are common at the initiation of OCPs. They tend to subside after a few cycles of pill use. If problems persist, taking the pill at night with a meal can help. Lowering the estrogen dose or changing to a progestin-only pill can be considered if the nausea and vomiting do not improve within a few cycles of pill use. If a woman vomits within 2 hours after taking the pill, she should take an extra pill.

Pregnancy. If a woman becomes pregnant and plans to continue the pregnancy, OCPs should be discontinued. There is no increased risk of malformations in the baby if a woman gets pregnant while on the pill.[22,82]

Weight gain. Although common belief is that OCPs lead to weight gain, it is most often minimal or absent.[83–85] If bothersome, pills containing desogestrel or norgestimate or low-dose estrogen pill can be tried. Weight gain related to OCPs responds to exercise and decreased caloric intake.

Recently Approved Combined Hormonal Contraceptives

INJECTABLE ESTROGEN-PROGESTIN
Injectable estrogen-progestin (Lunelle) was approved by the Food and Drug Administration in October 2000. A monthly (every 28 to 33 days) intramuscular injection of estradiol cypionate 5 mg and medroxyprogesterone acetate 25 mg is administered in the deltoid muscle by health care clinicians. Its 1-year failure rate is 0.2%, and it has similar side effects to the combination oral contraceptives.[86]

YASMIN
A combination oral contraceptive containing 30 μg ethinyl estradiol and 3 mg drospirenone (analogue of the aldosterone antagonist spironolactone). Its 1-year failure rate is 0.4 per 100 women-year.[87]

Progestin-Based Contraceptives

Progestin-based contraception relies on the inhibitory effect of progesterone on ovulation, as well as effects on cervical mucus, which becomes scant and thick. The effects of progesterone on the endometrial glands produce an atrophic endometrium. Under the influence of progestins, the fallopian tube cilia become less active. Progestins also interfere with corpus luteal function.

Progestins for contraception are a good choice in breast-feeding women,[88] women with compliance problems such as teenagers[89] and psychiatric patients, and women in their late reproductive years.[90] The lack of cardiovascular complications makes progestins a good alternative for women with contraindications to estrogen.[91] As with combined OCPs, progestins decrease menstrual cramps and flow and, therefore, indirectly the incidence of anemia, as well as mittelschmerz, PID, and endometrial and ovarian cancer. They also can be used to treat endometriosis-related pain.[92]

PRECAUTIONS
Progestin contraceptives should not be administered to pregnant women, women with unexplained abnormal vaginal bleeding, or breast cancer patients. In women with liver or cardiovascular disease, complicated diabetes, breast cancer in remission for more than 5 years, or on medications that induce the hepatic enzymes, progestins need to be used with caution.[3]

Progestins can be offered to women of all ages and body weights, smokers, and women who are postpartum if not breast-feeding, as well as lactating women more than 6 weeks postpartum.[85] Progestins also can be used in women with fibroids, endometriosis, benign breast disease, benign ovarian tumors, cervical neoplasia, PID, STDs, and chronic diseases such as hypertension, gallbladder disease, thyroid conditions, epilepsy, valvular heart disease, and headaches. Perioperative status is not a contraindication to progestin use, regardless of the duration of immobilization.

INJECTABLE PROGESTIN

Medroxyprogesterone acetate (Depo-Provera) 150 mg injected intramuscularly every 3 months is an effective method of contraception, with only 0.3% of its users experiencing pregnancy at 1 year of use.[3] Fertility can be delayed in some cases, with ovulation occurring at 6 to 12 months after the last dose.[93] It decreases the risk of ectopic pregnancy,[52] and it is especially useful in women with compliance problems and in seizure patients,[94] where better seizure control has been documented. It is associated with a decrease in high-density lipoprotein (HDL) cholesterol[89] and bone mineral density.[95,96] The effect on bone density is reversible after discontinuation of this method,[97] and it is similar to the one induced by lactation.[98] Menstrual cycle abnormalities, weight gain, depression, headache, nervousness, decreased libido, and mastalgia are the most common reasons for discontinuation of this method.[99] These side effects can last for up to 6 to 8 months after the last dose. Depo-Provera use does not increase the risk of breast and cervical cancers in humans, and it decreases the risk of ovarian and endometrial cancers.[100–102]

PROGESTIN PILLS

Norethindrone 0.35 mg (Micronor) and norgestrel 0.075 mg (Ovrette) are available for contraceptive use in the United States. For perfect users, the failure rate is 0.5% at 1 year of use; for typical users it is 5%.[3] The incidence of ectopic pregnancies is the same as in nonusers, but when pregnancy happens it is more likely to be ectopic.[91]

The pills have to be taken regularly, ideally at the same time each day. The main reasons for discontinuation are menstrual cycle abnormalities and the need for excellent compliance with pill taking.[103] It is a good contraceptive choice for postpartum lactating women, since it does not decrease milk production.[88]

SUBCUTANEOUS PROGESTIN IMPLANTS

Norplant is a subcutaneous implant, that consists of five rods containing 36 mg levonorgestrel released at 85 μg daily initially, then 50 μg daily at 9 months, 35 μg daily at 18 months, and 30 μg daily for 42 months. It is effective, with a 1-year pregnancy rate of 0.05%.[3,104] The cumulative rate of pregnancy at the end of the 5 years is 1.6%. The pregnancy rate is higher in heavier women. Removal of implants is associated with immediate return to fertility. Norplant use decreases the risk of ectopic pregnancy, and it does not affect lipid profile and bone density.[105]

The insertion and removal of Norplant require a small surgical procedure with its risks of local infection and pain. The more common side effects leading to implant removal are menstrual cycle abnormalities, headache, dizziness, mastalgia, nervousness, acne, and weight gain.[104,105]

Good candidates for this method are women who have completed their childbearing but do not desire sterilization, smokers over 35 years of age, women with compliance problems or contraindications to estrogen, and women who desire long-term birth spacing. Various studies show a good continuation rate among adolescents.[106,107]

Future Methods

Methods of contraception currently in development for the US market are described in Table 9–5.[108–117]

INTRAUTERINE CONTRACEPTIVE DEVICES

The IUDs available in the United States are the Paragard T380A copper IUD, which is effective for up to 10 years, and the Progestasert IUD, which requires annual replacement and MIRENA, which is effective for 5 years[118] (approved by FDA in December 2000). The Progestasert IUD releases progesterone at a rate of 65 μg/d, and MIRENA releases levonorgestrel at 20 μg/d, which diminishes menstrual blood loss.[119] The copper IUD use is associated with a 1-year pregnancy rate of 0.6%, and the Progestasert IUD with a 1-year pregnancy rate of 1.5%.[3,120]

Initially, IUDs were thought to prevent implantation, but more recently they have been shown to prevent fertilization by changing cervical mucus quality and by causing a local inflammatory reaction in the genital tract. This seems to affect the sperm's ability to reach the distal end of the fallopian tube and fertilize the egg. In studies, no sperm were identified in the fallopian tube at 30 minutes and 12 hours after intercourse in IUD users.[119] Users of IUDs have half the rate of ectopic pregnancy of nonusers, which implies that IUDs inhibit fertilization, since ectopic

TABLE 9-5. Future Methods of Hormonal Contraception

Vaginal rings
  Combination estrogen and progestin: left in the vagina for 21 d/mo[108]
  Nuvaring: releases 20 μg ethinyl estradiol and 1 mg norethindrone daily
  Progestin only[88,109]

Antiprogestins, eg RU 486: alone or in combination with prostaglandins to prevent follicular development and egg
  implantation[110–112] or incorporated in IUDs

Luteolytic agents: truncated LH receptors and LH binding protein administered monthly to interfere with LH supported luteal function[113]

Transdermal progestin applied daily (Nestorone cream)[3]

Transdermal patch: ethinyl estradiol and 17-dyacetyl norgestimate applied weekly for 3 weeks each month[114]

New implants
  Norplant 2 (2 rods effective for 3 yr)[115]
  Implanon (1 rod effective for 2 yr)[116,117]
  Capronor: biodegradable systems (effective for 1–2 yr)[116]

New injectables
  Progestins
  Norethisterone 200 mg every 8–10 wk[116]
  Levonorgestrel butanoate (more rapid return to fertility upon discontinuation)[116]
  Unijet: new device for self-injection of a progestin dose

  Estrogen/progestin combinations:
    Mesygina: norethisterone and estradiol[116]
    Cyclofem: medroxyprogesterone and estradiol[116]

IUD = intrauterine contraceptive device; LH = luteinizing hormone.

pregnancies develop before the egg reaches the uterus.[120] The progestin in Progestasert and MIRENA adds a hormonal mechanism to its contraceptive effect and can be used for the treatment of menorrhagia[121] and dysfunctional uterine bleeding,[122] which makes it an appealing alternative for older reproductive age women.

There were concerns in the past regarding the safety of IUDs in relation to the risk of PID; these concerns led to its withdrawal from the US market in the 1970s. Studies have shown that an increased risk is related specifically to the insertion process and the patient's own risk of acquiring STDs.[123] The rate of PID decreases from about 10 in 1,000 women—years within the first 20 days after insertion to 1 in 1,000 women—years after 21 days of IUD use.[123]

The IUD is inserted after a vaginal speculum is introduced in the vagina to visualize the cervix. Iodine or chlorhexidine are applied to the cervix, and local anesthesia can be used to make the procedure more comfortable for the patient. The anterior lip of the cervix is grasped with a tenaculum at about 1.5 to 2 cm from the os. The tenaculum is then closed, and traction is applied to straighten the axis of the uterus. The IUD is loaded into the inserter tube and the horizontal arms are folded and maneuvered into the end of the inserter tube, under sterile conditions. The other end of the inserter tube contains a solid rod. The inserter tube with the rod and the folded IUD are then inserted into the uterus to the depth marked on the tube. The outer tube is then withdrawn no more than 1.3 cm over the solid rod, which is kept still to release the horizontal arms of the IUD. The solid rod should be felt in contact with the vertical arm of the IUD. The solid rod is then withdrawn, the outer barrel of the insertion tube is withdrawn, and the IUD strings are clipped at 2.5 cm. The patient should be instructed in checking the IUD string.

The IUD expulsion rate is 5 to 6% during the first year, mostly in the 1-month postinsertion period, and 1 to 2% per year thereafter.[117] Women experience cramping, discharge, and spotting associated with IUD expulsion. Bleeding and pain lead to IUD removal in 12% of women within the first year and about 3% thereafter.[124] Nonsteroidal anti-inflammatories can be helpful in controlling pain and bleeding associated with IUDs. Uterine perforation is a rare complication (1 in 1,000 women-years)[125] related mostly to the insertion procedure and associated with immediate bleeding and severe pain.

Use of IUDs should be considered in women at low risk for STDs, women who have completed their childbearing or desire spacing of pregnancies, and women who have contraindications to other contraceptives and desire a coitus-independent method. Intrauterine contraceptive devices can be used post partum or post abortion and in lactating women.

Intrauterine contraceptive devices should not be used in women who are pregnant, have genital infections, a history of PID, an allergy to copper, Wilson's disease, pelvic malignancy (suspected or diagnosed) or anatomic abnormalities (eg, large fibroids) or in women with increased susceptibility to infections (eg, HIV or cancer patients, intravenous drug users, and women with multiple sexual partners) or a history of genital actinomycosis. It is advisable to avoid IUDs in women who have had previous problems with using such devices.

The return to fertility after removal of an IUD is similar to that with OCPs, with almost 90% of women conceiving within 12 months.[126,127] For rare cases of contraceptive failure, there is no increase in congenital abnormalities in babies conceived with an IUD in place.[128] The device should be removed after pregnancy is confirmed.[129,130]

In regard to IUDs and the risk of cancer, there seems to be no additional risk, and there might be a protective effect against endometrial cancer.[131,132]

Intrauterine contraceptive devices are a safe and effective method of contraception,[133] which have an excellent economic value over 5 years, the best in a comparison of 15 methods in 1995.[134]

There are new progesterone-releasing IUDs available in Europe, effective for up to 10 years after insertion.[135] Other future IUDs will be more flexible, easier to remove, and have lower expulsion rates (Flexigard,[136] Gynefix,[137] Cu-fix[138] frameless IUD) or they will be uterine-cavity shaped, without a string (UDCcu is a copper-plated uterine-cavity shaped IUD that comes in three sizes and prevents pregnancy for at least 3 years).

STERILIZATION

Female Sterilization

In the United States, there are almost 11 million reproductive-age women who have undergone **surgical sterilization** by tubal occlusion as a method of pregnancy prevention.[1] There are different sterilization techniques: suprapubic minilaparotomy or laparoscopy approach followed by tubal occlusion using Silastic bands, Falope rings, clips, electrocoagulation or fimbriectomy. The first-year pregnancy probability is 5.5 per 1,000 procedures, and the 10-year pregnancy probability is 18.5 for every 1,000 procedures,[139] with most of the failures happening in younger women. The use of electrocautery might be followed by fistula formation, which permits sperm passage. Clips are not as occlusive as are other methods, and account for some of the overall method failures.[139]

In the United States about one-third of female sterilization procedures are performed within 48 hours post partum.[140] The fatality rate for female sterilization procedures is 1 to 2 in 100,000, much lower than maternal mortality or the fatality rate for hysterectomy.[141]

The advantages of tubal occlusion are its high effectiveness, lack of side effects, permanence, lack of interference with intercourse, and ease of compliance, as there is no need to take daily pills or have periodic injections. There are also disadvantages that have to be considered—mostly the permanent nature of contraception, which, in some cases, can be associated with regret. Eventually, about 2% of women undergo tubal reanastomosis,[142] and the pregnancy rate following this procedure varies between 43 and 88% depending on the technique used to occlude the tubes, with a higher-than-normal risk of ectopic pregnancy (2 to 5%).[143] Also, tubal occlusion requires a surgeon, an operating room, and associated costs. It does not protect against sexually transmitted diseases, and, if it fails, the resulting pregnancy can be ectopic.

Before undergoing the procedure, the woman has to understand the nature of the operation, the risks associated, the permanence of this method, the possibility of reversal (including expense and need for surgery), and the risk of ectopic pregnancy in case of method failure. The main complications[144] associated with tubal occlusion are bleeding, infection, anesthesia complications, and instrumental trauma to the uterus, bladder, or intestines. The long-term problems[145] associated with this method are ectopic pregnancy, in cases of failure, a possible decline in serum progesterone levels, and possible menstrual changes. The issue of menstrual changes as a result of tubal ligation has been debated in the literature, but the evidence does not support it.[146–148] Many of the cases of dysmenorrhea, heavy bleeding or spotting, and cycle length changes are actually due to factors such as hormonal changes related to aging or to the fact that patients had been using oral contraceptives prior to having their tubes occluded.

Transcervical insertion of quinacrine pellets has been used for years in developing countries as a method of **chemical sterilization**. It is a simple procedure and is cost effective, but there are still unresolved issues regarding quinacrine toxicity that prevent its widespread use at this time.[149,150]

Male Sterilization

Surgical blockage of the vas deferens (vasectomy) is an effective method of pregnancy prevention, with a 1-year pregnancy rate of 0.1%, mainly due to spontaneous recanalization.[3] After the procedure, the time to achieve azoospermia correlates with 12 to 15 ejaculations or 6 weeks in 80 to 90% of men.[151] It is a safer procedure than is female sterilization. It is probably the most cost-effective contraceptive method, has no side effects, and does not disrupt intercourse. It is not associated with any change in sexual function or the volume of the ejaculate. The problems associated with vasectomy are the risk of bleeding or infection at the time of the procedure, permanence, and lack of protection against STDs.

Vasectomy reversal is associated with a pregnancy rate of about 50% and with an 81 to 98% rate of sperm presence in the ejaculate.[152–154] The development of sperm antibodies after vasectomy is common, but it does not seem to have any health consequences in humans.[155–157] The issue of vasectomy and prostate cancer has been debated highly, but there does not seem to be any convincing evidence that vasectomy leads to an increased risk.[158–160]

The "no-scalpel technique" for vasectomy was developed in China in the 1970s using a puncture and ring forceps,[161] but in the United States the traditional method, consisting of skin incision and vas deferens occlusion or resection, is more popular.[162,163]

Future Methods

Future methods of sterilization will likely employ transcervical methods for tubal occlusion, new techniques for vasectomy, reversible silicone occlusion of vas deferens,[164] and, ideally, the design of a one-way valve to prevent sperm/oocyte passage in the vas deferens or fallopian tube.

EMERGENCY CONTRACEPTION

Emergency contraception is used to prevent pregnancy after unprotected intercourse or the failure of a barrier method. Interestingly, 4 to 7% of US couples who use condoms over a 3-month period recognize condom failure.[165] Emergency contraception can be used up to 72 hours after intercourse, not just the "morning after." It is a method of primary pregnancy prevention, since pregnancy begins with implantation and not with fertilization.[166]

Only 1% of US women report ever using emergency contraception.[167] Its widespread use in the US could prevent 1 million abortions and 2 million unwanted pregnancies that end in childbirth each year.[168] Not only would this benefit the women in question, but it would also have a significant economic impact by avoiding pregnancy care costs.[169] Hormonal emergency contraception is available without prescription in certain countries. Self-administration without physician supervision does not seem harmful.[170,171] Methods of emergency contraception are summarized in Table 9–6.[172–179]

Hormonal emergency contraception interferes with ovulation,[180] fertilization[166] and implantation[181] and has no effect on an egg which is already implanted.[166] The IUD is toxic to sperm[182] and induces changes in the endometrium, which prevents implantation.[183] Mifepristone affects endometrial maturation (preventing implantation), can block ovulation,[176,184] and induces regression of the corpus luteum.[185,186] Danazol interferes with luteal-phase progesterone secretion[181] and inhibits or delays ovulation.[180]

Nausea and vomiting as well as menstrual abnormalities, including delayed or early menses following treatment, are the most common side effects of hormonal emergency contraception.[187] These side effects happen more often with high-dose estrogen, less often with estrogen-progesterone combination pills, and even less often with progestins alone and with mifepristone. Other less

TABLE 9–6. Methods of Emergency Contraception

Combination oral contraceptives

    Estrogen and progestin: 100 μg ethinyl estradiol and 0.5 mg levonorgestrel; 2 doses, 12 hours apart, within 72 h
        after intercourse (Yuzpe regimen).* Examples of this regimen include:

        Preven kit—2 doses of 2 pills

        Ovral—2 doses of 2 white pills

        Lo/Ovral—2 doses of 4 white pills

        Levlen—2 doses of 4 light orange pills

        Nordette—2 doses of 4 light orange pills

        Tri-Levlen—2 doses of 4 yellow pills

        Triphasil—2 doses of 4 yellow pills

        Alesse—2 doses of 5 pink pills

    Progestin: Plan B 2 tablets each dose or

    Levonorgestrel: 0.75 mg; 2 doses 12 h apart within 48 h after intercourse (20 Ovrette tablets each dose)[†]

High-dose estrogen: 5 mg ethinyl estradiol daily for 5 d[‡]

Mifepristone (RU 486): single 600-mg dose within 72 h after intercourse[176,177]§

Danazol: Two 400-800-mg doses 12 h apart or 3 doses of 400 mg every 12 h[178]‖

Intrauterine contraceptive devices: insertion within 5 d after intercourse[#]

*At least 75% effective in prevention of pregnancy.[172]
†Similar efficacy to Yuzpe regimen (or better) with fewer side effects.[173]
‡Similar efficacy to Yuzpe regimen[174] with more side effects (eg, nausea and vomiting).[175]
§Up to 100% effective;[176,177] not approved in the United States for emergency contraception but available for medical abortion.
‖Not in clinical use.
#Failure rate of less than 1%.[179]

common complaints are fatigue, breast tenderness, headache, abdominal pain, and dizziness. To reduce the chance of nausea, antiemetics can be administered 1 hour prior to the first dose of hormonal emergency contraception.

A backup method of contraception should be used until the onset of menses following emergency contraception. The patient should have a pregnancy test if menses are delayed after using emergency contraception. Clinicians should discourage frequent use of this method and discuss other long-term and more efficient contraceptive methods with the patient.

Emergency contraception has not been used widely in the United States because the general public is unaware of these methods. Only 36% of respondents of a study were aware that "anything could be done" within a few days after sex to prevent pregnancy, 55% "had heard" of emergency contraception, and only 1% had used it.[188] Some patients and medical clinicians regard it as a method of abortion; however, it is not abortion since there is no effect on a fertilized egg after implantation.

There has not been any documented harmful effect on the fetus when these methods have failed.[22,81]

CONTRACEPTION FOR SPECIAL POPULATIONS

Adolescents

The rate of childbirth by teenagers in the United States is four times higher than it is in Western Europe,[189] accounting for 13% of all births in the United States.[190] Most adolescents seek contraception months after becoming sexually active.[191] Contraception and prevention of STDs should be an important aspect of any clinical encounter with a teenager. A nonjudgmental, confidential, and concrete approach (ie, showing different methods and demonstrating their use) will likely be successful.

Oral contraceptives are most popular with teenagers,[192] and they are safe to use in this age group, even in the presence of smoking, uncomplicated diabetes, sickle cell disease, or cystic fibrosis. This is an excellent method when the noncontraceptive benefits are considered, such as improvement in dysmenorrhea and acne. The transient nature of most side effects should be emphasized. Simultaneous condom use should be advocated for STD prevention, and correct use of condoms should be demonstrated, since condom failures are frequent in this age group.

Condom use is a good contraceptive choice since it prevents both pregnancy and STDs and is available without a prescription. However, the high rate of failure in this age group should be considered.

Diaphragms, cervical caps, and vaginal spermicides are not popular among adolescents, mostly because of their interference with the act of intercourse. The IUD should be avoided in adolescents due to the high incidence of STDs in this age group.

Norplant and Depo-Provera are good contraceptive choices for adolescents since they do not require daily compliance. Irregular bleeding and acne are frequent reasons for discontinuation. These methods are also appropriate for women who have experienced pregnancies or who have had compliance problems with oral contraceptives. With good education, the continuation and failure rates with Norplant can be better than those with oral contraceptives.[192]

Emergency contraception counseling should accompany all discussions of long-term contraception.

Women of Older Reproductive Age

For women in the United States, the interval between their last delivery and menopause is about 20 years, which is more than half of their reproductive life. Effective and safe contraception is essential in the older reproductive age group (over 35 years).

Surgical sterilization is common in couples who have completed their families. Other popular methods are condoms and the diaphragm, mostly because of their lack of side effects. Recently, the use of oral hormonal contraception in this age group has increased, as low-dose estrogen pills have become available;[4,193] OCPs are safe to use until menopause in women without contraindications. Noncontraceptive benefits especially relevant for the older woman include prevention of ovarian and uterine cancers, increase in bone density, and prevention of perimenopausal symptoms. At the time of menopause, oral contraceptive therapy should be discontinued, and consideration should be given to hormone replacement therapy. This change should be prompted by an elevated FSH level after 7 to 14 days from the last active pill or by vasomotor symptoms in the pill-free interval.

In women over 35 years who are smokers or have contraindications to estrogen, long-acting progestins or the IUD should be considered. The progestin-releasing IUD is a good option since it also controls dysfunctional uterine bleeding, which is common in this age group.[121,122] The problem with this method is that it requires annual removal and re-insertion, but the introduction of the longer-lasting model MIRENA in the United States will probably increase the popularity of the IUD.

Women with Health Problems

Vasectomy should be discussed as a contraceptive option for women with health problems who are in a monogamous relationship.

CARDIOVASCULAR DISEASES
Hypertension. Nonsmokers with controlled blood pressure can use oral hormonal contraception. Nonestrogen methods should be used in hypertensive smokers or if the blood pressure is not adequately controlled.[65]

Congenital heart disease and valvular disease. Nonestrogen methods should be used if there is any associated risk of thrombosis. Women with mitral valve prolapse can use combined hormonal contraception in the absence of mitral regurgitation. If an IUD is considered, antibiotic prophylaxis should be used at the time of insertion.[68,194]

Thromboembolic disease. Women with a history of thromboembolic events or with a family history of idiopathic thrombosis should use nonestrogen methods of contraception.[70,71]

Ischemic heart disease. Non-estrogen methods should be used in women with a history of ischemic heart disease.[195]

DYSLIPIDEMIA
Oral hormonal contraception can alter the lipid profile, depending on the composition of the pill. The estrogen component increases total cholesterol, HDL cholesterol, and triglycerides, and the progestin component has the opposite effect. The third-generation progestins have less of an impact on the lipid profile. Women with very high triglycerides should not use oral hormonal contraception.[196]

Norplant is a hormonal method that does not affect the lipid profile.[105] The IUD and barrier methods can be used safely.

HEMORRHAGIC DISORDERS

Women with hemorrhagic disorders or who use anticoagulants should not use IUDs.[197] Any of the other methods can be used. The risk of bleeding associated with surgical sterilization should be considered.

DIABETES MELLITUS

Women with gestational diabetes can use oral contraceptives as well as any other method after delivery. Diabetics over 35 years of age and younger diabetics who are smokers or have vascular complications should use nonestrogen methods. Long-acting progestins and the IUDs are safe to use in these cases.[198]

ENDOCRINOPATHIES

Women with thyroid disorders can use any birth control method. Oral hormonal contraception can interfere with the results of some thyroid tests, such as increased total thyroxine, but the free thyroxine and thyroid stimulating hormone are unchanged. Oral contraception can be used in patients with prolactinomas and are an excellent choice for women with polycystic ovaries.[199]

NEUROLOGIC DISORDERS

Migraine headache. Oral hormonal contraception should not be used in patients who have aura or a vascular component to their migraines, focal neurologic and visual disturbances (such as aphasia, dysarthria, numbness, tingling, or motor deficits in a localized area), visual field defects, or luminous visual hallucinations.[94] In women with classic migraines, oral contraception can increase the frequency of the headache, mostly in the pill-free interval. In the case of premenstrual migraines, oral contraceptives can prove beneficial.

Epilepsy. Medroxyprogesterone acetate improves seizure frequency and severity,[94] which makes it an excellent choice for seizure patients. The IUD can be used safely, without impact on seizure activity or its treatment. Oral contraceptives do not influence seizure pattern, but they can interact with anticonvulsants, leading to contraceptive failure due to increased cytochrome P450 activity and increased metabolic clearance of the sex steroids. Low-dose

(under 35 µg estrogen) pills should not be used. Norplant should not be used in seizure patients because anticonvulsants lead to an increased clearance of the already low level of levonorgestrel used for contraception in this method.[94] Because of the teratogenicity of anticonvulsants, contraceptive methods with high failure rates (ie, some barrier methods and the rhythm method) should be avoided if possible.

Multiple sclerosis. Oral contraceptives do not seem to alter the natural course of multiple sclerosis. Women with sensory deficits in the abdominal area should avoid IUDs. Women with motor deficits can have difficulties with vaginal barrier methods.[195]

PULMONARY DISEASE

Women with asthma can use any contraceptive method. Patients on steroids should avoid IUDs, because of the risk of infection. Oral contraceptives can decrease the clearance of theophylline, requiring dose reduction. For women with cystic fibrosis, all methods can be used; there was an initial concern that the use of progesterone could increase mucus production, but this was not confirmed by subsequent studies.[200]

DIGESTIVE DISEASES

Women with active inflammatory disease might be served better by using contraceptive methods, that bypass the gastrointestinal tract. Intrauterine contraceptive devices should not be offered to patients on chronic steroids or immunosuppressives. Estrogen-containing methods should be avoided in women with gallbladder disease. Patients with active hepatitis or cirrhosis should not use hormonal contraception. Women with a history of intrahepatic cholestasis of pregnancy have a 50% chance of recurrence if they use oral contraceptives.[201] Patients who have acute hepatitis can use hormonal contraception when their liver enzymes return to normal; IUDs should be avoided in women with sexually acquired hepatitis B or C, since they are at risk for transmission of other sexually transmitted diseases. Progestin-only methods and tubal ligation are probably the best options for liver transplant patients.

RENAL DISEASE

Progestin methods are safe for women on dialysis. Depo-Provera is the preferred progestin contraceptive, since plasma progestin levels in patients on

Depo-Provera do not change significantly after dialysis. Depo-Provera is a good alternative since it also helps to reduce the anemia associated with renal disease. Progestin pills and Norplant are associated with a significant fall in the progestin level after dialysis. Intrauterine contraceptive devices should not be used due to the anemia and immune suppression associated with end-stage renal disease. For women who undergo renal transplant, ovulation usually returns to normal within 6 months after the operation.[202] Tubal ligation can be performed at the time of the transplant, if desired. Barrier methods are a good choice because they lack systemic effects, but their high failure rate can be problematic. Oral contraceptives can inhibit hepatic microsomal enzymes, decreasing the clearance of cyclosporine,[203] so cyclosporine levels should be monitored closely if oral contraceptives are used. The IUD should not be used in patients on immunosuppressives post transplant.

RHEUMATIC DISEASES

Systemic lupus erythematosus. Traditionally, women with systemic lupus erythematosus (SLE) have been advised to avoid estrogen due to its hypercoagulable effect. Studies of estrogen use in SLE are ongoing. Progestin-only methods are safe to use. Patients with SLE should avoid the use of IUDs since these patients can be immunosuppressed. Barrier methods are excellent because they lack systemic side effects, but their high failure rate can be problematic in these patients.

Rheumatoid arthritis. Patients with rheumatoid arthritis do well on oral contraceptives.[57,58] These patients can have an IUD placed if they are not immunosuppressed and they have the physical ability to check the string.

SKIN DISEASES

Melanoma. There is no conclusive evidence that estrogen or progestin can affect melanoma in humans, but animal studies show that melanoma cells grow faster when exposed to estrogen;[204] this may need to be considered when offering contraceptive counseling to a patient with diagnosed melanoma.

Acne. Women with acne generally find that their skin improves when they are using combined oral hormonal contraceptives.

HUMAN IMMUNODEFICIENCY VIRUS

Sexually active women who are infected with HIV can use hormonal contraceptives. There has been a concern regarding an alteration of the immune response and enhanced viral shedding in relation to hormonal contraceptives,[205] but the World Health Organization (WHO) considers all hormonal contraceptives as an acceptable option for HIV-infected women.[205] Drug interactions should be evaluated carefully in these patients, since they take multiple drugs that are metabolized by the liver. Barrier methods are a good choice; IUDs should definitely be avoided. Frequent spermicide use should be avoided due to increased local irritation that could increase transmission of the virus.[29] Tubal ligation also can be offered to HIV-infected women.

POSTPARTUM AND BREAST-FEEDING WOMEN

Women should begin contraception at 3 to 6 weeks postpartum if they do not fully breast-feed. Since full breast-feeding is rare in the United States, contraception should be offered to all women at their postpartum follow-up. Since estrogen interferes with milk production,[78] progestin-only methods are preferred.[79] The IUD is also a good choice and can be inserted 4 to 8 weeks postpartum.

FUTURE CONTRACEPTIVE APPROACHES

"The Male Pill"

A male pill is already being used in China. It contains gossypol (derived from cottonseed oil), which causes azoospermia.[206] It is administered daily until the ejaculate is sperm free, and weekly thereafter.[207] Animal studies in the United States were associated with significant hypokalemia and cardiac toxicity,[208] but studies of human use in China have reported high effectiveness and low toxicity.

Inhibition of FSH/LH secretion in males[207] can be achieved by administering a combination of progesterone and androgens or using FSH antagonists, truncated FSH receptors, gonadotropin-releasing hormone (Gn-RH) agonists/antagonists, or inhibins. These methods are still being researched. Also being studied are potential clinical applications of the toxic effect mifepristone and calcium channel blockers[209] have on sperm by inhibiting calcium influx.

Immune Contraception

The development of a contraceptive vaccine has been an appealing idea to researchers for decades.[210,211] The antigens used in the development of such a vaccine[212] would be the reproductive hormones,[213] egg/sperm antigens,[214–216] or immunogens of the early conceptus.[217] At this point in time, there are phase III clinical trials beginning for human chorionic gonadotropin (hCG) vaccines in India, sponsored by the WHO. Such vaccines would interrupt early pregnancy by blocking hCG secretion.[218,219] Obviously, such a vaccine would not be acceptable to many cultural and religious groups since it interrupts pregnancy.

Olfactory Contraception

The idea of developing olfactory contraception is based on Kallmann's syndrome and its features of anosmia and anovulation due to a lack of Gn-RH-producing hypothalamic cells, which originate in the olfactory placode during embryonic development. Ideally, a pheromone could regulate the pulse generator of Gn-RH to achieve an anovulatory state similar to the one induced by lactation.[113] Studies in rodents show that pheromones (urinary secretory products) of a "foreign" male mouse (other than the one impregnating the female) can inhibit the implantation of an early embryo.[113]

CONCLUSION

The option of pregnancy prevention is essential for the physical and emotional well-being of every woman. In the United States, the average woman has two children and will need contraception for the remainder of her reproductive life. There are a variety of available contraceptive methods to suit women of different ages and with different medical problems. In the practices of primary care clinicians caring for reproductive-age women in the United States, 1 of every 10 patients does not use contraception, and 6 of every 10 pregnancies are mistimed or unwanted. There is a stringent need for further patient education in the field of contraception. Providing contraceptive advice should be part of every clinical encounter with a reproductive-age patient. When offering contraceptive choices, the clinician should remember that many health plans in the United States do not pay for contraceptive services.[220] Promoting health while preventing unwanted pregnancy should be an intrinsic component in the primary care of women in the twenty-first century.

RESOURCE

Planned Parenthood Federation of America
810 Seventh Avenue
New York, New York 10019
Telephone: (212) 541-7800
          1-800-230-PLAN (1-800-230-7526)
Web site: www.plannedparenthood.org

This toll-free hotline provides answers to medical questions. Extensive information is available on the Web site in both English and Spanish, addressing all currently available methods of contraception in detail.

REFERENCES

1. Abma JC, Chandra A, Mosher WD, et al. Fertility, family planning and women's health: new data from the 1995 National Survey of Family Growth. Vital Health Stat 23 1997;19:1–114.

2. Henshaw SK. Unintended pregnancy in the United States. Fam Plann Perspect 1998;30:24–9,46.

3. Hatcher RA, Trussel J, Stewart F, et al. Contraceptive Technology. New York: Ardent Media Inc; 1998.

4. Piccinino LJ, Mosher WD. Trends in contraceptive use in the United States: 1982–1995. Fam Plann Perspect 1998;30(1):4–10, 46.

5. Schuster MA, Bell RM, Kanouse DE. The sexual prac-

tices of adolescent virgins: genital sexual activities of high school students who have never had vaginal intercourse. Am J Public Health 1996;86:1570–6.

6. Wilcox AJ, Weinberg CR, Baird DD. Timing of sexual intercourse in relation to ovulation. N Engl J Med 1995;333:1517–21.

7. Kambic RT, Lamprecht V. Calendar rhythm efficacy: a review. Adv Contracept 1996;12:123–8.

8. Trussel J, Grummer-Strawn L. Contraception failure of the ovulation method of periodic abstinence. Fam Plann Perspect 1990;22:65–75.

9. Frank-Hermann P, Freundl G, Baur S, et al. Effectiveness and acceptability of the symptothermal method of natural family planning in Germany. Am J Obstet Gynecol 1991;165:2052–4.

10. Population Action International. A guide to methods of birth control. Briefing paper No. 25. Washington (DC): PAI; 1991.

11. Pudney J, Oueta M, Mayer K, et al. Preejaculatory fluid as a potential vehicle for sexual transmission of HIV [letter]. Lancet 1992;340:1,470.

12. Ilaria G, Jacobs JL, Polski B, et al. Detection of HIV-1 DNA sequences in preejaculatory fluid [letter]. Lancet 1992;340:1,469.

13. Rogow D, Horowitz S. Withdrawal: a review of the literature and an agenda for research. Stud Fam Plann 1995;26(3):140–53.

14. Kennedy KI, Rivera R, McNeilly AS. Consensus statement on the use of breastfeeding as a family planning method. Contraception 1989;39:477–96.

15. Steiner M, Piedrahita C, Glover L, et al. The impact of lubricants on latex condoms during vaginal intercourse. Int J STD AIDS 1994;5:29–36.

16. Cates W Jr, Holmes KK. Condom efficacy against gonorrhea and nongonococcal urethritis. Am J Epidemiol 1996;143:843–4.

17. Centers for Disease Control and Prevention. Facts about condoms and their use in preventing HIV infection and other sexually transmitted diseases. Atlanta (GA): CDC; 1995.

18. Kestelman P, Trussel J. Efficacy of the simultaneous use of condoms and spermicides. Fam Plann Perspect 1991,23:226–7, 232.

19. Trussel J, Sturgen K, Strickler J, Dominik R. Comparative contraceptive efficacy of the female condom and other barrier methods. Fam Plann Perspect 1994;26:66–72.

20. Trussel J, Stricker J, Vaughan B. Contraceptive efficacy of the diaphragm, sponge and cervical cap. Fam Plann Perspect 1993;25:101–5.

21. Mauck C, Glover LH, Miller E, et al. Lea's Shield: a study of the safety and efficacy of a new vaginal barrier contraceptive used with and without spermicide. Contraception 1996;53:329–36.

22. Simpson JL, Phillips OP. Spermicides, hormonal contraception and congenital malformations. Adv Contracept 1990;6:141–67.

23. Strobino B, Kline J, Warburton D. Spermicide use and pregnancy outcome. Am J Public Health 1988;78;260–3.

24. Einarson TR, Koren G, Mattice D, Schecher-Tsafriri C. Maternal spermicide use and adverse reproductive outcome: a metaanalysis. Am J Obstet Gynecol 1990;162:655–60.

25. Centers for Disease Control and Prevention. What do we know about nonoxynol-9 for HIV and STD prevention? CDC update. Atlanta (GA): CDC 1997.

26. Hooton TM, Fennel CL, Clark AM, Stamm WE. Nonoxynol-9: differential antibacterial activity and enhancement of bacterial adherence to vaginal epithelial cells. J Infect Dis 1991;164:1216–9.

27. Wittowski KM, Susser E, Dietz K. The protective effect of condoms and nonoxynol-9 against HIV infection. Am J Public Health 1988;88:590–6.

28. Roddy RE, Zekeng L, Ryan KA, et al. A controlled trial of nonoxynol 9 to reduce male to female transmission of sexually transmitted diseases. N Engl J Med 1998;339:504–10.

29. Goeman J, Ndoye I, Sakho LM, et al. Frequent use of menfegol spermicidal vaginal foaming tablets associated with a high incidence of genital lesions. J Infect Dis 1995;171:1611–4.

30. Roddy RE, Cordero M, Cordero C, Fortney JA. A dosing study of nonoxynol-9 and genital irritation. Int J STD AIDS 1993;4:165–70.

31. Hooton TM, Scholes D, Hughes JP, et al. A prospective study of risk factors for symptomatic urinary tract infection in young women. N Engl J Med 1996;335:468–74.

32. Fihn SD, Boyko EJ, Normand EH, et al. Association between use of spermicide-coated condoms and *E. coli* urinary tract infection in young women. Am J Epidemiol 1996;144:512–20.

33. Garg S, Taluja V, Upadhayay SN, Talwar GP. Studies on the contraceptive efficacy of Praneem polyherbal cream. Contraception 1993;48:591–6.

34. Talwar GP, Raghuvanshi P, Mirsa R, et al. Plant immunomodulators for termination of unwanted pregnancy and for contraception and reproductive health. Immunol Cell Biol 1997;76:190–2.

35. Stone AB, Hitchcock PJ. Vaginal microbicides for preventing the sexual transmission of HIV. AIDS 1994;8(Suppl 1):S285–93.

36. Faundes A, Elias CC, Coggins C. Spermicides and barrier contraception. Curr Opin Obstet Gynecol 1994;6:552–8.

37. Sturgis SH, Albright F. Mechanism of estrin therapy in relief of dysmenorrhea. Endocrinology 1940;26: 102.

38. Peterson LS, Oakley D, Potter LS, Darroch JE. Women's efforts to prevent pregnancy: consistency of oral contraceptive use. Fam Plann Perspect 1998; 30(1):19–23.

39. Oakley D, Potter L, De Leon-Wong E, Visnes C. Oral contraceptive use and protective behavior after missed pills. Fam Plann Perspect 1997;29:277–9, 287.

40. Trussell J, Stewart F, Potts M, et al. Should oral contraceptives be available without a prescription? Am J Public Health 1993;83:1094–9.

41. Vessey MP, Smith MA, Yates D. Return to fertility after discontinuation of oral contraceptives: influence of age and parity. Br J Fam Plann 1986;11:120.

42. Bracken MB, Hellenbrand KG, Holford TR. Conception delay after oral contraceptive use: the effect of estrogen dose. Fertil Steril 1990;53:21–7.

43. Mortola JF. A risk-benefit appraisal of drugs used in the management of premenstrual syndrome. Drug Saf 1994;10:160–9.

44. Grimes DA, Economy KE. Primary prevention of gynecologic cancers. Am J Obstet Gynecol 1995; 172:227–35.

45. Schlesselman JJ. Net effect of oral contraceptive use on the risk of cancer in women in the United States. Obstet Gynecol 1995;85:793–801.

46. Harlap S, Kost K, Forrest JD. Preventing pregnancy, protecting health: a new look at birth control choices in the United States. New York: The Alan Guttmacher Institute; 1991.

47. Narod SA, Risch H, Moslehi R, et al. Oral contraceptives and the risk of hereditary ovarian cancer. N Engl J Med, 1998;339:424–8.

48. Rubin S. Chemoprevention of hereditary ovarian cancer. N Engl J Med 1998;339:469–71.

49. Broome M, Clayton J, Fotherhy K. Enlarged follicles in women using oral contraceptives. Contraception 1995;52:13–6.

50. Egarter CH, Putz M, Strohmer H, et al. Ovarian function during low dose contraceptive use. Contraception 1995;51:329–33.

51. Franks AL, Beral V, Cates W, Hogue CJR. Contraception and ectopic pregnancy risk Am J Obstet Gynecol 1990;163:1120–3.

52. Mol BWJ, Ankum WM, Bossuyt PMM, Van der Veen F. Contraception and the risk of ectopic pregnancy: a metaanalysis. Contraception 1995;52:337–41.

53. Redmond GP. Effectiveness of oral contraceptives in the treatment of acne. Contraception 1998,58 (3 Suppl):29–33S.

54. Thorneycroft IH. Update on androgenicity. Am J Obstet Gynecol 1999;180:288–94.

55. De Cherney A. Bone sparing properties of oral contraceptives. Am J Obstet Gynecol 1996;174:15–20.

56. Chaffarino P, Parazzini F, La Vecchia C, et al. Oral contraceptive use and benign gynecologic conditions. A review. Contraception 1998;57:11–8.

57. Pladevall-Villa M, Declos GL, Vargas C, et al. Controversy of oral contraceptive use and the risk of rheumatoid arthritis: metaanalysis of conflicting studies. Am J Epidemiol 1996;144:1–14.

58. Jorgewan C, Picot MC, Bologna C. Oral contraception, parity, breastfeeding and severity of rheumatoid arthritis. Ann Rheum Dis 1996;55(2):94–8.

59. Goldzicher JW, Fotherhy K, editors. Pharmacology of contraceptive steroids. New York: Raven Press; 1994. p. 335–44.

60. Graham CA, Ramos R, Bancroft J, et al. The effects of steroidal contraceptives on the well being and sexuality of women: a double blind, placebo controlled, two centre study of combined and progestogen-only methods. Contraception 1995;52:363–9.

61. Cutchlow CW, Wolner-Hanssen P, Eschenbach DA, et al. Determinants of cervical ectopia and of cervicitis: age, oral contraception, specific cervical infection, smoking and douching. Am J Obstet Gynecol 1995;173:534–43.

62. McGregor JA, Hammill HA. Contraception and sexually transmitted disease: interactions and opportunities. Am J Obstet Gynecol 1993;168:2033–41.

63. World Health Organization Scientific Group. Oral contraceptives and neoplasia. technical report series, no.817. Geneva: WHO; 1992.

64. Nichols M, Robinson G, Bounds W, et al. Effect of four combined oral contraceptives on blood pressure in the pill free interval. Contraception 1993;47: 367–76.

65. Qifang S, Deliang L, Xiurong J, et al. Blood pressure changes and hormonal contraception. Contraception 1994;50:131–4.

66. Rooks JB, Ory HW, Ishak KG, et al. Epidemiology of hepatocellular adenoma. The role of oral contraceptive use. JAMA 1979;242:644–8.

67. Waetjen LE, Grimes OA. Oral contraceptives and primary liver cancer: temporal trends in three countries. Obstet Gynecol 1996;88:945–9.

68. Rosenberg L, Palmer JR, Sands MI, et al. Modern oral contraceptives and cardiovascular disease. Am J Obstet Gynecol 1997;177:707–15.

69. Chasan-Taber L, Stampfer MJ. Epidemiology of oral contraceptives and cardiovascular disease. Ann Intern Med 1998;128:467–77.

70. Ory HW. Epidemiology of venous thrombembolic disease and oral contraceptive use. Dialogues in Contraception 1996;5:4–10.

71. Lidegaard O. Thrombotic disease in young women and the influence of oral contraceptives. Am J Obstet Gynecol 1998;179:S62–7.

72. Spitzer WO. Bias versus causality. Interpreting recent evidence of oral contraceptive studies. Am J Obstet Gynecol 1998;179:S43–50.

73. Westhoff CL. Oral contraceptives and thrombosis. An overview of study methods and recent results. Am J Obstet Gynecol 1998;179:S38–42.

74. Vandenbrouke JP, Koster T, Briet E, et al. Increased risk of venous thrombombolism in oral contraceptive users who are carriers of factor V Leiden mutation. Lancet 1997;349:1114–5.

75. Collaborative Group on Hormonal Factors in Breast Cancer. Breast Cancer and hormonal contraceptives: collaborative reanalysis of individual data on 53,297 women with breast cancer and 100,239 women without breast cancer from 54 epidemiological studies. Lancet 1996;347:1713–27.

76. Thomas DB, Ray DM, and the World Health Organization Collaborative Study of Neoplasia and Steroid Contraceptives. Oral contraceptives and invasive adenocarcinomas and adenosquamous carcinomas of the uterine cervix. Am J Epidemiol 1996;144:281–9.

77. Schiff I. Oral contraceptives and smoking, current considerations: recommendations of a consensus panel. Am J Obstet Gynecol 1999;180:S383–4.

78. Tankeyoon M, Dusitsin N, Chalapati S, et al. Effects of hormonal contraceptives on milk volume and infant growth. Contraception 1984;30:505–22.

79. World Health Organization. Progestogen-only contraceptives during lactation. Contraception 1994;50:35–53, 55–68.

80. Villegas-Salas E, Ponce de Leon R, Juares-Perez MA, Grubb GS. Effect of vitamin B6 on the side effects of a low dose combined oral contraceptive. Contraception 1997;55:245–8.

81. Masse PG, Van den Berg H, Duguay C, et al. Early effect of a low dose (30 mcg) ethinyl estradiol containing Triphasil on vitamin B6 state. A follow up study of six menstrual cycles. Int J Vit Nutr Res 1996;66(1):46–54.

82. Bracken MB. Oral contraception and congenital malformation in offspring: a review and metaanalysis of the prospective studies. Obstet Gynecol 1990;76:552–7.

83. Rosenberg M. Weight change with oral contraceptive use and during menstrual cycle. Results of daily measurements. Contraception 1998;58:345–9.

84. Moore LL, Valuck R, McDougall C, Fink W. A comparative study of one-year weight gain among users of medroxyprogesterone acetate, levonorgestrel implants and oral contraceptives. Contraception 1995;52:215–9.

85. Rubinoff BE, Grubenstein A, Meirow D, et al. Effects of low-dose estrogen oral contraceptives on weight, body composition and fat distribution in young women. Fertil Steril 1995;63:516–21.

86. Kaunitz AM, Garceau RJ, Cromie MA. Comparative safety, efficacy, and cycle control of Lunelle monthly contraceptive injection (medroxyprogesterone acetate and estradiol cypionate injectable suspension) and Ortho-Novum 7/7/7 oral contraceptive (norethindrone/ethinyl estradiol triphasic). Lunelle Study Group. Contraception 1999;60:179–87.

87. Parsey KS, Pong A. An open-label, multicenter study to evaluate Yasmin, a low-dose combination oral contraceptive containing drospirenone, a new progestogen. Contraception 1999;61:105–11.

88. Diaz S, Zepeda A, Maturana X, et al. Fertility regulation in nursing women. IX. Contraceptive performance, duration of lactation, infant growth and bleeding patterns during use of progesterone vaginal rings, progestin-only pills, Norplant implants and Copper T 380 intrauterine device. Contraception 1997;56:223–32.

89. Polaneczky M. Adolescent contraception. Curr Opin Obstet and Gynecol 1998;10:213–9.

90. Glasier A, Gebbie A. Contraception for the older woman. Baillieres Clin Obstet Gynaecol 1996;10(1):121–38.

91. McCann MF, Potter LS. Progestin-only oral contraceptives: a comprehensive review. Contraception 1994;Suppl 50:S1–19.

92. Mainwaring R, Hales HA, Stevenson K, et al. Metabolic parameter, bleeding and weight changes in US women using progestin-only contraceptives. Contraception 1985;51:149–53.

93. Garza-Flores J, Cardenas S, Rodriguez V, et al. Return to ovulation following the use of long acting injectable contraceptives: a comparative study. Contraception 1985;31:361–66.

94. Mattson RH, Rebar RN. Contraceptive methods for women with neurologic disorders. Am J Obstet Gynecol 1993;168:2027–32.

95. Cromer BA, Blair JM, Mahan JD, et al. A prospective comparison of bone density in adolescent girls receiving depot medroxyprogesterone acetate (Depo-Provera), levonorgestrel (Norplant) or oral contraceptives. J Pediatr 1996;129:671–6.

96. Taneepanichskul A, Intaraprasert S, Theppisai U, et al. Bone mineral density in long-term depot-medroxyprogesterone acetate acceptors. Contraception 1997;56:1–3.

97. Cundy T, Cornish J, Evans MC, et al. Recovery of bone density in women who stop using medroxyprogesterone acetate. Br Med J 1994;308:247–48.

98. Kaunitz AM. Long acting hormonal contraception: assessing impact on bone density, weight and mood. Int J Fertil Women's Med 1999;44(2):110–7.

99. Paul C, Skegg DC, Williams S. Depot medroxyprogesterone acetate. Patterns of use and reasons for discontinuation. Contraception 1997;56:209–14.

100. World Health Organization. WHO collaborative study of neoplasia and steroid contraceptives: depot medroxyprogesterone acetate (DMPA) and risk of endometrial cancer. Int J Cancer 1991;49:186–90.

101. World Health Organization. WHO collaborative study of neoplasia and steroid contraceptives: depot-medroxyprogesterone acetate (DMPA) and risk of epithelial ovarian cancer. Int J Cancer 1991;49:191–5.

102. World Health Organization. WHO collaborative study of neoplasia and steroid contraceptives: breast cancer and depot-medroxyprogesterone acetate: a multinational study. Lancet 1991;338:833–8.

103. Chi I. The safety and efficacy issues of progestin only oral contraceptives—an epidemiologic perspective Contraception 1993;47:1–21.

104. Conkell AJ, Balfour JA. Levonorgestrel subdermal implants. A review of contraceptive efficacy and acceptability. Drugs 1998;55:861–87.

105. Fraser IS, Tiitinen A, Affandi B, et al. Norplant consensus statement and background review. Contraception 1998;57:1–9.

106. Zibners A, Cromer BA, Hayes J. Comparison of continuation rates for hormonal contraception among adolescents. J Pediatr Adolesc Gynecol 1999;12(2):90–4.

107. Fleming D, Dane J, Glasier A. Continuation rates of long acting methods of contraception. A comparative study of Norplant implants and intrauterine devices. Contraception 1998;57:19–21.

108. Davies G, Feng L, Newton J, Dieben T. Ovarian activity and bleeding patterns during extended continuous use of a combined contraceptive vaginal ring. Contraception 1992;46:269–78.

109. WHO Task Force on Long Acting Systemic Agents for Fertility Regulation. Microdose intravaginal levonorgestrel contraception: a multicentre clinical trial. I. Contraceptive efficacy and side effects. Contraception 1990;41:105–24.

110. Van Look PF, Von Hertzen H. Clinical use of antiprogestogens. Hum Reprod Update 1995;1(1):19–34.

111. Chen X, Xiao B. Effect of once weekly administration of mifepristone on ovarian function in normal women. Contraception 1997;56:175–80.

112. Heikinheimo O, Archer DF. Mifepristone: a potential contraceptive. Clin Obstet Gynecol 1996;39:461–8.

113. Harrison PF, Rosenfield A, editors. Institute of Medicine. Contraceptive Research and Development. Washington DC: National Academy Press; 1996.

114. Archer DF. New contraceptive options. Clin Obstet Gynecol 2001;44(1):122–6.

115. Sivin I, Alvarez F, Mishell DR, et al. Contraception with two levonorgestrel rod implants. A five year study in the US and Dominican Republic. Contraception 1998;58:275–82.

116. Newton J. Long acting methods of contraception. Br Med Bull 1993;49:40–61.

117. Makarainen L, Van Beek A, Tuomivaara L, et al. Ovarian function during use of a single contraceptive implant: Implanon compared with Norplant. Fertil Steril 1998;69:714–21.

118. Bromham DR. Intrauterine contraceptive devices: a reappraisal. Br Med J 1993;49:100–23.

119. Pasquale S. Clinical experience with today's IUDs. Obstet Gynecol Surv 1996;51(Suppl 12):S25–9.

120. Xiong X, Buekens P, Wollast E. IUD users and the risk of ectopic pregnancy: a metaanalysis of case-control studies. Contraception 1995;52:23–34.

121. Luukkainen T, Toivonen J. Levonorgestrel-releasing IUD as a method of contraception with therapeutic properties. Contraception 1995;52:269–76.

122. Anderson K, Rybo G. Levonorgestrel-releasing intrauterine device in the treatment of menorrhagia. Br J Obstet Gynecol 1990;97:690–4.

123. Farley TMM, Rosenberg MJ, Rowe PJ, et al. Intrauterine devices and pelvic inflammatory disease: an international perspective. Lancet 1992;339: 785–8.

124. World Health Organization. The Tcu 380A, Tcu 220 C, Multiload 250 and Nova T IUD at 3, 5 and 7 years of use: results from three randomized multicentre trials. Contraception 1990;42:141–58.

125. American College of Obstetricians and Gynecologists. The intrauterine device [ACOG technical bulletin 164]. Washington (DC): ACOG: 1992.

126. Vessey MP, Lawless M, McPherson K, et al. Fertility after stopping the use of intrauterine contraceptive devices. Br Med J 1983;286:106.

127. Belhadj H, Sivin I, Diaz S, et al. Recovery of fertility after the use of the levonorgestrel 200 mcg/day or Copper T 380 A intrauterine device. Contraception 1986;34:261–7.

128. Guillebaud J. IUD and congenital malformation [letter]. Br Med J 1975;1:1016.

129. Tatum HJ, Schmidt FH, Jain AK. Management and outcome of pregnancies associated with the copper T intrauterine contraceptive device. Am J Obstet Gynecol 1976;869–79.

130. United Kingdom Family Planning Research Network. Pregnancy outcome associated with the use of IUDs. Br Fam Plann 1989;15:7–11.

131. Sturgeon SR, Brinton LA, Berman ML, et al. Intrauterine device and endometrial cancer risk. Int J Epidemiol 1997;26:496–500.

132. Hill DA, Weiss NS, Voigt LF. Endometrial cancer in relation to IUD use. Int J Cancer 1997;70:278–81.

133. Fortney JA, Feldblum PJ, Raymond EG. Intrauterine devices. The optimal long term contraceptive method? J Reprod Med 1999;44:269–74.

134. Trussel J, Levecque JA, Koening JD. The economic value of contraception: a comparison of 15 methods. Am J Public Health 1995;85:494–503.

135. Rybo G, Anderson K, Odlind V. Hormonal intrauterine devices. Ann Med 1993;25:143–7.

136. Wildemeersch D, Defoort P, Martens G. The Flexigard 330Icc, an ultrasound evaluation. Contraception 1992;46:471–6.

137. Van Kets H, Vrijens M, Van Trappen U, et al. The framelees Gynefix intrauterine implant: a major improvement in efficacy, expulsion and tolerance. Adv Contraception 1995;11(2):131–42.

138. Wilemeersch D, Van der Pas H, Thiery M, et al. The Copper-Fix (Cu-fix): a new concept in IUD technology. Adv Contracept 1988;4:197–205.

139. Peterson HB, Xia Z, Hughes JM, et al. The risk of pregnancy after tubal sterilization: findings from the US Collaborative Review of Sterilization. Am J Obstet Gynecol 1996;174:1161–70.

140. Schwartz DB, Wingo PA, Antarsh L, Smith JC. Female sterilizations in the US, 1987. Fam Plann Perspect 1989;21:209–12.

141. Escobedo LG, Peterson HB, Grubb GS, Franks AL. Case fatality rates for tubal sterilization in US hospitals 1979 to 1980. Am J Obstet Gynecol 1989; 160:147–50.

142. Wilcox LS, Chu SY, Eaker ED, et al. Characteristics of women who considered or obtained tubal reanastomosis: results from a prospective study of tubal sterilization. Obstet Gynecol 1990;75:661–5.

143. Siegler AM, Hulka J, Peretz A. Reversibility of female sterilization. Fertil Steril 1985;43:499–510.

144. Ryder RM, Vaughan MC. Laparoscopic tubal sterilization: methods, effectiveness and sequelae. Obstet Gynecol Clin North Am 1999;26(1):83–97.

145. Chi IC, Petta CA, McPheeters M. A review of safety, efficacy, pros and cons and issues of puerperal tubal sterilization: an update. Adv Contracept 1995; 11(3):187–206.

146. Rulin MC, Davidson AR, Philliber SG, Graves WL. Long term effect of tubal sterilization on menstrual indices and pelvic pain. Obstet Gynecol 1993;82: 118–21.

147. De Stefano P, Perlman JA, Peterson HB, et al. Long term risk of menstrual disturbances after tubal sterilization. Am J Obstet Gynecol 1985;152:835–41.

148. Wilcox LS, Martinez-Schnell V, Peterson HB, et al. Menstrual function after tubal sterilization. Am J Epidemiol 1992;135:1368–81.

149. Suhadi A, Anwar M, Soejoenos A. Four year clinical evaluation of quinacrine pellets for nonsurgical female sterilization. Adv Contraception 1998;14:69–77.

150. Kessel E. 100,000 quinacrine sterilizations. Adv Contraception 1996;12:69–79.

151. Speroff L, Darney P. A clinical guide for contraception. 2nd ed. Baltimore (MD): Williams & Wilkins; 1996.

152. Bagshaw HA, Masters JRW, Pryor JP. Factors influencing the outcome of vasectomy reversal. Br J Urol 1990;52:57–60.

153. Belker AM, Konnak JW, Sharlip ID, Thomas AJ. Intraoperative observations during vasovasostomy in 334 patients. J Urol 1993;149:524–7.

154. Hendry WF. Vasectomy and vasectomy reversal. Br J Urol 1994;73:337–44.

155. Giovannucci E, Tosteson TD, Speizer FE, et al. A long term study of mortality in men who have undergone vasectomy. N Engl J Med 1992;326:1392–8.

156. Schuman LM, Coulson AH, Mandel JS, et al. Health status of American men—a study of post-vasectomy sequelae. J Clin Endocrinol 1993;46:697–958.

157. Moller H, Knudsen LB, Lynge E. Risk of testicular cancer after vasectomy: cohort study of over 73,000 men. Br Med J 1994;309:295–9.

158. Giovannucci E, Asherio A, Rimm EB, et al. A prospective study of vasctomy and prostate cancer in US men. JAMA 1993;269:878–2.

159. Rosenberg L, Palmer JR, Zauber AG, et al. The relation of vasectomy to the risk of cancer. Am J Epidemiol 1994;140:431–8.

160. Lesko SM, Louik C, Vezina R. Vasectomy and prostate cancer. J Urol 1999;16:1848–52.

161. Li SQ, Goldstein M, Zhu J, Huber D. The no-scalpel vasectomy. J Urol 1992;145:341–4.

162. Magnani RJ, Haws JM, Morgan GT, et al. Vasectomy in the US 1991 and 1995. Am J Public Health 1999; 89:92–4.

163. Haws JM, Morgan GT, Pollack PE, et al. Clinical aspects of vasectomies performed in the US in 1995. Urology 1998;52:685–91.

164. Soebadi DM, Gardjito W, Mensink HJ. Intravasal injection of formed-in place medical grade silicone rubber for vas occlusion. Int J Androl 1995;18 Suppl 1:45–52.

165. Steiner M, Piedrahita C, Joanis C, et al. Condom breakage and slippage rates among study participants in eight countries. Int Fam Plann Perspect 1994; 20:55–8.

166. Glasier A. Emergency postcoital contraception. N Engl J Med 1997;337:1058–64.

167. Delbanco SF, Mauldon J, Smith MD. Little knowledge and limited practice: Emergency contraceptive pills; the public and the obstetrician-gynecologist. Obstet Gynecol 1997;89:1006–11.

168. Trussel J, Stewart F. The effectiveness of postcoital contraception. Fam Plann Perspect 1992;24:262–4.

169. Trussell J, Koenig J, Ellertson C, Stewart F. Preventing unintended pregnancy: the cost effectiveness of three methods of contraception. Am J Public Health 1997;87:932–7.

170. Glasier A, Baird D. The effects of self-administering emergency contraception. N Engl J Med 1998; 339:1–4.

171. Ellertson C, Trussel J, Stewart F, Winikoff B. Should emergency contraceptive pills be available without a prescription? JAMWA 1998;53 Suppl 2:S226–9.

172. Trussell J, Rodriguez G, Ellertson C. New estimates of the effectiveness of the Yuzpe regimen of emergency contraception. Contraception 1998;57: 363–9.

173. Task Force on Postovulatory Methods of Fertility Regulation. Randomised controlled trial of levonorgestrel versus the Yuzpe regimen of combined oral contraceptives for emergency contraception. Lancet 1998;352:428–33.

174. Glasier A, Ketting E, Ellertson C, Armstrong E. Emergency contraception in the United Kingdom and the Netherlands. Fam Plann Perspect 1996; 28:49–51.

175. Van Santen MR, Haspels AA. A comparison of high-dose estrogen versus low-dose ethinyl estradiol and norgestrel combination in postcoital contraception: a study in 493 women. Fertil Steril 1985; 43:206–13.

176. Glasier A, Thong KJ, Dewar M, et al. Mifepristone (RU 486) compared with high dose estrogen and progestogen for emergency postcoital contraception. N Engl J Med 1992;327:1041–4.

177. Webb AMC, Russell J, Elstein M. Comparison of the Yuzpe regimen, danazol and mifepristone (RU 486) in oral postcoital contraception. BMJ 1992;305: 927–31.

178. Zuliani G, Colombo UF, Molla R. Hormonal postcoital contraception with and ethinyl estradiol-norgestrel and two danazol regimens. Eur J Obstet Gynecol Reprod Biol 1990;37:253–60.

179. Trussell J, Ellertson C. Efficacy of emergency contraception. Fertil Control Rev 1995;4(2):8–11.

180. Rowlands S, Kubba AA, Guillebaud B, Bounds WA. A possible mechanism of action of danazol and an ethinyl estradiol/norgestrel combination used as postcoital contraceptive agents. Contraception 1986;33:539–45.

181. Swahn ML, Westlund P, Johannisson E, Bygdeman M. Effect of postcoital contraceptive methods on

the endometrium and the menstrual cycle. Acta Obstet Gynecol Scand 1996;75:728–44.

182. Alvarez F, Brache V, Fernandez E, et al. New insights on the mode of action of intrauterine contraceptive devices in women. Fertil Steril 1988;49:768–73.

183. Hagenfeldt K. Studies on the mode of action of the copper T device. Acta Endocrinol Suppl 1972; 169:3–37.

184. Ledger WL, Sweeting VM, Hillier H, Baird DT. Inhibition of ovulation by low-dose mifepristone (RU 486). Hum Reprod 1992;7:945–50.

185. Swahn ML, Bygdeman M, Cekan S, et al. The effect of RU 486 administered during the early luteal phase on the bleeding pattern, hormonal parameters and endometrium. Hum Reprod 1990;5: 402–8.

186. Gemzell-Danielsson K, Swahn ML, Svalander P, Bygdeman M. Early luteal phase treatment with mifepristone (RU 486) for fertility regulation. Hum Reprod 1993;8:870–3.

187. American College of Obstetricians and Gynecologists. Emergency oral contraception. ACOG Practice Patterns. Washington (DC): ACOG; 1996.

188. Delbanco S, Stewart FH, Koenig JD, et al. Are we making progress with emergency contraception? Recent findings on American adults and health professionals. JAMWA 1998;53 Suppl 2:S242–6.

189. Adamson P, editor. The progress of nations 1996. New York: Unicef; 1996.

190. Ventura SJ, Martin JA, Matthews TJ. Advance report of final natality statistics, 1996. Mon Vital Stat Rep 1998;46(11 Suppl):1–99.

191. The Alan Guttmacher Institute. Sex and America's teenagers, New York: The Alan Guttmacher Institute; 1994.

192. Centers for Disease Control and Prevention, Adolescent Health. State of the nation-pregnancy, sexually transmitted diseases and related risk behaviors among U.S. adolescents. Atlanta (GA): U.S. Department of Health and Human Services, Public Health Services; 1995 DHHS Publication No.: 099–4630.

193. Ortho Pharmaceutical Corporation. Annual birth control study, 1994.

194. Sullivan JM, Lobo RA. Consideration for contraception in women with cardiovascular disease. Am J Obstet Gynecol 1993;168:2006–11.

195. Neinstein L. Contraception in women with special medical needs. Compt Ther 1998;24:229–50.

196. Knopp RH, LaRosa JC, Burkman RT. Contraception and dyslipidemia. Am J Obstet Gynecol 1993; 168:1994–2004.

197. Comp PC, Zacur HA. Contraceptive choices in women with coagulation disorders. Am J Obstet Gynecol 1993;168:1990–3.

198. Kjos SL: Contraception in diabetic women. Obstet Gynecol Clin North Am 1996;23(1):243–58.

199. Corson SL. Contraception for women with health problems. Int J Fertil 1996;41(2):77–84.

200. Fitzpatrick SB, Stokes DC, Rosenstein BJ, Hubbard VS. Use of oral contraceptives in women with cystic fibrosis. Chest 1984;86:863–7.

201. Coonnolly TJ, Zuckerman AL. Contraception in the patient with liver disease. Semin Perinatol 1998; 22:178–82.

202. Merkatz IR, Schwartz GH, David DS, et al. Resumption of female reproductive function following renal transplantation. JAMA 1971;216:1749–54.

203. Shenfield GM, Griffin JM. Clinical pharmacokinetics of contraceptive steroids. An update. Clin Pharmacokinet 1991;10:15–37.

204. Lopez RE, Bhakoo H, Paolini NS, et al. Effect of estrogen on the growth of B-16 melanoma. Surg Forum 1978;29:153–4.

205. Korn AP, DeRemer Abercrombie P. Gynecology and family planning care for the woman infected with HIV. Obstet Gynecol Clin North Am 1997;24:855–72.

206. Coutinho EM, Melo JF, Barbosa I, Segal SJ. Antispermatogenic action of gossypol in men. Fertil Steril 1984;42:424–30.

207. Waites G. Male fertility regulation: the challenges for the year 2000. Br Med Bull 1993;49:210–21.

208. Wang C, Yeung RTT. Gossypol and hypokalemia. Contraception 1985;32:237–52.

209. Norwak R. Antihypertension drug may double as male contraceptive. J Natl Inst Health Res 1994; 6:27–30.

210. O'Rand MG, Lea IA. Designing an effective immunocontraceptive. J Reprod Immunol 1997;36:51–9.

211. Habenicht UF, Stock G. Development of new immunocontraceptives: industrial perspectives, Am J Reprod Immunol 1996;35:517–22.

212. Herr JC. Update on the Center for Recombinant Gamete Contraceptive Vaccinogens, Am J Reprod Immunol 1996;35:184–9.

213. Miller LA, Johns BE, Elias DJ, Crane KA. Comparative efficacy of two immunocontraceptive vaccines. Vaccine 1997;15:1858–62.

214. Diekman AB, Herr JC. Sperm antigens and their use in the development of an immunocontraceptive. Am J Reprod Immunol 1997;37:111–7.

215. Aitken RJ, Patterson M, Van Duin M. The potential of the zona pellucida as a target for immunocontraception. Am J Reprod Immunol 1996;35:175–80.

216. Skinner SM, Prasad SV, Ndolo TM, Dunbar BS. zona pellucida antigens: targets for contraceptive vaccines. Am J Reprod Immunol 1996;35:163–74.

217. Stevens VC. Progress in the development of human chorionic gonadotropin antifertility vaccines. Am J Reprod Immunol 1996;35:148–55.

218. Talwar GP, Singh O, Gupta SE, et al. The HSD-hCG vaccine prevents pregnancy in women: feasibility study of a reversible safe contraceptive vaccine. Am J Reprod Immunol 1997;37:153–60.

219. Coulam CB. Immunocontraception becomes a reality: the Talwar hCG vaccine. Am J Reprod Immunol 1997;37:151–2.

220. Gold RB, Richards CL. Managed care and unintended pregnancy. Womens Health Issues 1998; 8:134–47.

10

PRECONCEPTION COUNSELING

Karen A. Filkins, MD

Women who are planning a pregnancy often seek advice from friends, family, magazines, books, the Internet, and, occasionally, their physicians. Often patients do not discuss their plans to attempt a pregnancy with a physician unless there is some difficulty in achieving the pregnancy. Many women feel, perhaps justifiably, that their physician has no time to answer their questions or that their questions are too trivial to deserve attention. Furthermore, at least 50% of all pregnancies are unplanned,[1] so the opportunity for preconceptional planning is lost.

The predominant cause of infant mortality in the United States today is birth defects, with prematurity being a close second. Three percent of liveborn infants have a major malformation detectable at birth,[2] and approximately 6 to 8% of newborns are delivered preterm.

Although the majority of birth defects do not appear to result from specifically known causes, a subset of high-risk patients can be identified in the preconception period, and risk modification can be achieved.

IDENTIFYING THE PRECONCEPTIONAL PATIENT

The first challenge is to identify the cohort of women likely to become pregnant before their next health care visit. Asking the simple question, "Are you planning a pregnancy within the next year?" is a starting point. Most women will answer this question honestly if they trust their caregiver. However, in an occupational health setting, they may feel that their job security is being threatened and may even attempt to conceal an ongoing pregnancy for as long as possible. In the occupational health setting, a significant campaign is needed to promote the

TABLE 10–1. Birth Control Methods with High Accidental Pregnancy Rates within the First Year of Use

	Percent Pregnant	
Method	Typical Use	Perfect Use
Chance	85	85
Spermicides	21	6
Periodic abstinence, calendar method	20	9
Withdrawal	19	4
Cervical cap		
Parous women	36	9
Nulliparous women	18	6
Diaphragm	18	6
Condom		
Female	21	5
Male	12	2

Adapted from Hatcher RA, Trussel J, Stewart F, et al. Contraceptive technology. 16th ed. New York: Irvington Publishers, Inc.; 1994.

benefits of preconceptional planning in a nonthreatening atmosphere, so that cooperation can be gained.

Although one cannot predict an unplanned pregnancy, it is certainly possible to identify a group of women who have a high risk to become pregnant. Women who are planning marriage or who are recently married should certainly be offered preconceptional planning. The approximate risk of unintended pregnancy by method of birth control used can be estimated (Table 10–1), and those with a greater than 10% chance of pregnancy in the next year also could be offered preconceptional counseling.

IDENTIFYING THE RISKS

Once the group to be targeted has been identified, historic information can be reviewed and updated, either in conversation or by use of a questionnaire form. If a questionnaire form is used, it should be specific enough and, whenever possible, in lay terminology, so that the patient may recognize pertinent items in the checklist. Information about the patient's partner also is important in assessing genetic and lifestyle risks. Figure 10–1 is the current version of a genetic and exposures questionnaire form that the author developed and finds useful in her prenatal and perinatal service. This form can be used alone or in combination with an occupational history questionnaire (Figure 10–2) for those with significant occupational exposures.

ADDRESSING POSITIVE RISK FACTORS

Parental Age

While much attention has been given to the increased risk for chromosomal abnormalities with advancing maternal age, delayed childbearing raises other concerns as well. Table 10–2 illustrates the effect of delayed childbearing on fecundity (ie, the ability to conceive and carry a pregnancy to term). Older women also have a greater risk of chronic illness, diabetes, hypertension, and pregnancy complications related to placental abnormalities.[3] Advanced paternal age also is associated with a slight increase in the risk of new genetic mutations. At the other end of the spectrum, teenage mothers have an increased risk of having premature infants, low-birth weight infants, and infants who die before 1 year of age.[4]

While there may never be a perfect time for childbearing that fits all lifestyles, the advantages and disadvantages of both early and late childbearing should be considered. If a pregnancy is planned and detected early, first trimester screening by ultrasound and biochemistry can establish gestational age, viability, and number of fetuses, and be used to adjust a woman's risk for some chromosome abnormalities.[5] Chorionic villus sampling (CVS) can be done safely as early as 10 to 11 weeks' gestational age,[6] and amniocentesis can be provided after 13 to 14 weeks. Multiple-marker biochemical screening for neural tube defects and some chromosome abnormalities can be offered in the second trimester, along with detailed anatomic evaluation by ultrasound.

The screening tests can be offered to all pregnant women, with the diagnostic tests (CVS and amniocentesis) usually being reserved for women who have an increased risk due to advanced maternal age, a positive screening test result, or other high-risk factor.

Medical History

Of utmost importance is identification of women who are at risk for pregnancy and whose medical condition would be gravely affected by a pregnancy. An example is women with primary pulmonary hypertension, in which case the maternal mortality rate approaches 50%, and the fetal mortality rate exceeds 40%.[7] In such a case, it is appropriate to discuss the need for an adequate birth control method, and, if a pregnancy is desired, a frank discussion of the risks and medical management needed should be provided

A history of previously treated cancer[8,9] or a prior organ transplantation[10–12] may well be compatible with a successful pregnancy, but cancer therapy during pregnancy or the risks related to the possible immediate need for organ transplantation may make postponement of pregnancy the better option. Reproductive decisions for women with serious medical conditions should be made with a team approach involving appropriate specialists.

Infectious Diseases, Immunization, and History of Sexually Transmitted Disease

Preconception identification of rubella-susceptible women combined with a program of vaccination effectively prevents congenital rubella syndrome.[13]

TABLE 10–2. Effect of Delayed Childbearing on Fecundity, 1995

Age (yr)	Percent Impaired Fecundity (%)	
	All Women[†]	Married Women
15–44	10.2	24.8
15–24	6.1	11.7
25–34	11.2	19.7
35–44	12.8	42.1

[†]Includes single women and those who are married.
Adapted from Abma J, Chandra A, Mosher W, et al. Fertility, family planning, and women's health: new data from the 1995 National Survey of Family Growth. National Center for Health Statistics. Vital Health Stat 23 1997;19:1–114.

Genetic History Questionnaire

Name:_____   Partner's Name:_____

Date of Birth: ___/___/___   Date of Birth:___/___/___

Medical History

CHECK ANY CONDITIONS LISTED BELOW THAT APPLY TO YOU OR YOUR PARTNER

Self	Partner		Partner	Self
[ ]	[ ]	Diabetes	Infertility [ ]	[ ]
[ ]	[ ]	Seizures or epilepsy	Birth defects [ ]	[ ]
[ ]	[ ]	Kidney disease	Handicapping condition [ ]	[ ]
[ ]	[ ]	Cancer	Miscarriages: #._____ [ ]	[ ]
[ ]	[ ]	Skin changes	Stillbirths: #._____ [ ]	[ ]
[ ]	[ ]	Rheumatoid arthritis	Sexually transmitted disease (eg, [ ]	[ ]
[ ]	[ ]	PKU (needed special diet as child)	Herpes, chlamydia, syphilis, HIV) [ ]	[ ]
[ ]	[ ]	Heart disease	Other infections [ ]	[ ]
[ ]	[ ]	High blood pressure	Other_____ [ ]	[ ]

Family and Patient History

IS YOUR FAMILY OR YOUR BABY'S FATHER'S FAMILY...

Yes	No			Yes	No
[ ]	[ ]	From SE Asia, Taiwan or the Phillippines?	From Italy, Greece, or the Middle East?	[ ]	[ ]
[ ]	[ ]	African or African American (Black)?	Central Eastern European (Ashkenazi) Jewish?	[ ]	[ ]
[ ]	[ ]	Cajun or French Canadian?	Hispanic?	[ ]	[ ]
[ ]	[ ]	Caucasian?	Other?_____	[ ]	[ ]

CHECK ANY OF THE FOLLOWING BIRTH DEFECTS AND GENETIC DISEASES THAT MIGHT BE IN YOUR FAMILY

(Include brothers, sisters, parents, grandparents, aunts, uncles, nieces, nephews, cousins)

[ ]	Anencephaly (open skull)	Limb defects	[ ]
[ ]	Arthritis	Malformations or Birth Defects	[ ]
[ ]	Blindness or eye problems	Marfan syndrome, other Connective tissue disorder	[ ]
[ ]	Cancer ( ) Breast ( ) Ovarian	Mental illness	[ ]
[ ]	Bone disorder	Mental retardation	[ ]
[ ]	Cerebral palsy	Muscular dystrophy	[ ]
[ ]	Chromosome abnormality	Neurofibromatosis	[ ]
[ ]	Cleft lip/palate	Neurologic or degenerative disorder	[ ]
[ ]	Cystic fibrosis	Short Stature (under 5 ft)	[ ]
[ ]	Deafness	Sickle cell anemia	[ ]
[ ]	Down syndrome (mongolism)	Skeletal Problems (eg, easily broken bones or curvature spine)	[ ]
[ ]	Epilepsy or seizures	Skin disease (include dark or light patches)	[ ]
[ ]	Heart defect	Spina bifida (open spine)	[ ]
[ ]	Other heart, blood vessel problem	Tay Sachs / Canavan disease	[ ]
[ ]	Hemophilia (bleeding tendency)	Thalassemia	[ ]
[ ]	Hydrocephalus (water on brain)	Urinary tract abnormality	[ ]
[ ]	Infertility	Others:_____	[ ]
[ ]	Kidney disease	_____	[ ]

FIGURE 10–1. Genetic history and environmental exposures questionnaire. PKU = phenyketonuria; HIV = human immunodeficiency virus.

Environmental Exposures Questionnaire
Immune Status

Are you immune to rubella (German measles)?	[ ] immune	[ ] not immune	[ ] never tested
Are you immune to toxoplasmosis?	[ ] immune	[ ] not immune	[ ] never tested
Are you immune to cytomegalovirus (CMV)?	[ ] immune	[ ] not immune	[ ] never tested
Are you immune to parvovirus (Fifth disease)?	[ ] immune	[ ] not immune	[ ] never tested
Are you immune to varicella (chickenpox)?	[ ] immune	[ ] not immune	[ ] never tested
Are you exposed to children or infectious diseases at home or at work?	[ ] Yes	[ ] No	

Medications

Do you or your partner take any prescription drugs or over-the-counter medications? [ ] Yes [ ] No
If yes, describe and include dose_____

Self	Partner	DO YOU OR YOUR PARTNER TAKE ANY OF THE FOLLOWING?		Partner	Self
[ ]	[ ]	Accutane, dermatologic or acne medications	Epilepsy (seizure) medications	[ ]	[ ]
[ ]	[ ]	Antibiotics, eg, tetracycline, streptomycin	Folic acid	[ ]	[ ]
[ ]	[ ]	Anticoagulants (blood thinners to prevent blood clots)	Hormones	[ ]	[ ]
[ ]	[ ]	Antihypertensives (blood pressure medication)	Multivitamins	[ ]	[ ]
[ ]	[ ]	Asthma medications	Steriods	[ ]	[ ]
[ ]	[ ]	Birth control pills	Thyroid drugs	[ ]	[ ]
[ ]	[ ]	Chemotherapeutic drugs	Tranquilizers or antidepressants	[ ]	[ ]
[ ]	[ ]	Diet pills	Vitamin A supplements	[ ]	[ ]
			Other high-dose vitamins	[ ]	[ ]
[ ]	[ ]	List any other medications here_____			

Have you recently had any of the following? (Check any that apply)

[ ]	Fever	Viral illness		[ ]
[ ]	Surgery	X-rays		[ ]
[ ]	Other illnesses_____	Physical injuries		[ ]

If you checked any of the above, describe who, when, and give details_____

Yes	No	Do you		Yes	No
[ ]	[ ]	Exercise regularly?	Smoke?	[ ]	[ ]
[ ]	[ ]	Have any eating problems?	Are you a vegetarian?	[ ]	[ ]
[ ]	[ ]	Drink more than one glass of alcohol per week (including beer)?			
[ ]	[ ]	Use any drugs such as marijuana, cocaine, "crack," heroin (circle any that apply and list others)?_____			
[ ]	[ ]	Use saunas, hot whirlpool baths?	Eat raw or very rare meat?	[ ]	[ ]
[ ]	[ ]	Have a household cat? If there is a litterbox, who changes it?_____			
[ ]	[ ]	Engage in hobbies involving solvents, paint, heavy metals, or other potentially dangerous exposures? Describe_____			

Occupational Exposures

[ ]	[ ]	Are you or your partner exposed to toxic chemicals, anesthetic gases, lead, or other metals, paint, flea products, pesticides, solvents, radiation, or lifting more than 25 lbs. in your occupation? If yes, please complete Occupational Exposures Questionnaire.

Genetic History Questionnaire, Rev. 5/2000

FIGURE 10–1. (continued)

Occupational Exposures Questionnaire

Name	Sex	Date of Birth

Current Occupation

Job Title	Employer

Employment Dates	Hours per Week

Describe work assignments and conditions. _____

_____

Job/Occupational Exposures

List current and previous work exposures. Please attach copy of Material Safety Data Sheets (MSDS) to this form. Make sure that you keep a copy of your MSDS forms for your own use.

Product Name	Chemical Name	Type of Contact (resp, skin, etc.)	Past	Current

List any additional exposures on another sheet.

FIGURE 10–2. Questionnaire for history of occupational exposures. Reproduced with permission from Filkins K, Kerr M. Occupational reproductive health risks. Occup Med 1993;8:733–54.

Occupational Exposures Questionnaire *(continued)*

Symptoms

Have you had any symptoms that might be related to the exposures listed above?   ☐ Yes   ☐ No

If yes, list symptoms and possible causes. _____

_____

_____

Protective Measures

Have you been provided with a gown, a respirator, gloves, MSDSs, or have you taken any protective measures related to your occupational exposures?   ☐ Yes   ☐ No

If yes, list protective measures you use (eg, gloves, respirator, ventilation).

_____

_____

_____

Non-occupational Exposures

List vacation jobs, second jobs, temporary work, and other work exposures.

_____

_____

_____

List recreational exposures, crafts, hobbies, etc.

_____

_____

_____

If other family members work with hazardous materials (eg, solvents or metals) that may be brought home on clothing or in other ways, list possible exposures.

_____

_____

_____

FIGURE 10–2. (continued)

Women with social or occupational exposure risks for hepatitis B should be identified and offered vaccination. Although most adults are immune to varicella (even if they cannot recall having had chickenpox), immunization can now be offered to women who are not immune, especially if they have small children or frequent exposure to school-aged children.[14] Women whose occupations require travel to parts of the world where there is a high risk for a variety of diseases may want to postpone pregnancy to avoid risks from certain immunizations or illnesses. Reassessment of the method of birth control may be important to these women. Issues related to international travel before and during pregnancy are reviewed in detail in Chapter 71, "Approach to the International Traveler."

Those at risk for exposure to tuberculosis, cytomegalovirus (CMV) or toxoplasmosis can be offered preconceptional testing; in the case of tuberculosis, appropriate treatment can be started before initiating pregnancy, if indicated. Instructions can be given to those susceptible to CMV or toxoplasmosis to minimize their risk of exposure. Testing for HIV also can be offered, and, if positive, treatment and counseling can be provided to help prevent vertical transmission. Testing for and appropriate treatment of other STDs, including syphilis, gonorrhea, chlamydia, herpes, and human papillomavirus also should be considered at appropriate intervals.

History of Prior Pregnancy

A history of prior poor pregnancy outcome warrants further investigation. Couples who have experienced two or three prior losses in any trimester, or who have a history of a prior stillbirth (especially if anomalous), have an increased risk that one of the parents carries a balanced chromosomal translocation.[15] Referral for genetic counseling and parental chromosomal analysis is indicated. The genetic counselor also explores additional family, social, occupational, and other exposure history that may be contributing to the pattern of losses. Other possible factors, including infections and uterine anatomic, endocrine, autoimmune, and other medical concerns also should be explored.

Prior pregnancy complications such as preeclampsia or Rhesus factor sensitization have implications for increased recurrence risks in future pregnancies. These and other medical concerns can be discussed; a team approach involving the primary care physician, a high-risk-pregnancy specialist, and, depending on the condition, other medical specialists and nutritionists, for example, may be needed. The team approach often can provide the best possible plan of management, starting with the preconceptional period and continuing throughout pregnancy and the postpartum period. Additional information can be found in Chapter 15, "Common Medical Problems in Pregnancy."

Family History and History of Birth Defects

The questionnaire reproduced in Figure 10–1 can be used to elicit a history of birth defects and genetic disorders that may be present in the family. Most isolated birth defects follow a multifactorial pattern of inheritance with a 2 to 4 percent risk of recurrence. Early prenatal diagnosis is now possible for many of these defects, so preconceptional coun-

seling can offer reassurance about the relatively low recurrence risk and about the opportunity for early detection. In the case of neural tube defects, folic acid given at the higher dose of 4.0 mg daily before conception and throughout the first trimester, can significantly reduce the recurrence risk.[16]

A team approach, involving both obstetric and medical specialists, can be used in instances where treatment of maternal illness involves the use of teratogens, or when maternal illness itself is potentially teratogenic. Avoidance of specific teratogen exposures at the critical timing can reduce the risk of birth defects and often can be accomplished without compromising maternal medical care.

A history suggestive of an autosomal dominant or X-linked disorder in the family also warrants genetic counseling and discussion of alternatives. Alternatives include a decision not to procreate, presymptomatic testing for a dominant disorder (eg, Huntington's disease), or testing for X-linked carrier status. If the couple decide to pursue a pregnancy, the options of donor gametes, preimplantation genetic diagnosis, CVS, and early or standard amniocentesis also are discussed during the genetic counseling session, so an appropriate plan can be made.

The questionnaire reproduced in Figure 10–1 also identifies, based on population gene frequencies, those couples at increased risk for a variety of autosomal recessive disorders such as Tay-Sachs disease, sickle cell anemia, the thalassemias, and cystic fibrosis. Carrier screening for these and other recessive disorders is simple for some disorders, but can be quite complex for others such as cystic fibrosis. In cystic fibrosis, the detection rate varies by the ability to identify the specific mutations in a given population. As newer approaches are developed, screening protocols will most likely become easier. Laboratories generally can provide the primary care physician with a specific detection rate for the particular ethnic background of the couple. If a concern arises, genetic counseling often can clarify the results of screening.

Many common disorders, such as cardiovascular disease, thromboembolic disorders, diabetes, kidney disease, hypertension, and cancer, have genetic and environmental components, but in some families may follow an autosomal dominant pattern of inheritance with a 50% risk to first-degree relatives. In some cases, genetic testing for mutations or by linkage analysis may be available. In others, standard medical tests can be used to assess risks (eg, a lipid panel).

Breast, ovarian, and colon cancer risks can be assessed in some families but not all; this assessment is best done through services that have adequate counseling about the meaning of a negative or positive test.[17] For example, if a specific mutation is found in a given family but the individual does not have that mutation, the risk is similar to that of the general population risk, and no unusual follow-up would be required. This does not mean that there is no risk. It simply means that the individual should continue to receive standard care. It also means that the offspring have no increased risk. This removes the "burden" of transmitting the gene for the disorder (or susceptibility to the disorder) to the next generation.

Medication Exposure

Previous studies have indicated that the vast majority of pregnant women have an exposure to either a prescription or an over-the-counter medication.[18] Fortunately, most of these exposures are not associated with an increased risk for birth defects or adverse fetal effects. In fact, medication use may be essential in some cases to protect the fetus. The risk to a pregnancy from fever or infection usually outweighs the potential small unknown risk involved in treating the fever or in using most antibiotics for an infection.

Unfortunately, many physicians have a fear of prescribing *any* medication to a pregnant woman; yet, there are many circumstances in which the benefit clearly outweighs the risk. There are few known teratogens that will damage the vast majority of fetuses exposed. If a fetus is exposed to a category D or X drug, it does not automatically follow that ill effects will occur. It does mean that genetic or teratogen counseling should be considered, and that there may be appropriate ultrasound assessments available. The questionnaire in Figure 10–1 is designed to elicit specific categories of medication use along with certain conditions such as epilepsy, asthma, acne, or hypertension, for which a variety of medication choices exist. Some of the choices (eg, isotretinoin [Accutane]) are associated with a significant risk for birth defects, whereas other choices are much safer. In the preconceptional setting, the opportunity exists to modify medication

use (eg, to change from warfarin to heparin therapy) before the pregnancy, and, thus, avoid the potential risk. More detail on medication use during pregnancy can be found in Chapter 17, "Drugs in Pregnancy and Lactation," and Chapter 15, "Common Medical Problems in Pregnancy."

Social History

A history of alcohol or illicit drug use obtained in the preconceptional period provides the opportunity for education and, if needed, a structured rehabilitation program before initiation of the pregnancy. There is abundant educational material available relating to fetal alcohol syndrome.[19,20] Cocaine use is known to be associated with prematurity, abruption of the placenta, and other complications. Certain vascular disruptive forms of birth defects are also suspected to be linked to cocaine use.[21,22] Smoking is associated with low birth weight and should be discouraged before conception.[23] For more information on smoking and illicit drug use in pregnancy, refer to Chapter 12, "Smoking Cessation," and Chapter 18, "Substance Abuse and Pregnancy."

Domestic violence can result in placental abruption; hemorrhage and direct damage to the fetus; rupture of the uterus, liver, or spleen; and preterm labor.[24] Intervention before involvement of a pregnancy is certainly prudent. Information on screening and treatment can be found in Chapter 88, "Domestic Violence."

Nutritional Concerns and Exercise

Preconceptional dietary evaluation can be important, since high-risk situations may be identified and modified before pregnancy. Appropriateness of weight for height, eating disorders, habits such as vegetarianism, fasting, pica, and use of megavitamin supplementation (especially vitamin A)[25] should be addressed. In the questionnaire form shown in Figure 10–1, the history of need for a special diet as a child is primarily aimed at identifying pregnancies at risk for maternal phenylketonuria (PKU). Dietary restrictions should be initiated in this population before any attempt at conception, because infants born to women with elevated phenylalanine levels have an increased risk for microcephaly, mental retardation, congenital heart defects, and growth retardation. Dietary control can significantly decrease this risk.[26,27] A team involving a nutritionist and a metabolic geneticist should be provided for appropriate management of these patients.

For an otherwise healthy woman, exercise can be beneficial. A program of exercise can be continued with modifications during pregnancy, based on the individual situation.[28] In general, it is not desirable for a pregnant woman to become overheated, dehydrated, or exhausted, or to engage in a sport in which direct fetal trauma is a significant possibility. In addition, extended use of hot tubs or saunas, which result in a significant elevation of core body temperature, should be avoided.[29,30]

Occupational History and Hobbies

Fifty-eight percent of working-age women in the United States were in the work force in 1999,[31] and more than 53% of them had full-time employment.[32] Yet little focus has been placed on women's occupational reproductive risks. Appropriately used, the questionnaire form shown in Figure 10–2 elicits specific exposures to chemicals such as lead (a known teratogen), other heavy metals such as mercury, organic solvents, pesticides, x-rays, anesthetic gases, infectious diseases (especially relevant for day-care workers), and other potentially toxic substances.

Occupations that involve heavy lifting and long hours of standing appear to be associated with low-birth weight infants.[33,34] In all these instances, job modifications can improve safety conditions. If necessary, the Occupational Health and Safety Administration of the US Department of Labor (OSHA) can assist by monitoring the workplace environment and recommending use of special equipment, clothing, respirators, and other protective apparatus. A list of state and regional OSHA offices offering consultation services is provided at the OSHA Web site (see "Resources" in this chapter).

Hobbies also should not be overlooked as a potential source of exposure to teratogens. Some hobbies, such as working with lead solder to produce leaded glass or stained glass windows, represent obvious hazards. Painting, especially in poorly ventilated areas, may involve exposure to organic solvents. Gardening may involve direct and potentially hazardous exposure to pesticides, especially if the precautions on the labels are not followed. In addition, ingestion of unwashed garden produce may expose a pregnant woman to toxoplasmosis, because the parasite can persist in soil for a very long time.

Reproductive Planning Questionnaire*

Yes	No	
☐	☐	Are you using any method of birth control at the present time? List method(s). _____
☐	☐	Are you planning a pregnancy in the near future? If yes, ☐ In less than 3 months ☐ In less than 1 year
☐	☐	Do you think you could be pregnant now? If yes, list the date of your last menstrual period or length of pregnancy. _____
☐	☐	Are you currently breast-feeding an infant?
☐	☐	Do you plan to breast-feed your infant in the future?

List name, address, and telephone number of your obstetrician OR indicate if you have not had obstetric care.

_____

_____

_____

FIGURE 10–3. Reproductive planning questionnaire. *If patient is planning a pregnancy, or if patient is using a method of birth control with a higher than 10% failure rate, administer the genetics and teratology screening questionnaire. Reproduced with permission from Filkins K, Kerr M. Occupational reproductive health risks. Occup Med 1993;8:749.

SUMMARY

"Have you changed or are you planning to change your marital status, and are you considering becoming pregnant in the next year or two?" If this simple question is asked at every visit to a primary care center made by a woman of childbearing age, preconceptional planning could make a substantial impact. If the answer to this question is no, then it should be followed by a question about the method of birth control used (Figure 10–3). If the response indicates a greater than 10% chance of pregnancy within 1 year (see Table 10–1), further discussion is warranted. No single questionnaire form can address all risks; therefore, the type of assessment used has to be modified for the individual setting and for new information when it becomes available. However, one can be confident that when a high-risk situation is identified and addressed before a pregnancy, progress has been made.

RESOURCES

United States Department of Labor
Occupational Safety and Health Administration
Office of Public Affairs—Room N3647
200 Constitution Avenue
Washington, DC 20210
Telephone: (202) 693-1999
Web site: www.osha.gov

OSHA offers consultative services to address workplace issues relating to pregnancy. A list of state and regional offices is listed on the OSHA Web site.

The March of Dimes
1275 Mamaroneck Avenue
White Plains, New York 10605
Telephone: 1-888-MODIMES (1-888-663-4637)
Web site: www.modimes.org

The March of Dimes provides information about preconception planning and specific birth defects. It also maintains a resource center to answer specific questions from both clinicians and patients.

American College of Obstetricians and Gynecologists
409 12th Street Southwest
PO Box 96920
Washington, DC 20090-6920
Telephone: (202) 484-3321
Web site: www.acog.org

ACOG offers patient education pamphlets and a book for patients entitled "Planning Your Pregnancy and Birth" that address pregnancy planning issues. These may be ordered through the ACOG Web site.

REFERENCES

1. Leuzzi R, Scoles K. Preconception counseling for the primary care physician. Med Clin North Am 1996;80:337–74.
2. California Department of Health Services. Genetic Disease Branch. California Birth Defects Monitoring Program. The cost of birth defects. Sacramento (CA): Birth Defects Monitoring Program; April 1999.
3. Catanzarite V, Deutchman M, Johnson C, et al. Pregnancy after 35: what's the real risk? Patient Care 1995;29:41–51.

4. Fraser A, Brockert J, Ward R. Association of young maternal age and the risk of fetal death. N Engl J Med 1995;332:1113–7.

5. Orlandi F, Damiani G, Hallahan T, et al. First trimester screening for fetal aneuploidy: biochemistry and nuchal translucency. Ultrasound Obstet Gynecol 1997;10:381–6.

6. American College of Obstetricians and Gynecologists. Chorionic villus sampling. ACOG committee opinion 160. Washington (DC): ACOG; 1995.

7. American College of Obstetricians and Gynecologists. Preconceptional care. ACOG technical bulletin 205. Washington (DC): ACOG; 1995.

8. Roy M, Plante M. Pregnancies after radical vaginal trachelectomy for early-stage cervical cancer. Am J Obstet Gynecol 1998;179(6 Pt 1):1491–6.

9. Shiver S, Miller D. Preinvasive and invasive breast and cervical cancer prior to or during pregnancy. Clin Perinatol 1997;24:369–89.

10. Pruvot F, Noel C, Declerck Nvalat-Rigot A, et al. Consecutive successful pregnancies in a combined liver and kidney transplant recipient with type 1 primary hyperoxaluria. Transplantation 1997;63:615–6.

11. Fleschler R, Sala D. Pregnancy after organ transplantation. J Obstet Gynecol Neonatal Nurs 1995;24:413–22.

12. Riley E. Obstetric management of patients with transplants. Int Anesthesiol Clin 1995;33:125–40.

13. American College of Obstetrics and Gynecology. Rubella in pregnancy. ACOG technical bulletin 171. Washington (DC): ACOG; 1992.

14. American College of Obstetricians and Gynecologists. Immunization during pregnancy. ACOG technical bulletin 160. Washington (DC): ACOG; 1991.

15. DeWald G, Michels V. Recurrent miscarriages: cytogenetic causes and genetic counseling of affected families. Clin Obstet Gynecol 1986;29:865–8.

16. MRC Vitamin Study Research Group. Prevention of neural tube defects: results of the Medical Research Counsel Vitamin Study. Lancet 1991;338:131–7.

17. Burke W, Culver J, Bowen D, et al. Genetic counseling for women with an intermediate family history of breast cancer. Am J Med Genet 2000;90:361–8.

18. Nelson M, Forfar J. Association between drugs administered during pregnancy and congenital abnormalities of the fetus. Bri Med J 1971;1:523–7.

19. Clarren S. Recognition of fetal alcohol syndrome. JAMA 1981;245:2436–9.

20. Jones K, Smith D, Ulleland C, Streissguth A. Pattern of malformation in offspring of chronic alcoholic mothers. Lancet 1973;1:1267–71.

21. Bingol N, Fuchs M, Diaz V, et al. Teratogenicity of cocaine in humans. J Pediatr 1987;110:93–6.

22. Chavez G, Mulinare J, Codero J. Maternal cocaine use during early pregnancy as a risk factor for congenital urogenital anomalies. JAMA 1989;262:795–8.

23. Werler M. Teratogen update: smoking and reproductive outcomes. Teratology 1997;55:382–6.

24. Goodwin T, Breen M. Pregnancy outcome and fetomaternal hemorrhage after noncatastrophic trauma. Am J Obstet Gynecol 1990;162:665–71.

25. American College of Obstetricians and Gynecologists. Vitamin A supplementation during pregnancy. ACOG committee opinion 196. Washington (DC): ACOG; 1996.

26. Lenke R, Levy H. Maternal phenylkentonuria—results of dietary therapy. Am J Obstet Gynecol. 1982;142:548–53.

27. Drogari E, Smith I, Beasly M, Lloyd J. Timing of strict diet in relation to fetal damage in maternal phenylketonuria. Lancet 1987;2:927–30.

28. American College of Obstetricians and Gynecologists. Exercise during pregnancy and the postpartum period. ACOG technical bulletin 189. Washington (DC): ACOG; 1994.

29. Milunsky A, Ulcickas M, Rothman K, et al. Maternal heat exposure and neural tube defects. JAMA 1992;268:882–5.

30. Warkany J. Teratogen update: hyperthermia. Teratology 1986;33:365–71.

31. U.S. Department of Labor. Bureau of Labor Statistics. Current labor statistics. Monthly Labor Review 2001; May:70.

32. U.S. Department of Labor. Bureau of Labor Statistics. Issues in labor statistics. Summary 97–3. Washington (DC): Bureau of Labor Statistics; 1997.

33. Mozurkewich E, Luke B, Avni M, Wolf F. Working conditions and adverse pregnancy outcome: a meta-analysis. Obstet Gynecol 2000;95:623–35.

34. Ahlborg G Jr. Physical work load and pregnancy outcome. J Occup Environ Med 1995;37:941–4.

11

PREGNANCY AFTER AGE 35

Judith A. Mikacich, MD, and Alan H. DeCherney, MD

Through personal choice or because of life circumstances, more women in the United States are becoming first-time mothers after the age of 35 years. Many others are choosing to have subsequent pregnancies after age 35 years. Primary care clinicians are often asked to provide information about the possible risks of childbearing for older mothers and to care for older women during pregnancy.

STATISTICS AND TRENDS

Women who choose to delay childbearing until age 35 or later are a growing group. The percentage of live births to women ages 35 to 49 in the United States (compared with all live births) increased from 4.7% in 1974 to 12.6% in 1997. The median maternal age increased from 23.4 years in 1974 to 26.4 years in 1997.[1] According to current population survey data, the median age at first birth increased from 21.3 to 24.4 years from 1969 to 1994.[2] Similar trends have been noted throughout the industrialized world.[3,4]

In the United States, only in women aged 30 years and over has the birth rate consistently increased over the past two decades. In 1996 these rates were the highest ever recorded. Since 1984 pregnancy rates for women in their forties have increased as well. More of the increase in the pregnancy rates in women in their thirties and forties is attributable to first births rather than subsequent births, although both contribute.[5]

PSYCHOSOCIAL ISSUES

Myriad forces have encouraged delayed childbearing. The trend toward delayed childbearing has occurred most significantly among women with at least a high school education.[2] Delayed childbearing is more pronounced in those with the highest level of education. This is similar for African Americans and Caucasians.[6] Between 1969 and 1994, the median age at first birth rose by almost 4 years to 29.5 years for those with 16 or more years of education.[2] Women with more education have fewer unwanted births, use contraception more regularly, and use more effective means of birth control than their less educated counterparts.[5] Child care is more available and acceptable but costly; there may be a fertility delay in order to be more financially prepared.[2,6]

The trend toward delayed childbearing seems to confer some advantages to the children. Advantages include wealth, better performance on cognitive tests, and less problematic behavior patterns. In addition, women over 35 tend to have higher rates of early prenatal care and to smoke less during pregnancy than do younger mothers. Weight gain is more likely to be adequate. Marital discord occurs less frequently.[2] Children of better-educated mothers are more likely to be living with both parents.[6]

FERTILITY ISSUES

In the United States, 10 to 15% of all couples in the reproductive age group are diagnosed as infertile, defined as being unsuccessful at conception after a year of unprotected intercourse. About one-third of women who defer pregnancy until the mid- to late thirties have an infertility problem, as do at least half of women over age 40 years.[7] Ovarian function declines as oocytes decrease in number and quality with age. By 16 to 20 weeks' gestation, the female fetus has 6 to 7 million oogonia, and this number then begins to decrease. By puberty, only 300,000 are present, and by menopause, only a few hundred remain. At some point in a woman's late thirties, the number of follicles falls to about 25,000, and the rate of atresia doubles. At the same time, there is an increase in follicle-stimulating hormone (FSH) and a decrease in inhibin, a glycoprotein secreted by granulosa cells. Cycle lengths may shorten when these changes occur.[7,8]

The partners of women over age 35 are usually of a similar age or older. After age 30, male fertility begins to decline. Vascular changes in the testicle are associated with a decline in the number of spermatozoa and a decrease in sperm quality, as is evidenced by decreased sperm motility and an increase in abnormal sperm morphology. In artificial insemination programs, increasing age of the donor has been associated with decreased pregnancy rates.[3]

Some authors suggest that hormonal support of the endometrium and uterine vascularity decline in later life, decreasing uterine receptivity to fertilized oocytes.[8] However, one study comparing the live birth rates of in vitro fertilization/gamete intrafallopian transfer cycles for women using donor eggs versus their own oocytes found that whereas pregnancy rates did not differ based on donor age, the live birth rate did. They concluded that the risk of miscarriage is related to the age of the oocyte rather than uterine factors.[9] This has been demonstrated by the successful pregnancies of women up to age 63 years.[10]

The evaluation and treatment of infertility are discussed in detail in Chapter 19. Many older women without a diagnosis of infertility and without specific risk factors request information about fertility issues prior to attempting to conceive. Among women who report monthly periods accompanied by premenstrual symptoms and dysmenorrhea, only about 5% are not ovulating. Basal body temperature testing can be helpful as a preliminary indicator of ovulation. A significant increase in temperature is noted 2 days after the luteinizing hormone (LH) peak and is sustained for 11 to 16 days. Pregnancy is most likely if intercourse occurs on the day of ovulation or 1 or 2 days before.[11] Home urinary LH kits can also be used to assist in timing of intercourse.[7] Ovarian reserve can be tested by a baseline FSH. A value over 12 is associated with difficulties conceiving.

Because many older women contemplating pregnancy may anticipate needing assistance to achieve pregnancy, it is important to be able to counsel them about likely outcomes should they successfully undergo infertility treatment. Assisted reproductive technologies do result in more multiple gestations, increasing obstetric risk; however, among singleton gestations, a comparable obstetric course has been noted.[12] Expected obstetric risks with aging are discussed in more detail below.

GENETICS

It is well established that a maternal age greater than 35 is associated with higher risk for chromosomal abnormalities in the fetus.[13] Although the rates of such abnormalities increase consistently from age 20 to age 35, they increase almost exponentially thereafter. At age 25, the risk of any chromosomal abnormality is 1 in 476. At age 35, the risk rises to 1 in 204, and by age 45, it reaches 1 in 20. The most common abnormalities are Down syndrome, Edwards' syndrome (trisomy 18), Patau's syndrome (trisomy 13), and abnormalities of the sex chromosomes, including XXY genotype (Klinefelter's syndrome), XYY genotype, and XO genotype (Turner's syndrome).[13] A recent study of 100,000 pregnancies suggested that nonchromosomal malformations, including cardiac defects, clubfoot, and diaphragmatic hernia, may also be more frequent in infants born to women ages 25 years and older compared with those born to younger women.[14] Advancing paternal age, also a factor in the pregnancies of many older mothers, has been implicated as the source of increased risk of autosomal dominant mutations, such as achondroplasia, Apert's syndrome, Crouzon's disease, Marfan syndrome, and retinoblastoma.[3]

Genetic counseling with prenatal diagnosis through cytogenetic analysis has been offered since the 1970s to couples at increased risk for bearing a child with a chromosomal abnormality. It is the responsibility of obstetric clinicians to discuss options thoroughly early in pregnancy, as soon as the first prenatal visit. This includes the discussion of expectations after the testing is done, such as whether termination or continuation of the pregnancy would ensue.[15] Serum screening for three maternal serum biochemical markers, α-fetoprotein (AFP), human chorionic gonadotropin, and unconjugated estriol, is generally offered to all pregnant women between weeks 15 and 20. In the triple-marker screen, the levels of the markers differ quantitatively and predictably in women carrying a fetus with trisomy 21 or 18. The test is thought to detect about 60% of pregnancies with Down syndrome.[16]

Those considered at high risk for fetal chromosomal abnormalities include women with advanced maternal age, abnormal serum markers, a family history of chromosomal abnormalities, or an abnormal ultrasound scan. Such women should be offered further counseling and evaluation, including diagnostic ultrasonography and cytogenetic testing. As these services should be offered to any woman who will be 35 or older at the time of her child's delivery, the demand for genetic counseling and prenatal diagnosis is increasing as pregnancy rates among delayed childbearers rise.

Options for cytogenetic analysis include amniocentesis and chorionic villus sampling (CVS). The choice of which to recommend is based on multiple factors. Amniocentesis is more commonly performed. One advantage of amniocentesis is that amniotic fluid AFP levels provide a more reliable screening tool for neural tube defects than maternal serum AFP.[16,17] An important issue for some parents is that diagnostic information is not available from amniocentesis until well into the second trimester. Studies of early amniocentesis (performed before 14 completed weeks) have shown an increased risk of unintended fetal loss and talipes equinovarus.[17,18] Therefore, amniocentesis is generally performed after the first trimester, between 15 and 20 weeks.

Chorionic villus sampling is typically performed in weeks 10 to 13. Therefore, compared with amniocentesis, diagnostic information is available earlier in pregnancy. Preliminary CVS results may be available in 2 days, although, like amniocentesis, there is a delay of 1 to 3 weeks for the complete culture period. Attempts to obtain preliminary results from amniocentesis through the use of fluorescence in situ hybridization on uncultured amniocytes have not shown comparable accuracy to date.[19–21]

Chorionic villus sampling can be performed transcervically or transabdominally and has been shown to be safe in twin gestations.[22] Chorionic villus sampling offers the opportunity for DNA analysis to detect genetic diseases such as Tay-Sachs.[16] Of critical importance in choosing CVS is the availability of an expert in performing CVS. Reports of limb abnormalities published in the late 1980s and early 1990s were thought to be the result of the procedure being performed by nonexperts.[16] One study of 158 transcervical CVS cases, each performed by one of three experienced technicians, resulted in a miscarriage rate of 3.2%. As the natural miscarriage rate for women aged 35 to 39 years is 2.6% at 10 weeks, the rate attributable to the procedure was estimated at less than 1%.[23] Other studies have demonstrated similar spontaneous loss rates.[18,24]

Several centers have proposed alternatives to routine invasive genetic testing. These include combining maternal age, ultrasound findings, and serum or urinary markers. In particular, increased nuchal thickness by ultrasonography and serum inhibin A in the second trimester are used as indicators of Down syndrome risk.[1] A recently published analysis of US natality statistics estimated that 88.3% of pregnancies affected by Down syndrome would be identified by the triple test alone, obviating the need for amniocentesis.[1] Sensitivity rates of 92 to 100% have been achieved using a new screening algorithm for Down syndrome combining the urinary ß-core fragment/estriol ratio, maternal age, and nuchal thickness data.[25] Work is being done to develop studies on fetal cells in maternal blood as noninvasive screening for chromosomal abnormalities.[26]

HEALTH RISKS FOR MOTHER AND BABY

As for all women, preconception medical evaluation and counseling, as well as early prenatal care, are important factors in ensuring healthy outcomes of pregnancies for women over age 35 years. These are discussed in detail in Chapter 10, "Preconception Counseling," and Chapter 14, "Normal Pregnancy." Older mothers are more likely to have pre-existing chronic medical conditions. Management of common chronic medical conditions in pregnancy is discussed in detail in Chapter 15.

As the birth rate among women in their thirties has increased, there has been significant discourse concerning the potential increased risks to the mother and child associated with delayed childbearing. There is no question that older mothers are more likely to have a host of age-dependent risk factors for maternal and fetal complications, including hypertension, diabetes, high parity, uterine myomas, and a history of infertility. A gradual loss of compliance in the cardiovascular system has been demonstrated; an age-dependent decline in vascular responsiveness to endothelium-dependent vasodilators may explain the demonstrated increased risk of vascular complications of pregnancy in older women. This is found in both normotensive and hypertensive women.[27] There is a strong positive relationship between age and gestational diabetes, contributing to the increase in larger babies noted among the pregnancies of older mothers.

Increased maternal mortality in older mothers attributable to risk factors such as hypertension and diabetes has been seen primarily in African American, poor women over 40 years of age.[28] In contrast, studies of middle and upper-middle class women have shown that delayed childbearing, although not without some risk, does not usually adversely affect maternal health.[29,30] Most pregnancies proceed uneventfully. Older pregnant women have been found to have higher rates of gestational diabetes, pregnancy-induced hypertension, gestational bleeding, abruptio placentae, placenta previa, and postpartum hemorrhage.[29,31] Despite increases in maternal morbidity, maternal mortality among socioeconomically advantaged older mothers does not appear to be increased.[30,31]

Although the overwhelming majority of babies born to older mothers are healthy, neonatal morbidity is also increased in this age group, even among educated, socioeconomically advantaged women with good prenatal care.[29] Intrapartum hypertension, uterine bleeding, and fetal distress are more common during pregnancies of women over 35 years of age.[29] The risk of preterm birth, small-for-gestational-age newborns, and low birth weight is higher in the majority of studies of pregnancies among older mothers.[31,32] Increased rates of admission of newborns to the neonatal intensive care unit have also been consistently demonstrated for the babies of older mothers.[29,31,33,34] Older mothers who are primarily Caucasian married college-educated nonsmokers have consistently had better outcomes; in particular, one large study showed no increased risk of preterm delivery and small-for-gestational-age infants among this group.[29] In one study of such women, although fetal macrosomia was shown to be more common among the pregnancies of older mothers, associated complications were not.[30]

Unexplained fetal death in a woman 35 years of age or older without maternal or fetal risk factors is estimated to be approximately 1 in 440 births versus 1 in 1,000 births in those under 34 years.[35]

Increased fetal death rates persist even when age-associated comorbidities, such as hypertension, diabetes, and other maternal characteristics, are taken into account. Even so, less than 1% of pregnant women over the age of 35 who have undergone early screening for fetal anomalies experience stillbirth.[36] Being married seems to confer protection against fetal death, conceivably because these births are more often planned and accompanied by improved socioeconomic status.[37] After the first birth, women of advanced maternal age have less age-specific increased risk of fetal death during subsequent pregnancies.[38]

Multiple studies have demonstrated a higher rate of cesarean section delivery in older mothers.[28,30,33,34] However, only 8% of recent increases in the rate of cesarean section in the United States can be attributed to the changing distribution of maternal age at delivery.[39] In one study, the rate of cesarean section was 18% in younger women compared with 40% in those over 35 years. In those who did labor, twice the risk of cesarean section was demonstrated; in those who did not labor, the risk was 3.5 times that in younger women.[33] It is suggested that anxiety about pregnancy outcome in older women, especially those with a history of infertility, promotes the phenomenon of "premium" or "precious" pregnancies, which might influence the decision to undergo cesarean section electively or after a shorter period of labor.[33] In women over 44 years of age, known as very advanced maternal age, one study showed a 7.5 times higher rate of cesarean delivery. This was most pronounced in those who had received infertility treatment.[40]

SUMMARY

Women over age 35 are more frequently becoming pregnant. This trend is particularly marked among well-educated women. Motherhood at older ages can offer significant psychosocial advantages to both parents and child. Women considering delayed childbearing should be aware that fertility declines rapidly between ages 35 and 40 and that assisted reproduction is less successful with age, particularly after age 40 years. Preconception medical evaluation and counseling are particularly important in this group because of a greater prevalence of concomitant medical conditions. The overwhelming majority of older women who become pregnant have healthy pregnancies and good obstetric outcomes.

REFERENCES

1. Egan J, Benn P, Borgida A, et al. Efficacy of screening for fetal down syndrome in the United States from 1974 to 1997. Obstet Gynecol 2000;96:979–85.

2. Heck KE, Schoendorf MD, Ventura AM, Kiely JL. Delayed childbearing by education level in the United States, 1969–1994. Matern Child Health J 1997; 1:81–8.

3. Lansac J. Is delayed childbearing a good thing? Hum Reprod 1995;10:1033–5.

4. Breart G. Delaying childbearing. Eur J Obstet Gynecol Reprod Biol 1997;75:71–3.

5. Ventura SJ, Mosher WD, Curtin SC, et al. Trends in pregnancies and pregnancy rates by outcome: estimates for the United States, 1976–96. National Center for Health Statistics. Vital Health Stat 2000;21(56).

6. Rindfuss RR, Morgan SP, Offutt K. Education and the changing age pattern of American fertility: 1963–1989. Demography 1996;33:277–90.

7. Speroff L, Glass RH, Kase NG. Clinical gynecologic endocrinology and infertility. 6th ed. Baltimore (MD): Lippincott, Williams & Wilkins;1999.

8. Fitzgerald C, Zimon AE, Jones EE. Aging and reproductive potential in women. Yale J Biol Med 1998; 71:367–81.

9. Abdallah HI, Burton G, Kirkland A, et al. Age, pregnancy and miscarriage: uterine versus ovarian factors. Hum Reprod 1993;8:1512–7.

10. Paulson RJ, Thornton MH, Francis MM, Salvador HS. Successful pregnancy in a 63-year-old woman. Fertil Steril 1997;67:949–51.

11. Wolff KM, McMahon MJ, Kuller JA, et al. Advanced maternal age and perinatal outcome: oocyte recipiency versus natural conception. Obstet Gynecol 1997;89:519–23.

12. Wilcox AJ, Weinberg CR, Baird DD. Timing of sexual intercourse in relation to ovulation—effects on the probability of conception, survival of the pregnancy, and the sex of the baby. N Engl J Med 1998; 333:1517–21.

13. Hook EB. Rates of chromosomal abnormalities at different maternal ages. Obstet Gynecol 1981;58:282–5.

14. Hollier LM, Leveno KJ, Kelly MA, et al. Maternal age and malformations in singleton births. Obstet Gynecol 2000;96:701–6.

15. Bachu A, O'Connell M. Fertility of American women: June 1998. Current Population Reports, P20-526. Washington (DC): Census Bureau (US); 2000.

16. Olsen CL, Cross PK. Trends in the use of prenatal diagnosis in New York State and the impact of biochemical screening on the detection of Down syndrome: 1984–1993. Prenat Diagn 1997;17:1113–24.

17. Nagel HTC, Vandenbussche FPHA, Keirse MJNC, et al. Amniocentesis before 14 completed weeks as an alternative to transabdominal chorionic villus sampling: a controlled trial with infant follow-up. Prenat Diagn 1998;18:465–75.

18. Nicolaides KH, Brizot ML, Patel F, Snijders R. Comparison of chorion villus sampling and early amniocentesis for karyotyping in 1492 singleton pregnancies. Fetal Diagn Ther 1996;11:9–15.

19. Lewin P, Kleinfinger P, Bazin A, et al. Defining the efficiency of fluorescence in situ hybridization on uncultured amniocytes on a retrospective cohort of 27,407 prenatal diagnoses. Prenat Diagn 2000;20: 1–6.

20. Thein ATA, Abdel-Fattah SA, Kyle PM, Soothill PW. An assessment of the use of interphase FISH with chromosome specific probes as an alternative to cytogenetics in prenatal diagnosis. Prenat Diagn 2000;20:275–80.

21. Pergament E, Chen PX, Thangavelu M, Fiddler M. The clinical application of interphase FISH in prenatal diagnosis. Prenat Diagn 2000;20:215–20.

22. De Catte L, Liebaers I, Foulon W. Outcome of twin gestations after first trimester chorionic villus sampling. Obstet Gynecol 2000;96:714–20.

23. Salihu HM, Boos R, Schmidt W. A report on 158 cases of transcervical chorionic villus sampling. Arch Gynecol Obstet 1997;259:91–5.

24. Borrell A, Fortuny A, Lazaro L, et al. First-trimester transcervical chorionic villus sampling by biopsy forceps versus mid-trimester amniocentesis: a randomized controlled trial project. Prenat Diagn 1999; 19:1138–42.

25. Bahado-Singh R, Oz U, Kovanci E, et al. A high-sensitivity alternative to "routine" genetic amniocentesis: multiple urinary analyses, nuchal thickness, and age. Am J Obstet Gynecol 1999;180:169–73.

26. Bianchi D. A guest editorial: state of fetal cells in maternal blood: diagnosis or dilemma. Obstet Gynecol Surv 2000;55:665–7.

27. Taddei S, Virdis A, Mattei P, et al. Aging and endothelial function in normotensive subjects and

patients with essential hypertension. Circulation 1995;91:1981–7.

28. Van Katwijk C, Peeters LLH. Clinical aspects of pregnancy after the age of 35 years: a review of the literature. Hum Reprod Update 1998;4:185–94.

29. Berkowitz GS, Skovron ML, Lapinski RH, Berkowitz RL. Delayed childbearing and the outcome of pregnancy. N Engl J Med 1990;322:659–64.

30. Ales KL, Druzin ML, Santini DL. Impact of advanced maternal age on the outcome of pregnancy. Surg Gynecol Obstet 1990;171:209–16.

31. Prysakk M, Lorenz RP, Kisly A. Pregnancy outcome in nulliparous women 35 years and older. Obstet Gynecol 1995;85:65–70.

32. Cnattingius S, Forman MR, Berendes HW, Isotalo L. Delayed childbearing and risk of adverse perinatal outcome: a population-based study. JAMA 1992; 268:886–90.

33. Edge V, Laros RK Jr. Pregnancy outcome in nulliparous women aged 35 or older. Am J Obstet Gynecol 1993;168:1881–4.

34. Dollberg S, Seidman DS, Armon Y, et al. Adverse perinatal outcome in the older primipara. J Perinatol 1996;16(2 Pt 1):93–7.

35. Fretts RC, Usher RH. Causes of fetal death in women of advanced maternal age. Obstet Gynecol 1997; 89:40–5.

36. Cunningham FG, Leveno KJ. Childbearing among older women—the message is cautiously optimistic. N Engl J Med 1995;333:1002–4.

37. Fretts RC, Schmittdiel J, McLean FH, et al. Increased maternal age and the risk of fetal death. N Engl J Med 1995;333:953–7.

38. Cnattingius S, Berendes HW, Forman MR. Do delayed childbearers face increased risk of adverse pregnancy outcomes after the first birth? Obstet Gynecol 1993;81:512–6.

39. Taffel SM, Placek PJ, Liss T. Trends in the United States cesarean section rate and reasons for the 1980–85 rise. Am J Public Health 1987;77:955–9.

40. Dulitzki M, Soriano D, Schiff E, et al. Effect of very advanced maternal age on pregnancy outcome and rate of cesarean delivery. Obstet Gynecol 1998; 92:935–9.

12

SMOKING CESSATION

Edith Flores, MD

It is now proved beyond doubt that smoking is the leading cause of statistics.

—Fletcher Knebel

It is well established that cigarette smoking poses significant health hazards. It threatens multiple organ systems and increases the risks for many different types of cancers. Despite public warnings and labels, smoking continues to be the leading cause of premature morbidity and mortality in the United States. In the United States 430,000 deaths annually were attributable to tobacco smoking during the period from 1990 to 1994.[1] This accounted for approximately 1 in 5 deaths in the United States during this time. More than 140,000 women die from smoking-related diseases annually.

Cigarette smokers miss approximately 6.5 days more of work each year than do nonsmokers. Smokers visit health care facilities six more times per year and their dependents 4 times more per year than do nonsmokers. Monetary costs to society of smoking-related illnesses were estimated at 65 billion dollars annually in 1985, including health care costs and lost productivity. In addition, fires related to cigarette smoking are the leading cause of fire deaths in the United States.[2]

Smoking is a difficult addiction to overcome, especially for women. Because of the lag time between smoking initiation and morbidity and mortality, the full impact of the increased prevalence of smoking that began in the early and middle twentieth century in the United States is yet to be seen.

The emphasis of this chapter is on cigarette smoking, since it is the most common form of tobacco use among women. Other forms of tobacco use (cigars, snuff, pipes, and chewing tobacco), although also hazardous, are not addressed in this chapter.

EPIDEMIOLOGY

Forty-seven million adults in the United States smoked in 1995, including 22.5 million women.[3] The prevalence of smoking has been declining steadily since the 1960s, although more slowly for women than men (Figure 12–1).[4] In the 1990s, this decrease appeared to be leveling off, and in 1995 gender-specific smoking prevalences were similar: 26% and 23% for men and women, respectively,[3] compared with 52% and 34% in 1965. Unfortunately, this decline does not apply to high-school students (grades 9 to 12), whose prevalence of current smoking increased from 27.9% in 1991 to 36.4% in 1997.[5] Smoking prevalence is highest among the poor and the less educated.[6] This fact applies to both men and women (including pregnant women; Figures 12–2 and 12–3).

Smoking begins during adolescence for both men and women. About 80% of adults who have ever smoked began by age 18 years, and more than half of young adults have tried smoking tobacco by the age of 18 years.[7] Among US high-school students, 70% have tried smoking; 1.5 million adolescent girls smoked in 1994. The earlier a young women begins smoking, the more heavily she is likely to smoke as an adult.[8]

Once an adolescent begins smoking, it is difficult to stop. Tobacco has a high addictive potential, even when compared with the most addictive illicit drugs. Twenty-three percent of those who try smoking develop nicotine dependence. In comparison, 24% of persons who try cocaine become addicted, and 20% of persons who try heroin become addicted.[9]

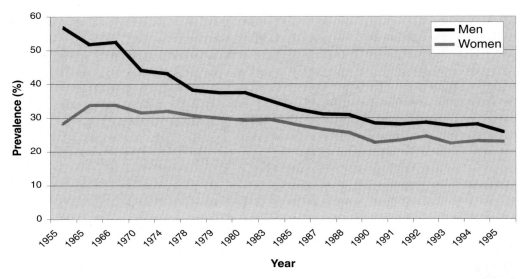

FIGURE 12–1. Smoking prevalence (%) among US adults >18 years of age by gender. Reproduced with permission from Centers for Disease Control and Prevention. Cigarette smoking among adults—United States, 1994. MMWR Morb Mortal Wkly Rep 1996;45:588–90.

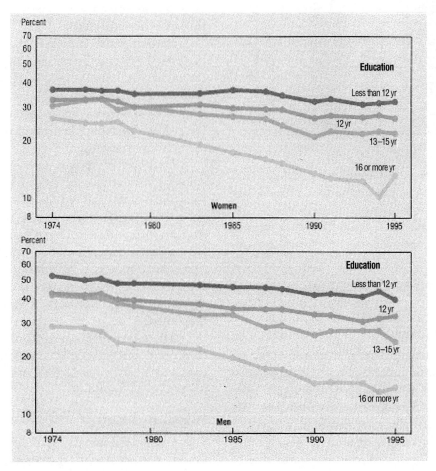

FIGURE 12–2. Cigarette smoking among adults 25 years of age and over by education and sex: United States, 1974–1995. Percents are age adjusted and plotted on a big scale. The definition of "current smoker" was revised in 1992 and 1993. Reproduced from Pamuk E, Makuc D, Heck K, et al. Socioeconomic status and health chartbook. Health, United States 1998. Hyattsville (MD): National Center for Health Statistics.

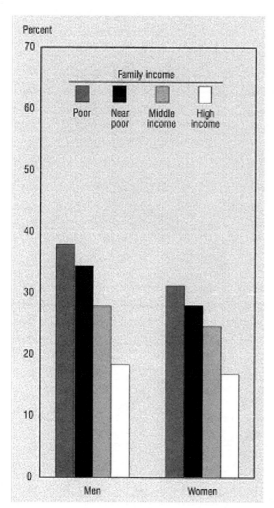

FIGURE 12–3. Cigarette smoking among adults 18 years or age and over, by family income and sex: United States, 1995. Reproduced from Pamuk E, Makuc D, Heck K, et al. Socioeconomic status and health chartbook. Health, United States 1998. Hyattsville (MD): National Center for Health Statistics.

HEALTH CONSEQUENCES OF SMOKING

Cardiovascular Effects

The majority of deaths associated with smoking are related to the cardiovascular system. Of the 418,690 deaths attributed to smoking in 1990, 43% were due to cardiovascular diseases (Figure 12–4).[10] By far the most significant cardiovascular effect of smoking is the increase in risk for coronary artery disease (CAD). Twenty percent of deaths due to coronary artery disease are attributable to smoking. Smoking also acts synergistically with other CAD risk factors. Furthermore, CAD death rates are higher for those who continue to smoke after a

myocardial infarction (MI) compared with rates for those who quit.[11]

It appears that women are more susceptible to the harmful cardiovascular effects of tobacco than are men. Several studies have shown that women smokers have a higher relative risk of MI than do men, despite similarities in lipid profiles and blood pressure.[12–14] Cardiovascular mortality increases by 18% in men and by 31% in women for each 10 cigarettes smoked per day.[15] Even small amounts of smoking pose an increased risk of disease: women who smoke one to four cigarettes per day increase their risk of fatal CAD and nonfatal MI by 2.5-fold.[8]

Smoking cessation can decrease the risk of dying of an MI by 50% in the first year.[16] After 3 years, the risk decreases to the level of never-smokers.[17] Clearly there is a benefit to urging smoking cessation among individuals with CAD, especially in women, who appear to be more susceptible to its harmful effects.

Smoking also increases the risk of strokes, peripheral vascular disease, and atherosclerotic aortic aneurysm.[11] Smoking is implicated in 15% of stroke deaths. Although smoking does not increase the risk of developing hypertension, it does increase the risk of developing malignant hypertension and dying from hypertension.[11]

Oral contraceptives act synergistically with smoking to increase the risk of MI. One study in the United States showed the risk of MI in women aged less than 45 years was 30 times greater for smokers using oral contraceptives, 8.7 times greater for smokers not using oral contraceptives, and not significantly increased for nonsmoking oral contraceptive users.[18] Women over the age of 35 years should be advised not to use oral contraceptives if they smoke.

The effect of progestin-only contraceptives (both oral and injectable) on cardiovascular disease, and in particular in association with smoking, has not been established.

Pulmonary Effects

The principal pulmonary morbidity (other than lung cancer) associated with cigarette smoking is chronic obstructive pulmonary disease (COPD). In the United States 80% of deaths from COPD are attributable to cigarette smoking.[11] Smoking leads to various derangements in pulmonary function including

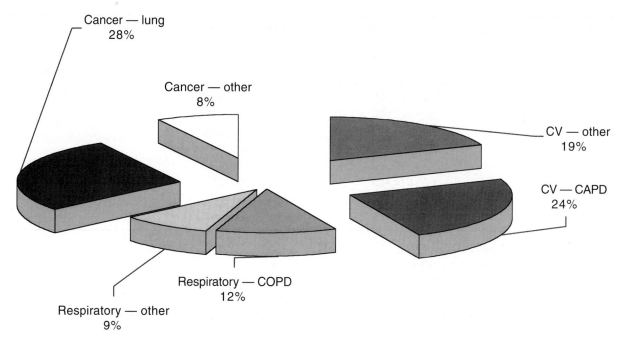

FIGURE 12–4. Smoking-attributable mortality in the United States in 1990. CV = cardiovascular; CAD = coronary artery disease; COPD = chronic obstructive pulmonary disease. Adapted from MacKenzie T, Bartecchi C, Schrier R. The human costs of tobacco use (first of two parts). N Engl J Med 1994;330:975–80.

a decrease in FEV₁ (forced expiratory volume in 1 second), mucus hypersecretion, inflammation of lung parenchyma and airways, and abnormalities in the mucociliary system.[19] Smokers experience many respiratory symptoms, including cough, dyspnea, and wheezing, that can improve rapidly with smoking cessation.

Smoking increases the risk of pulmonary infections. The risk of dying from influenza or pneumonia is 1.3 to 1.9 times higher in smokers compared to never-smokers.[19] It is estimated that the proportion of community-acquired pneumonia attributable to tobacco use is 23% in the general population and 34% in those with COPD.[20]

From the pulmonary standpoint, several studies suggest that women are more susceptible to the harmful effects of smoking than are men.[21–24] Women who are heavy smokers have a more rapid decline in pulmonary function compared with male heavy smokers. Further, women develop COPD with less cigarette exposure than do men. Female smokers also have higher rates of reactive airways, due to the smaller caliber of their airways.[25,26]

Death from COPD is higher in smokers than never-smokers, but intermediate in former smokers, suggesting a decreased risk of death with smoking cessation. Nevertheless, pulmonary function does not return to baseline; even after 20 years, former smokers have a higher mortality from COPD than do never-smokers.

Cancer

Smoking is the single most important cause of cancer deaths in the United States. It is a major cause of cancer of the lung, larynx, oral cavity, and esophagus, and also contributes significantly to bladder, kidney, pancreatic, stomach, and cervical cancers (Table 12–1).

Among women there is 20 to 30% excess in total cancer incidence when comparing smokers with never smokers.[27] Excess in total cancer incidence for men is higher and likely reflects a heavier tobacco burden (ie, men have been smoking longer and more heavily than women). Lung cancer is the leading cause of cancer deaths among men and women (overtaking breast cancer as the leading cause of cancer death in women since 1987). It is estimated that close to 89,300 men and 68,800 women died of lung cancer in 1999.[28] The proportion of these deaths attributable to smoking is 90% and 79% for men and women, respectively[11] (see Table 12–1).

Among women, lung cancer deaths rose slowly between the 1930s and the 1960s. A steep rise

TABLE 12–1. New Cases, Deaths, and Percentage of Deaths Attributable to Smoking[*]

Site	No. of New Cases Annually (Male/Female)	Deaths (Male/Female)	Percentage of Deaths Attributable to Smoking
Lung	94,000/77,600	90,900/68,000	90 (79)[†]
Larynx	8,600/2,000	3,300/900	82
Oral cavity	20,000/9,800	5,400/2,700	92 (61)[†]
Esophagus	9,400/3,100	9,400/2,800	80
Bladder/kidney	56,900/17,300	15,300/8,700	50/50 (37/12)[†]
Pancreas	14,000/14,600	13,900/14,700	30
Stomach	13,700/8,200	7,900/5,600	20
Uterine cervix	—/12,800	—/4,800	37

[*]By gender, in the United States.
[†]Figures in parentheses are for women, when a gender difference exists.
Adapted from Xu et al,[23] Mordlund et al,[27] and Taioli and Wynder.[32]

in lung cancer deaths then ensued, and as of 1995 there were 35 deaths per 100,000 women yearly. The peak of this increase in deaths has yet to be seen, given the lag time between smoking initiation and the development of lung cancer (women began smoking in significant numbers in the 1940s). Among men, the rise in cancer began in the 1930s and rose rapidly, peaking in the 1980s at 75 deaths per 100,000 men yearly. The 1995 death rate was about 69 deaths per 100,000 men annually. For women overall, age-adjusted lung cancer death rates have increased, paralleling those of men but lagging by about 20 years.[3]

Whether there are gender differences in susceptibility to cancer is controversial. There have been conflicting results from multiple studies.[11,29,30] It is unknown how other risk factors for developing lung cancer (eg, occupational exposures, family history, air pollution, and diet) interact with tobacco, or if there are gender differences associated with other risks that may explain the conflicting results of these studies.[11]

Smoking increases the risk of all histologic types of lung cancer, but the most common type in men is squamous cell cancer, and the most common type in women is adenocarcinoma. Women are also at a higher risk of developing small cell lung carcinoma than are men.[31] It has been suggested that hormonal factors contribute to the increased risk of adenocarcinoma in women. The risk of adenocarcinoma of the lung decreases in female smokers during menopause and increases if hormone replacement therapy is begun.[32]

Smoking cessation decreases the risk of developing lung cancer. This effect can be seen within 5 years, although the risk does not equal that of never-smokers, even after 25 years.[16]

Smoking is also thought to be responsible for about 30% of new cases of cervical cancer and 37% of cervical cancer deaths.[33] It is considered an independent risk factor for cervical cancer. Nicotine and cotinine, a major metabolite of nicotine, have been identified in the cervical mucus of smokers. Additionally, tobacco-related deoxyribonucleic acid damage has been found in cervical epithelium.[34,35] The incidence of cervical cancer for smokers is double that of never-smokers. Smoking cessation decreases the risk of developing cervical cancer to that of never-smokers; thus, it appears only current smokers are at increased risk.

There appears to be a negative association between smoking and endometrial cancer,[11] which occurs less frequently in cigarette smokers; cigarette smoking appears to involve a 30% reduction of risk.[36] Postmenopausal women are protected the most, and the antiestrogenic effect of tobacco is a probable mechanism for this protective effect. However, the adverse health effects of smoking greatly outweigh this small benefit—the number of lives lost due to smoking is 60 times greater than is the number lost due to endometrial cancer.[1,28]

Tobacco has not been shown conclusively to play a role in breast cancer, and there are conflicting studies in the literature.[11] However, postmenopausal women with *N*-acetyltransferase deficiency (ie, slow acetylators) who smoke may be at a higher risk of developing breast cancer, especially if they smoke more than 20 cigarettes per day and began smoking before age 16 years, according to one study.[37]

Effects on Pregnancy and Lactation

The health hazards associated with smoking in pregnancy also have been well documented. It is estimated that between 19 and 27% of women smoke throughout their pregnancy.[38] Smokers are more likely to experience ectopic pregnancy, spontaneous abortion, premature rupture of membranes, placenta previa, abruptio placentae, and infertility compared with nonsmokers.[11] The fetus is susceptible to intrauterine growth retardation, sudden infant death syndrome, and perinatal mortality.[11] Women who smoke during pregnancy should be strongly urged to stop. Pregnancy is a powerful motivator for smoking cessation. Women most likely to quit during pregnancy include light smokers, those with nonsmoking partners, primiparous women, and more educated women.[39] Heavy smokers (>1 pack per day) are less likely to quit during pregnancy, thus putting themselves and their fetuses at risk.

The nutritional benefits of breast milk for infants have been well described. Unfortunately, women who smoke during pregnancy tend not to breast-feed, and wean their babies sooner than do nonsmoking women.[40] Nicotine can reduce the basal prolactin levels and has been shown to decrease the milk supply as well as the fat levels in the milk.[40,41] Additionally, significant amounts of nicotine are excreted in the breast milk, and infant plasma levels of nicotine and cotinine are 2 to 3 times that found in maternal serum.[42] Although not absolutely contraindicated, the American Academy of Pediatrics considers nicotine potentially harmful, and suggests that breast-feeding should be avoided if possible.[43] Women who are heavy smokers and find it difficult to quit should be advised to avoid smoking 2 to 3 hours prior to breast-feeding, since the half-life of nicotine in maternal milk is 90 minutes. By the time of feeding, maternal levels will have fallen to one-quarter of their initial values.[40,42]

Other Health Effects

Many effects of cigarette smoking are related to its antiestrogenic effect. There are several mechanisms proposed, including altered hepatic metabolism, decreased production of estrogens, and increased circulating androgens.[44]

Female smokers undergo menopause approximately 1 to 1.5 years earlier than do nonsmokers.[11,45–51] This is due to direct toxicity causing premature egg cell death by polycyclic aromatic hydrocarbons found in tobacco smoke.[52] Cigarette smoking also has been linked to lower bone marrow density, osteoporosis, and fractures.[11,53–58] Decreased intestinal calcium absorption may contribute to this effect, in addition to lower levels of estrogen.[59] There is decreased risk of endometrial cancer, endometriosis, leiomyomas, and hyperemesis gravidarum in smokers.[60,61]

Smoking also has been shown to lead to premature skin wrinkling; this effect is independent of age, sex, and sun exposure.[62] Our society pressures women to maintain a youthful appearance. Although wrinkles are not a life-threatening condition, fear of developing crow's-feet may be more of a motivation to quit smoking than fear of illness or premature death.

BARRIERS TO SMOKING CESSATION

The health benefits of smoking cessation cannot be overstated. Smokers decrease their risk of morbidity and mortality from a myriad of diseases by this single action, whether or not they are currently suffering from a smoking-related illness. The US Surgeon General's 1990 report concluded that smokers who quit before age 50 years have half the risk of dying within the next 15 years compared with continuing smokers.[16]

The majority of people who smoke want to quit, but long-term success is elusive in the majority. Seventeen million smokers made an attempt to quit smoking in 1990, and, of those, only 1.2 million achieved long-term success.[63] About two-thirds of these attempts resulted in relapses within 48 hours. There are many barriers to smoking cessation, including addiction to nicotine, fear of weight gain, and psychosocial factors.

Nicotine Addiction

The Surgeon General has determined that smoking is an addiction and that nicotine is the addictive substance. As mentioned earlier, the addictive potential of nicotine is similar to that of cocaine and heroin. Withdrawal symptoms include insomnia, irritability, craving for nicotine, nervousness, restlessness, impaired concentration, increased appetite, and mood lability.[64,65] These symptoms peak after 24 to 48 hours and subside after 2 weeks, although cravings can persist for years. Pharmacologic methods of addressing nicotine addiction are discussed below.

Fear of Weight Gain

Fear of weight gain can play a role in smoking initiation, maintenance, and relapse. Concern about weight gain is a commonly cited barrier to smoking cessation, especially among women. General weight concerns predict initiation of smoking in adolescent girls but not in boys;[66] 40% of young female smokers specifically report that they smoke to control weight. Young women are three to four times as likely as men to report weight gain as a cause of smoking relapse. Compared to nonsmoking women, smokers are twice as likely to be concerned about weight, two to five times more likely to use diet pills, and more likely to view their body weight as important to self-esteem.[67] Further, smokers are less likely to try to quit and are less successful if they are worried about weight gain.[16]

Smoking cessation is, in fact, associated with subsequent weight gain; 75% of all smokers who quit gain weight.[16] The etiology of the weight gain appears to be increased food consumption, mainly in the form of between-meal snacking, and the negation of metabolic affects of nicotine (ie, the increase in the resting metabolic rate and energy expenditure).[67] The amount of weight gained averages from 3 to 5 kg, with the majority of smokers gaining less than 5 kg, but as many as 10% of quitters can gain up to 15 kg.[68] Groups who are at risk for significant weight gain include those who are at a heavier baseline weight, heavy smokers (> 25 cigarettes per day), women, and African Americans.[68]

Certain measures may attenuate weight gain. Exercise can attenuate the weight gain associated with smoking cessation and contributes to overall health.[69,70] Nicotine gum (but not other nicotine-replacement products) can delay weight gain, but this effect is nullified when the drug is discontinued.[71,72] Bupropion also has been shown to attenuate weight gain, but, again, the benefit disappears when the drug is discontinued.[73] Attempts at controlling weight by dieting during the smoking cessation attempt are associated with lower abstinence rates at 12 and 52 weeks.[74] Therefore, it is not recommended that patients try to control their weight by dieting while discontinuing their smoking.

It is clear that weight gain is an issue that must be addressed when counseling women about smoking cessation. It is important to acknowledge the likelihood of weight gain and not to minimize its importance to the patient. Countering exaggerated fears about weight gain is important. It should be explained to the patient that in the majority of cases, the weight gain is modest. The health effects of postcessation weight gain, even when large, are far outweighed by the health advantages of quitting.

Psychosocial Issues

Habituation, stressful situations, poor coping mechanisms, and living with a smoker are additional factors that form barriers to smoking cessation. Behavioral interventions may help with these issues and are discussed in more detail below.

STRATEGIES TO PROMOTE SMOKING CESSATION

The great majority of former smokers have quit without any assistance. Those who have quit using the "cold turkey" method represent the largest proportion of former smokers. This, however, is the least-efficient method, with a 95% failure rate at 1 year.[75] The high cessation failure rate together with the high smoking-related death rate demand intervention on the part of physicians to improve the odds of smoking cessation. Pharmacologic and behavioral therapies are known to increase the success rate for smoking cessation, but, unfortunately, these are the least-used methods.

First-Line Drug Therapies

Nicotine-replacement therapies can approximately double the success rate of smoking cessation.[75-78] Currently, there are four different nicotine-replacement delivery systems: transdermal patch, nasal spray, gum, and inhaler. All of these products alleviate the symptoms associated with nicotine withdrawal[79] but differ in side effect profiles (Table 12–2).

The nicotine transdermal patch can cause dermatitis, which generally resolves within 24 hours. Since it is used for 24 hours, nicotine levels may be higher at night in patients using the patch than in smokers. Nicotine gum can cause toxicity if used incorrectly (ie, chewed too rapidly or if more than one piece is chewed at a time).

TABLE 12–2. Pharmacologic Therapy for Smoking Cessation

Product	Brand	Dose	Advantages and Side Effects	Prescription Duration	Pregnancy Category
Gum	Nicorette—2 mg Nicorette DS—4 mg	9–12 pieces/d 9–12 pieces/d	Delays weight gain; acidic beverages interfere with absorption; local irritation, nicotine toxicity if chewed too rapidly	12 wk followed by ≤ 12-wk taper	D
Transdermal patch*	Habitrol Nicoderm Nicoderm CQ Nicotrol Prostep	21, 14, 7 mg/d 21 mg/d 14, 7 mg/d 15, 10, 5 mg/16h 22, 11 mg/d	Maximizes compliance; delivers steady predictable dose; sleep disturbances (fewer with Nicotrol); local irritation	6–8 wk followed by 2–4 wk taper	D
Nasal spray	Nicotrol NS	1–2 sprays/h†	Greater capacity for self-titration; highest abuse potential; local irritation	6–8 wk followed by 4–6 wk taper	D
Inhaler	Nicotrol R inhaler	6–16 cartridges/d	Mimics behavioral aspect of smoking; local irritation	12 wk followed by ≤ 12-wk taper	D
Bupropion SR	Zyban, Wellbutrin	150 mg × 3 d, then 300 mg/d	No nicotine; well tolerated; effective; contraindicated with seizure disorder	12 wk—no taper necessary	B
Clonidine	Catapress	0.1–0.75 mg/d*	No nicotine; hypotension, dry mouth, drowsiness and sedation, and constipation; may not be discontinued abruptly	10 wk followed by by taper	C
Nortriptyline	Pamelor, Aventyl	25–100 mg qhs	No nicotine; drowsiness, dry mouth, hypotension, headache, confusion, urinary retention	16 wk—no taper necessary	D

*Begin at higher dose for heavy smokers (> 20 cigarettes/d) for 4–6 wk; then use lower doses for taper. Lighter smokers may be started on lower doses.
†Maximum dose: 5 sprays/h or 40 sprays/d.

Symptoms of nicotine toxicity include nausea, vomiting, abdominal pain, flushing, dizziness, confusion, and weakness.

Nicotine nasal spray can cause nasal irritation,[65,80] which generally declines with continued use. Irritation is due to the rapid absorption through the nasal mucosa, which mimics the effects of cigarette smoking. The nicotine inhaler can cause local irritation of the mouth and throat and also can produce cough. Some patients have found it embarrassing to use the inhaler, limiting compliance.[65,80] This delivery system has not been studied in patients with asthma or COPD, and its safety in these patients is unknown. In addition, there is a dependency risk with the use of nicotine nasal spray that is intermediate between the other nicotine-delivery systems and cigarette smoking. All nicotine-containing products are rated by the US Food and Drug Administration (FDA) as use-in-pregnancy category D (demonstrated fetal risk, benefits of use may outweigh risk in some patients). The safety of nicotine-replacement therapy for patients with CAD was established in a randomized double-blind placebo-controlled trial that showed no significant increase in adverse events in patients with CAD who were treated with the transdermal nicotine patch for 10 weeks.[81]

Bupropion has been shown to have higher abstinence rates at 12 months than does nicotine replacement (16.4% for transdermal nicotine; 30.3% with bupropion; 35.5% for combination therapy with bupropion plus the patch, but the latter was not statistically significant).[82] The most common side effect with bupropion is insomnia and headache, and it is contraindicated in persons with seizure disorders. Bupropion is rated by the FDA as use-in-pregnancy category B (ie, no evidence of risk, but not proven safe by controlled studies).

Second-Line Drug Therapies

Second-line agents, while shown to be effective, have not been approved by the FDA for smoking cessation. Further, their side effect profiles are less favorable compared with first-line agents; therefore, they should only be used in persons who have failed first-line treatments or in those patients in whom contraindications preclude the use of first-line agents.

Combination nicotine replacement therapy (NRT), in the form of the nicotine patch and either gum or nasal spray is more effective than is mono-

therapy.[83,84] The patch provides a steady level of nicotine while the gum or nasal spray can be used for "breakthrough" cravings. Combination NRT produces higher long-term abstinence rates and is more effective at suppressing withdrawal symptoms. Combination therapy may increase toxicity associated with NRT, and safety data is lacking.[85]

Clonidine, an α_2 adrenergic antagonist, was originally developed to treat hypertension. For smoking cessation, the success rate is twice that for placebo.[86–88] It works primarily in the central nervous system to relieve tobacco withdrawal symptoms (craving, irritability, restlessness).[86] There is evidence that it may be more effective in women, although the reason for this is unclear.[86,87] The use of clonidine in doses ranging from 0.1 to 0.75 g/d can approximately double abstinence rates. Side effects include drowsiness, fatigue and rebound hypertension, dizziness, and tremor if discontinued abruptly. Clonidine can be administered transdermally and orally. The starting dosage is 0.1 mg bid orally, or 0.10 mg/d with the transdermal formulation for 3 to 10 weeks, starting 3 days prior to quit date.[85] Optimum dosing has not been established. Clonidine is rated by the FDA as use-in-pregnancy category C.[85] It is secreted into breast milk, and although hypotensive episodes have not been documented in infants, the long-term significance of exposure is unknown.

Nortriptyline is a tricyclic antidepressant, which has been shown to increase abstinence rates compared with placebo.[89,90] This may occur because withdrawal is often accompanied by depression, and depression is associated with smoking relapse. It should be started 10 to 28 days prior to quit date to allow it to reach steady state levels. Dosing begins at 25 mg/d, increasing gradually to a target of 75 to 100 mg/d.[85] It is rated by the FDA as use-in-pregnancy category D. Its safety in lactating women has not been established. Side effects include drowsiness, dry mouth, and hypotension.

Some studies suggest that women are less successful at quitting smoking than are men, although attempt rates are similar.[91,92] Quit ratios (defined as former smokers/ever-smokers) are higher for men than for women. Women are more likely to relapse at various stages after quitting. Many theories have been proposed to explain these findings including factors of stress, appetite and weight control, differing coping styles, and depression. Perkins[93] suggests that women are less responsive to nicotine replacement than are men. Gender differences in response to nicotine replacement have been documented showing that women are less likely to obtain relief from withdrawal symptoms than are men.[94] The reasons for gender differences are unknown, and more research needs to be done to improve smoking-cessation rates for women. Nevertheless, women do benefit from the smoking cessation strategies as outlined by the clinical practice guidelines Q[85] so the recommendations are the same for both men and women.

ROLE OF THE CLINICIAN

Although the health consequences of smoking are substantial and effective treatments are available, the treatments are underused. Only about half of smokers receive advice from a physician to quit smoking.[95] The Agency for Health Care Research and Quality (AHRQ) developed smoking cessation guidelines[75] for primary care physicians, smoking cessation specialists and health care administrators, insurers, and purchasers. These guidelines recognize that primary care physicians have limited time in which to deal with multiple issues and that smoking cessation is only one of these issues. Important steps for clinicians include inquiring about the smoking status of every patient, advising the patient to quit in a way that is clear and individualized, and offering assistance in the form of counseling, pharmacologic therapy, and follow-up (Table 12–3).

Ask

The smoking status of every patient should be established at each visit (except for never-smokers or long-term former smokers). This can be done easily by including smoking status (ie, current, former, or never-smoker) along with vital signs, or adding a check box to progress note forms.

Advise

Sending a strong, clear, and above all *personalized* message advising smokers to quit is effective in increasing quit rates.[75] Brief advice of less than 3 minutes has been shown to modestly increase quit rates.[75] Patients should be advised of the health risks of smoking as it relates to their personal medical history and/or its effects on family members at home. Self-help materials (eg, pamphlets and audio-

TABLE 12–3. Clinical Approach to Smoking Cessation

Ask about smoking
    Implement a system that documents smoking status at every visit
    Include smoking status with vital signs

Advise smokers to quit
    Be clear
    Speak strongly but do not be judgemental or argumentative
    Personalize advice
    Be emphatic
    Make quitting relevant

Assist smoker with a quit plan
    Emphasize rewards
    If smoker is willing to quit, assist
    If smoker is unwilling to quit, provide motivational intervention
    Set a quit date (ideally within 2 wk)
    Patient should inform family and friends and mobilize support
    Patient should remove cigarettes from work, home, car
    Review previous quit attempts (what worked or led to relapse)
    Anticipate challenges
    Warn about alcohol and other household smokers (increase relapse rate)
    Clarify that total abstinence is essential
    Offer pharmacologic therapy
    Offer intensive counseling if appropriate

Follow-up
    Follow up within 1–2 wk, then again within 1 mo (phone or visit)
    Congratulate success
    Identify problems and anticipate challenges

Prevent relapse
    Congratulate success
    Review health benefits of cessation
    Explore and anticipate problems that may threaten abstinence:
        Weight gain
        Negative mood/depression
        Prolonged nicotine withdrawal
        Lack of social support for cessation

cassettes) can be used as adjuncts to counseling, allowing the physician to spend less time on certain topics. However, self-help materials alone have not been shown to be effective in increasing smoking

---

TABLE 12–4. Enhancing Motivation to Quit Tobacco—the "5 Rs"

Relevance	Encourage the patient to indicate why quitting is personally relevant, being as specific as possible. Motivational information has the greatest impact if it is relevant to a patient's disease status or risk, family or social situation (eg, having children in the home), health concerns, age, gender, and other important patient characteristics (eg, prior quitting experience, personal barriers to cessation).
Risks	The clinician should ask the patient to identify potential negative consequences of tobacco use. The clinician may suggest and highlight those that seem most relevant to the patient. The clinician should emphasize that smoking low-tar/low-nicotine cigarettes or use of other forms of tobacco (eg, smokeless tobacco, cigars, and pipes) will not eliminate these risks. Examples of risks are: • Acute risks: shortness of breath, exacerbation of asthma, harm to pregnancy, impotence, infertility, increased serum carbon monoxide • Long-term risks: heart attacks and strokes, lung and other cancers (larynx, oral cavity, pharynx, esophagus, pancreas, bladder, cervix), chronic obstructive pulmonary diseases (chronic bronchitis and emphysema), long-term disability and need for extended care • Environmental risks: increased risk of lung cancer and heart disease in spouses; higher rates of smoking by children of tobacco users; increased risk for low birth weight, sudden infant death syndrome, asthma, middle ear disease, and respiratory infections in children of smokers
Rewards	The clinician should ask the patient to identify potential benefits of stopping tobacco use. The clinician may suggest and highlight those that seem most relevant to the patient. Examples of rewards follow: • Improved health • Food will taste better • Improved sense of smell • Save money • Feel better about yourself • Home, car, clothing, breath will smell better • Can stop worrying about quitting • Set a good example for children • Have healthier babies and children • Not worry about exposing others to smoke • Feel better physically • Perform better in physical activities • Reduced wrinkling/aging of skin
Roadblocks	The clinician should ask the patient to identify barriers or impediments to quitting and note elements of treatment (problem solving, pharmacotherapy) that could address barriers. Typical barriers might include: • Withdrawal symptoms • Fear of failure • Weight gain • Lack of support • Depression • Enjoyment of tobacco
Repetition	The motivational intervention should be repeated every time an unmotivated patient visits the clinic setting. Tobacco users who have failed in previous quit attempts should be told that most people make repeated quit attempts before they are successful.

From Nides M, Rand C, Dolce J, et al. Weight gain as a function of smoking cessation and 2 mg nicotine gum use among middle-aged smokers with mild lung impairment in the first 2 years of the Lung Health Study. Health Psychol 1994;13:354–61.

cessation rates. For those patients who are not ready to quit smoking, discussing the importance of cessation can lay the groundwork for future attempts.

Assess

Ask all tobacco smokers if they are willing to quit at the present time. For those who are willing, provide assistance (as outlined in the next section). For those who are unwilling to quit, use the opportunity to educate and motivate using the "5Rs" (Table 12–4). The physician is more likely to be successful in motivating a patient to quit if he/she is empathic, nonjudgmental, and not argumentive. The relevance of quitting should be emphasized. The risks, rewards, and roadblocks should be outlined, and this should be repeated in future visits.

Assist

For those smokers who are ready to attempt to stop, assistance comes in three forms: counseling, pharmacologic therapy, and follow-up. Patients should be advised to set a quit date, preferably within 2 weeks. Specific, practical advice should be given on how to live as a former smoker. Patient should advise friends and family of their decision and enlist their help. Homes, cars, and workspaces should be purged of cigarettes. Urges to smoke last 2 to 3 minutes; patients should be prepared and develop a strategy for distraction until the urge subsides. Patients should be encouraged to anticipate situations in which relapse might occur (eg, specific social or stressful situations) and develop coping strategies. Relapse is more common when a spouse also smokes, so patients should consider a joint cessation attempt or develop strategies on how to live with a current smoker. Patients should abstain from alcohol during the quit attempt, since the use of alcohol increases relapse rates.[96]

Patients can be referred for counseling. Both individual and group counseling are equally effective, and patient preference can be the guide to choosing which is most appropriate. Interpersonal contact increases cessation success rates, and it is equally effective whether it comes from a physician, nurse, dentist, social worker, or pharmacist. Optimal counseling programs use four to seven sessions over 8 weeks, lasting more than 10 minutes each session.[75]

Patients should be offered pharmacologic therapy. The AHRQ guidelines recommend trans-

dermal nicotine and nicotine gum; however, all forms of nicotine replacement are equally effective for smoking cessation and differ only in their side effect profiles.[79] As noted above, bupropion also has been shown to be effective for smoking cessation and should be offered where appropriate.

Follow-up should be scheduled within 1 week of cessation (office visit or telephone call), and then within 1 month. The majority of patients relapse within 3 months, and close follow-up during this time encourages abstinence. Follow-up visits should address lapses, response to pharmacologic therapy, and the identification of problems that may increase the risk of relapse. Abstinent patients should be congratulated. Referral to a smoking-cessation specialist should be considered for unsuccessful patients.

Finally, smoking cessation should be addressed with pregnant women and hospitalized patients. During pregnancy, counseling can increase the cessation rate by 70%.[97] Pregnant heavy smokers are less likely to respond to counseling, and pharmacologic therapy may be indicated. There are no studies of efficacy of either nicotine replacement or bupropion during pregnancy for smoking cessation. Benowitz argues for the use of nicotine-replacement therapy during pregnancy in heavy smokers who are unable to quit with intensive counseling alone.[75,98] Nicotine replacement during pregnancy does not expose the fetus to other toxins found in cigarettes and, if used as directed, exposes the fetus to less nicotine and at a slower rate compared with fetuses of mothers who smoke cigarettes.

The smoking cessation guideline does not specifically address the use of bupropion during pregnancy. Although no human studies have been conducted, this medication has not been shown to produce fetal abnormalities in animal studies. Another advantage is that it contains no nicotine. Its safety during lactation has not been established. As with any drug, the risks and the benefits must be carefully considered before prescribing.

Nursing women should be advised to stop smoking. If that is not possible, they should avoid nicotine gum or nasal spray for 2 to 3 hours before breast-feeding. If a transdermal system is used, it should be removed at night, since night-time levels of nicotine in women using a transdermal patch are higher than are levels in women who smoke.[42] Nicotine from replacement products is excreted into the breast milk, but the baby is exposed to less nicotine and at a slower rate than are babies of mothers who smoke cigarettes, with no exposure to additional toxins. Only women who smoke more than 20 cigarettes per day benefit from replacement therapy during lactation. The safety of bupropion during lactation has not been established, but it is excreted in breast milk. The American Academy of Pediatrics considers that antidepressants as a class have uncertain effect on infants.

Many patients are hospitalized for smoking-related (or other) illnesses and are thus in a smoke-free environment. This provides a unique opportunity for patients to begin cessation; encourage its continuance upon discharge.

SUMMARY

Cigarette smoking has a negative impact on health and is responsible for over 400,000 deaths annually in the United States. It impacts the cardiovascular and pulmonary systems, is a leading cause of cancer deaths, and negatively affects reproductive health. Women are more susceptible to the cardiopulmonary effects of cigarette smoking and are less successful at quitting. Clinicians must begin to address this health hazard more effectively and to use the interventions available to combat the most preventable cause of morbidity and mortality.

RESOURCES

The Agency for Health Care Research and Quality
Office of Health Care Information
Suite 501 Executive Office Center
2101 East Jefferson Street
Rockville, Maryland 20852
Telephone: (301) 594-1364
Web site: www.ahrq.gov

The Agency for Health Care Research and Quality (formerly The Agency for Health Care Policy and Research) makes available full guidelines information, quick clinical references, and patient information about smoking cessation.

The American Lung Association
1740 Broadway
New York, New York 10019
Telephone: (212) 315-8700
Web site: www.lungusa.org

The American Lung Association provides information for patients on smoking cessation, including referral to support programs.

The American Cancer Society
Greater Atlanta Office
Lenox Park
2200 Lake Boulevard
Atlanta, Georgia 90319
Telephone: (404) 816-4994
Web site: www.cancer.org

The American Cancer Society provides information on smoking cessation, including referral to support programs.

REFERENCES

1. Centers for Disease Control & Prevention Perspectives in disease prevention & health promotion smoking—attributable mortality and years of potential life lost. United States 1984. MMWR 1997; 46:444–51.

2. MacKenzie T, Bartecchi C, Schrier R. The human costs of tobacco use (second of two parts). N Engl J Med 1994;330:975–80.

3. Pamuk E, Makuc D, Heck K, et al. Socioeconomic status and health chartbook; Health, United States, 1998. Hyattsville (MD): National Center for Health Statistics; 1998.

4. Centers for Disease Control and Prevention. Cigarette smoking among adults—United States, 1994. MMWR Morb Mortal Wkly Rep 1996;45:588–90.

5. Centers for Disease Control and Prevention. Tobacco use among high school students—United States, 1997. MMWR Morb Mortal Wkly Rep 1998;47:229–33.

6. Pamuk E, Makuc D, Heck K, et al. Socioeconomic status and health chartbook. Health, United States 1998. Hyattsville (MD): National Center for Health Statistics.

7. US Department of Health and Human Services. Preventing tobacco use among young people: a report of the Surgeon General. Atlanta (GA): US Department of Health and Human Services, Public Health Services, CDC; 1994.

8. Bartecchi C, MacKenzie T, Schrier R. The human costs of tobacco use (first of two parts). N Engl J Med 1994;330:907–12.

9. Centers for Disease Control and Prevention. Selected cigarette smoking initiation and quitting behaviors among high school students—United States, 1997. MMWR Morb Mortal Wkly Rep 1998;47:386–9.

10. Centers for Disease Control and Prevention. Cigarette smoking–attributable mortality and years of potential life lost—United States, 1990.

11. Centers for Disease Control and Prevention. Reducing the health consequences of smoking; 25 years of progress: a report of the Surgeon General, 1989.

12. Vriz O, Nesbitt S, Krause L. Smoking is associated with higher cardiovascular risk in young women than in men: the Tecumseh Blood Pressure Study. J Hypertens 1997;15(2):127–34.

13. Prescott E, Hippe M, Schnohr P, et al. Smoking and risk of myocardial infarction in women and men: longitudinal population study. BMJ 1998;316: 1043–7.

14. Njolstad I, Arnesen E, Lund-Larsen PG. Smoking, serum lipids, blood pressure, and sex differences in myocardial infarction. A 12-year follow-up of the Finnmark Study. Circulation 1996;93:450–6.

15. Kannel WB, Higgins M. Smoking and hypertension as predictors of cardiovascular risk in population studies. J Hypertens Suppl 1990;8:S3–8.

16. Centers for Disease Control and Prevention. The health benefits of smoking cessation: a report of the Surgeon General, 1990. p. 1247–53.

17. Dobson AJ, Alexander HM, Heller RF, Lloyd DM. How soon after quitting smoking does risk of heart attack decline? J Clin Epidemiol 1991;44:1247–53.

18. Mishell D. Cardiovascular risks: perception vs. reality. Contraception 1999;59:21–24S.

19. Bone RC. Pulmonary and critical care medicine. St. Louis: Mosby Year Book; 1998.

20. Almirall J, Gonzalez CA, Balanzo X, Bolibar I. Proportion of community-acquired pneumonia cases attributable to tobacco smoking. Chest 1999;116: 375–9.

21. Carter R, Nicotra B, Huber G. Differing effects of airway obstruction on physical work capacity and ventilation in men and women with COPD. Chest 1994;106:1730–9.

22. Chen Y, Horne SI, Dosman JA. Increased susceptibility to lung dysfunction in female smokers. Am Rev Respir Dis 1991;143:1224–30.

23. Xu X, Li B, Wang L. Gender differences in smoking effects on adults pulmonary function. Eur Respir J 1994;7:477–83.

24. Prescott E, Bjerg AM, Andersen PK, et al. Gender difference in smoking effects on lung function and risk of hospitalization for COPD: results from a Danish longitudinal population study. Eur Respir J 1997;10:822–7.

25. Kanner RE, Connett JE, Altose MD, et al. Gender difference in airway hyperresponsiveness in smokers with mild COPD. The Lung Health Study. Am J Respir Crit Care Med 1994;150:956–61.

26. Gold DR, Wang X, Wypij D, et al. Effects of cigarette smoking on lung function in adolescent boys and girls. N Engl J Med 1996;335:931–7.

27. Mordlund LA, Carstennsen J, Pershagen G. Cancer incidence in female smokers: a 26-year follow-up. Int J Cancer 1997;73:625–8.

28. Landis S, Murray T, Bolden S, Wingo P. Cancer statistics, 1999. CA Cancer J Clin 1999;49:8–31.

29. Risch HA, Howe GR, Jain M, et al. Are female smokers at higher risk for lung cancer than male smokers? A case-control analysis by histologic type. Am J Epidemiol 1993;138:281–93.

30. Harris RE, Zang EA, Anderson JI. Race and sex differences in lung cancer risk associated with cigarette smoking. Int J Epidemiol 1993;22:592–9.

31. Baldini EH, Strauss GM. Women and lung cancer. Waiting to exhale. Chest 1997;112:229–34S.

32. Taioli E, Wynder EL. Re: endocrine factors and adenocarcinoma of the lung in women. J Natl Cancer Inst 1994;86:869–70.

33. Centers for Disease Control and Prevention. Smoking-attributable mortality and years of potential life lost—United States, 1984. MMWR Morb Mortal Wkly Rep 1999;48:131–8.

34. McCann MF, Irwin DE, Walton LA, et al. Nicotine and cotinine in the cervical mucus of smokers, passive smokers, and nonsmokers. Cancer Epidemiol Biomarkers Prev 1992;1:125–9.

35. Prokopczyk B, Cox JE, Hoffmann D, Waggoner SE. Identification of tobacco-specific carcinogen in the cervical mucus of smokers and nonsmokers. J Natl Cancer Inst 1997;89:868–73.

36. Newcomb PA, Carbone PP. The health consequences of smoking. Cancer. Med Clin North Am 1992; 76:305–31.

37. Ambrosone CB, Freudenheim JL, Graham S, et al. Cigarette smoking, *N*-acetyltransferase 3 genetic polymorphisms, and breast cancer risk. JAMA 1996;276:1494–501.

38. Centers for Disease Control and Prevention. Medical-care expenditures attributable to cigarette smoking during pregnancy—United States, 1995. MMWR Morb Mortal Wkly Rep 1997;Nov 7: 1048–50.

39. HaKansson A, Lendahls L, Petersson C. Which women stop smoking? A population based study of 403 pregnant smokers. Acta Obstet Gynecol Scand 1999;78:217–34.

40. Liston J. Breastfeeding and the use of recreational drugs—alcohol, caffeine, nicotine and marijuana. Breastfeed Rev 1998;6(2):27–30.

41. Hokinson JM, Schanler RJ, Fraley JK, Garza C. Milk production by mothers of premature infants: influence of cigarette smoking. Pediatrics 1992;90: 934–8.

42. Schatz B. Nicotine replacement products: implications for the breast-feeding mother. J Hum Lact 1998;14(2):161–3.

43. Pavers NG, Slusser W. Breastfeeding update 2: clinical lactation management. Pediatr Rev 1997;18:147–161.

44. Baron J, Vecchia C, Levi F. The antiestrogenic effect of cigarette smoking in women. Am J Obstet Gynecol 1990;162:502–14.

45. Cooper GS, Sandler DP, Bohlig M. Active and passive smoking and the occurrence of natural menopause. Epidemiology 1999;10:771–3.

46. Kaufman DW, Stone D, Rosenberg L, et al. Cigarette smoking and age at natural menopause. Am J Public Health 1980;70:420–2.

47. Jick H, Porter J. Relation between smoking and age of natural menopause. Report from the Boston Collaborative Drug Surveillance Program, Boston University Medical Center. Lancet 1977;1:1354–5.

48. Midgette AS, Baron JA. Cigarette smoking and the risk of natural menopause. Epidemiology 1990; 1:474–80.

49. Lindquist O, Bengtsson C. Menopausal age in relation to smoking. Acta Med Scand 1979;205:73–7.

50. Adena MA, Gallagher HG. Cigarette smoking and the age at menopause. Ann Hum Biol 1982;9(2):121–30.

51. Andersen FS, Transbol I, Christiansen C. Is cigarette smoking a promoter of the menopause? Acta Med Scand 1982;212:137–9.

52. Bradbury J. Mechanism found for smoking-induced early menopause. Lancet. 2001;358:215.

53. Cornuz J, Feskanich D, Willet WC, Colditz GA. Smoking, smoking cessation and risk of hip fracture in women. Am J Med 1999;106:311–4.

54. Grainge MJ, Coupland CA, Cliffe SJ, et al. Cigarette smoking, alcohol and caffeine consumption, and bond mineral density in postmenopausal women. The Nottingham EPIC Study Group. Osteoporos Int 1998;8:355–63.

55. Forsen L, Bjartveit K, Bjorndal A, et al. Ex-smokers and risk of hip fracture. Am J Public Health 1998; 88:1481–3.

56. la Vecchia C, Negri E, Levi F, Baron JA. Cigarette smoking, body mass and other risk factors for fractures of the hip in women. Int J Epidemiol 1991; 20:671–7.

57. Kiel DP, Baron JA, Anderson JJ, et al. Smoking eliminates the protective effect of oral estrogens on the risk for hip fracture among women. Ann Intern Med 1992;116:716–21.

58. Law MR, Hackshaw AK. A meta-analysis of cigarette smoking, bone mineral density and risk of hip fracture: recognition of a major effect. BMJ 1997;315: 841–6.

59. Krall E, Dawson-Hughes B. Smoking increases bone loss and decreases intestinal calcium absorption. J Bone Min Res 1999;14(2):215–20.

60. Little RE, Hook EB. Maternal alcohol and tobacco consumption and their association with nausea and vomiting during pregnancy. Acta Obstet Gynecol Scand 1979;58:15–7.

61. Spangler JG. Smoking and hormone-related disorders. Prim Care 1999;26:499–511.

62. Kadunce OP. Cigarette smoking: risk factor for premature facial wrinkling. Ann Intern Med 1991;114: 840–4.

63. Shiffman S, Mason KM, Henningfield JE. Tobacco dependence treatments: review and prospectus. Ann Rev Public Health 1998;19:335–58.

64. Benowitz N. Cigarette smoking and nicotine addiction. Med Clin North Am 1992;76(2).

65. Thompson GH, Hunter DA. Nicotine replacement therapy. Ann Pharmacother 1998;32:1062–75.

66. French SA, Perry CL, Leon GR, Fulkerson JA. Weight concerns, dieting behavior, and smoking initiation among adolescents: a prospective study. Am J Public Health 1994;84:1818–20.

67. Perkins KA, Levine MD, Marcus M, Shiffman S. Addressing women's concerns about weight gain due to smoking cessation. J Subst Abuse Treat 1997; 14:173–82.

68. Williamson DF, Madans J, Anda RF, et al. Smoking cessation and severity of weight gain in a national cohort. N Engl J Med 1991;324:739–45.

69. Marcus BH, Albrecht AE, King TK, et al. The efficacy of exercise as an aid for smoking cessation in women. A randomized controlled trial. Arch Intern Med 1999;159.

70. Marcus BH, King TK, Albrecht AE, et al. Rationale, design and baseline data for commit to quit: an exercise efficacy trial for smoking cessation among women. Prev Med 1997;26:586–97.

71. Gross J, Stitzer ML, Maldonado J. Nicotine replacement: effects on post-cessation weight gain. J Consult Clin Psychol 1989;57:87–92.

72. Nides M, Rand C, Dolce J, et al. Weight gain as a function of smoking cessation and 2 mg nicotine gum use among middle aged smokers with mild lung impairment in the first 2 years of the Lung Health Study. Health Psychol 1994;13:354–61.

73. Hurt RD, Sachs DP, Glover ED, et al. A comparison of sustained-release bupropion and placebo for smoking cessation. N Engl J Med 1997;337: 1195–202.

74. Hall SM, Tunstall CD, Vila KL, Duffy J. Weight gain prevention and smoking cessation: cautionary findings. Am J Public Health 1992;82:799–803.

75. Fiore MC, Bailey WC, Cohen SJ, et al. Treating tobacco use and dependence. Clinical practice guideline. Rockville (MD): U.S. Department of Health and Human Services. Public Health Service. June 2000.

76. Law M, Tang JL. An analysis of the effectiveness of interventions intended to help people stop smoking. Arch Intern Med 1995;155:1933–41.

77. Tang JL, Law M, Wald N. How effective is nicotine replacement therapy in helping people to stop smoking? BMJ 1994;308:21–6.

78. Silagy C, Mant D, Fowler G, Lodge M. Meta-analysis on efficacy of nicotine replacement therapies in smoking cessation. Lancet 1994;343:139–42.

79. Hajek P, West R, Foulds J, et al. Randomized comparative trial of Nicotine Polacrilex, a transdermal patch, nasal spray and an inhaler. Arch Intern Med 1999;159:2033–8.

80. Manufacturer's product information. Pharmaciq, Inc. Sweden. Approved 1996.

81. Joseph AM. The safety of transdermal nicotine as an aid to smoking cessation in patients with cardiac disease. N Engl J Med 1996;335:1792–8.

82. Jorenby D, Leischow SJ, Nides MA, et al. A controlled trial of sustained-release bupropion, a nicotine patch, or both for smoking cessation. N Engl J Med 1999;340:685–91.

83. Konitzer M, Boutsen M, Dramaiz M, et al. Combined use of nicotine patch and gum in smoking cessation: a placebo controlled clinical trial. Prev Med 1995;24:41–7.

84. Blondal T, Gudmundsson LJ, Olafsdottir I, et al. Nicotine nasal spray with nicotine patch for smoking cessation: randomised trial with six year follow up. BMJ. 1999;318:285–9.

85. Smoking cessation guideline.

86. Gourley SG, Benowitz NL. Is clonidine an effective smoking cessation therapy? Drugs 50(2):197–207.

87. Glassman AH, Stetner F, Walsh BT, et al. Heavy smokers, smoking cessation, and clonidine: results of a double-blind randomized trial. JAMA 1988;259: 2863–6.

88. Gourlay SG, Stead LF, Benowitz NL. Clonidine for smoking cessation (Cochrane Review). In: The Cochrane Library, 3, 2001. Oxford.

89. Hughes JR, Stead LF, Lancaster T. Antidepressants for smoking cessation (Cochrane Review). In: The Cochrane Library, 3, 2001. Oxford.

90. Prochazka AV, Weaver MJ, Keller RT. A randomized trial of nortriptyline for smoking cessation. Arch Intern Med 1998;158:2035–9.

91. Wetter D, Kenford SL, Smith SS, et. al. Gender differences in smoking cessation. J Consult Clin Psychol 1999;67:555–62.

92. Osler M. Gender and determinants of smoking cessation: a longitudinal study. Prev Med 1999;29:57–62.

93. Perkins K. Nicotine discrimination in men and women. Pharmacol Biochem Behav 1999;64:295–9.

94. Wetter DW, Fiore MC, Young TB, et al. Gender differences in reponse to nicotine replacement therapy: objective and subjective indexes of tobacco withdrawal. Exp Clin Psychopharmacol 1999;7:135–44.

95. Center for Disease Control and Prevention. Physician and other health care professional counseling of smokers to quit—United States, 1991. MMWR Morb Mortal Wkly Rep 1993;42:854–7.

96. Humfleet G, Munoz R, Sees S, et al. History of alcohol or drug problems, current use of alcohol or marijuana, and success in quitting smoking. Addict Behav 1999;24(1):149-54.

97. Mullen PD. Maternal smoking during pregnancy and evidence-based intervention to promote cessation. Prim Care 1999;26:577–89.

98. Benowitz N. Nicotine replacement therapy during pregnancy. JAMA 1991;265:3174–7.

13

GENETIC TESTING FOR CANCER

Joyce L. Seldon, MS, CGC, and Patricia A. Ganz, MD

For women, the lifetime risk of developing cancer (excluding nonmelanoma skin cancer) is approximately 1 in 3, and cancer is second only to heart disease as the leading cause of death among women. A woman's lifetime risk of developing breast or colon cancers is approximately 1 in 8 and 1 in 18, respectively.[1] As with any prevalent disease, distinguishing familial cancer from sporadic occurrences in a family is difficult. Inherited cancer syndromes usually are characterized by early age at onset and multiple affected family members in multiple generations with the same or associated cancers. With cancer usually occurring in middle-aged or older women, cancer aggregates at early ages are much less likely to be due to chance association.[1]

Cancer is not a single disease. It is a common set of diseases characterized by uncontrolled cellular growth. All cancer is "genetic" in that the uncontrolled proliferation of cells is the result of numerous genetic mutations. It is well established that carcinogenic agents cause genetic mutations. Furthermore, individuals belonging to cancer-prone families can "inherit" an increased susceptibility to the development of cancer. The malignant transformation of a cell is not the result of one mutation, but, rather, it is a complex process resulting from numerous molecular mutations. The rapid advancement of molecular biology has allowed a recognition that these molecular mutations fall into at least three distinct categories: oncogenes, tumor suppressor genes, and deoxyribonucleic acid (DNA) repair genes.

Proto-oncogenes are normal cellular genes that play an essential role in the normal life of a cell. When inappropriately activated as **oncogenes**, they cause disregulation of growth and differentiation pathways enhancing the probability of neoplastic transformation.[2] They can be seen as "gain-of-function" mutations that permanently signal the cell to divide.

Tumor suppressor genes are normal cellular genes that, when inactivated, lead to a disturbance of cell proliferation and the development of neoplasia. These "loss-of-function" genes usually impose some constraint on the cell cycle or cell growth, and the release of the constraint is tumorigenic.[3]

Deoxyribonucleic acid **mismatch repair genes** can recognize, excise, and correct mismatched DNA sequences caused by either DNA polymerase slippage on the template strand during replication or incorrect base pairings (eg, an incorrect A-C pairing rather than the correct A-T pairing). Heterozygous cells have normal or nearly normal mismatch repair activity; however, loss of heterozygosity of the wild-type allele results in cells with defective mismatch repair.[4–6]

It is important for physicians to identify high-risk individuals for primary and secondary breast, ovarian, and colon cancer. Genetic testing and counseling is complex for both affected and unaffected individuals who are considering testing for inherited cancer genes. In the absence of studies showing the lack of efficacy of surveillance in high-risk individuals, it is presumed that close cancer surveillance can possibly diagnose cancer at its early stages when prognosis and treatment options are best, decreasing the morbidity and mortality rate.[7,8] Knowledge of genetic risk also may provide motivation to consider chemopreventive interventions, which hopefully will prevent cancer rather than treat it. Predisposition testing also can have a significant impact on subsequent behavior and life decisions. For example, individuals from families with known mutations who are *not* carriers for these mutations might be spared unnecessary diagnostic and screening tests or extreme surgical procedures such as prophylactic mastectomy or oophorectomy.

BREAST AND OVARIAN CANCER

An estimated 5 to 10% of breast and ovarian cancers have an inherited component. Familial breast cancer is characterized by young age at diagnosis, bilateral tumors, multiple affected individuals in multiple generations, ancestry, and a strong association with ovarian cancer and male breast cancer. The most important contribution to inherited breast and ovarian cancers comes from mutations in the BRCA1 and BRCA2 genes, which account for an estimated 84% of hereditary breast and ovarian cancers.[9] The function of the BRCA1 and BRCA2 genes is not precisely known, but they may act as tumor suppressor genes.[10] In 1994 and 1995, the BRCA1 and BRCA2 genes, respectively, were isolated by positional cloning methods.[11–13] BRCA1 and BRCA2 have autosomal dominant inheritance with incomplete penetrance. Genetic linkage studies suggest that approximately 45 to 52% and 35% of breast cancer families are linked to BRCA1 and BRCA2, respectively.[9,14] However, the existence of other breast and ovarian cancer susceptibility genes (BRCA3, BRCA4, etc.) is suspected by the identification of a high incidence of breast cancer within families that do not show linkage to either BRCA1 or BRCA2.[9,15,16]

After the observation of a BRCA1 mutation (185delAG frameshift) in several Ashkenazi Jewish families with breast/ovarian cancer, a study was conducted in 858 individuals of Ashkenazi Jewish ancestry seeking genetic testing for conditions unrelated to cancer, and in 815 control individuals who were unselected for ethnic origin. The study found that almost 1% of the Ashkenazi Jewish population carried this mutation as compared with none of the controls. These results suggest that 1 in 100 women of Ashkenazi descent may be at increased risk of developing breast/ovarian cancer.[17] Subsequent large-scale population studies found that over 2% of Ashkenazi Jews carry mutations for BRCA1 or BRCA2 mutations (185delAG, 5382insC, and 6174delT) that confer increased risks for breast, ovarian, and prostate cancers.[18,19]

Risk of Cancer in Mutation Carriers

Women who carry a mutation for either BRCA1 or BRCA2 have a significantly increased risk of developing breast and ovarian cancers; however, estimates regarding the degree of risk for these women are still

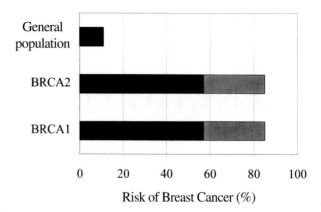

FIGURE 13–1. Approximate risk of breast cancer by age 70 years. Light grey shaded areas represent upper and lower limits of current breast cancer risk estimates for BRCA1 and BRCA2 carriers.

being refined, and they may vary depending on the specific mutation identified and other modifying factors. According to several different studies, the risk of breast cancer by age 70 years for a BRCA1 or BRCA2 carrier who is from a family with multiple affected members with breast/ovarian cancer ranges from 76 to 87%.[9,14,20–22] The risk for ovarian cancer in a woman with the same family history ranges from 44 to 63% for carriers of BRCA1 mutations, but it is much lower (approximately 27%) for those who carry BRCA2 mutations.[9,20–22] However, one large population-based study reported much lower estimates of risk. This study tested over 5,000 Ashkenazi Jewish participants for three common BRCA1 and BRCA2 mutations and found that the risk of breast cancer for carriers was 56% by age 70 years. The risk for ovarian cancer for BRCA1 and BRCA2 carriers of these three mutations was 16% by age 70 years.[19] Thus, risk estimates for breast and ovarian cancer are usually presented as ranges to patients; these ranges are illustrated in Figures 13–1 and 13–2, respectively.

Probability of Detecting a Mutation

Table 13–1 presents the modeled probability of carrying a BRCA1 or BRCA2 mutation in women with breast cancer before age 50 years or ovarian cancer at any age, and at least one first- or second-degree relative with either diagnosis.[23] These data could be useful in identifying women who are likely to carry a predisposing mutation in BRCA1 or BRCA2, as in Figure 13–3. Figure 13–3 illustrates an example of a three-generation pedigree with two affected women with breast cancer. Individual III:1 is a 30-year-old

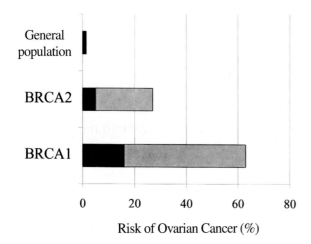

FIGURE 13–2. Approximate risk of ovarian cancer by age 80 years. Light grey shaded areas represent upper and lower limits of current ovarian cancer risk estimates for BRCA1 and BRCA2 carriers.

female who went to her doctor seeking genetic testing because she was concerned about her risk for breast/ovarian cancer and was considering prophylactic surgeries. We calculate her risk of being positive for a BRCA1/BRCA2 mutation by first calculating her mother's risk (because the data apply to affected women, not unaffected women). We find that her

mother, individual II:1, is alive at 53 years of age with a previous diagnosis of bilateral breast cancer at 46 years of age. Our patient's maternal grandmother died at 45 years of age from breast cancer that was diagnosed at 44 years of age. Looking at Table 13–1 we see that individual II:1 fits two risk factors ("Any relative with breast cancer < 50 years?" and "Proband: bilateral breast cancer or ovarian cancer?") from this modeled probability, which gives her a 51% chance of carrying a gene for BRCA1 or BRCA2. Therefore, given Mendelian autosomal dominant inheritance for BRCA1/BRCA2, individual III:1 has an approximate 25.5% risk of carrying a gene for BRCA1/BRCA2 (half of her mother's risk, which is 51%). Risk calculations, however, are not the only factors to discuss with this patient. She also needs a complete discussion of the risks, benefits, and limitations of cancer genetic susceptibility testing as well as informed consent and a discussion of who in her family should have testing first.

COLORECTAL CANCER

Colorectal cancer is the third most common cancer in women, affecting approximately 68,000 women yearly.[1] An estimated 5% of colon cancers can be

TABLE 13–1. Modeled Probabilities of Women with Breast Cancer Under 50 Years of Age Carrying a Mutation in BRCA1 or BRCA2[*]

Any Relative with Breast Cancer < 50 Yr?	Any Relative with Ovarian Cancer?	Proband: Bilateral Breast Cancer or Ovarian Cancer?	Proband: Breast Cancer < 40 Yr?	BRCA1 Mutation Probability (%)	BRCA2 Mutation Probability (%)	BRCA1 or BRCA2 Mutation Probability (%)
•				10.1	14.5	25
•			•	28.2	11.6	40
•		•		41.5	9.5	51
•		•	•	71.1	4.7	76
	•			22.9	12.5	35
	•		•	22.9	12.5	35
	•	•		65.0	5.7	71
	•	•	•	65.0	5.7	71
•	•			22.9	12.5	35
•	•		•	50.9	7.9	59
•	•	•		65.0	5.7	71
•	•	•	•	86.7	2.2	89

[*]Based on an analysis of women with at least one first- or second-degree relative with ovarian or breast cancer before 50 years of age. Reproduced with permission from Frank T, Manley SA, Olopade OI, et al. Sequence analysis of BRCA1 and BRCA2: correlations of mutations with family history and ovarian cancer risk. J Clin Oncol 1998;16:2417–25.

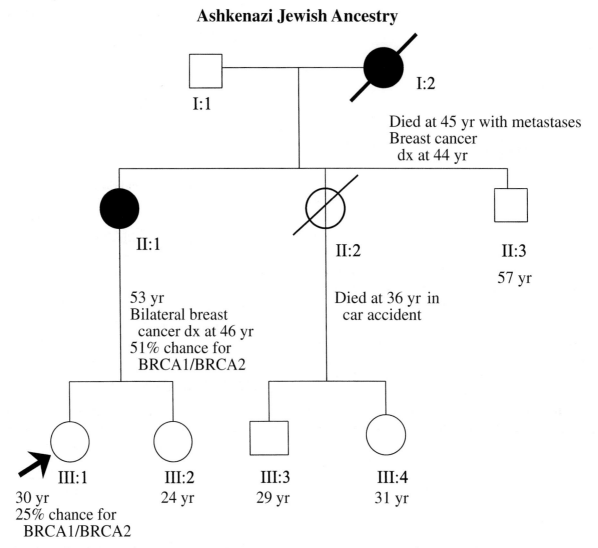

Ashkenazi Jewish Ancestry

FIGURE 13–3. A three-generation pedigree. Individual III:1 is the initial patient seeking genetic testing because she is concerned about her risk for breast and ovarian cancer and is considering prophylactic surgery. Note that testing should be done on an affected individual first, if possible, to establish informative testing for unaffected family members. The ideal individual to test first in this pedigree would be II:1 because she is still alive and is a first-degree relative to the initial patient. Also note that the modelled probability of detecting a BRCA1 or BRCA2 mutation (using Table 13–1) in individual II:1 is 51%. Therefore, the a priori chance of detecting a BRCA1 or BRCA2 mutation in her daughter is 25.5% (half of her mother's risk given autosomal dominant inheritance). If individual II:1 tests positive for a mutation in either BRCA1 or BRCA2, then the chance that either III:1 or her sister, III:2, are positive for the same mutation is 50% each. Additionally, a positive test result in II:1 would mean that the chances for II:3, III:3, and III:4 to test positive for the same mutation would be 50%, 25%, and 25%, respectively. dx = diagnosis.

attributed to highly penetrant autosomal dominant susceptibility syndromes.[24,25] The most common syndrome is hereditary nonpolyposis colorectal cancer syndrome (HNPCC), which is also known as Lynch syndrome. The rare familial adenomatous polyposis (FAP) also constitutes a small percent of inherited colon cancers.

Hereditary Nonpolyposis Colorectal Cancer
The HNPCC syndrome is characterized by early-onset colon cancer (the average age of onset is approximately 44 years) with a proximal predominance (approximately 70% are proximal to the splenic flecture), multiple synchronous and metasynchronous colorectal cancers (approximately 45%

TABLE 13–2. Amsterdam Criteria for Hereditary Nonpolyposis Colorectal Cancer

1. Three or more family members with colorectal carcinoma, two of whom are first-degree relatives
2. At least two generations represented
3. At least one individual younger than 50 yr at diagnosis

Adapted from Vasen HFA, Mecklin J-P, Meerakhan P, Lynch HT. The International Collaborative Group on Hereditary Non-polyposis Colorectal Cancer. Dis Colon Rectum 1991;34:424–5.

within 10 years after incomplete colonic resection), and other associated cancers such as breast, ovary, stomach, small bowel, urinary tract (ureter and renal pelvis), and endometrium.[26,27] In 1991 an international panel meeting in Amsterdam put forth a list of criteria (Table 13–2) for the diagnosis of HNPCC.[28] Limitations of the Amsterdam criteria are that they are too restrictive in that (1) other malignancies besides colon cancer are not considered and (2) small families are not likely to meet the criteria.

Hereditary nonpolyposis colorectal cancer shows genetic heterogeneity, and the syndrome is associated with mutations in the hMSH2 gene on chromosome 2p21–22,[29,30] the hMLH1 gene on chromosome 3p21,[31,32] the hPMS1 gene on chromosome 2q31–33,[33] and the hPMS2 gene on chromosome 7p22.[33] All genes cloned in association with HNPCC have been DNA mismatch repair genes. These four genes together account for nearly 70% of mutations found in HNPCC families (Table 13–3).[34]

The lifetime risks of cancer in HNPCC mutation carriers are approximated as follows: colorectal (78%), endometrial (43%), stomach (19%), biliary tract (18%), urinary tract (10%), and ovarian (9%).[35] The actual contribution of breast cancer to this syndrome is controversial, and risk estimates are not known. These risks are based on results from gene-positive HNPCC families and may be subject to ascertainment bias.

MICROSATELLITE INSTABILITY
Microsatellites are repetitive DNA sequences that naturally occur and vary from one individual to another. Microsatellite instability (MIN) refers to the expanded pattern of microsatellites found in tumor tissues. In colon cancers from patients with HNPCC it has been shown that microsatellites carry mutations that are not found in the germline. Microsatellite instability is found infrequently in

TABLE 13–3. DNA Mismatch Repair Genes Involved in Hereditary Nonpolyposis Colorectal Cancer

Gene	Chromosome Locus	HNPCC Families with Mutation (%)
hMLH1	3p21	33
hMSH2	2p21–22	31
hPMS1	2q31–33	2
hPMS2	7p22	4

DNA = deoxyribonucleic acid; HNPCC = hereditary nonpolyposis colorectal cancer.
Adapted from Liu B, Parsons R, Papadopoulos N, et al. Analysis of mismatch repair genes in hereditary non-polyposis colorectal cancer patients. Nat Med 1996;2:169–74.

sporadic colon cancers (10 to 15%),[36] but it is common in HNPCC kindreds (92%)[34] and young patients less than 35 years of age (58%).[37] Testing for MIN can be used to identify families at high risk for HNPCC. In 1997, the Bethesda criteria were established for testing colorectal tumors for MIN as follows: (1) individuals with cancer in families that meet the Amsterdam criteria (above);[28] (2) individuals with two HNPCC-related cancers, including synchronous and metachronous colorectal cancers or extracolonic cancers; (3) individuals with colorectal cancer and a first-degree relative with colorectal cancer and/or HNPCC-related extracolonic cancer and/or a colorectal adenoma—one of the cancers diagnosed at less than 45 years, and the adenoma diagnosed at less than 40 years; (4) individuals with colorectal cancer or endometrial cancer diagnosed at less than 45 years; (5) individuals with right-sided colorectal cancer with an undifferentiated pattern (solid/cribriform) on histopathology or signet-ring cell type diagnosed at less than 45 years; and (6) individuals with adenomas diagnosed at less than 40 years.[38]

Familial Adenomatous Polyposis
Familial adenomatous polyposis, also known as Gardner's syndrome, is a rare autosomal dominant condition with clinical heterogeneity that is expected to demonstrate complete penetrance. Classically, it is characterized by the progressive development of hundreds (sometimes thousands) of adenomatous colorectal polyps, some of which inevitably progress to cancer. Most of these polyps are usually less than 5 mm in diameter and so thickly grown that they carpet the entire surface of

TABLE 13–4. Other Inherited Cancer Syndromes

Syndrome	Features and Associated Cancers	Inheritance	Gene
Ataxia-telangiectasia	Neurologic degeneration, cerebellar ataxia, telangiectasia, immunodeficiency, sensitivity to ionizing radiation, leukemias, and lymphomas; breast cancer in heterozygotes	Autosomal recessive	ATM
Li-Fraumeni syndrome	Sarcoma, breast cancer, brain cancer, adrenocortical tumors, and leukemia	Autosomal dominant	p53
Cowden syndrome	Breast cancer, thyroid cancer, hamartomas, cerebellar gangliocytomas, macrocephaly, and mucocutaneous lesions	Autosomal dominant	MMAC1 PTEN
Peutz-Jeghers syndrome	Melanin spots of lips, buccal mucosa, and digits; GI hamartomatous polyps (especially in the jejunum); colon, breast, cervical, ovarian, testicular, and pancreatic cancers	Autosomal dominant	STK11

GI = gastrointestinal.

the colon. The clinical diagnosis of FAP is the finding of 100 or more colorectal adenomas.[39] Other diagnostic features include jaw and sebaceous cysts, osteomata, retinal lesion known as congenital hypertrophy of the retinal pigment, and desmoid tumors.

In 1991, the gene responsible for FAP, known as the adenomatous polyposis coli (APC) gene on chromosome 5q, was identified and characterized.[40–43] A study of 79 unrelated patients with FAP searched for germline mutations in the APC gene. Sixty-seven percent carried germline mutations, and, of the mutations found, 92% resulted in the truncation of the APC protein.[44] Given the high penetrance for this disorder and early age of onset, all affected individuals should be tested for mutations in the APC gene and appropriate relatives should be tested.

DIFFERENTIAL DIAGNOSIS OF INHERITED CANCER SYNDROMES

Several other rare syndromes also may contribute to hereditary colon, breast, and/or ovarian cancer. A patient's medical and family histories must be assessed for these syndromes since a differential diagnosis is necessary. The syndromes, patterns of inheritance, genetic locations, and typical features are listed in Table 13–4.[45]

Family History and Testing

In the context of cancer-susceptibility testing, the careful recording of the family history, both paternal and maternal, is crucial. A three-generation pedigree (see Figure 13–3) is important for the analysis of patterns of inheritance and should include the following at minimum: both affected and unaffected relatives, type of primary cancer, second primary tumors, age at diagnosis, current age of individual, and, if deceased, age and cause of death.[46] To the greatest extent possible, cancer history confirmation should be done by obtaining medical records, pathology or autopsy reports, or death certificates.[47] The interpretation of the family history is important to determine whether or not to suspect a possible hereditary cancer syndrome. Features of a family history such as early age at diagnosis and multiple affected individuals demonstrating autosomal dominant inheritance are some of the "red flags" for a possible hereditary syndrome (Table 13–5).

Genetic cancer susceptibility testing is complex, and, whenever possible, informative genetic cancer susceptibility testing should begin with an affected relative at high risk to carry a gene. A negative test result in an affected individual from a high-risk family has the following explanations: a false-negative result; a different (untested) gene(s) is responsible; the familial clustering is actually sporadic and due to chance event; or this is a family with a hereditary cancer syndrome, but the patient initially tested is a sporadic case. A positive test result allows for informative testing of other affected and unaffected relatives. Therefore, testing of an unaffected individual is most informative in the

TABLE 13–5. Family History Assessment: When to Suspect a Possible Hereditary Syndrome

Younger age of onset than is typical for type of cancer (eg, < 50 yr for breast and colon cancers)

Multiple affected family members (usually two or more) with the same type of cancer or cancers that are known to be related in certain syndromes (eg, colon, ovarian, and uterine cancers in HNPCC families)

Multiple generations of related affected individuals

Presence of rare cancers (eg, breast cancer in males)

Excess of multifocal or bilateral cancers

Multiple primary cancers in the same individual (eg, breast and ovarian cancer primaries in the same woman)

Physical findings that may suggest a hereditary syndrome (eg, macrocephaly and mucocutaneous lesions found in Cowden syndrome)

context of a known mutation; however, this is not always possible (see Figures 13–3 and 13–4). A negative test result in an unaffected individual is only a true-negative if a mutation is known in the family.

The American Society of Clinical Oncology, the National Society of Genetic Counselors, the American Society of Human Genetics, and the National Action Plan on Breast Cancer all have issued position papers on cancer genetic-susceptibility testing.[48–51] Cancer-susceptibility testing should only be performed after comprehensive genetic counseling and informed consent. Genetic counseling is the process of communicating genetic, medical, and scientific knowledge into understandable and practical information for the patient, so that he or she can make an educated and fully informed choice about testing. Genetic counseling should be provided before, during, and after susceptibility testing. The complexities and special nature of genetic cancer susceptibility testing also require the need for informed consent. Proper informed consent should include the following: discussion of basic principles of cancer biology; discussion of basic genetic concepts such as inheritance, genes, mutations, patterns of inheritance, variable expression of genes, heterogeneity, polymorphisms, and penetrance of genes; risk assessment; implications of a positive, negative, or ambiguous result and informative testing; limitations; possible benefits of testing; genetic risk to

relatives and transmission of mutation to offspring; accuracy of testing; costs; risk of psychological distress and strain on family relationships; risk of employment/insurance discrimination and stigmatization; confidentiality and sharing of results; options, risks, benefits, and limitations of medical surveillance, screening, prophylactic surgery, and chemoprevention; and alternatives to testing.

CANCER DETECTION AND RISK-REDUCTION OPTIONS

Individuals who test positive for a mutation in either the BRCA1/BRCA2 genes or for a mutation in one of the HNPCC genes have different options available to them, such as lifestyle changes, high-risk surveillance, chemoprevention, and prophylactic surgery, that need to be discussed (Figure 13–5).[7,8] Lifestyle modifications, although they have no proven benefit specifically for mutation carriers, have been associated with decreased risks for breast cancer in those with a family history, and they have a broad range of other health benefits.[52] For either BRCA1/BRCA2 or HNPCC mutations carriers, lifestyle modifications include low-fat high-fiber diets, adequate intake of fruits and vegetables, decreased alcohol consumption, and physical exercise. For BRCA1/BRCA2 mutation carriers, surveillance options based on expert opinion include monthly breast self-examinations, semiannual clinical breast examinations, annual mammography beginning at age 25 to 35 years (or 10 years younger than the youngest diagnosis in the family) and annual transvaginal ultrasound with color Doppler and CA-125 blood test for ovarian cancer surveillance.[7] The Breast Cancer Prevention Trial reported a 49% reduction in risk for invasive breast cancer and a 50% reduction in risk for noninvasive breast cancer in women at increased risk for breast cancer who took tamoxifen, a nonsteroidal antiestrogen.[53] Although data from this trial is not yet available on the effects of tamoxifen specifically on BRCA1/BRCA2 mutation carriers, this is a chemopreventive option that should be discussed with women who test positive for a deleterious mutation in BRCA1/BRCA2.[53,54] Prophylactic mastectomy has been associated with a significant reduction in the incidence of breast cancer among women with a family history of breast cancer and BRCA1/BRCA2 carriers.[55,56] Additionally, prophylactic oophorectomy has been

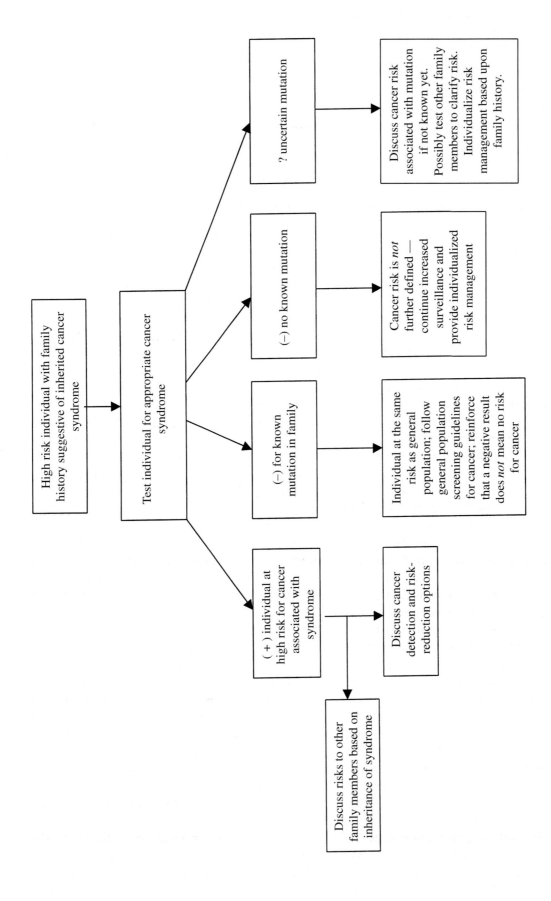

FIGURE 13–4. Cancer genetic susceptibility flow diagram.

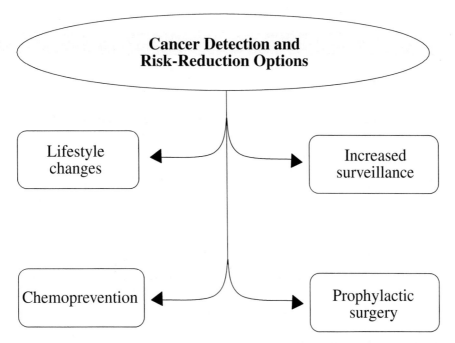

FIGURE 13–5. Cancer detection and risk-reduction options for mutation carriers.

shown to reduce the risk for breast cancer in BRCA1 carriers.[57] It should always be emphasized to patients considering a surgical option that although prophylactic mastectomy and oophorectomy may reduce the risk of breast and ovarian cancer, the risk is never zero.

For HNPCC carriers, experts recommend colonoscopy (as opposed to flexible sigmoidoscopy due to the characteristic right-sided colon cancers in HNPCC, which the sigmoidoscopy would not detect) every 1 to 3 years beginning at age 20 to 25 years. For women, annual endometrial cancer screening with transvaginal ultrasound and/or endometrial biopsy beginning at 25 to 35 years is recommended. Additionally, prophylactic subtotal colectomy, hysterectomy, and oophorectomy should be discussed as options for the patient, even though there is no recommendation at this time for or against these surgeries for HNPCC mutation carriers.[8]

SUMMARY

As genetic testing becomes more widespread, it is critical that physicians appreciate the complexities of genetic testing to accurately and responsibly interpret results for patients and their families. Further research is essential to fully understand the function of these genes and to develop effective prevention strategies and therapies. Access to research

protocols should be provided to all patients at risk for these cancer syndromes.

For physicians and health care clinicians who feel comfortable with genetic counseling for cancer-predisposition testing, it is important that they keep current with the literature, as testing for these inherited syndromes and options for known carriers are changing constantly in this particular area. Professionals who are not comfortable with genetic counseling, or do not have the time required to provide adequate genetic counseling, should refer patients to trained genetic counselors, medical geneticists, and oncologists who provide these specialized services.

REFERENCES

1. American Cancer Society. Cancer facts and figures 2001. Atlanta: American Cancer Society, Publication No.: 5008.01.2001.
2. Stehelin D, Varmus HE, Bishop JM, Vogt PK. DNA related to the transforming gene(s) of avian sarcoma viruses is present in normal avian DNA. Nature 1976;260:170–3.
3. Weinberg RA. Tumor suppressor genes. Science 1991;254:1138–46.
4. Parsons R, Li G, Longley MJ, et al. Hypermutability and mismatch repair deficiency in RER+ tumor cells. Cell 1993;75:1227–36.

RESOURCES

Online Mendelian Inheritance in Man
Web site: www.ncbi.nlm.nih.gov/Omim

Often the first place to check for the latest information about a particular genetic disease, this is an extensive database of virtually all inherited disorders, which is maintained by the Johns Hopkins University School of Medicine and developed for the World Wide Web by NCBI, the National Center for Biotechnology Information. The database contains textual information, pictures, and reference information. It also contains hyperlinks to MEDLINE articles and sequence information.

Gene Tests
Telephone: (206) 527-5742
Web site: www.genetests.org

This is an online directory, produced by the Children's Hospital and Regional Medical Center and University of Washington, of available diagnostic and/or research laboratories for a particular genetic disorder. This database is available to health professionals only.

National Society of Genetic Counselors
233 Canterbury Drive
Wallingford, Pennsylvania 19086-6617
Telephone: (610) 872-7608
Web site: www.nsgc.org

This Web site provides a listing of qualified genetic counselors who provide cancer risk genetic counseling.

The American Cancer Society
1599 Clifton Road Northeast,
Atlanta, Georgia 30329
Telephone: 1-800-ACS-2345 (1-800-227-2345) (Information for the public)
Web site: www.cancer.org

The American Cancer Society provides information about cancer, treatment options, and local programs and services.

National Cancer Institute Information Service
Building 31, Room 10A31
31 Center Drive, MSC 2580
Bethesda, Maryland 20892-2580
Telephone: 1-800-4-CANCER (1-800-422-6237)
Web site: www.cancernet.nci.nih.gov

The NCI maintains an online information center for both patients and physicians. It provides information on a variety of subjects such as cancer screening, treatment, and genetic testing. It also maintains a current listing of health professionals throughout the United States who provide cancer risk genetic counseling.

Publications
Offit K. Clinical cancer genetics: risk counseling and management. New York: Wiley-Liss, Inc.; 1998.
Volgelstein B, Kinzler K. The genetic basis of human cancer. New York: The McGraw-Hill Companies, Inc.; 1998.

5. Jass JR, Edgar S. Unicryptal loss of heterozygosity in hereditary nonpolyposis colorectal cancer. Pathology 1994;26:414–7.

6. Hemminki A, Peltomäki P, Mecklin J-P, et al. Loss of the wild type MLH1 gene is a feature of hereditary nonpolyposis colorectal cancer. Nat Genet 1994; 8:405–10.

7. Burke W, Daly M, Garber J, et al. Recommendations for follow-up care of individuals with an inherited predisposition to cancer: II. BRCA1 and BRCA2. JAMA 1997;277:997–1003.

8. Burke W, Peterson G, Lynch P, et al. Recommendations for follow-up care of individuals with an inherited predisposition to cancer: I. Hereditary nonpolyposis colon cancer. JAMA 1997;277:915–9.

9. Ford D, Easton DF, Stratton M, et al. Genetic heterogeneity and penetrance analysis of the BRCA1 and BRCA2 genes in breast cancer families. Am J Hum Genet 1998;62:676–89.

10. Holt JT, Thompson ME, Szabo C, et al. Growth retardation and tumour inhibition by BRCA1. Nat Genet 1996;12:298–302.

11. Miki Y, Swensew J, Shattuck-Eidens D, et al. A strong candidate for the breast and ovarian cancer susceptibility gene BRCA1. Science 1994;266:66–71.

12. Wooster R, Bignell G, Lancaster J, et al. Identification of the breast cancer susceptibility gene BRCA2. Nature 1995;378:789–92.

13. Tavtigian SV, Simard J, Rommens R, et al. The complete BRCA2 gene and mutations in chromosome 13q–linked kindreds. Nat Genet 1996;12:333–7.

14. Easton DF, Bishop T, Ford D, Crockford GP, and the Breast Cancer Linkage Consortium. Genetic linkage in familial breast and ovarian cancer: results from 214 families. Am J Hum Genet 1993; 52:678–701.

15. Rebbeck TR, Couch FJ, Kant J, et al. Genetic heterogeneity in hereditary breast cancer: role of BRCA1 and BRCA2. Am J Hum Genet 1996;59:547–53.

16. Serova OM, Mazoyer S, Puget N, et al. Mutations in BRCA1 and BRCA2 in breast cancer families: are there more breast cancer–susceptibility genes? Am J Hum Genet 1997;60:486–95.

17. Struewing JP, Abeliovich D, Peretz T, et al. The carrier frequency of the BRCA1 185delAG mutation is approximately 1 percent in Ashkenazi Jewish individuals. Nat Genet 1995;11:198–200.

18. Roa BB, Boyd AA, Volcik K, Richards CS. Ashkenazi Jewish population frequencies for common mutations in BRCA1 and BRCA2. Nat Genet 1996;14:185–7.

19. Struewing JP, Hartge P, Wacholder S, et al. The risk of cancer associated with specific mutations of BRCA1 and BRCA2 among Ashkenazi Jews. N Engl J Med 1997;336:1401–8.

20. Ford D, Easton DF, Bishop DT, et al. Risks of cancer in BRCA1 mutation carriers. Lancet 1994;343:692–5.

21. Wooster R, Neuhasuen SL, Mangion J, et al. Localization of a breast cancer susceptibility gene, BRCA2, to chromosome 13q12–13. Science 1994;265:2088–90.

22. Easton DF, Ford D, Bishop DT. Breast and ovarian cancer incidence in BRCA1 mutation carriers. Am J Hum Genet 1995;56:265–71.

23. Frank T, Manley SA, Olopade OI, et al. Sequence analysis of BRCA1 and BRCA2: correlation of mutations with family history and ovarian cancer risk. J Clin Oncol 1998;16:2417–25.

24. Mecklin J, Järvinen HJ, Hakkiluoto A, et al. Frequency of hereditary nonpolyposis colorectal cancer: a prospective multicenter study in Finland. Dis Colon Rectum 1995;38:588–93.

25. Ponz de Leon M, Sassatelli R, Benatti P, Roncucci L. Identification of hereditary nonpolyposis colorectal cancer in the general population. Cancer 1993; 71:3493–501.

26. Lynch HT, Smyrk T. Hereditary nonpolyposis colorectal cancer (Lynch syndrome): an updated review. Cancer 1996;78:1149–64.

27. Risinger JI, Barrett JC, Watson P, et al. Molecular genetic evidence of the occurrence of breast cancer as an integral tumor in patients with the hereditary nonpolyposis colorectal carcinoma syndrome. Cancer 1996;77:1836–43.

28. Vasen HFA, Mecklin J-P, Meerakhan P, Lynch HT. The International Collaborative Group on Hereditary Nonpolyposis Colorectal Cancer. Dis Colon Rectum 1991;34:424–5.

29. Fishel R, Lescoe MK, Rao MRS, et al. The human mutator gene homolog MSH2 and its association with hereditary nonpolyposis colon cancer. Cell 1993;75:1027–38.

30. Leach FS, Nicolaides NC, Papadopoulos N, et al. Mutations of a mutS homolog in hereditary nonpolyposis colorectal cancer. Cell 1993;75:1215–25.

31. Bronner CE, Baker SM, Morrison PT, et al. Mutation in the DNA mismatch repair gene homologue hMLH1 is associated with hereditary non-polyposis colon cancer. Nature 1994;368:258–61.

32. Papadopoulos N, Nicolaides NC, Wei Y, et al. Mutation of a mutL homolog in hereditary colon cancer. Science 1994;262:1625–9.

33. Nicolaides NC, Papadopoulos N, Liu B, et al. Mutations of two PMS homologues in hereditary non-polyposis colon cancer. Nature 1994;371:75–80.

34. Liu B, Parsons R, Papadopoulos N, et al. Analysis of mismatch repair genes in hereditary non-polyposis colorectal cancer patients. Nat Med 1996;2:169–74.

35. Aarnio M, Sankila R, Pukkala E, et al. Cancer risk in mutation carriers of DNA-mismatch-repair genes. Int J Cancer 1999;81:214–8.

36. Aaltonen LA, Peltomaki P, Leach FS, et al. Clues to the pathogenesis of familial colorectal cancer. Science 1993;260:812–6.

37. Lui B, Farrington SM, Petersen GM, et al. Genetic instability occurs in the majority of young patients with colorectal cancer. Nat Med 1995;1:348–52.

38. Rodriguez-Bigas MA, Boland CR, Hamilton SR, et al. A National Cancer Institute workshop on hereditary nonpolyposis colorectal cancer syndrome: meeting highlights and Bethesda guidelines. J Natl Cancer Inst 1997;89:1758–62.

39. Bussey HJ. Familial polyposis coli: family studies, histopathology, differential diagnosis, and results of treatment. Baltimore: Johns Hopkins University Press; 1975.

40. Kinzler KW, Nilbert MC, Su L-K, et al. Identification of FAP locus genes from chromosome 5q21. Science 1991;253:661–5.

41. Nishisho I, Nakamura Y, Miyoshi Y, et al. Mutations of chromosome 5q21 genes in FAP and colorectal cancer patients. Science 1991;253:665–9.

42. Groden J, Thliveris A, Samowitz W, et al. Identification and characterization of the familial adenomatous polyposis coli gene. Cell 1991;66:589–600.

43. Joslyn G, Carlson M, Thliveris A, et al. Identification of deletion mutations and three new genes at the familial polyposis locus. Cell 1991;66:601–13.

44. Miyoshi Y, Ando H, Nagase H, et al. Germ-line mutations of the APC gene in 53 familial adenomatous polyposis patients. Proc Natl Acad Sci U S A 1992;89:4452–6.

45. Lindor NM, Greene MH, and the Mayo Familial Cancer Program. The concise handbook of family cancer syndromes. J Natl Cancer Inst 1998;90:1039–71.

46. Bennett RL, Steinhaus KA, Uhrich SB, et al. Recommendations for standardized human pedigree nomenclature. Am J Hum Genet 1995;56:745–52.

47. Love RR, Evans AM, Josten DM. The accuracy of patient reports of a family history of cancer. J Chronic Dis 1985;38:289–93.

48. American Society of Clinical Oncology. Statement of the American Society of Clinical Oncology: genetic testing for cancer susceptibility. J Clin Oncol 1996; 14:1730–6.

49. National Society of Genetic Counselors. Predisposition genetic testing for late-onset disorders in adults. JAMA 1997;278:1217–20.

50. Statement of the American Society of Human Genetics on genetic testing for breast and ovarian cancer predisposition. Am J Hum Genet 1994; 55:i–iv.

51. National Action Plan on Breast Cancer. National Action Plan on Breast Cancer position paper: hereditary susceptibility testing for breast cancer. J Clin Oncol 1996;14:1738–40.

52. Egan KM, Stampfer MJ, Rosner BA, et al. Risk factors for breast cancer in women with breast cancer family history. Cancer Epidemiol Biomarkers Prev 1998;7:359–64.

53. Fisher B, Costantino JP, Wickerham DL, et al. Tamoxifen for prevention of breast cancer: report of the National Surgical Adjuvant Breast and Bowel Project P-1 Study. J Natl Cancer Inst 1998;90:1371–88.

54. King M-C, Hale K, Dalakishvili K, et al. A study of the association between inherited mutations and the effect of tamoxifen on breast cancer incidence (Protocol P-1G). Proceedings from the 37th Annual Meeting of the American Society of Clinical Oncology, May 2001.

55. Hartmann LC, Schaid DJ, Woods JE, et al. Efficacy of bilateral prophylactic mastectomy in women with a family history of breast cancer. N Engl J Med 1999;340:77–84.

56. Meijer-Heijboer H, van Geel B, van Putten WJ, et al. Breast cancer after prophylactic mastectomy in women with a BRCA1 or BRCA2 mutation. N Engl J Med 2001;345:159–64.

57. Rebbeck TR, Levin AM, Eisen A, et al. Breast cancer risk after bilateral prophylactic oophorectomy in BRCA1 mutation carriers. J Natl Cancer Inst 1999; 91:1475–9.

14

NORMAL PREGNANCY

Karen Kish, MD, Michael C. Lu, MD, MPH, and Jessica S. Lu, MPH

Over 90% of women in the United States expect to give birth at least once during their lifetime.[1] Pregnancy is a critical event in a woman's life that strongly affects her health and well-being.[2] Preconceptional and prenatal care is therefore an important part of women's health care.

EPIDEMIOLOGY

There are approximately 6 to 7 million pregnancies each year in the United States.[3] These result in 4 million live births, over 1 million legal induced abortions, at least 1 million spontaneous abortions (miscarriages), nearly 100,000 ectopic pregnancies, and about 30,000 fetal deaths each year.[3]

Of the 4 million babies born in the United States in 1998, 12% were born to women under 20 years of age, and 13% of babies were born to women 35 years and older. Three of 5 newborns (60%) were born to non-Hispanic white women; the proportions of newborns born to African American, Asian or Pacific Islander, Hispanic, and Native American women were 15%, 4%, 19%, and 1%, respectively. The fertility rate, which relates births to the number of women of childbearing age, was 65.6 births per 1,000 US women aged 15 to 44 years.[3]

Four of 5 (82.8%) women who gave birth in 1998 started prenatal care in the first trimester, and 3 of 4 (74.3%) women received adequate prenatal care; 3.9% of women had late or no prenatal care. One in 8 (12.9%) smoked cigarettes during pregnancy. Despite an overall improvement in prenatal care use, the proportions of low–birth weight (LBW) births and preterm births have been increasing gradually since the mid-1980s. In 1998 7.6% of babies were born with LBW, and 11.6% of babies were born premature. One in 5 (21.2%) infants were delivered by cesarean section. The proportion

of deliveries attended by midwives has increased to 7.4%; about 99% of births in 1998 were delivered in hospitals.[3]

As of 1997, the United States ranked 25th in infant mortality rate (7.6 infant deaths per 1,000 live births) and 21st in maternal mortality ratio (7.1 maternal deaths per 100,000 live births) among developed nations.[4] The leading causes of maternal deaths include thromboembolism, hemorrhage, infection, and preeclampsia.[5] About one-third to one-half of maternal deaths may be preventable. Maternal deaths are only the tip of the iceberg as 1 in 4 women experience complications during pregnancy,[6] many of which also may be preventable. The leading causes of infant deaths include congenital anomalies, LBW and prematurity, and sudden infant death syndrome.[7]

Significant disparities persist in pregnancy outcomes across racial-ethnic and other sociodemographic categories. For example, infant mortality, LBW, and prematurity are twice as common among African American infants as among Caucasian infants. Maternal mortality is five times higher among pregnant African American women than among pregnant Caucasian women.

PHYSIOLOGY

The human pregnancy lasts, on average, 266 days from conception to delivery. Conception occurs when the sperm fertilizes the ovum in the fallopian tube of the woman. The fertilized egg then travels through the fallopian tube into the uterus, where it implants about 7 days after conception. Between 2 and 8 weeks after conception, the developing conceptus is referred to as an embryo; thereafter, it is called a fetus until delivery. Development of major organs (organogenesis) begins during the embryonic period, about 17 days after conception.[8] Some of the major landmarks in this process include the beating of the heart at 21 days after conception and the closure of the neural tube at 28 days after conception. The fusion of the palate in the midline at 57 days after conception marks the end of organogenesis. Interference with this process may result in a birth defect. Women taking harmful substances or women with pre-existing diseases such as diabetes mellitus are at increased risk for having babies with birth defects.

Although most major organs are present by the end of the embryonic period, the development of their functions continues well into the fetal period, infancy, and early childhood. Interference with this process may lead to functional deficits. For example, undernutrition during this period of growth and differentiation has been associated with increased risk for coronary heart disease, diabetes mellitus, high blood pressure, and other chronic diseases in adulthood.[9] Maternal alcohol use during pregnancy has been linked to mental retardation and other birth defects.

Remarkable changes take place in the woman in adaptation to her pregnancy. Her cardiac output increases by about 30 to 50%. Her respiratory tidal volume increases by 30 to 40%. Her glomerular filtration rate also increases by 50%, which leads to increased creatinine clearance. Therefore, serum creatinine levels fall from a nonpregnant level of approximately 0.8 mg/dL to 0.5 to 0.6 mg/dL by term. Plasma volume expansion of 50% in normal pregnancy often contributes to physiologic anemia. Iron deficiency is the most common cause of anemia during pregnancy, defined as hemoglobin of 10.5 to 11 g/L. Pregnancy is a hypercoagulable state, characterized by an increase in fibrinogen and clotting factors XII, XIII, IX, and X. The gastrointestinal system slows down to enhance absorption but also causes problems such as heartburn and constipation. Relative immunosuppression during pregnancy is an adaptation to avoid rejection of the fetal semiallograft, while at the same time maintaining immune competence to defend against infections. Human placental lactogen is primarily responsible for the development of insulin resistance during pregnancy and gestational diabetes. The placenta also produces corticotropin-releasing hormone (CRH), which, in conjunction with the CRH from the fetal hypothalamus, signals the initiation of labor. Alveolar hypertrophy in the breasts is stimulated primarily by progesterone, ductal hypertrophy by estrogen, milk production and maintenance by prolactin, and let-down by oxytocin. A comprehensive review of maternal adaptations is beyond the scope of this chapter, and interested readers are referred to standard texts in obstetrics for further reading.[10,11] An understanding of these adaptations is essential for clinicians who care for pregnant women (Table 14–1).[4–25]

PRECONCEPTIONAL VISIT

Care of the pregnant woman should begin prior to conception.[12] Much of the impetus for preconception care is driven by fetal considerations, particularly for preventing congenital anomalies, although there may be important maternal benefits that are less well demonstrated. Because organogenesis begins around 17 days after conception, often before a woman starts prenatal care, steps to provide the ideal environment for the developing conceptus are most likely to be effective if they precede pregnancy. The primary care clinician should routinely ask every woman at her health maintenance visit whether she plans to conceive in the next year. Because approximately half of all pregnancies in the United States are unintended at conception,[13] preconceptional care is recommended for every woman of reproductive age during a routine visit to the health care clinician. All women, and particularly those with chronic medical illnesses, should be counseled about the importance of obtaining preconceptional counseling even if they have no immediate plans for pregnancy.

Preconceptional care should begin by obtaining detailed reproductive, family, and medical histories.[14] The preconceptional reproductive history helps identify factors that contributed to earlier poor pregnancy outcomes and that may be amenable to intervention. The risk of recurrent pregnancy losses may be reduced by diagnosis and treatment of factors such as uterine malformations, maternal autoimmune disease, endocrine abnormalities, or genital infections. Inquiry should be made about in utero exposure to diethylstilbestrol (DES).

Preconceptional assessment of family history allows for identification of genetic diseases such as fragile X or Down syndrome. Carrier screening can be offered based on family history or the racial-ethnic background of the couple. Examples include testing for Tay-Sachs disease for people of Eastern

TABLE 14–1. Maternal Physiology

System	Complications/Observations in Pregnancy	Physiology
Breasts	Tenderness, tingling, heaviness, enlargement	Alveolar hypertrophy stimulated by progesterone, ductal hypertrophy stimulated by estrogen[4]
Cardiac	Ankle edema	Increased venous pressure in the lower extremities and reduced plasma colloid pressure
	Lateralization of the point of maximal impulse	Elevation of the diaphram; S_3, exaggerated splitting, and systolic murmurs are also commonly found in normal pregnancy
	Decreased blood pressure (1st and 2nd trimesters)	Smooth muscle relaxation from elevated progesterone levels, leading to decrease peripheral vascular resistance[5]
ENT/pulmonary	Nasal congestion/epistaxis	Estrogen-related hypersecretion of mucus
	Increased minute ventilation with normal respiratory rate, dyspnea of pregnancy	Progesterone-related increase in tidal volume of 30–40%. Other pulmonary findings: expiratory reserve volume decreases 20%, total lung volume decreases 5%, and residual lung volume decreases 20%. FEV_1, FEV_1/FVC unchanged. Increased minute ventilation causes fall in maternal CO_2, increasing CO_2 transfer from fetus to mother. Arterial oxygenation remains unchanged.[6-9]
Endocrine	Increased cortisol levels (free and total)	Plasma levels of corticosteroid-binding globulin increase caused by estrogen-induced increased hepatic synthesis. Increased adrenal production and delayed plasma clearance cause an increase in free cortisol.[10]
	Increased maternal insulin levels	B cell hypertrophy and insulin resistance in the liver and peripheral tissues induced by increasing levels of human placental lactogen
	Pituitary gland enlargement	Proliferation of chromophobe cells in the anterior pituitary related to increased prolactin secretion[11]
	Enlargement of the thyroid gland	The thyroid gland increases in size during pregnancy owing to estrogen effects. TSH decreases early in gestation but returns to normal by the second trimester. Total T_4 and thyroid binding globulin increase, but free T_3 and T_4 remain unchanged.[12,13]
Eyes	Corneal thickening	Increased fluid retention
Gastrointestinal	Ptyalism	Increased saliva, inability to swallow normal amounts because of nausea[14]
	Nausea, vomiting of pregnancy	Uncertain; thought to be direct placental stimulation of the vomiting center in the CNS. Possible hormonal mediators: hCG or one of its isoforms, estradiol.[15]
	Acid reflux	Decreased lower esophageal sphincter tone[16]
	Reduced incidence of peptic ulcer disease	Thought to be caused by increase in gastric mucus secretion and protective effect of prostaglandins on gastric mucosa
	Constipation	Mechanical obstruction from the uterus, smooth muscle relaxation causing reduced motility, and enhanced water absorption

ENT = ear, nose, and throat; FEV = forced expiratory volume; FVC = forced vital capacity; TSH = thyroid-stimulating hormone; T_4 = thyroxine; T_3 = triiodothyronine; CNS = central nervous system; HCG = human chorionic gonadotropin; GFR = glomerular filtration rate.

TABLE 14–1. (continued)

System	Complications/Observations in Pregnancy	Physiology
Gastrointestinal (continued)	Hemorrhoids	Increased portal venous pressure and constipation
	Increased formation of liver proteins, including fibrinogen	Estrogenic effect[17]
	Increased gallstone formation	Saturation of biliary cholesterol increases and proportion of chenodeoxycholic acid decreases.[18] Increased residual and slower emptying time of gallbladder in 2nd and 3rd trimesters.[19]
Hematologic	Decreased hematocrit	"Physiologic anemia" caused by increase in plasma volume. Erythrocyte mass also increases, but not to the same extent.[20]
	Elevated white blood cell count	Pregnancy-related increase in polymorphonuclear cells[21]
	Hypercoagulable state	Increase in fibrinogen and factors XII, XIII, IX, and X. Clotting and bleeding times remain unchanged.
Musculoskeletal	Gait instability and falls	Thought to be a combination of effects of pregnancy-induced lordosis (including anterior convexity of the lumbar spine) and loosening of the pubic symphysis and sacroiliac joints by the hormone relaxin[22]
Renal	Pyelonephritis	Mechanical compression by the enlarging uterus leads to ureteral and renal pelvic dilation, and progesterone-induced smooth muscle relaxation causes an increase in vesiculoureteral reflux
	Decrease in blood urea nitrogen, creatinine, uric acid	Increased GFR during pregnancy; uric acid levels return to normal in the 3rd trimester because of increased renal tubular resorption of urate (uncertain mechanism)[23]
	Decreased plasma osmolality	Reset of osmoreceptor system
	Increased urine glucose	Increased GFR (urine glucose is not a reliable indicator of plasma glucose during pregnancy)
Skin	Spider angiomata, palmar erythema	Estrogen related, regress after delivery. Not reliable to diagnose liver disease in pregnancy as common in normal pregnant women.[17,24]
	Hyperpigmentation of nipples, areola, axilla, umbilicus, abdominal midline, forehead, cheeks, and nose	Increased levels of estrogen, progesterone, and α-melanocyte-stimulating hormone
	Striae	Appear to be genetically determined[25]
	Increased fullness of hair	In late pregnancy, amount of hair follicles in telogen (resting) phase increases—reversion to normal cycle causes hair loss postpartum
	Acne, hirsutism	Exaggerated luteinization of normal ovaries, regress after delivery

ENT = ear, nose, and throat; FEV = forced expiratory volume; FVC = forced vital capacity; TSH = thyroid-stimulating hormone; T_4 = thyroxine; T_3 = triiodothyronine; CNS = central nervous system; HCG = human chorionic gonadotropin; GFR = glomerular filtration rate.

European Jewish or French Canadian ancestry; ß-thalassemia for those of Mediterranean, Southeast Asian, Indian, Pakistani, or African ancestry; α-thalassemia for people of Southeast Asian or African ancestry; sickle cell anemia for people of African, Mediterranean, Middle Eastern, Caribbean, Latin American, or Indian descent; and cystic fibrosis for people of Northern European background.[15,16]

Preconceptional care for women with significant medical problems should include an assessment of potential risk not only to the fetus but also to the woman should she become pregnant. For example, primary pulmonary hypertension has a maternal mortality that approaches 50% and a fetal mortality that exceeds 40%.[17] For women with insulin-dependent diabetes mellitus, the risk of congenital malformations is significantly reduced in those who maintain euglycemic control during organogenesis.[18] These women should be counseled on the importance of preventing unintended pregnancies and should aim for the lowest possible glycosolated hemoglobin level prior to attempting to become pregnant.

Preconceptional care should include a detailed nutritional assessment. The assessment consists of four main parts: anthropometric, biochemical, clinical, and dietary.[19] Anthropometric evaluation includes the body mass index (BMI, or weight in kilograms divided by the square of height in centimeters). Women who are underweight (BMI < 19.8) are at risk for having an LBW or premature infant. The clinician should consider some correctable causes of being underweight, such as eating disorders, food insecurity, or use of medications or illicit drugs (eg, speed or cocaine). Women who are overweight (BMI > 29) are also at increased risk for pregnancy complications, including pregnancy-induced hypertension, diabetes, fetal macrosomia, and perinatal mortality. Although weight loss is an important goal in obese women, the emphasis should be on the dietary and physical activity behavioral changes for the long-term benefit of the woman. Weight loss should occur at a healthy rate of no more than a pound or two per week.

Biochemical assessment should include measurement of serum hemoglobin. Evaluation of serum folate, glucose, and lipids has been recommended by some experts, but data supporting the benefit of these preconceptional biochemical screening tests are lacking. Clinical assessment should include

determination of any history of chronic diseases that may affect a woman's nutritional status, such as inflammatory bowel disease or acquired immune deficiency syndrome. Infants born to women with phenylketonuria and a maternal blood level of phenylalanine > 20 mg/dL are at increased risk for microcephaly, mental retardation, intrauterine growth retardation, and congenital heart disease.[20] The risk of congenital malformation is significantly reduced by dietary restrictions during the earliest weeks of gestation. Dietary assessment should focus on dietary restrictions that interfere with adequate nutrition, such as veganism, and appropriate referral to a registered dietitian should be made.

Each year in the United States, about 2,500 infants are born with the neural tube defects such as spina bifida and anencephaly, and an unknown number are aborted.[21] Randomized controlled trials have shown that folic acid supplementation significantly reduces the risk of neural tube defects. The US Public Health Service recommends that all women capable of becoming pregnant should consume at least 0.4 mg of folic acid daily.[22] Women with a prior pregnancy affected by a neural tube defect should consume 4.0 mg of folic acid daily starting 1 month before conception and continuing through the first 3 months of pregnancy as a randomized trial has shown that use of such high-dose supplements significantly reduces the risk of recurrence.[23]

Preconceptional care also should include a detailed social assessment. Queries should be made about hobbies and habits, including use of tobacco, alcohol, and illicit drugs. All women should be screened preconceptionally for domestic violence, which presents a significant risk to both the mother and fetus during pregnancy.[24] These topics are discussed in detail in this text in Chapter 12, "Smoking Cessation," Chapter 18, "Substance Abuse and Pregnancy," and Chapter 88, "Domestic Violence." Routine assessment of occupational and environmental exposures may identify exposures that have been associated with adverse reproductive outcomes, such as organic solvents, vinyl monomers used in the manufacturing of plastics, pesticides, and heavy metals such as lead and mercury.[25] Efforts should be made to minimize unsafe exposures periconceptionally.

A complete physical examination should be performed if not done previously. Height, weight, and blood pressure should be measured. Auscultation of the heart may identify women with previously undiagnosed heart disease, such as mitral stenosis from childhood rheumatic heart disease, which may remain asymptomatic until pregnancy. A pelvic examination should be performed. A Pap test should be performed if one has not been done in the past 3 years (1 year for high-risk women).[26]

Recommended laboratory evaluation should include all tests that are recommended for the first prenatal visit, including hemoglobin and hematocrit, urinalysis and culture for asymptomatic bacteriuria, determination of blood groups and D (Rh) typing and antibody screen, hepatitis B surface antigen, syphilis testing, and rubella serology (if unknown).[27] Women who are found to lack immunity to rubella or hepatitis B virus can then be vaccinated prior to attempts to conceive as immunization is contraindicated during attempts to conceive or pregnancy. Patients who have not been immunized against tetanus in the last 10 years should receive a booster tetanus-diphtheria vaccination.[26] Many experts recommend that women who do not have a known history of varicella be tested by serology and, if nonimmune, vaccinated with varicella vaccine prior to attempts to conceive. Patients at risk for exposure to tuberculosis or cytomegalovirus (people who work in neonatal intensive care units, child care facilities, or dialysis units) or toxoplasmosis (cat owners and people who eat or handle raw meat) can be offered preconceptional tests for immunity.[14] Voluntary and confidential antibody testing for human immunodeficiency virus (HIV) should be offered to all women; tests for other sexually transmitted infections such as *Neisseria gonorrhoeae* or *Chlamydia trachomatis* may be offered based on risk factors. Additional testing should be guided by risk factors such as measuring fasting glucose in women with a history of gestational diabetes during prior pregnancy.[14]

PRENATAL CARE

The objectives of prenatal care are to promote the health and well-being of the pregnant woman, the fetus, the infant, and the family up to 1 year after the infant's birth.[28] Through early and continuing risk assessment, health promotion, and medical and psychosocial interventions and follow-up, prenatal care provides an opportunity to affect positively not only the immediate outcomes of pregnancy but also the continuing health of the woman, the infant, and the family.

The First Prenatal Visit

Ideally, early and continuing risk assessment, health promotion, and medical and psychosocial interventions should begin preconceptionally. However, many patients present without having had a preconceptional visit and, in many cases, having had no medical care for some time.

The first prenatal visit provides an opportunity to assess or review reproductive, family, medical, nutritional, and psychosocial histories as described above. Reproductive histories such as preterm birth, LBW, preeclampsia, stillbirth, congenital anomalies, or gestational diabetes are important to obtain because of substantial risk of recurrence. Women with prior cesarean delivery should be asked about the circumstances of the delivery, and discussion about options for the mode of delivery for the current pregnancy should be initiated. Women whose health may be seriously jeopardized by the pregnancy, such as those with Eisenmenger's syndrome or a history of peripartum cardiomyopathy, should be counseled about the option of terminating the pregnancy. Additionally, the importance of screening women for domestic violence cannot be overemphasized. As much as 20% of women are abused physically during pregnancy (the prevalence of abuse in most studies clusters around 4 to 8%), making abuse more common than preeclampsia, diabetes, and other conditions that are routinely screened for during prenatal care.[29]

A complete physical examination should be performed if not recently done. Clinicians should be familiar with physical findings associated with normal pregnancy, such as systolic murmurs, exaggerated splitting, and S_3 during cardiac auscultation, or spider angiomata, palmar erythema, linea nigra, and striae gravidarum on inspection of the skin.[11] During the breast examination, clinicians can initiate discussion about breast-feeding. In addition to assessment of the cervix, uterus, and adnexa, clinical pelvimetry may be performed during the pelvic examination. Any abnormality should be noted, such as a vaginal septum, uterine myoma, or cervical changes associated with in utero DES exposure, including cervical collar, Cock's comb, pancake cervix, pseudopolypoid appearance, and cervical hypoplasia. Women with in utero DES exposure are at increased risk for pregnancy loss and preterm delivery.[30]

Recommended standard laboratory testing includes hemoglobin and hematocrit, screening for asymptomatic bacteriuria, determination of blood groups and D (Rh) typing and antibody screen using indirect Coombs' test, hepatitis B surface antigen, syphilis testing, and rubella serology.[27] Screening for and treating asymptomatic bacteriuria have been shown in randomized trials to significantly reduce the risk of pyelonephritis and preterm delivery.[31] Women who are Rh negative may be at risk for isoimmunization during pregnancy and should receive Rh_O (D) immune globulin at 28 weeks of gestation and post partum, and at any time when sensitization may occur (eg, threatened abortion or amniocentesis). Voluntary and confidential HIV testing should be offered.[32] Other tests may be obtained based on risk factors, such as testing for tuberculosis, gonorrhea, and chlamydia.

Additionally, the clinician may use the first prenatal visit to confirm pregnancy and determine viability, estimate gestational age and due date, and provide advice on nutrition, lifestyle changes, coping with unpleasant symptoms during pregnancy, and breast-feeding.

CONFIRMING PREGNANCY AND DETERMINING VIABILITY

Women most commonly present to the clinician after missed menses. About 30 to 40% of all pregnant women have some bleeding during early pregnancy, which may be mistaken for a period.[33] Therefore, a pregnancy test should be performed in all women of reproductive ages presenting with abnormal vaginal bleeding.

The pregnancy test detects human chorionic gonadotropin (hCG) in the serum or the urine. The most widely used current standard is the First International Reference Preparation (First IRP). Human chorionic gonadotropin is first detectable 6 to 8 days after ovulation. A titer of less than 5 IU/mL is considered negative; a level above 25 IU/L is a positive result. Values between 6 and 24 IU/L are considered equivocal, and the test should be repeated in 2 days.[34] A concentration of 100 IU/L is reached about the date of expected menses. Most urine pregnancy tests have a sensitivity of 25 IU/L, but some may be less sensitive. Perimenopausal and post-

menopausal women have endogenous pituitary hCG secretion with luteinizing hormone that may lead to false-positive results. A negative pregnancy test in a woman not intending to get pregnant should be viewed as an opportunity to provide contraceptive counseling and family planning.

It is important to differentiate normal pregnancy from nonviable or ectopic pregnancy. In the first 30 days of a normal gestation, the level of hCG doubles every 2.2 days.[35] In patients whose pregnancies are destined to abort, the level of hCG rises more slowly, plateaus, or declines. The predictive value of a normal rise in hCG level for a successful pregnancy is 88%, and that of an abnormal rise in hCG level for fetal demise is 76%.[35] The use of transvaginal ultrasonography has improved the diagnostic accuracy of predicting viability in early pregnancies. Using transvaginal ultrasonography, the gestational sac should be seen at 5 weeks of gestation or a mean hCG level of 1,398 mIU/mL (First IRP). The fetal pole should be seen at 6 weeks or a mean hCG level of 5,113 mIU/mL. Fetal cardiac motion should be seen at 7 weeks or a mean hCG level of 17,208 mIU/mL.[36] The presence of a gestational sac of 8-mm mean sac diameter without a demonstrable yolk sac, or 16 mm without a demonstrable embryo,[37] or the absence of fetal cardiac motion in an embryo with a crown-rump length > 5 mm,[38] also indicates embryonic demise.

ESTIMATING GESTATIONAL AGE AND DATE OF CONFINEMENT

Gestational age should be determined during the first prenatal visit. Accurate determination of gestational age may become important later in pregnancy for the management of obstetric conditions such as preterm labor, intrauterine growth restriction, and postdate pregnancy. Clinical assessment to determine gestational age is usually appropriate for the woman with regular menstrual cycles and a known last menstrual period (LMP) that was confirmed by an early examination. Ultrasonography may be used to estimate gestational age. Measurement of fetal crown-rump length between 8 and 13 weeks of gestation can define gestational age to within 5 days. Thereafter, measurements, typically taken of the biparietal diameter, femur length, and abdominal and head circumferences, become less reliable with advancing gestation (± 3 weeks in the third trimester).[39]

Estimated date of confinement (or due date) may be determined from a known LMP by adding 9 months and 7 days to the LMP (Nägele's rule). This presupposes a 28-day menstrual cycle and may be subject to error, especially in those with longer or shorter menstrual cycles. The date of confinement can also be estimated based on ultrasonography.

ADVICE DURING PREGNANCY

One of the most important functions of prenatal care is to provide information and support to the woman for self-care. A pregnant woman is subject to a variety of prescriptions and proscriptions, many of which lack a scientific basis. The effectiveness of much of the advice given during pregnancy often goes unevaluated. A complete review of advice and interventions during pregnancy is beyond the scope of this chapter. The Cochrane pregnancy and childbirth database has compiled systematic reviews on the effectiveness of advice and interventions during pregnancy and can be a useful source of information for prenatal care clinicians.[40] The following sections examine advice given to alleviate unpleasant symptoms during pregnancy, nutritional counseling, lifestyle advice, and breast-feeding.

Alleviating unpleasant symptoms during pregnancy. Nausea and vomiting are common complaints during pregnancy, complicating up to 70% of pregnancies. Eating small frequent meals; avoiding greasy or spicy foods; and having protein snacks at night, saltine crackers at the bedside, and room-temperature sodas are nonpharmacologic approaches that may provide some alleviation. When medication is deemed to be necessary, antihistamines appear to be the drug of choice, although no single product has been satisfactorily tested for efficacy and safety. Small trials suggest that vitamin B_6 (pyridoxine) and accupressure (sea sickness arm bands) may be effective and should be further investigated. Patients with dehydration and electrolyte abnormalities from vomiting (hyperemesis gravidarum) should be evaluated for possible secondary causes and hospitalized for rehydration and antiemetic therapy.[41]

Heartburn affects about two-thirds of women at some stage of pregnancy, resulting from progesterone-induced relaxation of the esophageal sphincter. Avoiding lying down immediately after meals, avoiding eating spicy or greasy food, and elevating the head of the bed may help reduce heartburn.

When these simple and sensible measures fail, evidence suggests that antacids, such as calcium carbonate, should be used as first-line treatment.[42]

Constipation is a troublesome problem for many women in pregnancy, secondary to decreased colonic motility. Dietary modification, including increased fiber and water intake, can help lessen this problem. Stool softeners may be used in combination with bulking agents. Irritant laxatives should be reserved for short-term use in refractory cases.[43]

Hemorrhoids are caused by increased venous pressure in the rectum. In the absence of any sound research about the best means of preventing or treating this condition, advice similar to that given to nonpregnant sufferers may be appropriate, such as rest, elevation of the legs, and, most importantly, avoiding constipation.[44]

Leg cramps are experienced by almost half of all pregnant women, particularly at night and in the later months of pregnancy. The cause is unclear. Massage and stretching may afford some relief during an attack. Both calcium and sodium chloride appear to help reduce leg cramps in pregnancy.[45]

Backaches are common during pregnancy and are lessened by avoiding excessive weight gain. Additionally, exercise, posture, sensible shoes, and specially shaped pillows can offer relief. In cases of muscle spasm or strain, analgesics (such as acetaminophen), rest, and heat may lessen the symptoms.[46]

Nutritional counseling. Although the nutritional care plan should be individualized, every woman can benefit from nutritional education that includes counseling on weight gain, dietary guidelines, physical activity, avoidance of harmful substances and unsafe foods, and breast-feeding. The appropriate weight gain during pregnancy for a woman with a normal prepregnancy weight for height (BMI of 19 to 25) is 11 to 16 kg. Approximately 1 to 1.5 kg are gained in fluid volume, 1.5 to 2 kg in blood volume, 0.5 to 1 kg in breast enlargement, 1 kg in amniotic fluid, 2.5 to 3.5 kg for the fetus at term, 0.5 to 1 kg from the placenta, and 2 to 2.5 kg in maternal stores of fat and protein. The recommended weight gain is 12.5 to 18 kg for an underweight woman (BMI < 19) and 7 to 11 kg for an overweight or obese (BMI > 25) woman.[19] Recommended rates of weight gain per week during the second and third trimesters are 0.5 kg, 0.4 kg, and 0.3 kg for pregnant women who are underweight, normal weight, and overweight, respectively.[19] Inadequate weight gain has been associated with LBW, whereas excessive weight gain has been associated with fetal macrosomia.

Weight gain is of secondary importance to nutrition; the clinician should emphasize the right amount of nutrition over the right amount of weight gain. Normal pregnancy requires an increase in daily caloric intake by 300 kcal. Women should be advised to eat seven or more servings of bread, grains, and cereals per day; three to five servings each of vegetables and fruits; and three servings each of protein goods and milk products, and to minimize their intake of fats, oils, and sweets.[19] Prenatal vitamins are often prescribed during the first prenatal visit, but their benefits have not been conclusively established.[47] A comprehensive review of nutrition during pregnancy is beyond the scope of this chapter; prenatal care providers should become knowledgeable with guidelines for nutritional assessment and competent in providing nutritional counseling during pregnancy.[19]

Lifestyle advice. During the first trimester, increased fatigue is reported. Women should be advised to rest when tired and reassured that the fatigue usually abates by the fourth month of pregnancy. Normal pre-pregnancy activity levels are usually acceptable. General advice on work is clearly inappropriate; such advice should be individualized to the nature of the work, the health status of the woman, and the condition of the pregnancy. Work that requires prolonged standing, shift or night work, and high cumulative occupational fatigue has been associated with increased risk for LBW and prematurity.[48] Where working conditions involve occupational fatigue or stress, a request for a change in work during pregnancy should be supported by the prenatal care clinician.[40]

Women should be advised to continue to exercise during pregnancy unless it is complicated by pregnancy-induced hypertension, preterm labor or rupture of membranes, intrauterine growth retardation, incompetent cervix, persistent second- or third-trimester bleeding, or medical conditions that severely restrict physiologic adaptations to exercise during pregnancy.[49] They should avoid exercise in the supine position after the first trimester and should be encouraged to modify the intensity of their exercise according to maternal symptoms. Any type of exercise involving the potential for loss of balance or even mild abdominal trauma should be avoided.[49]

Travel is acceptable under most circumstances. Prolonged sitting increases the risk of thromboembolism; pregnant women should be encouraged to ambulate periodically (eg, walk for 10 minutes every 1 to 2 hours) when taking a long flight or car ride. Support stockings may help reduce lower extremity edema. International travel that places the patient at a high risk for infectious disease (such as travel to areas with a high rate of transmission of malaria or typhoid fever) should be avoided whenever possible.[50] When such travel cannot be avoided, appropriate vaccinations should be administered. Live attenuated virus vaccinations are contraindicated in pregnancy, but inactivated virus vaccines are acceptable.[51]

Women should be reassured that increased, unchanged, and decreased levels of sexual activity can be normal during pregnancy. Available evidence does not support any prohibition of sexual activity during normal pregnancy. Abstinence or condom use may be advisable in cases of preterm labor, repeated pregnancy loss, or persistent second- or third-trimester bleeding.[52,53]

Breast-feeding. Breast-feeding has been shown to significantly reduce morbidity and improve cognitive development during infancy and childhood.[54] Despite the well-known benefits of breast-feeding, 40% of women in the United States never initiate nursing, and only 22% breast-feed for longer than 6 months.[55] A recent study found that clinician encouragement significantly increases breast-feeding initiation among American women of all social and ethnic backgrounds.[56] Clinicians should discuss breast-feeding with the patient and her family during the first visit, including possible barriers to breast-feeding, such as prior poor experiences, misinformation, or a nonsupportive work environment. Partners, peers, and other family members or friends may also exert an important influence on the decision to breast-feed. Referrals to childbirth preparation classes or lactation consultations may provide additional encouragement to breast-feed.

Follow-up Visits

Additional prenatal visits are routinely scheduled every 4 weeks until 28 weeks' gestation, every 2 to 3 weeks until 36 weeks' gestation, and then weekly until delivery.[27] The schedule of these follow-up visits, however, should be tailored to the needs of individual patients.[28] The regularity of scheduled prenatal visits should be sufficient to allow the clinician to monitor the progress of the pregnancy, provide education and recommended screening and interventions, assess the well-being of the fetus and mother, reassure the mother, and detect and treat medical and psychosocial complications. During each regularly scheduled visit, the clinician should evaluate blood pressure, weight, urine protein and glucose, uterine size for progressive growth, and fetal heart rate. After the patient reports quickening (first sensation of fetal movement, on average at 20 weeks' gestation) and at each subsequent visit, she should be asked about fetal movement, contractions, leakage of fluid, and vaginal bleeding. Women are often instructed to perform routine fetal movement counting, although the benefit of such practice remains unsupported by current evidence. Between 24 and 34 weeks, women should be taught the warning symptoms of preterm labor (uterine contractions, leakage of fluid, vaginal bleeding, low pelvic pressure, or low back pain). Beginning in the late second trimester, they also should be taught to recognize the warning symptoms of preeclampsia (headache, visual changes, hand or facial swelling, or epigastric or right upper quadrant pain). Near term they should be instructed on the symptoms of labor.[27]

Additional laboratory and diagnostic testing may be recommended. Triple markers (serum unconjugated estriol, α-fetoprotein, and ß-hCG) may be offered, ideally between 15 and 18 weeks of gestation by menstrual dating, to detect Down syndrome and neural tube defects. Women aged 35 years or older and women with increased risk for Down syndrome or other chromosomal abnormalities may be offered cytogenetic diagnosis. This can be accomplished through chorionic villus sampling, typically performed at 11 to 12 weeks, or amniocentesis performed at 15 to 16 weeks by menstrual dating.[57]

Depending on the practice setting and population, either universal or selective screening for gestational diabetes should be performed between 24 and 28 weeks of gestation. Risk factors for selective screening include a family history of diabetes; previous birth of a macrosomic, malformed, or stillborn baby; hypertension; glycosuria; maternal age of 30 years or older; or previous gestational diabetes.[27] The cost-effectiveness of diabetic screening during pregnancy remains highly controversial. Repeat measurements of hemoglobin or hematocrit levels early in the third trimester have been recommended. Tests for sexually transmitted infections may also be repeated at 32 to 36 weeks of gestation if the woman has specific risk factors for these diseases. The Centers for Disease Control and Prevention recommend universal screening for maternal colonization of group B streptococcus at 35 to 37 weeks of gestation. Alternatively, women who were not previously screened should receive antibiotic prophylaxis during labor based on risk factors, which include a previous infant with invasive group B streptococcus disease, group B streptococcus bacteriuria during current pregnancy, delivery at < 37 weeks of gestation, duration of ruptured membrane ≥ 18 hours, and temperature of 38°C during labor.[58]

The value of selective ultrasonography for specific indications has been clearly established; that of routine ultrasonography in low-risk pregnancies remains undetermined. At present, there is no evidence that ultrasound examination during pregnancy is harmful. Controlled trials have failed to demonstrate that routine ultrasound examinations for dating in early pregnancy, anatomic survey in midpregnancy, or anthropometry in late pregnancy improve perinatal outcomes.[59,60] Varying levels of expertise make this a particularly difficult issue about which to make a general statement.

Postpartum Visit

Women should be advised to receive a check-up 4 to 6 weeks after childbirth and sooner after a cesarean delivery or a complicated gestation.[27,61] This postpartum visit is believed to offer an important opportunity to assess the physical and psychosocial well-being of the mother, counsel her about breast-feeding and family planning, initiate preconception care for the next pregnancy, and address nascent problems within the family. The optimal timing and content of the postpartum visit remain to be determined.

HEALTHY PREGNANCY

In the twentieth century, infant mortality declined by 90% and maternal mortality by 99%. Healthy pregnancy was hailed as one of the greatest achievements of public health in the twentieth century.[62] However, we still fall short of our goal to ensure that every pregnancy is healthy. Current efforts to ensure healthy pregnancy work at three different levels of prevention.[63]

Primary prevention refers to efforts to prevent diseases from occurring during pregnancy. Examples of primary prevention include family planning, preconceptional care, and health promotion during prenatal care. By preventing unintended pregnancies from occurring in the first place, family planning can prevent morbidity associated with these unintended pregnancies. Preconceptional care has been shown to reduce certain birth defects. Health education about proper nutrition and cessation of tobacco, alcohol, and drug use during pregnancy can prevent LBW and other complications.

Secondary prevention refers to efforts to facilitate early detection and treatment of diseases during pregnancy. Prenatal care provides an opportunity for secondary prevention through early and continuous assessment. Examples include early detection of preeclampsia, syphilis, and tuberculosis.

Tertiary prevention refers to efforts to avert severe complications resulting from diseases during pregnancy. Examples of tertiary prevention include the administration of antibiotics in the treatment of puerperal infection, magnesium to prevent eclampsia in women affected by severe preeclampsia, and transfusion of blood products in the setting of obstetric hemorrhage. Regionalization of perinatal health services, so that high-risk women deliver only in hospitals equipped to deal with potential complications, has played an important role in tertiary prevention.

Just as much of the improvement in maternal and infant health in the twentieth century was attributable largely to improved social conditions such as better sanitation, sewage control, and the cleaning up of the water supply, continued improvement is more likely to come from social and behavioral changes than from advancement in medical care.[64] For example, cigarette smoking is known to cause LBW and prematurity. Yet simply telling women to stop smoking may not be enough. Our challenge is to find out what factors cause women to continue to smoke during pregnancy (eg, stress, addiction) and to learn to address those biologic, psychological, behavioral, and social factors at the individual, community, and society levels.

Because the health of the baby is tied to the health of the mother, efforts to improve pregnancy outcome must begin with women's health. Our current efforts fall short by doing too little too late; to expect prenatal care to reverse all of the cumulative effects of risk exposures over the life course on the health of the woman may be expecting too much of prenatal care. Future efforts need to promote maternal health not only during pregnancy but throughout the life course of the woman if we are to make significant improvement in pregnancy outcomes.[65]

RESOURCES

March of Dimes Birth Defects Foundation
1275 Mamaroneck Avenue
White Plains, New York 10605
Telephone: 1-800-MODIMES (1-800-663-4637)
Web site: www.modimes.org

The March of Dimes is a national voluntary health agency whose mission is to improve the health of babies by preventing birth defects and infant mortality. The March of Dimes Web site includes The Mama Program, which provides information for mothers from pre-pregnancy planning through the postpartum period.

REFERENCES

1. Abma JC, Chandra A, Mosher WD. Fertility, family planning and women's health: new data from the 1995 National Survey of Family Growth. Vital Health Stat 1997;23:1–28.

RESOURCES (continued)

The American College of Obstetricians and Gynecologists
409 12th Street Southwest
PO Box 96920
Washington, DC 20090-6920
Web site: www.acog.org

ACOG has over 43,000 physician members. It offers patient education materials and a book for patients entitled Planning Your Pregnancy and Birth *that addresses pregnancy issues. ACOG also publishes guidelines for clinicians on care of the pregnant woman.*

American Academy of Pediatrics
601 13th Street Northwest
Suite 400 North
Washington, DC 20005
Web site: www.aap.org

AAP has 55,000 physician members from throughout North and South America. Its goal is to promote health, safety, and the well-being of infants and youth. The AAP Web site includes guidelines and information on breast-feeding.

---

2. Grason HA, Hutchins JE, Silver GB, editors. Charting a course for the future of women's and perinatal health. Volume I—concepts, findings and recommendations. Baltimore (MD): Women's and Children's Health Policy Center, Johns Hopkins School of Public Health; 1999.

3. Ventura SJ, Martin JA, Curtin SC, et al. Births: final data for 1998. National Vital Statistics Reports. Vol. 48, no. 3. Hyattsville (MD): National Center for Health Statistics; 2000.

4. Curtin SC, Martin JA. Births: preliminary data for 1999. National Vital Statistics Reports. Vol. 48, no. 14. Hyattsville (MD): National Center for Health Statistics; 2000.

5. Centers for Disease Control and Prevention (US). Maternal mortality—United States, 1982–1996. MMWR Morb Mortal Wkly Rep 1998;47:705–7.

6. Benett TA, Kotelchuck M, Cox CE, et al. Pregnancy-associated hospitalizations in the United States in 1991 and 1992: a comprehensive view of maternal morbidity. Am J Obstet Gynecol 1998;178:346–54.

7. Mathews TJ, Curtin SC, MacDorman MF. Infant mortality statistics from the 1998 period linked birth/infant death data set. National Vital Statistics Reports. Vol. 48, no. 12. Hyattsville (MD): National Center for Health Statistics; 2000.

8. Moore KL. Essentials of human embryology. Toronto: BC Decker; 1988.

9. Barker DJP. Mothers, babies and health in late life. 2nd ed. Edinburgh: Churchill Livingstone; 1998.

10. Cunningham FG, MacDonald PC, Gant NF, et al. Williams obstetrics. 19th ed. East Norwalk (CT): Appleton & Lange; 1993.

11. Cruikshank DP, Hayes PM. Maternal physiology in pregnancy. In: Gabbe SG, Niebyl JR, Simpson JL, editors. Obstetrics: normal and problem pregnancies. 3rd ed. New York: Churchill Livingstone; 1996. p. 125–46.

12. Cefalo RC, Moos MK. Preconceptional health care: a practical guide. St. Louis (MO): Mosby; 1995.

13. Henshaw SK. Unintended pregnancy in the United States. Fam Plann Perspect 1998;30(1):24–29, 46.

14. American College of Obstetricians and Gynecologists. Preconceptional care. ACOG Technical Bulletin #205. Washington (DC): American College of Obstetricians and Gynecologists; 1995.

15. Simpson JL. Genetic counseling and prenatal diagnosis. In: Gabbe SG, Niebyl JR, Simpson JL, editors. Obstetrics: normal and problem pregnancies. 3rd ed. New York: Churchill Livingstone; 1996. p. 215–48.

16. National Institutes of Health (US). NIH consensus statement: genetic testing for cystic fibrosis. Bethesda

(MD): Dept. of Health and Human Services (US); 1997;15:1–25.

17. Dawkins KD, Burke CM, Billingham ME, Jamieson SW. Primary pulmonary hypertension and pregnancy. Chest 1986;89:383–8.

18. Kitzmiller JL, Gavin LA, Gin GD, et al. Preconception care of diabetes. Glycemic control prevents congenital anomalies. JAMA 1991;265:731–6.

19. Institute of Medicine. Subcommittee on Nutritional Status and Weight Gain During Pregnancy, Subcommittee on Dietary Intake and Nutrient Supplements During Pregnancy, Committee on Nutritional Status During Pregnancy and Lactation, Food and Nutrition Board. Nutrition during pregnancy. Washington (DC): National Academy Press; 1990.

20. Platt LD, Koch R, Azen C, et al. Maternal phenylketonuria collaborative study, obstetric aspects and outcome; the first 6 years. Am J Obstet Gynecol 1992; 166:1150–62.

21. Centers for Disease Control and Prevention (US). Trends in infant mortality attributable to birth defects—United States, 1980–1995. MMWR Morb Mortal Wkly Rep 1998;47:773–7.

22. Centers for Disease Control and Prevention (US). Recommendations for the use of folic acid to reduce the number of cases of spina bifida and other neural tube defects. MMWR Morb Mortal Wkly Rep 1992;41:1–7.

23. Centers for Diseases Control and Prevention (US). Use of folic acid for prevention of spina bifida and other neural tube defects, 1983–1991. MMWR Morb Mortal Wkly Rep 1991;40:513–6.

24. Council on Scientific Affairs (US). Violence against women: relevance for medical practitioners. JAMA 1992;267:3184–9.

25. Sever LE, Mortensen ME. Teratology and the epidemiology of birth defects: occupational and environmental perspectives. In: Gabbe SG, Niebyl JR, Simpson JL, editors. Obstetrics: normal and problem pregnancies. 3rd ed. New York: Churchill Livingstone; 1996. p. 185–214.

26. American College of Obstetricians and Gynecologists. Guidelines for women's health care. Washington (DC): American College of Obstetricians and Gynecologists; 1996.

27. American Academy of Pediatrics and the American College of Obstetricians and Gynecologists. Guidelines for perinatal care. 4th ed. Elk Grove Village (IL): American Academy of Pediatrics; 1997.

28. Expert Panel on the Content of Prenatal Care. Caring for our future: the content of prenatal care. Washington (DC): Public Health Service (US); 1989.

29. Gazmararian JA, Lazorick S, Spitz AM, et al. Prevalence of violence against pregnant women. JAMA 1996;275:1915–20.

30. Barnes AB, Colton T, Gundersen J, et al. Fertility and outcome of pregnancy in women exposed in utero to diethylstilbestrol. N Engl J Med 1980;302:609–13.

31. Smaill F. Antibiotics for asymptomatic bacteriuria in pregnancy. Cochrane Database Syst Rev 2000;2: CD000490.

32. Centers for Disease Control and Prevention (US). U.S. Public Health Service recommendations for human immunodeficiency virus counseling and voluntary testing for pregnant women. MMWR Morb Mortal Wkly Rep 1995;44(RR-7):1–15.

33. Herbst AL, Mishell DR, Stenchever MA, et al. Comprehensive gynecology. St. Louis (MO): Mosby Year Book; 1992.

34. Speroff L, Glass RH, Kase NG. Clinical gynecologic endocrinology and infertility. 5th ed. Baltimore (MD): Williams & Wilkins; 1994.

35. Batzer FR, Schlaff S, Goldfarb AF. Serial B-subunit human chorionic gonadotropin doubling time as a prognosticator of pregnancy outcome in an infertile population. Fertil Steril 1981;35:307–12.

36. Fossum GT, Davajan V, Kletzky OA. Early detection of pregnancy with transvaginal ultrasound. Fertil Steril 1988;49:789–91.

37. Levi CS, Lyons EA, Lindsay DJ. Early diagnosis of nonviable pregnancy with endovaginal ultrasound. Radiology 1988;167:383–5.

38. Levi CS, Lyons EA, Zheng XH, et al. Endovaginal ultrasound: demonstration of cardiac activity in embryos of less than 5.0 mm in crown-rump length. Radiology 1990:176;71–4.

39. Iams JD, Gabbe SG. Intrauterine growth retardation. In: Iams JD, Zuspan FP, Quilligan EJ, editors. Manual of obstetrics and gynecology. 2nd ed. St Louis (MO): Mosby; 1990. p. 165–72.

40. Enkin M, Keirse MJNC, Renfrew M, Neilson J. A guide to effective care in pregnancy and childbirth. 2nd ed. Oxford: Oxford University Press; 1999.

41. Jewell D, Young G. Interventions for nausea and vomiting in early pregnancy. Cochrane Database Syst Rev 2000;2:CD000145.

42. Jewell D. Compound antacid preparations for heartburn in pregnancy. Cochrane Database Syst Rev No. 06858.

43. Jewell DJ, Young G. Interventions for treating constipation in pregnancy. Cochrane Database Syst Rev 2000;2:CD001142.

44. Brisanda G. How to treat hemorrhoids. Prevention is best; hemorrhoidectomy needs skilled operators. BMJ 2000;321:582.

45. Young GL, Jewell D. Interventions for leg cramps in pregnancy. Cochrane Database Syst Rev 2000;2:CD000121.

46. Young G, Jewell D. Interventions for preventing and treating backache in pregnancy. Cochrane Database Syst Rev 2000;2:CD001139.

47. Hemminki E, Starfield B. Routine administration of iron and vitamins during pregnancy: review of controlled clinical trials. Br J Obstet Gynaecol 1978;85:404–10.

48. Mozurkewich EL, Luke B, Avni M, Wolf FM. Working conditions and adverse pregnancy outcome: a meta-analysis. Obstet Gynecol 2000;95:623–35.

49. American College of Obstetricians and Gynecologists. Exercise during pregnancy and the postpartum period. ACOG Technical Bulletin #189. Washington (DC): American College of Obstetricians and Gynecologists, 1995.

50. Thomas RE. Preparing your patients to travel abroad safely. Part 3: reducing the risk of malaria and dengue fever. Can Fam Physician 2000;46:1126–31.

51. Thomas RE. Preparing patients to travel abroad safely. Part 2: updating vaccinations. Can Fam Physician 2000;46:646–52, 655–6.

52. Sayle AE, Savitz DA, Thorp JM Jr, et al. Sexual activity during late pregnancy and risk of preterm delivery. Obstet Gynecol 2001;97:283–9.

53. Bartellas E, Crane JM, Daley M, et al. Sexuality and sexual activity in pregnancy. Br J Obstet Gynaecol 2000;107:964–8.

54. American Academy of Pediatrics Work Group on Breastfeeding. Breastfeeding and the use of human milk. Pediatrics 1997;100:1035–7.

55. Ryan AS. The resurgence of breastfeeding in the United States. Pediatrics 1997;99:E12.

56. Lu MC, Lange L, Slusser W, et al. Provider encouragement of breast-feeding: evidence from a national survey. Obstet Gynecol 2000;97:290–5.

57. Simpson JL. Genetic counseling and prenatal diagnosis. In: Gabbe SG, Niebyl JR, Simpson JL, editors. Obstetrics: normal and problem pregnancies. 3rd ed. New York: Churchill Livingstone; 1996. p. 269–98.

58. Centers for Disease Control and Prevention (US). Prevention of perinatal group B streptococcal disease: a public health perspective. MMWR Morb Mortal Wkly Rep 1996;45:1–24.

59. Neilson JP. Ultrasound for fetal assessment in early pregnancy. Cochrane Database Syst Rev 2000;2:CD000182.

60. American College of Obstetricians and Gynecologists. Routine ultrasound in low-risk pregnancy. ACOG practice patterns #5. Washington (DC): American College of Obstetricians and Gynecologists; 1997.

61. Browne FJ. Antenatal and postnatal care. London: J & A Churchill; 1987. p. 511–26.

62. Centers for Disease Control and Prevention (US). Achievements in public health, 1900–1999: healthier mothers and babies. MMWR Morb Mortal Wkly Rep 1999;48:849–58.

63. Lu MC. Pregnancy. In: Breslow L, editor. Encyclopedia of public health. [In press]

64. Korenbrot CC, Moss NE. Preconception, prenatal, perinatal and postnatal influences on health. In: Smedley BD, Syme SL, editors. Promoting health: intervention strategies from social and behavioral research. Washington (DC): National Academy Press; 2000. p. 125–69.

65. Lu MC, Halfon N. Racial and ethnic disparities in birth outcomes: a life-course perspective. [Submitted]

15

COMMON MEDICAL PROBLEMS IN PREGNANCY

Donelle Laughlin, MD, and Brian Koos, MD

The majority of women deliver a healthy infant without complication. However, medical disorders or problems that arise in pregnancy may increase the risk for mother and/or fetus, and the likelihood of such medical complications increases as women delay pregnancy until the latter part of their reproductive life. Women with medical disorders should undergo preconception counseling and stabilization of the medical condition prior to pregnancy. The management of medical conditions in pregnancy is generally similar to that in the nonpregnant state, although therapy may have to be modified because of concerns for the developing fetus. This chapter highlights the management of some of the more common medical problems encountered in pregnancy.

DIABETES MELLITUS

Diabetes encompasses about 2 to 3% of the medical complications of pregnancy with about 90% of these representing gestation-induced insulin resistance. Diabetes in pregnancy has been classified traditionally on the basis of age of onset, duration of disease, and the existence of complications (Table 15–1), but diabetes also has been categorized based on the need for insulin to prevent ketoacidosis.[1] Type 1 patients are insulin dependent, whereas Type 2 diabetics do not require insulin to avoid ketoacidosis. Type 3 patients are gravidas with insulin resistance resulting from the hormonal changes of pregnancy. However, a classification based on the extent of metabolic control and vascular involvement would likely be a better predictor of pregnancy outcome

Insulin-Requiring Diabetes

PRECONCEPTION COUNSELING
The fetal malformation rate is about four times the normal rate in women who become pregnant and have poor glucose control. High glucose concentrations during embryogenesis have been linked to

TABLE 15–1. White Classification of Diabetes in Pregnancy

Class	Onset (yr)		Duration (yr)	Insulin Requirement	Vascular Involvement
A1	Any		Any	No	No
A2	Any		Any	Yes	No
B	> 20		< 10	Yes	No
C	10–19		10–19	Yes	No
D	< 10	or	> 20	Yes	Benign retinopathy
F	Any		Any	Yes	Nephropathy
R	Any		Any	Yes	Proliferative retinopathy
H	Any		Any	Yes	Heart disease

Adapted from Gabbe SG, Landon MB. Diabetes mellitus in pregnancy. In: Quilligan EJ, Zuspan FP, editors. Current therapy in obstetrics and gynecology. 5th ed. Philadelphia: Saunders; 2000. p. 263–8.

TABLE 15–2. Optimal Glucose Concentrations During Pregnancy

Time	Glucose Concentration (mg/dL)
Before	
Breakfast	60–95
Lunch, dinner, bedtime snack	60–105
After meals	
1 h	≤140
2 h	≤120
2:00 am–6:00 am	>60

Adapted from Metzger BE, Coustan DR. Summary and recommendations of the Fourth International Workshop-Conference on Gestational Diabetes Mellitus. Diabetes Care 1998;21:B164.

cardiac and neural tube defects, and relatively tight regulation of maternal glucose during this time has been associated with a malformation rate that approximates that of normal gravidas. Tight metabolic control established prior to pregnancy is critical to minimize the risk of congenital malformations. Thus, patients should be familiar with the techniques for monitoring glucose concentrations and with the therapy that is used to provide optimal glucose regulation.

The preconceptional visit should include an evaluation of arterial blood pressure, renal function (ie, creatinine clearance and protein excretion), and retinal vessels. Diabetic retinopathy may progress to proliferative changes requiring photocoagulation; however, diabetic renal disease may not be affected adversely by pregnancy if blood pressure is controlled. An electrocardiogram should be performed if the duration of the disease is at least 10 years or if there is reason to suspect the presence of vascular disease.

Postconception Management

Relatively tight regulation of maternal glycemia is important even after embryogenesis to reduce the risk of fetal hyperglycemia and hyperinsulinemia that have been associated with fetal macrosomia and stillbirth. The gravida should measure her glucose concentrations several times a day using portable reflectance or absorbence meters. When establishing glucose control, measurements may be taken before meals, 1 or 2 hours after meals, and at bedtime. Less intensive monitoring generally is

required if glucose is reasonably controlled. A common regimen involves measuring fasting and postprandial glucose concentrations. The target blood glucose levels for pregnant women with diabetes are shown in Table 15–2.

Diet. The average woman requires 2,200 to 2,400 kcal/d during pregnancy that is comprised of 50 to 60% carbohydrates, 20% protein, and 20% fat. The daily caloric intake is divided so that 25% are consumed at breakfast, 30% at lunch, 30% at dinner, and 15% in a bedtime snack. Proper nutrition is critical to glucose control, and dietary instruction should be given with preconception counseling and reinforced early in gestation.

Insulin. Insulin should be given in multiple doses to maintain maternal euglycemia. Two-thirds of the total daily insulin requirement is given before breakfast in the form of short-acting (one-third of dose) and intermediate-acting (two-thirds of dose) human insulin. The remaining insulin is given as short-acting (one-half of dose) and intermediate-acting (one-half of dose) preparations prior to dinner. Alternatively, the evening dose can be split so that short-acting insulin is given before dinner and the intermediate-acting agent is given at bedtime. This latter approach may help reduce the risk of nocturnal hypoglycemia. Long-acting insulin (eg, Ultralente) may also be given at bedtime and/or before breakfast with the administration of short-acting insulin prior to meals, but it should be used cautiously because of the greater risk of maternal hypoglycemia.[2] Insulin pump therapy also can be used, but careful consideration must be given to patient selection and management because of the increased risk of nocturnal hypoglycemia in pregnancy. If insulin lispro is used as the short-acting insulin, the injection should be given immediately before a meal rather than 30 minutes prior as is normally recommended for regular insulin. In general, the appropriate insulin dose is increased or decreased by about 20% when adjustments are necessary to maintain target plasma glucose concentrations.

Oral therapy. Glyburide, which does not enter the fetal circulation in appreciable quantities, has been used successfully to treat women with gestational diabetes.[3] Although the available information does not preclude no adverse effects on fetal development, clinical experience with glyburide suggests that this agent can be given safely to pregnant women after the first trimester. Sulfonylurea drugs that cross the placenta should not be given to pregnant women because of the potential for teratogenesis and neonatal hypoglycemia.

Outpatient management. Pregnant women with uncomplicated diabetes are commonly seen in the outpatient clinic every 2 weeks for the first 36 weeks of gestation. Insulin dosage can be adjusted based on home monitoring of maternal glucose concentrations, with the results communicated by phone to health care clinicians. Hospitalization may be necessary for those with poorly controlled diabetes, ketoacidosis, infection, preeclampsia, fetal growth retardation, poor clinic attendance, or other conditions that increase maternal and fetal risk. Gravidas with benign retinopathy should have funduscopic examinations during each trimester, and those with proliferative changes may require monthly examinations.[4]

FETAL ASSESSMENT
The fetus should be evaluated for neural tube defects, cardiac malformations, and other anomalies. This assessment should include a measurement of maternal serum α-fetoprotein concentrations at 16 weeks of gestation and obstetric ultrasonography with echocardiography at 18 to 22 weeks of gestation. Fetal assessment, which is normally started at 32 to 34 weeks of gestation, may be started as early as 26 to 28 weeks of gestation when the pregnancy is complicated by ketoacidosis, hypertension, preeclampsia, nephropathy, fetal growth retardation, or poor glucose control. Fetal surveillance may involve the nonstress test, computerized assessment of fetal heart rate variability (eg, Oxford Sonicaid, System 8000, Oxford Instruments, Clearwater, Florida), biophysical profile, or contraction stress test. The nonstress test commonly is performed, but measurements of fetal heart rate variability are more reproducible, often performed in less time, and accurately applied to young fetuses (< 32 weeks' gestation). Testing is usually performed weekly in uncomplicated cases and twice weekly in gravidas with complications, but more frequent testing may be indicated in unstable clinical conditions.

OBSTETRIC MANAGEMENT
Precautions should be taken in the management of obstetric complications. Magnesium sulfate is the drug of choice for preterm labor because it does not alter glucose homeostasis as do ß-sympathometics. The administration of glucocorticoids (eg, dexamethasone, betamethasone) to enhance fetal lung development may cause significant elevations in maternal glucose levels; thus, an intravenous insulin infusion may be necessary to control maternal glucose concentrations under these conditions.

The timing of delivery should be individualized according to maternal and fetal risk factors. Uncomplicated diabetics in good metabolic control generally can await the onset of spontaneous labor, with induction generally performed if the gestational age exceeds 40 weeks. Gravidas with poor glucose regulation, noncompliance, previous stillbirth, or vascular disease are candidates for delivery when the fetal lungs are sufficiently mature to minimize the risk of respiratory distress syndrome. Preterm delivery may be necessary with more severe complications, such as superimposed preeclampsia, fetal growth retardation, or nonreassuring fetal testing. An amniocentesis should be performed to establish fetal lung maturity when an elective delivery is planned before 39 weeks' gestation.

A vaginal delivery is anticipated unless there is an obstetric indication for cesarean delivery. The risk of shoulder dystocia is greater in pregnant women with diabetes because of disproportionate deposition of fat in the shoulders and trunk of the fetus. Therefore, cesarean delivery generally is recommended to avoid birth trauma when the fetal weight is estimated to exceed 4,000 to 4,500 g. Both clinical and ultrasonographic estimates of fetal weight may differ from birth weight by more than 20%, which is one important limitation of this approach. Cesarean delivery also should be considered strongly when the second stage is protracted.

Maternal hyperglycemia predisposes the newborn to hypoglycemia; thus, maternal glucose concentrations are monitored closely by measuring maternal capillary glucose levels every 1 to 2 hours during labor. Glucose (5% dextrose in Ringer's lactate or water) is infused at 125 mL/h with continuous intravenous administration of regular insulin (0.5 to 1.5 units/h) as required to keep maternal glucose levels within the target range of 80 to 120 mg/dL. Alternatively, insulin (10 units of regular) may be added to 1,000 mL of a 5% dextrose solution that is infused at 100 to 125 mL/h.[4] Many diabetics require no insulin during the active phase of labor.

Elective cesarean delivery is best performed early in the morning. Insulin is withheld on the morning of surgery, and maternal glucose levels are checked frequently. After surgery, a 5% dextrose solution is infused intravenously with blood glucose concentrations determined every 2 hours. The therapeutic goal is to keep maternal glucose levels to less than 200 mg/mL and to avoid hypoglycemia. Because insulin requirements fall significantly after delivery, insulin may not be required for several hours post partum. One-half the pregestational dose of NPH (Neutral Protamine Hagedorn) insulin may be given on the morning of the first day after a vaginal birth.[4]

Gestational Diabetes

About 90% of pregnant diabetics have gestational or Type III disease. This condition has been associated with fetal macrosomia, birth trauma, stillbirth, and neonatal hypoglycemia and hyperbilirubinemia.[5] Therefore, the identification and appropriate management of gestational diabetes may reduce perinatal morbidity and mortality in these patients.

The incidence of gestational diabetes is about 2 to 5%, but higher rates (~10%) are reported for some ethnic groups such as Africans, Mexicans, Puerto Ricans, and Cubans. The incidence is about 16% in Japanese and is 5 to 50% in Native Americans. Besides ethnicity, other risk factors include gestational diabetes in a previous pregnancy, obesity, hypertension, glycosuria, or a first-degree relative with diabetes. Fetal anomalies, macrosomia, and demise in a prior pregnancy are also risk factors.

DIAGNOSIS

Only about one-half of gestational diabetics have a traditional risk factor; consequently, provocative glucose testing (plasma glucose concentration measured 1 hour following 50 g of oral glucose) has been used as a screening test for pregnant women. Testing may target patients who have a high-risk factor, such as obesity (body mass index > 27 kg/m^2), older age (≥ 25 years of age), a first degree relative with diabetes mellitus, or being a member of an ethnic group with a high incidence ($> 5\%$) of diabetes.[1] Alternatively, screening may be performed for all pregnant women. Screening generally is performed at 24 to 28 weeks of gestation, although testing early in pregnancy is indicated if there is a prior history of gestational diabetes, glycosuria, or marked obesity. The 1-hour screen may be carried out in the nonfasting state. Women with 1-hour plasma glucose levels of 140 to 200 mg/dL should have a 3-hour oral glucose tolerance test (OGTT). This glucose threshold identifies about 90% of gestational diabetics and requires that about 15% of screened patients have an OGTT. Patients with a 1-hour screening glucose level of over 200 mg/dL generally are treated as diabetics.

The diagnosis of gestational diabetes requires that at least two plasma glucose measurements of the OGTT meet or exceed the upper limits of normal (Table 15–3). These criteria are based on glucose measurements in whole blood of over 700 women.[6] The criteria established in 1972 by the National Diabetes Data Group was an attempt to convert the whole blood glucose levels to equivalent plasma concentrations;[7] however, the more accurate Carpenter and Coustan conversion[8] has been embraced by the Fourth International Workshop-Conference on Gestational Diabetes Mellitus.[1]

GLUCOSE REGULATION

Women with gestational diabetes should be placed on a diet that is similar to that for pregestational

TABLE 15–3. Criteria for Diagnosis of Gestational Diabetes Mellitus[*]

| Timing | Venous Glucose Concentrations (mg/dL) | | |
	Whole Blood	Plasma	Corrected Plasma
Fasting	90	105	95
1 h after load	165	195	180
2 h after load	145	165	155
3 h after load	125	145	140

[*]Oral 100-g glucose load; diagnosis requires that two or more values of the 3-hour test meet or exceed these glucose concentrations. Plasma concentrations[7] are calculated from whole blood measurements.[6] Corrected plasma values,[8] which have been adjusted for systematic errors of whole blood glucose analysis, are to be used for diagnosis.

diabetes with a daily caloric intake of 30 kcal/kg (for those 80 to 120% of ideal body weight), 35 to 40 kcal/kg (for those <80% of ideal body weight), or 24 kcal/kg (for those 120 to 150% of ideal body weight). Markedly obese women (>150% of ideal body weight) have been successfully managed on 12 to 15 kcal/kg/d. Fasting and 1- or 2-hour postprandial glucose concentrations should be measured at least once per week. Although measurements can be taken in the office, it is often more convenient and informative to have the patient monitor her own glucose values on a daily basis using a portable reflectance/transmission meter. The physician reviews these measurements at clinic visits, while keeping in mind that a single measurement of glucose concentrations in capillary blood may vary up to 20 mg/dL or more from levels in venous blood.[9] The mean of several measurements taken at the same time of day tends to better approximate venous levels. Exercise also may improve glucose control. Insulin therapy should be initiated if maternal plasma glucose concentrations are frequently above 95 mg/dL for fasting and/or above 120 mg/dL for concentrations measured 2 hours after meals. The starting insulin dose is usually 0.7 units/kg maternal weight/d during the first trimester, with higher dosages required as pregnancy progresses, to a maximum of 1.0 unit/kg body weight/d at term. The oral agent glyburide also may be considered for the regulation of maternal glycemia for patients who are beyond the first trimester.

OBSTETRIC MANAGEMENT
Antepartum testing is normally started at 40 weeks of gestation in uncomplicated gestational diabetics. Fetal assessment should be started earlier as for pregestational diabetes if the gravida has hypertension, history of a stillbirth, or requires insulin.

In most cases, women with uncomplicated gestational diabetes who remain in good control can await the onset of spontaneous labor. Vaginal delivery in these patients poses a greater risk for shoulder dystocia and birth trauma; therefore, cesarean delivery is appropriate according to the guidelines presented for delivery of pregestational diabetics. Midpelvic deliveries by forceps or vacuum extractor generally should be avoided because of the associated increased risk of shoulder dystocia in this population.

POSTPARTUM ASSESSMENT
Patients with gestational diabetes have at least a 50% risk of developing Type 2 diabetes in later life; thus, they should be tested for diabetes about 6 to 12 weeks after delivery, with screening performed every 1 to 3 years thereafter.[5] Testing can be performed using either fasting glucose concentrations (>110 mg/dL are abnormal) or the 2-hour 75-g OGTT. In the latter test, diabetes is established if the fasting glucose is equal to or greater than 140 mg/dL or if two postglucose concentrations equal or exceed 200 mg/dL.

THYROID DISEASE

Thyroid disease is a common endocrinopathy seen during pregnancy that can adversely affect perinatal outcome.

Hypothyroidism
The common causes of hypothyroidism include thyroiditis (chronic or Hashimoto's), treatment for Graves' disease (surgery or radiation), nodular goiter, thyroid carcinoma, or primary (idiopathic) myxedema.[10]

PREGNANCY EFFECTS
Women on appropriate thyroid replacement can expect a normal pregnancy outcome, but untreated maternal hypothyroidism is associated with an increased risk of preeclampsia, spontaneous abortion, premature separation of the placenta, and low–birth weight or stillborn infants. Undiagnosed hypothyroidism in pregnant women also has been linked to lower intelligence levels in their offspring.[11] Hypothyroid women who remain fertile may have only mild symptoms, so that the condition may not be readily identified; thus, iodine supplementation of the general population or screening of pregnant women for this disorder may be appropriate.[11,12] Gravidas with insulin-dependent diabetes mellitus, who are at increased risk for hypothyroidism, should undergo thyroid testing.

LABORATORY FINDINGS
In primary hypothyroidism the thyroid-stimulating hormone (TSH) is elevated, and free thyroxine (T_4) is low; but in subclinical hypothyroidism a high TSH may be associated with a normal free T_4. In hypothyroid gravidas, total serum T_4 concentrations may be normal because of the estrogen-induced rise

in the levels of thyroid-binding globulin. Anti-thyroid microsomal antibodies, which are elevated in Hashimoto's thyroiditis, may be useful in predicting neonatal hypothyroidism and postpartum thyroiditis.[13]

THERAPY

Hypothyroidism during pregnancy is treated with replacement doses (0.1 to 0.15 mg/d) of levothyroxine. An increase in the dose may be necessary during the course of pregnancy, and these adjustments are made according to maternal TSH and free T_4 concentrations at the initial visit in the first trimester, and subsequently at 16 to 20 weeks and 28 to 32 weeks of gestation. Women in whom thyroid therapy is initiated during pregnancy should have monthly TSH measurements with levothyroxine adjustments until the TSH is within the normal range.

Hyperthyroidism

Graves' disease accounts for more than 90% of hyperthyroidism in pregnancy, but other disorders, such as toxic adenoma, toxic multinodular goiter, and thyroiditis, should be considered. Pregnant women also may be hyperthyroid as a result of gestational trophoblastic disease or hyperemesis gravidarum. High human chorionic gonadotropin (hCG) levels associated with the latter disorders may cause excessive thyroid stimulation.

PREGNANCY EFFECTS

Pregnant women with hyperthyroidism are predisposed to heart failure, and infants born to hyperthyroid mothers are at increased risk of preterm delivery, growth retardation, thyrotoxicosis (Graves' disease), and congenital anomalies.[14] Thus, it is critical that pregnant women who are hyperthyroid be identified and treated appropriately.

The symptoms of hyperthyroidism in pregnant women are less apparent than in nonpregnant women because many of the classic signs of hyperthyroidism resemble the physiologic adjustments of normal pregnancy, such as emotional lability, heat intolerance, palpitations, and tachycardia. Weight loss (~ 1 kg) is also normal during the first trimester. Some distinguishing features of pregnancy complicated by hyperthyroidism include progressive weight loss, onycholysis, and a pulse rate that persistently exceeds 100 beats per minute (bpm).[13] An elevated serum free T_4 concentration and a depressed

TSH level confirm the diagnosis. Levels of TSH may be depressed with a normal free T_4 in cases of T_3 hyperthyroidism; serum free T_3 concentrations should be measured if hyperthyroidism is suspected but the free T_4 is normal. Concentrations of TSH during the first 16 weeks of pregnancy must be interpreted with caution because these levels typically are suppressed in euthyroid women, as the result of high circulating levels of hCG.[14]

THERAPY

Hyperthyroidism during pregnancy usually is treated with propylthiouracil (100 to 150 mg q8h), although methimazole (10 to 20 mg q12h) also may be administered. Higher doses may be required in some cases, and ß-adrenergic receptor blockade with propranolol (10 to 40 mg q6–8h) may be used for rapid control of severe adrenergic symptoms. Clinical improvement begins within 2 weeks, with maximum benefit achieved within about 6 weeks. The dose of the antithyroid medication is reduced by 50% once the free T_4 starts to fall.[15] Antithyroid medication is tapered further when the patient becomes euthyroid, so as to give the lowest dose that maintains monthly free T_4 measurements within the upper range of normal, which reduces the risk of drug-induced fetal hypothyroidism. Levels of TSH should not be used to adjust therapy because the rise to normal values lags by several weeks the normalization of free hormone concentrations. Graves' disease often abates during pregnancy, which may permit the discontinuance of antithyroid therapy after 30 weeks of gestation.

Less than 5% of patients have reactions to antithyroid therapy; these may involve skin rash, pruritus, fever, arthralgias, or lymphadenopathy. A serious but uncommon complication is agranulocytosis, which should be suspected in the presence of sore throat, fever, or gingivitis. The drug should be discontinued if the granulocyte count is decreased.[15] Fetal goiter is more likely to occur with high doses of antithyroid medication.

Thyroidectomy may be necessary during pregnancy if the patient has poor compliance with medical therapy or has an allergy to both antithyroid drugs. Radioiodine ablates the thryoid in both the mother and fetus; therefore, radioiodine is reserved for the nonpregnant state. Thyroid storm during pregnancy is managed as for nonpregnant individuals. This is discussed further in Chapter 57.

FETAL HYPERTHYROIDISM

Placental transfer of thyroid-stimulating receptor antibodies (immunoglobulin [Ig] G) may induce hyperthyroidism in the fetus and newborn of women with a history of Graves' disease or Hashimoto's thyroiditis. Fetal thyrotoxicosis is suggested by a fetal heart rate that is persistently above 160 bpm, fetal growth retardation, and craniosynostosis.[13] High titers of TSH receptor antibodies at about 30 weeks' gestation may help identify fetuses at increased risk for hyperthyroidism.[13] When fetal hyperthyroidism is suspected, fetal growth and well-being should be assessed by ultrasonography and monitoring of the heart rate.

POSTPARTUM THYROIDITIS

About 5% of postpartum women develop a transient thyroiditis that is characterized by hyperthyroidism that begins 2 to 3 months post partum, and hypothyroidism that develops 4 to 8 months post partum. Most women become euthyroid after 5 months. The diagnosis is confirmed by abnormal TSH and free T_4 values and by the presence of antithyroperioxidase and antimicrosomal antibodies.[13] Treatment, which usually is not necessary, is based on severity of symptoms.

CHRONIC HYPERTENSION

Pregnant women may have hypertension as a result of a pregnancy disorder or a chronic condition that developed before conception. In chronic hypertension, arterial pressures are generally equal to or greater than 140/90 mm Hg during the first 20 weeks of pregnancy. Hypertension is considered mild if the systolic pressure is 140 to 159 mm Hg or the diastolic pressure is 90 to 109 mm Hg. The disorder is considered severe if the systolic pressure equals or exceeds 160 mm Hg or if the diastolic value equals or exceeds 105 to 110 mm Hg. Chronic hypertension has been associated with several pregnancy complications, including preeclampsia, abruptio placentae, fetal growth retardation, preterm delivery, and fetal demise. Most women with uncomplicated mild hypertension generally do well during pregnancy. The major risk for this group is superimposed preeclampsia, which occurs in up to 20% of these patients.

Maternal and fetal complications are greater when chronic hypertension is severe (> 160/110 mm Hg) or longstanding (> 15 years). Increased maternal

and fetal risk also are associated with diabetes mellitus, renal disorders, collagen vascular disease, cardiomyopathy, coarctation of the aorta, congestive heart failure, and prior cerebral hemorrhage.[16] These women should receive thorough preconception counseling and be followed up by a medical team that is experienced in managing gravidas with these disorders.

Management

TARGET PRESSURES

Pregnant women with uncomplicated chronic hypertension should monitor their pressures at home and generally should be seen in the office at 2-week intervals. The therapeutic goal should be to keep diastolic pressures below 105 mm Hg to reduce the risk of maternal and fetal complications. Antihypertensive therapy generally is started when the diastolic pressure or mean arterial pressure persistently exceeds 90 to 95 mm Hg or 110 to 112 mm Hg, respectively. Treatment should not be too aggressive because low arterial pressures (eg, diastolic pressure < 85 mm Hg) may be associated with decreased fetal growth. Such fetal effects may be related to reduced uteroplacental perfusion or alterations in the umbilical and/or fetal circulations. Lowering maternal diastolic blood pressure below 100 mm Hg does not improve maternal or fetal outcome,[17] but it may reduce end-organ damage[18] and decrease the risk of blood pressure fluctuations that reach severe levels. Because of the lack of good clinical studies in this area, there is some controversy regarding the threshold pressures for initiating antihypertensive therapy during pregnancy.

THERAPY

Several antihypertensive agents appear to be relatively safe during pregnancy. α-Methyldopa (up to 4 g/d) has been for many years a first-line medication for treating pregnant women with chronic hypertension. Labetalol (200 to 2,400 mg/d), which blocks $α_1$- and ß-adrenergic receptors, has the advantage of having fewer maternal side effects such as drowsiness and postural hypotension. Nifedipine (40 to 120 mg/d) also may be used in single-agent therapy, and nifedipine or hydralazine may be added to α-methyldopa or labetalol therapy, if multidrug therapy is required. Clonidine also has an acceptable side effect profile. The administration of some ß-adrenergic receptor blockers (eg, atenolol or propranolol) during pregnancy generally has been discouraged for the treatment of hypertension because these agents have been associated with restricted fetal growth,[19] although other antihypertensive agents apparently have this effect too.[20] Diuretics, which reduce plasma volume, may decrease uteroplacental blood flow; thus, diuretics generally are avoided except in patients who have salt-sensitive hypertension or myocardial dysfunction.[16] Inhibitors of angiotensin converting enzyme are contraindicated in pregnancy because their use has been associated with fetal growth restriction, oligohydramnios, neonatal hypotension, and neonatal renal failure.[21] Preconception counseling is particularly important to help ensure that blood pressure is stabilized with a relatively safe agent before conception.

MEDICAL ASSESSMENT

The etiology of hypertension should be determined if the gravida has not had a prior evaluation. Although most gravidas have essential hypertension, an investigation is more likely to identify a cause for hypertension in pregnant women than it is in the elderly. The physical examination should include an assessment of her general appearance, comparison of the arterial pressures and pulses in the upper and lower extremities, inspection of the ocular fundi, examination of the heart and lungs, auscultation of the flanks for bruits, and palpation of the abdomen for masses. Laboratory assessment generally should include a complete blood count, serum potassium, a screen for glucose intolerance, urine analysis, creatinine clearance, serum uric acid concentration, and an estimate of 24-h urinary excretion of protein. Electrocardiography is performed if there is evidence of cardiac hypertrophy or if the patient has a long history of hypertension. A chest radiograph may be helpful if aortic coarctation is suspected or if the disease is longstanding. Urinary excretion of vanillylmandelic acid and metanephrines should be performed if there is reason to suspect a pheochromocytoma, such as the abrupt onset of severe hypertension, headaches, anxiety attacks, sweating, or hyperglycemia. Laboratory studies for systemic lupus erythematosus should be conducted if the gravida has proteinuria, and tests for lupus anticoagulant and anticardiolipin antibodies should be performed if the patient has had recurrent pregnancy loss.[16] Evaluation for secondary causes of hypertension is discussed further in Chapter 31.

ARTERIAL PRESSURE

Because management depends on accurate blood pressure determinations, care must be taken to ensure that arterial pressure is measured properly. Blood pressure should be taken with the patient in the sitting position with the forearm supported at the heart level. The cuff should have a bladder length that is at least 80% of the circumference of the arm and a width that is at least 40% of the circumference. The fifth Korotkoff sound (disappearance of repetitive sounds) is more reflective of diastolic pressure (overestimates diastolic pressure by 4 to 7 mm Hg) than is the fourth Korotkoff sound (muffling of repetitive sounds), which cannot be identified consistently and which overestimates diastolic pressure by 9 to 11 mm Hg.[22] Thus, the fifth (rather than the fourth) Korotkoff sound should be used in pregnant women, except in rare cases when the fifth Korotkoff sound is audible at zero pressure due to the hyperdynamic circulation of pregnancy.[22] Care must be taken to avoid artifacts when taking blood pressure in the lateral position; the measurements must be either taken at or *corrected* to the level of the heart.

Systemic arterial pressure normally decreases during the first 24 weeks of gestation, as is reflected in a 5 to 10 mm Hg fall in systolic pressure and a 10 to 15 mm Hg drop in diastolic pressure. After 24 weeks systolic and diastolic pressures gradually rise and return to nonpregnant levels by term. Thus, pregnancy may result in a reduction in drug dosage required to control arterial pressure. Patients in whom arterial pressure fails to fall during the second trimester tend to have greater problems with the control of blood pressure later in the pregnancy.

FETAL ASSESSMENT

Fetal growth should be assessed by ultrasonography at 18 to 24 weeks' gestation and then monthly, starting at 26 to 28 weeks' gestation. The ultrasound evaluation should include an assessment of amniotic fluid volume and umbilical artery velocimetry. Fetal assessment by heart rate testing or the biophysical profile is initiated in women with uncomplicated hypertension if there is evidence of superimposed preeclampsia, abnormal umbilical artery velocimetry, or fetal growth restriction, or history of a prior stillbirth. Fetal monitoring also should be performed in pregnancies complicated by vascular disease or other conditions that increase fetal risk. This assessment is commonly started at 32 to 34 weeks of gestation, but it may be initiated as early as 25 to 26 weeks of gestation, depending on the clinical situation.

PREECLAMPSIA

Hypertensive gravidas with chronic hypertension should be closely followed up for symptoms and signs of superimposed preeclampsia, because this condition materially increases the risks for mother and fetus. Changes in management may include more intensive monitoring of the mother and fetus, the administration of magnesium sulfate, and early delivery. Superimposed preeclampsia is indicated by the development of generalized edema, proteinuria, and/or a rise in arterial pressure of at least 30 mm Hg systolic and/or 15 mm Hg diastolic above baseline values. Platelet counts and serum aminotransferase concentrations should be measured to determine the presence of thrombocytopenia or liver injury. Significant proteinuria (> 300 mg/24 h), high serum uric acid concentrations (> 5 mg/dL), and a low urine calcium/creatinine ratio (< 0.04) help establish the diagnosis.[23]

Hypertensive emergencies. Severe hypertension (arterial blood pressure > 160/105 mm Hg), which is common in superimposed preeclampsia, is a medical emergency that requires immediate therapy. However, treatment must be given in a way that avoids large falls in maternal arterial pressure, which can reduce uteroplacental blood flow and, thus, fetal oxygen delivery.

Hydralazine has been the traditional agent for lowering arterial pressure in women with severe preeclampsia. The initial intravenous dose is 5 mg; this is a test dose to determine maternal sensitivity to the drug. The agent (5 to 10 mg) is injected at 15- to 20-minute intervals until the diastolic pressure falls to 90 to 100 mm Hg. Hydralazine begins to act within about 15 minutes after administration, with maximum effects occurring within 60 minutes. Side effects include tachycardia and headache. This powerful vasodilator should be used cautiously so that maternal diastolic pressures do not fall below 90 mm Hg.

Compared with hydralazine, labetalol acts more rapidly and has a response that is less likely to produce hypotension. The initial dose is a 20-mg intravenous injection; this is followed up with doses of 40 and 80 mg, respectively, administered at 10-minute intervals until maternal diastolic pressure falls to target levels of 90 to 100 mm Hg. The maximum total dose should not exceed 220 mg.[24]

Calcium entry blockers, such as nifedipine, can be effective in lowering maternal blood pressure. The initial oral dose of nifedipine is 10 mg. Subsequent doses are taken at 20-to 30-minute intervals to a maximum of five doses. Compared with labetalol, nifedipine is advantageous because it has a more rapid onset of action, and it does not have the potential to blunt fetal cardiovascular responses to hypoxia. Diastolic pressure should not be decreased below 90 mm Hg. Oral nifedipine should be used with caution when administered with magnesium sulfate because of the potential for greater falls in arterial pressure under these conditions. Maternal side effects of nifedipine include headache and tachycardia. Overall, nifedipine compares favorably with labetalol in the management of acute hypertension in pregnancy.[25]

Sodium nitroprusside, a nonselective direct vasodilator of arterial and venous smooth muscle, is a short-acting agent that has an almost immediate onset of action. The drug dosage is controlled through careful titration of the continuous intravenous infusion rate (starting dose: 0.25 µg/kg/min) and frequent (if not continuous) monitoring of systemic arterial pressures. Prolonged sodium nitroprusside infusion to pregnant women has the potential for fetal cyanide toxicity, although this complication is unlikely with rates of infusion of < 3 µg/kg/min for less than 4 hours' duration.[26] Nitroprusside should not be administered to pregnant women unless hydralazine, labetalol, or nifedipine fail to control arterial pressures.[24]

DELIVERY

Gravidas with uncomplicated hypertension generally are delivered by 41 weeks of gestation. In other patients, management is individualized according to fetal growth, fetal well-being, the development of superimposed preeclampsia, difficulty in controlling arterial pressure, and other complications. Delivery after 34 weeks of gestation is preferred because the risks associated with preterm delivery at this age are small, but earlier delivery may be indicated in more severe conditions.

SYSTEMIC LUPUS ERYTHEMATOSUS

Systemic lupus erythematosus (SLE), an autoimmune disorder, requires the presence of at least four of the following: malar and/or discoid rash, photosensitivity, oral ulcers, arthritis, serositis, renal disorder, neurologic abnormalities, hematologic disorder, immunologic abnormalities, and antinuclear antibody (ANA).[27] Virtually all patients with lupus have a positive ANA test, but a positive test is not specific for lupus because it can occur in association with other conditions. Antibodies to double-stranded deoxyribonucleic acid (DNA) are more specific for SLE. These patients may have a false-positive test for syphilis, prolonged partial thromboplastin time, rheumatoid factors, anemia, thrombocytopenia, proteinuria, and renal insufficiency.[28]

Preconception Counseling

LUPUS FLARES

Systemic lupus erythematosus is characterized by exacerbations and remissions, which has made it difficult to determine whether pregnancy alters the clinical course of the disease. Most studies indicate that the pregnancy has little effect on lupus flares[29-31] or may even protect against exacerbations.[32] However, a recent study has indicated that women with lupus had significantly more flares (65% versus 42%) compared with a control group of nonpregnant age-matched patients with similar disease duration and autoantibodies. Flares were more likely to occur during the last two trimesters and the puerperium.[33] Prednisone administration did not prevent flares.

PREGNANCY OUTCOME

Pregnant women with SLE have an increased risk of spontaneous abortion, intrauterine demise, intrauterine growth retardation, heart block in the fetus, preeclampsia, and preterm delivery. High-risk factors for adverse outcome include active disease at or immediately prior to conception, lupus nephritis, antiphospholipid antibodies, and anti–SS-A antibodies. A good outcome (90% livebirth rate) can be expected if the disorder has been in remission for 6 months prior to conception and renal function has been good (serum creatinine ≤ 1.5 mg/dL, creatinine clearance ≥ 60 mg/dL, proteinuria < 3 g/d).[34,35] Lupus flares in pregnancy can lower the livebirth rate to 65%. Clinical or histologic evidence of glomerulonephritis is present in up to 90% of patients with SLE. Adverse pregnancy outcome is more likely with nephrotic syndrome (60% livebirth rate), serum creatinine > 1.5 mg/dL (50% livebirth rate), and hypertension (50% livebirth rate).[36]

Women with SLE should be tested for anti–SS-A and anti–SS-B antibodies, which are associated with fetal heart block. Although 25% of patients with SLE have anti–SS-A antibodies, only about 5% of pregnant women with these antibodies have fetuses with congenital heart block. Anti–SS-A antibodies also have been associated with nonimmune hydrops fetalis, stillbirth, and congenital SLE.[36]

ANTIPHOSPHOLIPID SYNDROME

Up to 30% of pregnant women with lupus have the antiphospholipid syndrome, which involves recurrent abortion (three or more) or unexplained stillbirth, thrombosis or thrombocytopenia in association with lupus anticoagulant, or medium to high levels of anticardiolipin IgG antibodies. Pregnant women who have the antiphospholipid syndrome are predisposed to recurrent abortion, fetal growth restriction, fetal demise, and early-onset preeclampsia.[37] Decidual vasculopathy and placental infarction, which are commonly associated with the syndrome, likely have a critical role in mediating the adverse effects on reproduction. These women are also at increased risk for venous and arterial thrombosis, hemolytic anemia, and thrombocytopenia. In addition to autoimmune disorders, testing for lupus anticoagulant and antiphospholipid antibodies should be considered prior to conception in cases of prior unexplained pregnancy loss or fetal growth restriction, early-onset preeclampsia, venous or arterial thrombosis, and false-positive tests for syphilis.

Management

LABORATORY ASSESSMENT

At the first prenatal visit, complete blood and platelet counts and serum aminotransferase (aspartate aminotransferase [AST], alanine aminotransferase [ALT]) levels should be determined. Serum creatinine clearance and urinary protein excretion should be determined, and tests should be performed for lupus anticoagulant, anticardiolipin antibodies, and anti–SS-A and anti–SS-B antibodies. Anti-DNA titers, ANA, and complement factors 3, 4, and CH_{50} also should be measured. Complement levels normally increase in pregnancy, which can hinder the diagnosis of active disease. Decreasing or low levels of complement are consistent with lupus flares, but active disease also may be associated with high concentrations.[28] Leukocyte and platelet counts, complement levels, aminotransferase activity, serum creatinine clearance, and urinary protein excretion should be determined based on the symptoms and signs of disease and are measured at least every 3 months during pregnancy and the puerperium.

FETAL ASSESSMENT

Fetal growth should be monitored monthly by ultrasonography after 18 weeks of gestation, and this evaluation should include Doppler velocimetry of the umbilical artery. Fetal assessment by heart rate monitoring or biophysical profile generally are performed starting at 36 weeks of gestation in uncomplicated cases or as early as 26 to 28 weeks gestation when the disorder is associated with a lupus flare, renal impairment, hypertension, fetal growth restriction, antiphospholipid syndrome, or abnormal Doppler studies. In women with anti–SS-A or anti–SS-B antibodies, fetal echocardiography is recommended at 4-week intervals for detecting heart block. Fetuses with incomplete heart block may benefit from maternal administration of dexamethasone, a corticosteroid that crosses the placenta and may prevent further injury to fetal conduction system and may be effective in treating hydrops associated with third-degree heart block.[38–40] Antepartum assessment in fetuses with heart block may be performed by an assessment of fetal behavior (biophysical profile) or heart rate triggered by atrial movement.

THERAPY

Lupus flares are usually treated with prednisone, 60 mg/d for 3 weeks, after which the dose is tapered to 10 mg/d. Higher doses (up to 200 mg/d) may be required for lupus glomerulonephritis; plasmapheresis or azathioprine also may be used.[36] Pregnant women treated with glucocorticosteroids should receive calcium supplementation, monthly screens for glucose intolerance, and stress doses of glucocorticosteroids at delivery.

Patients should be hospitalized with deterioration in renal or liver function, involvement of the central nervous system, worsening hypertension, superimposed preeclampsia, or fetal compromise. Delivery is indicated if the fetus is at least at 34 weeks of gestation. Medical management with glucocorticoids and antihypertensive agents may be attempted for gestational ages of less than 34 weeks. Dexamethasone or betamethasone may be administered to the gravida during the first couple of days to enhance pulmonary maturity of the fetus. Severe preeclampsia, fetal compromise, and maternal arterial pressures that are difficult to control are indications for delivery.[36] Magnesium sulfate should be administered to patients with superimposed preeclampsia, and vaginal delivery should be attempted if the fetus is able to tolerate labor.

An exacerbation of lupus nephropathy may be difficult to distinguish from superimposed preeclampsia. Lupus flares usually are associated with increased anti-DNA titer, whereas preeclampsia is not associated with a rise in this antibody. The decline in complement levels tends to be more severe with lupus flares, but complement levels may not be a consistent indicator of lupus activity.[28,36] When the diagnosis is uncertain, corticosteroids are administered to treat a possible flare while the patient is managed as for superimposed preeclampsia.[28]

ANTIPHOSPHOLIPID SYNDROME

The antiphospholipid antibody syndrome requires special management. If the syndrome has been associated with recurrent pregnancy loss (three or more) or an unexplained fetal demise in the second or third trimester, prophylactic heparin should be given either in the unfractionated (7,500 to 10,000 units bid) or low–molecular weight form, and low-dose aspirin (80 mg daily) should be administered.[37] Antiphospholipid antibody syndrome with prior thrombosis or stroke should receive heparin either for anticoagulation or prophylaxis in addition to low-dose aspirin therapy, and this treatment should extend until 6 to 8 weeks after delivery. Warfarin instead of heparin may be used postpartum. All patients on heparin should have daily calcium (1,500 mg calcium carbonate) and vitamin D supplementation to reduce the risk of heparin-induced osteoporosis.

Appropriate treatment is less certain in pregnant women who have antiphospholipid antibodies but no prior pregnancy losses or thrombosis. These women may receive no treatment, daily low-dose aspirin administration, or daily prophylactic heparin and low-dose aspirin.[37] The same management applies to pregnant women with antiphospholipid antibodies (lupus anticoagulant or medium to high titers of anticardiolipin IgG) but without the antiphospholipid antibody syndrome. Anticardiolipin IgM or IgA antibodies, low titers of anticardiolipin IgG, or the presence of other antiphospholipid antibodies have questionable clinical significance, and pregnant women who have these antibodies may receive either daily low-dose aspirin or no treatment.

GASTROINTESTINAL DISEASE

Pregnancy is associated with a number of changes that may lead the unwary to an erroneous diagnosis of liver disease. For example, edema, palmar erythema, and spider angiomata occur commonly during pregnancy. Other changes include increased circulating levels of complement (C3 and C4), α- and ß-globulins, binding globulins, fibrinogen, and angiotensinogen. Serum albumin concentrations are reduced by up to 60%, which results in part from increased catabolism. Cholesterol levels double, and heat-stable serum alkaline phosphatase activity increases two- to fourfold as the result of placental production of the enzyme. Alanine aminotransferase, AST, 5′-nucleotidase, γ-glutamyl transpeptidase, and bilirubin levels are unchanged by pregnancy.[41]

Jaundice and pruritus are always abnormal in pregnancy and may be the first indication of a liver abnormality. The physician also should be attuned to more subtle suggestions of an underlying liver disorder, such as abdominal pain, excessive fatigue, edema, and fever, that may be indications for laboratory tests of liver injury and function. Liver and spleen enlargement can be difficult to detect in late pregnancy.

Disorders of Pregnancy

Pregnancy may be complicated by a number of conditions that are associated with liver dysfunction, and the following summarizes the disorders that are related specifically to pregnancy.

HYPEREMESIS GRAVIDARUM

Nausea and vomiting commonly occur during the first 12 to 16 weeks of gestation and normally do not endanger the health of the mother or the fetus. Excessive vomiting can lead to hyperemesis gravidarum that is associated with weight loss, dehydration, ketonuria, hyponatremia, hypochloremia, and hypokalemia. Serum bilirubin and aminotransferase levels also may be mildly elevated. This condition normally responds to intravenous hydration, electrolyte replacement, vitamins, and antiemetics, such as promethazine, prochlorperazine, and metoclopramide. Intravenous droperidol and diphenhydramine also have been used successively.[42] Hyperemesis that persists despite these treatments may require psychotherapy, nasogastric feedings,[43] or hyperalimentation. Patients with persistent vomiting also should be evaluated for other diseases, such as gastroenteritis, cholecystitis, pancreatitis, hepatitis, peptic ulcer, pyelonephritis, hyperthyroidism, multifetal gestation, hydatidiform mole, and fatty acute liver of pregnancy.

INTRAHEPATIC CHOLESTASIS OF PREGNANCY

In susceptible women, the increased estrogen levels of pregnancy reduce canalicular transport of bile acids, leading to increased serum concentrations and generalized pruritus. This complication, which typically occurs during the third trimester, is not accompanied by skin lesions or abdominal pain. Elevated serum bile acid concentrations confirm the diagnosis. Aminotransferases and bilirubin may be mildly elevated, with jaundice present in up to 25% of cases.

The pruritus, which can be severe, is best treated with ursodeoxycholic acid (300 mg twice daily), a nontoxic bile acid that decreases the cytotoxicity of the bile acid mixture in the hepatocyte.[44] Pruritus and liver enzyme abnormalities generally respond to this therapy. Dexamethasone (12 mg daily for 7 days) is another effective treatment.[45]

Intrahepatic cholestasis of pregnancy increases the risk of fetal demise that may involve bile toxicity; thus, antepartum fetal heart rate testing is advocated for gravidas who have this disorder, and labor is commonly induced at about 38 weeks' gestation.[46]

PREECLAMPSIA AND ECLAMPSIA

Elevated serum aminotransferases and bilirubin levels may accompany severe preeclampsia and eclampsia. The liver pathology includes periportal lesions that consist of hemorrhage, fibrin deposition, and hepatocellular necrosis.[47] The exact mechanism of the injury is not known but probably involves ischemia associated with vasospasm and fibrin deposition periportal capillaries.

Women with preeclampsia/eclampsia usually present with hypertension, proteinuria, and/or generalized edema and may have headache, visual changes, or epigastric pain. Serum aminotransferase and bilirubin levels usually are elevated only moderately; hepatic failure is uncommon. The differential diagnosis includes acute fatty liver of pregnancy, which usually has greater liver dysfunction. Hepatitis also should be considered, but hypertension is not usually a feature of hepatitis.

The management of preeclampsia with liver dysfunction normally involves delivery, but, in cases of preterm presentation (< 32 weeks' gestation), patients are hospitalized for close observation by obstetricians who are trained to manage these difficult cases. Headache, epigastric pain, eclampsia, and other symptoms and signs of severe disease are indications for prompt delivery.

HELLP Syndrome

Up to 12% of patients with severe preeclampsia develop hemolysis, liver dysfunction, and thrombocytopenia that probably results from microangiopathic hemolysis.[47,48] The acronym "HELLP" encompasses the pathologic findings that include *h*emolysis, *e*levated *l*iver enzymes, and a *l*ow *p*latelet count. These patients may have nonspecific complaints of malaise, nausea, vomiting, and upper abdominal pain and also may have hypertension, hematuria, and seizures. About one-third of patients develop the syndrome after delivery.

In HELLP syndrome, serum lactate dehydrogenase levels usually are elevated as a result of liver injury and hemolysis; aminotransferases and indirect bilirubin may be moderately elevated. Hypertension, generalized edema, and proteinuria are present commonly in patients with HELLP syndrome, but they may be absent even in severe HELLP syndrome. The extent of thrombocytopenia varies and is a predictor of outcome. Platelet counts less than $50,000/\mu L$ are associated with most of the morbidity and mortality of this condition. Prothrombin and thromboplastin times become prolonged when the disorder is complicated by disseminated intravascular coagulation. Laboratory evaluation includes a complete blood count, liver aminotransferases, urinalysis, and serum concentrations of uric acid and creatinine. Cocaine and amphetamine testing also may be appropriate because these drugs can cause laboratory abnormalities that mimic HELLP syndrome.[48]

All patients with HELLP syndrome should be managed as for severe preeclampsia with careful surveillance for the major complications, which include disseminated intravascular coagulation, abruptio placentae, acute renal failure, and pulmonary edema.[47,48] Obstetric ultrasonography should be performed to estimate size and gestational age of the fetus, and heart rate monitoring or biophysical profile should be carried out to assess fetal health. Corticosteroids (eg, dexamethasone 10 mg, intravenously (IV) q12h) may be given to women with platelet counts less than $100,000/\mu L$. Besides enhancing fetal lung maturation, corticosteroids may attenuate the disease through effects on the vasculature. Delivery should be initiated for gravidas who have completed at least 34 weeks of gestation, have disease progression despite corticosteroid therapy, platelet counts declining toward $50,000/\mu L$, or significant maternal and/or fetal compromise. Delivery also should be considered for patients less than 34 weeks of gestation that have completed 48 hours of corticosteroid treatment.[48] Magnesium sulfate should be infused intravenously to prevent seizures, and antihypertensive agents (eg, hydralazine or labetalol) may be required to keep systolic pressures less than 160 mm Hg and diastolic values less than 100 mm Hg. Patients also should be monitored closely for hypotension, which can result from hepatic rupture, and for signs of pulmonary compromise.

Intravenous fluids should be administered at about 100 mL/h with adjustments in rate to keep urine output greater than 20 mL/h, and electrolytes and glucose concentrations should be monitored. Measurements of pulmonary wedge pressures generally are reserved for patients who remain oliguric despite a 1-L fluid challenge. Packed erythrocyte transfusions are reserved for patients with hematocrits less than 22% and hemodynamic instability, and platelet transfusions are given prior to cesarean delivery if the platelet count is less than $50,000 /\mu L$ and before vaginal delivery if the count is less than $20,000/\mu L$.[48] Platelet transfusion is also likely to benefit patients who have severe thrombocytopenia (< 20,000 platelets/μL) during labor. Platelet counts may be significantly increased for hours following such transfusions, which may reduce the risk of spontaneous bleeding in these patients with vascular injury and a predisposition to hemorrhage. Fibrinogen levels with measurement of prothrombin and partial thromboplastin times should be performed for patients with platelet counts less than 50,000 µL/mL or who are bleeding.

Patients with HELLP syndrome should be monitored carefully during the puerperium until the disorder shows signs of resolution, as indicated by a rising platelet count, a diuresis (> 100 mL/h), and arterial pressure controlled with oral agents. Magnesium sulfate therapy is normally continued post partum until the hemolytic process has abated. Dexamethasone therapy may be administered until the syndrome shows clear signs of resolution, with a tapering dose (5 mg IV q12h × 2) given during the last 24 hours of corticosteroid treatment.[48]

Acute Fatty Liver

Acute fatty liver of pregnancy is a rare disorder that is characterized by swollen hepatocytes filled with microvesicular lipid. It usually presents with malaise, anorexia, nausea, vomiting, and jaundice. Many women have signs of preeclampsia, such as hypertension, proteinuria, and edema, and all have laboratory abnormalities that may include hypofibrinogenemia, prolonged prothrombin and partial thromboplastin times, hyperbilirubinemia, and elevated aminotransferase activities. Mild thrombocytopenia, hemolysis, and hypoglycemia also may be present.

Acute fatty liver of pregnancy is associated with a high incidence of hepatic failure, severe hypoglycemia, coagulopathy, hypovolemia, acidosis, and renal failure. Not surprisingly, this syndrome has been associated with a high mortality rate for the fetus and the mother.[49] Maternal deaths have resulted from sepsis, aspiration, renal failure, pancreatitis, and bleeding. Management involves supportive care and delivery. In severe cases, cesarean delivery, after correction of coagulation abnormalities, may be considered to expedite delivery when a vaginal birth cannot be achieved within a reasonable time.[49] Liver transplantation may be considered for those in whom hepatic failure does not resolve post partum. The recurrence risk for survivors appears to be very low.

Hepatic Hematoma

Hepatic hemorrhage and subcapsular hematoma are the most serious liver complications of preeclampsia/eclampsia and HELLP syndrome. Other causes of intrahepatic hemorrhage include trauma, hepatic adenoma, hepatocellular carcinoma, liver abscess, acute fatty liver of pregnancy, and cocaine use. Patients usually present in the third trimester with right upper quadrant pain and tenderness; hemorrhagic shock and abdominal distention suggest hepatic rupture. Computed tomography with contrast is more sensitive than is ultrasonography for confirming the diagnosis, and magnetic resonance imaging has greater sensitivity than do other imaging techniques for the diagnosis of chronic hematomas.[50]

Microscopic inspection of maternal liver in cases associated with preeclampsia or HELLP syndrome reveals periportal necrosis and fibrin deposits in the periportal capillaries. Endothelial damage and vasospasm-induced ischemia are thought to predispose these patients to hepatic hemorrhage; trauma, which can be slight, is considered the immediate factor that ruptures the liver capsule.[50]

Management consists of close observation if the liver capsule is intact, with careful monitoring for delayed rupture. Shock and coagulation abnormalities, which are more likely to occur with rupture of the liver capsule, should be treated aggressively. Hemorrhage can be controlled surgically by packing and oversewing of lacerations, but persistent bleeding may require the ligation of the hepatic artery. Hepatic artery embolization also may be performed for continuing hemorrhage associated with ruptured or unruptured liver hematoma.

Disorders Coincident with Pregnancy

Hepatic abnormalities that develop in the nonpregnant population also may occur in pregnancy. The following summarizes some of the common disorders.

Viral Hepatitis

At least seven types of viral hepatitis may complicate pregnancy: hepatitis A, B, D, C, E, GB virus C, and G.[51] As in the nonpregnant state, infected patients typically present with malaise, headache, nausea, vomiting, low-grade fever, and jaundice. Subclinical infections may also occur. Peak aminotransferase and serum bilirubin concentrations may rise to very high levels. Serologic tests for acute hepatitis can determine the type based on IgM specific for hepatitis A, hepatitis B core antigen, and hepatitis C. Pregnant patients with hepatitis may be managed as outpatients if the disease is mild. In severe cases the woman should be given supportive care in the hospital until hepatic function has stabilized and she is able to eat. Pregnancy does not appear to make the mother more vulnerable to viral hepatitis. Fulminant hepatic necrosis, which is the most common cause of death, may be confused with acute fatty liver of pregnancy.

While rare for hepatitis A and B, transplacental transmission to the fetus apparently occurs more frequently with hepatitis C and E. Viral hepatitis apparently is not teratogenic, but fetal/neonatal exposure during delivery may result in neonatal infection. Hepatitis B infection in neonates, which may be fulminant, leads to a chronic carrier state that places them at risk for cirrhosis and hepatocellular carcinoma in about 85% of cases. Therefore, all prenatal patients are to be screened for hepatitis B surface antigen (HBsAg), with immunoprophylaxis (hepatitis Ig and vaccine) for newborns of women who test positive. Mothers who are at high risk for infection should receive the vaccine. Amniocentesis may be performed in gravidas with chronic active hepatitis because the risk of transmission is minimal.[51] Immunoglobulin should be given to pregnant women who are exposed to hepatitis A, and Ig and vaccination probably should be given to newborns of women with acute disease.[51] Immunoglobulin treatment is not recommended for neonates of mothers with anti-C antibody.

Table 15–4 summarizes the common hepatic disorders that may be encountered during pregnancy. The diagnosis depends on the symptoms, timing in pregnancy, and laboratory abnormalities. Thrombocytopenia accompanies several diseases that are outlined in this chapter, but the physician should remember that reduced platelet counts are a feature of other conditions, such as immune thrombocytopenia, gestational thrombocytopenia, viral infections, drug reactions, thrombotic thrombocytopenic purpura, hemolytic uremic syndrome, and disseminated intravascular coagulation.

THROMBOEMBOLISM

Thromboembolism, a leading obstetric cause of maternal mortality, has an incidence in pregnancy of about 0.5 to 2 in 1,000, a frequency that is about five times that in the nonpregnant state. Loss of venous tone and compression of the inferior vena cava by the gravid uterus increases venous distention and lowers the velocity of venous blood flow in the lower extremities. This reduction in venous flow is thought to be the major factor underlying the increased risk of thromboembolism during pregnancy.[52,53] Pregnancy is associated with increased levels of coagulation factors (I [fibrinogen], II, VII, VIII, X, and XII), normal or reduced (eg, protein S) levels of endogenous anticoagulants, and reduced fibrinolysis. The overall effect is to shift the coagulation system toward clot formation and stability.[54] The risk of thromboembolism, which is roughly the same for all three trimesters, is increased by prolonged bedrest, hemorrhage, sepsis, cardiac disease, diabetes, and instrument-assisted or cesarean delivery.[52,55] Deep venous thrombosis occurs most frequently in the left side.[55] The risk of thrombosis extends to the postpartum period, which poses the greatest risk for pulmonary embolism, particularly following cesarean delivery.[52,55]

Women who had thromboembolism during a previous pregnancy are particularly at risk, with a recurrence rate of up to 20%. Other high risk groups include those with antithrombin III, protein C, or protein S deficiencies; factor V Leiden; hyperhomocystinemia; prothrombin G20210A mutation, or lupus anticoagulant. Risk of maternal thromboembolism, which may be 9 to 15 times greater with heritable coagulopathies,[56] involves thrombosis in the lower extremities as well as unusual sites such as in the portal vein, sagittal sinus, mesenteric veins, and the uteroplacental and intervillous circulation.[54]

Diagnosis

Pain and swelling are classic symptoms associated with deep venous thrombosis. Physical findings may include tenderness, cyanosis, redness, increased leg circumference, and pain in the calf muscle following forceful dorsiflexion of the foot (positive Homan's sign). However, these presumptive findings are not specific and lead to a correct diagnosis of thrombophlebitis less than half the time.[57]

Doppler ultrasound methods, which are generally superior to impedance plethysmography, have become the first-line diagnostic tests when proximal deep venous thrombosis is suspected.[53] Compared with venography, this noninvasive test has a sensitivity of 91% and a specificity of 99% for detecting thromboses in popliteal and femoral veins.[58] Doppler flow studies are less useful for

TABLE 15–4. Common Gastrointestinal Diseases Encountered during Pregnancy

Disorder	Symptoms	Onset*	Laboratory Findings
Hyperemesis gravidarum	Nausea, vomiting	1, 2	Bilirubin < 4 mg/dL ALT < 200 U/L
Cholestasis of pregnancy	Pruritus	2, 3	Bilirubin < 6 mg/dL ALT < 300 U/L Bile acids increased
Acute fatty liver of pregnancy	Upper abdominal pain, nausea, vomiting	3	ALT < 500 U/L Glucose low DIC Bilirubin and ammonia increased late in disease
Preeclampsia/eclampsia	Upper abdominal pain, hypertension, edema	2, 3, P	ALT < 500 U/L Proteinuria Uric acid elevated Platelets may be decreased
HELLP syndrome	Upper abdominal pain, nausea, vomiting, malaise	3, P	ALT < 500 U/L Platelets < 100,000/mm³ Hemolysis LDH increased DIC in 20–40%
Biliary tract disease	Right upper abdominal pain, nausea, vomiting, fever	1, 2, 3, P	CBD stone Bilirubin GGT
Viral hepatitis	Nausea, vomiting, fever	1, 2, 3, P	ALT > 500 U/L Bilirubin

*Trimester of pregnancy; P = post partum.
ALT = alanine aminotransferase; DIC = disseminated intravascular coagulation; LDH = lactate dehydrogenase; CBD = common bile duct; GGT = γ-glutamyl transpeptidase.
Adapted from Knox TA, Olans LB. Liver disease in pregnancy. N Engl J Med 1996;335:569–75.

detecting clots in smaller veins of the calf, where sensitivity and specificity are only 36% and 95%, respectively. After the first trimester, the noninvasive tests should be performed with the uterus displaced laterally to reduce uterine compression of the inferior vena cava.[57]

Although expensive, magnetic resonance imaging is reasonably accurate in detecting thrombi and is particularly useful in the diagnosis of ovarian or pelvic venous thrombosis. Measurements of fibrin breakdown products are elevated in patients with thromboembolism, but these tests have little predictive value in women whose coagulation system has been activated by abruptio placentae, surgery, or delivery. Clinical suspicion with confirmation by a noninvasive study generally is sufficient evidence to start anticoagulation. However, venography may be performed when the noninvasive studies are equivocal or do not support strong clinical evidence of venous thrombosis.[57]

Pulmonary Embolism

Sudden unexplained dyspnea is the hallmark of pulmonary embolism; pleuritic chest pain and hemoptysis may occur with lung infarction. Tachycardia is the most consistent finding on cardiac examination; hypotension and right heart failure are present with massive embolism.

The electrocardiogram usually shows only a sinus tachycardia, but abnormalities consistent with right ventricular strain develop with extensive embolization. The chest radiograph is normal, in most cases, but infiltrates and effusion suggest infarction. Abnormal lucent areas and disproportionate vessel diameters are more subtle signs of embolization. Arterial partial pressure of oxygen (Pao_2) generally is reduced (< 90 torr) in pulmonary embolism, but a normal Pao_2 does not rule out the diagnosis. Thus, pulmonary embolism may be present even with a normal electrocardiogram, chest radiograph, and arterial blood gases.

A more definitive diagnostic test is the ventilation-perfusion (V/Q) scan, which has been the traditional initial test for pulmonary embolism. This test, which involves small amounts of radiation, can be performed safely during pregnancy. Helical pulmonary computed tomography has a sensitivity of 93% and a positive predictive value of 95% for emboli in the main, lobar, or segmental pulmonary arteries, but it has little ability to detect emboli in subsegmental branches. This may not be a major limitation for most patients because isolated subsegmental involvement occurs only about 6% of the time.[59] Helical computed tomography is less useful in the evaluation of patients with nondiagnostic V/Q scans, where the sensitivity is only 63 to 85%.[59] Pulmonary angiography should be considered if the diagnosis of pulmonary embolism cannot be established or excluded by noninvasive methods.

Therapy

Deep venous thrombosis or pulmonary embolism should be treated with therapeutic intravenous heparin, which, in combination with antithrombin III, is a potent inhibitor of thrombin formation. Heparin, which is the anticoagulant of choice during pregnancy, does not cross the placenta, produce developmental abnormalities, or cause fetal hemorrhage. In contrast, warfarin may have teratogenic effects (eg, nasal hypoplasia or stippling of epiphyses) and may cause fetal bleeding. Complete blood cell and platelet count, prothrombin and activated partial thromboplastin times, and urinalysis should be obtained before instigating therapy. Unfractionated heparin should be administered as a 100-unit/kg (5,000 units minimum) IV injection for deep venous thrombosis or as a 150-unit/kg IV injection for pulmonary embolism; either is followed by a continuous

infusion of 15 to 25 units/kg/h. An activated partial thromboplastin time (aPTT), a prothrombin time, and platelet and complete blood counts should be performed before initiating therapy. Blood for aPTT measurements should be drawn 4 hours after starting heparin or changing the infusion rate, and the dosage should be adjusted to keep the aPTT at 1.5 to 2 times the control value. The aPTT may be performed once daily when the results remain stable in the therapeutic range. After 5 days of IV therapy, treatment is changed to subcutaneous administration, in which one-half the total daily requirement of heparin is injected every 12 hours. The therapeutic goal is to maintain the aPTT at 1.5 to 2 times the control value (or a heparin level of 0.3 U/mL of plasma) for blood samples drawn 6 hours after a heparin injection. Compared with unfractionated heparin, low–molecular weight heparin has several advantages, including administration of intermittent injections instead of continuous IV, more predictable therapeutic dosing, lack of requirement of coagulation tests, reduced incidence of thrombocytopenia, and decreased risk of maternal hemorrhage. Because of these advantages, low–molecular weight heparin has become the first-line treatment for thromboembolism in many centers. Weight-adjusted dosing is recommended during pregnancy, and measurement of anti–factor Xa levels (therapeutic range, 0.5 to 1.2 units/L) about 4 hours after administration may help to guide therapy.[60]

Heparin may be stopped at the onset of labor or 24 hours prior to induction of labor; however, heparin is infused intravenously to those who have recently developed iliofemoral thromboses or pulmonary emboli, with the dose adjusted to maintain the aPTT at about 1.5 times the control value during labor and delivery.[53,60] Protamine sulfate may be administered if excessive bleeding occurs at delivery. Full heparin treatment should be initiated 6 hours after delivery and continued until about 6 weeks post partum. Warfarin also may be used for postpartum anticoagulation with the dosage adjusted to prolong the international normalized ratio to 2 to 2.5. Warfarin, dicumarol, and heparin are compatible with breast-feeding.

In uncomplicated deep venous thrombosis, full anticoagulation usually is maintained for at least 4 months[61] with either continued anticoagulation or lower-dose prophylactic treatment until 6 to 8 weeks post partum. Longer periods of anticoagulation (eg, 4 to 6 months) are indicated for pulmonary embolism and for high-risk conditions such as ilio-femoral venous thrombosis or recurrent deep venous thrombosis.

Inferior vena cava filters may be indicated for recurrent pulmonary embolism, major complications of anticoagulant therapy, and contraindications to anticoagulant treatment. Thrombolytic therapy should only be considered for patients with a life-threatening pulmonary embolus.[53]

Pregnant women with artificial heart valves should remain fully anticoagulated during pregnancy. Adjusted doses of subcutaneous heparin administered every 6 to 8 hours to keep the activated partial thromboplastin time at 1.5 to 2.5 times control failed to prevent fatal massive thrombosis of a mitral tilting prothesis in one gravida,[62] which has led some to favor warfarin anticoagulation in these patients.[63,64] However, the benefit of thrombosis prevention with warfarin must be balanced against the ~ 4% risk of warfarin embryopathy. Intravenous heparin should be substituted for warfarin during the last 2 weeks of gestation to avoid the risks of delivering an anticoagulated infant.[63] Low–molecular weight heparin can be administered subcutanously more easily and safely than can unfractionated heparin, but the efficacy of low–molecular weight heparin with monitoring of plasma anti–factor Xa concentrations has not been examined in pregnant women with prosthetic heart valves.

Prophylaxis

Subtherapeutic doses of heparin promote the activity of antithrombin III, the major inhibitor of factor Xa that is critically involved in thrombus formation. The usual prophylactic regimen is to administer subcutaneously 5,000 units of unfractionated heparin every 12 hours, although 7,500 to 10,000 units every 12 hours may be more appropriate for the second and third trimesters.[52] This low-dose heparin treatment, which does not require a PTT monitoring, may be considered for women who have a history of deep venous thrombosis (unrelated to trauma) or pulmonary embolism. Women with congenital thrombophilia but no prior thromboembolism should be managed individually based on the type of disorder and other risk factors.[65] Studies are needed to establish the optimal management of these cases.

Complications

Anticoagulant therapy poses several risks, of which the most common is hemorrhage (~ 2% incidence); thus, urinalyses should be performed periodically to detect microscopic hematuria. Heparin therapy may result in osteoporosis, particularly when the dosage of heparin exceeds 15,000 units/d for more than 6 months.[53] Calcium and vitamin D supplementation may reduce the risk of bone demineralization; the osteoporosis appears to be at least partly reversible upon terminating heparin therapy. Women receiving unfractionated heparin may develop thrombocytopenia during the first 3 weeks of therapy;[53] thus, platelet counts should be monitored during this time.

SEIZURE DISORDERS

Seizure disorders represent the most common neurologic disorder in pregnancy. The therapeutic goal in pregnancy is to prevent seizures while minimizing the risk of drug therapy on fetal development.

Preconception Counseling

Women with a seizure disorder generally can expect to have a good pregnancy outcome. The frequency of seizures is roughly the same during pregnancy in about 50% of women, and increases in about 45%. Those who have more than one seizure per month are more likely to have a worsening of the condition during pregnancy.[66] Therapy should be adjusted to control seizures prior to conception, particularly for those with tonic-clonic seizures. Those who have been free of seizures for more than 2 years may be candidates for a slow withdrawal of medication under the close supervision of a neurologist. About 50% of such patients remain seizure free and are able to conceive without the teratogenic concerns of anticonvulsant therapy. For women requiring therapy, a single agent is considered to pose less fetal risk than do multiple medications. Thus, consideration should be given to switching patients on multiple drugs to monotherapy.[66] In general, the goal is to have the seizures controlled on the lowest dosage and number of anticonvulsants before conception.

The risk of a seizure disorder in children of women with idiopathic epilepsy is about four times higher than that of unaffected women. The children of women who take anticonvulsants also have about a

6 to 8% chance of having a congenital malformation, which is about two to three times that of children of normal women, and part of this increased risk may be related to genetic factors associated with epilepsy, rather than drug treatment alone.[67] The fetal hydantoin syndrome, which occurs in about 11% of infants exposed in utero to phenytoin, is characterized by low birth weight, dysmorphic facies (eg, short nose, low nasal bridge, hypertelorism, and clefting), limb deformities (eg, hypoplasia of the distal phalanges and nails), and impairment of mental and/or motor development.

The anticonvulsant use of phenobarbital during pregnancy increases risk of minor malformations by two- to threefold, but the use of the drug for other indications has not been associated with a greater incidence of structural defects.[68] Hence, much of the apparent teratogenic effect of phenobarbital may be related to maternal epilepsy rather than to therapy. Phenobarbital has not been implicated in the fetal hydantoin syndrome.

The major fetal concern of valproic acid therapy during pregnancy is the 1 to 2% risk of a lumbar meningomyelocele, although facial dysmorphism, growth restriction, and abnormalities of the limbs and heart also have been described.[68] Carbamazepine use during pregnancy is associated with ~ 1% risk of spina bifida and ~ 12% risk of subtle minor malformations.

An interference with folic acid metabolism may underlie the teratogenic effect of anticonvulsants. Therefore, it has been suggested that woman taking these drugs should take 4 mg/d of folic acid before conception, which is the same dose recommended for women who have had a previous child with a neural tube abnormality.[69] Because folic acid may increase hepatic clearance of anticonvulsants, serum levels of these drugs should be monitored closely.

Pregnancy

The effective plasma levels of anticonvulsants are commonly reduced during pregnancy because of inability to take medications due to nausea and vomiting, delayed gastric emptying, accelerated hepatic metabolism, reduced concentration of plasma-binding proteins, and increased volume of distribution. During pregnancy, the free drug–to–protein-bound drug ratio increases, which blunts the fall in active drug levels in plasma resulting from increased metabolism.[66] Because of these changes, anticonvulsant dosage should be adjusted periodically according to the clinical condition, the half-life of the medication, and free serum levels that are drawn immediately before drug ingestion. Anticonvulsant levels usually are checked weekly when adjusting the dosage, and then monthly to ensure that the drug levels remain within the therapeutic range.

Pregnant women who require anticonvulsant therapy should be counseled regarding the risk of having a fetus with a neural tube defect; additionally, they should be offered maternal α-fetoprotein screening at 16 weeks' gestation and a comprehensive evaluation of the fetus by ultrasonography at 16 to 18 and 20 to 22 weeks' gestation. Targeted ultrasound examination by appropriately trained sonographers has sensitivity of ~ 97% for detecting neural tube defects in women with elevated maternal serum α-fetoprotein.[70]

During labor, anticonvulsants should be administered parenterally because of delayed and erratic absorption of oral medications. In patients with therapeutic drug levels, the usual dose of phenytoin may be infused intravenously, while phenobarbital (60 to 90 mg) may be injected intramuscularly.[67] Oral administration of carbamazepine may be tried because a parenteral form of carbamazepine is not available. However, a therapeutic dose of intravenous phenytoin (loading dose of 10 to 15 mg/kg) is a more prudent choice should seizures or preseizure aura develop.[67] The maternal electrocardiogram should be recorded continuously because intravenous infusion may evoke arrhythmias.

Recurrent seizures require immediate treatment because of the risk of hypoxic injury to the mother and fetus. The airway should be maintained, and the mother should be given oxygen and placed on her side to minimize compression of the inferior vena cava by the gravid uterus; this helps to maintain maternal cardiac output and uterine blood flow. Intravenous phenytoin therapy is recommended because this highly effective anticonvulsant has prolonged action and few serious side effects. Fosphenytoin sodium (loading dose of 15 to 20 mg phenytoin equivalents/kg), a water-soluble formulation, is best for IV infusions because it can be administered three times more rapidly than can phenytoin.[71] Intravenous diazepam (10 to 30 mg) or phenobarbital also may be used, but the health care team must be prepared to treat respiratory depression in the mother and the newborn. Other causes of seizures, including eclampsia, should be considered when evaluating a gravida in status epilepticus.

Primidone, phenobarbital, and phenytoin exposure to the fetus in utero may decrease vitamin K–dependent coagulation factors (ie, II, VII, IX, and X) in the newborn and, thus, predispose these infants to hemorrhage. Such neonates should receive vitamin K (1 mg) intramuscularly at birth.[67] Prophylactic administration of vitamin K_1 (10 mg daily) to the mother during the last month of pregnancy also may be beneficial.[72]

Postpartum Management

The levels of anticonvulsants typically increase following delivery, particularly if the dosage was raised during pregnancy. Therapy may be adjusted according to the anticonvulsant levels that are measured at discharge and at 2 and 6 weeks post partum. In the case of phenytoin, the patient may be take the daily dose prescribed prior to pregnancy plus one-half of the pregnancy increment, with the dose further reduced at 2 weeks and 6 weeks post partum.[66] Adjustments in the dosage of phenobarbital and carbamazepine may not be required until 2 weeks after delivery because the rise in free drug levels tends to be slower than with phenytoin.[66] Women on anticonvulsant therapy may breast-feed, although the infants should be watched for excessive sedation, particularly if the mother is taking primidone, phenobarbital, or benzodiazepines.

ASTHMA

Asthma is seen in 0.4 to 1.3% of all pregnant women and it is the most common obstructive pulmonary disease in pregnant women.[73] The severity of the disease ranges from mild disease requiring only ß-agonist therapy to severe disease necessitating multidrug therapy. Pregnancy has a variable effect on symptoms, with a worsening of symptoms in about 22%, an improvement in 29%, and no change in 49% of pregnant women.[74,75] Exacerbations, which may occur during labor and delivery, are particularly prevalent after cesarean delivery.[76] Maternal asthma has been associated with adverse pregnancy outcomes, such as preterm birth, small-for-gesta-tional-age infants, and hypertensive disorders of pregnancy.[77]

Pregnancy is associated with decreased total lung capacity, residual volume, functional residual capacity, and expiratory reserve volume. Inspiratory capacity and tidal volume increase, while vital capacity respiratory rate and peak expiratory flow remain unchanged. The rise in tidal volume increases minute ventilation, which decreases maternal $Paco_2$ to about 30 to 32 mm Hg.[78] Arterial pH remains in the normal range as a result of a fall in plasma bicarbonate.

Prior to conception women with asthma should have a flu vaccination and have baseline measurements of peak expiratory flow. Asthma should be well controlled before pregnancy. Most therapeutic agents have little impact on fetal development, although corticosteroid treatment may be associated with an increased risk of oral clefts.[79] Allergen immunotherapy may be continued during gestation, but initiating it during pregnancy is not recommended because of the potential for systemic reactions.[80]

Asthma therapy in pregnant women is generally similar to that for the nongravid woman. Mild asthma (symptoms < three times/wk, PEV_1 > 80% during attacks) requires only intermittent use of inhaled $ß_2$-agonists (albuterol or metaproterenol), whereas mild persistent disease (symptoms > two times/wk, nocturnal symptoms > two/mo, PEV_1 > 80% during attacks) may be treated with inhaled mast cell stabilizers (cromolyn, two puffs, three to four times/d). Inhaled nedocromil should be continued in women who have had a good response prior to pregnancy. Inhaled beclomethasone (two to four puffs, two to four times/d) may be substituted if these agents are ineffective. Moderate persistent asthma (daily symptoms and nocturnal symptoms > one time/wk, forced expiratory volume in 1 second [FEV_1] of 60 to 80%) is managed with inhaled beclomethasone or budesonide. Oral xanthine bronchodilators (theophylline) or inhaled salmeterol can be added for further control. Severe persistent asthma (continuous symptoms, frequent noctural symptoms, FEV_1 < 60%) require similar treatment as for moderate disease, with the addition of oral prednisone.[79,81] Methylprednisolone (rather than dexamethasone) is preferred for intravenous administration because the placenta converts methylprednisolone into less active metabolites that pass into the fetal circulation.

Pregnant women who cannot tolerate ß₂-agonists may benefit from inhaled anticholinergics (ipratropium), which can be used in conjunction with ß₂-agonists for status asthmaticus.[81] Tripelennamine and chlorpheniramine, which are sedating antihistamines, may be used in pregnancy; loratadine, a nonsedating antihistamine, appears to be safe (as determined by animal studies), although little information is available on its effects on human reproduction.[81] As with all drugs, these agents should be avoided during the first 12 weeks of gestation, unless they are essential for therapy.

In nonpregnant individuals, inhibitors of leukotriene synthesis (zileuton) or leukotriene receptors (montelukast, zarfirlukast) may be used in place of inhaled steroids for mild asthma and may be added to existing therapy for moderate and severe asthma.[82] Because of the paucity of human pregnancy data, montelukast and zarfirlukast should be administered during pregnancy only for severe persistent asthma that has responded uniquely well to these agents before pregnancy.[81] Zileuton, which can produce congenital anomalies in animals, should be avoided, particularly during the first trimester.

Acute exacerbations should be managed quickly and aggressively. Pulse oximetry and blood gas measurements should be used to monitor oxyhemoglobin concentrations, and therapy should be directed to keep the arterial oxyhemoglobin saturation above 70%. Because of the physiologic adjustments of pregnancy, maternal hypoxemia with a $PaCO_2 > 35$ mm Hg may indicate impending respiratory failure and the requirement for mechanical ventilation.

REFERENCES

1. Metzger BE, Coustan DR. Summary and recommendations of the Fourth International Workshop-Conference on Gestational Diabetes Mellitus. Diabetes Care 1998;21:B161–7.

2. Moore TR. Diabetes in pregnancy. In: Creasy RK, Resnick R, editors. Maternal-fetal medicine. 4th ed. Philadelphia: Saunders; 1999. p. 964–95.

3. Langer O, Conway DL, Berkus MD, et al. A comparison of glyburide and insulin in women with gestational diabetes mellitus. N Engl J Med 2000;343:1134–8.

4. Gabbe SG, Landon MB. Diabetes mellitus in pregnancy. In: Quilligan EJ, Zuspan FP, editors. Current therapy in obstetrics and gynecology. 5th ed. Philadelphia: W.B.Saunders; 2000. p. 263–8.

5. Kjos SL Buchanan TA. Gestational diabetes mellitus. N Engl J Med 1999;341:1749–56.

6. O'Sullivan JB, Mahan CM. Criteria for the oral glucose tolerance test in pregnancy. Diabetes 1964; 13:278–85.

7. National Diabetes Data Group. Classification and diagnosis of diabetes mellitus and other categories of glucose intolerance. Diabetes 1979;28:1039–57.

8. Carpenter MW, Coustan DR. Criteria for screening tests for gestational diabetes. Am J Obstet Gynecol 1982;144:768–73.

9. Teng F, Koos BJ. The predictive value of capillary whole blood glucose measurements during pregnancy. J Soc Gynecol Investig 1995;2:618–22.

10. Mestman JH. Hypothyroidism. In: Quilligan EJ, Zuspan FP, editors. Current therapy in obstetrics and gynecology. 5th ed. Philadelphia: W.B.Saunders; 2000. p. 303–5.

11. Haddow JE, Palomaki GE, Allan WC, et al. Maternal thyroid deficiency during pregnancy and subsequent neuropsychological development of the child. N Engl J Med 1999;341:549–55.

12. Utiger RD. Maternal hypothyroidism and fetal development. N Engl J Med 1999;341:601.

13. Seely BL, Burrow GN. Thyroid disease in pregnancy. In: Creasy RK, Resnick R, editors. Maternal-fetal medicine. 4th ed. Philadelphia: W.B.Saunders; 1999. p. 996–1014.

14. Burrow GN, Fisher DA, Larsen PR. Maternal and fetal thyroid function. N Engl J Med 1994;331:1072–8.

15. Mestman JH. Hyperthyroidism. In: Queenan JT, Hobbins JC, editors. Protocols for high-risk pregnancies. 3rd ed. Cambridge: Blackwell Science; 1996. p. 268–72.

16. Sibai BM: Chronic hypertension in pregnancy. In: Quilligan EJ, Zuspan FP, editors. Current therapy in obstetrics and gynecology. 5th ed. Philadelphia: W.B.Saunders; 2000. p. 256–61.

17. Sibai BM, Mabie WC, Shamsa F, et al. A comparison of no medication versus methyldopa or labetalol in chronic hypertension during pregnancy. Am J Obstet Gynecol 1990;162:960–1.

18. Fletcher AE, Bulpitt CJ. How far should blood pressure be lowered? N Engl J Med 1992;326:251–4.

19. Rubin PC. Beta blockers in pregnancy. N Engl J Med 1981;305:1323–6.

20. von Dadelszen P, Ornstein MP, Bull SB, et al. Fall in mean arterial pressure and fetal growth restriction in pregnancy: a meta-analysis. Lancet 2000;355:87–92.

21. Hanssens M, Keirse MJ, Vankelecom F, VanAssehe FA. Fetal and neonatal effects of treatment with ACE-inhibitors in pregnancy. Obstet Gynecol 1991;171:128–35.

22. de Swiet M, Shennan A. Blood pressure measurement in pregnancy. Br J Obstet Gynaecol 1996;103:862–3.

23. Rodriquez MH, Masaki DI, Mestman J, et al. Calcium/creatinine ratio and microalbuminuria in the prediction of preeclampsia. Am J Obstet Gynecol 1988;159:1452–5.

24. Cunningham FG, Gant NF, Leveno KJ, et al. Williams obstetrics. 21st ed. New York: McGraw-Hill; 2001. p. 604–5.

25. Vermillion ST, Scardo JA, Newman RB, et al. A randomized double-blind trial of oral nifedipine and intravenous labetalol in hypertensive emergencies of pregnancy. Am J Obstet Gynecol 1999;181:858–61.

26. Stoelting RK. Pharmacology and physiology in anesthetic practice. 3rd ed. New York: Lippincott-Raven; 1999. p. 317.

27. Tan EM, Cohen AS, Fries JF, et al. The 1982 revised criteria for the classification of systemic lupus erythematosus. Arthritis Rheum 1982;25:1271–7.

28. Cunningham FG, MacDonald PC, Gant NF, et al. Williams obstetrics. 20th ed. Stamford: Appleton & Lange; 1997. p. 1239–47.

29. Mor-Yosef S, Navot D, Rabinowitz R, Schenker JG. Collagen diseases in pregnancy. Obstet Gynecol Surv 1984;39:67–84.

30. Lochshin MD: Pregnancy does not cause systemic lupus erythematosus to worsen. Arthritis Rheum 1989;32:665–70.

31. Mintz G, Niz J, Gutierrez G, et al. Prospective study of pregnancy in systemic lupus erythematosus: results of a multidisciplinary approach. J Rheumatol 1986;13:732–9.

32. Urowitz MB, Gladman DD, Farewell VT, et al. Lupus and pregnancy studies. Arthritis Rheum 1993;36:1392–7.

33. Ruiz-Irastorza G, Lima F, Alves J, et al. Increased rate of lupus flare during pregnancy and the puerperium: a prospective study of 78 pregnancies. Br J Rheumatol 1996;35:133–8.

34. Burkett G. Lupus nephropathy and pregnancy. Clin Obstet Gynecol 1985;28:310–23.

35. Nicklin JL. Systemic lupus erythematosus and pregnancy at the Royal Women's Hospital, Brisbane 1979–1989. Aust N Z J Obstet Gynaecol 1991;31:128–33.

36. Lockwood CJ. Autoimmune disease. In: Queenan JT, Hobbins JC. Protocols for high-risk pregnancies. 3rd ed. Cambridge: Blackwell Science; 1996. p. 196–211.

37. American College of Obstetricians and Gynecologists. Educational bulletin, number 244. In: Antiphospholipid syndrome. 2000 compendium of selected publications. Washington (DC): ACOG; 2000. p. 302–11.

38. Fox R, Hawkins DF. Fetal-pericardial effusion in association with congenital heart block and maternal systemic lupus erythematosus: case report. Br J Obstet Gynaecol 1990;97:638–40.

39. Buyon JP, Waltuck J, Kleinman C, Copel J. In utero identification and therapy of congenital heart block. Lupus 1995;4:116–21.

40. Watson WJ, Katz VL. Steroid therapy for hydrops associated with antibody-mediated congenital heart block. Am J Obstet Gynecol 1991;165:553–4.

41. Knox TA, Olans LB. Liver disease in pregnancy. N Engl J Med 1996;335:569–75.

42. Nageotte MP, Briggs GG, Towers CV, Asrat T. Droperidol and diphenhydramine in the management of hyperemesis gravidarum. Am J Obstet Gynecol 1996;174:1801–6.

43. Hsu JJ, Clark-Glena R, Nelson DK, Kim CH. Nasogastric enteral feeding in the management of hyperemesis gravidarum. Obstet Gynecol 1996;88:343–6.

44. Diaferia A, Nicastri PL, Tartagni M, et al. Ursodeoxycholic acid therapy in pregnant women with cholestasis. Int J Gynaecol Obstet 1996;52:133–40.

45. Hirviorja ML, Tuimala R, Vuori J. The treatment of intrahepatic cholestasis of pregnancy. Br J Obstet Gynaecol 1992;99:109–111.

46. Davidson KM. Intrahepatic cholestasis of pregnancy. Semin Perinatol 1998;22:104–11.

47. Saphier CJ, Repke JT. Hemolysis, elevated liver enzymes, and low platelets (HELLP) syndrome: a review of diagnosis and management. Semin Perinatol 1998;22:118–33.

48. Martin JN, Magnann EF. HELLP syndrome. In: Quilligan EJ, Zuspan FP, editors. Current therapy in obstetrics and gynecology. 5th ed. Philadelphia: W.B. Saunders; 2000. p. 288–93.

49. Bacq Y. Acute fatty liver of pregnancy. Semin Perinatol 1998;22:134–40.

50. Sheikh RA, Yasmeen S, Riegler JL. Spontaneous intrahepatic hemorrhage and hepatic rupture in the HELLP syndrome. Clin Gastroenterol 1999;28:323–8.

51. Magriples U. Hepatitis in pregnancy. Semin Perinatol 1998;22:112–7.

52. Toglia MR, Weg JG. Venous thromboembolism during pregnancy. N Engl J Med 1996;335:108–14.

53. American College of Obstetricians and Gynecologists. Technical bulletin, number 234. Thromboembolism in pregnancy. In: 2000 compendium of selected publications. Washington (DC): ACOG; 2000. p. 839–47.

54. Lockwood CJ. Heritable coagulopathies in pregnancy. Obstet Gynecol Surv 1999;54:754–65

55. Gherman RB, Goodwin TM, Leung B, et al. Incidence, clinical characteristics, and timing of objectively diagnosed venous thromboembolism during pregnancy. Obstet Gynecol 1999;94:730–4.

56. Gerhardt A, Scharf RE, Beckmann MW, et al. Prothrombin and factor V mutations in women with a history of thrombosis during pregnancy and the puerperium. N Engl J Med 2000;342:374–80.

57. Toglia MR, Nolan TE. Venous thromboembolism during pregnancy: a current review of diagnosis and management. Obstet Gynecol Surv 1996;52:60–72.

58. Lensing AWA, Prandoni P, Brandjes D, et al. Detection of deep-vein thrombosis by real-time B-mode ultrasonography. N Engl J Med 1989;320:342–5.

59. Bates SM, Ginsberg JS. Helical computed tomography and the diagnosis of pulmonary embolism. Ann Intern Med 2000;132:240–2.

60. Ginsberg JS. Thromboembolism and pregnancy. Thromb Haemost 1999;82:620–5.

61. Kearon C, Gent M, Hirsh J, et al. A comparison of three months of anticoagulation with extended anticoagulation for a first episode of idiopathic venous thromboembolism. N Engl J Med 1999;340:901–7.

62. Salazar E, Izaguirre R, Verdejo J, Mutchinick O. Failure of adjusted doses of subcutaneous heparin to prevent thromboembolic phenomena in pregnant patients with mechanical cardiac valve prostheses. J Am Coll Cardiol 1996;27:1698–703.

63. Salazar E, Izaguirre R. Heart disease, anticoagulants and pregnancy. Rev Esp Cardiol 2001;54 Suppl 1:8–16.

64. Sbarouni E, Oakley CM. Outcome of pregnancy in women with valve prostheses. Br Heart J 1994;71:196–201.

65. Greer IA. The challenge of thrombophilia in maternal-fetal medicine. N Engl J Med 2000;342:424–5.

66. Donaldson JO. Seizure disorders in pregnancy. In: Quilligan EJ, Zuspan FP, editors. Current therapy in obstetrics and gynecology. 5th ed. Philadelphia: W.B.Saunders; 2000. p. 346–9.

67. American College of Obstetricians and Gynecologists. Technical bulletin, number 231. Seizure disorders in pregnancy. In: 2000 compendium of selected publications. Washington (DC): ACOG; 2000. p. 756–62.

68. Briggs GG, Freeman RK, Yaffe SJ. Drugs in pregnancy and lactation. 5th ed. Baltimore: Williams & Wilkins; 1998. p. 835–6.

69. Locksmith GJ, Duff P. Preventing neural tube defects: the importance of periconceptional folic acid supplements. Obstet Gynecol 1998;91:1027–34.

70. Lennon CA, Gray DL. Sensitivity and specificity of ultrasound for the detection of neural tube and ventral wall defects in a high-risk population. Obstet Gynecol 1999;94:562–6.

71. Aminoff MJ. Neurologic disorders. In: Creasy RK, Resnick R, editors. Maternal-fetal medicine. 4th ed. Philadelphia: W.B.Saunders; 1999. p. 1091–119.

72. Cornelissen M, Steegers-Theunnissen R, Kollee L, et al. Supplementation of vitamin K in pregnant women receiving anticonvulsant therapy prevents neonatal vitamin K deficiency. Am J Obstet Gynecol 1993;168:884–8.

73. Greenberger PA, Patterson R. Management of asthma during pregnancy. N Engl J Med 1985;312:897–902.

74. Turner ES, Greenberger JA, Patterson R. Management of the pregnant asthmatic patient. Ann Intern Med 1980;93:905–18.

75. White RJ, Coutts II, Gibbs CJ, MacIntyre C. A prospective study of asthma during pregnancy and the puerperium. Respir Med 1989;83:103–6.

76. Wendel PJ. Asthma in pregnancy. Obstet Gynecol Clin 2001;28:537–51.

77. Liu S, Wen SW, Demissie K, et al. Maternal asthma and pregnancy outcomes: a retrospective cohort study. Am J Obstet Gynecol 2001;184:90–6.

78. Puranik BM, Kaore SB, Kurhade GA, et al. A longitudinal study of pulmonary function test during pregnancy. Indian J Physiol Pharmacol 1994;38:129–32.

79. Schatz M. Asthma medications during pregnancy. Semin Perinatol 2001;25:145–52.

80. Terr AI. Asthma and reproductive medicine. Obstet Gynecol Surv 1998;53:699–707.

81. Luskin AT, Lipskowitz MA. The diagnosis and management of asthma during pregnancy. Immunol Allergy Clin North Am 2000;20:745–61.

82. Wood AJJ. Treatment of asthma with drugs modifying the leukotriene pathway. N Engl J Med 1999;340:197–206.

16

DEPRESSIVE DISORDERS IN PREGNANCY AND THE POSTPARTUM PERIOD

Anupama Kalsi, MD, and Vivien Burt, MD, PhD

The rate of depression is twice as high in women as in men,[1] and it is particularly common between the ages of 18 and 44 years.[2] As these are the years of childbearing, psychiatric disorders sometimes appear in pregnancy and postpartum. When they occur at these times, they have profoundly negative effects not only on patients but also on spouses or partners, children, and extended family. Cognitive development in children is largely dependent on maternal responsiveness,[3] which often is impaired in depressed mothers. Cognitive impairment has been documented in children raised by depressed mothers; these negative effects on cognition appear to persist even after the resolution of depression.[4] Further, children of depressed mothers tend to suffer from childhood depression.[5] Spouses of women with postpartum psychiatric disorders are themselves at increased risk for psychiatric illness. It may be that postnatal illness in mothers disrupts the expected "psychosocial flux" in new fathers, putting them at risk for psychiatric illness.[6]

In both men and women, a major risk factor for chronic mood disorders is a past history of affective illness.[7] In particular, women with a prior history of reproductive-related mood syndromes, such as premenstrual dysphoria or prior postpartum depression, are at increased risk for future reproductive-related affective disorders.[8] It is therefore important for primary care clinicians to identify women who are vulnerable to depression and to screen for affective illness at times of high risk, for example, during reproductive-life events.

Once diagnosed, treatment options for depressed women both in pregnancy and post partum include individual psychotherapy, medications, and, in rare cases, electroconvulsive therapy. The issue of medication management in pregnant and post partum women is complicated because of concerns regarding the well-being of the fetus and/or nursing infant. How does one decide which agent(s) is both efficacious for the depressed pregnant or postpartum woman and yet safe for the fetus/neonate? In addition to safety issues for a developing fetus or infant, consideration should be given to which medications have worked in the past, a family history of response, side effect profile, ease of delivery (eg, frequency of dosing), and lethality, if there is the possibility of suicide.

PREGNANCY AND DEPRESSION

Pre-pregnancy Planning for the Patient at Risk for Depression

In the past, pregnancy was thought to protect against psychiatric illness. However, more recent evidence suggests that this is not the case.[2] Because depressed women who are treated with antidepressants often tend to discontinue their medications abruptly upon discovering that they are pregnant, pregnancy may precipitate a relapse of depression. Furthermore, for women who become pregnant at later ages, prior depressive episodes are more likely to have occurred; this increases the risk for a recurrence, possibly in the setting of pregnancy. Women

TABLE 16–1. Possible Consequences of Untreated
Depression in Pregnancy

Preterm labor
Small-for-gestational-age babies
Impulsive behaviors: eg, cigarette smoking, illicit drug
  use, alcohol use
Suicide
Postpartum depression

with psychiatric illnesses should therefore be encouraged to plan their pregnancies in conjunction with their primary care clinicians, psychiatrists, and obstetricians so that pregnancy occurs when they are euthymic and stable. Treatment options in the event of a recurrence include medications with a good "track record" for safety in pregnancy.

Possible Consequences

Untreated depression occurring in the context of pregnancy carries with it potential risks both for the expectant mother and her fetus.[2] These are summarized in Table 16–1. Depressed pregnant women tend not to eat properly or to ingest enough fluids, increasing the chance of preterm labor and/ or small-for-gestational-age babies. Impaired concentration and judgment heightens the risk for motor vehicle accidents and other untoward events. Also, depression often is characterized by impulsive or reckless behavior, including cigarette smoking, illicit drug use, or alcohol use. These behaviors further threaten the health of the developing fetus. Carried to the extreme, this impulsivity may result in attempted or completed suicide. Finally, untreated depression in pregnancy invariably leads to depression post partum.

Assessment

Assessment of mood disorders in pregnancy is complicated by the fact that many of the neurovegetative signs and symptoms of depression are mimicked by the normative somatic and behavioral changes of pregnancy, such as decreased energy, insomnia or disturbed sleep, altered appetite, weight changes, and agitation or worry. Nevertheless, careful attention to the specific characteristics of sleep and appetite disturbances assists the clinician in identifying clinical depression in the setting of pregnancy. For instance, insomnia related to depression is more likely if the woman is unable to

sleep in spite of sufficient opportunity. Further, if the woman has no appetite in the absence of nausea or hyperemesis gravidarum, this may favor the diagnosis of depression.

Evaluation of depression in pregnancy therefore involves careful attention to both the report of the patient as well as the context of the current situation. In addition to monitoring changes in appetite, weight, sleep, and energy, women should be asked about symptoms of depressed mood or sadness, loss of interest in usually enjoyable activities, feelings of guilt or worthlessness, difficulties in concentration or sustained attention, and thoughts of suicide or passive but persistent thoughts of death. Additionally, the clinician should note behavioral changes such as psychomotor slowing or agitation. Because they are at increased risk of depressive recurrence, women with a history of depression, anxiety, and/or mood instability deserve special attention. Of even greater significance is a history of psychiatric illness associated with reproductive-life events, for example, mood disturbance associated with the premenstruum, pregnancy, and the postpartum period. Special circumstances that should be monitored are those in which psychotropic medication was abruptly withdrawn upon learning of pregnancy, there is no partner or a poor social support system, or there is a recent history of major stressors.

Treatment

Once the diagnosis of depression has been made, it is useful before any treatment is initiated to meet with both the woman and her partner to educate them as to the nature of the illness, prognosis with and without treatment, available treatment options, length of treatment, and risks and benefits of treatment options to mother and fetus. Options for treatment of depression in pregnancy are summarized in Table 16–2. Nonpharmacologic options that should be initiated include encouraging the discontinuation of alcohol, caffeine, and nicotine. Every opportunity should be made for adequate time for uninterrupted rest. Sometimes this requires assistance to care for small children in the household and reduction of duties at work. Relaxation techniques, cognitive-behavioral therapy (to change negative cognitions), interpersonal therapy (to examine current relationships and supports), and support groups are viable options for women whose illness is mild or moderate in severity and who wish to remain medication free.[9]

TABLE 16–2. Management of Depression in
Pregnancy

Educate patient and partner about depression

Inform patient and partner about risks and benefits to
mother and fetus of treatment options

Encourage rest

Psychotherapy: relaxation-training, cognitive-behavioral
therapy, interpersonal therapy, support group,
conjoint counseling

Psychopharmaco therapy

Electroconvulsive therapy (for severe, refractory, or
psychotic depression)

If the relationship between mother and partner is conflictual, couples therapy is also important.

Because major depression in pregnancy compromises the health and well-being of the expectant mother and also increases the likelihood of small-for-gestational-age and preterm babies, psychotropic medication should be considered to achieve resolution of depressive symptoms.[2] Efforts should be directed toward controlling symptoms to minimize any threats to the mother or the fetus.[9] Although not always possible, it is advisable to avoid psychotropic medication during the first trimester of pregnancy, the time of greatest vulnerability for organ teratogenesis.

Several studies to date have looked at the use of antidepressants in pregnant women. Most of these have focused on the use of tricyclic antidepressants and selective serotonin reuptake inhibitors (SSRIs). In the studies of tricyclic antidepressants, no significant association has been reported between fetal exposure and higher than expected rates of major congenital abnormalities. However, withdrawal syndromes including jitteriness, irritability, and convulsions have been noted in neonates exposed to tricyclic antidepressants near term. In addition, anticholinergic symptoms such as functional bowel obstruction and urinary retention have been noted. In utero exposure to tricyclic antidepressants has not been shown to have behavioral or developmental consequences for children studied up to age 7 years.[10]

Prenatal exposure to fluoxetine in the first trimester does not appear to be associated with an increase in the rate of major congenital organ malformations or with the clustering of any particular malformation.[11] Although a single case of possible fluoxetine toxicity in a newborn with symptoms of agitation and tachycardia has been reported,[12] two other studies[13,14] demonstrated no increased rate of neonatal or perinatal abnormalities. In another study, infants exposed to fluoxetine appeared to exhibit an increase in minor anomalies if exposed during the first trimester, and premature delivery if exposed during the third trimester.[15] However, this study failed to include a properly matched control group comprising untreated depressed pregnant women. In the same study, maternal exposure to fluoxetine later in pregnancy (after 25 weeks' gestation) was correlated to lower birth weights and lower maternal weight gain.[15] This finding was not corroborated in a recent study of neurobehavioral functioning of children up to age 7 years exposed in utero to fluoxetine; the study showed no adverse perinatal consequences or neurobehavioral abnormalities to age 7 years.[10] It is prudent, however, to monitor weight gain in pregnant women treated with antidepressants. Recent data consisting of a total of 420 deliveries of infants exposed to fluvoxamine, paroxetine, or sertraline during the first trimester did not reveal an increased risk for major malformations, miscarriages, or stillbirths.[16] Thus far, 375 documented cases of citalopram exposure during pregnancy revealed no evidence of teratogenicity.[17] To date, there are no published studies of the safety of venlafaxine, nefazodone, trazodone, mirtazapine, or citalopram in pregnancy.

Electroconvulsive therapy is not necessarily contraindicated in pregnancy; for severe, refractory, or psychotic depression, this may be an efficacious alternative or adjunct to psychotropic medications. Electroconvulsive therapy is relatively safe in pregnancy provided that the procedure is performed in the presence of a comprehensive treatment team (ie, psychiatrist, anesthesiologist, and obstetrician) and that appropriate safeguards and monitoring procedures are in place.[11,18]

DEPRESSION POST PARTUM

Identifying Postpartum Depressive Conditions

The postpartum period is a time of increased vulnerability for psychiatric illness in women. During the first postpartum month, the rate of inpatient psychiatric admissions is seven times higher than the pre-pregnancy rate.[19] Although postpartum depression arises during the first 4 weeks following childbirth, in practice, women with postpartum depression frequently present as late as 6 months and sometimes even 1 year post partum. Several reasons may explain the delayed presentation of postpartum depressed women. Women often feel ashamed of being depressed rather than joyful. In addition, many of the neurovegetative symptoms of depression are similar to expected postpartum disruptions in sleep, appetite, and energy. Finally, depressive symptoms that present beyond the first 2 postpartum weeks and fulfill criteria for major depression are often minimized and mistakenly diagnosed as "just the blues."

Course of Postpartum Mood Conditions

Postpartum mood conditions can be divided into three general categories based on severity and clinical characteristics. Affecting as many as 50 to 80% of new mothers, postpartum blues is the most common and least severe of these syndromes. The disturbance, comprising symptoms of irritability, anxiety, tearfulness, mood swings, and sleep disruption, usually begins on days 2 to 4 post partum and resolves by the end of the second postpartum week. Risk factors are work-related difficulties, conflicts with family and friends, stressful life events, history of prior depression, depression during pregnancy, and premenstrual dysphoria. However, there is no relation to obstetric complications.[20] Eighty percent of women with postpartum blues experience no psychological difficulties following resolution of their symptoms. For 20% of women who experience postpartum blues, symptoms persist and deepen such that the condition becomes postpartum depression.

Postpartum depression affects approximately 10 to 15% of women. In addition to symptoms consistent with major depression during other periods in a woman's life cycle, postpartum depression often is characterized by pronounced anxiety, ruminations, and, sometimes, obsessive worries regarding the health and well-being of the baby. Risk factors for postpartum depression are summarized in Table 16–3. Without a history of depression, the risk of postpartum depression is 10%; previous depression increases that risk to 25%, and prior postpartum depression increases it further to 50%.[20] Other risk factors include depression during the current pregnancy, unmarried status, and unplanned pregnancy.

As in depression occurring during pregnancy, one method of distinguishing depressive symptomatology from normative events is to assess whether

TABLE 16–3. Risk Factors for Postpartum Depression

Prior history of major depression
Prior postpartum depression
Depression during current pregnancy
Unmarried status
Unplanned pregnancy

sleep is difficult even when the new mother is provided with the opportunity to do so. Because of the overlap of symptoms, a useful screening method is the use of a rating scale such as the Edinburgh Postnatal Depression Scale (Figure 16–1). This instrument is a self-rated questionnaire that contains ten items, each with four possible responses. The first four items are scored zero points for the first response, one point for the second response, two points for the third response, and three points for the fourth response. The last six items are scored three points for the first response, two points for the second response, one point for the third response, and zero points for the fourth response. A score of 12 or more indicates likely depression.[21] This instrument can be introduced at weeks 6 to 8 post partum. Suprathreshold results should be confirmed by retesting 2 weeks later. It also can be used over time to monitor the effectiveness of treatment.

Postpartum psychosis is a rare but severe psychotic mood disorder occurring after 0.1% of births and almost always requiring acute hospitalization and treatment by psychiatric specialists. Postpartum psychosis may be considered a subcategory of bipolar disorder. Like bipolar disorder, symptoms include mood lability, confusion, agitation, paranoia, delusions, hallucinations, bizarre behavior, and sleep disruption.[20] Symptoms of postpartum psychosis appear early and rapidly, usually within 3 days of delivery. Of special concern for women with postpartum psychosis is the risk of suicide or infanticide. Risk factors for postpartum psychosis include a prior history of bipolar disorder, prior postpartum psychosis, and family history of bipolar disorder.[20]

Treatment

Treatment for the blues consists of reassurance, education, assistance with childcare and home duties, and monitoring for worsening or progression of symptoms. Since hypothyroidism is a fairly common postnatal condition that may mimic postpartum

Today's date _____ Baby's age _____

Baby's date of birth _____ Birth weight _____

Mother's age _____ Baby's place in family: 1 2 3 4 5 6 7

HOW ARE YOU FEELING?

As you have recently had a baby, we would like to know how you are feeling now. Please underline the answer which comes closest to how you have felt in the past 7 days, not just how you feel today.

Here is an example, already completed:

I have felt happy:
  Yes, most of the time
  Yes, some of the time
  No, not very often
  No, not at all

This would mean: "I have felt happy some of the time" during the past week. Please complete the other questions in the same way.

IN THE PAST SEVEN DAYS

1. I have been able to laugh and see the funny side of things:
  As much as I always could
  Not quite so much now
  Definitely not so much now
  Not at all

2. I have looked forward with enjoyment to things:
  As much as I ever did
  Rather less than I used to
  Definitely less than I used to
  Hardly at all

3. I have blamed myself unnecessarily when things went wrong:
  No, never
  Not very often
  Yes, some of the time
  Yes, most of the time

4. I have felt worried and anxious for no very good reason:
  No, not at all
  Hardly ever
  Yes, sometimes
  Yes, very often

5. I have felt scared or panicky for no very good reason:
  Yes, quite a lot
  Yes, sometimes
  No, not much
  No, not at all

6. Things have been getting on top of me:
  Yes, most of the time
  Yes, sometimes I haven't been coping as well as usual
  No, most of the time I have coped quite well
  No, I have been coping as well as ever

7. I have been so unhappy that I have had difficulty sleeping:
  Yes, most of the time
  Yes, sometimes
  Not very often
  No, not at all

8. I have felt sad or miserable:
  Yes, most of the time
  Yes, quite often
  Not very often
  No, not at all

9. I have been so unhappy that I have been crying:
  Yes, most of the time
  Yes, quite often
  Only occasionally
  No, never

10. The thought of harming myself has occurred to me:
  Yes, quite often
  Sometimes
  Hardly ever
  Never

FIGURE 16–1. Edinburgh Postnatal Depression Scale. Reproduced with permission from Cox JL, Holden JM, Sagovsky R. Detection of postnatal depression: development of the 10-item Edinburgh Postnatal Depression Scale. Br J Psychiatry 1987;150:782–6.

depression, it is essential to evaluate the thyroid status of all women who present with symptoms of postpartum depression. As with depression in pregnancy, treatment of depression post partum includes nonpharmacologic measures such as edu-cation, reassurance, conjoint meetings with the partner, and reduction of stressors and responsibilities in household tasks and in the care of the newborn to ensure adequate opportunity for rest. Additionally, advocacy and support groups such as Depression

After Delivery, Inc., and Postpartum Support International afford women the opportunity to share their experiences with other women in similar circumstances. Individual and group psychotherapy with mental health professionals well versed in postpartum mood disorders is also useful.

When depression is moderate to severe in intensity, medication may be required and should be instituted early to reduce the risk of refractoriness. For severe refractory postpartum depression, electroconvulsive therapy may be administered. For women with a history of depression post partum, consideration should be given to prophylactic treatment with medication. In a study of women with histories of postpartum depression, 7% of those who elected to take antidepressant medication prophylactically during the immediate postpartum period relapsed, compared with 63% of those who chose to monitor symptoms alone.[22] Prophylactic medication should be started within 24 hours of delivery. As in other periods of the woman's life cycle, selection of an antidepressant should be based on side effect profile, ease of dosing, prior response, family history of response, and patient preference. For nursing women, an additional consideration is safety for the nursing infant exposed to medication via ingested breast milk. Approaches to the treatment of postpartum depression are summarized in Table 16–4. An algorithm for diagnosis and treatment of postpartum depression is presented in Figure 16–2.

Breast-Feeding and Antidepressant Medication

About one-half of new mothers in the United States breast-feed.[9] Breast milk offers numerous advantages to mother and infant, including reduced cost, promotion of digestion and absorption of nutrients via nucleotides and enzymes, decreased incidence of infections, promotion of neurologic development, better performance on measures of intelligence, and bonding between mother and infant.[23] It is therefore not surprising that when women with postpartum depression are faced with the need to take medication, they often do not wish to stop breast-feeding. When considering psychotropic medication in breast-feeding women, it is important to analyze factors such as the benefits of breast-feeding and the adverse consequences of untreated mental illness on both maternal well-being and infant attachment and development. Discussions should be held with mother and partner and the baby's physician and

TABLE 16–4. Management of Postpartum Depression

Educate patient and partner about postpartum depression

Conjoint meetings to provide reassurance and, if needed, counseling

Strategize measures to achieve stress reduction: eg, childcare and household assistance

Supportive psychotherapy: group and individual

Psychopharmaco therapy

Electroconvulsive therapy for severe refractory depression

should be documented in the medical record. Since the data on the safety of breast-feeding while taking antidepressants is relatively sparse and generally arises from case reports and small studies, the decision to proceed with nursing while on medication must take into account the known benefits of breast-feeding to both infant and mother, the risk of adverse effects in the nursling, and the possibility that a depressed mother may refuse treatment rather than discontinue nursing. Since the postpartum period is a time of increased risk psychiatrically, and since depression post partum is a serious and debilitating illness that threatens the health and well-being of mother, baby, and other family members, it is best to provide new mothers with effective treatment to alleviate their depressive symptoms. This often entails the use of antidepressant medication.

Once the decision to continue breast-feeding with concomitant antidepressant administration has been made, prior to initiation of treatment, a thorough history and physical examination of the infant should be performed by a primary physician with special focus on feeding, temperament, sleep pattern, and activity level. Infants exposed to antidepressants via breast milk should be evaluated at regular intervals to ensure normal development without adverse effects.

It is not advisable for premature infants to be exposed to antidepressants via breast milk, as it is likely that their livers are immature and incapable of metabolizing the medications efficiently. As infants increase in age, their ability to metabolize medications improves, and the likelihood of accumulation of medication or active metabolites diminishes. In the event that adverse effects are noted, it is best to discontinue nursing. In some cases, infant serum levels of parent and metabolite

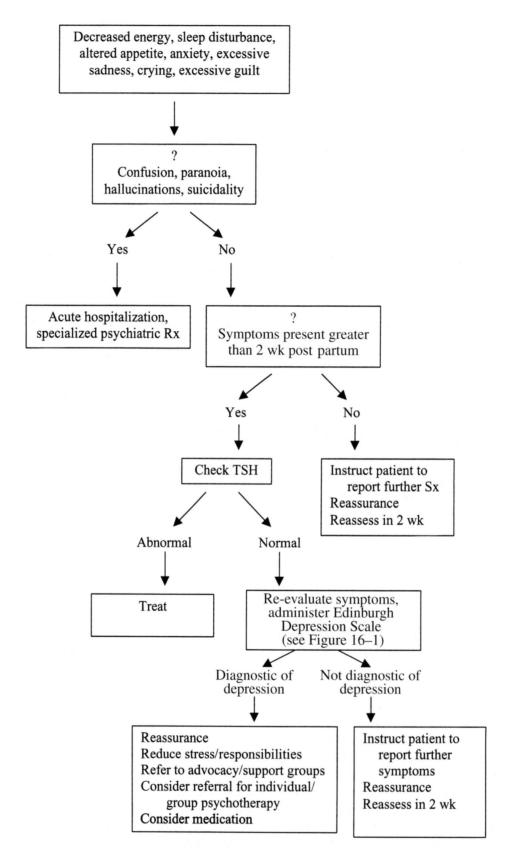

FIGURE 16–2. Evaluation of postpartum depressive symptoms. Rx = prescription; TSH = thyroid-stimulating hormone; Sx = symptoms.

compounds may be measured; where levels are high (eg, > 10 ng/mL) and the infant displays adverse effects, nursing should be discontinued.

Tricyclic antidepressants appear to be relatively safe in breast-feeding,[9] with the exception of doxepin, for which there is a single case of sedation and respiratory depression in an infant nursed by a doxepin-treated mother.[24] With one exception, infants exposed to fluoxetine via breast milk showed no adverse consequences;[25,26] in the exceptional case, a 6-week-old nursling exhibited colic and high serum levels that dissipated upon discontinuation of nursing.[27] Although nine other cases among three other studies reported adverse effects from fluoxetine exposure through breast milk, these cases were either unconfirmed by medical personnel, transient, or confounded by other medications.[28–30] Based on 16 cases, sertraline appears to be relatively safe in breast-feeding.[31–35] Although data are more sparse than for fluoxetine or sertraline, adverse consequences have not been reported for nursing infants exposed to paroxetine,[36–40] fluvoxamine,[41,42] or citalopram.[43–45] Case reports for bupropion[46] and venlafaxine[47] also revealed no adverse clinical consequences for breast-fed babies.

CONCLUSION

Mood disorders are often chronic and recurring in women, particularly of childbearing age. This raises the likelihood of illnesses such as depression occurring during pregnancy and the postpartum period. Not only does untreated illness pose significant morbidity for the woman, it also impacts greatly on maternal-fetal and maternal-infant bonding, spousal relationships, and risk for future episodes. With careful planning and monitoring, education, treatment, and, in some cases, prophylaxis, the burden of depression for pregnant and postpartum women and their families can be greatly ameliorated.

RESOURCES

Depression After Delivery, Inc.
91 East Somerset Street
Raritan, New Jersey 08869
Telephone: 1-800-944-4PPD (1-800-944-4773) (Information request line)
(215) 295-3994 (Professional inquiries)
Web site: www.depressionafterdelivery.com

Depression After Delivery, Inc., provides information about pregnancy and postpartum disorders, professional referral lists, and lists of volunteer telephone contacts and support groups.

Postpartum Support International
52 Sand Lana
Islandia, New York<None> 11749–1731
Telephone: (631) 582-2174
Web site: www.chss.iup.edu/postpartum

Postpartum Support International is an organization that works to increase awareness among the public and health professionals about peripartum, mood, and anxiety disorders. Their Web site includes information for both laypersons and health professionals on diagnosis and treatment of peripartum depression. The site includes state-by-state information on support groups and hotlines.

REFERENCES

1. Kessler RE, McGonagle KA, Chao S, et al. Lifetime and 12-month prevalence of DSM-III-R psychiatric disorders in the United States: results from the National Comorbidity Survey. Arch Gen Psychiatry 1994;54Suppl 1:8–19.
2. Burt VK, Hendrick V. Psychiatric assessment of

female patients. In: Hales RE, Yudofsky SC, Talbott JA, editors. The American Psychiatric Press textbook of psychiatry. 3rd ed. Washington (DC): American Psychiatric Press, Inc.; 1999. p. 1429–45.

3. Blehar MC, Lieberman AF, Ainsworth MDS. Early face-to-face interaction and its relation to later infant-mother interaction. Child Dev 1977;48:182–94.

4. Cogill K, Caplan HL, Alexandra H, et al. Impact of maternal postnatal depression on cognitive development of young children. Br Med J 1986;292:1165–7.

5. Rutter M, Quinton D. Parental psychiatric disorder: effects on children. Psychol Med 1984;14:853–80.

6. Lovestone S, Kumar R. Postnatal psychiatric illness: the impact on partners. Br J Psychiatry 1993;163:210–6.

7. Post RM. Transduction of psychosocial stress into the neurobiology of recurrent affective disorder. Am J Psychiatry 1992;149:999–1010.

8. Pajer K. New strategies in the treatment of depression in women. J Clin Psychiatry 1995;56Suppl 2:30–7.

9. Burt VK, Hendrick V. Concise guide to women's mental health. Washington (DC): American Psychiatric Press, Inc.; 1997.

10. Nulman I, Rouet J, Stewart DE, et al. Neurodevelopment of children exposed in utero to antidepressant drugs. N Engl J Med 1997;336:258–62.

11. Altshuler LL, Cohen L, Szuba MP. Pharmacologic management of psychiatric illness during pregnancy: dilemmas and guidelines. Am J Psychiatry 1996;153:592–606.

12. Spencer MJ. Fluoxetine hydrochloride (Prozac) toxicity in the neonate. Pediatrics 1993;92:721–2.

13. Goldstein DJ. Effects of third trimester fluoxetine exposure on the newborn. J Clin Psychopharmacol 1995;15:417–20.

14. McElhatton PR, Garbis HM, Elefant E, et al. The outcome of pregnancy in 689 women exposed to therapeutic doses of antidepressants: a collaborative study of the European network of teratology information services (ENTIS). Reprod Toxicol 1996;10:285–94.

15. Chambers CD, Johnson KA, Dick LM, et al. Birth outcomes in pregnant women taking fluoxetine. N Engl J Med 1996;335:1010–5.

16. Kulin NA, Pastuszak A, Sage SR, et al. Pregnancy outcome following maternal use of the new selective serotonin reuptake inhibitors: a prospective controlled multicenter study. JAMA 1998;279:609–10.

17. Ericson A, Kullen B, Wilholm BE. Delivery outcome after the use of antidepressants in early pregnancy. Eur J Clin Pharmacol 1999;55:503–8.

18. Miller LJ. Use of electroconvulsive therapy during pregnancy. Hosp Community Psychiatry 1994;45:444–50.

19. Kendell RE, Chalmers JC, Platz C. Epidemiology of puerperal psychoses. Br J Psychiatry 1987;150:662–73.

20. Suri R, Burt VK. The assessment and treatment of postpartum psychiatric disorders. J Pract Psychiatry Behav Health 1997;3:67–77.

21. Holden JM. Postnatal depression: its nature, effects, and identification using the Edinburgh Postnatal Depression Scale. Birth 1991;18:211–21.

22. Wisner KL, Wheeler SB. Prevention of recurrent postpartum major depression. Hosp Community Psychiatry 1994;45:1191–6.

23. Wisner KL, Perel JM, Findling RL. Antidepressant treatment during breast-feeding. Am J Psychiatry 1996;153:1132–7.

24. Matheson I, Pande H, Alertsen AR. Respiratory depression caused by *N*-desmethyldoxepin in breast milk [letter]. Lancet 1985;2:1124.

25. Burch KJ, Wells BG. Fluoxetine/norfluoxetine concentrations in human milk. Pediatrics 1992;89:676–7.

26. Isenberg KE. Excretion of fluoxetine in human breast milk. J Clin Psychiatry 1990;51:169.

27. Lester BM, Cucco J, Andreozzi L, et al. Possible association between fluoxetine hydrochloride and colic in an infant. J Am Acad Child Adolesc Psychiatry 1993;32:1253–5.

28. Moretti M, Sharma A, Bar-Oz B, et al. Fluoxetine and its effects on the nursing infant: a prospective cohort study [abstract]. Clin Pharmacol Ther 1989;65:141.

29. Kristensen JH, Ilett KI, Hacketty LP, et al. Distribution and excretion of fluoxetine and norfluoxetine in human milk. Br J Clin Pharmacol 1999;48:521–7.

30. Brent, Wisner K. Fluoxetine and carbamazepine concentrations in a nursing mother/infant pair. Clin Pediatr 1998;37:41–4.

31. Stowe ZN, Owens MJ, Landry JC, et al. Sertraline and desmethylsertraline in human breast milk and nursing infants. Am J Psychiatry 1997;154:1255–60.

32. Altshuler LL, Burt VK, McMullen M, et al. Breast-feeding and sertraline: a 24 hour analysis. J Clin Psychiatry 1995;56:243–5.

33. Mammen O, Perel JM, Rudolph G, et al. Sertraline and norsertraline levels in three breastfed infants. J Clin Psychiatry 1997;58:100–3.

34. Birnbaum CS, Cohen LS, Bailey JW, et al. Serum concentrations of antidepressants and benzodiazepines in nursing infants: a case series (electronic article). Pediatrics 1999;104:e11.

35. Kristensen J, Ilett KI, Dusci L, et al. Distribution and excretion of sertralene and *N*-desmethylsertraline in human milk. Br J Clin Pharmacol 1998;45:453–7.

36. Spigset O, Carleborg L, Norstrom A, et al. Paroxetine level in breast milk. J Clin Psychiatry 1996;57:39.

37. Ohman R, Hagg S, Carleborg L, Spigset O. Excretion of paroxetine into breast milk. J Clin Psychiatry 1999;60:519–23.

38. Stowe ZA, Cohen LS, Hostetter A, et al. Paroxetine in human breast milk and nursing infants. Am J Psychiatry 2000;157:185–9.

39. Begg EJ, Duffull SB, Saunders DA, et al. Paroxetine in human milk. Br J Clin Pharmacol 1999;48:142–7.

40. Hendrick VC, Stowe ZN, Altshuler LL, et al. Paroxetine use during breast feeding. J Clin Psychopharmacol 2000;20:587–8.

41. Wright S, Dawling S, Ashford JJ. Excretion of fluvoxamine in breast milk. Br J Clin Pharmacol 1991; 31:209.

42. Yoshida K, Smith B, Kumar RC. Fluvoxamine in breast-milk and infant development [letter]. Br J Clin Pharmacol 1997;44:210–1.

43. Spigset O, Carleborg L, Ohman R, et al. Excretion of citalopram in breast milk. Br J Clin Pharmacol 1997;44:295–8.

44. Schmidt K, Oleson OV, Jensen PN. Citalopram and breast-feeding: serum concentration and side effects in the infant. Biol Psychiatry 1999;47:164–5.

45. Jensen P, Oleson O, Bertelsen A, et al. Citalopram and desmethylcitalopram concentrations in breast milk and in serum of mother and infant. Ther Drug Monit 1997;19:236–9.

46. Briggs GG, Samson JH, Ambrose PJ, et al: Excretion of buproprion in breast milk. Ann Pharmacother 1985;27:431–3.

47. Ilett KF, Hackett LP, Dusci LJ, et al. Distribution and excretion of venlafaxine and O-desmethylvenlafaxine in human milk. Br J Clin Pharmacol 1998;45:459–62.

17

DRUGS IN PREGNANCY AND LACTATION

Karen A. Filkins, MD

Teratology is the study of abnormal fetal development, whether structural or functional. A teratogen is anything that can cause abnormal fetal development. When medications are used during pregnancy or lactation, concerns arise about teratogenic or toxic effects on the fetus or infant.

Exposures that occur prior to pregnancy or implantation generally are thought to have little or no effect, but, in reality, effects depend upon the metabolism or storage of the substance in the body. Exposures during organogenesis (days 17 to 56 post conception) occur at a most critical time with respect to malformations. Later exposures may result in damage to organ function, carcinogenesis, or even deformations of previously normal structures. Exposures through breast milk may result in mild but undesirable side effects to severe toxic effects that can produce permanent functional damage or even death.

In evaluating any exposure, timing is not the only critical factor. Dosage (ie, threshold levels for teratogenic or toxic effects), species and genetic differences (eg, metabolic pathways), and risks from lack of treatment and possible alternative treatments, have to be considered when weighing the risks and benefits of drug use in pregnancy and lactation.

NO TREATMENT

For physicians who are less accustomed to treating pregnant women, there is a natural tendency to want to stop or minimize all treatments once a woman becomes pregnant. Some physicians even fear ordinary diagnostic tests such as radiography in pregnant women, even when the benefit clearly outweighs the risk (eg, a chest radiograph in a pregnant woman suspected to have tuberculosis or pneumonia).

However, untreated maternal illness often presents a great risk to the fetus. Before the introduction of insulin in 1921, diabetic women rarely had successful pregnancies.[1,2] Fever, hypertension, and anything that may cause hypoxia (including seizures and asthma) all present obvious risks to pregnancies, if untreated. Depression may be exacerbated during pregnancy and especially in the postpartum period. If untreated, suicidal or infanticidal behavior can result in direct harm to the mother, fetus, or infant. Many other medical conditions (see Chapter 15, "Common Medical Problems in Pregnancy") can result in adverse pregnancy outcomes if left untreated.

DECISION TO TREAT

Teratologists evaluate exposures during pregnancy by comparing benefits versus risks, taking into account dosage, timing, and clinical effects. Once the decision is made to use medication during pregnancy, an effort should be made to devise a plan of treatment that presents the least possible risk to the fetus. Few drugs are known teratogens (Table 17–1). However, often one has a choice of several drugs for a given clinical indication, for which there may be more or less information or concern about teratogenicity. Ideally, one should choose drugs for which human data are available and for which the data are reassuring.

Sometimes a drug that is relatively safe in the first trimester is not a good choice later in pregnancy, and vice versa. For pregnancy-related drug information, one can consult books such as *Drugs in*

TABLE 17–1. Teratogenic Agents[*]

Drugs and chemicals
   Alcohol
   Androgens and testosterone derivatives (eg, danazol)
   Angiotensin-converting enzyme inhibitors (eg, enalapril, captopril)
   Angiotensin II receptor antagonists (eg, losartan)
   Busulfan
   Carbamazepine
   Chlorobiphenyls
   Cocaine
   Coumarin derivatives (eg, warfarin)
   Cyclophosphamide
   Diethylstilbestrol
   Diphenylhydantoin
   Disulfiram
   Folic acid antagonists (eg, methotrexate, aminopterin)
   Kanamycin
   Lead
   Lithium
   Methimazole
   Organic mercury
   Paramethadione
   Penicillamine
   Phenytoin
   Primidone
   Streptomycin
   Tetracycline
   Thalidomide
   Toluene (abuse)
   Trimethadione
   Valproic acid
   Vitamin A and its derivatives (eg, isotretinoin, etretinate, retinoids)

Infections
   Cytomegalovirus
   Herpesvirus
   Parvovirus B19
   Rubella
   Syphilis
   Toxoplasmosis
   Varicella
   Venezuelan equine encephalitis virus

Ionizing radiation
   Atomic weapons
   Radioiodine
   Therapeutic radiation

Metabolic imbalance
   Endemic cretinism
   Diabetes
   Folic acid deficiency
   Hyperthermia
   Phenylketonuria
   Rheumatic disease
   Virilizing tumors

[*]Broadly defined.
Adapted from ACOG[3] and Paul M. Occupational and environmental reproductive hazards. Baltimore: Williams & Wilkins; 1983. p. 51.

Pregnancy and Lactation (Briggs et al) or Shepard's *Catalog of Teratogenic Agents*, or computerized databases, or one can contact local geneticists or teratogen information services (hotlines). Specific sources of information are listed under "Resources" at the end of this chapter.

APPROACH TO THE PRECONCEPTIONAL PATIENT

Consultation with the preconceptional patient is the ideal situation for risk/benefit analysis. Unfortunately, more than 50% of all pregnancies are unplanned, so one needs to identify the group of patients likely to become pregnant in the next year and focus on them (refer to Chapter 10, "Preconception Counseling"). One should review the medications used by the patient including over-the-counter preparations, herbal remedies, and dietary supplements or restrictions.

A plan should be initiated for safe management of medical conditions—if possible, using medications that have been well studied and are without adverse effects. One should attempt to avoid the use of multiple medications because drug interactions may increase risk. If there is little human information about a drug that clearly is needed and for which there is no alternative, then the patient can be given two choices: she has the option of postponing pregnancy until more data become available, or becoming pregnant knowing that one cannot predict, even from excellent animal studies, the effects on a given human pregnancy. If the illness has a known adverse effect on pregnancy, then the treatment with its unknown potential effects may outweigh the known undesirable effects of lack of treatment.

INADVERTENT EXPOSURE

Consider the following scenario: a patient has had an exposure to a drug labeled category X by the US Food and Drug Administration (FDA), and someone has mistakenly informed her that this means she should immediately terminate her pregnancy. This situation is not so unusual, especially for those who handle hotline calls from patients. Category X drugs are drugs that have *no benefit* during pregnancy and, therefore, because the benefit is zero, the risk-benefit ratio is infinite, even if the risk is only theoretical. Oral contraceptives obviously fall into this category (ie, no benefit for a pregnant woman but probably minimal or no increased risk, especially with today's low-dose versions). Oral contraceptive failures, especially with low-dose pills, are a steady source of hotline calls regarding category X drugs.

Even with more serious exposures, one must assess the timing, dose, genetic background of the individual, and available human and animal data before determining the actual risk involved. For some known teratogens, the timing and percentage of defects to be expected have been documented clearly. Thalidomide, for example, resulted in defects of limbs, ears, heart, and gastrointestinal tract in 20% of children whose mothers were exposed between 34 and 50 days after the last menstrual cycle.[3,4] An experienced clinician may be able to detect the limb defects with ultrasound evaluation in the late first trimester. Ear, cardiac, and gastrointestinal defects may be detected in many cases in the second trimester. When presented with this information, even in an extreme case such as that of thalidomide exposure, women can make a rational choice about continuing or ending a pregnancy.

Some exposures present a greater problem because mental retardation may be part of the syndrome produced, and there may not be a physical change reasonably detectable by ultrasonography that is always associated with the mental retardation. Functional abnormalities often present a greater challenge for prenatal diagnosis than do structural defects, unless there is some metabolic change that can be measured. Isotretinoin (Accutane) exposure falls into this category, as mental retardation, especially borderline retardation, is not associated consistently with major malformations. Isotretinoin exposure is associated with a 35% risk for embryopathy if it continues beyond the 15th day after conception.[5] No affected babies have been born to women who stopped the drug prior to 15 days following conception. Therefore, in this case, accurate ultrasonographic dating may change the risk estimate from 35% to essentially zero for isotretinoin embryopathy (but still with about a 3% *background risk* for all pregnancies for major birth defects). Inadvertent exposure to topical applications of vitamin A derivatives, although not recommended during pregnancy, generally are not a cause of concern. However, etretinate, an oral retinoid used to treat psoriasis, is stored in the body for years and remains a concern even if the exposure occurs long before the pregnancy.[6]

Obviously, each exposure must be handled individually, using the most current information available. The FDA drug category classifications (Table 17–2), although helpful in considering risks versus benefits for treatment of pregnant women, have been less helpful in determining appropriate counseling for women who have had an inadvertent exposure. For this reason, the classifications are under revision to include more descriptive information rather than general categories. In addition, when risks are discussed with patients, information should be given with reference to the expected background rate for birth defects in general as well as the specific risks for the particular birth defect(s) of concern.

CHOOSING THE BEST TREATMENT DURING PREGNANCY

When a pregnant woman requires drug treatment, one usually has a choice of available medications. In general, it is best to compile a list of possible treatments and then to research each medication. One might start with a list of drugs in a particular pharmacologic category using the *Physicians' Desk Reference* or *Drugs in Pregnancy and Lactation* (Briggs et al; see "Resources" below). Some idea of the type of information available may be obtained by checking for the FDA category, but this is just a

TABLE 17–2. US Food and Drug Administration Pregnancy Risk Categories

Category	Definition
A	Controlled studies in women fail to demonstrate a risk to the fetus in the first trimester (and there is no evidence of a risk in later trimesters), and the possibility of fetal harm appears remote. Example: vitamin C when use does not exceed recommended daily allowance
B	Either animal reproduction studies have not demonstrated fetal risk but no controlled studies in pregnant women have been reported, or animal reproduction studies have shown an adverse effect (other than a decrease in fertility) that was not confirmed in controlled studies in women in the first trimester (and there is no evidence of risk in later trimesters). Example: ampicillin
C	Either studies in animals have revealed adverse effects on the fetus (teratogenic, embryocidal, or other) but no controlled studies in women have been reported, or studies in women and animals are not available; drugs should be given only if the potential benefit justifies the potential risk to the fetus. Example: diazepam
D	Positive evidence of human fetal risk exists, but the benefits from use in pregnant women may be acceptable despite the risk (eg, if the drug is needed for a life-threatening condition or for a serious disease for which safer drugs cannot be used or are ineffective). Example: phenytoin
X	Studies in animals or humans have demonstrated fetal abnormalities, or evidence exists of fetal risk based on human experience, or both, and the risk in pregnant women clearly outweighs any possible benefit; the drug is contraindicated in women who are or may become pregnant. Example: isotretinoin

Reproduced from US Food and Drug Administration. 1980.
Federal Register 44:37434-67.

starting point. Use of resources such as hotlines or databases can be helpful in providing recent information. If you are basing your decision on information that is more than 1 year old, you may be missing important adverse information that has recently become available.

The timing in pregnancy is extremely important in assessing teratogenic risk. For example, a drug such as carbamazapine (Tegretol) exerts its teratogenic potential very early in pregnancy by increasing the risk for spina bifida.[7,8] After neural tube closure, it may become the drug of choice in many cases. On the other hand, angiotensin converting enzyme inhibitors may not have significant adverse effects in the first trimester but are associated with a high (30%) risk of fetal morbidity, including in utero fetal hypotension, decreased renal blood flow, and renal failure, when used in the second and third trimesters.[9] Some exposures can exert teratogenic effects in the first trimester but can cause functional defects or (for warfarin[10,11] and cocaine[12,13]) vascular disruptive defects later in pregnancy.

The dose of drug also may affect the level of teratogenic risk and, in the case of topical agents, the degree of absorption may depend on a variety of factors, including integrity of the skin. One should not assume that all topical agents are automatically safe.

CHOOSING THE BEST TREATMENT DURING LACTATION

Because physicians are aware of the benefits of breast-feeding, they frequently assume that all women will or should breast-feed. The need to take a particular medication or, for that matter, to work in a particularly hazardous workplace (eg, high exposure to dry cleaning chemicals) may preclude breast-feeding because the risks to the newborn clearly outweigh the benefits.

The search for alternative medications during lactation is similar to that for medications to be used during pregnancy. Briggs et al's text and the American Academy of Pediatrics provide guidelines that are two good starting points. Some hotlines provide information about breast-feeding; others do not. Information also can be found in databases (see "Resources" below).

If there is no safe alternative, one must assess the need for treatment. If treatment is needed for a brief period only, the patient could bottle-feed the infant with formula, and pump and discard the breast milk until treatment has stopped and a reasonable time has passed (based on half-life), so there is no danger to the newborn; then, breast-feeding can resume. If treatment or exposure needs to continue for an extended period of time, and the risk of breast-feeding the infant outweighs the benefit, the patient *should not* breast-feed the infant.

Because it has become almost a social mandate to breast-feed today, it is imperative that the caregiver be supportive and reassuring when breast-feeding is contraindicated. One could point out that not long ago in the United States, most women did not breast-feed, and formula was considered a great advance for the freedom of women, especially those who intended to return to work. That generation of infants comprise a major portion of today's adults, and although there are good reasons to breast-feed, there are also times when there are good reasons not to breast feed an infant.

SUMMARY

Most of the time the use of medications during pregnancy and lactation is quite safe. One should become familiar with the relatively short list of known teratogens as well as a list of commonly used medications for which there has been a long history of safe use in pregnancy. When confronted with an unknown, many resources are available and should be consulted. One should use not only the FDA pregnancy categories but also information that is more specific in counseling patients about risks versus benefits. If a medication is needed in the postpartum period and it is known to produce serious adverse effects in the breast-fed infant, then breast-feeding, *not the medication*, is contraindicated. By following the guidelines detailed above, pregnant and lactating women are not deprived of appropriate treatment, and risks to the fetuses and newborns are minimized or eliminated.

RESOURCES

Organization of Teratology Information Services
UCSD Medical Center, Department of Pediatrics
200 West Arbor Drive
San Diego, California 92103-8446
Telephone: 1-800-532-3749
            (619) 543-2131
Web site: orpheus.ucsd.edu/otis

The OTIS lists hotline information services by region. Most services provide resources, including answers to specific questions, for both clinicians and patients.

March of Dimes
1275 Mamaroneck Avenue
White Plains, New York 10605
Telephone: 1-888-MODIMES (1-888-663-4637)
Web site: www.modimes.org

The March of Dimes provides information about preconception planning and specific birth defects. It also maintains a resource center to answer questions from both clinicians and patients.

RESOURCES (continued)

Publications and Computerized Information Databases

American Academy of Pediatrics. Committee on Infectious Disease. 1997 red book: report of the Committee on Infectious Diseases. Elk Village (IL): American Academy of Pediatrics; 1997.

American College of Obstetricans and Gynecologists. Seizure disorders in pregnancy. ACOG educational bulletin 231. Washington (DC): ACOG; 1996.

American College of Obstetricians and Gynecologists. Teratology. ACOG educational bulletin 236. Washington (DC): ACOG; 1997.

Briggs GC, Freeman RK, Yaffe SJ. Drugs in pregnancy and lactation. 5th ed. Philadelphia: Lippincott Williams & Wilkins; 1998.

Jones KL. Smith's recognizable patterns of human malformation. 5th ed. Philadelphia: W.B. Saunders Company; 1997.

Physicians' Desk Reference. Montvale (NJ): Medical Economics Company, Inc.; 2001.

Shepard TH. Catalog of teratogenic agents. 9th ed. Baltimore: Johns Hopkins University Press; 1998.

Micromedex, Inc.
Reprorisk (Reprotext, Reprotox, Shepard's Catalog of Teratogenic Agents, TERIS)
Englewood, Colorado
Telephone: 1-800-525-9083

Reproductive Toxicology Center
Reprotox
Columbia Hospital for Women Medical Center
Washington, DC
Telephone: (202) 293-5137

National Library of Medicine, MEDLARS Service Desk
Grateful Med (Toxline, Toxnet, and Medline)
Bethesda, Maryland
Telephone: 1-800-638-8480

Teratogen Information System
TERIS and Shepard's Catalog of Teratogenic Agents
Seattle, Washington
Telephone: (206) 543-2465

REFERENCES

1. Jovanovic L, Peterson C. Optimal insulin delivery for the pregnant diabetic patient. Diabetes Care 1982;5 Suppl 1:24–37.

2. Cunningham F, MacDonald P, Grant N, et al. Williams obstetrics. 19th ed. Norwalk (CN): Appleton & Lange; 1993. p. 1201.

3. American College of Obstetricians and Gynecologists. Teratology. ACOG educational bulletin, no. 236. Washington (DC): ACOG; 1997.

4. Miller M, Stromland K. Teratogen update: thalidomide: a review with focus on ocular findings and new potential uses. Teratology 1999;60:306–21.

5. Jones K. Smith's recognizable patterns of human malformation. 5th ed. Philadelphia: W.B. Saunders Company; 1997. p. 572–3.

6. Grote W, Harms D, Janig U, et al. Malformation of fetus conceived 4 months after termination of maternal etretinate treatment. Lancet 1985;1:1276.

7. Rosa FW. Spina bifida in infants of women treated with carbamazepine during pregnancy. N Engl J Med 1991;324:674–7.

8. Kallen A. Maternal carbamazepine and infant spina bifida. Reprod Toxicol 1994;8:203–5.

9. Feldkamp M, Jones K, Orneoy A, et al. Postmarketing surveillance for angiotensin-converting enzyme inhibitor use during the first trimester of pregnancy—United States, Canada and Israel, 1987–1995. JAMA 1997;277:1193–4.

10. Hall J, Pauli R, Wilson K. Maternal and fetal sequelae of anticoagulation during pregnancy. Am J Med 1980;68:122–40.

11. Iturbe-Alessio I, Fonseca M, Mutchinik O, et al. Risks of anticoagulant therapy in pregnant women with artificial heart valves. N Engl J Med 1986;315:1390–3.

12. Hoyme H, Jones K, Dixon S, et al. Prenatal ocaine exposure and fetal vascular disruption. Pediatrics 1990;85:743–47.

13. Hume R Jr, Gingras J, Martin L, et al. Ultrasound diagnosis of fetal anomalies associated with in utero cocaine exposure: further support for cocaine-induced vascular disruption teratogenesis. Fetal Diagn Ther 1994;9:239–45.

18

SUBSTANCE ABUSE
IN PREGNANCY

Carol Archie, MD

The use of social and illicit drugs represents a serious ongoing threat to the well-being of mothers and babies despite increased awareness among physicians and the public of this preventable risk. The National Institute of Drug Abuse reports that 70 to 90% of Americans between the ages of 15 and 40 years have used mood-altering chemicals, approximately half of whom are women with reproductive potential. Among women in this group, approximately 60% (34 million) are current drinkers, and 2.4 million of those admitted to heavy alcohol consumption in the past month; 32% (18 million) are smokers, and 11% (6 million) use marijuana.[1] Among women aged 15 to 44 years with no children and who were not pregnant, 9.3% were current drug users. Only 2.3% of pregnant women were current drug users,[2] which suggests that most women reduce drug use when they become pregnant. Unfortunately, women with a recent birth (nonpregnant women with a child under 2 years old) had a rate of use of 5.5%,[1] suggesting that many women resume drug use after giving birth. Similar patterns exist for alcohol and cigarette use. Rates of drug and cigarette use are highest during the first trimester and lowest in the third trimester among pregnant women. Nonetheless, screening a single urine sample for alcohol, cannabis, cocaine, and opiates in women presenting for delivery has revealed positive urine toxicology results in about 11% of cases in several large studies.[3-5] This finding has remained remarkably consistent in various populations, including patients from high and low socioeconomic backgrounds and multiple ethnic groups.

Substance use by an expectant mother can affect reproduction from fertility through pregnancy and lactation. In addition, this behavior can affect the developing fetus and neonate. Ideally, a woman's primary care clinician should take advantage of routine gynecologic examinations and pre-pregnancy and other office visits to provide information and counseling about substance use effects. These are valuable opportunities for informing women of the risks involved, especially since most congenital structural anomalies are induced in the 58 days following conception, which is often prior to recognition of pregnancy by the woman. Unfortunately, most women who use social and illicit substances do not have that optimal interaction before pregnancy. Hence, it is important for those providing prenatal care to be familiar with the possible adverse effects of commonly used and abused drugs. In most cases continued substance use beyond the period of embryogenesis carries risks for both the mother and the fetus. These are the risks that the obstetrician most frequently has the opportunity to reduce.

The purpose of this chapter is to outline an approach to the identification and effective treatment or referral of cases of substance abuse in pregnancy. Additionally, specific maternal and fetal effects of commonly abused social and illegal substances are reviewed.

PATIENT EDUCATION

Opportunities for substance use screening and patient education are presented by any patient encounter and include routine primary care, pre- and postnatal visits, and encounters during obstetric emergencies. The focus of patient education varies with the nature of the encounter.[6] During routine visits emphasis may be placed on the effects of various substances on fertility.[7–9] The woman also should be informed of potential fetal effects and obstetric problems should she become pregnant and continue substance use. When counseling a woman during routine prenatal visits, fetal and obstetric effects associated with initial or continued use should be discussed. At this time, the benefits to the mother and the fetus of treatment or abstinence should be emphasized. The risks of passive smoking should also be reviewed. The postnatal visit invites discussion of the effects of substance use on neonatal health through lactation or passive exposure (eg, tobacco or cocaine smoke may harm children). The potential harm, which may arise from impaired parental judgment while under the influence of psychoactive drugs, should not be overlooked. Substance abuse may interfere with a woman's contraceptive plans either through chemical interactions or by affecting the woman's ability to comply with the regimen. These issues should be discussed frankly.

SCREENING FOR SUBSTANCE ABUSE: ROLE OF THE CLINICAL INTERVIEW

The substance use interview should take place within the context of a comprehensive medical history. The quality of the substance use history obtained, like that of the general medical history, is frequently dependent on the quality of the relationship the clinician is able to establish with the patient.[10] In addition to reassuring the patient that all information will be treated with strict confidence, the following five specific steps have been shown to enhance the establishment of an optimal working relationship with patients:[11]

1. Establish a partnership with the patient: "We will work together throughout your pregnancy in order for you and your baby to have the best outcome possible."
2. Assure the patient that you intend to be supportive: "I will be available to work with you and answer any questions you might have."
3. Demonstrate respect for the patient: "I know it has been difficult, but it sounds as if you have been coping with the morning sickness and managing to get adequate nutrition."
4. Demonstrate empathy by identifying emotions expressed by the patient and expressing them in words: "You seem sad."
5. It can be important to legitimate the patient's concerns: "It is understandable that you might be concerned because of your last experience with childbirth."

Specific substance use screening is often best addressed while discussing other patient-controlled health issues such as nutrition and exercise. It is important to specifically address the use of prescription drugs. The dosage and indication as well as the frequency and duration of use should be carefully noted. Similarly, any nonprescription medication use must be carefully evaluated. The intake of caffeine, tobacco, and alcohol and the use of illicit drugs must be recorded.[12]

ADDRESSING SUBSTANCE ABUSE PROBLEMS

One commonly used screening test that can be easily integrated into the clinical interview is the CAGE questionnaire. For any alcohol or drug use mentioned in the initial interview, ask the following CAGE questions:[13]

1. Have you ever felt the need to *cut down* on your drinking or drug use? Why? When? What did you do? What happened?
2. Have you ever been *annoyed* by criticism of your drinking or drug use? Who criticized you? What happened? How often did this happen?
3. Have you ever felt *guilty* about your drinking or drug use? Under what circumstances? Did you try to change?
4. Have you ever had a morning *eye-opener* (used drugs first thing in the morning to get started)? How often? What were the feelings you had that made you think you needed it? Did the drug relieve these feelings?

One positive response indicates problem use and possible dependence. The follow-up questions provide important information for making a diagnosis of dependence or addiction and offer clues to the level of intervention that will be required. In pregnancy any substance use that is potentially harmful to the fetus is problematic and requires intervention. In addition to establishing the level of current use, it is important to assess the amount of alcohol and drug use at the time of conception.

PRESENTING THE DIAGNOSIS

When problematic substance use is discovered, the manner in which the diagnosis is presented to the patient becomes a factor in determining the level of cooperation with intervention that is likely to be obtained. It is crucial that a nonjudgmental approach be taken. Begin by providing valid factual information about substance use and its effects. Explain carefully the implications and consequences of future use, especially fetal effect and effects on the reproductive system. Describe the benefits of stopping or decreasing substance use or, in some cases, substituting medication (eg, methadone) for substances of abuse. Allow the patient to describe her understanding of the problem and check the patient's understanding of information provided. Finally, correct any misunderstandings.[12]

MANAGEMENT STRATEGIES

All obstetric patients can be categorized into one of three groups by the substance use interview. The majority are found to have no substance problems. Some are found to be currently using or abusing substances harmful to the mother, the fetus, or both. Others are found to have a previous substance abuse problem but to be currently in recovery. Each individual should be managed appropriately based on the outcome of the interview.

For those with no substance abuse problems, management should be directed toward prevention. As always, the physician should provide factual information about the effects of substance use, including prescription drugs, over-the-counter drugs, tobacco, and caffeine. The physician should re-inforce positive attitudes expressed by the patient regarding avoidance of damaging substances.[12] Additionally, it is important to recognize that some in this group are women who have become abstinent because they are now pregnant. It is therefore important to stress the importance of abstinence from tobacco, alcohol, and illicit drugs while breast-feeding, as well as the detrimental health effects of secondhand smoke on children reared in the homes of smokers.[14]

The management of those with a current substance use or abuse problem is more difficult. Once the diagnosis has been made and appropriately presented to the patient (see earlier), the urgency of treatment, especially in pregnancy, must be stressed. Where appropriate, referrals should be made. Whether the referral is for drug/alcohol treatment or support group only, the patient must understand that the primary clinician will continue to manage her medical and obstetric care while supporting her drug treatment.[15]

An effective treatment program must be and feel safe for the woman. Staff should express concern for and interest in both the mother and the fetus. A therapy team incorporating case management; nutritional support; high-risk obstetric evaluation; expertise in substance abuse, detoxification, and rehabilitation; and pediatric follow-up seems to offer the best approach. When the entire environment must be changed, residential facilities, which can accommodate the pregnant woman with other children and her newborn, are ideal, although hard to find. Additionally, the woman on methadone maintenance is often excluded from some residential communities and 12-step programs because she is not "drug free."

Many pregnant addicts respond well to being cared for because this has been lacking in their current environment or their background. Guilt reduction is often more effective than guilt induction. Group support from women in or from similar circumstances may help improve self-esteem and provide a better perspective on the situation. Pregnant women unable to benefit from such an environment may be suffering from concurrent severe psychopathology, which requires a more sophisticated mental health evaluation and intervention.[14,16]

When referral is not indicated or possible, the clinician should approach management by beginning with clear definite treatment recommendations. At times it may be necessary to make reasonable compromises in the treatment plan to secure the patient's acceptance. For example, if a woman consumes three drinks every night and smokes one pack of cigarettes each day, it may be necessary to accept a decrease in smoking while the woman attempts to achieve abstinence from alcohol. The specifics of the treatment plan should be reviewed with the patient, and the patient's verbal or written agreement should be obtained.

In whatever setting drug treatment is provided, it is important for the care clinician to maintain and express optimism about treatment. Treatment does work and can improve outcomes. The time invested will be returned in positive results for both the mother and baby, even if all treatment goals are not met. For example, the woman who smokes or drinks less but is unable to completely stop has decreased a dangerous exposure to the fetus and thereby decreased the potential damage to the child.

Pregnancy and parenting can be stressful for a woman in the best of circumstances, and for recovering substance users, this may be particularly true. This group of women requires close follow-up and monitoring. The physician should stress the importance of strict self-monitoring and of continuing in treatment or self-help group activities. Each patient should understand the risks to herself, the fetus, and her newborn of a full relapse.

EFFECTS OF RECREATIONAL AND ILLICIT DRUG USE ON PREGNANCY

In most cases the limitations of the data concerning substance use in pregnancy do not allow full assessment of either maternal or fetal risks. In many cases, the available information is confounded by complications that may arise from the lifestyle of the addicted woman. Malnutrition, frequently seen with the use of various substances including alcohol, opiates, and amphetamines, is associated with anemia and fetal growth retardation. Sexually transmitted and other infectious diseases occur more frequently in the pregnancies of substance abusers and cause complications. For example, intravenous drug use is associated with endocarditis, phlebitis, hepatitis, and acquired immune deficiency syndrome, all of which cause problems in pregnancy. Another important confounder when analyzing information on drug use in pregnancy is the fact that substance abusers rarely take a single drug. This makes it difficult to discern which drug is causing a given effect or whether the drugs are acting synergistically to cause a given finding.

SPECIFIC DRUGS FREQUENTLY COMPLICATING PREGNANCY

Tobacco

The chemically complex nature of tobacco smoke, which contains potentially harmful components such as nicotine, carbon monoxide, hydrogen cyanide, and potential carcinogens, makes specific identification of factors responsible for deleterious effects elusive. Nonetheless, several specific perinatal problems have been identified as complications of this addiction. Maternal smokers have a higher rate of pulmonary disease and lower weight gain in pregnancy. An increased frequency of spontaneous abortion, stillbirth, abnormal bleeding, fetal growth retardation, premature rupture of membranes, and lower birth weight, and an increased rate of preterm delivery complicate their pregnancies. These complications appear to be dose-related effects. Fortunately, smoking cessation by midpregnancy seems to reduce most of these risks. Long-term follow-up studies of children raised in a home in which either parent smokes have described a higher rate of respiratory infections and hospitalizations (contributing to poor school attendance), impaired growth, impaired intellectual development, and behavioral disorders, as well as a higher rate of infant death. The frequency of major structural congenital anomalies has not been shown consistently to be increased among neonates of mothers who smoked during pregnancy.[16]

Alcohol

An estimated 70% of Americans use alcohol socially. Typical periconceptual alcohol consumption (the period of maximum vulnerability to the anatomic defects of this recognized teratogen) is nearly as heavy as that in the nonpregnant state. During pregnancy, alcohol use varies considerably. Alcohol abuse has been defined as four or more drinks per day and has been found to occur in approximately 2% of pregnant women. As many as 1 in 300 infants born in the United States has some degree of stigmata of fetal alcohol exposure. Fetal alcohol syndrome is the most commonly identifiable cause of mental retardation in liveborn infants.[14]

The anatomic abnormalities detectable in the neonate are related in a dose-response fashion to prenatal alcohol exposure. Moreover, as would be expected embryologically, the critical period for precipitating these abnormalities is in the early first trimester.[17] The consumption of more than three cans of beer or three glasses of wine or mixed drinks per day and repetitive binge drinking greatly increase the risk of teratogenicity. A precise intake threshold has not been established, and lower doses may still be related to an increased incidence of cranial, facial, or other abnormalities.[18] Because of the uncertainty of how little alcohol is required to cause fetal disruption, and because many women may become aware of pregnancy after the possible effects of their drinking habit have occurred, women contemplating pregnancy should consider avoidance of all alcohol to eliminate the possibility of alcohol-related birth defects. Those women who conceive while maintaining their normal drinking patterns are advised to stop alcohol consumption as soon as they become aware of pregnancy.

There is a continuum of effects of alcohol on the fetus. The most severe complications of alcohol are abortion and stillbirth. Of lesser severity are fetal alcohol syndrome and alcohol-related birth defects, including abnormal growth and neurobehavioral development. The complex of newborn findings characterizing the diagnosis of fetal alcohol syndrome was defined by the Research Society on Alcoholism in 1980.[19] The diagnosis requires the presence of characteristic manifestations in each of three areas: (1) prenatal and postnatal growth retardation, (2) central nervous system involvement, and (3) characteristic facial morphology.[17]

Growth retardation of the fetus or neonate is defined as weight below the 10th percentile. Central nervous system abnormalities include tremulousness, poor suckling, abnormal muscle tone, hyperactivity, attention defects and mental retardation. At least two characteristic facial anomalies are required for the diagnosis. The range of possible dysmorphology includes microcephaly (head circumference less than the third percentile), thin upper lip vermilion, short upturned nose, flattened nasal bridge, and general underdevelopment of the midfacial area.

Alcohol-related birth defects are congenital anomalies attributable to alcohol but not meeting the criteria for fetal alcohol syndrome. Possible congenital anomalies include congenital heart defects and brain abnormalities. Other major congenital anomalies such as spina bifida, limb defects, and genitourinary defects are seen much less frequently.

Marijuana

Among women of reproductive age, marijuana is the most commonly used illicit substance and, after alcohol and tobacco, the most commonly used recreational drug in pregnancy. Epidemiologic studies show that women who use marijuana outside of and during early pregnancy are often young and tend to use other substances. The minority of women who continue to use marijuana throughout pregnancy tend to be less well educated, of lower social class, and much more likely to use other substances.

Studies on the use of marijuana in pregnancy have generated inconclusive data. None of the studies distinguishes between exposure in early versus late pregnancy, dosage is vaguely defined, and the potency of tetrahydrocannabinol (THC), the active ingredient in marijuana, varies greatly, if reported at all. Because women who use marijuana during pregnancy are more likely to use other substances as well, the effect of polydrug use and other factors that correlate with marijuana use during pregnancy needs to be addressed when analyzing data on the impact of THC on the fetus and infant. This has not been done consistently.

Some studies of marijuana use in pregnancy have reported intrauterine growth retardation, neurobehavioral effects, and increased prematurity. The results have not, however, been replicated consistently across studies. Most available data do not show an increased risk of major congenital anomalies among infants prenatally exposed to marijuana. The long-term effects of marijuana use in pregnancy have not been identified, but few studies have been reported.[19]

Cocaine

Cocaine is derived from the leaves of the *Erythroxylon coca* plant, which is native to South America. In addition to its local anesthetic properties, cocaine is a potential central nervous system stimulant through its sympathomimetic action. It blocks dopamine and norepinephrine uptake at nerve terminals. These actions are manifested physiologically as tachycardia, hypertension, and muscle twitching immediately after intake. The intense sense of euphoria experienced with intake and the decreasing cost of this drug over the past decade have contributed to its becoming one of the most widely abused recreational drugs. Cocaine use crosses all ethnic, geographic, and socioeconomic lines.[20] The prevalence in obstetric populations varies. Approximately 10% of an average obstetric population may be using the drug.

Cocaine may result in numerous maternal medical complications, including but not limited to acute myocardial infarction, arrhythmia, hyperthermia, hypertensive crisis, stroke, seizures, and sudden death. Cocaine use in pregnancy has been implicated in a wide spectrum of adverse pregnancy sequelae. Pregnancy complications include abruption, spontaneous abortion, intrauterine growth retardation, low birth weight, and prematurity.[21]

Embryo-fetal and neonatal adverse outcomes also have been found attributable to cocaine exposure prenatally. Many congenital anomalies such as segmental intestinal atresia, limb reduction defects, and disruptive brain anomalies have been thought to result from vascular disruption caused by cocaine exposure. Congenital heart defects, prune-belly syndrome, and urinary tract anomalies also have been reported in higher than expected numbers of cocaine-exposed neonates.[21]

Postnatal problems also have been associated with cocaine use in pregnancy. An increased risk of sudden infant death syndrome has been reported. Early neurobehavioral studies have suggested depression of interactive behavior and poor organizational responses to environmental stimuli. Studies are under way to evaluate this population for possible long-term sequelae.

Narcotics

Heroin and methadone are the two narcotics most frequently encountered in pregnancy.[22,23] Heroin is a widely abused illegal narcotic that is most often used intravenously but also may be smoked, sniffed, or injected subcutaneously. Methadone is taken orally, usually under medical supervision. The use of narcotics in pregnancy has not been associated with an increased incidence of congenital anomalies in prenatally exposed infants, but other morbidity is common. The ecology of the heroin addict includes dirty needles and other high-risk behaviors, including lack of prenatal care, that complicate pregnancy. These behaviors result in a high incidence of skin and subcutaneous tissue infections, phlebitis, endocarditis, urinary tract infections, and sexually transmitted diseases (including human immunodeficiency virus transmission) in heroin-addicted women. An increased incidence of inflammation or infection of the placenta, chorion, and amnion also has been reported. Adverse pregnancy effects include an increased incidence of premature labor and delivery, intrauterine growth retardation, low birth weight, fetal distress, and meconium passage, as well as neonatal infections.[24]

The pharmacologic effects of narcotic use in pregnancy are marked by the development of physical dependence in both mother and fetus when the drugs are used regularly. In these patients, failure to take the drug or use of a narcotic antagonist will precipitate the narcotic abstinence syndrome: agitation, lacrimation, rhinorrhea, yawning, mydriasis, and perspiration. Prolonged narcotic withdrawal may produce abdominal and uterine cramps, diarrhea, and myalgia. Although extremely uncomfortable, narcotic withdrawal is rarely injurious to the mother. Maternal withdrawal is, however, potentially fatal to the fetus. During the first trimester, abortion may occur during severe withdrawal. Later in pregnancy, maternal withdrawal is accompanied by fetal withdrawal, which results in hyperactivity, hypoxia, meconium passage, and possibly (rarely) intrauterine fetal death. Because of the risks to the fetus, narcotic withdrawal is not encouraged during pregnancy, and narcotic antagonists are used with caution.[24]

Some patients use heroin irregularly, and because the content of heroin available in the community is highly variable, physical dependence may not develop. Serious narcotic overdose is most likely to occur among these less tolerant users. The overdosed patient presents with respiratory depression or arrest with pinpoint pupils and may be comatose. Naloxone, a narcotic antagonist without respiratory depressive activity, should be given intravenously in a dose of 2 mg/kg. The same dose may be given intramuscularly, subcutaneously, or via an endotracheal tube.

Pregnant heroin addicts are most commonly managed in methadone maintenance programs. Methadone is a long-acting synthetic opiate that blocks heroin-induced euphoria and blunts heroin craving. Detection and treatment of infections, improved nutrition, provision of prenatal care, and psychosocial support all contribute to an improved outcome for the pregnancy.[25] Medication without prenatal care and psychosocial support is less effective.

Neonatal withdrawal syndrome in the children of heroin-addicted mothers tends to occur within the first 12 to 24 hours after birth. It is characterized by high-pitched crying, frantic fist sucking or searching for food, and tremulousness, and can be associated with seizures, disrupted sleep-wake cycles, and muscle hypertonia. Withdrawal in children of methadone-maintained mothers tends to be less severe (although this depends in part on the mother's dosage and use of other drugs) and occurs 2 to 4 weeks after birth. Subacute withdrawal of methadone-exposed infants may last for months.[26]

Postnatally, growth patterns in small-for-gestational-age children of narcotic addicts (heroin or methadone) tend to normalize. The long-term effects of narcotics have been difficult to identify because of numerous environmental confounders. Pregnant women who are found to have a narcotic use habit should be cared for and delivered in a high-risk obstetric and neonatal center with a methadone maintenance program. In this way, the special needs of both the mother and the neonate can be identified and optimally managed.

Amphetamines

Amphetamines are central nervous system stimulants that can be obtained by prescription or illegally acquired as street drugs. Amphetamines are traditionally ingested orally or administered intravenously. A form of methamphetamine known as "crystal," which is inhaled, is becoming increasingly popular as a recreational drug. Amphetamines may be used in cycles following binges of sedative and alcohol abuse. They also have been used to "cut" or mix with other street drugs. Therefore, amphetamine abusers should be screened for use of other substances.

Tolerance develops with regular use of amphetamines. Patients actively abusing amphetamines are hyperactive and paranoid, have insomnia and hallucinations, and, because of a lack of appetite, are usually badly malnourished. Patients who use amphetamines intravenously are subject to all of the complications of intravenous drug use. Amphetamine use may increase the risk of a serious arrhythmia during obstetric anesthesia. The abstinence syndrome of lethargy and profound depression, which should be closely monitored, characterizes withdrawal.[27]

Hallucinogens

Lysergic acid diethylamide (LSD; "acid") and phencyclidine hydrochloride (PCP; "angel dust") are the most commonly used agents in this class of drugs. The major maternal risks associated with their use are psychiatric and environmental: patients high on these drugs often place themselves in physically dangerous situations. Reports describing infants with congenital anomalies born to mothers who used LSD or PCP during pregnancy have shown no consistent pattern of anomalies. There is little evidence, based on available data, that these drugs are human teratogens. Studies of exposed neonates have suggested an association with decreased birth weight and head circumference, but well-controlled studies of use of other drugs and other environmental risk factors for these findings have not been done. Neonatal withdrawal characterized by tremors, jitteriness, and irritability has been described in some prenatally exposed children. Developmental delays are suggested by ongoing studies that seek to determine long-term effects.[28]

SUMMARY

The use of substances that are potentially harmful to both mother and fetus is widespread in pregnancy and involves both legal and illegal drugs. Efforts should be made to educate all pregnant and potentially pregnant women about the risks of substance use and to identify all patients who have a substance abuse problem. Women who are identified as users of potentially harmful drugs require intensified maternal and fetal surveillance as well as psychosocial support. Referral to a high-risk obstetric center is sometimes necessary and usually advisable.

RESOURCES

The National Clearinghouse for Alcohol and Drug Information
Web site: www.health.org/index.htm

The Substance Abuse and Mental Health Services Administration (SAMHSA) maintains a searchable Web site that provides information related to substance abuse. These include patient education materials and information for professionals on the screening, diagnosis, and treatment of the various aspects of substance abuse. Specific information relating to women is available at this site.

RESOURCES (continued)

The National Institute on Drug Abuse
6001 Executive Boulevard
Bethesda, Maryland 20892-9561
Telephone: (301) 443-0107
Web site: www.nida.nih.gov

The NIDA provides guidelines on the treatment of drug addiction and information on various drugs of abuse.

The National Council on Alcoholism and Drug Dependence, Inc.
12 West 21st Street
New York, New York 10010
Telephone: 1-800-NCA-CALL (1-800-622-2255) (24-hour referral line)
Web site: www.ncadd.org

NCADD provides education and information on addiction. Affiliates throughout the United States provide a program to help family members and others encourage women to seek treatment for addiction. NCADD also offers a video about educating children about drinking. Guidelines on drinking from a variety of organizations are also posted on the NCADD Web site.

The American Society of Addiction Medicine
4601 North Park Avenue, Arcade Suite 101
Chevy Chase, Maryland 20815
Telephone: (301) 656-3920
Web site: www.asam.org

ASAM is a professional organization dedicated to improving the treatment of individuals suffering from addiction. The ASAM Web site links to various Web sites of interest to those treating addiction patients.

REFERENCES

1. National Institute on Drug Abuse (US). National pregnancy and health survey. Rockville (MD): NIDA; 1994.

2. National Institute on Drug Abuse (US). Substance abuse among women and parents. Rockville (MD): NIDA; 1994.

3. Substance Abuse and Mental Health Services Administration, Office of Applied Studies. National Household Survey of Drug Abuse, preliminary estimates. Washington (DC): The Administration; 1993.

4. Vega WA, Kolody B, Hwang J, Noble A. Prevalence and magnitude of perinatal substance exposures in California. N Engl J Med 1993;329:850–4.

5. Chasnoff IJ, Landress HJ, Barrett ME. The prevalence of illicit drug or alcohol use during pregnancy and discrepancies in mandatory reporting in Pinellas County, Fla. N Engl J Med 1990;322:1202–6.

6. Dube CE, Lewis DC, editors. The Project ADEPT curriculum for primary care physician training. Vol. IV: special populations. Providence (RI): Brown University Center for Alcohol and Addiction Studies; 1994.

7. Halliday A, Bush B, Cleary P, et al. Alcohol abuse in women seeking gynecological care. Obstet Gynecol 1986;69:322–6.

8. Grodstein F, Goldman MB, Cramer DW. Infertility in women and moderate alcohol use. Am J Public Health 1994;84:1429–32.

9. Rasheed A, Tareen IA. Effects of heroin on thyroid function, cortisol and testosterone level in addicts. Pol J Pharmacol 1995;47:441–4.

10. Chasnoff IJ, Neuman K, Thornton C, Callaghan MA. Screening for substance use in pregnancy: a practical approach for the primary care physician. Am J Obstet Gynecol 2001;184:752–81.

11. Dube DE, Goldstein MG, Lewis DC, et al, editors. The Project ADEPT curriculum for primary care physician training. Vol I: core modules. Providence (RI): Brown University Center for Alcohol and Addiction Studies; 1989.

12. Alario AJ, Carr SR, Ogburn PL, Leipman MR. Substance use during pregnancy and lactation: the ob/gyn patient, instructor's guide. In: Dube CE, Goldstein MG, Lewis DC, et al, editors. The Project ADEPT curriculum for primary care physician training. Vol. II: special topics. Providence (RI): Brown University Center for Alcohol and Addiction Studies; 1989.

13. Hays JT, Spickard WA. Alcoholism: early diagnosis and intervention. J Gen Intern Med 1987;2:420–9.

14. Kandall SR, Chavkin W. Illicit drugs in America: history, impact on women and infants, and treatment strategies for women. Hastings Law J 1992;34:615–43.

15. Morrison CL. The development of health care services for drug misusers and prostitutes. Postgrad Med J 1995;71:593–7.

16. Schuckit MA. Biological vulnerability to alcoholism. J Consult Clin Psychol 1987;55:301–9.

17. Abel EL, Sokol RJ. A revised conservative estimate of the incidence of fetal alcohol syndrome and its economic impact. Alcohol Clin Exp Res 1991;15:514–24.

18. Hannigan JH, Armart DR. Alcohol in pregnancy and neonatal outcome. Semin Neonatal 2000;5:243–54.

19. Little RE, Wendt JK. The effects of maternal drinking in the reproductive period: an epidemiological review. J Subst Abuse 1991;3:187–204.

20. Hollister LE. Health aspects of cannabis. Pharmacol Rev 1986;38:1–20.

21. Gawin FH, Ellinwood EH. Cocaine and other stimulants: actions, abuse, and treatment. N Engl J Med 1988;318:1173–83.

22. Dube DE, Goldstein MG, Lewis DC, Cates-Wessel KL, editors. The Project ADEPT curriculum for primary care physician training. Vol III: AIDS and substance abuse. Providence (RI): Brown University Center for Alcohol and Addiction Studies; 1992.

23. Kamerow DB, Pincus HA, Macdonald DI. Alcohol abuse, other drug abuse, and mental disorders in medical practice: prevalence, costs, recognition, and treatment. JAMA 1986;255:2054–7.

24. Kandall SR, Doloerczak TM, Jantunen M, Stein J. The methadone-maintained pregnancy. Clin Perinatal 1999;26(1):173–83.

25. Joseph H, Stancliff S, Langrod J. Methadone maintenance treatment (MMT); a review of historical and clinical issues. Mt Sinai J Med 2000;67:347–64.

26. Wagner CL, Katikanon LD, Cox TH, Ryan RM. The impact of perinatal drug exposure on the neonate. Obstet Gynecol Clin North Am 1998;25(1):169–99.

27. Prenatal exposure to amphetamines. Risks and adverse outcomes in pregnancy. Obstet Gynecol Clin North Am 1998; 25(1):119–38.

28. Neurobehavioral consequences of early exposure to phencyclidine and related drugs. Clin Neuropharmacol 1998;21:320–32.

19

INFERTILITY

Vidya Nagaraj-Palta, MD

Infertility is defined as the inability to conceive after 1 year of unprotected intercourse, and it affects 10 to 15% of couples in the United States. Both partners must undergo assessment in an effort to identify whether treatment is needed for female infertility, male infertility, or unexplained infertility.[1]

In counseling patients about possible infertility, it is important to provide information about what is normal in terms of pregnancy rates, since even highly educated patients often have significant misconceptions. During the first month of trying to conceive, about 20% of normal couples are successful. After 3 months, 50% will have conceived, and, by 1 year, 90% will have conceived. Some subfertile couples, including those with oligospermia, infrequent ovulation, or mild endometriosis, conceive without treatment over a longer period of time. Others, including couples with azoospermia or tubal occlusion, are unlikely ever to conceive without intervention.[2]

Successful evaluation, treatment, and referral by the primary care clinician requires an understanding of the known causes of infertility, the basic precepts of infertility treatment, and the range of treatments available to infertile couples. Causes of infertility and an appropriate initial evaluation are outlined in this chapter.

MALE FACTOR INFERTILITY

Male infertility spans a spectrum of disorders from congenital to acquired, and from direct testicular damage to dysfunction at the hypothalamic/pituitary level. As male factor has been approximated to be the cause of 25 to 33% of infertility cases, a screening evaluation of male infertility is considered a basic and early part of the infertility evaluation.[3–5]

A complete history and physical examination must be performed on all infertile men. Information regarding in utero diethylstilbestrol (DES) exposure, the presence of ambiguous genitalia or inguinal hernias at birth, and chronic illnesses or testicular trauma in childhood should be elicited specifically. In addition to the medical history, other pertinent information includes duration of infertility, pregnancies with previous partners, occupational history (eg, exposure to hydrocarbons), social history (eg, smoking, alcohol, drugs, and recreational activity) and coital history. The physical examination should include evaluation for gynecomastia, varicocele, and testicular size. A varicocele often can be visualized or palpated when the patient is upright; one can increase palpability by having the patient perform Valsalva's maneuver. The testes should measure approximately 5 cm in diameter. They also may be compared in volume with precalibrated ovoids.[6]

Whether history and physical are normal or abnormal, a semen analysis is almost always indicated. A normal semen analysis, according to the World Health Organization guidelines, is as follows: volume greater than 2 mL; sperm concentration greater than 20 million/mL; motility greater than 50% with forward progression or greater than 25% with rapid progression less than 60 minutes after ejaculation; morphology greater than 30% with normal forms; and leukocytes less than 1 million/mL. However, men with much lower sperm counts have achieved pregnancy. In an effort to identify characteristics with better predictive value, investigators have looked into quantitative motility measurements, sperm function tests, and strict morphologic parameters. Authors have concluded that defective semen is likely to be the sole cause of a couple's failure to conceive if the conventional semen analysis is "severely abnormal" or if sperm have failed a functional test (such as a hamster oocyte penetration assay).[7]

When a semen sample is deemed inadequate in volume, motility, concentration, or morphology, intrauterine insemination may achieve pregnancy. Prior to insemination, the semen should be processed to remove seminal plasma from spermatozoa. For those patients who do not achieve pregnancy with intrauterine insemination, referral to a specialist in infertility for consideration of in vitro fertilization (IVF) may be warranted. Couples with male factor infertility with a >14% normal sperm morphology have a high rate of fertilization (85 to 88%) with IVF.[8] Those with lower sperm counts can undergo IVF along with intracytoplasmic sperm injection (ICSI), a method of injecting the sperm into the oocyte. An alternative to IVF is the use of cryopreserved donor sperm for insemination.

TUBAL DISEASE

Tubal diseases cause 25 to 35% of infertility in women. The fallopian tubes may either be obstructed (by inspissated material or spasm) or occluded by permanent organic pathology.[9] The prognosis for fertility depends both on the nature of the insult and the severity of tissue damage. Thus, the chance of achieving pregnancy following tuboplasty can range from 3 to 77%, depending on the degree of tubal damage. Damage can occur from infection (eg, venereal disease, tuberculosis, or ruptured appendix), surgical trauma leading to ischemia, inflammatory diseases such as endometriosis, foreign body reactions, salpingitis isthmica nodosa (SIN),(diverticia of tubal epithelium into the tubal musculature in the isthmus)[10] and polypoid lesions.

Hysterosalpingography (HSG) can detect non-patency of the fallopian tubes, as well as intraluminal defects characteristic of SIN or polyps. Intermittent obstruction detected by HSG may be genuine tubal disease or spasm of the tubes, depending on the presence or absence of elevated injection pressures. If spasm is suspected, a repeat examination with the use of spasmolytic agents is suggested.[11] If the results of the HSG are abnormal, the patient should be referred to an infertility specialist who can decide whether tubal surgery or IVF is warranted.

OVULATORY DYSFUNCTION

There have been tremendous advances in the treatment of anovulatory infertility. From hyperpro-lactinemia to hypogonadotropic hypogonadism, correct treatment of many causes of anovulation can lead to pregnancy rates close to those of normal couples. Successful treatment is predicated upon proper identification of the underlying abnormality. Common treatable and untreatable causes of ovulatory dysfunction are discussed in this section.

Polycystic Ovary Syndrome

Polycystic ovary syndrome (PCOS) is the most common cause of anovulation.[12] Polycystic ovary syndrome is diagnosed clinically, since no single group of laboratory tests has a high enough sensitivity and specificity to identify all women with PCOS. Criteria for the diagnosis include (1) menstrual irregularity, (2) clinical or biochemical evidence of hyperandrogenism, and (3) the exclusion of other diseases such as thyroid dysfunction, hyperprolactinemia, congenital adrenal hyperplasia, and androgen-secreting tumors. Although laboratory tests cannot definitively diagnose or exclude PCOS, women with PCOS tend to have increases in serum testosterone, androstenedione, dihydroepiandrosterone, mean luteinizing hormone (LH) levels, LH-to-FSH (follicle-stimulating hormone) ratio, and insulin. Mild elevations of serum prolactin also can be seen in women manifesting hyperandrogenism. This is of uncertain significance. A characteristic appearance (peripheral array of many small follicles) of ovaries on ultrasound examination is seen in almost 80% of women with PCOS.[13]

The most commonly used agent to induce ovulation in women with PCOS is clomiphene citrate. Clomiphene citrate, which is similar in structure to the synthetic estrogen DES, has effects at the hypothalamic, pituitary, and ovarian levels. At higher doses, it may confer antiestrogenic properties on the endometrium and cervical mucus. Clomiphene citrate acts on the hypothalamus to induce ovulation by increasing gonadotropin-releasing hormone (Gn-RH) pulse frequency. It acts on the pituitary to enhance the sensitivity of the gonadotrophs to Gn-RH. There is further evidence that it may enhance FSH-stimulated aromatase activity in the ovary.

Because of its mechanisms of action, clomiphene citrate can only be effective in the presence of an intact hypothalamic-pituitary-ovarian axis. Therefore, it is indicated in anovulatory women who either bleed spontaneously or in response to a progestin challenge. Its use extends beyond women with PCOS. It also has been used to treat women with luteal phase defects in the hope that progesterone concentrations will increase in the luteal phase; results have been variable, since luteal phase deficiencies are multifactorial in origin. Clomiphene citrate has also been used in unexplained infertility and to induce superovulation for a variety of assisted reproductive technologies (ART).[14]

Patients should attempt weight reduction prior to ovulation induction treatments, because they appear to be less effective when the body mass index is greater than 28 to 30 kg/m^2. The usual starting dose of clomiphene citrate is 50 mg daily for 5 days beginning on day 3 of the menstrual cycle. If there is no response (as monitored by basal body temperature, luteal phase progesterone levels, or urinary pregnanediol estimations), the dose is increased to 100 mg daily for 5 days during the next cycle, and then to 150 mg daily for 5 days in the subsequent cycle, if no result is seen from lower doses. Most experts do not increase the dose further, as doses higher than 150 mg may impose undesired antiestrogenic properties on the endometrial lining and cervical mucus. However, doses of up to 250 mg daily have been used, with the belief that heavier women need more medication to promote ovulation. When clomiphene is given without ultrasonographic monitoring, women should be advised to have intercourse from cycle days 9 or 10 for at least 1 week or until a rise in basal body temperature is observed.[14] It is advisable not to exceed six cycles in an attempt to conceive.

If treatment with clomiphene is ineffective, the patient should be referred to an infertility specialist for further evaluation and possible treatment with injectable gonadotropin preparations. As an example, clomiphene has been used in combination with human menopausal gonadotropins, but this requires monitoring with frequent ultrasonographic examination by experienced operators. For clomiphene-resistant patients, laparoscopic ovarian drilling is an alternative to gonadotropins. This can be done by creating multiple holes on the surface of the ovary with a laser or electrocautery. After surgery, there is a decrease in LH pulse amplitude and in serum gonadotropin levels. Although these changes appear to be temporary (lasting 2 to 6 years), they can allow ovulation and pregnancy to occur.[15]

Recently, metformin has been shown to ameliorate hyperandrogenic abnormalities, restore ovulation and regularity of menstrual cycles, and improve fertility in women with PCOS.[16] Randomized controlled trials comparing metformin to other agents are yet to be published.

Hyperprolactinemia

Hyperprolactinemia is associated with infertility in both men and women. Anovulation and luteal phase defects in hyperprolactinemic women are likely due to reduced Gn-RH pulse frequency. Treatment strategies vary depending on the underlying cause.

Assigning a diagnosis of hyperprolactinemia requires some caution as confounding factors induce a great deal of variability in prolactin levels. The serum level can be quite erratic and is influenced by stress, exercise, food and sleep, as well as some prescription drugs. It is best obtained in the morning after an overnight fast. Thyroid function tests should always be measured, since hypothyroidism causing an elevated thyrotropin-releasing hormone can lead to increased prolactin secretion.[17] Evaluation of elevated serum prolactin is discussed in detail in Chapter 59, "Hyperprolactinemia."

Once a thorough evaluation to rule out hypothalamic/pituitary tumors and systemic disorders is completed, it is important to determine whether treatment of the hyperprolactinemia is likely to improve fertility. Infertile women with idiopathic hyperprolactinemia are more likely to conceive with treatment only if they are anovulatory.

Bromocriptine has been the most widely used dopaminergic agent to re-establish ovulation. Cabergoline has received much attention recently, as it has a long duration of action, excellent efficacy, and tolerability. Pregnancies resulting from dopaminergic treatment to induce ovulatory cycles have not had an increased rate of spontaneous abortion, multiple pregnancies, or congenital anomalies.[18]

ENDOMETRIOSIS

Endometriosis can cause impaired steroidogenic capacity of the granulosa cells,[19] immune reactions possibly affecting oocyte passage and sperm function, and intense local fibrosis leading to adhesion and cyst formation.[20]

Whatever the mechanism, most couples with endometriosis have a relative reduction in the monthly probability of conception (1 to 3%). Since treatment-independent conceptions do occur, the proportion of couples who conceive because of treatment can only be identified if untreated control groups are included in the clinical trials. This has not been the case with the majority of trials, making it difficult to compare different treatments.[21]

Treatment may be medical or surgical. At the time of laparoscopy, if structural damage such as adhesions or cysts are noted, surgical correction should be undertaken; the pregnancy rates can increase to 50 to 60% in 2 years. If conception is not achieved by 1 to 2 years after surgery, it is appropriate to use assisted reproductive techniques managed by an infertility specialist (eg, controlled ovarian stimulation with intrauterine insemination, IVF and embryo transfer, or gamete intrafallopian transfer [GIFT]).[20]

When there is no distortion of the pelvic viscera noted on laparoscopy, treatment remains controversial. In such mild to moderate cases of endometriosis, neither surgical ablation nor medical suppression of endometriosis have demonstrated any improvement in fertility. If expectant management fails, assisted reproductive technology offers a substantial enhancement of monthly fecundity.[21]

CERVICAL FACTOR

Cervical factor infertility can result from anatomic defects, abnormal cervical mucus, or poor sperm-mucus interaction. Anatomic defects include cervical stenosis (most commonly due to conization for cervical dysplasia), obstructive lesions such as polyps and leiomyomas, and varicosities in the presence of a hypoplastic endocervical canal. The probability of conception may be improved by the removal of polyps and fibroids. Cryosurgery and lasers have been used for the treatment of varicosities. Patients with cervical anatomic defects also may improve their chance of pregnancy by undergoing intrauterine insemination using washed sperm.[22]

To evaluate cervical mucus and sperm-mucus interaction, the postcoital test (PCT) is used. Classically, it is scheduled slightly before or on the day of the expected rise in basal body temperature as determined by reviewing a temperature graph from the previous month. More reliable ways to time the postcoital test, which should be done just prior to ovulation, include urinary LH immunoassays, serum estradiol measurements, and ultrasound measurements of follicles.

Most physicians perform the PCT by evaluating cervical mucus 6 to 12 hours after coitus. Some clinicians advocate timing the test up to 24 hours after coitus. One study indicates that the functional integrity of spermatozoa can be better tested at 9 to 12 hours after intercourse. Microscopic evaluation should be used to determine if sperm are immotile, locally motile, or progressive.[23] Cervical mucus also is evaluated for quantity, viscosity, ferning, spinnbarkeit, and cellularity. If the PCT shows repeated abnormal results despite normal mucus and semen analysis, in vitro tests assessing sperm penetration should be performed. The recommended treatment for persistently abnormal tests is intrauterine insemination.[24]

LUTEAL PHASE DEFECTS

Luteal phase deficiency occurs when insufficient progesterone production during the luteal phase of the menstrual cycle results in inadequate development of the endometrium, compromising embryo implantation and pregnancy maintenance. The defect may occur occasionally in otherwise-normal women, and its diagnosis is difficult due to inconsistencies in diagnostic criteria. Basal body temperature charts, endometrial biopsies evaluating glandular maturation and stromal development, and serum progesterone levels all have been used to detect the deficiency.[25] Once detected, treatment can be approached either by stimulating normal folliculogenesis with clomiphene citrate and/or gonadotropins or by supporting luteal function with progesterone supplementation. If one treatment does not correct the problem, an empiric switch to the alternate treatment has been suggested.[26]

ANTISPERM ANTIBODIES

In both men and women, antisperm antibodies (ASAs) may be found systemically and in local secretions, including seminal and cervicovaginal fluids.[27] Several mechanisms have been proposed to explain how these antibodies cause subfertility. Studies have shown that the migration of spermatozoa coated with immunoglobulin A (IgA) ASA through cervical mucus is impaired.[28] Other proposed mechanisms include (1) disruption of the sperm oocyte recognition and fusion process, (2) prevention of sperm capacitation by immobilizing antibodies, (3) inhibition of penetration of the zona pellucida by blocking antibodies, and (4) deleterious affect on postfertilization early embryo development and implantation.[11]

Routine screening for ASAs in couples with unexplained infertility has not become standardized because there is no universally accepted assay. The immunobead and direct mixed agglutination reaction tests are two excellent screening methods for determining the presence of IgG and IgA on the surface of spermatozoa. These tests require motile sperm. If the reaction is negative or weakly positive, it is unlikely that the infertility is caused by ASA. If the tests are strongly positive, there is wisdom in determining levels in serum and seminal plasma, as high titers imply high levels on spermatozoa.

Intrauterine insemination to bypass the cervical mucus, IVF, and IVF with ICSI are the major acceptable treatments available to infertile couples with ASAs. One IVF center screens all male partners for direct ASA using immunobead tests prior to IVF. If there are more than 50% IgG or IgA antibodies, couples are counseled to undergo ICSI for half of the oocytes retrieved.[27]

AUTOANTIBODIES

Autoantibodies and their relation to infertility have been a source of controversy for several years. Published reports have noted a higher prevalence of antibodies to smooth muscle nuclear antigens, phospholipids, histones, and nucleotides in women with infertility. The populations of women studied in various reports have differed as to the cause of infertility and the types of antibodies tested. This may explain why there have been conflicting results from study to study regarding the link between certain types of antibodies and infertility.

One fairly consistent finding has been the identification of a high prevalence of antiphospholipid antibodies in infertile women when compared with controls. Although the mechanism of antiphospholipid antibody–associated infertility is not clear, impressive pregnancy rates have been reported in series describing the treatment of infertile antiphospholipid antibody–positive patients

with heparin and aspirin. There has not, however, been a randomized controlled trial with sufficient power to evaluate definitively the efficacy of such treatments. At present, it is not routine to screen infertility patients for antiphospholipid antibodies or other autoantibodies.[29]

EVALUATION

In this era of managed care, primary care clinicians can and should initiate a systematic work-up of infertility for patients who seek help. Women generally are assessed after 1 year of infertility if they are younger than age 35 years, and after 6 months if 35 years or older. A thorough history includes menstrual cycle lengths, symptoms of mittelschmerz, noted changes in cervical mucus, and questions regarding factors that might have led to anatomic distortion of the pelvis (eg, treatment for cervical dysplasia or other surgical procedures, pelvic inflammatory disease, prior use of intrauterine devices, maternal DES exposure). The physical examination should include evaluation for hirsutism or acne (which are suggestive of a hyperandrogenic state), obesity or abdominal striae (as are seen in Cushing's disease or PCOS), and a careful pelvic examination including palpation for pelvic masses or nodularity in the cul-de-sac (suggesting endometriosis).[1]

Useful blood tests include a serum progesterone to evaluate ovulation (performed 7 days after expected ovulation), FSH and estradiol levels (performed on day 3 of the menstrual cycle) to evaluate ovarian reserve in women suspected of diminished ovarian function, and thyroid-stimulating hormone and prolactin levels if menstrual cycles are irregular. Additional tests are warranted only if history and physical examination findings lead to a suspicion of other disorders.[1]

The male partner should be asked if he has ever fathered a child and about his general health. More specific questions to evaluate androgenic and sexual function include inquiring about shaving habits, morning erections, and any history of testicular damage, trauma, or surgery are appropriate. The semen analysis is essential to the evaluation for male infertility; semen should be collected after 2 to 3 days of sexual abstinence, with a prompt analysis to follow.[1]

In addition to blood tests for women and a semen analysis for men, an HSG may be warranted if tubal disease or uterine abnormalities are suspected. The HSG is performed 7 to 11 days after the onset of menses and may have a therapeutic effect by clearing the fallopian tubes of barriers such as mucous plugs. As with any invasive procedure, the patient should be made aware of risks (eg, infection or bleeding) and provided with prophylactic antibiotics if there is an increased risk of infection.[1]

Based on the results of the initial evaluation, the primary care clinician may elect to provide initial treatment for male infertility and/or anovulatory states, or to refer to an infertility specialist for further evaluation and treatment.

CONCLUSION

In addition to initiating the basic infertility workup in both partners, the primary care clinician is in the unique position of assisting couples through the emotionally straining process of infertility treatment. Clinicians with an understanding of the physiology and anatomy involved can suggest the most cost-effective strategies to maximize the possibility of pregnancy. Primary care clinicians may then decide which patients require more advanced investigation and treatment. Helping couples through this process can be a professionally rewarding experience.

RESOURCE

The American Society for Reproductive Medicine
1209 Montgomery Highway
Birmingham, Alabama 35216-2809
Telephone: (205) 978-5000
Web site: www.asrm.org
Fax: (205) 978-5005

The American Society for Reproductive Medicine provides information for patients and health professionals on issues relating to infertility diagnosis and treatment, including information about ongoing clinical trials.

REFERENCES

1. Hanson MA, Dumesic DA. Initial evaluation and treatment of infertility in a primary care setting. Mayo Clin Proc 1998;73:681–5.
2. Mishell DR. Infertility. In: Mishell DR, Brenner PF, editors. Management of common problems in obstetrics and gynecology. 3rd ed. Boston: Blackwell Scientific Publications; 1994. p. 387–93.
3. Sokol RZ. Male factor in infertility. In: Lobo R, Mishell DR Jr, Paulson R, Shoupe D, editors. Mishell's textbook of infertility, contraception and reproductive endocrinology. Malden (MA): Blackwell Science Inc.; 1997. p. 546–63.
4. Hull MGR, Glazener CMA, Kelly NJ, et al. Population study of causes, treatment and outcome of infertility. Br Med J 1985;291:1693–5.
5. Okabe M, Ikawa M, Ashkenas J. Male infertility and the genetics of spermatogenesis. Am J Hum Genet 1998;62:1274–81.
6. Winters SJ. Pathogenesis and medical management of male infertility. In: Seibel MM, editor. Infertility: a comprehensive text. Stamford (CT): Appleton & Lange; 1997. p. 261–9.
7. Ford WCL, Mathur RS, Hull MGR. Intrauterine insemination; is it an effective treatment for male factor infertility? Baillieres Clin Obstet Gynaecol 1997;11;691–710.
8. Kruger TF, Menkveld R, Stander FS, et al. Sperm morphologic features as a prognostic factor in in vitro fertilization. Fertil Steril 1986;46:1118–23.
9. Honore GM, Holden AEC, Schenken RS. Pathophysiology and management of proximal tubal blockage. Fertil Steril 1999;71:785–94.
10. Sauer MV. Tubal infertility: the role of reconstructive surgery. In: Lobo R, Mishell DR Jr, Paulson R, Shoupe D, editors. Mishell's textbook of infertility, contraception and reproductive endocrinology.

Malden (MA): Blackwell Science Inc.; 1997. p. 604–5

11. Mazumthar S, Levine AS. Antisperm antibodies: etiology, pathogenesis, diagnosis and treatment. Fertil Steril 1998;70:799–809.

12. Hamilton FD, Franks S. Common problems in induction of ovulation. Baillieres Clin Obstet Gynaecol 1990;4:609–25.

13. Taylor AE. Polycystic ovary syndrome. Endocrinol Metab Clin North Am 1998;27:877–95.

14. Glasier AF. Clomiphene citrate. Ballieres Clin Obstet Gynaecol 1990;4:491–501.

15. Tulandi T, al-Took S. Surgical management of polycystic ovarian syndrome. Ballieres Clin Obstet Gynaecol 1998;12:541–53.

16. Balen A. Endocrine methods of ovulation induction. Baillieres Clin Obstet Gynaecol 1998;12:521–33.

17. Vale W, Blackwell RE, Grant G, Guillemin R. TRF and thyroid hormones on prolactin secretion by rat anterior pituitary cells in vitro. Endocrinology 1973; 93:26–33.

18. Crosignani PG, Ferrari C. Dopaminergic treatments for hyperprolactinemia. Ballieres Clin Obstet Gynaecol 1990;4:446–9.

19. Cahill DJ, Wardle PG, Maile LA, et al. Ovarian dysfunction in endometriosis-associated and unexplained infertility. J Assist Reprod Genet 1997; 14:554–7.

20. Hull MGR, Cahill DJ. Female infertility. Endocrinol Metab Clin North Am 1998;27:851–79.

21. Haney AF. Endometriosis-associated infertility. Ballieres Clin Obstet Gynecol 1993;7:791–812.

22. Zegers F, Lenton E, Sulaiman R. The cervical factor in patients with ovulatory infertility. Br J Obstet Gynecol 1981;88:537–42.

23. Eimers JM, te Velde ER, Gerritse R, et al. The validity of the postcoital test for estimating the probability of conceiving. Am J Obstet Gynecol 1994;171:65–70.

24. Mezrow G. The cervical factor as a cause of infertility. In: Lobo R, Mishell DR Jr, Paulson R, Shoupe D, editors. Mishell's textbook of infertility, contraception and reproductive endocrinology. Malden (MA): Blackwell Science Inc.; 1997. p. 536–41.

25. McNeely MJ, Soules MR. The diagnosis of luteal phase deficiency; a critical review. Fertil Steril 1988; 50:1–13.

26. Daya S. Ovulation induction for corpus luteum deficiency. Semin Reprod Endocrinol 1990;8:156–64.

27. Kutteh WH. Do antisperm antibodies bound to spermatozoa alter normal reproductive function? Hum Reprod 1999;14:2426–8.

28. Hjort T. Antisperm antibodies and infertility; an unsolvable question? Hum Reprod 1999;14:2423–6.

29. Van Voorhis BJ, Stovall DW. Autoantibodies and infertility: a review of the literature. J Reprod Endocrinol 1997;33:239–56.

20

SPONTANEOUS ABORTION

Michael C. Lu, MD, MPH

"Spontaneous abortion" refers to the spontaneous loss of pregnancy before the 20th week of gestation. A spontaneous abortion can be missed, inevitable, incomplete, or complete. "Missed abortion" refers to the death of a fetus in utero without expulsion of any fetal or maternal tissue for at least 8 weeks. "Inevitable abortion" refers to uterine bleeding accompanied by cervical dilation but without expulsion of fetal or placental tissue. "Incomplete abortion" refers to the passage of some, but not all, fetal or placental tissue through the cervix. "Complete abortion" refers to the spontaneous expulsion of all fetal and placental tissues from the uterine cavity. When uterine bleeding occurs without any cervical dilation or effacement, it is called a "threatened abortion." At or beyond the 20th week, intrauterine fetal death is commonly referred to as a "stillbirth."[1]

About 1 in 6 (~ 15%) clinically recognized pregnancies are lost spontaneously before 20 weeks of gestation. The true pregnancy loss rate is probably higher, closer to 60 to 70%.[2-4] Most of these losses occur before the pregnancy is detected clinically.[5] Two-thirds of clinically recognized spontaneous abortions occur before 12 weeks of gestation, with the mean being 9 weeks. After 16 weeks (from LMP), fetal loss rate is less than 1%.[6]

The risk of spontaneous abortion increases with advancing maternal age, paternal age, parity, and prior history of spontaneous abortion.[7] One in 4 clinically recognized pregnancies in women over the age of 40 years is lost; the incidence is probably 75% if the loss of unrecognized pregnancies is included.[8] The risk of recurrence in the next pregnancy after a single early spontaneous abortion is 10 to 20%. After two or more spontaneous abortions, the recurrence risk is about 25 to 30% if the woman has had a previous liveborn baby, and 40 to 45% if the woman has never had a liveborn baby.[9]

PATHOPHYSIOLOGY

Overall, 30 to 50% of sporadic spontaneous abortions are cytogenetically abnormal.[10] Half of preimplantation embryos and one-third of implanted embryos are morphologically, and probably cytogenetically, abnormal.[11] One-fifth of losses occurring in the first 20 weeks of pregnancy, and one-third of those occurring at or before 8 weeks of pregnancy, are anembryonic;[11] that is, the embryo never developed. Of those losses where the embryo is present, only half appear to be morphologically normal.

Half of abortuses at 8 to 11 weeks, and nearly one-third of those at 16 to 19 weeks, are karyotypically abnormal.[10] The most common abnormalities are, in order of decreasing frequency, autosomal trisomy, sex chromosome monosomy (45X), and triploidy. Autosomal trisomy is found in 53% of all cytogenetically abnormal abortuses. The most common trisomy found is trisomy 16. Nearly 1 in 5 are found to carry 45X, and 1 in 6 are found to carry triploidy (69 XXY, 69 XXX, 69 XYX, or others).[12]

Infection has been implicated in spontaneous abortions. Bacteria such as *Ureaplasma urealyticum, Mycoplasma hominis, Treponema pallidum, Borrelia burgdorferi, Chlamydia trachomatis, Neisseria gonorrhoeae, Streptococcus agalactiae,* and *Listeria monocytogenes,* as well as some viruses, all have been identified in abortuses.[13] Certain drugs and chemical agents also have been implicated, including anesthetic gases, chloroquine, oral hypoglycemic agents, arsenic, heavy metals, ethanol, caffeine, and cigarette smoking. A causal relationship between exposure and abortion, however, has not been established clearly. Recent studies found no increased risk of spontaneous abortion among women exposed to video display terminals for more than 20 hours per week.[14]

DIAGNOSIS

About 30 to 40% of all pregnant women have some bleeding during the first 20 weeks. Half of them abort their pregnancies spontaneously, and half of them go on to have liveborn babies. The latter have a slightly increased risk of preterm delivery and fetal anomalies than do women who have no bleeding during the first half of pregnancy. One in 4 women who bleed for 3 or more days aborts her pregnancy, whereas only 7% abort if their bleeding lasts only 1 or 2 days.[15]

Commonly women present with vaginal spotting or bleeding, with or without pain. Threatened abortion that does not abort eventually is often painless. Inevitable or incomplete abortion often presents with heavy bleeding and painful uterine cramping. A brief history is taken and physical examination is performed. The clinician should obtain a menstrual history and estimate gestational age. Because an important differential diagnosis is ectopic pregnancy, inquiry about risk factors, particularly previous history of ectopic pregnancy, pelvic inflammatory disease, abdominal surgery, or tubal sterilization, should be made. Risk factors for spontaneous abortion should be assessed.

Physical examination should focus on monitoring vital signs, palpating the abdomen for tenderness, and performing the pelvic examination. The cervix is inspected for dilation and passage of tissue. In threatened or missed abortion, the cervix is closed. If the cervix is dilated, spontaneous abortion is inevitable. When fetal or placental tissue starts to pass through the cervical os, it is called an incomplete abortion. After complete passage of the product of conception, it is called a complete abortion. Uterine size is assessed with a bimanual examination. The adnexa are palpated for the presence of a mass or tenderness that may signify an ectopic pregnancy.

An ultrasound examination, in conjunction with serum human chorionic gonadotropin (B-hCG), can be helpful in differentiating an early viable pregnancy, a spontaneous abortion, and an ectopic pregnancy. The use of transvaginal ultrasonography has improved the diagnostic accuracy of predicting viability in early pregnancies. Using transvaginal ultrasonography, the gestational sac should be seen at 5 weeks of gestation or a mean hCG level of 1,398 mIU/mL (First International Reference Preparation). The fetal pole should be seen at 6 weeks or a mean hCG level of 5,113 mIU/mL. Fetal cardiac motion should be seen at 7 weeks or a mean hCG level of 17,208 mIU/mL.[16] The absence of a gestational sac at an hCG level of greater than 2,500 mIU/mL confirms nonviability. The presence of a gestational sac of 8-mm mean sac diameter without demonstrable yolk sac, or of 16-mm diameter without a demonstrable embryo,[17] or the absence of fetal cardiac motion in an embryo with crown-rump length of greater than 5 mm[18] also indicates embryonic demise.

If the hCG is less than 2,500 mIU/mL, viability cannot be predicted reliably sonographically. Serial quantitative hCG levels may be helpful in ascertaining viability. The patient is instructed to return for a repeat hCG test in 48 hours. In the first 30 days of a normal gestation, the level of hCG doubles every 2.2 days.[19] In patients whose pregnancies are destined to abort, the level of hCG rises more slowly, plateaus, or declines. The predictive value of a normal rise in hCG level for a successful pregnancy is 88%, and that of an abnormal rise in hCG level for fetal demise is 76%.[19]

MANAGEMENT

If the pregnancy is viable, only expectant management is warranted. Some clinicians prescribe bedrest and proscribe coitus for the duration of the bleeding, although the efficacy of these recommendations in preventing subsequent spontaneous abortion is unproven. Similarly, the use of a progesterone suppository in threatened abortion is of unproven clinical benefit.

If the pregnancy is nonviable, watchful waiting for a spontaneous abortion to take place is acceptable. One randomized trial found that expectant management of spontaneous abortion was comparable to dilatation and curettage (D & C) in outcomes.[20] The risk of disseminated intravascular coagulopathy developing from necrotic fetal tissue retained in utero in the first trimester is minimal, even up to 5 weeks after fetal death. Women who do not want expectant management can be offered a D & C. For an uncomplicated spontaneous abortion, a D & C can be performed in the office, similar to an induced abortion. The tissue must be examined for evidence of an intrauterine pregnancy.

In the case of an incomplete abortion, the loss of blood can be brisk and profuse. Attention should immediately be directed to the patient's hemodynamic stability. Volume replacement with crystalloids should be given through two large bore (18 gauge or larger) intravenous lines, and the patient's blood should be typed and cross-matched for possible replacement. A decrease in fibrinogen or platelets may indicate early disseminated intravascular coagulopathy and the need for replacement with platelets, fresh frozen plasma, and possibly cryoprecipitate.

The patient should undergo a D & C immediately. The cervix typically is dilated sufficiently, and minimal mechanical dilatation is required. A ring forceps may provide adequate traction on the cervix. Suction curettage is preferred over sharp curettage. Deep curettage should be avoided, especially in the setting of infection, to prevent the formation of uterine synechiae. Oxytocin infusion is advocated by some, but its clinical benefit in incomplete abortion during early pregnancy is unproven. The procedure may be performed safely under local anesthesia with sedation in the office or the emergency department, as long as hemodynamic stability can be maintained. Following curettage, the patient should be observed for 4 to 8 hours. She then is discharged home on bedrest for 24 hours and pelvic rest for 2 weeks. Rh_o (D) immune globulin (RhoGAM), 50 µg before 12 weeks' gestation and 300 µg thereafter, should be given to a woman who is Rhesus (Rh) factor negative to prevent isoimmunization.

Sometimes it may be difficult to differentiate between an incomplete and a complete abortion; the amount of bleeding, the aperture of the cervix, or the size of the uterus is unreliable in determining the completeness of the abortion. Ultrasonography can be used to detect retained tissues in utero. A D & C should be performed when the completeness of the spontaneous abortion is uncertain.

In the diagnosis and management of women with early pregnancy bleeding, the possibility of an ectopic pregnancy must be kept in mind. If an ectopic pregnancy is strongly suspected clinically (eg, due to presence of adnexal mass or tenderness), a D & C should be performed if the pregnancy is undesired to determine the location of the pregnancy. Absence of chorionic villi in the curettage specimen points to an extrauterine gestation. If the pregnancy is desired and viability cannot be deter-mined sonographically, the patient should undergo laparoscopy. Selected patients may be followed as outpatients with an hCG level test 48 hours later to ascertain viability, if deemed clinically safe to do so. Patients found to have nonviable pregnancies may then undergo a D & C and, if indicated, a laparoscopy. Selected patients may qualify for treatment with methotrexate.

POSTABORTION FOLLOW-UP

The patient should be seen after 1 to 2 weeks. Extensive work-up for the cause of pregnancy loss following a single sporadic episode of early spontaneous abortion probably is not necessary. Attention should be directed toward her emotional adjustment, as profound grief and guilt often follow the loss of pregnancy. Exoneration of her role in causing the spontaneous abortion, as many women often blame themselves, and reassurance about her future pregnancy outcome can greatly help the patient cope with the loss. Referral should be made for psychological counseling if clinically indicated. Family planning should be discussed, and the patient should be advised to wait at least 6 weeks and for the resumption of normal menses (preferably much longer), before reattempting to conceive.

RECURRENT SPONTANEOUS ABORTIONS

Recurrent abortion is defined as the loss of three or more consecutive pregnancies.[21] It affects 0.5 to 1% of pregnant women. Depending on the woman's age and wishes, work-up for recurrent spontaneous abortions may begin after two consecutive pregnancy losses. In up to 50% of couples with recurrent abortions, however, an evaluation does not identify a cause.

Genetic Abnormalities

Most cytogenetic abnormalities in abortuses arise sporadically. Genetically balanced structural chromosome rearrangements are found in 2 to 3% of couples with recurrent abortions.[22] The most common type of structural chromosomal rearrangement is balanced translocations. These include reciprocal translocation (exchange of chromatin between two nonhomologous chromosomes), simple translocation (addition of part of one chromosome to another nonhomologous chromosome), and robertsonian translocation (fusion of acrocentric chromosomes. ie, those whose centromeres are near terminal). The overall risk of miscarriage in couples with reciprocal or simple translocations is approximately 25 to 50%, and the overall risk of an offspring carrying an unbalanced translocation is approximately 10%. If a parent carries a 14:21 robertsonian translocation, over half of the conceptuses abort, and the observed risk for Down syndrome in the liveborn baby is 10 to 15% if the mother is the carrier and 2% if the father is the carrier. Studies of parental karyotypes may be offered to couples with recurrent abortions and, if one partner is found to have a chromosome abnormality, prenatal genetic studies in all future pregnancies should be offered.

Luteal Phase Defect

Luteal phase defect is believed by some investigators to be the cause of recurrent early pregnancy loss in up to one-quarter of patients,[23] although unequivocal supportive evidence is lacking. It is associated with a deficiency in progesterone during the luteal phase, which is necessary for successful implantation and the maintenance of early pregnancy. The diagnosis is made by an endometrial biopsy on day 23 of the menstrual cycle. If histologic dating lags menstrual dating by 3 days, a luteal phase defect is suspected. There is considerable interobserver variation in the interpretation of the biopsies, however, and 6 to 7% of normal fertile women are out of phase on a single biopsy.[24] The diagnosis of luteal phase defect, therefore, should be made on two out-of-phase biopsies in consecutive cycles. Uncontrolled studies have shown that treatment with supplemental progesterone increases the likelihood of achieving term pregnancy among women with luteal phase defect and recurrent abortions. However, a meta-analysis of randomized controlled trials found that progesterone therapy was ineffective.[25]

Uterine Abnormalities

Congenital uterine anomalies are found in 10 to 15% of women with recurrent first-trimester abortions.[26,27] Bicornis, septus, and didelphys uteri are among the most common associated malformations. Other abnormalities include uterine synechiae (Asherman's syndrome) and submucosal leiomyomata. These abnormalities are thought to cause inadequate placentation from poorly vascularized endometrium.

Diagnosis is made by hysterosalpingography, ultrasonography, hysteroscopy, and, as indicated, laparoscopy. Corrective surgery has been shown to lead to successful pregnancies in 70 to 85% of patients with a bicornis or septus uterus and recurrent abortions, although there are no well-controlled randomized clinical trials documenting the efficacy of corrective surgery.[28]

Infections

Although certain bacterial (*Ureaplasma urealyticum*), parasitic (*Toxoplasma gondii*), and viral (rubella virus, herpes simplex virus, cytomegalovirus, measles virus, coxsackievirus, and parvovirus) infections have been associated with spontaneous abortion, no infectious agent has been proven to cause recurrent pregnancy losses. The finding of higher rates of *Ureaplasma* and *Mycoplasma* colonization among women with recurrent abortions has led to recommendations for performance of endometrial culture and preconceptional empiric treatment with erythromycin, but there are no well-controlled trials to support these interventions. Serologic testing or cultures for TORCH syndrome (*t*oxoplasmosis, *o*ther agents, *r*ubella, *c*ytomegalovirus, *h*erpes simplex) and other infections should be guided by the patient's history.

Metabolic and Endocrinologic Disorders

Maternal metabolic and endocrinologic disorders (diabetes mellitus and hypothyroidism in particular) have been implicated in recurrent pregnancy loss. Although any disorder that results in moderate to severe systemic metabolic derangements may cause recurrent abortions, there is no evidence from controlled trials that *asymptomatic* disorders cause recurrent abortions, or that treatment improves pregnancy outcomes.

Immunologic Factors

AUTOIMMUNE DISORDERS

Several autoantibodies have been implicated in recurrent abortions, including antiphospholipid, antinuclear, anti–SS-A, and thyroid colloidal autoantibodies. The two antiphospholipid antibodies held responsible are lupus anticoagulant and anticardiolipin. The presence of one of these autoantibodies in clinically significant titers, along with one or more clinical features including pregnancy loss, thrombosis, autoimmune thrombocytopenia, Coombs'

TABLE 20–1. Factors to Be Considered in the Assessment of Recurrent Early Pregnancy Loss

History
　　Pattern, trimester, and characteristics of prior pregnancy losses
　　Exposure to environmental toxins and drugs
　　Gynecologic or obstetric infections
　　Features associated with antiphospholipid syndrome (ie, thrombosis, autoimmune phenomena, false-positive tests for syphilis)
　　Genetic relationship between reproductive partners (consanguinity)
　　Family history of recurrent spontaneous abortion or syndrome associated with embryonic or fetal loss
　　Previous diagnostic tests and treatments

General physical examination, including gynecologic examination
Tests to be considered*
　　Endocrine evaluation
　　Hysterosalpingography
　　Parental karyotypes
　　Endometrial biopsy
　　Identification of lupus anticoagulant and anticardiolipin antibodies

---

*The sequence of testing should take into consideration the costs, clinical circumstances, and indications. If other tests are negative, consider performing hysteroscopy.

test–positive hemolytic anemia, or livedo reticularis, confirms the diagnosis of antiphospholipid syndrome. Antiphospholipid antibodies are thought to cause 5 to 10% of recurrent abortions.[29] Successful pregnancy outcomes have been reported in approximately 55 to 85% of women with antiphospholipid syndrome treated with heparin or prednisone (with or without low-dose aspirin) in uncontrolled studies.[30] Heparin is preferred over prednisone because there are increased pregnancy complications associated with prednisone.

ALLOIMMUNE DISORDERS

Some reproductive immunologists believe that allogenic similarities between male and female partners may be associated with recurrent abortions. These partners may share human leukocyte antigens, and the female partner may fail to produce serum blocking factors or antileukocytotoxic antibodies against paternal leukocytes;[31] however the clinical relevance of these findings has been challenged.[32] Immunization of the female partner with the male partner's leukocytes have produced a clinically marginal but statistically significant benefit in two recent meta-analyses.[33]

Diagnosis and Management

Evaluation of patients with recurrent spontaneous abortions may include aspects listed in Table 20–1.[21] In couples with unexplained recurrent spontaneous abortions, no treatment of proven efficacy can be offered. In couples where one partner carries a structural chromosomal abnormality, prenatal genetic testing should be offered in all future pregnancies. Women with a luteal phase defect may be offered supplemental progesterone. Corrective surgeries may be offered to women with uterine abnormalities such as septus, bicornis, or didelphys uteri. Preconceptional diagnosis and treatment of infectious or metabolic diseases are recommended. Treatment with heparin and low-dose aspirin may benefit women with antiphospholipid syndrome. Treatment for alleged alloimmune causes remains unproven and expensive; they cannot be recommended outside an experimental protocol. None of these treatments has been proven effective through randomized clinical trials. Couples with recurrent spontaneous abortions may be vulnerable to interventions of unproven efficacy. The physician should offer a sympathetic approach that encourages appropriate evaluation and management.

REFERENCES

1. Herbst AL, Mishell DR, Stenchever MA, et al. Comprehensive gynecology. St. Louis: Mosby Year Book: 1992. p. 425–55.
2. Boklage CE. Survival probability of human conceptions from fertilization to term. Int J Fertil 1990; 35:74–94.
3. Edmonds DK, Lindsay KS, Miller JF, et al. Early embryonic mortality in women. Fertil Steril 1982; 38:447–53.
4. Leridon H. Human fertility. Chicago: University of Chicago Press; 1977.
5. Wilcox AJ, Weinberg CR, O'Connor JF, et al. Incidence of early loss of pregnancy. N Engl J Med 1988;319:189–94.
6. Tabor A, Philip J, Madsen M, et al. Randomized controlled trial of genetic amniocentesis in 1606 low-risk women. Lancet 1986;1:1287–93.

7. Shapiro S, Levine HS, Abramowicz M. Factors associated with early and late fetal loss. Adv Plann Parenth 1971;6:45.

8. Warburton D, Fraser FC. Spontaneous abortion risks in man: data from reproductive histories collected in a medical genetics unit. Am J Hum Genet 1964;16:1–5.

9. Poland BJ, Miller JR, Jones DC, et al. Reproductive counseling in patients who have had a spontaneous abortion. Am J Obstet Gynecol 1977;127:685–91.

10. Kline J, Stein Z. Epidemiology of chromosomal anomalies in spontaneous abortion: prevalence, manifestation and determinants. In: Bennett MJ, Edmonds DK, editors. Spontaneous and recurrent abortion. Oxford: Blackwell Scientific Publications; 1987. p. 1–28.

11. Fantel AG, Shepard TH. Morphological analysis of spontaneous abortuses. In: Bennett MJ, Edmonds DK, editors. Spontaneous and recurrent abortion. Oxford: Blackwell Scientific Publications; 1987. p. 29–50.

12. Simpson JL, Bombard AT. Chromosomal abnormalities in spontaneous abortion: frequency, pathology and genetic counseling. In: Bennett MJ, Edmonds DK, editors. Spontaneous and recurrent abortion. Oxford: Blackwell Scientific Publications; 1987. p. 51.

13. Sompolinsky D, Solomon F, Elikina L, et al. Infections with mycoplasma and bacteria: individual midtrimester abortion and fetal loss. Am J Obstet Gynecol 1975;121:610–16.

14. Schnorr TM, Grajewski BA, Hornung RW, et al. Video display terminals and the risk of spontaneous abortion. N Engl J Med 1991;324:727–33.

15. Herbst AL, Mishell DR, Stenchever MA, et al. Comprehensive gynecology. St. Louis: Mosby Year Book; 1992. p. 425.

16. Fossum GT, Davajan V, Kletzky OA. Early detection of pregnancy with transvaginal ultrasound. Fertil Steril 1988;49:789–91.

17. Levi CS, Lyons EA, Lindsay DJ. Early diagnosis of nonviable pregnancy with endovaginal ultrasound. Radiology 1988;167:383–5.

18. Levi CS, Lyons EA, Zheng XH, et al. Endovaginal ultrasound: demonstration of cardiac activity in embryos of less than 5.0 mm in crown-rump length. Radiology 1990;176:71–4.

19. Batzer FR, Schlaff S, Goldfarb AF, et al. Serial B-subunit human chorionic gonadotropin doubling time as a prognosticator of pregnancy outcome in an infertile population. Fertil Steril 1981;35:307–12.

20. Nielsen S, Hahlin M. Expectant management of first-trimester spontaneous abortion. Lancet 1995; 345:84–6.

21. American College of Obstetricians and Gynecologists. Early pregnancy loss. Technical bulletin, no. 212. Washington (DC): ACOG; 1995.

22. Simpson JL, Elias S, Meyers CM, et al. Translocations are infrequent among couples having repeated spontaneous abortions but no other abnormal pregnancies. Fertil Steril 1989;51:811–4.

23. Daya S, Ward S, Burrows E. Progesterone profiles in luteal phase defect cycles and outcome of progesterone treatment in patients with recurrent spontaneous abortion. Am J Obstet Gynecol 1988;158:225–32.

24. Davis OK, Berkeley AS, Naus GJ, et al. The incidence of luteal phase defect in normal, fertile women, determined by serial endometrial biopsy. Fertil Steril 1989;51:582–6.

25. Goldstein P, Berrier J, Rosen S, et al. A meta-analysis of randomized control trials of progestational agents in pregnancy. Br J Obstet Gynaecol 1989;96:265–74.

26. Harger JH, Archer DF, Marchese SG, et al. Etiology of recurrent pregnancy losses and outcome of subsequent pregnancies. Obstet Gynecol 1983;62:574–81.

27. Stray-Pedersen B, Stray-Pedersen S. Etiologic factors and subsequent reproductive performance in 195 couples with a prior history of habitual abortion. Am J Obstet Gynecol 1984;148:140–6.

28. Rock JA, Schlaff WD. The obstetric consequences of uterovaginal anomalies. Fertil Steril 1985;43:681–92.

29. Parazzini F, Acaia B, Faden D, et al. Antiphospholipid antibodies and recurrent abortion. Obstet Gynecol 1991;77:854–8.

30. Branch DW, Silver RM, Blackwell JL, et al. Outcome of treated pregnancies in women with antiphospholipid syndrome: an update of the Utah experience. Obstet Gynecol 1992;80:614–20.

31. Branch DW. Immunologic aspects of pregnancy loss: alloimmune and autoimmune considerations. In: Reece EA, Hobbins JC, Mahoney MJ, Petrie RH, editors. Medicine of the fetus and mother. Philadelphia: JB Lippincott Co,; 1992. p. 217–33.

32. Coulam CB. Immunologic tests in the evaluation of reproductive disorders: a critical review. Am J Obstet Gynecol 1992;167:1844–51.

33. Coulam CB, Clark DA, Collins J, et al. A worldwide collaborative observational study and meta-analysis on allogenic leukocyte immunotherapy for recurrent spontaneous abortion. Am J Reprod Immunol 1994;23:55–72.

21

INDUCED ABORTION

Michael C. Lu, MD, MPH

Induced abortion is the intentional termination of pregnancy. It is considered elective if performed for the woman's desires, and therapeutic if performed for reasons of maintaining the woman's health.[1]

Today induced abortion is the most frequently performed gynecologic surgery in the United States. In 1996, a total of 1,221,585 legal induced abortions were reported to the Centers for Disease Control and Prevention.[2] There were 314 induced abortions for every 1,000 live births. Nearly 1 in 3 (30%) women in the United States has had one or more induced abortions in her lifetime. One in 5 women who obtained legal abortions in 1996 was less than 20 years old; 1 in 3 was aged 20 to24 years. More than half of legal abortions (55%) were performed during the first 8 weeks of gestation, and approximately 88% of abortions were performed during the first 12 weeks of pregnancy.

Abortion was legalized in the United States by the Supreme Court in 1973. In *Roe v. Wade,* the Supreme Court held that women have a constitutional right of privacy that is "fundamental" and "broad enough to encompass a woman's decision . . . to terminate her pregnancy."[3] Specifically, the court ruled that states could not interfere with the physician-patient decision about abortion during the first trimester, and that a state could intervene during the second trimester only to ensure safe medical practices reasonably related to maternal health. For the third trimester, a state could regulate, or even proscribe, abortion unless medical judgment deemed the procedure necessary to preserve the life or health of the pregnant woman.

PREABORTION COUNSELING

Preabortion counseling should include a thorough discussion of options, risks, and benefits. The counseling should be unbiased and nonjudgmental. Clinicians who do not perform abortions should refer women to those who do. All women seeking an elective abortion should be offered the option of continuing with the pregnancy and assistance with adoption.

If a woman chooses to obtain an abortion, she should be informed of her options (see below). The clinician should describe the procedure, risks, and benefits to the woman. Informed consent should be obtained. Spousal consent or notification is never required,[4] but parental consent or notification may be required in some states, unless the minor can convince a judge that obtaining parental consent would not be in her best interest, as in the case of incest.[5,6] Patient confidentiality must be respected.

PATIENT HISTORY AND PHYSICAL EXAMINATION

A brief history is taken and a physical examination is performed. The clinician should obtain a menstrual history and estimate gestational age. Inquiry about contraceptive use should be made. History of valvular disease, active hepatic or renal disease, asthma, drug allergy, cervical stenosis, uterine anomalies, or any other condition that may complicate the abortion should be obtained. Physical examination should include the heart, lungs, and abdomen. In preparation for surgical abortion, special attention is paid to uterine size, shape, and position, and the presence of an adnexal mass or tenderness. The pregnancy is confirmed with a urine test. Sonographic confirmation of gestational age is recommended for medical abortion, advanced gestation, or discrepancy between gestational age and uterine size. Hematocrit and Rhesus (Rh) type are routinely obtained in all women.

MEDICAL ABORTION

Medical abortion may be accomplished in early pregnancy with methotrexate or mifepristone, in combination with a prostaglandin.[7] The advantages of medical abortion include privacy, autonomy, and avoidance of a psychologically and physically invasive procedure. The disadvantages include longer duration, noxious gastrointestinal side effects, prolonged bleeding with occasional hemorrhaging, higher failure rate, the inconvenience of several visits, and inability to immediately confirm success for some patients.[8] Labor induction is used in later gestation.

Methotrexate and Misoprostol

In early pregnancy, abortion may be accomplished with the administration of methotrexate, a folic acid antagonist, and misoprostol, a prostaglandin. Contraindications include active hepatic or renal disease, active asthma or hematologic disorder, inflammatory bowel disease, known allergy to methotrexate, or inability to adhere to a follow-up routine.[9,10] Thus, a complete blood count with platelets, aspartate aminotransferase, serum creatinine, and a ß-subunit of human chorionic gonadotropin (ß-hCG) are obtained in women undergoing medical abortion with methotrexate and misoprostol. The women should be advised to avoid taking prenatal vitamins or any other medications containing folate.

Methotrexate (50 mg/m[2] body surface area) is given by an intramuscular injection. Oral administration of methotrexate may be equally effective.[11] Giving methotrexate alone is less effective than is the combined methotrexate-misoprostol regimen.[12] Misoprostol (800 µg) is then inserted intravaginally 3 to 7 days later. Class I evidence (at least one properly done randomized controlled trial) supports waiting 7 days after methotrexate injection before inserting misoprostol; this was found to be more effective than waiting 3 days only.[13] Class II-2 (cohort studies) evidence supports giving 800 µg of misoprostol vaginally rather than 600 µg orally.[14] Women who are Rh negative and unsensitized to Rh antibodies are given Rh(D) immune globulin at this time.

Complete abortion was reported in 48 to 86% of women after the first dose, most within the first 24 hours following misoprostol insertion. A repeat ultrasonography is performed within 1 week if complete abortion has not occurred. A second dose of misoprostol (800 µg) is given to women with a persistent gestational sac. Serial ß-hCG levels are obtained weekly until it declines to less than 10 IU/L. If pregnancy continues after the second misoprostol dose, as demonstrated by the presence of fetal cardiac activity or a rising ß-hCG, a surgical abortion usually is performed.[10]

When administered within 54 to 63 days (8 to 9 weeks) from the last menstrual period, methotrexate and misoprostol achieve complete abortion in 88 to 100% of women in reported case series.[9–16] Common side effects include bleeding, cramping, headache, nausea, vomiting, and diarrhea. Clinically significant blood loss (a fall in hemoglobin of 20% or greater) occurs in fewer than 2% of women.[13] Stomatitis has been reported, but bone marrow toxicity, penumonitis, and hepatic damage have not. Congenital malformations have been associated with the use of both methotrexate and misoprostol in pregnancy.[17]

Mifepristone

Induced abortion may also be accomplished in early pregnancy with mifepristone (RU 486), an antiprogestin.[18] Mifepristone blocks the P receptor in the placenta, resulting in the termination of pregnancy.

Mifepristone given in combination with a prostaglandin was found to be more effective than mifepristone alone.[19] Class I evidence supports a class A (good) recommendation that 200 mg oral mifepristone is as effective as is 600 mg, when each is followed by a prostaglandin.[20,21] A single dose of mifepristone appears to be just as efficacious as is sequential dosing. Mifepristone is followed 48 hours later by intravaginal insertion of 800 µg of misoprostol. Class I evidence supports the superiority of the vaginal route over the oral route of equal doses of misoprostol.[22]

A review of nine randomized controlled trials of mifepristone and prostaglandin yielded a summary complete abortion rate of 94% when given at less than 64 days gestation.[23] In a more recent multicenter trial in the United States in which 600 mg of mifepristone and 400 µg of misoprostol were used, complete abortion was accomplished in 92% of women with an intrauterine gestation at 49 menstrual days or less, in 83% at 50 to 56 menstrual days, and in 77% at 57 to 63 menstrual days.[24] Abdominal pain, nausea, vomiting, diarrhea, and vaginal bleeding were the most common complaints; these increased with advanced gestational age. Class II evidence suggests that medical abortion with mifepristone and prostaglandin may be associated with higher failure rates than is suction curettage in early pregnancy.[25,26]

Mifepristone also may be used in combination with prostaglandin for midtrimester labor induction. Pretreatment with mifepristone has been shown to decrease the induction-to-abortion interval, as well as side effects, when compared with labor induction with prostaglandin alone.

Labor Induction

Labor induction should be offered as an option for second-trimester abortion. At between 13 and 16 weeks' gestation, dilatation and evacuation (D & E) should be the method of choice.[27] At or beyond 17 menstrual weeks, labor induction is comparable to D & E in safety.[28] It can be accomplished by instillation of hypertonic solutions (eg, hypertonic saline, hypertonic urea, or a prostaglandin-like carboprost tromethamine [Hemabate]) via amniocentesis, induction of labor with uterotonic agents such as prostaglandins (eg, vaginal PGE_2 or misoprostol), or both. The use of intravenous oxytocin and osmotic cervical dilators may accelerate the process. Prolonged induction may be concluded with D & E.

The advantages of labor induction include avoidance of surgery and less dependence on the skills of the clinician for its efficacy and safety. The disadvantages include longer duration and higher morbidity and mortality when compared with D & E prior to 17 menstrual weeks.[29,30] Complications include failed abortion, incomplete abortion, retained tissue, hemorrhage, infection, and embolic phenomenon.[31] The incidence of disseminated intravascular coagulopathy (DIC) is 191 per 100,000 following a midtrimester D & E, and 658 per 100,000 following saline instillation. Cervical laceration, cervicovaginal fistula, and annular detachment of the lower cervix have been reported with labor induction. Uterine rupture may occur when instillation is augmented with high-dose oxytocin infusion.

SURGICAL ABORTION

In 1996, 99% of all induced abortions were performed using dilatation and curettage (D & C; 96.5% suction curettage and 2.3% sharp curettage).[2] Menstrual regulation (also termed menstrual extraction) is used before 7 weeks' gestation; D & E and dilatation and extraction (intact D & X) are used for more advanced gestation.

Dilatation and Curettage

Dilatation of the cervix is facilitated with the use of osmotic dilators. Three types are available: *Laminaria* tents, the magnesium sulfate sponge (Lamicel), and synthetic tents of polyacrylonitrile (Dilapan). The use of *Laminaria* tents to facilitate cervical dilatation has been shown to reduce the risk of cervical laceration fivefold and uterine perforation threefold.[32,33] Following informed consent, an osmotic dilator is placed inside the cervical os 1 day prior to surgery. In practice, many women are not seen until the day of surgery, and an osmotic dilator may be placed 2 to 4 hours preoperatively to achieve sufficient dilatation. Lamicel and Dilapan produce cervical dilatation more quickly than do *Laminaria* tents.[34]

Prophylactic antibiotic is administered as 200 mg of doxycycline in two divided doses, or in a single dose immediately following the procedure. A meta-analysis of 12 randomized controlled trials found a 42% reduction in the risk of infection in women given periabortal prophylactic antibiotics.[35]

Premedication consists of a sedative (eg, lorazepam) and a nonsteroidal anti-inflammatory agent (eg, ketorolac) given 1 hour prior to the procedure. Adequate analgesia may be achieved with a paracervical block using a local anesthetic (eg, lidocaine). Because of its lower morbidity and mortality risks, local anesthesia is preferred over general anesthesia.[36,37]

Cervical dilatation is completed using dilators. Tapered dilators (eg, Pratt or Denniston) are less traumatic than are nontapered dilators (eg, Hegar). The cervix is dilatated to one size above the number of weeks' gestation. Sounding the uterus is unnecessary and increases the risk of uterine perforation.

Curettage may be accomplished with a suction or a sharp curet (eg, Sims curet). Suction curettage is associated with fewer complications than is sharp curettage. Suction curettage is performed using a suction cannula (eg, Berkeley) attached to a vacuum aspirator. The size of the cannula should match the number of weeks in gestation. The suction cannula is inserted into the lower uterine segment, and the product of conception is aspirated through a rotational motion. The tissue is examined immediately in water or under wet mount for presence of chorionic villi.

Following curettage, the patient is observed with serial vital signs and abdominal examinations for 1 hour prior to being discharged home. She is instructed to call if she experiences fever, heavy bleeding, nausea or vomiting, severe abdominal pain, or foul-smelling vaginal discharge.

Dilatation and Evacuation

Dilatation and evacuation differs from D & C in three important ways.[38] First, it is performed in later gestation. Dilatation and evacuation is performed at 13 or more weeks of gestation. It is the safest method between 13 and 16 weeks; at 17 weeks and beyond its safety is comparable to labor induction.

Second, because of the more advanced gestation and the larger size of the fetus, greater cervical dilatation is required. To achieve wider cervical dilatation safely, more osmotic dilators may be used. For example, placement of five *Laminaria* tents overnight, or one Lamicel for 4 hours, achieves an average dilatation of 1.5 to 2.0 cm. This cervical dilatation accommodates a cannula 14 mm in diameter, which can evacuate a pregnancy of up to 16 weeks' gestation. For more advanced gestations, serial placement of increasing numbers of osmotic dilators over a 2-day period facilitates greater cervical dilatation.

Third, forceps extraction of fetal parts is often needed, especially beyond 16 weeks of gestation. Specially designed forceps, such as the Sopher or the Bierer forceps, are used to extract fetal parts. Forceps require the cervix to be dilatated to 1.2 cm (small Foerrester forceps for 13 to 15 weeks' gestation) to 2 cm (Hern, Bierer, or Sopher forceps for more advanced gestation) for their passage into the uterine cavity. The use of intraoperative ultrasonography may be helpful in locating fetal parts and forceps. On occasion the fetal calvaria is retained. The use of oxytocin infusion for 2 hours prior to a reattempt at extraction may facilitate its evacuation. Fetal parts are examined immediately to ensure complete abortion.

Dilatation and Extraction

Dilatation and extraction, also known as "partial birth abortion" in the common vernacular, is a variant of D & E. It is used primarily for late-term abortion. It involves deliberate dilatation of the cervix, usually over a sequence of days, followed by internal podalic version of the fetus to a footling breech. Total breech extraction of the body is performed up to the head, and intracranial contents of the fetus are then partially evacuated to effect vaginal delivery of a dead but otherwise intact fetus. The decompression of the skull (cephalocentesis), accomplished typically by incising the cranium and then performing suction evacuation of its contents, is intended to reduce the diameter of the head and thereby reduce the risk of cervical injury during its passage through the cervix.[39–41] The morbidity and mortality of the procedure have not been established clearly.

Menstrual Regulation

Also known as menstrual extraction or minisuction, menstrual regulation is an early suction curettage typically performed prior to 7 completed weeks of gestation. Anesthesia and dilatation often are not required. A 4- to 6-mm flexible Karman cannula attached to a vacuum syringe is inserted inside the uterine cavity to evacuate its contents.[42] The instrument is rotated and moved in and out until the gritty endometrium is reached. Menstrual regulation is associated with a higher risk of incomplete abortion.

Hysterotomy and Hysterectomy

Hysterotomy is an archaic procedure that should no longer be used for abortion. It requires a laparotomy and a uterine incision to evacuate the pregnancy. Hysterectomy should be performed as a method of abortion only when a hysterectomy is indicated.

POSTABORTAL COUNSELING AND FOLLOW-UP

The patient should be followed up within 1 to 2 weeks after the abortion. A pelvic examination is performed. Family planning should be the focus of the follow-up visit; contraceptive counseling and services, including information about emergency contraception, should be provided (see Chapter 9, "Contraception").

COMPLICATIONS OF SURGICAL ABORTION

The risk of major complications requiring hospitalization or blood transfusion from an induced abortion was estimated to be 1 per 1,000 in 1990.[43] The incidence of major complications varies according to the gestational age and method of abortion.[30] At less than 8 weeks, major complications occur in 2 patients per 1,000 procedures, whereas the major complication rate for abortions at 20 weeks or later is 15 per 1,000. Overall, the incidence of major complications is 2 per 1,000 for suction curettage, 7 per 1,000 for D & E, and 21 per 1,000 for saline instillation.

Complications can be categorized as immediate (within 3 hours of the operation), delayed (> 3 hours and up to 28 days), or late (after 28 days).[38]

Immediate Complications

Immediate complications include hemorrhage, acute hematometra, cervical laceration, and uterine perforation. Clinically significant hemorrhage requiring blood transfusion occurs in 0.06% of early abortions and in 0.26% of D & Es. Acute hematometra (postabortal syndrome) occurs as a result of incomplete evacuation in 0.1 to 1% of abortions. Women develop severe cramps within 2 hours of procedure, with or without heavy bleeding. The uterus is enlarged and markedly tender. Treatment is re-evacuation with suction curettage and oxytocin infusion. The uterus then contracts down to its normal postabortal size.

Clinically significant cervical injury requiring sutures for repair occurs in 1.03% of abortions. Protective factors include the use of *Laminaria* and local anesthesia; risk factors include age less than 17 years, the use of general anesthesia, and performance of the abortion by a resident rather than by an attending physician.[31]

Perforation of the uterus occurs in 0.2% of suction curettage abortions. Multiparity and advanced gestational age increase the risk of uterine perforation, whereas the use of *Laminaria* and performance of the abortion by an attending physician decrease the risk.[44]

If the patient is awake during the procedure, she will complain of sudden upper abdominal pain upon perforation. The procedure should cease immediately. Most uterine perforations take place at the fundus, where they tend to go undetected. The uterine sound may be used as a probe to gently locate the defect. Observation of suspected perforations may be all that is required. Uterine perforations from dilators are often innocuous, but those caused by forceps and suction cannula can injure internal organs such as the bowel or bladder. Uterine perforations near the cornu or the cervicoisthmic junction can cause hemorrhage. In these cases of bowel injury or hemorrhage, immediate laparoscopy or laparotomy is advised.

Delayed Complications

Delayed complications include retained tissue and infection. Retained tissue can cause infection, bleeding, or both. It occurs in less than 1% of suction curettage. When women present with abdominal cramping, bleeding, and low-grade fever several days following an abortion, retained tissue must be suspected. Ultrasonography may be helpful in confirming the diagnosis. Treatment consists of immediate curettage and administration of broad-spectrum antibiotics, if indicated.

Septic abortion refers to an abortion associated with intrauterine infection.[45] Infection occurs in less than 1% of abortions. Risk factors include untreated endocervical gonorrhea or chlamydial infection, bacterial vaginosis, advanced gestation, use of instillation abortion, and retained tissue. Women may present with mild illness characterized by the triad of low-grade fever, mild lower abdominal pain, and moderate vaginal bleeding. Women who delay seeking treatment until sepsis is disseminated may present with altered mental status, high fever, prostration, tachycardia, tachypnea, respiratory difficulty, and hypotension. A delay in treatment also may lead to pelvic abscess, septic pelvic thrombophlebitis, DIC, septic shock, renal failure, and death. Adult respiratory distress syndrome occurs in 25 to 50% of women with septic shock.

Rapid initial assessment should focus on the timing and method of the abortion. Presence of guarding and rebound on abdominal examination suggests peritonitis. Foul-smelling pus or product of conception at cervical os, an enlarged tender uterus, and an adnexal mass (tubo-ovarian abscess) may be found upon pelvic examination. Blood, urine, and cervical cultures should be obtained. Endometrial biopsy may yield higher recovery of organisms. Radiographic studies may reveal the presence of free air or foreign body, and ultrasonography may help diagnose an abscess.

Treatment consists of eradicating the infection and evacuating the uterus. Most septic abortions are polymicrobial in origin, involving gram-positive and gram-negative aerobes and facultative or obligate anaerobes. *Neisseria gonorrhoeae, Chlamydia trachomatis,* and *Mycoplasma* are commonly found pathogens. Therefore, wide-spectrum antibiotics should be used. For outpatient treatment of mild septic abortion limited to the uterus, regimens recommended for outpatient treatment of pelvic inflammatory disease, such as ofloxacin plus either clindamycin or metronidazole, are appropriate. For treatment of severe septic abortion, high doses of intravenous broad-spectrum antibiotics, such as ampicillin, clindamycin, and an aminoglycoside, should be given immediately.

Any retained tissue should be evacuated without delay, typically within 2 hours after antibiotic therapy has been initiated. Waiting for the uterus to "cool down" or the patient to stabilize causes unnecessary delay that could prove fatal. The infected uterus should not be sounded. Suction curettage can be performed immediately under local anesthesia with minimal sedation in the emergency room or, if necessary, in the intensive care unit. Dilatation and evacuation or labor induction is used to abort a retained fetus of advanced gestation. Prompt hysterectomy may be indicated in clostridial sepsis with systemic manifestations such as hemolysis. Supportive care for postabortal septic shock is provided as with septic shock from any other causes.

Late Complications

Potential late complications include Rh sensitization, adverse psychological sequelae, and adverse future reproductive outcomes. The risk of Rh sensitization from suction curettage without Rh immunoglobulin prophylaxis is estimated to be 2.6%; the risk increases with increasing gestational age.[46] Postabortal Rh_o (D) immune globulin (RhoGAM) should be given, 50 μcg before 12 weeks gestation and 300 μcg thereafter, to women who are Rh negative.

Transient feelings of stress or sadness may follow an induced abortion, but long-term major psychiatric sequelae are rare.[47,48] A review of 225 studies found that most women reported feeling relief and reduced distress, depression, and anxiety after terminating an unwanted pregnancy.[49] Women with symptoms of distress or dysphoria after an induced abortion typically had those symptoms prior to the abortion.

Most women (70%) in the United States who have had an abortion want to have children in the future.[50] One first-trimester abortion does not appear to increase the risk of future adverse reproductive outcomes.[51] Women who have had one prior induced abortion in the first trimester experience no greater risk of infertility, ectopic pregnancy, spontaneous abortion, stillbirth, infant mortality, congenital anomalies, low–birth weight infants, or major complications during pregnancy or delivery than do women who have never had an abortion. The risk of adverse outcomes for women who have had more than one induced abortions has not been established clearly, but it appears to be increased with sharp curettage.[52] Dilatation and evacuation significantly increases the risk of subsequent spontaneous abortion, premature delivery, and low birth weight.[53]

The relation between induced abortion and breast cancer has not been established clearly. A review of five cohort and 39 case-control studies concludes that "any such relation is likely to be small or nonexistent."[54]

Death

Fewer than 1 in 100,000 women die from induced abortion. In contrast, nearly 5 women die from every 100,000 live births.[55,56] Abortion (both induced and spontaneous) accounted for less than 5% of the 2,644 maternal deaths in the United States from 1979 to 1986.

Prior to 1979, infection, embolism, and hemorrhage were the leading causes of death from legal induced abortions. Since 1983, however, anesthesia complications have become the most frequent cause, accounting for 29% of the deaths. Women aged 40 years or older have three times the risk of death as do teenagers. Black women have 2.5 times the risk of death as do Caucasian women. Abortions performed at or over 16 weeks of gestation carry 15 times the risk of material death as do abortions performed under 12 weeks. Abortions by instillation or other methods increase the risk of maternal death 10-fold, as compared with abortions by suction curettage.[29]

ILLEGAL ABORTION

An estimated 1 million illegal abortions were performed annually in the United States prior to liberalization of abortion laws in 1967.[57] Today illegal abortions continue to be performed frequently worldwide, but rarely in the United States. Illegal abortion can be accomplished by oral abortifacients and intrauterine instrumentation. Oral abortifacients include turpentine, laundry bleach, and quinine. Intrauterine instrumentation includes insertion of foreign objects (eg, clothes hangers) and injection of soap or phenol disinfectants through the cervix. Insertion of rigid foreign objects increases the risk of perforation, and instillation of solutions containing cresol or phenol may cause uterine necrosis, renal failure, central nervous system toxicity, cardiac depression, and respiratory arrest. The most common complication from illegal abortion is retained product of conception; the most frequent cause of death is infection and sepsis.[29] The death rate from illegal abortion is nearly 70 times higher than that from legal abortion.[58]

RESOURCES

Planned Parenthood
810 Seventh Avenue
New York, NY 10019
Telephone: (212) 541-7800
    1-800-230-PLAN (1-800-230-7526)
Web site: www.plannedparenthood.org

Planned Parenthood provides patient information, as well as schedules appointments with clinicians of induced abortion services throughout the United States.

The Alan Guttmacher Institute
120 Wall Street, 21st Floor
New York, New York 10005
Telephone: (212) 248-1111

1120 Connecticut Avenue Northwest, Suite 460
Washington, DC 20036
Telephone: (202) 296-4012
Web site: www.agi-usa.org

The Alan Guttmacher Institute's mission is to protect reproductive choice in the United States and worldwide. The AGI provides information, including statistics and policy information, on induced abortion, as well as information about laws and legal issues applicable in the various states.

The National Abortion and Reproductive Rights Action League
1156 15th Street Northwest
Washington, DC 20005
Telephone: (202) 973-3018
Web site: www.naral.org/home.html

The National Abortion and Reproductive Rights Action League educates about and lobbies for reproductive rights and health issues, as well as supports pro-choice candidates for elected office in the United States.

REFERENCES

1. Herbst AL, Mishell DR, Stenchever MA, et al. Comprehensive gynecology. St. Louis: Mosby Year Book; 1992. p. 425.

2. Centers for Disease Control and Prevention. Abortion surveillance: preliminary analysis—United States, 1996. MMWR Morb Mortal Wkly Rep 1998; 47:1025–8, 1035.

3. *Roe v. Wade*, 410 US 113 (1973).

4. *Danforth v. Planned Parenthood of Central Missouri*, 428 US 52 (1976).

5. *Bellotti v. Baird*, 443 US 622 (1989).

6. *Planned Parenthood of Southeastern Pennsylvania v. Casey* 505 US 833 (1992).

7. Grimes DA. Medical abortion in early pregnancy: a review of the evidence. Obstet Gynecol 1997; 89:790–6.

8. Henshaw RC, Naji SA, Russell IT, et al. A comparison of medical abortion (using mifepristone and gemeprost) with surgical vacuum aspiration: efficacy and early medical sequelae. Hum Reprod 1994;9:2167–72.

9. Hausknecht RU. Methotrexate and misoprostol to terminate early pregnancy. N Engl J Med 1995; 333:537–40.

10. Creinin MD, Vittinghoff E. Methotrexate and misoprostol vs misoprostol alone for early abortion: a randomized controlled trial. JAMA 1994;272:1190–5.

11. Wiebe ER. Oral methotrexate compared with injected methotrexate when used with misoprostol for abortion. Am J Obstet Gynecol 1999;181:149–52.

12. Wiebe ER. Comparing abortion induced with methotrexate and misoprostol to methotrexate alone. Contraception 1999;59:7–10.

13. Crenin MD, Vittinghoff E, Galbraith S, Klaisle C. A randomized trial comparing misoprostol three and seven days after methotrexate for early abortion. Am J Obstet Gynecol 1995;173:1578–84.

14. Crenin MD, Darney PD. Methotrexate and misoprostol for abortion at 57–63 days gestation. Contraception 1994;50:511–5.

15. Schaff EA, Eisinger SH, Franks P, et al. Methotrexate and misoprostol for early abortion. Fam Med 1996; 28:198–203.

16. Wiebe ER. Abortion induced with methotrexate and misoprostol. Can Med Assoc J 1996;154:165–70.

17. Gonzalez CH, Vargas FR, Perez ABA, et al. Limb deficiency with or without Möbius sequence in seven Brazilian children associated with misoprostol use in the first trimester of pregnancy. Am J Med Genet 1993;47:59–64.

18. Mahajan DK, London SN. Mifepristone (RU 486): a review. Fertil Steril 1997;68:967–76.

19. Cameron IT, Michie AF, Baird DT. Therapeutic abortion in early pregnancy with antiprogesterone RU 486 alone or in combination with prostaglandin analog (gemeprost). Contraception 1986;34:459–68.

20. McKinley C, Thong KJ, Baird DT. The effect of dose of mifepristone and gestation on the efficacy of medical abortion with mifepristone and misoprostol. Hum Reprod 1993;8:1502–5.

21. World Health Organization Task Force on Post-Ovulatory Methods of Fertility Regulation. Termination of pregnancy with reduced doses of mifepristone. Br Med J 1993;307:532–7.

22. El-Refaey H, Rajasekar D, Abdalla M, et al. Induction of abortion with mifepristone (RU 486) and oral or vaginal misoprostol. N Engl J Med 1995; 332:983–7.

23. Grimes DA. Medical abortion in early pregnancy: a review of the evidence. Obstet Gynecol 1997; 89:790–6.

24. Sptiz IM, Bardin CW, Benton L, et al. Early pregnancy termination with mifepristone and misoprostol in the United States. N Engl J Med 1998; 338:1241–7.

25. Henshaw RC, Naji SA, Russell IT, et al. A comparison of medical abortion (using mifepristone and gemeprost) with surgical vacuum aspiration: efficacy and early medical sequelae. Hum Reprod 1994; 9:2167–72.

26. Winikoff B, Sivin I, Coyaji KJ, et al. Safety, efficacy and acceptability of medical abortion in China, Cuba and India: a comparative trial of mifepristone-misoprostol versus surgical abortion. Am J Obstet Gynecol 1997;176:431–7.

27. Robbins J, Surrago EJ. Early midtrimester pregnancy termination: a comparison of dilatation and evacuation and intravaginal prostaglandin F2a. J Reprod Med 1982;27:415–9.

28. Kafrissen ME, Schulz KR, Grimes DA, et al. A comparison of intraamniotic instillation of hyperosmolar urea and prostglandin F2a vs dilatation and evacuation for midtrimester abortion. JAMA 1984; 251:916–9.

29. Atrash HK, Lawson HW, Smith JC. Legal abortion in the U.S.: trends and mortality. Contemp OB/GYN 1990;35:58–69.

30. Tietze C, Henshaw SK. Induced abortion: a world view, 1986. New York: The Alan Guttmacher Institute; 1986.

31. Stufflefield PG. Pregnancy termination. In: Gabbe SG, Niebyl JR, Simpson JL. editors. Obstetrics: normal and problem pregnancies. New York: Churchill Livingstone; 1991. p. 1323–7.

32. Schulz KF, Grimes DA, Cates W Jr. Measures to prevent cervical injury during suction curettage abortion. Lancet 1983;1:1182–5.

33. Gold J, Schulz KR, Cates W Jr, et al. The safety of *Laminaria* and rigid dilators for cervical dilatation prior to suction curettage for first trimester abortion:

a comparative analysis. In: Naftolin F, Stubblefield PG, editors. Dilatation of the uterine cervix: connective tissue biology and clinical management. New York: Raven Press; 1980. p. 363–75.

34. Darney PD, Dorward K. Cervical dilatation before first-trimester elective abortion: a controlled comparison of meteneprost, *Laminaria*, and hypan. Obstet Gynecol 1987;70:397.

35. Sawaya GF, Grady D, Kerlikowske K, et al. Antibiotics at the time of induced abortion: the case for universal prophylaxis based on a meta-analysis. Obstet Gynecol 1996;87:884–90.

36. Grimes DA, Schulz KR, Cates W Jr, et al. Local versus general anesthesia: which is safer for performing suction curettage abortions? Am J Obstet Gynecol 1979;135:1030–35.

37. Peterson HB, Grimes DA, Cates W Jr, et al. Comparative risk of death from induced abortion at 12 weeks or less gestation performed with local versus general anesthesia. Am J Obstet Gynecol 1981;141: 763–8.

38. Grimes DA. Surgical management of abortion. In: Thompson JD, Rock JA editors. Te Linde's operative gynecology. 7th ed. Philadelphia: J.B. Lippincott Company; 1992. p. 333–4.

39. American College of Obstetricians and Gynecologists: Statement on intact dilatation and extraction. Washington (DC): ACOG; 1997.

40. Grimes DA. The continuing need for late abortions. JAMA, 1998;280:747–50.

41. Annas GJ. Partial-birth abortion, congress, and the Constitution. N Engl J Med 1998;339:279–83.

42. Karman H, Potts M. Very early abortion using syringe as vacuum source. Lancet 1972;1:7759–62.

43. Council on Scientific Affairs, American Medical Association. Induced termination of pregnancy before and after *Roe v. Wade*. JAMA 1992;268:3235–9.

44. Grimes DA, Schulz KF, Cates W Jr. Prevention of uterine perforation during curettage abortion. JAMA 1984;251:2108–11.

45. Stubblefield PG, Grimes DA. Septic abortion. N Engl J Med 1994;331:310–4.

46. Simonovits I, Timar I, Bajtai G. Rate of Rh immunization after induced abortion. Vox Sang 1980;38: 161–4.

47. Stotland NL. The myth of the abortion trauma syndrome. JAMA 1992;268:2078–9.

48. Adler NE, David HP, Major BN, et al. Psychological response after abortion. Science 1990;248:41–4.

49. Dagg PKB. The psychological sequelae of therapeutic abortion—denied and completed. Am J Psychiatry 1991;148:578–85.

50. Henshaw SK, Silverman J. The characteristics and prior contraceptive use of US abortion patients. Fam Plann Perspect 1988;20:158–68.

51. Atrash HK, Hogue CJ. The effect of pregnancy termination on future reproduction. Baillieres Clin Obstet Gynaecol 1990;4:391–405.

52. Institute of Medicine. Legalized abortion and the public health. Report of a study committee of the Institute of Medicine. Washington (DC): National Academy of Sciences; 1975.

53. Frank PI. Sequelae of induced abortion. Ciba Found Symp 1985;115:67–82.

54. Michels KB, Willett WC. Does induced or spontaneous abortion affect the risk of breast cancer? Epidemiology 1996;7:521–8.

55. Atrash HK, Koonin LM, Lawson HW, et al. Maternal mortality in the United States, 1979–1986. Obstet Gynecol 1990;76:1055–60.

56. Lawson HW, Frye A, Atrash HK, et al. Abortion mortality, United States, 1972 through 1987. Am J Obstet Gynecol 1994;171:1365–72.

57. Tietze C. Abortion on request: its consequences for population trends and public health. Semin Psychiatry 1970;2:375–81.

58. Tietze C. The public health effects of legal abortion in the United States. Fam Plann Perspect 1984; 16:26–8.

22

APPROACH TO THE PATIENT
WITH BREAST PROBLEMS

Sherry Goldman, RN, NP

Breast cancer is diagnosed in an estimated 180,000 women in the United States per year. It is the most common nonskin cancer in US women, and it is second only to lung cancer as a cause of cancer mortality in US women. It is the leading cause of cancer mortality for women aged 15 to 54 years.[1]

Breast cancer can present clinically in many ways. This chapter reviews common clinical scenarios in which the primary care clinican must distinguish between benign and malignant causes of breast abnormalities. Included are algorithms that summarize the approach to palpable breast masses, abnormal results on mammograms, breast skin changes, and nipple discharge.

CAUSES OF GENERALIZED BREAST CHANGES AND SOLITARY LUMPS

Generalized Breast Changes: Fibrocystic Tissue

Also known as chronic cystic mastitis and mammary dysplasia, fibrocystic disease is a general term that does not represent any distinct entity, either physically or microscopically. Mostly, it is a generic term that is used to describe benign changes that do not fit into the other discrete categories. Recently, the term "physiologic nodularity" has been used, to emphasize that fibrocystic changes are not a "disease."

Fibrocystic tissue often is described as "lumpy" or "granular" and is felt most often around the nipple and areola or in the upper outer quadrant of the breast, where most of the breast tissue is located. It is most common in women approaching middle age. *It may affect 50% of women clinically and a higher number at autopsy.*[2] Most clinical symptoms disappear after menopause, unless the woman is using replacement hormones.

Fibrocystic disease is responsible for the lumpiness and tenderness that occurs in the breasts of many women during midmenstrual cycle, the time of maximal hormonal stimulation. Fibrocystic disease can be frustrating for the patient, as well as the clinicians who are trying to treat this condition. At times, stopping exogenous hormone therapy can be helpful. However, for the premenopausal woman, enough hormonal stimulation occurs with each menstrual cycle that eliminating exogenous hormones may not be helpful.

Methylxanthine ingestion from coffee, tea, and chocolate also is thought to stimulate fibrocystic disease and cause painful tender breasts. Women who eliminate caffeine from their diet may notice improved symptoms. Intake of vitamin E (400 to 1200 IU/d) also has helped women with painful breasts.[3] Danazol, bromocriptine, and tamoxifen have been used to treat fibrocystic breast disease, but side effects and risks outweigh benefits in most patients who would use these drugs for fibrocystic symptoms.[2] Reduction of fibrocystic symptoms is a possible beneficial side effect of using tamoxifen for another indication, such as reduction of risk of breast cancer in a high-risk woman. Most of the time, women with painful fibrocystic breasts who adhere to one of the above treatments continue to have some pain in their breasts, usually at midcycle.

Solitary Lumps

FIBROADENOMAS

Fibroadenomas are benign tumors that are solid and round. Composed of both solid ("fibro-") and glandular ("adenoma") tissue, these painless lesions feel rubbery and can be moved around easily by the patient. In fact most fibroadenomas are found during routine breast self-examination.

Fibroadenomas occur most commonly in young women in their late teens and early twenties and are reported twice as often in African American women as in other American women.[4] *Fibroadenomas rarely present after menopause.* Although fibroadenomas do not become malignant, they can enlarge with pregnancy and breast-feeding. Although fibroadenomas are benign, a tissue diagnosis to rule out the possibility of cancer generally should be obtained. Some may become tender or large enough to cause a cosmetic deformity. In this type of situation, the fibroadenoma usually is removed. If a fibroadenoma is small and painless and has been proven benign by pathology from a biopsy or a fine-needle aspiration (FNA), it can be followed up clinically.

CYSTS

Cysts are fluid-filled sacs that occur most frequently in women between the ages of 35 and 50 years. Cysts can become tender and painful before the menstrual period.

The size of any given cyst is variable, with some being so small that they cannot be felt and some being as large as several inches in diameter. Mammography and ultrasonography often can provide an accurate diagnosis. Cysts are treated with aspiration, which can be guided by ultrasound, if necessary. This usually gives instant relief from any physical symptoms such as pain.

Cysts are so rarely associated with breast cancer that cyst aspirates usually are not tested for cancer. However, if the fluid drawn from the cyst is bloody, sending the specimen to the cytopathologist to determine whether cancerous cells can be detected is recommended. The vast majority of cyst fluids do not need to be sent for cytology.[4]

FAT NECROSIS OR LIPOMA

Fat necrosis refers to painless round firm lumps formed by damaged and disintegrating fatty tissue. This condition typically occurs in obese women with very large breasts. Fat necrosis often develops in response to a bruise, a blow to the breast, or a previous surgery, even though a woman may not remember having been injured.[5] Sometimes, the skin around the lumps looks red or bruised. Because fat necrosis can easily be mistaken for cancer, surgical biopsy generally is needed for definitive diagnosis.

SCLEROSING ADENOSIS

Sclerosing adenosis is a benign condition involving the excessive growth of tissue in the breast. This can also be called a "pseudolump." It frequently causes breast pain. Usually the changes are microscopic. However, adenosis can produce lumps, and it can show up on mammography, often as calcification. Because adenosis is often difficult to distinguish from cancer, surgical biopsy usually is needed for diagnosis.[6]

CLINICAL EVALUATION OF SOLITARY BREAST MASSES

History and Physical Examination

Since abnormal breast findings may indicate cancer, the work-up needs to proceed in a timely manner. Important points in the clinical history of a woman presenting with a breast lump include current symptoms such as nipple discharge, lumps in the axilla, skin dimpling, ulceration, inflammation, and noncyclical pain. The clinician also should inquire about the presence of breast implants, which may affect the sensitivity of clinical breast examination (CBE) and mammography, as well as be a potential cause of a lump.

Other aspects of the medical history that may influence the women's personal risk of breast cancer also should be elicited, including current or prior use of hormonal therapy; history of previous breast cancer or other breast problems, including previous biopsy results; age at menarche and menopause; age at first live birth; history of radiation exposure; family history of breast cancer in a first-degree relative (ie, mother, sister, or daughter), including number of family members affected; and personal and family history of other types of cancer, particularly ovarian cancer. In the premenopausal patient, complete menstrual, pregnancy, and lactation history should be obtained. Breast cancer screening history should include the date of last CBE and/or mammography and the result(s).[7]

The CBE needs to be thorough and preferably performed in the follicular phase of the woman's menstrual cycle. A mass is three-dimensional, distinct from surrounding tissues, and usually asymmetric. Cysts are fluid filled, round, and vary in size. Clinical signs suggestive of benignity, but not diagnostic, include a mass that is soft and mobile. Normal glandular tissue generally is mirrored in the contralateral breast. Features suggestive of malignancy include a mass that feels firm or hard, has an irregular shape, is solitary, and feels different from surrounding breast tissue. Frequently, breast cancers are fixed and associated with other signs, such as skin tethering, dimpling, retraction, or peau d'orange. Regardless of the age of a woman, every clinically suspicious lesion requires complete evaluation.[8]

Evaluation of a New Palpable Mass in a Woman Under Age 50 Years

An approach to work-up of a new palpable mass in a woman under age 50 years is summarized in Figure 22–1. If the clinician suspects the mass is cystic, this may be confirmed by ultrasonography or FNA. A cyst that is completely resolved by FNA revealing non-bloody fluid can be considered benign if there are no signs of recurrence 4 to 6 weeks post aspiration. Typical cystic fluid should not routinely be sent for cytologic analysis, as the diagnostic yield is extremely low. A cyst that recurs more than twice, yields blood-stained fluid, or leaves a residual palpable mass post aspiration demands cytologic examination and further evaluation.[9] Excisional biopsy also may be performed in these situations. Although multiple cysts commonly occur, the woman with breast cysts needs advice to be particularly cautious and to seek medical advice every time a new lump arises. Neither the clinician nor the woman can automatically assume that a new mass is "just another cyst."

If the mass is suspected to be solid, and it is clinically not suspicious, it may be reassessed early in the next menstrual cycle. If it persists, and the woman is over 30 years, it should be evaluated with mammography, followed by clinical and pathologic evaluation described below for solid breast masses in the woman over 50 years. Clinically suspicious masses should be immediately referred for mammography and definitive tissue diagnosis. If the woman is under 30 years, ultrasonography to definitively rule out a cyst as a cause of the mass may be the test of first choice.

Evaluation of a New Palpable Mass in a Woman Aged 50 Years or Older

The risk of breast carcinoma increases with age. Generally, the older woman's breasts are less glandular, and nodularity is not as common. Thus, the clinician needs to be particularly suspicious of a dominant mass or asymmetric thickening in the breast of an older woman. An approach to the work-up of a new palpable mass in a woman aged 50 years or older is summarized in Figure 22–2.

Because of the widespread use of hormone replacement therapy, cysts are now not uncommonly found in the breasts of older women. If a mass is clinically cystic, and the woman has had normal results on a mammogram within the past 6 months, it can be evaluated with FNA as described for women under the age of 50 years.

If the mass is clinically cystic and the woman's last mammogram was more than 6 months prior, or if the mass is clinically solid, diagnostic mammography is the first-line investigation. Diagnostic mammography includes an additional view of the abnormal breast to better define any radiologic abnormalities. Ultrasonography also may be useful to better define the mass and to assess if it is cystic or solid.

If the results on the mammogram are normal (category 1) and do not reveal a mass at the palpable site, FNA should be performed, and evaluation by a physician who is knowledgeable and skilled in the diagnosis of breast cancer should be obtained. Unless the results of the FNA are definitely benign, excisional biopsy should be performed.

If the mammogram reveals a radiographically benign lesion at the same location as the palpable mass (category 2), and there are no other suspicious clinical findings, CBE should be repeated in 3 months.[5] If the mass persists or enlarges, further evaluation is warranted. Lesions that are shown to be cysts should then be evaluated and treated as described for women under age 50 years. All other lesions require excisional biopsy.

If the mammogram reveals any other findings (probably benign—category 3; suspicious abnormality—category 4; or suggestive of malignancy—category 5), referral for definitive tissue diagnosis is indicated. It may be obtained through the use of FNA, or core or excisional biopsy, depending on the clinical situation.

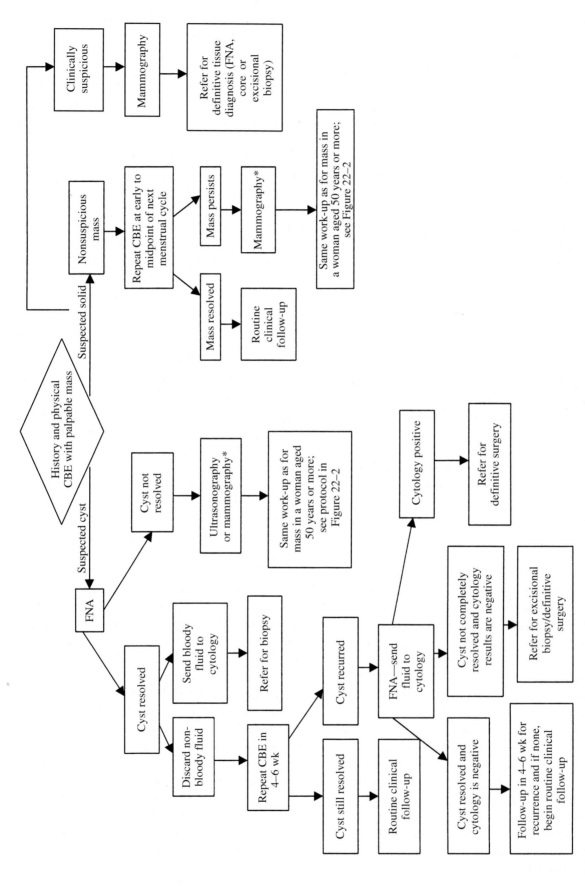

FIGURE 22–1. Work-up of a new palpable breast mass in a woman under age 50 years. *Consider ultrasonography as a first test if the patient is less than 30 years old. CBE = clinical breast examination; FNA = fine-needle aspiration. Adapted from California Department of Health Services, Cancer Detection Section. Work-up of a new palpable breast mass in a premenopausal woman age 30–50.

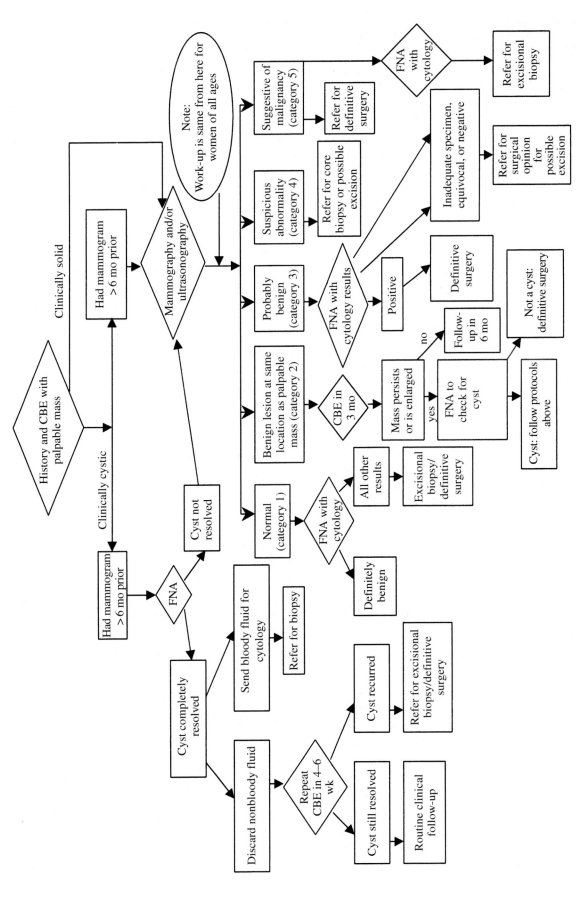

FIGURE 22–2. Work-up of a new palpable breast mass in a woman aged 50 years or older. CBE = clinical breast examination; FNA = fine-needle aspiration. Adapted from California Department of Health Services, Cancer Detection Section. Work-up of a new palpable breast mass in a premenopausal woman.

TABLE 22–1. Breast Imaging Reporting and Data Systems (BI-RADS) Classifications

Category	Description
0	Needs additional imaging evaluation
1	Negative
2	Benign finding with no mammographic evidence of malignancy
3	Probably benign finding—short-interval follow-up suggested
4	Suspicious abnormality—biopsy should be considered
5	Highly suggestive of malignancy—appropriate action should be taken

Adapted from American College of Radiology. Breast Imaging Reporting and Data Systems (BI-RADS™). 2nd ed. Reston (VA): ACR; 1995.

CLINICALLY OCCULT LESIONS

Mammographic reporting in the United States now has been standardized. All mammograms are reported using the Breast Imaging Reporting and Data Systems (BI-RADS) categories developed by the American College of Radiology. This system places all mammograms into one of six categories, as shown in Table 22–1.[10]

In a screening setting, an indeterminate or incomplete assessment (category 0) is sometimes reported. Immediate assessment with additional imaging is always required in this situation to determine the appropriate final category of the mammogram. Routine clinical follow-up is appropriate for patients with normal CBEs whose mammograms are classified as category 1 or 2. Patients whose mammograms are classified into category 3, 4, or 5 always require further evaluation, even when the mammographic findings are not associated with a palpable mass or other clinical breast abnormality.[10]

Ideally, further assessment of a CBE- and/or screening mammography-detected abnormality should be performed by a multidisciplinary team, including a skilled radiologic technologist, radiologist, surgeon, and pathologist. In some settings this cannot be accomplished practically within a single clinic; however, a coordinated evaluation can and should be achieved through a cooperative effort between the woman's primary clinician and these specialists.

A category 3 lesion indicates a lesion that the radiologist feels is probably benign. Generally, this lesion requires clinical evaluation at the time of mammography by a physician or surgeon experienced in breast disease, and again within 6 months as recommended by the radiologist and/or surgeon. Some of these cases are biopsied or excised, depending on the recommendations of the breast specialist and the preferences of the woman.[10]

A category 4 lesion is suspicious, and biopsy is recommended. Initial evaluation of the abnormality can often be accomplished by performance of a stereotactic core biopsy. Clinical decision making based on core biopsy results is summarized in Figure 22–3. Negative/benign findings should be interpreted cautiously, and excisional biopsy performed if results are inadequate, unclear, or discordant. Should a benign lesion be definitively diagnosed at core biopsy, however, and results are consistent with the radiologic findings, excisional biopsy may not be required. The decision to forgo excisional biopsy when core biopsy does not reveal a malignancy should only be made by an experienced assessment team.[10] Similarly, a category 5 lesion (highly suspicious of malignancy) demands tissue diagnosis. The methods of biopsy include stereotactic core biopsy and excisional biopsy after needle localization.[10] All clinically occult mammographic lesions undergoing excision must be confirmed to be completely excised by specimen radiology.

An algorithm for the approach to the clinically occult breast lesion is presented in Figure 22–4.

BREAST PAIN

Breast pain (mastalgia) is a common symptom. It is usually mild and cyclic, in phase with the menstrual cycle. The history must ascertain whether the pain has a cyclic pattern, and the physical examination should be used to determine whether there are physical signs present that require investigation on their own merit. Pain alone, without other symptoms or physical signs classic for cancer, is rarely associated with cancer, and, therefore, one must use

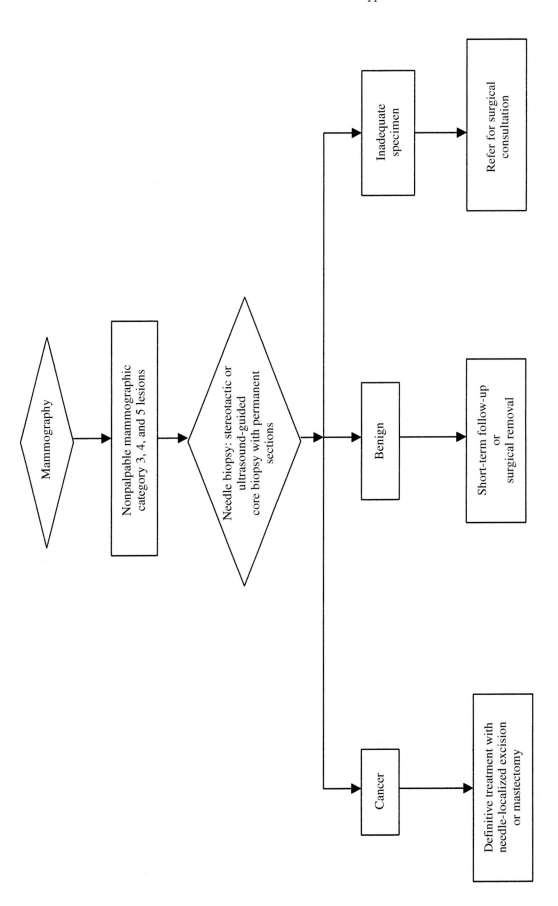

FIGURE 22–3. Stereotactic ultrasound-guided core biopsies of nonpalpable breast lesions. Adapted from California Department of Health Services, Cancer Detection Section. Stereotactic ultrasound guided core biopsies of nonpalpable breast lesions.

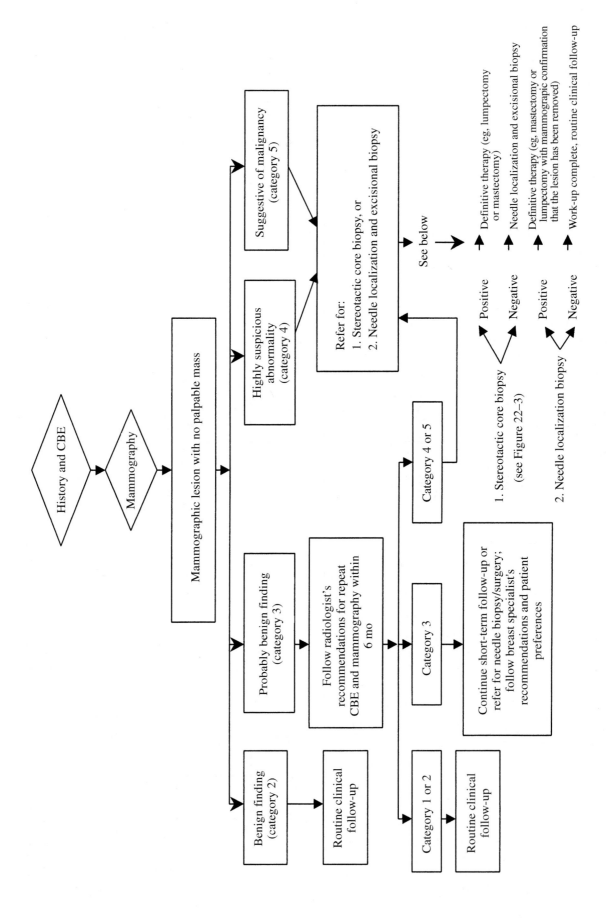

FIGURE 22–4. Work-up of new mammographic lesion that is clinically occult. CBE = clinical breast examination. Adapted from California Department of Health Services, Cancer Detection Section. Work-up of new mammographic lesion that is clinically occult.

clinical judgment before proceeding with mammography. Noncyclic pain initially is investigated with a bilateral mammography, but cyclic pain in the absence of other findings generally can be managed conservatively.

Interventions for mastalgia include birth control pills, danazol, a low-fat diet, and decrease of caffeine intake. Recently, homeopathic remedies such as oil of primrose, Chinese herbs, and acupuncture have been used with some success.[11]

Costochondritis also may present as breast pain. Thrombophlebitis of the thoracoepigastic vein (Mondor's disease) can manifest like a cord drawing in from the breast down the abdomen.[11] Measures such as the use of nonsteroidal anti-inflammatory drugs and ice packs usually are effective in relieving symptoms in these cases.

BREAST SKIN CHANGES, NIPPLE RETRACTION, AND MASTITIS

A thorough history and examination are fundamental in the appropriate assessment of the patient with skin changes in the breast such as scaling or nipple retraction. Timing of onset is of paramount importance; long-standing (for many years) nipple inversion is insignificant but recent, even slight, nipple retraction has serious implications. A change that is bilateral generally can be disregarded, but unilateral symptoms are worrisome.

Skin changes that may signify carcinoma include redness, skin retraction, and nipple excoriation or crustiness. Asymmetry of the breasts and previous biopsy scars also should be noted, and other signs, such as a mass, must be sought and managed appropriately. The differential diagnosis may include eczema and fungal infection, which are described in Chapter 52, "Common Skin Diseases." Often, the findings are most consistent with a bacterial skin infection. In these cases, patients may be treated empirically with cephalexin 250 to 500 mg qid for 10 days; if the skin changes are unresponsive, inflammatory carcinoma must be excluded by further work-up.

Bilateral mammography is the first-line investigation in the above situation, but negative results on the mammogram must not preclude surgical referral. A woman with any suggestive skin lesion in the nipple area that has not resolved after 2 weeks of conservative measures, such as steroid creams, observation, antibiotics, and/or warm compresses, should be considered to have breast cancer until proven otherwise.[12] The woman should be referred to a breast specialist. Punch biopsy is usually performed in this situation. An algorithm for the work-up of breast skin changes is presented in Figure 22–5.

Mastitis occurs in lactating women when milk-producing ducts become blocked. It often presents with skin changes including erythema and swelling. It also is characterized by increased temperature of the breast, firmness, and sometimes a palpable mass. It is treated by frequent breast-feeding or pumping, usually in conjuction with an antibiotic active against *Staphylococcus aureus,* such as dicloxacillin 500 mg qid or clindamycin 300 mg qid.[13] Stopping breast-feeding is not necessary. Ice packs can help the pain, but they decrease milk flow. Heat encourages milk flow but does not help the pain. If an abscess is present, discontinuation of nursing and surgical drainage should be considered.[13] If a patient with suspected mastitis is not improving, ultrasonography and/or mammography and biopsy may be necessary to investigate for breast cancer.

NIPPLE DISCHARGE

Approximately 3% of breast cancers present as nipple discharge.[14] Discharge that is spontaneous, bloody, or unilateral is particularly worrisome. However, nipple discharge is usually caused by a benign breast condition. Historic evaluation should include a thorough review of medications. Birth control pills, sedatives, and tranquilizers are common causes of medication-induced nipple discharge. Any associated breast skin changes or breast masses should be evaluated completely. Patients with bilateral nipple discharge should have a serum prolactin checked to exclude hyperprolactinemia.

Structural etiologies include intraductal papilloma, duct ectasia, fibrocystic changes, and carcinoma.[15] One of the most common causes of nipple discharge is an intraductal papilloma, which is a wart-like growth projecting from the breast duct near the nipple. Intraductal papillomas associated with discharge are usually single intraductal papillomas in woman nearing menopause. However, multiple intraductal papillomas usually present as a lump in younger women and, thus, need to be removed. If the discharge becomes extremely uncomfortable and

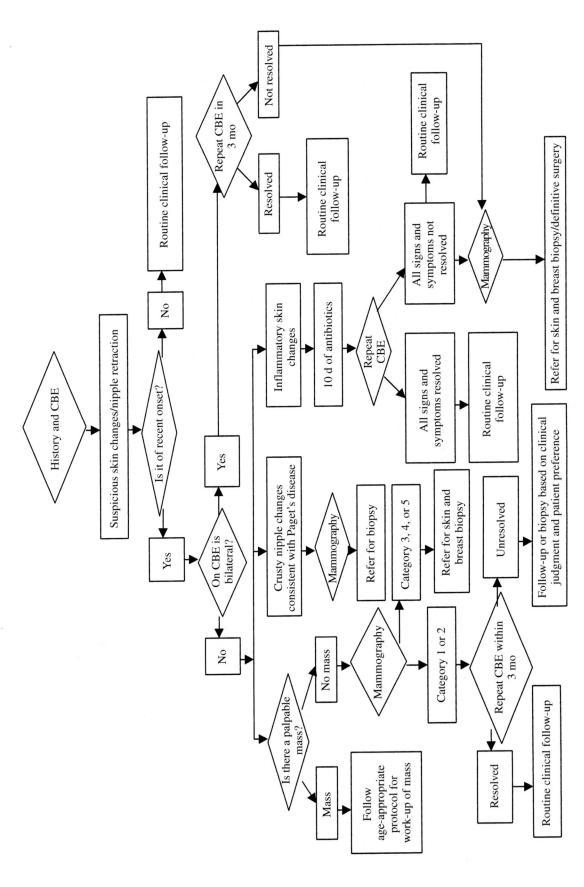

FIGURE 22–5. Work-up of breast skin changes/nipple retraction. CBE = clinical breast examination. Note: Clinical findings suggesting Paget's disease: edema of one breast; nipple deviation/asymmetry; nipple retraction; skin dimpling (peau d'orange). Adapted from California Department of Health Services, Cancer Detection Section. Work-up of breast skin changes/nipple retraction.

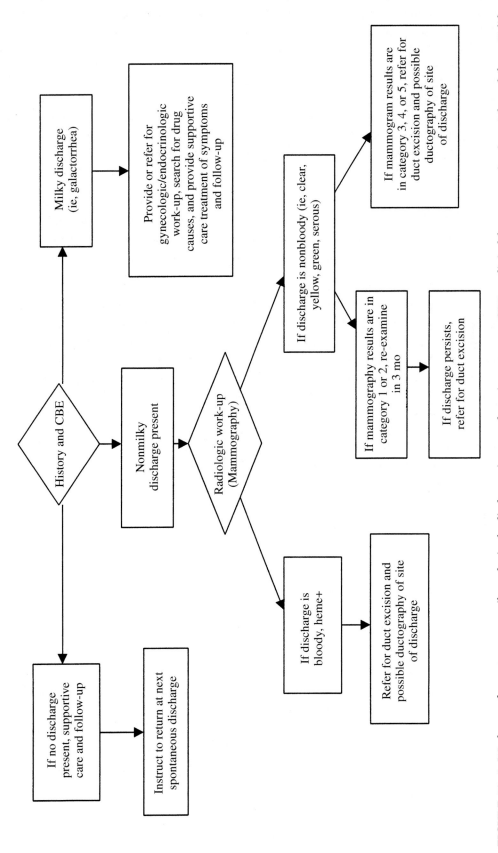

FIGURE 22-6. Work-up of spontaneous unilateral nipple discharge in a nonlactating woman. CBE = clinical breast examination. Adapted from California Department of Health Services, Cancer Detection Section. Work-up of spontaneous unilateral nipple discharge in a nonlactating woman.

an intraductal papilloma is present, the patient usually is given the option of having the duct removed. This type of surgery usually does not result in any substantial cosmetic change in appearance in the breast, but it may require an incision, which could result in numbness of the region.[15] Duct ectasia is a narrowing or blockage of the duct, that occurs most frequently in the peri- and postmenopausal period.

An approach to the evaluation of spontaneous unilateral nipple discharge is summarized in Figure 22–6.

REFERENCES

1. U.S. Preventive Services Task Force. Guide to clinical preventive services. 2nd ed. Baltimore: Williams & Wilkins; 1996.

2. Scott EB. Fibrocystic breast disease. Am Fam Physician 1987;36:119–26.

3. Vorherr H. Fibrocystic breast disease: pathophysiology, pathomorphology, clinical picture, and management. Am J Obstet Gynecol 1986;(154)1:161–79.

4. Hughes LE, Mansel RE, Webster DJT, et al. Benign disorders and diseases of the breast: concepts and clinical management. London: Bailliere Tindall; 1989.

5. Donegan WL. Evaluation of a palpable breast mass. N Engl J Med 1992;327:937–42.

6. Guiliano AE. Breast. In: Tierney LM Jr, McPhee SJ, Papadakis MA, editors. Current medical diagnosis and treatment 1995. 34th ed. Norwalk (CT): Appleton and Lange; 1995. p. 593–616.

7. Winchester DP. Evaluation and management of breast abnormalities. Cancer 1990;66 Suppl:1345–47.

8. Spratt JS, Spratt SW. Medical and legal implications of screening and follow-up procedures for breast cancer. Cancer 1990;66 Suppl:1351–62.

9. O'Grady LF, Lindfors KK, Howell LP, et al. The palpable breast mass. In: O'Grady LF, et al, editors. A practical approach to breast disease. Boston: Little, Brown; 1995. p. 107–18.

10. American College of Radiology. Breast Imaging Reporting and Data Systems (BI-RADS™). 2nd ed. Reston (VA): ACR; 1995.

11. Love SM, Linsey K. Dr. Susan Love's breast book. 2nd ed. Menlo Park: Addison-Wesley Pub. Co.; 1995.

12. Haagensen CD. Diseases of the breast. 3rd ed. Philadelphia: WB Saunders; 1986.

13. Gilbert DN, Moellering RC, Sande MA. The Sanford guide to antimicrobial therapy 1999. Hyde Park (VT): Antimicrobial Therapy, Inc.; 1999.

14. Lippman ME, Lichter AS, Danforth D. Diagnosis and management of breast disease. Philadelphia: WB Saunders; 1988. p. 65–9.

15. Osuch JR. Abnormalities on physical examination. In: Harris JR, Lippman ME, Morrow M, et al, editors. Diseases of the breast. Philadelphia: Lippincott-Raven; 1996. p. 110–4.

23

BREAST CANCER

Linnea I. Chap, MD

Breast cancer is the most common malignancy in American women and the second leading cause of cancer death (lung cancer being the first). In 1998 approximately 180,000 women were diagnosed with breast cancer and 43,500 died from the disease. The mortality rate for breast cancer has remained stable for several decades but recently appears to be taking a downward trend.

RISK FACTORS

The layperson frequently is surprised to learn that at least 70% of patients diagnosed with breast cancer have no identifiable risk factor. Unfortunately, a woman may mischaracterize herself at being "low risk" for breast cancer and delay mammographic screening or appropriate clinical evaluation. The primary risk factor for breast cancer is being of female gender. Additionally, the lifetime risk of breast cancer, which occurs in approximately 1 of 8 to 9 women, gradually increases with age. Greater than 50% of this risk occurs after age 65 years. Aside from age and gender, the other risk factors associated with breast cancer are listed below.

Personal History

A prior history of breast cancer increases a woman's risk for developing contralateral disease. The risk is slightly higher for patients with a diagnosis of infiltrating lobular breast cancer, and in a large cohort of patients was found to be 0.7% per patient-year of follow-up.[1] Benign breast disease, such as that labeled "fibrocystic breast disease" does not represent an increased risk for developing breast cancer. An exception is the category of atypical hyperplasia. In the Nurses' Health Study,[2] a prior biopsy of atypical ductal hyperplasia or atypical lobular hyperplasia was associated with an odds ratio of 2.4

and 5.3, respectively, for the future development of breast cancer.

Familial and Genetic Factors

A family history of breast cancer may significantly increase one's risk for breast cancer. The risk is highest if the affected person is a first-degree relative with bilateral premenopausal disease (risk is approximately 0.5).[3] However, given the high prevalence of breast cancer, one must not misconstrue a family with ≥ 1 cases of breast cancer as necessarily having a genetic predisposition. Therefore, it is important to do a family pedigree and to give equal weight to the paternal history.

Five to ten percent of patients with breast cancer have a pedigree consistent with hereditary disease. The majority of these patients are found to have mutation of either BRCA1 (*Breast Cancer*) and/or −2.[4] Both of these genes have been isolated, and each appears to encode for a tumor suppressor gene. The prevalence of these genetic mutations is quite high in certain subpopulations, such as Ashkenazi Jews in which 1 in 44 is found to have either mutation.[5] Both of these genetic abnormalities also are associated with an increased risk for ovarian cancer and an earlier age of onset of breast cancer. Additionally, BRCA2-linked breast cancer families appear to have an increased frequency of male breast cancer.[4] Although early epidemiologic data reported the risk of breast cancer with these genetic mutations to be $\geq 85\%$ by age 80 years,[6] in the Washington DC Area Ashkenazi Study, Ashkenazi women with either the BRCA1 or BRCA2 mutation had a 56% chance of developing breast cancer and a 16% chance of developing ovarian cancer by age 70 years.[7] Variable gene penetrance may partly explain this variation in risk. Overall, it appears that mutation of either of the BRCA genes results in a 40 to

85% risk of developing breast cancer. These high-risk families should be considered for aggressive screening, prevention trials, and possible prophylactic surgery.

Mutation of the p53 tumor suppressor gene is associated with the Li-Fraumeni syndrome, in which individuals are at an increased risk for breast cancer, soft tissue sarcomas, brain tumors, leukemia, and adrenal cortical tumors.

Genetic testing for cancer is discussed in further detail in Chapter 13.

Hormonal Factors

ENDOGENOUS FACTORS

Both early menarche and late menopause have been associated with an increased risk for breast cancer, which may relate to the number of years of endogenous estrogen exposure. Nulligravity and first pregnancy after the age of 30 years also increases an individual's risk, as may an early therapeutic or spontaneous abortion.

EXOGENOUS FACTORS

The data regarding oral contraceptive (OC) use and breast cancer risk is controversial, but OC use does not appear to increase the risk of breast cancer in most women.[8] Some studies have suggested that breast cancer risk may be increased in women who have used OC for extended periods and/or prior to a first full-term pregnancy. However, in reviewing the prospective data available from the U.S. Nurses' Health Study cohort,[9] these relationships were not observed (although data was limited to women over 40 years of age). Recent use of OCs (< 2 years) has been reported to have a modest association with breast cancer risk for women aged 35 to 45 years at diagnosis.[10,11]

Hormone replacement therapy (HRT) may affect the incidence of breast cancer in a dose-related fashion. The most recent meta-analysis of 51 studies of 52,705 women with breast cancer demonstrated a 31% increase in breast cancer for long-term HRT users.[12] The Nurses' Health Study[13] demonstrated a comparable elevated risk. Arguably, however, many of the women in these studies were treated with higher doses of estrogen than is currently prescribed. Additionally, in two large case-control studies in postmenopausal women in Los Angeles,[14] combined estrogen-progestin replacement therapy was associated with an approximate 24% increase in risk for

every 5 years of use (OR [odds ratio] = 1.24; 95% CI = 1.07 to 1.45). The risk was substantially lower for estrogen replacement alone (OR = 1.06; 95% CI = 0.97 to 1.15). The issue of HRT and breast cancer risk is being addressed by the Women's Health Initiative in a multicenter randomized trial comparing HRT with placebo in 27,500 postmenopausal women.[15]

In regard to lactation, it remains controversial as to whether it provides benefit; its effect probably relates to the length of associated amenorrhea.

Environmental Factors

DIET

Epidemiologic data suggests the importance of dietary factors in the etiology of breast cancer. For example, native Japanese women have a low risk of breast cancer until they move to the United States, when their risk increases. Dietary factors such as high soy consumption and low fat intake in Japan have been speculated as protective factors. However, thus far the data, such as that from the Nurses' Health Study, does not support a role for fat intake as a risk factor in adults. Ongoing studies are examining further the role of fat in adult women, but it may be that dietary fat intake is most carcinogenic during puberty rather than during adulthood. A reduced risk of breast cancer has been associated with high soy consumption in native Asians[16] and is supported by laboratory data.[17] The risk of breast cancer also appears to be increased with obesity.

Epidemiologic data generally has supported a positive association between breast cancer risk and alcohol intake, particularly an intake of ≥ two drinks per day.[18] In an update of the original Framingham Study, however, light alcohol consumption was not associated with an increased risk.[19]

Environment

Radiation, particularly when administered close to the time of puberty, is associated with an increased risk of breast cancer. Examples include women who receive radiation therapy for chest acne, or Hodgkin's disease.

Summary

Although several risk factors have been linked to an increased risk of breast cancer, it remains difficult to assess an individual's risk for developing breast cancer. One model for the prediction of breast cancer risk is the Gail Model.[20] This model is good for predicting breast cancer risk in women over 50 years, and it incorporates age, age at birth of first child, family history, age at menarche, and number of prior breast biopsies (and if atypia is noted). See resource section at the end of this chapter.)

PRESENTING SIGNS AND SYMPTOMS

Breast cancer may present clinically as a hard dominant mass or as a more subtle finding such as an area of asymmetric thickening, nipple retraction, or bloody nipple discharge. With the increasing use of screening mammography, however, the disease is now more frequently diagnosed while subclinical. Inflammatory breast cancer may mimic mastitis in the patient presenting with erythema ± peau d'orange dimpling of the skin. It is not infrequent for oncologists to see these patients only after multiple trials of antibiotics have failed. An important breast cancer misconception is "she is too young to have breast cancer." Although it is extremely rare prior to the age of 20 years, patients in their twenties can be diagnosed with this disease.

DIAGNOSIS

Chapter 22, "Approach to the Patient with Breast Problems," outlines the appropriate evaluation for both palpable and nonpalpable (ie, abnormal results on a mammogram) breast abnormalities. Generally speaking, core biopsy is both more sensitive and specific than is fine-needle aspiration (FNA). Although a FNA is relatively easy to perform, it must be done by a skilled cytopathologist, and it cannot distinguish invasive from noninvasive carcinoma. A core biopsy offers the advantage of providing tissue for biologic assays and surgical treatment planning (eg, whether to proceed with an axillary lymph node dissection at the time of the wide excisional surgery). A wide excisional biopsy (ie, lumpectomy) involves removal of the entire abnormality. Another important misconception is "she doesn't have cancer, the mammography results are normal." A palpable mass warrants follow-up.

PATHOLOGY

Carcinoma In Situ

Ductal carcinoma in situ (DCIS) is a noninvasive breast lesion that may become invasive in approximately 25 to 30% of untreated cases. It is detected most frequently by abnormal-appearing microcalcifications on a mammogram. The treatment consists of wide excision (usually followed by radiation) or mastectomy. Breast conservation usually is feasible unless the disease is widespread. Lobular carcinoma in situ (LCIS), in contrast to DCIS, does not appear to be a preinvasive disease. Instead, it is a marker for increased breast cancer risk and usually is managed with close follow-up or consideration for prophylactic surgery.

Infiltrating and Invasive Cancer

Infiltrating ductal cancer is the most common histologic subtype of breast cancer (~ 78% of occurrences), followed by infiltrating lobular cancer. A particularly high-grade subtype is inflammatory breast cancer (IBC). As described above, the breast is often erythematous and swollen due to tumor invasion of dermal lymphatics. Inflammatory breast cancer has a particularly high local as well as distant recurrence rate. Subtypes of favorable histology include classic medullary, tubular, and mucinous cancers. Paget's disease involves the nipple, which appears excoriated.

TREATMENT

The treatment of newly diagnosed breast cancer focuses on (1) local treatment, to minimize local recurrence via surgery ± radiation; and (2) systemic treatment, to minimize the chance of systemic (distant) recurrence.

Local Treatment

Several large studies have confirmed breast conservation (ie, lumpectomy) followed by radiation therapy (RT) to provide equivalent survival to that of a modified radical mastectomy. General contraindications to breast conservation are widespread disease in the breast and/or disease involving more than one quadrant, prior radiation to the breast or chest wall, and pre-existing connective tissue disease.

Traditionally, the surgical treatment of breast cancer has included a formal level I/II axillary lymph node dissection (ALND) to allow for pathologic assessment of axillary nodes. A relatively new alternative to a formal ALND, in selected patients, is a sentinel lymph node biopsy (SLNB). In simple terms, with SLNB, a blue dye ± a radioactive colloid is injected in the near vicinity of the primary tumor. The surgeon then removes the SLN, which has blue dye ± radioactive colloid uptake. In experienced hands a pathologically negative SLN predicts a negative formal ALND in 95% of patients. Thus, the procedure may spare some patients the morbidity of a formal ALND, which includes pain, decreased shoulder mobility, and lymphedema. Relative contraindications to SLNB are a large tumor (eg, > 3 cm) or a large hematoma/seroma in the breast.

Postmastectomy radiation is indicated for patients with tumors > 5 cm and/or ≥ 4 involved axillary lymph nodes. Although two recent randomized trials[21,22] suggest a survival advantage with postmastectomy RT in all lymph-node positive premenopausal patients, it remains controversial for patients with 1 to 3 involved lymph nodes. Radiation generally is done daily (except on Saturdays and Sundays) over a 6-week period.

Prognosis

Multiple pathologic and biologic factors aid the oncologist in estimating a woman's risk for distant systemic recurrence. Most important is the status and extent of axillary lymph node involvement. Women with lymph node involvement have a 50 to 60% long-term risk of relapse. Generally, all of these patients are offered systemic treatment if there are no significant comorbid conditions. Women without lymph node involvement have a 24 to 30% risk for systemic recurrence. In these patients tumor size is the most important prognostic feature. Tumors measuring < 1 cm reflect an 8 to 10% systemic recurrence rate versus a rate of 30% for a 2.5 to 3.0-cm tumor. Generally, patients with tumors of ≤ 5 mm are not offered systemic therapy, whereas most patients with tumors > 1 cm are appropriate candidates for systemic therapy. For patients with tumors of 0.6 to 1.0 cm and one or more unfavorable prognosis factors, adjuvant therapy should be considered. These factors include high histologic grade, hormone-receptor negativity, angiolymphatic invasion, and a high fraction of cycling cells. Her-2/neu overexpression also is considered by some to be an unfavorable feature in this group. The her-2/neu oncogene encodes a transmembrane growth factor receptor. It is overexpressed in 25 to 30% of breast tumors, and is associated with a worse prognosis.

Systemic Treatment

The Early Breast Cancer Trialists' (EBCT) Collaborative Group overview[23,24] analyses of adjuvant polychemotherapy and tamoxifen demonstrates approximately a ≥ 30% reduction in the odds of recurrence and death in all age groups of breast cancer patients under 70 years.

Because systemic adjuvant treatment involves significant risks and variable benefits, patient participation in the treatment decision process is important. Most medical oncologists offer chemotherapy to patients with lymph node–negative disease, tumors > 1 cm, and hormone-receptor-negative tumors. Patients with hormone-receptor-positive tumors usually are offered tamoxifen, and the addition of chemotherapy often is favored for tumors ≥ 2.0 cm, tumors 1 to 2.0 cm with ≥ 1 unfavorable prognostic feature(s), or lymph node involvement.

Chemotherapy Selection

In women without lymph node involvement, appropriate regimens include CMF (cyclophosphamide, methotrexate, and 5-fluorouracil), FAC/CAF (5-fluorouracil, doxorubicin, and cyclophosphamide), or AC (doxorubicin and cyclophosphamide). These treatments generally are administered in 21- or 28-day cycles over a 4 to 6-month period. In women with lymph node involvement, a doxorubicin-based regimen is favored, either alone or followed, sequentially, by CMF or paclitaxel (Taxol). In the EBCT overview,[24] anthracycline-containing regimens demonstrated a 12% further reduction in the annual odds of recurrence compared with that of CMF. Additionally, several retrospective reviews have suggested that doxorubicin may be superior to CMF in patients with her-2/neu overexpression.[25,26] For patients at high risk, for example, those with ≥ 10 involved lymph nodes, high-dose chemotherapy remains investigational.

Neoadjuvant Chemotherapy

Patients presenting with locally advanced breast cancer (eg, tumor size ≥ 5.0 cm, fixed lymph nodes, skin invasion, and/or inflammatory breast cancer) generally are treated with preoperative chemotherapy. In a substantial number of patients, significant tumor shrinkage occurs and may even permit breast conservation surgery. Surgery usually follows 4 to 5 chemotherapy treatments; after surgery postoperative chemotherapy and radiation are used.

TIMING OF TREATMENT

The patient diagnosed with breast cancer should not feel "rushed" or "pressured" to make a decision. Most breast tumors have, in all likelihood, been present for a few years at the time of diagnosis. There is time, therefore, for the patient to be educated and to seek out information.

The sequencing of chemotherapy and radiation is dependent on the choice of chemotherapeutic agents. If CMF is used, many oncologists choose to administer radiation concomitantly, whereas others recommend that it be "sandwiched" after 3 months of chemotherapy. Due to skin toxicity with concomitant doxorubicin and radiation, they are done sequentially.

SIDE EFFECTS OF TREATMENT

Although a careful review of chemotherapy's side effects can be daunting, the patient should be reassured that most patients experience few of these side effects. Common side effects include mild to moderate nausea, leukopenia, fatigue, hair loss (~ 99% with doxorubicin versus 10% with CMF), mouth sores, and cardiac toxicity (1 to 3% with doxorubicin).

Pretreatment Tests

Prior to treatment, patients generally undergo blood work, including a complete blood count and a chemistry panel, and a preoperative chest radiography. In general, bone scans and computed tomographic scans are reserved for patients with symptoms, abnormal laboratory results, and/or local advanced disease.

ROLE OF PREVENTION AND SCREENING

Screening: Genetic Testing

Before a patient opts to be tested for the BRCA1 and/ or –2 genetic mutations, it is strongly recommended that she seek genetic counseling. Only a small fraction of breast cancers are related to either of these mutations. Therefore, a negative test does not indicate a risk of zero. A genetic counselor can aid in determining the likelihood of a positive test and, most importantly, help to explore the issues posed by knowledge of a positive test, for example, impact on other family members and the possibility of insurance discrimination. The patient's options

of surgery, chemoprevention, and close surveillance also need to be discussed.

Risk Reduction and Prevention

CHEMOPREVENTION

Chemoprevention is an area of intense research in women at high risk for developing breast cancer. Most notable has been a study of tamoxifen. Based on earlier studies[27,28] that demonstrated a statistically lower risk of contralateral breast cancer in women treated with tamoxifen, in 1992 the National Surgical Adjuvant Breast and Bowel Project (NSABP) initiated a trial with tamoxifen in high-risk women.[29] Eligible women were those greater than 60 years and patients 35 to 59 years old with a 5-year predicted risk of breast cancer > 1.66% or a history of LCIS. A total of 13,388 women were randomized to tamoxifen 20 mg/d or placebo. At a median follow-up of 54.6 months, tamoxifen was found to have lowered the risk of breast cancer by 49% and of noninvasive disease by 50%, across all age groups. There was, however, a small but significant risk for endometrial cancer (2.3 vs 0.91 cases per 1,000 women), thromboembolism (0.69 vs 0.23 cases per 1,000 women), and stroke (1.45 vs 0.92 cases per 1,000 women). Two European studies[30,31] have been published that do not support the NSABP findings. However, both of these studies were much smaller, had fewer breast cancer events, and, amongst other differences, the women had different risks.

Raloxifene is a selective estrogen-receptor modulator (SERM) that has been associated with a reduced incidence of breast cancer in postmenopausal women treated for osteoporosis.[32] As reported with tamoxifen, there was an elevated risk of thromboembolism; there was no association with endometrical cancer. The next NSABP Prevention Trial, P-2, is comparing the toxicities and benefits of tamoxifen with those of raloxifene.

PROPHYLACTIC MASTECTOMY

Prophylactic mastectomy has been an option for women at high risk of developing breast cancer, but there have been relatively minimal data available regarding its long-term efficacy. Concern has focused on the inability to completely remove all of the breast tissue[33] and cases of local recurrence after prophylactic mastectomies. A recent retrospective analysis was published[34] that examined women with a family history of breast cancer who underwent prophylactic surgery at Mayo Clinic between 1960 and 1993. Risk assessment for these women was based on the Gail Model, and the control group was the patients' sisters. Overall, with a median follow-up of 14 years, prophylactic mastectomy was associated with approximately a 90% reduction in the incidence of breast cancer. The authors appropriately point out, however, the importance of individual counseling and risk assessment with patients who are considering this surgery.

BILATERAL OOPHORECTOMY

Researchers recently reported on 43 women who were known carriers of the BRCA1 mutation who underwent bilateral oophorectomy (BO) as a preventative measure. In comparison to appropriately matched controls who had not undergone BO, a statistically significant reduction of invasive breast cancer was demonstrated after 10 years of follow-up.[35] These results need to be confirmed in a larger study.

PREGNANCY

As more women are delaying childbearing into their thirties and forties, gestational breast cancer is seen more frequently. One of the primary problems with this situation is the frequent delay in appropriate work-up and diagnosis. Thus, many of these patients present with relatively advanced disease.[36,37] Breast ultrasonography and needle aspiration should be considered for the evaluation of a persistent breast lump during pregnancy or lactation. Mammography (with shielding of the abdomen) also can be used, particularly when the ultrasonography results are nondiagnostic.[37]

Regarding local treatment, mastectomy generally has been advocated due to the potential harm that radiation may pose to the fetus. However, when diagnosed in the second or third trimester, breast conservation and radiation initiated after delivery can be considered.[38] For systemic therapy, several studies have demonstrated that the use of chemotherapy during the second and third trimesters is generally safe.[38-40] There does not appear to be an elevated risk of fetal malformation, but there may be an increased risk for premature birth, fetal growth restriction, and myelosuppression of the fetus and mother.[40] The chemotherapy most frequently used is CAF.[39] Methotrexate should be avoided due to potential concentration in the amniotic fluid. Treatment with chemotherapy requires close communication between the obstetrician and the oncologist. When

possible, attempts should be made to avoid myelosuppression at the expected time of delivery. Although the data are limited, termination of pregnancy does not appear to improve survival.[36,41]

The literature is controversial regarding whether pregnancy associated breast cancer has a worse outcome. Some data suggest that pregnancy is an independent poor prognostic feature,[42] whereas other data support that lactation but not pregnancy is a poor prognostic feature.[43] Additionally, controversy surrounds the impact of subsequent pregnancy on breast cancer recurrence. Overall, the data do not support that subsequent pregnancy worsens a patient's prognosis,[43,44] even within 2 years of treatment[36] and after adjusting for age at diagnosis, stage of disease, and reproductive history before diagnosis.[45] A possible confounding variable, however, is the exclusion of patients who relapse quickly and are lost to any future risk assessment of pregnancy.

MENOPAUSE

In general, women diagnosed with breast cancer after menopause are more likely to be hormone-receptor positive (a favorable prognostic feature). When other prognostic features are taken into account, however, the prognosis in postmenopausal women does not differ from that in their premenopausal counterparts.

Use of Hormone Replacement Therapy after Breast Cancer

Given the possible association of breast cancer risk with HRT, there is general reluctance on the part of most physicians as well as patients to employ HRT after a diagnosis of breast cancer. Unfortunately, to date, there are no randomized trials to support or refute this reluctance. In 1997 at a Virginia-based conference of international experts,[46] all agreed that nonestrogen therapy should be used to address symptoms and osteoporotic concerns before the use of estrogen therapy is considered. The patient with severe continued problems of estrogen deficiency can consent to take HRT if she has been fully informed of the risks.

REFERENCES

1. Yeatman TJ, Lyman GH, Smith SK, et al. Bilaterality and recurrence rates for lobular breast cancer: considerations for treatment. Ann Surg Oncol 1997; 4:198–202.

2. Marshall LM, Hunter DJ, Connolly JL, et al. Risk of breast cancer associated with atypical hyperplasia of lobular and ductal types. Cancer Epidemiol Biomarkers Prev 1997;6:297–301.

3. Williams WR. In: Harris JR, editor. Breast diseases. Management of the high risk and the concerned patient. Philadelphia: JB Lippincott Co.; 1987. p. 109.

4. Narod SA, Ford D, Devilee P, et al. An evaluation of genetic heterogeneity in 145 breast-ovarian cancer families. Breast Cancer Linkage Consortium. Am J Hum Genet 1995;56:254–64.

5. Roa BB, Boyd AA, Volcik K, Richards CS. Ashkenazi Jewish population frequencies for common mutations in BRCA1 and BRCA2. Nat Genet 1996; 14:185–7.

6. Easton DF, Bishop DT, Ford D, Crockford GP. Genetic linkage analysis in familial breast and ovarian cancer: results from 214 families. Breast Cancer Linkage Consortium. Am J Hum Genet 1993;52:678–701.

7. Struewing JP, Hartge P, Wacholder S, et al. The risk of cancer associated with specific mutations of BRCA1 and BRCA2 among Ashkenazi Jews. N Engl J Med 1997;336:1401–8.

8. Lebow MA. The pill and the press: reporting risk. Obstet Gynecol 1999;93:453–6.

9. Hankinson SE, Colditz GA, Manson JE, et al. A prospective study of oral contraceptive use and risk of breast cancer (Nurses' Health Study, United States). Cancer Causes Control 1997;8:65–72.

10. Newcomb PA, Longnecker MP, Storer BE, et al. Recent oral contraceptive use and risk of breast cancer. Cancer Causes Control 1996;7:525–32.

11. Ursin G, Ross RK, Sullivan-Halley J, et al. Use of oral contraceptives and risk of breast cancer in young women. Breast Cancer Res Treat 1998;50:175–84.

12. Collaborative Group on Hormone Factors in Breast Cancer. Breast cancer and hormone replacement therapy: collaborative reanalysis of data from 51 epidemiological studies of 52,705 women with breast cancer and 108,411 women without breast cancer. Lancet 1997;350:1047–59.

13. Grodstein F, Stamfer MJ, Colditz GA, et al. The use of estrogen and progestins and the risk of breast cancer in postmenopausal women. N Engl J Med 1997;336: 1769–75.

14. Ross RK, Paganini-Hill A, Wan PC, et al. Effect of hormone replacement therapy on breast cancer risk: estrogen versus estrogen plus progestin. J Natl Cancer Inst 2000;92:328–32.

15. The Women's Health Initiative Study Group. Design of the Women's Health Initiative Clinical Trial and Oservational Study. Control Clin Trials 1998;19: 61–109.

16. Wu AH, Ziegler RG, Nomura AM, et al. Soy intake and risk of breast cancer in Asians and Asian Americans. Am J Clin Nutr 1998;68(6 Suppl):1437–43S.

17. Barnes S. The chemopreventive properties of soy isoflavonoids in animal models of breast cancer. Breast Cancer Res Treat 1997;46:169–79.

18. Swanson CA, Coates RJ, Malone KE, et al. Alcohol consumption and breast cancer risk among women under age 45 years. Epidemiology 1997;8:231–7.

19. Zhang Y, Kreger BE, Dorgan JF, et al. Alcohol consumption and risk of breast cancer: the Framingham Study revisited. Am J Epidemiol 1999;149:93–101.

20. Gail MH, Brinton DP, Corle DK, et al. Projecting individualized probabilities of developing breast cancer for white females who are being examined annually. J Natl Cancer Inst 1989;81:1879–86.

21. Overgaard M, Hansen PS, Overgaard J, et al. Postoperative radiotherapy in high-risk premenopausal

women with breast cancer who receive adjuvant chemotherapy. N Engl J Med 1997;337:949–955.

22. Ragaz J, Jackson SM, Le N, et al. Adjuvant radiotherapy and chemotherapy in node-positive premenopausal women with breast cancer. N Engl J Med 1997;337:956–62.

23. Early Breast Cancer Trialists' Collaborative Group. Tamoxifen for early breast cancer: an overview of the randomized trials. Lancet 1998;351:1451–67.

24. Early Breast Cancer Trialists' Collaborative Group. Polychemotherapy for early breast cancer: an overview of the randomized trials. Lancet 1998;90:1346–60.

25. Paik S, Bryant J, Park C, et al. Erb B-2 and response to doxorubicin in patients with axillary lymph node positive, hormone receptor-negative breast cancer. J Natl Cancer Inst 1998;90:1361–70.

26. Thor AD, Berry DA, Budman DR, et al. Erb B-2, p53, and efficacy of adjuvant therapy in lymph node—positive breast cancer. J Natl Cancer Inst 1998;90:1346–60.

27. Rutqvist LE, Cedermark B, Glas U, et al. Contralateral primary tumors in breast cancer patients in a randomized trial of adjuvant tamoxifen therapy. J Natl Cancer Inst 1991;83:1299–306.

28. Fisher B, Constantino J, Redmond C, et al. A randomized clinical trial evaluating tamoxifen in the treatment of patients with node-negative breast cancer who have estrogen-receptor tumors. N Engl J Med 1989;320:479–84.

29. Fisher B, Constantino J, Wickerman D, et al. Tamoxifen for prevention of breast cancer: report of the National Surgical Adjuvant Breast and Bowel Project P-1 Study. J Natl Cancer Inst 1998;90:1371–88.

30. Veronesi U, Maisunneuve P, Cost A, et al. Prevention of breast cancer with tamoxifen: preliminary findings from the Italian randomized trial among hysterectomized women. Italian Tamoxifen Prevention Study. Lancet 1998;352:93–7.

31. Powels T, Eeles R, Ashley S, et al. Interim analysis of the incidence of breast cancer in the Royal Marsden Hospital tamoxifen randomized chemoprevention trial. Lancet 1998;352:98–101.

32. Cauley JA, Norton L, Lippman ME, et al. Continued breast cancer risk reduction in postmenopausal women treated with raloxifene: 4-year results from the MORE trial. Multiple outcomes of raloxifene evaluation. Breast Cancer Res Treat 2001;65(2):125–34.

33. Hicken NF. Masectomy: clinical pathologic study demonstrating why most masectomies result in incomplete removal of mammary gland. Arch Surg 1940;40:6–14.

34. Hartman LC, Schaid DJ, Woods JE, et al. Efficacy of bilateral prophylactic mastectomy in women with a family history of breast cancer. N Engl J Med 1999;340:77–84.

35. Rebbeck TR, Levin AM, Eisen A, et al. Breast cancer risk after bilateral prophylactic oophorectomy in BRCA1 mutation carriers. J Natl Cancer Inst 1999;91:1475–9.

36. Sorosky JI, Scott-Conner CE. Breast disease complicating pregnancy. Obstet Gynecol Clin North Am 1998;25:353–63.

37. Samuels TH, Liu FF, Yaffe M, Haider M. Gestational breast cancer. Can Assoc Radiol J 1998;49:172–80.

38. Bernik SF, Bernik TR, Whooley BP, Wallack MK. Carcinoma of the breast during pregnancy: a review and update on treatment options. Surg Oncol 1998;7(1–2):45–9.

39. Berry DL, Theriault RL, Holmes FA, et al. Management of breast cancer during pregnancy using a standarized protocol. J Clin Oncol 1999;17:855–61.

40. Buekers TE, Lallas TA. Chemotherapy in pregnancy. Obstet Gynecol Clin North Am 1998;25:323–9.

41. Espie M, Cuvier C. Treating breast cancer during pregnancy: what can be taken safely? Drug Saf 1998;18:135–42.

42. Bonnier P, Romain S, Dilhuydy JM, et al. Influence of pregnancy on the outcome of breast cancer: a case-control study. Société Française de Sénologie et de Pathologie Mammaire Study Group. Int J Cancer 1997;72:720–7.

43. Lethaby AE, O'Neil MA, Mason BH, et al. Overall survival from breast cancer in women pregnant or lactating at or after diagnosis. Auckland Breast Cancer Study Group. Int J Cancer 1996;67:751–5.

44. Von Schoultz E, Johansson H, Wilking N, Rutqvist LE. Influence of prior and subsequent pregnancy on breast cancer prognosis. J Clin Oncol 1995;13:430–4.

45. Kroman N, Jensen MB, Melbye M, et al. Should women be advised against pregnancy after breast-cancer treatment? Lancet 1997;350:319–22.

46. Swain S, Santen R, Burser H, Pritchard K, editors. Executive Summary and Consensus Statement. Treatment of estrogen deficiency symptoms in women surviving breast cancer. Oncology 1999 June.

24

PRIMARY CARE OF THE BREAST CANCER SURVIVOR

Janet P. Pregler, MD

In the United States, approximately 180,000 women per year are diagnosed with breast cancer. The majority of these women are cured of their disease. Emphasis on screening is believed to be the cause of a recent increase in breast cancer cases with a tumor diameter < 2 cm and negative axillary nodes. Women diagnosed with early-stage breast cancer have over 90% 10-year survival.[1]

These statistics have important implications for the care of women diagnosed with early-stage breast cancer. Because they are very likely to survive and develop other medical problems, most will require care from generalist clinicians and/or specialists other than oncologists. Primary prevention of other diseases, such as heart disease and osteoporosis, is an important issue for the majority of women diagnosed with breast cancer. Women's health clinicians have an important role to play in ensuring medically appropriate and coordinated care for breast cancer survivors.

SURVEILLANCE FOR LOCAL RECURRENCE, SECOND PRIMARY CANCERS, AND METASTATIC DISEASE

Breast cancer survivors are at risk for local recurrence. Local recurrences are potentially curable. All breast cancer survivors should have frequent physical examinations of the operated and non-operated breasts. Mammography of mastectomy sites has been shown not to increase detection of locally recurrent breast cancer.[2] However, mammography of a "preserved" breast (after lumpectomy) does increase detection of locally recurrent potentially

curable cancer.[3] Women with a history of breast cancer are at high risk for a second primary breast cancer. They should undergo yearly clinical breast examination and mammography of the contralateral breast.

Prior to the end of the 1980s, most experts believed that following up breast cancer survivors with a battery of laboratory tests to detect metastasis in an asymptomatic stage improved survival. By the 1990s retrospective studies suggested that survival might not be improved by initiating treatment in asymptomatic women whose metastatic disease was detectable only by laboratory testing.[4,5] In 1994 the results of two large randomized controlled trials evaluating follow-up schemes for breast cancer survivors were published. The Gruppo Italiano Valotazione Interventi in Oncologia (GIVIO) investigators randomized over 1,300 women to two follow-up protocols. Both the control group and an intensive intervention group underwent periodic history and physical examination and yearly mammography. The intensive group additionally underwent laboratory testing consisting of measurement of γ-glutamyltransferase, liver ultrasonography, chest radiography, measurement of alkaline phosphatase, and bone scanning. Both symptomatic and asymptomatic recurrences were treated with standard regimens as soon as they were identified. At a median 5-year follow-up, there was no difference in overall survival.[6] A similar trial by Del Turco and colleagues, which randomized over 1,200 women, also showed identical survival between control and intensive monitoring groups over a 10-year period.[7,8] Some clinicians had suggested that although intensive fol-

TABLE 24–1. Recommended Follow-Up for Asymptomatic Early-Stage Breast Cancer Survivors

	American Society of Clinical Oncology	*Canadian Medical Association*
Frequency of history/physical examination	3–6 mo for 3 yr, then 6–12 mo for 2 yr, then annually*	4–6 wk after completion of therapy, 4–6 mo after completion of therapy, then annually†
Counseling	Breast self-examination, symptoms of recurrence	Breast self-examination, symptoms of recurrence, psychosocial support, participation in clinical trials
Mammography	6 mo after breast-conserving therapy if applicable, then annually	Annually
Complete blood count	Not recommended	Not recommended
Liver chemistries, albumin, calcium	Not recommended	Not recommended
Bone scan	Not recommended	Not recommended
Chest radiography	Not recommended	Not recommended
Tumor markers	Not recommended‡	Not recommended
Liver ultrasonography	Not recommended	Not recommended
Computed tomographic scans	Not recommended	Not recommended

*Includes specific recommendation for "pelvic examination at regular intervals," with statement that longer intervals may be appropriate for women who have had TAH/BSO.[10]
†Includes specific recommendation for "physical examination (of) both breasts, regional lymph nodes, chest wall, and abdomen, (as well as) arms…for lymphedema."[11]
‡Specifically, carcinoembryonic antigen, cancer antigen (CA) 15-3, and CA 27-29 are not recommended.[10]
Reproduced with permission from Pregler JP. Primary care of the breast cancer survivor. Fam Pract Recertification 2000;22(5):31–46.

low-up testing had no medical utility, patient satisfaction was improved by frequent laboratory testing. However, in the GIVIO trial, there was no difference between women who received frequent laboratory testing and those who did not on measures of satisfaction with medical care.[6] Routine laboratory testing of asymptomatic breast cancer survivors is no longer recommended (Table 24–1).

It is important to detect symptomatic metastatic disease as soon as possible to provide timely and appropriate palliative therapy. Most recurrences occur within 5 to 10 years after diagnosis, but breast cancer can recur 20 or more years after initial treatment. Seventy-five to 95% of recurrences are detected by patients between visits to the clinician.[9] Patients should be encouraged to report new symptoms such as persistent musculoskeletal pain, cough, breast lumps, mastectomy scar changes, fatigue, and anorexia promptly.[10,11]

TAMOXIFEN

Tamoxifen is by far the most commonly prescribed adjuvant treatment for breast cancer. Because of its frequent use and low toxicity, primary care clinicians often provide the majority of care for women using this drug once the recommendation has been made for adjuvant therapy by the treating oncologist.

Tamoxifen is an estrogen receptor agonist-antagonist. It is classified as a selective estrogen receptor modulator (SERM). Like raloxifene (Evista), it acts like estrogen on some body tissues and as an anti-estrogen at other sites. This explains many of its potential benefits and side effects (Table 24–2).[12,13] Common side effects of tamoxifen include hot flushes, night sweats, vaginal discharge, painful intercourse, and bladder control problems.[14]

Like estrogen and raloxifene, tamoxifen improves the lipid profile, lowering total cholesterol and low-density lipoproteins.[12] Unlike estrogen, it does not raise high-density lipoproteins. The overall effect of tamoxifen on pre-existing heart disease or the development of heart disease is still unclear. In a large study of tamoxifen use for prevention of breast cancer, there appeared to be no cardiac benefit for women using tamoxifen compared with placebo for an average of 4 years.[13]

Several studies have demonstrated that tamoxifen improves bone density and appears to reduce certain types of typical osteoporotic fractures, although this effect does not appear to be as strong as that for agents currently prescribed for the prevention and treatment of osteoporosis.[12,13]

Just as the use of unopposed estrogen increases the risk of endometrial cancer, tamoxifen has also been shown to increase the risk of endometrial cancer.[12,13] The overall incidence of endometrial cancer is still low, less than 2%.[15] Although there has been some interest in combining tamoxifen with progesterone to attempt to lower endometrial cancer risk, the use of oral progesterone with tamoxifen is not currently recommended as concerns exist that the use of progesterone might increase the recurrence risk of breast cancer.[16] All breast cancer survivors on tamoxifen should be instructed to report vaginal bleeding. Vaginal bleeding should be investigated by endometrial biopsy.[10,11]

Tamoxifen also increases the risk of venous thrombosis in a manner similar to estrogen.[12,13] Clinicians should be alert for signs and symptoms of deep venous thrombosis and pulmonary embolism in patients taking tamoxifen. Also, any personal or family history of blood clots should be investigated. Many oncologists would not recommend adjuvant tamoxifen to a woman at increased risk for blood clots, particularly if the woman had a small tumor with a low likelihood of recurrence.

A recent study of the use of tamoxifen for breast cancer prevention showed an increased risk of cataracts and cataract surgery, especially in older tamoxifen users.[13] Because of the ease of treatment of these cataracts, pre-existing cataracts are not considered a contraindication to the use of tamoxifen. However, patients should be instructed to receive regular ophthalmologic checks.

Recommended Length of Treatment

Tamoxifen use to prevent recurrence of breast cancer has been studied extensively in both the United States and Europe. In 1989 the results of a US study of over 2,000 women with node-negative, estrogen receptor–positive tumors showed less recurrence in women who took tamoxifen for 5 years.[17] At that time many clinicians wondered if using tamoxifen for longer periods, or even for life, might prevent even more cancer recurrences. In practice many clinicians were already recommending this. The National Cancer Institute (NCI) supported a study that compared women who took only 5 years of tamoxifen, and then switched to placebo, with women who continued on tamoxifen. To the surprise of many experts, after 9 years, the women who continued on tamoxifen had more breast cancer recurrences than did those who stopped after 5 years. Similar results were suggested by a smaller Scottish study.[18,19]

In 1995 the NCI stopped this study and issued a clinical alert warning that tamoxifen for the adjuvant treatment of breast cancer should not be continued for more than 5 years.[20] The authors of the NCI study postulated that the worst outcomes seen in women who took tamoxifen beyond 5 years might have resulted from the development of tumor resistance or by the tumor being stimulated to grow by the estrogenic properties of the tamoxifen. It had been noted previously that some breast tumors actually grow with the administration of tamoxifen and regress with stopping the drug.[18]

TABLE 24–2. Tamoxifen Therapy

Benefits
  Improved lipid profile
    Decreased low-density lipoproteins
    Decreased total cholesterol
  Increased bone density

Risks
  Endometrial hyperplasia
  Endometrial cancer
  Deep venous thrombosis/pulmonary embolism
  Cataracts

Common side effects
  Hot flushes
  Vaginal dryness/discharge
  Irregular menses

Reproduced with permission from Pregler JP. Primary care of the breast cancer survivor. Fam Pract Recertification 2000; 22(5):31–46.

Others have postulated that, with time, breast cancer cells "switch" from recognizing tamoxifen as an estrogen antagonist to an estrogen agonist and are thus stimulated to grow by it after prolonged use.[21] Currently the standard of practice is to use adjuvant tamoxifen for 5 years and to stop tamoxifen in disease-free breast cancer survivors who have used it for more than 5 years.

COMMON COMPLICATIONS OF BREAST CANCER TREATMENT

Local Complications

Soft tissue swelling, hematomas and seromas, numbness and stiffness of the upper arm, and pain, tingling, or numbness of the surgical site may occur after lumpectomy or mastectomy. Erythema, tenderness, and skin edema are common during radiation therapy.[11] In the case of symptoms in and around the surgical site, the primary care clinician should perform a careful examination to exclude recurrence as an etiology of symptoms, referring the patient for further evaluation as indicated.

Lymphedema

Lymphedema may first occur immediately after surgery or months or even years later. A small amount of swelling postsurgically can be normal and does not necessarily mean that the patient will have chronic lymphedema. Precursors to the development of lymphedema can include infection (cellulitis or lymphangitis), muscle fatigue from overuse of the arm, vasodilation following exposure to local or systemic heat, local trauma, vigorous massage, and prolonged standing and sitting. Airplane flights and stays at higher elevations also can provoke the development of lymphedema because of the effect of decreased atmospheric pressure, increasing filtration from capillaries into the tissues. Lymphedema not infrequently is experienced as pain; patients also may describe heaviness, fullness, or fatigue of the arm.[22]

Evaluation of the initial presentation of lymphedema should include a thorough evaluation of other possible causes of arm swelling, including deep venous thrombosis and recurrent malignancy. No consensus about the treatment of lymphedema exists. Physical therapy and teaching of home exercises for shoulder range of motion and massage for lymphedema treatment are most effective when

initiated as soon as symptoms develop. Elevation of the limb may be of benefit. External compression bandages and garments for treatment of lymphedema should be provided at the first sign of swelling. The use of pneumatic pumps is controversial. Drugs (such as coumarin and diuretics) are not of benefit. Surgical procedures are of questionable efficacy and carry a significant risk of postoperative complications. All patients should be counseled to avoid trauma to the arm, muscle fatigue, and vigorous massage and to report signs and symptoms of infection immediately. Medical procedures on the involved arm, including injections, blood draws, and blood pressure readings, should be avoided whenever possible.[11,22]

Weight Gain

Weight gain is common after treatment for breast cancer and may predispose women to recurrence and second breast cancers, as well as other complications, such as type 2 diabetes.[23,24] Women who undergo adjuvant chemotherapy, as well as those who enter menopause during treatment, are at particular risk. Tamoxifen does not appear to cause weight gain.[14] The reasons for weight gain are probably multifactorial; most breast cancer survivors do not increase caloric intake after breast cancer diagnosis. Changes in metabolic rate and physical activity may play a role.[24] Breast cancer survivors should be counseled about the risk of weight gain with treatment. Nutrition counseling should be provided to breast cancer survivors who gain weight.

Psychosocial Distress

Psychosocial distress is particularly common and persistent in breast cancer survivors who may have had a past history of psychological distress, as well as those with limited social support.[25] Breast cancer survivors should be screened for depression and treated if depression is diagnosed. Recently a randomized controlled trial found that educational groups were effective in improving the perceptions of breast cancer survivors regarding both their physical and mental health. In this study, educational groups presented women with detailed information on topics such as nutrition, exercise, future health care issues, and sexuality.[26] Referral to such programs should be strongly considered for all breast cancer survivors. Aerobic exercise may be of particular benefit in reducing depression and anxiety in breast cancer survivors. A specific recommendation from their clinician to exercise improves compliance.[27]

Menopausal Symptoms

Menopausal symptoms are particularly troubling for many breast cancer survivors. Younger women undergoing chemotherapy may have an abrupt onset of menopause. Older women may develop menopausal symptoms when hormone replacement therapy is discontinued at the time of breast cancer diagnosis.

HORMONAL TREATMENT OF MENOPAUSAL SYMPTOMS IN BREAST CANCER SURVIVORS

Estrogen therapy is the most effective treatment for menopausal symptoms. However, a large body of evidence from epidemiologic and case-control studies has led most US oncologists to advise against its use in breast cancer survivors. Factors that increase women's exposure to estrogen, including early menarche, late menopause, obesity, and the use of hormone replacement therapy, have been associated with increased breast cancer risk. Factors that decrease a woman's exposure to estrogen, such as late menarche, early menopause, and oophorectomy before natural menopause, have been associated with a decreased risk of breast cancer.[28] Tamoxifen, which acts as an antiestrogen on breast tissue, prevents breast cancer.[14] Oophorectomy and use of tamoxifen decrease breast cancer recurrence.

No long-term double-blind randomized studies of sufficient numbers of breast cancer survivors exist to define whether estrogen use promotes breast cancer recurrence. Many studies have been reported following small numbers of breast cancer survivors taking estrogen over a period of years, but since over 90% of women with early-stage tumors are cured, recurrence risk with the use of estrogen could have been missed in these studies because of their small size.[16]

A consensus conference of American and Canadian oncologists, endocrinologists, and other experts has recommended nonhormonal treatment of menopausal symptoms and complications whenever possible. In cases in whom quality of life is severely affected and nonhormonal treatments are ineffective, this conference panel recommended the use of estrogen "in the lowest dose for the shortest duration of time and only after full discussion of concerns regarding potential risks with respect to breast cancer outcomes (with the patient)."[16]

Megestrol acetate (Megace) has been used in the treatment of breast cancer. It is a type of progesterone. In a double-blind randomized trial, megestrol acetate 20 mg orally twice a day for 4 weeks caused an 85% reduction in hot flushes, significantly different from placebo.[29] However, because the long-term effects of using this drug in breast cancer survivors are unknown, it is considered by most American oncologists to be indicated only when non-hormonal alternatives fail, and its prolonged use is not recommended.[16]

NONHORMONAL TREATMENT OF HOT FLUSHES

In clinical practice, non-hormonal treatments, when used correctly, are very often effective in reducing vasomotor symptoms to tolerable levels. Venlafaxine extended release 75 mg daily has been shown in a randomized controlled trial to reduce hot flushes by 60%. Side effects include mouth dryness, anorexia, nausea, and constipation. Higher doses were not more effective but did cause more side effects.[30] Paroxetine, sertraline, and fluoxetine may have similar effectiveness.[30,31]

The α-adrenergic agonist clonidine is also an effective treatment for hot flushes.[32] It can be given orally or by patch. Studies suggest that many patients need 0.15 mg/d or more for it to be effective.[33,34] Side effects that occur with relative frequency include orthostatic hypotension and dry mouth and eyes. These often become less noticeable with time. In clinical practice, these only rarely limit its use, particularly at lower doses. Patients may be started on a 0.1 mg/d transdermal patch, with reassessment of symptoms in 1 month to 6 weeks. Those who experience significant side effects may benefit from taking the clonidine orally before bed instead of using a patch. Younger women often require a 0.2 mg/d or 0.3 mg/d patch for relief of symptoms.

Bellergal contains a combination of ergotamine tartrate, belladonna, and phenobarbital. It often has been used for the treatment of hot flushes. The evidence for its effectiveness is limited, with reported benefits no different than placebo. It is usually given twice daily.[35]

UROGENITAL SYMPTOMS

Treatment of vaginal dryness and other urogenital symptoms often can be accomplished with local nonhormonal measures. Vaginal lubricants (Replens, Astroglide, Gyne Moistrin) can be effective in ameliorating vaginal dryness, particularly when used on a regular basis.[36] Some women notice vaginal dryness only with intercourse and prefer to use a lubricant only at that time.

Nonhormonal treatment of urogenital symptoms is not always sufficient to relieve symptoms. In this case, topical estrogen therapy is sometimes used. Estring, a Silastic silicone vaginal ring containing micronized estradiol-17ß, is placed intravaginally by the woman or her clinician and is replaced at 12-week intervals. Because it has been felt to minimally affect systemic estrogen levels and is clearly effective in treating urogenital symptoms,[37,38] many clinicians have advocated its use in breast cancer survivors. However, product labeling still advises against the use of this device in women with hormone-dependent tumors, such as breast cancer. This is the best studied low-dose local estrogen treatment available, but questions still exist as to its safety in breast cancer survivors. Low-dose vaginal estrogen cream (estriol 0.5 mg twice weekly) and estradiol-17ß vaginal tablets also appear to have minimal effects on systemic estrogen levels but probably raise them slightly.[39,40]

COMPLEMENTARY AND ALTERNATIVE TREATMENTS FOR MENOPAUSAL SYMPTOMS

Many breast cancer survivors have questions about the use of complementary or alternative treatments for menopausal symptoms and complications. In counseling breast cancer survivors about the use of such treatments, it should be emphasized in particular that no long-term studies of their use exist. It also should be emphasized that, theoretically, those that contain "natural" hormones may present risk for causing recurrence as it is clear that a woman's own natural hormones can cause the growth of breast cancer cells.

Clinicians should be aware that there is a significant placebo effect demonstrated consistently in studies of the treatment of hot flushes. Patients taking placebo typically report around a 25% reduction of hot flushes at 8 to 12 weeks. Because of this placebo effect, women may anecdotally report as efficacious compounds that, in clinical trials, are no better than placebo in improving vasomotor symptoms.

In one study, vitamin E at a dosage of 400 IU twice daily was found to be minimally effective in relieving hot flushes, reducing hot flushes by one per day compared with placebo. However, patients did not prefer vitamin E to placebo in this study, suggesting that the reduction of one hot flush per day was not clinically significant.[41]

Much interest has been present recently in the use of soy phytoestrogens for the treatment of menopausal symptoms in breast cancer survivors. Soy phytoestrogens are a collection of compounds found in soy that affect estrogen receptors, in effect, "natural" SERMs.[42] Epidemiologic data suggest that the use of soy phytoestrogens may be safe as populations that eat diets high in soy generally have lower rates of breast cancer than do populations who eat little or no soy.[43] However, laboratory studies suggest that, under certain conditions, the phytoestrogens found in soy can stimulate estrogen-dependent gene expression in breast cancer tumor cells in vitro.[44]

The efficacy of soy in treating menopausal symptoms is now being studied systematically. Although some studies have suggested that soy supplements are efficacious in the treatment of hot flushes,[45,46] a recent trial in breast cancer survivors showed them to be no more effective than placebo.[47] Soy phytoestrogens do not improve urogenital atrophy.[48,49]

Dong quai, at a dosage equivalent to 4.5 g of root daily, oil of primrose, and black cohosh have been found in randomized double-blind placebo-controlled trials to be no better than placebo in relieving hot flushes.[50–52] Some physicians and other practitioners have recommended the use of topical "natural" progesterones (such as those derived from yams) for treatment of menopausal symptoms in breast cancer survivors. Topical progesterone has been shown to be effective in relieving hot flushes.[53] However, such treatment has theoretic risks of stimulating breast cancer cell lines. Further, nonstandard preparations of progesterone are of unknown efficacy. Red clover, a herbal remedy that may have estrogenic and progestigenic properties, has not been studied systematically.[54]

Long-Term Complications of Menopause in Breast Cancer Survivors

Long-term health concerns for menopausal breast cancer survivors, as for all menopausal women, include coronary artery disease and osteoporosis. Fasting lipid profile and bone density should be measured. Because both may be improved with tamoxifen treatment, it is important that they be remeasured once tamoxifen treatment is completed. Lifestyle-related risk factors, including smoking, obesity, and hypertension, should be addressed. Calcium supplements should be recommended. Cardiovascular risks of adverse lipid profiles are best managed with nonhormonal alternatives to improve lipid profile, such as 3-hydroxy-3-methyl-glutaryl (HM6) coenzyme A inhibitors. Prophylactic treatment with daily aspirin also should be considered for women at increased risk of coronary artery disease.

Osteoporosis treatment and prevention may be accomplished by the use of alendronate (Fosamax) or risedronate (Actonel). Alendronate and risedronate are similar to pamidronate, another bisphosphonate, which has been shown to treat and prevent bony lesions in women with metastatic breast cancer, a theoretic advantage to their use.[55] Raloxifene, is currently also approved by the US Food and Drug Administration for prevention and treatment of osteoporosis. However, because it is structurally similar to tamoxifen, and because of the dangers of long-term tamoxifen use, its long-term use in breast cancer survivors should be avoided until it has been studied further in this population.

ISSUES FOR SURVIVORS OF REPRODUCTIVE AGE: OVARIAN FUNCTION, CONTRACEPTION, AND PREGNANCY

Seven percent of breast cancers are diagnosed before the age of 40 years, and 25% of women diagnosed with breast cancer are premenopausal.[56] For these patients, special issues include contraception and family planning. As previously discussed, because of a large body of evidence that increased exposure to estrogen (and possible progestins) is associated with an increased risk of breast cancer, hormonal contraception is not recommended for premenopausal breast cancer survivors.

Breast cancer does not cause changes in ovarian function. Adjuvant chemotherapy, however, causes well-documented changes in ovarian function, including oligomenorrhea, temporary amenorrhea, and menopause. Most studies address outcomes in women treated with cyclophosphamide,

methotrexate, and 5-fluorouracil- or doxorubicin-containing regimens. Amenorrhea in reports of breast cancer treatment trials has been variably defined, but most studies required cessation of menses for at least 3 months. About 40% of women aged 40 years and younger and over 70% of those over age 40 who undergo chemotherapy for breast cancer experience amenorrhea.[56] Reports of rates of return of menses for women under age 40 years have varied greatly, from 12 to more than 50%.[56,57] Less than 10% of women older than 40 years can be expected to menstruate again. Return of menstruation has been reported over 2 years after cessation of menses.[56] Because of the possibility of return of ovarian function, breast cancer survivors of reproductive age who develop amenorrhea and do not desire pregnancy should be counseled to continue to use contraception. This is particularly important for women under the age of 40 years.

Amenorrhea and menopause are unusual in women under the age of 35, at least during the first year after diagnosis.[57] However, younger women who continue to ovulate and menstruate during and immediately after treatment may still be at risk for early menopause.[58] Breast cancer survivors treated with chemotherapy should be aware that they may reach menopause at an early age, so that if pregnancy is desired, it may be advisable to attempt it at the youngest age that is practical. Because tamoxifen causes urogenital abnormalities in laboratory animals, it should be stopped for several months before a woman attempts to conceive.[59]

The study of pregnancy outcomes and the risk of breast cancer recurrence after pregnancy in breast cancer survivors has been hampered by a lack of large studies and the impossibility of conducting a randomized trial. Little can be conclusively stated about pregnancy outcomes, other than that chemotherapy treatment completed prior to conception does not appear to increase the risk of major congenital malformations. Rates of miscarriage, premature birth, and low birth weight may be higher.[60]

Data on maternal outcomes have been somewhat reassuring in that rates of breast cancer recurrence in women who give birth after breast cancer treatment do not appear to be increased when compared with rates of recurrence in similar breast cancer survivors who did not become pregnant.[60,61] However, some experts remain concerned that pregnancy, and its concomitant high estrogen state, may increase the risk of recurrence. A criticism of available studies is that women who are somehow "healthier" after breast cancer diagnosis (and therefore less likely to recur) may be more likely to be those who become pregnant. Therefore, similar rates of recurrence compared with all breast cancer survivors of similar age, stage, receptor status, and treatment may actually represent a poorer outcome since these women, had they not become pregnant, may have been destined to have better than average outcomes.[60] Studies are ongoing, but this issue is unlikely ever to be resolved definitively. The effect of hormonally assisted reproduction on the risk of breast cancer recurrence is unknown.

RESOURCES

American Society of Clinical Oncology (ASCO)
1900 Duke Street, Suite 200
Alexandria, Virginia 22314
Telephone: (703) 299-0550
Web site: www.asco.org

ASCO is a professional organization with over 15,000 members worldwide. It publishes guidelines for follow-up of breast cancer survivors, available on-line at its Web site. Information on breast cancer treatment and research is also available for clinicians and patients.

American Cancer Society
PO Box 102454
Atlanta, Georgia 30368
Telephone: 1-800-ACS-2345 (1-800-227-2345)
Web site: www.acs.org

ACS provides information on a wide variety of issues for breast cancer survivors, as well as access to support group information.

REFERENCES

1. NIH Consensus Development Conference statement of the treatment of early-stage breast cancer. Oncology 1991;5:120–4.
2. Fajardo LL, Roberts CC, Hunt KR. Mammographic surveillance of breast cancer patients: should the mastectomy site be imaged? AJR. Am J Roentgenol. 1993;161:953–5.
3. Dershaw DD, McCormick B, Osborne MP. Detection of local recurrence after conservative therapy for breast carcinoma. Cancer 1992;70:493–6.
4. Rutgers EJT, van Slooten EA, Kluck HM. Follow-up after treatment of primary breast cancer. Br J Surg 1989;76:187–90.
5. Tomin R, Donegan WL. Screening for recurrent breast cancer—its effectiveness and prognostic value. J Clin Oncol 1987;5:62–7.
6. The GIVIO Investigators. Impact of follow-up testing on survival and health-related quality of life in breast cancer patients: a multicenter randomized controlled trial. JAMA 1994;271:1587–92.
7. Roselli Del Turco M, Palli D, Carridi A, et al. Intensive diagnostic follow-up after treatment of primary breast cancer: a randomized trial. JAMA 1994;271:1593–7.
8. Palli D, Russo A, Saieva C, et al. Intensive vs. clinical follow-up after treatment of primary breast cancer: a 10-year update of a randomized trial. JAMA 1999;281:1586.
9. Schapira DV, Urban N. A minimalist policy for breast cancer surveillance. JAMA 1991;265:380–2.
10. Smith TJ, Davidson NE, Schapira DV, et al. American Society of Clinical Oncology 1998 update on recommended breast cancer surveillance guidelines. J Clin Oncol 1999;17:1080–2.
11. The Steering Committee on Clinical Practice Guidelines for the Care and Treatment of Breast Cancer.

Follow-up after treatment of breast cancer. Can Med Assoc J 1998;158 Suppl 3:S9–14.

12. Osborne CK. Tamoxifen in the treatment of breast cancer. N Engl J Med 1998;339:1609–18.

13. Fisher B, Constantino JP, Wickerham DL. Tamoxifen for prevention of breast cancer: report of the National Surgical Adjuvant Breast and Bowel Project P-1 Study. J Natl Cancer Inst 1998;90:1371–88.

14. Day R, Ganz PA, Costantino JP, et al. Health-related quality of life and tamoxifen in breast cancer prevention: a report from the National Surgical Adjuvant Bowel Project P-1 Study. J Clin Oncol 1999;17:2659–69.

15. Shapiro CL, Recht R. Side effects of adjuvant treatment of breast cancer. N Engl J Med 2001;344:1997–2008.

16. The Hormone Foundation, Canadian Breast Cancer Research Initiative, National Cancer Institute of Canada, Endocrine Society, and the University of Virginia Cancer Center and Women's Place. Treatment of estrogen deficiency symptoms in women surviving breast cancer. J Clin Endocrinol Metab 1998;83:1993–2000.

17. Fisher B, Constantino J, Redmond C, et al. A randomized clinical trial evaluating tamoxifen in the treatment of patients with node-negative breast cancer who have estrogen receptor positive tumors. N Engl J Med 1989;320:479–84.

18. Fisher B, Dignam J, Bryant J, et al. Five versus more than five years of tamoxifen therapy for breast cancer patients with negative lymph nodes and estrogen receptor positive tumors. J Natl Cancer Inst 1996;88:1529–42.

19. Stewart HJ, Forrest AP, Everington D, et al. Randomised comparison of 5 years of adjuvant tamoxifen with continuous therapy for operable breast cancer. Br J Cancer 1996;74:297–9.

20. Clinical alert: adjuvant therapy of breast cancer—tamoxifen update. Clinical announcement released by the National Cancer Institute, November 30, 1995.

21. Norris JD, Paige LA, Christensen DJ, et al. Peptide antagonists of the human estrogen receptor. Science 1999;285:744–6.

22. Cohen SR, Payne DK, Tunkel RS. Lymphedema: strategies for managment. Cancer 2001;92 Suppl 4:980–7.

23. Huang Z, Hankinson, SE, Colditz GA, et al. Dual effects of weight and weight gain on breast cancer risk. JAMA 1997;278:1407–11.

24. Goodwin PJ, Ennis M, Pritchard KI, et al. Adjuvant treatment and the onset of menopause predict weight gain after breast cancer diagnosis. J Clin Oncol 1999;17:120–9.

25. Schag CAC, Ganz PA, Polinsky ML, et al. Characteristics of women at risk for psychosocial distress in the year after breast cancer. J Clin Oncol 1993;11:783–93.

26. Helgeson VS, Cohen S, Schulz R, et al. Education and peer discussion interventions and adjustment to breast cancer. Arch Gen Psychiatry 1999;56:340–7.

27. Segar ML, Katch VL, Roth RS, et al. The effect of aerobic exercise on self-esteem and depressive and anxiety symptoms among breast cancer survivors. Oncol Nurs Forum 1998;25:107–13.

28. Clemons M, Goss P. Estrogen and the risk of breast cancer. N Engl J Med 2001;344:276–85.

29. Loprinzi CL, Michalak JC, Quella SK, et al. Megestrol acetate for the prevention of hot flashes. N Engl J Med 1994;331:347–52.

30. Loprinzi CL, Kugler JW, Sloan JA, et al. Venlafaxine in the management of hot flashes in survivors of breast cancer: a randomised controlled trial. Lancet 2000;356:2059–63.

31. Stearns V, Isaacs C, Rowland J, et al. A pilot trial assessing the efficacy of paroxetine hydrochloride (Paxil) in controlling hot flashes in breast cancer survivors. Ann Oncol 2000;11:17–22.

32. Pandya K, Raubertas R, Plynn P, et al. Oral clonidine in postmenopausal patients with breast cancer experiencing tamoxifen-induced hot flashes: a University of Rochester Cancer Center Community Clinical Oncology Program study. Ann Intern Med 2000;132:788–93.

33. Miller KL. Alternatives to estrogen for menopausal symptoms in women surviving breast cancer symptoms. Clin Obstet Gynecol 1992;35:884–93.

34. Hammar M, Berg G. Clonidine in the treatment of menopausal flushing. Acta Obstet Gynecol Scand Suppl 1985;132:29–31.

35. Ginsberg ES. Hot flashes—physiology, hormonal therapy, and alternative therapies. Obstet Gynecol Clin North Am 1994;21:381–90.

36. Nachtigall LE. Comparative study: Replens versus local estrogen in menopausal women. Fertil Steril 1994;61:178–80.

37. Henriksson L, Stjernquist M, Boquist L, et al. A one-year multicenter study of efficacy and safety of a continuous, low-dose, estradiol-releasing vaginal ring (Estring) in postmenopausal women with symptoms and signs of urogenital aging. Am J Obstet Gynecol 1996;174:85–92.

38. Barentsen R, van de Weijer PHM, Schram JHN. Continuous low dose estradiol release from a vaginal ring versus estriol vaginal cream for urogenital atrophy. Eur J Obstet Gynecol Reprod Biol 1997; 71:73–80.

39. Mettler L, Olsen PG. Long-term treatment of atrophic vaginitis with low-dose oestradiol vaginal tablets. Maturitas 1991;14:12–31.

40. Vooijs GP, Geurts TBP. Review of the endometrial safety during intravaginal treatment with estriol. Eur J Obstet Gynecol Reprod Biol 1995;62:101–6.

41. Barton DL, Loprinzi CL, Quella SK, et al. Prospective evaluation of vitamin E for hot flashes in breast cancer survivors. J Clin Oncol 1998;16:495–500.

42. Clarke R, Hilakivi-Clarke L, Cho E, et al. Estrogens, phytoestrogens, and breast cancer. Adv Exp Med Biol 1996;401:63–85.

43. Ingram D, Snaders K, Kolybaba M, et al. Case-control study of phyto-oestrogens and breast cancer. Lancet 1997;350:990–4.

44. Willard ST, Frawley LS. Phytoestrogens have agonistic and combinatorial effects on estrogen-responsive gene expression in MCF-7 human breast cancer cells. Endocrine 1998;8:117–21.

45. Albertazzi P, Pansini F, Bonaccorsi G, et al. The effect of dietary soy supplementation on hot flushes. Obstet Gynecol 1998;91:6–11.

46. Washburn S, Burke GL, Morgan T, et al. Effect of soy protein supplementation on serum lipoproteins, blood pressure, and menopausal symptoms in perimenopausal women. Menopause 1999;6:7–13.

47. Quella S, Loprinzi C, Barton D, et al. Evaluation of soy phytoestrogens for the treatment of hot flashes in breast cancer survivors: a North Central Cancer Treatment Group trial. J Clin Oncol 2000;18:1068–74.

48. Baird DD, Umbach DM, Lansdell L, et al. Dietary soy intervention study to assess estrogenicity of dietary soy among postmenopausal women. J Clin Endocrinol Metab 1995;80:1685–90.

49. Cline JM, Obasanjo IO, Paschold JC, et al. Effects of hormonal therapies and dietary soy phytoestrogens on vaginal cytology in surgically postmenopausal macaques. Fertil Steril 1996;65:1031–5.

50. Hirata JD, Small R, Swiersz L, et al. Does dong quai have estrogenic effects in postmenopausal women? A double-blind, placebo-controlled trial. Fertil Steril 1997;68:981–6.

51. Chenoy R, Hussain S, Tayob Y, et al. Effect of oral gamolenic acid from evening primrose oil on menopausal flushing. BMJ 1994;308:501–3.

52. Jacobson JS, Troxel AB, Evans J, et al. Randomized trial of black cohosh for the treatment of hot flashes among women with a history of breast cancer. J Clin Oncol 2001;19:2739–45.

53. Leonetti HB, Longo S, Anasti JN. Transdermal progesterone cream for vasomotor symptoms and postmenopausal bone loss. Obstet Gynecol 1999;94:225–8.

54. Zawa D, Dollbaum CM, Blen M, et al. Estrogen and progestin bioactivity of foods, herbs, and spices. Prog Soc Exp Biol Med 1998;217:369.

55. Hortobagyi GN, Theriault RL, Porter L, et al. Efficacy of pamidronate in reducing skeletal complications in patients with breast cancer and lytic bone metastases. N Engl J Med 1996;335:1785–41.

56. Bines J, Oleske DM, Cobleigh M. Ovarian function in premenopausal women treated with adjuvant chemotherapy for breast cancer. J Clin Oncol 1996; 14:1718–29.

57. Goodwin PJ, Ennis M, Pritchard KI, et al. Risk of menopause during the first year after breast cancer diagnosis. J Clin Oncol 1999;17:2365–70.

58. Byrne J, Fears TR, Gail M, et al. Early menopause in long-term survivors of cancer during adolescence. Am J Obstet Gynecol 1992;166:788–93.

59. Burstein HJ, Winer EP. Primary care for survivors of breast cancer. N Engl J Med 2000;343:1086–94.

60. Surbone A, Petrek J. Childbearing issues in breast carcinoma survivors. Cancer 1997;79:1271–6.

61. Velentgas P, Daling JR, Malone KE, et al. Pregnancy after breast carcinoma: outcomes and influence on mortality. Cancer 1999;85:2424–31.

25

ALLERGIC RHINITIS

Ricardo A. Tan, MD, and Sheldon Spector, MD

Allergic rhinitis shows a prevalence of 10 to 20% in various population studies.[1] It is more common in males than in females during childhood and adolescence, but it appears to be generally equal in prevalence in adult men and women.[2] In a study of an entire 10,000-person community, the prevalence was 8.2% in women and 7.5% in men.[3] In another study the prevalence was 14% in women and 15% in men.[4] Although it is often dismissed by nonsufferers as being a minor condition, it significantly affects the quality of life of sufferers.[5] When symptoms are severe or when complications such as sinusitis are present, patients frequently miss days of work, school, or other regular activities. The evergrowing array of over-the-counter medications and herbal supplements directed toward alleviating allergy symptoms is a sign of the magnitude of this problem.

PATHOPHYSIOLOGY

When a genetically predisposed person is first exposed to an allergen, a process of sensitization is initiated with the presentation of the allergen by an antigen-presenting cell to a CD4+ or helper T lymphocyte. T helper cells are classified as T helper 1 (Th1) or T helper 2 (Th2) cells depending on the cytokines they produce. The Th2 cells play a major role in allergic disease with a characteristic cytokine profile that includes interleukin (IL)-4 and IL-5. Interleukin-4 released from Th2 cells stimulates B cell differentiation into plasma cells and promotes isotype switching to immunoglobulin E (IgE) synthesis.[6] Then IgE attaches to the surface of mast cells, basophils, and other cells in the nasal mucosa. When the patient is re-exposed, the allergen causes surface IgE molecules to undergo cross-linking, which leads to mast cell or basophil degranulation and release of preformed and newly formed mediators. The pre-formed mediators include histamine, chymase, tryptase, heparin, and tosyl arginine methyl esteresterase (TAME). The newly formed mediators include leukotrienes (LTs) and prostaglandins (PGs).[7]

Histamine and other mediators act on receptors in the mucosa, glands, and blood vessels to produce the characteristic symptoms of allergic rhinitis. Sneezing results from stimulation of itch receptors. Edema from increased vascular permeability and dilated blood vessels produces nasal congestion. Rhinorrhea is caused by increased production of mucus from glands.

The response to an allergen can be biphasic with an early-phase response due to the effects of mediators released from mast cells or basophils and a late-phase response produced partly by the influx of inflammatory cells including neutrophils, macrophages, T lymphocytes, and eosinophils. Nasal congestion is commonly the predominant symptom in the late phase. The absence of PGD_2, released only by mast cells, in the late-phase response suggests that basophils have a larger role in this response. The early-phase response occurs within minutes, whereas the late-phase response can happen 4 to 8 hours after allergen exposure.[8] Eosinophils play a major role in the late-phase response and chronic allergic inflammation through the effects of products such as major basic and eosinophil cationic proteins. The presence of numerous eosinophils in a nasal smear is a diagnostic feature of allergic rhinitis. A complex network of cells and cellular products influence inflammation. Cytokines, including IL-1, IL-2, IL-4, IL-5, IL-6, tumor necrosis factor α (TNF-α), and granulocyte-macrophage colony-stimulating factor (GM-CSF) all contribute to allergic inflammation. Chemokines are cytokines involved in chemotaxis, and those important in the allergic process include IL-8, RANTES (regulated

267

on activation, normal T expressed and secreted), macrophage inflammatory protein 1α (MIP-1α), and macrophage chemoattractant proteins 1, 2, and 3 (MCP-1, -2 and -3).[9]

The "priming" phenomenon refers to the observation that regular exposure to an allergen "primes" patients so that the amount of allergen needed to produce symptoms decreases with time. This was first noted when patients reported exacerbation of symptoms with less allergen exposure toward the end compared with the beginning of the allergy season.[10]

DIAGNOSIS

History

The symptoms of allergic rhinitis can start as early as 1 year of age or may not manifest until decades later. In the majority of patients, symptoms are present by the second decade.[1] Sneezing, nasal congestion, and rhinorrhea are the most common symptoms of allergic rhinitis. Tearing and itching cause patients to rub their eyes for relief. Itching in the throat and palate also may be present. Ear fullness, plugging, and even pain often can be present and are signs of blockage of the eustachian tube. Facial pressure is felt when the ostia or openings of the sinuses, especially the maxillary sinuses, are blocked due to nasal congestion. Facial pressure suggests a sinus infection, especially if green or yellow purulent nasal discharge is seen. Headaches, myalgias, fatigue, and irritability can be nonspecific presenting symptoms. Symptoms can be present only during certain seasons (seasonal) or throughout the year (perennial). In many patients symptoms are initially seasonal, but they progressively become perennial. This may be due to progression of untreated seasonal allergy with chronic nasal allergic inflammation or the addition of new sensitivities. The presence of associated atopic conditions such as asthma and atopic dermatitis strongly point to an allergic etiology for rhinitis. A family history of atopy is a risk factor for developing allergic rhinitis.[1]

Seasonal allergic rhinitis is characterized by exacerbation of symptoms due to pollen or outdoor molds present in the air during certain seasons, especially the spring and fall. The lay term "hay fever" was coined when a temporal association was first noted between hay field pollination seasons and allergy symptoms. There are wide regional variations in the seasonal fluctuations in pollen count, but, in general, trees pollinate in the early spring, grasses in the spring and summer, and weeds in the fall. Clinicians and patients should contact the local pollen bureau or pollen count center to determine the prevailing pollen types and counts during a specific time of year. Patients with seasonal allergic rhinitis may be completely free of symptoms or have low-grade symptoms during the off-season. Airborne mold allergens often are increased in areas with high humidity and are responsible for many cases of allergic rhinitis in places such as Florida and the Gulf Coast of Texas. *Alternaria* and *Cladosporium* are common airborne outdoor molds in many regions. Seasonal exacerbations of mold allergy usually occur in the summer and fall.[11]

Perennial allergic rhinitis is associated with symptoms throughout the year and is due most commonly to dust mites, indoor molds, or animal dander. Cockroaches, rabbits, mice, and rats also can be sources of allergen. Patients often will volunteer the information that their symptoms appear around animals such as cats or dogs. Animal dander on other people's clothes or remaining in the air after the animals are removed also can trigger symptoms.[12] *Dermatophagoides farinae* and *Dermatophagoides pteronyssinus* are the two dust mite species associated with human allergic rhinitis. Feather pillows and mattresses as well as increased humidity favor the growth of dust mites. It is important to check for this allergy because dust mites are microscopic and are present even in the most well-cleaned houses. If patients have more symptoms inside than outside the home, dust mite allergy should be suspected. *Aspergillus* and *Penicillium* frequently are responsible for indoor mold growth and perennial symptoms.[13] In the home moisture under carpets and in the walls can promote the proliferation of molds. Shower curtains, trash cans, and basements are common sites of mold growth.

Infectious rhinitis is commonly viral in etiology (the common cold) and can be differentiated from allergic rhinitis by more prominent systemic symptoms of headache, occasional fever, minimal sneezing, and virtually no itching. **Vasomotor rhinitis** results from vasomotor instability in the mucosal blood vessels and presents with nasal congestion or rhinorrhea mainly triggered by changes in temperature and irritants such as strong perfume or cigarette smoke.[14]

The syndrome of **nonallergic rhinitis with eosinophilia** (NARES) is distinguished from allergic rhinitis mainly by the absence of evidence of an IgE-mediated process resulting from testing in the skin and serum. The syndrome of NARES is clinically identical to allergic rhinitis except for negative results on skin testing and radioallergosorbent test (RAST; see below). The mechanism of this syndrome is unclear. Symptoms include sneezing and rhinorrhea. This condition is treated primarily with intranasal steroid therapy.

Nasal polyps commonly cause nasal obstruction with loss of smell or anosmia seen more often than in allergic rhinitis. Use of topical decongestants such as oxymetazoline for more than 5 days at a time can cause rebound congestion due to down-regulation of α-adrenergic receptors.[2] Although topical decongestants are the most common cause of medicamentous rhinitis (**drug-induced rhinitis**), oral medications including reserpine, methyldopa, guanethidine, and phentolamine also can be responsible.

In women, **oral contraceptives and oral estrogens** often are reported to cause nasal symptoms as a side effect. Increased glandular hyperplasia, histiocytic infiltration, and interepithelial edema in the nasal mucosa are believed to contribute to the nasal congestion seen.[15] In most cases, symptoms are mild, and lowering the dosage of estrogen may lead to improvement. The comparative nasal side effects from different oral contraceptive and estrogen preparations have not been studied. However, switching to an alternative preparation has clinically been observed to help and may be done if symptoms are persistent.

Physical Examination

Dark circles under the eyes, also known as "allergic shiners," are common. These are due to hyperpigmentation in the lower lid areas due to pooling of fluid caused by chronic nasal congestion. Allergic patients frequently rub their noses upwards with the medial side of their hands in a gesture known as an "allergic salute." This frequent motion eventually causes a horizontal skin crease to form on the bridge of the nose, commonly called the "allergic crease." Allergic conjunctivitis is associated with eye redness, itching, and tearing with clear secretions. Eyelids can be edematous or puffy. Ear examination may show tympanic membranes that are retracted or

appear to be pulled inward. This is due to eustachian tube blockage associated with nasal congestion.

If present, nasal polyps are visible on inspection of the nasal passages and appear as whitish grape-like structures commonly filling the nasal passages. The nasal mucosa appears swollen, pale and boggy in allergic rhinitis. In contrast, medicamentous rhinitis causes the nasal mucosa to have a beefy red appearance. In severe cases of rhinitis, the nasal passages may be obstructed completely. Rhinorrhea can be profuse, causing patients to blow their noses constantly. Secretions usually are clear but may be purulent if infection is present. Purulent nasal discharge or crusting suggest sinusitis. The nasal mucosa often is red in nonallergic rhinitis syndromes including vasomotor rhinitis and NARES. Structural abnormalities such as septal deviation or tumors can cause persistent nasal obstruction, especially only on one side, and should be looked for carefully, particularly when symptoms are described as being predominantly unilateral.

Procedures

Nasal Smear
The nasal smear can be useful in the differential diagnosis of rhinitis. The procedure is most commonly performed by having a patient blow out nasal secretions into a piece of wax paper. Secretions are then transferred onto a slide and stained, usually with Hansel stain. A nasal probe also may be used to collect secretions by scraping it against the inferior turbinate. Numerous eosinophils are found in allergic rhinitis and NARES, whereas infectious rhinitis shows predominantly neutrophils on microscopic examination. In clinical practice, the nasal smear is an inexpensive readily performed procedure that can help to determine diagnosis.

Skin Test
Skin testing is the primary form of diagnostic testing for allergic rhinitis. A positive response is a wheal-and-flare skin reaction to an allergen. Percutaneous skin testing can be done by either a prick-puncture or a scratch method, both of which introduce the allergen into the epidermis. Intradermal testing consists of injecting allergen into the dermis. The latter is more sensitive but less specific.[16] Many practitioners perform the percutaneous test first and use the intradermal test to confirm equivocal responses. Many convenient plastic devices such as the Multitest (Lincoln

Diagnostics, Decatur, IL) and Greerpick (Greer Laboratories, Lenoir, NC) now are being used for percutaneous testing instead of needles. The test is preferably performed on the skin of the back because it is the widest flat surface available on the body. The back is also more reactive to histamine than is the forearm.[17] Up to 70 percutaneous and 40 intradermal tests can be done.[18] There are several methods of grading the responses. For example, responses may be graded on a scale of 0 to 4 based on the comparative size of the reaction to the histamine control.[19] Recording the actual wheal and flare diameters of each response is the most accurate method, and it enables comparison of results with repeat skin tests in the future. The response is evaluated 15 to 20 minutes after application. Histamine is applied as the positive control, and saline is the negative control. Patients must avoid all antihistamines for at least 3 days before the skin test. Astemizole (Hismanal), which has a longer half-life, should be avoided for 3 to 6 weeks. Corticosteroids do not significantly affect the immediate skin test responses and do not have to be withheld.[1]

RADIOALLERGOSORBENT TEST

Skin testing is considered to be more sensitive than is serum testing for IgE antibodies.[20] However, when the allergic sensitivity is significant, both methods are reliable.[21] Skin testing has the advantage of being less expensive with immediate results, but it may not be possible in patients who refuse it or have extensive skin conditions such as dermatographism or atopic dermatitis. The RAST, also known as the IgE antibody test, uses radio- or enzyme-labeled anti-IgE antibodies to detect specific IgE antibodies. The RAST can be done for most known allergens, including pollen, mold, animals, and food. Panels of allergens grouped by type or regional distribution can be considered as an inexpensive screening test.[22] The IgE antibody or RAST results correlate well with skin test results and clinical history when symptoms are significant, but not necessarily when they are mild. This makes it difficult to establish an absolute sensitivity and specificity for RAST.[21]

TREATMENT

Avoidance Measures

POLLEN

Pollen counts are available in most areas through phone hotlines to help patients and clinicians determine the prevailing allergens in the air. Patients with grass pollen sensitivity should try not to mow the grass or wear a mask if this is unavoidable. In general trees pollinate in the early spring, grasses in the late spring and early summer, and weeds in the late summer and fall in North America.[1] Patients should keep the windows closed in the car to minimize exposure. In the summer, air conditioning is recommended so that windows can be kept closed at home as well.[11] Pollen levels generally decrease during and after rain for a short period. Pollen should be removed from skin and hair by showering immediately after being outdoors to avoid increasing indoor levels of pollen.

ANIMALS

Allergy to pets, especially cats and dogs, can be a difficult issue for many patients. Sensitivity to cats appears to be more common than is sensitivity to dogs.[23] Strong emotional attachment to their pets causes patients to adamantly refuse or be quietly noncompliant with avoidance measures. For patients who agree to remove animals from their environment, it is important to inform them that the major cat allergen, *Fel d* I, and major dog allergen, *Can f* I, have been detected for up to 6 months after removal of the animal and a thorough cleaning.[12] Patients may experience symptoms on moving into a home whose previous owner had a pet. Animal dander in the clothes of co-workers or classmates also can invoke symptoms. Previously thought to be a salivary protein, *Fel d* I actually is synthesized predominantly in the skin and is shed in fur or dander.[24] Carpets and upholstered furniture are reservoirs for cat and dog allergens. Different degrees of decreasing cat or dog exposure, short of complete removal, have been shown to have benefits and may be the best option for those who cannot part with their pets. Keeping the pet outside the house may decrease the amount of allergen in reservoirs such as the carpet. If patients insist on keeping the pet inside the house, keeping it outside the bedroom in an uncarpeted room that has a high-efficiency particulate air (HEPA) filter has been recommended.[1] Some clinicians recommend weekly washings of pets but efficacy studies are inconclusive.[25–27]

Patients unable to avoid pets can be started on immunotherapy, commonly referred to as "cat or dog allergy vaccine." This decreases sensitivity and induces long-term improvement in symptoms.

Immunotherapy usually is given for at least 3 to 5 years (see below).

DUST MITES

Dermatophagoides pteronyssinus and *D. farinae* can be present in rooms that appear to be completely clean and dust free. The major mite allergens, *Der p* I, *Der f* I, *Der p* II, and *Der f* II, are derived from mite feces.[28] The mites are microscopic and feed primarily on skin scales. This makes objects and materials in close contact with human skin, such as carpets, pillows, mattresses, and sofas, especially those containing feather or down, conducive to dust mite growth. One of the most effective measures to lessen dust mite exposure is the use of impermeable covers for pillows and mattresses.[29] These are now available in a variety of comfortable textures and thickness and no longer give the sensation of lying on a plastic sheet. Sheets and beddings should be washed at 54°C every week.[30] Heavy curtains, stuffed toys, and rugs that gather dust should be removed from the environment. Carpets should be cleaned (preferably not by the allergic person) regularly with a vacuum cleaner equipped with a HEPA filter or a double-thickness bag.[11] Removal of wall-to-wall carpeting also may be helpful. Mite growth is encouraged by humidity, so it is important to keep humidity below 50% inside the house.[11] Acaricides such as benzyl benzoate kill mites; denaturing solutions, such as tannic acid, only temporarily neutralize mite allergen.[31]

MOLDS

Both indoor and outdoor molds and fungi can trigger allergic rhinitis symptoms. Outdoor leaks can create damp and moist areas inside walls or underneath carpets that encourage mold growth. Kitchens, showers, garages, and trash cans are common areas of mold growth. These areas should be cleaned with fungicides available as household cleaning solutions and dried to prevent further mold growth. Airborne outdoor mold is highest in the late summer and fall but may have high levels all year round in regions with high humidity such as Florida. Molds and fungi are present in the soil and on vegetation and often become airborne with activities such as plowing or mowing the lawn. Avoidance of these activities is important for mold-sensitive individuals.[1]

Pharmacologic Measures

ANTIHISTAMINES

Antihistamines block histamine effects by binding to H_1 receptors in the nasal mucosa; they improve symptoms of sneezing and rhinorrhea. Itching in the nose, ears, eyes, palate, and skin also are improved. However, antihistamines do not significantly affect nasal congestion. The so-called first-generation antihistamines, including diphenhydramine (Benadryl) and hydroxyzine (Atarax), are effective in treating symptoms but cause significant sedation and/or affect performance. Second-generation antihistamines are effective but are either nonsedating or considerably less sedating due to poor penetration of the blood-brain barrier.[32] Loratadine (Claritin), fexofenadine (Allegra), and cetirizine (Zyrtec) have half-lives of up to 24 hours. Astemizole (Hismanal) has a half-life of up to 19 days.[1] The possible induction of a prolonged Q–T interval and a fatal torsades de pointes arrhythmia has been associated with the use of terfenadine (Seldane, no longer available in the United States) or astemizole with (1) concomitant liver disease or hypokalemia or (2) an interaction with drugs metabolized in the hepatic cytochrome p450 system, including ciprofloxacin, erythromycin, and imidazole antifungals such as fluconazole (Diflucan) and ketoconazole (Nizoral).[33,34] Fexofenadine is a modified form of terfenadine that is not metabolized extensively in the cytochrome p450 system and has not been associated with cardiac side effects.[35] Antihistamines also are available in the form of topical nasal sprays and eye drops. Azelastine (Astelin), the first topical nasal antihistamine spray introduced, is dosed as two sprays each side twice a day as needed and may serve as an effective alternative to oral preparations.[36] Opthalmic antihistamines, including levocabastine (Livostin) and olopatadine (Patanol), may be used when symptoms are limited to the eyes, or added when oral antihistamines are inadequate for relief. Oral antihistamine-decongestant combinations improve compliance and are more convenient for patients to take than are separate preparations (see below).

DECONGESTANTS

Decongestants offer the only fast-acting relief for nasal congestion and can be used both orally and topically. Topical decongestant sprays such as oxymetazoline (Afrin) cause vasoconstriction of dilated blood vessels in the nasal mucosa and provide almost immediate relief of obstructed passages. However, these sprays should not be used for more than 3 to 5 days at a time to avoid rebound congestion. Rebound congestion results from downregulation of α-adrenergic receptors and is characterized by worsening nasal congestion every time use of the spray is stopped. Oral decongestants are widely available over the counter or with prescriptions. Pseudoephedrine is commonly used in many over-the-counter and prescription preparations. Extended-release antihistamine-decongestant combinations (eg, Claritin-D 24 hour and Allegra-D) can be taken conveniently only once or twice daily with good control of symptoms. Oral decongestants are α-adrenergic agents and can have side effects of insomnia, palpitations, or elevated blood pressure.

CORTICOSTEROIDS

Intranasal steroids improve symptoms of allergic rhinitis including nasal congestion. After 1 week of regular use, intranasal steroids can inhibit both the early- (priming) and late-phase allergic responses.[37] Both oral and intranasal steroids have multiple anti-inflammatory effects including diminishing the influx of inflammatory cells into the nose. Initially patients should be told to use the spray regularly, whether they have symptoms or not, for at least 6 to 8 weeks. Regular use of intranasal steroids decreases chronic inflammation in the nasal mucosa and leads to long-term improvement. It is important to inform patients not to expect the immediate relief of congestion that results with use of decongestant sprays. Oral antihistamines can be used on an as-needed basis while patients use intranasal steroids regularly. Budesonide (Rhinocort), fluticasone (Flonase), mometasone (Nasonex), triamcinolone (Nasacort), beclomethasone (Vancenase), and flunisolide (Nasarel, Nasalide) are all effective preparations. The intranasal steroids generally are safe to use with minimal suppression of the hypothalamic-pituitary-adrenal axis.[1] The incidence of septal perforation is low and may be avoided by directing the nasal spray away from the septum.[38] Biopsy studies after 5 years of intranasal steroid use have shown no atrophy or tissue damage.[39] There have been reports of posterior subcapsular cataracts with intranasal and inhaled steroid use, but the studies are not conclusive.[40]

Oral steroids should not be used routinely in allergic rhinitis as the risk of side effects outweighs the benefits. A short burst of prednisone 30 to 40 mg/d for 4 to 5 days is effective in promptly improving severe symptoms.

ANTICHOLINERGIC AGENTS

Ipratropium bromide (Atrovent) nasal spray is available in 0.03 and 0.06% solutions for patients whose main complaint is rhinorrhea. It is a quaternary ammonium muscarinic-receptor antagonist that blocks rhinorrhea from cholinergic stimulation.[41] The recommended dosage is two sprays each nostril three to four times per day. It may be used as an adjunct for patients who have persistent rhinorrhea even when taking antihistamines, decongestants, or intranasal steroids. Side effects are minimal compared with older anticholinergic agents because it penetrates the blood-brain barrier poorly and has no significant systemic absorption.[42]

CROMOLYN

Intranasal sodium cromoglycate (Nasalcrom) is now available to buy without a prescription. It is a mast cell stabilizer and prevents degranulation of mast cells and mediator release on allergen exposure. It probably has the fewest side effects of all the medications used for allergies.[43] The recommended dosage is one to two sprays each nostril three to four times per day. It is effective when used prophylactically before allergen exposure or before the allergy season. It has been shown to inhibit both the early- and late-phase responses.[44] Intranasal cromolyn is not as effective as are intranasal steroids, but it may be used as maintenance preventive therapy when safety is an issue, such as in pregnancy.[1]

ANTILEUKOTRIENES

The cysteinyl leukotrienes LTC_4, LTD_4, and LTE_4, previously known as SRS-A (slow-reacting substance of anaphylaxis), have been shown to increase vascular permeability, mucus production, and influx of inflammatory cells in many organs including the nose. Although presently indicated only for asthma, they are actively being studied in allergic rhinitis. Zafirlukast (Accolate), montelukast (Singulair), and zileuton (Zyflo) are the preparations now available.

IMMUNOTHERAPY

Immunotherapy is the process of exposing allergic patients to gradually increasing doses of specific allergen extracts to decrease their sensitivity and improve symptoms. It is indicated in patients who show specific IgE responses by skin testing or RAST. Patients who have responded poorly to other therapy, are unable to avoid allergens, or who would prefer not to use medications are all candidates for immunotherapy. The efficacy of immunotherapy has been confirmed for symptoms from a variety of allergens including ragweed, cat, and birch tree.[45] Many immunologic changes occur with immunotherapy that are thought to contribute to its efficacy including increased specific IgG1 and IgG4, declined specific IgE, decreased lymphocyte proliferation, increased CD8+ T lymphocytes, and decreased serum IL-2 receptor.[46] The introduction of standardized allergens has made the preparation of immunotherapy extracts more consistent. Allergy injections are commonly started at a frequency of once or twice weekly until a maintenance dose is reached. When the maintenance dose is reached (eg, at 6 months), the patient can receive immunotherapy less frequently—eventually just once per month. Immunotherapy generally is given for at least 3 to 5 years for long-term benefit.[47] Lack of improvement after 1 year may be an indication for discontinuation. Prolonged immunotherapy for up to 10 years is no longer necessary. Reactions can range from small local reactions to anaphylaxis and death. For this reason, injections should be given only in a medically supervised setting where emergency resuscitation equipment is available. Serious or fatal reactions can develop rapidly, so practitioners should no longer allow the old practice of home administration of allergen immunotherapy.[16]

Relative contraindications to immunotherapy include use of ß-blockers, uncontrolled asthma, and uncontrolled underlying chronic disease (eg, coronary artery disease).[16] Immunotherapy should not be initiated or the dose increased in pregnancy, due to the risk to the fetus if a systemic reaction occurs. However, it may be continued on a stable dose throughout pregnancy.[48,49]

Treatment of the Patient with Allergic Rhinitis

An algorithm detailing the treatment of a patient with allergic rhinitis is presented in Figure 25–1. Avoidance of specific allergens and triggers is the cornerstone of the treatment of allergic rhinitis. Patients should be given specific instructions on avoidance measures, especially for dust mites.

Pharmacologic therapy should include as-needed antihistamines for sneezing and rhinorrhea, and decongestants for nasal congestion. Intranasal cromolyn may be successful for patients with mild symptoms, whereas intranasal steroids are preferred in patients who require daily antihistamines or decongestants for relief of symptoms. A short course of oral corticosteroids may be necessary for those who present with severe symptoms not responsive to other medications. Immunotherapy should be recommended especially for those patients not responsive to avoidance and pharmacologic therapy.

PREGNANCY AND LACTATION

Allergic rhinitis may improve, worsen, or remain the same during pregnancy. In one study the symptoms of 45% of women with pre-existing rhinitis remained the same in pregnancy, whereas 34% worsened, and 15% improved.[50] Nasal congestion that starts during pregnancy, usually during the second month, and resolves soon after delivery also is seen and is believed to be vasomotor rather than allergic in etiology.[51] The incidence of sinusitis appears to increase in pregnancy.[52] Histologic and electron microscopic examination of the nasal mucosa in pregnant women has shown increased glandular activity, phagocytic activity, and amount of acid mucopolysaccharides in the ground substance. These changes have been attributed to increased levels of estrogen and progesterone.[53] Increased blood volume and the effects of vasoactive intestinal peptide and oxytocin also may be involved in worsening nasal congestion during pregnancy.[54]

Nonpharmacologic measures such as saline irrigation or inhalation of steam often are effective in relieving nasal obstruction and thinning secretions. If symptoms are persistent, chlorpheniramine and tripelennamine traditionally have been used safely in pregnancy.[1] Of the newer sedating antihistamines, loratadine and cetirizine have a US Food and Drug Administration category B classification for use in pregnancy, whereas fexofenadine is in category C. In one large study the use of asthma and allergy medications by 824 asthmatic and 678 nonasthmatic pregnant women was monitored prospectively. Although an association was seen between the use of oral steroids and preeclampsia, no significant association was found between major congenital malformations

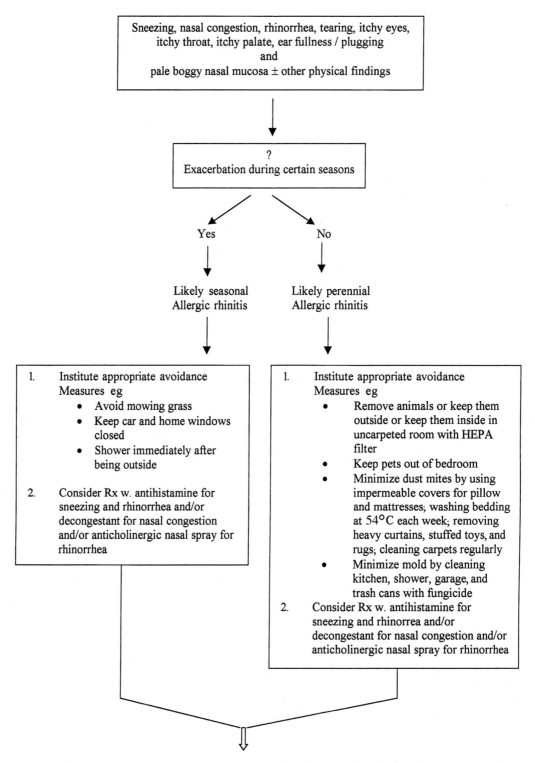

FIGURE 25–1. Treatment of symptoms of allergic rhinitis. Rx = prescription; HEPA = high-efficiency particulate air.

and exposure to topical and systemic steroids, cromolyn, antihistamines, or decongestants in all trimesters.[55] Two hundred sixty-nine subjects took chlorpheniramine, 192 took tripelennamine, and 193 took other antihistamines; pseudoephedrine was the decongestant most commonly used. The risk-benefit ratio should be weighted for the use of decongestants since an association between maternal use of decongestants and infant gastroschisis has been seen in at least two studies.[56,57] If maintenance

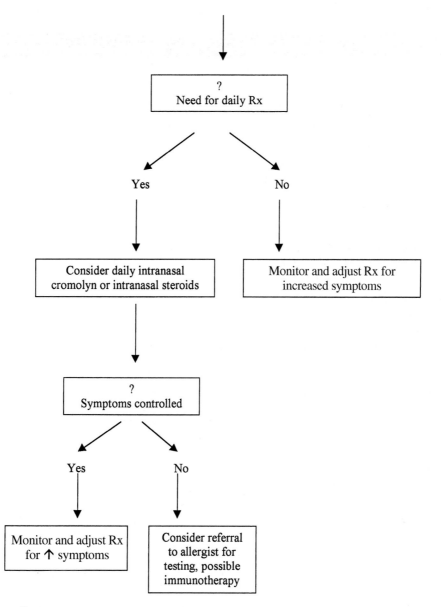

FIGURE 25–1. *(continued)*

anti-inflammatory therapy is needed for recurrent symptoms, intranasal cromolyn, or intranasal beclomethasone may be used.[1] As in asthma, oral steroids may be used if severe allergic rhinitis is not responsive to other therapy. Efforts still continue to add to the inadequate data available on the safety of agents used for allergy in pregnancy. This includes the Registry for Allergic, Asthmatic Pregnant Patients (RAAPP) established by the American College of Allergy, Asthma and Immunology to provide data that aggressive therapy for allergy and asthma results in positive outcomes for both mother and child.[58] Immunotherapy may be continued during pregnancy, but no increase in dose should be made

because of the potential harm of a systemic reaction to the fetus.[49]

The first-generation antihistamines may cause sedation or irritability in infants if taken by their nursing mothers. This has not been observed with the second-generation antihistamines.[35]

REFERRAL TO SPECIALISTS

Allergy specialists can assist primary care clinicians when there is a need to identify or confirm specific allergies by skin or serum IgE antibody testing. Referral to allergists also is indicated when symptoms are refractory to conventional treatment, concomitant

RESOURCES

The following organizations provide resources for primary care clinicians as well as specialists:

American Academy of Allergy, Asthma and Immunology
611 East Wells Street
Milwaukee, Wisconsin 53202
Telephone: (414) 272-6071
          1-800-822-2762 (Physician referral and information line)
Fax: (414) 272-6070
Web site: www.aaaai.org

American College of Allergy, Asthma and Immunology
85 West Algonquin Road, Suite 550
Arlington Heights, Illinois 60005
Telephone: (847) 427-1200
Fax: (847) 427-1294
Web site: www.acaai.org
Web site: allergy.mcg.edu (Information for the public)

The following lay organizations offer support groups and educational materials (eg, videos, brochures, and books) for patients and their families:

Allergy and Asthma Network/Mothers of Asthmatics, Inc
2751 Prosperity Avenue, Suite 150
Fairfax, Virginia 22031
Telephone: 1-800-878-4403
          (703) 385-4403
Fax: (703) 352-4354
E-mail: aanma@aol.com
Web site: www.aanma.org

National Allergy Bureau
(sponsored by American Academy of Allergy, Asthma and Immunology; see address and Web site above)
Telephone: 1-877-9-ACHOOO (1-877-922-4666) (Year-round indoor allergies)
          1-800-9-POLLEN (1-800-976-5536) (Pollen and mold report)

Asthma and Allergy Foundation of America
1125 Fifteenth Street, Northwest, Suite 502
Washington, DC 20005
Telephone: 1-800-727-8462
          (202) 466-7643
Fax: (202) 466-8940
Web site: www.aafa.org

conditions such as asthma are present, recurrent complications such as sinusitis occur, medication side effects impair patient's work or school performance, or immunotherapy is indicated.[1]

REFERENCES

1. Dykewicz MS, Fineman S, Skoner DP, et al. Diagnosis and management of rhinitis: complete guidelines of the joint task force on practice parameters in allergy, asthma and immunology. Ann Allergy Asthma Immunol 1998;81(Pt 2):478–518.

2. Druce HM. Allergic and non-allergic rhinitis. In: Middleton EJ, Reed CE, Ellis EF, et al, editors. Allergy: principles and practice. 5th ed. St. Louis: Mosby; 1998. p. 1005–16.

3. Broder I, Higgins MW, Mathews KP, et al. Epidemiology of asthma and allergic rhinitis in a total community, Tecumseh, Michigan. J Allergy Clin Immunol 1974;54:100–10.

4. Edfors-Lubs ML. Allergy in 7000 twin pairs. Acta Allergol 1971;26:249–85.

5. Bousquet J, Bullinger M, Fayol C, et al. Assessment of quality of life in patients with perennial allergic rhinitis with the French version of the SF-36 Health Status Questionnaire. J Allergy Clin Immunol 1994; 94:182–8.

6. Del Prete G, Maggi E, Parronchi P, et al. IL-4 is an essential co-factor for the IgE synthesis induced in vitro by human T-cell clones and their supernatants. J Immunol 1988;140:4193–8.

7. Naclerio RM. Allergic rhinitis. N Engl J Med 1991; 325;860–9.

8. Naclerio RM, Proud D, Togias AG, et al. Inflammatory mediators in late antigen-induced rhinitis. N Engl J Med 1985;313:65–70.

9. White M. Mediators of inflammation and the inflammatory process. J Allergy Clin Immunol 1999; 103:S37–81.

10. Connell JT. Quantitative intranasal pollen changes. III. The priming effect in allergic rhinitis. J Allergy 1969;50:43–4.

11. Solomon WR, Platts-Mills TAE. Aerobiology and inhalant allergens. In: Middleton EJ, Reed CE, Ellis EF, et al, editors. Allergy: principles and practice. 5th ed. St. Louis: Mosby; 1998. p. 367–403.

12. Wood RA, Chapman MD, Adkinson NF Jr, et al. The effect of cat removal on allergen content in household-dust samples. J Allergy Clin Immunol 1989; 83:730–4.

13. Burge HA. Fungus allergens. Clin Rev Allergy 1989; 3:319–29.

14. Mygind N, Naclerio RM, editors. Allergic and non-allergic rhinitis. Philadelphia: 1993.

15. Toppozada H, Toppozada M, El-Ghazzawi I, et al. The human respiratory nasal mucosa in females using contraceptive pills. J Laryngol Otol 1984;98:43–51.

16. Creticos PS, Lockey RF, editors. Immunotherapy: a practical guide to current procedures. Milwaukee: American Academy of Allergy, Asthma and Immunology; 1994.

17. Demoly P, Michel F, Bousquet J. In vivo methods for the study of allergy: skin tests, techniques and interpretation. In: Middleton EJ, Reed CE, Ellis EF, et al, editors. Allergy: principles and practice. 5th ed. St. Louis: Mosby; 1998. p. 430–9.

18. Bernstein IL, Storms WW, et al. Practice parameters for allergy diagnostic testing: complete guidelines of the joint task force on practice parameters in allergy, asthma and immunology. Ann Allergy Asthma Immunol 1995;75(Pt 2):543–625.

19. Dreborg S, Backman A, Basomba A, et al. Skin tests used in type I allergy testing. Position paper of the European Academy of Allergy and Clinical Immunology. Allergy 1989;44:1–4.

20. Berg TLO, Johannson SGO. Allergy diagnosis with the radioallergosorbent test: a comparison with the results of skin and provocation tests in an unselected group of children with asthma and hay fever. J Allergy Clin Immunol 1974;54:209–21.

21. Homburger HA. Methods in laboratory immunology. In: Middleton EJ, Reed CE, Ellis EF, et al, editors. Allergy: principles and practice. 5th ed. St. Louis: Mosby; 1998. p. 417–29.

22. Ownby DR, Anderson JA, Jacob GL, et al. Development and comparative evaluation of a multiple-antigen RAST as a screening test for inhalant allergy. J Allergy Clin Immunol 1984;73:466–72.

23. Kjellman B, Peterson R. The problem of furred pets in childhood atopic disease. Allergy 1983;38:65–73.

24. Charpin C, Mata P, Charpin D, et al. Fel d I allergen distribution in cat fur and skin. J Allergy Clin Immunol 1991;88:77–82.

25. Glinert R, Wilson P, Wedner HJ. Fel d I is markedly reduced following sequential washing of cats. J Allergy Clin Immunol 1990;85:327–9.

26. Klucka CV, Ownby DR, Green J, et al. Cat shedding of Fel d I is not reduced by washings, Allerpet-C spray, or acepromazine. J Allergy Clin Immunol 1995;95:1164–71.

27. Avner DB, Perzanowski MS, Platts-Mills TAE. Evaluation of different techniques for washing cats: quantitation of allergen removed from the cat and the effect on airborne Fel d I. J Allergy Clin Immunol 1997;100:307–12.

28. Tovey ER, Chapman MD, Platts-Mills TAE. Mite feces are a major source of house dust allergens. Nature 1981;289:592–3.

29. Owen S, Morganstern M, Hepworth J, et al. Control of house dust mite antigen in bedding. Lancet 1990;335:396–7.

30. McDonald LG, Tovey E. The role of water temperature and laundry procedures in reducing house dust mite populations and allergen content of bedding. J Allergy Clin Immunol 1992;90:599–608.

31. Woodfolk JA, Hayden ML, Couture N, et al. Chemical treatment of carpets to reduce allergen: comparison of the effects of tannic acid and other treatment on proteins derived from dust mites and cats. J Allergy Clin Immunol 1995;96:325–33.

32. Meltzer EO, Welch MJ. Adverse effects of H1 receptor antagonists in the central nervous system. In: Simons FER, editor. Histamine and H1 receptor antagonists in allergic disease. New York: Marcel Dekker; 1996. p. 357–81.

33. Woosley RL, Chen Y, Freiman JP, et al. Mechanism of the cardiotoxic actions of terfenadine. JAMA 1993;269:1532–6.

34. Simons FER, Kesselman MS, Giddins NG, et al. Astemizole-induced torsades de pointes. Lancet 1988;2:624–7.

35. Simons FER. Antihistamines. In: Middleton EJ, Reed CE, Ellis EF, et al, editors. Allergy: principles and practice. 5th ed. St. Louis: Mosby; 1998. p. 612–37.

36. Ratner PH, et al. A double-blind, controlled trial to assess the safety and efficacy of azelastine nasal spray in seasonal allergic rhinitis. J Allergy Clin Immunol 1994;94:818–25.

37. Pipkorn U, Proud D, Lichtenstein LM, et al. Inhibition of mediator release in allergic rhinitis by pretreatment with topical glucocorticosteroids. N Engl J Med 1987;316:1506–10.

38. La Force C, Davis V. Nasal septal perforation with intranasal beclomethasone. J Allergy Clin Immunol 1985;75:186–8.

39. Brown HM, Storey G, Jackson FA. Beclomethasone diproprionate aerosol in treatment of perennial and seasonal rhinitis: a review of five years' experience. Br J Clin Pharmacol 1977;4:283–6S.

40. Barenholtz H. Effect of inhaled steroids on the risk of cataract formation in patients with steroid-dependent asthma. Ann Pharmacother 1996;30:1324–7.

41. Meltzer EO. Intranasal anticholinergic therapy of rhinorrhea. J Allergy Clin Immunol 1992;90:1055–70.

42. Grossman J, Banov C, Boggs P, et al. Use of ipratropium bromide nasal spray in chronic treatment of nonallergic perennial rhinitis, alone or in combination with other perennial rhinitis medications. J Allergy Clin Immunol 1995;95:1123–7.

43. Norris AA, Holgate ST. Cromolyn sodium and nedocromil sodium. In: Middleton EJ, Reed CE, Ellis EF, et al, editors. Allergy: principles and practice. 5th ed. St. Louis: Mosby; 1998:661–7.

44. Pelikan Z, Snoek WJ, Booij-Noord H, et al. Protective effect of disodium cromoglycate on the allergen provocation of the nasal mucosa. Ann Allergy 1970;28:548–53.

45. Norman PS, Lichtenstein LM. The clinical and immunologic specificity of immunotherapy. J Allergy Clin Immunol 1978;61:370–7.

46. Nelson HS. Immunotherapy for inhalant allergens. In: Middleton EJ, Reed CE, Ellis EF, et al, editors. Allergy: principles and practice. 5th ed. St. Louis: Mosby; 1998. p. 1050–62.

47. World Health Organization/IUIS (International Union of Immunological Societies) Working Group Report. Current status of allergen immunotherapy. Lancet 1989;1:259–366.

48. Metzger WJ, Turner E, Patterson R. The safety of immunotherapy during pregnancy. J Allergy Clin Immunol 1978;61:268–72.

49. Mawhinney H, Spector SL. Allergy diagnosis, environmental control and immunotherapy during pregnancy. In: Schatz M, Zeiger R, Claman H, editors. Lung biology in health and disease. New York: Marcel Dekker; 1998.

50. Schatz M, Zeiger RS. Diagnosis and management of rhinitis during pregnancy. Allergy Proc 1988;9:545–54.

51. Bende M, Hallgarde U, Sjogren C, Uvnas-Moberg K. Nasal congestion during pregnancy. Clin Otolaryngol 1989;14:385–7.

52. Sorri M, Hartikainen-Sorri A, Karja J. Rhinitis during pregnancy. Rhinology 1980;18:83–6.

53. Toppozada H, Michaels L, Toppozada M, et al. The human respiratory nasal mucosa in pregnancy. J Laryngol Otol 1982;96:613–26.

54. Bende M, Hallgarde U, Sjogren C. Occurrence of nasal congestion in pregnancy. Am J Rhinol 1989; 3:217–20.

55. Schatz M, Zeiger RS, Harden K, et al. The safety of asthma and allergy medications during pregnancy. J Allergy Clin Immunol 1997;100:301–6.

56. Werler MM, Mitchell AA, Shapiro A. First trimester maternal medication use in relation to gastroschisis. Teratology 1992;45:361–7.

57. Torfs CP, Katz EA, Bateson TF, et al. Maternal medications and environmental exposure as risk factors for gastroschisis. Teratology 1996;54:84–92.

58. Lipkowitz MA. The American College of Allergy, Asthma and Immunology Registry for Allergic, Asthmatic Pregnant Patients (RAAPP). J Allergy Clin Immunol 1999;103:S364–72.

26

OTITIS, PHARYNGITIS, AND SINUSITIS

Marilene B. Wang, MD

OTITIS

There are three components to the ear: the external ear, comprised of the cartilaginous auricle and bony portions of the external ear canal; the middle ear, including the tympanic membrane, ossicles, and middle ear space; and the inner ear, which is composed of the cochlea and the vestibular system (ie, semicircular canals, saccule, and utricle). The most common infections of the ear involve the external or middle ears. External ear infections are seen in those of all ages, whereas middle ear infections are more common in the pediatric population. Genders are affected equally by ear infections.

Otitis externa is defined as inflammation of the external ear, including the auricular cartilage, skin, and appendages of the external ear canal (Figure 26–1). External ear infections are characterized by exquisite warmth and tenderness of the pinna upon palpation, discharge from the external auditory canal, and, occasionally, fever.

There are many predisposing factors to the development of otitis externa, some of which are more common in women. Trauma from injudicious removal of cerumen or injury with a cotton-tipped swab may cause abrasion of the epithelial covering of the external auditory canal and allow entrance of bacteria. Accumulation of moisture from frequent swimming or scuba diving can lead to otitis externa. Piercing of the earlobe under nonsterile conditions can lead to a cellulitis of the auricle and extension into the external ear canal. Finally, many

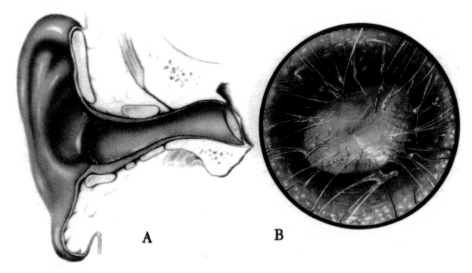

FIGURE 26–1. Otitis externa. *A*, The external ear canal is erythematous and swollen. *B*, Otoscopic examination may also reveal exudate. Reproduced with permission from Cummings CW, ed. Onlaryngology: Head and Neck Surgery. Mosby: St. Louis; 1986.

systemic conditions, such as nutritional deficiencies, endocrine abnormalities, and seborrheic dermatitis or psoriasis, can predispose an individual to developing otitis externa.

In most cases of otitis externa, bacterial cultures yield a mixed flora, with predominant presence of *Pseudomonas aeruginosa*.[1] Occasionally fungal elements can be seen in otitis externa, often after previous treatment with topical antibiotics.

The treatment for otitis externa includes pain relievers, cleansing of the ear canal, acidification of the ear canal, and topical and/or systemic antibiotics. Pain relief may require the short-term use of narcotics. Initial cleansing of the ear canal may be impossible due to edema of the external auditory canal. In such cases a wick may need to be placed in the ear by an otolaryngologist and saturated with an antibiotic/steroid solution. This allows penetration of the medication into ear canal, which results in a decrease in inflammation. Topical antibiotics (Cortisporin suspension or solution [hydrocortisone, neomycin sulfate, and polymyxin B sulfate]) or acidic solutions (VōSoL HC [acetic acid, benzethonium chloride, hydrocortisone, and 1, 2-propanediol diacetate]) should be given as two drops in the affected ear three times daily for 7 to 10 days. Systemic antibiotics are not always needed for cases of otitis externa. They should be reserved for use when there are signs of systemic infection, such as surrounding cellulitis, cervical lymphadenopathy, or an accompanying otitis media. Otitis externa with surrounding cellulitis generally is caused by *Pseudomonas* species and requires intravenous antibiotic therapy. Specialty consultation should be considered.

Otitis media is defined as an inflammatory condition of the middle ear, including the tympanic membrane, ossicles, and middle ear space. Although the disease most commonly affects infants and children, it may occur at any age, and the clinician must be alert to the different etiologies and management strategies pertaining to a particular age group.

Acute otitis media is characterized by a rapid onset of signs and symptoms of inflammation in the middle ear. Otalgia, fever, fullness in the ear, and decreased hearing acuity are common symptoms in the adult. On examination, an erythematous or perforated tympanic membrane is often seen, accompanied by a purulent discharge. There may be an accompanying upper respiratory infection or influenza-like syndrome as well.

In the adult population, certain factors predispose an individual to the development of otitis media. The most common cause of middle ear infections in the adult is dysfunction of the eustachian tube. The eustachian tube is composed of one-third bony and two-thirds cartilaginous material. Weakness of the eustachian tubes may be congenital or may develop later in life associated with aging and cartilage degeneration. More commonly, edema and inflammation of the nasopharynx cause eustachian tube dysfunction (ETD). The symptoms of ETD include intermittent popping and/or plugging of the ear, fullness or pain in the ear, and fluctuating hearing loss. Eustachian tube dysfunction allows a pressure differential to develop between the middle and the external ears. The resulting negative pressure in the middle ear results in an accumulation of a sterile effusion. Bacteria from the respiratory tract can then ascend and flourish in the middle ear.

Temporary ETD can occur during an upper respiratory infection or common cold. The edema and mucus from the nasal cavity and nasopharynx cause obstruction of the exit of the eustachian tubes, with the development of a resulting otitis media. Patients with allergic rhinitis and postnasal drip also have excess edema and mucus in the nasopharynx, causing obstruction of their eustachian tubes. Women in the second trimester of pregnancy sometimes experience an estrogen-induced rhinitis. Estrogens affect the ground substance in nasal mucosa, resulting in increased tissue edema and increased secretory activity in the mucous glands.[2,3] As in allergic rhinitis, this edema and mucous in the nasopharynx lead to obstruction of the eustachian tubes and predisposition to development of otitis media. In the absence of otitis media, ETD can be treated with oral or topical decongestants such as pseudoephedrine or oxymetazoline. The use of decongestants is described further in Chapter 25, "Allergic Rhinitis."

Otitis media is best treated empirically with antibiotics that are effective against the most common pathogens. Whereas in children under age 5 years, *Haemophilus influenzae* is a frequent pathogen, in older children and adults, *Streptococcus pneumoniae* is seen more commonly.[4] Amoxicillin, ampicillin, amoxicillin/clavulanate, cefuroxime, and trimethoprim/sulfamethoxazole are some useful antibiotics for acute otitis media (Table 26–1). A 10-day course of therapy should be completed to ensure resolution of the infection. A patient who fails one or

---

TABLE 26–1. Selected Oral Antibiotics for Otitis Media in Adults[*]

Amoxicillin 500 mg PO tid for 5–7 d[†]
Amoxicillin/clavulanate 875 mg/125 mg bid for 5–7 d
Cefuroxime axetil 500 mg PO bid for 5–7 d[†]

---

[*]Note: clarithromycin 500 mg PO bid for 10 d can be used for multiallergic patients, it is not known to be safe during pregnancy and breast-feeding.
[†]Considered safe for use during pregnancy and breast-feeding in nonallergic patients.
Adapted from Berkowitz et al,[5] Briggs et al,[6] and Gilbert DN, et al. The Sanford guide to antimicrobial therapy 2001. Hyde Park (VT): Antimicrobial Therapy Inc.

more courses of antibiotic therapy should be referred to an otolaryngologist for further work-up. Chronic mastoid disease, tympanic membrane perforation, and/or ETD may be an underlying etiology for the otitis media and may need to be addressed surgically.

PHARYNGITIS AND TONSILLITIS

Acute pharyngitis usually accompanies a viral upper respiratory infection (URI). Known as the common "sore throat," it is self-limited and requires no specific treatment other than symptomatic relief, which may be obtained from over-the-counter preparations, lozenges, and topical sprays. A sore throat that does not resolve within 7 to 10 days may require further work-up to determine etiologies other than a viral URI. Referral to an otolaryngologist may be indicated, particularly in a patient with a significant smoking history, for fiberoptic examination of the hypopharynx and larynx.

Although most cases of acute pharyngitis are viral in etiology, a significant number of sore throats are caused by ß-hemolytic streptococcus. The symptoms and signs of "strep throat" are essentially the same as those for viral pharyngitis. Microbiologic culture is the definitive method for diagnosis of streptococcal pharyngitis. A properly performed throat culture detects streptococcal infection in a symptomatic patient. A patient with frequent episodes of sore throat and/or acute tonsillitis should undergo a throat culture to determine whether a ß-hemolytic streptococcal infection is present. The antibiotic treatment of choice is penicillin administered orally (penicillin V 500 mg bid or 250 mg qid for 10 days) or intramuscularly (penicillin G benza-

thine 1.2 million units given once). Erythromycin can be used in patients who are allergic to penicillin (erythromycin base 500 mg qid for 10 days). Both are considered safe for use in pregnancy and breast-feeding in the nonallergic patient, except for the use of the estolate ester of erythromycin.[5,6]

Acute and chronic tonsillitis affect all ages and both sexes equally. In the pediatric population the large size of the tonsils relative to the oropharynx makes them susceptible to swelling and inflammation during the frequent URIs that occur in this age group. Sore throat, dysphagia, odynophagia, and referred otalgia are common symptoms of tonsillitis. A purulent exudate may form on the surface of the tonsils or a peritonsillar abscess may accumulate deep to the tonsils and appear as an asymmetric swelling of the soft palate. Peritonsillar abscess should be suspected when there is bulging of the tonsil and tonsillar pillar on one side of the oropharynx as well as asymmetry and fullness of the soft palate on one side. These symptoms indicate a submucosal collection of pus underneath the tonsil.

Treatment for acute tonsillitis includes oral antibiotics, fluids, analgesics, and antipyretics as needed. In severe cases of acute tonsillitis in which the patient is unable to tolerate oral intake, intravenous hydration and antibiotics are necessary. Peritonsillar abscesses should be evaluated by an otolaryngologist; they may be drained in the outpatient setting to prevent extension of the abscess to the parapharyngeal and prevertebral spaces. Patients should be given a course of antibiotics for 7 to 10 days for acute tonsillitis or after drainage of a peritonsillar abscess.

There are several indications for tonsillectomy, as recommended by the American Academy of Otolaryngology—Head and Neck Surgery[7]:

1. Patient experiencing three or more infections of tonsils and/or adenoids per year in spite of adequate medical therapy
2. Hypertrophy, of one or both tonsils, resulting in dental malocclusion or adverse effects on orofacial growth documented by an orthodontist
3. Hypertrophy, which results in upper airway obstruction, difficulty swallowing, sleep disturbances, or cardiopulmonary problems
4. Peritonsillar abscess that does not resolve after medical management and drainage
5. Persistent foul taste or halitosis due to chronic infection not responsive to medical therapy
6. Chronic or recurrent tonsillitis in a patient who is a streptococcal carrier and who does not respond to appropriate antibiotics
7. Asymmetric tonsil hypertrophy suspicious for malignancy

A patient with any of the above conditions should be referred to an otolaryngologist for evaluation for a tonsillectomy.

SINUSITIS

Normal Physiology

The sinus epithelium forms a mucociliary system that supplies the nose with a mucus covering to warm and humidify inspired air. Both parasympathetic and sympathetic nerves supply this mucous blanket, which is renewed every 10 to 15 minutes.[8] The cilia beat 10 to 15 times per second and move the mucous blanket toward the natural ostia of the sinuses. Environmental factors influence ciliary function; humidity increases the activity, whereas dehydration and cold temperatures decrease flow.[9] Bacterial and viral proliferation may increase when there is dysfunction of the cilia and relative stasis of the mucous blanket.

In addition to mucociliary dysfunction, any condition that obstructs the drainage of the sinuses (eg, polyps or inflammation and edema of the nasal mucosa) leads to sinusitis. Benign and malignant tumors of the nasal cavity, paranasal sinuses, and skull base also can lead to a postobstructive sinusitis of one or more of the paranasal sinuses.

Inflammatory Conditions

Acute rhinosinusitis is one of the most common healthcare problems afflicting the population, and it is increasing in both incidence and prevalence.[10]

Costs associated with this disease are enormous and include significant loss of productivity at work and school.[11,12] Acute rhinosinusitis affects all age groups, including the pediatric population. One study from Denmark indicated that women may be more frequently afflicted with acute sinusitis than are men.[13] Acute rhinosinusitis is found often in conjunction with a viral URI and generally lasts 4 weeks or less.[14] Edema and inflammation of the nasal mucosa, including the turbinates, result in symptoms of nasal congestion, rhinorrhea, postnasal drip, and fever. Inflammation can extend to involve the mucosa of the paranasal sinuses. Edema and mucus production within the sinuses lead to partial or complete blockage of the natural ostia. This, in turn, can result in further fluid accumulation, causing pain and pressure of the involved sinus. Stasis of mucus and fluid in the sinuses leads to bacterial overgrowth and sinus infection. Bacterial etiologies of acute rhinitis and sinusitis include the common upper respiratory pathogens: *Streptococcus pneumoniae*, *Staphylococcus aureus*, and *Haemophilus influenzae*, among others.[15–17] Without treatment, the sinusitis may progress to a cellulitis and/or abscess of the orbit and eventually a cavernous sinus thrombosis.[18] Patients with recurrent episodes of acute rhinosinusitis may be candidates for surgery.

No specific treatment is necessary for uncomplicated **acute rhinitis** associated with a URI. Symptomatic relief may be obtained with antihistamines, decongestants, and nonsteroidal anti-inflammatory drugs.

Fungal sinusitis is less common and may be classified as invasive or allergic. Invasive fungal sinusitis usually afflicts diabetics and other immunocompromised hosts. Mucormycosis is a life-threatening invasive fungal sinusitis with a propensity to spread to the central nervous system via blood vessels.[19] Thrombosis of the tissue vessels results in a necrotic-appearing black nasal mucosa. A patient suspected of having mucormycosis requires immediate biopsy of the nasal tissue and crusts. Emergency surgical débridement is mandatory once the diagnosis of mucormycosis is obtained. Aggressive resection of all affected tissue may necessitate radical maxillectomy, orbital exenteration, or even craniotomy. *Aspergillus*, *Blastomyces*, and other fungi are involved less commonly in invasive sinusitis.

Allergic fungal sinusitis usually affects a younger population of patients. These patients often

TABLE 26–2. Selected Oral Antibiotic Regimens for Acute Sinusitis[*]

Amoxicillin 500 mg PO tid for 10 d[†]
Amoxicillin/clavulanate 875/125 mg bid for 10 d
Cefuroxime axetil 250 mg PO bid for 10 d [†]

[*]Regimens should be accompanied by the use of decongestants, such as pseudoephedrine extended release 120 mg bid.
Note: clarithromycin 500 mg PO bid for 10 d can be used in multiallergic patients, but is not known to be safe in pregnant and breast-feeding patients.
[†]Considered safe for use during pregnancy and breast-feeding in nonallergic patients.
Adapted from Berkowitz et al,[5] Briggs et al,[6] and Gilbert DN, et al. The Sanford guide to antimicrobial therapy 2001. Hyde Park (VT): Antimicrobial Therapy Inc.

have concurrent asthma and nasal polyps and do not respond to repeated courses of antibiotics. They often have elevated total IgE levels and are atopic to both fungal and nonfungal antigens.[20,21] Their sinuses are filled with thick mucoid secretions that contain eosinophils and fungal elements.[22,23] In contrast to the fungal sinusitis of immunocompromised patients, these fungal elements are not angioinvasive, and radical surgical intervention is not required.

Acute sinusitis is difficult to differentiate from acute rhinitis. The presence of purulent nasal secre-tions has been the only reliable clinical predictor of sinusitis in several studies.[24] Acute sinusitis is treated initially with decongestants and oral antibiotics (Table 26–2). Severe refractory sinusitis may require intravenous antibiotics. Surgical drainage is neces-sary for sinusitis that fails to respond to medical ther-apy, or if there is concomitant orbital or brain involvement or fungal sinusitis. Endoscopic drainage is appropriate for most cases of sinusitis, except when débridement of tissue is necessary as in mucormy-cosis. Allergic fungal sinusitis is best treated by

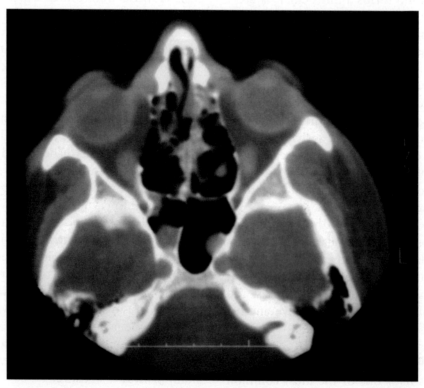

FIGURE 26–2. Chronic rhinosinusitis. Typical findings of mucosal thickening in the ethmoid, maxillary, and sphenoid sinuses bilaterally are demonstrated on this computed tomographic scan.

TABLE 26–3. Selected Nasal Steroids for Chronic Sinusitis

Triamcinolone (Nasacort, Nasacort AQ) 2 puffs in each nostril qd

Fluticasone (Flonase) 2 puffs in each nostril qd

Beclomethasone 1–2 puffs in each nostril bid (Beconase Aq, Vancenase AQ) or qd (Vancenase AQ DS)

Mometasone (Nasonex) 2 puffs in each nostril qd

DS = double strength

endoscopic surgical drainage of the sinuses, followed by systemic and intranasal corticosteroids.[25,26]

Chronic rhinosinusitis is most often allergic in etiology and lasts longer than 12 weeks. Symptoms are similar to those in acute rhinosinusitis and include nasal congestion, rhinorrhea, facial pressure and pain, postnasal drip, halitosis, hyposmia, and headache. Nasal polyps may be present as well. Other concurrent conditions should be sought, including cystic fibrosis, aspirin sensitivity, and asthma. Computed tomographic scans in chronic rhinosinusitis reveal mucoperiosteal thickening or complete opacification of one or more sinuses (Figure 26–2).

Medical treatment for chronic rhinosinusitis includes antibiotics, antihistamines, nasal steroid sprays, and short courses of oral steroids.[27] Amoxicillin-clavulinic acid may be superior to other commonly used antibiotics.[28] A typical regimen consists of amoxicillin-clavulinic acid 500 mg tid for 6 weeks. Nasal steroid regimens are summarized in Table 26–3. In addition, the underlying allergies should be addressed, and immunotherapy for allergies may be of benefit. Referral to an otolaryngologist is indicated when a patient fails medical treatment for chronic rhinosinusitis. Surgery may be indicated when medical treatment has not resulted in satisfactory improvement of symptoms. Following surgery, medical treatment for the underlying allergic condition should be continued, including nasal steroids, nasal irrigation with normal saline, and systemic antihistamines.

REFERENCES

1. Feinmesser R, Wiesel YM, Argaman M, Gay I. Otitis externa—bacteriological survey. ORL J Otorhinolaryngol Relat Spec 1982;44:121–5.

2. Weisskopf A. Connective tissue: a synthesis of modern thought and its impact on the understanding of nasal disease. Laryngoscope 1960;70:1029–59.

3. Toppozada H, Toppozada M, El-Ghazzawi I, Elwany S. The human respiratory nasal mucosa in females using contraceptive pills. J Laryngol Otol 1984;98:43–51.

4. Klein JO, Daum RS. The diagnosis and management of the patient with otitis media. New York: Biomedical Information Corp.; 1985.

5. Berkowitz RL, Coustan DR, Mochizuki TK. Handbook for prescribing medications during pregnancy. 2nd ed. Boston: Little, Brown; 1986.

6. Briggs GG, Freeman RK, Yaffe SJ. Drugs in pregnancy and lactation. 5th ed. Baltimore: Williams & Wilkins; 1998.

7. The American Academy of Otolaryngology—Head and Neck Surgery. 2000 clinical indicators compendium. Alexandria (VA): AAO-HNS; 2000.

8. Hilding AC. The role of the respiratory mucosa in health and disease. Minn Med 1967;50:915–9.

9. Grossan M. The saccharin test of nasal mucociliary function. Eye Ear Nose Throat 1975;54:415–7.

10. Benson V, Marano MA. Current estimates from the 1993 National Health Interview Survey. National Center for Health Statistics. Vital Health Stat 1994;190:1–22.

11. Collins JG. Prevalence of selected chronic conditions: United States, 1986–88. National Center for Health Statistics. Vital Health Stat 1993;10:1–87.

12. Hahn B, Lefkowitz D. Annual expenses and sources of payment for health care services. Rockville (MD): Public Health Service, National Expenditure Survey Research Findings 14, Agency for Health Care Policy and Research; 1994. AHCPR Publication No.: 93–0007, 1994.

13. Mabeck CE. Prescription of antibacterial drugs for treatment of otitis media and upper respiratory tract infections in general practice in Denmark. Acta Otolaryngol 1982;93:69–72.

14. Lanza D, Kennedy D. Adult rhinosinusitis defined. Otolaryngol Head Neck Surg 1997;117 Suppl:S1–7.

15. Gwaltney JM, Scheld WM, Sande MA, et al. The microbial etiology and antimicrobial therapy of adults with acute community-acquired sinusitis: a

fifteen-year experience at the University of Virginia and review of other selected studies. J Allergy Clin Immunol 1992;90:457–62.

16. Gwaltney JM, Sydnor A, Sande MA. Etiology and antimicrobial treatment of acute sinusitis. Ann Otol Rhinol Laryngol 1981;90:68–71.

17. Jousimies-Somer HR, Savolainen S, Ylikoski JS. Bacteriological findings of acute maxillary sinusitis in young adults. J Clin Microbiol 1988;26:1919–25.

18. Chandler JR, Langenbruner DJ, Stevens ER. The pathogenesis of orbital complications in acute sinusitis. Laryngoscope 1970;80:1414–28.

19. Peterson KL, Wang M, Canalis RF, Abemayor E. Rhinocerebral mucormycosis: evolution of the disease and treatment options. Laryngoscope 1997; 107:855–62.

20. Manning SC, Mabry RL, Shaefer SD, et al. Evidence of IgE-mediated hypersensitivity in allergic fungal sinusitis. Laryngoscope 1992;103:717–21.

21. Mabry RL, Manning SC. Radioallergosorbent microscreen and total immunoglobulin E in allergic fungal sinusitis. Otolaryngol Head Neck Surg 1995; 113:721–3.

22. Bent JP III, Kuhn FA. Diagnosis of allergic fungal sinusitis. Otolaryngol Head Neck Surg 1994; 111:580–5.

23. Morpeth JF, Rupp NT, Dolen WK, et al. Fungal sinusitis: an update. Ann Allergy Asthma Immunol 1996;76:128–40.

24. Hueston WJ, Eberlein C, Johnson D, et al. Criteria used by clinicians to differentiate sinusitis from viral upper respiratory tract infection. J Fam Pract 1998; 46:487–92.

25. Goldstein MF, Atkins PC, Cogen FC, et al. Allergic *Aspergillus* sinusitis. J Allergy Clin Immunol 1985; 76:515–24.

26. DeShazo RD, Swain RE. Diagnostic criteria for allergic fungal sinusitis. J Allergy Clin Immunol 1995;96: 24–35.

27. Benninger MS, Anon J, Mabry RL. The medical management of rhinosinusitis. Otolaryngol Head Neck Surg 1997;117 Suppl:S41–9.

28. Brook I. Microbiology and management of sinusitis. J Otolaryngol 1996;25:249–56.

27

APPROACH TO

THE PATIENT WITH COUGH

Jeffrey Goldsmith, MD, and Eric Kleerup, MD

Cough serves as an important defense mechanism by helping to clear secretions and foreign material from the airways. Among nonsmoking adults, the prevalence of chronic cough in the United States is reported to range from 14 to 23%.[1,2] Cough is the most common chief complaint and is mentioned by patients as the principle reason for the visit in 25.8 million ambulatory care visits in 1996 in the United States.[3] The expenditure for over-the-counter cough suppressants, which modify rather than eliminate cough, is approximately $1 billion per year.[4]

The complications of cough include retching, exhaustion, hoarseness, insomnia, urinary incontinence, excessive sweating, and dizziness. Chronic cough is associated with deterioration in a patient's quality of life, and the patient may be most troubled by the psychosocial complications. Most patients that seek medical attention are needing reassurance that nothing is serious, are concerned that something is wrong, feel that others think something is wrong with them, or are embarrassed and self-conscious.[4] It is therefore inappropriate to minimize this complaint and important to have a comfortable grasp on the most common etiologies of the cough. Evaluation of chronic cough requires a careful history and physical examination, attention to previous treatment successes and failures, diagnostic testing, therapeutic trials, and persistence.

Cough is divided into two overlapping categories. Acute cough is defined as that lasting 3 or fewer weeks. Chronic cough lasts longer than 3 to 8 weeks.[5] Acute cough is most often due to the common cold but may be associated with pneumonia, congestive heart failure, pulmonary embolism, and other more serious acute illnesses. Chronic cough is most often caused by one (38 to 82% of cases) or a combination (18 to 62% of cases) of three processes: postnasal drip syndrome (PNDS), asthma, and/or gastroesophageal reflux disease (GERD), if the patient is a nonsmoker who is not medicated with an angiotensin converting enzyme inhibitor (ACEI) and has normal or stable scarring patterns on a chest radiograph (Table 27–1, Figure 27–1).[1,5] More serious illnesses also may present with chronic cough. Cough is present in 79% of patients with non–small cell lung cancer at presentation.[6] The character, timing, or complications of cough are not likely to be useful in diagnosing the cause of cough.[4]

ANATOMY AND PHYSIOLOGY OF COUGH

Cough involves a complex reflex arc including stimulation of an irritant receptor, transmission to the central nervous system, pattern generation in the brain, transmission to the effector muscles, and action of the muscles to produce a cough.

Irritant Receptors

Rapidly adapting irritant receptors in the epithelium act as mechanical (pressure and displacement) and chemical sensors. Mechanical sensors are most numerous on the posterior wall of the trachea, the carina, and the branching points of the larger airways.[5,7–9] Chemical sensors are sensitive to noxious gases and fumes and are localized primarily in the larynx and bronchi. Bronchioles and subsegmental

---

TABLE 27–1. Causes of Chronic Cough

Common causes

　　Chronic obstructive pulmonary disease; tobacco smoking
　　Drugs: angiotensin converting enzyme inhibitors
　　Postnasal drip syndrome: allergic rhinitis, vasomotor rhinitis, sinusitis
　　Asthma
　　Gastroesophageal reflux

Uncommon causes

　　Bronchiectasis
　　Recurrent aspiration
　　Occupational exposure to irritants
　　Carcinoma: lung, laryngeal, lymphoma, metastatic
　　Foreign-body aspiration
　　Habit or psychogenic cough
　　Interstitial pulmonary fibrosis: idiopathic, pneumonoconiosis, hypersensitivity pneumonitis, sarcoidosis
　　Pulmonary-vascular conditions: embolism, infarction, hypertension, vasculitis, edema
　　Chronic infections: tuberculosis, coccidioidomycosis, histoplasmosis, pertussis, ascariasis

---

bronchi appear to be devoid of these afferent nerve complexes.[10] Outside the lower respiratory tract, mechanical sensing cough receptors have been identified in the pharynx and are inferred in the external auditory canal and eardrums, paranasal sinuses, diaphragm, pleura, pericardium, and stomach. Adaptation (decreased sensitivity after repetitive stimulation) of mechanical receptors is more rapid and complete than that of chemical receptors.

Experimentally, cough can be induced by inhalation of capsaicin, tartaric acid, citric acid, or distilled water. Women demonstrate a three- to five-fold heightened sensitivity to capsaicin compared to men.[11,12]

Cough receptors are innervated primarily by branches of the vagus nerve. The superior laryngeal nerves carry the majority of sensory innervations from the larynx. This area provides the greatest protection against aspiration of foreign material.[9] Mucosal receptors in the distal esophagus may contribute to afferent cough reflex in patients with GERD; they also travel via the vagus nerve.[13] Other inputs that may have less significance include trigeminal, glossopharyngeal and phrenic nerves.

Central Pattern Generation

Cough is a centrally mediated event with origins in the medulla oblongata of the brain stem. **Afferent** nerve inputs are initially received by the nucleus tractus solitarii.[14] An integrated cough response is coordinated in diffuse areas of the medulla oblongata; this is blocked by opiates, if present. **Efferent** nerve outputs from the ventral respiratory group (nucleus retroambigualis) feed to the inspiratory and expiratory respiratory muscles, the larynx, and the bronchial tree. These efferent outputs are carried both by the phrenic and other spinal motor nerves, and recurrent laryngeal branches of the vagus nerve.[15]

Mechanical Elements of Cough

Cough is a critical defense mechanism that aids in clearing excessive secretions and foreign material from the airways. The sudden explosive force of air through the glottis can exceed 12 L/s through the tracheobronchial tree and enhances the removal of mucus adhering to the walls of the airway.[16] The intrathoracic pressures generated during a cough can be as high as 300 mm Hg, and velocities of up to 85% of the speed of sound can be created.[5] The hemodynamic changes of a vigorous cough are similar to that of a chest compression; in the expiratory phase, systolic pressures can approach 140 mm Hg.[17]

VIRAL UPPER RESPIRATORY TRACT INFECTIONS

Acute cough usually is due to the common cold. The common cold, influenza, and other acute upper respiratory infections (URIs) are the most frequent

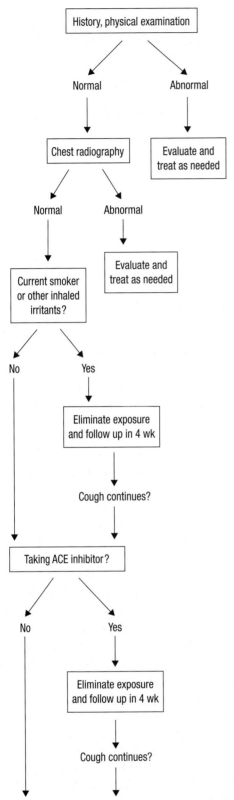

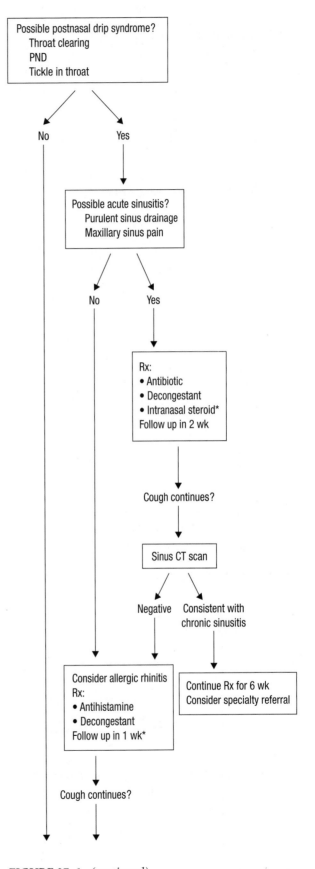

FIGURE 27–1. Evaluation of chronic cough.* See text for details. PND = postnasal drip; URI = upper respiratory infection; GERD = gastroesophageal reflux disease; Rx = prescription; CT = computed tomography.

FIGURE 27–1. *(continued)*

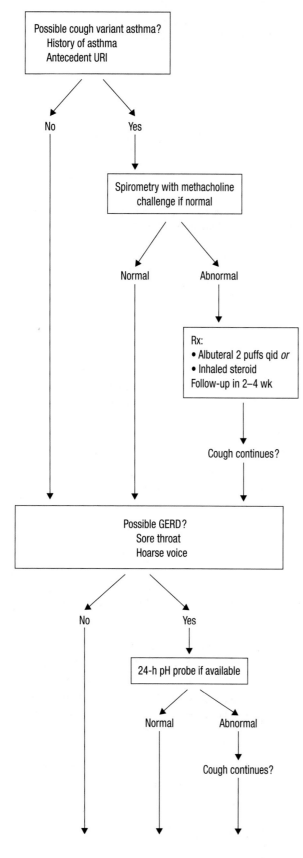

FIGURE 27–1. (continued)

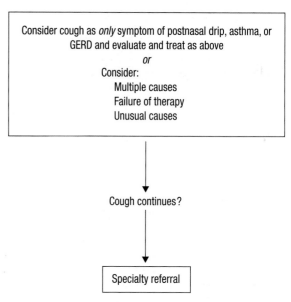

FIGURE 27–1. (continued)

acute ailments known to mankind, with 200 million cases reported annually in the United States.[18] Viral upper respiratory tract infections cause the majority of "colds." Cough is present in 83% of patients with the common cold within the first 48 hours and persists in 26% on day 14.[19] Postviral rhinitis often causes a postnasal drip-associated cough (see section below). *Mycoplasma pneumoniae, Chlamydia pneumoniae,* and *Bordetella pertussis* in adults and *Chlamydia trachomatis, Ureaplasma urealyticum,* cytomegalovirus, and *Pneumocystis carinii* in children also produce prolonged coughs. Increased sensitivity to inhaled capsaicin develops during URIs without increase in methacholine sensitivity.[20] This implies a role for substance P postviral cough. Increased degrees of airway hyper-responsiveness have been demonstrated in both asthmatics and nonasthmatics following viral respiratory tract infections.[21]

Treatment with an antihistamine/decongestant (eg, dexbrompheniramine maleate 6 mg/pseudoephedrine 120 mg PO bid) or an intranasal anticholinergic spray, (eg, ipratropium nasal spray 0.03% two sprays in each nostril qid) reduces postnasal drip and cough.[19,22,23] Antihistamines alone, such as terfenadine, chlorpheniramine maleate, and diphenhydramine hydrochloride, do not. In 86% of cases, inhaled ipratropium is effective in relieving or improving persistent cough (>2 months) following URI in patients with a negative methacholine challenge test.[24] Asthma or cough variant asthma exacerbation also must be considered following

URI. The diagnosis and treatment of asthma are discussed below and in Chapter 28.

DRUG-INDUCED COUGH

The Drugdex Adverse Drug Reactions Index (Micromedex) reports 137 drugs causing cough. The frequency, severity, and clinical significance of cough varies with each drug. In determining the cause of chronic cough, ACEIs are the most clinically important drugs to consider. Treatment with ACEIs is associated with cough as a side effect in about 10% of patients (Table 27–2). The ACEIs probably cause an inhibition of the degradation of kinins, particularly bradykinin, in the airway.[25] Inhibition of prostaglandin (PG) and thromboxane synthesis by cyclooxygenase inhibitors (eg, indomethacin and sulindac) or antagonism of thromboxane (eg, with picotamide) inhibits ACEI-induced cough.[26] Bradykinin, PGE_2, substance P, or other tachykinins might accumulate in tissues after use of ACEIs, and thromboxane may amplify their cough-inducing potential. In one randomized trial women treated with the ACEI lisinopril reported cough three times more often than did men.[27] Cough resolves within 1 month of stopping the ACEI.[28] Angiotensin II–receptor antagonists such as irbesartan, losartan, and valsartan have a low incidence of inducing cough, even in patients with ACEI induced cough.[29]

POSTNASAL DRIP SYNDROME

"Postnasal drip syndrome" (PNDS) is best understood as an umbrella term describing the end point of a number of etiologies. The variety of causes of PNDS all result in the movement of secretions from the nose or sinuses into the hypopharynx and stimulation of the afferent limb of the cough reflex. Therefore, any process resulting in mucus drainage along this pathway may result in PNDS–postviral

TABLE 27–2. Frequency of Drug-Induced Cough[*]

	Frequency (%)	
Treatment	Women	Men
Lisinopril	19.0	7.3
Nifedipine	−1.4	1.0

[*]As compared with frequency during treatment with placebo. Adapted from Os I, Bratland B, Dahleof B, et al. Female preponderance for lisinopril-induced cough in hypertension. Am J Hypertens 1994;7:1012–5.

rhinitis (discussed above), allergic seasonal and perennial rhinitis, vasomotor rhinitis, or sinusitis. Collectively, this group is the most common etiology of chronic cough, with a range in prevalence of up to 87%.[1]

The most common historic features of PNDS include a sensation of material in the back of the throat with an associated tickle, clearing of mucopurulent secretions from the oropharynx, and cough.[30] Further evaluation of the timing, character, or complications experienced with the chronic cough has been found to be of little use in defining its etiology.[31] The most common findings on physical examination include mucus on the posterior oropharynx or submucosal lymphoid follicle hyperplasia on the oropharyngeal mucosa ("cobblestoning"). Neither are specific for the etiology of PNDS.

Allergic Rhinitis

There are 25.7 million cases of allergic rhinitis reported annually in the United States.[18] Symptoms classically experienced by patients with this disorder are the result of an array of bioactive mediators, cytokines, and cells in nasal mucosa that result in an inflammatory reaction and excess mucus production.[32] In fact, rhinitis may share a common pathophysiology with asthma; it is characterized by similar inflammatory events and responds to similar treatment modalities.[33] Postviral rhinitis is best distinguished from that of the allergic variant by its duration and association with a recent URI.

The treatment of allergic rhinitis–associated cough consists of a combination of a first-generation antihistamine and a decongestant.[1,5] The anticholinergic side effects of first-generation antihistamines may be their greatest advantage. The data supporting the use of newer less-sedating antihistamines is sparse; in most studies they have been found to be ineffective in decreasing cough associated with PNDS but can be considered for patients unable to tolerate drowsiness from first-generation antihistamines.[34] Nasal corticosteroids can be added if an antihistamine-decongestant regimen is unsuccessful after 1 week or they can be an alternate treatment for patients experiencing side effects.[1] The evaluation and treatment of allergic rhinitis is reviewed in detail in Chapter 25.

Vasomotor Rhinitis

"Vasomotor rhinitis" or "nonallergic noninfectious perennial rhinitis" refers to a syndrome of sinus

---

TABLE 27–3. Treatment of Sinusitis

Acute sinusitis

Antibiotic (3–10 d): eg, amoxicillin/clavulanate, trimethoprim/sulfamethoxazole, doxycycline, loracarbef, cefuroxime, or erythromycin/sulfisoxazole[*]

Decongestant[†]

Possibly, inhaled nasal corticosteroids and/or antihistamines[‡]

Chronic sinusitis

Antibiotic (3–6 wk) preferably based on culture results: amoxicillin/clavulanate, loracarbef, cefuroxime[*]

Decongestant, at least initially[†]

Inhaled nasal corticosteroids[291]

Saline irrigation of the nasal passages

Surgical drainage if above measures fail, if sinusitis is recurrent, or if fungal sinusitis is present

---

[*]Dosages of antibiotics in sinusitis: amoxicillin/clavulanate 875 mg/125 mg bid; trimethoprim/sulfamethoxazole 160 mg/800 mg (double strength) bid; doxycycline 100 mg qd; loracarbef 400 mg bid; cefuroxime 250 mg bid; erythromycin/sulfisoxazole 500 mg/500 mg bid.
[†]Dosages of decongestants in sinusitis: pseudoephedrine extended-release 120 mg PO bid; oxymetazoline nasal spray 2 puffs in each nostril bid.
[‡]Dosages of inhaled nasal corticosteroids: budesonide 1–2 puffs bid; beclomethasone 1–2 puffs bid; flunisolide 2 puffs bid; triamcinolone 2 puffs qd; fluticasone 2 puffs qd.

---

complaints for which an etiology cannot be found. The symptoms resemble those of allergic rhinitis; however, there are fewer pruritus, sneezing, and conjunctival symptoms and more sinus symptoms. Irritants such as cigarette smoke and environmental changes seem to be common triggers.[35] The exact mechanism of vasomotor rhinitis is still in debate; however, it appears that inflammatory cells do not play a major role in the pathogenesis of this disorder.[36] It is possible that abnormalities in either the mucosa or nerve endings, resulting in various forms of nasal hyper-reactivity, may be responsible for this condition.

Studies of the use of nasal ipratropium bromide (an anticholinergic) are limited, but it may have benefit alone or in combination with first-generation antihistamines, decongestants, or intranasal steroids in patients with vasomotor rhinitis.[37,38]

Sinusitis

Sinusitis is a less common cause of PNDS-associated cough.[1] Acute sinusitis usually is associated with a bacterial infection and is defined as being no longer than 3 weeks in duration. It is most often a complication of viral or allergic inflammation of the upper respiratory tract resulting in obstruction of sinus drainage, and it most often is associated with complaints of sinus pressure, maxillary headaches, and nasal discharge discoloration.[39] The physical finding of sinus tenderness is correlated strongly with this disorder, but it is absent in many patients.[40, 41] In one study it was not possible to distinguish those patients who had PNDS as a result of sinusitis from those who did not. Sinusitis could only be diagnosed by use of sinus radiography.[30]

Streptococcus pneumoniae, Haemophilus influenzae, and *Moraxella catarrhalis* are the bacterial pathogens to consider when there is a high index of clinical suspicion for sinusitis.[41] In addition to killing/suppressing microorganisms (antimicrobial therapy), treatment must reduce tissue edema, facilitating drainage and maintaining ostial patency (decongestant therapy) (Table 27–3). Intranasal corticosteroids can effectively reduce the duration and severity of cough associated with acute sinusitis, at least in children.[42]

Chronic sinusitis should be considered in patients with symptoms such as those described for acute sinusitis but lasting more than 8 to 12 weeks. In patients with presumptive allergic or vasomotor rhinitis unresponsive to therapy, a limited sinus computed tomography or radiography should be considered for evaluation of occult chronic sinusitis. Anaerobic bacteria, coagulase-negative staphylococci, and *Staphylococcus aureus* are predominant in chronic sinusitis.[41,43] In addition to a prolonged course of antibiotics, decongestants, and intranasal steroids, patients may require surgical drainage procedures to eradicate symptoms.

ASTHMA

Cough is a frequent symptom of asthma. Most commonly, asthma is accompanied by dyspnea, wheezing, expiratory obstruction, and/or chest tightness; however, it is clear that some individuals have only cough as the only symptom of asthma.[44] Twenty-four to 29% of patients with chronic cough have cough variant asthma as two contributory causes, but only 6 to 7% have chronic cough, without other signs, symptoms, or findings of asthma, that is responsive to asthma-specific therapy alone.[1,30, 45] Asthma is an inflammatory process of the airways. Inflammation of the airways results in nonspecific hyper-reactivity to a variety of stimuli including methacholine, cold air, and hypertonic saline. Bronchoconstriction, a drop of about 20% in FEV_1 (forced expiratory volume in 1 second) to a provocative challenge with < 10 mg/mL of inhaled methacholine is considered a positive result of a challenge test. Bronchoconstriction with between 10 and 25 mg/mL of methacholine is considered intermediate and may be present in patients with allergic rhinitis. The methacholine challenge test has a positive predictive value of between 60 to 82% and a negative predictive value of nearly 100% for cough variant asthma.[1] Symptoms of asthma including cough often are exacerbated by viral URIs. A childhood history of asthma, onset of chronic cough following viral URI, or a typical history of prolonged cough following viral URI is suggestive of, but not specific for, cough variant asthma as the cause of chronic cough.

Response to asthma-specific therapy is necessary to confirm the diagnosis of cough variant asthma. Usually therapy is initiated with an inhaled ß₂-agonist, such as albuterol two puffs four times daily. Of patients with a positive methacholine challenge, 60% resolve after 1 week of ß₂-agonist therapy; no additional patients improve after a supplementary 2 to 6 weeks of low-dose inhaled corticosteroids.[46] However, inhaled corticosteroids also have been demonstrated to be of use in the treatment of cough variant asthma.[47] A diagnostic trial of inhaled corticosteroids may require several weeks to be effective. A diagnostic trial of oral corticosteroids might incidentally treat some patients with allergic rhinitis; it is, therefore, nonspecific. Long-term therapy for cough variant asthma is usually successful with low-dose inhaled corticosteroids, but presumably long-acting bronchodilators such as salmeterol also would be successful. Escalation of asthma treatment, as is used for asthma with dyspnea, may be necessary for refractory cases. This is described further in Chapter 28, "Asthma." Cough may be made worse by the cold temperature of the inhaler spray, the droplets impacting on the oropharynx, or the added excipients such as oleic acid (in beclomethasone and albuterol).

Twenty-four percent of women report subjective and objective (peak flow measurements) worsening of asthma in relation to their menstrual cycle, most commonly in the premenstrual and/or the menstrual week.[48] Presumably menstrual cycle–phase variation in severity also may be present in cough variant asthma. Although treatment of asthma exacerbations related to the menstrual cycle has not been extensively studied, the use of oral contraceptives appears to have been useful in at least one case.[49]

GASTROESOPHAGEAL REFLUX

The movement of acid and other gastric contents into the esophagus is a normal asymptomatic event. When it results in symptoms or physical complications, GERD is diagnosed. Reflux also may be a sequelae of cough.[50] Distinguishing normal asymptomatic reflux from pathologic reflux causing cough is difficult (Table 27–4).[51] A successful therapeutic trial is considered the gold standard.

Gastroesophageal reflux disease is found in up to 21% of patients with chronic cough.[52] In addition 80% of patients with asthma have documented GERD when examined by 24-hour ambulatory esophageal pH monitoring.[5] Cough was found to be caused by GERD 11% of the time in one frequently cited study but always in combination with either asthma or PNDS or both.[1]

The mechanism of GERD and its relation to cough is thought to be due to either irritation of vagal receptors found in the distal esophagus or microaspiration. As few as 25% of patients have complaints of heartburn (dyspepsia), sour eructations, bitter taste, or regurgitation in those cases in which cough is mediated by vagal sensory nerves in the esophagus.[13,52–54] It may be that acid reflux produces chronic irritation of the mucosa, resulting in hypersensitivity to a variety of stimuli. Acid-induced cough is inhibited experimentally by inhalation but not esophageal instillation of ipratropium bromide

TABLE 27–4. Reflux Events* in Patients with or without Gastroesophageal Reflux Disease–Associated Cough†

Characteristic	Subjects with Cough (n = 12): % Positive for GERD (mean ± SD)	Asymptomatic Normal Subjects with Reflux (95th percentile)
Reflux symptoms	25	—
Reflux events (distal)	Total 42 (53 ± 56) Upright (48 ± 50), supine (5 ± 7)	< 51 events
Reflux events lasting ≥ 5 min (distal)	Total 25 (3 ± 4) Upright (3 ± 4), supine (0±0)	≤ 4 events
% of time pH < 4 (distal)	25 (4 ± 5)	< 4.4% of study time
Reflux preceding and during cough	93 (12 ± 12)	—

*Found on 24-h pH monitoring.
†Successfully treated with antireflux measures.
SD = standard deviation.
Adapted from Irwin RS, French CL, Curley FJ, et al. Chronic cough due to gastroesophageal reflux. Clinical, diagnostic, and pathogenetic aspects. Chest 1993;104:1511–7.

(an anticholinergic) and by topical anesthesia of the esophagus with lidocaine.[13,52–54] Microaspiration, however, usually is associated with more classic symptoms–most notably hoarseness and sore throat.[52,55]

The initial investigation to assess for GERD is a 24-hour pH probe to evaluate the extent of reflux and its temporal relationship to cough. An empiric trial of therapy for GERD-associated cough is appropriate in patients with symptomatic GERD, those who do not have another cause for cough (eg, asthma or PND), those who fail therapy for another cause of cough, or if 24-hour pH probe monitoring is not available.[5,56,57] Empiric therapy usually begins with the use of a proton pump inhibitor. Omeprazole 20 mg PO qd or lansoprazole 15 mg qd is a usual initial starting dosage. Higher doses (eg, omeprazole 40 mg bid or lansoprazole 30 mg bid) may be required. In addition to gastric acid supression, dietary and lifestyle changes and possibly prokinetic agents are recommended as initial therapy, with

clinical response taking up to 6 months (Table 27–5).[1,58] If initial therapy is unsuccessful, a further evaluation of GERD with a 24-hour pH probe on therapy is warranted, because treatment may not have adequately suppressed the reflux. When specific antireflux medications have successfully alleviated the symptoms of cough, then the diagnosis of GERD as the cause of cough can be made.

CHRONIC OBSTRUCTIVE PULMONARY DISEASE

Chronic bronchitis is defined clinically as production of any sputum (whether expectorated or swallowed), usually accompanied by chronic cough, occurring on most days for at least 3 months of the year for at least 2 consecutive years.[59] Specifically excluded from this definition are bronchiectasis and chronic bronchopulmonary infections or other identified causes of cough. Pathologically, chronic

TABLE 27–5. Therapy for Gastroesophageal Reflux Disease–Associated Cough

Dietary changes: high-protein low-fat (45 g) foods; omit acidic foods and beverages; omit caffeine

Limitation of eating and drinking between meals and 2 h before bed

Raising of head of bed frame by 10 cm

Gastric acid suppression with H_2 antagonist or proton pump inhibitor

Prokinetic agent: metoclopramide

Surgical intervention; to be performed only with failure of maximal medical therapy documented on 24-h pH probe on medications cough from smoking is due to mucus hypersecretion. Fifteen to 36% of continuing smokers have chronic cough, and 8% continue to have chronic cough after quitting.[60] In spite of the prevalence of cough from smoking, smoking is the cause of chronic cough in only about 5% of patients who seek medical attention for cough. However, chronic obstructive pulmonary disease (COPD) which should be considered as a diagnosis in any smoker with a chronic cough, is a leading cause of death in women. The diagnosis of COPD is suggested by findings of hyperinflation on chest radiographs, and is confirmed by pulmonary function testing.

SUMMARY

Cough is a common and frustrating disease. It can be trivial or devastating. In chronic cough one or more specific causes can be found and treated, with resolution of the cough in nearly all cases. The most common causes are tobacco smoking, use of ACEIs, PNDs (eg, allergic rhinitis, vasomotor rhinitis, sinusitis), cough variant asthma, and gastroesophageal reflux. A great deal of persistence is necessary to diagnose and treat a patient with two or three contributory causes of cough. Specific therapy, based on the cause(s) of chronic cough, is preferential to chronic use of cough suppressants such as narcotics or expectorants. A positive test is only presumptive evidence of the cause of the cough—therapeutic success is the gold standard.

REFERENCES

1. Pratter MR, Bartter T, Akers S, et al. An algorithmic approach to chronic cough. Ann Intern Med 1993; 119:977–83.
2. Wynder EL, Lemon FR. Epidemiology of persistent cough. Am Rev Respir Dis 1965;91:679–700.
3. Schappert SM. Ambulatory care visits to physician offices, hospital outpatient departments, and emergency departments: United States, 1996. Data from the National Health Survey. Vital Health Stat 13 1998;134:1–37.
4. French CL, Irwin RS, Curley FJ, et al. Impact of chronic cough on quality of life. Arch Intern Med 1998;158:1657–61.
5. Irwin RS, Boulet LP, Cloutier MM, et al. Managing cough as a defense mechanism and as a symptom. A consensus panel report of the American College of Chest Physicians. Chest 1998;114:133–81S.
6. Dudgeon DJ, Rosenthal S. Management of dyspnea and cough in patients with cancer. Hematol/Oncol Clin North Am 1996;10:157–71.
7. Widdicombe JG. Sensory neurophysiology of the cough reflex. J Allergy Clin Immunol 1996;98:S84–90.
8. Widdicombe JG. Afferent receptors in the airways and cough. Respir Physiol 1998;114:5–15.
9. Sant'Ambrogio G, Tsubone H, Sant'Ambrogio FB. Sensory information from the upper airway: role in the control of breathing. Respir Physiol 1995; 102:1–16.
10. ten Berge RE, Zaagsma J, Roffel AF. Muscarinic inhibitory autoreceptors in different generations of human. Am J Respir Crit Care Med 1996;154:43–9.
11. Fujimura M, Kasahara K, Kamio Y, et al. Female gender as a determinant of cough threshold to inhaled capsaicin. Eur Respir J 1996;9:1624–6.
12. Dicpinigaitis PV, Rauf K. The influence of gender on cough reflex sensitivity. Chest 1998;113:1319–21.
13. Ing AJ, Ngu MC, Breslin AB. Pathogenesis of chronic persistent cough associated with gastroesophageal reflux. Am J Respir Crit Care Med 1994;149:160–7.
14. Shannon R, Baekey DM, Morris KF, et al. Ventrolateral medullary respiratory network and a model of cough motor pattern generation. J Appl Physiol 1998;84:2020–35.
15. Widdicombe JG. Neurophysiology of the cough reflex [comments]. Eur Respir J 1995;8:1193–202.
16. Mahajan RP, Singh P, Murty GE, et al. Relationship between expired lung volume, peak flow rate and peak velocity time during a voluntary manoeuvre. Br J Anaesth 1994;72:298–301.
17. Schultz DD, Olivas GS. The use of cough cardiopulmonary resuscitation in clinical practice. Heart Lung 1986;15:273–82.
18. Benson V, Marano MA. Current estimates from the National Health Interview Survey, 1995. National Center for Health Statistics. Vital Health Stat 10 1998;199:1–136.
19. Curley FJ, Irwin RS, Pratter MR, et al. Cough and the common cold. Am Rev Respir Dis 1988;138:305–11.
20. O'Connell F, Thomas VE, Studham JM, et al. Capsaicin cough sensitivity increases during upper respiratory infection. Respir Med 1996;90:279–86.
21. Aubier M, Cockcroft DW. [Bronchial hyperreactivity other than that seen in asthma]. Rev Mal Respir 1994;11:179–87.
22. Gaffey MJ, Hayden FG, Boyd JC, et al. Ipratropium bromide treatment of experimental rhinovirus infection. Antimicrob Agents Chemother 1988;32:1644–7.

23. Gaffey MJ, Gwaltney JM Jr, Sastre A, et al. Intranasally and orally administered antihistamine treatment of experimental rhinovirus colds. Am Rev Respir Dis 1987;136:556–60.

24. Holmes PW, Barter CE, Pierce RJ. Chronic persistent cough: use of ipratropium bromide in undiagnosed cases following upper respiratory tract infection. Respir Med 1992;86:425–9.

25. Lalloo UG, Barnes PJ, Chung KF. Pathophysiology and clinical presentations of cough. J Allergy Clin Immunol 1996;98:S91–7.

26. Malini PL, Strocchi E, Zanardi M, et al. Thromboxane antagonism and cough induced by angiotensin-converting-enzyme inhibitor. Lancet 1997;350:15–8.

27. Os I, Bratland B, Dahleof B, et al. Female preponderance for lisinopril-induced cough in hypertension. Am J Hypertens 1994;7:1012–5.

28. Yeo WW, Chadwick IG, Kraskiewicz M, et al. Resolution of ACE inhibitor cough: changes in subjective cough and responses to inhaled capsaicin, intradermal bradykinin and substance-P. Br J Clin Pharmacol 1995;40:423–9.

29. Paster RZ, Snavely DB, Sweet AR, et al. Use of losartan in the treatment of hypertensive patients with a history of cough induced by angiotensin-converting enzyme inhibitors. Clin Ther 1998;20: 978–89.

30. Irwin RS, Curley FJ, French CL. Chronic cough. The spectrum and frequency of causes, key components of diagnostic evaluation, and outcome of specific therapy. Am Rev Respir Dis 1990;141:640–7.

31. Mello CJ, Irwin RS, Curley FJ. Predictive values of the character, timing, and complications of chronic cough in diagnosing its cause. Arch of Intern Med 1996;156:997–1003.

32. Levenson T, Greenberger PA. Pathophysiology and therapy for allergic and nonallergic rhinitis: an updated review. Allergy Asthma Proc 1997;18:213–20.

33. Durham SR. Mechanisms of mucosal inflammation in the nose and lungs. Clin Exp Allergy 1998;28 Suppl 2:11–6.

34. Gaffey MJ, Kaiser DL, Hayden FG. Ineffectiveness of oral terfenadine in natural colds: evidence against histamine as a mediator of common symptoms. Pediatr Infect Dis J 1988;7:223–8.

35. Sanico A, Togias A. Noninfectious, nonallergic rhinitis (NINAR): considerations on possible mechanisms. Am J Rhinol 1998;12:65–72.

36. Blom HM, Van Rijswijk JB, Garrelds IM, et al. Intranasal capsaicin is efficacious non-allergic, non-

infectious rhinitis. A placebo-controlled study. Clin Exper Allergy 1997;27:796–801.

37. Finn AF Jr, Aaronson D, Korenblat P, et al. Ipratropium bromide nasal spray 0.03% provides additional relief from rhinorrhea when combined with terfenadine in perennial rhinitis patients; a randomized, double-blind, active-controlled trial. Am J Rhinol 1998;12:441–9.

38. Grossman J, Banov C, Boggs P, et al. Use of ipratropium bromide nasal in chronic treatment of non-allergic perennial rhinitis, alone and in combination with other perennial rhinitis medications. J Allergy Clin Immunol 1995;95:1123–7.

39. Diaz I, Bamberger DM. Acute sinusitis. Semin Respir Infect 1995;10:14–20.

40. Hueston WJ, Eberlein C, Johnson D, et al. Criteria used by clinicians to differentiate sinusitis from viral upper respiratory tract infection. J Fam Pract 1998;46:487–92.

41. Brook I. Microbiology and management of sinusitis. J Otolaryngol 1996;25:249–56.

42. Barlan IB, Erkan E, Bakir M, et al. Intranasal budesonide spray as an adjunct to oral antibiotic therapy acute sinusitis in children. Ann Allergy Asthma Immunol 1997;78:598–601.

43. Biel MA, Brown CA, Levinson RM, et al. Evaluation of the microbiology of chronic maxillary sinusitis. Ann Otol Rhinol Laryngol 1998;107:942–5.

44. Corrao WM, Braman SS, Irwin RS. Chronic cough as the sole presenting manifestation of bronchial asthma. N Engl J Med 1979;300:633–7.

45. Johnson D, Osborn LM. Cough variant asthma: a review of the clinical literature. J Asthma 1991; 28:85–90.

46. Irwin RS, French CT, Smyrnios NA, et al. Interpretation of positive results of a methacholine inhalation challenge and 1 week of inhaled bronchodilator use in diagnosing and treating cough-variant asthma. Arch Intern Med 1997;157:1981–7.

47. Cheriyan S, Greenberger PA, Patterson R. Outcome of cough variant asthma treated with inhaled steroids. Ann Allergy 1994;73:478–80.

48. Agarwal AK, Shah A. Menstrual-linked asthma. J Asthma 1997;34:539–45.

49. MatsuoN, Shimoda T, Matsuse H, Kohno S. A case of menstruation-associated asthma, treatment with oral contraceptives. Chest 1999;116:252–3.

50. Laukka MA, Cameron AJ, Schei AJ. Gastroesophageal reflux and chronic cough: which comes first? J Clin Gastroenterol 1994;19:100–4.

51. Irwin RS, French CL, Curley FJ, et al. Chronic cough due to gastroesophageal reflux. Clinical, diagnostic, and pathogenetic aspects. Chest 1993;104:1511–7.

52. Koufman JA. The otolaryngologic manifestations of gastroesophageal reflux disease (GERD): a clinical investigation of 225 patients using ambulatory 24-hour pH monitoring and an experimental investigation of the role of acid and pepsin in the development of injury. Laryngoscope 1991;101:1–78.

53. Ing AJ, Ngu MC, Breslin AB. Chronic persistent cough and gastro-oesophageal reflux. Thorax 1991; 46:479–83.

54. Ing AJ, Ngu MC, Breslin AB. Chronic persistent cough and clearance of esophageal acid. Chest 1992; 102:1668–71.

55. Waring JP, Lacayo L, Hunter J, et al. Chronic cough and hoarseness in patients with severe gastroesophageal reflux disease. Diagnosis and therapy. Dig Dis Sci 1995;40:1093–7.

56. Richter JE. Extraesophageal presentations of gastroesophageal reflux disease [published erratum appears in Semin Gastrointest Dis 1997;8:210]. Semin Gastrointest Dis 1997;8:75–89.

57. DeVault KR, Castell DO. Guidelines for the diagnosis and treatment of gastroesophageal reflux disease. Practice Parameters of the American College of Gastroenterology. Arch Intern Med 1995; 155:2165–73.

58. Smyrnios NA, Irwin RS, Curley FJ. Chronic cough with a history of excessive sputum production. The spectrum and frequency of causes, key components of the diagnostic evaluation, and outcome of specific therapy. Chest 1995;108:991–7.

59. American Thoracic Society. Standards for the diagnosis and care of patients with chronic obstructive pulmonary disease. Am J Respir Crit Care Med 1995;152:S77–120.

60. Krzyzanowski M, Robbins DR, Lebowitz MD. Smoking cessation and changes in respiratory symptoms in two populations followed for 13 years. Int J Epidemiol 1993;22:666–73.

28

ASTHMA

Eric Kleerup, MD

EPIDEMIOLOGY

In the United States, 5.9% of the population has been given the diagnosis of asthma by a physician.[1] The overall prevalence of asthma is higher, as many cases of asthma go undiagnosed. The incidence of asthma is highest in those under the age of 18 years. Between the ages of 45 and 64 years, there is a greater incidence in women (7.4%) compared with men (3.1%). In response to rising reported rates of asthma and increased deaths due to asthma, a series of national and international guidelines for diagnosis and treatment have been developed. In 1997, the National Heart, Lung, and Blood Institute published revised clinical practice guidelines.[2–4] Treatment of asthma following these guidelines has been highly successful.

Poorly controlled asthma increases hospitalizations, emergency department visits, urgent care visits, sick days, and limitation of activity. Unfortunately, in a 1998 survey 7% of adult asthmatics were hospitalized in the previous year, 19% were treated in an emergency department, 25% had unscheduled urgent care visits, and 25% had lost work days.[5] Fifty-three percent of responders indicated that activities were impaired somewhat or "a lot" for sports and recreation, 40% for normal physical exertion, and 37% for sleeping. Quality asthma care can be simple and effective. Mortality and morbidity can be reduced or nearly eliminated in all but the most severe asthmatics.

PATHOGENESIS AND DEFINITION

Asthma is caused by inflammation of the lungs. This inflammation is present to some degree regardless of the level of asthma severity. Many cells, cellular elements, and products contribute to multiple pathways that result in airway inflammation. There are many inciting triggers including allergens, irritants, and viruses. These triggers contribute to a cycle of self-perpetuating inflammation in the airways. The severity of the inflammatory infiltrate reflects the severity of the airway's hyper-responsiveness (as evidenced by response to irritant challenge, such as that with methacholine) but not symptoms or lung function.[6] Airway narrowing (obstruction) and, therefore, many of the symptoms of asthma are caused by bronchoconstriction, airway edema, chronic mucous plug formation, and airway remodeling—all of which are due to inflammation. The inflammation also causes an increase in the existing bronchial hyper-responsiveness to a variety of stimuli such as allergens, irritants, cold air, and viruses.

DIAGNOSIS

For the patient, asthma is manifested by the symptoms perceived. Most commonly, cough, wheezing, dyspnea, and chest tightness are present episodically or continuously. Nocturnal symptoms or symptoms on awaking in the morning are common. The key to the diagnosis of asthma is the variable nature of the airway obstruction and symptoms. Documenting a history of symptoms that vary through the day or in episodes is an important step toward establishing the diagnosis. Many women report fluctuations in symptoms throughout their menstrual cycle.[7] To confirm the diagnosis, airflow obstruction is measured using spirometry. A forced expiratory volume in 1 second (FEV_1) of less than 80% predicted or an FEV_1-to-FVC (forced vital capacity) ratio of less than 65% is diagnostic of obstructive lung disease. Reversibility of the obstruction can be documented by an increase in FEV_1 of 12% and at least 200 mL after using a short-acting inhaled ß$_2$-agonist (eg, albuterol).

TABLE 28–1. Assessment of Asthma Severity at Presentation

Clinical Features before Treatment	Asthma Severity			
	Mild Intermittent	Mild Persistent	Moderate Persistent	Severe Persistent
Symptoms	Intermittent and brief (≤ 2 /wk), asymptomatic and normal PEF between exacerbations	> 2/wk but < 1/d	Daily, requiring use of inhaled short-acting ß₂ agonists	Continuous
Nocturnal asthma	≤ 2/mo	> 2/mo	> 1/wk	Frequent
Limitation of physical activity	None	Exacerbations may affect activity	Exacerbations affect activity	Activity limited by symptoms
Exacerbations	Brief (from a few hours to a few days); intensity may vary	May affect sleep and activity	Affect sleep and activity≥ 2/wk; may last days	Frequent
PEF or FEV₁	≥ 80% predicted; variability < 20%	≥ 80% predicted; variability 20–30%	> 60 ≤ 80% predicted; variability > 30%	60% predicted; variability > 30%

*The presence of one of the features of severity is sufficient to place the patient in that category.[3]
PEF = peak expiratory flow, FEV₁ = forced expiratory volume in 1 s.

Some patients present without symptoms and with normal airflow at the time of examination. Peak expiratory flow (PEF) monitoring twice a day for 2 weeks at home may show either episodes of obstruction (PEF, 80% predicted) or ≥ 20% diurnal variation of peak flow, as shown in the equation below, to support the diagnosis of asthma:

$$\frac{\text{(PEF between 12:00 and 2:00 pm)} - \text{(PEF on awaking)}}{[\text{(PEF between 12:00 and 2:00 pm)} + \text{(PEF on awaking)}]/2}$$

Bronchoprovocation with methacholine, histamine, or exercise challenge testing can be performed by trained individuals in select cases with normal or near-normal spirometry (eg, methacholine challenge testing).

MEASURES OF ASTHMA SEVERITY AND CONTROL

For any given patient, a particular symptom may be most prevalent or bothersome—a sentinel symptom. Because of the often gradual onset of asthma and its chronic nature, it is not unusual for patients to assume that even marked symptoms are "normal" for them. This makes objective measures of lung function, FEV₁ and PEF, vitally important. Frequency and severity of symptoms, exercise limitation, exacerbations, and objective measures of obstruction define the severity of asthma at presentation (Table 28–1). Control of asthma is indicated by a minimum of symptoms and near-normal lung function. The first goal of therapy (Table 28–2) is to relieve symptoms. The goal is to make the patient's symptoms match those of a mild intermittent asthmatic (see Table 28–1). After the initiation of therapy, disease severity is best judged by the medication necessary to maintain good control (Table 28–3). Inadequate control of asthma may be manifested by symptoms similar to mild, moderate, or severe persistent asthma at diagnosis. When symptoms occur, they are primarily treated by as-needed use of quick-relief medications (relievers) (see below). The amount of quick relief medication a patient is using is an excellent measure of symptom control. A canister of albuterol should last about 1 year for a well-controlled asthmatic, indicating it is used for symptoms about two times per week. Patients who require a new canister every 3 months

TABLE 28–2. General Goals of Asthma Therapy

Prevent chronic and troublesome symptoms

Maintain near-normal pulmonary function

Maintain normal activities of daily living including work (or school) and exercise

Prevent recurrent exacerbations of asthma, and minimize the need for emergency department visits and hospitalizations

Provide optimal pharmacotherapy with minimal or no adverse effects

Meet patients' and families' expectations of asthma care

are using it daily, on average. Patients averaging the maximum recommended dose of 2 puffs every 4 hours use two canisters per month. Use of two canisters per month of rescue medication is consistent with severe asthma and is associated with an increased risk of death due to poorly controlled asthma. In general poor control also is characterized by a large diurnal variation in PEF; exacerbations are characterized by a decline in consecutive PEF values over several days.[8]

Patients with moderate-to-severe persistent asthma should learn to monitor their PEF and have a peak flow monitor at home. Monitoring of PEF during exacerbations determines the severity of the exacerbation and can guide therapeutic decisions. Long-term monitoring of PEF provides objective evidence of changing airflow obstruction. Falls in PEF may occur before perceived symptoms in some individuals. Degree of control in the short term can be related to the patient's personal best maximal PEF, and in the longer-term to the predicted PEF (Figure 28–1).

To facilitate patient understanding and compliance, an analogy can be made between a stoplight using either symptoms or objective measurements. Red, equivalent to severe persistent symptoms, indicates that immediate action is needed. Yellow, equivalent to mild- and moderate-persistent symptoms, indicates that a review of potential triggers, exacerbating factors, medication use, and adherence to the treatment plan is in order. Green, equivalent to mild-intermittent symptoms, indicates good control. Similarly, exacerbations can be graded as mild, moderate, and severe (Table 28–4). Patients can be

TABLE 28–3. Stepped Therapy of Asthma*

Severity	Long-Term Control	Quick Relief
4 Severe persistent	High-dose inhaled corticosteroids[†] *and* salmeterol 2 puffs bid *and* daily or alternate-day oral corticosteroids	Short-acting inhaled ß₂-agonists as needed for symptoms[‡]
3b Moderate persistent	Medium-to-high dose inhaled corticosteroids[†] *and* salmeterol 2 puffs bid	Short-acting inhaled ß₂-agonists as needed for symptoms[‡]
3a Moderate persistent	Medium-dose inhaled corticosteroids[†] *Or* low-dose inhaled corticosteroids[†] *and* salmeterol 2 puffs bid	Short-acting inhaled ß₂-agonists as needed for symptoms
2 Mild persistent	Low-dose inhaled corticosteroids[†] *Or* cromolyn 2 puffs qid *Or* nedocromil 2 puffs qid *Or* antileukotrienes: montelukast 10 mg qhs or zafirlukast 20 mg bid, zileuton 600 mg qid	Short-acting inhaled ß₂-agonists as needed for symptoms
1 Mild intermittent	None needed	Short-acting inhaled ß₂-agonists as needed for symptoms

*Initial severity (see Table 28–1) dictates initial therapy above. As asthma increases in severity or patients remain poorly controlled, patients proceed up the above steps from 1 to 4. With improvement, decreases in therapy may be possible and should be attempted on a regular basis (eg, every 3 mo).
†For doses of inhaled corticosteroids see Figure 28–2.
‡Patients with severe asthma may require frequent bronchodilators to control symptoms. Salmeterol in the discus or formoterol fumarate, one dose bid, may be substituted for salmeterol.

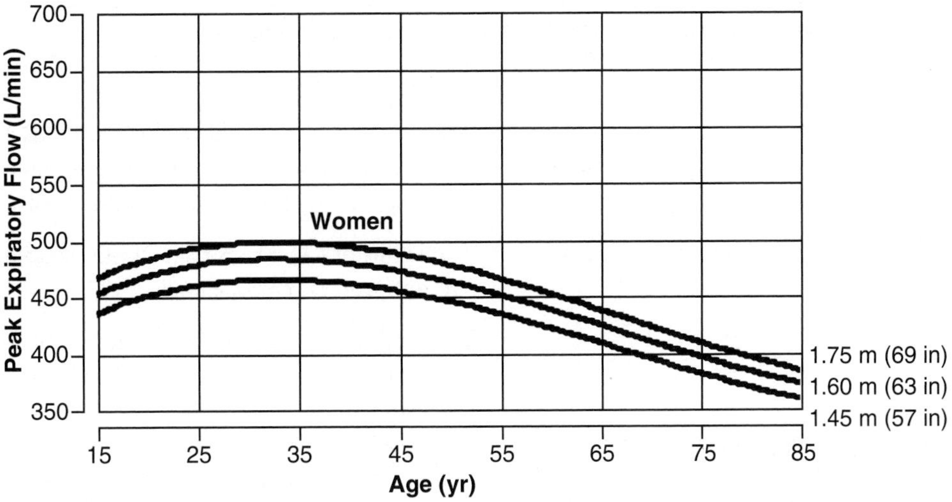

FIGURE 28–1. Predicted peak expiratory flow (PEF). The lower 90% confidence interval (below which only 5% of the values from normal subjects are expected to fall) is 70 to 80 L/min below predicted PEF. Adapted from Nunn AJ, Gregg I. New regression equations for predicting peak expiratory flow in adults. BMJ 1989;298:1068–70.

given specific instructions for self-treatment based on their own assessment of the level of control they are achieving or the severity of an exacerbation.

MIMICS OF ASTHMA

All that wheezes is not asthma, but all that wheezes is airway obstruction. Additional tests may be necessary to rule out alternative causes of airway obstruction (Table 28–5), particularly in patients who present atypically or fail to respond to therapy.

INTEGRATED THERAPY AND EDUCATION

Involvement of the patient in asthma therapy is essential for success. The patient's personal goals for therapy should be determined first. They should

---

TABLE 28–4. Assessment of the Severity of an Exacerbation

Severe exacerbations
  Characterized by rapid onset, lack of response to initial therapy, and previous history of severe attacks
  Patient is breathless at rest, hunching forward, speaking only single words, agitated or confused
  Respiratory rate > 30, pulse > 120 bpm or bradycardia, loud wheezes or absent breath sounds due to severely reduced flow rates insufficient to generate wheezing sounds, accessory muscle use, respiratory muscle fatigue, paradoxic thoracoabdominal movement, pulsus paradoxus >25 mm Hg, cyanosis, hypoxemia ($SaO_2 < 90\%$), PEF after initial bronchodilators < 60% predicted or personal best or <100 L/min.

Moderate exacerbations
  Patient is breathless while talking, prefers sitting, speaks in phrases, is agitated
  Respiratory rate is increased, pulse 100–120 bpm, loud wheezes, accessory muscle use, pulsus paradoxus 10–25 mm Hg, mild hypoxemia (SaO_2 90–95%), PEF 60–80% predicted or personal best after initial bronchodilators

Mild exacerbations
  Patient is breathless while walking, can lie down, speaks in sentences, may be agitated
  Respiratory rate is increased, pulse < 100 bpm, mild to moderate wheezes or wheezes present only on forced expiration, no accessory muscle use, no abnormal pulsus paradoxus (< 10 mm Hg), no hypoxemia (SaO_2 >95%), PEF >80% predicted or personal best after initial bronchodilators

---

bpm = beats per minute; SaO_2 = arterial oxygen saturation; PEF = peak expiratory flow.

TABLE 28–5. Differential Diagnosis of Airway Obstruction other than Asthma*

Diagnosis	Tests and Comments
Chronic obstructive pulmonary disease (eg, emphysema, chronic bronchitis, and obstructive bronchiolitis)	Etiology—tobacco smoking; slow insidious onset; average age = 55 yr; slow progressive decline—does not reverse to normal but may respond to bronchodilators; DLCO reduced
α_1-Antiprotease deficiency (hereditary emphysema)	Family history, increases risk; DLCO reduced; screen with α_1-antiprotease enzyme level
Pulmonary embolism	Acute release of bronchospastic mediators results in wheezing (or triggers a refractory asthma attack in an asthmatic)
Congestive heart failure and pulmonary edema	Airway edema results in narrowing and wheeze, orthopnea, and other signs and symptoms of failure
Pulmonary infiltrates with eosinophilia	Uncommon; chest radiograph shows migratory but persistent infiltrates; difficult to control asthma; has many causes; not all have peripheral eosinophilia—it is more prevalent in asthma patients in general
Bronchiolitis (constrictive or obliterative)	Uncommon; many idiopathic; often history of toxic fume exposure; high-resolution CT of the chest may be helpful in diagnosis
Bronchiectasis, cystic fibrosis	Large amounts of purulent sputum; limited reversibility
Large airway masses, narrowing, and foreign bodies	Flow volume curves flattened, low peak inspiratory and/or expiratory flow; chest radiography, CT, and bronchoscopy may be useful in diagnosis
Vocal cord dysfunction (spasm)	An excellent mimic of asthma; often inspiratory and expiratory obstruction and wheeze—may have monotone wheeze at neck; difficult to obtain reproducible spirometry with smooth flow volume curves; usually intermittent, may be severe; usual cause is acid reflux; confirm with direct laryngoscopy

*In adults and children over 12 years.
DLCO = diffusing capacity for carbon monoxide; CT = computed tomography.

then be integrated with the general (clinician's) goals of asthma therapy (see Table 28–2). Education should occur during all phases of therapy and involve a variety of health care professionals, including physicians, other primary care clinicians, nurses, and pharmacists (Table 28–6).

NONPHARMACOLOGIC INTERVENTIONS

Nonpharmacologic interventions, particularly avoidance of asthma triggers, should be attempted by all patients being treated for asthma. The extent to which specific environmental triggers of asthma can be identified and avoided varies from patient to patient. The simplest approach to identifying triggers is taking a careful history. Patients often associate worsening of symptoms with certain activities, locations, or seasons. Skin testing may be useful for perennial allergens (eg, house dust mite, cat, and cockroach) for which environmental modification is possible. The ability to avoid triggers varies depending on the nature and prevalence of the trigger. Avoidance of triggers such as dust mites for 2 to

TABLE 28-6. Sample Plan for Patient Education

Knowledge	Skills	Clinician Intervention
Disease process		
Inflammation	—	Diagnosis
Bronchospasm		Assessment of severity
Hypersensitivity		Determination of goals of therapy with patient
Controlling asthma triggers		
Infections	Dust-proofing	Identification of triggers
Miscellaneous aeroallergens	Environmental controls	Instruction in avoidance and home/
Drugs	Dietary limitations	environmental controls
Lung irritants		
Drug therapy		
Long-term control and quick relief medications	Inhaler technique	Implementation of stepped therapy
	Use of spacers/holding chambers	Instruction in use of aerosol delivery devices
Guidelines to taking medications	Nebulizers	and auxiliary devices
	Cleaning of devices	Immunotherapy
Monitoring		
Peak flow monitoring	Symptom monitoring/diary maintenance	Determination of personal best or predicted PEF
Warning signs and symptoms		
When to go to school/work	Recognition of early signs of deterioration	Teaching about "green, yellow, and red" zones
When to call clinician	Use of PEF meters	
	Keeping of PEF diary	
Management		
Treatment of exacerbations	—	Establishment of exacerbation treatment
Action plan		protocol
Complicating factors		
Allergic rhinitis, sinus disease	—	Identification and treatment
Gastroesophageal reflux		
Nasal polyps		

HCP = health care professional; PEF = peak expiratory flow.

9 months may result in a decrease in symptoms, medication use, and specific and nonspecific bronchial hyper-responsiveness.[9] Measures to control or limit exposure to triggers of inflammation and/or bronchospasm may require major lifestyle changes, which the patient or family may not be willing or able to make. Expensive interventions such as removing carpeting may not be possible, and most patients resist removing a beloved pet from their home.

PHARMACOLOGIC THERAPY

Pharmacologic therapy of asthma can be divided into two broad categories: long-term-control med-

ications used routinely to continually prevent or relieve symptoms, and quick-relief medications taken intermittently for short-term relief of symptoms (see Table 28–3).[10] Ideally, patients unperturbed by an exacerbation of their asthma have all of their signs and symptoms of asthma continually prevented and/or relieved by their anti-inflammatory long-term-control medications (eg, one or more of medications including inhaled corticosteroids, cromolyn, nedocromil, or leukotriene modifiers). Symptoms or signs resulting from exposure to a trigger (eg, cat dander, smoke, or viral infection) ideally resolve a short time after the use of quick-relief medication (eg, an inhaled short-acting ß₂-agonist).

Quick-relief medications also may be used to prevent symptoms before exposure to a known trigger (eg, exercise).

It is important to start long-term anti-inflammatory medications as soon as they are clinically indicated (see below). A 2-year delay in initiating inhaled corticosteroid therapy results in incomplete response when they are begun.[11] Early initiation of anti-inflammatory therapy prevents irreversible airway obstruction, which is likely due to airway remodeling. After prolonged anti-inflammatory therapy it usually is possible to reduce the dosage of inhaled corticosteroids but not to eliminate them completely.[11]

Treatment of Acute Asthma Symptoms and Exacerbations

SHORT-ACTING SELECTIVE ß₂-AGONISTS

The major role of bronchodilators is the temporary relief of symptoms, primarily those caused by bronchoconstriction. Regularly scheduled around-the-clock use of short-acting or long-acting bronchodilators may mask the severity of asthma, resulting in undertreatment of the underlying inflammation. Short-acting selective ß₂-agonists are ideal for acute control of bronchospasm and prevention of exercise-induced bronchospasm. Such agents include albuterol and albuterol sulfate (Proventil, Proventil HFA, Ventolin), terbutaline sulfate (Brethaire), metaproterenol sulfate (Alupent), bitolterol mesylate (Tornalate), and pirbuterol acetate (Maxair); all are available as metered-dose inhalers (MDIs). For mild symptoms, two puffs as needed should be sufficient. Frequent use indicates a significant exacerbation or poor chronic control, and requires further investigation. Acute exacerbations may be treated at home with up to three treatments of two to four puffs of short-acting ß₂-agonist at 20-minute intervals (Table 28–7).

When used in higher doses, all selective ß₂-agonists exhibit some ß₁-agonist effects, most often manifested by tachycardia in addition to tremor and/or anxiety (the latter two are ß₂-agonist effects). Less selective ß-agonists (epinephrine bitartrate [Primatene], isoproterenol hydrochloride [Isuprel], and isoetharine mesylate [Bronkometer]) may cause a greater degree of cardiac side effects. In large doses inhaled ß₂-agonists may result in a slight lowering of serum potassium.

IPRATROPIUM BROMIDE

The anticholinergic medication ipratropium bromide (Atrovent) is a second-line choice for acute bronchodilator therapy in asthmatics who are intolerant of the side effects associated with ß₂-agonists. The onset of action is somewhat slower than that of ß₂-agonists, with a peak response in 20 to 30 minutes.

ORAL CORTICOSTEROIDS

Oral corticosteroid use in bursts of 7 to 14 days is appropriate for treatment of acute exacerbations and poorly controlled chronic asthma, either at the initiation of therapy or when response to maintenance inhaled anti-inflammatory therapy is inadequate. Oral or parenteral corticosteroids probably require 6 to 24 hours to begin to act. Little residual effect on the hypothalamic-pituitary-adrenal (HPA) axis occurs after bursts, and tapering is not necessary to prevent adrenal insufficiency. During a burst, however, it may be useful to taper the corticosteroid dose to evaluate the effect of withdrawal on the patient's asthma. An example of a burst is prednisone qAM 60 mg days 1 to 3, 50 mg day 4, 40 mg day 5, 30 mg day 6, 20 mg day 7, and 10 mg day 8 (dispense 33 tablets, 10 mg each). Prepackaged tapering doses of methylprednisolone that decrease by 4 mg/d from 24 mg also are available (Medrol Dosepak). In general the requirement for a prednisone burst necessitates a temporary or long-standing increase of the patient's long-term control (anti-inflammatory) regimen. Inhaled corticosteroids should be resumed or begun before completion of an oral corticosteroid taper.

SUMMARY

Acute exacerbations usually are due to intercurrent viral infections or unexpected exposure to triggers. Rapid relief of symptoms reduces the impact of asthma on the patient and may be lifesaving. Therapy of acute exacerbations is simply an intensification of routine rescue therapy (see Table 28–7). In the emergency department or inpatient hospital unit, additional assessment tools are available, but the mainstay of therapy is still inhaled albuterol and oral or parenteral corticosteroids. Additional therapy may include oxygen for hypoxemia, antibiotics for evidence of bacterial infection, and intubation and mechanical ventilation for respiratory failure.

Medications for Long-Term Control

Anti-inflammatory agents administered on a regularly scheduled basis treat the underlying inflammation of

TABLE 28–7. Treatment of Acute Asthma Exacerbations

Assessment and initial treatment

Assess severity.*

Take 2–4 puffs of albuterol by MDI; repeat at 20-min intervals for 3 dosages.

Good response: PEF = 80% personal best on predicted, resolution of dyspnea and wheezing, bronchodilator response sustained for 4 h.

Continue albuterol q3–4h for 24–48 h.
Take double dose of inhaled corticosteroids for 7–10 d.

Incomplete response: PEF 50–80%, persistent dyspnea and/or wheezing

Continue albuterol q3–4h for as long as needed.
Initiate burst and taper of oral corticosteroid (prednisone); contact clinician same day.

Poor response: PEF < 50%, marked dyspnea and/or wheezing

Repeat 4 puffs of albuterol immediately.
Begin burst and taper of oral corticosteroid (prednisone).
Proceed to Emergency Department; consider calling ambulance or 911.

*Patients with severe exacerbations not immediately responsive to inhaled albuterol (or other short-acting ß₂-agonist) should be transported to the Emergency Department.
MDI = metered-dose inhaler; PEF = peak expiratory flow.

asthma, resulting in reduced airway hyper-reactivity and decreased frequency of acute bronchospasm and symptoms. The addition of long-acting bronchodilators to anti-inflammatory regimens may provide further relief of bronchospastic symptoms—wheezing, chest tightness, and dyspnea.

INHALED CORTICOSTEROIDS

Inhaled corticosteroids (ICSs) are nonspecific suppressors of bronchial inflammation.[12,13] Their use results in decreased frequency of acute exacerbations, symptoms, and need for concurrent medications.[14] The effects of ICS use are superior to those of regular use of ß₂agonists in the treatment of frequent asthma symptoms. Delay in instituting ICSs results in prolonged and perhaps permanent airways remodelling.

The relative strength of the different types of ICSs used in the treatment of asthma is poorly defined. As a surrogate measure of topical anti-inflammatory activity, topical skin blanching efficacy has been used, although this measure of efficacy does not take into account the variation in aerosol delivery of medication to the lungs that occurs with different devices and different inhaler techniques. As a rough approximation, however, estimated relative skin-blanching potency has been converted to puffs in Figure 28–2.

Side effects from low-dose ICSs are unusual. Detectable HPA axis suppression is uncommon at doses below 1,000 to 1,260 µg of beclomethasone daily (24 to 30 puffs/d, 42 µg/puff; "high dose" in Figure 28–2).[15] Even if HPA axis suppression occurs, the degree of suppression is less than that caused by the amount of daily oral prednisone required to produce comparable asthma control.[16] Localized infections with *Candida albicans* may occur in the mouth, the pharynx, or, occasionally, the larynx. Clinically significant infection may be treated with topical antifungal agents and reduction in dosage or discontinuation of the ICS. The incidence of local oral effects may be reduced by the use of a spacer or holding chamber and by rinsing the mouth following use. Indirect laboratory studies indicate that ICSs in high doses (1,500 µg of beclomethasone daily or the equivalent) may decrease bone density. Bone densitometry should be considered for patients using high-dose ICSs, particularly if other risk factors are present. Inhaled corticosteroid use, mainly in high doses administered over long periods of time, leads to an increased risk for cataracts[17] and glaucoma.[18] Therefore, regular eye examinations are recommended for patients on high-dose ICSs.

Frequent exacerbations indicate a failure of the chronic regimen and are an indication to inten-

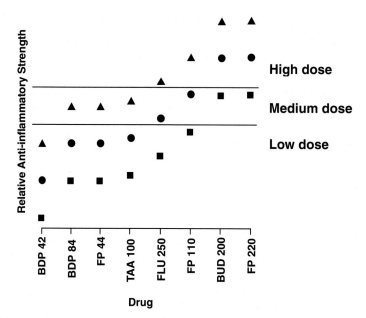

FIGURE 28–2. Relative anti-inflammatory strength of inhaled corticosteroids. Relative strength is an estimate based on skin blanching data adjusted for dose per puff. *Squares* represent doses of 2 puffs qd; *circles,* 2 puffs bid; and *triangles,* 4 puffs bid. BDP 42-beclomethasone dipropionate (Beclovent, Vanceril 42 μg/puff); BDP 84-beclomethasone dipropionate (Vanceril DS 84 μg/puff, approximately equivalent to beclomethasone HFA at half the dose [QUAR 40 μg/puff]); BUD-budesonide (Pulmicort 200 μg/puff); TAA-triamcinolone acetonide (Azmacort 100 μg/puff); FLU-flunisolide (AeroBid 250 μg/puff); FP-fluticasone propionate (Flovent 44 μg/puff, 110 μg/puff, or 220 μg/puff, or 2 puffs of each of the preceding is equivalent to Advair as a combination product with salmeterol 100 μg/50 μg/puff, 250 μg/50 μg/puff, and 500 μg/50μg/puff, respectively).

sify chronic therapy. Before increasing ICS dosages, it is important to review inhaler technique and compliance. After asthma control is achieved, a stepwise decrease in anti-inflammatory therapy may be possible and is advisable. The ideal dosage of ICSs is the minimum dosage necessary to attain and maintain the goals of therapy. Patients not controlled on high dosages of ICSs should be referred to an asthma specialist.

CHRONIC ORAL CORTICOSTEROIDS

Every effort should be made to minimize the use of chronic oral corticosteroids. Any patient requiring chronic oral corticosteroids should be managed by a specialist. In patients previously on chronic maintenance therapy with oral corticosteroids, withdrawal of oral corticosteroids may result in adrenal insufficiency for up to 1 year. This complication is not prevented by the substitution of ICSs.

INHALED NONSTEROIDAL ANTI-INFLAMMATORIES

Cromolyn sodium and nedocromil sodium are nonsteroidal but less potent anti-inflammatory agents. Cromolyn sodium (Intal) is available as an

MDI that delivers 800 μg/puff (as well as a dry powder inhaler and a solution for use with a powered nebulizer). Nedocromil sodium (Tilade) is available as an MDI that delivers 1.75 mg/puff. Nedocromil may be slightly more effective than is cromolyn.[19] Effects of nedocromil two puffs qid are approximately equivalent to those of beclomethasone two puffs bid. Because both nedocromil and cromolyn have favorable side-effect profiles and no HPA axis suppression, they should be considered for patients with mild persistent asthma. No studies of the effectiveness of higher dosages are available. Nedocromil and cromolyn are generally well tolerated.

LONG-ACTING INHALED AND ORAL BRONCHODILATORS

Ultra-long-acting bronchodilators, such as salmeterol xinafoate (Serevent, an ultra-long-acting inhaled ß₂-agonist with a 12-hour duration of bronchodilation) or as a combination product with fluticasone-Advair), formatorol fumarate (Foradil, also with a 12-hour duration), controlled-release oral albuterol (Proventil Repetabs, Volmax), and sustained-release theophylline, all relieve bronchospasm for extended periods of time. Their role in the chronic therapy of asthma is unclear. In mild disease they may mask increasing symptoms that would be treated more appropriately with inhaled anti-inflammatory agents. In poorly controlled moderate or severe disease, they may lull the patient and clinicians into acceptance of less-than-optimal anti-inflammatory therapy. Nonetheless, around-the-clock bronchodilator therapy may be required in addition to relatively high or maximal dosages of ICSs for adequate control of symptoms in moderate to severe asthmatics. Long-acting bronchodilators are not appropriate for acute symptoms or exacerbations.

METHYLXANTHINES: PHOSPHODIESTERASE INHIBITORS

With the current emphasis on the use of anti-inflammatory drugs for chronic asthma therapy and fast-acting inhaled ß2-agonists for acute treatment of asthma, theophylline has been relegated to a minor role in the treatment of asthma. Superior bronchodilation is provided by ß2-agonists and by anticholinergics, avoiding the attendant side effects that often are seen with theophylline use. During acute asthma exacerbations, the addition of intravenous aminophylline to treatment with an inhaled ß2-agonist and intravenous corticosteroids increases the risk of side effects but does not provide improvement in objective measures of airflow.

Adverse effects from theophylline may be seen at therapeutic levels (8 to 15 μg/mL), and severe side effects are common at higher levels. Inter- and intraindividual variations in metabolism and absorption of theophylline are complicated by interactions with common drugs. The narrow therapeutic window and multiple drug interactions necessitates careful monitoring, including serum theophylline levels. Many clinicians now rarely use theophylline to treat asthma. If it is to be used in an individual patient, objective benefit that is clearly attributable to the theophylline therapy should be documented.

LEUKOTRIENE ANTAGONISTS

The leukotriene pathway represents one of several inflammatory pathways in asthmatic patients. Blocking of 5-lipoxygenase prevents metabolism of arachidonic acid to leukotrienes. Blocking the leukotriene receptor inhibits the action of leuko-triene (LTD4). Leukotriene modifiers may be considered as alternative therapy to low dosages of inhaled anti-inflammatory medications in mild persistent asthma. Zafirlukast (Accolate 20 mg bid) and montelukast (Singulair 10 mg qhs if age ≥ 15 years, 5 mg qhs for those 6 to 14 years old) are leukotriene-receptor antagonists. Zileuton (Zyflo 600 mg qid) is a 5-lipoxygenase inhibitor. Liver function monitoring is recommended in zileuton use due to reported elevation of liver enzymes, reversible hepatitis, and hyperbilirubinemia.

IMMUNOTHERAPY

In contrast to its efficacy in allergic rhinitis, the role of immunotherapy in asthma is unclear. In carefully selected cases, a few specific well-defined antigens (eg, grass pollen, house dust mite, and *Alternaria*) may provide antigen-specific reduction in sensitivity. This mild benefit (7.1% improvement in FEV_1) must be weighed against the potential for systemic reactions (5 to 30% risk) including anaphylaxis, and the cost and inconvenience of weekly physician visits.[20–22]

Other Therapies

In women hormonal manipulation may improve asthma control. Menstruation-associated asthma may respond to use of oral contraceptives.[23] A case report of acute severe life-threatening asthma was reversed within hours following termination of a first trimester pregnancy.[24]

Use of alternative (complementary) medications in asthma is common and often is not reported to clinicians. Various derivatives from specific medicinal plants and other materials are the basis of some current asthma medications.[25] Many alternative medications are less selective pharmacologically than are their pharmaceutic derivatives. For example, *Ephedra sinica* (ma huang) contains L-ephedrine, a nonselective ß-agonist, *Datura stramonium* (d'hatura) contains an anticholinergic compound, and *Ammi visnaga* (khellin) contains a chromone related to cromolyn. Due to severe potential side effects, patients should be questioned specifically about the use of alternative compounds containing animal adrenal extracts, which often are promoted to treat asthma and carry the attendant risks of oral corticosteroid use. Patient attitudes and expectations can significantly affect their lung function. Therefore, it is particularly important to account for placebo effects in evaluating both individual reports of response to treatment and formal clinical trials.

DISEASES COMPLICATING THE MANAGEMENT OF ASTHMA

Allergic rhinitis occurs in many, if not most, asthmatics and may share a common etiologic pathway. Topical treatment of rhinitis may improve asthma symptoms, pulmonary function, and bronchial responsiveness.[26] Systemic treatment of rhinitis also may affect asthma directly (see Chapter 25).

Gastroesophageal reflux, with or without acid aspiration into the lung, may make asthma difficult to control. Increased airways inflammation and bronchospasm may be mediated neurologically through irritant receptors in the upper esophagus. Behavioral, pharmacologic, or surgical reduction of acid reflux may improve asthma control (see Chapters 27 and 39).

Continuous internal exposure to allergens from fungal colonization of airways (allergic bronchopulmonary aspergillosis) or parasitic infections (tropical pulmonary infiltrates with eosinophilia), or mediator release from carcinoid tumors (eg, bradykinin) or pulmonary emboli (eg, platelet acti-vating factor) may make asthma symptoms nearly impossible to control without steroids and/or specific treatment of the underlying condition.

PREGNANCY

In patients with asthma, preparation for pregnancy should begin well in advance of conception, with achievement of good asthma control. In approximately equal proportions of patients, asthma improves, worsens, or remains unchanged during pregnancy. The effect of pregnancy on asthma is often the same in subsequent pregnancies and returns to the nonpregnant baseline about 3 months post partum.[27] The same stepped approach used for general asthma care is appropriate for care during pregnancy.[28,29] No therapy has been proven absolutely safe for use during pregnancy. The clinical experience with terbutaline, albuterol, and metaproterenol is reassuring. For patients requiring anti-inflammatory therapy, the use of inhaled beclomethasone or cromolyn is supported by human studies and long experience. Use of higher-potency ICSs likely carries a proportionally higher risk but remains preferable to use of chronic oral corticosteroids during pregnancy. Treatment of exacerbations with bursts of oral corticosteroids is preferable to the deleterious physiologic effects of withholding treatment.

RESOURCE

The National Heart, Lung, and Blood Institute
PO Box 3105
Bethesda, Maryland 20824-010
Telephone: (301) 592-8573
Web site: www.nhlbi.nih.gov

The NHLBI of the National Institutes of Health provides patient information in English and Spanish. It also supports the development of clinical guidelines. Of particular interest to clinicians is "Expert Panel Report 2: Guidelines for the Diagnosis and Management of Asthma" (NIH 97-4051), April 1997, available at the NHLBI Web site. The NHLBI also published the report of the Working Group on Asthma and Pregnancy, "Management of Asthma During Pregnancy" (NIH 93-3279), September 1993.

REFERENCES

1. Benson V, Marano MA. Current estimates from the National Health Interview Survey, 1995. National Center for Health Statistics. Vital Health Stat 10 1998;199:1–136.

2. Murphy S. National Asthma Education and Prevention Program. Expert panel report II: guidelines for the diagnosis and management of asthma. Washington (DC): National Heart, Lung, and Blood institute; 1997. NIH Publication No.: 97-4051.

3. Murphy S. Highlights of the expert panel report 2: guidelines for the diagnosis and management of asthma. Bethesda 9MD): National Institutes of Health, National Heart, Lung, and Blood Institute; 1997. NIH Publication No.: 97-4051.

4. Murphy S. National Asthma Education and Prevention Program. Practical guide for the diagnosis and management of asthma. Washington (DC): National Heart, Lung, and Blood Institute; 1997. NIH Publication No.: 97-4053.

5. Sander N, Weiss S. Asthma in America, a landmark survey, executive summary. Research Triangle Park (NC): GlaxoWellcome; 1998.

6. Sont JK, Han J, van Krieken JM, et al. Relationship between the inflammatory infiltrate in bronchial biopsy specimens and clinical severity of asthma in patients treated with inhaled steroids. Thorax 1996; 51:496–502.

7. Agarwal AK, Shah A. Menstrual-linked asthma. J Asthma 1997;34:539–45.

8. Reddel H, Ware S, Marks G, et al. Differences between asthma exacerbations and poor asthma control. Lancet 1999;353:364–9.

9. Platts-Mills TAE, Tovey ER, Mitchell EB, et al. Reduction of bronchial hyperreactivity during prolonged allergen avoidance. Lancet 1982;2:675–8.

10. Drugs for asthma. Med Let Drugs Ther 1999;41:5–10.

11. Haahtela T, Järvinen M, Kava T. Effects of discontinuing inhaled budesonide in patients with mild asthma. N Engl J Med 1994;331:700–5.

12. Laitinen LA, Laitinen A, Haahtela T. A comparative study of the effects of an inhaled corticosteroid, budesonide, and a beta-2-agonist, terbutaline, on airway inflammation in newly diagnosed asthma: a randomized, double-blind, parallel-group controlled trial. J Allergy Clin Immunol 1992;90:32–42.

13. Trigg CJ, Manolitsas ND, Wang J, et al. Placebo-controlled immunopathologic study of four months of inhaled corticosteroids in asthma. Am J Respir Crit Care Med 1994;150:17–22.

14. Barnes PJ, Pedersen S, Busse WW. Efficacy and safety of inhaled corticosteroids, new developments. Am J Respir Crit Care Med 1998;157:S1–53.

15. Lipworth BJ. Systemic adverse effects of inhaled corticosteroid therapy. Arch Intern Med 1999;159:941–55.

16. Bosman HG, van Uffelen R, Tamminga JJ, et al. Comparison of inhaled beclomethasone dipropionate 1000 micrograms twice daily and oral prednisone 10 mg once daily in asthmatic patients. Thorax 1994; 49:37–40.

17. Cumming RG, Mitchell P, Leeder SR. Use of inhaled corticosteroids and the risk of cataracts. N Engl J Med 1997;337:8–14.

18. Gasarbe E, LeLorier J, Boivin J, et al. Inhaled and nasal glucocorticoids and the risk of ocular hypertension or open-angle glaucoma. JAMA 1997;277:722–7.

19. Lal S, Dorow PD, Venho KK, et al. Nedocromil sodium is more effective than cromolyn sodium for the treatment of chronic reversible obstructive airways disease. Chest 1993;104:438–47.

20. Frew AJ. Conventional and alternative allergy immunotherapy: do they work? Are they safe? Clin Exp Allergy 1994;24:416–22.

21. Bousquet J, Michel FB. Specific immunotherapy in asthma: is it effective? J Allergy Clin Immunol 1994; 94:1–11.

22. Abramson MJ, Puy RM, Weiner JM. Is allergen immunotherapy effective in asthma? Am J Respir Crit Care Med 1995;151:969–74.

23. Matsuo N, Shimoda T, Matsuse H, et al. A case of menstruation associated asthma, treatment with oral contraceptives. Chest 1999;116:252–3.

24. Shanies HM, Venkataraman MT, Peter T. Reversal of intractable acute severe asthma by first-trimester termination of pregnancy. J Asthma 1997;34:169–72.

25. Bielory L, Lupoli K. Herbal interventions in asthma and allergy. J Asthma 1999;36:1–65.

26. Casale TB. Immunobiology of asthma and rhinitis: pathogenic factors and therapeutic options, Montreal, Canada; American Thoracic Society; 1999.

27. Venkataraman MT, Shanies HM. Pregnancy and asthma. J Asthma 1997;34:265–71.

28. Luskin AL. Report of the Working Group on Asthma and Pregnancy. Management of asthma during pregnancy. Bethesda (MD): National Institutes of Health, Heart, Lung, and Blood Institute, National Asthma Education Program; 1993.

29. Clark SL, National Asthma Education Program Working Group on Asthma and Pregnancy. Asthma in pregnancy. Obstet Gynecol 1993;82:1036–40.

29

APPROACH TO THE PATIENT WITH DYSPNEA

Farhad Melamed, MD, David Ahdoot, MD, FACOG, and Christopher Cooper, MD

One of the most common complaints with which a patient presents to their physician is that of dyspnea. Unfortunately, it is also a nonspecific symptom. Patients often present to their clinician after starting a new exercise program, as dyspnea frequently limits exercise capacity.[1] Although the majority of patients have a pulmonary or cardiac etiology,[2] the differential diagnosis is quite extensive (Table 29–1). Most studies of dyspnea have been done with subjects of both genders. However, there are special issues in the evaluation of women with dyspnea, particularly during pregnancy.

A meticulous history and physical examination (H & P) is the single most important factor in directing the evaluation of dyspnea. It has been shown that the H & P is most useful in ruling out certain common etiologies, and thus carries a high negative predictive value;[2] the low positive predictive value of the H & P makes imaging studies and further testing an integral part of the complete evaluation.

DEFINITION

"Dyspnea" has become the medical term that encompasses a variety of symptoms relating to breathlessness;[3] several of these terms can be correlated into clusters. Table 29–2 reviews some descriptive clusters that are commonly associated with certain diagnoses.[3] As shown, certain descriptors are specific to certain conditions; for example, in a group of patients asked to describe their breathlessness, difficulty with exhalation and chest tightness were described only with asthma, the feeling of suffocation was noted only with congestive heart failure (CHF), and shallow breathing was described with only

neuromuscular disease. Pregnancy was only associated with a feeling of air hunger, although this symptom was shared by people who had chronic obstructive pulmonary disease (COPD) and CHF as well. Conversely, some symptoms such as increased work of breathing were nonspecific.

SENSATION

The sensation of dyspnea is a complex phenomenon whereby the central nervous system integrates neurologic inputs from chemoreceptors, mechanoreceptors, and higher centers. Dyspnea has been described as unsatisfied inspiratory effort and is presumed to be related to an imbalance between respiratory drive and the resulting tidal volume.

Acid-base homeostasis is one of the most prominent factors in the control of ventilation.[4] The respiratory drive to breathe is affected more by hypercapnea than by hypoxia; however, the role of hypoxia and hypercapnea with relation to the sensation of dyspnea is unclear.[4] Studies have shown that some patients with hypercapnea report a greater degree of dyspnea, as well as more anxiety and depression,[5-7] than do those with hypoxia alone.

Chemoreceptors, both central and peripheral, are important in the regulation of acid-base state and maintenance of normal oxygenation. The arterial partial pressure of carbon dioxide ($PaCO_2$) is tightly coupled to alveolar ventilation, and its control is mainly mediated via the central chemosensitive area in the ventral medulla oblongata. The carotid bodies, which are the functional peripheral chemoreceptors in humans, account for 20 to 30% of CO_2 sensitivity but mainly defend the body against

TABLE 29–1. Common Causes of Dyspnea

Pulmonary
  Obstructive
    Asthma
    Chronic obstructive pulmonary disease
      Chronic bronchitis
      Emphysema
    Foreign body aspiration
  Restrictive
    Interstitial lung disease
    Pulmonary fibrosis
    Chest wall deformities: scoliosis and kyphosis
  Parenchymal
    Pneumonia
    Malignancy
    Pneumonitis
    Pulmonary edema
      Cardiogenic
      Adult respiratory distress syndrome
      High altitude
      Neurogenic
  Pleural
    Pneumothorax
    Effusion
    Malignancy

Cardiac
  Acute myocardial infarction/coronary artery disease
  Arrhythmia
  Congestive heart failure
  Pulmonary edema
  Pericardial disease
  Valvular disease
  Right-to-left intracardiac shunt

Vascular/hematologic
  Anemia
  Pulmonary embolism
  Pulmonary hypertension
  Deconditioning/obesity

Endocrine
  Thyroid dysfunction
  Diabetic ketoacidosis
  Pheochromocytoma

Gastroenterologic
  Gastroesophageal reflux
  Ascites

Infectious
  Pneumonia
  Sepsis

Medications
  ß-blockers

Metabolic
  Acidosis
  Uremia

Neuromuscular
  Amyotropic lateral sclerosis
  Myasthenia gravis

Pregnancy

Psychiatric
  Anxiety
  Hyperventilation syndromes

acidemia and hypoxemia. Peripheral chemoreceptor activation is highly dyspnogenic, as is evidenced in patients with metabolic acidosis or hypoxemia and oxyhemoglobin desaturation. Interestingly, patients with ventilatory failure and chronic hypercapnia (increased Pa_{CO_2}) develop metabolic compensation with increases in blood and cerebrospinal fluid bicarbonate levels, which renders them less sensitive to carbon dioxide. Patients with COPD with carbon dioxide retention tend to be less dyspneic than do those with hypoxemia and increased respiratory drive.

Mechanoreceptors undoubtedly play an important role in the perception of dyspnea. These include stretch receptors in the intercostal muscles, Golgi organs in the diaphragm, and a variety of sensory receptors in the pleura, lung parenchyma, and larger airways.[3,8] These include C fiber receptors in lung parenchyma and bronchi, irritant receptors, and respiratory muscles themselves, which respond to the mechanical displacements of the respiratory system.[1,8,9]

HISTORY

Onset

Factors such as the acute versus chronic onset help to narrow the differential diagnosis for dyspnea. Acute onset usually is associated with arrhythmia, anxiety

TABLE 29–2. Different Types of Dyspnea Associated with Specific Conditions

Clusters	Asthma	COPD	ILD	CHF	Neuro	Pregnancy	PVD
Rapid breathing				x			x
Incomplete exhalation	x						
Shallow breathing					x		
Breathing with excess effort	x	x	x		x		
Feeling of suffocation				x			
Air hunger		x		x		x	
Chest tightness	x						

COPD = chronic obstructive pulmonary disease; ILD = interstitial lung disease; CHF = congestive heart failure; Neuro = neuro-muscular and chest wall diseases; PVD = pulmonary vascular disease.
Adapted from Simon PM, Schwartzstein RM, Weiss JW, et al., Distinguishable types of dyspnea in patients with shortness of breath. Am Respir Dis 1990;142:1009–14.

and panic attacks, myocardial infarction, pneumonia, pneumothorax, and pulmonary embolism.[10]

Most patients who present to the clinician present with dyspnea of a subacute or chronic nature. In evaluating 85 patients who presented to a pulmonary clinic for chronic dyspnea,[2] 75% of patients were found to have a respiratory disorder, most commonly asthma, interstitial lung disease, or COPD. A cardiac etiology was found in 10% of patients, most notably cardiomyopathy. The remaining 15% of patients were diagnosed as having psychogenic factors (5%), deconditioning (5%), and gastroesophageal reflux (5%) as the etiology of their dyspnea.[2] By having the patient use the specific descriptors in Table 29–2, the physician can gain a better idea as to the likely etiology.[2]

Although duration and severity of dyspnea are believed to be important factors in the evaluation, one study found that these factors provided no diagnostic value.[11] This was supported by another study that found that the *quality* of the sensation of dyspnea, rather than the *quantity* or severity, was the distinguishing feature.[3]

Posture

The effect of position on dyspnea can be helpful in diagnosing its cause. "Orthopnea" refers to dyspnea in the recumbent position, which is relieved by sitting upright. Orthopnea is commonly associated with left ventricular failure, but it also is seen with diaphragm weakness or obstructive airway disease. "Platypnea" describes dyspnea in the upright position relieved by lying recumbent. Platypnea is commonly seen with intracardiac, vascular, or pulmonary parenchymal shunts. "Trepopnea" is dyspnea associated with one lateral position but not the other. Trepopnea is commonly a sign of unilateral pulmonary disease, such as pleural effusion or bronchial tree obstruction; with the patient lying on the affected side, increased perfusion of the affected lung segment in addition to the poor ventilation of that area results in dyspnea.[4]

Associated Symptoms

Frequency, presence at rest, and precipitating factors are integral to the elucidation of the cause of dyspnea. Table 29–3 reviews some of the more salient points of the history and associated findings. Furthermore, in addition to being asked about a personal and family history of cardiac or pulmonary disease, patients should be evaluated with regard to risk factors for cardiopulmonary disease, anxiety, or depression. In women there is a higher incidence of thromboembolic etiologies and lower incidence of pulmonary disease due to job-related chemical exposures. In evaluating dyspnea in women, important historic factors include current or recent pregnancy, use of birth control pills, history of smoking, and prior or current use of diet medication.

A pulmonary etiology is suggested by the presence of wheezing, cough, sputum production, pleuritic chest pain, history of tobacco and/or marijuana smoking, exposure to chemicals or inhalants, or exposure to animals, especially birds. In one study, for the diagnosis of COPD, a negative smoking history ruled out the diagnosis in all patients (100% negative predictive value); however, smoking had only a 20% positive predictive value for the diagnosis of COPD as the etiology of dyspnea.[2] The absence of throat clearing or postnasal drip strongly argues against an upper airway etiology.[2]

TABLE 29–3. Common Causes of Dyspnea and Related Findings on Evaluation

Diagnosis	History	Physical Findings	Findings of Diagnostic Studies
Acute/chronic asthma	Episodic acute dyspnea Atopic disease Family history	Wheezing Resonance on percussion Prolonged expiration	Pulmonary function test reversible obstructive pattern Hyperinflation seen on chest radiography Positive methacholine challenge cbc may show eosinophilia
Interstitial lung disease	Connective tissue disease Industrial exposures	Dry bibasilar rales Clubbing Signs of systemic vasculitis	Chest radiograph shows ground glass pattern, possible effusion Chest CT scan, biopsy Lymphocytosis and elevated ESR with connective tissue diseases
COPD	Progressive dyspnea Smoking Chronic cough, sputum production	Increased AP diameter Distant breath sounds Resonance to percussion May have cyanosis	PFTs with obstructive defect not responsive to ß-agonist Hyperinflation with flattening of diaphragms seen on chest radiograph Cor pulmonale may be seen on chest radiograph Right axis deviation on ECG
Cardiomyopathy/ acute MI	Orthopnea, PND, nocturia Chest pain, angina CAD Diet pills, drug use	Crackles, rales S_3, displaced PMI JVD, hepatomegaly Ankle edema	Edema on chest radiograph Echocardiogram ECG (variable) Hyponatremia
Pneumonia	Cough, sputum, fever, pleuritic chest pain	Bronchial breath sounds Increased fremitus Egophony, Fever	Infiltrate seen on chest radiograph Sputum gram stain/culture Leuckocytosis
Pulmonary embolism	Immobilization, travel Recent surgery, trauma Pregnancy Oral contraceptives Smoking Hematologic disorders	Variable, nonspecific Loud P_2 Pleural rub Rales, splinting (rare)	Spiral CT or V/Q scan D-dimer test Pulmonary angiography S1Q3T3 on ECG

cbc = complete blood count; CT = computed tomography; ESR = erythrocyte sedimentation rate; COPD = chronic obstructive pulmonary disease; AP = anteroposterior; PFT = pulmonary function test ECG = electrocardiogram; MI = myocardial infarction; PND = paroxysmal nocturnal dyspnea; CAD = coronary artery disease; S_3 = third heart sound; PMI = point of maximal impulse; JVD = jugular venous distention. P_2 = pulmonic second sound; V/Q = ventilation-perfusion; S = wave in lead I; Q = wave in lead II; T = wave inversion in lead III.

TABLE 29–3. (continued)

Diagnosis	History	Physical Findings	Findings of Diagnostic Studies
Pneumothorax	Acute onset dyspnea Chest pain Trauma Interstitial lung disease (eg, eosinophilic granuloma)	Tall, thin individual Decreased breath sounds Resonance to percussion Decreased fremitus Tracheal deviation	Typical findings on chest radiograph
Gastroesophageal reflux	Dyspepsia "Heartburn" Morning cough, sore throat	Epigastric tenderness	Confirmed esophageal pH probe symptoms relieved by therapeutic trial of anti-GERD medication
Hyperventilation/anxiety	Young age Recent emotional stress Perioral tingling, carpopedal spasm	Tachypnea Tachycardia (variable)	Normal studies

cbc = complete blood count; CT = computed tomography; ESR = erythrocyte sedimentation rate; COPD = chronic obstructive pulmonary disease; AP = anteroposterior; PFT = pulmonary function test ECG = electrocardiogram; MI = myocardial infarction; PND = paroxysmal nocturnal dyspnea; CAD = coronary artery disease; S₃ = third heart sound; PMI = point of maximal impulse; JVD = jugular venous distention. P₂ = pulmonic second sound; V/Q = ventilation-perfusion; S = wave in lead I; Q = wave in lead II; T = wave inversion in lead III.

A cardiac etiology is suggested by dyspnea on exertion, association with chest pain or pressure, radiation of discomfort to the left arm or jaw, and, especially, the presence of diaphoresis. A personal history of peripheral vascular disease, diabetes, hypertension, obesity, or smoking, and a personal or family history of coronary artery disease (CAD) are suggestive. Patients with a history of obesity treated with certain diet medications, such as fenfluramine and dexfenfluramine, need to be evaluated for cardiac valvular abnormalities and pulmonary hypertension. The use of certain ß-blockers also can be associated with dyspnea on exertion, and their relation to the onset of symptoms is an important factor.[10]

Both acute and chronic pulmonary embolism can cause dyspnea. In the acute setting Pulmonary embolism is associated with a deep venous thrombus, immobility, recent trauma or surgery, pregnancy, or smoking while on hormone therapy. In the chronic setting small recurrent pulmonary emboli can result in pulmonary hypertension, leading to dyspnea.

Certain endocrinologic conditions can cause dyspnea. These include thyroid dysfunction, pheochromocytoma, and diabetic ketoacidosis. Given the higher incidence of thyroid dysfunction in women, a history of hair loss, palpitations, and involuntary weight loss may suggest thyrotoxicosis (see Chapter 57, "Hyperthyroidism").

Panic attacks commonly present with acute dyspnea, palpitations, chest discomfort, and a feeling of impending doom. Furthermore, circumoral and carpopedal dysesthesias and carpopedal spasm may occur. In the patient with appropriate risk factors, a cardiac or pulmonary etiology needs to be ruled out; however, most young patients who are otherwise healthy need to be carefully evaluated for anxiety. One study showed that age younger than 40 years at symptom onset had an 81% positive predictive value and a 77% negative predictive value for the etiology being either bronchial hyperreactivity or hyperventilation.[11]

Finally, anemia and renal disease need to be considered in the patient who complains of dyspnea, especially on exertion. In the female patient heavy menstrual bleeding can lead to significant chronic blood loss, with fatigue and dyspnea on exertion as the common presenting symptoms. Furthermore, a history of gastrointestinal blood loss and melena is significant in the older patient. Conversely, renal disease can present with a history of metallic taste, pruritis, and swelling of the ankles, in association with dyspnea on exertion; patients often may note that their shoes no longer fit well. Renal disease can cause dyspnea due to either volume overload or metabolic acidosis; both must be ruled out.

PHYSICAL EXAMINATION

In the patient with a suggestive history, the physical examination is helpful in diagnosing an upper respiratory cause, asthma, pneumonia, pneumothorax, or congestive heart failure. The presence of sinus congestion, tenderness, and a cobblestone pattern on examination of the pharynx is suggestive of rhinitis, which, if left chronically untreated, can be associated with asthma. Furthermore, wheezing on pulmonary examination is suggestive of an obstructive defect, such as asthma or COPD. Clubbing of extremities is associated with chronic respiratory or cardiovascular diseases causing chronic hypoxemia, and with lung cancer.[10]

One study found that if crackles were noted on pulmonary auscultation, the patients had either interstitial lung disease (ILD) (79%) or left ventricular dysfunction (21%);[2] the absence of crackles had a 91% negative predictive value for either ILD or cardiomyopathy. Elevated jugular venous pressure, hepatic congestion, and peripheral edema are suggestive of right ventricular failure. In the evaluation of dyspnea, cardiac gallops and murmurs were uncommon findings with low predictive value.[10]

An excellent way to assess *severity* of the dyspnea is to note the use of accessory muscles.[7] Accessory muscles are recruited to assist with ventilation when the work of breathing is increased. Commonly used accessory muscles include the sternocleidomastoids, the scalenes, other neck muscles, and the pectoral muscles. Hence, the severely dyspneic patient might brace the arms against furniture to allow the pectoral muscles to participate in rib cage expansion. Work of breathing is increased by three factors: (1) airflow obstruction, as in asthma or COPD; (2) reduced lung compliance, as in pulmonary edema, inflammation, or fibrosis; and (3) reduced chest wall compliance, as in kyphoscoliosis. The exaggerated intrathoracic pressure fluctuations that accompany accessory muscle use may manifest as intercostal recession during exertion or even during breathing at rest.

If the patient's symptoms are not explained by the history and physical examination, further evaluation is required, and chest radiography is the first test recommended.

FURTHER EVALUATIONS

Chest radiography is the most commonly ordered test in the evaluation of dyspnea; it is most useful for diagnosing patients with ILD.[2] However, there is evidence that the clinician's assessment after taking a history, performing a physical examination, and evaluating a chest radiograph is accurate in only two-thirds of cases.[2] Thus, further evaluation with specific diagnostic tests is necessary to confirm the clinical suspicion of specific diagnoses. Furthermore, given that studies show that almost 7 of 10 patients are eventually noted to have asthma, COPD, ILD, or cardiomyopathy,[2] initial evaluation should focus on these conditions.

Spirometry and pulmonary function tests are used to further evaluate pulmonary disease. The diagnosis of asthma is made by demonstrating reversible obstruction on pulmonary function tests. However, more than two-thirds of patients with asthma have normal pulmonary function tests. Bronchoprovocation challenge testing with methacholine help to confirm this diagnosis,[2] but it does not always give a definite answer.

Some patients obviously have asthma as determined by history and physical examination, and others clearly do not. It is the ambiguous ones in whom the bronchial challenge test might be useful. Unfortunately, a single methacholine challenge test is not always definitive. Giving the patients a peak flow meter and a chart and having them document airway function four times per day for 2 weeks, especially at times when they are symptomatic, may be the best diagnostic test.

Spirometry is also a useful test for the diagnosis of COPD;[2] such patients show evidence of obstruction, with an FEV_1-to-FVC (forced vital capacity) ratio of < 0.7. More than 90% of cases of COPD have some reversibility, especially if tested with ipratropium, the anticholinergic bronchodilator.

A ventilation-perfusion (V/Q) or spiral computed tomography (CT) scan is recommended to assess for pulmonary embolism in the patient with an appropriate history. These patients also have decreased diffusion capacity (DLCO) but normal flow rates, normal lung volumes, and no parenchymal abnormalities seen on the chest radiography.[10]

For the patient suspected to have a cardiac etiology, electrocardiography gives some insight into the presence of current arrhythmia and the possibility of myocardial infarction, pericarditis, and abnormal chamber size. However, echocardiography is necessary to evaluate a patient for cardiomyopathy or valvular disease, as in patients with a history of diet medication use. Echocardiography is also diagnostic for patients with intracardiac shunts; for patients with platypnea and arterial hypoxemia, echocardiography may have to be performed with the patient in an upright position to diagnose a patent foramen ovale.[12]

Given that somatization disorder is strongly correlated with self-rating scales of chest symptoms,[13-15] this diagnosis needs to be considered for patients without any objective evidence of cardiac pathology.

One study evaluated 72 patients who had dyspnea unexplained by initial history, physical examination, chest radiography, and spirometry.[11] The noninvasive test that had the highest diagnostic yield was the methacholine bronchoprovocation;[11] in 75% of such patients, it confirmed bronchial hyper-reactivity. The same study found that the majority of such patients who presented to a pulmonary clinic for consultation had respiratory tract disease (36%)—most of whom had asthma. In 19% of the total patients, hyperventilation syndrome was the eventual diagnosis. Another 19% of the patients had dyspnea of unexplained etiology. Finally, 10% of the patients were found to have cardiac disease; lower percentages of patients were diagnosed with thyroid dysfunction, gastroesophageal reflux, and poor conditioning.[11]

Exercise Testing

Integrative exercise testing that examines pulmonary ventilation and gas exchange, as well as cardiovascular and musculoskeletal factors, is extremely valuable in defining physiologic causes of dyspnea and exercise limitation.[16] This is particularly true when other investigations fail to distinguish pulmonary from cardiovascular etiologies.

The bicycle ergometer is favored for diagnostic exercise testing because the increment of external work rate can be controlled carefully. A successful integrative exercise test can distinguish cardiovascular limitation, ventilatory limitation, gas exchange abnormalities, abnormal symptom perception, and suboptimal effort. A normal physiologic response with distorted symptom perception suggests psychogenic factors contributing to exercise intolerance. Taking measurements of gas exchange at maximum exercise is often the most sensitive method for identifying early pulmonary parenchymal abnormalities such as pulmonary vascular disease or fibrosing alveolitis.[16]

Psychogenic dyspnea should be diagnosed only after other causes have been ruled out. It should be considered for patients with multiple somatic complaints, breathlessness with no association to exertion, an unremarkable examination, and normal diagnostic studies.[10] There is evidence that patients with COPD can distinguish dyspnea from the anxiety and distress associated with it during exercise.[17]

Patients who stop exercise due to leg discomfort at submaximal exercise intensities, who have reduced maximum oxygen uptake, and who have a normal ventilating reserve of about 30% of their ventilating capacity usually are limited by deconditioning or musculoskeletal factors.[10] For patients with ILD, the most common cause of exercise limitation is dyspnea (62%), whereas, for patients with COPD, fatigue is the limiting factor in the majority of patients (46%).[1] This may be explained by the fact that in those with COPD, pulmonary artery pressures increase rapidly with exercise, whereas, in normal subjects, only a minimal increase in these pressures is seen with increased cardiac output.[18] In patients with COPD, this associated pulmonary hypertension leads to decreased oxygen transport to peripheral muscles due to an increased afterload imposed on the right ventricle; clinically, this results in a reduction of exercise capacity.[18]

For patients suspected of a neuromuscular disease, the negative inspiratory force should be measured[4] along with vital capacity. Patients with myasthenia gravis or amyotrophic lateral sclerosis are not able to develop high inspiratory pressures and are expected to have a restrictive ventilatory abnormality with reduced respiratory muscle strength.

Additional Laboratory Evaluation

Additional laboratory testing should be guided by history and physical examination findings. Evalua-tion of thyroid function (usually thyroid-stimulating hormone and free thyroxine index), a complete blood count, and urine pregnancy tests should be performed in the patients with a history of fatigue, weight change, and/or menstrual irregularities. A basic electrolyte panel and creatinine are needed if metabolic acidosis or renal insufficiency is suspected.

The arterial blood gas (ABG) is used to assess hypoxemia and hypercapnea, two factors related to dyspnea; the ABG also provides useful information in patients with acid-base disorders. The pulse oximeter is noninvasive and gives an approximation of the O_2 saturation of blood. However, it does not give any information about hypercapnea or acid-base status, and it needs to be calibrated by simultaneous co-oximetry on arterial blood. Although various laboratories have different ranges, usually PaO_2 values of 70 to 103 mm Hg, with an O_2 saturation of 95% or higher, are considered normal. Moderate hypoxemia generally is defined as a PaO_2 of between 55 and 60 mm Hg. Severe hypoxemia is characterized by a $PaO_2 < 40$ mm Hg.[19]

In the hypoxemic patient, the following five major causes need to be considered: decreased inspired oxygen tension, hypoventilation, diffusion impairment, V/Q mismatch, and extrapulmonary shunt. For patients with a V/Q mismatch, the alveolar-arterial pressure gradient ($P[A-a]O_2$) is increased.[4] Severe V/Q mismatch is the most common cause of hypoxemia and usually can be corrected with administration of 100% O_2. Abnormal extrapulmonary shunts, the most common of which are the intracardiac shunts, should be considered in patients who remain hypoxemic despite adequate O_2 supplementation.[4,19] In one study of patients with symptom onset prior to age 40 years, an intermittent pattern of dyspnea, and a normal $P(A-a)O_2$ gradient of < 20 mm Hg, 100% of patients were found to have either bronchial hyper-reactivity or hyperventilation.[11] These patients were then distinguished with the use of a methacholine bronchoprovocation challenge to diagnose those with asthma.

DYSPNEA DURING PREGNANCY

Dyspnea of pregnancy is an isolated and common physiologic symptom that is not associated with specific disease indicators. Changes in the pulmonary system resulting from physiologic adaptations during

TABLE 29–4. Common Symptoms and Physical Findings and Their Mechanisms in Normal Pregnancy

Finding	Mechanism
Dyspnea	Physiologic changes
Hyperventilation	Progesterone effect on respiratory center
Decreased exercise capacity/fatigue	Anemia of pregnancy, increased body weight
Orthopnea/paroxysmal nocturnal dyspnea	Uterine mechanical effects on diaphragm
Jugular venous distention	Hypervolemia
Pulmonary basilar crackles	Raised diaphragm, compression of lungs
Continuous murmur	Cervical venous hum, mammary souffle (systematic murmur heard over the breasts)
Peripheral edema	Reduced osmotic pressure, increased femoral venous pressure

Adapted from Zeldis SM. Dyspnea during pregnancy: distinguishing cardiac from pulmonary causes. Clin Chest Med 1992;13:567–85.

pregnancy produce some of the most common symptoms. About 70% of normal healthy women with no history of cardiopulmonary disease complain of dyspnea during pregnancy. Fifty percent of gravidas experience these symptoms before the 19th week of gestation, and 76% complain of dyspnea by 31 weeks.[20] Dyspnea typically does not interfere with daily activities; however, because the effects of pregnancy pose a particular burden on the cardiovascular system, the presence of dyspnea may be a sign of decompensation of underlying heart or lung disorders. The challenge for the clinician is to differentiate between physiologic and pathologic dyspnea.

It is important to appreciate the anatomic and physiologic adaptations in pregnancy to accurately diagnose and treat cardiopulmonary disease states in the gravid woman. During pregnancy anatomic changes occur in the chest. The lower ribs tend to flare, and the subcostal angle enlarges, but the respiratory muscles are unaffected. Although the diaphragm may be elevated 4 to 5 cm, the enlarged uterus does not usually hamper its excursions. Despite these anatomic changes, the ability to move air in and out of the lungs is not impeded by pregnancy. Table 29–4 outlines the clinical features and mechanism of action of symptoms of dyspnea in normal pregnancy. The increased levels of estrogen and progesterone during pregnancy produce several changes in the respiratory system. Progesterone derived from the placenta appears to stimulate the respiratory centers in the brain to induce hyperventilation and a sensation of dyspnea. Hyperventilation decreases the alveolar CO_2 tension and the arterial P_{CO_2}, producing respiratory alkalosis. Thus normal pregnancy is a state of compensated respiratory alkalosis.

Most, but not all, studies have found airway conductance and lung compliance to be slightly increased secondary to progesterone-induced bronchial smooth muscle relaxation. Resulting changes are an increase in tidal volume and a decrease in functional residual capacity. By the second trimester, tidal volume is increased by almost 40%, and the respiratory rate has increased slightly (10 to 15%). The increased ventilation leads to a mild respiratory alkalosis, resulting in physiologic dyspnea—a perception of shortness of breath. Normal heart and respiratory rates during pregnancy are 80 to 100 beats and 16 breaths per minute, respectively.[20,21] Table 29–5 lists indicators of heart or lung disease that are *not* anticipated during pregnancy.

Symptoms of orthopnea and paroxysmal nocturnal dyspnea occasionally are reported in the later stages of pregnancy and may mimic symptoms of heart disease.[22] Of consideration in the evaluation of dyspnea during pregnancy is peripartum cardiomyopathy. Patients with poor systolic function are at risk for CHF in the peripartum period. Indications from the history, physical examination, chest radiography, and echocardiography are usually sufficient to diagnose these patients. Invasive monitoring guides fluid management, inotropic therapy, and afterload reduction, and prepares patients for hemodynamic changes during labor and in the postpartum period[23] (see Chapter 33, "Congestive Heart Failure").

MANAGEMENT

In the acutely dyspneic patient, stabilization of the airway and hemodynamic support is required, followed by the transfer of the patient to an appropriate medical care setting, as indicated. In the more

TABLE 29–5. Indicators of Pulmonary or Cardiac Disease during Pregnancy

Indicator	Pulmonary Disease	Cardiac Disease
Symptoms		
Cough	x	
Sputum production	x	
Wheezing	x	
Pleuritic chest pain	x	
Hemoptysis	x	x
Severe or progressive dyspnea	x	x
Progressive orthopnea		x
Syncope with exertion		x
Signs		
Wheezes, ronchi, or diffuse rales	x	
Hyperventilation with splinting	x	
Cyanosis	x	x
Clubbing	x	x
Prominent jugular venous distention	x	x
Evidence of pulmonary hypertension	x	x
Systolic murmur > grades III–VI		x
Diastolic murmur		x
Significant arrhythmia		x
Cardiomegaly (general or chamber specific)		x

Adapted from Zeldis SM. Dyspnea during pregnancy: distinguishing cardiac from pulmonary causes. Clin Chest Med 1992;13:567–85.

stable patient with chronic dyspnea, therapy needs to be directed at the specific cause. The reader is directed to the appropriate chapters in this textbook for the detailed management of such patients.

Psychological factors can affect the sensation of dyspnea in both normal and chronically ill patients.[13] Both anxiety and depression can exacerbate dyspnea caused by other illness.[4,7] Depression has been found to be a significant predictor of self-rated breathlessness.[13] Appropriate management may require supplementation with anxiolytics such as benzodiazepines, treatment with buspirone,[24] and/or long-term therapy with antidepressants. For the patient in whom obesity and deconditioning are the major factors, comprehensive diet counseling and a graded exercise program may be therapeutic without pharmacologic intervention. Morphine has been beneficial for the nonspecific treatment of dyspnea of any cause,[4] and is used most commonly for comfort in patients with a poor prognosis and in those with congestive cardiac failure. Benzodiazepines and phenothiazines have been studied for the treatment of dyspnea itself, rather than for anxiety, with conflicting results.[4,25]

CONCLUSION

Evaluation of dyspnea requires consideration of a broad differential diagnosis. However, the majority of patients who present with this complaint are found to suffer from asthma, COPD, ILD, or cardiomyopathy. The clinical evaluation should commence with a detailed history and physical examination followed by chest radiography. In appropriate individuals empiric therapy may have both diagnostic and therapeutic benefits at only a modest cost, precluding the need for extensive evaluation. However, in more enigmatic cases, appropriate evaluation is recommended to elucidate the specific etiology and to rule out potentially life-threatening conditions. In the patient with a negative evaluation despite an adequate H & P, chest radiography, and other diagnostic studies, the possibility of hyperventilation, anxiety, or depression should be considered. Once a diagnosis is made, therapy should by directed toward that specific etiology, although in about 10% of patients, a specific condition is not identified. In such patients consultation with specialists may be indicated if empiric therapy fails.

Although physiologic dyspnea of pregnancy is probably an unusual awareness of hyperventilation, dyspnea due to heart and lung disease is the result of specific pathophysiologic conditions. By understanding the physiology and clinical findings of pregnancy, the clinician is able to effectively identify pathologic states. Management of respiratory disorders during pregnancy is not markedly different from management in the nonpregnant state, but to optimize treatment, the clinicians must be aware of the respiratory changes in pregnancy and how they affect the fetus. With an awareness of specific disease indicators and knowledge of the more common causes of cardiac and pulmonary dyspnea, an appropriate evaluation can be initiated and a therapeutic plan derived.

REFERENCES

1. Rampulla C, Baiocchi S, Dacosto E, Ambrosino N. Dyspnea on exercise: Pathophysiologic mechanisms. Chest 1992;101:248–52S.

2. Pratter MR, Curley FJ, Dubois J, Irwin, RS. Cause and evaluation of chronic dyspnea in a pulmonary disease clinic. Arch Intern Med 1989;149:2277–82.

3. Simon PM, Schwartzstein RM, Weiss JW, et al. Distinguishable types of dyspnea in patients with shortness of breath. Am Rev Respir Dis 1990;142:1009–14.

4. Seamens CM, Wrenn K. Breathlessness: strategies aimed at identifying and treating the cause of dyspnea. Postgrad Med 1995;98:215–27.

5. Castle RJ, Connors AG, Altose MD. Effects of changes in CO_2 partial pressure on the sensation of respiratory drive. J Appl Physiol 1985;59: 1747–51.

6. Clagnaz P, Braun S, Dixon R. Psychological and physiological correlates in COPD patients. Chest 1982; 82:240–1.

7. Gift AG, Cahill CA. Psychophysiologic aspects of dyspnea in chronic obstructive pulmonary disease: a pilot study. Heart Lung 1990;19:252–7.

8. Killian KJ, Jones NL. Respiratory muscles and dyspnea. Clin Chest Med 1988;9:237–48.

9. Tobin MJ. Dyspnea: pathophysiologic basis clinical presentation, and management. Arch Intern Med 1990;150:1604–13.

10. Mahler DA, Horowitz MB. Clinical evaluation of exertional dyspnea. Clin Chest Med 1994;15:259–69.

11. DePaso WJ, Winterbauer RH, Lusk JA, et al. Chronic dyspnea unexplained by history, physical examination, chest roentgenogram, and spirometry. Chest 1991;100:1293–9.

12. Khouzaie TA, Busser JR. A rare cause of dyspnea and arterial hypoxemia. Chest 1997;112:1681–2.

13. Kellner R, Samet J, Pathak D. Dyspnea, anxiety, and depression in chronic respiratory impairment. Gen Hosp Psychiatry 1992;14(1):20–8.

14. Gift AG, Plaut M, Jacox A. Psychologic and physiologic factors related to dyspnea in subjects with chronic obstructive pulmonary disease. Heart Lung 1986;12:595–601.

15. Agle DP, Baum G. Psychological aspects of chronic obstructive pulmonary disease. Med Clin North Am 1977;61:749–58.

16. Cooper CB. Determining the role of exercise in patients with chronic pulmonary disease. Med Sci Sports Exerc 1995;27:147–57.

17. Carrieri-Kohlman V, Gormley JM, Douglas MK, et al. Differentiation between dyspnea and its affective components. West J Nurs Res 1996;18:626–42.

18. Fujii T, Kurihara N, Fujimoto S, et al. Role of pulmonary vascular disorder in determining exercise capacity in patients with severe chronic obstructive pulmonary disease. Clin Physiol 1996;16:521–33.

19. Ventriglia WJ. Arterial blood gases. Emerg Med Clin North Am 1986;4:235–51.

20. Elkus R, Popovich J Jr. Respiratory physiology in pregnancy. Clin Chest Med 1992;13:555–65.

21. Zeldis SM. Dyspnea during pregnancy: distinguishing cardiac from pulmonary causes. Clin Chest Med 1992;13:567–85.

22. Metcalfe J, Ueland K. Maternal cardiovascular adjustments to pregnancy. Prog Cardiovasc Dis 1974; 16:363–74.

23. Dec GW, Fuster V. Idiopathic dilated cardiomyopathy. N Engl J Med 1994;331:1564–75.

24. Argyropoulou P, Patakas D, Koukou A, et al. Buspirone effect on breathlessness and exercise performance in patients with chronic obstructive pulmonary disease. Respiration 1993;60:216–20.

25. Stark RD. Dyspnea: assessment and pharmacological manipulation. Eur Respir J 1988;1:280–7.

30

PNEUMONIA

Robert Shpiner, MD

BACKGROUND

Acute infectious illness of the upper and lower respiratory tracts is the most common acute medical problem in the US population.[1-3] The peak frequency seems to be within the first 2 years of life (up to eight per year) and "typical" adults may have two to four episodes of acute respiratory illness per year. In adults 37% of these illnesses lead to physician evaluation and are classified as being "lower respiratory" with productive cough and signs/symptoms indicating respiratory dysfunction.[4,5]

Community-acquired pneumonia is defined loosely as infection of the lower respiratory tract acquired outside of hospital or institutions, as evidenced by acute signs and symptoms and new changes on chest radiograph. Using this definition, there are approximately 2 to 4 million cases per year in the United States,[6] leading to nearly 1,000,000 hospitalizations[7-9] and a cost of 4 billion dollars.[10] Pneumonia and influenza are the sixth leading cause of death in the United States.

DEFINITIONS

Terminologies for infections of the upper and lower respiratory system are overlapping and are often imprecise. "Lower respiratory infections" usually are confined to infections involving the lung parenchyma itself, the pleural space, or the tracheobronchial tree below the level of the glottis or vocal cords. Further breakdown of the type and location of the apparent infection can be "anatomically" classified: laryngitis, tracheitis, tracheobronchitis, bronchitis, and bronchiolitis, as the process may involve more "distal" parts of the tracheobronchial tree.

The term "pneumonia" usually is considered to define an infection of the lungs, but such infections often affect distal components of the respiratory tract, proximal and distal alveolar spaces, and the adjacent pleural space. Pneumonia is understood to connote an acute *infectious* process to differentiate it from other forms of inflammation of the tracheobronchial tree. "Pneumonitis" refers also a process involving the distal alveolar spaces, but it is noninfectious in nature and tends to be scattered throughout the entire lung. Etiologic causes include inhalational agents, systemic diseases with secondary pulmonary involvement, and drug or radiation reaction. Pathologically, pneumonia can be *necrotizing*, with liquefaction of the lung parenchyma, formation of air-fluid levels, and, often, associated infection of the pleural space (empyema). Organization of this process can lead to lung abscesses. "Empyema" is defined as pus in the pleural space, usually caused by an infectious etiology.

"Lobar pneumonia" refers to an air space disease involving a large segment (lobe) of the lung with adjacent airway involvement. It usually represents the "classic" pneumonia, with sudden onset of cough, chills, purulent sputum, and dense changes on radiograph. "Interstitial pneumonia" involves the areas around the alveolar spaces (ie, connective tissue, lymphatics) with alveolar filling a less prominent feature. "Chronic pneumonia" is essentially a radiographic diagnosis, and it is usually present for weeks to months, with subclinical findings and progressive radiographic changes. Etiologies can be either infectious or inflammatory.

"Atypical pneumonia" was first described in 1983[11] as an acute infection of the respiratory tract with atypical features. It has come to encompass a clinical syndrome of pneumonia with different radiographic and clinical manifestations than those of "classic" pneumococcal pneumonia. In 1960. *Mycoplasma pneumoniae* was described as a primary cause

321

of atypical pneumonia.[12] *Legionella* was isolated in 1976, and *Chlamydia pneumoniae* in 1986. With the descriptions of these organisms and the diseases associated with them, it became apparent that there was great overlap in the manifestations of typical and atypical pneumonia. This overlap precludes the possibility of accurately predicting the microbiologic cause of an individual clinical or radiographic presentation.

PATHOGENESIS

Seasonal increase of respiratory infections during the winter and early spring may be due to the concomitant increase in viral respiratory infections as prodromal illnesses and the increased contact of individuals due to increased indoor confinement. Infections with viruses precedes up to 21% of cases of bacterial pneumonia.[13] Viral infection may cause loss of ciliated epithelium and secondary loss of mucociliary clearance. Impairment of host defenses also may occur with increased mucus production and increased aspiration risk;[14] alteration of normal nasopharyngeal flora; or changes in the phagocytic function of mono- and polymorphonuclear cells.[15,16]

Pathogenic mechanisms for infection include inhalation, aspiration, hematogenous spread, and contiguous spread. **Inhalation** involves the translocation of the infectious agent by aerosol, dust, or particulate matter. Substances between 0.5 and 5 μm in size are able to lodge in the alveolar spaces and avoid the upper respiratory tract's normal defenses.[17] Once in the distal air space, these organisms (viruses, legionella, fungi) are able to survive, multiply, and initiate infection.

Aspiration of upper oral particles or saliva and infectious microorganisms is a primary event in nosocomial pneumonia and may be important in community-acquired processes as well.[18,19] Sequentially, oral colonization is the initial event, followed by aspiration. This may be due to alteration in normal oral or neural function, impaired gag reflex (as in alcoholism and drug use or associated with dental procedures), gastroesophagel reflux, or emesis. Aspiration may occur in normal individuals without predisposition and is a common event during sleep.[20] Gum disease and/or poor dentition increases the number of anaerobic or microaerophilic organisms within the oral flora. If these organisms are aspirated, there is a risk of developing mixed flora pneumonia or lung abscess.

Hematogenous spread is an unusual cause of pneumonia, especially in the outpatient setting. It may occur with right-sided endocarditis or thrombophlebitis of the pelvic or lower extremity venous system. **Contiguous spread** is also a fairly rare form of pathogenesis for lower respiratory tract infections. It may occur from extension from abdominal infections (eg, hepatic bacterial abscesses, hepatic amebic abscesses, peritonitis) or through lymphatic spread. Respiratory viruses usually gain access to the lower airway via direct mucosal extension from initial pharyngeal or nasopharyngeal infection. Reactivation of latent infection can occur in fungal infections (eg, *Coccidioides immitis*, *Toxoplasma gondii*) and in mycobacterial disease (eg, tuberculosis).

PRESENTATION

Presentation of acute infection of the lower respiratory tract/community-acquired pneumonia has many common features, although variation may occur with different "host" factors (see below); in the "normal" host the following often are found:

- Respiratory distress: such as tachypnea, dyspnea, and decreased oxygen saturation
- Increased secretions, with cough and purulent sputum production
- Systemic symptoms such as fever, chills, heart rate changes (ie, tachycardia or paradoxical bradycardia), joint and muscle symptoms, alteration in central nervous system function, and gastrointestinal symptoms

At time of presentation, noninfectious causes of pneumonia-like illnesses with similar signs and symptoms must be considered and evaluated. Noninfectious causes are summarized in Table 30–1.

EVALUATION AND DIAGNOSIS

Once the diagnosis of community-acquired pneumonia has been made, the health care professional must determine whether initial treatment should commence with antibiotics on an out- or inpatient basis. This decision is based on objective findings, assessment of the severity of illness, comorbid factors, and psychosocial factors that may impact on morbidity or mortality. The American Thoracic Society has identified a series of risk factors for complications from community-acquired pneumonia.

TABLE 30–1. Noninfectious Causes of Pneumonic-Like Illnesses

Condition	Diagnostic Features
Drug-induced pneumonitis	Known exposure, allergic presentation with cutaneous findings and eosinophilia
Bronchoalveolar carcinoma	Nonresolving infiltrate with treatment, bronchorrhea
Radiation pneumonitis	Often demarcated to area of exposure, signs/symptoms within 6–12 wk of treatment, prodromal dry cough and dyspnea
Collagen vascular disease	Previous history, extrapulmonary involvement, active disease
Bronchiolitis obliterans with organizing pneumonia (BOOP)	History of known rheumatologic disease, known viral/mycoplasma infection, toxin exposure, organ transplantation
Hypersensitivity pneumonitis	Recurrent episodes, known exposures, rapid onset of symptoms
Alveolar hemorrhage	Hemoptysis, concurrent glomerulonephritis
Wegener's granulomatosis	Concurrent renal and sinus disease, hemoptysis with patchy infiltrates
Eosinophilic pneumonia	Acute exposure to helminths with eosinophilia, chronic peripheral infiltrates ("reverse negative effect")

The at-risk population has changed over the past years, as the type of immunocompromised status has expanded (Table 30–2). If multiple risk factors are present, hospitalization is recommended.

Diagnostic Testing

A large prospective multicenter observational study (the Pneumonia Patient Outcomes Research Team [PORT] Study) was performed in the early 1990s to describe the processes of care and to assess medical outcomes for patients with community-acquired pneumonia.[21] More than 2,000 patients over the age of 18 years were identified who fulfilled criteria for community-acquired pneumonia, including signs and symptoms of lower respiratory tract infection and abnormal chest radiograph. Extensive information about risk stratification, laboratory evaluation, and morbidity and mortality was gathered.

This study demonstrated that microbiologic tests often are not performed in patients treated as outpatients; more elaborate and invasive tests are obtained from patients requiring hospitalization. Examples of testing modalities included chest radiography, sputum gram stain, sputum culture, blood cultures, complete blood count, human immunodeficiency virus (HIV) testing, thoracentesis, and pathogen-specific serologies (serum and urine). Recent guidelines from the Infectious Diseases Society of America (IDSA)[22] emphasize awareness of resistance patterns and agent-specific etiology by presentation for guiding diagnostic and treatment decisions. The majority of patients treated on an outpatient basis do not require extensive diagnostic testing.

CHEST RADIOGRAPY

Diagnosis of pneumonia often is based on the presence of parenchymal or air space disease at time of presentation, although the presence of dehydration, neutropenia, or early onset of illness may render the initial radiograph unremarkable. Infiltrates may "blossom" with time and hydration, often in the area of abnormal physical examination findings. As with clinical presentation, radiographic findings, are nonspecific and do not correlate with etiologic diagnosis. The overlap of pathogenic etiologies and radiographic findings is great. Although nonspecific, the chest radiograph can contain useful information: the degree of consolidation, the presence of pleural effusions, evidence of cavitary disease, and evidence of prior lung disease (eg, granulomatous changes, chronic obstructive pulmonary disease [COPD]); these findings are important to consider in making management decisions. Also, there are some clinical correlations with radiographic changes that are useful:

- Segmental or lobar air space/alveolar disease is more common with pyogenic bacteria.[23]
- Diffuse interstitial infiltrates tend to suggest viral or pneumocystis pneumonia in the appropriate host or setting.

TABLE 30–2. Risk Factors for Complications of Community-Acquired Pneumonia

Historic factors

    Age > 65 yr

    Suspicion of aspiration of gastric or oropharyngeal secretions

    Congestive heart failure

    Chronic obstructive pulmonary disease/bronchiectasis

    Diabetes

    Chronic alcohol abuse

    Malnutrition

    Chronic renal failure

    Chronic liver disease (any etiology)

    Hospitalization during the prior 12 mo

    Previous splenectomy

    Altered mental status

Physical findings

    Temperature > 38.3°C

    Ventilatory rate 30/min or more

    Blood pressure < 90 mm Hg systolic or < 60 mm Hg diastolic

    Evidence of extrapulmonary sites of disease, eg, septic arthritis or meningitis

    Confusion or decreased level of consciousness

Laboratory abnormalities

    WBC < 4,000 or > 30,000

    Hematocrit < 30% or hemoglobin < 9 g/dL

    Po_2 < 60 mm Hg or Pco_2 > 50 mm Hg on room air

    Unfavorable chest radiograph: multilobe involvement, caviation, rapid radiographic spreading, or pleural effusion

    Abnormal renal function with BUN ≥ 20 mg/dL or creatinine ≥ 1.2 mg/dL

    Metabolic acidosis

    Increased prothrombin or partial thromboplastin time, decreased platelets, or positive tests for disseminated intravascular coagulopathy

Other: other evidence of sepsis or organ dysfunction

WBC = white blood cell count; Po_2 = partial pressure of oxygen; Pco_2 = partial pressure of carbon dioxide; BUN = blood urea nitrogen.

- Pleural effusions in community-acquired pneumonia are usually benign and uncomplicated, and are relatively common (see Table 30–1).[15,24,25]
- Cavitary disease suggests infection with *Staphylococcus aureus*, *Klebsiella pneumoniae*, mixed anaerobic organisms (possible aspiration), tuberculosis (especially in an upper lobe distribution), or fungi.
- Hilar adenopathy is unusual in community-acquired pneumonia and, if present, may suggest tuberculosis, malignancy, fungal infection, or sarcoidosis.

SPUTUM EXAMINATION

There is significant controversy in the medical literature regarding the usefulness of the sputum Gram stain in the diagnosis of pneumonia.[26,27] Guidelines for obtaining and examining sputum samples have been published (Table 30–3). The major confusion arises with differentiation of colonization and true infection, and interpretation of inadequate samples. Additional stains may be applied to facilitate diagnosis. These include acid-fast (tuberculosis), modified acid-fast (*Nocardia*, *Legionella*), and direct fluorescent antibody stains (*Legionella*, influenza, respiratory syncytial virus). Also, potassium hydroxide

TABLE 30–3. Infectious Diseases Society of America's Guidelines for Obtaining and Examining Sputum Samples

1. The specimen should be obtained by deep cough and be grossly purulent; it should be obtained before treatment with antimicrobial agents and in the presence of a physician or nurse.
2. The specimen should be immediately transported to the laboratory for prompt processing. Delays of 2–5 h at room temperature result in reduced isolation rates for *Streptococcus pneumoniae, Staphylococcus aureus,* and gram-negative bacilli with increased numbers of indigenous flora.
3. A purulent portion is selected for Gram's stain and culture. Quellung test should be done when available.
4. Cytologic screening should be done under low-power magnifications (× 100) to determine the cellular composition. Criteria for culture are variable: the "classic study" required < 10 squamous epithelial cells and > 25 polymorphonuclear neutrophils per low-power field. Cytologic assessment is not useful for screening specimens for detection of *Legionella* or mycobacteria.
5. Culture should be performed by using standard techniques and reporting with semiquantitative assessment. Most pathogens are recovered in 3 to 4 + growth, indicating more than five colonies in the second streak.

Reproduced with permission from Gotfried MH. Community acquired pneumonia. J Crit Illness 1999;14:S20–1.

stain for fungal hyphae and silver stain for pneumocystis can be used. Although potential problems exist, information gained from an adequate or high-quality Gram-stained specimen is extremely useful in diagnosis and selection of initial treatment.

BLOOD CULTURES

Isolation of pathogens from the blood establishes an etiologic cause for the presenting pneumonia. Two sets of cultures are suggested before the institution of therapy in patients who are ill enough to require hospitalization. The rate of positivity ranges by pathogen: 70% of patients with *Klebsiella* pneumonia demonstrate positive blood cultures, compared with 33% of patients with *S. aureus* pneumonia, 24% of patients with pneumococcal pneumonia, 10% of patients with *Haemophilus influenzae* pneumonia, and only 1 to 2% of patients with pneumonia caused by *Legionella*, anaerobes, or viral pathogens. Positive blood cultures are often a bad prognostic finding and are associated with up to a fourfold increase in mortality.[14]

SPECIAL TESTS

Small effusions can occur in up to 50% of pneumonia cases.[28] Generally, these can be managed conservatively with observation alone. The failure to respond to empiric therapy, the possibility of empyema, and significant respiratory compromise are indications for diagnostic and therapeutic thoracentesis. In large effusions associated with significant pneumonia, positive cultures are found up to 12% of the time, establishing the diagnosis. Additional studies of secretions include polymerase

chain reaction tests which currently are available to detect presence of *Chlamydia, Mycoplasma,* and *Legionella.* Complement fixation serologies are available for *Chlamydia, Mycoplasma,* and *Coccidioides.* Additional studies for *Legionella* include urinary antigen analysis and direct fluorescent antibody, and enzyme immunoassay for sputum. The urinary test for *Legionella* is sensitive but only detects one serogroup.

Etiology

Numerous articles have been written about the classification of etiologic causes of community-acquired pneumonia.[9,29,30] However, there are a number of reasons why the specific diagnosis of pneumonia by etiologic organism is difficult, if not impossible. Factors influencing whether a specific causative organism can be identified include prior antibiotic usage before presentation, inability to obtain adequate sputum sampling, lack of test sensitivity or specificity once sputum stain and culture have been obtained, infrequency of positive blood cultures, inability to culture viruses, or atypical agents such as *Mycoplasma* and *Chlamydia,* and the time delay in waiting for changes in serum antibody titers. The etiologic diagnosis is unknown in 30 to 60% of cases of outpatient pneumonia because of these problems. Table 30–4 demonstrates the changing etiology of community-acquired pneumonia in adults.

STREPTOCOCCUS PNEUMONIAE

Twenty to 75% of community-acquired pneumonias are caused by *S. pneumoniae,* and it is recovered in up to two-thirds of hospitalized patients

TABLE 30–4. Microbiologic Pathogens in Community-Acquired Pneumonia

Organism/Cause	Prevalence (%)*
Bacteria	
Streptococcus pneumoniae	20–75
Haemophilus influenzae	3–10
Staphylococcus aureus	3–5
Gram-negative bacilli	3–10
Miscellaneous†	3–5
Atypical agents	10–20
Legionella	2–8
Mycoplasma pneumoniae	1–6
Chlamydia pneumoniae	4–6
Viruses	2–15
Aspiration	6–10

*Based on 15 published North American studies.
†Includes *Moraxella catarrhalis*, group A streptococci, and *Neisseria meningitidis* (each accounting for 1 to 2% of cases). Reproduced with permission from Gotfried MH. Community acquired pneumonia. J Crit Illness 1999;14:S20–1.

with community-acquired pneumonia. Pneumococcus is identified in approximately 65% of patients who die from community-acquired pneumonia.[31] It is gram-positive, "lancet shaped," and often seen in pairs.[14,32]

There is a 10 to 70% *asymptomatic* carrier rate in the adult population. This pathogen does not usually cause disease unless there is some impairment of the host defenses, often occurring post viral respiratory infection. Therefore, pneumococcal pneumonia is not considered highly contagious.

Symptoms usually begin suddenly after a 1- to 3-day incubation period. Shaking chills and rigors occur in 80% of cases. Purulent sputum production is the rule, as is sustained high fevers over 39°C. Single-lobe involvement occurs up to 90% of the time, two lobes are involved in 25% of cases, and multilobar abnormalities are unusual. In addition, pleuritic symptoms occur in 75% of patients, with associated effusions in about 25% of cases; these are usually small and uncomplicated.

Bacteremia during the acute infection occurs about 25% of the time and rarely seeds sites outside the lung, including the meninges, pericardium, and joints. The incidence of bacteremia tends to increase in winter and early spring months and is more common in patients with underlying malignancies such as leukemia or lymphoma, lack of a functioning spleen, and HIV infection.

Antibiotic treatment has attenuated the prolonged course of pneumococcal disease, but the rate of mortality within the first 24 hours has remained unchanged despite treatment. Fulminant disease with sepsis, and disseminated intravascular coagulopathy, is rare in the normal host, but this form of overwhelming disease may be seen in asplenic patients.

MYCOPLASMA PNEUMONIAE

Community-acquired pneumonia caused by *Mycoplasma* is usually a relatively mild disease. It is the most frequent cause of pneumonia in the 5 to 20-year-old age group, representing 1 to 6% of outpatient pneumonias,[33] and up to 50% of cases of upper respiratory infection in the summer months. This agent is very contagious, with symptoms occurring in up to 80% of children and 60% of adult family members of index cases.[34]

In contrast to other agents, *Mycoplasma* affects otherwise healthy individuals, often manifesting as pharyngitis or tracheobronchitis. Pneumonia develops in 33% of patients, with one-third requiring hospitalization. Attempts to distinguish infection with this organism on clinical grounds alone on an individual patient basis are not successful.[35] Nonspecific symptoms include fever, malaise, headache, and a nonproductive cough; they usually begin after a 2- to 3-week incubation period. Bullous myringitis is seen in 15% of cases and otitis in 20%. Although considered the "prototype for walking pneumonia." fulminant disease can be seen rarely with encephalitis, myopericarditis, and frank sepsis; it appears that these complications tend to be underdiagnosed and underappreciated. In patients with sickle cell disease, fatalities have been reported.

LEGIONELLA

Although retrospective isolation of *Legionella* has demonstrated occurrences of pneumonia as far back as 1947, it was not until 1976 that clinical recognition, isolation, and identification of the agent causing the famous Philadelphia outbreak among conventioning state Legionnaires was possible. This organism is ubiquitous in nature and generally is thought to infect susceptible persons via aerosolization from cooling towers, air conditioners, condensers, and showerheads. Infection is not thought to be contagious and clinical disease tends to occur in patients with concomitant illnesses.

The incubation period is 2 to 10 days and systemic symptoms are the rule. High sustained temperatures up to 40.5°C are seen in 20% of cases. Gastrointestinal (eg, diarrhea or abnormal liver tests), neurologic (eg, alteration in the level of consciousness), and other systemic involvement (eg, hypophosphatemia or hyponatremia) may occur. Results of chest radiograpy are nonspecific but usually show rapid progression of infiltrates and air space disease. Although at initial presentation differentiation of this agent from other causes of pneumonia can be difficult, the rapid progression of radiographic abnormalities and systemic findings in susceptible hosts should alert the clinician to legionella infection.

HAEMOPHILUS INFLUENZAE

Haemophilus influenzae has been identified in 5 to 15% of cases of community-acquired pneumonia and tends to affect adults with underlying lung disease and the elderly. The incubation period is 1 to 3 days, and acute onset of symptoms is common, although not as dramatic as that with pneumococcus. Purulent blood-tinged sputum is the rule, and pleural symptoms often are seen. The chest radiograph usually shows lobar consolidation, with pleural effusion in half of cases.

STAPHYLOCOCCUS AUREUS

Staphylococcus aureus can be found to reside in the anterior nasal passage of 20 to 35% of healthy adults, and has been shown to cause up to 10% of community-acquired pneumonia cases. This organism tends to affect patients with underlying systemic diseases, or lung disease, the elderly, and intravenous-drug users. Healthy adults usually are not affected except during influenza epidemics, in which *S. aureus* is found to cause 50% of the cases of secondary pneumonia. This organism tends to cause extensive lung tissue destruction with multilobar involvement. Pleural fluid can be detected in 50% of cases, with frank empyema occurring in one-half of these cases. Abscess formation occurs in up to 20% of cases, and results of blood cultures are positive in about one-third of cases. The documented mortality rate from fulminant staphylococcal pneumonia is up to 50%.

CHLAMYDIA PNEUMONIAE

Chlamydia pneumoniae previously was known as "TWAR," and is probably responsible for up to 13% of cases of community acquired pneumonia.[36] There has been no natural reservoir discovered for this organism, and infection seems to occur from person to person. It is possible that *C. pneumoniae* may act more as a cofactor that causative pathogen, and mixed infections with *C. pneumoniae* and pneumococcus appear to be common. There is not enough information to establish the degree of transmissibility, but serologic antibody testing of young adults often demonstrates previous exposure. This suggests a wide range of possible clinical manifestations including mild upper respiratory infection and pharyngitis, as well as frank pneumonia. As with mycoplasma, low grade fever and nonproductive cough are common. Radiographs are non-specific, and pleural involvement is seen in 25% of cases. Because of susceptibility patterns, this agent should be considered when "atypical" pneumonia occurs in adults with poor response to penicillin or cephalosporin antibiotics.

KLEBSIELLA PNEUMONIAE AND OTHER GRAM-NEGATIVE RODS

The classic clinical presentation of *Klebsiella* pneumonia is rapid onset of symptoms, often in the alcoholic population, with thick "currant-jelly" sputum. Previously thought to be a common cause of pneumonia, its incidence has dropped to 3 to 10% overall. Populations at risk include persons with COPD, alcoholics, and malnourished individuals. The classic "bowing" fissure is seen in over half of the cases, but it can be caused by other agents. Early cavitation suggests an etiology of *Klebsiella* and can be seen in up to 60% of cases. Overall, enteric gram-negative rods are rare causes of community-acquired pneumonia, even in the alcoholic population.

MORAXELLA CATARRHALIS

Previously termed "*Branhamella catarrhalis*," *Moraxella catarrhalis* is more likely to cause sinusitis and otitis media than pneumonia. The population most at risk seems to be smokers and patients with COPD. Most isolates are penicillin resistant; therefore, the possibility of *Moraxella* infection may affect the initial choice of antibiotic, especially in the seriously ill patient.

VIRUSES

Viral organisms are a more common cause of pneumonia in young children and infants than in adults. Mixed infections with viruses and bacteria can be seen in adults, making accurate diagnosis difficult. Viruses can be isolated in up to 10% of patients hospitalized with community-acquired pneumonia and are more common in nosocomial pneumonia, especially in immunocompromised patients.

The most commonly isolated viruses in the adult population with community-acquired pneumonia are influenza A and B and respiratory syncytial virus. The peak season seems to be the winter months, and patients requiring hospitalization are ones with prior cardiac or pulmonary disease. A study of the impact of influenza on pregnant women demonstrated that women in their third trimester of pregnancy were hospitalized at a rate comparable with that of nonpregnant women with high-risk medical conditions.[37] Other pathogenic viruses described in patients with community-acquired pneumonia include herpes simplex virus 1, parainfluenza virises 1, 2, and 3, adenovirus, and rhinovirus. Organ transplantation seems to increase the risk of contracting these viral pneumonias as well as cytomegalovirus.

Cases of primary influenza pneumonia are associated with a high mortality rate, but the most common presentation is the postviral bacterial pneumonia with *Pneumococcus* or *S. aureus;* this also is associated with a high mortality rate. Tissue culture, enzyme immunoassay, and polymerase chain reaction are used to establish a diagnosis. These tests are not available routinely. There are only a few approved antiviral agents available, and these have not been shown to be effective in preventing or treating associated viral or bacterial pneumonia.[37] Vaccination programs seem to be effective in reducing severe influenza cases.

TREATMENT

Initial antibiotic choices are based upon the most likely pathogen, results of laboratory testing, severity of illness, and suspected resistance pattern. Treatment and testing can then be modified in response to the patient's clinical course. Although the etiology of community-acquired pneumonia has changed over the past two decades, *Pneumococcus* still remains the most common pathogen. Clearly, selection of treatment regimens is based on numerous factors including the specific population (eg, elderly, or immunocompromised), socioeconomic factors, local and seasonal variation, and degree of illness based on compiled risk factors at presentation. The increased prevalence of atypical pathogens and the emergence of multidrug-resistant pathogens require significant attention. If an atypical pathogen seems to be a possible etiology, the choices for treatment include macrolides or the newer quinolones. Although the significance of drug-resistant *Pneumococcus* is still debated, it is clear that this strain is associated with increased mortality. Vancomycin and the newer fluoroquinolones remain the treatment of choice in this circumstance (Table 30–5).

Special Populations

ELDERLY PATIENTS

There is a clearly documented increase in pneumonia-associated morbidity and mortality in the elderly compared with that in the younger adult population, with up to a fourfold increase in case-specific mortality;[28] this has significant impact on diagnosis and management. Causes more common in the elderly include impaired cough reflex and aspiration risk.

Clinical signs such as fever may be absent, with altered respiratory pattern or changes in the level of consciousness being the only demonstrable change, making diagnosis difficult and possibly delayed. In addition, obtaining adequate samples from the lower respiratory tract can be difficult, limiting diagnostic accuracy. *Pneumococcus* remains the most likely pathogen, but enteric gram-negative organisms may be responsible for 20% of the cases of pneumonia in this population. Up to 50 to 60% of cases community-acquired pneumonia in the elderly require hospitalization. This stems from the associated comorbid conditions and the impact of hypoxia. In fact, in hospitalized elderly patients mortality from pneumonia often results from underlying disease and respiratory failure rather than microbiologic causes. The mortality rate approaches 40%.[38] Initial empiric treament should include a broad-spectrum ß-lactam or newer fluoroquinolones and a macrolide.

IMMUNOCOMPROMISED PATIENTS

The spectrum of immunosuppression includes HIV infection, organ transplantation, and cytotoxic and corticosteroid treatments. Any of these factors

TABLE 30–5. Empiric Antibiotic Selection for Patients with Community-Acquired Pneumonia

Outpatients
  Generally preferred: macrolides*, fluoroquinolones†, or doxycycline
  Modifying factors
    Suspected penicillin-resistant *Streptococcus pneumoniae:* fluoroquinolones†
    Suspected aspiration: amoxicillin/clavulanate
    Young adult (17–40 yr): doxycycline

Hospitalized patients
  General medical ward
  Generally preferred: ß-lactam† with or without a macrolide* *or* a fluoroquinolone† (alone)
  Alternatives: cefuroxime with or without a macrolide* *or* azithromycin (alone)
  Hospitalized in the intensive care unit for serious pneumonia
  Generally preferred: erythromycin, azithromycin, or a fluoroquinolone† *plus* cefotaxime, ceftriaxone,
    or a ß-lactam-ß-lactamase inhibitor§
  Modifying factors
    Structural disease of the lung: antipseudomonal penicillin, a carbapenem, *or* cefepime plus a macrolide*
      or a fluoroquinolone† *plus* an aminoglycoside
    Penicillin allergy: a fluoroquinolone† with or without clindamycin
    Suspected aspiration: a fluoroquinolone plus either clindamycin or metronidazole or a ß-lactam-ß-lactamase
      inhibitor§ (alone)

*Azithromycin, clarithromycin, or erythromycin.
†Levofloxacin, sparfloxacin, grepafloxacin, or another flururoquinolone with enhanced activity against *S. pneumoniae.*
‡Cefotaxime, ceftriaxone, or a ß-lactam-ß-lactamase inhibitor.
§Ampicillin/sulbactam, ticarcillin/clavulanate, or piperacillin/tazobactam (for structural disease of the lung, ticarcillin/clavulanate or piperacillin).
Reproduced with permission from Bartlett JG, Breiman RF, Mandell LA, File TM Jr. Community-acquired pneumonia in adults: guidelines for management. The Infectious Diseases Society of America. Clin Infect Dis 1998;26:811–38.

makes determination of etiologic causes of pneumonia difficult. The type and duration of the immunocompromised state impacts on all facets of community-acquired pneumonia. The rate of progression of infection and dissemination is increased, and the signs and symptoms often are blunted or more difficult to interpret due to the impact of impaired immunologic response reflected in physical findings and laboratory evaluation. It becomes increasingly challenging to determine if a recovered organism is merely a colonizing bacteria or true pathogen. Noninfectious causes of respiratory findings are more prevalent, also confounding diagnosis and treatment. Aside from the differences in possible pathogens, drug interactions and toxicity are more complex and common in this population.

Each population of immunocompromised patients has specific etiologies, diagnostic considerations, and therapeutic approaches for pneumonia. This heterogeneity emphasizes the need to adjust initial evaluation in each specific population. In the HIV population, *Pneumococcus* remains the most common pathogen in community-acquired pneumonia. *Pneumocystis carinii* and *H. influenzae* are less common, as are atypical pathogens. The use of trimethoprim/sulfamethoxazole as prophylaxis increases the risk of drug-resistant pneumococcus.

PREVENTION

Vaccination is effective in reducing the risk of community-acquired pneumococcal pneumonia. Pneumococcal vaccine should be given to all women who are 65 years of age or older, as well as those who are immunocompromised or who have chronic illnesses that increase their risk of pneumococcal disease. Routine revaccination is not recommended. However, revaccination is recommended for severely immunocompromised persons, such as those with functional or anatomic asplenia, HIV infection, or cancer, or those on long-term immunosupressive therapy, if they have not received the vaccine for at least 5 years. Elderly persons who received the vaccine before age 65 years should be revaccinated if they have not received the vaccine for at least 5 years. Optimal revaccination strategies are being studied. Currently, revaccination following a second dose is not recommended, because safety data are lacking.[39]

Vaccination is effective in reducing the risk of illness, respiratory complications, and death from influenza. New influenza virus variants occur frequently, resulting from mutations that occur during viral replication. Vaccination against one influenza virus type does not necessarily provide protection against another virus type. Therefore, new strains are incorporated yearly into the influenza vaccine, and yearly vaccination is recommended. Vaccination generally is advised in the fall, prior to the beginning of the winter influenza season.[37]

Influenza vaccination is recommended for all women aged 50 years and above, those with chronic medical illnesses, and women who will be in the second or third trimester of pregnancy during the influenza season. Many experts consider influenza vaccination safe at any stage of pregnancy. A study of influenza vaccination in more than 2,000 pregnant women showed no adverse fetal outcomes. Some experts, however, prefer to defer vaccination until after the first trimester. Pregnant women with medical conditions such as asthma that present a high risk for complications from influenza should be vaccinated before the influenza season begins, regardless of the stage of pregnancy.[37]

Although a vaccine is available for *H. influenzae*, there is limited data on its efficacy in adults. Its use in adults is not currently recommended.[40]

RESOURCES

Infectious Diseases Society of America
99 Canal Center Plaza, Suite 210
Alexandria, Virginia 22314
Telephone: (703) 299-0200
Web site: www.idsociety.org

The IDSA provides on-line guidelines for the diagnosis, treatment, and management of pneumonia, as well as other infectious diseases.

Centers for Disease Control
1600 Clifton Road
Atlanta, Georgia 30333
Telephone: 1-800-311-3435
Web site: www.cdc.gov

The CDC provides on-line access to guidelines for vaccination and other measures to prevent pneumonia. Free on-line subscription to the CDC's Morbidity and Mortality Weekly Report (MMWR) *is available at the CDC Web site; the journal provides yearly information about influenza vaccination and updates on other measures, such as chemoprophylaxis, to prevent influenza.*

REFERENCES

1. Garbaldi RA. Epidemiology of community-acquired respiratory tract infections in adults. Am J Med 1985;78 Suppl 6B:32–7.

2. Klein JO. Emerging perspectives in management and prevention of infections of the respiratory tract in infants and children. Am J Med 1985;78 Suppl 6B:38–44.

3. Monto AS. Acute respiratory infection in children of developing countries—challenge of the 1990s. Rev Infect Dis 1989;11:498–505.

4. Monto AS, Napier JA, Metzner HL. The Tecumseh study of repiratory illness. I. Plan of study and observations of acute respiratory disease. Am J Epidemiol 1971;94:269–79.

5. Monto AS, Ulman BM. Acute respiratory illness in an American community. JAMA 1974;227:164–9.

6. Bartlett JG, Mundy LM. Current concepts: community-acquired pneumonia. N Engl J Med 1995;333: 1618–24.

7. Adams PF, Marano MA. Current estimates from the National Health Interview Survey, 1994, National Center for Health Statistics. Vital Health Stat 1995;10.

8. Graves EJ, Gillum BS. 1994 summary: National Hospital Discharge Survey, Advance Data, No. 278. National Center for Health Statistics; 1996.

9. Marrie TJ, Durant H, Yates L. Community-acquired pneumonia requiring hospitalization: 5-year prospective study. Rev Infect Dis 1989;11:586–99.

10. Dixon RE. Economic costs of respiratory tract infections in the United States. Am J Med 1985;7888 Suppl 6B:45–51.

11. Guzzetta P, Toews GB, Robertson KJ, et al. Rapid diagnosis of community-acquired bacterial pneumonia. Am Rev Respir Dis 1983;128:461–4.

12. Austrian R. The Gram stain and the etiology of lobar pneumonia, a historical note. Bacteriol Rev 1960; 24:261–4.

13. Glezen WP. Viral pneumonia as a cause and result of hospitalization. J Infect Dis 1983;147:765–70.

14. Coonroud J. Pneumococcal pneumonia. Semin Respir Infect 1989;4:4–11.

15. Abramson JS, Mills EL. Depression of neutrophil function induced by viruses and its role in secondary microbial infections. Rev Infect Dis 1988;10:326–41.

16. Rouse BT, Horohov DW. Immunosuppression in viral infections. Rev Infect Dis 1986;8:850–73.

17. Mitchell RI. Retention of aerosol particles in the respiratory tract. Am Rev Respir Dis 1960;82:627–39.

18. DePaso WJ. Aspiration pneumonia. Clin Chest Med 1991;12:269–84.

19. LaForce FM. Hospital-acquired gram-negative rod pneumonias—an overview. Am J Med 1981;70:664–9.

20. Huxley EJ, Viroslav J, Gray WR, et al. Pharyngeal aspiration in normal adults and patients with depressed consciousness. Am J Med 1978;64:564–8.

21. Fine MJ, Auble TE, Yealy DM, et al. A prediction rule to identify low-risk patients with community-acquired pneumonia. N Engl J Med 1997;336: 243–50.

22. Bartlett JG, Breiman RF, Mandell LA, File TM Jr. Community-acquired pneumonia in adults: guidelines for management. The Infectious Diseases Society of America. Clin Infect Dis 1998;26:811–38.

23. Levy M, Dromer F, Brion N. Community acquired pneumonia. Chest 1988;92:43–8.

24. Addiss DG, Davis JP, LaVenture M, et al. Community-acquired legionnaires' disease associated with a cooling tower. Am J Epidemiol 1989;130:557–68.

25. Alexander HE. *Haemophilus influenzae*. In: Dubos RJ, editor. Bacterial and mycotic infections of man. Philadelphia: JB Lippincott; 1958. p. 470–85.

26. Geckler RW, Gremillion DH, McAllister CK, et al. Microscopic and bacteriological comparison of paired sputa and transtracheal aspirates. J Clin Microbiol 1977;6:396–9.

27. Gleckman R, Devita J, Hibert D, et al. Sputum gram stain in the assessment of community acquired bacteremic pneumonia. J Clin Microbiol 1988:26:846–9.

28. Light RW. Clinical manifestations and useful tests. In: Light RW, editor. Pleural diseases. Philadelphia: Lea & Febiger; 1983. p. 33–60.

29. Berntasson E, Blombert J, Lagergard T, et al. Etiology of CAP in patients requiring hospitalization. Eur J Clin Microbiol 1985;4:268–72.

30. Holmberg H. Aetiology of CAP in hospital treated patients. Scand J Infect Dis 1987;19:491–501.

31. Fine MJ, Smith MA, Carson CA, et al. Prognosis and outcomes of patients with community-acquired pneumonia: a meta-analysis. JAMA 1996;275:134–41.

32. Mufsan SA. *Streptococcus pneumoniae*. In: Mandell GL, Douglas RG, Bennett JE, editors. Principles and practice of infectious diseases. 3rd ed. New York: Churchill Livingstone; 1990. p. 1539–50.

33. Foy HM, Kenny GE, McMahan R, et al. *Mycoplasma pneumoniae* pneumonia in an urban area. JAMA 1970;214:1666–72.

34. Couch RB. *Mycoplasma* pneumonia. In: Mandell GL, Douglas RG, Bennett JE, editors. Principles and practice of infectious diseases 3rd ed. New York: Churchill Livingstone; 1990. p. 1446–58.

35. Boerner DF, Zwadyk P. The value of the sputum Gram's stain in the community-acquired pneumonia. JAMA 1982;247:642–5.

36 Schaffner W. TWAR. In: Mandell GL, Douglas RG, Bennett JE, editor. Principles and practice of infectious diseases. 3rd ed. New York: Churchill Livingstone; 1990. p. 1443–4.

37. Advisory Committee on Immunization Practices. Prevention and control of influenza. MMWR Morb Mortal Wkly Rep 2000;49(RR03):1–38.

38. Marrie TJ. Epidemiology of community-acquired pneumonia in the elderly. Semin Respir Infect 1990; 5:260–8.

39. Advisory Committee on Immunization Practices. Prevention of pneumococcal disease: recommendations of the Advisory Committee on Immunization Practices MMWR Morb Mortal Wkly Rep 1997; 46(RR-08):1–24.

40. Advisory Committee on Immunization Practices. Recommendation of the Immunization Practices Advisory Committee: polysaccharide vaccine for prevention of *Haemophilus influenzae* type b disease. MMWR Morb Mortal Wkly Rep 1985;34(15):201–5.

31

HYPERTENSION

Michael P. Brousseau, MD

Cardiovascular disease is the most common cause of death for both women and men in the United States.[1] More than 230,000 women die annually from acute myocardial infarction, and more than 87,000 die from stroke. Hypertension has been identified in epidemiologic studies to be a major risk factor for the development of cardiovascular disease in both women[2-4] and men.[5,6] Meta-analyses of large randomized controlled trials have demonstrated that treatment of hypertension with pharmacologic therapy reduces cardiovascular morbidity and mortality as well as overall mortality.[7,8] Subgroup analysis has confirmed that these reductions occur similarly in men and women.[9]

Efforts to treat hypertension have contributed to the decline in age-adjusted death rates of nearly 60% from stroke and 53% from coronary heart disease over the last 22 years.[10] Yet despite increasing awareness of the cardiovascular risks associated with hypertension, only 53% of the hypertensive population is receiving treatment, and only 27% of hypertensives are controlled on therapy.

The Nurses' Health Study found that women with hypertension have an increased relative risk of 3.5 for coronary artery disease and 2.6 for stroke as compared with normotensive women.[2] Although coronary artery disease is the leading cause of death in women overall, in women under the age of 65 years the incidence is less than that of men.[11] Until this age, women are less likely to develop coronary artery disease even when equally exposed to the same known cardiovascular disease risk factors (ie, smoking, hypertension, higher body mass index, and lower socioeconomic class).[12]

INCIDENCE

The National Health and Nutrition Examination Survey III (1988 to 1991)[10] reported the overall prevalence of hypertension in women aged 18 to 74 years to be 18%. The prevalence of hypertension increased with age. Women aged 65 to 74 years had a prevalence of 52%. Black women had a higher prevalence of hypertension than did white women in all age groups. Men with hypertension outnumber women with hypertension during young adulthood and early middle age, but after the age of menopause, women outnumber men. The reason for this increase after menopause remains speculative.

CLINICAL EVALUATION

Hypertension is defined as a systolic blood pressure (SBP) of greater than or equal to 140 mm Hg, or a diastolic blood pressure (DBP) of greater than or equal to 90 mm Hg on three or more occasions.[13-15] This definition applies to all ages. Normal blood pressure and the stages of hypertension are defined in Table 31–1.

Measurement of Blood Pressure

The patient should refrain from caffeine intake and smoking 30 minutes prior to measurement. Also, the patient should rest for several minutes prior to the recording.

Measurements of blood pressure should be taken while the patient is seated in a chair with back support, with the cuff placed over a bare arm at the level of the heart. The measurement should be taken with a mercury sphygmomanometer. If this is unavailable, then a calibrated aneroid manometer or validated electronic devise can be used. A wrist or forearm cuff should not be used. The cuff's bladder should encircle at least 80% of the arm. Larger cuffs may be required for some patients.

The systolic pressure is defined as the first sound audible, and the diastolic pressure as the

TABLE 31–1. Classification of Blood Pressure for Adults Aged 18 Years and Older*

Category	Blood Pressure (mm Hg)		
	Systolic		Diastolic
Optimal[†]	<120	and	<80
Normal	<130	and	<85
High-normal	130–139	or	85–89
Hypertension[‡]			
Stage 1	140–159	or	90–99
Stage 2	60–179	or	100–109
Stage 3	≥180	or	≥110

*Not taking antihypertensive drugs and not acutely ill.
[†]Optimal blood pressure with respect to cardiovascular risk is less than 120/80 mm Hg. However, unusually low readings should be evaluated for clinical significance.
[‡]Based on the average of two or more readings taken at each of two or more visits after an initial screening.
Adapted from The sixth report of the Joint National Committee on Prevention, Detection, Evaluation, and Treatment of High Blood Pressure. Arch Intern Med 1997;157:2413–46.

disappearance of sound. The blood pressure should be taken in both arms, and, if they are different, the highest reading should be used as the measurement.

WHITE COAT HYPERTENSION

White coat hypertension is a phenomenon whereby blood pressures measured in the presence of a physician or clinical personnel exceed those taken in more familiar surroundings. Up to 80% of patients have higher clinic pressures than home blood pressures. A significant portion of patients can have clinic readings >20/10 mm Hg higher than home readings.[16]

Clinicians should encourage their patients to record blood pressure measurements at home or in the workplace with a 24-hour ambulatory blood pressure monitor, digital cuff, or mercury sphygmomanometer.[17,18] Patients can bring their blood pressure machine to the clinic to have their readings validated. This is particularly important when home readings are very different from those obtained in clinic. Although there are no long-term studies assessing the efficacy of hypertensive treatment based on home readings, home readings can serve as an adjunct in making treatment decisions. A home

blood pressure reading of 135/85 mm Hg or greater is considered elevated.[19]

Clinical History

The clinical history should determine the duration of pre-existing hypertension, risk stratify the patient for cardiovascular disease, determine if target organ damage has occurred, and evaluate for secondary causes of hypertension. Approximately 90 to 95% of patients with hypertension have essential hypertension. Many of these patients have a family history of hypertension or environmental risks such as obesity, increased salt sensitivity, occupational stressors, and alcohol use that may contribute to increased blood pressure. The majority of these patients have no symptoms referable to their elevated blood pressure and are diagnosed upon measurement of their blood pressure during routine physical examination. Therefore, a prior history of normal or abnormal blood pressure measurements is essential in identifying the duration of hypertension. In the absence of documentation of prior readings, it may be impossible to know how long a patient has been hypertensive.

The presence of additional risk factors for coronary artery disease and/or target organ damage mandates a more aggressive approach to the treatment of hypertension. The major risk factors for cardiovascular disease include a history of cigarette smoking, diabetes, a family history of cardiovascular disease among first-degree relatives (particularly women <65 years and men <55 years), dyslipidemia, and age >45 years for men and >55 years for women.[13] Target organ damage can be obtained by inquiring about a history of angina, myocardial infarction, congestive heart failure, transient ischemic attack, stroke, peripheral artery disease, sexual dysfunction, nephropathy, and retinopathy.

A discussion of the patient's lifestyle is important in determining whether nonpharmacologic therapies for the treatment of mild hypertension may be indicated. A dietary assessment of the use of fats, alcohol, caffeine, and salt should be made. Exercise duration and frequency should be discussed, and any recent changes in weight documented.

Physical Examination

All patients undergoing evaluation for the diagnosis and treatment of hypertension need to have a thorough physical examination to assess for the presence

TABLE 31–2. Physical Examination Assessment of Hypertensive Patients

Vital signs: blood pressure, pulse, height, weight

Eyes: retina examination for hypertensive retinopathy[*]

Neck: evaluation for jugular venous distension, thyromegaly, and carotid bruits

Chest: auscultation for rales and wheezes, palpation for collateral vessels that may occur in patients with coarctation of the aorta

Heart: palpation for precordial heave, and location and duration of the apical impulse, auscultation for rate, rhythm, murmurs, and third and fourth heart sounds

Abdomen: auscultation for presence of renal bruits consistent with renal artery stenosis[†], palpation for presence of enlarged kidneys consistent with polycystic kidney disease and abdominal aortic aneurysm

Extremities: inspection for edema, palpation for diminished pulses[‡], auscultation for bruits

Neurologic: complete examination to assess for prior cerebrovascular accident

[*]Arteriolar narrowing, focal arterial spasm, hemorrhages, exudates, papilledema.
[†]Usually best appreciated right or left of the midline above the umbilicus or over the flanks.
[‡]A diminished femoral pulse compared with the radial pulse in a patient less than 30 yr old suggests coarctation of the aorta.

of target organ damage and secondary causes of hypertension (Table 31–2).

Laboratory Evaluation

Laboratory evaluation of patients with hypertension further assesses for target organ damage and secondary causes of hypertension. Laboratory data also should be used to evaluate the presence of other cardiovascular risk factors. Routine laboratory tests should include a serum hematocrit; a urinalysis; electrolytes including sodium, potassium, creatinine, and fasting glucose; a fasting lipid profile; and 12-lead electrocardiography for detection of left ventricular hypertrophy.[13,14] Optional tests include a thyroid-stimulating hormone test for evaluation of hyper- and hypothyroidism; a glycated hemoglobin; a 24-hour assessment of proteinuria and creatinine clearance; a check for microalbuminuria to more sensitively screen for nephropathy; uric acid test to assess the risk of diuretic-induced gout and renal stones; and a limited echocardiography to more sensitively screen for left ventricular hypertrophy.

SECONDARY HYPERTENSION

The percentage of patients that have a definable cause of their hypertension has been debated widely. Studies are quite variable in the methods used to identify secondary hypertension, and many were published from specialty clinics, in which patients were referred particularly for evaluation of secondary forms of hypertension (Table 31–3).

Because secondary hypertension is rare, not all hypertensive patients require testing for secondary causes. In general, if a patient exhibits any of the following clinical characteristics, then a secondary cause of hypertension should be considered: (1) hypertension diagnosed at an age less than 30 years or older than 55 years, (2) the sudden development of severe hypertension, and (3) hypertension refractory to aggressive treatment with three or more antihypertensive agents.

Renal parenchymal disease and **renovascular hypertension** are the most common forms of secondary hypertension. Renal parenchymal disease induces hypertension through sodium retention and volume expansion as well as activation of the renin-angiotensin system. Hypertension is observed commonly in patients with a glomerular filtration rate of less than 50 mL/min or a serum creatinine of greater than 1.5.

Renovascular disease activates the renin-angiotensin system and, over time, causes ischemic nephropathy.[20] Causes of renovascular disease include atherosclerotic narrowing of the renal arteries and narrowing caused by fibromuscular dysplasia. Atherosclerotic renal artery stenosis is more

TABLE 31–3. Frequency of Various Diagnoses in Hypertensive Subjects

Study (N)	Frequency of Diagnosis (%)							
	EH	CRD	RD	CA	PA	CS	P	OC
Gifford, 1969 (4,339)	89	5	4	1	0.5	0.2	0.2	—
Berglund et al, 1976 (689)	94	4	1	0.1	0.1	—	—	—
Rudnick et al, 1977 (665)	94	5	0.2	0.2	—	0.2	—	0.2
Danielson and Dammström, 1981 (1,000)	95.3	2.4	1	—	0.1	0.1	0.2	0.8
Sinclair et al, 1987 (3,783)	92.1	5.6	0.7	—	0.3	0.1	0.1	1.0

EH = essential hypertension; CRD = chronic renal disease; RD = renovascular disease; CA = coarctation of the aorta; PA = primary aldosteronism; CS = Cushing's syndrome; P = pheochromocytoma; OC = oral contraceptive use.
Adapted from: Kaplan. Clinical hypertension. 7th ed. 1998; p. 13.

common in the elderly with diffuse atherosclerotic disease; fibromuscular hyperplasia is more common in patients under the age of 30 years, particularly females. Renovascular disease should be suspected in a patient with (1) new-onset stage 3 hypertension (blood pressure > 180/110 mm Hg) who previously did not have hypertension, (2) poorly controlled hypertension with three or more hypertensive agents, (3) clinical examination findings of a renal systolic-diastolic bruit lateralizing to a single kidney, (4) moderate stage 2 hypertension (blood pressure > 160/100 mm Hg) and peripheral vascular disease, or (5) a sustained increase of creatinine to > 1.5 mg/dL.[21–25] The diagnosis of renovascular disease can be made radiographically with captopril renography, renal ultrasonography, renal angiography, intravenous pyelography, or magnetic resonance angiography.[23] Figure 31–1 demonstrates an algorithm for evaluation of patients with suspected renovascular disease.

Endocrine disease is a more rare cause of secondary hypertension. Endocrine causes include hyperaldosteronism, Cushing's syndrome, pheochromocytoma, acromegaly, and hyperparathyroidism. Hyperaldosteronism from either an adrenal tumor or bilateral adrenal hyperplasia induces hypertension by excessively stimulating renal tubular sodium retention in exchange for potassium depletion. The subsequent increased plasma volume suppresses the renin-angiotensin system. Clinically, patients with hyperaldosteronism display low serum potassium levels, high urinary potassium levels, hypernatremia, high aldosterone levels, and suppressed renin levels.

Cushing's syndrome should be suspected in patients with difficult-to-treat hypertension who also display glucose intolerance, truncal obesity, hirsutism, striae, moon facies, osteopenia, muscle weakness, decreased libido, or menstrual disorders, or who bruise easily. A screening 1-mg dexamethasone suppression test followed by a confirmatory 24-hour urinary cortisol or a low-dose dexamethasone suppression test can be used to diagnose Cushing's syndrome.[25,26] The short overnight dexamethasone suppression test is performed by administering 1-mg PO dexamethasone between 11:00 pm and midnight, and drawing a serum cortisol at between 8:00 and 9:00 the following morning. Normal individuals display a supressed morning cortisol level of ≤ 5 mg/mL. If the serum cortisol level is > 5 mg/mL then the possiblity of Cushing's syndrome should be explored further.

Pheochromocytoma often causes paroxysmal symptoms of adrenergic excess. More than 50% of patients with pheochromocytoma have sustained hypertension. However, the hypertension can be paroxysmal with periods of normotension, or it can be superimposed on chronic hypertension. Other accompanying symptoms include headache, sweating, palpitations, anxiety, pallor and flushing, nausea and vomiting, and weight loss. The episodes vary in frequency and duration and may occur several times per day or only every few months. In patients with pheochromocytoma, a 24-hour collection of catecholamines is almost always elevated. To evaluate for possible pheochromocytoma, a 24-hour urine test for metanephrines, vanillylmandelic acid, and free catecholamines should be ordered along

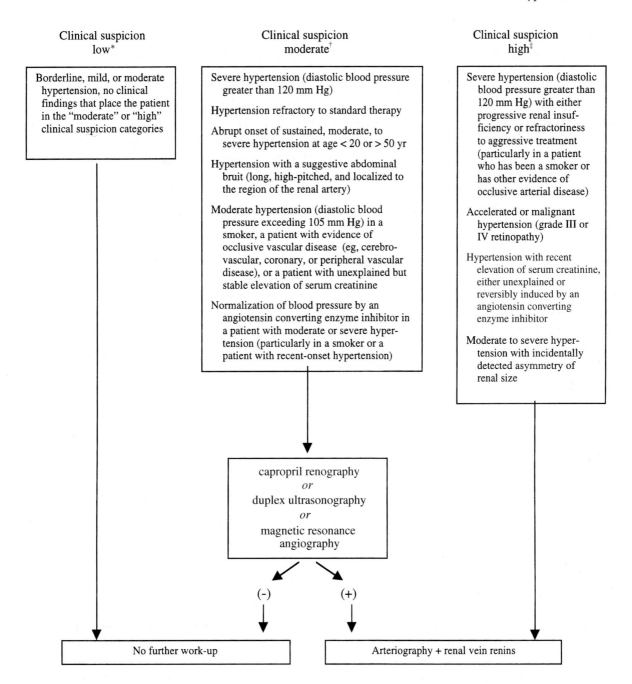

FIGURE 31–1. Suggested work-up for renovascular hypertension. Patients with these clinical characteristics have a prevalence of renovascular hypertension of:[*] < 1%;[†] 5 to 15%;[‡] > 25%. Adapted from Mann SJ, Pickering T. Detection of renovascular hypertension. State of the art 1992. Ann Intern Med 1992;117:845.

with the urine creatinine.[27,28] Plasma catecholamine measurements often yield a false-positive result and are therefore not recommended as part of an initial diagnostic evaluation.[29]

Acromegaly frequently is complicated by hypertension.[30] The clinical changes of acromegaly are subtle, slow, and progressive for years but lead to a dramatic presentation. The effects of hyper-

secretion of growth hormone are mediated through somatomedin. This insulin-like growth factor causes tissue growth that is accentuated in the acral areas. The most obvious growth occurs in the hands, feet, nose, and jaw. Somatomedin C levels are elevated and correlate with disease activity.

Hyperparathyroidism also may induce hypertension, particularly in patients with nephrocalcinosis.

It is more common in older patients. Hyperparathyroidism should be suspected in patients with persistent hypercalcemia in the absence of other causes of hypercalcemia, most notably, neoplastic disease. An elevated serum parathyroid level is diagnostic. Other biochemical studies that are helpful but not diagnostic include hypophosphatemia (<3.0 mg/dL), serum chloride >106, and a serum chloride-to-serum phosphorus ratio >33.

Coarctation of the aorta is a more rare cause of hypertension in adults. Constriction can occur anywhere along the lumen but is appreciated most commonly just distal to the origin of the left subclavian artery. Coartation should be suspected in any patient with hypertension in the upper extremities and diminished or absent femoral pulses. Often the heart is large and shows left ventricular strain on an electrocardiogram, and a chest radiograph demonstrates dilation of the aorta above and below the constriction, and rib notching from collateral vessels. Echocardiography is diagnostic.

HORMONES AND HYPERTENSION

Oral Contraceptives

Blood pressure increases slightly in women taking oral contraceptives. Both estrogen and progesterone are responsible for the blood pressure effect, but the mechanism remains speculative.[31] This small rise in blood pressure raises the blood pressure to beyond 140/90 mm Hg in approximately 5% of women who continue oral contraceptive use over a period of 5 years. The risk of developing hypertension with use of oral contraceptives increases significantly after age 35 years,[32] and with a longer duration of use. Blood pressures also are significantly higher in women taking oral contraceptives who also have a family history of hypertension or a history of hypertension during pregnancy.[31] The incidence may be lower in women receiving lower-dose (30 to 35 µg of estrogen) oral contraceptives.[33]

In more than half of women who develop hypertension while using oral contraceptives, blood pressure returns to normal with cessation of the pill. In a small minority of women, oral contraceptives can cause the development of malignant hypertension.[34] If use of the pill is stopped and underlying renal disease is avoided, the long-term prognosis for patients with oral contraceptive-induced malignant hypertension is excellent.

Hormone Replacement Therapy

Randomized prospective trials and epidemiologic studies have demonstrated that postmenopausal hormone replacement therapy does not increase blood pressure. The largest randomized controlled trial to date, the Postmenopausal Estrogen/Progestin Interventions (PEPI) Trial,[35] enrolled 875 healthy postmenopausal women aged 45 to 64 years and randomly assigned them to receive placebo, conjugated equine estrogen, or a combination of conjugated equine estrogen and various combinations of progesterone. The subjects were followed up for 3 years. No significant changes in blood pressure were demonstrated at the termination of the trial.

A prospective analysis of a large group of older women found that hormone replacement therapy did not increase blood pressure. Compared with nonusers over a period of 5 months, women of an average age of 70 years who were using hormone replacement therapy had lower systolic pressures but did not differ in diastolic blood pressures.[36]

NONPHARMACOLOGIC THERAPY

Nonpharmacologic therapy has been successful in preventing hypertension and reducing blood pressure in patients with mild hypertension. It also reduces other atherosclerotic risk factors at a low cost and with minimal adverse effects. However, nonpharmacologic treatment should be used only as adjunctive therapy in patients with moderate to severe hypertension. There are currently no studies that show a reduction in cardiovascular events from nonpharmacologic therapy for hypertension.

Lifestyle modification recommendations are summarized in Table 31–4. Exercise, weight loss, and the avoidance of excess alcohol are the cornerstones of nonpharmacologic management of hypertension. Exercise not only reduces blood pressure in hypertensive patients, but it also reduces left ventricular hypertrophy in patients with severe hypertension. Exercise should be encouraged for at least three to four sessions per week, with a goal that each session should last 30 minutes to 1 hour. A target heart rate of 60 to 80% of maximal heart rate should be achieved.

TABLE 31–4. Lifestyle Modifications for Hypertension Prevention and Management in Women

Lose weight if overweight

Limit alcohol intake to no more than 15 mL of ethanol/d (eg, 360 mL of beer, 150 mL of wine, or 60 mL of 100-proof whiskey)

Increase aerobic physical activity to 30–45 min most days of the week

Reduce sodium intake to no more than 100 mmol/d (2.4 g of sodium or 6 g of sodium chloride)

Maintain adequate intake of dietary potassium (approximately 90 mmol/d)

Maintain adequate intake of dietary calcium and magnesium for general health

Stop smoking*

Reduce intake of dietary saturated fat and cholesterol*

*For overall cardiovascular health.
Adapted from The sixth report of the Joint National Committee on Prevention, Detection, Evaluation, and Treatment of High Blood Pressure. Arch Intern Med 1997;157:2413–46.

Weight loss should be advised for those patients with a body mass index of over 27.[37–39] Even small reductions in weight of 3.5 to 4.5 kilograms have a significant blood pressure–lowering effect.[40–42] Alcohol should be restricted to one or fewer drinks per day in women with mild hypertension.[43–46] Randomized trials have found that alcohol reduction reduces blood pressure by 5/3 mm Hg. This reduction in blood pressure occurs within 3 weeks of alcohol cessation, independent of changes in weight.

Salt restriction has been studied extensively, and an intake of less than 2 g/d has a significant effect on lowering blood pressure. Salt restriction has a greater effect on reduction of blood pressure in the elderly.[40,41,47,48] Potassium intake should be maintained at 80 mmol or greater per day during the treatment of mild hypertension.[49] This is supported by a large meta-analysis of 33 randomized controlled trials that found potassium supplementation decreased blood pressure by 3/2 mm Hg. This small effect may be more dramatic in those with a high salt intake. Less impressive antihypertensive benefits are derived from calcium- and magnesium-rich diets or supplements. At this time a diet with only the regular recommended daily allowances of magnesium and calcium is suggested.[50–53]

Recently a particular diet rich in fruits, vegetables, and low-fat dairy products with reduced saturated and total fat (Table 31–5) has been shown to be effective for the primary prevention of hypertension and the treatment of mild hypertension, even in the absence of weight loss.[54]

PHARMACOLOGIC THERAPY

Clinical Considerations

Large randomized controlled trials have demonstrated that the treatment of hypertension with pharmacologic agents reduces cardiovascular morbidity, cardiovascular mortality, and overall mortality. Meta-analyses of these trials enrolling over 15,000 patients have demonstrated a 36% reduction in stroke-related mortality and a 35% reduction in stroke-related morbidity. Cardiac morbidity and mortality were reduced by 25% and 15%, respectively. Overall mortality was reduced 12%. These dramatic results occurred in only 4 years of follow-up.[7]

The decision to initiate drug therapy for the treatment of hypertension depends on several clinical considerations. These include the stage of hypertension, the presence of target organ damage, the number of cardiovascular risk factors in the particular patient, and the failure of nonpharmacologic therapy. Patients with diabetes whose blood pressure exceeds 130/80 mm Hg should always receive pharamacotherapy of hypertension, because of their high risk of renal and cardiovascular complications (Table 31–6). A treatment algorithm is provided in Figure 31–2.

Initial Therapy

When pharmacologic therapy is required for the treatment of hypertension, several considerations should influence the choice of the initial therapeutic agent. Longer-acting once-daily or twice-daily

TABLE 31–5. The DASH (Dietary Approaches to Stop Hypertension) Diet[*]

Food Group	Daily Servings	Serving Sizes	Examples and Notes	Significance to the DASH Diet Pattern
Grains and grain products	7–8	1 slice bread 120 mL dry cereal cooked rice, pasta, or cereal	Whole wheat bread, English muffin, pita bread, bagel, cereals, grits, oatmeal	Major sources of energy and fiber
Vegetables	4–5	240 mL raw leafy vegetable 120 mL cooked vegetable 180 mL vegetable juice	Tomatoes, potatoes, carrots, peas, squash, broccoli, turnip greens, collards, kale, spinach, artichokes, beans, sweet potatoes	Rich sources of potassium, magnesium, and fiber
Fruits	4–5	180 mL fruit juice 1 medium fruit 60 mL dried fruit 120 mL fresh, frozen, or canned fruit	Apricots, bananas, dates, grapes, oranges, orange juice, grapefruit, grapefruit juice, mangoes, melons, peaches, pineapples, prunes, raisins, strawberries, tangerines	Important sources of potassium, magnesium and fiber
Low-fat or nonfat dairy foods	2–3	240 mL milk 240 mL yogurt 45 g cheese	Skim or 1% milk, skim or low-fat buttermilk, nonfat or low-fat yogurt, partly skimmed mozzarella cheese, nonfat cheese	Major sources of calcium and protein
Meats, poultry, and fish	≤2	84 g cooked meats, poultry, or fish	Select only lean meats; trim away visible fats; broil, roast, or boil, instead of frying; remove skin from poultry	Rich sources of protein and magnesium
Nuts, seeds, and legumes	4–5/wk	42 g or 80 mL nuts 14 g or 30 mL seeds 120 mL cooked legumes	Almonds, filberts, mixed nuts, peanuts, walnuts, sunflower seeds, kidney beans, lentils	Rich sources of magnesium, potassium, protein, and fiber

[*]The DASH eating plan shown above is based on 2,000 calories a day (8,400 J/d). Depending on energy needs, the number of daily servings in a food group may vary from those listed.
Adapted from The sixth report of the Joint National Committee on Prevention, Detection, Evaluation, and Treatment of High Blood Pressure. Arch Intern Med 1997;157:2413–46.

TABLE 31–6. Risk Stratification and Treatment of Hypertension[*]

Blood Pressure[†]	Risk Group A[‡]	Risk Group B[§]	Risk Group C[‖]
High-normal	Lifestyle modification	Lifestyle modification	Drug therapy[**]
Stage 1	Lifestyle modification (up to 12 mo)	Lifestyle modification (up to 6 mo)[#]	Drug therapy
Stages 2 and 3	Drug therapy	Drug therapy	Drug therapy

[*]For example, a patient with diabetes and a blood pressure of 142/94 mm Hg plus left ventricular hypertrophy should be classified as having stage 1 hypertension with target organ disease (left ventricular hypertrophy) and with another major risk factor (diabetes). This patient would be categorized as "Stage 1 Risk Group C," and recommended for immediate initiation of pharmacologic treatment. Lifestyle modification should be adjunctive therapy for all patients recommended for pharmacologic therapy.
[†]See Table 31–1 for blood pressure measurements of various stages.
[‡]No risk factors; no target organ disease (TOD) or clinical cardiovascular disease (CCD).
[§]At least one risk factor, not including diabetes; no TOD or CCD.
[‖]TOC/CCD and/or diabetes, with or without other risk factors.
[#]For patients with multiple risk factors, clinicians should consider drugs as initial therapy plus lifestyle modifications.
[**]For those with heart failure, renal insufficiency, or diabetes. Drug therapy should be initiated in diabetic patients whose blood pressure exceeds 130/80 mm Hg.
Adapted from The Sixth Report of the Joint National Committee on Prevention, Detection, Evaluation, and Treatment of High Blood Pressure. Arch Intern Med/Vol 157, Nov. 24, 1997

medication should be chosen over short-acting agents, unless there is documentation regarding the need for agents that require more frequent dosing. This enhances patient compliance and decreases abrupt increases in the blood pressure in the morning, when patients are at an increased risk of stroke or myocardial infarction.[55,56]

Diuretics and ß-blockers are the most extensively studied medications for the treatment of hypertension and the first-line agents for the treatment of essential hypertension. Drugs from these antihypertensive classes should be used unless there are contraindications to the use of these agents or alternative drugs are chosen as a consequence of special indications (Table 31–7). In a recent meta-analysis of 10 large randomized controlled trials, the benefits of diuretic therapy exceeded those of ß-blocker treatment.[57] Diuretics were significantly effective in reducing nonfatal cerebrovascular accidents, fatal cerebrovascular accidents, coronary artery disease, cardiovascular mortality, and all cause mortality, whereas ß-blockers as monotherapy were significantly effective only in preventing nonfatal cerebrovascular accidents.

Unless there exist special indications are calcium channel blockers should be chosen as the third-line of therapy. Two long-term randomized controlled trials demonstrated that long-acting dihydropyridine calcium channel blockers significantly decreased the rate of stroke and reduced cardiovascular disease in elderly patients with essential hypertension.[58,59]

Consensus statements advocate the use of angiotensin converting enzyme (ACE) inhibitors and α-blockers as other initial therapies for the treatment of essential hypertension.[15] These classes have never been studied in patients with essential hypertension in long-term randomized controlled trials.

Combination Therapy

Combination therapy of different classes of antihypertensive agents often is more effective in reducing blood pressure than monotherapy. However, combination therapy is more likely to result in side effects. The physician should attempt lower blood pressure to < 140/90 mm Hg with a single agent. If this is not achieved at the full dose of a single drug then one of two options may be implemented: either a second agent must be added or another agent can be substituted as monotherapy.

Diuretics are effective in enhancing the effects of other classes of medications. If a diuretic is not chosen as a first-line agent, then it should be added as the next agent.[13] If the second medication lowers the blood pressure to the target level, then the initial agent may be withdrawn slowly to assess the efficacy of the second agent alone.

Many classes now have been combined into single formulations to improve patient compliance (Table 31–8). At this time, there are no available

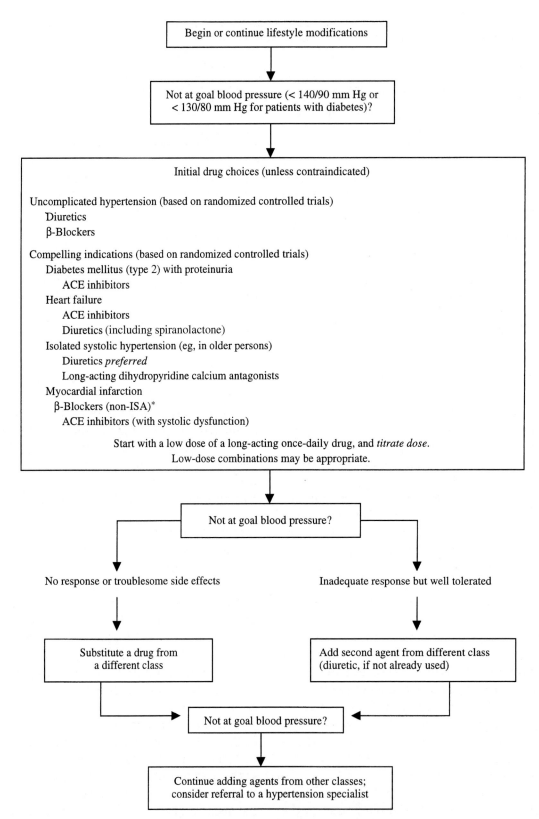

FIGURE 31–2. Algorithm for the treatment of hypertension. ACE = angiotesin converting enzyme; ISA = intrinsic sympathomimetic activity. Adapted from The sixth report of the Joint Committee on Prevention, Detection, Evaluation, and Treatment of High Blood Pressure. Arch Intern Med 1997;157:2430.
*Non-ISA ß-blockers may another be appropriate.

TABLE 31–7. Considerations for Individualizing Antihypertensive Drug Therapy[*]

Indication	Drug Therapy
Compelling Indications Unless Contraindicated	
Diabetes mellitus (type 1) with proteinuria	ACEIs
Heart failure	ACEIs, diuretics
Isolated systolic hypertension (older patients)	Diuretics (preferred), CA (long-acting DHP)
Myocardial infarction	ß-Blockers (non-ISA), ACEIs (with systolic dysfunction)
May Have Favorable Effects on Comorbid Conditions[†]	
Angina	ß-Bblockers, CA
Atrial tachycardia and fibrillation	ß-Blockers, CA (non-DHP)
Cyclosporine-induced hypertension (caution with the dose of cyclosporine)	CA
Diabetes mellitus (types 1 and 2) with proteinuria	ACEIs (preferred), CA
Diabetes mellitus (type 2)	Low-dose diuretics
Dyslipidemia	α-Blockers
Essential tremor	ß-Blockers (non-CS)
Heart failure	Carvedilol, losartan potassium
Hyperthyroidism	ß-Blockers
Migraine	ß-Blockers (non-CS), CA (non-DHP)
Myocardial infarction	Diltiazem verapamil
Osteoporosis	Thiazides
Preoperative hypertension	Portal hypertension
Prostatism (BPH)	ß-Blockers
Renal insufficiency (caution in renovascular hypertension and creatinine level ≥ 265.2 μmol/L [≥ 3 mg/dL])	α-Blockers ACEIs
May Have Unfavorable Effects on Comorbid Conditions[†‡]	
Bronchospastic disease	ß-Blockers[§]
Coronary artery disease	α-Blockers
Depression	ß-Blockers, central α-agonists, reserpine[§]
Diabetes mellitus (types 1 and 2)	ß-Blockers, high-dose diuretics
Dyslipidemia	ß-Blockers (non-ISA), diuretics (high-dose)
Gout	Diuretics
2° or 3° heart block	ß-Blockers[§], CA (non-DHP)[§]
Heart failure	ß-Blockers (except carvedilol), CA (except amlodipine besylate; felodipine)
Liver disease	Labetalol hydrochloride, methyldopa[§]
Peripheral vascular disease	ß-Blockers
Pregnancy	ACEIS[§], angiotensin II receptor blockers[§]
Renal insufficiency	Potassium-sparing agents
Renovascular disease	ACEIs, angiotensin II receptor blockers

[*]For initial drug therapy recommendations, see Figure 31–8. For references, see Section 4 of the Physicians' Desk Reference (51st ed), and Kaplan and Gifford. [†]Conditions and their respective drugs are listed in alphabetical order. [‡]These drugs may be used with special monitoring unless contraindicated. [§]Contraindicated.

ACEI = angiotensin converting enzyme inhibitor; BP = benign prostatic hyperplasia; CA = calcium antagonists; DHP = dihydropyridine; ISA = intrinsic sympathomimetic activity; non-CS = noncardioselective.

Adapted from The sixth report of the Joint National Committee on Prevention, Detection, Evaluation, and Treatment of High Blood Pressure. Arch Intern Med 1997;157:2413–46.

data in long-term trials that show any reductions in cardiovascular end points with any particular combination treatment.

Follow-Up

After initiating antihypertensive therapy, a follow-up visit to assess the effectiveness of the medication and any side effects should occur in 3 to 4 weeks.[13-15] If a diuretic, ACE inhibitor, or angiotensin receptor blocker is prescribed for therapy, then a measurement of potassium, blood urea nitrogen, and creatinine should be made in 7 days.[60-66] This same follow-up regimen should be followed after any change in medication classes or doses until the blood pressure has been lowered to < 140/90 mm Hg. Once the blood pressure has been appropriately controlled, then follow-up visits can be made 3 to 6 months apart.

Hypertensive Crisis

Hypertensive urgency and hypertensive emergency are distinct clinical entities with different treatment modalities. Hypertensive urgency is common and may account for up to one-quarter of medical emergencies in a community emergency room. Hypertensive emergency is less common and accounts for less than one-quarter of all hypertensive crises.[67] Implementing the appropriate therapy for hypertensive emergency can reverse target organ damage. Unfortunately, mismanagement can precipitate a cerebrovascular accident.

Hypertensive urgency is defined as a severe elevation of blood pressure, generally considered as a resting systolic blood pressure > 200 mm Hg or a diastolic blood pressure > 120 mm Hg.[3] Most patients with hypertensive urgency have a previous history of hypertension. Hypertensive emergency is diagnosed with the clinical presence of hypertension-induced target organ damage. Target organ damage can include hypertensive encephalopathy, intracranial hemorrhage, subarachnoid hemorrhage, cerebral infarction, unstable angina, acute myocardial infarction, acute left ventricular failure with pulmonary edema, dissecting aortic aneurysm, acute renal insufficiency, microangiopathic hemolytic anemia, grade III or grade IV Keith-Wagener fundoscopic changes, or eclampsia.

Patients with chronic hypertension often can withstand higher blood pressures than can those with an acute rise in blood pressure. For example, patients with chronic hypertension rarely develop encephalopathy until the diastolic blood pressure exceeds 150 mm Hg.[68]

The initial history and physical examination should rapidly distinguish between hypertensive urgency and hypertensive emergency. The patient with suspected hypertensive emergency should immediately be placed on a cardiac monitor. An arterial line should be placed to confirm the sphygmomanometer readings and to help guide antihypertensive therapy, and intravenous access should be established. Admittance to the intensive care unit should then be arranged.

The history and physical examination should assess the degree of target organ damage and define the precipitating cause of the crisis. The history should concentrate on any history of hypertension, medication use (ie, prescription, over-the-counter, and illicit drugs as well as herbal remedies), previous end-organ damage, coexistent disease processes, and any symptoms consistent with end-organ damage. Symptoms most commonly described in hypertensive crisis include headache, chest pain, dyspnea, faintness, nausea, and vomiting.[69] The focus of the physical examination should be the detection of end-organ damage, including signs of congestive heart failure, aortic aneurysm, neurologic deficits, and retinopathy.

Of note, the symptoms of hypertensive encephalopathy are nebulous, and it is a diagnosis of exclusion that requires intracranial pathology to be ruled out. Symptoms may include headache, nausea, vomiting, visual disturbances, confusion, and focal or generalized weakness. Signs that may be present are generalized or focal seizures, disorientation, obtundation, focal neurologic signs, asymmetric reflexes, and nystagmus.[68] Renovascular hypertension rarely manifests reliable signs or symptoms, but must be considered carefully, as it may account for up to one-third of the cases of hypertensive emergency.

Basic laboratory tests should include electrocardiography (to assess for ischemic changes), a complete blood count (to assess for hemolysis), a urinalysis (to detect hematuria or red blood cell casts), chest radiography (to detect pulmonary edema), and serum electrolytes and creatinine.

Once the clinician has distinguished between urgency and emergency, therapy can be initiated. Hypertensive urgency can be treated in the clinic with the use of short-acting oral medications. A number of short-acting oral medications are available including loop diuretics (furosemide), ß-blockers

TABLE 31–8. Oral Antihypertensive Drugs

Classification and Generic Name	Trade Name	Usual Dosage Range, Total mg/d* (Frequency per Day)	Selected Side Effects and Comments†
Diuretics (partial list)			Increases cholesterol and glucose levels; biochemical abnormalities: decreased potassium, sodium, and magnesium levels, increased uric acid and calcium levels. Rare: blood dyscrasias, photosensitivity, pancreatitis, hyponatremia
Chlorthalidone (G)	Hygroton	12.5–50 (1)	
Hydrochlorothiazide (G)	Hydrodiuril, Microzide, Esidrix	12.5–50 (1)	
Indapamide	Lozol	1.25–5 (1)	(Less or no hypercholesterolemia)
Metolazone	Mykrox	0.5–1.0 (1)	
	Zaroxolyn	2.5–10 (1)	
Loop diuretics			
Bumetanide (G)	Bumex	0.5–4 (2–3)	(Short duration of action, no hypercalcemia)
Ethacrynic acid	Edecrin	25–100 (2–3)	(Only nonsulfonamide diuretic, ototoxicity)
Furosemide (G)	Lasix	40–240 (2–3)	(Short duration of action, no hypercalcemia)
Torsemide	Demadex	5–100 (1–2)	
Potassium-sparing agents			
Amiloride hydrochloride (G)	Midamor	5–10 (1)	Hyperkalemia
Spironolactone (G)	Aldactone	25–100 (1)	(Gynecomastia)
Triamterene (G)	Dyrenium	25–100 (1)	
Adrenergic inhibitors			
Peripheral agents			
Guanadrel sulfate	Hylorel	10–75 (2)	(Postural hypotension, diarrhea)
Guanethidine monosulfate	Ismelin	10–150 (1)	(Postural hypotension, diarrhea)
Reserpine (G)‡	Serpasil	0.05–0.25 (1)	(Nasal congestion, sedation, depression, activation of peptic ulcer)
Central α-agonists			
Clonidine hydrochloride (G)	Catapres	0.2–1.2 (2–3)	Sedation, dry mouth, bradycardia, withdrawal hypertension
Guanabenz acetate (G)	Wytensin	8–32 (2)	(More withdrawal)
Guanfacine hydrochloride (G)	Tenex	1–3 (1)	(Less withdrawal)
Methyldopa (G)	Aldomet	500–3,000 (2)	(Hepatic and "autoimmune" disorders)
α-Blockers			
Doxazosin mesylate	Cardura	1–16 (1)	Postural hypotension
Prazosin hydrochloride (G)	Minipress	2–30 (2–3)	
Terazosin hydrochloride	Hytrin	1–20 (1)	

TABLE 31–8. (continued)

Drug — Classification and Generic Name	Trade Name	Usual Dosage Range, Total mg/d* (Frequency per Day)	Selected Side Effects and Comments†
ß-Blockers			Bronchospasm, bradycardia, heart failure, may mask insulin-induced hypoglycemia; less serious: impaired peripheral circulation, insomnia, fatigue, decreased exercise tolerance, hypertriglyceridemia (except for agents with intrinsic sympathomimetic activity)
Acebutolol‖	Sectral	200–800 (1)	
Atenolol (G)§	Tenormin	25–100 (1–2)	
Betaxolol hydrochloride§	Kerlone	5–20 (1)	
Bisoprolol fumarate§	Zebeta	2.5–10 (1)	
Carteolol hydrochloride‖	Cartrol	2.5–10 (1)	
Metoprolol tartrate (G)§	Lopressor	50–300 (2)	
Metoprolol succinate§	Toprol-XL	50–300 (1)	
Nadolol (G)	Corgard	40–320 (1)	
Penbutolol sulfate‖	Levatol	10–20 (1)	
Pindolol (G)‖	Visken	10–60 (2)	
Propranolol hydrochloride (G)	Inderal	40–480 (2)	
	Inderal-LA	40–480 (1)	
Timolol maleate (G)	Blocadren	20–60 (2)	
Combined α- and ß-blockers			Postural hypotension, bronchospasm
Carvedilol	Coreg	12.5–50 (2)	
Labetalol hydrochloride (G)	Normodyne, Trandate	200–1,200 (2)	
Direct vasodilators			Headaches, fluid retention, tachycardia
Hydralazine hydrochloride (G)	Apresoline	50–300 (2)	(Lupus syndrome)
Minoxidil (G)	Loniten	5–100 (1)	(Hirsutism)
Calcium antagonists			
Nondihydropyridines			Conduction defects, worsening of systolic dysfunction, gingival hyperplasia
Diltiazem hydrochloride	Cardizem SR	120–360 (2)	(Nausea, headache)
	Cardizem CD, Dilacor XR, Tiazac	120–360 (1)	
Mibefradil dihydrochloride (T-channel calcium antagonist)	Posicor	50–100 (1)	(No worsening of systolic dysfunction; contraindicated with terfenadine [Seldane], astemizole [Hismanal], and cisapride [Propulsid])

TABLE 31–8. (continued)

Drug		Usual Dosage Range, Total mg/d* (Frequency per Day)	Selected Side Effects and Comments†
Classification and Generic Name	Trade Name		
Verapamil hydrochloride	Isoptin SR, Calan SR, Verelan, Covera HS	90–480 (2) 120–480(1)	(Constipation)
Dihydropyridines			Peripheral edema, flushing, headache, gingival hypertrophy
Amlodipine besylate	Norvasc	2.5–10 (1)	
Felodipine	Plendil	2.5–20 (1)	
Isradipine	DynaCirc	5–20 (2)	
	DynaCirc CR	5–20 (1)	
Nicardipine hydrochloride	Cardene SR	60–90 (2)	
Nifedipine	Procardia XL, Adalat CC	30–120 (1)	
Nisoldipine	Sular	20–60 (1)	
Angiotensin-converting enzyme inhibitors			Common: cough; Rare: angioedema, hyperkalemia, rash, loss of taste, leukopenia
Benazepril hydrochloride	Lotensin	5–40 (1–2)	
Captopril (G)	Capoten	25–150 (2–3)	
Enalapril maleate	Vasotec	5–40 (1–2)	
Fosinopril sodium	Monopril	10–40 (1–2)	
Lisinopril	Prinivil, Zestril	5–40 (1)	
Moexipril	Univasc	7.5–15 (2)	
Quinapril hydrochloride	Accupril	5–80 (1–2)	
Ramipril	Altace	1.25–20 (1–2)	
Trandolapril	Mavik	1–4 (1)	
Angiotensin II receptor blockers			Angioedema (very rare), hyperkalemia
Losartan potassium	Cozaar	25–100 (1–2)	
Irbesartan	Avapro	150–300 (1)	
Valsartan	Diovan	80–320 (1)	

*These dosages may vary from those listed in the *Physicians' Desk Reference*, 51st ed, which may be consulted for additional information. †The listing of side effects is not all-inclusive, and side effects are for the class of drugs except where noted for individual drug (in parentheses); clinicians are urged to refer to the package insert for a more detailed listing.
‡Also acts centrally.
§Cardioselective.
‖Has intrinsic sympathomimetic activity.
G = generic version availability.
Adapted from Joint Committee on Prevention, Detection, Evaluation, and Treatment of High Blood Pressure. The sixth report of the Joint National Committee on Prevention, Detection, Evaluation, and Treatment of High Blood Pressure. Arch Intern Med 1997;157:2426.

TABLE 31–9. Oral Antihypertensive Agents for Treating Hypertensive Urgencies

Drug	Dosage	Onset of Action	Adverse Effects	Reported Complications
Captopril	25 mg, repeat as required	15–30 min	Angioneurotic edema, acute renal failure in patients with bilateral renal artery stenosis or unilateral stenosis in solitary kidney	Renal failure
Clonidine	0.1–0.2 mg, repeat qh as required to a total dose of 0.6 mg	30–60 min	Drowsiness, sedation, dry mouth	Hypotension
Labetalol	200–400 mg, repeat q2–3h	30–120 min	Bronchoconstriction, heart block	Orthostatic hypotension
Prazosin	1–2 mg, repeat qh as necessary	30–60 min	Syncope (first dose), palpitations, tachycardia, headache	Orthostatic hypotension
Nimodipine	60 mg q4h for 21 days	30–120 min	Edema, headache	Hypotension

(propanolol), combination α- and ß-blockers (labetalol), central-acting agents (clonidine), ACE inhibitors (captopril), and calcium channel blockers (isradipine and nicardipine). The more commonly used regimens are highlighted in Table 31–9.

The use of short-acting nifedipine for treatment of hypertensive urgency is controversial. Currently it should be avoided. Once the blood pressure has been stabilized, the patient can be sent home and a follow-up arranged for within 48 hours.

Hypertensive emergency requires the administration of parenteral medication. Therapy should be given with an arterial line placed, and the patient should be observed with a cardiac monitor. The goal of therapy is to reduce mean arterial pressure by no more than 25%, or to reduce diastolic blood pressure to between 100 and 110 mm Hg, in the first several hours. The ultimate goal is to achieve normotension; however, this should be achieved over the ensuing weeks.[70] If blood pressure is lowered too quickly, cerebral hypoperfusion can induce ischemia and a stroke. Parenteral therapy may involve any of the agents listed in Table 31–10. Sodium nitroprusside is the drug of choice for most hypertensive emergencies as it allows for a controlled reduction in blood pressure.

SPECIAL CONSIDERATIONS

Pregnancy

High blood pressure complicates approximately 10% of all pregnancies. High blood pressure during pregnancy can be the result of pre-existing essential or secondary hypertension, hypertension that develops during pregnancy, or preeclampsia. Essential hypertension complicates 1 to 5% of all pregnancies,[71] increasing the risk of preeclampsia and abruptio placentae. Women with longstanding severe hypertension, those with pre-existing cardiovascular disease or renal disease, and those with a diastolic blood pressure exceeding 110 mm Hg during the first trimester have a higher maternal and fetal morbidity than do normal pregnant women. Conversely, women with mild chronic hypertension (ie, diastolic blood pressure 90 to 110 mm Hg) during pregnancy have similar outcomes to normal pregnant women.[72]

Preeclampsia represents a greater risk to the fetus and the mother than does essential hypertension and can result in life-threatening complications. The incidence of preeclampsia is unclear, but one estimate from an indigent population is 13%, and among nulliparous women, estimates from 10 to 20% have been noted.[71]

The American College of Obstetrics and Gynecology in 1972[71] classified hypertension during

TABLE 31–10. Parenteral Drugs for Treatment of Hypertensive Emergencies

Drug	Dosage*	Onset of Action	Duration of Action	Adverse Effects[†]	Special Indications
Vasodilators					
Sodium-nitroprusside	0.25–10 µg/min as IV infusion[‡] (maximal dose for 10 min only)	Immediate	1–2 min	Nausea, vomiting, muscle twitching, sweating, thiocyanate and cyanide intoxication	Most hypertensive emergencies; caution with high intracranial pressure or azotemia
Nicardipine hydrochloride	5–15 mg/h IV	5–10 min	1–4 h	Tachycardia, headache, flushing, local phlebitis	Most hypertensive emergencies; except acute heart failure; caution with coronary ischemia
Fenoldopam mesylate	0.1–0.3 µg/kg/min IV infusion	< 5 min	30 min	Tachycardia, headache, nausea, flushing	Most hypertensive emergencies; caution with glaucoma
Nitroglycerin	5–100 µg/min as IV infusion[‡]	2–5 min	3–5 min	Headache, vomiting, methemoglobinemia, tolerance with prolonged use	Coronary ischemia
Enalaprilat	1.25–5 mg q6h IV	15–30 min	6 h	Precipitous fall in pressure in high-renin states; response variable	Acute left ventricular failure; avoid in acute myocardial infarction
Hydralazine hydrochloride	10–20 mg IV / 10–50 mg IM	10 min / 20–30 min	3–8 h	Tachycardia flushing, headache vomiting, aggravation of angina	Eclampsia
Diazoxide	50–100 mg IV bolus repeated *or* 15–30 mg/min infusion	2–4 min	6–12 h	Nausea, flushing, tachycardia, chest pain	Now obsolete; when no intensive monitoring available
Adrenergic inhibitors					
Labetalol hydrochloride	20–80 mg IV bolus q10min *or* 0.5–2.0 mg/min IV infusion	5–10 min	3–6 h	Vomiting, scalp tingling, burning in throat, dizziness, nausea, heart block, orthostatic hypotension	Most hypertensive emergencies except acute heart failure
Esmolol hydrochloride	250–500 µg/kg/min for 1 min, then 50–100 µg/kg/min for 4 min; may repeat sequence	1–2 min	10–20 min	Hypotension, nausea	Aortic dissention; perioperative
Phentolamine	5–15 mg IV	1–2 min	3–10 min	Tachycardia, flushing, headache	Catecholamine excess

*Dosages may vary from those in the Physicians' Desk Reference, 51st ed.
[†]Hypotension may occur with all agents.
[‡]Requires special delivery system.
IV = intravenous; IM = intramuscular.
Adapted from Joint National Committee on Prevention, Detection, Evaluation, and Treatment of High Blood Pressure. Blood Pressure and Intern Med 1997;157:2413–46.

pregnancy into four categories: (1) chronic hypertension, (2) transient hypertension, (3) preeclampsia, and (4) preeclampsia superimposed on chronic hypertension. Chronic hypertension is defined as hypertension (blood pressure > 140/90 mm Hg) present before pregnancy or that is diagnosed before the twentieth week of gestation. Hypertension diagnosed during pregnancy and continuing after the 42nd week is also classified as chronic hypertension. Transient hypertension can develop during pregnancy or in the first 24 hours post partum without other evidence of preeclampsia. The occurence of transient hypertension during pregnancy often is predictive of the eventual development of essential hypertension. Generally, the outcome of pregnancy in these patients is good without drug therapy.

Preeclampsia-associated hypertension by definition occurs after 20 weeks' gestation and is accompanied by proteinuria, edema, or both. To meet preeclampsia criteria, either systolic blood pressure must increase by 30 mm Hg or more, or diastolic blood pressure must increase by 15 mm Hg or more as compared with average blood pressures prior to 20 weeks' gestation. Many women may never reach a blood pressure that exceeds 140/90 mm Hg yet still are diagnosed with preeclampsia. Proteinuria is defined as the excretion of 0.3 g or greater over 24 hours, which correlates to a 1+ dipstick value. Edema can occur peripherally with pedal edema, or centrally with a rapid weight gain. Preeclampsia can develop in those diagnosed with chronic hypertension, and the prognosis for the mother and fetus is worse than if either condition occurs independently

It is important to distinguish between preeclampsia and chronic hypertension because the treatment is different. The distinction between these entities can be confusing because of the normal changes of blood pressure that occur during pregnancy. During early gestation diastolic blood pressure often falls 7 to 10 mm Hg, with a rise occurring toward the third trimester.[71] There may be a greater reduction in patients with pre-existing hypertension. Systolic blood pressure remains relatively stable throughout pregnancy.

The need to distinguish preeclampsia from the other disorders is particularly important in the management of women in mid-pregnancy (prior to gestational week 28). Although chronic hypertension may be managed conservatively even with moderate to severe degrees of hypertension, preeclampsia must be treated aggressively. In a study of 60 women between the 18th and 27th week of gestation, those with severe preeclampsia treated with conservative therapy experienced an 87% perinatal mortality.[73]

LABORATORY ANALYSIS AND MONITORING

Patients found to have hypertension prior to gestational week 20 often have chronic hypertension. Initial laboratory tests should include those that are ordered regularly for a patient newly diagnosed with hypertension, with the addition of a platelet count and uric acid test to assist in the screening for the superimposed development of preeclampsia. These help to assess the chronicity of the hypertension, the presence of target organ damage, and the possibility of a secondary cause of hypertension. Baseline fetal ultrasonography also is suggested to assess intrauterine growth.

Pregnant women with a normal blood pressure but who are at high risk for the development of hypertension include (1) women with an increased blood pressure when not pregnant, (2) those that have had hypertension in a previous pregnancy other than the first, and (3) those with diabetes, collagen vascular disorders, or underlying renal vascular disease or renal parenchymal disease. These women should be screened to determine baseline hemoglobin, hematocrit, platelet count, urinalysis, serum creatinine, and uric acid levels.[71] Hemoconcentration, thrombocytopenia, and reduced glomerular filtration rate are markers for preeclampsia. Baseline ultrasonography can assist with the evaluation of subsequent fetal growth.

Patients that develop hypertension after the 20th week of gestation need to be assessed on at least a biweekly basis.[71] A hemoglobin test; hematocrit; blood smear; platelet count; urinalysis; and determination of serum creatinine, serum uric acid, lactate dehydrogenase, albumin, and hepatic transaminase levels are helpful in evaluating for the presence of severe preecalmpsia and for the development of the life-threatening HELLP (*h*emolysis, *e*levated *l*iver enzymes, and *l*ow *p*latelet count) syndrome.

TREATMENT

Nonpharmacologic therapy is the treatment of choice for most pregnant women with chronic hypertension. The goal is to achieve a diastolic blood pressure < 100 mm Hg. Nonpharmacologic therapy in pregnant individuals is different than that in nonpregnant individuals. Restriction of physical activity with occasional daily bed rest has been shown to reduce premature labor, lower blood pressure, and promote diuresis in patients with mild to moderate hypertension.[71] Weight loss should not be encouraged.[71] Some studies suggests that the severity of the hypertension correlates to the degree of plasma contraction, and, therefore, sodium restriction is not recommended for all individuals.[71] Salt restriction should be advocated only in those that have been successfully treated with salt restriction in the past. As for all pregnant women, alcohol and cigarette use should be discouraged.

Pharmacologic therapy for the treatment of chronic hypertension must be undertaken cautiously. Two retrospective trials have shown that antihypertensive therapy reduces the risk of stroke and cardiovascular complications among pregnant women with a diastolic blood pressure above 110 mm Hg.[74,75] However, the benefits of treatment of mild hypertension remain speculative. The decision to initiate pharmacologic therapy in pregnant women must take into account the history of pre-existing cardiovascular disease and the risk of developing target organ damage. Caution must be exercised to avoid a significant decrease in placental blood flow.

The antihypertensive drug of choice is methyldopa.[76–81] Methyldopa is the most extensively studied medication in pregnant women with hyperetension. If methyldopa is not tolerated or does not effectively lower blood pressure, then any other antihypertensive agent may be chosen, with the exception of the ACE inhibitor and angiotensin receptor blocker classes. Although angiotensin receptor blockers have not been well studied, ACE inhibitors have been shown to reduce uterine blood flow and fetal survival in sheep and rabbits and are associated with renal failure in neonates.[82]

The treatment of preeclampsia-induced hypertension is early detection, close medical monitoring, and delivery of the fetus. Patients must be followed up carefully under the supervision of an obstetrician. Bed rest with close scrutiny of the mother's blood pressure, weight, urinary protein excretion, platelet count, and fetal status is reasonable treatment for patients with mild preeclampsia. If there is any progression of the disease, then hospitalization is warranted.

Antihypertensive therapy has not been proven to be an effective treatment for the treatment of preeclampsia, except under conditions of acute hypertension (diastolic blood pressure >105 to 110 mm Hg) during delivery. In this situation, intravenous hydralazine given in 5-mg bolus doses is the treatment of choice.[71] Diastolic blood pressure should be lowered to between 90 and 104 mm Hg. Sodium nitroprusside should be used only when it is needed to preserve maternal well being. Cyanide toxicity from nitroprusside has been demonstrated to precipitate fetal death in laboratory animals.[71]

Acute hypertensive changes induced by pregnancy often dissipate rapidly after pregnancy. If severe hypertension persists, the likelihood of underlying chronic hypertension is increased. These patients should be treated with antihypertensive therapy and followed up in the outpatient setting.

Coronary Artery Disease

Patients that have experienced a myocardial infarction should have immediate treatment within the first several hours with a ß-blocker and an ACE inhibitor.[83] Patients with stable angina should have symptomatic treatment with a ß-blocker, calcium channel blocker, or nitrate medication.[84]

ß-Blockers, without intrinsic sympathomimetic activity, administered within several hours after a myocardial infarction have been shown to reduce morbidity and mortality over the weeks, months, and years following an infarction. ß-Blockers reduce the magnitude of the infarction, the rate of re-infarction, and the incidence of sudden cardiac death from ventricular tachycardia. They also slow the ventricular response in ischemia-induced tachyarrhythmias such as atrial fibrillation.

Relative contraindications to ß-blockers include (1) heart rate less than 60, (2) systolic pressure < 100 mm Hg, (3) moderate or severe left ventricular failure, (4) signs of peripheral hypoperfusion, (5) pulse rate interval greater than .24 seconds, (6) second- or third-degree heart block, (7) severe obstructive lung disease, (8) severe peripheral vascular disease, and (9) insulin-dependent diabetes mellitus. ACE inhibitors of have shown a similar reduction in mortality if given within the first 24 hours of a myocardial infarction. They are particularly effective in reducing mortality in patients with ischemic cardiomyopathy and a left ventricular ejection fraction of < 40%.

Patients with stable angina may be treated with medication therapy to alleviate their chest discomfort. Patients with unstable angina should be admitted to a hospital for a cardiology evaluation and monitoring. ß-Blocker therapy is the agent of choice in a patient with anginal symptoms. Calcium channel blocker therapy for the treatment of angina is controversial. Short-acting calcium channel blockers should not be used for the treatment of angina. Longer-acting dihydropyridine calcium channel blockers have been used safely in the treatment of ischemic and nonischemic cardiomyopathy; however, mortality was decreased in only the nonischemic cohort.[85] Verapamil or diltiazem can be given to patients with ongoing ischemia or rapid venticular response with atrial fibrillation in the absence of congestive heart failure, left ventricular dysfunction, or atrioventricular block.

Congestive Heart Failure

Despite improved treatment of hypertension over the last two decades, the prevalence of cardiomyopathy is on the rise.[10] Patients with chronic hypertension can develop a reduced left ventricular function from either ischemic or nonischemic mechanisms. These patients are defined as having a left ventricular ejection fraction of < 40% on echocardiogram or cardiac catheterization. Patients with chronic hypertension also may develop congestive heart failure with a preserved left ventricular dysfunction, implying a diastolic dysfunction. The development of concentric ventricular hypertrophy in these patients impairs left ventricular relaxation and filling.[86]

Therapy with an ACE inhibitor is the treatment of choice for patients with poor left ventricular function. Total mortality and hospitalizations for congestive heart failure are significantly reduced with ACE inhibitor therapy.[87] Many studies have included concurrent treatment with diuretics and digoxin. If ACE inhibitor therapy is not tolerated secondary to cough, angioedema, hyperkalemia, or worsening renal function, then angiotensin receptor blockers may be substituted. A small study has validated that angiotensin receptor blockers reduce mortality and hospitalizations.[88] If neither of these treatments is tolerated, the use of combination hydralazine and nitrates can be initiated.[89]

ß-Blocker therapy also has reduced mortality and hospitalizations in studies of patients with systolic dysfunction.[90,91] These studies were conducted in patients already on therapy with diuretics, digoxin, and ACE inhibitors. Worsening heart failure as an adverse reaction to therapy with ß-blocker treatment was less frequent than that in the placebo groups.

Dihydropyridine calcium channel blockers have been shown to be safe in patients with cardiomyopathy. These patients were treated previously with ACE inhibitors, diuretics, and digoxin. Only treatment of nonischemic cardiomyopathy produced a significant survivial benefit.[85]

Nephropathy

The incidence of end-stage renal disease has increased linearly over the last 20 years despite improvement in the treatment of hypertension.[10] There is a direct correlation between both systolic blood pressure and diastolic blood pressure and the development of end-stage renal disease.[92,93] There also is strong evidence that aggressive treatment of blood pressure in patients with diabetic and nondiabetic nephropathy can delay the progression of renal disease.

The natural course of chronic renal disease is a gradual decline in glomerular filtration rate with time, as defined by the slope of 1/creatinine. This rate of decline can be slowed with aggressive treatment of the blood pressure.[94,95] The target blood pressure for an individual patient with diabetic or nondiabetic nephropathy is dependent on the degree of proteinuria over a 24-hour time period. A spot urine albumin-to-creatinine ratio can be used to accurately screen for the presence of proteinuria. A test for microalbuminuria (30 to 300 mg/d or 20 to 200 µg/min) is a good marker for early nephropathy and should be ordered for all diabetic patients. At this time, a test for microalbuminuria has not been recommended for all patients with hypertension, although a regular urinalysis should be ordered.

In patients with < 1 mg/d of proteinuria and an elevated creatinine level, a target blood pressure of < 130/80 mm Hg should be achieved with whatever therapy is necessary. In patients with > 1 g of proteinuria, this target blood pressure is lowered to < 125/75 mm Hg. These lower blood pressures have been shown in large studies to be tolerated by elderly subjects.[96]

ACE inhibitors are the antihypertensive agents of choice for treating patients with chronic renal disease and proteinuria. Large randomized trials have demonstrated their efficacy in delaying the progression of end-stage renal disease.[97–99] The major side effect of these agents is hyperkalemia, and this should be monitored closely in patients with chronic renal disease.[60–66] In patients with diffuse atherosclerotic disease, the renal function should be monitored closely after initiation of ACE inhibitor therapy, as the pre-existance of bilateral renal artery stenosis in these patients can precipitate renal failure with the addition of ACE inhibitors.[100]

If tolerated, ACE inhibitors should be used throughout the entire course of chronic renal disease, even in patients with a very low creatinine clearance. Although there are no long-term trials with angiotensin receptor blockers in patients with chronic renal disease, these blockers should be used as a second-line agent if ACE inhibitors are not tolerated. The benefit of calcium channel blockers for the treatment of chronic renal disease is controversial. Calcium channel blockers and any other antihypertensive class should be added as adjunctive therapy to further reduce blood pressure in patients that have not achieved target goals.[101]

Patients with renovascular-induced hypertension and chronic renal disease can be treated with antihypertensive medication, angioplasty, or surgery.[102–112] ACE inhibitors are the medical therapy of choice for treatment of refractory hypertension in these patients. Some of the patients may have bilateral renal artery stenosis, and, therefore, the physician should monitor for sudden declines in renal function after initiation of an ACE inhibitor.

Surgery

There are numerous studies that have shown that mild to moderate hypertension is not an independent risk factor for perioperative cardiovascular complication. However, patients with preoperative hypertension tend to develop electrocardiographic evidence of intraoperative ischemia when wide fluctuations of blood pressure occur during surgery. Since intraoperative ischemia is a predictive marker for postoperative cardiovascular complications, it is prudent to control hypertension prior to surgery.[113]

Patients with mild to moderate hypertension can be sent for surgical intervention without delay.

If blood pressure exceeds 180/110 mm Hg, then elective surgery should be delayed for several weeks until the blood pressure is better controlled.[113]

Blood pressure medication should be continued throughout the perioperative course. Rebound hypertension is a common phenomenon that is observed with the sudden discontinuation of clonidine and ß-blocker therapy. Patients taking these medications should be continued on intravenous ß-blocker therapy and transdermal clonidine if they are unable to take oral pills. Patients on diuretic therapy should be monitored closely for hypokalemia and dehydration after surgery. The large fluid shifts that occur during surgery, particularly during vascular surgery, may further exacerbate intravascular dehydration and cause blood pressure shifts in those on diuretic therapy.

ß-Blocker therapy is the agent of choice for control of blood pressure in the perioperative period. ß-Blockers are the only class of hypertensive agent to demonstrate a reduced postoperative cardiovascular complication rate and mortality in patients with a history of coronary artery disease or two or more risk factors for cardiovascular disease.[114]

Chronic Obstructive Pulmonary Disease

In patients with coexistant hypertension and obstructive lung disease, ß-blocker therapy must be used with caution. If ß-blocker therapy is necessary to manage their hypertension or cardiovascular disease, then a cardioselective ß-antagonist should be selected. The selective β_1-antagonists metoprolol and atenolol have demonstrated less bronchoconstriction than have other ß-blockers.[115–117]

Gout

Hyperuricemia is a frequent finding in patients with hypertension and may reflect a decreased renal blood flow. Thiazide diuretics decrease uric acid clearance and cause a secondary increase in uric acid levels. In those with pre-existing gout, there is an increased frequency of gouty attacks with the initiation of thiazide diuretic therapy. However, this occurs in less than half of these patients. Without prior history, gout occurs in less than 1 per 1,000 patient years.[118]

RESOURCES

The American Heart Association
7272 Greenville Avenue
Dallas, Texas 75231
Telephone: 1-800-242-8721
Web site: www.americanheart.org

The American Heart Association is an objective, comprehensive, and current source of information on hypertension. It is useful for both clinicians and patients.

The National Heart, Lung, and Blood Institute
PO Box 3105
Bethesda, Maryland 20824-0105
Web site: www.nhlbi.nih.gov

The NHLBI, a division of the National Institutes of Health, provides information on hypertension for clinicians and patients, including patient education materials, through the NHLBI Web site.

REFERENCES

1. National Center for Health Statistics. Vital statistics of the United States, 1988. Vol. II: Mortality, part A. Hyattsville (MD): US Department of Health and Human Services, Public Health Service, Centers for Health Disease Control; 1991.

2. Fiebach NH, Hebert PR, Stampfer MJ, et al. A prospective study of high blood pressure and cardiovascular disease in women. Am J Epidemiol 1989; 130:646–54.

3. Sigurdsson JA, Bengtsson C, Lapidus L, et al. Morbidity and mortality in relation to blood pressure and antihypertensive treatment: a 12-year follow-up study of a population sample of Swedish women. Acta Med Scand 1984;215:313–22.

4. Johnson JL, Heineman EF, Heiss G, et al. Cardiovascular disease and factors and mortality among black women and white women aged 40–64 years in Evans County, Georgia. Am J Epidemiol 1986; 123:209–20.

5. Stamler J, Stamler S, Newton JD. Blood pressure, systolic and diastolic, and cardiovascular risks. US population data. Arch Intern Med 1993;153:598–615.

6. Kannel WB, McGee D, Gordon T. A general cardiovascular risk profile: the Framingham study. Am J Cardiol 1976;38:46–51.

7. Insua JT, Sacks HS, Lau TS, et al. Drug treatment of hypertension in the elderly: a meta-analysis. Ann Intern Med 1994;121:355–62.

8. MacMahon S, Rodgers A. The effect of blood pressure reduction in older patients: an overview of five randomized controlled trials in elderly hypertensives. Clin Exp Hypertens 1993;15:967–78.

9. Gueyffier F, Boutitie F, Boissel JP, et al. Effect of antihypertensive drug treatment on cardiovascular outcomes in women and men. A meta-analysis of individual patient data from randomized, controlled trials. Ann Intern Med 1997;126:761–7.

10. National Center for Health Statistics. Third National Health and Nutrition Examination Survey, 1988–91. Hyattsville, (MD): US Department of Health and Human Services; 1994.

11. Kuhn FE, Rackley CE. Coronary artery disease in women: risk factors, evaluation, treatment and prevention. Arch Intern Med 1993;153:2626–56.

12. Isles CG, Hole DJ, Hawthorne VM, et al. Relation between coronary risk and coronary mortality in women of the Renfrew and Paisley survey: comparison with men. Lancet 1992;339:702–6.

13. Joint National Committee on Prevention, Detection, Evaluation, and Treatment of High Blood Pressure. The sixth report of the Joint National Committee on Prevention, Detection, Evaluation, and Treatment of High Blood Pressure. Arch Intern Med 1997;157:2413–46.

14. National High Blood Pressure Education Program Working Group. Report on hypertension in the elderly. Hypertension 1994;23:275–85.

15. Report of the World Health Organization Expert Committee. Hypertension control. WHO Technical Report Series;1996. p. 862.

16. Hall CL, Higgs CM, Notarianni L. Home blood pressure recording in mild hypertension: value of distinguishing sustained from clinic hypertension and effect on diagnosis and treatment. Bath Health District Hypertension Study Group. J Hum Hypertens 1990; 4:501–7.

17. Kleinert HD, Harshfield GA, Pickering TG, et al. What is the value of home blood pressure measurement in patients with mild hypertension? Hypertension 1984;6:574–8.

18. Cox J, et al. Relationship between blood pressure measured in the clinic and by ambulatory monitoring and left ventricular size as measured by electrocardiogram in elderly patients with isolated systolic hypertension. J Hypertens 1993;11:269–76.

19. Lutgarde T, et al. Reference values for self-recorded blood pressure. A meta-analysis of summary data. Arch Intern Med 1998;158:481–8.

20. Dean RH, Kieffer RW, Smith BM, et al. Renovascular hypertension: anatomic and renal function changes during drug therapy. Arch Surg 1981;116:1408–15.

21. Horvath JS, Waugh RC, et al. The detection of renovascular hypertension: a study of 490 patients by renal angiography. QJM 1982;51(202):139–46.

22. Simon N, Tiller DJ, Franklin SS, Bleifer KH, et al. Clinical characteristics of renovascular hypertension. JAMA 1972;220:1209–18.

23. Mann SJ, Pickering T. Detection of renovascular hypertension. State of the art 1992. Ann Intern Med 1992;117:845–53.

24. Hollenberg NK. Medical therapy for renovascular hypertension: a review. Am J Hypertens 1988;4 (Pt 2):338–43S.

25. Danese RD, Aron DC. Cushing's syndrome and hypertension. Endocrinol Metab Clin N Am 1994; 23:299–324.

26. Ross EJ, Linch DC. Cushing's syndrome-killing disease: discriminatory value of signs symptoms aiding early diagnosis. Lancet 1982;Sept: 646–9.

27. Héron E, Chatellier G, Billaud E, et al. The urinary metanephrine-to-creatinine ratio for the diagnosis of pheochromocytoma. Ann Intern Med 1996; 125:300–3.

28. Werbel SS, Ober KP. Pheochromocytoma. Med Clin N Am 1995;79:131–53.

29. Ross EJ, Griffith DNW. The clinical presentation of phaeochromocytoma. QJM 1989;71;485–96.

30. Gomberg-Maitland, Frishman WH. Recombinant growth hormone: a new cardiovascular drug therapy. Am Heart J 1996;132:1244–66.

31. Khaw KT, Peart WS. Blood pressure and contraceptive use. Br Med J 1982;2:403–7.

32. Woods JW. Oral contraceptives and hypertension. Hypertension 1988;11:II11–5.

33. Malantino LS, et al. The effects of low-dose estrogen-progestogen oral contraceptives on blood pressure and the renin-angiotensin system. Curr Ther Res 1988;43:743–9.

34. Lim KG, Isles CG, Hodsman GP, et al. Malignant hypertension in women of childbearing age and its relation to the contraceptive pill. Br Med J 1987; 294:1057–9.

35. The Writing Group for the PEPI Trial. Effects of estrogen or estrogen/progestin regimens on heart disease risk factors in postmenopausal women. The Postmenopausal Estrogen/Progestin Interventions (PEPI) Trial. JAMA 1995;273:199–208.

36. Pfeffer RI, Kurosaki TT, Charlton SK. Estrogen use and blood pressure in later life. Am J Epidemiol 1979;110:469–78.

37. Kelley G, McClellan P. Antihypertensive effects of aerobic exercise. A brief meta-analytic review of randomized controlled trials. Am J Hypertens 1994;7:115–9.

38. Physical exercise in the management of hypertension: a consensus statement by the World Hypertension League. J Hypertens 1991;9:283–7.

39. Kokkinos PF, Narayan P, Colleran JA, et al. Effects of regular exercise on blood pressure and left ventricular hypertrophy in African-American men with severe hypertension. New Engl J Med 1995;333: 1462–7.

40. Whelton PK, Appel LJ, Espeland MA, et al. Sodium reduction and weight loss in the treatment of hypertension in older persons: a randomized controlled trial of nonpharmacologic interventions in the elderly (TONE). JAMA 1998;279:839–46.

41. The Trials of Hypertension Prevention Collaborative Research Group. Effects of weight loss and sodium reduction intervention on blood pressure and hypertension incidence in overweight people with high-normal blood pressure. The Trials of Hypertension Prevention. Phase II. Arch Intern Med 1997;157: 657–67.

42. Wassertheil-Smoller S, et al. The Trial of Antihypertensive Interventions and Management (TAIM) Study. Arch Intern Med 1992;152:131–6.

43. Cushman WC, Cutler JA, Hanna E, et al. Prevention and Treatment of Hypertension Study (PATHS): effects of an alcohol treatment program on blood pressure. Arch Intern Med 1998;158:1197–207.

44. Puddey IB, Beilin LJ, Vandongen R, et al. Regular alcohol use raises blood pressure in treated hypertensive subjects. A randomised controlled trial. Lancet 1987;1:647–51.

45. Puddey IB, Beilin LJ, Vandongen R, et al. Evidence for a direct effect of alcohol consumption on blood pressure in normotensive men. A randomized controlled trial. Hypertension 1985;7:707–13.

46. Bulpitt CJ, Shipley MJ, Semmence A. The contribution of a moderate intake of alcohol to the presence of hypertension. J Hypertens 1987;5:85–91.

47. Midgley JP, Matthew AG, Greenwood CM, et al. Effect of reduced dietary sodium on blood pressure: a meta-analysis of randomized controlled trials. JAMA 1996; 275:1590–7.

48. Elliott P, et al. Intersalt revisited; further analyses of 24 hour sodium excretion and blood pressure within and across populations. BMJ 1996;312:1249–53.

49. Whelton P, et al. Effects of oral potassium on blood pressure. JAMA 1997;277:1624–32.

50. Allender S, Cher DJ, Cook RJ, et al. Dietary calcium and blood pressure. A meta-analysis of randomized clinical trials. Ann Intern Med 1996;124:825–831.

51. The Trials of Hypertension Prevention Collaborative Research Group. The effects of nonpharmacologic interventions on blood pressure of persons with high normal levels. JAMA 1992;267:1213–20.

52. Kawano Y, Matsuoka H, Takishita S, et al. Effects of magnesium supplementation in hypertensive patients: assessment by office, home and ambulatory blood pressures. Hypertension 1998;32(2):260–5.

53. Witteman J, Grobbee DE, Derkx FH, et al. Reduction of blood pressure with oral magnesium supplementation in women with mild to moderate hypertension. Am J Clin Nutr 1994;60(1):129–35.

54. Appel LJ, Moore TJ, Obarzanek E, et al. A clinical trial of the effects of dietary patterns on blood pressure. N Engl J Med 1997;336:1117–24.

55. Eisen SA, Miller DK, Woodward RS, et al. The effect of prescribed daily dose frequency on patient medication compliance. Arch Intern Med 1990;150: 1881–4.

56. Monane M, Bohn RL, Gurwitz JH, et al. Compliance with antihypertensive therapy among elderly Medicaid enrollees: the roles of age, gender and race. Am J Public Health 1996;86:1805–8.

57. Messerli H, Grossman, Goldbourt U. Are ß-blockers efficacious as first-line therapy for hypertension in the elderly? JAMA 1998;279:1903–7.

58. Staessen J, Fagard R, Thijs L, et al. Randomized double-blind comparison of placebo and active treatment for older patients with isolated systolic hypertension. Lancet 1997;350:757–63.

59. Gong L, Zhang W, Zhu Y, et al. Shanghai trial of nifedipine in the elderly (STONE). J Hypertens 1996; 14;1237–45.

60. Savage PJ, Pressel SL, Curb JD, et al. Influence of long-term, low-dose, diuretic-based, antihypertensive therapy on glucose, lipid, uric acid, and potassium levels in older men and women with isolated systolic hypertension. Arch Intern Med 1998;158:741–51.

61. Curb J, Borhani NO, Blaszkowski TP, et al. Long-term surveillance for adverse effects of antihypertensive drugs. JAMA 1985;253:3263–8.

62. Widner P, et al. Diuretic-related hypokalemia: the role of diuretics, potassium supplements, glucocorticoids and ß2-adrenoceptor agonists. Br J Clin Pharmacol 1995;49:31–6.

63. Morgan DB, Davidson C. Hypokalaemia and diuretics: an analysis at publications. Br Med J 1980;905–8.

64. Greenblatt DJ, Koch-Wesser J. Adverse reactions to spironolactone. JAMA 1973;225(1):40–3.

65. Hansen KB, Bender D. Changes in serum potassium levels occurring in patients treated with triamterene and a triamterene-hydrochlorothiazide combination. Clin Pharmacol Ther 1966;8:392–9.

66. Whiting G, McLaran CJ, Bochner F. Severe hyperkalaemia with Moduretic. Med J Aust 1979;1:409.

67. Zampaglione B, Pascale C, Marchisio M, et al. Hypertensive urgencies and emergencies. Prevalence and clinical presentation. Hypertension 1996;27(1):144–7.

68. Gifford RW, Westbrook E. Hypertensive encephalopathy: mechanisms, clinical features and treatment. Prog Cardiovasc Dis 1974;XVII:115–24.

69. Joint National Committee on Prevention, Detection, Evaluation, and Treatment of High Blood. The fifth report of the Joint National Committee on Prevention, Detection, Evaluation, and Treatment of high blood pressure (JNC V). Arch Intern Med 1993; 153:154–83.

70. Calhoun DA, Oparil S. Treatment of hypertensive crises. N Engl J Med 1990;323:1177–83.

71. National High Blood Pressure Education Program Working Group. Report on high blood pressure in pregnancy. Consensus report. Am J Obstet Gynecol 1990;163(Pt 1):1689–710.

72. Sibai BM, Abdella TN, Anderson GD, et al. Pregnancy outcome in 211 patients with mild chronic hypertension. Obstet Gynecol 1983;61:571–6.

73. Sibai BM, et al. Maternal and perinatal outcome of conservative management uteroplacental and fetal umbilical placental circulations. Am J Obstet Gynecol 1985;65:301–6.

74. Sibai BM, Anderson GD. Pregnancy outcome of intensive therapy in severe hypertension in first trimester. Obstet Gynecol 1986;67:517–22.

75. Kincaid-Smith P, Bullen M, Mills J. Prolonged use of methyldopa in severe hypertension in pregnancy. BMJ 1966;1:274–6.

76. Leather HM, Humphreys DM, Baker PB, Chadd MA. A controlled trial of hypotensive agents in hypertension in pregnancy. Br Heart J 1968;30:871.

77. Redman CWG. Fetal outcome in trial of antihypertensive treatment in pregnancy. Lancet 1976; 2:753–6.

78. Arias F, Zamora J. Antihypertensive treatment and pregnancy outcome in patients with mild chronic hypertension. Obstet Gynecol 1979;53:489–94.

79. Weitz C, Khouzami V, Maxwell K, et al. Treatment of hypertension in pregnancy with methyldopa: a randomized double blind study. Int J Gynaecol Obstet 1987;25(1):35–40.

80. Sibai BM, Mabie WC, Shamsa F, et al. A comparison of no medication versus methyldopa or labetalol in chronic hypertension during pregnancy. Am J Obstet Gynecol 1990;162:960–6.

81. Montan S, Anandakumar C, Arulkumaran S, et al. Effects of methyldopa on uteroplacental and fetal hemodynamics in pregnancy-induced hypertension. Am J Obstet Gynecol 1993;168(1 Pt 1):152–6.

82. Rosa FW, Bosco LA, et al. Neonatal anuria with maternal angiotensin-converting enzyme inhibition. Obstet Gynecol 1989;74(3 Pt 1):371–4.

83. Ryan TJ, Graham CF, Antman EM, Brooks NH, et al. ACC/AHA guidelines for the management of patients with myocardial infarction. A report of the American College of Cardiology/American Heart Association Task Force on Practice Guidelines (Committee on Management of Acute Myocardial Infarction). J Am Coll Cardiol 1999;28:1328–428.

84. Packer M, O'Connor CM, Ghali JK, et al. Effect of amlodipine on morbidity and mortality in severe chronic heart failure. N Engl J Med 1996;335:1107–14.

85. Ramachandran SV, Levy D. The role of hypertension in the pathogenesis of heart failure. Arch Intern Med 1996;156:1789–96.

86. Garg R, Yusuf S. Overview of randomized trials of angiotensin-converting enzyme inhibitors on mortality and morbidity in patients with heart failure. JAMA 1995;273:1450–6.

87. Pitt B, Segal R, Martinez FA, et al. Randomised trial of losartan versus captopril in patients over 65 with heart failure (Evaluation of Losartan in the Elderly Study, ELITE). Lancet 1997;349:747–52.

88. Cohn JN, Archibald DS, Ziesche S, et al. Effect vasodilator therapy on mortality in chronic congestive heart failure. N Engl J Med 1986;314:1547–52.

89. Australia/New Zealand Heart Failure Research Collaborative Group. Randomised, placebo-controlled-trial of carvedilol in patients with congestive heart failure due to ischaemic heart disease. Lancet 1997; 349:375–80.

90. Packer M, Coats AJ, Fowler MB, et al. Effect of carvedilol on severe chronic heart failure. N Engl J Med 2001;344:1051–8.

91. Klagg MJ, Whelton PK, Randall BL, et al. Blood pressure and end-stage renal disease in men. N Engl J Med 1996;334:13–18.

92. Perry HM Jr, Miller P, Fornoff JR, et al. Early predictors of 15-year end-stage renal disease in hypertensive patients. Hypertension 1995;25(4 Pt 1): 587–94.

93. Mahboob R, Smith MC. Chronic renal insufficiency. A diagnostic and therapeutic approach. Arch Intern Med 1998;158:1743–52.

94. National High Blood Pressure Education Program Working Group. 1995 update of the working group reports on chronic renal failure and renovascular hypertension. Arch Intern Med 1996;156:1938–47.

95. Peterson JC, Adler S, Burkart JM, et al. Blood pressure control, proteinuria, and the progression of renal disease. Ann Intern Med 1995;123:754–62.

96. Ioannis G, Lau J, Levey AS. Effect of angiotensin-converting enzyme inhibitors on the progression of nondiabetic renal disease: a meta-analysis of randomized trials. ACP J Club 1997;127:337–45.

97. Lewis EJ, et al. The effect of angiotensin-converting-enzyme inhibition on diabetic nephropathy. N Engl J Med 1993;329:1456–62.

98. Ravid M, Lang R, Rachmani R, et al. Long-term renoprotective effect of angiotensin-converting enzyme inhibition in non-insulin-dependent diabetes mellitus. Arch Intern Med 1996;156:286–9.

99. Hricik DE, Browning PJ, Kopelman R, et al. Medical intelligence. Captopril-induced functional renal insuffiency in patients with bilateral renal-artery

stenoses or renal-artery stenosis in a solitary kidney. N Engl J Med 1983;308:373–6.

100. ter Wee PW, de Micheli AG, Epstein M. Effects of calcium antagonists on renal hemodynamics and progression of nondiabetic chronic renal disease. Arch Intern Med 1994;154:1185–202.

101. Hollenberg NK. Medical therapy for renovascular hypertension: a review. Am J Hyperts 1988;1(4 Pt 2): 338–43S.

102. Dean RH, Kieffer RW, Smith BM, et al. Renovascular hypertension: anatomic and renal function changes during drug therapy. Arch Surg 1981; 116:1408–15.

103. Rimmer J, Gennari JF. Atherosclerotic renovascular disease and progressive renal failure. Ann Intern Med 1993;118:712–9.

104. Ramsay LE, Waller PC. Blood pressure response to percutaneous angioplasty for renovascular hypertension: an overview of published series. BMJ 1990; 3:569–72.

105. Aurell M, Jensen G. Treatment of renovascular hypertension. Nephron 1997;75:373–83.

106. Harden PN, Macleod MJ, Rodgers RS, et al. Effect of renal-artery stenting on progression of renovascular renal failure. Lancet 1997;349:1133–6.

107. Hannequinn L, et al. Renal artery stent placement: long-term results with the wallstent endoprosthesis. Radiology 1994;191:713–9.

108. Novick AC, et al. Trends in surgical revascularization for renal artery disease. Ten years experience. JAMA 1987;257:498–501.

109. Hansen KJ. Contemporary surgical management of renovascular disease. J Vasc Surg 1992;16:319–31.

110. Plouin PF, et al. Blood pressure outcome of angioplasty in atherosclerotic renal artery stenosis. A randomized trial. Hypertension 1998;31:823–9.

111. Webster J, et al. Randomized comparison of percutaneous angioplasty vs. continued medical therapy for hypertensive patient with atheromatous renal artery stenosis. J Hum Hypertens 1998;12:329–35.

112. Weibull H, et al. Percutaneous transluminal renal angioplasty versus surgical reconstruction of atherosclerotic renal artery stenosis: a prospective randomized study. J Vasc Surg 1993;18:841–52.

113. Mangano DT, et al. Effect of atenolol on mortality and cardiovascular morbidity after non-cardiac surgery. Multicenter Study of Perioperative Ischemia Research Group. N Engl J Med 1996;335:1717–20.

114. Lammers H, Foldering HT, van Herwaarden CLA. Ventilatory effects of long-term treatment with pindolol and metoprolol in hypertensive patients with chronic obstructive lung disease. Br J Clin Pharmacol 1985;20:205–10.

115. Patakas D, et al. Beta-blockers in bronchial asthma: effect of propranolol and pindolol on large and small airways. Thorax 1983;38:108–12.

116. Benson MK, et al. A comparison of four ß-adrenoceptor antagonists in patients with asthma. Br J Clin Pharmacol 1978;5:415–9.

117. Perks WH, Chatterjee SS, Croxson RS, et al. Comparison of atenolol and oxprenolon in patients with angina or hypertension and co-existent chronic airways obstruction. Br J Clin Pharmacol 1978;5: 101–6.

118. Nader PC, Thompson JR, Alpern RJ. Complications of diuretic use. Semin Nephrol 1998;8365–87.

32

APPROACH TO THE PATIENT WITH CHEST PAIN

Barbara Natterson, MD

The complaint of chest pain is one of the most common presenting symptoms encountered by the primary care clinician. The differential diagnosis for chest pain is extensive and various organ systems need to be considered before arriving at a diagnosis. Indeed, the complaint of chest pain presents unique challenges for the clinicians. In both women and men it may herald a life-threatening process requiring rapid invasive intervention or represent a benign process requiring no intervention other than reassurance. Quickly and accurately identifying and differentiating these processes from one another is essential. Often a focused and thorough history and physical examination is all that is required to arrive at a proper diagnosis. At other times diagnostic testing is required to identify treatable processes and to rule out potentially life-threatening conditions.

The approach to the woman with chest pain requires knowledge of the disease processes that may affect a woman at various stages in the life cycle. The complaint of chest pain in both premenopausal and postmenopausal women requires consideration of a broad differential diagnosis. Diagnoses to consider in all women include, but are not limited to, coronary artery disease (ischemic heart disease); musculoskeletal disorders; neurologic disorders; gastrointestinal disorders such as gallbladder and esophageal disease; mitral valve prolapse syndrome; pulmonary processes including pneumonia, bronchitis, pleuritis, pulmonary embolism, and pneumothorax; and nonischemic cardiac conditions including pericarditis. A summary of historical information that can be helpful in differentiating different types of chest pain is presented in Table 32–1. In addition, conditions

associated with pregnancy and delivery including amniotic fluid embolus, aortic dissection, and thromboembolic events should be considered in women who are or could be pregnant.

Recently much attention has been focused on the underdiagnosis of coronary artery disease and related syndromes in women. In fact women may present with clinical syndromes, ischemic and non-ischemic, in ways that are unique and different from the classic male presentation of these disorders. The clinician is challenged with accurately identifying and treating these disorders in a timely manner.

This chapter provides an approach to the woman with chest pain. The major clinical syndromes for which chest pain may be the presenting symptom are reviewed. An approach to differentiating the various types of chest pain is provided. Finally, issues unique to the woman with chest pain are discussed.

CARDIAC CHEST PAIN

Cardiovascular disease is the leading killer of women in the United States. Despite the prevalence of **coronary artery disease** in postmenopausal women, angina and acute myocardial infarction (MI) too often are misdiagnosed or are not diagnosed in a timely manner in women. Many factors contribute to this problem. One factor is the difference in the ways women and men experience and describe ischemic syndromes such as angina or MI. Inadequate awareness of the ways in which women present with acute coronary syndromes results in delayed diagnosis and therapy. It is well known that early intervention with thrombolytics or revascularization

TABLE 32–1. Differential Diagnosis of Episodic Chest Pain Resembling Angina Pectoris

	Duration	Quality	Provocation	Relief	Location	Comment
Effort angina	5–15 min	Visceral (pressure)	During effort or emotion	Rest, nitroglycerin	Substernal, radiates	First episode vivid
Rest angina	5–15 min	Visceral (pressure)	Spontaneous (? with exercise)	Nitroglycerin	Substernal, radiates	Often nocturnal
Mitral valve prolapse	Minutes to hours	Superficial (rarely visceral)	Spontaneous (no pattern)	Time	Left anterior	No pattern, variable charcter
Esophageal reflux	10 min–1 h	Visceral	Recumbency, lack of food	Food, antacid	Substernal, epigastric	Rarely radiates
Esophageal spasms	5–60 min	Visceral	Spontaneous, cold liquids, exercise	Nitroglycerin	Substernal, radiates	Mimics angina
Peptic ulcer	Hours	Visceral (burning)	Lack of food, "acid" foods	Food, antacids	Epigastric, substernal	—
Biliary disease	Hours	Visceral (waxes and wanes)	Spontaneous, food	Time, analgesia	Epigastric, ? radiates	Colic
Cervical disc	Variable (gradually subsides)	Superficial	Head and neck movement, palpation	Time, analgesia	Arm, neck	Not relieved by rest
Hyperventilation	2–3 min	Visceral	Emotion, tachypnea	Removal of stimulus	Substernal	Facial paresthesia
Musculoskeletal	Variable	Superficial	Movement, palpation	Time, analgesia	Multiple	Tenderness
Pulmonary	30+ min	Visceral (pressure)	Often spontaneous	Rest, time, bronchodilator	Substernal	Dyspneic

Reproduced with permission from Christie LG Jr, Conti CR. Systematic approach to the evaluation of angina-like chest pain. Am Heart J 1981;102:897.

has a profound impact on survival in acute MI.[1] Therefore, any factor that delays prompt diagnosis and treatment has an impact on the clinical outcome following acute MI.

Eighty percent of men and women presenting with angina or MI will complain of some kind of chest pain.[1] Women often present with "atypical" chest pain, that is, chest pain that is unlike the classic descriptions of anginal pain. Women often describe "discomfort," "unease in the chest," "breathlessness," "fatigue," and "weakness" when presenting with ischemic syndromes.[2] These differ from the complaints of chest pressure, chest heaviness, squeezing, constriction, and diaphoresis that are classically associated with acute coronary syndromes. Women are more likely than men to describe back, jaw, and/or neck pain, nausea, and shortness of breath when presenting with an acute MI. Women are more likely than men to experience angina at rest, during sleep, or in conjunction with episodes of psychological stress.[3] Women are less likely than are men to have diaphoresis associated with their chest pain when presenting with an acute MI.[4] These differences may be related to the ways women experience pain or the ways women communicate about their pain. Notably women themselves may not believe they are experiencing an MI when these atypical symptoms occur at home. They may not associate these symptoms with heart disease and they may believe erroneously that coronary artery disease is a condition that primarily affects men.[4] Delayed and missed diagnosis of coronary syndromes in women undoubtedly is due at least partially to the differences in the presenting symptoms described above.

The suspicion of coronary artery disease should be strongest in postmenopausal women, especially those with significant risk factors for coronary artery disease. In women, possibly more than in men, low high-density lipoprotein levels, cigarette smoking, hypertension, diabetes, and possibly hyperglycemia significantly increase the risk of coronary artery disease. Determining which patients should proceed to stress testing and which should proceed to diagnostic angiography can be difficult. Exercise treadmill testing can be unreliable in women due to a high incidence of false-positive tests.[5] The addition of an imaging procedure can increase the sensitivity and specificity of the stress test. However, the gold standard for the diagnosis of coronary artery disease remains diagnostic angiography (cardiac catheterization). Assessing a woman's pretest probability of coronary artery disease using risk factor analysis is advised when making decisions about further testing. This approach is described further in Chapter 34, "Coronary Artery Disease."

Ischemic chest pain may occur in the absence of obstructive coronary artery disease. **Coronary vasospasm** is a condition resulting in ischemic chest pain that is seen more commonly in women than in men. Coronary vasospasm presents with a symptom complex similar to that of an acute MI. It is seen at rest, in response to mental stress, and may be a cardiac manifestation of systemic vasospasm in patients with migraine headache and Raynaud's disease.[6]

Another ischemic syndrome that typically presents with chest pain and is seen primarily in postmenopausal women is **syndrome X**. Syndrome X is diagnosed when a patient presents with anginal chest pain, has a positive exercise treadmill test, and has no angiographic evidence of obstructive coronary artery disease. Indeed, at least 10% of all patients with typical anginal chest pain have normal results on coronary angiograms. Patients with syndrome X have a good long-term prognosis but experience significant morbidity and disability related to their chest pain.[7] The chest pain associated with syndrome X is similar to that experienced with ischemia due to obstructive coronary artery disease. However, the pain associated with syndrome X may be more prolonged, is more likely to occur at rest, and is poorly responsive to nitrates. Patients with syndrome X have significant coronary artery calcification despite "normal" results on angiograms. The syndrome may be caused by endothelial dysfunction related to coronary arterial calcification resulting in inappropriate constriction of the epicardial arteries with exercise or stress.[8] Other possible factors include estrogen deficiency[9] or increased intracardiac sensitivity.

MUSCULOSKELETAL, NEUROLOGICAL AND PSYCHOGENIC CHEST PAIN

The most common form of musculoskeletal chest pain is costochondritis, a syndrome characterized by inflammation of the costal cartilages with resulting pain and tenderness over the costochondral joints. It generally affects the second through fifth ribs and associated cartilage.[10] Patients typically complain of anterior chest wall pain or tenderness to palpation. The pain may be described as "sore," "aching," or "knife-like" and may be pleuritic. It may occur spontaneously or in association with systemic inflammatory conditions. There may be an increased incidence of costochondritis among patients with fibromyalgia.[11] Young women who participate in athletics may present with this syndrome following upper body weight training sessions.

Neurologic conditions presenting with chest pain include radiculopathies, nerve root disorders, herpes zoster, cervical spine lesions, and herniated discs.[6]

Chest pain syndromes also may be psychogenic in origin. Neurocirculatory asthenia (Da Costa's syndrome) is diagnosed more commonly in women than in men. It is characterized by a stabbing or aching pain of the left breast region. The pain may be of variable duration and intensity. It often is accompanied by hyperventilation and palpitations. It occurs most often in association with stressful life events and is seen in individuals with a history of anxiety disorders with or without depression.[6,12]

GASTROINTESTINAL CHEST PAIN

Gastrointestinal disorders represent a common cause of chest pain in the general population. Cystic or bile duct obstruction, cholecystitis, and pancreatitis may result in epigastric pain that often radiates to the back. Associated symptoms including indigestion, nausea, vomiting, and fatty food intolerance may accompany the chest pain complaint. Ultrasonography and/or other imaging procedures may be necessary to make this diagnosis.[6] Other gastrointestinal causes of chest pain include esophageal disorders including esophageal reflux, esophageal spasm, and rarely esophageal dissection or rupture. Reflux of acidic gastric contents may result in a "heartburn-like" pain in the epigastrium that can mimic the symptoms of ischemic chest pain. Similarly esophageal spasm may present as epigastric chest pain with or without associated symptoms of nausea, vomiting, and diaphoresis and may be nitrate responsive, making it difficult to distinguish from ischemic pain.

MITRAL VALVE PROLAPSE

Mitral valve prolapse often is identified as the "cause" of atypical chest pain in young women. It is said to affect between 1 and 2% of the population,[13] and is characterized by myxomatous changes/thickening of the mitral valve leaflets, superior systolic displacement of the leaflets into the left atrium, and usually mitral regurgitation. The diagnosis has historically been made by performing auscultation and/or echocardiography. A constellation of symptoms including nonanginal chest pain, palpitations, exertional dyspnea, intense anxiety, and panic attacks have been attributed to the "mitral valve prolapse syndrome." In fact a clear association between these symptoms and the echocardiographic diagnosis of mitral valve prolapse is lacking.[14] Although a syndrome does seem to exist linking symptoms of atypical chest pain, palpitations, and anxiety, the relationship of these symptoms to structural mitral valve prolapse remains uncertain.[13,14]

PULMONARY CHEST PAIN

Pulmonary processes often present with chest pain. Severe pulmonary hypertension of any etiology can result in exertional chest pain that can be difficult to distinguish from ischemic chest pain. **Primary pulmonary hypertension** is a specific idiopathic disorder that affects primarily young to middle-aged women.

The chest pain associated with this condition likely results from ischemia of a hypertrophied right ventricle facing markedly elevated pulmonary pressures.[15] It may be described as "feeling like pressure" or "heaviness," usually is exertional, and often is accompanied by shortness of breath.

Pulmonary embolism should always be considered as a possible cause of chest pain any patient. Many factors may predispose patients to venous thromboembolism. Those factors specific to young and middle-aged women include use of oral contraception, cigarette smoking, and pregnancy. Women confined to bed due to preeclampsia or who have undergone cesarean section are at increased risk for venous thromboembolism. Hypercoagulability and increased predisposition toward venous thromboembolism may occur in the setting of malignancy as well. Chest pain may be part of the initial presentation of pulmonary embolism or it may develop over time, particularly if pulmonary infarction occurs. Common associated symptoms include dyspnea, apprehension or anxiety, cough, diaphoresis, hemoptysis, and syncope.[6] Early consideration of this diagnosis, prompt testing, and timely therapy may prevent serious and even life-threatening complications.

Pneumonia, pneumothorax, pleuritis, and bronchitis are other pulmonary conditions to consider in a woman presenting with chest pain. Patients generally present with pleuritic chest pain with associated symptoms. A physical examination, focused history, and possibly a chest radiography may be all that is required to properly make these diagnoses.

PREGNANCY

The differential diagnosis of chest pain in the pregnant woman must include all the conditions that may affect nonpregnant women plus several processes that are unique to the pregnant woman. Pulmonary embolism should be considered given the increased incidence of venous thromboembolism in pregnancy. Amniotic fluid emboli should be considered when a woman presents with acute onset of chest pain, hemodynamic collapse, and shortness of breath. This condition is seen in conjunction with ruptured membranes and is associated with the use of uterine stimulants.[16] Aortic dissection should be considered in a pregnant or delivering woman who presents with acute onset of chest pain, especially if there is radiation to the back. Dissection occurs most commonly in the third trimester and in the peripartum period and occurs most commonly in multiparous women with a history of Marfan syndrome, connective tissue diseases, or coarctation of the aorta.[17]

The possibility of ischemic heart disease should be considered when a pregnant woman presents with chest pain suggestive of an acute coronary syndrome. Acute myocardial infarction due to obstructive coronary disease is an uncommon occurrence during pregnancy. Typically, coronary artery disease does not present clinically until after the age of 50 years. However, rarely a younger women with strong risk factors for premature coronary artery disease including an adverse lipid profile, diabetes, hypertension, and cigarette smoking may present with an ischemic coronary syndrome during pregnancy. Polycystic ovaries also may predispose a woman to premature coronary artery disease.[18] Acute chest pain during the peripartum period should raise the possibility of related diagnoses including coronary dissection, coronary vasospasm, or acute coronary thrombosis.[17]

Chest pain also may be associated with the syndrome of pulmonary edema seen occasionally in conjunction with the administration of tocolytic agents to pregnant women.[16]

CONCLUSION

The complaint of chest pain should be investigated thoroughly by the primary care clinician. The conditions reviewed in this chapter represent some, but by no means all, possible disorders that may present with chest pain. The clinician should start with a broad differential diagnosis and narrow the possibilities down based on the history, physical examination, and diagnostic testing. Recognition of the types of disease processes that affect women at varying stages in the life cycle is of assistance in determining appropriate diagnosis.

REFERENCES

1. Foster S, Mallik M. A comparative study of differences in the referral behaviour patterns of men and women who have experienced cardiac-related chest pain. Intensive Crit Care Nurs 1998;14:192–202.

2. Swahn E. The card of patients with ischaemic heart disease from a gender perspective. Eur Heart J 1998; 19:1758–65.

3. Douglas P, Ginsburg G. The evaluation of chest pain in women. N Engl J Med 1996;334:131–5.

4. Goldberg R, O'Donnell C, Yarzebski J, et al. Sex differences in symptom presentation associated with acute myocardial infarction; a population-based study. Am Heart J 1998;136:189–95.

5. Alexander K, Shaw L, De Long E., et al. The value of exercise treadmill testing in women. J Am Coll Cardiol 1998;32:1657–64.

6. Braunwald E, Rutherford J. Chronic ischemic heart disease. In: Braunwald E, editor. Heart disease: a textbook of cardiovascular medicine. 4th ed. Boston: W.B. Saunders; 1992. p. 1292–364.

7. Atienza F, Velasco J, Brown S. Assessment of quality of life in patients with chest pain and normal coronary arteriograms (syndrome X) using a specific questionnaire. Clin Cardiol 1999;22:283–90.

8. Shemesh J, Fisman E, Tenenbaum A, et al. Coronary artery calcification in women with syndrome X: usefulness of double helical CT for detection. Radiology 1997;205:697–700.

9. Rosano G, Peters N, Lefroy D, et al. 17 beta-estradiol therapy lessens angina in postmenopausal women with syndrome X. J Am Coll Cardiol 1996;28:1500–5.

10. Lum-Hee N, Abdulla A. Slipping rib syndrome: an overlooked cause of chest and abdominal pain. Int J Clin Pract 1997;57:252–3.

11. Disla E, Rhim H, Reddy A, et al. Costochondritis: a prospective analysis in an emergency department setting. Arch Intern Med 1994;154:2466–9.

12. Sonino N, Fava G, Boscaro M, et al. Life events and neurocirculatory asthenia. J Intern Med 1998;244: 523–8.

13. Freed L, Levy D, Levine R, et al. Prevalence and clinical outcome of mitral valve prolapse. N Engl J Med 1999;341:1–7.

14. Devereux R, Kramer-Fox R, Brown WT, et al. Relation between clinical features of mitral prolapse syndrome and echocardiographically documented mitral valve prolapse. J Am Coll Cardiol 1986;8:763–72.

15. Rubin L. Pathology and pathophysiology of primary pulmonary hypertension. Am J Cardiol 1995; 75:51–4A.

16. Pisani R, Rosenow E. Pulmonary edema associated with tocolytic therapy. Ann Intern Med 1989; 110:714–8.

17. Elkayam U. Pregnancy and heart disease. In: Braunwald E, editor. Heart disease: a textbook of cardiovascular medicine. 4th ed. Boston: W.B. Saunders; 1992. p. 1790–809.

18. Birdsall M, Farquhar C, White H. Association between polycystic ovaries and extent of coronary artery disease in women having cardiac catheterization. Ann Intern Med 1997;126:32–5.

33

CONGESTIVE HEART FAILURE

Michele A. Hamilton, MD, FACC

EPIDEMIOLOGY

Congestive heart failure affects almost 5 million Americans, with the prevalence in women slightly exceeding that in men.[1] It is responsible for more than 11 million clinician office visits and is the leading cause of hospitalization in people over 65 years old. Although women with heart failure generally live longer than do men, the National Heart, Lung, and Blood Institute's Framingham Heart Study found that the median survival for women was only 3.2 years.[2] As the population ages, the incidence of both new cases of heart failure and heart failure deaths has been increasing in women of all races and is expected to continue to rise.

Unfortunately, women have not only a higher early mortality rate than do men following acute myocardial infarction,[3] they also have a higher probability of developing heart failure within 6 months post infarction. Women with heart failure generally have more severe symptoms and a worse quality of life than do their male counterparts.[4] Women also have been greatly under-represented in clinical research trials,[5] making it difficult to be certain of the most appropriate diagnostic and therapeutic options for them.

ETIOLOGIES

Congestive heart failure, defined as the inability of the heart to provide adequate circulation (and, thus, oxygen and nutrients) to the rest of the body, has many different causes. Hypertension is the most frequent culprit for women.[6] Longstanding hypertension generally leads to left ventricular hypertrophy and diastolic dysfunction, followed later by systolic dysfunction. Diabetes[7] and obesity[8] also have been found to be more important factors in the development of heart failure in women than in men. Although coronary artery disease and subsequent ventricular impairment from infarcts is a more common cause of heart failure in men, its incidence in women is common and is increasing. Valvular abnormalities, either congenital, rheumatic, or due to calcification or myxomatous degeneration, also can cause heart failure.

CARDIOMYOPATHIES

Cardiomyopathies (ie, abnormalities of cardiac muscle) frequently lead to symptoms of heart failure in both men and women. They are divided into three categories: restrictive, hypertrophic, and dilated.

Dilated cardiomyopathy, with thinned endocardium, enlarged ventricles, and impaired systolic function, occurs most commonly (Figure 33–1). It can be caused by alcohol, hypothyroidism, collagen vascular diseases, or nutritional deficiencies, but most often is declared idiopathic, possibly of viral origin. Viral cardiomyopathies are caused by common viruses (including coxsackie B and echovirus) or the human immunodeficiency virus, so far with no explanation for the predilection in some individuals to have cardiac involvement from a viral syndrome. Interestingly the incidence of alcohol-related cardiomyopathy is similar in men and women, despite the lower alcohol intake in women.[9] This may relate to women's generally smaller body size.

Peripartum cardiomyopathy also is part of the dilated cardiomyopathy group.[10] Women with this illness develop symptoms of heart failure within a few weeks before delivery or up to 6 months postpartum. It occurs with a higher incidence in those who bear twins or women who are multiparous, over 30 years old, or African American. The etiologic mechanism remains unknown but may be related to

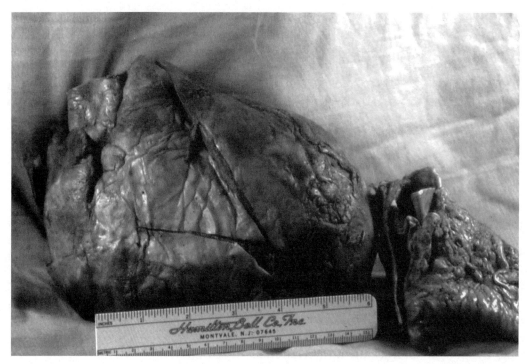

FIGURE 33–1. This photograph of a heart with a dilated cardiomyopathy (*left*) demonstrates how long-term exposure to high resistance (afterload) and filling pressures (preload) leads to markedly enlarged ventricles compared with those of a normal heart (*right*).

immunologic factors or hormones associated with pregnancy, myocarditis, or the marked cardiovascular stress of pregnancy and delivery on a previously asymptomatic cardiac abnormality. The prognosis is variable, ranging from full recovery in approximately half of the patients to chronic dysfunction in the others, sometimes with progressive heart failure leading to death or the need for transplantation. Recurrences are common in subsequent pregnancies, with the highest risk and greatest potential for maternal mortality (as high as 50%) in those women who do not demonstrate complete recovery of ventricular function between pregnancies. Guidelines for therapy of peripartum cardiomyopathy are generally the same as for other forms, which are described below. However, if diagnosis is made before delivery, angiotensin converting enzyme inhibitors should be avoided and ß-blockers used with caution.

Restrictive cardiomyopathy is characterized by decreased compliance of the ventricles that impedes filling and leads to progressive congestive symptoms.[11] Systolic function generally is preserved until advanced stages. This type of cardiomyopathy can be caused by infiltrative disorders such as amyloidosis, hemochromatosis, or sarcoidosis. It also may be precipitated by radiation therapy or anthracyclines[12] (eg, doxorubicin). Therapy is difficult and focuses on treatment of the underlying disorder, if possible. Symptomatic patients with a restrictive cardiomyopathy typically do not respond to traditional vasodilator therapy due to the development of hypotension; often they require aggressive diuresis to challenge the progressive right ventricular failure.

Hypertrophic cardiomyopathy, often familial and less common in women than in men, involves hypertrophy of the myocardium—usually most marked in the interventricular septum. This leads to decreased compliance causing diastolic dysfunction and symptoms of congestive heart failure despite normal or hyperdynamic systolic function.[13] In approximately one-fourth of patients the septal hypertrophy also leads to left ventricular outflow obstruction. Distinct from the familial type of hypertrophic cardiomyopathy, there is a form seen in elderly patients, frequently those with longstanding hypertension, that occurs more commonly in women. Patients with a hypertrophic cardiomyopathy may be asymptomatic, but many are at risk for exercise-induced syncope, sudden death, or progression to systolic dysfunction. Therapy focuses on reducing myocardial contractility and any outflow gradient with ß-blockers and calcium antagonists, and severe cases may be addressed with surgical ventricular myotomy-myomectomy. The roles of amiodarone, biventricular pacing, and catheter-directed alcohol-induced septal infarction remain controversial.[14]

HEART FAILURE WITH PRESERVED SYSTOLIC FUNCTION

Congestive heart failure can occur in the absence of systolic dysfunction when compliance (passive filling) and relaxation (an active process) are affected. This "stiff" ventricle leads to elevated end-diastolic pressure and pulmonary congestion, contributing to both dyspnea on exertion and orthopnea. The most common cause of diastolic dysfunction is hypertrophy from hypertension or aortic stenosis. Women have a greater degree of hypertrophy than do men in response to these problems,[15] leading to greater prevalence of diastolic dysfunction–related heart failure.[16] Diastolic dysfunction also can be caused by ischemia, often in conjunction with impaired systolic function.

PATHOPHYSIOLOGY OF HEART FAILURE

When myocardial contractility is reduced by infarctions or some form of cardiomyopathy, forward cardiac output decreases. To maintain output and blood pressure, a system of compensatory mechanisms occurs (Figure 33–2). Although initially helpful in achieving these goals, ultimately these compensatory processes are maladaptive and lead to further progression of ventricular dysfunction and worsening of heart failure symptoms. Stimulation of the sympathetic nervous system increases heart rate and contractility, while activation of the renin-angiotensin-aldosterone axis and arginine-vasopressin system leads to vasoconstriction and fluid retention. Over time these neurohumoral systems exacerbate heart failure hemodynamically by increasing afterload and filling pressures. They also cause fibrosis and deleterious cardiac remodeling. Direct cellular toxicity leads to myocyte elongation and slippage and programmed cell death (apoptosis).[17] Elevated levels of cytokines[18] (eg, tumor necrosis factor) and endothelin[19] (a potent vasoconstrictor) also likely contribute to cardiac failure. Although concurrent endogenous

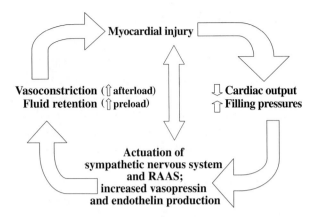

FIGURE 33–2. Progression of heart failure. Myocardial injury (eg, from infarctions, alcohol, or a viral infection) leads to reduced cardiac output and elevated filling pressures, causing activation of multiple neurohumoral factors, including the sympathetic nervous system and the renin-angiotensin-aldosterone system (RAAS). The subsequent vasoconstriction and fluid retention initially maintain blood pressure but ultimately lead to further myocardial damage.

release of natriuretic factors, kinins, prostaglandins, and endothelium-derived relaxing factors would be expected to provide vasodilation, they appear to be overwhelmed by the vasoconstricting systems in heart failure patients.

APPROACH TO THE PATIENT WITH HEART FAILURE

In caring for a patient with congestive heart failure, one must complete a thorough assessment,[20] addressing multiple issues. First, the diagnosis must be confirmed, excluding noncardiac conditions that cause similar signs and symptoms. The specific structural problem must be determined in terms of etiology, degree of left ventricular impairment, relative contributions from systolic and diastolic dysfunction, and valvular function. The patient's functional status needs to be assessed in regard to New York Heart Association (NYHA) class (I–IV, mild to severe limitation) and "congestive" versus "low-output" symptoms (see below). The physiologic manifestations (eg. fluid retention) also need to be identified prior to the initiation of therapy. Successful treatment of heart failure is multidimensional and requires long-term involvement by health care clinicians, with extensive patient education and active patient participation.

SYMPTOMS AND SIGNS

Heart failure symptoms generally can be divided into two categories, one caused by low forward output (ie, low-output failure) and the other by elevated filling pressures (ie, congestion). Low-output symptoms include exertional fatigue and generalized weakness. Congestion from left ventricular dysfunction and elevated left-sided filling pressures leads to orthopnea, paroxysmal nocturnal dyspnea, cough, and exertional dyspnea. Right-sided congestion causes anorexia, early satiety, and abdominal bloating as well as peripheral edema. Patients with severe heart failure may have impaired mental function related to low output. Other symptoms such as chest pain and palpitations may provide clues as to etiology and other possible associated problems such as arrhythmias.

Patients with congestive heart failure are likely to have tachypnea, tachycardia, and diaphoresis, but blood pressure can range from high to low, depending on the etiology. The other major findings on physical examination include jugular venous distention, pulmonary basilar rales, a laterally displaced and possibly diffuse left ventricular apical impulse (frequently in conjunction with an S_3 and a systolic murmur of mitral regurgitation, a common abnormality in heart failure), hepatomegaly with ascites, and peripheral edema. Patients with chronic congestive heart failure, even in the setting of a very low ejection fraction, may have clear lung fields on examination because they develop collateral lymphatic drainage that removes the fluid from the alveoli but not the interstitial tissues. In these patients one must rely on the symptom of orthopnea as the best predictor of elevated left ventricular diastolic pressure.[21]

DIAGNOSTIC TESTING

Simple initial evaluation with electrocardiography and chest radiography can provide important information as to cardiac rhythm, possible prior infarctions, cardiac size, pulmonary vascular congestion, and parenchymal lung disease. In patients with chronic advanced heart failure, chest radiographs may show deceptively normal lung fields because of the increased lymphatic drainage (as in lungs on physical examination, as mentioned above). Echocardiography has been proven to be a valuable tool

in the assessment of a patient with congestive heart failure. It details left and right ventricular size, wall thickness, and contractility (ie, regional wall motion as well as overall ejection fraction). It also is useful in identifying any valvular abnormalities, apical thrombi, diastolic dysfunction, or associated pulmonary hypertension.

It is critical to determine whether impaired systolic function is caused by coronary ischemia, since this could potentially be addressed via mechanical revascularization, including coronary artery bypass graft surgery or percutaneous transluminal coronary angioplasty (PTCA) and its related procedures. Traditional exercise treadmill testing is less accurate in women than in men, necessitating an imaging modality such as echocardiography or nuclear imaging with sestamibi in conjunction with the electrocardiographic monitoring. For patients who are unable to perform enough exercise to raise their heart rate to target levels, stress may be imposed pharmacologically with dobutamine, or coronary flow assessed with dipyridamole or adenosine. In some cases it may be appropriate to proceed to cardiac catheterization with coronary angiography for a definitive diagnosis. Positron emission tomography (PET) scan has become a valuable tool (available, however, only in centers with access to a cyclotron) for identifying areas of potential myocardial viability in patients with ischemic cardiomyopathy for whom surgical revascularization is being considered.[22]

Right heart catheterization should be performed in patients with severe heart failure or a complex clinical presentation to assess hemodynamic status and to optimize therapy. Endomyocardial biopsy is seldom indicated but may be useful when diagnoses of infiltrative diseases or active myocarditis are suspected.

Cardiopulmonary exercise testing consists of bicycle ergometer or treadmill exercise with simultaneous measurement (via a mouth piece) of parameters of ventilation, oxygen consumption, and carbon dioxide production. This test has multiple applications in the area of congestive heart failure, including differential diagnosis of pulmonary versus cardiac causes of dyspnea and assessment of functional class and prognosis. Cardiopulmonary exercise testing has been shown to be as valuable in women as in men for these tasks.[23] It now is used commonly in major heart failure centers and transplantation programs not only in the initial evaluation, but also as a follow-up to assess response to an intervention or potential need for cardiac transplantation. A 6-minute walk test (simple and inexpensive) also has been shown to be useful to judge functional impairment and prognosis.

THERAPY

The ideal therapy for congestive heart failure is prevention. For example, aggressive lowering of cholesterol and control of hypertension and diabetes all would be expected to reduce the development of congestive heart failure. Healthy lifestyle measures including cessation of smoking, moderation of alcohol consumption, regular exercise, and maintenance of ideal body weight also are beneficial.

Once a patient has had an episode of congestive heart failure, it is likely that it will recur and that the underlying cause will progress unless intensive interventions are made. Until recently, heart failure therapy targeted the reduced contractility and fluid retention, with digoxin and diuretics serving as the major drug treatments. The emphasis then changed to the hemodynamic abnormalities, adding vasodilators (such as hydralazine and nitrates) as "unloading therapy." The mainstay of therapy now also targets the neurohumoral pathways that contribute to the development and progression of heart failure, such as the renin-angiotensin-aldosterone axis (treated with angiotensin converting enzyme [ACE] inhibitors, angiotensin receptor blockers [ARBs], and spironolactone) and the sympathetic nervous system (treated with ß-blockers) (Table 33–1). New medications (eg, cytokine and endothelin antagonists) that aim at other specific biochemical abnormalities are being studied.[24,25]

We know now (see below) that medical therapy (ACE inhibitors and ß-blockers) in asymptomatic patients with reduced systolic function can prevent the development of heart failure, a fact that emphasizes the importance of early aggressive intervention.

Nonpharmacologic Interventions and Education

Salt restriction (< 2 g sodium/d) and fluid restriction (generally < 2 quarts total daily fluid intake), in conjunction with daily weight measurements and a flexible diuretic regimen, are important in reducing heart failure exacerbations. A low-fat and low-cholesterol diet is particularly important for those

TABLE 33–1. Heart Failure Therapy

Medications
    Angiotensin converting enzyme inhibitors
    Glycosides (digoxin)
    Diuretics
    ß-Blockers
    Aldosterone antagonists
    Direct vasodilators (hydralazine, nitrates)
    Angiotensin receptor blockers

Nonpharmacologic interventions
    Sodium and fluid restriction, daily weight
       measurements
    Abstinence from smoking and alcohol
    Initiation of aerobic exercise program
    Low-fat and low cholesterol diet, weight loss

patients with an ischemic cardiomyopathy. Heart failure patients were advised previously to reduce physical activity, but now a progressive aerobic exercise program generally is recommended. Exercise rehabilitation programs have been equally effective in both women and men, improving functional capacity and quality of life.[26] Smoking cessation (and avoidance of alcohol for those with an alcohol-related cardiomyopathy or very low ejection fraction of any etiology) also must be encouraged. Patients with advanced heart failure also should be advised to avoid nonsteroidal anti-inflammatory agents since they may adversely affect their renal function.

Pharmacologic Interventions

ANGIOTENSIN CONVERTING ENZYME INHIBITORS
Angiotensin converting enzyme inhibitors form the foundation of therapy for congestive heart failure. Some commonly prescribed agents for heart failure include captopril, lisinopril, and enalapril. This family of medications has been proven to reduce the progression of heart failure, improve functional status, and reduce hospitalizations and mortality.[27,28] In postinfarction patients with a reduced ejection fraction, ACE inhibitors decrease re-infarction rate and mortality.[29] Even in asymptomatic patients with impaired systolic function, ACE inhibitors provide clinical benefit.[30] Although the actual number of women in each of the clinical trials has been quite low, meta-analysis does suggest a survival benefit from ACE inhibitors for women.[31]

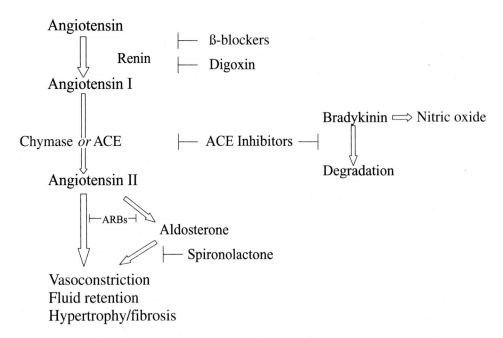

FIGURE 33–3. This figure shows the different sites in the renin-angiotensin-aldosterone axis at which medications act. ACE = angiotensin converting enzyme; ARB = angiotensin receptor blocker.

Inhibitors of ACE have several mechanisms of action (Figure 33–3). They block the conversion of angiotensin I to angiotensin II, reducing vasoconstriction and fluid retention. They also block the degradation of bradykinin, an action that may contribute to the favorable hemodynamic and remodeling effects.

All patients with reduced left ventricular systolic function should be started on an ACE inhibitor, with the dose gradually titrated as tolerated. Higher doses have better clinical efficacy (with a similar side effect profile) and should be achieved when possible.[32] The most common side effects include cough, hypotension, hyperkalemia, and renal insufficiency. Angioedema is rare. With careful monitoring, few patients are truly ACE inhibitor intolerant. Use of ACE inhibitors must be avoided during pregnancy as their use has been associated with oligohydramnios and other possible birth defects.

DIURETICS

Diuretics lead to excretion of sodium and water by blocking their reabsorption in the renal tubules. Loop diuretics (eg, furosemide and torsemide) are more effective than are the thiazide diuretics (eg, hydrochlorothiazide), especially in patients with impaired renal function.

Diuretics are required for the treatment of fluid retention in most patients with heart failure. All patients on diuretics need careful monitoring of electrolytes, creatinine, and blood urea nitrogen, and usually require potassium, and sometimes magnesium, supplementation. Addition of a potassium-sparing diuretic (see "Aldosterone Antagonists," below) may be helpful in patients with high potassium requirements. For patients with refractory fluid retention, addition of a specific thiazide diuretic, such as metalazone, potentiates the effect of the loop diuretic (usually with a need for additional potassium supplementation). Patients with massive fluid retention and consequent bowel edema are unlikely to absorb their oral medications and often require intravenous diuretics until this problem is resolved, at which time they can be switched to an oral diuretic regimen. The optimal way to manage diuretics in heart failure patients is with daily weight measurements and an adjustable diuretic regimen based on targeting an individual patient's "dry weight."

ß-BLOCKERS

Although ß-blockers were once considered contraindicated in heart failure because of their negative inotropic effects, they now have been found to have substantial clinical benefit in this population when used carefully. ß-blockers counteract the adverse effects of the activated sympathetic nervous system, specifically the vasoconstriction, tachyarrhythmias, and cellular changes, including calcium overload and programmed cell death.[33] They also reduce renin release from the kidney (see Figure 33–3) and have beneficial effects on diastolic relaxation and ischemia.[34]

Several trials of ß-blockers added to conventional therapy with an ACE inhibitor have demonstrated significant clinical improvement, including substantial reductions in mortality. Specifically carvedilol,[35] a combined nonselective ß- and α-blocker, was found in a combination of trials in the United States to reduce mortality by 65% (equally effective in men and women and in both ischemic and nonischemic disease). Metoprolol[36] and bisoprolol,[37] both ß₁ selective agents, also have demonstrated significant mortality reductions in patients with NYHA classes II and III heart failures.

Since there is a risk of heart failure exacerbation with ß-blockers, especially in patients with severe heart failure or volume overload, these drugs should be started in clinically stable euvolemic patients only. The starting dosages must be very low, and dosages should be titrated carefully every few weeks to find the optimal dose. ß-blockers should be avoided in patients with bronchospasm, bradycardia, or major depression.

DIGITALIS

Digitalis leads to a mild increase in contractility via inhibition of myocardial Na+–K+ adenosine-triphosphatase and also attenuates activation of the sympathetic nervous system and renin-angiotensin axis. Digoxin, the most commonly used cardiac glycoside, has been proven to improve symptoms and exercise tolerance.[38,39] Although it does not appear to provide a significant survival benefit, digoxin does reduce heart failure hospitalizations.[40] It should therefore be used as an adjunct to ACE inhibitors and ß-blockers in symptomatic patients. Since digoxin is excreted in the kidneys and its levels can be affected by other medications such as the anti-amythmic amiodarone, serum digoxin levels should be monitored closely and maintained in the 0.5 to 1.2 range to reduce toxicity risk. Digoxin should be avoided in patients with bradycardia or significant conduction disease.

ANGIOTENSIN RECEPTOR BLOCKERS

Angiotensin receptor blockers, such as losartan, irbesartan, and valsartan, that directly block the angiotensin II receptors are useful for the treatment of hypertension and heart failure. Angiotensin receptor blockers provide a more complete blockade of the renin-angiotensin system than do ACE inhibitors[41] (see Figure 33–3), and they do not have the bradykinin-related cough side effect; however, they also do not have the potential benefit (increased nitric oxide) of bradykinin. Small trials have demonstrated hemodynamic and neurohumoral benefits;[42,43] however, until large survival studies using the ARBs are completed, ACE inhibitors should be used as a first-line agent, with ARBs reserved for those patients with unacceptable cough from ACE inhibitor use. Potential side effects of hypotension, hyperkalemia, and renal insufficiency must still be considered with use of ARBs.

OTHER VASODILATORS

Hydralazine (a direct arterial vasodilator, effective for afterload reduction) can be used in addition to an ACE inhibitor in a hypertensive patient or a patient with persistent symptoms of low output. Nitrates (venodilators) are used commonly to lower left ventricular filling pressures in patients with orthopnea (or documented elevated pulmonary capillary wedge pressure); they also are used as antianginal therapy for ischemic cardiomyopathy patients. Calcium channel blockers generally should be avoided in heart failure patients because of their negative inotropic effects and possible adverse neurohumoral properties; however, amlodipine has been found not to increase mortality[44] and may be appropriate in an occasional patient for whom further afterload reduction or antianginal therapy is needed.

ALDOSTERONE ANTAGONISTS

Aldosterone, the final element in the renin-angiotensin-aldosterone axis, is known to cause fluid retention with potassium and magnesium wasting, hypertrophy, and fibrosis. Its production may not be completely blocked by ACE inhibitors or ARBs. Aldosterone antagonists such as spironolactone, in addition to having mild to moderate diuretic effects, may reduce the progression of heart failure. The RALES trial[45] showed a reduction in mortality and hospitalizations when spironolactone was added to conventional therapy in patients with class IV heart failure. Its role in patients with less severe heart failure is unknown. Potassium supplementation requirements usually diminish over the first week or two after the initiation of an aldosterone antagonist; serum potassium levels must be monitored closely.

Inotropic Therapy

Inotropic agents, such as ß-agonists (eg, dobutamine) and phosphodiesterase inhibitors (eg, milrinone, amrinone), can increase contractility and are used frequently to improve hemodynamic status in patients hospitalized with decompensated heart failure. However, all studies of outpatient use of oral inotropic agents (not including digoxin) have demonstrated an increase in mortality.[46,47] In addition, no study has ever proven a survival benefit for outpatient intermittent infusions of inotropic medications. These agents should therefore be avoided for outpatient use except for the rare patient who is too ill to be discharged home on conventional therapy and is not a candidate for any other intervention, such as heart transplantation.

Treatment of Diastolic Dysfunction

Unfortunately there have been few studies regarding treatment of patients with heart failure predominantly caused by diastolic dysfunction. The therapy for diastolic dysfunction is difficult and must focus on aggressive treatment of the underlying problem, such as hypertension or ischemia. Diuretics and venodilators such as nitrates are helpful in reducing elevated filling pressures. Calcium channel blockers and ß-blockers may help relaxation theoretically, but fibrosis limits their effectiveness. Digoxin may have an adverse effect in this setting and generally should be avoided in isolated diastolic dysfunction.

Antiarrhythmic Therapy

Patients with congestive heart failure are susceptible to both ventricular and supraventricular arrhythmias. In advanced heart failure populations, an arrhythmia is responsible for approximately half of the mortality, evenly distributed between bradyarrhythmias and ventricular arrhythmias.[48]

Type I antiarrhythmic agents, such as procainamide, quinidine, and flecainide, have been shown to *increase* mortality in patients with impaired ventricular function and should therefore be avoided.[49] Amiodarone (a class III agent) is the drug of choice for the treatment of atrial fibrillation in such patients; a meta-analysis has suggested a possible small mortality benefit.[50] The role of implantable cardiac defibrillators is still being defined. To date

their use has proven survival benefit for survivors of sudden death or a sustained arrhythmia, and in patients with an ischemic cardiomyopathy who have both ambient ectopy and inducible ventricular tachycardia on electrophysiology testing.[51]

Anticoagulation

Patients with reduced left ventricular function have an increased risk of thromboembolic events because of stasis within the ventricle and common prevalence of atrial fibrillation. There have been no large controlled clinical trials to direct the use of anticoagulants in patients with congestive heart failure. Using the guideline of warfarin use for patients with depressed left ventricular function who have either a thrombus evident on echocardiogram, atrial fibrillation, or a prior embolic event, leads to a very low risk of embolization.[52]

Cardiac Transplantation

Cardiac transplantation is now a standard treatment option for advanced heart failure and is indicated for those patients with either an unacceptable quality of life or a poor prognosis despite maximal medical therapy.[53] Women have had excellent outcomes with transplantation, usually resuming active lifestyles, although they do have a somewhat higher rate of cardiac rejection than do men because of presensitization related to prior pregnancies.[54]

WHEN TO REFER

Referral to a cardiologist may be necessary for assistance in the diagnosis of heart failure when the case is complex or if cardiac catheterization is contemplated. A patient with persistent heart failure symptoms, syncope, or symptomatic arrhythmias needs referral for optimization of the medical regimen and consideration of possible electrophysiologic study or defibrillator use. Patients with progressive heart failure or recurrent hospitalizations often benefit from a specialized comprehensive heart failure management program. These programs can provide aggressive medical management and multidisciplinary care, and have been shown to dramatically reduce rehospitalizations and overall costs.[55]

The author thanks Drs. Joshua Goldhaber and Gregg Fonarow for their editorial assistance and Ms. Kim Einhorn and Ms. Stephanie Kagimoto for their secretarial help.

RESOURCES

The American Heart Association
7272 Greenville Avenue
Dallas Texas 75231
Telephone: 1-800-242-8721
Web site: www.americanheart.org

The American Heart Association Web site contains patient education materials as well as information on compliance tools and continuing medical education for practitioners. The "Living with Heart Failure" site has extensive information for patients and caregivers.

The National Heart, Lung, and Blood Institute
PO Box 3105
Bethesda, Maryland 20824-0105
Telephone: (301) 496-4236
Web site: www.nhlbi.nih.gov

The National Heart, Lung, and Blood Institute of the National Institutes of Health provides patient education materials, clinical guidelines, and risk-reduction strategies.

REFERENCES

1. American Heart Association. 1999 heart and stroke statistical update. Dallas (TX): AHA 1998.

2. Ho KKL, Anderson KM, Kanel WB, et al. Survival after the onset of congestive heart failure in Framingham Heart Study subjects. Circulation 1993;88:107–15.

3. Vaccarino V, Parsons L, Every N, et al. Sex-based differences in early mortality after myocardial infarction. N Engl J Med 1999;341:217–25.

4. Petric M, Dawson N, Murdoch D, et al. Failure of women's hearts. Circulation 1999;99:2334–41.

5. Moser DK. Heart failure in women. Crit Care Nurs Clin North Am 1997;9:511–9.

6. Johnstone D, Limacher M, Rousseau M, et al. Clinical characteristics of patients in studies of left ventricular dysfunction (SOLVD). Am J Cardiol 1992;70:894–900.

7. Shindler DM, Kostis JB, Jusuf S, et al. Diabetes mellitus: a predictor of morbidity and mortality in the Studies of Left Ventricular Dysfunction (SOLVD) Trials and Registry. Am J Cardiol 1996;77:1017–20.

8. Kannel WB, Belanger AJ. Epidemiology of heart failure. Am Heart J 1991;121:951–7.

9. Urbano-Marquez A, Estruch R, Fernandeez-Sola J, et al. The greater risk of alcoholic cardiomyopathy and myopathy in women compared with men. JAMA 1995;274:149–54.

10. Lampert MB, Lange RM. Peri-partum cardiomyopathy. Am Heart J 1995;130:860–70.

11. Kushwaha SS, Fallon JT, Fuster V. Restrictive cardiomyopathy. N Engl J Med 1997;336:267–76.

12. Feenstra J, Grobbel D, Remme W, Stricker B. Drug-induced heart failure. J Am Coll Cardiol 1999;33:1152–62.

13. Maron BJ. Hypertrophic cardiomyopathy. Lancet 1997;350:123–33.

14. Spirito P, Seidman CE, McKenna WJ, Maron BJ. The management of hypertrophic cardiomyopathy. N Engl J Med 1997;3369:775–85.

15. Carroll J, Carroll E, Feldman T, et al. Sex-associated differences in left ventricular function in aortic stenosis of the elderly. Circulation 1992;86:1099–107.

16. Aronow WS, Ahn C, Kronzon I. Normal left ventricular ejection fraction in older persons with congestive heart failure. Chest 1998;113:867–9.

17. Sabbah HN, Sharov VG. Apoptosis in heart failure. Prog Cardiovasc Dis 1998;40:549–62.

18. Levine B, Kalman J, Mayer L, et al. Elevated circulating levels of tumor necrosis factor in severe chronic heart failure. N Engl J Med 1990;323:236–41.

19. Mulder P, Richard V, Derumeaux G, et al. Role of endogenous endothelin in chronic heart failure:

effect of long-term treatment with an endothelin antagonist on survival, hemodynamics, and cardiac remodeling. Circulation 1997;96:1976–82.

20. Packer M, Cohn JN. Consensus recommendations for the management of chronic heart failure [abstract]. Am J Cardiol 1999;83:2A.

21. Stevenson LW, Perloff JP. The limited reliability of physical signs for estimating hemodynamics in chronic heart failure. JAMA 1989;261:884–98.

22. Tillisch J, Brunken R, Marshall R, et al. Rerversibility of cardiac wall-motion abnormalities predicted by positron emission tomography. N Engl J Med 1986; 314:884–8.

23. Richards DR, Mehra MR, Ventura HO, et al. Usefulness of peak oxygen consumption in predicting outcome of heart failure in women versus men. Am J Cardiol 1997;80:1235–6.

24. Silwa K, Studicky D, Candy G, et al. Randomized investigation of effects of pentoxifylline on left ventricular performance in idiopathic dilated cardiomyopathy. Lancet 1998;351:1091–3.

25. Drexler H. Endothelium as a therapeutic target in heart failure. Circulation 1998;98:2652–5.

26. Tyni-Lenne R, Gordon A, Europe E, Sylven C. Exercise-based rehabilitation improves skeletal muscle capacity, exercise tolerance, and quality of life in both women and men with chronic heart failure. J Card Fail 1998;1:9–17.

27. The Studies of Left Ventricular Dysfunction (SOLVD) Investigators. Effect of enalapril on survival in patients with reduced left ventricular ejection fractions and congestive heart failure. N Engl J Med 1991;325:293–302.

28. The CONSENSUS Trial Study Group. Effects of enalapril on mortality in severe congestive heart failure: results of the Cooperative North Scandinavian Enalapril Survival Study (CONSENSUS). N Engl J Med 1987;316:1429–35.

29. Pfeffer MA, Braunwald E, Moy LA, et al on behalf of the SAVE Investigators. Effect of captopril on mortality and morbidity in patients with left ventricular dysfunction after myoocardial infarction: results of the survival and ventricular enlargement trial. N Engl J Med 1995;333:1670–6.

30. The Studies of Left Ventricular Dysfunction (SOLVD) Investigators. Effect of enalapril on mortality and the development of heart failure in asymptomatic patients with reduced left ventricular ejection fractions. N Engl J Med 1992;327:685–91.

31. Garg R, Yusuf S. Overview of randomized trials of angiotensin-converting enzyme inhibitors on mortality and morbidity in patients with heart failure. JAMA 1995;273:1450–6.

32. Packer M, Poole-Wilson P, Armstrong P, et al. Comparative effects of low and high doses of the angiotensin-converting enzyme inhibitor lisinopril on morbidity and mortality in chronic heart failure. ATLAS Study Group. Circulation 1999;100:2312–8.

33. Communal C, Singh K, Pimentel DR, Colucci WS. Norepinephrine stimulates apoptosis in adult rat ventricular myocytes by activation of the α-adrenergic pathway. Circulation 1998;98:1329–34.

34. Lechat P, Packer M, Chalon S, et al. Clinical effects of α-adrenergic blockade in chronic heart failure: a meta-analysis of double-blind, placebo-controlled, randomized trials. Circulation 1998;98:1184–91.

35. Packer M, Bristow MR, Cohn JN, et al. The effect of carvedilol on morbidity and mortality in patients with chronic heart failure. N Engl J Med 1996;334: 1349–55.

36. Pih B, Zannad F, Remme W, Cody R. Metoprolol CR/XL Randomized Intervention Trial In Congestive Heart Failure (MERIT-HF). Lancet 1999;353:2001–7.

37. CIBIS II Investigators and Committees. The Cardiac Insufficiency Bisoprolol Study (CIBIS-II): a randomized trial. Lancet 1999;353:9–13.

38. Packer M, Gheorghiade M, Young JB, et al for the RADIANCE Study. Withdrawal of digoxin from patients with chronic heart failure treated with angiotensin-converting enzyme inhibitors. N Engl J Med 1993;329:1–7.

39. Guyatt GH, Sullivan MJ, Fallen EL, et al. A controlled trial of digoxin in congestive heart failure. Am J Cardiol 1988;61:371–5.

40. The Digitalis Investigation Group. The effect of digoxin on mortality and morbidity in patients with heart failure. N Engl J Med 1997;336:525–33.

41. Struthers AD. Angiotensin II receptor antagonists for heart failure. Heart 1998;80:5–6.

42. Gottlieb SS, Dickstein K, Fleck E, et al. Hemodynamic and neurohormonal effects of the angiotensin II antagonist losartan in patients with congestive heart failure. Circulation 1993;88:1602–9.

43. Pitt B, Segal R, Martinez FA, et al on behalf of ELITE Study Investigators. Randomized trial of losartan versus captopril in patients over 65 with heart failure (Evaluation of Losartan in the Elderly Study, ELITE). Lancet 1997;349:747–52.

44. Packer M, O'Connor CM, Ghali JK, et al for the Prospective Randomized Amlodipine Survival Evaluation Study Group. Effect of amlodipine on morbidity and mortality in severe chronic heart failure. N Engl J Med 1996;335:1107–14.

45. Pitt B, Zannad F, Remme WJ, et al. RALES Trial. The effect of spironolactone on morbidity and mortality in patients with severe failure. N Engl J Med 1999; 341:709–17.

46. Packer M, Carver JR, Rodeheffer RJ, et al for the PROMISE Study Research Group. Effect of oral milrinone on mortality in severe chronic heart failure. N Engl J Med 1991;325:1468–75.

47. Feldman AM, Bristow MR, Parmley WW, et al for the Vesnarinone Study Group. Effects of vesnarinone on morbidity and mortality in patients with heart failure. N Engl J Med 1993;329:149–55.

48. Luu M, Stevenson WG, Stevenson LW, et al. Diverse mechanisms of unexpected cardiac arrest in advanced heart failure. Circulation 1989;80:1675–80.

49. Stevenson WG, Stevenson LW, MiddleKauff HR, et al. Improving survival for patients with atrial fibrillation and advanced heart failure. J Am Coll Cardiol 1996;28:1458–63.

50. Amiodarone Trial Meta-analysis Investigators. Effect of prophylactic amiodarone on mortality after acute myocardial infarction and in congestive heart failure: meta-analysis of individual data from 6500 patients in randomized trials. Lancet 1997;350:1417–24.

51. Moss AJ, Hall WJ, Cannom DS, et al for the Multicenter Automatic Defibrillator Implantation Trial Investigators. Improved survival with an implanted defibrillator in patients with coronary disease at high risk for ventricular arrhythmias. N Engl J Med 1996;335:1933–40.

52. Natterson PD, Stevenson WG, Saxon LA, et al. Risk of arterial embolization in 224 patients awaiting cardiac transplantation. Am Heart J 1995;129:564–70.

53. Kobashigawa JA, Laks H, Marelli D, et al. The University of California at Los Angeles experience in heart transplantation. In: Cecka JM, Terasaki PI, editors. Clinical transplants. Los Angeles: UCLA Tissue Typing Laboratory; 1998. p. 303–10.

54. Esmore D, Keogh A, Spralt P, et al. Heart transplantation in females. J Heart Lung Transplant 1991;10: 335–41.

55. Fonarow GC, Stevenson LW, Walden JA, et al. Impact of a comprehensive heart failure management program on hospital readmission and functional status of patients with advanced heart failure. J Am Cardiol 1997;30:725–32.

34

CORONARY ARTERY DISEASE

Cynthia Thaik, MD, FACC

Coronary artery disease (CAD) is defined by a spectrum of clinical manifestations, including various forms of angina pectoris, myocardial infarction (MI), sudden cardiac death, and chronic ischemic heart disease. The pathophysiology underlying this syndrome involves acute or chronic disorder of myocardial function caused by insufficient blood supply due to narrowing of the coronary arteries (coronary arteriosclerosis), with severe obstruction leading to myocardial cell necrosis (myocardial infarction).[1] The basic mechanism underlying the atherosclerotic process involves chronic multifactorial injury to the vessel wall leading to the formation of an atherosclerotic plaque. The atherosclerotic plaque is characterized by atherogenic lipoproteins, macrophage foam cells, monocytes, and lipid-laden smooth muscle cells comprising the lipid core, surrounded by a thick layer of fibrous connective tissue capsule. It is usually the disruption of this atherosclerotic plaque by endothelial injury, with influx of blood components, platelet accumulation, and aggregation, that leads to nonocclusive or occlusive thrombus, resulting in the clinical syndrome of acute coronary ischemia and MI.[2]

It has long been believed that cardiovascular disease (CVD) is a disease of men. This belief is borne out by the fact that, until recently, most of the basic research and clinical trials on CVD focused exclusively on men. This prevailing false belief extends from the medical community to the lay public. A Gallup poll in 1995 surveying American women aged 45 to 75 years found that 4 of 5 women and 1 of 3 primary care clinicians were unaware that heart disease is the number one cause of death in women. Far more women are afraid of dying from breast cancer, even though only 1 in 26 women dies of breast cancer and 1 in 2 women dies of cardiovascular diseases, including CAD and stroke. In fact,

cardiovascular diseases claim more lives than the next 16 leading causes of death combined (Figure 34–1). According to the 1998 National Center for Health Statistics computations, if all forms of major CVD were eliminated, 10 years would be added to life expectancy in the United States, as opposed to a gain of 3 years for the elimination of all forms of cancer.[3]

Since 1984, CVD mortality in women has exceeded that of men, and this gap continues to widen (Figure 34–2). Although the CVD death rate for Americans is declining, the rate of decline in women is slower than that in men, with the smallest rate of decline observed in African American women.[4] In 1989 the age-adjusted death rate for CAD in black women was 28% higher than that for white women in the United States; death from MI for black women was twice that of white women.

Over 58 million Americans have some form of cardiovascular disease.[5] These diseases account for 5.9 million hospitalizations, 51.6 million clinician office visits, 4.4 million hospital outpatient visits, and 4.2 million hospital emergency room visits. The financial burden is tremendous, with the cost of CVD and strokes in 1998 estimated at 274 billion dollars. This estimate includes total health expenditures such as hospital and nursing home care, clinician and allied health services, pharmaceutical costs, and home health and other medical durables, as well as the indirect costs from lack of productivity due to the morbidity and mortality of these diseases.[3]

To assist the health care community to be more cognizant of the unique medical and psychosocial aspects of women's care, the American Heart Association has published a scientific statement on cardiovascular disease in women.[6] In 1993 the National Institutes of Health sponsored the Women's Health Initiative, the largest study funded

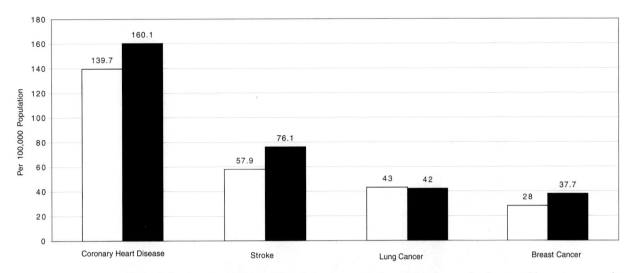

FIGURE 34–1. Age-adjusted death rates (2000 standard) for coronary heart disease, stroke, lung and breast cancers for white (☐) and black (■) females in the United States, 1997. Reproduced with permission from the Centers for Disease Control and Prevention/National Center for Health Statistics and the American Heart Association. 2000 heart and stroke statistical update. Dallas (TX): AHA; 1999. © Copyright American Heart Association.

by this institution to address the negligence of women's health by major federal research agencies. This important 10-year follow-up study is scheduled for completion in 2007 and will address prevention of heart disease, breast and colon cancers, and osteoporosis in 164,500 postmenopausal women, using three distinct interventions: a low-fat eating pattern, hormone replacement therapy, and calcium and vitamin D supplementation.[7]

PRESENTING SIGNS AND SYMPTOMS

Midsternal chest discomfort, occurring with activity or at rest, is the typical presentation of CAD and is the predominant symptom reported by both men and women. However women tend to have more associated atypical features related to their discomfort, and, often, these symptoms are attributed to arthritic pain, musculoskeletal discomfort, anxiety, psychological and emotional stress, heartburn, and other noncardiac etiologies. In community-based studies of patients hospitalized with confirmed acute MIs, there

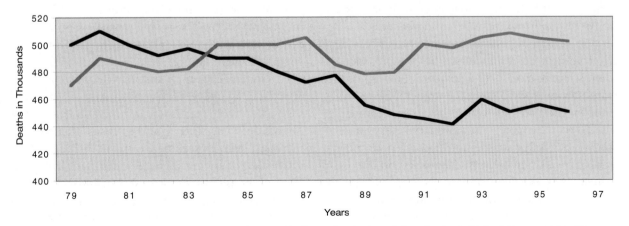

FIGURE 34–2. Cardiovascular disease mortality trends for males (—) and females (—), United States, 1979–97. (Reproduced with permission from the Centers for Disease Control and Prevention/National Center for Health Statistics and the American Heart Association. 2000 heart and stroke statistical update. Dallas (TX): AHA; 1999. © Copyright American Heart Association.)

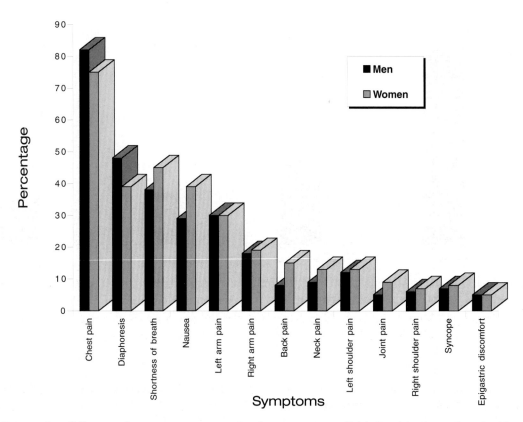

FIGURE 34–3. Sex differences in symptom presentation in acute myocardial infarction. Reproduced with permission from Goldberg RJ, O'Donnell C, Yarzebski J, et al. Sex differences in symptom presentation associated with acute myocardial infarction: a population-based perspective. Am Heart J 1998;136:189–95.

were no gender differences in the reporting of chest pain; however women were significantly more likely to complain of neck pain, back pain, jaw pain, abdominal discomfort, nocturnal dyspnea, nausea, or anorexia, and were less likely to report diaphoresis (Figure 34–3).[8,9] Commonly associated signs and symptoms for both men and women include fatigue, pain at rest, shortness of breath, and weakness.[10]

In general, chest discomfort is a far less discriminating feature in women for the presence of atherosclerotic disease. In a 26-year follow-up of the Framingham Study, 31% of the women initially evaluated for chest pain died of cardiac disease compared with 70% of the men.[11] The Coronary Artery Surgery Study (CASS) Registry demonstrated a poor angiographic correlation between chest pain and the presence of CAD with 50% women versus only 17% men evaluated for chest pain showing little or no CAD.[12] These findings contributed to the misperception that CAD affects predominantly the male population.

Women with established CAD tend to manifest anginal symptoms as their first presentation, whereas men are more likely to have an MI as their initial presentation. Women, however, have more unrecognized infarctions than do men. In patients presenting to the emergency room with symptoms suggestive of acute coronary syndrome, after adjusting for patients' demographic and clinical characteristics, men were twice as likely to have acute MI as were women.[13] This gender effect was eliminated in patients with ST segment elevations on electrocardiogram and in patients presenting with signs of congestive heart failure.

Women have their first manifestation of CAD at an older age, have more concomitant diseases, and seek attention later in the clinical course of the infarction.[14] Variables found to be associated with increased delay in seeking treatment include a medical history of angina, diabetes mellitus, or hypertension; older age; black race; seeking advice from a family member or a clinician; symptom onset on a weekday; and attempts at self treatment. Variables associated with reduced delay times are pain recognized as of cardiac origin, hemodynamic instability, severe chest pain, younger age, and consultation with a co-worker.[15] As delay in seeking treatment has a significant impact on the success of the therapeutic intervention and the subsequent prognosis, appropriate attention must be paid to the education of the public and the medical community about signs and symptoms of MI.

DIAGNOSIS

The first step in the diagnosis of coronary artery disease involves establishing it clinical likelihood based on the patient history, physical examination, and electrocardiography. Important factors to consider in this assessment include the age and sex of the patient, and the presence of known cardiac risk factors, such as hypertension, dyslipidemia, diabetes mellitus, a history of smoking, family history of CAD, physical inactivity, and obesity. Careful attention must be paid to the nature of the chest pain (ie, the location, severity, and duration) and associated symptoms. An approach to this evaluation of chest pain is described further in Chapter 32. Based on this information, the clinician should establish a pretest probability for the presence of CAD. It is this clinical likelihood of CAD (low, intermediate, or high) that helps to dictate whether noninvasive testing is required to establish the presence of disease or if more aggressive intervention is needed (Table 34–1).

Early detection and accurate diagnosis are the goals of diagnostic testing. These often are a more difficult task in women because of atypical presentation, lower pretest probability, lower age-matched prevalence of significant CAD, higher presence of single-vessel disease, and time lag in the onset of the disease. Given the higher morbidity and mortality observed in women after an MI, noninvasive testing must be sensitive and specific enough to provide accurate diagnosis early in the course of the disease, prior to the development of more severe clinical disease when therapeutic interventions have high risk and poor outcome.

The standard noninvasive test, which is widely available and relatively inexpensive, is the **exercise (stress) treadmill test**.[16] This test, unfortunately has a relatively low sensitivity and specificity, with a false-positive rate as high as 40% in women compared with 10% in men.[17–20] Given its limited accuracy, this test is best used to exclude functionally significant CAD in younger patients, with good exercise capacity, and a low clinical suspicion for the presence of CAD. Given its high false-positive

and false-negative rates, it is neither an adequate screening test nor a sensitive diagnostic test for women with multiple coronary risk factors or for women with clinical symptoms dictating a higher index of suspicion for the presence of CAD.

Stress echocardiography provides an added level of specificity by providing information regarding cardiac structures and function, with an anatomic analysis of the size and severity of the ischemia. As the functional abnormalities manifested are dependent on the degree of luminal narrowing and the resultant supply-and-demand mismatch, it is imperative that exercise testing be performed to the maximal tolerable level to identify the full degree of myocardium at risk. This is often the limiting feature of the test, as patients often are not able to achieve target heart rate, or the physician performing the test stops the exercise at the first sign of symptoms or wall motion abnormalities. Another difficulty with stress echocardiography is that visualization and imaging is inadequate in 10 to 15% of the patients due to factors such as obesity, large breasts or breast implants, and chronic obstructive pulmonary disease. This accounts for the rather wide range of sensitivity (70 to 93%) and specificity (37 to 96%) reported in the literature.[21–23] Stress echocardiography has widespread availability and convenience of performance in community based cardiology offices; however, the sensitivity, specificity, and diagnostic accuracy of the test reported in the tertiary care centers may not be achieved unless careful attention is paid to patient selection and strict analysis criteria are met.

Nuclear perfusion imaging is less subject to operator variability, especially with new computerized acquisition systems. The same requirement holds that an adequate treadmill stress test be performed to achieve the metabolic demands to induce flow limiting ischemia. However, because imaging usually is confined to medical centers with a trained nuclear radiologist and a cardiologist, there is greater standardization and quality control of the process and the interpretation. There are two frequently used radiotracers. The traditional tracer, thallium-201, is taken up by the myocardium via the potassium pump in proportion to the regional blood flow, and requires the integrity of a viable cell membrane. Nonviable myocardium (ie, a fixed scar demonstrating prior myocardial injury) does not take up the thallium tracer, whereas cells with reversible ischemia

---

TABLE 34–1. Factors Indicating Likelihood of Short-Term Nonfatal Myocardial Infarction or Death[*]

High likelihood of significant CAD

One or more of the following:

> Known history of CAD
>
> Symptoms definitely consistent with angina in a woman ≥70 yr of age
>
> Hemodynamic or ECG changes with pain
>
> Variant angina[†]
>
> ST increase or decrease ≥1 mm
>
> Symmetrical T wave inversion in multiple precordial leads

High likelihood of short-term death or nonfatal myocardial infarction

One or more of the following:

> Pulmonary edema
>
> Angina with any of the following features:
>
> > New or worsening murmur of mitral regurgitation
> >
> > Rest pain ≥20 min in duration, ongoing without relief
> >
> > S_3 or rales
> >
> > Hypotension

Intermediate likelihood of significant CAD

No high likelihood features and one or more of the following:

> Symptoms **definitely** consistent with angina in a woman <70 yr old
>
> Symptoms **probably** consistent with angina in a woman ≥70 yr old
>
> Diabetes mellitus
>
> Two or all of the following: hypertension, smoking, or elevated cholesterol
>
> ST depression 0.05–1 mm
>
> T wave inversion ≥1 mm in leads with dominant R waves

Intermediate likelihood of short-term death or nonfatal myocardial infarction

No high likelihood features and one or more of the following:

> Age >65 yr
>
> Q waves or ST depression ≥1 mm in multiple leads
>
> Angina with any of the following features:
>
> > Rest angina now resolved and intermediate or high likelihood of CAD
> >
> > Rest angina >20 min, better with rest or nitroglycerin
> >
> > Dynamic T wave changes
> >
> > Nocturnal angina
> >
> > New onset of angina that limits ordinary activity and an intermediate or high likelihood of CAD

Low likelihood of significant CAD

No high or intermediate likelihood features, but may have:

> Chest pain not typical of angina
>
> Only one of the following: hypertension, smoking, or elevated cholesterol
>
> Normal results on ECG or T wave flat or inverted <1 mm in leads with dominant R waves

Low likelihood of short-term death or nonfatal myocardial infarction

No high or intermediate likelihood features, but may have:

> Increasing angina frequency, severity, or duration or angina provoked by a lower degree of activity than that previously required
>
> New-onset angina within 2 wk–2 mo
>
> Normal or unchanged results on ECG

---

[*]In women with symptoms suggestive of unstable angina.
[†]Rest pain with reversible ECG changes without subsequent enzyme evidence of acute myocardial infarction.
CAD = coronary artery disease; ECG = electrocardiogram.
Adapted from Braunwald E, Mark DB, Jones RH, et al. Unstable angina diagnosis and management, clinical practice guideline, number 10. Rockville (MD): Agency for Health Care Policy and Research, National Heart, Lung and Blood Institute, US Department of Health and Human Services, Public Health Service; 1994. AHCPR Publication No.:94-0602.

manifest a deficiency of tracer injected at peak exercise but show redistribution uptake during delay imaging. There is a reported sensitivity of 84 to 90% and a specificity of 75 to 87% in women.[24] The diagnostic accuracy of the thallium imaging is limited by scatter and attenuation, which obscure the inferior wall in obese patients, and by breast attenuation artifact, which limits the visualization of the anterior wall. Technetium 99m sestamibi, because of its higher energy emission, has less scatter and attenuation artifact than does thallium. Technetium does not redistribute within the cells and requires a second injection of the tracer to obtain rest images. In addition to evaluating regional blood flow, technetium 99m sestamibi can evaluate wall motion abnormalities and left ventricular ejection fraction using gated single-photon emission computer tomographic (SPECT) imaging. These added features improve the specificity of technetium compared with thallium, especially when SPECT imaging is used to improve diagnostic accuracy.[25]

For patients unable to perform an adequate exercise protocol, either because of limited exercise capacity, deconditioned state, obesity, or physical limitation, various pharmacologic stress tests are available. Dobutamine is most often used with echocardiographic imaging to increase myocardial workload by increasing heart rate and force of contractility. Drugs such as dipyridamole and adenosine often are used with nuclear perfusion imaging to achieve a hyperemic state, with differential perfusion secondary to coronary vasodilatory state (coronary steal phenomenon). Dipyridamole side effects (ie, flushing, hypotension, and shortness of breath) occur more frequently in women. Pharmacologic means are more often necessary in women (55 to 60%) than in men (40%), probably due to limited exercise capacity.[20]

Other noninvasive tests that are not widely applicable include **electron-beam computed tomography (EBCT)**, **magnetic resonance imaging (MRI)**, **and positron emission tomography (PET)**. Electron-beam CT uses a sweeping electron beam that acquires images 10 times faster than does the fastest slip-ring CT system; it therefore allows imaging of a beating heart. The system quantifies coronary calcification in the major coronary vessels. The absence of coronary calcification has important prognostic implications to exclude the presence of significant CAD. Early imaging of calcium deposits in the coronary arteries can allow aggressive preventive measures to be implemented, particularly with respect to lipid modification. The differences in prevalence and extent of coronary calcium appear to parallel the clinical incidence of CAD in both men and women, with one study showing the prevalence of calcium in women to be half that of men until the age of 60 years, when this difference diminishes.[26] A review of several studies suggests that EBCT sensitivity ranges between 80 and 100% and specificity ranges between 47 and 62%. The American College of Cardiology and the American Heart Association still consider the role of EBCT scanning to be controversial, with insufficient data to support the use of EBCT as a screening tool in assessing risk of developing CAD.[27]

Cardiac MRI can give functional information on cardiac valves and chambers by gated CINE acquisition. Magnetic resonance angiography to assess coronary anatomy and techniques to determine sufficiency of myocardial blood and oxygen flow (and therefore viability) are being developed and improved upon continually. Magnetic resonance angiography is not widely applicable at this time. Scans with PET are useful in the evaluation of chronic ischemic heart disease to distinguish irreversibly injured myocardium from viable, but hypoperfused, hibernating myocardium with reversible contractile dysfunction. Myocardial perfusion imaging with PET has demonstrated enhanced sensitivity and specificity compared with SPECT studies for detection of CAD, leading some authors to refer to this test as "the woman's test for CAD."[28] However the expense of purchasing a PET camera, and the expertise required to run a cyclotron have limited use of PET to academic centers, and have led many to question its cost effectiveness compared with other more readily available diagnostic tests.

Coronary angiography remains the gold standard in the assessment of CAD. However, the anatomic presence of atherosclerotic plaques does not necessarily correlate with clinical syndromes of coronary ischemia. In fact myocardial infarction is more likely to result from plaque rupture of a previously stable seemingly insignificant 30% lesion than from a chronically stable more significant plaque, which is more likely to cause chronic, but stable, angina. Therefore, it is imperative to keep in mind that coronary angiogram provides a static picture of the coronary anatomy at that point in time and cannot necessarily predict future coronary events. This fact underlies the importance of risk factor modification in any patient displaying even slight evidence of coronary atherosclerosis.

There remains a divergence of opinions, even among experts, regarding the indications for cardiac catheterization in older women with suspected CAD. Figure 34–4 is an algorithm for assessing the need for coronary angiography. Much has been quoted in the literature regarding the apparent gender bias in the application of coronary angiography. Various studies showed a two- to 10-fold lower

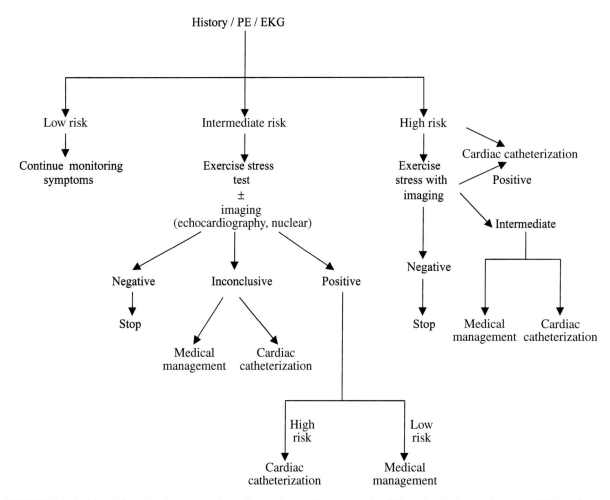

FIGURE 34–4. Algorithm for the evaluation of a patient with chest pain. PE = physical examination; EKG = electro-cardiography.

*Imaging should be strongly considered in all postmenopausal women, as well as women with other cardiac risk factors

referral rate for women following an abnormal result of nuclear stress testing.[29,30] This referral bias is partly due to the misperception among physicians that chest pain in women carries a more benign prognosis (based on the Framingham Study, which showed that 86% of women presenting with chest pain did not suffer an MI).[11] It is now believed that the Framingham population included many women with noncardiac chest pain.

The misperception regarding the benign nature of chest pain was further supported by angiographic studies that showed a high presence of normal coronary anatomy (41 to 48%) in women referred for catheterization.[31,32] Given this high rate of normalcy, other authors have suggested that the lower referral rate for angiography is appropriate in women, given the significantly lower pretest probability of coronary disease and the lower rate of pos-

itive exercise test results.[33,34] In fact the apparent gender difference in case management might reflect overuse of angiography in men at low risk for coronary disease and an appropriate conservative treatment in women. Once a diagnosis of CAD is established, revascularization procedures, including percutaneous transluminal coronary angioplasty and coronary artery bypass grafting, are used with equal frequency in men and women.[32]

Normal results of a coronary angiography do not exclude the presence of myocardial ischemia. Women are more likely than are men to have coronary spasm or clinical syndrome X as the cause of their chest pain, and myocardial ischemia in the absence of major stenosis of the coronary arteries. Variant (Prinzmetal's) angina refers to a syndrome of cardiac pain that often occurs at rest, with associated ST segment elevation rather than depression on the electrocardiogram; the condition resolves spontaneously or when treated with antianginals. Coronary artery spasm is the underlying mechanism for cardiac ischemia and can occur in the presence or absence of obstructive coronary lesions.[35] "Syndrome X" describes symptoms of angina pectoris with positive noninvasive evidence of ischemia but normal results on coronary angiograms and no other cardiac cause (eg, epicardial coronary spasm or ventricular hypertrophy) for the angina. It is speculated that increases in microvascular tone in the prearteriolar coronary vessels might be the cause of the myocardial ischemia.[36] Although symptoms associated with ischemia are present in these two conditions, the prognosis for these conditions is far better than is that for atherosclerotic CAD.

TREATMENT IN THE OUTPATIENT SETTING

The initial treatment and urgency of establishing a definitive diagnosis in a patient presenting with chest pain are determined by the primary physician's assessment of the clinical likelihood of CAD and the perceived severity of the disease. Chest pain can be categorized as noncardiac pain, new-onset angina, chronic stable angina, unstable angina, or acute myocardial ischemia/injury. Given that the clinical history in women is more difficult to assess and qualify, unless the symptoms are highly atypical or have another obvious diagnosis, the patient should be referred for a diagnostic evaluation and/or referred to a cardiologist.

The therapies that have been shown to lower the risk of subsequent mortality in patients with established CAD include aspirin, cholesterol-lowering medication, smoking cessation, and exercise. In addition, the therapies that have been shown to lower the risk of recurrent MI and to prolong survival after an MI are ß-blockers and angiotensin converting enzyme (ACE) inhibitors. There are limited roles for nitrates and calcium channel blockers for symptom relief. In treatment of unstable angina and acute MI, intravenous heparin, subcutaneous low-molecular weight heparin, glycoprotein IIb/IIIa receptor antagonist, and thrombolytic therapy confer significant benefit. All patients with unstable angina or MI should be evaluated and considered for catheter-based revascularization or coronary artery bypass graft (CABG).

Aspirin should be recommended to patients presenting with chest pain, unless the clinician is convinced that the pain is of a noncardiac etiology or there is an absolute contraindication. In patients with CAD, aspirin confers a 51% reduction in risk of death, a 48% reduction in risk of myocardial infarction, a 23% reduction in vascular mortality, and a 46% reduction in nonfatal strokes.[37–39] The Physicians' Health Study showed that regular use of aspirin decreased the risk for MI by approximately half in healthy male physicians with no history of CVD, suggesting a potential role for aspirin in the primary prevention of heart disease.[40] However, another study concluded that evidence was insufficient to recommend for or against prophylactic aspirin use for primary prevention of MI in asymptomatic men or women.[41]

There are a few absolute contraindications to the use of aspirin. These include history of an allergic anaphylactic reaction, severe bleeding diathesis, and active peptic ulcer disease with recent documented gastrointestinal bleeding requiring transfusion or surgery. Patients with minor symptoms of dyspepsia or even heme-occult-positive stool usually can tolerate low-dose aspirin (81 mg) when combined with H_2 blockers, such as ranitidine or famotidine, or antacids and careful monitoring. Low-dose aspirin confers the needed benefit in chronic stable angina, however full-dose aspirin (160 to 324 mg) should be administered to patients with unstable angina or acute MI.

ß-blockers limit myocardial oxygen demand by decreasing heart rate, blood pressure, and contractility. ß-Blockers improve anginal symptoms and limit the risk of unstable angina and MI. Theoretic benefits after MI include antiarrhythmic effects and prevention of sudden death, reduction in infarct size, attenuation of the remodeling process, and reduction of ventricular wall tension. ß-blockers have been studied in 50 clinical trials involving 50,000 patients with MI. Pooled results show a 23% overall reduction in mortality, with confidence intervals of 16 to 30%.[42] Early ß-blocker therapy confer a 15% reduction in mortality within 24 hours after an MI.[43] Cardioselective ß-blockers (eg, acebutolol, atenolol, betaxolol, bisoprolol, celiprolol, esmolol, metoprolol) should be used preferentially over ß-blockers with intrinsic sympathomimetic activity (eg, carteolol, penbutolol, pindolol). Commonly used dosages are metoprolol 25 to 50 mg bid or atenolol 50 to

100 mg qd. Side effects of ß-blockers include fatigue, bradycardia, heart block, hypotension, heart failure, bronchospasm, altered glucose metabolism, impotence, depression, peripheral vasoconstriction, claudication, and Raynaud's phenomenon.

ACE inhibitors prevent the formation of angiotensin II, a potent vasoconstrictor and stimulator of aldosterone secretion. They have been shown to prolong survival post myocardial infarction and should be started within 24 hours of presentation.[44] ACE inhibitors limit postinfarction left ventricular dilatation and hypertrophy and improve symptoms and mortality from heart failure. They also have been shown to reverse endothelial dysfunction and to lower the risk of atherosclerosis. ACE inhibitors are contraindicated in patients with severe hypotension, or a history of angioedema. They should be used with caution in patients with renal artery stenosis. Side effects include hypotension, cough, skin rash, angioedema, dysgeusia, proteinuria, hyperkalemia, glomerulonephritis, neutropenia, and agranulocytopenia.

Nitrates cause arterial, arteriolar, and collateral vessel dilatation and venodilatation, thus improving myocardial oxygen delivery and lowering metabolic demand. Nitrates also inhibit platelet aggregation and abolish paradoxic vasoconstriction due to endothelial dysfunction. Sublingual nitroglycerin tablets or spray (0.2 to 0.4 mg) repeated 5 minutes apart for three doses can relieve pain from myocardial ischemia. Intravenous nitroglycerin is available for titration at 10 μg/min every 5 minutes until symptom relief or until limited by hypotension (systolic blood pressure < 90). Chronic prophylactic therapy is available in oral (Isordil 10 to 40 mg tid, Imdur 30 to 120 mg qd) or transdermal (ointment or patch) form. Tolerance to nitrate therapy can be prevented by a nitrate-free period. Nitrates do not have a mortality benefit. Side effects include flushing, hypotension, headache, and reflex tachycardia. Nitrates should be avoided in patients with critical aortic stenosis or hypertrophic obstructive cardiomyopathy.

Calcium channel blockers reduce myocardial contractility and promote vasodilatation resulting in a lower blood pressure and improved coronary blood flow and, thus, a significant improvement in myocardial supply-and-demand mismatch. Calcium channel blockers have been studied in over 20,000 patients with MI, with pooled results showing no mortality benefit. Subgroup analysis showed that short-acting dihydropyridines, such as nifedipine increase mortality and re-infarction,[45] whereas diltiazem and verapamil have no mortality benefit but reduce re-infarction by 21%.[42,43] Diltiazem and verapamil should not be used in patients with significant left ventricular dysfunction. Use of calcium channel blockers should be reserved for patients with refractory angina not responsive to nitrates, ß-blockers, or revascularization procedures. Side effects include hypotension, heart block, flushing, headache, peripheral edema, gingival hyperplasia, and constipation.

Any patient with a change in the nature, severity, or frequency of her symptoms should be referred to a specialist for further evaluation. The severity of presentation of unstable angina can predict the patient's short-term risk of death or nonfatal MI. The Agency for Health Care Policy and Research has published guidelines for the diagnosis and risk stratification of patients with symptoms suggestive of unstable angina (see Table 34–1).[46] Based on the patient's clinical history, physical examination, and electrocardiogram results, the physician can make a decision regarding the safety of an outpatient work-up versus the necessity of an expedited inpatient evaluation.

Heparin should be administered to patients with high-risk unstable angina and considered for patients at intermediate risk.[47] Once initiated, it should be continued for 3 to 5 days, unless revascularization has been achieved. There are two recent studies showing greater efficacy of low–molecular weight heparin in preventing recurrent angina and MI, with the option to maintain therapy long-term in an outpatient setting.[48,49] Glycoprotein IIb/IIIa receptor antagonists have been approved for use in unstable angina with or without percutaneous coronary intervention, and in MI with catheter-based intervention. This molecule selectively inhibits the platelet glycoprotein surface receptor, preventing platelet aggregation and thrombus formation.

Patients at high risk for significant CAD should be referred promptly for **cardiac catheterization**. Those at intermediate risk may be referred for catherization or an exercise imaging study. Those at low risk can be managed medically (see Figure 34–4). After excluding patients with definite unstable angina or MI, the respective disease prevalence in the 8,157 patients in the CASS who underwent angiography with definite angina, probable angina, and nonspecific chest pain was 93%, 66%, and 14%

in men and 72%, 36%, and 6% in women ($p < .001$). Left main disease ($> 50\%$) or significant ($> 70\%$) three-vessel disease occurred in more than 50% of middle-aged men and older women with definite angina and in more than 50% of men over age 60 years with probable angina, but it was found in less than 2% of men and less than 1% of women with nonspecific chest pain, regardless of age.[12] Those patients with left main or significant three-vessel disease with depressed left ventricular function should be referred for CABG. Patients with significant one- or two-vessel proximal disease should be referred for percutaneous transluminal coronary angioplasty (PTCA) or CABG, depending on the nature, complexity, and location of the lesion. Those with more diffuse or distal disease might be successfully managed medically, depending on the severity of the symptoms.

Patients presenting with an acute ST elevation MI should immediately receive oxygen supplementation, full-dose aspirin, intravenous ß-blocker, and antithrombotic therapy. Intravenous nitroglycerin and morphine sulfate may be used for the relief of symptoms; however, these drugs do not confer mortality benefit. The decision of whether to proceed with reperfusion therapy with thrombolytic therapy (tissue plasminogen activator, streptokinase, anistreplase) or primary PTCA should be made by the cardiologist. Primary PTCA is the preferred mode of reperfusion if facilities and personnel are readily available. However, as myocardial salvage is dependent on the speed of reperfusion, if there is a foreseeable delay in performing the procedure, thrombolytic therapy should be administered.

PROGNOSIS

Compared with their age-matched male counterparts, women have a worse prognosis after MI; there are higher in-hospital and 1-year morbidity and mortality rates. Multivariate analyses have shown that gender alone has no independent predictive value. Rather, variables such as older age at presentation and greater comorbidities (including a higher incidence of diabetes mellitus and systemic hypertension), later presentation in the course of infarction, less aggressive intervention, and greater incidence of heart failure are responsible for the worse outcomes seen in women.[50,51] These factors, along with smaller body size and smaller coronary artery lumen dimensions,

are responsible for higher operative mortality, less graft patency, and greater rates of recurrent angina, perioperative MI, congestive heart failure, incomplete revascularization, and need for revascularization after CABG in women. After PTCA, success rates and survival rates are similar in both sexes, with no difference observed in subsequent MI rates. Women are more likely to have recurrent severe angina but are less likely to undergo CABG.[52]

In an evaluation of 5,362 patients with suspected CAD, the 1- and five-year mortality rates were 11% and 25.6% in men and 10% and 25.7% in women, respectively. The development of MI occurred in more men than women (25% versus 16%, $p < .001$); whereas women had a higher prevalence of known congestive heart failure and hypertension.[53,54] In the Framingham study, 1-year mortality after a first myocardial infarction was 20% in men versus 45% in women. A second MI occurred in 13% of men and 40% of women within 5 years of the first infarction.[55] The Myocardial Infarction Triage and Intervention Project Registry found that women were half as likely to undergo acute catheterization, angioplasty, thrombolysis, or CABG than were men, and had almost twice the risk of hospital mortality.[56]

Sudden death is a prominent feature of coronary heart disease in both men and women. Women with CAD have a risk of sudden death that is half that of men with CAD. The presence of heart failure increases the sudden death risk of women by fivefold, but this risk remains a fraction (one-fourth) of the risk in men with heart failure or CAD. The risk of sudden death increases incrementally with a greater burden of coronary risk factors; however, this risk is always less in women than in men. Sudden death occurring in the absence of prior overt heart disease is more frequent in women than in men.[57]

In a single-institution study of outcome post CABG in 1,979 women and 6,972 men, there was a higher operative mortality in women than in men (2.7% versus 1.9%, $p = .2$). This difference was more marked in patients with left main or three-vessel disease and an abnormal left ventricular function (5.4% versus 2.8%, $p = .009$). The 5-, 10-, 15-, and 18-year survival rates for women versus men were 86% versus 88%, 70% versus 73%, 50% versus 54%, and 37% versus 42%, respectively ($p = .03$). Women were older, with a higher incidence of

---

TABLE 34–2. Pulmonary Prevention: Coronary Artery Disease Risk Reduction*

Lifestyle factors

Stop smoking

Engage in ≥ 30 min of moderate-intensity physical activity most or all days

Eat a low-fat and low-cholesterol diet (≥ 30% fat, 8–10% saturated fat, < 300 mg/d cholesterol)

Limit salt intake (≤ 6 g/d)

Maintain dietary fiber (25–30 g/d from foods)

Consume ≥ 5 servings of fresh fruits and vegetables daily

Limit alcohol intake to ≤ 114 mL wine, 341 mL beer, or 43 mL spirits daily

Maintain a healthy weight (BMI 18.5–24.9 kg/m²); waist circumference < 88 cm

Avoid social isolation, treat depression and anxiety

Medical risk factors

Blood pressure screening at every visit (< 140/90 = acceptable, < 120/80 optimal)

Blood cholesterol screening every 5 yr if normal, more frequently if not

(LDL level < 160 mg/dL is goal for women without other cardiac risk factors)

Diabetes screening for women at high risk (family history; personal history of gestational diabetes; hypertension; African American, Latina, Native American, or Asian-Pacific Islander; age ≥ 45 yr, HDL level ≥ 35 mg/dL, triglyceride levels ≥ 250 mg/dL, delivery of baby > 4 kg, prior history of elevated blood sugar, or abnormal glucose tolerance test)

Pharmacologic interventions

Hormone replacement therapy (role unclear in primary prevention)

Aspirin (consider–role in women without known CAD still unclear)

Avoid OCPs in women over 35 yr who smoke; counsel younger women who use OCPs to stop smoking

---

*For women at average risk for CAD and no known CAD. All interventions listed here are discussed in detail in chapters elsewhere in this text.

BMI = body mass index; LDL = low-density lipoprotein; HDL=high-density lipoprotein; CAD = coronary artery disease; OCP = oral contraceptive pill.

Adapted from Mosca et al[62] and American Diabetes Association.[67]

---

diabetes, systemic hypertension, and unstable angina, and with a smaller body surface area and smaller coronary artery lumens. More men were smokers, and men had a higher incidence of prior MI, previous bypass surgery, and greater extent of CAD and severe left ventricular dysfunction. The differences were small but statistically significant, with patient-related factors, rather than gender, being independent predictors of worse outcome and survival.[58] In the CASS Registry, the 15-year survival rate was 50% in men and 49% in women ($p = .53$) with initial medical management, and 52% in men and 48% in women ($p = .004$) with initial surgical treatment. Much of the difference in the long-term surgical survival can be explained by higher operative mortality in women (2.5% of men versus 5.3% of women, $p < .0001$).[59]

PREVENTION AND SCREENING

Risk factors for coronary artery disease are well established, with recommendations for both primary and secondary prevention of CAD supported by compelling data from epidemiologic studies and randomized clinical trials (Table 34–2).[60–62] In light of the poor prognosis in women once CAD is established, early screening, assessment, and management of risk factors for CAD have been shown to be cost effective.[63] Despite the volumes of published data supporting risk factor modification and screening, clinicians have been woefully lacking in addressing these issues, particularly with women. Data shows that the smoking rate is declining less in women than in men and the prevalence of obesity is increasing, with 25% of women reporting no regular sustained physical activity. In middle-aged and older women, 52% have hypertension and 40% have hypercholesterolemia.[62]

In the Centers for Disease Control and Prevention National Ambulatory Medical Care Survey, women were counseled less often than were men about exercise, nutrition, and weight reduction in routine office visits.[64] In the multicenter Heart and Estrogen/Progestin Replacement Study (HERS), only 10% of women with documented CAD had a baseline low-density lipoprotein (LDL) cholesterol level below the National Cholesterol Education Program (NCEP) guideline of 100 mg/dL.[65]

The 27th Bethesda Conference sponsored by the American College of Cardiology met in 1995 to address the issue of risk factor management for the prevention of coronary disease events.[63] Based on the clinical epidemiologic data, the trial data, and basic research, these experts proposed four categories of risk factors:

1. Category I—risk factors for which interventions have been proven to reduce the incidence of CAD events. These risk factors include cigarette smoking, a high level of LDL cholesterol, hypertension, left ventricular hypertrophy, and thrombogenic factors, such as abnormalities of thrombin and fibrinogen.
2. Category II—risk factors for which interventions are likely to lower CAD events. Diabetes falls into this category because the benefit of therapy to lower vascular risk is less well established, despite the proven causal relationship between diabetes and atherosclerosis. Other risk factors in this category include physical inactivity, low levels of high density lipoprotein (HDL) cholesterol and obesity.
3. Category III—risk factors clearly associated with an increase in CAD risk, which, if modified, might lower the incidence of CAD events. Psychosocial factors, oxidative stress, and high levels of triglycerides, lipoprotein(a), and homocysteine are included in this group.
4. Category IV—risk factors associated with increased risk but that cannot be modified or whose modification would be unlikely to change the incidence of CAD events. Age, gender, and family history fall into this category.

Several unique aspects of risk factor modification are important for women. Diabetes mellitus is a particularly powerful risk factor, negating the protective effect of estrogen in premenopausal women. Diabetes increases CAD risk by three- to sevenfold in women, compared with two- to threefold in men, due to its potentiation of the deleterious effect of lipid abnormalities and hypertension. A patient with diabetes has the same risk and prognosis for an MI as does a patient with a history of CAD or a prior MI. The current recommendation by the American Diabetes Association is to treat patients with diabetes to a target LDL level < 100 mg/dL, the same target as for those patients with established CAD.[66] A low level of HDL cholesterol appears to be a stronger predictive risk factor for CAD in older women than in men of the same age group. There are also some data suggesting that high triglyceride levels might be an isolated risk factor for CAD in women, independent of HDL levels.

Estrogen deficiency and the postmenopausal state is an important risk factor to consider in all older patients. Previously, the NCEP recommended the use of estrogen replacement therapy (ERT) prior to the initiation of lipid-lowering drugs. However, in light of the recent HERS Study, which failed to show an overall mortality difference with ERT in women with established CAD due to a higher thrombotic risk in the first 2 years of the therapy, HMG-CoA (3-hydroxy-3-methylglutaryl coenzyme A) reductase inhibitors should be the first-line approach to secondary prevention and lipid modification. This recommendation also applies to the primary prevention of CAD in women without established CAD. There are volumes of epidemiologic data supporting the cardioprotective and mortality benefits of ERT, for which no randomized trials have shown benefits.

PREGNANCY

Many cardiovascular changes occur during pregnancy that can impact on underlying CAD. The hemodynamic effects of pregnancy include an increase in blood volume, heart rate, and cardiac output. Blood pressure tends to fall during the first and second trimesters prior to returning to pre-pregnancy level before term; this leads to symptoms of postural hypotension and syncope. Some women are predisposed to hypertension and preeclampsia late in their pregnancy. During labor, stroke volume increases. This effect, combined with anxiety and pain, can lead to marked increases in blood pressure. Immediately post partum, there is an increase in blood volume and venous return, due to the expelling of blood from the contracting uterus and the release of the mechanical obstruction on the vena cava. In combination these effects can provoke ischemia in patients with significant CAD. However, CAD is rare in women of childbearing age.

Pregnancy leads to a hypercoagulable state due to an increase in blood clotting factors, fibrinogen, and platelet turnover, and a decrease in the deformity of red cells, combined with the local static effects. This hypercoagulable state predisposes the pregnant women to coronary, pulmonary, and deep venous thrombosis. The hypercoagulable state is particularly accentuated if a woman continues to smoke during her pregnancy. The risk of an MI is increased during pregnancy, and the risk of mortality of an infant born to mothers who have suffered an MI during the pregnancy is increased.[67]

If a pregnant woman presents with an acute MI, certain modifications must be made to the usual acute MI care. Although aspirin and heparin are safe to use, thrombolytic therapy is clearly contraindicated. Nitrates and ß-blockers can be used, especially in this emergent setting, although there are some concerns about intrauterine growth retardation with ß-blocker use. Angiotensin converting enzyme inhibitors are contraindicated due to their association with spontaneous abortions and fetal anomalies. If the patient presents with a small MI without evidence of ongoing ischemia or hemodynamic instability, this patient should be treated conservatively, with more definitive therapy planned for after the delivery. However if the patient is having a large infarction, has unstable angina, or is hemodynamically unstable, then coronary angiography and intervention must be used, despite the risk of radiation exposure to the fetus (of special concern during the first trimester). Precautions may be taken by using lead shields and minimizing the exposure time. In rare incidences in which the mother's life is at stake, CABG might be indicated. The risk of significant morbidity and mortality to the fetus is as high as 50%, but is lessened by shorter bypass time and good postoperative condition of the mother. Whenever possible, surgery should be postponed until the fetus is viable, with delivery taking place prior to bypass surgery.

MENOPAUSE

The incidence of CAD rises dramatically in women 10 to 15 years after menopause, due to the hypoestrogenemic state and associated changes in the lipoprotein profile. The Framingham Study showed a 10-fold increase in the incidence of coronary events in women older than age 55 years, such that the risk equals or exceeds that of men.[11] Menopausal status influences the development of CAD independently of age. After menopause, the total and LDL cholesterol and triglyceride levels increase, whereas the HDL cholesterol level tends to decrease. There is also evidence of a possible shift in the lipid composition to produce smaller-density LDL particles and increased concentration of lipoprotein(a) in the menopausal women.[68,69] There appears to be an enhanced stress-induced cardiovascular response with higher ambulatory blood pressures and a higher prevalence of hypertension in the postmenopausal woman. In addition, menopause increases fibrinogen factor VII and tissue plasminogen activator inhibitor 1 plasma concentration, which may cause a prothrombotic effect.[70]

USE OF ORAL CONTRACEPTIVE PILLS AND HORMONE REPLACEMENT

Use of combination oral contraceptive pills (OCPs) has been linked to venous thrombosis, strokes, and MIs.[71,72] In response to epidemiologic research that illustrates these links, newer OCPs have been developed with lower estrogen doses and different steroid contents (third-generation progestins), resulting in a lowering of venous thromboembolism and MI risks.[73,74] The relative risk is higher in women who smoke cigarettes; OCPs should not be prescribed for any women with established CAD, or who have significant risk factors for CAD, or who are over the age of 35 years.

Several mechanisms have been proposed to explain the increased risk of MI in women using OCPs, including damage to the arterial intima leading to atherosclerosis, adverse effects on lipid profile, and increased thrombogenicity. It generally is believed that the increased risk of MI is solely a thrombotic event, with the effects on the arterial walls and lipids being weak contributing factors. This belief is supported by studies that demonstrate that risk of an MI returns to baseline levels soon after stopping OCP use; otherwise, one would expect increased risk from intimal damage and atherosclerotic plaque formation to persist. Lowering the dosage of ethinyl estradiol within the OCP favorably lowers the hemostatic balance of the coagulation and the fibrinolytic system.

Use of OCPs increases systolic and diastolic pressures slightly, but this is probably of little clinical significance. The estrogen component of OCPs increases fasting serum triglyceride levels in a dose-dependent manner. It remains to be determined whether elevated triglycerides alone is an independent risk factor for coronary events in women. Nonetheless, OCPs are contraindicated in women with moderate hypertriglyceridemia (200 to 500 mg/dL). Use of OCPs causes little change in the LDL level, however, they have been shown to induce compositional changes and to shift the particle distribution to the smaller dense particles.[75] It is the androgenic effects of progestins that lower the protective HDL cholesterol concentration and elevate the total cholesterol level. The atherogenic effects of these adverse alterations in serum lipoproteins is minimized when a potent estrogen is coadministered. Use of OCP is contraindicated in patients with severe hypercholesterolemia (>300 mg/dL) and should be used with high caution in those patients with moderate cholesterol levels and other cardiac risk factors. Use of OCPs alters carbohydrate metabolism by decreasing insulin sensitivity. This minor effect does not induce clinical diabetes; however, the increased insulin level might adversely affect the vascular endothelium, predisposing it to thrombosis and atherogenesis.[76]

There is a wealth of epidemiologic cross-sectional studies, case-control studies, and prospective studies demonstrating possible beneficial effects of hormone replacement therapy (HRT). Non-randomized studies have suggested reduction in the risk of death from cardiovascular and cerebrovascular complications by up to 50%. The beneficial effects include favorable modification of the lipid profile, reduction of severe coronary stenosis in various angiographic studies, and reduction of the relative risk of MI to 0.3 (confidence interval

0.2 to 0.6) in current HRT users compared with nonusers in the Nurses' Health Study and other trials.[77-79] The recent HERS has called into question the mortality benefit of ERT in women with established CAD. This appears to be due to the thrombogenic effect of estrogen, which appears to be most prominent in the period immediately after initiation of HRT.[80]

Several mechanisms have been suggested to explain possible cardioprotective effect of estrogen after menopause. In the postmenopausal woman, estrogen increases HDL and decreases LDL levels. Estrogen inhibits LDL oxidation, thereby reducing atheroma formation. Although the beneficial effect on lipid profile is an important contributing factor, its role was overstated in earlier reports. The lipoprotein effect probably accounts for only 30% of the observed reduction in the incidence of CAD in estrogen users.[81] Estrogen has direct and indirect effects on the different vascular layers, reducing peripheral vascular resistance and increase blood flow by inducing the release of vasoactive substances such a prostacyclin and endothelial-derived relaxing factor (nitric oxide). Estrogen has been reported to decrease arterial LDL uptake and/or degradation and to decrease arterial smooth muscle cell migration and proliferation, thereby modulating the atherosclerotic process.[82] The use of estrogen to prevent CAD (pulmonary prevention) is currently controversial. Data from a large randomized study (the Women's Health Institute) should be available in the next few years.

CONCLUSION

When addressing women's health issues, both the medical and lay community tend to focus on matters that effect exclusively or primarily women. In the past, less emphasis was placed on diseases and conditions that are common in both men and women. Even though CAD affects both genders, there are gender-specific issues that make the presentation, diagnosis, and treatment of CAD unique for women. Despite our vast knowledge, much still needs to be learned about the biology and pathophysiology of CAD in women. Increasing public and clinician awareness of the importance of CAD in women is the first step toward achieving this goal.

RESOURCES

The American Heart Association
7272 Greenville Avenue
Dallas, Texas 75231
Telephone: 1-800-242-8721
Web site: www.americanheart.org

The American Heart Association is considered the most objective, comprehensive, and current source of information on cardiovascular risk and diseases. It is useful for both clinicians and patients.

The National Heart, Lung, and Blood Institute
PO Box 3105
Bethesda, Maryland 20824-0105
Telephone: (301) 496-4236
Web site: www.nhlbi.nih.gov

The NHLBI, a division of the National Institutes of Health, has sponsored the periodic generation of guidelines for management of cholesterol and other coronary artery disease risk factors. Information for both clinicians and patients, including patient education materials, is available through the NHLBI Web site.

REFERENCES

1. Willerson JT, Hillis LD, Buja LM. Ischemic heart disease: clinical and pathophysiological aspects. New York: Raven Press; 1982.
2. Willerson JT. Treatment of heart diseases. London: Gower Medical Publishing; 1992.
3. American Heart Association. 1998 heart and stroke statistical update. Dallas (TX): American Heart Association; 1997.
4. Cardiovascular Health Branch, Division of Chronic Disease Control and Community Intervention, National Center for Chronic Disease Prevention and Health Promotion, CDC. Trends in ischemic heart disease mortality—United States, 1980–1988. MMWR Morb Mortal Wkly Rep 1992;41:545–56.
5. National Center for Health Statistics and the American Heart Association. Phase I, National Health and Nutrition Examination Survey III (NHANES III), 1988–91. NCHS and AHA. www.cdc.gov/nchs/nhanes.htm.
6. Mosca L, Manson JE, Sutherland SE, et al for the American Heart Association Writing Group. Cardiovascular disease in women: a statement for healthcare professionals from the American Heart Association (AHA scientific statement). Circulation 1997;96:2468–82.
7. The Women's Health Initiative Study Group. Design of the Women's Health Initiative clinical trial and observational study. Control Clin Trials 1998; 19:61–109.
8. Goldberg RJ, O'Donnell C, Yarzebski J, et al. Sex differences in symptom presentation associated with acute myocardial infarction: a population-based perspective. Am Heart J 1998;136:189–95.
9. Meischke H, Laresen MP, Eisenberg MS. Gender differences in reported symptoms for acute myocardial infarction: impact on prehospital delay time interval. Am J Emerg Med 1998;16:363–6.
10. Penque S, Halm M, Smith M, et al. Women and coronary disease: relationship between descriptors of signs and symptoms and diagnostic and treatment course. Am J Crit Care 1998;7:175–82.
11. Lerner DJ, Kannel WB. Patterns of coronary heart disease morbidity and mortality in the sexes: a 26-year follow-up of the Framingham population. Am Heart J 1986;111:383–90.
12. Chaitman BR, Bourassa MG, Davis K, et al. Angiographic prevalence of high-risk coronary artery disease in patient subsets (CASS). Circulation 1981;64:360–7.

13. Zuker DR, Griffith JL, Beshansky JR, Selker HP. Presentation of acute myocardial infarction in men and women. J Gen Intern Med 1997;12:79–87.

14. Mendelson MA, Hendel RC. Myocardial infarction in women. Cardiology 1995;86:272–85.

15. Dracup K, Moser DK. Treatment-seeking behavior among those with signs and symptoms of acute myocardial infarction. Heart Lung 1991;20:570–5.

16. Gibbons RJ, Balady GJ, Beasley JW, et al. ACC/AHA guidelines for exercise testing: a report of the American College of Cardiology/American Heart Association Task Force on Practice Guidelines (Committee on Exercise Testing). J Am Coll Cardiol 1997;30:260–315.

17. Curzen N, Patel D, Clarke D, et al. Women with chest pain: is exercise testing worthwhile? Heart 1996; 76:156–60.

18. Sketch MD, Mohiuddin SM, Lynch JD, et al. Significant sex differences in the correlation of electrocardiographic exercise testing and coronary arteriograms. Am J Cardiol 1975;36:169–73.

19. Guiteras VP, Chaitman BR, Water DD, et al. Diagnostic accuracy of exercise ECG lead systems in clinical subsets of women. Circulation 1982;65:1465–73.

20. Judelson DR. Examining the gender bias in evaluating coronary artery disease in women. Medscape Women's Health 1997;2(2).

21. Sawada SG, Ryan T, Fineberg NS, et al. Exercise echocardiographic detection of coronary artery disease in women. Am J Cardiol 1989;4:1440–7.

22. Quinones MA, Verani MS, Haichin RM, et al. Exercise echocardiography versus thallium-201 single photon emission computed tomography in evaluation of coronary artery disease: analysis of 292 patients. Circulation 1992;85:1026–31.

23. Roger VL, Pellikka PA, Bell MR, et al. Sex and test verification bias: impact on the diagnostic value of exercise echocardiography. Circulation 1997;95: 405–10.

24. Beller GA. Radionuclide exercise testing for coronary artery disease. Cardiol Clin 1984;2:367–78.

25. Taillefer R, DePuey EG, Udelson J, et al. Comparative diagnostic accuracy of Tl-201 and Tc-99m sestamibi SPECT imaging (perfusion and gated SPECT) in detecting coronary artery disease in women. J Am Coll Cardiol 1997;29:69–77.

26. Janowitz WR, Agatston AS, Kaplan G, Viamonte M Jr. Differences in prevalence and extent of coronary artery calcium detected by ultrafast computed tomography in asymptomatic men and women. Am J Cardiol 1993;72:247–54.

27. American College of Cardiology/American Heart Association. Expert consensus document on electron-beam computed tomography for the diagnosis and prognosis of coronary artery disease. J Am Coll Cardiol 2000;36:324–40.

28. Churchwell KB, Pilcher WC, Eisner RL, et al. Quantitative analysis of PET: the woman's test for coronary disease [abstract]. J Nucl Med 1995;36:79.

29. Tobin JN, Wassertheil SS, Wexler JP, et al. Sex bias in considering coronary bypass surgery. Ann Intern Med 1987;107:19–25.

30. Shaw LJ, Miller DD, Romeis JC, et al. Gender differences in the noninvasive evaluation and management of patients with suspected coronary artery disease. Ann Intern Med 1994;120:559–66.

31. Sullivan AK, Holdright DR, Wright CA, et al. Chest pain in women: clinical, investigative, and prognostic features. Br Med J 1994;308:883–6.

32. Bell MR, Berger PB, Holmes DR Jr, et al. Referral for coronary artery revascularization procedures after diagnostic coronary angiography: evidence for gender bias? J Am Coll Cardiol 1995;25:1650–5.

33. Mark DB, Shaw LK, DeLong ER, et al. Absence of sex bias in the referral of patients for cardiac catheterization. N Engl J Med 1994;330:1101–6.

34. Hachamovitch R, Berman DS, Kiat H, et al. Gender-related differences in clinical management after exercise nuclear testing. J Am Coll Cardiol 1995;26:1457–64.

35. Prinzmetal M, Kennamer D, Merliss R, et al. A variant form of angina pectoris. Am J Med 1959;27:375–88.

36. Kemp HG. Left ventricular function in patients with the anginal syndrome and normal coronary arteriograms. Am J Cardiol 1973;32:375–6.

37. Theroux P, Ouimet H, McCans J, et al. Aspirin, heparin, or both to treat acute unstable angina. N Engl J Med 1988;319:1105–11.

38. Smith SC Jr, Blair SN, Criqui MH, et al. Preventing heart attack and death in patients with coronary disease. Circulation 1995;92:2–4.

39. Antiplatelet Trialists' Collaboration. Secondary prevention of vascular disease by prolonged antiplatelet treatment. Br Med J 1988;296:320–31.

40. Anonymous. Final report on the aspirin component of the ongoing Physicians' Health Study. N Engl J Med 1989;321:129–35.

41. US Preventive Services Task Force. Aspirin prophylaxis for the primary prevention of myocardial infarction. In: US Preventive Services Task Force. Guide to clinical preventive services. 2nd ed. Baltimore (MD): Williams and Wilkins; 1996. Ch. 69.

42. Held PH, Yusuf S. Effects of ß-blockers and calcium channel blockers in acute myocardial infarction. Eur Heart J 1993;14 Suppl F:18–25.

43. Yusuf S, Anand S, Avenzum A, et al. Treatment of acute myocardial infarction. Overview of randomized clinical trials. Eur Heart J 1996;17 Suppl F:16–29.

44. Gutstein DE, Fuster V. Pathophysiologic basis for adjunctive therapies in the treatment and secondary treatment of acute myocardial infarction. Clin Cardiol 1998;21:161–8.

45. Furberg CD, Psaty BM, Meyer JV. Nifedipine. Dose-related increase in mortality in patients with coronary heart disease. Circulation 1995;92:1326–31.

46. Braunwald E, Mark DB, Jones RH, et al. Unstable angina: diagnosis and management, clinical practice guideline, number 10. Rockville (MD): Agency for Health Care Policy and Research, National Heart, Lung, and Blood Institute, US Department of Health and Human Services, Public Health Service; 1994. AHCPR Publication No.: 94-0602.

47. RISC Group. Risk of myocardial infarction and death during treatment with low dose aspirin and intravenous heparin in men with unstable coronary artery disease. Lancet 1990;336:827–30.

48. Gurfinkel EP, Manos EJ, Mejaíl RI, et al. Low molecular weight heparin versus regular heparin or aspirin in treatment of unstable angina and silent ischemia. J Am Coll Cardiol 1995;26:313–8.

49. Fragmin During Instability in Coronary Artery Disease (FRISC) Study Group. Low molecular weight heparin during instability in coronary artery disease. Lancet 1996;347:561–8.

50. Dittrich H, Gilpin E, Nicod P, et al. Acute myocardial infarction in women: influence of gender on mortality and prognostic variables. Am J Cardiol 1998;62:1–7.

51. Vaccarino V, Krumholz HM, Berkman LF, Horwitz RI. Sex differences in mortality after myocardial infarction. Is there evidence for an increased risk for women? Circulation 1995;91:1861–71.

52. Keelan ET, Nunez BD, Grill DE, et al. Comparison of immediate and long-term outcome of coronary angioplasty performed for unstable angina and rest pain in men and women. Mayo Clin Proc 1997;72:5–12.

53. Karlson BW, Herlitz J, Hartford M, Hjalmarson A. Prognosis in men and women coming to the emergency room with chest pain or other symptoms suggestive of acute myocardial infarction. Coron Artery Dis 1993;9:761–7.

54. Herlitz J, Karlson BW, Lindqvist J, Sjolin M. Long-term prognosis in men and women coming to the emergency room with chest pain or other symptoms suggestive of acute myocardial infarction. Eur J Emerg Med 1997;4:196–203.

55. Kannel WB, Sorlie P, McNamara PM. Prognosis after initial myocardial infarction: the Framingham study. Am J Cardiol 1979;44:53–9.

56. Kudenchuk PJ, Maynard C, Martin JS, et al. Comparison of presentation, treatment, and outcome of acute myocardial infarction in men versus women. Am J Cardiol 1996;78:9–14.

57. Kannel WB, Wilson PF, D'Agostino RB, Cobb J. Sudden coronary death in women. Am Heart J 1998;136:205–12.

58. Rahimtoola SH, Bennet AJ, Grunkemeier GL, et al. Survival at 15–18 years after coronary bypass surgery for angina in women. Circulation 1993;88(5 Pt 2):1171–8.

59. Davis KB, Chaitman B, Ryan T, et al. Comparison of 15-year survival for men and women after initial medical or surgical treatment for coronary artery disease: a CASS Registry Study. Coronary Artery Surgery Study. J Am Coll Cardiol 1995;25:1000–9.

60. Grundy SM, Balady GJ, Criqui MH, et al. Guide to primary prevention of cardiovascular diseases: a statement for healthcare professionals from the Task Force on Risk Reduction. Circulation 1997;95:2329–31.

61. Smith SC Jr, Blair SN, Criqui MH, the Secondary Prevention Panel, et al. Preventing heart attack and death in patients with coronary disease. Circulation 1995;92:2–4.

62. Mosca L, Grundy SM, Judelson D, et al. Guide to preventive cardiology for women. AHA/ACC scientific statement: consensus panel statement. J Am Coll Cardiol 1984;33:1751–5.

63. Goldman L, Garber A, Grover S, et al. 27th Bethesda conference: matching the intensity of risk factor management with the hazard for coronary disease events. Task force 6: cost effectiveness of assessment and management of risk factors. J Am Coll Cardiol 1996;27:1020–30.

64. Missed opportunities in preventive counseling for cardiovascular disease: United States. MMWR Morb Mortal Wkly Rep 1995;47:91–5.

65. Schrott HG, Bittner V, Vittinghoff E, et al for the HERS Research Group. Adherence to National Cholesterol Education Program treatment goals in postmenopausal women with heart disease: the Heart and Estrogen/progestin Replacement Study (HERS): the HERS Research Group. JAMA 1997;277:1281–6.

66. The American Diabetes Association. Clinical practice recommendations. Diabetes Care 2000;23:S32–42.

67. Hawkins GD, Wendal GD, Leveno KJ, et al. Myocardial infarction during pregnancy: a review. Obstet Gynecol 1985;65:139–46.

68. Meilahn EN, Kuller LH, Mathews KA, et al. Lp(a) concentrations among pre- and post-menopausal women over time. The Healthy Woman Study. Circulation 1991;84 Suppl II:546.

69. Campos H, McNamara JR, Ordovas JM, et al. Differences in low density lipoprotein subfractions and apolipoproteins in premenopausal and postmenopausal women. J Clin Endocrinol Metab 1988;67:30–5.

70. Scarabin PY, Plu-Bureau G, Bara L, et al. Haemostatic variables and menopausal status: influence of hormone replacement therapy. Thromb Haemost 1993;70:584–7.

71. Lidegaard O. Oral contraceptives and the risk of a cerebral thromboembolic attack: the results of a case-controlled study. Br Med J 1993;306:956–63.

72. Wynn V. Oral contraceptives and coronary heart disease. J Reprod Med 1991;36:19–25.

73. Meade TW, Greenberg G, Thompson SG. Progestogens and cardiovascular reactions associated with oral contraceptives and a comparison of the safety of 30 and 50 mcgs oestrogen preparations. Br Med J 1980;280:1157–61.

74. La Vecchia C. Sex hormones and cardiovascular risk. Hum Reprod 1992;7:62–167.

75. De Graaf J, Swinkels DW, Demacker PNM, et al. Differences in the low density lipoprotein subfraction profile between oral contraceptive users and controls. J Clin Endocrinol Metab 1993;78:197–202.

76. Skouby SO, Andersen O, Petersen KR, et al. Mechanism of action of oral contraceptives on carbohydrate on the cellular level. Am J Obstet Gynecol 1990;163:343–8.

77. The Writing Group for the PEPI Trial. Effects of estrogen or estrogen/progestin regimens on heart disease risk factors in postmenopausal women. The Postmenopausal Estrogen/Progestin Interventions (PEPI) Trial. JAMA 1994;273:199–208.

78. Gruchow H, Anderson A, Barboriak, et al. Postmenopausal oestrogen and occlusion of coronary arteries. Am Heart J 1988;115:954–63.

79. Stampfer M, Willett W, Colditz G, et al. A prospective study of postmenopausal estrogen therapy and coronary heart disease. N Engl J Med 1985;313:756–62.

80. Hulley S, Grady D, Bush T, et al, for the Heart and Estrogen/progestin Replacement Study (HERS) Research Group. Randomized trial of estrogen plus progestin for secondary prevention of coronary heart disease in postmenopausal women. JAMA 1998; 280:605–13.

81. Barrett-Conor E. Presentation to the Food and Drug Administration Advisory Committee on Estrogen and Arterial Disease Risk. Washington (DC): FDA; 1990.

82. Soma MR, Baetta R, Crosignani P. The menopause and lipid metabolism: strategies for cardiovascular disease prevention. Curr Opin Lipidol 1997;8:229–35.

35

MITRAL VALVE PROLAPSE

Jan H. Tillisch, MD

From Barlow's classic description of the association of abnormal coaption of the mitral valve, with the physical findings of a systolic click or murmur and various symptomatic presentations,[1] to the present careful delineation of anatomic mitral valve prolapse,[2] confusion has persisted regarding the clinical significance and natural history of the entity called "mitral valve prolapse" or "mitral valve prolapse syndrome," as some authors have named it.[3] This subtle difference in name is a key to understanding the confusion about this clinical entity. Indexing affected patients by the presence of anatomic mitral valve leaflet prolapse on random screening echocardiograms has resulted in a clinical focus on mitral valve pathology and its consequences—progressive mitral regurgitation, valve-based thromboembolic disease, and infective endocarditis. Determining incidence and clinical features from a population presenting with "cardiac" symptoms and/or the midsystolic click and systolic murmur gives a very different picture; yet these two diagnoses are grouped customarily as a single clinical entity.

In contrast to most chapters of this text, the first task of this chapter is to define and differentiate the clinical presentation of these two overlapping diagnoses—anatomic mitral valve prolapse (MVPa) and mitral valve prolapse syndrome (MVPs)—and to offer insight into potential pathophysiologic mechanisms that affect diagnosis and therapy.

ANATOMIC MITRAL VALVE PROLAPSE

The incidence, natural history, and contributing factors of MVPa have been described well in several studies[2,4,5] that used echocardiographic examination of large referred and nonreferred populations with stringent criteria for echocardiographic evidence of MVPa. It should be mentioned that, as with most

tests, the more rigorous are the criteria for positivity, the more severe or advanced are the pathologic process identified and its consequences. The criteria chosen in the above studies are biologically arbitrary in the sense that the degree of leaflet prolapse is a continuous, not dichotomous, variable. Thus, in those with positive tests, the incidence of secondary changes in valve architecture, such as thickening of the leaflets that predispose to infection or valve disruption and the severity of mitral regurgitation leading to hemodynamic consequences, are greater as the number of positive tests become smaller through more strict criteria for test positivity. Additionally, population-based studies, although free of ascertainment bias, necessarily describe a population with a lower incidence of clinically evident disease than do studies based on a referral population in which patients may already manifest some evidence of the disease process being studied.

With those caveats, studies focusing on anatomic mitral valve prolapse have found an incidence of 2 to 6% in the general population.[6] Sixty percent of patients were women, with that percentage rising with advancing age at diagnosis. Two subgroups can be identified: those with and those without mitral leaflet thickening or redundancy. Those with thickening/redundancy (termed "classic" prolapse by some[2,4]) had a greater incidence of mitral valve endocarditis, need for valve replacement, and sudden death or embolic event—the total affected percentage ranging from 10 to 30% of the "classic" group.[2,4,5,7]

The incidence of serious complications in the MVPa group is greater in men (relative risk, 2 to 3), particularly with regard to the need for valve replacement and infective endocarditis. Males more often present with mitral regurgitant murmurs, symptoms of congestive heart failure, or cardiac arrhythmias. Cerebral ischemic events occur evenly in men and women in those studies, using MVPa as the inclusion criterion.

The incidence of cerebral ischemic events determined prospectively in the population identified to have MVPa by screening echocardiography is statistically the same as incidence for those without MVPa,[8] whereas in referral based studies of either MVPa or stroke, the relative risk of cerebrovascular events with MVPa ranges from 1 to 9, with a higher risk in younger patients (< 45 years) or those with additional risk factors for stroke.[9,10]

Population-based studies have not conclusively supported a genetic influence, at least in classic MVPa.[11]

In summary MVPa, defined by rigid and dichotomous criteria, occurs relatively uncommonly (in approximately 2% of the general population), without gender preponderance, and is associated with a low incidence of severe complications of infective endocarditis, need for mitral valve surgery, and cerebrovascular events. Evidence for a genetic pattern is weak when associated collagen diseases known to be associated with valve leaflet abnormalities (eg, Marfan or Ehlers-Danlos syndromes) are excluded.

MITRAL VALVE PROLAPSE SYNDROME

Barlow's early work[1,3] described the association of mitral valve prolapse (ie, MVPa) with certain physical findings of a midsystolic click, often followed by a late systolic murmur, abnormalities of the thoracic skeleton, and cardiac symptoms of breathlessness, atypical chest pain, and palpitations as well as anxiety. Subsequent investigators focused on an etiologic concept of a primary collagen abnormality leading to progressive deterioration of valve architecture ("myxomatous degeneration") and linked that with physical findings of skeletal abnormalities. Symptoms were felt due to mitral regurgitation and its hemodynamic consequence or to ischemia secondary to pathologic tension induced by a "billowing" or sail-like valve tensing the chordal tendineae and papillary muscles.[12] The current controversy regarding etiology, incidence, and management of MVPs derives from these earlier descriptions.

Again stressing the caveat that the criteria for enrolling patients in any study profoundly affects the data and conclusions, the studies that delineate the clinical characteristics and natural history of MVPs are largely composed of patients referred for evaluation of either the physical findings of a midsystolic click and/or late systolic murmur or for cardiac symptoms including chest pain, palpitations, breathlessness, and near syncope. It is therefore particularly important to describe the findings in *this patient population*, who represent not a general population but, rather, a population seeking medical advice and care.

The incidence in the general population of those with MVPs as defined by the presence of a midsystolic click and/or murmur has been variously cited as 5 to 10%, with an incidence of up to 17% in young women.[13] Generally MVPs is thought to be three to four times as common in women than in men, with the gender difference being greatest in the young.

Other physical components of the syndrome to be discussed include thoracic skeletal abnormalities and certain other anthropomorphic characteristics. These features have led some investigators and clinicians to consider MVPs as a forme fruste of Marfan syndrome, but careful differentiation of the two show quite different skeletal abnormalities[14] and no evidence of other cardiac structural abnormalities in MVPs other than occasional mild tricuspid valve prolapse. No evidence for a structural collagen abnormality has been found in MVPs.[15]

In contrast to classic MVPa, MVPs in general behaves as an autosomal dominant trait;[16] family studies of affected patients have uncovered a high incidence of mitral leaflet prolapse and thoracic skeletal abnormalities, often in asymptomatic patients.

The symptom complex of MVPs has been attributed by many to exaggerated neurohormonal responses. Studies of these responses in symptomatic patients have shown an increased response to ß-receptor stimulation as well as an increased catecholamine response to exercise and early "fatigue" of adrenergic responses.[17,18] This "hyperadrenergic" response seems likely to be pathophysiologically important in the generation of many, if not all, of the symptoms and signs of MVPs.

The finding that echocardiographic mitral valve prolapse may accompany hyperthyroid states,[19] may occur transiently in anorexia nervosa[20] and dehydrated states,[21] and is clearly dependent on ventricular volume with increasing prolapse seen with diminished ventricular size (as evidenced by the positional variation of both click/murmur intensity and timing) all suggest that relative hypovolemia may contribute to or even cause mitral valve leaflet prolapse, particularly of the modest degree that the rigorous definition of MVPa might exclude. Mid-systolic clicks with normal variant echocardiographic leaflet motion or billowing of the mitral leaflets are common.[22] Prolapse is associated with a lower body mass index, supporting the notion that patients with aesthenic habitus and/or those with an adren-ergically stimulated metabolic rate may be more prone to hypovolemia and, thus, prolapsing of the mitral leaflets. Males may be more resistant to hypo-volemia for a variety of reasons,[21] but in men with MVPs, an attenuation in the volume-conserving aldosterone response to upright exercise was noted, despite an increase in plasma renin activity.[23] How-ever, this may only partially explain the gender dif-ference in incidence.

A unitary etiologic hypothesis in MVPs, albeit still speculative, would be that individuals with exaggerated adrenergic responsiveness are more prone to hypovolemia (as noted, for example, in pheochromocytoma) and, thus, develop the "non-classic" form of mitral valve prolapse. This valvular abnormality has nothing to do with their sympto-matic state, which is due to the exaggerated adren-ergic responsiveness (eg, palpitations, postural hypotension, breathlessness, chest pain, and cuta-neous flushing). If adrenergic hyper-responsiveness is coupled either genetically or by chance to a devel-opmental predisposition to low body weight or to environmental contributions to decreased volume, mitral valve prolapse might occur.

Patients presenting with systolic click/mur-mur or with cardiac symptoms consistent with increased adrenergic response may have echo-cardiographically "negative" mitral valve prolapse or prolapse below the current degree required to define MVPa.

Rigorous criteria for MVPa identify a different population without the high incidence of neuro-hormonally mediated symptoms but with a greater predisposition to true cardiac events, particularly infective endocarditis or the need for valve replace-ment. The two entities of MVPa and MVPs may well overlap, particularly through the role of an abnormal hemodynamic effect on the valve leaflets inducing thickening and abnormal function of the mitral valve apparatus. Thus, even patients with MVPs, after long periods of functional mitral regur-gitation, may infrequently develop severe regurgita-tion requiring valve repair or replacement.

The diagnostic approach and subsequent therapeutic plan should be based on both the dis-tinct difference between MVPa and MVPs and the potential for overlap. That differentiation depends on the manner in which the patient presents and the nature of symptoms and physical findings (dis-cussed below).

PRESENTING SYMPTOMS AND SIGNS

Cardiac Symptoms

Patients presenting only with primary MVPa often are asymptomatic at presentation but have had a cardiac murmur auscultated. Older patients may present with atrial fibrillation secondary to enlarge-ment of the left atrium from mitral regurgitation, even in the absence of symptoms of congestive heart failure.

Congestive heart failure symptoms may be slowly progressive as the degree of mitral regurgita-tion worsens *or* as the ability of the left ventricle to accommodate to the continuous volume load is exceeded. Alternatively, the congestive symptoms may be acute, suggesting an acute ischemic event, but, in fact, due to sudden disruption of one or more chordal attachments. This leads to acute onset of, or worsening of pre-existing, mitral regurgita-tion. These patients may present with acute pul-monary edema. This most frequently occurs in women in their sixties to seventies,[24] whereas more slowly progressive heart failure with onset in the forties or fifties is slightly more common in men.

Patients with MVPs may present with similar acute or chronic cardiac symptoms, but they occur less frequently. Congestive heart failure is generally a late presentation, due either to acute or long-standing chordal rupture or to progressive mitral regurgitation from valve thickening and abnormal coaption of the leaflets.

Palpitations are more frequent in those with MVPs, although sustained atrial fibrillation more often tracks with the degree of mitral regurgitation and, thus, is more frequent with MVPa or the over-lap of the two entities. Palpitations in MVPs are caused by either atrial or ventricular premature contractions or reentrant atrial tachycardia. Serious ventricular arrhythmias are much less common, but incidence figures are highly dependent on patient referral bias.[2,7] No published series of sufficient size has examined arrhythmias and outcomes in patients enrolled for MVPs criteria (midsystolic click/murmur and clinical symptoms). Extrapolating from large follow-up studies, the risk of sudden death or ventricular tachycardia is slightly higher than in a comparable control population but is still very low.

Chest pain, often sharp and localized, is a common symptom in MVPs. The discomfort/pain is rarely exertional, is not positional or pleuritic, and has been ascribed to focal ischemia, pulmonary vascular congestion, hysteria, or a somatization disorder but seems logically to be a consequence of increased adrenergic stimulation, analogous to the discomfort noted after an injection of epinephrine for other therapeutic indications. Adrenergic stimulation in patients with MVPs reproduces the chest pain and other symptoms of fatigue, dyspnea, and a "lightheaded" feeling.[18]

"Extracardiac" Symptoms

Dyspnea, often described after initial vigorous effort but not imposing exercise limitation, is common although less so than previously described symptoms. More gradual initiation of effort, "working through" the dyspnea, or slower pace are self-adopted modes of reducing the impact. Worsening of the dyspnea in the second trimester of pregnancy has been noted. This is indirect evidence of the adrenergic cause of this symptom; the valvular prolapse diminishes as the ventricle enlarges during the course of pregnancy, while catecholamine excretion rises.

Postural hypotension leading to feelings of lightheadedness with rare true syncope is common in MVPs but is largely mentioned by the patient without direct questioning.

Easy fatigability and sustained fatigue often are described, despite evidence of energy and active lifestyle. The association between neurally mediated hypotension and chronic fatigue syndrome has been described, although not in MVPs.[25] The most classic, although exaggerated, description of this and other symptoms of MVPs is Charles Dickens's, description of Mrs. Wititterly in *Nicholas Nickleby*.

Panic attacks have been noted repeatedly in association with MVPs, but careful examination of this association has not validated it. The indexing of the study population and the definition of panic attacks (usually neither is well defined) may lead to the variable association noted.

Clinical Signs

In both MVPa and MVPs, the cardinal physical finding is the midsystolic click(s), ascribed to the tensing of the redundant valve leaflets as they fill during systolic contraction. A mid- to late systolic murmur, variable in length, intensity, and even presence in a given patient, follows the click. Both are best auscultated between the lower left sternal border and the left ventricular apex. Conditions that alter ventricular filling alter both the length and intensity of the murmur with an inverse relation to ventricular volume. Thus, the click and the murmur occur earlier and the murmur is longer with short diastolic filling cycles (relative tachycardia or during short cycles of a sinus arrhythmia), during standing, or in conditions leading to decreased venous return (venodilation or hypovolemia) or more complete ventricular ejection (vasodilation or inotropic stimulation). Although the Valsalva maneuver has been advocated as a way to diagnostically alter the murmur, it has complex effects on ventricular volume, heart rate, and impedance to ejection and is less useful than is standing (to bring on the click earlier in systole and prolong the murmur) and squatting (to increase vascular resistance, impede ejection, delay the click, and shorten the murmur).

The presence of the murmur has been advocated as an indication for infective endocarditis prophylaxis. Unfortunately the murmur may be so variable in its presence and intensity to be of no use in that decision.

Postural hypotension is common as is a marked sinus arrhythmia, which some have attributed to an increase in vagal tone as well as adrenergic response. Localized cutaneous flushing with stress also is often noted. Cool fingers and toes are often found and are a frequent symptomatic complaint.

The symptoms and, to a lesser extent, the signs of MVPs often vary inexplicably, disappearing for months and even years, only to reappear without discernible cause. A careful history taking often uncovers potential alterations in adrenergic "tone." Although mental stress is an obvious factor, stressors are not always easy for the patient to identify or to admit. Decreases in exercise routine often lead to worsening of symptoms, which are attributed by the patient to some stress that caused them to decrease frequency/duration of exercise (eg, examinations, a new job, or moving). The increase in adrenergic response associated with decreased conditioning may well be the actual modifier. As mentioned, pregnancy may increase adrenergic tone and, thus, symptoms. Many patients with MVPs note exacerbation of their symptoms in the premenstrual period, with relief following the onset of menstruation (despite the hypovolemia that accompanies the latter). Fatigue, alcohol ingestion, and sympathomimetic drugs all adversely affect the symptoms in MVPs, and caffeine intake is noted frequently to increase palpitations and often chest pain and dyspnea as well.

DIAGNOSTIC APPROACH

In MVPa, the diagnostic approach is, by definition, echocardiography. The finding of mitral regurgitation *and* leaflet thickening defines a population at higher risk for symptomatic valvular incompetence or infective endocarditis.

In patients with MVPs who *may* have significant or classic leaflet prolapse, echocardiography is indicated. The difficulty lies in determining which patient should undergo routine screening echocardiography. Although outcome models have been developed for antibiotic prophylaxis based on the presence of a murmur of mitral regurgitation (a problematic approach, as previously described), a cost/benefit analysis of echocardiography was not performed.[26]

In lieu of clear outcome studies, it seems prudent to perform echocardiography as an initial diagnostic tool in all female MVPs patients with symptoms of congestive heart failure, atrial fibrillation or flutter, holosystolic apical murmurs, and increasing murmur length and intensity over several examinations, and in patients with MVPs who are over the age of 60 years. In those with more than trivial mitral regurgitation or with valve thickening, serial echocardiography annually or at least biannually is warranted. In patients with only a click or a click/midsystolic murmur, initial echocardiographic evaluation is not required.

Other diagnostic studies such as Holter monitoring, stress testing, or tilt-table studies should be reserved for the specific indications of symptomatic or sustained arrhythmias, chest pain of an anginal character associated with coronary risk factors, and unexplained recurrent syncope, respectively.

TREATMENT

In those patients with hemodynamically significant mitral regurgitation, mitral valve repair by a surgical team that has wide experience with the technique is the preferred approach.

Allusions to the issue of infective endocarditis prophylaxis have been made. Given the low risk of prophylaxis in nonpenicillin-allergic patients and the poor negative predictive value of the absence of a midsystolic murmur on initial examination, amoxicillin prophylaxis for dental procedures and appropriate antibiotic prophylaxis for other surgical procedures is recommended.[27] Recent guidelines for antibiotic prophylaxis are summarized in Tables 35–1 and 35–2. Information about prophylactic antibiotics in pregnant and breast-feeding women is presented in Table 35–3. When multidrug allergy is present, echocardiography is indicated to determine relative risk; however, those interpreting the echocardiogram results also can miss or underestimate prolapse or mitral regurgitation.[28]

In those patients with MVPs, attempts to decrease adrenergic responsivity are indicated, although outcome studies are lacking. The simplest and safest way to achieve this decrease is with a sustained low-level aerobic exercise program that employs walking, bicycling, swimming, or similar exercises that permit a sustained submaximal level. Burst exercises such as tennis, basketball, or gym aerobics are less successful and also less well tolerated by this population.

Increasing blood volume by generous salt and water consumption may also decrease symptoms by decreasing adrenergic compensatory responses. Obviously patients with a tendency toward hypertension are not good candidates for this approach, but, fortunately, few patients with MVPs are hypertensive.

A number of European investigators have described a relation between MVPs and hypomagnesemia in humans; this has been described in animals as well. Treatment with magnesium supplementation may decrease MVPs symptoms and lower catecholamine excretion.[29] No large clinical studies have confirmed these conclusions.

A logical pharmacologic approach, based on the hypothesis that increased adrenergic response is responsible for the symptom complex, is a ß-blockade; indeed, this class of agents has been effective in modifying symptoms, particularly palpitations, chest

---

TABLE 35–1. Mitral Valve Prolapse: Procedures for which Endocarditis Prophylaxis is Recommended*

Dental procedures: many dental procedures, including prophylactic cleaning of teeth where bleeding is anticipated, dental extractions, and intraligamentary local anesthetic injections[†]

Surgical procedures
    Tonsillectomy/adenoidectomy
    Operations that involve respiratory mucosa
    Operations that involve intestinal mucosa[‡]
    Biliary tract surgery[‡]

Other procedures
    Cystoscopy, urethral dilatation
    Bronchoscopy with a rigid bronchoscope
    Sclerotherapy for esophageal varices[‡]
    Esophageal stricture dilation[‡]
    Endoscopic retrograde cholangiography during biliary obstruction[‡]

---

*The American Heart Association recommends prophylaxis for patients with valvular regurgitation and/or thickened leaflets.
[†]For a list of dental procedures for which antibiotic prophylaxis is not recommended, see reference outlined below.
[‡]Prophylaxis is stated to be "optional" for these procedures.
Adapted from Dajani AD, Taubert KA, Wilson W, et al. Prevention of bacterial endocarditis: recommendations by the American Heart Association. JAMA 1997;277:1794–801.

TABLE 35–2. Antibiotics for Endocarditis Prophylaxis for Patients with Mitral Valve Prolapse*

Dental, oral, respiratory tract, or esophageal procedures
    Standard regimen: amoxicillin 2.0 g PO 1 h before the procedure
    Regimen for penicillin-allergic patients[†]
        Clindamycin 600 mg PO 1 h before the procedure, or
        Azithromycin 500 mg PO 1 h before the procedure, or
        Clarithromycin 500 mg PO 1 h before the procedure
    Regimen for patients unable to take oral medications: ampicillin 2.0 g IM or IV within 30 min before the procedure
    Regimen for patients unable to take oral medications and who are penicillin allergic[‡]: clindamycin 600 mg IV within 30 min before the procedure

Gastrointestinal (excluding esophageal) and genitourinary procedures
    Standard regimen
        Amoxicillin 2.0 g PO 1 h before the procedure, or
        Ampicillin 2.0 g IM or IV within 30 min before the procedure
    Regimen for penicilli-allergic patients: vancomycin 1.0 g IV over 1–2 h, complete infusion within 30 min of starting the procedure

---

*The American Heart Association recommends prophylaxis for patients with valvular regurgitation and/or thickened leaflets.
[†]Cephalexin 2.0 g or cefadroxil 2.0 g 1 h before the procedure is also acceptable in patients without immediate-type hypersensitivity reaction (eg, urticaria, angioedema, anaphylaxis) to penicillins
[‡]Cefazolin 1.0 g IM or IV within 30 min of the procedure is also acceptable in patients without immediate-type hypersensitivity reaction (eg, urticaria, angioedema, anaphylaxis) to penicillins
IM = intramuscularly; IV = intravenously.
Adapted from Dajani AD, Taubert KA, Wilson W, et al. Prevention of bacterial endocarditis: recommendations by the American Heart Association. JAMA 1997;277:1794–1801.

TABLE 35–3. Antibiotics Used for Endocarditis
Prophylaxis Considered Safe during Pregnancy
and Breast-Feeding*

Amoxicillin
Ampicillin
Cephalexin
Cefadroxil
Cefazolin

*Assuming the mother is not allergic to the drug(s).
Adapted from Berkowitz RL, et al. Handbook for prescribing
medications during pregnancy. 2nd ed. Boston: Little, Brown;
1986, and Briggs GG, et al. Drugs in pregnancy and lactation.
5th ed. Baltimore, Williams & Wilkins.

pain, and near syncope. Despite their efficacy, these
agents often are poorly tolerated by patients who
are accustomed to the increased energy level or tendency to hyperactivity that is characteristic of the
syndrome. For some, however, this hyperactive state
is both emotionally and physically fatiguing, and ß-
blockade offers some relief from this symptom. As
with most receptor-blocking agents, the increased
stimulation and/or responsiveness of ß-receptors
translates into an increased sensitivity to the receptor blockers. ß₁-specific agents with low lipophilia
are preferable, initiated at low doses such as
atenolol 25 mg or the equivalent. ß-blockade
should be an interval therapy, pending the effects of
exercise modification of adrenergic tone; if symptoms recur after cessation of drug therapy, re-insti-
tution of therapy may be indicated, recognizing
that the drug only modifies symptoms.

ß-blocking agents are the first choice for prevention of paroxysmal atrial arrhythmias or for
symptomatic frequent ventricular ectopy. Class I
antiarrhythmic drugs should be avoided because of
proarrhythmic effects and an adverse risk-to-benefit ratio when the arrhythmias themselves are benign
(as is usually the case).

Calcium channel–blocking drugs increase
sympathoadrenal activation and generally are ineffective in treating the paroxysmal atrial arrhythmias.

For more serious arrhythmias such as nonsus-
tained ventricular tachycardia, recurrent sustained
atrial fibrillation/flutter, or frequent prolonged atrial
tachycardia, sotalol or amiodarone are effective.
Sotalol has significant proarrhythmic effects, and
amiodarone has infrequent, but significant, extra-
cardiac toxicity, so their use should follow a trial of a

ß-blockade and the nonpharmacologic therapies
previously discussed.

SCREENING AND REFERRAL

Screening for mitral valve prolapse with echocardiography has no demonstrated benefit. As mentioned,
routine echocardiography to screen all MVPs is also
unnecessary. Careful history and physical examination at the patient's initial contact with a clinician is
sufficient screening. The click and murmur are
rarely subtle, particularly when the clinician is looking for them on the basis of clues derived from the
history. It has been said that MVPs is a "20-foot
diagnosis," with some truth; the positive predictive
value of aesthenic habitus, increased leg-to-torso
ratio, and a somewhat energetic manner is unstud-
ied but is probably above 50%. Family studies often
confirm a similar appearance and manner, not surprisingly, but with variable incidence of the mitral
valve prolapse itself.

From the diagnostic standpoint, referral is
rarely necessary for asymptomatic or symptomatic
MVPs. However, patients with MVPa or MVPs with
prominent systolic murmurs should be examined by
a cardiologist annually, and referral for echocardiography should be dependent on that assessment.
Referral for cardiologic consultation is useful when
cardiac symptoms become frequent or sustained and
require a more intensive approach than nonpharmacologic therapy or use of low-dose ß-blockers.

EFFECTS OF PREGNANCY, MENOPAUSE, AND HORMONE REPLACEMENT

Pregnancy poses no particular risk for those with
MVPa or MVPs in the absence of hemodynamically
symptomatic mitral regurgitation. As mentioned
previously, adrenergically mediated symptoms, particularly palpitations, chest pain, and dyspnea, may
become more prominent. Rarely, supraventricular
tachycardia may occur during pregnancy or delivery; adenosine for conversion has been used safely
even during delivery. ß-blockade has been used
safely during pregnancy, but, as with all medications,
the benefits of therapy should be substantial and
nonpharmacologic alternatives exhausted before
instituting such therapy.

Menopause may reduce adrenergically mediated symptoms in some patients; in others, little change is seen. Hormone replacement therapy has no demonstrated effect on symptoms or the course of either MVPa or MVPs.

PROGNOSIS

In general, MVPs is a systemic syndrome that may almost be considered a variant of normal. Its prognosis is, with few exceptions, benign. Several authors experienced in this area have felt that it should not be considered a disease entity, and patients should not be told they have an abnormality. However, this often leads patients to continue to be concerned about their symptoms without adequate explanation for the genesis of symptoms. Indeed, many patients are told that their symptoms are psychogenic or frankly hysterical. It is profoundly reassuring to patients to receive a logical explanation for their symptoms (some of which they have considered to be their particular burden in life), to be reassured as to the benign nature of the symptoms, and to have a nonpharmacologic therapy available with a high chance of benefit.

The requisite intermittent examinations for progression of mitral regurgitation and antibiotic prophylaxis for infective endocarditis, with appropriate explanation, need not be considered an indication of important cardiac disease.

The patient with MVPa has a different prognosis, although recent studies suggest that MVPa is more benign than was previously thought.[2] The line between MVPa and MVPs is ill defined. The hyperadrenergic character of patients with MVPs often is present without any abnormalities of mitral leaflet coaption; conversely, many patients with MVPa, particularly men, have no evidence of increased adrenergic response. In the former, attention should be paid to the symptomatic patient who seeks insight into the cause of the symptoms, and safe, well-tolerated, and effective therapy (including reassurance) should be provided. In the latter, the focus is on serial assessment for the development of significant mitral valve incompetence, careful prophylaxis against infective endocarditis, and aggressive treatment of sustained or frequent cardiac arrhythmias. When the syndromes overlap, so, too, must the diagnostic and therapeutic approaches.

RESOURCES

The American Heart Association
7272 Greenville Avenue
Dallas, Texas 75231
Telephone: 1-800-AHA-USA1 (1-800-242-8721) (Patient information line)
Web site: www.americanheart.org

The American Heart Association Web site contains patient information on mitral valve prolapse. Full-text guidelines for endocarditis prophylaxis are also available on-line for the use of clinicians. A toll-free phone line is maintained to provide consumer health information.

The National Society for Mitral Valve Prolapse and Dysautonomia
c/o Baptist Health Foundation
PO Box 83060
Birmingham, Alabama 35283-0605
Web site: www.mvprolapse.com

The society's Web site, maintained by a private clinic that treats mitral valve prolapse patients, contains patient information and a list of support group contacts throughout the United States.

REFERENCES

1. Barlow JB, Bosman CK. Aneurysmal protrusion of the posterior leaflet of the mitral valve. An auscultatory-electrocardiographic syndrome. Am Heart J 1966; 71:166–78.

2. Freed LA, Levy D, Levine RA, et al. Prevalence and clinical outcome of mitral-valve prolapse. N Engl J Med 1999;341:1–7.

3. Pocock WA, Barlow JB. Etiology and electrocardiographic features of the billowing posterior mitral leaflet syndrome. Am J Med 1971;51:731–9.

4. Marks AR, Choong CY, Sanfilippo AJ. Identification of high-risk and low-risk subgroups of patients with mitral-valve prolapse. N Engl J Med 1989;320: 1031–6.

5. Nishimura RA, McGoon MD, Shub C, et al. Echocardiographically documented mitral-valve prolapse. N Engl J Med 1985;313:1305–9.

6. Procacci PM, Savran SV, Schreiter SL, et al. Prevalence of clinical mitral-valve prolapse in 1169 women. N Engl J Med 1976;294:1086–8.

7. Duren DR, Becker AE, Dunning AJ. Long-term follow-up of idiopathic mitral valve prolapse in 300 patients: a prospective study. J Am Coll Cardiol 1988; 11:42–7.

8. Gilon D, Buonano FS, Joffe MM, et al. Lack of evidence of an association between mitral-valve prolapse and stroke in young patients. N Engl J Med 1999;341:8–13.

9. Orencia AJ, Petty GW, Khandheria BK, et al. Risk of stroke with mitral valve prolapse in population-based cohort study. Stroke 1995;26:7–13.

10. Barnett HJM, Roughner DR, Taylor DW, et al. Further evidence relating mitral-valve prolapse to cerebral ischemic events. N Engl J Med 1980; 302:139–44.

11. Zuppiroli A, Roman MJ, O'Grady M, et al. A family study of anterior mitral leaflet thickness and mitral valve prolapse. Am J Cardiol 1998;82:823–6.

12. Devereux RB, Perloff JK, Reichek N, et al. Mitral valve prolapse. Circulation 1976;54:3–14.

13. Markiewicz W, Stoner J, London E, et al. Mitral valve prolapse in one hundred presumably healthy young females. Circulation 1976;53:464–73.

14. Roman MJ, Devereux RB, Kramer-Fox R, et al. Comparison of cardiovascular and skeletal features of primary mitral valve prolapse and Marfan syndrome. Am J Cardiol 1989;63:317–21.

15. Wordsworth P, Ogilvie D, Akhras F, et al. Genetic segregation analysis of familial mitral valve prolapse shows no linkage to fibrillar collagen genes. Br Heart J 1989;61:300–6.

16. Devereux RB. Recent developments in the diagnosis and management of mitral valve prolapse. Curr Opin Cardiol 1995;10:107–16.

17. Davies AO, Mares A, Pool JL, et al. Mitral valve prolapse with symptoms of beta-adrenergic hypersensitivity. Am J Med 1987;82:193–201.

18. Boudoulas H, Reynolds J, Mazzaferri E, et al. Mitral valve prolapse syndrome: the effect of adrenergic stimulation. J Am Coll Cardiol 1983;2:638–44.

19. Klein M, Pascal V, Aubert V, et al. Heart and thyroid. Ann Endocrinol 1995;56:473–86.

20. De Simone G, Scalfi L, Galderisi M, et al. Cardiac abnormalities in young women with anorexia nervosa. Br Heart J 1994;71:287–92.

21. Aufderheide S, Lax D, Goldberg SJ. Gender differences in dehydration-induced mitral valve prolapse. Am Heart J 1995;129:83–6.

22. Weis AJ, Salcedo EE, Stewart WJ et al. Anatomic explanation of mobile systolic clicks: implications for the clinical and echocardiographic diagnosis of mitral valve prolapse. Am Heart J 1995;129:314–20.

23. Zdrojewski TR, Wyrzykowski B, Krupa-Wojciechowska B. Renin-aldosterone regulation during upright posture in young men with mitral valve prolapse syndrome. J Heart Valve Dis 1995;4:236–41.

24. Naggar CZ, Pearson WN, Seljan MP. Frequency of complications of mitral valve prolapse in subjects aged 60 years and older. Am J Cardiol 1986;58:1209–12.

25. Bou-Holaigah I, Rowe PC, Kan J, et al. The relationship between neurally mediated hypotension and the chronic fatigue syndrome. JAMA 1995;274:961–7.

26. Devereux RB, Frary CJ, Kramer-Fox R, et al. Cost-effectiveness of infective endocarditis prophylaxis for mitral valve prolapse with or without a mitral regurgitant murmur. Am J Cardiol 1994;74:1024–9.

27. Committee on Rheumatic Fever, Endocarditis, and Kawasaki Disease. Prevention of bacterial endocarditis: recommendations by the American Heart Association. Circulation 1997;96:358–66.

28. Noble LM, Dabestani A, Child JS, et al. Mitral valve prolapse. Cross sectional and provocative M-mode echocardiography. Chest 1982;82:158–63.

29. Lichodziejewska B, Klos J, Rezler J, et al. Clinical symptoms of mitral valve prolapse are related to hypomagnesemia and attenuated by magnesium supplementation. Am J Cardiol 1997;79:768–72.

36

HYPERLIPIDEMIA

Benjamin J. Ansell, MD

As coronary heart disease (CHD) is the leading killer of American women, identification and correction of modifiable risk factors such as hyperlipidemia is crucial. Other prevalent conditions associated with elevated serum cholesterol include ischemic stroke and peripheral vascular disease. Vascular disease accounts for nearly 1 in 2 female deaths in the United States, more than the next 16 leading causes of death combined. While the death rates have declined among men with cardiovascular disease since 1979, vascular death rates among women have been stable or increased over the same time period.[1]

PRESENTING SIGNS AND SYMPTOMS

In severe hyperlipidemia, patients may develop cutaneous xanthomas. These are typically on extensor surfaces (tuberous xanthomas), adjacent to the eyes (xanthelasmas), or in association with the Achilles' tendon and extensor tendons of the knuckles.[2] However, despite underlying development of atherosclerosis, most cases of hyperlipidemia are asymptomatic until late in the pathogenesis of the disease. This is more evident in women than in men; nearly two-thirds of females who die suddenly from CHD had no previous clinical evidence of the disease.[1] The need to identify and treat patients at risk before an event occurs presents a challenge for health clinicians, given the lack of symptoms accompanying development of vascular disease in many instances. In addition to educating themselves about varied (so-called atypical) presentations of CHD in women, health professionals should be aware of the latest information on CHD prevention.

The disparity between symptomatic presentation and, thus, identification of CHD in female and male patients tends to delay diagnosis of myocardial infarction (MI) and contributes to worse outcomes in women. In the Global Use of Strategies to Open Occluded Coronary Arteries (GUSTO) IIb Trial, for example, women were less likely to have characteristic ECG changes at the time of their infarction, more likely to suffer complications after their infarction, and more likely to die after their infarction, than were the men in the study.[3] The study also suggested a significantly better outcome for women with unstable angina than for men. Although this report confirmed previous observations that women tend to be older than men at the time of MI, another study showed that women less than 50 years of age had twice the MI case-fatality rate as did age-matched men in a large registry of postinfarct patients.[4] This evidence suggests that there may be underlying differences in pathophysiology in men and women presenting with acute coronary syndromes.

Some lipid risk factors for CHD differ between men and women. For example, triglycerides (TGs) predict CHD better in women, especially older women, than they do in men.[5] Also, low levels of high-density lipoproteins (HDLs) are more predictive of coronary events in women over age 65 years than in men of similar age.[6] In the Lipid Research Clinics Trial, low HDL levels were more predictive for CHD than were any other lipid parameter in women.[7]

DIAGNOSIS

Characterization and diagnosis of hyperlipidemia has been improved by the wide availability of quantitative measurements of low-density lipoprotein (LDL), HDL, and TG fractions. However, according to a survey by the National Heart, Lung, and Blood Institute, 26% of Americans without CHD are unaware of their cholesterol levels.[8]

There is some disparity in public health recommendations regarding when to begin screening for dyslipidemia in females. The National Cholesterol Education Program (NCEP) recommends that all individuals over the age of 20 have a full fasting lipoprotein panel (including total, HDL, LDL and TG levels) measured at least every 5 years. If the testing is obtained on a nonfasting basis, a full lipoprotein panel should be obtained if total cholesterol is greater than 200 mg/dL and/or HDL is less than 40 mg/dL.[9] The American Heart Association (AHA), the American College of Cardiology (ACC), and the American College of Obstetricians and Gynecologists (AHOG) all have endorsed the NCEP screening recommendations.[5] This type of early screening is supported by evidence that total cholesterol is positively associated with both short-term and long-term all-cause mortality in women under age 55 years.[10]

There is concern by some that this approach might lead to expensive drug therapy in younger low-risk patients. Therefore, guidelines from the U.S. Preventive Services Task Force and the American College of Physicians recommend delaying cholesterol screening in women without risk factors until age 45 years (as opposed to age 35 years in men).[11] These two groups also suggest caution in screening asymptomatic patients of either sex over age 65 years. This recommendation is based on the lack of association between hyperlipidemia and cardiovascular events in the elderly.[12]

TREATMENT

Nonpharmacologic means to improve lipid parameters, including reduction of dietary saturated fat and cholesterol, engaging in regular aerobic exercise, and weight loss (if appropriate), should be recommended to *all* patients with dyslipidemia, even if drug therapy is also to be used. Smoking cessation benefits HDL levels in women, especially when accompanied by exercise training.[13] Exercise is also important to achieve lipid benefit in women with dietary modification; a study of a cholesterol-lowering diet in dyslipidemic women found that the diet failed to reduce LDL cholesterol levels unless the study participants also engaged in aerobic exercise.[14] Another study reported that the combination of intensive diet and exercise in postmenopausal women led to LDL level reduction, as well as reduced susceptibility of LDLs to oxidation.[15] If nonpharmacologic means fail to achieve lipid targets in patients without CHD or diabetes within a few months, then drug therapy should be considered.

There is considerable evidence to support the use of 3-hydroxy-3-methylglutaryl coenzyme A (HMG-CoA) reductase inhibitors ("statins") as first-line therapy for the treatment and prevention of CHD in women. Analyses of the carotid arteries (Asymptomatic Carotid Progression Study [ACAPS] Trial) and coronary bypass grafts (Post CABG Trial) in women treated with lovastatin have shown improvement in the size of atherosclerotic plaques compared with those in women on placebo treatment.[16,17] In the Scandinavian Simvastatin Survival Study, there was a 35% reduction in major coronary events in hypercholesterolemic women with CHD treated with simvastatin versus those treated with placebo.[18] In the Cholesterol and Recurrent Events (CARE) Trial, women with CHD and "average" cholesterol levels (mean total cholesterol 215 mg/dL) experienced a 43% reduction in coronary events with pravastatin compared with those on placebo treatment. In this trial there was also a 56% reduction in stroke, a 48% reduction in coronary angioplasty, and 40% reduction in coronary bypass surgery in treated women; all of these effects were superior for the female compared with the male subjects.[19] Women without overt CHD also benefit with comparable relative risk reduction in coronary events when treated with statins (Table 36–1). For example, in the Air Force/Texas Coronary Atherosclerosis Prevention Study (AF/TexCAPS) Trial, lovastatin reduced the risk of first major coronary event by 46% versus placebo in women with average cholesterol levels.[20]

Recently published guidelines recommend statins as first-line therapy for most female patients requiring medical therapy for dyslipidemia.[21] This includes virtually all patients with CHD/known atherosclerotic disease or Type 2 diabetes patients who have LDL levels > 130 mg/dL, and any coronary or diabetic patient unable to reach her LDL goal of 100 mg/dL by nonpharmacologic means.

With the advent of high-potency statins, the vast majority of patients with elevated LDL levels can be managed by the generalist, using nonpharmacologic therapy alone or in combination with a statin. Before beginning statin therapy, complete lipid and hepatic panels should be obtained. All patients should be warned of potential toxicities of

TABLE 36–1. Mean Pretreatment Serum Lipid Concentrations and Relative Risk Reduction in Coronary Events[*]

| | | Cholesterol Levels | | | | Reduction in |
Trial	Known CHD?	Total	LDL	HDL	Drug Used	Coronary Events (%)
4S[18]	Yes	268	190	53	Simvastatin	34
CARE[19]	Yes	215	140	45	Pravastatin	43
LIPID[22]	Yes	218	150	36	Pravastatin	26
AF/TexCAPS[20]	No	221	150	40	Lovastatin	46

[*]In female subjects treated with statins in randomized placebo-controlled coronary heart disease (CHD) prevention trials.
CHOL = cholesterol; LDL = low-density lipoprotein; HDL = high-density lipoprotein; 4S = Scandinavian Simvastatin Survival Study; CARE = Cholesterol and Recurrent Events; LIPID = Long-Term Intervention with Pravastatin in Ischemic Disease; AF/TexCAPS = Air Force/Texas Coronary Atherosclerosis Prevention Study.

therapy, including myositis (characterized by generalized muscle pain, tenderness, or weakness) and hepatitis, which is usually asymptomatic. Statins can be started safely at a dose expected to achieve the degree of LDL-level reduction necessary to achieve targets. Patients should avoid combining statins with other agents that have the potential to increase the risk of these toxicities, including fibrates, niacin (at doses of greater than 250 mg/d), cyclosporine, macrolide antibiotics, and alcohol in large quantities. Lipid and hepatic panels should be reassessed at 6 to 8 weeks from the start of therapy and doses adjusted as necessary to achieve LDL targets (Table 36–2).[22] In general, doubling a statin dose further reduces LDL levels by 5 to 8%.[23] If possible, the secondary targets for HDL and TG levels also should be reached by increasing statin doses, but there is insufficient evidence to support adding of a second agent if statin monotherapy fails to achieve these

secondary goals. Once targets are reached, the lipid and hepatic panels should be rechecked annually, or sooner if the underlying risk profile changes (eg, if CHD or type 2 diabetes is diagnosed, and the LDL target changes as a result). Muscle enzyme tests such as creatinine phosphokinase (CPK) do not need to be measured unless symptoms consistent with myositis occur.

Resins, such as cholestyramine, and niacin are second-line options to reduce LDL levels. The combination of statins or niacin with resins is safe and is more efficacious than either drug alone. Other combinations, such as statin-niacin or statin-fibrate carry increased risk of myopathy and hepatic dysfunction. Those patients with the inability to reach target lipid levels with a single drug or a safe combination of drugs merit consideration of referral to a lipid specialist. In severe, usually familial, forms of the disease, when two or three drugs are used to control the

TABLE 36–2. Lipid Goals for Women

| | Goals for Prevention | |
Lipid Parameter	Primary CHD	Secondary CHD/High Risk
LDL	< 160 mg/dL (optimal < 130 mg/dL) if 0 or 1 other risk factor[*] < 130 mg/dL if ≥ 2 other risk factors[*]	< 100 mg/dL
HDL	> 35 mg/dL (optimal ≥ 45 mg/dL)	NS
TG	< 200 mg/dL (optimal < 150 mg/dL)	NS

[*]Coronary heart disease (CHD) risk factors as defined by the National Cholesterol Education Program[9] are as follows: female aged > 55 years, or having premature menopause without estrogen replacement therapy; family history of first-degree relative with coronary event prior to 55 years (male) or 65 years (female); current smoking; hypertension; high-density lipoprotein (HDL) levels < 40 mg/dL. Note: HDL > 60 mg/dL is considered protective and negates a risk factor. The NCEP recommends patients with any form of clinical atherosclerosis, diabetes mellitus, and/or 10-yr CHD risk exceeding 20% be treated to secondary prevention targets, ie, LDL-C < 100 mg/dL.
LDL = low-density lipoprotein; TG = triglycerides.
Adapted from Mosca L, Grundy SM, Judelson D, et al. Guide to preventive cardiology for women. Circulation 1999;99:2480–4.

dyslipidemia, the technique of LDL apheresis is sometimes used to further reduce LDL levels.

There is no consensus on the best means by which to treat hypertriglyceridemia and/or low HDL levels when LDL cholesterol is at the NCEP target. Severe forms of hypertriglyceridemia (TGs >700 to 1,000) almost always require a fibrate to minimize risk of pancreatitis. Milder elevations (200 to 400) should be treated with a statin or niacin. Hormone replacement therapy (HRT) and resins tend to exacerbate hypertriglyceridemia.

Female patients with low HDL levels (<45 mg/dL) and TGs <150 can be considered for use of statins (given efficacy in such patients in the AF/TexCAPS Study) or niacin, and/or HRT, given the HDL-raising abilities of each of these therapies. Fibrate monotherapy, although able to improve HDL levels, has been associated with increased non-cardiovascular mortality in clinical trials[24] and, as such, should not be used in this setting.

PREGNANCY AND BREAST-FEEDING

Typically, serum lipid levels rise during pregnancy, and the upper limit of a normal cholesterol level during the third trimester is approximately double that for an age-matched nonpregnant woman.[25] This makes pregnancy and the early postpartum period an inappropriate time to assess for hyperlipidemia. Furthermore, except in the most unusual of circumstances such as a severely hypertriglyceridemic (serum TG >1,000) woman suffering from pancreatitis, *cholesterol-lowering medication should not be given to pregnant or nursing women.* The likely interference with the central role played by cholesterol in steroid hormone biosynthesis during embryonic development serves as the basis for this recommendation. The statins are categorized by the U.S. Food and Drug Administration as category X—contraindicated in pregnancy. Therefore, statins *should not be prescribed to pregnant women or those who are likely to become pregnant soon.* Gemfibrozil, cholestyramine, and niacin are classified as category C—risk in pregnancy cannot be ruled out. Gemfibrozil has been linked with increasing rates of spontaneous abortion in female rats treated at comparable doses to those used for humans. Cholestyramine may impede absorption of fat-soluble vitamins, which greatly limits its utility in pregnancy/lactation as well.

ORAL CONTRACEPTION

There is relatively little information on the lipid effects or long-term cardiovascular implications associated with use of oral contraceptives. In one report, a monophasic formulation of ethinyl estradiol and norgestimate had similar improvement in lipid parameters as do triphasic ethinyl estradiol and gestodene. The increase in total cholesterol, HDL, and TG levels reflect a predominance of estrogen over the progestin effect. Concentration of LDLs also decreased on both therapies.[26] The increased TG levels associated with oral contraceptive use do not appear to confer excess cardiovascular risk if LDL levels are not increased.[26]

POSTMENOPAUSAL TREATMENT AND HORMONE REPLACEMENT

Adverse changes in the lipid profile have been documented within 3 months of surgical menopause, and these are reversed by estrogen replacement.[27] Historically, many public health guidelines have recommended that HRT be considered first-line treatment of dyslipidemia in postmenopausal women. These recommendations were based in part on the benefits of hormone replacement on serum lipid parameters: reduction of the atherogenic LDL cholesterol concentration along with an increase in the beneficial HDL cholesterol level. The Postmenopausal Estrogen/Progestin Interventions (PEPI) Trial demonstrated that conjugated estrogen raised HDL cholesterol levels by as much as 12%, but that the effect was markedly reduced by the coadministration of progestins.[28] Micronized progesterone caused less attenuation of estrogen HDL improvement than did medroxyprogesterone acetate in the trial.[29] However, conjugated estrogen and the estrogen/progestin combinations in the trial produced an approximately 10% reduction in LDL cholesterol concentration. Recent evidence suggests that the LDL reduction with HRT is seen only in women with ApoE4-negative genotype.[30] Both oral and transdermal estrogen treatment reduce the serum concentration of lipoprotein(a), a particularly atherogenic form of LDL.[31,32] The reduction in lipoprotein(a) level is diminished by the addition of progesterone.[33] All of the HRT regimens in PEPI unfortunately raised the levels of TG, which also are considered a potential CHD risk factor.[34] This estrogen-induced increase in triglycerides is accompanied by an increase in small dense LDL particles, also believed to have increased atherogenic potential.[35]

Some have argued that the combination of hormone replacement with statins offers potential benefit over either therapy alone. In one study, both simvastatin and a combined continuous HRT regimen increased HDL comparably, but simvastatin reduced LDL levels to a greater extent than did HRT.[36] Another study demonstrated that the increase in triglycerides associated with HRT can be offset by the addition of pravastatin.[37] Adding to the appeal of HRT in CHD prevention were the results of the large observational Nurses' Health Study, which suggested that ever having taken any form of HRT was associated with a significant reduction in major coronary events.[38]

To date, the only major prospective placebo-controlled coronary prevention trial of HRT was the Heart and Estrogen/Progestin Replacement Study (HERS) Trial, in which 2,763 postmenopausal women with established CHD and intact uteri were randomized to receive either conjugated estrogen/medroxyprogesterone acetate or placebo for 4 years. No difference was noted between the groups in any cardiovascular end points including coronary events, MIs, transient ischemic attacks, strokes, and death, despite a reduction of LDL cholesterol levels by 11% and increase in HDL cholesterol levels by 10% in the HRT group.[39] It is worth noting that the majority of women enrolled in the HERS Trial did not reach the LDL treatment goal (< 100 mg/dL in CHD patients) in the 1993 NCEP/Adult Treatment Panel II guidelines that were in force at the time the trial was conducted.[9] Moreover, fewer than half of the women (47%) were taking lipid-lowering medications.[40]

Some recent evidence suggests that selective estrogen response modulators (SERMs) might potentially have a role in therapy of dyslipidemia. Raloxifene therapy, for example, lowers LDL cholesterol levels by about 11% and total cholesterol levels by about 7%. In contrast with HRT though, raloxifene does not appear to raise either HDL cholesterol or TG levels.[41] In another trial, breast cancer patients treated with tamoxifen had a significant reduction in LDL levels and an increase in HDL levels compared with those who did not receive the medication.[42] However, it remains to be seen whether these lipid effects yield any benefit in the prevention of CHD.

RESOURCES

The American Heart Association
7272 Greenville Avenue
Dallas, Texas 75231
Telephone: 1-800-242-8721
Web site: www.americanheart.org

The American Heart Association is considered the most objective, comprehensive, and current source of information on cardiovascular risk and diseases. It is useful for both clinicians and patients.

National Cholesterol Education Program
NCEP Information Center
PO Box 30105
Bethesda, Maryland 20824-0105
Telephone: (301) 251-1222
Web site: www.nhlbi.nih.gov/about/ncep/index.htm

The National Heart, Lung, and Blood Institute, a division of the National Institutes of Health, has sponsored the periodic generation of guidelines for management of cholesterol and other coronary risk factors through the National Cholesterol Education Program. Cholesterol information for both clinicians and patients, including patient education materials, are available through the NCEP website.

CONCLUSION

Although the future holds promise for the discovery of other means to reduce women's risk of cardiovascular events, there is considerable evidence that the majority of women with dyslipidemia in this country are not receiving proper dietary instruction or medical therapy. This seems unjustifiable given the large trial data demonstrating profound cardiovascular benefits with statin therapy. Lipid lowering should be part of an evidence-based treatment plan for virtually all women with atherosclerotic disease, and for most women with hyperlipidemia and other CHD risk factors.

REFERENCES

1. American Heart Association. 1999 heart and stroke facts: statistical update. Dallas (TX): AHA; 1999.

2. Ginsberg HN, Goldberg IJ. Disorders of lipoprotein metabolism. In: Fauci AS, editor. Harrison's principles of internal medicine. 14th ed. New York: McGraw Hill; 1998.

3. Hochman JS, Tamis JE. Thompson TD, et al. Sex, clinical presentation, and outcome in patients with acute coronary syndromes. N Engl J Med 1999;341: 226–32.

4. Vaccarino V, Parsons L, Every NR, et al. Sex-based differences in early mortality after myocardial infarction. N Engl J Med 1999;341:217–25.

5. Mosca L, Grundy SM, Judelson D, et al. Guide to preventive cardiology for women. Circulation 1999;99: 2480–4.

6. Manolio TA, Pearson TA, Wenger NK, et al. Cholesterol and heart disease in older persons and women: review of an NHLBI workshop. Ann Epidemiol 1992;2:161–76.

7. Jacobs DR Jr, Meban IL, Bangdiwala SI, et al. High density lipoprotein cholesterol as a predictor of cardiovascular risk in men and women. The follow-up study of the Lipid Research Clinics Prevalence Study. Am J Epidemiol 1990;131:32–47.

8. National Heart, Lung, and Blood Institute. 1995 cholesterol awareness surveys. Bethesda (MD): National Institutes of Health; 1995.

9. Expert Panel on Detection, Evaluation and Treatment of High Blood Cholesterol in Adults. Executive summary of the National Cholesterol Education Program (NCEP) Expert Panel on Detection, Evaluation and Treatment of High Blood Cholesterol in Adults (Adult Treatment Panel III). JAMA 2001;285: 2486–97.

10. Edmond MJ, Zareba W. Prognostic value of cholesterol in women of different ages. J Womens Health 1997;6:295–307.

11. U.S. Preventive Services Task Force. Guide to clinical preventive services. 2nd ed. Washington (DC): Dept. of Health and Human Services, Office of Disease Prevention and Health Promotion; 1996.

12. Benfante R, Reed D. Is elevated serum cholesterol a risk for coronary heart disease in the elderly? JAMA 1990;263:393–6.

13. Niaura R. Marcus B, Albrecht A, et al. Exercise, smoking cessation, and short-term changes in serum lipids in women: a preliminary investigation. Med Sci Sports Excerc 1998;30:1414–8.

14. Stefanik ML, Mackey S, Sheehan M, et al. Effects of diet and exercise in men and postmenopausal women with low levels of HDL cholesterol and high LDL cholesterol. N Engl J Med 1998;339:12–20.

15. Barnard RJ, Inkeles SB. Effects of an intensive diet and exercise program on lipids in postmenopausal women. Womens Health Issues 1999;9:155–61.

16. Byington RP, Evans GW, Espeland MA, et al. Effects of lovastatin and warfarin on early carotid atherosclerosis: sex-specific analysis. Asymptomatic Carotid Progression Study (ACAPS) Research Group. Circulation 1999;100:e14–7.

17. Forrester JS, Geller NL, Gobel FL, et al, Post CABG Trial Investigators. Aggressive cholesterol lowering delays saphenous vein atherosclerosis in women, the elderly, and patients with associated risk factors. NHLBI Post Coronary Artery Bypass Graft Clinical Trial. Circulation 1999;99:3241–7.

18. Miettinen TA, Pyorala K, Olsson AG, et al. Cholesterol-lowering therapy in women and elderly patients with myocardial infarction or angina pectoris. Findings from the Scandinavian Simvastatin Survival Study (4S). Circulation 1997;96:4211–8.

19. Lewis SJ, Sacks FM, Mitchell JS, et al. Effect of pravastatin on cardiovascular events in women after myocardial infarction: the Cholesterol and Recurrent Events (CARE) Trial. J Am Coll Cardiol 1998; 32:140–6.

20. Downs JR, Clearfield M, Weis S, et al. Primary prevention of acute coronary events with lovastatin in men and women with average cholesterol levels. JAMA 1998;279:1615–22.

21. Ansell BJ, Watson KE, Fogelman AM. The National Cholesterol Education Program/Adult Treatment

Panel II guidelines: an evidence-based assessment. JAMA 1999;282:2051–7.

22. The Long-Term Intervention with Pravastatin in Ischemic Disease (LIPID) Study Group. Prevention of cardiovascular events and death with pravastatin in patients with coronary heart disease and a broad range of initial cholesterol levels. N Engl J Med 1998; 339:1349–57.

23. Jones P, Kafonek S, Laurora I, Hunninghake D. Comparative dose efficacy study of atorvastatin versus simvastatin, pravastatin, lovastatin, and fluvastatin in patients with hypercholesterolemia (the CURVES study). Am J Cardiol 1998;81:582–7.

24. Gould AL, Rossouw JE, Santanello NC, et al. Cholesterol reduction yields clinical benefit. A new look at old data. Circulation 1995;91:2274–82.

25. Fallon HJ, Riely CA. Liver diseases. In: Burrow GN, Ferris TF, editors. Medical complications during pregnancy. 4th ed. Philadelphia: WB Saunders; 1995. p. 309.

26. Wiegratz I, Jung-Hoffman C, Gross W, Kuhl H. Effect of two oral contraceptives containing ethinyl estradiol and gestodene or norgestimate on different lipid and lipoprotein parameters. Contraception 1998;58: 83–91.

27. Bruschi F, Meschia M, Soma M, et al. Lipoprotein(a) and other lipids after oophorectomy and estrogen replacement therapy. Obstet Gynecol 1996;88:950–4.

28. Barrett-Connor E, Slone S, Greendale G, et al. The Postmenopausal Estrogen/Progestin Interventions Study: primary outcomes in adherent women. Maturitas 1997;27:261–74.

29. The Writing Group for the PEPI Trial. Effects of estrogen or estrogen/progestin regimens on heart disease risk factors in postmenopausal women. JAMA 1995;273:199–208.

30. Heikkinen AM, Niskanen L, Ryyanen M, et al. Is the response of serum lipids and lipoproteins in postmenopausal hormone replacement therapy modified by ApoE genotype? Arteriosclerosis Thromb Vasc Biol 1999;19:402–7.

31. Meschia M, Bruschi F, Soma M, et al. Effects of oral and transdermal hormone replacement therapy on lipoprotein(a) and lipids: a randomized controlled trial. Menopause 1998;5:157–62.

32. Sacks FM, McPherson R, Walsh B. Effect of postmenopausal estrogen replacement on plasma Lp(a) lipoprotein concentrations. Arch Intern Med 1994; 154:1106–10.

33. Kim CJ, Min YK, Ryu WS, et al. Effect of hormone replacement therapy on lipoprotein(a) and lipid levels in postmenopausal women. Influence of various progestogens and duration of therapy. Arch Intern Med 1996;156:1693–700.

34. The Writing Group for the PEPI Trial. Effects of hormone replacement therapy on endometrial histology in postmenopausal women. The Postmenopausal Estrogen/Progestin Interventions (PEPI) Trial. JAMA 1996;275:370–5.

35. Wakatsuki A, Ikenoue N, Sagara Y. Estrogen-induced small low-density lipoprotein particles in postmenopausal women. Obstet Gynecol 1998; 91:234–40.

36. Darling GM, Johns JA, McCloud PI, Davis SR. Estrogen and progestin compared with simvastatin for hypercholesterolemia in postmenopausal women. N Engl J Med 1997;337:595–601.

37. Davidson MH, Testolin LM, Maki KC, et al. A comparison of estrogen replacement, pravastatin, and combined treatment for the management of hypercholesterolemia in postmenopausal women. Arch Intern Med 1997;157:1186–92.

38. Stampfer MJ, Colditz GA, Willett WC, et al. Postmenopausal estrogen therapy and cardiovascular disease. Ten-year follow-up from the Nurses' Health Study. N Engl J Med 1991:325:756–62.

39. Hulley S, Grady D, Bush T, et al. Randomized trial of estrogen plus progestin for secondary prevention of coronary heart disease in postmenopausal women. Heart and Estrogen/Progestin Replacement Study (HERS). JAMA 1998;280:605–13.

40. Schrott HG, Bittner V, Vitinghoff E, et al, the HERS Research Group. Adherence to the National Cholesterol Education Program treatment goals in postmenopausal women with heart disease. The Heart and Estrogen/Progestin Replacement Study (HERS). JAMA 1997;277:1281–6.

41. Walsh, BW, Kuller LH, Wild RA, et al. Effects on raloxifene of serum lipids and coagulation factors in healthy postmenopausal women. JAMA 1998;279:1445–51.

42. Wasan KM, Ramaswamy M, Haley J, Dunn BP. Administration of long-term tamoxifen therapy modifies the plasma lipoprotein-lipid concentration and lipid transfer protein I activity in postmenopausal women with breast cancer. J Pharm Sci 1997; 86:876–9.

37

APPROACH TO THE PATIENT WITH PALPITATIONS

Zenaida Feliciano, MD

Palpitations are a common complaint in the general medical setting. As many as 16% of patients may report palpitations, making it one of the 10 most common complaints in the primary care setting.[1] Palpitations are defined as an unpleasant awareness of the heartbeat, and are described by the patient in myriad ways. They may be described as extra or skipped beats, fast heartbeats, irregular heart rate, heart fluttering, racing, pounding, and/or a "flip-flopping" sensation in the chest. Palpitations are a nonspecific symptom, and although they may suggest the presence of an abnormality of the cardiac rhythm, this subjective symptom is not always associated with cardiac arrhythmias. "Arrhythmia" is defined as any cardiac rhythm that deviates from normal sinus rhythm; it can refer to a fast (tachyarrhythmia) or a slow (bradyarrhythmia) heartbeat.

Gender differences in patients with palpitations have not been well studied, but 57 to 88% of outpatients presenting with palpitations are female.[1,2] It has been noted that women of all ages complain of palpitations. Palpitations frequently are reported during the luteal phase of the menstrual cycle, pregnancy, and the perimenopausal period. Electrocardiographic and electrophysiologic differences between men and women have been noted.[3] Women have a higher intrinsic heart rate than do men after autonomic blockade, and their sinus node function recovers more quickly after autonomic blockade than does sinus node function in men.[4,5]

Palpitations are usually benign, but occasionally they are the manifestation of potentially life-threatening conditions. An evaluation is required to exclude potentially life-threatening conditions and to differentiate between organic and psychological issues. In this chapter a diagnostic algorithm for the evaluation of patients with palpitations is discussed.

PATHOPHYSIOLOGY

Arrhythmias are due to disturbances in the formation or the conduction of the cardiac impulse. Cardiac impulse formation normally starts in the sinus node, which is located in the high right lateral atrium, and is transmitted through both atria down to the atrioventricular node located in the septal area between the atria and the ventricles. Normally the atrioventricular node is the only electrical connection between the atrium and the ventricles, and the impulse is transmitted down to the ventricular muscle using the specialized conduction system of the heart comprised by the bundle of His and the right and left bundle branches.

Cardiac impulse propagation occurs via electrical conduction due to the depolarization of the myocardial and specialized conduction system cells. All cells activated by depolarization enter a refractory period during which they are not excitable. Therefore, once all the cardiac tissue is depolarized, the conduction impulse cannot be further propagated and extinguishes. However, if a group of cells are not activated during depolarization or recover excitability before the impulse dies out, they may be reactivated by the extinguishing impulse and can themselves re-excite areas that have recovered. This results in a reentrant excitation that can result in tachyarrythmias. Alternatively, cardiac impulse propagation can be interrupted and produce bradyarrhythmias. Other mechanisms of arrythmias are

410

enhanced or abnormal automaticity and trigger activity, which may arise either in the cardiac conduction system and/or the atrial or ventricular myocardium.

DIFFERENTIAL DIAGNOSIS OF PALPITATIONS

The differential diagnosis of palpitations is extensive and ranges from cardiac causes to psychiatric causes[6] (Table 37–1). Common cardiac causes of arrhythmias leading to palpitations are structural abnormalities including coronary artery disease, valvular heart disease, congenital heart disease, cardiomyopathies, and conduction system abnormalities such as sick sinus syndrome and Wolff-Parkinson-White syndrome.

The diagnostic evaluation of patients with palpitations requires detailed history taking, physical examination, and 12-lead electrocardiography (ECG). A recent study found that an etiology could be determined in 84% of patients presenting with palpitations.[6] Forty percent of these diagnoses were established with a complete history, physical examination, 12-lead ECG, and basic laboratory data. Figure 37–1 summarizes the diagnostic approach to a patient with palpitations.

History

A detailed history is essential in the evaluation of patients with palpitations. The history should include the patient's age at onset of the palpitations, the frequency and severity of palpitations, a detailed description of any associated symptoms, the mode of onset and termination of the palpitations, and any precipitating or alleviating factors that the patient may have recognized.

The patient who has had palpitations that are rapid since childhood is more likely than those with adult-onset palpitations to have a supraventricular tachycardia as the etiology of the palpitations. Rare episodes in healthy patients that last only a few seconds and are not associated with hemodynamic compromise such as syncope, dizziness, or presyncope may not need further evaluation. In patients with episodes that are frequent, debilitating, and associated with presyncope or syncope, as well as in patients with associated underlying cardiovascular disease, immediate evaluation is usually necessary.

The examiner should elicit the rate and degree of regularity of the palpitations. It is helpful for the

TABLE 37–1. Differential Diagnosis of Palpitations

Cardiac causes
  Structural heart disease
    Coronary artery disease
    Valvular heart disease
    Cardiomyopathy
    Congenital heart disease

  Conduction system abnormalities
    Acquired
      Sick sinus syndrome
      Mobitz type I and type II AV block
      Complete heart block
    Congenital
      Lone atrial fibrillation
      Wolff-Parkinson-White syndrome
      Long QT syndrome

Noncardiac causes
  Anxiety
  Stress
  Caffeine
  Nicotine
  Hyperthyroidism
  Electrolyte disturbances
  Drugs
    Antiarrhythmics
    Decongestants
    Contraceptives
    Herbal remedies
    Others

AV = atrioventricular.

examiner to ask the patient to "tap out" the rhythm with his or her fingers.[7] Rapid and regular rhythms are suggestive of paroxysmal supraventricular tachycardias or ventricular tachycardias, whereas rapid and irregular rhythms suggest atrial fibrillation, atrial flutter, or atrial tachycardia with variable block. Reid[8] has indicated that, in his experience, only one-third of the patients with palpitations are able to describe the cadence of the palpitations. He has suggested that if patients are asked to tap out what is felt, they are better able to describe the regularity and rate of onset and offset of the palpitations.

Inquiring for any concomitant medical history is important when evaluating patients with palpitations. Patients with a history of significant ventricular dysfunction or significant coronary artery disease

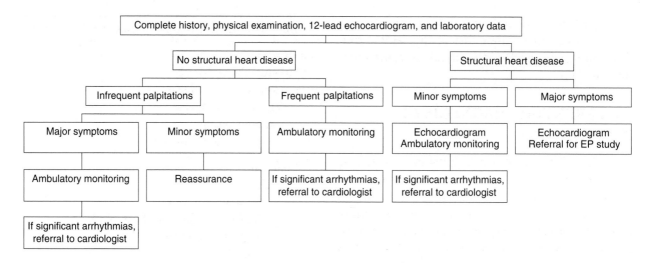

FIGURE 37–1. Approach to diagnosing the patient with palpitations. EP = electrophysiologic.

are more likely to have life-threatening arrhythmias as the cause of palpitations. Frequently the initial presentation of life-threatening arrythmias is not palpitations but hypotension, presyncope, syncope, or cardiovascular collapse without antecedent palpitations. Arrythmias may present as angina in patients with clinically significant coronary artery disease. A pre-existing underlying psychiatric, panic, or somatization disorder history is also important. Individuals with a prior history of these disorders are more likely to have palpitations that do not correlate with cardiac arrythmias.[7]

The severity of the symptoms associated with palpitations is important and may be characterized as minor, such as the sensation of an abnormal heartbeat in the absence of any other symptoms, or major, such as palpitations associated with angina, diaphoresis, presyncope, or syncope. The patient with associated major symptoms presents a greater urgency for evaluation, since the palpitations are more likely to be a manifestation of life-threatening arrythmia.

Knowledge of specific symptoms and circumstances during which palpitations occur is helpful in narrowing the differential diagnosis of palpitations. The mode of onset and termination of the palpitations is helpful in identifying their cause. Most patients are unable to identify what initiates the palpitations, or any aggravating factors. It is important to search for this information since, in the few patients in whom initiating factors can be identified, the avoidance of these factors may result in resolution of the palpitations. The search for precipitating factors should include a careful history of any substances that the patient may have ingested before the symptoms occurred, including caffeinated beverages, chocolate, alcohol, over-the-counter medications, illicit drugs, and tobacco. In addition, the differential diagnosis can be narrowed down if the palpitations occur with activity. Palpitations related to organic heart disease usually occur at all times, despite distractions associated with daily living activities. Patients that terminate their arrhythmia with carotid sinus massage or other vasovagal maneuvers are likely to have an atrioventricular (AV) nodal–dependent arrhythmia as the cause of the palpitations. The relationship between the description of palpitations and the underlying arrhythmia mechanisms has been studied. Zimetbaum and Josephson[7] describe a correlation between symptoms and mechanisms, as described below.

RAPID HEART BEATS OR FLUTTERING

Rapid heart beats or fluttering usually are caused by a type of tachyarrythmia, atrial or ventricular, including sinus tachycardia. The rhythm of the palpitations may indicate the source of the arrythmia: irregular and sustained rapid flutterings without hemodynamic deterioration suggest atrial fibrillation with rapid ventricular response, whereas a regular rapid fluttering suggests reentrant tachyarrhythmia, either atrial or ventricular in origin.

FLIP-FLOPPING SENSATION

The sensation of a flip-flop in the chest usually is associated with premature ventricular contractions followed by a compensatory pause. In patients with normal cardiac physiology, the cardiac contraction after a pause is stronger or more notable, following Starling's law.

NECK POUNDING

When associated with palpitations, neck pounding suggests the presence of AV dissociation. The pounding sensation is usually the result of an atrial contraction against the closed tricuspid and mitral valve. If the neck pounding is regular and rapid, it suggests a reentrant supraventricular arrythmia, most commonly AV nodal reentry tachycardia. If the pulsations are more irregular and less sustained, they are suggestive of dissociation secondary to either premature ventricular contractions or ventricular tachycardia. Atrioventricular nodal reentry tachycardia is the most common form of paroxysmal supraventricular tachycardia, and it is three times as common in women than in men.

PALPITATIONS ASSOCIATED WITH ANXIETY

It is often difficult to discern whether a patient felt the sensation of anxiety or panic before or after feeling palpitations. There is a tendency to ascribe palpitations to anxiety, particularly when they occur in young women.[7] Psychiatric disorders have been diagnosed as a cause of palpitations in up to 31 to 45% of patients.[6] Many patients who frequently report palpitations have a history of panic attacks. Despite the fact that psychiatric disorders are a common cause of palpitations, a psychiatric etiology of palpitations should not be assumed until an arrythmic cause for the symptoms has been excluded. In a recent study 67% of patients with electrophysiologically documented reentrant supraventricular tachycardia met the criteria for panic disorders detailed in the diagnostic and statistical manual of mental disorders.[9] A median of 3.3 years between the initial presentation to a physician and a definite diagnosis of supraventricular tachycardia was noted.[7] Approximately 50% of the patients in whom supraventricular tachycardia was not recognized at the initial medical evaluation received a diagnosis of panic, stress, or anxiety disorder; 65% of these patients were women.[7]

PALPITATIONS ASSOCIATED WITH CATECHOLAMINE EXCESS

The presence of palpitations during conditions of catecholamine excess such as exercise or emotional stress suggests several etiologies. In patients with structurally normal hearts, right ventricular outflow tract tachycardia usually occurs in the setting of catecholamine excess. This disorder most often produces palpitations in teenagers and persons in their twenties. Atrial fibrillation also may be induced during exercise or immediately after termination of activity. This occurs particularly in athletic men, in their twenties to fifties. Catecholamine surges also may produce palpitations in patients with the long QT syndrome. The long QT syndrome is an inherited abnormality of myocardial repolarization that results in polymorphic ventricular tachycardia during periods of emotional stress or vigorous exercise. An exaggerated response to catecholamine excess can be seen in patients with inappropriate sinus tachycardia. This is an extremely rare disorder that usually presents with the feeling of palpitations during minimal exertion or emotional stress. Inappropriate sinus tachycardia is seen most frequently in young women and may result from a hypersensitivity to ß-adrenergic stimulation.

PALPITATIONS TRIGGERED BY POSITIONAL CHANGES

Palpitations that often appear when the patient stands up after bending over suggest the presence of AV nodal reentrant tachycardia. The palpitations usually terminate when the patient assumes the supine position.

Physical Examination

The focus of the physical examination is to identify the presence of potential cardiovascular or other systemic abnormalities that can serve as a substrate for arrythmias. During the physical examination, the patient's mental status also should be assessed to identify the presence of depression, panic disorders, or other psychiatric disorders that may be the cause of or exacerbate the symptoms. The clinician is rarely able to examine the patient during an episode of palpitations; most patients are free of symptoms at the time of presentation. If the clinician has the opportunity to examine the patient as symptoms occur, then attention should be focused on the patient's heart rate and rhythm. If the palpitations are associated with a normal sinus rhythm, then a cardiac cause for the symptoms is unlikely. The physical examination should include a careful cardiovascular evaluation and auscultation, as certain findings are suggestive of specific etiologies for the palpitations. For example, if a midsystolic click of mitral valve prolapse is heard then it is likely that the symptoms are secondary to a cardiac arrhythmia as many supraventricular as well as ventricular arrhythmias have been associated with the presence of mitral valve prolapse. A harsh holosystolic murmur heard along the left exsternal border that increases with a Valsalva maneuver suggests the possibility of hypertrophic cardiomyopthy. This disorder normally is associated with atrial fibrillation, as well as with ventricular tachycardias.

A careful cardiovascular evaluation during the examination may disclose signs of dilated cardiomyopathy and congestive heart failure. These conditions are described further in Chapter 33, "Congestive Heart Failure." If signs of congestive heart failure and dilated cardiomyopathy are present, then an important consideration is the possibility of ventricular tachycardias as the cause of the palpitations. Such patients also have an increased risk of developing atrial fibrillation. If the patient is in chronic atrial fibrillation during the physical examination, then the patient should be instructed to take a brisk walk, after which the patient's pulse should be examined—many of these patients have a rapid ventricular response during activity that is not present at rest and that results in the symptom of palpitations.

Twelve-Lead Electrocardiography

Even when patients present with normal sinus rhythm, the 12-lead electrocardigraphy is often helpful in narrowing the differential diagnosis of palpitations. If there is presence of a short P–R interval (<0.12 seconds) and a prolonged QRS complex (>0.12 seconds) associated with a slur on the upstroke of the QRS, then the presence of Wolff-Parkinson-White (WPW) syndrome should be entertained and, with this, a substrate for supraventricular tachycardias (Figure 37–2). Evidence of left atrial abnormality (Figure 37–3) on the electrocardiogram, as indicated by a terminal P wave force in V1 that is more negative than 0.04 milliseconds or a notched P wave in lead 2, suggests a substrate for possible atrial fibrillation.

Evidence for marked left ventricular hypertrophy with deep septal Q waves in leads I, aVL, and V4 through V6 suggests septal hypertrophy, as is seen in hypertrophic cardiomyopathy. The presence of Q waves is a characteristic of a prior myocardial infarction. In both cases a more extensive search for an unsustained or sustained ventricular arrythmias is warranted. An elongation of the Q–T interval and abnormal T wave morphology may suggest the presence of long QT syndrome, and further evaluation is warranted to rule out the possibility of unsustained ventricular arrythmias (Figure 37–4).

Isolated atrial or ventricular premature beats may be the etiology of the palpitations, or they could be the trigger for more sustained supraventricular or ventricular arrythmias. There are two types of idiopathic ventricular tachycardias in normal hearts; one that originates in the right ventricular outflow tract with a left bundle branch block, inferior axis morphology, and one that originates in the left ventricle basilar septum with a right bundle branch block left axis morphology. Therefore, when isolated ventricular premature beats with the above morphologies are detected in patients with palpitations and a normal heart, the presence of an idiopathic ventricular arrhythmia should be suspected. If there is evidence of a bradycardic rhythm during the 12-lead ECG, it is important to evaluate for the presence of a specific conduction block or coexisting ventricular arrhythmia that may result from the bradycardia.

The presence or absence of a cardiac etiology for palpitations should be clear in the few patients in which the 12-lead ECG is performed while the patient is symptomatic. Since this happens infrequently, further cardiac evaluation usually is required when the etiology of the palpitations remains unclear after a detailed history, physical examination, and interpretation of the 12-lead ECG are completed. The next section reviews the additional diagnostic tests that are recommended for further evaluation of these patients.

Additional Studies

Especially in high-risk patients, when the history, physical examination, and 12-lead ECG are unrevealing, additional studies should be considered. Patients are considered to be at high risk if there is any evidence of organic heart disease found in the history, in the physical examination, or on the 12-lead ECG. Evidence of organic heart disease includes any evidence of myocardial abnormalities, myocardial infarction, dilated cardiomyopathy, clinically significant valvular lesions, or hypertrophic cardiomyopathy,

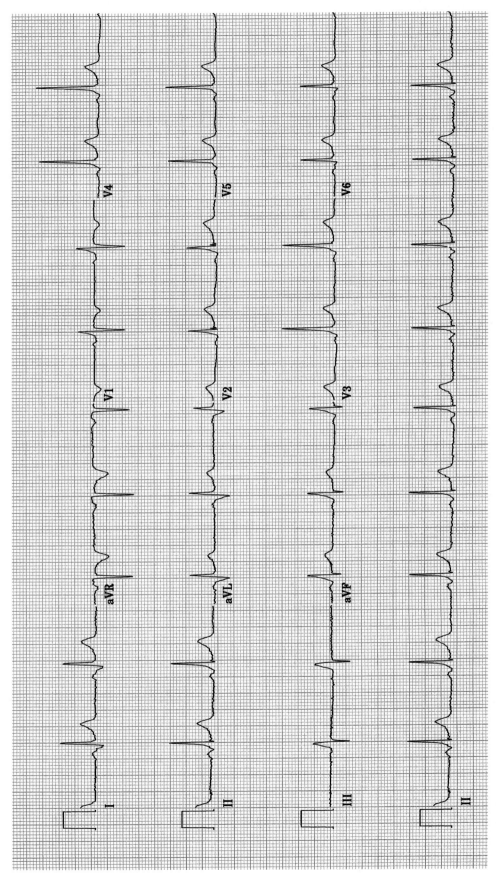

FIGURE 37-2. Twelve-lead electrocardiogram indicating the presence of Wolff-Parkinson-White syndrome. A slurred upstroke of the QRS is noted particularly in leads V1 and V2.

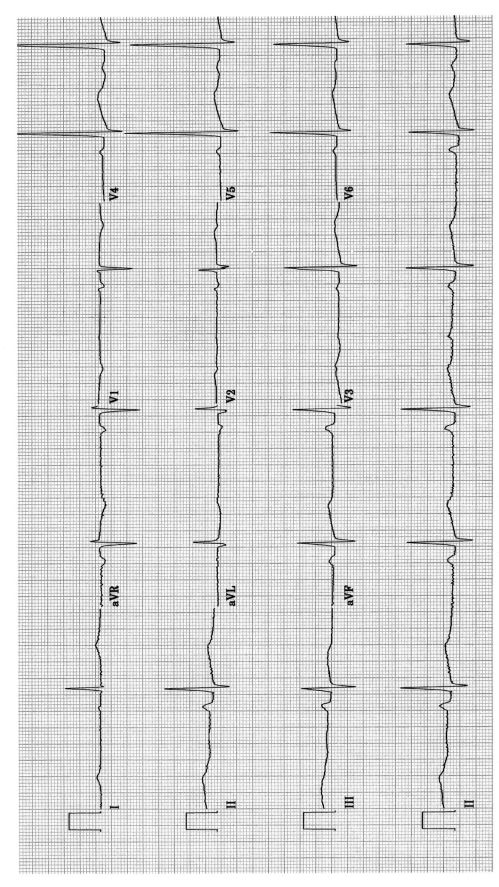

FIGURE 37–3. Twelve-lead electrocardiogram indicating a left atrial abnormality. Biphasic P waves in V1 and V2 are indicated an abnormality of the atrium, possibly providing a substrate for atrial fibrillation.

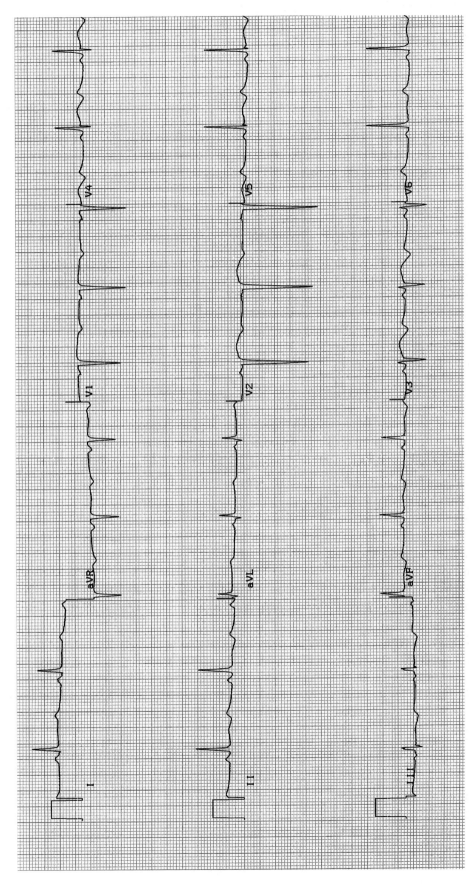

FIGURE 37–4. Twelve-lead electrocardiogram indicating a prolonged Q–T interval. Long QT syndrome is associated with unsustained ventricular arrythmias.

or a significant family history of arrythmias or sudden death. Low-risk patients are those without evidence of significant organic heart disease and who have a normal physical examination.

BLOOD TESTS

The additional studies should be chosen to investigate the presence of the most likely etiology based on the history and physical examination. For example, if a patient is receiving diuretics then an electrolyte disturbance is possible and serum potassium and magnesium levels should be obtained. If during the physical examination there is any suggestion of the possibility of anemia or thyroid dysfunction, then a blood count or thyroid function test should be obtained, respectively. Serum glucose levels at the time of the symptoms should be obtained in any patient who has palpitations with other features that suggest hypoglycemia such as tremulousness and diaphoresis, especially if the symptoms improve after meals. In a patient who has these symptoms and is not seen at the time of palpitations, a glucose tolerance test should be obtained to evaluate for hypoglycemia.

AMBULATORY ELECTROCARDIOGRAPHIC MONITORING

Intermittent palpitations are best evaluated using ambulatory electrocardiographic monitoring devices. Options for ambulatory monitoring devices include a 24-hour Holter monitor that can be worn for 1 or 2 days versus a continuous loop event recorder. The 24-hour Holter monitoring system records and saves data continuously; the rhythm of the heart of the patient can be recorded for 1 to 2 days. The disadvantage of this system is that unless the patient has the symptoms during these 1 or 2 days, no clear diagnosis can be achieved. On the other hand, continuous loop event recorders continuously record data but save data only when the patient manually activates the monitor. The yield for the use of these ambulatory monitoring devices is higher when the patient wears the device for 2 to 4 weeks, as an episode of palpitations is likely to occur during that prolonged period of time. This system typically saves data from at least 1 minute preceding the activation of the system through the subsequent 2 minutes after activation of the system. Continuous loop recorders have been shown to be more cost effective and efficacious in the diagnosis of cardiac arryth-

mias and the evaluations of palpitations than are traditional 24-hour Holter monitors.[10]

For low-risk patients, many experts suggest use of ambulatory monitoring only if the history and/or electrocardiogram suggest the possibility of a sustained arrythmia, or if the patient needs reassurance of the absence of a cardiac arrythmia associated with their symptoms. However, an aggressive approach to the diagnosis of cardiac arrythmias in high-risk patients is recommended. If the palpitations are short-lived and are not associated with hemodynamic compromise, then ambulatory monitoring devices can be used. On the other hand if the patient's palpitations are sustained or poorly tolerated (as evidenced by associated dizziness, presyncope, or syncope), then an electrophysiologic study (see below) should be performed for further evaluation of the palpitations and to rule out the possibility of a life-threatening arrhythmia.

ECHOCARDIOGRAPHY AND STRESS TESTING

If the physical examination suggests the possibility of mitral valve prolapse or other structural abnormalities such as valvular heart disease or hypertrophic cardiomyopathy, an echocardiogram should be obtained to confirm the diagnosis. If there is evidence of a dilated heart or congestive heart failure, an echocardiogram is recommended to evaluate left ventricular function. In patients with premature ventricular contractions as the cause of palpitations, the evaluation of left ventricular function is critical, since the likelihood of the development of a sustained life-threatening ventricular arrhythmia is directly associated with the presence of left ventricular dysfunction or ischemic heart disease. In patients with structurally normal hearts and no ischemia, the presence of premature ventricular contractions is not associated with a decrease in survival rate or an increase in the possibility of a sustained ventricular arrhythmia. These patients should be reassured of the benign nature of the palpitations and should only be treated if symptoms are unbearable. In contrast, patients with left ventricular dysfunction and premature ventricular contractions, especially if frequent (> 10/h), have an associated increased risk of a sustained ventricular arrhythmia and a decrease in survival rate and should be investigated further. If the palpitations are provoked by exertion, an exercise stress test should be performed to evaluate for exercise-induced arrhythmia.

ELECTROPHYSIOLOGIC TESTING

A cardiac electrophysiologic study is an invasive procedure that evaluates the mechanism of arrythmias. Treatment may be performed during the procedure. A blunt catheter is advanced under fluoroscopic guidance into the heart. Intracardiac electrograms are obtained, and the heart is paced in both the atrium and ventricles in an attempt to induce arrhythmias. Often the origin and mechanism of the arrythmia can be established, and, during the same procedure, radiofrequency energy can be used to cause small endocardial burns that ablate the tissue that is the source of the arrythmia. Most supraventricular tachycardias and many types of ventricular tachycardias can be cured with radiofrequency ablation.[11–13]

Basic electrophysiology studies are indicated in patients in whom palpitations occur in association with syncope, near syncope, seizures, sudden death, or any other hemodynamic compromise, such as pulmonary edema.[8,14,15] Electrophysiologic studies also are useful in patients with documented paroxysmal supraventricular tachycardias as an etiology for palpitations, to further evaluate the mechanism of the arrhythmia and to pursue a cure for the arrhythmia with radiofrequency ablation.

MANAGEMENT

Normal Sinus Rhythm and Benign Ectopy

Normal sinus rhythm during episodes of palpitations is found in up to one-third of the patients with palpitations who undergo cardiovascular evaluation. When arrhythmias are excluded as the cause of palpitations, then panic disorders, somatization disorders, and depression must be considered.

Supraventricular Arrhythmias

ATRIAL PREMATURE BEATS

In symptomatic patients with atrial premature beats, a careful history taking may reveal the presence of a precipitating factor, such as caffeine intake, cigarette smoking, excessive alcohol intake, drug abuse, prescription drug therapy, or use of over-the-counter sympathomimetic compounds such as nasal decongestants. This precipitating factor should be removed,

and the patient should be reassured of the benign nature of this arrhythmia. If, despite removing the precipitating factors and reassuring the patient, the patient remains significantly symptomatic and anxious about the palpitations, consideration can be given to the use of ß-blocking agents. Atenolol 25 mg PO qd or metoprolol 25 mg PO bid frequently are used.

ATRIOVENTRICULAR NODAL REENTRANT TACHYCARDIAS

Atrioventricular nodal reentrant tachycardia is the most common sustained arrhythmia in young females as well as in pregnant patients. It often occurs in patients without heart disease. In patients with a previous history of these arrhythmias, the number and frequency of the episodes of supraventricular tachycardia increase during pregnancy, especially in the third trimester.[16]

Paroxysms of AV nodal reentrant tachycardia often respond to vagal maneuvers, rest, and sedation. Vagal maneuvers include having the patient take a deep breath and hold it for a few seconds, cough, or bear down. If no carotid bruits are present, carotid massage can be used. If these measures fail to terminate the arrhythmia, then intravenous (IV) medications such as adenosine 6 mg IV push can be used to terminate the arrhythmia. If 6 mg of adenosine is unsuccessful in terminating the arrhythmia, then the IV push can be repeated at higher doses of 12 mg and up to 18 mg. This infusion terminates the arrhythmia in over 90% of incidences, but it can produce transient clinically insignificant complete heart block and bronchospasm. If the patient has a prior history of bronchial asthma or evidence of bronchospasm, adenosine should be withheld, as it is known to cause bronchoconstriction. The advantage of IV adenosine is that its half-life is short, and the drug's effect lasts only seconds.

If adenosine is contraindicated, then IV verapamil or diltiazem can be given for their AV nodal blocking effects. Intravenous verapamil can be given in 5 to 10 mg doses or IV diltiazem 10 mg both can be given over 5 to 10 minutes. Careful monitoring of the blood pressure in the patients receiving these drugs is required as both drugs can produce hypotension. If these treatments are not successful in terminating or controlling the tachycardia, IV digoxin can be given at 0.5 mg followed by 0.25 mg every

2 to 4 hours for a total of 1 mg. Intravenous propranolol also can be used at 0.1 mg/kg of body weight given at a rate of 1 mg/min.

If cardiac decompensation occurs prior to the arrhythmia termination or effective treatment with drug therapy, then external electrical cardioversion with low energy (50 to 100 J) can be used. This therapeutic option requires the use of significant sedation or anesthesia. Alternatively, rapid atrial pacing, which does not require anesthesia, can be used as a therapeutic approach. This pacing can be done safely at the bedside without the need for use of fluoroscopy, even in pregnant patients.

The long-term therapy of patients with paroxysmal AV nodal reentrant tachycardia depends on the frequency of the attacks. If the attacks are infrequent, well tolerated hemodynamically, and terminate spontaneously or reliably with vagal maneuvers, then no prophylactic therapy is necessary. In contrast, if these episodes are associated with significant hemodynamic compromise and/or occur with a high frequency, particularly in the setting of organic heart disease, then daily preventive therapy with AV nodal–blocking drugs such as digitalis, ß-blockers, or calcium channel blockers should be considered.

PAROXYSMAL ATRIAL TACHYCARDIA

Paroxysmal atrial tachycardia may be seen in patients with cardiomyopathy, chronic lung disease, coronary artery disease, or drug toxicities such as alcohol or digoxin toxicities. It also is seen with a variety of metabolic abnormalities. Therapy should be designed to correct the underlying condition. Digitalis toxicity is a frequent cause for atrial arrhythmias, and digoxin levels should be obtained in patients taking digoxin that present with arrhythmias. Hypomagnesemia, hyperkalemia, and hypokalemia should be corrected if present.

If hemodynamic compromise ensues, use of electrical cardioversion should be considered to terminate the arrhythmia. ß-Blocker therapy may be used in patients without heart failure and used carefully in those with heart failure to slow the ventricular response of the automatic atrial tachycardia until the underlying condition can be stabilized.

WOLFF-PARKINSON-WHITE SYNDROME

Most of the patients with WPW or preexcitation syndrome have an otherwise normal heart and a high incidence of paroxysmal supraventricular tachycardias, usually AV reentrant tachycardia. WPW syndrome can be seen with a variety of acquired and congenital cardiac defects.[16] In females with WPW syndrome, there is a higher incidence of arrhythmias during pregnancy.

The termination of an acute episode of narrow complex supraventricular tachycardia usually requires the use of IV adenosine, verapamil, or propranolol as described above for the treatment of AV nodal tachycardia. If the patient has a very rapid ventricular rate, wide complex tachycardia, and hemodynamic compromise, then electrical cardioversion should be the treatment of choice. It is important to avoid the use of digitalis in patients with WPW syndrome as it may increase the conduction velocity of the accessory pathway and consequently increase the ventricular response to atrial fibrillation, as well as the rate of AV reentrant tachycardia.

Wolff-Parkinson-White syndrome can be cured with radio frequency ablation. Use of this invasive electrophysiologic evaluation and treatment should be considered for females with frequent episodes of paroxysmal supraventricular tachycardia during the childbearing years to avoid recurrent episodes during future pregnancies. If the patient is already pregnant at the time of the diagnosis, propranolol and quinidine can be used to prevent recurrent attacks. Quinidine has been used in the obstetric patient since the early 1930s, and, despite its extensive use, there have been no reported teratogenic or other adverse fetal effects (see below).

ATRIAL FIBRILLATION AND ATRIAL FLUTTER

Atrial fibrillation may be paroxysmal or chronic. When it occurs in females during the childbearing years, it usually is associated with coexistent heart disease, such as rheumatic heart disease, hypertensive heart disease, cardiomyopathy, ostium secundum atrial septal defect, and Ebstein's anomaly. Noncardiac causes for atrial fibrillation such as thyrotoxicosis and pulmonary embolism also can occur in this patient population. Initially the ventricular response to the atrial fibrillation or flutter should be controlled with IV ß-blockers, calcium channel blockers (verapamil or diltiazem), or digitalis, as discussed above.

If the atrial fibrillation is of recent onset, restoration of sinus rhythm should be the objective. The mode of conversion depends on the patient's hemodynamic status. If the patient is hemodynamically compromised, immediate electrical cardioversion is necessary, whereas, in those who are hemodynamically stable, the ventricular rate should be controlled first. Subsequently either chemical or electrical cardioversion should be pursued.

Transthoracic electrical cardioversion of atrial fibrillation requires energy levels of 100 to 360 J for termination. Chemical cardioversion in the nonpregnant patient can be obtained using IV ibutilide 1 mg over 10 minutes under continuous cardiac monitoring with transthoracic patches in place; IV procainamide at 0.5 mg/kg over approximately 30 minutes is an alternate therapy. In the pregnant patient, chemical cardioversion can be pursued with quinidine sulfate 200 to 400 mg PO four times per day. If atrial fribillation persists for more than 48 hours, anticoagulation is recommended to decrease the risk of cardiac embolism and stroke during spontaneous, chemical, or electrical conversion; this is especially important in patients with history of mitral stenosis.

Patients with chronic longstanding atrial fibrillation for more than 1 year usually have a structural abnormality with an enlarged atrium and are unlikely to be converted to sinus rhythm. The goal of therapy in such patients is to control the ventricular response and to prevent cardiac embolism and stroke with chronic anticoagulation. It is important to know that warfarin cannot be given to pregnant patients as it is known to be teratogenic; anticoagulation must be achieved with either IV or subcutaneous heparin. More recently a low–molecular weight heparin, enoxaparin (Lovenox), has been approved; this drug can be used for anticoagulation during pregnancy. The ventricular response can be controlled using combined or single therapy with digitalis, ß-blockers, or calcium channel blockers, as detailed in the next section.

Atrial flutter generally occurs in patients with coexisting heart disease. Electrical cardioversion for these patients requires a lower energy (50 to 100 J) and is effective. It is considered the therapy of choice in nonpregnant patients. In pregnant patients, pharmacologic conversion is preferable, using digitalis and/or propranolol and quinidine sulfate therapy, as detailed above.

Ventricular Arrhythmias

In general, ventricular premature beats are of no concern in patients without organic heart disease. If they are seen in the presence of organic heart disease, a careful evaluation should be completed to rule out the possibility of sustained or unsustained episodes of ventricular arrhythmia. There is a tendency for an increased frequency of isolated ventricular premature beats to occur during normal pregnancy.[16]

Ventricular arrhythmias often are seen in patients with significant organic heart disease. They are worrisome as they can become a sustained ventricular tachycardia, which can deteriorate into life-threatening ventricular fibrillation. When ventricular tachycardia occurs in the presence of organic heart disease, an aggressive work-up and therapy should be pursued, as these patients are at high risk for sudden death. Patients with evidence of organic heart disease and ventricular tachyarrhythmias that are recurrent should be referred to a cardiologist or electrophysiologist for further diagnostic and therapeutic interventions, including implantable cardioverter-defibrillator implantation, radio frequency ablation, or antiarrhythmic drugs. The termination of a sustained ventricular arrhythmia usually can be achieved with IV lidocaine or procainamide or by electrical cardioversion. Electrical cardioversion of sustained ventricular arrhythmias requires energy levels of 100 to 360 J. The mode of cardioversion (chemical versus electrical) depends on the hemodynamic status of the patient.

Ventricular tachyarrhythmias occurring in patients with normal hearts are hemodynamically better tolerated, even when sustained. There are different idiopathic ventricular tachycardias seen in patients with normal hearts that can be cured with radio frequency ablation; therefore, patients with normal hearts and recurrent sustained monomorphic ventricular tachycardia should be referred to a cardiac electrophysiologist. When ventricular tachycardia occurs in response to activity, ß-blockers usually are successful in controlling the ventricular arrhythmia, especially in patients without organic heart disease.

If the patient has ventricular tachyarrhththymias associated with the hereditary long QT syndrome, medical therapy with ß-blockers has been associated with a decreased risk of cardiac events. Several gender differences have been found in regard to the Q–T interval. The Q–T interval is usually longer in females than in males, and, therefore, females are more likely to develop tachyarrhythmias, such as torsades de pointes, associated with the use of drugs that prolonged the Q–T interval. However the Q–T dispersion (ie, the time period from the end of the T wave in the lead with the shortest Q–T interval to the end of the T wave in the lead with the longest Q–T interval) in males is higher than that in females, and this may explain the increased risk of sudden cardiac death in males.[3] A retrospective analysis of women affected with the long QT syndrome who had one or more pregnancies revealed that there is a significant increase in the risk of cardiac events in the postpartum period but not during pregnancy.[17]

If ß-blocker therapy fails to control recurrent episodes of unsustained polymorphic ventricular tachycardia that are associated with presyncope or syncope in a patient with long QT syndrome, the patient should be referred to a cardiologist, and the implantation of a permanent pacemaker should be considered. If the combination of permanent pacemaker implantation and ß-blocker therapy are unsuccessful in controlling these symptoms, the implantation of an internal cardioverter-defibrillator should be considered. Use of an internal cardioverter-defibrillator also should be considered for high-risk patients with a strong family history of sudden death. Please note that the implantation of these devices (permanent pacemakers and implantable cardioverter-defibrillators) requires fluoroscopy exposure; therefore, these treatment modalities are not ideal for use in the pregnant patient.

In the pregnant patient, digitalis toxicity can aggravate ventricular arrhythmias, and the level of digoxin should be assessed in these patients if digitalis therapy is used. If a digitalis-induced ventricular tachycardia is diagnosed, IV lidocaine should be used, followed by electrical cardioversion in patients who are unresponsive to lidocaine. If the digitalis-induced ventricular arrhythmia recurs, then the use of digoxin immune Fab (Digibind) should be considered. Phenytoin should not be used as it has a significant to teratogenic effect. In pregnant patients with ventricular tachycardia refractory to drugs such as quinidine or procainamide, amiodarone therapy may be considered (see drugs below).

Bradyarrhythmias

Significant bradyarrythmias as a cause of palpitations are seen infrequently. Sinus bradycardia of less than 40 beats per minute may be secondary to sick sinus syndrome and may require permanent pacemaker implantation if associated with significant symptoms. If the patient is asymptomatic, clinical follow-up without intervention is recommended. Underlying causes, such as drug-induced bradycardia, hypothyroidism, and carotid sinus hypersensitivity, should be ruled out.

Heart block in young females or pregnant patients may be congenital, with a presentation of dizziness or syncope as the first manifestation during pregnancy, or it may be acquired—usually secondary to rheumatic heart disease, endocarditis, sarcoidosis, scleroderma, or a primary degenerative process following a previous cardiac surgery. Clinically significant bradyarrhythmias in pregnant females are rare. The treatment of choice for congenital or acquired symptomatic heart block is implantation of a permanent pacemaker, especially if the resultant bradyarrhythmia is hemodynamically significant and a causal relationship between the patient's symptoms and the bradyarrhythmia is found. In the asymptomatic pregnant patient, one should establish the patient's ability to meet the increasing demands of gestation prior to making the decision to implant a permanent pacemaker.

PREGNANCY

In the evaluation of female patients, it is important to know that there is an increased risk for both the exacerbation and the new onset of supraventricular tachycardias during pregnancy.[3] The relative risk of supraventricular tachycardia during pregnancy in female patients was 5.1 in one study and was not affected by the stage of pregnancy.[3] New-onset ventricular tachycardia during pregnancy is rare but has been reported in a review article by Brodsky et al;[18] most patients were found to have no evidence of structural heart disease. The mechanisms responsible for this apparent increase in the incidence of arrhythmias during pregnancy are unknown. Several hypotheses for this increased arrhythmia incidence have been proposed, including changes in autonomic tone, hormonal effects, and hemodynamic alterations that occur during pregnancy. Further studies are needed to determine the etiology of the increased incidence of tachyarrhythmias and palpitations during pregnancy.

During pregnancy if there is no identifiable organic abnormality and there are sporadically occurring episodes of unsustained arrhythmias, the patient should be reassured that the arrhythmia is unlikely to have a significant clinical importance. As an example, during pregnancy atrial premature beats have been noted to become more prevalent, but they usually do not require therapy. In these cases, if benign arrhythmias are associated with any specific precipitating factors, such as an excessive ingestion of caffeine, alcohol, cigarette smoking, or any other drug therapy or abuse, then the precipitating factor should be removed. Antiarrhythmic drug therapy should not be started in any patient, especially if pregnant, unless there is evidence of persistent symptomatic and hemodynamically significant arrhythmias.

In patients with underlying heart disease, palpitations frequently are associated with cardiac arrhythmias. The arrhythmias can occur for the first time in the patient's life during pregnancy, presumably secondary to the increased hemodynamic burden during gestation. The occurrence of the sustained cardiac arrhythmia during pregnancy places both the mother and the fetus at risk. In cases in which palpitations are associated with a cardiac arrhythmia and underlying organic heart disease, combined therapy for both the underlying heart disease and the arrhythmia is indicated. Continued antiarrhythmic therapy is required in cases in which the arrhythmia persists despite the stabilization of the underlying heart disease. Continued therapy also can be used as a prophylactic measure to avoid serious arrhythmias that may occur upon discontinuation of the treatment.

The choice of antiarrhythmic therapy depends on the patient and the type of arrhythmia that is being treated—supraventricular or ventricular. Virtually all antiarrhythmic drugs can be transferred across the placenta; therefore, special consideration must be given to the selection of drugs with proven safety during pregnancy when significant arrhythmias occur. In addition the smallest effective dose should be used in pregnant patients, and the indication for continued therapy should be reassessed periodically.

Antiarrhythmic Drugs Shown to Be Relatively Safe during Pregnancy

DIGITALIS

Digitalis preparations, both digoxin and digitoxin, are transferred freely across the placenta. In mothers treated with digoxin, serum digoxin concentrations at term were found to be similar in the newborn and the mother. No significant adverse effects have been noted in the fetus or neonate despite extensive prenatal exposure to digitalis preparations.[16] However, adverse fetal effects including fetal death have been reported in babies of mothers with digitalis toxicity.[16] Digoxin also is secreted into human breast milk at a concentration comparable to that of the maternal serum concentration at steady state.[19] The total daily secretion of digoxin in breast milk does not exceed 1 to 2 μg, which is an amount unlikely to be of pharmacologic significance in the infant.[19]

QUINIDINE

Quinidine has been used in the obstetric population since the early 1930s. No reported teratogenic or other adverse fetal effects have been seen. Quinidine readily crosses the placenta and also is excreted into breast milk.[20] Maternal and neonatal plasma concentrations of quinidine are comparable, whereas levels in breast milk are somewhat lower than those in plasma. Uncommonly quinidine may cause minimal uterine contractions, but usually these do not occur until spontaneous uterine contractions have begun. In therapeutic doses quinidine is unlikely to cause premature labor,[21] but toxic doses may result in abortions.[22] Quinidine has been known to cause adverse cardiovascular effects including ventricular tachyarrhythmias associated with prolonged Q–T interval, postural hypertension, and, rarely, AV block. Quinidine may be used relatively safely throughout pregnancy when antiarrhythmic therapy is considered absolutely necessary.

PROCAINAMIDE

Procainamide readily crosses the placenta and has been used recently for transplacental cardioversion of fetal supraventricular tachycardia.[23] Procainamide use in the early stages of pregnancy does not appear to have teratogenic effects. Procainamide is metabolized to *N*-acetylprocainamide (NAPA), which is then eliminated by the kidneys. Therefore, in patients with diminished renal function, a dose reduction is necessary to prevent accumulation of active NAPA.

Procainamide is considered to be relatively safe to use during pregnancy, but among its side effects is a "lupus-like syndrome" associated with chronic therapy. Since congenital complete heart block has been associated with the maternal lupus syndrome, procainamide therapy should be limited to those patients that are unresponsive to quinidine therapy when antiarrhythmic therapy is deemed necessary.

ß-ADRENORECEPTOR-BLOCKING AGENTS

Nonselective and selective ß-blockers readily cross the placenta.[24–26] At delivery maternal and fetal cord blood concentrations of these drugs are comparable. Propranolol has been the most widely used of these drugs, and many favorable reports have been published regarding its use. Occasional reports have described the association of propranolol with intrauterine growth retardation, bradycardia, apnea, hypoglycemia, and hyperbilirubinemia in the fetus.[26] The incidence of these complications is so low that propranolol use during pregnancy is considered safe. Other ß-blockers, such as atenolol, metoprolol, and labetalol also have been used during pregnancy without significant adverse effects in the newborn. Most ß-blockers are secreted in breast milk, and their concentration in milk is approximately five times higher than that in maternal plasma. Despite this, they have not been found to cause any signs of ß-blockade in the breast-feeding infant.[27]

LIDOCAINE

Lidocaine crosses the placenta after epidural or IV administration to the mother.[28,29] Fetal blood concentrations at delivery are approximately 50 to 60% of maternal levels. There are data that suggest that exposure to lidocaine during pregnancy is not related to an increased risk of malformations or other fetal adverse effects.[16] Administration in the presence of fetal acidosis is not recommended, as it may result in cardiac and central nervous system toxicity for the fetus.[30] In pregnant patients with diminished hepatic blood flow, such as those with congestive heart failure, the lidocaine dose should be reduced to avoid toxicity. Signs of toxicity include somnolence, confusion, euphoria, and seizures.

Antiarrhythmic Drugs Requiring More Study to Determine Their Safety in Pregnancy

DISOPYRAMIDE

Disopyramide readily crosses the placenta and also is secreted in breast milk. Fetal serum concentrations at birth are approximately 40% of those found in the mothers.[16] There is limited experience with disopyramide use during pregnancy, and, at

this time, it cannot be recommended as routine therapy in the obstetric patient.

MEXILETINE

In one patient with recurrent ventricular tachycardia who received mexiletine for the last 7 weeks of her pregnancy, maternal and cord blood concentrations were equal at delivery, and breast milk concentrations were somewhat higher.[31] No adverse effects were reported in the fetus during the course of labor or the postpartum period. However, the experience with mexiletine during pregnancy is too limited to assess its safety during pregnancy.

VERAPAMIL

Verapamil crosses the placenta readily and has been used recently to successfully treat maternal as well as fetal supraventricular tachycardias during pregnancy.[29] Limited information is available about the use of verapamil during pregnancy; most data is derived from studies of the use of verapamil for the treatment of premature labor and severe preeclampsia. There have been no associated deleterious results from the use of verapamil, but attention must be given to the potential development of significant hypotension when it is injected intravenously.[32] Again, the data available is too limited to establish the safety of verapamil for long-term use during pregnancy.

AMIODARONE

Amiodarone has been used successfully in the prevention of recurrent life-threatening supraventricular and ventricular arrhythmias in patients during pregnancy.[33–35] Importantly, transplacental passage of amiodarone or its metabolite, desethyl-amiodarone, appears to be limited—approximately 10% and 25%, respectively. In contrast, the breast milk concentrations of both the parent compound and the metabolite have been found to be similar or significantly higher than are maternal blood concentrations.[33,35] In the limited reported use of amiodarone during pregnancy, there are no reported adverse effects on fetal outcome or clinically significant cardiac or thyroid dysfunction. These reports are encouraging, but are insufficient to recommend amiodarone use during pregnancy. Amiodarone therapy during pregnancy and breast-feeding must be restricted to those patients who are resistant to other antiarrhythmic therapies, such as quinidine and procainamide, that have better established safety during pregnancy.

Antiarrhythmic Drug Known to Be Unsafe during Pregnancy: Phenytoin

Phenytoin readily crosses the placenta, and maternal and neonatal serum concentrations are equal at birth.[36] Long-term therapy with phenytoin has been associated clearly with significant fetal side effects, including birth defects known as the fetal hydantoin syndrome.[37,38] In addition genital abnormalities, cardiopulmonary malformation, and life-threatening bleeding as well as neuroblastomas and mesenchymomas have been described in infants exposed to phenytoin in utero.

Phenytoin must be avoid during pregnancy. The only potential use of phenytoin during pregnancy is for the short-term therapy of digitalis-induced arrhythmia that is unresponsive to other agents. The recent advent of digoxin immune Fab (Digibind) should abolish the need for phenytoin use during pregnancy.

The concentration of phenytoin in breast milk is low, and no adverse responses have been reported in children following breast-feeding.[36]

Anticoagulant Known to Be Safe during Pregnancy: Heparin

Heparin has been used successfully during pregnancy. It does not cross the placenta due to its large molecular weight and high negative charge. Heparin use during pregnancy has not been associated with negative teratogenic or adverse effects to the fetus. There have been no reported increases in bleeding complications during delivery or cesarean sections. Heparin is safe to use in nursing mothers as it is not excreted in breast milk, again due to its large molecular weight.[39] If anticoagulant therapy is required, heparin intravenously or subcutaneously should be the drug of choice.[40] Patients should be treated with a continuous IV infusion of heparin during the acute stage of their illness, followed by 5,000 U subcutaneously every 6 to 12 hours until the desired anticoagulation effect has been achieved.

Anticoagulant Requiring More Study to Determine Its Safety in Pregnancy: Enoxaparin

Enoxaparin does not cross the placenta and has been used safely during pregnancy for the treatment of acute thromboembolic events (or in those with a history of thromboembolic events), antiphospholipid syndrome, and active lupus disease. In a review of 41 pregnancies, patients received enoxaparin 40 mg subcutaneously daily, and no bleeding disorders were reported, despite continued therapy during cesarean deliveries.[41] Further studies are required to determined the teratogenicity of the drug and its safety during breast-feeding.

Anticoagulant Known to Be Unsafe during Pregnancy: Warfarin

Use of warfarin is contraindicated in patients that may become pregnant or who are in their first trimester of pregnancy.[42] It crosses the placental barrier and can cause bleeding (including fatal hemorrhage) in the fetus in utero. There have been reports of birth malformations in children born to mothers who received warfarin therapy during pregnancy. There is a relationship between the warfarin dose and fetal complications.[43] The reported fetal malformations include nasal hypoplasia with or without stippled epiphyses, if the mother is exposed to warfarin during the first trimester; and mental retardation, blindness, and other central nervous system abnormalities, if the mother is exposed during the second or third trimester.[44] Women of childbearing potential who are candidates for warfarin therapy should be advised to avoid pregnancy while taking the drug. If a patient becomes pregnant while taking the drug, she should be apprised of the potential risk to the fetus, and the option of termination of the pregnancy should be discussed.

Warfarin therapy is safe for use by nursing mothers. It is secreted in the breast milk but in an inactive form; prothrombin times of nursing infants have not been found to be prolonged.[45]

REFERENCES

1. Barsky JA, Cleary PD, Coeytaux RR, Ruskin JN. The clinical course of palpitations in medical outpatients. Arch Intern Med 1995;155:1782–8.
2. Kinlay S, Leitch JW, Neil A, et al. Cardiac event recorders yield more diagnoses and are more cost-effective than 48 hour Holter monitoring in patients with palpitations. Ann Intern Med 1996;124:16–20.
3. Wolbrette D, Patel H. Arrhythmias and women. Curr Opin Cardiol 1999;14:36–43.

4. Jose A, Collison D. The normal range and determinants of the intrinsic heart rate in man. Cardiovasc Res 1970;4:160–7.

5. Larsen JA, Kadisch AH. Effects of gender in cardiac arrhythmias. J Cardiovasc Electrophysiol 1998; 9:655–64.

6. Weber BE, Kapoor WN. Evaluation and outcomes of patients with palpitations. Am J Med 1996;100:138–48.

7. Zimetbaum P, Josephson ME. Evaluation of patients with palpitations. N Engl J Med 1998;338:1369–73.

8. Reid P. Indications for intracardiac electrophysiologic studies in patients with unexplained palpitations. Circulation 1987;75 Suppl III:154–8.

9. Lessmeier TJ, Gamperling D, Johnson-Liddon V, et al. Unrecognized paroxysmal supraventricular tachycardia: potential for misdiagnosis as panic disorder. Arch Intern Med 1997;157:537–43.

10. Fogel RI, Evans JJ, Prystowsky EN. Utitlity and cost of event recorders in the diagnosis of palpitations, presyncope and syncope. Am J Cardiol 1997; 79:207–8.

11. Swartz J, Tracy C, Fletcher R. Radiofrequency and catheter ablation of accessory atrioventricular pathway atrial insertion sites. Circulation 1993;87:487–99.

12. Jackman WM, Bechman KJ, McClelland JH, et al. Treatment of supraventricular tachycardia due to atrioventricular nodal reentry by radio frequency catheter ablation of slow pathway conduction. N Engl J Med 1992;327:313–8.

13. Calkins H, Langberg J, Sousa J, et al. Radiofrequency catheter ablation of accessory atrioventricular connections in 250 patients. Circulation 1992;327:313–8.

14. Mason J. Cardiac arrhythmias and clinical electrophysiology. In: Lewis R, editor. Adult clinical cardiology self assessment program. Bethesda (MD): American College of Cardiology; 1993. p. 5.3–5.24.

15. Schlant R. Electrophysiologic studies and unexplained palpitations. Circulation 1987;75 Suppl III:159–60.

16. Rotmensch HH, Rotmensch S, Elkayam U. Management of cardiac arrhythmias during pregnancy. Drugs 1987;33:623–33.

17. Rashba EJ, Zareba W, Moss AJ, et al. for the LQTS Investigators. Influence of pregnancy on the risk for cardiac events in patients with hereditary long QT syndrome. Circulation 1998;97:451–6.

18. Brodsky M, Doria R, Allen B, et al. New onset ventricular tachycardia during pregnancy. Am Heart J 1992;123:933–41.

19. Levey M, Granit L, Laufer N. Excretion of drugs in human milk. N Engl J Med 1978;299:845.

20. Colin A, Lambotte R. Influence teratogene des medicaments administres a la femme enceinte. Rev Med Liege 1972;27 Suppl 1:39–45.

21. Bellet S. Essentials of cardiac arrhythmias diagnosis and management. Philadelphia: W.B. Saunders Co.; 1972.

22. Merx W, Rotmensch HH, Rotmensch S, et al. Management of cardiac arrhythmias during pregnancy—current concepts. Drugs 1987;33:623–33.

23. Dumesic DA, Silverman NH, Tobias S, et al. Transplacental cardioversion of fetal supraventricular tachycardia with procainamide. N Engl J Med 1982;307:1128–31.

24. Sandstrom B. Antihypertensive treatment with the adrenergic beta receptor blocker metoprolol during pregnancy. Gynecol Obstet Invest 1978;9:195–204.

25. Teuscher A, Bossi E, Imhof P. Effect of propranolol on fetal tachycardia in diabetic pregnancy. Am J Cardiol 1978;42:304–7.

26. Gladstone GR, Hordof A, Gersony WM. Propranolol administration during pregnancy: effects on the fetus. J Pediatr 1975;86:962–4.

27. Liedholm H, Melander A, Bitzen P-O, et al. Accumulation of atenolol and metoprolol in human breast milk. Eur J Clin Pharmacol 1971;20:229–31.

28. Ulmsten U. Inhibition of myometrial hyperactivity by Ca antagonist. Dan Med Bull 1979;26:125–6.

29. Wolff F, Breuker KH, Schlensker KH, et al. Prenatal diagnosis and therapy of fetal heart rate anomalies: with a contribution on the placental transfer of verapamil. J Perinat Med 1980;8:203–8.

30. Brown WW, Bell GG, Alper MH. Acidosis local anaesthesia and newborn. Obstet Gynecol 1976;48:23–30.

31. Timmis AD, Jackson G, Holt DW. Mexiletine for control of ventricular dysrrhythmias in pregnancy. Lancet 1980;2:647–8.

32. Buxton AE, Marchlinski FE, Doherty JU, et al. Hazards of intravenous verapamil for sustained ventricular tachycardia. Am J Cardiol 1987;59:1107–10.

33. McKenna WJ, Harris L, Rowland E, et al. Amiodarone therapy during pregnancy. Am J Cardiol 1983;51:1231–3.

34. Robson DJ, Jeeva-Raj MV, Storey GC, et al. Use of amiodarone during pregnancy. Postgrad Med J 1985;61:75–7.

35. Pitcher D, Leather HM, Storey CGA, et al. Amiodarone in pregnancy. Lancet 1983;1:597–8.

36. Shapiro S, Hortz SC, Siskind V, et al. Anticonvulsants and parental epilepsy in the development of birth defects. Lancet 1976;1:272–5.

37. Hanson JW, Myrianthopoulos NC, Harvey MAS, et al. Risks of offspring of women treated with hydantoin anticonvulsants and emphasis of fetal hydantoin syndrome. J Pediatr 1976;89:662–8.

38. Monson RR, Rosenberg L, Hartz SC, et al. Diphenylhydantoin and selected congenital malformations. N Engl J Med 1973;189:1049–52.

39. Rylance G, Plant N. Drugs and breast milk. Practitioner 1991;235:692–4.

40. Nishimura H, Tanimura T. Clinical aspects of the teratogenicity of drugs. New York: Exerpta Medica 1976.

41. Dulitzki M, Pauzner R, Langevitz P, et. al. Low–molecular weight heparin during pregnancy and delivery: preliminary experience with 41 pregnancies. Obstet Gynecol 1996;87:380–3.

42. Briggs GG, Freeman RK, Yaffee SJ. Drugs in pregnancy and lactation. Baltimore (MD):Williams and Wilkins; 1994.

43. Vitale N, De Feo M, De Santo LS, et al. Dose dependent fetal complications of warfarin in pregnant women with mechanical heart valves. J Am Coll Cardiol 1999;33:1637–41.

44. Wellesley D, Moore I, Heard M, Keeton B. Two cases of warfarin embryopathy: a re-emergence of this condition? Br J of Obstet Gynecol 1998;105:805–6.

45. McKenna R, Cole ER, Vasan U. Is warfarin therapy contraindicated in the lactating mother? J Pediatr 1983;103:325–7.

38

APPROACH TO THE PATIENT WITH CONSTIPATION

Bennett E. Roth, MD

Transient constipation is a frequent occurrence for most of us. It can occur as a result of temporary change in lifestyle such as vacationing away from home, or as a reaction to brief use of medications, transient illness, or stress. However, its presentation as a chronic condition may affect 20 to 30% of adults, and it is not an uncommon presenting complaint among patients seen by primary care clinicians. One of the difficulties encountered by clinicians is defining what really constitutes a problem with constipation. It can mean different things to different people. Many individuals believe that the absence of a daily bowel movement constitutes an abnormality. Therefore, it is helpful to have a formal definition upon which to base a diagnosis and to formulate a treatment plan.

DEFINITION

Epidiomologic studies have indicated that 98% of adults in Western countries have three or more bowel movements per week.[1-3] Therefore, in estimating what constitutes an "abnormality," a history of fewer than three bowel movements per week has been chosen to represent constipation. However, some patients may have daily bowel movements but report having hard or small stools, difficulty passing stool, and the need to strain with a sensation of incomplete evacuation. Using these symptom criteria an international working group developed a standardized definition for constipation.[4] This includes (1) patients not taking laxatives who complain of two or more of the following for 12 months or more: stools less frequent than three per week, straining with at least 25% of stools, hard or pellet stools at least 25% of time, a feeling of incomplete evacuation 25% of time; and (2) patients who have fewer than two bowel movements per week for at least 12 months.

The above definition is useful for identifying individuals with significant problems; it aids in distinguishing real constipation from unrealistic perceptions of patients, and it is helpful in the conduct of clinical studies for management of the problem. It may be too restrictive in daily clinical practice. It is helpful for the primary care clinician to recognize what is within the realm of normal and what variances may represent the need for simple reassurance versus the need for investigation and treatment.

CAUSES

Constipation is the result of an abnormality of stool movement through the colon and/or the anorectal region. Slow colonic transit occurs as a primary motor disorder or may be associated with a variety of diseases or result from medication side effects (slow-transit constipation). Anorectal disorders include pelvic floor dysfunction or dyssynergia (also known as "anismus").[5] Although there are many identifiable causes for constipation, the vast majority of patients have no obvious etiology and are best classified as having idiopathic chronic constipation or irritable bowel syndrome. An overview of the causes of constipation can be seen in Table 38–1.

Irritable bowel syndrome is a common disorder that often presents with abdominal pain and/or bloating and is relieved with passage of stool or flatus. In some patients the complaint of constipation and/or straining may predominate.

TABLE 38–1. Causes of Constipation

Structural conditions
   Obstructive disease: neoplasm, stricture, volvulus
   Rectal prolapse, rectocele, anal fissure, and stricture

Systemic conditions
   Hypokalemia
   Hypercalcemia
   Hyperparathyroidism
   Diabetic neuropathy
   Hypopituitarism
   Addison's disease
   Pheochromocytoma
   Porphyria
   Uremia
   Amyloidosis
   Scleroderma
   Polymyositis
   Mixed connective tissue disease
   Pregnancy

Neurologic conditions
   Parkinson's disease, multiple sclerosis, autonomic
     neuropathy, Hirschsprung's disease
   Sacral nerve trauma or tumor

Medications
   Opiates
   Anticholinergics
   Antidepressants
   Anticonvulsants
   Antipsychotics
   Antacids (Ca, Al)
   Calcium channel blockers
   Ganglionic blockers
   Iron supplements
   Cholestyramine
   Sucralfate

Idiopathic conditions
   Intestinal pseudo-obstruction
   Irritable bowel syndrome
   Slow transit constipation
   Pelvic floor dysfunction

Adapted from Stark ME. Challenging problems presenting as constipation. Am J Gastroenterol 1999;94:567–74.

Slow-transit constipation, also termed "colonic inertia," occurs almost exclusively in young women with symptoms usually beginning before age 25 years.[6] Patients complain of infrequent stools (perhaps less than once per week) and often com-plain of abdominal pain and bloating. The colonic diameter is usually normal. Slow transit usually occurs as an isolated abnormality; however, it may be associated with concomitant pelvic floor dysfunction or, rarely, with a more generalized motor disorder such as chronic intestinal pseudo-obstruction. A significant number of these patients have psychological disorders.[7]

Anorectal disorders may be divided into those associated with pelvic floor dysfunction and structural problems. Pelvic floor dyssynergia or anismus is defined as an inappropriate contraction or failure to relax the pelvic floor and/or anal sphincter during attempts to defecate, resulting in the impedence of stool passage. The classic example of this is Hirschsprung's disease which is usually diagnosed in childhood but sometimes presents in varying degrees in adulthood. More commonly, lack of synergistic relaxation of the pelvic floor or anal sphincter is responsible. Structural problems of the pelvic floor occur much more commonly in women than in men and frequently are related to a history of vaginal deliveries. These problems include rectal prolapse, rectocele, and abnormal perineal descent. It must be remembered that many patients may be found to have these structural abnormalities without significant functional impairment, necessitating a careful correlation of symptoms with these findings.

Rectal prolapse may be difficult to diagnose. Patients may report a sensation of internal pressure or heaviness with the urge to defecate. They may indicate the presence of a protrusion from the anal canal with straining that they presume is hemorrhoidal but, in reality, is the prolapsed segment. Rectal bleeding may occur if the disorder is complicated by solitary rectal ulcers.

Rectoceles are present in many women but are usually asymptomatic. However, if the rectocele is large, it may fill preferentially as stool descends through the rectal canal, and it can lead to retention and incomplete evacuation. The diagnosis should be suspected if patients report improved defecation following digital pressure on the posterior vaginal wall.

The descending perineum syndrome usually results from weakness in the pelvic floor, resulting from multiple vaginal deliveries. It may be readily apparent during a physical examination if the perineum is observed during straining.

It is important to recognize the possibility of psychiatric issues resulting from or precipitating the problems or complaints of constipation. Although psychiatric issues may develop as a result of chronic constipation, it is not uncommon that psychological issues may translate into somatic complaints or be the underlying reasons for the seeking of health care. These may include unusual attitudes toward bowel function. Some patients may have a fear of building up toxins if they do not evacuate daily. Some have rigid schedules often developed in childhood that, if altered, create emotional concern and result in somatic symptomatology. Constipation is a frequent complaint among patients suffering from depression or somatoform disorders. There is a well-recognized association of physical or sexual abuse among women with irritable bowel syndrome.[5,8] Abuse also has been observed in association with anismus.[9] Last, constipation is a frequent complaint of patients with eating disorders.[5]

EVALUATION

Figure 38–1 presents an algorithm for evaluation and management of patients with constipation. The initial evaluation of patients with constipation begins with a careful history. This must address the stool pattern, whether patients experience an urge to defecate and/or must strain to evacuate, the duration of symptoms, and any changes in lifestyle that might explain the problem, for example, medication use, dietary changes, or a job change, possibly with new hours and increased stress. Patients should be asked if they voluntarily withhold bowel movements despite an urge, due to job or social situations that make a visit to the bathroom difficult. Any family history of colorectal cancer should be elicited. In addition, women should be questioned about history of pregnancies and types of delivery. Alarm signals must be sought, such as bleeding, weight loss, fever, or new onset of abdominal pain. A significant change in bowel habits without a possible reason such as medication side effects should prompt an evaluation to exclude obstruction. For many patients this evaluation requires the use of a flexible sigmoidoscope. For older patients (over age 50 years), colonoscopy should be considered. It is often helpful to have patients keep a diary of bowel activity for at least a 2-week period to exclude the misperception of constipation. It is also helpful to know what, if any, medications or home remedies the patients have used to treat their constipation.

In performancing the physical examination, one should be alert for any signs of hypothyroidism, and any evidence of abdominal mass or tenderness, and pay particular attention to the rectal and perineal examination. In addition to searching for a palpable rectal mass and testing for occult blood, visual inspection of the perineum during straining may reveal evidence of prolapse or descending perineum syndrome. During the digital examination, the patient should be asked to squeeze the lower anal sphincter and also to strain as if passing stool. This might give clues indicating disorders of the pelvic floor or sphincter.

Routine laboratory profiles are helpful in excluding metabolic causes such as hypothyroidism, hypercalcemia, and diabetes. In addition, it is important to check the stool for stigmas of iron deficiency anemia and occult blood.

TREATMENT

If no systemic or metabolic disease or alarm signs are found during the initial evaluation, it is quite reasonable to offer a treatment trial such as increased fluid consumption and fiber intake. Fiber may be in the form of natural food fiber (eg, cereal, citrus fruit, and wheat and oat bran) or fiber laxatives such as psyllium or methylcellulose; 30 to 85 mL of unprocessed bran can be added to each meal and supplemented with increased fluids. Patients should be warned that bran may produce symptoms of gaseousness, and that they may benefit from a gradual introduction of this product into their diet. Any medications suspected of contributing to the problem should be stopped. For those patients who give a history of withholding bowel movements because of job or social constraints, it is often helpful if they set aside a specific time each day (often in the morning) when they can relax and, if needed, use a glycerine suppository to help initiate a bowel movement. This regimen provides relief for many patients suffering from constipation.

For those patients who fail to respond to the above regimen, clinicians must decide whether to proceed with the use of stimulant laxatives or consider further evaluation. The use of a mild stimulant two to three times a week, if successful, is a reasonable approach in most instances. Choices include emollients, osmotic agents, saline laxatives, traditional stimulants, and promotility agents, or drugs

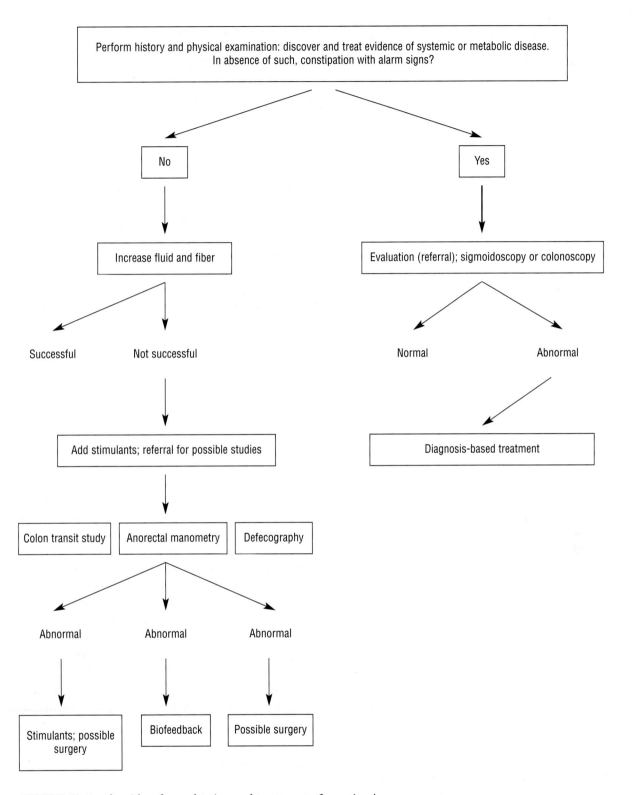

FIGURE 38–1. Algorithm for evaluation and treatment of constipation.

TABLE 38–2. Medications Used for Constipation

Bulk agents
    Psyllium
    Methylcellulose
    Bran

Emollients
    Docusates
    Mineral oil

Osmotic agents
    Polyethylene glycol
    Lactulose
    Sorbitol
    Glycerin

Saline laxatives
    Magnesium sulfate
    Magnesium citrate

Stimulant laxatives
    Castor oil
    Phenolphthalein
    Bisacodyl
    Cisapride
    Misoprostol
    Colchicine

Anthraquinones
    Cascara sagrada
    Senna
    Aloe

*Available only for compassionate use
Adapted from Wald A. Chronic constipation: pathophysiology, diagnosis, and management. Gastrointest Dis Today 1997;6(2):8–17.

traditionally used for other purposes whose side effects include diarrhea. Examples of these treatments may be found in Table 38–2.

There remains a small group of patients (< 1%) who fail to respond to initial measures and continue to complain of persistent constipation or difficulty passing stools. These patients are predominantly adult women. If these patients are experiencing abdominal pain, they may suffer from elements of irritable bowel syndrome in addition to pure constipation. They may report worsening of their symptoms with fiber supplements or stimulants. At this point, the primary care clinician must consider referral for further evaluation to aid in distinguishing slow-transit constipation from anorectal disorders. The subsequent diagnostic evaluation usually begins with a colonic transit study, during which patients ingest radiopaque markers that are observed with on abdominal radiographs over a 5-day period in the absence of laxative use. If the markers are essentially gone by the end of that period, the patient probably does not have significant constipation and may suffer from irritable bowel syndrome or significant psychological problems that are being manifested by the inappropriate perception or complaint of constipation. If the markers are retained throughout the colon, colonic inertia can be diagnosed. If the markers accumulate in the left colon or rectal area, it is likely that there is an anorectal problem causing outlet delay.[10,11] In this scenario patients often require anorectal manometry to search for evidence of anismus or pelvic floor dysfunction, and/or defecography to identify rectoceles, prolapse, or other anatomic abnormalities. The former group often responds to biofeedback.[12] The latter group may require surgical intervention. For those patients with colonic inertia, the use of more potent promotility agents and laxatives may suffice. If the use of laxatatives such as senna, polyethylene glycol, or lactulose are not successful, one may resort to the use of agents such as misoprostol or colchicine. It must be remembered that misoprostol has the potential to cause uterine contractions and is relatively contraindicated in women of childbearing age for fear of inducing abortions. If medical therapy is not successful, abdominal colectomy with low ileorectal anastomosis must be considered. When patients are selected properly for this procedure, the results are satisfactory. However, failure to exclude outlet dysfunction, significant psychological problems, or more generalized intestinal motor disorders leads to complications and poor outcomes.[5]

In certain clinical circumstances such as bedridden or demented patients or those with serious neurologic or muscular diseases, mechanical disimpaction followed by a regimen of oral laxatives and/or enemas on a standard schedule is needed to maintain colonic cleansing.

PREGNANCY

The actual frequency of problematic constipation during pregnancy is uncertain. Studies have estimated its occurrence as being from 1.5 to 33%.[13] This wide variation in prevalence probably reflects differences in social, cultural, and dietary customs. Several factors probably contribute to constipation in pregnancy, including prolongation of small and large intestinal transit times and mild obstructive effects from the gravid uterus.

The treatment of constipation in pregnancy requires knowledge of the potential side effects and safety of laxatives. The safest agents are fiber supplements such as psyllium or methylcellulose. Lactulose, sorbitol, and glycerin are safe, although the first two may produce excessive gaseousness. Certain anthraquinones such as alon and danthron are potentially teratogenic, whereas use of senna may lead to diarrhea in the neonate. Castor oil may induce uterine contractions leading to premature labor. Saline laxatives such as milk of magnesia are not recommended since they may induce sodium retention. Excessive use of mineral oil can result in decreased maternal absorption of fat-soluble vitamins. Stimulant laxatives can be used, but some, such as phenolphthalein, are excreted in breast milk and can cause colic in infants.

REFERENCES

1. Ashraf W, Park F, Lof J, et al. An examination of the reliability of reported stool frequency in the diagnosis of idiopathic constipation. Am J Gastroenterol 1996; 91:26–32.

2. Drossman DA. The functional gastrointestinal disorders: a multinational consensus. Boston: Little Brown; 1994.

3. Sandler RS, Drossman DA. Bowel habits in young adults not seeking health care. Dig Dis Sci 1987; 32:841–5.

4. Thompson WG, Creed F, Drossman DA, et al. Functional bowel disorders and functional abdominal pain. Gastroenterol Int 1992;5:75–91.

5. Stark M. Challenging problems presenting as constipation. Am J of Gastroenterol 1999;94:568–74.

6. Preston DM, Lennard-Jones JE. Severe chronic constipation of young women: "Idiopathic slow transit constipation". Gut 1986;27:41–8.

7. Wald A, Hinds JP, Caruana BJ. Psychological and physiological characteristics of patients with severe idiopathic constipation. Gastroenterology 1989;97:932–7.

8. Drossman DA, Leserman J, Nachman G, et al. Sexual and physical abuse in women with functional or organic gastrointestinal disorders. Ann Intern Med 1990;113:828–33.

9. Leroi AM, Duval V, Roussignol C, et al. Biofeedback for anismus in 15 sexually abused women. Int J Colorectal Dis 1996;11:187–90.

10. Floch MH, Wald A. Clinical evaluation and treatment of constipation. Gastroenterologist 1994;2:50–60.

11. Wald A. Chronic constipation: pathophysiology, diagnosis, and management. Gastrointest Dis Today 1997; 6(2):8–17.

12. Rao SS, Enck P, Loening-Baucke V. Biofeedback therapy for defecation disorders. Dig Dis 1997;15:78–92.

13. Barron TH, Ramirez B, Richter J. Gastrointestinal motility disorders during pregnancy. Ann Intern Med 1993;118:366–75.

39

GASTROESOPHAGEAL REFLUX DISEASE

Andrew Ippoliti, MD

Gastroesophageal reflux disease (GERD) is a symptom complex that results from the chronic reflux or retrograde movement of gastric contents into the esophagus. Chronic exposure of the esophageal mucosa to gastric juices produces heartburn and regurgitation, and may lead to mucosal inflammation and erosive esophagitis. In addition reflux can produce a number of nonesophageal symptoms and lesions, such as cough, hoarseness, asthma, and vocal cord inflammation. Although reflux disease affects men and women equally, there are important gender differences in some of the complications of reflux disease, such as Barrett's esophagus (discussed below). Men are nine times more likely to suffer from Barrett's esophagus than are women. On the other hand, heartburn is the single most common gastrointestinal complication of pregnancy.

PATHOGENESIS

Acid reflux is defined as a decrease in esophageal pH from a usual range of 6 to 7 to less than 4. It is not always pathologic. It occurs in healthy asymptomatic individuals during about 2% of the day, or roughly a half-hour, usually within 1 hour of mealtime.[1] This physiologic reflux consists of 50 episodes that are transient, last about 1 minute per episode, and are rare during sleep. Several factors limit the frequency and duration of reflux in healthy patients. The pathophysiology of GERD is outlined in Table 39–1.

The most important factor limiting reflux is the competence of the lower esophageal sphincter. For years, sphincter competence was thought to be determined by the resting sphincter tone or pressure.

Normal resting sphincter pressure is 15 to 30 mm Hg. It generally was thought that the majority of reflux patients had low pressures, less than 10 mm Hg. However, studies by the late Wylie J. Dodds, conducted from 1980 to 1986, indicated otherwise. He found that resting pressures were in the normal range in 50% of reflux patients, and that the resting pressure varied widely throughout the day in individual subjects.[2]

In 1980 Dent reported that reflux events were more likely to occur when the sphincter was relaxed or open, that is, when the pressure was 0 mm Hg.[3] When the sphincter is closed, even at relatively low pressures, it is an adequate barrier to reflux. The majority of reflux events are found when the sphincter is relaxed. Relaxation is the physiologic response to swallowing. The sphincter remains open or relaxed for 6 to 7 seconds after a swallow to permit passage of the food bolus into the stomach. During

---

TABLE 39–1. Pathophysiology of GERD

Increased frequency of reflux episodes
    Lower esophageal sphincter pressure (< 5 mm Hg)
    Increased frequency transient lower esophageal
        sphincter relaxations
    Nonreducing hiatal hernia
    Delayed gastric emptying

Increased duration of reflux episodes
    Loss of esophageal contraction amplitude or peristalsis
    Loss of afferent stimulation of secondary peristalsis
    Loss of salivary ouput

Increased exposure to mucosal irritants: acid, pepsin,
    bile, and certain drugs

this time, reflux can happen. Dent also observed that the sphincter could relax transiently without a prior swallow, and that reflux could follow.

Therefore, the two abnormalities of the sphincter that are important in reflux pathogenesis are a very low resting tone and an increased frequency of transient relaxations. In some patients with more severe gastroesophageal reflux disease, the resting lower esophageal sphincter pressure is so low (< 5 mm Hg) that it no longer functions as an anti-reflux barrier. Increases in intra-abdominal pressure, such as those produced by straining or bending, can overcome the competency of a weak sphincter and cause reflux. In addition, the number of transient sphincter relaxations and the number associated with reflux events are both increased in patients with GERD as compared with healthy controls.

The presence of a hiatal hernia is a common finding in patients with reflux. In fact, patients and physicians sometimes refer to gastroesophageal reflux disease as "hiatal hernia." In patients without hiatal hernia, the distal esophagus is below the diaphragm, in the abdomen. Increasing abdominal pressure actually raises lower esophageal sphincter tone to help prevent reflux in patients with normal anatomy. A hiatal hernia is a protrusion of the fundus of the stomach through the diaphragmatic hiatus into the chest. The larger the hernia, the more likely it is to remain above the diaphragm, forming a nonreducible hernia. When the distal esophagus remains above the diaphram, increasing intra-abdomial pressure can provoke reflux. Thus, when the herniated stomach has displaced the distal esophagus into the chest, reflux is frequent when the intra-abdominal pressure is raised.

Once gastric contents reflux into the esophagus, a series of peristaltic contractions proceed through the esophageal body to clear the reflux. Also, contractions of the esophageal body promote mixing of the gastric acid reflux with saliva. Saliva has a neutral pH and buffers gastric acid. The daily salivary output can neutralize about 300 mL of gastric acid. Defects in these mechanisms can delay acid clearance, leading to esophageal inflammation. Most reflux patients have normal esophageal body contractions, that is, the amplitude or strength of the body contractions and the frequency of peristaltic sequences are the same as those in persons without reflux. Patients with scleroderma or Raynaud's disease alone may have weak body contractions that do not generate a peristaltic sequence. Severe reflux with esophagitis is a common complication. The volume and buffering capacity of saliva is sometimes abnormal in patients with reflux, leading to severe esophageal inflammation. This is particularly true in patients with xerostomia due to Sjögren's syndrome or after radiation therapy.

Delayed gastric emptying can contribute to reflux. As the postprandial period lengthens, there is a greater likelihood of reflux of food as well as gastric acid. A mild delay in emptying of solid food has been found in about 40% of reflux patients.[4]

Since GERD is primarily a motility disorder, there has been speculation that physiologic increases in progesterone might further inhibit esophageal muscle contractions and cause reflux. However, in a recent study of healthy women between the ages of 21 and 39 years, there were no changes in esophageal motility and acid reflux throughout the menstrual cycle.[5]

PREVALENCE

Reflux symptoms occur daily in about 10% of the U.S. population. Overall the symptom of weekly to monthly heartburn is a regular event in one-third of adults.[6] There is no clear association between the incidence of reflux symptoms and gender. However, there is a significant association between Barrett's esophagus and the male sex.

Barrett's esophagus represents the most severe form of reflux disease. It is defined by the presence of specialized (ie, metaplastic) columnar epithelium within the esophagus. The degree of reflux is higher in patients with Barrett's esophagus than in other patients with GERD. The frequency of complications, including ulcers and stricture, are also greater, and about 10% of patients with Barrett's esophagus develop adenocarcinoma of the esophagus.[7]

Barrett's esophagus and adenocarcinoma of the esophagus are found almost exclusively in Caucasian males. The cause for this association is unknown, but there is emerging evidence that females may not be "protected" from developing Barrett's esophagus. Traditionally, an extent of ≥ 2 cm of metaplastic epithelium has been used to define the presence of Barrett's esophagus. Recently a number of groups have studied short-segment (< 2 cm) Barrett's esophagus, and have found that can occur in females as well as non-Caucasians.[8] Even these short

---

TABLE 39–2. Typical and Atypical Reflux Symptoms

Typical symptoms
    Retrosternal burning
    Regurgitation
    Association with meals and sleep
    Relief with antacids
    Dysphagia
    Water brash

Atypical symptoms
    Nonburning chest pain
    Nausea, epigastric fullness
    Cough, wheezing
    Hoarseness, throat pain, frequent throat clearing
    Halitosis
    Hiccups

---

segments can develop malignant change, resulting in adenocarcinoma at the gastroesophageal junction.

PRESENTATION

There are no differences between symptoms of GERD in men and women. Complaints can be grouped as being esophageal or typical, and as extra-esophageal or atypical (Table 39–2). The most common symptom is retrosternal burning, which usually occurs after meals; this can be relieved by acid neutralizing with an antacid, or by acid diluting with water. Regurgitation of a sour-tasting fluid often is reported. In fact, even after adequate suppression of acid secretion, some patients continue to note regurgitation of food. Water brash is the sudden filling of the mouth with a bland-tasting fluid and represents the reflex stimulation of salivary gland secretion. Dysphagia may result from esophageal stenosis or stricture but also can occur from esophageal spasm. Reflux symptoms generally are noted during the day and may be associated with certain foods or beverages. Citrus juices, coffee, and spicy or fried foods commonly are reported as precipitating heartburn.

Chief among nonesophageal symptoms are pulmonary and throat complaints. In about 20% of patients with chronic cough, reflux is the trigger.[9] Reflux is an important cause of adult-onset nonallergic asthma. Nocturnal symptoms are extremely important because they indicate the potential for aspiration. Sudden awakening with heartburn or regurgitation can be associated with cough and wheezing, heralding chronic pulmonary damage. Reflux is also frequently the cause of throat complaints, such as hoarseness, pain, a globus sensation, frequent throat clearing, and postnasal drip. It also may produce a nonburning substernal pain, often confused with angina, that may similarly follow exercise. Nausea alone may be attributed to GERD and also can be found in the setting of delayed emptying with early satiety and vomiting. Finally, hiccups, halitosis, and ear pain are potential reflux symptoms.

The physical examination by medical doctors is usually unrevealing in GERD, but dentists often identify dental erosions that are caused by reflux.

DIAGNOSIS

Gastroesophageal reflux disease is a clinical diagnosis suggested by history and confirmed by the response to treatment. There is little need for any confirmatory tests unless the symptoms are atypical or the patient fails to improve. However, upper gastrointestinal series and/or upper endoscopy ultimately are indicated in many patients.

The role of the upper gastrointestinal series in the diagnosis of reflux is limited. The presence of a hiatal hernia, although an important factor in the pathogenesis of reflux, is nonspecific, and frequently is seen in subjects with few or no reflux symptoms. The report of spontaneous reflux of barium is useful since it correlates well with other measures of reflux, but it is an uncommon finding. Reflux-induced by maneuvers such as the Valsalva, abdominal compression, or the water siphon test, is an insensitive, nonspecific finding. A barium study can be useful to exclude reflux complications such as ulcer, stricture, and erosive esophagitis. It also identifies peptic ulcers and esophageal or gastric cancers.

Upper endoscopy usually is used to investigate alarm symptoms (Table 39–3), and it is used to diagnose superficial erosive esophagitis, Barrett's esophagus, and cancer. All patients, regardless of gender, should undergo a screening endoscopy when symptoms are present for 1 year or more. Up to 50% of patients with GERD have erosive esophagitis, characterized by linear or circumscribed lesions in the distal esophagus. This finding is associated with chronicity. At long-term follow-up, persistent symptoms and the need for medication is greatest in those patients with erosive changes. The

TABLE 39–3. GERD: Alarm Symptoms*

Hematemesis, occult blood in stool, iron deficiency
Dysphagia, odynophagia
Early satiety, vomiting
Weight loss

*Should generally precipitate specialty referral

diagnosis of Barrett's esophagus can only be made by performing a biopsy. The location and appearance of the squamocolumnar junction clues the endoscopist to perform a biopsy. The reduction in reimbursements for endoscopic procedures has eliminated much of the cost differential between endoscopy and radiography.

pH monitoring is a more sensitive indicator of reflux than is radiography. The test is performed by placing a pH-sensitive electrode in the distal esophagus transnasally. The electrode is connected to a small tape recorder, worn at the belt, that records the esophageal pH level continuously over a 24-hour period, and that can be signaled whenever symptoms are present. Thus, it provides both an objective measure of the frequency and duration of reflux events and determines the association between symptoms and reflux. pH monitoring can be performed prior to initiating treatment to establish the diagnosis of GERD, or to assess refractory symptoms while the patient is receiving therapy. Throat and nose discomfort are common complaints, but most patients are willing to repeat the test if needed.[10]

Two other esophageal tests are esophageal biopsy and manometry. There is not much value in performing a biopsy in a normal-appearing esophagus; specific biopsy findings for the diagnosis of reflux such as acute inflammation are uncommon. Manometry is valuable in the assessment of candidates for antireflux surgery but has little diagnostic value. Table 39–4 lists an approach to the diagnostic evaluation of the patient with GERD.

TREATMENT

Treatment of GERD can be divided into four categories: (1) lifestyle modifications and use of nonprescription drugs, (2) antisecretory drugs, (3) promotility and other medications, and (4) antireflux surgery. In general, less is more. In other words, in a chronic disease such as GERD, long-term treatment is best accomplished through cost-

TABLE 39–4. Diagnostic Approach

Empiric trial of treatment unless alarm symptoms are present

Barium swallow—screening test for esophageal complications

Endoscopy—screen for erosive esophagitis or Barrett's esophagus

24-h pH monitoring—typical symptoms or symptoms refractory to medical therapy

Confirm reflux in patient with negative endoscopy

Biopsy to confirm Barrett's esophagus or esophagitis

Gastric emptying to evaluate symptoms of gastric stasis

Motility—pre-operative assessment of body peristalsis

effective strategies. The financial burden of altering the diet, abstaining from food for 3 hours before bed, and the "as-needed" use of antacids or over-the-counter histamine 2–receptor antagonists (H_2RAs) is modest. However, some patients may opt for the convenience and freedom from dietary restrictions afforded by a once-daily proton-pump inhibitor, despite the higher cost of this therapy.

Lifestyle modifications are listed in Table 39–5. The most useful behavioral modifications are "not to eat too much, too fast, or too late." Meal size and fat content are correlated with postprandial reflux. Air swallowing is associated with gulping one's meal, which enhances transient sphincter relaxations and reflux. The time at which 50% of a standard meal has emptied the stomach is 90 minutes, so 3 hours are required to achieve an empty stomach at bedtime. There are no therapeutic benefits to eliminating specific foods as a general rule. Patients usually identify their own food intolerances and behave accordingly. In the patient with occasional symptoms, over-the-counter antacids or H_2-receptor antagonists usually provide prompt relief.

TABLE 39–5. Lifestyle Modifications

Fast for 3 h before bedtime
Sleep with head of bed elevated by 15 cm
Avoid large meals
Avoid specific foods that repeatedly cause symptoms
Avoid smoking, excessive alcohol, aspirin, and nonsteroidal anti-inflammatory drugs
Reduce body weight

TABLE 39–6. Medical Therapy for Gastroesophageal Reflux Disease

Drug Category	Examples and Dosages
H₂RA	Cimetidine (Tagamet) 400–800 mg bid
	Ranitidine (Zantac) 150–300 mg bid
	Famotidine (Pepcid) 20–40 mg bid
	Nizatidine (Axid) 150–300 mg bid
PPI	Omeprazole (Prilosec) 20–40 mg qd–bid
	Lansoprazole (Prevacid) 15–30 mg qd–bid
	Rabeprazole (Aciphex) 20–40 mg qd–bid
	Pantoprazole (Protonix) 40 mg qd–bid
	Esomeprazole (Nexium) 20–40 mg qd
Promotility	Metoclopramide (Reglan) 10–20 mg qid
	Bethanecol (Urecholine) 10–25 mg qid

H_2RA = histamine 2–receptor antangonist; PPI = proton-pump inhibitor.

Inhibition of acid secretion is the mainstay of GERD treatment. The two classes of secretory inhibitors are H_2RAs and proton-pump inhibitors (PPIs) (Table 39–6). Histamine, gastrin, and acetylcholine are direct stimulants of parietal cell acid secretion. Inhibition of any of these stimulants is sufficient to reduce acid production. Thus, an H_2RA decreases fasting and meal-stimulated secretion. A hydrogen-potassium adenosinetriphosphatase is responsible for the secretion of hydrogen ions from the parietal cell, and it is the target of PPIs. The only clinical difference between H_2RAs and PPIs is their relative potency in suppressing gastric acid secretion. A once-daily dosage of a PPI generally normalizes esophageal pH, relieves symptoms, and heals esophagitis after 4 to 8 weeks of treatment in 80 to 90% of patients.[11] Standard dosages of H_2RAs are about half as effective.[12]

For most patients there are two phases of treatment—an acute phase and a maintenance phase. The acute phase represents the initial control of symptoms and the healing of erosive esophagitis. Erosive esophagitis is found only in 25 to 40% of patients and, generally, responds well to treatment. The primary end point of treatment is symptom control. After the first 6 to 8 weeks of treatment, it is advisable to use low-dose maintenance therapy to prevent relapse. Recurrence of symptoms off treatment is the rule for both erosive and nonerosive disease.

The role of promotility drugs in the treatment of GERD is controversial. Theoretically, since GERD is primarily a disorder of impaired motor function, these agents should be useful. However, the improvement in esophageal motor function during treatment is modest. Nonetheless, there is evidence of symptomatic improvement and endoscopic healing to a degree.[13] Patients with symptoms suggestive of delayed gastric emptying or those with nonacid regurgitation may be especially benefited. In the patient with refractory reflux symptoms on standard PPI therapy, a common practice is to increase the PPI dosage before prescribing a promotility drug. The most widely prescribed agent was cisapride (Propulsid), but it has been withdrawn due to cardiac abnormalities. The other available promotility drugs, metoclopramide (Reglan) and bethanechol (Urecholine), frequently produce side effects and are not as effective as was cisapride.

Sucralfate (Carafate) is a topically active agent that is cytoprotective. It has no antisecretory activity, but it does bind bile acid to a degree. It can be helpful in the patient with nonacid reflux.

Antireflux surgery is gaining popularity since the development of a laparoscopic technique. The principle component of the surgery is the creation of a high-pressure zone at the gastroesophageal junction by wrapping the fundus of the stomach around the distal esophagus. When the stomach completely encircles the esophagus (a 360° wrap), it is called a Nissen fundoplication. Modifications of the operation include 270° and 180° wraps. Patient selection is critical, but, with proper screening, the immediate results (12 to 24 months post surgery) are excellent to good in 85 to 90% of patients.[14] The best candidates are patients with objective evidence of reflux by endoscopy or pH monitoring, and a high association between reflux and their symptoms. An example is a patient with satisfactory control of symptoms on medical treatment but with an unwillingness to continue medication indefinitely. Patients with refractory symptoms are less optimal candidates because of the strong possibility that the symptoms or a portion of them are not due to reflux.

It is important to recognize that the response to medical or surgical treatment is less satisfactory for patients with atypical symptoms, as compared with those patients who have typical complaints. Cough, hoarseness, and other extraesophageal symptoms require 4 to 6 months of medical treatment at two to three times the usual dosages of medications to respond. Results after fundoplication are not as impressive for these patients.

PROGNOSIS

There are three potential outcomes of GERD: intermittent nonprogressive disease, esophageal complications, and esophageal carcinoma. Complications, including ulcers and strictures, are limited to those patients with erosive esophagitis. About 25 to 40% of patients develop erosive esophagitis, and most heal completely with medical treatment. Overall, the complication risk is about 10%. The risk of esophageal cancer is low. It is associated with a lengthy history of frequent symptoms and underlying Barrett's esophagus. At most, 1% of reflux patients develop esophageal cancer.

The majority of GERD patients have uncomplicated nonerosive disease. The notion that GERD is a lifelong chronic disease requiring constant medical treatment surgery is unfounded. Long-term follow-up studies indicate that most of these patients require only intermittent medication and do not ultimately have antireflux surgery.

PREVENTION AND SCREENING

There is no clear evidence that diet or behavior influences the onset of GERD. Recent weight gain may be associated with the onset of symptoms in some cases, albeit infrequently. Smoking has multiple inhibitory effects on esophageal and gastric motility and is associated with reflux. Certain medications are either injurious to esophageal mucosa or increase the frequency of reflux (Table 39–7). Avoiding these precipitating factors may lessen the chance that a patient will develop GERD.

Screening with upper endoscopy to detect Barrett's esophagus and erosive esophagitis is advisable in patients who have frequent symptoms for 1 year or more. The prevalence of Barrett's esophagus in women is lower than that in men by a ratio of about 1:9. Because Barrett's esophagus is so much more frequent in Caucasian men, some authorities do not favor screening in women or non-Caucasians.

PREGNANCY AND BREAST-FEEDING

Daily heartburn has been reported by 25% of pregnant women. Another 25% have weekly or monthly

TABLE 39–7. Drugs to Avoid in Gastroesophageal Reflux Disease

Esophageal irritants
    Antibiotics
    Potassium
    Iron
    Aspirin and nonsteroidal anti-inflammatory drugs
    Quinidine
    Alendronate

Reflux stimulants
    Anticholinergics
    ß-blockers
    Calcium channel blockers
    Nitrates
    Theophylline
    Diazepam

symptoms.[6] The onset is usually early in pregnancy, as 52% of women who develop heartburn first experience it in the first trimester. Forty percent of heartburn occurrences develop during the second trimester. Heartburn is rarely felt initially in the third trimester;[15] however, the severity of heartburn generally worsens throughout the course of the pregnancy. Predisposing factors, in addition to greater gestational age, are pre-pregnancy reflux and increased parity.[16] The onset of reflux is not related to pre-pregnancy weight or the amount of weight gain, nor are there racial or ethnic predispositions. The presumed etiologies are hormonal and mechanical. Van Thiel et al described a steady significant fall in resting lower esophageal sphincter pressure during pregnancy due to the increased levels of estrogen and progesterone.[17] In addition, the mechanical effect of increased abdominal pressure is a significant contributor. Heartburn is likely to be a recurrent problem in subsequent pregnancies.

The safest therapies are lifestyle modifications and antacids. Small meals and fasting 3 hours before bedtime are desirable. Antacids generally are considered safe to use during the last two trimesters of pregnancy. Magnesium-aluminum antacids with or without alginate (Gaviscon) are preferred. However, high doses of magnesium may retard labor and should be avoided late in pregnancy. Sodium bicarbonate should not be used as an antacid because of the risk of metabolic alkalosis. Sucralfate is also quite safe to use during pregnancy since it has minimal absorption. The H$_2$RAs cimetidine, ranitidine, and famotidine, like antacids and sucralfate, are US Food and Drug Administration category B drugs. That is, there is no demonstrated risk in human studies or, if human studies are not adequate, animal studies have shown no risk.[18] There is less information available about proton-pump inhibitors. In one study of omeprazole use, there was no difference in fetal outcome compared with that in controls. Omeprazole and other PPIs should be reserved for the patient refractory to H$_2$RAs in the last trimester. Metoclopramide is a category B drug, but it still is of concern because of maternal side effects. Endoscopy with sedation to investigate bleeding or dysphagia is reasonable in the second and third trimesters. In the breast-feeding mother, safety data is only established regarding antacids, sucralfate, and H$_2$RAs.

MENOPAUSE

The influence of menopause on the onset or the course of reflux disease has never been studied. It has been shown that hormonal changes during the menstrual cycle do not affect esophageal motility or acid reflux.[5] Consequently, cessation of the cycle would not be expected to impact reflux on a hormonal basis. However, the emotional impact of menopause, as well as other physiologic changes, could conceivably exacerbate reflux.

Aging does change the clinical picture of reflux. Although the condition is quite common in the geriatric population, the symptoms are likely to be atypical, (eg, cough, or chest, or throat pain), rather than heartburn.[19] Coexisting pulmonary and heart disease more frequently cause diagnostic confusion in older patients. Reflux contains more nonacid compounds, such as bile, in the older individual. Antisecretory and bile-binding agents may be necessary for treatment.

ORAL CONTRACEPTIVE PILLS AND HORMONE REPLACEMENT

Theoretically, since replacement estrogen/progesterone and contraceptives relax esophageal smooth muscle, they should provoke reflux. Clinically, however, this seems to be an uncommon association. In general, the severity of symptoms, the response to antisecretory or promotility drugs, and the healing of esophagitis are not affected by hormone replacement or use of oral contraceptives. Oral contraceptives have been responsible for pill-induced esophageal injury on a few occasions.[20]

RESOURCE

The American Gastroenterological Association
7910 Woodmont Avenue, Suite 700
Bethesda, Maryland 20814
Telephone: (310) 654-2055
Web site: www.gastro.org

The American Gastroenterological Association offers information about a wide variety of gastrointestinal diseases, including GERD, through its Web site. Brochures and videotapes also are available.

REFERENCES

1. Johnson LF, Demeester TR. Twenty-four-hour pH monitoring of the distal esophagus. Am J Gastroenterol 1974;62:325–32.

2. Dodds WJ, Dent J, Hogan WJ, et al. Mechanisms of gastroesophageal reflux in patients with reflux esophagitis. N Engl J Med 1982;307:1547–52.

3. Dent J, Dodds WJ, Friedman RH, et al. Mechanism of gastroesophageal reflux in recumbent asymptomatic human subjects. J Clin Invest 1980;65:256–67.

4. McCallum RW, Berkowitz DM, Lerner E. Gastric emptying in patients with gastroesophageal reflux. Gastroenterology 1981;80:285–91.

5. Mohiuddin MA, Pursnani KG, Katzka DA, et al. Effect of cyclic hormonal changes during normal menstrual cycle on esophageal motility. Dig Dis Sci 1999;44:1368–75.

6. Nebel OT, Fornes MF, Castell DO. Symptomatic gastroesophageal reflux: incidence and precipitating factors. Am J Dig Dis 1976;21:953–6.

7. Tytgat GNJ, Hameeteman W. The neoplastic potential of columnar-lined (Barrett's) esophagus. World J Surg 1992;16:308–12.

8. Lembo T, Ippoliti AF, Ramers C, et al. Inflammation of the gastro-oesophageal junction (carditis) in patients with symptomatic gastro-oesophageal reflux disease: a prospective study. Gut 1999;45:484–8.

9. Irwin RS, Corrao WM, Pratter MR. Chronic persistent cough in the adult: the spectrum and frequency of causes and successful outcome of specific therapy. Am Rev Respir Dis 1981;123:413–7.

10. Fass R, Hell R, Sampliner RE, et al. Effect of ambulatory 24-hour esophageal pH monitoring on reflux-provoking activities. Dig Dis Sci 1999;44:2263–9.

11. Castell DO, Richter JE, Robinson M, et al. Efficacy and safety of lansoprazole in the treatment of erosive reflux esophagitis. Am J Gastroenterol 1996;91:1527–31.

12. Chiba N, de Gara CJ, Wilkinson JM, et al. Speed of healing of grade II to IV gastroesophageal reflux disease. A meta-analysis. Gastroenterology 1997;112:1798–810.

13. Galmiche JP, Fraitag B, Filoche B, et al. Double-blind comparison of cisapride and cimetidine in the treatment of reflux esophagitis. Dig Dis Sci 1990;35:649–55.

14. Rattner DW, Brooks DC. Patient satisfaction following laparoscopic and open anti-reflux surgery. Arch Surg 1995;130:289–94.

15. de Paula Castro L. Reflux esophagitis as the cause of heartburn of pregnancy. Am J Obstet Gynecol 1967;98:1–10.

16. Marrero JM, Goggin PM, de Caestecker JS, et al. Determinants of pregnancy heartburn. Br J Obstet Gynaecol 1992;99:731–4.

17. Van Thiel DH, Gavaler JS, Joshi SN, et al. Heartburn of pregnancy. Gastroenterology 1977;72:666–8.

18. Baron TH, Ramirez B, Richter JE. Gastrointestinal motility disorders during pregnancy. Ann Intern Med 1993;118:366–75.

19. Raiha I, Hietanen E, Sourander L. Symptoms of gastro-esophageal reflux in the elderly people. Age Aging 1991;20:365–70.

20. Kikendall JW. Pill esophagitis. J Clin Gastroenterol 1999;28:298–305.

40

APPROACH TO THE PATIENT WITH DYSPEPSIA

Eric Strom, MD

Dyspepsia is a persistent or recurrent abdominal pain or discomfort that is centered in the upper abdomen.[1] Derived from the Greek *dys* meaning "bad" and *peptein* meaning "to digest," it also may encompass symptoms of nausea, bloating, heartburn, and early satiety.

PREVALENCE

Dyspeptic symptoms are seen commonly. The prevalence of dyspepsia varies throughout the world, with a range from 26% in the United States to 41% in Great Britain.[2] Symptoms occur more commonly in younger patients, but the proportion of patients with dyspepsia who seek medical advice increases with age, perhaps due to concern of serious illness.[3] With a few notable exceptions, dyspepsia occurs equally in men and women. Gastric ulcers not associated with use of nonsteroidal anti-inflammatory drugs (NSAIDs) occur more frequently in men than in women, whereas the increasingly common use of these anti-inflammatory agents, especially in the elderly female population, has resulted in a female preponderance of NSAID-associated gastric ulcer.[4] A history of abuse, sexual, physical and/or emotional, is associated with gastrointestinal illnesses. These illnesses include irritable bowel syndrome, nonulcer ("functional") dyspepsia, and chronic abdominal pain.[5] Pregnancy also may present with gastrointestinal symptoms including dyspepsia.

EVALUATION OF THE PATIENT WITH DYSPEPSIA

The clinical evaluation of a patient with complaints of dyspepsia should include a comprehensive history and physical examination. The history in particular, should be used to *exclude* the following:

- Gastroesophageal reflux disease—an approach to evaluation for this disease is described in Chapter 39.
- Biliary type pain—abdominal ultrasonography should be performed to look for stones, sludge, and dilated ducts
- Irritable bowel syndrome—an approach to evaluation for irritable bowel syndrome is described in Chapter 41.
- Medication-induced symptoms—stop offending agent if possible

Additional pertinent history includes the patient's age, recurrent vomiting, significant unintentional weight loss, radiation of pain to the back, dysphagia, drug use (ie, aspirin, NSAID), heavy alcohol or cigarette use, family history of cancer or peptic ulcer disease, and evidence of bleeding from the gastrointestinal tract, such as the presence of bright red blood in stool, hematemesis, or melena. The complete physical examination should include checking for abdominal masses, organomegaly, stool positive for occult blood, and jaundice.

Laboratory tests should include a complete blood count, liver function and amylase tests, and evaluation of renal function with a blood urea nitrogen and creatinine measurements.

DIFFERENTIAL DIAGNOSIS

Approximately 40% of cases of dyspepsia have organic or structural etiologies. Most of these are due to peptic ulcer disease (duodenal and gastric ulcers), with a variety of disorders accounting for the rest (Table 40–1). The remaining 60% of cases comprise a heterogeneous group of patients with nonulcer dyspepsia (NUD).

Peptic Ulcer Disease

Peptic ulcer disease is a common disorder, with more than 10% of adult Americans claiming a positive past history.[6] Symptoms of peptic ulcer vary widely, with the "classic" presentation described as a "burning," "gnawing," or "hunger-like" epigastric pain, usually lessened by food or antacids, and often waking the patient from sleep between 1:00 am and 3:00 am Although food is usually emptied from the stomach within 2 to 3 hours of eating, food-stimulated acid production continues for 4 to 5 hours. This accounts for the night-time discomfort when food, usually an excellent buffer of acid, is no longer present in the stomach. Despite this description of typical symptoms it should be remembered that both gastric and duodenal ulcers can remain asymptomatic for long periods of time.[7]

PATHOGENESIS OF PEPTIC ULCER DISEASE

The maintenance of gastric and duodenal mucosal integrity depends on a balance of "aggressive" factors, including acid, pepsin, and drugs, among others, and "defensive" factors, such as gastric mucus, bicarbonate secretion, prostaglandin production, and blood flow. Stimulation of acid production may be caused by coffee (caffeine-containing and caffeine-free), alcohol, calcium, and pepper. Pepsin is a proteolytic agent, that, in concert with the corrosive action of gastric acid, produces the tissue injury seen in peptic ulcer disease. The activity of

---

TABLE 40–1. Differential Diagnosis of Dyspepsia

Duodenal ulcer
Gastric ulcer
Atypical gastroesophageal reflux disease
Gastroparesis
Gastric cancer
Parasitic infections
Carbohydrate maldigestion
Drug side effects
Biliary disease
Pregnancy
Nonulcer (functional) dyspepsia

---

pepsin is maximal at a pH of approximately 2 and is significantly inhibited at a pH above 4.

DUODENAL ULCER

Duodenal ulcer disease is a chronic recurrent condition ("*Helicobacter pylori*," below). More than 95% of all duodenal ulcers occur in the first portion of the duodenum (the duodenal bulb) and are usually less than 1 cm in diameter. Prevalence in the United States is estimated to be between 6 and 15%. Duodenal ulcers are seen with equal frequency in males and females.

Although acid is a prerequisite for the development of a duodenal ulcer, there are other contributing factors. These include genetic factors, blood type, and cigarette smoking.[8] Several chronic medical conditions also are associated with the development of duodenal ulcers, including renal failure, alcoholic cirrhosis, chronic obstructive pulmonary disease, and rheumatoid arthritis (independent of aspirin use). Recent data indicates that the adverse effect of smoking might not be present in those patients who have been cured of an *H. pylori* infection.[9]

Helicobacter pylori. Evidence now firmly establishes gastric colonization with *H. pylori* as a causative factor for duodenal ulcer disease. The chronic inflammation caused by *H. pylori* infection leads to changes in gastric secretory physiology and chronic gastritis. In most individuals this change is asymptomatic, but, in some, the combination of tissue injury and gastric acid leads to peptic ulcer disease. In others, gastritis leads to atrophy and, in rare cases, gastric carcinoma or lymphoma. Although a duodenal ulcer can be "healed" with appropriate acid-reducing medications in the presence of untreated *H. pylori* infection, the recurrence rate of duodenal ulcer after 1 year is less than 10% if *H. pylori* is eradicated, compared with a 60 to 80% recurrence rate if the bacteria are not eradicated.[10]

Clinical features. Duodenal ulcers most commonly present with epigastric pain, variably described as "burning," "gnawing," "sharp," or "hunger-like." Night-time awakening is common, and the pain usually is relieved within several minutes if food or antacids are ingested. Other symptoms may include nausea and/or vomiting. If bleeding is present, the emesis may be red or black ("coffee-ground" emesis). Alternatively, bleeding may present with the passage of a black tarry stool (melena) or with red blood, if the bleeding is massive. Physical examination usually reveals tenderness in the midline, midway between the xyphoid process and the umbilicus.

Diagnosis. Upper gastrointestinal series demonstrate approximately 80 to 90% of duodenal ulcers. Endoscopic evaluation (gastroscopy) is the gold standard for diagnosis, however, providing not only greater sensitivity and specificity than radiography, but also the potential for therapy via electrocoagulation or sclerotherapy of bleeding vessels.

Medical therapy. Current therapy is based on the use of acid-reducing medications. Antacids are inexpensive, safe, and readily available but of limited value due to side effects, including diarrhea and unpleasant taste. Histamine 2 blockers (cimetidine, ranitidine, famotidine and nizatidine) are prescribed widely and are effective, with healing rates of 70 to 80% after 4 weeks of treatment and 87 to 94% after 8 weeks.[11]

The current data linking *H. pylori* with peptic ulcer disease has led to a rethinking of the management of this disease. Numerous studies have documented the efficacy of treatment with powerful antisecretory agents, together with combination antibiotic therapy for patients with *H. pylori*–associated peptic ulcer disease. Although the eradication of *H. pylori* helps with ulcer healing to a small degree,[12] the most significant benefit is the decreased recurrence rate when eradication is successful.[13] In support of the eradication of *H. pylori* is the evidence supporting a relationship between chronic *H. pylori* infection and the development of gastric cancer.[14] The diagnosis of *H. pylori* infection can be established in several ways. A serum antibody test for immunoglobulin G is highly sensitive but remains positive for long periods of time. This persistence of the antibody makes it difficult to determine treatment success, failure, or re-infection (which is a rare event). A radioactive carbon–labeled urea breath test, the gold-standard, is positive only in cases of active infection, but it is expensive, cumbersome, and not always readily available. A recent report has demonstrated that a stool antigen test for *H. pylori* gives results equal in specificity and sensitivity to the breath test.[15] Several treatment regimens have been approved (Table 40–2). They

TABLE 40–2. Treatment Regimens for *Helicobacter pylori* Eradication

Regimen	Drug and Dosage	Duration
1	Proton-pump inhibitor (lansoprazole 30 mg bid or omeprazole 20 mg bid)	10–14 d
	Amoxicillin 1 g bid	10–14 d
	Clarithromycin 500 mg bid	10–14 d
2	Substitute metronidazole 500 mg bid in penicillin-allergic patients	
3	Proton-pump inhibitor	14 d
	Metronidazole 500 mg qid	14 d
	Tetracycline 500 mg qid	14 d
	Bismuth subsalicylate 525 mg qid	14 d

usually include two antibiotics and a proton-pump inhibitor (omeprazole or lansoprazole), with the duration of treatment lasting 7 to 14 days.

Less commonly used regimens in the treatment of peptic ulcer disease include coating agents (sulcrafate) and prostaglandin therapy (misoprostol). Misoprostol is particularly effective in preventing NSAID-associated peptic disease, but use is limited by a high incidence of diarrhea.

GASTRIC ULCER

Much of the information relating to gastric ulcer is similar to that mentioned above for duodenal ulcer. Some significant differences include the following:

- The peak age of incidence for gastric ulcer is approximately 10 years later than that for duodenal ulcer (ie, sixth decade of life as compared with the fifth decade).
- There is a slight male predominance for gastric ulcer except for that associated with NSAID use, which is more common in women
- Gastric ulcer patients generally have acid secretory rates that are equal to or lower than those of nonulcer patients.
- Ten to 20% of gastric ulcer patients also have duodenal ulcers.
- Gastric ulcer patients often get little relief by eating; many have increased pain with eating.
- Weight loss is more common in patients with gastric ulcer than in those with duodenal ulcer.

- Whereas nausea and vomiting frequently indicate a degree of obstruction in duodenal ulcer patients, these symptoms often are seen in gastric ulcer patients without evidence of obstruction.
- Hemorrhage is more commonly associated with gastric ulcer than duodenal ulcer.
- Gastric ulcers have a small but definite incidence of malignancy, whereas duodenal ulcers are rarely malignant.
- Healing usually occurs more slowly with gastric ulcers.
- Use of NSAID is the cause of a large proportion of gastric ulcers, with between 10 and 30% of those on chronic NSAID therapy being affected.
- Gastric ulcers are associated with an *H. pylori* infection 60 to 70% of the time, compared with a higher percentage (85 to 90%) of *H. pylori* association with duodenal ulcer.
- Due to the small but definite incidence of malignancy associated with gastric ulcers, endoscopy may be indicated to ensure complete healing after a course of therapy. This may not always be necessary, however, especially if the patient's history contains a likely cause for the gastric ulcers (NSAID use).

Gastroesophageal Reflux

Gastroesophageal reflux disease may present with epigastric discomfort, usually associated with retrosternal burning and increased symptoms when bending or assuming a supine position; it is discussed in detail in Chapter 39, "Gastroesophageal Reflux Disease."

Gastroparesis

Gastroparesis is a condition characterized by impaired gastric emptying, often associated with diabetes mellitus, scleroderma, use of drugs such as high-dose tricyclic antidepressants, prior gastric surgery, and some neurologic disorders such as parkinsonism. Drugs also may impair gastric motility. Examples include some drugs used in the treatment of parkinsonism, anticholinergics, and some psychiatric medications. Symptoms commonly include nausea, vomiting, postprandial bloating, early satiety, and anorexia. Prokinetic agents, including metaclopramide, and low-dose erythromycin, are used commonly in the treatment of gastroparesis.

Gastric Cancer

Gastric cancer rarely occurs before the age of 45 years. Thereafter the incidence slowly rises, reaching a peak in the seventh decade with men affected at twice the rate of women. In the United States the incidence of gastric cancer has decreased significantly over the past 50 years.[16] Due to its high case fatality rate, however, gastric cancer remains among the top 10 causes of cancer-related death, with African American, Latino, and Native American rates from 1.5 to 2.5 times higher than Caucasian Americans.[17]

Dyspepsia rarely is a presenting sign of gastric cancer, unless it is associated with weight loss, anemia, or some other alarm sign.[18]

Parasitic Infections

Parasitic infection, such as giardiasis or strongyloidiasis, has been known to present with typical dyspeptic symptoms. A travel history in patients who have gone to parts of the world where these infections are endemic may be helpful, although a history of travel is not a prerequisite for suspecting these conditions.

Carbohydrate Maldigestion

Maldigestion or malabsorption of various carbohydrates can lead to upper abdominal pain and bloating. These symptoms are common in patients with lactase deficiency (lactose intolerance) and also may be seen with the ingestion of increased amounts of fructose, sorbitol, and mannitol. These nonabsorbable sugars are found in sodas, dietetic foods, sugarless chewing gum, and some liquid medications.

Drug Side Effects

Some drugs have the potential to produce dyspeptic symptoms; examples include digoxin, tetracycline, theophylline, erythomycin, and NSAIDS.

Biliary Disease

Patients who develop distinct episodes of moderate to severe upper abdominal pain (epigastric and/or in the right upper quadrant) that last for 1 hour or more may be suffering from biliary type pain. This pain often may radiate to the back or scapula and may be associated with sweating, nausea, and vomiting. By definition these patients are not classified as having dyspepsia.

Gallbladder disease is common in the United States, with a prevalence of gallstones approaching 10 to 20% in women under age 50 years and as high as 30% in women over age 50 years. Several studies have addressed the issue of the role of gallbladder disease causing dyspepsia; there is no convincing evidence to support this relationship.

Pregnancy

Dyspeptic symptoms during pregnancy are most often a result of increased acid reflux (see Chapter 39, "Gastroesophageal Reflux Disease").

Nonulcer Dyspepsia

The criteria for diagnosing NUD are "chronic or recurrent upper abdominal pain or discomfort for a period of a least one month, with symptoms present more than 25% of the time, and an absence of clinical, biochemical, endoscopic, and ultrasonographic evidence of organic disease that would account for the symptoms."[1]

PATHOPHYSIOLOGY

The 60% of dyspeptic patients in whom no organic pathology can be found are considered to have nonulcer or functional dyspepsia. The cause of functional dyspepsia is not known at this time. It is likely a heterogeneous disorder with multiple etiologies, characterized by frequent relapses and remissions.[18] Patients with NUD represent a large population. Therefore, a complete medical evaluation in all of those affected represents a significant expenditure of time and money. Many strategies have been suggested for the evaluation of this patient population, in an effort to distinguish patients that may be treated safely empirically for a specified period of time and those that should be referred immediately for more intensive investigation.[11,19–22] A common approach has been to group these patients according to symptoms. Four main groups have been described:[2]

1. Reflux type—heartburn, regurgitation, cough
2. Dysmotility type—belching, bloating, distention, and absence of nocturnal symptoms
3. Ulcer type—pain improves with food intake; night-time symptoms; localized pain
4. Essential type—episodic, unlocalized, occurs night and day

It has been suggested that the patients with reflux-type symptoms are significantly different from the others. It may be appropriate to consider them to have gastroesophageal reflux disease and not to include them with the other three groups.

Hopes were that this approach would allow for a rational and systematic treatment plan, using drugs designed to target specific symptoms. However, numerous studies have shown such a substantial overlap, with patients having symptoms in two or three of the groups, that the approach is of little discriminating value.[2,8] In addition, there is generally a poor correlation between symptoms and physiologic measurements. Recent attention has focused on the following factors: gastric motility, augmented visceral perception, *H. pylori* infection, and psychosocial factors.

Gastric motility. Between 35 and 80% of patients with NUD have demonstrable abnormalities of gastric emptying.[23] Therapy with prokinetic agents such as metaclopramide may improve gastric emptying, but this often fails to correlate with improvement in symptoms. Likewise, symptoms may improve with no change in gastric emptying.[24] Gastric compliance refers to the ability of the stomach to distend and accommodate a meal. Studies have demonstrated decreased compliance in the proximal stomach in patients with functional dyspepsia. Clinical evaluation of several agents designed to correct this disturbance are in progress. These are described further in the section "Treatment," below.

Visceral sensitivity. Increased visceral sensitivity refers to a lower threshold for pain during gastric or bowel distention. Patients with NUD have shown a consistent visceral hypersensitivity, a finding that is independent of abnormalities in gastric emptying.[25] A recent study by Mertz et al has demonstrated that, although patients with severe functional and organic dyspepsia have a similar prevalence of dyspeptic symptoms, only those with functional disease show evidence of altered visceral perception in the form of a lowered perception threshold.[26]

Helicobacter pylori. *Helicobacter pylori* is a well-known cause of chronic active gastritis. However, a consistent link between the finding of gastritis on upper endoscopy and symptoms of dyspepsia has not been established.[27] Up to 50% of patients with NUD harbor *H. pylori*. Several recent reviews on the relationship of *H. pylori* to dyspepsia have come to different conclusions as to the role of this organism in producing dyspeptic symptoms, but the weight of evidence seems to support a minimal (5% or less) benefit of treatment of *H. pylori* in these patients.[28,29]

Psychosocial factors. Although no specific personality profile has been found in patients with functional dyspepsia, this group of patients demonstrates an increased incidence of depression, anxiety, and neurotic behavior. In general, they have multiple somatic complaints, and a previously noted link between childhood abuse and irritable bowel syndrome has now been shown to exist in patients with functional dyspepsia as well.[5,30]

APPROACH TO MANAGEMENT

For many, the symptoms of dyspepsia are mild and of short enough duration that they do not seek medical attention. It has been estimated that less than 50% of affected individuals seek medical care.[2,18] Views differ on the management strategy for this patient population, but strategies can be divided into four main groups.[31]

1. Empiric therapy with antisecretory (proton-pump inhibitors [PPI]) and/or prokinetic (metaclopramide) agents—therapy may be started with a PPI for a 4-week duration and, if ineffective, switched to the prokinetic agent for an additional 4 weeks; failure to respond or rapid relapse after treatment warrants further investigation
2. Testing for *H. pylori* with a locally validated serologic test and treating all positive cases with one of the accepted regimens
3. Testing for *H. pylori* and having all patients with positive results undergo upper gastrointestinal endoscopy to search for ulcer disease or malignancy
4. Early endoscopy to distinguish cases with organic causes from functional dyspepsia

If the decision is made to pursue a definitive early diagnosis, endoscopy has been shown to provide greater accuracy in detecting organic causes than does radiography.[22,32] Analyses based on cost savings, ability to perform biopsies, documentation of *H. pylori* status, and overall risks have supported the recommendation that, if investigation of a patient with dyspepsia is to be done, endoscopy should be the first diagnostic test performed.[18]

The decision to treat empirically and thus avoid a more costly and invasive work-up raises concern about the possibility of missing a serious organic disorder. If attention is paid to signs and symptoms (alarm signs), this rarely occurs. Patients who are presenting with new dyspeptic symptoms and are over the age of 45 years are candidates for referral for more intensive evaluation (ie, endoscopy). In addition, any patient, regardless of age, with any of the other signs and symptoms presented in Table 40–3 should be evaluated similarly.

TREATMENT

No definitive treatment exists for functional dyspepsia at this time.[33,34] A realistic goal is to diminish symptoms and help the patient cope with them, rather than eliminate them completely. A review by Talley[35] examined the efficacy or lack thereof of many agents that were chosen on the basis of "assumed" physiologic disturbances in functional dyspepsia (Table 40–4). These drugs, despite the absence of proven efficacy, are used, with varying degrees of success, to mitigate dyspeptic symptoms, once endoscopy has firmly established the diagnosis of nonulcer dyspepsia. Motility agents are appropriate for a short empiric trial, as described above.

Despite the lack of strong evidence linking *H. pylori* to dyspeptic symptoms, the small (5%) gain that may be achieved makes treatment a reasonable choice.[18] Several regimens have been evaluated with a range of success from 85 to 93% (see Table 40–2).

Despite conflicting data, it is likely that a small percentage of dyspeptic patients respond to acid-reducing medications and/or prokinetic agents.[35]

TABLE 40–3. Symptoms and Signs that May Suggest Serious Organic Disease[*]

Age ≥ 45 yr at symptom onset
Undesired weight loss
Anemia
Positive fecal occult blood test
Dysphagia
Odynophagia
Strong family history of cancer
Past history of cancer or peptic ulcer disease
Failure of prior treatment

[*]Alarm signs.

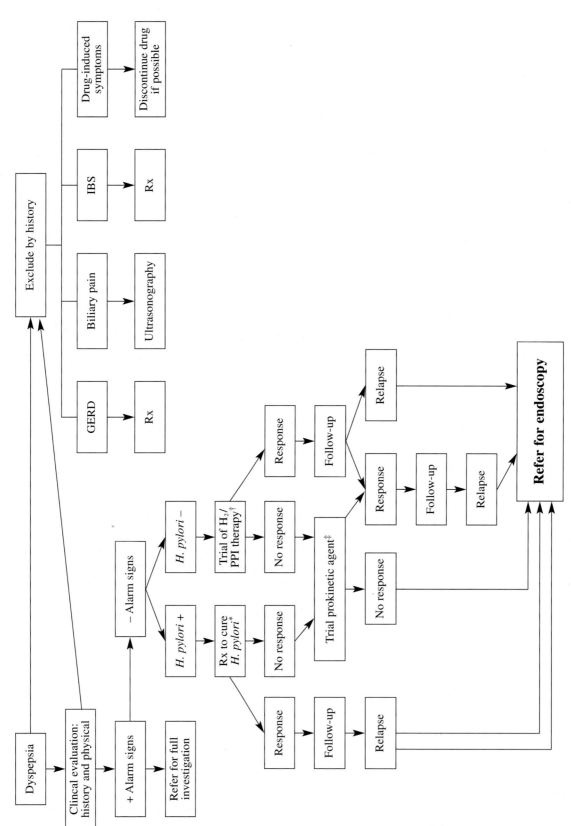

FIGURE 40–1. Evaluation and treatment of dyspepsia in patients < 45 years old. *See Table 40–2 for regimens. †For example, famotidine 20 mg PO bid or omeprazole 20 mg PO qam or lansoprazole 15 mg PO qam. ‡Metaclopramide 10 mg ac and qhs. Rx = prescription; H₂ = histamine 2; PPI = proton-pump inhibitor; GERD = gastroesophageal reflux disease.

TABLE 40–4. Treatment Candidates for Nonulcer Dyspepsia

Drugs of limited value
  H2 blockers (eg, ranitidine)
  PPI agents (eg, omeprazole)
  Prokinetic agents (eg, metaclopramide)

Drugs of uncertain value
  Antidepressants
    Tricyclic-type (eg, amitriptyline)
    SSRI-type (eg, fluoxetine)
  Anti–*H. pylori* therapy (see Table 40–2)
  5-HT$_3$-receptor antagonists (eg, alosetron)
  Prokinetics (eg, domperidone)
  GRH analogues (eg, leuprolide acetate)
  κ-receptor opiate agonists (eg, fedotozine)

Drugs of unlikely value
  Anticholinergics (eg, dicyclomine)
  Macrolides (eg, erythromycin)
  Prostaglandin analogues (eg, misoprostol)
  Somatostatin analogues (eg, octreotide)
  Mucosal protectants (eg, sulcralfate)

PPI = proton-pump inhibitor; SSRI = selective serotonin reuptake inhibitor; GRH=gonadotropin-releasing hormone; 5-HT = serotonin.

A study evaluating the use of prokinetic agents, including metaclopramide and cisapride, showed some short-term improvement in symptoms.[25,36]

Medications directed toward the hypothesized mechanism of "visceral hypersensitivity" currently are being advocated, with many clinical trials now underway to confirm their effectiveness. These include amitriptyline (a tricyclic antidepressant), fedotozine[37,38] (a κ-receptor opiate agonist), sumatriptan and buspirone[39] (5-HT-receptor agonists that affect proximal gastric compliance, and cyproheptadine (an antihistamine and serotonin antagonist).

Preliminary data has supported the value of some herbal preparations, including a caraway oil–peppermint oil combination and other preparations with multiple ingredients. Additional data is needed to validate these findings.[40,41]

If the patient is less than 45 years of age with no alarm signs, any of several treatment strategies may be employed (Figure 40–1). Although results of investigations vary, it is reasonable to test for *H. pylori* and treat it if positive.[18,42] If treatment fails

to relieve symptoms, a 4-week course with a prokinetic agent should be tried. If the *H. pylori* test is negative, a trial of acid-reducing therapy (histamine 2 blocker or proton-pump inhibitor) for 4 weeks may be initiated. Failure to alleviate symptoms with any of the above is an indication for a definitive investigation. If investigation confirms the diagnosis of nonulcer dyspepsia, drug therapy listed in Table 40–4 should be prescribed.

Some patients are resistant to all currently available therapies. Traditional psychotherapy is usually of little benefit, but behavioral modification to optimize the doctor-patient interaction and to reduce abnormal illness behaviors can be helpful.[43]

REFERENCES

1. Talley NJ, Colin-Jones D, Koch KL, et al. Functional dyspepsia: a classification with guidelines for diagnosis and management. Gastroenterol Int 1991;4:145–60.
2. Talley NJ, Zinsmeister AR, Schleck CD, Melton LJ III, Dyspepsia and dyspepsia subgroups: a population-based study. Gastroenterology 1992;102:1259–68.
3. Jones R, Lydeard Susan. Prevalence of symptoms of dyspepsia in the community. Br Med J 1989;298:30–2.
4. Walt RP, Katschinski B, Logan R, et al. Rising frequency of ulcer perforation in elderly people in the United Kingdom. Lancet 1986;i:489–92.
5. Drossman DA, Talley, NJ, Leserman J, et al. Sexual and physical abuse and gastrointestinal illness. Ann Intern Med 1995;123:782–94.
6. Sonnenberg A, Everhart JE, Health impact of peptic ulcer disease in the United States. Am J Gastroenterol 1997;92:614–20.
7. Jorde R, Bostad L, Burhol PG. Asymptomatic gastric ulcer: a follow-up study in patients with previous gastric ulcer disease. Lancet 1986;1:119–21.
8. Korman MG, Hansky J, Eaves ER, Schmidt GT. Influence of cigarette smoking on healing and relapse in duodenal ulcer disease. Gastroenterology 1983; 85:871–4.
9. Chan FKL, Sung JJY, Lee YT, et al. Does smoking predispose to peptic ulcer relapse after eradication of *Helicobacter pylori*? Am J Gastroenterol 1997;92:442–5.
10. Hopkins RJ, Girardi LS, Turney EA. Relationship between *H. pylori* eradication and reduced duodenal and gastric ulcer recurrence: a review. Gastroenterology 1996;110:1244–62.
11. Fendrick M, Chernew ME, Hirth RA, Bloom BS. Alternative management strategies for patients with

suspected peptic ulcer disease. Ann Intern Med 1995; 123:260–8.

12. Hosking SW, Ling TK, Chung SC, et al. Duodenal ulcer healing by eradication of *Helicobacter pylori* without anti-acid treatment: randomised controlled trial. Lancet 1994;343:508–10.

13. Walsh JH, Peterson WL, The treatment of *Helicobacter pylori* infection in the management of peptic ulcer disease. N Engl J Med 1995;333:984–91.

14. The Eurogast Study Group. An international association between *Helicobacter pylori* infection and gastric cancer. Lancet 1993;341:1359–62.

15. Vairu D, Malfertheiner P, Megraud F, et al. Non invasive tests for monitoring *Helicobacter pylori* (HP). European multicentre study [abstract]. Gastroenterology 1999;116:A341.

16. National Cancer Institute. Annual cancer statistics review: 1973–1991. Bestheda (MD): Department of Health and Human Services; 1994. DHHS Publication No.: 94-2789.

17. Wiggins CL, Becker TM, Key CR, et al. Stomach cancer among New Mexico's American Indians, Hispanic whites, and non-Hispanic whites. Cancer Res 1989;49:1595–9.

18. Talley NJ, Silverstein MD, Agreus L, et al. AGA technical review: evaluation of dyspepsia. Gastroenterology 1998;114:582–95.

19. Health and Public Policy Committee, American College of Physicians. Position paper. Endoscopy in the evaluation of dyspepsia. Ann Intern Med 1985; 102:266–9.

20. Bytzer P, Hansen JM, Schaffalitzky de Muckadell OB. Empirical H_2-blocker therapy or prompt endoscopy in management of dyspepsia. Lancet 1994;343:811–16.

21. Anthony TR. Axon chronic dyspepsia: who needs endoscopy? Gastroenterology 1997;112:1376–80.

22. Longstreth GF. Long-term costs after gastroenterology consultation with endoscopy versus radiography in dyspepsia. Gastrointest Endosc 1992;38(1):23–6.

23. Malagelada JR. Functional dyspepsia. Insights on mechanisms and management strategies. Gastroenterol Clin North Am 1996;25:103–12.

24. Jian R, Ducrot F, Ruskone A, et al. Symptomatic, radionuclide and therapeutic assessment of chronic idiopathic dyspepsia. A double-blind placebo-controlled evaluation of cisapride. Dig Dis Sci 1989;34:657–64.

25. Mearin F, Cucala M, Azpiroz F, Malagelada JR. The origin of symptoms on the brain-gut axis in functional dyspepsia. Gastroenterology 1991;101: 999–1006.

26. Mertz H, Fullerton S, Naliboff B, Mayer BA. Symptoms and visceral perception in severe functional and organic dyspepsia. Gut 1998;42:814–22.

27. Johnsen R, Bernersen B, Straume B, et al. Prevalences of endoscopic and histological findings in subjects with and without dyspepsia. BMJ 1991;302:749–52.

28. McColl K, Murray L, El-Omar E, et al. Symptomatic benefit from eradicating *Helicobacter pylori* infection in patients with nonulcer dyspepsia. N Engl J Med 1998;339:1869–74.

29. Blum AL, Talley NJ, O'Morain C, et al. Lack of effect of treating *Helicobacter pylori* infection in patients with nonulcer dyspepsia. N Engl J Med 1998; 339:1875–81.

30. Haug TT, Svebak S, Wilhelmsen I, et al. Psychological factors and somatic symptoms in functional dyspepsia. A comparison with duodenal and healthy controls. J Psychosom Res 1994;38:281–91.

31. Colin-Jones DG. Report of a working party. Management of dyspepsia. Lancet 1988; March 12:576–9.

32. Martin TR, Vennes JA, Silvis SE, Ansel HJ. A comparison of upper gastrointestinal endoscopy and radiography. J Clin Gastroenterol 1980;2:21–5.

33. Veldhuyzen van Zanten SJO, Cleary C, Talley NJ, et al. Drug treatment of functional dyspepsia: a systematic analysis of trial methodology with recommendations for design of future trials. Am J Gastroenterol 1996;91:660–73.

34. Fisher RS, Parkman HP. Management of nonulcer dyspepsia. N Engl J.Med 1998;339:1376–80.

35. Talley NJ. Review article: functional dyspepsia—should treatment be targeted on disturbed physiology? Aliment Pharmacol Ther 1995;9:107–15.

36. Dobrilla G, Comberlata M, Steele A, Vallaperta P. Drug treatment of functional dyspepsia. A meta-analysis of randomized controlled trials. J Clin Gastroenterol 1989;11:169–77.

37. Read NW, Abitbol JL, Bardhan KD, et al. Efficacy and safety of the peripheral kappa agonist fedotozine versus placebo in the treatment of functional dyspepsia. Gut 1997;41:664–8.

38. Fraitag B, Homerin M, Hecketsweiler P. Double-blind dose-response multicenter comparison of fedotozine and placebo in treatment of nonulcer dyspepsia. Dig Dis Sci 1994;39:1072–7.

39. Tack J, Leuven KU, Piessevaux H, et al., A placebo-controlled trial of buspirone, a fundus-relaxing drug,

in functional dyspepsia: effect on symptoms and gastric sensory and motor function [abstract]. Gastroenterology 1999;116:A325.

40. Holtmann G, Madisch A, Hotz J, et al. A double-blind, randomized, placebo-controlled trial on the effects of a herbal preparation in patients with functional dyspepsia [abstract]. Gastroenterology 1999; 116:A65.

41. May B, Koehler S, Schneider B, Pharms WS, Efficacy and tolerability of a fixed peppermint oil/caraway oil combination in non-ulcer dyspepsia [abstract]. Gastroenterology 1999;116:A248.

42. The European *Helicobacter pylori* Study Group. Current European concepts in the management of *Helicobacter pylori* infection: the Maastricht consensus report. Gut 1997;41:8–13.

43. Drossman DA, Thompson WG. The irritable bowel syndrome: review and a graduated multicomponent treatment approach. Ann Intern Med 1992; 116:1009–16.

41

IRRITABLE BOWEL SYNDROME

Britta Dickhaus, MD, Max J. Schmulson, MD, and Lin Chang, MD

Irritable bowel syndrome (IBS) is a chronic functional bowel disorder characterized by abdominal pain or discomfort and alterations in bowel habits. The syndrome affects up to 20% of the population of the United States, producing considerable costs to society in terms of work lost, consultations, unnecessary tests, inappropriate management, and even unnecessary surgery.[1,2]

Irritable bowel syndrome is the most common functional gastrointestinal (GI) disorder, with worldwide prevalence rates ranging from 9 to 23%.[3] Several population-based studies have demonstrated IBS symptoms to be more common in women, with prevalence ratios ranging from 2:1 to 3:1.[2,4] It is not known if this increased prevalence represents a reporting bias (ie, if female patients are more willing than men to disclose that they have IBS-related symptoms) or if it represents a biologic difference. Not all individuals seek medical care for their IBS symptoms. Based on different epidemiologic studies performed in different countries, 20 to 75% of individuals meeting symptom criteria for IBS seek medical care for their symptoms at some point in their lives.[1,5,6] The wide range in these numbers appears to be related, in part, to differences in national health care systems and access to medical care.

The diagnosis of IBS is based on identifying characteristic symptoms and excluding organic disease. Although the cause of IBS is not well understood, visceral hypersensitivity and altered brain-gut interactions are postulated as contributing causes. Currently, novel therapies are being developed to broaden treatment options, which presently include pharmacotherapy and psychotherapy.

CLINICAL FEATURES

The hallmark symptoms of IBS are chronic abdominal pain and/or discomfort.[7] Approximately 40% of IBS patients report abdominal pain when asked for their most bothersome symptom.[8] Alterations in bowel habits also are commonly present. Irritable bowel syndrome has a chronic relapsing course and overlaps with other functional GI disorders.[2] However, IBS is a heterogeneous disorder with numerous different symptom presentations. In addition to symptoms from the digestive system, clinical experience and recent reports in the literature have demonstrated a variety of extraintestinal symptoms in these patients, including sexual dysfunction,[9] sleep disturbances,[10,11] urinary bladder dysfunction,[12] and other pain syndromes, such as fibromyalgia (FMS).[13–15]

Gastrointestinal Symptoms

ABDOMINAL PAIN OR DISCOMFORT

Abdominal pain usually is characterized as being primarily crampy or as a generalized ache with superimposed periods of abdominal cramps, although sharp, dull, gas-like, and nondescript pains are also common.[16] The intensity and location of abdominal pain in IBS are highly variable, even at different times within a single patient. Although it may be so mild as to be ignored, the abdominal pain of IBS patients is often severe enough to interfere with daily activities. Although sleep deprivation solely as a result of IBS is unusual because abdominal pain is mostly present during waking hours, some patients have reported that GI symptoms wake them from sleep.[11]

Several factors exacerbate or reduce the pain of IBS. Many IBS patients report increased symptoms during periods of stress or emotional upset such as job or marital difficulties.[17] Defecation may provide temporary relief from the abdominal pain of IBS, whereas ingestion of food may exacerbate the discomfort, usually 60 to 90 minutes after the meal. Despite this, malnutrition caused by inadequate caloric intake is exceedingly rare with painful IBS. Abdominal pain, that is progressive, leads to anorexia, or is associated with weight loss is not consistent with IBS and warrants evaluation for organic disease.

From surveys of different populations, evidence has been provided to suggest that abdominal pain is not only the most predominant symptom in IBS patients, it also predicts physicians visits and correlates highly with GI symptom severity and the presence of psychiatric comorbidity.[2,17–20]

ALTERED BOWEL HABITS

The range of normal defecatory patterns is broad. In a combined series of 1,455 subjects from a British industrial community and general medical practice, 99% reported a defecation frequency between three stools per week and three stools per day, documenting a wide range in an unselected population.[21]

Based on bowel habits, patients commonly are subclassified into those having diarrhea-predominant IBS (IBS-D) or constipation-predominant IBS (IBS-C).[22,23] In many patients the predominant bowel habit is not stable over time but may alternate between the two patterns (constipation or diarrhea). If this alternation occurs within a short cycle period, the pattern is referred to as alternating bowel habit IBS (IBS-A). Among the IBS "subtypes," IBS-D is the most commonly treated, although it accounts for about 30% of cases, whereas IBS-C is the least frequent, and also accounts for about 30% of IBS cases. Approximately 30 to 50% of IBS cases alternate between bouts of constipation and diarrhea.[1,2,24] Preliminary results from a recent drug intervention study suggest that differences in the predominant bowel habit can have profound influences on responses to certain treatments.[25]

In patients with IBS-C, stools usually are hard and may be scyballous or pellet-like. Long periods of straining on the toilet may be required to achieve a satisfactory stool passage, especially in constipation-predominant cases but also with some diarrhea-prone patients.[26] Constipation can persist for weeks to months. A sensation of incomplete fecal evacuation may lead the IBS patient to make multiple attempts at stool passage over a short period of time.

In patients with IBS-D, the stools characteristically are loose and frequent but of normal total daily volume. Usually, diarrheal stools occur only during waking hours, often early in the day, and an urgent desire to defecate after a meal often is noted. Mucus discharge has been reported in up to 50% of IBS patients.[27] Patients may experience fecal urgency and loose stools during periods of stress. Complaints that are noted more frequently in IBS than in organic GI disease include relief of abdominal pain with defecation, looser stools at the onset of pain, and more frequent stools at the onset of pain.[28]

Symptoms that are not associated with IBS include nocturnal diarrhea, rectal bleeding, malabsorption, and weight loss. The presence of any of these symptoms should prompt a thorough evaluation for organic disease.

OTHERS

Symptoms of upper GI dysfunction are common in IBS, with 25 to 50% of patients reporting heartburn, early satiety, nausea, abdominal fullness, bloating, and vomiting; and up to 87% noting intermittent dyspepsia.[29] It is possible for individuals to have upper abdominal pain or discomfort exclusively related to IBS. If upper abdominal pain or discomfort is relieved exclusively by defecation and/or is associated with a change in bowel pattern, IBS is the diagnosis by definition.[30]

Many IBS patients note a sensation of increased gas production and abdominal distention, although the majority do not, in fact, produce excessive amounts of gas.[31] Nonpainful symptoms referred to the upper abdomen, such as early satiety and abdominal fullness and bloating, are reported commonly by IBS patients, particularly those who are predominantly constipated.[32]

Extraintestinal Symptoms

Although symptoms referable to the GI tract predominate, IBS patients commonly report extraintestinal complaints. Compared with healthy individuals, patients with functional GI disorders visit primary care physicians three times as often for non-GI problems.[18–33] Additionally, patients with functional GI complaints are more likely to have undergone hysterectomy or appendectomy.[34]

TABLE 41–1. ROME II Diagnostic Criteria for Irritable Bowel Syndrome

---

At least 12 weeks, which need not be consecutive, in the preceding 12 months of abdominal discomfort or pain that has two of three features:
• Relieved with defecation
• Onset associated with a change in frequency of stool
• Onset associated with a change in form (appearance) of stool

---

Adapted from Thompson WG, Longstreth GF, Drossman DA, et al. Functional bowel disorders and functional abdominal pain. Gut 1999;45 Suppl II:1143–7.

In IBS a high incidence of genitourinary dysfunction, including dysmenorrhea, dyspareunia, impotence, urinary frequency, nocturia, and a sensation of incomplete bladder emptying has been reported. One study showed that 83% of IBS patients experienced impaired sexual function, compared with 30% of inflammatory bowel disease patients and 16% of peptic ulcer patients.[17,35,36] Sleep-related disturbances, such as constant fatigue, difficulty falling asleep, or repeated awakening from sleep, occurred in up to two-thirds of IBS patients.[11,37] Patients with IBS also have a high prevalence of psychiatric diagnoses, which include most commonly depression and anxiety.[38] In a telephone survey, patients with functional bowel disorders reported a higher incidence of peptic ulcer disease, hypertension, low back pain, headaches, and rashes than did the general population.[39] Finally, IBS patients often report nonspecific fatigue, loss of concentration, headache, prostatism, insomnia, palpitations, and an unpleasant taste in the mouth.[37]

A series of epidemiologic studies have confirmed in a cross-sectional analysis the clinical impression that IBS and other functional disorders typically overlap in the same patient, and that the same patient may present with different symptoms when studied over time. These observations strongly suggest shared pathophysiologic mechanisms.[14,40] In particular there appears to be a significant overlap of FMS, a chronic somatic pain disorder, and IBS. Fibromyalgia syndrome occurs in up to 60% of patients with functional bowel disorders[41] and in 32 to 70% of patients with IBS.[42,43] Fifty percent of patients with a diagnosis of FMS complain of nausea, abdominal pain, gas, and bloating, which are symptoms characteristic of functional dyspepsia.[41] A study of 80 patients demonstrated that 70% of those with FMS also had symptoms of IBS, and 65% of those with IBS suffered from FMS symptoms.[15]

APPROACH TO DIAGNOSIS

According to Drossman et al and Sandler et al,[1,2] less than half of individuals with IBS seek medical care. Reasons for seeking care include symptom severity, fear about serious illness, disability, and psychosocial factors.[44] An early confident diagnosis permits tests to be minimized and reassures the patient that there is no lethal disease.[45]

There are no physical findings or diagnostic tests that confirm the diagnosis of IBS. Therefore, diagnosis involves identifying certain symptoms consistent with the disorder and excluding other medical conditions that may have a similar clinical presentation.[46] The symptom-based Rome II criteria (Table 41–1),[47] emphasize a "positive diagnosis" rather than exhaustive tests to exclude other diseases.[21] The original Rome criteria was established in 1994 but was considered to be relatively complex for widespread use.[48] Although the accuracy and pathophysiologic significance have yet to be reported, the Rome criteria is probably the most reasonable approach for clinical diagnosis and research purposes. A validation study of the Rome I criteria after excluding patients with warning features (Table 41–2) showed a sensitivity of 63%, a specificity of 100%, and, more importantly, a positive predictive value of 100% and a negative predictive value of 76%.[49]

History and Physical Examination

A careful history of pain and/or discomfort and stool characteristics is the most important step in recognizing IBS.[50] A detailed history using the established symptom criteria often can exclude most organic diseases that can cause symptoms similar to IBS. In typical IBS, abdominal pain or discomfort is related to defecation. Pain associated with exercise, movement, urination, or menstruation is atypical and requires further evaluation. The

TABLE 41–2. Findings in Patients with Possible IBS Tract Need Further Investigation

Documented weight loss
Nocturnal symptoms
Blood mixed in stools
Recent antibiotic use
Family history of colon cancer
Physical examination findings that suggest an alternative diagnosis
Perianal bleeding[†]

[†]Defined as blood streaked on the outside of the stool or on toilet paper. This finding is common in IBS patients and is usually the result of bleeding from hemorrhoids. Patients with this finding but no others generally should undergo flexible sigmoidoscopy to confirm the presence of hemorrhoids and absence of alternative causes of bleeding, but usually no other specific work-up is needed. Adapted from Vanner SJ, Depew WT, Paterson WG, et al. Predictive value of the Rome criteria for diagnosing the irritable bowel syndrome. Am J Gastroenterol 1999;94:2912.

presence of GI bleeding, fever, weight loss, anemia, palpable masses, or other warning features of organic disease should trigger further evaluation for organic illness.[51] Although the presence of a palpable tender sigmoid colon and discomfort with rectal examination is sometimes found (because of visceral sensitivity),[52] physical examination is usually unremarkable in IBS and serves primarily to exclude other diagnoses.[3] A careful physical examination often is helpful in reassuring the patient.[46]

Differential Diagnosis

The differential diagnosis of common symptoms of IBS is quite small; it includes inflammatory bowel disease, GI infections, lactose intolerance, thyroid disease, endocrine tumors, microscopic colitis, and malabsorption syndromes[45,53] (Table 41–3). It is important to note that a common condition such as IBS that affects up to 20% of the population often coexists with organic diseases. As an example, the presence of diverticula on a barium enema does not rule out the diagnosis of IBS.[54]

Diagnostic Evaluation

Care should be taken to avoid unnecessary investigations that are costly and harmful. So far, no test has been established as a diagnostic standard for IBS, and there currently is no specific treatment available that relies on the result of any diagnostic procedure. Thus, minimal diagnostic procedures have been advocated in the initial diagnostic approach to reasonably exclude structural lesions and to assure the patient of the diagnosis of IBS.[55,56] Groups of patients diagnosed with IBS by symptom

criteria and limited diagnostic studies have been prospectively followed up for up to 9 years. These studies have found that fewer than 5% of patients were diagnosed subsequently with organic disease related to their symptoms.[49,57]

As shown in Figure 41–1, minimal diagnostic procedures include complete blood count (CBC), erythrocyte sedimentation rate (ESR), blood chemistries, thyroid panel, and stool testing for occult blood, ova, and parasites.[58] Flexible sigmoidoscopy and barium enema or colonoscopy in patients older than 50 years have a yield of approximately 1% for identifying structural lesions such as polyps, colon

TABLE 41–3. Differential Diagnosis of IBS

Inflammatory bowel disease

Colorectal carcinoma

Constipating medications

Gastrointestinal infections (eg, *Giardia, Entamoeba histolytica, Yersinia, Strongyloides*)

Lactose intolerance

Endocrine disorders (hypo- or hyperthyroidism, diabetes)

Medications (eg, laxatives, magnesium-containing antacids)

Microscopic colitis

Bacterial overgrowth

Malabsorption syndromes (eg, celiac sprue, pancreatic insufficiency)

Chronic intestinal idiopathic pseudo-obstruction

Endocrine tumors (eg, gastrinoma, VIPoma)

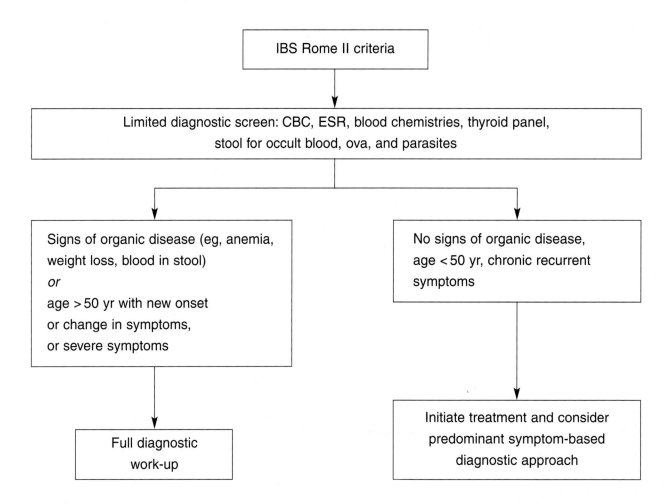

FIGURE 41–1. Diagnostic approach of patients with irritable bowel syndrome (IBS). CBC = complete blood count; ESR = erythrocyte sedimentation rate.

cancer, and colitis.[59] Other tests such as abdominal ultrasonography do not appear to change treatment.[60] The simple persistence of symptoms does not justify suspicion of another diagnosis. Indeed, such persistence is to be expected, and further investigation only serves to undermine the patient's confidence in the diagnosis and the physician.[50]

A more detailed diagnostic evaluation (see Figure 41–1) should be considered for those individuals who present with recent onset of symptoms, particularly patients who are 50 years of age or older, have more severe or disabling symptoms, or experience a clinical change over time. A family history of colon cancer, particularly in individuals younger than 55 years of age, should trigger structural evaluation by colonoscopy in most cases. Patients with psychosocial difficulties report more symptoms of IBS. Clinicians should consider this when designing a diagnostic approach but remem-

ber that patients with psychiatric illness also may have concomitant organic gastrointestinal disease.[47]

Psychological Assessment

A psychosocial assessment is essential in the evaluation of patients with IBS.[51] Patients with IBS who seek medical attention have a high frequency of psychosocial disturbances as well as a higher frequency of psychiatric diagnoses than do other groups.[61] Patients with IBS who have psychosocial problems have a poorer clinical outcome.[62] Also, presentation with IBS symptoms can be the first clinical clue to the diagnosis of important concomitant psychological conditions and psychosocial problems. It is known that stressful life events such as physical or sexual abuse, death, divorce, or other major traumas frequently precede the onset of IBS symptoms.[63]

A recent survey of 206 women patients with functional bowel disorders reports a 44% incidence of physical or sexual abuse in childhood, which was 3 to 11 times the rate in a control population.[64] Abuse history leads to poorer health outcome: more GI and non-GI pain symptoms and days spent in bed, greater psychological dysfunction, and more physician visits and surgical procedures.[62]

Further Testing Based on Predominant Symptoms

Further testing should be based on the predominant symptom of presumptive IBS. If the initial diagnostic approach does not reveal organic pathology, the physician should initiate symptomatic treatment for IBS and reassess in 3 to 6 weeks. Should an initial trial of therapy fail, it is useful to decide on further diagnostic studies based on whether constipation, diarrhea, or abdominal pain is the predominant symptom.[65,66]

PATIENTS WITH CONSTIPATION-PREDOMINANT IBS
Patients with IBS-C mainly complain of infrequent bowel movements, hard or lumpy stools, and a sensation of incomplete evacuation or excessive straining, with no loose or watery stools unless laxatives are taken. Further evaluation is warranted if they do not respond to general treatment measurements.[65] In those with low-frequency defecation, measurement of colonic transit using radiopaque markers is recommended.[67] Patients with colonic inertia usually have prolonged transit time, predominantly in the right colon. In patients with left-side colon delay or normal colonic transit, excessive straining, or sensation of constant rectal fullness, flexible sigmoidoscopy is recommended to rule out structural abnormalities. If this study results are negative, functional rectal outlet obstruction should be suspected.[52,68] The causes of functional rectal outlet obstruction include anismus (pelvic floor dyssynergia), rectocele, rectal prolapse, and intussusception. These coexist with IBS. These disorders can be evaluated by several diagnostic tests.

Anorectal manometry is helpful in the evaluation of constipation by measuring rectal compliance (accommodation of the rectal wall) and sensations.[69] In constipated patients lower rectal sensory thresholds have been reported,[24] although, in patients with increased rectal compliance, elevated volume thresholds may be found.[70] Anorectal manometry also can evaluate anal sphincter relaxation, which may be abnormal in constipated patients. Loss of

the rectoanal inhibitory reflex (ie, failure of the internal anal sphincter to relax normally during rectal balloon distention) has been used as diagnostic criteria for Hirschsprung's disease. Anorectal manometry also includes the use of two tests that aid in the diagnosis of functional rectal outlet obstruction: rectal balloon expulsion and electromyography. Rectal balloon expulsion is probably the simplest test to rule out anismus.[71,72] Electromyography evaluates the function of the striated muscle of the anal sphincter and can detect paradoxic contraction of the puborectal muscles during defecation.[67] This finding in the setting of an abnormal rectal balloon expulsion test supports the diagnosis of anismus.[67,70]

Defecography (defecating proctography), in which the rectum and anus are imaged while the patient strains and expels barium inserted into the rectum, is the best available technique to visualize the pelvic floor and rectal wall motions during rectal emptying. It is useful in the diagnosis of rectal prolapse, rectocele, and anismus, all of which can present with constipation.[67]

PATIENTS WITH DIARRHEA-PREDOMINANT IBS
Patients with IBS-D complain of frequent bowel movements, loose or watery stools, and urgent bowel movements. On presentation, testing should be performed to rule out inflammatory bowel disease, other causes of bleeding from the GI tract, infectious diarrhea, and hyperthyroidism; CBC, ESR, blood chemistries, thyroid function tests, and stool examination for occult blood, bacterial infection, ova and parasites (including *Giardia*), and *Clostridium difficile* (if the patient has recent antibiotic exposure), generally are indicated.[73] Human immunodeficiency virus antibody testing should be considered in patients with a history of multiple sexual partners, intravenous drug abuse, or blood transfusions, as well as in patients whose sexual partner has one or more of these risk factors.

Other tests can be performed to exclude structural diseases and infections that may present with diarrhea. These should be considered when patients have abnormal initial tests or other symptoms such as fever or weight loss. Flexible sigmoidoscopy or colonoscopy with mucosal biopsies allow the exclusion of neoplasms, inflammatory bowel disease, and microscopic or collagenous colitis. Radiographic examination of the small intestine (small bowel follow-through) is useful in evaluating intestinal disorders such as celiac sprue, lymphoma, and Crohn's disease. Abnormal findings such as excess luminal fluid and irregular mucosal surface guide in the diagnosis of malabsorption.[74] Upper endoscopy with biopsy specimens from the distal duodenum or proximal jejunum are helpful in ruling out Crohn's disease, celiac sprue, Whipple's disease, intestinal lymphoma, and infections. If bacterial overgrowth is suspected, an aspirate of small intestinal contents can be sent for aerobic and anaerobic bacterial culture. More than 10^5 organisms per milliliter is diagnostic for bacterial overgrowth.[75,76] *Giardia lamblia* infection can be diagnosed by small bowel biopsies and aspirate.[77] Analysis of laxatives in stool or urine should be done in patients with diarrhea of unknown causes to rule out factitious diarrhea.[78]

PATIENTS WITH PAIN-PREDOMINANT IBS

A subgroup of patients complain mainly of abdominal pain, which may be associated with symptoms such as bloating, gas, and abdominal distention. Prior to the diagnosis of IBS in such patients, other etiologies of these symptoms, including gastrointestinal or gynecologic cancer, should be investigated. Breath tests are used to rule out lactose malabsorption and bacterial overgrowth.[79] Small bowel follow-through is indicated to investigate mechanical obstruction, chronic intestinal idiopathic pseudo-obstruction, and inflammatory diseases.[74] Chronic pancreatitis can be diagnosed by abdominal radiography, abdominal ultrasonography, or computerized tomography. Unexplained abdominal pain is an indication for antroduodenal manometry to investigate small intestinal motor disorders and to differentiate intestinal myopathies from neuropathies.[80]

PATHOPHYSIOLOGY

Although psychological and physiologic abnormalities have been described, the overall pathophysiology of IBS is not well understood. Initially, psychological factors inducing illness behavior, ineffective coping styles, and affective comorbidity were thought to be the major factors responsible for the transition from a symptomatic individual ("non-patient") to a healthcare-seeking patient.[2] However, a series of other factors have been identified, including the presence and frequency of abdominal pain,[7] the presence of rectal bleeding,[81] stressful or traumatic life events,[82,83] and a history of enteric infections.[84] Furthermore, clinical evidence strongly suggests a role for genetic factors. For example, it is conceivable that although IBS symptoms are experienced by a high percentage of the healthy population, they develop into a medical syndrome only in a subset that has other risk factors that make such a transition likely.

Similar to other chronic illnesses, a multicomponent conceptual model of IBS, which involves physiologic, affective, cognitive, and behavioral factors, has been formulated (Figure 41–2). Although all factors are closely interconnected, the importance of individual factors in the generation of IBS symptoms may vary greatly between individuals. Previously, IBS was considered primarily a disorder of altered gut motility. Currently, visceral hypersensitivity and altered brain-gut interactions are felt to play a principal role in the pathophysiology of IBS.

Altered Intestinal Motor Responses

The principal motility abnormalities seen in IBS are increased rectal and sigmoid motility in response to rectal or sigmoid distention; increased ileal motility in response to ileal balloon distention, meals, or stress; increased frequency of discrete clustered contractions of the small intestine,[85] and exaggerated

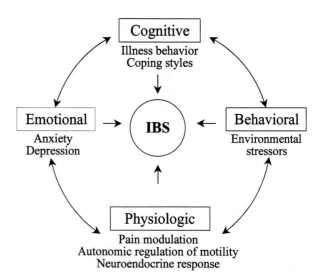

FIGURE 41–2. Multicomponent model of irritable bowel syndrome (IBS). Development of IBS symptoms can be explained by the inter-relation of cognitive, behavioral, emotional, and physiologic components. Reproduced with permission from Mayer EA. Emerging disease model for functional gastrointestinal disorders. Am J Med 1999;107(5A):13S.

phasic sigmoid motor responses to laboratory anger stressors[75] and food intake ("gastrocolonic response").[76] These alterations may explain why many IBS patients experience typical IBS symptoms following meals and develop exacerbations during stressful life events. Studies have reported different colonic motility findings based on the predominant bowel habit, with constipation-predominant patients displaying few gut contractions and diarrhea-predominant patients displaying more.[18,23,86–89]

In a study of small bowel motility, 61% of clustered contractions were associated with symptoms in patients with IBS, whereas only 17% of these contractions were associated with symptoms in healthy controls. However, all of the contractions were qualitatively normal, suggesting that an abnormality in visceral sensitivity rather than a primary dysmotility disorder of the small intestine is present in the majority of patients with IBS.[85]

Altered Perception of Visceral Events

Over the past two decades, there has been compelling evidence that enhanced perception of visceral stimuli develops in IBS patients.[90–92] The initial clinical observations that led to the hypothesis that patients with IBS have visceral hypersensitivity included the presence of recurring abdominal pain as a principal symptom, the presence of tenderness during palpation of the sigmoid colon during physical examination in many patients, and excessive pain often reported by patients during endoscopic examination of the sigmoid colon. Published experimental evidence from studies assessing visceral sensitivity suggest that a variety of perceptual abnormalities to GI stimuli may be more frequent in IBS patients. At least two perceptual alterations can be distinguished; a hypervigilance toward expected aversive events arising from the viscera, and a hyperalgesia that is inducible by sustained noxious visceral stimulation.[93]

HYPERVIGILANCE

Mertz et al found that IBS patients had a significantly lower median discomfort threshold for phasic rectal balloon distentions compared with that of a normal population.[94] Other studies also have found significant perceptual alterations in IBS populations, including lowered discomfort thresholds for balloon distention of the small intestine, the colon, and the rectosigmoid. Similar findings of hypersensitivity also have been reported for patients with functional dyspepsia[94] and noncardiac chest pain.[95,96] These findings are paralleled by similar findings of target system hypersensitivity in other disorders such as FMS and myofascial pain disorder.

HYPERALGESIA

A series of studies have demonstrated that patients with functional GI disorders, including those with IBS, show enhanced perception to repeated noxious distention of the viscera.[97–99] In contrast to their enhanced perception of visceral pain, most IBS patients have normal[100] or even increased thresholds[101] for painful stimulation of somatic neuroreceptors. However, patients with IBS who also have FMS (a disorder of somatic hypersensitivity) demonstrate somatic hypersensitivity as well.[14] Preliminary evidence from brain-imaging studies suggests a compromised ability of IBS patients to activate brain regions that play a prominent role in that activation of the inhibitory symptoms that modulate endogenous pain.

Altered Autonomic Regulation of Intestinal Function

Converging evidence suggests that the different patterns of bowel habits observed in IBS patients may be related to different patterns of autonomic outflow to the intestinal tract. For example, in IBS-D a relative predominance of parasympathetic over sympathetic influences on the colon may result in reduced compliance,[97] increased phasic motor activity,[88,89] reduced colonic transit time,[102] and decreased net water absorption.[103] By contrast, in IBS-C a relative predominance of sympathetic over parasympathetic influences may be related to the increased rectal compliance,[97] decreased phasic colonic motor activity,[104] increased mucus secretion,[105] and prolonged colonic transit time.[106]

Altered Neuroendocrine Response

In contrast to numerous reports on GI motility alterations and enhanced visceral sensitivity, there are few published reports on alterations in neuroendocrine responses to stress or visceral stimulation in IBS. Several studies have reported increased plasma and urinary epinephrine levels in IBS-D patients,[107,108] which is consistent with an increase in sympathoadrenal output.

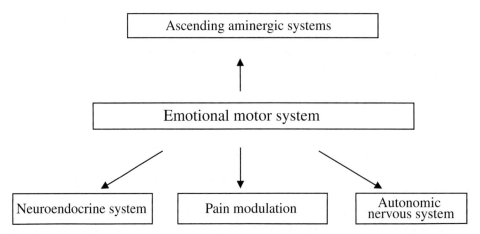

FIGURE 41–3. Major outputs of the emotional motor system. The emotional motor system refers to a set of parallel output pathways that are activated in response to perceived threat or fear. Alterations in the four pathways shown have been demonstrated in patients with irritable bowel syndrome. Reproduced with permission from Mayer EA. Emerging disease model for functional gastrointestinal disorders. Am J Med 1999;107(5A):13S.

There is some evidence that alterations in the hypothalamic-pituitary-adrenal axis may play a role in the pathogenesis of chronic functional syndromes. Preliminary data suggest that patients with IBS-D have blunted adrenocorticotropin hormone and plasma cortisol responses to a sustained noxious sigmoid stimulus.[109] Similar findings have been reported in FMS.[110] However, it remains to be determined whether these neuroendocrine alterations play a direct role in symptom generation.

The Brain-Gut Connection and the Emotional Motor System

The interesting observation that the prevalence of IBS in treatment-seeking psychiatric patients with panic disorder, generalized anxiety disorder, and major depression is much higher than in the general population[111–113] supports the hypothesis of shared pathophysiology between these disorders and IBS. It is not surprising that seemingly distinct syndromes such as IBS and panic disorder, appearing in the same individuals, are made worse by stress and improve when effective pharmacologic (or psychological)[114] treatment for the central nervous system (CNS) neuronal dysfunction is accomplished.[115] Emerging evidence shows that cognitive-behavioral techniques and hypnosis, both of which clearly involve the CNS, have been shown to have distinct benefits in the treatment of IBS. The beneficial effect of psychological treatment in functional bowel disorders supports the observation that psychosocial factors exert effects on gut physiology, modulate the symptom experience, influence illness behavior, and impact outcome and treatment approach.

A unifying hypothesis to explain the functional GI disorders is that they result from a dysregulation of the brain-gut neuroenteric system. The brain-gut neurotransmitters associated with symptoms are not site specific; they have varied influences on GI, endocrine, and immune function, and human behavior. An evolving theory is that normal GI function results from an integration of intestinal motor, sensory, autonomic, and CNS activity, and that GI symptoms may relate to dysregulation of these systems (Figure 41–3).[91] Neuroimaging studies such as positron emission tomography (PET) have been performed in IBS patients to measure CNS responses to visceral stimuli. These studies suggest that the CNS response to rectal distention is altered in patients with IBS compared with response in controls.[116] The findings implicate differences in the way the brain of a patient with IBS functions in response to visceral pain.

Effects of Stress on Symptom Exacerbation

PSYCHOLOGICAL STRESSORS

Psychological stress is widely believed to play a major role in IBS by precipitating exacerbation of symptoms. The varied influences of environmental stress, thoughts, and emotions on gut function help to explain the variation in symptoms of patients with this disorder. They also help to explain how psychosocial trauma (eg, history of physical or sexual abuse)[117] or poor coping style (eg, "catastrophizing") profoundly affects symptom severity, daily function, and health outcome. When directly asked, more than half of IBS patients[118] and nonpatients with symptoms compatible with IBS[119] report that psychologically stressful events exacerbate their bowel symptoms, and 51% report that a stressful event preceded the onset of their IBS.[120] In laboratory studies, the acute induction of pain[121] and emotional arousal[122] elicits increased motility in the distal colon, and the magnitude of the response is greater in IBS patients than in asymptomatic controls. An analysis of the relationship between daily life stress and GI symptoms in women with IBS showed higher mean GI symptoms and stress in IBS patients relative to controls.[123]

Physical Stressors

Symptoms suggestive of IBS occur in approximately one-third of patients following acute GI infections, often persisting for years following complete resolution of the infection. On the other hand only a small percentage of all IBS patients present such a history. A prospective study found that psychometric scores for anxiety, depression, somatization, and neurotic traits were higher in those individuals who developed prolonged IBS symptoms following their acute gastroenteritis than in those patients who later returned to normal bowel function.[84] This suggests that only in predisposed individuals can enteric infection and presumably other causes of mucosal irritation precipitate ongoing IBS symptoms that may persist long after the infection (or inflammation) has resolved. The fact that affective disorders appear to be part of this predisposition is consistent with a role of CNS alterations in the etiology of IBS.

Gender Differences

In addition to IBS, many functional GI disorders and other chronic visceral pain disorders such as interstitial cystitis[124,125] and chronic pelvic pain are more common in women than in men. Although the reason for this female predominance is not clear, it is consistent with gender-based differences in the reporting of other GI diseases such as inflammatory bowel disease.[126] Female IBS patients are more likely to be constipated, and to complain of abdominal distention and certain extracolonic symptoms.[127] Although animal studies have clearly demonstrated gender-related differences in pain perception and antinociceptive mechanisms, unequivocal evidence for gender-related differences in human pain perception or modulation has been provided only recently.[128,129]

Gender-related differences may be related to constant differences in the physiology of pain perception, such as structural or functional differences in the visceral afferent pathways involved in pain transmission or modulation, and/or they may be related to fluctuations in female sex hormones. Several investigators have reported a variation in GI symptoms during different phases of the menstrual cycle, suggesting altered motility and/or enhanced visceral sensitivity to normal GI events.[36,129–131] More women, both with and without GI symptoms, report abdominal pain during the perimenstrual phase compared to nonmenses phases.[131] Abdominal pain, pelvic cramping pain, nausea and diarrhea, but not back pain were rated higher at menses in women with IBS than in women without IBS, suggesting enhanced visceral sensitivity during the perimenstrual period. Preliminary evidence suggests that female IBS patients show specific perceptual alterations in regard to rectosigmoid balloon distention,[132] and that they show differences in regional brain activation measured by PET.[133] These studies were performed using $H_2^{15}O$ PET evaluating regional brain activation in response to rectosigmoid distention. This preliminary evidence suggests that gender-related differences in symptoms and in the perceptual responses to visceral stimuli exist in IBS patients and can be detected using specific stimulation paradigms and neuroimaging techniques.

There also exists a gender difference in treatment efficacy in IBS patients. In female patients with predominant diarrhea or alternating constipation and diarrhea, alosetron, a 5-HT_3-receptor antagonist subsequently withdrawn because of side effects, produced improvement in both pain and bowel-related functions, but it showed less of a treatment effect in male IBS patients.[65]

TREATMENT

Because attempts to treat the IBS patient can be frustrating to the clinician and the patient, the clinician should strive to gain the patient's confidence with a concise appropriate work-up and by offering reassurance and education that IBS is a functional disorder without significant long-term health risk.

A fraction of IBS patients, especially those presenting with new onset of symptoms, express relief that their symptoms are not caused by a serious condition such as malignancy. Despite the pessimistic reports from long-term studies,[134] the quality of life for IBS patients can be enhanced by appropriate clinician intervention. The treatment of IBS includes the following interventions: education, reassurance, diet recommendations, lifestyle modifications, pharmacotherapy, and psychosocial intervention.

Patients with mild IBS symptoms comprise the most prevalent group and usually are treated by primary care clinicians, rather than specialists. These patients have less significant functional impairment or psychological disturbance. Their symptoms closely correlate with gut-related physiologic events (eg, pain/diarrhea worse after meals or during stressful times and menses), and they occur intermittently. These patients do not see a clinician often and usually maintain normal daily activities. Treatment is directed toward education, reassurance, and achievement of a healthier lifestyle. Education involves explaining that the symptoms of IBS are real. The clinician can explain that the intestine is overly sensitive to a variety of stimuli, such as food, hormonal changes, medication, and stress. These stimuli can produce spasms or stretching of the gut, enhanced sensitivity of nerves, or both; these are experienced as pain, diarrhea, constipation, bloating, or any combination anywhere in the abdomen.

Because IBS is a symptom complex without clear pathophysiologic markers, the efficacy of drug therapy is difficult to measure. Drug therapy is best used in patients with severe symptoms that are refractory to clinician counseling and dietary manipulations. First-line treatment usually is aimed at treating the most bothersome symptom because of the lack of effective treatment resulting in overall improvement of multiple symptoms in IBS patients. Whenever possible, the clinician should resist the temptation to try a broad range of medications, which might have limited efficacy and diminish the patient's confidence.

Dietary Measures

Occasionally, a meticulous dietary history reveals foods that exacerbate symptoms in an individual patient; however, most studies of dietary exclusion as a treatment of IBS have yielded negative results. A subset of patients with excess gas with or without diarrhea, after lactase deficiency is ruled out, should be considered for dietary modification to reduce excess gas. Analysis of patients in this group has revealed that a low–molecular weight fraction containing mono-, di-, and oligosaccharides is responsible for the excess gas production. High levels of dietary fiber also induce intestinal gas production. However, most IBS patients with complaints of excess flatus produce normal amounts of gas of which they may have an enhanced perception. One study indicated that a history of patient perception of increased gas production does not reliably identify those who truly produce excess gas.[32]

Subsequent studies led to lists of food associated with increased flatulence, including beans, onions, celery, carrots, raisins, bananas, apricots, prunes, Brussels sprouts, wheat germ, pretzels, and bagels.[135] Exclusion of these foods should be considered in some patients with excess gas. Furthermore, the presence of a food allergy or food intolerance should be considered in certain patients.

Fiber

The most widely recommended agents for treatment of IBS are fiber preparations that serve to enhance the water-holding properties of the stool, form gels to provide stool lubrication, provide bulk for the stool, and bind agents such as bile acids that may be responsible for some of the symptoms in IBS.[136] Soluble fibers, such as pectin, psyllium, and oat bran, offer the theoretic advantage of enhancing water-retentive properties of the stool, whereas insoluble fibers, such as cellulose or lignin, are likely to be more effective bulking agents.[136]

Increased dietary fiber or psyllium products frequently are recommended for patients with IBS-C, even though, as a group, these patients do not consume less dietary fiber than do control subjects.[137] In patients with IBS-C, fiber accelerates colonic or oroanal transit,[138] and if a sufficient quantity of fiber (20 to 30 g/d) is consumed, a significant improvement in constipation can be effected.[138,139]

There is evidence that fiber also may decrease intracolonic pressures, which could reduce pain, because it is recognized that wall tension is one of the factors that contributes to visceral pain.[140–142] However, many patients complain of abdominal bloating with higher fiber intake. Fiber induces bloating because it increases loading of residue and bacterial fermentation in the colon without accelerating the onward movement of the increased residue.[143] Thus, whereas fiber has a role in treating constipation, its value in IBS or, specifically, in the relief of abdominal pain and diarrhea associated with IBS is controversial.[111,144] The uncertain benefits reported in several clinical studies have led to a call for a formal reappraisal of the effectiveness of fiber in IBS.[145]

Antispasmodic Agents

After fiber preparations, antispasmodic agents are the next most commonly prescribed group of medications for the treatment of IBS. Included in the antispasmodic class are anticholinergics (eg, dicyclomine, prifinium, and cimetropium) and calcium channel blockers (eg, verapamil, diltiazem, and octylonium bromide). A meta-analysis by Poynard et al concluded that as a therapeutic class, smooth muscle relaxants or antispasmodics were significantly better than was placebo for global assessment (62% versus 35% improvement) and abdominal pain (64% versus 45% improvement). However, only 3 of 8 drugs had efficacy in comparison with placebo: cimetropium bromide (Alginor), dicyclomine hydrochloride (Bentyl), and octylonium (Spasmomen).[146] Of these agents, only dicyclomine is available currently in the United States.

ANTICHOLINERGICS

Anticholinergic agents represent the major class of antispasmodic medications used in the United States. Several studies do not provide firm evidence that anticholinergic agents are efficacious in the IBS population as a whole;[147,148] however, because of their physiologic effects on the gastrocolonic response, it is possible that IBS patients with abdominal pain or fecal urgency, especially after a meal, may benefit from their use. Cimetropium bromide has been reported to reduce symptoms in IBS compared with placebo, improving both fecal urgency and pain.[149] Antispasmodics and anticholinergic agents are best used on an as-needed basis up to two times per day for acute attacks of pain, distention, or bloating. Dicyclomine generally is dosed at 10 to 20 mg four times daily, up to a maximum of 160 mg in divided doses. Such agents seem to retain efficacy when used on an as-needed basis, but they become less effective with chronic use. It is possible that these compounds work in a subset of patients, in which

enhanced, more frequent, or prolonged intestinal motor activity contributes to symptoms. Alternatively, it is conceivable that the CNS effects of these compounds, which include sedation, plays a role in symptom relief in some patients.

CALCIUM CHANNEL BLOCKERS

Calcium channel blockers have been proposed for the treatment of IBS by virtue of their smooth muscle–relaxant properties and their inhibitory effects on the gastrocolonic response. There is little data on the use of most calcium channel blockers in IBS. A new agent, pinaverium, a purported gut selective slow calcium channel blocker with minimal systemic effects, may inhibit colonic contractile activity and affect colonic transit.[150] Peppermint oil is a naturally occurring carminative that relaxes GI smooth muscle by reduction of calcium influx.[151] More well-designed and executed studies are needed to determine if peppermint oil is truly efficacious in treating IBS. As with anticholinergics, there are no controlled studies to support the use of calcium channel blockers in the treatment of IBS as a whole.

Antidiarrheal Agents

There is an association between IBS-D and acceleration of small bowel and proximal colonic transit.[152,153] Loperamide (2 to 4 mg up to four times daily), a synthetic opioid, decreases intestinal transit, enhances intestinal water and ion absorption, and increases anal sphincter tone at rest. These physiologic actions seem to account for the improvement in diarrhea, urgency, and fecal soiling observed in patients with IBS.[152] The effect on resting anal sphincter tone[103,154] may help reduce fecal soiling at night-time, when internal anal sphincter function is the predominant mechanism of continence and is not enhanced by the voluntary contraction of the external anal sphincter. Because it does not traverse the blood-brain barrier, loperamide (Imodium) generally is preferred to other opiates, such as diphenoxylate (Lomotil), codeine, or other narcotics, for treating patients with IBS-D and/or incontinence. Clinically, loperamide (Imodium) also can be used to reduce postprandial urgency associated with a prominent colonic response to eating or as a means of improving control at times of anticipated stress or other colonic stimuli (eg, exercise or social gatherings). Patients whose diarrhea does not respond to loperamide may benefit from the use of cholestyramine. Evidence for its efficacy in IBS is limited.[155,156] Cholestyramine may be dosed at one packet one to three times daily, and should be titrated according to stool form and frequency.

Prokinetic Agents

Medications that stimulate GI motor function, known as prokinetic agents, have been proposed for use in IBS-C patients. Additionally because many IBS patients experience dyspepsia, prokinetic agents have been proposed for patients with upper gut symptoms. Agents studied in IBS include domperidone, a selective dopamine-receptor antagonist, and cisapride, which acts through cholinergic, serotonergic, and direct smooth muscle effects. Domperidone is most effective as a prokinetic agent in the upper GI tract, having been demonstrated to enhance gastric emptying and small bowel transit.[157] The usefulness of domperidone in IBS remains to be established, but patients with dyspepsia may benefit. At the time of publication, domperidone was not available in the United States.

Cisapride, a GI motility stimulant and 5-HT_4-receptor agonist, has been used in treating constipation. Recently several studies have shown that cisapride can induce dose-dependent cardiac adverse effects, including lengthening of the electrocardiographic Q–T interval, syncopal episodes, and ventricular dysrhythmias.[158,159] Therefore, it generally is not recommended for the treatment of non-life-threatening conditions such as IBS. In contrast to domperidone, cisapride exhibits motor stimulatory effects in the colon. In IBS-C patients, an increase in stool frequency and acceleration of whole gut transit was noted with cisapride.[160] Although the drug accelerates colonic transit and is beneficial in a subset of constipated patients, its effects in the colon are only moderate, and, therefore, it is not considered to be a standard treatment.

Novel, more selective, 5-HT_4-receptor agonists, such as prucalopride and tegaserod are currently in advanced clinical development for the treatment of various forms of constipation.[161,162] There are encouraging signs that these newer prokinetic agents may have therapeutic use in patients with constipation.

Psychotropic Agents

Because many IBS patients exhibit abnormal psychiatric features that predate the onset of their bowel symptoms, many investigators have evaluated the use of antidepressant and anxiolytic medications in IBS.

Among the classes of antidepressant medications, the tricyclics have been evaluated most extensively IBS. Tricyclic agents (eg, amitriptyline, imipramine, and doxepin) are now used frequently to treat patients with IBS, particularly those with more severe or refractory symptoms, impaired daily function, and associated depression or panic attacks. Initially their use was based on the fact that a high proportion of patients with IBS reported significant depression.[163,164] However, amitriptyline at lower dosages than those usually used to treat depression (up to 75 mg nightly) has been found to be significantly more effective than is placebo in reducing abdominal pain and producing global improvement in patients with IBS.[165]

Antidepressants have neuromodulatory and analgesic properties, which may benefit patients independently of the psychotropic effects of the drugs.[166] Although the effects of amitriptyline on esophageal and rectal sensory thresholds and compliance are not significant,[167] it is suggested that central effects predominate. Neuromodulatory effects may occur sooner and with lower dosages than those used in the treatment of depression (eg, 10 to 25 mg amitriptyline or 50 mg desipramine).

Psychotropic agents typically have been reserved for those patients with diarrhea- or pain-predominant IBS,[19,90] with no improvement being noted in constipated patients,[168] although this may reflect their anticholinergic effects that aggravate constipation. There is increasing interest in the potential application of selective serotonin reuptake inhibitors (SSRIs), which tend not to cause constipation and may even induce diarrhea in some patients; the role of SSRIs is currently the focus of prospective randomized placebo-controlled studies.[169]

Because antidepressants must be used on a continual rather than an as-needed basis, they generally are reserved for patients having frequently recurrent or continual symptoms. To encourage compliance (most patients feel stigmatized by taking a "psychotropic" drug), the patient should be informed that even at low doses the medication acts as a central analgesic that reduces pain by facilitating descending inhibitory pain pathways; at higher doses it also helps to treat depressive symptoms encumbered by the illness. To determine efficacy, treatment should be continued for at least 3 to 4 weeks up to full therapeutic dosages and, if effective, continued for 3 to 12 months before tapering. A poor clinical response may be due to noncompliance or a lower-than-adequate dosage.[170]

Several groups have evaluated the use of benzodiazepines in the treatment of IBS. Narducci et al demonstrated prevention of stress-induced increases in rectosigmoid motility with chlordiazepoxide.[171] In another investigation diazepam led to greater relief of anxiety and related symptoms than did placebo.[172] However, because of the clear abuse potential of these medications and the rapid development of tolerance to their anxiolytic effects, the use of sedatives in IBS is not indicated in most patients.

Other Psychological Treatments

Psychological treatments used to treat IBS include psychotherapy (dynamic and cognitive-behavioral therapy), relaxation therapy, hypnotherapy, and biofeedback therapy. Psychological treatments also can be combined. Because it is not yet known if one form of psychological treatment is superior to another, or which patients are likely to benefit from which of the psychological treatments, the choice of treatment depends on patient preference, cost, and availability. Hypnotherapy or psychotherapy has been advocated for patients with significant pain, but, generally, practicing clinicians are less likely to be able to offer these services.[173,174]

Psychotherapy has shown promise of reduced symptoms in patients who do not show improvement on medications. In a population of 101 IBS patients, 3 months of dynamically orientated psychotherapy, in addition to medications, provided greater improvement in somatic symptoms than did medical treatment alone.[174] A second psychotherapy study in 102 patients who had failed medications showed improvement in depression and reduced abdominal pain and diarrhea, but not reduced constipation.[175] Factors indicating a favorable response to psychotherapy include predominant diarrhea or pain, association of IBS with overt psychiatric symptoms, and intermittent pain exacerbated by stress.[175,176] In contrast, patients with constant abdominal pain do poorly with psychotherapy or hypnotherapy.

Cognitive-behavioral therapy helps patients identify stressors and cognition that may increase their physical distress. Once identified, effective and rational coping strategies are then developed, thought processes are restructured, and actions are modified to reduce health care use. Cognitive-behavioral therapy, which uses diaries and exercises to modify maladaptive thoughts, eventually produces a sense of increased control over the symptoms.[177]

Biofeedback and stress-reduction techniques have been employed by some clinicians. Muscle relaxation training and education into means of decreasing stress was used successfully by Blanchard to reduce bowel symptoms in an uncontrolled study, especially in those individuals who exhibited improvement in depression and anxiety.[178] At a follow-up after 4 years, 50% of those studied reported sustained improvement in pain, diarrhea, nausea, and flatulence.[179] In another study, patients were trained to reduce bowel symptoms by listening to their bowel sound pattern through a stethoscope and attempting to modify their borborygmus.[180] This bowel sound biofeedback led to improved symptomatology in 3 of 5 patients enrolled, with long-term success in 2 of the 5. Mollen et al showed in a study that the trend toward reduced postprandial colonic tone in patients with evacuation disorders was normalized after biofeedback training.[181] Ford et al reported that stress (induced by a dichotic listening task) increased the intensity of gas and pain sensations in the sigmoid colon, and relaxation (progressive muscle relaxation training) significantly decreased the intensity of gas sensations in the sigmoid.[182] Relaxation training attempts to counterpart the physiologic effects of stress. Reduction in skeletal muscle tension decreases autonomic arousal and subjective tension/anxiety, and may improve gut motility.

Hypnosis has been proposed for refractory cases of IBS. In an initial study of 30 patients with refractory IBS randomized to hypnosis or psychotherapy, the hypnosis group showed a small improvement in abdominal pain, distention, and well-being, but not in bowel pattern, after 3 months of treatment.[173]

Novel Therapies

The pharmaceutical industry has identified agents with visceral analgesic properties, and this has stimulated much interest in the field of IBS therapy. It is recognized that 5-HT$_3$-receptor antagonists slow colonic transit and enhance fluid and electrolyte absorption, leading to a decrease in stool frequency and a firming of stool consistency.[183–185] Alosetron (Lotronex), which is a 5-HT$_3$-receptor antagonist, is effective in relieving pain, normalizing bowel frequency, and reducing urgency in nonconstipated IBS female patients.[183] In studies alosetron significantly improved abdominal pain or discomfort in IBS females, but not in males. However, postmarketing reports of serious complications requiring hospitalization, including severe constipation and ischemic colitis, prompted withdrawal of alosetron from clinical use. 5-HT$_4$-receptor partial agonists such as tegaserod currently are undergoing clinical trials.[186–188]

Approaches to Different Subsets of Patients

There is compelling evidence from treatment trials that it is useful to distinguish patients with IBS-C from patients with IBS-D or those with more variable bowel habits; these subgroups respond differently to treatment.

PATIENTS WITH CONSTIPATION-PREDOMINANT IBS

The principles of management of the IBS-C patient are to increase stool water and bulk and to reduce the effort needed for defecation. The previous sections indicate that the most widely used and most efficacious compounds for this purpose are bulking agents (eg, bran, psyllium, carboxymethylcellulose) in concert with a high-fiber diet. Additionally, any medications that cause constipation should be discontinued. Patients should be cautioned that fiber supplementation may take several weeks to produce a satisfactory result and that fiber should be introduced gradually to prevent excess distention and gas. The bulking agents usually are not effective in severe chronic constipation and can even cause fecal impaction. Patients with severe constipation may benefit from the use of stool softeners (eg, docusate sodium), which facilitate the expulsion of the bolus of stool.

Those patients with an inadequate response should be given an osmotic agent such as milk of magnesia, polyethylene glycol (Miralax), or lactulose in addition to the fiber program. Stimulant laxatives should be avoided because of the potential for long-term damage to colonic motor function.

Other novel agents include prokinetic agents (5-HT$_4$ agonists), which are not yet available for patient use except in clinical research studies.

PATIENTS WITH DIARRHEA-PREDOMINANT IBS

The management of the IBS-D patient centers on reduction of defecation frequency or urgency and improvement in stool consistency. The agents most commonly employed and the drugs shown to be most effective are the opiate derivatives such as loperamide or diphenoxylate. Many clinicians prescribe agents such as fiber to add bulk to the stool, but controlled trials do not show a greater response to this therapy in IBS-D than to placebo. Other drugs with efficacy in diarrhea-prone patients include cholestyramine and antidepressant medications. A careful dietary history should screen for foods containing compounds such as lactose, sorbitol, or fructose that cause diarrhea. Other dietary manipulations usually are without benefit and are not encouraged in most individuals. The use of disodium chromoglycate, directed at treatment of food hypersensitivity, is unsubstantiated in most diarrhea-prone patients. Unfortunately, antidiarrheal medications may cause constipation or be ineffective in relieving abdominal pain.

PATIENTS WITH PAIN-PREDOMINANT IBS

Severe abdominal pain represents one of the most difficult symptoms to treat in IBS and is compounded by the lack of convincingly effective medications for this complaint. Perhaps the most useful treatment that can be offered by the physician is reassurance and counseling about the nonthreatening nature of IBS. Use of addictive pain killers should be avoided because their use is counterproductive. Many clinicians recommend bulking agents for painful IBS, although the data supporting efficacy for this symptom is weak. Antispasmodic drugs, especially the anticholinergics, are most commonly employed in pain-predominant IBS, and some patients, especially those with postprandial pain, may benefit from such therapy. Antidepressant medications, such as low-dose tricyclics and SSRIs, may benefit an additional subset of patients, especially those with constant pain. Antigas agents or low-gas diets are sometimes recommended for bloating, with variable results.

Psychological/behavioral treatments are useful when the symptoms (particularly abdominal pain) are moderate to severe, more constant, and associated with psychological distress and impaired quality of life.[189] The benefits are greatest when patients are motivated and able to associate symptoms with stressors.[175] Behavioral treatments reduce anxiety, encourage health-promoting behaviors, give the patient some control in the treatment, and improve pain tolerance.

CONCLUSION

Irritable bowel syndrome is a common chronic disorder characterized by exacerbations and remissions, that presents with symptoms of abdominal pain and/or discomfort and altered bowel habits. It has a chronic relapsing course and can overlap with other functional GI (eg, dyspepsia) and non-GI (eg, FMS) disorders.

The clinical diagnosis of IBS is based on identifying symptom criteria with a "positive diagnosis" and excluding organic disease with minimal diagnostic evaluation. Clinicians should feel secure with the diagnosis of IBS, if made properly, because it is rarely associated with other explanations for symptoms. Although there are many expensive and sophisticated tests available for the evaluation of IBS symptoms, these generally are not needed for patients with typical symptoms and no features suggestive of organic diseases.

An integrated diagnostic and treatment approach first requires an effective clinician-patient relationship. A careful history identifies the need for diagnostic studies and treatments as determined by the nature and severity of the predominant symptoms, and the degree and extent of influencing psychosocial and other factors.

The fact that definite structural or biochemical abnormalities for these disorders can be detected with conventional diagnostic techniques does not rule out the possibility that neurobiologic alterations eventually are identified to explain fully the symptoms of most functional disorders. Examples of such a shift in perspective from symptom-based disorders without detectable abnormalities to medically treatable diseases based on specific neurobiologic alterations include affective disorders (eg, depression and anxiety) and migraine headaches.

Similar to other chronic illnesses, a multicomponent model that involves physiologic, affective, cognitive, and behavioral factors can be formulated for IBS. Although all factors are closely interconnected, the importance of individual factors in the generation of IBS symptoms may vary greatly between individuals. Physiologic factors implicated in the generation of IBS symptoms include hypersensitivity of the GI tract to normal events, autonomic dysfunction including altered intestinal motility response to stress and food intake, alterations in fluid and electrolyte handling by the bowel, and alterations in sleep. Future studies will further enhance our understanding of this condition and lead to newer more effective treatments.

RESOURCE

National Institute of Diabetes and Digestive and Kidney Diseases
United States National Institutes of Health
Office of Communications and Public Liaison
31 Center Drive, MSC 2560
Bethesda, Maryland 20892-2560
Telephone: (301) 496-3583
Web site: www.niddk.nih.gov

The NIDDK provides patient information and information about clinical trials on IBS that can be accessed or printed from the World Wide Web.

REFERENCES

1. Sandler RS, Drossman DA, Nathan HP, McKee DC. Symptom complaints and health care seeking behavior in subjects with bowel dysfunction. Gastroenterology 1984;87:314–8.

2. Talley NJ, Zinsmeister AR, Van Dyke C, Melton LJ III. Epidemiology of colonic symptoms and irritable bowel syndrome. Gastroenterology 1991;101: 927–34.

3. Drossman DA, Whitehead WE, Camilleri M. Irritable bowel syndrome: a technical review for practice guideline development. Gastroenterology 1997; 112:2120–37.

4. Drossman DA, Li Z, Andruzzi E, et al. U.S. household survey of functional GI disorders: prevalence, sociodemography and health impact. Dig Dis Sci 1993; 38:1569–80.

5. Heaton KW, O'Donnell LJD, Braddon FEM, et al. Symptoms of irritable bowel syndrome in a British urban community: consulters and non-consulters. Gastroenterology 1992;102:1962–7.

6. Talley NJ, Boyce PM, Jones M. Predictors of health care seeking for irritable bowel syndrome: a population based study. Gut 1997;41:394–8.

7. Schuster MM. Irritable bowel syndrome. In: Sleisenger MH, Fordtran JS, editors. Gastrointestinal disease. New York: Saunders; 1989. p. 1402–18.

8. Elliott R, Frith CD, Dolan RJ. Differential neural response to positive and negative feedback in planning and guessing tasks. Neuropsychologia 1997; 247:1395–404.

9. Stryker SJ, Phillips SF, Dozois RR, et al. Anal and neorectal function after ileal pouch–anal anastomosis. Ann Surg 1986;1:55–61.

10. Fass R, Fullerton S, Tung S, Mayer EA. Sleep disturbance in clinic patients with functional bowel disorders. Am J Gastroenterol 2000;95:1195–2000.

11. Elsenbruch S, Harnish MJ, Orr WC. Subjective and objective sleep quality in irritable bowel syndrome. Am J Gastroenterol 2000;95:37–42.

12. Marshall BJ, Warren JR. Unidentified curved bacilli in the stomach of patients with gastritis and peptic ulceration. Lancet 1984;1:1311–5.

13. Chang L, Mayer EA, Johnson T, et al. Differences in somatic perception in female patients with irritable bowel syndrome with and without fibromyalgia. Pain 2000;84:257–307.

14. Veale D, Kavanagh G, Fielding JF, Fitzgerald O. Primary fibromyalgia and the irritable bowel syndrome: different expressions of a common pathogenetic process. Br J Rheumatol 1991;30:220–2.

15. Triadafilopoulos G, Simms RW, Goldenberg DL. Bowel dysfunction in fibromyalgia syndrome. Dig Dis Sci 1991;36:59–64.

16. Chaudhary NA, Truelove SC. The irritable colon syndrome: a study of the clinical features, predisposing causes, and prognosis in 130 cases. Q J Med 1962; 616:307–22.

17. Whitehead WE, Crowell MD, Robinson JC, et al. Effects of stressful life events on bowel symptoms: subjects with irritable bowel syndrome compared with subjects without bowel dysfunction. Gut 1992; 33:825–30.

18. Drossman DA, McKee DC, Sandler RS, et al. Psychosocial factors in the irritable bowel syndrome. A multivariate study of patients and nonpatients with irritable bowel syndrome. Gastroenterology 1988;95:701–8.

19. Drossman DA, Thompson GW, Talley NJ, et al. Identification of subgroups of functional gastrointestinal disorders. Gastroenterol Int 1990;3:159–72.

20. Stuart GJ, Dodt H-U, Sakmann B. Patch-clamp recordings from the soma and dendrites of neurons in brain slices using infrared video microscopy. Pflugers Arch 1993;423:511–8.

21. Connell AM, Jones FA, Rowlands EN. Motility of the pelvic colon: pain associated with colonic hypermotility after meals. Gut 1965;6:105–12.

22. Talley NJ, Zinsmeister AR, Melton III LJ. Irritable bowel syndrome in a community: symptom subgroups, risk factors, and health care utilization. Am J Epidemiol 1995;142:76–83.

23. Schmulson M, Lee OY, Chang L, et al. Symptom differences in moderate to severe IBS patients based on predominant bowel habit. Am J Gastroenterol 1999; 94:2929–35.

24. Kay L, Jorgensen T, Jensen KH. The epidemiology of irritable bowel syndrome in random population: prevalence, incidence, natural history and risk factors. J Intern Med 1994;236:23–30.

25. Northcutt AR, Camilleri M, Mayer EA, et al. Alosetron, a 5-HT$_3$-receptor antagonist, is effective in the treatment of female irritable bowel syndrome patients. Gastroenterology 1998;114:812.

26. Kellow JE, Gill RC, Wingate DL. Prolonged ambulant recordings of small bowel motility demonstrate abnormalities in the irritable bowel syndrome. Gastroenterology 1990;98:1208–18.

27. Kalser MH, Zion DE, Bockus HL. Functional diarrhea: an analysis of the clinical and roentgen manifestations. Gastroenterology 1956;31:629.

28. Manning AP, Thompson WD, Heaton KW, Morris AF. Towards positive diagnosis in the irritable bowel syndrome. Br Med J 1978;2:653–4.

29. Mayer EA, Gebhart GF. Basic and clinical aspects of visceral hyperalgesia. Gastroenterology 1994; 107:271–93.

30. Talley NJ, Colin-Jones DG, et al. Functional gastroduodenal disorders. In: Drossman DA, Richter JE, Talley NJ, et al, editors. The functional gastrointestinal disorders. Boston: Little, Brown and Company; 1994. p. 71–113.

31. Lasser RB, Bond JH, Levitt MD. The role of intestinal gas in functional abdominal pain. N Engl J Med 1975;293:524–6.

32. Schmulson M, Lee OY, Chang L, et al. Differences in viscerosensory processing between IBS patients with constipation and diarrhea. Am J Gastroenterol 1999; 94:2929–35.

33. Maxton DG, Martin DF, Whorwell PJ, Godfrey M. Abdominal distension in female patients with irritable bowel syndrome: exploration of possible mechanisms. Gut 1991;32:662–4.

34. Whitehead WE, Cheskin LJ, Heller BR, et al. Evidence for exacerbation of irritable bowel syndrome during menses. Gastroenterology 1990;98:1485–9.

35. Guthrie E, Creed FH, Whorwell PJ. Severe sexual dysfunction in women with the irritable bowel syndrome: comparison with inflammatory bowel disease and duodenal ulceration. Br Med J 1987;295:577–8.

36. Fass R, Fullerton S, Naliboff BD, et al. Sexual dysfunction in patients with irritable bowel syndrome (IBS) and non-ulcer dyspepsia (NUD). Digestion 1998;43:388–94.

37. Whorwell PJ, McCallum M, Creed FH, Roberts CT. Non-colonic features of irritable bowel syndrome. Gut 1986;27:37–40.

38. Whitehead WE, Bosmajian L, Zonderman AB, et al. Symptoms of psychological distress associated with irritable bowel syndrome. Gastroenterology 1988; 95:709–14.

39. Whitehead WE, Winget C, Fedoravicius AS, et al. Learned illness behavior in patients with irritable bowel syndrome and peptic ulcer. Dig Dis Sci 1982; 27:202–8.

40. Moldofsky H, Franklin LA. Disordered sleep, pain, fatigue, and gastrointestinal symptoms in fibromyalgia, chronic fatigue and irritable bowel syndromes. In: Mayer EA, Raybould HE, editors. Basic and clinical aspects of chronic abdominal pain. New York: Elsevier; 1993. p. 249–56.

41. Barton A, Whorwell PJ, Marshall D. Increased prevalence of sicca complex and fibromyalgia in patients with irritable bowel syndrome. Am J Gastroenterol 1999;94:1898–901.

42. Sivri A, Cindas A, Dincer F, Sivri B. Bowel dysfunction and irritable bowel syndrome in fibromyalgia patients [comments]. Clin Rheumatol 1996;15: 283–6.

43. Sperber A, Atzmon Y, Weitzman I, et al. Fibromyalgia in the irritable bowel syndrome: studies of prevalence and clinical implications. Am J Gastroenterol 1999;94:3541–6.

44. Coremans G, Dapoigny M, Muller-Lissner SA, et al. Working team report. Diagnostic procedures in irritable bowel syndrome. Digestion 1995;56:76–84.

45. Thompson GW. Pathogenesis and management of the irritable bowel syndrome. In: Champion MC, Orr WC, editors. Evolving concepts in gastrointestinal motility. Oxford: Blackwell Science; 1996. p. 200–20.

46. American Gastroenterological Association. Medical position statement: irritable bowel syndrome. Gastroenterology 1997;112:2118–9.

47. Hammer J, Talley NJ. Diagnostic criteria for irritable bowel syndrome. Am J Med 1999;157:5–11S.

48. Drossman DA, Richter J, Talley N, et al. The functional gastrointestinal disorders: diagnosis, pathophysiology, and treatment. Boston: Little Brown; 1994.

49. Vanner S, Depew WT, Paterson WG, et al. Predictive value of the Rome criteria for diagnosing the irritable bowel syndrome. Am J Gastroenterol 1999;94: 2912–7.

50. Thompson WG, Longstreth GF, Drossman DA, et al. Functional bowel disorders and functional abdominal pain. Gut 1999;45 Suppl II:1143–7.

51. Lembo T, Mayer EA. Irritable bowel syndrome. In: Brandt LJ, editor. Clinical practice of gastroenterology; current medicine. Philadelphia: 1998. p. 19–29.

52. Whorwell PJ, Prior A, Colgan SM. Hypnotherapy in severe irritable bowel syndrome: further experience. Gut 1987;28:423–5.

53. Barnard LOB, Grantham WG, Lamberton P. Treatment of resistant acromegaly with a long-acting somatostatin analogue (SMS 201-995). Ann Intern Med 1986;105:856–61.

54. Thompson GW. Do colonic diverticula cause symptoms? Am J Gastroenterol 1986;81:613–4.

55. Holtmann G. Treatment stategies for functional gastrointestinal disorders. In: Goebell H, Holtmann G, Talley NJ, editors. Functional dyspepsia and irritable bowel syndrome. Dordrecht: Kluwer Academic Publishers; 1997. p. 217–23.

56. Camilleri M, Prather CM. The irritable bowel syndrome: mechanisms and a practical approach to management. Ann Intern Med 1992;116:1001–8.

57. Svendsen JH, Munck LK, Andersen JR. Irritable bowel syndrome: prognosis and diagnostic safety. A 5-year follow-up study. Scand J Gastroenterol 1985;20:415–8.

58. Barrett JN, Magleby KL, Pallotta BS. Properties of single calcium-activated potassium channels in cultured rat muscle. J Physiol 1982;331:211–30.

59. McIntosh DG, Thompson GW, Patel DG. Is rectal biopsy necessary in irritable bowel syndrome? Am J Gastroenterol 1992;87:1407–9.

60. Francis CY, Duffy JN, Whorwell PJ, Martin DF. Does routine abdominal ultrasound enhance diagnostic accuracy in irritable bowel syndrome? Am J Gastroenterol 1996;91:1348–50.

61. Palmer RL, Stonehill E, Crisp AH, et al. Psychological characteristics of patients with the irritable bowel syndrome. Postgrad Med J 1974;50:416–9.

62. Whitehead WE, Crowell MD, Heller BR, et al. Modeling and reinforcement of the sick role during childhood predicts adult illness behaviour. Psychosom Med 1994;6:541–50.

63. Drossman DA, Creed FH, Fava GA. Psychosocial aspects of the functional gastrointestinal disorders. Gastroenterol Int 1995;8:47–90.

64. Drossman DA, Leserman J, Nachman G, et al. Sexual and physical abuse in women with functional or organic gastrointestinal disorders. Ann Intern Med 1990;113:828–33.

65. Camilleri M, Mayer EA, Drossman DA, et al. Improvement in pain and bowel function in female irritable bowel patients with alosetron, a 5-HT$_3$ receptor antagonist. Aliment Pharmacol Ther 1999;13:1149–59.

66. Drossman DA, Thompson WG. Irritable bowel syndrome: a graduated multicomponent treatment approach. Ann Intern Med 1992;118:1001–8.

67. Whitehead WE, Wald A, Diamant NE, et al. Functional disorders of the anus and rectum [review]. Gut 1999;45 Suppl 2:1155–9.

68. Wald A. Evaluation and management of constipation. Clinical Perspect Gastroenterol 1998;1:106–15.

69. Mertz H. Constipation. Curr Opin Gastroenterol 1997;13:5–10.

70. Lee OY, Schmulson M, Mayer EA. Common functional gastrointestinal disorders: nonulcer dyspepsia and irritable bowel syndrome. Clin Cornerstone 1999;1:57–68.

71. Kuijpers HC, Bleijenberg G. The spastic pelvic floor syndrome: a cause of constipation. Dis Colon Rectum 1985;28:669–72.

72. Fleshman J, Dreznik Z, Cohen E, et al. Balloon expulsion test facilitates diagnosis of pelvic floor obstruction due to nonrelaxing puborectalis muscle. Dis Colon Rectum 1992;35:1019–25.

73. Fine KD, Fordtram JS. The effect of diarrhea on fecal fat excretion. Gastroenterology 1992;102:1936–9.

74. Ott DJ, Chen YM, Gelfand DW, et al. Detailed per-oral small bowel examination vs. enteroclysis. Radiology 1985;155:29–31.

75. Egger G, Wolfenden K, Pares J, Mowbray G. "Bread: it's a great way to go." Increasing bread consumption decreases laxative sales in an elderly community. Med J Aust 1991;155:820–1.

76. Dent J, Dodd WJ, Friedman RH. Mechanism of gastroesophageal reflux in recumbent asymptomatic human subjects. J Clin Invest 1980;65:256–7.

77. Perera DR, Weinstein WM, Rubin CE. Small intestine biopsy. Hum Pathol 1975;6:157–217.

78. American Gastroenterological Association. Technical review on the evaluation and management of chronic diarrhea. Gastroenterology 1999;116:1464–86.

79. Solomons NW. Evaluation of carbohydrate absorption: the hydrogen breath test in clinical practice. Clin Nutr 1984;3:71–8.

80. Byrne KG. Antroduodenal manometry: an evaluation of an emerging methodology. Dig Dis 1997;15:53–63.

81. Jones R, Lydeard S. Irritable bowel syndrome in the general population. BMJ 1992;304:87–90.

82. Bennett EJ, Tennant CC, Piesse C, et al. Level of chronic life stress predicts clinical outcome in irritable bowel syndrome. Gut 1998;43:256–61.

83. Gwee KA. The role of psychological and biological factors in postinfective gut dysfunction. Gut 1999;44:400–6.

84. Collins S. Inflammation in the irritable bowel syndrome. In: Mayer EA, Raybould HE, editors. Basic and clinical aspects of chronic abdominal pain. Amsterdam: Elsevier; 1993. p. 62–70.

85. Kellow JE, Phillips SF. Altered small bowel motility in irritable bowel syndrome is correlated with symptoms. Gastroenterology 1987;92:1885–93.

86. Bassotti G, Gaburri M, Imbimbo BP, et al. Colonic mass movements in idiopathic chronic constipation. Gut 1988;29:1173–9.

87. Bueno L, Fioramonti J, Ruckebusch Y, et al. Evaluation of colonic myoelectrical activity in health and functional disorders. Gut 1980;21:480–5.

88. Choi M-G, Camilleri M, O'Brien MD, et al. A pilot study of motility and tone of the left colon in patients with diarrhea due to functional disorders and dysautonomia. Am J Gastroenterol 1997;92:297–302.

89. Bazzocchi G, Ellis J, Villanueva-Meyer J, et al. Effect of eating on colonic motility and transit in patients with functional diarrhea. Simultaneous scintigraphic and manometric evaluations. Gastroenterology 1991;101:1298–306.

90. Camilleri M, Choi M-G. Review article: irritable bowel syndrome. Aliment Pharmacol Ther 1997;11:3–15.

91. Mayer EA, Gebhart GF. Basic and clinical aspects of visceral hyperalgesia. In: Tache Y, Wingate D, Burks T,

editors. Innervation of the gut: pathophysiological implications. Boca Raton (FL): CRC Press; 1993. p. 211–34.

92. Gracely RH, McGrath P, Dubner R. Validity and sensitivity of ratio scales of sensory and affective verbal pain descriptors: manipulation of affect by diazepam. Pain 1976;2:19–29.

93. Petersen CC, Petersen OH, Berridge MJ. The role of endoplasmic reticulum calcium pumps during cytosolic calcium spiking in pancreatic acinar cells. J Biol Chem 1993;268:22262–4.

94. Mertz H, Fullerton S, Naliboff B, Mayer EA. Symptoms and visceral perception in severe functional and organic dyspepsia. Gut 1998;42:814–22.

95. Cannon RO, Benjamin SB. Chest pain as a consequence of abnormal visceral nociception. Dig Dis Sci 1993;38:193–6.

96. Sakar S, Aziz Q, Woolf CJ, et al. Contribution of central sensitization to the development of non-cardiac chest pain. Lancet 2000;356:1154–9.

97. Mertz H, Naliboff B, Munakata J, et al. Altered rectal perception is a biological marker of patients with irritable bowel syndrome. Gastroenterology 1995; 109:40–52.

98. Naliboff BD, Munakata J, Fullerton S, et al. Evidence for two distinct perceptual alterations in irritable bowel syndrome. Gut 1997;41:505–12.

99. Munakata J, Naliboff B, Harraf F, et al. Repetitive sigmoid stimulation induces rectal hyperalgesia in patients with irritable bowel syndrome. Gastroenterology 1997;112:55–63.

100. Whitehead WE, Holtkotter B, Enck P, et al. Tolerance for rectosigmoid distention in irritable bowel syndrome. Gastroenterology 1990;98(5 Pt 1):1187–92.

101. Cook IJ, Van Eeden A, Collins SM. Patients with irritable bowel syndrome have greater pain tolerance than normal subjects. Gastroenterology 1987; 93:727–33.

102. Vassallo M, Camiller M, Phillips SF, et al. Transit through the proximal colon influences stool weight in the irritable bowel syndrome. Gastroenterology 1992;102:102–8.

103. Sun WM, Read NW, Verlinden M. Effects of loperamide oxide on gastrointestinal transit time and anorectal function in patients with chronic diarrhoea and faecal incontinence. Scand J Gastroenterol 1997;32:34–8.

104. Bassotti G, Crowell M, Whitehead W. Contractile activity of the human colon: lessons from 24 hour studies. Gut 1993;34:129–33.

105. Furness J, Costa M. The enteric nervous system and the control of the mucosal epithelium and glands. In: Furness J, Costa M, editors. The enteric nervous system. London: Churchill Livingstone; 1987. p. 190–206.

106. Chaussade S, Khyari A, Roche H, et al. Determination of total and segmental colonic transit time in constipated patients. Dig Dis Sci 1989;34:1168–72.

107. Heitkemper M, Jarrett M, Cain K, et al. Increased urinary catecholamines and cortisol in women with irritable bowel syndrome. Am J Gastroenterol 1996;91:906–13.

108. Munakata J, Mayer EA, Chang, L et al. Autonomic and neuroendocrine responses to recto-sigmoid stimulation [abstract]. Gastroenterology 1998;114:808.

109. Munakata J, Silverman DHS, Naliboff B, et al. Evidence for cortical visceral autonomic dysregulation in irritable bowel syndrome [abstract]. Neurogastroenterol Motil 1998;10:362.

110. Chang L. The association of functional gastrointestinal disorders and fibromyalgia [review]. Eur J Surg 1998;Suppl 583:32–6.

111. Cook IJ, Irvine EJ, Campbell D, et al. Effect of dietary fiber on symptoms and rectosigmoid motility in patients with irritable bowel syndrome. A controlled, crossover study. Gastroenterology 1990;98:66–72.

112. Kaplan DS, Masand PS, Gupta S. The relationship of irritable bowel syndrome (IBS) and panic disorder. Ann Clin Psychiatry 1996;8:81–8.

113. Dewsnap P, Gomborone J, Libby G, Farthing M. The prevalence of symptoms of irritable bowel syndrome among acute psychiatric inpatients with an affective diagnosis. Psychosomatics 1996;37:385–9.

114. Toner BB, Stuckless N, Ali A, et al. The development of cognitive scale for functional bowel disorders. Psychosom Med 1998;60:492–7.

115. Lydiard RB, Fossey MD, Marsh W, Ballenger JC. Prevalence of psychiatric disorders in patients with irritable bowel syndrome. Psychosomatics 1993;34:229–34.

116. Silverman DHS, Munakata J, Hoh CK, et al. Regional cerebral activity in normal and pathologic perception of visceral pain. Gastroenterology 1997;112:64–72.

117. Drossman DA, Li Z, Leserman J, et al. Health status by gastrointestinal diagnosis and abuse history. Gastroenterology 1996;110:997–1110.

118. Ford MJ, Miller PM, Eastwood J, Eastwood MA. Life events, psychiatric illness and the irritable bowel syndrome. Gut 1987;28:160–5.

119. Drossman DA, Sandler RS, McKee DC. Bowel patterns among subjects not seeking health care. Gastroenterology 1982;83:529–34.

120. Hislop IG. Psychological significance of the irritable colon syndrome. Gut 1971;12:452–7.

121. Almy TP, Hinkle LE, Berle B, Kern F. Alterations in colonic function in man under stress. Gastroenterology 1949;12:437–49.

122. Welgan P, Meshkinpour H, Beeler M. The effect of anger on colon motor and myoelectric activity in irritable bowel syndrome. Gastroenterology 1988; 94:1150–6.

123. Levy RL, Cain KC, Jarrett M, Heitkemper MM. The relationship between daily life stress and gastrointestinal symptoms in women with irritable bowel syndrome. J Behav Med 1997;20:177–93.

124. Berkley KJ. Sex differences in pain. Behav Brain Sci 1997;20:371–80.

125. Mayer EA, Naliboff B. Review: gender-related differences in functional gastrointestinal disorders. Aliment Pharmacol Ther 1999;13 Suppl 2:65–9.

126. Zarling EJ, Bernsen MB. The effect of gender on the rates of hospitalization for gastrointestinal illnesses. Am J Gastroenterol 1997;92:621–3.

127. Lee OY, Mayer EA, Schmulson M, et al. Gender-related differences in IBS symptoms. Am J Gastroenterol 2001;96:2184–93.

128. Aziz Q, Andersson J, Valind S, et al. Identification of human brain loci processing esophageal sensation using positron emission tomography. Gastroenterology 1997;113:50–9.

129. Naliboff B, Munakata J, Kodner A, Mayer EA. IBS non-patients do not differ from healthy controls on visceral sensitivity [abstract]. Gastroenterology 1996;110:A723.

130. Bouhassira D, Gall O, Chitour D, LeBars D. Dorsal horn convergent neurones: negative feedback triggered by spatial summation of nociceptive afferents. Pain 1995;62:195–200.

131. Heitkemper MM, Jarrett M. Patterns of gastrointestinal and somatic symptoms across the menstrual cycle. Gastroenterology 1992;102:505–13.

132. Toner BB, Akman D. Gender role and irritable bowel syndrome: literature review and hypothesis. Am J Gastroenterol 2000;95:11–6.

133. Berman S, Munakata J, Naliboff BD, et al. Gender differences in regional brain response to visceral pressure in IBS patients. Eur J Pain 2000;4:157–72.

134. Harvey RF, Mauad EC, Brown AM. Prognosis in the irritable bowel syndrome: a 5-year prospective study. Lancet 1987;1:963–5.

135. Van Ness MM, Cattau EL Jr. Flatulence: pathophysiology and treatment. Am Fam Phys 1985;31:198–208.

136. Friedman G. Diet and irritable bowel syndrome. Gastroenterol Clin North Am 2000;20:313–24.

137. Jarrett M, Heitkemper MM, Bond EF, Georges J. Comparison of diet composition in women with and without functional bowel disorder. Gastroenterol Nurs 1994;16:253–8.

138. Cann PA, Read NW, Holdsworth CD. What is the benefit of coarse wheat bran in patients with irritable bowel syndrome? Gut 1984;25:168–73.

139. Voderholzer WA, Schatke W, Muhldorfer BE, et al. Clinical response to dietary fiber treatment of chronic constipation. Am J Gastroenterol 1997;92: 95–8.

140. Distrutti E, Azpiroz F, Soldevilla A, Malagelada JR. Gastric wall tension determines perception of gastric distension. Gastroenterology 1999;116: 1035–42.

141. Thumshirn M, Camilleri M, Choi M-G, Zinsmeister AR. Modulation of gastric sensory and motor functions by nitrergic and α_2-adrenergic agents in humans. Gastroenterology 1999; 116:573–85.

142. Malcolm A, Phillips SF, Camilleri M, Hanson RB. Pharmacological modulation of rectal tone alters perception of distension in humans. Am J Gastroenterol 1997;92:2073–9.

143. Hebden JM, Blackshaw PE, Perkins AC, et al. Small bowel transit of a bran meal residue in humans: sieving of solids from liquids and response to feeding. Gut 1998;42:685–9.

144. Lucey MR, Clark ML, Lowndes J, Dawson AM. Is bran efficacious in irritable bowel syndrome? A double-blind, placebo-controlled crossover study. Gut 1987;28:221–5.

145. Francis CY, Whorwell PJ. Bran and the irritable bowel syndrome: time for reappraisal. Lancet 1994;344:39–40.

146. Poynard T, Naveau S, Mory B, Chaput JC. Meta-analysis of smooth muscle relaxants in the treatment of irritable bowel syndrome. Aliment Pharmacol Ther 1994;8:499–510.

147. Klein KB. Controlled treatment trials in the irritable bowel syndrome: a critique. Gastroenterology 1988; 95:232–41.

148. Piai G, Mazzacca G. Prifinium bromide in the treatment of the irritable colon syndrome. Gastroenterology 1979;77:500–2.

149. Centonze V, Imbimbo BP, Campanozzi F, et al. Oral cimetropium bromide, a new antimuscarinic drug, for long-term treatment of irritable bowel syndrome. Am J Gastroenterol 1988;83:1262–6.

150. Christen MO. Action of pinaverium bromide, a calcium-antagonist, on gastrointestinal motility disorders. Gen Pharmacol 1990;21:821–5.

151. Hills JM, Aaronson PI. The mechanism of action of peppermint oil on gastrointestinal smooth muscle. An analysis using patch clamp electrophysiology and isolated tissue pharmacology. Gastroenterology 1991;101:55–65.

152. Cann PA, Read NW, Holdsworth CD, Barends D. Role of loperamide and placebo in management of irritable bowel syndrome (IBS). Dig Dis Sci 1984; 29:239–47.

153. Lembeck F, Donnerer J, Bartho L. Inhibition of neurogenic vasodilatation and plasma extravasation by substance P antagonists, somatostatin and [D-Met2,Pro5] enkephalinamide. Eur J Pharmacol 1982;85:171–6.

154. Hallgren T, Fasth S, Delbro DS, et al. Loperamide improves anal sphincter function and continence after restorative proctocolectomy. Dig Dis Sci 1994; 39:2612–8.

155. Luman W, Williams AJ, Merrick MV, Eastwood MA. Ideopathic bile acid malabsorption: long-term outcome. Eur J Gastroenterol Hepatol 1995;7:641–5.

156. Brydon WG, Nyhlin H, Eastwood MA, Merrick MV. Serum 7α-hydroxy-4-cholesten-3-one and seleno-homocholyltaurine (SeHCAT) whole body retention in the assessment of bile acid induced diarrhoea. Eur J Gastroenterol Hepatol 1996;8:117–23.

157. Baeyens R, Van de Velde E, De Schepper A, et al. Effects of intravenous and oral domperidone on the motor function of the stomach and small intestine. Postgrad Med J 1979;55:19–23.

158. Tonini M, De Ponti F, Di Nucci A, Crema F. Review article: cardiac adverse effects of gastrointestinal prokinetics. Aliment Pharmacol Ther 1999;13:1585–91.

159. Walker AM, Szneke P, Weatherby LB, et al. The risk of serious cardiac arrhythmias among cisapride users in the United Kingdom and Canada. Am J Med 1999;107:356–62.

160. Scarpignato C, Pelosini I. Management of irritable bowel syndrome: novel approaches to the pharmacology of gut motility [review]. Can J Gastroenterol 1999;18 Suppl A: 50–65A.

161. Zhou H, Khalilieh S, Lau H, et al. Effect of meal timing not critical for the pharmacokinetics of tegaserod (HTF 919). J Clin Pharmacol 1999;39:911–9.

162. Scott LJ, Perry CM. Tegaserod. Drugs 1999;58:491–6.

163. Heefner JD, Wilder RM, Wilson JD. Irritable colon and depression. Psychosomatics 1978;19:540–7.

164. Lancaster-Smith MJ, Prout BJ, Pinto T, et al. Influence of drug treatment on the irritable bowel syndrome and its interaction with psychoneurotic morbidity. Acta Psychiatr Scand 1982;66:33–41.

165. Rajagopalan M, Kurian G, John J. Symptom relief with amitriptyline in the irritable bowel syndrome. J Gastroenterol Hepatol 1998;13:738–41.

166. Onghena P, Van Houdenhove B. Antidepressant-induced analgesia in chronic non-malignant pain: a meta-analysis of 39 placebo-controlled studies. Pain 1992;49:205–19.

167. Gorelick AB, Koshy SS, Hooper FG, et al. Differential effects of amitriptyline on perception of somatic and visceral stimulation in healthy humans. Am J Physiol 1998;275:G460–6.

168. Greenbaum DS, Mayle JE, Vanegeren LE, et al. Effects of desipramine on irritable bowel syndrome compared with atropine and placebo. Dig Dis Sci 1987;32:257–66.

169. Gram L. Fluoxetine. N Engl J Med 1994;331:1354–61.

170. Callies AL, Popkin MK. Antidepressant treatment of medical-surgical inpatients by nonpsychiatric physicians. Arch Gen Psychiatry 1987;44:157–60.

171. Narducci F, Snape WJ, Battle WM, et al. Increased colonic motility during exposure to a stressful situation. Dig Dis Sci 1985;30:40–4.

172. Deutsch E. Relief of anxiety and related emotions in patients with gastrointestinal disorders: a double-blind controlled study. Am J Dig Dis 1971;16:1091–4.

173. Whorwell PJ, Prior A, Faragher EB. Controlled trial of hypnotherapy in the treatment of severe refractory irritable-bowel syndrome. Lancet 1984; 2:1232–4.

174. Svedlund J. Psychotherapy in irritable bowel syndrome: a controlled outcome study. Acta Psychiatr Scand 1983;306:1–86.

175. Guthrie E, Creed F, Dawson D, Tomenson B. A controlled trial of psychological treatment for the irritable bowel syndrome. Gastroenterology 1991; 100:450–7.

176. Hellman CJ, Budd M, Borysenko J, et al. A study of the effectiveness of two group behavioral medicine interventions for patients with psychosomatic complaints. Behav Med 1990;16:165–73.

177. Colwell LJ, Prather CM, Phillips SF, Zinsmeister AR. Effects of an irritable bowel syndrome educational class on health-promoting behaviors and symptoms. Am J Gastroenterol 1998;93:901–5.

178. Blanchard EB, Radnitz C, Schwarz SP, et al. Psychological changes associated with self-regulatory

treatments of irritable bowel syndrome. Biofeedback Self Regulation 1987;12:31–7.

179. Schwarz SP, Taylor AE, Scharff L, Blanchard EB. Behaviorally treated irritable bowel syndrome patients: a four-year follow-up. Behav Res Ther 1990;28:331–5.

180. Radnitz CL, Blanchard EB. Bowel sound feedback as a treatment for irritable bowel syndrome. Biofeedback Self Regulation 1988;13:169–79.

181. Mollen RM, Salvioli B, Camilleri M, et al. The effects of biofeedback on rectal sensation and distal colonic motility in patients with disorders of rectal evacuation: evidence of an inhibitory rectocolonic reflex in humans? Am J Gastroenterol 1999;94:751–6.

182. Ford MJ, Camilleri M, Zinsmeister AR, Hanson RB. Psychosensory modulation of colonic sensation in the human transverse and sigmoid colon. Gastroenterology 1995;109:1772–80.

183. Camilleri M. Therapeutic approach to the patient with irritable bowel syndrome. Am J Med 1999; 107:27–32S.

184. Gore S, Gilmore IT, Haigh CG, et al. Colonic transit in man is slowed by ondansetron (GR38032F), a selective 5-hydroxytryptamine receptor (type 3) antagonist. Aliment Pharmacol Ther 1990;4:139–44.

185. Talley NJ, Phillips SF, Hadddad A, et al. GR 38032F (Ondansetron), a selective $5HT_3$ receptor antagonist, slows colonic transit in healthy man. Dig Dis Sci 1990;35:477–80.

186. Muller-Lissner SA, Fumagalli I, Bardhan KD, et al. Tegaserod, a 5-HT4 receptor partial agonist, relieves symptoms in irritable bowel syndrome patients with abdominal pain, bloating and constipation. Aliment Pharmacol Ther 2001;15:1655–66.

187. Camilleri M. Review articles: tegaserod. Aliment Pharmacol Ther 2001;15:277–89.

188. Prather CM, Camilleri M, Zinsmeister AR, et al. Tegaserod accelerates orocecal transit in patients with constipation-predominant irritable bowel syndrome. Gastroenterology 2000;118:463–8.

189. Whitehead WE. Behavioral medicine approaches to gastrointestinal disorders. J Consult Clin Psychol 1992;60:605–12.

42

APPROACH TO THE PATIENT

WITH DIFFUSE JOINT

AND MUSCULAR PAIN

David J. Klashman, MD

A common presentation to clinicians in the ambulatory setting is the patient with a chief complaint of "hurting all over." Given that most rheumatic conditions have a female predominance, the ability to make the proper diagnosis takes on enhanced significance in women's health.

Diffuse pain syndromes can be categorized into three broad groups: inflammatory polyarthritis, degenerative arthrosis, and nonarticular disease. Although the history plays a major role in formulating the final working differential diagnosis, it is the physical examination that plays the decisive role in this first important step of sorting clinical presentations into one of these three groups. The ability to identify inflammatory joint synovitis allows the clinician to focus on potentially crippling or life-threatening entities. The ability to sort out articular pain from nonarticular pain enables the clinician to further narrow down the list of diagnostic possibilities.

The recognition of synovitis is the key physical diagnostic skill in the evaluation of the diffuse pain patient. Proper identification of inflamed joints directs the clinician toward diagnoses that may involve high levels of morbidity and mortality, such as rheumatoid arthritis, systemic lupus erythematosus, and other autoimmune connective tissue diseases. Synovitis is characterized by erythema, swelling, warmth, and tenderness (rubor et tumor cum calor et dolor). Note that tenderness has a potentially large subjective component, whereas the other three findings are purely objective observations on the part of

the examiner. Knowledge of the locations of "true articular" regions of each joint facilitates identification of polyarthritis by the examiner. For example, the finding of swelling in the humeral-ulnar articulation (the "true elbow") implicates inflammatory arthritis, whereas a swollen olecranon bursa directs the examiner toward a completely different differential list related to bursitis. An inflamed "true joint" also is tender to motion throughout the entire range of the involved joint. This is to be contrasted with a nonarticular condition such as bursitis, which is tender at the extremes of flexion and extension motion, but not between them. Examination of the metacarpophalangeal (MCP) joints of the hands takes on additional significance given the high frequency of involvement of this joint in inflammatory arthritis and the rarity of MCP involvement in degenerative arthritis (Figure 42–1).

POLYARTHRITIS

Polyarthritis refers to multiple inflamed joints. For the purpose of separating the discussion from that of monoarthritis, polyarthritis may be defined as involving two or more joints. The differential diagnosis of polyarthritis involves multiple conditions (Table 42–1). These range from relatively benign conditions (self-limited viral arthritis) to those with potentially high morbidity (eg, rheumatoid arthritis) to those with possible mortality (eg, the vasculitides).

Virtually all categories of infectious organisms have been associated with polyarthritis. Viral arthritis

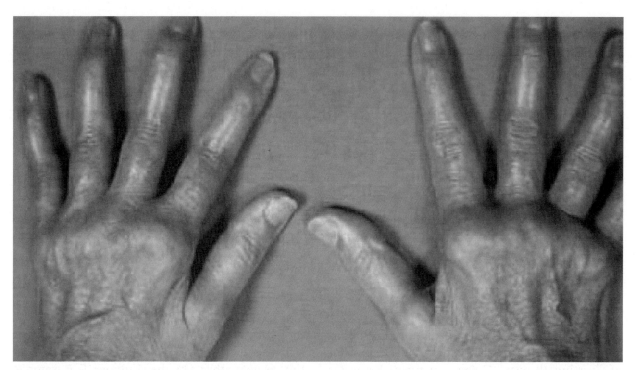

FIGURE 42–1. Inflammatory polyarthritis. Synovitis as evidenced by swollen metacarpophalangeal joints typically is seen in inflammatory arthritides such as rheumatoid arthritis. Reproduced from the Clinical Slide Collection on the Rheumatic Diseases, copyright 1991, 1995, 1997. Used by permission of the American College of Rheumatology.

can be relatively benign and self-limited (eg, parvovirus) or may be a consequence of a more dangerous systemic condition such as chronic viral hepatitis or human immunodeficiency virus (HIV).[1] Hepatitis C virus can produce polyarthritis secondary to cryoglobulinemia.[2] Pyogenic bacteria are associated more often with monoarthritis but, on occasion, can affect more than one joint in a patient via direct joint invasion. Streptococcal-induced rheumatic fever represents an immune-mediated polyarthritis in reaction to the nonarticular streptococcal infection. Immune-mediated polyarthritis also can be seen with bacterial endocarditis. Gonococcus may disseminate from the genitourinary tract and involve one or more joints. Atypical bacteria such as chlamydia and spirochetes (syphilis, Lyme disease) may cause polyarthritis.[3] Controversy exists as to whether reactive arthritis from organisms such as chlamydia represents an immunologic reaction to the organism or direct invasion of the joint by the organism. Chronic indolent infections with acid-fast or mycotic organisms, although more commonly associated with directly infected single joints, also may be associated with an immune-mediated polyarthritis.

Metabolic disorders resulting in crystal deposition (eg, urate gout or calcium pyrophosphate pseudogout), although more commonly associated with mono- or oligoarthritis, may produce a diffuse relatively symmetric polyarthritis.[4] Infiltrative conditions such as hemachromatosis and amyloidosis, neoplastic conditions, and endocrine conditions (eg, hypothyroidism) all may produce a clinical picture of polyarthritis. Osteoarthritis, although generally a degenerative disorder, may involve a component of secondary inflammation and rarely appear as an inflammatory condition.

Autoimmune conditions account for the majority of chronic arthritides. Swollen peripheral joints can be a component of multiple diseases. These include rheumatoid arthritis (RA), juvenile-onset rheumatoid arthritis (JRA), seronegative spondyloarthropathies (ie, ankylosing spondylitis, psoriatic arthritis, Reiter's syndrome, inflammatory bowel disease), systemic lupus erythematosus (SLE), myositis (dermatomyositis/polymyositis), progressive systemic sclerosis (PSS, also called "scleroderma"),[5] mixed or undifferentiated connective tissue diseases (MCTD or UCTD), Sjögren's syndrome, sarcoidosis, and various vasculitides.

Sorting out the diagnosis from this large differential can be a formidable task (Figure 42–2). The cornerstone to diagnostic strategy is a thorough

TABLE 42–1. Differential Diagnosis of Polyarthritis

Infectious
  Viral
    Parvovirus
    Rubella virus
    Hepatitis associated (B and C)
    Human immunodeficiency virus associated
  Bacterial
    Pyogenic (via direct invasion or immune reaction)
    Gonococcus
    Chlamydia
    Spirochete (syphilis, Lyme disease)
    Acid-fast bacteria
  Fungal
  Parasitic

Metabolic—crystalline
  Urate
  Calcium pyrophosphate dihydrate

Infiltrative
  Hemachromatosis
  Amyloidosis
  Hypothyroidism

Neoplastic
  Direct invasion
  Paraneoplastic immune reaction

Inflammatory osteroarthritis

Autoimmune
  Rheumatoid arthritis
  Seronegative spondyloarthropathies
    Ankylosing spondylitis
    Psoriatic arthritis
    Reactive arthritis/Reiter's syndrome
    Inflammatory bowel disease
  Systemic lupus erythematosus
  Myositis
  Scleroderma
  Mixed or undifferentiated connective tissue disease
  Sjögren's syndrome
  Sarcoidosis
  Vasculitis

history and physical examination. The history can provide clues to narrow down diagnostic possibilities.[6–8] For instance, duration of symptoms of less than a few weeks is suggestive of viral infection, whereas prolonged duration points toward the chronic arthritides. Patterns of joint involvement may be somewhat helpful in disease distinction but may be nonspecific given the overlap of joint involvement among the different conditions. Asymmetric or pauciarticular involvement suggests diagnoses of seronegative spondyloarthropathy or crystalline disease. Associated nonarticular musculoskeletal signs may be helpful: spinal involvement especially in the sacroiliac region points toward the seronegative spondyloarthropathies. Involvement of tendinous insertions (enthesitis) also suggests the group of seronegative spondyloarthropathies. Nonmusculoskeletal or systemic manifestations may be diagnostic clues (eg, malar rash or oral ulcers in SLE; fevers, weight loss, and foot drop in systemic vasculitis). Temporal patterns of arthritis onset may be useful. A migratory pattern of joint involvement, consisting of arthritis beginning in one joint then shifting to another with resolution in the first joint, is suggestive of gonococcal arthritis or rheumatic fever. An additive pattern (newly involved joints adding on to previous disease involvement without resolution) points toward RA, SLE, seronegative spondyloarthropathies, and rubella. A palindromic pattern involving periods of spontaneous remission between arthritis episodes suggests crystalline disease, familial Mediterranean fever (FMF), sarcoidosis, or seronegative spondyloarthropathy. Finally, marked therapeutic responses to certain medications can be diagnostic. Rheumatic fever responds markedly well to aspirin; improvement with colchicine suggests a crystalline disease or, less likely, sarcoidosis, Behçet's disease, or FMF.

Laboratory work-up should include a complete blood count (CBC), comprehensive chemistry panel, and urinalysis. The CBC may show nonspecific leukocytosis or may reveal leukopenia, anemia, or thrombocytopenia, suggestive of autoimmune destruction such as that seen in SLE. In many situations there are no obvious clinical clues to these laboratory findings—most patients do not clinically manifest symptoms from a platelet count of 48K, yet this is ominously abnormal. The chemistry panel can shed light on renal and hepatic function. Routine urinalysis is highly useful in detecting early renal abnormalities. Serum uric levels may direct diagnostic work-up toward (or away from) a diagnosis of gout. A Westergren erythrocyte sedimentation rate (ESR), although nonspecific, may be helpful in some patients with disease activity correlating with ESR elevation. Thyroid function tests

BASIC WORK-UP

History and Physical Examination

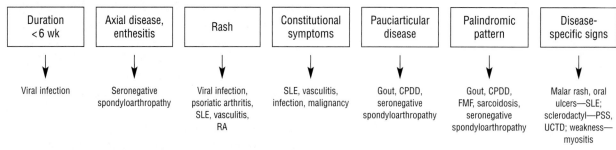

Basic Laboratory Tests

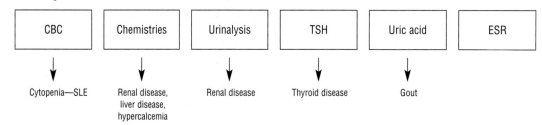

Radiography of affected joints: Specific disease patterns—RA, seronegative spondyloarthropathy, gout, sarcoidosis

Screening serologies: Rheumatoid factor—RA, immune-complex disease
ANA—SLE, other connective disease

IF CLINICALLY INDICATED

Radiography of asymptomatic areas: SI joints—seronegative spondyloarthropathies, CXR—sarcoidosis, RA—lung lesions, vasculitis, SLE

Laboratory Tests

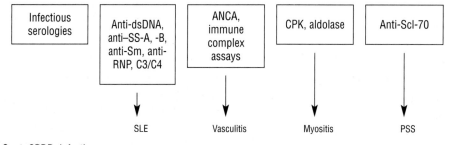

Joint aspiration: Gout, CPDD, infection

FIGURE 42–2. Diagnostic approach to the patient with inflammatory polyarthritis. The work-up of the polyarthritis patient includes a thorough history and physical examination, basic laboratory tests, radiography of affected joints and screening antinuclear antibody (ANA) and rheumatoid factor. When indicated by findings in the basic work-up, radiography of asymptomatic regions, specific serologies, and joint aspiration may be helpful. SLE = systemic lupus erythematosus; RA = rheumatoid arthritis; CPDD = calcium pyrophospate deposition disease; FMF = familial Mediterranean fever; PSS = progressive systemic sclerosis; UCTD = undifferentiated connective tissue disease; CBC = complete blood count; TSH = thyroid-stimulating hormone: ESR = erthrocyte sedimentation rate; SI = sacroiliac; CXR = chest radiography; anti-dsDNA = anti-double-stranded deoxyribonucleic acid; anti-Sm = anti-Smith antibody; RNP = anti-ribonucleoprotein antibody; C3/C4 = complement 3/complement 4; ANCA = antinuclear cytoplasmic antibody; CPK = creatine phosphokinase.

may help to differentiate components of musculoskeletal symptomatology related to thyroid dysfunction either as the primary diagnosis or as an associated diagnosis. Increased incidence of autoimmune thyroid disease has been noted in association with autoimmune polyarthritides such as RA and SLE. If appropriate as directed by information in the history and physical examination, infectious work-up is indicated (eg, blood cultures; viral serology—parvovirus, hepatitis, HIV; spirochetal serology).

Basic serologies for the polyarthritis patient include rheumatoid factor (RF) and antinuclear antibody (ANA). Rheumatoid factor is technically an anti-immunoglobulin antibody. It is ultimately found in 75 to 80% of patients with RA.[9] It also may be found in other conditions involving immune complexes such as vasculitides, SLE, or infections. There is also an increased incidence of positive RF in the normal aging population. Thus, the test entails a significant degree of nonspecificity. Antinuclear antibody is found in ~95% of SLE patients. It is also somewhat nonspecific: ANA is found in a number of non-SLE autoimmune conditions, as well as with advancing age, infection, or even secondary to certain medications.[10]

If a diagnosis of SLE is suggested, other serologies may be useful in confirming the diagnosis, categorizing the disease, and assessing risk for potential involvement of specific organs.[11] Anti-double-stranded deoxyribonucleic acid (anti-dsDNA) antibody correlates with renal involvement and may fluctuate in titer with disease activity. Anti–SS-A (anti-Ro antibody) has been associated with SLE skin manifestations, ANA-negative lupus, Sjögren's syndrome, and the congenital lupus syndrome resulting from maternal transmission of the antibody to the fetus. Anti-Sm antibody is highly specific for a diagnosis of SLE, although with limited sensitivity. Anti-RNP antibody may be seen in SLE as well as in the mixed connective tissue disease. C3 and C4 complement levels may be useful in monitoring disease activity; some patients have decreased levels during disease flare.

If a diagnosis of vasculitis is entertained, antinuclear cytoplasmic antibody (ANCA) can be useful.[12] A cytoplasmic pattern (c-ANCA) suggests a diagnosis of Wegener's granulomatosis. A perinuclear pattern (p-ANCA) is more nonspecific, being found in other vasculitides such as microscopic polyangiitis, as well as other autoimmune conditions (eg, SLE, inflammatory bowel disease). Circulating immune-complex assays and complement levels may be useful in some individuals with vasculitis.

Antibodies seen in PSS include the anti-Scl-70 antibody, more commonly found in the diffuse form, and the anticentromere antibody, seen in the limited form (or CREST [*c*alcinosis cutis, *R*aynaud's phenomenon, *e*sophageal dysfunction, *s*clerodactyly, and *t*elangiectasia] variant).

Radiologic work-up includes radiography of clinically affected joints. Patterns of erosion, joint space narrowing, and localized changes in bone density may help differentiate RA from other diagnoses such as seronegative spondyloarthropathies, crystalline disease, infection, or classically nonerosive arthritic diseases such as SLE or vasculitis. Following the progression of bony changes is extremely valuable in long-term monitoring of therapeutic efficacy. In certain situations, films of unaffected areas may have diagnostic use. Sacroiliac joint involvement suggests the category of seronegative spondyloarthropathies. A chest radiograph may show hilar adenopathy in sarcoidosis, or pulmonary lesions in RA, or Wegener's granulomatosis in patients without respiratory symptoms.

Joint aspiration and synovial fluid analysis, although more useful in monoarthritis to diagnose crystalline disease or infection, can be of some value in the work-up of polyarthritis. Unfortunately the high degree of overlap of findings between fluids of different disease categories limits the usefulness of this procedure (Table 42–2). In practicality, the major purpose for doing this procedure in polyarthritis is to evaluate for polyarticular crystalline disease.

Because the work-up of polyarthritis may take weeks or longer, it is usually necessary to prescribe treatment empirically until a definitive diagnosis can be made. Appropriate therapy involves local/mechanical measures such as advising rest in the involved joints and a trial of application of ice or heat to affected painful areas. In terms of pharmacologic management, nonsteroidal anti-inflammatory drugs (NSAIDs) are the drugs of choice because of their anti-inflammatory properties in addition to their analgesic effects. Pure analgesics such as acetaminophen and/or narcotics also may be used as supplemental therapy. If NSAIDs are

TABLE 42–2. Synovial Fluid Analysis*

Group	Diagnosis	Appearance	White cell Count/mm³	% PMNs
Normal	None	Clear, pale yellow	0–200	< 10
Noninflammatory	Osteoarthritis	Clear to slightly turbid	50–2,000	< 30
Mildly inflammatory	Systemic lupus erythematosus	Clear to slightly turbid	0–9,000	< 20
Severely inflammatory (noninfectious)	Gout	Turbid	100–160,000	~ 70
	Pseudogout	Turbid	50–75,000	~ 70
	Rheumatoid arthritis	Turbid	250–80,000	~ 70
Severely inflammatory (infectious)	Bacterial infections	Very turbid	150–250,000	~ 90
	Tuberculosis	Turbid	2,500–100,000	~ 60

*Classification of synovial fluid by appearance, white blood count, and percentage polymorphonuclear neutrophil leukocytes (PMNs) may have some diagnostic use, but it is limited by a large degree of overlap.

contraindicated in individual patients, analgesics alone have to suffice. Empiric therapy with glucocorticoids should be avoided unless the clinical presentation strongly suggests the diagnosis of a steroid-responsive condition. Acknowledging that pain is decreased to some degree in virtually all conditions with steroid therapy, the potential long-term complications vastly outweigh the initial short-term benefit. Immunosuppressive steroid agents can worsen some conditions such as infections. Patients may become physically dependent to the pain-relieving properties of steroids and ultimately become long-term steroid users. Specifically, in polyarticular gout, steroid therapy may mask the ability to make the diagnosis, resulting in chronic steroid therapy for a patient with a condition better managed with other interventions.

DEGENERATIVE ARTHRITIS

Global pain secondary to degenerative disease occurs most commonly secondary to primary generalized osteoarthritis (OA). This presentation is described in detail in Chapter 46, "Osteoarthritis." The majority of individuals with this condition begin to develop signs and symptoms some time after the age of 40 years. Rare familial syndromes have been reported, with victims of the condition developing severe symptomatology as early as the second decade of life.[13] Obesity may predispose to early development of OA in weight-bearing as well as non-weight-bearing joints. Mechanical factors

such as multiple trauma and hypermobility syndromes may predispose to premature OA. Previous inflammatory arthritides (eg, JRA) may predispose to secondary OA. Calcium pyrophosphate deposition disease (CPDD) has been associated with osteoarthritis. The role of CPDD in the pathogenesis of OA is controversial.[14] Endocrine/metabolic diseases such as acromegaly and hemachromatosis can result in diffuse degenerative arthritis in multiple joints.

History usually reveals pain that worsens with activity and is relieved with rest. In the long-term, pain gradually worsens. Patients may be stiff in the morning but for a relatively short duration of 15 to 20 minutes. Physical examination may reveal palpable joint line crepitus, tenderness, and decreased joint range of motion. Sometimes bony osteophytes are palpable. Occasionally a joint effusion is noted.

Laboratory parameters are all essentially normal in osteoarthritis, the only exception being when OA is precipitated by an underlying metabolic condition (eg, hemachromatosis). Radiography of affected joints is indicated to confirm the diagnosis of OA, to obtain a baseline to monitor disease course, and possibly to identify clues suggestive of an underlying etiology (eg, chondrocalcinosis in CPDD).

NONARTICULAR DISEASE

Nonarticular disease may involve arthralgia, myalgia, and/or neuralgia (Table 42–3). Subacute disease

TABLE 42–3. Differential Diagnosis of Nonarticular Disease

Infectious
  Viral
  Indolent bacterial, fungal

Thyroid disease

Drug/toxin exposure

Myopathy
  Autoimmune myositis
  Hereditary metabolic myopathy

Polymyalgia rheumatica

Early autoimmune connective tissue disease

Painful peripheral neuropathy

Paraneoplastic syndrome

Fibromyalgia

Seronegative spondyloarthropathy

duration (less than 6 weeks) suggests infection (eg, viral myalgia), drug or toxin exposure, or an overuse syndrome. Chronic symptomatology may be secondary to endocrinopathies such as thyroid disease, indolent infections, painful peripheral neuropathy, myopathy (either metabolic or autoimmune), drugs/toxins, autoimmune disease such as ankylosing spondylitis (or other seronegative spondyloarthropathies with axial involvement), polymyalgia rheumatica (PMR),[15] vasculitis or overlap syndromes, paraneoplastic disease, or poorly characterized conditions such as the fibromyalgia syndrome.[16]

History and physical examination provide the major clues toward making a specific diagnosis (Figure 42–3). A thorough medication history is required and should include inquiry regarding prescriptions, over-the-counter products, herbal and holistic products, and recreational drugs. Documented fevers, anorexia, and weight loss point toward infectious, autoimmune, or paraneoplastic etiologies. Nonpainful weakness suggests myopathy or motor neuropathy. Focal numbness and/or paresthesia warrant consideration of neuropathy. Morning stiffness for greater than 1 hour is suggestive of PMR. Functional syndromes typically involve the subjective nonspecific complaint of "slowing down."

During examination findings of thyroid and adrenal disease should be sought carefully. Skin lesions or rashes may point toward SLE, dermatomyositis, vasculitis, sarcoidosis, autoimmune overlap syndromes, or infectious etiologies. Eye, ear, nose, and throat; lung; cardiac; and abdominal findings may help narrow down the list of systemic diseases. Neurologic examination is important. A nonpainful weakness usually is characterized by a smooth loss of strength throughout the tested resisted motion, whereas an intermittently "breaking" weakness is suggestive of decreased effort either secondary to pain or noncooperatiion. Loss of sensation is difficult to evaluate due to an inherent component of subjectivity; reflex evaluation may be useful given the involuntary nature of this finding. Functional syndromes are characterized by benign physical examination results, without evidence of progression or deformity. Distribution of muscle tenderness may help to delineate overuse pathology. Presence of classic "tender points" may help to determine the diagnosis of fibromyalgia. Sacroiliac tenderness points toward a diagnosis of seronegative spondyloarthropathy.

Laboratory work-up includes CBC, routine chemistries, creatine phosphokinase (CPK), thyroid-stimulating hormone (TSH), and serologies. Leukocyte count abnormalities may be a clue to infection, hematologic malignancy, or autoimmune disease (eg, leukopenia in SLE). Anemia of chronic inflammatory disease is a nonspecific clue that justifies an aggressive search for an inflammatory systemic etiology. Thrombocytopenia may be seen in autoimmune disease, drug- or toxin-related conditions, infections, marrow disease, or splenic sequestration. Thrombocytosis may be a nonspecific sign of systemic inflammation. A chemistry panel may be helpful in sorting conditions involving the liver, kidney, thyroid, and adrenal gland. Alkaline phosphatase may be abnormal in conditions involving bone. Hypercalcemia of various etiologies may be noted in patients with nonspecific aching. Testing for TSH is a useful screen for thyroid disease. Levels of CPK are necessary to search for myopathy or even neuropathy. In patients over the age of 50 years, a Westergren ESR is important to evaluate for PMR. Positivity for ANA may suggest early autoimmune disease. A rheumatoid factor may be helpful in suggesting non-RA immune-complex disease (including cryoglobulinemia), even in the absence

BASIC WORK-UP

History and Physical Examination

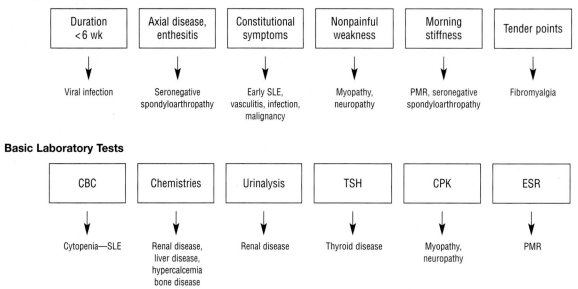

Duration <6 wk	Axial disease, enthesitis	Constitutional symptoms	Nonpainful weakness	Morning stiffness	Tender points
↓	↓	↓	↓	↓	↓
Viral infection	Seronegative spondyloarthropathy	Early SLE, vasculitis, infection, malignancy	Myopathy, neuropathy	PMR, seronegative spondyloarthropathy	Fibromyalgia

Basic Laboratory Tests

CBC	Chemistries	Urinalysis	TSH	CPK	ESR
↓	↓	↓	↓	↓	↓
Cytopenia—SLE	Renal disease, liver disease, hypercalcemia bone disease	Renal disease	Thyroid disease	Myopathy, neuropathy	PMR

IF CLINICALLY INDICATED

Radiography of sites of deep bony pain: SI joints—seronegative spondyloarthropathies

Laboratory Tests

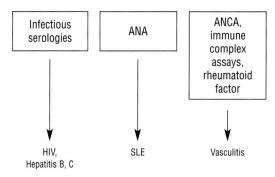

Infectious serologies	ANA	ANCA, immune complex assays, rheumatoid factor
↓	↓	↓
HIV, Hepatitis B, C	SLE	Vasculitis

EMG-NCV study: Myopathy, neuropathy

Muscle biopsy: Myopathy

FIGURE 42–3. Diagnostic approach to the patient with nonarticular pain. The work-up includes a thorough history and physical examination, basic laboratory tests, including thyroid-stimulating hormone (TSH), creatine phosphokinase (CPK), and erythrocyte sedimentation rate (ESR). When indicated by findings in the basic work-up, radiography, serologies, and electromyography–nerve conduction velocity (EMG-NCV) may be helpful. SLE = systemic lupus erythematosus; PMR = polymyalgia rheumatica; CBC = complete blood count; SI = sacroiliac; HIV = human immunodeficiency virus; ANA = antinuclear antibody; ANCA = antinuclear cytoplasmic antibody.

of synovitis. If indicated by findings in the history and physical examination, infectious serologies (eg, for hepatitis or HIV) may be helpful.

If pain is deep, bony tenderness is noted, or range of motion is limited, radiography of affected areas may be helpful. Axial morning stiffness suggestive of seronegative spondyloarthropathies warrants radiographic evaluation of not only affected spinal areas but the sacroiliac joints as well. Even if asymptomatic, abnormal radiographic involvement of the sacroiliac joints may have diagnostic significance.[17]

Electromyography–nerve conduction velocity testing may shed light on possible diagnoses involving myopathy or neuropathy. Ultimately a muscle biopsy may be necessary to diagnose the underlying cause of pain.

As in polyarthritis, the work-up may take weeks to complete, and patients may require empiric therapy. Analgesics are preferable; NSAIDs may be helpful. Local modalities such as heat or ice may be of benefit. Rest may be helpful, although the use of this strategy may run the risk of causing deconditioning, which can have long-term adverse consequences. An empiric trial of low-dose corticosteroids (eg, prednisone 10 mg/d) may have diagnostic benefit in patients with possible PMR. A marked response in symptom relief is suggestive of the PMR diagnosis. Otherwise empiric courses of steroids are not indicated, given their potential for side effects.

REFERENCES

1. Ytterberg SR. Viral arthritis. Curr Opin Rheumatol 1999;11:275–80.
2. Rivera J, Garcia-Monforte A, Pineda A, Millan Nunez-Cortes J. Arthritis in patients with chronic hepatitis C virus infection. J Rheumatol 1999;26:420–4.
3. Keat A. Sexually transmitted arthritis syndromes. Med Clin North Am 1990;74:1617–31.
4. Schumacher HR. Crystal-induced arthritis: an overview. Am J Med 1996;100:46–52S.
5. Baron M, Lee P, Keystone EC. The articular manifestations of progressive systemic sclerosis (scleroderma). Ann Rheum Dis 1982;41:147–52.
6. Schumacher HR. Arthritis of recent onset. A guide to evaluation and initial therapy for primary care physicians. Postgrad Med 1995;97:52–63.
7. Barth WF. Office evaluation of the patient with musculoskeletal complaints. Am J Med 1997;102:3–10S.
8. Weiss TE, Gum OB, Biundo JJ. Rheumatic diseases. 1. Differential diagnosis. Postgrad Med 1976; 60:141–50.
9. Shmerling RH, Delbanco TL. The rheumatoid factor: an analysis of clinical utility. Am J Med 1991; 91:528–34.
10. Forslid J, Heigl Z, Jonsson J, Scheynius A. The prevalence of antinuclear antibodies in healthy young persons and adults, comparing rat liver tissue sections with Hep-2 cells as antigen substrate. Clin Exp Rheumatol 1994;12:137–41.
11. Quismorio FP. Clinical applications of serologic abnormalities in systemic lupus erythematosus. In: Wallace DJ, Hahn BH, editors. Dubois' lupus erythematosus. 5th ed. Baltimore: Williams and Wilkins; 1997:925–42.
12. Schultz DR, Tozman EC. Antineutrophil cytoplasmic antibodies: major autoantigens, pathophysiology, and disease associations. Semin Arthritis Rheum 1995;25:143–59.
13. Bleasel JF, Poole AR, Heinegard D, et al. Changes in serum cartilage marker levels indicate altered cartilage metabolism in families with the osteoarthritis-related type II collagen gene COL2A1 mutation. Arthritis Rheum 1999;42:39–45.
14. Schumacher HR. Synovial inflammation, crystals, and osteoarthritis. J Rheumatol Suppl 1995;43:101–3.
15. Evans JM, Hunder GG. Polymyalgia rheumatica and giant cell arteritis. Clin Geriatr Med 1998;14:455–73.
16. Buskila D. Fibromyalgia, chronic fatigue syndrome, and myofascial pain syndrome. Curr Opin Rheumatol 1999;11:199–26.
17. McEniff N, Eustace S, McCarthy C, et al. Asymptomatic sacroliliitis in inflammatory bowel disease. Assessment by computed tomography. Clin Imaging 1995;19:258–62.

43

RHEUMATOID ARTHRITIS

Alan H. Gorn, MD

Rheumatoid arthritis (RA) is characterized by generally persistent inflammatory synovitis with a predilection for peripheral joints in a symmetric distribution. The synovitis is typically severe and frequently leads to cartilage destruction, periarticular erosions of bone, and tendon displacement or ruptures. This destruction leads to the joint deformities that characterize severe RA. Although the hallmark of RA is its inflammatory synovitis (joint disease), it is, in fact, a chronic disease of unknown cause that involves multiple organ systems over time.

The prevalence of RA is estimated at approximately 1% of the population.[1] Women are affected three to four times more frequently than are men, although the difference in prevalence by sex diminishes in older-aged populations.[2] Onset of RA may occur at any age, from infancy to advanced old age, but most frequently between the ages of 35 and 50 years.[3] Genetics plays a role in predisposition to disease. Rheumatoid arthritis is approximately four times more frequent than is otherwise expected among first-degree relatives of patients with seropositive (rheumatoid factor [RF] positive) disease. Even so, only about 10% of patients have a first-degree relative with disease.[4]

The histocompatibility complex gene human leukocyte antigen (HLA)-DR4 is expressed in up to 70% of patients with RA, compared with 28% of control individuals.[5] In some populations, other HLA-DR alleles that encode a similar amino acid motif to one found in the DR4 allele are associated with RA, implicating these amino acid sequences as possible genetic diatheses to disease, even in patients without the HLA-DR4 allele.[6] The HLA encoded molecules play a role in presentation of peptide antigens to CD4-positive T cells and are involved in the initial selection of the individual's CD4-positive T cell repertoire in the thymus, per-

haps influencing recognition of an antigen that initiates or perpetuates the disease process. Genetic risk factors do not fully account for the incidence of RA, leading to theories that a relatively ubiquitous infectious organism may trigger disease in a genetically susceptible host. Infectious etiology theories have long been proposed and investigated, without conclusion.[7]

Microvascular injury and hypertrophy of the synovial lining cells with increasing mononuclear cell infiltration results over time in grossly thickened edematous synovia that protrudes into the joints. The synovia produces a number of cytokines secreted from infiltrating lymphocytes and monocyte-macrophages. These include interleukin (IL)-1, IL-2, IL-6, tumor necrosis factor (TNF), and granulocyte-macrophage colony-stimulating factor (GM-CSF). These factors drive much of the pathologic response that leads to cartilage and bone destruction and the systemic features of RA. There is a correlation between active arthritis and the histologic presence of macrophages and monocyte-macrophage products such as TNF-α and IL-6. Therapeutic agents that specifically target some of these monocyte-macrophage-produced factors are quite effective in reducing disease manifestations.[7,8]

T lymphocytes also produce a number of B cell promoting factors that result in production of immunoglobins (Igs), including RFs, which are autoantibodies that react with the Fc portion of IgG. This feature is the basis of the widely used clinical tests that typically detect IgM RFs. Such RFs are present in perhaps 80% of RA patients, although they may be detected in as little as 50% at disease onset. Rheumatoid factors are not specific for RA and are found in approximately 5% of healthy individuals, increasing to 10 to 20% in the elderly. Many other conditions also result in positive RF tests, including viral syndromes such as mononucleosis, chronic hepatitis, tuberculosis, subacute bacterial endocarditis and other chronic infections, and other connective tissue diseases. Rheumatoid factors may occasionally occur transiently after vaccination.[9]

PRESENTING SIGNS AND SYMPTOMS

Rheumatoid arthritis may present with fatigue, anorexia, and vague musculoskeletal complaints before the appearance of synovitis is apparent. Such a prodrome may persist for weeks or a few months and defy diagnosis, particularly if the evaluating clinicians are not attuned to checking for evidence of early synovitis. Characteristically, RA ultimately becomes a chronic polyarthritis, as detectable synovitis gradually appears over several joints, especially those of the hands, wrists, knees, and feet. Over time, a symmetric pattern of joint involvement is most typical, but symptoms initially may be limited to one or a few joints at presentation. In some patients (perhaps 10%) the onset is more acute with rapid development of severe polyarthritis, and it may include constitutional symptoms, lymphadenopathy, and splenomegaly.[10]

Pain, swelling, and tenderness in affected joints, aggravated by movement and stiffening with inactivity, is characteristic of established inflammatory arthritis such as RA. Morning stiffness of 1 hour or more helps to distinguish inflammatory arthritis such as RA from noninflammatory joint disease such as osteoarthritis (OA). The pattern of joints involved in RA also helps to distinguish RA from OA, and other forms of inflammatory arthritis. As compared to OA, RA is much more likely to affect the proximal metacarpophalangeal joints, wrists, and elbows. The distal interphalangeal joints are typically not involved in RA. Axial involvement usually is limited to the upper cervical spine. Low back pain is not a feature of rheumatoid arthritis.

Over time, a number of deformities develop from destruction and weakening of the joint capsule, tendons, ligaments, cartilage, and juxta-articular bone. Deformities include ulnar deviation of the digits and hyperextension of the proximal interphalangeal joints with flexion of the distal interphalangeal joints (the "swan neck" deformity), but these changes should not be expected on presentation of early disease.[11] Typical deformities also occur in the feet, including lateral deviation and dorsal

subluxation of the toes with plantar subluxation of the metatarsal heads.[12] Synovitis at the wrist causes swelling that may lead to carpal tunnel syndrome. The knees commonly are involved, and inflamed synovia may extend into the popliteal space and produce pain and swelling behind the knee, called a "Baker's cyst." A Baker's cyst may rupture, resulting in calf swelling and sometimes bruising around the ankle. A ruptured Baker's cyst may be mistaken as a sign of deep vein thrombosis.[13] Inflammation of the joints ultimately leads to erosive changes at the joint margins in most patients, to a greater or lesser degree.[10]

Inflammation of the synovial tissue and bursae of the upper cervical spine may lead to instability and subluxation at the atlantoaxial joint. This may present as pain over the occiput and can lead to compression of the spinal cord, generally as a late complication of disease. Atlantoaxial subluxation can be detected by obtaining cervical spine radiographs that include flexion and odontoid views. When compared to neutral and extension views, the flexion view shows a widened gap between the posterior margin of the anterior arch of the atlas and the anterior margin of the odontoid. This distance is generally greater than 7 mm in symptomatic patients, who should be evaluated by a neurosurgeon.[14]

Rheumatoid nodules develop in 20 to 35% of patients as a manifestation of extra-articular disease thought to arise as focal small vessel vasculitis. They occur most frequently on areas around joints subject to mechanical pressure, but they can develop anywhere, including tendons, pleura, and lung. Nodules almost always occur in patients who are positive for RF. In general, extra-articular manifestations are found in patients with high-titer RF.[10]

Other extra-articular manifestations include anemia of chronic disease, thrombocytosis, weight loss, and serositis including pleural effusions and pericarditis. Pleural fluid demonstrates predominantly a mononuclear exudate with very low glucose levels and low complement levels, suggesting immune-complex disease.[15] Interstitial pulmonary disease initially tends to affect the bases toward the pleura. Intrapulmonary rheumatoid nodules may sometimes cavitate and can mimic malignancy radiographically. Bronchiectasis and bronchiolitis obliterans with and without organizing pneumonia occur. All forms of rheumatoid lung disease are more frequent in smokers but occur as a complication of the disease itself.[10] Patients with RA may rarely suffer methotrexate-induced inflammatory lung complications. Although the frequency of methotrexate pneumonitis may be as low as 2.5%, it may occur at any dosage and at any point during treatment.[16] Ocular involvement in RA is uncommon but includes episcleritis and the serious complication of nodular scleritis with necrotic rheumatoid granuloma that may lead to eye perforation. Perhaps 20% of RA patients experience keratoconjunctivitis sicca or Sjögren's syndrome.[17] Osteoporosis is common, resulting from disease-related inflammatory cytokines that adversely affect bone mass, and from corticosteroid treatment.

Rheumatoid vasculitis generally occurs late in the disease course and can affect many organs. Vasculitis presents most commonly as cutaneous purpuric lesions that may lead to ulcerations, digital infarcts, and gangrene. A few small brown spots near the nail beds or on the digital pulp are the first signs of this vasculitis. Neurovascular disease may lead to distal sensory neuropathy or mononeuritis multiplex. Unlike polyarteritis nodosa, rheumatic arteritis virtually always lacks renal involvement, although it can rarely involve the gut. Felty's syndrome occurs occasionally as a late manifestation of RA, even after joint inflammation has receded ("burned-out"). This syndrome consists of leuko-cytopenia with predominant neutropenia, often with splenomegaly. These patients demonstrate increased risk of infections associated with neutropenia and also from inhibited neutrophil function. Thrombocytopenia occurs occasionally.[10,17]

DIAGNOSIS

The diagnosis of RA may initially require a period of observation at disease onset before confirmation can be made. Rheumatoid arthritis may present with constitutional symptoms and arthralgias. Initial arthritis may be in an asymmetric distribution before evolving into the typical bilateral symmetric inflammatory polyarthritis that includes both small and large joints.[18] Generally the disease declares itself with characteristic clinical features within 6 months to 1 year of onset, but it may vary in severity. The arthritis must persist for more than 6 weeks before satisfying criteria for the diagnosis of RA (Table 43–1). The finding of an isolated RF test, particularly in an older patient, does not constitute evidence of RA without other criteria.[9] The diagnosis of RA is generally easy to establish in a patient with longstanding disease. Early in disease, radiographs may show normal or subtle results and somewhat subjective findings such as radiographic evidence of soft tissue swelling or periarticular osteopenia. The

---

**TABLE 43–1. The 1987 American Rheumatism Association Revised Criteria for Classification of Rheumatoid Arthritis*

1. Morning stiffness—in and around joints, lasting at least 1 h before maximal improvement.
2. Arthritis of three or more joint areas—at least three joint areas simultaneously having soft tissue swelling or fluid (not bony overgrowth alone); the 14 possible joint areas (right or left) are PIP, MCP, wrist, elbow, knee, ankle, and MTP joints
3. Arthritis of hand joints—at least one joint area, swollen as above in wrist, MCP, or PIP joint
4. Symmetric arthritis—simultaneous involvement of the same joint areas (as in criterion 2) on both sides of the body (bilateral involvement)
5. Rheumatoid nodules—subcutaneous nodules over bony prominences or extensor surfaces, or in juxta-articular regions
6. Rheumatoid factor—demonstration of abnormal amounts of serum "rheumatoid factor"
7. Radiographic changes—changes typical of RA on hand and wrist radiographs, which must include erosions or unequivocal bony decalcification localized to or adjacent to the involved joints (osteoarthritis changes alone do not qualify)

---

*Guidelines for classification: A patient that satisfies at least 4 of 7 criteria has RA. Criteria 1 to 4 must be present for at least 6 weeks. Patients with two clinical diagnoses are not excluded.
PIP = proximal interphalangeal; MCP = metacarpophalangeal; MTP = metatarsophalangeal; RA = rheumatoid arthritis.
Reproduced with permission from Arnett FC, Edworthy SM, Block DA, et al. The American Rheumatism Association 1987 revised criteria for the classification of rheumatoid arthritis. Arthritis Rheum 1988;31:319.

physical examination by an examiner accustomed to discerning evidence of synovitis is often more sensitive than is radiography. Nevertheless, early radiographs of the hands and feet may be helpful both to establish the diagnosis and to identify cartilage and bone erosions. The presence of bone and cartilage destruction are important considerations when choosing medications that may modify the disease course and assessing the need for possible surgical intervention. Studies of early radiographic changes in RA reveal that a disproportionate degree of damage occurs in the first 2 years of the disease.[19]

In addition to positive RF at a relatively high or high titer in an individual with a clinical picture suggestive of RA, the patient generally demonstrates an elevated erythrocyte sedimentation rate and C-reactive protein.[20] If RA is active, normochromic normocytic anemia frequently is found, sometimes with thrombocytosis. These later laboratory features may correlate with disease activity and recede toward normal with disease-modifying treatments. Approximately 20 or 25% of RA patients have a positive antinuclear antibody.[21]

The American Rheumatism Association (American College of Rheumatology) classification criteria for RA (see Table 43–1), were developed as a research instrument but are helpful guidelines in making the diagnosis of RA. One must remember that RA patients sometimes fail to meet these criteria, particularly early in their disease course. The criteria are 91 to 94% sensitive and 89% specific for diagnosing patients with RA as opposed to controls with other rheumatic diseases.[22]

PROGNOSIS

The course of RA is variable, particularly due to the potential for fluctuating disease activity and a varying degree of ultimate joint deformity. More than 10 years after disease onset, more than 80% of patients show significant deformities, and 50% may be unable to work.[23] Predictors of a worse prognosis include female sex, the presence of high-titer RF, nodules, evidence of radiographic bone erosions at the time of initial evaluation, and sustained disease activity of more than 1 year's duration.[24] The most rapid period of joint damage generally occurs in the first 1 to 3 years of disease, although perhaps 15% of patients may have a remitting course that does not lead to major deformity. These later patients are more likely to be seronegative (RF negative). The median life expectancy of RA patients is shortened by 3 to 7 years.[25] Increased mortality is due to the disease itself or, often, to infection and gastrointestinal bleeding. Early death correlates with disease severity and duration, corticosteroid use, male sex, low level of formal education, and earlier age of onset. Prompt diagnosis and treatment with aggressive disease-modifying therapies within the first 3 months is often important, particularly in patients with rapidly destructive disease ("malignant RA").[26] In general, RA patients fare better when followed up by a rheumatologist throughout their disease course.[27] Early referral to a rheumatologist helps to avoid frequently encountered delays in the diagnosis of RA and to allow earlier initation of effective therapy.[28]

TREATMENT

No currently available therapeutic agents are curative; however, effective treatments often can deliver gratifying responses that can retard aspects of disease destruction and disability and improve the quality of life. Clinical experience and emerging research support the concept that a number of agents can alter the course of RA.[26] Most of these drugs have delayed onset of action and may require "bridging" with more rapid relievers of inflammation and pain, such as nonsteroidal anti-inflammatory drugs (NSAIDs) or corticosteroids. For the purpose of bridging therapy, synovitis often can be rendered tolerable with corticosteroid dosages of 5 to 15 mg/d; subsequently, the dosage of corticosteroid should be tapered as the chosen disease-modifying antirheumatic drug (DMARD) exerts its effects and ultimately replaces the corticosteroid. Corticosteroids and NSAIDs must not be considered effective treatment by themselves once the diagnosis of RA has been established. Ideally corticosteroid treatment should be avoided or limited to low doses for early control of disease symptoms, severe flares, and certain serious complications. Toxicity and increased complications from long-term corticosteroid use in RA are well known, particularly in dosages above 5 to 7.5 mg/d. A possible exception to avoidance of corticosteroids occurs in a small subset of patients with a form of elderly-onset rheumatoid arthritis, who demonstrate a marked response to low dosages of corticosteroids. In these patients, few, if any, other medications appear to be as effective.

Treatment with NSAIDs[29] alone is appropriate during an initial period of diagnostic uncertainty that sometimes occurs while sorting out whether a patient has RA or another arthritic condition, and NSAIDs are often used as an adjunct to disease-modifying medications. They are not, by themselves, adequate therapy once RA has been diagnosed. These agents have both analgesic and anti-inflammatory effects but do not alter disease progression. There are many NSAIDs, none proven to be more effective than are others, including aspirin. Some of these agents may present certain increased risk for toxicity. For example, aspirin may pose more significant risk of gastrointestinal toxicity, whereas NSAIDs with very long half-lives (eg, piroxicam) may be inappropriate for use by the elderly or for intermittent use. Inhibition of cyclooxygenase by NSAIDs in general may pose significantly increased risk to the kidneys in patients who are treated with a combination of diuretics and angiotensin converting enzyme inhibitors. Elderly patients are also more sensitive to NSAID side effects, including potential central nervous system effects such as mental confusion. The new highly selective cyclooxygenase-2 (COX-2) inhibitor NSAIDs, such as celecoxib (Celebrex) and rofecoxib (Vioxx), may offer significantly reduced capacity to injure gastroduodenal mucosa, based on theoretic factors and short-term studies; however, this needs to be proven during long-term trials and use.[30] These COX-2 selective agents do not inhibit platelet function and can be used with warfarin. All NSAIDs may cause renal complications.

Early rheumatologic consultation is strongly recommended to confirm the diagnosis of RA and to make an early decision on DMARD treatment before joints are damaged.[26] Generally, once RA is diagnosed, and particularly if periarticular bone erosions are present, methotrexate should be administered unless there are contraindications. Contraindications include significant alcohol use, evident hepatitis, significant pulmonary disease, or renal disease. The initial dose is typically 7.5 to 10 mg taken 1 day per week as a single dose or in divided doses over 24 hours. Methotrexate typically takes 4 to 6 weeks before any effect is noted and maximal effect takes 6 months or more. The starting dosage should be increased in 2.5-mg increments at 4 to 6 week intervals until a satisfactory result has been achieved or a dose of 20 mg/wk is reached. If patients fail to respond or do not tolerate higher oral dosages (usually due to gastrointestinal side effects), weekly intramuscular administration may improve the response and tolerability. Folic acid should be supplemented at a dosage of 1 mg/d with methotrexate. Patients treated with methotrexate require a relatively recent baseline chest radiography; baseline complete blood count, differential, and platelet counts; and liver and renal function tests, with follow-up blood testing performed every 4 to 8 weeks. Common side effects include mucositis (oral sores), gastrointestinal complaints, and mild alopecia. Mild elevations of alkaline phosphatase may occur, but significant persistent transaminase elevations or suppression of albumin synthesis (in a patient with RA under good control) are indications of liver toxicity. Pneumonitis is uncommon but can occur at any time at any dose level. Complaints of cough and shortness of breath need thorough evaluation.[31]

Alternatives to methotrexate historically have included intramuscular gold and azathioprine (Imuran).[31,32] Mild RA may be treated with sulfasalazine at a dosage of 1.5 to 3 g/d.[32] Gastrointestinal intolerance is common, and sulfasalazine should not be given to patients with glucose 6-phosphate dehydrogenase (G6PD) deficiency or sulfa allergy. Patients should be monitored for potential bone marrow suppression.[31] Hydroxychloroquine (Plaquenil) has also been used to treat mild RA, and both hydroxychloroquine and sulfasalazine have been combined with methotrexate for increased effect.[32] Myelosuppression (particularly leukopenia) must be monitored carefully in patients receiving combined methotrexate and sulfasalazine; generally laboratory tests should be performed every 4 weeks.[31] Treatment with hydroxychloroquine should be monitored by an ophthalmologist every 6 months to 1 year, although serious ophthalmologic side effects are rare.[31] Regular follow-up by a rheumatologist is recommended strongly for a patient treated with combined DMARD treatments.

Three recently approved DMARD treatments appear to offer significant new alternatives or additions. Leflunomide (Arava) appears to exert clinical responses and effects comparable to methotrexate, including preventing or slowing bone erosions. Leflunomide inhibits pyrimidine synthesis and appears to cause cell cycle arrest of stimulated lymphocytes that may decrease the autoimmune response without a significant incidence of opportunistic infection. Leflunomide side effects include diarrhea and gastrointestinal reactions, liver enzyme elevations, rash, hypertension, and reversible alopecia. The onset of effect generally is evident in the first 4 weeks.[33]

The second new agent is etanercept (Enbrel). Etanercept is a soluble TNF-α receptor fused to the Fc portion of human IgG1 that inhibits TNF-α-mediated proinflammatory effects. This agent requires twice-weekly 25-mg subcutaneous injection, but it often results in a rapid and excellent response beginning after a few injections, and is generally well tolerated.[34] Erythematous injection site reactions are the most common side effects. Combination treatment using methotrexate and etanercept is effective without apparent potentiation of known toxicities and with rapid and apparently sustained improvement over methotrexate alone.[35] Etanercept also has been shown to slow radiographically evident joint damage.[36]

The third new agent is infliximab (Remicade). Infliximab, like etanercept, is a TNF-α inhibitor, but it is a chimeric mouse-human monoclonal antibody composed of a high-affinity mouse antihuman TNF-α antibody variable region coupled to the constant regions of human IgG1κ. This chimeric monoclonal antibody neutralizes TNF-α. Unlike etanercept, infliximab does not also bind lymphotoxin. Because of the mouse origin of part of the infliximab antibody, patient-produced antichimeric (anti-infliximab) antibodies develop with repeated dosing. The frequency of these antichimeric antibodies decreases with methotrexate coadministration.[37] Because these antichimeric antibodies decrease the duration of response and may contribute to possible allergic reactions, current recommendations call for infliximab to be administered concomitantly with methotrexate. Infliximab is given by intravenous infusion starting at 3 mg/kg on weeks 0, 2, and 6, followed by maintenance dosing every 8 weeks. If the clinical response is incomplete or of insufficient duration, doses may be increased to 5 mg/kg to 10 mg/kg given every 8 weeks, or administered at a maximum of every 4 weeks.[38] The safety and efficacy of infliximab together with methotrexate has been demonstrated in a large clinical trial over 54 weeks, with better results than the methotrexate-only group, including significantly less

progression of radiographically evident joint damage. Infusion reactions, such as headache or nausea, are the most common side effects and may be ameliorated by pretreatment with acetaminophen and antihistamines and by slowing the infusion rate.

Anti-TNF-α treatment with either etanercept or infliximab raises concerns about possible increased frequency or severity of infections since studies in both humans and animals point to the importance of TNF-α in defense against infection.[39,40] In a human clinical trial of anti-TNF-α treatment for septic shock (in patients without RA), the TNF-α-inhibitor-treated group demonstrated increased mortality in patients infected with gram-positive organisms.[40] Despite these concerns, initial controlled trials of etanercept did not seem to show increased infectious complications.[34,35] Generally, patients in initial infliximab trials did not demonstrate a significantly higher rate of serious infections compared to that with methotrexate alone, but certain infections were seen in somewhat greater numbers (upper respiratory tract infections, sinusitis, and pharyngitis).[41] One particular infectious concern is latent tuberculosis reactivation. As of July 2001, over 270,000 patients have been treated with etanercept or infliximab worldwide.[42] (A high proportion of infliximab use has been in patients with Crohn's disease, another indicated use for this agent.) Mycobacterium tuberculosis (TB) infection has been reported in 82 infliximab-treated and 11 etanercept-treated patients worldwide.[42] (Eighty percent of the cases of TB in infliximab-treated patients were from outside the United States) Other opportunistic infections, including fungal and atypical mycobacterial infections, have also been reported.[42] There is concern among clinicians that these risks are class effects for anti-TNF agents, but so far only the infliximab package insert has been revised by Centocor, warning that TB and other opportunistic infections have been observed in infliximab-treated patients.[38] Clinicians should consider PPD skin testing in patients who will be or who are receiving infliximab. Clinicians should also be aware of the potential for anti-TNF treatment to suppress cardinal signs of infection such as fever or malaise. Treatment with anti-TNF agents should be held if significant infection is present, but the long half-life of these agents limits the practical effectiveness of treatment withdrawal in dealing with infection.

PREGNANCY AND BREAST-FEEDING

Some RA patients may tend to improve during pregnancy, but most of the improved patients relapse within 6 months post partum.[43] There has not been a consistently observed effect of oral contraceptives in the prevention or treatment of RA. There is no significant infertility in RA patients, and generally there are no increased fetal or maternal complications.

Aspirin and NSAIDs have been used in pregnancy. These medications cross the placenta and have resulted in fetal cutaneous and intracranial bleeding and premature closure of the ductus arteriosus. Maternal complications include increased peripartum bleeding, prolonged labor, and maternal anemia. Although best avoided entirely, aspirin and other NSAIDs have been used during the first two trimesters, but should particularly be avoided in the third trimester due to bleeding and hemorrhagic complications in mother and fetus, and the risk for pulmonary circulatory complications in the fetus.[44] When more aggressive treatment is needed during pregnancy, low-dose corticosteroids are preferred.

Nonsalicylate NSAIDs with short half-lives are compatible with breast-feeding in selected patients, but aspirin in anti-inflammatory doses is not. Aspirin is excreted into breast milk and can cause neonatal metabolic acidosis, bleeding, altered pulmonary circulation, and Reye's syndrome. Because NSAIDs displace bilirubin, they increase the risk of kernicterus.[44]

Corticosteroids can be used in pregnancy in low to moderate doses; prednisone or prednisolone are preferred since placental metabolism by 11-ß-dehydrogenase limits the amount of steroid delivered to the fetus. Intrauterine growth retardation and premature rupture of membranes are more frequent when corticosteroids are used in pregnancy. Exacerbation of maternal diabetes and hypertension may occur.[44]

Low to moderate doses of prednisone also appear safe to use while lactating, although breast-feeding should be avoided if high-dose corticosteroid are used for long periods (eg, 1 mg/kg/d), since 5 to 20% of the drug is excreted in milk. Patients should wait 4 hours after a corticosteroid dose before breast-feeding if the dose is greater than 20 mg.[44]

Methotrexate clearly increases the risk of birth defects, particularly during the first trimester. These include cleft palate, hydrocephalus, growth retardation, fetal death, and spontaneous abortions. The appropriate interval after discontinuing methotrexate before attempting conception is at least one ovulatory cycle, although longer intervals such as 4 to 6 months often are recommended. Males should wait 3 months due to methotrexate-induced decreased sperm count.[31] Small amounts of methotrexate are excreted in breast milk, and its use during lactation is contraindicated.

Sulfasalazine can be used during pregnancy without apparent risk of congenital malformations, but it should be avoided near term due to the increased risk of kernicterus.[44] When sulfasalazine is used in pregnancy, folic acid should be supplemented. Sulfasalazine is excreted in significant amounts in breast milk and should be avoided in breast-feeding women. Sulfasalazine apparently does not affect female fertility, although it may decrease sperm counts in men, requiring 2 to 3 months to return to normal.

Leflunomide cannot be taken during pregnancy or in women who may become pregnant. It has caused serious teratogenic effects in animals. A drug-elimination procedure must be followed using cholestyramine 8 g three times daily for 11 days before attempting to become pregnant. If the drug-elimination procedure is not used, it may take up to 2 years for the drug level to fall below minimal risk levels. Women of childbearing potential should be treated with the drug-elimination procedure after leflunomide use, even if pregnancy is not planned. Leflunomide should not be used by nursing mothers.[45]

Etanercept does not cause fetal or maternal toxicity in animals, but its use has not been studied in pregnant women (US Food and Drug Administration [FDA] category B drug). It is not known whether etanercept is excreted in human milk, or whether this protein product is absorbed after ingestion, but due to potential risk, it is recommended that it be discontinued in nursing mothers.[46]

Infliximab (Remicade) is also considered a pregnancy category B drug and should generally not be given to pregnant women. Infliximab does not cross-react with TNF-α in other species, so animal reproduction studies were not conducted with infliximab. Analogous antibodies for antimouse TNF-α did not cause maternal or embryonic toxicity or teratogenic effects in mice. The need for methotrexate use together with infliximab in RA precludes use of this treatment combination in pregnancy, given the clear teratogenic potential of methotrexate. The same warnings apply to the use of infliximab in nursing as for etanercept, and infliximab should generally be withdrawn during nursing.[38]

Hydroxychlorquine use in pregnancy is controversial. Most infants born to mothers exposed to chloroquine salts either for malaria prophylaxis or rheumatic disease appear normal. Nevertheless, hydroxychloroquine crosses the placenta and may accumulate in fetal tissues, particularly the eyes and

ears. Sensorineural hearing loss has been reported as a suspected fetal association, and hydroxychloroquine is listed as an FDA pregnancy category C drug. Although the benefits of hydroxychloroquine treatment during pregnancy in patients with severe manifestations of systemic lupus erythematosus may, in some circumstances, outweigh the risk, hydroxychloroquine's relatively modest effect in RA does not outweigh its possible risk to the fetus. If conception is planned, hydroxychloroquine should be stopped at least 2 months in advance. Hydroxychloroquine also is contraindicated in breast-feeding women due to its potential to accumulate in infant tissues.[44]

RESOURCES

Arthritis Foundation
1300 West Peachtree Street
Atlanta, Georgia 30309
Telephone: 1-800-283-7800 (Arthritis information for patients)
Web site: www.arthritis.org

The Arthritis Foundation provides patient and clinician information about rheumatoid arthritis, including information about support groups and clinical research.

National Institute of Arthritis and Musculoskeletal and Skin Diseases
31 Center Drive, MSC 2350
Building 31/Room 4C05
Bethesda, Maryland 20982-2350
Telephone: (301) 496-8188
Web site: www.nih.gov/niams

The NIAMS of the National Institutes of Health provides patient and clinician information about rheumatoid arthritis, as well as information about clinical research.

REFERENCES

1. Wolfe AM. The epidemiology of rheumatoid arthritis: a review. Bull Rheum Dis 1968;19:518–23.
2. Ahmed SA, Penhale WJ, Talal N. Sex hormones, immune responses, and autoimmune disease. Am J Pathol 1985;121:531–51.
3. Wiles N, Symmons DPM, Harrison B, et al. Estimating the incidence of rheumatoid arthritis: trying to hit a moving target? Arthritis Rheum 1999;42:1339–46.
4. Wordsworth P, Bell J. Polygenic susceptibility in rheumatoid arthritis. Ann Rheum Dis 1991;50:343–6.
5. Stastny P. Association of the B-cell alloantigen DRw4 with rheumatoid arthritis. N Engl J Med 1978;298:869–71.
6. Weyand CM, Hicok KC, Conn DL, et al. The influence of HLA-DRBl genes on disease severity in rheumatoid arthritis. Ann Intern Med 1992;117:801–6.
7. Firestein GS. Etiology and pathogenesis of rheumatoid arthritis. In: Kelley WN, et al, editors. Textbook of rheumatology. 5th ed. Philadelphia: W.B. Saunders Co; 1997. p. 851–97.
8. Breedweld FC. New insights in the pathogenesis of rheumatoid arthritis. J Rheumatol 1998;25 (Suppl 53):3–7.
9. Tighe H, Carson DA. Rheumatoid factors. In: Kelley WN, et al, editors. Textbook of rheumatology. 5th ed. Philadelphia: W.B. Saunders Co; 1997. p. 241–9.

10. Harris ED Jr. Clinical features of rheumatoid arthritis. In: Kelley WN, et al editors. Textbook of rheumatology. 5th ed. Philadelphia: W.B. Saunders Co; 1997. p. 898–932.

11. Brewerton DA. Hand deformities in rheumatoid disease. Ann Rheum Dis 1957;16:183.

12. Vidigal E, Jacoby R, Dixon A St J, et al. The foot in chronic rheumatoid arthritis. Ann Rheum Dis 1975; 34:292–7.

13. Hench PK, Reid RT, Reames PM. Dissecting popliteal cyst stimulating thrombophlebitis. Ann Intern Med 1966;64:1259–64.

14. Meijers KA, Cats A, Kremer HPH, et al. Cervical myelopathy in rheumatoid arthritis. Clin Exp Rheumatol 1984;2:239–45.

15. Delcambre B, Tomel AB, et al. Rheumatoid pleurisy. Rev Rheum 1980;47:621–9.

16. Carroll GJ, Thomas R, Phatouros C, et al. Incidence, prevalence and possible risk factors for pneumonitis in patients with rheumatoid arthritis receiving methotrexate. J Rheumatol 1994;21:51–4.

17. Bacon PA. Extra-articular rheumatoid arthritis. In: McCarty DJ, Kooperman WJ, eds. Arthritis and allied conditions. 12th ed. Philadelphia: Lea & Febiger, 1993. p. 811–40.

18. Jacoby RK, Jayson MI, Cosh JA. Onset, early stages and prognosis of rheumatoid arthritis: a clinical study of 100 patients with 11-year follow-up. Br Med J 1973;2:96–100.

19. Fuchs HA, Kaye JJ, Callahan LF, et al. Evidence of significant erosion in rheumatoid arthritis within the first 2 years of disease. J Rheumatol 1989;16:585–91.

20. Gabay G, Kushner I. Acute phase proteins and other systemic responses to inflammation. N Engl J Med 1999;340:448–54.

21. Baum J, Zwillich SM, Ziff M. Laboratory findings in rheumatoid arthritis. In: McCarty DJ, Kooperman WJ, editors. Arthritis and allied conditions. 12th ed. Philadelphia: Lea & Febiger; 1993. p. 841–60.

22. Arnett FC, Edworthy SM, Block DA, et al. The American Rheumatism Association 1987 revised criteria for the classification of rheumatoid arthritis. Arthritis Rheum 1988;31:315–24.

23. Yelin E, Henke C, Epstein W. The work dynamics of the person with rheumatoid arthritis. Arthritis Rheum 1987;30:507–12.

24. Sherrer YS, Bloch DA, Mitchell DM, et al. The development of disability in rheumatoid arthritis. Arthritis Rheum 1986;29:494–500.

25. Vandenbrouke JP, Hazevoet HM, Cats A. Survival and cause of death in rheumatoid arthritis: a 25 year prospective follow-up. J Rheumatol 1984;11:158–61.

26. Weinblatt ME. Rheumatoid arthritis: treat now, not later. Ann Intern Med 1996;124:773–4.

27. Ward MM, Leigh JP, Fries JF. Progression of function disability in patients with rheumatoid arthritis. Associations with rheumatology subspecialty care. Arch Intern Med 1993;153:2229–37.

28. Chan KW, Felson DT, Yood RA, Walker AM. The lag time between onset of symptoms and diagnosis of rheumatoid arthritis. Arthritis Rheum 1994; 37:814–20.

29. Clements PJ, Paulus HE. Clinical pharmacology for rheumatic diseases. In: Kelley WN, et al, editors. Textbook of rheumatology. 5th ed. Philadelphia: W.B. Saunders Co; 1997. p. 707–40.

30. Wolfe MM, Lichtenstein OR, Singh G. Medical progress: gastrointestinal toxicity of non-steroidal antiinflammatory drugs. N Engl J Med 1999;340: 1888–99.

31. American College of Rheumatology ad Hoc Committee on Clinical Guidelines. Guidelines for monitoring drug therapy in rheumatoid arthritis. Arthritis Rheum 1996;39:723–31.

32. Harris ED Jr. Treatment of rheumatoid arthritis. In: Kelley WN, et al, editors. Textbook of rheumatology. 5th ed. Philadelphia: W.B. Saunders Co; 1997. p. 933–50.

33. Rozman B. Clinical experience with leflunomide in rheumatoid arthritis. J Rheumatol 1998;25 Suppl 53:27–32.

34. Moreland LW, Schiff MH, Baumgartner SW, et al. Etanercept therapy in rheumatoid arthritis: a randomized, controlled trial. Ann Intern Med 1999; 130:478–86.

35. Weinblatt ME, Kremer JM, Bankhurst AD, et al. A trial of etanercept, a recombinant tumor necrosis factor receptor: Fc fusion protein, in patients with rheumatoid arthritis receiving methotrexate. N Engl J Med 1999;340:253–9.

36. Barthon JM, Martin RW, Fleischmann RM, et al. A comparison of etanercept and methotrexate in patients with early rheumatoid arthritis. N Engl J Med 2000;343:1586–93.

37. Maini RN, Breedveld FC, Kalden JR, et al. Therapeutic efficacy of multiple intravenous infusions of anti-tumor necrosis factor monoclonal antibody combined with low-dose weekly methotrexate in

rheumatoid arthritis. Arthritis Rheum 1998;41: 1552–63.

38. Centocor, Inc. Remicade (infliximab) prescribing information (package insert); revised 12/1/2000. Malvern: Centocor, Inc.; 2000.

39. Bazzoni F, Beutler B. The tumor necrosis factor ligand and receptor families. N Engl J Med 1996; 334:1717–25.

40. Fisher CJ Jr, Agosti JM, Opal SM, et al. Treatment of septic shock with tumor necrosis factor receptor: Fc fusion protein. N Engl J Med 1996;334:1697–1702.

41. Lipsky PE, van der Heijde DMFM, St Clair EW, et al. Infliximab and methotrexate in the treatment of rheumatoid arthritis. N Engl J Med 2000;343: 1594–602.

42. Cush JJ, Matteson EL. ACR hotline: FDA advisory committee reviews safety of TNF inhibitors. Atlanta: ACR Hotline, American College of Rheumatology; Sept. 2001.

43. Banett JH, Brennan P, Fiddler M, Silman AJ. Does rheumatoid arthritis remit during pregnancy and relapse postpartum? Arthritis Rheum 1999;42: 1219–27.

44. Soscia PN, Zurier RB. Drug therapy of rheumatic diseases during pregnancy. Bull Rheum Dis 1992; 41(2):1–3.

45. Hoechst Marion Roussel. Prescribing information (package insert) as of September 1998: Arava (leflunomide). Kansas City, (MO): Hoechst Marion Roussel Pharmaceutical Co.

46. Immunex and Wyeth-Ayerst. Enbrel (etanercept) prescribing information (package insert); issue date 11/1998. Seattle: Immunex Corporation; 1998.

44

SYSTEMIC LUPUS

ERYTHEMATOSUS

Alan H. Gorn, MD

Systemic lupus erythematosus (SLE) is an autoimmune disease characterized by multisystem inflammation and a relapsing course. Organ involvement in SLE may include skin, joints, muscle, serosas, lungs, kidney, heart, the blood elements and coagulation system, and the central and peripheral nervous systems. The potential of SLE to attack multiple organ systems results in a broad spectrum of possible clinical presentations varying in severity from merely nagging to catastrophic. Tissue damage in SLE results largely from tissue deposition of complement-fixing immune complexes and autoantibodies.

Systemic lupus erythematosus most typically presents in women between menarche and menopause, with a female-to-male preponderance of approximately 10:1. Before puberty and after menopause this female preponderance declines, perhaps approaching 3:1.[1] The prevalence of SLE in women of childbearing age suggests that sex steroid hormones or gonadotropin play an as-yet undefined role in the pathogenesis of SLE; however, the pathogenesis appears to result from an interplay of factors that include genetic predisposition and environmental factors as well. Among environmental factors, drug treatment history must be considered since drug-induced lupus may account for as many as 10% of lupus cases (often cases involving older patients and men) and is a reversible cause of disease.[2] Drug history also must be considered in evaluating patients with a positive antinuclear antibody test (ANA)—the most prevalent, but nonspecific, immunologic marker for SLE. Genetic factors are important in the pathogenesis of SLE.[3] Multiple genetic loci have been associated with the disease, suggesting that the co-inheritance of a number of

interacting loci are required for the disease phenotype. Approximately 10 to 12% of SLE patients have a first-degree relative with the disease. Dizygotic twins have a 2 to 9% concordance rate, compared with a 25 to 58% rate for monozygotic twins.[3] The current genetic evidence, including the results of these twin studies, leaves room for probable environmental factors in the triggering of disease expression.

The prevalence of SLE has been estimated at between 14.6 to 50.8 cases per 100,000. The incidence appears to be higher among certain ethnic or racial groups, with an increased incidence among Blacks and Hispanics, for example. Overall, an 80 to 90% survival rate at 10 years appears to be a reasonable estimate, with early deaths (less than 5 years from diagnosis) typically resulting from active SLE or infection, and late deaths from infection, premature vascular disease, and organ failure.[1,4]

PRESENTING SIGNS AND SYMPTOMS

Characteristically, patients with lupus may present with general symptoms that often are attributed initially to other causes, since, by themselves, many of these symptoms are not disease specific. Fatigue is the most common symptom and can reach debilitating proportions during flares of disease activity. Fever also may occur; typically it is of low grade but sometimes is a prominent feature. Since infection itself may instigate a flare in SLE activity, fever must never be taken for granted and must always trigger appropriate investigations for infection until evidence suggests otherwise. Many lupus patients are at increased risk for infection due to immunosuppressive treatments, or possibly from the disease itself. Weight loss is not usually prominent in SLE but can occur in severe disease.

Mild SLE comprises the majority of SLE cases in the primary care setting. In addition to malaise and fatigue, these patients may have rash, arthralgias, pleuritic pain, alopecia, and recurrent oral or nasal ulcers (most often painless). Complaints of migraines, Raynaud's phenomenon and decreased memory are relatively frequent. The rash may be over the malar region of the cheeks and the bridge of the nose ("butterfly rash"), and it tends to spare the nasolabial folds, in contrast to seborrheic dermatitis. Discoid lupus rashes (raised, irregularly outlined lesions with central scaling, atrophy, and scarring, often involving the scalp) may occur but are relatively uncommon in SLE (10 to 20% of patients). Conversely, most patients with discoid lupus skin disease do not have SLE. Patients with SLE may report macular or macular-papular eruptions over the cheeks or other areas after sun exposure (photosensitivity). Sun exposure (UV-B radiation in particular) also may precipitate a flare in systemic disease. Subtle mottled palmar and digital erythema or livedo reticularis rashes may occur (particularly in patients with the antiphospholipid antibody syndrome). Arthritis, often arthralgia and tenosynovitis, usually occurs without erosions or deformities and often without significant joint swelling. Leukopenia, lymphopenia, or a slightly decreased platelet count may occur in mild SLE. Immunologic studies should, on most occasions, be positive for ANA, which is more reliable if found at a titer of > 1:160. Additional serologic evidence such as anti-double-stranded deoxyribonucleic acid (anti-dsDNA) antibodies may be present, but "mild" SLE patients do not have significant renal, central nervous system (CNS), pulmonary, or hematologic disease.

In the persistent absence of a positive ANA result or other more specific SLE disease markers,[5] such as anti-Smith (Sm) antibody or anti-dsDNA, the diagnosis of SLE should be questioned. Using current techniques, an ANA is manifest by > 98% of lupus patients.[6] Conversely, a patient with a low-titer ANA result (eg, 1:40 or 1:80) without other convincing criteria should not be diagnosed as having SLE, particularly if other causes of a positive ANA result can be found (eg, thyroid disease, ANA-associated drug use history, chronic hepatitis, or another connective tissue disease). Management of all patients with SLE requires persistent monitoring for more severe manifestations of disease that may require aggressive treatment to preserve organ function or life.

Approximately 40% of patients with SLE develop renal disease.[7] The majority of patients with SLE have at least subclinical renal involvement, as seen in renal biopsy (if performed). Most often these pathologic findings are limited to mild mesangial changes without glomerulonephritis (GN). Typically renal disease is the result of immune-complex deposition with more serious disease secondary to subendothelium deposits in focal and diffuse proliferative GN, or subepithelial deposits in membranous GN.[8] Patients with renal disease may have any of the other clinical features of SLE as well as renal disease, but patients with high-titer dsDNA antibodies are at greatest risk of developing lupus nephritis, often in the setting of depressed serum C3 or C4 complement levels. Serum creatinine levels and even creatinine clearance do not initially reflect the potential renal damage. Keep in mind that even high "normal" range serum creatinine in a young woman is atypical in the normal population and may reflect the presence of subclinical nephritis in a patient with SLE. Due to the high incidence of renal involvement in SLE, patients should be treated effectively for even mild hypertension.

Patients with SLE should be monitored frequently with urine analysis and sedimentation checks at every visit to monitor for pyuria and hematuria, and, in particular, proteinuria and red cell casts. These findings, particularly the more active sediment changes, require renal biopsy to classify the type of involvement and the potential reversibility of the nephritis. Clinical renal function measures lag behind the disease and do not accurately reflect damage, although it may be reversible. Patients with SLE without evident renal disease 3 or more years after diagnosis probably have a reduced chance of developing significant renal disease. Active renal lesions that may require aggressive immunosuppressive treatment to avoid renal failure include glomerular necrosis, cellular epithelial crescents, interstitial inflammatory infiltrates, hyaline thrombi, and necrotizing vasculitis. Glomerular sclerosis, interstitial fibrosis, fibrous crescents, and tubular atrophy are not reversible with immunosuppression.

The nervous system is frequently involved in SLE.[9] As many as 80% of SLE patients demonstrate CNS abnormalities in diagnostic testing such as brain magnetic resonance imaging (MRI) and electroencephalography, or elevated cerebrospinal fluid (CSF) protein levels.[10] However, probably less than one-third of patients have severe neuropsychiatric manifestations. Serious CNS manifestations include seizures of any type, cerebral vascular accidents (CVA), Guillain-Barré-like syndromes, transverse myelitis, optic neuritis, organic brain syndromes, pseudotumor cerebri, and peripheral sensorimotor neuropathy. Mild cognitive dysfunction such as short-term memory deficit is frequent, particularly during flares in disease activity. Migraine headaches (often with somewhat atypical or incomplete migraine-like features) appear fairly commonly, sometimes associated with antiphospholipid antibodies and Raynaud's phenomenon. Cognitive defects from SLE may be defined or identified by neuropsychiatric testing. Depression and anxiety are common in lupus patients. Some neuropsychiatric manifestations may result from lupus complications involving other organ systems, such as CVA in the setting of arterial hypertension from renal disease, thromboembolic events associated with the antiphospholipid antibody syndrome, or embolization from Libman-Sacks endocarditis lesions. Iatrogenic complications also may result in neuropsychiatric problems, such as psychosis from corticosteroids or CNS infections from immunosuppression. Treatment with NSAIDs (eg, ibuprofen) may occasionally lead to aseptic meningitis in SLE patients.

Clearly, CNS events occur directly as the result of lupus activity but often present a diagnostic dilemma as to their cause. Diagnostic tests to rule out causes other than lupus (eg, infection) often are essential. An MRI is the most sensitive radiologic test for CNS lupus, revealing small, or occasionally large, high-intensity lesions on T2-weighted scans. Such findings are found in as many as 80% of SLE patients, but they can be quite nonspecific and are also found in many normal controls. A higher number of lesions (eg, > 5) may be more suggestive of SLE, and lupus-associated lesions are sometimes reversible. Abnormalities of CSF are present in up to 50% of patients with CSF lupus, particularly increased protein, mononuclear cells, and increased IgG synthesis.[10] Antineuronal antibodies and antiribosomal P antibodies have been associated with diffuse neuropsychiatric SLE.[11] Antiphospholipid antibodies also are associated with CNS lupus with-

out overt stroke, presumably by perturbating microvascular coagulation and by producing reactive endothelial hyperplasia.[12] The outcome and treatment of neuropsychiatric SLE varies with the nature of the CNS lesion. Severe focal lesions may require high doses of corticosteroids, whereas seizures generally respond primarily to antiseizure medications. Thromboembolic events associated with antiphospholipid antibodies require chronic anticoagulation. Cognitive impairment or even psychosis may, at times, respond to high doses of corticosteroids during flares, but many times do not. Relatively short trials of high-dose corticosteroids are sometimes tried for these later symptoms, but if they are ineffective, they should be withdrawn.

Hematologic manifestations of SLE commonly include anemia of chronic disease, which may fluctuate with disease activity. Leukopenia, thrombocytopenia, and lymphopenia constitute potential criteria for the diagnosis of SLE. A positive Coomb's test for hemolytic anemia also is included as a lupus diagnostic criterion, but hemolytic anemia occurs in a relatively small proportion of lupus patients. Lymphopenia accounts for much of the leukopenia seen in SLE and apparently does not result in recurrent infection. Severe thrombocytopenia leading to bleeding complications occurs and requires treatment, usually in the form of high-dose corticosteroids, sometimes with the use of intravenous γ-globulin, or splenectomy in unresponsive cases.

Thrombocytopenia also may occur in the setting of the antiphospholipid (anticardiolipin) antibody syndrome in SLE or in patients who may have SLE-like disease. The presence of anticardiolipin antibodies accounts for the presence of a false-positive Venereal Disease Research Laboratory (VDRL) or rapid plasma reagin (RPR) test for syphilis in some patients with SLE. The VDRL and RPR tests are relatively insensitive tests for the presence of lupus-associated antiphospholipid antibodies; however, the presence of these false-positive tests were identified as disease criteria before the widespread use of more sensitive and specific tests for antiphospholipid antibodies, or the use of certain indirect tests for these antibodies in the form of "lupus anticoagulant" testing such as the dilute Russell viper venom test (DRVVT). The term "lupus anticoagulant" is a misnomer based on the ability of such antibodies to produce an in vitro artifactual elevation of partial thromboplastin time (PTT) testing. The usual clinical manifestation of these anticoagulants is not bleeding (despite possible elevated PTT tests); it is thrombosis. The PTT test is a relatively insensitive test for lupus anticoagulant, however, and such antibodies can exist with normal range PTT testing. No single test for lupus anticoagulant detects all such antibodies due to the heterogeneity and polyclonality of lupus anticoagulants in different patients.[13] Other relevant laboratory tests for this condition are antiphospholipid antibodies directed against B_2 glycoprotein I. These latter antibodies, in particular, may adhere to endothelium and provoke a prothrombotic surface. Clinical conditions associated with antiphospholipid antibodies, in addition to thromboembolic disease and thrombocytopenia, include recurrent fetal loss and valvular heart disease (Libman-Sacks endocarditis). Only rarely, in the presence of antibodies to clotting factors, or in association with hypoprothrombinemia or severe thrombocytopenia, does hemorrhagic disease occur in the presence of antiphospholipid antibodies. Clotting syndromes associated with these antibodies are treated with indefinite anticoagulation.

Cardiopulmonary SLE manifestations commonly include pleuritis and pericarditis. Cardiac tamponade and constrictive pericarditis are rare. Pleural effusions are a relatively common manifestation, and lupus pneumonitis may cause fever, dyspnea, cough, and pulmonary infiltrates or atelectasis that responds to corticosteroids once infectious causes for pulmonary infiltrates have been ruled out. Pleural fluid in SLE is typically an exudate with mononuclear cells predominating later in the course of disease. Lupus erythematosus cells (polymorphonuclear neutrophil leukocytes with phagocytized nuclei that have been opsinogenized by antinuclear antibodies) are found frequently in lupus pleural effusions, if sought. Pulmonary hemorrhage with hemoptysis occurs infrequently but can be severe and life threatening. Chronic interstitial lung disease and pulmonary hypertension occur in SLE rarely. Recurrent pulmonary embolism associated with antiphospholipid antibodies also may lead to pulmonary disease and pulmonary hypertension. Libman-Sacks endocarditis only rarely leads to valvular insufficiency (usually aortic or mitral). Women with SLE do have an appreciably increased incidence of artherosclerosis, congestive heart failure, and coro-

nary artery disease, and they occasionally present with myocardial infarction at young ages.[14,15]

Gastrointestinal manifestations of lupus may result commonly from peritoneal serositis presenting as abdominal pain, nausea, and vague abdominal discomfort. Vasculitis of the intestine can occur more rarely with similar but more severe symptoms and is a serious problem that may lead to bowel infarction.[16] Mesenteric thrombosis and Budd-Chiari syndrome have occurred in patients with antiphospholipid antibodies.[17] Pancreatitis or elevations in liver enzymes can occur in lupus, although both liver function test abnormalities and pancreatitis are probably associated more frequently with therapies such as corticosteroids, azathiaprine, and NSAIDs.

Cutaneous disease is a hallmark of SLE, but in some patients cutaneous disease is minimal or absent.[18] The malar (butterfly) rash is not seen in all lupus patients and can be mistaken for seborrheic dermatitis or rosacea. It does not scar. Discoid lupus erythematosus (DLE) lesions are distinct, occurring as single or multiple indurated plaques, often over the face, scalp and ears, and associated with epidermal atrophy, scarring and follicular plugging with both hypo- and hyperpigmented areas. In the hair, DLE may produce sites of scarring alopecia. Patients with DLE may have lesions below the neck or, occasionally, lesions involving the pannus (panniculitis, also termed "lupus profundus"). Most patients with DLE do not have SLE, and most are ANA negative. Only 15 to 20% of SLE patients develop DLE. A subset of SLE patients, typically with high titers of SS-A (Ro) antibodies, have subacute cutaneous lupus erythematosus (SCLE) and demonstrate extreme photosensitivity with papulosquamous, psoriasiform, or polycyclic/annular skin lesions that usually do not scar, although they may become hyperpigmented.[19]

Musculoskeletal complaints, particularly arthritis or arthralgias, are the most commonly occurring symptoms and presenting complaints in patients with SLE. The most common joint manifestations are stiffness and pain, often in a waxing-and waning-pattern that includes morning stiffness. Commonly, the wrists and hands are involved, but there is usually no overt joint deformity or even localized swelling. A subset of patients may develop synovial thickening resembling rheumatoid arthritis, rarely with periarticular erosions. Hand deformities in such patients can include ulnar deviation and subluxation, and "swan neck" deformities, but these deformities usually are reducible, unlike those seen in patients with rheumatoid arthritis. Such hand deformities in SLE patients have been termed "Jaccoud's arthropathy"; function and grip strength usually are preserved. Tenosynovitis can lead to carpal tunnel syndrome and other entrapment neuropathies in SLE.

Generalized myalgia is a common complaint during lupus flares, but true inflammatory myositis occurs in only 5 to 11% of patients.[20] Elevated serum creatinine phosphokinase (CPK), abnormal electromyographic results, and muscle biopsies reveal true myositis, which may present as proximal weakness. Myositis in SLE is generally corticosteroid responsive.

Avascular necrosis (AVN) of bone (ischemic or aseptic necrosis of bone) may occur in up to 5% of SLE patients and causes necrosis of subchondral bone leading to secondary osteoarthritis or joint destruction.[20] Although small vessel vasculopathy in SLE patients may play a role, high-dose corticosteroid treatment is implicated in most cases. Avascular necrosis may present with dull aching pain localizing to the hip or knee, for example, sometimes with joint effusion. It may occur months or years after corticosteroid treatment. Occasionally AVN may be polyarticular. Early AVN, or small AVN lesions, may not show up on plain radiographs. An MRI of the involved joint is the most sensitive and specific diagnostic test when plain radiographs show negative findings. Significant AVN lesions may require surgical orthopedic intervention, including joint replacement.

Drug-induced lupus can be the cause of a reversible syndrome with features of SLE. Use of procainamide or hydralazine is by far the most frequent cause, but many medications have been associated with drug-induced lupus, including isoniazid, chlorpromazine, ß-blockers, minocycline, methyldopa, and antiepileptic medications.[21] Positive ANA test results are more common than are clinical symptoms of drug-induced lupus after exposure to these and certain other medications. Patients with drug-induced lupus may develop ANAs to histones,[22] but such antibodies are also relatively frequent in patients with SLE.[23] The most common manifestations of drug-induced lupus are arthralgias or arthritis, pleuritis or pericarditis, nonspecific rashes, and leukopenia. Renal and CNS disease typically do not occur in drug-induced lupus, and many patients fail to meet full American College of Rheumatology (ACR) classification criteria for SLE. Most symptoms of drug-induced lupus improve within weeks or a few months of discontinuing the drug; occasionally a short course of corticosteroids is required for more severe manifestations. Positive ANA results may persist for years after drug exposure. Drugs that can cause drug-induced lupus generally are not contraindicated in idiopathic/spontaneous SLE patients.

DIAGNOSIS

The diagnosis of SLE is made primarily on clinical grounds with the support of laboratory tests such as antinuclear antibodies (ANA) that are obtained when there is reasonable suspicion of disease; ANA tests are not for general screening of patients with low-pretest probability of the disease.

The American Rheumatism Association (now the American College of Rheumatology) criteria for classification of SLE (Table 44–1) were devised to identify patients for clinical studies.[24] In common practice these criteria often are used as guidelines for the clinical diagnosis of SLE. When 4 of 11 of these criteria are present, they are 96% sensitive and specific when evaluated against the patient database from which they were devised.[24] In practice the sensitivity and specificity of these criteria are probably somewhat lower. It should be remembered that these criteria may be satisfied over time, and that 4 manifestations need not be present at the same time. Many patients who have lupus do not demonstrate 4 of 11 active criteria at the time of presentation, either initially or when presenting subsequently with a flare. The diagnosis also is established occasionally with fewer than 4 criteria ever being present. For example, a patient with positive ANA results, dsDNA antibodies, and red cell casts in the urine sediment (nephritis) can be confidently diagnosed as having SLE without any additional criteria. The term "lupus-like syndrome" is sometimes reserved for a patient who does not meet a full 4 of 11 criteria. Of course, alternative diagnoses that can mimic SLE must be ruled out. These often include conditions that may present with arthritis and a rash, such as parvovirus B19 infection, acute infectious mononucleosis, subacute bacterial endocarditis, and acute or chronic active hepatitis—all of which may result in positive ANA test results.

TABLE 44–1. The 1982 American Rheumatism Association Criteria for Classification of Systemic Lupus Erythematosus[*]

1. Malar rash—fixed malar erythema, flat or raised
2. Discoid rash—erythematous raised patches with adherent keratotic scaling and follicular plugging; atrophic scarring may occur
3. Photosensitivity—an unusual skin rash reaction to sunlight
4. Oral ulcers—oral and/or nasopharyngeal ulcers (usually painless), observed by physician
5. Arthritis—nonerosive arthritis involving two or more peripheral joints, characterized by tenderness, swelling, or effusion
6. Serositis—pleuritis or pericarditis documented by ECG, rub, or pericardial effusion
7. Renal disorder—proteinuria > 0.5 g/d or > 3+, or cellular casts
8. Neurologic disorder—seizures without other cause, or psychosis without other cause
9. Hematologic disorder—hemolytic anemia or leukopenia (< 4,000/mm³ on ≥ 2 occasions) or lymphopenia (< 1,500/mm³ on ≥ 2 occasions) or thrombocytopenia (< 100,000/mm³ in the absence of offending drugs)
10. Immunologic disorder—positive LE cell preparation or anti-dsDNA or anti-Sm antibodies or false-positive VDRL test
11. Antinuclear antibodies—an abnormal titer of ANAs by immunofluorescence or an equivalent assay at any point in time in the absence of drugs known to induce ANAs

[*]For identifying patients in clinical studies, a patient is said to have systemic lupus erythematosus if any four or more of these criteria are present at any time during the course of disease.
ECG = electrocardiography; LE = lupus erythematosus; dsDNA = double-stranded deoxyribonucleic acid; Sm = Smith; VDRL = Venereal Disease Research Laboratory; ANA = antinuclear antibody.
Reproduced with permission from Tan EM, Cohen AS, Fries, JF, et al. Special article: the 1982 revised criteria for the classification of systemic lupus erythematosus. Arthritis Rheum 1982;25:1274.

TREATMENT

The goal of treatment in SLE[25] is to suppress acute severe flare-ups in disease activity, particularly organ- or life-threatening disease, and to suppress more general symptoms to a tolerable degree. In mild SLE, this often requires a reasonable trade-off juxtaposing symptom suppression against medication toxicity. Many lupus manifestations are quite responsive to corticosteroids, but mild disease activity that is not life threatening or disabling, such as arthralgias, fatigue, and relatively mild serositis, may improve with use of nonsteroidal anti-inflammatory drugs and hydroxychloroquine, sparing glucocorticoid toxicity. Corticosteroid toxicity is both dose and treatment duration dependent. Life-threatening or disabling manifestations of SLE that are responsive to immunosuppression include active lupus nephritis, severe pleuropulmonary disease, severe cytopenias, severe systemic manifestations (prolonged fever, weight loss, severe arthritis), and CNS disease (eg, cerebritis). These presentations may require decisive treatment with moderately high or high dosages of glucocorticoids (≥ 1 to 2 mg/kg/d),

sometimes in divided dosages. Certain disease manifestations, such as active nephritis, require the addition of cytotoxic drugs (eg, cyclophosphamide or azathioprine) for effective control. At times, more mild but refractory disease, such as prominent joint pain, fatigue, or serositis, may reasonably require corticosteroids in lower dosages, in the range of 10 to 30 mg/d.

Although SLE activity often responds rapidly to appropriate doses of corticosteroids, a frequently observed characteristic of SLE is the flares that can occur if steroids are tapered too rapidly. This is often true when dosages are tapered to less than approximately 20 mg/d, but it varies from patient to patient. At times a level is found at which a decrease of 1 or 2 mg/d precipitates a flare. More often, a larger decrement of 5 or 10 mg/d, particularly in the range below 20 mg/d, leads to a flare. For this reason, some patients require dosage decreases of only 1 or 2 mg /d at intervals of 1 to 2 weeks after reaching dosages of approximately 20 mg/d. Likewise, many patients with SLE may tolerate "dose pack" tapers poorly, flaring rapidly as the corticosteroid dosage is inflexibly tapered according to the instructions of these prepackaged products. This cycle of suppression and flare may be repeated if the clinician is unaware of the potential need to taper corticosteroids slowly in some patients. Many patients with SLE do not tolerate every-other-day corticosteroid tapering schedules and flare on the day off corticosteroids. Despite these caveats, corticosteroids must always be tapered as disease activity permits to avoid undue toxicity, as no chronic dose of corticosteroids is truly preventive or curative.

Other treatment may be employed to avoid or minimize corticosteroid use and to improve outcome. Lupus nephritis patients are significantly less likely to develop renal failure when cyclophosphamide is added to corticosteroid treatment, with azathioprine (and occasionally other drugs) used as second-line treatment. Other manifestations may not respond well, or even at all, to immunosuppression. The presence of antiphospholipid antibodies associated with thromboembolic disease requires anticoagulation, seizures require antiseizure medications, and psychoactive drugs are often more effective than is immunosuppression for other neuropsychiatric manifestations of disease. Low-dose methotrexate has been used to spare corticosteroid use in lupus patients with severe arthritis. Hydroxychloroquine treatment is discussed below.

PREVENTION AND SCREENING

Preventive measures include the need to avoid sun exposure or other sources of ultraviolet light by wearing a hat, long-sleeved clothes, and high-potency sun block (eg, SPF 30). Hydroxychloroquine should strongly be considered in most patients with SLE; it is particularly beneficial for skin and joint disease, serositis, and fatigue.[26] Hydroxychloroquine is a slow-acting treatment, and little benefit may be expected for 6 weeks to 3 months or more after initiating treatment. Likewise, disease flares frequently occur 1 to 3 months after stopping hydroxychloroquine. Dosages are generally 200 mg twice per day, sometimes decreasing to 200 mg once per day after a couple years of treatment. Patient should receive a baseline ophthalmologic examination which should be repeated every 6 to 12 months to monitor possible, but uncommon, ophthalmologic toxicity. Patients with SLE should be cautioned to avoid becoming over fatigued. Precautions should be taken to minimize corticosteroid toxicity, such as the addition of a calcium supplement (1,000 to 1,500 mg/d), often with vitamin D supplement (eg, 400 to 800 IU of D_3 per day).[27] At doses of more than 5 mg/d of prednisone or an equivalent, additional osteoporosis preventive treatment should be strongly considered; alendronate (Fosamax) or nasal calcitonin (Miacalcin) may be added to prevent or diminish corticosteroid-associated osteoporosis.

If disease activity is stable, the benefits of certain vaccinations such as pneumococcal and influenza vaccines outweigh theoretic risks of inducing disease flares or postvaccination syndromes and should be given. Immunotherapy (allergy shots) is not recommended for SLE patients.[28] The use of estrogen has remained somewhat controversial in SLE. Although estrogen in birth control pills may slightly increase the risk of SLE activity, this must be balanced against a likely much higher risk of pregnancy exacerbating SLE. However, estrogen-containing birth control preparations generally should not be a first-choice birth control method in SLE patients. Perimenopausal and postmenopausal use of estrogen appears somewhat less likely to aggravate SLE, and the general health benefits of such hormone replacement may perhaps outweigh the risk.[28] In both indications, estrogen should be administered at the lowest effective dose and should be avoided in the setting of significant titers of antiphospholipid antibodies to avoid additional risk for thromboembolic disease.

An ANA test should not be used to screen patients for SLE without significant pretest probability of disease.

PREGNANCY AND BREAST-FEEDING

Lupus patients generally do not suffer from decreased fertility, although certain medications used in lupus treatment significantly affect fertility. Cyclophosphamide is associated with ovarian failure in about 25% of patients. Spontaneous abortions and stillbirths are clearly more frequent in SLE.[29,30] Normal pregnant women may suffer fetal loss approximately 10% of the time, whereas fetal loss may occur with an incidence of about 30 to 40% in patients with SLE. Active renal disease clearly is associated with increased frequency of fetal loss.[29,30] Pregnant SLE patients also carry increased risk of prematurity and intrauterine growth retardation.[30]

Patients with antiphospholipid antibodies are more likely to have spontaneous abortions, particularly in the second trimester. If patients with antiphospholipid antibodies have suffered recurrent fetal loss, options include daily subcutaneous heparin or daily low-dose aspirin until the last month of pregnancy.[13,30] The combination of prednisone and aspirin has been used, although this approach has been disappointing in studies.[31] Maternal SS-A (Ro) antibodies transfer across the placenta and may react with fetal antigen present in skin or the cardiac conduction system, leading to the neonatal lupus syndrome. Fortunately, only perhaps 3 to 7% of infants born to antiSS-A (Ro) antibody–positive mothers develop heart block, with a higher risk correlating with a high titer of antibody.[30]

Lupus pregnancy is a "high risk" pregnancy. Disease activity may flare during pregnancy, particularly early in pregnancy, or after delivery.[32] Also, pregnancy-related findings may be mistaken for SLE activity (eg, malar erythema, alopecia, hypertension, thrombocytopenia). Poorly controlled SLE at the time of pregnancy (particularly active nephritis) portends a significant risk of maternal and fetal complications.[30,32] A patient with active or recently active lupus should be advised to avoid pregnancy. Ideally a patient should demonstrate quiescent SLE for 6 months or more before conception. Lupus activity during pregnancy is best managed by low doses of corticosteroids, or high-dose corticosteroids for lupus nephritis. Prednisone is used as it is inactivated by placental enzymes (Chapter 43,

"Rheumatoid Arthritis"). Pregnant lupus patients should be followed up by an obstetrician and a rheumatologist, perhaps as often as alternating 2-week intervals during the last trimester. A pregnant lupus patient who has received significant periods of systemic corticosteroid treatment in the 1 to 2-year period before the due date may be adrenal insufficient and may need stress doses of corticosteroids at the time of delivery. Careful, frequent rheumatologic follow-up should continue for at least 3 months post partum due to increased risk of flare after delivery. Despite all this, most patients with SLE have successful pregnancies and deliver normal infants.

Hydroxychloroquine for mild SLE typically is withdrawn at least 2 months prior to pregnancy, although some experts consider continuing its use in patients at a high risk for serious flares, after informing the patient of the existence of some inconclusive reports of congenital abnormalities associated with its use during pregnancy.[32] Nevertheless, hydroxychloroquine deposits in fetal tissues and is listed by the US Food and Drug Administration as a pregnancy category C drug (see Chapter 43, "Rheumatoid Arthritis"), and it generally is discontinued in pregnancy. The use of NSAIDs in pregnancy is discussed in Chapter 43 in the section on the treatment of rheumatoid arthritis; NSAIDs may be similarly used in SLE patients during the first two trimesters, although prednisone is preferred. The use of antirheumatic drugs in breast-feeding also is discussed in Chapter 43.

RESOURCES

Arthritis Foundation
1300 West Peachtree Street
Atlanta, Georgia 30309
Telephone: 1-800-283-7800 (Arthritis information for patients)
Web site: www.arthritis.org

The Arthritis Foundation provides patient and clinician information about lupus, including information on support groups and clinical research.

REFERENCES

1. Hochberg MC. The epidemiology of systemic lupus erythematosus. In: Wallace DJ, Hahn BH, editors. Dubois' lupus erythematosus. 5th ed. Baltimore: Williams & Wilkins; 1997. p. 49–65.

2. Cush JJ, Goldings EA. Drug induced lupus: clinical spectrum and pathogenesis. Am J Med Sci 1985;290:36–45.

3. Tan FK, Arnett FC. The genetics of lupus. Curr Opin Rheumatol 1998;10:399–408.

RESOURCES (continued)

National Institute of Arthritis and Musculoskeletal and Skin Diseases
31 Center Drive, MSC 2350
Building 31/Room 4C05
Bethesda, Maryland 20982-2350
Telephone: (301) 496-8188
Web site: www.nih.gov/niams

The NIAMs of the National Institutes of Health provides patient and clinician information about lupus, as well as information about clinical research.

Lupus Foundation of America
4 Research Place, Suite 180
Rockville, Maryland 20850-3226
Telephone: (301) 670-9292
Web site: www.lupus.org

The Lupus Foundation of America maintains a network of local chapters throughout the United States, providing information and support for patients with lupus.

---

4. Uramoto KM, Clement MJ, Thumboo J, et al. Trends in the incidence and mortality of systemic lupus erythematosus, 1950–1992. Arthritis Rheum 1999; 42:46–50.

5. Cabral AR, Alarcon-Segovia D. Autoantibodies in systemic lupus erthythematosus. Curr Opin Rheumatol 1998;10:409–16.

6. Reichlin R, Harley JB. Antinuclear antibodies: an overview. In: Wallace DJ, Hahn BH, editors. Dubois' lupus erythematosus. 5th ed. Baltimore: Williams & Wilkins; 1997. p. 397–405.

7. Wallace DJ, Hahn BH, Klippel JH. Lupus nephritis. In: Wallace DJ, Hahn BH, editors. Dubois' lupus erythematosus. 5th ed. Baltimore: Williams & Wilkins; 1997. p. 1053–65.

8. Wener MH, Mannik M, Schwartz MM. Relationship between renal pathology and the size of circulating immune complexes in patients with systemic lupus erythematosus. Medicine 1987;66:85–97.

9. Wallace DJ, Metzger AL. Systemic lupus erythematosus and the nervous system. In: Wallace DJ, Hahn BH, editors. Dubois' lupus erythematosus. 5th ed. Baltimore: Williams & Wilkins; 1997. p. 723–54.

10. West SG, Emlen W, Wener MH, Kotzin BL. Neuropsychiatric lupus erythematosus: a 10-year prospective study on the value of diagnostic tests. Am J Med 1995;99:153–63.

11. Isshi K, Hirohata S. Differential roles of the anti-ribosomal P antibody and antineuronal antibody in the pathogenesis of central nervous system involvement in systemic lupus erythematosus. Arthritis Rheum 1998;41:1819–27.

12. Toubi E, Khamashta MA, Panarra A, et al. Association of antiphospholipid antibodies with central nervous system disease in systemic lupus erythematosus. Am J Med 1995;99:397–401.

13. Petri M. 1998 update on antiphospholipid antibodies. Curr Opin Rheumatol 1998;10:426–30.

14. Ward MM. Premature morbidity from cardiovascular and cerebrovascular disease in women with systemic lupus erythematosus. Arthritis Rheum 1999; 42:338–46.

15. Manzi S, Selzer F, Sutton-Tyrell K, et al. Prevalence and risk factors of carotid plaque in women with systemic lupus erythematosus. Arthritis Rheum 1999; 42:51–60.

16. Zizic TM, Classen JN, Stevens MB. Acute abdominal complications of systemic lupus erythematosus and polyarteritis nodosa. Am J Med 1982;73:525–31.

17. Simon LS, Gorn AH. A 38-year-old woman with fever, skin lesions, thrombocytopenia, and venous thromboses. Case records of the Massachusetts General Hospital. Scully RE, editor. N Engl J Med 1990;322:754–69.

18. Wallace DJ. Cutaneous and cutaneovascular manifestations of systemic lupus erythematosus. In: Wallace DJ, Hahn BH, editors. Dubois' lupus erythematosus. 5th ed. Baltimore: Williams & Wilkins; 1997. p. 693–721.

19. Callen J, Klein J. Subacute cutaneous lupus erythematosus: clinical, serologic, immunogenetic, and therapeutic considerations in seventy-two patients. Arthritis Rheum 1988;31:1007–13.

20. Wallace DJ. The musculoskeletal system. In: Wallace DJ, Hahn BH, editors. Dubois' lupus erythematosus. 5th ed. Baltimore: Williams & Wilkins; 1997. p. 635–51.

21. Rubin RL. Drug induced lupus. In: Wallace DJ, Hahn BH, editors. Dubois' lupus erythematosus. 5th ed. Baltimore: Williams & Wilkins; 1997. p. 871–901.

22. Craft JE, Radding JA, Harding MW, et al. Autoantigenic histone epitopes: a comparison between procainamide and hydrolazine-induced lupus. Arthritis Rheum 1987;30:689–94.

23. Hardin JA, Thomas JO. Antibodies to histones in systemic lupus erythematosus: localization of prominent autoantigens on histones H1 and H2B. Proc Natl Acad Sci U S A 1983;80:7410–4.

24. Tan EM, Cohen AS, Fries JF, et al. Special article: the 1982 revised criteria for the classification of systemic lupus erythematosus. Arthritis Rheum 1982;25:1271–7.

25. Godfrey T, Khamashta MA, Hughes GRV. Therapeutic advances in systemic lupus erythematosus. Curr Opin Rheumatol 1998;10:435–41.

26. Canadian Hydroxychloroquine Study Group. A randomized study of the effect of withdrawing hydroxychloroquine sulfate in systemic lupus erythematosus. N Engl J Med 1991;324:150–4.

27. Buckley LM, Leib ES, Cartularo KS, et al. Calcium and vitamin D3 supplementation prevents bone loss in the spine secondary to low dose corticosteroids in patients with rheumatoid arthritis. Ann Intern Med 1996;125:961–8.

28. Wallace DJ, Hahn BH. Adjunctive measures and issues: allergies, antibiotics, vaccines, hormones, and osteoporosis. In: Wallace DJ, Hahn BH, editors. Dubois' lupus erythematosus. 5th ed. Baltimore: Williams & Wilkins; 1997. p. 1203–12.

29. Rahman P, Gladman DD, Urowitz M. Clinical predictors of fetal outcome in systemic lupus erythematosus. J Rheumatol 1998;25:1526–30.

30. Kitridou C. The fetus in systemic lupus erythematosus. In: Wallace DJ, Hahn BH, editors. Dubois' lupus erythematosus. 5th ed. Baltimore: Williams & Wilkins; 1997. p. 1003–21.

31. Laskin CA, Bombardier C, Hannah ME, et al. Prednisone and aspirin in women with autoantibodies and unexplained recurrent fetal loss. N Engl J Med 1997;337:148–53.

32. Kitridou RC. The mother in systemic lupus erythematosus. In: Wallace DJ, Hahn BH, editors. Dubois' lupus erythematosus. 5th ed. Baltimore: Williams & Wilkins; 1997. p. 967–1002.

45

SJÖGREN'S SYNDROME AND RAYNAUD'S PHENOMENON

Alan H. Gorn, MD

SJÖGREN'S SYNDROME

Sjögren's syndrome (SS) is characterized by dry eyes and dry mouth resulting from lymphocytic infiltrate and destruction of the lacrimal and salivary exocrine glands. Primary SS often includes systemic symptoms such as arthralgias, fatigue, Raynaud's phenomenon, or small vessel vasculitis. Secondary SS accompanies the diagnosis of another differentiated connective tissue disease such as rheumatoid arthritis, systemic lupus erythematosus, or scleroderma. Chronic infections such as human immunodeficiency virus[1] and hepatitis C[2] also are associated with secondary SS. Sjögren's syndrome predominantly affects women of middle age and has a female-to-male ratio of 9:1.[3] The disease is considered relatively common with most cases going undiagnosed. Approximately 20% of rheumatoid arthritis patients have secondary SS. Patients with SS often demonstrate autoantibodies such as rheumatoid factors, antinuclear antibodies, and SS-A (Ro) and SS-B (La). The presence of SS-A and SS-B antibodies in particular is associated with earlier onset and increased severity, including salivary gland enlargement and extraglandular involvement such as lymphadenopathy and small vessel vasculities.[4] A small proportion of Sjögren's patients develop malignant lymphoma, sometimes preceded by benign lymphomatous growths designated as pseudolymphomas.[5] (HLA) genotypes for HLA-B8, -DR3, and -DRw52 are prevalent in primary SS patients.[6]

Presenting Signs and Symptoms

The majority of patients with SS complain of dry eyes and/or dry mouth and have a prolonged slowly progressive disease course. Symptoms may be expressed (or elicited) as difficulty in swallowing dry foods, increased dental caries, or increasing difficulty in wearing dentures. Patients may show dry mouth or an increase in the viscosity of oral secretions resulting in a sticky oral mucosa and increased oral erythema. Symptoms may worsen due to an increased incidence of oral candidiasis, which sometimes manifests as an exacerbation in symptoms of oral discomfort or "burning" and erythema, with only minimal plaque and sometimes angular cheilitis.[7] Sinusitis and bronchitis are more frequent. Eyes may feel gritty or film covered. Eye irritation is exacerbated easily by a dry environment. Corneal ulcerations and opacifications may occur later in the course of disease. Nasal and vaginal dryness are also significant complaints, but usually need to be elicited. Parotid gland enlargement may be present on examination or imaging studies, as well as lymphadenopathy and thyroid enlargement. Arthralgias or arthritis, which is usually nonerosive and nondeforming, may be present, or the patient may suffer from fibromyalgia symptoms.[4] Neurologic manifestations occur, including symmetric peripheral neuropathies and mononeuritis multiplex, and may be associated with hypergammaglobulinemic purpura or leukocytoclastic vasculitis.[8]

Diagnosis

The definitive diagnosis of SS is made by performing a minor salivary gland biopsy, typically of the inner lower lip. This biopsy must show more than one focus of at least 50 lymphocytes/4 mm[2].[9] Schirmer's test and rose bengal staining of the cornea and sclerae can be done to confirm dry eyes. The presence of SS-A or SS-B antibodies also is supportive of the diagnosis.

Treatment

Treatment and management of SS generally requires the support of an ophthalmologist, frequent dental care follow-up, and a rheumatologist. Once the diagnosis is in place and the need for treatment established and initiated, the primary care clinician may continue follow-up. Regular ophthalmology follow-up is important for monitoring for corneal ulcers, eyelid infections, the possible need for tear duct ligation procedures (a palliative treatment), and hydroxychloroquine treatment, if used. Hydroxychloroquine is beneficial for systemic symptoms such as malaise and arthralgias in particular. Prednisone may be needed occasionally. Sinusitis or bronchitis symptoms may require antibiotics after upper respiratory infections. Anticholineric medications should be avoided when possible. Sjögren's patients undergoing general anesthesia should be treated with particularly rigorous use of occular lubricating ointment and occular occlusion during anesthesia. Thyroid stimulating hormone levels should be checked yearly due to increased risk of thyroid disease. Local symptomatic treatments such as artificial tears (sometimes several preparations must be tried before one is found that is acceptable to the patient) and the use of lip balms, special chewing gums (eg, Biotene or Xylifresh), and oral moisturizers (eg, Salivart spray or ORALbalance gel) can be used. Oral pilocarpine (eg, Salagen) is approved by the US Food and Drug Administration for treatment of SS although cardiopulmonary side effects must be considered in susceptible patients.

The clinician must monitor patients with SS for signs of malignant lymphoma that may occasionally develop, at a frequency perhaps exceeding 20 to 30 times normal. Lymphoma may present (often in a patient with longstanding stable disease) as rapid development of massive parotid gland enlargement or, even more ominously, as lymphoproliferative masses in extraglandular sites such as lymph nodes, spleen, lung, kidney, skin, gastrointestinal tract, or bone marrow. Such lesions may be difficult to differentiate from the associated "benign" pseudolymphomas, but the clinical course of such extraglandular lymphoproliferation in SS often is found to be that of fatal lymphoma.[4,5]

RAYNAUD'S PHENOMENON

Presenting Signs and Symptoms

Raynaud's phenomenon (RP) is a vasospastic condition resulting in episodic attacks of reversible digital ischemia leading to generally well-demarcated blanching of the digits and hands or the feet. The blanching color change (white) often is followed by cyanosis (blue) and subsequently by the rubor (red) of hyperemia. The usual trigger is exposure to cold, but some events may be triggered by emotion. Raynaud's phenomenon often is precipitated by direct exposure of the hands or feet to cold (eg, grasping a cold object or drink). Chilling of the body in general also may precipitate an attack, even when the hand is encased in mittens. Although the triphasic response (ie, white, blue, red) is typical, many patients recall only pallor or cyanosis. The sensation of cold digits or distal extremities, numbness, or throbbing may accompany attacks.

Raynaud's phenomenon most commonly exists without an associated underlying disease (primary Raynaud's phenomenon or Raynaud's disease). It is quite common, probably occurring in at least 10% of women.[10] If patients with infrequent bouts are included, particularly those living in cold climates, the prevalence is probably higher.[11] Primary RP predominately occurs in women, with 60 to 90% of affected patients being female.[12]

Raynaud's phenomenon also may occur secondary to connective tissue disease, particularly systemic sclerosis (scleroderma), which almost never occurs in the absence of RP. Patients with scleroderma often initially present for medical attention with complaints of RP and such patients should always be evaluated carefully for signs of sclerodactyly and other stigmas of scleroderma. Raynaud's phenomenon occurs in about 85% of patients with mixed connective tissue disease, and it is associated with the presence of anti-RNP antibodies.[13] Raynaud's phenomenon also is relatively frequent in SLE and dermatomyositis or polymyositis, and it is sometimes seen in rheumatoid arthritis.

Nonconnective tissue disorders have been associated with secondary RP. These associations include hyperviscosity syndromes such as polycythemia, cryoglobulinemia, paraproteinemia, thrombocytosis, leukemia, and occasionally other malignancies. Certain medications may precipitate or worsen RP, including ß-blockers, ergot, methylsergide, vinblastine, bleomycin, cisplatin, and clonidine. In postmenopausal women, unopposed estrogen supplements may increase the prevalence of RP, as compared with prevalence in those not taking supplements or in those taking estrogen-plus-progesterone supplements (which did not appear to significantly increase the prevalence of RP).[14] Tobacco use is probably a contributing factor, although some studies have not demonstrated this association.[10] Atheroemboli may be a factor in older patients but most often involve one or two digits only. Patients with primary hypertension also may demonstrate RP, and it may be seen more frequently in patients with migraine syndromes.[15] Raynaud's phenomenon may occur more frequently in the setting of thoracic outlet syndrome. Occupations requiring the use of vibrating hand tools such as chain saws, grinders, and jackhammers may predispose workers to RP, as may previous frostbite injury.

Diagnosis

Primary Raynaud's phenomenon typically occurs in a young woman who may generally tend to have cold hands and feet. One or more fingers of both hands usually are involved with the feet being somewhat less frequently involved, and the ears and nose occasionally involved. Attacks may occur infrequently or at multiple times per day. These patients do not develop ischemic fingertips or ulcers, although livedo reticularis and some diffuse mottling of the skin may be noted, sometimes in association with migraine-like headaches and antiphospholipid antibodies.

Patients with underlying connective tissue disease, particularly limited scleroderma, are likely to demonstrate dilated capillary loops or avascularity of the nail fold capillaries (ie, the capillaries at the base of the nail bed just proximal to the cuticle) These capillaries can be visualized with the use of an ophthalmoscope set at +40 diopters and, preferably, with a drop of immersion oil placed on the cuticle. Normal nail fold capillaries are relatively uniform with a confluent span of fine capillary loops. Dilated or tortuous loops, or areas of avascularity ("drop out") are suggestive of an underlying connective tissue disease, particularly scleroderma.[16] These capil-

lary changes may be seen before the appearance of clear sclerodactyly in scleroderma.

In addition to abnormal nail fold capillaries, warning signs of secondary causes of RP include the presence of autoantibodies such as antinuclear antibodies (ANAs), particularly ANAs with a nucleolar pattern or antibodies against certain antigens such as RNP ("mixed connective tissue disease") or scl-70, or the presence of antiphospholipid antibodies. Other warning signs of secondary RP include onset after age 30 years, unilateral involvement, color changes involving the whole hand, and trophic changes of the digits such as pits and ulcers, gangrene, or rashes.

Treatment

Most patients with RP phenomenon experience relatively infrequent episodes. These patients should be advised of the need to stop tobacco use and to dress warmly, wearing gloves or mittens, enclosed shoes and stockings, and overall warm dress to the entire body. In cold temperatures hats and scarves should be worn, as chills over parts of the body besides the hands may precipitate episodes of RP. Patients in warm climates may need protective dress on exposure to air conditioning, or the use of gloves for grocery shopping in freezer compartments, for example. Use of a handled mug or insulated glass may be important when drinking cold drinks. Drugs that may aggravate RP (eg, ß-blockers or ergot) should be replaced with alternatives.

Drug treatment is reserved for severe RP, with episodes typically occurring on at least a daily basis. Unfortunately drug therapy is only partially effective and often is frustrating. A good response may be a 50% reduction in frequency. The best-tolerated drug therapy is the use of calcium channel blockers, particularly nifedipine 10 to 30 mg tid, or the use of long-acting nifedipine preparations or other calcium channel blockers such as diltiazem. Surgical sympathectomy is sometimes used for severe refractory RP but its benefit may be transient, perhaps lasting only a few months. It is generally reserved for situations involving threatened severe digital ischemia.

RESOURCES

The Arthritis Foundation
1300 West Peachtree Street
Atlanta, Georgia 30309
Telephone: 1-800-283-7800 (Arthritis information for patients)
Web site: www.arthritis.org

The Arthritis Foundation provides patient and clinician information about Sjögren's syndrome and Raynaud's phenomenon, including information on support groups and clinical research.

National Institute of Arthritis and Musculoskeletal and Skin Diseases
31 Center Drive, MSC 2350
Building 31/Room 4C05
Bethesda, Maryland 20982-2350
Telephone: (301) 496-8188
Web site: www.nih.gov/niams

The NIAMS of the National Institutes of Health provides patient and clinician information about Sjögren's syndrome and Raynaud's phenomenon, as well as information about clinical research.

Sjögren's Syndrome Foundation
333 North Broadway
Jericho, New York 11753
Telephone: (516) 933-6365
Web site: www.sjogrens.com

The Sjögren's Syndrome Foundation provides a newsletter and handbook for patients, as well as a network of local support organizations.

REFERENCES

1. Itescu S. Diffuse infiltrative lymphocytosis syndrome in human immunodeficiency virus infection: a Sjögren's-like disease. Rheum Dis Clin North Am 1991;17:99–115.
2. Jorgensen C, Legouffe MC, Perney P, et al. Sicca syndrome associated with hepatitis C virus infection. Arthritis Rheum 1996;39:1166–71.
3. Talal N, Montsopoulos HM, Kassan SS, editors. Sjögren's syndrome: clinical and immunologic aspects. New York: Springer Verlag; 1987.
4. Fox RI, Tornwall J, Maruyama T, Stern M. Evolving concepts of diagnosis, pathogenesis, and therapy of Sjögren's syndrome. Curr Opin Rheumatol 1998; 10:446–56.
5. Diss TC, Wotherspoon AC, Speight P, et al. B-cell monoclonality, Epstein-Barr virus and t(14;18) in myoepithelial sialadenitis and low-grade B-cell MALT lymphoma of the parotid gland. Am J Surg Pathol 1995;19:531–6.
6. Mann D, Moutsopoulous H. HLA-DR alloantigens in different subsets of patients with Sjögren's syndrome and in family members. Ann Rheum Dis 1983; 42:533–6.
7. Rhodus NL, Bloomquist C, Liljemark W, Bereuter J. Prevalence, density, and manifestations of oral *candida albicans* in patients with Sjögren's syndrome. J Otolaryngol 1997;26:300–5.
8. Grant IA, Hunder GG, Homburger HA, Dyck PJ. Peripheral neuropathy associated with sicca complex. Neurology 1997;48:855–62.
9. Daniels TE. Labial salivary gland biopsy in Sjögren's syndrome. Arthritis Rheum 1984;27:147–56.

10. Fraenkel L, Zhang Y, Chaisson CE, et al. Different factors influencing the expression of Raynaud's phenomenon in men and women. Arthritis Rheum 1999;42:306–10.

11. Kallenberg CG. Connective tissue disorders in patients presenting with Raynaud's phenomenon alone. Ann Rheum Dis 1991;50:666–7.

12. Seibold JR, Sturgill MG. Rational use of calcium-channel antagonists in Raynaud's phenomenon. Curr Opin Rheumatol 1998;10:584–8.

13. Sharp GC, Singsen BH. Mixed connective tissue disease. In: McCarty DJ, Koopman WJ, editors. Arthritis and allied conditions. 12th ed. Philadelphia, Lea & Febinger; 1993. p. 1213–24.

14. Fraenkel L, Zhang Y, Chaisson CE, et al. The association of estrogen replacement therapy and the Raynaud phenomenon in post-menopausal women. Ann Intern Med 1998;129:208–11.

15. O'Keefe ST, Tsapatsaris NP, Beecham WP Jr. Association between Raynaud's phenomenon and migraine in a random population of hospital employees. J Rheumatol 1993;20:1187–8.

16. McGill NW, Gow PJ. Nailfold capillaroscopy: A blinded study of its discriminancy value in scleroderma, systemic lupus erythematosus, and rheumatoid arthritis. Aust N Z J Med 1986;16:457–60.

46

OSTEOARTHRITIS

Andrew Concoff, MD

Osteoarthritis (OA) is the most common form of arthritis in humans. It has an enormous economic impact, estimated at 15.5 billion dollars in the United States in 1994,[1] and ranks among the leading causes of disability and dependence.[2] Osteoarthritis is notoriously more easily recognized than defined. Specifically, OA is a disturbance in the metabolic pathways of the cartilage, subchondral bone, and synovium of a joint that is manifested by a characteristic constellation of pathologic features including softening, fibrillation, loss of volume, and degradation of the articular cartilage; formation of new bone at the joint surfaces and margins; and a specific pattern of hypertrophic inflammation of the synovium. Osteoarthritis likely represents a final common pathway for joint failure of several etiologies, rather than a single disease entity.

Several potent inflammatory cytokines including interleukin-1 (IL-1) and tumor necrosis factor α trigger cartilage degradation and extracellular matrix depletion.[3] Cartilage degradation is achieved primarily through the stimulation of a single family of enzymes termed matrix metalloproteinases.[4] Cytokines including transforming growth factor ß and insulin-like growth factor 1 induce anabolic processes in cartilage and inhibit the actions of the proinflammatory cytokines. Animal models suggest that in both sexes, sex hormones decrease cartilage damage in response to IL-1[5] and that cartilage from female animals is more sensitive to IL-1-induced degradation than is that of males.[6]

The pathologic changes of OA may ultimately give rise to characteristic radiographic and clinical features, but the correlation is far from complete. Thus, only a subset of patients with pathologic changes typical of OA bear radiographic evidence of OA (Figure 46–1), seen as joint space narrowing, presence of osteophytes, subchondral cysts, and sclerosis. Similarly, those with both pathologic and radiographic evidence of OA may or may not have symptoms referrable to the joint pathology. Because cartilage is aneural, OA pain is not directly related to cartilage destruction. Thus, the cartilage changes that are thought to be primary in OA pathogenesis may occur in the absence of symptoms. Cartilage damage must trigger changes in other structures including the synovia, joint capsule, or underlying bone before symptoms result. Ultimately, however, function is dependent on the presence and integrity of the articular cartilage. Of note, women appear to have smaller knee cartilage volumes than do men, even after adjusting for age, height, weight, and bone volume, a factor which may contribute to the development of OA in women.[7]

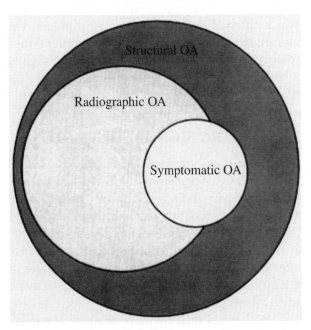

FIGURE 46–1. Correlation between structural, radiographic, and symptomatic osteoarthritis (OA).

The epidemiology of OA is complicated by the lack of a standardized definition of the disease and by the lack of correlation between symptoms, radiographs, and structural change.[8] Prevalence estimates vary greatly between studies using radiographic criteria alone and those investigating symptomatic OA. Further complexity is added by the variation in risk factors, including gender predilection, for the joint assessed.

If clinical symptoms and signs are required, the prevalence of osteoarthritis among Americans 25 years or older has been estimated to be 12.1%.[8] Before age 50 years, the prevalence of osteoarthritis in men exceeds that of women.[9] However, the overall prevalence of OA is higher among women than men, specifically because of an increased incidence in women over 50 years of age. It has been postulated that postmenopausal estrogen withdrawal or estrogen deficiency may be responsible for the increase in OA prevalence among women over 50 years. Women are more likely to bear evidence of radiographic and symptomatic knee OA than are men but are less likely to manifest radiographic or symptomatic hip OA.[8] Both radiographic and symptomatic OA of the hands and feet appear to be more common in women than men. Less data is available regarding the incidence of OA, but one study[10] showed that elderly women developed incident knee OA at a rate of 2% per year when defined radiographically and 1% per year when defined symptomatically and that 4% per year progressed significantly. Women with knee OA also are recognized to be more likely to suffer symptoms referrable to OA than are men.[9] Finally, slightly higher rates of disability and use of medical services have been noted for women than for men with OA.[11]

PRESENTING SIGNS AND SYMPTOMS

Pain and stiffness are the principle symptoms associated with OA. The pain of OA is typically exacerbated by activity and relieved by rest. As the disease advances, progressively less exertion is tolerated before pain is triggered. Eventually, pain may occur at rest or recur at night. Stiffness typically is worse after prolonged rest and is noted upon waking in the morning or after prolonged daytime inactivity, when it is termed "gelling."

With established disease several objective manifestations of OA become apparent. Tenderness to palpation of the affected joint may be noted and is variably attended by inflammation and effusion. Crepitus is also common, reflecting the disruption of the normally smooth articulating cartilage surfaces. Bony enlargement appreciated at the joint margins reflects osteophyte formation. With advanced disease, range of motion deficits, gross malalignment, and instability typically are noted.

Osteoarthritis bears a predilection for certain joints, including the hips, knees, and proximal and distal interphalangeal joint of the fingers, as well as the cervical and lumbar spine. Other joints typically are spared including the elbow, wrist, metacarpophalangeal joints, and ankle. Local differences in biomechanics and sensitivity to metalloproteinases likely explain why certain joints are relatively more susceptible to OA than are others. When OA changes are seen in atypical joints, consideration must be given to a variety of causes of so-called secondary OA. These include trauma, congenital abnormality, coexistent crystalline arthritis, and systemic diseases including acromegaly and hemachromatosis.

The specific set of joints involved with OA tends to conform to one of several recognized clinical patterns. Younger adults may suffer OA in a single joint as a result of a congenital anomaly or trauma. A pauciarticular form affecting the hips and/or knees is recognized in middle age. The most common form, however, generalized OA, is seen in greatest frequency among middle-aged to elderly women.

The expression of OA differs between men and women in certain respects. One such variant is erosive OA. An inflammatory form of the disease usually affecting the hand joints of middle-aged women, erosive OA bears a female-to-male ratio of between 10:1 and 28:1.[12] This form of OA often is recognized radiographically by its "gull wing" deformities. A second genetic form of the disease, nodal OA, causes Heberden's and Bouchard's nodes of the distal and proximal interphalangeal joints, respectively. For over half a century, this form of OA has been recognized to be passed in an autosomal dominant pattern with a strong female predominance, from mother to daughter.[13]

DIAGNOSIS

Numerous classification schemes and diagnostic criteria have been developed for OA. The clinical features and risk factors differ for each joint, necessitating different methods for each site. The classification and diagnostic criteria most widely followed are those of the American College of Rheumatology (ACR).[14-16] According to this scheme, patients are classified according to whether the OA found is idiopathic or secondary (Table 46–1).[14] Within the idiopathic group, patients are further subdivided according to whether the joint involvement is localized to one area or is generalized. The area of joint involvement in those with localized disease is then identified (eg, hand, foot, or knee) and is further differentiated by the nature of involvement at that site (eg, eccentric, concentric, or diffuse involvement of the hip). Generalized disease is defined as involvement of three or more of the following areas: hands, feet, knees, hips, spine, and other single joints. Generalized OA is further delineated according to whether the involvement affects small joints and the spine, large joints and the spine, or both peripheral joints and central joints in addition to the spine. Secondary involvement is divided according to cause including post-traumatic, congenital, or developmental diseases; calcium-deposition diseases; other bone and joint diseases; and a group of miscellaneous disorders.

The ACR classification criteria for OA of the knee were developed in 1986.[14] The criteria were developed by analyzing the consensus expert opinion regarding index cases and control cases with other diseases relevant to the differential diagnosis and then applying stepwise logistic regression and recursive partitioning to the results. Three separate criteria were developed based on the presence of knee pain in association with clinical and laboratory data, with clinical and radiographic data, or with clinical findings alone (Table 46–2). The clinical and laboratory criteria, requiring knee pain in association with five of nine parameters, were found to be 92% sensitive and 75% specific. The clinical and radiographic criteria require knee pain with osteophytes and one of the following: age over 50 years, morning stiffness less than 30 minutes, or the presence of crepitus on physical examination. The clinical and laboratory criteria were found to be 91% sensitive and 86% specific. Finally, the clinical criteria alone require knee pain with three of six items and were determined to be 95% specific and 69% specific.

Similar analysis has been performed at the hip[15] and hand.[16] At the hip, pain in combination with two of the following three clinical parameters was established: erythrocyte sedimentation rate less than 20 mm/h, radiographic osteophytes, or radiographic joint space narrowing (Table 46–3). This combination yields a sensitivity of 89% and specificity of 91%. With hand OA, the clinical examination has proved to be of greater importance than is radiography. In the presence of pain, patients were required to meet three of the following four criteria: swelling of fewer than three metacarpophalangeal joints, hard enlargement of at least two distal interphalangeal joints, bony enlargement of two of 10 other selected joints of the hand, and deformity of at least one of the 10 selected joints (Table 46–4). The hand OA criteria bear a sensitivity of 94% and a specificity of 87%.

Although useful for ensuring homogeneity among study samples, the ACR criteria are not employed routinely in the clinical setting. As the disease is likely a common end point to a series of biomechanical and metabolic derangements, efforts should be made to chronicle an individual patient's demographics, pattern of involvement, likely relevant etiologic factors, and clinical features including the presence of inflammation. This descriptive approach may be of greater use clinically than the formal criteria described above.

Radiography is indicated in a variety of instances in patients with OA. When performed upon initial presentation, radiographic results confirm the diagnosis and provide an assessment of the severity of disease. A single view of each of the hands and feet may help to discriminate between OA and its mimics. Atypical presentations, including involvement of the metacarpophalangeal joints, wrists, or shoulders, should prompt radiographic assessment for secondary causes of OA. Evidence of chondrocalcinosis should, in turn, lead to a laboratory investigation based on the clinical picture. Systemic disorders including acromegaly, hemachromatosis, hypothyroidism and hyperparathyroidism, must be considered.

MANAGEMENT IN THE OUTPATIENT SETTING

No intervention has been demonstrated to alter the slowly progressive loss of articular cartilage associated with osteoarthritis.[17] Accordingly, approaches to treating osteoarthritic patients have been directed at limiting pain and functional disability. Various algorithms and guidelines have been developed for the management of OA.[17-19]

TABLE 46–1. Classification of Subsets of Osteoarthritis

I. **Idiopathic**

  A. Localized

    1. Hands: eg, Heberden's and Bouchard's nodes (nodal), erosive interphalangeal arthritis (non-nodal), scaphometacarpal, scaphotrapezial

    2. Feet: eg, hallux valgus, hallux rigidus, contracted toes (hammer/cock-up toes), talonavicular

    3. Knee:

      a. Medial compartment

      b. Lateral compartment

      c. Patellofemoral compartment (eg, chondromalacia)

    4. Hip

      a. Eccentric (superior)

      b. Concentric (axial, medial)

      c. Diffuse (coxae senilis)

    5. Spine (particularly cervical and lumbar)

      a. Apophyseal

      b. Intervertebral (disc)

      c. Spondylosis (osteophytes)

      d. Ligamentous (hyperostosis [Forestier's disease or diffuse idiopathic skeletal hyperostosis (DISH)]

    6. Other single sites: eg, shoulder, temporomandibular, sacroiliac, ankle, wrist, acromioclavicular

  B. Generalized: includes 3 or more areas listed above

    1. Small (peripheral) and spine

    2. Large (central) and spine

    3. Mixed (peripheral and central) and spine

II. **Secondary**

  A. Post-traumatic

  B. Congenital or developmental disease

    1. Localized

      a. Hip diseases: eg, Legg-Calvé-Perthes, congenital hip dislocation, slipped capital femoral epiphysis, shallow acetabulum

      b. Mechanical and local factors: eg, obesity (?), unequal lower extremity length, extreme valgus/varus deformity, hypermobility syndromes, scoliosis

    2. Generalized

      a. Bone dysplasias: eg, epiphyseal dysplasia, spondyloapophyseal dysplasia

      b. Metabolic diseases: eg, hemachromatosis, ochronosis, Gaucher's disease, hemoglobinopathy, Ehlers-Danlos syndrome

  C. Calcium deposition disease

    1. Calcium pyrophosphate deposition disease

    2. Apatite arthropathy

    3. Destructive arthropathy (shoulder, knee)

    Other bone and joint disorders: eg, avascular necrosis, rheumatoid arthritis, gouty arthritis, septic arthritis, Paget's disease, osteopetrosis, osteochondritis

  D. Other diseases

    1. Endocrine diseases: eg, diabetes mellitus, acromegaly, hypothyroidism, hyperparathyroidism

    2. Neuropathic arthropathy (Charcot's joints)

    3. Miscellaneous: eg, frostbite, Kashin-Bek disease, caisson disease

---

Reproduced with permission from Altman R, Asch E, Bloch D, et al. Development of criteria for the classification and reporting of osteoarthritis of the knee. Arthritis Rheum 1986;29:1039–49.

TABLE 46–2. Criteria for Classification of Idiopathic Osteoarthritis of the Knee

Clinical and Laboratory[*]	Clinical and Radiographic[†]	Clinical[‡]
Knee pain +	Knee pain + osteophytes +	Knee pain +
at least 5 of the following:	at least 1 of the following:	at least 3 of the following:
Age > 50 y	Age > 50 y	Age > 50 y
Stiffness < 30 min	Stiffness < 30 min	Stiffness < 30 min
Crepitus	Crepitus	Crepitus
Bony tenderness		Bony tenderness
Bony enlargement		Bony enlargement
No palpable warmth		No palpable warmth
ESR < 40 min/h		
RF < 1:40		
SF OA		

[*]Criteria are 92% sensitive and 75% specific.
[†]Criteria are 91% sensitive and 86% specific.
[‡]Criteria are 95% sensitive and 69% specific.
ESR = erythrocyte sedimentation rate (Westergren); RF = rheumatoid factor; SFOA = synovial fluid signs of osteoarthritis (clear, viscous, or white blood cell count < 2,000/mm^3).
Adapted from Altman R, Asch E, Bloch D, et al. Development of criteria for the classification and reporting of osteoarthritis of the knee. Arthritis Rheum 1986;29:1039–49.

One recent approach to the management of OA[19] emphasizes the importance of differentiating between inflammatory and noninflammatory osteoarthritis (Figure 46–2). Nonpharmacologic interventions are first-line therapy for early or mild OA. These interventions include patient education, exercise, weight loss if appropriate, topical rubifacients (eg, capsaicin), orthoses, and formal physical and/or occupational therapy addressing deficits in range of motion, atrophy, joint protection, assistive devices, and ultrasound treatments. If these measures fail, therapy diverges based upon the presence or absence of inflammation. Inflammation is assessed using a simple analysis.[20] If a patient suffers two or three of the following criteria, inflammatory osteoarthritis is considered to be present: morning stiffness lasting greater than 30 minutes, night pain rated greater than 2.5 on a five-point scale, and joint-line tenderness rated greater than 2 on a five-point scale. For patients without such evidence of inflammation, anti-inflammatory effects associated with nonsteroidal anti-inflammatory drugs (NSAIDs)

TABLE 46–3. Combined Clinical[*] and Radiographic Classification Criteria for Osteoarthritis of the Hip[†]

Hip pain and at least 2 of the following 3 features:
    ESR < 20 mm/h
    Radiographic femoral or acetabular osteophytes
    Radiographic joint space narrowing (superior, axial and/or medial)

[*]History, physical examination, and laboratory findings.
[†]This classification method yields a sensitivity of 89% and a specificity of 91%.
ESR = erythrocyte sedimentation rate (Westergren).
Reproduced with permission from Altman R, Alarcon G, Appelrouth D, et al. The American College of Rheumatology criteria for the classification of osteoarthritis of the hip. Arthritis Rheum 1991:34:505–14.

TABLE 46–4. Clinical Classification Criteria for Osteoarthritis of the Hand[*]

Hand pain, aching, or stiffness and at least 3 of the following 4 features:
    Hard tissue enlargement of 2 or more DIP joints
    Hard tissue enlargement of 2 of the following 10 joints: second and third DIP, second and third PIP, trapeziometacarpal (base of the thumb)
    Swelling of fewer than 3 metacarpophalangeal joints
    Deformity of at least 1 of 10 selected joints

[*]This classification method yields a sensitivity of 94% and a specificity of 87%.
DIP = distal interphalangeal; PIP = proximal interphalangeal.
Reproduced with permission from Altman R, Alarcon G, Appelrouth D, et al. The American College of Rheumatology criteria for the classification of osteoarthritis of the hand. Arthritis Rheum 1990;33:1601–10.

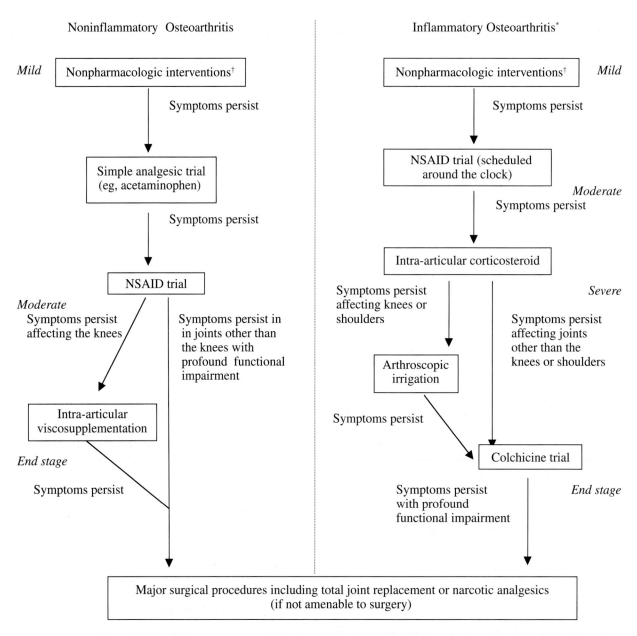

FIGURE 46–2. Therapeutic algorithms for osteoarthritis. *Patient suffers from 2 of 3 criteria: morning stiffness >30 min; night pain >2.5; joint pain >2 on five-point scales. †Patient education, weight loss, exercise, topical rubifacients (eg, capsaicin), orthoses, physical and/or occupational therapy. NSAID = nonsteroidal anti-inflammatory drug. Reproduced with permission from Concoff AL, Kalunian KC. What is the relation between crystals and osteoarthritis? Curr Opin Rheumatol 1999;11:436–40.

and intra-articular corticosteroids are not likely to be of benefit and, when combined with potential side effects, generate unfavorable risk-to-benefit ratios. In such patients the safety of simple analgesics, such as acetaminophen 1,000 mg PO every 6 hours, makes them appropriate first-line pharmacologic therapy. In patients with moderate knee OA without inflammation, intra-articular viscosupplementation (eg, three weekly injections of 2 mL of

hylan G-F 20) is less likely to induce a pseudogout attack than in the presence of inflammatory disease and may be pursued if an adequate trial of non-pharmacologic intervention, simple analgesics, and NSAIDs has failed.

The converse is true for those with inflammatory OA, where the anti-inflammatory and analgesic effects of NSAIDs are relevant to pain perception; NSAIDs (eg, ibuprofen 600 mg PO three times daily) become the pharmacologic first-line therapy. If the patient has a significant risk for or history of gastropathy or bleeding diathesis, the NSAID chosen should be a selective inhibitor of the cyclooxgenase isoform 2 (eg, celecoxib 200 mg/d PO). Elderly women have a particular risk for NSAID-induced gastropathy. If patients fail NSAIDs, control of synovitis and pain is next attempted though intra-articular corticosteroid injection (eg, methylprednisolone acetate 60 mg and lidocaine 1% without epinephrine 2 cc). Patients with severe inflammatory OA of the knee may undergo arthroscopic irrigation. Arthroscopic irrigation is most effective in patients with inflammatory symptomatology and represents a third-line treatment for refractory cases. Finally, a trial of colchicine (0.6 mg PO twice daily) is warranted in inflammatory OA that remains recalcitrant. By decreasing neutrophil response to crystalline material, colchicine may limit pain in a subset of severe OA patients with coexisting occult crystalline disease. Major surgical approaches are used if the above approaches fail and profound functional impairment is noted. Narcotic analgesics are used in patients with contraindications to surgery.

A sudden increase in pain in a single osteoarthritic joint should prompt a careful physical examination of ligamentous integrity and periarticular structures. Arthrocentesis should be performed if the diagnosis remains in doubt to assess for the presence of infection or crystalline disease. The interpretation of the results of arthrocentesis are described further in Chapter 42, "Approach to the Patient with Diffuse Joint and Muscular Pain." Repeat radiographs should be obtained if this fails to identify a cause for the change in symptoms. The appropriate interval for repeat radiographs in patients without a change from baseline symptoms is the subject of debate. In most cases intervals of less than 1 year are unlikely to provide useful information regarding OA disease progression.

Referral to a rheumatologist should be pursued if the diagnosis of OA remains in question following an initial work-up including radiography. Patients with atypical presentations and those refractory to simple analgesics, NSAIDs, and intra-articular injection also may benefit from referral to a rheumatologist. For those refractory to all nonsurgical interventions, orthopedic referral should be pursued. Appropriate referral patterns may change in the event of development of chondroprotective agents that require more frequent monitoring to assess for efficacy or side effects.

PROGNOSIS

Osteoarthritis is typically a slowly progressive disorder,[21] and no therapy has been recognized to slow progression of the disease.[17] However, some 35% of patients with OA of the hip or knee experience sustained reduction is symptomatology.[22] Risk factors for progression of OA include older age, diffuse articular involvement, neuropathy, associated crystalline disease, and obesity among patients with knee OA. Thirty-four percent of women with osteoarthritis of one knee, develop radiographic evidence of knee OA in the contralateral previously unaffected knee after 2 years, and 22% suffer radiographic evidence of disease progression.[23]

PREVENTION AND SCREENING

Investigation of methods for the prevention of osteoarthritis have begun only recently.[9] Several risk factors for osteoarthritis have been identified including increasing age, female gender, obesity, higher bone mass, occupational overuse, previous injury, and genetic factors. Of these, age is the single greatest risk factor for osteoarthritis. Primary prevention strategies should focus on the modifiable risk factors from among this group, namely obesity, occupational overuse, and knee injury. Quadriceps muscle weakness and deficits in knee proprioception, each of which is common in established knee OA, may antedate the development of knee OA and may, therefore, serve as additional targets for primary prevention. Secondary prevention may eventually focus on developing strategies to prevent patients with early asymptomatic OA (noted radiographically) from becoming symptomatic. To date no such strategies are known. Similarly, long-term tertiary prevention strategies to decrease pain and disability among patients with existing OA are not yet available.

PREGNANCY AND BREAST-FEEDING

The only study to date of the relationship between pregnancy and osteoarthritis indicates that a previous successful pregnancy is negatively associated with the development of generalized OA involving the hands.[24] Because it is a disease strongly associated with older age, the incidence of OA among women of childbearing years is quite small, and few women with OA become pregnant. Thus, the effects of OA on pregnancy and breast-feeding are not known, nor are the effects of pregnancy and breast-feeding on OA.

MENOPAUSE

Several lines of evidence implicate the estrogen withdrawal of menopause with an increase in incidence of OA.[25] The demographics of patients with OA change during the fourth decade reflecting a change in the predominant gender, with men predominating before 50 years and women predominating after 50 years. This change occurs because of a dramatic increase in the prevalence, incidence, and female predominance of OA of the hand, knee, and hip that begins at age 50 years and increases thereafter. Additional evidence of the importance of estrogen withdrawal to the development of OA is seen in "menopausal arthritis," a particularly aggressive form of hand OA associated with the rapid formation of Heberden's nodes at the distal interphalangeal joints.[26] Postmenopausal women exhibit more rapid OA progression at the hip and report symptoms with greater frequency at a given level of knee OA than do men.[25] Finally, older women may experience a more rapid deterioration, as age is a risk factor for progression of OA.[22]

Hormone Replacement Therapy

Six cross-sectional studies have evaluated the impact of postmenopausal estrogen replacement therapy (ERT) on the development of OA.[25] Each study demonstrates a decrease in prevalence of OA in women who have ever used ERT. The first prospective cohort study recently revealed a trend toward a decrease in incidence and progression of

---

RESOURCES

Arthritis Foundation
1300 West Peachtree Street
Atlanta, Georgia 30309
Telephone: 1-800-283-7800 (Arthritis information for patients)
Web site: www.arthritis.org

The Arthritis Foundation provides patient and clinician information, including text of recent treatment guidelines and information on support groups and clinical research.

National Institute of Arthritis and Musculoskeletal and Skin Diseases
31 Center Drive, MSC 2350
Building 31/Room 4C05
Bethesda, Maryland 20982-2350
Telephone: (301) 496-8188
Web site: www.nih.gov/niams

The NIAMS of the National Institutes of Health provides patient and clinician information, as well as information about clinical research.

The American College of Rheumatology
1800 Century Place, Suite 250
Atlanta, Georgia 30345
Telephone: (404) 633-3777
Web site: www.rheumatology.org

The American College of Rheumatology is the national organization for specialists in rheumatology. It provides patient information, Web links, and information about clinician educational opportunities.

radiographic OA among patients receiving ERT.[27] Since no prospective randomized clinical trials have yet been conducted, ERT cannot be recommended as a treatment for OA. Further research is needed in this area.

REFERENCES

1. Yellin E. The economics of osteoarthritis. In: Brandt K, Doherty M, Lohmander LS, editors. Osteoarthritis. New York: Oxford University Press; 1998. p. 23–30.

2. Guccione AA, Felson DT, Anderson JJ, et al. The effects of specific medical conditions on functional limitations of elders in the Framingham Study. Am J Public Health 1994;84:351–8.

3. Lotz M, Blanco FJ, von Kempis J, et al. Cytokine regulation of chondrocyte functions. J Rheumatol 1995; 22 Suppl 43:104–7.

4. Emonard H, Grimaud J-A. Matrix metalloproteinases. A review. Cell Molecular Biol 1990;36(2):131–53.

5. da Silva JA, Colville-Nash P, Spector TD, et al. Inflammation-induced cartilage degradation in female rodents. Protective role of sex hormones. Arthritis Rheum 1993;36:1007–13.

6. Larbre JP, da Silva JA, Moore AR, et al. Cartilage contribution to gender differences in joint disease progression. A study with rat articular cartilage. Clin Exp Rheumatol 1994;12:401–8.

7. Cicuttini F, Forbes A, Morris K, et al. Gender differences in knee cartilage volume as measured by magnetic resonance imaging. Osteoarthritis Cartilage 1999;7:265–71.

8. Lawrence RC, Helmick CG, Arnett FC, et al. Estimates of the prevalence of arthritis and selected musculoskeletal disorders. Arthritis Rheum 1998;41:778–99.

9. Felson DT, Zhang Y. An update on the epidemiology of knee and hip osteoarthritis with a view to prevention. Arthritis Rheum 1998;41:1343–55.

10. Felson DT, Zhang Y, Hannan MT. The incidence and natural history of knee osteoarthritis in the elderly: the Framingham Study. Arthritis Rheum 1995;38:1500–5.

11. Verbrugge LM. Women, men, and osteoarthritis. Arthritis Care Res 1995;8:212–20.

12. Belhorn LR, Hess EV. Erosive osteoarthritis. Semin Arthritis Rheum 1993;22:298–306.

13. Stecher RM. Heberden's nodes. Heredity in hypertrophic arthritis of the finger joints. Am J Med Sci 1941;201:801–4.

14. Altman R, Asch E, Bloch D, et al. Development of criteria for the classification and reporting of osteoarthritis of the knee. Arthritis Rheum 1986;29: 1039–49.

15. Altman R, Alarcon G, Appelrouth D, et al. The American College of Rheumatology criteria for the classification of osteoarthritis of the hip. Arthritis Rheum 1991;34:505–14.

16. Altman R, Alarcon G, Appelrouth D, et al. The American College of Rheumatology criteria for the classification and reporting of osteoarthritis of the hand. Arthritis Rheum 1990;33:1601–10.

17. Hochberg MC, Altman RD, Brandt KD, et al. Guidelines for the medical management of osteoarthritis. Part I. Osteoarthritis of the hip. Arthritis Rheum 1995;38:1535–40.

18. Hochberg MC, Altman RD, Brandt KD, et al. Guidelines for the medical management of osteoarthritis. Part II. Osteoarthritis of the knee. Arthritis Rheum 1995;38:1541–46.

19. Concoff AL, Kalunian KC. Crystal and osteoarthritis: what is their relationship? Curr Opin Rheumatol 1999;11:436–40.

20. Concoff A, Singh R, Klashman D, et al. A clinical algorithm for identifying occult crystalline disease in patients with knee osteoarthritis [abstract]. Arthritis Rheum 1997;40:S239.

21. Hernborg JS, Nilsson BE. The natural course of untreated OA of the knee. Clin Orthop 1977;123:130–7.

22. Felson DT. The course of osteoarthritis and factors that affect it. Rheum Dis Clin North Am 1993;19: 607–15.

23. Spector TD, Hart DJ, Doyle DV. Incidence and progression of osteoarthritis in women with unilateral knee disease in the general population: the effect of obesity. Ann Rheum Dis 1994;53:565–8.

24. Samanta A, Jones A, Regan M, et al. Is osteoarthritis in women affected by hormonal changes or smoking? Br J Rheumatol 1993;32:366–70.

25. Felson DT, Nevitt MC. The effects of estrogen on osteoarthritis. Curr Opin Rheumatol 1998;10:269–72.

26. Stecher RM, Beard EE, Hersh HH. Development of Heberden's nodes and menopause. J Lab Clin Med 1949;34:1193–202.

27. Zhang Y, McAlindon TE, Hannan M, et al. Estrogen replacement therapy and worsening of radiographic knee osteoarthritis. The Framingham study. Arthritis Rheum 1998;41:1867–73.

47

OSTEOPOROSIS

Jennifer M. Grossman, MD

Osteoporosis is defined as a systemic disease characterized by low bone mass and microarchitectural deterioration of bone tissue, with a consequent increase in bone fragility and fracture risk.[1] It results from an imbalance in the constant process of bone remodeling. In remodeling, osteoclasts first resorb the bone, forming a lacune. Osteoblasts then lay down the next bone matrix. In osteoporosis, resorption is greater than is formation, although the ratio of mineral to matrix remains normal.

There are two types of bone: trabecular and cortical. The peripheral skeleton is composed primarily of cortical bone, whereas the axial skeleton is composed of trabecular bone. Trabecular bone is more active metabolically, and, therefore, it is more likely to be the first site to become osteoporotic. A variety of cytokines and hormones influence this process.

The degree of osteoporosis is related to the peak bone mass, which is reached around the third decade. The peak bone mass is primarily a function of genetic, hormonal, and lifestyle factors such as weight bearing activities and diet. Women with the greatest bone mass are less likely to develop osteoporosis. After peak bone mass is achieved, bone loss begins to occur at a rate of 0.3 to 0.5% per year.[2] This rate can increase by 10-fold during the years around menopause. Lifetime losses can be 30 to 40% of the peak bone mass for women, and 20 to 30% for men.[1] This accelerated loss of bone as well as a lower peak bone mass explains in large part the increased prevalence of this disease in women as compared with that in men. During the early postmenopausal phase, the rate of bone loss is greatest in the trabecular bone, which explains the clinical finding that vertebral fractures tend to occur at a younger age than do hip fractures.

Osteoporosis is a common condition. The National Osteoporosis Foundation (NOF) estimates that over 8 million women and 2 million men in the United States have osteoporosis, and another 15 million women and 3 million men have low bone mass.[3] Calculations suggest that 54% of women aged 50 years and over sustain an osteoporotic fracture during their lifetime.[4] Patients over age 50 years who experience a hip fracture have a 4% in-hospital mortality rate and an average mortality rate of 24% for the year following the fracture.[5] This mortality rate increases with age and is higher in men, perhaps because of a higher prevalence of concomitant illness. Morbidity is also significant with hip fracture. Approximately 40% of patients suffering a hip fracture are discharged to a nursing home, with one-third of these patients still residing in a nursing home 1 year later.[5] Furthermore, two longitudinal studies suggest that hip fracture is more likely to lead to functional impairment than are other serious medical conditions such as myocardial infarctions and cerebrovascular accidents.[5] Women with any type of osteoporotic fracture have increased physical and functional limitations.[6] For example, women with vertebral fractures have an increased risk of back pain and loss of function.[7] Furthermore, vertebral fractures are associated with increased mortality.[8,9] This association with mortality may be stronger for men.[9] Last, osteoporotic fractures cost an estimated 13.8 billion dollars in the United States in 1995.[10] As the general population ages, osteoporosis becomes an even greater health concern.

PRESENTING SIGNS AND SYMPTOMS

Like hypertension, osteoporosis is often silent, presenting only after a fracture has occurred. Therefore, it is important to think about this diagnosis even in women who are asymptomatic. It should be considered in all women under age 65 years with one or

TABLE 47–1. Risk Factors for the Development of Osteoporosis

Epidemiology
    Caucasian or Asian ancestry
    Female gender
    Advancing age
    History of a fracture in a first-degree relative
    Low body mass
    Early menopause
    Prolonged premenopausal amenorrhea
    Cigarette smoking
    Alcoholism
    Low calcium intake
    Inactive lifestyle or history of immobilization

Medications
    Corticosteroids
    Anticonvulsants
    Heparin
    Gonadotropin-releasing hormone agonists
    Excess thyroid hormone replacement

Comorbid conditions
    Chronic obstructive pulmonary disease
    Severe liver disease
    Gastrectomy
    Rheumatoid arthritis
    Hyperparathyroidism
    Lymphoma, leukemia, and multiple myeloma
    Chronic renal insufficiency/failure
    Nutritional disorders

more risk factors for osteoporosis and for all women over age 65 years. Risk factors for osteoporosis are presented in Table 47–1.

The symptoms of osteoporosis, in addition to acute fracture, include loss of height, back pain, development of thoracic kyphosis (dowager's hump), and an accentuated lumbar lordosis. These physical deformities can cause abdominal discomfort, restrictive lung disease, sleep disorders, early satiety, weight loss, and poor self-esteem.

DIAGNOSIS

Osteoporosis too often is discovered after a fracture has occurred; early diagnosis is important so that therapeutic interventions can be undertaken. However, an operational definition of osteoporosis is problematic. Bone mineral density (BMD) reflects fracture risk just as blood pressure reflects risk of stroke. In fact, BMD is a better predictor of fracture risk than is blood pressure of stroke risk.[11] Bone mineral density accounts for approximately 75 to 85% of bone strength.[3] Although BMD is a continuous variable with significant overlap between patients with fragility fractures and those without, it has become the standard method of diagnosing osteoporosis. However, there is no absolute level of BMD that necessitates treatment. The risk factors and medical history as well as the cost/benefits of a treatment must be taken into account on an individual basis.

Usually, BMD is reported as a standard deviation (SD) from the norm, either as a T score, in which the norm is young healthy sex-matched controls, or as a Z score, in which the norm is age- and sex-matched controls. The World Health Organization (WHO) has defined osteopenia as a T score between –1 and –2.5, osteoporosis as a T score < -2.5, and established or severe osteoporosis as a T score < -2.5 and a history of at least one minimal trauma fracture (Table 47–2).[12] There are multiple techniques for measuring BMD; all except ultrasonography use radiation. Techniques for peripheral measurements include single photon absorptiometry (SPA), single x-ray absorptiometry (SXA), peripheral quantitative computed tomography (QCT), and ultrasonography, whereas central *and* peripheral measurements are done with dual x-ray absorptiometry (DXA), dual photon absorptiometry (DPA), and QCT. Because of the relatively shorter scan times, minimal radiation exposure, precision, and accuracy, DXA has become the procedure of choice. Limitations of its use include inaccuracies that can result if osteoarthritis, scoliosis, or calcification of the aorta are present.

Numerous prospective studies have found that BMD predicts fracture risk, even when controlling for other risk factors.[13–16] It has been estimated that for every 1 SD below the normal T score, the age-adjusted relative risk of hip fracture is increased by 1.5 to 2.8, depending on the site measured—the highest risk related to bone loss is in Ward's triangle.[17] The recommendations by the NOF for a bone density measurement[18] are shown in Table 47–3. Furthermore, the NOF has suggested an algorithm for the initial evaluation of a patient (Figure 47–1). In addition to instituting treatment based on a history of fracture and low BMD, the NOF also recommends treatment of women over

TABLE 47–2. Defining Osteoporosis by Bone Mineral Density According to World Health Organization Guidelines

Condition	Bone Mineral Density
Normal	T score ≥−1
Osteopenia (low bone mass)	T score between −1 and −2.5
Osteoporosis	T score of <−2.5
Severe or established osteoporosis	T score <−2.5 and a history of minimal trauma fracture

Adapted from Kanis JA, Melton JL III, Christiansen C, et al. The diagnosis of osteoporosis. J Bone Miner Res 1994;9:1137–41.

age 70 years who have multiple risk factors, regardless of the BMD results.

There has been interest in the use of markers of bone formation and resorption from both serum and urine for the diagnosis and monitoring of disease. Markers of bone formation include serum alkaline phosphatase, bone specific alkaline phosphatase, osteocalcin, and type I procollagen peptide. Fasting urinary calcium, urinary pyridinoline and deoxypyridinoline cross-links, N-telopeptides, and C-terminal cross-linked collagen telopeptides are markers of bone resorption. These markers may be useful in determining response to therapy and in identifying patients who are fast losers of bone who might warrant more aggressive treatment. One study using crude markers of resorption and formation demonstrated that women who were fast losers at the time of menopause had lost 50% more bone by 12 years post menopause than had those who were designated as slow losers.[19] The combination of markers of resorption and the measurement of BMD has been found to predict hip fracture risk better than either measure alone.[20] At this point, however, these markers are not recommended as part of routine clinical practice.

Once a patient is diagnosed with osteoporosis, the clinician needs to consider whether this is a primary condition or the result of an underlying medical condition. Numerous guidelines.[21–23] recommend performing the following tests: complete blood count, serum calcium, phosphate, liver function tests, creatinine, and electrolytes. These tests can be useful in detecting occult renal and liver disease, hyperparathyroidism, and nutritional deficiency. Some guidelines[22,23] also recommend routine testing with a urinalysis and serum protein electrophoresis to screen for renal disease and multiple myeloma, respectively. Any abnormality detected on these tests warrants further evaluation. The clinician also should perform a careful history and physical examination, with laboratory testing as indicated, to evaluate for any other associated conditions, particularly hyperthyroidism.

PREVENTION AND SCREENING

Preventative measures are an important component of the treatment of this condition. Prevention can occur at three stages: maximization of peak bone density, maintenance during the premenopausal years, and the minimization of postmenopausal and age-related bone loss. Regular weight-bearing exercise, dietary adequacy of calcium and vitamin D intake, maintenance of an adequate weight, early

TABLE 47–3. Recommendations for Testing of Bone Mineral Density

Women under age 65 years with one or more risk factors for osteoporosis*
All women aged 65 years and over
Postmenopausal women with a history of fracture
Women who would consider therapy for osteoporosis based on the BMD results
Women who have been on hormone replacement therapy for a prolonged period of time

*See Table 47–1.
BMD = bone mineral density.
Adapted from National Osteoporosis Foundation. Physician's guide to prevention and treatment of osteopososis. Belle Mead (NJ): Excerpta Medica; 1998.

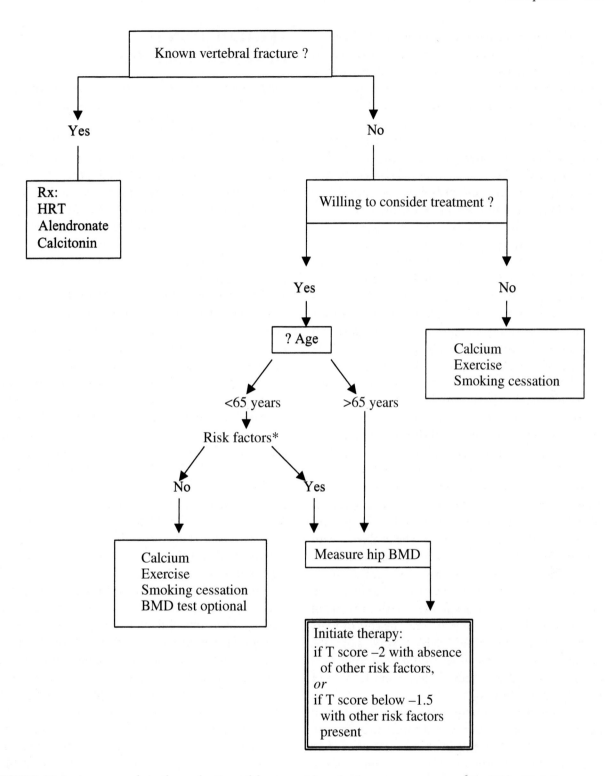

FIGURE 47–1. An approach to the evaluation of fracture risk and subsequent treatment. *See Table 47–1. Rx = prescription; HRT = hormone replacement therapy; BMD = bone mineral density. Adapted from the National Osteoporosis Foundation. Physician's guide to prevention and treatment of osteoporosis. Belle Mead [NJ]: Excerpta Medica; 1998. © National Osteoporosis Foundation, DC 20036, 1997.

mobilization after periods of bed rest, and avoidance of activities associated with bone loss such as smoking are steps that can be taken at any point. Women with irregular menstrual cycles may benefit from treatment with oral contraceptives. The elderly should be assessed for adequate sun exposure and, if insufficient, be considered for vitamin D supplementation. Factors such as visual acuity, the need for assistive devices such as canes and walkers, and medications associated with falls also should be assessed in an attempt to reduce fracture risk.

At this time, there is no screening test for osteoporosis that is recommended for the general population. As noted earlier, bone mineral density can be a useful test, and it meets many of the requirements of a screening test such as ability to detect a disease that is relatively common with a known natural history, reasonable cost and acceptability, and treatment options for a positive screening test. However, there is a lack of consensus regarding the age at which the test should be done and whether a mass screening program would indeed result in a reduction in fractures and in improved morbidity and mortality. Most experts do agree that BMD measurement is warranted for glucocorticoid usage greater than 2 months and for conditions related to osteoporosis such as hyperparathyroidism.[24] Screening of perimenopausal women has been proposed since identification of women at risk would allow for greater preservation of their bone mass. The problems with this approach include poor compliance with long-term therapy (most women would not experience a fracture until age 70 years or more), the increased risk of breast cancer associated with long-term hormone replacement therapy, and the cost of years of therapy.[25] Furthermore, 750 BMD studies of Caucasian women in their fifties would need to be performed followed by 5 years of treatment to prevent one hip or vertebral fracture.[24]

There are arguments that screening women aged 65 years and older would target more of the population at risk, result in fewer cases needed to treat for a briefer period of time, and thus be more efficient and effective.[25] However, until well-designed clinical trials are performed, it is unlikely that there will be a consensus on screening for osteoporosis. Decisions for BMD testing should be made on an individual basis. The guidelines for the use of BMD testing, as put forth by the National Osteoporosis Foundation, are shown in Figure 47–1.

TREATMENT IN THE OUTPATIENT SETTING

All patients with osteoporosis should be encouraged to participate in weight-bearing exercises. Weight-bearing activity earlier in life contributes to a higher peak BMD, which decreases the risk for osteoporosis.[26] Exercise, defined by self-reported walking, was associated with a 30% reduction in the risk of fractures (relative risk of fracture, 0.7; 95% confidence interval [CI], 0.5 to 0.9) in the prospective Study of Osteoporotic Fractures.[27] Furthermore, the US Preventive Task Force Guidelines note that both randomized and nonrandomized controlled trials provide evidence that exercise can retard bone loss.[28] Physical activity that promotes balance also has been found to decrease the risk of falls.[29] Last, a prospective study has demonstrated that exercise can improve quality of life by decreasing the pain associated with osteoporosis.[30]

All patients with osteoporosis should be encouraged to take calcium and vitamin D supplements. Two randomized controlled trials in postmenopausal women suggest that calcium supplementation alone may exert an attenuating effect on bone loss.[31,32] The NOF recommends that all adults intake at least 1,200 mg/d of elemental calcium.[18] The average American diet provides only 600 mg/d of calcium. There are a variety of calcium preparations that are available, and there is no convincing evidence that any one formulation is superior. Numerous studies have found that vitamin D improves bone mineral density; however, the dosage and preparation of vitamin D varied significantly making the results difficult to compare. A systematic review of randomized controlled trials of vitamin D with fracture as an outcome concluded that the use of vitamin D was controversial; however, several of the trials did show limited evidence of fracture reduction.[33] A recent review, however, felt that the data on vitamin D supplementation or treatment with synthetic vitamin D analogs such as calcitriol had too wide a range of uncertainty to make definitive recommendations for those who were not vitamin-D deficient.[3] Several guidelines do recommend vitamin D supplementation, at a dose of 400 to 800 IU/d, for elderly persons and those with inadequate intake.[18,21,34]

After these initial steps are taken, treatment options include hormone replacement therapy

(HRT), selective estrogen-receptor modulators (SERMs), bisphosphonates, and calcitonin. Bisphosphonates have the strongest data from randomized placebo-controlled trials supporting their use in the treatment of osteoporosis. Bisphosphonates are compounds that bind permanently to mineralized bone surfaces and inhibit osteoclasts, thus decreasing bone resorption. Alendronate is one bisphosphonate that has demonstrated efficacy in fracture reduction. One of the largest studies, the Fracture Intervention Trial, which is a multicenter randomized placebo-controlled 4-year study of postmenopausal Caucasian women with low BMD, evaluated fracture reduction risk in patients with prior vertebral fractures and those without. For those with a prior vertebral fracture, alendronate use resulted in a decreased incidence of vertebral as well as hip fractures (relative risk, 0.53, 95% CI, 0.41 to 0.68; and relative hazard, 0.49, 95% CI, 0.23 to 0.99, respectively).[35] For women with low bone density but no vertebral fractures, alendronate use resulted in improved BMD at all sites measured; however, the reduction in fractures was only significant in the subgroup analysis of women with a T score of the femoral neck < −2.5 at baseline.[36] A meta-analysis of five different trials of alendronate in women with low BMD found that the relative risk of nonvertebral fractures compared with risk in those using placebo was 0.71 ($p = .048$).[37] Risedronate is the second bisphosphonate approved by the US Food and Drug Administration (FDA) for the treatment of osteoporosis. Risedronate has been shown to reduce the risk of vertebral fracture in women with established osteoporosis[38] and to reduce the risk of hip fracture in elderly women aged 70 to 79 years with a T score at the hip of ≤ −4 or a T score at the hip of ≤ −3 with at least one additional risk factor for fracture.[39] Interestingly, in this second study, women of at least 80 years who were selected primarily on the basis of risk factors did not have a reduced fracture risk associated with risedronate use. Alendronate is given at a dosage of 5 mg/d for the prevention of osteoporosis for those with osteopenia or multiple risk factors, and at 10 mg/d for the treatment of those with osteoporosis. Because alendronate is poorly absorbed, it should be taken at least 30 minutes before breakfast with a large glass of water, and patients are instructed to remain upright for 30 minutes after taking the medication to decrease the risk of esophageal ulceration. More recently BMD

data suggest that a weekly dosage of 70 mg of alendronate is as effective as is a daily dosage of 10 mg, and it has fewer gastrointestinal side effects.[40] There is no fracture data for the weekly dosing. The dosage of risedronate is 5 mg by mouth daily with the same precautions as for alendronate.

Etidronate is another bisphosphonate that has been used in the treatment of osteoporosis. Although the FDA has only approved its use in the treatment of Paget's disease and hypercalcemia of malignancy, and the prevention of heterotopic bone formation after hip replacement, its use in osteoporosis is approved in many countries. Studies[41,42] have shown a significant decrease in the risk of vertebral fractures associated with cyclic etidronate for those with established vertebral fractures or osteopenia at baseline. Etidronate needs to be given cyclically to avoid adverse effects on bone mineralization. A common regimen for etidronate is 400 mg/d for 2 weeks of every 13 weeks.

A recent review calculates that bisphosphonates decrease vertebral fractures by 50% and that alendronate also can reduce hip and wrist fractures by 50%.[3] Their safety and efficacy in children and young adults has not been evaluated. The optimal duration of treatment also is not established. It has been shown that discontinuation of alendronate results in bone loss at a similar rate to loss in those given placebo.[43] The addition of bisphosphonates to HRT has been shown to have additive benefits in terms of BMD.[44]

Hormone replacement therapy has been a standard approach for the prevention and treatment of osteoporosis. Randomized clinical trials have shown that HRT improves BMD.[45,46] Numerous case-control[47–49] and cohort studies[50–52] demonstrated a reduced fracture risk with the use of HRT. A pooled estimate of the relative risk of having a hip fracture for ever-users of estrogen compared with that of never-users is 0.75 (95% CI, 0.68 to 0.84).[53] A recent review estimates that 5 years of HRT decreases the risk of vertebral fractures by 50 to 80% and of other fractures by 25%.[3] One randomized placebo-controlled trial[54] demonstrated a reduced risk in the number of new vertebral fractures associated with HRT; however, when the data was reanalyzed for the number of women with new fractures, the results were no longer significant.[55] A recent meta-analysis of randomized trials of HRT for the prevention of nonvertebral fractures found a significant reduction of 27% for nonvertebral fractures in women randomized to HRT with a mean age younger than 60 years. The results were not significant for women with a mean age of 60 years and older.[56] This meta-analysis is limited studies designed to test HRT on outcomes other than fracture. Therefore many of the participants did not have low BMD at baseline, especially in the studies with older participants. It should be noted that the only population in which a reduction in fracture risk has been demonstrated is one with osteoporosis by BMD or fracture history at baseline. Nonetheless, with the lack of strong data from randomized controlled trials with fracture as an outcome, the FDA has changed its indications for HRT to the prevention of osteoporosis only. A recent consensus statement from the NIH[24] and the National Osteoporosis Foundation[18] still considers HRT a treatment option.

There has been further controversy regarding benefits of HRT in terms of the timing of its initiation. The Study of Osteoporotic Fractures found that estrogen use must be ongoing to prevent fractures. Previous use of estrogen, even for more than 10 years, did not provide a significant reduction in fracture risk.[57] This study also suggested that fracture reduction was less effective if HRT was begun more than 5 years after menopause. The Rancho Bernardo Study also found that the greatest benefit of HRT on BMD occurred when treatment was initiated early in menopause and continued; however, they also found benefit with initiation after age 60 years and continued use.[58] The Heart and Estrogen/progestin Replacement Study (HERS) Trial in which the initiation of HRT in women with established coronary artery disease resulted in an increased risk of coronary events has generated additional controversy regarding HRT.[59] The Women's Health Initiative, a large ongoing randomized trial of HRT, published a press release of similar interim results (National Institutes of Health press release). Data from the Nurses' Health Study found that HRT decreased the risk for coronary events in women without pre-existing disease, but that the risk of stroke may be increased.[60] For any individual woman, the risks and potential benefits of HRT must be considered carefully.

A dose equivalent to 0.625 mg of conjugated estrogen has been suggested to be the most effective for increasing BMD.[61] The most commonly used preparations are conjugated estrogen (0.625 mg),

micronized estradiol (1 mg), and transdermal estradiol (0.05 mg). For those with an intact uterus, progesterone is given to reduce the risk of endometrial cancer. The progesterone (usually medroxyprogesterone acetate) can be give continuously at a dosage of 2.5 to 5 mg daily with the estrogen, or cyclically with a common regimen using estrogen day 1 through 30 and medroxyprogesterone acetate (5 to 10 mg) on days 1 to 13. It has been shown that in women over age 65 years, low-dose HRT (conjugated estrogen dosage 0.3 mg/d) resulted in a similar improvement in BMD as compared with results with higher-dose regimens, and it was well tolerated.[62]

Raloxifene is a SERM that has been shown to improve BMD, albeit not as much as do conjugated estrogens, without adverse effects on the endometrium.[63] It further has been shown to decrease the rate of vertebral fractures.[64] In a recent osteoporosis trial of 3 years, raloxifene was associated with a reduced risk of invasive breast cancer.[65] Raloxifene does not treat the symptoms of menopause, such as hot flashes, and its cardiovascular benefits remain to be determined. These may be factors to consider when selecting a treatment regimen. The dosage of raloxifene is 60 mg/d.

Calcitonin, a hormone produced by the follicular cells of the thyroid gland, has the ability to suppress osteoclast activity. It is available in several forms including injectable salmon and human calcitonin, and nasal spray salmon calcitonin. Because of the increased side effects such as flushing and nausea associated with the subcutaneous injections, and decreased acceptability with the injectable forms, the nasal spray has been used more widely. It is administrated as one spray (200 IU) daily, alternating the nostril used to decrease irritation. Although it may be somewhat less effective than are other agents, studies have shown that it stabilizes or improves bone mass of the spine and radius; however, fracture data are limited.[3] One randomized trial did demonstrate a reduction of vertebral fractures associated with intranasal salmon calcitonin, although the absence of a dose response and the high dropout rate make the conclusions suspect.[66] Calcitonin may have the additional benefit of controlling the pain of acute vertebral fracture;[67,68] one controlled study also has found it to be effective in the treatment of chronic back pain from osteoporotic fractures.[69]

A new agent, parathyroid hormone (1-34), has been recommended for approval by the the Endocrinologic and Metabolic Drug Advisory Committee to FDA. If approved, this will be the first drug that stimulates bone growth; the other drugs are antiresorptive agents. Parathyroid hormone (1-34) was shown in a randomized placebo-controlled trial of postmenopausal women with prior vertebral fractures to decrease the rate of new vertebral and nonvertebral fractures more effectively than do the bisphosphonates or raloxifene.[70]

Although not considered a treatment for osteoporosis, hydrochlorothiazide use has been associated with a reduced risk of hip fracture.[71] Thiazide diuretics decrease urinary calcium excretion. In a randomized placebo-controlled trial, low-dose (12.5 to 25 mg) hydrochlorothiazide maintained bone density at the hip and spine.[72] This information can be useful when choosing therapy for women with concomitant hypertension.

Most of the trials for osteoporosis therapy have been performed in postmenopausal women. This limits their generalizability in regard to the treatment of men. Androgen therapy has been used in men with osteoporosis, although trials are limited. Osteoporosis in men is associated with an underlying condition in 26 to 78% of cases;[73] this could potentially guide therapy.

Monitoring of osteoporosis is a controversial issue. Because the natural history of bone loss in 1 year is less than is the precision in the measurement of BMD, repeat BMD monitoring more frequently than every 2 to 3 years is not recommended. Numerous guidelines do recommend follow-up bone density studies at varying intervals;[21–23] however, there are no clinical trials demonstrating the efficacy of this intervention. The potential benefits of follow-up bone density studies include improved compliance with medical regimens and alterations in therapy if further loss is documented. Because of a statistical phenomenon called "regression to the mean," whereby patients who have lost large amounts of BMD gained more in both the treatment and placebo groups, it is not recommended that changes in therapy be based only on BMD results.[24] Biochemical markers for osteoporosis also may be useful in monitoring response to therapy, but their use at this time is experimental.[74]

TREATMENT IN THE INPATIENT SETTING

Treatment of osteoporosis in the inpatient setting occurs most frequently with hip fractures and with intractable pain from compression fractures. These situations present opportunities to initiate or modify the treatment of osteoporosis, as a history of an osteoporotic fracture is a risk factor for future fractures.[27] Consultation by a specialist is helpful for patients with severe unexplained osteoporosis to rule out an underlying cause, and for patients with persistent bone loss despite therapy.

PROGNOSIS

The average 50-year-old Caucasian woman has an approximate 15% chance of hip fracture and a 40% chance of any type of fracture by age 85 years.[75] In comparison, for a 50-year-old Caucasian male, the lifetime risk of hip fracture has been estimated at 5 to 6%.[76] Women with low bone density are at increased risk, with each reduction of 1 SD in the BMD associated with a 1.5 to twofold increase in risk of a peripheral fracture.[75] Women age 65 years and over with a BMD T score of < -2.5 are five times more likely to experience a hip fracture than are women whose BMD is higher.[76] Bone mineral density is not the only factor accounting for fracture risk; numerous other factors such as body mass, current cigarette smoking, history of a prior fracture, history of a hip fracture in a first-degree relative, and gait disturbances contribute to the risk of fracture.[3] With a population-based effort, it is estimated that smoking cessation would reduce an individual's risk of hip fracture by 40% and the population's hip fracture rate by 0.2%; walking for exercise would reduce an individual's risk of hip fracture and the population's hip fracture rate by 30% and 6%, respectively. Screening and initiation of treatment for osteoporosis (BMD T score < -2.5) would reduce the risk of hip fracture by 50% for the individual and hip fracture rates by 11% for the population.[76]

PREGNANCY AND BREAST-FEEDING

In normal pregnancy and lactation, data suggest that there is significant bone turnover due to the increased calcium demands of the fetus; however, these requirements are met predominantly by increased maternal calcium absorption in the intestines. Despite this increased turnover, most studies do not suggest that pregnancy and lactation result in a significant net loss of bone mass.[77] On the other hand, pregnancy and lactation in adolescents who have not yet achieved a peak BMD may be a risk factor for lower BMD.[77]

Osteoporosis has been described as a rare complication of pregnancy. This topic has been reviewed by Khovidhunkit and Epstein.[78] There is controversy as to whether this illness is a distinct entity or an incidental finding in women with predisposing risk factors. It typically presents during the first pregnancy in the third trimester or post partum, with back pain and/or a vertebral fracture. The etiology is unknown. The course is variable, with most patients experiencing recovery or stabilization of their BMD shortly post partum. Recurrences are rare but have been reported.

Another rare condition in pregnancy is transient osteoporosis of the hip. This typically presents with groin and anterior leg pain. The cause is unknown. Radiography should be avoided if possible, but, if necessary, a fetal shield can be used. Osteopenia often is noted on the film. Ultrasonography can be helpful in identifying a hip effusion, which can be aspirated both for symptomatic relief and to rule out the possibility of an infection. Treatment is conservative and consists of limited weight-bearing and pain medications. Resolution with return to normal density usually occurs in 2 to 6 months.[79]

USE OF ORAL CONTRACEPTIVE PILLS

There is limited information on the use of oral contraceptive pills in osteoporosis. Although the studies are variable in design and are not consistent in their results, several do suggest that oral contraceptives have a beneficial effect on BMD.[80] The optimal daily dose appears to be between 25 and 35 μg of ethinyl estradiol; norethindrone also may improve bone mass.[80]

REFERENCES

1. Consensus Development Conference. Diagnosis, prophylaxis, and treatment of osteoporosis. Am J Med 1993;94:646–50.
2. Manolagas SC, Jilka RL. Bone marrow, cytokines, and bone remodeling. Emerging insights into the pathophysiology of osteoporosis. N Engl J Med 1995;332:305–11.

3. Osteoporosis: review of the evidence for prevention, diagnosis and treatment and cost-effectiveness analysis. Osteoporos Int 1998;8 Suppl 4:S7–80.

4. Chrischilles EA, Butler CD, Davis CS, Wallace RB. A model of lifetime osteoporosis impact. Arch Intern Med 1991;151:2026–32.

5. US Congress, Office of Technology Assessment. Hip fracture outcomes in people age 50 and over—Background Paper, OTA-BP-H-120. Washington (DC): US Government Printing Office; 1994.

6. Greendale GA, Barret-Connor E, Ingles S, Haile R. Late physical and functional effects of osteoporotic fractures in women: the Rancho Bernardo Study. J Am Geriatr Soc 1995;43:955–61.

7. Nevitt MC, Ettinger B, Black DM, et al. The association of radiographically detected vertebral fractures with back pain and function. A prospective study. Ann Intern Med 1998;128:793–800.

8. Kado DM, Browner WS, Palermo L, et al. Vertebral fractures and mortality in older women: a prospective study. Arch Intern Med 1999;159:1215–20.

9. Center JR, Nguyen TV, Schneider D, et al. Mortality after all major types of osteoporotic fracture in men and women: an observational study. Lancet 1999; 353:878–82.

10. Ray NF, Chan JK, Thamer M, Melton LJ. Medical expenditures for the treatment of osteoporotic fractures in the United States in 1995: report from the National Osteoporosis Foundation. J Bone Miner Res 1997;12:24–35.

11. Kanis JA. Diagnosis of osteoporosis. Osteoporos Int 1997;7 Suppl 3:S108–16.

12. Kanis JA, Melton JL III, Christiansen C, et al. The diagnosis of osteoporosis. J Bone Miner Res 1994; 9:1137–41.

13. Gardsell P, Johnell O, Nilsson BE. Predicting fractures in women by using forearm bone densitometry. Calcif Tissue Int 1989;44:235–42.

14. Ross PD, Wasnich RD, Heilbrun LK, Vogel JM. Definition of a spine fracture threshold based upon prospective fracture risk. Bone 1987;8:271–8.

15. Hui SL, Slemenda CW, Johnston CC Jr. Baseline measurement of bone mass predicts fracture in white women. Ann Intern Med 1989;111:355–61.

16. Cummings SR, Black DM, Nevitt MC, et al. Appendicular bone density and age predict hip fracture in women. The Study of Osteoporotic Fractures Group. JAMA 1990;263:665–8.

17. Cummings SR, Black DM, Nevitt MC, et al. Bone density at various sites for prediction of hip fractures. The Study of Osteoporotic Fractures Research Group. Lancet 1993;341:72–5.

18. National Osteoporosis Foundation. Physician's guide to prevention and treatment of osteoporosis. Belle Mead (NJ): Excerpta Medica; 2000.

19. Hansen MA, Overgaard K, Riis BJ, Christiansen C. Role of peak bone mass and bone loss in postmenopausal osteoporosis: 12 year study. BMJ 1991;303:961–4.

20. Garnero P, Hausherr E, Chapuy MC, et al. Markers of bone resorption predict hip fracture in elderly women: the EPIDOS prospective study. J Bone Miner Res 1996;11:1531–8.

21. American Association of Clinical Endocrinologists clinical practice guidelines for the prevention and treatment of osteoporosis. 1996, 1998. Available at www.aace.com. Accessed on 3/24/98.

22. Kanis JA, Delmas P, Burckhardt P, et al. Guidelines for diagnosis and management of osteoporosis. Osteoporos Int 1997;7:390–406.

23. Clinical practice guidelines for the diagnosis and management of osteoporosis. Scientific Advisory Board, Osteoporosis Society of Canada. Can Med Assoc J 1996;155:1113–33.

24. Osteoporosis prevention, diagnosis, and therapy. NIH Consensus Development Panel on Osteoporosis Prevention, Diagnosis and Therapy. JAMA 2001; 285:785–95.

25. Torgerson DJ. Is there a future for non-menopausal screening strategies for osteoporosis prevention? Osteoporos Int 1998;8 Suppl 1:S57–61.

26. Welten DC, Kemper HC, Post GB, et al. Weight bearing activity during youth is a more important factor for peak bone mass than calcium intake. J Bone Miner Res 1994;9:1089–96.

27. Cummings SR, Nevitt MC, Browner WS, et al. Risk factors for hip fracture in white women. Study of Osteoporotic Fractures Research Group. N Engl J Med 1995;332:767–73.

28. U.S. Preventive Services Task Force. Guide to clinical preventive services: report of the U.S. Preventive Services Task Force. Baltimore: Williams & Wilkins; 1996. http://text.nlm.nih.gov.

29. Province MA, Hadley EC, Hornbrook MC, et al. The effects of exercise on falls in elderly patients. A preplanned meta-analysis of the FICSIT Trials. Frailty and Injuries: Cooperative Studies of Intervention Techniques. JAMA 1995;273:1341–7.

30. Harrison JE, Chow R, Dornan J, et al. Evaluation of a program for rehabilitation of osteoporotic patients (PRO): 4-year follow-up. Osteoporos Int 1993;3:13–7.

31. Reid IR, Ames RW, Evans MC, et al. Effect of calcium supplementation on bone loss in postmenopausal women. N Engl J Med 1993;328:460–4.

32. Dawson-Hughes B, Dallal GE, Krall EA, et al. A controlled trial of the effect of calcium supplementation on bone density in postmenopausal women. N Engl J Med 1990;323:878–83.

33. Gillespie WJ, Henry DA, O'Connell DL, Robertson J. Vitamin D and vitamin D analogues in the prevention of fractures in involutional and postmenopausal osteoporosis. The Cochrane Database System Review 2000; CD000227.

34. Murray TM. Prevention and management of osteoporosis. Consensus statement from the Scientific Advisory Board of the Osteoporosis Society of Canada. 4. Calcium nutrition and osteoporosis. Can Med Assoc J 1996;155:935–9.

35. Black DM, Cummings SR, Karpf DB, et al. Randomised trial of effect of alendronate on risk of fracture in women with existing vertebral fractures. Fracture Intervention Trial Research Group. Lancet 1996; 348:1535–41.

36. Cummings SR, Black DM, Thompson DE, et al. Effect of alendronate on risk of fracture in women with low bone density but without vertebral fractures. Results from the Fracture Intervention Trial. JAMA 1998;280:2077–82.

37. Karpf DB, Shapiro DR, Seeman E, et al. Prevention of nonvertebral fractures by alendronate: a meta-analysis. Alendronate Osteoporosis Treatment Study Groups. JAMA 1997;277:1159–64.

38. Harris ST, Watts NB, Genant HK, et al. Effects of risedronate treatment on vertebral and nonvertebral fractures in women with postmenopausal osteoporosis. Vertebral Efficacy with Risedronate Therapy (VERT) Study Group. JAMA 1999;282:1344–52.

39. McClung MR, Geusens P, Miller PD, et al. Effect of risedronate on the risk of hip fracture in elderly women. Hip Intervention Program Study Group. N Engl J Med 2001;344:333–40.

40. Schnitzer T, Bone HG, Crepaldi G, et al. Therapeutic equivalence of alendronate 70 mg once-weekly and alendronate 10 mg daily in the treatment of osteoporosis. Alendronate Once-Weekly Study Group. Aging (Milano) 2000;12:1–12.

41. Harris ST, Watts NB, Jackson RD, et al. Four-year study of intermittent cyclic etidronate treatment of postmenopausal osteoporosis: three years of blinded therapy followed by one year of open therapy. Am J Med 1993;95:557–67.

42. Storm T, Thamsborg G, Steiniche T, et al. Effect of intermittent cyclical etidronate therapy on bone mass and fracture rate in women with postmenopausal osteoporosis. N Engl J Med 1990;32:1265–71.

43. Ravn P, Bidstrup M, Wasnich RD, et al. Alendronate and estrogen-progestin in the long-term prevention of bone loss: four-year results from the Early Postmenopausal Intervention Cohort Study. A randomized, controlled trial. Ann Intern Med 1999; 131:935–42.

44. Lindsay R, Cosman F, Lobo RA, et al. Addition of alendronate to ongoing hormone replacement therapy in the treatment of osteoporosis: a randomized, controlled clinical trial. J Clin Endocrinol Metab 1999;84:3076–81.

45. Lindsay R, Hart DM, Aitken JM, et al. Long-term prevention of postmenopausal osteoporosis by oestrogen. Evidence for an increased bone mass after delayed onset of oestrogen therapy. Lancet 1976; I:1038–41.

46. Munk-Jensen N, Pors Nielsen S, Obel EB, et al. Reversal of postmenopausal vertebral bone loss by oestrogen and progestogen: a double blind placebo controlled study. Br Med J (Clin Res Ed) 1988;296:1150–2.

47. Ettinger B, Genant HK, Cann CE. Long-term estrogen replacement therapy prevents bone loss and fractures. Ann Intern Med 1985;102:319–24.

48. Paganini-Hill A, Ross RK, Gerkins VR, et al. Menopausal estrogen therapy and hip fractures. Ann Intern Med 1981;95:28–31.

49. Weiss NS, Ure CL, Ballard JH, et al. Decreased risk of fractures of the hip and lower forearm with postmenopausal use of estrogen. N Engl J Med 1980; 303:1195–8.

50. Naessen T, Persson I, Adami HO, et al. Hormone replacement therapy and the risk for first hip fracture: a prospective, population-based cohort study. Ann Intern Med 1990;113:95–103.

51. Cauley J, Seeley DG, Ensrud K, et al. Estrogen replacement therapy and fractures in older women. Ann Intern Med 1995;122:9–16.

52. Kiel DP, Felson DT, Anderson JJ, et al. Hip fracture and the use of estrogens in postmenopausal women. The Framingham Study. N Engl J Med 1987;317: 1169–74.

53. Grady D, Rubin SM, Petitti DB, et al. Hormone therapy to prevent disease and prolong life in postmenopausal women. Ann Intern Med 1992;117: 1016–37.

54. Lufkin EG, Wahner HW, O'Fallon WM, et al. Treatment of postmenopausal osteoporosis with transdermal estrogen. Ann Intern Med 1992;117:1–9.

55. Windeler J, Lange S. Events per person year. A dubious concept. BMJ 1995;310:454-6.

56. Torgerson DJ, Bell-Syer SEM. Hormone replacement therapy and prevention of nonvertebral fractures. A meta-analysis of randomized trials. JAMA 2001;285: 2891–7.

57. Cauley JA, Seeley DG, Ensrud K, et al. Estrogen replacement therapy and fractures in older women. Study of Osteoporotic Fractures Research Group. Ann Intern Med 1995;122:9–16.

58. Schneider DL, Barrett-Connor EL, Morton DJ. Timing of postmenopausal estrogen for optimal bone mineral density. The Rancho Bernardo Study. JAMA 1997;277:543–7.

59. Hulley S, Grady D, Bush T, et al. Randomized trial of estrogen plus progestin for secondary prevention of coronary heart disease in postmenopausal women. Heart and Estrogen/progestin Replacement Study (HERS) Research Group. JAMA 1998;280:605–13.

60. Grodstein F, Manson JE, Colditz GA, et al. A prospective, observational study of postmenopausal hormone therapy and primary prevention of cardiovascular disease. Ann Intern Med 2000;133:933–41.

61. Lindsay R, Hart DM, Clark DM. The minimum effective dose of estrogen for prevention of postmenopausal bone loss. Obstet Gynecol 1984;63:759–63.

62. Recker RR, Davies M, Dowd RM, Heaney RP. The effect of low-dose continuous estrogen and progesterone therapy with calcium and vitamin D on bone in elderly women. A randomized, controlled trial. Ann Intern Med 1999;130:897–904.

63. Delmas PD, Bjarnason NH, Mitlak BH, et al. Effects of raloxifene on bone mineral density, serum cholesterol concentrations, and uterine endometrium in postmenopausal women. N Engl J Med 1997;337: 1641–7.

64. Ettinger B, Black DM, Mitlak BH, et al. Reduction of vertebral fracture risk in postmenopausal women with osteoporosis treated with raloxifene. Results from a 3-year randomized clinical trial. Multiple Outcomes of Raloxifene Evaluation (MORE) Investigators. JAMA 1999;282:637–45.

65. Cummings SR, Eckert S, Krueger KA, et al. The effect of raloxifene on risk of breast cancer in postmenopausal women. Results from the MORE randomized trial. JAMA 1999;281:2189–97.

66. Chestnut CH, Silverman S, Andriano K, et al. Prospective, randomized trial of nasal spray calcitonin in postmenopausal women with established osteoporosis. The PROOF study. Am J Med 2000; 109:267–76.

67. Pun KK, Chan LWL. Analgesic effect of intranasal salmon calcitonin in the treatment of osteoporotic vertebral fractures. Clin Ther 1989;11:205–9.

68. Lyritis GP, Tsakalalos N, Magiasis B, et al. Analgesic effect of salmon calcitonin in osteoporotic vertebral fractures: a double-blind placebo-controlled clinical study. Calcif Tissue Int 1991;49:369–72.

69. Ljunghall S, Gardsell P, Johnell O, et al. Synthetic human calcitonin in postmenopausal osteoporosis: a placebo-controlled, double-blind study. Calcif Tissue Int 1991;49:17–9.

70. Neer RM, Arnaud CD, Zanchetta JR, et al. Effect of parathyroid hormone (1-34) on fractures and bone mineral density in postmenopausal women with osteoporosis. N Engl J Med 2001;344:1434–41.

71. Cauley JA, Cummings SR, Seeley DG, et al. Effects of thiazide diuretic therapy on bone mass, fractures and falls. The Study of Osteoporotic Fractures Research Group. Ann Intern Med 1993;118:666–73.

72. LaCroix AZ, Ott SM, Ichikawa L, et al. Low-dose hydrochlorothiazide and preservation of bone mineral density in older adults. A randomized, double-blind, placebo-controlled trial. Ann Intern Med 2000; 133:516–26.

73. Kelepouris N, Harper KD, Gannon F, et al. Severe osteoporosis in men. Ann Intern Med 1995;123: 452–60.

74. Garnero P, Delmas PD. New developments in biochemical markers for osteoporosis. Calcif Tissue Int 1996;59 Suppl 1:S2–9.

75. Lindsay R. Risk assessment using bone mineral density determination. Osteoporos Int 1998;8 Suppl 1: S28–31.

76. Cummings SR. Prevention of hip fractures in older women: a population-based perspective. Osteoporos Int 1998;8 Suppl 1:S8–12.

77. Sowers M. Pregnancy and lactation as risk factors for subsequent bone loss and osteoporosis. J Bone Miner Res 1996;11:1052–60.

78. Khovidhunkit W, Epstein S. Osteoporosis in pregnancy. Osteoporos Int 1996;6:342–54.

79. Schapira D. Transient osteoporosis of the hip. Semin Arthritis Rheum 1992;22:98–105.

80. DeCherney A. Bone-sparing properities of oral contraceptives. Am J Obstet Gynecol 1996;174:15–20.

48

FIBROMYALGIA

Samuel A. Skootsky, MD

The first significant attempt to understand the clinical entity we now call fibromyalgia was a report on the "fibrositis" syndrome by Smythe and Moldofsky in 1977.[1] Previously, the term "fibrositis" had been used widely for a plethora of ill-defined entities associated with soft tissue pain. In their report Smythe and Moldofsky stated, "It seems to us that there is a definable entity to which traditional clinical descriptions of the 'fibrositis syndrome' may be applied." This initial report emphasized a syndrome that included widespread chronic pain, characteristic tender points, and nonrestorative sleep. Four years later, Yunus et al[2] redefined this clinical entity under the term "fibromyalgia"—a term that seemed more fitting, since no inflammation could be demonstrated.

In 1990, Frederick Wolfe[3] published the results of a landmark multicenter study that developed reliable criteria for the diagnosis of fibromyalgia under the auspices of the American College of Rheumatology (ACR). The diagnosis of fibromyalgia is now straightforward and is based on a clinical history and examination that can be done easily in the office setting. However, the etiology and pathogenesis of fibromyalgia remain unknown, and the treatment is empiric and symptomatic.

CLINICAL EPIDEMIOLOGY

At least 85% of cases of fibromyalgia occur in women. Both patients and nonpatients (ie, persons in the general population who exhibit symptoms of fibromyalgia but who have not sought medical treatment for these symptoms) have been studied. In the general population the median age of women reporting a new onset of fibromyalgia symptoms is 49 years. The prevalence of fibromyalgia peaks in the seventh decade.[4] Although most patients with

fibromyalgia are perimenopausal or older, the onset of symptoms also can occur in the teenage years or young adulthood.

Historically there was felt to be an association between psychiatric disorders and fibromyalgia. This perceived increased prevalence of psychiatric disorders in fibromyalgia patients has been determined to be the result of referral bias. Patients self-referred or sent for evaluation to specialized clinics are not the same as unselected persons with symptoms of fibromyalgia. Subjects with fibromyalgia who are nonpatients (ie, not in contact with the health care system) have the same number of lifetime psychiatric disorders as do control subjects. Patients with fibromyalgia (who therefore do have contact with the health care system) have a higher number of lifetime psychiatric diagnoses and higher levels of distress[5] when compared with control subjects.Common psychiatric problems identified in fibromyalgia patients include depression and/or anxiety.

Although the symptoms of fibromyalgia often can suggest other rheumatologic conditions, long-term studies[6] have clarified that fibromyalgia patients who are appropriately diagnosed do not generally develop subsequent connective tissue disease. This is supported by a recent report that found no clinical differences between fibromyalgia patients with or without positive results in antinuclear antibody tests.[7]

Fibromyalgia is best considered a chronic illness that undergoes cycles of exacerbation and remission. Furthermore, there is a spectrum of severity. Long-term follow-up studies show that in patients being followed up in specialty clinics, complete remission is rare. A cohort of fibromyalgia patients has been surveyed in 1983, 1985, and 1993 following diagnosis in 1982.[6] Eleven years following diagnosis (by the criteria of Yunus et al[2]), no patient in this cohort was free of symptoms. Fifty-five percent reported moderate to severe pain or stiffness; 48% had sleep disturbance, 59% had moderate to severe fatigue. In spite of this, 55% of patients rated their fibromyalgia symptoms as "doing well" (45% rated their symptoms fair or poor), and 66% felt that they were a little or a lot better (24% felt they were a little or a lot worse). Alternative medical therapies were used by 62%. These findings have been confirmed by another study of 538 patients in which pain, fatigue, sleep disturbance, anxiety, depression, and health status were unchanged over a 7-year period.[8]

EFFECTS OF PREGNANCY, PERI-MENOPAUSE, AND SEX HORMONES

Little information exists concerning the effect of pregnancy, menopause, or sex hormones on fibromyalgia. One retrospective study of 26 women with a total of 40 pregnancies reported worsening of fibromyalgia symptoms during pregnancy, particularly during the last trimester.[9] These women also had increased postpartum depression and anxiety. These pregnancies were otherwise uneventful, there were no fetal abnormalities, and breast-feeding was successful. This one retrospective study should be interpreted with caution, and, at present, there is no reason to suggest that patients with fibromyalgia who wish to get pregnant should not do so.

There are no prospective studies published concerning the effect of exogenous sex-hormone replacement or the perimenopause on fibromyalgia. The age of diagnosis of fibromyalgia can overlap with the expected age of menopause, and some of the symptoms of menopause also can be seen in fibromyalgia, especially fatigue. But the perimenopause generally is not associated with significant widespread pain. At present there is no evidence that alterations in sex hormones have a significant relationship to the development of fibromyalgia.

DIAGNOSIS

The 1990 ACR criteria for the diagnosis of fibromyalgia is outlined in Table 48–1.[3] One of the key diagnostic criteria is the presence of tender points. The location of characteristic tender point areas is presented in more detail in Figure 48–1. A positive

TABLE 48–1. American Rheumatology Criteria for the Diagnosis of Fibromyalgia

1. History of widespread pain for > 3 mo: widespread pain is defined as pain that is present on both sides of the body (left and right) *and* above and below the waist *and* has an axial component (cervical, low back, anterior chest, or thoracic spine)
2. Pain in 11 of 18 specific tender point sites on digital palpation: there are nine paired sites (see Figure 48–1)—occiput, low cervical, trapezius, supraspinatus, second anterior rib, lateral epicondyle, gluteal, greater trochanter, and medical knee

Adapted from Wolfe F, Smythe HA, Yunus MB, et al. The American College of Rheumatology 1990 criteria for the classification of fibromyalgia. Arthritis Rheum 1990;33:160–72.

response at a tender point site is defined by the patient stating that palpation at that site is painful. In the ACR study defining fibromyalgia, palpation was done with the thumb or first two or three fingers with a pressure of 4 kg/cm^2. This is firm, not light, pressure. The examination is best done with the patient sitting on the examining table and the examiner standing in front, facing the patient.

The 1990 ACR criteria were developed to separate fibromyalgia from other rheumatologic conditions with which it may be confused. No distinction was made between primary and secondary (associated with other conditions) fibromyalgia. The ACR criteria are solely widespread pain and the number of tender points because it was found that these features alone provided the greatest degree of diagnostic accuracy. However, patients with fibromyalgia routinely do have other symptoms. Therefore, the clinical evaluation should also screen for the presence of these other features. Although these other symptoms and problems are not part of the ACR criteria, if they are completely absent, the presence of fibromyalgia is unlikely. Almost all of these associated features were used as "minor criteria" in the Yunus classification that was used widely prior to 1990. These features are listed in Table 48–2.

One problem with use of the 1990 ACR criteria in routine clinical practice is that the criteria do not take into account the waxing and waning of manifestations that typically occur in patients with fibromyalgia. A patient with 9 or 10 tender points may have more tender points at another time of examination. It is therefore necessary in clinical

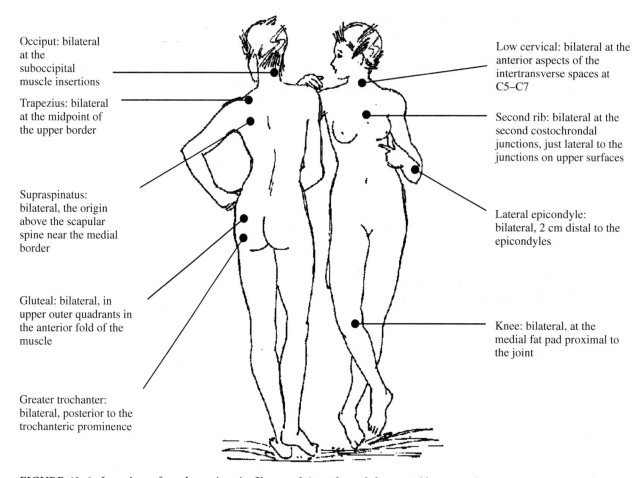

Occiput: bilateral at the suboccipital muscle insertions

Trapezius: bilateral at the midpoint of the upper border

Supraspinatus: bilateral, the origin above the scapular spine near the medial border

Gluteal: bilateral, in upper outer quadrants in the anterior fold of the muscle

Greater trochanter: bilateral, posterior to the trochanteric prominence

Low cervical: bilateral at the anterior aspects of the intertransverse spaces at C5–C7

Second rib: bilateral at the second costochrondal junctions, just lateral to the junctions on upper surfaces

Lateral epicondyle: bilateral, 2 cm distal to the epicondyles

Knee: bilateral, at the medial fat pad proximal to the joint

FIGURE 48–1. Location of tender points in fibromyalgia. Adapted from Wolfe F, Smythe HA, Yunus MB, et al. The American College of Rheumatology 1990 criteria for the classification of fibromyalgia. Arthritis Rheum 1990; 33:160–72.

TABLE 48–2. Symptoms and Problems Commonly Associated with Fibromyalgia

Sleep disturbance[*]

Fatigue[*]

Morning stiffness[*]

Paresthesia[*]

Chronic headache[*]

Irritable bowel syndrome[*]

Anxiety[*]

Modulation by noise, temperature, stress, or physical activity[*]

Subjective swelling[*]

Current or prior depression

[*]Features described in Yunus MB, Masi AT, Calabro JJ, et al. Primary fibromyalgia (fibrositis): clinical study of 50 patients with matched controls. Semin Arthritis Rheum 1981;11:151–71.

practice to recognize that even though some patients may not fit the 1990 ACR criteria exactly, they nonetheless should be treated similarly to patients who fulfill both criteria for the diagnosis of fibromyalgia. On the other hand, it is reasonable to strictly use the criteria of widespread pain in the diagnosis of fibromyalgia, because *that* feature helps distinguish fibromyalgia from other regional (nonwidespread) pains such as myofascial pain.

While the differential diagnosis of diffuse pain is extensive, the primary care approach of systematic evaluation is appropriate. First the patient should be evaluated by taking a history and performing a physical examination. Laboratory tests should be ordered selectively. There is no laboratory test for fibromyalgia, and no laboratory tests are required for the diagnosis. However, it is logical to consider certain tests to screen for more serious diseases. These include a thyroid panel, complete blood count, creatine phosphokinase level, and erythrocyte sedimentation rate. An antinuclear antibody and rheumatoid factor tests should be ordered if there are features that specifically suggest systemic lupus or rheumatoid arthritis. Regardless of whether other features of systemic lupus are present, women with symptoms suggestive of rheumatic disease frequently undergo antinuclear antibody testing. It is important not to misinterpret low-titer positive results; these results are common and are unlikely to represent systemic lupus in the absence of other characteristic symptoms, signs, and laboratory findings. Women who fulfill the criteria for fibromyalgia and who lack the typical features of systemic lupus should not be labeled as having lupus even if their antinuclear antibody test is positive.[7]

ETIOLOGY AND PATHOGENESIS

The etiology of fibromyalgia is unknown. The finding that sleep in fibromyalgia is disturbed (nonrestorative sleep) and is associated with the specific electroencephalogram (EEG) abnormality of "α wave intrusion" into stages of sleep usually free of α waves led to speculation that this intrusion was causal.[1] However, this EEG abnormality is not specific to fibromyalgia and is associated with chronic pain states generally. In a subgroup of chronic pain patients with disturbed sleep, it was found that increased body pain, physical disability, depression, and anxiety were more common in fibromyalgia.[10] A transient condition clinically similar to fibromyalgia can be induced in healthy volunteers by noise disruption of stage 4 sleep. Interestingly, sedentary subjects are more susceptible, compared with those who are well-conditioned physically.[1] It is now felt that the disturbed sleep and EEG abnormalities in some patients with fibromyalgia are secondary phenomena, possibly caused by sleep disruption due to stress.

Traumatic injury has been suggested to play a role in some patients with fibromyalgia. There is an association between injury and the development of fibromyalgia.[11] Injury is associated with pain, stress, anxiety, and depression. In one study, 2 to 4 months following initial traumatic insult, fibromyalgia developed in 22% of subjects.

A recent study has demonstrated that the deep tissues of fibromyalgia patients have a lower pain threshold than do those of normal subjects.[12] There-fore the widespread pain that characterizes fibromyalgia may be the result of central sensitization to nociceptive input. This results in allodynia, a clinical state in which pain is experienced at levels of nociception (eg, palpation) that normal subjects would not find painful.

Central sensitization may be related to abnormalities and responses in the central nervous system, particularly with neuropeptides (eg, substance P)[13] and the neuroendocrine system. Patients with fibromyalgia have a neuroendocrine response pattern that is associated with stress,[14] with upregulation of the hypophyseal-pituitary axis. There are low levels of serotonin and insulin-like growth hormone. A recent study suggests that patients with fibromyalgia may have reduced cortical or subcortical inhibition of nociception.[15] Recently, decreased regional blood flow in the thalamus and caudate nucleus has been described. Although progress is being made in our understanding of fibromyalgia, it is not yet clear which abnormalities are important.

EVALUATION STRATEGIES IN PRIMARY CARE

The initial focus when evaluating a patient with possible fibromyalgia should be on (1) establishing trust with the patient, (2) establishing the diagnosis, (3) screening for psychological disturbance, and (4) understanding the patient's level of physical and social functioning. It is assumed that if the diagnosis is fibromyalgia, at least one of the chief complaints will be widespread pain. However, patients also can present with other features (see Table 48–2).

The first step is establishing the diagnosis by taking a history and performing a physical examination (see Table 48–1 and Figure 48–1), taking time to elicit the commonly associated features of fibromyalgia that are not necessary for diagnosis (see Table 48–2). Performing a complete evaluation of the patient's symptoms indicates to the patient that her complaints are being taken seriously and that her clinician is knowledgeable about her illness. It is important to keep in mind that many patients have read materials in books, pamphlets, or on the World Wide Web that are full of misinformation. Alternative disease processes that could explain or contribute to the patient's complaints, including thyroid and inflammatory rheumatologic illnesses, should be considered. An approach to this evaluation is described in Chapter 42, "Approach to the Patient with Diffuse Joint and Muscular Pain."

It is useful to maintain a written record of perceived pain. A visual analog scale or other rating system is most useful and can be incorporated into a patient diary.

It is essential to screen for psychological dysfunction, especially depression and anxiety. Sometimes the primary care physician can successfully treat psychiatric illness in patients with fibromyalgia, but there should be a very low threshold for an evaluation by a competent psychologist or psychiatrist. This is especially true if there is dysfunction at home or work or with social activities. Ideally, this mental health clinician would have an interest in patients with chronic pain. A psychological evaluation also is needed for patients who require or insist on any opiate or opiate-containing compounds—not because opiate use is intrinsically harmful, but because in the United States opiate use is associated with dysfunctional behaviors. Commonly, fibromyalgia patients who request or require narcotics are found to have depression and/or anxiety disorders. Screening for sleep disturbance is logically done during the psychological screen, since depression and anxiety so commonly impact on sleep. Regardless of the cause, poor sleep intensifies the pain symptoms and causes fatigue.

Physical and social functioning should be evaluated. Patients so debilitated that they cannot fulfill the basic activities of daily living are rare and need referral to a specialist. Basic, intermediate, and advanced levels of functional status should be investigated. Can she get up in the morning, dress, eat, and groom herself? Can she take care of more extended needs such as shopping, finances, and getting to work? Can she function in society, for example, at work and within the community? Is there anything that she doesn't do now that she used to do? What is her immediate family structure, and how has it been impacted?

TREATMENT

Table 48–3 lists pharmacologic and nonpharmacologic treatments shown to be useful.[16–37] In addition, several other treatments and strategies have shown some promise but are unproven or are not practical for treatment of outpatients. These treatments and strategies include lidocaine, tramadol, ketamine, regional sympathetic blockers, odensetron,[38] and growth hormone.[39]

As important as knowing effective therapies is knowing which therapies have been shown to be ineffective. These include acupuncture, trigger point injection, imipramine, calcitonin, prednisone, naproxen, guaifenesin, *S*-adenosylmethionine, and maprotiline.

The following conclusions can be drawn from treatment trials in fibromyalgia:

- There is no cure for fibromyalgia, but in many patients symptoms can be ameliorated.
- Anti-inflammatory agents (ie, nonsteroidal anti-inflammatory agents and corticosteroids) are ineffective.
- Amitriptyline and cyclobenzaprine have demonstrated short-term effectiveness (amitriptyline is more effective).
- Patients with fibromyalgia *can* exercise and improve their cardiovascular fitness.
- There is benefit associated with cardiovascular fitness.
- Some patients may benefit from psychopharmacology directed toward depression or anxiety.
- Cognitive behavioral therapy may be useful, especially when combined with exercise.

Treatment Strategies in Primary Care

After an understanding of the biopsychosocial status of the patient has been obtained, a plan of treatment can be developed.

Some patients with very mild disease, no psychological disturbance, and good social functioning are relieved to have a diagnosis made by a knowledgeable physician and do not require any specific therapy. Patients with very severe symptoms, polypharmacy, and poor functional status may require more specialized care than a primary care clinician can reasonably provide.

All fibromyalgia patients should participate in an exercise program. Assisting the patient in developing daily aerobic exercise and light weight–training routines is a worthwhile goal. Although initial studies of therapeutic exercise to improve fibromyalgia symptoms emphasized enhanced cardiovascular fitness[30] by having patients undergo supervised training, other reports have shown benefit obtained from walking 20 minutes three times

TABLE 48–3. Useful Treatment Strategies for Fibromyalgia

Treatment Strategy	Agent	Improvement in Pain?	References	Comment
Pharmacologic	Amitriptyline	Yes	16–19	Proven short-term benefit
	Cyclobenzaprine	Yes	20–24	Proven short-term benefit
	Alprazolam	—	25	May be useful when symptoms of anxiety predominate
	Venlafaxine	—	26	May be useful when symptoms of depression predominate
	Fluoxetine	—	27, 28	May be most useful when symptoms of depression predominate; some reports showed no effect
	Zolpidem	No	29	Improved sleep but not pain
Nonpharmacologic	Cardiovascular fitness training	—	30,31	Proven benefit, especially if patient is motivated
	Electromyographic biofeedback	—	32	Limited information
	Electroacupuncture	—	33	Limited information
Psychodynamic	Cognitive behavioral therapy	—	34,35	Usually combined with exercise
	Hypnotherapy	—	36	May be useful when mental distress predominates
	Meditation-based stress reduction	—	37	Program was pyscho-dynamically based

weekly.[31] A reasonable initial goal might be at least 20 minutes of significant aerobic exercise at least three days a week—more is probably better. Having the patient keep diaries and logs may enhance compliance. Some patients benefit from physical therapy as a way to break out of a sedentary lifestyle. A brief course of physical therapy can be used to develop an individualized home exercise program.

Alternative medicine therapies are being studied for use in fibromyalgia. For example, a recent report suggested that electroacupuncture may be effective,[33] but more studies are needed.

For patients who need drug therapy, a low dose of amitriptyline or cyclobenzaprine usually is used initially. Amitriptyline is the agent most commonly used, and it is more effective than is cyclobenzaprine. The starting dose is 10 mg PO at bedtime. This dose can be increased approximately every week in 10 mg increments to about 30 to 50 mg, as long as side effects do not develop. Patients rarely need more than 30 mg of either drug. In clinical practice amitriptyline is prescribed indefinitely if it is helpful and well tolerated, even though long-term treatment studies are lacking. This initial pharmacologic therapy should be combined with attention to sleep hygiene, which is described in further detail in Chapter 60, "Approach to the Patient with Insomnia."

Any psychological issues should be assessed early and treated in parallel with other interventions. When patients require pharmacotherapy for psychiatric issues, it is best to use the drugs listed in Table 48–3, which have been studied in fibromyalgia patients. The only exception might be to substitute citalopram (Celexa) for fluoxetine (Prozac), as it seems to be much better tolerated. In some cases, when sleep is improved due to treatment of the psychologic disturbance, the patient may obtain enough clinical improvement from her pain that she is satisfied with the results. These are the cases in which the symptoms of depression or anxiety pre-

dominate. In such cases, it makes sense to delay the trial of amitriptyline to determine the initial benefit of psychological treatment alone.

If the patient fails to find any satisfaction with these strategies, referral to a rheumatologist (or other clinician) with a special interest in fibromyalgia is the next step.

RESOURCE

As is true for other chronic conditions that are poorly understood, much misinformation exists, including that on the World Wide Web.

The American Fibromyalgia Association, Inc.
6380 East Tanque Verde, Suite D
Tuscon, Arizona 85715
Telephone: (520) 733-1570
Web site: www.afsafund.org

The American Fibromyalgia Association is a nonprofit organization with a well-organized Web site that provides a good deal of accurate information and links to other related sites. Brochures, books, and videos can be located through this site.

REFERENCES

1. Smythe HA, Moldofsky H. Two contributions to understanding of the "fibrositis" syndrome. Bull Rheum Dis 1977;28:928–31.
2. Yunus MB, Masi AT, Calabro JJ, et al. Primary fibromyalgia (fibrositis): clinical study of 50 patients with matched controls. Semin Arthritis Rheum 1981; 11:151–71.
3. Wolfe F, Smythe HA, Yunus MB, et al. The American College of Rheumatology 1990 criteria for the classification of fibromyalgia. Arthritis Rheum 1990; 33:160–72.
4. Wolfe F, Ross K, Anderson J, et al. The prevalence and characteristics of fibromyalgia in the general population. Arthritis Rheum 1995;38:19–28.
5. Aaron LA, Bradley LA, Alarcon GS, et al. Psychiatric diagnoses in patients with fibromyalgia are related to health care–seeking behavior rather than to illness. Arthritis Rheum 1996;39:436–45.
6. Kennedy M, Felson DT. A prospective long-term study of fibromyalgia syndrome. Arthritis Rheum 1996;39:682–5.
7. Zonana-Nacach A, Alacron GS, Reveille JD, et al. Clinical features of ANA-positive and ANA-negative patients with fibromyalgia. Clin Rheumatol 1998; 4:52–6.
8. Wolfe F, Anderson J, Harkness D, et al. Health status and disease severity in fibromyalgia: results of a six-center longitudinal study. Arthritis Rheum 1997; 40:1571–9.
9. Ostensen M, Rugelsjoen A, Wigers SH. The effect of reproductive events and alterations of sex hormone levels on the symptoms of fibromyalgia. Scand J Rheumatol 1997;26:355–60.
10. Pilowsky I, Crettenden I, Townley M. Sleep disturbance in pain clinic patients. Pain 1985;23:27–33.
11. Buskila D, Neumann L, Vaisberg G, et al. Increased rates of fibromyalgia following cervical spine injury. Arthritis Rheum 1997;40:466–52.
12. Kosek E, Ekholm J, Hansson P. Modulation of pressure pain thresholds during and following isometric contraction in patients with fibromyalgia and in healthy controls. Pain 1996;64:415–23.
13. Russell IJ. Neurochemical pathogenesis of fibromyalgia syndrome. J Musculoskeletal Pain 1999;7:183–91.
14. Crofford LJ. Neuroendocrine findings in patients with fibromyalgia. J Musculoskeletal Pain 1998;6:69–76.

15. Lorenz J, Grasedyck K, Bromm B. Middle and long latency somatosensory evoked potentials after painful laser stimulation in patients with fibromyalgia syndrome. Electroencephalogr Clin Neurophysiol 1996;100:165–8.

16. Carette S, McCain GA, Bell DA, Fam AG. Evaluation of amitriptyline in primary fibrositis. A double-blind, placebo-controlled study. Arthritis Rheum 1986; 29:655–9.

17. Goldenberg DL, Felson DT, Dinerman H. A randomized, controlled trial of amitriptyline and naproxen in the treatment of patients with fibromyalgia. Arthritis Rheum 1986;29:1371–7.

18. Jaeschke R, Adachi J, Guyatt G, et al. Clinical usefulness of amitriptyline in fibromyalgia: the results of 23 N-of-1 randomized controlled trials. J Rheumatol 1991;18:447–51.

19. Scudds RA, McCain GA, Rollman GB, Harth M. Improvements in pain responsiveness in patients with fibrositis after successful treatment with amitriptyline. J Rheumatol 1989;16 Suppl 19:113–9.

20. Reynolds WJ, Moldofsky H, Saskin P, Lue FA. The effects of cyclobenzaprine on sleep physiology and symptoms in patients with fibromyalgia. J Rheumatol 1991;18:452–4.

21. Bennett RM, Gatter RA, Campbell SM, et al. A comparison of cyclobenzaprine and placebo in the management of fibrositis. Arthritis Rheum 1988; 31:1535–42.

22. Quimby LG, Gratwick GM, Whitney CA, Block SR. A randomized trial of cyclobenzaprine for the treatment of fibromyalgia. J Rheumatol 1989;16 Suppl 19:140–3.

23. Santandrea S, Montrone F, Sarzi-Puttini P, et al. A double-blind crossover study of two cyclobenzaprine regimens in primary fibromyalgia syndrome. J Int Med Res 1993;21:74–80.

24. Hamaty D, Valentine JL, Howard R, et al. The plasma endorphin prostaglandin and catecholamine profile in patients with fibrositis treated with cyclobenzaprine and placebo. J Rheumatol Suppl 1989; 19:S164–8.

25. Russell IJ, Fletcher EM, Michalek JE, et al. Treatment of primary fibrositis/fibromyalgia syndrome with ibuprofen and alprazolam: a double-blind, placebo-controlled study. Arthritis Rheum 1991;34:552–60.

26. Dwight MM, Arnold LM, O'Brien H, et al. An open clinical trial of venlafaxine treatment of fibromyalgia. Psychosomatics 1998;39:14–7.

27. Goldenberg D, Mayskiyy M, Mossey C, et al. A randomized, double-blind crossover trial of fluoxetine and amitriptyline in the treatment of fibromyalgia. Arthritis Rheum 1996;39:1852–9.

28. Wolfe F, Cathey MA, Hawley DJ. A double-blind placebo controlled trial of fluoxetine in fibromyalgia. Scand J Rheumatol 1994;23:255–9.

29. Moldofsky H, Lue FA, Mously C, et al. The effect of zolpidem in patients with fibromyalgia: a dose ranging, double-blind, placebo controlled, modified crossover study. J Rheumatol 1996;23:529–33.

30. McCain GA, Bell DA, Mai F, Halliday PD. A controlled study of the effects of a supervised cardiovascular fitness training program on the manifestations of the primary fibromyalgia syndrome. Arthritis Rheum 1988;31:1135–41.

31. Nichols DS, Glenn TM. Effects of aerobic exercise on pain perception, affect, and level of disability in individuals with fibromyalgia. Phy Ther 1994;74:327–32.

32. Furaccioli G, Chirelli L, Scita F, et al. EMG-biofeedback training in fibromyalgia syndrome. J Rheumatol 1987;14:820–5.

33. Deluze C, Bosia L, Zirbs A, et al. Electroacupuncture in fibromyalgia: results of a controlled trial. Br Med J 1992;305:1249–52.

34. White KP, Nielson WR. Cognitive behavioral treatment of fibromyalgia syndrome: a follow-up assessment. J Rheumatol 1995;22:717–21.

35. Bradley LA. Cognitive behavioural therapy for fibromyalgia. J Rheumatol Suppl 1989;19:131–6.

36. Hannen HCM, Hoenderdos HTW, Van Romunde LKJ, et al. Controlled trail of hypnotherapy in the treatment of refractory fibromyalgia. J Rheumatol 1991;18:72–5.

37. Kaplan KH, Goldenberg DL, Galvin-Nadeau M. The impact of a meditation-based stress reduction program on fibromyalgia. Gen Hosp Psychiatry 1993; 15:284–9.

38. Hrycaj P, Stratz T, Mennet P, Muller W. Pathogenetic aspects of responsiveness to ondansetron (5-hydroxytryptamine type 3 receptor antagonist) in patients with primary fibromyalgia syndrome—a preliminary study. J Rheumatol 1996;23:1418–23.

39. Bennett RM, Clark SC, Walczyk J. A randomized, double-blind, placebo-controlled study of growth hormone in the treatment of fibromyalgia. Am J Med 1998;104:227–31.

49

APPROACH TO THE PATIENT WITH LOW BACK PAIN

Thomas O. Staiger, MD, Dawn E. DeWitt, MD, MSc, and Richard A. Deyo, MD, MPH

Low back pain is a common, generally self-limited, problem produced by numerous conditions that can affect the back. It is one of the most frequent reasons for visits to a primary care clinician.[1] Over two-thirds of adults experience low back pain at some time during their life, with a yearly prevalence in the US population of 15 to 20%.[2,3] About 14% of individuals experience an episode during their life of back pain lasting longer than 2 weeks.[4] Approximately 2% of patients with back pain experience lower extremity nerve root symptoms (radiculopathy) lasting greater than 2 weeks.[5]

Most patients improve considerably during the first 4 weeks after an episode of low back pain. Approximately two-thirds of patients are either pain free or have mild pain at 4 weeks, whereas 20 to 25% have pain that continues to limit their activities. Recurrences of pain are common during the first year following an episode of acute low back pain.[6] The majority of patients with radicular symptoms experience substantial improvement within 6 weeks. Five to 10% of patients who have radicular pain from a disk herniation fail to improve with conservative treatment and eventually require surgery.[5]

Most causes of back pain are seen in both women and men. Causes of back pain seen exclusively in women include back pain associated with pregnancy, endometriosis, or dysmenorrhea. Osteoporotic compression fractures are much more common in women than in men. On the other hand, ankylosing spondylitis is less common in women.[7]

ETIOLOGIES AND CLASSIFICATION OF BACK PAIN

Approximately 98% of back pain is related to injuries, or other mechanical factors, affecting the muscles, ligaments, vertebrae, and disks. Only 2% of patients in a typical primary care practice are found to have back pain due either to systemic causes such as cancer or infections, or to visceral causes, such as renal stones, pyelonephritis, aortic aneurysms, or gynecologic disorders.[8] In up to 85% of patients with low back pain, a definitive diagnosis of the cause is not possible. Strains and sprains involving back muscles or ligaments and degeneration of facet joints or disks, for which there is no definitive diagnostic test, appear to be responsible for many instances of back pain. Because improvement with conservative therapy is usual, making a specific diagnosis does not affect treatment or prognosis for most patients with back pain.

Intervertebral Disk Herniation

Disk herniations are present on imaging studies in 20 to 30% of adults without back pain.[9] Back pain and sciatica can be caused by compression or inflammation of a nerve root due to a herniated intervertebral disk. Sciatica is a sharp or burning radicular pain radiating into the buttock and down the leg below the knee, often with paresthesia of the lower leg. Since sciatica is present in 95% of symptomatic disk herniations, the absence of sciatica makes a clinically important disk herniation unlikely.[10] Approximately 95% of clinically important disk herniations occur at the lumbar vertebrae (L)4–5 or the L5–sacral vertebra (S) 1 disk level.[5] Herniations of

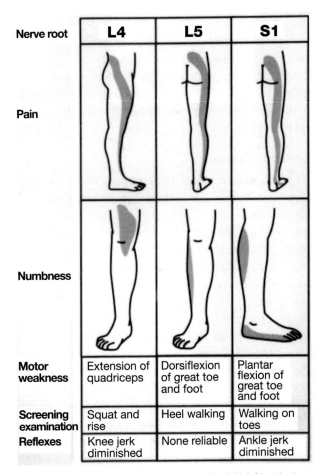

Nerve root	L4	L5	S1
Pain			
Numbness			
Motor weakness	Extension of quadriceps	Dorsiflexion of great toe and foot	Plantar flexion of great toe and foot
Screening examination	Squat and rise	Heel walking	Walking on toes
Reflexes	Knee jerk diminished	None reliable	Ankle jerk diminished

FIGURE 49–1. Examples of intervertebral disk herniation.

L4–5 (L5 root) cause pain and/or numbness in the posterior thigh, lateral leg, medial foot, and great toe (Figure 49–1).[11] Examination may show weakness of ankle and great toe dorsiflexion. The L5–S1 (S1 root) disk herniations cause pain and/or numbness of the posterior thigh, posterolateral foot, and lateral toes. There may be weakness of plantar flexion of the foot and toes and a decrease in the ankle reflex.[12] Impingement at the L2–3 or L3–4 disk level is seen in 2 to 5% of disk herniations. These patients present with pain/numbness of the posterolateral or anterior thigh radiating to the anteromedial knee. Most patients with disk herniations improve in 4 to 6 weeks. If a patient who would be a candidate for surgery fails to improve with 4 to 6 weeks of conservative treatment and has an obvious level of nerve root dysfunction on examination, a surgical consultation and/or imaging (magnetic resonance imaging [MRI] or computed tomography [CT]) are warranted. If an examination is equivocal for a discreet level of nerve-root dysfunction, an electromyogram (EMG) can be helpful.[13]

Large midline disk herniations (as well as tumors or epidural abscesses) can cause the cauda equina syndrome. Patients characteristically present with back pain, urinary retention, and bilateral radicular symptoms.[14] Urinary retention and overflow incontinence are the most consistent finding, being present in about 90% of patients. Seventy-five percent of patients experience saddle anesthesia of the perineum and posterior thighs due to compression of S3 and S4. Patients with the cauda equina syndrome or who have rapidly progressing neurologic deficits require emergent surgical consultation.

Compression Fractures and Osteoporosis

About 4% of patients with back pain in primary care are found to have vertebral compression fractures.[10] Compression fractures usually are due to osteoporosis but also can occur with significant axial trauma or with myeloma or other metastatic neoplasms. Most osteoporotic compression fractures occur spontaneously or with minimal trauma.[15] Among Caucasian women 5% of 50-year-olds and 25% of 80-year-olds have compression fractures. African American and Latino women have 75% fewer osteoporotic fractures than do Caucasian women.[16] In addition to age and gender, long-term corticosteroid use is a strong risk factor for vertebral compression fractures. New vertebral fractures are an important cause of back pain and functional limitation, as women with new compression fractures have a twofold risk of back pain compared with women without fractures.[17] An estimated 26 to 50% of acute osteoporotic fractures are asymptomatic.[18] Women whose osteoporotic fractures are over 3 years old have rates of back pain similar to those who have never had osteoporotic fractures. There is moderately good evidence that calcitonin nasal spray leads to improvement in pain after a recent osteoporotic compression fracture.[19] No comparisons of calcitonin and nonsteroidal anti-inflammatory drugs (NSAIDs) or analgesics for the treatment of osteoporotic compression fractures have been published. Treatment of osteoporosis should include calcium and vitamin D, regular weight-bearing exercise, and hormone replacement therapy, raloxifene, alendronate, risjdronate or calcitonin as appropriate. This is discussed in detail in Chapter 47, "Osteoporosis."

Spinal Stenosis

Spinal stenosis is caused by nerve impingement in the spinal canal due to degeneration of the disks, facet joints, and/or ligaments of the spine. Spondylolisthesis is a common underlying factor. Patients with spinal stenosis typically have persistent back pain along with lower extremity pain or numbness that is worsened by walking and decreased by spine flexion or by sitting. These lower extremity symptoms, called "neurogenic claudication" or "pseudoclaudication," are similar to peripheral vascular disease symptoms. Patients with spinal stenosis have intact peripheral pulses and may have pain in a radicular distribution in contrast to the calf cramping with exercise and decreased pulses seen in peripheral vascular disease. Radicular symptoms in spinal stenosis may be bilateral and poorly localized if the central canal is stenosed, or they may be well localized to the distribution of one or more nerve roots. Only a few studies have compared outcomes of surgical and nonsurgical treatments for spinal stenosis. Some patients respond to NSAIDs and physical therapy directed at strengthening abdominal muscles and reducing lumbar lordosis; however, rigorous clinical trials of these treatments have not been reported.[20] Since some patients improve spontaneously, surgery should be considered only after 3 months of symptoms.[13] Patients with severe pain often improve after surgery; however, recurrence of pain is common. In patients with severe refractory symptoms who are candidates for surgery, an EMG with sensory evoked potentials can help identify patients in whom a surgical referral is warranted.[13]

Spondylolisthesis and Spondylolysis

Spondylolisthesis, a forward displacement of one or more lumbar vertebra with respect to the vertebra below, can be caused by degenerative changes, congenital factors, or trauma. It is unclear how often spondylolisthesis causes low back pain. Two studies found higher rates of spondylolisthesis (4.9% versus 1.5% and 3.1% versus 0%) in patients with back pain compared with asymptomatic individuals.[13,21] Three other studies found no significant difference in the prevalence of spondylolisthesis between patients with and without back pain.[13] It seems clear, however, that at least severe spondylolisthesis can produce back pain and even radiculopathy. Approximately 15 to 20% of patients with spondylolisthesis have nerve root irritation with radicular symptoms.[22] Degenerative spondylolisthesis can cause spinal stenosis. Patients with spondylolisthesis and radicular symptoms who fail to respond to conservative treatment

may benefit from surgery. One randomized controlled trial found that surgery was moderately effective in reducing pain and disability in back pain associated with spondylolisthesis.[23] Spondylolysis, an interarticular defect of the posterior vertebral arch, generally does not cause low back pain and requires no treatment.[13]

Systemic Causes

Approximately 1% of back pain is due to malignancy, infection, or inflammatory arthropathy.[10] Carcinoma of the breast, lung, prostate, kidney, thyroid, and gastrointestinal tract are the most frequent malignancies to metastasize to the spine. Other malignancies that cause back pain include multiple myeloma, leukemia, lymphoma, primary tumors of the spinal cord, and extradural tumors.[14] Pain unrelieved by bedrest is virtually always present when cancer is responsible for patients' back pain, but it is a nonspecific symptom that is also common in patients with back pain from nonmalignant causes.[24] Fever and back pain suggests vertebral osteomyelitis, diskitis, an epidural abscess, or pyelonephritis. Forty percent of patients have identifiable risk factors for osteomyelitis, such a history of injection drug use, recent urinary tract infection, or skin infection.[25] Spine tenderness to percussion is 86% sensitive for patients with osteomyelitis but is a nonspecific finding.[10] *Staphylococcus aureus* is the most common organism associated with vertebral osteomyelitis. Gram-negative organisms cause osteomyelitis in injection-drug users and the elderly.

Ankylosing spondylitis is an inflammatory arthropathy found in about 0.3% of patients with back pain. It is characterized by intermittent or continuous back pain, progressive reduction in range of motion, onset of symptoms over weeks to months, and improvement with exercise. Women often have more peripheral joint symptoms than do men. Symptoms typically begin prior to age 40 years. Clinically apparent disease is three times more common in men than in women, and the diagnosis is frequently missed or delayed in women.[7] Ankylosing spondylitis by the presence of sacroiliitis on an anteroposterior film of the pelvis. Other inflammatory arthropathies, including psoriatic arthritis, Reiter's syndrome, and arthritis associated with inflammatory bowel disease or bacterial dysentery, can cause back pain, often with associated polyarthritis.

Visceral Causes

Uncommon, but potentially serious causes of referred back pain can arise from disorders of the abdomen, retroperitoneum, and pelvis. Rupturing abdominal aortic aneurysms typically cause acute back pain, occasionally with pain radiating to the groin. Rarely aortic aneurysms can cause chronic back pain. Patients over 50 years or those known to have vascular disease should receive a careful abdominal examination to search for a pulsatile abdominal mass. Back pain due to kidney stones commonly begins abruptly in the flank and radiates to the groin. Most, but not all, patients have hematuria. A family history of kidney stones is common. Subclinical pyelonephritis generally produces unilateral flank pain associated with dysuria frequency or hesitancy, but urinary symptoms may be absent, especially in older patients. Posterior penetrating peptic ulcers or diseases of the pancreas (eg, pancreatitis, tumors) sometimes produce back pain that is more prominent than is the patient's abdominal pain. Sudden onset of back pain in a patient using anticoagulants suggests a retroperitoneal hemorrhage.

Dysmenorrhea

Low backache resulting from dysmenorrhea is extremely common. Primary dysmenorrhea, symptoms without underlying pathology such as endometriosis or pelvic inflammatory disease, usually presents at the onset of menarche. Symptoms often improve following pregnancy. Cramps caused by prostaglandin-induced uterine contractions result in low back or pelvic discomfort. Timing can help distinguish between primary dysmenorrhea, which usually begins with or right before bleeding and stops after several days, and secondary dysmenorrhea, which begins several days before the onset of menses.

Diagnosis is based on history confirming symptoms with menses since menarche, and excluding risk factors for secondary dysmenorrhea, such as a history suggestive of endometriosis, multiple sexual partners, use of an intrauterine contraceptive device, vaginal discharge, and fever. Pelvic examination should include cervical cultures if the history discloses risk factors for sexually transmitted diseases. A pregnancy test is indicated for recent onset discomfort since pregnancy also causes low backache. Nonsteroidal antiinflammatory medications, such as ibuprofen 400 to 600 mg PO qid, block prostaglandin synthesis and prevent associated cramps and backache. Therapy is best begun either at the first sign of bleeding or, for severe cramps, 1 to 2 days prior to the likely onset of menses. Use of oral contraceptive pills also can reduce dysmenorrhea.

Endometriosis and Adenomyosis

Endometriosis almost never presents as isolated low back pain. More frequently, patients present with the classic triad of dysmenorrhea, deep dyspareunia, and infertility. Vague (usually cyclical) pelvic pain, pain with bowel movements or urination during menstruation, and menorrhagia are also common. Characteristically, symptoms begin several days before menstrual flow. Endometriosis is caused by ectopic functioning endometrium implanted in the pelvic or peritoneal cavities. Adenomyosis, endometrium embedded in the myometrium, causes dysmenorrhea with low back or rectal discomfort, and tends to affect older women (40 to 50 years old). Physical examination may be normal, or it may reveal a retroverted or fixed uterus or palpable adnexal nodules in endometriosis, and an enlarged painful uterus in adenomyosis. The imaging study of choice for documenting endometriomas is MRI, but laparoscopy remains the gold standard for diagnosis. Evaluation and treatment of pelvic pain and endometriosis are discussed in detail in Chapters 75 and 79.

Pregnancy

Low back pain is experienced by approximately 50 to 70% of women during pregnancy (compared with 11% of the general population who have low back pain severe enough to require sick leave).[26,27] Identified risk factors for low back pain during pregnancy include history of low back pain, greater body weight at the first trimester and the third trimester, and lack of control over the pace of activities at work.[28,29] Women with a prior history of back pain during pregnancy are more likely to refrain from becoming pregnant, to experience low back pain in subsequent pregnancies, and to have low back pain at other times.[26] Pain is usually worst in the third trimester and resolves soon after pregnancy, dropping to only 16% at 6 years (comparable to 18% pre-pregnancy).[27] Lumbar disk herniation is rare in pregnancy, but progressive back pain with paresthesias radiating below the knee, weakness, absent knee or ankle reflexes, or urinary retention should prompt evaluation with MRI and referral to a surgeon. Case reports confirm that patients undergoing MRI and surgery tolerate both well with deliveries near term.[30] Some treatments for back pain are contraindicated during pregnancy. These include use of NSAIDs during the third trimester, prolonged use of narcotics, use of muscle relaxants other than cyclobenzaprine, and hot tub use. The Ozzlo pillow, a pillow designed to support the pregnant abdomen, has been evaluated as safe and effective.[31]

HISTORY AND PHYSICAL EXAMINATION

A focused history and physical examination are sufficient to evaluate most patients with acute low back pain of less than 4 weeks' duration.[13] The possibility of a fracture is suggested by major trauma—such as a fall from height, a high speed motor vehicle accident, or blunt trauma; or minor trauma in a patient at risk for osteoporosis. The possibility of infection or neoplasm is raised in patients who are over 50 years, have a history of cancer, have constitutional symptoms (eg, fever or unexplained weight loss), have had a recent bacterial infection, have a history of injection drug use, or have pain unrelieved by rest. Saddle anesthesia, recent onset of bladder dysfunction (ie, urinary retention or incontinence), or major or progressive motor weakness suggests a cauda equina syndrome and requires urgent surgical consultation. The history may suggest nonspinal causes of back pain, such as abdominal, pelvic, or thoracic etiologies, or avoidable precipitants for pain, such as a history of lifting heavy or unwieldy items. Symptoms of depression may influence a patient's response to treatment, particularly in patients with chronic back pain. Other elements of the history that may influence treatment include a history of substance abuse, a history of peptic ulcer disease, or pain resulting from a work injury.

A directed examination is sufficient for most patients with low back pain of less than 4 weeks' duration. This should include inspection for anatomic abnormalities such as scoliosis or kyphosis. Assessment of spine flexion generally does not influence a diagnosis, but it can be helpful in following a patient's response to treatment. Also, patients with herniated disks usually have increased pain with flexion, whereas those with spinal stenosis have increased pain on extension. Soft tissue tenderness suggests pain in muscles or ligaments, but interobserver agreement about soft tissue tenderness and

muscle spasm is poor.[10] Palpation of the abdomen should be performed in patients with risk factors for vascular disease to assess for an aortic aneurysm. Patients with pain persisting for more than 4 weeks and those with risk factors for systemic disease should receive a screening general physical examination.

In patients with back pain and radicular symptoms, a lower extremity neurologic examination can identify evidence of nerve root impingement. If sciatica is present, the examination should focus on the L5 and S1 nerve roots (see Figure 49–1). Only 2% of symptomatic disk herniations occur at higher nerve roots. These generally cause thigh pain or numbness, which is more prominent than calf symptoms. In such patients patellar reflexes and quadriceps and psoas strength should be tested.[10]

Straight leg raising (SLR) is useful in assessing patients with sciatic symptoms. The examiner lifts the patient's leg with the patient supine. A positive test reproduces the patient's sciatic pain when the leg is lifted between 30° and 60°. Ipsilateral SLR is moderately sensitive for the presence of a disk herniation, but it is a nonspecific finding. Crossed SLR, in which sciatica on the affected side is caused by lifting the leg on the unaffected side, is highly specific but only 25% sensitive for a disk herniation.[10] When the diagnosis is in doubt or symptom magnification is suspected, the sitting SLR (straightening the knee when the patient is sitting) can help to confirm the diagnosis.

IMAGING AND LABORATORY TESTS

There is wide variation among physicians in the tests ordered to evaluate patients with low back pain. Based on evidence-based guidelines published by the Agency for Health Care Policy and Research (AHCPR), imaging studies often are performed unnecessarily.[13,32] Among the disadvantages of overusing imaging in patients with low back pain are gonadal radiation exposure and the cost of imaging studies. Furthermore, irrelevant findings may lead to inappropriate diagnoses or treatment. Degenerative changes on plain films and disk herniations on MRI are present in 20 to 30% of asymptomatic adults.[9]

The AHCPR guidelines suggest that after an initial history and physical examination, patients with low back pain can be categorized as having (1) a potentially serious spinal condition such as a

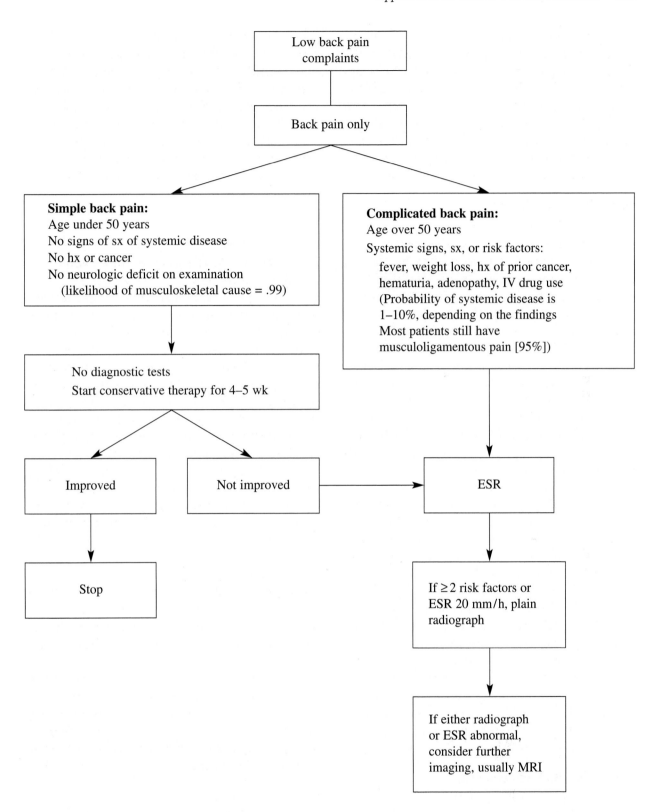

FIGURE 49–2. Algorithm for the treatment of patients with nonradicular low back pain. sx = symptoms; hx = history; IV = intravenous; ESR = erythrocyte sedimentation rate; MRI = magnetic resonance imaging. Adapted from Wipf JE, Deyo RA. Low back pain. In: Branch WT, editor. The office practice of medicine. 3rd ed. Philadelphia: WB Saunders; 1994. p. 646.

malignancy, infection, fracture, or severe neurologic compromise, (2) sciatic symptoms suggestive of a nerve root impingement, or (3) nonspecific symptoms, primarily in the back, that are not suggestive of a serious underlying disease or of nerve root impingement. Most patients with acute low back pain belong to the third group. These patients experiences improvement with conservative treatment within 4 weeks and requires no diagnostic studies.

Nonradicular Back Pain

In patients without "red flags" for a serious underlying condition, diagnostic studies generally are unnecessary in the first 4 weeks after the onset of symptoms. Anteroposterior and lateral lumbar spine radiographs should be obtained in patients with risk factors for a potentially serious condition and should be considered for anyone who fails to improve with 4 weeks of conservative treatment (Figure 49–2).[33] A careful history and a pregnancy test, if necessary, should be performed to ensure that radiography is not performed on a woman who might be pregnant. Since a pregnancy test is negative during the first 8 to 10 days after conception, radiography should be avoided from the middle to the end of the menstrual cycle in any sexually active woman not using reliable contraception.

In patients with risk factors for malignancy or infection, or who fail to improve with conservative treatment, a test of erythrocyte sedimentation rate (ESR) is useful. An elevated ESR is sensitive for detecting osteomyelitis, and has been found to be 78% sensitive and 33% specific for detecting occult malignancies.[23] A urinalysis should be obtained in any patient with urinary symptoms or flank pain. In patients who fail to improve with conservative treatment, a bone scan is moderately sensitive for detecting a malignancy or osteomyelitis. If there is sufficient clinical suspicion for an occult malignancy or infection, MRI provides a greater sensitivity and specificity than does a bone scan, at approximately twice the cost.[34]

Back Pain with Radiculopathy

The rare patient with cauda equina syndrome or with major neurologic compromise requires emergent surgical consultation and imaging. However, most patients with low back pain and radicular symptoms should be treated conservatively for the first 4 to 6 weeks. If a patient is a candidate for sur-

gery, has not improved in 4 to 6 weeks, and has a clear level of nerve root impingement on examination, an MRI or CT is warranted (Figure 49–3).[33] If a patient with nerve root symptoms has an equivocal neurologic examination for nerve root impingement, an EMG can be useful to determine whether nerve root impingement is present. In patients over 50 years, sensory evoked potentials along with an EMG can help diagnose spinal stenosis (Figure 49–4).[33]

TREATMENT

Pharmacologic Treatment

Nonsteroidal Anti-inflammatory Drugs and Acetaminophen

There is good evidence that NSAIDs can effectively treat acute uncomplicated back pain.[35] No difference has been found in the efficacy of different NSAIDs, but individual patients may respond better to one NSAID than to another. If a patient has not improved after 1 to 2 weeks of treatment, changing to another NSAID is warranted.[13] Ketorolac should be avoided due to a much higher risk of gastrointestinal bleeding than is associated with other NSAIDs. Nonsteroidal anti-inflammatory drugs have not been shown to be effective for treating patients with sciatica symptoms.[36] Acetaminophen has fewer gastrointestinal side effects than do NSAIDs and may be effective in some patients with back pain.

Muscle Relaxants

There is good evidence that muscle relaxants can be effective for short-term improvement in patients with acute back pain.[35] No difference in efficacy among muscle relaxants has been found. Most studies have shown that benefits last for only 4 to 7 days.[13] Drowsiness is seen in up to 30% of patients using muscle relaxants. Unless patients have severe spasms, nonbenzodiazepine muscle relaxants (cyclobenzaprine, methocarbamol, chlorzoxazone) are preferable to benzodiazepines, to reduce the risk of medication dependence.

Narcotic Analgesics

There is limited evidence that codeine is no more effective than are NSAIDs for patients with acute low back pain.[13] Time-limited courses of narcotic analgesics for acute low back pain may be appropriate for some patients with pain poorly controlled by

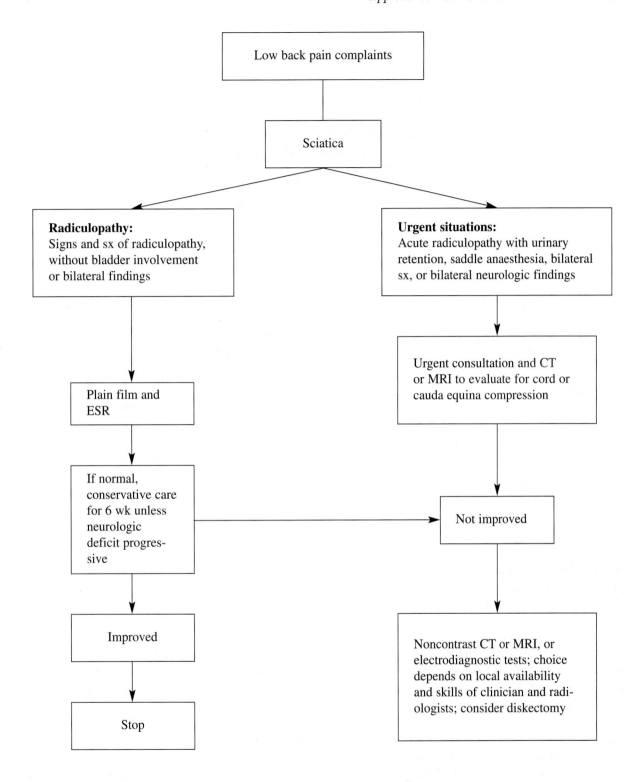

FIGURE 49–3. Algorithm for the treatment of patients with sciatica. sx = symptoms; ESR = erythrocyte sedimentation rate; CT = computed tomography; MRI = magnetic resonance imaging. Adapted from Wipf JE, Deyo RA. Low back pain. In: Branch WT, editor. The office practice of medicine. 3rd ed. Philadelphia: WB Saunders; 1994. p. 646.

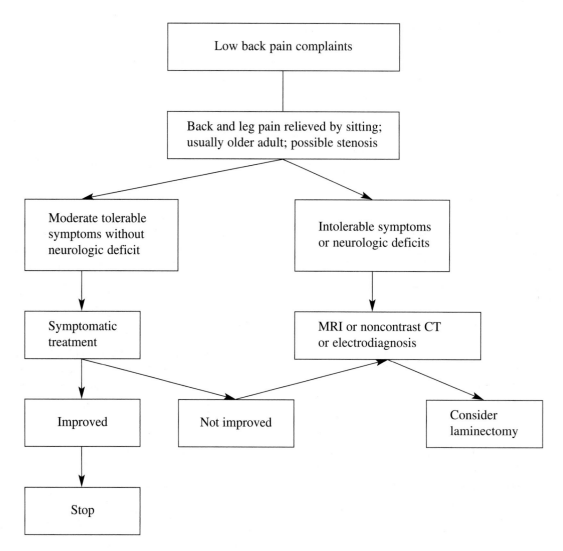

FIGURE 49–4. Algorithm for the treatment of patients with possible stenosis. MRI = magnetic resonance imaging; CT = computed tomography. Adapted from Wipf JE, Deyo RA. Low back pain. In: Branch WT, editor. The office practice of medicine. 3rd ed. Philadelphia: WB Saunders; 1994. p. 646.

NSAIDs. The potential benefits of narcotic analgesics should be weighed against side effects such as somnolence, decreased reaction time, and the risk of physical dependence.[13]

CALCITONIN
There is moderately good evidence that calcitonin, available in a nasal spray, reduces pain in patients with acute osteoporotic fractures.[19] Improvement occurs with as little as 3 days of treatment.

EPIDURAL STEROIDS
There is limited evidence that injection of epidural steroids is helpful in patients with acute low back pain associated with nerve root pain and a radicular

neurologic deficit.[13,35] There is no evidence to support epidural steroids in patients with acute back pain without symptoms or signs of nerve root impingement.

MEDICATIONS FOR THE PREGNANT PATIENT
Acetaminophen is generally considered safe (US Food and Drug Administration category B) throughout pregnancy.[37] Nonsteroidal anti-inflammatory drugs such as ibuprofen and naproxen appear to be safe (category B) during the first and second trimesters but are contraindicated during the third trimester because they may lead to premature closure of the ductus arteriosus. Narcotic analgesics such as codeine, hydrocodone, and oxycodone are

reported by their manufacturers to be category C (avoid, if possible, during pregnancy, due to a possible association with fetal malformations).[38] The author of Chapter 17, "Drugs in Pregnancy and Lactation," considers hydrocodone and oxycodone to be category B drugs but states that they are contraindicated for long periods or in high doses close to term. Cyclobenzaprine (category B) may be preferred to other muscle relaxants during pregnancy.

Nonpharmacologic Treatment

BED REST AND EXERCISE

Gradually returning to normal activities is safer and more effective than is prolonged bed rest for patients with acute back pain.[13] Prolonged bed rest (> 4 days) may lead to deconditioning and debilitation. Most patients with back pain do not require bed rest, although some patients with severe pain experience transient symptom relief from 2 to 4 days of bed rest. The majority of studies have shown no advantage for exercise therapy in acute low back pain; however, there is limited evidence that low-stress aerobic exercise during the first month of symptoms may prevent debilitation and facilitate an earlier return to usual activities.[13,35] Clinical trials suggest that exercise is effective in preventing recurrences after the acute episode and for treating chronic back pain.

CHIROPRACTIC

There is limited evidence that chiropractic manipulation may benefit some patients with nonradicular back pain of less than 1 month's duration.[13] Chiropractic or physical therapy have produced marginally better short-term outcomes with greater costs compared with an educational booklet in patients with acute low back pain.[39]

SURGERY

Patients with symptoms suggestive of the cauda equina syndrome or with severe or progressive lower extremity weakness should be referred for immediate surgical consultation. Patients who have severe sciatica symptoms that have not responded to 4 to 6 weeks of conservative treatment and who have evidence upon examination or an EMG of nerve root compromise may benefit from a surgical referral. Among patients with sciatica undergoing a diskectomy, 65 to 85% are free of sciatica at 1 year, compared with 36% of controls.[40] Diskectomy is less

successful for relieving back pain than it is for leg pain. Outcomes at 4 to 10 years are similar with diskectomy and conservative care. Patients with severe pain due to spinal stenosis that fails to respond to conservative treatment and persists beyond 3 months also may benefit from surgery.[13] Symptoms may recur following initial improvement after surgery for spinal stenosis. Treatment decisions regarding back surgery should incorporate patients' preferences, health status, and surgical risks.

Treatments to Avoid

Based on an evidence-based guideline published by AHCPR, there is good evidence to avoid the following treatments for acute low back pain: oral steroids, transcutaneous electrical nerve stimulation (TENS), trigger point or facet joint injections, traction, and prolonged bed rest.[13]

Treatments for Chronic Back Pain

Several treatments are available for chronic back pain:

- Exercise therapy. In patients with chronic back pain there is good evidence that exercise therapy can lead to improvements in pain and in level of activity.[35]
- Nonsteroidal anti-inflammatory drugs. There is moderately good evidence that NSAIDs are effective in chronic back pain, and good evidence that the various available NSAIDs are equally effective.[35]
- Chiropractic. Six of nine randomized controlled trials identified in a recent systematic review found that chiropractic was more effective than was placebo treatment or usual care in patients with chronic low back pain.[35]
- Acupuncture. Based on a limited number of high-quality studies, there is no evidence that acupuncture is more effective than is no treatment in patients with chronic low back pain.[41]
- Tricyclic antidepressants. Three of the four randomized controlled trials of tricyclic antidepressants in chronic back pain reported improvements in pain or functional status, although the degree of improvement was generally modest.[35,42] Depression is three to four times more common in patients with chronic low back pain than it is in the general population, and it warrants treatment when present.[43]
- Back schools. Most studies have shown that an intensive "back school" program can lead to reductions in pain for patients with chronic back pain.[35]

RESOURCE

The Agency for Health Care Research and Quality
Office of Health Care Information
Suite 501, Executive Office Center
2101 East Jefferson Street
Rockville, Maryland 20852
Telephone: (301) 594-1364
Web site: www.ahcpr.gov

The Agency for Health Care Research and Quality (formerly The Agency for Health Care Policy and Research) makes available full guidelines, quick clinical references, and patient information about the diagnosis and treatment of low back pain.

REFERENCES

1. Cypress BK. Characteristics of physician visits for back symptoms: a national perspective. Am J Public Health 1983;73:389–95.
2. Loeser JD, Volinn E. Epidemiology of low back pain. Neurosurg Clin N Am 1991;2:713–8.
3. Andersson GBJ. The epidemiology of spinal disorders. In: Frymoyer JW, editor. The adult spine: principles and practice. New York: Raven Press, Ltd.; 1991. p. 107–46.
4. Deyo RA, Tsui-Wu JY. Descriptive epidemiology of low back pain and its related medical care in the United States. Spine 1987;12:264–8.
5. Deyo RA, Loeser JD, Bigos SJ. Herniated lumbar intervertebral disk. Ann Intern Med 1990;112:598–603.
6. Von Korff M, Saunders K. The course of back pain in primary care. Spine 1996;21:2833–7.
7. Rodnan GP, Schumacher HR, editors. Primer of rheumatic diseases. 8th ed. Atlanta: Arthritis Foundation; 1983.
8. Deyo RA. Low back pain. Sci Am 1998;279:48–53.
9. Jensen MC, Brant-Zawadzki MN, Obuchowski N, et al. Magnetic resonance imaging of the lumbar spine in people without low back pain. N Engl J Med 1994; 331:69–73.
10. Deyo RA, Rainville J, Kent DL. What can the history and physical exam tell us about low back pain? JAMA 1992;268:760–5.
11. Bigos SJ, Bowyer OR, Braein GR, et al. Acute low back problems in adults: assessment and treatment. Quick reference guide for clinicians. Rockville (MD): US Dept. of Health and Human Services, Public Health Service, Agency for Health Care Policy and Research; 1994. AHCPR Publication No.: 95-0643.
12. Finneson BE. Low back pain. 2nd ed. Philadelphia: JB Lippencott; 1980.
13. Bigos SJ, Bowyer OR, Braein GR, et al. Acute low back problems in adults. Rockville (MD): US Dept. of Health and Human Services, Public Health Service, Agency for Health Care Policy and Research; 1994. AHCPR Publication No.: 95-0642.
14. Wifp JE, Deyo RA. Low back pain. Med Clin North Am 1995;79:231–46.
15. Patel U, Skingle S, Cambell GA, et al. Clinical profile of acute vertebral compression fractures in osteoporosis. Br J Rheumatol 1991;30:418–21.
16. Bauer RL, Deyo RA. Low risk of vertebral fracture in Mexican-American women. Arch Intern Med 1987; 147:1437–9.
17. Nevitt MC, Ettinger B, Black DM. The association of radiographically detected vertebral fractures with back pain and function. Ann Intern Med 1998; 128:793–800.
18. Kanis JA, McCloskey EV. Epidemiology of vertebral osteoporosis. Bone 1992;13:S1–10.
19. Wallach S. The role of calcitonin treatment in postmenopausal osteoporosis. Orthop Rev 1992;21:1034–42.
20. Ciricillo SF, Weinstein PR. Lumbar spinal stenosis. West J Med 1993;158:171–7.
21. Torgesson WR, Dotter WE. Comparative roentgenographic study of the asymptomatic and symptomatic lumbar spine. J Bone Joint Surg 1976;58:850–3.
22. Stillerman CB, Schneider JH, Gruen JP. Evaluation and management of spondylolysis and spondylolisthesis. Clin Neurosurg 1993;40:384–415.

23. Moller H, Hedlund R. Surgery versus conservative management in adult isthmic spondylolisthesis—a prospective randomized study. Spine 2000;25:1711–5.

24. Deyo RA, Diehl AK. Cancer as a cause of back pain. J Gen Intern Med 1988;3:230–8.

25. Waldvogel FA, Vesey H. Oseomyelitis: the past decade. N Engl J Med 1980;303:360–70.

26. Brynhildsen J, Hansson A, Persson A, Hammar M. Follow-up of patients with low back pain during pregnancy. Obstet Gynecol 1998;91:182–6.

27. Ostgaard HC, Zetherstrom G, Roos-Hansson E. Back pain in relation to pregnancy: a 6-year follow-up. Spine 1997;22:2945–50.

28. Sihvonen T, Huttunen M, Makkonen M, Airaksinen O. Functional changes in back muscle activity correlate with pain intensity and prediction of low back pain during pregnancy. Arch Phys Med Rehabil 1998;79:1210–2.

29. Wergeland E, Strand K. Work pace control and pregnancy health in a population-based sample of employed women in Norway. Scand J Work Environ Health 1998;24:206–12.

30. Garmel SH, Guzelian GA, D'Alton JG, D'Alton ME. Lumbar disk disease in pregnancy. Obstet Gynecol 1997;89:821–2.

31. Thomas IL, Nicklin J, Pollock H, Faulkner K. Evaluation of a maternity cushion (Ozzlo pillow) for backache and insomnia in late pregnancy. Aust N Z J Obstet Gynaecol 1989;29:133–8.

32. Schroth WS, Schectman JM, Elinsky EG, et al. Utilization of medical services for the treatment of acute low back pain. J Gen Intern Med 1992;7:486–91.

33. Wipf JE, Deyo RA. Low back pain. In: Branch WT, editor. The office practice of medicine. 3rd ed. Philadelphia: WB Saunders; 1994. p. 646–59.

34. Algra PR, Bloem JL, Tissing H, et al. Detection of vertebral metastases: comparison between MR imaging and bone scintigraphy. Radiographics 1991;11:219–32.

35. van Tulder MW, Koes BW, Bouter LM. Conservative treatment of acute and chronic low back pain. Spine 1997;22:2128–56.

36. Weber H, Holme I, Amlie E. The natural course of acute sciatica with nerve root symptoms in a double-blind placebo-controlled trial evaluating the effect of piroxicam. Spine 1993;18:1433–8.

37. Briggs GG, Freeman RK, Yaffe SJ. Drugs in pregnancy and lactation. 4th ed. Baltimore: Williams & Wilkins; 1994.

38. Physicians desk reference. Montvale (NJ): Medical Economics; 1999.

39. Cherkin DC, Deyo RA, Battie M, et al. A comparison of physical therapy, chiropractic manipulation, and provision of an educational booklet for the treatment of patients with low back pain. N Engl J Med 1998;339:1021–9.

40. Hoffman RM, Wheeler KJ, Deyo RA. Surgery for herniated lumbar discs. J Gen Intern Med 1993;8:487–96.

41. van Tulder MW, Cherkin DC, Berman B, et al. Acupuncture for low back pain. Cochrane Database of Systematic Reviews. 1999. The Cochrane Library, Issue 3, 2001. Oxford: Update Software; updated Feb. 24, 1999.

42. Atkinson JH, Slater MA, Williams RA, et al. A placebo-controlled randomized controlled clinical trial of nortriptyline for chronic low back pain. Pain 1998;76:287–96.

43. Sullivan MJ, Reeser K, Mikail S, Fisher R. The treatment of depression in chronic low back pain. Pain 1992;50:5–13.

50

APPROACH TO THE PATIENT WITH KNEE PAIN

Jeffrey K. Shimoyama, MD, and Karen Cheng, MD

The knee is the largest joint in the body and one of the most commonly injured. A systematic approach allows the primary care clinician to determine diagnosis, treatment, and the need for referral.

BASIC KNEE ANATOMY

Understanding the basic anatomy of the knee is essential in evaluating the patient complaining of knee pain (Figure 50–1). Pertinent anatomic structures are soft tissue, bony and cartilagenous structures.

Soft tissue structures include the following:

- Prepatellar bursa—superficial to the patella and often inflamed by repetitive kneeling
- Anterior and posterior cruciate ligaments (ACL/PCL)—important for anterior and posterior stability

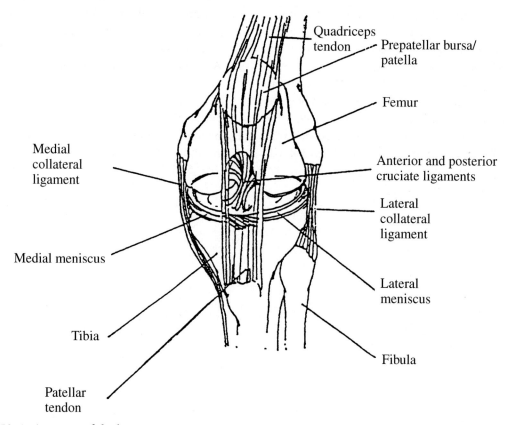

FIGURE 50–1. Anatomy of the knee.

TABLE 50–1. Common Causes of Acute and Chronic Knee Pain

Acute pain
    Patellofemoral disorders[*]
    Meniscal injury
    Ligamentous injury[†]
    Osseous injury

Chronic pain
    Patellofemoral disorders
    Meniscal injury
    Dengenerative changes
    Collateral ligament injury
    Loose body
    Bursitis

[*]The patellofemoral joint is the most commonly injured compartment of the knee.
[†]Particularly anterior cruciate ligament injuries.
Adapted from Jensen JE, Conn RR, Hazelrigg G, et al. Systemic evaluation of acute knee injuries. Clin Sports Med 1985;4:295–312.

- Medial and lateral collateral ligaments (MCL/LCL) —important for lateral stability
- Quadriceps and patellar tendon—vital for knee extension and patellar stability

Bony structures are the patella/patellofemoral joint, femur, tibia, and fibula. Cartilagenous structures are the medial and lateral menisci, which are important as shock absorbers and anterior stabilizers.

COMMON CAUSES OF KNEE PAIN

Table 50–1[1] lists some of the most common causes of acute and chronic knee pain, which are detailed below. The clinical presentation is important in discerning the most likely cause of knee pain.

Common causes of acute knee pain include the following:

- Patellofemoral disorders—those resulting from acute injury often present with anterior knee pain which is noted particularly when ascending or descending stairs
- Meniscal (cartilagenous) injury—usually accompanied by pain in the knee, often exacerbated by pivoting-type motions, swelling, decreased range of motion, and sometimes "locking" (the inability to fully extend and flex the knee)

- Ligamentous (particularly ACL) injury—presents with an acute onset of pain accompanied by a perceived or audible "pop;" it is associated with immediate swelling, which is perceptible within minutes to hours after the traumatic event
- Osseous injury—characterized by pain associated with significant bony tenderness

Common causes of chronic knee pain are as follows:

- Chronic patellofemoral disorders—present similarly to those caused by acute injury, being characterized by anterior knee pain worse when ascending or descending stairs
- Chronic meniscal injury—tends to present with pain, swelling, decreased range of motion, and sometimes "locking" (see above)
- Degenerative knee pain—presents with pain and stiffness
- Collateral ligament injury—associated with pain on the side of the injured ligament noted by the patient with twisting or cutting motions
- A loose body in the knee joint—presents with pain associated with "locking"
- Bursitis of the knee—characterized by localized swelling and tenderness of an overlying knee bursa with exacerbation of pain on full flexion; the overall range of motion, however, is essentially normal

ANATOMIC AND STRUCTURAL FACTORS PREDISPOSING WOMEN TO KNEE INJURIES

Recently, as women have become more active in sports, it has become apparent that they are at increased risk for certain types of knee injuries.[2,3] Factors thought to contribute to this difference in knee injury rates include:

- Suboptimal physical conditioning—increases overall risk of injury
- Smaller size/less body weight—important when participating in contact sports with men
- Increased ligamentous laxity—may predispose to patellar subluxation and various ligamentous injuries.[4]

In addition to these factors, anatomic differences mentioned in Table 50–2[3,5] are thought to

TABLE 50–2. Lower Extremity Alignment and Developmental Differences in Women*

Wider pelvis
Greater genu valgum
Femoral anteversion
Less muscular development of the vastus medialis
    obliquus[†]
Decreased ACL size[‡]
Smaller muscle fiber size

---

*As compared with men.
[†]This tends to increase lateral forces on the patellofemoral joint, predisposing to subluxation and maltracking of the patella in the trochlear groove.
[‡]This is thought to contribute to the increased rate of anterior cruciate ligament (ACL) injuries in many women athletes, particularly in basketball and soccer.[5]
Adapted from Hutchinson MR, Ireland ML. Knee injuries in female athletes. Sports Med 1995;19:288–302.

predispose some women to an increased risk for knee injuries.

HISTORY

It is important to obtain the following historic data in evaluating a patient presenting with knee pain:

- *Age.* Older patients are at higher risk for fractures and degenerative knee problems.
- *Occupation and lifestyle including recreational activities.* The patient's usual activities are important to consider during both acute treatment and rehabilitation.
- *Timing of the onset of pain.* Sudden onset of pain with inability to carry on current activity may suggest serious internal derangements such as an ACL tear, patellar dislocation, or a large meniscal tear. Gradual onset of pain may suggest a meniscal tear, collateral ligament injury, or a patellofemoral disorder.
- *Location of pain.* Retropatellar/peripatellar pain may be suggestive of a patellofemoral disorder. Lateral/medial joint line pain may suggest a meniscal or collateral ligament injury.
- *Mechanism of any current or past injury.* Forced hyperextension may cause an ACL tear. Forced hyperflexion or blunt trauma to the anterior knee may impose a posterior force sufficient to injure the PCL. Blunt trauma to the lateral or medial knee may impose sufficient stresses to cause medial or lateral collateral ligamentous or menis-

cal injuries. Twisting injuries may damage the ACL, menisci, and collateral ligaments, or even dislocate or sublux the patella.

- *Exacerbating/alleviating factors.* Pain after prolonged sitting with flexed knees ("theater sign") or with climbing or descending stairs may suggest a patellofemoral disorder. Discomfort with the performance of twisting or cutting actions may suggest a meniscal or ACL injury.
- *History of an audible pop.* A hyperextension injury with an audible pop may suggest an ACL tear. Tears of the PCL are much less common.
- *Onset of swelling.* If atraumatic, infection of the joint, monoarticular arthritides, bursitis, and degenerative meniscal tear should be considered. If post-traumatic, an immediate-onset (within hours of injury) swelling is highly suggestive of a hemarthrosis and a cause of pain that may require orthopedic consultation. These causes include ligamentous (particularly ACL) or large meniscal tears, acute patellar dislocation or subluxation, and osteochondral fractures. Delayed-onset (within a few days) swelling often indicates a meniscal tear or less serious injury.
- *Associated mechanical symptoms.* The persistence of locking may suggest a significant meniscal injury or loose body and warrants an orthopedic referral. Buckling, characterized by a "giving way" of the knee, may be associated with ACL and meniscal tears, patellar subluxation, and loose bodies.
- *Medications.* As an example, the use of corticosteroids may increase the risk for avascular necrosis of the knee.
- *Rheumatologic, orthopedic, or systemic disorders*
- *Past surgeries*
- *Past diagnostic studies or attempted treatments*

PHYSICAL EXAMINATION

In examining the knee, it is advisable to have patients disrobe to allow direct visualization of both knees. The asymptomatic side should be examined first, so that a basis for comparison with the symptomatic knee can be established.

The patient's gait when standing should be observed to assess the functional limitation imposed by the knee pain. Lower extremity alignment problems, muscular atrophy, and signs of inflammation should be noted.

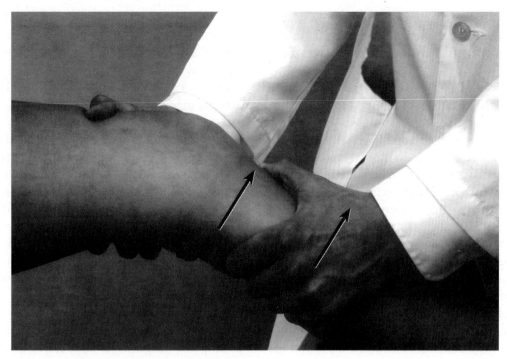

FIGURE 50–2. Lachman's test (see text for description).

The position of the patellae should be observed while the patient is sitting. The examiner should passively flex and extend both knees as tolerated, and then the patient should actively flex and extend both knees. Normal knee flexion is approximately 135°, and normal extension is 0°. Inability to actively flex or extend the knee may be indicative of serious derangement such as meniscal tear or patellar tendon rupture.

The patient should assume the supine position for the following examinations:

- The neurovascular status of the leg should be determined by assessing pedal pulses and by performing a neurologic examination in patients who have sustained significant trauma.
- Extra-articular soft and bony structures should be systematically palpated. Tenderness of the anterior patella is suggestive of possible prepatellar bursitis. If the infrapatellar tendon is tender, patellar tendonitis is likely. Tenderness along the joint line may indicate collateral ligamentous, meniscal, or bony injury.
- Evidence of effusion should be elicited by performing the patellar ballotment test. With the legs fully extended, the patella is pushed into the trochlear groove, then released. A positive test is one in which the patella readily rebounds, implying

significant effusion and possible significant intra-articular derangement.
- Patellofemoral irritability should be assessed by performing the patellofemoral "grinding test." With the patient supine and knees fully extended, the patella is pushed distally, while the patient firmly extends her knees. A positive test in which this maneuver elicits pain is suggestive of a femoral pathology.
- The ACL and PCL should be assessed by performance of Lachman's test (Figure 50–2). This is considered to be the most sensitive test for assessing the integrity of the ACL, with a sensitivity of over 98% in one study.[6] The knee is flexed to 30°. The distal thigh is braced with one of the examiner's hands, while the proximal tibia is held in the examiner's other hand. An attempt is made to sharply pull the tibia forward. The test is positive if there is either excessive anterior tibial translation (laxity) relative to the asymptomatic knee, or if there is lack of a firm end point to the forward motion of the tibia. The anterior and posterior drawer tests assess the ACL and PCL, respectively. With the patient supine and her knee flexed to 90°, the examiner sits on the ipsilateral foot and wraps his/her fingers around the posterior aspect of the proximal gastrocnemius, sharply pulling anteriorly (anterior drawer test) and then pushing posteriorly (posterior drawer

test). A positive test is either excessive laxity, relative to the asymptomatic knee, or lack of a firm end point to either anterior or posterior movement of the tibia.

- The MCL and LCL are assessed by applying stress to each ligament. To test the right MCL, the right ankle is secured under the examiner's right arm, and the examiner's left hand is placed against the proximal fibula. A medially directed (valgus) force is applied in an attempt to open the medial joint line. Increased laxity or lack of a firm end point relative to the asymptomatic side constitutes a positive test. This procedure is reversed to check the left MCL. To test the right LCL, the examiner's right hand is placed on the medial aspect of the right knee and pushed laterally, while the right ankle is secured with the examiner's left hand in an attempt to open the joint line laterally (varus stress). Increased laxity or lack of a firm end point constitutes a positive test and suggests ligamentous injury. This procedure is reversed to check the left LCL.
- The medial and lateral menisci are evaluated by performance of the McMurray test. To test the right knee, the right heel is grasped by the examiner's right hand, and the top of the right knee enveloped by the examiner's left hand, with the fingertips placed along the medial joint line. To test the medial meniscus, the knee is rotated externally and slowly brought into extension, while a valgus (medially directed) stress is applied. A palpable or audible click and the eliciting of pain constitute a positive test. To test the lateral meniscus, the knee is rotated internally and slowly brought into extension as varus (laterally directed) stress is applied. A positive test is the same as that for the medial maneuver. This procedure is reversed to test the left knee. The sensitivity of the McMurray test has been reported to range from 20 to 29%. Its specificity is as high as 91 to 96%.[7]
- Hip range of motion is assessed by the examiner passively moving the hip; this joint can refer pain to the knee.

DIAGNOSTIC MODALITIES

Plain radiographs of the knee can be useful in evaluating patients for fracture, dislocation, infection, neoplasm, ligamentous injury, osteoarthritis, loose bodies, and systemic disorders.

Recently the "Ottawa Rules," a set of validated guidelines for assessing patients for possible traumatic fractures of the knee in an emergency room setting, were published.[8] In the emergency room setting, fractures were almost exclusively seen in patients in whom one or more of the following criteria were met: (1) 55 years of age or older, (2) tenderness to palpation at the head of the fibula, (3) bony tenderness to palpation isolated to the patella, (4) inability to flex the knee to 90°, and (5) inability to bear weight immediately and in the emergency room. Patients were excluded from the study if they were younger than 18 years old, were paraplegic or pregnant, or had multiple injuries or injuries more than 7 days old. Although clinically useful, caution must be observed when attempting to apply the "Ottawa Rules" to patients presenting with knee pain in the clinic setting.

According to the American Academy of Orthopedic Surgeons, anteroposterior, lateral, and patellar tangential views often are useful in radiographically evaluating the knee.[9] Additional special views may be indicated, depending on the clinical presentation of the patient. Consultation with a radiologist or orthopedist often is helpful prior to ordering radiography, and it is encouraged.

The soft tissues of the knee, including the menisci and ligaments, are best imaged by magnetic resonance imaging (MRI). Some authors have reported an 88% overall sensitivity (confidence interval [CI], 86 to 90%) and a 94% overall specificity (CI, 93 to 94%) for meniscal and cruciate ligament tears.[10,11] In addition to meniscal and ligamentous injuries, MRI is useful when occult fracture or avascular necrosis are suspected clinically but are not apparent on plain radiographs. Although not a routinely ordered test, the MRI can be useful in patients with knee pain that is not improving with an adequate course of appropriate conservative therapy, or in assisting with surgical planning. Orthopedic consultation prior to ordering this study may be prudent.

Diagnostically, aspiration is indicated if infection is the suspected etiology of a joint effusion. In addition, analysis of aspirated joint fluid can be useful if crystal-induced inflammation, such as that from gout or pseudogout (rheumatic conditions), or hemarthrosis is suspected. A hemarthrosis can result from a cruciate ligament tear, meniscal/patellar injury, or a fracture. Information on interpretation of the results of joint fluid analysis is provided

TABLE 50–3. Indications for Orthopedic Referral

ACL/PCL tear
Collateral ligament instability
Dislocation
Fracture
Joint infection
Neurovascular compromise
Persistent locking
Neoplasm
Large effusion

ACL = anterior eruciate ligament; PCL = posterior cruciate ligament.

in Chapter 42, "Approach to the Patient with Diffuse Joint and Muscular Pain."

In addition to diagnostic utility, therapeutically, aspiration of joint fluid may provide significant pain relief. This may facilitate more active participation in a knee rehabilitation program.

INDICATIONS FOR ORTHOPEDIC REFERRAL

Indications for referral to an orthopedist are summarized in Table 50–3. In addition, any patient who is not improving, or who has an uncertain diagnosis, is a candidate for referral.

CONSERVATIVE MANAGEMENT OF KNEE PAIN

Many patients with knee pain, particularly those with small meniscal tears, osteoarthritis, and patellofemoral disorders can be successfully treated with the following nonsurgical treatment modalities: (1) rest and avoidance of aggravating activities, (2) exercise, (3) use of analgesics, and (4) icing of the painful area.

In exercise the focus is on strengthening the vastus medialis oblique, the quadriceps muscle that helps to prevent excessive lateral displacement of the patella. Daily performance of two to three sets of 10 repetitions of each of the following exercises (which emphasize quadriceps strengthening) may be useful in alleviating knee pain (Figure 50–3).

- Quadriceps setting. The patient sits on the ground with the knees in full extension and the feet in dorsiflexion. The quadriceps are tightened, pushing the knees onto the floor for 5 seconds, and then relaxed.

Quadriceps setting

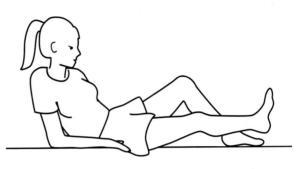

Straight leg raise

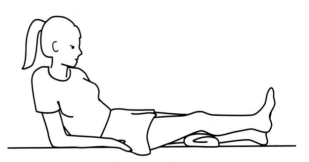

Terminal arc extension

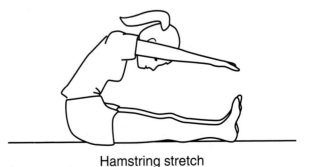

Hamstring stretch

FIGURE 50–3. Quadriceps strengthening exercises (see text for description).

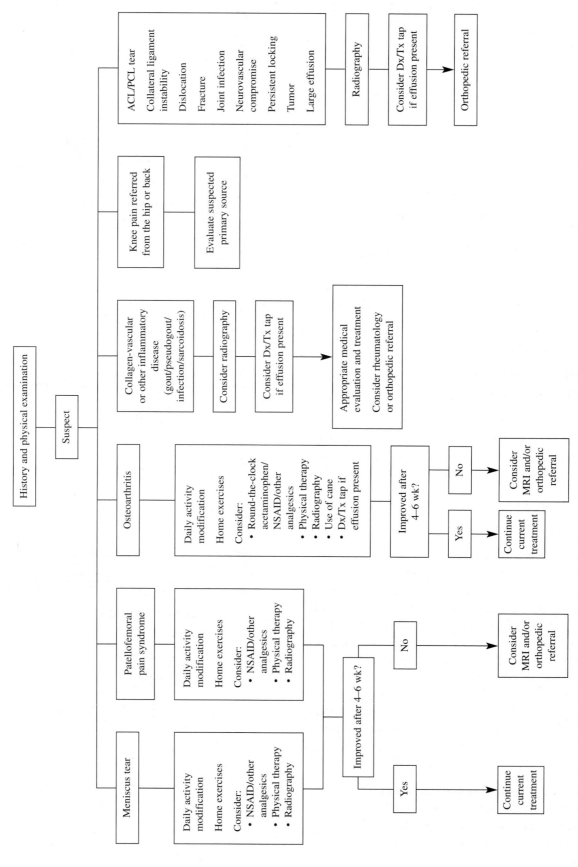

FIGURE 50–4. A suggested primary care approach to knee pain. NSAID = nonsteroidal anti-inflammatory drug; MRI = magnetic resonance imaging; Dx = diagnosis; Tx = treatment; ACL = anterior cruciate ligament; PCL = posterior cruciate ligament.

- Straight leg raise. From the sitting position with the affected knee in extension and the other bent at 90°, the leg is slowly raised off the floor until it is parallel with the other thigh. It is held for 5 seconds.
- Terminal arc extensions. While sitting on the floor, a rolled towel (about 15 cm in diameter) is placed under the knee. The knee is brought into full extension and is held for 5 seconds.
- Hamstring stretch. The patient sits on the floor with knees in full extension. While actively tightening the quadriceps, the upper body is slowly lowered forward until significant hamstring stretching is felt. Without bouncing, the position is held for about 15 seconds.

Especially in patients afflicted with osteoarthritis, aerobic activities such as walking and aquatic exercises may help decrease knee pain and improve functional status.[12] Physical therapy may be useful in patients who are unmotivated, have significant functional or strength deficits, or who do not improve after several weeks of home exercises.

Acetaminophen, aspirin, and nonsteroidal anti-inflammatory medications may be helpful when not contraindicated. Therapy with any of these agents must be appropriately monitored.

Applying ice may be useful in controlling pain and swelling after certain activities.

Figure 50–4 summarizes a systematic approach to the patient presenting with knee pain.

We gratefully acknowledge the following individuals for the contributions they have made in the preparation of this chapter: Steven T. Shimoyama, MD, Clinical Associate Professor of Orthopedic Surgery, University of Southern California School of Medicine and orthopedist in private practice; Matthew S. Shapiro, MD, Assistant Professor of Orthopedic Surgery, University of California at Los Angeles School of Medicine; Gerald Finerman, MD, Professor and Chair of Orthopedic Surgery, University of California at Los Angeles School of Medicine; Lawrence Yao, MD, musculoskeletal radiologist; Gregory Saccone, MD, internal medicine, Kaiser-Permanente, Woodland Hills; and Dina R. Shimoyama, DDS, for typing this manuscript. Also, we would like to thank Mrs. Tula Pregler for providing us with some of the drawings included in this manuscript.

REFERENCES

1. Jensen JE, Conn RR, Hazelrigg G, et al. Systematic evaluation of acute knee injuries. Clin Sports Med 1985;4:295–312.
2. Beck JL. The female athlete's knee. Clin Sports Med 1985;4:345–66.
3. Hutchinson MR, Ireland ML. Knee injuries in female athletes. Sports Med 1995;19:288–302.
4. Powers JA. Characteristic features of injuries in the knee of women. Clin Orthop 1979;143:120–4.
5. Miller MD. The medical care of athletes. In: Beaty JH, editor. Orthopaedic knowledge update 6. Rosemont (IL): American Academy of Orthopedic Surgeons; 1999. p. 107–8.
6. Kim SJ, Kim HK. Reliability of the anterior drawer, pivot shift, and Lachman. Clin Orthop 1995;317:237–42.
7. Stratford PW, Binkley J. A review of the McMurray test: definition, interpretation and clinical usefulness. J Orthop Sports Phys Ther 1995;22:116–20.
8. Steill IG. Prospective validation of a decision rule for the use of radiography in acute knee injuries. JAMA 1996;275:611–5.
9. Ivey FM. Acute knee injuries. In: Griffin LY, editor. Orthopaedic knowledge update: sports medicine. Rosemont (IL): American Academy of Orthopedic Surgeons; 1994. p. 255.
10. Munk B, Madsen F, Lundorf E, et al. Clinical magnetic resonance imaging and arthroscopic findings in knees: a comparative prospective study of meniscus, anterior cruciate ligament and cartilage lesions. J Arthroscopic Relat Surg 1998;14:171–5.
11. MacKenzie R, Palmer CR, Lomas DJ, et al. Magnetic resonance imaging of the knee: diagnostic performance studies. Clin Radiol 1996;51:251–7.
12. Hochberg MC, Altman RD, Brandt KD, et al. Guidelines for the medical management of osteoarthritis. Arthritis Rheum 1995;38:1541–6.

51

ANKLE SPRAINS

Karen Cheng, MD

Ankle injuries are the most common musculoskeletal injury associated with sports. The majority of ankle injuries are sprains. Of these, 85% are lateral sprains, only 5% are medial, and 10% are combined injuries. While most ankle sprains can be managed by the primary care clinician, 15% are associated with fractures and up to 30 to 40% of all ankle sprains lead to chronic symptoms.[1-4] The ability to accurately diagnose an ankle injury and then prescribe appropriate treatment, including rehabilitation, gives the patient the best chance for complete functional recovery.

ANATOMY AND DIFFERENTIAL DIAGNOSIS

The ankle joint consists of the distal tibia and fibula composing the mortise, which articulates with the talar dome (Figure 51–1).[1] The talar dome is wider anteriorly giving the ankle the most stability when the foot is dorsiflexed. Its surrounding ligaments and musculotendinous units also stabilize the ankle.[3] There are three groups of ligamentous structures: medial, lateral, and tibiofibular. The

tibiofibular ligament stabilizes the ankle mortise. The medial complex consists of a thick fan-shaped deltoid ligament, which is a strong medial stabilizer (Figure 51–2). The lateral complex consists of three separate ligaments: anterior talofibular, calcaneofibular, and posterior talofibular (Figure 51–3). In plantar flexion the anterior talofibular ligament (ATFL) is the main lateral stabilizer. Thus, the ATFL is the ligament first injured when an inversion stress occurs in plantar flexion. If the stress continues, studies have shown that, next, the calcaneofibular and then the posterior talofibular ligaments are injured.[1]

With this anatomy in mind, it is easier to understand the differential diagnosis for ankle injury. The most common injury is lateral ankle sprain. Various grading systems have been used to assess the integrity of the ATFL. A common grading system defines grade 1 as a stretch injury with minimal swelling and little loss of function. Grade 2 is defined as a partial tear that involves more pain and swelling but the ability to walk is maintained. Grade 3 injury is a complete tear with instability and inability to bear weight. The grading system is helpful in determining prognosis, with patients being able to return to usual activities in 1 to 2 weeks with a grade 1 injury, while grade 3 injuries may take more than 1 to 2 months.[1,3,5]

Medial eversion sprains are far less common but more often associated with fractures.[6] Syndesmosis (high ankle) sprains occur with the ankle in eversion and dorsiflexion. The syndesmosis consists of the thick ligaments connecting the distal tibia and fibula. These sprains take longer to heal (about 2 months) but are unlikely to recur.[6,7] Peroneal tendon subluxation or dislocation is not common but does occur with inversion injuries. This tendon lies in a groove posterior to the fibula. It can be palpated by

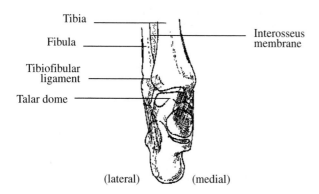

FIGURE 51–1. Essential anatomy of the ankle: anterior view.

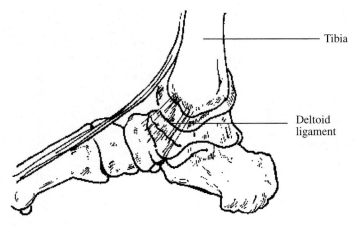

FIGURE 51–2. Ankle (medial view).

having the patient actively dorsiflex and evert the ankle, which may cause pain.[6]

A discussion of the various ankle fractures is beyond the scope of this chapter. They include malleolar fractures, avulsion fractures of the calcaneus and talus, and fractures of the base of the fifth metatarsal as well as the tibia and fibula. Also, osteochondral injury to the talus can cause prolonged pain.[2,7]

HISTORY AND PHYSICAL EXAMINATION

Key historic questions include the following:[1,3]

1. What was the mechanism of injury? This includes details of the sport or recreational activity and the position of the foot when the patient landed. Most often, the ankle undergoes an inversion injury because the lateral ligaments are weaker.

2. What is the quality and severity of the pain? In other words, did the pain occur suddenly (often associated with immediate swelling, which is more worrisome)? Was she able to walk or continue her activity after the injury?

3. Has the ankle been injured before? If so, what treatment was prescribed? Previous injury increases the risk for recurrent or chronic pain.

Key components to the physical examination include the following:[1,6]

1. **Inspection.** To assess functional status, the patient's gait should be observed to see if she can walk. Areas of swelling and ecchymosis can help to localize the injury. With significant injury, the swelling may be symmetric, indicating a joint effusion. The patient should also be assessed for evidence of concomitant injury to other parts of the body (eg, wrist, elbow, knee).

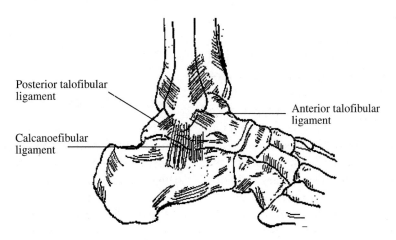

FIGURE 51–3. Ankle (lateral view).

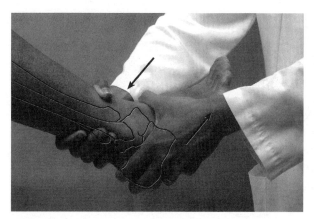

FIGURE 51–4. Anterior drawer test.

2. **Palpation.** Palpating the ligaments and tendons (including the Achilles and peroneal tendons) is helpful for determining areas of injury. It is especially important, however, to palpate three particular bony areas—the lateral and medial malleoli, the proximal fifth metatarsal, and the fibula along its entire length. These areas are particularly susceptible to fracture with an ankle injury. Neurovascular status should be assessed by palpation of pulses and tests of sensation, especially if there is a history of significant trauma.

3. **Range of motion.** The patient and then the examiner should move the ankle through plantar and dorsiflexion, as well as inversion and eversion in plantar and dorsiflexion. It is useful to compare the ankle with the uninjured side.

4. **Stress testing.** The anterior drawer test stresses the ATFL. This is done by placing one hand anterior to the tibia and the other hand around the heel and drawing the foot toward the examiner (Figure 51–4). A shift of >3 to 4 mm is worrisome for a tear in the ATFL. The talar tilt test places the ankle in inversion and then eversion to assess the calcaneofibular and deltoid ligaments respectively (Figure 51–5). A >5 to 10% difference between ankles is indicative of ligamentous injury. The side-to-side test assesses the integrity of the tibiofibular ligament. The ankle is placed in neutral position and the tibia and fibula are grasped with one hand while medial and lateral forces are applied to the heel with the other hand. Pain and an audible sound secondary to widening of the ankle mortise characterize a positive test. The squeeze or compression test is often neglected but is a quick and easy way to diagnose the important syndesmosis injury, especially if

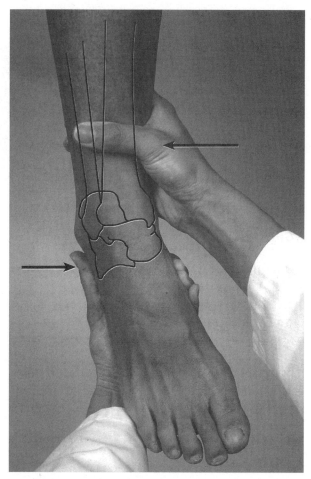

FIGURE 51–5. Talar tilt test.

the injury occurred with the ankle in eversion and external rotation. This test is performed by grasping the anterior tibia and fibula at midshaft and squeezing them together. Pain is suggestive of syndesmotic injury or a fracture. Finally, the Thompson's test assesses Achilles tendon integrity. The patient is placed in a prone position with the knee flexed to 90°, and the midcalf is squeezed. Lack of plantarflexion of the foot indicates a rupture of the Achilles tendon.

RADIOGRAPHY

In the setting of acute recent ankle injury, the decision to order radiographs is aided by using a set of prospectively validated criteria called the "Ottawa rules."[8] These rules have been tested in an emergency department in thousands of patients over the age of 18 years. The authors of the rules caution against the application of these rules in patients with altered sensorium, intoxication, paraplegia, or bone disease, or delay in seeking care as such patients were excluded from participation in the study. According to this study, an ankle radiographic series is indicated if any one of the two clinical features is present:

1. Inability to bear weight, both immediately and for four steps, including limping, at the time of the examination
2. Bone tenderness at the posterior edge or tip of either malleolus

These criteria had a sensitivity of 100% in this study. No patients had clinically significant fractures who did not meet at least one of the two clinical criteria for radiography.

An ankle series consists of anteroposterior, oblique or mortise, and lateral views of the ankle. These should be examined carefully for fractures and defects, including avulsion fractures over the distal fibula and talus, distal tibia, and osteochondral fractures. Stress radiographs as well as magnetic resonance imaging (MRI) and computed tomography (CT) have limited indications and are best ordered by the orthopedist.

TREATMENT

After ruling out other diagnoses, including fractures, most ankle sprains can be managed by the primary care clinician. Grades 1 and 2 sprains can be treated similarly, while grade 3 sprains should be referred to the orthopedist.

The first phase of treatment involves minimizing local pain and swelling.[9–11] The modalities that are helpful for this include rest, ice, compression, and elevation (RICE). Cryotherapy's benefits include vasoconstriction, reduced inflammation and swelling, and analgesia. Ice packs are convenient and can be applied for up to 20 minutes every hour for 24 to 48 hours. Ice application for longer than 20 minutes may result in reflex vasodilatation and concomitant swelling. Compression can be achieved with an elastic bandage wrap. This, along with raising the ankle above the level of the heart, helps to decrease swelling. Resting the ankle with crutches for the first few days helps to decrease pain. In addition, nonsteroidal anti-inflammatory drugs can be effective analgesics when not contraindicated and their usage is properly monitored. For grades 1 and 2 sprains, immobilization with an air-stirrup orthosis prevents talar tilting (Figure 51–6). For some grade 2

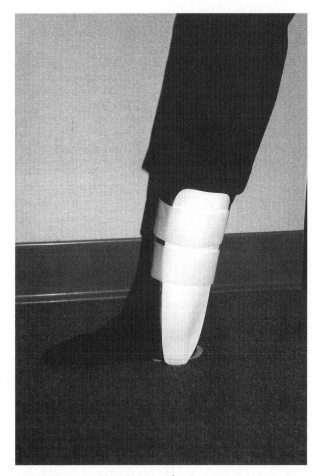

FIGURE 51–6. Air-stirrup orthosis.

and most grade 3 sprains, immobilization can be achieved with a posterior splint or removable walking boot. Short leg casts are commonly used for fractures but rarely used for sprains alone.

The most common cause for chronic pain after an ankle sprain is incomplete rehabilitation; thus, the last two phases of treatment are critical.[4] The second phase of treatment involves range-of-motion exercises and can begin as early as the second day. Plantar and dorsiflexion are initially recommended followed by inversion and eversion exercises. One way of achieving this is to have the patient inscribe the letters of the alphabet in the air. Athletes, in particular, can be referred to physical therapy for range-of-motion exercises incorporating a wobble board or a biomechanic ankle platform system (BAPS). In addition, heel cord stretches can decrease the tightness of the posterior structures.

The third phase of treatment, which is usually 4 to 6 weeks following injury, incorporates strengthening and proprioceptive exercises. Initially, isometric

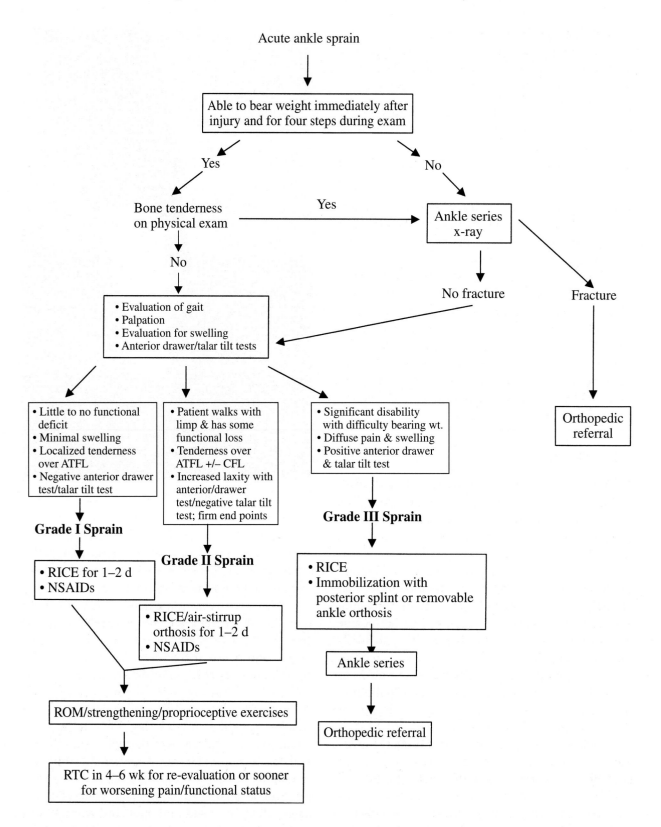

FIGURE 51–7. Ankle sprain algorithm. ATFL = anterior talofibular ligament; RICE = rest, ice, compression, elevation; CFL = calcanofibular ligament; NSAID = nonsteroidal anti-inflammatory drug; ROM = range of motion; wt = weight.

Step 1   <u>R</u>est
              <u>I</u>ce
              <u>C</u>ompression
              <u>E</u>levation

              For 1–2 days, anti-inflammatory drugs are helpful. Speak to your physician.

Step 2   Range-of-motion exercises. (Repeat two to three times a day.)

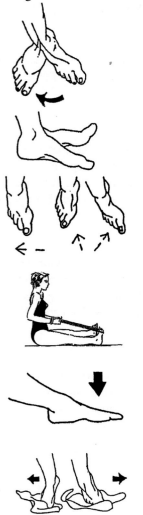

Ankle circles: rotate ankle in clockwise and then counterclockwise direction for 10 repetitions.

Ankle pumps: pump ankles up and down in a seated position with legs extended for 10 repetitions.

Alphabet: use foot to draw the letters of the alphabet in the air.

Dorsiflexion stretch: place a towel around foot and grasp the ends with your hands; pull the foot toward your body and hold for a count of 10. Repeat 3 times.

Plantarflexion stretch: push foot down pointing toes and hold for a count of 10. Repeat 3 times.

Towel slides: place towel on floor and with heel in place, move the towel side to side with the foot for 10 repetitions.

FIGURE 51–8. Ankle sprain treatment and exercises.

exercises are started in plantar and dorsiflexion, again followed by inversion and eversion exercises. Rubber tubing or a Theraband can be used to provide resistance as the patient progresses in isokinetic exercises. This should be done in two to three sets of 10 to 15 repetitions. Toe raises are also helpful in achieving muscle strength, starting, of course, with the help of the uninjured leg.

Finally, ankle injuries can lead to loss of proprioception. Proprioceptive ankle exercises can, indeed, reduce the incidence of chronic ankle sprains and ankle pain. At this point in the rehabilitation phase, especially for athletes, formal physical therapy is very helpful. The BAPS board is used with progression to partial weight bearing. Single leg stork stands assisted and unassisted, teeterboards, and foursquare

Step 3   Strengthening exercises. (Repeat two to three times a day.)

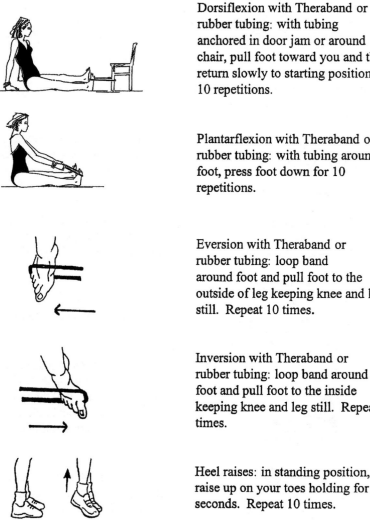

Dorsiflexion with Theraband or rubber tubing: with tubing anchored in door jam or around chair, pull foot toward you and then return slowly to starting position for 10 repetitions.

Plantarflexion with Theraband or rubber tubing: with tubing around foot, press foot down for 10 repetitions.

Eversion with Theraband or rubber tubing: loop band around foot and pull foot to the outside of leg keeping knee and leg still. Repeat 10 times.

Inversion with Theraband or rubber tubing: loop band around foot and pull foot to the inside keeping knee and leg still. Repeat 10 times.

Heel raises: in standing position, raise up on your toes holding for 2 seconds. Repeat 10 times.

FIGURE 51–8. (continued).

hopping are some of the exercises utilized. Prophylactic ankle stabilizers appear to reduce the incidence of acute ankle sprains and should be especially considered in athletes in high-risk sports.[12]

Figure 51–7 presents an algorithm for evaluation and treatment of ankle sprains. Figure 51–8 is a handout that may be given to patients.

REFERENCES

1. Buddecke D, Mandracchia V, Pendarvis J, Yoho R. Is this "just" a sprained ankle? Hosp Med 1998;46–52.
2. American Academy of Orthopedic Surgeons. The essentials of musculoskeletal care. Rosemont (IL): American Academy of Orthopedic Surgeons; 1997. p. 371, 390–4, 402–4, 424–6.
3. Birrer R, Cartwright T, Denton J. Immediate diagnosis of ankle trauma. Phys Sportsmed 1994;22:95–102.
4. Grana W. Chronic pain after ankle sprain. Phys Sportsmed 1995;23:67–79.
5. Baker C, Todd J. Intervening in acute ankle sprain and chronic instability. J Musculoskel Med 1995; 51–68.
6. Swain R, Holt W. Ankle injuries—tips from sports medicine physicians. Postgrad Med 1993;93:91–100.
7. Trojian T, McKeag D. Ankle sprains—expedient assessment and management. Phys Sportsmed 1998;26:29–40.

8. Stiell I, Greenberg G, McKnight D, et al. Decision rules for the use of radiography in acute ankle injuries. JAMA 1993;269:1127–32.

9. Losito J, O'Neil J. Rehabilitation of foot and ankle injuries. Sports Med Rehab 1997;14:533–57.

10. Vegso J, Harmon L. Nonoperative management of athletic ankle injuries. Clin Sports Med 1982;1:85–98.

11. Birrer R, Cartwright T, Denton J. Primary treatment of ankle trauma. Phys Sportsmed 1994;22:33–42.

12. Sitler M, Horodyski M. Effectiveness of prophylactic ankle stabilisers for prevention of ankle injuries. Sports Med 1995;20:53–7.

52

COMMON SKIN DISEASES

Kathleen Behr, MD

Women frequently seek medical care for skin problems. This chapter describes the various common dermatologic diseases seen in general practice and reviews current treatment strategies appropriate for the primary care clinician.

ACNE VULGARIS

Acne vulgaris is a common disease of the pilosebaceous unit. The cause of acne is multifactorial, including blockage of the pilosebaceous canal with keratin, increased sebum production behind the plug, and proliferation of anaerobic bacteria. This leads to a wide range of clinical lesions including comedones, papules, pustules, and cysts.

Acne affects more than 17 million persons in the United States. The start of acne correlates more with pubertal stage than with age.[1] In women acne often starts a year or more before menarche. The highest percentage of acne is seen in middle to late teenage years, but acne may persist through the third decade or later, especially in women.

The major burden of acne is the psychiatric morbidity associated with the disease. This can cause impaired self-image, social impairment, anger, and depression.[2] It can profoundly impair the patient's academic, social, and vocational functioning.

Presenting Signs and Diagnosis

The patient usually makes the diagnosis of acne and then comes to the clinician for therapy. Presenting signs are often noninflammatory open and closed comedones, but may include more severe inflammatory papules and cysts. Later, the patient may present with scars or pigmentation changes.

In women, a history of irregular menses or hirsutism should lead to consideration of an endocrine disorder. In these patients laboratory work-up should include serum dehydroepiandrosterone (DHEA-S) and free testosterone. Among patients with acne it has been shown that mean serum levels of DHEA-S and testosterone are higher but still within normal range compared with those without acne.[3] A history of lotion and cosmetic use is also important, since some of these products can be comedogenic.

Treatment

There are great fluctuations in the natural course of acne, so the efficacy of medications can be difficult to evaluate. Table 52–1 is a guideline of therapy, which is explained in further detail below.

Therapy depends on the severity of disease and the patient's skin type (ie, oily, dry, or sensitive). All patients should wash with mild soap and avoid

TABLE 52–1. Acne Therapy

Type of Acne	Treatment
Mild comedonal	Retinoid, glycolic acid, or benzoyl peroxide
Mild-moderate comedonal and inflammatory	Add topical antibiotic
Moderate inflammatory	Add oral antibiotic and consider OCP
Resistant	Check hormones and consider spironolactone or isotretinoin (Accutane)
Severe with scarring	Refer to specialist for isotretinoin

OCP = oral contraceptive.

scrubbing, which can irritate lesions. Picking at lesions also should be avoided. Since the comedone is the primary lesion, almost all patients require a comedolytic agent. These include topical retinoids (tretinoin [Retin-A], adapalene [Differin], tazarotene [Tazorac]) and agents containing benzoyl peroxide and azelaic acid.

Tretinoin is available as a cream, gel (more drying), or solution (most drying). A pea-sized amount should be applied nightly to the entire face or affected area, not just individual lesions. For patients who are particularly sensitive to Retin-A, Retin-A micro 0.1 is available in a microsponge formulation to help decrease irritation from the 0.1 concentration. Patients should be made aware that increased sun sensitivity can occur with retinoid usage.

Benzoyl peroxides are comedolytics and powerful antibacterial agents.[4] Benzoyl peroxide is the active ingredient in many acne preparations among the most prescribed topical medications. Dryness can be a problem with the benzoyl peroxides. Rarely, an allergic reaction can develop. Benzoyl peroxides are available in strengths ranging from 2.5 to 10% .

Azelaic acid 20% reduces keratinization and decreases the follicular bacterial population; it is therefore another useful comedolytic agent.

When inflammatory lesions are present, a topical antibiotic is added, usually erythromycin or clindamycin. These are available as creams, gels, and solutions. Two popular combinations are benzoyl peroxide and erythromycin (Benzamycin) or clindamycin (Benzadin).

For more severe inflammatory acne, oral antibiotics are added to the topical regime. The antibiotics act by an anti-inflammatory effect as well as a direct effect on *Proprinobacterium acnes*. Tetracycline is effective in dosages of 250 to 500 mg bid taken on an empty stomach. Doxycycline 50 to 100 mg bid or minocycline 50 to 100 mg bid also are commonly used, and they can be taken with food. Side effects include increased photosensitivity with doxycycline and bluish-black pigmentation in scars and on the gums with minocycline. Minocycline also has been reported rarely to cause autoimmune hepatitis and a lupus-like syndrome.[5] Erythromycin 500 mg bid also is used sometimes. However, increasing bacterial resistance to erythromycin has been noted.

Hormonal therapy often is useful in women to counteract effects of androgens on the sebaceous gland. Estrogens help to decrease sebum production.

Birth control pills with second-generation progestins such as desogestrel and norgestimate have low androgenic activity. Ortho Tri-Cyclen has been studied for the treatment of acne and was statistically significantly effective compared with placebo.[6] It often takes 3 to 4 months of therapy to notice improvement.

Spironolactone reduces sebum production and acne through its effects as an androgen receptor blocker and an inhibitor of 5α-reductase.[7,8] Dosages are 50 to 100 mg bid. Side effects include menstrual irregularities, breast tenderness, headaches, fatigue, and hyperkalemia. It cannot be given during pregnancy, since there is a risk of feminization of the male fetus.

Isotretinoin (Accutane) is useful in cystic acne or resistant acne vulgaris that is scarring. This therapy involves counseling and close monitoring by the dermatologist. Side effects are common, especially cheilitis and xerosis, which occur in all patients. Other possible side effects include conjunctivitis, pruritis, joint pain, hair loss, headache, and symptoms of increased intracranial pressure (pseudotumor cerebri), palmarplantar desquamation, nausea and vomiting, and depression. Thrombocytopenia, leukopenia, hypertriglyceridemia, and increases in erythrocyte sedimentation rate and liver-associated enzymes often occur. Initial dosage is often 0.5 mg/kg/d to prevent flares. This is increased gradually up to 1 to 2 mg/kg/d. Therapy is continued for 16 to 20 weeks. Total dosage of about 100 mg/kg is important for successful therapy. Prevention of pregnancy is of utmost importance to avoid teratogenic effects on the developing fetus.

Prognosis

Acne usually lasts several years followed by spontaneous remission. The main physical sequela is scarring that often can be improved with cosmetic procedures.

Prevention and Screening

No preventive treatment exists, but screening for family history of severe acne often can help guide therapy.

Pregnancy and Breast-Feeding

Acne can flare or remit during pregnancy. Treatment is limited since tetracyclines, spironolactone, and isotretinoin must be avoided due to possible adverse

TABLE 52–2. Hair Loss Classification of Hair Loss

Nonscarring
    Focal
        Alopecia areata
        Trichotillomania
        Tinea capitis
    Diffuse
        Broken hairs (hair treatments or tinea)
        Telogen effluvium (loss of > 100 hairs/d)
        Androgenetic alopecia (decreased production)

Scarring*
    Alopecia cutis congenita
    Lupus
    Lichen planopilaris
    Pseudopelade de Brocq
    Follicular degeneration syndrome
    Folliculitis decalvans
    Dissecting folliculitis

*Patients should be referred for biopsy.

effects on the fetus. Topical benzoyl peroxides, retinoids, and clindamycin also are not used since they are classified as US Food and Drug Administration (FDA) category C drugs. Commonly used agents are glycolic acids, topical erythromycin, and azelaic acid. Oral erythromycin can be used in more severe cases. Acne that flares during pregnancy usually remits within a few months post partum.

ALOPECIA

Hair loss is a common complaint in women. History and physical examination findings allow classification of alopecia into several types (Table 52–2). Diagnosis and treatment strategies are then developed based on the clinical type.

Alopecia Areata

Alopecia areata presents with coin-shaped areas of patchy alopecia that may progress to become confluent. The pathogenesis is obscure, but most authors believe it is an autoimmune disease. Alopecia areata affects 0.2% of the population at any given time.[9]

Presenting Sign and Diagnosis

Alopecia areata presents with hair loss in a coin-shaped distribution (Figure 52–1). Alopecia areata is diagnosed by this clinical appearance and can be

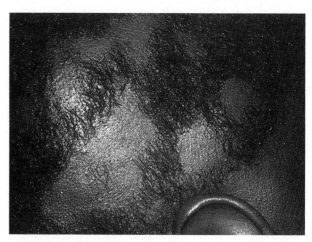

FIGURE 52–1. Alopecia areata.

confirmed by biopsy, when necessary. The differential diagnosis includes trichotillomania and tinea capitis (described below).

Treatment

Topical steroids class I to V (Table 52–3) or 5% minoxidil (Rogaine) are effective treatments for alopecia areata, but it may take several months for regrowth to be apparent. Intralesional steroid therapy is performed commonly by dermatologists, with a response usually seen in a few weeks. For extensive disease, psoralen photochemotherapy (psoralen plus ultraviolet A), oral steroids, or immunostimulation (anthralin or dinitrochlorobenzene) can be used.

Prognosis

Spontaneous remission is common with patchy alopecia areata but less so with more extensive disease. Remission usually occurs within months of onset. Focal disease usually responds well to therapy, but relapses are common both acutely and over a lifetime. More extensive cases are difficult to treat and require both combination therapy and emotional counseling.

Trichotillomania

Trichotillomania is an impulse control disorder in which a patient pulls, plucks, or cuts her hair.[10,11]

Presenting Signs and Diagnosis

Patients generally present with bizarre patterns of hair loss. Patients usually deny any role in their hair loss (Figure 52–2). Trichotillomania is suspected clinically based on this pattern of hair loss, and is confirmed with biopsy.

TABLE 52–3. Selected Topical Steroids

High potency

    Class I

        Clobetasol propionate cream and ointment 0.05%
            (Temovate)*

        Betamethasone dipropionate ointment 0.05%
            (Diprolene)

Medium potency†

    Class II

        Amcinonide ointment 0.1% (Cyclocort)

        Halcinonide cream 0.1% (Halog)

        Desoximetasone cream and ointment 0.25%
            (Topicort)

        Desoximetasone gel 0.5% (Topicort)

    Class III

        Triamcinolone acetonide 0.5% cream and
            ointment (Aristocort)

        Amcinonide cream and lotion 0.1% (Cyclocort)

    Class IV

        Mometasone furoate 0.1% cream and lotion
            (Elocom)

        Fluocinolone acetonide 0.025% ointment
            (Fluonide, Synalar)

    Class V

        Fluocinolone acetonide 0.025% cream
            (Fluonide, Synalar)

        Hydrocortisone 0.2% cream (Westcort)

        Desonide 0.05% ointment (Desocort)

    Class VI

        Fluocinolone acetonide 0.01% cream and lotion
            (Fluonid, Synalar)

        Triamcinolone acetonide 0.025% cream
            (Aristocort)

Low potency

    Class VII

        Hydrocortisone 2.5% cream, lotion, and ointment
            (Hytone, Synacort)

*More potent than are others in this class.
†Steroids in lower numbered classes are of higher potency.
Adapted from Habif TP. Clinical dermatology. 2nd ed.
St. Louis: Mosby; 1990. p. 708–9.

TREATMENT

Psychiatric referral generally is indicated. Treatment is focused on ameliorating obsessive-compulsive behavior.

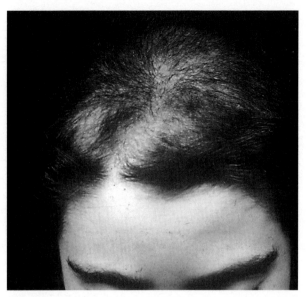

FIGURE 52–2. Trichotillomania.

Tinea Capitis

Tinea capitis is a common cause of hair breakage or loss. In the United States, the current most common pathogenic cause is *Trichophyton tonsurans*.

PRESENTING SIGNS AND DIAGNOSIS

Tinea capitis commonly presents with breakage of hair shaft ("black dot ringworm") and scaling of the scalp. Some areas can be very inflamed and pus filled. These areas are termed "kerions."

    Tinea capitis is diagnosed by culture of the hair shafts or by microscopic KOH examination.

TREATMENT

Oral therapy is required and contacts should be sought to prevent re-infection. Griseofulvin is the standard therapy. Patients are treated with 15 to 20 mg/kg/d of micronized griseofulvin or 10 to 15 mg/kg/d of ultramicronized griseofulvin for 6 to 8 weeks until hair shaft culture is negative. Recent data suggest itraconazole (Sporanox) or terbinafine (Lamisil) are effective alternative treatments. Itraconazole may be used at a dosage of 200 mg qd for 6 to 8 weeks. Terbinafine can be used at a dosage of 250 mg qd, also for 6 to 8 weeks.[12] For all these drugs, caution should be used in patients with pre-existing liver disease. It is prudent to check liver-associated enzyme levels prior to therapy.

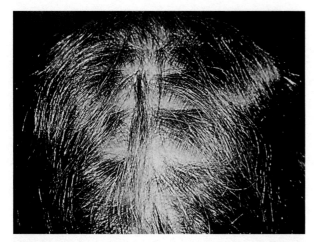

FIGURE 52–3. Alopecia caused by hair rollers.

PROGNOSIS

There is an excellent cure rate with therapy. Inflammatory scarring is seen in those patients with kerions.

Hair Breakage

Nonscarring alopecia due to breakage of the hair shaft can be due to weakening of the hair shaft by chemical factors (eg, permanent waves, bleaching, dyes) or physical factors (hot combs, or blow dryers with high heat).

PRESENTING SIGNS AND DIAGNOSIS

Alopecia caused by chemical or physical factors presents as broken hair shafts temporally associated with hair treatment (Figure 52–3). Diagnosis is made by clinical examination, which reveals broken hair shafts and damaged weakened dry hair.

TREATMENT

Treatment consists of avoidance of the suspected trauma or chemical. Patients should be reassured that the hair will regrow, at a rate of about 1 cm/mo.

PROGNOSIS

The prognosis for hair breakage alopecia is excellent, since the hair follicle itself is not damaged.

Telogen Effluvium

Telogen effluvium is a common type of hair loss that may occur at any age due to a variety of physical or mental stressors. These stressors are listed in Table 52–4.[12,13] Telogen effluvium occurs when a larger than normal amount of anagen hairs (hairs in the growth phase) are shifted into the telogen (resting) phase.

TABLE 52–4. Etiologies of Telogen Effluvium

Endocrine causes
    Thyroid abnormalities
    Postpartum state
    Peri- or postmenopausal state

Nutritional deficiencies

Drugs (especially anticoagulants, ACE inhibitors, antimitotic drugs, ß-blockers, lithium, OCPs, retinoids, valproic acid, excess vitamin A)

Physical stressors
    Anemia
    Systemic illness
    Surgery

Psychological stress

ACE = angiotensin converting enzyme; OCP = oral contraceptive.

PRESENTING SIGNS

Patients with telogen effluvium notice increased hair loss over the normal 100 hairs lost per day. This usually occurs 3 to 4 months after the inciting event and lasts for several months.

DIAGNOSIS

Diagnosis is made by history taking and physical examination to eliminate other causes of hair loss. History of any significant physical stressors, such as surgery, delivery, systemic illness, and death of close friend or relative, should be sought. Questions regarding diet are important, since caloric, protein, essential fatty acid, zinc, biotin, and iron deficiency can be causes. Laboratory testing for thyroid abnormalities, anemia, and menopause (when appropriate) should be obtained. Drug history is important, since many drugs can cause telogen effluvium.

TREATMENT

Treatment consists of evaluation and correction of any identifiable cause, as well as reassurance. Appropriate therapy of endocrine or nutritional abnormalities should be pursued. If a drug is suspected as the cause, it should be discontinued, if possible. If there is a history of a physical or physiological event that is the likely etiology, the patient should be reassured that telogen effluvium will revert. To help quicken hair regrowth, minoxidil 2% bid for 6 months can be used.

PROGNOSIS

Recovery of hair loss is good after an episode of telogen effluvium. However, it may take 6 to 12 months for hair density to return to the baseline level.

PREGNANCY AND BREAST-FEEDING, MENOPAUSE, AND ORAL CONTRACEPTIVES

Telogen effluvium is commonly noticed 3 to 4 months post partum. It is treated by reassurance. Hormonal changes in the peri- and postmenopausal period can stimulate telogen effluvium, as can hormonal changes temporarily invoked by oral contraceptives (OCPs).[14]

Androgenetic Alopecia

The decline in hair production termed androgenetic alopecia is a genetically mediated type of alopecia, which occurs in 50% of both men and women. It usually begins in the third or fourth decade. The basic etiology is the same in men and women, and it is mediated by androgens. There is a greater androgen-receptor content in the dermal papilla cells of balding scalps compared to nonbalding scalps.[15] Hair loss is dihydrotestosterone dependent. Dihydrotestosterone is produced by the conversion of testosterone at the skin and sebaceous gland level by 5α-reductase. The effect of dihydrotestosterone stimulation of the androgen receptor is progressive miniaturization of follicles, leading to the loss of hair.

PRESENTING SIGNS

Women present with gradual hair loss, characterized by thinning on the top of the scalp and preservation of the frontal hairline. In contrast, men demonstrate bitemporal and vertex predominance of hair loss.

DIAGNOSIS

Androgenetic alopecia is a diagnosis of exclusion. A family history of hair loss is suggestive. The causes of hair loss associated with telogen effluvium should be ruled out. Finally, the patient should be tested for androgenic abnormalities, including increased free testosterone or elevated DHEA-S. If no other cause of hair loss is identified and the pattern of hair loss is correct, the diagnosis of androgenetic alopecia is made.

TREATMENT

For women with androgenetic alopecia, the use of medications that block production or receptors of androgens is helpful. Topical minoxidil 2% is a nonspecific hair growth promotor that helps stabilize hair loss. It must be used twice a day for at least 6 months to produce a visible response.[16]

Oral contraceptives that contain a nonandrogenic progestin can be useful to decrease ovarian and adrenal production of androgens, helping to decrease hair loss and promote new growth.[17]

Spironolactone 50 to 100 mg bid is an antiandrogen that can stabilize hair loss. In some cases patients note hair regrowth with the use of spironolactone. Flutamide in a dosage of 250 to 500 mg bid is effective, but it is seldom used due to potential hepatotoxicity.

PROGNOSIS

Women with androgenetic alopecia continue to experience gradual thinning without treatment.

MENOPAUSE

Although patients often first note androgenetic alopecia during menopause, it is age, not menopausal status, that determines the degree of hair loss in these cases.

DERMATITIS

Allergic Contact Dermatitis

Allergic contact dermatitis is one of the most frequently encountered dermatologic problems. Often it is an occupational-related illness, which accounts for an annual cost of 250 million dollars in lost productivity, medical care, and disability payments in the United States.[18] Common causes of allergic contact dermatitis differ between women and men, owing to a differing prevalence of exposure to causative agents.

PRESENTING SIGNS

The clinical presentation of contact dermatitis varies, depending on the location and duration of exposure to the offending agent. Acute eruptions are characterized by erythema, papules, vesicles, and edema. Chronic allergic contact dermatitis presents as a lichenified, scaling, and erythematous dermatitis. The rash is almost always exceedingly pruritic.

DIAGNOSIS

Taking a complete history of contact exposures is important for diagnosis. Cosmetics are often culprits in women, including hair dye, cosmetic creams (eg, vehicles, preservatives, emulsifiers, and fragrances), and nail products. Nickel is another common allergen and is frequently found in jewelry.

The only useful and reliable test for allergic contact dermatitis is the patch test. A prepared patch test is placed on the back, and readings are performed at 48 and 72 hours to identify and confirm the offending allergen.

TREATMENT
Avoidance of the allergic agent is necessary. Therapy of the reaction is with topical or oral steroids depending on the severity of the reaction. Antihistamines are also of benefit. If the wound is weeping, Domeboro solution compresses are recommended for 15 to 30 minutes two to four times per day.

PROGNOSIS
The prognosis is excellent if contact with the allergen is stopped. However, some agents are so ubiquitous that they are difficult to avoid.

Atopic Dermatitis

Atopic dermatitis is a chronic relapsing skin disease frequently associated with a family history of atopic dermatitis, allergic rhinitis, or asthma. It is a common disorder in infancy and childhood but can persist into adulthood.

PRESENTING SIGNS
Patients present with pruritus, flexural erythema, and lichenification that is chronic or relapsing. Nearly 80% of patients with atopic dermatitis develop allergic rhinitis or asthma.

DIAGNOSIS
The diagnosis of atopic dermatitis is based on the presence of a combination of clinical features, family history, and associated hay fever or asthma.

TREATMENT
Successful therapy involves preventing flares with regular skin hydration and avoidance of irritants. Skin care involves avoidance of hot water, which is drying. Bathing in a lukewarm tub for 15 to 20 minutes should be followed immediately by application of an occlusive emollient such as Aquaphor or a heavy cream such as Cetaphil or Eucerin. Therapy with topical cortisones is a mainstay of treatment.

Potent fluorinated glucocorticoids must be avoided on the face, axilla, and genitalia, or thinning and striae will result. Topical steroids should be applied twice per day to lesions, and emollients to the rest of the skin. Strong potency steroids should be used for only 1 to 2 weeks. Medium and low-potency steroids can be used for prolonged periods (see Table 52–3).

Dust mites and animal danders are common allergens in atopic patients. They can be identified with selective skin prick tests, usually performed by an allergist.

Secondary infections with *Staphylococcus aureus* should be considered in patients with crusted and moist lesions; appropriate antibiotic therapy should be given.

Antihistamines can be helpful in relieving some of the pruritus associated with atopic dermatitis. Nonsedating antihistamines used during the day have shown variable results. Pruritus is usually worse at night. The use of doxepin or hydroxyzine is recommended.

A new topical therapy with FK 506 has been proven promising. Preliminary data of FK 506 in an ointment base (tacrolimus) show marked decrease in pruritus within 3 days of initiation of therapy.[19] Currently it is available as Protopic Oil and 0.03% ointment, to be applied twice a day. Patients should be warned that stinging or itching may occur with the first few applications.

For more severe atopic disease, therapy by the dermatologist includes systemic steroids, ultraviolet light, cyclosporine, or interferon.

PROGNOSIS
The course of atopic dermatitis is difficult to predict, but spontaneous resolution or lessening of the disease occurs in many children. Others may have persistent or relapsing dermatitis.

Intertrigo

Intertrigo is a superficial dermatitis in the folds of the skin, which are often colonized with *Candida*. It can be submammary, gluteal, or in folds of skin of the abdominal pannus. Predisposing factors include obesity, occlusive clothing, and diabetes.[20]

PRESENTING SIGNS AND DIAGNOSIS
The diagnosis is made clinically from appearance of an erythematous macerated area of skin with satellite vesicopustules. In particular, satellite

vesicopustules are classic for *Candida* infection. Microscopic KOH examination of skin scrapings confirms the diagnosis.

TREATMENT AND PROGNOSIS
Treatment consists of keeping the area dry. Domeboro compresses may be used if areas are weeping or moist. Topical antifungal preparations (eg, clotrimazole 1%, ketoconazole 2%) should be used twice daily. Adding a low-potency steroid for a short period of 1 to 2 weeks helps to relieve symptoms, but patients must be warned to avoid chronic use due to the risk of developing atrophy.

Prognosis is excellent with treatment.

PREVENTION AND SCREENING
Patients with a history of intertrigo should keep their skin dry and avoid occlusive clothing. Regular use of nystatin powder to fold areas can prevent infection.

Perioral Dermatitis

Perioral dermatitis is a facial dermatosis predominately affecting females of childbearing age. It affects perioral areas, classically sparing a rim of skin at the vermillion border. It also can affect the eyelids at the lateral canthus.

Many factors have been implicated in the etiology of perioral dermatitis, including infections, steroids, and hormones. Some women report a premenstrual flare or the development of perioral dermatitis during pregnancy.[21] Topical steroids often are implicated in causing or exacerbating perioral dermatitis.

PRESENTING SIGNS
Patients usually report a short history of a perioral facial eruption consisting of erythema, micropapules, and fine scale. An sensation of burning or irritation is common, but pruritus is mild. The severity of symptoms generally runs a chronic fluctuating course (Figure 52–4).

DIAGNOSIS
Perioral dermatitis is diagnosed by clinical appearance. The differential diagnosis includes acne rosacea, seborrheic dermatitis, contact dermatitis, acne, and papular sarcoidosis.

TREATMENT AND PROGNOSIS
Treatment of perioral dermatitis is highly successful. It is responsive to tetracycline 250 mg bid, doxy-

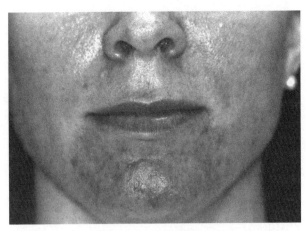

FIGURE 52–4. Perioral dermatitis.

cycline 50 mg bid, or minocycline 50 mg bid. Significant improvement often occurs within the first month of treatment. Treatment usually is continued for 2 to 3 months.

If patient is using a topical cortisone, it should be stopped by a slow taper. A sudden discontinuation of topical cortisone often results in a flare.

Untreated perioral dermatitis can persist for years. With therapy, prognosis is excellent and recurrence is uncommon.[22]

PREVENTION
Perioral dermatitis can sometimes be prevented by avoiding the use of topical cortisones on the face.

PREGNANCY AND BREAST-FEEDING, MENOPAUSE, AND ORAL CONTRACEPTIVES
Pregnant patients with perioral dermatitis can be treated with oral erythromycin, which, although less effective, is safe during pregnancy.

Perioral dermatitis is unusual during menopause, as it is seldom seen after age 45 years.

Despite epidemiologic evidence of a hormonal link, there is little evidence to implicate OCPs as a cause of perioral dermatitis.

Seborrheic Dermatitis

Seborrheic dermatitis is a chronic dermatitis of the sebaceous follicle–rich areas of the scalp, face, and trunk. The incidence of seborrheic dermatitis has two peaks: one in infancy and the other in the fourth through seventh decades of life. It affects 2 to 5% of the population, with women being less commonly affected than are men. The etiology is unknown.

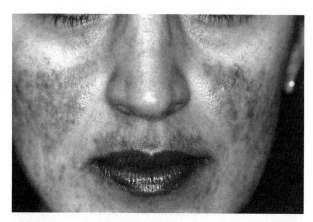

FIGURE 52–5. Melasma.

PRESENTING SIGNS

The skin lesions are characterized by a yellow greasy appearance with underlying erythema and superficial scales and crusts. Particular areas of involvement are the scalp, ears, inner parts of the eyebrows, nasolabial folds, and chest.

DIAGNOSIS

Clinical examination is usually diagnostic. Differential diagnosis should include psoriasis, atopic dermatitis, allergic contact dermatitis, and rosacea. An acute onset of seborrheic dermatitis may serve as a clue of the presence of human immunodeficiency virus infection.[23]

TREATMENT

Therapy for seborrheic dermatitis of the scalp includes the daily use of a medicated shampoo containing zinc, selenium sulfide, tar, salicylic acid, or ketoconazole. On the face and trunk, ketoconazole creams and zinc soap (ZNP bar) are useful for maintenance therapy. Mild topical steroids can be added to control flares.

PROGNOSIS

Usually, seborrheic dermatitis lasts for years to decades, with periods of remission and exacerbation.

MELASMA

Melasma is a common disorder of acquired hypermelanosis that occurs in sun-exposed areas, most notably the cheeks.[24] It is common in women of childbearing age but has been reported rarely in men. It is seen in all races but is more commonly diagnosed in Latins and Asians. The majority of cases are related to pregnancy or oral contraceptive use.

Presenting Signs and Diagnosis

Melasma presents as macular areas of hypermelanosis on the face with serrated geographic borders that are more apparent after sun exposure (Figure 52–5). Diagnosis is made by clinical examination.

Treatment

Therapy for melasma involves the use of an opaque or broad-spectrum SPF 30 sunblock. Topical bleaching creams that contain hydroquinone 2 to 4% should be used twice daily. Tretinoin or glycolic acid preparations can be added to therapy. Azelaic acid 20% daily or twice daily also may be effective. In more severe cases, the dermatologist may perform a chemical peel.

Prognosis

Melasma appears to be a chronic process exacerbated by sunlight; it often resolves with discontinuation of OCPs or following childbirth.

Prevention

Broad-spectrum sunscreens of SPF 30 are helpful in lessening the appearance of melasma.

Pregnancy and Breast-Feeding, Menopause, and Oral Contraceptives

Melasma often begins or is exacerbated during pregnancy. Therapy during pregnancy and breast-feeding is limited to sun protection.

Melasma is uncommon in postmenopausal women. However, hormonal replacement therapy containing estrogen can cause melasma, even in those women who did not experience melasma during their pregnancies.

Patients taking OCPs should understand that it may not be possible to clear their melasma while they are using OCPs.

ROSACEA

Rosacea, or acne rosacea, is an inflammatory condition that consists of papules and papulopustules on a background of erythema. It starts in early stages as blushing, progressing in later stages to dark red erythema on the nose and cheeks. Rosacea often starts in the twenties and peaks between the ages of 40 and

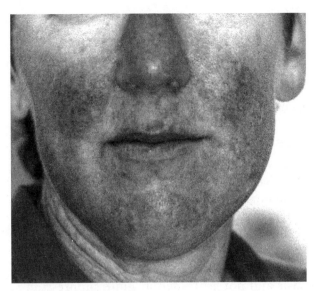

FIGURE 52–6. Rosacea.

50 years. Women are more commonly affected than are men by a 3:1 ratio, but they often have less severe disease.[25] Men develop grotesque deformities and sebaceous gland hyperplasia much more frequently.

The precise etiology of rosacea is not known but it is much more common in fair-skinned people of Celtic or other Northern European heritage. Sunlight, heat, and certain spicy foods are contributing factors to flares.

Presenting Signs

Rosacea is a disease of the centrofacial regions. Hallmarks are papules and papulopustules on a base of erythema and telangiectasias. Comedones are absent. The disease presents in stages. The beginning stage consists of erythema and telangiectasias. The intermediate stage has erythema, increased telangiectasias, papules, and pustules. Late-stage rosacea has deep erythema, dense telangiectasias, papules, pustules, nodules, and variable edema (Figure 52–6).

Diagnosis

The diagnosis of rosacea is based on clinical appearance. The differential diagnosis includes acne vulgaris, seborrheic dermatitis, lupus erythematosus, dermatomyositis, perioral dermatitis, carcinoid syndrome, and polymorphous light eruption. Rosacea fulminans is a variant with sudden severe onset seen almost exclusively in postadolescent women. The appearance can be extremely distressing to the patient, and immediate treatment by a dermatologist is recommended.

Treatment and Prognosis

Rosacea is difficult to treat. Cures are often not possible, but the disease can be controlled. Skin irritants should be avoided, since rosacea patients often have sensitive skin. These include alcoholic cleansers, astringents, harsh soaps, and peeling agents. It is important to provide sun protection that does not irritate the skin. Physical blockers that have zinc oxide or titanium dioxide are chemical free and thus are often recommended.

The topical therapy most commonly used is metronidazole 0.75% gel or cream applied bid for papules and papulopustules, but this only minimally helps erythema. Noritate is a newer preparation for once-a-day use. Old-time remedies are creams with 2 to 5% sulfur qhs. Tretinoin A 0.025% qhs can help over months, if the patient can tolerate an initial flare.

Oral antibiotics are effective due to their anti-inflammatory effects and are used in more severe papular and pustular disease. These are used in combination with topical therapy. Oral antibiotics are tapered as control is achieved. Tetracycline 500 mg bid, doxycycline 50 mg bid, and minocycline 50 mg bid are most commonly used for 2 to 3 weeks. Subsequently, the doses are often halved for a few months and then stopped. Exacerbations may require intermittent oral therapy. More severe disease may require treatment with isotretinoin by a dermatologist.

Adjunctive therapy includes dietary avoidance of alcoholic beverages, hot drinks, and spicy foods. Laser therapy with the pulsed dye laser for persistent telangiectasias is effective and can help decrease the number of pustules.

Prevention

Sun avoidance and protection are helpful in preventing rosacea in predisposed individuals.

Pregnancy, Menopause, and Oral Contraceptives

During pregnancy and breast-feeding many treatments are contraindicated. Topically, azelaic acid 20% often is used. It is an FDA category B drug. In more severe cases erythromycin is given orally 500 mg bid for 3 weeks and then tapered to a dose of 500 mg daily.

Rosacea may first occur in women experiencing the hormonal changes associated with menopause, but it usually is unaffected by birth control pill use.

URTICARIA

Urticaria is a vascular reaction characterized by the eruption of wheals of pruritic hives. Individual lesions arise suddenly and resolve within 24 to 48 hours. Episodes of urticaria of less than 6 to 8 weeks' duration are called "acute," and those lasting longer are termed "chronic." Urticaria affects persons of any age, but it is most common in young adulthood. Chronic urticaria is more common in women.

Presenting Signs and Diagnosis

Circumscribed raised erythematous plaques of edema that are pruritic are characteristic of urticaria. The diagnosis of uriticaria is made by clinical examination. Acute urticaria is differentiated from chronic urticaria only by the time course of the eruption. Acute urticaria was found to be the result of an upper respiratory tract infection in 40% and drugs in 9% of patients in one study, with the remaining cases being idiopathic.[26]

In most patients with chronic urticaria, no underlying disorder or cause can be found. Evaluation of patients with chronic urticaria should include a complete history and physical examination, with laboratory testing as indicated. In addition to a drug reaction, possible, although rare, causes of chronic urticaria include parasitic infection, hepatitis B, thyroid autoimmune disease, cryoproteinemia, necrotizing vasculitis, lupus, and acquired complement 1 inhibitor (C1 INH) deficiency.

Treatment

Removal of the cause of urticaria is essential; however, the cause often is not identifiable. Treatment of symptoms in acute and chronic urticaria with antihistamines is the mainstay of therapy. Nonsedating antihistamines generally are used during the day and combined with traditional sedating antihistamines at night. These should be given on a regular basis and not as needed. If more suppression is needed, doxepin, a tricylic antidepressant with H_1 and H_2 antihistamine blockers, can be added.

Prognosis

By definition, acute urticaria resolves in 6 to 8 weeks. Chronic urticaria resolves within 1 year in about 50% of cases. However, 20% of patients continue to have episodes of urticaria for 20 years or more.

RESOURCES

The National Alopecia Areata Foundation
710 C Street, Suite 11
San Rafael, California 94901
Telephone: (415) 546-4644
Web site: www.alopeciaareata.com

The National Alopecia Areata Foundation provides information for patients through their Web site.

The National Rosacea Society
800 South Northwest Highway, Suite 200
Barrington, Illinois 60010
Telephone: (847) 382-8971
        1-888- NO BLUSH (1-888-662-5874)
Web site: www.rosacea.org

The National Rosacea Society offers information for patients, a patient newsletter, and brochures and other written information about rosacea.

REFERENCES

1. Lucky AW, Biro FM, Huster GA, et al. Acne vulgaris in premenarchal girls. Arch Dermatol 1994;130:308–14.
2. Koo J. The psychosocial acne. The psychosocial impact of acne: patient's perceptions. J Am Acad Dermatol 1995;32:526–30.
3. Lucky A, McGuire J, Rosenfield RL, et al. Plasma androgens in women with acne vulgaris. J Invest Dermatol 1983;81:70–4.
4. Fulton JE Jr, Farzad-Bakshandeh A, Bradely S. Studies on the mechanism of action of topical benzoyl peroxide and vitamin A in acne vulgaris. J Cutan Pathol 1974;1:191–200.
5. Knights SE, Leando MJ, Khamashta MA, et al. Minocycline induced arthritis. Clin Exp Rheumatol 1998; 16:587–90.
6. Redmond GP, Olson WH, Lippman JS, et al. Norgestimate and ethinyl estradiol in the treatment of acne vulgaris: a randomized placebo controlled trial. Obstet Gynecol 1997;89:615–22.
7. Goodfellow A, Alaghband-Zadeh J, Carter G, et al. Oral spironolactone improves acne vulgaris and reduces sebum excretion. Br J Dermatol 1984;111:209–14.
8. Goodman DS. Vitamin A and retinoids in health and disease. N Engl J Med 1984;310:1024–31.
9. Safovi KH, Muller SA, Suman VJ, et al. Incidence of alopecia areata in Olmsted County, Minnesota, 1975 through 1989. Mayo Clin Proc 1995;70:628–33.
10. Rothbaum BO, Ninan PT. The assessment of trichotillomania. Behav Res Ther 1994;32:651–2.
11. Stein DJ, Simeon D, Cohen DJ, et al. Trichotillomania and obsessive compulsive disorder. J Clin Phychiatry 1995;56:28–34.
12. Lopez-Gomez S, Del Palacio S, Van Cutsem J, et al. Itraconazole versus griseofulvin in the treatment of tinea capitis: a double-blind randomized study in children. Int J Dermatol 1994;33:743–7.
13. Fiedler VC, Hafeez A. Diffuse alopecia: telogen hair loss. In: Olsen EA, editor. Disorders of hair growth: diagnosis and treatment. New York: McGraw-Hill; 1994. p. 241–55.
14. Pillans PI, Woods DJ. Drug associated alopecia. Int J Dermatol 1995;34:149–58.
15. Sawaya ME, Price VH. Different levels of 5 alpha-reductase type I and II, aromatase, and androgen receptor in hair follicles of women and men with androgenetic alopecia. J Invest Dermatol 1997; 109:296–300.
16. Olsen EA. Androgenetic alopecia. In: Olsen EA, editor. Disorders of hair growth: diagnosis and treatment. New York: McGraw-Hill; 1994. p. 257–83.
17. Mestman JH, Anderson GV, Nelson DH. Adrenal pituitary responsiveness during therapy with an oral contraceptive. Obstet Gynecol 1968;31:378–86.
18. Proposed national strategy for the prevention of leading work-related diseases and injuries, Part 2. Washington (DC): Association of Schools of Public Health and National Institutes of Occupational Safety and Health: 1988. p. 65–95.
19. Nakagawa H, Etoh T, Ishibashi Y, et al. Tacrolimus ointment for atopic ointment dermatitis [letter]. Lancet 1994;344:883.
20. Pariser DM. Cutaneous candidiasis. Postgrad Med 1990;87:101–3, 106–8.
21. Hogan DJ, Epstein JD, Lane PR, et al. Perioral dermatitis: an uncommon condition? J Calif Med Assoc 1986;134:1025–8.
22. Hogan DJ. Perioral dermatitis. Curr Probl Dermatol 1995;22:98–104.
23. Mathes BM, Douglass MC. Seborrheic dermatitis in patients with acquired immunodeficiency syndrome. J Am Acad Dermatol 1985;13:947–51.
24. Sanchez NP, Pathak MA, Sato S, et al. Melasma: a clinical, light, microscopic, ultrastructural and immunofluorescence study. J Am Acad Dermatol 1981; 4:698–710.
25. Chalmers DA. Roseacea. Recognition and management for the primary care provider. Nurse Pract 1997;22:23–8, 30.
26. Soter NA. The investigation of urticaria and angiooedema. Clin Exp Dermatol 1995;20:266–76.

53

COMMON BENIGN SKIN GROWTHS, PRECANCER AND CANCER OF THE SKIN

Kathleen Behr, MD

Concern about skin growths is a common reason women visit the primary care clinician. This chapter provides illustrations and descriptions of common skin growths, including precancerous and cancerous lesions.

COMMON BENIGN SKIN GROWTHS

Cherry Angiomas

Cherry angiomas appear clinically as red papules 1 to 5 mm in diameter (Figure 53–1). They are benign vascular lesions, which occur commonly on the trunks of middle-aged and elderly women. No treatment is required. However, if irritated, they can be removed by electro-dessication with cautery or laser therapy.

Dermatofibromas

Dermatofibromas are firm brown, red, or yellowish papules or nodules with a propensity for the lower extremities (Figure 53–2). They dimple when pinched. They are more common in women than in men. The etiology of dermatofibromas is thought to be secondary to a bite or ingrown hair. No therapy is necessary. Surgery is avoided since the scar is more apparent than the lesion.

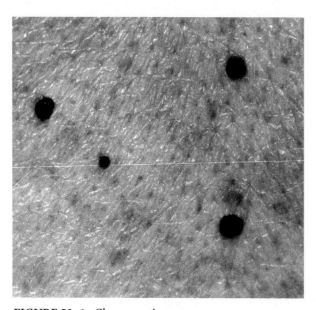

FIGURE 53–1. Cherry angiomas.

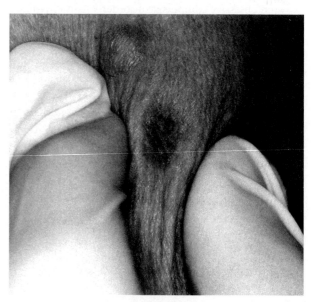

FIGURE 53–2. Dermatofibroma.

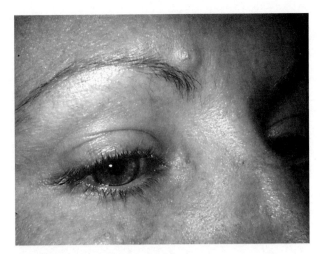

FIGURE 53–3. Epidermal inclusion cyst.

Epidermal Inclusion Cysts

Epidermal inclusion cysts are keratin-containing cysts with an epithelial lining (Figure 53–3). They affect women and men equally. Clinically, they present as firm intradermal freely mobile tumors, often with a visible puncta in the overlying epidermis. If the cysts rupture, they become inflamed due to a foreign body reaction and can become secondarily infected. Therapy of inflamed cysts involves incision and drainage, intralesional cortisone 5 mg/cc, and oral antibiotics. The cysts can only be completely removed when noninflamed.

Solar Lentigines

A solar lentigo is an acquired circumscribed light brown macule induced by ultraviolet light (Figure 53–4). Once present, it persists for an indefinite period, even in the absence of further sun exposure. It is more common in fair-skinned individuals.[1] Treatment includes sunblock, light liquid nitrogen, laser therapy, or chemical peels. If a lesion becomes dark or irregular, lentigo maligna must be ruled out by biopsy.

Lipomas

Lipomas are the most common tumor of the mesenchmyal tissue.[2] Clinically, they are dermal nodules that are well circumscribed. They are often slowly growing and asymptomatic but can easily be removed, if tender.

Milia

Milia are small 1 to 3 mm superficial keratin cysts (Figure 53–5). They are superficial pearly white papules that occur primarily on the face. Milia can be easily removed with a comedone extractor after the surface is nicked with a no. 11 blade.

Nevi

The common nevus is a collection of nevomelanocytes in the epidermis (junctional), causing a flat brown macule; in the dermis (intradermal), causing fleshy papule; or in both areas (compound), resulting in brown papule (Figures 53–6 to 53–8). In a series from Australia, the average number of nevi peaked during second and third decades and decreased to very few in the sixth and seventh decades.[3] There is evidence that the size and distribution patterns of nevi tend to aggregate in families. This is well documented for dysplastic nevi

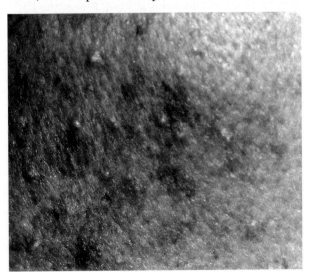

FIGURE 53–4. Solar lentigines.

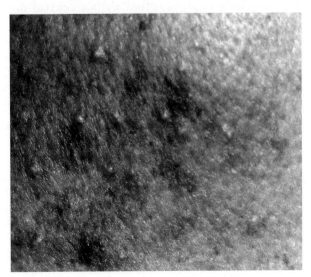

FIGURE 53–5. Milia.

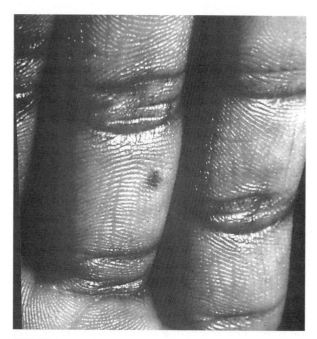

FIGURE 53–6. Nevus.

associated with familial melanoma.[4] Nevi may be removed for cosmetic purposes, but specimens should always be sent for histopathology. Nevi should be removed if irritated, itchy, changing, or atypical in appearance. Benign-appearing nevi can be shaved off. Atypical lesions may represent melanoma. Therefore, they should be excised so that the depth of the lesion can be ascertained to guide therapy and prognosis.

Sebaceous Hyperplasia

Sebaceous hyperplasia occurs on the face as 1- to 3-mm yellow papules, often with a central del

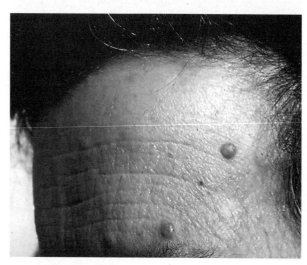

FIGURE 53–7. Nevi.

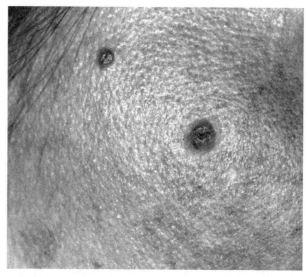

FIGURE 53–8. Nevi.

(indentation) (Figure 53–9). Lesions tend to increase with age, with most occurring past middle age. The differential diagnosis often includes basal cell carcinoma, but the yellowish color and del are distinguishing features. Therapy involves light electrocautery or laser. Lesions often recur.

Seborrheic Keratoses

Seborrheic keratoses are extremely common benign growths. Clinically, seborrheic keratoses can range in color from flesh-colored to dark brown and appear as rough or warty papules that are well demarcated and have a "stuck on" appearance (Figure 53–10). They occur anywhere on the body but are most common on the trunk. Most women have at least one during their lifetime. Some develop hundreds. There

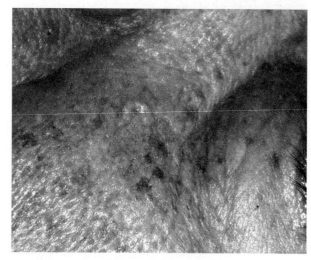

FIGURE 53–9. Sebaceous hyperplasia.

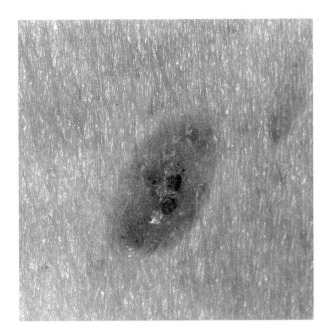

FIGURE 53–10. Seborrheic keratosis.

is often a positive family history in patients with numerous lesions.

Variants include dermatosis papulosa nigra, seen in darker-skinned persons. These present as small facial papules, especially on the cheeks. Stucco keratoses are 3- to 4-mm light-colored lesions located on the legs, particularly the ankles. These are usually multiple.

Seborrheic keratoses may become irritated in areas of friction. Removal is performed if lesions become irritated or for cosmetic purposes. Treatment includes cryotherapy in lighter-skinned individuals, but this is not recommended in darker skin types because it often causes postinflammatory hyperpigmentation. Other treatments include electro-dessication, curettage, and excision. A seborrheic keratosis should only be treated with destructive techniques if it is clinically typical. If its appearance is atypical, a shave excision should be done, and the specimen should be sent for histologic examination.

Acrochordons

Acrochordons, commonly referred to as "skin tags," are very common benign tumors that present as flesh-colored, pedunculated papules. These lesions are common in the body folds, such as those found in the neck, axilla, eyelids, and groin. Irritated lesions are treated by cryotherapy, electro-dessication, or snip excision.

PRECANCEROUS SKIN LESIONS: ACTINIC KERATOSES

The most common precancerous skin growth among fair-skinned individuals is the actinic keratosis.[5] Risk factors include blue eyes, freckling, old age, and sun exposure.

PRESENTING SIGNS AND SYMPTOMS

Actinic keratoses present on sun-exposed body regions as red-brown ill-defined scaling macules or plaques. Actinic keratoses are usually asymptomatic but may be mildly itchy or painful.

DIAGNOSIS

The diagnosis of actinic keratosis is made clinically, on the basis of the finding of a typical-appearing lesion in a fair-skinned patient with background solar damage. Squamous cell carcinoma should be suspected if the lesion is indurated at the base, tender, or unresponsive to therapy, and, in this case, a biopsy should be performed.

TREATMENT

Cryosurgery with liquid nitrogen is the most common therapy for isolated lesions. In patients with multiple lesions, topical 5-fluorouracil is used twice daily for 2 to 3 weeks. During this treatment, the actinic keratoses become very inflamed and then regress.[6]

PROGNOSIS

Actinic keratoses have the potential to develop into squamous cell carcinoma, but the exact probability of an individual lesion developing into a squamous cell carcinoma is not known.[7] The risk of progression is higher in immunosuppressed patients.

PREVENTION

Solar protection may prevent the development of new actinic keratoses.[8] Reducing sunlight exposure in childhood may substantially decrease the incidence of actinic keratoses later in life.[9]

SKIN CANCER

Basal Cell Carcinoma

Basal cell carcinoma is the most common malignancy in humans. It is a locally aggressive tumor

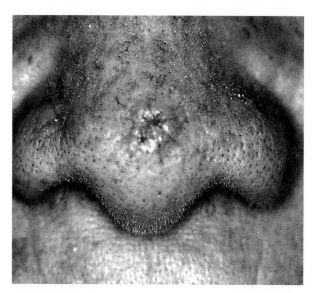

FIGURE 53–11.   Basal cell carcinoma.

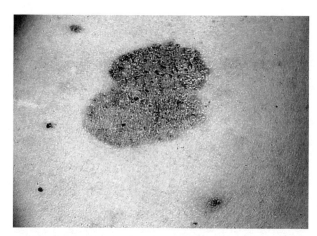

FIGURE 53–12.   Basal cell carcinoma.

that can invade the fascia, muscle, perichrondrium, cartilage, bone, and nerve but rarely metastasizes.[10] The incidence of basal cell carcinoma in the United States is about 600,000 new cases annually, but the exact number is difficult to determine since most cases are treated in private offices and not reported. Approximately 85% of basal cell carcinomas occur in the head and neck area. There are several types of basal cell carcinoma based on histopathology, including superficial, nodular, micronodular, and morpheaform cancers.

PRESENTING SIGNS AND SYMPTOMS
Clinically, basal cell carcinoma most often presents as a pink pearly patch or papule with rolled borders and telangiectasias, with or without a central ulceration (Figures 53–11 and 53–12). The morpheaform type presents as an indurated scar with ill-defined borders.

DIAGNOSIS
The diagnosis is confirmed by biopsy and histologic examination.

TREATMENT
Treatment is usually provided by a dermatologist or plastic surgeon. Surgical treatment options include electro-dessication and curettage, cryosurgery, excision, and Mohs' micrographic surgery.[11] All methods of treatment have a 90% or better cure rate. Basal cell carcinomas can also be treated nonsurgically with radiation therapy. The choice of therapy

is based on tumor type, size, location, and the patient's general health status.

PROGNOSIS
Prognosis is excellent as basal cell carcinoma has a rate of metastasis of only 0.01 to 0.1%.[12] Close follow-up is important since a patient with a skin cancer has a 22 to 50% chance of developing a new or recurrent lesion.[13]

PREVENTION AND SCREENING
Minimization of sun exposure with avoidance and proper usage of sunscreen from the age of 6 months is effective in reducing the risk of basal cell carcinoma. Screening of all patients with a complete skin examination during routine physical examinations is recommended by the American Cancer Society.

Squamous Cell Carcinoma
Squamous cell carcinoma (SCC) is the second most common skin cancer, with a yearly estimated incidence of 100,000 new cases in the United States. Etiologic factors include skin type; exposure to sun (ultraviolet light); radiation; carcinogens, such as arsenic and coal tar; infection with human papilloma virus (HPV); immunosuppression; and chronic ulcers or inflammation.[14]

Rates of metastasis vary from 0.5 to 16%.[15] Metastases are more common in men. This may be due to the fact that tumors with the highest rate of metastases are those on the lip and ear, and those that are > 2 cm in diameter. Women often have protection from acquiring lip and ear lesions due to use of lipstick and hairstyles that cover the ears.

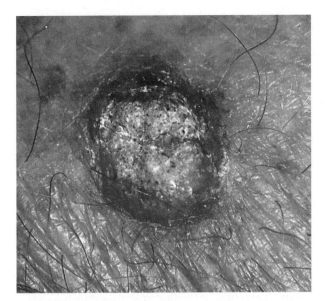

FIGURE 53–13. Squamous cell carcinoma.

PRESENTING SIGNS AND SYMPTOMS

Squamous cell carcinoma presents as a red indurated papule, plaque, nodule, or ulceration, most commonly on sun-exposed surfaces (Figure 53–13). The growth rate of these lesions is highly variable.

DIAGNOSIS

The diagnosis of SCC is confirmed by biopsy and histologic examination.

TREATMENT

Therapy for SCC is provided by a specialist, usually a dermatologist or plastic surgeon. Treatment options include electro-dessication and curettage (for very superficial lesions), excision, and Mohs' micrographic surgery. The choice of therapy is based on tumor size, location, histology, and the patient's general health status.

PROGNOSIS

The cure rate for SCC is excellent, well over 90% for most lesions. Lesions of concern for higher risk of metastases are those on the lip and ears, large lesions, and lesions with perineural invasion. Primary spread of SCC is first to the regional nodes, then it progresses to widespread metastatic disease. The 5-year survival of metastatic SCC is only 25%, so early detection and therapy are essential.[16]

Melanoma

Malignant melanoma is the most aggressive of the skin cancers. The incidence rate is growing faster

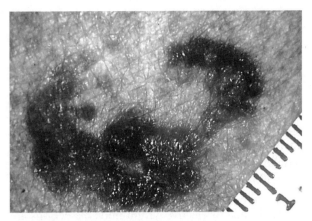

FIGURE 53–14. Melanoma.

than that of any other cancer in the United States. Currently, 1 in 87 persons is be afflicted during their lifetime.[17] There are 32,000 new cases annually and approximately 6,500 deaths due to melanomas.[18] Melanoma is the most common cancer in women 25 to 29 years of age and is second only to breast cancer in women aged 30 to 35 years. Risk factors include fair skin type, a history of sunburns, a family history of melanoma, and the presence of atypical moles. Gender differences in melanoma distribution are according to sun exposure patterns, with melanomas more common on the backs of men and the legs of women.[19]

There are four types of melanoma. Superficial spreading melanoma represents 70% of lesions. Nodular melanoma represents 15 to 30% of melanomas. Lentigo maligna occurs in elderly individuals, mostly on the face as a brown stain. Acral lentiginous melanoma is rare in the general population but is the most common type of melanoma in African Americans.

PRESENTING SIGNS AND SYMPTOMS

Melanomas are characterized by asymmetry, irregular border, and color variation (Figure 53–14). It is important to instruct all the patients to watch for changes in moles or the development of new lesions, and to report them immediately. It is also important to promptly evaluate itchy or tender nevi.

DIAGNOSIS

Melanoma is diagnosed by excisional biopsy of the lesion with a 1- to 3-mm margin of normal skin and including underlying fat.[20] Stage I localized melanomas are those < 1.5 mm in thickness. Stage II melanomas are localized deeper lesions. Stage III melanomas have limited nodal metastases. Stage IV melanomas are those with advanced regional or distant metasteses.

TREATMENT

Therapy comprises excision of the lesion with margins that depend on depth (Breslow thickness). Most early melanomas are cured with wide excision. A baseline chest radiograph and liver function tests are often obtained even for early lesions, but there are no universally accepted guidelines. For deeper lesions, sentinel node or elective lymph node dissections are often recommended. These patients should be evaluated by an oncologist. Adjuvant therapy for deeper lesions is high-dose interferon-α-2b.[21] Therapy for lymph node metastasis includes therapeutic lymph node dissection. Therapies for stage IV disease with distant metastasis include surgical removal of isolated metastases, radiation, chemotherapy with dacarbazine (DTIC), interferon, interleukin-2, and monoclonal antibodies, as well as melanoma vaccines,[22] which are currently being developed.

PROGNOSIS

Survival with melanoma has many prognostic factors, the most important of which is depth of the lesion. Patients diagnosed with stage I and II melanomas of < .75 mm thickness have a 99% long-term survival rate. Those with lesions 0.76 to 1.49 mm thickness have an 80 to 90% long-term survival rate. For lesions 1.50 to 4 mm in depth, patients have a 60 to 75% survival rate. Patients with lesions > 4 mm in depth have a < 50% survival rate.[23]

Other key prognostic factors include the anatomic location of the lesion and the age and gender of the patient. Patients whose lesions are on an extremity have a better prognosis than do those whose lesions are found on the trunk, head, or neck. Women have a better prognosis than do men, independent of the site and thickness of the lesion.[24] Advanced age leads to a poorer prognosis. Finally, there is poor prognosis for lesions that are clinically ulcerated or have a high mitotic rate histologically. Stage III disease with lymph node metastasis has a 5-year survival rate of 30%.[25] Stage IV disease has a 5-year survival rate of 6%.[26]

PREVENTION AND SCREENING

While basal cell and squamous cell carcinoma incidences correlate with chronic sun exposure, the incidence of melanoma correlates with intense blistering sunburns.[27] Sun avoidance and protection should start from childhood. Avoiding peak hours of sun exposure and using sunscreen and sun-protective clothing are important preventive measures. Screening of all first-degree relatives of patients with melanoma and individuals with multiple dysplastic nevi should be performed. Performing a skin examination of all patients during routine physical examination and providing education on the "ABCDs" (*a*ssymetry, *b*order irregularity, *c*olor variation, and *d*iameters > 0.6 mm) of melanoma detection to patients have been recommended as further measures to facilitate early diagnosis.

PREGNANCY AND BREAST-FEEDING

The prognosis for women diagnosed with melanoma during pregnancy appears to be the same as for nonpregnant women diagnosed with melanoma, according to recent reviews.[28] This is in contrast to earlier studies that showed a poorer prognosis for melanoma diagnosed during pregnancy. However, these studies were often not controlled for lesion thickness and site.[29] Two studies have demonstrated shorter disease-free survival among pregnant patients who went on to develop recurrent disease.

Many experts recommend avoiding pregnancy during the first 2 years after the diagnosis and treatment of melanoma. This is the period of greatest risk for recurrence.[30] For low-risk patients with thin lesions, this may not be necessary. Therefore, counseling about the timing of pregnancy should be individualized.

ORAL CONTRACEPTIVE PILLS AND HORMONE REPLACEMENT THERAPY

Many clinicians recommend that women diagnosed with melanomas with > 1.5 mm thickness avoid oral contraceptives for the first 2 years of follow up.[30] This is because estrogen receptors have been identified on some melanoma specimens. There have been no randomized controlled trials on the use of either oral contraceptive pills or hormone replacement therapy in melanoma survivors.

RESOURCE

The American Academy of Dermatology
930 North Meacham Road
PO Box 4014
Schaumberg, Illinois 60168-4014
Telephone: 1-888-462-DERM ext. 22 (1-888-462-3376)
Web site: www.aad.org

The American Academy of Dermatology provides patient education materials on a variety of skin conditions, which can be purchased or accessed through its Web site. The AAD also has an on-line listing of advocacy groups for patients with various skin conditions.

REFERENCES

1. Rhodes AR, Stern RS, Melski JW. The PUVA lentigo: an analysis of predisposing factors. J Invest Dermatol 1983;81:459–63.

2. Benign lipomatous tumors. In: Enzinger FM, Weiss SW, editors. Soft tissue tumors. 3rd ed. St. Louis (MO): Mosby; 1995. p. 381.

3. Nicholls EM. Development and elimination of pigmented moles, and the anatomical distribution of primary malignant melanoma. Cancer 1973;32: 191–5.

4. Reimer RR, Clark WH Jr, Greene MH, et al. Precursor lesions in familial melanoma: a new genetic preneoplastic syndrome. JAMA 1978;239:744–6.

5. Marks R. Solar keratoses. Br J Dermatol 1990;122 Suppl 35:49–54.

6. Klein E, Stoll HL, Milgrom H, et al. Tumors of the skin: topical 5-flurouracil for epidermal neoplasms. J Surg Oncol 1971;3:331–49.

7. Swartz RA. Premalignant keratinocytic neoplasms. J Am Acad Dermatol 1996;35:223.

8. Lookingbill DP, Lookingbill GL, Leppard B. Actinic damage and skin cancer in albinos in northern Tanzania. J Am Acad Dermatol 1995;32:653.

9. Marks R, Jolley D, Lectsa S, Foley P. The role of childhood exposure to sunlight in the development of solar keratosis and nonmelanoma skin cancer. Med J 1990;152:62–6.

10. Hanke CW, Wolf RL, Hochman SA, O'Brian JJ. Chemosurgical reports: perineural spread of basal cell carcinoma. J Dermatol Surg Oncol 1983;9:742–7.

11. Freeman RG, Knox JM, Heaton CL. The treatment of skin cancer: a statistical study of 1,341 skin tumors comparing results obtained with irradiation surgery, and curettage followed by electrodesiccation. Cancer 1964;17:535–8.

12. Domarus HV, Stevens PJ. Metastatic basal cell carcinoma: report of 5 cases and review of 170 cases in the literature. J Am Acad Dermatol 1984;10:1043–60.

13. Robinson JK. Risk of developing another basal cell carcinoma. Cancer 1987;60:118–20.

14. Aubrey F, MacGibbon P. Risk factors of squamous cell carcinoma of the skin: a case-control study in the Montreal region. Cancer 1985;55:907–11.

15. Dinehart SM, Pollack SV. Metastases from squamous cell carcinoma of the skin and lip. J Am Acad Dermatol 1992;26:467–84.

16. Moller R, Reymann F, Hou-Jensen K. Metastases in dermatological patients with squamous cell carcinoma. Arch Dermatol 1979;115:703–5.

17. Sober AJ, Lew RA, Koh HK, Barnhill RL. Epidemiology of cutaneous melanoma: an update. Dermatol Clin 1991;9:617–29.

18. Rigel DS, Friedman RJ, Kopf AW, Silverman MK. Factors in influencing survival in melanoma. Dermatol Clin 1991;9:631–42.

19. Cress RD, Hollyea Ahn DK, et al. Cutaneous melanoma in women: anatomical distribution to sun exposure and phenotype. Cancer Epidemiol Biomarkers Dev 1995;4:831–6.

20. Urist MM. Management of patients with intermediate thickness melanoma. Ann Rev Med 1996;47:211–7.

21. De Takets PG, Williams MV, Howkins R. Adjuvant therapy for melanoma: how should we respond to high-dose interferon? Br J Cancer 1998;77:1287–7.

22. Meyers ML, Balch CM. Diagnosis and treatment of metastatic melanoma. In: Balch CM, Houghton AN,

Sober AJ, et al, editors. 3rd ed. Philadelphia (PA): JB Lippincott; 1998. p. 325–72.

23. Brown TJ, Nelson BR. Malignant melanoma: a clinical review. Cutis 1999;63:275–84.

24. Sondergaard K, Schou G. Survival with primary cutaneous malignant melanoma, evaluated from 2,012 cases. Virchows Arch [A] 1985;406:179–95.

25. Balch CM, Soong SJ, Murad TM, et al. A multifactorial analysis of melanoma III. Ann Surg 1981;193:377–88.

26. Barth A, Wanek LA, Maorton DL. Prognostic factors in 1,521 melanoma patients with distant metastases. J Am Coll Surg 1995;181:193–201.

27. Lang PG Jr. Malignant melanoma. Med Clin North Am 1998;82:1325–58.

28. Driscoll MS, Grin-Jorgensen CM, Grant-Kels JM. Does pregnancy influence the prognosis of malignant melanoma? J Am Acad Dermatol 1993;29:619.

29. Holly EA. Melanoma and pregnancy. Recent Results Cancer Res 1986;102:118–26.

30. Mackie RM. Pregnancy and exogenous female sex hormones in melanoma patients. In: Balch CM, Houghton AN, Sober AJ, et al, editors. Cutaneous melanoma. Philadelphia (PA): JB Lippincott; 1998. p. 187–93.

54

APPROACH TO THE PATIENT WITH HIRSUTISM

Jesse Hade, MD

Hirsutism is a hormonal problem, that usually results from a subtle excess of circulating androgens. For a woman, it is defined as an excess of body hair in a male pattern distribution.[1] Hirsutism can result from either an elevation in circulating androgen concentrations due to hormone overproduction or from an increase in the sensitivity of target organs to normal plasma androgen levels.[2] Some women who become hirsute have a combination of these two factors.[3]

Often, women with hirsutism experience excessive hair growth on the face, chest, abdomen, inner thighs, back, and upper arms. This hair is usually coarse and dark in nature. Two physicians, Ferriman and Gallwey, quantified hirsutism and created a scale to determine the extent of hair growth in women. This scoring method is based on assessing nine body areas that contain hairs that are sensitive to androgens and their actions. Each individual body area is then graded from 1 (minimal terminal hair) to 4 (frank virilization). The score from each individual body area is then summed. A total score of 8 or more indicates the presence of hirsutism (Figure 54–1).[4] Menstrual irregularity, infertility, and obesity can be symptoms associated with a syndrome or disease that is associated with hirsutism. Thus, a complete evaluation and workup should be performed on all hirsute women who manifest these symptoms and signs.

Acne is another sign of hyperandrogenism and is often associated with severe degrees of hirsutism. Other skin disorders associated with elevations in circulating androgen levels include seborrhea and alopecia. **Virilization** is the extreme

form of excess androgen production and represents the masculinization of a woman. It is characterized by hirsutism, acne, as well as temporal balding, clitoromegaly, deepening of the voice, and the development of a male muscle pattern.

The rate of development of the signs of hyperandrogenism should influence a clinician's level of concern and urgency for making a diagnosis. When excessive hair growth occurs over a short period of time, evaluation for an ovarian or adrenal tumor should be pursued. In addition to laboratory tests, pelvic ultrasonography or abdominal computed tomography (CT) may be required.

Variations in hair growth patterns vary among different racial, ethnic, and genetic groups. Women of Mediterranean descent naturally have increased hair growth in the sex hormone–dependent regions, whereas women of Asian descent have less hair growth in the sex hormone–dependent regions of the body. However, it is important to realize that a woman can have increased hair growth on a few androgen-sensitive regions of her body without it being hirsutism.[5] True hirsutism is relatively rare; only 5% of premenopausal women fit the criteria for the diagnosis of true hirsutism.

Hypertrichosis is the term used to describe excessive hair growth on non–sex hormone–dependent parts of the body, such as the forehead, forearms, or lower legs. This type of increased hair growth pattern, although disturbing to an individual, is not related to elevated levels of androgens or the metabolism of androgens. However, this condition may be caused by medications, such as dilantin, diazoxide, and corticosteroids. It may also arise from longstanding anorexia or hypothyroidism or may be familial in origin. Typically, the hair growth that is associated with this process is fine vellus hair and not coarse hair like that associated with hirsutism.

ANDROGEN PRODUCTION, SECRETION, AND TRANSPORTATION

Androgens originate from either the ovary or the adrenal gland. Biologically, only androgens that circulate in the plasma free and unbound diffuse across the plasma membrane to interact with androgenic receptors. However, some peripheral tissues can convert testosterone into dihydrotestosterone (DHT), a more potent and biologically active androgen than testosterone, allowing local effects on androgen receptors to occur without altering plasma androgen levels.

During the reproductive years, a woman's ovary produces about 25% of circulating testosterone and 50% of plasma androstenedione.[6] In the ovary, androgens are considered obligate intermediates in the formation of estrogen. They are produced by the theca cells of a growing follicle and by the interstitial compartments of the ovary.[7] Luteinizing hormone (LH) is the gonadotropin responsible for stimulating the production of androgens within these cells of the ovary.

The adrenal glands are responsible for the production of the remaining 50% of androstenedione, as well as 25% of the testosterone in circulation.[8] There is no negative feedback control between circulating androgen levels and the pituitary and

	1	2	3	4	SCORE
UPPER LIP	few hairs at outer margin	small moustache at outer margin	moustache extending halfway from outer margin	moustache extending to midline	
CHIN	a few scattered hairs	scattered hair with small concentrations	light complete cover	heavy complete cover	
CHEST	circumareolar hairs	circumareolar and midline hairs	fusion of these areas with 3/4 cover	complete cover	
UPPER BACK	a few scattered hairs	more scattered hairs	light complete cover	heavy complete cover	
LOWER BACK	a sacral tuft of hair	a sacral tuft of hair with some lateral extension	three quarter cover	complete cover	
UPPER ABDOMEN	a few midline hairs	more midline hairs	half cover	full cover	
LOWER ABDOMEN	a few midline hairs	a midline streak of hair	a midline band of hair	an inverted v-shaped growth	
UPPER ARM	sparse growth affecting not more than 1/4 of the limb surface	heavy growth, still incomplete	light complete cover	heavy complete cover	
THIGH	sparse growth affecting not more than 1/4 of the limb surface	heavy growth, still incomplete	light complete cover	heavy complete cover	
				TOTAL	

FIGURE 54–1. Ferriman and Gallwey method for assessment of hirsutism. Clinical hirsutism is defined by a score of 8 or higher. Scoring: 0 = absence of terminal hair. Adapted from Ferriman D, Gallwey JD. Clinical assessment of body hair growth in women. J Clin Endocrinol Metab 1961;21:1440.

hypothalamus in women. Therefore, elevated plasma androgen levels cannot regulate and suppress further androgen synthesis and secretion.[9]

Nearly 50% of the circulating testosterone found in the plasma of women is formed by peripheral conversion of precursor hormones. Peripheral organs responsible for this conversion include the liver, skin, and fat cells.[10] These tissues possess the aromatase enzyme and can further convert androgens into estrone. Adipose tissue is the most important source of peripheral aromatization of androstenedione into estrone.[11] Other tissues that can convert androstenedione into estrone include the bone, brain, breast, hair follicles, muscle, prostate, and skin.[12–17]

The 17-ketosteroids include dehydroepiandrosterone (DHEA) and its sulfate (DHEAS) as well as androstenedione. They are the most ubiquitous androgenic hormones circulating in the plasma of women but demonstrate weak bioactivity. DHEA is a 19-carbon steroid that is secreted by both the adrenal glands and the ovaries. Most circulating DHEA comes from the conversion of DHEAS in peripheral tissues.[18] DHEAS is the major source of circulating DHEA in the peripheral circulation. The conversion of DHEAS to DHEA occurs readily; however, the conversion of DHEA back to DHEAS occurs to a much smaller degree.

The enzyme 17-hydroxy reductase is responsible for converting the 17-ketosteroids into 17ß-hydroxysteroids. These 17ß-hydroxysteroids are more potent and bioactive than their predecessors. These biologically active androgens include the steroids androstenediol, androstanediol, testosterone, and DHT.[19]

Hormones are transported in the plasma bound to either sex hormone–binding globulin (SHBG) or albumin. Approximately 66% of the circulating testosterone is bound to SHBG, and another 33% is bound to albumin.[20] The remaining portion is free within the circulation. The biologically active hormone is the portion that is free and not bound. Production of SHBG is inversely related to androgen production and insulin concentrations. Thus, elevations in androgen levels results in a decline in SHBG production and an increase in free circulating androgens.[21]

Aromatase activity is absent in the stroma of normal postmenopausal ovaries. As a result, only androgenic hormones, particularly dehydroepian-

drosterone, androstenedione, and testosterone, can be produced. The ovaries of postmenopausal women produce mainly testosterone and androstenedione.[22] The postmenopausal ovary produces 30% of the total circulating pool of androstenedione. The remaining 70% is produced by the adrenal glands.[23]

HAIR GROWTH AND RESPONSE TO ANDROGENS

The number of hair follicles on the body of an individual is genetically determined and fixed prior to birth. It is for this reason that hirsutism is more pronounced in specific ethnic and racial groups than in others. **Vellus hair** is the fine, slightly pigmented hair that is found covering the majority of the body. During puberty, this fine type of hair is replaced by terminal hair, which is coarser and darker. The rise in androgen levels at puberty is responsible for the replacement of vellus hair by terminal hair in the axilla, mons and pubic area, stomach, inner aspect of the thigh, chest, chin, and upper lip. Once vellus hair is converted into terminal hair, the pattern of growth becomes cyclical and, in part, independent of hormonal stimulation.

The **pilosebaceous unit** is composed of the sebaceous gland and the hair follicle. Generally, the sebaceous gland is more sensitive to androgens than is the hair follicle. As a result, acne is commonly the initial presentation of hyperandrogenism. In the adult female, there are four different classes of pilosebaceous units. These include the terminal pilosebaceous unit, the apo-pilosebaceous unit, the vellus pilosebaceous unit, and the sebaceous pilosebaceous unit.[24,25] Of these different pilosebaceous units, only the last three are influenced by circulating androgen concentrations.

There are three stages of the hair follicles-growth cycle. The active growth stage (**anagen phase**), followed by a regressive or dying stage (**catagen phase**) and finally a resting phase (**telogen phase**). Terminal hair follicles spend nearly 90% of their time in the anagen phase and only a minority of the time in the catagen and telogen phases. During the anagen stage, the hair matrix cells actively divide to lengthen the hair shaft. This process is subdivided into six stages, the first five being the proanagen and the last the metanagen. The position of the tip of the hair shaft within the skin determines the precise proanagen stage, and when the tip finally erupts above the level of the skin, the term "metanagen" is used.[26]

The hair follicle contains histologic derivatives from both dermal and epidermal origins. The dermal papilla and connective tissue sheath comprise the dermal components, and the matrix and inner and outer root sheaths make up the epidermal components. Interestingly, androgen receptors have been identified only on the cells of the outer root sheath and the dermal papilla.[27,28] When present, testosterone and DHT are transported from the cytosol of these cells and into the nucleus, where mRNA production is upregulated and hair growth is initiated.

Variations in hormone concentrations can influence hair patterns and growth. In the skin and hair follicles, the enzyme 5α-reductase is responsible for converting testosterone into DHT. DHT is a more biologically potent androgen than testosterone. There are two isoenzymes for 5α-reductase (type 1 and type 2). Genital skin contains more of the type 2 isoenzyme, and the 5α-reductase isoenzyme type 1 is mostly abundant in nongenital skin.[29] Hyperactivity of this enzyme, regardless of the total circulating level of androgens, may cause hirsutism and signs of virilization.

Other hormones can influence the growth cycle of hair follicles. Estrogen lengthens the anagen phase of the hair cycle, whereas thyroid hormone increases the resting phase of the hair follicle cycle.[30] In addition to hormonal factors, environmental and local neurovascular factors can both significantly influence hair growth and development.[31]

DISEASES THAT CAUSE HIRSUTISM

Polycystic ovary syndrome (PCOS) is the most common cause of anovulatory infertility and hirsutism in women.[32] It accounts for more than 35% of the anovulation and amenorrhea experienced by women. This syndrome is characterized by hyperandrogenic chronic anovulation beginning at menarche. Although symptoms may vary among different individuals, all patients have a history of oligomenorrhea with episodes of amenorrhea associated with hyperandrogenism.

The spectrum of clinical problems faced by women with PCOS includes menstrual irregularities, androgen excess, infertility, insulin resistance, and obesity. There are no specific diagnostic tests for PCOS. Thus, it must be suspected on the basis of the patient's history and clinical symptoms. Clinical work-up of patients with suspected PCOS is warranted to exclude other serious and potentially life-threatening conditions, such as functional and neoplastic processes, and should be performed prior to making a diagnosis of PCOS.

Over 40% of all patients with PCOS demonstrate symptoms related to hyperinsulinemia. These can include the development of acanthosis nigricans. Acanthosis nigricans is a velvety, verrucous hyperpigmented skin change that develops in the intertriginous areas, such as the neck, axilla, under the breasts, and on the perineum and inner aspects of the thighs. It is a common finding in women with hirsutism and is most commonly seen on the vulva.[33] Its presence usually indicates that elevated levels of insulin are present and that the patient possibly is insulin resistant.[34]

Obesity alone can be a cause of elevated androgen levels. Women who have a body mass index (BMI) > 29 kg/m² are considered to be obese. Obese women often are insulin resistant and manifest problems associated with elevated insulin and insulin-like growth factors. Weight loss often improves the insulin resistance and hirsutism experienced by these individuals.[35]

Congenital adrenal hyperplasia (CAH) can be recognized at birth or manifest signs and symptoms only after puberty. When the latter occurs, the term "nonclassic CAH" is used. Women with late-onset or nonclassic adrenal hyperplasia represent between 2 and 4% of all women with hyperandrogenic chronic anovulation.[36] A mutation in one of the five enzymes responsible for the conversion of cholesterol into cortisol is responsible for the altered steroidogenesis within these individuals (Figure 54–2). Currently, only three of the enzymes in the cortisol pathway have been identified as being responsible for the majority of cases of CAH.

Abnormalities in 11ß-hydroxylase and 3ß-hydroxy-Δ⁵-steroid dehydrogenase-isomerase are less common causes of CAH. An abnormality in the 11ß-hydroxylase gene accounts for < 1% of all women who experience symptoms of hyperandrogenism. It usually presents at a young age and is associated with hypertension in addition to hirsutism and signs of virilization.[37]

Individuals who have a heterozygous defect in the 21-hydroxylase gene generally manifest symptoms with the onset of puberty. When a defect in the

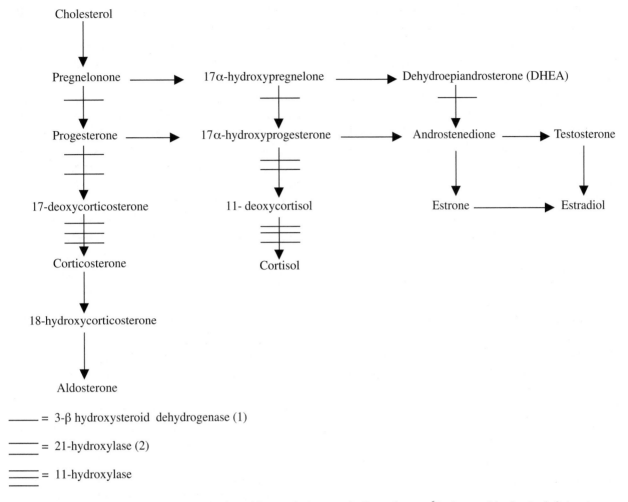

Cholesterol

Pregnelonone ——→ 17α-hydroxypregnelone ——→ Dehydroepiandrosterone (DHEA)

Progesterone ——→ 17α-hydroxyprogesterone ——→ Androstenedione ——→ Testosterone

17-deoxycorticosterone   11- deoxycortisol   Estrone ——→ Estradiol

Corticosterone   Cortisol

18-hydroxycorticosterone

Aldosterone

——— = 3-β hydroxysteroid dehydrogenase (1)

⸗ = 21-hydroxylase (2)

≡ = 11-hydroxylase

FIGURE 54–2. Nonclassical congenital adrenal hyperplasia: metabolic pathways. *Patients with classic deficiencies are generally identified at birth or in early childhood. Less severe nonclassic presentations probably represent partial enzyme defects.

1. Diagnostic criteria for nonclassic deficiency: following values 60 minutes after cortrosyn 25U IV: Δ^5-17 hydroxpregnelone ≥ 49.2 nmol/L, DHEA ≥ 63.1 nmol/L, $\Delta^5$17- hydroxyprogesterone ≥ 6.4 and Δ^5-17P/cortisol ≥ 52.
2. Diagnostic criteria for nonclassic deficiency are described in the text.

Adapted from Speroff L, Glass RH, Kase, Nater G. Clinical gynecologic endocrinology and infertility. Baltimore (MD): Williams & Wilkins; 1994; and Schram P, et al. Nonclassical 3-ß hydroxysteroid dehydrogenase deficiency. Fertil Steril 1992;58:1, 129.

21-hydroxylase gene occurs, 17α-hydroxyprogesterone levels rise, since it cannot be converted into 11-deoxycorticosterone. Consequently, a decrease in cortisol production occurs resulting in an increase in corticotropin (adrenal corticotropic hormone [ACTH]) secretion and a further increase in the production of 17α-hydroxyprogesterone. Thus, more precursors are available for conversion into androgens. Patients with nonclassic adrenal hyperplasia usually present with symptoms of chronic anovulation, hirsutism, and menstrual irregularities.

Cushing's syndrome, or hypercortisolemia, should be considered in the differential diagnosis for all patients with signs of cortisol excess. Characteristic features include centripetal obesity, purple abdominal striae, peripheral muscle wasting, hypertrichosis, moon facies, hypertension, buffalo hump, and a history of spontaneous ecchymoses. Patients diagnosed with hypercortisolemia require additional evaluation to identify the cause. Cushing's syndrome can result from pituitary, hypothalamic, or adrenal dysfunction, from ACTH- or cortisol releasing hormone CRH-producing non-endocrine tumors, or as a result of exogenous steroid administration.

Some patients with **hyperprolactinemia** may present with signs of hyperandrogenic chronic anovulation. The adrenal gland contains prolactin receptors and, as a result, can produce excessive amounts of androgens when stimulated by high plasma concentrations of prolactin.[38] Despite an increase in adrenal androgen production, the peripheral action of androgens is limited because prolactin blocks the peripheral conversion of testosterone to dihydrotestosterone. Therefore, hirsutism is uncommon in a patient with hyperprolactinemia but is relatively mild when present.

Lastly, **ovarian hyperthecosis** is a condition in which the ovaries produce a disproportionate amount of androgens due to excessive proliferation of luteinized theca cells. Normally, theca cells are scattered throughout the ovarian stroma in nests. However, in this condition, these nests of theca cells become luteinized and proliferate in abundance, resulting in an enlarged firm ovary. It is believed that these theca cells are extremely sensitive to gonadotropin stimulation, since LH levels are commonly in the normal range.[39] These patients are severely hirsute and often demonstrate signs of virilization.

TESTING FOR ANDROGEN EXCESS

Tests that are performed to determine the etiology of androgen elevation in a hirsute woman may include a total testosterone, free testosterone, DHEAS, 3ß-diol G, 17-OH progesterone, cortisol, and prolactin levels. If testing is limited to the 17-ketosteroids, only 15% of hirsute women will demonstrate an elevation in these hormones.[40] When a total testosterone level is obtained from a woman with hirsutism, an abnormal value is obtained almost 40% of the time.[41] However, the single test that is most often abnormal is the plasma free testosterone level. A plasma free testosterone level is elevated in nearly 80% of women with hirsutism.[42]

Levels of SHBG are depressed in almost 50% of hirsute women.[43] Free and albumin-bound testosterone are the biologically active forms of testosterone in the circulation. When SHBG levels fall, as a consequence of increased androgens on hepatic synthesis, the amount of free testosterone found in the plasma increases, thus worsening the patients' predicament.

Many hirsute women encountered in primary care practice fit the clinical criteria for the diagnosis of PCOS. Some, in fact, have nonclassic adrenal hyperplasia. Hirsute women of Ashkenazi Jewish or Eskimo descent should be strongly considered for screening for this disorder, since they are at high risk for having an enzymatic defect leading to excess circulating androgens. Screening and testing are generally done for the most common (21-hydroxylase) deficiency. 3ß-Hydroxysteroid dehydrogenase deficiency causes more subtle symptoms, and so the approach to these patients can be the same general approach to patients with hirsutism of other causes. 11-Hydroxylase deficiency very rarely presents in adult women. Testing for these rarer disorders is summarized in Figure 54–2.

An 8 am 17-OH progesterone level can be used as the initial screening test for nonclassic CAH caused by 21-hydroxylase deficiency. This level should be obtained during the early follicular period, since levels are falsely elevated during the luteal phase in a menstruating woman. If this value is > 4 ng/mL, it is likely that the patient has nonclassic adrenal hyperplasia. A value of < 2 ng/mL indicates that a diagnosis of CAH is unlikely.

However, values between 2 and 4 ng/mL are indeterminate, and an ACTH stimulation test needs to be performed to confirm a diagnosis. This 1-hour test is performed by administering 0.25 mg of cosyntropin (ACTH) intravenously and measuring a 17-OH progesterone level 60 minutes later. Levels that are > 10 ng/mL after ACTH stimulation suggest the presence of a 21-hydroxylase deficiency.[44]

Normal testosterone levels for women range between 30 ng/dL to 115 ng/dL. Women with mild hyperandrogenism often have a total testosterone level > 200 ng/dL. When testosterone levels are > 200 ng/dL, a work-up should be done to rule out an androgen-producing ovarian or adrenal tumor. Likewise, an elevation in DHEAS above 700 µg/dL may indicate the presence of an adrenal tumor. Although nearly all the DHEAS that is produced is of adrenal origin, patients who have nonclassic CAH do not have markedly elevated levels of this hormone.[45]

Testing for Cushing's syndrome begins by screening for hypercortisolemia. This can be done by obtaining either a 24-hour urine free cortisol level or by an overnight dexamethasone suppression test. An overnight dexamethasone supression test is performed by administering 1 mg of dexamethasone orally at bedtime and then measuring a plasma cortisol level at 8 am the next day. If circulating cortisol levels are >5 µg/dL, the patient is considered to exhibit excess cortisol production.

If this screening test is positive, then a 2-day low-dose dexamethasone suppression test should be performed to establish a definitive diagnosis. The patient is given dexamethasone 0.5 mg every 6 hours for 2 days, and plasma cortisol is remeasured. If the circulating cortisol levels are still >5 µg/L then Cushing's syndrome is confirmed. All patients diagnosed with Cushing's syndrome should undergo further evaluation to define the cause of excess cortisol, which can be caused by ACTH-, CRH-, or cortisol-producing benign or malignant tumors, or adrenal hyperplasia.[46]

TREATMENTS FOR HIRSUTISM

Dietary Management

Weight loss of only 5% of an obese individual's initial weight can lead to a 50% rise in SHBG levels and a 40% reduction in the patients Ferriman-Gallwey score.[47] Therefore, weight loss is associated with a lowering of insulin, testosterone, androstenedione, and LH levels.[48] A small reduction in weight can also restore monthly ovulation and menstruation.[49]

Drug Therapy

The pharmacologic approach to treating this androgen-dependent disease aims at interrupting the mechanism involved in causing unwanted hair growth and symptoms of hyperandrogenism. Thus, interrupting the source of androgen secretion is aimed either at the level of the ovaries and adrenal glands or peripherally at the target organs.

The combined **oral contraceptive pill** (OCP) is the most commonly used agent to manage hirsutism. Since the OCP contains both estrogen and progesterone, it inhibits gonadotropin releases and reduces LH-dependent ovarian androgen production. Therefore, this method of treatment is best for women with an ovarian source of excess androgen production. Levels of SHBG also rise from the elevation in circulating estrogen provided by the pill.

This decreases the amount of free testosterone found in the circulation. Women who are anovulatory derive additional benefit from treatment with the OCP, since the progesterone contained within the pill prevents the deleterious effects of continuous unopposed estrogen on the endometrium.

Spironolactone is a synthetic steroid that acts both as an aldosterone and androgen antagonist. Its antiandrogenic activity occurs as a result of several different mechanisms. This drug can act as a competitive inhibitor of DHT at the receptor site, and it can inhibit androgen production by decreasing cytochrome P450 activity.[50] Since spironolactone has diuretic properties, it can also increase the metabolic clearance rate of testosterone.

Effective and safe dosages of spironolactone range between 50 and 400 mg orally daily. However, the most commonly prescribed regimen is 200 mg daily for the initial treatment of hirsutism and 100 mg daily for maintenance therapy. Although side effects are an uncommon reason for the discontinuation of this medication, they do occur, particularly when the drug is prescribed at higher dosages. Side effects include nausea, vomiting, diarrhea, abdominal discomfort, drowsiness, mental confusion, headache, and dizziness. Gastrointestinal problems occur in nearly 20% of the patients who use this medication. In addition, more than 40% of women may complain of breast tenderness and enlargement when doses of 200 mg or more per day are used.[51]

Because spironolactone has a mild progestational activity, 80% of women who use this drug as monotherapy for the treatment of hirsutism experience menstrual irregularities, including menorrhagia. This occurs regardless of whether the patient uses the medication in a cyclic or continuous fashion. Therefore, combination therapy with an OCP is often prescribed, as this improves the abnormal bleeding pattern caused by spironolactone, and also synergistically improves symptoms of androgen excess.

Patients who use spironolactone should have their blood pressure and plasma potassium levels checked before initiating treatment, 2 weeks after starting their medication, and after each dose change. A build-up of potassium within the bloodstream can occur, but is rarely clinically important when an individual's underlying renal function is normal.[52]

Flutamide is a selective nonsteroidal drug with pure peripheral antiandrogen activity. The active metabolite of flutamide is hydroxy-flutamide, which acts by competitively inhibiting androgen binding to both cytoplasmic and nuclear receptors.[53] Flutamide also inhibits adrenal 17,20 desmolase activity. However, it does not have any progestogenic or antigonadotropic action and, thus, does not cause any menstrual disturbances.[54]

Flutamide is generally prescribed in doses of 250 to 750 mg orally four times daily. Most randomized clinical trials have found that flutamide is as effective as spironolactone and other antiandrogen drugs for the treatment of hirsutism. This drug is tolerated well but can be associated with such side effects as dry skin, reduced libido, nausea, vomiting, increased appetite, and other effects associated with decreased androgen levels. Severe complications from liver toxicity can arise in a small number of flutamide users (0.4%). These problems include cholestatic jaundice, hepatic necrosis, hepatic encephalopathy, and even death.[55] Most authorities do not recommend the use of flutamide for hirsutism, since the potential side effects outweigh the benefit of treatment. However, if flutamide is used as treatment, liver function tests should be performed routinely.

Finasteride is a 5α-reductase inhibitor, that blocks the conversion of testosterone to the more potent androgen DHT.[56] It has no progestational activity and consequently can be used as monotherapy for the treatment of hirsutism. This agent does not bind to the androgen receptor and has no effect on testosterone secretion. It can reduce DHT concentrations by nearly 80% when used in doses of 5 to 400 mg orally per day. A reduction in the metabolite 3α-diol glucuronide (3α-diol G) and a rise in plasma testosterone levels accompany the fall in serum DHT. Although two types of 5α-reductase isoenzymes exist, finasteride is more effective against the type 2 than the type 1 isoenzyme.[57]

The recommended daily dose of finasteride is 5 mg, but doses as high as 400 mg/d can be used with minimal side effects. The use of a combined oral contraceptive pill is recommended with finasteride because of its potential teratogenicity in male fetuses. When fertility is desired, finasteride should be discontinued for a total of 3 months prior to attempting conception.

Gonadotropin-releasing hormone agonist (Gn-RH agonist) can be used to suppress gonado-tropin production and, ultimately, ovarian production of androgens. Women with increased production of ovarian androgens, such as in PCOS, benefit from ovarian suppression with this treatment modality.[58] Gn-RH agonist administration suppresses ovarian androgen production better than OCP therapy alone. Nearly 75% of women who use a Gn-RH agonist to treat their hirsutism demonstrate an improvement in their Ferriman-Gallwey score.[59] This treatment modality is ideal for those patients who demonstrate functional ovarian hyperandrogenism.

However, long-term treatment with Gn-RH agonists can result in a hypoestrogenic state. The problems associated with this "chemical menopause" include hot flushes, decreased libido, moodiness, headache, dizziness, and eventually osteoporosis. Bone demineralization can be prevented by concomitant estrogen replacement therapy with either combination OCP or hormone replacement therapy (HRT). The addition of this "add-back" therapy may act synergistically with Gn-RH agonist therapy in reducing hirsutism.[60]

Methods of drug administration include daily subcutaneous injections of 0.2 mg/d or daily intranasal inhalation. When a monthly depot injection is preferred, a dose of 3.75 mg intramuscularly can be used and continued for at least 6 months. After this time, the risk of osteopenia and osteoporosis increases, and add-back therapy with OCP or HRT should be started.

Glucocorticoid therapy can decrease circulating androgen concentrations in women who have elevated adrenal androgen production.[61] A dose of dexamethasone 0.5 mg orally qhs is enough to reduce early morning ACTH secretion to reduce adrenal androgen production. Side effects from this therapy include depression, weight gain, and an increase in insulin resistance. Some patients develop adrenal suppression and failure after prolonged administration of this therapy. Therefore, adrenal suppression with glucocorticoid therapy should be reserved for only severe cases of adrenal androgen overproduction (ie, severe CAH). Women with hirsutism as a result of increased adrenal androgen secretion respond better to peripheral androgen blockade, compared with adrenal suppression.[62]

Ketoconazole is an imidazole derivative that has both antifungal and antiandrogen activity. Ketoconazole inhibits cytochrome P450 enzyme activity, reducing the activity of 17α-hydroxylase, 17,20 lyase, and 11ß-hydroxylase.[63] This drug is effective for the treatment of hirsutism when prescribed at doses of 400 to 1,200 mg/d. Side effects include nausea, hair loss, dry skin, fatigue, headache, and menstrual irregularities. Serious side effects include hepatotoxicity, alterations in liver function, and even liver failure.

Cimetidine is a histamine type 2 blocker, which also binds to the androgen receptor to inhibit its function.[64] However, this antiandrogen activity of cimetidine is weak, and the clinical benefit of its use in women with hirsutism is minimal. Thus, this drug is not recommended for the treatment of hyperandrogenism.

Cyproterone acetate (CPA), although not available in the United States, is a commonly used agent throughout the rest of the world. This progestational agent is derived from 17-hydroxyprogesterone and has antigonadotropic and antiandrogenic properties.[65] CPA inhibits both testosterone and DHT action by binding to intracellular receptors and blocking their actions. It inhibits the activity of 5α-reductase and, therefore, reduces the transformation of testosterone into dihydrotestosterone.[66] Since it is a progesterone, it also acts to inhibit LH release from the pituitary, thus reducing ovarian testosterone production. Lastly, CPA increases the cytochrome P450 enzyme cascade to promote hepatic clearance of circulating androgens.[67]

Generally, CPA is administered in a cyclic fashion on days 5 to 15 in conjunction with oral ethinylestradiol on cycle days 5 to 26. Since the half-life of CPA is long, dosing occurs in the first half rather than in the second half of the cycle. The initial dose of CPA is between 50 and 100 mg, followed by a gradual reduction to a maintenance dose of 2 mg when an adequate reduction of hirsutism is achieved.[68]

Side effects of CPA include edema, weight gain, headache, nausea, fatigue, mood swings, and decreased libido.[69] It is contraindicated in pregnancy and should be discontinued for several months prior to attempting conception. Hepatotoxicity is a major concern for users of CPA. Several cases of hepatocellular carcinoma have been reported in patients who used cyproterone acetate; however, these individuals consumed dosages >200 mg/d.[70] Long-term use of CPA is still considered acceptable therapy, but it is recommended that the lowest effective dose possible be used for maintenance therapy.

The success of hirsutism therapy is determined by the change in the Ferriman-Gallwey score. Studies that have compared treatment with finasteride, flutamide, and CPA have demonstrated a significant decrease in hair growth and hirsutism in women with either hyperandrogenic disorders or with idiopathic hirsutism. All three drugs were equally capable of decreasing the Ferriman-Gallwey score; however, flutamide took up to twice as long to accomplish this.[71] The use of these agents improved a patient's Ferriman-Gallwey score by approximately 50%.

Cosmetic Measures

There are a variety of temporary methods to remove unwanted hair. These methods include depilatory creams, shaving, plucking, and waxing. Permanent methods of hair removal include electrolysis and laser therapies. However, the last two methods usually require multiple treatment regimens for permanent hair removal.

When hair is removed by **electrolysis**, an electrode is inserted into each hair follicle, which is then electrocuted by a small charge. This method is not only invasive but also extremely tedious. Often, multiple treatments are required to achieve permanent hair removal. Yet, the regrowth of hair after therapy can be as high as 50%.[72]

Hair removal with the use of a **laser light source** is rapid and less invasive than electrolysis. The principle of selective photothermolysis allows specific hair follicles to be targeted for destruction and removal.[73] This is accomplished either by targeting the endogenous chromophores in the hair shaft (melanin) or by applying an exogenous chromophore to the hair follicle and then irradiating the follicle with a wavelength of light, which matches its absorption peak.[74]

Lasers, which target endogenous chromophores, include the long-pulse ruby laser, long-pulse alexandrite laser, pulsed diode laser, and the Q-switched Nd:YAG laser. These lasers work best when the patient's hair follicles are darker than the patient's skin. Hence, patients with dark skin or light hair have better results when an exogenous chromophore is applied, moving the peak absorption of light into the infrared portion of the light spectrum. This method reduces injury to epidermal tissue with high melanin concentration.

Hair loss always occurs for the first 3 months after laser treatment, regardless of the patient's hair color and type of laser used. However, this hair loss is often temporary. Permanent hair removal is positively correlated with the patient's skin pigmentation, hair color, and type of laser used. Patients with dark color hair are more likely to have a permanent loss of hair, compared with patients with blonde, red, gray, or white colored hair.

The probability of permanent hair removal in a patient with fair skin and dark hair is about 80% after a single treatment.[75] Other patients can anticipate a 20% loss of hair with each treatment cycle. Thus, multiple laser cycles are needed to produce longlasting and permanent hair removal.

Side effects from laser therapy include mild discomfort of exposed skin, perifollicular erythema and edema, transient and at times permanent skin pigment changes. More severe adverse outcomes include scarring, bacterial infection, and a recurrence of a herpes simplex virus outbreak. However, most of these side effects occur infrequently.

CONCLUSION

Although hirsutism can be a common complaint among patients presenting to the primary care clinician, only a small percent of these patients have true hirsutism. Understanding the etiology of a patient's hyperandrogenism is important in order to create a plan to effectively treat the patient.

REFERENCES

1. Conn JJ, Jacobs HS. The clinical management of hirsutism. Eur J Endocrinol 1997;136:339–48.
2. Toscano V. Hirsutism: pilosebaceous unit dysregulation. Role of peripheral and glandular factors. J Endocriol Invest 1991;14:153–70.
3. Rittmaster RS. Clinical relevance of testosterone and dihydrotestosterone metabolism in women. Am J Med 1995;98 Suppl 1A:17S–21S.
4. Ferriman D, Gallwey JD. Clinical assessment of body hair growth in women. J Clin Endocrinol Metab 1961;21:1440.
5. Hamilton JB, Terada H. Interdependence of genetic, aging, and endocrine factors in hirsutism. In: Breenblatt RB, editor. The hirsute woman. Spring-
field (IL): 1962, Charles C Thomas, Publisher; 1962. p. 20.
6. Rosenfield RL. Role of androgens in growth and development of the fetus, child and adolescent. Adv Pediatr 1972;19:171.
7. Tsang BK, Armstrong DT, Whitfield JF. Steroid biosynthesis by isolated human ovarian follicular cells in vitro. J Clin Endocrinol Metab 1980;51:1407.
8. Rosenfield RL, Ehrlich EN, Cleary RE. Adrenal and ovarian contributions to the elevated free plasma androgen levels in hirsute women. J Clin Endorcrinol Metab 1972;34:92.
9. Ganong WF, Alpert LC, Lee TC. ACTH and the regulation of ACTH secretion. N Engl J Med 1974;290:1006.
10. Nimrod A, Ryan KJ. Aromatization of androgens by human abdominal and breast fat tissue. J Clin Endocrinol Metab 1975;40:367.
11. Perel E, Killinger DW. The interconversion and aromatization of androgens by human adipose tissue. J Steroid Biochem 1979;10:623–7.
12. Frisch RE, Canick JA, Tulchinsky D. Human fatty marrow aromatizes androgen to estrogen. J Clin Endocrinol Metab 1980;51:394–6.
13. Naftolin F, Tyan K, Petro Z. Aromatization of androstenedione by the diencephalon. J Clin Endocrinol Metab 1971;33:368–70.
14. Perel E, Wilkins D, Killinger DW. The conversion of androstenedione to estrone, estradiol and testosterone in breast tissue. J Steroid Biochem 1980; 13:89–94.
15. Schweikert HU, Milewich L, Wilson JD. Aromatization of androstenedione by isolated human hairs. J Clin Endocrinol Metab 1975;40:413–7.
16. Longcope C, Pratt JH, Schneider SH, et al. Aromatization of androgens by muscle and adipose tissue in vivo. J Clin Endocrinol Metab 1978;46:146–52.
17. Schweikert HU. Conversion of androstenedione to estrone in human fibroblasts cultured from prostate, genital and nongenital skin. Horm Metab Res 1979;11:635–40.
18. Longcope C. Adrenal and gonadal androgen secretion in normal females. Clin Endocrinol Metab 1986:15;213–28.
19. Rosenfield RL. Studies of the relation of plasma androgen levels to androgen action in women. J Steroid Biochem 1975;6:695.
20. Pardridge WM. Transport of protein-bound hormones into tissues in vivo. Endocr Rev 1981;2:103–23.
21. Moll GW Jr, Rosenfield RL. Testosterone binding and free plasma androgen concentrations under physio-

logical conditions: characterization by flow dialysis technique. J Clin Endocrinol Metab 1979;49:730.

22. Adashi EY. The climacteric ovary as a functional gonadotrope driven androgen-producing gland. Fertil Steril 1994;62:20–7.

23. Vermeulen A. The hormonal activity of the post-menopausal ovary. J Clin Endocrinol Metab 1976; 42:247.

24. Wilson JD. Metabolism of testicular androgens. In: Greep RO, Astwood EB editors. Handbook of physiology. Washington (DC): American Physiological Society; 1975. p. 491–508.

25. Rosenfield R, Deplewski D. Role of androgens in the developmental biology of the pilosebaceous unit. Am J Med 1995;98 Suppl 1A:81–5S.

26. Littler CM. Hair removal using an Nd:YAG laser system. Dermatol Clin 1999;17:401–30.

27. Blauer M, Vaalasti A, Pauli SL, et al. Location of androgen receptor in human skin. J Invest Dermatol 1991;97:264–8.

28. Choudhry A, Hodgins MB, Van der Kwast TH, et al. Localization of androgen receptors in human skin by immunohistochemistry. J Endocrinol 1992; 133:467–75.

29. Jenkins EP, Andersson S, Imperato-McGinley J, et al. Genetic and pharmacological evidence for more than one human steroid 5α-reductase. J Clin Invest 1992;89:293–300.

30. McCarthy JA, Seibel MM. Physiologic hair growth. Clin Obstet Gynecol 1991;34:799–804.

31. Schriock EA, Schrioc ED. Treatment of hirsutism. Clin Obstet Gyecol 1991;34:852–63.

32. Hull MGR. Epidemiology of infertility and polycystic ovarian disease: endocrinological and demographic studies. Gynecol Endocrinol 1987;1:235–45.

33. Grsinger CC, Wild RA, Parker IJ. Vulvar acanthosis nigricans: a marker for insulin resistance in hirsute women. Fertil Steril 1993;59:583–6.

34. American College of Obstetricians and Gynecologists. Hyperandrogenic chronic anovulation. ACOG Technical Bulletin 202. Washington (DC): ACOG; 1995.

35. Franks S. Polycystic ovary syndrome: a changing perspective. Clin Endocrinol 1989;31:87–120.

36. Azziz R, Zacur HA. 21-hydroxylase deficiency in female hyperandrogenism: screening and diagnosis. J Clin Endocrinol Metab 1989;69:577–84.

37. Azziz R, Boots LR, Parker CR Jr, et al. 11ß-hydroxylase deficiency in hyperandrogenism. Fertil Steril 1991; 55:733–41.

38. Glickman SP, Rosenfield RL, Bergenstal RM, Helke J. Multiple androgenic abnormalities, including elevated free testosterone, in hyperprolactinemic women. J Clin Endorcrinol Metab 1982;55:251–7.

39. Chang RJ, Katz SE. Diagnosis of polycystic ovary syndrome. Endocrinol Metab Clin North Am 1999; 28:397–408.

40. Maroulis GB, Manlimos FS, Abraham GE. Comparison between urinary 17-ketosteroids and serum androgens in hirsute patients. Obstet Gynecol 1977; 49:454.

41. Rosenfield RL. Plasma testosterone binding globulin and indexes of the concentration of unbound androgens in normal and hirsute subjects. J Clin Endocrinol Metab 1971;32:717.

42. Vermeulen A, Stoica T, Verdonck F. The apparent free testosterone concentration, an index of androgenicity. J Clin Endocrinol Metab 1971;33:759.

43. Judd HL, McPherson RA, Rekoff JS, Yen SSC. Correlation of the effects of dexamethasone administration on urinary 17-ketosteroids and serum androgen levels in patients with hirsutism. Am J Obstet Gynecol 1977;128:408.

44. New MI, Lorenzen F, Lerner AJ, et al. Genotypig steroid 21-hydroxylase deficiency: hormonal reference data. J Clin Endocrinol Metab 1983;57:320–6.

45. Siegel SF, Finegold DN, Lanes R, Lee PA. ACTH stimulation test and plasma dehydroepiandrosterone sulfate levels in women with hirsutism. N Engl J Med 1990;323:849–54.

46. Kaye TB, Crapo L. The Cushing syndrome: an update on diagnostic tests. Ann Intern Med 1990;112:434–44.

47. Kiddy DS, Hamilton-Fairley D, Bush A, et al. Improvement in endocrine and ovarian function during dietary treatment of obese women with polycystic ovary syndrome. Clin Endocrinol 1992;36:105–11.

48. Bates GW, Whitworth NS. Effect of body weight reduction on plasma androgens in obese, infertile women. Fertil Steril 1982;38:406–9.

49. Guzick DS, Wing R, Smith D, et al. Enocrine consequences of weight loss in obese, hyperandrogenic anovulatory women. Fert Steril 1994;61:598–604.

50. Lobo RA, Shoupe D, Serafini P, et al. The effects of two doses of spironolactone on serum androgens and anagen hair in hirsute women. Fert Steril 1985;43:200–5.

51. Shaw JC. Spirinolactone in dermatologic therapy. J Am Acad Dermatol 1991;24:236–43.

52. Crosby PDA, Rittmaster RS. Predictors of clinical response in hirsute women treated with spironolactone. Fertil Steril 1991;55:1076–81.

53. Cuson L, Dupont A, Gomez JL, et al. Comparison of flutamide and spironolactone in the treatment of hirsutism: a randomized controlled trial. Fertil Steril 1994;61:281–7.

54. Couzinet B, Pholsena M, Young J, Schaison G. The impact of a pure anti-androgen (flutamide) on LH, FSH, androgens and clinical status in idiopathic hirsutism. Clin Endocrinol 1993;39:157–62.

55. Wallace C, Lalor EA, Chik CL. Hepatotoxicity complicating glutamide treatment of hirsutism. [letter]. Ann Intern Med 1993;119:1150.

56. Rittmaster RS. Finasteride. N Engl J Med 1994; 330:120–5.

57. Dallob AL, Sadick NS, Unger W, et al. The effect of finasteride, a 5α-reductase inhibitor, on scalp skin testosterone and dihydrotestosterone concentrations in patients with male pattern baldness. J Clin Endocrinol Metabol 1994;79:703–6.

58. Carr BR, Breslau NS, Givens C, et al. Oral contraceptive pills, gonadotropin-releasing hormone agonists or use in combination for the treatment of hirsutism: a Clinical Research Center study. J Clin Endocrinol Metab 1995;80:1169–78.

59. Ciotta L, Cianci A, Giuffrida G, et al. Clinical and hormonal effects of gonadotropin-releasing hormone agonist plus an oral contraceptive in severely hirsute patients with polycystic ovary disease. Fertil Steril 1996;65:61–7.

60. Carmina E, Janni A, Lobo RA. Physiological estrogen replacement may enhance effectiveness of the gonadotropin-releasing hormone agonist in the treatment of hirsutism. J Clin Endocrinol Metab 1994;78:126–30.

61. Carmina E, Lobo RA. Peripheral androgen blockade versus glandular androgen suppression in the treatment of hirsutism. Obstet Gynecol 1991;78:845–9.

62. Spritzer P, Billaud L, Thalabard JC, et al. Cyproterone acteate versus hydrocortisone treatment in late-onset adrenal hyperplasia. J Clin Endocrinol Metab 1990; 70:642–6.

63. Venturoli S, Fabbri R, Dal Prato L, et al. Ketoconazole therapy for women with acne and/or hirsutism. J Clin Endocrinol Metab 1990;71:335–9.

64. Vigersky RA, Mehlman I, Glass AR, Smith CE. Treatment of hirsute women with cimetidine. N Engl J Med 1980;303:1042.

65. Herxheimer A. Management of hirsutism. Drugs Ther Bull 1989;27:49–51.

66. Dorfman RI. Biological activity of antiandrogens. Br J Dermatol 1970;82 Suppl 6:3–8.

67. Rittmaster RS. Medical treatment of androgen-dependent hirsutism. J Clin Endocrinol Metab 1995;80:2559–63.

68. Miller JA, Jacobs HS. Treatment of hirsutism and acne with cyproterone acetate. Clin Endocrinol Metabol 1986;15:373–89.

69. Belisle S, Love EJ. Clinical efficacy and safety of cyproterone acetate in severe hirsutism: results of a multicentered Canadian study. Fertil Steril 1986; 46:1015–20.

70. Committee on Safety of Medicines. Current problems. 1995;21:1.

71. Fruzzetti F, Bersi C, Parrini D, et al. Treatment of hirsutism: comparisons between different antiandrogens with central and peripheral effects. Fertil Steril 1999;71:445–51.

72. Wagner RF. Physical methods for the management of hirsutism. Cutis 1990;45:319–26.

73. Anderson RR, Parrish JA. Selective photothermolysis: precise microsurgery by selective absorption of pulsed radiation. Science 1983;220:524–7.

74. Dierickx C, Beatrice A, Dover JS. A clinical overview of hair removal using lasers and light sources. Dermatol Clin 1999;17:357–66.

75. Dierickx CC, Grossman MC, Farinelli WA, et al. Hair removal by a pulsed, infrared laser system. Lasers Surg Med 1998;S10:199.

55

DIABETES MELLITUS

Christine Darwin, MD, and Willa A. Hsueh, MD

Diabetes mellitus is a major health problem affecting over 16 million Americans. It is currently the seventh leading cause of death in the United States. Most of the morbidity and mortality of diabetes is caused by its long-term complications. In the United States, diabetes is the most common cause of blindness and end-stage renal disease. It is associated with a two- to fourfold increase in the risk of cardiovascular disease and stroke. Diabetic patients are also at risk for neuropathy and peripheral vascular disease. Diabetes is the cause of over 50,000 limb amputations in the United States annually. Diabetes imposes a substantial socioeconomic burden because of its complications and the large number of affected individuals. Recent estimates indicate that the economic cost of diabetes exceeds $100 billion annually.[1] The socioeconomic cost of diabetes is expected to escalate with the increase in its prevalence because of the aging of American society, the increase in visceral obesity, and the rapid growth of minority population at high risk for the disease.

Several aspects of diabetes are unique to women. Pregnancy predisposes women to the development of insulin resistance and diabetes. Diabetes puts women at risk for pregnancy complications, including miscarriage and congenital malformations. Although diabetes is a risk factor for the presence and severity of coronary heart disease in both men and women, it carries a greater incremental risk in women. Diabetes is the major cause of premature cardiovascular disease in women.

The presence of diabetes in women appears to eliminate the cardiovascular protective effects afforded premenopausal women. Diabetes causes a greater incremental risk of cardiovascular disease in older women as well.[2] After accounting for the effects of hypertension, dyslipidemia, smoking, age, and obesity, the relative risk of death from coronary artery disease in women with diabetes compared with nondiabetic women is 3.3, and in women between 30 and 50 years, the risk is increased sevenfold. In comparison, the relative risk of death from coronary artery disease for diabetic men is only 1.9 that of nondiabetic men.[3]

The mechanism by which diabetes abrogates the cardiovascular protective effects of female sex hormones is not well understood. Some authors have suggested that interactions between insulin and androgens may adversely effect lipid physiology.[3] One recently described mechanism involves the interaction between hyperglycemia and estradiol in regulation of endothelial cell nitric oxide production. Hyperglycemia reduces the estradiol-mediated production of nitric oxide from vascular endothelial cells, which may contribute to accelerated atherosclerosis in diabetic women.[4]

CLASSIFICATION, EPIDEMIOLOGY, AND PATHOGENESIS

Diabetes mellitus is a syndrome that includes a heterogeneous group of disorders (Table 55–1), all of which are characterized by hyperglycemia and absolute or relative insulin deficiency. Approximately 10% of cases are attributable to type 1, and more than 85% belong to type 2 diabetes.[5] All other types of diabetes account for less than 5% of the cases and are not discussed further here.

Type 1 Diabetes

Type 1 diabetes was previously known as insulin-dependent diabetes mellitus or juvenile-onset diabetes. This type of diabetes is characterized by absolute insulin deficiency caused by autoimmune destruction of the Beta cells of the pancreas. The great majority of cases occur before the age of 35, with a

TABLE 55–1. Classification of Diabetes Mellitus

Type 1 diabetes (because of absolute insulin deficiency
    from beta cell destruction)
    Immune mediated
    Idiopathic

Type 2 diabetes (associated with insulin resistance and
    progressive beta cell deficiency)

Other specific types
    Genetic defects of beta cell function (maturity-onset
        diabetes of the young)
    Genetic defects in insulin action
    Disease of the exocrine pancreas
    Endocrinopathies
    Drug or chemical induced
    Infections
    Uncommon forms of immune-mediated diabetes
    Other genetic syndromes associated with diabetes

Gestational diabetes

peak onset during the second decade of life. Unlike most other common autoimmune disorders, type 1 diabetes mellitus does not show a female predominance and has about a 3:2 male-to-female ratio of incidence. Fathers are more likely to transmit type 1 diabetes to their offspring than are mothers.[6] These sex-based differences in the incidence of diabetes remain unexplained.

Genetic factors play an important role in the predisposition to type 1 diabetes. In Caucasians, the disease is strongly associated with histocompatibility antigens HLA-DR3, -DR4, -DQA, -DQB, and -DRB, which are located on chromosome 6. These genetic factors are necessary but not sufficient for the development of the disease. Environmental factors such as certain viruses (eg, retrovirus, rubella, cytomegalovirus), dietary proteins (eg, cow's milk), or toxic agents trigger the immune response that leads to beta cell destruction. An inflammatory destructive process, mediated by humoral and cellular factors, is associated with the appearance of autoantibodies to islet cells (ICAS), insulin (IAAS), glutamic acid decarboxylase (GAD 65), and tyrosine phosphates IA-2 and IA-2B in the circulation. One or more of these autoantibodies is usually present in 70% or more of individuals at the time of initial diagnosis of type 1 diabetes.[7–9] The rate of beta cell destruction is quite variable. Most commonly, it follows a slow progressive course, with clinical disease occurring months or years later.[9,10]

Type 2 Diabetes

Type 2 diabetes was previously known as non–insulin-dependent, adult-onset, or maturity-onset diabetes. The prevalence among women and men is about equal. Women may be more likely to transmit the tendency to type 2 diabetes to their children than are men.[6]

Type 2 diabetes is a disease of affluent societies. Obesity appears to be the strongest risk factor for the development of type 2 diabetes in women. Lack of exercise, smoking, and a poor diet are also risk factors for the development of type 2 diabetes, even after adjusting for the effect of obesity.[11] The incidence of type 2 diabetes is increasing worldwide because of the adoption of "Western" habits, including high caloric intake and a sedentary lifestyle. Type 2 diabetes occurs in older subjects, usually presenting after the age of 40, although recently the incidence of type 2 diabetes has been rising among younger obese individuals. Type 2 diabetes is more prevalent among women of color, including African Americans, Latinas, Asian-Pacific Islanders, and Native Americans.[12]

Type 2 diabetes is generally preceded by a clinically silent phase of impaired fasting glucose or impaired glucose tolerance. In the great majority of cases, insulin resistance is the primary pathophysiologic feature as it precedes the development of the disease. Insulin resistance is defined as a defect in the ability of insulin to drive glucose into its main target issues. The mechanism of insulin resistance in type 2 diabetes is unknown but appears to be caused mainly by a postreceptor defect that is genetically determined. Environmental factors such as obesity, aging, and physical inactivity can, however, worsen insulin resistance, and thus are important issues in both treatment and prevention of Type 2 diabetes. Hyperinsulinemia reflects insulin resistance, especially in the presence of normoglycemia, and is common in populations with a high prevalence of type 2 diabetes. It is also an early abnormality that characterizes subjects who subsequently develop abnormal glucose tolerance or type 2 diabetes.[13]

Although insulin resistance is the primary pathophysiologic defect in the majority of patients with type 2 diabetes, beta cell dysfunction plays an essential role. Not all subjects with insulin resistance

TABLE 55–2. Risk Factors for Type 2 Diabetes

Evidence of a tendency to glucose intolerance
  Previous diagnosis of impaired fasting glucose or impaired glucose tolerance
  History of gestational diabetes mellitus or history of delivery of a baby weighing more than 9 lb

Medical conditions associated with a high prevalence of type 2 diabetes mellitus
  Obesity ($\geq$20% over ideal body weight or body mass index $\geq$ 27 kg/m^2)
  Polycystic ovary syndrome
  Hypertension ($\geq$ 140/90 mm Hg in adults)

Abnormal lipid levels associated with a high prevalence of type 2 diabetes mellitus
  High-density lipoprotein cholesterol $\leq$ 35 mg/dL and/or triglycerides $\geq$ 250 mg/dL

Lifestyle habits associated with a high prevalence of type 2 diabetes mellitus
  Physical inactivity

Race/ethnicity with a high prevalence of type 2 diabetes mellitus
  African American
  Latina
  Native American
  Asian-Pacific Islander

From American Diabetes Association. Screening for diabetes. Diabetes Care 2001;24 Suppl 1:521–4.

develop diabetes. Among insulin-resistant subjects with normal or impaired glucose tolerance, those with a lower insulin secretion are more likely to develop diabetes. Whether this beta cell dysfunction is primary or secondary is controversial. Studies in Pima Indians showed a mild decrease in the acute insulin response to glucose prior to development of impaired glucose tolerance.[13] Impaired beta cell function may result from long-term exposure to insulin resistance and prolonged increased demand for insulin secretion that eventually exceeds beta cell capacity (exhaustion). In addition, the minimal elevation of plasma glucose during deterioration of glucose tolerance could impair beta cell function (glucose toxicity). Some subjects can maintain high levels of insulin secretion for prolonged periods. Others may have acquired or inherited abnormalities that make beta cells susceptible to exhaustion or glucose toxicity. Such defects could include reduced islet-cell mass, limited replicative capacity, and more rapid age-related demise or intrinsic functional or structural abnormalities.[14]

PRIMARY PREVENTION, SCREENING, AND DIAGNOSIS

Primary prevention programs that aim to limit the onset or incidence of a disease are the most desirable and often the most cost-effective way to reduce the burden of a major disease. Currently, no known interventions prevent type 1 diabetes. However, type 2 diabetes is preventable. Exercise and modest improvements in diet can reduce the incidence of diabetes in persons at high risk.[11] Factors that place women at high risk for diabetes are reviewed in Table 55–2.[15] Treatment of obesity is discussed in Chapter 89.

Classic symptoms of diabetes mellitus include polydipsia, polyuria, and polyphagia. Blurry vision and persistent yeast infections, including yeast vaginitis, are also common complaints. Patients with type 1 or type 2 diabetes may present with acute metabolic decompensation and dehydration, nausea, vomiting, abdominal pain, confusion, or coma. On the other hand, many patients with type 2 diabetes are often asymptomatic for years or present with subtle signs and symptoms, such as neuropathy.

All patients with signs or symptoms suggestive of diabetes mellitus should be tested. In addition, because type 2 diabetes is often unrecognized, the American Diabetes Association recommends that all persons age 45 and above with one or more risk factors for type 2 diabetes should be screened every 3 years with a fasting plasma glucose level. Younger persons who are overweight (> 120% of ideal body weight) and have any two additional risk factors should be screened every 2 years starting at age 10 or puberty, whichever comes first.[15]

Normal fasting plasma glucose should be less than 110 mg/dL. According to the American Diabetes Association, diabetes is diagnosed when fasting plasma glucose concentration is 126 mg/dL or more, 2-hour postload plasma glucose is 200 mg/dL, or random plasma glucose is 200 mg/dL or more on two separate occasions.[12]

Some people do not meet the criteria for a diagnosis of diabetes but have blood sugar levels that are still somewhat higher than normal. Individuals with impaired fasting glucose and impaired glucose tolerance are at increased risk for subsequent development of diabetes and have higher rates of cardiovascular disease. A fasting plasma glucose of 110 to 125 mg/dL is described as "impaired fasting glucose," whereas impaired glucose tolerance is defined by a fasting plasma glucose < 126 mg/dL and a 2-hour postload plasma glucose of 140 to 199 mg/dL (Table 55–3).[12]

APPROACH TO THE DIABETIC PATIENT

Treatment of diabetic patients aims to avoid a wide variety of symptoms and complications. The cornerstone of treatment is avoidance of hyperglycemia. Mild hyperglycemia can cause blurred vision, polyuria, polydipsia, and fatigue. Yeast infections, including vaginitis, are also more common in hyperglycemic patients. Severe hyperglycemia can cause life-threatening metabolic disturbances.

Treatment of hyperglycemia has been proven to decrease the risk of development and progression of microvascular complications of diabetes, including diabetic retinopathy, nephropathy, and neuropathy. Treatment of hyperglycemia has a more

TABLE 55–3. Classification of Glucose Tolerance According to the American Diabetes Association Criteria

	Plasma Glucose (mg/dL)		
	Fasting		2 Hour
Normal	<110	and	<140
Impaired fasting glucose	110–125		
Impaired glucose tolerance	<126	and	140–199
Diabetes mellitus	≥126	or	≥200

modest effect to reduce the risk of coronary artery disease, and it results in a less atherogenic lipid profile.[16] Importantly, control of hyperglycemia prior to conception results in a decreased risk of miscarriage and birth defects.[17] Diabetes care also includes using multiple modalities in addition to glycemic control to monitor, prevent, and treat complications of diabetes. These are discussed in more detail below.

Important elements of the initial historic evaluation of a diabetic patient are summarized in Table 55–4. A complete physical examination also should be performed. Initial laboratory testing should include a fasting plasma glucose, hemoglobin A_{1C}, fasting lipid profile, and an electrocardiogram. Dipstick urinalysis and serum creatinine should be performed. If urinalysis is negative for proteinuria, a test for microalbuminuria (usually a urine albumin-to-creatinine ratio) should be done. Patients should be referred for an annual comprehensive dilated eye examination. Pneumonococcal vaccination (if not previously done) should be performed. Annual influenza vaccination is also indicated.[16]

Aspirin has been shown to reduce significantly the risk of cardiovascular and cerebrovascular events in diabetic women. Enteric-coated aspirin 81 to 325 mg daily should be considered for all diabetics without contraindications. Absolute contraindications include aspirin allergy. Relative contraindications include bleeding tendency, anticoagulant therapy, recent gastrointestinal bleeding, and clinically active liver disease.[18]

TREATMENT

Goals of Treatment and Standards for Follow-Up Care

Goals of treatment for all diabetic patients are summarized in Tables 55–5 and 55–6. Type 1 diabetic patients require insulin treatment. Type 2 diabetic patients often can be managed by lifestyle changes alone or in combination with oral medications. Insulin treatment is indicated for type 2 diabetic patients when lifestyle changes and oral medications fail.

Frequency of follow-up examinations depends on whether treatment goals have been reached. Women who have reached all treatment goals may be seen every 6 months. Patients who have not yet reached treatment goals or who are experiencing diabetic complications should be seen frequently, at least every 3 months. Consultation with a specialist

TABLE 55–4. Initial Evaluation of Women with Diabetes Mellitus

History of present illness, including (when applicable)
  Age at diagnosis
  Presenting symptoms
  Results of prior tests, including hemoglobin A_{1c} levels
  Details of previous nutritional and self-management education
  Current treatment of diabetes, including medications, meal plan, and results of prior self-glucose testing and
    self-management
  Frequency, severity, and cause of acute complications such as ketoacidosis and hypoglycemia

Medications, with a focus on those that affect blood glucose levels

Past medical history, including
  Hypertension
  Dyslipidemia
  Infections
  Ophthalmologic complications
  Neuropathic complications, including diabetic gastropathy, neurogenic bladder, autonomic dysfunction,
    and peripheral neuropathy
  Renal complications, including proteinuria
  Atherosclerotic complications, including cerebrovascular disease, coronary artery disease, and peripheral
    vascular disease
  Endocrine disease, including thyroid
  Eating disorders

Social history, including
  Tobacco use
  Alcohol use
  Exercise history
  Lifestyle, cultural, psychosocial, educational, and economic factors that might influence the management of diabetes

Family history, particularly of
  Endocrine disorders
  Coronary artery disease

Reproductive history, with a focus on
  Family planning, including contraceptive use and plans for future pregnancy (if applicable)
  Gestational history, including hyperglycemia, delivery of an infant weighing > 9 lb, toxemia, stillbirth, polyhydramnios,
    or other complications, fetal malformations

Current symptoms, including symptoms of
  Hyperglycemia
  Hypoglycemia
  Thyroid dysfunction
  Visual disturbances
  Bladder dysfunction
  Gastrointestinal dysfunction
  Sexual dysfunction
  Skin, foot, dental, and/or genitourinary infections
  Coronary artery disease
  Peripheral vascular disease
  Cerebrovascular disease

From American Diabetes Association. Standards of medical care for patients with diabetes mellitus. Diabetes Care 2001;24 Suppl 1: 521–4.

TABLE 55–5. Recommended Laboratory Evaluation and Treatment Goals and Therapeutic Triggers for Diabetic Patients

Laboratory Test	Goal	Level at Which Action Is Recommended	Recommended Action
Hemoglobin A_{1c} (%)	< 6.5%	> 8%	Type 1 diabetes: adjust insulin Type 2 diabetes: lifestyle changes, oral medications, insulin[*]
Low-density lipoprotein cholesterol	< 100 mg/dL	≥ 100 mg/dL	Lifestyle changes (saturated fat < 7% of total calories, cholesterol < 200 mg/d, weight reduction, increased physical activity), HMG-CoA reductase inhibitors[†‡]
Microalbumin[§]			
24-h collection	NA[//]	> 30 mg/24 h	Angiotensin-converting enzyme inhibitors[#**]
Timed collection	NA[//]	> 20 μg/min	
Spot collection	NA[//]	> 30 μg/mg creatinine	
Blood pressure	< 120/80 mm Hg	> 130/80 mm Hg	Angiotensin-converting enzyme inhibitors[**], additional agents as needed to reach target[††]

[*]See text.
[†]See chapter on hyperlipidemia in this textbook.
[‡]High-density lipoprotein cholesterol < 45 mg/dL and triglyceride levels ≥ 200 mg/dL are also considered risk factors for atherosclerotic disease. There is no consensus on the best approach to treating these factors.
[§]Patients with proteinuria or elevated creatinine should be further evaluated; specialty consultation should be considered.
[//]Goals for reduction in albuminuria have not been established.
[#]Controversial in type 2 diabetic patients who are normotensive. All others should receive an angiotensin-converting enzyme inhibitor (ACE). Most experts would treat a normotensive type 2 diabetic patient with microalbuminuria with an ACE.
[**]Contraindicated in pregnancy.
[††]See Chapter 31, "hypertension."
From American Diabetes Association. Standards of medical care for patients with diabetes mellitus. Diabetes Care 2001;24 Suppl 1: 521–4.

is recommended for type 1 diabetic patients and for type 2 diabetic patients who are not responding to an oral regimen or who demonstrate progressive diabetic complications. Such patients may benefit from a team approach involving the primary care clinician, diabetologist, nutritionist, diabetes educator, and other specialists as indicated.

During follow-up visits, the frequency and severity of hyperglycemic and hypoglycemic episodes should be reviewed, along with the results of glucose self-monitoring. Adherence to diet, lifestyle, and medication recommendations should be discussed, focusing in particular on psychosocial issues that may limit compliance. A review of systems focused on possible complications should be completed.

TABLE 55–6. Goals of Glycemic Therapy

Biochemical	NI	Goal	Action Suggested
Fasting plasma glucose (mg/dL)	< 110	< 110	< 80 or > 140
Bedtime plasma glucose (mg/dL)	< 120	100–140	< 100 or > 160
Hemoglobin A_{1c} (%)	< 6	< 6.5	> 8
NI range	4 to 6%		

At a minimum, diabetic patients should have an annual complete physical examination, including a foot examination. At every visit, weight and blood pressure should be checked, along with examination of any systems found to be abnormal previously (eg, foot checks in patients with known neuropathy). A dilated eye examination should be performed annually by an ophthalmologist. Hemoglobin A_{1C} should be checked at least every 6 months in patients who have met glycemic goals and quarterly in all others. Fasting lipid profile and testing for microalbuminuria should be performed annually.[16]

Education and Self-Monitoring

Education and self-monitoring are essential elements of successful diabetes management. Diabetes education often is accomplished using a multidisciplinary approach. Diabetic nurse educators and registered dieticians can provide in-depth education for patients, supplementing that provided by primary care clinicians and medical specialists. The National Certification Board for Diabetes Educators is recognized by the American Diabetes Association and has certified over 10,000 diabetes educators in the United States.[19]

Patients should be instructed in the diabetes disease process and treatment options. They should understand the importance of lifestyle in the treatment of diabetes, including nutrition, smoking cessation, and physical activity. Diabetic patients should be trained to monitor blood glucose and understand how to use the information obtained to help prevent acute and chronic complications. They should be aware of the signs and symptoms of chronic complications of diabetes (such as retinopathy, neuropathy, and foot ulcers) and the importance of reporting these promptly. Women of reproductive age should be counseled about contraception and preconception care (see below).[19]

Diet

Caloric restriction is indicated in obese patients to promote weight loss. Moderate weight loss (5 to 9 kg [10 to 20 lb]) has been shown to improve blood sugar levels, lower blood pressure, and improve the cholesterol profile of patients with type 2 diabetes.[20] 10–20% of the diet should come from protein.

Complex carbohydrates such as starches and cereals, have a positive effect on blood sugar and lipid profiles. Simple sugars should be avoided. Fat intake should be limited to 30 to 35% of total calories; saturated animal fats should be restricted and replaced by mono- and unsaturated fats. Cholesterol intake should be reduced to less than 300 mg/d; further reduction to less than 200 mg/d is indicated in patients with hypercholesterolemia. As for all women, alcohol intake is recommended not to exceed one drink per day (12 oz beer, 5 oz wine, or 1½ oz liquor).[20]

Lifestyle Modification

Regular physical exercise is recommended. Exercise increases insulin sensitivity, lowers plasma glucose concentration, promotes weight loss, and improves the lipid profile by increasing high-density lipoprotein cholesterol and decreasing total and low-density lipoprotein cholesterol, lowering blood pressure, and increasing physical working capacity. However, patients should be evaluated carefully, and the exercise program should be individualized to fit the patient's lifestyle and physical condition. Patients with longstanding diabetes (> 10 to 15 years), additional risk factors for coronary artery disease, or evidence of retinopathy, neuropathy, or peripheral vascular disease may benefit from cardiac testing prior to undertaking a moderate- to high-intensity exercise program. A moderate- to high-intensity exercise program can be defined as any program expected to achieve 55% or more of the patient's maximal heart rate (defined as 220 bpm minus the patient's age).[21]

Poorly controlled diabetes, proliferative retinopathy, and overt diabetic nephropathy are contraindications to strenuous physical exercise. Peripheral neuropathy may increase the risk of traumatic lesions, and autonomic neuropathy may limit physical performance. For patients with these diabetic complications, mild to moderate physical activity such as brisk walking for 30 to 45 minutes for 3 to 5 days per week should be suggested. Patients on insulin or sulfonylureas are at risk for hypoglycemia during exercise. They should be aware of the signs and symptoms of hypoglycemia and have carbohydrate-based foods available during and after exercise. Patients who experience hypoglycemia should perform glucose monitoring before and after exercise and adjust their diet (and insulin, if applicable) as necessary.

Smoking compounds the diabetic patient's risk of heart attack, cerebrovascular disease, peripheral vascular disease, and death. All diabetic patients who smoke should be encouraged to stop.[22] Approaches to smoking cessation are discussed in Chapter 12.

Oral Agents

Many patients with type 2 diabetes can be managed effectively with diet, lifestyle changes, and weight loss. If these measures fail, oral hypoglycemic drugs are recommended. Generally, one agent is chosen and titrated to maximum dose, unless side effects develop. If one agent is ineffective in reaching hemoglobin A_{1C} goals, then a second agent is added. Some patients require therapy with three oral hypoglycemics. For patients who do not reach hemoglobin A_{1C} goals despite maximum oral therapy, insulin is recommended. Insulin can be combined with oral agents (Tables 55–7 and 55–8).

SULFONYLUREAS

Sulfonylureas act primarily by increasing insulin levels. Sulfonylureas stimulate insulin release from beta cells and also decrease hepatic insulin clear-

TABLE 55–8. Options for Oral Hypoglycemic Therapy in Type 2 Diabetes: Combination Therapy

Dual therapy
   Sulfonylurea + biguanide*
   Sulfonylurea + thiazolidinedione
   Sulfonylurea + α-glucosidase inhibitor
   Biguanide + meglitinide
   Biguanide + α-glucosidase inhibitor

Triple combination therapy
   Sulfonylurea + biguanide + thiazolidinedione
   Sulfonylurea + biguanide + α-glucosidase inhibitor

*Available in single-pill form (glyburide/metformin) as Glucovance.
From Luna B, Feinglas MN. Oral agents in the management of type 2 diabetes mellitus. Am Fam Physician 2001;63:1747–56, 1759–80.

ance.[23–25] They may decrease peripheral insulin resistance, although whether this effect is of clinical importance is not clear.[23]

Hypoglycemia is the major side effect of sulfonylureas. Older first generation sulfonylureas (acetohexamide, chlorpropamide, tolazamide, and tolbutamide) generally have been supplanted by second-generation agents (glyburide, glipizide, and glimepiride) because second-generation agents are,

TABLE 55–7. Options for Oral Therapy in Type 2 Diabetes

Class	Reduction in Hemoglobin A_{1C} (%)	Generic Names	Dose Range (mg/d)	Brand Names	Generic Available?
Sulfonylureas	0.8–2.0	Glyburide	5–20	Diabeta, Micronase	Yes
		Glyburide (micronized)	0.75–12	Glynase	Yes
		Glipizide	10–40	Glucotrol	Yes
		Glipizide (XL)	5–20	Glucotrol XL	No
		Glimepiride	1–8	Amaryl	No
Meglitinides	0.5–2.0	Repaglinide	1.5–16	Prandin	No
		Nateglinide	180–360	Starlix	No
Biguanides	1.5–2.0	Metformin	1,500–2,550	Glucophage	No
		Metformin (XR)	1,000–2,000	Glucophage XR	No
Thiazolidinediones	0.5–1.5	Pioglitazone	15–45	Actos	No
		Rosiglitazone	4–8	Avandia	No
α-Glucosidase Inhibitors	0.7–1.0	Acarbose	150–300	Precose	No
		Miglitol	150–300	Glyset	No

From Luna B, Feinglas MN. Oral agents in the management of type 2 diabetes mellitus. Am Fam Physician 2001;63:1747–56,1759–80.

in general, associated with less hypoglycemia and other side effects. Patients with impaired renal function are at particular risk of hypoglycemia with the use of glyburide because it is metabolized to an active metabolite excreted by the kidney. Sulfonylureas are the least expensive of available oral agents. However, they are associated with weight gain, making their use in the obese patient problematic.[26,27]

MEGLITINIDES

Meglitanides, like sulfonylureas, increase the release of insulin from pancreatic beta cells. Meglitinides bind to a different receptor on the pancreatic beta cell than sulfonylureas. They have a shorter onset of action and a shorter half-life than sulfonylureas. Therefore, a dose must be taken before each meal and skipped if a meal is not eaten. The role of meglitinides in the treatment of type 2 diabetes is not yet well defined, although they may offer certain advantages to patients with unpredictable meal schedules or who suffer hypoglycemia on sulfonylureas.[28]

BIGUANIDES

Biguanides lower blood sugar by decreasing hepatic glucose production and inhibiting intestinal glucose absorption. They also increase insulin sensitivity in the liver and, to a lesser extent, in peripheral tissues.[29] The use of biguanides is not associated with weight gain.[26,27] Some obese patients lose weight while taking biguanides.[27] Therefore, they are often first-line therapy in obese patients with type 2 diabetes. The side effects of biguanides are mainly gastrointestinal (anorexia, nausea, abdominal discomfort, and diarrhea). They are usually transient, dose dependent, and minimized by taking the drug with meals.

Biguanides can precipitate lactic acidosis, a rare but potentially fatal side effect. The incidence of lactic acidosis with metformin, the only biguanide currently marketed in the United States, is about 3 cases per 100,000 patient-years. This rare complication occurs in the settings of renal insufficiency, hepatic dysfunction, and alcoholism. It also has been reported in severe infection and severe cardiac dysfunction with decreased tissue perfusion.[29] The creatinine of patients with diabetes should be monitored and biguanide therapy discontinued if it exceeds 1.4 mg/dL.[30] In addition, because radiocontrast materials often cause transient renal insufficiency in patients with diabetes, biguanide therapy should be held prior to radiologic examinations with intravenous contrast. It is prudent to discontinue biguanides when a patient is hospitalized for any acute illness because of the increased risk of decreased tissue perfusion and/or acute renal and hepatic dysfunction in the setting of severe illness of almost any cause.

THIAZOLIDINEDIONES

Thiazolidinediones treat insulin resistance by enhancing the effect of insulin in the liver and peripheral tissues.[31] They are very well tolerated generally, but weight gain sometimes occurs.[28] The weight gain is due in part to fluid retention. They should be used with caution in patients with advanced heart failure or in patients taking insulin, which can also cause fluid retention.[31]

Troglitazone, the first thiazolidinedione marketed in the United States, was withdrawn because of reports of severe, sometimes fatal, liver toxicity. Similar patterns of liver toxicity have not been reported with newer agents. Studies have found no difference in aminotransferase levels compared with placebo in patients treated with rosiglitazone and pioglitazone.[28] However, the manufacturers recommend a baseline alanine aminotransferase level for all patients prior to initiating either pioglitazone or rosiglitazone, with follow-up levels every other month for 2 years and periodically thereafter.[30] Until further information is available, these agents probably should be avoided in patients with liver disease.

α-GLUCOSIDASE INHIBITORS

α-Glucosidase is an enzyme that hydrolyzes disaccharides and oligosaccharides at the intestinal brush border. α-Glucosidase inhibitors block the breakdown, and therefore absorption, of dextrins, maltose, sucrose, and starch in the gut. The absorption of glucose and lactose is not affected. α-Glucosidase inhibitors do not raise insulin levels and, when taken alone, do not cause hypoglycemia. However, should hypoglycemia occur during combined therapy with other agents (eg, sulfonylureas, insulin), glucose should be given, as sugar (sucrose) will not be effective.[32]

Common side effects associated with these agents are increased flatulence, abdominal pain, and diarrhea. These side effects may be reduced by beginning therapy at a low dose and slowly increasing to the maximum dose. These agents are contraindicated in patients with inflammatory bowel disease. Because of rare reports of liver toxicity, they should not be used in patients with liver disease.[33]

Insulin Therapy

Insulin therapy is indicated for all type 1 diabetic patients, as well as the relatively small proportion of type 2 diabetic patients who cannot be adequately controlled with lifestyle modification and oral agents. Because of the immunogenicity of animal insulin, synthetic human insulin is preferred. To maintain glucose control throughout the day and night, combinations of short- and longer-acting insulin generally should be used.

When injected subcutaneously, synthetic human (regular) insulin forms dimers, retarding its diffusion. It reaches peak plasma concentrations in about 1½ hours, with a duration of action of about 5 hours. Combining insulin with zinc causes it to form hexamers, retarding diffusion further. This produces longer-acting insulin with a longer time to peak serum concentration and a longer duration of action. Older forms of longer-acting insulin work by this principle. NPH and Lente insulin begin to lower blood sugar in about 2½ hours and have a peak action of about 11 hours and a total period of action of around 25 hours. Ultralente insulin has an onset of action of about 5 hours, a peak action between 18 and 24 hours, and a duration of action of 2 to 3 days.[34]

Recently, there has been an interest in genetically altering the insulin molecule to shorten or prolong the onset and duration of action of insulin. Insulin lispro is an analog of human insulin in which the sequence of proline and lysine at the B28 and B29 positions of human insulin have been reversed. It remains a monomer when injected subcutaneously. Because it diffuses faster, it attains peak serum concentration in about 45 minutes, and its duration of action is about 5 hours. Regimens containing insulin lispro have not been proven superior to regimens containing regular insulin in achieving hemoglobin A_{1C} goals, and insulin lispro is more expensive. However, since it can be injected right at the time of meals, it is useful for patients who eat irregularly. Because of its short duration of action, it also may be useful in patients who experience hypoglycemia.[35] Insulin aspart, another short-acting insulin analog, also was approved recently by the US Food and Drug Administration.

Insulin glargine differs from human insulin in that glycine has been substituted for asparagine at position 21, and two arginine molecules have been added to the C-terminus of the ß-chain. When injected subcutaneously, it maintains a relatively constant serum concentration over 24 hours with no pronounced peak. Therefore, it can be used as a once-daily bedtime injection to maintain a basal insulin level.[36] Some have advocated a regimen of night-time insulin glargine and insulin lispro or aspart before each meal. Whether such a regimen would result in superior outcomes compared with established regimens is under investigation.

Of note, genetically altered insulin molecules may have affinities for receptors in the body other than insulin. This is a theoretic concern during fetal development. Synthetic insulins have not been studied systematically in human pregnancy.[35,36]

In type 2 diabetic patients, addition of a bedtime dose of long-acting insulin to oral regimens can sometimes lead to adequate glycemic control.[30] Type 1 diabetic patients and type 2 diabetic patients who have failed all other measures are generally treated with a mixed-split insulin regimen. Typical insulin regimens include NPH and regular insulin twice daily and Ultralente and regular insulin before breakfast, with supplemental regular insulin injected before lunch and dinner. Regular insulin should be injected about 30 minutes before eating; longer-acting insulins may be injected at the same time in the same syringe. Adults of average size are usually started on 20 units per day (eg, NPH 10 units subcutaneously before breakfast and dinner, with regular insulin added as the results of blood sugar monitoring are known). Insulin doses should be adjusted based on home glucose monitoring; readings before breakfast, lunch, dinner, and bedtime are generally most important. For multi-dose insulin regimens to be adjusted effectively, patients generally must eat three meals a day and a bedtime snack to avoid hypoglycemia, particularly at night.[34]

Most adults who experience morning hyperglycemia require increased evening long-acting insulin to control it. Morning hyperglycemia may be caused by the nocturnal release of growth hormone. This has been termed the "dawn phenomenon." The "Somogyi phenomenon" refers to rebound hyperglycemia caused by the release of counter-regulatory hormones in response to hypoglycemia. Although rare in adults, it should be suspected when patients report increased blood sugar readings (particularly morning fasting blood sugar readings) despite escalating doses of insulin. A trial of decreased insulin dosage is diagnostic.[34]

Hypoglycemic episodes on standard insulin therapies are the main indication for the use of more complex regimens, such as those including insulin lispro and/or continuous subcutaneous insulin infusion (insulin pumps). Such regimens generally are formulated with subspecialty consultation. Insulin pumps carry a high risk of complications, including both hypoglycemia and ketoacidosis, if not carefully managed. Persistently elevated hemoglobin A_{1C} on standard insulin regimens generally is not improved by the use of such complex regimens, particularly in type 2 diabetic patients.[35] For patients who remain hyperglycemic despite large doses of medications, compliance issues (such as diet, exercise, and use of medications as prescribed) should be investigated thoroughly.

GESTATIONAL DIABETES MELLITUS

Gestational diabetes mellitus (GDM) is defined as glucose intolerence that begins or is recognized first during pregnancy. In the United States, about 7% of pregnancies are complicated by GDM.[12]

Risk assessment for GDM should be performed at the first prenatal visit. Patients with marked obesity, a personal history of GDM, glucosuria, or a strong family history should undergo a screening 1-hour glucose tolerance test (serum glucose measurement after a 50-g oral glucose load) as soon as feasible. Women at normal risk, as well as high-risk women with normal tests earlier in pregnancy, are tested between 24 and 28 weeks' gestation. Those whose value exceeds 130 mg/dL should then undergo a 3-hour glucose tolerance test with a 100-g oral glucose load, performed in the morning after an overnight fast. The diagnosis of GDM is made if any two of four threshold values are met or exceeded (Table 55–9).[12]

Clinical recognition of GDM is important because appropriate treatment with diet and exercise and insulin, when necessary, combined with antepartum fetal surveillance, can reduce the associated perinatal morbidity and mortality. Treatment of GDM is discussed in Chapter 15, "Common Medical Problems in Pregnancy." Glucose tolerance commonly returns to normal after delivery. Nonetheless, women with a history of GDM have an increased risk for subsequent development of type 2 diabetes. They should undergo standard 2-hour glucose tolerance testing 6 weeks after delivery or

TABLE 55–9. Diagnostic Criteria* for Gestational Diabetes Mellitus

	Plasma Glucose (mg/dL)
Fasting	≥105
1 h	≥195
2 h	≥165
3 h	≥145

*Two or more must be met.

when they stop breast-feeding. Women with a history of GDM and a normal postpartum glucose tolerance test should subsequently be screened annually with a fasting plasma glucose level.

PRECONCEPTION CARE AND PREGNANCY

Prepregnancy counseling for diabetic women should begin at the onset of puberty and continue until menopause. Pregnancy in diabetic women carries a risk of increased maternal and infant morbidity. Hyperglycemia is associated with an increase in spontaneous abortions and major congenital malformations.[17]

Ideally, pregnancy in diabetic women should be planned. Unfortunately, unplanned pregnancies occur in about two-thirds of reproductive aged women with diabetes. Every effort should be made to optimize glycemic control prior to conception. Consequently, effective contraception is imperative if pregnancy is not planned and when glycemic control is not optimal. Preconception care of diabetic women also should include genetic counseling, education about the impact of pregnancy on glycemic control and diabetes complications, and avoidance of teratogenic medications (eg, angiotensin-converting enzyme inhibitors).[17]

Preconception care should include a careful evaluation for complications of diabetes and treatment of all associated conditions prior to conception. Diabetic women with established complications and associated medical conditions face special concerns when contemplating pregnancy. Diabetic retinopathy may worsen with pregnancy. Hypertension is more likely to occur. Peripheral neuropathy may be exacerbated. Untreated coronary artery disease is associated with a high maternal mortality rate.[17]

The care of the pregnant women with diabetes is discussed in Chapter 15, "Common Medical Problems in Pregnancy."

Contraception

Adequate contraception is an integral part of pre-pregnancy planning so that pregnancy occurs during a period of good glycemic control. Providing contraceptive services to diabetic women involves balancing the risks and benefits of each form of birth control. There is no form of birth control that is specifically contraindicated in diabetic women.[17] Because of significant risks to both the mother and the fetus of unplanned pregnancy, methods likely to be highly effective based on each woman's individual circumstances are preferred. Available methods of birth control are discussed in more detail in Chapter 9, "Contraception." After a woman with diabetes has completed her family, sterilization (vasectomy for her partner or tubal ligation) should be offered because this eliminates the risks and failures of the other contraceptive methods.

Of particular concern to patients and clinicians are questions about the use of oral hormonal contraceptives. Oral contraceptives have been associated with a small increased risk of myocardial infarction and stroke. These risks are increased in diabetic patients.[37,38] Because diabetic retinopathy can worsen during pregnancy, many experts have advised against the use of oral contraceptives in women with retinopathy. A recent retrospective study, however, showed no difference in the incidence or worsening of retinopathy in diabetic women related to oral contraceptive use.[39]

Low-dose oral contraceptives with 20- to 35-mg ethinyl estradiol and a low-dose progestin (such as norethindrone 0.35 to 0.40 mg), the progestin-only pill, and long-acting progestins (depot medroxyprogesterone acetate, subcutaneous levonorgestrel implants) can be considered, but medical status, blood glucose, and lipids should be monitored. Patients with established macrovascular atherosclerotic complications, including coronary artery disease, should avoid the use of hormonal contraception.

Of note, the use of progestin-only oral contraceptives has been associated with an increased risk of diabetes in breast-feeding Latino women with a history of GDM. Combination oral contraceptives do not seem to increase the risk of diabetes in breast-feeding Latinas with a history of GDM.[40]

HORMONE REPLACEMENT THERAPY

Decisions about the use of hormone replacement therapy in diabetic patients are difficult because of a lack of data from long-term randomized controlled trials. Available information about hormone replacement therapy and glycemic control is reassuring. Hormone replacement does not appear to alter serum insulin levels in normal women.[41] It has not been associated with poorer glycemic control in type 2 diabetic patients.[42,43]

Postmenopausal women with diabetes are at very high risk for coronary artery disease. Because hormone replacement therapy was believed previously to reduce the risk of coronary events, it often has been recommended to diabetic women. Recent studies in women with established coronary artery disease suggest that hormone replacement therapy may not reduce the risk of subsequent cardiac events and may place a subset of women at increased risk for cardiac events, particularly within the first few years of treatment.[44,45]

At the current time, hormone replacement therapy is not recommended routinely for women with diabetes. Women with diabetes who have compelling reasons to use hormone replacement (such as symptoms not manageable with alternative treatments) should be monitored closely. In general, hormone replacement therapy should not be started in patients with established coronary artery disease. Diabetic women who are currently using hormone replacement therapy should thoroughly discuss the potential risks and benefits of continuing with their clinician. These are outlined in Chapter 4, "Approach to the Menopausal Patient."

RESOURCE

American Diabetes Association
1701 North Beuregard
Alexandria, Virginia 22311
Telephone: 1-800-DIABETES (1-800-342-2383)
Web site: www.diabetes.org

The American Diabetes Association provides information for patients and clinicians, including on-line, updated guidelines on most aspects of diabetes management.

REFERENCES

1. American Diabetes Association. Facts and figures: the impact of diabetes [on-line]. www.diabetes.org (accessed. Sept 12, 2001).

2. Hanes DS, Weir MR, Sowers JR. Gender considerations in hypertension pathophysiology. Am J Med 1996;101 Suppl 3A:10–21S.

3. Barrett-Connor EL, Cohn BA, Wingard DL, et al. Why is diabetes mellitus a stronger risk factor for fatal ischemic heart disease in women than in men? JAMA 1991;265:627–31.

4. Xu R, Morales JA, Muniyappa R, et al. Interleukin-1beta-induced nitric oxide production in rat aortic endothelial cells: inhibition by estradiol in normal and high glucose cultures. Life Sci 1999;64:2451–62.

5. Screening for Diabetes Mellitus in US Preventative Services Task Force. Guide to clinical preventive services. 2nd ed. Baltimore (MD): Williams & Wilkins; 1996.

6. Gale EA, Gillespie KM. Diabetes and gender. Diabetologia 2001;44(1):3–15.

7. Kaufman DL, Erlander MG, Clare-Salzler M, et al. Autoimmunity to two forms of glutamate decarboxylase in insulin-dependent diabetes mellitus. J Clin Invest 1992;89:283–92.

8. Atkinson MA, Maclaren NK, Riley WJ, et al. Are insulin autoantibodies markers for insulin-dependent diabetes mellitus? Diabetes 1986;35:894–8.

9. Schott M, Schatz D, Atkinson M, et al. GAD autoantibodies increase the predictability but not the sensitivity of islet cell and insulin autoantibodies for developing insulin dependent diabetes mellitus. J Autoimmun 1994;7:865–72.

10. Atkinson MA, Maclaren NK. The pathogenesis of insulin-dependent diabetes mellitus. N Engl J Med 1994;331:1428–36.

11. Hu FB, Manson JE, Stampfer MJ, et al. Diet, lifestyle, and the risk of type 2 diabetes mellitus in women. N Engl J Med 2001;345:790–7.

12. American Diabetes Association. Report of the Expert Committee on the Diagnosis and Classification of Diabetes Mellitus. Diabetes Care 2001;24 Suppl 1:S5–20.

13. Banerji MA, Lebovitz HE. Insulin-sensitive and insulin-resistant variants in NIDDM. Diabetes 1989; 38:784–92.

14. Porte D Jr. Clinical importance of insulin secretion and its interaction with insulin resistance in the treatment of type 2 diabetes mellitus and its complications. Diabetes Metab Res Rev 2001;17:181–8.

15. American Diabetes Association. Screening for diabetes. Diabetes Care 2001;24 Suppl 1:S21–4.

16. American Diabetes Association. Standards of medical care for patients with diabetes mellitus. Diabetes Care 2001;24 Suppl 1:S33–43.

17. American Diabetes Association. Clinical practice recommendations 2001: preconception care of women with diabetes. Diabetes Care. 2001;24 Suppl 1:S3–5.

18. Aspirin therapy in diabetes. Diabetes Care 2001; 24 Suppl 1:S62–3.

19. Mensing C, Boucher J, Cypress M, et al. National standards for diabetes self-management education. Diabetes Care 2000;23:682–9.

20. American Diabetes Association. Nutrition recommendations and principles for people with diabetes mellitus. Diabetes Care. 2001;24 Suppl 1:S44–7.

21. American Diabetes Association. Diabetes mellitus and exercise. Diabetes Care 2001;24 Suppl 1:S51–5.

22. American Diabetes Association. Smoking and diabetes. Diabetes Care 2000;23:93–4.

23. Marshall A, Gringereich RL, Wright PH. Hepatic effect of sulfonylureas. Metabolism 1970;19:1046–52.

24. Groop L, Groop PH, Stenman S, et al. Do sulfonylureas influence hepatic insulin clearance? Diabetes Care 1988;11:689–90.

25. Kolterman OG, Gray RS, Shapiro G, et al. The acute and chronic effects of sulfonylurea therapy in type II diabetic subjects. Diabetes 1984;33:345–6.

26. Hermann LS, Schersten B, Bitzen PO. Therapeutic comparison of metformin and sulfonylureas, alone and in various combinations. Diabetes Care 1994; 17:1100–9.

27. Campbell IW, Menzies DG, Chalmers J, et al. One year comparative trial of metformin and glipizide in type 2 diabetes mellitus. Diabetes Metab 1994;20: 394–400.

28. Luna B, Feinglos MN. Oral agents in the management of type 2 diabetes mellitus. Am Fam Physician 2001;63:1747–56, 1759–80.

29. Bailey CJ, Turner RC. Metformin. N Engl J Med 1996;334:574–9.

30. Harrigan RA, Nathan MS, Beattie P. Oral agents for the treatment of type 2 diabetes mellitus: pharmacology, toxicity, and treatment. Ann Emerg Med 2001; 38:68–78.

31. Henry RR. Thiazolidinediones. Endocrinol Metab Clin North Am 1997;26:553–73.

32. Yee HS, Fong NT. A review of the safety and efficacy of acarbose in diabetes mellitus. Pharmacotherapy 1996;16:792–805.

33. Andrade RJ, Lucena M, Vega JL et al. Acarbose-associated hepatotoxicity. Diabetes Care 1998;21: 2029–30.

34. Foster DW. Diabetes. In: Fauci AS, Braunwald E, Isselbacher, et al, editors. Harrison's principles of internal medicine. 14th ed. p. 2060–80.

35. Holleman F, Hoekstra JBL. Insulin lispro. N Engl J Med 1997;337:176–83.

36. Product information, insulin glargine. 2000.

37. Rosenberg L, Palmer JR, Sands MI, et al. Modern oral contraceptives and cardiovascular disease. Am J Obstet Gynecol 1997;177:707–15.

38. Chasan-Taber L, Stampfer MJ. Epidemiology of oral contraceptives and cardiovascular disease. Ann Intern Med 1998;128:467–77.

39. Klein BE, Klein R, Moss SE. Exogenous estrogen exposures and changes in diabetic retinopathy. Diabetes Care 1999;22:1984–7.

40. Kjos SL, Peters RK, Xiang A, et al. Contraception and the risk of type 2 diabetes mellitus in Latina women with prior gestational diabetes mellitus. JAMA 1998;280:533–8.

41. The writing group for the PEPI trial. Effects of estrogen or estrogen/progestin regimens on heart disease risk factors in postmenopausal women. JAMA 1995;273:199–208.

42. Ferrara A, Karter AJ, Ackerson LM, et al. Hormone replacement therapy is associated with better glycemic control in women with type 2 diabetes: The Northern California Kaiser Permanente Diabetes Registry. Diabetes Care 2001;24:1144–50.

43. Manning PJ, Allum A, Jones S, et al. The effect of hormone replacement therapy on cardiovascular risk factors in type 2 diabetes: a randomized controlled trial. Arch Intern Med 2001;161:1772–6.

44. Hulley S, Grady D, Bush T. Randomized trial of estrogen plus progestin for secondary prevention of coronary heart disease in postmenopausal women. JAMA 1998;280:605–13.

45. Herrington DM, Reboussin DM, Brosnihan BK, et al. Effects of estrogen replacement on the progression of coronary-artery atherosclerosis. N Engl J Med 2000; 343:522–9.

56

HYPOTHYROIDISM

Thuy T. Tran, MD, and Inder J. Chopra, MD

The insufficient production of thyroid hormone results in hypothyroidism. Euthyroidism, a state of normal function of the thyroid, depends on a negative feedback system. When there is insufficient production of thyroid hormone, the anterior pituitary gland compensates by increasing the production of thyroid stimulating hormone (TSH). TSH helps restore normal thyroid function by increasing the production of thyroid hormone. A breakdown in any of these steps can cause hypothyroidism.

Hypothyroidism is a relatively common disease, especially in older women. Estimates show that the prevalence of overt hypothyroidism is 1.5 to 2% in females and 0.2% in males. The incidence increases with age. Approximately 10% of postmenopausal women show signs of hypothyroidism.[1]

There are primary thyroidal and secondary pituitary or hypothalamic types of hypothyroidism. Primary hypothyroidism accounts for 95% of the cases of hypothyroidism. Chronic autoimmune thyroiditis (Hashimoto's thyroiditis), radioactive iodine treatment for hyperthyroidism (eg, Graves' disease), and thyroidectomy are common causes of primary hypothyroidism. Secondary hypothyroidism is uncommon; some of its causes are listed in Table 56–1.

TABLE 56–1. Causes of Hypothyroidism

Primary Hypothyroidism	Secondary Hypothyroidism
Hashimoto's thyroiditis	Pituitary macroadenoma
Subtotal thyroidectomy	Infection
Postirradiation	Infiltrative disease
Postpartum thyroiditis	Surgery/irradiation
Idiopathic atrophy	
Development defect	
Drug-induced	
Iodide deficiency	

PATHOPHYSIOLOGY

Hashimoto's thyroiditis, the most common cause of hypothyroidism, causes an immune system–mediated injury to the thyroid, compromising its ability to produce thyroid hormone. Thyroglobulin and microsomal enzymes (thyroid peroxidase) are common target antigens, and their antibodies serve as laboratory markers for the disease. Approximately 90% of patients with Hashimoto's thyroditis have antimicrosomal antibodies, and antithyroglobulin antibodies are detectable in about 50% of patients.[2] Not all patients with Hashimoto's thyroiditis have hypothyroidism when first seen. Some experience transient hyperthyroidism followed by hypothyroidism, while others remain euthyroid for many years before the occurrence of hypothyroidism.

Postpartum thyroiditis is a variant of Hashimoto's thyroiditis, affecting 5 to 10% of postpartum women 3 to 6 months after delivery. A period of transient hyperthyroidism may precede hypothyroidism. Most of these patients return to the euthyroid state within a year but are at risk for recurrence of thyroiditis and thyroid dysfunction with subsequent pregnancies.

Hypothyroidism occurring after iodine-131 (^{131}I) is seen in almost 20% of Graves' disease patients in the first year after treatment (usually 2 to 6 months), and an additional 3% of patients develop hypothyroidism every year thereafter. External radiation to the neck for various conditions can also cause hypothyroidism. Subtotal thyroidectomy for Graves' disease causes hypothyroidism in approximately 5% of patients at 1 year and in about 2.5% more patients every year thereafter.

SUBCLINICAL HYPOTHYROIDISM

When serum TSH is elevated and free thyroxine (free T_4) concentration is normal, the patient has subclinical hypothyroidism. Five to 10% of adult women have elevated TSH but normal free T_4.[3] Most patients with subclinical hypothyroidism are asymptomatic, and therapy is controversial. Potential complications of subclinical hypothyroidism include hyperlipidemia, fatigue, weight gain, depression, coronary artery disease, and progression to overt hypothyroidism. Populations that may benefit from treatment include the elderly, patients with hypercholesterolemia, patients with TSH level above 10 mc'U/L, and those who have had ^{131}I treatment or thyroid surgery.[4] It is desirable to treat subclinical hypothyroidism in patients who have detectable antithyroid autoantibodies, since this population is very prone to develop overt hypothyroidism.[5] Patients with subclinical hypothyroidism who do not receive treatment should be monitored closely.

SYMPTOMS AND SIGNS

Most organ systems require thyroid hormone for normal functioning. The deficiency of thyroid hormone slows down these systems. Patients with early hypothyroidism often present with vague symptoms, and the diagnosis may be overlooked until serum TSH is abnormal on a screening test. Common early symptoms of hypothyroidism are fatigue, weight gain, and constipation. However, these nonspecific symptoms are also noted in some euthyroid individuals. Other symptoms of hypothyroidism are hoarseness, mental slowing, joint pains, depression, constipation, and cold intolerance. Menstrual disorder is common in women, especially menorrhagia. Infertility is also common and may be related to anovulatory cycles. See Table 56–2 for a list of symptoms and signs of hypothyroidism.

Performing a comprehensive physical examination is essential in the evaluation of hypothyroidism. The thyroid gland may be diffusely enlarged, rubbery, and nodular in autoimmune thyroiditis. There may be edema, slow speech, and cool and dry skin. The tongue is sometimes enlarged. The heart rate may be slow, while the heart size may appear enlarged due to dilation or pericardial effusion. The deep tendon reflexes show delay in the relaxation phase. Coarsened hair, sparse eyebrows, especially the lateral third, and hair loss are also

TABLE 56–2. Common Signs and Symptoms of Hypothyroidism

Symptoms	Signs
Dry skin	Slow movements
Cold intolerance	Coarse skin and hair
Hoarseness	Cold skin
Constipation	Periorbital puffiness
Decreased sweating	Bradycardia
Weakness/fatigue	Slow relaxation of tendon reflexes
	Increased hair loss

common. Hydrophilic mucopolysaccharides accumulate in the subcutaneous tissues in late stages, producing myxedematous changes. The skin may appear thickened and "doughy," not only periorbitally but peripherally as well. In more severe cases, patients may complain of symptoms indicating carpal tunnel syndrome and decreased hearing. Left untreated, hypothyroid patients may progress into the serious condition of myxedema coma.

Myxedema coma is life threatening and typically occurs in longstanding hypothyroid and elderly patients. These patients often present with a concurrent acute medical illness, and without treatment, many die. Symptoms may include lethargy, bradycardia, hypothermia, respiratory failure, cardiovascular collapse, and coma. Treatment includes intravenous levothyroxine, glucocorticoids, care in the intensive care unit (ICU), and consultation with an endocrinologist.

DIAGNOSIS

Symptoms may suggest the diagnosis of hypothyroidism, but laboratory tests are necessary to detect early disease and to confirm the diagnosis. Although both serum TSH and free T_4 are useful for diagnosing hypothyroidism, serum TSH is a more sensitive indicator of primary hypothyroidism. It should be measured first when hypothyroidism is suspected.[6] When TSH is elevated and free T_4 is low, the patient has primary hypothyroidism. An elevated TSH and normal free T_4 indicate subclinical disease. When TSH is low, inappropriately normal, or only slightly elevated and free T_4 is low, the patient may have secondary hypothyroidism. An endocrinology consultation and radiographic imaging of the sella turcica are recommended for patients with secondary hypothyroidism. In autoimmune thyroiditis, such as Hashimoto's thyroiditis or postpartum thyroiditis, measurement of the antimicrosomal or antithyroid peroxidase (TPO) and antithyroglobulin antibodies is useful for diagnosis.[7]

TREATMENT

The goal of the treatment of hypothyroidism is to normalize the patient's clinical state and the serum TSH and free T_4 levels. The treatment of hypothyroidism is summarized in Table 56–3. Typical treatment consists of synthetic l-thyroxine (levothyroxine, l-T_4). After ingesting thyroxine, serum T_4 level peaks at about 4 hours. Circulating T_4 is converted in part (~ 30 to 40%) to T_3, which is the predominant thyroid hormone regulating some tissues. The daily requirement of thyroxine is related to body mass. Monitoring serum TSH level and keeping it in the normal range prevent the potential risk of overtreatment with levothyroxine. Even mild hyperthyroidism over a period of several years, such as that caused by overtreatment with levothyroxine, can result in decreased bone mineral density and increased bone loss and will worsen osteoporosis.[8] The purpose for estimating appropriate replacement doses of levothyroxine for patients with secondary hypothyroidism resulting from hypothalamic–pituitary dysfunction is to relieve patient's symptoms and normalize free T_4 level;[9] serum TSH is not an appropriate test for adjusting treatment of secondary hypotension.

The average daily dose of levothyroxine for adult patients with primary hypothyroidism is 1.6 µg/kg body weight.[10] It approximates 75 to 100 µg/d for most women. After 2 months of therapy, the patient's serum TSH level should be checked. Once normal, this level should be monitored every 4 to 6 months.

Biannual monitoring of thyroid function is important in treated hypothyroid patients to evaluate compliance, drug interactions, and changes related to diet, weight, or age. If the serum TSH level is below normal, the dosage should be reduced slightly and serum TSH measured again in 2 months. When serum TSH has normalized, the level of free thyroxine is usually normal or slightly elevated. Certain drugs, such as ferrous sulfate, cholestyramine, sucralfate, aluminum hydroxide, and antacids, interfere with levothyroxine absorption.[5] In the experience of some clinicians, calcium and fiber preparations also diminish the absorption of levothyroxine. Levothyroxine should be taken about 4 hours apart from these drugs. It is recommended that patients should use the same brand of thyroid preparation. When there is a change in the levothyroxine brand, serum TSH and free T_4 levels need to be monitored more closely.

The starting dose of levothyroxine should be lower for geriatric patients and cardiac patients. A typical starting dosage for such patients is 25 µg/d with increases in 25 µg increments each 2 months, until the serum TSH level and clinical state are normal.

SCREENING

Screening for hypothyroidism[3,5] can detect overt or subclinical disease. However, screening of populations for hypothyroidism has not been recommended. It is preferable to target the groups at increased risk. For example, many experts recommend screening women ≥ 50 years old, patients with a history of thyroidectomy or radioiodine treatment for hyperthyroidism or thyroid nodules, and those with autoimmune diseases, depression, cognitive dysfunction, or hypercholesterolemia.

Serum TSH can identify persons with abnormal thyroid function before other clinical or laboratory abnormalities occur. If the serum TSH level is > 10 mcIU/L, a free T_4 level should be obtained. A patient with a low free T_4 level has overt hypothyroidism that requires treatment. There is no clear consensus on the frequency with which screening should be repeated; some experts evaluate high-risk populations at 6-month intervals or if new symptoms are observed.

ISSUES PERTAINING TO PREGNANCY AND BREAST-FEEDING

Pregnancy is infrequent in women with untreated hypothyroidism as they often suffer from anovulation. Some recent publications report an incidence

TABLE 56–3. Treatment of Hypothyroidism

Initial dosage:
   75–100 µg/d *or* 1.6 µg/kg of actual weight

Re-adjustments:

TSH elevated by < 20	Add 25 µg/d
TSH > 20	Add 50 µg/d

Check TSH every 6 to 8 wk until level is normal.

of pregnancy in this population of 1 in 1,600 to 2,000.[11] The most common cause of hypothyroidism during pregnancy is autoimmune thyroiditis, but previous treatment for Graves' disease and thyroid ablation therapies are also common causes.[12] Pregnant women with untreated hypothyroidism have an increased risk for preeclampsia, placental abruption, heart failure, low–birth weight baby, and stillbirths. Thus, women with hypothyroidism should be informed of these risks.[13] Studies have shown a higher rate of complications in patients who are more severely hypothyroid initially and still hypothyroid at delivery than patients who are euthyroid throughout treatment.[14]

Currently, there is no universal screening for hypothyroidism in pregnancy. However, high-risk patients should be evaluated with routine screening. Such patients include those with a history of previous treatment for hyperthyroidism, neck irradiation, postpartum thyroiditis, menstrual irregularity, other (nonthyroidal) autoimmune diseases, or a family history of hypothyroidism. Serum TSH is measured when there is suspicion of hypothyroidism. When it is elevated, serum FT_4 and antithyroid peroxidase antibody (TPO) titers should be measured. Women with high titers of antithyroid antibodies, regardless of their thyroid function status, have an increased risk of miscarriage.[15]

Appropriate treatment improves the outcome of the pregnancies of hypothyroid patients (see Table 56–3). Whenever possible, it is important to establish and maintain a euthyroid state before pregnancy. Close monitoring during pregnancy is vital, and serum TSH and free T_4 levels should be normalized as soon as possible when they are found to be abnormal. Serum TSH levels should be checked routinely each trimester and appropriate treatment instituted as needed. In patients taking thyroxine, serum TSH should be checked at 6- to 8-week intervals during pregnancy and within a few weeks after delivery.

Most patients require an increase in their replacement dose of levothyroxine during pregnancy, but the need for the drug returns to pre-pregnancy dosage soon after delivery.[16] Pregnant women should take levothyroxine in the morning on an empty stomach, unless they are experiencing nausea or vomiting. Levothyroxine should not be taken concomitantly with iron, calcium, or vitamin supplements. As noted above, thyroxine should be ingested at least 2 and preferably 4 hours away from these agents. Women who breast-feed secrete small amounts of thyroid hormone in their milk. However, no significant adverse reactions have been reported with the use of thyroid hormone when breast-feeding.[17]

MENOPAUSE, AGING, AND HYPOTHYROIDISM

As women age, the incidence of hypothyroidism increases. Older people may present with subtle nonspecific signs and symptoms of thyroid dysfunction, often similar to the normal aging process. Thus, the cause of symptoms may be overlooked unless serum TSH is measured. Symptoms of hypothyroidism in older age include deafness, confusion, dementia, and ataxia. Some authors suggest measuring serum TSH even on slight suspicion of hypothyroidism in an older person.[18] Many experts feel that it is reasonable to screen for hypothyroidism in women ≥ 50 years old because available evidence suggests an association between hypothyroidism and such disorders as coronary heart disease, hypercholesterolemia, and depression.

About 10% of postmenopausal women have subclinical hypothyroidism. Current information is incomplete to recommend or discourage treatment of these patients. However, subclinically hypothyroid elderly women with autoimmune thyroiditis become overtly hypothyroid at a high rate of 20%.[19] If treatment of subclinical hypothyroidism is deferred, patients should be monitored closely. It is worth noting that the requirement for levothyroxine usually declines with age, apparently secondary to its diminished degradation.[20] One should be very careful not to overtreat hypothyroidism in the elderly, as this can precipitate or worsen cardiac dysfunction, bone loss, and osteoporosis.

RESOURCES

The American Thyroid Association
6066 Leesburg Pike, Suite 650
Falls Church, Virginia 22041
Telephone: (703) 998-8890
Web site: www.thyroid.org

Founded in 1923, this association consists of clinicians and scientists dedicated to the research and treatment of thyroid pathophysiology. An annual meeting is held in the fall. The society publishes the monthly journal Thyroid *that covers topics ranging form molecular biology to clinical management. It also publishes guidelines on topics of diagnosis and treatment of thyroid disorders.*

Thyroid Foundation of America, Inc.
350 Ruth Sleeper Hall-RSL 350
Parkman Street
Boston, Massachusetts 02114
Telephone: 1-800-832-8321
Web site: www.clark.net/pub/tfa

Created in 1986, this nonprofit organization provides educational brochures and a quarterly newsletter for thyroid patients and health professionals, as well as support group information.

The Thyroid Society
7515 South Main Street, Suite 250
Houston, Texas 77030
Telephone: 1-800-THYROID (1-800-849-7643)
Web site: www.the-thyroid-society.org

This organization is recommended to patients. Its main mission is educating both patients and the public about thyroid disease. The Thyroid Society publishes patient education materials.

Publications
Surks MI. The thyroid book: what goes wrong and how to treat it. Yonkers (NY): Consumer Reports Books; 1994.

This book is informative for patients.

REFERENCES

1. Tunbridge WM, Evered DC, Hall R, et al. The spectrum of thyroid disease in a community: the Whickham Survey. Clin Endoc 1977;7:481–93.
2. Baker BA, Gharib H. Correlation of thyroid antibodies and cytologic features in suspected autoimmune thyroid disease. Am J Med 1983;74:941.
3. Helfand M, Redfern CC. Screening for thyroid disease: ACP-ASIM. Ann Intern Med 1998;129(2):144–58.
4. Toft AD. Thyroxine therapy. N Engl J Med 1994; 331:174–80.
5. Singer PA, Cooper DS, Levy EG, et al. Treatment guidelines for patients with hyperthyroidism and hypothyroidism. JAMA 1995;273:808–12.
6. Schectman JM, Pawlson LG. The cost-effectiveness of three thyroid function testing strategies for suspicion of hypothyroidism in a primary care setting. J Gen Intern Med 1990;5:9–15.
7. Klee GG, Hay ID. Biochemical testing of thyroid function. Endocrin Metab Clin North Am 1997; 26:763–74.

8. Stall GM, Harris S, Sokoll LJ, et al. Accelerated bone loss in hypothyroid patients overtreated with L-thyroxine. Ann Int Med 1990;113:265–9.

9. Surks MI, Chopra IJ, Mariash CN, et al. American Thyroid Association guidelines for use of laboratory tests in thyroid disorders. JAMA 1990;263:1529–32.

10. Mandel SJ, Brent GA, Larsen PR. Levothyroxine therapy in patients with thyroid disease. Ann Intern Med 1993;119:492–502.

11. Montoro MN. Management of hypothyroidism during pregnancy. Clin Obstet Gynecol 1997;40:65–80.

12. Mestman JH, Goodwin M, Montoro MM. Thyroid disorders of pregnancy. Endocrinol Metab Clin North Am 1995;24:41–70.

13. Pregler JP. Common chronic medical illnesses: effects on fertility and principles of preconception counseling. Clin of North Am 1998;9:4635–46.

14. Leung AS, Millar LK, Koonings PP, et al. Perinatal outcome in hypothyroid pregnancies. Obstet Gynecol 1993;81:349–53.

15. Lejeune B, Grun JP, De Nayer P, et al. Thyroid antibodies underlying thyroid abnormalities and miscarriage or pregnancy induced hypertension. Br J Obstet Gynecol 1993;100:669–72.

16. Kaplan MM. Monitoring thyroxine therapy treatment during pregnancy. Thyroid 1992;2:147.

17. Mizuta H, Amino N, Ichihara K, et al. Thyroid hormones in human milk and their influence on thyroid function of breast-fed babies. Pediatr Res 1983; 17:468–71.

18. Sawin CT. Thyroid dysfunction in older persons. Adv Intern Med 1991;37:223–48.

19. Rosenthal MJ, Hunt WC, Garry PJ, Goodwin JS. Thyroid failure in the elderly: microsomal antibodies as discriminant for therapy. JAMA 1987;258:209–13.

20. Rosenbaum RL, Barzel OS. Levothyroxine replacement dose for primary hypothyroidism decrease with age. Ann Intern Med 1982;96:53–5.

57

HYPERTHYROIDISM

Michael Malamed, MD, and Inder J. Chopra, MD

Hyperthyroidism is a common endocrinologic abnormality, affecting approximately 2% of women. It is 10 times more common in women than in men.[1] Clinically unrecognized hyperthyroidism is relatively common and can have significant long-term sequelae, including osteoporosis and an increased risk of atrial fibrillation. This chapter reviews the clinical presentation, diagnosis, and treatment of hyperthyroidism, with a particular emphasis on issues of importance when treating women.

SIGNS AND SYMPTOMS

The signs and symptoms of hyperthyroidism are summarized in Table 57–1. It is worth noting that some of the symptoms of hyperthyroidism may mimic those of other conditions common in primary care practice, including anxiety disorder, irritable bowel syndrome, and menopause. For this reason, it is important to maintain a high level of suspicion for hyperthyroidism and to test appropriately when patients present with suggestive or unexplained symptoms.

Of note, hyperthyroidism can be the cause of various menstrual abnormalities. The reason thyroid hormone levels affect menstruation is only partly understood. Hyperthyroidism occurring in childhood prior to puberty may be associated with a delayed onset of menarche. High levels of thyroid hormone may cause menstrual disorders, such as oligomenorrhea or amenorrhea. Anovulatory cycles are common.[2]

A comprehensive physical examination needs to be performed in all patients suspected to have hyperthyroidism. Table 57–2 summarizes the important aspects of the physical examination. Physical findings fall into two categories: (1) those due to hyperthyroidism per se, and (2) those related to the

TABLE 57–1. Sign and Symptoms Associated with Hyperthyroidism

Nervousness and irritability
Increased resting heart rate causing palpitations
Heat intolerance and increased sweating
Tremor
Weight loss or alterations in appetite
Frequent bowel movements (hyperdefecation, rather than diarrhea)
Sudden paralysis
Thyroid enlargement
Pretibial myxedema
Thin, delicate skin and irregular fingernail and hair growth
Menstrual disturbance (decreased flow)
Impaired fertility
Mental disturbances, confusion, mania
Loss of libido
Sleep disturbances (including insomnia)
Changes in vision, eye irritation, or exophthalmos

From Surks MI, Chopra IJ, Mariash CN, et al. American Thyroid Association guidelines for use of laboratory tests in thyroid disorders. JAMA 1990;263:1529–32.

TABLE 57–2. Physical Examination of the Hyperthyroid Patient

Weight and height
Blood pressure
Temperature
Pulse rate and rhythm
Thyroid (to determine size, nodularity, and vascularity)
Neuromuscular examination
Eye examination (to detect evidence of exophthalmos or ophthalmopathy)
Skin
Cardiovascular system
Lymph nodes

From Surks MI, Chopra IJ, Mariash CN, et al. American Thyroid Association guidelines for use of laboratory tests in thyroid disorders. JAMA 1990;263:1529–32.

cause of hyperthyroidism. Warm, moist skin, palmar erythema, tremor, and tachycardia can be found in hyperthyroidism from any cause. A characteristic "stare" with widened palpebral fissures, infrequent blinking, and associated lid lag is also characteristic, but nonspecific. Physical findings associated with specific causes of hyperthyroidism are discussed below.[3]

LABORATORY EVALUATION

The recent development of sensitive thyroid stimulating hormone (TSH) assays has greatly facilitated the diagnosis of hyperthyroidism. The sensitive TSH test includes many of the second-generation and all of the third-generation or "ultrasensitive" TSH assays. The sensitive TSH is the single best screening test for hyperthyroidism. Hyperthyroidism from any cause generally results in a clearly suppressed TSH. The only exceptions occur in rare cases of excess TSH production from the pituitary or an extrapituitary tumor.[4]

If the TSH is suppressed, additional blood tests are needed to confirm the diagnosis and to determine the severity of the hyperthyroid condition (see Table 57–3 for normal ranges). The best tests for this are measurents of the free T_4 and T_3 levels (by dialysis) in the blood, since the more overactive the thyroid gland is, the higher these levels are. In mild cases of hyperthyroidism, the free T_4 and T_3 may be only slightly above normal, whereas, in severe cases, they may be over twice the upper limit of normal.

Older tests include measurement of free T_4 by indirect measures and T_3 resin uptake. Not all elevations of T_4 and T_3 and not all suppressed TSH levels are associated with hyperthyroidism. Estrogen administration and pregnancy raise the level of thyroid-binding globulin, resulting in a high total T_4 and T_3 by radio-immunoassay (RIA) but normal free T_4 and sensitive TSH. Euthyroid hyperthyroxinemia may also be due abnormal levels of other binding proteins, including albumin and prealbumin. Similarly, thyroid hormone resistance states can produce elevations of the T_4 without hyperthyroidism. Glucocorticoids, severe illness, and pituitary dysfunction can be associated with suppressed TSH in the absence of hyperthyroidism.[5]

Other tests, such as TSH receptor antibodies (thyroid-stimulating immunoglobulins [TSIs] or TSH receptor antibodies [TRAbs]) and radioactive

TABLE 57–3. Normal Values of Thyroid Function Tests

Test	Normal Range (Laboratory Specific)
TSH	0.3–5 mcIU/mL
Free T_4*	0.7–2.2 ng/dL
Free T_4 Index	5.8–10.6
Plasma T_4†	5–12 μg/dL
Plasma T_3†	80–160 ng/dL

From Surks MI, Chopra IJ, Mariash CN, et al. American Thyroid Association guidelines for use of laboratory tests in thyroid disorders. JAMA 1990;263:1529–32.
*By dialysis   †Total

iodine uptake thyroid scanning, are useful in some cases for diagnosis and management of hyperthyroidism and are discussed below.

CAUSES

The most common cause of hyperthyroidism is **Graves' disease** (diffuse toxic goiter), possibly a genetically linked disease, which is caused by circulating immunoglobulins that bind to and stimulate the thyrotropin (TSH) receptor, resulting in sustained thyroid overactivity. It is by far the most likely cause of hyperthyroidism in patients under the age of 50 years. Graves' disease can manifest with diffuse goiter, ophthalmopathy, and dermopathy. The presence of a diffusely enlarged nontender goiter is highly suggestive of Graves' disease, as is the presence of a thyroid bruit. Graves' ophthalmopathy is characterized by proptosis, which can be accompanied by periorbital swelling. Dermopathy is rarer and consists of areas of raised erythematous skin, usually over the dorsum of the legs, that are commonly thickened and have a peau d'orange appearance.[6]

The diagnosis of overt Graves' disease with ophthalmopathy is usually obvious. In elderly individuals, however, Graves' disease may be more difficult to diagnose and may present only with cardiac manifestations and weight loss. Some patients may present with a normal-sized thyroid gland. The T_4, T_3 resin uptake, free T_4 index, free T_4, T_3 RIA, and free T_3 are usually and variably elevated, although some individuals may have elevations of only T_3 RIA or free T_3 (T_3 toxicosis). In Graves' disease the serum TSH is suppressed. When the diagnosis of Graves' disease is in doubt, radioactive iodine uptake and scan, using iodine-123 (^{123}I) or technetium-99m (^{99m}Tc), may be useful. In Graves' disease, uptake is increased. The presence of TSI or TRAb confirms Graves' disease.[7]

Toxic nodular goiter is a clinical condition in which individual thyroid nodules are responsible for excess thyroid hormone production. A toxic adenoma (hot nodule) is associated with a high T_4 and/or a high T_3, and a suppressed TSH. The thyroid scan reveals a functioning nodule with suppression of the remaining thyroid tissue. Toxic multinodular goiter has the same characteristics and similar laboratory findings as those associated with a toxic nodule, but the gland is variably enlarged and composed of multiple nodules. In both cases, radioactive iodine uptake is usually elevated but may be in the normal range.[8]

Subacute thyroiditis is a self-limited inflammation of thyroid tissue, most likely triggered by a viral infection. The gland is usually painful. Hyperthyroidism is due to the release of stored thyroid hormone from the inflamed gland. Frequently, the early hyperthyroid phase is followed by a 2- or 3-month hypothyroid phase before resolution.[9]

Silent thyroiditis, apparently an autoimmune disorder, has a similar course and is particularly common post partum. Five to 10% of women develop thyroid inflammation within a few months after delivery, termed "**postpartum thyroiditis**".[10] Usually, this occurs in women who have never had a thyroid problem before. It is more common in Asian women and those with a history of diabetes. This form of thyroid inflammation is painless and causes little or no gland enlargement. Leakage of thyroid hormone from the inflamed gland may cause hyperthyroidism that lasts for several weeks. As the injured gland recovers, it may not be able to make enough thyroid hormone, resulting in temporary hypothyroidism, which may last up to a year. Symptoms of hyperthyroidism and hypothyroidism may not be recognized when they occur in a new mother and may simply be attributed to lack of sleep, nervousness, or depression. Women who have had an episode of postpartum thyroiditis are very likely to develop the problem again after future pregnancies. One of 4 women with postpartum thyroiditis goes on to develop permanent hypothyroidism.[11]

Iodine-induced hyperthyroidism occurs most often in older populations and is seen typically in the setting of a pre-existing nontoxic nodular goiter. An iodine load, from oral medications or supplements or from intravenous contrast agents, induces the hyperthyroidism, which does not readily resolve and may require specific treatment. **Factitious hyperthyroidism** is caused by exogenous thyroid hormone ingestion. It is important to note that animal thyroid preparations are available without prescription and are sometimes included in "natural" treatments in amounts that can result in hyperthyroidism. **Ectopic thyroid tissue** (struma ovarii) is also an infrequent cause of hyperthyroidism.[12]

A low radioiodine uptake with poor thyroid gland imaging on the thyroid scan characterizes subacute thyroiditis, silent thyroiditis, and factitious thyroxine-induced hyperthyroidism. Subacute thyroiditis and silent thyroiditis have variably elevated T_3 and T_4 levels during the hyperthyroid phase.[13]

Excessive pituitary TSH or trophoblastic disease producing TSH-like materials or excess human chorionic gonadotropin (hCG; which has some TSH activity) are rare causes of hyperthyroidism.

SUBCLINICAL HYPERTHYROIDISM

Subclinical hyperthyroidism is defined by a suppressed TSH with normal serum T_4 and T_3 levels. Other causes of TSH suppression, such as glucocorticoid use, severe illness, and pituitary dysfunction, should be excluded. The development of sensitive TSH assays allows for the identification of many patients with subclinical hyperthyroidism resulting from excessive production or excessive replacement of thyroid hormone. Subclinical hyperthyroidism associated with toxic goiter, toxic adenoma, or toxic multi-nodular goiter frequently require treatment.[14]

TREATMENT

The treatment of hyperthyroidism depends on the cause of the condition. For all types of hyperthyroidism, ß-blockers are helpful in controlling the symptoms. Propranolol, metoprolol, and atenolol are commonly used. It should be noted that these drugs do not have any effect on the thyroid gland per se, but, rather, they rapidly diminish the effects of the high hormone levels. Hyperthyroid patients may be relatively resistant to the effects of ß-blockers such that larger frequent doses may be necessary. Using propanolol as an example, many patients require dosages of 160 mg/d, which can be taken as 40 mg every 6 hours. This can be adjusted, depending on patient symptoms. These drugs are tapered and discontinued once the patient is no longer hyperthyroid.[15]

For patients who have a thyroiditis-associated hyperthyroidism, a ß-blocker is usually the only treatment that is needed, since the hyperthyroidism is temporary. In subacute thyroiditis, aspirin or, rarely, steroids are needed to help control the pain and tenderness in the thyroid gland. Oral cholecystography agents, such as ipodate and tyropanoate, are potent inhibitors of peripheral conversion of T_4 to T_3 (the more active thyroid hormone). Because of this, they have been used with benefit in patients with severely symptomatic hyperthyroidism ("thyroid storm," see below). In addition, some patients with thyroiditis may temporarily develop hypothyroidism and may need at least temporary replacement therapy.[16]

There are three major modalities of treatment of Graves' disease and toxic nodular or multinodular goiter: antithyroid drugs, surgery, and radioactive iodine therapy. All are effective, but no method is without limitations. Patients with Graves' disease may be prescribed antithyroid drugs over a period of 12 to 24 months in an attempt to induce long-term remission (Table 57–4). These drugs block thyroid hormone synthesis. Serum T_4 level should be checked after a month of treatment and every 2 to 3 months thereafter. After 18 to 24 months of therapy, approximately 40% of Graves' disease patients go into remission. Unfortunately, Graves' disease recurs in some 60% of patients, who subsequently need to restart the antithyroid drugs or have radioiodine therapy.[17]

For patients with toxic nodules, antithyroid drugs must be continued long term because the overactivity in the nodule almost always flares up again if the medication is stopped, even for a short period. These drugs are also often given for a limited period to render the patient euthyroid before definitive therapy with radioiodine or thyroidectomy.[17]

Most patients do well on antithyroid medications, which can be continued long term. The most common side effect is a rash, occurring in approximately 5% of patients, while rarer side effects include hepatitis, arthritis, and agranulocytosis. It is, extremely important that all patients taking antithyroid drugs be advised that they should stop their medication and contact their clinician immediately if they develop a fever, sore throat, rash, jaundice, or arthritis.[3]

Propylthiouracil (PTU) and methimazole can be used during pregnancy and by nursing mothers; however, it is important that the clinician monitor the woman taking these drugs closely so that the smallest effective dose is prescribed, maintaining serum T_4 at a high normal level. All clinicians caring for the mother, fetus, and neonate need to be aware that the mother is taking these drugs, so that the baby's thyroid status can be monitored. PTU is the preferred drug for pregnant women, since it crosses the placenta and gets into the breast milk less easily than does methimazole.[3] Methimazole has also been associated with a skin disorder in the fetus (cutis aplasia).[1] Often Graves' disease improves as pregnancy progresses, but it often flares up again in the postpartum period.

The use of radioiodine (^{131}I) as a first-line therapy for Graves' disease is growing. It is well tolerated; the only long-term sequela is hypothyroidism. Studies have shown no increased risk of cancer or problems with future pregnancies. Radioiodine can be used in all age groups other than in children, although it needs to be avoided in pregnancy and during lactation. Radioactive iodine is contraindicated during pregnancy because it may ablate the thyroid in the fetus. It has been advocated that pregnancy should be avoided for 3 to 5 months following its administration. Radioactive iodine therapy should be deferred in women who are breast-feeding because it appears in the breast milk. The treatment of choice for toxic nodular goiter is radioiodine.[13]

Usually, the treatment with ^{131}I is entirely painless, though an occasional patient notices mild soreness over the thyroid gland for a few days after the treatment. A radioactive iodine treatment takes about 2 to 4 months to work, after which most patients are euthyroid or hypothyroid. The radioactive iodine treatment is effective about 90 to 95%

TABLE 57–4. Dosage Recommendations for Treatment of Hyperthyroidism

Initial therapy
    Propylthiouracil 100–150 mg every 8 h
    Methimazole 20–30 mg every 12 h

Maintenance therapy
    Propylthiouracil 50–100 mg twice a day
    Methimazole 5–10 mg once or twice a day

From Surks MI, Chopra IJ, Mariash CN, et al. American Thyroid Association guidelines for use of laboratory tests in thyroid disorders. JAMA 1990;263:1529–32.

of the time; a few patients may require a second dose. Elderly or cardiac patients with Graves' disease may require treatment with antithyroid drugs prior to radioactive iodine, to deplete the gland of stored hormone and reduce the risk of exacerbation of hyperthyroidism secondary to [131]I- induced thyroiditis.[13]

After treatment with radioactive iodine, patients should be seen at frequent intervals until they are euthyroid and stable. The visits can vary from 4 to 6 weeks, but each case should be individualized. Some patients require thyroid hormone replacement therapy. Patients often become hypothyroid within 3 months after treatment and may require replacement doses of levothyroxine approximately 2 to 3 months after receiving radioactive iodine. During the early follow-up period, it is important to monitor clinical symptoms and free T_4 as well as TSH. At this stage, TSH may not be a good indicator of function because it fails to rise quickly. It may take several months before there is recovery of TSH responsiveness.[13]

Surgery, either subtotal or near-total thyroidectomy, has a limited but specific role to play in the treatment of hyperthyroidism; this approach is rarely used in patients with Graves' disease, unless radioiodine has been rejected by the patient or there is a large goiter causing symptoms of compression in the neck. It is also used during pregnancy when antithyroid drugs cannot be used for reasons of side effects or failure to comply. Thyroidectomy is typically considered only during the second trimester of pregnancy because of concerns about risks of surgery to the fetus during the first and third trimesters.[16]

THYROID STORM

Thyroid storm is a rare but potentially life-threatening syndrome characterized by exaggerated manifestations of hyperthyroidism, including hyperthermia, severe tachycardia with or without cardiac failure, severe agitation, and mental disorientation escalating to stupor and coma. In addition to general supportive measures, therapy should be directed at the underlying cause of the hyperthyroidism as well as the accompanying hypermetabolism and tachycardia.

Propylthiouracil, 150 to 200 mg every 4 to 6 hours as starting dosage, is given to inhibit thyroid hormone synthesis. It is preferred to methimazole, as it also inhibits peripheral conversion of T_4 to T_3.

The first dose should precede iodine administration. Iodine, as Lugol's iodine, three to eight drops 8 hourly (1 drop = 3 mg iodine) is given to inhibit release of preformed T_3 and T_4. Iodine alone is potentially hazardous as its withdrawal results in the massive release of T_4 and T_3.

Propranolol, 60 to 120 mg every 6 hours diminishes the effect of high thyroid hormone levels, but ß-adrenergic blockade should not be used in patients with cardiac failure. Calcium channel blockers, for example, diltiazem, may be used in that situation. Glucocorticoids, for example, hydrocortisone 300 mg followed by 100 mg every 8 to 12 hours, seem to reduce the mortality rate of thyroid storm when given in conjunction with the above therapy.[6]

PREGNANCY

The prevalence of hyperthyroidism in pregnancy is about 0.2%. The most common cause is Graves' disease. Maternal, fetal, and neonatal morbidity and mortality rates may be reduced to a minimum with careful attention to the clinical symptoms and interpretation of thyroid tests. Ideally, hyperthyroid women should achieve euthyroidism before considering conception. The incidence of maternal and neonatal morbidity is significantly higher in those patients whose hyperthyroidism is not medically controlled. Even the incidence of thyroid storm is high in women who are under poor medical supervision in the presence of a medical or obstetric complication. Maternal morbidity includes a higher incidence of toxemia, premature delivery, placenta abruptio, congestive heart failure, and thyroid crisis. In some series, anemia and infections were also reported. Neonatal morbidity includes intrauterine growth retardation, prematurity, and low birth weight. Fetal goiter and transient neonatal hypothyroidism is occasionally reported in infants of mothers who have been overtreated with antithyroid drugs.[16]

Propylthiouracil and methimazole are equally effective in controlling the disease, although propylthiouracil has usually been preferred for the reasons discussed above. In most patients, symptoms improve and thyroid tests return to normal in 3 to 8 weeks after initiation of therapy. Resistance to antithyroid drugs is extremely rare; most cases are caused by poor compliance is the most common cause of persistent hyperthyroidism despite treatment. Surgery for the treatment of hyperthyroidism is reserved for the unusual patient who is allergic to both propylthiouracil and methimazole; those who have large goiters; those who require large doses of antithyroid drugs; or those patients with poor compliance. Fetal and neonatal hyperthyroidism can be predicted in the majority of cases by the previous maternal medical and obstetric histories and by the proper interpretation of thyroid tests, including the finding of a high level of TSH receptor antibodies in the mother. Finally, hyperthyroidism may recur in the postpartum period.[5]

PRECONCEPTION CARE

Women who plan to have children should have their thyroid condition adequately controlled before conceiving. Antithyroid medications alone may not be the best approach in cases of Graves'

disease because hyperthyroidism often returns when medication is stopped. Radioactive iodine is the most widely recommended permanent treatment, with surgical removal being the second choice. Radioactive iodine cannot be given to a pregnant woman, since it can cross the placenta and destroy normal thyroid cells in the fetus. As noted above, the only common side effect of radioactive iodine treatment is hypothyroidism, and this can be easily and safely treated with levothyroxine. There is no evidence that radioactive iodine treatment of hyperthyroidism interferes with a woman's future chances of becoming pregnant and delivering a healthy baby. If hyperthyroidism during pregnancy is not treated, there is an increased risk of miscarriage. Euthyroid pregnant patients treated for Graves' disease prior to the pregnancy may still have stimulating thyroid autoantibodies in the circulation, which can cross the placenta and affect fetal thyroid function.[12]

RESOURCES

The American Thyroid Association, Inc.
Townhouse Office Park
55 Old Nyack Turnpike, Suite 661
Nanuet, New York 10954
Telephone: (914) 623-1800
Fax: (914) 623-1800
Web site: www.thyroid.org

Founded in 1923, this association consists of clinicians and scientists dedicated to the research and treatment of thyroid pathophysiology. An annual meeting is held in the fall. The society publishes the monthly journal Thyroid *that covers topics ranging from molecular biology to clinical management. It also publishes guidelines on topics of diagnosis and treatment of thyroid disorders.*

Thyroid Foundation of America, Inc.
350 Ruth Sleeper Hall-RSL 350
Parkman Street
Boston, Massachusetts 02114
Telephone:1-800-832-8321
Web site: www.clark.net/pub/tfa

Created in 1986, this nonprofit organization provides educational brochures and a quarterly newsletter for thyroid patients and health professionals, as well as support group information.

RESOURCES

The Thyroid Society
7515 South Main Street, Suite 250
Houston, Texas 77030
Telephone:1-800-THYROID (1-800-849-7643)
Web site: www.the-thyroid-society.org

The Thyroid Society's main mission is educating both patients and the public about thyroid disease. The Thyroid Society publishes patient education materials for professionals.

Publications
Surks MI. The thyroid book: what goes wrong and how to treat it. Yonkers (NY): Consumer Reports Books; 1994.

This book is a good source of information for patients.

REFERENCES

1. Sakiayama R. Common thyroid disorders. Am Fam Phys 1988;38:227–38.
2. Foley TP. Goiter in adolescence. Adolesc Endocrinol 1993;22:593–606.
3. Surks MI, Chopra IJ, Mariash CN, et al. American Thyroid Association guidelines for use of laboratory tests in thyroid disorders. JAMA 1990;263:1529–32.
4. Borst GC, Eil C, Burman KD. Euthyroid hyperthyroxemia. Ann Intern Med 1983;98:366–78.
5. McIver B, Morris JC. The pathogensis of Grave's disease. Endocrinology and metabolism. Clin North Am 1998;27(1):73–89.
6. Singer PA, Cooper DS, Levy EG, et al. Treatment guidelines for patients with hyperthyroidism and hypothroidism. JAMA 1995;273:808–12.
7. Baker JR Jr. Autoimmune endocrine diseases. JAMA 1997;278:1931–7.
8. Siegel RD, Lee SL. Toxic nodular goiter: toxic adenoma and toxic multinodular goiter. Endocrinol Metab Clin North Am 1998;27(1):151–68.
9. Lazarus JH. Clinical manifestations of postpartum thyroid disease. Thyroid 1999;9:685–9.
10. Franklyn JA. The management of hyperthyroidism. N Engl J Med 1994;330:1731–7.
11. Hay ID. Thyroiditis: a clinical update. Mayo Clin Proc 1985;60:836–43.
12. McDougal IR. Grave's disease: current concepts. Med Clin North Am 1991;75:79.
13. Araham GD, Burman KD. Radioiodine treatment of Graves' disease. Ann Intern Med 1986;105:900.
14. Utiger RD. Beta-adrenergic antagonist therapy for hyperthyroid Grave's disease. N Engl J Med 1984; 310:1597–8.
15. Dillman WH. Thyroid storm. Current therapy in endocrinology and metabolism 1997;6:81–5.
16. Mestman JH. Hyperthyroidism in pregnancy. Clin Obstet Gynecol 1997;40(1):45–64.
17. Hall R, Richards CJ, Lazarus JH. The thyroid and pregnancy. Br J Obstet Gynecol 1993;100:512–5.

58

APPROACH TO THE PATIENT WITH A THYROID MASS

Katja Van Herle, MD, and Andre J. Van Herle, MD

The management of thyroid nodules is becoming an increasingly common clinical issue. The advent of sophisticated imaging techniques has led to early and incidental discovery of thyroid nodules, which are sometimes termed "thyroid incidentalomas." Incidentally found thyroid nodules, which frequently are nonpalpable, have added to the large

TABLE 58–1. Common Thyroid Disorders with Nodules

Cyst (pure or mixed)

Multi-nodular goiter

Adenoma (autonomous or nonautonomous)

Graves' disease

Carcinoma (primary thyroid and secondary metastases)

Colloid nodule

Thyroiditis
  Acute
    Bacterial
    Absesses
    Granulomatous
  Subacute thyroiditis
  Chronic thyroiditis
    Hashimoto's
    Riedel's struma
Developmental anomalies
  Unilateral lobe agenesis (with hypertrophy of contra-
    lateral side)
  Cystic hygroma
  Dermoid cyst, branchial cleft cyst
  Teratoma

burden of palpable nodules which are clinically identifiable, making the number of thyroid nodules requiring evaluation substantially greater than in past years. Imaging techniques that lead to the discovery of incidental thyroid nodules include duplex ultrasonography for the study of arterial stenosis and plaque formation, and computer tomography (CT) and magnetic resonance imaging (MRI) of the neck performed in the evaluation of patients with neck injuries, neuropathic pain, or other neurologic abnormalities.

Moreover, recent studies have shown that malignancies are present with the same frequency in multinodular goiters as in single nodules, necessitating a more extensive evaluation of the patient with multinodular goiter, something that has not been deemed necessary in the past. For these reasons, the clinician is faced with having to rethink the approach to palpable as well as nonpalpable nodules in clinical practice. This chapter attempts to summarize the most current management guidelines for thyroid nodules in an attempt to simplify the clinician's approach to a growing health care problem.

DEFINITION

A thyroid nodule is not a single disorder but represents an external sign of a multitude of thyroid disorders that manifest as a single nodule or as a multinodular goiter. These thyroid disorders are summarized in Table 58–1.

It is clear that a thyroid gland can be affected simultaneously by more than one disorder, making evaluation and treatment more challenging. It is not unusual, for example, to encounter a patient with Hashimoto's thyroiditis or Graves' disease who has also associated thyroid cancer. Similarly, a patient could be affected by Graves' disease and have benign colloid nodules. In such cases, for example, it is sometimes difficult to establish whether the thyrotoxicosis is due to Graves' disease or due to the nodular goiter. This distinction is not entirely academic, since patients with thyrotoxicosis due to Graves' disease go into remission when treated with antithyroid drugs, such as propylthiouracil or methimazole, in approximately 60% of the cases. This is in contrast to patients with toxic multinodular goiter, in whom permanent remission never occurs when they are treated with antithyroid drugs alone.

INCIDENCE OF THYROID NODULES IN POPULATION STUDIES

In the earliest population study, the incidence of thyroid nodules was estimated to be 4.2%,[1] and the incidence in men and women was approximately 1.5% and 6.4%, respectively. A second study performed by Tunbridge et al, in the United Kingdom, revealed a clinical incidence of 2.5% in persons 25 to 54 years of age.[2] Autopsy series suggest that thyroid nodules exist in almost 50% of people who have not been clinically diagnosed with thyroid nodules during their lifetime.[3]

In the American adult population, one study estimated the annual incidence of thyroid nodules to be roughly 0.1%, with a prevalence of 4 to 7%.[4,5] In this study, the incidence of thyroid carcinoma was 2.1%. An autopsy study performed in Michigan, reported the incidence of thyroid nodules to be 51%, with a cancer incidence of 13%. Thyroid glands from persons aged 16 to 85 years were included in this study.[6]

The incidence of thyroid abnormalities in the normal adult population, based on ultrasound imaging, increases with age and has been reported to be as high as 27%.[7,8] It is clear from these studies that thyroid nodules represent a monumental clinical problem in the United States. The sheer number of thyroid nodules that need a work-up represents a challenging medical-economic problem as well. In many cases, it is up to the primary care clinician to perform the work-up to uncover possible thyroid malignancies in the thyroid nodules found. How to go about achieving this goal is the subject of the remainder of this chapter.

ETIOLOGY: FACTORS FAVORING A MALIGNANCY IN THYROID NODULES

Besides a history of radiation exposure in childhood or adulthood and a genetic predisposition to medullary carcinoma as seen in the multiple endocrine neoplasia syndromes (MEN IIA + MEN IIB), a number of other clinical findings are frequently associated with thyroid cancer. These are summarized in Table 58–2.

The characteristics listed in Table 58–2 are not uniquely seen in patients with thyroid cancer. For example, other thyroid conditions can be associated with lymph nodes, such as Hashimoto's disease. Hoarseness can also be caused by benign lesions of the thyroid. A firm tender nodule is occasionally seen in patients with subacute thyroiditis, a benign process in which the nodule has a tendency to spontaneously resolve with time.

As part of the primary care clinician's work-up, a detailed history must be obtained regarding any possible exposure the patient may have had to external radiation. It is well known that thyroid tissue is very sensitive to the effects of radiation and that significant past exposures to radiation carry with them a lifetime risk to the patient of developing a thyroid tumor. Table 58–3 summarizes the most common forms of radiation exposure which pose an increased risk for carcinoma of the thyroid.

TABLE 58–2. Signs, Symptoms, and Laboratory Findings Frequently Associated with Thyroid Cancer

Presence of very firm nodules
Presence of palpable cervical or supraclavicular lymph nodes
Presence of hoarseness or vocal cord paralysis
Fixation of the thyroid to the trachea
Presence of stippled calcifications on plain radiograph
Rapid growth of a nodule
Pain in the thyroid bed
Elevated serum calcitonin level

TABLE 58–3. Common Forms of Radiation Exposure

Frequent fluoroscopic procedures[*]

External radiation therapy for
  Acne vulgaris
  Ringworm
  Tonsillitis
  Skin hemangiomas
  Hodgkin's lymphoma
  Thymic enlargement

Shoe-sizing machines of the 1940s–1960s

Nuclear radiation exposure[†]

[*]Including frequent cardiac catheterization for congenital heart disease.
[†]Including visiting areas of recent nuclear accidents, eg, Chernobyl.

WORK-UP OF THYROID NODULES

Thyroid Function and Thyroid Autoantibodies

Most patients with thyroid nodules are euthyroid. However, it is important to establish the status of the thyroid function in any given patient presenting with a thyroid nodule. A serum thyroid stimulating hormone (TSH) level is usually sufficient as a routine test. However, if the TSH level is below or above the normal limit, then free T_4 and free T_3 indices should be obtained in addition. High estrogen states, as seen associated with pregnancy or the use of oral contraceptive estrogen-containing pills, cause an elevation in thyroxine-binding globulin, which, in turn, may falsely elevate the total thyronine levels, (TT_4, TT_3). Consequently, a correction factor must be applied in these situations by performing a T_3 resin uptake and then calculating the FT_4 index. Recently, it has become possible to measure free T_3 and free T_4 levels directly by dialysis methods. These tests are not affected by the level of thyroxine-binding globulin.

Hyperthyroid and hypothyroid states are only rarely caused by a malignancy of the thyroid. Widespread functioning metastatic thyroid carcinoma can cause hyperthyroidism. Anaplastic thyroid carcinoma can cause complete destruction of the thyroid gland, resulting in increased TSH levels and clinical hypothyroidism. These clinical scenarios are extremely rare.[9–11]

It is not uncommon to find nodules in the thyroid of patients with Graves' disease, which is commonly associated with a hyperthyroid state. Nodules have been reported to occur in 10 to 15% of these patients.[8,9] In a recent study, it was noted that thyroid cancer occurs in 10% of these nodules; thus, a thorough work-up is mandatory in patients with a nodular gland and Graves' disease.

Thyroid autoantibodies (antithyroglobulin, [anti-Tg] and antithyroid peroxidase [anti-TPO]) should be measured in all patients presenting with thyroid abnormalities. They are frequently associated with thyroid nodules due to Hashimoto's disease, especially anti-TPO antibodies. Positive anti-Tg antibodies are seen in 12 to 23% of patients with thyroid cancer. Although anti-Tg antibody levels are not useful for the diagnosis of malignancy, their presence makes the interpretation of serum thyroglobulin as a marker for recurrent disease unreliable. Occasionally, patients with autoimmune thyroiditis, such as Hashimoto's disease, have no anti-TPO antibodies but do have anti-Tg antibodies. Therefore, both titers are indicated in the evaluation of patients with thyroid abnormalities.

Thyroid Scans

The iodine-123 (^{123}I) scan of the thyroid is nonspecific in terms of defining whether a nodule comprises thyroid cancer or benign thyroid tissue. Consequently, the scan is not considered a useful test in the work-up of thyroid nodules in the euthyroid patient. However, in patients who have hyperthyroidism, whether it is secondary to a multinodular goiter or a single nodule, a thyroid scan is still indicated. It is important to note that patients with a single toxic adenoma rarely have a malignant process in the thyroid. The incidence of malignancy in these cases is reported to be 4%, according to recent studies.[12,13] The precise incidence of thyroid malignancies in multinodular toxic goiter is not known. A thyroid scan does not provide any additional information in this situation.

Thyroid Ultrasonography

Thyroid ultrasonography has become a very valuable tool in the evaluation of the patient with thyroid nodules. Ultrasonography is a relatively inexpensive technique and has a high degree of accuracy in the identification and localization of nodules as small as 3 mm.

Ultrasonography of the thyroid has four definitive indications. They can be summarized as follows:

1. To differentiate between the presence of a thyroid nodule and a lymph node when there is a clinically suspect area in the cervical neck
2. To assist the clinician in performing a fine-needle aspiration biopsy (FNAB) of nonpalpable thyroid nodules or of a palpable nodule when past aspiration biopsy samples were judged insufficient for diagnosis
3. To screen for the presence of thyroid nodules in patients who have been exposed to radiation
4. To determine if there is recurrencein patients who were thyroidectomized for thyroid cancer

Tumor Markers

SERUM THYROGLOBULIN

Serum Tg is used in the evaluation and treatment of patients with well-differentiated thyroid cancer. Serum Tg rises in patients with recurrence of tumor or with development of metastatic disease. The test, however, is nonspecific, since serum Tg levels may also be elevated in other benign thyroid conditions. This test should only be used as a tumor marker in patients with firmly established differentiated cancers or undifferentiated thyroid cancer, *after* thyroidal surgery and radioablation have been performed, in order to monitor the disease course.[14]

Elevation of serum Tg levels after thyroidectomy is a concern as it points to the possibility of recurrent tumor growth. Generally, once serum Tg levels fall after thyroidectomy and stay low in follow-up evaluations, the patient is considered to be at low risk for recurrent disease. There are two caveats to this. The first is in the case of de-differentiated thyroid carcinoma (papillary or follicular carcinomas that have lost their differentiation) or in anaplastic thyroid cancer (a specific histologic type). In these cases, the tumor cells have often lost their ability to produce Tg despite the fact that they are still able to grow and metastasize. Serum Tg levels in these cases may be low and remain low despite increasing tumor bulk. The second caveat applies when evaluating Tg in the thyroidectomized thyroid cancer patients who have positive anti-Tg antibodies. In these patients, as mentioned earlier, the anti-Tg autoantibodies preclude the reliable interpretation of the Tg level, and it becomes useless in tracking the disease course.

SERUM THYROCALCITONIN

Serum thyrocalcitonin (TCT), also referred to as calcitonin, is frequently positive in patients with medullary carcinoma of the thyroid gland. This marker is elevated in patients with MEN IIA and IIB syndromes as well as in patients with familial medullary thyroid carcinoma.[15] In some of these patients, serum calcitonin levels are elevated only after the intravenous administration of pentagastrin or calcium infusion. Normal baseline serum calcitonin levels are not sufficient to exclude the presence of a medullary carcinoma. At the present time, familial screening for these tumors can be effectively done by using genetic screening for the RET–proto-oncogene mutations. Currently, 95% of the familial cases can be picked up by this technique.[16–18] Patients with a familial history of thyroid cancers should be referred to an endocrinologist for consideration of genetic testing.

Fine-Needle Aspiration Biopsy of the Thyroid Gland

FNAB of the thyroid has gained general acceptance in the diagnostic work-up of a thyroid nodule. The accuracy rate of the technique exceeds 90%.[19] The technique should be carried out by clinicians expert in the technique, often a trained endocrinologist or cytopathologist. It is the responsibility of the primary care clinician to decide which patients need referral for FNAB.

INDICATIONS FOR FNAB

1. All single nodules in a thyroid gland
2. All multinodular goiters, especially dominant nodules ≥ 1 cm
3. All lymph nodes or recurrent neck masses in patients who underwent thyroidectomy for a previous thyroid cancer
4. All dominant nodules ≥ 1 cm in the thyroid glands of patients with Graves' disease, Hashimoto's disease, or a history of radiation exposure
5. All nodular lesions whose initial biopsy results were considered insufficient for final diagnosis; these should be rebiopsied in 3 months under ultrasound guidance
6. Any nodules that have increased in size, regardless of past FNAB results

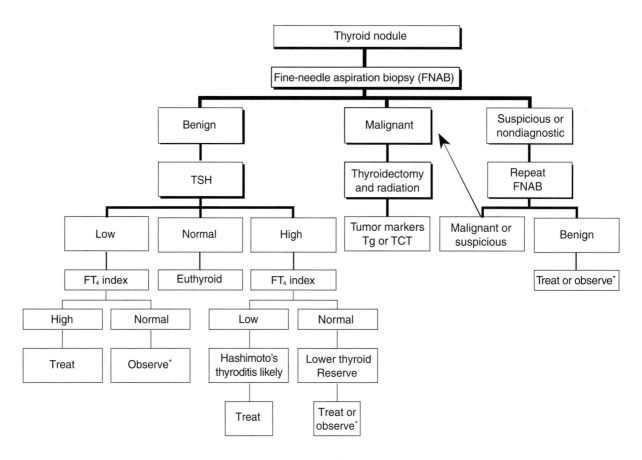

FIGURE 58–1. Approach to evaluation of the thyroid nodule. *See text for details.

LIMITATIONS OF FNAB

1. Biopsy of lesions < 1 cm in diameter is difficult without ultrasound guidance.
2. Biopsy of calcified lesions is difficult.
3. Findings of follicular neoplasm are difficult to evaluate. Approximately 20% are follicular carcinomas, and an FNAB does not allow the distinction between a benign follicular adenoma and a follicular carcinoma. Therefore, those with FNABs of the thyroid yielding a diagnosis of "follicular neoplasm" should be referred for surgery.
4. Substernal nodules or goiters cannot be reached via FNAB in most cases and require surgical biopsy for final evaluation.

Please refer to Figure 58–1 for an algorithm for the approach to the thyroid nodule.

TREATMENT OPTIONS

Thyroxine Suppression Therapy

In the past, patients with thyroid nodules often were treated with suppressive doses of thyroid hormone.

Previously, suppression therapy was promoted as effective in reducing nodule size and in differentiating benign from malignant nodules. However, the results were disappointing.[15] Only approximately 10% of patients responded to this therapy with a reduction in the size of the nodule, and some individuals with thyroid cancer also had a decrease in the size of their tumor. This approach cannot be used safely without first knowing the exact cytologic nature of the thyroid lesion. Furthermore, enthusiasm for T_4 suppression has diminished not only because of its low success rate but also because it requires a patient to be closely monitored via regular thyroid function testing to avoid over-repletion and the risks of osteoporosis and cardiac dysrhythmias.

Observation

If FNAB yields a diagnosis, such as Hashimotos's thyroiditis or a colloid goiter, the patient should be observed, and the thyroid function studies should be performed every 6 months. Treatment should only be initiated if abnormal thyroid function studies develop, signaling hyper- or hypothyroidism.

Observation of a thyroid nodule in a subject with a past history of radiation exposure should not be advocated, unless the lesion has been established by cytopathology to be unquestionably benign. Again, in these cases, as with any thyroid nodule, repeat FNAB is recommended if the patient develops any increase in size of the lesion or develops symptoms, such as pain, dysphagia, or hoarseness.

Surgical Therapy

Surgical therapy with total thyroidectomy is indicated in the following situations:

1. If a lesion is malignant or suspicious for malignancy as determined by FNAB
2. If recurrence of a malignancy is established and if the growing mass is amenable to surgery
3. If a patient's FNAB reveals the presence of a follicular neoplasm
4. If an FNAB of a lymph node in an established thyroid cancer indicates the presence of metastatic involvement
5. If a thyroid nodule or a nodular goiter is benign as established by FNAB, but the patient has symptoms of compression, manifested by swallowing difficulties, breathing problems or hoarseness
6. If a large goiter's appearance is cosmetically unacceptable

If a pregnant women is found to have a thyroid nodule and FNAB reveals a malignancy, surgery is recommended in the second trimester of pregnancy. Subsequent iodine-131 (^{131}I) treatment is *never* given during pregnancy and is usually deferred until well after the postpartum period, to allow the mother to breast-feed. During this period, the patient must be closely monitored clinically. If surgical, clinical, or pathologic evaluation reveals an aggressive carcinoma, ^{131}I treatment is undertaken as soon as possible after delivery, and the mother is then advised not to initiate breast-feeding.

CONCLUSION

The primary care clinician plays a critical role in the detection of thyroid nodules. A multidisciplinary approach is required to ensure early diagnosis and to treat thyroid conditions appropriately. The role of the primary care clinician is to guide the patient through the correct test combinations and then refer the patient in a timely fashion to the endocrinologist. Although it may appear that a large amount of health care dollars are spent on diagnosing and treating thyroid cancer, it is clear from every study that *early* diagnosis and treatment of differentiated thyroid cancer are associated with a normal life span. Thyroid cancer, as manifested by the focal thyroid nodule, is a curable disease if found early and treated aggressively from the onset.

REFERENCES

1. Vander JB, Gaston EA, Dawber TR. The significance of nontoxic thyroid nodules. Ann Intern Med 1968;69:537–40.
2. Tunbridge WMG, Evered DC, Hall R, et al. The spectrum of thyroid disease in a community: the Whickham survey. Clin Endocrinol (Oxf) 1977;7:481–93.
3. Mortensen JD, Woolner LB, Bennet WA. Gross and microscopic findings in clinically normal thyroid glands. J Clin Endocrinol Metab 1955;15:1270–80.
4. Rojeski MT, Gharib H. Nodular thyroid disease: evaluation and management. N Engl J Med 1985;313:428–36.
5. Van Herle AJ, Rich P, Ljung B-ME, et al. The thyroid nodule. Ann Intern Med 1982;96:221–32.
6. Nishiyama RH, Ludwig GK, Thompson NW. The prevalence of small papillary thyroid carcinoma in 100 consecutive necropsies in the American population. In: Degroot LJ, editor. Radiation-associated thyroid carcinoma. New York (NY): Grune and Straton; 1977. p. 123–35.
7. Blum M. Thyroid sonography, computer tomography, and magnetic resonance imaging. In: Becker KL, editor. Principles and practice of endocrinology and metabolism. Philadelphia (PA): JB Lippincott; 1995. p. 313.
8. Brander A, Viikinkoski P, Nickels J, Kivisaari L. Thyroid gland: US screening in a random adult population. Radiology 1991;181:683–7.
9. Dobyns BM, Sheline GE, Workman JB, et al. Malignant and benign neoplasms of the thyroid in patients treated for hyperthyroidism: a report of the cooperative thyrotoxicosis therapy follow-up study. J Clin Endocrinol Metab 1974;38:976–98.
10. Pacini F, DiCosci PC, Anelli S, et al. Thyroid carcinoma in thyrotoxicosis patients treated by surgery. J Endocrinol Invest 1988;11:107–12.

11. Carnell NE, Valente WA. Thyroid nodules in Graves' disease: classification, characterization and response to treatment. Thyroid 1998;8:571–6.

12. Ashcraft MW, Van Herle AJ. Management of thyroid nodule I: history and physical examination, blood tests, x-ray tests, and ultrasonography. Head Neck Surg 1981;3:216–30.

13. Ashcraft MW, Van Herle AJ. Management of thyroid nodule II: scanning techniques, thyroid suppressive therapy and fine-needle aspiration. Head Neck Surg 1981;3:297–322.

14. Van Herle AJ, Uller RP, Matthews NI, Brown J. Radio-immunoassay for measurement of thyroglobulin in human serum. J Clin Invest 1973;52:1320–7.

15. Melvin KEW, Tashjian AH Jr. The syndrome of excessive thyrocalcitonin produced by medullary carcinoma of the thyroid. Proc Natl Acad Sci USA 1968;59:1216.

16. Simpson NE, Kidd KK, Goodfellow PJ, et al. Assignment of multiple endocrine neoplasia type 2A to chromosome 10 by linkage. Nature 1988;328:527.

17. Mulligan LM, Kwok JBJ, Healey CS, et al. Germline mutations of the ret protooncogene in multiple endocrine neoplasia type 2A. Nature 1993;363:458–60.

18. Donis-Keller H, Dou S, Chi D, et al. Mutations in the ret protooncogene are associated with MEN2A and FMTC. Hum Mol Genet 1993;2:851.

19. Baloch ZW, Sack MJ, Yu GH, et al. Fine-needle aspiration of the thyroid: an institutional experience. Thyroid 1998;8:565–9.

59

HYPERPROLACTINEMIA

Jenell S. Coleman, MD, Marsha K. Guess, MD, Jeanie Rahimian, MD, and
Alan H. DeCherney, MD

Hyperprolactinemia is the most common endocrine disorder of the hypothalamic pituitary axis and is estimated to occur in approximately 0.4% of the general population.[1] The incidence of hyperprolactinemia is higher in women than in men, and in certain high-risk populations may approach 17%.[1] This chapter reviews the signs and symptoms that may be associated with hyperprolactinemia, the clinical evaluation necessary when hyperprolactinemia is suspected, the differential diagnosis, and the treatment options and prognosis of some of the more common causes of this disorder.

PHYSIOLOGY OF PROLACTIN

Prolactin is a peptide hormone that was first identified as a distinct hormone in the 1970s. Normal serum concentrations of prolactin range between 5 and 20 ng/mL. Values exceeding this are considered abnormal. Prolactin is synthesized and secreted by the lactotroph cells of the anterior pituitary gland and regulated at the level of the hypothalamus. Dopamine, which is secreted by the hypothalamus, travels to the pituitary via the hypophyseal portal system and binds dopaminic D_2 receptors on the surface of the lactotropes; this results in tonic inhibition of prolactin synthesis and secretion.[2,3] Physiologic and pathologic processes that decrease the supply of dopamine to the anterior pituitary relieve the inhibition of prolactin production and secretion by lactotropes, resulting in increased serum concentrations of prolactin.

In the basal state, prolactin is secreted in a pulsatile diurnal fashion as monomers, dimers, or polymers. Maximal prolactin release occurs during sleep.[4] The monomeric form, also known as "little" prolactin, is thought to represent more than 50% of secreted prolactin and exerts the greatest physiologic activity.[5] Any alterations in the relative concentrations of the different types of prolactin molecules or disruptions in the inhibition of prolactin may result in the pathologic condition of hyperprolactinemia.

SIGNS AND SYMPTOMS

When mild to moderate elevations in prolactin are present, clinical signs and symptoms may be subtle and may include infertility, luteal phase insufficiency, decreased libido, and possibly an increased rate of spontaneous abortions.[6] Galactorrhea is the most common symptom of hyperprolactinemia. However, in up to two-thirds of patients, hyperprolactinemia occurs in the absence of galactorrhea.[5] Hyperprolactinemia has been shown to produce mild hirsutism and acne. Several investigators have reported increased dehydroepiandrosterone sulfate levels in women with hyperprolactinemia, likely resulting from adrenal stimulation by excess prolactin.[7]

As the severity of hyperprolactinemia increases, evidence of hypogonadism typically ensues.[6] Although no clear cause of this hypogonadotropic condition has been elucidated, it is thought to result from direct suppression of pulsatile secretion of gonadotropin-releasing hormone by prolactin molecules.[8,9]

Oligomenorrhea or amenorrhea is reported in about 15% of women with hyperprolactinemia and is associated with osteopenia in up to 50% of cases.[10,11] About 9% of women presenting with adult-onset amenorrhea are found to be hyperprolactinemic.[12–14] In women presenting with both amenorrhea and galactorrhea, more than two-thirds are ultimately diagnosed with hyperprolactinemia.[6]

Less commonly, women may present with visual disturbances from optic nerve compression

---

TABLE 59–1. Causes of Hyperprolactinemia

Physiologic
   Anesthesia
   Idiopathic
   Intercourse
   Major surgery and disorders of chest wall
      (burns, herpes, chest percussion)
   Nipple stimulation
   Pregnancy
   Postpartum (non-nursing: days 1–7; nursing:
      with suckling)
   Sleep
   Stress

Pharmacologic
   α-Methyldopa
   Antidepressants
   Cimetidine
   Dopamine antagonists
   Estrogen therapy
   Narcotics
   Neuroleptics
   Reserpine
   Thyrotropin-releasing hormone administration
   Verapamil

Pathologic
   Hypothalamic
      Arachnoid cyst
      Craniopharyngioma
      Cystic glioma
      Dermoid cyst
      Epidermoid cyst
      Pineal tumors
      Pseudotumor cerebri
      Sarcoidosis
      Suprasellar cysts
      Tuberculosis
      Polycystic ovary syndrome

   Pituitary
      Acromegaly
      Addison's disease
      Cushing's syndrome
      Hypothyroidism
      Lymphoid hypophysitis
      Metastatic tumors
      Multiple endocrine neoplasia
      Pituitary adenoma
      Trauma to stalk
      Tuberculosis

   Metabolic
      Hepatic cirrhosis
      Renal failure

---

by microadenomas and macroadenomas of the pituitary. Prolactin levels in excess of 100 ng/mL are typically found in this setting. Frequently, other clinical signs precede this finding.

CLINICAL EVALUATION AND DIFFERENTIAL DIAGNOSIS

The initial evaluation of the patient in whom hyperprolactinemia is suspected should include a thorough history, a careful review of medications, and a physical examination. Elevated levels of prolactin are normal during pregnancy. Therefore, all women of reproductive age suspected of hyperprolactinemia should undergo a urine pregnancy test.

If the urine pregnancy test is negative, a prolactin level should then be drawn, midmorning, in a fasting state, and prior to any physical activity.[5] If the prolactin level is elevated, it should be confirmed using the same laboratory because there may be some variations between laboratories. When tested as outlined above, if the prolactin level is above normal on two separate occasions, the diagnosis of hyperprolactinemia can be made with confidence.

Causes of hyperprolactinemia are physiologic, pharmacologic, and pathologic (Table 59–1). Certain physiologic conditions may result in a transient elevation of prolactin levels. The diurnal release of prolactin results in increasing levels beginning with the onset of sleep and peaking in the early morning. There is also an increase from the early follicular phase of the menstrual cycle to the luteal phase. Additionally, stress, exercise, food intake, and repeated contact to the chest wall along the dermatome innervating the nipples (eg, herpes zoster or sexual activity) may result in physiologic increases in the serum prolactin level. One study determined that prolactin levels may be elevated for as long as 2 years post partum when lactation is prolonged, with resolution commonly correlating with the resumption of menses.[15] Performing the prolactin level test after fasting, midmorning, and before exercise eliminates many physiologic causes of elevation. The remainder usually can be accounted for by a careful history and physical examination.

Pharmacologic causes of hyperprolactinemia are often predictable and usually result from the ingestion of drugs that interfere with dopamine secretion or action. Examples include neuroleptics, which are dopamine receptor blockers,[16] selective serotonin reuptake inhibitors, dopamine antagonists, exogenous estrogens, and antihypertensive medications such as α-methyldopa,[17] reserpine,[18] and verapamil.[19] Correction of the hyperprolactinemia is usually prompt and complete with cessation of these drugs.

If hyperprolactinemia cannot be explained by physiologic or pharmacologic causes, a thyroid-stimulating hormone level should be obtained. Thyroid-releasing hormone (TRH) is a known stimulator of prolactin synthesis and secretion.[9] In the presence of primary hypothyroidism, TRH levels are increased, and this may result in hyperprolactinemia. When adequate therapy renders the patient euthyroid, prolactin values decrease to normal levels.

Mildly elevated prolactin levels may occur in up to 17% of women with polycystic ovary syndrome.[12–14] Renal failure is a rare cause of hyperprolactinemia. Studies of renal failure patients suggest that there is decreased renal clearance of prolactin and increased production of prolactin secondary to disordered hypothalamic regulation.[20] A serum creatinine level within the normal range excludes this diagnosis in patients without a known history of renal disease. If serum creatinine levels are high, a 24-hour urine evaluation of protein and creatinine clearance and a radiologic evaluation of the renal collecting system may be warranted.

The most common cause of hyperprolactinemia is a pituitary adenoma or hyperplasia. Approximately one-third of women with hyperprolactinemia have a pituitary adenoma, most of which are microadenomas measuring < 1 cm.[21,22]

Macroadenomas, which are masses > 1 cm, and other stalk lesions also may be present but are less common. Magnetic resonance imaging (MRI) is the diagnostic modality of choice.[23] Newer studies have confirmed the superiority of contrast-enhanced MRI over computed tomography for diagnosing pituitary masses. The sensitivity and specificity are both increased using MRI, with sensitivity approaching 90%.[21] Evaluation for panhypopituitarism by an endocrinologic expert is indicated when macroadenomas are identified. A thorough evaluation of visual fields when lesions are identified near the optic chiasm or when vision impairment is reported is recommended.[1]

When the etiology remains unclear or patients complain of neurologic symptoms, visual impairment, or headaches, a radiologic evaluation of the pituitary is indicated. Lesions that interfere with dopamine secretion from the hypothalamus or the hypophyseal portal system can lead to elevated prolactin levels via release of the tonic inhibition of lactotropes. Central nervous system abnormalities, such as lesions in the suprasellar region, infundibular stalk, adjacent bone, dura, cranial nerves, vessels, and nasopharynx, can potentially disrupt dopamine release.

The term idiopathic hyperprolactinemia implies an unknown etiology. Patients with this diagnosis are thought to have microadenomas too small to visualize by current imaging techniques or an altered hypothalamic regulation of prolactin secretion.[9]

TREATMENT

Indications for treatment of hyperprolactinemia should be based on symptoms and the underlying etiology. Physiologic etiologies generally result in transient increases in prolactin levels, and therapy is not warranted. Similarly, patients with hypothyroidism typically experience normalization in their prolactin level when a euthyroid state is achieved. Hence, thyroid replacement therapy is the only therapy required. Cessation of drugs commonly known to cause hyperprolactinemia corrects the level. In many instances, continuation of the drug may be more beneficial to the patient, particularly when symptoms of hyperprolactinemia are mild or absent. However, hyperprolactinemia can be associated with a progressive decrease in bone mass, particularly in women who are amenorrheic, so if drug treatment is continued, patients should be monitored for bone loss.[24,25]

In patients with idiopathic hyperprolactinemia, long-term follow-up has revealed that in about one-third of patients, prolactin levels return to normal; in 10 to 15%, there is a rise in prolactin levels to > 50% over the baseline, and in the remaining patients, prolactin levels remain stable.[26,27] During a 2- to 6-year follow-up of 199 patients, evidence of microadenomas developed in 23 patients. No macroadenomas were diagnosed in this group of patients.[21]

Patients with asymptomatic or minimally symptomatic microadenomas may be managed conservatively. The natural history of microadenomas has been evaluated in several series. Ninety to 95% of microadenomas remain stable without any form of treatment.[25] In many cases, serum prolactin levels spontaneously decrease. It is estimated that 7 to 10% of microadenomas progress to macroadenomas. Therapy is indicated in these cases.[21,28]

Patients with symptoms including galactorrhea, decreased libido, prolonged amenorrhea, evidence of osteopenia, and infertility, as well as those with macroadenomas, require therapy. Prolonged amenorrhea is particularly associated with progressively decreasing bone mass and the risk of osteoporosis.[24,25] Evidence suggests that treatment of hyperprolactinemia prevents bone loss.[24] Thin women may be at highest risk for progressive bone loss and should be monitored closely.[29]

Dopamine agonists are effective in decreasing prolactin levels in virtually all forms of hyperprolactinemia.[30] Prolactin concentrations generally normalize within days of exposure to therapeutic levels of dopamine agonists. Once a patient has been asymptomatic and has maintained a normal prolactin level for 2 years, tapering and discontinuation of therapy may be considered.[1] Most patients retain normal levels of prolactin after discontinuation of therapy.[31]

Dopamine agonist drugs used in the treatment of hyperprolactinemia in the United States include bromocriptine and cabergoline. Bromocriptine is a short-acting agonist, dosed once or twice daily. The medication is started at 1.25 mg daily for the first 3 days and slowly titrated to 2.5 mg two times daily. This helps minimize side effects, which can include nausea, dizziness, and headaches.[32] Patients who experience primarily gastrointestinal side effects may be able to tolerate bromocriptine treatment when administered vaginally.[33] A study in which women inserted a 2.5-mg tablet of bromocriptine intravaginally before bed (using a tampon to hold the tablet in place overnight during menses) demonstrated a prolonged effect of prolactin suppression with a single daily dose, a very low rate of gastrointestinal side effects, and no significant local complications.[34]

Cabergoline has a longer duration of action than bromocriptine. It is usually started at 0.25 mg weekly and increased in increments of 0.5 mg to a maximum of 2 mg twice weekly.[32] The results of comparative studies suggest that cabergoline is superior to bromocriptine in prolactin suppression, restoration of gonadal function, and tolerability.[30,35] Additionally, cabergoline has been used successfully in patients who were resistant to bromocriptine or who showed poor tolerance to bromocriptine.[36,37] Recent studies suggest that cabergoline can be considered the first-line agent in the medical treatment of microprolactinomas and macroprolactinomas. In this setting, cabergoline has been proven to induce tumor shrinkage, normalize prolactin levels, and improve clinical symptoms, including visual field abnormalities. These beneficial effects were associated with a very high compliance rate and minimal side effects.[35]

Up to 90% of premenopausal patients have return of ovulatory menses and fertility after starting therapy.[30,37] Since fertility may return prior to menses, a barrier method is recommended for contraception with the initiation of treatment or until menses becomes regular or pregnancy is desired. Bromocriptine is the treatment of choice in this setting of attempting pregnancy because it is the most widely studied.[38] Bromocriptine use in early pregnancy has been studied in numerous clinical trials. To date, no studies have convincingly shown this drug to be associated with an increased risk of congenital abnormalities, fetal wastage, or mental development when used in early pregnancy.[39–41] Generally, these medications are discontinued once pregnancy is confirmed unless worsening symptoms or significant tumor growth is noted. Recent studies suggest a similar safety profile for cabergoline.[39]

Dopamine agonists can be used to decrease both tumor size and serum prolactin levels in patients with macroadenomas. Most tumors decrease in size rapidly, within 1 to 3 months, with 30% of tumors shrinking by more than 50% in size.[37] As occurs with microprolactinomas, most premenopausal women regain cyclic menses. With shrinkage of tumor size, 90% of patients have improvement of abnormal visual fields. If visual field defects are not corrected within 3 months of initiation of medical therapy, surgical correction is recommended. When bromocriptine therapy is discontinued in patients with macroprolactinomas, prolactin levels often return to pretreatment concentrations, and tumors also may increase in size over a period of months or years.

Surgical correction involves trans-sphenoidal or transcranial resection and is appropriate treatment for prolactinomas in women who desire pregnancy, who are intolerant to the side effects of dopamine agonist drugs, or who have visual field defects unresponsive to medical treatment. Surgical decompression also is indicated in cases of tumors with cystic or hemorrhagic components or for relief of headaches. The procedure has low morbidity and mortality, and prolactin levels initially return to normal in 85 to 90% of patients with microadenomas and 25 to 80% of macroadenomas. Cure rates are highest in patients with prolactin levels lower than 200 ng/mL and smaller (< 2 cm) tumors.[42] Only a minority of patients with very high prolactin levels (> 500 ng/mL) are cured. Recurrences may occur years after surgery.[43]

Radiation therapy results in a slow decline in serum prolactin levels with normalization in approximately 30% of patients over 2 to 10 years after treatment. However, radiation therapy usually is regarded as salvage therapy given the high risk of panhypopituitarism.

SUMMARY

Hyperprolactinemia is a relatively common endocrinopathy in women that can present with subtle symptoms, including oligomenorrhea, acne, and hirsuitism. More classic symptoms include amenorrhea and galactorrhea. Diagnosis is based on careful measurement of serum prolactin levels. Physiologic factors, as well as hypothyroidism and certain drugs, can raise prolactin levels. Treatment of pathologic causes of hyperprolactinemia, including pituitary microadenoma and macroadenoma, is based primarily on the degree of symptomatology and whether the patient desires childbearing.

REFERENCES

1. Cosigning PG, Molitch M, Olive D, et al. Guidelines for the diagnosis and treatment of hyperprolactinemia. J Reprod Med 1999;44:1075–84.
2. Molitch ME. Medical treatment of prolactinomas. Endocrinol Metab Clin North Am 1999;28:143–69.
3. Ford SM, Peters JR, Dieguez C, et al. Dopamine receptors on intact anterior pituitary cells in culture: functional association with the inhibition of prolactin and thyrotropin. Endocrinology 1983;112:1567–77.
4. Katznelson L, Riskind PN, Saxe VC, Klibanski A. Prolactin pulsatile characteristics in postmenopausal women. J Clin Endocrinol Metab 1998;83:761–4.
5. Hershlag A, Peterson CM. Endocrine disorders. In: Berek JS, Adoshi EY, Hillard PA, edtiros. Novak's gynecology. 12th ed. Baltimore (MD): Williams & Wilkins; 1996. p. 833–86.
6. Luciano AA. Clinical presentation for hyperprolactinemia. J Reprod Med 1999;44:1085–90.
7. Glickman SP, Rosenfield RL, Bergenstal RM, Helke J. Multiple androgenic abnormalities, including elevated free testosterone, in hyperprolactinemic women. J Clin Endocrinol Metab 1982;55:251–7.
8. Cohen-Becker IR, Selmanoff M, Wise PM. Hyperprolactinemia alters the frequency and amplitude of pulsatile luteinizing hormone secretion in the ovariectomized rat. Neuroendocrinology 1986;42:328–33.
9. Molitch ME. Anterior pituitary. In: Goldman L, Bennett JC, editors. Cecil's textbook of medicine. 21st ed. Orlando (FL): WB Saunders; 2000.
10. Frank S, Murray MAF, Jequier AM, et al. Incidence and significance of hyperprolactinemia in women with amenorrhea. Clin Endocrinol 1975;4:597–607.
11. Biller BMK, Baum HB, Rosenthal DI, et al. Progressive trabecular osteopenia in women with hyperprolactinemic amenorrhea. J Clin Endocrinol Metab 1992;75:692–7.
12. Reindollar RH, Novak M, Thos SPT, et al. Adult-onset amenorrhea: a study of 262 patients. Am J Obstet Gynecol 1986;155:531–43.
13. Luciano AA, Chapler FK, Sherman BM. Hyperprolactinemia in polycystic ovary syndrome. Fertil Steril 1984;41:719–25.
14. Minakami H, Abe N, Oka N, et al. Prolactin release in polycystic ovarian syndrome. Endocrinol J 1988;

35:3031–41.

15. Delvoye P, Demaegd M, Uwayiitu-Nyampeta, Robyn C. Serum prolactin, gonadotropins, and estradiol in menstruation and amenorrheic mothers during two years' lactation. Am J Obstet Gynecol 1978;130:635–9.

16. Langer G, Sachar EJ. Dopaminergic factors in human prolactin regulation: effects of neuroleptics and dopamine. Psychoneuroendocrinology 1977;2:373–8.

17. Steiner J, Cassar J, Mashiter K, et al. Effect of methyldopa on prolactin and growth hormone. BMJ 1976; 1:1186–8.

18. Lee PA, Kelly MR, Wallin JD. Increased prolactin levels during reserpine treatment of hypertensive patients. JAMA 1976;235:2316–7.

19. Gluskin LE, Strasberg B, Shah JH. Verapamil-induced hyperprolactinemia and galactorrhea. Ann Intern Med 1981;95:66–7.

20. Hou SH, Grossman S, Molitch ME. Hyperprolactinemia in patients with renal insufficiency and chronic renal failure requiring hemodialysis or chronic ambulatory peritoneal dialysis. Am J Kidney Dis 1985;6:245–9.

21. Schlechte J, Dolan K, Sherman B, et al. The natural history of untreated hyperprolactinemia: a prospective analysis. J Clin Endocrinol Metab 1988;67: 124–30.

22. Sisan DA, Sheehan JP, Sheeler LR. The natural history of untreated microprolactinomas. Fertil Steril 1987; 48:67–71.

23. Naidich MJ, Russell EJ. Advances in pituitary tumor therapy: current approaches to imaging the sellar region and pituitary. Endocrinol Metab Clini 1999; 28(1):45–76.

24. Klibanski A, Greenspan SL. Increase in bone mass after treatment of hyperprolactinemic amenorrhea. N Engl J Med 1986;315:542–6.

25. Klibanski A, Biller BMK, Rosenthal DI, et al. Effects of prolactin and estrogen deficiency in amenorrheic bone loss. J Clin Endocrinol Metab 1988;67:124–30.

26. Martin TL, Kim M, Malarkey WB. The natural history of idiopathic hyperprolactinemia. J Clin Endocrinol Metab 1985;60:855–8.

27. Sluijmer AV, Lappohn RE. Clinical history and outcome of 59 patients with idiopathic hyperprolactinemia. Fertil Steril 1992;58:72–7.

28. Weiss MH. Natural history of microprolactinomas: six-year follow-up. Neurosurgery 1983;12:180–3.

29. Miller KK, Klibanski A. Amenorrheic bone loss. J Clin Endocrinol Metab 1999;84:1175–83.

30. Webster J. A comparison of cabergoline and bromocriptine in the treatment of hyperprolactinemic amenorrhea. Cabergoline Comparative Study Group. N Engl J Med 1994;6:904–9.

31. Ciccarelli E. Effectiveness and tolerability of long term treatment with cabergoline, a new long-lasting ergoline derivative, in hyperprolactinemic patients. J Clin Endocrinol Metab 1989;64:725–8.

32. Webster J. Dopamine agonist therapy in hyperprolactinemia. J Reprod Med 1999;44:1105–10.

33. Vermesh M, Fossum GT, Kletzky OA. Vaginal bromocriptine: pharmacology and effect on serum prolactin in normal women. Obstet Gynecol 1988; 72:693–8.

34. Kletzky OA, Vermesh M. Effectiveness of vaginal bromocriptine in treating women with hyperprolactinemia. Fertil Steril 1989;51:269–72.

35. Pontikides N, Krassas GE, Nikopoulou E, Kaltsas A. Cabergoline as a first-line treatment in newly diagnosed macroprolactinomas. Department of Endocrinology and Metabolism, Panagia Hospital, Thessaloniki, Greece. Pituitary 2000;2:277–81.

36. Delgrange E. Effects of dopamine agonist cabergoline in patients with prolactinoma intolerant or resistant to bromocriptine. Eur J Endocrinol 1996; 134:454–6.

37. Verhelst J, Abs R, Maiter D, et al. Cabergoline in the treatment of hyperprolactinemia: a study in 455 patients. J Clin Endocrinol Metab 1999;84:2518–22.

38. Molitch ME. Management of prolactinomas during pregnancy. J Reprod Med 1999;44:1121–6.

39. Robert E. Pregnancy outcome after treatment with the ergot derivative, cabergoline. Reprod Toxicol 1996;10:333–7.

40. Krupp P. Bromocriptine in pregnancy:safety aspects. Klin Wochenschr 1987;65:823–7.

41. Raymond JP. Follow-up children born of bromocriptine-treated mothers. Horm Res 1985;22: 239–46.

42. Aron DC, Tyrrell JB, Wilson CB. Pituitary tumors—current concepts in diagnosis and management. West J Med 1995;162:340–52.

43. Andrews DW. Pituitary adenomas. Curr Opin Oncol 1997;9:55–60.

60

APPROACH TO THE PATIENT WITH INSOMNIA

Frisca Yan-Go, MD, and Rosa Elena Garcia, MPH

Sleep and wakefulness are part of the human 24-hour circadian rhythm regulated by one's own internal biologic clock. Sleep is a recurrent reversible behavioral state of perceptual disengagement from and unresponsiveness to the environment. While asleep, the body undergoes a vast number of physiologic changes that affect every major system and include physiologic changes in the central nervous, respiratory, cardiovascular, and neuromuscular systems and the gastrointestinal tract. It has two separate and distinct states based on behavioral and physiologic characteristics: nonrapid eye movement (NREM) and rapid eye movement (REM). REM sleep is most often associated with vivid dreaming and a high level of brain activity. NREM sleep, which accounts for 75 to 80% of sleep time and is divided into four distinct states, is usually associated with reduced neuronal activity; thought content during this state in humans, unlike dreams, are typically nonvisual and consisting of ruminative thoughts.[1-3] Although the normal sleep needs of individuals can vary from 6 to over 9 hours, normal sleep needs average about 7.5 hours. Synchronization with one's own circadian rhythm and meeting one's sleep needs, in quantity and quality, are necessary for optimal functioning to maintain health and a sense of well-being. Excessive daytime sleepiness can occur when the quantity and quality of sleep are inadequate.

A disruption in sleep may have serious consequences on a woman's health and well-being, particularly if the problems persist and go without management. Insufficient sleep, primary sleep disorders, other medical, neurologic, psychological conditions, lifestyle factors, medications (prescribed and over-the-counter), and substance abuse (eg, caffeine and nicotine) can cause excessive daytime sleepiness.[4-6] Poor or disordered sleep can affect an individual's work, concentration, and ability to interact with others and can have serious health consequences for the individual and others. Sleep problems can lead to or exacerbate other serious medical, neurologic, and psychiatric disorders; contribute to impaired academic or occupational performance;[7-10] result in accidents at work or while driving;[11-13] cause or exacerbate disturbances of mood and social adjustment; and bring about decreased marital satisfaction.

Among women, some of the factors that may contribute to altered sleep patterns include the menstrual cycle,[14] pregnancy,[15,16] menopausal status, and contraceptive/hormonal use. The bloating, tender breasts, headaches, and cramps experienced by some women before and during menses can disrupt sleep and lead to trouble falling asleep, nocturnal awakenings, and feeling less refreshed on awakening. Pregnant women also experience insomnia,[17] which is usually associated with weight gain, physiologic changes occurring during pregnancy, low back pain,[18] and leg cramps.[19] Women with preeclampsia experience increased amounts of wakefulness and periodic movements in sleep.[20] Sleep apnea[21,22] and restless legs syndrome (RLS) may increase during the third trimester, contributing to insomnia and excessive daytime somnolence (EDS).[23] These symptoms continue into the first 3 months post partum.[17,24] Menopause can also cause negative changes in sleep patterns.[25] Since about one-third of women are menopausal and about 40% of menopausal women in the general population suffer from sleep problems, the clinician should inquire of peri- and

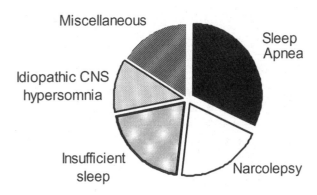

FIGURE 60–1. Causes of excessive daytime sleepiness (EDS) are multifactorial. Many primary sleep conditions can contribute to EDS as well other medical, neurologic, psychiatric conditions and environmental factors and drug and substance use. CNS = central nervous system.

postmenopausal women if they have any sleep complaints and find out if they are on hormone replacement therapy. Many women report that hot flashes during sleep, increased night waking, and increased nocturia affect their daytime functioning.

Although sleep is essential for normal functioning, more than 100 million Americans of all ages regularly fail to get a good night's sleep.[26] Approximately 84 disorders of sleeping and waking result in diminished quality of life and personal health and endanger public safety through their contribution to traffic and industrial accidents. These disorders include those leading to problems falling asleep and staying asleep, difficulties staying awake or adhering to a consistent sleep/wake cycle, sleepwalking, nightmares, and other problems that interfere with sleep. Some sleep disorders are potentially fatal. As noted in Figure 60–1, various sleep conditions can cause EDS. In the general population, the most common causes of EDS are due to insufficient sleep, insomnia, sleep apnea, restless legs syndrome and periodic limb movement disorder (RLS/PLMD), and narcolepsy. Other causes of EDS include drug effects, including withdrawal, and psychiatric and neurologic conditions.

In this chapter, we provide information on the general epidemiology, evaluation and differential diagnosis, and treatment for insomnia and also briefly highlight some information about sleep apnea, RLS and PLMD, and narcolepsy.

GENERAL EVALUATION OF VARIOUS SLEEP CONDITIONS

Female patients with sleep complaints usually have one or more of three types of problems that may not be mutually exclusive: (1) insomnia, (2) EDS, and (3) abnormal movements or behaviors or sensations during sleep or during nocturnal awakenings. However, many women with other health concerns may not complain to their primary care clinicians about their sleep concerns and only focus on their other health problems. The clinician has an important role in identifying sleep problems and providing diagnosis, treatment, and referral for sleep conditions.

Clinical Interview

Accurate identification of all causes of a patient's sleep complaints is crucial for effective diagnosis and treatment. An assessment usually begins with a thorough review of the patient's sleep condition, which can be obtained via the clinical interview in the office or by using a sleep questionnaire or log that includes questions on the following components and which can be answered by the patient herself and supplemented by the spouse or partner:

- **Sleep history** should include information on the patient's age, her psychosocial situation, occupational or academic status, marital status and living arrangements, and information on sleep habits. This should include information during the entire 24 hours, not just at sleep onset or during sleep at night, which includes bedtime, sleep onset, awakenings, particular behaviors noted during sleep, such as kicking or twitching, pauses in breathing, and snoring.[27]
- **Onset, frequency, duration, and severity of the sleep complaint;** its progression, evolution, and fluctuation over time; and any events that could have initiated it. In addition, it is important to ask about a woman's sleep patterns during various points of the menstrual cycle (if premenopausal); use of birth control or hormone replacement therapy and pregnancy status.
- **Medical diseases.** The degree of sleep disturbance usually varies with the severity of an underlying illness. Medical conditions that can cause insomnia include cardiovascular, pulmonary, gastrointestinal, renal, rheumatic, and allergic disorders.

Neurologic conditions that may lead to insomnia include toxic metabolic disorders, trauma, tremor, infection, epilepsy, peripheral neuropathies, degenerative-demyelinating diseases, muscle diseases, and movement disorders.

- **Possible psychiatric or psychophysiologic factors** should be considered, since treating these conditions can alleviate sleep problems. If a psychological/psychiatric condition is suspected, depression screening may be performed.

- **Drug use.** Particular attention should be paid to drugs (both prescribed and over-the-counter) that could cause insomnia and/or sleepiness as well as withdrawal-induced insomnia. Intake of caffeine, alcohol, and cigarettes as well as natural food supplements should be noted as well.[5,6]

Sleep Laboratory Testing

Sleep laboratory testing is indicated when such conditions as sleep apnea, RLS/PLMD, or narcolepsy are suspected. These conditions are discussed in detail below. Specialized tests, such as the polysomnogram (PSG) and multiple sleep latency test (MSLT), can be conducted, which allow the clinician to confirm the diagnosis and determine the severity of the sleep condition. **Polysomnography** (PSG) is an invaluable test for the diagnosis and treatment of sleep disorders.[28,29] The polysomnograph measures various physiologic parameters using such tests as the electroencephalography (EEG), electro-oculography (EOG), electromyography (EMG), electrocardiography (ECG). The following are also recorded: nasal and buccal air flow, chest and abdominal movements, and oximetry. These recordings allow the sleep specialist to determine the sleep stages, sleep efficiency, and latency periods and note any abnormalities found during the study. The **MSLT** is a test that documents the latency of sleep onset and the appearance of REM episodes, within a standardized sleep-conducive setting, repeated at 2-hour intervals throughout the day.[30] The MSLT uses standard sleep-recording methods to document both the latency of sleep onset and the appearance of REM episodes at sleep onset and is essential for documenting pathologic sleepiness and diagnosing narcolepsy. In many laboratories, a routine drug screen may be performed during the MSLT.

DIFFERENTIAL DIAGNOSIS AND MANAGEMENT

Insomnia

Insomnia, which is not a specific illness or disease, but rather a symptom of more specific disorders, is defined by the 4th edition of the *Diagnostic and Statistical Manual of Mental Disorders* (DSM-IV)[31] as the "presence of difficulty initiating sleep, difficulty maintaining sleep—be it in the form of disrupted sleep or early morning awakenings—or nonrestorative sleep lasting at least 1 month, occurring at least three times a week, and causing either distress or daytime consequences."

PREVALENCE

Insomnia is the most prevalent sleep-related complaint; approximately 30% of American adults report occasional insomnia, and nearly 10 to 20% report chronic insomnia.[32–36] Women, the elderly, and individuals with poor education and socioeconomic status, recent stress, and alcohol or drug abuse are more likely to have insomnia.[37–40] Although it is a very common complaint, < 5% of those with sleep problems seek professional help.

CAUSES

Potential factors that may affect the development of insomnia are (1) **predisposing factors**, such as a woman's basic sleep-wake cycle, her circadian rhythm, personality, coping mechanisms, and age; (2) **precipitating factors**, which can exacerbate a sleep problem include medical and/or neurologic conditions, use of prescription and nonprescription drugs, psychological, psychiatric, situational, and environmental factors, menstrual cycle, pregnancy, menopausal status, and hormonal/contraceptive use; and (3) **perpetuating factors**, which can include conditioning and maladaptive behaviors, poor sleep hygiene, performance anxiety, and substance abuse—all of which affect a woman's quality and quantity of sleep and ultimately can impact her health and sense of well-being.[41]

DIAGNOSIS

Insomnia is a sleep complaint, not a specific disorder, resulting from multiple causes. The differential diagnosis of insomnia must focus on the factors that may contribute to insomnia as well as on the duration and timing of this condition. A clinician needs to note the duration of the insomnia, whether it is *transient* (lasting only a few days, usually due to acute stress or change in one's environment); *short term* (has a duration of up to 4 weeks and is often precipitated by more severe situational changes), or *chronic* (has duration of more than 4 weeks and precipitating factors include physical or emotional illness, use of medications, abuse of drugs and/or chemicals like alcohol, caffeine, and cigarettes). Treatment should be tailored on the basis of the cause and duration of insomnia.

MANAGEMENT

Insomnia is complex and multidetermined and often requires both specific and general interventions for adequate treatment.[42,43] Within the context of treatment, the clinician must take a holistic approach to the problem and help the patient with stress management, improving coping skills, and establishing more satisfactory interpersonal relationships. The goals of treatment should be to (1) resolve underlying problems, (2) prevent progression of insomnia from transient to chronic, and (3) improve the quality of life. The choice of treatment is based on the type and the duration of the insomnia and the underlying causal factors. Transient and intermittent insomnia may not require treatment, since episodes last only a few days at a time. Treatment approaches can include treating the underlying disorder, nonpharmacologic approaches, and pharmacologic intervention (when appropriate). Studies have shown that behavioral and drug treatments alone or in combination, can reduce symptoms of insomnia. A specific description of treatment approaches that can be used for insomnia (and other sleep conditions) are described below. Referral to a sleep specialist should be considered if a primary sleep condition, such as sleep apnea or periodic limb movement disorder, is suspected.

Behavioral/cognitive/lifestyle changes. Often, it is appropriate for the primary care clinician to provide counseling on simple lifestyle changes patients can make in their activities to increase their sleep. Table 60–1 includes a list of things to help patients deal with the habits, practices, or conditions that may be contributing to sleep problems. The clinician can also help the patient with sleep management skills and improved coping skills. Nonpharmacologic

---

TABLE 60–1. Healthy Sleep Tips for Patients with Sleep Problems

The following guidelines can be useful in alleviating all types of sleep disorders and will help most people sleep well:

- Get up about the same time every day.
- Go to bed only when sleepy.
- Establish relaxing presleep rituals, such as a warm bath, light bedtime snack, or 10 minutes of reading.
- Exercise regularly. Confine vigorous exercise to early hours, at least 6 hours before bedtime, and do mild exercise, such as stretching or walking, at least 4 hours prior to bedtime.
- Keep a regular schedule. Regular times for meals, medication, chores, and other activities help keep the inner clock running smoothly. Plan regular hours of sleep time: have a regular time to go to bed and to get up each day, even on weekends.
- Avoid the use of caffeine within 6 hours of bedtime. Avoid alcohol in the evening. Although alcohol causes sleepiness, it disrupts sleep later, often causing early morning awakenings. Avoid stimulants and drugs that disturb sleep: caffeine and nicotine are prime culprits as are some cold remedies and over-the-counter diet aids.
- Avoid smoking close to bedtime.
- Try to nap at the same time every day; midafternoon is the best time for most people.
- Avoid sleeping pills, or use them conservatively. Most doctors avoid prescribing sleeping pills for periods longer than 3 weeks. Do not drink alcohol while taking sleeping pills.
- Use the bedroom for sleeping and sex only.
- There should be no reminders of work or stresses at bedtime.
  If you cannot fall asleep, don't lie in bed awake, but get up and go to another room.
  Do something boring until you feel sleepy, then go back to bed. If you still cannot get to sleep, get up again.
- Don't go to bed hungry or immediately after eating a large meal. A light snack or glass of warm milk before bedtime may be appropriate.
- Minimize light, noise, and extremes in temperature.

management of insomnia can also include cognitive and behavior therapies, including such techniques as guided imagery, meditation, breathing exercises, and other relaxation techniques (eg, yoga). These can help patients reduce the amount of hyperarousal and anxiety that may contribute to their insomnia.

Pharmacologic management. Pharmacologic management, although not a cure, does provide symptomatic relief. As shown in Table 60–2, the pharmacologic properties of hypnotics must be considered in choosing an agent, and the use of short-acting agents are usually preferred in order to minimize daytime "hangover." Patients should be counseled to avoid chronic daily use of hypnotics as much as possible to prevent tolerance and dependence. Medications should be reviewed and proper adjustments made to dosages and times of intake, with consideration given to effects, side effects, and drug interactions. The benzodiazepine and imidazopyridine sedative-hypnotics have been shown to be rapidly and reliably effective for insomnia over the course of short-term use. These medications should not be used during pregnancy because of their potential teratogenic effects. In breast-feeding women, the potential risks and benefits of pharmacologic therapy should be carefully weighed.

Combination strategy. A dual approach combining early pharmacologic therapy with behavioral strategies can also be used. Hypnotic agents can provide relief from wakefulness while behavioral strategies are being learned and/or implemented. For short-term insomnia, drug therapy can be used, using the lowest dose and for not more than 4 weeks, along with sleep hygiene and coping skills management. For patients with chronic insomnia, the mainstay of treatment is to identify the underlying conditions and to pursue treatment using nonpharmacologic strategies. Medication is to be used as a "rescue," given only intermittently, at most two to three times a week. Medication dependence and hypnotic rebound sleeplessness should be prevented.

Sleep Apnea

Sleep apnea is a serious potentially life-threatening condition, characterized by repetitive episodes of upper airway obstruction that occur during sleep, which are associated with sleep disruption and

---

TABLE 60–2. Pharmacologic Management of Patients with Insomnia

General guidelines for pharmacologic management:

- Pharmacologic management is not a cure but provides symptomatic relief only (40% of patients self-medicate with alcohol or over-the-counter medication like antihistamines, which are all minimally effective and can further decrease quality of life and affect daytime performance).
- Pharmacologic properties of hypnotics must be considered in choosing an agent.
- Short-acting agents are usually preferred in order to minimize daytime "hangover."
- Avoid chronic daily use of hypnotics as much as possible to prevent tolerance and dependence.

Pharmacologic agents that can be used:
- Imidazopyridine
- Benzodiazepines
  Zolpidem (*Ambien*)
  Temazepam (*Restoril*)
  Triazolam (*Halcion*)
- Sedating antidepressants
  Tricyclics (eg, amitriptyline)
  Trazadone
- Chloralhydrates
- Melatonin
- Over-the-counter antihistamines

---

oxygen desaturations during the night and result in chronic daytime sleepiness or fatigue. There is usually a history of snoring. There are two types of sleep apnea: central and obstructive. Central sleep apnea, which is less common, occurs when the brain fails to send the appropriate signals to the breathing muscles to initiate respiration during sleep. Obstructive sleep apnea (OSA), which is far more common, occurs when air cannot flow into or out of the person's nose or mouth although efforts to breathe continue.

PREVALENCE
Sleep apnea is found in approximately 4% of middle-aged men and 2% of middle-aged women.[33] Sleep apnea occurs in all age groups and is more common in men, obese individuals, and older people.[44–46] Recent studies, however, indicate that obstructive

sleep apnea is much more prevalent in women than previously recognized and is underdiagnosed.[47–51]

PATHOPHYSIOLOGY

The pathophysiology of upper airway occlusion during sleep has been elucidated. The size of the pharyngeal upper airway is dependent on the balance of forces between the upper airway dilator, which maintains upper airway patency, and the negative pharyngeal intraluminal pressure created during thoracic expansion as a result of inspiration. Certain mechanical and structural problems, such as craniofacial abnormalities, high arched hard palate, long soft palate placement and redundant tissue, and a moderately retroplaced mandible in the airway, cause interruption in breathing during sleep, leading to apnea.[52]

SYMPTOMS AND SIGNS

Symptoms of obstructive sleep apnea include chronic loud snoring, gasping or choking episodes during sleep, excessive daytime sleepiness, drowsiness while driving, automobile- or work-related accidents, and personality changes or cognitive difficulties. These factors should be assessed if the clinician suspects that a patient may have OSA. The severity of symptoms dictates the urgency of the need for referral or testing.

Clinicians should specifically elicit whether the patient or partner has noted the patient gasping or choking during sleep. Other associated symptoms may include waking up with nocturnal esophageal acid reflux and heartburn, bruxism, and a history of seasonal allergies. Cognitive complaints may include poor memory and difficulties concentrating or making decisions, and personality changes, such as irritability, anxiety, aggression, or depression. Hypertension, angina, symptoms of right heart failure, peripheral edema, and transient ischemic symptoms should also be assessed, since they may be related to OSA.

PHYSICAL EXAMINATION

Indicators of OSA are obesity, a thick neck, systemic hypertension, and nasopharyngeal narrowing. The physical examination should include the patient's height and weight to determine the patient's body mass index. Examination of the neck and throat should include evaluation of the lateral facial profile and the temporomandibular joint to determine dental occlusion and whether jaw misalignment exists. The oral cavity should be inspected for dental prostheses, the size of the tongue, soft palate tissue size and appearance, and the shape of the hard palate. The nose should be assessed for septal deviation, polyps, flaring of the nostrils, and patency of either vestibule with the opposite nares occluded. The thyroid should be examined for evidence of enlargement. Evidence of upper airway obstruction is obtained by evaluating breathing with the patient in the supine position, with the jaw slackened slightly open and nares occluded, to simulate oral breathing during sleep. If snoring or labored breathing results, this is good evidence that even greater difficulties occur during sleep.

DIFFERENTIAL DIAGNOSIS

Obstructive sleep apnea lies along a continuum of sleep-disordered breathing, ranging from pure snoring without daytime sleepiness, to upper airway resistance syndrome, through progressive degrees of obstructive apnea based on respiratory disturbance index (RDI—average number of respiratory disturbances per hour of sleep) and oxyhemoglobin desaturations. The upper airway resistance syndrome (UARS) may be present without associated snoring and is associated with daytime sleepiness or fatigue.[53] Sleep apnea is definitively diagnosed by a sleep study, or nocturnal polysomnogram (NPSG). In some laboratories, "split night protocols" are performed. Under this method, patients are first diagnosed, and then treatment is evaluated the same night. This method tends to underestimate the severity of disease because treatment occurs in the latter half of the night when apnea is usually at its worst. Treatment is tailored to the type and severity of the patient's OSA on the basis of clinical history, sleep complaints, and results of polysomnography.

MANAGEMENT

Once OSA is diagnosed, specific therapy for sleep apnea should be tailored to the individual patient on the basis of her medical history, physical examination, and results of polysomnography. Treatment can include one of the interventions below.

Lifestyle changes. Lifestyle changes may help reduce or eliminate sleep apnea among some individuals, particularly if sleep apnea is mild. Because obesity is associated with many cases of sleep apnea, exercise and weight loss are usually recommended to the patient. For the morbidly obese patient, surgical interventions for weight loss may be recommended. Improvements in sleep hygiene (see Table 60–1) are recommended along with the use of sleep position training, in which individuals can use wedge pillows or other devices to help them sleep on their sides rather than on their backs.

Physical or mechanical interventions. Positive airway pressure machines, which keep the respiratory tract open while a patient sleeps, and oral/dental appliances can be very effective in treating sleep apnea, but patient concerns and consideration need to be addressed, since they may affect compliance. Various machines and masks are available, allowing each person to find the combination of equipment that works best. Most patients first try machines that deliver continuous positive airway pressure (CPAP); some prefer bilevel positive airway pressure (BIPAP) machines. Properly set and used whenever the patient sleeps, these machines can eliminate sleep apnea and snoring in many patients. The pressure settings should be determined by an overnight titration study in a sleep laboratory, to ensure that the settings are appropriate in all sleep positions. Patient tolerance is one key factor that needs to be considered with this treatment option, since patients often have a hard time getting used to these machines and some patients develop nasal and mouth discomfort; sore, dry, or red eyes; and other discomforts that reduce compliance. The use of nasal sprays and humidifiers can help diminish these side effects and increase the use of the machines. Oral appliances that hold the tongue or jaw forward and increase the airway space behind the tongue, tongue-retaining devices, and jaw-advancement devices are other mechanical interventions used in the patient with mild to moderate OSA.

Surgical interventions. Surgical options may be considered, if the patient has obvious airway obstruction or if more conservative treatments have not worked. Surgical options for treating sleep apnea include nasal operations, laser-assisted uvulopalatoplasty (LAUP), uvulopalatopharyngoplasty (UPPP), inferior sagittal mandibular osteotomy (ISO) and geniohyoid advancement with hyoid myotomy (GAHM), maxillomandibular advancement (MMO), and tra-

cheostomy. Referral to specialists must be made to determine if surgical options should be considered and, if so, what surgical option would be best for the patient, given her symptoms, the severity of her condition, and determination of risks and side effects.

Restless Legs Syndrome and Periodic Limb Movement Disorder

RLS and PLMD are two intrinsic disorders in which leg symptoms lead to difficulties with sleep initiation and may disrupt sleep.[54]

SYMPTOMS AND SIGNS

Most people with RLS have PLMD, but patients with PLMD do not always have RLS. RLS is characterized by "creepy, crawly, pulling, and tingling" sensations that occur in the lower extremities usually prior to sleep onset or during sedentary activities in the daytime and cause an almost irresistible urge to move.[55–57] This results in difficulty falling asleep or getting back to sleep after nocturnal awakenings. In severe cases, patients frequently have nights when sleep is delayed for several hours because of their symptoms, and many may also have difficulty maintaining sleep. Usually, patients complain of daytime fatigue and excessive daytime somnolence. Patients with PLMD have periodic episodes of repetitive stereotypical movements of the lower limb, characterized by rhythmic extension of the big toe, together with an upward bending of the ankle, knee, or hip. The movements usually do not occur continuously during the night but, instead, cluster in the first half of the night. These movements, which many individuals with PLMD may not be aware of, can lead to excessive insomnia or daytime sleepiness and can disrupt the partner's or spouse's sleep patterns as well. These leg movements are often associated with partial or complete awakening, although patients are usually unaware of either their movements or the arousals.

CAUSES

There are no clear causes for the development of RLS/PLMD, but a familial history has been noted in approximately 30% of cases.[58] In addition, although PLMD may occur as an isolated condition, it may also be associated with a large number of other medical (eg, iron or vitamin deficiency, uremia, rheumatoid arthritis, diabetes), neurologic (peripheral neuropathy), or sleep disorders or with medications and other pharmacologic agents. Other factors that can trigger RLS are excessive consumption of caffeine, smoking, fatigue, a very warm environment, or prolonged exposure to cold temperatures. Pregnancy is a known precipitant of RLS/PLMD; symptoms usually first appear later in the pregnancy and then subsequently remit, only to reappear in a more chronic form in later years. Because RLS is associated with pregnancy and perhaps with other hormonally changing states in women (eg, the menstrual cycle, surgical menopause), some studies have suggested that there may be some hormonal influence on RLS.

Pathophysiology

Researchers have hypothesized that abnormal excitability within the central nervous system, increased reflexes or damaged peripheral nerves, and abnormalities of the cerebral structure or blood flow may lead to RLS/PLMD, although studies have not been consistent. Others have found that either condition was associated with bilateral cerebellar activation and thalamic activation contralateral to the affected leg.[59] Finally, other studies have found a possible connection among dopaminergic and opioid, circadian, and activity-dependent physiologic changes in the pathogenesis of RLS and PLMD.

Diagnosis

The diagnosis of RLS can often be made on the basis of the patient's description of her symptoms and a review of her clinical history. A diagnosis of PLMD, however, requires additional extensive evaluation for proper diagnosis, since patients are often unaware of their night-time movements and may instead complain only of excessive daytime sleepiness or restless sleep. Nocturnal polysomnography can diagnose RLS in this situation.

Management

Because effective therapies are multiple and only recently developed, there is no fixed consensus on appropriate treatment. In mild cases of RLS, lifestyle changes and such activities as taking a hot bath, massaging the legs, using a heating pad or ice pack, exercising, and eliminating caffeine intake can help alleviate symptoms. In more severe cases, drugs are prescribed to control symptoms. Unfortunately, no one drug is effective for everyone with RLS. Patients respond differently to medications, depending on

the severity of symptoms, other medical conditions, and other drugs being taken. A drug that is initially found to be effective may lose its effectiveness with nightly use; thus, it may be necessary to alternate between different categories of drugs in order to keep symptoms under control.

Patients with PLMD should be treated when their movements seem to be the sole or a clearly major cause of their sleep disruption that is related to significant subjective complaints. Patients with RLS and PLMD should be treated pharmacologically when their symptoms are bothersome and cannot be managed by lifestyle changes. Since RLS tends to get worse as pregnancy proceeds, it may be possible to avoid medication until the last trimester, when it should do the least harm. Iron levels should be measured in all women and corrected, if at all low, since this too can lead to RLS.

Treatment choices for RLS and PLMD can be broken down into several categories. **Ancillary treatments**, which include lifestyle changes and other behavioral changes, are often used as the principal treatment for more stoic patients or patients with mild symptoms and are usually the first choice of treatment before going to pharmacologic treatment for other patients as well. **Primary treatment** is used to reduce patients' subjective complaints, as well as their objective findings. Primary treatment is with three classes of medication whose effectiveness in RLS has been established: dopaminergic agents (eg, carbidopa, levodopa, pergolide, pramipexol [Mirapex]), opioids (eg, propoxyphene), and benzodiazepines (eg, clonazepam). **Secondary treatment** is considered when primary treatments fail to control symptoms and includes the use of drugs whose efficacy is not well established or whose usefulness is restricted or more modest. The most promising of the secondary therapies are currently anticonvulsants, such as gabapentin (Neurontin).

Narcolepsy

Narcolepsy is a disorder of unknown etiology, characterized by excessive sleepiness that typically is associated with cataplexy and other REM sleep phenomena, such as sleep paralysis and hypnagogic hallucinations. The sleep episodes of narcolepsy are sometimes brought on by highly stressful situations and are not completely relieved by any amount of sleep. Although narcolepsy is a fairly uncommon condition, its impact on a person's life can be serious and, if not recognized and appropriately managed, can become a disabling condition.

PREVALENCE

Narcolepsy is not a rare condition. Its prevalence was calculated as 0.05% in the San Francisco bay area[60] and 0.067% in the Los Angeles area.[61] Approximately 200,000 Americans suffer from narcolepsy, yet fewer than 50,000 are diagnosed correctly. It can affect men and women of any age, with onset peaking between 15 and 25 years of age.[62,63] Special circumstances, such as an abrupt change of sleep-wake schedule or a severe psychological stress, precede the occurrence of the first symptom in half the cases. There is strong evidence that narcolepsy may run in families, since 8 to 12% of people with narcolepsy have a close relative with the disease. In addition, the risk of narcolepsy in first-degree relatives is 6 to 18 times that of unrelated individuals.

SIGNS, SYMPTOMS, AND ETIOLOGY

The four most common symptoms of narcolepsy include excessive daytime somnolence, cataplexy (sudden loss of muscle strength usually brought about by intense emotions), sleep paralysis, and hypnagogic hallucinations (hallucinations that occur just before falling asleep, during naps, and/or on waking up).[54] The symptoms of narcolepsy can appear all at once or can develop gradually over many years. Although the exact cause is not known, narcolepsy appears to be a disorder of the part of the central nervous system that controls sleep and wakefulness. Cataplexy and sleep paralysis are similar to the loss of muscle tone that accompanies normal dreaming during REM stage, although in narcoleptics these events occur at inappropriate times.

DIFFERENTIAL DIAGNOSIS

The first step in the diagnosis of narcolepsy should include evaluation (noted above) by the clinician to rule out any underlying medical/neurologic condition that may be contributing to the patient's EDS, cataplexy, and hallucinations. A definitive diagnosis of narcolepsy usually requires objective testing using NPSG as well as an MSLT the following day and evaluation by a sleep specialist. Human leukocyte antigen (HLA) tissue typing is sometimes done, although it should not be solely used for the definitive diagnosis of narcolepsy. The major conditions in the differential diagnosis of narcolepsy are idiopathic hypersomnia and other symptoms that present as EDS with one or more sleep-onset REM periods. The presence or history of both EDS and cataplexy are required for the unequivocal diagnosis of narcolepsy, although some patients may not have cataplexy. Idiopathic hypersomnia should be considered as a possible diagnosis only when a thorough evaluation has been completed.

MANAGEMENT

Although there is no cure for narcolepsy, treatment options include pharmacologic, behavioral, and supportive therapies, which help control the narcoleptic symptoms and allow the patient to continue full participation in familial and professional daily activities. Treatment should be individualized on the basis of the severity of the symptoms, and it may take weeks or months for an optimal regimen to be worked out. Pharmacologic treatments have focused on decreasing excessive daytime somnolence by using stimulants (eg, amphetamine and methylphenidate) and also on alleviating auxiliary effects with the use of tricyclic antidepressants (eg, imipramine, desipramine). More recently, modafinil (Provigil) has been recognized as the first specific drug for narcolepsy.[64] Clinicians prescribing drugs for narcolepsy must take into account all possible side effects, keeping in mind the fact that narcolepsy is a lifelong illness and patients will have to receive medication for years. Tolerance or addiction may be seen with some compounds. In addition, hypertension, abnormal liver function, and psychosis are the most commonly reported complications associated with long-term prescriptions of stimulant medications. Treatment of narcolepsy should take into account avoidance of secondary side effects, avoidance of tolerance, and maintenance of an active life. All these drugs are contraindicated during pregnancy and should be carefully evaluated for use in lactating women.

An important adjunct to pharmacologic treatment is scheduling short daytime naps (10 to 15 minutes) two to three times per day to help control excessive daytime sleepiness and help the person stay as alert as possible. In addition, counseling of patients with narcolepsy and their families is essential. For their own safety and that of their co-workers and communities, patients with narcolepsy should be counseled to avoid jobs that require driving long distances, handling hazardous equipment, and maximal alertness for lengthy periods.

Narcolepsy is a disabling disorder, leading, in many instances, to loss of gainful employment because of daytime sleepiness. It is often ill understood by patients, family members, and peers. It can result in rejection from family and other social groups, in divorce, loss of self-esteem, and depressive reactions. For these reasons, it is important that narcolepsy patients be put in contact with support groups, as they can help patients and their families cope with the physical and psychological burdens of this lifelong condition. Most importantly, patients with narcolepsy should be reassured that with appropriate medical care, they can lead active productive satisfying lives.

CONCLUSION

Sleep problems are very common in the general population. They can have a tremendous impact on an individual's health and well-being and have tremendous social and public health implications as well. Many women who experience sleep problems do not bring them to the attention of their health care clinicians. Sleep problems, however, are correctable, when recognized. The primary care clinician is in an ideal position not only to identify signs and symptoms of sleep disorders among patients who seek help for sleep problems but also to help identify them among patients who may present for other medical, neurologic, psychiatric conditions that affect the circadian rhythm and sleep. It is most effective to use a holistic approach, including recommending lifestyle changes, instructing on coping behaviors, providing pharmacologic treatment, when necessary, and providing referral to sleep specialists for more detailed evaluation, if clinically indicated. This will not only help the patients improve their sleep condition but may improve other areas of their life, which may ultimately help patients lead active productive satisfying lives.

RESOURCES

American Sleep Apnea Association
2025 Pennsylvania Avenue Northwest, Suite 905
Washington, DC 20006
Telephone: (202) 293-3650
Web site: asaa.nicom.com

The ASAA is a nonprofit organization that promotes awareness of sleep apnea in order to reduce injury, disability, and death from this common, but treatable, disorder. The ASAA serves as an advocate for people affected by sleep apnea, sponsors the ASAA A.W.A.K.E. Network for support groups, and publishes an educational newsletter.

Narcolepsy Network
PO Box 42460
Cincinnati, Ohio 45242
Telephone: (513) 891-3522
Web site: www.websciences.org/narnet

The Narcolepsy Network is a national nonprofit patient-based organization, whose members are people who have narcolepsy (or related sleep disorders), their families and friends, and professionals involved in treatment, research, and public education.

RESOURCES (continued)

National Center on Sleep Disorders Research
Two Rockledge Centre, Suite 7024
6701 Rockledge Drive, MSC 7920
Bethesda, Maryland 20892-7920
Telephone: (301) 435-0199
Web site: www.nhlbi.nih.gov.about/ncsdr

The National Center on Sleep Disorders Research is located in the National Heart, Lung, and Blood Institute of the National Institutes of Health. It supports research, scientist training, dissemination of health information, and other activities on sleep disorders and related concerns. The NCSDR also coordinates sleep research activities with other federal agencies and with public and nonprofit organizations.

NHLBI Information Center
PO Box 30105
Bethesda, Maryland 20824-0105
Telephone: (301) 251-1222
Web site: www.nhlbi.nih.gov

This center acquires, analyzes, promotes, maintains, and disseminates programmatic and educational information related to sleep disorders and sleep-disordered breathing. A list of publications is available.

National Sleep Foundation
1367 Connecticut Avenue Northwest, Suite 200
Washington, DC 20030
Telephone: (202) 785 2300
Web site: www.sleepfoundation.org

The NSF is a national nonprofit organization dedicated to improving the lives of the millions of Americans who suffer from sleep disorders and to the prevention of catastrophic accidents caused by sleep deprivation, sleep disorders, and disturbed sleep.

Restless Legs Syndrome Foundation, Inc.
819 Second Street Southwest
Rochester, Minnesota 55902
Telephone: (507) 287-6465
Web site: www.rls.org

The Restless Legs Syndrome Foundation, Inc., is a nonprofit organization dedicated to achieving universal awareness, developing effective treatments, and finding a definite cure for restless legs syndrome.

REFERENCES

1. Rechtschaffen A, Kales A. A manual of standardized terminology, techniques, and scoring systems for sleep stages of human subjects. Los Angeles (CA): UCLA Brain Information Service/Brain Research Institute; 1968.

2. William RL, Agnew HW Jr, Webb WB. Sleep patterns in young adults: an EEG study. Electroencephalogr Clin Neurophysiol 1964;17:376–81.

3. Williams RL, Karacan I, Hursch CJ. Electro-encephalography (EEG) of human sleep: clinical

applications. New York (NY): John Wiley and Sons; 1974.

4. Nicholson AN, Bradley CM, Pascoe PA. Medications: effect on sleep and wakefulness. In: Kryger MH, Roth T, Dement WC, editors. Principles and practice of sleep medicine. 2nd ed. Philadelphia (PA): WB Saunders; 1994. p. 364–71.

5. Stradling JR. Recreational drugs and sleep. In: Shapiro CM, editor. ABC of sleep disorders. London (UK): BMJ Publishing; 1993. p. 74–6.

6. Phillips BA, Danner FJ. Cigarette smoking and sleep disturbance. Arch Intern Med 1995;155:734–7.

7. Lee KA. Self-reported sleep disturbances in employed women. Sleep 1992;15:493–8.

8. Lee KA, DeJoseph JF. Sleep disturbances, vitality and fatigue among a select group of employed childbearing women. Birth 1992;19:208–13.

9. Rotenberg VS. Sleep and memory. I: The influence of different sleep stages on memory. Neurosci Biobehav Rev 1992;16:497–502.

10. Dinges DF. An overview of sleepiness and accidents. J Sleep Res 1995;4 Suppl 2:4–14.

11. Pack AI, Pack AM, Rodgman E, et al. Characteristics of crashes attributed to the driver having fallen asleep. Accident Ana Prev 1995;27:769–75.

12. Findley L, Unverzagt M, Guchu R, et al. Vigilance and automobile accidents in patients with sleep apnea or narcolepsy. Chest 1995;108:619–24.

13. Wu H, Yan-Go. Self-reported automobile accidents involving patients with obstructive sleep apnea. Neurology 1996;46:1254–7.

14. Chuong CJ, Kim SR, Taskin O, et al. Sleep pattern changes in menstrual cycles of women with premenstrual syndrome: a preliminary study. Am J Obstet Gynecol 1997;177:554–8.

15. Nishihara K, Horiushi S. Changes in sleep patterns of young women from late pregnancy to postpartum: relationships of their infants' movements. Percept Motor Skills 1998;8 (3 Pt 1):1043–56.

16. Sugihara K, Kobayashi T. Sleep behavior of pregnant women using sleep log. Psychiatr Clin Neurosci 1998;52:201–2.

17. Driver HS, Shapiro CM. A longitudinal study of sleep stages in young women during pregnancy and post partum. Sleep 1992;15:449–53.

18. Fast A, Shapiro D, Ducommun EJ, et al. Low back pain in pregnancy. Spine 1987;12:368–71.

19. Hertz G, Fast A, Feinsilver SH, et al. Sleep in normal late pregnancy. Sleep 1992;15:246–51.

20. Ekholm E, Polo O, Sjoholm T, et al. Body movements during sleep in normal and preeclamptic pregnancies. Sleep Res 1991;20A:419.

21. Hastie Sj, Prowse K, Perks WH, et al. Obstructive sleep apnea during pregnancy requiring tracheostomy. Aust NZ J Obstet Gynaecol 1989;29(Pt 2):365–7.

22. Kowall J, Clark G, Nino-Murcia G, et al. Precipitation of obstructive sleep apnea during pregnancy. Obstet Gynecol 1989;74(Pt 2):453–5.

23. Charbonneau M, Falcone T, Cosio MG, et al. Obstructive sleep apnea during pregnancy. Therapy and implications for fetal health. Am Rev Respir Dis 1991;144:461–3.

24. Swain AM, O'Hara MW, Starr KR, et al. A prospective study of sleep, mood, and cognitive function in postpartum and nonpartum women. Obstet Gynecol 1997;90:381–6.

25. Bliwise NG. Factors related to sleep quality in healthy elderly women. Psychol Aging 1992;7(1);83–8.

26. National Commission on Sleep Disorders. Wake up America. Washington (DC): U.S. Government Printing Office; 1993.

27. Kales A, Soldatos CR, Kales JD. Taking a sleep history. Am Fam Phys 1980;22(2):101–7.

28. American Sleep Disorders Association, Standards of Practice Committee. Indications for Polysomnography Task Force. Practive parameters for the indication for polysomnography and related procedures. Sleep 1997;20:406–22.

29. Standards of Practice Committee of the American Sleep Disorders Association. Practice parameters for the use of polysomnography in the evaluation of insomnia. Sleep 1995;18:55–7.

30. Carskadon MA, Dement WC, Mitler M, et al. Guidelines for the multiple sleep latency test (MSLT): a standard measure of sleepiness. Sleep 1986;9:519–24.

31. American Psychiatric Association. Diagnostic and Statistical Manual of Mental Disorders. 4th ed. Washington (DC): American Psychiatric Association; 1994.

32. Costa e Silva JA, Chase M, Sartorius N, et al. Special report from a symposium held by the World Health Organization and the World Federation of Sleep Research Societies: an overview of insomnias and related disorders—recognition, epidemiology, and rational management. Sleep 1996;19:412–6.

33. Young T, Palta M, Dempsey J, et al. The occurrence of sleep-disordered breathing among middle-aged adults. N Engl J Med 1993;328:1230–5.

34. Ford DE, Kamerow DB. Epidemiological study of sleep disturbances and psychiatric disorders. An opportunity for prevention? JAMA 1989;262:1479–84.

35. Bixler EO, Kales A, Soldatos CR, et al. Prevalence of sleep disorders in the Los Angeles metropolitan area. Am J Psychiatry 1979;136:1257–62.

36. Ohayon MM, Caulet M, Guilleminault C. Complaints about nocturnal sleep: how a general population perceives its sleep, and how this relates to the complaint of insomnia. Sleep 1997;20:715–23.

37. Radecki SE, Brunton SA. Management of insomnia in office-based practice. National prevalence and therapeutic patterns. Arch Fam Med 1993;2:1129–34.

38. Weyerer S, Dilling H. Prevalence and treatment of insomnia in the community: results from the Upper Bavarian Field Study. Sleep 1991;14:392–8.

39. Gallup Organization. Sleepiness in America: a national survey of U.S. adults. National Sleep Foundation; 1995.

40. Ohayon M. Epidemiological study on insomnia in the general population. Sleep 1996;19 Suppl 3:S7–15.

41. Buysse DJ, Reynolds CF III. Insomnia In: Thorpy MJ, editor. Handbook of sleep disorders. New York (NY): Marcel Dekker Inc.; 1990. p. 375–433.

42. Gilin J, Byedey WF. The diagnosis and management of insomnia. N Engl J Med 1990,322:239–48.

43. Kupfer DJ, Reynolds CF III. Management of insomnia. N Engl J Med 1997;36:341–6.

44. Leech JA, Onal E, Dulberg C, et al. A comparison of men and women with occlusive sleep apnea syndrome. Chest 1988;94(5):983–8.

45. Fletcher EC, DeBehnke RD, Lovoi MS, et al. Undiagnosed sleep apnea in patients with essential hypertension. Ann Intern Med 1985;103:190–5.

46. Block AJ, Boysen PG, Wynne JW, et al Sleep apnea, hypopnea, and oxygen desaturation in normal subjects: a strong male predominance. N Engl J Med 1979;300:513.

47. Ambrogetti A, Olson LG, Saunders NA. Differences in the symptoms of men and women with obstructive sleep apnea. Aust NZ J Med 1991;21(6):863–6.

48. Young T, Evans L, Finn L, et al. Estimation of the clinically diagnosed proportion of sleep apnea syndrome in middle-aged men and women. Sleep 1997; 20:705–6.

49. Young T, Hutton R, Finn L, et al. The gender bias in sleep apnea diagnosis. Are women missed because they have different symptoms? Arch Intern Med 1996;156:2445–51.

50. Halvorson DJ, Porubsky ES. Obstructive sleep apnea in women. Otolaryngol Head Neck Surg 1998; 119:497–501.

51. Guilleminault C, Quera-Salva MA, Partinen M, et al. Women and the obstructive sleep apnea. Chest 1988; 93:104–9.

52. Kribbs NB, Pack AI, Kline LR, et al. Effects of one night without nasal CPAP treatment on sleep and sleepiness in patients with obstructive sleep apnea. Am Rev Resp Dis 1993;147:1162–8.

53. Guilleminault C, Kim YD, Stoohs R. Upper airway resistance syndrome. Oral Maxillofacial Clin North Am 1995;7:243–7.

54. American Sleep Disorders Association, Diagnostic Classification Steering Committee, MJ Thorpy, Chairperson. The International Classification of Sleep Disorders: Diagnostic and Coding Manual. Rochester (MN): American Sleep Disorders Association; 1990.

55. Aldrich MS. Cardinal manifestation of sleep disorders. In: Kryger M, Roth T, Dement W, editors. Principles and practice of sleep medicine. 2nd ed. New York: W.B. Saunders Co.; 1994. p. 418–25.

56. Hening WA, Allen R, Walters AS, et al. Motor functions and dysfunctions of sleep. In: S Chokroverty editor Sleep disorders medicine: basic science, technical considerations and clinical aspects. 2nd ed. Boston (MA): Butterworth-Heinemann; 1999. p. 441–507.

57. Krueger BR. Restless legs syndrome and periodic movements of sleep. Mayo Clin Proc 1990;65:999–1006.

58. Silber MH. Restless legs syndrome. Mayo Clin Proc 1997;72:261–4.

59. Bucher SF, Seelos KC, Oertel WH, et al. Cerebral generators involved in the pathogenesis of the restless leg syndrome. Ann Neurol 1997;41:639–45.

60. Dement WC, Zarcone V, Varner V, et al. The prevalence of narcolepsy. Sleep Res 1972;1:148.

61. Dement WC, Carskadon MA, Ley R. The prevalence of narcolepsy. Sleep Res 1973;2:147.

62. Robinson A, Guilleminault C. Narcolepsy. S. Chokroverty, editor. Sleep disorders medicine: basic science, technical considerations and clinical aspects. 2nd ed. Boston (MA): Buttenworth-Heinemann; 1999. p. 427–39.

63. Choo KL, Guilleminault C. Narcolepsy and idiopathic hypersomnolence. Clin Chest Med 1998;19:169–81.

64. Broughton RJ, Flemin JA, George CF, et al. Randomized, double-blind, placebo-controlled crossover trial of modafinil in the treatment of excessive daytime sleepiness in narcolepsy. Neurology 1997;49:444–51.

61

DEPRESSION AND DYSTHYMIA

Natalia Rasgon, MD, PhD, and Co T. Truong, BS

DEPRESSION

Major depressive disorder (MDD) is the most common psychiatric diagnosis in primary care. The Diagnostic and Statistical Manual for Psychiatric Disorders[1] characterizes depressive disorders as mood changes of protracted periods of low mood which return to normal functioning. The criteria for MDD (unipolar depression) is at least 2 weeks of depressed mood or loss of interest in addition to other symptoms of depression. Analysis of 83 studies conducted between 1975 and 1990 showed that the prevalence of MDD ranges from 5 to 10% of primary care patients and that up to three times as many patients have some depressive disorder.[2] The lifetime prevalence of depression is 21% in women, compared with 12% in men. Women are less likely to commit suicide, but twice as likely to make a suicide attempt.[3] Caucasian women are twice as likely to commit suicide as African American women.[4]

Dysthymic disorder (chronic depression) is characterized by at least 2 years of depressed mood for most of the day, more days than not, and does not meet the full diagnostic criteria of a major depressive episode. The lifetime prevalence rate for dysthymia is 8% in women and 4.8% in men.

Bipolar disorder is characterized by alternating periods of depression and mania with normal mood. A manic episode is a period where there is an unusually expansive or irritable mood, lasting at least a week and causing impairment in daily functioning.[1] Bipolar I disorder is characterized by one or more manic episodes, whereas bipolar II disorder is characterized by hypomanic episodes, which are not as severe as to cause marked impairment in functioning. The lifetime prevalence rate for bipolar disorder is 1.0% in women and 0.8% in men,

indicating no gender difference for bipolar disorder. However, women tend to experience more depressive episodes, whereas men experience more manic episodes.[5] Dysphoric mania is also more common in women.[6] Women have a greater likelihood than men to be rapid cyclers.[6,7] A possible explanation is that because women experience depression more than men do, they are also more likely to take antidepressants, which may precipitate rapid cycling.[8] Women are more likely to develop lithium-induced hypothyroidism, which has been implicated in rapid cycling. Women with bipolar disorder are also at greater risk for postpartum affective episodes.[9] Some studies have shown an increased vulnerability to bipolar disorder in menopausal women.[10] Thus, the treatment of bipolar disorder is a formidable task. Such patients should be referred to a psychiatrist.

A recent study reported by the National Depressive and Manic-Depressed Association estimated the annual cost of depression to be approximately $43 billion, which includes cost of work absenteeism and reduced productive capacity. Bipolar disorder, dysthymia, and MDD are estimated to account for more than 85% of this cost.[11] However, these figures underestimate the true cost of these illnesses because they do not take into account the effects of reduced quality of life of the depressed individual or the out-of-pocket expenses for their families. Early recognition and adequate treatment are estimated to reduce the cost of the illnesses by more than $4 billion.[11]

Gender differences in unipolar depression and dysthymia may be due to both psychosocial and biologic factors. Although depressive disorders have strong familial predisposition, genetic factors do not appear to significantly contribute to the female preponderance in this illness.[12]

The *psychosocial hypothesis* suggests that sex-role stresses may play a role in the higher prevalence of depression in women.[13,14] Disadvantaged social status, lower wages, and pressure to balance family and career have led to increased vulnerability to depression for women.[15] In addition, sexual and domestic violence has also contributed to higher rates of depression in women.[16] Girls being taught to be dependent and internalize stress at an early age may also account for the high prevalence of depression in women.[17]

The *biologic hypothesis* identifies a hormonal basis for the female preponderance in the prevalence of MDD. Throughout their lifetime, women undergo hormonal changes from the start of puberty to the time of menopause. The fluctuation of hormones is implicated in premenstrual dysphoric disorder, postpartum depression, and possibly the increase in the vulnerability to depression present throughout a woman's lifetime.[18]

Further, many studies have shown that estrogen may enhance serotonin function, a neurotransmitter implicated in the pathophysiology of depression, consequently influencing mood positively. Also, estrogen has been shown to decrease monoamine oxidase (MAO) activity.[19,20] The role of female reproductive hormones on mood is also supported by gender differences in rates of depression first arising during puberty.[9] Depression is twice as prevalent in females, compared with males, starting at puberty and throughout the reproductive life span. In postmenopausal women, higher estradiol levels have also been associated with higher mood scores.[21]

DIAGNOSIS AND INITIAL ASSESSMENT

Symptom Inventory

Depression is not one symptom but a combination of mood disturbances, physical disturbances and cognitive disturbances, for the duration of at least 2 weeks. Overall, men and women are similar in the presentation and course of depression. However, women tend to have more severe depression. Also, subtle pattern differences, such as younger age, increased psychomotor retardation, and increased anxiety and somatization are observed in women. Higher substance abuse rates are observed in men.

The differential diagnosis of primary mood disorders is presented in Figure 61–1.

DSM-IV Diagnostic Criteria for MDD

At least one of the following abnormal moods, *which significantly interfere with a person's life*, must be present for a diagnosis of MDD:

- Depressed mood, present most of the day, nearly every day for ≥ 2 weeks
- Anhedonia (loss of pleasure and interest in most activities), present most of the day, nearly every day for ≥ 2 weeks

In addition, four of the following symptoms should be present during the same 2-week depression period:

- Abnormal weight loss (without dieting or other identifiable cause)
- Sleep disturbance, for example, abnormal insomnia or hypersomnia
- Abnormal fatigue or loss of energy
- Abnormal self-reproach or inappropriate guilt
- Activity disturbance, that is, either abnormal agitation or slowing
- Abnormally poor concentration or indecisiveness
- Abnormally morbid thoughts of death or suicide

Symptoms of depression represent a change from previous functioning and cause clinically significant distress or impairment in social/occupational or other important areas of functioning. Symptoms are not due to bereavement, a medical condition, medication, or effects of substance abuse. In addition, these symptoms should not meet the criteria for a mixed episode (ie, there should not be symptoms of mania).

A careful review of prior episodes of depression, including any depression relating to premenstrual episodes, oral contraceptive usage, and symptoms related to pregnancy must first be taken into consideration when assessing a female patient. Also, psychosocial stressors and past and current drug and alcohol usage should be explored. A complete history and physical examination should be performed to evaluate concomitant medical conditions. In particular, hypothyroidism should be ruled out as the cause of the depression episode.

The suicidality of the patient should be assessed by inquiring about future plans, current mood, and suicidal thoughts. Suicidal patients require emergent

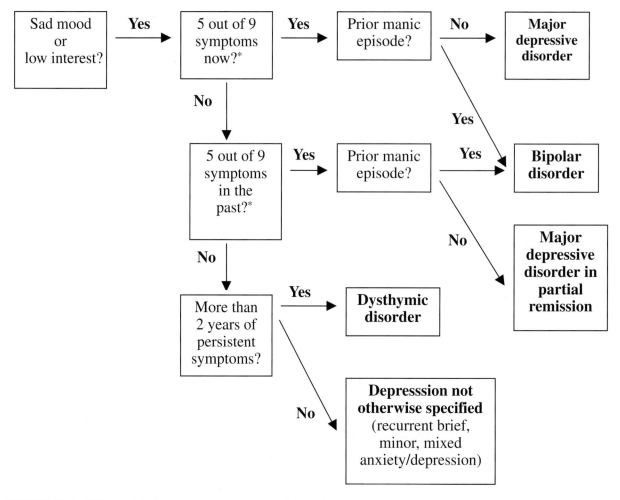

FIGURE 61–1. Differential diagnosis of primary mood disorders.

*1. Depressed mood	6. Fatigue
2. Markedly diminished interest or pleasure	7. Feelings of worthlessness/guilt
3. Significant weight loss/gain	8. Impaired concentration/indecisiveness
4. Insomnia/hypersomnia	9. Recurrent thoughts of death or suicide
5. Psychomotor agitation/retardation	

Adapted from Depression in primary care. Rockville (MD): Agency for Health care Policy and Research; April 1993. Publication No.: 93-0550.

psychiatric consultation to determine the need for hospitalization. A history of mania or hypomania should prompt a consultation with a psychiatrist prior to prescribing antidepressant treatment, as inducement of mania or hypomania can be caused by the antidepressants.

DYSTHYMIA

The DSM-IV categorizes dysthymic disorder as having fewer symptoms than MDD and persisting for at least 2 years.[1] Dysthymia usually begins early in life, and in more than 90% of these patients,

major depressive episodes occur, resulting in "double depression." The disorder is classified into four subtypes: early onset (before age 21 years), late onset (after age 21 years), and primary or secondary (presence or absence of other nonaffective disorders). Significantly more physical and sexual abuse and poorer relationships with parents are reported by patients with early onset dysthymia than nondepressed patients.[22]

DSM-IV Criteria for Diagnosing Dysthymia

• Depressed mood for most days

- Presence of at least two of the following:
    Poor appetite or overeating
    Insomnia or hypersomnia
    Low energy or fatigue
    Low self-esteem
    Poor concentration, indecisiveness
    Feelings of hopelessness
- Symptoms present during 2-year period without a 2-month remission
- No major depressive episode during first 2 years of disturbance
- No history of manic episode
- Does not occur only during a chronic psychotic disorder (eg, schizophrenia)
- Not due to substance abuse, medication, or general medical condition

OUTPATIENT TREATMENT OF DEPRESSION BY THE PRIMARY CARE CLINICIAN

Once MDD is diagnosed, interventions to decrease symptoms and morbidity are important. The key initial objectives of treatment, in order of priority, are

1. to reduce and, ultimately, remove all signs and symptoms of the depressive syndrome (acute treatment);
2. to restore occupational and psychosocial function to that of the asymptomatic state; and
3. to reduce the likelihood of relapse (continuation treatment) and recurrence (maintenance treatment).

Initial treatments can include pharmacotherapy and psychotherapy, either alone or in combination (Table 61–1). Many clinicians choose to begin therapy with selective serotonin reuptake inhibitors (SSRIs) due to their effectiveness and good safety profile. The choice of an SSRI is first made by assessing the side effect profile.

The typical treatment for a young healthy woman suffering from mild to moderate depression is prescribing the standard dosage of an SSRI and assessing the patient at 6 weeks. If the patient opts for nonpharmacologic treatment, cognitive-behavioral therapy (CBT) has been shown to have similar effectiveness to antidepressants.[23] Patients should be referred to a therapist trained in CBT for 15 to 20 sessions. Combinations of SSRIs and CBT produce the best results.

Consultation with a psychiatrist should occur if an initial medication trial by the primary care clinician is ineffective. Other options for treatment include light therapy. Hospitalization may be required in severe cases. Electroconvulsive therapy (ECT) can be effective when other treatments fail.

The possibility of pregnancy in women of the reproductive age must be taken into consideration when providing pharmacologic treatment. Prescribing an antidepressant that is safe during pregnancy will preclude the need to change medication following conception.[24] In particular, monoamine oxidase inhibitors (MAOIs) should be avoided during pregnancy due to their teratogenicity. Lithium, carbamazepine, and valproate are often prescribed by psychiatrists for mania. These also have been shown to be teratogens and should be avoided during pregnancy.[25]

Women are more at risk for eating disorders than are men. Patients with anorexia or bulimia are at higher risk for seizures because of electrolyte imbalances. Therefore, drugs reducing the seizure threshold (bupropion, clomipramine, maprotiline) should be avoided in these patients.[24] Women also tend to be less responsive to tricyclic antidepressants than men.[25]

A recommended protocol for assessment, continuation, and maintenance of pharmacotherapy for depression is presented in Figure 61–2. Response to antidepressant therapy should be assessed after 6 to 8 weeks. If the patient is clearly better, treatment should be continued and reassessed in 6 weeks. If the patient is somewhat better, treatment should be continued and dosage adjustment considered. If the patient has not improved, the dosage should be adjusted, or the treatment changed. For the first 12 weeks, patients should be monitored every 1 to 2 weeks until they are clearly better. If after 12 weeks, significant symptoms persist, referral to a psychiatrist should be considered. Once the patient is in complete remission, treatment should be continued for 4 to 9 months.

REASONS FOR CONSULTATION AND REFERRAL

Psychiatric consultation should be considered when the diagnosis or appropriate treatment is unclear, when comorbid conditions raise medication dilemmas or when the patient is not responding to medication or is noncompliant.

TABLE 61–1. Medication Recommendations for Depression/Dysthymia

Tricyclic Antidepressants (TCAs)	*Average Dosage (mg/d)*
Tertiary amine tricyclic drugs	
Amitriptyline (Elavil, Endep, Amitril)	75–300
Doxepin (Sinequan, Adapin)	75–300
Imipramine (Tofranil, Janimine, SK-Pramine)	75–300
Trimipramine (Surmontil)	75–300
Secondary amine tricyclic drugs	
Desipramine (Norpramin, Pertrofrane)	100–300
Nortriptyline (Aventyl, Pamelor)	25–150
Protriptyline (Vivactil)	15–60
Serotonin selective reuptake inhibitors (SSRIs)	
Fluoxetine (Prozac)	20–80
Paroxetine (Paxil)	20–50
Sertraline (Zoloft)	50–200
Citalopram (Celexa)	20–60
Atypical antidepressants	
Amoxapine (Asedin)	200–300
Bupropion (Wellbutrin)	200–300
Mirtazapine (Remeron)	15–45
Maprotiline (Ludiomil)	25–225
Nefazodone (Serzone)	100–600
Trazodone (Desyrel)	150–600
Venlafaxine (Effexor)	75–375

Adapted from Kaplan HI, Sadock BJ. Comprehensive textbook of psychiatry. 6th ed. Baltimore (MD): Williams & Wilkins; 1995. p. 1146, 2055, 2060–1, 2104, 2109.

Patients should be referred for care by a psychiatrist if they show signs of bipolar disorder, suicidal ideation, or psychosis, which is usually manifested by hallucinations and delusions. Patients with suicidal ideation or active psychosis should receive emergent psychiatric evaluation. Patients with severe functional impairment or who respond to medication but have residual significant psychosocial problems should also be referred.

PROGNOSIS

The efficacy rates of acute antidepressant treatment is 50 to 75% in reducing symptom severity by at least half. Analysis of randomized controlled trials of pharmacologic treatments of MDD in patients who achieve adequate initial treatment exposure show response rates of 65 to 70%.[26,27] These findings support the importance of adherence to antidepressant regimens in achieving initial treatment response. Higher response rates can be achieved in patients with a partial response to an initial antidepressant by switching to another medication or augmenting the existing treatment agent.

The risk of relapse is reduced from 40 to 60% to 10 to 20% by continuing treatment.[26] The primary reason for unsuccessful therapy is noncompliance. Untreated episodes of depression can last from 6 to 24 months.

PREVENTION AND SCREENING

Early recognition of depression is crucial in managing the disorder quickly and appropriately. It is important to monitor patients with subthreshold depressive symptoms in order to detect a potential emerging MDD. A greater likelihood of recurrence is associated with the length of the initial depressive episode.[27]

In terms of preventative measures, stress-reducing techniques may be useful in alleviating areas of a patient's life that are creating distress.

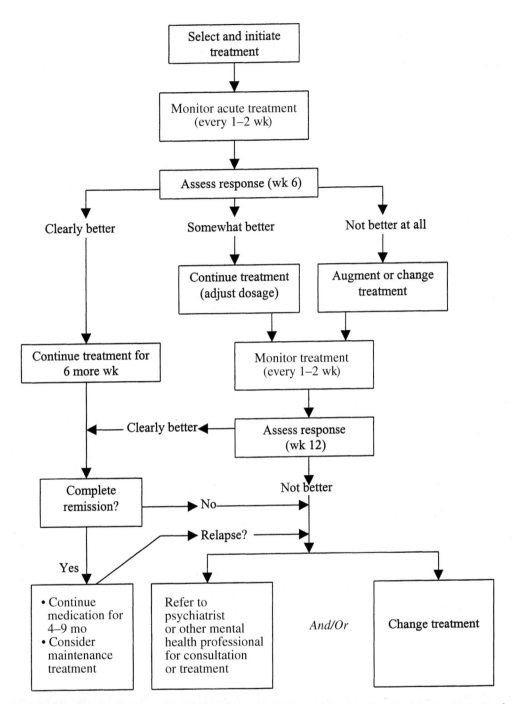

FIGURE 61–2. Overview of treatment for depression. Adapted from Depression in primary care. Rockville (MD): Agency for Health Care Policy and Research; April 1993. Pub. No.: 93-0550.

MENOPAUSE

Natural or surgical menopause has not been shown to increase the rate of depression in most women.[28–32] One of the most comprehensive epidemiologic surveys, the Massachusetts Women's Health Study,[28,33] concluded that although the new onset of depression may be linked to perimenopause, the symptoms are usually transitory and related to the physical discomforts of perimenopause. A history of prior depression and social circumstances are considered better predictors of depression onset than the menopause status. The rate of depression decreases as women go through menopause.

The Manitoba Project on Women and Their Health in the Middle Years[29] conducted a longitudinal investigation of the relationship between menopause and depression and found that natural menopause did not increase the chances that a woman would become depressed. They suggest that health problems or life stressors appearing during the late middle age should be considered as possible etiologies for women who develop depression during the perimenopausal period. A study conducted by Stewart and Boydell[34] found that women with affective disorders during a reproductive event (oral contraceptive–related dysphoria, premenstrual dysphoric syndrome, and postpartum depression) are at greater risk for recurrences during other times of hormonal change, such as menopause.

USE OF ORAL CONTRACEPTIVES AND HORMONE REPLACEMENT

Prior studies have reported an association between oral contraceptive pills and clinical depression.[35,36] These studies involved high-dose oral contraceptives that are no longer in use. Recent controlled studies using lower-dosage birth control pills do not show an association between oral contraceptives and depression.[37] However, recurrence of depression with oral contraceptive usage has been reported in women with a history of depression.[35,36] Further, it is unclear if subclinical depressive symptoms are associated with birth control pills. Mood changes alleviated with vitamin B_6 supplementation (25 to 50 mg) have been associated with the use of oral contraceptives.[38]

Previous research on the effects of estrogen on mood in naturally menopausal women revealed mixed results.[23] In a study of the effect of estrogen on clinically depressed and nondepressed women attending a menopause clinic, estrogen treatment was associated with improved scores on the Beck Depression Inventory (BDI) for nondepressed women but not for clinically depressed women.[23] Other studies suggest that estrogen may play a role in enhancing mood in surgically menopausal women.[39] Hormone replacement therapy should also be considered for relieving vasomotor symptoms in perimenopausal women. An improvement in depressive symptomatology has been shown following treatment with estrogen.[40] Thus, while estrogen may improve depressive symptoms in women whose distress is not of clinical proportions, hormone replacement therapy alone is an insufficient treatment modality for depression in menopause.[41] Therefore, the primary care clinician should treat depression in menopause with the standard recommended treatment modalities.

TREATMENT OF DYSTHYMIA

Historically, patients with dysthymia received no treatment or were seen as candidates for long-term insight-oriented psychotherapy. The current view is that a combination of cognitive or behavioral therapy with the use of medication may be the best approach to treatment. SSRIs remain the drugs of choice for dysthymia (see Table 61–1). A therapeutic trial of an antidepressant in maximal tolerated doses for a minimum of 8 weeks is necessary to determine the effectiveness of any chosen medication. Often, a long-term medication trial of a year or more is necessary to achieve remission.

RESOURCE

The National Institute of Mental Health
6001 Executive Boulevard
Room 8184, MSC 9663
Bethesda, Maryland 20892-9663
Telephone: 1-800-421-4211 (To order free brochures)
Web site: www.nimh.nih.gov

The NIMH of the National Institutes of Health offers free brochures on depression and its treatment. It also offers on-line information about depression, specific to women and in Spanish, as well as English.

REFERENCES

1. Diagnostic and Statistical Manual of Mental Disorders. 4th ed. Washington (DC): American Psychiatric Association; 1994.

2. Spitzer RL, Williams JBW, Kroenke K, et al. Utility of a new product for diagnosing mental disorders in primary care: the PRIME-MD 1000 study. JAMA 1994;272:1749–56.

3. Vieta E, Nieto E, Gastó C, Cirera E. Serious suicide attempts in affective patients. J Aff Dis 1992;9:75.

4. Ghosh TB, Victor BS. Suicide. In: Hales RE, Yudovsky SC, Talbot JA, editors. Textbook of psychiatry. Washington (DC): American Psychiatric Press; 1985: 1251–72.

5. Perugi G, Musetti L, Simonini E, et al. Gender-mediated clinical features of depressive illness: the importance of temperamental differences. Br J Psychiatry 1990;157:835–41.

6. Liebenluft E. Women with bipolar illness: clinical and research issues. Am J Psychiatry 1996;153:163–73.

7. Alarcon RD. Rapid cycling affective disorders: a clinical review. Compr Psychiatry 1985;26:522–40.

8. Wehr TA, Goodwin FK. Rapid cycling in manic depressives induced by tricyclic antidepressants. Arch Gen Psychiatry 1979;36:555–9.

9. Kendell RE, Chalmers JC, Platz C. Epidemiology of puerperal psychoses. Br J Psychiatry 1987;150:662–73.

10. Angst J. The course of affective disorders: typology of bipolar manic-depressive illness. Arch Psychiatry Nervenkr 1978;226:65–73.

11. Hirschfeld RMA, Keller MB, Panico S, et al. The National Depressive and Manic-Depressive Association consensus statement on the undertreatment of depression. JAMA 1997;277:333–40.

12. Merikangas KR, Leckman JF, Prusoff BA, et al. Familial transmission of depression and alcoholism. Arch Gen Psychiatry 1985;42:367.

13. Barnett RC, Baruch GK. Social roles, gender and psychological distress. In: Barnett RC, Biener L, Baruch GK, editors. Gender and stress. New York (NY): The Free Press. p. 122–43.

14. Wilhelm K, Parker G. Is sex necessarily a risk factor to depression? Psychol Med 1989;19:401–13.

15. Pajer K. New strategies in the treatment of depression in women. J Clin Psychiatry 1995;56 Suppl 2:30–7.

16. Council on Scientific Affairs, American Medical Association. Violence against women. Relevance for medical practitioners. JAMA 1992;267:3184–9.

17. Seligman M. Helplessness. San Francisco (CA): WH Freeman; 1975.

18. Parry B. Reproductive factors affecting the course of affective illness in women. Psych Clin North Am 1989;12:207–20.

19. Klaiber El, Kobayashi Y, Broverman DM, et al. Plasma monoamine oxidase activity in regularly menstruating women and in amenorrheic women receiving cyclic treatment with estrogen and a progestin. J Clin Endocrinol Metab 1971;33:630–8.

20. Klaiber EL, Broverman DM, Vogel W, et al. Estrogen therapy for severe persistent depression in women. Arch Gen Psychiatry 1979;36:550–4.

21. Sherwin BB. The impact of different doses of estrogen and progestin on mood and sexual behavior in postmenopausal women. J Clin Endocrinol Metab 1991;72:336–43.

22. Lizardi H. Klein DN, Quimette PC, et al. Reports of childhood home environment in early-onset dysthymia and episodic major depression. J Abnorm Psychol 1995;104:132–9.

23. Burt VK, Hendrick VC. Gender issues in the treatment of major mental illness. Perimenopause and menopause. In: Hales RE, editor. Women's mental health. Washington (DC): American Psychiatric Press; 1997. p. 112, 122–23.

24. Altshuler LL, Cohen L, Szuba MP, et al. Pharmacologic management of psychiatric illness during pregnancy: dilemmas and guidelines. Am J Psychiatry 1996;153;592–606.

25. Beck AT, Rush AJ, Shaw BF, et al. Cognitive therapy of depression. New York (NY): Guilford Press; 1979.

26. Agency for Healthcare Policy and Research. Depression in primary care: detection and diagnosis. Clinical practice guideline. Vol. 1, No. 5. Washington (DC): UC Dept of Health and Human Services, 1993. USPHS Publication No.: 93-0551.

27. Thase ME, Kupfer DJ. Recent developments in the pharmacotherapy of mood disorders. J Consult Clin Psychiatry 1996;64:646–59.

28. Avis NE, McKinlay SM. A longitudinal analysis of women's attitudes towards menopause: results from the Massachusetts Women's Health Study. Maturitas 1991;13:65–79.

29. Kaufert PA, Gilbert P, Tate R. The Manitoba Project: a re-examination of the link between menopause and depression. Maturitas 1992;14:143–55.

30. McKinlay JB, McKinlay SM, Brambilla D. The relative contributions of endocrine changes and social circumstances to depression in mid-aged women. J Health Soc Behavior 1987;28:345–63.

31. Van Hall EV, Verdel M, Van der Velden J. "Perimenopausal" complaints in women and men: a comparative study. J Women's Health 1994;3:45–8.

32. Weissman MM, Bland R, Joyce PR, et al. Sex differences in rates of depression: cross-national perspectives. J Aff Dis 1993;29:77–84.

33. Avis NE, McKinlay SM. The Massachusetts Women's Health Study: an epidemiologic investigation of the menopause. JAMA 1995;50:45–9, 63.

34. Stewart DE, Boydell KM. Psychological distress during menopause: association across the reproductive life cycle. Int J Psychiatry Med 1993;23:157–62.

35. Bancroft J, Sartorius N. The effects of oral contraceptives on well-being and sexuality. Oxford Rev Reprod Biol 1990;12:57–92.

36. Kendler KS, Martin NS, Heath AC, et al. A twin study of the psychiatric side effects of oral contraceptives. J Nerv Ment Dis 1998;176:153–60.

37. Cho JT, Bone S, Dunner DL, et al. The effects of lithium treatment on thyroid function in patients with primary affective disorder. Am J Psychiatry 1979;136:115.

38. Winston F. Oral contraceptives, pyridoxine, and depression. Am J Psychiatry 1973;130:1217–21.

39. Sherwin BB. Affective changes with estrogen and androgen replacement therapy in surgically menopausal women. J Aff Dis 1988;44:177–87.

40. Burt VK, Altshuler LL, Rasgon N. Depressive symptoms in the perimenopause: prevalence, assessment, and guidelines for treatment. Harvard Rev Psychiatry 1998;6:121–32.

41. Schneider MA, Brotherton PL, Hailes J. The effect of exogenous estrogens on depression in menopausal women. Med J Aust 1977;2:162–3.

62

ANXIETY AND PANIC DISORDERS

Meir Steiner, MD, PhD, FRCPC, and Leslie Born, MSc

Anxiety is defined as "the apprehensive anticipation of future danger or misfortune accompanied by a feeling of dysphoria or somatic symptoms of tension."[1] More than one in four women suffer from an anxiety disorder in their lifetime,[2] and most patients with anxiety initially consult their primary care clinician. Yet, despite this high prevalence, less than half the women with anxiety may receive treatment. A proclivity of patients with anxiety to report physical or somatoform (ie, physically unexplained) symptoms may hinder accurate diagnosis and the initiation of treatment.[3,4] Anxiety is associated with a notable impact on mental health and quality of life, with significant impairment in social and occupational functioning and greater utilization of health care services.[5] The National Institute of Mental Health has estimated that in 1990, the direct and indirect costs of anxiety disorders—the most common type of mental illness in the United States—added up to US $46.6 billion.

Anxiety disorders predominant in women include panic disorder, agoraphobia, social phobia, generalized anxiety disorder (GAD), and post-traumatic stress disorder (PTSD).[6] Prior to adolescence, the rate of anxiety disorders in girls is approximately 18%—more than double the rate in boys.[7] This has led to the examination of gender-specific pathophysiologic mechanisms in the etiology of anxiety.[8] Anxiety-related personality traits may be associated with the occurrence of anxiety disorders. In studies of humans and primates, researchers have found that personality attributes related to low assertiveness and low risk taking are associated with anxiety; these attributes are common in women. The relationship between age and onset of anxiety disorder in young girls is particularly pertinent as there is evidence to suggest that having an anxiety disorder prior to or around menarche is a potent risk factor for the onset of major depression in adolescence.[7] Increasing age, in general, appears to have a moderating effect on the lifetime rate of anxiety disorders in adult women, with the exception of generalized anxiety disorder.[9]

Anxiety and panic disorders are viewed as a psychophysiologic response to stress. Stress is defined an as event that is *perceived* as beyond personal control, threatening, unexpected, undesirable, or aversive. The stressor may be acute (eg, car accident, disruption of secure attachment) or chronic (eg, domestic violence, living in poverty). The nature of the response to stress can vary. For example, a panic attack may represent a "fight or flight" reaction to an acute stressor, while chronic stress may induce a general state of tension or helplessness. The connection between a stressor and anxiety or panic, however, may not be readily apparent to the individual or to the health care clinician.[3]

Others have examined the relationship between neuroendocrine functioning and behavior. The γ-aminobutyric acid (GABA), noradrenergic, and serotonergic neurotransmitter systems appear to be involved in the manifestations of anxiety. Much of the literature to date, however, stems from treatment studies, and causality cannot be implied.[8] Changes in the severity of symptoms around reproductive events, for example, premenstrual or postpartum exacerbation, in women with pre-existing anxiety disorders also suggests a modulating effect of ovarian hormones.[6] The etiology of anxiety disorders is likely multifactorial, and the relationships among gender, biology, stress, and anxiety are more complex than can be described in this brief chapter; the interested reader is referred to our sources and to additional literature.[10]

PRESENTING SIGNS AND SYMPTOMS

Panic Disorder and Agoraphobia

A **panic attack** is an episode of intense fear or discomfort that is accompanied by symptoms which may include pounding heart, sweating, shaking, shortness of breath or choking, chest pain, nausea, feeling dizzy or faint, feelings of unreality or being detached from oneself, fear of losing control or going crazy, fear of dying or having a life-threatening illness, and numbness. **Panic disorder** denotes recurrent panic attacks that strike often and without warning.[1] Panic disorder may occur with or without **agoraphobia**—anxiety about being in places or situations from which escape might be difficult or in which help might not be available in the event of having a panic attack. The patient may also complain of insomnia or sleep-related panic attacks.[11]

In the adult American population, about 5% of women have a lifetime occurrence of panic disorder, and 7% have agoraphobia without panic disorder.[2] The age of onset is typically between late adolescence and the mid-thirties. Women with panic disorder, with or without concurrent agoraphobia, frequently present with a comorbid psychiatric condition, especially major depression or another anxiety disorder, in particular, generalized anxiety disorder, simple phobia, PTSD, or social phobia.[1,12] Comorbid alcohol abuse or somatization disorder (a pattern of recurring multiple clinically significant somatic complaints) is also common.[6] Adolescent girls who have experienced at least one panic attack appear to present with a similar profile, that is, concurrent depression, anxiety sensitivity, and alcohol use, although less avoidance behavior.[13] Compared with men, women may endorse more catastrophic thoughts and judge their body sensations as more frightening and also report more severe agoraphobic avoidance when facing phobic situations alone.[12]

Generalized Anxiety Disorder

GAD manifests as constant, excessive tension and worry about everyday routine life events and activities, lasting at least 6 months. It is accompanied by such symptoms as restlessness or feeling keyed up or on edge, easily fatigability, difficulty concentrating, irritability, muscle tension, or sleep disturbance. The patient finds it difficult to control the worry and always anticipates the worst, even though there is little reason to expect it.[1] In children

and adolescents, GAD is also referred to as **overanxious disorder**.[14]

GAD can develop at any time during the life span. The lifetime prevalence of GAD in American women is estimated at 6.6%;[2] from the age of 24 years, the prevalence of GAD in women rises—to an estimated prevalence of 10.3% in those over the age of 44 years.[15] Significant sociodemographic correlates of GAD include marital (separated, widowed, divorced) and occupational status (unemployed, homemaker).[15] Women with GAD frequently have concurrent chronic (at least 2 years) depressed mood also known as **dysthymic disorder**.[6] Adolescents with GAD typically present with unrealistic worry about future catastrophic events or school performance; other characteristics include perfectionism, overzealousness in seeking approval, and requiring excessive reassurance about performance.[1] Patients with comorbid anxiety and depression may be at greater risk for suicide and overall greater functional disability—the indicators include absenteeism from work, higher utilization health services and medication, higher numbers of unexplained symptoms, and poorer treatment response.[16]

Post-traumatic Stress Disorder and Acute Stress Disorder

PTSD denotes a cluster of symptoms that arise following exposure to an extremely traumatic stressor, such as rape or other criminal assault, war, abuse, natural disaster, or accident. The trauma may have been personally experienced or witnessed, or the patient may have learned of an event that involved injury, death, or a threat to the physical integrity of herself or others. The individual's response is marked by intense fear, helplessness, or horror. The symptoms typically include nightmares or flashback dreams, daytime flashbacks, numbing of emotions, depression, and feeling angry or irritable and easily distracted or startled.[1]

PTSD can occur at any age, and, in women, it is frequently associated with the aftermath of a physical or sexual assault or threat, childhood abuse, or the experience of or witnessing a life-threatening event. Patients commonly endorse feelings of guilt, shame, social withdrawal, or hostility and may report disruptions in intimate and social relationships and loss of their job or work role. Women suffering from PTSD may have comorbid phobia, generalized anxiety, or panic; other comorbid conditions can include depression, low self-esteem, dissociation (a disturbance of integrated consciousness, memory, or identity), somatization, eating disorders, and substance abuse. There is evidence to suggest an increased vulnerability to PTSD in women who were exposed to trauma under the age of 15 years.[6] Women with a history of both childhood and adult abuse may have more severe psychological and physical symptoms.[17] Women with PTSD or subthreshold PTSD (one to four PTSD symptoms) are at high risk for suicide attempts.[18]

Acute stress disorder denotes a similar cluster of symptoms that develop after exposure to a traumatic event; however, the onset of the symptoms is within weeks of the trauma, and the symptoms usually do not last long. PTSD, on the other hand, can manifest itself months (usually within 3 months), even years, after the trauma and last much longer.

Social Phobia (Social Anxiety Disorder) and Specific Phobia

The foremost feature of **social phobia** is an overwhelming and disabling fear of scrutiny, embarrassment, or humiliation in social situations. The anxiety can manifest as panic attack, and it usually leads to avoidance of meaningful social activities. Social anxiety can interfere with an individual's social development and/or occupational function; for example, individuals with social phobia are more likely to underachieve in school or at work (including dropping out or remaining unemployed), have few friends, or cling to unfulfilling relationships. It is frequently comorbid with depression, panic disorder, or substance abuse.[1] **Specific phobia**, on the other hand, is a disabling, irrational fear of a specific object or situation. Common examples of specific phobia include fear of a specific animal or insect, heights, water, elevators, flying, or driving.[1] The lifetime prevalence of specific phobia in women has been estimated at 15.7%.[2]

The age of onset of social phobia is typically in the mid-teens. There may be a childhood history of shyness. Despite a relatively high lifetime prevalence of social phobia in the American adult population, that is, 11.1% of males and 15.5% of females,[2] there is little published literature on gender differences. Women with this disorder may be more likely than men to develop agoraphobia, to avoid using public restrooms, or to avoid speaking or performing in public.[6,19] Women with more severe social phobia

who are pregnant may be reluctant to visit their clinicians and, thus, receive less than adequate prenatal care.

Obsessive-Compulsive Disorder

The distinctive features of obsessive-compulsive disorder (OCD) include persistent unwanted thoughts, impulses, or images that cause marked anxiety or distress (obsessions), or repetitive behaviors or mental acts that an individual feels driven to perform (compulsions). The thoughts or behaviors seem impossible to stop or control.[1] Common themes in obsessions include contamination, doubts, excessive tidiness, or a need to have things in a particular order, as well as explicit sexual imagery or an aggressive impulse to shout or strike something/someone. Typically, the patient tries to suppress or neutralize the obsession by some other thought or action. Common compulsions include hand washing or cleaning; praying, counting, or repeating words silently; ordering or checking; and demanding assurance.

The clinical presentation can also include reporting of avoidance actions, hypochondriacal concerns, an excessive sense of responsibility or guilt, sleep disturbance, or attempt at self-sedation with medication or alcohol. The obsessions or compulsions significantly interfere with the normal daily routine, for example, being unable to leave the home because of repeated checking of the doors or the stove.

Women typically develop OCD in their twenties. Aggressive obsessions or cleaning rituals are common, and OCD in women is frequently comorbid with eating disorders, depression, and panic attacks.

Anxiety Disorders Comorbid with Other Physical or Mental Conditions

Anxiety disorders can arise due a *general medical condition*, such as an endocrine (especially hyper- and hypothyroidism, hypercortisolism or Cushing's syndrome, diabetes mellitus, hypoglycemia, hyperprolactinemia, pheochromocytoma), cardiovascular (ischemic heart disease, congestive heart failure, pulmonary embolism, arrhythmia, mitral valve prolapse), respiratory (chronic obstructive pulmonary disease, pneumonia, hyperventilation, asthma), metabolic (vitamin B_6 or B_{12}, or folate deficiencies), or neurologic (brain tumors, cerebral vascular disorders, epilepsy, encephalopathies) condition. The medical condition may be masked by the patient's complaints of persistent worrying, tension, fear, autonomic hyperactivity, sleep disturbance, or emotional lability.[1,20,21] Women who seek treatment for premenstrual syndrome may suffer from an anxiety disorder with premenstrual exacerbation.[22] Anxiety in women can also be associated with sexual dysfunction,[23] and infertility,[24] and, last but not least, clinically significant anxiety can be triggered by the diagnosis of an acute medical condition, such as breast cancer.

Prominent anxiety symptoms can be *substance induced* due to the direct physiologic effects of a medication, drug abuse, or toxin exposure, either in association with overuse or intoxication (especially caffeine, alcohol, cannabis, cocaine, hallucinogens, inhalants, amphetamines) or in association with withdrawal from the same.[1]

SCREENING AND DIAGNOSIS

An anxiety disorder may underlie persistent psychological and/or physical complaints, and in the primary care setting, patients with anxiety frequently couch their feelings in somatic terms. Assessment of female patients should therefore include the following:

- A retrospective history of the presenting symptoms and an inquiry about any current life stressors or recent changes
- A complete review of physical systems including endocrinologic, respiratory, cardiovascular, metabolic, neurologic, and medical conditions; rapid pulse, elevated blood pressure, change in bowel function, increased sweating, difficulty breathing, and sleep and/or appetite disturbance may be indicative of an underlying organic cause for anxiety symptoms, although they also may relate to anxiety disorders themselves
- A review of diet and lifestyle, including detailed questioning about alcohol and/or drug use (prescribed, nonprescribed, herbal) and caffeine intake

A brief screening system for the detection of anxiety in the primary care setting can assist with the differential diagnosis. The current emphasis is on a series of short questions that target common somatic symptoms of anxiety in addition to typical psychological complaints; the patient provides a "yes" or "no" response. Two easy-to-administer examples include the Goldberg scales for anxiety

Anxiety scale
(Score one point for each "Yes")

1. Have you felt keyed up, on edge?
2. Have you been worrying a lot?
3. Have you been irritable?
4. Have you had difficulty relaxing?

(If "Yes" to two of the above, go on to ask:)

5. Have you been sleeping poorly?
6. Have you had headaches or neck aches?
7. Have you had any of the following: trembling, tingling, dizzy spells, sweating, urinary frequency, diarrhea?
8. Have you been worried about your health?
9. Have you had difficulty falling asleep?

Depression scale
(Score one point for each "Yes")

1. Have you had low energy?
2. Have you had loss of interests?
3. Have you lost confidence in yourself?
4. Have you felt hopeless?

(If "Yes" with ANY question, go on to ask:)

5. Have you had difficulty concentrating?
6. Have you lost weight (due to poor appetite)?
7. Have you been waking up early?
8. Have you felt slowed up?
9. Have you tended to feel worse in the mornings?

Interpretation: Add the anxiety score. Add the depression score. Patients with anxiety score of 5 or depression score of 2 have a 50% chance of having a clinically important disturbance; above these scores, the probability rises sharply.

FIGURE 62–1. Short screening scales for anxiety and depression. Reproduced with permission from Goldberg D, Bridges K, Duncan-Jones P, Grayson D. Detecting anxiety and depression in general medical settings. Br Med J 1988;297:897–9.

and depression[25] and the SWIKIR anxiety scale (Figures 62–1 and 62–2).[26] Given the high comorbidity of depression with anxiety, a screen for both may be useful. Patients who score above the cutoff on either scale can then complete a standardized anxiety self-rating instrument (eg, the Duke Anxiety-Depression Scale) to gauge the severity of

Somatic complaints
Worries
Irritability
Keyed up, on edge
Initial insomnia
Relaxation difficulties

Interpretation: 1 point is scored for each item in the scale that applies to the patient. Patients with SWIKIR anxiety scale scores of at least 3 are assumed to have a significant probability of a clinically important anxiety disorder.

FIGURE 62–2. SWIKIR anxiety scale. Reproduced with permission from Baughman OL. Rapid diagnosis and treatment of anxiety and depression in primary care. The somaticizing patient. J Fam Pract 1994;39:373–8 (by permission).

their anxiety (Figure 62–3).[27] The latter provides a baseline evaluation of symptom severity and a means to evaluate the patient's response to treatment.

Given the indications of the presence of an anxiety disorder, a detailed psychiatric history should be elicited (consultation with a psychiatrist may be required). In this review, the female patient should be asked about a history of premenstrual syndrome, occurrence of trauma (to herself, family or friends, or learned about in the news), suicide ideation or plan, and interference of the symptoms with daily function or lifestyle. In addition, the clinician should also obtain a detailed review of any family history of mental illness (a simple sketch of the family tree—including first and second degree relatives—can assist with this process). The *Diagnostic and Statistical Manual of Mental Disorders,*

INSTRUCTIONS:

Here are a number of questions about your health and feelings. Please read each question carefully and check (√) your best answer. You should answer the questions in your own way. There are no right or wrong answers.

	Yes, describes me exactly	Somewhat describes me	No, doesn't describe me at all
1. I give up too easily	2	1	0
2. I have difficulty concentrating	2	1	0
3. I am comfortable being around people	0	1	2

DURING THE <u>PAST WEEK</u>:
How much trouble have you had with:

	None	Some	A lot
4. Sleeping?	0	1	2
5. Getting tired easily?	0	1	2
6. Feeling depressed or sad?	0	1	2
7. Nervousness?	0	1	2

HOW TO SCORE

1. Add the scores next to each of the blanks you checked.
2. If your total score is 5 or greater, then your symptoms of anxiety and/or depression may be excessive.

FIGURE 62–3. Duke Anxiety-Depression Scale (DUKE-AD). Reproduced with permission from the Department of Community and Family Medicine, Duke University Medical Center, Durham, N.C., U.S.A. Copyright © 1994.

TABLE 62–1. DSM-IV Criteria for Selected Anxiety Disorders and Panic (modified)[*]

Panic Attack

A discrete period of intense fear or discomfort, in which four or more of the following symptoms developed abruptly and reached a peak within 10 minutes: accelerated heart rate, sweating, trembling, sensation of shortness of breath, feeling of choking, chest pain, nausea or abdominal distress, feeling dizzy or faint, derealization or depersonalization, fear of losing control or going crazy, fear of dying, numbness or tingling, chills or hot flushes.

Agoraphobia

Anxiety about being in places or situations from which escape might be difficult or embarrassing, or in which help may not be available in the event of having a panic attack or panic symptoms.
The situations are avoided or are endured with marked distress, or require the presence of a companion.

Generalized Anxiety Disorder

Excessive anxiety and worry (apprehensive expectation), occurring more days than not for at least 6 months, about a number of events or activities (eg, work or school performance). The person finds it difficult to control the worry. The anxiety and worry are associated with three or more of: restlessness or feeling keyed up or on edge, easily fatigued, irritability, muscle tension, sleep disturbance.

Post-traumatic Stress Disorder

The person has been exposed to a traumatic event in which she experienced, witnessed, or was confronted with an injury or events that involved serious injury or threatened death or a threat to the physical integrity of herself or others. The person's response involved intense fear, helplessness, or horror. The traumatic event is persistently re-experienced in one or more of: visual or thought recollections, distressing dreams, feeling as if the trauma were recurring (eg, flashbacks), or intense emotional distress or physiologic reactivity at exposure to cues that resemble an aspect of the event. The patient reports persistent avoidance of stimuli associated with the trauma and numbing of general responsiveness as indicated by three of: efforts to avoid thoughts, feelings, or conversations about the trauma; avoiding activities, places, or people that arouse recollections; unable to recall an important aspect of the trauma; decreased interest or participation in significant activities; feeling detached or estranged from others; restricted range of affect; sense of foreshortened future. Two or more symptoms of increased arousal are present: sleep disturbance, irritability or anger, difficulty concentrating, hypervigilance, or exaggerated startle response. The symptoms last more than 1 month.

Social Phobia

A marked persistent fear of one or more social or performance situations in which the person is exposed to unfamiliar people or to possible scrutiny by others. The individual fears that she will act in a way or show anxiety symptoms that will be humiliating or embarrassing. Exposure to the feared social situation provokes anxiety, which may be in the form of a panic attack. The person recognizes that the fear is excessive or unreasonable. The feared situations are avoided or endured with intense anxiety or distress. The social anxiety interferes significantly with the person's role or social function, or emotional well-being. In individuals under age 18 years, the duration is at least 6 months.

---

[*]Note: We have included only those disorders that are frequently seen in women. The reader is referred to the DSM-IV for a comprehensive discussion in the anxiety disorders section.[1]

4th edition, (DSM-IV) diagnostic criteria for panic attack, agoraphobia, GAD, PTSD, and social phobia are shown in Table 62–1.

TREATMENT IN THE OUTPATIENT SETTING

As the majority of women with anxiety disorders present either to their family clinician or to their gynecologist, the role of the primary care clinician in the assessment and treatment of anxiety disorders is paramount. At the minimum, this role can include the initial general medical evaluation as well as a rapid screening and an indication of symptom severity. A tentative differential diagnosis can be reached. The clinician can discuss with the patient her goals for treatment, and if indicated and/or preferred, a referral to an allied mental health clinician for further diagnostic evaluation and/or treatment can be made. A strong treatment alliance with the patient and her other health clinicians is essential, as is providing a supportive environment for the patient to talk about sensitive issues. Continued medical monitoring can be provided as necessary. The patient can be counseled on the importance of lifestyle changes, including regular exercise (eg, rhythmic aerobics and yoga), adequate rest, and good nutrition. Adjunctive interventions, such as group therapy (cognitive behavior therapy or mindfulness meditation), marital and family therapy, or support groups, can also be recommended (see the section on resources).

Anxiety disorders can be successfully treated in the primary care setting. The first-line treatment option for anxiety disorders is combined medication and cognitive behavioral therapy. In remote areas or in other settings where patients have difficulty obtaining formal psychological therapy, treatment can include medication alone plus a support group (community-based or on-line). The use of telephone counseling for treatment of anxiety is currently being studied.

Anxiety is often comorbid with depression, and the first-line options for medication are antidepressants, including the selective serotonin reuptake inhibitors (SSRIs), and the serotonin norepinephrine reuptake inhibitors (SNRIs) (Table 62–2). In women, hormonal and neurotransmitter fluctuations during the menstrual cycle, pregnancy, puerperium, perimenopause, and postmenopause may affect the pharmacokinetics of psychotropic medication.

Benzodiazepines should be used only for the symptomatic relief of acute anxiety and/or sleep disturbance. Patients taking antidepressant agents (ie, SSRIs, SNRIs, tricyclics, or buspirone) may experience a temporary period of increased anxiety. These agents also have a relatively slow onset of therapeutic action, with their full effects often not seen for 4 to 6 weeks after initiation of therapy. Therefore, a benzodiazepine may be of benefit during the initiation phase of antidepressant therapy.[28–30] To avoid side effects, the starting dose of the antidepressant should be small with gradual increase in titration, and gradual tapering off is recommended when discontinuing the medication. It is essential to monitor patients with suicidal ideation, especially those with concurrent depression. Also, in women, attention should be paid to the concomitant use of oral contraceptives and benzodiazepines (see below).

Augmentation strategies using pindolol or topiramate have had a marked and rapid effect on treatment-refractory patients with panic disorder and PTSD respectively.[31,32]

Cognitive behavior therapy (CBT)—both individual and group formats—has been well documented to be effective in the treatment of anxiety disorders. The efficacy of CBT group therapy in general practice has been recently published.[33] Other effective nondrug therapies include variations of cognitive or behavioral therapy, psychodynamic therapy, interpersonal psychotherapy (especially in the treatment of GAD), systematic desensitization (especially in the treatment of phobias and PTSD), breathing retraining, and massage therapy.[34,35]

The duration of therapy varies; psychotherapy usually consists of 4 to 20 weeks of "acute" therapy plus booster sessions to prevent recurrence of symptoms. The typical length of a randomized controlled trial of an SSRI in the treatment of anxiety is 12 weeks (note that some patients may not realize a full response before 12 weeks). A suggested regimen is 6 to 12 months, with intermittent review of response to treatment.

PROGNOSIS

Clinically significant symptoms can and do recur (ie, anxiety symptoms that last for at least 1 week) in some of those successfully treated for anxiety disorders. The severity and chronicity of the presenting symptoms, the type of anxiety disorder, and comorbid medical and/or psychiatric illnesses (especially comorbid major depression, severe personality disorders, and ongoing substance abuse) all influence the prognosis. For example, in a 5-year follow-up of 412 patients treated for panic disorder, mostly those with concurrent agoraphobia, the cumulative probability of symptom recurrence 3 years after remission was 65% for women with panic disorder and 75% for women with panic disorder/agoraphobia. The rate of recurrence of panic symptoms in women was nearly double the rate in men.[36] Nevertheless, without treatment, improvement in clinically significant symptoms of anxiety is not likely. There is some evidence to suggest that cognitive-behavior therapy in the intensive stage of treatment may be of lasting benefit long after treatment has terminated.[37]

TABLE 62–2. Pharmacotherapy for Anxiety Disorders in Women

Disorder	Drug	Dosage	Nondrug Therapies
Panic disorder with or without agoraphobia	Paroxetine	10–40 mg/d	Cognitive behavior therapy (CBT), bibliotherapy
	Sertraline	50–200 mg/d (start dose 25 mg/d)	
	Fluoxetine	5–20 mg/d	
	Fluvoxamine	50–300 mg/d	
	Citalopram	20–60 mg/d	
	Clomipramine	25–150 mg/d	
	Venlafaxine	50–150 mg/d	
	Clonazepam	0.5–2 mg/d	
	Nefazodone	200–500 mg/d	
Social phobia	Paroxetine	10–40 mg/d	CBT, systematic desensitization, hypnosis, exposure therapy
	Sertraline	50–200 mg/d (start dose 25 mg/d)	
	Fluvoxamine	50–300 mg/d	
GAD	Buspirone	20–30 mg/d (start dose 5 mg/d)	CBT, IPT, stress management, biofeedback
	Alprazolam	maximum 3 mg/d (start dose 0.25 mg 2 to 3 times daily)	
	Venlafaxine-XR	75–225 mg/d	
PTSD	Sertraline	50–200 mg/d (start dose 25 mg/d)	CBT (individual or group), systematic desensitization, imagery rehearsal therapy, exposure therapy
	Fluoxetine	10–60 mg/d	
	Paroxetine	10–40 mg/d	
	Fluvoxamine	50–300 mg/d	
OCD	Fluoxetine	20–60 mg/d	CBT
	Sertraline	50–200 mg/d	
	Paroxetine	40–60 mg/d	
	Fluvoxamine	100–300 mg/d	
	Clomipramine	150–300 mg/d	

GAD = generalized anxiety disorder; PTSD = post-traumatic stress disorder; OCD = obsessive-compulsive disorder.

Regular patient contact (visit or telephone) increases patients' use of and adherence to recommended pharmacotherapy, and results in greater clinical and functional improvements.[38]

PREGNANCY, PUERPERIUM, AND BREAST-FEEDING

The emergence of anxiety symptoms during pregnancy and especially in the third trimester in women *without pre-existing anxiety disorders*—for example, worries about the baby's health, concerns about labor, or uncertainties about finances or the relationship with the baby's father—is common. Stressful life events (eg, unplanned pregnancy, loss of a job, financial constraints, moving), poor social adjustment to pregnancy, or perceived lack of social support (from partner, parents, confidant), however, may exacerbate anxiety and tension ante partum.[39] Moreover, persistent complaints of insomnia or severe fatigue, high levels of anxiety, worrying, dysphoric mood, irritability, or anger during pregnancy may be associated with increased risk for postpartum depression.[40] Pregravid patients with anxiety that does not meet the criteria for a full disorder may benefit from individual supportive counseling or from a pregnancy support group. Massage therapy has demonstrated benefits, such as reduction of anxiety, improved mood, and improved sleep, in pregnant women.[41]

The course of *pre-existing anxiety disorders* during pregnancy is variable. Retrospective case studies indicate that many women with OCD (about 78%) may have no change in symptoms during pregnancy.[42] Up to 40% of women with pregravid panic disorder may experience improvement in their symptomatology during pregnancy or remain stable, especially if they have milder forms of panic disorder; however, up to 20% may experience more severe panic. Pregnancy is not associated with the likelihood of successful discontinuation of antipanic medication in women with moderate-to-severe panic disorder.[43]

Parturition, for some women, can be a stressful time, and the circumstances around delivery can impact early puerperal psychological adjustment. For example, the experience of parturition may provoke recall of earlier sexual trauma, and the patient may disclose the onset of PTSD-like symptomatology. Moreover, the early postpartum phase is typically wrought with disrupted sleep and the stress of caring for a newborn. In women with *existing anxiety disorders*, the early postpartum period (the first 3 months, in particular) seems to be associated with worsening of panic and OCD symptoms.[6] Women who have a history of panic attack or GAD may be at risk for the onset of OCD several weeks after delivery.[44]

Women *without pre-existing anxiety or psychiatric disorders* can experience the first onset of panic disorder or OCD post partum—usually within the first 6 weeks.[44–46] In the presentation of OCD, the content of the obsessions (gruesome thoughts and/or visual images) frequently pertains to harming the baby. The women usually become depressed, and they may also develop panic attacks; however, the onset of associated compulsions has not been reported.[44] Conversely, women with major depression with postpartum onset may also experience disturbing aggressive obsessional thoughts—about something harmful happening to the baby—with related compulsive checking behavior.[47]

The potential risks versus the benefits of using psychotropic medication during pregnancy and the postpartum period should be carefully considered in consultation with the patient.[48–50] When possible (ie, the patient is not deemed to be at high risk for relapse and/or suicide), pharmacotherapy should be stopped or delayed until the beginning of the second trimester. Gradual tapering of the medication following a decision to discontinue is advised. If, on the other hand, there is an absolute indication for pharmacotherapy, antidepressants are effective and mostly safe and should be the first line of treatment; the preferred drugs during pregnancy include fluoxetine (starting dose 20 mg/d) or sertraline (starting dose 25 mg/d), as well as the tricyclic antidepressants. Benzodiazepines are indicated only when the target symptoms are severe and immediate relief is required; the duration of use should be as brief as possible, with the minimum effective dose. Lorazepam is recommended because of its slower rate of placental transfer.[51]

Patients with milder forms of *panic disorder* on medication prior to conception are more likely than the more severely ill patients to successfully discontinue medication during pregnancy.[52] Any patient with panic disorder who discontinues medication should be closely monitored during pregnancy. Patients with panic disorder are at risk for postpartum exacerbation or re-emergence of symptoms, and there is some evidence to suggest that the use of antipanic medication during pregnancy may be prophylactic.[53]

For those with *OCD,* behavioral strategies should be considered (as an alternative to medication) in the first trimester. Women who have postpartum onset of OCD or worsening of OCD symptoms usually initiate or restart pharmacotherapy, and they may require hospitalization.

MENOPAUSE

Some of the emotional and physical symptoms associated with the menopausal transition include features of anxiety, such as tension, nervousness, fearfulness, panic, restlessness, sleep disturbance, and irritability, as well as dizziness, palpitations, and headache.[54] In some women, these symptoms may result in significant psychic and/or somatic distress (although the reporting and experience of these symptoms may be culturally influenced).

The current thinking suggests that there may be a subgroup of women who are vulnerable to exacerbation of mood/anxiety symptomatology due to a heightened sensitivity to the decline in gonadal hormones; this does not necessarily reflect the emergence of specific menopause-related psychiatric syndromes.[55,56] This can include women with a history of premenstrual syndrome or perinatal mood disturbance and those with a history of cyclic affective disorder.[57] Indeed, a review of major community-based epidemiologic studies has indicated that the prevalence of anxiety disorders in general—with the exception of GAD—*declines* with advancing age, that is, over 65 years. The gender differences in the prevalences of anxiety disorders also diminish.[9]

There is little literature on existing anxiety disorders and the perimenopause. Further, the psychological effects of adding hormone replacement therapy (HRT) to an existing psychotropic regimen for anxiety has not been well delineated. The clinician should be aware of possible pharmacokinetic changes in anxiety reduction medication (see below). The treatment protocol for women presenting with minor psychological symptoms—with or without concurrent physical complaints—might include a trial of HRT. A psychotropic drug can be considered first with (new) presentations of more severe symptoms or be added subsequently if the patient does not have relief of minor anxiety symptoms from HRT alone.[57] Preliminary evidence suggests that HRT combined with 100 mg/d of Kava extract (55% Kavain) is a highly tolerable rapid treatment for menopausal anxiety.[58]

USE OF ORAL CONTRACEPTIVE PILLS AND HORMONE REPLACEMENT

The metabolism of the benzodiazepines and several serotonergic agents may be affected when used in combination with hormonal therapies. Concomitant administration of an oral contraceptive along with lorazepam, oxazepam, or temazepam may cause the latter to be more rapidly metabolized. Conversely, an oral contraceptive in combination with alprazolam, triazolam, or diazepam may result in higher benzodiazepine plasma concentrations.[6]

Doses of HRT doses may need to be reduced if fluoxetine, fluvoxamine, or nefazadone are coadministered; these antidepressant agents inhibit CYP 3A4, the same cytochrome P450 enzyme involved in the metabolism of HRT.[6]

SUMMARY

More than one in four women suffer from an anxiety disorder in their lifetime, and most women with anxiety initially consult their primary care clinician. Anxiety disorders predominant in women include panic disorder, agoraphobia, social phobia, generalized anxiety disorder, and post-traumatic stress disorder. An anxiety disorder can underlie affective or somatic complaints in women who present to their clinician for consultation concerning premenstrual syndrome, during pregnancy or post partum, and during the menopausal transition. The assessment plan optimally includes a general medical evaluation, followed by rapid screening for anxiety and an indication of symptom severity. Patients can be encouraged to instigate lifestyle changes and support groups, or structured therapy can be recommended. The first-line treatment option for anxiety disorders is combined medication and cognitive behavioral therapy. Regular patient contact during the treatment period appears to enhance patients' adherence to the treatment regimen, as well as their overall clinical and functional improvement.

The authors would like to thank Ms. Janice Rogers and Ms. Carol Ballantyne for their help in the preparation of this manuscript.

RESOURCES

National Institute of Mental Health
6001 Executive Boulevard, Room 184, MSC 9663
Bethesda, MD 20892-9663
Telephone: 1-800-64-PANIC (1-800-647-2642)
              (301) 443-4513
Web site: www.nimh.nih.gov

The NIMH Information Resources and Inquiries Branch Web site has a comprehensive list of mental health organizations (including most of those listed below) to help clinicians and patients to find more information about anxiety disorders and related issues. In addition, the NIMH has informative brochures for clinicians and patients, which include overviews of specific anxiety disorders, brief screening instruments, referral resources, and reference materials. For professionals, a list of relevant conferences is also available.

The American Psychiatric Association
1400 K Street Northwest
Washington, DC 20005
Telephone: (202) 682-6220
Web site: www.psych.org

The Web site provides practice guidelines for the treatment of patients with panic disorder, and also material on social anxiety disorder awareness, criteria for short-term treatment of acute psychiatric illness, and information for the public.

MOTHERISK
555 University Avenue
Toronto, Ontario
Canada MSG 1X8
Telephone: (416) 813-6780
Web site: www.motherisk.org

Located at the Hospital for Sick Children in Toronto and affiliated with the University of Toronto (Ontario, Canada), the MOTHERISK program was initiated to provide evidence-based information to pregnant women concerning potential risks to the developing fetus from the ingestion of various drugs. The program offers immediate telephone counseling to patients and can assist in the decision about optimal therapy during pregnancy.

Anxiety Disorders Association of America
11900 Parklawn Drive, Suite 100
Rockville, Maryland 20852
Telephone: (301) 231-9350
E-mail: anxdis@adaa.org
Web site: www.adaa.org

The AADA promotes the prevention and cure of anxiety disorders. In addition to general information about anxiety disorders, the Web site includes consumer resources (including insightful accounts, by patients, of the road to recovery), information exchange for health professionals, and referrals by zip code.

RESOURCES   (continued)

Association for Advancement of Behavior Therapy (AABT)
305 Seventh Avenue, 16th Floor
New York, New York 10001
Telephone: (212) 647-1890
Web site: www.aabt.org

The AABT is a centralized resource and network for all facets of behavior therapy and cognitive behavior therapy. The Web site offers a referral service to the general public and third-party payers, educational programs for the public and professionals, and fact sheets.

Freedom From Fear (FFF)
308 Seaview Avenue
Staten Island, New York 10305
Telephone: (718) 351-1717
Web site: www.freedomfromfear.org

FFF is a not-for-profit mental health advocacy association, whose primary concern is to direct aid to sufferers of anxiety and their families. In addition to an on-line screening program, the Web site offers information on a referral program, publications and other educational resources, and the FFF Friends Club.

Pocket Books and Guides for Clinicians
Nutt D, Bell C, Potokar J. Depression, anxiety and the mixed conditions. London (UK): Martin Dunitz; 1997. [ISBN: 1-85317-461-0]
Montgomery SA, editor. Pocket reference to social phobia. London (UK): Science Press; 1995. [ISBN: 1-85873-078-3]
Andrews G, Crino R, Hunt C, et al. The treatment of anxiety disorders. Clinician's guide and patient manuals. Cambridge (UK): Cambridge University Press; 1994. [ISBN: 0-521-46927-9 paperback; 0-521-46958-9 set of 5 manuals].

REFERENCES

1. American Psychiatric Association. Diagnostic and statistical manual of mental disorders. Washington (DC): American Psychiatric Association; 1994.

2. Kessler RC, McGonagle KA, Zhao S, et al. Lifetime and 12-month prevalence of DSM-III-R psychiatric disorders in the United States. Results from the National Comorbidity Survey. Arch Gen Psychiatry 1994;51:8–19.

3. Frank JB, Weihs K, Minerva E, Lieberman DZ. Women's mental health in primary care: depression, anxiety, somatization, eating disorders, and substance abuse. Med Clin North Am 1998;82: 359–89.

4. Kroenke K, Spitzer RL. Gender differences in the reporting of physical and somatoform symptoms. Psychosom Med 1998;60:150–5.

5. Spitzer RL, Kroenke K, Linzer M, et al. Health-related quality of life in primary care patients with mental disorders. Results from the PRIME-MD 1000 Study. JAMA 1995;274:1511–7.

6. Pigott TA. Gender differences in the epidemiology and treatment of anxiety disorders. J Clin Psychiatry 1999;60 Suppl 18:4–15.

7. Breslau N, Schultz L, Peterson E. Sex differences in depression: a role for preexisting anxiety. Psychiatry Res 1995;58:1–12.

8. Shear MK. Anxiety disorders in women: gender-related modulation of neurobiology and behavior. Semin Reprod Endocrinol 1997;15:69–76.

9. Krasucki C, Howard R, Mann A. The relationship between anxiety disorders and age. Int J Geriatr Psychiatry 1998;13:79–99.

10. Chrousos GP, McCarty R, Pacák K, et al, editors. Stress: basic mechanisms and clinical implications. Ann N Y Acad Sci 1995;771.

11. Benca RM. Sleep in psychiatric disorders. Neurol Clin 1996;14:739–64.

12. Turgeon L, Marchand A, Dupuis G. Clinical features in panic disorder with agoraphobia: a comparison of men and women. J Anxiety Disord 1998;12:539–53.

13. Hayward C, Killen JD, Kraemer HC, et al. Assessment and phenomenology of nonclinical panic attacks in adolescent girls. J Anxiety Disord 1997;11:17–32.

14. Bernstein GA, Shaw K. Practice parameters for the assessment and treatment of children and adolescents with anxiety disorders. J Am Acad Child Adolesc Psychiatry 1997;36 Suppl 10:69–84S.

15. Wittchen H-U, Zhao S, Kessler RC, Eaton WW. DSM-III-R generalized anxiety disorder in the National Comorbidity Survey. Arch Gen Psychiatry 1994;51:355–64.

16. Roy-Byrne PP, Katon W. Generalized anxiety disorder in primary care: the precursor/modifier pathway to increased health care utilization. J Clin Psychiatry 1997;58 Suppl 3:34–8.

17. McCauley J, Kern DE, Kolodner K, et al. Clinical characteristics of women with a history of childhood abuse: unhealed wounds. JAMA 1997;277:1362–8.

18. Marshall RD, Olfson M, Hellman F, et al. Comorbidity, impairment, and suicidality in subthreshold PTSD. Am J Psychiatry 2001;158:1467–73.

19. Weinstock LS. Gender differences in the presentation and management of social anxiety disorder. J Clin Psychiatry 1999;60 Suppl 9:9–13.

20. Pennington A. Women's health. Anxiety disorders. Prim Care 1997;24:103–11.

21. Geffken GR, Ward HE, Staab JP, et al. Psychiatric morbidity in endocrine disorders. Psychiatr Clin North Am 1998;21:473–89.

22. Bailey JW, Cohen LS. Prevalence of mood and anxiety disorders in women who seek treatment for premenstrual syndrome. J Womens Health Gend Based Med 1999;8:1181–4.

23. Dunn KM, Croft PR, Hackett GI. Association of sexual problems with social, psychological, and physical problems in men and women: a cross-sectional population survey. J Epidemiol Community Health 1999;53:144–8.

24. Oddens BJ, den Tonkelaar I, Nieuwenhuyse H. Psychosocial experiences in women facing fertility problems —a comparative survey. Hum Reprod 1999;14:255–61.

25. Goldberg D, Bridges K, Duncan-Jones P, Grayson D. Detecting anxiety and depression in general medical settings. Br Med J 1988;297:897–9.

26. Baughman OL 3rd. Rapid diagnosis and treatment of anxiety and depression in primary care: the somatizing patient. J Fam Pract 1994;39:373–8.

27. Parkerson GR Jr, Broadhead WE. Screening for anxiety and depression in primary care with the Duke Anxiety-Depression Scale. Fam Med 1997;29:177–81.

28. Argyropoulos SV, Nutt DJ. The use of benzodiazepines in anxiety and other disorders. Eur Neuropsychopharmacol 1999;9 (Suppl 6):S407–12.

29. Uhlenhuth EH, Balter MB, Ban TA, Yang K. Trends in recommendations for the pharmacotherapy of anxiety disorders by an international expert panel, 1992-1997. Eur Neuropsychopharmacol 1999;9 Suppl 6:S393–8.

30. Godard AW, Brouette T, Almai A, et al. Early co-administration of Clonazepam with sertraline for panic disorder. Arch Gen Psychiatry 2001;58:681–6.

31. Hirschmann S, Dannon PH, Iancu I, et al. Pindolol augmentation in patients with treatment-resistant panic disorder: double-blind, placebo-controlled trial. J Clin Psychopharmacol 2000;20:556–9.

32. Berlant JL. Topiramate in posttraumatic stress disorder: preliminary clinical observations. J Clin Psychiatry 2001;62 Suppl 17:60–3.

33. Martinsen EW, Olsen T, Tonset E, et al. Cognitive-behavioral group therapy for panic disorder in the general clinical setting: a naturalistic study with 1-year follow-up. J Clin Psychiatry 1998;59:437–42.

34. Harvey AG, Rapee RM. Cognitive-behaviour therapy for generalized anxiety disorder. Psychiatr Clin North Am 1995;18:859–70.

35. Shear MK. Psychotherapeutic issues in long-term treatment of anxiety disorder patients. Psychiatr Clin North Am 1995;18:885–94.

36. Yonkers KA, Zlotnick C, Allsworth J, et al. Is the course of panic disorder the same in women and men? Am J Psychiatry 1998;155:596–602.

37. Liebowitz MR, Heimberg RG, Schneier FR, et al. Cognitive-behavioral group therapy versus phenelzine in social phobia: long-term outcome. Depress Anxiety 1999;10:89–98.

38. Roy-Byrne PP, Katon W, Cowley DS, et al. A randomized effectiveness trial of collaborative care for patients with panic disorder in primary care. Arch Gen Psychiatry 2001;58:869–76.

39. O'Hara MW. Adjustment, social support, and life events across pregnancy and the puerperium. In, Postpartum depression: causes and consequences. New York (NY): Springer-Verlag; 1995. p. 93–109.

40. Affonso DD, Mayberry LJ. Common stressors reported by a group of childbearing American women. Health Care Women Int 1990;11:331–45.

41. Field T, Hernandez-Reif M, Hart S, et al. Pregnant women benefit from massage therapy. J Psychosom Obstet Gynaecol 1999;20:31–8.

42. Williams KE, Koran LM. Obsessive-compulsive disorder in pregnancy, the puerperium, and the premenstruum. J Clin Psychiatry 1997;58:330–4.

43. Hertzberg T, Wahlbeck K. The impact of pregnancy and puerperium on panic disorder: a review. J Psychosom Obstet Gynaecol 1999;20:59–64.

44. Sichel DA, Cohen LS, Dimmock JA, Rosenbaum JF. Postpartum obsessive compulsive disorder: a case series. J Clin Psychiatry 1993;54:156–9.

45. Sholomskas DE, Wickamaratne PJ, Dogolo L, et al. Postpartum onset of panic disorder: a coincidental event? J Clin Psychiatry 1993;54:476–80.

46. Wisner KL, Peindl KS, Hanusa BH. Effects of childbearing on the natural history of panic disorder with comorbid mood disorder. J Affect Disord 1996;41:173–80.

47. Wisner KL, Peindl KS, Gigliotti T, Hanusa BH. Obsessions and compulsions in women with postpartum depression. J Clin Psychiatry 1999;60:176–80.

48. Diket AL, Nolan TE. Anxiety and depression. Diagnosis and treatment during pregnancy. Obstet Gynecol Clin North Am 1997;24:535–58.

49. Suri RA, Altshuler LL, Burt VK, Hendrick VC. Managing psychiatric medications in the breastfeeding woman. Medscape Women's Health 1998; 3:1–13.

50. Cohen LS, Rosenbaum JF. Psychotropic drug use during pregnancy: weighing the risks. J Clin Psychiatry 1998:59 Suppl 2:18–28.

51. Wisner KL, Perel JM. Psychopharmacologic agents and ECT during pregnancy and the puerperium. In: Cohen RL, editor. Psychiatric consultations in childbirth settings. New York (NY): Plenum Publications; 1988. p. 165–74.

52. Cohen LS, Sichel DA, Dimmock JA, Rosenbaum JF. Impact of pregnancy on panic disorder: a case series. J Clin Psychiatry 1994;55:284–8.

53. Cohen LS, Sichel DA, Dimmock JA, Rosenbaum JF. Postpartum course in women with preexisting panic disorder. J Clin Psychiatry 1994;55:289–92.

54. Baram DA. Physiology and symptoms of menopause. In: DE Stewart, Robinson GE, editors. A clinician's guide to menopause. Washington (DC): American Psychiatric Press; 1997. p. 9–27.

55. Charney DA, Stewart DE. Psychiatric aspects. In: DE Stewart, Robinson GE, editors. A clinician's guide to menopause. Washington (DC): American Psychiatric Press; 1997. p. 129–44.

56. Becker D, Lomranz J, Pines A, et al. Psychological distress around menopause. Psychosomatics 2001;42: 252–7.

57. Pearlstein T, Rosen K, Stone AB. Mood disorders and menopause. Endocrinol Metab Clin North Am 1997;26:279–94.

58. De Leo V, la Marca A, Morgante G, et al. Evaluation of combining Kava extract with hormone replacement therapy in the treatment of postmenopausal anxiety. Maturitas 2001;39:185–8.

63

EATING DISORDERS

Joel Yager, MD

Eating disorders are common afflictions among women today. They include anorexia nervosa and bulimia nervosa, the well-delineated eating disorders of the American Psychiatric Association's *Diagnostic and Statistical Manual* (DSM-IV), and several other conditions grouped together as "Eating Disorders Not Otherwise Specified" (EDNOS), including binge eating disorder, a condition akin to compulsive overeating that is still being delineated, and a variety of other ill-defined syndromes consisting of varying types and intensities of eating disorder–related symptoms.

PATHOPHYSIOLOGY

The pathogenesis of eating disorders is complex. Social pressures for women to overvalue unnatural degrees of thinness are so ubiquitous that the majority of women are, to at least some degree, dissatisfied with their bodies. The much smaller percentage who develop clinical eating disorders are further predisposed to these disorders by certain biologic, psychological, and social vulnerabilities. Eating disorders are familially transmitted and are much more commonly shared by monozygotic than dizygotic twins; thus, some individuals may be genetically predisposed, seemingly through certain childhood temperaments and behavioral predilections that have been loosely linked to serotonin-mediated brain processes. Those who develop anorexia nervosa often show prior tendencies to be overanxious, depressed, obsessional, compulsive, perfectionistic, and shy and to avoid novel situations. Some of these tendencies are also seen among those who develop bulimia nervosa; however, at least one subgroup of those who develop bulimia nervosa may actually be stimulus or novelty seeking, not avoidant. Furthermore, individuals prone to bulimia nervosa and binge eating disorder have greater tendencies to be obese and have more obesity in their families. Certain family and social environments, those that overvalue physical appearance, competitiveness, and strenuous physical exercise, for example, and in which psychological, physical, and sexual abuse occur more commonly, may promote the development of eating disorders in otherwise predisposed women.

Once dieting and excessive caloric expenditure via exercise results in malnutrition, the semi-starved state itself contributes significantly to the pathophysiology. In the brains of underweight anorexia nervosa patients, decreases in the volume of both white and gray matter and increases in cerebrospinal fluid (CSF) space are seen. Furthermore, although white matter changes seem to be completely reversible with weight recovery, some residual gray matter deficits apparently persist. The skeletal growth retardation that occurs in malnourished children and adolescents is not entirely reversible, nor are the deficiencies in bone calcium storage that occur at any age.[1]

EPIDEMIOLOGY

Lifetime rates in community samples for anorexia nervosa range from about 0.5 to 3.7%; bulimia nervosa from 1.1 to 4.2%; and binge eating disorder about 2%, depending on how strictly the conditions are defined, so that about 8 to 10% of women have some degree of clinically significant impairment during their lives.[2–5] Rates may be higher among women seeking help in women's health clinics and infertility clinics. Anorexia nervosa and bulimia nervosa are estimated to be about 10 times more prevalent in women than in men; binge eating disorder is twice as frequent in women than in men. Although previously associated primarily with the upper and

675

upper-middle social classes and almost exclusively with Caucasians, these disorders are now well represented among middle and lower-middle class women, including non-Caucasians.

CLINICAL AND SOCIAL IMPACT

The clinical and social significance of anorexia nervosa is considerable. Death rates for anorexia nervosa are estimated to be at least twice those for any other psychiatric disorder in women, including depression and drug abuse, and have been estimated at up to 12 times higher than for aged-matched community controls.[6] Anorexia nervosa may account for the second highest number of bed-days for a psychiatric condition paid for by private insurance, second only to schizophrenia. In addition to a substantial enduring psychiatric burden related to anorexia nervosa itself and the very common comorbid psychiatric disorders that frequently accompany it, anorexia nervosa often carries a significant ongoing health burden as well. As described below, women with chronic anorexia nervosa show greatly increased risks for early-onset osteopenia and osteoporosis. They also have higher rates of difficulties with fertility, pregnancy, delivery, and child rearing.

Bulimia nervosa is often accompanied by considerable psychiatric impairment, since most patients have at least one concurrent major mood or anxiety disorder and often have other psychiatric comorbidity as well.[7,8] Similarly, rates of mood and anxiety disorders are elevated among individuals with binge eating disorder, compared with the general population.[9]

PRESENTING SIGNS AND SYMPTOMS

Individual symptoms of eating disorders—body image distortion; excessive negative self-evaluation based on weight and shape; extreme fear of being fat, out of line with health concerns; the desire to reduce body fat to levels below those ordinarily considered healthy; restrictive and fad dieting; excessive compulsive exercise among normal-weight and even underweight individuals; and even purging by means of vomiting, laxative abuse, and diuretic abuse—are relatively common.[9] Some of these symptoms may even occur in most women within certain subgroups, as in select college sororities or among female dance majors.

Because these concerns and symptoms are so common, these diagnoses should be kept in mind for virtually every female patient. The age of onset is typically the teens and early adult years, but prepubertal onset and initial onset in the forties and older ages have been reported.

Particular thought regarding anorexia nervosa and bulimia nervosa should be given in young weight-preoccupied women who have mood, anxiety, and self-esteem problems, are perfectionistic and compulsive, overvalue thinness, are prone to severe dieting and exercise, experiment with their diets by eliminating entire classes of food, and/or have menstrual irregularities, bowel complaints and preoccupations, or infertility.

Binge eating disorder is quite common among individuals seeking medical treatment for obesity. About 70% of participants in Overeaters Anonymous and 30% in weight loss programs are estimated to suffer from binge eating disorder.[10,11]

DIAGNOSIS

The DSM-IV diagnostic criteria for anorexia nervosa and bulimia nervosa are given in Tables 63–1 and 63–2. Suggested criteria for binge eating disorders are listed in Table 63–3. Patients with both anorexia nervosa and bulimia nervosa are almost always preoccupied with weight and the desire to be thinner. The two disorders are not mutually exclusive, and there appears to be a continuum among patients of the two symptom complexes of self-starvation and the binge-purge cycle.

The diagnosis of anorexia nervosa is made clinically, is usually straightforward, and is rarely in question. The differential diagnosis includes other conditions associated with weight loss, including endocrine, infectious, and neoplastic conditions associated with anorexia and weight loss, as well as other psychiatric conditions associated with loss of appetite and/or lack of intake, such as major depressive disorders, delusional states, and conversion disorders.

Anorexia Nervosa

Although the diagnosis of anorexia nervosa requires a weight loss of at least 15% below normal weight, many patients lose considerably more before coming to medical attention, and weight loss of 30 to 40% below normal weight are not unusual. Patients engage

---

TABLE 63–1. Diagnostic Criteria for Anorexia Nervosa

A. Refusal to maintain body weight at or above a minimally normal weight for age and height (eg, weight loss leading to maintenance of body weight < 85% of that expected; or failure to make expected weight gain during period of growth, leading to body weight < 85% of that expected)

B. Intense fear of gaining weight or becoming fat, even though underweight

C. Disturbance in the way in which one's body weight or shape is experienced, undue influence of body weight or shape on self-evaluation, or denial of the seriousness of the current low body weight

D. In postmenarcheal females, amenorrhea, that is, the absence of at least three consecutive menstrual cycles. (A woman is considered to have amenorrhea if her periods occur only following hormone, eg, estrogen, administration).

Subcategorized into:

Restricting type: During the current episode of anorexia nervosa the person has not regularly engaged in binge eating or purging behavior (ie, self-induced vomiting or the misuse of laxatives, diuretics, or enemas).

Binge-eating/purging type: During the current episode of anorexia nervosa the person has regularly engaged in binge eating or purging behavior (ie, self-induced vomiting or the misuse of laxatives, diuretics, or enemas).

Adapted from American Psychiatric Association. Diagnostic and statistical manual of mental disorders. 4th ed. Washington (DC): APA; 1994.

in a variety of behaviors to lose weight, including markedly reduced caloric intake, usually in the range of 300 to 600 calories per day, avoiding entire classes of food, and, not unusually, compulsive hard exercise for hours each day. Other frequent, disturbing, and odd behaviors may include refusal to eat in front of others, rituals concerning food preparation and consumption, and unusual flavoring practices (such as putting huge quantities of pepper or lemon juice on all foods). Although patients may initially seem cheerful and energetic, about half develop an accompanying major depression, and all ultimately become moody and irritable. After several years, many patients complain of having no real sense of themselves apart from the anorexia nervosa. Accompanying the weight loss are signs and symptoms indicative of the physical complications of semi-starvation: depletion of fat, muscle wasting (including cardiac muscle loss in severe cases), bradycardia and other arrhythmias, constipation, abdominal pains, leukopenia, hypercortisolemia, osteoporosis, renal complications, and, in extreme cases, the development of cachexia and lanugo (fine, baby hair–like hair over the body). Metabolic alterations that conserve energy are seen in thyroid function (low T_3 syndrome) and reproductive function.

TABLE 63–2. Diagnostic Criteria for Bulimia Nervosa

A. Recurrent episodes of binge eating. An episode of binge eating is characterized by both of the following:
    1. Eating, in a discrete period of time (eg, within any 2-hour period), an amount of food that is definitely larger than most people would eat during a similar period of time and under similar circumstances
    2. A sense of lack of control over eating during the episode (eg, a feeling that one cannot stop eating or control what or how much one is eating)

B. Recurrent, inappropriate compensatory behavior in order to prevent weight gain, such as self-induced vomiting; misuse of laxatives, diuretics, enemas, or other medication; fasting; or excessive exercise

C. The binge eating and inappropriate compensatory behaviors both occurring, on average, at least twice a week for 3 months

D. Self-evaluation unduly influenced by body shape and weight

E. The disturbance not occurring exclusively during episodes of anorexia nervosa

---

Adapted from American Psychiatric Association. Diagnostic and statistical manual of mental disorders. 4th ed. Washington (DC): APA; 1994.

TABLE 63–3. Diagnostic Criteria for Binge Eating Disorder

A. Recurrent episodes of binge eating. An episode of binge eating is characterized by both of the following:
1. Eating, in a discrete period of time (eg, within any 2-hour period), an amount of food that is definitely larger than most people would eat in a similar period of time under similar circumstances
2. A sense of lack of control over eating during the episode (e.g., a feeling that one cannot stop eating or control what or how much one is eating)

B. The binge eating episodes are associated with three (or more) of the following:
1. Eating much more rapidly than normal
2. Eating until feeling uncomfortably full
3. Eating large amounts of food when not feeling physically hungry
4. Eating alone because of being embarrassed by how much one is eating
5. Feeling disgusted with oneself, depressed, or very guilty after overeating

C. Marked distress regarding binge eating

D. The binge eating occurring, on average, at least 2 days a week for 6 months

  Note: The method of determining frequency differs from that used for bulimia nervosa; future research should address whether the preferred method of setting a frequency threshold is counting the number of days on which binges occur or counting the number of episodes of binge eating

E. The binge eating not associated with the regular use of inappropriate compensatory behaviors (eg, purging, fasting, excessive exercise) and not occurring exclusively during the course of anorexia nervosa or bulimia nervosa

Specific type:
Purging type: During the current episode of bulimia nervosa, the person has regularly engaged in self-induced vomiting or the misuse of laxatives, diuretics, or enemas.

Nonpurging type: During the current episode of bulimia nervosa, the person has used other inappropriate compensatory behaviors, such as fasting or excessive exercise, but has not regularly engaged in self-induced vomiting or in the misuse of laxatives, diuretics, or enemas.

Adapted from American Psychiatric Association. Diagnostic and statistical manual of mental disorders. 4th ed. Washington (DC): APA; 1994.

Virtually all female patients stop menstruating; up to a third stop menstruating even before losing sufficient body fat to account for the onset of amenorrhea. A few may retain skimpy periods in spite of advanced malnutrition. Secretion of luteinizing hormone (LH) and follicle-stimulating hormone (FSH) is impaired, and serum estradiol is severely diminished. Consequently, of considerable concern, both bone calcium resorption and retention are impaired, and osteopenia may be noted after only several months of amenorrhea. Since anorexia nervosa often begins in the early to mid-teens, during the peak age of bone formation, the risk of early onset osteoporosis is significant. Anorexia nervosa patients in their mid-twenties have seven times more pathologic stress fractures than have age-matched controls.[12]

Concurrent major depressive disorders and/or generalized anxiety disorders, with or without panic, occur in 50% or more; frank obsessive-compulsive disorder (dealing with non-eating-related issues) occurs in up to 25% of patients. Avoidant and obsessive-compulsive personality disorders are common.

Anorexia nervosa appears in two general varieties, the **restricting** and **binge eating/purging** subtypes, although these may occasionally alternate in the same patient. The restricted patient tends to exert maximal self-control regarding food intake and tends to be socially avoidant, withdrawn, and isolated, with an obsessional thinking style and ritualistic behavior in nonfood areas. In contrast, the binge eating/purging subtype purges by means of vomiting or ingesting extremely large quantities of laxatives and/or diuretics to further the weight loss; sometimes, but not always, purging is preceded by large eating binges. Patients of the binge eating/purging subtype also tend to be depressed and self-destructive, often display the emotional, dramatic, and erratic personality cluster, and not infrequently abuse alcohol and drugs.

Bulimia Nervosa

This disorder occurs predominantly in weight-preoccupied females who engage in substantial eating binges and purging episodes at least twice per week for 3 consecutive months. Eating binges are usually stimulated by hunger because the patient ingests too few calories for their non–binge eating meals. Up to 40% of patients also report that eating binges may be provoked by negative emotional states, such as shame, hurt, or frustration, rather by than hunger. Patients are embarrassed by bulimic behaviors and often are reluctant to voluntarily report them to their primary care clinician. Therefore, in order to make the diagnosis, the clinician who suspects that bulimia nervosa is present has to actively inquire about these behaviors. Certain suggestive physical signs should increase suspicion (see below). Two subtypes of bulimia nervosa are recognizable: patients with the **purging type** use self-induced vomiting or misuse laxatives or diuretics; those with the **nonpurging type** use other inappropriate compensatory behaviors, such as excessive exercise or fasting, but do not ordinarily self-induce vomiting or misuse laxatives or diuretics. Patients frequently consume 2,000 to 10,000 calories per binge, and the binge-purge cycles may occur multiple times per day. Patients always feel that their eating is out of control, feel ashamed, and are often secretive about their problems. Concurrent major depression or anxiety disorders occur in up to 75% of cases.[13] Substantially increased rates of chemical dependency and personality disorders are also seen in these patients.

Binge Eating Disorder

Patients with binge eating disorder typically manifest many of the psychological and behavioral aspects of patients with bulimia nervosa, but they do not employ compensatory behaviors, such as vomiting, use of laxatives, or excessive exercise. Consequently, they tend to be obese. Onset usually occurs in the teens or twenties, often after attempts at severe dieting. As the condition is currently construed, to meet diagnostic criteria, binge eating must occur at least twice a week for at least a 6-month period. Eating binges are triggered by feelings of tension, distress, boredom, habit, or attempts to crash-diet. Some individuals eat to numb themselves emotionally. In comparison with non–binge eaters of similar weights, including non–binge-eating obese individuals, those with binge eating disorders ordinarily have more symptoms of self-loathing, depression, anxiety, and interpersonal sensitivity, and more diagnosable comorbid depressive, substance abuse, and personality disorders than comparison groups of non–binge eating obese persons; but they are less likely than patients with bulimia nervosa to have these comorbid conditions.[4,5]

TREATMENT IN THE OUTPATIENT SETTING

Detailed practice guidelines for treating eating disorders, initially published by the American Psychiatric Association,[14] have just been revised, with considerable input from primary care clinicians.[15] Roles for the generalist clinician in the outpatient management include diagnosis, assessment for appropriate level and site of treatment, coordination of a comprehensive team of medical and mental health personnel, basic counseling and support, medical monitoring, and, at times, initiation and monitoring of psychotropic medication. The extent of involvement varies from case to case, depending on the clinician's familiarity and comfort in dealing with patients with eating disorders, relationship with the particular patient and family, and access to specialty eating disorder services in the community. For outpatient management, frequent contact and discussions among team members is necessary to prevent patients from falling between the cracks or from "splitting" team members against one another. Specific indications for mandatory consultation with a psychiatrist or psychologist with special competence in treating eating disorders include failure of the patient to respond to treatment efforts, severe depression with suicidality or other complex psychiatric disorders, and/or marked family problems.

Anorexia Nervosa

Assessment includes a full history, physical examination, and selective laboratory examinations. The clinician should inquire about the presence of clinical signs and symptoms mentioned above, with special attention to the onset and duration of restrictive eating, the extent and rate of weight loss, exercise patterns, purging by means of self-induced vomiting, laxatives or diuretics, the ingestion of other substances to promote purging or weight loss, and assessment of the patient's attitudes regarding her weight, shape, dieting behaviors, and motivational state with respect to normalizing eating and achieving a healthy weight (defined for menarcheal women as the weight at which normal menstruation and ovulation occurs or resumes). Patients should also be assessed for pathologic shifts in mood, anxiety (with panic), emotional sensitivity, obsessional thoughts, compulsive behaviors, and the use of illicit substances.

Physical examinations should always include height and weight (preferably postvoiding, gowned weight), vital signs (including orthostatic blood pressure changes), and body temperature.

Laboratory tests should routinely include a complete blood count (CBC) including red blood cell (RBC) indices and differential, urinalysis (including specific gravity), blood urea nitrogen (BUN), creatinine, electrolytes, magnesium, phosphorus, calcium, liver function tests, protein and albumin, and thyroid-stimulating hormone (TSH). For those who weigh < 25% below expected healthy weight for height, and/or who are purging, and/or who are eating less than maintenance requirement for protein (minimum of 20 g/d), an electrocardiogram (EKG) should be obtained. For patients amenorrheic for 3 months or more or who have had chronic spotty menstrual periods, bone densitometry by dual-energy x-ray absorptiometry (DEXA) should be performed, both for purposes of obtaining a baseline value and, in the many cases where bone densities fall below the mean for age, for purposes of informing patients and their families. Extensive endocrinologic work-up and brain radiography or imaging studies should not performed, unless there are other specific indications and concerns.

Treatment should be planned in consultation with health professionals who are knowledgeable about the assessment and management of anorexia nervosa. Decisions regarding whether the patient can be treated as an outpatient rest on several factors. Patients should be hospitalized if they show rapid weight loss, before they become physiologically unstable (eg, orthostatic changes of ≥ 30 mm Hg blood pressure; temperature of < 97°F), or if there

are other behavioral indications, such as suicidality or inability to improve eating behaviors or stop compulsive exercise without the ongoing presence of external (ie, nursing) support. Patients who weigh < 25% below expected healthy weights (based on their prior histories and/or extrapolation from their prior growth charts) are likely to require hospital care, at least initially, especially if there is any question of their motivation and/or the quality of family support. Such patients should be hospitalized until they are medically safe *and* are able to maintain and continue weight gain as outpatients; this rarely occurs before the patient has achieved a minimum of 90% of expected healthy weight. Insurance companies may need to be convinced of the seriousness of the problems and the need for ongoing treatment to reduce risks of relapse or chronicity.[16]

Outpatient treatment for anorexia nervosa requires an interdisciplinary team that includes the primary care clinician, a psychiatrist and/or psychologist familiar with treating eating disorders, and a registered dietician. The comprehensive outpatient treatment program usually includes some form of ongoing counseling and psychotherapy for the patient (and often family counseling as well), dietary counseling, medical monitoring, and sometimes psychotropic medication.

Medical monitoring by the generalist clinician initially entails having the patient visit the office at least weekly, and sometimes twice weekly, for postvoiding, gowned weights early in the day, usually obtained by a nurse. Initially, patients may or may not be told their weights, depending on their ability to withstand the shock of hearing the actual numbers. The treatment team should establish a minimum weight below which hospitalization is required, and an expected rate of weight gain, about < 0.5 to 1 lb/wk for outpatients. Primary clinicians should stress the importance of weight gain as a prerequisite for psychological, behavioral, and attitudinal recovery. Laboratory tests, including items from the panel mentioned above, may be repeated on a variable schedule, depending on the course of the patient's condition. For purging patients, frequent serum potassium and EKG rhythm strip assessments should be performed. Monitoring should continue until the patient is at a healthy and stable weight.

Primary care clinicians should make decisions concerning the use of psychiatric medication in conjunction with a knowledgeable psychopharma-cologist. No drug works for anorexia nervosa in the absence of adequate food intake, and selective sero-tonin reuptake inhibitors (SSRIs) have not been shown to speed up weight gain or reduce the length of hospitalization when added to a program of good nutritional rehabilitation and nursing care. Once the patient is achieving adequate intake and, partic-ularly, once weight has been regained, SSRIs may help prevent relapse, weight loss, return of depres-sion, and rehospitalization. Fluoxetine (Prozac) in dosages of about 40 mg/d has been useful for these purposes.[17] However, anorexia nervosa outpatients receiving citalopram (Celexa) together with psy-chotherapy actually lost weight, compared with those receiving psychotherapy alone.[18] Clinicians often use SSRIs to treat residual mood, anxiety, and obsessive-compulsive problems in ambulatory patients with anorexia nervosa. Although no con-trolled studies yet exist for these practices, for treat-ment-resistant patients, some clinicians also use low doses of buspirone (eg, 5 to 15 mg bid or benzodi-azepines (eg, clonazepam 0.5 mg bid) or even atypi-cal antipsychotics (eg, risperidone 0.5 mg/d) or olanzapine 2.5 to 10 mg/d) to help patients deal with anticipatory anxieties concerning food intake.

Osteopenia and osteoporosis present formida-ble problems. Unfortunately, although many clini-cians employ supplemental estrogens, calcium, and vitamin D to combat osteopenia and early osteo-porosis, these interventions have not been shown to be effective in reversing these conditions in anorexia nervosa.[12] In practice, virtually all clinicians pre-scribe supplemental calcium and vitamin D. How-ever, they are divided in their opinions regarding recommendation of supplemental estrogens or oral contraceptives. Various treatments for promoting bone growth and retarding bone resorption are now being studied, but no data yet exist to guide clinical practice on this point.

Bulimia Nervosa

The principles of assessment for bulimia nervosa are similar to those described for anorexia nervosa. The key issues for the primary care clinician are to assess for the presence of the disorder, motivate patients to seek and continue with outpatient treat-ment, monitor medical issues that may emerge, and sometimes prescribe and monitor psychotropic medication in conjunction with psychotherapy pro-

vided by a psychologist. The clinician should assess the patient's overall weight and menstrual history (since patients may not be in good health status with regard to these parameters, even though they may be within a statistically healthy range), usual nonbinge dietary intake, nature and frequency of eating binges, and nature and frequency of purges. The clinician should also ask the patient how many pounds she may be willing to gain as the price of recovery from bulimia nervosa, to assess her moti-vation, since a small degree of weight gain may be necessary to reduce the physiologic pressure to binge. Patients should also be assessed regarding adverse life stressors, pathologic shifts in mood, anxiety (with panic), emotional sensitivity, obses-sional thoughts, compulsive behaviors, and the use of alcohol and illicit drugs, including diet pills and other stimulants.

Physical examination should include height and weight and examination for "squirrel" or "chipmunk cheeks" due to salivary gland hyperplasia, erosion of dental enamel, particularly involving the incisors and canines, and scarring on the dorsum of the fin-gers and hands, often a sign of self-induced vomit-ing. Complaints may indicate esophageal and gastric irritation and rectal bleeding or constipation due to the effects of chronic laxative abuse on the colon.

Routine laboratory tests for bulimia nervosa should be based on the frequency and severity of purging. Generally, these should include a CBC, electrolytes, magnesium, phosphorus, calcium, and TSH. Serum amylase is occasionally useful as a marker of purge frequency and severity. Common abnormalities include hypochloremic hypokalemic alkalosis and hyperamylasemia of about 25 to 40% over normal values due to excessive salivary gland stimulation.[19]

Treatment should be planned in consultation with mental health professionals who are knowl-edgeable about assessing and managing bulimia nervosa. Inpatient treatment is rarely indicated for bulimia nervosa and is recommended only when patients continue to be considerably impaired after having failed competent attempts at outpatient care or have other behavioral indications, such as serious suicidality. For uncomplicated bulimia nervosa, about 12 to 16 sessions of cognitive behavior psycho-therapy is the most effective short-term intervention. This approach includes considerable attention to careful monitoring of eating behaviors as well as the emotional and situational contexts that trigger binge eating and purging, education about the physiology and psychology of bulimia nervosa, dietary assessment, meal planning, challenges to maladaptive and negative thoughts that contribute to maintaining the disorders, planned behavior changes, and suggestions for alternative forms of coping. Many patients find value in "guided self-help," using workbooks that provide cognitive behavior programs, and clinicians should direct patients to these sources. Controlled studies have also shown interpersonal psychotherapy to be helpful in bulimia nervosa. This approach focuses on recent actual and imagined losses and traumas, interpersonal disputes, and, to some extent, personality deficits.

Studies have shown that patients who also take certain antidepressant drugs do better than those receiving psychotherapy alone. The SSRI fluoxetine is the best studied and the only drug to receive the US Food and Drug Administration (FDA) approval for treating bulimia nervosa. Studies have shown that 60 mg/d, about three times higher than the usual antidepressant doses, is the most effective dosage for reducing bulimic symptoms, even in the absence of depression. In addition to being an antidepressant, the medication has antianxiety and antipanic effects and, at the higher doses, antiobsessive-compulsive effects as well. Although no studies are available, other SSRIs are likely to be effective in treating bulimia nervosa as well. Some other heterocyclic antidepressant drugs, including imipramine, desipramine, trazodone, and the monoamine oxidase inhibitor tranylcypromine, have been shown to be effective in reducing the symptoms of bulimia nervosa. However, because of their side effects and potential toxicities, most clinicians no longer use these older agents as first-line treatment for bulimia nervosa. Because of its propensity to induce seizures in individuals who have recently purged, bupropion (Wellbutrin) is contraindicated in patients with active bulimia nervosa.

After symptom remission, which occurs in about 60 to 70% of patients receiving these treatments, most authorities suggest that at least 1 more year of "booster session" psychotherapy and medication be continued to diminish the risk of relapse.

Binge Eating Disorder

The principles for treating bulimia nervosa apply to binge eating disorder as well. Since many patients seeking treating for binge eating disorder are overweight, issues regarding the assessment and management of obesity also apply. This is discussed in detail in Chapter 89. Most authorities suggest that the binge eating aspects of the disorder be controlled before weight reduction programs are undertaken. Treatment programs using combinations of cognitive behavioral therapy and dietary management, some of which include SSRIs, have been most effective for short-term treatment. Long-term outcomes research studies regarding any current programs using cognitive behavior therapies, controlled low-calorie diets, currently permissible pharmacologic treatments, and other interventions for binge eating disorder are sparse. Some patients have been helped by guided self-help manuals for controlling binge eating.[20]

PROGNOSIS

Anorexia Nervosa

On average, full recovery within a few years is seen in 30 to 50% of patients. Younger-age-onset patients and those with the restricted rather than bulimic subtype appear to have a better prognosis, and of such patients, up to 85% may recover, but, for many, full recovery takes 6 to 7 years.[8] Death from starvation, sudden cardiac arrhythmias, and suicide occurs in 5 to 10% of patients within 10 years and in almost 20% of patients within 20 years of onset.[21] As mentioned above, death rates for anorexia nervosa are much higher than for community comparison groups and for women with other psychiatric illnesses.

Bulimia Nervosa

Short-term outcomes for patients treated with cognitive behavior therapy and/or medication are usually favorable, with about 60 to 70% of patients experiencing substantial symptom remission. However, about 30% of patients experience some degree of relapse within the first year, indicating that ongoing treatment to maximize relapse prevention should be conducted for a minimum of 1 year following symptom remission. Some studies indicate that well-treated patients have good rates of ongoing and sustained improvement 10 to 15 years after their initial presentation.[22]

Binge Eating Disorder

Long-term outcome data are not available.

PREVENTION AND SCREENING

Efforts at screening and prevention have been undertaken in numerous school programs (kindergarten through Grade 12) as well as in women's health programs in colleges and universities. A National Eating Disorders Awareness Week providing education, screening, and referral has been in existence for several years, conducting programs on hundreds of college campuses. Although many preventive intervention efforts have been attempted at the elementary, high school, and college levels, the results are, at best, mixed. Authorities differ as to whether these interventions have been helpful or even harmful by virtue of glamorizing eating disorders in susceptible populations. Carefully targeted screening efforts in particularly vulnerable populations, for example, gymnasts, ballet students, female runners, and younger female relatives of women with eating disorders, might be of conceivable aid in early detection. But such efforts should be linked to readily available and accessible education and treatment programs, if they are to actually help and avoid negative unintended consequences.

PREGNANCY AND BREAST-FEEDING

Although eating disorders may occasionally first begin during pregnancy, many patients get pregnant in the midst of actively symptomatic disorders or during early recovery. Although fertility is decreased in anorexia nervosa during episodes of malnutrition, on the whole, women with lifetime histories of anorexia nervosa may not have reduced fertility. However, women who are actively anorectic at the time of pregnancy as well as women with a prior history of anorexia nervosa appear to be at risk of a greater number of birth complications and of giving birth to babies of lower birth weight than are controls.[23] Women with anorexia nervosa who become pregnant may be able to eat in a more healthy fashion during pregnancy for the sake of the fetus. However, many often revert to a more symptomatic state following delivery. Changes in body shape that occur during pregnancy may be particularly distressing to women with eating disorders. Attention should be paid to the mothering skills of those whose mothers have, and have had, eating disorders in order to minimize the risk of transmitting their eating disorders to their children.[24–26] Clinicians should apply cautions generally used regarding the use of SSRIs and other psychotropic drugs during pregnancy and breast-feeding. This is discussed in further detail in Chapter 16, "Depressive Disorders in Pregnancy and the Postpartum Period."

USE OF ORAL CONTRACEPTIVE PILLS AND HORMONE REPLACEMENT

In the absence of clear-cut data to show that oral contraceptive pills and hormone replacement are useful to prevent or reverse calcium loss in anorexia nervosa, authorities are divided regarding recommending their use for these purposes. Some routinely prescribe estrogen, assuming that positive effects on bone calcium stores may be facilitated. Others believe that this is unwise, since the pseudomenses induced by oral contraceptives may lull patients and clinicians into unwarranted complacency regarding menstrual function and/or obscure the potential return of healthy physiologic menses.

RESOURCES

The American Psychiatric Association
1400 K Street Northwest
Washington, DC 20005
Telephone: 1-888-357-7924
Web site: www.psych.org

The American Psychiatric Association has produced authoritative practice guidelines for the treatment of eating disorders. A revision of the 1993 guidelines was published in 2000. See www.psych.org/clin_res/guide.bk.cfm.

RESOURCES (continued)

The Academy for Eating Disorders
6728 Old McClean Village Drive
McLean, Virginia 22101-3906
Telephone: (703) 556-9222
Web site: www.aedweb.org

The Academy for Eating Disorders provides information about eating disorders, including a position statement regarding medical insurance for treatment of severe eating disorders. The site also has a directory of mental health professionals who have special interest and experience in treating patients with eating disorders.

Eating Disorders Awareness and Prevention, Inc.
603 Stewart Street, Suite 803
Seattle, Washington 98101
Telephone: (206) 382-3587
        1-800-931-2237 (Information for patients and the public)
Web site: www.edap.org

EDAP is devoted to the awareness and prevention of eating disorders. The EDAP Web site contains information for patients and families, as well as information about patient education materials and modules, which can be ordered through the site.

Publications
Of particular note are several guided self-help manuals for bulimia nervosa and binge eating disorders that many patients and clinicians have found useful:
Fairburn C. Overcoming binge eating. New York (NY): Guilford; 1995.
Apple R, Agras WS. Overcoming eating disorders: a client's guide. San Antonio (TX): Psychological
        Press; 1998.
Agras WS, Apple R. Overcoming eating disorders: therapist's guide. San Antonio (TX): Psychological
        Press; 1998.

REFERENCES

1. Katzman DK, Zipursky RB. Adolescents with anorexia nervosa: the impact of the disorder on bones and brains. Ann NY Acad Sci 1997;817:127–37.

2. Walters EE, Kendler KS. Anorexia nervosa and anorexic-like syndromes in a population based female twin sample. Am J Psychiatry 1995;152:64–71.

3. Sullivan PF, Bulik CM, Kendler KS. Genetic epidemiology of bulimia nervosa. Br J Psychiatry 1998;173:75–9.

4. Spitzer RL, Devlin MC, Walsh BT, et al. Binge eating disorder: a multisite field trial of the diagnostic criteria. Int J Eating Disorders 1992;11:191–203.

5. Spitzer RL, Yanovski S, Wadden T, et al. Binge eating disorder: its further validation in a multisite study. Int J Eating Disorders 1993;13:137–53.

6. Sullivan PF. Mortality in anorexia nervosa. Am J Psychiatry 1995;152:1073–4.

7. Lilenfeld LR, Kaye WH, Greeno CG, et al. Psychiatric disorders in women with bulimia nervosa and their first-degree relatives: effects of comorbid substance dependence. Int J Eating Disorders 1997;22:253–64.

8. Lilenfeld LR, Kaye WH, Greeno CG, et al. A controlled family study of anorexia nervosa and bulimia nervosa: psychiatric disorders in first-degree relatives and effects of proband comorbidity. Arch Gen Psychiatry 1998;55:603–10.

9. Drewnowski A, Hopkins SA, Kessler RC. The prevalence of bulimia nervosa in the US college student population. Am J Public Health, 1988;78:1322–5.

10. de Zwaan M, Nutziger DO, Schoenbeck G. Binge eating in overweight women. Comprehensive Psychiatry 1992;33:256–61.

11. Devlin M. Assessment and treatment of binge eating disorder. Psychiatr Clin North Am 1996;19:761–72.

12. Rigotti NA, Nussbaum SR, Herzog DB, et al. The clinical course of osteoporosis in anorexia nervosa: a longitudinal study of cortical bone mass. JAMA 1991;265:1133–8.

13. Johnson C, Connors ME. The etiology and treatment of bulimia nervosa. New York (NY): Basic Books;1987.

14. American Psychiatric Association. Practice guidelines for eating disorders. Am J Psychiatry 1993;150:207–28.

15. American Psychiatric Association. Practice guidelines for eating disorders, Revised edition. Am J Psychiatry 2000;157 Suppl:1–39.

16. Kaye W, Kaplan AS, Zucker ML. Treating eating disorders in a managed care environment. Psychiatr Clin North Am 1996;19:793–810.

17. Kaye WH, Weltzin TE, Hsu LK, Bulik CM. An open trial of fluoxetine in patients with anorexia nervosa. J Clin Psychiatry 1991;52:464–71.

18. Bergh C, Eriksson M, Lindberg G, Södersten P. Selective serotonin reuptake inhibitors in anorexia. Lancet 1996;348:1459–60.

19. Mitchell JE, Pyle RL, Eckert ED, et al. Electrolyte and other physiological abnormalities in patients with bulimia. Psychol Med 1988;13:273–8.

20. Fairburn C. Overcoming binge eating. New York (NY): Guilford; 1995.

21. Steinhausen H-CH, Rauss-Mason C, Seidel R. Follow-up studies of anorexia nervosa: a review of four decades of outcome research. Psychol Med 1991;21:447–54.

22. Keel PK, Mitchell JE. Outcome in bulimia nervosa. Am J Psychiatry 1997;154:313–21.

23. Bulik CM, Sullivan PF, Fear JL, et al. Fertility and reproduction in women with anorexia nervosa: a controlled study. J Clin Psychiatry 1999;60:130–5.

24. Stein A, Woolley H, Cooper S, et al. An observational study of mothers with eating disorders and their infants. J Child Psychol Psychiatry Allied Disciplines 1994;35:733–48.

25. Russell GFM, Treasure J, Eisler I. Mothers with anorexia nervosa who underfeed their children: their recognition and management. Psychol Med 1998;28(1):93–108.

26. Agras WS, Hammer L, McNicholas F. A prospective study of the influence of eating-disordered mothers on their children. Int J Eating Disorders 1999;25:253–62.

64

SUBSTANCE ABUSE

Karen Miotto, MD, and Elizabeth Suti, MFT

Addiction is a chronic relapsing disease involving the misuse or compulsive use of drugs or alcohol. "Substance abuse and dependence" describe the use of drugs or alcohol despite adverse consequences in health, social, family, occupational, or legal functioning. Patterns of drug and alcohol use are variable, and people with addictive disease cannot predict when they will lose control and use to excess. Addictive disease is a major public health problem in this country, impacting women across the life cycle. This chapter reviews recent studies on women and addiction and provides the primary care clinician with information on epidemiology, signs and symptoms, and medical and behavioral treatments.

Differences in how men and women are affected by addictive disorders have only recently become a focus of study by the United States National Institute of Drug Abuse (NIDA). Historically, studies of substance abuse disorders have been done on cohorts of men, with the assumption that women's and men's substance abuse had a common etiology and progression. Recent research on substance abuse in women has disproved these assumptions, with disturbing findings. With less use of alcohol, tobacco, and many illicit drugs, women may proceed more rapidly to drug dependence and may suffer greater medical consequences than men. This quickened progression has been termed "telescoping."[1] The National Center on Addiction and Substance Abuse (CASA) at Columbia University analyzed data from thousands of sources for their 1996 report, "Substance Abuse and the American Woman." The following statement from the report summarizes its findings: "Women who smoke, abuse alcohol or use illegal drugs suffer the same consequences as men, but the harsh reality of women's addiction is that illness, violence and death come more quickly, and the social stigma is more severe."[2]

Inaccurate stereotypes of addicted women may prevent clinicians from detecting the disorder and making early interventions. For most women, addiction is so inconsistent with their image of themselves as homemakers, members of the work force, and mothers that it is often out of their own scope of recognition. This view of addiction as a hidden disease, combined with societal stigma of the "fallen woman," fuels a sense of guilt and shame that impedes women of all racial, geographic, and socioeconomic backgrounds when seeking addiction treatment.

Generally, women are more likely to seek medical treatment than are men. This provides an opportunity for diagnosis and treatment by primary care clinicians. Women are more comfortable seeking help for the medical or psychiatric symptoms associated with their substance abuse rather than for the actual substance abuse problem.[3] The physical and emotional complaints with which substance-abusing women present include fatigue, headaches, gastric distress, sexual and fertility problems, insomnia, depression, and anxiety. This illustrates the importance of regular substance abuse screening by clinicians. When substance abuse problems are overlooked, inappropriate tests or psychoactive medications may be prescribed, and the opportunity to refer the patient to treatment is lost.

EPIDEMIOLOGY

Results from the 1997 National Household Survey on Drug Abuse (NHSDA) indicate that substance use is greater in men than in women. However, women's substance use and abuse have been on the rise. The following are some of the results of the 1997 survey:

- Alcohol and tobacco are the most frequently used substances by women.
- Fifty percent of women reported alcohol use in the previous month.
- More than 27% of women had used tobacco in the previous month.[4]
- Thirty-four percent of women reported that they had used marijuana, cocaine, hallucinogens, heroin, or inhalants at some point in their lifetime.[2]

Notably, the most intense use of drugs and alcohol by women is during the childbearing years, which include the adolescent years. There is grave concern that the gender gap between adolescent girls and boys has been closing in regard to their use of all substances. Girls and boys are now equally likely to smoke and use alcohol,[5] and there is a narrowing gap for the use of other drugs. The onset of substance use is occurring at an earlier age. Alcohol or drug use at age 15 years or younger is an important predictor of progression to substance dependence.[6]

Women's consumption of alcohol has been increasing over the past 50 years. A recent household survey found that 2.6% of all women reported consuming 60 drinks per month.[7] This is a measure of heavy drinking as established by the National Institute of Alcohol Abuse and Alcoholism (NIAAA), which defines moderate drinking as no more than two drinks per day for men and no more than one drink a day for women (as women are more susceptible to the effects of alcohol).[8] Young women are now drinking to the point of intoxication more frequently. College women are still less likely to "binge" drink than men (30% versus 50%), but this is another area in which the gender gap is closing.[9] It has been documented that heavy drinking by women during their college years predicts alcohol abuse problems for those women later in life.[10,11]

Women's abuse of drugs also has been rising steadily over the past 50 years. Today, 3.1 million women regularly use illicit drugs, and 3.5 million misuse prescription drugs.[2] Men and women equally misuse psychoactive drugs such as stimulants, tranquilizers, sedatives, and analgesics. The greater prevalence of depression and anxiety in women accounts for the fact that two-thirds of all prescriptions for tranquilizers and antidepressants are written for women.[2] Women often have difficulty identifying the misuse of prescription drugs sanctioned by their clinicians. Two common forms of prescription drug misuse are drinking alcohol while on psychoactive medications and combining different types of psychoactive medications (to achieve intoxication or to relieve stress).

ASSOCIATED FACTORS

The etiology of drug abuse by women often lies in a psychiatric disorder that has a bidirectional relationship with the substance abuse disorder. Women frequently report the coexistence of psychiatric conditions such as depression, anxiety, panic disorder, agoraphobia, and eating disorders.[2,11] Women often experience a significant loss of social, familial, financial, or occupational support prior to (or in association with) their drug use.[12] They may describe a series of failed relationships, often patterned after childhood abuse and family dysfunction.

Another significant psychosocial factor that increases a woman's risk for substance abuse is having a partner who is a substance abuser. Many women report that they were introduced to drugs by their boyfriends or husbands whereas men typically begin their drug use with other male friends. Women are strongly influenced by their primary relationships. In fact, women report that using substances provides a sense of connection to partners who are also abusing substances.[13,14] Alcoholic women often have male partners who drink heavily. This is a concern because heavy drinking by men is highly correlated with domestic violence.[2] A self-perpetuating cycle is observed as batterers and survivors turn to substance abuse to escape from the pain of their situation.

Female alcoholics are more likely than male alcoholics to have a family history of alcoholism.[12] In a small study by Lex, women with a family history of alcoholism were found to have decreased impairment in motor and cognitive tasks after alcohol intake, compared to controls. It is hypothesized that individuals with a family history of alcoholism have a higher tolerance for alcohol, which allows them to drink more and which increases their susceptibility to developing alcohol-related problems.[1]

Abuse and trauma have been strongly correlated with later substance abuse in women.[15] Both physical and sexual abuse in childhood are as significant as genetic risk factors for developing a substance abuse disorder. Various studies report that nearly 70% of women undergoing substance abuse treatment have been sexually abused as children, compared with 12% of men.[16,17] The long-term effects of child abuse include post-traumatic stress disorder (PTSD), depression, anxiety, and increased vulnerability to other forms of trauma such as domestic violence, rape, and physical assault.

A troubling connection exists between women's desire to control their weight and the use of tobacco, stimulants, and opiates. Many women who quit tobacco and stimulants quickly relapse due to fears of increased appetite and weight gain. The media and advertising portray ideals of youth, thinness, and sexuality in association with tobacco, alcohol, and other drugs. These standards of beauty and thinness are a factor in some women's initiation and continued use of certain substances.

MEDICAL ASPECTS

Gender differences in susceptibility to the medical consequences of drugs and alcohol is an evolving area of research. Alcohol-dependent women have a higher age-adjusted mortality rate than non-alcohol-dependent men. This increased mortality is associated with liver disease, accidents, and a five-fold increased rate of suicide.[18] There is a greater incidence of severe liver disease in women with a lower alcohol intake and a shorter duration of use than in men. The increased bioavailability of alcohol in women is associated with women's higher fat-to-water ratio in body composition, which results in a less diluted alcohol dose per drink. Lower levels of gastric activity of alcohol dehydrogenase contribute to higher and faster peak levels of alcohol in the blood, compared with similar alcohol consumption per body weight in men. Both alcoholic men and women have very low levels of alcohol dehydrogenase; this allows most of the alcohol to be absorbed before it is metabolized, contributing to toxicity.[19] Oral contraceptive use is also associated with decreased rates of alcohol metabolism. These metabolic differences may account for the quickened progression to pathologic effects of alcohol, such as fatty liver, hypertension, anemia, malnutrition, gastric hemorrhage, and ulcer.[20] In addition, a greater susceptibility to cardiomyopathy and decline in cardiac function has been reported in alcoholic women, compared with men.[21]

Gender differences exist in the metabolism of nicotine as well. Women generally smoke fewer cigarettes than do men but metabolize nicotine more slowly, thus achieving nicotine levels similar to those found in men. Smoking is clearly associated with cardiovascular morbidity. Smoking reduces estrogen levels, which further increases the risks of heart disease and osteoporosis.[2] Oral contraceptive use combined with smoking greatly increases the risk of a heart attack, especially for women over the age of 35 years.[2]

Alarm signs for alcohol and drug abuse are the same for both men and women (Table 64–1). Alcohol organ system toxicity includes diseases of the liver and pancreas; cancer of the esophagus, nasopharynx and larynx; and neurologic disorders. Laboratory abnormalities associated with alcoholism include elevated γ-glutamyl transpeptidase (GGT) and increased aspartate aminotransferase (AST) relative to alanine aminotransferase (ALT). Mean corpuscular volume (MCV) and triglycerides can also be elevated.

The effects of drinking and drug use on sexuality and reproduction are complex. Some women use drugs and alcohol with the expectation of enhanced sexual enjoyment. Others may attempt to remedy sexual dysfunction through the use of such substances. However, the chronic use of such substances has been shown to exacerbate sexual dysfunction. Women addicted to alcohol, stimulants, and opiates report a high prevalence of amenorrhea, dysmenorrhea, anorgasmia, infertility, and early menopause.

Female drug users are at higher risk than men for contracting acquired immunodeficiency syndrome (AIDS) and other sexually transmitted

TABLE 64–1. Observable Evidence of Substance Abuse

Tremor/perspiring/tachycardia

Evidence of current intoxication

Prescription drug seeking behavior

Frequent falls; unexplained bruises

Diabetes, elevated BP, ulcers; nonresponsive to treatment

Frequent hospitalizations

Inflamed eroded nasal septum

Dilated pupils

Track marks/injection sites

Gunshot/knife wounds

Suicide talk/attempt; Depression

diseases (STDs). This higher risk is due to unsafe sexual practices with multiple partners, human immunodeficiency virus (HIV)–positive drug-using sexual partners, and injection drug use. The Centers for Disease Control and Prevention report that approximately two-thirds of women with AIDS contracted the disease either by intravenous drug use or through sexual contact with an intravenous (IV) drug user.[8] The relationship between injection drug use and HIV infection is important; however, there is also growing evidence of a connection between the use of alcohol and illicit drugs and high-risk sexual activity. The practice of "unsafe sex" among women who use crack cocaine results in an equal or greater risk of contracting AIDS and other STDs, compared with users of IV drugs.[2]

In addition to sexual dysfunction and the contraction of STDs, female stimulant users may present with burns on their hands or lips from crack pipes or with rhinorrhea after intranasal ingestion. Extensive intranasal use of drugs results in an inflamed and eroded nasal septum. Pulmonary edema and pneumomediastinum may develop abruptly after crack is smoked. Mortality results from arrhythmia, myocardial infarction, stroke, subarachnoid hemorrhage, or drug-induced seizure.

Due to a sensation of bugs or impurities under the skin (known as formication), amphetamine users often present with self-inflicted skin lesions. Drug-induced psychosis or paranoia is also a common presentation. Toxicity includes hypertension, hyperpyrexia, arrhythmia, diarrhea, and vomiting. Less frequent toxic effects are rhabdomyolysis, seizure, myocardial infarction, and coma.

As the purity of heroin has increased, there is a growing number of heroin users who are smoking heroin or using it intranasally. These users do not present with "track" marks or abscesses, but they develop the same physical dependence and withdrawal as IV heroin users. Toxic opiate complications include hypotension, bradycardia, respiratory depression, pulmonary edema, and overdosage.

The development of medication for addictive disorders is an active area of research at the NIDA. Currently there are FDA-approved medications to help with recovery from alcohol, opiate, and nicotine dependence. Naltrexone is an opiate antagonist used to decrease alcohol craving and to prevent relapse in detoxified opiate-dependent individuals. Opiate agonist medications such as methadone and levo-α-acetylmethadol (LAAM) are provided at licensed opiate treatment facilities. Buprenorphine, a partial agonist medication, is currently in development for use by clinicians in a less restrictive setting, for opiate detoxification or detoxification maintenance. Many medications are available for nicotine-dependent individuals. These include nicotine preparations (gums, patches, and nasal sprays) and bupropion (Wellbutrin SR and Zyban), which are described in more detail in Chapter 12, "Smoking Cessation."

The clinical signs and symptoms of withdrawal from alcohol, sedatives, stimulants, nicotine and opiates are listed in Table 64–2. Severe withdrawal from alcohol and sedative/hypnotic drugs is considered medically dangerous due to the risk of autonomic hyperactivity and seizures. The flulike withdrawal associated with opiate use is medically distressing and frightening for patients, however, it is not considered dangerous. Seizures do not occur in opiate withdrawal, and autonomic changes are mild. Stimulant withdrawal is described as a "crash" and is marked by dysphoria, increased appetite, and somnolence. It can usually be managed without medical intervention or hospitalization. Detoxification protocols are provided by the Substance Abuse and Mental Health Service Administration Treatment Improvement Protocol Series (TIPS) No. 19 (see "Resources").

COSTS TO SOCIETY

The consequences of substance abuse include deterioration of physical health, family dysfunction, job loss, poverty, and criminal behavior. Approximately 140,000 women die from smoking-related illnesses each year. Illnesses related to tobacco use kills half of all women smokers.[2] Lung cancer now surpasses breast cancer as the leading cancer killer of American women. Death rates for female alcoholics are almost twice as high as those for male alcoholics in the same age group. The higher death rate is due to alcohol-related illness, accidents, violence, and suicide.[18]

Another social consequence of addiction is women in prison. Substance abuse problems are adding significantly to the female prison population. Between 1980 and 1994, the number of women inmates quintupled. By 1989 one-third of incarcerated women were serving time for drug-related

TABLE 64–2. Clinical Signs and Symptoms of Substance Withdrawal

Substance	Signs and Symptoms
Alcohol, sedative/hypnotic, or anxiolytic	2 of the following: Autonomic hyperactivity (eg, sweating or pulse > 100 bpm) Increased hand tremor Insomnia Nausea or vomiting Transient visual, tactile, or auditory hallucinations or illusions Psychomotor agitation Anxiety Grand mal seizures
Amphetamine (or related substance) or cocaine	Dysphoric mood and 2 of the following: Fatigue Vivid unpleasant dreams Insomnia or hypersomnia Increased appetite Psychomotor retardation or agitation
Nicotine	4 of the following: Dysphoric or depressed mood Insomnia Irritability, frustration, or anger Anxiety Difficulty concentrating Restlessness Decreased heart rate Increased appetite or weight gain
Opioid	3 of the following: Dysphoric mood Nausea or vomiting Muscle aches Lacrimation or rhinorrhea Pupillary dilatation, piloerection, or sweating Diarrhea Yawning Fever Insomnia

offenses, and 40% of female inmates reported being on drugs at the time they committed their crimes.[2]

A study that analyzed factors resulting in the "disruption of primary caregiving" by mothers found that children born to substance-abusing women are at great risk for being placed in foster care.[22] Between 1985 and 1994 the incidence of child abuse and neglect increased by 64%; in many areas of the country, more than 75% of these abuse cases were associated with alcohol and drug use.[23]

Such costs to society as family disruption, poverty, missed workdays, homelessness, and accidents are difficult to quantify.

SCREENING

Primary care clinicians are in a key position to identify substance abuse disorders in their patients. Nonjudgmental questions can be asked about all classes of substances—alcohol, tobacco, marijuana,

TABLE 64–3. Alcoholism Screening and Assessment

Screen*

At each visit, ask about alcohol use (drinks per week; maximum number of drinks per occasion in previous month).

Use CAGE questions to probe for alcohol problem:

Have you ever tried to **C**ut down on your drinking?

Do you get **A**nnoyed when people talk about your drinking?

Do you feel **G**uilty about your drinking?

Have you ever had an **E**ye-opener (a drink first thing in the morning)?

Assessments:

Medical problems (eg, blackouts, depression, hypertension, trauma, abdominal pain, liver dysfunction, sexual problems, sleep disorders)

Laboratory tests (elevated GGT or other LFTs; elevated MCV; +positive blood alcohol level)

Behavioral problems (work, family, school, accidents)

Alcohol dependence (3+ on CAGE questions, or one or more of the following: compulsion to drink, impaired control, withdrawal symptoms, increased tolerance, relief drinking)

*Screen is positive if alcohol consumption is >7 drinks per week or >3 drinks per occasion (in women) and if CAGE question score >1 (Each "yes" = one point)
GGT = γ-glutamyl transpeptidase; LFT = liver function test; MCV = mean corpuscular volume.

stimulants (cocaine, amphetamines, and cold or diet preparations), opiates (heroin and prescription and pain medications), sedatives (sleeping pills and tranquilizers), hallucinogens (lysergic acid diethylamide [LSD], mescaline, and peyote), "designer" drugs (ecstasy and GHB), and inhalants (gases, glue, and fumes). It is best to ask first about legal substances. Such questions can be asked as routinely as questions about other behavioral and lifestyle patterns. The likelihood of getting honest answers to assessment questions is increased if questions are asked in a matter-of-fact and unthreatening manner. This kind of focus and concern communicates to the patient that the clinician is informed about substance abuse and that she or he is in a position to provide understanding and assistance.

The screening instrument shown in Table 64–3 was adapted by the American Society of Addiction Medicine from the CAGE questionnaire. The CAGE questionnaire (the name of which is an acronym formed from key words of its principal questions [see Table 64–3]) is a simple assessment tool that can assist primary care clinicians in determining if a patient is at risk for developing a substance abuse problem or if such a problem already exists. The CAGE questions can

be modified to include an assessment of licit and illicit drug use.

Screening for prescription drug abuse can be a sensitive and challenging process for both clinician and patients. Prescription drug–seeking behavior by women may occur in the course of treatment of comorbid anxiety, depression, and chronic pain. Screening for prescription drug misuse includes questions about the number of health care clinicians the patient has, emergency room visits, and medication use patterns. Additional questions include a history of medication overdose and termination of care by health care clinicians. Collateral information is often necessary for a diagnosis of prescription drug abuse. A spectrum of prescription medication problems can be seen in women; these problems range from the use of medication as a means of coping with illness, pain, and stress to the use of medication for the purpose of intoxication.

If a diagnosis of substance abuse or dependence cannot be made on the basis of the results of the screening process, the primary care clinician can get collateral information, with the patient's permission, from family members. If a substance abuse disorder is diagnosed, the patient ideally should be referred to an addiction specialist or a substance abuse program. If the screening results are negative for substance abuse, periodic screening is still indicated as a person's drug and alcohol use can change over time.

APPROACH TO THE ADDICTED PATIENT

The screening assessment may be the first step in motivating the patient to think about changing her substance use behavior. Prochaska and DiClemente sought to understand how and why people change smoking behaviors. They described a series of six stages, from precontemplation and contemplation to action and beyond, that discriminate different stages of a patient's readiness to change.[24] Miller and Rollnick wrote extensively about a model for moving substance users through the stages of change.[25] Individuals with a substance abuse disorder are always ambivalent about changing their behavior. The hallmarks of addiction are denial and shame, making it very difficult for most addicted people to ask for help.

During the precontemplation stage, the individual does not even see a problem and therefore does not recognize a need for change. In the period that follows, called contemplation, there is some awareness that a problem may exist, yet there is a great deal of vacillation between admitting and dismissing that possibility. There is a tension between awareness and denial that forces the individual to think about the issue of substance abuse in a new way.[25] Miller showed that patients are more resistant to change if the clinician uses a highly confrontational approach as such an approach can evoke feelings of shame, guilt, defensiveness, or anger. It is more effective to give feedback in a supportive way.

Miller and Sanchez identified six elements or techniques that are recommended as an effective way to intervene on a substance-using patient with a brief intervention. The acronym "FRAMES" represents standard elements of the motivational interviewing method of providing feedback:[25]

- **F**eedback of personal risk and impairment
- **R**esponsibility for change
- **A**dvice to change
- **M**enu of alternative change options
- **E**mpathy
- **S**elf-efficacy or optimism

This directive approach conveys a sense of responsibility and hope to the patient, as clinician and patient come up with a plan for treating the substance abuse problem.

TREATMENT

The continuum of care in the treatment of substance abuse disorders includes a range of services. The three basic treatment settings are inpatient, residential, and outpatient treatment. A biopsychosocial model is used in many of the most progressive treatment programs today. The treatment curriculum at all levels of care should include education of the patient about the disease of addiction, family involvement and education, an introduction to 12-step programs, cognitive-behavioral relapse prevention strategies, and pharmacotherapy when indicated. Random urine testing and breath analysis (eg, by Breathalyzer) should be standard in outpatient treatment settings.

Criteria for admission to different levels of care are based on the degree of intoxication or withdrawal, biomedical conditions and complications, chronic relapse, and the availability of psychosocial support.[26] Inpatient hospitalization is the most restrictive form of care and is used to treat patients who require medical detoxification and those with compromising medical conditions or serious psychiatric comorbidity. Detoxification can take up to 1 week or longer for benzodiazepines and other prescription medications. Residential treatment settings are appropriate for women with severe substance abuse problems who are not able to remain abstinent on an outpatient basis and who require a structured environment for a longer period. These services can last 30 days to 1 year or longer. Sober-living homes are less restrictive residential programs in which individuals can gradually make the transition back into the community.

The therapeutic community, popularized in the 1950s, is another form of residential treatment. Historically, therapeutic communities were designed for men and were traditionally highly confrontational. Today many therapeutic communities have incorporated less confrontational techniques for both men and women, with good results.

Intensive outpatient treatment programs became more prevalent in the 1980s, because managed care organizations refused to pay for traditional 28-day inpatient treatment programs unless they were medically necessary. With the necessary treatment components, outpatient treatment is as successful as inpatient treatment. Intensive outpatient treatment generally requires a minimum of 9 hours of weekly attendance, lasts from 30 days to a year, and uses a structured chemical-dependency focus. This level of care is appropriate for patients making the transition from inpatient settings or for those with severe addictions who have adequate structure and support in their lives. The least intensive form of outpatient treatment consists of regular psychotherapy sessions delivered in a therapist's office.

The continuum of treatment options should begin at the least intensive level and increase until the drug or alcohol use can be effectively curtailed, as measured by objective testing. As previously noted, it is important to have a thorough assessment to give the most appropriate referral. Patients with extensive drug and alcohol problems require more intensive and structured care.

Substance abuse treatment has become more specialized in the last 20 years. Treatment for women is most successful when it addresses gender-specific issues and needs of women, including pregnancy, parenting skills, child care (and other support services), psychiatric comorbidity, partners who are substance abusers, domestic violence, and past physical or sexual abuse.[27] A woman-centered model includes a female staff, a curriculum that responds to women's emotional needs and psychological development, a stages-of-change model, and flexible programming with child care. Functioning well in relationships is pivotal to a woman's mental health. Relational and self-esteem issues must be integrated into the overall treatment approach. Making lifestyle changes and improving psychological and social functioning is integral to relapse prevention. When these issues are not addressed in treatment, relapse may be more likely. However, comparative research outcomes between mixed-gender and women-only programs have produced mixed findings so far.[28]

Individuals who are abusing drugs or alcohol and who are at risk for developing an addiction disorder are considered "hazardous drug and alcohol users."[29] Obert et al designed a brief-intervention model to meet the needs of this "at-risk" group. A series of sessions help patients to identify the degree of disruption that substance abuse is creating in their lives and to set some goals for change. This brief-intervention model can be provided in an outpatient clinic as well as by individual mental health clinicians who have expertise in treating substance abuse.[29]

From the inception of substance abuse treatment programs, mutual-help groups such as Alcoholics Anonymous (AA) and other 12-step programs have been one of the major foundations for people struggling to get sober and stay sober. Many treatment programs initiate recovering addicts into the 12-step philosophy and fellowship. Alcoholics Anonymous was founded in 1935 for people suffering from the disease of alcoholism. Since that time many other 12-step programs have been formed, such as Narcotics Anonymous (NA) and Cocaine Anonymous (CA). There are thousands of self-help meetings that take place daily across the world. Often women are more comfortable in women-only meetings, where their special concerns can be addressed. Another self-help group, Women for Sobriety (WFS), was founded in 1976 to address issues of women's substance abuse.

Substance abuse treatment needs to be readily available, and this is not the case for many women. Barriers to treatment include lack of resources, fears of social stigmatization, unavailability of child care, and lack of support from spouses and family members. For women of color, women with disabilities and concurrent psychiatric disorders, lesbians, and older women, there are even greater challenges in meeting their treatment needs. Women living with HIV infection and other life-threatening illnesses also have special needs that must be addressed within a comprehensive treatment program. Community outreach is essential to reach these individuals effectively.

CONCLUSION

Substance abuse in women is a major public health issue. Research findings on addicted males cannot be generalized to the female population. In response to this fact, there is currently more research being done on women, which will determine future changes in education, prevention, and treatment.

Primary care clinicians have an enormous impact on the preventive health choices of their patients. Doctors who routinely give advice about smoking cessation have a direct impact on their

---

RESOURCES

The National Clearinghouse for Alcohol and Drug Information
5600 Fishers Lane
Rockville, Maryland 20857
Telephone: 1-800-729-6686
Web site: www.health.org

The Substance Abuse and Mental Health Services Administration maintains a searchable Web site that provides information related to substance abuse. This includes education materials for patients, as well as information for professionals on screening, diagnosis, and treatment of the various aspects of substance abuse. Specific information related to women is available at this site.

The National Institute on Drug Abuse
6001 Executive Boulevard
Bethesda, Maryland 20892-9561
Telephone: (301) 443-0107
Web site: www.nida.nih.gov

The National Institute on Drug Abuse provides guidelines on the treatment of drug addiction, as well as information on various drugs of abuse.

---

patients' chances of stopping smoking.[30] Inquiring about other drugs and alcohol increases opportunities for diagnosis and treatment. As doctors become more informed about the disease of addiction in women, they will be better equipped to diagnose the disorder and intervene at an earlier stage of the illness.

Educating adolescents about the realities of substance abuse is crucial to preventing addictive disorders. Adolescents need alternatives to drugs and alcohol as means of coping with their problems. The media and advertising industries contribute to one perception of a "quick fix" for life's problems (eg, the use of alcohol and tobacco to relieve stress and increase sociability).

Societal attitudes toward women with addictive disorders are slowly changing. Betty Ford challenged pervasive stereotypes by acknowledging her own history of addiction. Her dedication to the special needs of women is reflected in the Betty Ford Treatment Center, which has separate programming for women.

Finally, in every setting in which substance abuse information is disseminated, a sense of hope must be conveyed about recovery. Patients with addictive disorders can elicit moral judgments and negative attitudes from others. Clinicians must be aware that such attitudes do not foster positive change in their patients. Doctors take important steps in minimizing the shame and stigma surrounding the disease of addiction when they ask their patients about substance abuse. Treatment of addiction is as successful as treatment of other chronic diseases such as diabetes, hypertension, and asthma. This disorder needs to be treated with the same compassion and hope as other chronic relapsing illnesses seen in primary care.

The authors wish to thank Jeanne Obert, MFT, MSM, executive director of the Matrix Center in Los Angeles, for her helpful suggestions on this chapter. The authors also wish to thank Janice Basch, BA, for her research and editorial assistance.

RESOURCES (continued)

The National Council on Alcoholism and Drug Dependence, Inc.
12 West 21st Street
New York, New York 10010
Telephone: 1-800-NCA-CALL (1-800-622-2255) (24-hour referral line)
Web site: http://www.ncadd.org

The National Council on Alcoholism and Drug Dependence, Inc., provides education and information on addiction. Affiliates throughout the United States provide programs to help family members and others encourage women to seek treatment for addiction. The council also offers a video that educates children about drinking. Guidelines on drinking from a variety of organizations are also posted on the NCADD Web site.

The American Society of Addiction Medicine
4601 North Park Avenue, Arcade Suite 101
Chevy Chase, Maryland 20815
Telephone: (301) 656-3920
Web site: www.asam.org

The American Society of Addiction Medicine is a professional organization that is dedicated to improving the treatment of individuals suffering from addiction. The ASAM Web site links to various Web sites of interest to those who treat addiction patients.

Alcoholics Anonymous
PO Box 459
New York, New York 10163
Telephone: (212) 870-3400
Web site: www.aa.org

REFERENCES

1. Lex BW. Some gender differences in alcohol and poly-substance users. Health Psychol 1991;10(2):121–32.
2. Reid J. Substance abuse and the American woman. The National Center on Addiction and Substance Abuse at Columbia University. New York (NY): Columbia University; 1996. p. 45.
3. McCrady BS, Raytek H. Women and substance abuse: treatment and outcome modalities. In: Gomberg EL, Nirenberg TD, editors. Women and substance abuse. Norwood (NJ): Ablex Publishing; 1993. p. 314–38.
4. 1997 National Household Survey on Drug Abuse. Main Findings. Rockville (MD): Substance Abuse and Mental Health Service Administration. 1997.
5. Johnston LD, O'Malley PM, Bachman JG. National survey results on drug use from the Monitoring the Future study. Vol. I. National Institute on Drug Abuse 1975–1994. Washington (DC): US Dept of Health and Human Services, National Institute of Health.
6. Substance Use among Women in the United States. Analytic Series:A-3. Office of Applied Studies. Rockville (MD): Substance Abuse and Mental Health Service Administration; 1997. p. 4–8.
7. Grant BF. IDC-10 harmful use of alcohol and the alcohol dependence syndrome: prevalence and implication. Addiction 1993;88:413–20.
8. Blumenthal SJ. Women and substance abuse: a new national focus. In: Wetherington CL, Roman AB, editors. National Institute on Drug Abuse. Rockville (MD): 1998. p. 13–32.
9. Wechsler H, Dowdall G, Davenport A, Castillo S. Correlates of college student binge drinking. Am J Public Health 1995;85:921–6.

10. Gomberg ESL. Women and alcoholism: psychosocial issues. In: Women and alcohol: health-related issues. Research Monograph 16. Washington (DC): National Institute on Alcohol and Alcoholism, 1986. Dept. of Health and Human Services Publication No.: ADM 86-1139. p. 78–120.

11. Schuckit MA, Tipp JE, Anthenelli RM, et al. Anorexia nervosa and bulimia nervosa in alcohol-dependent men and women and their relatives. Am J Psychiatry 1996;153:74–82.

12. Zerbe KJ. Women's mental health in primary care. Philadelphia (PA): W.B. Saunders Company; 1999. p. 78–80.

13. Grella CE, Vandana J. Gender differences in drug treatment careers among clients in the National Drug Abuse Treatment Outcome study. Am J Drug Alcohol Abuse 1999;23:385–406.

14. Kilbourne J, Surrey JL. Women, addiction and codependency [audio tape]. Wellesley (MA): The Stone Center; 1996.

15. Harvey EM, Rawson RA, Obert JL. History of sexual assault and the treatment of substance abuse disorder. J Psychoactive Drugs 1994;26:361–7.

16. Brady KT, Randall CT. Gender differences in substance use disorders. Psychiatr Clin North Am 1999; 22:241–52.

17. Windle M, Windle RC, Scheidt DM, Miller GB. Physical and sexual abuse and associated mental disorders among alcoholic inpatients. Am J Psychiatry 1995;152:1322–8.

18. Smith EM, Cloninger R, Bradford S. Predictors of mortality in alcoholic women: a prospective follow-up study. Alcohol Clin Exp Res 1983;7:237–41.

19. Frezza M, di Padova C, Pozzato G, et al. High blood alcohol levels in women: the role of decreased gastric alcohol dehydrogenase activity and first-pass metabolism. N Engl J Med 1990;322:95–9.

20. Ashley MG, Olin JS, leRiche WH, et al. Morbidity in alcoholics: evidence for accelerated development of physical disease in women. Arch Intern Med 1977; 883–7.

21. Urbano-Marquez A, Estruch R, Fernandez-Sola J, et al. The greater risk of alcoholic cardiomyopathy and myopathy in women compared with men. JAMA 1995;274:149–54.

22. Nair P, Black MM, Schuler M, et al. Risk factors for disruption in primary caregiving among infants of substance abusing women. Child Abuse Negl 1997; 21:1039–51.

23. Weise D, Daro D. The National Center on Child Abuse Prevention Research. Current trends in child abuse reporting and fatalities: the results of the 1994 annual fifty state survey. Chicago (IL): National Committee to Prevent Child Abuse, 1995.

24. DiClemente CC, Prochaska JO. Towards a comprehensive, transtheoretical model of change: stages of change and addictive behaviors. In: Miller WR, Heather N, editors. Treating addictive behaviors. 2nd ed. New York (NY): Plenium Press; 1998 p. 3–24.

25. Miller WR, Rollnick S. Motivational interviewing: preparing people to change addictive behavior. New York: Guilford, 1991.

26. US Department of Health and Human Services. A guide to substance abuse services for primary care clinicians. Treatment Improvement Protocol (TIP) Series No.: 24. Washington (DC): The Department; 1997.

27. Grella CE, Polinsky ML, Hser YL, Perry SM. Characteristics of women-only and mixed-gender drug abuse treatment programs. J Subst Abuse Treat 1999;17:37–44.

28. Martin K, Giannandrea P, Rogers B, Johnson J. Group intervention with pre-recovery patients. J Subst Abuse Treat 1996;1333–44.

29. Obert JL, Rawson RA, Miotto K. Substance abuse treatment for "hazardous users": an early intervention. J Psychoactive Drugs 1997;29:291–8.

30. Center for the Future of Children. The future of children: low birth weight. Los Altos (CA): David and Lucile Packard Foundation, Center for the Future of Children; 1995.

65

DEMENTIA

Verna R. Porter, MD, and Jeffrey L. Cummings, MD

As the world's population continues to increase and age, estimates suggest that by the year 2030, 17 to 20% of the US population will be over the age of 65 years.[1] This increase in elderly individuals is expected to cause a concomitant increase in the number of patients with dementia. Estimates of prevalence rates for dementia range from 5 to 10% for persons over the age of 65 years, and the prevalence roughly doubles with each 5-year increase in age, reaching frequencies of 35 to 50% for all persons over the age of 85 years.[2] Among centenarians, almost 60% reportedly demonstrate dementia.[3] The substantial potential impact of dementia on public health underscores the importance of accurate detection, diagnosis, and treatment. Although many etiologies of dementia have been described (Table 65–1),[4] the majority of patients suffer from Alzheimer's disease (AD), vascular dementia (VaD), or a combination of AD and cerebrovascular disease.

It is increasingly recognized that women are at greater risk than men for certain forms of dementia (eg, AD). This is due both to the greater relative longevity of women and to increased age-specific incidence rates for women. For example, in the Rotterdam Study, prior to the age of 85, the age-specific incidence rates for dementia of all causes were similar for men and women under the age of 85 years; however, after the age of 85 years, the incidence rates in men stabilized (eg, 29.6 for ages 85 to 89 years) whereas the rates for women continued to increase (eg, 68.3 for ages 85 to 89 years), reflecting both their higher life expectancy and greater risk for dementia in very old age.[5] This study also suggested higher incidence rates of AD in women than in men and a tendency to higher incidence rates of VaD in men, findings that agree with those of previous studies.[6,7] The contribution of gonadal steroids and gender-specific factors must therefore be considered in relationship to the etiology and age-specific incidence rates of dementia. In addition, the potential therapeutic role of hormones in the prevention and treatment of dementia is being increasingly recognized. Thus, to permit early therapeutic intervention, it is of fundamental importance to identify those factors that may be contributing to a woman's risk of developing dementia and to be able to diagnose the onset of dementia early. The objectives of this chapter are to (1) describe potential risk factors contributing to the development of dementia in women; (2) describe a general approach to the diagnosis and evaluation of dementia, based on established assessment methods; and (3) present an overview of current treatment modalities.

DEFINITIONS

Dementia is a clinical syndrome characterized by an acquired persistent decline in cognitive functioning from previous higher levels of premorbid functioning, affecting multiple domains of cognitive performance and interfering with an individual's ability to function independently in activities of daily living (ADLs). This deterioration occurs in an otherwise alert individual and is not accompanied by any acute confusional state or alteration of consciousness (eg, delirium). The intellectual deterioration may affect some areas of cognitive functioning while sparing others and thus does not necessarily result in "global" cognitive impairment.[4] By criteria established in the fourth edition of the *Diagnostic and Statistical Manual of Mental Disorders* (DSM-IV),[8] the diagnosis of dementia involves compromise of at least two discrete domains of cognitive function, one of which must be memory (Table 65–2). Other domains that may be affected include language, perception, visuospatial skills, calculation, judgment,

---

TABLE 65–1. Classification of Dementias by Etiology

Degenerative dementias
  Alzheimer's disease
  Frontotemporal dementia
  Huntington's disease
  Dementia with Lewy bodies
  Parkinson's disease
  Progressive supranuclear palsy
  Corticobasal ganglionic degeneration
  Spinocerebellar degeneration

Vascular dementias
  Cardiac disorders (eg, atrial fibrillation)
  Central nervous system vasculitis
  Postradiation necrosis and vasculitis
  Hemorrhage (intraparenchymal, subarachnoid,
    subdural, arteriovenous malformation)
  Hypoperfusion (cardiac arrest, profound hypotension)
  Multiple infarcts (amyloid angiopathy, large complete
    infarcts, lacunae of the basal ganglia and pons,
    frontal white matter lacunae)
  Strategic single infarct (thalamic, posterior cerebral
    artery, bilateral carotid occlusion, parietal infarct)
  Senile leukoencephalopathy (also related to amyloid
    angiopathy)

Infectious etiologies
  Bacterial meningitis
  Whipple's disease of CNS
  Creutzfeldt-Jakob disease
  Fungal or tuberculous meningitis
  Neurosyphilis
  Viral encephalitis (herpes, HIV infection)

Inflammatory diseases
  Demyelinating disease (multiple sclerosis)
  Limbic encephalitis
  Lupus erythematosus
  Sarcoidosis
  Sjögren's syndrome

Neoplastic processes
  Carcinomatosis, meningeal lesions
  Primary tumors (frontal or corpus callosal tumors)
  Metastatic lesions

Traumatic etiologies
  Hypoxemic anoxia (respiratory failure, pure asphyxia)
  Subdural hematoma
  Traumatic brain injury

Toxic etiologies
  Alcohol
  Heavy metals (arsenic, lead, mercury)
  Histotoxic anoxia (carbon monoxide, cyanide)
  Medications (anticholinergic, antihistaminic,
    polypharmacy)

Metabolic etiologies
  Vitamin B_{12} deficiency
  Cushing's disease
  Hypopituitarism
  Parathyroid disease
  Porphyria
  Thyroid disease (hyperthyroidism, hypothyroidism)
  Uremia
  Wilson's disease

Psychiatric disorders
  Depression

Hydrocephalus
  Nonobstructive vs obstructive
  Normal-pressure hydrocephalus

CNS = central nervous system; HIV = human immunodeficiency virus.
Adapted from Fleming KC, Adams AC, Peterson RC. Dementia: diagnosis and evaluation. Dementia 1994;5:106–9.

---

abstraction, and problem-solving skills.[4] As a result of the intellectual deterioration and progressive social, occupational, and functional impairment, an individual's capacity to maintain employment, manage household affairs, and handle finances may become severely impaired. Dementia is thus one of the main causes of institutionalization among elderly individuals.[9]

The most commonly used clinical diagnostic criteria for the diagnosis of **AD** were developed in 1984 by the joint task force of the National Institute of Neurological and Communicative Disorders and Stroke and the Alzheimer's Disease and Related Disorders Association (NINCDS-ADRDA). The NINCDS-ADRDA diagnostic criteria further classify AD into possible, probable, or definite AD,

TABLE 65–2. Diagnostic Criteria for Dementia

A. The development of multiple cognitive deficits manifested by both of the following:
   1. Memory impairment (impaired ability to learn new information or to recall previously learned information)
   2. One or more of the following cognitive disturbances:
       a. Aphasia (language disturbance)
       b. Apraxia (impaired ability to perform motor activities despite intact motor function)
       c. Agnosia (failure to recognize or identify objects despite intact sensory function)
       d. Disturbance in executive functioning (planning, organization, sequencing, and abstracting)

B. The cognitive deficits in criteria A1 and A2 each cause severe impairment in social or occupational functioning and represent a major decline from a previous level of functioning.

C. The cognitive deficits in criteria A1 and A2 are not due to any of the following:
   1. Other central nervous system conditions that cause progressive deficits in memory and cognition (eg, cerebrovascular disease, Parkinson's disease, Huntington's disease, subdural hematoma, normal-pressure hydrocephalus, brain tumor)
   2. Systemic conditions known to cause dementia (eg, hypothyroidism, vitamin B_{12} and folic acid deficiency, niacin deficiency, hypercalcemia, neurosyphilis, HIV infection)

D. The deficits do not occur exclusively during the course of a delirium.

E. The disturbance is not better accounted for by another axis I disorder (eg, major depressive disorder, schizophrenia).

HIV = human immunodeficiency virus.
Reproduced with permission from American Psychiatric Association. Diagnostic and statistical manual of mental disorders. 4th ed. Washington (DC): The Association; 1994. p. 129–33.

based on clinical criteria or pathologic findings at autopsy (Table 65–3).[10]

The World Health Organization International Classification of Diseases 10th edition (ICD-10) diagnostic criteria for **VaD** are summarized in Table 65-4.[11] Difficulties in the diagnosis of VaD have been related to problems in determining whether vascular disease is a causal factor, a contributing factor, or an incidental condition in a patient with dementia. Vascular dementia may encompass such diverse etiologies as hemorrhage, ischemic stroke, and hypoxic-ischemic cerebral injury (eg, during cardiac arrest).

Mild cognitive impairment (MCI) is a condition characterized by memory test performance that is more than 1.5 standard deviations below age-matched norms, but with the preservation of other cognitive abilities.[12] Such patients do not meet DSM-IV criteria for a dementing syndrome since the cognitive impairment is confined to deficits in memory. Emerging literature from longitudinal studies suggest that in a subset of patients with MCI, mild episodic memory complaints represent the earliest harbingers of AD.[12,13]

RISK FACTORS

Alzheimer's Disease

Identified risk factors for AD include advanced age, lower intelligence levels, a family history of disease, small head size, a history of head trauma, and female gender.[14] In women, the absence of estrogen replacement therapy (ERT) in the postmenopausal period further increases the risk for the subsequent development of AD.[15,16]

Susceptibility genes may contribute an additional risk of developing AD when they are combined with other epigenetic phenomena but are not themselves causative for the disease. Among the susceptibility genes that have been identified, the ε4 allele of the apolipoprotein E (ApoE) gene on chromosome 19 has been shown to be an age- and dose-related risk factor.[17] The three common alleles of the ApoE gene are ε2, ε3, and ε4; the most common of these is ε3, followed by ε4 and ε2.[14] Subjects with the ε4 allele are at increased risk for developing AD and have an earlier age of onset as compared to individuals without the allele. The ε4 allele has been shown to be three to four times more prevalent in AD

TABLE 65–3. Classification of Alzheimer's Disease[*]

Classification: Levels of Diagnostic Certainty	Diagnostic Requirements
Definite	Clinical features of probable AD; and histopathologic confirmation by biopsy or autopsy
Probable	Onset between the ages of 40 to 90 yr
	Presence of dementia documented by standardized mental status assessment and confirmed by neuropsychological tests
	Gradually progressive deficits in two or more areas of cognition (including memory)
	Absence of delirium
	No other systemic or brain diseases that could account for the progressive deficits in memory and cognition
Possible	Typical clinical syndrome present, but variations exist in onset, presentation, or clinical course
	A second systemic brain disease may be present but is not considered the cause of the dementia
	A single cognitive deficit (eg, memory) may be identified in the absence of another identifiable cause

[*]Criteria of the National Institute of Neurological and Communicative Disorders and Stroke and the Alzheimer's Disease and Related Disorders Association (NINCDS-ADRDA criteria).
Reproduced with permission from McKhann G, Drachman DD, Folstein M, et al. Clinical diagnosis of Alzheimer's disease: report of the NINCDS-ADRDA Work Group under the auspices of the Department of Health and Human Services Task Force on Alzheimer's disease. Neurology 1984;34:939–44.

TABLE 65–4. World Health Organization (ICD-10) Diagnostic Criteria for Vascular Dementia[*]

Classification	Description
G1	There is evidence of dementia of a specified level of severity.
G2	There is an unequal distribution of deficits in higher cognitive functions, with some affected and others relatively spared. Thus, memory may be profoundly affected, whereas thinking, reasoning, and information processing may show only mild decline.
G3	Focal brain damage is evident, manifest as at least one of the following: unilateral spastic weakness of the limbs, unilateral increased tendon reflexes, an extensor plantar response, and pseudobulbar palsy.
G4	The history, examination, or tests disclose severe cerebrovascular disease that may reasonably be judged to be etiologically related to the dementia (history of stroke, evidence of cerebral infarction).

[*]From the World Health Organization International Classification of Diseases, 10th edition (ICD-10).
Reproduced with permission from Wetterling T, Kanitz RD, Borgis KJ. The ICD-10 criteria for vascular dementia. Dementia 1994;5:185–8.

(including the most common category of late-onset disease with no known family history), as compared with individuals who are not demented.[18] When used in conjunction with conventional diagnostic evaluations, the finding of an ε4 allele may serve to augment the clinical impression of AD but should not be considered a diagnostic marker for the presence of the disease. Moreover, the presence of the ε4 allele is not a predictive test that can forecast the development of AD. However, a recent study demonstrated that for patients with MCI, the presence of the ε4 allele may be an important predictive variable for the subsequent development of AD.[4]

Vascular Dementia

Identified risk factors for the development of VaD include transient ischemic attacks (TIAs), hypertension, heart disease, hyperlipidemia, smoking, excessive alcohol consumption, lower educational status, a family history of cerebrovascular disease, and (in women) the absence of estrogen replacement therapy. These risk factors have been suggested to accelerate cerebral atrophy, ventricular enlargement, leukoaraiosis (a radiologic finding probably caused by cerebral ischemia), and cortical perfusion declines that may contribute to the susceptibility to hypoxic-ischemic events.[19] Vascular dementia is often divided into cortical and subcortical syndromes;[20,21] cortical vascular dementia is characterized predominantly by cardioembolic or atherothrombotic vascular events, and subcortical vascular dementia is characterized by hypertensive small vessel and lacunar disease with prominent white matter ischemia.

DIAGNOSIS

History

A thorough medical, neurologic, and psychiatric history from a knowledgeable informant is essential to the evaluation of dementia. The pattern of onset (eg, acute versus subacute) and temporal characteristics (eg, fluctuating course versus gradual decline) may suggest an etiology and direct further investigations. An insidious onset is more consistent with a degenerative process such as AD, whereas a stepwise deterioration suggests the presence of cerebrovascular disease. In contrast, an abrupt deterioration in attention and cognition, accompanied by an acute confusional state, is more suggestive of a delirium. Changes in cognition should be assessed with respect to the particular cognitive domains compromised and the pattern of intellectual decline. In AD, recent memory is lost first, with a relative preservation of remote memories and overlearned tasks. The dementia then progresses to involve remote memory and other cognitive and behavioral domains (eg, executive dysfunction, visuospatial compromise, language difficulties, and changes in mood and behavior).

The assessment of functional changes should be reviewed carefully with respect to a patient's ability to independently manage ADLs (bathing, feeding, dressing, transferring, and toileting) and instrumental activities of daily living (IADLs) (eg, doing housework, preparing food, driving or using other forms of transportation, using the telephone, taking medication, shopping, and managing finances). To evaluate a deterioration from a previous level of functioning, a gender-appropriate assessment of ADLs is required. To help establish the rate of cognitive decline, additional questions should be directed to the timing of functional losses.

Changes in mood, personality, and behavior may be prominent signs of a dementia and are often among the most disabling features of the disease (Table 65–5). Common personality changes include indifference, impulsivity, and agitation.[22] Behavioral alterations may include lack of insight, impaired planning and judgment, aggression, restlessness, delusions, hallucinations, wandering, paranoia, and sleep disturbances.[4,23]

Additional features of importance in the history include drug and alcohol use, a past medical history of a systemic illness capable of influencing cognition (eg, chronic renal insufficiency or systemic vasculitis), and any family history of dementia.[4] An evaluation of the past medical history should include any risk factors for stroke (eg, TIAs, hypertension, coronary artery disease, and atrial fibrillation). The patient's social and occupational history should be assessed, with particular attention to toxic exposures in relation to the timing and onset of the compromise in cognition.

Mental Status

An appropriate assessment of the patient's mental status is essential to a complete dementia evaluation. Simple tests of orientation in three spheres (person, place, and date) are not sufficient to exclude the presence of cognitive compromise. Mental status questionnaires (eg, the Mini Mental State Examination [MMSE] or the Short Test of Mental Status) are important as primary screening tests and should be used routinely in clinical examinations of elderly patients at risk for dementia. (The MMSE is reproduced in Chapter 5, "Approach to the Geriatric Patient." The MMSE is the most widely used primary screening test in clinical examinations.[24] This 30-point measurement tool is adequate for detecting cognitive impairment, establishing a baseline, and measuring mental decline over time. Although the

TABLE 65–5. Neuropsychiatric Evaluation of the Patient with Possible Dementia

Psychiatric Feature	Clinical Implications for Dementia Diagnosis
Depression	May cause impairment of cognition in the absence of a dementing process (ie, pseudodementia). Complaints of deficit may be disproportionate to the actual deficit. May accompany a dementing process (eg, vascular dementia or early Alzheimer's disease [AD]).
Apathy	Most common behavioral change in AD.
Paranoia	May suggest underlying psychotic disorder or may accompany later stages of dementing process (eg, AD).
Anxiety	May suggest underlying anxiety disorder or may accompany dementing process, especially in the initial stages.
Delusions	May accompany primary psychotic disorder or dementing diseases (eg, dementia with Lewy bodies; later stages of AD).
Hallucinations	May accompany primary psychotic disorder or dementing disease (eg, late stages of AD).
Personality changes or disinhibited behavior	May accompany primary dementing process (eg, frontotemporal dementia).

Reproduced with permission from Cummings JC, Vinters HV, Cole GM, Khachaturian ZS. Alzheimer's disease: etiologies, pathophysiology, cognitive reserve, and treatment opportunities. Neurology 1998;51 Suppl 1:S2–17.

interpretation of the MMSE may be influenced by language, socioeconomic status, ethnicity, age, and education, the use of age- and education-specific cutoff scores has been shown to improve the sensitivity to 82% with a retained specificity of 99% for distinguishing normal from abnormal cognition (Table 65–6).[24] However, the MMSE is insensitive to MCI and is not useful in patients with severe dementia.

Neurologic and Physical Examination

A neurologic examination is essential to rule out potential deficits that may contribute to cognitive compromise (eg, visual or hearing deficits). Although the examination may be normal and nonspecific in early dementia, primitive reflexes (eg, glabellar, palmomental, snout, and grasp) may be present. The diagnosis of VaD is supported by focal deficits identified on examination (eg, hemiparesis, unilateral extensor plantar response, gait abnormalities). In advanced stages of either AD or VaD, abnormalities of posture, balance, and urinary function may be present. Abnormalities in muscle tone may be informative with respect to the localization of lesions. For example, the presence of cogwheel rigidity suggests dysfunction of the extrapyramidal system (eg, basal ganglia) whereas rigidity suggests involvement of the pyramidal or upper

motoneuron tracts. Extensive extrapyramidal signs (eg, bradykinesia and rigidity) accompanied by gait disturbances may be found in Parkinson's disease, dementia with Lewy bodies, progressive supranuclear palsy, and advanced stages of AD. The

TABLE 65–6. Revised Cutoff Scores for Mini–Mental State Examination, Stratified by Age and Education*

Age (yr)	Education (no. of yr)					
	6–8	9–11	12	13–16	17–18	>19
60–64	26	27	27	28	29	29
65–69	25	26	27	27	28	29
70–74	24	25	26	27	27	28
75–79	23	24	25	26	27	27
80–84	23	23	24	24	25	26
85–89	23	23	23	24	25	26
90–95	23	23	23	23	24	25

*Scores less than or equal to those shown suggest that further evaluation for dementia is needed. Scores > 23 are based on being 1 residual standard deviation (SD) below age- and education-appropriate mean (23 was adopted as a minimal cutoff score on the basis of sensitivity and specificity analyses). Reproduced with permission from Tangalos EG, Smith GE, Ivnik RJ, et al. The Mini Mental State Exam in general medical practice: clinical utility and acceptance. Mayo Clin Proc 1996;71:829–37.

presence of a sensory peripheral neuropathy may suggest an underlying toxic or metabolic process (eg, vitamin B_{12} deficiency or hypothyroidism).

Some disorders of cognition have well-established clinical characteristics. Normal-pressure hydrocephalus is characterized by the triad of cognitive impairment, gait disturbance, and urinary incontinence. Creutzfeldt-Jakob disease features generalized myoclonus, with an accentuated startle response motor disorders, and a rapidly progressive dementia. In patients with VaD, cardiac abnormalities (atrial fibrillation, congestive heart failure, or valvular disease) or physical examination findings suggestive of peripheral vascular disease (eg, carotid bruit) may be informative as to the etiology of the cerebrovascular disease.

Neuropsychological Evaluation

In selected patients, a formal neuropsychological evaluation, performed by a licensed psychologist, may be valuable when a baseline assessment is needed to document the presence and severity of compromise in specific cognitive domains or to monitor disease progression over time. Additional testing also may be useful for patients in whom a "ceiling effect" is noted on screening tests (ie, on routine office screening evaluations, the patient scores in the normal range despite the clinical suspicion of dementia).

Neuropsychological testing also may be useful when the diagnosis of dementia is unclear due to equivocal test results or confounding processes such as the presence of depression. An accurate diagnosis of dementia is essential when decisions about the patient's competence with respect to driving, occupation, and safety must be made. In some cases, serial testing may allow an assessment of the patient's response to medication.

Laboratory Evaluation

Laboratory evaluation is routinely performed to screen for potentially reversible causes of dementia (eg, thyroid dysfunction, hyponatremia, syphilis, vitamin B_{12} deficiency). Although the usefulness of performing screening tests on all patients with dementia has been debated, a recent study assessing the diagnostic usefulness of the American Academy of Neurology Practice Parameters suggested an added value of laboratory testing of 9% for changing the diagnosis and 12.6% for changing the management of patients with dementia.[25] In another prospective study, 5% of elderly outpatients with suspected dementia had underlying metabolic abnormalities (eg, hypothyroidism, hypoparathyroidism, hyponatremia, or hypoglycemia) that were suspected of being contributory or causative factors in their dementia.[26] An exhaustive search for reversible causes of dementia (eg, by using urine heavy-metal evaluations) is not indicated for all patients; a suggested standard battery of laboratory tests is presented in Table 65–7.[27]

Neuroimaging

Neuroimaging may be performed to exclude potentially treatable causes of dementia, such as strokes, tumors, and normal-pressure hydrocephalus. Many patients with AD may show structural changes

---

TABLE 65–7. Suggested Standard Laboratory Screening Tests for Patients with Dementia*

Routine laboratory tests
  Blood chemistry profile (SMA-7 and LFTs)
  Complete blood count with differential
  Thyroid function tests
  Erythrocyte sedimentation rate (ESR):
    Westergren or Wintrobe
  Vitamin B_{12} levels
  Syphilis serology
  Urinalysis

Tests to be done when risk factors for immune
  dysfunction are present:
  Human immunodeficiency virus (HIV)
    antibody tests

Specialized investigations based on clinical suspicion:
  Drug screening (toxicology panel)
  Urinalysis for heavy metals
  Cobalamin levels
  Folate levels
  Fluorescent treponemal antibody absorption
    (FTA-Ab) test
  Examination of spinal fluid

---

*Based on the 1995 American Academy of Neurology Practice Parameters.
SMA-7 = electrolytes, blood urea nitrogen, creatinine, glucose; LFT = liver function test.
Reproduced with permission from Chui H, Zhang Q. A systematic study of the usefulness of the American Academy of Neurology's Practice Parameters. Neurology 1997;49:925–35.

(atrophy) in a pattern suggestive of the underlying neurodegenerative disease. Magnetic resonance imaging (MRI) has been shown to be more sensitive than computed tomography (CT) for evaluating atrophy, vascular lesions, and lesions adjacent to bone.[28]

Positron emission tomography (PET) and single-photon emission computed tomography (SPECT) may demonstrate decreased glucose metabolism or blood flow in the temporoparietal regions in early-stage AD.[29] The current National Institute on Aging Task Force[30] recommendation for imaging in the evaluation of dementia is to perform a neuroimaging procedure once in the course of an evaluation, for all cases of dementia (a recommendation regarding CT versus MRI is not specified).

Ancillary Testing

Analysis of cerebrospinal fluid (CSF) is an additional ancillary test that may be indicated in certain circumstances (eg, in cases of fever, nuchal rigidity, or suspected infection of the central nervous system [CNS]; atypical or rapidly progressive courses; dementia in persons under the age of 55 years; or evidence of demyelinating disease, vasculitis, or immunosupression).[4] An imaging study (eg, CT) should be performed prior to collecting CSF, to ensure the safety of the procedure.

Electroencephalography (yielding a conventional electroencephalogram [EEG] or quantitative brain mapping) may be useful in specific circumstances, for example, to document the presence of generalized background slowing (eg, in metabolic encephalitis) or the presence of focal or epileptiform discharges that might implicate a localized process. Electroencephalography may be useful in the diagnosis of specific disease processes such as Creutzfeldt-Jakob disease, complex partial seizures, or infectious encephalitides.[4]

THERAPEUTIC INTERVENTIONS

Alzheimer's disease is characterized by the presence of progressive neuronal loss, gliosis, deposition of amyloid extracellular neuritic plaques, and intracellular neurofibrillary tangles. Much attention has been focused on neurotransmitters and neuromodulators (eg, acetylcholine and cholinergic enzymes) because these substances are depleted in AD.[14] Antioxidants (such as vitamin E), monoamine oxidase inhibitors (such as selegiline), estrogen replacement therapy, and nonsteroidal anti-inflammatory drugs (NSAIDs) have also been investigated.[16,31–33] Other neurotransmitters, including serotonin and norepinephrine, may be affected. To date, the majority of clinical pharmaceutic agents have been directed at the relief of symptoms rather than alteration of the basic pathophysiology of the disease. Table 65–8 outlines the principal drugs that are in current use for the treatment of AD.[15,16,31–35]

Most agents used in VaD are designed to ameliorate risk factors such as hypertension (eg, antihypertensive medications), etiologic events such as thrombosis (eg, antiplatelet agents—aspirin, clopidogrel bisulfate, ticlopidine), or further vascular events (such as carotid stenosis) in patients with known vascular disease (eg, anticoagulation with warfarin) (see Table 65–8).

Of particular interest in regard to dementia in women is the role of gonadal hormones, such as estrogen, in preventing or delaying the onset of cognitive decline and dementia. One possible mechanism by which postmenopausal declining estrogen may contribute to the risk and severity of cognitive decline associated with AD has been suggested by recent studies linking the long-term loss of ovarian function with an associated decline in the functioning of basal forebrain cholinergic neurons.[36] Several studies that have suggested beneficial effects of ERT in preventing progression to AD and preserving cognitive function. In addition, a recent prospective cohort study of ERT and the risk of developing AD (the Baltimore Longitudinal Study of Aging) demonstrated a protective influence of estrogen in AD patients.[16] Although such studies support the use of ERT in postmenopausal women for decreasing the risk of developing AD and delaying the time to onset of the disease, the therapeutic efficacy of ERT in established cases of AD remains under investigation.

A woman's estrogen status may also affect treatment outcome with respect to certain therapeutic agents in AD. For example, ERT enhances clinical and cognitive responses to tacrine therapy.[37] Nevertheless, the decision to initiate ERT should be made in the context of a women's medical and family history (eg, a familial history of breast cancer) and her desire for relief of postmenopausal symptoms, and not solely for the purpose of preventing or delaying progression to dementia.

TABLE 65–8. Pharmacologic Therapies for Alzheimer's Disease and Vascular Dementia

Therapy for Alzheimer's disease

    Cholinergic agents

        Tacrine (Cognex). Centrally acting reversible acetylcholinesterase inhibitor. Adverse effects: elevation of serum transaminases, nausea, vomiting, diarrhea, dyspepsia, myalgias, and anorexia.

        Donezepil (Aricept). A new piperdine derivative that inhibits acetylcholinesterase potently. Compared to tacrine, donezepil has better results on cognitive tests and clinician's global impression of change ratings with less cholinergic side effects and no significant elevation of transaminases.

        Rivastigmine (Exelon). A carbamate acetylcholinesterase inhibitor. A useful option for patients with mild to moderate AD. Pooled results from clinical trials indicate that 6–12 mg/d produces less deterioration in cognitive, global, and functional changes than placebo. Side effects are related to actions as acetyl cholinesterase inhibitor.

        Galantamine (Reminyl). A selective long-acting acetylcholinesterase inhibitor. A 6-month trial comparing maintenance doses of 24 and 32 mg daily with placebo demonstrated that patients receiving the higher dosage had an improvement on a disability assessment for dementia scale when compared with patients receiving placebo.

    Monoamine oxidase B inhibitor

        Selegiline (Deprenyl). A large multicenter trial comparing selegiline and vitamin E (α-tocopherol) with placebo suggested a benefit of selegiline on preserving functional independence and dementia rating scales. Effect size was similar to that of vitamin E alone. Combination therapy (selegiline plus vitamine E) did not enhance effectiveness.

        Vitamin E (α-tocopherol). Indication of benefit at higher dosages (1,000 IU twice per day) on dementia rating scales. Adverse effects: alteration of vitamin K–dependent coagulation factors with mild bleeding diasthesis and easy bruising.

        Estrogens. A prospective cohort study of estrogen replacement therapy (Baltimore Longitudinal Study of Aging) suggested a protective effect of estrogen replacement therapy on the relative risk of developing AD.

        Nonsteroidal anti-inflammatory drugs (NSAIDs). Some studies suggest that prolonged use of NSAIDs may prevent decline in cognition associated with aging. High-dose use is contraindicated due to known risks of NSAIDs.

Therapy for vascular dementia

    Primary prevention. Control of vascular risk factors through modification of hypertension, diabetes, coronary artery disease, peripheral vascular disease, obesity, etc.

    Prophylactic use of antiplatelet agents (eg, aspirin, clopidogrel bisulfate, ticlopidine).

AD = Alzheimer's disease.

Adapted from Scheltens et al,[15] Kawas et al,[16] Sano et al,[31] Fleming et al,[32] Karplus et al,[33] Spencer et al,[34] Wilcock et al.[35]

CONCLUSION

Due to the aging of the world's population, dementia will become an increasingly prevalent health care problem. Accurate assessment, diagnosis, recognition of risk factors, and therapeutic decision making are important tools for the primary care clinician. In addition, it is important to be aware of particular risk factors that are relevant to women, such as declining gonadal hormone levels with age. Since recent research suggests a potential modulatory influence of ERT on the development and rate of progression of AD, therapeutic consideration of the use of hormone replacement therapy is particularly important for the postmenopausal woman. There is also evidence to suggest that ERT may influence responses to other treatment modalities (such as tacrine) in patients with AD. Continued research should clarify whether the use of ERT is justified as primary treatment in established cases of AD.

RESOURCE

Alzheimer's Association
919 North Michigan Avenue, Suite 1000
Chicago, Illinois 60611-1676
Telephone: 1-800-272-3900
           (312) 335-8700
Web site: www.alz.org

Through a network of local chapters throughout the United States, the Alzheimer's Association offers information, support, and assistance on issues related to Alzheimer's disease. The Alzheimer's Association also maintains an extensive Web site with information on a variety of issues for patients and caregivers.

REFERENCES

1. Schoenberg BS. Epidemiology of Alzheimer's disease and other dementing illnesses. J Chron Dis 1986; 39:740–3.

2. Graves AB, Kukull WA. The epidemiology of dementia. In: Morris JC, editor. Handbook of dementing illnesses. New York (NY): Marcel Dekker; 1994. p. 23–69.

3. Powell AL. Senile dementia of extreme aging: a common disorder of centenarians. Dementia 1994;5:106–9.

4. Fleming KC, Adams AC, Peterson RC. Dementia: diagnosis and evaluation. Mayo Clin Proc 1995; 70:1093–107.

5. Ott A, Breteler MB, van Harskamp F, et al. Incidence and risk of dementia. Am J Epidemiol 1998;147: 574–80.

6. Letenneur L, Commenges D, Dartigues JF, et al. Incidence of dementia and Alzheimer's disease in elderly community residents of south-western France. Int J Epidemiol 1994;23:1256–61.

7. Yoshitake T, Kiyohara Y, Kato I, et al. Incidence and risk factors of vascular dementia and Alzheimer's disease in a defined elderly Japanese population: the Hisayama Study. Neurology 1995;45:1161–8.

8. American Psychiatric Association. Diagnostic and statistical manual of mental disorders. 4th ed. Washington (DC): American Psychiatric Association; 1994. p. 129–33.

9. Lanska DJ, Schoenberg BS. The epidemiology of dementia: methodologic issues and approaches. In: Whitehouse PJ, editor. Dementia. Philadelphia (PA): F.A. Davis; 1993. p. 3–33.

10. McKhann G, Drachman DD, Folstein M, et al. Clinical diagnosis of Alzheimer's Disease: report of the NINCDS-ADRDA Work Group under the auspices of the Department of Health and Human Services Task Force on Alzheimer's disease. Neurology 1984; 34:939–44.

11. Wetterling T, Kanitz RD, Borgis KJ. The ICD-10 criteria for vascular dementia. Dementia 1994;5: 185–8.

12. Almkvist O, Basun H, Backman L, et al. Mild cognitive impairment—an early stage of Alzheimer's disease? J Neur Transm Suppl 1998;54:21–9.

13. Peterson RC, Smith GE, Tangalos EG, et al. Longitudinal outcome of patients with mild cognitive impairment [abstract]. Ann Neurol 1993;34:294–5.

14. Cummings JC, Vinters HV, Cole GM, Khachaturian ZS. Alzheimer's disease: etiologies, pathophysiology, cognitive reserve, and treatment opportunities. Neurology 1998;51 Suppl 1:S2–17.

15. Scheltens P, van Gool WA. Emerging treatments in dementia. Eur Neurol 1997;38:184–9.

16. Kawas C, Resnick S, Morrison A, et al. A prospective study of estrogen replacement therapy and the risk of developing Alzheimer's disease: the Baltimore Longitudinal Study on Aging. Neurology 1997;48:1517–21.

17. Ganguli M, Cauley JA, DeKosky ST, Kamboh MI. Dementia among elderly apolipoprotein E Type 4/4 homozygotes: a prospective study. Genet Epidemiol 1995;12:309–11.

18. Growdon JH. Biomarkers of Alzheimer's disease. Arch Neurol 1999;56:281–2.

19. Meyer JS, Terayama Y, Konno S, et al. Risk factors for cerebral degenerative changes and dementia. Eur Neurol 1998;39 Suppl 1:7–16.

20. Stuss DT, Cummings JL. Vascular dementia. In: Cummings JL, editor. Subcortical dementia. New York (NY): Oxford University Press; 1990. p. 145–63.

21. Wolfe N, Linn R, Babikian VL, et al. Frontal systems impairment following multiple lacunar infarcts. Arch Neurol 1990;47:129–32.

22. Petry S, Cummings JL, Hill MA, Shapira J. Personality alterations in dementia of the Alzheimer's type. Arch Neurol 1988;45:1187–90.

23. Patterson MB, Bolger JP. Assessment of behavioral symptoms in Alzheimer's disease. Alzheimer's Dis Assoc Disord 1994;8 Suppl 3:4–20.

24. Tangalos, EG, Smith GE, Ivnik RJ, et al. The Mini Mental State Exam in general medical practice: clinical utility and acceptance. Mayo Clin Proc 1996;71:829–37.

25. Chui H, Zhang Q. A systematic study of the usefulness of the American Academy of Neurology's Practice Parameters. Neurology 1997;49:925–35.

26. Larson EB, Reifler BV, Sumi SM, et al. Diagnostic tests in the evaluation of dementia: a prospective study of 200 elderly outpatients. Arch Intern Med 1986;146:1917–22.

27. Corey-Bloom J, Thal LJ, Galasko D, et al. Diagnosis and evaluation of dementia. Neurology 1995;45:211–8.

28. Xanthakos S, Krishnan KR, Kim DM, Charles HC. Magnetic resonance imaging of Alzheimer's disease. Progress in Neuropsychopharmacol Biol Psychiatry 1996;20:597–626.

29. Masterman DL, Mendez MF, Fairbanks LA, Cummings JL. Sensitivity, specificity, and positive predictive value of technetium 99-HMPAQ SPECT in discriminating Alzheimer's disease from other dementias. J Geriatr Psychiatry Neurol 1997;10:15–21.

30. National Institute on Aging Task Force. Senility reconsidered: treatment possibilities for mental impairment in the elderly. JAMA 1980;244:259–63.

31. Sano M, Ernesto C, Thomas RG, et al. A controlled trial of selegiline, alpha-tocopherol, or both as treatment for Alzheimer's disease. The Alzheimer's Disease Cooperative Study. N Engl J Med 1997;336:1216–22.

32. Fleming KC, Evans JM. Pharmacologic therapies in dementia. Mayo Clin Proc 1995;70:1116–23.

33. Karplus TM, Saag KG. Nonsteroidal anti-inflammatory drugs and cognitive function: do they have a beneficial or deleterious effect? Drug Saf 1998;19:427–33.

34. Spencer CM, Nobel S. Rivastigmine. A review of its use in Alzheimer's disease. Drugs Aging 1998;13:391–411.

35. Wilcock GK, Lilienfeld S, Gaens E. Efficacy and safety of galantamine in patients with mild to moderate Alzheimer's disease: multicenter randomized controlled trial. Galantamine International-1 Study Group. BMJ 2000;321:1445–9.

36. Gibbs RB. Impairment of basal forebrain cholinergic neurons associated with aging and long-term loss of ovarian function. Exp Neurol 1998;151:289–302.

37. Schneider LS, Farlow MR, Henderson VW, Pogoda JM. Effects of estrogen replacement therapy on response to tacrine in patients with Alzheimer's disease. Neurology 1996;46:1580–4.

66

DIZZINESS

Giselle Cabello Namazie, MD, and Robert W. Baloh, MD

Dizziness is a symptom that can stem from a wide variety of causes. Although most patients who present to the primary care clinician have causes of dizziness that are not life-threatening, dizziness can be a symptom of a serious neurologic or cardiac illness. Although both men and women can have a psychological cause for dizziness, in the past, women were more likely to have their dizziness symptoms labeled inappropriately as "hysterical."

The spectrum of causes of dizziness is wide and includes both benign self-limiting conditions and potentially life-threatening ones. The most effective evaluation of dizziness focuses on obtaining a thorough history, focusing on specific aspects that differentiate the various underlying causes of dizziness. Most diagnoses are made after carefully eliciting the patient's descriptive complaints. A focused physical examination, which can be performed in a few minutes, is generally all that is necessary to confirm the diagnosis of most of the common causes of dizziness. In many cases, the clinician can offer simple remedies and maneuvers, some of which result in immediate relief of the patient's symptoms.

EVALUATION

Differentiation of Types

The first step in the evaluation of dizziness is to define whether the dizziness is vestibular (vertiginous) or nonvestibular. Vestibular dizziness stems from central or peripheral neurologic causes and is experienced as vertigo. Nonvestibular dizziness can be caused by cardiac arrhythmia, orthostatic hypotension, and psychiatric illness, among other causes. These are described in further detail below.

The patient's own description of the dizziness can be an important clue to its origin. Dizziness is a broad nonspecific term that patients commonly use to describe their symptoms. It is important to carefully determine whether patients are experiencing vertigo when they complain of dizziness. However, this can often be difficult as some patients cannot adequately describe vertigo.[1] In many cases, patients may have to be prompted with cues. Ascertaining the duration of symptoms and identifying associated symptoms and triggers can also assist the clinician in making the distinction between vertigo and nonvertiginous dizziness.

Patients with vertigo use expressions such as "spinning," "falling to one side," "sense of movement," and "everything around me turns."[2] Patients who describe their dizziness in this way are more likely to have a vestibular cause of their complaint. Vertigo is usually episodic.[3] However, it is not unusual for vertigo to be interspersed with a persistent sense of imbalance between attacks. Thus, patients should be prompted to determine whether their continuous symptoms actually consist of discrete vertiginous attacks with nonspecific dizziness between attacks.

Changes in head position trigger benign paroxysmal positional vertigo (BPPV), a disorder of the peripheral vestibular system and the cause of about 25% of all cases of dizziness. Typically, craning of the neck upward, such as when grabbing a book from a bookshelf ("top-shelf vertigo"), triggers BPPV. Patients with BPPV may also note that symptoms suddenly may occur after they turn in bed in the morning or bend down to put on their shoes.

Patients with migraine-related vertigo may have common migraine triggers, such as sleep disturbances, alcohol, chocolate, or stress. Vertigo and nonvertiginous dizziness may both be manifested and either can occur with or without headache. Migraine headaches may have occurred years earlier or may not be recognized by the patient as such. As many as 40% of patients who describe typical migraine symptoms on a questionnaire do not know they have migraines.[4]

Otosclerosis, an inherited conductive hearing loss, is more common in women than in men and can be associated with vertigo. A family and personal history of early-onset hearing loss is frequent.

Patients with psychophysiologic dizziness describe it with terms such as "lightheaded," "spinning in my head—everything around me stays still," "floating," "disorientated," "feel faint," "out-of-body sensation," and "don't think clearly."[2] Patients who describe their dizziness in this way are unlikely to have a vestibular cause. Nonvestibular dizziness may be continuous from morning to night; exceptions to this include dizziness experienced during postural hypotension (which patients identify as occurring with changes in position) and dizziness experienced during cardiac arrhythmias (which may be abrupt and without premonitory symptoms). Situational dizziness, such as that which occurs while one is driving on a freeway, entering a crowded room, or working in an office, suggests nonvestibular dizziness, especially if is reliably reproduced by entering the same situations and alleviated by leaving them.[3] Pregnancy may increase occurrences of paroxysmal supraventricular tachycardia, causing dizziness and syncopal episodes. There is an increased incidence of arrhythmias in pregnancy.[5] Women with a prior history of paroxysmal supraventricular tachycardia are more likely to experience exacerbations during pregnancy.[6]

Patients are frequently asked if stress affects their symptoms, presumably to ascertain if it is psychogenic in origin. Unfortunately, stress can aggravate both vestibular and nonvestibular dizziness; it can be used to distinguish them only if stress consistently gives rise to dizziness, implying a nonvestibular cause.[7]

VESTIBULAR DIZZINESS

Vertigo accounts for 50% of all cases of dizziness.[8] There are two main types of vertigo: central vertigo, which is caused by abnormalities in the brain, and peripheral vertigo, which is caused by abnormalities in the inner ear, the vestibular nerve (cranial nerve[CN] VIII), and the nerve root entry zone up to but not including the brain. Once it is established that a patient has vertigo, distinguishing between central and peripheral vertigo is the next

TABLE 66–1. Causes of Central Vertigo

Acoustic neuroma
Internuclear ophthalmoplegia
Intracranial tumors (brain stem, cerebellum)
Cerebellar atrophy
Multiple sclerosis
Vascular lesions and stroke
Vertebrobasilar insufficiency
Vertigo with migraine
Vertiginous epilepsy

important step in deciding whether further tests or subspecialty referrals are needed.

The causes of central vertigo include acoustic neuromas, brain tumors, transient ischemic attacks, cerebrovascular accidents, multiple sclerosis, and migraines (Table 66–1). Migraine-related dizziness is far more common in women than in men, constituting up to 80% of cases in women in some series.[4] Causes of peripheral vertigo include BPPV (which alone accounts for up to one-half of cases of vertigo overall), labyrinthitis, and Meniere's disease (a disease of the cochlea) (Table 66–2). Women develop BPPV twice as often as men.[9]

Both the duration of the attacks and the presence of associated symptoms help distinguish central from peripheral vertigo. In the acute phase of any vertiginous illness, it is common for patients to have persistent nonspecific feelings of dizziness between attacks of vertigo. For example, BPPV

TABLE 66–2. Causes of Peripheral Vertigo

Acute and chronic otitis media

Autoimmune

Benign paroxysmal positional vertigo

Cholesteatoma

Labyrinthitis (vestibular neuronitis)
    Bacterial
    Viral

Meniere's syndrome

Ototoxicity

Syphilis

Trauma
    Cranial nerve VIII
    Labyrinthine
    Perilymph fistula

patients reveal that, rather than days of continuous vertigo, they in fact have short 10- to 30-second attacks of vertigo, followed by an unremitting sensation of imbalance. Attacks that last for seconds are characteristic of BPPV. Those which last for minutes are often due to vertebral basilar insufficiency or migraine. Attacks that last for hours are often caused by Meniere's disease. Symptoms that last for days to weeks are most often associated with viral labyrinthitis, labyrinthine trauma, and infarcts involving the labyrinth, brain stem, or cerebellum.

Central disorders that cause vertigo usually have associated focal neurologic findings.[7] These may include dysarthria, focal numbness, focal weakness, and incoordination, which is usually severe. Diplopia by itself can occur transiently in peripheral vertigo due to malalignment of the eyes and cannot be used to distinguish central from peripheral vertigo unless the symptoms are persistent. Nausea or vomiting may be minimal or (rarely) severe.

A history of vascular risk factors may be a clue to some central causes of vertigo, including vertebrobasilar insufficiency, transient ischemic attack (TIA), and cerebrovascular accident (CVA). These factors include age greater than 60 years, known coronary artery disease or peripheral vascular disease, a known history of CVA or TIA, and a history of smoking. Vertebrobasilar insufficiency presents with ischemic symptoms of the posterior circulation: diplopia, dysarthria, ataxia, Horner's syndrome, hemianopia, hemiparesis, and numbness of the face or limbs.[10] Infarct and TIA rarely occur in young healthy individuals. Older patients at risk often already have a previous diagnosis of cerebrovascular disease, coronary artery disease, or peripheral vascular disease. If there is any doubt about the diagnosis when such patients present with vertigo, brain imaging should be performed at an early stage to evaluate for possible infarct.

Peripheral vertigo is provoked by the position of the head and especially by turning the head. It may be accompanied by severe nausea and vomiting, unilateral hearing loss, tinnitus, ear fullness, and ear pain. Meniere's syndrome is typically associated with a fluctuating hearing loss and tinnitus. These peripheral signs almost always confirm the diagnosis of peripheral vertigo; however, cerebellar infarction and hemorrhage can (rarely) mimic peripheral vertigo. The absence of such signs does not exclude a peripheral cause.

Nonvestibular Dizziness

If it is determined by history that the patient does not have vertigo, then causes of nonvestibular dizziness should be pursued. Because cardiac causes of dizziness can be life threatening, evaluating for cardiac causes takes priority. Even after extensive evaluation, the underlying pathology remains unidentified in up to 10% of patients with dizziness.[8]

Presyncope accounts for 5% of all cases of dizziness.[8] Patients state, "I feel faint, like I'm going to pass out; vision tunnels or narrows." They may describe light-headedness, nausea, diaphoresis, pallor, or coldness in the minutes preceding the episode. A postural component is often noted, as when dizziness only occurs when the patient goes from lying to sitting and from sitting to standing. **Vasovagal episodes** occur with prolonged standing or with intense fear or pain; in young patients, this is the most common cause of syncope.[11] A variant of this is the **visceral reflex syncope** that typically affects elderly persons; this can occur after micturation, defecation, or eating. **Orthostatic hypotension** may be caused by gastrointestinal illness or diuretics, medications such as antihypertensives or antiarrhythmics, prolonged bed rest, or autonomic neuropathies (including those caused by diabetes). Palpitations occurring simultaneously with dizziness, or a sudden onset of dizziness, suggest arrhythmia as a cause. Orthostatic hypotension and cardiac abnormalities are typically marked by presyncopal or frank syncopal episodes. Associated true syncope almost always excludes a noncardiac cause of dizziness.[12] A patient presenting with dizziness and true syncope generally requires urgent cardiac evaluation.

Psychiatric illness is responsible for up to 20% of cases of dizziness.[8] All patients with dizziness should be questioned regarding the use of psychiatric medications, alcohol, and street drugs. They should be questioned about symptoms of depression and anxiety, panic attacks, and the amount of stress they experience at home or at work. Fatigue and an inability to concentrate may be described as dizziness by some patients.

Dysequilibrium causes 5% of all dizziness.[8] This is a condition described primarily among geriatric patients, who have multifactorial sensory deficits that lead to a perception of imbalance.[13] Dysequilibrium usually is attributed to vision impairments such as cataracts and macular degeneration and to somatosensory deficits such as peripheral neuropathies, arthritis, and stroke. Vitamin B_{12} deficiency is more common in elderly patients and may present as dysequilibrium from peripheral neuropathy. Vestibular disorders and orthostatic hypotension can be superimposed on these problems. Patients describe symptoms only with walking, irrespective of sudden changes in position. It is common for their symptoms to worsen in the dark because patients lose their visual cues for balance.

Physical Examination

The general physical examination should focus on identifying signs associated with causes of dizziness, such as orthostatic hypotension and stigmas of vascular and neurologic disease. The key elements of the neurologic examination that are specific to the evaluation of dizziness include the evaluation of nystagmus and positional testing, as well as tests of balance and gait.

For defining the cause of dizziness, the presence of nystagmus is the most useful part of the neurologic examination because its presence suggests vestibular dizziness. Nystagmus is described as having a "slow component" and a "fast component." The direction of the nystagmus is defined by the direction of the fast component. Nystagmus in central vertigo changes with the direction of the patient's gaze. With or without fixation, the nystagmus remains prominent. Nystagmus in peripheral vertigo always beats in one direction. Typically, the nystagmus goes away in 1 to 2 days and is strongly inhibited by visual fixation on a stationary object. The nystagmus typically intensifies in the same direction if the patient looks toward the direction of the fast component.

For example, in a patient complaining of vertigo with nystagmus beating to the right (the fast component), central lesions can be differentiated from peripheral ones by having the patient look to her left and right. With a peripheral defect, the patient's right-beating nystagmus worsens if she looks toward her right; if she looks to her left, the nystagmus lessens. This has been called "Alexander's law." With a central defect, the patient's right-beating nystagmus also worsens if she looks to the right. However, if she looks to her left, the nystagmus often changes directions and becomes a left-beating nystagmus (the fast component is now to the left).

There are two maneuvers that helps confirm the presence of positional vertigo: a rapid change from a sitting position to head-hanging position (Hall-Pike maneuver) and a rapid turn of the head to each side while the patient is supine (Figure 66–1). Prior to the examination, it is important to warn the patient that it is important to keep her eyes open at all times and that the maneuver may cause vertigo. If the patient presents with nausea as a prominent symptom, an oral or intramuscular dose of an antiemetic should be considered, to lessen the patient's discomfort and to avoid emesis during testing. The patient should be asked to state when the vertigo begins and ends.

Three aspects of the positional examination are important at this stage: latency, fatigue, and direction of nystagmus. Latency refers to a delay in the onset of the nystagmus after reaching the critical position (usually 5 to 15 seconds). Fatigue describes whether or not the nystagmus extinguishes with repetition of the positional testing. Direction, as mentioned above, refers to the fast component of the nystagmus.

Central positional nystagmus has no latency, begins abruptly, and lasts longer than 60 seconds. Despite further repositioning of the patient, the nystagmus does not fatigue. Nystagmus direction is variable, but the down beat is the most common. Peripheral positional nystagmus usually has a 3- to 10-second latency before onset. The nystagmus is brief, lasting less than 30 seconds. With repeated testing, the severity of the patient's response will lessen or fatigue until the vertigo and nystagmus disappears. The nystagmus typically has vertical and torsional components, with the upper pole of the eyes beating toward the ground in the head-hanging position.

If the typical fatigable torsional/vertical nystagmus is seen on the Dix-Hall–pike maneuver, the diagnosis of BPPV is clear, and one can proceed directly to the particle repositioning maneuver (modified Epley). Less than 20% of patients need further testing after these steps are followed.

Patients with peripheral vertigo may prefer to lie down but can walk when asked to. They often walk into the office, albeit veering to one side. Patients with central vertigo suffer a severe imbalance and often cannot stand up; they typically present to the emergency room. Tests such as the Romberg and tandem gait tests do not help to distinguish central

A   **B**

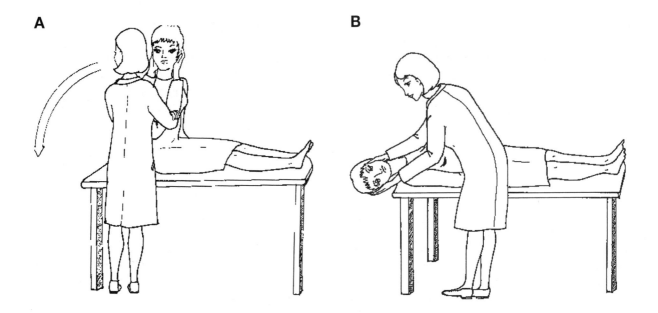

FIGURE 66–1. The Hall-Pike maneuver. The patient sits upright with her head turned to one side and is then rapidly lowered to the table so that her head is below the horizontal plane of the table. The patient should be instructed to keep her eyes open throughout the procedure so that nystagmus can be observed. The nystagmus may correlate with the patient's report of vertigo symptoms. The patient's head is maintained in position until the nystagmus resolves. The direction of the "fast component" of nystagmus, the latency to onset of vertigo, and the duration are noted (see text). Then, the patient is instructed to sit up, her head is turned to the opposite direction, and the maneuver is repeated (there may be a repeat onset of vertigo as the patient sits up). Typically, the symptoms of a patient with benign paroxysmal positional vertigo (BPPV) are worse when her head is turned toward the affected ear.

from peripheral vertigo. Romberg's test is insensitive for chronic unilateral vestibular lesions.[14] Closed-eye tandem gait testing is more accurate for vestibular function whereas tandem with eyes open is a better test of cerebellar function.[4] Acute vestibular lesions may impair tandem walking, however. In some situations, even normal older persons can fail.

Additional Procedures and Tests

Blood tests are rarely helpful, except in two instances. When blood loss or a metabolic cause of orthostasis is suspected, blood tests may support the diagnosis. Also, in the presence of hearing loss or suspected Meniere's disease, a syphilis test should be performed. A Holter monitor or event recorder is required when cardiac arrhythmia is suspected.

A formal complete audiologic examination by a qualified audiologist is necessary for any patient complaining of hearing loss or tinnitus in the presence of vertigo. An office-based audiometric test cannot give the detail necessary to differentiate between conductive or sensorineural hearing loss, nor can it yield other details that are required by

the specialist in this clinical situation. In acoustic neuroma, hearing loss typically affects only one side. In Meniere's disease, low-frequency hearing loss may start on one side and then progress to the other, corresponding to the common clinical history of fluctuating hearing loss associated with intermittent attacks of vertigo. It is important to differentiate these types of hearing loss from presbycusis, which is the normal high-frequency hearing loss associated with aging.

Brain-stem auditory-evoked response (BAER) testing is used to evaluate abnormal audiometry results, usually to differentiate between peripheral and central auditory disease. Electronystagmography (ENG) can help diagnose vestibular disease, although normal results do not rule out disease. The caloric testing may be uncomfortable for some patients. Rotary-chair or dynamic posturography may be more sensitive than ENG for vestibular disease. Computerized tomography (CT) and magnetic resonance imaging (MRI) are useful only if primary neurologic disease (such as tumor, multiple sclerosis, or stroke) is suspected by history and

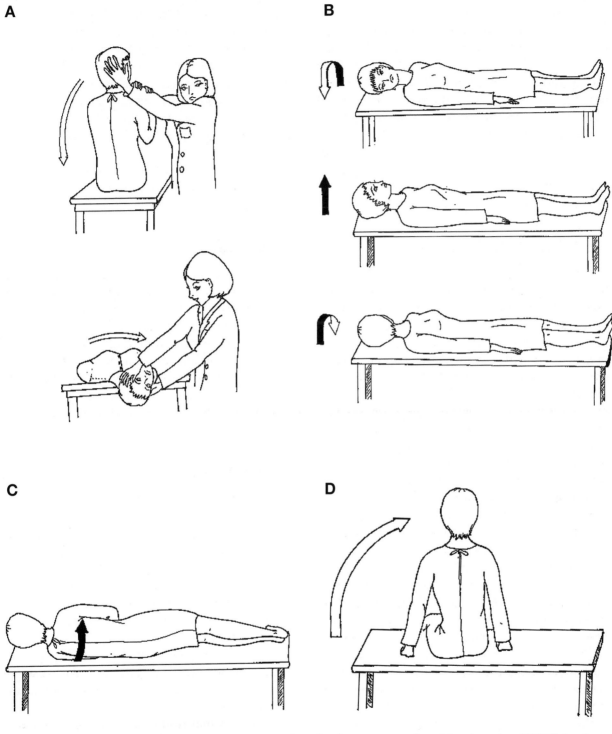

FIGURE 66–2. The canalith repositioning maneuver. Once benign paroxysmal positional vertigo (BPPV) has been established as the diagnosis by the Hall-Pike maneuver, this maneuver can then follow and be taught to the patient. Each position change occurs rapidly. *A*, As with the Hall-Pike maneuver, the upright patient's head is turned to the affected ear (here, the affected ear is on the right). Then the patient drops back to the table and waits until the vertigo resolves. *B*, The patient then turns her head in the opposite direction and again waits until the vertigo resolves. *C*, The patient then turns her body so that her head and back are aligned. *D*, In the final move, the patient sits up. Ideally, the patient's head should be below the plane of the bed until the final move, but this may be difficult for elderly patients.

physical examination or if audiologic or vestibular testing suggests a central disorder.

Neurologists, otolaryngologists, and specialists in the newer fields of neuro-otolaryngology and neuro-ophthalmology are all qualified to help in the diagnostic evaluation of dizziness. If an ear lesion requiring surgery is suspected, a head and neck surgeon may be the appropriate consultant. Suspected or diagnosed stroke requires emergent radiologic evaluation and consultation with a neurologist. When presyncopal symptoms are present and are not due to orthostatic hypotension, consultation with a cardiologist is most useful.

MEDICAL MANAGEMENT

Benign paroxysmal positional vertigo is best treated by the canalith repositioning maneuver (modified Epley). This maneuver is very effective, is simple to perform in the office, and produces immense patient satisfaction (Figure 66–2). Patients can be taught to perform this maneuver at home; this is useful because patients with BPPV may have multiple recurrences.

Meclizine (25 mg every 6 hours as needed for acute symptoms) is the treatment of choice for viral labyrinthitis. Neurorehabilitation may help the patient compensate for vestibular deficits. Meniere's disease is also treated with meclizine (as needed) as well as with a salt-restricted diet (1 to 2 g of sodium per day) and with diuretics for chronic symptoms.

Basilar migraines are much more common in women than in men, by a ratio of 5:1.[1] Vertigo typically occurs independently of headache; patients may have a distant history of headache, if any at all. Agents typically used for acute headache, such as sumatriptan, do not work for a vertiginous attack. The emphasis rather should be on prophylaxis and on identifying migraine triggers. (This is discussed further in Chapter 67, "Approach to the Patient with Headache.") Selective serotonin reuptake inhibitors (SSRIs) and tricyclic amine antidepressants are often useful in preventing basilar migraines, especially when combined with lifestyle changes. The lowest dose should be started for 1 week and then advanced according to symptoms. Improvement is gradual over 6 to 8 weeks.

For patients with presyncope, medications that may be exacerbating their symptoms should be discontinued when possible. For diabetics with autonomic neuropathies, other treatments may include elevation of the head of the patient's bed, compression stockings, and fludrocortisone.

Patients who suffer from dysequilibrium should have sensory or orthopedic problems that impair balance perception corrected. Assistive devices such as single-point canes, four-point canes, or walkers may be useful. Physical therapy for gait and balance training is also appropriate.

For patients suspected of having anxiety or panic as the cause of their dizziness, psychiatric referral or counseling is appropriate. Tricyclic amines and SSRIs are often useful.

CONCLUSION

Dizziness is a common complaint in primary care practice. Migraine and BPPV, the two most common causes of dizziness in women, often can be successfully diagnosed and treated by the primary care clinician. A careful history and a focused physical examination usually leads rapidly to diagnosis. Clinicians should be alert to rarer and potentially life-threatening causes of dizziness, such as cardiac arrhythmias, brain tumors, and cerebrovascular disease.

REFERENCES

1. Baloh RW. Dizzy patients: the varieties of vertigo. Hosp Pract 1998;15:55–77.
2. Kroenke K. Dizziness: a focused 5-minute workup. Consultant 1996;Aug:1715–21.
3. Baloh RW. Approach to the evaluation of the dizzy patient. Head Neck Surg 1995;112:3–7.
4. Johnson JD. Medical management of migraine-related dizziness and vertigo. Laryngoscope 1998;108 Suppl:1–28.
5. Shotan A, Ostrezega E, Mehra A, et al. Incidence of arrhythmias in normal pregnancy and relation to palpitations, dizziness, and syncope. Am J Cardiol 1997;79:1061–4.
6. Lee S, Chen S, Wu T, et al. Effects of pregnancy on first onset and symptoms of paroxysmal supraventricular tachycardia. Am J Cardiol 1995;76:675–8.
7. Baloh RW. Dizziness: neurological emergencies. Neurol Clin North Am 1998;16:305–21.
8. Kroenke K. Causes of persistent dizziness: a prospective study of 100 patients in ambulatory care. Ann Intern Med 1992;117:898.

9. Katsarkas A, Kikham TH. Paroxysmal positional vertigo: a study of 255 cases. J Otolaryngol 1978;7:320–30.

10. Fife TD, Baloh RW, Duckwiler GR. Isolated dizziness in vertebrobasilar insufficiency: clinical features, angiography, and follow-up. J Stroke Cerebrovasc Dis 1994;4:4.

11. Manoli AS, Linzer M, Salem D, Estes NA 3rd. Syncope: current diagnostic evaluation and management. Ann Intern Med 1990;112:850.

12. Froehling DA, Silverstein MD, Mohr DN, Beatty CW. Does this patient have a serious form of vertigo? JAMA 1994;271:385–8.

13. Baloh RW. Dizziness in older people. J Am Geriatr Soc 1992;40:713–21.

14. Baloh RW, Honrubia V. Clinical neurophysiology of the vestibular system. 2nd ed. Philadelphia (PA): F.A. Davis, 1990. p. 1–301.

67

APPROACH TO THE PATIENT WITH HEADACHE

Anh Kieu, MD, and Ernestina Saxton, MD

Migraine and other syndromes of head pain have been recognized for centuries. References to headache appear in the written record of most civilizations, and treatment has evolved from trepanation (evidence of which has been found in neolithic skulls dating from 7000 BC) to the modern development of the triptans, a family of chemicals with properties similar to serotonin.[1]

EPIDEMIOLOGY AND SOCIETAL IMPACT

Although it is the seventh most common reason for seeking medical care and is second only to acquired immunodeficiency syndrome (AIDS) in its adverse effects on quality of life and function, recurrent headache disorders have been addressed only rarely in education and research in women's health. Women experience headaches with a higher prevalence than men. The tension-type headache is the most common primary headache, with a lifetime prevalence of 78%, compared with 16% for migraine and 0.1 to 0.4% for cluster headache.

The American Migraine Study estimates migraine prevalence to be 17.6% for women and 6% for men.[2] Women are twice as likely to seek medical care and to receive prescriptions than are men. They also report more frequent and debilitating headaches than do men and are twice as likely as men to lose time from work.[3]

The gender ratio of migraine varies with age. Before puberty, migraine prevalence is higher in boys than in girls; as puberty approaches, the ratio begins to shift, and by the age of 25 to 45 years (the peak of migraine prevalence), three times as many women as men are affected. Hormonal changes may account partially for this difference, but even after menopause, the female-to-male migraine prevalence remains greater than 2:1.[1]

COMMON TYPES OF HEADACHE

The International Headache Society (IHS) system is widely accepted as the standard for classifying headaches. It distinguishes between primary and secondary headache.[4] In primary headache syndromes, by definition, there are no underlying structural or systemic causes for the headache. Secondary headaches are caused by underlying diseases, many of which have significant associated morbidity or mortality. Primary headache syndromes include migraine, tension-type, and cluster headaches, as well as miscellaneous headaches unassociated with structural lesions. Primary headaches are significantly more common than secondary headaches, particularly in primary care practice.[5]

Migraine

Migraine is a primary episodic headache disorder associated with varying combinations of neurologic, gastrointestinal, and autonomic changes. The diagnosis is based on the reporting of the headache's characteristics and associated symptoms. The specific cause of migraine is not known. Clearly, the brain responds to external triggers, resulting in a migraine attack. There are several proposed mechanisms of migraine; the most favored model is the trigeminovascular hypothesis. Trigeminal nerve axons supply extracranial arteries, meningeal tissues, dural arteries, and the dural sinuses. It is postulated that the local release of peptides from the trigeminal nerve terminals causes neurogenic inflammation, which is a pain-sensitive state. This leads to local vasodilation and sensitization of trigeminal nerve endings, which creates the pain phenomenon.[6-8] Sumatriptan and the other newly developed antimigraine drugs (zolmitriptan, naratriptan, and rizatriptan) are selective agonists of the serotonin (5-HT1) receptors localized on peripheral trigeminal nerve terminals. The triptans block presynaptic neuropeptide release by binding to 5-HT1 receptors; they also bind to 5-HT1B receptors on intracranial vessels, with resultant vasoconstriction.[1]

Patients may experience migraine with or without aura. The course of a migraine headache can be divided into four phases: the prodrome phase, the aura phase (in migraine with aura), the headache phase, and the headache resolution phase. Except for the absence of aura, the headache and associated symptoms of migraine without aura are the same as those of migraine with aura. By IHS criteria, two attacks are needed for a diagnosis of migraine with aura, and five attacks are needed for a diagnosis of migraine without aura.[4]

PRODROME PHASE
The prodrome phase occurs several hours to days before the onset of the headache in about 60% of migraine patients. It occurs with equal frequency in migraine with and without aura. There are often changes in mood and behavior, including depression or elation, cognitive dysfunction, and food cravings.[9]

AURA PHASE
Migraine with aura is associated with neurologic symptoms that occur before or during the headache. The aura lasts 60 minutes or less and usually precedes the headache by less than 60 minutes. Visual phenomena are the most common auras: scintillating lines, figures, or dots; scotomata (areas of decreased vision in the visual field) with or without scintillating phenomena (scintillating scotomata); photopsia (unformed flashes of light); or distortion of shape and size of objects. Tingling is the most common sensory aura. Motor symptoms include hemiparesis and aphasia (or dysphasia). Brain-stem symptoms include ataxia, diplopia, dysarthria, visual field disturbances, and changes in level of consciousness.

The aura of migraine is associated with cerebral blood flow changes that are consistent with vasoconstriction (vasospasm). Woods et al demonstrated that cerebral vasospasm also precedes headache in patients experiencing migraine without aura. Reduction in blood flow, or spreading oligemia, begins in the occipital region and moves across the cortex, with no respect to vascular territories. The rate of spread is characteristic of the phenomenon known as "spreading depression" that occurs with noxious stimulation of the cerebral cortex.[6]

HEADACHE PHASE
During the headache phase, patients generally describe a throbbing pulsatile pain that is usually unilateral but that may be bilateral. The pain is usually reported to feel like an internal pressure inside the head, like a balloon blowing up. Nausea, vomiting, photophobia, and phonophobia may be present. Routine physical activity aggravates migraine symptoms. The headache may last from 4 to 72 hours.[9]

HEADACHE RESOLUTION PHASE
For 1 day after the headache, migraine patients may experience nonspecific but recognizable symptoms that include cravings for certain foods, fatigue or increased activity, euphoria or dysphoria, yawning, and gastrointestinal discomfort. After the attack, many patients describe feeling "hung over."[9]

Tension-Type Headaches
Tension-type headaches have also been described as tension headaches, muscle contraction headaches, and psychogenic headaches. Tension-type headaches may or may not be associated with disorders of the pericranial muscles. Patients generally describe a pressing nonpulsatile pain that is viselike in nature, like a tight cap on the head. The pain is usually bilateral although it may be described as unilateral. Pain lasts from 30 minutes to 7 days and is not aggravated by activity. Nausea is generally not present. Photophobia or phonophobia may be associated but not both at the same time. The pain of a tension-type headache is usually worse at the end of the day.[10]

A distinction is made between episodic and chronic forms of tension-type headaches. The episodic form occurs with a frequency of less than

15 days per month, and the chronic form occurs 15 or more days per month. Patients may report a family history. Tension-type headaches are more common in women than in men. The prevalence of tension-type headaches varies from 1.3 to 65.0% in men and from 2.7 to 86.0% in women.[10,11]

The pathophysiology of tension-type headaches is not directly related to muscle contraction. Electromyography studies have not shown a correlation between the amount of muscle contraction and the amount of pain. Tension-type headache pain is postulated to be related to abnormal neuronal sensitivity and pain facilitation, such that pain sensitivity is increased.[10]

Serotonin is also thought to play a role in chronic tension-type headaches. Plasma and platelet serotonin levels are low in patients with chronic tension-type headaches, and this is postulated to be a reflection of abnormal serotonin metabolism that also may be occurring in the brain.[12]

Cluster Headaches

Cluster headache is rare, having a prevalence of 0.1 to 0.4% in the general population. The pain is severe and debilitating and is often described as boring and penetrating. The pain is usually unilateral, and is located in the orbital, supraorbital, or temporal region. Associated symptoms include conjunctival injection, lacrimation, nasal congestion, rhinorrhea, miosis, and facial sweating. Attacks occur in series lasting for days to weeks to months, separated by remissions lasting for months to years. Approximately 10% of patients have chronic symptoms with no remission periods. Attack frequency varies from one every other day to eight attacks per day. Each attack lasts 15 to 180 minutes if untreated. Cluster headaches are nine times more common in men than in women.[13]

The pathophysiology and etiology of cluster headaches is unknown. Cluster headaches incorporate four different elements—pain, vasodilation, autonomic features, and periodicity—and no one mechanism has been able to account for all components.

Pain is usually centered about the eye, suggesting involvement of the ophthalmic branch of the trigeminal nerve. Associated pain, vasodilation, Horner's syndrome, and parasympathetic overactivity are thought to be related to the activation of nociceptive fibers of the trigeminal nerve in the cavernous sinus where sympathetic and parasympathetic fibers join. The periodicity of cluster headaches has been attributed to a defect in the central pacemaker, which is located in the suprachiasmatic nuclei in the hypothalamus. There are also connections from the suprachiasmatic nuclei to the nuclei of the trigeminal nerve, and disturbances in the pacemaker are thought to lead to the activation of the trigeminovascular system.[13,14]

DIAGNOSIS

Accurate headache diagnosis depends on a thorough history and on complete general physical and neurologic examination. The primary aim of the evaluation is to distinguish between benign primary headache conditions and secondary headache conditions caused by systemic illness or other ominous factors (Tables 67–1 and 67–2).

A careful description of current headache symptoms should be elicited. The quality, location, intensity, duration, and frequency of pain are important clues to diagnosis. Premonitory and associated symptoms, aura, triggers, and alleviators can form a pattern that can classify the type of headache the patient is experiencing. Throbbing and pressure are more consistent with migraine; squeezing pain is more apt to be a tension-type headache.[5] Pain localized to only one side is usually cause for alarm since migraine pain usually changes sides, albeit not equally.

A complete knowledge of the patient's past and current use of medication, including over-the-

---

TABLE 67–1. Signs Indicative of Possible Secondary Causes of Headache

Onset after age 50 yr
New headache or change in headache pattern
"Worst" headache of life
Increasing intensity of headache over time
Headaches from coughing, sneezing, exertion, or sexual activity
Headaches with focal neurologic signs or symptoms
Headaches associated with signs or symptoms of systemic illness

Adapted from Solomon GD, Cady RK, Klapper JA, Ryan RE Jr. Standards of care for treating headache in primary care practice. National Headache Foundation. Cleve Clin J Med 1997;64:373–83.

TABLE 67–2. Evaluation and Diagnostic Testing for Secondary Headaches

Headache Characteristic	Underlying Illness/Condition	Diagnostic Test/Imaging
Headache with fever, stiff neck, systemic illness	Meningitis, encephalitis, systemic infection, collagen vascular disease (eg, temporal arteritis)	Neuroimaging, lumbar puncture (in that order); ESR
New-onset headache after age 50 yr	Temporal arteritis, mass lesion	ESR, neuroimaging
Change in headache	Mass lesion, subdural hematoma	Neuroimaging
New-onset headache in patient with cancer or HIV infection	Metastasis, meningitis (infectious or carcinomatous), abscess	Neuroimaging, lumbar puncture
Sudden or worse headache	Subarachnoid hemorrhage, pituitary apoplexy, AVM	Neuroimaging, lumbar puncture
Headache with focal symptoms or signs (including change in consciousness)	Mass lesion, AVM, stroke, collagen vascular disease, venous sinus thrombosis, subarachnoid hemmorrhage, subdural or intracerebral hematoma	Neuroimaging, collagen vascular evaluation
Papilledema	Mass lesion, pseudotumor cerebri, venous sinus thrombosis	Neuroimaging, lumbar puncture (opening pressure)
Headache associated with constant eye pain, blurred vision	Acute angle closure glaucoma	Tonometry for intraocular pressure, eye examination (fixed, dilated pupil, steamy cornea)
Continuous severe unilateral pain lasting for days	Internal carotid artery dissection	Neuroimaging
Recent-onset severe bilateral headache	Sinusitis	CT of sinuses

AVM = arteriovenous malformation; CT = computed tomography; ESR = erythrocyte sedimentation rate; HIV = human immuno-deficiency virus. Adapted from Silberstein et al[1] and Marks et al.[5]

counter medications, is important in formulating a treatment plan. The history of caffeine, alcohol, tobacco, and recreational drug use is especially important in the treatment of headache patients. A family history of migraine is suggestive of migraine headache as up to 80% of migraine headache patients have a first-degree relative who experiences migraines.[1] Coexisting medical and psychiatric conditions can determine the diagnosis as well as the choice of medications for treatment and should be evaluated by a thorough history, a review of systems, and physical examination.

The physical examination should focus on findings indicative of the primary or secondary causes of headache (Table 67–3). The neurologic examination should evaluate for secondary causes of headache. Any abnormality should be thoroughly investigated. At minimum, this should consist of (1) a brief examination of mental status to determine if altered consciousness is present; (2) examination of the fundus to look for papilledema; and (3) evaluation of pupillary size and light response, strength and gait, and deep tendon reflexes, with testing of plantar responses to rule out a Babinski response.[5,15]

APPROACH TO HEADACHE TREATMENT

Managing patients with migraine and other headache syndromes is a challenging task. To find the

TABLE 67–3. Physical Examination in the Evaluation of Headache

Assess vital signs

Evaluate for head trauma

Palpate temporal arteries for tenderness

Inspect oral cavity for dental disorders

Assess temporomandibular joint mobility, alignment, crepitus

Evaluate neck for cervical motion, thyromegaly, lymphadenopathy

Auscultate carotid arteries

Palpate suboccipital and sternocleidomastoid regions for trigger points

Examine ears, throat, heart, lungs, and abdomen for systemic disease

Neurologic testing
    Mental status examination
    Cranial nerves
    Fundoscopic examination and visual field testing
    Upper- and lower-extremity strength
    Deep tendon reflexing
    Test for Babinski's reflex

Adapted from Silberstein DS, Lipton RB, Goadsby PJ, editors. Headache in clinical practice. Oxford: Isis Medical Media; 1998.

right therapy for each patient, the clinician relies primarily on trial and error. This empiric treatment must take into consideration the type of headache, the patient's age, the presence of comorbid conditions, and the ratio of benefit to risk.

Trigger Prevention

The avoidance of headache triggers is an important step in the prevention and treatment of headache. A "headache diary" is an important tool that allows the patients to participate fully in their care. The recognition of precipitants assists the patient in making lifestyle changes that include changes in sleep, diet, and exercise patterns.

Migraine triggers are myriad and include the menstrual cycle, stress and/or poststress letdown, too much or too little sleep, skipped meals, changes in weather and barometric pressure, light, heat, and odors. Food triggers include chocolate, cheeses, alcoholic beverages, citruses, monosodium glutamate (MSG), and nitrates in cured meats. Allergies and

sinus disease as well as temporomandibular joint dysfunction are migraine triggers in some patients (Table 67–4). Tension-type headaches are triggered by stress. Cluster headaches may be triggered by the ingestion of alcohol during a cluster period.[13]

Abortive Therapy

Abortive or acute therapy is used for infrequent headaches and for breakthrough headaches in patients

TABLE 67–4. Triggers of Migraine Headache

Foods
    Cheese
    Chocolate
    Alcohol (especially red wine)
    Citrus fruits
    Cured meats
    Nuts
    Pickled, fermented, or marinated food
    Freshly baked yeast products, sourdough bread

Chemicals
    Monosodium glutamate (MSG)
    Nitrates
    Aspartame

Drugs
    Caffeine (and caffeine withdrawal)
    Cocaine (and cocaine withdrawal)
    Oral contraceptives, hormone replacement

Environmental factors
    Weather changes
    High altitude
    Exposure to flickering or bright light
    Chemical fumes or perfumes
    Loud noises

Physical factors/comorbidities
    Menstruation, ovulation, pregnancy
    Lack of sleep or too much sleep
    Stress
    Fatigue
    Dehydration
    Skipping of meals
    Exercise
    Temporomandibular joint disease, musculoskeletal disorders of the head and neck
    Sinus disease

Adapted from Marks DR, Rapoport AM. Practical evaluation and diagnosis of headache. Semin Neurol 1997;17:307–12.

on prophylactic regimens. The type of headache, the intensity of the pain, and the associated symptoms all influence the choice and route of administration of abortive medication (Table 67–5).

Acute therapy should be instituted as early in the attack as possible. Most drugs work best when given in the early stages. When attacks are treated later or at the height of the migraine, the triptans (sumatriptan, naratriptan, rizatriptan, and zolmitriptan) and dihydroergotamine (DHE) are more likely to work. These vasoconstrictors, however, should not be used during the aura. If these fail, a narcotic such as a butorphanol nasal spray can provide effective pain relief. The highest tolerable dose of a selected medication should be administered as early as possible in the attack. The patient's preference and prior experience must be taken into consideration at all times since patients may have idiosyncratic or paradoxic responses to certain medications.

The severity of the attack determines the type of medication selected. A mild attack may respond to aspirin, acetaminophen, nonsteroidal anti-inflammatory drugs (NSAIDs), or other over-the-counter or prescription combination drugs such as Excedrin or Fiorinal/Fioricet. A moderate attack may respond to NSAIDs or compounds such as Midrin. A severe attack often requires a specific antimigraine drug such as ergotamine tartrate, DHE, or the highly specific triptans. An extremely severe attack may require a combination of a specific antimigraine drug along with any of the above, or it may require corticosteroids.[8]

Associated symptoms contribute to migraine severity and determine the type of drug and the route of administration. Severe nausea with vomiting is associated with gastric stasis and inhibits the absorption of oral medications; subcutaneous or intramuscular drug administration is required under these circumstances. An antiemetic given parenterally or as a rectal suppository may be used in combination with a specific antimigraine drug. In many instances, an antiemetic suppository taken 15 to 20 minutes before oral medication enhances gastric motility and allows better drug absorption. An intranasal narcotic such as butorphanol can provide effective pain relief and obviate the need for a visit to an emergency room.

Cluster headaches are so painful and debilitating that every attack should be treated. Because the attacks are of rapid onset, it is important to use agents that work quickly. Oxygen at 7 to 10 L/min for 15 minutes can be effective if given early in the attack. Sumatriptan, DHE, and ergotamine can be used at the same dosage as used for migraine headache. These agents are effective within 30 minutes of treatment.

Preventive Therapy

The major indication for prophylactic therapy is attack frequency. Daily preventive medication for migraine headache should be used when attacks occur two or more times per month and produce disability lasting for 3 or more days. Mild migraine attacks that occur four or five times per month but are easily aborted do not require prophylactic therapy. However, severe migraine attacks that are physically or psychologically disabling and that are unresponsive to abortive medications may warrant preventive therapy even if they occur only once or twice per month. There is no standard medication or set dosage. Preventive therapy should be tailored to the patient's comorbid conditions and response.

Prophylactic treatment for tension-type headaches should be considered if they occur more than two times per week and last more than 3 or 4 hours. Tricyclic antidepressants or the selective serotonin reuptake inhibitors are usually tried first. However, any of the migraine-preventing drugs may be used empirically for tension-type headaches as well (see Table 67–5).

Preventive treatment for cluster headaches is almost always required because of the high frequency and severity of the attacks. Verapamil is the drug of first choice. There is no standard dose, but effective dosages generally range from 120 to 480 mg daily. If verapamil is ineffective or contraindicated, prednisone (60 to 80 mg for about 10 days) can be used in an attempt to lessen or terminate a cluster headache attack. Ergotamine (1 mg tid), methysergide (6 to 16 mg daily), lithium carbonate (600 to 1,200 mg daily), and divalproex sodium (Depakote) (750 to 2,000 mg daily) have also been used.

Nonpharmacologic Approach to Recurrent Headache

"Recurrent headache" refers to migraine or tension-type headaches that have been a continuing problem for a period of at least 6 months and that have been adequately diagnosed by a clinician to rule out

TABLE 67–5. Drugs Used in the Acute Treatment and Prophylaxis of Migraine and Tension Headaches*

Drug Class	Example (with Dose)	Migraine: Acute Rx	Migraine: Prophylaxis	Tension: Acute Rx	Tension: Prophylaxis†	Common Side Effects	Therapeutic Opportunity	Therapeutic Caution
Analgesics								
NSAIDS	Ibuprofen (OTC or Rx) Naproxen (OTC or Rx) Indomethacin (50 mg PO) Diclofenac (50 mg, 75 mg PO) Many others	•	•	•	•	GI irritation, drowsiness (rare)	Other pain	May worsen hypertension, relatively contraindicated if pt has hx/o upper or lower GI bleeding
Acetaminophen	Acetaminophen 1000 mg PO (OTC)	•		•		—	—	Liver toxicity
Opioids	Codeine 30 mg PO Others	•		•		CNS and respiratory depression, nausea, vomiting	—	Habituation, addiction
Opiate antagonist	Butorphanol 1 mg NS	•		•		Dizziness, drowsiness	—	—
Combination analgesics	Esgic 1–2 tabs PO Butalbital 50 mg Acetaminophen 500 mg Caffeine 40 mg Fioricet 1–2 tabs PO Butalbital 50 mg Acetaminophen 325 mg Caffeine 40 mg Others	•		•		Sedative, CNS stimulation	—	Tolerence, physical and psychological dependence to barbiturate component
Vasoactive agents								
DHE	Dihydroergotamine 1 mg IM, SQ, IV	•				Nausea, diarrhea	—	—
Other combination agents	Midrin 2 PO then 1 each hour up to 6 Isometheptene muscate 65 mg Dichloralphenazone 100 mg Acetaminophen 325 mg	•				Dizziness, drowsiness	—	Contraindicated in pregnancy, hypertension, coronary, cerebral, vascular disease, renal and liver failure, basilar migraine, uncontrolled HTN, or concomitant use of MAOI.
5 HT- agonists‡	Sumatriptan 6 mg SQ 25–100 mg PO, 20 mg NS Naratriptan 2.5 mg PO Rizatriptan 5–10 mg PO Zolmitriptan 25–50 mg PO	•				Chest pain	—	Avoid taking within 24 hours of using other vasoactive agents, may be used with butorphanol concurrently
Ergotamine	Ergotamine 2 mg PO Various combinations of ergotamine and caffeine PO and PR	•				Nausea, CNS stimulation	—	—

*Consult manufacturer or other information for a complete list of theraputic precautions, contraindications, and drug interactions
†Preferred drugs for tension headache prophylaxis are indicated with "•"—all drugs listed for migraine prophylaxis may have some efficacy.
The maximum dose in 24 hours is two of any formula with at least two hours between doses.
‡The maximum dose in 24 hours is two of any formula with at least two hours between doses.

NSAID = nonsteroidal anti-inflammatory drug; OTC = over the counter; Rx = prescription; GI = gastrointestinal; pt = patient; CNS = central nervous system; MAOI = monoamine oxidase inhibitor.

TABLE 67-5. (continued)

Drug Class	Example (with Dose)	Migraine: Acute Rx	Migraine: Prophylaxis	Tension: Acute Rx	Tension: Prophylaxis†	Common Side Effects	Therapeutic Opportunity	Therapeutic Caution
Muscle relaxants	Diazepam 2–10 mg PO Cyclobenzaprine 10 mg PO Others			•		Dizziness, drowsiness	—	Habituation, dependence
ß-Blockers	Propranolol 80–480 mg PO qd Metoprolol 50–200 mg PO qd Nadolol 80–240 mg PO qd Others		•			Fatigue, depression	Concomitant hypertension, coronary artery disease, congestive heart failure (CHF), certain cardiac arrythmias	May be contraindicated in asthma, brittle diabetes, certain cardiac arrythmias, depression. Although indicated in most patients with CHF, may worsen CHF in some patients
Antidepressants Tricyclic antidepressants	Amitriptyline 25–75 mg PO qd Doxepin 30–150 mg PO qd Others		•		•	Orthostatic hypotension, dry mouth, constipation	Depression, neuropathy fibromyalgia	Contraindicated in some cardiac arrythmias. Side effects may be particularly troublesome in elderly patients.
Selective serotonin reuptake inhibitors	Fluoxetine 20–80 mg PO qd (Others may be effective)		•		•	Decreased sex drive, insomnia	Depression, PMS	Contraindicated in patients using/ with recent use of MAOI
Others	Trazodone 50–300 mg PO qd Others		•			—	Depression, insomnia	—
Calcium channel blockers	Verapamil 80–320 mg PO qd Nimodipine 40 mg PO tid Others		•			Constipation, peripheral edema	Hypertension, Raynaud's phenomenon	Cardiac conduction defects, constipation
Anticonvulsants	Valproic acid 250–500 mg PO bid (Others may be effective)		•			Sedation, may cause peripheral neuropathy	Epilepsy, manic–depressive illness	Pregnancy, liver disease
Serotonin peripheral antagonist/central agonist	Methysergide		•			Hallucinations, weight gain, nausea	—	Irreversible retroperitoneal fibrosis (1/250)—should be used only in consultation with a migraine specialist; drug holidays recommended. Avoid taking within 24 hours of vasoactive agents; concomitant use of other serotonin agents not recommended
Adjunctive agents	Metoclopramide 10 mg Prochlorperazine 50 mg Prednisone 60 mg	•						—

*Consult manufacturer or other information for a complete list of theraputic precautions, contraindications, and drug interactions.
†Preferred drugs for tension headache prophylaxis are indicated with "•"—all drugs listed for migraine prophylaxis may have some efficacy.
CHF = congestive heart failure; MAOI = monoamine oxidase inhibitor; PMS = premenstrual syndrome; Rx = prescription.

structural abnormality and disease states. Non-pharmacologic therapies for recurrent headache include relaxation training, biofeedback training, and cognitive-behavioral (stress management) therapy.

Progressive muscle relaxation is the most widely used form of relaxation training. It involves alternately tensing and relaxing selected muscle groups throughout the body while simultaneously attending to the feelings associated with tension and relaxation. It works best in the prevention of headaches. Autogenic relaxation training involves the use of self-instructions of warmth and heaviness to promote a state of deep relaxation. Meditation or passive relaxation involves the use of a silently repeated word or sound to promote mental calm and relaxation. Thermal biofeedback or hand-warming training is used mainly for migraine. Electromyography biofeedback gives feedback of electrical activity from selected muscles. It is most often used in the treatment of tension-type headaches. Relaxation and EMG biofeedback training, individually or in combination, have been shown to produce up to a 50% reduction in tension headaches.

Cognitive-behavioral (stress management) therapy focuses on the cognitive and affective components of headache disorders. Behavioral treatments tend to emphasize prevention of headache episodes as opposed to alleviation to suffering once an episode has become severe. The goals of treatment are to identify stressful circumstances that precipitate or aggravate headaches, to develop effective coping strategies for dealing with stressors, to assist patients in coping more effectively with the pain and distress of headache, and to limit negative psychological consequences of recurrent headache.

MEDICATION-INDUCED CHRONIC DAILY HEADACHE

Patients with migraine or tension-type headaches can develop chronic daily headaches from the misuse of abortive medications. It is estimated that 3% of the general population have daily headaches, and 50 to 80% of these headaches are related to analgesic abuse. Commonly abused analgesics that are implicated in chronic daily headache include acetaminophen, aspirin, butalbital, caffeine, ergotamine, and sumatriptan. Patients with medication-induced chronic daily headaches are most commonly

between 30 and 40 years of age. Many report depression and gastrointestinal disturbance as comorbid conditions. Abuse of other substances, including caffeine, alcohol, and tobacco, is also common. Women are 3.5 times more likely to be affected than are men.[16,17]

Patients with analgesic rebound headaches report having a daily or near-daily headache that is refractory to treatment. The headache often varies with respect to intensity, type of pain, and location. Early morning headaches are common. Patients often have a previously diagnosed primary headache disorder and give a history of using abortive medications in excess. They report tolerance to headache medication, with requirements for increasing doses over time. Prophylactic medications may have been ineffective during periods of heavy abortive-medication use. The abrupt cessation of abortive medications is usually associated with withdrawal symptoms, including worse headaches. Headaches can be associated with depression, irritability, decreased concentration, restlessness, and asthenia.[18]

The treatment of choice is complete withdrawal of medications (unless the patient has been abusing barbiturates, opioids, or benzodiazepines, which should be tapered over time). Patients experience an increase in headaches during the immediate withdrawal period (2 to 10 days). For patients who require pain medications during this time, NSAIDs, triptans, or DHE can be used if these were not the agents of abuse. Cessation without analgesics is often necessary. Antiemetics, anxiolytics, and neuroleptics can be used if needed for symptoms of nausea, vomiting, sleep disturbance, restlessness, and anxiety. Other treatment modalities include amitriptyline, valproate, oxygen, and electrical stimulation. Treatment regimens should be individualized for each patient.[19]

If prophylaxis for migraines is indicated, it should be started immediately or within several days of medication withdrawal. Amitriptyline is the agent of choice. Patients may respond to prophylactic agents that were unsuccessful previously.[19]

The most important aspect of the treatment of medication-induced headaches is their prevention. Patients should be educated about the risk of developing analgesic rebound headaches, and they should monitor the frequency and amount of drugs used. Prophylaxis should be started early for management of frequent headaches.[16,19]

MIGRAINES AND THE HORMONAL MILIEU

Migraine and Menses

Depending on the study, 10 to 30% of migraines begin at menarche. True menstrual migraine occurs exclusively with the menstrual cycle (between −2 and +3 days of the period) in 10% of migraine sufferers. Menses-related migraines may occur at any time during the cycle, with an increased frequency and/or severity during menstruation in 50 to 70% of patients. Estrogen withdrawal may be the cause of the headache. Some studies suggest that administering estrogen perimenstrually may delay the onset of headache without affecting menstruation whereas progesterone treatment may delay menstruation without preventing headache.[20,21]

Menstrual migraines tend to be less responsive to treatment. Patients with true menstrual migraine can be treated perimenstrually with any of the prophylactic categories of medications, including antidepressants, calcium channel blockers, or ß-blockers. In addition, perimenstrual treatment can be combined with an NSAID. Oral magnesium (360 mg of magnesium pyrolidone carboxylic acid) at the time of menses decreases the severity of premenstrual syndrome symptoms. Acute attacks can be treated with any of the recommended abortive medications (see Table 67–5).

A sequence of treatment for menstrual migraine may include NSAIDs, the triptans, and other vasoactive drugs (DHE, Midrin), opioids, opiate agonist/antagonists, and a short course of steroids. Hormone therapy can be considered in cases of severe refractory migraines. Estrogen replacement therapy can provide a stable plasma level when administered several days before menstruation and during menses. Hormonal therapy may include estrogens alone or in combination with progestins, including mono- or multiphasic birth control pills. The antiestrogen tamoxifen or the androgen derivative danazol may be considered for resistant menstrual migraine. Bromocriptine, a dopamine D2 agonist, used at a dose of 2.5 to 5 mg/d during the luteal phase of the menstrual cycle may decrease the premenstrual symptoms.[20,21]

Migraine in Pregnancy

Migraines may improve in pregnant patients with a history of pre-existing migraine. Complete cessation is estimated to occur in 15 to 20% of pregnant patients, and less frequent headaches occur in 50 to 60% of pregnant patients. However, 20 to 30% experience no improvement. Up to 65% of women who have a history of menstrually related migraines improve during the course of pregnancy, presumably due to high estrogen levels.[20] Patients who do not experience aura are more likely to improve; 40 to 50% of women who experience migraine without aura note an improvement during pregnancy, compared with 25 to 30% of women who suffer from migraine with aura. When migraine headaches appear for the first time during pregnancy, they more often occur during the first trimester. Many women are headache-free in the second and third trimester.[22]

Due to potential risks to the fetus, nonpharmacologic techniques (massage, biofeedback, relaxation) and reassurance that symptoms improve with pregnancy should be the first interventions. In cases of headaches that do not respond to nonpharmacologic treatment, abortive therapy such as acetaminophen and NSAIDs alone or with codeine can be tried. The use of NSAIDs in the third trimester should be limited to less than 48 hours because NSAIDs can inhibit labor, decrease the volume of amniotic fluid, cause pulmonary hypertension, or induce premature closure of the ductus arteriosus in the newborn. Aspirin should be avoided due to its effects on hemostasis in mother and baby; in the newborn, it can cause hyperbilirubinemia and a narrowing of the ductus arteriosus. Narcotics of greater potency should be used cautiously due to addicting properties. For severe acute attacks, patients should be admitted for intravenous (IV) hydration and narcotics. Occasionally, prednisone is used adjunctively. Ergots and sumatriptan are contraindicated.[20,23]

In general, acetaminophen, nonsteroidal drugs, caffeine, and butorphanol are safe in the first and second trimesters. Narcotics are safe throughout pregnancy, except during labor.[20,23] Preventive therapy may be used if patients have three to four severe attacks per month that are not adequately treated with abortive therapy. ß-Blockers, antidepressants, and calcium channel blockers may be considered.

Although the use of any medication during pregnancy should be carefully considered, studies show that the incidence of adverse pregnancy outcomes (miscarriage, toxemia, congenital anomalies, or stillbirth) of patients with migraines does not differ from that of patients without migraines or patients who have used medications for their headaches.[24]

Migraine Post Partum

Migraines can re-start in the postpartum period or can begin during this time. Patients who have used nonpharmacologic techniques to control their headaches during pregnancy can observe continuing improvement of symptoms for up to a year post partum.[25] For patients who need medications to control their migraines while breast-feeding, acetaminophen (Tylenol), butorphanol, caffeine, narcotics, NSAIDs, and prochlorperazine are safe to use for abortive therapy. Prophylactic medications may include ß-blockers, calcium channel blockers, valproic acid, and prednisone.[23]

Migraines and Oral Contraceptive Use

Oral contraceptive pills (OCPs) have been reported to induce, alleviate, or change headaches. Some women with menstrual migraine benefit from OCPs. Other women with a family history of migraines may experience, with OCP use, the onset of their first migraine or an exacerbation of existing migraine. Stopping the use of OCPs may not alleviate symptoms for 6 months to a year.[20]

Due to the controversy concerning the risk of stroke associated with oral contraceptive use in migraineurs, pills containing less than 30 to 40 µg of ethinyl estradiol are recommended. Migraine patients who are starting to use OCPs should be closely observed for the development of neurologic symptoms and aggravation of headache. Other options for hormonal contraception include progestin-only methods since these have not been shown to affect blood clotting or platelet aggregation.[20]

Migraines and Menopause

Migraine prevalence decreases with advancing age. At menopause, symptoms can remain unchanged, regress, or worsen. Natural menopause results in improved migraines in approximately two-thirds of cases whereas the converse is true for surgical menopause, after which symptoms worsen in approximately two-thirds of cases.[20]

Estrogen replacement can exacerbate migraine in some patients; in others, estrogen replacement (alone or with testosterone) can relieve migraines. For women for whom estrogen replacement is indicated for the alleviation of menopausal symptoms but for whom it leads to worsening migraine symptoms, reducing the dose or changing the type of estrogen may be of benefit.[20]

INDICATIONS FOR REFERRAL

Referral to a headache specialist should be considered when attempted therapies fail or when the patient has progressive symptoms, rebound headaches that limit outpatient treatment, or comorbid conditions requiring polypharmacy.[15]

RESOURCES

National Institute of Neurological Disorders and Stroke
PO Box 5801
Bethesda, Maryland 20824
Telephone: (301) 496-6334
Web site: www.ninds.nih.gov

The National Institute of Neurological Disorders and Stroke, of the National Institutes of Health, provides information on headache for patients.

National Headache Foundation
420 West St. James Place, Second Floor
Chicago, Illinois 60614-2750
Telephone: 1-888-643-5552
Web site: www.headaches.org

The National Headache Foundation offers members newsletters, information about ongoing headache research, and access to information about local support groups.

REFERENCES

1. Silberstein SD, Lipton RB, Goadsby PJ, editors. Headache in clinical practice. Oxford: Isis Medical Media; 1998.

2. Stewart WF, Lipton RB, Celentano DD, Reed ML. Prevalence of migraine headache in the United States. JAMA 1992;267:64–9.

3. Lipchik GL, Rains JC, Penzien DB, et al. Recurrent headache: a neglected women's health problem. Womens Health Issues 1998;8(1):60–4.

4. Classification and diagnostic criteria for headache disorders, cranial neuralgias and facial pain. Headache Classification Committee of the International Headache Society. Cephalalgia 1988;8 Suppl 7:1–96.

5. Marks DR, Rapoport AM. Practical evaluation and diagnosis of headache. Semin Neurol 1997;17: 307–12.

6. Welch KM. Pathogenesis of migraine. Semin Neurol 1997;17:335–41.

7. Sharfman M. Update on headache. Compr Ther 1998;24:194–7.

8. Maizels M. The clinician's approach to the management of headache. West J Med 1998;168:203–12.

9. Freilich D. Is it migraine? Aust Fam Physician 1998; 27:591–6.

10. Silberstein SD. Tension-type headaches. Headache 1994;34(8):S2–7.

11. Schwartz BS, Stewart WF, Simon D, Lipton RB. Epidemiology of tension-type headache. JAMA 1998; 279:381–3.

12. Kunkel RS. Diagnosis and treatment of muscle contraction (tension-type) headaches. Med Clin North Am 1991;75:595–603.

13. Mathew NT. Cluster headache. Semin Neurol 1997; 17:313–23.

14. Mendizabal JE, Umana E, Zweifler RM. Cluster headache: Horton's cephalalgia revisited. South Med J 1998;91:606–17.

15. Solomon GD, Cady RK, Klapper JA, Ryan RE Jr. Standards of care for treating headache in primary care practice. National Headache Foundation. Cleve Clin J Med 1997;64:373–83.

16. Zed PJ, Loewen PS, Robinson G. Medication-induced headache: overview and systematic review of therapeutic approaches. Ann Pharmacother 1999; 33(1):61–72.

17. Rapoport A, Stang P, Gutterman DL, et al. Analgesic rebound headache in clinical practice: data from a physician survey. Headache 1996;36(1):14–9.

18. Mathew NT. Medication misuse headache. Cephalalgia 1998;18 Suppl 21:34–6.

19. Antonaci F. Drug abuse headache: recognition and management. Cephalalgia 1998;18 Suppl 22:47–55.

20. Silberstein SD. Migraine and women. The link between headache and hormones. Postgrad Med 1995; 97:147–53.

21. Kornstein SG, Parker AJ. Menstrual migraines: etiology, treatment, and relationship to premenstrual syndrome. Curr Opin Obstet Gynecol 1997;9:154–9.

22. Maggioni F, Alessi C, Maggino T, Zanchin G. Headache during pregnancy. Cephalalgia 1997;17:765–9.

23. Miles CB. Treatment of migraine during pregnancy and lactation. S D J Med 1995;48:373–7.

24. Wainscott G, Valans GN. The outcome of pregnancy in women suffering from migraine. Postgrad Med J 1978;54:98.

25. Scharff L, Marcus DA, Turk DC. Maintenance of effects in the nonmedical treatment of headaches during pregnancy. Headache 1996;36:285–90.

68

ANEMIA

Gary J. Schiller, MD

Anemia is a decrease in the quantity of hemoglobin in the peripheral blood due to a decrease in the number of red blood cells (RBCs) or erythrocytes.[1,2] It is present when there are fewer than 4 million erythrocytes per cubic millimeter.[3,4] This simple description of anemia is true regardless of age or gender.[2,3,5,6] Although women tend to have a lower hemoglobin level than men, latent iron deficiency due to menstrual blood loss may partly contribute to a lower "normal range" for women than for men.[7-10] Further, although the red blood cell number tends to be lower in older people, there is no information to suggest that the criteria by which anemia is defined should be altered in any way on the basis of age.[3,11,12] Since most clinicians are not used to dealing with an erythrocyte count, anemia is defined more often as a hemoglobin level < 12 g/dL in women and < 13 g/dL in men.[4] Thus, hemoglobin and the derivative calculation, hematocrit, are surrogate markers for a decreased number of erythrocytes.[2]

PATHOPHYSIOLOGY

The precursors of erythrocytes are derived from pluripotenital hematopoietic precursors.[13,14] Mature erythrocytes are metabolically underprivileged cells that lack a nucleus and most of the enzymatic machinery required to maintain prolonged cell survival.[15-17] Their purpose is to carry hemoglobin, which, in turn, carries oxygen. Only a tiny fraction of the erythrocyte is devoted to the plasma membrane, which contains the metabolic machinery necessary for RBC survival. Erythrocytes circulate for about 120 days but remain dependent on simple sources of energy to maintain membrane integrity, protect hemoglobin from oxidative denaturation, and synthesize glutathione and adenine nucleotides.[17-19]

Because about 1% of the erythrocytes are replaced daily, erythrocyte production must be a well-controlled process responsive to stresses such as anemia and hypoxemia. The major humoral factor responsible for inducing changes in erythrocyte production is erythropoietin, a protein manufactured in the kidneys and (to a lesser extent) in the liver.[20-22] A so-called normal erythropoietin level (ie, a level within the normal range) cannot be considered normal in a patient with anemia. As an example, patients with chronic renal failure have a serum erythropoietin level that is often higher than the level in normal nonanemic individuals, indicating continued responsiveness to the anemic state.[23,24] However, the erythropoietin level is invariably decreased in the uremic patient with respect to the degree of anemia. This continues to be a major cause of confusion among those who do not understand the basics of erythrocyte production.

To produce large numbers of erythrocytes, the pluripotent hematopoietic progenitor cell differentiates in a predictable manner. In the final step of differentiation, reticulocytes mature to anucleate mature erythrocytes. Reticulocytes are young erythrocytes that have residual ribosomal ribonucleic acid (RNA) in their cytoplasm. They are identified by basophilic dyes, such as methylene blue, which stain ribonucleotides.[25] Reticulocytes usually live for 2 days in the bone marrow after extruding their nucleus and are then released into the bloodstream, where they live for 1 day before maturing into erythrocytes, losing all their residual ribosomal RNA. There are approximately 3.0×10^{11} mature erythrocytes per kilogram in normal individuals; about 1% of these cells are replaced daily by the bone marrow production of reticulocytes.[26,27] Thus, erythrocyte production is a high-output process, and anemia can be considered from the perspective of the factory responsible for erythrocyte production.

DIFFERENTIAL DIAGNOSIS

In the primary care setting, the differential diagnosis of anemia usually begins by evaluating information obtained from the peripheral blood smear. Two tests, the reticulocyte count and the mean corpuscular volume (MCV), can be particularly useful in determining possible causes of anemia.

Reticulocyte production by the bone marrow may increase by an absolute factor of 10 in response to anemia. In a patient with normal bone marrow, the reticulocyte count increases in response to anemia. Therefore, in an anemic patient, a reticulocyte count that falls within the normal range is not normal. The measured reticulocyte count on the peripheral blood smear is determined by counting the number of cells that pick up basophilic dye and dividing that number by the number of RBCs counted in a field. To assess bone marrow production more accurately, one takes the uncorrected reticulocyte percentage and normalizes it by a factor that takes into account the severity of the patient's anemia. A second correction is done if there is evidence that marrow reticulocytes are being released into the bloodstream 1 day early, thus potentially being counted twice (thereby not reflecting a single day's erythrocyte production) (Figure 68–1). The highest corrected reticulocyte count that one can expect in bone marrow that is actively responsive to anemia is about 10.

Based on the correction of the measured reticulocyte count, erythroid production in the bone marrow can be considered as either "noncompensatory" or "compensatory." When the corrected reticulocyte count is abnormally low, the anemia is called noncompensatory. Noncompensatory anemias are due to either a hypoproliferative state in the bone marrow or a process of ineffective hematopoiesis. When the corrected reticulocyte count falls within the normal range or is high, the anemia is called "compensatory." Compensatory erythroid production occurs in the setting of hemolytic anemia.

The MCV can be used to further differentiate noncompensatory anemias into those that are hypoproliferative and those that are ineffective. In hypoproliferative anemias, the bone marrow does not respond to anemia appropriately by increasing erythrocyte production adequately. In this case, the MCV of the erythrocytes is normal or low. In contrast, in anemias that result from ineffective erythrocyte production, maturation of erythroid precursors into erythrocytes does not proceed normally, leading to abnormally large erythrocytes with a higher-than-normal MCV.

Bone marrow cellularity is assessed by bone marrow biopsy. Bone marrow biopsy usually is not needed to establish the cause for anemia in most patients in the outpatient setting. The differential diagnosis of anemia is summarized in Table 68–1 and Figure 68–2.

HYPOPROLIFERATIVE ANEMIAS

Iron Deficiency Anemia

The most common form of hypoproliferative anemia is that produced by iron deficiency.[14]

Iron is transported from its site of absorption by transferrin, a protein responsible for the transport of iron from the intestine to sites of storage and utilization.[14,28–31] Iron is required for the normal synthesis of heme by erythroid cells. When erythroid cells are deficient in iron, heme synthesis does not occur, indicating an absolute dependency of hemoglobin synthesis on transferrin-bound iron. All iron for hemoglobin synthesis comes from transferrin, and there is almost no nonheme iron present in mature erythrocytes.

$$\text{Measured reticulocyte count} \times \left(\frac{\text{Hemoglobin patient}}{\text{Hemoglobin control}} \right)^{*} \div 2^{\dagger} = \text{Corrected reticulocyte count}$$

$$^{*}\text{First correction} \qquad ^{\dagger}\text{Second correction—only if nRBCs are present on the blood smear}$$

FIGURE 68–1. Method of calculating the reticulocyte count. nRBC = nucleated red blood cell.

TABLE 68–1. Differential Diagnosis of Anemia

Bone Marrow Histology	Hypoproliferative	Ineffective	Compensatory
Bone marrow cellularity	↓	↑	↑
Reticulocyte count	↓	↓	↑
MCV	↓, —	↑	↓, —, ↑
Etiologies	Iron deficiency	Deficiencies of vitamin B$_{12}$, folate	Physical agents
	Chronic inflammation	Myelodysplasia	Trauma
	Renal failure	Chemotherapy	Vasculopathy
	Aplastic anemia	Inborn errors of metabolism	Membranopathy
	Pure RBC aplasia		Hemoglobinopathy
	Blockade of heme syntheis		Enzymopathy
	Sideroblastic anemia		Infection
	Marrow infiltration		Osmotic

MCV = mean corpuscular volume; RBC = red blood cells.

Common causes of iron deficiency include diminished dietary iron intake, chronic blood loss, and increased utilization of iron.[32] Other causes of iron deficiency include extracorporeal dialysis, genitourinary losses related to chronic intravascular hemolysis, and malabsorption often associated with protein-losing enteropathy.[33–35]

A combination of both iron loss and diminished iron intake is often found in patients with iron deficiency.[32] The average daily iron intake for most people in the United States is 5 to 7 mg per 1,000 calories. Many individuals, however, especially children and young women, have a dietary intake that is below the recommended daily allowance. Without any bleeding at all, about 1 mg of iron must be replaced daily. Absorption is approximately 10% of oral intake. Even iron-enriched foods such as bread products have poorly absorbable iron. However, dietary iron suffices in most adults who do not have chronic blood loss.

Women who have a chronic source of blood loss related to menses may have an unstable iron balance and may quickly become iron deficient. The average menstrual blood loss is about 40 cc per cycle, or about 15 mg of iron.[36,37] Iron requirements in menstruating women are considerably higher than for other adults, and iron supplementation to the diet is often required. In pregnancy, iron loss results from the diversion of iron to the fetus for its erythropoiesis. Lactation causes further iron depletion. Therefore, all pregnant women should receive oral iron before they develop overt signs of iron deficiency anemia.

In postmenopausal women and in men, iron deficiency is most commonly caused by chronic bleeding from the gastrointestinal tract. Bleeding related to gastroesophageal reflux disease, linear gastic erosions, gastritis related to drugs, enteritis, and colonic lesions accounts for most causes of chronic gastrointestinal blood loss. All patients with iron deficiency anemia should be evaluated for signs and symptoms of gastrointestinal blood loss. Further, otherwise asymptomatic postmenopausal women who present with iron deficiency anemia should always be evaluated for sources of occult gastrointestinal bleeding, including colonic malignancy.

Regardless of the cause of iron deficiency, this reticulocytopenic anemia is typically associated with microcytosis (low MCV), anisocytosis (variations in cell size, characterized by high red cell distribution width [RDW]), and (often) severe poikilocytosis (variations in cell shape seen on peripheral blood smears). Typically, there is an elevation in the platelet count, and some patients have leukopenia as well. The bone marrow shows a marked decrease in erythrocyte progenitors, which tend to be smaller than normal and to have an abnormal shape. The cells are poorly hemoglobinized, and there is a virtual absence of iron granules in precursors and in macrophages.

Serum chemistries demonstrate a low serum iron concentration and an elevated iron-binding

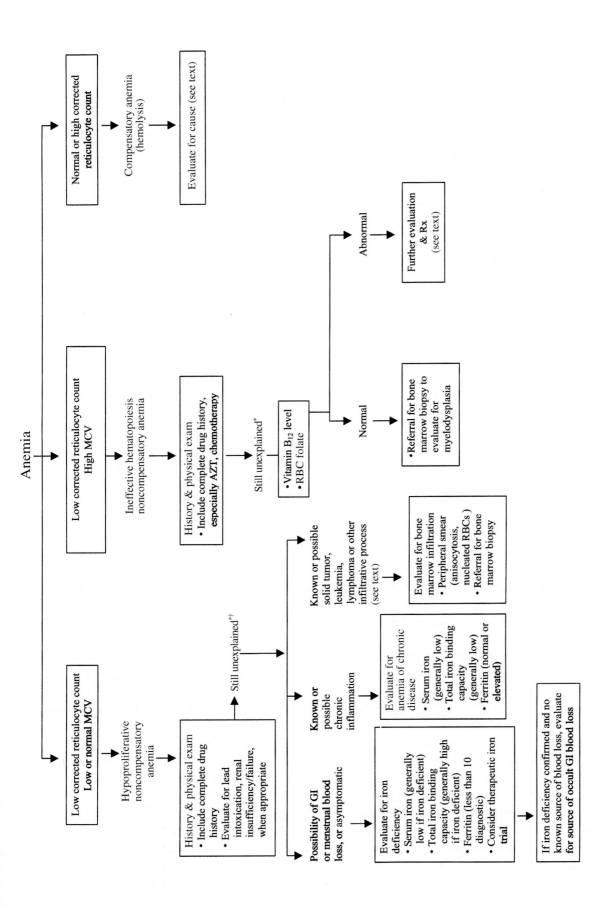

FIGURE 68–2. Evaluation of anemia. *Patients may have more than one cause of anemia. Evaluate for multiple causes if clinically indicated. †If listed common causes are excluded, referral for evaluation of uncommon causes should be considered (see text). MCV = mean corpuscular volume; GI = gastrointestinal; RBC = red blood cell; AZT = zidovudine; Rx = prescription.

$$\text{Deficit of hemoglobin iron (g)} = [\text{Desired hemoglobin (g/dL)} - \text{Actual hemoglobin (g/dL)}] \div 100 \times$$
$$\text{Weight of patient (kg)} \times \text{Blood volume} \times 0.0034$$

FIGURE 68–3. A method of calculating the total hemoglobin iron deficit. The blood volume is equal to 65 mL/kg in adults. Adapted from Fairbanks VR, Beutler E. Williams hematology. 5th ed. New York: McGraw-Hill; 1995.

capacity.[38,39] However, the measurement of serum iron concentration is subject to many variables that can cause errors in interpretation. Iron concentration has a diurnal variation, reaching its maximum early in the morning. Elevated concentrations of serum iron may also occur if patients are treated with oral iron before the blood test is done.[38] Iron-binding capacity also is variable. A normal value may be associated with low serum iron concentration in the anemia of chronic disease or in a combination of iron deficiency and anemia related to chronic inflammation.[40–44]

Even less reliable is the serum ferritin concentration, which is responsive to inflammatory conditions.[45–48] Serum ferritin concentrations < 10 µg/L are characteristic of iron deficiency anemia, and those < 20 µg/L should be considered as supportive of that diagnosis. However, higher ferritin levels may reflect chronic inflammation and may not rule out concomitant iron deficiency.[49,50] Other serum chemistries that have been used to diagnose iron deficiency include erythrocyte ferritin and free erythrocyte protoporphyrin;[51] the former is decreased in patients with iron deficiency whereas the latter is increased. Finally, response to a therapeutic trial of iron is often used as a diagnostic test of iron deficiency.

Once it has been established that a patient is deficient in iron, replacement therapy should be initiated not only for treatment of anemia but also for repletion of diminished iron stores. The preferred form of replacement therapy is oral, and the iron preparation used should contain between 50 and 100 mg of elemental iron. Ascorbic acid may increase iron absorption. The side effects of oral iron replacement, however, may preclude compliance. These include nausea, anorexia, and constipation. To avoid some of these side effects, some iron preparations are given in enteric-coated tablets, which diminish the iron available for absorption. One regimen that is often effective is 150 to 200 mg of elemental iron daily, taken in divided doses three or four times a day for several months. Parenteral iron is indicated only in the setting of malabsorption, severe intolerance to oral iron, or a need that

exceeds the amount that can be delivered orally.[52] Parenteral iron is usually given as iron dextran, in doses of 2 mL (100 mg), intramuscularly or intravenously. A method for calculating the dose of the total hemoglobin iron deficit can be found in Figure 68–3.

Anemia of Chronic Inflammation

Another hypoproliferative anemia is the anemia of chronic inflammation.[53–56] Also known as the anemia of chronic disease, this microcytic reticulocytopenic anemia may be very difficult to distinguish from iron deficiency. This form of anemia is typically a response to infection, malignancy, or chronic inflammatory disease and is characterized by impaired iron metabolism and release from reticuloendothelial stores. It is also associated with a shortened RBC survival and a decrease in RBC production. A reduced concentration of transferrin is typical in anemia of chronic inflammation although serum iron is typically low as well. Unlike iron deficiency anemia, in which transferrin is elevated, transferrin is decreased in the anemia of chronic inflammation, such that the percent saturation (serum iron divided by the iron-binding capacity) may be close to normal. The serum ferritin is typically elevated or in the normal range and iron staining of the bone marrow reveals adequate tissue iron. Some patients may also have diminished endogenous erythropoietin.[54,57]

Therapy for anemia associated with chronic inflammation is usually directed at the underlying disease. However, some patients may respond to treatment with erythropoietin. Trials in renal failure, rheumatoid arthritis, chronic lymphocytic leukemia, multiple myeloma, and acquired immunodeficiency syndrome (AIDS) have demonstrated that supplemental erythropoietin may be successful in treating anemia of chronic disease.[58–60]

Marrow Infiltrative or Myelophthisic Disorders

A discussion on the differential diagnosis of hypoproliferative anemias is not complete without a discussion about at least one more set of disorders, namely, the marrow infiltrative or myelophthisic disorders. A variety of solid tumors, leukemia, lymphoma, intracellular infections such as tuberculosis and histoplasmosis, storage diseases such as Gaucher's disease, osteopetrosis, myelofibrosis, and sarcoidosis may all cause the replacement of marrow elements.[61–63] These disorders are typically characterized by a reticulocytopenic anemia, with distinctive findings on the peripheral blood smear. Anisocytosis (particularly, tear-drop-shaped RBCs) may be present. Occasionally, early nucleated RBCs and early myeloid elements are present in the peripheral blood as well. This leukoerythroblastic blood picture is typical of disorders involving the bone marrow. Also common is extramedullary hematopoiesis in the liver and spleen. Depending on the underlying disease, patients may have serum chemistry features similar to those of patients with anemia of chronic inflammation.

Other Causes of Hypoproliferative Anemia

Aplastic anemia is pancytopenia with an empty bone marrow.[64] Its pathology is simple although the underlying causes are complex and often do not yield to a diagnostic investigation. Patients typically present with signs and symptoms related to pancytopenia. Agranulocytosis and acute bacterial infection typically present as fever and less commonly as septic shock.[65] Severe thrombocytopenia may be associated with petechial hemorrhage, ecchymosis, and spontaneous bleeding. Sustained microscopic gastrointestinal bleeding associated with reticulocytopenia may produce very severe anemia at presentation, with signs of high-output congestive heart failure. The most common etiology of aplastic anemia is iatrogenic due to chemical agents, drugs, or radiation therapy.[64] Immune-mediated causes include pregnancy, aplastic anemia associated with viral hepatitis, and idiopathic immune-mediated destruction of the bone marrow.[66–68]

A similar disorder confined to erythroid progenitors is pure red blood cell aplasia.[69–73] Pure erythrocyte aplasia may occur as a result of a low-grade lymphoproliferative disease (such as chronic lymphocytic leukemia and small cell non-Hodgkin's lymphoma) or may be a result of an infection with human parvovirus B19. Unlike aplastic anemia, the bone marrow in pure RBC aplasia is typically quite cellular, with the presence of myeloid and megakaryocyte elements, but the absence of all RBC precursors. Therapy often includes intra-venous immunoglobulin and treatment directed against the underlying lymphoproliferative disorder (if present).

Finally, hypoproliferative anemia may result from lead intoxication, drug-induced blockage of heme synthesis (due to isoniazid or pyrazinamide), or sideroblastic anemia.

ANEMIAS CAUSED BY DISORDERS OF INEFFECTIVE HEMATOPOIESIS

A very different form of reticulocytopenic anemia occurs in disorders of ineffective hematopoiesis. These disorders are characterized by abnormal cellular DNA synthesis due to a block in the production of nucleotides.[74,75] This block prevents chromosomal replication and division of the nucleus. The cytoplasm, however, may continue to mature since protein synthesis is not affected. Thus, in the bone marrow (the site of blood cell production), there is dysynchrony in the maturation of the nucleus and the cytoplasm; the nucleus appears to be immature, but the cytoplasm contains elements of mature blood cells. Because the replication of DNA is impaired and cell division is thus decreased, the cells in the bone marrow remain large and are incapable of leaving the marrow microenvironment. Thus, disorders of ineffective hematopoiesis are characterized by bone marrow hypercellularity but pancytopenia in the peripheral blood. The cells in the bone marrow that are unable to enter the peripheral blood are destroyed, and this cellular destruction is called intramedullary hemolysis. Those blood cells that do manage to leave the bone marrow remain large and have a variety of distinctive features. The RBC series is macrocytic and contains large oval-shaped RBCs called macro-ovalocytes. The morphologic features of ineffective hematopoiesis are not confined to the bone marrow but occur in all rapidly proliferating cells. These features are termed "megaloblastic" and may be found in the gastrointestinal tract and in the skin.

Laboratory features that can be identified consistently in megaloblastic anemias include a high MCV, a low reticulocyte count, an increased lactate dehydrogenase (LDH) level due to intramedullary hemolysis, and the morphologic features described above. Neutropenia and thrombocytopenia are typical as well, and the neutrophils have characteristic hypersegmentation.

The etiologies of ineffective hematopoiesis include disorders of vitamin B_{12} metabolism, folate deficiency, cytotoxic chemotherapy, drugs (such as zidovudine [AZT]) that produce nucleotide deficiency, and inborn errors of nucleic acid metabolism. Myelodysplasia, an intrinsic disorder of the bone marrow, also may produce ineffective hematopoiesis.

Vitamin B_{12} Deficiency and Folic Acid Deficiency

Vitamin B_{12} deficiency may occur in patients who have a strict vegetarian diet and are unable to maintain the normal daily dietary requirement of 1 to 2 μg. Since the body stores of vitamin B_{12} are on the order of 3 to 5 mg, a sustained strict vegetarian diet is necessary to develop vitamin B_{12} deficiency. On the other hand, folic acid is much more rapidly depleted in the setting of dietary deficiency. The minimum daily folate requirement is at least 100 to 150 μg, and it has been suggested that higher doses may offset risks of cerebrovascular disease. There are minimal body stores of folic acid, and diminished intake or increased utilization can rapidly lead to its deficiency.

Besides dietary deficiency, intestinal malabsorption may produce deficiencies of both folic acid and vitamin B_{12}. A specific deficiency of gastric intrinsic factor in pernicious anemia is responsible for vitamin B_{12} deficiency that may be associated with both megaloblastic anemia and neuropsychiatric disorders.

In patients with vitamin B_{12} deficiency, a decrease in that enzymatic cofactor is usually associated with an increase in methylmalonic acid and homocysteine. The measurement of these metabolites from two vitamin B_{12}–dependent pathways may be sensitive detectors of vitamin B_{12} deficiency.[76,77] In patients with vitamin B_{12} deficiency, the elevated levels of both serum methylmalonic acid and total homocyteine decrease with vitamin B_{12} therapy. In folate-deficient patients, however, only homocysteine levels return to normal after the replacement of folic acid.

Vitamin B_{12} deficiency of any cause is confirmed by the finding of a low serum vitamin B_{12} level. The diagnosis of pernicious anemia requires the demonstration of both vitamin B_{12} deficiency and antibodies to either parietal cells or intrinsic factors (the latter are much more specific). The Schilling test is a nuclear medicine study to determine vitamin B_{12} absorption. It is carried out in two stages. In the first, radioactive vitamin B_{12} is ingested after a large dose of parenteral unlabeled vitamin B_{12} is given. Malabsorption of the radioactive vitamin B_{12} is shown by the absence of the labeled compound in the urine during a 24-hour period. The second stage of the test involves administering radiolabeled vitamin B_{12} with intrinsic factor.

Once the diagnosis is established, vitamin B_{12} can be given either intramuscularly at a dose of 1,000 μg monthly or orally at a dosage of 2 mg daily.[78] As in other metabolic deficiencies, treatment should be directed toward correcting the anemia and repleting the body stores. The reticulocyte response is usually dramatic and occurs within 1 or 2 days after a single dose of parenteral vitamin B_{12}.

Folic acid deficiency is confirmed by the finding of a low RBC folate level. Repletion is usually accomplished by prescribing a dose of 1 mg of folic acid daily.

Myelodysplasia

The diagnosis of myelodysplasia should be considered in any patient, particularly any older patient, who presents with macrocytic anemia and normal vitamin B_{12} and folate levels and who is not taking any drugs known to cause ineffective hematopoesis. Such patients should be referred to a hematologist for consideration of bone marrow biopsy.

COMPENSATORY (HEMOLYTIC) ANEMIAS

The hemolytic syndromes are a complicated set of disorders characterized by shortened RBC survival and compensatory reticulocytosis. Premature erythrocyte destruction produces a compensatory increase in bone marrow production and an increase in reticulocytes. This is generally associated with distinctive findings on the peripheral blood smear, such as polychromatophilia (large grey-blue cells) and morphologic abnormalities such as spherocytosis, sickle cells, or fragmented erythrocytes. The bone marrow exhibits nonspecific hypercellularity, and a physical examination may or may not reveal splenomegaly. Serum chemistries may show only an elevation in LDH, but many patients have an elevation in indirect bilirubin. A finding of bilirubinuria suggests concomitant cholelithiasis, hepatitis, or other hepatic dysfunction.

There are many ways to categorize hemolytic anemias; the most common way is to classify them as either intravascular or extravascular. The former are fragmentation-hemolysis syndromes usually characterized by vascular disease. The latter are associated with RBC spherocytosis, most often due to a congenital or acquired membrane abnormality, which induces reticuloendothelial cell–mediated destruction of the erythrocyte.

Another way to categorize hemolytic anemia is from the point of view of the erythrocyte. If one considers the erythrocyte as it flows in a blood vessel, one may divide causes of hemolysis from the vascular endothelium through the circulating plasma to red blood cell membrane disorders and intracytoplasmic disorders. Vascular disorders commonly associated with fragmentation hemolysis include physical agents (such as burns, trauma, and march hemoglobinuria), valvular heart disease, and prosthetic heart valves. As well, large vascular abnormalities such as hemangiomas also may contribute to fragmentation hemolysis, often with associated thrombocytopenia. Microrangiopathies such as disseminated intravascular clotting or thrombotic thrombocytopenia are typically associated with thrombocytopenia. Plasma disorders caused by snake or insect envenomations, *Clostridium perfringens* toxin, and chemical agents such as benzene or hypotonic solution all may induce intravascular hemolysis. In these disorders, hemoglobin is released into the plasma and is bound by haptoglobin. The free haptoglobin concentration is therefore markedly depleted when hemolysis is active. Any additional free hemoglobin ends up in the urine, as does any associated heme iron. This heme iron is taken up by renal tubular cells, where it is converted to hemosiderin; when the epithelium is shed, the centrifuged urinary sediment contains cells that stain positive for hemosiderin. If there is sufficient intravascular hemolysis, iron deficiency anemia may develop.

Disorders of the erythrocyte membrane are the most common causes of hemolytic anemia. They may be either extravascular or intravascular. More often than not, changes in the RBC membrane decrease deformability, and these changes are processed by the reticuloendothelial system to produce a cell of maximum volume called a spherocyte. Spherocytic disorders may be congenital or acquired. Many abnormalities of the RBC cytoskeleton are inherited in an autosomal dominant fashion.[79,80]

Hereditary spherocytosis may present in a family as lifelong anemia, cholelithiasis, or splenomegaly. These subtle clinical abnormalities may defy early diagnosis.

Idiopathic or drug-induced autoimmune diseases also may be considered RBC membrane abnormalities.[81–84] When immunoglobulin G (IgG) is bound to the erythrocyte membrane, the immunoglobulin's Fc component is bound by reticuloendothelial cells in the spleen, liver, and bone marrow, and portions of the membrane are removed. Again, the resultant erythrocyte assumes its critical hemolytic volume in the form of a spherocyte. Like the hereditary disorders of the erythrocyte membrane, warm antibody–mediated hemolytic anemia is typically characterized by spherocytes and enhanced osmotic fragility. Unlike the congenital disorders, however, patients with warm antibody–mediated hemolytic anemia typically have circulating antibodies directed against nearly all human erythrocytes (panagglutinins), making it very difficult to find crossmatch-compatible red cells for transfusion. Most drug-induced hemolytic anemias operate similarly, with an antibody against a drug-hapten complex on the RBC membrane, or a drug-circulating protein complex that fixes on the RBC membrane, or a drug-induced autoantibody to erythrocytes. All these mechanisms may be associated with immune-mediated membrane changes inducing extravascular hemolysis.

Antibodies that are capable of initiating the complement cascade may produce intravascular hemolysis. Paroxysmal nocturnal hemoglobinuria (PNH) is a rare syndrome associated with an abnormal RBC sensitivity to complement. In this disorder, cells produced by a dysfunctional clone fail to possess the normal membrane proteins that normally inhibit the action of complement. Hemolysis and PNH may be overt or chronic and inconspicuous, associated with secondary renal-associated iron deficiency. Because PNH is a stem cell disorder, patients often develop leukopenia and thrombocytopenia. Another intravascular hemolytic syndrome is cold agglutinin disease, in which an antibody, usually of IgM type, induces RBC agglutination in the extremities upon exposure to cold. Another immune-mediated disorder is associated with the Donath-Landsteiner antibody, an IgG antibody capable of inducing intravascular hemolysis upon exposure to cold.[85–87]

Disorders of the erythrocyte cytoplasm are heterogeneous and include hemoglobinopathies, enzyme deficiencies, and intracellular infections. The presence of irreversibly sickled cells indicates a type of sickle hemoglobinopathy usually associated with predominant extravascular hemolysis. Target cells indicate thalassemia but may also be present in sickle hemoglobinopathies, including hemoglobin S and hemoglobin C.[88]

The most common enzyme disorder is glucose-6-phosphate dehydrogenase (G6PD) deficiency, a disorder related to more than 300 isotypes of the glycolytic enzyme.[89] This X-linked disorder may occur in women because of unbalanced lyonization and often occurs in the setting of an oxidant stress such as a drug or infection. Common offending agents include sulfonamides or other antibiotics such as nalidixic acid, analgesics such as phenacetin or aspirin in large doses, and antimalarials. Many other drugs may induce hemolysis through non-G6PD pathways. Heinz bodies are intraerythrocytic inclusions composed of denatured hemoglobin and are present in patients with G6PD deficiency and hemoglobinopathies characterized by unstable hemoglobins.

Hemolytic disorders are almost always associated with compensatory reticulocytosis unless something else is going on.[90] Concomitant infection, folic acid deficiency, or iron deficiency may impair bone marrow compensation and be associated with very severe anemia. Due to their heterogeneity, the treatment of the hemolytic anemias depends on the treatment of the underlying disease. Transfusion is limited to those with severe symptomatic anemia. Iron replacement therapy is given to patients who have sustained iron loss through the urinary tract. Folic acid in dosages of at least 1 mg/d is a rational supportive care measure.

CONCLUSION

When considered from the point of view of the bone marrow—the site of erythrocyte production—the anemias neatly fall into three pathophysiologic categories. Peripheral blood findings, erythrocyte indices, LDH, reticulocyte count, and erythropoietin level are useful for narrowing down the differential diagnosis within a category determined by history, physical examination, and clinical findings.

REFERENCES

1. Coles A. The blood: how to examine and diagnose its diseases. London: J & A Churchhill; 1898.
2. Patterson KG, Carter AB. Automated differential counting. Blood Rev 1991;5:78–83.
3. Izaks GJ, Westendorp RG, Knook DL. The definition of anemia in older persons. JAMA 1999;281:1714–7.
4. World Health Organization. Nutritional anaemias: report of a WHO Scientific Group. Geneva (Switzerland): World Health Organization; 1968.
5. Salive ME, Cornoni-Huntley J, Guralnik JM, et al. Anemia and hemoglobin levels in older persons: relationship with age, gender, and health status. J Am Geriatr Soc 1992;40:489–96.
6. Timiras ML, Brownstein H. Prevalence of anemia and correlation of hemoglobin with age in a geriatric screening clinic population. J Am Geriatr Soc 1987; 35:639–43.
7. Pate R, Miller B, Davis J, et al. Iron status of female runners. Int J Sport Nutr 1993;3:222.
8. Buetler E, Robson M, Buttenwiesser E. A comparison of the plasma iron, binding capacity, sternal marrow iron and other methods in the clinical evaluation of iron stores. Ann Intern Med 1958;48:60.
9. Uchida T, Yoshida M, Sakai K, et al. Prevalence of iron deficiency in Japanese women. Nippon Ketsueki Gakkai Zasshi 1988;51(1):24–7.
10. Scott D, Pritchard J. Iron deficiency in healthy young college women. JAMA 1967;199:897.
11. Ania BJ, Suman VJ, Fairbanks VF, et al. Incidence of anemia in older people: an epidemiologic study in a well defined population. J Am Geriatr Soc 1997; 45:825–31.
12. Joosten E, Pelemans W, Hiele M, et al. Prevalence and causes of anaemia in a geriatric hospitalized population. Gerontology 1992;38(1–2):111–7.
13. Shivdasani R, Orkin S. The transcriptional control of hematopoiesis. Blood 1996;87:4025–39.
14. Ponka P. Tissue-specific regulation of iron metabolism and heme synthesis: distinct control mechanisms in erythroid cells. Blood 1997;89(1):1–25.
15. Valentine WN. Hemolytic anemia: diagnosis and management. Compr Ther 1980;6(7):30–6.
16. Valentine WN. Metabolismo de los globulos rojos y de las anemias hemoliticas hereditarias debidas a deficiencias enzimaticas. Hematologia 1972;II(5): 11–7.
17. Valentine WN, Tanaka KR, Paglia DE. Hemolytic anemias and erythrocyte enzymopathies. Ann Intern Med 1985;103:245–57.

18. Beutler E. Hemolytic anemia in disorders of red cell metabolism. New York: Plenum Medical Book Co.; 1978.

19. Beutler E. Glucose-6 phosphate dehydrogenase deficiency. In: Stanbury J, Wyngaarden J, Frederickson D, et al, editors. The metabolic basis of inherited disease. New York: McGraw-Hill Book Co.; 1983. p. 1629–53.

20. Adamson J. The erythropoietin/hematocrit relationship in normal and polycythemic man: Implications of marrow regulation. Blood 1968;3:597.

21. Erslev A. Erythropoietin. N Engl J Med 1991;324: 1339.

22. Jelkmann W. Erythropoietin: structure, control of production, and function. Physiol Rev 1992;72: 449–89.

23. Schiller GJ, Berkman SA. Hematologic aspects of renal insufficiency. Blood Rev 1989;3:141–6.

24. Eschbach J. Correction of the anemia of end-stage renal disease with recombinant human erythropoietin. N Engl J Med 1987;316:73–8.

25. Mel H, Prenant M, Mohandas N. Reticulocyte motility and form: studies on maturation and classification. Blood 1977;49:1001.

26. Young NS, Maciejewski J. The pathophysiology of acquired aplastic anemia. N Engl J Med 1997; 336:1365–72.

27. Hillman R, Finch C. Erythropoiesis: normal and abnormal. Semin Hematol 1967;4:327.

28. Edwards JA, Hoke JE. Red cell iron uptake in hereditary microcytic anemia. Blood 1975;46:381–8.

29. Shahidi NT, Nathan DG, Diamond LK. Nutrition classics: the Journal of Clinical Investigation, volume 43, 1964. Iron deficiency anemia associated with an error of iron metabolism in two siblings. Nutr Rev 1983;41:315–7.

30. Buchanan GR, Sheehan RG. Malabsorption and defective utilization of iron in three siblings. J Pediatr 1981;98:723–8.

31. Hartman KR, Barker JA. Microcytic anemia with iron malabsorption: an inherited disorder of iron metabolism. Am J Hematol 1996;51:269–75.

32. Finch CA, Deubelbeiss K, Cook JD, et al. Ferrokinetics in man. Medicine (Baltimore) 1970;49(1):17–53.

33. Kis AM, Carnes M. Detecting iron deficiency in anemic patients with concomitant medical problems. J Gen Intern Med 1998;13:455–61.

34. Boutry M, Needlman R. Use of diet history in the screening of iron deficiency. Pediatrics 1996;98(6 Pt 1): 1138–42.

35. Nasolodin VV, Rusin VI, Dvorkin VA, et al. Relationship of vitamins and microelements and their role in the prevention of iron deficiencies. Gig Sanit 1996; 6:26–9.

36. Bini EJ, Micale PL, Weinshel EH. Evaluation of the gastrointestinal tract in premenopausal women with iron deficiency anemia. Am J Med 1998;105:281–6.

37. Milsom I, Andersson K, Jonasson K, et al. The influence of the Gyne-T 380S IUD on menstrual blood loss and iron status. Contraception 1995;52:175–9.

38. Beard JL, Dawson H, Pinero DJ. Iron metabolism: a comprehensive review. Nutr Rev 1996;54:295–317.

39. Smieja MJ, Cook DJ, Hunt DL, et al. Recognizing and investigating iron-deficiency anemia in hospitalized elderly people. Can Med Assoc J 1996;155:691–6.

40. Roberts GT, El Badawi SB. Red blood cell distribution width index in some hematologic diseases. Am J Clin Pathol 1985;83:222–6.

41. Flynn MM, Reppun TS, Bhagavan NV. Limitations of red blood cell distribution width (RDW) in evaluation of microcytosis. Am J Clin Pathol 1986;85: 445–9.

42. Beck JR, Cornwell GG, Rawnsley HM. Multivariate approach to predictive diagnosis of bone-marrow iron stores. Am J Clin Pathol 1978;70:665–70.

43. Hamilton LD, Gubler CJ, Cartwright GE, Wintrobe MM. Diurnal variation in the plasma iron level of man. Proc Soc Exp Biol Med 1964;61:44.

44. Zilva JF, Patston VJ. Variations in serum-iron in healthy women. Lancet 1966;1:459–62.

45. Fairbanks VF, Klee GG. Ferritin. Prog Clin Pathol 1981;8:175–203.

46. Jacobs A, Miller F, Worwood M, et al. Ferritin in the serum of normal subjects and patients with iron deficiency and iron overload. BMJ 1972;4:206–8.

47. Jacob RA, Sandstead HH, Klevay LM, Johnson LK. Utility of serum ferritin as a measure of iron deficiency in normal males undergoing repetitive phlebotomy. Blood 1980;56:786–91.

48. Lipschitz DA, Cook JD, Finch CA. A clinical evaluation of serum ferritin as an index of iron stores. N Engl J Med 1974;290:1213–6.

49. Galan P, Sangare N, Preziosi P, et al. Is basic red cell ferritin a more specific indicator than serum ferritin in the assessment of iron stores in the elderly? Clin Chim Acta 1990;189:159–62.

50. Balaban EP, Sheehan RG, Demian SE, et al. Evaluation of bone marrow iron stores in anemia associated with chronic disease: a comparative study of serum and red cell ferritin. Am J Hematol 1993;42:177–81.

51. Jensen BM, Sando SH, Grandjean P, et al. Screening with zinc protoporphyrin for iron deficiency in non-anemic female blood donors. Clin Chem 1990; 36:846–8.

52. Burns DL, Pomposelli JJ. Toxicity of parenteral iron dextran therapy. Kidney Int Suppl 1999;69:S119–24.

53. Bertero MT, Caligaris-Cappio F. Anemia of chronic disorders in systemic autoimmune diseases. Haematologica 1997;82:375–81.

54. De Marchi S, Pirisi M, Ferraccioli GF. Erythropoietin and the anemia of chronic diseases. Clin Exp Rheumatol 1993;11:429–44.

55. Means RT Jr, Krantz SB. Progress in understanding the pathogenesis of the anemia of chronic disease. Blood 1992;80:1639–47.

56. DeRienzo DP, Saleem A. Anemia of chronic disease: a review of pathogenesis. Tex Med 1990;86(10):80–3.

57. Pinevich AJ, Petersen J. Erythropoietin therapy in patients with chronic renal failure. West J Med 1992; 157:154–7.

58. Eschbach JW, Kelly MR, Haley NR, et al. Treatment of the anemia of progressive renal failure with recombinant human erythropoietin. N Engl J Med 1989;321:158–63.

59. Miles SA, Mitsuyasu RT, Moreno J, et al. Combined therapy with recombinant granulocyte colony-stimulating factor and erythropoietin decreases hematologic toxicity from zidovudine. Blood 1991; 77:2109–17.

60. Cazzola M, Mercuriali F, Brugnara C. Use of recombinant human erythropoietin outside the setting of uremia. Blood 1997;89:4248–67.

61. Gaucher disease. Current issues in diagnosis and treatment. NIH Technology Assessment Panel on Gaucher Disease. JAMA 1996;275:548–53.

62. Weinstein IM. Idiopathic myelofibrosis: historical review, diagnosis and management. Blood Rev 1991;5(2):98–104.

63. Pangalis GA, Poziopoulos C, Angelopoulou MK, et al. Effective treatment of disease-related anaemia in B-chronic lymphocytic leukaemia patients with recombinant human erythropoietin. Br J Haematol 1995;89:627–9.

64. Nissen C. The pathophysiology of aplastic anemia. Semin Hematol 1991;28:313–8.

65. Abe T, Komiya M. Some clinical aspects of aplastic anemia. In: Hibino S, et al, editors. Aplastic anemia. Baltimore (MD): University Park Press, 1978. p. 197–206.

66. Brown KE, Tisdale J, Barrett AJ, et al. Hepatitis-associated aplastic anemia. N Engl J Med 1997; 336:1059–64.

67. Young NS. Autoimmunity and its treatment in aplastic anemia [published erratum appears in Ann Intern Med 1997 Oct 15;127(8 Pt 1):658]. Ann Intern Med 1997;126:166–8.

68. Gale RJ, Champlin RE, Feig SA, Fitchen JH. Aplastic anemia: biology and treatment. Ann Intern Med 1981;95:477–94.

69. Sieff C. Annotation: pure red cell aplasia. Br J Haematol 1983;54:331–6.

70. Kurtzman GJ, Ozawa K, Cohen B, et al. Chronic bone marrow failure due to persistent B19 parvovirus infection. N Engl J Med 1987;317:287–94.

71. Kurtzman G, Frickhofen N, Kimball J, et al. Pure red-cell aplasia of 10 years' duration due to persistent parvovirus B19 infection and its cure with immunoglobulin therapy. N Engl J Med 1989;321:519–23.

72. Mangan KF. Immune disregulation of hematopoiesis. Annu Rev Med 1987;38:61–70.

73. Steinberg MH, Coleman MF, Pennebaker JB. Diamond-Blackfan syndrome: evidence for T-cell mediated suppression of erythroid development and a serum blocking factor associated with remission. Br J Haematol 1979;41(1):57–68.

74. Stabler SP, Allen RH, Savage DG, Lindenbaum J. Clinical spectrum and diagnosis of cobalamin deficiency. Blood 1990;76:871–81.

75. Chanarin I. Folate and cobalamin. Clin Haematol 1985;14:629–41.

76. Allen RH, Stabler SP, Savage DG, Lindenbaum J. Diagnosis of cobalamin deficiency I: usefulness of serum methylmalonic acid and total homocysteine concentrations. Am J Hematol 1990;34(2):90–8.

77. Carmel R. Subtle and atypical cobalamin deficiency states. Am J Hematol 1990;34(2):108–14.

78. Kuzminski AM, Del Giacco EJ, Allen RH, et al. Effective treatment of cobalamin deficiency with oral cobalamin. Blood 1998;92:1191–8.

79. Hassoun H, Palek J. Hereditary spherocytosis: a review of the clinical and molecular aspects of the disease. Blood Rev 1996;10:129–47.

80. Fournier CM, Nicolas G, Gallagher PG, et al. Spectrin St Claude, a splicing mutation of the human alpha-spectrin gene associated with severe poikilocytic anemia. Blood 1997;89:4584–90.

81. Engelfriet CP, Overbeeke MA, dem Borne AE. Autoimmune hemolytic anemia. Semin Hematol 1992; 29(1):3–12.

82. Patten E. Immunohematologic diseases. JAMA 1987;258:2945–51.

83. Domen RE. An overview of immune hemolytic anemias. Cleve Clin J Med 1998;65(2):89–99.

84. Winkelstein A, Kiss JE. Immunohematologic disorders. JAMA 1997;278:1982–92.

85. Moore JA, Chaplin H Jr. Autoimmune hemolytic anemia associated with an IgG cold incomplete antibody. Vox Sanguinis 1973;24:236–45.

86. Freedman J, Newlands M. Autoimmune haemolytic anaemia with the unusual combination of both IgM and IgG autoantibodies. Vox Sang 1977;32(2):61–8.

87. Silberstein LE, Berkman EM, Schreiber AD. Cold hemagglutinin disease associated with IgG cold-reactive antibody. Ann Intern Med 1987;106:238–42.

88. Davies SC, Brozovic M. The presentation, management and prophylaxis of sickle cell disease. Blood Rev 1989;3(1):29–44.

89. Valentine WN. Hereditary hemolytic anemias associated with specific erythrocyte enzymopathies. Calif Med 1968;108:280–94.

90. Pirofsky B. Clinical aspects of autoimmune hemolytic anemia. Semin Hematol 1976;13:251–65.

69

ANTIPHOSPHOLIPID ANTIBODY SYNDROME

Hyunah Poa, MD, and Kenneth Kalunian, MD

DEFINITION

Antiphospholipid antibody syndrome (APS) currently is defined as a disorder of recurrent arterial or venous thromboses, recurrent fetal loss, or thrombocytopenia in association with persistently elevated levels of antiphospholipid (aPL) antibodies (anticardiolipin antibodies or lupus anticoagulant).[1] Antiphospholipid antibody syndrome may occur as a primary (idiopathic) entity in otherwise healthy individuals or as a secondary form associated with autoimmune disease (most commonly systemic lupus erythematosus [SLE] or lupus-like diseases), malignancy, syphilis, human immunodeficiency virus (HIV) infection, drug ingestion, or other medical conditions.[2,3] Clinical and laboratory features of APS appear to be the same in either primary or secondary APS.

EPIDEMIOLOGY

An apparent female predominance of APS may be due to the fact that the diagnostic criteria include recurrent pregnancy loss. Also, APS often is diagnosed in patients with SLE, a disorder that affects predominantly women.[4,5] Although there are some genetic studies finding an increased incidence of human leukocyte antigen (HLA)-DR4, -DR7, and -Drw53 in patients with APS, data are limited at this time.[6-8]

The prevalence of APS is uncertain, because it is not clear whether patients followed up due to the presence of aPL antibodies alone will eventually acquire the clinical syndrome. Positive aPL antibody tests have been detected in patients with no medical disorder, including no evidence of SLE or related autoimmune disorders, infection, or history of use of drugs known to induce aPL antibodies. These patients may not have evidence of the clinical APS. Preliminary studies suggest that antibody isotype and titer may help predict whether patients will develop APS. Antiphospholipid antibodies are reported to be present in up to 50% of SLE patients and in up to 14% of healthy older people.[3,9-11]

PATHOPHYSIOLOGY

Phospholipids are a class of polar lipids that are formed in essentially all cells in the body. They function primarily as structural support in plasma membranes and can change configuration. There are several pathogenic mechanisms that may be important for the development of APS. These include the effects of autoantibodies on endothelial cells, the coagulation cascade, and platelet membranes.

Endothelial cell membranes may serve as a phospholipid template and a procoagulant surface. Sera-containing aPL antibodies have high reactivity with endothelial cells. Antiphospholipid antibodies binding endothelial cells have been associated with increased interleukin (IL)-6 expression and adhesion molecule upregulation, suggesting activation of endothelium by antibodies in a procoagulant direction.[12] Other evidence of endothelial activation by endothelium-binding autoantibodies includes increased release of von Willebrand's factor and the observation that membrane lipid turnover may be triggered by these antibodies.[13,14]

Phospholipids are critical at several points in the extrinsic, intrinsic, and common pathways of the coagulation cascade. Antiphospholipid antibodies appear to have effects on the anticoagulant activity of proteins C and S.[15-21] Protein C acts as an anticoagulant within the coagulation cascade by degrading activated clotting factors Va and VIIIa. Inhibition of protein C activity appears to be a chronic function of aPL antibodies, leading to a predisposition for thrombosis. In one study decreased rates of protein C–mediated factor Va degradation were noted in patients with lupus anticoagulants as compared with rates in controls.[22] Protein S is a regulatory component in an anticoagulant feedback system. Transient reversible episodes of acquired protein S deficiency have been reported during thrombotic events in patients with aPL antibodies.[23-29] Acquired protein S deficiency has been associated with both aPL antibodies and procoagulant laboratory measures in SLE patients and patients with primary APS.[26,30-32]

Antiphospholipid antibodies are known to bind to platelet membrane structure leading to either thrombocytopenia or hemostatic activation.[22,33-37] An association between aPL antibodies and immune-mediated thrombocytopenia (ITP) has been noted.[33] In ITP, antibodies to phospholipid membrane–bound glycoproteins have been pathogenically linked to the development of thrombocytopenia. Antiplatelet glycoprotein antibodies have been detected in a high proportion of plasma samples containing lupus anticoagulant activity; however, clinical correlations with antiplatelet glycoprotein antibodies appear to be specific for thrombocytopenia and not thrombosis.[33,34] Activation of platelets by a thrombotic stimulus causes a membrane phospholipid turnover that exposes surface anionic phospholipids. β_2-Glycoprotein 1 preferentially binds to activated platelets, and β_2-glycoprotein 1-dependent aPL antibodies have been found to increase their adhesion to platelet surfaces sixfold when the platelets are activated with thrombin.[35]

CLINICAL FEATURES

Antiphospholipid antibody syndrome is a disorder of recurrent vascular thrombosis, pregnancy losses, and thrombocytopenia associated with persistently elevated levels of aPL antibodies. A variety of other abnormalities of the skin, cardiac valves, and central nervous system have been described.[38-40] Many clinical presentations of APS relate to thrombosis of

large, medium, or small blood vessels. Other features, such as thrombocytopenia, Coombs' positive hemolytic anemia, and cardiac valve abnormalities are less clearly described pathophysiologically.

Many patients with APS have clinical and laboratory features of other autoimmune diseases, particularly SLE (Table 69–1). It is clinically important to determine whether a patient has a primary autoimmune disorder or other medical problem, as complications of thrombosis may be caused by the primary disorder, and different treatment strategies may be required.

Cutaneous Manifestations

Various cutaneous manifestations have been associated with aPL antibodies (Table 69–2). Cutaneous abnormalities may develop early in the course of APS and may be the first sign of the underlying cause of APS. Livedo reticularis is well described in association with APS.[41,42] Other cutaneous descriptions include superficial thrombophlebitis, evidence of deep venous thrombosis, cutaneous necrosis (most commonly involving the legs, face, and ears, but may be generalized),[41,43] digital gangrene, leg ulcers, Degos' disease (malignant atrophic papulosis),[43] and splinter hemorrhages.[43] Sneddon's syndrome is a finding of livedo reticularis with cerebrovascular accident.[44]

Neurologic Findings

Most of the neurologic abnormalities in APS relate to cerebrovascular thrombosis of large and small vessels, including cerebral ischemia (infarction, transient ischemic attacks, and retinal occlusive disease). Other nonthrombotic neurologic disorders have been reported in limited numbers of patients. Epilepsy has been reported, but it is unusual in APS without concurrent cerebral infarction.[45] Migraine headaches,[45] chorea,[46] multiple sclerosis, myasthenia gravis,[44] and transverse myelopathy[47] have been suggested as features in a few reported cases.[48]

Venous Thrombosis

Thrombosis of the venous system occurs more commonly than does arterial thrombosis in APS and usually occurs in areas common for thrombophlebitis—the deep and superficial veins of the legs. Some patients have pulmonary embolism, and pulmonary hypertension from recurrent emboli or intrapulmonary thrombosis has been reported.[49]

TABLE 69–1. Conditions and Medications Associated with Antiphospholipid Antibodies

Immunologic diseases	**Infectious diseases**
Systemic lupus erythematosus	Syphilis
Autoimmune thrombocytopenic purpura	Leprosy
Autoimmune hemolytic anemia	Tuberculosis
Adult/juvenile rheumatoid arthritis	Mycoplasma
Primary/secondary Sjögren's syndrome	Lyme disease
Polymyalgia rheumatica/giant cell arteritis	Human immunodeficiency virus infection
Dermatomyositis/polymyositis	Other viral infections[*]
Mixed connective tissue disease	Bacterial infections[†]
Systemic sclerosis	
Behçet's disease	**Neurologic diseases**
Polyarteritis nodosa	Sneddon's syndrome
Chronic active hepatitis	Myasthenia gravis
	Multiple sclerosis
Malignancies	Migraine headache
Solid tumors	
Leukemia	**Medications**
Hodgkin's disease/lymphoproliferative disorders	Chlorpromazine
Multiple myeloma	Phenothiazines
Mycosis fungoides	Phenytoin
	Hydralazine
	Procainamide
Hematologic diseases	Quinidine
Myelofibrosis	Streptomycin
von Willebrand's disease	Clozapine
Paraproteinemias	

[*]Hepatitis A, varicella, mononucleosis, adenovirus, parvovirus, measles, mumps.
[†]Endocarditis, sepsis.
Adapted from Nahass GT.[4] Antiphospholipid antibodies and the antiphospholipid antibody syndrome. J Am Acad Dermatol 1997;36:149–68.

Less common venous thrombosis sites include the inferior vena cava and pelvic, renal, mesenteric, portal, hepatic, iliofemoral, axillary, and retinal veins.[4,50–52]

Arterial Thrombosis

The most common manifestations of arterial thrombosis are stroke and transient ischemic attacks. Cerebral infarctions can be silent. If multiple events are undetected at first, the initial presentation can be seizure or dementia from extensive brain damage. In addition, coronary, retinal, renal, mesenteric, or peripheral arteries also may become occluded.[53] Renal dysfunction can result from renal artery, vein, or glomerular capillary thrombosis. The degree of renal dysfunction can vary from mild asymptomatic involvement to severe proteinuria, renal insufficiency, and hypertension. Cardiac valve thickening or vegetative lesions have been reported in up to one-third of patients with primary APS and in over two-thirds of patients with the SLE-associated syndrome.[40,54] Some evidence suggests that valvular lesions are as frequent in patients with SLE who are aPL antibody negative as it is in those with APS.

Thrombocytopenia

Patients with APS often have some degree of thrombocytopenia. Bick et al noted that moderate to severe thrombocytopenia occurs in 50% of patients with secondary APS, but in less than 10% of those with primary APS. The autoimmune pathophysiology is thought to be platelet sensitization by antibodies attached to surface phospholipids. A high correlation between immunoglobulin (Ig) A anticardiolipin antibodies and thrombocytopenia has been described.

TABLE 69–2. Cutaneous Manifestations Associated with Antiphospholipid Antibodies

Livedo reticularis
Acrocyanosis
Ulceration
Necrosis
Raynaud's phenomenon
Capillaritis
Purpuric/cyanotic macules
Nodules
Digital ischemia/gangrene
Blue toe
Thrombophlebitis
Hemorrhage/splinter hemorrhages
Porcelain-white scars/atrophie blanche

Reproduced with permission from Nahass GT.[4] Antiphospholipid antibodies and the antiphospholipid antibody syndrome. J Am Acad Dermatol 1997;36:149–68.

In addition IgG and IgM antibodies may be present. Regardless of the degree of thrombocytopenia, thrombosis and not bleeding is the major clinical consequence. Treatment with intravenous Ig or plasma exchange may be beneficial in addition to standard management in those patients with severe thrombocytopenia and thrombosis.[50,55,56]

Obstetric Manifestations

Recurrent pregnancy loss is well described in association with APS, but early-onset pre-eclampsia, placental abruption, and intrauterine growth retardation are also associated.[57,58] Women harboring anticardiolipin antibodies may have a 50 to 75% chance of fetal loss, but this may approximate the rate of pregnancy loss in the general population. There is no clear increase in fetal loss in asymptomatic normal healthy women with an incidental finding of aPL antibodies. It is uncertain what the risk of pregnancy or fetal complications is in a woman with clinical features suggestive of APS, but not completely fulfilling criteria, for example, women with one or two previous spontaneous abortions or symptoms suggestive of but not diagnostic for autoimmune disease.

Fetal complications can occur at any stage of pregnancy. The cause of fetal death related to APS appears to be hypoxia from insufficient uteroplacental blood flow.[59] Histologic studies of placentas reveal a vasculopathy of the maternal spiral arteries that leads to placental infarction.[60,61]

Catastrophic Antiphospholipid Syndrome

In 1992 Asherson used the term "catastrophic antiphospholipid syndrome" to describe a case of rapid deterioration associated with multisystem coagulation vasculopathy in a patient with APS.[7] Several similar cases have been described involving malignant hypertension, acute respiratory distress syndrome, pulmonary hypertension, central nervous system deterioration, progressive renal failure, and widespread thrombosis.[62] High-titer IgG anticardiolipin antibodies or lupus anticoagulant appears to be associated with this clinical syndrome. The clinical presentation may be similar to that of a spectrum of disorders that includes thrombotic thrombocytopenic purpura, disseminated intravascular coagulation, and active SLE. Morbidity and mortality rates are quite high. The optimal treatment strategy is unclear but may include anticoagulation, plasmapheresis,[7,63] and immunosuppression.

LABORATORY INVESTIGATIONS

There is no one single screening test sensitive enough to be used alone for the detection of lupus anticoagulant activity. The lupus anticoagulant test is a functional assay that measures the ability of serum containing aPL antibodies to prolong in vitro measures of clotting. Three findings are helpful in demonstrating the presence of lupus anticoagulant in platelet poor plasma: (1) prolongation of activated plasma thromboplastin time, kaolin clotting time, or dilute Russell viper venom time (dRVVT); (2) demonstration that the test is not corrected by mixing patient plasma with an equal volume of normal plasma; and (3) correction of the test to normal or near-normal by the addition of freeze-thawed platelets or a phospholipid preparation.[64,65] The dRVVT has been used as a confirmatory test because it is a sensitive assay, is accurate in pregnancy, and is unaffected by antibodies to factors VIII, IX, and XI.[66] However, very low levels of factor V or X (less than 0.4 U/mL) will prolong the dRVVT.[64] A suggested approach to laboratory diagnosis of APS is summarized in Figure 69–1.

Anticardiolipin antibodies can be differentiated by isotype (IgG, IgM, and IgA) and quantification of these antibodies can be measured by enzyme-linked immunosorbent assay (ELISA) testing. The IgA isotype alone appears less commonly, but it also may be associated with APS. The concentration of

Clinical evidence for antiphospholipid antibody syndrome[*]

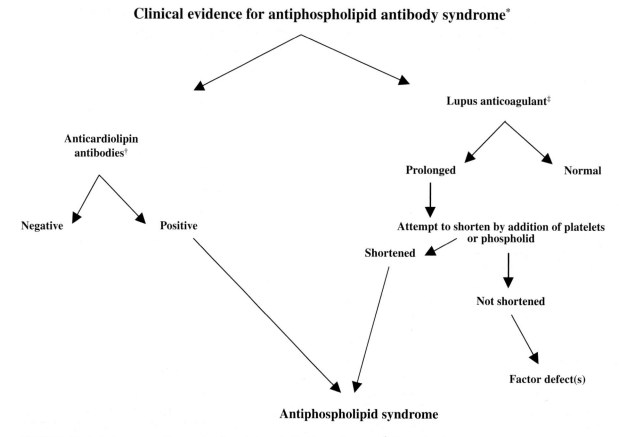

Antiphospholipid syndrome

FIGURE 69–1. Laboratory diagnosis of antiphospholipid syndromes. [*]Thrombosis, recurrent spontaneous abortion; [†]determined by ELISA (enzyme-linked immunosorbent assay) for immunoglobulins M, G, and A; [‡]dilute Russell viper venom time is the preferred test. (Adapted from Bick RL, Kaplan H. Syndromes of thrombosis and hypercoagulability. Curr Concepts Thrombosis 1998;82:409–55.)

IgG anticardiolipin antibodies can be measured in standard units as defined by the International Symposium on Antiphospholipid Antibodies. One G phospholipid (GPL) unit is the binding activity of 1 microgram/mL of affinity-purified IgG anticardiolipin antibody. The symposium recommends that results for IgG/IgM should be expressed semiquantitatively. These guidelines are summarized in Table 69–3.[67]

Generally, most clinical investigators and clinicians with extensive experience with APS feel that GPL units greater than 40, MPL units greater than 50, and APL units greater than 40 are clinically significant and may warrant therapy, depending on the clinical presentation of the individual patient.[68]

Anti-β_2-glycoprotein 1 antibodies, other phospholipid-binding cofactors, and antibodies directed against different phospholipids can be measured commercially. Data on the clinical significance of these measurements is emerging. The definition of

APS may be modified in the future as our knowledge of associated cofactors and antibodies evolves.

Some patients with APS do not test positive for antiphospholipid antibodies but have other serologic abnormalities. For example, patients whose clinical

TABLE 69–3. Interpretation of Results of Anticardiolipin Antibody Titers

	Immunoglobulins	
Category	G (GPL units)	M (MPL units)
Low positive	5–15	< 6.0
Medium positive	15–80	6–50
High positive	> 80	> 50

GPL = immunoglobulin (Ig) G phospholipid unit;
MPL = IgM phospholipid unit.
Adapted from Biasiolo A, Rampazzo P, Brocco T, et al. [Anti-beta 2 glycoprotein IObeta 2 glycoprotein I] immune complexes in patients with antiphospholipid syndrome and other autoimmune diseases. Lupus 1999;65:193–213.

picture fits APS but who have negative lupus anticoagulant tests and anticardiolipin antibody assays may have detectable anti-ß$_2$-glycoprotein 1 antibodies.[67] Some preliminary findings suggest that measurement of anti-ß$_2$-glycoprotein 1 increases the sensitivity and possibly the specificity of testing in patients highly suspected of having APS.[20]

MANAGEMENT

The treatment approach to a patient with APS depends on the clinical manifestations and presence or absence of underlying disease. There are no data to justify screening healthy pregnant women for aPL antibodies without previous recurrent fetal loss; the presence of aPL antibodies in healthy women without recurrent fetal loss does not require therapeutic intervention.

In non-pregnant patients who have never had thrombosis but who have high IgG anticardiolipin or unequivocally positive lupus anticoagulant tests, prophylaxis with aspirin (325 mg) is recommended. Usual risk factors for atherosclerosis should be addressed, such as hyperlipidemia, diabetes, smoking, hypertension, obesity, homocystinemia, anemia, and inactivity. Avoidance of oral contraceptives and probably estrogen replacement in menopause would appear advisable until further data become available.

Acute management of venous thrombosis or arterial thrombosis in patients with APS is no different than in other patients. Treatment with heparin followed by warfarin to achieve an international normalized ratio (INR) of 2.5 to 3.0 appears to prevent recurrences or future venous thromboses.[69] Treatment of a concurrent illness with steroids or immunosuppression is an issue separate from thrombosis and does not prevent recurrence of thrombosis. Although not proven in prospective studies, it seems advisable to prescribe lifelong anticoagulation for patients with APS and thrombosis. Although its use is indicated to treat thrombosis during pregnancy, long-term use of heparin generally is avoided because of associated osteoporosis, heparin-induced thrombocytopenia, and difficulties due to the discomfort and inconvenience of administration. Low–molecular weight heparins have a reduced risk of heparin-induced thrombocytopenia, but they are still associated with osteoporosis.[70] However, because warfarin is teratogenic, women with a history of thrombosis who take warfarin should stop a few

months prior to attempting to conceive; they should then be placed on subcutaneous heparin twice daily through conception and pregnancy (see below).

Several retrospective studies suggest that the majority of patients with APS and thrombosis of vessels have recurrent events even when treated with anticoagulation at all therapeutic INR ranges of 2.0 to 3.0, often within 6 months of stopping anticoagulation. Some advocate anticoagulation for recurrence or for arterial thrombosis in the INR range of 3.0 to 3.5 indefinitely.[69]

Studies of pregnant women with APS have demonstrated that subcutaneous heparin, intravenous immunoglobulin (IVIG), or prednisone may prevent fetal loss.[71] Treatment depends on the clinical scenario and the risk of side effects. In women with a history of recurrent fetal loss, treatment with subcutaneous heparin (5,000 to 10,000 units bid) is recommended throughout pregnancy and for 3 months after delivery. Women with a prior history of thrombosis may benefit from a higher dose of heparin (15,000 units bid), as the risk of recurrent thrombosis may be increased during pregnancy. A woman with pregnancy loss despite adequate treatment with heparin may be offered IVIG (0.4 g/kg/d × 4 days each month). This is expensive, but it has been found to be a safe and effective treatment.[72–76] Prednisone in dosages of 20 to 40 mg/d is effective, but it is associated with many significant side effects and should be considered for only those women who have failed heparin and IVIG. Successful anticoagulant therapy, depending on the clinical problem, can increase the chances of normal term delivery to about 80%.[77]

REFERENCES

1. Asherson RA, Cervera R. "Primary", "secondary" and other variants of antiphospholipid syndrome. Lupus 1994;3:293–8.
2. Boumpas DT, Fessler BJ, Austin HA, et al. Systemic lupus erythematosus: emerging concepts. Part 2: dermatologic and joint disease, the antiphospholipid antibody syndrome, pregnancy and hormonal therapy, morbidity and mortality, and pathogenesis. Ann Intern Med 1995;123:42–53.
3. Cervera R, Khamashta MA, Font J, et al. Morbidity and mortality in systemic lupus erythematosus during a 5-year period. A multicenter prospective study of 1,000 patients. European Working Party on

Systemic Lupus Erythematosus. Medicine (Baltimore) 1999;78:167–75.

4. Asherson RA, Khamashta MA, Ordi-Ros J, et al. The "primary" antiphospholipid syndrome: major clinical and serological features. Medicine (Baltimore) 1989;68:366–74.

5. Belilos E, Carsons S. Rheumatologic disorders in women. Med Clin North Am 1998;82:77–101.

6. Abu-Shakra M, Gladman DD, Urowitz MB, et al. Anticardiolipin antibodies in systemic lupus erythematosus: clinical and laboratory correlations. Am J Med 1995;99:624–8.

7. Asherson RA. The catastrophic antiphospholipid syndrome. J Rheumatol 1992;19:508–12.

8. Goldstein R, Moulds JM, Smith CD, Sengar DP. MHC studies of the primary antiphospholipid antibody syndrome and of antiphospholipid antibodies in systemic lupus erythematosus. J Rheumatol 1996;23:1173–9.

9. Fields RA, Toubbeh H, Searles RP, et al. The prevalence of anticardiolipin antibodies in a healthy elderly population and its association with antinuclear antibodies. J Rheumatol 1989;16:623–5.

10. Love PE, Santoro SA. Antiphospholipid antibodies: Anticardiolipin and the lupus anticoagulant in systemic lupus erythematosus (SLE) and in non-SLE disorders. Ann Intern Med 1990;112:682–8.

11. Petri M. Diagnosis of antiphospholipid antibodies. Rheum Dis Clin North Am 1994;20:443–69.

12. Del Papa N, Raschi E, Catelli L, et al. Endothelial cells as a target for antiphospholipid antibodies: role of anti-beta2 glycoprotein I antibodies. Am J Reprod Immunol 1997;38:212–7.

13. Dueymes M, Levy Y, Ziporen L, et al. Do some antiphospholipid antibodies target endothelial cells? Ann Med Interne (Paris) 1996;147 Suppl 1:22–3.

14. Ferro D, Pittoni V, Quintarelli C, et al. Coexistence of anti-phospholipid antibodies and endothelial perturbation in systemic lupus erythematosus patients with ongoing prothrombotic state. Circulation 1997;95:1425–32.

15. Triplett DA. Antiphospholipid antibodies and thrombosis. A consequence, coincidence or cause? Arch Pathol Lab Med 1993;117:78–88.

16. Marciniak E, Romond E. Impaired catalytic function of activated protein C: a new in vitro manifestation of lupus anticoagulant. Blood 1989;74:2426–32.

17. Tsakiris DA, Settas L, Makris PC, et al. Lupus anticoagulant, antiphospholipid antibodies and thrombophilia. Relation to protein C–protein S-thrombomodulin. J Rheumatol 1990;17:705–7.

18. Amer L, Kisiel W, Searles R, et al. Impairment of the protein C anticoagulant pathway in a patient with systemic lupus erythematosus, anticardiolipin antibodies and thrombosis. Thromb Res 1990;57:247–58.

19. Freyssinet JM, Wiesel MI, Gauchy J. An IgM lupus anticoagulant that neutralized the enhancing effect of phospholipid on purified endothelial thrombomodulin activity—a mechanism for thrombosis. Thromb Haemost 1986;55:309–13.

20. Cariou G, Tobelem G, Soria C, et al. Inhibition of protein C activation by endothelial cells in the presence of lupus antocoagulant. N Engl J Med 1986;314:1193–4.

21. Cariou R, Tobelem G, Belluci S. Effect of lupus anticoagulant on antithrombogenic properties of endothelial cells—inhibition of thrombomodulin-dependent protein C activation. Thromb Haemost 1988;380–6.

22. Machin SJ. Platelets and antiphosphlipid antibodies. Lupus 1996;5:386–7.

23. Moreb J, Kitchens CS. Acquired functional protein S deficiency, cerebral venous thrombosis and coumarin skin necrosis in association with antiphospholipid syndrome: report of two cases. Am J Med 1989;87:207–10.

24. Sthoeger ZM, Sthoeger D, Mellnick SD. Transient anticardiolipin antibodies, functional protein S deficiency and deep vein thrombosis. Am J Hematol 1991;36:206–7.

25. Ruiz Arguelles CJ, Ruiz Arguelles A, Alarcon Segovia D. Natural anticoagulants in systemic lupus erythematosus. Deficiency of protein S bound to C4bp associates with recent history of venous thromboses, antiphospholipid antibodies and the antiphospholipid syndrome. J Rheumatol 1991;10:552–8.

26. Ginsberg JS, Demers C, Brill-Edwards P, et al. Acquired free protein S deficiency is associated with antiphospholipid antibodies and increased thrombin generation in patients with systemic lupus erythematosus. Am J Med 1995;98:379–83.

27. Amster MS, Conway J, Zeid M, et al. Cutaneous necrosis resulting from protein S deficiency and increased antiphospholipid antibody in a patient with systemic lupus erythematosus. J Am Acad Dermatol 1993;29:853–7.

28. Wattiaux MJ, Herve R, Robert A, et al. Coumarin-induced skin necrosis associated with acquired protein S deficiency and antiphospholipid antibody syndrome. Arthritis Rheum 1994;37:1096–100.

29. Hill VA, Whittaker SJ, Hunt BJ, et al. Cutaneous necrosis associated with the antiphospholipid syndrome and mycosis fungoides. Br J Dermatol 1994; 130:92–6.

30. Reverter JC, Tassies D, Font J, et al. Hypercoagulable state in patients with antiphospholipid syndrome is related to high induced tissue factor expression on monocytes and to low free protein S. Arterioscler Thromb Vasc Biol 1996;16:1319–26.

31. Forastiero RR, Kordich L, Basilotta E, et al. Differences in protein S and C4b-binding protein levels in different groups of patients with antiphospholipid antibodies. Blood Coagul Fibrinolysis 1994;5: 609–16.

32. Parke AL, Weinstein RE, Bona RD. The thrombotic diathesis associated with the presence of antiphospholipid antibodies may be due to low levels of free protein S. Am J Med 1992;9:49–56.

33. Galli M, Daldossi M, Barbui T. Anti-glycoprotein Ib/IX and Iib/IIIa antibodies in patients with antiphospholipid antibodies. Thromb Haemost 1994;71: 571–5.

34. Panzer S, Gschwandtner ME, Hutter D, et al. Specificities of platelet autoantibodies in patients with lupus anticoagulants in primary antiphospholipid syndrome. Ann Hematol 1997;74:239–42.

35. Vazquez-Mellado J, Llorente L, Richaud-Patin Y, et al. Exposure of anionic phospholipids upon platelet activation permits binding of beta 2 glycoprotein I and through it that of IgG antiphospholipid antibodies. Studies in platelets from patients with antiphospholiped syndrome and normal subjects. J Autoimmun 1994;7:335–48.

36. Amengual O, Atsumi T, Khamashta MA, et al. Specificity of ELISA for antibody to beta 2-glycoprotein I in patients with antiphospholipid syndrome. Br J Rheumatol 1996;35:1239–43.

37. Stewart MW, Etches WS, Gordon PA. Antiphospholipid antibody–dependent c5b-9 formation. Br J Haematol 1997;96:451–7.

38. Cabiedes J, Cabral AR, Alarcon-Segovia D. Clinical manifestations of the antiphospholipid syndrome in patients with systemic lupus erythematosus associate more strongly with anti-beta 2-glycoprotein-I than with antiphospholipid antibodies. J Rheumatol 1995; 22:1899–906.

39. Feldmann E, Levine SR. Cerebrovascular disease with antiphospholipid antibodies: immune mechanisms, significance, and therapeutic options. Ann Neurol 1995;37 Suppl 1:S114–30.

40. Grondin F, Giannoccaro JP. Antiphospholipid antibody syndrome associated with large aortic valve vegetation and stroke. Can J Cardiol 1995;11: 133–5.

41. Abernathy ML, McGuinn JL, Callen JP. Widespread cutaneous necrosis as the initial manifestation of the antiphospholipid antibody syndrome. J Rheumatol 1995;22:1380–3.

42. Aronoff DM, Callen JP. Necrosing livedo reticularis in a patient with recurrent pulmonary hemorrhage. J Am Acad Dermatol 1997;37:300–2.

43. Nahass GT. Antiphospholipid antibodies and the antiphospholipid antibody syndrome. J Am Acad Dermatol 1997;36:149–68.

44. Geschwind DH, FitzPatrick M, Mischel PS, et al. Sneddon's syndrome is a thrombotic vasculopathy: neuropathologic and neuroradiologic evidence [comments]. Neurology 1995;45:557–60.

45. Angelini L, Granata T, Zibordi F, et al. Partial seizures associated with antiphospholipid antibodies in childhood. Neuropediatrics 1998;29:249–53.

46. Asherson RA, Hughes GRV. Antiphospholipid antibodies and chorea. J Rheumatol 1988;15:377–9.

47. Brey RL, Escalante A. Neurological manifestations of antiphospholipid antibody syndrome. Lupus 1998;7 Suppl 2:S67–74.

48. Levine SR, Brey RL, Sawaya KL, et al. Recurrent stroke and thrombo-occlusive events in the antiphospholipid syndrome. Ann Neurol 1995;38:119–24.

49. Asherson RA, Cervera R. Review: antiphospholipid antibodies and the lung. J Rheumatol 1995;22:62–5.

50. Bick RL. Antiphospholipid thrombosis syndromes: etiology, pathophysiology, diagnosis and management. Int J Hematol 1997;65:193–213.

51. Gul A, Inanc M, Ocal L, et al. Primary antiphospholipid syndrome associated with mesenteric inflammatory veno-occlusive disease. Clin Rheumatol 1996;15:207–10.

52. Lee HJ, Park JW, Chang JC. Mesenteric and portal venous obstruction associated with primary antiphospholipid antibody syndrome. J Gastroenterol Hepatol 1997;12:822–6.

53. Ho YL, Chen MF, Wu CC, et al. Successful treatment of acute myocardial infarction by thrombolytic therapy in a patient with primary antiphospholipid antibody syndrome. Cardiology 1996;87:354–7.

54. Vianna JL, Khamashta MA, Ordi-Ros J, et al. Comparison of the primary and secondary antiphospholipid syndrome: a European multicenter study of 114 patients. Am J Med 1994;96:3–9.

55. Bick RL. The antiphospholipid thrombosis syndromes: lupus anticoagulants, and anticardiolipin antibodies. Adv Pathol Lab Med 1995;8:391.

56. Bick RL. Disseminated intravascular coagulation. Hematol Oncol Clin North Am 1992;6:1259–85.

57. Rai R, Regan L. Obstetric complications of antiphospholipid antibodies. Curr Opin Obstet and Gynecol 1997;9:387–90.

58. Branch DW, Silver R, Pierangeli S, et al. Antiphospholipid antibodies other than lupus anticoagulant and anticardiolipin antibodies in women with recurrent pregnancy loss, fertile controls, and antiphospholipid syndrome. Obstet Gynecol 1997;89:549–55.

59. Borrelli AL, Brillante M, Borzacchiello C, et al. Hemocoagulative pathology and immunological recurrent abortion. Clin Exp Obstet Gynecol 1997;24:39–40.

60. Branch DW. Thought on the mechanism of pregnancy loss associated with the antiphospholipid syndrome. Lupus 1994;3:275–80.

61. De Wolf F, Carrerra LO, Moerman P, et al. Decidual vasculopathy and extensive placental infarction in a patient with repeated thromboembolic accidents, recurrent fetal loss and a lupus anticoagulant. Am J Obstet Gynecol 1982;142:829–34.

62. Hayem G, Kassis N, Nicaise P, et al. Systemic lupus erythematosus–associated catastrophic antiphospholipid syndrome occurring after typhoid fever: a possible role of *Salmonella* lipopolysaccharide in the occurrence of diffuse vasculopathy-coagulopathy. Arthritis Rheum 1999;42:195–200.

63. Greisman SG, Thayaparan R-S, Godwin TA, et al. Occlusive vasculopathy in systemic lupus erythematosus. Association with anticardiolipin antibody. Arch Intern Med 1991;151:389–92.

64. Harris NE. Antiphopholipid syndrome. In: Klippel JH, Dieppe PA, editors. Rheumatology. 2nd ed. London: Mosby; 1998;35:1–6.

65. Bick RL, Kaplan H. Syndromes of thrombosis and hypercoagulability. Curr Concepts Thrombosis 1998;82:409–55.

66. Pengo V, Biasiolo A, Rampazzo P, et al. dRVVT is more sensitive than KCT or TTI for detecting lupus anticoagulant activity of anti-beta2-glycoprotein I autoantibodies. Thromb Haemost 1999;81:256–8.

67. Biasiolo A, Rampazzo P, Brocco T, et al. [Anti-beta2 glycoproteinimmune complexes in patients with antiphospholipid syndrome and other autoimmune diseases. Lupus 1999;65:193–213.

68. Lakos G, Kiss E, Regeczy N, et al. Isotype distribution and clinical relevance of anti-beta2-glycoprotein I (beta-GPI) antibodies: importance of IgA isotype. Clin Exp Immunol 1999;117:574–9.

69. Khamashta MA, Cuadrado MJ, Mujic F, et al. The management of thrombosis in the antiphospholipid-antibody syndrome. N Engl J Med 1995;332:993–7.

70. Dulitzki M, Pauzner R, Langevitz P, et al. Low-molecular-weight heparin during pregnancy and delivery: preliminary experience with 41 pregnancies. Obstet Gynecol 1993;87:380–3.

71. Khamashta MA. Management of thrombosis and pregnancy loss in the antiphospholipid syndrome. Lupus 1998;7 Suppl 2:S162–5.

72. Spinatto JA, Clark AL, Pierangeli SS, et al. Intravenous immunoglobulin therapy for the antiphospholipid syndrome in pregnancy. Am J Obstet Gynecol 1995;172:690–4.

73. Carreras LO, Perez GN, Vega HR, et al. Lupus anticoagulant and recurrent fetal loss: successful treatment with gammaglobulin. Lancet 1988;2:393–4.

74. Scott JR, Branch DW, Kochenour NK, et al. Intravenous globulin treatment of pregnant patients with recurrent pregnancy loss due to antiphospholipid antibodies and Rh disease. Am J Obstet Gynecol 1988;159:1055–6.

75. Clark AL. Clinical uses of intravenous immunoglobulin in pregnancy. Clin Obstet Gynecol 1999;42-368–80.

76. Gordon C, Kilby MD. Use of intravenous immunoglobulin therapy in pregnancy in systemic lupus erythematosus and antiphospholipid antibody syndrome. Lupus 1998;7:429–33.

77. Bick RL, Laughlin HR, Cohen B, et al. Fetal wasting syndrome due to blood protein/platelet defects: results of prevalence studies and treatment outcome with low-dose heparin and low-dose aspirin. Clin Appl Thromb Hemost 1995;1:286.

70

SCREENING AND PRIMARY CARE OF THE HIV-POSITIVE WOMAN

Ardis Moe, MD

One-fourth of all acquired immunodeficiency syndrome (AIDS) cases in the United States involve women,[1] yet most drug treatment research and studies on pathophysiology of disease are derived from studies of men. Only recently has sufficient evidence accumulated to demonstrate that men and women have important differences in the epidemiology and presentation of illness, psychosocial issues, and transmission rates associated with human immunodeficiency virus (HIV).

EPIDEMIOLOGY

The epidemiology of HIV in women in the United States differs markedly from that of men. Women with HIV are more likely to be African American or Latina than are men, and they are more likely to have HIV as a heterosexually acquired disease than are men.[1] Forty-nine percent of all reported male cases of AIDS involve Caucasians, whereas 77% of all cases of AIDS in women occur in Latina or African American women.[1,2] Approximately half of all AIDS cases reported are in men who have sex with men, with the rest attributed mainly to injection drug use (IDU). In contrast 38% of women with AIDS acquired it from a male partner, and another 32% do not report any known risk. When cases with no known risk are investigated, the majority are ultimately shown to involve heterosexual contact with a high-risk partner.[1,2] Overall, 29% of all AIDS cases in women come from IDU,[1] a risk factor that varies by location. In one cohort of 724 HIV-infected women from the East Coast, IDU was identified as the source of infection in 53% of cases. In contrast, in Los Angeles, a similar group of 240 HIV-infected women had IDU identified as the source of infection in only 12% of cases.[3,4] Less than 10 cases of isolated woman-to-woman transmission of HIV have been reported in the literature.[1,5]

The median age of women with AIDS is the mid-thirties, the same as that for men with AIDS. However, because of the prolonged asymptomatic period in many persons with HIV infection, these statistics translate into a high rate of HIV infection among teenagers. In one survey of clients recruited from sexually transmitted disease clinics, 28% of the HIV-positive women were less than 20 years of age.[6]

DIAGNOSIS

Testing

Both patients and clinicians may have misconceptions about what behaviors are associated with a high risk for HIV infection in women. These misconceptions have led to undertesting of women patients. One misperception about HIV risk is the idea that only women with multiple sexual partners or IDU are at risk of contracting HIV. In fact studies indicate that one-half of at-risk women with no history of IDU have had two or fewer sexual partners in the previous 12 months.[6] Since 1993 the most common way women have been infected is through sex with a male partner.[1] Their partner's behaviors and risks are of high importance in determining which women are at risk for infection, but determining the partner's risks has not been part of most routine clinical practice.

Denial plays a large part in why women are not tested for HIV. For example, one half of newly diagnosed HIV-positive women attending a clinic for sexually transmitted diseases (STDs) did not believe they were at high risk for HIV.[7] Denial occurs in clinicians as well: only 17% of HIV-positive women in a British clinic recalled having a conversation about HIV testing with their medical clinician in the year prior to diagnosis, even though one-half of those women were born in sub-Saharan Africa, an area of high HIV prevalence, and 46% presented with symptomatic HIV infection or AIDS.[8] In one Los Angeles study, black women were four times more likely to be offered an HIV test by medical clinicians than were Caucasian women, even though the Caucasian women in this study were as likely as were the black women to practice IDU, 6.7 times as likely to have a partner who practiced IDU, and 5 times more likely to partcipate in anal intercourse.[5] Only one-third of HIV-infected women with private gynecologists in this study recalled a conversation about HIV testing.[5]

Women with HIV may have difficulties with disclosure of their HIV risk factors and their HIV status to medical clinicians, fearing denial of medical services; in one study of HIV-infected women, one-fifth of those who had a private gynecologist did not reveal their HIV status to their gynecologist.[5] Twenty-eight percent of pregnant women refused HIV testing in one survey, with the most common reason being a perception of no HIV risk.[9] Removing the stigma of disease and educating women on the benefit of treatment increases the likelihood of accepting an HIV test; those pregnant women who were comfortable with finding a positive HIV result and who knew of the benefits of treatment during pregnancy were much more likely to accept HIV testing.[9]

The onus is therefore on medical clinicians to offer HIV testing, emphasizing to the patient the benefits of knowing one's HIV status in this new era of treatment options for persons who do test positive. There are currently fourteen licensed anti-HIV medications, and they can be combined in a variety of potent triple-drug therapies; studies have repeatedly demonstrated improved survival with triple-drug therapy in persons with AIDS.[10] State and federal funding sources such as the Ryan White Act have permitted uninsured persons with HIV infection to obtain the new medications for free.[11] As a result AIDS has dropped from the number one cause of death for young people to the fifth greatest cause of death—in just 2 years following the licensure of the

protease inhibitors, the most powerful class of anti-HIV medications.[12] Unfortunately women are less likely than are men to be offered antiviral therapy[13] and, as a result, AIDS is still the second greatest cause of death for African American women and the third greatest cause of death for Latina women aged 25 to 44 years.[12]

Rapid HIV testing is now available; this can improve the likelihood of appropriately diagnosing and treating HIV in some populations. For example up to 40% of HIV-positive persons do not return for their HIV results.[14] One rapid HIV-screening kit has been licensed by the US Food and Drug Administration and can provide clinicians with results in minutes. These test systems have unique clinical applications: for example, the SUDS-HIV-1 test (Abbott Laboratories, Abbott Park, Illinois) has equivalent sensitivity to the routine ELISA (enzyme-linked immunosorbent assay) screening of current HIV-testing systems, with a positive predictive rate of 88% in STD clinics. A negative SUDS-HIV-1 test result has the same sensitivity in excluding HIV as does a negative HIV ELISA test; a positive SUDS-HIV-1 test requires confirmation with routine HIV testing because of decreased specificity when compared with Western blot test for HIV.[14,15]

In select populations, a rapid testing system can be an impetus to counsel the patient on the high likelihood of HIV positivity and to initiate HIV medical care immediately, such as in the situation of a high-risk woman presenting in labor with no prenatal care. Some anti-HIV medications have immediate protective benefits on the unborn child (eg, intravenous zidovudine or oral nevirapine), and these medications can cut HIV transmission by at least half when given during labor and delivery and when given to the infant post delivery.[16,17] A positive rapid HIV test can give presumptive diagnosis to a pregnant woman in labor and can allow the use of medications during delivery, even in cases in which the woman's HIV status was previously unknown.

When rapid HIV testing is not available, or when confirmatory results are necessary, clinicians should counsel the patients on the need for a follow-up visit to review results. As a part of HIV counseling, clinicians and patients should be aware of the "window" period after infection when the standard HIV tests results can be negative despite the fact that the patient is actively growing HIV and can infect others. This window period of seroconversion can last for up to 6 months, so two or more HIV tests at least 6 months apart after a risky event are necessary to determine whether someone is infected with HIV. The patient should be counseled on safe sex techniques and to avoid behaviors that may transmit HIV, until the possibility of infection has been eliminated definitively.[18]

Typical Signs and Symptoms

Since survival is so closely linked to early diagnosis and treatment of this disease, primary care clinicians should be cognizant of typical and less typical HIV signs, symptoms, and risk factors that become apparent during primary care. A list of some of these risk factors and symptoms of HIV are listed in Table 70–1.[19–28]

At the time of their diagnosis, HIV-positive women tend to have constitutional complaints, including fatigue, shortness of breath, and chronic pain requiring prescription medications for relief, and they may be advanced in their disease.[8,29] Skin disorders are common in women with HIV infection, with molluscum contagiosum, atopic dermatitis, xerosis, seborrheic dermatitis, nongenital warts, and eosinophilic pustular folliculitis ("itchy red bump disease") being the most common problems.[30] With the exception of Kaposi's sarcoma and cervical cancer, men and women present with similar AIDS-defining illnesses, with tuberculosis, *Pneumocystis carinii* pneumonia, and *Candida* esophagitis accounting for 70% of the current AIDS-defining illnesses.[29] Risk category also affects the presentation of illness: women who acquire HIV through IDU are more likely to develop thrush, anemia, weight loss, and abnormal liver function than are women who acquire their disease heterosexually.[29] Increasing degrees of immunosuppression from HIV lead to the development of progressive *Candida* infections: women first develop recurrent vaginal yeast infections, then oral thrush, and finally *Candida* esophagitis.[31]

In addition to vaginal yeast infections, other gynecologic complications are common in HIV-infected women. Infection with HIV complicates treatment of salpingitis by doubling the risk of tubo-ovarian abscess.[32] Women who are positive for HIV are more likely to have cancer-causing human papillomavirus serotypes, particularly with high amounts of circulating HIV virus (HIV load).[33,34] Abnormal results of Papanicolaou (Pap) smears are common, with up to 25% of initial Pap smears indicating dysplasia.[34,35] Women infected with HIV who have abnormal results of Pap smears should undergo colposcopy, and should be monitored closely by a clinician experienced in evaluating and treating HPV.

INITIAL EVALUATION

The primary care clinician can perform the initial evaluation of an HIV-positive woman, including obtaining baseline laboratory data and performing basic primary care procedures such as vaccination and counseling. Referral to social work services, women's support groups, and case management should be part of the evaluation of the newly diagnosed woman, as these women often suffer from poverty, lack of medical insurance, and lack of social supports—factors that interfere with care.[3] The initial medical history, physical examination, and laboratory work-up of the HIV-positive[18,36,37] woman is listed in Table 70–2.[19,36,37]

CD4 Count and HIV Load Interpretation

The CD4 count is the best indicator of current immune status and immediate risk of disease; few opportunistic infections occur with CD4 counts >200.[20] If the CD4 count is <200, there is a high risk of infectious complications of HIV such as *Pneumocystis carinii* pneumonia. A woman with a CD4 count of <200 is therefore classified as having AIDS.[20] Several studies indicate that the CD4 count decline predicts progression to AIDS equally well in men and women.[38]

The HIV viral load is the best indicator for the likelihood of decline of CD4 cell number and overall survival.[39] For this reason HIV load is used to decide when to start antiretroviral medication in otherwise asymptomatic persons. The commonly used cutoff points for beginning antiretroviral medications are based on information from a large study of men.[39] Interpretation of HIV load in women has become an area of controversy, with several studies indicating that women progress to AIDS at lower HIV loads than do men.[40,41] This suggests that the HIV load may be less reliable as a threshold for starting therapy with anti-HIV medications in women. However, much of the controversy is confounded because, compared with the men in studies

TABLE 70–1. Clinical Indications for HIV Testing in Women

Clinical situations specific to women
  Risk factors that are often present in HIV-positive women
    Pregnancy
    Domestic violence
    Bisexual male partner

  Illnesses that may be caused by HIV
    Recurrent vaginal yeast infections (> 3/yr) in nondiabetic women
    Persistent or recurrent HPV infection of cervix
    Invasive cervical cancer in young women (< 40 yr)

Other situations
  Risk factors that are often present in HIV-positive persons
    History of cocaine abuse
    History of IDU
    Blood transfusions prior to 1985
    History of STDs, especially genital warts and syphilis
    Partner with history of IDU
    Homelessness
    Hepatitis C
    Hepatitis B
    History of incarceration
    Receptive anal intercourse
    Victim of rape
    Needlestick injury or other occupational exposure

  Illnesses/clinical presentations that may be caused by HIV
    Idiopathic thrombocytopenic purpura
    Tuberculosis
    Unexplained persistent weight loss
    Unexplained persistent diarrhea
    Fever of unknown origin
    Unexplained generalized lymphadenopathy
    B cell lymphoma
    Kaposi's sarcoma
    Unexplained thrush
    Shingles in persons < 60 yr
    Hemophilia
    Oral hairy leukoplakia
    Persistent herpes simplex infections
    Aseptic meningitis*
    Pneumocystis carinii pneumonia, *Mycobacterium avium* complex infections, invasive CMV disease,
      or other opportunistic infections not otherwise explained by immunosuppressive therapy

Potential donors of organs, blood, or human eggs

---

*Include HIV RNA PCR testing with routine HIV testing.
HIV = human immunodeficiency virus; HPV = human papillomavirus; STD = sexually transmitted disease; IDU = injection drug use; RNA = ribonucleic acid; PCR = polymerase chain reaction; CMV = cytomegalovirus.
Adapted from Bartlett,[19] Schuman et al,[20,21] Chin et al,[22] Ho et al,[23] Eisenstat and Bancroft,[24] Axelrod et al,[25] Inciardi,[26] Fogel and Belya,[27] and Opravil et al.[28]

TABLE 70–2. Evaluation and Primary Care Follow-Up of the Newly Diagnosed HIV-Positive Woman

Medical history: Review symptoms; be sure to inquire about weight loss, fevers, diarrhea, cough, and other signs of acute infection.

Psychosocial factors: Evaluate for substance abuse, depression, and domestic violence.

Physical examination: Perform oral examination for thrush and hairy leukoplakia, complete skin examination for lesions, palpation for lymphadenopathy, and pelvic examination including a Papanicolaou (Pap) smear and examination for signs of STDs, and gonorrhea and chlamydia testing. An HIV-positive woman with a normal Pap smear result at baseline and at 6-mo follow-up can be followed up with annual Pap smears.[36]

Blood tests: VDRL test, hepatitis B surface antigen test, hepatitis B surface antibody test, hepatitis C antibody test, toxoplasmosis antibodies (IgG) test[*], liver and kidney function tests, CBC with platelets and differential, glucose 6-phosphate level[*],[19] HIV RNA PCR "HIV load"(—determined by Roche Amplicor assay or Chiron branched-chain DNA assay), and CD4 cell count.

Vaccines: Pneumococcal and annual influenza vaccinations should be offered to all HIV-positive persons. Persons negative for hepatitis B surface antigen and surface antibody should be offered a series of hepatitis B vaccines. Other vaccines should be given when indicated (eg, before travel or occupational risks); note that live vaccines should *not* be used in HIV-positive persons.[19]

TB testing: An annual PPD skin test should be offered to all HIV-positive persons who are not already known to have a positive PPD. Persons with at least 5 mm of reactivity on their PPD should undergo chest radiography and be evaluated for the need for prophylactic TB treatment, or a full course of TB therapy for acute disease.

Estrogen replacement: Women who are perimenopausal or menopausal should receive evaluation and counseling regarding estrogen replacement therapy, since there may be a trend toward greater survival in older women with HIV who take estrogen replacement.[37]

[*]Toxoplasmosis titers are checked to determine if patients require prophylactic therapy against toxoplasmosis. Levels of G6PD are checked to determine if sulfa drugs may be used for prophylaxis and treatment of active AIDs-related infections, as sulfa drugs are contraindicated in G6PD-deficient persons.

HIV = human immunodeficiency virus; STD = sexually transmitted disease; VDRL = Venereal Disease Research Laboratory; CBC = complete blood count; RNA = ribonucleic acid; PCR = polymerase chain reaction; DNA = deoxyribonucleic acid; TB = tuberculosis; PPD = purified protein derivative.

of HIV load, women in studies of HIV load generally have had additional risk factors for poor prognosis, such as IDU.[40]

TRANSMISSION FROM THE HIV-POSITIVE WOMEN TO PARTNERS AND UNBORN CHILDREN

Issues of transmission from HIV-positive women to their unborn children or their partners are common areas of concern for both clinicians and patients. Women may want to have children despite their illness, and they may want to continue sexual relations with their partners. They may have difficulty notifying partners and family of their HIV risk due to a fear of rejection or discrimination.[42] A frank discussion on the relative risks of transmission may be helpful in counseling HIV-positive women. A table of approximate risks by exposure category is presented in Table 70–3.[43–51]

Some European and American studies indicate that men are eight times more likely to transmit HIV to women than are women to men.[46,47] In one recent African study of mostly uncircumcised men and women, however, HIV load was the major determinant in transmission risk, not gender. An HIV-infected partner, regardless of gender, with high viral loads was much more likely to transmit HIV than was a partner with low viral loads. In addition, circumcision appeared to be protective of HIV uninfected men and may account for the difference in Africa and European studies of heterosexual transmission risk.[50] Sex during menses, genital ulcers, anal intercourse without condoms, untreated HIV infection, and advanced HIV disease all contribute to an increased risk of transmission from one partner to another.[45–49] In couples who choose to continue sexual relations, consistent use of condoms has been shown to provide significant protection, with an estimated annual transmission

---

TABLE 70–3. Risks of Transmission by Various Types of Exposure to HIV

Type of Exposure	Risk of Transmission
Pregnancy and lactation	
Untreated HIV-infected pregnant mother to infant	22.5%
HIV-infected pregnant mother on antiretrovirals* to infant	2% or less
Breastfeeding mother to infant	12%
Sexual intercourse	
Vaginal intercourse	1 in 1,000 per sex act
Oral sex	1 in 10,000 per sex act
Anal receptive intercourse	1 in 100 per sex act
Anal insertive intercourse	1 in 250 per sex act
Direct blood exposure	
Needlestick injury	1 in 300
Shared IDU from HIV-infected person	1 in 100 per act of IDU
Recipient of a unit of infected blood	>95% risk

*Including oral zidovudine during second and third trimesters, intravenous zidavudine during labor and delivery, and zidovudine for 6 wk post partum for the infant.

HIV = human immunodeficiency virus; IDU = injection drug use.

Adapted from Fiscus et al,[43] Mofenson et al,[44] Nicolosi et al,[45] Saracco et al,[46] Padian et al,[47] Vincenzi,[48] Royce et al,[50] and Bertolli et al.[51]

---

rate of 1% in serodiscordant heterosexual couples. Heterosexual couples who do not use condoms consistently have an estimated annual transmission rate of 10%.[45–50] Counseling of both partners helps couples to use condoms consistently.[52] Use of condoms often is linked to ethnic perceptions of effectiveness and acceptability; Latina and African American women may have particular difficulty in negotiating condom use.[53]

Women who are HIV positive are twice as likely to have relationship violence as are HIV-negative women,[25] and cases of physical abuse arising from partner notification have occurred.[42,54,55] Clinicians should be sensitive to the possibility of physical harm to the woman if her HIV status is disclosed to her partner. If a clinician discovers that her patient may be at risk for physical harm from disclosure of her HIV status, counseling and referral for domestic violence should be done before partner notification procedures are begun.

Transmission of HIV during pregnancy appears to be closely linked to maternal HIV load. In one study women who had an HIV load > 80,000 copies/mL at delivery had > 90% of infants infected; of 107 women who had an HIV load < 500 copies/mL at delivery, none transmitted HIV to their infants.[44,56] Elective cesarean section may have a limited use in prevention of transmission in selected pregnant women.[57] For example, those women who are intolerant of anti-HIV medications, or who have a detectable HIV load during pregnancy despite treatment, may be able to decrease their likelihood of delivering an infected child by undergoing this procedure. One large meta-analysis indicated that cesarean section may have cut the incidence of HIV transmission from mother to infant from 7 to 1% in women who were taking zidovudine as single-drug therapy—but only in those women who had elective cesarean section prior to the onset of labor.[58]

Cesarean section in HIV-infected women doubles the risk of postoperative complications, including bleeding, sepsis, and pneumonia.[59] In discussions of pregnancy and delivery issues, HIV-infected women should be informed of the risks to themselves associated with cesarean section, particularly since aggressive anti-HIV therapy may drop the risk of transmission to the infant to nearly zero, rendering cesarean section unnecessary.

INDICATIONS FOR REFERRAL TO A SPECIALIST

Asymptomatic women with CD4 counts > 500 and HIV loads of < 5,000 with no other HIV-related issues do not require antiretroviral therapy and can be followed up with repeated laboratory studies of CD4 counts and HIV loads every 4 to 6 months.[18] Women who have CD4 counts < 500, have higher HIV loads, or who are symptomatic from their HIV should be referred to an HIV specialist, since treatment by an HIV-experienced clinician can increase survival by over 40%.[59]

Pregnancy in an HIV-positive woman is also an indication for referral, even though pregnancy is not associated with more rapid progression to AIDS.[60] Referral is needed in this situation to manage the anti-HIV medications to prevent transmission to the unborn infant, while preserving the mother's health.

CONCLUSION

When fear and denial are overcome by both clinicians and female patients, women with HIV have the potential not only to achieve the same survival benefit as men, but also to return to a near-normal lifestyle that can include motherhood, career, and marriage. This represents the fruit of two decades of AIDS research, but these benefits can be obtained only when social and financial barriers are removed. There are medical differences between men and women with HIV, but they are minor when compared with the issues of testing, medical access, and information. Primary care of women includes the need to diagnose HIV early in the course of the disease, and to direct HIV-infected women to the resources, both medical and psychosocial, that are needed to maintain health and preserve the opportunities of living.

REFERENCES

1. Center for Disease Control. Fact sheet: HIV/AIDS among US women: minority and young women at continuing risk. Atlanta (GA): CDC; August 1999.

2. Center for Disease Control. HIV/AIDS surveillance by race/ethnicity. Atlanta (GA): CDC; August 4, 1999.

3. Palacio H, Shiboski CH, Yelin EH, et al. Access to and utilization of primary care services among HIV-infected women. J Acquir Immune Defic Syndr 1999; 21:293–300.

4. Wyatt GE, Moe A, Guthrie D. The gynecological, reproductive, and sexual health of HIV-positive women. Cultural Diversity Ethnic Minority Psychol 1999;5:183–96.

5. Rich JD, Buck A, Tuomala RE, et al. Transmission of human immunodeficiency virus infection presumed to have occurred via female homosexual contact. Clin Infect Dis 1993;17:1003–5.

6. Quinn TC, Glasser D, Cannon RO, et al. Human immunodeficiency virus infection among patients attending clinics for sexually transmitted diseases. N Engl J Med 1988;318:197–204.

7. McCombs SB, McCray E, Frey RL, et al. Behaviors of heterosexual sexually transmitted disease clinic patients with sex partners at increased risk for human immunodeficiency virus infection. Sex Transm Dis 1999;24:461–8.

8. Madge S, Olaitan A, Mocroft A, et al. Access to medical care one year prior to diagnosis in 100 HIV-positive women. Fam Pract 1997;14:255–7.

9. Carusi D, Learman LA, Posner SF. Human immunodeficiency virus test refusal in pregnancy: a challenge to voluntary testing. Obstet Gynecol 1998; 91:540–4.

10. Palella FJ Jr, Delaney KM, Moorman AC, et al. Declining morbiditiy and mortality among patients with advanced human immunodeficiency virus infection. N Engl J Med 1998;338:853–60.

11. Marx R, Chang SW, Park MS, Katz MH. Reducing financial barriers to HIV-related medical care: does the Ryan White CARE Act make a difference? AIDS Care 1988;10:611–6.

12. Center for Disease Control. AIDS mortality. Atlanta (GA): CDC; March 11, 1999.

13. Stern MD, Piette J, Mor V, et al. Differences in access to zidovudine (AZT) among symptomatic HIV-infected persons. J Gen Intern Med 1991;6:35–40.

14. Irwin K, Olivo N, Schable CA, et al. Performance characteristics of a rapid HIV antibody assay in a hospital with a high prevalence of HIV infection. Ann Intern Med 1996;125:471–5.

15. Rapid HIV testing. MMWR Morb Mortal Wkly Rep 1998;47:211–4.

16. Public Health Service Task Force recommendations for the use of antiretroviral drugs in pregnant women infected with HIV-1 for maternal health and for reducing perinatal HIV-1 transmission in the United States. MMWR Morb Mortal Wkly Rep 1998 Apr 17;47(14): 287 and Apr 24;47(15):315.

17. Stephenson J. Perinatal HIV prevention. JAMA 1999;282:625.

18. Demeter LM, Reichman RC. Detection of human immunodeficiency virus infection. In: Mandell GL, Bennett JE, Dolin R, editors. Principles and practice

of infectious diseases. 5th ed. Churchill Livingston; 2000. p. 1369–74.

19. HIV/AIDS. In: Bartlett JG, editor. Pocket book of infectious diseases. Lippincott Williams and Wilkins; 2000. p. 319–22.

20. Schuman P, Sobel JD, Ohmit SE, et al. Mucosal candidal colonization and candidiasis in women with or at risk for human immunodeficiency virus infection. Clin Infect Dis 1998;27:1161–7.

21. Schuman P, Capps L, Peng G, et al. Weekly fluconazole for the prevention of mucosal candidiasis in women with HIV infection. Ann Intern Med 1997;126: 689–96.

22. Chin KM, Sidhu JS, Janssen RS, et al. Invasive cervical cancer in human immunodeficiency virus–infected and uninfected hospital patients. Obstet Gynecol 1998;92:83–6.

23. Ho GYF, Bierman R, Beardsley L, et al. Natural history of cervicovaginal papillomavirus infection in young women. N Engl J Med 1998;338:423–8.

24. Eisenstat SA, Bancroft L. Domestic violence. N Engl J Med 1999;341:886–92.

25. Axelrod J, Myers HF, Durvasula RS, et al. The impact of relationship violence, HIV, and ethnicity on adjustment in women. Cultural Diversity Ethnic Minority Psychol 1999;5:263–75.

26. Inciardi JA. Crack, crack house sex, and HIV risk. Arch Sex Behav 1995;24:149–69.

27. Fogel CI, Belya M. The lives of incarcerated women: violence, substance abuse, and at Risk for HIV. J Assoc Nurses AIDS Care 1999;10(6):66–74.

28. Opravil M, Pechare M, Spreich R, et al. HIV associated primary pulmonary hypertension. A case control Study. Swiss HIV cohort study.

29. Rompalo AM, Astemborski J, Schoenbaum E, et al. Comparison of clinical manifestations of HIV infection among women by risk group, CD4 cell count, and HIV-1 plasma viral load. J Acquir Immune Defic Syndr Hum Retrovirol 1999;20:448–54.

30. Barton JC, Buchness MR. Nongenital dermatologic disease in HIV-infected women. J Am Acad Dermatol 1999;40:938–48.

31. Iman N, Carpenter CC, Mayer KH, et al. Hierarchical pattern of mucosal *Candida* infections in HIV-seropositive women. Am J Med 1990;89:142–6.

32. Cohen CR, Sinei S, Reilly M, et al. Effect of human immunodeficiency virus type 1 infection upon acute salpingitis: a laparoscopic study. J Infect Dis 1998; 178:1352–8.

33. Sun XW, Kuhn L, Ellerbrock TV, et al. Human papillomavirus infection in women infected with the human immunodeficiency virus. N Engl J Med 1997; 337:1343–58.

34. Luque AE, Demeter LM, Reichman RC. Association of human papillomavirus infection and disease with magnitude of human immunodeficiency virus type 1 (HIV-1) RNA plasma level among women with HIV-1 infection. J Infect Dis 1999;179:1405–9.

35. Rugpao S, Nagachinta T, Wanapirak C, et al. Gynaecological conditions associated with HIV infection in women who are partners of HIV-positive Thai blood donors. Int J STD AIDS 1998;9:677–82.

36. Goldie SJ, Weinstein MC, Kuntz KM, et al. The costs, clinical benefits, and cost-effectiveness of screening for cervical cancer in HIV-infected women. Ann Intern Med 1999;130:97–106.

37. Clark RA, Bessinger R. Clinical manifestations and predictors of survival in older women infected with HIV. J Acquir Immune Defic Syndr Hum Retrovirol 1997;15:341–5.

38. Webber MP, Schoenbaum EE, Gourevitch MN, et al. A prospective study of HIV disease progression in female and male drug users. AIDS 1999;13: 257–62.

39. Mellors JW, Rinaldo CR Jr, Gupta P, et al. Prognosis in HIV-1 infection predicted by the quantity of virus in plasma. Science 1996;272:1167–70.

40. Farzadegan H, Hoover DR, Astemborski J, et al. Sex differences in HIV-1 viral load and progression to AIDS. Lancet 1998;352:1510–4.

41. Angstos K, Gange SJ, Law B, et al. Gender specific differences in quantitative HIV RNA levels [abstract]. Presented at the 6th Conference in Retrovirus and Opportunistic Infections. 1999 Jan 31–Feb 4; Chicago (IL). p. 274.

42. Gielan AC, O'Campo P, Faden RR, et al. Women's disclosure of HIV status: experiences of mistreatment and violence in an urban setting. Women Health 1997;25(3):19–31.

43. Fiscus SA, Adimora AA, Schoenbach VJ, et al. Trends in human immunodeficiency virus (HIV) counseling, testing, and antiretroviral treatment of HIV-infected women and perinatal transmission in North Carolina. J Infect Dis 1999;180:99–104.

44. Mofenson LM, Lambert JS, Stiehm R, et al. Risk factors for perinatal transmission of human immunodeficiency virus type 1 in women treated with zidovudine. N Engl J Med 1999;341:385–92.

45. Nicolosi A, Musicco M, Saracco A, et al. Risk factors for woman-to-man sexual transmission of the human immunodeficiency virus. J Acquir Immune Defic Syndr 1994;7:296–300.

46. Saracco A, Musicco M, Nicolosi A, et al. Man-to-woman sexual transmission of HIV: longitudinal study of 343 steady partners of infected men. J Acquir Immune Defic Syndr 1993;6:497–502.

47. Padian NS, Shiboski SL, Glass DD, et al. Heterosexual transmission of human immunodeficiency virus (HIV) in Northern California results from a ten-year study. Am J Epidemiol 1997;146:350–7.

48. Vincenzi I. A longitudinal study of human immunodeficiency virus transmission by heterosexual partners. N Engl J Med 1994;331:341–6.

49. Quinn TC, Wawer MJ, Sewankambo N, et al. Viral load and heterosexual transmission of human immunodeficiency virus type 1. Rakai Project Study Group. N Engl J Med 2000;342:921–9.

50. Royce RA, Sena A, Cates William Jr, et al. Sexual transmission of HIV. N Engl J Med 1997;336:1072–8.

51. Bertolli J, St. Louis ME, Simonds RJ, et al. Estimating the timing of mother-to-child transmission of human immunodeficiency virus in a breast-feeding population in Kinshasa, Zaire. J Infect Dis 1996; 174:722–6.

52. Padian NS, O'Brien TR, Chang Y, et al. Prevention of heterosexual transmission of human immunodeficiency virus through couple counseling. J Acquir Immune Defic Syndr 1993;6:1043–8.

53. Choi KH, Rickman R, Catania JA. What heterosexual adults believe about condoms. N Engl J Med 1994; 331:406–7.

54. Rothenberg KH, Paskey SJ. The risk of domestic violence and women with HIV infection: implications for partner notification, public policy, and the law. Am J Public Health 1995;85:1569–76.

55. Gilchrest BA. Partner notification and the threat of domestic violence against women with HIV infection. N Engl J Med 1993;329:1194.

56. Dickover RE, Garratty EM, Herman SA, et al. Identification of levels of maternal HIV-1 RNA associated with risk of perinatal transmission. Effects of maternal zidovudine treatment in viral load. JAMA 1996; 275:599–608.

57. Stringer JSA, Rouse DJ, Goldenberg RL. Prophylactic cesarean delivery for the prevention of perinatal human immunodeficiency virus transmission: the case for restraint. JAMA 1999;281:1946–9.

58. Andiman W, Boucher M, Burns D, et al. The mode of delivery and the risk of vertical transmission of human immunodeficiency virus type 1. N Engl J Med 1999;240:977–86.

59. Kitahata MM, Koepsell TD, Deyo RA, et al. Physicians' experience with the acquired immunodeficiency syndrome as a factor in patients' survival. N Engl J Med 1996;334:701–6.

60. Deschamps MM, Pape JW, Desvarieux M, et al. A prospective study of HIV-seropositive asymptomatic women of childbearing age in a developing county. J Acquir Immune Defic Syndr1993;6:446–51.

71

APPROACH TO THE

INTERNATIONAL TRAVELER

Claire Panosian, MD

Your patient is a professional in her mid-thirties, recently married and hoping to start a family soon. But before she does, she and her husband are planning their adventure-of-a-lifetime, an African safari. She breezes into your office. "Can I get shots and malaria pills next week?" she asks. "And oh, by the way," she adds, "I hope it's okay if we conceive on the trip."

Sound familiar? It should. In recent years, international travel has increased dramatically. In 1993, for example, roughly 27 million North Americans and 18 million Europeans traveled to developing countries in Asia, Africa, and Latin America. Worldwide, annual international tourist arrivals number close to 500 million.

This boom in overseas travel has had medical by-products. In the past decade, travel medicine has become a bona fide specialty complete with journals, textbooks, and an international certifying examination. In recent years, global disease surveillance and communications have also improved, yielding rapid intelligence to clinicians and patients. In practicing travel medicine, there is just one caveat: stay on top of new information. Fortunately, with modern computer links, the tools are here.

This chapter highlights some modern ABCs of pretravel health care for adults and pregnant women, as well as current strategies to thwart microbial stowaways in patients visiting a far-off land.

BEFORE YOU GO: GENERAL RESOURCES FOR PATIENT AND CLINICIAN

The starting point for designing health advice for travel is a database that details the itinerary, pro-

jected length of stay, style of travel, medications and allergies, immunization history, and medical history of the patient, as well as current or anticipated pregnancy in women of childbearing age. After listing destinations, travelers or their clinicians may then review country-specific regulations and health risks by consulting the Centers for Disease Control and Prevention (CDC) Web site. Another standard reference on the worldwide distribution of infectious diseases is an annual CDC publication, *Health Information for International Travel* (available for purchase from the US Government Printing Office by calling 202-512-1800). A third set of resources offering general medical information for travel are recent manuals, reviews, and book chapters.[1-3]

Travel Immunization

Throughout the twentieth century, immunization has been a mainstay of travel disease prophylaxis. Over time, the design and manufacture of biologic products has improved, yielding products of increasing purity and efficacy.[4] When recommending a list of immunizations for travel, three categories of vaccines should be considered: (1) routine childhood and adult vaccines (eg, tetanus-diphtheria, poliomyelitis, measles, varicella, pneumococcal, and influenza), (2) required vaccines (eg, yellow fever, meningococcal meningitis, and cholera), and (3) recommended vaccines (eg, hepatitis A, hepatitis B, typhoid, rabies, and Japanese encephalitis). The following summaries highlight major clinical and epidemiologic indications for most of these vaccines. For more in-depth prescribing information on travel immunization, the reader is directed to several excellent reviews.[1-6]

Travel vaccinations should be entered in the yellow booklet entitled "International Certificates of Vaccination." This document is recognized by the World Health Organization (WHO) and provides a convenient lifelong immunization record for adults. It should be carried and stored with the traveler's passport.

Routine Childhood and Adult Immunizations

TETANUS-DIPHTHERIA

A single booster of tetanus-diphtheria (Td) vaccine should be given to all adults traveling overseas who have not received a booster within the preceding 5 to 10 years. Recent serologic surveys indicate that roughly 50% of senior citizens in the United States are susceptible to tetanus and diphtheria.[7] Between 1990 and 1996 a diphtheria outbreak in the former Union of Soviet Socialist Republic (USSR) caused more than 125,000 cases and 4,000 deaths, highlighting the potential risk of diphtheria to travelers.[8] Tetanus immunization circumvents the risk of exposing patients to vaccines and needles of dubious sterility following minor injuries overseas.

POLIOMYELITIS

Although the last case of poliomyelitis in the Americas occurred in 1991 and although global eradication is proceeding (an 85% reduction in cases over the last decade), wild-type poliovirus still circulates in many tropical and developing countries. As of 1996, WHO estimated the annual worldwide incidence of clinical infection at 90,000 cases per year. Adults visiting countries that continue to register significant poliovirus activity should either complete a series of enhanced inactivated poliovirus vaccine (eIPV) injections or receive a single eIPV booster. Oral poliovirus vaccine (OPV), which contains live virus, is no longer used in adults and should not be given to patients who are immunosuppressed or patients with family or household contacts who are immunosuppressed.

MEASLES

Between 1991 and 1994, 20% of measles (rubeola) cases in the United States were imported. Travelers who are nonimmune to measles by history or serologic testing should receive a single dose of live attenuated measles or measles-mumps-rubella (MMR) vaccine before leaving for a developing country. Patients born in the United States after 1957 generally are assumed to be nonimmune to measles and are now advised to receive two lifetime immunizations. Contraindications to adult measles vaccination are immunosuppression, pregnancy, or a history of anaphylactic allergy to eggs. In addition, pregnancy must be avoided for at least 3 months following MMR vaccination and for 1 month after monovalent measles vaccination. Measles and MMR vaccines are both ineffective if given concurrently with immune globulin.

Required Vaccines

SMALLPOX

The last case of naturally acquired smallpox is believed to have occurred in Somalia in 1977. In 1979, WHO declared the world to be smallpox free, and in the early 1980s WHO ceased its regulation of smallpox vaccine. Today, smallpox vaccine, which is available from CDC on a case-by-case basis, is administered only to selected laboratory and military personnel. Smallpox vaccination is not required for international travel.

YELLOW FEVER

Yellow fever (YF) virus is found in tropical South America and equatorial Africa between 15° south latitude and 15° north latitude. In general, visitors traveling outside of urban areas in these regions should receive YF vaccination. However, regulations regarding vaccination vary among countries within and beyond the endemic zone. Some African nations require a current certificate of YF vaccination of all entering travelers whereas other non-endemic countries in Africa, South America, and Asia require vaccination of travelers who have recently visited an endemic locale, even in transit. For re-entry into the United States, no requirements exist. For further information, consult the CDC Web site or CDC's annual publication, *Health Information for International Travel*.

Yellow fever vaccine consists of live attenuated virus grown in eggs. It should be given to pregnant women and patients with altered cellular immunity or known hypersensitivity to eggs only when exposure is completely unavoidable. The vaccine must be administered by an approved YF vaccine center, accompanied by a signed and validated International Certificate of Vaccination. Boosters are required every 10 years.

MENINGOCOCCAL MENINGITIS

Epidemics of meningococcal infection are common in the sub-Saharan "meningitis belt" that stretches from Senegal to Ethiopia; recently, outbreaks have also occurred in Kenya, Tanzania, Burundi, Mongolia, northern India, Nepal, and Saudi Arabia. Saudi Arabia requires a certificate of meningococcal immunization of all pilgrims to Mecca. The current meningococcal polysaccharide vaccine protects against *Neisseria meningitidis* serogroups A, C, Y, and W135; it does not protect against serogroup B. The vaccine should be considered for travelers who anticipate significant respiratory contact in high-risk areas, particularly during dry or winter months.

CHOLERA

Although cholera remains a global problem, the risk of cholera in travelers is extremely low (less than 1 per 100,000), with a case fatality rate of less than 2%. The traditional phenol-killed whole-cell cholera vaccine administered by injection has a short-term efficacy of less than 50%; most authorities agree that it is now obsolete. Newer vaccines not yet licensed in the United States provide 60 to 80% protection for 6 months to 1 year but are not effective against *Vibrio cholerae* serotype 0139, the cholera strain currently spreading throughout Asia. Consequently, most overseas travelers neither need nor benefit from cholera vaccine. Rare exceptions include individuals who are post-gastrectomy or otherwise hypochlorhydric, and health care workers and other volunteers whose work exposes them to epidemic conditions.

Although no country officially requires cholera vaccination for entry, documentation is periodically requested at certain borders. A clinician-signed waiver in the International Certificate of Vaccination usually satisfies this demand.

Recommended Vaccines

HEPATITIS A

Hepatitis A is the most common vaccine-preventable disease of overseas travelers. Between 1977 and 1981 the mean attack rate in Swiss travelers was 80 per 100,000 for visitors to North and sub-Saharan Africa; the Near, Middle, and Far East; and Central and South America. The mortality rate from hepatitis A increases with age, reaching 2% or higher in patients over 40 years of age.

Although immune globulin has traditionally been used to protect travelers against hepatitis A, its disadvantages include discomfort with administration and a theoretic risk of transmitting blood-borne viruses. Consequently, the recent licensing of two highly immunogenic formalin-inactivated vaccines prepared from whole hepatitis A virus has made prophylactic immune globulin virtually obsolete. A single dose of either vaccine administered 2 weeks before travel confers protection in 70 to 85% of vacinees; seroconversion approaches 100% following a second dose given 6 to 12 months later.

HEPATITIS B

Of the current world population, more than 2 billion people have been infected with hepatitis B, and 350 million are chronic carriers. Carriers are concentrated in Asia, sub-Saharan Africa, and the Amazon basin of South America. Visitors to these (and other) areas who will have an increased risk of exposure to hepatitis B (for example, through medical work, through receiving local medical or dental care, or through engaging in sex with local residents), as well as visitors who plan to stay for more than 3 months, should undergo hepatitis B vaccination. The currently available recombinant vaccines are highly effective and may provide lifelong protection.

In addition, many experts now believe that hepatitis B vaccination should be administered universally, regardless of travel itinerary or individual risk of infection.

TYPHOID FEVER

Three commercial typhoid vaccines are currently available in the United States: (1) an oral live attenuated vaccine made from the noninvasive Ty21a strain of *Salmonella typhi*; (2) a parenteral purified polysaccharide vaccine called Vi CPS, which contains the cell surface virulence (Vi) antigen of *S. typhi*; and (3) parenteral heat/phenol-killed whole-cell vaccine. The oral vaccine, taken as four enteric-coated capsules over 7 days, is contraindicated in immunosuppressed hosts or for patients with gastrointestinal disease. Administration of oral typhoid vaccine with concurrent antibiotics or mefloquine should also be avoided. Among parenteral vaccines, a single dose of Vi CPS is preferred over whole-cell vaccine because of the decreased local and systemic side effects and enhanced immunogenicity of Vi CPS.

Of all cases of typhoid fever reported in the United States each year, more than half are acquired abroad. The average risk of typhoid is 1 per 30,000 per month of stay in most developing countries; the risk is higher in India and parts of Africa. Although no typhoid vaccine provides more than 80% protection, immunization is recommended, especially for expatriates returning home to high-risk countries and for travelers with itineraries that are "off the beaten path."

RABIES

At least 50,000 deaths from rabies are reported annually to WHO, primarily due to dog and cat bites. Dog rabies is endemic in Mexico, El Salvador, Guatemala, Peru, Colombia, Ecuador, India, Nepal, the Philippines, Sri Lanka, Thailand, and Vietnam, and is well established in most other countries of Africa, Asia, and Central and South America. Pre-exposure vaccination with three injections of human diploid cell vaccine (HDCV) or purified chick embryo cell vaccine (PCECV) is recommended for expatriates residing in high-risk countries, as well as for long-stay visitors engaging in activities (for example, field research, bicycling, or jogging) that increase the risk of animal bites. Chloroquine and mefloquine interfere with the immune response to HDCV given intradermally but not with the immune response to HDCV given intramuscularly.

After being bitten or scratched by a potentially rabid animal, immunized travelers still need intramuscular boosters on days 0 and 3 following exposure.

JAPANESE ENCEPHALITIS

Although most infections caused by the mosquito-borne Japanese encephalitis (JE) virus are asymptomatic, up to 30% of the minority of patients who develop encephalitis die, and 50% experience severe neurologic sequelae. A three-dose series of formalin-inactivated mouse brain–derived JE vaccine is therefore advised for mid- or long-stay travelers to rural Asia who anticipate frequent mosquito bites. In contrast, short-stay travelers to Asian cities have minimal risk and are rarely candidates for JE vaccination.

Countries endemic for JE virus are Bangladesh, Cambodia, China, India, Indonesia, Korea, Laos, Malaysia, Myanmar, Nepal, Pakistan, the Philippines, Singapore, Sri Lanka, Taiwan, Thailand, Vietnam, and eastern Russia. In temperate areas, JE is transmitted in summer and fall; in tropical areas, JE transmission occurs year-round or varies with local patterns of rainfall, irrigation, and rice and pig cultivation.

The side effects of JE vaccination include local reactions at the site of vaccination in 20% of recipients, systemic reactions in 10% of recipients, and severe allergic reactions (including urticaria and angioedema) in 0.1% of vaccinees.

OVERSEAS HEALTH HAZARDS

Malaria

At the end of the twentieth century, malaria remains the single most important parasitic disease of humans. Throughout the tropics, it causes 1 to 2 million deaths per year, primarily in children, and up to 500 million symptomatic infections in persons of all ages. *Plasmodium falciparum*, which causes the greatest malaria mortality, is still transmitted in Africa, East Asia, Oceania, Papua New Guinea, Haiti, and parts of South America. *Plasmodium vivax* predominates in Central America, North Africa, the Middle East, and the Indian subcontinent. The remaining two species of malarial parasites that infect humans—*Plasmodium ovale* and *Plasmodium malariae*—are rare outside of Africa.

Although a comprehensive review of malaria is beyond the scope of this chapter, every clinician who provides pretravel counsel should be familiar with the transmission, parasite life cycle, and clinical manifestations of malaria, as well as its chemoprophylaxis. In brief, the vector of malaria is the *Anopheles* mosquito, which feeds between dusk and dawn. After an infected mosquito inoculates a human with malaria sporozoites, the parasite matures in the liver (this takes a minimum of 7 to 10 days) prior to its release into the bloodstream, an event corresponding with the onset of fever and hemolysis. Although infections due to *Plasmodium vivax*, *Plasmodium ovale*, and *Plasmodium malariae* can remain latent for months to years, most cases of *Plasmodium falciparum* infection in nonimmune travelers become symptomatic within 1 to 3 months of exposure. (For further information on the clinical manifestations and treatment of malaria, the reader is directed to the recent review article by N. J. White.[9])

Travelers visiting malaria-endemic areas can decrease anopheline bites by applying insect repellants containing 20 to 35% N,N-diethyl-*m*-toluamide

TABLE 71–1. Drugs Used for Prevention of Malaria

Drug	Adult Dosage
Mefloquine (Lariam)	228 mg base (250 mg salt) every wk*
Doxycycline (Vibramycin)	100 mg qd†
Atovaquone/proguanil (Malarone)	250 mg atovaquone 1100 mg proguanil qd‡
Chloroquine phosphate (Aralen)	300 mg base (500 mg salt) every wk*
Hydroxyquine chloroquine sulfate (Plaquenil)	310 mg base (400 mg salt) every wk*
Primaquine§	15 mg base (26.3 mg salt) qd × 14

*Begin 1 to 2 weeks before exposure to malaria and continue 4 weeks beyond.
†Begin 1 to 2 days before exposure to malaria and continue 4 weeks beyond.
‡Begin 1 to 2 days before exposure and continue 7 days beyond. Take with food or milky drink.
§Terminal prophylaxis for latent infections due to *Plasmodium vivax* and *Plasmodium ovale* following prolonged exposure in malaria-endemic regions.

(DEET) to exposed skin and permethrin-based insecticide spray to their clothing, tents, and/or bed-nets. Malaria chemoprophylaxis is given according to known geographic patterns of antiplasmodial-drug susceptibility and resistance. Currently, chloroquine-resistant strains of *P. falciparum* are prevalent in all *P. falciparum*–endemic regions, with the exception of Hispaniola, Egypt, most countries of the Middle East, and Central America west of the Panama Canal Zone. Chloroquine- and primaquine-resistant strains of *Plasmodium vivax* are established in Papua New Guinea, Southeast Asia, and the Amazon basin. As a result, mefloquine (a quinoline-methanol compound), since the late 1980s, has largely replaced chloroquine as the preventive drug of choice for at-risk travelers to Africa, Asia, and tropical South America.

Although mefloquine is effective, there are important restrictions on its use. Mefloquine is contraindicated for patients with epilepsy, severe depression, psychosis, cardiac arrhythmia, or cardiac conduction disorders. Because it is metabolized by the liver, it also should be avoided in patients with hepatic dysfunction. Mefloquine can be used with caution in patients on ß-blockers for hypertension and in women in their second or third trimester of pregnancy (it is still contraindicated in the first trimester). Prescribers should alert all mefloquine users of possible dysphoria, dizziness, insomnia, nightmares, nausea, and headache and should advise discontinuation if severe side effects occur while overseas. One alternative to mefloquine is doxycycline, except for pregnant women and for children under 8 years of age, for whom doxycycline

is contraindicated. Malarone, a newly approved combination of atovaquone and proguanil, also protects against *P. falciparum* malaria, including chloroquine-resistant strains. In the few areas where mefloquine-resistant *Plasmodium falciparum* has been documented (eg, the Thai-Cambodian and Thai-Burmese borders), either doxycycline or malarone is an effective preventative drug.

Some travelers may also need empiric standby treatment for malaria. This treatment usually consists of three tablets of pyrimethamine-sulfadoxine (Fansidar) and is prescribed when an individual is taking a less effective prophylaxis (eg, chloroquine or proguanil) or has limited access to health care overseas. Patients should take pyrimethamine-sulfadoxine only if professional medical care is not available within 24 hours of the onset of fever, and they should seek attention soon after. In patients allergic to sulfa, pyrimethamine-sulfadoxine is strictly contraindicated because it induces Stevens-Johnson syndrome.[10] Malarone is now another option for presumptive self-treatment for travelers not taking Malarone for prophylaxis.

Table 71–1 lists the drugs and dosing schedules most commonly used for the prevention of malaria worldwide.

Other Vector-Borne Infections

Overseas travelers need to know that insect bites can transmit infections other than malaria. Day-biting *Aedes* and *Culex* mosquitoes, for example, are vectors of dengue fever and JE. In Africa, hard-backed ticks transmit the rickettsial pathogens

Rickettsia conorii and *Rickettsia africae*. Mites in Southeast Asia transmit another rickettsial pathogen, *Rickettsia tsutsugamushi*, the agent of scrub typhus. Tsetse flies and kissing or cone-nosed bugs are the respective vectors of African and South American trypanosomiasis, also known as Chagas' disease. Both in the Old World and the New World, sandflies transmit cutaneous leishmaniasis, an ulceronodular skin infection especially troublesome among visitors to the coastal jungles of Costa Rica and other parts of tropical Latin America.

With the exception of JE vaccination, insect repellents and insecticide sprays are the sole means of preventing the vector-borne infections listed above.

Travelers' Diarrhea

Diarrhea is the most common medical ailment of international travelers, typically affecting 20 to 50% of all European and North American visitors to developing countries.[11] The incidence of travelers' diarrhea is highest in infants and children (probably related to their decreased output of gastric acid and immature intestinal host defenses), followed by young adults (whose adventurous eating practices often place them at increased risk). Although etiologic agents are numerous and include bacteria, viruses, and parasites, enterotoxigenic *Escherichia coli* (ETEC) is the most common causative pathogen, followed in many adult series by *Campylobacter* spp, Norwalk virus, and the protozoan *Giardia lamblia*.

Prevention of travelers' diarrhea begins with common-sense food and water precautions. Bismuth subsalicylate (Pepto-Bismol) taken at a dosage of 2 tablets or 4 tablespoons (60 mL) four times a day also significantly decreases the likelihood of diarrhea, although clinicians should remember that this regimen includes an amount of salicylate roughly equivalent to eight 325-mg aspirin tablets per day. Rarely, antibiotic prophylaxis (eg, daily doxycycline, trimethoprim-sulfamethoxazole [TMP/SMX], or a quinolone antibiotic) is indicated for short trips when even a single day of illness might interfere with the intended purpose of travel. However, for most travelers, empiric self-treatment at the onset of diarrhea is most useful. Depending on the severity and the nature of symptoms, treatment may include oral rehydration, antimotility drugs, bismuth subsalicylate, and/or a 1- to 3-day course of antibiotics aimed at ETEC (quinolones are preferred, followed by TMP/SMX). Ciprofloxacin (500 mg one PO twice daily for 1 to 3 days) is commonly prescribed for this purpose.

Any intestinal illness acquired overseas that includes high fever (>38.9°C), severe abdominal pain, or the passage of grossly bloody stools merits prompt medical evaluation. However, if self-treatment is the only option in this circumstance, antibiotics should be taken, and antimotility treatment should be avoided.

Sexually Transmitted Infections

Statistically, the anonymity of international travel enhances the risk and opportunity of acquiring a sexually transmitted infection.[12] In two recent surveys, 5% of British travelers and 6% of Swiss travelers acknowledged having had casual sex while abroad.[3] Rates rise even higher for long-term visitors. In a study of 2,000 Dutch expatriates working in Africa (of whom only 25% reported consistent condom use), 31% of the men and 13% of the women had sex with local partners.[3]

Sexual restraint (in particular, abstinence), limiting sexual contact to a known partner, and safe sex practices are appropriate pretravel counsel for young adults, in particular. In addition, depending on the country, pretravel screening for human immunodeficiency virus (HIV) or in-country testing for HIV may be required of returning nationals, applicants for long-term residence or citizenship, and foreign students, residents, and guest-workers.

Environmental Infectious Hazards and Noninfectious Hazards

Exposure to freshwater in parts of South America, the Caribbean, Africa, the Middle East, and Southeast Asia can result in schistosomiasis, a helminthic disease that currently infects more than 200 million people worldwide. If complete avoidance of infested waters is not possible, the risk of schistosomiasis decreases if swimming is restricted to fast-moving water and if bathers towel themselves promptly after emerging, thus hindering skin penetration by parasite larvae. Another infection associated with freshwater and freshwater activities (including river rafting) is leptospirosis. In high-risk settings, leptospirosis can be prevented by taking prophylactic doxycycline (200 mg weekly). Walking barefoot or in sandals can lead to skin penetration by human and animal hookworm larvae and by *Strongyloides*; additional hazards of walking barefoot include tungiasis (skin infestation by burrowing sand fleas), snakebites, and plant and marine trauma predisposing to both typical and atypical bacterial infections.

Although infectious diseases are a significant source of travel-associated morbidity, they actually account for only 1 to 4% of deaths among travelers. Cardiovascular disease, accidents, and injuries are the most frequent causes of death among travelers.[3]

TRAVEL ADVICE FOR PREGNANT WOMEN

The benefits of travel should always be weighed against the potential risk to a pregnant mother or her baby. In addition to seeking advice regarding immunization, malaria prevention, and travelers' diarrhea, pregnant women should also prepare for overseas travel by identifying available overseas medical services, health insurance coverage for pregnancy-related complications or delivery overseas, and a checklist of signs and symptoms for which emergency obstetric care might be required. (For a detailed referenced discussion on all of the above, the reader is directed to the recent review by Samuel and Barry.[13])

Vaccination

Live-virus vaccines are contraindicated during pregnancy, except for YF vaccine for patients at special risk for this infection. Killed vaccines are generally safe although the benefits of vaccination should always outweigh potential risks. In every case it is recommended to defer immunization until after the first trimester.

Malaria Prophylaxis

Whenever possible, pregnant women should avoid travel to areas of chloroquine-resistant malaria because the most effective antimalarial regimens for these regions have neither been adequately studied nor sanctioned, especially during the first trimester of pregnancy. Moreover, maternal malaria during pregnancy causes anemia and placental insufficiency and can promote intrauterine growth retardation, prematurity, low birth weight, abortion, and stillbirth. When travel to malarious areas during pregnancy is unavoidable, the safest (although not fully protective) chemoprophylaxis is weekly chloroquine (see Table 71–1 for dosage); in addition, weekly mefloquine can now be used, with caution, during the second and third trimesters of pregnancy in high-risk patients. Since there is insufficient data regarding Malarone during pregnancy, Malarone is not currently recommended for prevention of malaria in pregnant women. The use of insect repellants and bednets are important adjunct measures. Primaquine (the only agent that eradicates latent *Plasmodium vivax* and *Plasmodium ovale* in the liver) and doxycyline are both contraindicated during pregnancy.

Travelers' Diarrhea

Since treatment of travelers' diarrhea in pregnant women is complicated by several relative contraindications, adherence to safe food and water precautions is imperative. In particular, pregnant women traveling overseas should drink only boiled or bottled beverages. If necessary, short-term use (< 3 weeks) of iodine-purified water is also permissible; however, prolonged use of iodine-treated water in pregnancy can adversely affect the fetal thyroid gland.

In preventing and treating travelers' diarrhea during pregnancy, bismuth subsalicylate should be used conservatively since high doses of bismuth are teratogenic in sheep and because large quantities of salicylates in humans are both teratogenic and promote fetal bleeds.

With respect to antibiotic treatment of travelers' diarrhea, TMP/SMX use is restricted to the second trimester, and doxycycline and quinolone antibiotics are contraindicated throughout pregnancy. Safe antibiotic alternatives in pregnancy are erythromycin and third-generation cephalosporins, which are effective against some bacterial causes of travelers' diarrhea. In addition, the antimotility drugs loperamide and diphenoxylate have been used in pregnancy. Neither is teratogenic although both exert a mild narcotic effect that could enhance neonatal respiratory depression if taken near term.

Other Issues

Since pregnancy predisposes to venous and thromboembolic disease, pregnant women traveling long distances should avoid prolonged immobilization and should wear elastic support hose from foot to waist. Air travel during the last month of pregnancy should be avoided altogether. Both domestic and international airline regulations stipulate no travel by pregnant women beyond a fixed period of gestation, usually 35 or 36 weeks. In the later months of pregnancy, a note signed by the patient's clinician specifying the expected date of delivery is also required by many carriers.

RESOURCE

The Centers for Disease Control and Prevention
1600 Clifton Road
Atlanta, Georgia 30333
Telephone: (404) 639-3311
          1-800-311-3435 (Public inquiries)
Fax: 1-888-232-3299 (Travel information)
Web site: www.cdc.gov

The Centers for Disease Control and Prevention (CDC) Web site provides detailed regional information (including updates on disease outbreaks) for international travelers and their health care clinicians. Recommended vaccinations and malaria prophylaxis are included, as well as other health advice. Information for international travelers can also be requested via phone and fax.

REFERENCES

1. Jong EC, McMullen R, editors. The travel and tropical medicine manual. 2nd ed. Philadelphia: WB Saunders Company; 1995.

2. Wolfe MS. Protection of travelers. Clin Infect Dis 1997;25:177–84.

3. Keystone JS, Kozarsky PE. Health advice for international travel. In: Guerrant RL, WalkerDH, Weller PF, editors. Tropical infectious diseases. Philadelphia: Churchill Livingstone; 1999.

4. McDonnell WM, Askari FK. Immunization. JAMA 1997;278:2000–7.

5. Jong EC. Immunizations for international travel. Infect Dis Clin North Am 1998;12:249–66.

6. Thanassi WT. Immunizations for international travelers. West J Med 1998;168:197–202.

7. Weiss BP, Strassburg MA, Feeley JC. Tetanus and diphtheria immunity in an elderly population in Los Angeles County. Am J Public Health 1983;73:802–4.

8. Update. Diphtheria epidemic—new independent states of the former Soviet Union, January 1995-March 1996. MMWR Morb Motility Mkly Rep 1996;45:693–7.

9. White NJ. The treatment of malaria. N Engl J Med 1996;335:800–6.

10. Miller KD, Lobel HO, Satriale RF, et al. Severe cutaneous reactions among American travelers using pyrimethamine-sulfadoxine (Fansidar) for malaria prophylaxis. Am J Trop Med Hyg 1986;35:451–8.

11. Passaro DJ, Parsonnet J. Advances in the prevention and management of traveler's diarrhea. Curr Clin Top Infect Dis 1998;18:217–36.

12. Mulhall BP. Sex and travel: studies of sexual behaviours, disease and health promotion in international travelers—a global review. Int J STD AIDS 1996; 7:455–65.

13. Samuel BU, Barry M. The pregnant traveler. Infect Dis Clin North Am 1998;12:325–54.

72

SEXUALLY TRANSMITTED DISEASES

Joseph Russo, MD

Sexually transmitted diseases (STDs) are among the most common infectious diseases in the United States today. More than 20 STDs have now been identified, and they affect more than 13 million men and women in the United States each year. Chlamydial infection is now the most common of all bacterial STDs, with 607,602 infections reported to US Centers for Disease Control and Prevention (CDC) in 1998. Genital herpes affects an estimated 60 million Americans. Approximately 500,000 new cases of this incurable viral infection develop annually. Genital warts infect an estimated 1 million Americans each year. In 1998, 355,642 cases of gonorrhea were reported to the CDC. The incidence of syphilis has decreased dramatically in recent years; 6,993 cases of primary and secondary syphilis were reported in 1998. Other diseases that may be sexually transmitted include chancroid, granuloma inguinale, hepatitis B, lymphogranuloma venereum, molluscum contagiosum, scabies, pubic lice, and human immunodeficiency virus (HIV) infection. The annual comprehensive cost of STDs in the United States is estimated to be well in excess of $10 billion.[1]

Sexually transmitted diseases affect men and women of all backgrounds and economic levels. They are most prevalent among teenagers and young adults. Nearly two-thirds of all cases of STDs occur in people younger than 25 years of age. The incidence of STDs is rising, partly because in the last few decades, young people have become sexually active earlier yet are marrying later. In addition, divorce is more common. The net result is that sexually active people today are more likely to have multiple sex partners during their lives and are potentially at risk for developing STDs.

Most of the time, STDs cause no symptoms, particularly in women. When and if symptoms develop, they may be confused with those of other diseases not transmitted through sexual contact. Even when an STD causes no symptoms, however, a person who is infected may be able to pass the disease on to a sex partner. That is why many experts recommend periodic testing or screening for people who have more than one sex partner.

Health problems caused by STDs tend to be more severe and more frequent for women than for men, partly because the frequency of asymptomatic infection means that many women do not seek care until serious problems have developed. When diagnosed and treated early, many STDs can be treated effectively. Some infections have become resistant to the drugs used to treat them and now require newer types of antibiotics.[2] The Centers for Disease Control and Prevention publish STD treatment guidelines.[3] The most recent were published in 1998 and are quoted in this chapter. Human immunodeficiency virus is discussed separately in Chapter 10.

Many STDs are uncomplicated. Many have long-term consequences. Some are life threatening. Therefore, prevention should be the primary focus when dealing with them. Individuals at risk for transmitting or acquiring infections must change their behaviors to prevent the spread of STDs. The health care clinician has an opportunity to deliver prevention messages with respect, compassion, and a nonjudgmental attitude. Pre-exposure vaccination is available for potential exposure to hepatitis B. When used correctly, male condoms prevent the transmission of many STDs.[4] Although no clinical studies have been completed to evaluate the effectiveness of female condoms, laboratory studies indicate that the female condom is an effective mechanical barrier to viruses and should therefore reduce the risk for STDs. Vaginal spermicides reduce the risk of cervical gonorrhea and chlamydial infection. Diaphragm use provides protection against cervical gonorrhea and infection with *Chlamydia* and *Trichomonas*.[5]

The accurate and timely reporting of STDs is an important part of infection control. Syphilis, gonorrhea, and acquired immunodeficiency syndrome (AIDS) are reportable diseases in every state. Chlamydial infection is reportable in most states. The requirements for reporting other STDs differ by state.

GENITAL ULCER SYNDROMES

The genital ulcer syndromes include herpes simplex, syphilis, chancroid, and lymphogranuloma venereum. The most common sexually transmitted cause of genital ulcers is herpes simplex.

Herpes Simplex Virus

Genital herpes is a recurrent and incurable viral disease. The herpes simplex virus (HSV) is transmitted by direct contact with infected secretions. There are two serotypes: HSV-1, usually associated with lesions above the umbilicus or oral/facial lesions, and HSV-2, associated with genital and neonatal lesions.

Initial infection with HSV may be mild, presenting with a flulike syndrome. Two-thirds of infected women have dysuria and vulvar tenderness. Not all cases have the classic symptoms of painful vesicular lesions and bilateral inguinal adenopathy.[6] Symptoms usually appear within a week of exposure to the virus, and viral shedding continues for 7 to 10 days. Lesions may take 2 to 6 weeks to resolve completely. Many cases of genital herpes are transmitted by persons who are unaware that they have the infection or who are asymptomatic when transmission occurs.[7,8] Occasionally, the primary infection is severe, and patients can require hospitalization due to complications.

Approximately one-half of patients infected with HSV have a recurrence of symptoms within 6 months.[9] Recurrent disease is localized, with fewer and less painful lesions that resolve more rapidly than primary lesions (7 days).

Infection with HSV can sometimes be difficult to diagnose. Physical examination of the vulva is helpful when characteristic lesions are present. The lesions initially are fluid-filled vesicles, but they quickly ulcerate and coalesce, covering most of the vulva. The definitive diagnosis is made by culture. The false-negative rate is lowest when the culture is taken from the base of a vesicle within the first 24 to 48 hours and decreases significantly as the lesions ulcerate and become crusted. Serologic testing for HSV antibodies documents past infection but has no value for diagnosing primary infections.

Systemic antiviral drugs partially control the symptoms and signs of herpes episodes when used to treat first clinical episodes or recurrent episodes or when used as daily suppressive therapy. Suppressive therapy should be considered for patients suffering from frequent symptomatic recurrences. Topical therapy is substantially less effective, and its use is discouraged. Recommended treatment regimens are summarized in Table 72–1.

Syphilis

Syphilis is caused by a spirochete, *Treponema pallidum*. It is transmitted primarily by sexual contact.[10] There is a high transmission rate after one unprotected contact with an infected partner. The signs and symptoms of syphilis infection differ depending on whether the patient presents in the primary, secondary, latent, or tertiary stage of infection.

Patients who have syphilis may seek treatment for signs or symptoms of a primary infection (ulcer or chancre at the infection site), but this is not common because the chancre is painless. The chancre is indurated, with a smooth base and raised firm borders. It occurs at the entry point of the spirochete (cervix, vagina, vulva, or oropharynx). It appears from 10 to 90 days after infection, depending on inoculum size,[11] and resolves spontaneously within 3 to 6 weeks.

With the onset of low-grade fever, mucocutaneous lesions, rash (macular, papular, or papulosquamous) seen especially on the palms and soles, and adenopathy 6 weeks to 6 months later, the secondary stage of infection occurs. If untreated, the symptoms and signs resolve spontaneously, but tertiary infection follows after a latent phase that is quite variable. Latent syphilis is defined as syphilis diagnosed by serologic testing alone in a patient

TABLE 72–1. Treatment of Genital Herpes Simplex[*]

First episode	Acyclovir 400 mg PO tid × 7–10 d
	or
	Acyclovir 200 mg PO 5 times per day × 7–10 d
	or
	Famciclovir 250 mg PO tid × 7–10 d
	or
	Valacyclovir 1 gram PO bid 7–10 d
Episodic recurrent infection	Acyclovir 400 mg PO tid × 5 d
	or
	Acyclovir 200 mg PO 5 times per day × 5 d
	or
	Acyclovir 800 mg PO bid × 5 d
	or
	Famciclovir 125 mg PO bid × 5 d
	or
	Valacyclovir 500 mg PO bid × 5 d
Daily suppressive	Acyclovir 400 mg PO bid
	or
	Famciclovir 250 mg PO bid
	or
	Valacyclovir 250 mg PO bid
	or
	Valacyclovir 500–1000 mg qd
Severe disease[†]	Acyclovir 5–10 mg/kg IV q8h × 5–7 d

[*]The safety of these medications in pregnancy has not been established. Current registry findings do not support an increased risk of major birth defects from acyclovir use. Life-threatening maternal herpes simplex virus infection should be treated with IV acyclovir.
[†]Treatment length may be extended if healing is incomplete after completing recommended course.
Reproduced from Centers for Disease Control and Prevention. 1998 guidelines for treatment of sexually transmitted diseases. MMWR Morb Mortal Wkly Rep 1998;47(RR-1):1–111.

without any clinical manifestations. Latent syphilis is generally diagnosed in patients undergoing syphilis testing because of a history suspicious for previous syphilitic lesions or because of known high-risk sexual behavior or exposure to other STDs. Tertiary syphilis generally presents with neurologic or cardiovascular manifestations.

Darkfield examination demonstrating *T. pallidum* and direct fluorescent antibody tests of lesion exudate or tissue are the definitive methods for diagnosing early (primary or secondary) syphilis. When it is not possible to demonstrate directly the presence of *T. pallidum* (because cutaneous lesions are not present or dry and/or other involved tissue is unavailable), two types of serologic tests for syphilis are used.

All clinical serologic tests for syphilis test for antibodies produced during treponemal infection. The nontreponemal (nonspecific reaginic antibody) tests for syphilis are the Venereal Disease Research Laboratory (VDRL) test and rapid plasma reagin (RPR). These are generally used as screening tests. The VDRL and RPR test results are reported as titers and reflect the activity of disease. A fourfold rise in antibody titer in a previously treated patient indicates re-infection.

The use of a nontreponemal test alone to confirm the diagnosis of syphilis is insufficient because false-positive nontreponemal test results occasionally occur secondary to various medical conditions, including viral illness and after immunizations. The treponemal (specific antitreponemal antibody) tests are the fluorescent treponemal antibody absorbtion (FTA-Abs) test and the microhemagglutination assay for antibody to *T. pallidum* (MTA-TP). These are generally used as confirmatory tests once a positive VDRL or RPR test has been obtained. If a positive treponemal test is obtained first, a VDRL or RPR titer should then be obtained to provide a baseline for monitoring therapy.

No single test can be used to diagnose all cases of neurosyphilis. The diagnosis of neurosyphilis can be made on the basis of various combinations of reactive serologic test results, abnormalities of cerebrospinal fluid cell count of protein, or a reactive VDRL cerebrospinal fluid with or without clinical manifestations.

Because of a significant risk of fetal loss and malformation, pregnant women with syphilis should receive treatment with the most effective agent available, which is penicillin. Pregnant women with a confirmed penicillin allergy by skin testing should undergo desensitization in an intensive care unit setting and then should be treated with penicillin.

Treatment regimens are summarized in Table 72–2. Patients should be warned of the Jarisch-Herxheimer reaction (characterized by fever, headache, and myalgia), which may occur in the first 24 hours after any therapy for syphilis. There is

TABLE 72–2. Treatment of Syphilis

Stage	Preferred Treatment	Alternate if Allergic to Penicillin*
Primary, secondary, early latent	Benzathine penicillin 2.4 million units IM	Doxycycline 100 mg PO bid × 2 wk *or* Tetracycline 500 mg qid × 2 wk
Late latent, tertiary[†]	Benzathine pencillin 2.4 million units IM every wk × 3 wks	Doxycycline 100 mg PO bid × 4 wk *or* Tetracycline 500 mg PO qid × 4 wk
Neurosyphilis[†]	Aqueous penicillin G 3–4 million units IV q4h × 10–14 d *or* Procaine penicillin 2.4 million units IM *and* probenicid 500 mg PO qid, both for 10–14 d[‡]	

*Pregnant women who are allergic to penicillin should be desensitized (see text).
[†]Specialty consultation recommended.
[‡]Only if compliance is assured.
Reproduced from Centers for Disease Control and Prevention. 1998 guidelines for treatment of sexually transmitted diseases. MMWR Morb Mortal Wkly Rep 1998;47(RR-1):1–111.

no proven therapy to prevent this reaction, which may induce premature labor or fetal distress in pregnant women. However, this concern should not prevent or delay therapy of syphilis in pregnancy.

Follow-up assessment is difficult because there are no definitive criteria for treatment success. After treatment of primary and secondary syphilis, clinical and serologic examination at 6 and 12 months is recommended. Failure of nontreponemal test titers to decline fourfold within 6 months after therapy suggests treatment failure. Re-treatment with three weekly injections of benzathine penicillin G (2.4 million units IM) is recommended. For patients with early latent and late latent syphilis, quantitative nontreponemal serologic tests should be repeated at 6, 12, and 24 months. For patients with neurosyphilis, cerebrospinal fluid examination should be repeated every 6 months until the cell count is normal.

Sex partners who were exposed within 90 days preceding the diagnosis of primary, secondary, or early latent syphilis should be treated presumptively. Sex partners who were exposed more than 90 days prior to the diagnosis should be tested serologically. Sex partners of patients with latent syphilis should be evaluated clinically and serologically and treated on the basis of the findings.

Granuloma Inguinale

Granuloma inguinale is a rare disease in the United States. It is caused by the intracellular gram-negative bacterium *Calymmatobacterium granulomatis*. It presents as painless progressive ulcerative lesions without regional lymphadenopathy. The ulcer bleeds easily. The most common sites are the labia and fourchette. It spreads to the groin, causing inguinal swelling. Healing is accompanied by scarring. It is transmitted by sexual trauma to the infected sites, but repeated exposures are needed. The incubation period is 7 days to 12 weeks.[12]

The diagnosis is made clinically with observation of characteristic lesions. The presence of intracellular Donovan bodies on histologic examination of scrapings from the edges of the lesion (stained with Wright's or Giemsa stain) can be confirmatory.

The recommended treatment regimen is trimethoprim-sulfamethoxazole (one double-strength tablet orally two times a day for 3 weeks) or doxycycline (100 mg orally two times a day for 3 weeks) (Table 72–3). An alternative regimen is ciprofloxacin (750 mg two times a day for 3 weeks) or erythromycin (500 mg four times a day for 3 weeks). Relapse can occur 6 to 18 months later despite effective initial treatment. Treatment in pregnancy is summarized in Table 72–3.

TABLE 72–3. Treatment of Sexually Transmitted Diseases in Pregnancy*

Chancroid	Erythromycin (base) 500 mg PO qid × 7 d
Granuloma inguinale	Erythromycin (base) 500 mg PO qid × 21 d
Lymphogranuloma venereum	Erythromycin (base) 500 mg PO qid × 21 d
Chlamydia[†]	Erythromycin (base) 500 mg PO qid × 7 d
	or
	Amoxicillin 500 mg PO tid × 7 d
Gonorrhea[‡]	Ceftriaxone 125 mg IM × one dose plus erythromycin (base) 500 mg PO qid × 7 d
Pediculosis pubis	Permethrin 1% cream applied to affected area and washed off after 10 minutes × one dose
	or
	Pyrethrins with piperanyl butoxide applied to affected area and washed off after 10 minutes × one dose
Scabies	Permethrin 5% cream applied to all areas of the body from the neck down and washed off after 8–14 hours × one dose

*See text and Tables 72–1 and 72–2 for treatment of syphilis and herpes simplex virus infection.
[†]Repeat testing 3 wk after completion of this regimen is recommended. Alternative regimens include erythromycin (base) 250 mg PO qid × 7 d or erythromycin ethylsuccinate 800 mg PO qid × 7 d or erythromycin ethylsuccinate 400 mg PO qid × 14 d.
[‡]Spectinomycin 2 g IM × one dose may be used in cephalosporin intolerant patients.
Reproduced from Centers for Disease Control and Prevention. 1998 guidelines for treatment of sexually transmitted diseases. MMWR Morb Mortal Wkly Rep 1998;47(RR-1):1–111.

Patients should be observed clinically until signs and symptoms have resolved. Sex partners should be examined and treated if they had sexual contact during the 60 days preceding the patient's onset of symptoms.

Lymphogranuloma Venereum

Lymphogranuloma venereum (LGV) is a rare disease in the United States. It is caused by the invasive serovars L1, L2,or L3 of *Chlamydia trachomatis*. The incubation period from exposure to the appearance of a painless vesiculopustular eruption is 4 to 21 days. The primary chancre is transient. In women, the lesion occurs most commonly on the posterior area of the vulva. One to 4 weeks later, there is tender inguinal adenopathy, which is often unilateral, followed by painful ulceration and draining abscesses. Untreated infection progresses with continued tissue destruction and scarring, leading to the development of sinuses, fistulae, and strictures involving the vulva, perineum, and rectum.[13] The clinical diagnosis is difficult in the early stages of the infection because the findings are nonspecific. A serologic titer of > 1:64 for acute infection or isola-

tion of *Chlamydia* from infected individuals is helpful after the exclusion of other causes of inguinal lympadenopathy or genital ulcers.

The recommended treatment regimen for LGV is doxycycline (100 mg orally twice a day for 21 days) or erythromycin base (500 mg orally four times a day for 21 days) (Table 72–3).

Patients should be observed until signs and symptoms have resolved. Sex partners should be examined, tested, and treated if they had sexual contact with the patient within 30 days of the onset of symptoms.

Chancroid

Chancroid is rare in the United States, but outbreaks have been reported recently.[14] Ten percent of patients have HSV infections or syphilis, and there is an increased rate of HIV infection in patients with chancroid.[15] Chancroid is caused by the gram-negative bacillus *Haemophilus ducreyi*.

The incubation period is 5 to 7 days, when small papules appear and ulcerate. The lesions are painful but are not indurated. The lesions are found in the vagina, fourchette, and anal area.[16] About one-half of patients have unilateral tender inguinal adenopathy, and one-fourth of the patients develop a bubo that if left untreated will rupture, forming an ulcer.

Clinical diagnosis is difficult, and other causes of genital ulcers must be excluded. Culture is definitive but difficult. The specimen must be obtained from a ruptured bubo. The sensitivity of a Gram stain is low. Polymerase chain reaction (PCR) testing is in development.

The recommended treatment regimens are azithromycin (1 g orally in a single dose), ceftriaxone (250 mg IM in a single dose), ciprofloxacin (500 mg orally twice a day for 3 days), or erythromycin base (500 mg orally four times a day for 7 days) (Table 72–3).

Successful treatment cures the infection, resolves the clinical symptoms (although scarring occurs in some cases), and prevents transmission. A follow-up examination 3 to 7 days after the initiation of therapy should show symptomatic improvement within 3 days and objective improvement in 7 days. If the sex partner had sexual contact with the patient during the 10 days preceding the onset of symptoms, he should be examined and treated.

CERVICAL INFECTION SYNDROMES

Two infections are grouped under cervical infections: gonorrhea and chlamydial infection. Although pelvic inflammatory disease (PID) is a polymicrobial infection, it is included in this section because it is most frequently associated with *Neisseria gonorrhoeae* and *Chlamydia trachomatis*, which ascend to the upper genital tract during or shortly after menstruation.

Gonorrhea

Gonorrhea is caused by the bacterium *Neisseria gonorrhoeae*. It is a major cause of cervicitis and PID. The majority of infected women are asymptomatic.[17] Each year in the United States, 600,000 new infections occur.[3] There is a very high risk of transmission (80 to 90%) from male to female.[18] The incubation period is 3 to 5 days.

The main presenting sign of *N. gonorrhoeae* infection is a mucopurulent discharge from an infection of the endocervical canal. This is present in 20% of women. Other sites of infection include Skene's glands, Bartholin's gland, and the anus. About 10% of women have a pharyngeal infection.[19] There are serious sequelae such as PID, chronic pelvic pain, ectopic pregnancy, and infertility. Occasionally, the infection is disseminated, causing arthritis, meningitis, and perihepatitis. The clinical examination is nonspecific and therefore not diagnostic. Diagnosis is made by culture, deoxyribonucleic acid (DNA) probe, or PCR test. Gram's stain is not a reliable diagnostic test for women. *Neisseria gonorrhoeae* and *Chlamydia* often coexist, and it is recommended that both be treated without confirming the presence of *Chlamydia*.[20]

Treatment regimens are summarized in Table 72–4. Testing for cure is not necessary. Patients who have persistent symptoms after treatment should be recultured, and the isolated gonococci should be tested for antimicrobial susceptibility. Sex partners should be evaluated and treated.

Chlamydial Infection

Chlamydial infection is the most common sexually transmitted infection. It caused by an intracellular obligate, *Chlamydia trachomatis*. It is most highly prevalent among teenagers and young adults.[21]

The incubation period for chlamydial infection is 1 to 3 weeks. Chlamydial infections in women are associated with cervicitis, acute urethral syndrome, salpingitis, PID, infertility, and perihepatitis. Women with clinically localized cervical infections may have subclinical salpingitis. Asymptomatic infections are common. It is recommended that sexually active teenagers and young adults (20 to 24 years of age) be screened routinely during annual examinations.[3]

The diagnosis cannot be made on clinical grounds alone because the symptoms are not specific. Infection with *Chlamydia* is best diagnosed by culture or rapid diagnostic tests with DNA probes. Polymerase and ligase chain reaction tests are particularly helpful for nongenital sites.[22] Cytology and serology are not helpful. Women with chlamydial infections should be cultured for gonorrhea as well.

Treatment regimens are summarized in Table 72–4. Follow-up cultures are not recommended for patients treated with azithromycin or doxycycline unless symptoms persist, but are recommended for those treated with erythromycin. Sex partners should be evaluated, tested, and treated.

TABLE 72–4. Treatment of Gonorrhea, *Chlamydia* Infection, and Pelvic Inflammatory Disease

Uncomplicated gonorrhea: infections of the urethra, cervix, and rectum[†]	Cefixime 400 mg PO × one dose *or* cefriaxone 125 mg IM × one dose *or* ciprofloxacin 500 mg PO × one dose *or* ofloxacin 400 mg PO × one dose *plus* Azithromycin 1 g PO × one dose or doxycycline 100 mg PO bid × 7 d
Uncomplicated gonorrhea: pharyngitis	Ceftriaxone 125 mg IM × one dose *or* ciprofloxacin 500 mg PO × one dose *or* ofloxacin 400 mg PO × one dose *plus* Azithromycin 1 g PO × one dose *or* doxycycline 100 mg PO bid × 7 d
Chlamydial infection[‡]	Azithromycin 1 gm PO × one dose *or* doxycycline 100 mg PO bid × 7 d
Pelvic inflammatory disease (oral regimen)[§]	Ofloxacin 400 mg PO bid × 14 d *and* metronidazole 500 mg po bid × 14 days *or* ceftriaxone 250 mg IM × one dose *and* probenecid 1 g orally × one dose *or* cefoxitin 2 g IM × one dose *and* probenecid 1 g orally × one dose *plus* Doxycycline 100 mg PO bid × 14 d
Pelvic inflammatory disease[‖][#] (parental regime)[‡]	Cefotetan 2 g IV q12h *or* cefoxitin 2 g IV q6h *plus* Doxycycline 100 mg IV or PO q12h *or* Clindamycin 900 mg IV q8h *and* Gentamicin 2 mg/kg IM *or* IV × one dose, followed by 1.5 mg/kg q8h *and* (when patient switched to oral therapy) Doxycycline 100 mg PO bid *or* clindamycin 450 mg PO qid to complete 14 d of antibiotics

[*]See Table 72–3 for treatment regimens in pregnancy.
[†]Other acceptable regimens include spectinomycin 2 g IM or ceftizoxime 500 mg IM *and* probenecid 1 g PO or cefotetan 1 g IM *and* probenecid 1 g PO or cefoxitin 2 g IM and probenecid 1 g PO.
[§]See text for indications.
[‡]Other acceptable regimens include erthromycin (base) PO 500 mg qid × 7 days or erythromycin ethylsuccinate 800 PO qid × 7 d or ofloxacin 300 mg PO bid × 7 d.
[‖]Alternative parenteral regimens include ofloxacin 400 mg IV q12h *and* metronidazole 500 mg IV q8h or ampicillin/sulbactam 3 g IV q6h *and* doxycycline 100 mg IV or PO q12h or ciprofloxacin 200 mg IV q12h *and* doxycycline 100 mg IV or PO q12h *and* metronidazole 500 IV q8h.
[#]The patient should complete 14 d of therapy, with a switch to oral therapy when patient improves clinically.
IM = intramuscularly; IV = intravenously; PO = orally.
Reproduced from Centers for Disease Control and Prevention. 1998 guidelines for treatment of sexually transmitted diseases. MMWR Morb Mortal Wkly Rep 1998;47(RR-1):1–111.

Pelvic Inflammatory Disease

Pelvic inflammatory disease presents with a spectrum of inflammatory disorders of the female upper genital tract. The disorders include endometritis, salpingitis, tubo-ovarian abscess, and pelvic peritonitis. The sequelae include infertility, chronic pelvic pain, dyspareunia, and ectopic pregnancy.

Acute PID is difficult to diagnose clinically because many women have subtle or mild symptoms, which delays diagnosis and treatment. Laparoscopy has increased the accuracy of diagnosis.[23] A low threshold for the diagnosis of PID is recommended. Delay in treatment increases the potential damage to the reproductive health of women. The diagnosis and management of other causes of lower-abdominal pain are not impaired by empiric antimicrobial therapy.[3]

If a sexually active young woman presents with lower-abdominal pain, adnexal tenderness, and cervical motion tenderness, she should be treated empirically. Additional criteria for diagnosis include an oral temperature of > 38.3°C, abnormal cervical or vaginal discharge, elevated erythrocyte sedimentation rate, elevated C-reactive protein, and positive cultures for gonorrhea or *Chlamydia*. The definitive criteria include endometritis on biopsy, ultrasonography showing thickened fallopian tubes or a tubo-ovarian complex, or laparoscopic abnormalities. Because parenteral therapy is no longer synonymous with hospitalization, hospitalization should be considered if the patient is pregnant; may have appendicitis; does not respond to oral antimicrobial therapy; is unable to follow or tolerate an outpatient oral regimen; has nausea, vomiting, or high fever; may have a tubo-ovarian abscess; or is immunodeficient.

Treatment regimens are summarized in Table 72–4. Patients usually show a clinical improvement of symptoms within 3 days. If there is no improvement within 3 days, the patient should be re-evaluated. Sex partners should be treated empirically.

EPIDERMAL SYNDROMES

The epidermal syndromes include human papillomavirus infection, molluscum contagiosum viral infection, and itch mite and crab louse infestations.

Human Papillomavirus

Human papillomavirus (HPV) may be the most common sexually transmitted viral infection, occurring in about one-third of sexually active individuals.[24] Infections of HPV may be symptomatic, subclinical, or unrecognized. They are caused by a slow growing DNA virus of the papovavirus family. Of the more than 60 types identified, 20 have been associated with genital infections.[25] Types 6 and 11 are associated with genital warts (condyloma accuminata) whereas types 16, 18, 31, 33, 35, and 39 have been associated with dysplasias and carcinomas.[26] They are spread by sexual contact. There is an incubation period of 3 to 6 months. Condyloma accuminata are the clinical manifestations of infection. These cauliflower-shaped warty lesions are visible mostly in the vulva, perineal body, perianal region, introitus, and lower third of the vagina.[27] Usually the diagnosis is made on physical examination, but biopsies may be performed on questionable lesions. Patients with visible genital warts can be infected simultaneously with multiple HPV types. The primary goal of treatment is the removal of the warts. Treatment can result in wart-free periods, but there is no evidence that treatments eradicate the HPV infection.

The recommended treatment regimens for genital warts are patient-applied therapies (podofilox, imiquimod) and clinician-administered therapies (cryotherapy, podophyllin resin, trichloroacetic acid [TCA], bichloroacetic acid [BCA], interferon, and surgery). The patient applies either podofilox 0.5% solution or gel to visible genital warts twice a day for 3 days, followed by 4 days of no therapy (this cycle may be repeated for a total of four cycles), or imiquimod 5% cream three times a week for as long as 16 weeks. The clinician-administered therapies are (1) cryotherapy with liquid nitrogen or cryoprobe, with repeat applications at 1 to 2 weeks; (2) podophyllin resin, 10 to 25% in a compound tincture of benzoin, applied to each wart and allowed to dry, washed off after 1–6 hours; (3) TCA or BCA applied until a white frosting develops; or (4) surgical removal by sharp excision or electrosurgery. Alternative therapies for external genital warts are intralesional interferon and laser surgery.

After visible genital warts have cleared, a follow-up evaluation is not mandatory, and an examination of sex partners is not necessary.

The subclinical manifestions of HPV infection are found most frequently on the cervix.[28] Infection often is indirectly diagnosed on the cervix by Pap test, colposcopy, or biopsy. Upon the application of acetic acid, infected areas appear white (undergoing what are called acetowhite changes) under green-filtered light and magnification. Acetowhitening is not a specific test for HPV infection. A definitive diagnosis of HPV infection requires the detection of viral nucleic acid (DNA or ribonucleic acid [RNA]) or capsid protein. Pap test diagnosis of HPV infection does not always correlate with detection of HPV DNA in cervical cells. Cell changes attributed to HPV in the cervix are similar to those of mild dysplasia and often regress spontaneously without treatment. Tests that detect several types of HPV DNA or RNA in cells scraped from the cervix are available, but the clinical usefulness of these tests for managing patients is unclear. Management decisions should not be made on the basis of HPV tests. Screening for subclinical genital HPV infection using DNA or RNA tests or acetic acid testing is not recommended.[3]

Treatment is not recommended for subclinical HPV infections. The presence of cervical dysplasia does require follow-up and treatment. Examination of sex partners is not necessary because they probably are infected subclinically with HPV. Cervical HPV is discussed further in Chapter 81.

Molluscum Contagiosum

Molluscum contagiosum is a poxvirus infection of the vulvar skin. It is spread by direct contact, but it is not highly contagious. It is asymptomatic. The incubation period is weeks to months. On physical examination, there are 1- to 5-mm domed papules with umbilicated centers. The nodule can be opened, with the expression of a white waxy material. The presence of intracytoplasmic molluscum bodies seen with Wright's or Giemsa stain confirms the diagnosis.[29]

Treatment of the individual papules requires unroofing each with a fine-gauge needle and removing the caseous material from the central core. The base of the papule is chemically treated with Monsel's solution or TCA. Alternatively, they may be treated with cryotherapy, electrocautery, or laser therapy.

Scabies

Scabies is transmitted by direct contact. It is caused by *Sacropies scabieri*, the itch mite. It is a highly contagious obligate parasite that burrows into the skin, where it resides and reproduces. Patients complain of intense pruritus that is worse at night. It is found in pelvic area as well as many other areas of the body. The examination generally shows short wavy-line burrows. The diagnosis is confirmed by the microscopic examination of scrapings of the skin over the burrows.[30]

The recommended treatment regimen is permethrin cream (5%), applied to all areas of the body from the neck down and washed off after 8 to 14 hours. Alternate treatment regimens include lindane (1 oz of lotion or 30 g of cream applied thinly to all areas of the body from the neck down and thoroughly washed off after 8 hours) and sulfur (6%) (precipitated in ointment and applied thinly to all areas nightly for 3 nights). Applications should

be washed off before each new application and 24 hours after the last application. Persons who have had sexual or household contact with the patient within the preceding month should be examined and treated. Clothes and bedding should be machine-washed and machine-dried using the hot cycle, or they should be dry-cleaned. The pruritus may persist for several weeks after treatment.

Pediculosis Pubis

Phthirus pubis is the crab louse that causes pediculosis pubis. It is highly contagious and is spread by direct contact or by fomites.[31] The incubation period is 30 days. The patient complains of pruritus. Dark brown spots are seen moving along the pubic hairs, and the eggs or nits are seen as white spots at the bases of hair follicles. Microscopic examination confirms their presence.

The recommended treatment regimens are permethrin (1%) cream rinse applied to affected areas and washed off after 10 minutes, or lindane (1%) shampoo applied for 4 minutes to the affected areas and thoroughly washed off, or pyrethrins with piperonyl butoxide applied to the affected areas and washed off after 10 minutes. If there is evidence of infestation 7 days later, the patient should be re-treated with an alternative regimen. Bedding and clothing should be machine-washed and machine-dried using the heat cycle, or they should be dry-cleaned. Sex partners within the preceding month should be treated.

HEPATITIS B

Hepatitis B virus (HBV) is spread sexually as well as parenterally and perinatally. It is a common STD. During the past 10 years, sexual transmission accounted for approximately 30 to 60% of the estimated 240,000 new cases of HBV infection that occur annually in the United States. Chronic HBV infection develops in 1 to 6% of infected adults, and these individuals transmit it to others.[3]

Hepatitis B causes an inflammation of the liver, but it is often asymptomatic or presents as a nonspecific viral syndrome. Some patients have jaundice, low-grade fever, or right upper-quadrant pain. Acute hepatitis B is diagnosed by the presence of hepatitis B surface antigen and/or hepatitis B core antibody. Patients generally have elevated serum transaminases and bilirubin. If the patient is found to have hepatitis B, then prothrombin time, serum bilirubin, and aminotransferases are followed weekly until improvement. If the symptoms and laboratory abnormalities persist after 3 months, monthly testing should be performed. If the antigen persists after 6 months, then a liver biopsy should be considered.[32] There is no specific treatment available for the acute infection. Chronic hepatitis B is diagnosed by the persistent presence of hepatitis B surface antigen. Numerous antiviral agents have been investigated for treating chronic HBV. A complete discussion of the evaluation and treatment of chronic hepatitis B is beyond the scope of this text.

Hepatitis B immune globulin should be given to those who have had sexual contact with individuals with an acute infection. Hepatitis B vaccine should be given to patients at risk for acquiring hepatitis B, including women diagnosed with other STDs. Immunity from vaccine develops after three injections (initial, 1 month, and 6 months) and lasts for 5 years.

RESOURCE

Centers for Disease Control and Prevention
1600 Clifton Road
Atlanta, Georgia 30333
Telephone: (404) 639-3534
           1-800-311-3435
Web site: www.cdc.gov

The Centers for Disease Control and Prevention (CDC) publish guidelines on screening, evaluating, and treating of sexually transmitted diseases. These are available on-line at the CDC Web site. The Web site also contains information appropriate for health care clinicians on a wide range of illnesses, including STDs.

REFERENCES

1. US Department of Health and Human Services. Division of STD Prevention. Sexually transmitted disease surveillance, 1998. Atlanta (GA): Centers for Disease Control and Prevention (CDC); September 1999.

2. Office of Communications and Public Liaison. Fact sheet. Bethesda (MD): National Institute of Allergy and Infectious Diseases, National Institutes of Health, Public Health Service, US Department of Health and Human Services; July 1999.

3. Centers for Disease Control and Prevention. 1998 guidelines for treatment of sexually transmitted diseases. MMWR Morb Mortal Wkly Rep 1998;47 (RR-1):1–111.

4. American College of Obstetricians and Gynecologists (ACOG). Condom availability for adolescents. ACOG Committee Opinion No. 154. Washington (DC): American College of Obstetricians and Gynecologists;1995 Apr.

5. Update: barrier protection against HIV infection and other sexually transmitted diseases. MMWR Morb Mortal Wkly Rep 42:589–91, 597.

6. Corey L, Adams H, Brown Z, et al. Genital herpes simplex viral infection: clinical manifestations, course, and complications. Ann Intern Med 1983;98:958.

7. Koelle DM, Benedetti J, Langenberg A, et al. Asymptomatic reactivation of herpes simplex virus in women after the first episode of genital herpes. Ann Intern Med 1992;116:433.

8. Koutsky LA, Stevens CE, Holmes KK, et al. Underdiagnosis of genital herpes by current clinical and viral-isolation procedures. N Engl J Med 1992; 326:1533.

9. Spruance SL, Overall JC Jr, Kern ER, et al. The natural history of recurrent herpes simplex labialis: implications for antiviral therapy. N Engl J Med 1977; 297:69.

10. Rolfs RT, Nakashima AK. Epidemiology of primary and secondary syphilis in the United States, 1981 through 1989. JAMA 1990;264:1432.

11. Magnuson HJ, Thomas EW, Olansky S, et al. Inoculation of syphilis in human volunteers. Medicine 1956;35:33.

12. Richens J. The diagnosis and treatment of donovanosis (granuloma inguinale). Genitourin Med 1991; 67:441.

13. Bolan RK, Sands M, Schacter J, et al. Lymphogranuloma venereum and acute ulcerative proctitis. Am J Med 1982;72:703.

14. Schmid GP, Sanders LL, Blount JH, et al. Chancroid in the United States: reestablishment of an old disease. JAMA 1987;258:3265.

15. Flood JM, Sarafian SK, Bolan GA, et al. Multistrain outbreak of chancroid in San Francisco, 1989-1991. J Infect Dis 1993;167:1106.

16. Albritton WL. Biology of *Haemophilus ducreyi*. Microbiol Rev 1989;53:377.

17. Judson FN. Gonorrhea. Med Clin North Am 1990; 74:1353.

18. Dans PE. Gonococcal anogenital infection. Clin Obstet Gynecol 1975;18:103.

19. Bro-Jornensen A, Jensen T. Gonococcal pharyngeal infections. Report of 110 cases. Br J Vener Dis 1973; 49:491–9.

20. Stamm WE, Guinan ME, Johnson C, et al. Effect of treatment regimens for *Neisseria gonorrhoeae* on simultaneuous infection with *Chlamydia trachomatis*. N Engl J Med 1984;310:545.

21. Randall J. New tools ready for chlamydia diagnosis, treatment, but teens need education most. JAMA 1993;269:2716.

22. Krieger JN. New sexually transmitted diseases treatment guidelines. J Urol 1995;154:209.

23. Chaparro MV, Ghosh S, Nashed A, et al. Laparoscopy for confirmation and prognostic evaluation of pelvic inflammatory disease. Int J Gynecol Obstet 1978; 15:307.

24. Heaton CL. Clinical manifestations and modern management of condylomata acuminata: a dermatologic perspective. Am J Obstet Gynecol 1995;172:1344.

25. American College of Obstetricians and Gynecologists (ACOG). Genital human papillomavirus infections. Washington (DC): American College of Obstetricians and Gynecologists; 1994. ACOG Technical Bulletin No. 194. 1994.

26. Chuang TY. Condylomata acuminata (genital warts). An epidemiologic view. J Am Acad Dermatol 1987; 16:376.

27. Ferenczy A. Epidemiology and clinical pathophysiology of condylomata acuminata. Am J Obstet Gynecol 1995;172:1331.

28. Lorincz AT, Reid R, Jenson AB, et al. Human papillomavirus infection of the cervix: relative risk association of 15 common anogenital types. Obstet Gynecol 1992;79:328–37.

29. Felman YM, Nikitas JA. Sexually transmitted molluscum contagiosum. Dermatol Clin 1983;1:103.

30. Amer M, El-Garib I. Permethrin vs crotamiton and lindane in the treatment of scabies. Int J Dermatol 1992;31:357.

31. Faber BM. The diagnosis and treatment of scabies and pubic lice. Prim Care Update Ob/Gyn 1996; 3:20–2.

32. Dienstag JL. Management of hepatitis. In: Goroll AH, May LA, Mulley AG, editors. Primary care medicine: office evaluation and management of the adult patient. 3rd ed. Philadelphia: JB Lippincott; 1995.

73

AMENORRHEA

T.C. Jackson Wu, MD, PhD

Normal menstrual cycles require a dynamic and coordinated control among hypothalamic, pituitary, and gonadal hormones as well as a normal genital tract. Amenorrhea, or absence of menstruation, is a symptom that is more commonly physiologic than pathologic. Amenorrhea is defined as the absence of menstruation for 6 consecutive months in a woman or girl who was previously menstruating, lack of menarche by the age of 16, or lack of menarche and no development of secondary sex characteristics by age 14 years.[1,2]

Traditionally, amenorrhea is classified as primary in women or girls who have never experienced menarche or as secondary when menses cease after the occurrence of menarche. Although many causes of secondary amenorrhea also may cause primary amenorrhea, making this distinction is nonetheless clinically useful in guiding initial evaluation. Patients with primary amenorrhea have a 35 to 40% probability of having either primary ovarian failure or developmental defects of the reproductive tract involving the fallopian tubes, uterus, or vagina. In contrast, most secondary amenorrhea is caused by pregnancy or polycystic ovary syndrome (PCOS).[1–4] A list of the diseases that may be associated with amenorrhea is summarized in Table 73–1.

HYPOTHALAMIC-PITUITARY-OVARIAN FEEDBACK REGULATION OF THE MENSTRUAL CYCLE

The menstrual cycle is associated with cyclic changes in gonadotropins, estradiol, and progesterone, which are closely related to the development of ovarian follicles, ovulation, and corpus luteum formation. Understanding hypothalamic-pituitary-ovarian feedback regulation is helpful to the diagnosis and treatment of menstrual dysfunction.

TABLE 73–1. Causes of Amenorrhea

Disorders of the outflow tract
  Asherman's syndrome
  Transverse vaginal septum
  Imperforate hymen
  Mayer-Rokitansky-Küster-Hauser syndrome
    (müllerian agenesis)
  Androgen insensitivity (testicular feminization)

Disorders of ovaries
  Gonadal dysgenesis
  Turner's syndrome, mosaicism, pure gonadal uterus
    dysgenesis, true gonadal dysgenesis
  Premature ovarian failure
  Autoimmune disorders, oophoritis, irradiation,
    chemotherapy, post-surgical, idiopathic
  Polycystic ovary syndrome
  Androgen-secreting tumor of the ovary

Disorders of the pituitary
  Laurence-Moon-Biedl syndrome
  Prader-Willi syndrome
  Tuberculoma
  Gumma
  Empty sella syndrome
  Sheehan's syndrome
  Pituitary adenoma
  Prolactinoma

Disorders of the hypothalamus
  Craniopharyngioma
  Infection
  Infiltrative disease (sarcoidosis)
  Kallmann's syndrome
  Anorexia nervosa
  Idiopathic
  Functional causes: weight changes, intense exercise,
    physical or mental stress

The hypothalamus regulates pituitary gonadotropin secretion and thus the menstrual cycle through the decapeptide gonadotropin-releasing hormone (Gn-RH). Gonadotropin-releasing hormone is synthesized in the arcuate nucleus and released in a pulsatile fashion via the portal circulation. The half-life of Gn-RH is 2 to 3 minutes. Constant release of Gn-RH is required to maintain the menstrual cycle. Secretion of Gn-RH is regulated by feedback from pituitary gonadotropins and ovarian sex steroids.[5]

Gonadotropin-releasing hormone stimulates pituitary gonadotrophs, which synthesize and secrete follicle-stimulating hormone (FSH) and luteinizing hormone (LH). Studies measuring serum LH and FSH levels have concluded that Gn-RH is released in a pulsatile fashion, approximately every 60 minutes. Both the amplitude and pulse frequency of Gn-RH are important for stimulation of FSH and LH release. Shorter intervals between Gn-RH pulses are observed during the follicular phase compared with the luteal phase. A decrease in Gn-RH pulse frequency increases FSH secretion but decreases LH secretion. Significant decreases in Gn-RH pulse frequency and amplitude result in a decrease or complete absence of FSH and LH secretion, as seen in hypothalamic amenorrhea. On the other hand, high pulse frequency of Gn-RH secretion results in high serum LH levels, such as those found in patients with PCOS.[5–7]

Both FSH and LH are important for the development of ovarian follicles and the production of ovarian steroid hormones. Normal development of ovarian follicles depends mainly on FSH stimulation. Only a minute amount of endogenous LH is needed for ovarian follicular development to occur. Estrogen is converted from androgen in the granulosa cells of the follicles under FSH stimulation. High serum LH levels (as seen in PCOS) stimulate excessive androgen production from the theca cells and ovarian stroma, resulting in follicular atresia and anovulation.[8]

Ovarian steroids and peptides regulate pituitary gonadotropins through feedback mechanisms. In the preovulatory phase, constantly high serum estrogen levels (estradiol levels greater than 200 pg/mL lasting for 48 hours) augmented by a small increase in progesterone levels trigger pituitary FSH and LH surges (positive feedback). Estrogen secreted by the growing follicles appears to inhibit basal FSH secretion, whereas progesterone from the corpus luteum suppresses both FSH and LH secretions from the pituitary (negative feedback). The secretion of FSH is inhibited by ovarian inhibins, peptides secreted by the granulosa layer of developing follicles and the corpus luteum after ovulation. The endocrine role of the other ovarian peptide, activins, in the regulation of pituitary gonadotropins has not been established.

Gonadotropin-releasing hormone secretion also is controlled by neurotransmitters released from higher centers in the central nervous system. Control of ovulation through higher centers in the central nervous system is, in general, less well described than mechanisms of hypothalamic and target organ feedback. Controlling neurotransmitters appear to include dopamine, norepinephrine, endorphin, serotonin, and melatonin. Pulsatile activity of Gn-RH appears to be stimulated by norepinephrine and inhibited by dopamine. The catecholaminergic system in the hypothalamus appears to have dual effects on Gn-RH secretion through norepinephrine and dopamine. The catecholamine system also can be influenced by endogenous opiate activity.[2,9]

DISORDERS OF THE OUTFLOW TRACT OR UTERUS

Asherman's Syndrome

Asherman's syndrome is defined as amenorrhea caused by intrauterine synechia. This syndrome is often a complication of uterine curettage, such as excessive curetting of the uterine lining, incomplete abortion, or associated endometritis. Asherman's syndrome also can occur after myomectomies, metroplasty, or cesarean section. Very often infection obliterates the endometrial cavity. If Asherman's syndrome is suspected as a cause of amenorrhea, either hysterosalpingography (HSG) or hysteroscopy can be used to evaluate the uterine cavity. In severe cases, HSG may not be helpful in making the diagnosis.

The treatment is surgically resecting adhesions under direct visualization with a hysteroscope. Following this procedure, an intrauterine device or Foley catheter can be placed in the uterine cavity for several weeks to prevent scar formation. Endometrial proliferation can be maintained with high-dose estrogen (Premarin 2.5 mg daily) for up to 2 months before menstrual withdrawal with medroxyprogesterone acetate (10 mg daily for 7 to 10 days).[3,4]

TABLE 73–2. Differences between Müllerian Agenesis and Testicular Feminization

	Müllerian Agenesis	*Testicular Feminization*
Karyotype	46,XX	46,XY
Hereditary	Unknown	X-linked recessive
Gonads	Ovaries	Testes
Serum testosterone level	Normal female	Normal to high male
Pubic and axillary hair	Normal female	Sparse
Height	Normal female	Taller than average
Abnormalities	Renal, skeletal	Rare inguinal hernia, renal, underdeveloped labia minora

Transverse Vaginal Septum and Imperforate Hymen

Patients with transverse vaginal septum or imperforate hymen present with primary amenorrhea associated with monthly abdominal or pelvic pain caused by retrograde menstruation into the abdominal cavity (hemoperitoneum). These patients have a high incidence of pelvic endometriosis. All other sexual development is normal. Hematometra and hematocolpos may develop from the accumulated menstrual blood. Very often a diagnosis can be made through careful pelvic examination. Imaging studies such as ultrasonography or magnetic resonance imaging (MRI) can be helpful. Hematocolpos should not be aspirated as pyocolpos may occur.

Surgical removal of the transverse vaginal septum or imperforate hymen corrects the problem. Since patients have retrograde menstruation and pelvic endometriosis, concurrent laparoscopy is recommended. The fertility outcome is good; 60 to 70% of affected women are able to conceive.[2-4]

Mayer-Rokitansky-Küster-Hauser Syndrome (Müllerian Agenesis)

Defects of müllerian development are the second most common cause of primary amenorrhea, resulting in abnormalities of the fallopian tubes, uterus, or vagina. Patients with congenital absence of the uterus and vagina may have associated urinary tract abnormalities (in one-third of the patients) and skeletal abnormalities. Urinary tract anomalies include ectopic kidney, renal agenesis, and horseshoe kidney.[10]

Because of the presence of normal functioning ovaries, serum gonadotropin levels are normal and the patient has normal secondary sex characteristics. Serum testosterone and progesterone levels are in the normal female range. Dilation of the vagina can be accomplished through the use of progressively larger dilators (Frank's procedure) or surgical creation of a neovagina (McIndoe's procedure).

Androgen Insensitivity (Testicular Feminization)

Psychologically and phenotypically female, patients with testicular feminization are 46,XY karyotype and possess both testes. The basic defect of testicular feminization is either a lack of androgen receptors in target tissues or, in some cases, inactive androgen receptors. This defect is caused by mutation of a gene responsible for the androgen receptor located on the long arm of the X chromosome.

Normal breasts exist because of the small amount of estrogen secreted by the adrenal glands and testes and the aromatase activity in peripheral tissue. Patients have female-type external genitalia because of androgen resistance. Pubic and axillary hair is sparse. Since the functional testes secrete a normal müllerian inhibiting factor during fetal life, patients have no ovaries, uterus, or fallopian tubes.

Testes are often located in the abdomen, inguinal canal, or labia majora. The size of the testes is normal. Serum testosterone level is normal or slightly higher than the normal male level. Because malignant tumors may arise from these nondescended testes after puberty, these gonads should be removed after puberty when the patient may be given hormone replacement therapy. Distinctions between testicular feminization and müllerian agenesis are summarized in Table 73–2.[1-4]

DISORDERS OF OVARIES

Gonadal Dysgenesis

Gonadal dysgenesis is the most common cause of primary amenorrhea. It can also, in some cases, be a cause of secondary amenorrhea. Approximately 30 to 40% of women with primary amenorrhea have some type of gonadal dysgenesis. Turner's syndrome is the most common cause, followed by mosaicism, ringed X chromosome, and pure gonadal dysgenesis. Patients have high serum gonadotropin levels and extremely low estrogen levels (hypergonadotropic hypogonadism). Patients with gonadal dysgenesis who are phenotypically female may, in some cases, have gonadal cells that possess Y chromosomes. This places them at risk for malignant transformation. Therefore, it is important to consider gonadal dysgenesis in the differential diagnosis of amenorrhea and (when indicated) to perform karyotyping to identify individuals who might benefit from removal of gonads.

Turner's Syndrome

Turner's syndrome (45,X) was first described by Dr. Henry Turner in 1838 as a syndrome characterized by primary amenorrhea, short stature (less than 60 inches in height), and genital infantilism. Patients with Turner's syndrome not only suffer from ovarian dysgenesis but also have coexisting abnormalities of the skeletal, cardiovascular, and nervous systems. Multiple abnormalities such as web neck, epicanthal folds, low-set ears, low posterior hairline, high arched palate, shield-like chest with widely spaced nipples, cubitus valgus, scoliosis, coarctation of the aorta, and renal anomalies may exist. Transient edema of dorsum of hands and feet may be observed at birth.

The ovaries of females with Turner's syndrome usually show a thin elongated firm whitish thickening on gross examination. Histologic section of the adult gonads reveals complete absence of the follicular structure with spindle-shaped cells in the ovarian stroma. It is postulated that a normal cohort of primordial follicles develops in utero, but these follicles undergo accelerated atresia; therefore, no or very few follicles exist around the time of menarche.

There also are some other variant forms of this type of gonadal dysgenesis caused by deletions of chromatin material from the X chromosome (deletions of the long arm 46,XXq⁻ or deletion of the short arm 46,XXp⁻). Patients with 46,XXq⁻ usually do not have somatic abnormalities of Turner's syndrome, but are sterile. Patients with 46,XXp⁻ present clinically like Turner's syndrome.

Mosaicism

Mosaicism is the second most common cause of gonadal dysgenesis. Patients with mosaicism have populations of cells with more than one karyotype. The most common form of mosaicism in gonadal dysgenesis is 45,X/46,XX. The phenotypic characteristics and clinical presentation may vary depending on the degree of mosaicism. Some patients have normal stature and functional ovarian tissue but eventually have premature menopause caused by accelerated follicular atresia.

Some of these Y chromosome–carrying individuals may show signs of virilization. However, about 30% of patients with Y chromosome do not develop signs of virilization. Therefore, all patients with hypergonadotropic hypogonadism who are younger than 30 years old require karyotyping to rule out the presence of any Y chromosome. Patients with gonadal dysgenesis caused by mosaicism with Y chromosome detected by karyotyping require gonadectomy as malignant transformation may occur, even prior to puberty.

Pure and Mixed Gonadal Dysgenesis

Patients with pure gonadal dysgenesis have a normal karyotype. Patients with pure gonadal dysgenesis with 46,XY (Swyer syndrome) have gonadal failure but do not have any somatic abnormalities. Swyer syndrome is probably X-linked recessive. The testes in patients with Swyer syndrome fail to develop during fetal life (vanishing testis). The presence of a uterus and vagina in Swyer syndrome is attributable to the absence of müllerian inhibiting substance. The absence of male external and internal genitalia is attributable to a lack of testosterone production. Serum testosterone concentration in these patients is of a normal female level. The gonadal streaks in patients with Swyer syndrome should be removed. On the other hand, 46,XX pure gonadal dysgenesis is inherited through an autosomal recessive mode and may be associated with neurosensory deafness. Patients usually present with primary amenorrhea with infantile sex characteristics.

Patients with mixed gonadal dysgenesis have a gonadal streak on one side and testes on the other side. The common karyotypes are 46,X/46,XY and rarely 46,XX/46,XY. These individuals may exhibit ambiguous genitalia, ranging from mild clitoral hypertrophy to hypospadia.[2–4]

Premature Ovarian Failure

Premature ovarian failure (POF) is defined as failure of ovarian estrogen production with hypergonadotropic state before age 40 years. Premature menopause or POF is caused by abnormally early depletion of the primordial follicles in the ovaries caused by either destruction of the follicles or an increased rate of follicular atresia.

Although gonadal dysgenesis is the most common cause of primary amenorrhea, it is not a comon cause of secondary amenorrhea. Nevertheless, patients diagnosed with POF prior to age 30 should undergo karyotyping to rule out the presence of a Y chromosome (including fragments). Patients with a Y-chromosome karyotype require removal of the gonads because of the risk of malignant transformation.

Other causes of POF include autoimmune disorders, infection (such as mump oophoritis), and prior ovarian surgery such as ovarian cystectomy, ovarian drilling, or other forms of adnexal surgeries. Some patients with autoimmune disorders have elevated levels of antinuclear antibody, rheumatoid factor, thyroid, adrenal, or ovarian antibodies. In recent years, the increased use of cytotoxic drugs in the treatment of malignancies in women of reproductive age has resulted in a higher prevalence of drug-induced ovarian failure. Irradiation in gynecologic malignancies such as endometrial cancer also may induce POF. Radiation doses > 500 rad to the abdomen result in ovarian failure and amenorrhea in about 60% of patients. There is an inverse relationship between the dose required to cause ovarian failure and the age of the patient. In most patients with POF, no cause can be identified. These cases are considered idiopathic.

Symptoms in women with POF are similar to those of normal menopause, although the severity can be greater because of the precipitous drop of the ovarian steroid hormones experienced by women who experience ovarian failure at relatively younger ages. Common symptoms include hot flushes and dyspareunia caused by atrophic vaginal mucosa and dryness. Psychological changes include mood swings, emotional instability, insomnia, and depression. The adverse psychological impact of POF is often more profound in women who have not completed their childbearing.

The spontaneous return of menses and conception occasionally occurs in patients with POF following chemotherapy or irradiation; therefore, follow-up serum FSH and estradiol levels are advised. For most patients with POF who desire childbearing, oocyte donor programs are the only available treatment option.[11,12]

Polycystic Ovary Syndrome

Polycystic ovary syndrome is defined as the perimenarche onset of hyperandrogenic chronic anovulation in the absence of any other identifiable cause. It is the most common cause of ovarian androgen hypersecretion and the most common endocrinologic cause of infertility. Stein and Leventhal first identified this syndrome in 1935. They described a triad of hirsutism, obesity, and amenorrhea in association with enlarged polycystic ovaries (Stein-Leventhal syndrome).

Although the pathophysiology of PCOS is still a subject of controversy, the clinical and biochemical features of women with PCOS have been well studied. Multiple small antral follicles are present at the outer layer of the ovary, but these follicles fail to reach the stage of preovulatory graafian follicles; therefore, patients do not ovulate. The lack of ovulation and cyclic hormonal changes results in amenorrhea. The characteristic polycystic ovary is the result of chronic anovulation. Some patients with PCOS present with dysfunctional uterine bleeding instead of amenorrhea. In these patients, unopposed estrogen causes endometrial proliferation and is responsible for unpredictable heavy bleeding episodes.

In patients with PCOS, elevated levels of androgen result in hirsutism and acne. The androgen excess noted in patients with PCOS arises from both the ovaries and the adrenal glands. Ovarian-related androgen excess results from LH-dependent hypersecretion of androgen from hyperplastic theca cells and ovarian stroma. Serum concentration of androstenedione is elevated. Total testosterone level may be normal or slightly increased, but free (unbound) testosterone is often increased because of an androgen-dependent decrease in sex hormone–binding globulin. Levels of dehydroepiandrosterone sulfate (DHEAS), an androgen exclusively of adrenal source, are either normal or elevated in PCOS.[8]

Total estrogen levels are increased because of peripheral conversion of increased amounts of androstenedione to estrone. In addition, free estradiol levels are increased because of decreases in sex

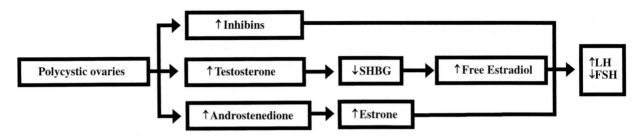

FIGURE 73–1. Hormonal regulation in polycystic ovary syndrome. LH=luteinizing hormone; FSH=follicle-stimulating hormone; SHBG = steroid hormone binding globulin.

hormone–binding globulin. The increase in androgen and estrone, as well as ovarian inhibins, may be responsible for alterations in pituitary gonadotropin secretion in patients with PCOS: high LH and low FSH levels are usually present, reflecting an increase in Gn-RH pulse activity. The LH-to-FSH ratio is increased and positively correlated with the increase in free estradiol level. Hormonal changes associated with PCOS are summarized in Figure 73–1.

The clinical manifestations of patients with PCOS are highly variable; therefore, using strict criteria to diagnose PCOS is not clinically practical. Only about 60% of patients with PCOS have ultrasonographic findings of polycystic ovary. Since many clinical conditions such as Cushing's syndrome and androgen-secreting tumors of the ovary or adrenal cortex also may cause anovulation and polycystic appearance of the ovary, initial work-up to rule out these diseases is important. Particularly in patients with significant findings of androgen excess, total testosterone and DHEAS levels should be measured. Total testosterone levels greater than 200 ng/dL are associated with a high incidence of androgen-producing tumors in the ovaries. Levels of DHEAS > 700 µg/dL may indicate an adrenal tumor. In patients with significantly elevated testosterone or DHEAS, MRI of the ovaries or adrenal glands is indicated.[2,8,10,13,14]

PITUITARY CAUSES

Pituitary tumors are the most common pituitary disorder that causes amenorrhea. Although pituitary tumors may secrete adrenocorticotropic hormone or growth hormone, prolactin-secreting adenomas are the most common. An elevated prolactin level is found in one-third of women with amenorrhea. Serum prolactin levels > 60 µg/mL are often associated with amenorrhea.

A serum prolactin level is a sensitive but not specific test for screening for pituitary tumors. Serum prolactin levels can be mildly elevated for a variety of reasons. Mildly elevated prolactin levels can be associated with PCOS. Primary hypothyroidism may cause prolactin to be elevated by increasing thyrotropin-releasing hormone. Extremely high prolactin levels (> 100 µg/mL) are often associated with prolactin-secreting pituitary adenomas (prolactinomas).

An elevated prolactin level in the absence of hypothyroidism warrants an imaging study, either MRI or computed tomography (CT), of the pituitary gland to rule out pituitary adenoma. Autopsy studies have shown that as many as 9 to 27% of individuals have pituitary adenomas and that the incidence of pituitary adenomas increases with age. However, most of these adenomas are small, < 5 mm in diameter. An unexplained elevated prolactin level with a normal pituitary imaging is termed idiopathic hyperprolactinemia.

Patients with a mildly elevated serum prolactin level are likely to have normal imaging of the pituitary gland or microadenomas (tumors < 1 cm in diameter). Serum prolactin levels > 100 ng/dL with a pituitary adenoma detected by MRI or CT are more likely to be associated with prolactin-secreting tumor (prolactinoma). Occasionally, macroadenomas can be associated with mild elevations of serum prolactin levels caused by compression of the pituitary stalk and interruption of dopamine delivery to pituitary lactotropes.

Elevated prolactin levels appear to suppress Gn-RH secretion by increasing opioid activity; thus, patients may have oligomenorrhea or amenorrhea. Because only one-third of patients have clinical signs of galactorrhea, all patients with oligomenorrhea should have serum prolactin levels tested. For more information on hyperprolactinema and prolactinomas, please consult Chapter 59, "Hyperprolactinemia."

Some rare congenital syndromes, such as Laurence-Moon-Bardet-Biedl syndrome and Prader-Willi syndrome, are associated with pituitary failure. Patients with these syndromes, which are associated with specific autosomal genetic defects, generally present in infancy or early childhood with obesity and other associated abnormalities. Other causes of pituitary dysfunction, such as tuberculoma, gumma, empty sella syndrome, and Sheehan's syndrome (pituitary failure secondary to infarction caused by postpartum hemorrhage), can also cause amenorrhea.[1-4]

HYPOTHALAMIC CAUSES

Hypothalamic amenorrhea is a diagnosis of exclusion and usually reflects a functional defect of the hypothalamic-pituitary axis. It is the most common cause of hypogonadotropic amenorrhea. Patients with a diagnosis of hypothalamic amenorrhea may have low or normal LH and FSH levels, and serum prolactin levels are normal. It is postulated that increased corticotropin-releasing hormone levels stimulate opioid secretion to inhibit gonadotropin secretion. As a result, serum estradiol levels are extremely low (often < 30 pg/mL), and there is no menstrual withdrawal with progesterone challenge.

Functional causes of hypothalamic amenorrhea include rapid weight loss or weight gain, systemic diseases, intense exercise, and physical or mental stress. Tumors (most commonly craniopharyngioma), infections, and infiltrative diseases (eg, sarcoidosis) of the hypothalamus are less common causes. Patients with Kallmann's syndrome have amenorrhea caused by congenital deficiency of Gn-RH release associated with anosmia.[15]

Patients with eating disorders such as anorexia nervosa may present initially with amenorrhea. In these patients, FSH and LH levels are low, cortisol levels are elevated, and thyroxine level is normal, but the 3,5,3'-triiodothyronine (T_3) level is low and reverse T_3 level is high. Competitive female athletes, especially professional ballet dancers and runners, have a significantly higher incidence of menstrual irregularities and amenorrhea. In women who exercise strenuously, both decreases in body fat and increases in stress levels are responsible for the suppression of Gn-RH pulse activity.

EVALUATION

A detailed medical history and careful physical examination provide important clues to possible causes of amenorrhea. The history should include age of menarche, menstrual pattern or any recent changes, development of secondary sex characteristics, weight changes, exercise, current medication, and detailed medical history such as irradiation or surgeries involving the reproductive tract. It is important to specifically elicit symptoms of androgen excess (hirsutism or acne), estrogen deficiency (hot flashes or vaginal dryness), hypothyroidism, and adrenal hyperfunction and to ask about galactorrhea and visual disturbances. A complete pelvic examination to rule out outflow blockage caused by Asherman's syndrome or congenital müllerian anomaly should be performed at the first visit. Since 70% of secondary amenorrhea is caused by pregnancy, a sensitive urine pregnancy test should be performed before other work-up.

The goal of evaluating amenorrhea is to identify the level of pathology in the hypothalamus-pituitary-ovary axis or in the target organs. Following a negative pregnancy test, a progesterone challenge test is often performed. Medroxyprogesterone acetate (Provera) 10 mg is given orally once a day for 7 to 10 days or by a single progesterone 100-mg intramuscular injection. A positive progesterone challenge test is uterine withdrawal bleeding following progesterone administration (usually within 1 week).

A positive progesterone challenge test confirms the presence of intrinsic estrogen, a functioning uterine endometrium, and indicates that there is no blockage of uterine outflow. A negative progesterone challenge (no withdrawal bleeding) suggests either outflow occlusion or an extremely low estrogen state caused by ovarian failure or hypothalamic amenorrhea. Estradiol levels greater than 60 pg/mL correlate well with a normal estrogen state but do not rule out the possibility of uterine outflow blockage. Additional laboratory tests are ordered based on the findings of the initial history and physical examination. Laboratory tests should include thyroid-stimulating hormone, prolactin, estradiol, FSH, and LH.

Serum FSH and LH levels are important in determining the cause of amenorrhea because gonadotropin levels reflect the activities of the hypothalamus, pituitary, and ovaries. It is crucial

TABLE 73–3. Hormonal Levels in Various Causes of Amenorrhea

	Estradiol	*FSH*	*LH*	*Prolactin*
Outflow occlusion	Normal	Normal	Normal	Normal
Polycystic ovary syndrome	Normal or high	Normal	High	Normal or high
Ovarian failure	Low	High	High	Normal
Pituitary disease	Low	Normal or low	Normal or low	High
Hypothalamic disorder	Low	Normal or low	Normal or low	Normal

FSH = follicle-stimulating hormone; LH = luteinizing hormone.

that FSH and LH results are interpreted together with the estradiol level (Table 73–3). High FSH and LH levels (LH level higher than FSH level) with an estradiol level greater than 60 pg/mL is indicative of preovulatory gonadotropin surges. If this pattern is found, the tests need to be repeated.

Low estradiol levels (less than 30 pg/mL) and high FSH and LH levels (hypergonadotropic hypogonadism) imply gonadal dysgenesis or POF. Usually, the FSH level is higher than the LH level in these patients. Elevated levels of both FSH and LH should be documented before a patient is given the diagnosis of POF. For patients with POF who are younger than 30 years of age, chromosome evaluation is mandatory to detect any Y-chromosome fragment as the gonads of these patients are prone to develop malignant tumors. If the karyotype is normal, screening for autoimmune disorders and systemic illnesses is indicated.

A normal FSH level and a high LH level (LH-to-FSH ratio > 1) with normal or slightly elevated estradiol levels are consistent with PCOS. In patients with hirsutism, total testosterone and DHEAS levels can distinguish the source of androgen excess and rule out androgen-secreting tumors of the ovary and the adrenal-gland, respectively. Serum 17-hydroxyprogesterone levels < 300 ng/dL rule out 21-hydroxylase deficiency, the most common cause of congenital adrenal hyperplasia, another relatively common cause of hirsutism. The evaluation of women with hyperandrogenism is discussed in further detail in Chapter 54.

A low estradiol level with low or normal FSH and LH levels (hypogonadotropic hypogonadism) implies either a pituitary or hypothalamic cause of amenorrhea. Generally, if prolactin levels are normal, no pituitary imaging is needed. If FSH and LH levels are extremely low (< 2 mIU/mL), pituitary MRI or CT is advised. Hypogonadotropic hypo-

gonadism with a normal pituitary imaging study confirms hypothalamic amenorrhea.

Although both patients with hypothalamic amenorrhea and with POF have extremely low estrogen levels, patients with hypothalamic amenorrhea do not experience hot flashes. The vasomotor flashes observed in POF patients coincide with the elevated LH level and are not directly caused by low estrogen.[1–4,16]

TREATMENT

Successful management of amenorrhea depends on the accurate diagnosis and patients' needs and complaints. Underlying diseases such as ovarian or adrenal tumors, pituitary adenomas, hypothyroidism, anorexia nervosa, and autoimmune disorders should be treated. Most patients are concerned about both fertility and the long-term health implications of amenorrhea. It is important to counsel patients on these two issues after the diagnosis is made.

Women with amenorrhea and high or normal estrogen levels, such as patients with PCOS, have an increased incidence of endometrial hyperplasia and cancer because of unopposed estrogen exposure. Patients with PCOS also have an increased risk of ovarian and breast cancer. Periodic menstrual withdrawal is important in preventing endometrial hyperplasia and can be accomplished by administering oral medroxyprogesterone acetate 10 mg/d for 12 to 14 days each month. Alternatively, oral contraceptive pills can be used and are especially helpful for women with signs of androgen excess. For women with hirsutism, spironolactone, at a dose up to 200 mg/d (together with oral contraceptive pills), achieves good results after about 6 months of continuous treatment and can be used long term. Ovulation can be induced with oral clomiphene citrate in 85% of patients. Fertility approaches the level of the normal population among patients with PCOS who undergo ovulation induction.

Patients who have low estrogen levels require hormone replacement therapy to prevent osteoporosis. These patients include those with POF of all causes and those with hypothalamic amenorrhea. Either sequential estrogen and progesterone therapy or continuous combined estrogen and progesterone preparation can be used. In women with hypothalamic amenorrhea, the comparatively low dosage of standard hormone replacement allows detection of the return of ovarian cycles. Oral contraceptive pills are an ideal substitute for young patients as these patients may require more estrogen than provided by hormone replacement. Oral contraceptive pills also provide contraception should ovarian cycles return. Calcium supplementation is recommended for these patients. For women with hypothalamic amenorrhea, ovulation and pregnancy can be achieved by pulsatile administration of Gn-RH agonist (via a pump) or by daily injection of gonadotropins. Patients with POF desiring pregnancy should be referred to a donor oocyte program.

REFERENCES

1. American College of Obstetricians and Gynecologists. Amenorrhea. ACOG Technical Bulletin 128. Washington (DC): ACOG; 1989.
2. Speroff L, Glass RH, Kase NJ. Amenorrhea. In: Speroff L, Glass RH, Kase NJ, editors. Clinical gynecologic endocrinology and infertility. 5th ed. Baltimore (MD): Williams & Wilkins; 1994. p. 401–56.
3. Salama MM, Casson P. Amenorrhea. In: Stovall TG, Ling FW, editors. Gynecology for the primary care physician. 1st ed. Philadelphia (PA): Current Medicine; 1999. p. 349–59.
4. Vaitukaitis JL. Anovulation and amenorrhea. In: Seibel MM, editor. Infertility. 2nd ed. Stamford (CT): Appleton & Lange; 1996. p. 111–9.
5. Carmel PW, Araki S, Ferin M. Pituitary stalk portal blood collection in rhesus monkeys: evidence for pulsatile release of gonadotropin-releasing hormone (GnRH). Endocrinology 1976;99:243–8.
6. Burger CW, Korsen T, van Kessel H, et al. Pulsating luteinizing hormone patterns in the follicular phase of the menstrual cycle, polycystic ovarian disease (PCOD) and non-PCOD secondary amenorrhea. J Clin Endocrinol Metab 1985;61:1126–32.
7. Veldhuis JD, Beitins I, Johnson ML, et al. Biologically active luteinizing hormone is secreted in episodic pulsations that vary in relation to stage of the menstrual cycle. J Clin Endocrinol Metab 1984;58:1050–8.
8. DeVane GW, Czekala NM, Judd HL, Yen SSC. Circulating gonadotropins, estrogen and androgens in polycystic ovarian disease. Am J Obstet Gynecol 1975;121:496–500.
9. Chrousos GP, Torpy DJ, Gold PW. Interactions between the hypothalamic-pituitary-adrenal axis and the female reproductive system: clinical implications. Ann Intern Med 1998;129:229–40.
10. Petrozza JC, Gray MR, Davis AJ, et al. Congenital absence of the uterus and vagina is not commonly transmitted as a dominant genetic trait: outcomes of surrogate pregnancies. Fertil Steril 1997;67:387–9.
11. Alper MM, Garner PR, Seibel MM: Premature ovarian failure: current concept. J Reprod Med 1986;31:699–708.
12. Anasti JN. Premature ovarian failure: an update. Fertil Steril 1998;70:1–15.
13. Barnes RB, Lobo RA. Endogenous opioids in polycystic ovary syndrome. Semin Reprod Endocrinol 1987;5:185.
14. Polson DW, Adams J, Wadsworth J, Franks S. Polycystic ovaries: a common finding in normal women. Lancet 1988;1:870–2.
15. Warren MP. Amenorrhea in endurance runners. J Clin Endocrinol Metab 1992;75:1393–7.
16. Warren MP. Evaluation of secondary amenorrhea. J Clin Endocrinol Metab 1996;81:437–42.

74

ABNORMAL MENSES AND DYSMENORRHEA

Lawrence Kagan, BS, and Alan H. DeCherney, MD

From menarche to menopause women can be afflicted with abnormal menses and/or dysmenorrhea. Menstrual symptoms generally occur because of an associated abnormality of the reproductive system. Therefore, a systematic approach to diagnosis is required to rule out any potential uterine pathology. In primary care practice, any significant alteration in the menstrual pattern or amount of discharge should be evaluated. When the cause is accurately diagnosed, most causes of abnormal uterine bleeding and excessive cramping can be treated effectively.

Perimenopausal women and women on hormone replacement therapy with abdominal bleeding require specific evaluation. This is discussed in Chapter 82.

HORMONES AND THE MENSTRUAL CYCLE

To accurately define disorders of the menstrual cycle, it is first necessary to discuss normal menses. Hormones control and coordinate the menstrual cycle, which normally lasts from 21 to 35 days with 2 to 6 days of flow and an average blood loss of 20 to 60 mL.[1] The ovarian cycle can be divided into two main phases: the follicular phase and the luteal phase. From the perspective of changes within the uterus, the phases are termed proliferative and secretory phases, respectively.

Follicular (Proliferative) Phase

The ovaries are in the follicular phase beginning on the first day of menstruation and ending on the day of ovulation. This period usually lasts between 10 and 14 days. During this time, follicle-stimulating hormone (FSH) and luteinizing hormone (LH) are released by the anterior pituitary, stimulating the development of a dominant Graafian follicle. As follicles grow, the granulosa cells gradually increase their production of estradiol (the primary estrogen) stimulating the development and maintenance of the endometrium. Toward the end of the follicular phase, increasing levels of FSH and estradiol also stimulate the production of LH receptors on the maturing follicle. At about day 13, a rapid increase in estradiol secretion exerts positive feedback on the anterior pituitary, initiating an LH surge that is responsible for follicular rupture approximately 24 hours later. During ovulation, the secondary oocyte is released into the uterine tube marking the end of the follicular phase.

Luteal (Secretory) Phase

Stimulated by high levels of LH, the luteal phase begins with the conversion of the empty follicle into the corpus luteum. The new corpus luteum secretes both progesterone and estradiol, whereas the Graafian follicle was only capable of secreting estradiol. The high levels of ovarian hormones serve two main functions: (1) they exert negative feedback on the production of FSH and LH ensuring no further follicular maturation, and (2) they stimulate further development of the uterine lining by converting the proliferative endometrium to secretory endometrium. The endometrium becomes thick and vascular to allow implantation and nourishment of a blastocyst should fertilization occur. If not, luteolysis (degeneration of the corpus luteum) occurs on about day 26 of the cycle. The drop in the ovarian hormone secretion by the degenerating corpus luteum initiates necrosis and sloughing of the stratum functionale of the endometrium, and menstruation occurs.

Menstruation

The fall in the progesterone and estrogen levels at the end of the luteal phase initiates a cascade of events leading to contractions of the myometrium, vasoconstriction followed by vasodilation of the vascular system of the endometrium, and the maintenance of hemostasis. Classic experiments by Markee, using the rhesus monkey as a model, shed light on the various endocrinologic states of the menstrual cycle. He found that the vasculature of the endometrial tissue constricts and dilates rhythmically and concluded that vasoactive substances initiate menstrual bleeding.[2]

Prostaglandins are a large group of vasoactive, 20-carbon, unsaturated fatty acid metabolites of arachidonic acid that have been found to be of importance to the reproductive tract. Two of these, PGE_2 and $PGF_{2\alpha}$, are such potent stimulators of the myometrium that they are widely used for induction of labor. They are also known to be vasodilators and vasoconstrictors, respectively. The decline in progesterone immediately before menstruation causes lysosomal labilization and the release of activated phospholipase A_2 generating arachidonic acid from phospholipids, triglycerides, and cholesterol of the endometrial cells. The arachidonic acid produced is converted to cyclic endoperoxides by cyclooxygenase, and finally isomerase and reductase converts it to PGE_2 and $PGF_{2\alpha}$.[3] In women, concentrations of PGE_2 and $PGF_{2\alpha}$ peak in the late luteal and menstrual phases. Hormones, such as vasopressin and oxytocin, are also known to cause contractions of the myometrium and are involved in the stimulation of PGE_2 and $PGF_{2\alpha}$ synthesis. These findings coincide with observations that fluctuations in plasma hormonal levels regulate endometrial $PGF_{2\alpha}$ production during the menstrual cycle.[4]

Using uteri extirpated during menstruation, Christiaens and associates revealed that up to 5 days preceding menstruation, shrinkage of the stratum functionale and vascular lesions in the walls of the spiral arterioles lead to endothelial degeneration and bleeding into the uterine cavity.[2,5] Hemostasis is established initially by hemostatic plug formation, which consists of degranulated platelets regularly seen at the vessel lesion, but seldom occluding the lesion. Fibrin is almost never seen in association with the initial hemostatic plugs but is found in the capillaries and stroma. With the onset of menstruation, massive extravasation of red blood cells into the compact layer has occurred.[5] During sloughing of the endometrium, hemostasis is maintained by the vasoconstriction of the basal layer until prompt proliferation of the functional layer occurs when menstruation ceases.

MENSTRUAL HISTORY

Obtaining a menstrual history is necessary for the diagnosis of any menstrual abnormality. The cycle is counted from the first day of menstrual flow to the first day of the following menstrual flow. Because the length of cycles varies widely from 22 to 35 days, any recent change in pattern is a more reliable indicator of a problem than the interval.

The amount of menstrual flow is difficult to measure. The brand and size of the tampon used can vary widely in its absorption capabilities leading to inaccurate estimations of menstrual volume. Despite this, it is worthy to note that the average blood loss during menstruation is 35 mL and repetitive loss of 80 mL/cycle can result in anemia.[1] If significant anemia is not present, variability in the menstrual patterns of adolescents and perimenopausal women is acceptable, provided it does not exceed 7 days of bleeding, with cycles longer than 42 days, or shorter than 21 days.

An indirect quantitative assessment of menstrual volume can be obtained by measuring hemoglobin concentration, serum iron levels, and serum ferritin levels. Furthermore, the passage of many large blood clots and saturation of more than one tampon per hour for 6 hours should be considered excessive. Any intermenstrual bleeding or that which occurs after intercourse should be noted because its presence may indicate cervical cancer, polyps, fibroids, or infections.[2]

ABNORMAL MENSES

The intricacies of the vascular and hemostatic events associated with menstruation are so precise that even subtle alterations to the associated physiologic events may lead to abnormal menses. Abnormal menses are a common complaint; approximately 10 to 15% of all gynecologic patients undergo evaluation for abnormal menses. Examples of some common abnormal menstrual patterns include:

- Oligomenorrhea: irregular, scanty menstrual flow at intervals of 40 days or more

- Polymenorrhea: regular or irregular menstrual flow at intervals of 21 days or less
- Menorrhagia: regular excessive bleeding, in duration or amount
- Metrorrhagia: irregularly timed menses with a normal amount of flow
- Menometrorrhagia: irregular, frequent, excessive bleeding
- Hypomenorrhea: regular bleeding with a decreased amount of flow
- Intermenstrual bleeding: bleeding occurring between normal menstrual cycles
- Dysmenorrhea: pain in association with menstruation

The age of a patient is a factor that must be considered when evaluating her menstrual pattern. The 5 to 7 years after menarche, the 20 to 25 intermediate years of reproductive life, and the 5 to 7 years prior to menopause have distinct variations in their pattern. Both perimenopausal and adolescent years are marked by irregularly timed menses. Generally longer intervals are observed (≥ 36 days) than shorter intervals (< 20 days). This can be attributed to varying patterns of gonadotropin-releasing hormone (Gn-RH) release resulting in suboptimal follicle development as well as poor corpus luteum development.[6] Although more commonly seen at the extremes of the reproductive years, abnormal menses can occur throughout reproductive life. Of patients evaluated for menstrual disorders, 50% are over the age of 45 years, 20% are adolescents, and the remaining 30% are in their intermediate reproductive years.[7]

The etiology of abnormal menses can be divided into two main categories: organic and dysfunctional. Organic systemic diseases that manifest abnormal uterine bleeding include coagulation disorders, such as von Willebrand disease; platelet deficiency disorders, such as leukemia, severe sepsis, idiopathic thrombocytopenic purpura, and hypersplenism; thyroid dysfunction; diabetes mellitus; hyperandrogenism; malnutrition; and cirrhosis.[8] Organic reproductive tract diseases are also common causes of abnormal menses. Submucous myomas, endometrial polyps, endometriosis, and adenomyosis frequently cause menorrhagia and intermenstrual spotting. Furthermore, malignancies of the reproductive tract can manifest as abnormal menses.[9]

Dysfunctional uterine bleeding can be either ovulatory or anovulatory. Most causes of abnormal bleeding patterns in ovulatory cycles are either idiopathic or caused by an insufficient luteal phase. Evidence of anovulatory cycles consists of prolonged menstrual irregularity, presence of cystic glandular hyperplasia of the endometrium, impaired follicular development, an absent positive feedback mechanism or other forms of endocrinopathy. Menorrhagia is common in women who are obese, have polycystic ovarian syndrome, or are anovulatory adolescents with an immature hypothalamic-pituitary axis and in perimenopausal women.[10] In the case of adolescents, maturation of the hypothalamic-pituitary unit establishes regular ovulatory menstrual cycles approximately 2 years following menarche.[11]

There are other pathophysiologic conditions that can lead to anovulation and abnormal bleeding. Anovulatory cycles in patients with polycystic ovarian disease have functional feedback mechanisms but inadequate estradiol signals. Eating disorders, such as anorexia nervosa or bulimia nervosa, stress, and excessive physical exercise can lead to dysfunction of the hypothalamus, resulting in lower FSH and LH secretion by the anterior pituitary and, finally, suboptimal follicle and corpus luteum development. Hyperandrogenemia involves the gonadotrophic action of the adrenals causing suppression of the hypothalamic and hypophyseal axis due to an increased supply of androgens. Hyperandrogenemia is a result of hyperplasia, adenomas, or enzyme defects in the adrenals. Diabetes mellitus, thyroid dysfunction, and endometriosis are also common causes of anovulation and abnormal menses.[12]

Symptoms and Diagnosis

The accurate clinicopathologic diagnosis of abnormal uterine bleeding should begin with a sensitive pregnancy test, a complete menstrual history (including distinguishing between ovulatory or anovulatory cycles), a Papanicolaou (Pap) smear, and a pelvic examination. Should the pregnancy test be positive, abnormal uterine bleeding could indicate an ectopic gestation. Women with a menstrual cycle length > 42 days are assumed to be anovulatory. Women with shorter cycles can also be anovulatory. Ovulation can be confirmed by basal body temperature monitoring. The presence of a temperature increase of 0.5°F over baseline for at least 10 days indicates the presence of a luteal phase. Lack of a temperature rise does not definitively rule out ovulation. In women with a monophasic basal body temperature cycle, documentation of a serum progesterone level of 4 ng/mL or less 5 to 7 days before the beginning of menstruation can confirm anovulation.

Common causes of abnormal uterine bleeding in women with regular ovulatory cycles are pelvic infection or anatomic abnormalities. The presence of gonorrhea or chlamydia can be determined with a cervical culture. The specific treatment for anatomic abnormalities depends on the anomaly that is present. The palpation of uterine or adnexal pathology during the pelvic examination warrants evaluation by hysterography or transvaginal ultrasonography, and further histologic diagnosis may be necessary. Endometriosis is more common in older women but should not be ruled out as a cause of abnormal bleeding in adolescents. A hysteroscopy combined with an endometrial biopsy is a highly accurate means of diagnosis and is the recommended course of evaluation of women in whom uterine pathology is suspected. It has been estimated that blind dilation and curettage gives false-negative results in 10 to 25% of women.[8] In the hands of a skilled clinician, a hysteroscope is capable of revealing submucous leiomyoma, endometrial polyps, and an embedded intrauterine device (IUD). An operating hysteroscope can also remove anatomic lesions. An endometrial biopsy identifies whether or not malignancy is present.

Menorrhagia is common in women with anovulatory cycles and is usually caused by estrogen withdrawal or estrogen breakthrough bleeding. Anovulatory uterine bleeding is a symptom of underlying endocrinopathy, and therefore, the dysfunction within the endocrine system must be determined. Testing for thyroid and hypothalamic dysfunction should be routinely performed in women with anovulatory cycles. Such women should also be tested for hyperprolactinemia.[2] Women who manifest signs of hyperandrogenism should be evaluated for underlying endocrinopathies. This evaluation is described in Chapter 53.

If there is any concern regarding endometrial cancer, aspiration curettage is in order because the progression from atypia to cancer is short. Hyper-plasia without atypia is not a precursor of carcinoma, but lesions exhibiting cytonuclear atypia usually progress to endometrial carcinoma. The latter condition, endometrial intraepithelial neoplasia, is characterized by enlargement, rounding, and pleomorphism of the nuclei with aneuploid DNA content.[10]

When a thorough evaluation does not lead to a specific diagnosis for abnormal menses, testing for a coagulation disorder should be performed. Von Willebrand disease is by far the most common inherited coagulation disorder in women, affecting up to 1.5% of women in the United States. Women with von Willebrand disease often report excessive menses, including simultaneous use of two pads or tampons, changing pads or tampons every 30 minutes to 2 hours, frequently staining clothes or bedsheets, and time lost from work or school because of excessive menstruation. Patients may also report excessive bleeding with surgical procedures or childbirth, sometimes requiring transfusion. Von Willebrand disease is underdiagnosed, in part because the routine coagulation tests (prothrombin time [PT], partial thromboplastin time [PTT], platelet count) are usually normal. Because it is inherited in an autosomal-dominant fashion, patients may not complain of symptoms because their menstrual pattern is considered by family members to be "normal." Patients with symptoms consistent with von Willebrand disease should be referred to a hematologist for further testing. Von Willebrand disease or another coagulation disorder can be treated with intranasal desmopressin acetate, a vasopressin analogue.[13,14]

Finally, if all tests are normal, adenomyosis, a cause of abnormal menses that is diagnosed by exclusion, should be considered. An approach to abnormal menses is summarized in Figure 74–1.

Treatment

The treatment of abnormal menses depends on the diagnosis. Anovulatory women without pelvic pathology or a specifically treatable endocrinopathy experiencing menorrhagia, oligomenorrhea, or polymenorrhea can be successfully treated with progestin therapy or standard dose combination oral contraceptives. Progestational regimens for use when hyperplasia and neoplasia are not present include 10 mg of medroxyprogesterone acetate or 2.5 to 5 mg of norethindrone for 10 days of the

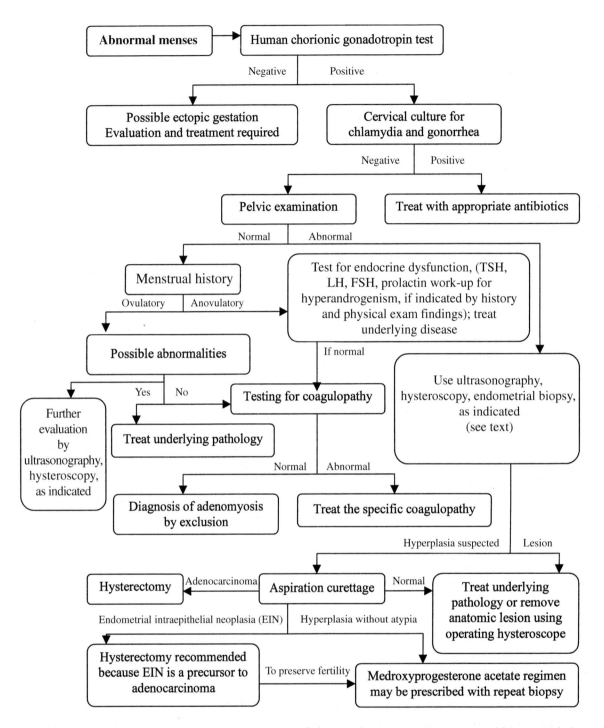

FIGURE 74–1. Algorithm for the diagnosis and treatment of abnormal menses, assuming general history and physical examination do not include asystemic causes. TSH = thyroid-stimulating hormone; LH = luteinizing hormone; FSH = follicle-stimulating hormone.

month.[2] Progestin therapy can prevent or reverse hyperplasia without atypia, whether it be architecturally simple or complex.[10] The recommended treatment for endometrial hyperplasia without atypia is 10 to 20 mg of medroxyprogesterone acetate daily for 2 to 3 months, followed by repeat endome-trial aspiration curettage to confirm resolution of the hyperplasia.

Another form of progestin therapy is the progestin-releasing IUD. The levonorgestrel-releasing system Mirena has a 7-year lifetime, and Progestasert has a 1-year lifetime. Both are considered effective contraceptives and means to control menorrhagia, causing an 80% reduction in menstrual blood loss in 3 months and 100% within 1 year.[8]

Nonsteroidal anti-inflammatory drugs (NSAIDs) are another treatment modality shown to be effective in the treatment of mild menorrhagia when no organic pelvic pathology is present.[15] A 20 to 50% reduction in menstrual blood loss can be expected from the following regimens given either for the first 3 days of menses or the duration: 500 mg three times per day of mefenamic acid; 400 mg three times per day of ibuprofen; 100 mg three times per day of meclofenamate sodium; or 275 mg every 6 hours of naproxen sodium after a loading dose of 550 mg.[8]

Danazol is an isoxazole derivative of the synthetic steroid 17α-ethinyltestosterone. It acts as an antigonadotrophic androgen, with weak progestogenic effects on the endometrium. It is commonly used as a treatment for endometriosis, but it is also very effective in reducing the blood loss associated with menorrhagia; 200 to 300 mg twice daily for 12 weeks is recommended. The side effects of danazol include weight gain and fluid retention, acne, decreased breast size, and hot flashes. Most of the side effects are due to danazol's androgenic actions, and therefore, this course of treatment should not be considered if there is a possibility of pregnancy.[10]

Endometrial ablation is an effective alternative to hysterectomy in cases of severe menorrhagia or menometrorrhagia in premenopausal women for whom fertility is not an issue and when endometrial pathology is not present. Uterine balloon therapy is often used. After a 1-year follow up, reduction of blood flow to normal levels or less was achieved in 81% of 125 patients treated in the American clinical trials. Only 3 cases of probable endometritis and 1 case of urinary tract infection occurred, all of which responded to oral antibiotic therapy.[16]

Uterine balloon therapy has been shown to be safer and as efficacious as hysteroscopic rollerball ablation. The ablation procedure can be performed in the outpatient setting, with a reduced need for general anesthesia. In one study, 84% of women undergoing rollerball ablation required general anesthesia, while only 53% of uterine balloon therapy patients were anesthetized.[16]

Gynecare's Thermachoice system is a software-controlled device designed to ablate uterine tissue, using thermal energy. A single-use balloon catheter is inserted through the cervix and is then filled with a sterile fluid consisting of 5% dextrose in water until a pressure of 160 to 180 mm of mercury is achieved. The fluid temperature is then raised to 87°C (188°F) and maintained for 8 minutes, at which time it is deflated and discarded. The procedure can be completed in less than 30 minutes, with only 2.3% of cases taking longer than 50 minutes, compared with 18% of rollerball cases.[16]

While the simplicity and short duration of endometrial ablation makes it an attractive alternative, it does not come without potential complications. Although the procedure decreases the likelihood of pregnancy, it should not be considered a means of sterilization. Pregnancy is possible and can be dangerous for both mother and fetus; therefore, alternative forms of contraception should be employed. Another potential complication of the ablation procedure is that it may mask an accurate diagnosis of hyperplasia or adenocarcinoma. Furthermore, the procedure is contraindicated in women with weakness of the myometrium, such as a history of cesarian sections or transmural myomectomy. Besides a normal Pap smear and endometrial biopsy, a uterine cavity depth of 6 to 10 cm is also required.[17]

Submucous fibroids, endometrial polyps, or an embedded IUD can be removed by an operating hysteroscope. Should endometrial intraepithelial neoplasia be identified, most clinicians recommend hysterectomy because the neoplasia can quickly progress to adenocarcinoma; but if fertility is an issue, 30 mg medroxyprogesterone acetate daily, with repeat biopsy in 3 to 4 months, can be an effective treatment.[10]

DYSMENORRHEA

Dysmenorrhea is derived from the Greek word for difficult monthly flow, but today it is defined as excessive pain in association with menstruation. Two classifications exist: (1) primary dysmenorrhea, which is an isolated disorder; and (2) secondary dysmenorrhea, in which an organic alteration can be ascertained. A finding of secondary dysmenorrhea is unlikely during the teenage years, but an organic cause must be sought when severe cramping begins after the age of 20 years in a patient with a history of regular ovulatory cycles.

In one study involving 19-year-old women in Sweden, the prevalence of dysmenorrhea was found to be as high as 72.4%.[18] As well as being very painful to the afflicted, at least 10% of those afflicted are incapacitated for several days each month, costing over 140,000,000 work hours each year in the United States alone.

Primary Dysmenorrhea

Primary dysmenorrhea is idiopathic in that no visible pathologic abnormality of the reproductive system exists. It is most common among nulliparous young women with a normal pelvic examination. Primary dysmenorrhea is characterized by cramping lower abdominal pain, which may radiate to the back and thighs and may be accompanied by gastrointestinal, cardiovascular, and neurologic symptoms. Premenstrual syndrome may also be present.

The historical theory that cervical obstruction may be the underlying cause of primary dysmenorrhea has been widely rejected. The size of the cervical canal has not been shown to be any smaller in women with dysmenorrhea, provided no cervical abnormalities or stenosis exists that may occlude menstrual flow.[19]

Experimental evidence implicates myometrial hypercontractility, prostaglandins, and abnormal uterine blood flow in the pathophysiology of primary dysmenorrhea. Tests have shown that the intrauterine pressure between the contractions, the amplitude, and the frequency of the contractions were all higher for women suffering from dysmenorrhea.[20] In ovulatory cycles, the production of prostaglandins peaks during the first 48 hours of menstrual flow, which is consistent with the occurrence of primary dysmenorrhea. Furthermore, PGE_2 and $PGF_{2\alpha}$ concentrations are elevated in the endometrium of dysmenorrheic women.[21] Vasopressin concentrations are also higher in women with dysmenorrhea. Using a thermister probe to measure the menstrual volume, Akerlund found that blood flow to the uterus was decreased during exacerbations of pain.[15] These data coincide with the exposure of $PGF_{2\alpha}$ to endometrial tissue, resulting in vasoconstriction and contraction.[22]

SYMPTOMS AND DIAGNOSIS

Primary dysmenorrhea often presents in adolescence. Careful evaluation requires not only a detailed history and appropriate physical examination but also an approach that is sensitive to adolescent psychosocial needs. The physician or other health care clinician should try to maintain a sympathetic concern for detail, exhibit understanding and empathy for the condition, and offer reassurance to the patient without minimizing her concerns.[23] As with most adolescent evaluations, it is best to ask potentially sensitive questions, such as those related to sexual activity, in confidence.

Since primary dysmenorrhea usually begins with the onset of ovulatory menstruation, it may not occur until 2 years following menarche. Cramping usually occurs just before or at the onset of bleeding in both the left and right lower quadrants of the suprapubic region, radiating down the thighs and throughout the lumbosacral region. Other typical symptoms include nausea, vomiting, diarrhea, sweating, irritability, and, rarely, syncopal episodes.[24] Patients frequently become apprehensive near the time of the menses, describing the pain as sharp and severe, unremitting, erosive, and discouraging and depressing.[23] By the time a patient has come to see a clinician, she has usually attempted self-medication with standard analgesics. However, standard analgesics are not effective treatment for severe dysmenorrhea.

Contraindications to estrogen-progestin therapy should be noted, as well as whether the patient is sexually active . If the patient is sexually active, cervical studies for chlamydia and gonorrhea, as well as a complete blood count with erythrocyte sedimentation rate, should be obtained to rule out subacute pelvic inflammatory disease. Furthermore, a sensitive pregnancy test should always be obtained. Following a complete history, a complete physical examination should be carried out. Secondary sexual characteristics should be noted. Vital sign abnormalities or a markedly tender abdominal examination mandate evaluation for alternative causes of pelvic pain.[24]

It is important to explain the necessity of a pelvic examination, even though the modern adolescent probably expects it. In all examinations of patients with dysmenorrhea, a pelvic examination with a finger and a bimanual examination should be carried out. A speculum examination is only required if the patient is sexually active.[24] Severe pain with movement of the cervix or palpation of the adnexal structures suggests possible pelvic infection or other pelvic pathology, and if present, further diagnostic evaluation should be pursued. Nodularity of the uterosacral ligaments and cul-de-sac suggests endometriosis, which also requires further evaluation.[10] If the pelvic examination is normal, rectal examination is not routinely necessary. Provided the patient responds to treatment and no visible pathologic abnormality exists, ultrasonography or laparoscopy is not necessary. A follow-up visit in 3 months should be scheduled to ascertain the effectiveness of the prescribed therapy (see below).

TREATMENT

Therapies designed to inhibit elevated levels of prostaglandin production are the most effective treatments for primary dysmenorrhea. NSAIDs inhibit the enzyme cyclooxygenase, which is necessary in the biosynthetic pathway of prostaglandins (Figure 74–2). NSAID treatment is also sometimes effective in reducing excessive uterine bleeding. It is worth noting that NSAIDs are also known to increase bleeding time in the skin. This paradox has yet to be fully explained.[25]

Treatment is usually initiated with NSAIDs from the arylpropionic acid family, such as flurbiprofen, ibuprofen, or naproxen. Although aspirin is often prescribed, evidence suggests that the uterus is relatively insensitive to aspirin. The most effective NSAIDs for relieving dysmenorrhea are the fenamates. The fenamate family acts antagonistically, competing for prostaglandin-binding sites.[10] Typical dosages include flufenamic acid 100 to 200 mg three times daily, mefenamic acid 250 to 500 mg four times daily, or tolfenamic acid 133 mg three times daily. The patient should receive a stronger medication, such as Darvocet or Fiorinal, for severe crises.

The side effects associated with NSAIDs are usually minimal in young women but can include blurred vision, headaches, dizziness, and gastrointestinal discomfort, which can be often alleviated by taking the medication with food or milk.[10] Patients who experience gastrointestinal discomfort or who have a history of NSAID-induced gastritis or peptic

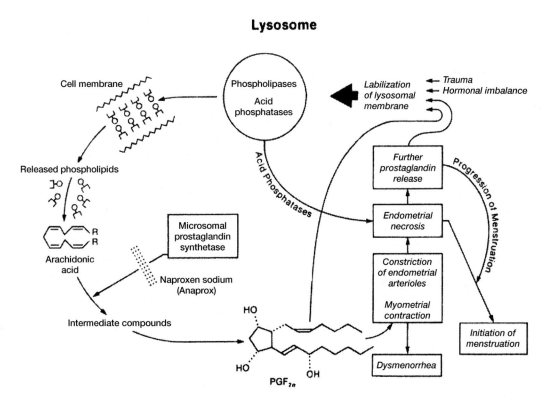

FIGURE 74–2. Theoretical concept of the synthesis of prostaglandins (PGs) and the mechanism of naproxen sodium action. Reproduced with permission from Rosenwaks Z, Jones GS. J Reprod Med 1980;252:207.

ulcer disease may benefit from the use of an NSAID that specifically inhibits cyclooxygenase-2 (COX-2), and, thus, has less gastrointestinal side effects. In a randomized controlled trial, the COX-2 inhibitor rofecoxib provided analgesic efficacy greater than that with the placebo. The recommended initial dosage of rofecoxib is 25 to 50 mg, followed by 25 mg every 24 hours, as needed.[26]

Combination oral contraceptives are the most widely used and most effective form of treatment for dysmenorrhea. Combination oral contraceptives have been shown to decrease uterine contractual response to vasopressin and $PGF_{2\alpha}$. The relief of dysmenorrhea may require a higher-dose pill over the long term, but it makes good clinical sense to use the lowest-dose pill that is effective with the greatest possible safety margin. Although there is little data indicating a preference of monophasics over multiphasics, a 30 to 35 μg estrogen monophasic has been shown to be effective in treating dysmenorrhea.[27] Patients and parents should be informed of the lack of association of long-term adverse medical events, the fact that oral contraceptives do not accelerate the initiation of sexual activity, the potential non-contraceptive benefits of these medications (eg, alleviation of acne, lessening and regulating the menstrual flow) but also warned of the rare risk of serious complications, such as deep venous thrombosis, pulmonary embolism, and stroke.[2]

Progestins have been found to decrease the sensitivity of the myometrium to prostaglandins and are known to restore an adequate luteal phase. In the adolescent, progesterone at doses of 20 mg/d from day 15 to day 25 of the cycle can be effective. Progestins, such as norethisterone, lynestrenol, nomegestrol acetate, or promegestone, have been used with success.

Additional modalities include the use of hot compresses or heating pads applied to the external genitalia or abdomen. Self-help groups can help some patients cope with the psychological effects of dysmenorrhea. Transcutaneous electrical nerve stimulation is also effective in relieving primary dysmenorrhea. This treatment may be used in addition to other therapies and should be considered for patients who have adverse reactions to medications.

In patients with severe dysmenorrhea, it may be necessary to use antigonadotrophic agents for 15 to 20 days per cycle.[28] Women with severe dysmenorrhea who are free of pathophysiologic abnormalities but are unresponsive to therapy may consider a presacral neurectomy. At least 50% pain relief has been obtained with this procedure. No notable additional benefit occurred when uterosacral transection was performed. Most women with primary dysmenorrhea are adolescents and, therefore, are not candidates for hysterectomy. As a last resort, this procedure is effective if fertility is not an issue and all other treatment modalities have failed.

Secondary Dysmenorrhea

Secondary dysmenorrhea is symptomatically similar to primary dysmenorrhea, but it is caused by an underlying pathology. A secondary cause of dysmenorrhea should be suspected when dysmenorrhea presents years after menarche, especially in women with anovulatory cycles. In general, women over the age of 20 years who present with dysmenorrhea and younger women who fail treatment with NSAIDs and combination oral contraceptives should undergo more extensive evaluation for secondary causes.

Ectopic pregnancy, endometriosis, pelvic inflammation and infection, intrauterine contraceptive devices, uterine myoma, endometrial polyps, submucous uterine fibroids, endometrial carcinoma, ovarian cysts, and extragenital lesions can all present with dysmenorrhea. Adenomyosis, another cause of secondary amenorrhea, is often referred to as endometriosis interna because of its similarity to endometriosis. In this case, the benign endometrial glands and stroma penetrate into the myometrium, instead of the peritoneum, causing pain.

Older women may shed their endometrium in large fragments causing occlusion of the cervix, a condition termed membranous dysmenorrhea. Powerful and painful uterine myometrium contractions ensue until the uterine contents are expelled. Pelvic congestion syndrome results from engorgement of the pelvic vasculature and may present as dymenorrhea.

Congenital malfusion of the Müllerian system and cervical stenosis are also causes of dysmenorrhea. The pathogenesis of these conditions are similar; in both cases, uterine distension, retention of menstrual fluids, and increased absorption of prostaglandins may occur. The pain associated with cervical stenosis may be similar to membranous dysmenorrhea due to partial occlusion of the cervix and can be relieved by dilation of the cervical canal.[24,29] Women with an embryonic maldevelopment will experience dysmenorrhea beginning at menarche, but stenosis can occur at any time due to an inflammatory disorder or excessive development of fibrous tissue.

DIAGNOSIS

Associated symptoms may provide historical clues to the underlying pathology in secondary amenorrhea. Uterine fibroids are typically manifested by menorrhagia, dysmenorrhea, urinary disturbances, and constipation. Adenomyosis can cause abnormal menstrual bleeding, dysmenorrhea, dyspareunia, dyschezia, uterine enlargement, and, occasionally, infertility.[9] Dysmenorrhea associated with adenomyosis usually occurs 1 week prior to the onset of menstruation in women over the age of 40 years. Pelvic congestion syndrome often causes low back pain and dyspareunia. The condition is often accompanied by headache and breast tenderness.[29]

As in patients with primary dysmenorrhea, a sensitive pregnancy test and a thorough pelvic examination are the initial steps in evaluation. Cervical cultures for gonorrhea and chlamydia should be obtained. Nonpregnant patients with uterine enlargement should undergo transvaginal ultrasonography to evaluate for uterine myomata.

A specific diagnosis for many cases of secondary dysmenorrhea can be obtained with laparoscopy and/or hysteroscopy. When acute pelvic inflammatory disease, cervical stenosis, normal pregnancy, or certain coagulopathies are present, dilatation and curettage (D & C) is usually contraindicated.[6] The diagnosis and removal of an embedded IUD, endometrial polyps, or submucous fibroids can be done with a hysteroscope. Laparoscopy, D & C, and hysteroscopy can all be performed in the outpatient surgical setting and should always be performed before committing to a specific course of therapy or surgery.[29]

Pelvic congestion syndrome is principally a clinical diagnosis of exclusion. Physical findings can include an enlarged and bluish appearance of the vaginal walls and cervix due to venous stasis. Pelvic congestion syndrome can be diagnosed using rapid-sequence radiography and injection of a dye into the cervical venous system. The size and configuration of the venous drainage plexus on the left and right side of the cervix can then be obtained.[27] However, uterine venograms are not readily available in the United States. Adenomyosis is also generally a clinical diagnosis, as definitive diagnosis is by hysterectomy. Extragenital causes of secondary dysmenorrhea are discussed in Chapter 75 on pelvic pain.

TREATMENT

Treatment of secondary dysmenorrhea is aimed at the underlying pathology. Patients with pain related to ectopic pregnancy should receive emergency evaluation and treatment. Patients with suspected IUD-related dysmenorrhea should have the IUD removed, by hysteroscopy, if necessary. Endometrial polyps should be removed by D & C or an operating hysteroscope. Treatment of endometriosis, uterine myomata, endometrial cancer, and pelvic inflammatory disease are discussed in detail in other chapters on endometriosis, uterine fibroids, endometrial cancer, and sexually transmitted diseases. As in the case of endometriosis, menstrual suppression with progestins has been found to be effective in the treatment of adenomyosis.

Powerful NSAIDs can lessen the severity of the contractions in patients with membranous dysmenorrhea. The surgical approach to correct müllerian anomalies is dependent on the specific anomaly present. Treatment of pelvic congestion syndrome is discussed further in Chapter 75. An approach to dysmenorrhea is summarized in Figure 74–3.

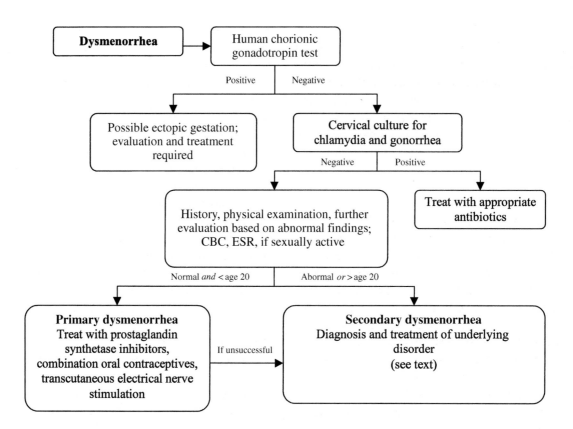

FIGURE 74–3. Algorithm for the diagnosis and treatment of dysmenorrhea. CBC = complete blood count; ESR = erythrocyte sedimentation rate.

REFERENCES

1. Berek JS. Novak's gynecology. 12th ed. Baltimore (MD): Williams & Wilkins; 1996.

2. Hammond CB, Riddick DH. Menstruation and disorders of menstrual function. In: Scott JR, Di Saia PJ, Hammond CB, Spellacy WN, editors. Danforth's obstetrics and gynecology. 8th ed. Philadelphia (PA): Lippincott Williams & Wilkins; 1999. p. 38.

3. Dawood MY. Dysmenorrhea. Baltimore (MD): Williams & Wilkins; 1981. p. 2.

4. Chaudhuri G. Biosynthesis and function of eicosanoids in the uterus. In: Carsten ME, Miller JD, editors. Uterine function molecular and cellular aspects. New York (NY): Plenum Press; 1990. p. 14.

5. Christiaens GCML, Sixma JJ, Haspels AA. Vascular and haemostatic changes in menstrual endometrium. In: Baird DT, Michie EA, editors. Mechanism of menstrual bleeding. Vol. 25. New York (NY): Raven Press; 1985.

6. Sherman BM, Wallace RB. Menstrual patterns: menarche through menopause. In: Baird DT, Michie EA, editors. Mechanism of menstrual bleeding. Vol. 25. New York (NY): Raven Press; 1985.

7. Zaino RJ. Interpretation of endometrial biopsies and curettings. Philadelphia (PA): Lippincott-Raven Publishers; 1996.

8. Mishell DR. Abnormal uterine bleeding. In: Mishell DR Jr, Stenchever MA, Droegemueller W, Herbst AL, editors. Comprehensive gynecology. 3rd ed. St. Louis (MO): Mosby-Year Book Inc.; 1997. p. 36.

9. Gompel C, Silverberg SG. Pathology in gynecology and obstetrics. Philadelphia (PA): J.B. Lippincott Company; 1994. p. 4.

10. Speroff L, Glass RH, Kase NG. Clinical gynecologic endocrinology and infertility. 4th ed. Baltimore (MD): Williams & Wilkins; 1989.

11. Baird DT. Endocrine basis of menstruation and its disorders. In: Baird DT, Michie EA, editors. Mechanism of menstrual bleeding. Vol. 25. New York (NY): Raven Press; 1985.

12. Runnebaum B, Rabe T. Pathophysiology of the corpus luteum function. In: Genazzani AR, Petraglia F, Volpe A, Facchinetti F, editors. Advances in gynecological endocrinology. Vol. 1. Park Ridge (NJ): The Parthenon Publishing Group; 1988. p. 41.

13. Kouides, PA. Females with von Willebrand disease: 72 years as the silent majority. Haemophilia 1998;4:665–76.

14. Dilley A, Crudder Sally. Von Willebrand disease in women: the need for recognition and understanding. Women's Health Gender-Based Med 1999;8:443–5.

15. De Cecco L, Venturini PL, Remorgida V, et al. Non-steroidal anti-inflammatory drugs in pelvic pain. In: Genazzani AR, Nappi G, Facchinetti F, Martignoni E, editors. Pain and reproduction. Park Ridge (NJ): The Parthenon Publishing Group; 1988. p. 30.

16. Meyer WR, Walsh BW, Grainger DA, et al. Thermal balloon and rollerball ablation to treat menorrhagia: a multicenter comparison. Obstet Gynecol 1998; 92:98–103.

17. Amso NN, Stabinsky SA, McFaul P, et al. Uterine thermal balloon therapy for the treatment of menorrhagia: the first 300 patients from a multi-centre study. Br J Obstet Gynaecol 1998;105:517–23.

18. Kinch RAH. Dysmenorrhea: a historical perspective. In: Dawood MY, McGuire JL, Demers LM, editors. Premenstrual syndrome and dysmenorrhea. Baltimore (MD): Urban & Schwarzenberg, Inc.; 1985. p. 7.

19. Lumsden MA. Dysmenorrhoea. In: Baird DT, Michie EA, editors. Mechanism of menstrual bleeding. Vol. 25. New York (NY): Raven Press; 1985.

20. Lamb EJ. Clinical features of primary dysmenorrhea. In: Dawood MY, editor. Dysmenorrhea. Baltimore (MD): Williams & Wilkins; 1981. p. 6.

21. Massobrio M, Benedetto C, Rosi A, Marozio L. Prostaglandins in dysmenorrhea. In: Genazzani AR, Petraglia F, Volpe A, Facchinetti F, editors. Advances in gynecological endocrinology. Vol. 1. Park Ridge (NJ): The Parthenon Publishing Group; 1988. p. 19.

22. Fraser IS, Peek MJ. Effects of exogenous hormones on endometrial capillaries. In: Alexander NJ, d'Arcangues C, editors. Steroid hormone and uterine bleeding. Washington (DC): American Association for the Advancement of Science; 1992. p. 8.

23. Astrachan JM. Psychiatric treatment of primary dysmenorrhea. In: Dawood MY, editor. Dysmenorrhea. Baltimore (MD): Williams & Wilkins; 1981. p. 6.

24. Dawood MY. Overall approach to the management of dysmenorrhea. In: Dawood MY, McGuire JL, Demers LM, editors. Premenstrual syndrome and dysmenorrhea. Baltimore (MD): Urban & Schwarzenberg, Inc.; 1985. p. 14.

25. Cowan BD. Dysfunctional uterine bleeding: clues to efficacious approaches. In: Alexander NJ, d'Arcangues C, editors. Steroid hormone and uterine bleeding. Washington (DC): American Association for the Advancement of Science; 1992. p. 2.

26. Morrison BW, Daniels SE, Kotey P, et al. Rofecoxib, a specific cyclooxygenase-2 inhibitor, in primary dysmenorrhea: a randomized controlled trial. Obstet Gynecol 1999;94:504–8.

27. Maxson SW, Rosenwaks Z. Dysmenorrhea, premenstrual syndrome, and other menstrual disorders. In: Copeland LJ, editor. Textbook of gynecology. Philadelphia (PA): W.B. Saunders Company; 2000. p. 23

28. Sitruk-Ware R. Therapeutic use of progestins: practical recommendations. In: Sitruk-Ware R, Mishell DR, editors. Progestins and antiprogestins in clinical practice. New York (NY): Marcel Dekker; 2000. p. 19.

29. Laros RK Jr. Secondary dysmenorrhea (excluding endometriosis). In: Dawood MY, editor. Dysmenorrhea. Baltimore (MD): Williams & Wilkins; 1981. p. 8.

75

APPROACH TO THE PATIENT WITH PELVIC PAIN

Andrea J. Rapkin, MD, and Marsha K. Guess, MD

General knowledge about pelvic pain and its pathophysiology and management is essential when providing health care to women. Pelvic pain is one of the most common complaints of women. Specifically, chronic pelvic pain is estimated to impair the lives of up to 15% of all women in the United States. The purpose of this chapter is to recapitulate briefly the basic neuroanatomy and physiology of the pain response, to review the pathologic conditions associated with acute and chronic pelvic pain, to provide information on how to evaluate patients with acute or chronic pain complaints, and to present an overview of the disorder-specific treatment options available. Given the extensive list of pathologies associated with pelvic pain in women, it is also suggested that the reader review specific chapters that provide more detailed information about individual diagnoses as well as disorders of the gastrointestinal (GI) and genitourinary (GU) tracts.

NEUROANATOMY

The proper evaluation and treatment of pelvic pain requires an understanding of the innervation of the pelvic viscera and the overlying somatic structures. The reproductive organs are innervated primarily by the thoracolumbar and sacral autonomics, with contributions from the somatic sensory nervous system.[1,2] The thoracolumbar and sacral afferents were formerly called the sympathetic and parasympathetic afferents; however, the latter terms now refer to efferents only. The pelvic visceral afferent fibers travel via three pathways.[3] First, fibers travel with sympathetic nerve bundles through the vaginal, cervical, and uterine plexuses to the inferior hypo-

gastric plexus (paracervical ganglia) and hypogastric nerve. They continue on to the superior hypogastric plexus and proceed to the lower thoracic and lumbar splanchnic nerves, which enter the spinal cord at thoracic 10–lumbar 1 (T10–L1).[1] Alternatively, afferent fibers may travel in the pelvic splanchnic nerve (nervi erigentes), via sacral autonomics (pelvic parasympathetics), through the uterosacral plexus to sacral spinal segments 2 to 4 (S2–4).[1] Finally, afferent fibers travel with the ovarian artery and enter the sympathetic nerve chain at L4. They then ascend with the sympathetic chain and penetrate the spinal cord at T9–10, bypassing the superior hypogastric plexus.[1] The specific organs and their corresponding pathways are as follows:

1. Thoracolumbar (T10–L1): upper vagina, cervix, uterine corpus, inner one-third of the fallopian tube, broad ligament, upper bladder, proximal urethra, distal ureter, terminal ileum, and terminal large bowel
2. Thoracolumbar (T10–L1) and sacral (S2–S4): urogenital sinus structures, including the vagina, rectum, and lower bladder
3. Thoracolumbar (T9–T10) bypassing the superior hypogastric plexus: ovary, outer fallopian tube, and upper ureter

The somatic sensory nervous system also has an important role in the genesis and localization of pelvic pain. First, mixed (motor and sensory) somatic nerves derived from L1–2 (iliohypogastric, ilioinguinal) supply the lower abdominal wall, anterior vulva, urethra, and clitoris. Second, somatic branches of the pudendal nerve, derived from S2–4, innervate the anal canal, urethra, perineum, lower vagina, and

TABLE 75–1. Nerves Carrying Painful Impulses from the Pelvis

Organ	Spinal Segments	Nerves
Perineum, vulva, lower vagina	S2–4	Pudendal, inguinal, genitofemoral, posterofemoral cutaneous
Upper vagina, cervix, lower uterine segment, posterior urethra, bladder trigone, uterosacral and cardinal ligaments, rectosigmoid, lower ureters	S2–4	Pelvic autonomics via pelvic nerve
Uterine fundus, proximal fallopian tubes, broad ligament, upper bladder, caecum, appendix, terminal large bowel	T11–12, L1	Lumbosacral autonomics via hypogastric plexus
Outer two-thirds of fallopian tubes	T9–10	Thoracolumbar autonomics via renal and aortic plexus and celiac and mesenteric ganglia
Abdominal wall	T12–L1	Iliohypogastric
	T12–L1	Ilioinguinal
	LI–2	Genitofemoral

clitoris. Finally, the lower back receives its innervation from the dorsal rami of L1–2. Ultimately, the perception of pain (1) depends on the structures involved in the insult and (2) results from the complex central processing of peripheral activity of the corresponding visceral and somatic fibers[3] (Table 75–1).

THE PAIN RESPONSE

The neurophysiology of pain transmission from somatic structures differs from that of the viscera. Pelvic viscera include bowel, bladder, ureters, uterus, ovaries, and fallopian tubes. Somatic structures include skin, fascia, muscles, parietal peritoneum, mesentery, external genitalia, anus, and urethra. Somatic pain is usually superficial and localizable because second-order neurons receive only somatic input and are numerous. Conversely, visceral pain is usually deep and difficult to localize, probably because there are no second-order neurons that receive only visceral input; instead, visceral fibers converge with somatic fibers upon arriving at the dorsal horn. Thus, the pain response is a result of this combined input. Moreover, somatic second-order neurons far outnumber visceral/somatic neurons, allowing for less than adequate localization of the original visceral stimulus.[2] Additionally, unlike somatic pain, acute visceral pain is frequently associated with autonomic reflexes such as restlessness, nausea, vomiting, and diaphoresis.[4]

In some instances, however, visceral pain appears to be superficial and well localized. This "referred pain" results when the pain is perceived to arise from somatic structures that share a common innervation or dermatome with the stimulated or damaged viscera. Referred pain occurs with both acute and chronic gynecologic conditions.[5–7] Referred visceral pain can easily be confused with somatic pain, and given the tremendous overlap in innervation between the reproductive, GU, and GI systems, the cause of the pain cannot always be inferred from the symptoms described by the patient. Consequently, a thorough history and physical examination should be undertaken, with an emphasis on both peripheral (somatic and visceral) and central factors leading to the modulation of ascending and descending sensory input.

DIAGNOSIS

History

The history of present illness is one of the most important elements in the diagnosis of pelvic pain.

This should begin with questions about the timing of the onset of pain as well as the nature, severity, duration, radiation, and aggravating and alleviating factors of the pain. First and most important, one must differentiate between acute and chronic processes as acute processes are often life threatening and require close observation or immediate medical or surgical therapy. Pain present for greater than 6 months is termed chronic, by definition. Specifically, the patient should be questioned about changes in menstrual cycle, abnormal bleeding, abnormal vaginal discharge, febrile episodes, nausea or vomiting, dizziness, right shoulder pain, acute changes in bowel function, acute urinary symptoms, sexual contacts, and method of contraception. Additional questions about ill contacts, exposure to animals, and recent travel may be important in some clinical settings, particularly when the symptoms appear to be gastrointestinal in origin. A careful menstrual history and complete review of symptoms, especially with reference to the GI, GU, abdominal, neurologic, and musculoskeletal systems, must be obtained. Pain exacerbation around the time of menses (cyclic pelvic pain), before or after eating, or at the time of micturition or bowel movements may provide vital clues regarding the organ system primarily involved.

Figure 75–1 provides an example of a comprehensive chronic pelvic pain assessment form that can be completed by the patient and elaborated upon by directed questions from the clinician if pain is deemed to be chronic in nature.

The patient should also be asked to quantify their pain. This is often done by providing a patient with a verbal visual analogue pain scale: "On a scale of 0 to 10, if 0 is no pain and 10 is the most severe pain imaginable, how severe is your pain?" Since this assessment is subjective, it is affected by an individual's pain threshold and tolerance. For women with chronic pain, it should therefore be accompanied by an objective assessment obtained by inquiring about the impact the pain has had on the patient's normal level of functioning.

An inquiry should be made regarding any history of multiple partners, sexually transmitted diseases (STDs), dyspareunia, infertility, or prior or current physical or sexual abuse. A brief psychological assessment should be conducted to rule out depression or anxiety. Additionally, past medical and surgical history is pertinent. Finally, if the pain is chronic, it is important to obtain information regarding past hospital admissions, diagnostic tests, treatments, and operative reports of previous evaluations of the pain.

Physical Examination

Once the history is complete, a comprehensive and systematic physical examination should be performed, with emphasis on the areas that appear to be of primary concern. The examination should focus on the vital signs and the general appearance of the patient and should include the inspection, auscultation, percussion, and palpation of the abdomen and pelvis and an examination of the genitalia, urethra, rectum, anus, and lower extremities. An attempt should be made to reproduce the symptoms with specific palpation. Initially, auscultation should be performed to determine if normal bowel sounds are present. Next, all four quadrants of the abdomen should be palpated to identify the most sensitive area and the presence of masses or organomegaly. When a focal tender point is identified, further investigation is necessary to determine if the pain is superficial or deep and if rebound or guarding is present. Tensing of the abdominal muscles with leg elevations or partial sit-ups helps one to discriminate between abdominal wall (cutaneous, musculoskeletal, or neuropathic) pain and visceral pain since abdominal wall pain is exacerbated and visceral pain eliminated when a straight leg elevation is performed.[8] Additionally, when a musculoskeletal problem is suspected, a more extensive examination of the abdominal, back, and pelvic floor musculature and skeleton is indicated. This should include an evaluation of the axial skeleton in the supine and standing positions, an evaluation of the gait, a determination of the range of motion at specific joints, and an evaluation of specific abdominal and pelvic floor muscles.

The external genitalia, urethra, Skene's and Bartholin's glands, hymen, vagina, and cervix should be thoroughly examined. Next, a gentle cotton-swab digital examination of the vestibule and labia should be performed. The goal of this examination should be to identify the presence of allodynia (pain with gentle palpation) without stimulating significant amounts of unnecessary pain. When palpating the vulva, vagina, cervix, uterus, ovaries, rectum, rectovaginal septum, or pouch of Douglas, an attempt should be made to identify abnormal masses, tender

Pelvic Pain Assessment Form

Physician: _____

Initial History and Physical Exam   Date:

_____

Contact Information

Name:_____ Birth Date: _____ Chart Number: _____

Phone: Work: _____ Home: _____ _____

Is there an alternate contact if we cannot reach you? _____

Alternate contact phone number: _____

Information About Your Pain

Please describe your pain problem: _____

What do you think is causing your pain? _____

What does your family think is causing your pain? _____

Do you think anyone is to blame for your pain? ☐ Yes ☐ No If so, who? _____

Do you think surgery will be necessary? ☐ Yes ☐ No

Is there an event that you associate with the onset of pain? ☐ Yes ☐ No If so, what? _____

How long have you had this pain? ☐ <6 months ☐ 6 months–1 year ☐ 1–2 years ☐ >2 years

For each of the symptoms listed below, please "bubble in" your level of pain over the last month using a 10-point scale:
              0 – no pain   10 – the worst pain imaginable

How would you rate your present pain?

	0	1	2	3	4	5	6	7	8	9	10
Pain at ovulation (mid-cycle)	○	○	○	○	○	○	○	○	○	○	○
Pain level just before period	○	○	○	○	○	○	○	○	○	○	○
Pain (not cramps) with period	○	○	○	○	○	○	○	○	○	○	○
Deep pain with intercourse	○	○	○	○	○	○	○	○	○	○	○
Pain in groin when lifting	○	○	○	○	○	○	○	○	○	○	○
Pelvic pain lasting hours or days after intercourse	○	○	○	○	○	○	○	○	○	○	○
Pain when bladder is full	○	○	○	○	○	○	○	○	○	○	○
Muscle/joint pain	○	○	○	○	○	○	○	○	○	○	○
Ovarian pain	○	○	○	○	○	○	○	○	○	○	○
Level of cramps with period	○	○	○	○	○	○	○	○	○	○	○
Pain after period is over	○	○	○	○	○	○	○	○	○	○	○
Burning vaginal pain with sex	○	○	○	○	○	○	○	○	○	○	○
Pain with urination	○	○	○	○	○	○	○	○	○	○	○
Backache	○	○	○	○	○	○	○	○	○	○	○
Migraine headache	○	○	○	○	○	○	○	○	○	○	○

What would be an acceptable level of pain? ○ ○ ○ ○ ○ ○ ○ ○ ○ ○

What is the worst type of pain that you have ever experienced?
☐ Kidney stone ☐ Bowel obstruction ☐ Migraine headache
☐ Labor & delivery ☐ Current pelvic pain ☐ Backache
☐ Broken bone ☐ Surgery
☐ Other

Demographic Information

Are you (check all that apply):
☐ Married ☐ Widowed ☐ Separated ☐ Committed relationship
☐ Single ☐ Remarried ☐ Divorced

Who do you live with? _____

Education: ☐ Less than 12 years ☐ High school graduate
           ☐ Bachelor's degree ☐ Postgraduate degree

What kind of work are you trained for? _____

What kind of work are you doing? _____

FIGURE 75–1. Pelvic pain assessment form. The format of this assessment form has been modified. © 1999, The International Pelvic Pain Society. This document may be freely reproduced and distributed as long as this copyright notice remains intact. Telephone (205) 877-2950; (800) 624-9676 (if in the US). Web site: www.pelvicpain.org

Health Habits

Do you get regular exercise? ☐ Yes ☐ No   Type: _____

What is your diet like? _____

What is your caffeine intake (number per day, include coffee, tea, soft drinks, etc.)? ☐ 0 ☐ 1–3 ☐ 4–6 ☐ >6

How many cigarettes do you smoke per day? _____ How many years? _____

Have you ever felt the need to cut down on your drinking? ☐ Yes ☐ No

Have you ever felt annoyed by criticism of your drinking? ☐ Yes ☐ No

Have you ever felt guilty about your drinking, or about something you said or did while you were drinking? ☐ Yes ☐ No

Have you ever taken a morning "eye-opener" drink? ☐ Yes ☐ No

What is your use of recreational drugs? ☐ Never used ☐ Used in past, but not now ☐ Presently using ☐ Choose not to answer
 ☐ Heroin ☐ Amphetamines ☐ Marijuana
 ☐ Barbiturates ☐ Cocaine ☐ Other _____

Have you ever received treatment for substance abuse? ☐ Yes ☐ No

Coping Mechanisms

What are the people you talk to concerning your pain, or during stressful times?
 ☐ Spouse/Partner ☐ Relative ☐ Support Group ☐ Clergy
 ☐ Friend ☐ Doctor/Nurse ☐ Mental Health Professional ☐ I take care of myself

How does your partner deal with your pain?
 ☐ Doesn't notice when I'm in pain ☐ Takes care of me ☐ Not applicable
 ☐ Withdraws ☐ Feels helpless
 ☐ Distracts me with activities ☐ Gets angry

What helps your pain?
 ☐ Meditation ☐ Relaxation ☐ Lying down ☐ Music
 ☐ Massage ☐ Ice ☐ Heating pad ☐ Hot bath
 ☐ Pain medication ☐ Laxatives/enema ☐ Injection ☐ TENS unit
 ☐ Bowel movement ☐ Emptying bladder ☐ Nothing
 ☐ Other _____

What makes your pain worse?
 ☐ Intercourse ☐ Orgasm ☐ Stress ☐ Full meal
 ☐ Bowel movement ☐ Full bladder ☐ Urination ☐ Standing
 ☐ Walking ☐ Exercise ☐ Time of day ☐ Weather
 ☐ Contact with clothing ☐ Coughing/sneezing ☐ Not related to anything
 ☐ Other _____

Of all of the problems or stresses in your life, how does your pain compare in importance?
 ☐ The most important problem ☐ Just one of several/many problems

Menses

 How old were you when your menses started? _____
 Are you still having menstrual periods? ☐ Yes ☐ No

Answer the following only if you *are* still having menstrual periods:

Periods are: ☐ Light ☐ Moderate ☐ Heavy ☐ Bleed through protection
 How many days between your periods? _____
 How many days of menstrual flow? _____
 Date of last menses? _____
 Do you have any pain with your periods? ☐ Yes ☐ No
 Does pain start the day flow starts? ☐ Yes ☐ No
 Starts _____ days before flow starts: ☐ Yes ☐ No
 Are periods regular? ☐ Yes ☐ No
 Do you pass any clots in menstrual flow? ☐ Yes ☐ No

FIGURE 75–1. (continued). © 1999, The International Pelvic Pain Society. This document may be freely reproduced and distributed as long as this copyright notice remains intact. Telephone (205) 877-2950; (800) 624-9676 (if in the US). Web site: www.pelvicpain.org

Bladder

Do you experience any of the following:

Loss of urine when coughing, sneezing, or laughing? ☐ Yes ☐ No
Frequent urination? ☐ Yes ☐ No
Need to urinate with little warning? ☐ Yes ☐ No
Difficulty passing urine? ☐ Yes ☐ No
Frequent bladder infections? ☐ Yes ☐ No
Frequency of nighttime urination: ☐ 0–1 ☐ 2 or more   Volume: ☐ Small ☐ Medium ☐ Large
Frequency of daytime urination: ☐ 8 or less ☐ 9–15 ☐ >16   Volume: ☐ Small ☐ Medium ☐ Large
Do you still feel full after urination? ☐ Yes ☐ No

Bowel

Is there discomfort or pain associated with a change in the consistency of the stool (i.e., softer or harder)? ☐ Yes ☐ No
Would you say that at least one-fourth (¼) of the occasions or days in the last 3 months you have had any of the following?

(Check *all* that apply)
☐ Fewer than three bowel movements *a week* (0–2 bowel movements)
☐ More than three bowel movements *a day* (4 or more bowel movements)
☐ Hard or lumpy stools
☐ Loose or watery stools
☐ Straining during a bowel movement
☐ Urgency—having to rush to the bathroom for a bowel movement
☐ Feeling of incomplete emptying after a bowel movement
☐ Passing mucus (white material) during a bowel movement
☐ Abdominal fullness, bloating, or swelling

[1] *The Functional Gastrointestinal Disorders*, Drossman, et al. Chapter 4, "Functional Bowel Disorders and Functional Abdominal Pain". 1994.

Gastrointestinal/Eating

Do you have nausea? ☐ No ☐ With pain ☐ Taking medications
☐ With eating ☐ Other _____

Do you have vomiting? ☐ No ☐ With pain ☐ Taking medications
☐ With eating ☐ Other _____

Have you ever had an eating disorder such as anorexia or bulimia? ☐ Yes ☐ No

Short-Form McGill

The words below describe average pain. Place a check mark (✓) in the column which represents the degree to which you feel that type of pain. Please limit yourself to a description of the pain in your pelvic area *only*.
What does your pain feel like?

Type	None (0)	Mild (1)	Moderate (2)	Severe (3)
Throbbing	_____	_____	_____	_____
Shooting	_____	_____	_____	_____
Stabbing	_____	_____	_____	_____
Sharp	_____	_____	_____	_____
Cramping	_____	_____	_____	_____
Gnawing	_____	_____	_____	_____
Hot-Burning	_____	_____	_____	_____
Aching	_____	_____	_____	_____
Heavy	_____	_____	_____	_____
Tender	_____	_____	_____	_____
Splitting	_____	_____	_____	_____
Tiring-Exhausting	_____	_____	_____	_____
Sickening	_____	_____	_____	_____
Fearful	_____	_____	_____	_____
Punishing-Cruel	_____	_____	_____	_____

Melzack, R: The Short-Form McGill Pain Questionnaire, Pain 30:191–197, 1987

Which statement(s) below best describes how you cope with the pain? (Check all that apply)

☐ I count numbers in my head or run a song through my mind
☐ I just think of it as some other sensation, such as numbness
☐ I pray to God it won't last long
☐ I do something active, like household chores or projects
☐ I ignore it as best I can

☐ I tell myself to be brave and carry on despite the pain
☐ I tell myself that it really doesn't hurt
☐ I worry all the time about whether it will end
☐ I take pain medication
☐ Other

FIGURE 75–1. (continued). © 1999, The International Pelvic Pain Society. This document may be freely reproduced and distributed as long as this copyright notice remains intact. Telephone (205) 877-2950; (800) 624-9676 (if in the US). Web site: www.pelvicpain.org

SF-36

In general, would you say your health is: ☐ Excellent ☐ Very Good ☐ Good ☐ Fair ☐ Poor

Compared to one year ago, how would you rate your health in general now?

- ○ Much better now than one year ago
- ○ Somewhat better now than one year ago
- ○ About the same as one year ago
- ○ Somewhat worse now than one year ago
- ○ Much worse than one year ago

The following items are about activities you might do during a typical day. *Does your health now limit you in these activities? If so, how much?*

	Yes, limited a lot	Yes, limited a little	No	Not limited at all
Vigorous activities, such as running, lifting heavy object, participating in strenuous sports	☐	☐	☐	☐
Moderate activities, such as moving a table, pushing a vacuum cleaner, bowling, or playing golf	☐	☐	☐	☐
Lifting or carrying groceries	☐	☐	☐	☐
Climbing several flights of stairs	☐	☐	☐	☐
Climbing on flight of stairs	☐	☐	☐	☐
Bending, kneeling, or stooping	☐	☐	☐	☐
Walking more than a mile	☐	☐	☐	☐
Walking several blocks	☐	☐	☐	☐
Walking one block	☐	☐	☐	☐
Bathing or dressing yourself	☐	☐	☐	☐

During the *past 4 weeks*, have you had any of the following problems with your work or other regular daily activities *because of your physical health?*

Cut down the amount of time you spent on your work or other activities	○ Yes	○ No
Accomplish less than you would like	○ Yes	○ No
Were limited in the kind of work or other activities	○ Yes	○ No
Had difficulty performing the work or other activities (for example, it took extra effort)	○ Yes	○ No

During the *past 4 weeks*, have you had any of the following problems with your work or other regular daily activities *because of any emotional problems* (such as feeling depressed or anxious)?

Cut down the amount of time you spent on work or other activities	○ Yes	○ No
Accomplished less than you would like	○ Yes	○ No
Didn't do work or other activities as carefully as usual	○ Yes	○ No

During the *past 4 weeks*, to what extent has your physical health or emotional problems interfered with your normal social activities with family, friends, neighbors, or groups?

○ Not at all   ○ Slightly   ○ Moderately   ○ Quite a bit   ○ Extremely

How much bodily pain have you had during the *past 4 weeks*?

○ None   ○ Very mild   ○ Mild   ○ Moderate   ○ Severe   ○ Very severe

During the past 4 weeks how much did pain interfere with your normal work (including both work outside the home and housework)?

○ Not at all   ○ A little bit   ○ Moderately   ○ Quite a bit   ○ Extremely

These questions are about how you feel and how things have been with you *during the past 4 weeks*. For each question, please give the one answer that comes closest to the way you have been feeling. How much of the time during *the past 4 weeks*:

	All of the time	Most of the time	A good bit of the time	Some of the time	A little of the time	None of the time
Did you feel full of pep?	☐	☐	☐	☐	☐	☐
Have you been a very nervous person?	☐	☐	☐	☐	☐	☐
Have you felt so down in the dumps that nothing could cheer you up?	☐	☐	☐	☐	☐	☐
Have you felt calm and peaceful?	☐	☐	☐	☐	☐	☐
Did you have a lot of energy?	☐	☐	☐	☐	☐	☐
Have you felt downhearted and blue?	☐	☐	☐	☐	☐	☐
Did you feel worn out?	☐	☐	☐	☐	☐	☐
Have you been a happy person?	☐	☐	☐	☐	☐	☐
Did you feel tired?	☐	☐	☐	☐	☐	☐

During the *past 4 weeks*, how much of the time has your *physical health or emotional problems* interfered with your social activities (like visiting with friends, relatives, etc.)?

○ All of the time   ○ Most of the time   ○ Some of the time   ○ A little of the time   ○ None of the time

FIGURE 75–1. (continued). © 1999, The International Pelvic Pain Society. This document may be freely reproduced and distributed as long as this copyright notice remains intact. Telephone (205) 877-2950; (800) 624-9676 (if in the US). Web site: www.pelvicpain.org

How TRUE or FALSE is each of the following statements for you?

	Definitely true	Mostly true	Don't know	Mostly false	Definitely false
I seem to get sick a little easier than other people	☐	☐	☐	☐	☐
I am as healthy as anybody I know	☐	☐	☐	☐	☐
I expect my health to get worse	☐	☐	☐	☐	☐
My health is excellent	☐	☐	☐	☐	☐

Personal History

What would you like to tell us about your pain that we have not asked? Comments: _____
_____
_____

What types of treatments have you tried in the past for this pain?

☐ Acupuncture
☐ Anesthesiologist
☐ Anti-seizure medications
☐ Antidepressants
☐ Biofeedback
☐ Birth control pills
☐ Danazole (Danocrine)
☐ Depo-Provera
☐ Family Practitioner
☐ Herbal medication

☐ Homeopathic medicine
☐ Lupron, Zoladex, Synarel
☐ Massage
☐ Meditation
☐ Narcotics
☐ Naturopathic medications
☐ Nerve blocks
☐ Neurosurgeon
☐ Nonprescription medicine
☐ Nutrition/diet

☐ Physical therapy
☐ Psychotherapy
☐ Rheumatologist
☐ Skin magnets
☐ Surgery
☐ TENS unit
☐ Trigger point injections
☐ Other _____

What physicians or health care providers have evaluated or treated you for chronic pelvic pain? Include all healthcare professionals, whether they were physicians or not. Do you have any objections to me contacting these healthcare providers?   ☐ Yes   ☐ No

Physician/Provider	City, State
_____	_____
_____	_____
_____	_____
_____	_____

Who is your primary care physician?_____

Please list *all* surgical procedures you've had (*related to this pain*):

Year	Procedure	Surgeon
_____	_____	_____
_____	_____	_____
_____	_____	_____
_____	_____	_____

Please list all *other* surgical procedures:

Year	Procedure	Year	Procedure
_____	_____	_____	_____
_____	_____	_____	_____
_____	_____	_____	_____

Please list pain medications you've taken for pain condition in the past 6 months, and the physicians who prescribed them (use separate page if necessary):

Medication	Physician	Did it help?
_____	_____	☐ Yes ☐ No
_____	_____	☐ Yes ☐ No
_____	_____	☐ Yes ☐ No
_____	_____	☐ Yes ☐ No
_____	_____	☐ Yes ☐ No
_____	_____	☐ Yes ☐ No
_____	_____	☐ Yes ☐ No
☐ I have written more medications on a separate page		

FIGURE 75–1. (continued). © 1999, The International Pelvic Pain Society. This document may be freely reproduced and distributed as long as this copyright notice remains intact. Telephone (205) 877-2950; (800) 624-9676 (if in the US). Web site: www.pelvicpain.org

Have you ever been hospitalized for anything besides surgery or childbirth? ☐ Yes   ☐ No   If yes, explain _____

_____

Have you had major accidents such as falls or back injury? ☐ Yes   ☐ No

Have you ever been treated for depression? ☐ Yes   ☐ No   ☐ Treatments: ☐ Medication   ☐ Hospitalization   ☐ Psychotherapy

Birth control method: ☐ Nothing   ☐ Pill   ☐ Vasectomy   ☐ Hysterectomy
                         ☐ IUD   ☐ Rhythm   ☐ Diaphragm   ☐ Tubal ligation
                         ☐ Condom   ☐ Other: _____

Is future fertility desired? ☐ Yes   ☐ No

How many pregnancies have you had? _____

Resulting in (#): _____ Full 9 months _____ Premature _____ Abortions (miscarriage) _____ # living children

Any complications during pregnancy, labor, delivery, or postpartum period?
        ☐ Episiotomy   ☐ C-section   ☐ Postpartum hemorrhaging
        ☐ Vaginal lacerations   ☐ Forceps   ☐ Medication for bleeding
        ☐ Other: _____

Has anyone in your family ever had: ☐ Fibromyalgia   ☐ Chronic pelvic pain   ☐ Scleroderma
                                       ☐ Endometriosis   ☐ Lupus   ☐ Interstitial cystitis
                                       ☐ Cancer   ☐ Depression   ☐ Irritable bowel syndrome
                                       ☐ Recurrent urinary tract infections

Place an "X" at the point of your most intense pain.
Shade in all other painful areas.

Sexual and Physical Abuse History

Have you ever been the victim of emotional abuse? This can include being humiliated or insulted. ☐ Yes   ☐ No   ☐ No answer
Circle an answer for *both* as a child and as an adult.

	As a child (13 years and younger)		As an adult (14 and over)	
1. a. Has anyone every exposed the sex organs of their body to you when you did not want it?	Yes	No	Yes	No
b. Has anyone ever threatened to have sex with you when you did not want it?	Yes	No	Yes	No
c. Has anyone ever touched the sex organs of your body when you did not want this?	Yes	No	Yes	No
d. Has anyone ever made you touch the sex organs of their body when you did not want this?	Yes	No	Yes	No
e. Has anyone ever forced you to have sex when you did not want this?	Yes	No	Yes	No
f. Have you had any other unwanted sexual experiences not mentioned above? If yes, please specify: _____	Yes	No	Yes	No
2. When you were a child (13 or younger), did an older person do the following?				
a. Hit, kick, or beat you?	Never	Seldom	Occasionally	Often
b. Seriously threaten your life?	Never	Seldom	Occasionally	Often
3. Now that you are an adult (14 or older), has any other adult done the following:				
a. Hit, kick, or beat you?	Never	Seldom	Occasionally	Often
b. Seriously threatened your life?	Never	Seldom	Occasionally	Often

Leserman, J., Drossman, D., Li, Z: The Reliability and Validity of a Sexual and Physical Abuse History Questionnaire in Female Patients with Gastrointestinal Disorders. Behavioral Medicine 21:141-148, 1995.

FIGURE 75–1. (continued). © 1999, The International Pelvic Pain Society. This document may be freely reproduced and distributed as long as this copyright notice remains intact. Telephone (205) 877-2950; (800) 624-9676 (if in the US). Web site: www.pelvicpain.org

Physical Examination – For Physician Use Only

Name: _____   Chart Number: _____

Height: _____   Weight: _____   BP: _____   LMP: _____   Temp: _____   Resp: _____

ROS, PFSH Reviewed: ☐ Yes   ☐ No   Physician Signature _____

General
☐ WNL   ☐ Walk   ☐ Facial expression
☐ Color   ☐ Alterations in posture   ☐ Other _____

HEENT ☐ WNL _____   ***Chest*** ☐ WNL _____

Heart ☐ WNL _____   ***Breasts*** ☐ WNL _____

Abdomen
☐ Non-tender   ☐ Incisions   ☐ Trigger points   ☐ Ovarian point tenderness
☐ Inguinal tenderness   ☐ Inguinal bulge   ☐ Suprapubic tenderness   ☐ Other _____

Back
☐ Non-tender   ☐ Tenderness   ☐ Altered ROM   ☐ Alterations in posture

Extremities
☐ WNL   ☐ Edema   ☐ Varicosities   ☐ Neuropathy   ☐ Range of motion

Neuropathy
☐ Iliohypogastric   ☐ Ilioinguinal   ☐ Genitofemoral   ☐ Pudendal   ☐ Altered sensation

EGBUS/Vagina
☐ WNL
☐ Lesions
☐ Wet prep:
☐ Local tenderness:
☐ Vaginal mucosa:
☐ Posterior fourchette:
☐ Discharge:
Cultures:
　☐ GC   ☐ Chlamydia
　☐ Fungal   ☐ Herpes

Patient rates allodynia produced by Q-tip for each circle (0–4).

Total Score: _____

Unimanual pelvic exam
☐ WNL   ☐ Cervix   ☐ R inguinal
☐ Introitus   ☐ Cervical motion   ☐ L inguinal
☐ Pelvic floor   ☐ Parametrium   ☐ R piriformis
☐ Urethra   ☐ Vaginal cuff   ☐ L piriformis
☐ Bladder   ☐ Cul de sac   ☐ Uterine-cervical junction
☐ R ureter   ☐ L ureter   ☐ R pubococcygeus
☐ R obturator   ☐ L obturator   ☐ L pubococcygeus

Bimanual pelvic exam

Uterus:			
Position	☐ Tender	☐ Non-tender	
Size	☐ Anterior	☐ Posterior	☐ Midplane
Contour	☐ Normal	☐ Other _____	
Consistency	☐ Regular	☐ Irregular	☐ Other _____
Mobility	☐ Firm	☐ Soft	☐ Hard
Support	☐ Mobile	☐ Hypermobile	☐ Fixed
	☐ Well supported	☐ Prolapse	

Adnexae

Right
☐ WNL
☐ Tender
☐ Fixed
☐ Enlarged _____ cm

Left
☐ WNL
☐ Tender
☐ Fixed
☐ Enlarged _____ cm

Rectovaginal
☐ WNL   ☐ Nodules   ☐ Guaiac positive
☐ Tenderness   ☐ Mucosal pathology

FIGURE 75–1. (continued). © 1999, The International Pelvic Pain Society. This document may be freely reproduced and distributed as long as this copyright notice remains intact. Telephone (205) 877-2950; (800) 624-9676 (if in the US). Web site: www.pelvicpain.org

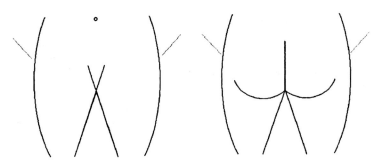

Trigger Points

Assessment (Controlled [C], Inactive [I], Resolved [R])	*Diagnostic Plan*	*Therapeutic Plan*
_____	_____	_____
_____	_____	_____
_____	_____	_____
_____	_____	_____
_____	_____	_____
_____	_____	_____
_____	_____	_____
_____	_____	_____
_____	_____	_____
_____	_____	_____

FIGURE 75–1. (continued). © 1999, The International Pelvic Pain Society. This document may be freely reproduced and distributed as long as this copyright notice remains intact. Telephone (205) 877-2950; (800) 624-9676 (if in the US). Web site: www.pelvicpain.org

areas or trigger points, and irregular surfaces. Specifically, the uterus and ovaries should be manipulated to determine if they are fixed or mobile and if they are abnormally positioned or enlarged. One method employed to identify the focus of pain is to compare the pain that is elicited when digital pressure is applied to the maximally tender points by the abdominal finger and the pelvic finger. When this procedure is employed, one can often deduce the area of primary pain. Similarly, if the pain is simulated when digital pressure is applied suprapubically or over the anterior vaginal epithelium, a genitourinary source should be considered. After the history and physical examination, the information obtained should be used to formulate a differential diagnosis.

ACUTE PELVIC PAIN: DIFFERENTIAL DIAGNOSIS

When developing a differential diagnosis for the patient with pelvic pain, several factors must be taken into consideration. First, acute pain must be differentiated from chronic pain since the etiologies and treatments are different. Second, an attempt should be made to determine the most likely system primarily involved. In general, when the symptoms in a specific organ system predominate, higher suspicion should be given to that system. Although the diagnosis cannot always be made with certainty prior to performing laboratory and imaging studies, an attempt should be made to narrow the diagnosis and thus decrease the unnecessary time and money that are spent when excessive tests and consults are done. Last, a mental review of the numerous causes of acute or chronic pelvic pain and their typical presentations should be undertaken to hone in on the most likely diagnosis in the patient being evaluated.

Typically, acute pain is characterized by a sudden onset or rapid escalation of intense pain.[9] It is often associated with autonomic-reflex responses such as nausea, emesis, diaphoresis, and apprehension. Moreover, when an infectious process is present, signs of inflammation (such as fever and leukocytosis) are usually present. Concurrent pregnancy usually suggests an acute process. In most instances, an acute process is heralded by a vague discomfort that is poorly localized. This is a result of the initial visceral response to the noxious stimuli. Over time, however, the pain is referred to a dermatome of shared innervation, and a more focal and superficial pain is produced. Once the pain is localized, an expedient evaluation is crucial to minimize permanent undesired sequelae. Table 75–2 provides a list of various pathologic causes of acute pelvic pain, grouped according to the involved organ system. For complete discussions of the evaluation and treatment of the disorders outlined below, the reader is referred to the appropriate chapters in this text.

Gynecologic Disorders

ECTOPIC PREGNANCY

An ectopic pregnancy is one in which the conceptus implants outside the uterine cavity. These pregnancies can occur anywhere within the abdominal cavity, including the fallopian tubes, the ovaries, the cervix, or the abdomen. Most commonly, however, they are found in the ampullary region of the fallopian tube; approximately 95 % of ectopic pregnancies are tubal pregnancies. A woman of childbearing age typically presents with a 6- to 8-week history of oligomenorrhea and unilateral lower-quadrant abdominal pain. Most patients report a recent history of spotting as a result of the abnormally fluctuating ß–human chorionic gonadotropin (ßhCG) levels and low progesterone levels. A ruptured tubal pregnancy is a surgical emergency. Such patients usually present with diffuse peritoneal signs and (depending on the time course) positional hypovolemia, obvious hypovolemia, or shock. Despite the availability of pregnancy tests that are more sensitive, ectopic pregnancies still account for a significant number of maternal deaths, and many of these patients have been seen at least once by a clinician. Hence, this diagnosis should be considered in any woman of childbearing age who presents with acute pain. The history, examination, hCG testing, and pelvic ultrasonography generally can provide the diagnosis although laparoscopy or serial hCG testing is sometimes required. Management of a small unruptured ectopic pregnancy can be medical. If the criteria for medical management are not met, an ectopic pregnancy should be surgically managed.

TABLE 75–2. Differential Diagnosis of Acute Pelvic Pain

Gynecologic disorders
   Ectopic pregnancy
   Spontaneous abortion
   Leaking/ruptured ovarian cyst
   Adnexal torsion
   Salpingo-oophoritis
   Endomyometritis
   Tubo-ovarian abscess
   Degenerating leiomyoma

Gastrointestinal disorders
   Appendicitis
   Gastroenteritis
   Diverticulitis
   Intestinal obstruction
   Endometriosis
   Inflammatory bowel disease
   Irritable bowel syndrome

Genitourinary disorders
   Cystitis
   Pyelonephritis
   Urethral lithiasis

Neurologic and musculoskeletal disorders
   Abdominal wall hematoma
   Hernia

Other disorders
   Acute porphyria
   Pelvic thrombophlebitis
   Aneurysm
   Sickle cell crisis
   Abdominal angina

SPONTANEOUS ABORTION

The term "spontaneous abortion" refers to the loss of a conceptus prior to 20 weeks of gestation. Losses in the first trimester are the most common, and frequently the loss is so early in the gestation that the woman has not yet missed a period. Thus a woman may present with a history of normal cycles or oligomenorrhea associated with severe pelvic cramping commonly described as resembling labor pains. Most women also report varying degrees of vaginal bleeding. Diagnosis is again based on history, examination, hCG testing, and ultrasonography. Evaluation and treatment of spontaneous abortion is discussed further in Chapter 20.

LEAKING OR RUPTURED OVARIAN CYSTS

Ovarian cysts may be functional cysts, benign neo-plasms, malignant neoplasms, or inflammatory cysts, all of which have the potential to leak or rupture. More frequently, leaking or ruptured cysts are functional and are either follicular or corpus luteum cysts. Follicular cysts are usually found incidentally during a routine gynecologic examination. Spontaneous resolution typically results in 4 to 8 weeks. However, follicular cysts may rupture prior to that time, producing mild to moderate self-limited abdominal pain.

Conversely, patients with a leaking or ruptured corpus luteum cyst typically present during the luteal phase of their cycle, with a sudden onset of progressive, unilateral, or generalized abdominal pain. Moreover, as corpus luteum cysts are vascular, they are more prone to produce a hemoperitoneum with rupture, and patients with coagulation deficits are at highest risk for this sequela. When this occurs, patients may show signs of hypovolemia (such as dizziness or syncope) and can be misdiagnosed with ectopic pregnancy. Diagnosis is determined by clinical history, physical examination, and ultrasonography. Treatment may be observation or surgery via laparoscopy or laparotomy, depending on the patient's clinical stability and hematocrit.

Benign and malignant neoplasms and inflammatory cysts may leak or rupture in a similar fashion. When this occurs, the presentation is not unlike that of patients with functional cysts. The abnormalities typically found are cystic teratomas (dermoids), cystadenomas, and endometriomas. Surgical treatment via laparoscopy or laparotomy is required.

ADNEXAL TORSION

Torsion reflects a dynamic change in adnexal anatomy, caused by the twisting of the vascular pedicle of an ovary, a fallopian tube, or a paratubal cyst. The result is decreased vascular perfusion and ensuing ischemia. Typically, torsion occurs in the presence of an adnexal mass, most commonly a benign cystic teratoma. Polycystic ovaries may also cause torsion. Ovarian carcinomas and inflammatory masses rarely torse because of the numerous adhesions that often form in these settings, making adnexal mobility and subsequent torsion less likely.

Patients with torsion have varied presentations. Some patients may present with severe, constant pain whereas others may have intermittent pain as a result of partial or intermittent twisting. In addition, autonomic-reflex responses are usually present (eg, nausea, emesis, apprehension). Ultrasonography will confirm the mass and often shows an absence of vascular flow (Doppler flow) to the adnexa. Treatment is surgical.

ACUTE SALPINGO-OOPHORITIS AND ENDOMETRITIS

Salpingo-oophoritis is an infectious process that originates in the cervix (cervicitis) and ascends to include the fallopian tubes and ovaries. The term "pelvic inflammatory disease" (PID) connotes an infection anywhere in the upper genital tract secondary to the ascending spread of microorganisms from the vagina or endocervix in situations unrelated to surgical intervention, pregnancy, or the puerperium; the term includes salpingo-oophoritis and endometritis. In the case of menstruating and sexually active young women, the diagnosis of PID should be considered whenever such individuals present with lower-quadrant abdominal pain since failure to recognize and treat this disorder may result in irreversible infertility. Gonococci, *Chlamydia*, or *Mycoplasma* (which are sexually transmitted) are the bacteria that are initially involved, and ultimately the normal genital flora (including gram-negative and gram-positive aerobic and anaerobic bacteria) become involved as well, in a polymicrobial process. In certain populations, patients should be evaluated for less common organisms. For example, in individuals with a current or recent history of intrauterine device (IUD) use, *Actinomyces* may be the causative agent. Similarly, in certain less developed nations, individuals may need to be evaluated for tuberculosis and for parasitic and fungal infections.

The typical presentation for patients with salpingo-oophoritis is the presence of fever, lower abdominal pain, leukocytosis, and an elevated erythrocyte sedimentation rate; however, reliance on these criteria may fail to identify many infected individuals. In gonococcal infections, patients usually complain of an acute onset of pain at the time of menses, such pain being exacerbated by movement; chlamydial pain is often reported to be more insidious. The presence of purulent vaginal discharge or of nausea or vomiting also argues more favorably for a gonococcal infection. The diagnosis and treatment of PID is discussed in Chapter 72.

Endometritis unassociated with PID results from the infection and subsequent inflammation of the endometrium or of the endometrium and myometrium (endomyometritis). Most patients report a recent history of a vaginal or (more commonly) a cesarean delivery, a surgical procedure involving the endometrium, current IUD use, cervical brachytherapy, or (less commonly) tuberculosis. Symptoms may include fever, abdominal pain, abnormal discharge, or abnormal uterine bleeding.

Tubo-ovarian Abscess

Tubo-ovarian abscesses are the natural sequelae of the lack of treatment, the incomplete treatment, or the delayed treatment of pelvic inflammatory disease or endomyometritis or salpingo-oophoritis. Bilaterality is typically the rule, and most patients present with prolonged symptoms of lower-quadrant abdominal pain and tender palpable masses in both adnexa. Fever, leukocytosis, and an elevated erythrocyte sedimentation rate (ESR) are also common, and the ultrasonographic picture is fairly characteristic. Prompt diagnosis is essential since a ruptured abscess can result in gram-negative sepsis and shock requiring immediate surgical attention.

Degenerating Uterine Leiomyomas

Acute pain resulting from leiomyomas (myomas) occurs when the myoma degenerates or undergoes torsion. When exposed to highly estrogenic environments, as occurs with pregnancy, myomas experience rapid growth; in the face of a limited blood supply, degeneration occurs and produces symptoms of acute pelvic pain. Myoma degeneration is exceedingly rare outside the context of pregnancy or uterine artery embolization. Similarly, pedunculated subserosal myomas may undergo torsion, causing ischemia and subsequent necrosis with resultant symptoms not unlike those of adnexal torsion.

Gastrointestinal Disorders

Appendicitis

Appendicitis accounts for most cases of acute abdominal pain of intestinal etiology. In the early stages the pain is a more diffuse periumbilical discomfort associated with nausea and anorexia. Over time the pain becomes more localized to the right lower quadrant (McBurney's point) and is often accompanied by fever, chills, vomiting, and obstipation.

Moreover, the pain may be reproduced with forced hip flexion or passive hip extension (psoas sign) or with passive internal rotation of the flexed thigh (obturator sign). When appendicitis is suspected, rapid surgical intervention is warranted to avoid the undesirable sequela of death or infertility, which may occur in the presence of a ruptured appendix.

Gastroenteritis

Gastroenteritis is an inflammation of the GI tract; it may be caused by bacterial, viral, or protozoan pathogens. In adults, enterotoxemic *Escherichia coli* contributes to the majority of cases of symptomatic disease. *Rotavirus* is implicated in most childhood infections. There is no typical presentation since the illness may range from subacute disease to fulminant life-threatening illness. When symptoms are present, however, patients invariably complain of diarrhea and abdominal cramping. In addition, vomiting and low-grade fevers are common, and bloody diarrhea may be reported when invasive organisms are involved.

Diverticulitis

Diverticulitis results from an acute inflammation of a diverticulum, which is an anatomic defect resulting in a small protrusion from the colon wall, usually involving the sigmoid colon. This defect usually occurs in older women and is generally asymptomatic. During acute inflammatory processes, however, the patient may present with an exacerbation of left lower-quadrant tenderness, associated with bloating, constipation, and diarrhea. Moreover, the patient may report a recent history of fever and chills. In this setting, deriving the accurate diagnosis is of utmost importance since perforation and or gastrointestinal bleeding may result.

Intestinal Obstruction

Intestinal obstruction is a pathologic process that prevents the normal passage of ingested material to the rectum. The obstruction can occur anywhere along the GI tract and results in distension of the bowel proximal to the area of obstruction. Clinically, patients present with colicky abdominal pain with associated abdominal distention. If the obstruction occurs in the stomach or proximal small bowel, nausea and vomiting usually occur earlier whereas, constipation, absent flatus, or obstipation may be the initial complaints when there is distal small bowel and colon involvement. Intestinal obstruction, if complete, is a surgical emergency.

Genitourinary Disorders

Acute pain from the GU tract may result from cystitis, pyelonephritis, or ureteral lithiasis. Although cystitis pain is typically confined to the suprapubic region, patients with pyelonephritis often have associated unilateral costovertebral-angle tenderness, and those with ureteral stones often report severe crampy pain radiating from the costovertebral angle to the groin. Frequently, a disorder in this region presents with symptoms of urgency, dysuria, and frequency of urination; in the case of lithiasis, hematuria is usually present. A pitfall in the diagnosis of acute cystitis in females is the failure to collect a "clean-catch" urine specimen. A urinalysis result with squamous epithelial cells suggests vaginal contamination. A catheterized specimen may have to be obtained if a clean-catch specimen cannot be produced. The diagnosis and treatment of urinary tract infection is discussed further in Chapter 84.

APPROACH TO THE PATIENT WITH ACUTE PELVIC PAIN

As previously stated, acute pelvic pain is often characterized by a sudden onset and a rapid progression of the pain over time. Moreover, it is usually localizable and is associated with autonomic symptoms such as nausea, vomiting, restlessness, anorexia, and diaphoresis or with systemic symptoms such as fever, dizziness, or syncope. When acute pain is suspected, the physical examination should be used as a guide for determining the appropriate management strategy. Specifically, evidence of pregnancy, hemodynamic instability, or significant peritonitis warranting surgical exploration should be assessed primarily. First, the vital signs with orthostatic changes should be assessed for signs of infection, acute bleeding, or other hypovolemia. The abdominal examination should carefully assess bowel sounds. Next, signs of peritoneal involvement (including rebound and guarding) should be investigated. Finally, signs of an impending viscous perforation, such as abdominal distention, absent or abnormal bowel sounds, or intractable nausea or vomiting, must be addressed. Delayed or failed identification of the cause of acute pelvic pain will directly impair the patient's outcome. Table 75–3

provides information on the signs and symptoms that are most commonly seen in the listed disease processes that are associated with acute pelvic pain.

The treatment of acute pelvic pain depends on the underlying cause, and the reader is referred to relevant chapters in this book. It is of utmost importance to recognize a surgical emergency since delayed intervention may result in life-threatening or permanent sequelae.

CHRONIC PELVIC PAIN: DIFFERENTIAL DIAGNOSIS

Chronic pelvic pain (CPP) is defined as pelvic pain that persists for more than 6 months. In contrast to acute pelvic pain, CPP is usually difficult to localize and lacks the associated autonomic-reflex responses seen with acute pelvic pain. The exact incidence of CPP is unknown; however, its impact on society is striking. In the United States alone, it is estimated that 12 to 15% of women report signs and symptoms of CPP or have been diagnosed with the disorder.[10,11] In this same population more than $881.5 million is spent on outpatient medical visits related to CPP.[10] Moreover, the etiology of CPP is frequently unidentified; expensive tests and treatments may be implemented, but these may yield inconclusive information and subtherapeutic results, thus increasing the financial deficit incurred without improving the overall results.[12–14]

The initial approach to the patient with CPP is not unlike the initial approach to the patient with acute pelvic pain; thorough history (see Figure 75–1), physical examination, and the judicious use of imaging studies allow the creation of a differential diagnosis. Figures 75–2 and 75–3 provide algorithms that can be used to guide the management of CPP. The patient should keep a "pain diary" for at least 2 months, documenting the date, the presence or absence of menstrual bleeding, a pain rating on a visual analogue scale of 1 to 10, and comments regarding aggravating and alleviating factors. The pain diary allows a more conclusive determination of whether the pain is cyclic or acyclic. Cyclic pain is premenstrual or menstrual or both. Table 75–4 shows a differential diagnosis of CPP according to the involved organ system. The gynecologic causes of CPP should be divided into cyclic and noncyclic causes as the former often represent diseases dependent on changes in the hormonal milieu

TABLE 75–3. Guide to Diagnosing Acute Pelvic Pain

Sign or Symptom	Ectopic Pregnancy	Spontaneous Abortion	Ruptured Cyst	Ovarian Torsion	PID	Tubo-ovarian Abscess
Abdominal pain	unilateral (generalized if tubal rupture has occurred)	crampy, midline	sudden onset, generalized	constant or intermittent	acute (gonococcal) insidious (*Chlamydia*)	Bilateral adnexal
Vaginal bleeding	irregular	persistent	absent	absent	absent	absent
Vaginal discharge	absent (malodorous if infection present)	absent	absent	absent	purulent	purulent
Menses	absent	absent	regular	regular	regular	regular
Nausea/vomiting	±	absent	absent	present	±	±
Anorexia	absent	absent	absent	absent	absent	absent
Constipation/obstipation	absent	absent	absent	absent	absent	absent
Dysuria	absent	absent	absent	absent	absent	absent
Urinary frequency	absent	absent	absent	absent	absent	absent
Flank pain	absent	absent	absent	absent	absent	absent
Fever	rare	±	rare	±	present	present
Chills	rare	±	absent	absent	±	±
Dizziness	±	±	±	±	absent	absent
Syncope	±	±	±	±	absent	absent
Orthostatic hypotension	present	±	±	±	absent	absent
Rebound	±	absent	present	present	present	present
Guarding	±	absent	present	present	present	present
Bowel sounds	normal / ↓	normal	decreased	normal	present	present
Cervical motion tenderness	present	±	absent	absent	present	present
Uterine tenderness	absent	±	absent	absent	±	±
Adnexal tenderness	unilateral	absent	unilateral	unilateral	bilateral	bilateral
Palpable pelvic mass	± (if present, usually represents corpus luteum)	absent (if present, usually represents corpus luteum)	± (if leaking without complete rupture, mass may be palpated)	present	absent	bilateral
Serum ßhCG	positive	positive	negative	negative	negative	negative
Leukocytosis	rare	rare	rare	±	±	present
Hematocrit	progressive anemia	stable/decreasing	stable/decreasing	stable/decreasing	stable	stable
Erythrocyte sedimentation rate	normal / ↑	nondiagnostic	nondiagnostic	nondiagnostic	elevated	elevated
Urine WBCs	normal	normal	normal	normal	normal	normal
Urine RBCs	absent	absent	absent	absent	normal	normal
Colpotomy fluid	bloody	clear	bloody (corpus luteum) chocolate (endometrioma) sebaceous (teratoma)	clear/bloody	purulent	purulent
Ultrasonography	no IUP (if ßhCG > 1,500, ectopic pregnancy may be visualized)	IUP (fetal heart tones usually absent)	adnexal-mass fluid in pelvis	unilateral adnexal mass	absent	bilateral adnexal masses

ßhCG = ß-human chorionic gonadotropin; CT = computed tomography; IUP = intrauterine pregnancy; PID = pelvic inflammatory disease; RBCs = red blood cells; UTZ = ultrasound; WBCs = white blood cells; ± = may or may not be present.

TABLE 75–3. (continued)

Sign or Symptom	Appendicitis	Gastroenteritis	Diverticulitis	Intestinal Obstruction	Urinary Tract Infection	Urinary Lithiasis
Abdominal pain	right lower quadrant (McBurney's point) suprapubic (if retrocecal location)	crampy, diffuse	left lower quadrant	colicky	suprapubic (cystitis) ipsilateral flank (pyelonephritis)	ipsilateral flank or groin
Vaginal bleeding	absent	absent	absent	absent	absent	absent
Vaginal discharge	absent	absent	absent	absent	absent	absent
Menses	regular	regular	regular (absent if postmenopausal)	regular	regular	regular
Nausea/vomiting	present	present	absent	present	±	±
Anorexia	present	absent	absent	±	absent	absent
Constipation/obstipation	absent	absent	present	present	absent	absent
Dysuria	absent	absent	absent	absent	present	present
Urinary frequency	absent	absent	absent	absent	present	±
Flank pain	absent	absent	present	absent	present	present
Fever	low grade	±	present	absent	± (consider pyelonephritis if present)	±
Chills	present	±	absent	absent	±	±
Dizziness	± (present with rupture)	±	± (present with rupture)	absent	absent	absent
Syncope	± (present with rupture)	± (present with dehydration)	± (present with rupture)	absent	absent	absent
Orthostatic hypotension	± (present with rupture)	± (present with dehydration)	± (present with rupture)	absent	absent	absent
Rebound	present	absent	present	±	absent	absent
Guarding	present	absent	present	±	absent	absent
Bowel sounds	hypoactive	hyperactive	hypoactive	initially ↑ then ↓	present	present
Cervical motion tenderness	absent	absent	absent	absent	absent	absent
Uterine tenderness	absent	absent	absent	absent	absent	absent
Adnexal tenderness	±—right sided	absent	±—left sided	absent	absent	absent
Palpable pelvic mass	±—right sided	absent	±—left sided	absent	absent	absent
Serum ßhCG	negative	negative	negative	negative	negative	negative
Leukocytosis	left shift	±	present	absent	± (consider pyelonephritis if present)	±
Hematocrit	stable/decreasing	stable/decreasing	stable/decreasing	stable	stable	stable
Erythrocyte sedimentation rate	nondiagnostic	nondiagnostic	nondiagnostic	nondiagnostic	nondiagnostic	nondiagnostic
Urine WBCs	normal	normal	normal	normal	normal	normal
Urine RBCs	absent	absent	absent	absent	normal	normal
Colpotomy fluid	clear (purulent/bloody with rupture)	clear	clear (bloody with rupture)	clear	clear	clear
Radiologic studies	fecolith/ inflammation/ abnormal filling	negative	diverticula/ inflammation on CT	dilated bowel/ air-fluid levels on x-ray	absent	renal/ureteral lithiasis on UTZ or x-ray

ßhCG = ß–human chorionic gonadotropin; CT = computed tomography; IUP = intrauterine pregnancy; PID = pelvic inflammatory disease; RBCs = red blood cells; UTZ = ultrasound; WBCs = white blood cells; ± = may or may not be present.

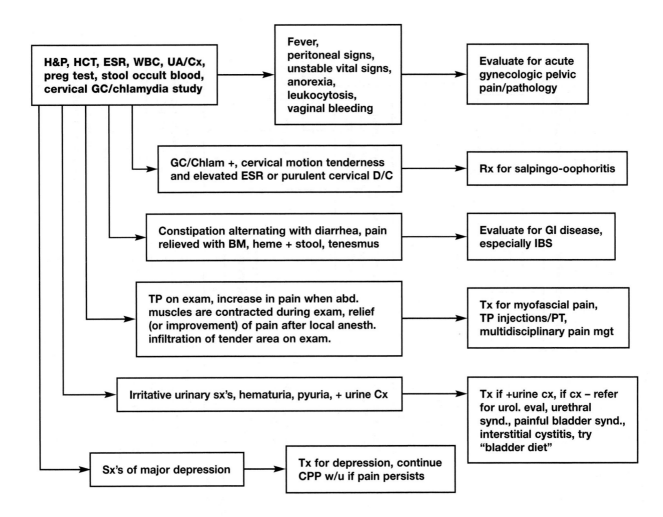

FIGURE 75–2. Algorithm for the evaluation of pelvic pain.

associated with the menstrual cycle and can be affected by altering that hormonal milieu. (Table 75–5 provides information on the symptoms, signs, test results, and imaging findings commonly seen in the listed disease processes that are associated with CPP.)

Cyclic Gynecologic Disorders

DYSMENORRHEA

Dysmenorrhea, simply defined as pain during menses, is the most common cause of cyclic pelvic pain and affects approximately 50% of menstruating females.[15] Patients with no demonstrable pathology associated with their symptoms are subclassified as having primary dysmenorrhea whereas those with coexisting anatomic abnormalities such as endometriosis, adenomyosis, or leiomyomas are subclassified as having secondary dysmenorrhea.

Several mechanisms have been suggested as causative factors, including myometrial contractions resulting in uterine hypoxia, hypersecretion of leukotrienes and other hormonal factors, altered central nervous system (CNS) processing, and environmental and behavioral factors.[16]

Patients with primary dysmenorrhea typically present with symptoms approximately 1 year after menarche, when ovulatory cycles begin. The pain is usually suprapubic and crampy, radiating to the thighs and the lumbosacral region; it classically begins with the onset of menses and lasts 48 to 72 hours. Moreover, gastrointestinal symptoms such as nausea, vomiting, and diarrhea are often reported. Conversely, pain associated with secondary amenorrhea may occur in the absence of ovulation. Typically, these patients present with suprapubic or uterine pain occurring years after menarche. The

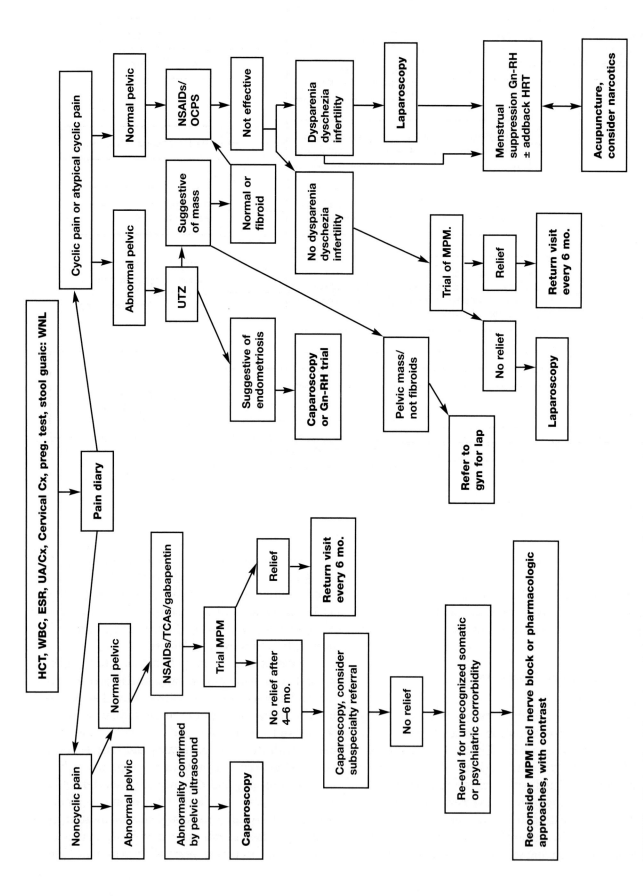

FIGURE 75–3. Algorithm for the management of chronic pelvic pain.*FIGURE 75–2.* Algorithm for the evaluation of pelvic pain. HCT = hematocrit; WBC = white blood cells; ESR = sedimentation rate; UA = urinalysis; Cx = culture

TABLE 75–4. Differential Diagnosis of Chronic Pelvic Pain

Gynecologic disorders
    Cyclic
        Dysmenorrhea
        Mittleschmertz
        Endometriosis
        Adenomyosis

    Noncyclic
        Endometriosis
        Adenomyosis
        Adhesions
        Pelvic congestion
        Ovarian-remnant syndrome
        Chronic pelvic infection
        Tumors
        Cysts

Gastrointestinal disorders
    Irritable bowel syndrome
    Endometriosis
    Appendicitis
    Diverticular disease
    Inflammatory bowel disease
    Tumors

Genitourinary disorders
    Interstitial cystitis
    Urethral syndrome
    Chronic calculi
    Carcinoma

Neurologic and musculoskeletal disorders
    Myofascial pain syndrome
    Fibromyalgia
    Hernias
    Nerve entrapment or injury
    Arthritis
    Disc disease
    Lordosis/scoliosis

Psychological disorders/syndromes
    Depression
    Abnormal personality profile
    Sexual and physical abuse
    Somatization
    Factitious pain
    Drug seeking

pain can begin up to 2 weeks before menses, and symptoms persist until menses have ceased. Abnormal uterine bleeding is often noted as well.

ENDOMETRIOSIS

Endometriosis is a disease process characterized by the implantation of endometrial glands and stroma in sites other than the uterine cavity, most commonly the ovaries, broad ligament, and cul-de-sac. Typically, this results in a sharp pressurelike pain in the abdomen, back, or rectum, with exacerbations noted during menses. Other common symptoms include abnormal bleeding and deep dyspareunia. When the bowel and bladder are involved, patients may present with dyschezia, cyclic hematochezia, urinary frequency or urgency bladder pain, hematuria, or (less commonly) bowel or ureteral obstruction. Importantly, the extent of endometriosis does not usually correlate with the pain.

Classic findings on physical examination include a fixed retroverted uterus, uterosacral nodularity, and focal tenderness on rectovaginal examination, all more commonly found with severe disease. In some patients one or more adnexal masses may be present, consistent with endometriomas. Although endometriosis has been reported in all age groups (including adolescents), women in their thirties to forties are more commonly afflicted with the disease than are younger women. However, a diagnosis of endometriosis does not rule out other peripheral or central factors as a cause of pain, especially if the pain is not cyclic, is very severe and disabling, and is not improved by traditionally effective medical or surgical therapies. These issues are discussed further in Chapter 79, "Endometriosis."

Noncyclic Gynecologic Disorders

ADHESIONS

Adhesions are unusual formations of connective tissue between two structures and typically result from a prior abdominal surgery or pelvic infection. Studies reporting adhesions as a cause of CPP are controversial and inconclusive. Numerous retrospective and prospective studies have demonstrated the presence of adhesions in up to 51% of patients undergoing laparoscopy for CPP.[17–21] One retrospective study showed adhesions to be present in 51% of patients undergoing laparoscopy for CPP, compared to 14% of patients whose surgery was for sterilization.[18]

TABLE 75–5. Guide to Diagnosing Chronic Pelvic Pain

Sign or Symptom	Primary Dysmenorrhea	Endometriosis	Adhesions	Pelvic Congestion	Ovarian-Remnant Syndrome	Leiomyoma
Abdominal pain	begins with menses; continues 48–72 h; crampy	dysmenorrhea; sharp or pressurelike suprapubic	noncyclic	bilateral lower pelvic dysmenorrhea	cyclic	pressurelike suprapubic or rectal
Vaginal bleeding	absent	present	absent	menorrhagia	absent	menorrhagia
Vaginal discharge	absent	absent	absent	absent	absent	absent
Dyspareunia	absent	deep	present	present	absent	±
Menses	regular	irregular	regular	regular	absent	irregular
Nausea/vomiting	present	absent	±	absent	absent	absent
Anorexia	absent	absent	±	absent	absent	absent
Constipation/obstipation	absent	may develop with severe disease	±	absent	absent	±
Dysuria	absent	absent	absent	absent	absent	absent
Urinary frequency	absent	±	absent	absent	present	±
Flank pain	absent	absent	absent	absent	absent	absent
Cervical motion tenderness	absent	absent	absent	absent	absent	absent
Uterine findings	tenderness with menses	fixed, retroverted uterosacral nodularity	immobility	bulky tender	normal	enlarged irregular surface
Adnexal tenderness	absent	±	±	±	absent	absent
Palpable pelvic mass	absent	± endometrioma	±	± functional ovarian cysts	tender mass in lateral pelvis	enlarged uterus
Leukocytosis	absent	absent	absent	absent	absent	absent
Hematocrit	normal	normal or ↓	normal	normal	absent	normal or ↓
Erythrocyte sedimentation rate	normal	normal or ↑	normal	normal	normal	normal or ↑
Urine WBCs	absent	absent	absent	absent	absent	normal
Urine RBCs	absent	± (+ when bladder involvement)	absent	absent	absent	normal
Radiologic studies	normal	UTZ reveals endometriomas	noncontributory	UTZ/CT/MRI show dilated tortuous parauterine tubular structures	UTZ confirms mass with ovarian characteristics	UTZ is diagnostic
Laparoscopy/laparotomy	nondiagnostic	definitive diagnosis	adhesions identified "pain mapping"	not indicated for diagnosis	not indicated for diagnosis	not indicated for diagnosis

CT = computed tomography; MRI = magnetic resonance imaging; UTZ = ultrasound; ± = may or may not be present.

Conversely, another study showed a similar incidence of adhesions in patients with CPP when compared to a group of infertile women, and there was no difference between the two groups in the density or location of adhesions.[19] The pitfall of assuming that adhesions are the only convincing etiology to explain the patient's symptoms can lead to multiple surgical procedures and further nerve damage. A double-blind prospective study of lysis of adhesions failed to show an improvement with lysis.[22] The patients who report symptoms that are consistent with partial or complete bowel obstruction do benefit from lysis of adhesions.[22] Furthermore, as shown by a prospective nonrandomized study, women with various "red flags" fail to have an improvement of symptoms after lysis of adhesions.[23] The red flags include at least four of the following: (1) pain duration of ≥ 6 months, (2) incomplete relief by previous treatments (eg, analgesics, prior operations), (3) impaired physical functioning (work, recreation, etc), (4) at least one vegetative sign of depression (sleep disturbance aside from being awakened by pain; loss of appetite; or psychomotor retardation), and (5) altered family roles.[23]

PELVIC CONGESTION

Pelvic congestion is a condition in which blood pools in the pelvic venous system. The association between CPP and pelvic congestion dates back to the 1950s, when Taylor proposed that emotional stress could result in autonomic dysfunction, thus leading to smooth muscle spasms and congestion of the ovarian and uterine venous plexuses.[24] More recently, Beard and colleagues conducted a blinded study of patients with CPP. When transuterine venography was performed, a larger mean ovarian diameter, delayed disappearance of contrast medium, and greater ovarian plexus congestion were found in patients with CPP when compared with controls.[25,26]

The typical presentation of patients was best characterized by Beard and colleagues, who performed a retrospective evaluation of 35 women with pelvic congestion on venography and compared them to women with pelvic pain of classic pathology. In general, the pain associated with congestion is often described as a dull aching bilateral pain exacerbated by postural changes, ambulation, menstruation, and coitus. Moreover, patients may report anxiety, chronic fatigue, breast tenderness, or an irritable bowel.[26] Uterine venography is not readily available in the United States and the diagnosis remains clinical. Treatment is surgical or menstrual suppression with cognitive behavioral therapy.

OVARIAN-REMNANT SYNDROME

Ovarian-remnant syndrome occurs when residual ovarian cortical tissue is left in situ after a bilateral salpingo-oophrectomy, usually as the result of a technically difficult operation. In the presence of a normally functioning hypothalamic-pituitary axis, this tissue may be stimulated and cysts may develop, with subsequent pelvic pain.[27,28] A cyclical pain of variable character typically begins 2 to 5 years after surgery and may be accompanied by flank pain or gastrointestinal or gastrourinary symptoms.[29] A normal level of follicle-stimulating hormone (FSH) in a patient who has not received hormonal therapy within at least 1 month in the setting of a prior bilateral salpingo-oophorectomy suggests an ovarian remnant. A small mass may be seen by ultrasonography.

VULVODYNIA

Vulvodynia is a syndrome that results in chronic burning, stabbing pain, or soreness over the vulva, for which no pathologic cause can be found. The term connotes the presence of symptoms for at least 6 months, and vulvodynia is often accompanied by psychological stress and sexual dysfunction.[30–32] Typically, the syndrome begins with an acute phase thought to be possibly secondary to a yeast infection; attenuation with persistence follows.[30,31] Vulvovaginitis and vulvar dermatoses must be ruled out first (see Chapter 80). Vulvar vestibulitis is the most common cause of vulvadynia. Vestibulitis is a nonspecific inflammatory condition of the vestibule. The key factors include allodynia (sensitivity to normally nonpainful stimuli) and hyperalgesia (severe pain from uncomfortable stimuli). Patients describe pain with sexual penetration or tampon placement; on examination, there is erythema and tenderness to gentle Q-Tip probing outside the hymenal ring in the region of the vestibule.

Gastroenterologic Disorders

IRRITABLE BOWEL SYNDROME

Irritable bowel syndrome (IBS) is classically defined by the Rome diagnostic criteria and is a diagnosis of exclusion (Table 75–6).[33] Symptomatic exacerbation is associated with eating, stress, anxiety, and

TABLE 75–6. The Rome II Diagnostic Criteria for Irritable Bowel Syndrome

At least 12 weeks, which need not be consecutive, in the preceding 12 months of abdominal discomfort or pain that has two of three of the following features:

  Relieved with defecation

  Onset associated with a change in frequency of stool

  Onset associated with a change in form (appearance) of stool

Adapted from Drossman DA, Corazziari E, Talley NJ, et al. Rome II: a multinational consensus document on functional gastrointestinal disorders. Gut 1999;45 Suppl II:II1–81.

depression, as well as intercourse and the premenstrual and menstrual phases of the monthly cycle.[34,35] Irritable bowel syndrome is discussed in detail in Chapter 41.

INFLAMMATORY BOWEL DISEASE

Inflammatory bowel disease (IBD) is associated with two distinct disease entities: ulcerative colitis and Crohn's disease. Despite the chronicity of both of these disorders, their presentation is unique in that the associated pain is acute in nature, unrelated to the menstrual cycle, and associated with severe gastrointestinal symptoms, the most prominent of which is bloody diarrhea. Febrile episodes may also accompany acute exacerbations.

DIVERTICULAR DISEASE

Diverticula are small outpouchings of the bowel mucosa and are usually found in the sigmoid colon.[36] Diverticulosis is found in 5 to 40% of individuals over 40 years of age. However, the majority of those afflicted are asymptomatic. In rare instances, diverticula became infected (diverticulitis), and patients may present with fever and acute, severe, or (rarely) subacute pain, usually in the left lower quadrant.

GASTROINTESTINAL TUMORS

Gastrointestinal tumors are more prevalent in older women. These tumors can cause pain by intestinal obstruction or by pressure on other pelvic structures. Abdominal pain and changes in bowel habits may suggest the diagnosis; however, many patients go undiagnosed until more obvious symptoms such as weight loss or rectal bleeding are noticed, when advanced disease is likely to be found.

Hernias

Inguinal, femoral, spigelian, incisional, and umbilical hernias are an uncommon cause of CPP in women.[36] Indirect inguinal hernias are found adjacent to the round ligament whereas direct hernias occur at Hesselbach's triangle. Spigelian hernias are found just lateral to the rectus muscle at the level of the semicircular line of Douglas and result from a defect in the transversalis facia.[37] Incisional hernias are usually the result of facial separation of a surgical incision. Patients may identify a groin or abdominal mass and correlate their pain with periods of increased intra-abdominal pressure. Additionally, sciatic hernias and vaginal hernias (specifically cystoceles, rectoceles, or enteroceles) may cause similar symptoms.[38] Symptoms of the latter can be ameliorated by a pessary; if this is successful, the hernia can be treated with a pessary or surgery.

Genitourinary Disorders

RECURRENT CYSTITIS

Recurrent urinary tract infections may result from incomplete treatment, a resistant organism, estrogen deficiency, or regular intercourse. Typically, symptoms mimic those of a primary infection and include suprapubic pain, dysuria, urgency, and urinary frequency.

URETHRAL SYNDROME

Differentiating urethral syndrome from cystitis is often done after laboratory evaluation since most patients with urethral syndrome also have symptoms of suprapubic tenderness, dysuria, and urinary frequency. Dyspareunia and slow and painful micturition may also be associated with this syndrome.[14,39]

Urethral syndrome lacks a definitive explanation; however, subclinical infection, chronic inflammation of periurethral glands, and urethral spasticity have been proposed as possible causative factors. Because of its uncertain etiology, the diagnosis of urethral syndrome should be reserved for those patients in whom no other pathology can be found. Cultures for gonococci, *Chlamydia*, and *Mycoplasma* should be done in addition to urinalysis, urine culture, and sensitivity.

INTERSTITIAL CYSTITIS

Interstitial cystitis is an inflammation-mediated process that results in pelvic pain, urgency, urinary

TABLE 75–7. The National Institutes of Health Consensus Criteria for Interstitial Cystitis (1998)

At least two of the following criteria must be met:[*]
1. Pain on bladder filling; relieved by emptying
2. Pain in the suprapubic, pelvic, urethral, vaginal, or perineal region
3. Glomerulations on endoscopy
4. Decreased compliance on cystometrography

[*]In the absence of these criteria, the diagnosis of urgency/frequency syndrome should be appointed.

frequency, and nocturia.[40] Dyspareunia and premenstrual exacerbations are also common. Differentiating interstitial cystitis from urgency-frequency syndrome is based on the National Institutes of Health (NIH) Consensus Criteria (Table 75–7) since patients with both syndromes have similar complaints and normal laboratory studies.[41,42] Cystoscopy is necessary for diagnosis.

INFILTRATING CARCINOMAS

Carcinomas originating from the bladder, cervix, uterus, or rectum may cause severe suprapubic pain, owing to their close proximity within the pelvis. Symptoms of pain may be accompanied by frank hematuria, vaginal bleeding, occult or frank rectal bleeding, and oliguria.

Neurologic and Musculoskeletal Disorders

MYOFASCIAL PAIN

The term "myofascial pain" implies that the pain originates from the muscles and fascia. In general, myofascial pain is described as a dull aching pain that is difficult to localize, is worse with menses and intercourse, and is exacerbated by positional changes of the lower extremities. "Pelvic floor muscle tension" is a term given to pain originating from the pelvic floor muscles (levator ani, obturator, piriformis, and coccygeus).

It has been reported that myofascial pain represents 15 to 89% of cases of CPP. However, the concept of referred pain and the tremendous overlap in innervation between the musculoskeletal and visceral structures make a definitive etiologic distinction quite difficult.[8,13,43]

NERVE ENTRAPMENT OR INJURY

Patients with nerve entrapment or injury in the pelvic area typically describe a sharp colicky pain in the region along the lateral edge of the rectus muscle, with radiation to the hip or sacroiliac region. Nerve entrapment syndrome usually develops after a laparoscopy with lateral ports or Pfannenstiel's skin incision. The ilioinguinal, iliohypogastric, and genitofemoral nerves (see Table 75–1) are vulnerable to compression or injury, and resultant lower abdominal and perineal pain may occur.[44] Alternatively, spontaneous entrapment may occur after physical trauma or repetitive activity or as a result of poor posture. Exacerbations occur with exercise, menstruation, nausea, a full bladder, and constipation, with relief noted after bed rest.[44,45] Confirmation of the diagnosis is provided by increased localized pain with palpation of the tender point after straight leg raising, and prolonged relief is provided by injection of local anesthetics.

Other Disorders

Nonmalignant and malignant neoplastic tumors and recurrent or persistent infections may also result in CPP. In such cases, the patient may describe vague lower abdominal discomfort, gastrointestinal or genitourinary symptoms, or a history of prior infection. Careful history, examination, and pelvic ultrasonography or computed tomography (CT) should be performed to rule out a neoplastic or chronic infectious process of the reproductive, GI, GU, musculoskeletal or lymphatic systems.

The etiology of CPP often remains obscure, and treatment should be geared toward improved functioning rather than cure in refractory cases.[12] Still, an attempt should be made to provide patients with the best chance for symptomatic improvement, depending on the working differential diagnosis.

LABORATORY TESTING AND ADDITIONAL STUDIES

All female patients of reproductive age with acute or chronic pelvic pain should have the following laboratory evaluations: urine or serum hCG (to rule out pregnancy), complete blood count with differential, routine urinalysis, and (if indicated) urine culture. Additionally, for patients who are sexually active, chlamydial and gonococcal cultures should be done, as well as an erythrocyte sedimentation rate assessment. Although the specificity of the latter test is low, a negative result argues strongly against PID.

As stated previously, superfluous testing is costly and time-consuming and should be avoided. Additional testing should be recommended on the basis of the findings of history, physical examination, and initial laboratory testing. For instance, pelvic ultrasonography is necessary to rule out an ectopic pregnancy; it may also be helpful in evaluating (1) the adnexa of obese patients or those whose pain precludes an adequate pelvic examination or (2) a pelvic mass or an abnormal pelvic examination. As described above, in certain instances, a vaginal wet mount specimen, pap smear, or stool guaiac test or culture are indicated.

An abnormal appendix may be identified by ultrasonography or CT. Similarly, patients with peritonitis may benefit from culdocentesis to help elucidate the cause. In patients suspected of having gastrointestinal abnormalities, abdominal radiography series or imaging studies using CT with contrast should be performed. In patients with an acute abdomen, barium studies should be delayed until there is confirmation that a bowel perforation does not exist. Computed tomography is often the imaging modality of choice for diagnosing retroperitoneal masses, pelvic or gastrointestinal abscesses, and pelvic congestion.[46] Finally, when gastrourinary sources such as ureteral lithiasis are suspected, an intravenous pyelography or CT urography is usually indicated.

CYCLIC PAIN

Medical Therapy

When implementing treatment for a patient with chronic cyclic pain, medical therapy is considered the first line of management. Prostaglandin synthetase inhibitors (nonsteroidal anti-inflammatory drugs [NSAIDs])have been used successfully for dysmenorrhea. These medications may be effective in up to 80% of patients with primary dysmenorrhea.[47] Despite the lack of clinical evidence confirming their success, positive patient feedback has prompted their continued use as a mainstay of therapy for CPP patients with secondary dysmenorrhea as well.[47] Typically, NSAIDs are initiated on a continuous basis every 6 to 8 hours for 1 to 2 days before menses or before the pain generally begins.

When symptomatic relief is not adequate with the use of NSAIDs alone, the addition of a cyclic oral contraceptive pill (OCP) to NSAIDs may increase the efficacy of dysmenorrhea treatment to more than 90%.[48] Oral contraceptives can also be used continuously without a withdrawal bleed. The best oral contraceptive for this approach is a monophasic 30-µg ethinyl estradiol continuous oral contraceptive. If breakthrough bleeding occurs, the patient should stop the oral contraceptives for 5 days and then restart.

High-dose progestins (medroxyprogesterone acetate 20 to 30 mg/d or depot medroxyprogesterone acetate 150 mg every 3 months or norethindrone acetate 15 mg/d), danazol, and gonadotropin-releasing hormone (Gn-RH) agonists act like oral contraceptives, suppressing endogenous hormones and the physiologic menstrual cycle. These medications may also offer relief for patients with cyclic pain when oral contraceptives fail or are contraindicated. Additionally, small studies have shown high-dose medroxyprogesterone acetate to be beneficial for pelvic congestion and Gn-RH agonists to be superior to OCPs, progestins, and danazol in the treatment of ovarian-remnant syndrome.[49–51] Moreover, several studies have confirmed significant symptomatic improvement when progestins, danazol, and Gn-RH agonists are used to treat endometriosis.[52–54]

When stronger analgesics are required, relief may be obtained by using narcotics for the duration of the painful monthly episodes. However, given the potential for the development of drug dependency, alternative forms of therapy or the implementation of a more intensive evaluation is recommended for patients requiring this level of analgesia.

Alternative/Complementary Therapy

As the trend toward employing alternative and complementary therapies increases, more and more data are available to defend their use in managing patients. It is therefore prudent to offer patients such therapy, particularly when traditional methods have failed. Acupuncture and transcutaneous electrical nerve stimulation (TENS) are the most widely used therapies for dysmenorrhea.[55–57]

In a study conducted by Kaplan et al, patients with primary dysmenorrhea were evaluated after undergoing TENS. In this population, 90% of patients showed benefit, 30% reported marked relief, and 60% reported moderate relief.[55] These results suggest that these remedies may provide results comparable to those reported with the combination of NSAIDs and oral contraceptives.

Surgical Therapy

Laparoscopy and/or hysteroscopy may be performed in an attempt to localize the source of pain.[58] In the setting of cyclic pelvic pain, laparoscopy should be reserved for patients who are refractory to medical therapies or for when there is a suspected pelvic pathology.

Presacral neurectomies (PSNs) and **laparoscopic uterine nerve ablation** (LUNA) are two surgical options offered to patients with severe cyclic pelvic pain that is unresponsive to medical management. During a PSN, the superior hypogastric nerve plexus is resected at the level of the sacrum. The procedure was initially described in 1937 as a treatment for intractable dysmenorrhea.[59] The LUNA procedure is a newer method in which the uterine nerves are transected at the uterosacral ligaments bilaterally. Despite limited data, these procedures may be beneficial in up to 80% of patients with primary dysmenorrhea; decreased efficacy usually is reported in patients with secondary dysmenorrhea.[59–64] Typically, these techniques are reserved for patients with deep central pain secondary to dysmenorrhea or endometriosis.

Patients should be carefully selected. In general, PSN and LUNA should be used only for patients for whom nonsurgical management has failed, whose activities of daily living are compromised as a result of their pain, and who have no identifiable structural pathology contributing to their symptoms. In addition, patients should have demonstrated an improvement in symptoms after fluoroscopically guided superior hypogastric nerve block (for PSN) or paracervical block (for LUNA). Patients should be counseled about the potential risks to the bowel, ureter, and pelvic blood vessels.

These procedures should be avoided in patients whose pain is thought to be somatic, GI, adnexal, or lateral pelvic in origin. Since the ovarian afferents enter the spinal cord at T9–T10, above the level of transection, patients with pain of this origin would not be expected to benefit from these procedures.

In selected instances, a **hysterectomy** may be indicated, especially in women with endometriosis, adenomyosis, or pelvic congestion syndrome who have completed childbearing and for whom less radical approaches have failed.

NONCYCLIC PAIN

Pain management therapy in this setting generally falls into one or more of five categories: pharmacologic, surgical, physical, behavioral, and alternative. Because of the multiple therapeutic modalities, multidisciplinary pain management by a team of physicians and other clinicians is often recommended. An overview of each therapeutic category is provided below, with general recommendations on their use in various clinical scenarios. Table 75–8 and Figure 75–4 summarize common treatment regimens.

Pharmacologic Therapy

Tricyclic antidepressants, anticonvulsants, and selective serotonin uptake inhibitors (SSRIs) are common treatments employed for patients with noncyclic CPP. Low-dose tricyclics and anticonvulsants raise the pain threshold and alter neural transmission via unknown mechanisms. They are useful for most chronic pain conditions. However, just as oral contraceptives, NSAIDs, and narcotics have not been systematically studied for the treatment of cyclic pelvic pain, no randomized controlled studies have evaluated the use of tricyclic antidepressants for noncyclic pelvic pain. However, successful use has been reported. Side effects include somnolence, dry mouth, constipation, and an increased fatigue threshold for tricyclics and somnolence, dizziness, and ataxia for anticonvulsants. Amitriptyline, nortriptyline, and desipramine (in order of most to least sedating) are administered at bedtime, starting initially with 10 mg and increasing to 50 to 75 mg hs as tolerated. Gabapentin is used in doses of 300 to 600 mg tid up to 2,800 mg/d. Side effects generally become tolerable over time.

If clinical depression is present, the use of a SSRI or other serotoninergic antidepressant is preferable to an increase in the dose of the tricyclic unless there are no significant side effects from the low-dose tricyclic.

Local anesthetic injection may benefit patients with abdominal wall nerve entrapment or trigger points identified by point tenderness and increased pain from palpation of the point on straight leg raising. These injections are thought to interfere with the transmission of the pain impulse and to eliminate the positive feedback arc.[8] An injection of local anesthetic (3 to 5 cc of bupivacaine 0.025%) is made into the tender point or trigger

TABLE 75–8. Treatment Regimens for Disorders of Chronic Pelvic Pain

Diagnosis	*Treatment*
Reproductive disorders	
Dysmenorrhea, cyclic pelvic pain	First line
	Prostaglandin synthetase inhibitors
	Adjuvant therapy
	Oral contraceptives
	Oral or depo progestins
	Gn-RH agonist with addback HRT
	Acupuncture
	TENS
	Second line
	Narcotic analgesia
	Laparoscopy with LUNA or PSN
	Hysterectomy
Adhesions	Adhesiolysis
Pelvic congestion	MPA or Gn-RH agonist
	Hysterectomy with bilateral salpingo-oophrectomy (rare)
	Embolization of involved veins?
	Bilateral ovarian vein ligation?
	Excision or ligation of collateral vessels?
Ovarian Remnant syndrome	Gn-RH agonist
	Laparotomy with removal of ovarian remnants
Vulvar vestibulitis	Topical anti-inflammatory creams (5% ASA in acid mantle)
	Behavioral therapy
	Pelvic floor muscle biofeedback or physical therapy
	Surgical excision of vestibule (Woodruff procedure)
Gastrointestinal disorders	
Irritable bowel syndrome	Medical
	Bulk forming agents
	Anxiolytics
	Anticholinergics
	Antispasmodics
	Low dose tricyclic antidepressants
	Behavioral
	Reassurance; high fiber diet; stress reduction; education
Diverticular disease	Antibiotics for diverticulitis
	Surgical resection
Hernia	Surgical repair
	Pessary
Genitourinary disorders	
Recurrent cystitis	Prophylactic antibiotics
	Vaginal estrogen cream

TABLE 75–8. (continued)

Diagnosis	Treatment
Urethral syndrome	Medical
	Antibiotics; urethral dilation; vaginal estrogen cream
	Behavioral
	Education; biofeedback
Interstitial cystitis	First line
	Antihistamines
	Tricyclic antidepressants
	Pentosan polysulfate sodium (PPS)
	Behavioral
	Bladder diet
	TENS
	Physical therapy
	Biofeedback
	Second line
	Dimethyl sulfoxide (DMSO)
	BCG
	Interferon
	Hyalluronic acid (Cystistat)
	Hypogastric plexus block
Neurologic-musculskeletal disorders	
Myofascial pain	First line
	Physical therapy
	Trigger point injections
	Second line
	Low-dose tricyclic antidepressants
	Anticonvulsants
Nerve entrapment	Medical
	Peripheral nerve block
	Cryoneurolysis
	Low-dose tricyclic antidepressants
	Anticonvulsants
	Behavioral
	Physical therapy
	Acupuncture
	Second line
	Neuroma excision

Gn-RH = gonadotropin-releasing hormone; HRT = hormone replacement therapy; LUNA = laparoscopic uterine nerve ablation; MPA = medroxyprogesterone acetate; PSN = presacral neurectomy; TENS = transcutaneous electrical nerve stimulation.

point. The points are then palpated again with the straight leg raise test and re-injected if still painful. Aspiration before injection should be performed to avoid an intravascular injection. Three or five weekly or biweekly injections are then performed.[65] Improvement may be noted in up to 95% of patients, with reported symptom-free intervals of up to 3 years.[8]

In patients with multiple vaginal wall, sacrum, and abdominal wall trigger points, **caudal or epidural anesthesia** or **physical therapy** may provide good results without the need for multiple

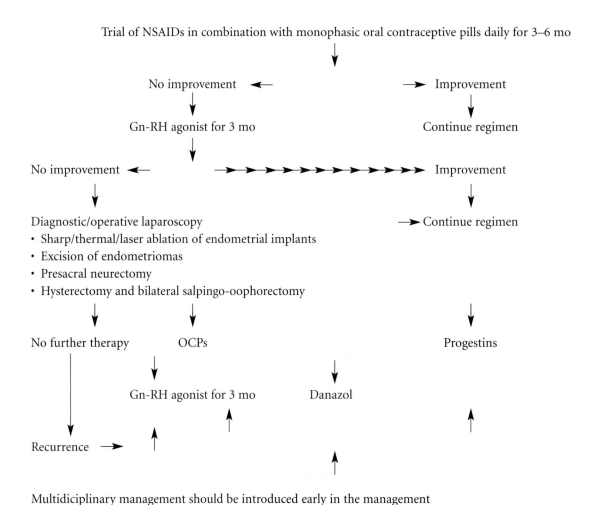

Multidiciplinary management should be introduced early in the management

FIGURE 75–4. Algorithm for the treatment of endometriosis. Gn-RH = gonadotropin-releasing hormone; NSAIDs = nonsteroidal anti-inflammatory drugs; OCPs = oral contraceptive pills.

injections.[8,66] Finally, a **superior hypogastric plexus block**, either CT-guided or during laparoscopy, has been proposed as a possible therapeutic technique[67,68] for midline visceral pain of T12–L2 dermatomal origin.

Surgical Therapy

The routine use of surgical interventions for patients with noncyclic CPP is quite controversial. Specifically, studies have not consistently confirmed a benefit in this setting.

LAPAROSCOPY

Currently, 40% of all laparoscopies are performed for patients with CPP.[11] However, studies have shown that 14 to 77% of these patients have no pathology and that up to two-thirds have only adhesions, for which a definitive correlation with

pain is often impossible.[69,70] Furthermore, nonsurgical multidisciplinary management of CPP is successful in 65 to 90% of patients, despite the presence or absence of pathology.[8,71,72] Although Howard found that patients with CPP are twice as likely to have pathology at the time of laparoscopy, as compared with the non-CPP patient,[11] "pathology" such as adhesions or mild endometriosis often is no longer (if it ever was) the cause of the pain.[73–77] Laparoscopies have shown an association with pathology in 70 to 90% of patients with an abnormal pelvic examination and up to one-half of patients with normal pelvic examinations.[11]

Consequently, it is generally recommended that laparoscopy be reserved for patients for whom the procedure may alter the management regimen. Typically, this includes patients with CPP who have failed medical or multidisciplinary management after a minimum of 3 to 6 months, patients with suspected endometriosis or adhesions who have not failed to have relief with previous surgical therapy, and patients with CPP undergoing infertility evaluation.

LAPAROTOMY

In certain settings, a laparotomy may be necessary. Given the widespread use and knowledge of laparoscopic techniques among gynecologists, laparotomies are generally reserved for patients in whom technical difficulties occur or are anticipated to occur during laparoscopy. This group includes patients suspected to have widespread disease, those with large pelvic masses or extensive endometriosis or adhesions, and patients suspected of having ovarian-remnant syndrome, in which potential complications (including hemorrhage and ureteral bladder or bowel damage) often preclude the application of a safe and effective laparoscopy.[78]

HYSTERECTOMY

Hysterectomy is another surgical intervention widely used in patients with CPP. Approximately 12% of all hysterectomies are performed for this diagnosis.[11] Unfortunately, symptoms may persist in up to 30% of patients who have undergone hysterectomy for CPP.[79–81] Moreover, after the hysterectomy, patients are at risk for nerve entrapment, adhesions, vaginal cuff pain, bladder and bowel irritability, and the development of new trigger points; all of these factors can result in persistent or worsened postoperative pain.[27] In light of these findings, the American College of Obstetricians and Gynecologists (ACOG) recommends that hysterectomies be limited to patients with CPP who meet the criteria listed in Table 75–9.[79]

Typically, patients with cyclic pain or those with associated abnormal uterine bleeding, uterine pathology, or endometriosis (in appropriately selected cases) are the best candidates. Even in these settings, however, it is generally recommended that nonsurgical management be attempted before opting for a hysterectomy. Additionally, any patients desirous of future fertility should be excluded from this group.[80,81]

Physical Therapy

Physical therapy is frequently employed in the multidisciplinary approach to CPP, particularly when myofascial pain or syndrome is suspected. No controlled studies are yet available to evaluate this component of therapy for CPP. A TENS or transvaginal electric nerve stimulator unit may be used as a supplement in this setting.[55,82] One study noted moderate to marked improvement in pain in 90% of the patients receiving TENS.[55]

Psychological Therapy

An emotional and psychological evaluation is mandatory when treating patients with noncyclic CPP and is best conducted by a psychologist experienced in working with CPP patients. Patients with CPP typically report a higher incidence of marital and family dysfunction, sexual or physical abuse, and depression.[30,83–88] Specifically, sexual or physical abuse is thought to accompany up to 50% of cases of CPP.[86–88] No randomized trials have been done to confirm the direct affect of psychological therapy on CPP. However, significant improvements in pain and a decreased incidence of hysterectomies for CPP have been reported from programs that use psychological evaluation and treatment as part of a multidisciplinary approach.[71,89,90]

The goals of psychological management include decreased pain levels, decreased reliance on

TABLE 75–9. American College of Obstetricians and Gynecologists (ACOG) Criteria for Hysterectomy for Patients with Chronic Pelvic Pain

All of the following:*
   Pain present for more than 6 months
   Impaired quality of life as a result of pain
   No remediable pathology present after appropriate evaluation
   Pain is felt to be of uterine origin

*Many patients who fit these criteria are not appropriate for hysterectomy. However, patients who do not meet these criteria should generally not be considered for hysterectomy.
Adapted from ACOG criteria set. Hysterectomy, abdominal or vaginal for chronic pelvic pain. Number 29, November 1997.
Committee on Quality Assessment. American College of Obstetricians and Gynecologists. Int J Gynaecol Obstet 1998;60:316–7.

pain medication, increased activity, and reduction of the toll pain takes on a woman's overall lifestyle, as well as enhanced opportunity for control. The pain management model maximizes overall functioning and reduces suffering and irritability. The therapy teaches specific skills and is active, directive, and time limited, in contrast to traditional psychotherapy. Techniques include relaxation, stress management, cognitive-behavioral modification, sexual and marital counseling, and (if appropriate) discussion of past traumas.[91]

Alternative/Complementary Therapy

Chiropractic therapy, hypnosis, and acupuncture are alternative/complimentary techniques available for the treatment of CPP.[56,57] Acupuncture is particularly useful for dysmenorrhea, but these techniques have been less well studied as therapies for noncyclic CPP. Despite the paucity of evidence in clinical trials, these methods have proven beneficial in small prospective studies, and the trend toward nontraditional approaches to medicine suggests their having an even larger role in the near future.[16,90]

MULTIDISCIPLINARY THERAPY

Typically, a multidisciplinary approach is recommended for the treatment of patients with CPP.[89,90,92,93] This type of treatment regimen combines the efforts of numerous specialists in order to achieve beneficial results for the patients involved. The team typically includes a gynecologist or internist as the pain manager, working together with a psychologist, and (if possible) an anesthesiologist, a dietitian, and a physical therapist. Together they use NSAIDs, narcotics, tricyclic antidepressants, anticonvulsants, trigger-point injections, and nerve blocks in an attempt to achieve favorable results. One program accomplished a 50% reduction in pain symptoms in 85% of their patients through the combined use of behavioral therapy, acupuncture, and tricyclic antidepressants.[90] Other studies suggested similar results with this type of approach.[22,23,70,89,92,93] In fact, one prospective study reported superior symptomatic improvement when a multidisciplinary approach was used, compared to a traditional gynecologic approach that used only medical and surgical interventions to obtain a cure.[89]

RESOURCE

International Pelvic Pain Society
Women's Medical Plaza, Suite 402
2006 Brookwood Center Drive
Birmingham, Alabama 35209
Telephone: (205) 877-2950
            1-800-624-9676
Web site: www.pelvicpain.org.

The International Pelvic Pain Society offers resources for both patients and clinicians, including patient education materials and access to scientific articles.

REFERENCES

1. Kumazawa T. Sensory innervation of reproductive organs. In: Cervero F, Morrison J, editors. Visceral sensation. New York: Elsevier Science Publications; 1986. p. 115–31.
2. Cervero F, Tattersall JEH. Somatic and visceral sensory integration in the thoracic spinal cord. In: Cervero F, Morrison J, editors. Visceral sensation. New York: Elsevier Science Publications; 1986. p. 189–205.
3. Cervero F. Sensory innervation of the viscera: peripheral basis of visceral pain. Physiol Rev 1994; 74:95–138.
4. Hughes JM. Psychological aspects of pelvic pain. In: Rocker I, editor. Pelvic pain in women. Diagnosis and management. London: Springer-Verlag; 1990. p. 13–20.
5. Procacci P, Aoppi M, Maresen M. Clinical approach to visceral sensation. In: Cervero F, Morrison J, editors.

Visceral sensation. New York: Elsevier Science Publications; 1986. p. 21–36.

6. Wesselmann U, Lai J. Mechanisms of referred visceral pain: uterine inflammation in the adult virgin rat results in neurogenic plasma extravasation in the skin. Pain 1997;73:209–317.

7. Giamberardino MA, Berkley KJ, Lezzi S, et al. Pain threshold variations in somatic wall tissues as a function of the menstrual cycle, segmental site, and tissue depth in nondysmenorrheic women, dysmenorrheic women, and men. Pain 1997;71:187–97.

8. Slocumb JC. Neurological factors in chronic pelvic pain: trigger points and the abdominal pelvic syndrome. Am J Obstet Gynecol 1984;149:536–43.

9. Thomson H, Francis DM. Abdominal-wall tenderness: a useful sign in the acute abdomen. Lancet 1977;2: 1053–4.

10. Walker EA, Katon WJ, Alfrey H, et al. The prevalence of chronic pain and irritable bowel syndrome in two university clinics. J Psychosom Obstet Gynaecol 1991;12 Suppl:65–75.

11. Howard FM. The role of laparoscopy in chronic pelvic pain: promise and pitfalls. Obstet Gynecol Surv 1993;48:357–87.

12. Mathias SD, Kuppermann M, Liberman RF, et al. Chronic pelvic pain: prevalence, health-related quality of life, and economic correlates. Obstet Gynecol 1996;87:321–7.

13. Reiter RC. Occult somatic pathology in women with chronic pelvic pain. Clin Obstet Gynecol 1990 b;33: 154–60.

14. Summit RL. Urogynecologic causes of chronic pelvic pain. In: Ling FW, editor. Obstetrics and gynecology of North America: contemporary management of chronic pain. Philadelphia: WB Saunders; 1993. p. 685–98.

15. American College of Obstetricians and Gynecologists. Dysmenorrhea. ACOG Technical Bulletin 1983;68.

16. Rapkin AJ, Rasgon NL, Berkley KJ. Dysmenorrhea. In: Yaksh TL, Lynch C, editors. Anesthesia: biologic foundations. Philadelphia: Lippincott-Raven; 1997. p. 785–93.

17. Hughes JM. Psychological aspects of pelvic pain. In: Rocker I, editor. Pelvic pain in women. Diagnosis and management. London: Springer-Verlag; 1990. p. 13–20.

18. Kresch AJ, Seifer DB, Sachs LB, Barrese I. Laparoscopy in 100 women with chronic pelvic pain. Obstet Gynecol 1984;64:672–4.

19. Rapkin AJ. Adhesions and pelvic pain: a retrospective study. Obstet Gynecol 1986;68:13–5.

20. Lundberg WI, Wall JE, Mathers JE. Laparoscopy in the evaluation of pelvic pain. Obstet Gynecol 1973; 42:872–6.

21. Liston WA, Bradford WP, Downier J, Kerr MG. Laparoscopy in a general gynecologic unit. Am J Obstet Gynecol 1972;113:672–7.

22. Peters AAW, Trimbos-Kemper GCM, Admiral C, Trimbos JB. A randomized clinical trial on the benefit of adhesiolysis in patients with intraperitoneal adhesions and chronic pelvic pain. Br J Obstet Gynaecol 1992;99:59–62.

23. Steege JF, Stout AL. Resolution of chronic pelvic pain after laparoscopic lysis of adhesions. Am J Obstet Gynecol 1991;165:278–83.

24. Taylor HC Jr. Pelvic pain based on a vascular and autonomic nervous system disorder. Am J Obstet Gynecol 1954;67:1177–96.

25. Beard RW, Reginald PW, Wadsworth J. Clinical features of women with chronic lower abdominal pain and pelvic congestion. Br J Obstet Gynaecol 1988;95:153–61.

26. Beard RW, Highman JH, Pearce S, Reginald PW. Diagnosis of pelvic varicosities in women with chronic pelvic pain. Lancet 1984;2:946–9.

27. Steege JF. Pain after hysterectomy. In: Steege JF, Metzger DA, Levy BS, editors. Chronic pelvic pain—an integrated approach. Philadelphia: WB Saunders Co.; 1998. p. 135–44.

28. Siddall-Allum J, Rae T, Rogers V, et al. Chronic pain caused by residual ovaries and ovarian remnants. Br J Obstet Gynaecol 1994;101:979–85.

29. Lafferty HW, Angioli R, Rudolph J, Penalver MA. Ovarian remnant syndrome: experience at Jackson Memorial Hospital, University of Miami, 1985 through 1993. Am J Obstet Gynecol 1996;174:641–5.

30. Bodden-Heidrich R, Kuppers V, Beckmann MW, et al. Psychosomatic aspects of vulvodynia: comparison with the chronic pelvic pain syndrome. J Reprod Med 1999;44:411–6.

31. Lynch PJ. Vulvodynia: a syndrome of unexplained vulvar pain, psychologic disability and sexual dysfunction. J Reprod Med 1986;31:773–80.

32. Paavonen J. Vulvodynia: a complex syndrome of vulvar pain. Acta Obstet Gynecol Scand 1995;74:243–7.

33. Hammer J, Talley NJ. Diagnostic criteria for irritable bowel syndrome. Am J Med 1999;157:5–11S.

34. Rapkin AJ, Mayer EA. Gastroenterologic causes of chronic pelvic pain. In: Ling FW, editor. Obstetrics and gynecology clinics of North America: contemporary

management of chronic pain. Philadelphia: WB Saunders; 1993. p. 663–84.

35. Drossman DA, Thompson WG. The irritable bowel syndrome: review and a graduated multicomponent treatment approach. Ann Int Med 1992;116;1009–16.

36. Hightower NC, Roberts JW. Acute and chronic lower abdominal pain of enterologic origin in chronic pelvic pain. In: Renaer MR, editor. Chronic pelvic pain in women. New York: Springer-Verlag; 1981. p. 110–37.

37. Spangen L. Spigelian hernia. Surg Clin North Am 1984;64:351–66.

38. Miklos JR, O'Reilly MJ, Saye WB. Sciatic hernia as a cause of chronic pelvic pain in women. Obstet Gynecol 1998;91:998–1001.

39. Bergman A, Darram M, Bhatia NN. Urethral syndrome: a comparison of different treatment modalities. J Reprod Med 1989;34:157–60.

40. Nigro DA, Wein AJ, Foy M, et al. Associations among cystoscopic and urodynamic findings in women enrolled in the Interstitial Cystitis Data Base (ICDB) Study. Urology 1997;49 Suppl 5A:86–92.

41. Gillenwater JY, Wein AJ. Summary of the National Institute of Arthritis, Diabetes, Digestive and Kidney Diseases Workshop on Interstitial Cystitis. National Institutes of Health, Bethesda, MD, August 28–29. J Urol 1988;140:203–6.

42. Karram MM. Frequency, urgency and painful bladder syndrome In: Walters MD, Karram MM, editors. Clinical urogynecology. St. Louis: Mosby; 1993. p. 285–98.

43. Slocumb JC. Chronic somatic myofascial and neurogenic abdominal pelvic pain. In: Porreco RP, Reiter RC, editors. Clinical obstetrics and gynecology. Philadelphia: JB Lippincott & Co; 1990. p. 145–53.

44. Sippo WC, Burghardt A, Gomez AC. Nerve entrapment after Pfannensteil incision. Am J Obstet Gynecol 1987;157:420–1.

45. Hammeroff SR, Carlson GL, Brown BR. Ilioinguinal pain syndrome. Pain 1981;10:253–7.

46. Coakley FV, Varghese SL, Hricak H. CT and MRI of pelvic varices in women. J Comput Assist Tomogr 1999;23:429–34.

47. Drugs for dysmenorrhea. Med Lett Drugs and Ther 1979;21:81–4.

48. Chan WY, Dawood MY. Prostaglandin levels in menstrual fluid of dysmenorrheic and of dysmenorrheic subjects with and without oral contraceptive or ibuprofen therapy. Adv Prostaglandin Thromboxane Res 1980;8:1443–7.

49. Farquhar CM, Rogers V, Franks S, et al. A randomized controlled trial of medroxyprogesterone acetate and psychotherapy for the treatment of pelvic congestion. Br J Obstet Gynaecol 1990;63:710–1.

50. Reginald PW, Adams J, Franks S, et al. Medroxyprogesterone acetate in the treatment of pelvic pain due to venous congestion. Br J Obstet Gynaecol 1989;96:1153–62.

51. Carey MP, Slack MC. GnRH analogue in assessing chronic pelvic pain in women with residual ovaries. Br J Obstet Gynaecol 1996;103:150–3.

52. Vercellini P, Cortesi I, Crosignani PG. Progestins for symptomatic endometriosis: a critical analysis of the evidence. Ferti Steril 1997;68:393–401.

53. D'Hooghe TM, Hill JA. Endometriosis. In: Berek JS, Adashi EY, Hillard PA, editors. Novak's gynecology. 12th ed. Baltimore: Williams & Wilkins; 1996. p. 887–914.

54. Berqvist A, Bergh T, Hogstrom L, et al. Effects of Triptorelin versus placebo on symptoms of endometriosis. Fertil Steril 1998;69:702–8.

55. Kaplan B, Peled Y, Pardo J, et al. Transcutaneous electrical nerve stimulation (TENS) as a relief for dysmenorrhea. Clin Exp Obstet Gynecol 1994;21:87–90.

56. Helms JM. Acupuncture for the management of primary dysmenorrhea. Obstet Gynecol 1987;69:51–6.

57. Hawk C, Long C, Azad A. Chiropractic care for women with chronic pelvic pain: a prospective single-group intervention study. J Manipulative Physiol Ther 1997;20:73–9.

58. Nezhat F, Nezhat C, Nezhat CH, et al. Use of hysteroscopy in addition to laparoscopy for evaluating chronic pelvic pain. J Reprod Med 1995;40:431–4.

59. Cotte G. Resection of the presacral nerves in the treatment of obstinate dysmenorrhea. Am J Obstet Gynecol 1937;33:1034–40.

60. Candiani GB, Fedele L, Vercellini P, et al. Presacral neurectomy for the treatment of pelvic pain associated with endometriosis: a controlled study. Am J Obstet Gynecol 1992;167:100–3.

61. Ingersoll FM, Meigs JV. Presacral neurectomy for dysmenorrhea. New Engl J Med 1948;238:357–60.

62. Polan ML, DeCherney A. Presacral neurectomy for pelvic pain in infertility. Fertil Steril 1980;34:557–60.

63. Vercellini P, Fedele L, Bianchi S, Candiani GB. Pelvic denervation for chronic pain associated with endometriosis: fact or fancy? Am J Obstet Gynecol 1991;165:745–9.

64. Nezhat CH, Seidman DS, Nezhat FR, Nezhat CR. Long-term outcome of laparoscopic presacral neurectomy for the treatment of central pelvic pain attributed to endometriosis. Obstet Gynecol 1998;91:701–4.

65. Hammeroff SR, Crago BR, Blitt CD, et al. Comparison of bupivacaine, etidocaine and saline for trigger point therapy. Anesth Analg 1981;60:E752–7.

66. Arner S, Lindblom U, Meyerson BA, Molander C. Prolonged relief of neuralgia after regional anesthetic blocks. A call for further experimental and systemic clinical studies. Pain 1990;43:287–97.

67. Steege JF. Superior hypogastric block during micro-laparoscopic pain mapping. J Am Assoc Gynecol Laparosc 1998;5:265–7.

68. Wechsler RJ, Maurer PM, Halpern EJ, Frank ED. Superior hypogastric plexus block for chronic pelvic pain in the presence of endometriosis: CT techniques and results. Radiology 1995;196:103–6.

69. Stout AL, Steege JF, Dodson WC, Hughes CL. Relationship of laparoscopic findings to self-report of pelvic pain. Am J Obstet Gynecol 1991;164:73–9.

70. Reese KA, Reddy S, Rock JA. Endometriosis in an adolescent population: the Emory experience. J Pediatr Adolesc Gynecol 1996;9:125–8.

71. Reiter RC, Gambone JC, Johnson SR. Availability of a multidisciplinary pelvic pain clinic and frequency of hysterectomy for pelvic pain. J Psychosom Obstet Gynaecol 1991;12 Suppl:109.

72. Reiter RC. A profile of women with chronic pelvic pain. Clin Obstet Gynecol 1990;33:130–6.

73. Duffy DM, DiZerega GS. Adhesions contoversies: pelvic pain as a cause of adhesions, crystalloids on preventing them. J Reprod Med 1996;41:19–26.

74. Saravelos HG, Le T-C, Cooke ID. An analysis of the outcome of microsurgical and laparoscopic adhesiolysis for chronic pelvic pain. Hum Reprod 1995; 10:2895–901.

75. Chan CLK, Wood. Pelvic adhesiolysis: the assessment of symptom relief by 100 patients. Aust N Z J Obstet Gynaecol 1985;25:295–8.

76. Fayez JA, Clark RR. Operative laparoscopy for the treatment of localized chronic pelvic-abdominal pain caused by postoperative adhesions. J Gynecol Surg 1994;10:79–83.

77. Daniell JP. Laparoscopic enterolysis for chronic abdominal pain. J Gynecol Surg 1989;5:61–6.

78. Pettit PD, Lee RA. Ovarian remnant syndrome: diagnostic dilemma and surgical challenge. Obstet Gynecol 1988;71:580–3.

79. ACOG criteria set. Hysterectomy, abdominal or vaginal for chronic pelvic pain. Number 29, November 1997. Committee on Quality Assessment. American College of Obstetricians and Gynecologists. Int J Gynaecol Obstet 1998;60:316–7.

80. Stovall TG, Ling FW, Crawford DA. Hysterectomy for chronic pelvic pain of presumed uterine etiology. Obstet Gynecol 1990;75:676–9.

81. Hillis SD, Marchbanks PA, Peterson HB. The effectiveness of hysterectomy for chronic pelvic pain. Obstet Gynecol 1995;86:941–5.

82. Morris L, Newton RA. Use of high voltage pulsed galvanic stimulation for patients with levator ani syndrome. Phys Ther 1987;67:265.

83. Magni G, Salmi A, deLeo D, Ceola A. Chronic pelvic pain and depression. Psychopathology 1984;17:132–6.

84. Walker E, Katon W, Harrop-Griffiths J. Relationship of chronic pelvic pain of psychiatric diagnoses and childhood sexual abuse. Am J Psychiatry 1988; 145:75–80.

85. Gross RJ, Doerr H, Caldirola D, et al. Borderline syndrome and incest in chronic pelvic pain patients. Int J Psychiatry Med 1980;10:79–96.

86. Harrop-Griffiths J, Katon W, Walker E, et al. The association between chronic pelvic pain, psychiatric diagnoses and childhood sexual abuse. Obstet Gynecol 1988;71:589–94.

87. Rapkin AJ, Kames LD, Darke LL. History of physical and sexual abuse in women with chronic pelvic pain. Obstet Gynecol 1990;76:90–6.

88. Walling MK, Reiter RC, O'Hara MW, et al. Abuse history and chronic pain in women: I. Prevalence of sexual abuse and physical abuse. Obstet Gynecol 1994; 84:193–4.

89. Peters AA, Van Dorst E, Jellis B, et al. A randomized clinical trial to compare two different approaches in women with chronic pelvic pain. Obstet Gynecol 1991;77:740–4.

90. Kames LD, Rapkin AJ, Naliboff BD, et al. Effectiveness of an interdisciplinary pain management program for the treatment of chronic pelvic pain. Pain 1990;41:41–6.

91. Rapkin AJ, Reading AE. Chronic pelvic pain. In: Barbieri RL, Berek JS, Creasy RK, et al, editors. Current problems in obstetrics, gynecology and fertility. Littleton (MA): Mosby Year Book; 1991. p. 102–37.

92. Milburn A, Reiter RC, Rhomberg AT. Multidisciplinary approach to chronic pelvic pain. In: Ling FW, editor. Obstetrics and gynecology clinics of North America: contemporary management of chronic pelvic pain. Philadelphia: WB Saunders; 1993. p. 643–61.

93. Gambone JC, Reiter RC. Nonsurgical management of chronic pelvic pain: a multidisciplinary approach. Clin Obstet Gynecol 1990;33:205–11.

76

PREMENSTRUAL SYNDROME AND PREMENSTRUAL DYSPHORIC DISORDER

Natalie Driessen, BSc, and Natalia Rasgon, MD, PhD

Premenstrual syndrome (PMS) is defined by a constellation of physical and psychological symptoms present in the late luteal phase of the menstrual cycle. The exact definition of PMS is controversial but usually includes a combination of somatic and psychiatric symptoms that occur reproducibly prior to menses and are relieved by the onset of menstruation. Many criteria for identifying women with premenstrual syndrome have been proposed. Using more inclusive definitions, 95% of reproductive age women may be identified as suffering from PMS.[1] This in itself has generated controversy as some have questioned defining as a "syndrome" symptoms common to the vast majority of menstruating women. However, it also is clear that PMS symptoms have an adverse effect on functioning at home and work for a minority of women. These women should be carefully evaluated, and some may require pharmacologic treatment.

Premenstrual dysphoric disorder (PMDD) affects a much smaller percentage of women. It has sometimes been referred to as "severe PMS" and as late luteal phase dysphoric disorder. Studies estimate that between 5 and 10% of reproductive age women are affected.[1] Premenstrual dysphoric disorder is characterized by more severe psychiatric symptoms than PMS, and its consequences to those affected are unquestionable. For this reason, it is essential that clinicians be able to identify and treat women with PMDD.

DEFINITIONS AND PATHOPHYSIOLOGY

American College of Obstetricians and Gynecologists diagnostic criteria for PMS are summarized in Table 76–1. Key features include the presence of both somatic and psychiatric complaints prior to

TABLE 76–1. ACOG Diagnostic Criteria for Premenstrual Syndrome, 2000

All of the following criteria must be met:

- At least one of the following physical symptoms present during the 5 days before menses for three consecutive menstrual cycles: breast tenderness, swelling of the extremities, headache, abdominal bloating
- At least one of the following psychological symptoms present during the 5 days before menses for three consecutive menstrual cycles: depression, angry outbursts, irritability, anxiety, confusion, social withdrawal
- Symptoms relieved within 4 days of menses, not recurring until at least the 13th day of the next cycle
- Symptoms adversely affect work performance and/or family or social life
- Symptoms cannot be explained by the use of hormones or other medications, or drug or alcohol use
- Symptoms occur reproducibly during two cycles of prospective recording

Adapted from American College of Obstetricians and Gynecologists. Premenstrual syndrome. Washington (DC): American College of Obstetricians and Gynecologists; April 2000, ACOG Practice Bulletin No. 15.

TABLE 76–2. DMS IV Criteria for Premenstrual Dysphoric Disorder

All of the following criteria must be met:

- At least one of the following symptoms present during the week before menstruation, and remitting within a few days of the onset of menstruation:
  1. Markedly depressed mood, feelings of hopelessness, or self-deprecating thoughts
  2. Marked anxiety, tension, feelings of being "keyed up" or "on edge"
  3. Marked affective lability (eg, feeling suddenly sad or tearful or increased sensitivity to rejection)
  4. Persistent or marked anger or irritability or increased interpersonal conflicts

- At least five of the following symptoms present during the week before menstruation, and remitting within a few days of the onset of menstruation:
  1. Markedly depressed mood, feelings of hopelessness, or self-deprecating thoughts
  2. Marked anxiety, tension, feelings of being "keyed up" or "on edge"
  3. Marked affective lability (eg, feeling suddenly sad or tearful or increased sensitivity to rejection)
  4. Persistent or marked anger or irritability or increased interpersonal conflicts
  5. Decreased interest in usual activities (eg, work, school, friends, hobbies)
  6. Subjective sense of difficulty in concentrating
  7. Lethargy, easy fatigability, or marked lack of energy
  8. Marked change in appetite, overeating, or specific food cravings
  9. Hypersomnia or insomnia
  10. Subjective sense of being overwhelmed or out of control
  11. Other physical symptoms, such as breast tenderness or swelling, headaches, joint or muscle pain, a sensation of "bloating" or weight gain

- Symptoms interfere with economic or social functioning

- Symptoms occur reproducibly during two cycles of prospective recording

- Symptoms are not only an exacerbation of an underlying psychiatric disorder (eg, major depression, panic, dysthymia or personality disorders) (although PMDD may be superimposed on other disorders)

Adapted from American Psychiatric Association (1994). Diagnostic and Statistical Manual of Mental Disorders. Fourth edition (PSM IV) Washington, DC.

menses, relief with onset of menstruation, identifiable social or economic dysfunction caused by the symptoms of PMS, and reproducibility of symptoms over several menstrual cycles. Although symptoms used for diagnosis are few, over 150 physical and psychological symptoms have been documented to worsen significantly during the late luteal phase.[2] *Diagnostic and Statistical Manual of Mental Disorders*, 4th edition, (DSM-IV) criteria for PMDD are summarized in Table 76–2. Features include multiple psychiatric symptoms occurring in the late luteal phase, with other aspects similar to the definition of PMS. It is particularly important when diagnosing PMS and PMDD to demonstrate prospectively, through the use of a diary (Figures 76–1 and 76–2), that the symptoms primarily occur or worsen during the late luteal phase. In clinical practice, psychiatric conditions such as major

depression and panic disorder often are misdiagnosed as PMS when they occur in reproductive age women because clinicians fail to recognize that symptoms are persistent throughout the menstrual cycle rather than occurring primarily around the time of menstruation.

Until the mid-twentieth century, most clinicians believed the PMS was a psychosomatic condition. Subsequently, researchers hypothesized that symptoms were related in some way to the ovaries because PMS typically occurs only in women with regular ovulatory menstrual cycles. Initial pathophysiologic theories about the cause of PMS implicated excess estrogen, deficient progesterone, an inappropriate ratio of the two sex steroids, or inadequate corpus luteal function.[3–6] More recent clinical studies have not consistently implicated abnormal estrogen or progesterone levels in PMS, although

Premenstrual Daily Symptom Chart—Assessment for PMS

1. Put a check mark in each box that best describes the degree of your symptoms.
2. Circle the days you menstruate.

Check: S = Severe   M = Moderate
m = mild   If no symptoms, DO NOT mark

Day of Month		1	2	3	4	5	6	7	8	9	10	11	12	13	14	15	16	17	18	19	20	21	22	23	24	25	26	27	28	29	30	31
Irritability	S																															
	M																															
	m																															
Angry outbursts	S																															
	M																															
	m																															
Sadness/ depression	S																															
	M																															
	m																															
Decreased interest in usual activities	S																															
	M																															
	m																															
Anxiety	S																															
	M																															
	m																															
Difficulty concentrating	S																															
	M																															
	m																															
Bloating	S																															
	M																															
	m																															
Breast tenderness	S																															
	M																															
	m																															
Headache	S																															
	M																															
	m																															
Swelling	S																															
	M																															
	m																															

FIGURE 76–1. Patient diary useful for diagnosing premenstrual syndrome.

Premenstrual Daily Symptom Chart—Assessment for PMDD

1. Put a check mark in each box that best describes the degree of your symptoms.
2. Circle the days you menstruate.

Check: S = Severe   M = Moderate
m = mild   If no symptoms, DO NOT mark

Day of Month		1	2	3	4	5	6	7	8	9	10	11	12	13	14	15	16	17	18	19	20	21	22	23	24	25	26	27	28	29	30	31
Depression	S																															
	M																															
	m																															
Anxiety	S																															
	M																															
	m																															
Irritability/ angry outbursts	S																															
	M																															
	m																															
Decreased interest in usual activities	S																															
	M																															
	m																															
Suddenly sad/ tearful/sensitive to rejection	S																															
	M																															
	m																															
Difficulty concentrating	S																															
	M																															
	m																															
Fatigue	S																															
	M																															
	m																															
Overeating/ cravings	S																															
	M																															
	m																															
Insomnia or sleeping too much	S																															
	M																															
	m																															
Overwhelmed or out of control	S																															
	M																															
	m																															
Swelling/breast tenderness/bloating headache/body aches	S																															
	M																															
	m																															

FIGURE 76–2. Patient diary useful for diagnosing premenstrual dysphoric disorder.

certain PMS symptoms can be reproduced through hormonal manipulation. Exogenous estradiol does not seem to mimic PMS.[7,8] Exogenous progesterone administration can mimic PMS symptoms.[8,9] Women with late luteal phase defects have somatic symptoms similar to PMS but less severe psychological symptoms than women with normal luteal function.[10] Androgens, prolactin, and aldosterone have been considered as possible mediators of PMS, but research has not supported such a relationship.[11]

Some have theorized that declining estradiol levels in the late luteal phase may affect dopamine neurotransmission.[12] The link between the hypothalamic-pituitary-ovarian axis, central nervous system neurotransmitters, and psychiatric disorders is an area of active research. Several epidemiologic observations support a possible link between sex steroid levels and mood disorders. At least 30% of women with primary recurrent depression experience their first depressive episode during a time of significant hormonal change. It also has been shown that a history of major depression is more common among women reporting PMS than those not reporting PMS symptoms.[13] Serotonin is strongly implicated as a mediator in PMDD. Fenfluramine, which releases serotonin and blocks its reuptake, decreases premenstrual depression and suppresses premenstrual rises in calorie, carbohydrate, and fat intake.[14] Sertraline, fluoxetine, citalopram, and paroxetine, all selective serotonin reuptake inhibitors, reduce premenstrual psychiatric symptoms.[15]

There may be a genetic predisposition to PMS. A study of monozygotic twins demonstrated that over 90% exhibited similar PMS symptoms to their twin. In contrast, only about 50% of dizygotic twins and non-twin siblings had similar PMS symptoms.[16] Familial and cultural factors influence a woman's experience of PMS. American, Turkish, and Nigerian women report more premenstrual symptoms than Japanese women. Baharani women also report relatively fewer PMS symptoms. However, swelling, irritability, breast pain, mood swings, and fatigue appear to be common symptoms of PMS worldwide, consistently reported by about 30% of menstruating women from a variety of cultures. Therefore, although PMS is not culture specific, some symptoms, or the reporting of some symptoms, may be more frequent in one culture than another.[17]

DIAGNOSIS

The diagnosis of PMS and/or PMDD is appropriate only for women with ovulatory menstrual cycles who report that their social or work functioning is adversely affected by menstrually associated symptoms. Diagnostic evaluation for PMS and PMDD should include a retrospective review of symptoms, a comprehensive medical history and physical examination, a psychiatric history, and at least a 2-month prospective daily rating of symptoms, initially most strongly focusing on those pertinent to diagnosis.

A retrospective history consists of a list of a woman's premenstrually related symptoms and how they interfere with her daily life. The timing of each symptom in relation to menses should be reviewed carefully. Other important aspects include the age at which symptoms began, whether there is a family history of PMS, how the patient has managed symptoms in the past, and whether any interventions have seemed to help.

Medical history should include a thorough review of the signs and symptoms of conditions that can mimic PMS, including primary and secondary dysmenorrhea (especially fibroids and endometriosis), thyroid disease, and hypoglycemia. Other illnesses associated with generalized fatigue, including anemia, autoimmune disorders, and fibromyalgia, can sometimes be confused with PMS. Diabetes also can sometimes mimic PMS as patients report symptoms of polyphagia and polydipsia. Rarely, temporal lobe seizures with premenstrual exacerbation can be confused with PMS.[18]

The clinician should identify whether drugs that can affect mood or hormone levels, including birth control pills, thyroid medications, and tranquilizers, are being used by the patient. This entails not only asking about prescription medications but also the ingestion of "alternative/complementary" preparations, which may contain animal thyroid extracts and/or herbs with possible estrogenic or progestogenic effects. A thorough psychiatric history and review of systems is essential. Excessive alcohol use can mimic PMS. A family history of alcoholism is associated with a genetic tendency toward depression. A psychosocial history, including past or current sexual and/or domestic abuse, also should be part of a routine evaluation for PMS and PMDD. Psychosocial functioning must be understood to diagnose PMS and PMDD. Abuse is a risk factor for psychiatric illness.

If PMS or PMDD is suspected, the patient should be asked to complete at least 2 months of a symptoms diary. For diagnosis, emphasis is placed on symptoms fulfilling diagnostic criteria for PMS and/or PMDD. However, for treatment, other bothersome symptoms also should be mapped. Patients with concomitant mood disorders, such as major depression, should receive treatment as soon as they are identified.

TREATMENT

Lifestyle modification is the cornerstone of treatment for most women with PMS. There are few data on efficacy, but expert opinion supports measures such as reducing caffeine intake, eating multiple small meals and not skipping meals, eating complex carbohydrates, increasing aerobic exercise, and engaging in relaxation techniques, such as meditation. Planning ahead, by knowing when symptoms are likely to occur and avoiding additional stress during that time when possible, also is recommended. Some of these measures are supported by data suggestive of their efficacy, at least for avoiding worsening of underlying symptoms. Caffeine can increase breast tenderness and cause headaches and anxiety. Hypoglycemia can exacerbate many of the symptoms of PMS. Aerobic exercise has been shown to reduce premenstrual symptoms.[19,20] A low-fat (10% of total calories) vegetarian diet decreased monthly PMS symptom duration in one study.[21]

Many women ask about the use of nonprescription supplements for the treatment of PMS. Data suggesting some efficacy for a number of vitamins, minerals, and supplements exist. Such treatments may be used as first-line therapy in women with milder symptoms or as an adjunct to the treatment of moderate or severe PMS or PMDD. A large randomized controlled trial of over 400 women showed that 1,200 mg of calcium carbonate daily reduced total symptom scores for women with PMS.[22] Magnesium supplements may afford relief of some symptoms. Magnesium pyrrolidone carboxylic acid (360 mg/d, administered with three times daily dosing) has been shown superior to placebo in improving the symptoms of premenstrual pain and

emotional distress.[23] Vitamin B_6 (50–100 mg/d), long recommended for PMS, has limited data to support its effectiveness.[24] Vitamin E (400 IU daily) may improve some physical and affective symptoms of PMS.[25] A randomized study showed improvement in affective symptoms and carbohydrate craving in women with PMS given a carbohydrate supplement formulated to increase serum tryptophan levels. Women given an isocaloric placebo had no improvements in PMS measures.[26] Evening primrose oil does not appear to be effective in treating PMS.[27] Black cohosh and other herbs with purported hormonal effects have not been studied effectively.

Women with severe PMS or who fulfill criteria for PMDD generally require cognitive behavioral therapy and/or pharmacologic treatment. Cognitive behavoiral therapy consisting of training in coping skills has been shown to improve symptoms of severe PMS in several studies.[28–31] The most extensively studied pharmacologic treatments for PMS are the selective serotonin reuptake inhibitors. Fluoxetine 20 mg and sertraline 50 to 100 mg have been proven in effective randomized, controlled trials and are the most commonly prescribed.[32] Paroxetine, citalopram, clomipramine, and nefazodone also have demonstrated effectiveness.[27] Anxiolytics, such as alprazolam and buspirone, sometimes have a role in the treatment of PMS but should not be considered first-line therapy because of side effects and the potential for dependency.[33] Medications may be prescribed continuously or intermittently during the luteal phase (day 15 of the menstrual cycle until menstruation begins).[33–36]

Historically, PMS has been treated by hormonal manipulation. Although frequently prescribed, hormonal therapy is less well studied than the use of antidepressants.[27] Oral progesterone and progesterone suppositories have been ineffective in a number of studies.[27,33,37] The results of studies of combination oral contraceptives have been mixed. Further study is needed.[38,39] Gonadotropin-releasing hormone agonists appear to be effective in eliminating premenstrual symptoms, but have significant associated morbidity and generally should be considered only in severe cases for which diagnostic criteria are strictly met and other therapies have failed.[27,40] Prior to such treatment, psychiatric consultation should be strongly considered.

SUMMARY

Physical and psychiatric symptoms in the late luteal phase are common. Only women who report that these significantly interfere with their activities should be diagnosed with PMS. Most women with PMS can be treated nonpharmacologically. For those requiring pharmacologic treatment, selective serotonin reuptake inhibitors have been shown to be effective in multiple studies. Ovulation suppression with oral contraceptives is also a treatment option but is less well studied. Approximately 5% of women suffer from recurrent severe psychiatric symptoms prior to menses, a syndrome now most commonly termed PMDD. These women generally require pharmacologic therapy. The mainstay of treatment for women with PMDD are serotonin-modulating antidepressants. Oral contraceptives are not currently recommended for the treatment of PMDD but are undergoing further study. Gonadotropin-releasing hormone agonists, although effective, should be used very rarely and only as a last resort.

REFERENCES

1. Logue C, Moos R. Perimenstrual symptoms: prevalence and risk factors. Psychosom Med 1986; 48:388–414.

2. Hamiltom JA, Parry B, Alagna S, et al. Premenstrual mood changes; a guide to evaluation and treatment. Psychiatr Ann 1984;14:426.

3. Israel RS. Premenstrual tension. JAMA 1938;110: 1721–3.

4. Greene R, Dalton K. The premenstrual syndrome. Br Med J 1953;1:1007–14.

5. Reid RL, Yen SSC. Premenstrual syndrome. Am J Obstet Gynecol 1981;139:85–104.

6. Frank RT. The hormonal basis of premenstrual tension. Arch Neural Psychiatry 1931;26:1053–9.

7. De Lignieres B. Two different kinds of PMS symptoms: high E2 and low E2 linked [abstract #23]. Paper presented at the 2nd International Symposium: Premenstrual, Postpartum and Menopausal, Mood Disorders, Kiawah Island, Charleston, SC, September 10, 1987.

8. Hammarback S, Backstrom T, Hoist J, von Schowltz B. Lyrenas in the premenstrual tension syndrome during sequential estrogen-progestagen postmenopausal replacement therapy. Acta Obstet Gynecol Scand 1985;64:393–7.

9. Backstrom T, Mattson B. Correlation of symptoms in pre-menstrual tension to estrogen and progesterone concentrations in blood plasma. Neuropsychobiology 1975;1:80–6.

10. Ying Y, Soto-Albors CE, Randolph JF, et al. Luteal phase defect and premenstrual syndrome in an infertile population. Obstet Gynecol 1987;69:96–8.

11. Majewska MD. Steroids and brain activity: essential dialogue between body and mind. Biochem Pharmacol 1987;22:3781–8.

12. Brockington IF, Kelly A, Hall P, Deakin W. Premenstrual relapse of puerperal psychosis. J Affective Disord 1988;14:287–92.

13. Halbreich U, Endicott J. Relationship of dysphoric premenstrual changes to depressive disorders. Acta Psychiatr Scand 1985;71:331.

14. Brzezinsk AA, Wurtmann JJ, Wurtman R, et al. D-Fenfluramine suppresses the increased calorie and carbohydrate intake and improves the mood of women with premenstrual depression. Obstet Gynecol 1990;76:296.

15. Dimmock P, Whatt K, Jones P, et al. Efficacy of selective serotonin-reuptake inhibitors in premenstrual syndrome: a systematic review. Lancet 2000;356: 1131–6.

16. Dalton K. The premenstrual syndrome and progesterone therapy. 2nd ed. Chicago: Yearbook Medical Publishers; 1984.

17. Gold JH, Severino SK, editors. Premenstrual dysphoria: myths and realities. Washington (DC): American Psychiatric Press; 1994.

18. Backstrom T. The menstrual cycle and epilepsy. Acta Neurol Scand 1976;54:321.

19. Steege J, Blumenthal J. The effects of aerobic exercise on premenstrual symptoms in middle-aged women: a preliminary study. J Psychosom Res 1993;37: 127–33.

20. Prior J, Vigna Y, Sciarretta D, et al. Conditioning exercise decreases premenstrual symptoms: a prospective, controlled 6-month trial. Fertil Steril 1987;47:402–8.

21. Barnard N, Scialli A, Hurlock D, et al. Diet and sex-hormone binding globulin, dysmenorrhea, and premenstrual symptoms. Obstet Gynecol 2000;95: 245–50.

22. Thys-Jacobs S, Starkey P, Bernstein D, et al. General obstetrics and gynecology. Am J Obstet Gynecol 1998;179:444–52.

23. Facchinetti F, Borella P, Sances G, et al. Oral magnesium successfully relieves premenstrual mood changes. Obstet Gynecol 1991;78:177–81.

24. Wyatt K, Dimmock P, O'Brien M. Efficacy of vitamin B-6 in the treatment of premenstrual syndrome: systematic review. BMJ 1999;318:1375–81.

25. London R, Murphy L, Kitlowski K, et al. Efficacy of alpha-tocopherol in the treatment of the premenstrual syndrome. J Reprod Med 1987;32:400–4.

26. Sayegh R, Schiff I, Wurtman J. The effect of a carbohydrate-rich beverage on mood, appetite, and cognitive function in women with premenstrual syndrome. Obstet Gynecol 1995;86:520–8.

27. Freeman E. Premenstrual syndrome: current perspective on treatment and etiology. Obstet Gynecol 1997;9:147–53.

28. Kirkby R. Changes in premenstrual symptoms and irrational thinking following cognitive-behavioral coping skills training. J Consult Clin Psychol 1994; 62:1026–32.

29. Christensen A, Oei T. The efficacy of cognitive behaviour therapy in treating premenstrual dysphoric changes. J Affect Disord 1995;33:57–63.

30. Morse C, Dennerstein L, Farrell E. A comparison of hormone therapy, coping skills training, and relaxation for the relief of premenstrual syndrome. J Behav Med 1991;14:469–89.

31. Blake F, Salkovskis P, Gath D, et al. Cognitive therapy for premenstrual syndrome: a controlled trial. J Psychosom Res 1998;45:307–18.

32. Steiner M, Pearlstein T. Premenstrual dysphoria and the serotonin system: pathophysiology and treatment. J Clin Psychiatry 2000;61:17–21.

33. Freeman E, Rickels K, Sondheimer S, et al. A double-blind trial of oral progesterone, alprazolam, and placebo in treatment of severe premenstrual syndrome. JAMA 1995;274:51–7.

34. Steiner M, Korzekwa M, Lamont J. Intermittent fluoxetine dosing in the treatment of women with premenstrual dysphoria. Psychopharmacology 1997; 33:771–4.

35. Sundblad C, Hedberg M, Eriksson E. Clomipramine administered during the luteal phase reduces the symptoms of premenstrual syndrome: a placebo-controlled trial. Neuropsychopharmacology 1993;9: 133–45.

36. Wikander I, Sundblad C, Andersch B. Citalopram in premenstrual dysphoria: is intermittent treatment during luteal phases more effective than continuous medication throughout the menstrual cycle? J Clin Psychopharmacol 1998;18:390–8.

37. Freeman E, Rickels K, Sondheimer S, et al. Ineffectiveness of progesterone suppository treatment for premenstrual syndrome. JAMA 1990;264:349–53.

38. Freeman E, Kroll R, Rapkin A, et al. Evaluation of a unique oral contraceptive in the treatment of premenstrual dysphoric disorder. J Womens Health Gender Based Med 2001;10:561–9.

39. Graham C, Sherwin B. A prospective treatment study of premenstrual symptoms using a triphasic oral contraceptive. J Psychosom Res 1992;36:257–66.

40. Schmidt P, Nieman L, Danaceau M, et al. Differential behavioral effects of gonadal steroids in women with and in those without premenstrual syndrome. N Engl J Med 1998;338:209–16.

77

SEXUAL DYSFUNCTION

Natalie Driessen, BSc, and Alan H. DeCherney, MD

Sexual dysfunction is a common clinical problem that often goes untreated. Survey studies show that on average, nearly 40% or more of women experience sexual dysfunction.[1-3] In a large survey of men and women under the age of 60 years, women described sexual dysfunction more frequently than did men. Studies have shown that there is a significant correlation between attitude toward sexuality and sexual function; a more conservative attitude toward sexual matters is associated with more sexual dysfunction.[3] Poor physical health and emotional health are risk factors for sexual dysfunction. Further, sexual dysfunction is associated not only with disappointment in sexual relationships but also with a decreased sense of well-being.[1]

Sexual dysfunction may be underdiagnosed, in part because clinicians believe that patients would be uncomfortable addressing the topic. When surveyed, however, 70% of patients considered sexual matters to be an appropriate topic for their primary care clinician to discuss.[2] Other studies have shown that patients may avoid discussing sexual issues because their clinician appeared either uncomfortable or disinterested in the topic.[4]

Female sexual dysfunction generally falls into four areas: general sexual dysfunction, anorgasmia, vaginismus, and dyspareunia (Table 77–1). General sexual dysfunction may be further subdivided into sexual desire disorders, including lack of desire or aversion to sexual contact, and sexual arousal disorders. The most common complaint among women is the loss of interest or arousal. The second most common complaint is the inability to reach an orgasm.[2,3,5] Vaginismus and dyspareunia are experienced by a minority of affected women.[2,3] Noncoital sexual stimulation may also cause genital pain in some women.

As is true with many medical conditions affecting both women and men, clinical research on sexual dysfunction has focused almost exclusively on male sexual dysfunction, specifically erectile dysfunction. Much remains unknown about the pathophysiology of female sexual dysfunction, and the study of pharmacologic treatments for female sexual dysfunction is still in its infancy. This chapter reviews female sexual function and what is known about evaluation and treatment of the most common types of female sexual dysfunction found in primary care practice.

SEXUAL EXCITEMENT AND ORGASMIC STATE

On the basis of data collected by Masters and Johnson, sexual response has been divided into four successive stages: excitement, plateau, orgasm, and resolution.[6] More recently, some experts have advocated combining the plateau and orgasm state into

TABLE 77–1. Female Sexual Dysfunction: Classifications

Sexual desire disorder*
Sexual arousal disorder*

Orgasmic disorder*

Sexual pain disorders
    Dyspareunia
    Vaginismus
    Noncoital sexual pain disorder

*To be considered a disorder, symptoms must be persistent or recurrent and cause personal distress.
Adapted from Report of the International Consensus Development Conference on female sexuality dysfunction: definitions and classifications. J Urol 2000;163:888.

one stage. For simplicity and a better understanding of the physiologic changes, all four stages are explained here. External genital changes during sexual excitement are relatively easily observed. The internal changes are where the major physiologic changes occur during sexual response, and it is extremely hard to observe these using ordinary methods. Illuminated speculum, cinematography, and electromyographic monitoring of the uterus have been able to provide most of the information currently available about internal changes that occur during sexual response.

There are a variety of nongenital normal physiologic responses during sexual arousal. There is an increase in the respiratory rate, heart rate, and blood pressure. Facial muscles tend to contract involuntarily, sometimes resembling a frown or grimace. All the muscles in the body contract. There may be gasping and hyperventilation, involuntary pelvic thrusting, and muscle spasms throughout the body. The nipples stand out, and the veins of the breast become visible during the excitement state. A pinkish tint, which can be referred to as a "sex flush," appears. This is more noticeable in Caucasians. The upper abdomen may become pink in color as well.

Directly following sexual stimulation, the excitement state occurs. There is a notable variation among women in their responses to particular stimuli. Some have suggested that there are identifiable erogenous zones, which act as sex buttons. When these zones are stimulated, the labia majora engorges with blood and spreads outward, exposing the labia minora and the introitus. The labia minora also fills with blood and increases in size due to vasoengorgement and also extends outward. Lastly, the clitoris lengthens, again due to vasoengorgement, to an approximate 12 to 15 mm in length, about three times its normal size.

Internally, the excitement state is marked by lubrication of the vagina. The lubrication is produced similar to the physiologic process in which sweating is produced. This lubrication is found in the outer two-thirds of the vagina, where small beads of fluid from along the vaginal fold. These small beads join to form larger drops indicating more arousal and lubrication. It is important to understand that depending on the position the woman is in, the lubrication may or may not be available to the introitus. If a woman is lying on her back the lubrication may drain away from the introitus and collect about the cervix, this may cause a false appearance of dryness or a lack of sexual arousal. At the same time lubrication is occurring, there is a pulling of the uterus away from the bladder; pulling the cervix away from the vagina. This pulling allows the vagina to expand and lengthen to accommodate the erect penis.

The plateau stage follows during continued sexual stimulation. The engorgement of blood during this state is extremely intense. The labia minora and majora continue to fill with blood causing a change in their color. Normally, 1 to 2 minutes after the color change has occurred, an orgasm usually occurs. Another distinct characteristic of this state is that the clitoris becomes extremely sensitive to the touch. In order to protect itself from pain or discomfort, it retracts under the prepuce or clitoral hood. During penile thrusting, the labia minora is moved by the penis causing the clitoral hood to move back and forth producing indirect stimulation on the clitoris. This indirect stimulation plays an important role in orgasm.

During the plateau stage, the uterus continues to pull away from the bladder to allow complete elevation at the time of the orgasm. It is also at this stage where the vagina reaches its maximum length. A swelling may also appear in the outer third of the vagina, forming a seal around the penis to prevent the loss of seminal fluid after ejaculation. This swollen cuff is where contractions occur during orgasm.

The orgasm stage is the next stage. During this stage, many events are occurring at once in a synchronized fashion. When the vagina is contracting, the uterus is contracting, beginning at the fundus and moving toward the cervix. Eight to 12 contractions may be considered intense, whereas three to five may be considered mild or a weak orgasm, but this is still subjective depending on the individual. This event is physiologically similar to the contractions at the time of labor but is rarely experienced as being painful.

It has been shown that some women, mostly those who are postmenopausal, do experience pain due to these contractions. It is thought that this pain is due to low amounts of estrogen or lack of estrogen. It is also important to realize that those women who have had a hysterectomy may have different orgasmic responses from those prior to the hysterectomy.

The sensation of an orgasm is very different from any other body sensation. If a woman does not know whether she has experienced an orgasm, the chances are she has not. Some women fail to accept the orgasm she is experiencing as a "true" orgasm because there is a large amount of fantasy and misconception about the feelings one would have while having an orgasm. Describing an orgasm is difficult because the experience is so subjective and the specifics are individual, but an orgasm does have some general characteristics. During an orgasm, there is a heightened feeling of excitement and tension, as well as an intense awareness of all body sensations, especially genital sensations. Another common characteristic is a loss of awareness of the surroundings and a sensation of everything stopping, followed by a feeling of relief and elation that is very pleasurable. A warm wave or tingling sensation followed by an intense throbbing and pulsating in the genital area is also another common characteristic of an orgasm. A woman may also feel an intense awareness of her genital area and warmth that spreads throughout the pelvis, vaginal area, and radiates throughout the body.

During the orgasm stage, there are no physical changes that occur in the external genitalia. The clitoris remains hidden under the hood. The only physiologic change that may occur is a slight dilation of the urethra. Women may note that during an orgasm they feel that they might be incontinent of bowel or bladder. During a normal orgasm, the sphincter muscles surrounding the meatus of the urethra close and the anal sphincter contracts preventing any spillage of waste.

The last stage is the resolution state. Unlike a man, who is forced into the resolution stage, a woman has complete control as to when she wants to reach this state. Most women enter the resolution stage because they are sleepy, psychologically disinterested, or no stimulus is continued to be provided. The labia minora and majora return to their unstimulated physiologic state. The regular color returns, as they become nonengorged with blood. The clitoral hood retracts exposing the clitoris allowing it to return to its normal state through the loss of vasocongestion. The external genitalia return to a more midline position because they are no longer swollen and subsequently cover the introitus.

Internally, a pocket or reservoir is created in the later two-thirds of the vagina for the seminal fluid. The uterus relaxes, allowing the cervix to come in contact with the seminal pool. The outer one-third of the vagina almost immediately begins to lose swelling. The inner two-thirds of the vagina remain distended for about 8 minutes after orgasm to allow the sperm to enter the cervix. Vasocongestion immediately begins to subside following orgasm. Without an orgasm, vasocongestion does not subside rapidly, causing a continued increase in uterine size. Women who complain of vague pains in the pelvic area during or after sexual intercourse should be questioned thoroughly to determine if the pain may be due to a nonorgasmic response.

INITIAL EVALUATION

Although some patients with sexual dysfunction present it as a primary complaint, many such patients in primary care practice do not volunteer this information. Therefore, it is recommended to include a few brief screening questions about sexual health as part of the overall patient history. For otherwise healthy patients in whom there is no reason to suspect sexual dysfunction, this can be as simple as asking if they are currently sexually active, and if so, whether with one or more partners and whether with men, women, or both. Patients should also be asked if sex is satisfying for themselves and their partners and/or if they have questions or concerns about their sexual functioning. Women with illnesses or situations known to affect sexual function should be asked specifically whether their interest and/or comfort during sex has changed.

Women who present with or endorse sexual dysfunction require more extensive historical evaluation. As described further below, complete medical and medication histories are essential. Although most women with sexual dysfunction have not been sexually abused, it is important to ask about this, as well as any other family or childhood influences that might be affecting the patient's sexuality. Previous and current partner relationships and gender and sexual orientation should be explored. Pertinent questions also include discerning the patient's desire for sex and sexual fantasies, whether she reaches orgasm when she wants to, and whether she experiences pain during sex. It is particularly important to identify whether sexual dysfunction occurs in all situations or only in certain situations (for example, some women can reach orgasm with masturbation but not with a particular partner).[7] One alternative is to use the Female Sexual Function Index (Figures 77–1 to 77–3), which can be easily scored to pinpoint various aspects of sexual dysfunction.

GENERAL SEXUAL DYSFUNCTION

General sexual dysfunction may be associated with physical or mental illness, psychological distress, medication, or hormonal abnormalities or changes, including aging. The most common reported causes of sexual dysfunction are mental illness, alcoholic neuropathy, diabetes mellitus, multiple sclerosis, hypertension, thyroid deficiency, chronic interstitial cystitis, injury to the labia or labial pathology, vulvovaginitis, endometriosis, lower bowel disease, musculoskeletal disorders, antidepressant drugs, and surgical procedures.[8–12]

Although scientific understanding of the female sexual response at the molecular and genetic levels remains extremely limited, it is believed that human female sexual behavior is mediated by gonadal steroids acting at the level of the central nervous system.[13] Female hormones that may play a part in sexual behavior are thought to be estrogen, progesterone, and androgens. While testosterone is also believed to have a major effect on woman's sexual libido, studies, to date, have shown an overall modest effect of testosterone supplementation on female sexual function.[14]

Treatment of general sexual dysfunction should be based on evaluation of the underlying factors that can be addressed. These may include a history of prior sexual abuse, relationship issues, partner's decreased motivation or capability, anatomic or physiologic genital dysfunction (including atrophic vaginitis), medication-related sexual dysfunction, and depression. Some specific causes of general sexual dysfunction are discussed below.

Physical Illness

Many women with medical illnesses suffer from physical symptoms that may inhibit sexual functioning, such as decreased lubrication and dyspareunia, as well as decreased libido. Diseases that affect the brain or parts of the body that regulate sexual activity have a direct effect on sexual function.[15] The most problematic diseases that effect sexual activity are those that are neurologic, neuromuscular, or endocrinologic because they directly influence the peripheral and central nervous systems. This is a direct effect on the hypothalamic-pituitary-gonadal axis that correlates to dysfunction in the vulva, vagina, cervix, and uterus. It is important to assess for thyroid dysfunction and hyperprolactinemia in women with general sexual dysfunction, particularly if it is of abrupt or recent onset.

Sexual dysfunction is a symptom of multiple sclerosis that is often overlooked. Sexual dysfunction was found in 73.1% of patients with definite multiple sclerosis in one study. The symptoms of sexual dysfunction more commonly reported in these patients with multiple sclerosis were anorgasmia or hyporgasmia (37.1%), decreased vaginal lubrication (35.7%), and reduced libido (31.4%).[16] There is an association between sexual dysfunction and sphincteric dysfunction in patients with multiple sclerosis. This suggests that central nervous system damage in multiple sclerosis may directly affect sexual function in some patients.[17]

Sexual dysfunction has also been well documented in stroke patients. A study has shown a marked decline in sexual activity in both the stroke patient and their spouses. It was shown that a stroke has an impact on the libido, sexual arousal, coital frequency, vaginal lubrication, orgasm, and overall satisfaction with sexual life. Sexual dysfunction correlated significantly ($p < .05$) with the presence of the sensory hemisyndrome.[18]

The diagnosis of breast cancer can also affect sexual health. An increase in sexual problems, including an absence of sexual desire, dyspareunia, lubrication problems, vaginismus, and orgasmic disorders, has been documented in breast cancer survivors. A study showed that 36% of breast cancer patients suffered from sexual dysfunction before treatment, which worsened in about 27%, while in 49% of women, sexual problems arose mainly after chemotherapy (26%) or surgery (12%).[19]

Gastrointestinal (GI) disorders have been shown to have an impact on quality of life relating to sexual function. In one study, over 40% of patients with GI disorders reported sexual dysfunction. Decreased libido was reported by 28.4% of female patients and dyspareunia by 16.4%.[20] There was a definitive positive association of sexual dysfunction with perceived GI symptom severity but not with psychological symptom severity, suggesting that organic, not psychological, factors were the principal determinants of sexual dysfunction.

Subject Identifier _____   Date _____

INSTRUCTIONS: These questions ask about your sexual feelings and responses <u>during the past 4 weeks</u>. Please answer the following questions as honestly and clearly as possible. Your responses will be kept completely confidential. In answering these questions the following definitions apply:

<u>Sexual activity</u> can include caressing, foreplay, masturbation and vaginal intercourse.

<u>Sexual intercourse</u> is defined as penile penetration (entry) of the vagina.

<u>Sexual stimulation</u> includes situations like foreplay with a partner, self-stimulation (masturbating), or sexual fantasy.

CHECK <u>ONLY</u> ONE BOX PER QUESTION.

<u>Sexual desire</u> or <u>interest</u> is a feeling that includes wanting to have a sexual experience, feeling receptive to a partner's sexual initiation, and thinking or fantasizing about having sex.

1. Over the past 4 weeks, how **often** did you feel sexual desire or interest?
   - ☐ Almost always or always
   - ☐ Most times (more than half the time)
   - ☐ Sometimes (about half the time)
   - ☐ A few times (less than half the time)
   - ☐ Almost never or never

2. Over the past 4 weeks, how would you rate your **level** (degree) of sexual desire or interest?
   - ☐ Very high
   - ☐ High
   - ☐ Moderate
   - ☐ Low
   - ☐ Very low or none at all

Sexual arousal is a feeling that includes both physical and mental aspects of sexual excitement. It may include feelings of warmth or tingling in the genitals, lubrication (wetness), or muscle contractions.

3. Over the past 4 weeks, how **often** did you feel sexually aroused ("turned on") during sexual activity or intercourse?
   - ☐ No sexual activity
   - ☐ Almost always or always
   - ☐ Most times (more than half the time)
   - ☐ Sometimes (about half the time)
   - ☐ A few times (less than half the time)
   - ☐ Almost never or never

4. Over the past 4 weeks, how would you rate your **level** of sexual arousal ("turn on") during sexual activity or intercourse?
   - ☐ No sexual activity
   - ☐ Very high
   - ☐ High
   - ☐ Moderate
   - ☐ Low
   - ☐ Very low or none at all

5. Over the past 4 weeks, how **confident** were you about becoming sexually aroused during sexual activity or intercourse?
   - ☐ No sexual activity
   - ☐ Very high confidence
   - ☐ High confidence
   - ☐ Moderate confidence
   - ☐ Low confidence
   - ☐ Very low or no confidence

6. Over the past 4 weeks, how **often** have you been satisfied with your arousal (excitement) during sexual activity or intercourse?
   - ☐ No sexual activity
   - ☐ Almost always or always
   - ☐ Most times (more than half the time)
   - ☐ Sometimes (about half the time)
   - ☐ A few times (less than half the time)
   - ☐ Almost never or never

7. Over the past 4 weeks, how **often** did you become lubricated ("wet") during sexual activity or intercourse?
   - ☐ No sexual activity
   - ☐ Almost always or always
   - ☐ Most times (more than half the time)
   - ☐ Sometimes (about half the time)
   - ☐ A few times (less than half the time)
   - ☐ Almost never or never

8. Over the past 4 weeks, how **difficult** was it to become lubricated ("wet") during sexual activity or intercourse?
   - ☐ No sexual activity
   - ☐ Extremely difficult or impossible
   - ☐ Very difficult
   - ☐ Difficult
   - ☐ Slightly difficult
   - ☐ Not difficult

9. Over the past 4 weeks, how often did you **maintain** your lubrication ("wetness") until completion of sexual activity or intercourse?
   - ☐ No sexual activity
   - ☐ Almost always or always
   - ☐ Most times (more than half the time)
   - ☐ Sometimes (about half the time)
   - ☐ A few times (less than half the time)
   - ☐ Almost never or never

10. Over the past 4 weeks, how **difficult** was it to maintain your lubrication ("wetness") until completion of sexual activity or intercourse?
    - ☐ No sexual activity
    - ☐ Extremely difficult or impossible

- ☐ Very difficult
- ☐ Difficult
- ☐ Slightly difficult
- ☐ Not difficult

11. Over the past 4 weeks, when you had sexual stimulation or intercourse, how **often** did you reach orgasm (climax)?
    - ☐ No sexual activity
    - ☐ Almost always or always
    - ☐ Most times (more than half the time)
    - ☐ Sometimes (about half the time)
    - ☐ A few times (less than half the time)
    - ☐ Almost never or never

12. Over the past 4 weeks, when you had sexual stimulation or intercourse, how **difficult** was it for you to reach orgasm (climax)?
    - ☐ No sexual activity
    - ☐ Extremely difficult or impossible
    - ☐ Very difficult
    - ☐ Difficult
    - ☐ Slightly difficult
    - ☐ Not difficult

13. Over the past 4 weeks, how **satisfied** were you with your ability to reach orgasm (climax) during sexual activity or intercourse?
    - ☐ No sexual activity
    - ☐ Extremely satisfied
    - ☐ Moderately satisfied
    - ☐ About equally satisfied and dissatisfied
    - ☐ Moderately dissatisfied
    - ☐ Very dissatisfied

14. Over the past 4 weeks, how **satisfied** have you been with the amount of emotional closeness during sexual activity between you and your partner?
    - ☐ No sexual activity
    - ☐ Extremely satisfied
    - ☐ Moderately satisfied
    - ☐ About equally satisfied and dissatisfied
    - ☐ Moderately dissatisfied
    - ☐ Very dissatisfied

15. Over the past 4 weeks, how **satisfied** have you been with your sexual relationship with your partner?
    - ☐ No sexual activity
    - ☐ Extremely satisfied
    - ☐ Moderately satisfied
    - ☐ About equally satisfied and dissatisfied
    - ☐ Moderately dissatisfied
    - ☐ Very dissatisfied

16. Over the past 4 weeks, how satisfied have you been with your overall sexual life?
    - ☐ No sexual activity
    - ☐ Extremely satisfied
    - ☐ Moderately satisfied
    - ☐ About equally satisfied and dissatisfied
    - ☐ Moderately dissatisfied
    - ☐ Very dissatisfied

17. Over the past 4 weeks, how **often** did you experience discomfort or pain <u>during</u> vaginal penetration?
    - ☐ Did not attempt intercourse
    - ☐ Almost always or always
    - ☐ Most times (more than half the time)
    - ☐ Sometimes (about half the time)
    - ☐ A few times (less than half the time)
    - ☐ Almost never or never

18. Over the past 4 weeks, how **often** did you experience discomfort or pain <u>following</u> vaginal penetration?
    - ☐ Did not attempt intercourse
    - ☐ Almost always or always
    - ☐ Most times (more than half the time)
    - ☐ Sometimes (about half the time)
    - ☐ A few times (less than half the time)
    - ☐ Almost never or never

19. Over the past 4 weeks, how would you rate your **level** (degree) of discomfort or pain during or following vaginal penetration?
    - ☐ Did not attempt intercourse
    - ☐ Very high
    - ☐ High
    - ☐ Moderate
    - ☐ Low
    - ☐ Very low or none at all

Thank you for completing this questionnaire
Copyright ©2000 All Rights Reserved

FIGURE 77–1. Female Sexual Function Index (FSFI) ©.

Question	**Response Questions**
1. Over the past 4 weeks, how **often** did you feel sexual desire or interest?	5 = Almost always or always 4 = Most times (more than half the time) 3 = Sometimes (about half the time) 2 = A few times (less than half the time) 1 = Almost never or never
2. Over the past 4 weeks, how would you rate your **level** (degree) of sexual desire or interest?	5 = Very high 4 = High 3 = Moderate 2 = Low 1 = Very low or none at all
3. Over the past 4 weeks, how **often** did you feel sexually aroused ("turned on") during sexual activity or intercourse?	0 = No sexual activity 5 = Almost always or always 4 = Most times (more than half the time) 3 = Sometimes (about half the time) 2 = A few times (less than half the time) 1 = Almost never or never
4. Over the past 4 weeks, how would you rate your **level** of sexual arousal ("turn on") during sexual activity or intercourse?	0 = No sexual activity 5 = Very high 4 = High 3 = Moderate 2 = Low 1 = Very low or none at all
5. Over the past 4 weeks, how **confident** were you about becoming sexually aroused during sexual activity or intercourse?	0 = No sexual activity 5 = Very high confidence 4 = High confidence 3 = Moderate confidence 2 = Low confidence 1 = Very low or no confidence
6. Over the past 4 weeks, how **often** have you been satisfied with your arousal (excitement) during sexual activity or intercourse?	0 = No sexual activity 5 = Almost always or always 4 = Most times (more than half the time) 3 = Sometimes (about half the time) 2 = A few times (less than half the time) 1 = Almost never or never
7. Over the past 4 weeks, how **often** did you become lubricated ("wet") during sexual activity or intercourse?	0 = No sexual activity 5 = Almost always or always 4 = Most times (more than half the time) 3 = Sometimes (about half the time) 2 = A few times (less than half the time) 1 = Almost never or never
8. Over the past 4 weeks, how **difficult** was it to become lubricated ("wet") during sexual activity or intercourse?	0 = No sexual activity 5 = Extremely difficult or impossible 4 = Very difficult 3 = Difficult 2 = Slightly difficult 1 = Not difficult
9. Over the past 4 weeks, how often did you **maintain** your lubrication ("wetness") until completion of sexual activity or intercourse?	0 = No sexual activity 5 = Almost always or always 4 = Most times (more than half the time) 3 = Sometimes (about half the time) 2 = A few times (less than half the time) 1 = Almost never or never
10. Over the past 4 weeks, how **difficult** was it to maintain your lubrication ("wetness") until completion of sexual activity or intercourse?	0 = No sexual activity 5 = Extremely difficult or impossible 4 = Very difficult 3 = Difficult 2 = Slightly difficult 1 = Not difficult
11. Over the past 4 weeks, when you had sexual stimulation or intercourse, how **often** did you reach orgasm (climax)?	0 = No sexual activity 5 = Almost always or always 4 = Most times (more than half the time) 3 = Sometimes (about half the time) 2 = A few times (less than half the time) 1 = Almost never or never
12. Over the past 4 weeks, when you had sexual stimulation or intercourse, how **difficult** was it for you to reach orgasm (climax)?	0 = No sexual activity 5 = Extremely difficult or impossible 4 = Very difficult 3 = Difficult 2 = Slightly difficult 1 = Not difficult
13. Over the past 4 weeks, how **satisfied** were you with your ability to reach orgasm (climax) during sexual activity or intercourse?	0 = No sexual activity 5 = Extremely satisfied 4 = Moderately satisfied 3 = About equally satisfied and dissatisfied 2 = Moderately dissatisfied 1 = Very dissatisfied
14. Over the past 4 weeks, how **satisfied** have you been with the amount of emotional closeness during sexual activity between you and your partner?	0 = No sexual activity 5 = Extremely satisfied 4 = Moderately satisfied 3 = About equally satisfied and dissatisfied 2 = Moderately dissatisfied 1 = Very dissatisfied
15. Over the past 4 weeks, how **satisfied** have you been with your sexual relationship with your partner?	0 = No sexual activity 5 = Extremely satisfied 4 = Moderately satisfied 3 = About equally satisfied and dissatisfied 2 = Moderately dissatisfied 1 = Very dissatisfied
16. Over the past 4 weeks, how satisfied have you been with your overall sexual life?	0 = No sexual activity 5 = Extremely satisfied 4 = Moderately satisfied 3 = About equally satisfied and dissatisfied 2 = Moderately dissatisfied 1 = Very dissatisfied
17. Over the past 4 weeks, how **often** did you experience discomfort or pain <u>during</u> vaginal penetration?	0 = Did not attempt intercourse 5 = Almost always or always 4 = Most times (more than half the time) 3 = Sometimes (about half the time 2 = A few times (less than half the time) 1 = Almost never or never
18. Over the past 4 weeks, how **often** did you experience discomfort or pain <u>following</u> vaginal penetration?	0 = Did not attempt intercourse 5 = Almost always or always 4 = Most times (more than half the time) 3 = Sometimes (about half the time 2 = A few times (less than half the time) 1 = Almost never or never
19. Over the past 4 weeks, how would you rate your **level** (degree) of discomfort or pain during or following vaginal penetration?	0 = Did not attempt intercourse 5 = Very high 4 = High 3 = Moderate 2 = Low 1 = Very low or none at all

FIGURE 77–2. Female Sexual Function Index scoring appendix.

Domain	Questions	Score Range	Factor	Minimum Score	Maximum Score	**Score**
Desire	1, 2	1 – 5	0.6	1.2	6.0	
Arousal	3, 4, 5, 6	0 – 5	0.3	0	6.0	
Lubrication	7, 8, 9, 10	0 – 5	0.3	0	6.0	
Orgasm	11, 12, 13	0 – 5	0.4	0	6.0	
Satisfaction	14, 15, 16	0 (or 1) – 5	0.4	0.8	6.0	
Pain	17, 18, 19	0 – 5	0.4	0	6.0	
			Full Scale Score Range	2.0	36.0	

FIGURE 77–3. Female Sexual Function Index (FSFI) domain scores and full-scale score. The individual domain scores and full scale (overall) score of the FSFI can be derived from the computational formula outlined in the table. For individual domain scores, add the scores of the individual items that comprise the domain and multiply the sum by the domain factor (see above). Add the six domain scores to obtain the full-scale score. It should be noted that within the individual domains, a domain score of zero indicates that the subject reported having no sexual activity during the past month. Subject scores can be entered in the right-hand column.

Specific physiologic impairments of vasculogenic female sexual dysfunction included vaginal engorement and clitoral erectile insufficiency syndromes. These syndromes exist when, during sexual stimulation, abnormal arterial circulation into the vagina or clitoris interferes with normal vascular physiologic processes. This may occur in patients with atherosclerotic vascular disease. Clinical symptoms may include delayed or diminished vaginal lubrication, delayed vaginal engorgement, pain or discomfort during sexual intercourse, lack of vaginal orgasm, and a loss of clitoral sensation or clitoral orgasm.[21]

Mental Illness

Mental disorders may cause a decrease or increase in sexual desire and orgasmic function. As an example, patients with bipolar disorder may be hypersexual when manic but suffer from a diminished libido when depressed. Patients with post-traumatic stress disorder may suffer from sexual dysfunction due to fear. The best treatment for these patients is continued therapy and education revolving around sexual function.

There is growing evidence of a variety of sexual side effects caused by commonly used antidepressant drugs. Sexual dysfunction is associated with several classes of antidepressant drugs, including tricyclic antidepressants, selective serotonin reuptake inhibitors (SSRIs), and venlafaxine. Side effects to antidepressant treatment can include decreased sexual desire as well as orgasmic delay or anorgasmia[22,23] Bupropion, mirtazapine, and nefazodone are antidepressant drugs that have

proven acute and long-term efficacy and appear less likely to cause sexual dysfunction.

Some patients elect or are advised to continue treatment with a specific antidepressant despite sexual side effects. For this reason, there has been great interest in drugs that might reverse sexual dysfunction caused by the use of antidepressants. Unfortunately, data from large randomized double-blinded controlled trials are lacking. Nonrandomized nonblinded prospective and retrospective studies have suggested that suldenifil (50 to 100 mg 1 hour before sexual activity), yohimbine (5.4 mg three times daily), and buproprion (75 or 150 mg 1 to 2 hours before sexual activity, or 75 mg tid) may be effective in alleviating sexual side effects of SSRIs in women.[23-25] Clinical experience shows that none of these remedies is universally effective.

Substance Abuse

The long-term use of substances may also cause a significant diminishment in sexual desire and pleasure. The severity of this effect depends on the type of substance and duration of use. Chronic narcotic opiates inhibit sexual arousal in women.[26] One study revealed 95.2% of women who were alcoholics experienced symptoms of dyspareunia and vaginal dryness.[27]

Medication

The effect of most drugs on female sexual function is poorly understood. Until very recently, the possible impact of drugs on female sexual function was rarely discussed, although the impact of many medications on male sexual function was understood and considered integral to the evaluation of male sexual disorders.

In addition to the now well-known effects of SSRIs and some other antidepressants, a variety of drugs have been implicated in female sexual dysfunction. In general, drugs that affect male sexual function commonly have also been found to have effects in women. Some drugs currently implicated in female sexual dysfunction are listed in Table 77–2.

Hormonal Factors

The impact of hormonal factors on female sexuality, and most specifically libido, is not well understood. In males, decreases in androgen are directly related to loss of libido. However, despite the strong sentiment of many clinicians, based on observation and a few clinical studies, that androgens are also integral to female sexuality, their exact role remains undefined. This is, in large part, because the androgen receptor has not been well characterized.[28]

TABLE 77–2. Some Medications Shown to Cause Sexual Dysfunction in Women*

Class	Examples
Appetite suppressants	Amphetamines and related drugs
Antidepressants	Selective serotonin reuptake inhibitors (SSRIs)
	Venlafaxine
	Monoamine oxidase inhibitors
	Imipramine, clomipramine
	Trazadone
Antihypertensives	Propranolol, timolol
	Methyldopa
	Reserpine
	Clonidine
	Spironolactone
Benzodiazepines	Diazepam
H₂ receptor blockers	Cimetidine
Endocrine agents	Bromocriptine
	Spironolactone

*Most drugs have not been systematically studied. Similar drugs not listed here may have similar effects on female sexuality. Others may have a beneficial effect (see text).
Adapted from ACOG Technical Bulletin-Sexual Dysfunction. No 211 Sept 1995, Int J Gynecol Obstet 1995;51:65–77; Mestan CM. Aging and sexuality. West J Med 1997;167: 285–90.

A study of adolescent women found that sexually active pubescent women had higher testosterone levels than controls.[29] Randomized, placebo-controlled studies of hormone replacement after bilateral salpingo-oophrectomy have found that women treated with testosterone alone or testosterone and estrogen have improved sexual function, compared with those receiving estrogen alone or a placebo.[14,30] In one such study, women who received estrogen alone or a placebo had a significant decrease in sexual fantasies and arousal, compared with their baseline state prior to surgery.[30]

Sexual dysfunction in women undergoing cytotoxic chemotherapy and/or bilateral salpingo-oophrectomy was found to be predicted by low testosterone levels, with women who maintained normal levels of testosterone significantly less likely to report problems with libido or sexual responsiveness. Testosterone replacement was found to restore libido and sexual responsiveness in these patients.[31] Unfortunately, the types of testosterone replacement used in recent studies are neither US Food and Drug Administration (FDA) approved nor readily available for use in women in the United States. It should also be noted that testosterone is metabolized to estrogen in the body. Because of this, its long-term safety in survivors of hormone-dependent cancers in uncertain.[31]

The role of birth control pills on sexual function is hormonally complex. Some combination oral contraceptives have been shown to decrease sexual interest in some women.[32] Oral contraceptives raise sex hormone–binding globulin levels, resulting in less bioavailable testosterone. They also lower luteinizing hormone levels, thereby decreasing testosterone production in the ovary. However, some oral contraceptives contain progestins that have androgenic effects so that all oral contraceptives might not have the same effect on libido.

Menopause and Aging

Numerous anatomic and physiologic changes have been demonstrated in postmenopausal women. These include atrophy of the vaginal epithelium, reduction of pubic hair, loss of fat and subcutaneous tissue from the mons pubis, atrophy of the labia majora, shortening and loss of elasticity of the vaginal barrel, and atrophy of the Bartholin glands.[33] The impact of these changes on sexual function is, in large part, uncertain, although clearly treatment that improves vaginal elasticity and lubrication can improve women's enjoyment of vaginal intercourse.

Masters and Johnson noted many changes in sexual response after menopause, including absence of increased breast size during stimulation, delayed or absent Bartholin gland secretion and vaginal lubrication, decreased vaginal congestion and expansion, and fewer uterine contractions with orgasm.[33] These factors may reduce sexual enjoyment or cause intercourse to be painful.

The exact role that menopause and aging play in female sexual function is unclear. Multiple studies have failed to show an association between estrogen levels in postmenopausal women and sexual function.[34] Levels of all plasma steroids, including androgens, decrease after menopause, however.[35] Epidemiologic data are limited.[33] Decreased sexual desire in postmenopausal women has been frequently demonstrated. However, menopausal status may not affect the frequency of sexual intercourse or orgasm.[34] On the other hand, urogenital atrophy clearly makes intercourse painful and difficult for many women, and treatment with local or systemic estrogens or vaginal lubricants can alleviate symptoms. This type of treatment is discussed in detail in Chapter 4 on menopause.

Although biologic, including hormonal, mediators of sexual function in older women are of great current scientific interest, other factors may be of equal or greater importance from a clinical perspective in determining an individual woman's sexual function as she ages. As women age, they are less likely to have an available and acceptable male partner. Sexual partners, when available, are also often frequently experiencing their own sexual difficulties. Particularly for elderly women, sexual issues may have never been addressed in the clinical setting. Although surveys have shown that three-quarters of women over the age of 65 years are sexually active, elderly women, like disabled women, are often presumed to be asexual.[7,33] Routine questions about sexuality should be asked of all women, including the elderly.[7]

Treatments for General Sexual Dysfunction

Many times, sexual dysfunction persists despite thorough evaluation and treatment for contributing causes. As noted above, some clinicians treat these patients with androgens, but the appropriate route

and dosing of androgen replacement in women with sexual dysfunction have yet to be established. Possible complications include acne, hirsutism, edema, deepening of the voice, and lipid and liver function abnormalities, although these have not been observed to a significant degree in recent short-term studies.[14] Oral methyltestosterone is available in pill form as Estratest (1.25 mg estrogen and 2.5 mg methyltestosterone) or in a half-strength formulation, but the usefulness of oral testosterone in female sexual dysfunction is unclear. Recent trials have used transdermal testosterone or intramuscular testosterone, but the transdermal and intramuscular formulations of testosterone available in the United States have not been studied with regard to dosage or long-term safety in women.[14,31] Dehydroepiandrosterone (DHEA) is available as a food supplement and is not FDA regulated. Its effectiveness is uncertain.

The EROS-CTD (clitoral therapy device) is an FDA-approved device marketed for treatment of sexual dysfunction. It is a small hand-held battery-operated device consisting of a small plastic cup that fits over the clitoris and provides gentle suction, simulating the stimulation of oral sex. Studies of its use in general sexual dysfunction were ongoing at the time of publication of this text.[21] It is also being studied as part of treatment for orgasmic dysfunction.

ORGASMIC DYSFUNCTION

Female orgasmic disorder is defined as persistent or recurrent delay in or absence of attaining orgasm following sufficient sexual stimulation and arousal, which causes personal distress.[36] This can be present in all situations or only in specific settings and cause marked distress or interpersonal difficulty. This diagnosis is not appropriate if the difficulty in reaching orgasm is due to sexual stimulation that is not adequate in focus, intensity, and duration.[37]

In order to understand why sexual dysfunction may occur, it is important to understand what is meant by a normal orgasm. An orgasm is described as the peaking of sexual pleasure. Many women do not reach orgasm solely through intercourse because penile thrusting is not direct enough or not intense enough to produce an orgasm.

Orgasmic dysfunction has been categorized as lifelong/generalized (primary), lifelong/situational (secondary), and acquired/generalized.[38,39] Each one of these categories has a distinct history, etiology, and treatment. Lifelong/generalized (primary) orgasmic dysfunction is characterized by the inability to have ever experienced an orgasm, regardless of circumstances or the stimulation that is received.[40] Various studies have reported that anywhere from 5 to 20% of women have never reached or experienced an orgasm. Most of these women do enjoy sexual experiences; they are just unable to reach an orgasm. Lack of information and experience is the most common cause of primary orgasmic dysfunction.

Although it might be supposed that a woman who had never reached orgasm might be refractory to treatment, in fact, primary orgasmic dysfunction is considered among the most treatable forms of sexual dysfunction.[41] It is extremely important that the clinician be supportive and encouraging with patients who have never reached an orgasm; however, the emphasis of treatment is on positive steps the woman herself can take to achieve orgasm. Many women benefit from self-help books that allow them to become more familiar with their own anatomy and the understanding of sexual intimacy and why an orgasm is or is not reached, due to stimulation or lack thereof. Self-exploration and body awareness are encouraged, allowing the patient to first experience an orgasm by herself before she tries to expect one during sexual interaction with a partner.[37] Couple's sex therapy can also be useful.[42]

Lifelong/situational (secondary) orgasmic dysfunction refers to the woman who has an inability to experience an orgasm in certain situations. Many times, this is in reference to a failure to reach an orgasm during sexual intercourse. It may also be specific to the location of intercourse, a specific partner, or a combination of all factors.[43] Most women with this problem have experienced orgasm at one time in their life through self-stimulation, oral sex, petting, sexual intercourse, heterosexual activity, or homosexual activity. Most often, secondary orgasmic dysfunction results from psychological issues, which may include poor self-esteem, a feeling of not being desired by their partner, a feeling that sexual intercourse is mundane, or excessive feelings of guilt associated with pleasure. A traumatic event may also lead to this type of orgasmic dysfunction.

Patients with secondary orgasmic dysfunction should be reassured that they can begin to achieve orgasm again. As with primary orgasmic dysfunction, education of the patient and her partner is the cornerstone of therapy. The patient should be encouraged to communicate to her partner which aspects of foreplay and intercourse are helpful to her achieving orgasm. The performance of pubococcygeal (Kegel) exercises may also improve a woman's understanding of her genital sensations. However, studies have not consistently shown improvement in coital orgasm frequency in women performing pubococcygeal exercises.[44–46] Couple's therapy is also useful. It is particularly important that partners not attempt to assign blame within their relationship for sexual dysfunction, but rather work together to resolve the problem.

Acquired/generalized orgasmic dysfunction is characterized by a woman's recent inability to achieve orgasm by any method with or without a partner. Another form of this may be a change in her sexual response pattern, which only allows her to reach orgasm after an extensive length of time. The cause of this type of dysfunction can many times be attributed to drugs that the patient is taking, illness, or substance abuse. If any of these factors are playing a role, they should be addressed. If not, the approach is similar to that for secondary orgasmic dysfunction.

VAGINISMUS

Vaginismus involves an involuntary contraction of the pelvic muscles surrounding the outer third of the vagina. The muscles that are directly affected include the perineal muscles, the levator ani muscles, possibly the adductor muscles in the thighs, the gluteus muscles, and the rectus abdominis muscle. In order to diagnose vaginismus, the spasms that occur must be recurrent and persistent and must interfere with intercourse.

Patients with vaginismus are either unable to have intercourse or experience extreme pain with penetration. A critical review disputes the widely held belief that vaginismus is an easily diagnosed and easily treated sexual dysfunction; instead, it is now more widely thought of as either an aversion/phobia of vaginal penetration or a genital pain disorder.[47] A history of genital trauma or sexual violence in the histories of women with vaginismus is unusual. More commonly, phobias, including fear of pain and fear of intimacy, are found in patients with vaginismus.[37]

Any complaint of persistent pain associated with vaginal entry requires a complete physical examination, but in the case of vaginismus, this may be impossible. In patients in whom vaginal examination is not possible at the initial visit, it is important to build a strong relationship with the patient and to establish trust and comfort over time so that ultimately a complete evaluation is possible. A thorough explanation of the process and rationale of pelvic examination, using diagrams and a mirror for the patient to view her genitals, may suffice. Other patients may need to touch and explore the areas to be examined in private before they are able to submit to a clinical examination.

The treatment of vaginismus is multifaceted and usually involves a psychotherapeutic approach in combination with behavioral therapy.[48] Both partners should be involved. A key aspect of therapy is reassuring the couple that their problems can be resolved. As with other types of sexual dysfunction, it is important to emphasize that both members are working toward a common goal, rather than assign blame to one partner for previous problems.

Treatment for vaginismus previously focused on helping women gain voluntary control of their vaginal muscles. However, a study comparing normal controls with women with vaginismus demonstrated that overall, women with vaginismus do not have less voluntary control of vaginal muscles.[49] Some women may benefit from the use of a vaginal dilator during treatment. Use of a vaginal dilator can allow the woman the opportunity to become used to having something in her vagina without fear or pain, as she can practice in a situation in which she is always in control. The dilator should be inserted daily, and the patient encouraged to leave it inside as long as can be managed. Progression to the next larger-size dilator should be considered only when there is no pain associated with the size the patient is using.

DYSPAREUNIA

Dyspareunia describes pain associated with sexual intercourse. The pain can be at the time of vaginal entry, during the movement that is associated with the back and forth motion of intercourse, or deep within the patient's vagina. It is a common complaint among women of reproductive age. The causes of dyspareunia may be structural, psychological, or a combination of factors. Therefore, patients with dyspareunia require comprehensive gynecologic and psychosocial assessment to determine the best treatment strategy.[50]

Although dyspareunia is categorized as a disorder of sexual dysfunction, like vaginismus, its presentation and treatment are most commonly like that of a chronic pain syndrome.[50] Compared with controls, women with dyspareunia have more psychological symptomatology, including a more negative attitude toward sexuality, higher levels of impairment of sexual function, and lower levels of marital adjustment. Aging does not appear to be a risk factor for dyspareunia, but low income may be. Women with dyspareunia have not been found to be more likely than control women to have suffered previous personal violence or sexual abuse.[51]

Many patients with dyspareunia suffer from vulvar vestibulitis syndrome (VVS). VVS is characterized by severe pain on vestibular touch or attempted vaginal entry, tenderness to pressure within the vulvar vestibule, and physical findings confined to vestibular erythema of varying degrees. The etiology of VVS is unknown. It is thought that infectious agents may be one cause, as many women with VVS have been noted clinically to have a high number of vaginal and/or urinary tract infections. This condition is most prevalent in Caucasians between the ages of 20 and 30 years. Most women feel initial discomfort due to a tampon and not sexual intercourse.

Vulvar vestibulitis may be a risk factor for developing psychosexual complications, including vaginismus, low libido, and orgasmic dysfunction. A study of psychological and psychosexual morbidity of patients with vulvar vestibulitis demonstrated that patients experienced considerable psychological dysfunction, compared with controls.[52]

VVS has been treated medically, surgically, or with cognitive-behavioral/pain management therapy. Medical management strategies have included the use of topical preparations, including anesthetics, capsaicin, progesterone, antifungals, antivirals, and antibiotics. Systemic drugs, including antivirals, antibiotics, and isotretinoin and injected α-interferon, have also been used. Studies of these strategies have been retrospective series or quasiexperimental; there is a lack of data from controlled studies to guide therapeutic choices. Isotretinoin and topical progesterone do not appear to be of benefit. Some patients may benefit from capsaicin or oral acyclovir. No strategy has been reported to provide complete relief for a majority of patients with VVS. Although not well studied in VVS, tricyclic antidepressants may have a role in some patients because of their proven efficacy in other chronic pain syndromes.[53]

Surgical interventions include vestibulectomy and laser therapy. The best outcomes have been associated with vestibulectomy, which is described as a modified perineoplasty, with a success rate of about 60%. A posterior crescent-shaped vestibular excision followed by vaginal advancement was performed in 12 women suffering from VVS for longer than 6 months. After an 8-month follow-up, 6 patients reported painless sexual intercourse, and 4 patients improved significantly.[54] Another prototype of surgical treatment for VVS has been the Woodruff vulvoplasty. This is thought to be a simpler surgery that can be performed under local anesthesia. A study, again involving 12 women, showed a decrease in tenderness and ease of healing with this procedure. Ten of the 12 women had complete resolution of vestibulitis.[55] Combining sexual counseling with surgery improves outcomes. Postoperatively, reflex vaginismus often occurs and needs therapy to complement the surgical treatment.

RESOURCES

American Psychological Association
750 First Street Northeast
Washington, DC 20002-4242
Telephone: 1-800-374-2721
Web site: www.apa.org

The American Psychological Association provides referrals to board-certified psychologists.

American Association of Sex Educators, Counselors, and Therapists
PO Box 5488
Richmond, Virginia 23220-0488
Telephone: (804) 644-3288
Web site: www.aasect.org

AASECT provides information and referrals for certified sex therapists throughout the United States.

Books for Patients
Because patients vary in their experiences and views of sexuality, no single book is "right" for all patients experiencing sexual dysfunction. Listed below are three that provide factual information and an approach to improving sexual function. Clinicians should assess whether the tone and approach of each book matches the outlook of an individual patient. Patients may also be advised to feel free to use the portions of a given book they find useful, even if the entire book does not always seem relevant to their experience.

Barbach L. For yourself: the fulfillment of female sexuality. New York: Signet; 2000.

This book outlines a straightforward approach to improving sexual function. Some psychosocial commentary may seem outdated to some women.

RESOURCES (continued)

Berman J, Berman L. For women only. New York: Henry Holt and Company; 2001.

"State of the art" describing many of the newest information and trends in the treatment of sexual dysfunction. May be particularly good for more highly educated "information-seeking" patients.

Heiman JR, LoPiccolo J. Becoming orgasmic: a sexual and personal growth program for women. Prentice-Hall; 1988.

A book that is especially good for women from sexually conservative backgrounds.

REFERENCES

1. Laumann EO, Paik A, Rosen RC. Sexual dysfunction in the United States: prevalence and predictors. JAMA 1999;281:537–44.
2. Read S, King M, Watson J. Sexual dysfunction in primary medical care: prevalence, characteristics and detection by general practitioner. J Public Health Med 1997;19:387–91.
3. Shokrollahi P, Mirmohamadi M, Mehrabi F, Babae G. Prevalence of sexual dysfunction in women seeking services at family planning centers in Tehran. J Sex Marital Ther 1999;25:211–5.
4. Morrison J. The first interview: revised from DSM-IV. New York (NY): The Guildford Press; 1995.
5. Hite S. The Hite report: a nationwide study on female sexuality: sexual practice in the United States. Chicago (IL): The University of Chicago Press; 1994. p. 35–73.
6. Masters WH, Johnson VE. Human sexual response. Boston (MA): Little Brown and Company; 1996.
7. Andrews WC. Approaches to taking a sexual history. J Women's Health Gender-Based Med 2000;9 Suppl 1: 21–4.
8. Cocores JA, Miller NS, Pottash AC, Gold MS. Sexual dysfunction in abusers of cocaine and alcohol. Am J Drug and Alcohol Abuse 1988;14:169–73.
9. Newman AS, Bertelson AD. Sexual dysfunction in diabetic women. J Behav Med 1986;9:261–70.
10. Papadopoulos C. Sexual aspects of cardiovascular disease. New York (NY): Praeger; 1989.
11. Sacks EL, Gerstein OG, Mann SG. Conservative surgery and radiation therapy for breast cancer. Frontiers Radiat Ther Oncol 1983;17:23–32.
12. Schover LR, Jensen SB. Sexuality and chronic illness: a comprehensive approach. New York (NY): Guildford Press; 1988.
13. Riley AJ, Peet M, Wilson C. Sexual pharmacology. Oxford (UK): Clarendon Press; 1993.
14. Shifren JL, Braunstein GD, Simon JA, et al. Transdermal testosterone treatment in women with impaired sexual function after oophorectomy. N Engl J Med 2000;343:682–8.
15. Malatesta VJ, Adams HE. The sexual dysfunctions. In: Adams HE, Sutker PB, editors. Comprehensive handbook of psychopathology. New York (NY): 1984. p. 725–75.
16. Zorzon M, Zivadinov R, Bosco A, et al. Sexual dysfunction in multiple sclerosis: a case-control study. I. Frequency and comparison of groups. Mult Scler 1999;5(6):418–27.
17. Zivadinov R, Zorzon M, Bosco A, et al. Sexual dysfunction in multiple sclerosis: II. Correlation analysis. Mult Scler 1999;5:428–31.
18. Korpelainen JT, Kauhanen ML, Kemola H, et al. Sexual dysfunction in stroke patients. Acta Neurol Scand 1998;98:400–5.
19. Barni S, Mondin R. Sexual dysfunction in treated breast cancer patients. Ann Oncol 1997;8:149–53.
20. Fass R, Fullerton S, Naliboff B, et al. Digestion 1998; 59:79–85.
21. Berman J, Berman L. For women only: a revolutionary guide to overcoming sexual dysfunction and reclaiming your sex life. New York (NY): Henry Holt and Company; 2001.
22. Segraves RT. Antidepressant-induced sexual dysfunction. J Clin Psychiatry 1998;59 Suppl 4:48–54.
23. Keller AA, Hamer R, Rosen RC. Serotonin reuptake inhibitor-induced sexual dysfunction and its treatment: a large-scale retrospective study of 596 psychiatric outpatients. J Sex Marital Ther 1997;23:165–75.

24. Fava M, Rankin MA, Alpert JE, et al. An open trial of oral sildenafilin antidepressant-induced sexual dysfunction. Psychother Psychosom 1998;67:328–31.

25. Ashton AK, Rosen RC. Bupropion as an antidote for serotonin reuptake inhibitor-induced sexual dysfunction. J Clin Psychiatry 1998;59:112–5.

26. Buffum J. Pharmacosexology: The effects of drugs on sexual function. J Psychoactive Drugs 1982;14:5–44.

27. Seki M, Yoshida K, Kashimura M. A study on sexual dysfunction in female patients with alcoholics. Nippon Rinsho 1997;55:3035–9.

28. DeCherney AH. Hormone receptors and sexuality in the human female. J Women's Health Gender-Based Med 2000;9 Suppl 1:9–13.

29. Halpern CT, Udry JR, Suchindran C. Testosterone predicts initiation of coitus in adolescent females. Pyschosom Med 1997;59:161–71.

30. Sherwin BB, Gelfand M, Brender W. Androgen enhances sexual motivation in females: a prospective, crossover study of sex steroid administration in the surgical menopause. Pyschosom Med 1985;47:339–51.

31. Kaplan HS, Owett T. The female androgen deficiency syndrome. J Sex Marital Ther 1993;19(1):3–24.

32. Bancoft J, Davidson DW, Warner P, Tyrer G. Androgens and sexual behaviour in women using oral contraceptives. Clin Endocinol 1980;12:327–40.

33. Gelfand MM. Sexuality among older women. J Women's Health Gender-Based Med 2000;9 Suppl 1: 15–20.

34. Avis NE, Stellato R, Crawford S, et al. Is there an association between menopause status and sexual functioning? Menopause 2000;7:297–309.

35. Shifren JL, Schiff I. The aging ovary. J Women's Health Gender-Based Med 2000;9 Suppl 1:3–7.

36. Basson R, Berman J, Burnett A, et al. Report of the International Consensus Development Conference on Female Sexual Dysfunction: definitions and classifications. J Urol 2000;163:888–93.

37. Maurice WL. Sexual medicine in primary care. St. Louis (MO): Mosby; 1999.

38. Diagnostic and Statistical Manual of Mental Disorders. 4th ed. Primary care version. Washington (DC): American Psychiatric Association; 1995.

39. Spector IP, Carey MP. Incidence and prevalence of the sexual dysfunction, Arch Sex Behav 1990;19:389–408.

40. LoPiccolo J, Stock WE. Treatment of sexual dysfunction. J Consult Clin Psychol 1986;54:158–67.

41. Wincze JP, Carey MP. Sexual dysfunction: a guide for assessment and treatment. New York (NY): Guilford Press; 1991.

42. Sudman S, Bradburn NM. Asking questions: a practical guide to questionnaire design, San Francisco (CA): Jossey-Bass Inc.; 1982.

43. Kentsmith D, Eaton M. Treating sexual problems in medical practice. New York (NY): Arco Publishing, Inc.; 1997.

44. Kegel AH. Sexual functions of the pubococcygeus muscle. West J Surg Obstet Gynecol 1952;60:521–4.

45. Chambless DL, Sultan FE, Stern TE, et al. Effect of pubococcygeal exercise on coital orgasm in women. J Consult Clin Psychol 1984;52:114–8.

46. Messe MR, Geer JH. Voluntary vaginal musculature contractions as an enhancer of sexual arousal. Arch Sex Behav 1985;14:13–28.

47. Reissing ED, Binik YM, Khalife S. Does vaginismus exist? A critical review of the literature. J Nerv Ment Dis 1999;187:261–74.

48. Harrison CM. Vaginismus. Contracept Fertil Sex 1996;24:223–8.

49. Van der Velde J, Everaerd W. Voluntary control over pelvic floor muscles in women with and without vaginistic reactions. Int Urogynecol J Pelvic Floor Dysfunct 1999;10:230–6.

50. Meana M, Binik YM, Khalife S, Cohen DR. Biopsychosocial profile of women with dyspareunia. Obstet Gynecol 1997;90:583–9.

51. Jamieson DJ, Steege JF. The prevalence of dysmenorrhea, dyspareunia, pelvic pain, and irritable bowel syndrome in primary care practices. Obstet Gynecol 1996;87:55–8.

52. Nunns D, Mandal D. Psychological and psychosexual aspects of vulvar vestibulitis. Genitourin Med 1997;73:541–4.

53. Bergeron S, Binik Y, Khalife S, Pagidas K. Vulvar vestibulitis syndrome: a critical review. Clin J Pain 1997;13:27–42.

54. Berville S, Moyal-Barracco M, Paniel BJ. Treatment of vulvar vestibulitis by posterior vestibulectomy. Twelve case reports. J Gynecol Obstet Biol Reprod (Paris) 1997;26:71–5.

55. Goetsch MF. Simplified surgical revision of the vulvar vestibule for vulvar vestibulitis. Am J Obstet Gynecol 1996;174:1701–5.

78

UTERINE FIBROIDS

Michael Broder, MD, MSHS

SCOPE OF THE PROBLEM

Uterine leiomyomas, often called fibroids, are the most common benign tumors of the female reproductive tract. Leiomyomas are a common cause of significant gynecologic symptoms and major gynecologic surgery. They have been identified in 4 to 40% of women between the ages of 25 and 45 years (Table 78–1).[1] Symptoms related to fibroids are responsible for a substantial minority of gynecologic office visits. These muscular tumors most commonly present with bleeding, pain, or abdominal/pelvic fullness. The bleeding may be symptomatic due to excess blood loss and anemia, or it may interfere with a woman's normal activities strictly because of the timing and frequency of bleeding episodes. Medical treatments for fibroids suffer from low success rates and many unacceptable side effects. As a result, fibroids lead to as many as 360,000 hysterectomies and 35,000 to 60,000 myomectomies each year in the United States (Table 78–2).

Despite the prevalence of both symptomatic and asymptomatic fibroids, there are no adequate estimates of the burden of disease from uterine myomas in the literature. Recent studies have shown that most patients who undergo hysterectomy for fibroids are significantly impaired in their ability to perform their usual activities, often taking 2 or more days per month off from work or usual activities.[2] These women often have symptoms for at least 6 months before surgery.

There are approximately 600,000 hysterectomies performed each year in the United States; between 30 and 60% are done to relieve symptoms of uterine fibroids.[3] If the average woman misses 2 days per month from her usual activities for 6 months before hysterectomy, then between 2 to 4 million person-days per year are lost before surgery, and an additional 3 to 7 million person-days per year are lost during recovery from surgery. Of course, many women do not seek medical care for their symptoms; of those that do, an unknown number are not offered or do not accept hysterectomy as treatment, making this estimate of time lost a lower bound only.

Because of the paucity of data, it is difficult to make direct comparisons between the burden of fibroids to that of other conditions. One estimate can be made based solely on the annual number of days women are hospitalized due to leiomyomas. Hysterectomy results in over 900,000 hospital days per year (based on the midpoint of the estimated number of hysterectomies performed for uterine myomas, a 1:4 ratio of vaginal to abdominal hysterectomy, and a stay of 2 days for vaginal hysterectomy and 4 days for abdominal hysterectomy). Using this conservative estimate, leiomyomas are responsible for more hospital days than acquired immunodeficiency syndrome (AIDS), breast cancer, dementia, cirrhosis, prostate cancer, or epilepsy.[4]

Calculations based on the number of surgical procedures done to treat this condition can provide a lower-bound estimate of the direct cost to health care payers. In the United States, 600,000 hysterectomies are done every year; 180,000 to 360,000 are done for symptoms of uterine myomas. As a hysterectomy costs approximately $6,000, the direct costs for hysterectomy amount to $1 billion to 2 billion per year. A myomectomy costs approximately $5,000; 37,000 to 44,000 myomectomies are done each year in the United States, resulting in $200 million per year in direct costs for myomectomy.

Thus, the minimum estimated direct cost of treating uterine myomas is over $1 billion per year (in 1999 dollars). Including office visits and procedures done to treat or diagnose myomas (eg, ultrasonog-

TABLE 78–1. Incidence of Uterine Leiomyoma among Premenopausal Women

	Woman-Years	Incidence*		Confirmation by Ultrasonography or Hysterectomy		Confirmation by Hysterectomy	
		Cases	Rate† (95% CI)	Cases	Rate† (95% CI)	Cases	Rate† (95% CI)
Age (yr)							
25–29	49,730	212	4.3 (3.7,4.8)	165	3.3 (2.8,3.8)	10	0.2 (0.1,0.3)
30–34	103,521	941	9.0 (8.4,9.6)	706	6.8 (6.3,7.3)	89	0.9 (0.1,1.0)
35–39	110,730	1,630	14.7 (14.0,15.4)	1,144	10.3 (9.7,10.9)	273	2.5 (2.2,2.8)
40–44	62,084	1,398	22.5 (21.3,23.7)	991	16.0 (15.0,17.0)	295	4.8 (4.3,5.3)
Age-standardized by race/ethnic group‡							
White	300,899	3,785	12.5 (12.1,12.9)	2,679	8.9 (8.6,9.2)	609	2.0 (1.9,2.2)
Black	4,367	174	37.9 (32.3,43.6)	140	30.6 (25.5,35.7)	21	4.5 (2.5,6.4)
Hispanic	4,654	66	14.5 (11.0,18.0)	50	11.0 (8.0,14.1)	6	1.3 (0.3,2.4)
Asian	6,007	65	10.4 (7.9,13.0)	50	8.0 (5.8,10.3)	1	1.9 (0.8,3.0)

*Cases confirmed by hysterectomy, by ultrasonography, or by pelvic examination only.
†Rate per 1,000 woman-years.
‡Incidence rates were standardized to the age distribution of the woman-years at risk in the entire study population. The 11,139 woman-years and 118 cases occurring among women of unknown race are not included.
CI = confidence interval.
Reproduced with permission from Marshall LM, Spiegelman D, Barbieri RL, et al. Variation in the incidence of uterine leiomyoma among premenopausal women by age and race. Obstet Gynecol 1997;90:967–73.

TABLE 78–2. Annual Volume: Procedures to Treat Uterine Leiomyomata, 1990 to 1996

| | *Hysterectomy for Fibroids* | | | |
Year	*Total Hysterectomy*	*Lower Bound*[*]	*Upper Bound*[*]	*Myomectomy*
1990	586,000	175,800	363,320	38,000
1991	540,000	162,000	334,800	46,000
1992	574,000	172,200	355,880	45,000
1993	546,000	163,800	338,520	44,000
1004	556,000	166,800	344,720	39,000
1995	583,000	174,900	361,460	38,000
1996	591,000	177,300	366,420	37,000

[*]Upper and lower bounds are calculated from estimates of the proportion of hysterectomies performed to treat uterine fibroids. Data from National Hospital Discharge Surveys 1990–1996.

raphy, dilation and curettage [D & C], and endometrial biopsy), researchers have estimated the direct cost of care as up to $3 billion per year.[5] These estimates do not include any indirect costs, such as time lost from work or the cost of care provided by relatives.

ANATOMY AND PATHOPHYSIOLOGY

Uterine leiomyomas arise from the neoplastic transformation of a single smooth muscle cell.[6] Myomas may arise throughout the body (eg, from smooth muscle cells in arterioles found in lungs or other organs) but most commonly present in the uterus and range from several millimeters to >20 cm in diameter. They contain predominately smooth muscle cells but also may have components of collagenous and degenerated tissue. The tumors are firm, spherical, and usually white to gray on cut section. They have a typical whorled appearance (Figure 78–1), making them easily identifiable at the time of surgery.

Myomas are described on the basis of their location with respect to the uterine body (Figure 78–2). Tumors located within the muscular wall of the uterus are referred to as intramural. Subserosal fibroids are found on the outer portion of the uterus, deforming its normal ovoid shape. Subserosal fibroids that protrude from the uterine body on a stalk are referred to as pedunculated. Myomas protruding into the uterine cavity are called submucosal myomas. Pedunculated myomas may become detached from the uterus and become

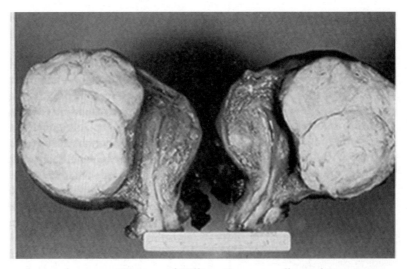

FIGURE 78–1. Large subserosal myoma. Courtesy of William Droegemueller and Vern L. Katz.

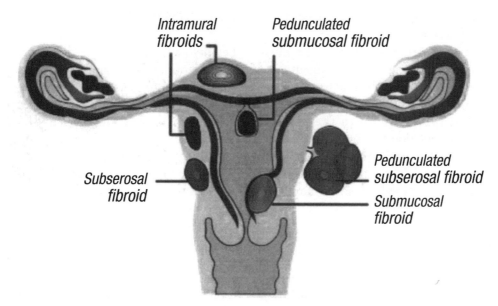

FIGURE 78–2. Types of fibroids.

parasitic, deriving their blood supply from adjacent structures (most commonly the broad ligament).

Although the mechanisms that control leiomyoma growth are not fully understood, such growth appears to be regulated by steroid hormones (estrogen and progesterone), peptide growth factors (such as epidermal growth factor), and the availability of adequate vascular perfusion.[7] Ovarian hormones are implicated both by work showing the presence of receptors for such hormones on myoma cells and by the natural history of leiomyomas. These tumors are rarely seen before age 20 years, and symptoms predominate in women in their thirties to fifties. At menopause, fibroids often shrink, and a new onset of suspected uterine fibroids after menopause should call the diagnosis into question. Increasing density of progesterone receptors within a myoma has been shown to correlate with an increased likelihood of myoma growth although estrogen receptor density has not.[8]

Myomas are said to undergo various types of degeneration, depending on their surgical pathologic appearance. "Red" or carneous degeneration occurs when the myoma loses adequate blood supply and becomes necrotic. This event is clinically significant as it can often produce severe pain and peritonitis. "Cancerous degeneration" appears to be a misnomer as it seems likely that individual myomas do not become cancerous. Rather, uterine leiomyosarcoma is a rare tumor that does not appear to be related to uterine leiomyomas. Recent evidence suggests that women with leiomyomas are not at increased risk for sarcoma. However, because of its rarity and lack of clear symptoms, leiomyosarcoma is often discovered at the time of surgery for what are believed to be leiomyomas. This occurs in approximately 0.1 to 0.3% of such surgeries in women of reproductive age, and as high as 1% of such procedures in postmenopausal women.[9]

CLINICAL PRESENTATION

The typical patient with symptomatic fibroids is in her thirties or forties although fibroids have been reported in girls as young as 13 years of age.[10] Risk factors for myoma development include earlier menarche, family history, and race (African American women are found to have a higher incidence of fibroids than do Caucasian women, even after correction for known risk factors)[11] (see Table 78–1). Women with uterine fibroids most commonly present with bleeding. However, because ultrasonography has become more common in clinical practice, many women are now diagnosed with myomas in the absence of any significant symptoms.[7] Some studies estimate that between 60 and 90% of fibroids fail to cause any symptoms.[9] Those that do produce symptoms typically do so during the late reproductive years to the perimenopausal period. Size and location may play a role in determining which myomas will become symptomatic, but these two factors alone do not explain the variation in symptomatology seen in clinical practice.

Abnormal menstrual bleeding is the most common symptom causing women with uterine fibroids to seek medical care although both leiomyomas and menstrual disorders (in the absence of myomata) are so common in the general reproductive-age population that some of the association between bleeding problems and leiomyomas is probably coincidental. The exact mechanism by which fibroids cause increased menstrual blood loss is not known although several theories have been advanced. Myomas located within the walls of the uterus (intramural myomas) may compress uterine veins as they grow, leading to venular ectasia and perhaps impairment of normal hemostatic mechanisms. Submucosal myomas (ie, those protruding into the endometrial cavity) have been postulated to cause increased bleeding as a result of ulcerations developing over the tumor. Finally, uterine myomas may increase the surface area of the endometrium, thereby increasing the area from which menstrual blood loss may be expected. However, the existence of a relationship between endometrial surface area and blood loss has been disputed.[7,11]

Leiomyomas may also cause pelvic pain, either through a mass effect or by the spontaneous necrosis of the tumor. Acute-onset pelvic pain may occur when a myoma outgrows its blood supply, producing a necrotic central core, or when a pedunculated fibroid undergoes torsion on its stalk and becomes ischemic. Pelvic discomfort, pressure, or pain may also result from compression of adjacent organs by an enlarging fibroid uterus. Frequent urination or constipation may result from compression of bladder or bowel, respectively.

The link between uterine leiomyomas and infertility, while frequently discussed, has not been convincingly established. In certain cases, such as when blockage of the cervix or fallopian tubes by myomata is demonstrated, the tumors certainly may impede normal fertility. In other cases, when myomas distort the uterus and infertility has developed, the association may be purely coincidental. There are multiple case series demonstrating improved individual fertility after myomectomy (ie, a previously subfertile couple conceiving after myomectomy), but there are no data comparing myomectomy to other treatments (such as watchful waiting or medical therapy) with regard to pregnancy rates or outcomes.[7]

DIAGNOSIS

Leiomyomas are generally diagnosed on physical examination, by finding an enlarged or irregularly shaped uterus in the absence of other abnormalities (eg, ovarian masses) that would suggest another diagnosis. Diagnosis may be supported by radiologic studies (typically ultrasonography), hysteroscopy, or laparoscopy.

Whether or not to pursue diagnostic modalities other than examination alone depends on the clinical setting and on clinician and patient preferences. Because uterine fibroids are the most common cause of an enlarged uterus in the absence of pregnancy, and because an enlarged or irregularly shaped uterus in a woman with typical symptoms is rarely a sign of malignancy, radiologic studies are often dispensed with entirely.

Although not always necessary, both ultrasonography and magnetic resonance imaging (MRI) can help confirm the diagnosis of myomas if history and physical examination are equivocal. Ultrasonography is currently the more common imaging technique because of its lower cost, greater availability, and high patient acceptance. Pelvic ultrasonography commonly involves both transabdominal and transvaginal scanning; transabdominal scanning yields superior views of enlarged uteri, and transvaginal scanning produces better views of adnexal structures. Saline infusion ultrasonography, in which a small amount of saline is infused through a catheter into the uterus, can identify intrauterine abnormalities that may contribute to the presenting complaint. Specifically, saline ultrasonography is highly sensitive for identifying subserosal myomas and intrauterine polyps, both of which may cause abnormal bleeding.[12]

In some cases, diagnostic imaging is vital to the patient's proper treatment. A patient with abnormal bleeding and whose symptoms have not responded to medical management may desire uterine-conserving treatment. Determining the most appropriate surgical treatment often depends on a clear understanding of the size, location, and number of myomas. The presence of submucosal fibroids, for example, may indicate that hysteroscopic resection will reduce symptoms. Depending on the skill and patience of the surgeon, a large number of fibroids may make myomectomy a less attractive surgical option than hysterectomy. Finally,

MRI or ultrasonography can aid in the diagnosis of adenomyosis.[13,14] If adenomyosis (rather than myomas), is found to be the cause of an enlarged uterus, surgical treatment short of hysterectomy is unlikely to reduce symptoms.

Diagnostic imaging can also be invaluable in determining the size of the ovaries when the uterus is grossly enlarged. Traditional teaching held that a uterus larger than it would be at 14 weeks of pregnancy should be removed to prevent ovarian cancer from going undetected by physical examination.[15,16] With high-resolution ultrasonography and MRI, this consideration is no longer valid. Ultrasonography and MRI are both more sensitive to ovarian enlargement than is physical examination—whether the uterus is enlarged or not. Ovarian cancer screening using imaging techniques (see Chapter 83) is insufficiently advanced to be used routinely. However, confirmation of uterine fibroids as the cause of uterine enlargement in the presence of normal-size ovaries should reassure the patient and physician that surgery is not indicated simply due to the presence of an enlarged uterus.

OUTPATIENT MANAGEMENT

Bleeding

Because of the frequency with which uterine myomas occur and the infrequency with which they are found to be malignant, treatment for these tumors generally should be based strictly on symptoms. There is little role for surgical management in the absence of significant symptoms, and as a result, first-line treatment consists of medical management directed at the primary symptoms.

Before beginning treatment for uterine bleeding with the assumption that fibroids are the cause, it is imperative that other causes of bleeding be ruled out. Causes of abnormal bleeding are discussed in detail in Chapter 82. In premenopausal women, ovulation should be confirmed either by history or by laboratory findings. A history of regular menses, occurring every 21 to 35 days and accompanied by moliminal symptoms (tenderness of breasts, bloating, and cramping), can be taken as presumptive evidence of ovulation. Menses occurring without any discernable pattern suggests anovulation although a confirmation of anovulation can be made by finding a progesterone level of < 3 ng/mL on menstrua cycle day 21 or by noting

the absence of secretory endometrium at a similarly timed endometrial biopsy.

Physical examination should reveal other potential causes of abnormal bleeding, including cervical polyps or vaginal abrasions. A Pap test, if not known to be normal in the previous year, should also be part of the routine evaluation of a patient with uterine fibroids and bleeding. In those women with a higher-than-average risk of endometrial cancer or hyperplasia, an assessment of the endometrium risk should be made before treatment is initiated. In premenopausal women, this assessment can best be performed by an endometrial biopsy in the office. Ultrasonography can be used to rule out endometrial cancer, but its sensitivity is not sufficient to replace biopsy in postmenopausal women.[17]

A standard cutoff point for determining when a biopsy is or is not needed cannot be established on the basis of the available evidence; thus, the decision to do a biopsy must be individualized. Most women less than 35 years of age have a very low risk of endometrial cancer, and biopsy can often be avoided in this group. However, prolonged anovulation, obesity, and smoking raise the risk of endometrial cancer such that biopsy may be appropriate in the presence of such risk factors, even at ages of less than 35 years.

There are no high-quality studies examining the use of medical therapy to treat bleeding associated with myomas. Medical therapy may be successful and is certainly less dangerous than surgery; therefore, primary therapy for bleeding (which accounts for the bulk of symptoms related to fibroids) is medical and includes the use of hormonal agents such as progestins, combined oral contraceptives, and (less commonly and for short-term treatment) gonadotropin-releasing hormone (Gn-RH) analogues. Nonhormonal treatments include nonsteroidal anti-inflammatory drugs (NSAIDs), and—in the United Kingdom but not in the United States, where they lack Food and Drug Administration (FDA) approval—antifibrinolytic agents. Progestin-releasing intrauterine devices (IUDs) are used in the United Kingdom and other countries to treat menorrhagia, but their use for this purpose remains rare in the United States. None of these agents plays a role in the genesis of endometrial cancer. As a result, treatment can usually be initiated before the results of endometrial biopsies are available.

Cyclic hormone therapy is usually initiated either with oral contraceptives or with progestins alone. Dosing depends on whether there is concurrent heavy bleeding. For patients with ongoing bleeding, oral contraceptives (OCPs) usually provide immediate control of symptoms. This is initiated as follows: a low-dose (estrogen 35 μg) monophasic pill is taken four times a day for 5 days. The use of prophylactic antiemetics is recommended because this regimen frequently causes nausea or vomiting. After 5 days, a new pill package is started, skipping the placebo pills from the first pack. This regimen has several advantages, not the least of which is the easy availability of OCPs. Oral contraceptives are inexpensive and conveniently packaged, and the regimen has a high success rate for controlling acute bleeding episodes. In addition the regimen provides an easy transition to combined OCs should the patient desire ongoing contraception. This OC-based regimen can also be given with a tapering dosing schedule, beginning with four pills a day and tapering to one pill per day as the bleeding abates.

Alternatives to this regimen include the use of progestins—usually medroxyprogesterone acetate (MPA)—in a cyclic fashion, typically initiated as 10 mg of MPA in the 10 days before menses each month for several months. Initiation with a higher dose (30 mg/d) can often control ongoing bleeding. This dose is then tapered to 10 mg/d for 10 days and is repeated monthly.

The immediate effect of high-dose OCPs is to stabilize the endometrium, preventing further hemorrhage. When the standard dose is initiated, the progestin dominance of the pills causes endometrial atrophy. Progestins produce similar effects on the endometrium. Notwithstanding our lack of understanding of the mechanism of fibroid-induced bleeding, it appears that inducing endometrial atrophy effectively decreases such bleeding. Furthermore, as the most common age range for symptomatic fibroids overlaps significantly with the range for women experiencing anovulatory bleeding, it is reasonable to surmise that some element of "fibroid-related bleeding" is actually anovulation, which these regimens are well suited to treating.

The use of NSAIDs has also been shown to decrease menstrual bleeding, by inhibiting prostaglandin synthesis. Although this reduction was not specifically found in women with uterine fibroids, a reduction in bleeding in these patients is commonly seen in clinical practice when NSAIDs are used. Furthermore, the pain relief provided by these medications is a welcome side effect for women who suffer concurrently from bleeding and dysmenorrhea. In the United States, ibuprofen is commonly chosen as first-line treatment as it is available without prescription. Other NSAIDs, including mefenamic acid and naproxen, have a similar effect on blood loss.

The progestin-releasing IUD (Progestasert, ALZA Corporation Mountain View, California) also effectively reduces blood loss and provides contraception. Intrauterine devices in general are not as popular in the United States as in some other countries, and (perhaps as a result) this treatment does not appear to be commonly used in the United States. The local release of progesterone induces endometrial effects that are similar to those of systemic progestin, but it does not require the daily ingestion of medication and therefore has better compliance. Inserting an IUD in a fibroid uterus can be complicated, particularly if the cervix or lower portion of the uterus contains submucosal or intramural myomas that distort the uterine cavity. Such insertions are best handled by an experienced operator.

Whereas hormones and hormone receptors clearly play a role in myoma growth, the use of OCPs containing estrogen and progestin does not appear to cause increased myoma growth. Indeed, some investigators have identified a protective effect of OCP use on leiomyoma growth although this has not been a consistent finding of all such studies.[18–20] A case-control study of depot-medroxyprogesterone acetate (Depo-Provera) also demonstrated a protective effect of DMPA with regard to the development of myomas requiring surgical intervention.[21] Given the frequency of uterine myomas and the widespread use of oral contraception and other hormonal birth control methods, the paucity of data on their interaction is somewhat surprising. In clinical practice, such birth control methods do not seem to cause myoma growth in most cases.

Pain

Pain related to uterine fibroids results from a variety of mechanisms. In the absence of menorrhagia, intracavitary myomata may induce uterine contractions and cramping as the uterus tries to expel the "foreign" body. These contractions can be effective enough to actually cause vaginal expulsion of pedunculated intracavitary myomata, usually with a great deal of pain. Pain also results from the necrosis of the myoma, either when the tumor becomes large enough that the central core is relatively hypovascular or when a pedunculated myoma twists on its stalk, effectively cutting off its blood supply. Finally, if menorrhagia is present, the elevated prostaglandin levels in the menstrual blood, combined with the uterine contractions used to expel blood clots, can cause severe dysmenorrhea.

Regardless of the cause of pain, initial treatment for pain usually involves NSAIDs, followed by an escalation to narcotic-containing compounds such as acetaminophen with codeine or hydrocodone. Of course, the long-term risks of using such agents must be balanced against the risk of surgical intervention to relieve pain.

Infertility

Outpatient management of infertility related to uterine myomata consists primarily of proper diagnosis. In the subfertile couple presenting with a history of more than 1 year of unprotected intercourse without conception, careful attention must be paid to the presence of reasons other than myomas for their infertility. During the course of such evaluation, additional information that increases or decreases the likelihood that the problem is related to fibroids may be revealed. For example, hysterosalpingography (HSG) may demonstrate tubal obstruction from the presence of a cornual myoma, suggesting that a myomectomy could improve fertility. Alternatively, HSG that demonstrates tubal patency and a normal uterine contour would make myomectomy seem less likely to improve outcomes.

In many couples, however, a thorough evaluation may reveal no specific cause of infertility. The proper course of action in this case cannot be prescribed on the basis of high-quality data. There are no controlled trials comparing myomectomy to other treatments in cases like this, but case series do indicate that myomectomy may improve fertility in a patient with a negative infertility work-up and uterine fibroids.[7]

Other Medical Treatments

GONADOTROPIN-RELEASING HORMONE ANALOGUES

Gonadotrophin-releasing hormone analogues (Gn-RHAs) mimic the action of Gn-RH on the pituitary. After causing a transient increase in gonad-atrophins (luteinizing hormone [LH] and follicle-stimulating hormone [FSH]), they competitively inhibit native Gn-RH, causing LH and FSH levels to drop. This results in a drop in circulating estrogens and "pseudomenopause." The Gn-RHAs have been found to substantially reduce uterine size after use for several months.[22] However, myomas return to their pretreatment size within months after cessation of therapy. Furthermore, prolonged use of Gn-RHAs results in bone loss although this can be reduced or eliminated with supplemental hormone "add-back" therapy.[23]

MIFEPRISTONE

Mifepristone (RU 486) is a synthetic antiprogesterone that was shown to cause a decrease in fibroid volume in early clinical trials.[24] Mifepristone did not cause decreased bone density in these short-term trials; however, the clinical use of this drug must await a fuller elucidation of its method of action and long-term side effects.

SURGICAL TREATMENT

Hysterectomy

Medical therapy may fail to control symptoms in up to two-thirds of patients with bleeding and in a higher proportion of those with mass-related symptoms. Those women who fail or refuse medical therapy are candidates for more invasive treatments such as hysterectomy or myomectomy. Hysterectomy remains the predominant invasive treatment of uterine fibroids in the United States; between 177,000 and 366,000 hysterectomies are performed each year for this problem.[3,25] Hysterectomy is a relatively safe procedure (with a major complication rate of 1 to 2% and a death rate of 0.1%) and guarantees permanent relief from the symptoms of myomas.[26] It is, however, a major abdominal surgery and requires a substantial recovery period.

Although hysterectomy can be considered the definitive therapy for symptoms related to myomas, there are important groups of patients for whom it is not appropriate treatment. Women desiring fertility, for example, are not appropriate candidates for hysterectomy. Even among women who are past their childbearing years or for whom the desire to have children is not a consideration, there are many who reject the option of hysterectomy.[27] In this age of "patient activation" and informed decision making, there is no place for the paternalistic approach, taken by some gynecologists, that views hysterectomy as the only reasonable treatment option for women who no longer desire pregnancy.

There remains considerable debate about the role of the uterus in sexual functioning, with some physicians arguing that hysterectomy results in significant sexual dysfunction and others arguing that it does not. A recent study of sexual functioning after hysterectomy lends support to the idea that hysterectomy results in significant improvements in sexual function for most women, including an improved ability to achieve orgasm and increased satisfaction from sexual intercourse.[28] Hysterectomy cannot be said to be uniformly beneficial with regard to sexual function since the same study found that a significant minority of women have new problems with the enjoyment of sexual activity after hysterectomy.

Regardless of its measured effects on sexual function, hysterectomy has important psychological implications for many women, affecting their feelings of sexual identity, completeness, and sexual attractiveness. For many women, excessive bleeding that is untreatable by medical treatments is ample reason to have a hysterectomy. For others, only the presence of a known or suspected cancer seems an adequate reason for this surgery. Since uterine fibroids rarely cause subclinical medical problems, the decision to have a hysterectomy should be made by the clinician and patient in collaboration and should be based on the level of symptoms, response to other treatments, the patient's desired degree of assuredness that the symptoms will not recur, and other patient-specific considerations.[29]

Myomectomy

Myomectomy, or the surgical removal of a leiomyoma, may provide relief from symptoms without requiring hysterectomy. In particular, since the uterus is conserved, future childbearing may be possible; the sexual and psychological implications of hysterectomy may also be avoided. It is difficult to estimate the total number of myomectomies performed in the United States since these procedures often are not coded as being performed for uterine fibroids, but at least 35,000 to 40,000 transabdominal myomectomies are done in US hospitals each year.[3]

Myomectomy was first described in 1864 by Eugene Koeberle but it was not in common use until the 1940s. The most common current technique for myomectomy involves a low transverse abdominal incision made to gain access to the uterus. The myomas are individually identified and excised, after which the cut sections of the uterus are reapproximated. There have been no randomized trials comparing hysterectomy to myomectomy with regard to either efficacy or risks.[30] A literature-based comparison (Table 78–3),[7,25,31–35] relying on case series and nonrandomized trials, demonstrates that myomectomy has both advantages and disadvantages as compared to hysterectomy, with the principal advantage being retention of the uterus and the principal disadvantage being the relatively high rate of recurrent symptoms.

Laparoscopic Myomectomy

Myomectomy can sometimes be accomplished via laparoscopy although such an approach often limits the size and number of myomata that can be removed successfully as the procedure tends to be more technically demanding than open myomectomy. In the hands of skilled operators, however, even large myomas can be excised via laparoscopy, morcellated, and removed without abdominal incision. A small randomized trial and a second nonrandomized trial demonstrated similar short-term outcomes and a more rapid recovery with laparoscopic myomectomy than with open myomectomy.[36,37] Participants in the randomized trial could have no more than four myomas with a maximum diameter of 6 cm for each, so the generalizability of the results may be limited.[36]

Myolysis and Cryomyolysis

Myolysis, a laparoscopic procedure in which electric current is used to cause local necrosis of myomatous tissue, was introduced in the 1980s. It is not widely used, partly because of concern that electrocautery of the uterine surface might lead to postoperative adhesions. Cryomyolysis uses a liquid nitrogen probe to cause myoma necrosis but is otherwise similar to myolysis. Reports of uterine rupture during pregnancy after these procedures have led some clinicians to abandon their use.

Uterine Artery Embolization

Uterine artery embolization (UAE) is an emerging minimally invasive technique for reducing symptoms from uterine fibroids.[38] An angiography

TABLE 78–3. Comparative Outcomes of Hysterectomy and Myomectomy

Outcome	Hysterectomy[*]	Myomectomy[*]
Symptoms		
Menorrhagia (% of patients improved)	100	81 (40–93)
Anemia (% of patients improved)	100	ND
Pelvic pain (% of patients improved)	92–95	ND
Complications		
Death (per 10,000 procedures)	11 (4–36)	ND
Transfusion (% of patients receiving at least 1 unit)	(2–13)	(20–32)
Reoperation (embolization, myomectomy, hysterectomy)	(0.2–1.0)	1
Operative injury (% of patients experiencing injury to bowel, bladder, or ureter)	<1	<1
Venous thrombosis or pulmonary embolism (%)	<1	ND
Febrile morbidity (%)	15	13 (10–25)
Urinary tract infection (%)	(3–10)	3
Operative site infection (%)	7	<1
Wound infection (%)	(2–10)	<1
Recurrence of fibroids		
Not requiring surgical treatment (%)	0	15 (4–30)
Requiring hysterectomy or myomectomy (%)	0	10 (3–32)
Cost		
Charges		
Hospital ($)	5,400	4,900
Physician ($)	2,300	2,100
Indirect cost: lost workdays ($)	5,600	4,800
Length of hospital stay (days)	Abdominal: 4.2; vaginal: 2.8	3.3

[*]Estimates presented as a point estimate and range (in parentheses), with the point estimate representing a weighted average of the various studies.
If study measures were heterogeneous, estimates are given as range (in parentheses) only.
ND = No data or data inadequate to present meaningful estimates.
Adapted from Buttram and Reiter,[7] Lepine et al,[25] LaMorte et al,[31] Iverson et al,[32] Carlson et al,[33] Schofield et al,[34] and Graves.[35]

catheter is inserted into the patient's femoral artery, and a single uterine artery is then catheterized. Embolic material is released until the uterine vessel is occluded. The catheter is then maneuvered to the contralateral uterine artery, and the process is repeated. During the procedure, the patient is exposed to approximately 20 rads (20 cGy) of ionizing radiation to the ovaries (compared to 2 to 3 rads during a computed tomography [CT] scan of the pelvis; this exposure may fall with continued experience with UAE). Patients are observed for up to 24 hours post procedure. While this technique is still maturing, at least 4,000 such procedures have been performed in the United States to date. A literature review and uncontrolled comparison of the results of UAE to those of myomectomy showed a rough equivalence in terms of complications and short-term success.[39] Long-term outcomes have not been studied, and it is unclear if myomas will begin to grow again after the procedure, leading to recurrent symptoms.

PREGNANCY

Although the incidence of fibroids in the population of women of reproductive age is high, the incidence of uterine fibroids presenting in or complicating pregnancy appears to be quite low. In one study, only 2% of patients who had ultrasonographic evaluations during pregnancy were noted to have myomas.[40] This relatively low incidence of myomas found during pregnancy lends some support to the claim that fibroids commonly impair fertility. Approximately 10% of pregnant patients with uterine fibroids are admitted to a hospital during pregnancy for problems related to fibroids.[40]

The most common problem caused by fibroids during pregnancy is pain from infarction of the myoma. Patients with infarcted myomas usually present with focal abdominal pain, tenderness of the uterus on palpation, and (sometimes) low-grade fever and leukocytosis. Ultrasonography demonstrating the presence of a myoma at the site of pain usually confirms the diagnosis. However, irritation from the infarcted myoma can lead to peritonitis, mimicking other conditions such as appendicitis and ovarian torsion. Treatment is usually symptomatic, and opioids are often needed to provide adequate pain control. Pain usually subsides within days after the initial infarctive episode but may recur in up to 25% of cases. Infection of necrotic myomas may also occur, requiring broad-spectrum antibiotics or even delivery and hysterectomy, in refractory cases.[41]

Myomas, particularly the larger ones, are also associated with preterm delivery and midtrimester abortion although the specific level of risk is not clear. Lev-Toaff and colleagues found a correlation between placental implantation site and level of risk for preterm labor and abortion, with 9 of 35 patients with myomas under the implantation site having abortions, compared to 1 abortion among 54 patients with no contact between the placenta and the myoma.[42] Myomas, particularly those located in the lower uterine segment, may increase the likelihood of cesarean delivery. Care in these cases must be individualized as it is often difficult to predict the impact of even large fibroids on the course of labor.

MENOPAUSE

Because leiyomomas tend to grow during the reproductive years, many women enter menopause with an existing diagnosis of a fibroid uterus. For these women, menopause usually brings relief from symptoms. For asymptomatic women, simple pelvic examinations help to determine whether the myomatous uterus is decreasing in size. If a new diagnosis of fibroids is made after menopause or if a previously diagnosed fibroid uterus begins to enlarge after menopause, additional investigations should be performed to rule out other causes of uterine enlargement. In particular, ultrasonography or possibly MRI should be considered to distinguish an enlarging uterus from an adnexal mass. Although there is good evidence that premenopausal uterine growth is not a marker for uterine sarcoma, no such evidence exists for the post-menopausal-age group.[43] For this reason, invasive procedures (laparoscopy with biopsy or hysterectomy) may be reasonable in the clinical setting of fibroid enlargement after menopause.

Many women, having been told that their fibroids would shrink with menopause, are understandably reluctant to begin hormone replacement therapy (HRT), worrying that hormones will delay or prevent this shrinkage. Although the data are far from overwhelming, it does not appear that standard HRT causes uterine fibroids to grow. Some regimens may be more likely to cause fibroid growth than others. For those women for whom HRT is indicated but who are concerned about myoma growth, a trial period of HRT with pelvic examinations every 6 months may be a reasonable approach. If the uterus begins to enlarge or if symptoms (bleeding or bulk-related symptoms) worsen, either an alternative HRT regimen can be tried or the hormones can be discontinued and alternative treatments (either for menopausal symptoms or for reducing cardiovascular or osteoporotic risk) initiated.

RESOURCE

The American College of Obstetricians and Gynecologists
409 12th Street Southwest
PO Box 96920
Washington, DC 20090-6920
Telephone: (202) 863-2518
Web site: www.acog.org

The American College of Obstetricians and Gynecologists is the main professional organization of gynecologists in the United States. This organization collects and distributes information for both patients and clinicians on a wide variety of gynecologic topics, including uterine fibroids.

REFERENCES

1. Marshall LM, Spiegelman D, Barbieri RL, et al. Variation in the incidence of uterine leiomyoma among premenopausal women by age and race. Obstet Gynecol 1997;90:967–73.

2. Rowe M, Kanouse D, Mittman B, Bernstein S. Quality of life among women undergoing hysterectomies. Obstet Gynecol 1999;93:915–20.

3. National Center for Health Statistics. Ambulatory and inpatient procedures in the United States, 1996. Hyattsville (MD): Public Health Service; 1998. DHHS Publication No.: (PHS) 99-1710. Sponsored by the Dept. of Health and Human Services (US).

4. Gross, CP, Anderson GF, Powe NR. The relation between funding by the National Institutes of Health and the burden of disease. N Engl J Med 1999; 340:1881–7.

5. Greenberg MD, Tarek IG. Medical and socioeconomic impact of uterine fibroids. Obstet Gynecol Clin North Am 1995;22:625–37.

6. Townsend DE, Sparkes RS, Baluda MC, McClelland G. Unicellular histogenesis of uterine leiomyomas as determined by electrophoresis of glucose-6-phosphate dehydrogenase. Am J Obstet Gynecol 1970;107: 1168–73.

7. Buttram V, Reiter R. Uterine leiomyomata: etiology, symptomatology, and management. Fertil Steril 1981;36:433–45.

8. Ichimura T, Kawamura N, Ito F, et al. Correlation between the growth of uterine leiomyomata and estrogen and progesterone receptor content in needle biopsy specimens. Fertil Steril 1998;70:967–71.

9. Uterine leiomyomata. ACOG Technical Bulletin 1994;192:863–70.

10. Fields KR. Uterine myomas in adolescents: case reports and a review of the literature. J Pediatr Adolesc Gynecol 1996;9:195.

11. Parazzini F, La Vecchia C, Negri E. Epidemiologic characteristics of women with uterine fibroids: a case-control study. Obstet Gynecol 1988;72: 853–7.

12. Chimbira TH, Anderson AB, Turnbull AC. Relation between measured menstrual blood loss and patient's subjective assessment of loss, duration of bleeding, number of sanitary towels used, uterine weight and endometrial surface area. Br J Obstet Gynaecol 1980;87:603–9.

13. Schwarzler P, Concin H, Bosch H, et al. An evaluation of sonohysterography and diagnostic hysteroscopy for the assessment of intrauterine pathology. Ultrasound Obstet Gynecol 1998;11:337–42.

14. Reinhold C, Tafazoli F, Mehio A, et al. Uterine adenomyosis: endovaginal US and MR imaging features with histopathologic correlation. Radiographics 1999;19:S147–60.

15. Herbst A, Mishell D, Droegemueller W. Comprehensive gynecology. 2nd ed. St. Louis: Mosby; 1992.

16. Thompson JD, Rock JA. Te Linde's operative gynecology. 7th ed. Philadelphia: JB Lippincott; 1992.

17. Smith-Bindman R, Kerlikowske K, Feldstein VA, et al. Endovaginal ultrasound to exclude endometrial cancer and other endometrial abnormalities. JAMA 1998;280:1510–7.

18. Marshall LM, Spiegelman D, Goldman MB, et al. A prospective study of reproductive factors and oral contraceptive use in relation to the risk of uterine leiomyomata. Fertil Steril 1998;70:432–9.

19. Chiaffarino F, Parazzini F, La Vecchia C, et al. Use of oral contraceptives and uterine fibroids: results from a case-control study. Br J Obstet Gynaecol 1999; 106:857–60.

20. Chiaffarino F, Parazzini F, La Vecchia C, et al. Oral contraceptive use and benign gynecologic conditions. Contraception 1998;57(1):11–8.

21. Lumbiganon P, Rugpao S, Phandhu-fung S, et al. Protective effect of depot-medroxyprogesterone acetate on surgically treated uterine leiomyomas: a multi-centre case-control study. Br J Obstet Gynaecol 1996; 103:909–14.

22. Vercellini P, Maddalena S, De Giorgi O, et al. Abdominal myomectomy for infertility: a comprehensive review. Hum Reprod 1998;13:873–9.

23. Hornstein MD, Surrey ES, Weisberg GW, Casino LA. Leuprolide acetate and hormonal add-back in endometriosis: a 12-month study. Obstet Gynecol 1998; 91:16–24.

24. Murphy AA, Morales AJ, Kettel LM, Yen SS. Regression of uterine leiomyomata to the antiprogesterone RU486: dose-response effect. Fertil Steril 1995; 64(1):187–90.

25. Lepine LA, Hillis SD, Marchbanks PA, et al. Hysterectomy surveillance—United States 1980–1993. MMWR CDC Surveill Summ 1997;46(4):1–15.

26. Bernstein S, Fiske M, McGlynn E, Gifford D. Hysterectomy: A review of the literature on indications, effectiveness, and risks. Santa Monica (CA): RAND; 1997. Publication No.: MR-592/2-AHCPR.

27. Scialli A. Alternatives to hysterectomy for benign conditions. Int J Fertil Womens Med 1998; 43:186–91.

28. Rhodes JC, Kjerulff KH, Langenberg PW, Guzinski GM. Hysterectomy and sexual functioning. JAMA 1999;282:1934–41.

29. Sutton C. Treatment of large uterine fibroids. Br J Obstet Gynaecol 1996;103:494–6.

30. Wilcox L, Lepine L, Kieke B. Comparisons of hysterectomy or myomectomy for uterine leiomyoma among US women. AHSR and FHSR Ann Mtg Abstract Book 1995;12:119.

31. LaMorte A, Lalwani S, Diamond M. Morbidity associated with abdominal myomectomy. Obstet Gynecol 1993;82:897–900.

32. Iverson R, Chelmow D, Strohbehn K, et al. Relative morbidity of abdominal hysterectomy and myomectomy for management of uterine leiomyomas. Obstet Gynecol 1996;88:415–9.

33. Carlson KJ, Miller BA, Fowler FJ Jr. The Maine women's health study: I. Outcomes of hysterectomy. Obstet Gynecol 1994;83:556–65.

34. Schofield MJ, Bennett A, Redman S, et al. Self-reported long-term outcomes of hysterectomy. Br J Obstet Gynecol 1991;98:1129–36.

35. Graves EJ. National hospital discharge summary: annual summary. 1990. Vital Health Stat 1992; 13:112–24.

36. Mais V, Ajossa S, Guerriero S, et al. Laparoscopic versus abdominal myomectomy: a prospective, randomized trial to evaluate benefits in early outcome. Am J Obstet Gynecol 1996;174:654–8.

37. Stringer N, Walker J, Meyer P. Comparison of 49 laparoscopic myomectomies with 49 open myomectomies. J Am Assoc Gynecol Laparosc 1997;4:457–64.

38. Goodwin S, Vedantham S, McLucas B, et al. Preliminary experience with uterine fibroid embolization for uterine fibroids. J Vasc Interv Radiol 1997;8:517–26.

39. Broder MS, Harris K, Morton S, et al. Uterine Artery Embolization: a systematic review of the literature and proposal for research Santa Monica (CA): RAND; 1999 Aug. RAND Report No.: MR-1138.

40. Katz VL, Dotters DJ, Droegemueller W. Complications of uterine leiomyomas in pregnancy. Obstet Gynecol 1989;73:593-6.

41. Cunningham FG, MacDonald PC, Gant NF, editors. Williams obstetrics. 18th ed. Norwalk (CT): Appleton & Lange; 1989. p. 387–91

42. Lev-Toaff AS, Coleman BG, Arger PH, et al. Leiomyomas in pregnancy: sonographic study. Radiology 1987;164:375.

43. Parker WH, Fu YS, Berek JS. Uterine sarcoma in patients operated on for presumed leiomyoma and rapidly growing leiomyoma. Obstet Gynecol 1994; 83:414–8.

79

ENDOMETRIOSIS

Alan H. DeCherney, MD, and Gayane Ambartsumyan, MD

Endometriosis was first described in the medical literature in 1690 by the German physician Daniel Shroen.[1] However, it was not until the twentieth century that it was recognized as a relatively common condition. In 1921 J.A. Sampson described lesions of ectopic tissue functionally similar to endometrium and called them "adenomas of the endometrial type." In 1927 Sampson first used the term "endometriosis" to describe functional endometrial tissue outside the uterus.[2]

Endometriosis is almost always diagnosed in women of reproductive ages, the mean age of diagnosis being from 25 to 29 years although endometriosis has been reported in postmenopausal women and adolescents.[3,4] Endometriosis is commonly confined to the pelvis. The most frequently involved sites are the ovaries, uterosacral ligaments, cul de sac, and uterovesicular peritoneum. Endometriosis can extend beyond the pelvis, as well as into the myometrium. Myometrial endometriosis is termed "adenomyosis."

The exact incidence of endometriosis is difficult to establish because it is often asymptomatic and therefore undiagnosed. The limited number of studies available report a prevalence of 1.8 to 6.2% in the general population and 2 to 11.2% in women of reproductive ages undergoing surgery for genitourinary problems.[5–7] Endometriosis has been reported in 25% of women undergoing laparoscopy for pelvic pain, 20% of women with infertility, and 4.1% of women undergoing tubal ligation.[8]

PATHOPHYSIOLOGY

The pathophysiologic mechanism of endometriosis is still debated. The direct transplantation theory, originally proposed by Sampson, remains the most clinically accepted. Sampson believed that viable endometrial cells in menstrual effluate transplant to ectopic sites and cause endometriosis.[9] In support of this theory, viable endometrial cells have been demonstrated both in menstrual discharge and in the peritoneal fluid of the majority of menstruating women.[10,11]

But how do endometrial cells disseminate to cause endometriosis? Transtubal dissemination appears to be the most likely route, as was first proposed by Sampson[2] in the 1920s and later supported by many others. This hypothesis is supported by evidence that retrograde menstruation does in fact occur in almost all women,[12,13] that there is an association between obstructed menstrual flow and endometriosis,[13] that women with short menstrual cycles and long flows have an increased incidence of endometriosis,[14] and that endometriosis is most commonly found in dependent parts of the pelvis. Another possible route of endometrial cell dissemination is through vascular and lymphatic channels;[15] this is supported by rare occurrences of endometriosis in distant sites such as the brain and lungs. It also appears that endometriosis can be induced iatrogenically via mechanical transplantation, based on numerous reports of endometriosis in episiotomy and laparotomy scars after gynecologic and obstetric procedures.[16]

Others have proposed that endometriosis occurs because multipotential coelomic epithelial cells undergo metaplastic transformation into endometrial glandular cells. This could account for the occurrence of endometriosis anywhere in the abdominal and thoracic cavity. The theory is supported by rare reports of endometriosis in men on high-dose estrogen,[17] in prepubertal girls,[18] and in women who have never menstruated.[19] Evidence for this theory remains scanty.

Immunologic factors have also been implicated in the pathophysiology of endometriosis. Retrograde menstruation is a nearly universal phenomenon in almost all women, yet not everyone develops endometriosis. Since normal immune surveillance involves the disposal of tissue fragments, endometriosis could be caused by decreased immunologic clearance of viable endometrial cells during menstruation. This immune derangement might be either humoral, with increased circulating autoantibodies, or cell mediated, with increased peritoneal macrophage activation, decreased T-lymphocyte reactivity, and decreased natural killer (NK) cell activity.[20,21] In fact, correlations between endometriosis and immune alterations have been described many times in literature; however, there is still not enough evidence to determine whether these changes cause endometriosis, result from it, or are merely coincidental.

Genetic factors may also influence susceptibility to endometriosis. Simpson et al demonstrated a sevenfold increase in the risk of endometriosis in first-degree relatives of patients as compared to a control group.[22] Furthermore, two different studies demonstrated a 75 to 87% concordance in monozygotic twins.[23,24] There is no specifically identified mendelian inheritance pattern. In fact, many scientists have postulated a multifactorial inheritance pattern, implying that endometriosis is caused by an interaction between multiple genes and the environment.[25,26] The Oxford Endometriosis Gene (OXE-GENE) Study is an international collaborative project that seeks to identify a susceptibility locus by using linkage analysis.[25] If the gene can be identified, functional analysis of it may lead to a better understanding of the pathophysiology of this disease.

HISTORY AND PHYSICAL EXAMINATION

There are a number of clinical signs and symptoms that are associated with endometriosis, the classic triad being dysmenorrhea, dyspareunia, and infertility (Table 79–1). Some women with endometriosis are asymptomatic.

Dysmenorrhea, generally a nonspecific symptom, is more suggestive of endometriosis when it begins after several years of relatively pain-free menses.[27] The pain is typically cyclical and progressive, starting within a couple of days of the onset of the menstrual flow and extending through menses for several days afterwards.[28] Patients with severe endometriosis may have constant pain throughout the menstrual cycle.

The usual location of pain is in the low abdominal and deep pelvic area but can be elsewhere, depending on the anatomic location of disease. Although there is a strong correlation between deep infiltrating endometriosis and severe pelvic pain,[29] there is no other correlation between the extent of the disease and the severity of pain. In fact, some women with extensive disease may have minimal or no pain whereas others with only minimal disease may have severe pelvic pain.[30] Dyspareunia is mainly associated with deep penetration and may become severe enough to preclude vaginal intercourse. It is usually associated with endometriosis in the cul-de-sac, uterosacral ligament, or vagina.[28]

Studies report that 20 to 50% of women with infertility have endometriosis.[8,31] Given such high association, many studies have addressed possible mechanisms of infertility in endometriosis. In fact, in moderate to severe disease, the mechanism of infertility is easily explained by the mechanical effects of adhesions or ovarian cysts that block tubo-ovarian motility and migration of the ovum.

TABLE 79–1. Common Symptoms and Signs of Endometriosis

Symptoms
    Dysmenorrhea
    Chronic pelvic pain
    Dyspareunia
    Infertility
    Extrapelvic
        Gastrointestinal: cyclical abdominal pain, dyschezia, hematochezia, bowel obstruction
        Genitourinary: hematuria, dysuria, obstruction
        Pulmonary: chest pain, hemoptysis, shortness of breath
        Neural: headaches, seizures, sciatica
Signs
    Cul-de-sac nodularity and tenderness
    Fixed ovarian mass
    Retroverted, fixed, and tender
    Unilateral ovarian enlargement uterus
    Diffuse or focal abdominal tenderness

The association between minimal or mild disease and infertility, however, is more difficult to explain and is still controversial. Some investigators believe that the relationship is merely casual whereas other believe it is causal. If the relationship is causal, however, its mechanism still needs to be elucidated since adhesions are unlikely to occur in mild disease. The postulated mechanisms are various and include pituitary-ovarian dysfunction, ovum uptake inhibition, oviduct dysfunction, recurrent abortion, decreased implantation, modified response of the immune system, and endoperitoneal inflammation.[32–35] The exact mechanism of infertility in mild endometriosis, however, is yet to be determined due to the lack of strong evidence in support of these theories.

Endometriosis may also affect nongynecologic organs. The gastrointestinal tract is the most common extrapelvic site,[36] but the disease can also manifest in the genitourinary tract, the thorax,[28] and the nervous system.[37,38] Associated symptoms are described in more detail in Table 79–1.

Physical examination is most informative if performed while the patient is symptomatic. Therefore, examination during menstruation may be best for detecting and localizing areas suspected of endometriosis.[28] The external genitalia should be examined for endometriosis, although occurrence here is very rare. On bimanual examination, tender nodules and fibrosis may be detected in the upper vagina, cul-de-sac, uterosacral ligament, or rectovaginal septum. Unilateral ovarian enlargement may also be noted. The uterus may be retroverted, fixed, and tender in more advanced cases. Abdominal examination may also demonstrate tenderness. It is extremely important to remember, however, that *many women with endometriosis have a completely normal clinical examination.*

DIAGNOSTIC TESTS

The diagnosis of endometriosis cannot be established from history and physical examination alone.[28] The differential diagnosis of endometriosis is extensive; a typical presentation includes pelvic inflammatory disease (PID), ectopic pregnancy, ovarian tumors, adenomyosis, myomas, hernias, interstitial cystitis, and irritable bowel syndrome (IBS). Atypical presentations may mimic a wide range of illnesses. Certain tests, such as ultrasonography, magnetic resonance imaging (MRI), and assays of CA 125 levels may aid in diagnosing endometriosis, but a definite diagnosis is established only by direct visualization and by biopsy of lesions during laparoscopy or laparotomy.

Currently available laboratory tests do not have the necessary sensitivity to serve as reliable screening tests for endometriosis. Many studies suggest that serum levels of CA 125, a marker found on derivatives of the coelomic epithelium and used for the prognosis of epithelial ovarian carcinoma, are higher in women with moderate to severe endometriosis. Some studies suggest that reliable results can be obtained during the late luteal phase,[39] some studies refute this[40] whereas others suggest using increased levels of CA 125 during menstruation and a ratio of 1.5 of menstrual to follicular phase CA 125 to increase the sensitivity for detecting endometriosis.[41] Nevertheless, none of these methods have been proven to be reliable for initial diagnosis as only 20 to 50% of women with endometriosis are identified by CA 125 testing.[42]

However, CA 125 levels can be used as markers for response to treatment and recurrence[43] and, when combined with transvaginal ultrasonography, may be helpful in differentiating endometriomas from benign adnexal cysts.[44] Finally, a recent meta-analysis suggested that the routine use of CA 125 testing in subfertile women may be justified because it can identify a subgroup of patients who are likely to benefit from laparoscopy. In the meantime, the quest for a reliable marker continues and has been extended to various proteins, including CA 72, CA 19-9, placental protein 14, and antiendometrial antibodies.[42]

Transvaginal ultrasonography, computed tomography (CT), or MRI can also provide additional information, but only laparoscopy can be used to determine the primary diagnosis. Indications for laparoscopy depend on the presenting symptoms. Patients who have been infertile for more than 1 year without symptoms or for more than 6 months with symptoms or who are older than 35 years of age are candidates for laparoscopy. Other indications for laparoscopy include pelvic pain unresponsive to nonsteroidal anti-inflammatory drugs (NSAIDs) and/or oral contraceptive pills (OCPs) for 3 months and an adnexal mass suspected of being an endometrioma (if the lesion has not resolved within 3 months).[45]

During laparoscopy, the pelvic and abdominal cavity is systematically inspected for peritoneal or retroperitoneal implants, adhesions, and endometriomas. Typical implants are pigmented and are dark "powder-burn" "gunshot" nodules surrounded by a thick fibrotic patch of peritoneum. Interestingly, histologic evaluation of these typical lesions is reported to be negative in 7 to 24% of cases, thus demonstrating the need for biopsy.[46,47] Endometriosis can also appear as atypical nonpigmented lesions as described in Table 79–2.[48] Adhesions induced by endometriosis may be encountered anywhere in the peritoneal cavity. Once identified, adhesions are assessed and mobilized. It is particularly important to evaluate adhesions on the ovaries and fallopian tubes of infertility patients.

Endometriomas are identified by a careful inspection of both ovaries. If adhesions are present, they are lysed to help in visualizing the ovary. In fact, a 97% sensitivity and a 95% specificity are reported for the visual diagnosis of endometriomas,[49] which are dark smooth-walled brownish cysts. Upon incision, a viscous "chocolate fluid" composed of hemosiderin derived from old intraovarian hemorrhage is released. Despite the high specificity of these typical lesions, biopsy is necessary because of the possibility of a hemorrhagic corpus luteum cyst or a malignancy. Finally, the bowel should be carefully inspected, given the possibility of implants on the rectum, sigmoid colon, caecum, appendix, and terminal ileum.

CLASSIFICATION

Once the diagnosis of endometriosis is made, the extent of the disease should be properly documented since both treatment and prognosis is determined by the severity of the disease. A uniform classification system was developed by the American Society for Reproductive Medicine (ASRM) in 1979.[50] It was revised in 1985 and again in 1996 to make it more standardized, based on (1) the appearance, size, and depth of peritoneal and ovarian implants; (2) the presence, extent, and type of adnexal adhesions; and (3) the degree of cul-de-sac obliteration[51,52] (Tables 79–3 and 79–4). While this classification system is a good predictor of the extent and the location of disease, also taking into account atypical lesions of endometriosis, it still remains of limited use in predicting both pain and the likelihood of pregnancy.[53,54] In addition, there is also a high intra- and interobserver variability in using this classification system. Therefore, as experience accumulates along with an improved understanding of the disease

TABLE 79–2. Endometriotic Lesions: Type and Specificity

Type of Visualized Lesion	% True Endometriosis*
Peritoneal or retroperitoneal implants	
Typical (pigmented)	76–93
"Powder burn" "gunshot" nodules	—
Black, dark brown, or bluish nodules	—
Atypical (nonpigmented)	45–81
Red flamelike lesions	81
Translucent glandular lesions	57
White opacified peritoneum (often thickened and raised)	81
Serous and clear vesicles	—
Subovarian adhesions	—
Yellow-brown peritoneal patches	47
Circular peritoneal defects	45
Endometriosis-induced adhesions	—
Endometriomas	
Viscous dark-brown "chocolate cyst"	95

*Confirmed by histology.
Adapted from JansenRP, Russell P. Nonpigmented endometriosis: clinical laparoscopic and pathologic definition. Am J Obstet Gynecol 1986;155:1154–9.

TABLE 79–3. American Society for Reproductive Medicine Revised Classification of Endometriosis

Finding	No. of Points
Peritoneal lesions	
< 1 cm	
Superficial	1
Deep	2
1–3 cm	
Superficial	2
Deep	4
> 3 cm	
Superficial	4
Deep	6
Ovarian lesions[*]	
< 1 cm	
Superficial	1
Deep	4
1–3 cm	
Superficial	2
Deep	16
> 3 cm	
Superficial	4
Deep	20
Ovarian adhesions[*]	
< ⅓ enclosure	
Filmy	1
Dense	4
⅓–⅔ enclosure	
Filmy	2
Dense	8
> ⅔ enclosure	
Filmy	4
Dense	16
Tubal adhesions[†]	
< ⅓ enclosure	
Filmy	1
Dense	4
⅓–⅔ enclosure	
Filmy	2
Dense	8
> ⅔ enclosure	
Filmy	4
Dense	16
Posterior cul-de-sac obliteration	
Partial	4
Complete	40

[*]Both the right and the left ovary should be scored.
[†]Both the right and the left tube should be scored.
Adapted from Revised American Society for Reproductive Medicine Classification of endometriosis: 1996. Fertil Steril 1997;67:817.

TABLE 79–4. American Society for Reproductive Medicine Revised Staging of Endometriosis

Stage	Points
I (minimal)	1–5
II (mild)	6–15
III (moderate)	16–40
IV (severe)	> 40

process, there will be a need for an improved classification system.

TREATMENT

The indications for treatment of endometriosis are pelvic pain, pelvic pathology (such as an ovarian cyst), abnormal bleeding, and infertility. The severity of symptoms, the stage of the disease, and the woman's desire for future fertility should be considered when planning therapy. The objectives of therapy are to relieve symptoms, improve or destroy implants, maintain or restore fertility, and avoid or delay the recurrence of the disease.[45] Despite numerous developments in medical and surgical approaches for treating endometriosis, an optimal therapy has yet to be established. Several management options are available; these can be categorized as observational, medical, surgical, or a combination of the latter two.

Observation

Expectant management may be appropriate in an asymptomatic patient. Many suggest that prophylactic treatment of endometriosis should be considered in young women, to preserve future reproductive function.[55] However, there is no evidence to suggest that such treatment has an impact on future fertility or that the lack of such treatment is associated with any future decline in fertility.[56]

Analgesic Therapy

Dysmenorrhea and pelvic pain associated with endometriosis have been postulated to be secondary to prostaglandin synthesis by the ectopic endometrium.[55] Because they inhibit the synthesis of prostaglandins, NSAIDs can alleviate the symptoms of pain. These drugs are inexpensive and are generally well tolerated without any significant side effects. Therefore, they can be used as first-line treatment for women with minimal symptoms. Ibuprofen (up to 2,400 mg/d) or naproxen sodium (up to 1,100 mg/d) are used with most patients.[57]

Hormonal Therapy

Both uterine endometrium and endometriotic tissue contain estrogen and progesterone receptors and respond to hormonal stimulation through these receptors.[58] Although the biochemical and histologic distribution, enzyme activity, and receptor levels of endometriotic tissue often are different from those of normal endometrium,[43] hormonal medications that suppress endometrial growth remain the basis of effective therapy for endometriosis.

ORAL CONTRACEPTIVES

Based on the observation that endometriosis seems to regress during pregnancy and the fact that endometriotic tissue contains binding sites for estrogen and progesterone, a "pseudopregnancy" regimen of daily oral contraceptives was introduced to create an anovulatory acyclic hormonal environment for the resolution of endometriotic implants.[59] The aim of the therapy was to create an environment of constantly high levels of progestins, such as seen in pregnancy, to thin the ectopic endometrium and cause its regression with progressive decidualization, necrobiosis, and resorption. High-dose regimens were used initially, but with experience, low-dose oral contraceptives were recognized to have similar desired effects, but fewer side effects. Currently, the accepted regimen is 20 to 35 µg of an ethinyl estradiol–containing oral contraceptive, used continuously for 6 to 9 months. The treatment is started at one daily tablet, with an objective to induce amenorrhea, and is increased to two tablets if breakthrough bleeding occurs.[55] The maximum dose should not exceed two tablets because of increased side effects.

Symptomatic relief of endometriosis has been reported in 75 to 100% of cases, although some patients may experience increased pelvic pain secondary to the estrogenic component of the treatment within the first 2 months. This therapy, unfortunately, is supportive rather than curative and has a first-year recurrence rate of almost 20% following the termination of therapy.[60] The most common side effects include depression, weight gain, breakthrough bleeding, and bloating. This treatment is currently reserved for short-term management of mild endometriosis or postoperative management in women who do not desire immediate fertility and who cannot tolerate other treatments.

PROGESTINS

Because of the side effects associated with the use of estrogen-containing oral contraceptives, progestogen-only regimens have been used for the past two decades.[55] Progestogens work by suppressing gonadotropin release, which in turn inhibits ovarian steroidogenesis and produces amenorrhea. In addition, these pills are effective because they cause decidualization and subsequent atrophy of endometrial tissue.[61] Vercellini et al showed that the efficacy of progestins was comparable to that of other treatments for the temporary relief of pelvic pain associated with endometriosis. Furthermore, they have the advantage of being inexpensive. Breakthrough bleeding (the principal side effect of progesterone regimens) has limited their use.

Many options for progestin treatment currently exist, and there are no data to suggest that any particular agent or dose is preferable to another. Medroxyprogesterone acetate (MPA) at a starting dosage of 30 mg/d for 3 months has been shown to be effective in both managing pain and infertility associated with stage I and II endometriosis.[62] The most common side effect with this regimen is spotting and breakthrough bleeding. Other side effects are depression, weight gain, and bloating. Larger doses of MPA have also been used but without any improvement in effectiveness. An injection of MPA at 150 mg every 3 months for 1 year has resulted in significant improvement of pain symptoms.[63] However, because of the prolonged interval of resumption of menstruation after the discontinuation of therapy, this regimen is not recommended for younger women who desire pregnancy. Several other progestin regimens, including lynestrenol, megestrol acetate, and dydrogesterone, have been used to treat endometriosis (Table 79–5).

DANAZOL

Danazol is a derivative of 17α-ethinyl testosterone that acts via several mechanisms to treat endometriosis. The pharmacologic properties of danazol include (1) direct inhibition of gonadotropin release and steroidogenesis, (2) binding to sex hormone binding and corticosteroid binding globulin to free native testosterone for acting against implants,

TABLE 79–5. Effective Medical Regimens for Endometriosis-Associated Pain

Type of Medication	Route	Dosage	Duration of Use
NSAIDs			—
Ibuprofen	PO	Max 2,400 mg/d	
Naproxen sodium	PO	Max 1,100 mg/d	
Oral contraceptives			6–9 mo
Ethinyl estradiol	PO	20–35 μg/d	
Progestogens			3 mo
MPA	PO	30 mg/d	
Megestrol acetate	PO	40 mg/d	
Lynestrenol	PO	10 mg/d	
Dydrogesterone	PO	20–30 mg/d	
Antiprogestins			6 mo
Mifepristone (RU-486)	PO	50 mg/d	
Danazol	PO	600 mg/d	6 mo
Gn-RH agonists[*]			3 mo
Leuprolide	SQ	500 μg/d	
	IM	3.75 mg/mo or 11.24 mg/3 mo	
	IN	400 μg × 4/d	
Nafarelin	IM	3 mg/mo	
	IN	200 μg × 2/d	
Goserelin	SQ	3.6 mg/mo or 10.8 mg/3 mo	
Histrelin	SQ	100 μg/d	
Buserlin	SQ	200 μg/d	
	IN	300 μg × 4/d	
Decapeptyl	IM	3 mg/mo	
Tryptorelin	IM	2–4 mg/mo	
Add-back regimen 1			
Leuprolide	IM	3.75 mg/mo	24 mo
Estrogen	PO	0.625 mg/d	3–24 mo
MPA	PO	2.5 mg/d	3–24 mo
Add-back regimen 2			
Nafarelin	PO	400 mg/d	6 mo
Norethisterone	PO	1.2 mg/d	Cont over 12 mo
Gestrinone	PO	1.25 or 2.5 mg × 2/week	6 mo

[*]The biologic efficacy of Gn-RH agonists administered by a nasal formulation is only 2 to 5% of that obtained through the subcutaneous route.
PO = per os (oral); SQ = subcutaneous; IM = intramuscular; IN = intranasal; NSAIDs = nonsteroidal anti-inflammatory drugs; Max = maximum; MPA = medroxyprogesterone acetate; Gn-RH = gonadotropin-releasing hormone; Cont = continue.

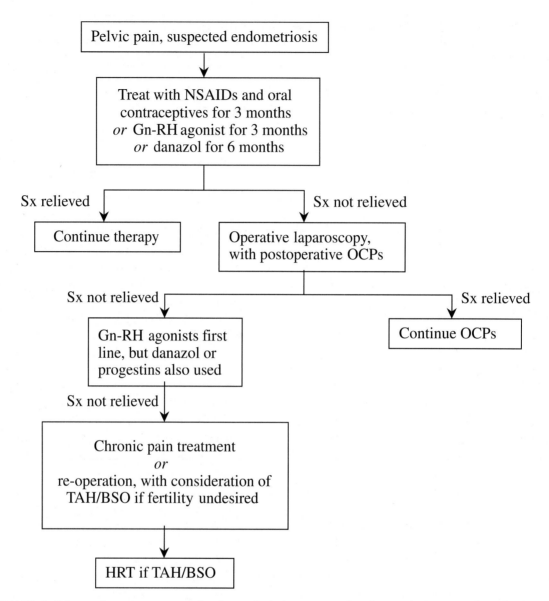

FIGURE 79–1. Schema for management of endometriosis in women who do not desire immediate fertility. BSO = bilateral salpingo-oophorectomy; Gn-RH = gonadotropin-releasing hormone; HRT = hormone replacement therapy; NSAIDs = nonsteroidal anti-imflammatory drugs; OCPs = oral contraceptive pills; Sx = symptoms; TAH = total abdominal hysterectomy.

(3) direct inhibition of implant growth by binding to its androgen and progesterone receptors, and (4) increased metabolic clearance of estradiol and progesterone.[55,60] Through these multiple effects, this drug creates an anovulatory, amenorrheic, high-androgen, and low-estrogen environment similar to menopause and hostile to the growth of the endometrial implants.

The hormonal changes that result from the administration of danazol produce significant pain relief in patients with endometriosis. An improve-ment of pelvic pain in up to 90% of women with mild to moderate endometriosis has been reported after 6 months of therapy.[64] The effect of danazol on endometrial implants also has been studied. Data collected from several second-look laparoscopic studies revealed 100% resolution of minimal to mild endometriosis and 50 to 70% resolution in severe cases.

Danazol is not, however, effective in treating pain that is secondary to pelvic adhesions. Further-more, it has no benefit in treating endometriomas

>1 cm in diameter.[65] Pregnancy rates after danazol therapy vary, depending on the population, the presence of other factors, and the severity of disease. In fact, for minimal or mild disease, danazol therapy has no advantage over expectant management.[66] Combining medical and surgical treatments may maximize the benefits of danazol.

Initially, danazol was prescribed at a dosage of 800 mg/d for 6 months or longer, but dosages of 400 to 600 mg/d were later shown to be equally effective. Currently, 600 mg/d for 6 months is recommended although therapeutic levels should be adjusted individually, depending on side effects and the extent of the disease. Danazol may cause virilization of the external genitalia of female fetuses when it is given during pregnancy. For this reason, most clinicians start therapy immediately after a normal menstrual period. Women receiving danazol therapy should also use barrier contraceptives during the course of their treatment.[55]

Danazol is associated with a variety of side effects that limit its use for endometriosis. The most common side effects include weight gain, fluid retention, acne, hirsutism, flushing, decreased breast size, and mood changes.[66] Breakthrough bleeding may also occur at dosages below 400 mg/d. Danazol also adversely affects the lipid profile, decreasing high-density lipoprotein (HDL) and increasing low-density lipoprotein (LDL). Hepatic dysfunction with elevated liver enzymes has also been reported with danazol use. Fortunately, these side effects are reversible within a few months of the discontinuation of therapy.

Gonadotropin-Releasing Hormone Agonist

Gonadotropin-releasing hormone (Gn-RH) is produced and released from the anterior hypothalamus in a pulsatile fashion. It then reaches the anterior pituitary through the portal system, where it stimulates the synthesis and secretion of leutenizing hormone (LH) and follicle-stimulating hormone (FSH). It is this pulsatile release of Gn-RH that results in the release of LH and FSH from the anterior pituitary.

Endogenous Gn-RH is rapidly cleaved by peptidases at positions 6 and 9; thus it has a very short half-life of 3.5 minutes.[43] Agonists with an increased potency and half-life are synthesized by altering the amino acids at these locations. The continuous administration of these much stronger agonists results in a paradoxic downregulation of LH and FSH release from the pituitary, leading to the suppression of ovarian steroid production and a medically induced state of "pseudomenopause."

Various Gn-RH agonists have been synthesized for treating endometriosis (see Table 79–5). They all produce amenorrhea and anovulation, which provides the basis for their use in endometriosis. Analogues of Gn-RH were first used in 1981 in clinical trials for the treatment of endometriosis,[67] nafarelin being the first analogue to be introduced in the United States.[55] Since the introduction of these drugs, several large well-designed studies have compared them with danazol. Both medications are equally effective in improving the symptoms of endometriosis and reducing the extent of the disease as determined by the ASRM classification score,[68-70] yet Gn-RH agonists do not produce the weight changes, fluid retention, and changes in lipid profiles often associated with danazol therapy.

The adverse effects observed with Gn-RH agonists are limited to the hypoestrogenic state and include hot flushes, vaginal dryness, and loss of vertebral trabecular bone. It is important to note that all these side effects are reversible although restoration of bone density may sometimes take over a year.[71] As with danazol, Gn-RH agonists therapy does not improve fertility in patients with minimal to mild endometriosis.[72]

Initial trials of Gn-RH agonist therapy were a 6-month course based on the traditional regimen for danazol, which relieved symptoms within 4 to 8 weeks of the initiation of therapy. To reduce the effect of the drug on bone metabolism, a shorter duration of therapy was evaluated. A comparison of 3 months versus 6 months of therapy in several clinical trials showed no significant differences in relief of pain between the two regimens.[73]

To further reduce the undesirable side effects of hypoestrogenism on bone metabolism and the vasomotor system, the possibility of administering a progestational agent and/or estrogen in addition to Gn-RH has been entertained. The rationale is based on the differences in threshold of serum estradiol levels for the suppression of endometriosis and the maintenance of normal bone metabolism.[74] Bone loss starts at serum estradiol levels <15 pg/mL, whereas preliminary evidence suggests that supressing serum estradiol to levels of up to 30 pg/mL may still be clinically effective to treat pelvic pain associated with endometriosis. The goal, therefore, is to use Gn-RH to treat endometriosis while maintaining the estradiol levels in the range of 15 to 30 pg/mL to prevent bone loss. This can be achieved either by low-dose progestin or estrogen/progestin "add-back" regimens or by the adjustment of the Gn-RH agonist dose to achieve the desired levels.

Add-back therapy to Gn-RH with a combination of estrogen and progestogen has been shown to be as effective as Gn-RH agonists alone for relieving pelvic symptoms of endometriosis and for attenuating both the loss of bone mineral density and the physiologic side effects of hot flushes and vaginal dryness.[75,76] In fact, because of the add-back therapy, a longer duration of Gn-RH therapy may be tolerated by women, without side effects (see Table 79–5).

Low-dose Gn-RH agonist therapy, also known as "draw-back" therapy, has also been evaluated; full-dose Gn-RH therapy is administered for several weeks to downregulate the pituitary, then a lower dose of the same agonist is administered for the remainder of 6 months. Studies show favorable results with decreased side effects, but more controlled clinical trials are needed to confirm the findings.[77,78]

ANTIPROGESTINS

Antiprogestins are steroid compounds that bind to progesterone receptors and exert antiprogesterone and antiglucocorticoid activities. Mifepristone, also known as RU 486, is the only clinically available antiprogestin. Mifepristone works by inhibiting ovulation and disrupting endometrial integrity. Administration of RU 486 at a dose of 100 mg/d for 3 months and 50 mg/d for 6 months has been evaluated in two pilot studies.[79,80] Both studies reported significant decreases in pelvic pain lasting throughout the therapy, decreased implants on follow-up laparoscopic assessment, and maintenance of bone mineral density.

The side effects of RU 486 use include atypical flushes, anorexia, and fatigue. Increased serum cortisol levels have been demonstrated at the 100-mg/d dosage. A study of a 50-mg/d dosage documented no changes in serum cortisol levels, with preservation of the normal circadian rhythm. These preliminary results demonstrate that the administration of RU 486 at a daily dosage of 50 mg may provide a safe treatment for endometriosis. Larger clinical

trials, however, are necessary to confirm these reports.

GESTRINONE

Gestrinone is a progesterone agonist/antagonist (derived from 19-nortestosterone) that decreases the secretion of FSH and LH.[66] The actions of gestrinone are similar to those of danazol, and so are some of the side effects.[81] However, gestrinone does not affect the lipid profile nor does it change the liver function test. Gestrinone thus compares favorably to danazol, but with decreased side effects. Its impact on patients with infertility is also similar to that of danazol.[82] Currently, gestrinone is used extensively in Europe to treat endometriosis, but it is not yet available in the United States.

Surgical Therapy

While the role of surgery in managing minimal to mild endometriosis is controversial, there is little doubt that surgery is the treatment of choice for moderate to severe endometriosis. This is because the elimination of large endometriomas and extensive adhesions is difficult to accomplish by hormonal therapy alone. Since endometriosis occurs in reproductive age groups, preservation of reproductive function is desirable for most women with the disease. As a result, the least invasive approach should be used initially. And since the most definitive way to diagnose endometriosis is laparoscopy, laparoscopy is now the most common therapeutic choice for treating women with endometriosis.[83]

When endometriosis is suspected, a trial of NSAIDs and OCPs is started. If the symptoms are not alleviated within 3 months, laparoscopy is performed. During laparoscopy, the endometriotic lesions are removed by sharp excision, electrocoagulation, or vaporization.[84] The goal of this surgery is to excise or coagulate all visible lesions, remove adhesions, and restore normal anatomy while preserving the reproductive organs.[60] If endometriomas are present, they should be aspirated. The cyst wall should then be removed from the ovarian cortex (to prevent recurrence) while trying to leave behind as much ovarian tissue as possible. Preservation of even one-tenth of an ovary is enough to maintain function and fertility.[85] More extensive surgery, including total abdominal hysterectomy and bilateral salpingo-oophorectomy (TAH/BSO), is reserved for women with very severe disease or for when the patient does not desire to maintain fertility and wants definitive therapy. (Figure 79–1).

Postoperative hormone replacement with estrogen after TAH/BSO is recommended because the risk of reactivation of endometriosis is very negligible and is a far smaller risk than that associated with prolonged estrogen deficiency. To further reduce the risk of recurrence, hormone replacement therapy (HRT) is withheld until 3 months after surgery.[60] The addition of a progestational agent is also recommended because of reported cases of adenocarcinoma in endometriotic tissue.

Studies of outcomes after surgery are even more varied and controversial than those of medical therapy. Most studies report significant improvement in pain symptoms in up to 70% of women with minimal to moderate endometriosis.[86,87] Surgical treatment is least effective for minimal endometriosis and is most beneficial for severe disease, with pain relief in as many as 80% of patients who previously had not responded to medical management. The rates of recurrence, however, are very similar to those observed after medical therapy alone.

The success of surgery in relieving infertility is directly related to the severity of the disease. The rate of pregnancy is approximately 60% for moderate disease but only 35% with severe disease.[88] Postoperative hormonal treatment is not recommended because it prevents pregnancy, of which the highest rate of occurrence is during the first 6 to 12 months after surgery.[61] When surgery is for symptomatic relief rather than for fertility, medical treatment may maximize the relief of pain symptoms, but studies are still limited and controversial. Several studies reveal added benefits and increased pain-free intervals with postoperative treatment with Gn-RH agonist for 3 to 6 months[89,90] whereas others report no advantage over expectant management with postoperative treatment with danazol for 3 months.[91] Further studies are needed.

PROGNOSIS

Prognoses with respect to pain relief, pregnancy rates, and recurrence are similar among the different methods of medical therapy. Treatment regimens thus should be individualized on the bases of clinician and patient preferences, and the side effect profiles of the available options. Recurrence rates with medical therapy have been reported to be between 5 and 20% within the first year but to be as much as 37 to 74% in 5 years, depending on the severity of the disease.[43,92] Lower rates of recurrence are reported with surgical therapy, ranging from 10% within a year following conservative surgery to 20% within 5 years;[93,94] TAH/BSO is curative. There are insufficient data for the reporting of recurrence rates for combined surgical and medical treatment of endometriosis.

The cumulative pregnancy rate after 5 years without therapy in women with minimal to mild disease is 90%, which is comparable to the rates with medical therapy and only slightly lower than the rates obtained from surgical ablation.[60,95] Nevertheless, it is currently recommended that resection or ablation be performed for all stages of endometriosis, including minimal or mild disease, at the time of laparoscopic diagnosis for infertility. Pregnancy rates after surgical therapy depend on the stage of disease but range from 35 to 63%. If pregnancy is not achieved following surgery, infertility should be treated with superovulation with intrauterine insemination and then with in vitro fertilization.

PREVENTION AND SCREENING

No strategies that can be used for screening or preventing endometriosis have been identified. A reduced incidence has been reported in women who engage in aerobic exercise, but this association has not been investigated extensively. Endometriosis is at times found incidentally at surgery in a young woman who has no immediate interest in pregnancy. Here, immediate surgical treatment of visible endometriosis is recommended, to be followed by the use of low-dose oral contraceptives to prevent further seeding and adhesions. Consideration has also been given to the prophylactic use of oral contraceptives in women with a family history of endometriosis. This theory, however, has not been evaluated in clinical trials.[96]

PREGNANCY AND BREAST-FEEDING

Even though endometriosis is a common cause of infertility, it poses no problems once the woman is actually pregnant. There was speculation that endometriosis was associated with an increased risk of spontaneous abortions. This was later refuted by appropriately controlled studies, which revealed no such relationship.[97,98] Pregnancy is beneficial for a woman with endometriosis because it creates an anovulatory and acyclic hormonal environment leading to the resolution of endometriotic implants. There is no evidence to suggest that breast-feeding is contraindicated in women with endometriosis.

MENOPAUSE

Since endometriotic implants depend on estrogen and progesterone for growth, they regress in menopausal women due to the absence of these hormones. In fact, endometriosis universally regresses after both natural and surgical menopause. Since endometriosis is estrogen responsive, there have been case reports in which endometriosis has recurred during HRT. This risk, however, is thought to be very low, and HRT may be given to women with a past diagnosis of endometriosis.[99]

RESOURCE

Endometriosis Association
8585 North 76th Place
Milwaukee, Wisconsin 53223
Telephone: 1-800-992-3636
Web site: www.endometriosisassn.org

The Endometriosis Association provides information and a local support group network for patients with endometriosis.

REFERENCES

1. Knapp VJ. How old is endometriosis? Late 17th- and 18th-century European descriptions of the disease. Fertil Steril 1999;72:10–4.

2. Sampson JA. Peritoneal endometriosis due to the menstrual dissemination of the endometrial tissue into the peritoneal cavity. Am J Obstet Gynecol 1927; 14:422–69.

3. Olive DL, Haney AF. Endometriosis. In: DeCherney AH, ed. Reproductive failure. New York: Churchill Livingstone; 1986. p. 153–4.

4. Propst AM, Laufer MR. Endometriosis in adolescents. Incidence, diagnosis and treatment. J Reprod Med 1999;44:751–8.

5. National Center for Health Statistics, McCarthy E. Inpatient utilization of short-stay hospitals by diagnosis: United States, 1980. Hyattsville (MD): National Center for Health Statistics; 1982.

6. Velebil P, Wingo PH, Xia Z, et al. Rate of hospitalization for gynecologic disorders among reproductive-age women in the United States. Obstet Gynecol 1995;86:764–9.

7. Wheeler JM. Epidemiology of endometriosis-associated infertility. J Reprod Med 1989;34:41–6.

8. Eskenazi B, Warner ML. Epidemiology of endometriosis. Obstet Gynecol Clin North Am 1997; 24:235–58.

9. Sampson JA. Heterotopic of misplaced endometrial tissue. Am J Obstet Gynecol 1925;10:649–54.

10. Keettel WC, Stein FJ. The viability of the cast-off menstrual endometrium. Am J Obstet Gynecol 1951; 61:440–4.

11. Kruitwagen RFPM, Poels LG, Willemsen WNP, et al. Endometrial epithelial cells in peritoneal fluid during the early follicular phase. Fertil Steril 1991;55:297–303.

12. Liu DT, Hitchcock A. Endometriosis: its association with retrograde menstruation, dysmenorrhea and tubal pathology. Brit J Obstet Gynecol 1986;93:859–62.

13. Olive DL, Henderson DY. Endometriosis and mullerian anomalies. Obstet Gynecol 1987;69:412–5.

14. Darrow SL, Vena JE, Batt RE, et al. Menstrual cycle characteristics and the risk of endometriosis. Epidemiology 1993;4:135–42.

15. Scot RB, Nowak RJ, Tindale RM. Umbilical endometriosis and Cullen's sign: study of lymphatic transport from pelvis to umbilicus in monkeys. Obstet Gynecol 1958;11:556–60.

16. Kale S, Shuster M, Sahmgold I. Endometrioma in cesarean scar: case report and review of the literature. Am J Obstet Gynecol 1971;111:596–7.

17. Schrodt GR, Alcorn MO, Ibanez J. Endometriosis of the male urinary system: a case report. J Urol 1980; 124:722–3.

18. Clark AH. Endometriosis in a young girl. JAMA 1948;136:690–2.

19. El-Mahgoub S, Yaseen S. A positive proof for the theory of coelomic metaplasia. Am J Obstet Gynecol 1980;137:137–40.

20. Oral E, Arici A. Pathogenesis of endometriosis. Obstet Gynecol Clin North Am 1997;24:219–33.

21. Hill JA. Immunology and endometriosis: fact, artifact or epiphenomenon? Obstet Gynecol Clin North Am 1997;24(2):291–306.

22. Simpson JL, Elias S, Malinak LR, Buttram VC Jr. Heritable aspects of endometriosis. I. Genetic studies. Am J Obstet Gynecol 1980;137:327–31.

23. Moen MH. Endometriosis in monozygotic twins. Acta Obstet Gynecol Scand 1994;73:59–62.

24. Hadfield RM, Mardon JH, Barlow DH, Kennedy SH. Endometriosis in monozygotic twins. Fertil Steril 1997;68:941–2.

25. Kennedy S. The genetics of endometriosis. Eur J Obstet Gynecol Reprod Biol 1999;82:129–33.

26. Kennedy S. The genetics of endometriosis. J Reprod Med 1998;43(3S):263–8.

27. Fedele L, Bianchi S, Bocciolone L, et al. Pain symptoms associated with endometriosis. Obstet Gynecol 1992;79:767–9.

28. Duleba AJ. Diagnosis of endometriosis. Obstet Gynecol Clin North Am 1997;24:331–46.

29. Koninckx PR, Meuleman C, Demeyere S, et al. Suggestive evidence that pelvic endometriosis is a progressive disease, whereas deeply infiltrating endometriosis is associated with pelvic pain. Fertil Steril 1991;55:759–65.

30. Bonner J. Clinical manifestations and diagnosis of endometriosis. Ir J Med Sci 1983;152:5–9.

31. Giudice LC, Tazuke SI, Swiersz L. Status of current research on endometriosis. J Reprod Med 1998; 43(3S):252–62.

32. Cahill DJ, Hull MG. Pituitary-ovarian dysfunction and endometriosis. Hum Reprod Update 2000; 6(1):56–66.

33. Garcia-Velasco JA, Arici A. Is the endometrium or oocyte/embryo affected in endometriosis? Hum Reprod 1999;14(2S):77–89.

34. Mulayim N, Arici A. The relevance of the peritoneal fluid in endometriosis-associated infertility. Hum Reprod 1999;14(2S):67–76.

35. Somigliana E, Viaganao P, Vignali M. Endometriosis and unexplained recurrent spontaneous abortion: pathological states resulting from aberrant modulation of natural killer cell function? Hum Reprod Update 1999;5(1):40–51.

36. Shah M, Tager D, Feller E. Intestinal endometriosis masquerading as common digestive disorders. Arch Intern Med 1995;155:977–80.

37. Descamps P, Cottier JP, Barre I, et al. Endometriosis of the sciatic nerve: case report demonstrating the value of MR imaging. Eur J Obstet Gynecol Reprod Biol 1995;58:199–202.

38. Thibodeau LL, Prioleau GR, Manuelidis EE, et al. Cerebral endometriosis: case report. J Neurosurg 1987;66:609–10.

39. Koninckx PR, Riittinen L, Seppala M, et al. CA-125 and placental protein 14 concentrations in plasma and peritoneal fluid of women with deeply infiltrating pelvic endometriosis. Fertil Steril 1992;57:523–30.

40. Hornstein MD, Thomas PP, Gleason RE, et al. Menstrual cyclicity of CA-125 in patients with endometriosis. Fertil Steril 1992;58:279–83.

41. O'Shaughnessy A, Check JH, Nowroozi K, et al. CA-125 levels measured in different phases of the menstrual cycle in screening for endometriosis. Obstet Gynecol 1993;81:99–103.

42. Mol BWJ, Bayram N, Lijmer J, et al. The performance of CA-125 measurement in the detection of endometriosis: a meta analysis. Fertil Steril 1998;70:1101–8.

43. Speroff L, Glass RH, Kase NG. Endometriosis. In: Speroff L, Glass RH, Kase NG. Clinical gynecologic endocrinology and infertility. 6th ed. Baltimore: Lippincott Williams & Wilkins; 1999. p. 1057–74.

44. Alcazar JL, Laparte C, Jurado M, Lopez-Garcia G. The role of transvaginal ultrasonography combined with color velocity imaging and pulsed Doppler in the diagnosis of endometrioma. Fertil Steril 1997;67:487–91.

45. Adamson D. Endometriosis. In: Rakel L. Conn's current therapy 2000. 52nd ed. St. Louis: W.B. Saunders Company; 2000. p. 1029–37.

46. Moen MH, Halvorsen TB. Histologic confirmation of endometriosis in different peritoneal lesions. Acta Obstet Gynecol Scand 1992;71:337–42.

47. Nisolle M, Paindaveine B, Bourdon A, et al. Histologic study of peritoneal endometriosis in infertile women. Fertil Steril 1990;53:984–8.

48. Jansen RP, Russell P. Nonpigmented endometriosis: clinical, laparoscopic and pathologic definition. Am J Obstet Gynecol 1986;155:1154–9.

49. Vercellini P, Vendola N, Bocciolone L, et al. Reliability of visual diagnosis of ovarian endometriosis. Fertil Steril 1991;56:1198–200.

50. American Fertility Society. Classification of endometriosis. Fertil Steril 1979;32:633–4.

51. Revised American Fertility Society classification: 1985. Fertil Steril 1985;43:351–2.

52. Revised American Society for Reproductive Medicine classification of endometriosis: 1996. Fertil Steril 1997;67:817–21.

53. Guzick DS, Silliman NP, Adamson GD, et al. Prediction of pregnancy in infertile women based on the American Society for Reproductive Medicine's revised classification of endometriosis. Fertil Steril 1997;67:822–9.

54. Hoeger KM, Guzick DS. Classification of endometriosis. Obstet Gynecol Clin North Am 1997; 24:347–59.

55. Moghissi KS. Medical treatment of endometriosis. Clin Obstet Gynecol 1999;42:620–32.

56. The American College of Obstetricians and Gynecologists. 2000 compendium of selected publications.Washington (DC): The College; 2000. p. 962.

57. Hornstein MD, Barbieri RL. Endometriosis. In: Ryan A, editor. Kistner's gynecology & women's health, 7th ed. St. Louis: Mosby; 1999. p. 492–518.

58. Lessey BA, Metzger DA, Haney AF, et al. Immunohistochemical analysis of estrogen and progesterone receptors in endometriosis: comparison with normal endometrium during the menstrual cycle and the effect of medical therapy. Fertil Steril 1989;51:409–15.

59. Kistner RW. Management of endometriosis in the infertile patient. Fertil Steril 1975;26:1151–66.

60. D'Hooghe TM, Hill JA. Endometriosis. In: Berek JS, Adashi EY, Hillard PA, editors. Novak's gynecology. 12th ed. Baltimore: Williams & Wilkins; 1996. p. 887–914.

61. Vercellini P, Cortesi I, Crosignani PG. Progestins for synthetic endometriosis: a critical analysis of the evidence. Fertil Steril 1997;68:393–401.

62. Hull ME, Moghissi KS, Magyar DF, Haves MF. Comparison of different treatment modalities of endometriosis in infertile women. Fertil Steril 1987;47:40–4.

63. Vercellini P, De Giorgi O, Oldani S, et al. Depot medroxyprogesterone acetate versus an oral contraceptive combined with very-low-dose danazol for long-term treatment of pelvic pain associated with endometriosis. Am J Obstet Gynecol 1996; 175:396–401.

64. Bayer SR, Seibel MM, Saffan DS, et al. Efficacy of danazol treatment for minimal endometriosis in infertile women: a prospective, randomized study. J Reprod Med 1988;33:179–83.

65. Salat-Baroux J, Giacomini P, Antoine JM. Laparoscopic control of danazol therapy on pelvic endometriosis. Hum Reprod 1988;3:197–200.

66. Kettel LM, Hummel WP. Modern medical management of endometriosis. Obstet Gynecol Clin North Am 1997;24:361–73.

67. Meldrum DR, Chang RJ, Vale W, et al. Medical oophorectomy using long-acting GnRH agonist: a possible new approach to the treatment of endometriosis. J Clin Endocrinol Metab 1982;54:1081–3.

68. Henzl M, Corson S, Moghissi K, et al. Administration of nasal nafarelin as compared with oral danazol for endometriosis. A multicenter double-blind comparative clinical trail. N Engl J Med 1988;318:485–9.

69. Wheeler JM, Knittle JD, Mier JD, for the Lupron Endometriosis Study Group. Depot leuprolide acetate versus danazol in the treatment of women with symptomatic endometriosis: a multicenter, double-blind randomized clinical trial. II. Assessment of safety. Am J Obstet Gynecol 1993;169: 26–33.

70. Shaw RW. An open randomized comparative study of the effect of goserelin depot and danazol in the treatment of endometriosis. Zoladex Endometriosis Study Team. Fertil Steril 1992;58:265–72.

71. Paoletti AM, Serra GG, Cagnacci A, et al. Spontaneous reversibility of bone loss induced by gonadotropin-releasing hormone analog treatment. Fertil Steril 1996;65:707–10.

72. Fedele L, Parazzini F, Radici E, et al. Buserelin acetate versus expectant management in the treatment of infertility associated with minimal or mild endometriosis: a randomized clinical trial. Am J Obstet Gyncol 1992;166:1345–50.

73. Heinrichs WL, Henzel MR. Human issues and medical economics of endometriosis. Three versus six months GnRH agonist therapy. J Reprod Med 1998; 43S:299–308.

74. Barbieri RL. Endometriosis and the estrogen threshold theory. Relation to surgical and medical treatment. J Reprod Med 1998;43S:287–92.

75. Surey ES. Add-back therapy and gonadotropin-releasing hormone agonists in the treatment of patients with endometriosis: can a consensus be reached? Add-Back Consensus Working Group. Fertil Steril 1999;71:420–4.

76. Moghissi KS, Schlaff WD, Olive DL, et al. Goserelin acetate (Zoladex) with or without hormone replacement therapy for the treatment of endometriosis. Fertil Steril 1998;69:1056–62.

77. Tahara M, Matsuoka T, Yokoi T, et al. Treatment of endometriosis with a decreasing dosage of a gonadotropin-releasing hormone agonist (nafarelin): a pilot study with low-dose agonist therapy ("draw-back" therapy). Fertil Steril 2000;73:799–804.

78. Uremura T, Shirasu K, Katagiri N, et al. Low-dose GnRH agonist therapy for the management of endometriosis. J Obstet Gynaecol Res 1999;25:295–301.

79. Kettel LM, Murphy AA, Mortola JF, et al. Endocrine responses to long-term administration of the anti-progesterone RU-486 in patients with pelvic endometriosis. Fertil Steril 1991;56:402–7.

80. Kettel LM, Murphy AA, Morales AJ, Yen SSC. Preliminary report on the treatment of endometriosis with low dose mifepristone (RU-486). Am J Obstet Gynecol 1998;178:1151–6.

81. Fedele L, Bianchi S, Viezzoli T, et al. Gestrinone versus danazol in the treatment of endometriosis. Fertil Steril 1989;51:781–5.

82. Hughes EG, Fedorkow DM, Collins JA. A quantitative overview of controlled trials in endometriosis-associated infertility. Fertil Steril 1993;59:963–70.

83. Winkel CA. Combined medical and surgical treatment of women with endometriosis. Clin Obstet Gynecol 1999;42:645–63.

84. Pouly JL, Drolet J, Canis M, et al. Laparoscopic treatment of symptomatic endometriosis. Hum Reprod 1996;11(S3):67–88.

85. Heaps JM, Berek JS, Nieberg RK. Malignant neoplasms arising in endometriosis. Obstet Gynecol 1990;75:1023–8.

86. Sutton C, Hill D. Laser laparoscopy in the treatment of endometriosis. A 5-year study. Br J Obstet Gynaecol 1990;97:181–5.

87. Sutton CJG, Ewen SP, Whitelaw N, Haines P. Prospective, randomized, double-blind, controlled trial of laser laparoscopy in the treatment of pelvic pain associated with minimal, mild, and moderate endometriosis. Fertil Steril 1994;62:696–700.

88. Olive DL, Lee KL. Analysis of sequential treatment of protocols for endometriosis-associated infertility. Am J Obstet Gynecol 1986;154:613–9.

89. Winkel CA, Bray M. Treatment of women with endometriosis using excision alone, ablation alone, or ablation in combination with leuprolide acetate. Proceedings of the Fourth World Congress on Endometriosis; 1996; Yokahama, Japan. p. 55–7.

90. Audebert A, Descamps P, Marret H, et al. Pre- or post-operative medical treatment with nafarelin in stage III-IV endometriosis: a French multicenter study. Eur J Obstet Gynecol Reprod Biol 1998; 79(2):145–8.

91. Bianchi S, Busacca M, Agnoli B, et al. Effects of 3 month therapy with danazol after laparoscopic surgery for stage III/IV endometriosis: a randomized study. Hum Reprod 1999;14:1335–7.

92. Waller KG, Shaw RW. Gonadotropin-releasing hormone analogues for the treatment of endometriosis: long-term follow-up. Fertil Steril 1993;59:511–5.

93. Redwine DB. Conservative laparoscopic excision of endometriosis by sharp dissection: life table analysis of reoperation and persistence of recurrent disease. Fertil Steril 1991;56:628–34.

94. Sutton CJG, Pooley AS, Ewen SP, Haines P. Follow-up report on a randomized controlled trial of laser laparoscopy in the treatment of pelvic pain associated with minimal to moderate endometriosis. Fertil Steril 1997;68:1070–4.

95. Badawy SZA, Elbakry MM, Samuel F, Dizer M. Cumulative pregnancy rates in infertile women with endometriosis. J Reprod Med 1988;33:757–60.

96. Vessey MP, Villard-Mackintosh L, Painter R. Epidemiology of endometriosis in women attending family-planning clinics. BMJ 1993;306:182–4.

97. Matorras R, Rodraiquez F, Guiterrez de Teraan F, et al. Endometriosis and spontaneous abortion rate: a cohort study in infertile women. Eur J Obstet Gynecol Reprod Biol 1998;77(1):101–5.

98. FitzSimmons J, Stahl R, Gocial B, Shapiro SS. Spontaneous abortion and endometriosis. Fertil Steril 1987;47:696–8.

99. Johnson SR. The clinical decision regarding hormone replacement therapy. Endocrinol Metab Clin North Am 1997;26:413–35.

80

VAGINAL AND VULVAR DISORDERS

Emily Wong, MD, Mary B. Migeon, MD, and David Eschenbach, MD

Primary care clinicians find that symptoms of vulvar and vaginal disorders are relatively nonspecific and often overlap. In addition, considerable variation exists between patients in terms of perception, ability to tolerate symptoms, and comfort level in reporting symptoms. Thus, physical examination is key to the diagnosis of both disorders. In the case of vaginitis, simple office analysis of vaginal fluid is also critical to establishing the correct diagnosis. Provided that the diagnosis is correct, treatment of infection and inflammatory conditions is usually straightforward.

VAGINAL CONDITIONS

At some point during their lifetime, most women experience symptoms that arise in the vagina. These symptoms are relatively nonspecific and thus cannot be used for diagnosis. Common vaginal symptoms include increased, yellow, or odorous discharge; burning; dyspareunia; irritation; and slight bleeding. Table 80–1 lists the more frequent causes.

Normal Vaginal Physiology and Vaginal Infection and Inflammation

"Normal" physiologic discharge varies between women and with hormonal state. Throughout the menstrual cycle the quality and quantity of discharge changes. Just prior to ovulation, many women experience a thin ropey cervical discharge caused by maximum estrogen levels. After ovulation and throughout the rest of the cycle, the discharge tends to be thicker and white, a so-called flocculent discharge. Normal vaginal fluid contains mostly serum transudate together with squamous cells from the vagina, a few white blood cells (WBCs), and

a wide variety of bacteria, predominantly of *Lactobacillus* species. The normal vaginal pH is acidic (< 4.5). *Candida albicans* is present as a nonpathologic colonizer in 10 to 25% of women.

Infection is the most common pathologic cause for vaginal symptoms. The most common infections are bacterial vaginosis (40 to 50%), candidal vaginitis (20 to 25%), and trichomonal vaginitis (15 to 20%).[1]

Bacterial vaginosis (BV) is an overgrowth of vaginal bacteria. Although previously thought to be due to *Gardnerella vaginalis* bacteria, *G. vaginalis* is in fact a normal vaginal inhabitant in 50% of women. Most cases of BV have a relative paucity of the protective *Lactobacillus* species, particularly

---

TABLE 80–1. Common Causes of Vaginal Symptoms

Vaginal infections
  Bacterial vaginosis
  Candidiasis
  Trichomonal vaginitis

Vaginal inflammation
  Atrophic vaginitis
  Allergic/hypersensitivity vaginitis
  Foreign body
  Desquamative inflammatory vaginitis

Nonvaginal causes
  Cervicitis (gonorrhea, chlamydia)
  Oral contraceptive use (with increased benign
    cervical discharge)
  Urinary incontinence (mimicker of vaginal
    discharge)
  Vulvovestibulitis

---

those that produce hydrogen peroxide and the overgrowth of other normal vaginal flora to as much as 1,000 times normal levels. Although BV is rarely diagnosed in individuals who have never been sexually active, the treatment of male sex partners has not been effective in preventing recurrences of BV.[2]

Although asymptomatic in up to 50% of cases, classic BV can cause a profuse watery discharge, a fishy odor (particularly after intercourse), and itching. The symptoms often wax and wane; 6 weeks after treatment for BV, up to 30% of women may have recurrent episodes. Spontaneous resolution is not uncommon. Factors that may predispose to BV include trichomonal infection, a new sexual partner, douches, and antibiotics.

Candida albicans is the most common cause of yeast vaginitis although other *Candida* species have also been implicated as pathogens. *Candida albicans* may be normal flora in 10 to 25% of asymptomatic women of childbearing age. *Candida* is more common in poorly controlled diabetes, human immunodeficiency virus (HIV) or other immune suppression, and malignancy. The most common symptoms of *Candida* vaginitis are vaginal itching and burning and a cheesy white discharge.

Trichomonal vaginitis, caused by the protozoan *Trichomonas vaginalis*, is the most common nonviral sexually transmitted disease (STD) in the world. Although a discharge is typically present, trichomonal infection can be asymptomatic in as many as 50% of female carriers and 90% of male carriers. *Trichomonas* alters the normal vagina, and thus bacterial vaginosis is a common accompanying condition. Symptoms include itching or burning, and a yellow-green vaginal discharge.[3]

Although inflammation and WBCs are common with infection, inflammation can also occur without infectious etiology. **Atrophic vaginitis** results from low estrogen levels, most commonly in menopausal women. However, this condition also can be present in lactating women who are amenorrheic or in other low-estrogen states such as hypothalamic hypopituitarism. The squamous lining of the vagina and the introitus becomes smooth and pale. Women may experience burning, urinary frequency, slight vaginal bleeding, and dyspareunia.

Hypersensitivity vaginitis is less common and results from a local reaction to topical soaps, lubricants, commercial douche products, and even some topical antifungal treatments. Inflammatory reactions to spermicidal ingredients such as nonoxynol-9 are quite common. **Desquamative inflammatory vaginitis** is a rare condition that can present in women at all ages. Women have a profuse and exceedingly uncomfortable yellow vaginal discharge and extreme vulvar irritation. Intercourse is often painful, and vaginal bleeding may be present. The cause is unknown.[4]

Evaluation of Vaginal Symptoms

Symptoms are not predictive of the diagnosis. Therefore physical examination and laboratory testing are required, to secure the diagnosis before treatment.[5] However, in up to 50% of women the etiology for vaginitis cannot be definitively identified. When patients present with recurrent vaginal symptoms, it should not be assumed that similar symptoms are being caused again by the same pathogen as previously documented. Repeated examination and testing are necessary.

Vaginal fluid analysis is quick and is critical for an accurate diagnosis. Easily performed in-office tests include pH tests, the "whiff" test, and microscopy. Gram's stain is not necessary for routine evaluation of vaginal discharge. Although a Pap test may identify specific organisms, it is neither sensitive nor specific enough to use diagnostically.

First, the perineum is examined for vesicles, ulcers, inflammation, atrophy, or other lesions. During the speculum examination, purulent cervical discharge suggestive of cervicitis of gonorrhea or *Chlamydia* infection (or of other bacterial infection) should be identified. Vaginal pH is tested by placing pH paper against the vaginal wall or by swabbing vaginal discharge onto pH paper.

Next, a sample of vaginal discharge is obtained via a cotton swab and placed in a test tube with a few drops of saline solution. At the microscope, the swab is used to place a drop of the vaginal fluid onto each of two clean glass slides. The first slide is prepared as a saline wet mount and is ready to examine after a glass coverslip is placed. One drop of 10% KOH solution is added to the second slide.

Immediately after adding KOH solution to the sample, the clinician performs the whiff test by smelling just above the slide. An obvious fishy odor is a positive whiff or "amine" test. (Anaerobic bacteria release amines when treated with an alkaline solution. Amines are present in abundance in bacterial vaginosis and sometimes with trichomonal infection. The postcoital odor that is often described by women with bacterial vaginosis occurs because ejaculate, like the KOH, is an alkaline solution.)

A coverslip should be placed on the KOH slide immediately after the amine test. Both the saline and KOH preparations are examined with the microscope, initially at 10× power to locate the sample plane, then increased to 40× for a closer view. Oil-field microscopy is not needed.

Diagnosis and Treatment

COMMON VAGINAL CONDITIONS IN NONPREGNANT WOMEN

The diagnosis and treatment of common types of vaginitis are summarized in Table 80–2.

Bacterial vaginosis is most commonly diagnosed by using Amsel's criteria, which require three of the following four findings: a thin homogeneous appearance of the vaginal discharge, pH > 4.5 to 4.7, a positive whiff test, and clue cells seen on the microscopic examination. Clue cells are granular-appearing squamous cells that are so covered with bacteria that the cell border is no longer sharp but has a serrated appearance. A culture of the discharge is not helpful. Bacterial vaginosis is not inflammatory, and if many WCBs are present on the wet mount, additional infections may be present.

Whether or not to treat bacterial vaginosis depends largely on the patient's symptoms and preference. Special considerations during pregnancy and prior to gynecologic procedures are discussed below. Although initial cure rates are > 90% for most regimens, recurrence is common.

Women with symptomatic bacterial vaginosis should be treated. Metronidazole and clindamycin are both effective and may be given orally or locally (by vaginal applicator). Metronidazole causes an Antabuse-like reaction to alcohol; patients should be warned to avoid alcohol while taking it. Other therapeutic options include one dose of metronidazole, amoxicillin-clavulanic acid, and triple sulfa cream; however, these regimens tend to be less effective. Ineffective therapies include lactate gel, chlorhexidine and povidone-iodine suppositories,

TABLE 80–2. Diagnosis and Treatment of Common Vaginal Conditions in Nonpregnant Women

Diagnosis	pH	Wet Mount	Treatment
Normal	< 4.5	Rare WBCs; normal squamous cells	None
Bacterial vaginosis	> 4.7	Rare WBCs; clue squamous cells[*]; positive "whiff" test[*]	Clindamycin oral 300 mg bid × 7d topical cream 2% qhs × 7d Metronidazole oral 500 mg bid × 7d topical gel 0.075% bid × 5d
Vaginal candidiasis	< 4.5	Moderate WBCs; normal squamous cells; hyphae on KOH slide	(see Table 80–3)
Vaginal trichomoniasis	> 5.0	Moderate to heavy WBCs; normal squamous cells; motile protozoa (1.5 × size of WBCs)	Metronidazole oral 2 g × 1 dose oral 500 mg bid × 7d
Atrophic vaginitis	> 5.5	Moderate WBCs; "fried-egg" squamous cells[†]	Estrogen (see text) Nonhormonal lubricants

[*]Bacterial vaginosis is diagnosed on the basis of Amsel's criteria. Three of the following four factors must be present: a thin grey discharge in the vagina, a positive "whiff" test (see text), pH > 4.7, and the presence of clue cells (granular-appearing squamous cells that are coated with copious bacteria).
[†]"Fried egg" squamous cells have enlarged nuclei and rounded cell margins. These consist of parabasal and basal vaginal epithelial cells.
KOH = potassium hydroxide; prn = pro re nata (as circumstances may require); WBCs = white blood cells.

intravaginal yogurt, and douching with hydrogen peroxide. Although treatment of the sex partner is not indicated, some clinicians recommend abstention from sex or the use of condoms until treatment is complete, particularly in cases of refractory BV.

Trichomonal vaginitis infection is diagnosed by finding motile trichomonads on microscopic examination of vaginal discharge. Copious WBCs are also typically seen. The incidence of false-negatives may be as high as 50%. Therefore, if clinical suspicion is high and the microscopic examination is negative, the vaginal discharge should be cultured for *Trichomonas.*

Trichomonal vaginitis is treated with metronidazole, either 2 g orally in a single dose or 500 mg orally twice daily for 7 days. Sexual partners must be treated simultaneously, regardless of whether the man has symptoms, as *Trichomonas* infection may recur if the sexual partner is not adequately treated. For men, the full 7-day course is more reliable than single-dose therapy although compliance is improved with single-dose therapy. For patients whose initial treatment of *Trichomonas* infection fails, re-treatment with the same regimen is adequate. For recalcitrant *Trichomonas* infection, continued therapy with metronidazole for 10 to 14 days is recommended. Resistance of *T. vaginalis* to metronidazole is rare, but, if suspected, the patient may require specialty consultation.

Candidal vaginitis is diagnosed by finding branching hyphae or buds on the KOH slide. It is usually caused by *Candida albicans* although occasionally *Torulopsis* spp, other *Candida* spp, or other yeasts are responsible.[2] Up to one-half of women with symptomatic candidiasis have negative KOH wet mounts; *Candida glabrata* and other yeasts usually do not form hyphae, and buds can be difficult to identify on wet mounts. Culture for yeast is indicated only (1) if clinical suspicion is high and KOH is negative or (2) in recurrent infection, when the specific identification of the yeast species may guide treatment. A positive culture may reflect nonpathogenic colonization; therefore, cultures should be performed only in symptomatic women.

A 3- to 7-day course of vaginal azoles is usually effective for treating vaginal candidiasis. A single dose of oral fluconazole at 150 mg may also be given to women using effective birth control. The effect lasts at least 72 hours following dosing. For symptoms that persist beyond 72 hours, an additional dose is usually needed. Women with significant vulvar itching and burning might prefer topical antifungal therapy, such as clotrimazole. The currently available therapies for vaginal candidiasis are summarized in Table 80–3.

Recurrent candidal vaginitis can be difficult to clear. Long-term intravaginal antifungal suppressive therapy for 6 to 12 months is effective, but high rates of recurrence develop when suppressive therapy is discontinued. Maintenance therapy (ketoconazole, 100 mg orally once daily for up to 6 months) has also reduced the frequency of recurrent episodes.[2] Patients may prefer the option of intravaginal boric acid. Boric acid powder is dosed in "0"-size gelatin capsules, which are inexpensive and available over the counter. Eating 8 oz of yogurt with live *Lactobacillus acidophilus* daily may also reduce re-infection.

Atrophic vaginitis is suggested by a pH > 5.5, moderate WBCs, and the atypical "fried-egg" appearance of squamous cells characterized by an enlarged nucleus and a round cell outline typical of parabasal and basal squamous epithelial cells. A variety of oral, transcutaneous, and local topical estrogen delivery systems are available for treatment. Oral and transdermal estrogen preparations have systemic effects and are discussed in detail in Chapter 4, "Approach to the Menopausal Patient." Local topical estrogen is most commonly given as estradiol cream (Estrace 0.1 mg/g, 2 to 4 g nightly for 1 to 2 weeks, followed by 1 g nightly three times weekly) and conjugated equine estrogen (Premarin 0.625 mg/g, 2 to 4 g nightly three times weekly). Both regimens result in significantly increased estrogen levels and therefore should not be used in the long term without the use of concomitant progestins in a woman with an intact uterus.

Low-dose (0.3 mg of conjugated equine estrogen) vaginal estrogen cream administered three times weekly has been shown to relieve symptoms and rarely causes endometrial changes.[6] Vaginal estrogen tablets (Vagifem, 25 µg of estradiol per tablet, one tablet vaginally for 2 weeks, then one tablet twice weekly) and indwelling reservoirs that deliver estrogen locally (Estring, inserted once every 3 months) have been shown to result in very low systemic estrogen levels and are used without the addition of systemic progestins. Women who wish to avoid estrogen may choose symptomatic treatment with lubricating agents such as Replens or Astroglide.

TABLE 80–3. Treatment of Vaginal Candidiasis

Medication	Dosage	Examples
Vaginal creams		
Tioconazole 6.5%	4.6 g intravaginally qhs × 1 d	Monistat 1, Vagistat-1
Butoconazole 2%	5 g intravaginally qhs × 3 d	Femstat 3, Mycelex-3
Terconazole 0.8%*	5 g intravaginally qhs × 3 d	Terazol 3
Terconazole 0.4%*	5 g intravaginally qhs × 7 d	Terazol 7
Miconazole 2%	5 g intravaginally qhs × 7 d	Femizol-M, Monistat 7
Clotrimazole 1%	5 g intravaginally qhs × 7–14 d	Gyne-Lotrimin, Mycelex-7
Vaginal tablets and suppositories		
Terconazole 80-mg suppository*	1 intravaginally qhs × 3 d	Terazol-3
Clotrimazole 200-mg tablet	1 intravaginally qhs × 3 d	Gyne-Lotrimin-3
Miconazole 100-mg suppository	1 intravaginally qhs × 7 d	Monistat-7
Clotrimazole 100-mg tablet	1 intravaginally qhs × 7 d	Gyne-Lotrimin, Mycelex- 7
Nystatin 100,000-U tablet*	1 intravaginally qhs × 14 d	Generic, various
Oral medications		
Fluconazole 150-mg tablet*	1 PO (1-time dose only)	Diflucan

*Requires a prescription.
Adapted from Drugs for vulvovaginal candidiasis. Med Lett Drugs Ther 2001 Jan 8;43(1905):3–4.

Hypersensitivity vaginitis is typically treated by avoiding contact with the offending agent. Patients should be counseled regarding risks associated with douching, such as pelvic inflammatory disease. **Desquamative inflammatory vaginitis** is confirmed by history and by physical findings of varying amounts of vaginal inflammation, from patchy erythema to ulcers.[4] The vaginal discharge has an elevated pH, increased neutrophils, and no lactobacilli. Parabasal or basal cells may be present from the vaginal mucosal sloughing. Prolonged treatment (at least 3 to 6 weeks) with 2% clindamycin vaginal cream is recommended.

CONSIDERATIONS FOR PREGNANT WOMEN
An increase in vaginal discharge during pregnancy is normal. Nonetheless, all symptomatic pregnant women should be screened for vaginal infections. Bacterial vaginosis has been associated with premature delivery, amniotic-fluid infection, postpartum endometritis, and salpingitis following the termination of pregnancy. Treatment of BV is indicated prior to the termination of pregnancy in both symptomatic and asymptomatic patients. Intravaginal clindamycin is the treatment of choice. All symptomatic patients should be treated, and asymptomatic pregnant patients with BV must be treated in order to prevent preterm delivery.

In the case of trichomonal infection, the use of oral metronidazole during the first trimester of pregnancy is controversial. Under these circumstances, topical clindamycin, although rarely curative, may provide relief until the pregnancy progresses further. For patients with vaginal candidiasis, topical vaginal antifungal preparations are safe to use at any time in pregnancy.

VULVAR CONDITIONS

Common vulvar complaints fall into four general categories: (1) a mass in the vulva, (2) raised or pigmented lesions (Table 80–4), (3) vulvar rashes, and (4) painful or pruritic conditions. Although infrequent, vulvar malignancies have a myriad of appearances; therefore, the clinician should have a very low threshold for the biopsy of vulvar lesions. This section covers a few of the most frequently encountered problems and provides a basic framework from which to approach these complaints.

Vulvar Masses

The most common etiologic factors for vulvar masses in premenopausal women are Bartholin's cysts and abscesses. Bartholin's glands are paired structures that are located in the labia majora and that produce mucus (Figure 80–1). If the narrow ducts that drain

TABLE 80–4. Common Raised Vulvar Lesions

	Painful	*Painless*
Ulcerative	HSV infection Chancroid	Syphilis
Nonulcerative	Follliculitis	Venereal warts Vulvar intraepithelial neoplasia (VIN) Bowen's disease Invasive vulvar carcinoma Verrucous carcinoma Paget's disease Basal cell carcinoma

HSV = herpes simplex virus.

into the vagina become occluded, mucus-filled cysts or an infection with an abscess forms.

Bartholin's cysts typically present as a painless mass in the labia majora. The differential diagnosis includes hidradenoma, lipoma, fibroma, endometrioma, sebaceous cyst, and adenocarcinoma. A biopsy should be performed on any vulvar mass whose diagnosis is in doubt. Bartholin's gland cyst formation is rarer in the postmenopausal patient; adenocarcinoma is more common. In general, women over the age of 40 years should be evaluated with a biopsy, to rule out malignancy.

The diagnosis is confirmed by the finding of unilateral swelling on palpation in the area of

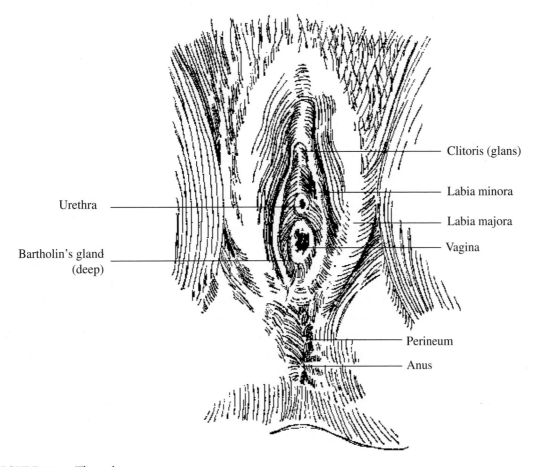

FIGURE 80–1. The vulva.

Bartholin's glands. If the patient is asymptomatic, no treatment is required; warm soaking baths can help clear the ductal occlusion. However, the recurrence rate is high, and definitive surgical treatment with marsupialization may thus be required (see below). Antibiotics are not indicated in this setting.

Bartholin's gland abscess formation results from infection of the duct and glands, and is usually accompanied by surrounding cellulitis. The abscess is generally extremely painful, often interfering with sitting or walking. Bacterial causes include organisms found in vaginal flora, as well as gonococcus and *Chlamydia*. Treatment consists of empiric broad-spectrum antibiotic therapy directed toward likely pathogens; culture of the abscess (including testing for gonococcal and chlamydial infection); and drainage of the infection, with the establishment of a new duct.

Simple incision and drainage of the abscess (or even cyst) should never be done because this is an abscess of a functioning gland to which continued drainage needs to be provided. Drainage is best accomplished through marsupialization, with the patient under anesthesia if necessary. With this surgical procedure, the cyst wall is attached to the vaginal mucosa, creating a new opening for gland drainage. Marsupialization also prevents recurrence.[7] Word catheters are a simple alternative to surgical marsupialization but require considerable technical experience to make the entrance small enough for the catheter to remain in place and not fall out. The catheter must be placed in the correct anatomic position such that inflation of the balloon fills the potential space and prevents further abscess formation. Further, women need to wear the Word catheters for about 6 weeks to ensure that the space over the catheter has formed a mature epithelial lining so as to properly drain the Bartholin abscess.

Raised or Pigmented Lesions of the Vulva

Pseudofolliculitis manifests as tender follicle-based inflammatory papules or pustules that result when hair tips penetrate the skin. Shaving is a common cause of pseudofolliculitis, and the use of depilatories rather than shaving may prevent recurrence.

Vulvar hidradenitis suppurativa develops with repeated blockage of sweat glands that then rupture and become superinfected, forming skin abscesses and (eventually) superficial fistulous tracts. Hidra-

denitis is difficult to treat and often requires surgical intervention. Consultation with a specialist familiar with its treatment is recommended.

Painful ulcerative lesions of the labia majora are usually caused by STDs such as herpes simplex or (occasionally) chancroid. Primary syphilis usually causes a painless ulcer. The ulcerative lesions have a varied vesicular, erosive, or ulcerated appearance. (Genital ulcers are discussed further in Chapter 72.)

The most common raised nonpigmented lesions of the vulva are venereal warts. Venereal warts are usually caused by the type 6 and type 11 strains of the human papillomavirus (HPV). Warts vary in appearance, from flesh-colored verrucous and cauliflower-like lesions to a flat surface. Warts can occur anywhere in the vulvar or perianal region. Their formation is generally asymptomatic although burning, itching, or pain can occur from the immune inflammatory response to HPV. Papillary fronds in the posterior fourchette are normal and should not be confused with warts. Various treatment strategies are available for genital HPV infection: (1) destruction with cryotherapy and topical podophyllin and trichloroacetic acid preparations, or (2) increasing the immune response by the topical application of imiquimod. (The diagnosis and treatment of HPV infection are discussed further in Chapter 81.)[8]

A biopsy for pathologic examination should be performed on any raised vulvar lesions with atypical features such as friability, ulceration, or refractoriness to treatment. Although vulvar neoplasms are relatively rare, no gross physical appearance is diagnostic of vulvar dysplasia or cancer, which can appear as pigmented lesions, white lesions, or red papules.[9] Vulvar venereal warts are strongly linked to vaginal and cervical warts, which may be identified on speculum examination as flat white raised lesions. Evidence of cervical or vaginal HPV infection requires further evaluation. (see Chapter 81)

Benign pigmented skin lesions such as nevi (moles), lentigines (freckles), or seborrheic keratoses may appear on the vulvar skin. Despite the fact that most women have limited exposure to sunlight in this area, there is a greater tendency for junctional and dysplastic nevi to become neoplastic in this area than in other skin areas. Fair-skinned and older individuals have a higher risk of dysplastic or malignant lesions. A full-thickness biopsy is indicated for lesions >5 mm in diameter, particularly those with atypical features such as irregular borders, heterogeneous pigmentation, very dark brown or black pigment, evidence of inflammation, changing features, or rapid growth.

Dermatoses of the Vulva

Vulvar dermatoses are relatively uncommon in primary care practice. However, the differential diagnosis is broad. The most common conditions are vulvar candidiasis and contact dermatitis. Other conditions may be specific to the vulva, such as lichen sclerosus and squamous cell hyperplasia or more generalized cutaneous conditions with vulvar manifestations, such as psoriasis and lichen planus. Examples of systemic conditions with cutaneous vulvar manifestations include morphea and Crohn's disease. Acanthosis nigricans presents with velvety dark pigmentation in skinfolds, including the vulva. It is associated with diabetes, obesity, and polycystic ovary disease.

The most common cause for an itching rash of the vulva is candidiasis. Vulvar candidiasis is usually accompanied by vaginal *Candida* infection. Vulvar candidiasis appears as an erythematous geographic rash typically associated with satellite lesions. Diagnosis is confirmed by the finding of fungal elements on KOH examination of vaginal discharge or even of skin scrapings. Topical antifungals are generally effective in treating this condition although chronic cases may require 2 to 3 months of therapy. Contact dermatitis is also frequently a cause of vulvar itching. The avoidance of possible offending agents is the key to treatment and prevention.

Other frequent causes of pruritic vulvar rashes include lichen sclerosus and squamous cell hyperplasia. Lichen sclerosus is an idiopathic chronic inflammatory dermatosis characterized by an atrophic parchment-like symmetric appearance to the skin and typically distributed in a figure eight–shaped area surrounding the vulva and the perianal region.[10] Although lichen sclerosus is most commonly seen as a genital lesion in adult women, it can affect any skin site and is also found in men and children. Affected patients may be asymptomatic but often report itching and soreness. Dysuria,

dyspareunia, and pain on defecation are also among the presenting complaints.

The diagnosis should be confirmed by a punch biopsy to rule out premalignant or malignant conditions that may have a similar appearance or presentation. The risk of squamous cell carcinoma of the vulva is increased in women with lichen sclerosus, but it is unknown whether lichen sclerosus represents a premalignant lesion. Lichen sclerosus does not appear to be related to HPV-associated premalignant or malignant lesions of the vulva although it can exist concurrently with these lesions. Factors such as autoimmunity, infection, and trauma may play a role in the etiology of lichen sclerosus in some patients, but no single etiologic factor can be invoked in all cases.[10]

There is no cure for lichen sclerosus. Because of the association with vulvar irritants and trauma, patients should be advised to avoid topical irritants (including tight-fitting clothing) and to use nonallergenic soaps and emollients. Patients with severe symptoms can be treated with clobetasol proprionate 0.05% ointment twice daily initially, then tapered to a minimum frequency that controls symptoms (this may be once a week, twice a month, or less).[11] Although often prescribed, topical testosterone and progesterone have proven minimally beneficial in a randomized clinical trial.[12] As in other chronic pain conditions, amitriptyline may be helpful if pain persists. Oral retinoids and surgery may have a limited role for some patients.[13] Surgery in women is useful mainly to treat complications of scarring. Recurrence after the ablation of lichen sclerosus by any technique is common.[10] Long-term follow-up is recommended because of the association with vulvar malignancy.

Squamous cell hyperplasia generally presents as a single vulvar plaque but may present as multiple simultaneous lesions. Lesions appear thickened and hyperkeratotic. Pruritus, burning, dyspareunia, or pain may be present. Biopsies should be performed on lesions suspected of being of squamous cell hyperplasia. The goals of treatment are to confirm the diagnosis, eliminate symptomatic itching, protect the skin from damage due to scratching, and improve sexual function. Treatment is similar to that of lichen sclerosus, with potent topical steroids being a mainstay of therapy. Surgical vulvectomy is indicated only for suspected malignant change.

Long-term follow-up surveillance is essential to detecting cancer in patients with squamous cell hyperplasia.[14]

Other Painful and Pruritic Vulvar Conditions

Clinicians often find that vulvar pain or pruritus persists despite multiple attempts at diagnosis and treatment. Recurrent symptoms can be extremely frustrating for both the patient and clinician. There is a growing recognition of a number of chronic painful and pruritic vulvar syndromes. These disorders are poorly defined, with limited data to guide diagnosis or therapy. They are most likely to consist of a heterogeneous group of conditions that share overlapping clinical manifestations.

The terms "vulvar pruritus," "vulvodynia," and "vulvar vestibulitis" have been used to describe these syndromes, depending on which symptoms predominate. Vulvar pruritus is by far the most common and may be related to cutaneous inflammation in response to the trauma of chronic scratching (leading to a cycle of itching and scratching). Vulvodynia is characterized by a chronic burning or stinging vulvar pain that is persistent and unrelated to specific stimuli. Vestibulitis manifests as tenderness to touch and as erythema or tenderness of the minor vestibular gland area that occurs with gentle pressure from a cotton-tipped applicator.

Other causes for these symptoms should be ruled out through careful history and physical examination. Treatment is generally directed at stopping the itch-scratch cycle, using topical corticosteroids and antihistamines at night. Vulvodynia is treated with oral tricyclic antidepressants (eg, nortriptyline, 10 mg qhs) although symptom relief is often minimal. Vestibulitis is treated with anti-inflammatory agents such as steroids or estradiol and tricyclic antidepressants. Surgical excision of affected tissue (vulvectomy) is rarely necessary.[15] Unfortunately, these treatments often can be unsatisfactory, perhaps reflecting the multifactorial etiology of these complaints.

Women with chronic vulvar symptoms typically see several clinicians and undergo many therapeutic trials. These patients may become depressed as a result of the chronic nature of these disruptive disorders. A multidisciplinary approach to diagnosis and treatment by specialists in a supportive environment is often necessary.

REFERENCES

1. Sobel JD. Vaginal infections in adult women. Med Clin North Am 1990;74:1573–99.
2. 1998 guidelines for treatment of sexually transmitted diseases. Centers for Disease Control and Prevention. MMWR Morb Mortal Wkly Rep 1998;47(RR-1):1–118.
3. Fleury FJ. Adult vaginitis. Clin Obstet Gynecol 1981;24:407–38.
4. Foster DC. Vulvitis and vaginitis. Curr Opin Obstet Gynecol 1993;5:726–32.
5. Schaaf VM. The limited value of symptoms and signs in the diagnosis of vaginal infections. Arch Intern Med 1990;150:1929–33.
6. Nathan L. Vulvovaginal disorders in the elderly woman. Clin Obstet Gynecol 1998;34:933–45.
7. Hill DA, Lense JJ. Office management of Bartholin gland cysts and abscesses. Am Fam Physician 1998;57:1611–20.
8. Ho GY, Bierman R, Beardsley L, et al. Natural history of cervicovaginal papillomavirus infection in young women. N Engl J Med 1998;338:423–8.
9. Herbst AL. Premalignant and malignant diseases of the vulva. In: Herbst AL, Mishell DR, Stenchever MA, Droegemueller W, editors. Comprehensive gynecology. 2nd ed. St. Louis (MO): Mosby Year Book; 1992.
10. Powell J, Wojnarowska F. Lichen sclerosus. Lancet 1999;353:1777–83.
11. Dalziel KL, Millard PR, and Wojnarowska F. The treatment of vulval lichen sclerosus with a very potent topical steroid (clobetasol propionate 0.05%) cream. Br J Dermatol 1991;124:461–4.
12. Bracco GL, Carli P, Sonni L, et al. Clinical and histologic effects of topical treatments of vulval lichen sclerosus: a critical evaluation. J Reprod Med 1993;38(1):37–40.
13. Bousema MT, Romppanen U, Geiger JM, et al. Acitretin in the treatment of severe lichen sclerosus et atrophicus of the vulva: a double-blind, placebo-controlled study. J Am Acad Dermatol 1994;30 (2 Pt l)225–31.
14. Hillard PA. Benign diseases of the female reproductive tract: symptoms and signs. In: Berek JS, Adashi EY, Hilliard PA, editors. Novak's gynecology. 12th ed. Baltimore (MD): Williams & Wilkins; 1996.
15. Davis GD, Hutchison CV. Clinical management of vulvodynia. Clin Obstet Gynecol 1999;42:221–33.

81

HUMAN PAPILLOMAVIRUS, CERVICAL DYSPLASIA, AND CERVICAL CANCER

Andrew John Li, MD

Cervical carcinoma is a preventable disease that remains the number one cancer killer of women worldwide. Despite widespread screening, approximately 16,000 cases of invasive carcinoma of the uterine cervix are diagnosed each year in the United States, making it the sixth most common malignant neoplasm in American women, behind breast, lung, colorectal, endometrial, and ovarian cancer. However, because of screening and treatment programs, only approximately 5,000 women die each year of this disease in the United States.[1] In contrast, cervix carcinoma is the most common cause of cancer-related death in women in developing countries. Worldwide, high cervical carcinoma death rates generally correlate with the absence of successful screening mechanisms.

Recently there has been a suggestion that the decline in the incidence and mortality of cervix cancer is slowing and may actually be rising slightly in young women.[2] The National Cancer Institute's Surveillance, Epidemiology, and End Results (SEER) program reported an increase in the incidence of high-grade cervical cancer precursors that began in the early 1980s in Caucasian women younger than 50 years of age.[3] The incidence of carcinoma in situ of the cervix increased from 27 to 45 per 100,000 women from 1980 to 1990, and currently 1.5 to 6% of all Pap tests demonstrate a neoplastic precursor.[4,5] More than 2,500,000 women are diagnosed with low-grade cervical cancer precursors each year in the United States.[6]

The human papillomavirus (HPV) has been identified as a key factor in cervical carcinogenesis. Epidemiologic studies conclusively demonstrate that there is a strong and consistent association between specific genotypes of HPV deoxyribonucleic acid (DNA) and premalignant and invasive cervix cancer and that exposure to HPV precedes the development of cervical dysplasia. Although not all women infected with HPV develop cervical neoplasia and not all cervix cancers are linked to HPV infection, the role of HPV in the malignant transformation of the cervical tissue is undisputed.

This chapter reviews the etiology, diagnosis, management, and treatment of cervical dysplasia and carcinoma, and the role of HPV in cervical cancer. New screening technologies also are discussed, and their efficacy and cost-effectiveness is compared with that of the traditional Papanicolaou smear test.

PREINVASIVE DISEASE

Anatomy

The location of the cervix in the upper vagina allows direct accessibility for detecting and treating cervical dysplasia. A routine pelvic examination includes visualization of the uterine cervix with the aid of a speculum, allowing the examination of the anterior and posterior lips of the cervix, the portio, and the external cervical os.

The squamocolumnar junction is an important landmark where dysplastic changes potentially

891

leading to carcinoma may arise. In young women, this junction is the intersection of the cervical glandular (or columnar) epithelium and the mucosal squamous epithelium of the vagina; it is usually located on the exocervix, just distal to the external os. During pregnancy this area may evert and move distally from its usual location. After menopause the junction recedes and is frequently located in the endocervical canal. During puberty and throughout reproductive life, the exposed columnar epithelium undergoes a gradual metaplastic change to squamous epithelium, and the areas of columnar epithelium and squamous metaplasia constitute the normal transformation zone.[7]

Etiology

A number of risk factors have been identified for the development of premalignant precursors and invasive carcinoma. The majority of risk factors are markers of sexual behavior, including multiple sexual partners, early age of first pregnancy and coitarche, a history of sexually transmitted diseases, and increased parity. In addition, lower socioeconomic class, cigarette smoking, and immunosuppression are also linked to cervical cancer.[8]

Initial epidemiologic observations suggested an association between cervical cancer and sexually transmitted diseases. Cancer was seen much more frequently in married women than in celibate nuns, was more common in prostitutes than in the general population, and was closely linked to the lifetime number of male partners.[9-11] Furthermore, the subsequent wife of a man whose first wife died of cervical cancer had a threefold increased risk of contracting the disease.[12] These findings led investigators to consider a wide variety of infectious agents as possible etiologic agents in cervical cancer; these included *Treponema pallidum*, *Trichomonas vaginalis*, *Candida albicans*, *Chlamydia trachomatis*, and the herpes simplex viruses. After intense study, however, all of these have subsequently been discarded as causative agents.[8]

Several other risk factors, including cigarette smoking, the use of oral contraceptives, and diet, are also associated with the development of cervical cancer. These risk factors have been linked more specifically with cervical cancers of squamous cell histology. Cigarette smoke may act through the secretion of nicotine and cotinine by-products in the cervical mucus, either from direct tobacco

inhalation or from passive exposure. These by-products may have a direct mutagenic effect on the cervical epithelium, as evidenced by the increased level of structurally altered DNA.[13] Since the number of Langerhans' cells is reduced in the cervical epithelium of smokers,[14] there may also be a local immunologic effect. Even after controlling for sexual behavior and Pap test screening, studies have indicated an approximate twofold increase in risk among oral contraceptive users.[15] However, the effect of these exogenous hormones on the cervix is unclear and controversial, and this association may be due to study bias or other confounding variables. Finally, some studies have demonstrated that diets low in vitamin A, vitamin C, and folate may be associated with increased cancer risk.[16,17]

Clear cell adenocarcinoma of the cervix is associated with prenatal exposure to diethylstilbestrol (DES), a synthetic steroid that was given to pregnant women from the late 1930s to the early 1970s for presumptive prevention of spontaneous abortions.[7] The overall incidence is low, at approximately 0.14 to 1.4 cases per 1,000 DES-exposed women. Risk factors for adenocarcinomas and adenosquamous carcinomas are less clearly defined.

Human Papillomavirus

Over the past decades a significant number of data have implicated HPV as a key factor in the pathogenesis of cervical cancer and its preinvasive precursors.[18] Epidemiologic studies clearly demonstrate a strong and consistent association between specific types of HPV and invasive cervix cancer and its precursor lesions. A case-control study reported that 75% of dysplasia was attributed to HPV infection and that traditional risk factors became irrelevant when HPV infection was controlled for.[19] Other studies demonstrate odds ratios of greater than 20 linking HPV infection and invasive cervical carcinoma.[20] Molecular studies have confirmed the presence of HPV DNA in neoplastic tumors and high-grade lesions.[21,22]

Human papillomavirus belongs to a family of double-stranded DNA viruses that are epitheliotropic, that is, they preferentially infect epithelial cells of the skin and mucous membranes.[23] Human papillomavirus is categorized into genotypes based on the extent of their DNA homology. Over 20 of these HPV types have been reported in the anogenital tract, and these have been further subdivided into three different groups. The first group consists of the low- or no-oncogenic-risk viruses, including HPV types 6, 11, 42, 43, and 44. These viruses are rarely linked with invasive genital tract cancer but are commonly associated with condyloma acuminatum and may sometimes be found in low-grade dysplastic lesions. The second group of viruses is the high-oncogenic-risk viruses, principally HPV 16, 18, and 31. These high-risk viruses are commonly found associated with high-grade dysplastic lesions and invasive cancers of the cervix. The remaining HPV types are often classified as of intermediate oncogenic risk since they are found in association with dysplastic states, but they are uncommonly associated with invasive cervical cancers. Intermediate-oncogenic-risk types include HPV types 33, 35, 39, 51, 52, and 56.[8]

Studies have recently elucidated the carcinogenic mechanisms of HPV. The genome of the virus includes transcriptional units that encode proteins, two of which are referred to as E6 and E7. These are the proteins important in the immortalization and transformation of HPV-infected cervical cells. The E7 protein is the dominant oncogenic protein and acts by binding to the protein encoded by the retinoblastoma (Rb) gene, an endogenous tumor suppressor that functions in regulating cell proliferation.[24] The weaker oncogenic HPV protein is E6, which acts by binding to the p53 protein tumor suppressor gene that functions in cellular DNA repair.[25] In HPV-positive invasive cervical carcinoma cell lines, p53 levels are low and Rb appears normal whereas in HPV-negative cervical carcinoma cell lines, p53 and Rb are mutated, suggesting that these tumor suppressor genes are targeted by the E6 and E7 proteins of HPV and that they function in the malignant transformation of cervical tissue.[26]

Screening Techniques

THE PAPANICOLAOU TEST

Dr. George Papanicolaou first introduced the concept of cervical cytologic evaluation in the 1940s as a means for detecting invasive and preinvasive cervical neoplasms.[27] The medical community has since realized that the Pap test is the most efficacious and cost-effective tool for cancer screening currently available.[28] Significant reductions in incidence and mortality from cervix cancer have been seen since widespread cervical cytology screening programs were implemented in Canada, Europe,

and the United States.[29,30] Conversely, in developing countries (where more than 80% of cervix cancers occur worldwide), only 5% of the female population has had a screening Pap test.[31]

The Pap test is a highly specific test for the detection of high-grade squamous intraepithelial lesions (SILs) and cancers; it is somewhat less specific for low-grade SILs. Although this specificity indicates that overdiagnoses are made infrequently, Pap tests are not very sensitive; false-negative rates are estimated to be 8 to 50%.[32-34] However, because an invasive cervical cancer takes 10 to 17 years to develop from a low-grade SIL and 5 to 10 years to develop from a carcinoma in situ, it is unlikely that cervical dysplasia will not be found before invasion to cancer occurs.[35] Thus the current recommendation from the American College of Obstetrics and Gynecology and the American Cancer Society is that "all women who are or have been sexually active, or have reached the age of 18 years, have an annual Pap test and pelvic examination. After a woman has had three or more consecutive satisfactory normal annual examinations, the Pap test may be performed less frequently in a low-risk woman at the discretion of her physician."[36] The carrying out of this recommendation has resulted in the reduction of cervical cancer by almost 80% in the United States over the last 30 years.[2]

Proper technique in obtaining a Pap smear is paramount in maintaining the quality of the test and reducing the false-negative rate. Smears should be obtained before any digital examination, and women should refrain from intercourse and the use of lubricants or douches for 24 hours before the test. Pap tests should be postponed if there is vaginal bleeding from menses or when there is evidence of cervicitis or vaginitis. An ectocervical scraping should be performed with an Ayres spatula, and an endocervical sample should be taken with a cytobrush. Moistening these tools may prevent air-drying artifacts. After the sample is smeared onto a glass slide, it should be sprayed immediately with a fixative.

TERMINOLOGY OF CYTOLOGIC FINDINGS

The original classification of cytologic smears, proposed by Dr. Papanicolaou, was modified by the World Health Organization in 1973 and then by the National Institutes of Health in 1988. This classification system was re-evaluated in 1991 and was revised again to form the present-day Bethesda System (Table 81–1).[37] This system incorporates the

---

TABLE 81–1. The 1991 Bethesda System

Adequacy of the specimen
    Satisfactory for evaluation
    Satisfactory for evaluation but limited by (specify reason)
    Unsatisfactory for evaluation (specify reason)

General categorization
    Within normal limits
    Benign cellular changes (see descriptive diagnosis)
    Epithelial cell abnormality (see descriptive diagnosis)

Descriptive diagnoses
    Benign cellular changes
        Infection
            Trichomonas vaginalis
            Fungal organisms morphologically consistent with *Candida* sp
            Predominance of coccobacilli, consistent with shift in vaginal flora
            Bacteria morphologically consistent with *Actinomyces* sp
            Cellular changes associated with herpes simplex virus
            Other

        Reactive changes

        Reactive cellular changes associated with:
            Inflammation (includes typical repair)
            Atrophy with inflammation ("atrophic vaginitis")
            Radiation
             Intrauterine contraceptive device (IUD)
            Other
    Epithelial cell abnormalities
        Squamous cell
            Atypical squamous cells of undetermined significance (ASCUS) (qualify)
            Low-grade squamous intraepithelial lesion (SIL) encompassing HPV, mild dysplasia/cervical intraepithelial
                neoplasia (CIN) 1
            High-grade SIL encompassing moderate and severe dysplasia, carcinoma in situ (CIS), CIN 2, and CIN 3
            Squamous cell carcinoma

        Glandular cell
            Endometrial cells, cytologically benign, in a postmenopausal woman
            Atypical glandular cells of undetermined significance (qualify)
            Endocervical adenocarcinoma
            Endometrial adenocarcinoma
            Extrauterine adenocarcinoma
            Adenocarcinoma, not otherwise specified

        Other malignant neoplasm (specify)
        Hormonal evaluation (applies to vaginal smears only)

        Hormonal pattern compatible with age and history

        Hormonal pattern incompatible with age and history (specify)

        Hormonal evaluation not possible due to (specify)

HPV = human papillomavirus.
Reproduced with permission from Luff RD. The Bethesda System for reporting cervical/vaginal cytologic diagnoses: report of the 1991 Bethesda Workshop. Hum Pathol 1992;23:719.

older categories of mild, moderate, and severe dysplasia (including cervical intraepithelial neoplasias 1, 2, and 3) and allows direct cytohistologic correlations to be made. The strengths of this classification are that (1) it requires an estimation of the adequacy of the specimen for diagnostic evaluation; (2) it describes a general categorization of either being within normal limits or showing an epithelial abnormality; and (3) it gives a diagnosis that includes evidence of infection, inflammation, and reactive changes and a description of epithelial cell abnormalities.

Squamous intraepithelial lesions describe features associated with premalignant states. These can include increased nucleocytoplasmic ratios due to enlarged nuclei, nuclear hyperchromatism, irregular nuclear membranes, halos, or perinuclear clearing. In a low-grade SIL cytologic changes are seen predominantly in superficial (or more mature) cell types. In a high-grade SIL the cytologic changes are seen in basal and parabasal cells (or less mature cell types) as well.

The term "atypical squamous cells of undetermined significance" (ASCUS) represents a group of cytologic findings in which cells have abnormalities characterized as atypical but not diagnostic of an SIL. Cytologists often may favor a reactive or neoplastic process, to indicate their degree of concern. Reports of ASCUS should be limited to less than 5% of all Pap test diagnoses.[6] Studies indicate that 19 to 56% of patients diagnosed with ASCUS subsequently developed an SIL or invasive cancer.[38,39]

Management

Numerous algorithms describe different strategies of management for disorders diagnosed from the abnormal Pap test. Most agree that cytology diagnosed as ASCUS may be managed with repeat tests in 3 to 6 months in reliable patients. Those patients with benign cellular changes suggesting inflammation or infection should be treated appropriately after evaluation for infectious agents such as *Chlamydia* or *Trichomonas*. Postmenopausal women diagnosed with reactive changes favoring atrophy may benefit from a course of intravaginal estrogen cream before repeating the test. An endometrial biopsy should be considered when atypical endometrial cells are found in a postmenopausal or irregularly menstruating woman.[6]

The presence of endocervical cells on a Pap smear is regarded as evidence of adequate sampling of the tranformation zone. When the cells are absent, the endocervix may not have been sampled; the Bethesda System classifies these smears as satisfactory but limited. Studies in which these tests have been immediately repeated indicate that the discovery of premalignant lesions has been rare. The American College of Obstetrics and Gynecology (ACOG) recommends that repeat Pap tests for patients who have no high-risk factors, who have had three consecutive annual normal Pap tests, and whose current Pap tests are otherwise normal may be deferred until the next annual examination. Women at any increased risk should undergo repeat endocervical sampling.[40]

All low- and high-grade SILs, as well as two consecutive ASCUS reports, should be evaluated with colposcopy and directed cervical biopsies. A dilute (4%) acetic acid solution is applied to the cervix; this solution dissolves any cervical mucus and dehydrates the cytoplasm of the epithelial cells. The SILs become whiter than the surrounding normal epithelium due to their increased nucleocytoplasmic ratios. The cervix is examined at a magnification of about 16 times with a microscope with a long focal length, and the identification of acetowhite lesions directs a biopsy of these lesions. High-grade SILs and invasive cancer may also be identified from punctate or mosaic patterns representing angiogenic blood vessel patterns. Except in pregnant patients, endocervical curettings should always be obtained to evaluate the endocervical canal, which cannot be visualized on examination.

In some patients, colposcopic evaluation cannot provide an adequate evaluation. Colposcopy is termed unsatisfactory when the transformation zone is not fully visualized, a visible lesion extends into the endocervical canal, the endocervical curettings reveal dysplastic fragments, or there is a discordance of more than one grade between the Pap test and the results of a colposcopically directed biopsy.

Treatment

A biopsy of a lesion provides a histologic diagnosis rather than a cytologic diagnosis of a suspected SIL. Cervical intraepithelial neoplasia (CIN) 1 describes dysplastic cells occupying less than one-third of the epithelium. Atypical cells occupying less than two-thirds of the epithelium is described as CIN 2, and CIN 3 describes atypical cells occupying more than two-thirds of the epithelium. Carcinoma in situ

(CIS) describes atypical cells occupying all of the epithelium but not invading through the basement membrane.

Not all CINs progress to invasive cancer. In a large group of women observed for more than 20 years, regression from mild dysplasia (CIN 1) to normal occurred in 62% of cases.[41] Similarly, a review of the world literature on cervical precursors demonstrated a 57% regression of CIN 1 to normal and regression rates of 43% and 32% for CIN 2 and CIN 3, respectively.[42] This data is summarized in Table 81–2. Conversely, a large study of more than 17,000 women demonstrated a risk of progression from mild to severe dysplasia of only 1% per year, but the risk of progression from moderate dysplasia was 16% within 2 years and 25% within 5 years.[43]

These findings shape treatment guidelines for CIN. In low-risk healthy women, CIN 1 may be managed conservatively with observation and heightened surveillance, with Pap tests and colposcopy every 3 to 6 months. However, in high-risk women, such as those with compliance problems or immunosuppression, definitive treatment should be considered more strongly.

Treatment consists of ablative or excisional therapy. A popular ablative technique is cryotherapy, in which destruction of superficial cervical epithelium is achieved by a freezing process. Carbon dioxide or nitrous oxide is released into a probe that is placed directly on the cervix. An ice ball forms and should extend 3 to 4 mm beyond the edge of the lesion; maximum freezing usually occurs between 3 to 5 minutes. After the probe thaws, a second application is usually performed. Cryotherapy is highly effective for small lesions, and its cure rates approach 90%.[44] The higher failure rates seen with CIN 3 may be due to the greater size of the lesions or the glandular involvement of cervical crypts associated with higher degrees of dysplasia.

Laser therapy is also used for ablation of dysplastic epithelium. The energy from a laser beam is applied to dysplastic cervical tissue, with absorption by water and resultant vaporization. The laser should be applied to a depth of 5 to 7 mm, with an approximate power density of 600 W/cm². Success rates are comparable to those of cryotherapy, and a CIN 3 resolution as high as 83 to 88% was seen in one study.[45] An advantage of the laser therapy, compared to cryotherapy, is easier post-treatment visualization of the transformation zone where the squamocolumnar junction usually relocates into the endocervical canal.

Excisional therapy is performed for both diagnostic and therapeutic reasons. Conization is indicated when (1) colposcopic examination is unsatisfactory, (2) histology and cytology results differ by two grades, (3) adenocarcinoma in situ is reported on the Pap smear, (4) an endocervical cancer is suspected, or (5) there is uncertainty regarding the presence of invasive disease. The technique involves the excision of a cone-shaped specimen from the cervix, to include the outer limits of the lesion. The apex of the cone is placed at a depth that varies with the visualization of the transformation zone and positivity of the endocervical curettage.

Conization may be performed with a scalpel in the operating room (cold-knife conization) or with a loop electroexcisional procedure (LEEP). Cold-knife conization may have an advantage in evaluating margins for residual disease. Ahlgren et al found 98% cure rates after 5 years when the specimen margins were free of dysplasia; this rate fell to 70% when margins were positive.[46] Loop electroexcisional procedures are also effective excisional modalities that have gained wide acceptance in recent years. The advantages of the LEEP include allowing the excision to be done in an office setting (at a considerably lower cost than cold-knife conization and with

TABLE 81–2. Natural History of Cervical Intraepithelial Neoplasia

N	CIN Type	Regress (%)	Persist (%)	Progress to CIN 3 (%)	Progress to Invasion (%)
4,504	1	57	32	11	1
2,247	2	43	35	22	5
767	3	32	56	—	12

CIN = cervical intraepithelial neoplasia; N = number of subjects.
Reproduced with permission from Ostor AG. Natural history of cervical intraepithelial neoplasia: a critical review. Int J Gynecol Pathol 1993;12:186.

the use of local anesthesia) and a low incidence of perioperative complications. Recent studies indicate that this technique is just as effective and reliable as cold-knife conization and yields similar diagnostic and therapeutic results.[47]

After conization, women still require surveillance with frequent Pap tests and pelvic examinations. Hysterectomy may be considered for women with residual disease at the margins of their conization specimen. However, yearly cytology is still indicated postoperatively as these patients are at risk for the development of vaginal dysplasia.

New Screening Techniques

Even patients who undergo annual screening Pap smears occasionally develop invasive carcinoma because of false-negative results. Concerns about false-negative results with the Pap technique have led to the development of new technologies to enhance the detection of cervical cancer precursors; these include fluid-based cytologic smear techniques and tests to detect cervical HPV infection.

Fluid-based technologies work by optimizing the collection and preparation of cells. ThinPrep (Cytyc Corporation, Boxborough, Massachusetts) is one such technique that is approved by the Food and Drug Administration. The specimen is collected in the same manner as the Pap smear, using the spatula and cytobrush. It is not smeared on a slide but is rinsed into a vial of preservative solution instead. This solution preserves epithelial cells and strengthens the bonds between cells to limit disaggregation. Fresh red blood cells are lysed, and microbiologic elements are killed. The sample is mixed by high-speed rotation of the vial and is drawn through a polycarbonate filter by vacuum pressure, with monitoring by a microprocessor to control how many cells are deposited on the filter. The cells are then transferred to a glass slide and stained.[48]

The advantages of fluid-based techniques include the removal of most mucus, protein, and fresh red blood cells from the preparation; uniform distribution of the cells; improved fixation and preservation of cellular structure; maintenance of diagnostic clusters; and uniform sampling of the specimen removed from the cervix.[48] Disadvantages may involve the need for retraining cytotechnologists and cytopathologists in the interpretation of a monolayer preparation. Also, the preservation of aggregates makes the evaluation of diagnostic features both at the center and in the periphery of these clusters more difficult. Finally, the estimated costs of the ThinPrep system may be twice that of conventional cytologic techniques after all variables are considered, including the greater cost of supplies, the longer slide preparation time, and the shorter slide evaluation time for ThinPrep.[49]

Comparisons between ThinPrep and conventional techniques have indicated equivalent specificities for low-grade and high-grade squamous lesions, but ThinPrep was found to be significantly more sensitive in predicting the presence of dysplasia in one study of high-risk women in Costa Rica.[50] However, another study found that the ThinPrep method was significantly less specific in predicting adenocarcinoma in situ.[51] Consistent evidence does not exist to suggest that fluid-based monolayers significantly improve the detection of dysplastic abnormalities. Similarly, there are insufficient data to indicate a reduction in cervical carcinoma morbidity and mortality with fluid-based techniques, versus the conventional Pap test.[49]

Testing for HPV is another new technique that has been proposed to enhance screening for cervical cancer. Hybrid Capture (Digene, Silver Spring, Maryland) is a highly sensitive commercial HPV DNA detection kit that detects five low-risk and nine high-risk HPV types from tissue swabs taken from the transformation zone of the cervix. Testing for HPV has been shown to be more sensitive but less specific than conventional Pap tests for detecting high-grade SILs or cancer, leading to almost twice the referral rate for colposcopy.[52] Futhermore, although it is clear that HPV has an outstanding role in cervical carcinogenesis, its presence in cervical infections in young women is more of a marker of sexual activity than of cervical cancer risk. Evidence indicates that HPV infection is often transient and is cleared in the first 12 to 24 months in many women.[53] The persistence of HPV infection in an older population, however, may be an indication of increased cancer risk.[49]

Current data do not demonstrate that HPV testing improves the overall efficacy of cervical cancer screening programs. Studies that used HPV testing in screening protocols found that only 22% of high-grade lesions were HPV DNA positive.[54] Other authors found similar sensitivities for high-grade lesions but determined that the predictive value of HPV testing was almost twice as high as that of the cytologic testing.[55] However, there may be a role for HPV testing in the triage of women with ASCUS or low-grade SILs. Studies demonstrate significant correlations between high-risk HPV types and the findings of CIN 2 and CIN 3 in women with repeated low-grade cervical cytologic abnormalities, suggesting that HPV testing may obviate the need for repeated colposcopic examinations.[56] Furthermore, the results from the ALTS trial (ASCUS/LSIL Triage Study) suggest that triaging ASCUS lesions to colposcopy based on HPV results has greater sensitivity to detect CIN 3 or above, and specificity comparable with a single additional cytologic test indicating ASCUS or above.[57]

The use of HPV testing in developing countries has also been suggested. A recent study compared conventional Pap smears with self-collected and clinician-collected swabs for HPV testing. Although the self-collected swabs had sensitivities similar to those of the Pap smears, they had higher false-positive rates. Furthermore, the self-collection was performed in an examination room, just after patients were given specific instructions.[58] Self-collection of samples in more realistic conditions was not evaluated.

In summary, new technologies have raised the awareness of the limitations of the Pap test as a screening tool for cervical dysplasia and cancer but have not been shown to be more effective than the conventional cytologic evaluation. Studies suggest that they may have an important adjunctive role in screening, but as yet they should not be substituted for the annual Pap test and pelvic examination.

INVASIVE CERVICAL CARCINOMA

Presenting Signs and Symptoms

Early invasive carcinoma of the cervix is usually asymptomatic and is diagnosed by a Pap test or a pelvic examination. The cervix may be grossly normal in appearance, or the only clinical finding may be a small exophytic or ulcerative lesion. In more advanced disease an ulcerative or necrotic tumor may present with abnormal vaginal bleeding, especially after sexual activity. There may be a malodorous serosanguinous or yellow discharge. Some patients present with low back or pelvic pain, or patients may report hematuria or rectal bleeding due to invasion of the bladder or rectum.

The physical examination is usually normal, except for cervical lesions visualized with a speculum. The bimanual pelvic examination may reveal a bulky endocervical mass, and the diameter of the tumor should be measured. An assessment of pelvic side-wall involvement should be done, and the inguinal and supraclavicular nodes should be evaluated for suspicious masses.

A biopsy should be performed on any ulcerative or exophytic cervical lesion to confirm the diagnosis of invasive carcinoma. When such a diagnosis is made, referral to a gynecologic oncologist for evaluation and treatment should be made immediately.

Staging and Prognostic Factors

The staging of cervical carcinoma is clinical, based on pelvic and rectal examination. Examination under anesthesia affords the benefits of muscular relaxation. When possible, examination under anesthesia should include as many members of the treating team as possible, including radiation oncologists. The staging system is described in Table 81–3.

The extent of disease may be further evaluated by chest radiography, intravenous pyelography, cystoscopy, and proctoscopy. Lymphangiography, computed tomography, and ultrasonography are not included in standard clinical staging but may assist in individual therapy.

A review of surgically treated early cervical cancers revealed that lymph node status, parametrial involvement, status of the surgical margins, capillary lymphatic-space involvement, tumor size, and depth of invasion were all significantly related to the occurrence of recurrent disease.[59] Other multivariate analyses indicate that clinical tumor size, depth of invasion, and grade are the main predictors for prognosis.[60]

Treatment

The main treatments of cervical carcinoma are surgery (in early-stage cancers) and radiation with adjuvant chemotherapy (in more advanced disease). The presence or absence of microinvasion is important in clinical decision making. In 1974 the Society of Gynecologic Oncologists defined microinvasion as basement membrane penetration with little or no risk of nodal involvement, dissemination, or recurrence. Women whose cancers show invasion of 3 mm or less may undergo total extrafascial

TABLE 81–3. Staging of Cervical Carcinoma[*]

Carcinoma is strictly confined to the cervix (extension to the corpus should be disregarded).

IA.   Invasive cancer identified only microscopically; all gross lesions even with superficial invasion are stage IB cancers

IA1. Measured invasion of stroma no greater than 3.0 mm in depth and no wider than 7.0 mm

IA2. Measured invasion of stroma greater than 3.0 mm and no greater than 5.0 mm in depth and no wider than 7.0 mm

IB.   Clinical lesions confined to the cervix or preclinical lesions greater than IA

IB1. Clinical lesions no larger than 4.0 cm

IB2. Clinical lesions larger than 4.0 cm

Carcinoma extends beyond the cervix but has not extended to the pelvic wall. Carcinoma involves the vagina but not as far as the lower third.

IIA. No obvious parametrial involvement

IIB. Obvious parametrial involvement

Carcinoma has extended to the pelvic wall. On rectal examination, there is no cancer-free space between the tumor and the pelvic wall. Tumor involves the lower third of the vagina. All cases with a hydronephrosis or nonfunctioning kidney are included.

IIIA. No extension to the pelvic wall

IIIB. Extension to the pelvic wall and/or hydronephrosis or nonfunctioning kidney

Carcinoma has extended beyond the true pelvis or has clinically involved the mucosa of the bladder or rectum, excluding bullous edema.

IVA. Spread of the growth to adjacent organs

IVB. Spread to distant organs

[*]International Federation of Gynecology and Obstetrics (FIGO) staging criteria.
Reproduced with permission from Jones H, Benedet J, Creasman W, et al, editors. SGO handbook: staging of gynecologic malignancies. 2nd ed. Princeton (NJ): Bristol-Myers Squibb; 1997. p. 15–20.

hysterectomy or conization without lymph node evaluation. Early invasive carcinoma (stage IA2) may be treated with a total hysterectomy or a modified radical hysterectomy.[61]

For bulky tumors staged as IB to IIA, both radiation and radical hysterectomy are standard treatment modalities that have comparable survival rates.[61] The choice of one over the other is based on the general condition of the patient as well as on surgeon and institution biases. Most gynecologic oncologists favor the surgical approach in younger women, for whom ovarian function may be more important. A recent study confirmed that ovarian conservation is safe in early-stage cancers and that the occurrence of subsequent complications in ovaries retained in situ is rare.[62] The desire to preserve sexual function may also influence the choice of a surgical approach over radiation therapy.

The extent of the hysterectomy often varies with the surgeon, and the decision in regard to

extent takes into consideration the size of the tumor. The class II modified radical hysterectomy removes the cervix and upper vagina, including paracervical tissues. The ureters are dissected in the paracervical tunnel to the point of entry into the bladder. The class III radical hysterectomy consists of a resection of the parametrial tissues to the pelvic wall, with complete dissection of the ureters from their beds and mobilization of the bladder and rectum to allow for more extensive removal of tissues. A vaginal cuff of at least 2 to 3 cm is always included in the procedure, and a bilateral pelvic lymphadenectomy is usually carried out. As expected, the class II procedure is less morbid and is well suited for tumors with 3 to 5 mm of invasion and for small lesions that do not distort anatomy.[61]

In young women with early-stage disease who want their fertility preserved, vaginal trachelectomy (removing the cervix while sparing the uterus) may be considered. Roy and Plante reviewed their experience of 30 cases in 1998 and described comparable morbidity and mortality with radical trachelectomy and laparoscopic lymphadenectomy, as well as healthy babies delivered by cesarean section at 39, 38, 34, and 25 weeks of gestation.[62] Certainly this new technique is a valuable procedure in well-selected patients with early-stage cancers; further evaluation is under way to determine precise indications.

Radiation is the standard treatment for more advanced disease. In February 1999 the National Cancer Institute issued a clinical announcement regarding concurrent chemoradiation for cervical cancer, based on the results of five randomized phase III trials. Each trial demonstrated overall survival advantages when cisplatin-based chemotherapy was given concurrently with radiation therapy. The patient populations in these studies included women with International Federation of Gynecology and Obstetrics (FIGO) stage IB2 to IVA cervical carcinomas treated with standard radiation and women with FIGO stage I to IIA disease with poor prognostic factors at the time of radical hysterectomy. Although the trials varied in terms of stage of disease, dose of radiation, and schedule of cisplatin and radiation, they all demonstrated significant survival benefits for this combined apporoach. Concurrent chemoradiation reduced the risk of death from cervical cancer by 30 to 50%.[62–65]

SPECIAL CONSIDERATIONS IN PREGNANCY

The evaluation of an abnormal Pap test result in pregnancy is complicated due to a number of factors, including increased vascularity and edema of the cervix, as well as the presence of the fetus. However, the natural eversion of the squamocolumnar junction that occurs during pregnancy allows better visualization of the transformation zone and easier colposcopy. Therapy usually is delayed until after delivery; the prime objective in the prepartum period is to exclude invasive carcinoma.

Cervical screening and management of cytological abnormalities is modified for pregnant patients. Cases of low- and high-grade SILs should be followed with colposcopy and biopsies as indicated; endocervical curettage should be postponed. In the absence of CIN 3 or carcinoma in situ, colposcopy should be repeated each trimester. It should be noted that CIN may have higher regression rates when detected in pregnancy. It may be that low-grade intraepithelial findings may represent cytologic changes that occur as a consequence of pregnancy or that the trauma of vaginal delivery may remove superficial cervical epithelium harboring preinvasive cells.[66]

If microinvasion is suspected, conization or an LEEP should be performed. A summary of reported conizations in the literature revealed that 9% of 448 patients required blood transfusions for procedural blood losses, but no adverse pregnancy outcomes occurred.[7]

Prior to fetal viability, invasive cervical cancer should be treated stage-for-stage as in the nonpregnant patient, with the understanding that this will result in the death of the fetus. Patients with cervical cancer in early stages can be treated by radical hysterectomy and pelvic lymphadenectomy or by pelvic irradiation followed by intrauterine and vaginal irradiation. Patients in the first trimester of pregnancy who are treated by the latter method may spontaneously abort the fetus prior to receiving 4,000 cGy of pelvic radiation. In second-trimester previable pregnancies, termination should be considered prior to treatment since spontaneous abortion frequently does not occur during radiation at this time. Vaginal delivery should be avoided; the major risk is hemorrhage secondary to tumor trauma from cervical dilation.[7]

With the increasing success of neonatal care in achieving the survival of neonates at 24 weeks or beyond, the management of cervical cancer in later pregnancy presents a more difficult decision. Prior to fetal pulmonary maturity, patients should be treated individually, and the concerns for infant survival must be weighed against the risks of delayed therapy. When fetal maturity is established, cesarean delivery should be performed prior to the initiation of therapy.

CONCLUSION

Many advances have been made recently in the etiology, diagnosis, management, and treatment of cervical dysplasia and invasive cancer. The success of contemporary efforts to identify and treat dysplastic precursors has made cervical cancer a more manageable disease in the United States, yet attention must be focused also on developing countries, where the morbidity and mortality of this disease continues to affect women who are without access to health care. As research better characterizes HPV and its role in cervical cancer, improved screening methods and (ultimately) a vaccine against cervical cancer may become feasible. The medical community must translate the results of new studies and technology into care for all women at risk for cervical carcinoma.

REFERENCES

1. Wingo PA, Tong T, Bolden S. Cancer statistics, 1995. CA Cancer J Clin 1995;45:8–30.
2. Devesa SS. Descriptive epidemiology of cancer of the uterine cervix. Obstet Gynecol 1984;63:605–12.
3. Larsen N. Invasive cervical cancer arising in young white females. J Natl Cancer Inst 1994;86:6–7.
4. Larsen N, Jones MA. The management of the mildly dyskaryotic smear. Br J Obstet Gynaecol 1994;101:474–6.
5. Sadeghi SB, Sadeghi A, Robboy SJ. Prevalence of dysplasia and cancer of the cervix in a nationwide Planned Parenthood population. Cancer 1988;61:2359–61.
6. Kurman RJ, Henson DE, Herbst AL, et al. Interim guidelines for management of abnormal cervical cytology. The 1992 National Cancer Institute workshop. JAMA 1994;271:1866–9.
7. Herbst AL. Intraepithelial neoplasia of the cervix. In: Mishell DR, Stenchever MA, Droegemueller W, Herbst AL, editors. Comprehensive gynecology. St. Louis: Mosby; 1997.
8. Wright TC, Richart RM. Pathogenesis and diagnosis of preinvasive lesions of the lower genital tract. In: Hoskins WJ, Perez CA, Young RC, editors. Principles and practice of gynecologic oncology. Philadelphia: Lippincott-Raven; 1997.
9. Brinton LA, Fraumeni JF. Epidemiology of uterine cervical cancer. J Chron Dis 1986;39:1051–65.
10. Buckley JD, Harris RW, Doll R, et al. Case-control study of the husbands of women with dysplasia or carcinoma of the cervix uteri. Lancet 1981;2:1010–5.
11. Franceschi S, LaVecchia C, Decarli A. Relation of cervical neoplasia with sexual factors, including specific veneral diseases. In: Peto R, zur Hausen H, editors. Viral etiology of cervical cancer. Cold Spring Harbor (NY): Cold Spring Harbor Laboratory; 1986.
12. Kessler II. Venereal factors in human cervical cancer: evidence from marital clusters. Cancer 1977;39:1912–9.
13. Ali S, Astley SB, Sheldon TA, et al. Detection and measurement of DNA adducts in the cervix of smokers and non-smokers. Int J Gynaecol Cancer 1994;4:188.
14. Barton SE, Jenkins D, Cuzick J, et al. Effect of cigarette smoking on cervical epithelial immunity: a mechanism for neoplastic change? Lancet 1988;2:652–4.
15. Gram IT, Macaluso M, Stalsberg H. Oral contraceptive use and the incidence of cervical intraepithelial neoplasia. Am J Obstet Gynecol 1992;167:40–4.
16. Verreault R, Chu J, Mandelson M, Shy K. A case control study of diet and invasive cervical cancer. Int J Cancer 1989;43:1050–4.
17. Butterworth CE, Hatch KD, Macaluso M, et al. Folate deficiency and cervical dysplasia. JAMA 1992;267:528–33.
18. Wallboomers JM, Jacobs MV, Manos MM, et al. Human papillomavirus is a necessary cause of invasive cervical cancer worldwide. J Pathol 1999;189:12–9.
19. Schiffman MH, Bauer HM, Hoover RN, et al. Epidemiologic evidence that human papillomavirus infection causes most cervical intraepithelial neoplasia. J Natl Cancer Inst 1993;85:958–64.
20. Bosch FX, Munoz N, de SanJose S, et al. Risk factors for cervical cancer in Colombia and Spain. Int J Cancer 1992;52:750–8.
21. Wright TC, Richart RM. Role of human papillomavirus in the pathogenesis of genital tract warts and cancer. Gynecol Oncol 1990;37:151–64.
22. zur Hausen H. Human papillomviruses in the pathogenesis of anogenital cancer. Virology 1991;184:9–13.
23. Taichman LB, La Porte RF. The expression of papillomaviruses in epithelial cells. New York: Plenum, 1987. p. 109.
24. Barbosa MS, Edwards C, Fisher C, et al. The region of the HPV E7 oncoprotein homologous to adenovirus E1A and SV40 large T antigen contains separate domains for Rb binding and casein kinase II phosphorylation. EMBO J 1990;9:153–60.
25. Werness BA, Levine AJ, Howley PM. Association of human papillomavirus types 16 and 18 E6 proteins with p53. Science 1990;248:76–9.
26. Syrjanen SM, Syrjanen KJ. New concepts on the role of human papillomavirus in cell cycle regulation. Ann Med 1999;31:175–87.

27. Papanicoloau G. Atlas of exfoliative cytology. Boston: Massachusetts Commonwealth Fund, University Press; 1954.

28. Guzick DS. Efficacy of screening for cervical cancer: a review. Am J Public Health 1978;68:125–34.

29. Fidler HK, Boyes DA, Worth AJ. Cervical cancer detection in British Columbia. Obstet Gynaecol Br Comm 1968;75:392–404.

30. Miller AB, Lindsay J, Hill GB. Mortality from cancer of the uterus in Canada and relationship to screening for cancer of the cervix. Int J Cancer 1976;17:602–12.

31. Parkin MD. Estimates of the worldwide frequency of sixteen major cancers in 1980. Int J Cancer 1988;41:184–97.

32. Coppleson LW, Brown B. Estimation of screening error rate from the observed detection rates in repeated cervical cytology. Am J Obstet Gynecol 1974;119:953–8.

33. Dehner LP. Cervicovaginal cytology, false-negative results, and standards of practice. Am J Clin Pathol 1993;99:45–7.

34. Figge DC, Bennington JL, Schweid AI. Cervical cancer after initial negative and atypical vaginal cytology. Am J Obstet Gynecol 1970;108:422–8.

35. Barron BA, Richart RM. A statistical model of the natural history of cervical carcinoma. Estimates of the transition from dysplasia to carcinoma in situ. J Natl Cancer Inst 1970;45:1025.

36. American College of Obstetrics and Gynecology. Committee opinion: recommendations on frequency of Pap test screening. Int J Gynaecol Obstet 1995;49:210–1.

37. Luff RD. The Bethesda System for reporting cervical/vaginal cytologic diagnoses: report of the 1991 Bethesda Workshop. Hum Pathol 1992:23:719–21.

38. Paavonen J, Kiviat NB, Wolner-Hanssen P, et al. Significance of mild cervical cytologic atypia in a sexually transmitted disease clinic population. Acta Cytol 1989;33:831–8.

39. Wright TC, Sun XW, Koulos J. Comparison of management algorithms for the evaluation of women with low-grade cytologic abnormalities. Obstet Gynecol 1995;35:202–10.

40. American College of Obstetricians and Gynecologists. Absence of endocervical cells on a Pap test. ACOG Committee Opinion 153. Washington (DC): The College; 1995.

41. Nasiell K, Roger V, Nasiell M. Behavior of mild cervical dysplasia during long-term follow-up. Obstet Gynecol 1986;67:665–9.

42. Ostor AG. Natural history of cervical intraepithelial neoplasia: a critical review. Int J Gynecol Pathol 1993;12:186–92.

43. Holowaty P, Miller AB, Rohan T, To T. Natural history of dysplasia of the uterine cervix. J Natl Cancer Inst 1999;91:252–8.

44. Charles EH, Savage EW. Cryosurgical treatment of cervical intraepithelial neoplasia. Obstet Gynecol Surv 1980;35:539–48.

45. Wetchler SJ. Treatment of cervical intraepithelial neoplaisa with the CO2 laser: laser versus cryotherapy. A review of effectiveness and cost. Obstet Gynecol Surv 1984;39:469–73.

46. Ahlgren M, Ingemarsson I, Lindberg LG, et al. Conization as treatment of carcinoma in situ of the uterine cervix. Obstet Gynecol 1975;46:135–9.

47. Duggan BD, Felix JC, Muderspach LI, et al. Cold-knife conization versus conization by the loop electrosurgical excisional procedure: a randomized, prospective study. Am J Obstet Gynecol 1999;180:276–82.

48. Zahniser DJ, Sullivan PJ. Cytyc Corporation. Acta Cytol 1996;40:37–44.

49. Spitzer M. Cervical screening adjuncts: recent advances. Am J Obstet Gynecol 1998;179:544–66.

50. Hutchinson ML, Zahniser DJ, Sherman ME, et al. Utility of liquid-based cytology for cervical carcinoma screening: results of a population-based study conducted in a region of Costa Rica with a high incidence of cervical carcinoma. Cancer 2000;87(2):48–55.

51. Roberts JM, Thurloe JK, Bowditch RC, et al. Comparison of ThinPrep and Pap smear in relation to prediction of adenocarcinoma in situ. Acta Cytol 1999;43(1):74–80.

52. Schiffman M, Herrero R, Hidesheim A, et al. HPV DNA testing in cervical cancer screening: results from women in a high-risk province of Costa Rica. JAMA 2000;283:87–93.

53. Herrington CS, Evans MF, Charnock FM, et al. HPV testing in patients with low grade cervical cytological abnormalities: a follow-up study J Clin Pathol 1996;459:493–6.

54. Cuzick J, Szarewski A, Terry G, et al. Human papillomavirus testing in primary cervical screening. Lancet 1995;345:1533–6.

55. Reid R, Greenberg MD, Lorincz A, et al. Should cervical cytologic testing be augmented by cervicography or human papillomavirus deoxyribonucleic acid detection? Am J Obstet Gynecol 1991;165:1461–71.

56. Fait G, Daniel Y, Kuperminc MJ, et al. Does typing of human papillomavirus assist in the triage of women with repeated low-grade, cervical cytologic abnormalities? Gynecol Oncol 1998;70:319–22.

57. Solomon D, Schiffman M, Tarone R. Comparison of three management strategies for patients with atypical squamous cells of undetermined significance: baseline results from a randomized trial. J Natl Cancer Inst 2001;93:293–9.

58. Wright TC, Denny L, Kuhn L, et al. HPV DNA testing of self-collected vaginal samples compared with cytologic screening to detect cervical cancer. JAMA 2000;283:81–6.

59. Hellebrekers BW, Zwinderman AH, Kenter GG, et al. Surgically-treated early cervical cancer: prognostic factors and the significance of depth of tumor invasion. Int J Gynecol Cancer 1999;9:212–9.

60. Kristensen GB, Abeler VM, Risberg B, et al. Tumor size, depth of invasion, and grading of the invasive tumor front are the main prognostic factors in early squamous cell cervical carcinoma. Gynecol Oncol 1999;74:245–51.

61. Windbichler GH, Muller-Holzner E, Nicolussi-Leck G, et al. Ovarian preservation in the surgical treatment of cervical carcinoma. Am J Obstet Gynecol 1999;180:963–9.

62. Roy M, Plante M. Pregnancies after radical vaginal trachelectomy for early-stage cervical cancer. Am J Obstet Gynecol 1998;179:1491–6.

63. Whitney CW, Sause W, Bundy BN, et al. A randomized comparison of fluorouracil plus cisplatin versus hydroxyurea as an adjunct to radiation therapy in stages IIB-IVA carcinoma of the cervix with negative para-aortic lymph nodes. A Gynecologic Oncology Group and Southwest Oncology Group study. J Clin Oncol 1999;17:1339–48.

64. Keys HM, Bundy BN, Stehman FB, et al. Cisplatin, radiation and adjuvant hysterectomy compared with radiation and adjuvant hysterectomy for bulky stage IB cervical carcinoma. New Engl J Med 1999; 340:1154–60.

65. Morris M, Eifel PJ, Lu J, et al. Pelvic radiation with concurrent chemotherapy compared with pelvic and para-aortic radiation for high-risk cervical cancer. N Engl J Med 1999;340:1137–43.

66. Yost NP, Santoso JP, McIntyre DD, Il a FA. Postpartum regression rates of antepartum cervical intraepithelial neoplasia II and III lesions. Obstet Gynecol 1999;93:359–62.

82

PERIMENOPAUSAL AND POSTMENOPAUSAL BLEEDING AND UTERINE CANCER

Christine H. Holschneider, MD, and Parul Gupta, MD

The evaluation and treatment of abnormal peri- and postmenopausal bleeding presents a distinct challenge to women's health care clinicians. Causes encompass a broad spectrum, ranging from endometrial atrophy to polyps, submucosal leiomyomata, hyperplasia and cancer. While only 10 to 20% of women with postmenopausal bleeding have endometrial cancer, 75 to 90% of patients with endometrial cancer have a history of abnormal bleeding.

The recognition of the etiologic significance of estrogen has lead to substantial improvements in the prevention of endometrial neoplasia. However, endometrial cancer continues to be the most common gynecologic malignancy in the United States. About 2 to 3% of women in the United States develop endometrial cancer at some point during their lives. With approximately 36,000 new cases diagnosed annually, it is the fourth most common of all cancers in women. Endometrial cancer tends to result in abnormal vaginal bleeding early in the course of disease reflected in the fact that about 70% of patients have stage I disease at presentation. Endometrial cancer is primarily treated surgically. The use of adjuvant radiation or chemotherapy is individualized based on the stage of the disease, histologic subtype of the tumor, and performance status of the patient. While women with early stage endometrial cancer have an excellent prognosis, the outcome for women with advanced disease remains poor.

MENOPAUSE AND DEFINITIONS OF ABNORMAL UTERINE BLEEDING

Menopause is the permanent cessation of menstruation following the decline of ovarian estrogen production. Clinically, menopause is diagnosed after 12 months of amenorrhea. The average age of menopause in the United States is 51.3 years, based on the Massachusetts Women's Health study.[1]

Most women experience some signs and symptoms of the menopausal transition prior to the cessation of menses. Only about 10% of women cease menstruating without a preceding prolonged period of bleeding abnormalities. The perimenopause lasts about 4 years and is characterized by markedly altered ovarian function and menstrual irregularity. It generally occurs between the ages of 45 and 55 years. Although uterine neoplasia is the greatest concern evoked by these symptoms, atrophy and the effects of unopposed estrogen are the most common causes. Terminology to describe menstrual bleeding abnormalities is summarized in Table 82–1.

CAUSES OF POSTMENOPAUSAL ABNORMAL UTERINE BLEEDING

Causes of postmenopausal bleeding are summarized in Table 82–2.[2] The likelihood of malignancy also increases with age in women with postmenopausal bleeding so that the farther away from her reproductive years a women is, the more

TABLE 82–1. Nomenclature of Abnormal Menses

Oligomenorrhea	Intervals between menses > 35 d
Polymenorrhea	Intervals between menses < 21 d
Menorrhagia	Regular, normal intervals between menses, but excessive flow (> 80 mL) and prolonged duration (> 7 d)
Metrorrhagia	Irregular intervals between menses with variable flow
Menometrorrhagia	Prolonged, excessive uterine bleeding occurring at irregular intervals
Intermenstrual bleeding	Bleeding of variable amounts occurring between regular menstrual periods

seriously the symptom should be viewed. While the reported incidence of malignancy is 15% for the 50 to 59-year-old, it rises above 40% for women age 70 years or older.[3]

HORMONE REPLACEMENT THERAPY, ABNORMAL VAGINAL BLEEDING, AND THE RISK OF ENDOMETRIAL HYPERPLASIA OR CANCER

Understanding the expected bleeding patterns and relative risks for the development of endometrial hyperplasia or cancer associated with various regimens of hormone replacement therapy is critical to identification of patients who require further evaluation.

The Postmenopausal Estrogen/Progestin Interventions (PEPI) Trial showed that 62% of women on unopposed estrogen (0.625 mg conjugated equine estrogen) developed endometrial hyperplasia after up to 3 years of treatment, 23% of whom had complex and 12% atypical hyperplasia. The baseline incidence of hyperplasia was 2% for women who received placebo.[4] Since 1975, more than 30 epidemiologic studies have been published, linking unopposed exogenous postmenopausal estrogen replacement to endometrial cancer. Recently, a meta-analysis of these studies has been published, which found a relative risk (RR) among

TABLE 82–2. Causes of Postmenopausal Bleeding

Atrophic changes (30%)
Exogenous estrogens (30%)
Endometrial cancer (15%)
Endometrial or cervical polyps (10%)
Endometrial hyperplasia (5%)
Miscellaneous causes (10%), such as cervical cancer, uterine sarcoma, urethral caruncle, or trauma

Adapted from Rubin SC.[3]

ever-users of 2.3 (95% confidence interval [CI] 2.1 to 2.5). There is an appreciably increasing risk with prolonged duration of unopposed estrogen use, with the RR for endometrial cancer being 1.4 (95% CI 1.0 to 1.8) with < 1 year use, 2.8 (95% CI 2.3 to 3.5) for 1 to 5 years use, 5.9 (95% CI 4.7 to 7.5) for 5 to 10 years use, and 9.5 (95% CI 7.4 to 12.3) for > 10 years unopposed estrogen exposure.[5]

The addition of progesterone either cyclically or daily decreases that risk dramatically. In the past, the dose of progestin for endometrial protection was derived empirically.[6] Randomized controlled trials have since tested various progestins.[7] The following progestin regimens are suggested for adequate endometrial protection:

- On a cyclic progestin regimen, medroxyprogesterone acetate in a dosage of 10 mg/d,[4] micronized progesterone at 200 mg/d,[4] or norethindrone acetate at 1 to 2.5 mg/d,[8] should be given each month for a minimum of 12 days.
- Continuous daily low-dose progestins, which are equally effective, include medroxyprogesterone at 2.5 to 5.0 mg/d,[4] or norethindrone acetate at dosages as low as 0.1 to .05 mg daily,[9] with 0.5 mg norethindrone acetate producing the lowest incidence of bleeding.[10]

With a hormone replacement regiment using a monthly cycled progestin, 70 to 90% of women have regular monthly vaginal bleeding. With this regimen, the bleeding should start some time after the 9th day of progestin use.[11] Endometrial assessment is recommended if the bleeding starts prior to this time or if there is a relative increase in the duration or amount of flow. The absence of vaginal bleeding is not a problem.

With continuous combined hormone replacement therapy, using daily estrogen plus progestin, bleeding is generally light to moderate, but the timing tends to be more erratic and unpredictable.

While in the beginning, about 50% of women have unpredictable bleeding, 75 to 86% are reported to be amenorrheic after 1 year.[12] For patients who have vaginal bleeding on a continuous combined hormone replacement therapy regimen, endometrial assessment is recommended during the first year only if the bleeding is unusually heavy or extended. The endometrium should be evaluated if there is bleeding after 1 year.

EVALUATION OF PERIMENOPAUSAL AND POSTMENOPAUSAL ABNORMAL UTERINE BLEEDING

Evaluation for the exclusion of endometrial hyperplasia or cancer should be performed in the following patients who have abnormal bleeding, spotting, or brownish discharge:

- Premenopausal women age 35 years or older, once pregnancy has been excluded; this should be extended to younger women with high risk factors, especially those with a history of anovulatory cycles or episodes of amenorrhea lasting longer than 6 to 12 months
- Perimenopausal women with intermenstrual bleeding or increasingly heavy periods
- Postmenopausal women who are not on hormone replacement with bleeding or spotting
- Postmenopausal women on hormone replacement who have bleeding that differs from the pattern expected for the patient's hormone regimen
- Postmenopausal women with a hemometra or pyometra

Options for the evaluation of abnormal uterine bleeding include an office endometrial biopsy, dilation and curettage (D & C), hysteroscopy, or transvaginal ultrasonography. An office endometrial biopsy to evaluate the endometrium may eliminate the need for most D & C procedures, which are usually done in the operating room. The accuracy of office endometrial biopsy for identifying endometrial hyperplasia or cancer approaches that of a D & C,[13] with a sensitivity of 85 to 95%. However, endometrial biopsy is a poor test for diagnosing other benign endometrial abnormalities as causes of abnormal bleeding, such as polyps or submucosal leiomyomata.

Insertion of the plastic endometrial sampling device (3-mm diameter: ie, Pipelle[7], Gyno sampler[7]) or a Novak or Kevorkian curette generally requires no cervical dilatation. In many patients, insertion can be accomplished without placement of a tenaculum. Occasionally, a second or third pass is needed. Most patients tolerate an office endometrial sampling with mild to moderate discomfort. The induced cramping usually passes within 5 minutes. Administration of a prostaglandin synthesis inhibitor 30 minutes prior to the procedure may be helpful. For repeat endometrial biopsies in patients known to cramp, consideration should be given to the use of a paracervical block.

About 6 to 18% of peri- and postmenopausal women cannot be adequately evaluated by office endometrial biopsy. Most commonly, the reason is the inability to enter the endometrial cavity due to cervical stenosis.[14] In such cases, transvaginal ultrasonography may provide additional information and aid in selecting those patients who require further evaluation with D & C.

Transvaginal ultrasonography is being increasingly used to assess the risk for endometrial cancer. One patient group who may benefit most from this evaluation tool are women in whom office sampling is not possible due to a stenotic os. In postmenopausal patients, there is a strong association between the thickness of the endometrial echo complex and the presence of endometrial disease, with an endometrial stripe measuring 4 mm or less being normal. In a large multi-institutional study of 1,168 women with postmenopausal bleeding, all 114 patients with endometrial cancer and 95% of 112 women with hyperplasia had an endometrial thickness of 5 mm or more.[15]

For postmenopausal women on unopposed estrogen, the negative predictive value of an endometrial echo complex of 4 mm or less on transvaginal ultrasonography is excellent, but the occurrence of a measurement this thin is rare in this patient group. Using an endometrial echo complex cutoff to 4 mm or less, the specificity of transvaginal ultrasonography for endometrial hyperplasia or cancer detection is only 10% for women on unopposed estrogen and only about 50% for women on combination hormone replacement therapy.[16] Thus, transvaginal ultrasonography is an inefficient first step in the evaluation of postmenopausal bleeding in women on hormone replacement therapy, and an office endometrial biopsy is generally preferred. Transvaginal ultrasonography may, however, be helpful in postmenopausal women with a stenotic cervical os which precludes office biopsy and may reduce the need for a uterine curettage.

D & C is the traditional gold standard for evaluating peri- and postmenopausal bleeding. A D & C should be performed in the following settings:

- Patients with a negative or nondiagnostic office endometrial biopsy who have persistent symptoms
- Patients with an abnormal endometrial echo complex on ultrasonography in whom an office endometrial biopsy is not possible

Commonly, hysteroscopy is performed along with the D & C. The addition of hysteroscopy does not add to the diagnostic accuracy for endometrial cancer or hyperplasia.[17] However, hysteroscopy may significantly increase the sensitivity for sessile or pedunculated intraluminal masses[18] and may allow for immediate therapeutic intervention by resecting the polyp or submucosal leiomyoma.

MANAGEMENT OF PERIMENOPAUSAL AND POSTMENOPAUSAL ABNORMAL BLEEDING AND ENDOMETRIAL HYPERPLASIA

The common pathologic findings on endometrial sampling fall into four categories: benign, hyperplasia without atypia, hyperplasia (simple or complex) with atypia, and endometrial carcinoma. Benign endometrial findings include proliferative, secre-

tory, and atrophic endometrium, at times with mixed hormonal effects.

The management of perimenopausal and postmenopausal abnormal bleeding in the absence of endometrial hyperplasia or cancer depends on the cause. Atrophic vaginitis is managed with topical and/or systemic estrogens. Cervical polyps can be easily removed in the office. Submucosal leiomyomata or endometrial polyps are often managed hysteroscopically.

For patients with endometrial hyperplasia, the presence of atypia is the major determinant of an increased risk of malignancy. In a long-term follow-up study of 170 patients with endometrial hyperplasia, Kurman and colleagues reported a 1.6% risk progression to cancer in cases of hyperplasia without atypia, compared with a 23% risk for patients with atypical hyperplasia.[19] Endometrial hyperplasia is further subdivided into cases without significant architectural alterations of the glands, which are referred to as simple hyperplasia, and into those cases where endometrial glands have complex configuration, thus called complex hyperplasia (Table 82–3).

Management of endometrial hyperplasia depends on several factors, such as the type of hyperplasia, the patient's age, the patient's desire to preserve her fertility, or whether the hyperplasia developed while the patient was receiving hormone replacement therapy. Identifying and addressing the underlying problem is central to the management of patients with endometrial hyperplasia. This may include weight reduction in the obese patient or long-term therapy with cyclic progestins or oral contraceptives for the anovulatory patient. Occasionally, endometrial hyperplasia is due to an estrogen-

TABLE 82–3. Endometrial Hyperplasia and the Risk of Malignancy

Histology	N	Progression to Carcinoma	Time Interval to the Development of Carcinoma
Nonatypical hyperplasia	122	2 (2%)	9.5 (8–11) yr
Simple hyperplasia without atypia	93	1 (1%)	
Complex hyperplasia without atypia	29	1 (3%)	
Atypical hyperplasia	48	11 (23%)	4.1 (1–11) yr
Simple hyperplasia with atypia	13	1 (8%)	
Complex hyperplasia with atypia	35	10 (29%)	

Adapted from Kurman RJ, Kaminski PF, Norris HJ. The behavior of endometrial hyperplasia: a long-term study of "untreated" hyperplasia in 170 patients. Cancer 1985;56:403–12.

producing adnexal tumor, such as a granulosa cell tumor.

In premenopausal women, hyperplasia without atypia can be managed with cyclic progestins for 12 days per month or with combination oral contraceptives. Patients desirous of childbearing may be treated effectively by ovulation induction. If endometrial hyperplasia without atypia develops on hormone replacement therapy, acceptable management options include changing from a cyclical to a continuous progestin, increase in the progestin dose, or cessation of the hormone replacement therapy. Following any of the above interventions, the patient, unless pregnant, should undergo repeat endometrial sampling after 3 to 6 months or if abnormal bleeding recurs. Endometrial hyperplasia without atypia generally resolves after 3 months of therapy.

Atypical hyperplasia is an indication for hysterectomy. Premenopausal patients who desire to preserve fertility may undergo a trial of progestin therapy. Though the optimal dose and regimen remain to be determined in this setting, progestins should generally be given at a higher dose and continually. Recommendations for the initial dosing of the progestin vary from 40 to 160 mg of megestrol acetate orally daily or an equivalent, such as 10 to 40 mg of medroxyprogesterone acetate daily. The patient should have repeat endometrial sampling performed every 3 months.

Atypical hyperplasia frequently requires prolonged therapy for as long as 9 months.[20] There should be some evidence of treatment response at the 3-month endometrial sampling. If the atypical hyperplasia resolves, maintenance therapy is frequently required with either cyclic progestins or oral contraceptive pills, unless the patient desires childbearing or the underlying cause has been resolved. Patients who do not respond to progestin therapy may be at significant risk for progressing to cancer and should be advised to have a hysterectomy.

Endometrial ablation is being increasingly used for the treatment of some women with dysfunctional uterine bleeding. There have been several reports of subsequent development of endometrial cancer in women who have undergone endometrial ablation.[21] It is important to stress that endometrial ablation is not a treatment for endometrial hyperplasia, and a previous endometrial ablation does not protect against endometrial neoplasia. Therefore, women undergoing endometrial ablation for abnormal bleeding should undergo careful evaluation for endometrial hyperplasia or cancer prior to ablation. Hormone replacement therapy for women who have undergone endometrial ablation should include a progestin to protect against the development of endometrial hyperplasia or cancer.

PATIENTS ON TAMOXIFEN

On the basis of The National Surgical Adjuvant Breast and Bowel Project (NSABP) B-14, there is a 7.5-fold increase in the risk of developing endometrial cancer among breast cancer patients on tamoxifen, compared with those on placebo, with an annual incidence of endometrial cancer of 1.6 per 1,000 in the tamoxifen group, compared with 0.2 per 1,000 among placebo users.[22] In the same study, the survival benefit from breast cancer associated with tamoxifen was 38% higher than with placebo and, by far, outweighed the small risk increase for endometrial cancer. A review of several other studies suggests a two- to threefold risk increase for the development of endometrial cancer.[23] While earlier studies suggested that tamoxifen-associated endometrial cancers had high-risk histologies,[24] this could not be confirmed by several more recent studies.[22,25] In the NSABP breast cancer trial (P1), 36 patients developed invasive endometrial cancer, all of whom had stage I disease; 32 of the 36 (89%) had vaginal bleeding.[26] Thus, the vast majority of women who develop cancer on tamoxifen are symptomatic with abnormal bleeding.

The use of routine screening endometrial biopsies or transvaginal ultrasonography in asymptomatic patients on tamoxifen cannot be recommended, given the unproven efficacy and the associated false-positive results leading to procedures with potentially significant morbidity.[27,28] However, women receiving tamoxifen should be informed of the increased risk of endometrial cancer and instructed to report any abnormal bleeding, spotting, or brownish discharge immediately. These patients should undergo annual gynecologic examinations. Any abnormal vaginal bleeding or discharge should be promptly evaluated by office endometrial biopsy, or D & C and hysteroscopy. Of note, there is no known increase in the risk of endometrial cancer for patients taking raloxifene, a related selective estrogen receptor modulator.

ENDOMETRIAL CANCER

Epidemiology

In the United States, endometrial cancer is the most common malignancy of the female genital tract, with an annual incidence of 36,100 new cases and approximately 6,500 deaths per year.[29] The mortality of endometrial cancer has more than doubled in the past decade. Endometrial cancer is most frequently diagnosed in Western industrialized countries (lifetime risk 2.4%); it is least common in southeast Asia and Japan.[30] African American women have an approximately 40% reduced incidence, but a 54% increased mortality from endometrial cancer compared with Caucasian women in the United States.[31]

Screening for Endometrial Cancer or Its Precursors in Asymptomatic Patients

Population-based screening is economically not feasible. Therefore, it is essential to assess the risk of individual patients to reduce the morbidity and mortality of endometrial cancer. Screening for endometrial cancer or hyperplasia is indicated in selected groups of asymptomatic patients, including

- premenopausal women with anovulatory cycles,
- premenopausal women with endometrial cells on a cervical cytology smear obtained during the luteal phase of the menstrual cycle,
- postmenopausal women with endometrial cells on a Pap smear at any time,
- postmenopausal women on estrogen replacement without progestins, and
- women who may have a genetic predisposition for endometrial cancer (hereditary nonpolyposis colorectal cancer [HNPCC]; Lynch II syndrome).

While cervical cytology smears are not a good screening tool for endometrial cancer, the presence of endometrial cells on a Pap smear in a postmenopausal women or in a premenopausal women during the luteal phase of the cycle is associated with a substantially increased incidence of endometrial pathology and should be further evaluated. The presence of cytologically normal endometrial cells on a cervical cytology smear in postmenopausal women carries a 6% risk for carcinoma and a 13% risk for hyperplasia.[32] The risk for carcinoma rises to 25% if the endometrial cells are morphologically abnormal.[33]

Risk Factors and Prevention

Adenocarcinoma of the endometrium is predominantly a disease of postmenopausal women; however, 30% of cases occur prior to menopause, and 5% occur prior to age 40 years.[34] Any characteristics that increase exposure to unopposed estrogen are associated with an increased risk of endometrial cancer (Table 82–4). When endometrial cancer occurs in women younger than 40 years of age, it is generally associated with anovulation or obesity.[35] As discussed above, prolonged unopposed exogenous postmenopausal estrogen replacement is associated with an eightfold increased incidence of endometrial cancer;[36] tamoxifen with a 2- to 7.5-fold risk increase.[22,23] Family history also contributes to the risk of endometrial cancer. For women with HNPCC, or Lynch II syndrome, endometrial cancer is the second most common malignancy with an incidence of 22 to 43%.[37]

Conversely, decreasing the exposure to unopposed estrogen decreases the risk of endometrial cancer, either by decreasing estrogen exposure, for example, in cigarette smokers, or by increasing exposure to progestins, such as through the use of oral contraceptives. Combination oral contraceptives decrease the risk of endometrial cancer by as much as 50%.[30] Protective effects from oral contraceptives are found to persist even 15 years after they are stopped.[38]

Pathology and Pathogenesis

There appear to be two main types of endometrial cancer, although clinically an overlap between the two types is not uncommon: type I tumors arise in a hyperestrogenic environment, are generally well-differentiated endometrioid tumors, and carry an excellent prognosis. Approximately 85% of all uterine cancers are endometrioid adenocarcinomas. Type II tumors appear to be due to other oncogenic processes, as they frequently arise in an environment of atrophy. They are associated with a higher rate of metastatic disease at the time of surgery and a lower overall survival rate. Uterine papillary serous carcinomas are the most common histologic subtype of type II tumor.[39]

Routes of Dissemination

There are four principal routes of spread for endometrial cancer:

TABLE 82–4. Risk Factors for the Development of Endometrial Cancer

Risk Factor	RR
Exogenous unopposed estrogen use	
< 1 year	1.0–1.8
1–5 years	2.3–3.5
5–10 years	4.7–7.5
> 10 years	7.4–12.3
Tamoxifen use	2–7.5
Obesity	
21–50 lb overweight	3
> 50 lb overweight	10
Nulliparity	2–3
Late menopause (> age 52 vs < age 49 yr)	1.7–2.4
Diabetes mellitus	1.2–2.8

Risk Factor	AR
Atypical hyperplasia	23%
HNPCC / Lynch II syndrome	20–40%

Adapted from Grady et al;[5] Aarnio et al;[37] Fisher et al;[22] Parazzini et al;[30] Rubin et al;[3] and Kurman et al.[19]
RR = relative risk; AR = absolute risk.

- Direct extension to adjacent structures, which is the most common route of dissemination
- Transtubal passage of exfoliated cells, as suggested by the presence of endometrial cells in washings and the development of disseminated intra-adominal metastases in some patients with endometrial cancer that appears early in the uterine specimen, that is, confined to endometrium or superficial myometrium. This appears to be a particularly common occurrence in uterine papillary serous carcinomas
- Lymphatic dissemination, which results in spread to pelvic and paraaortic lymph nodes. Furthermore, vaginal metastasis frequently appear to result from lymphatic spread
- Hematogenous dissemination, which most commonly results in metastases to the lung but may also involve the liver, bone, brain, and other sites

Signs and Symptoms

Ninety percent of patients with endometrial cancer have abnormal vaginal bleeding, which can take the form of menorrhagia or menometrorrhagia in a premenopausal woman and spotting or menses-like bleeding in a postmenopausal woman. Occasionally, the presenting symptom is pain, especially in elderly women, who have been estrogen deficient for many years and may present with a hematometra (blood entrapped in the uterine cavity) due to cervical stenosis or with purulent vaginal discharge resulting from a pyometra (pus entrapped in the uterine cavity). While one should have a high index of suspicion for endometrial cancer in women who are postmenopausal, obese, chronic hypertensive diabetics, it is important to note that 35% of patients with endometrial cancer show no signs of obesity or hyperestrogenism.

Examination

Findings on abdominal examination are generally normal; however, ascites, omental caking, or a palpable suprapubic mass may be present with advanced disease. Any suspicious lesions on the vulva, vagina, or cervix should be carefully inspected and biopsied. One should note the size, shape, consistency, mobility, and position of the uterus. This information

TABLE 82–5. FIGO Surgical Staging for Endometrial Carcinoma

Stage	Grade*	Definition
Stage I	1, 2, 3	Tumor limited to the uterine corpus
Ia		Limited to the endometrium
Ib		Invasion to less than 50% myometrium
Ic		Invasion to more than 50% myometrium
Stage II	1, 2, 3	Cervical involvement
IIa		Endocervical gland involvement only
IIb		Cervical stroma involvement
Stage III	1, 2, 3	Disease limited to pelvis and/or lymph nodes
IIIa		Invasion of uterine serosa, adnexa
		Positive cytology
IIIb		Vaginal metastases
IIIc		Metastases to pelvic or para-aortic lymph nodes
Stage IV	1, 2, 3	Extrapelvic disease
IVa		Invasion of bladder and/or bowel mucosa
IVb		Distant metastases, including intra-abdominal and inguinal metastases

Histopathologic grade of differentiation: grade 1: 5% or less of nonsquamous or nonmorular solid growth pattern; grade 2: 6–50% of nonsquamous or nonmorular solid growth pattern; grade 3: more than 50% of nonsquamous or nonmorular solid growth pattern.
Notes on grading: Notable nuclear atypia inappropriate for the architectural grade raises the grade of a grade 1 or 2 tumor by 1 grade. Nuclear grading takes precedence in serous adenocarcinoma, clear cell adenocarcinoma, and squamous cell carcinoma. Adenocarcinoma with squamous differentiation is graded according to the nuclear grade of the glandular component.
FIGO = International Federation of Gynecology and Obstetrics.

may be particularly helpful in determining the risk for complications from diagnostic testing, such as endometrial biopsy, and the possibility of metastatic or locally advanced disease. The adnexal examination is important because endometrial hyperplasia or cancer may be the result of an estrogen-secreting ovarian neoplasm, or there may be metastatic or synchronous disease.

Diagnosis

Any patient suspected of having endometrial cancer should have an office endometrial biopsy or uterine curettage. An endometrial biopsy positive for endometrial cancer confirms the diagnosis and allows for initiation of the appropriate treatment. If the endometrial biopsy is negative for malignancy in a patient who continues to be symptomatic, it should be followed by D & C. While hysteroscopy has not been shown to increase the sensitivity of a uterine curettage for the diagnosis of endometrial cancer, it may provide helpful information on benign disease leading to abnormal bleeding, such as polyps or submucosal leiomyomata.[17,40]

Staging

In 1988 the International Federation of Gynecology and Obstetrics (FIGO) introduced a surgical staging system for endometrial cancer (Table 82–5).[41] It is only the occasional patient who is unsuitable for surgical therapy whose disease would be staged according to the former FIGO clinical staging. On the basis of 5,281 patients staged surgically between 1990 and 1992, 72.8% of patients presented with stage I endometrial cancer, whereas 10.9% had stage II, 13.1% stage III, and 3.2% stage IV disease.[42]

Referral

Referral to a gynecologic oncologist should be considered for all women with proven or suspected endometrial cancer. While early endometrial cancer may not require full surgical staging and may be adequately treated with a hysterectomy and bilateral salpingo-oophorectomy, the immediate availability of surgical staging, if needed, should be offered to every patient. This should include patients with apparent grade 1 disease, as up to 20% experience an upgrade of their histology,[43] and 17% of patients

TABLE 82–6. FIGO Stage of Endometrial Cancer: Associated Prevalence and Survival

Stage	Prevalence (%)	5-Year Survival (%)
I	72.8	87.0
II	10.9	71.1
III	13.1	51.4
IV	3.2	8.9

FIGO = International Federation of Gynecology and Obstetrics. Adapted from Creasman W, Odicino F, Masionneuve P, et al. Carcinoma of the corpus uteri. Annual report on the results of treatment in gynecologic cancer. J Epidermiol Biostat 1998;3:35–61.

TABLE 82–7. Overall Survival by FIGO Stage of Uterine Cancer in Patients Treated Between 1990 and 1992

Stage	Patients (N)	Overall Survival at 1 Year (%)	2 Years (%)	5 Years (%)
I	3,845			
Ia	833	98.4	95.6	90.9
Ib	2,011	98.0	95.2	88.2
Ic	951	97.1	92.2	81.0
II	575			
IIa	269	93.6	88.5	76.9
IIb	306	93.6	85.5	67.1
III	694			
IIIa	453	87.3	74.9	60.3
IIIb	72	76.2	54.9	41.2
IIIc	169	78.4	58.2	31.7
IV	167			
IVa	41	58.5	29.3	20.1
IVb	126	58.2	30.2	5.3

FIGO = International Federation of Gynecology and Obstetrics. Adapted from Creasman W, Odicino F, Masionneuve P, et al. Carcinoma of the corpus uteri. Annual report on the results of treatment in gynecologic cancer. J Epidermiol Biostat 1998;3:35–61.

with exhibit deep myometrial invasion.[42] The importance of exact surgical staging is underscored by the fact that extrauterine disease is present in 28% of patients who are thought to have disease clinically confined to the uterus. Palpation or excision of enlarged lymph nodes alone is inadequate, as only 10% of involved lymph nodes are palpably enlarged. Detailed guidelines for the referral of patients to a gynecological oncologist have recently been put forth by the Society of Gynecologic Oncologists (see "Resources").[34]

Prognostic Variables

Knowledge of the prognostic variables pertinent to each patient is important if an appropriate, individualized treatment plan is to be instituted. Stage of disease is the most important prognostic variable (Tables 82–6 and 82–7).

There is a strong correlation between histologic grade and depth of myometrial invasion and prognosis. The incidence of lymphvascular space invasion increases with depth of myometrial invasion: 5% of patients with inner one-third myometrial invasion demonstrate lymphvascular invasion. In comparison, 70% of patients with outer one-third myometrial invasion have lymphvascular invasion.[44] In a review of 1,974 patients, the 5-year survival was 83.5% for patients without lymphvascular space invasion, which dropped to 64.5% for those with lymphvascular space invasion.[45] Histologic grade and depth of myometrial invasion are strong predictors of pelvic and para-aortic lymph node metastases (Table 82–8), adnexal metastases, positive peritoneal cytology, and hematogenous spread.

While patients with an endometrioid carcinoma have an overall good prognosis, survival for patients with other histologic subtypes, such as clear cell or papillary serous carcinomas, is reduced. Positive peritoneal cytology is most common in patients with grade 3 tumors, deep myometrial invasion, or lymph node metastases. In a study of 895 patients, the disease recurred in 29% of patients with positive washings, compared with 11% of patients with negative washings.[46] It appears, however, that the poor prognosis associated with positive washing is largely a reflection of other adverse prognostic factors.

Patients whose tumors are positive for estrogen and/or progesterone receptors have a longer survival, compared with patients whose tumors do not express these hormone receptors. Molecular tumor characteristics independently linked to prognosis include microvessel density, Ki-67, and p53 protein expression.[47]

Age and performance status appear to be independent prognostic variables. Based on Gynecologic Oncology Group data, 5-year relative survival rates

TABLE 82–8. Risk of Pelvic and Para-aortic Lymph Node Metastases Based on Histologic Grade and Depth of Myometrial Invasion

	Histologic Grade					
	Grade 1 (N=180)		Grade 2 (N=288)		Grade 3 (N=153)	
Depth of Myometrial Invasion	Pelvic	Para-aortic	Pelvic	Para-aortic	Pelvic	Para-aortic
Endometrium	0 / 44	0 / 44	1 / 31	1 / 31	0 / 11	0 / 11
only (N = 86)	(0%)	(0%)	(3%)	(3%)	(0%)	(0%)
Inner third	3 / 96	1 / 96	7 / 131	5 / 131	5 / 54	2 / 54
(N = 281)	(3%)	(1%)	(5%)	(4%)	(9%)	(4%)
Middle third	0 / 22	1 / 22	6 / 69	0 / 69	1 / 24	0 / 24
(N = 115)	(0%)	(5%)	(9%)	(0%)	(4%)	(0%)
Outer third	2 / 18	1 / 18	11 / 57	8 / 57	22 / 64	15 / 64
(N = 139)	(11%)	(6%)	(19%)	(14%)	(34%)	(23%)
Total	5 / 180	3 / 180	25 / 288	14 / 288	28 / 153	17 / 153
	(3%)	(2%)	(9%)	(5%)	(18%)	(11%)

Adapted from Creasman WT, Morrow CP, Bundy BN, et al. Surgical pathologic spread patterns of endometrial cancer: a Gynecologic Oncology Group study. Cancer 1987;60:2035–41.

progressively decline with advancing age from 96% for patients 40 years of age or younger, to 78% for the 60- to 70-year-old patient, to 54% for the 80-year-old or older patient.[48]

Treatment

Treatment for endometrial cancer is generally surgical and includes total hysterectomy and bilateral salpingo-oophorectomy. This also applies to patients in whom there is microscopic cervical involvement at fractional D & C. When there is macroscopic clinical involvement of the cervix, radical hysterectomy is indicated.

The specimen is opened in the operating room to determine the need for surgical staging in patients with grade 1 and 2 tumors. Surgical staging can be tailored to the individual patient and generally includes the collection of peritoneal cytology, pelvic and para-aortic lymph node sampling, and an omental biopsy. Surgical morbidity can be minimized by use of the laparoscope in selected patients and by modifying the extent of tissue sampling on the basis of histopathologic risk factors. Widely accepted criteria for the performance of complete surgical staging include all grade 3 tumors, >50% myometrial invasion, cervical extension, >2 cm tumor diameter, high-risk histologic subtypes, and grossly suspicious lymph nodes or adnexa.

Postoperatively, patients should be selected for adjuvant therapy on the basis of the risk of recurrent disease. Evidence for the optimal role of postoperative brachy- and teletherapy is still evolving. The following are general guidelines regarding the use of adjuvant postoperative radiation therapy:

- Low-risk patients (< 5% recurrence risk) are those with grade 1 or 2 tumors, confined to the upper two-thirds of the uterus, with no or only superficial (< one-third) myometrial invasion, and no lymphvascular space invasion. These patients require no further treatment. Their disease-free survival is 95%.[49,50]
- Intermediate-risk patients (5–10% recurrence risk) are those with grade 1 or 2 tumors with middle one-third myometrial invasion or with extension to the lower uterine segment or cervix, and with no lymphvascular space invasion. These patients should be given postoperative brachytherapy to the vaginal cuff. The reported 5-year survival after brachytherapy in this patient group is 97%.[51]
- High-risk patients (> 10% recurrence risk) are those with grade 3 tumors with any degree of myometrial invasion, with grade 1 or 2 tumors with outer one-third myometrial invasion, lymphvascular space invasion, adnexal spread, or pelvic

lymph node metastases. These patients are likely to benefit from adjuvant postoperative whole-pelvis radiation therapy. In patients with pelvic lymph node involvement alone, 5-year survival rates of 67 to 72% have been reported following surgery and postoperative whole-pelvis radiation therapy. If para-aortic lymph node metastases are present, in the absence of other distant metastases, extended field radiation therapy is recommended, since approximately 40% of these patients can be expected to live 5 years or longer.[46]

For women with advanced disease, treatment should be individualized. In younger patients with good performance status, debulking surgery, followed by chemotherapy and/or radiation, conveys a survival advantage. Median survival of 34 months has been reported after optimal cytoreduction (< 1 cm residual disease), compared with 11 months with > 1 cm residual tumor ($p = .0001$).[52] Progestins or chemotherapy are also indicated as primary treatment in selected cases of inoperable patients or for the palliative management of recurrent disease, although results are generally disappointing, and long-term disease control is the exception.[53,54] The most active cytotoxic agents in endometrial cancer include liposomal doxorubicin, platinum-based compounds, and paclitaxel.

Hormonal Therapy in the Young Patient Desirous to Preserve Fertility

There is expanding experience using progestins to treat women with presumed stage Ia, grade 1 endometrial cancer who wish to preserve their fertility.[55] However, the optimal progestin dose is unknown, and the therapy may take up to 9 months to take full effect.[20] Thus, this treatment should be offered only to selected highly motivated patients under close medical surveillance.

Estrogen Replacement Therapy in the Patient with Early Endometrial Cancer

There are no definitive prospective data to support specific recommendations regarding estrogen replacement in patients with a history of endometrial cancer. However, retrospective data suggest no difference in progression-free or overall survival associated with hormone replacement therapy in patients with surgical stage I or II endometrial cancer.[56] Of note, in this study, more than 50% of patients received progestins also. Other retrospective reviews find improved overall survival associated with hormone replacement, with no increase in tumor recurrence.[57]

Currently, a randomized placebo-controlled trial of estrogen replacement following surgery in patients with early endometrial cancer is being conducted. Until these data mature, it appears that the selection of appropriate candidates for hormone replacement should follow the same guidelines as those for patients without endometrial cancer and should, in addition, factor in prognostic indicators of the disease, the patient's symptoms, and risk for persistent disease based on tumor grade and stage, as well as the risk the patient is willing to assume.

RESOURCE

Society of Gynecologic Oncologists
401 North Michigan Avenue
Chicago, Illinois 60611
Telephone: (312) 644-6610
Web site: www.sgo.org

The Society of Gynecologic Oncologists publishes information and guidelines about the treatment of gynecologic cancers. Their Web site provides on-line access to referral guidelines, as well as links to other resources for clinicians and patients.

REFERENCES

1. McKinlay SM, Brambilla DJ, Posner JG. The normal menopause transition. Maturitas 1992;14:103–15.

2. Heaps JM, Leuchter RS. Uterine corpus cancer. In: Hacker NF, Moore JG, editors. Essentials of obstetrics and gynecology. 3rd ed. Philadelphia (PA): W.B. Saunders; 1998. p. 635.

3. Rubin SC. Postmenopausal bleeding: etiology, evaluation, and management. Med Clin North Am 1987; 71:59–69.

4. The Writing Group for the Postmenopausal Estrogen/Progestin Interventions (PEPI) Trial. Effects of hormone replacement therapy on endometrial histology in postmenopausal women. JAMA 1996;275:370–5.

5. Grady D, Gebretsadik T, Kerlikowske K, et al. Hormone replacement therapy and endometrial cancer risk: a meta-analysis. Obstet Gynecol 1995; 85:304–13.

6. Gambrell RD. Strategies to reduce the incidence of endometrial cancer in postmenopausal women. Am J Obstet Gynecol 1997;177:1197–207.p. 2000.

7. Lethaby A, Farquhar C, Sarkis A, et al. Hormone replacement therapy in postmenopausal women: endometrial hyperplasia and irregular bleeding (Cochrane Review). The Cochrane Library. Oxford (UK): Update Software; 2000.

8. Obel EB, Munk-Jensen N, Svenstrup B, et al. A two-year double-blind controlled study of the clinical effect of combined and sequential postmenopausal replacement therapy and steroid metabolism during treatment. Maturitas 1993;16:13–21.

9. Kurman RJ, Felix JC, Archer DF, et al. Norethindrone acetate and estradiol-induced endometrial hyperplasia. Obstet Gynecol 2000;96:373–9.

10. Archer DF, Dorin MH, Heine W, et al. Uterine bleeding in postmenopausal women on continuous therapy with estradiol and norethindrone acetate. Obstet Gynecol 1999;94:323–9.

11. Greendale GA, Lee NP, Arriola ER. The menopause. Lancet 1999;353:571–80.

12. Archer DF, Pickar JH, Bottiglioni F. Bleeding patterns in postmenopausal women taking continuous combined or sequential regimens of conjugated estrogens with medroxyprogesterone acetate. Menopause Study Group. Obstet Gynecol 1994;83:686–92.

13. Grimes DA. Diagnostic dilation and curettage: a reappraisal. Am J Obstet Gynecol 1994;83:686–92.

14. Koss LG, Schreiber K, Oberlander SG, et al. Screening of asymptomatic women for endometrial cancer. Obstet Gynecol 1981;57:681–91.

15. Karlsoon B, Granberg S, Wikland M, et al. Transvaginal ultrasonography of endometrium in women with postmenopausal bleeding: a Nordic multicenter study. Am J Obstet Gynecol 1995;172:1488–94.

16. Langer RD, Pierce JJ, O'Hanlan KA, et al. Transvaginal ultrasonography compared with endometrial biopsy for the detection of endometrial disease. N Engl J Med 1997;337:1792–8.

17. Ben-Yehuda OM, Kim YB, Leuchter RS. Does hysteroscopy improve upon sensitivity of dilatation and curettage in the diagnosis of endometrial hyperplasia or carcinoma? Gynecol Oncol 1998;68:4–7.

18. Gimpelson RJ, Rappold HO. A comparative study between panoramic hysteroscopy with directed biopsies and dilatation and curettage. Am J Obstet Gynecol 1988;158:489–92.

19. Kurman RJ, Kaminski PF, Norris HJ. The behavior of endometrial hyperplasia: a long-term study of "untreated" hyperplasia in 170 patients. Cancer 1985; 56:403–12.

20. Randall TC, Kurman RJ. Progestin treatment of atypical hyperplasia and well-differentiated carcinoma of the endometrium in women under age 40. Obstet Gynecol 1997;90:434–40.

21. Valle RF, Baggish MS. Endometrial carcinoma after endometrial ablation: high-risk factors predicting its occurrence. Am J Obstet Gynecol 1998;179:569–72.

22. Fisher B, Constantino JP, Redmond CK, et al. Endometrial cancer in tamoxifen-treated breast cancer patients: findings from the National Surgical Adjuvant Breast and Bowel Project (NSABP) B-14. J Natl Cancer Inst 1994;86:527–37.

23. ACOG. Committee Opinion. Tamoxifen and endometrial cancer. Washington (DC): Compendium of Selected Publications; 2000.

24. Magriples U, Naftolin F, Schwartz PE, Carcangiu ML. High-grade endometrial carcinoma in tamoxifen-treated breast cancer patients. J Clin Oncol 1993; 11:485–90.

25. Barakat RR, Wong G, Curtin JP, et al. Tamoxifen use in breast cancer patients who subsequently develop corpus cancer is not associated with a higher incidence of adverse histologic features. Gynecol Oncol 1994;55:164–8.

26. Runowicz CD. Gynecologic surveillance of women on tamoxifen: first do not harm. J Clin Oncol 2000; 18:3457–8.

27. Gerber B, Krause A, Müller H, et al. Effects of adjuvant tamoxifen on the endometrium in postmenopausal women with breast cancer: a prospective long-term study using transvaginal ultrasound. J Clin Oncol 2000;18:3464–70.

28. Barakat RR, Gilewski TA, Almadrones L, et al. Effect of tamoxifen on the endometrium in women with breast cancer: a prospective study using office endometrial biopsy. J Clin Oncol 2000;18:3459–63.

29. Greenlee RT, Murray T, Bolden S, Wingo PA. Cancer statistics, 2000. CA Cancer J Clin 2000;50:7–33.

30. Parazzini F, La Vecchia C, Bocciolone L, Franceschi S. The epidemiology of endometrial cancer. Gynecol Oncol 1991;41:1–16.

31. Madison T, Schottenfeld D, Baker V. Cancer of the corpus uteri in white and black women in Michigan. Cancer 1998;83:1546–54.

32. Ng ABP, Reagan JW, Hawliczek S, Wentz BW. Significance of endometrial cells in the detection of endometrial carcinoma and its precursors. Acta Cytol 1974;18:356–61.

33. Zucker PK, Kasdon EJ, Feldstein ML. The validity of Pap smear parameters as predictors of endometrial carcinoma and its precursors. Cancer 1985;56: 2256–63.

34. Society of Gynecologic Oncologists. Guidelines for referral to a gynecologic oncologist: rationale and benefits—endometrial cancer. Gynecol Oncol 2000; 78:S2–4.

35. Gallup DG, Stock RJ. Adenocarcinoma of the endometrium in women 40 years of age or younger. Obstet Gynecol 1984;64:417–20.

36. Mack TM, Pike MC, Henderson BE, et al. Estrogens and endometrial cancer in a retirement community. N Engl J Med 1976;294:1262–7.

37. Aarnio M, Mecklin JP, Aaltonen LA, et al. Life-time risks of different cancers in hereditary non-polyposis colorectal cancer (HNPCC) syndrome. Int J Cancer 1995;64:430–3.

38. The Cancer Steroid Hormone Study (CASH) of the Centers for Disease Control and the National Institute of Child Health and Human Development. Combination oral contraceptive use and the risk of endometrial cancer. JAMA 1987;257:796–800.

39. Sherman ME. Theories of endometrial carcinogenesis: a multidisciplinary approach. Mod Pathol 2000; 13:295–308.

40. Loffer FD. Hysteroscopy with selective endometrial sampling compared with D&C for abnormal uterine bleeding: the value of a negative hysteroscopic view. Obstet Gynecol 1989;73:16–20.

41. FIGO News. Annual report on the results of treatment in gynecological cancer. Int J Gynecol Obstet 1989;28:189–93.

42. Creasman W, Odicino F, Masionneuve P, et al. Carcinoma of the corpus uteri. Annual report on the results of treatment in gynecologic cancer. J Epidemiol Biostat 1998;3:35–61.

43. Daniel AG, Peters WA. Accuracy of office and operating room curettage in the grading of endometrial carcinoma. Obstet Gynecol 1988;71:612–14.

44. Hanson MB, Van Nagell JR, Powell DE, et al. The prognostic significance of lymph-vascular space invasion in stage I endometrial cancer. Cancer 1985;55:1753–7.

45. Abeler VM, Kjørstad KE, Berle E. Carcinoma of the endometrium in Norway: a histopathological and prognostic survey of a total population. Int J Gynecol Cancer 1992;2:9–22.

46. Morrow CP, Bundy BN, Kurman RJ, et al. Relationship between surgical-pathological risk factors and outcome in clinical stage I and II carcinoma of endometrium: a Gynecologic Oncology Group Study. Gynecol Oncol 1991;40:55–65.

47. Salvesen HB, Iversen OE, Akslen LA. Prognostic significance of antiogenesis and Ki-67, p53, and p21 expression: a population-based endometrial carcinoma study. J Clin Oncol 1999;17:1382–90.

48. Zaino RJ, Kurman RJ, Diana KL, Morrow CP. Pathologic models to predict outcome for women with endometrial adenocarcinoma. Cancer 1996;77: 1115–21.

49. Hørding U, Hansen U. Stage I endometrial adenocarcinoma: a review of 140 treated by surgery only. Gynecol Oncol 1985;22:51–8.

50. Carey MS, O'Connell GJ, Johanson CR, et al. Good outcome associated with a standardized treatment protocol using selective postoperative radiation in patients with clinical stage I adenocarcinoma of the endometrium. Gynecol Oncol 1995;57:138–44.

51. Orr JW, Holimon JL, Orr PF. Stage I corpus cancer: is teletherapy necessary? Am J Obstet Gynecol 1997; 176:777–89.

52. Bristow RE, Zerbe MJ, Rosenshein NB, et al. Stage IVB endometrial carcinoma: the role of cytoreductive surgery and determinants of survival. Gynecol Oncol 2000;78:85–91.

53. Hancock CK, Freedman RS, Edwards CL, Rutledge FN. Use of cisplatin, doxorubicin, and cyclophosphamide to treat advanced and recurrent adenocarcinoma of the endometrium. Cancer Treat Reports 1986;70:789–91.

54. Podratz KC, O'Brien PC, Malkasian GDJ, et al. Effects of progestational agents in treatment of endometrial carcinoma. Obstet Gynecol 1985;66:106–10.

55. Kim YB, Holschneider CH, Ghosh K, et al. Progestin alone as primary treatment of endometrial carcinoma in premenopausal women: report of seven cases and review of the literature. Cancer 1997;79:320–7.

56. Chapman JA, DiSaia PJ, Osann K, et al. Estrogen replacement in surgical stage I and II endometrial cancer survivors. Am J Obstet Gynecol 1996;175: 1195–200.

57. Creasman WT, Henderson D, Hinshaw W, Clarke-Pearson DL. Estrogen replacement therapy in the patient treated for endometrial cancer. Obstet Gynecol 1986;67:326–30.

83

OVARIAN CANCER

Fikret Atamdede, MD

Ovarian cancer is the most deadly gynecologic cancer. Although it is the sixth most common cancer in women, it is the fourth most common cause of death from cancer in women. Ovarian cancer causes more deaths in the United States than cervical and endometrial cancer combined. It is estimated that 25,000 new cases of ovarian cancer were diagnosed in the United States in 1999 and that approximately 15,000 of these women will ultimately die from ovarian cancer.[1] This chapter reviews epithelial ovarian cancer, the most common form of ovarian cancer. Epidemiology, prevention, screening, diagnosis, and treatment are discussed.

INCIDENCE AND EPIDEMIOLOGY

Ovarian cancer is diagnosed in women of all ages and ethnic backgrounds. However, most ovarian cancer occurs in women between the ages of 45 and 79 years.[2] In the United States, African American women have a lower lifetime risk of ovarian cancer (0.8%) compared with Caucasian women (1.8%). Cancer statistics from the period 1920 to 1991 reveal minimal change in the overall death rate from ovarian cancer.[3] However, during the period from 1973 to 1994, a slight increase in the incidence of ovarian cancer in older women and a slight decrease in the incidence of ovarian cancer in younger women occurred.[4]

Risk factors for the development of epithelial ovarian cancer include nulliparity, family history, early menarche, and late menopause.[5] Recent studies suggest that long-term postmenopausal estrogen use (> 10 years) may approximately double ovarian cancer risk.[6] Of the risk factors, parity is the most important; if one defines the risk of ovarian cancer at 1 in a nulliparous woman, having one to two children reduces this risk by approximately one half. Having three to four children reduces this risk by approximately two thirds. Having more than five children reduces this risk by approximately three-fourths.[7]

The use of oral contraceptives also has a significant modifying effect on the overall risk of ovarian cancer. Women who use oral contraceptives for 5 or more years reduce their risk of developing ovarian cancer by one half. The protective effects of childbearing and oral contraceptive use appear to be additive. As an example, if a woman has at least two children and uses oral contraceptives for 5 or more years, the relative risk of ovarian cancer is reduced by 70%.[8]

Only about 5 to 10% of ovarian cancer patients report a family history of ovarian cancer. However, a family history of ovarian cancer significantly increases a patient's risk of developing the disease. The overall incidence of ovarian cancer in the general population is approximately 1 in 80, which translates to be about 1.8%. However, if a patient has a first-degree relative within the family with an ovarian cancer, that individual's risk of ovarian cancer rises to approximately 5%. If there are two relatives with ovarian cancer within the family, this risk rises to approximately 7%.[9]

Originally, it was felt that there were three ovarian cancer syndromes: a site-specific ovarian cancer, a breast-ovarian cancer syndrome, and a familial cancer syndrome, otherwise known as the Lynch II syndrome. Recent studies have suggested that the site-specific and hereditary breast-ovarian cancer syndrome are the same and are really dependent on a mutation along the same gene with different penetrance for the different types of cancers.[10]

For the hereditary breast-ovarian cancer syndrome, the most commonly associated mutation in this syndrome is in the BRCA-1 gene, which is located on chromosome 17. A second gene, the BRCA-2, is associated with a somewhat lesser risk of ovarian cancer and is located on chromosome 13. Both of these mutations are inherited in an autosomal dominant fashion, although there is incomplete penetrance for the mutations of these genes. Therefore, the risk for the individual patient may be less than the implied 50% risk. Because of this incomplete penetrance, women who have a mutation of the BRCA-1 gene may have a lifetime risk of ovarian cancer of 28 to 44%, and if they have the BRCA-2 mutation, the risk may be as high as 27%.[11]

The inheritance in nonpolyposis colorectal syndrome is also an autosomal dominant genetic syndrome and is sometimes referred to as the Lynch II syndrome. Patients with this syndrome tend to have a predilection to early onset of colorectal cancer, especially in the proximal colon, and also a predisposition for several other tumors, including cancers of the endometrium, ovaries, and stomach. These patients have a 5 to 10% risk of ovarian cancer.[12]

Environmental factors clearly play a role in the development of ovarian cancer, although the role of individual environmental exposures is yet to be defined. Epithelial ovarian cancer has the highest incidence in industrialized countries, except in Japan, which has a low incidence of ovarian cancer. Japanese immigrants to the United States do have a higher risk of ovarian cancer than the native Japanese; however, the incidence does not approach that of Caucasians. Several dietary factors have been investigated in their contribution of ovarian cancer. Coffee and tobacco use have not been associated with an increased incidence of ovarian cancer, although excessive alcohol consumption may contribute to a slight increased risk for this cancer.[13] The use of talcum powder also has been associated with a slight increased risk of ovarian cancer, although a definitive correlation is yet to be shown.[14]

SCREENING

Since the vast majority of women who are diagnosed with ovarian cancer have no significant risk factors other than living in the industrialized world, and since this cancer tends to become symptomatic only at a late and usually incurable stage, finding an effective screening method is of paramount importance. Unfortunately, a cost-effective, highly sensitive, and specific screening method has yet to be found for ovarian cancer.

Multiple methods of screening for ovarian cancer have been suggested, including pelvic examination, abdominal and transvaginal ultrasonography, and analysis of cancer antigen (CA) 125 levels in the serum. Pelvic examination, although relatively inexpensive and commonly performed, is not an effective screening method. The sensitivity of pelvic examination is highly dependent on the experience of the examiner, and the specificity of the examination is quite poor at best. The vast majority of abnormal pelvic masses are benign and/or functional in nature, especially in the premenopausal woman.

Use of the CA 125 blood test presents its own set of complications. CA 125 is elevated in 80% of epithelial cancers. However, only half of women with stage I cancers have elevated levels. Additionally, there is a high false-positive rate for pre- or perimenopausal women as multiple nonmalignant conditions may elevate CA 125. Among women not undergoing treatment for gynecologic conditions and not subsequently diagnosed with ovarian cancer, one study found that approximately 4% were found to have elevated CA 125 levels.[15,16] The prevalence of false-positive CA 125 levels is higher in premenopausal women.

The use of ultrasonography also has been suggested as a screening method for ovarian cancer. Originally, abdominal ultrasonography was proposed as a screening method; however, the false-positive rate for abdominal ultrasonography was considered to be unacceptably high. Transvaginal and color flow Doppler ultrasonography are more sensitive tests; however, the number of false-positive tests when these modalities are used for screening is still unacceptably high.[17–19]

In an attempt to increase the specificity of these screening methods, combined modality screening, such as combining pelvic examinations with transvaginal ultrasonography and a CA 125 level, have been suggested. However, even in combination modality screening, the specificity and sensitivity of these studies are such that the risk-to-benefit ratio does not warrant screening the general population. Since the only definitive method of evaluating an abnormal screening test is to perform some form of invasive procedure, either in the form of a laparotomy or a laparoscopy, the low specificity of the current screening methods would result in an unacceptable number of unnecessary surgeries.

In 1994, the National Institutes of Health convened a consensus development conference on the topic of ovarian cancer. The expert panels agreed that, based on the limitations of currently available screening methods, screening of the general population for ovarian cancer is not indicated at this time. Screening of patients with a single first-degree relative with ovarian cancer also was not routinely recommended, although the decision whether to screen in this case was felt best left to the woman and her clinician.[20]

It was, however, recommended by the same consensus panel that patients who are at high risk for ovarian cancer (patients with familial ovarian cancer syndromes) should be screened by a combination of pelvic examination, CA 125, and transvaginal ultrasonography. Unfortunately, there is no clear evidence that even with this screening program any significant impact can be made in the overall survival of these patients.[21] The use of oral contraceptives in high-risk patients also has been advocated since oral contraceptives are associated with a decreased risk of ovarian cancer. This strategy requires additional study.

Patients who are no longer desirous of childbearing and who have pedigree-proven familial ovarian cancer syndromes may be offered prophylactic bilateral salpingo-oophorectomy. Although not definitively proven effective, observational studies suggest that prophylactic oophorectomy may significantly reduce cancer risk in these patients. Patients should be counseled that this procedure does not reduce their risk of ovarian cancer completely as the risk of primary peritoneal carcinoma remains.

DIAGNOSIS

Clinical diagnosis of ovarian cancer is problematic at best. Ovarian cancers, especially in their early stages, tend to be silent tumors. This is best evidenced by the fact that approximately 75 to 85% of ovarian cancers are diagnosed at an advanced stage. Most symptoms of ovarian cancer also are reported frequently by patients who do not have cancer. Patients frequently report that symptoms such as abdominal discomfort, abdominal fullness, and early satiety were present for 3 to 6 months prior to diagnosis. Other signs and symptoms include fatigue, increasing abdominal girth, urinary frequency, shortness of breath, and lower gastrointestinal upset.

Staging of ovarian cancer is summarized in Table 83–1. When early-stage ovarian cancer is found, it is usually found serendipitously on the basis of a mass detected during pelvic examination. However, most abnormal findings on pelvic examination do not represent ovarian cancer. The main goal of a diagnostic work-up in a patient who is diagnosed with an adnexal mass is to decide which patients require surgical intervention. During this evaluation, special attention should be given to possible nongynecologic etiologies of pelvic masses. Metastatic lesions from gastrointestinal urinary tract sources, along with more distant lesions need to be ruled out. Since the vast majority of adnexal masses regress in premenopausal women within one to three menstrual cycles, it is suggested that any premenopausal woman with a palpable adnexal mass of less than 8 cm in size and no other concerning findings be followed up for 1 to 2 months to see if the mass regresses in size.

Postmenopausal women, as well as premenopausal women with concerning or persistent findings, should have pelvic masses evaluated by transvaginal ultrasonography. Patients who have bilateral masses, solid and cystic components, excrescences, thick septations, or the presence of excessive peritoneal free fluid are at higher risk of having a malignant finding. If necessary, a computed tomographic (CT) scan also can be used to further characterize the mass and evaluate the rest of the abdomen. A CT scan offers the advantage of being able to evaluate the liver and the retroperitoneum. The use of magnetic resonance imaging (MRI) does not seem to have improved specificity or sensitivity within the abdomen, although it may provide a somewhat better view of the deep pelvic structures.

Other studies such as the barium enema, upper gastrointestinal series, colonoscopy, upper gastrointestinal endoscopy, and intravenous pyelogram may be indicated for patients with specific symptomatology to further identify the mass and to better prepare the patient for surgery. Screening mammography is generally recommended if it has not been done within 6 months as metastatic breast

TABLE 83–1. FIGO Staging for Ovarian Cancer

Stage I	Growth limited to the ovaries
IA	Growth limited to one ovary with capsule intact, no external tumor, no malignant cells in ascites or detected by peritoneal washings
IB	As in stage 1A, but involving both ovaries
IC	All other stage I (includes patients with malignant ascites or positive peritoneal washings)
Stage II	Growth involving one or both ovaries with pelvic extension
IIA	Extension to uterus and/or tubes only, with capsule intact, no external tumor on the surface of one or both ovaries, no malignant cells detected in ascites or peritoneal washings
IIB	As in stage IIA, but extending to other pelvic tissue types
IIC	All other stage II (includes patients with malignant ascites or positive peritoneal washings)
Stage III	Growth in one or both ovaries with extension beyond the pelvis, no distant metastasis. Includes one or more of the following: peritoneal implants outside the pelvis, retroperitoneal and/or inguinal nodes, superficial liver metastasis, tumor limited to the true pelvis but with biopsy-proven extension to bowel and/or omentum
IIIA	Tumor limited to the true pelvis with negative nodes but biopsy-proven microscopic seeding of abdominal peritoneum
IIIB	As in stage IIIA, but macroscopic implants of abdominal peritoneum, none exceeding 2 cm
IIIC	All other stage III
Stage IV	Distant metastasis: includes cytologically proven malignant pleural effusion and parenchymal liver metastasis, as well as all other distant metastasis

FIGO = International Federation of Gynecology and Obstetrics.
Adapted from Berek JS, Yao SF, Hackel NF. Ovarian cancer. In: Berek JS, Adashi EG, Hillard PA, editors. Novak's gynecology. 12th ed. Williams & Williams; Baltimore (MD): 1996. p. 1155–230.

cancer can present as a pelvic mass. Chest radiography or CT of the chest also may be indicated to evaluate for mediastinal and hilar masses.

Although CA 125 is not a good tool for general screening, it may be helpful in evaluating some patients with a documented pelvic mass. Sustained elevation of CA 125 levels occurs in more than 80% of patients with nonmucinous epithelial ovarian cancers but is elevated in only approximately 1% of the general population.[22] In postmenopausal women with a pelvic mass, CA 125 levels in serum greater than 65 U/mL are predictive of malignancy in approximately 75% of cases. On the other hand, in premenopausal women, there is a much higher incidence of nonmalignant conditions that can produce elevated CA 125 levels such as pregnancy, endometriosis, uterine fibroids, and pelvic inflammatory disease. Therefore, CA 125 in this setting is much less useful.

Other serum tumor markers occasionally may be useful; however, in most cases, serum tumor markers alone will not be definitive diagnostically.

Cancer antigen 19-9, which is generally used as a marker for gastrointestinal tumors, especially of the upper gastrointestinal and biliary tract, occasionally may be present in patients with mucinous epithelial cancer and can be elevated by nonmalignant gastrointestinal processes. The level of carcinoembryonic antigen (CEA) is sometimes helpful in distinguishing whether a mass is arising from the gastrointestinal or the reproductive tract; however, both ovarian cancers and gastrointestinal tumors can elevate CEA levels. If the possibility of a germ cell tumor is present, then other tumor markers such as α-fetoprotein, human chorionic gonadotropin, and lactic acid dehydrogenase also can be used in an attempt to better identify and treat identified pelvic masses.

Other invasive diagnostic studies, although commonly used in the diagnosis of many types of cancer, generally are not recommended for evaluation of pelvic masses. A negative diagnostic paracentesis does not necessarily rule out the presence of a malignant ovarian cancer, and a negative cytology would not preclude the need for an exploratory laparotomy/laparoscopy. A confined unruptured ovarian cancer of a lower grade has a very good prognosis, whereas the release of malignant cells has an unknown but theoretical potential for disseminating the disease; therefore, transabdominal biopsies generally are not recommended, except in special circumstances such as a medically inoperable patient.

Once a decision is made to take a patient to surgery, an assessment should be made as to the malignant potential of the mass. In any patient in whom malignancy is suspected, aggressive measures should be taken to prepare the patient for what could be a rather extensive surgery. Gynecologic oncologists receive training in intestinal and urologic surgery and are prepared to debulk extensive ovarian tumors, which frequently involve the bowel and the urinary system. Should a gynecologic oncologist not be available, consultation with general and urologic surgeons is recommended.

Aggressive management of other medical conditions that the patient may have preoperatively, perioperatively, or postoperatively is essential. Should the patient present with severe nutritional depletion, measures may need to be taken preoperatively to bring the patient into a positive nitrogen balance. The more stable a patient is in regard to her medical condition, the more aggressive a surgery may be performed. Mechanical and/or antibiotic bowel preparation and prophylaxis against infection and deep venous thrombosis are also usually recommended.

PRIMARY TREATMENT

Principles of Primary Treatment

Primary treatment for ovarian cancer begins with an aggressive surgical approach in those patients whose medical condition allows it. If, on initial surgical exploration, the patient has extensive disease, then aggressive attempts at reduction in tumor volume need to be undertaken. On the other hand, if the patient has minimal disease, then every attempt should be made to rule out metastases.

Ovarian epithelial cancer is spread primarily by exfoliation of cells into the peritoneal cavity and secondarily by lymphatic dissemination and hematogenous spread. The earliest mode of dissemination of ovarian cancer is by direct exfolia-

tion of cells from the ruptured capsule of the ovarian cancer. These cells are spread by the normal circulatory pattern of peritoneal fluid, which is generally in a clockwise manner, ending in the right hemidiaphragm. Ovarian cancer spread in this manner usually manifests itself as a surface epithelial cancer and generally does not invade intraperitoneal organs.

Lymphatic spread of ovarian cancer is more commonly seen in patients with advanced-stage disease.[23] It is reported that 78% of patients with stage III disease have metastasis to the pelvic lymph nodes. Hematogenous spread is much less common at initial presentation. Distal systemic spread, such as into the lung or into the parenchyma of the liver, is seen more commonly in patients who have received prior treatment and now are showing signs of recurrence.

A thorough surgical staging technique is especially important for patients who are presumed to have an early-stage disease. If patients do, indeed, have an early stage of disease, they are frequently considered for postoperative observation only rather than adjuvant therapy. Therefore, inadequate surgical staging can lead to undertreatment. Approximately 10% of the patients who are thought to have stage I or II disease preoperatively actually have involvement of retroperitoneal lymph nodes, 15% of patients have disease in the omentum, and 10% have microscopic disease on their diaphragm.[24] The statistics for periaortic lymph node involvement are summarized in Table 83–2.

If at the time of initial surgical exploration the patient is found to have obvious metastatic ovarian cancer, then the context of the surgery changes somewhat.[25] In this setting, instead of trying to prove that the patient has extensive disease, the focus of the surgery is toward excision and removal of as much disease as possible. Unlike many other cancers, ovarian cancer responds to a debulking or cytoreductive procedure. One of the most important overall prognostic factors in the treatment of ovarian cancer is residual disease at the completion of the procedure. Indeed, the volume of residual disease is correlated directly with survival. Both the largest size of residual mass and the number of residual masses are felt to be important prognostic factors. Several studies have shown that with decreasing the size of residual nodules, increasing survival benefits are obtained, with patients having

TABLE 83–2. Aortic Lymph Node Metastases in Epithelial Ovarian Cancer

Series	Stage I		Stage II		Stages III–IV		
	Positive Lymphangiography	Positive Biopsy	Positive Lymphangiography	Positive Biopsy	Positive Lymphangiography	Positive Biopsy	Total Positive Lymphangiography
Hanks and Bagshawe (1969)	2/9	—	2/6	—	4/7	—	8/22
Parker et al (1974)	3/13	—	2/29	—	12/27	—	17/69
Knapp and Friedman (1974)	—	5/26	—	—	—	—	—
Delgado et al (1977)	1/5	—	1/5	—	—	3/5	2/10
Buchsbaum et al (1989)*	—	4/95	—	8/41	—	7/46	—
Burghardt (1991)	—	1/20	—	4/7	—	51/78	—
Total		10/141		12/48		61/129	

*All patients had optimal carcinoma with metastatic lesions less than 3 cm. Reproduced with permission from DiSaia, Creasman, editors. Clinical gynecologic oncology. 5th ed. St. Louis (MO): Mosby; 1997. p. 298.

complete cytoreductive surgery having the best overall prognosis.

Surgical Approach and Technique

In initially approaching the surgery, care should be taken to decide on which type of abdominal incision should be made. In those patients in whom a malignancy is highly suspected, a midline or a paramedian incision is highly recommended since access to the upper abdomen is paramount to appropriate surgical staging or tumor reduction. A low transverse incision, although cosmetically appealing and somewhat less morbid, severely limits access to the upper abdomen in the majority of cases. Should a malignancy be encountered, then a more disfiguring incision such as a T incision, a secondary upper abdominal vertical incision, or a muscle-splitting incision may need to be performed if a standard midline incision has not been performed.

Once the abdomen is entered, and prior to any manipulation of the tissues, washings should be obtained from all four quadrants and set aside for possible cytologic evaluation. Should any free fluid be encountered, this also should be aspirated and set aside for cytologic evaluation. Once the pelvic mass is encountered, every attempt should be made to remove the mass intact, and this mass should be sent for frozen histologic examination.

Once a diagnosis of ovarian malignancy is made, a thorough exploration of the abdomen is necessary with a systematic exploration of all intraperitoneal surfaces. It is generally recommended that a systematic examination of both hemidiaphragms,

the liver serosal surfaces, the splenic area, both pericolic gutters, and the pelvic peritoneum be performed carefully. Once this inspection is concluded, careful inspection of the ascending transverse and descending colon should be performed with careful palpation of the omentum. The small bowel should be examined carefully from the ligament of Treitz all the way to the terminal ileum, with great care taken to palpate and visualize the mesentery of the small bowel throughout its entire length. Special attention should be paid to the appendix since this is a frequent site of metastasis.

Once the bowel is examined thoroughly, palpation of the retroperitoneum and the periaortic and the pelvic lymph node regions also should be carried out, with careful evaluation of both kidneys being performed at the same time. Any suspicious nodules or adhesions should be biopsied. If there are no suspicious areas, then consideration should be given to obtaining multiple random biopsies from the pelvis, colic gutters, intestinal mesentery, and diaphragm. Since the omentum is a frequent site of metastasis, an omentectomy should be performed. If there is no obvious tumor, then an infracolic omentectomy is adequate. However, if there are obvious tumors involving the omentum, then, of course, every attempt should be made to remove as much of the disease as possible. If there is still no obvious evidence of disease, then a retroperitoneal lymph node dissection needs to be carried out, sampling both the left and right periaortic nodal chain along with the pelvic lymph node chain. Using this technique, adequate staging of the ovarian cancer can be obtained.

During the surgical approach, every attempt should be made to reduce residual disease to as low a volume as possible, with the goal being complete resection. If this is not achievable, then every attempt should be made to reduce the volume of disease, with an attempt to leave no nodule greater than 2 cm behind. This aggressive surgical resection, however, should be tempered by surgical judgment and avoidance of significant surgical morbidity. If maximal cytoreductive surgery results in a patient who is so severely debilitated that adjuvant therapy cannot be administered, or who takes such a significant amount of time recovering from the surgery that adjuvant therapy is delayed, then the benefits of maximal cytoreductive surgery will have been lost. It has been shown that cytoreductive surgery, when performed by gynecologic oncologists, is feasible in approximately 70% of patients, with acceptable levels of morbidity and mortality.[26]

A bilateral salpingo-oophorectomy, hysterectomy, bowel resection, and colostomy should be considered if optimal cytoreduction can be obtained by using these techniques. Extensive involvement of the splenic region may result in consideration of splenectomy, and cytoreductive surgery of an enlarged retroperitoneal lymph node should be considered if this can be performed safely. Every attempt should be made to reduce the amount of tumor as much as possible, even in patients who have stage IV disease.

Indications for Conservative Surgery

"Conservative" surgical approaches can be considered in special settings. One of these is the diagnosis of a low-grade stage IA ovarian cancer, in a woman of childbearing age, who wishes to preserve her fertility. In this setting, the patient must have a surgically documented stage IA grade 1 tumor. A thorough staging procedure needs to be performed to rule out higher stage disease. Once shown to be a stage I disease, a total abdominal hysterectomy and removal of the contralateral ovary are not absolute requirements. However, once the patient has finished childbearing, removal of the remaining ovary should be strongly encouraged to exclude any occult contralateral lesion.

Another setting in which conservative surgery can be considered is when an ovarian tumor is found to be of low malignant potential. Low malignant potential tumors are a distinct subset of ovarian tumors. Tumors of low malignant potential account for approximately 15% of all epithelial ovarian cancers and occur predominantly in premenopausal women These tumors carry a much more favorable prognosis and generally show a much more indolent course of disease. Overall, patients with ovarian tumors with low malignant potential have an excellent prognosis, with a greater than 95% survival at 10 years in patients with stage I disease and a greater than 85% survival at 10 years in patients who have stage III disease.

The principal treatment of ovarian tumors of low malignant potential is surgical resection of the primary tumor.[27] Adjuvant therapy, either in the form of chemotherapy or radiotherapy, does not seem to significantly improve the prognosis for these tumors.[28] Once a diagnosis of a "borderline" ovarian cancer is made at the time of frozen section, consideration could be given to conservative surgery in those patients who desire future childbearing or maintenance of ovarian function. On the other hand, patients should be thoroughly staged both for prognostic and treatment purposes.

ADJUVANT THERAPY

Aggressive surgical techniques are rarely, if ever, curative alone in advanced ovarian cancer. Therefore, these patients usually require adjuvant therapy. Prior to the mid-1970s, single-agent alkylating therapy was the most commonly used adjuvant chemotherapy. Acceptable, although low, response rates were encountered with the use of these agents.[29] Beginning in the mid- to late 1970s, platinum compounds generally became available and showed a significant incremental increase in overall response and duration of response. In the 1980s combination chemotherapy was tested and was shown to be superior to single-agent therapy for most patients with ovarian cancer. A combination of cisplatin with an alkylating agent such as cyclophosphamide became the standard of care in the late 1980s and early 1990s.

In the mid- to late 1980s, paclitaxel (Taxol) was shown to be an active agent in ovarian cancer.[30] Rapidly after the introduction of paclitaxel, multiple trials were begun comparing a combination of cisplatin and paclitaxel to what was then considered the standard of care, cisplatin and cyclophosphamide. A seminal Gynecologic Oncology Group study (protocol 111) showed that treatment regimens containing paclitaxel achieved a significant reduction in mortality and improvement in progression-free interval as compared with standard therapy.[31] This study was confirmed by a similar study performed in Europe and Canada.[32]

Because of the rather significant renal, neural, and ototoxicity of cisplatin, the platinum analog carboplatin was introduced into the treatment regimen and was shown to have a lower toxicity profile.[33] Studies comparing paclitaxel and carboplatin with paclitaxel and cisplatin have shown efficacy rates that are virtually identical to one another. The standard of care in adjuvant therapy for ovarian cancer is now paclitaxel and carboplatin combination therapy.[34]

Other chemotherapy agents also are available against ovarian cancer and could be considered either for second-line therapy or in the initial treatment for patients who cannot tolerate paclitaxel or a platinum compound. These agents include cyclophosphamide, topotecan, hexamethylmelamine, doxorubicin, etoposide, ifosfamide, gemcitabine, liposomal doxorubicin, and 5-fluorouracil therapy.

Dose-density trials with the use of autologus bone marrow transplant or stem cell support have not shown any significant increases in overall survival, and substantial morbidity and mortality have been shown. Radiation therapy in the treatment of ovarian cancer generally is not used in the United States. Whole abdominal radiation therapy in patients with microscopic metastatic disease or completely resected disease can be useful; however, data suggest that if the patient is left with macroscopic disease, radiation therapy is not as effective as combination chemotherapy.[35]

POST-THERAPY SURVEILLANCE

Just as ovarian cancer is insidious and very difficult to diagnose, the recurrence of ovarian cancer after treatment also can be very difficult to detect. Follow-up after primary therapy is clinician specific. Generally, the follow-up examination consists of a detailed history and physical examination, including a bimanual pelvic examination, CA 125 levels, and other appropriate tumor markers. Imaging studies such as CT scans, sonograms, and MRIs, as well as chest radiographs, are generally liberally performed. Surgical reassessment or "second-look laparotomy" is frequently considered.

Of these follow-up modalities, CA 125 has been studied extensively as a modality for assessing the effectiveness of treatment and for recurrence of the tumor. It is generally accepted that a rapid decay of CA 125 to normal levels portends a good prognosis, whereas a slow decay or a failure to return to normal generally portends a poorer prognosis.[36] Virtually all patients with an elevated CA 125 of greater than 35 U/mL prior to second-look laparotomy have residual tumor. Unfortunately, 50% of patients who have a normal CA 125 level also have disease present.[37] Overall, elevated CA 125 has a 44% sensitivity and 95% specificity to detect residual disease in a patient prior to second-look laparotomy.[38] Sequential elevation of CA 125 proceeds clinical recurrence of disease by approximately 3 to 4 months. However, significant controversy exists as to whether treatment for increasing CA 125 levels, without clinical recurrence, improves survival or response.

Computed tomography also is used frequently and generally is recommended in the follow-up of patients who have been treated for ovarian cancer. Unfortunately, the CT scan is limited in its ability to detect tumor nodules < 1 cm in size. Furthermore, CT scans frequently miss relatively large omental metastases because of difficulties in differentiating normal tissues of varying density within the abdomen and those associated with tumor.[39] Overall, CT scans detect recurrent ovarian cancer in about 65% of cases. Clinicians generally combine CA 125 and CT scanning in follow-up assessment, and the combination of a negative CA 125 and CT scan can be reassuring, although not definitive.

Although MRI seems to have somewhat better soft tissue resolution compared with CT scans, there does not seem to be any significant advantage to the use of MRI except in evaluating the deep pelvis. Transvaginal ultrasonography is limited by its relative insensitivity for peritoneal disease and its inability to reliably detect lymph nodes < 2 to 3 cm in diameter.[40] New imaging modalities such as positron emission tomography (PET) also show promise for visualizing metabolically active areas such as would be evidenced by persistent or recurrent disease. However, this is a relatively new imaging modality, and extensive studies as to its usefulness are not available. Therefore, PET cannot be recommended as a general follow-up study at this time.

Second-look laparotomy provides the most accurate method of assessing recurrence of the tumor. Unfortunately, to date, there are no studies that indicate that the use of the second-look laparotomy influences the overall survival of patients with ovarian cancer.[41] However, the information obtained at second-look surgery is highly prognostic. If the patient has a negative second-look laparotomy, she has an approximately 50% risk of recurrence within 5 years.[42] Because of the limitations of second-look surgery, at the present time, this procedure is not considered standard of care in the follow-up of ovarian cancer. On the other hand, the second-look laparotomy may be useful in patients who are being considered for investigational second-line chemotherapy, either on a consolidation basis for patients who have a negative second-look surgery or for continuing therapy for patients who have a positive second-look surgery.

RECURRENT OR PROGRESSIVE OVARIAN CANCER

Unfortunately, despite aggressive surgical therapy, precise chemotherapy, and/or radiotherapy, most patients with ovarian cancer eventually succumb to their disease. Patients who have recurrence of disease following a complete course of chemotherapy, who show progression, or who have a poor response during therapy generally have a very poor prognosis in terms of ultimate cure of disease.

When a woman has a poor response to initial therapy, salvage therapy is generally considered. The course of an individual patient's disease predicts her response to salvage therapy. Patients who have refractory disease to initial therapy showing tumor growth or plateau of response while undergoing therapy generally have the worst response to salvage therapy. The second worst prognosis is found in the group of patients who have a good response to primary therapy but who recur within 6 months.

Generally, patients who recur at less than 6 to 12 months are considered platinum refractory, and the use of the original agents usually is not recommended. These patients can be treated with a variety of newer agents, such as topotecan, liposomal doxorubicin, gemcitabine, and ifosfamide, or older agents such as hexamethylmelamine and cytoxan. Response also can be obtained from hormonal manipulation, with agents such as tamoxifen or progestational agents. With the judicious use of these second-line agents, protracted response rates frequently can be obtained, with a reasonable quality of life for the patient. Novel techniques such as intraperitoneal chemotherapy or whole abdominal radiation therapy are sometimes used, although low response rates and complications preclude generalized recommendation for their use in the setting of recurrence.

Patients who have had a treatment interval of at least > 6 months and preferably > 12 months prior to recurrence or progression seem to have the best response to salvage therapies. Indeed, if the patient has shown a disease-free interval of at least 12 months, consideration also can be given to secondary cytoreductive surgery with follow-up chemotherapy using the initial agents.[43] However, at this point, there is little, if any, evidence suggesting that secondary cytoreductive surgery makes any significant impact in the overall survival of these patients, although patients in whom residual disease is completely resected do have a significantly longer progression-free survival than those patients in whom complete resection is not achievable.[44]

TERMINAL CARE

Since the vast majority of patients who present with ovarian cancer have advanced disease, and the vast majority of these patients eventually succumb to their disease, it is imperative on anyone who is taking care of a patient with ovarian cancer to be fully conversant in palliative and terminal care. Quality of life, patient dignity, independence, and free will always must be kept in mind. In considering secondary, tertiary, or quarternary treatments, there always should be a discussion with the patient and her family/significant others that revolves around the risk-to-benefit ratio and quality-of-life issues. Also, when discussions of potential benefits of treatment include references to response rates, it should be clear to the patient how response is defined. Compassionate support by the clinician and health care team is required in these patients who frequently have a slow and protracted course of events.

Generally, ovarian cancer progresses as an abdominal disease, causing multiple episodes of incomplete small bowel obstruction that may need to be treated either surgically or conservatively. Since gastrointestinal symptomatology for patients with recurrent ovarian cancer is a progressive and cumulative problem, and since most patients who undergo surgery for intestinal obstruction usually succumb to their disease within 2 to 3 months, it is generally recommended that every attempt be made to treat patients medically prior to resorting to surgical intervention. Thus, conservative therapy with nasogastric tube suction and intravenous hydration, for protracted amounts of time if necessary, is usually recommended.

The use of parenteral nutrition in this setting is somewhat controversial. Ovarian cancer, because of its multiple gastrointestinal complications, causes progressive muscle wasting and malnutrition in most patients. However, whether parenteral nutritional support improves the quality of life in such patients is controversial.

Progressive and debilitating ascites also can become a significant issue in the patient's quality of life. Malignant ascites also is frequently an issue and should be treated as conservatively as possible. Massive ascites can cause significant patient discomfort, intermittent small bowel obstruction, or respiratory compromise. When ascites reaches that point, paracentesis may be highly palliative and, depending on the extent of disease and progression of the ascites, may be palliative for a significant amount of time. If the patient has plural effusions, consideration could be given to drainage of these effusions with subsequent installation of a sclerosing agent.

SURVIVAL

The overall prognosis for patients with ovarian cancer is dependent on multiple factors that have been discussed already. Stage of disease and residual disease after cytoreductive surgery are the most signifi-

cant prognostic factors for patients. The average 5-year survival for stage I disease is approximately 85%; for stage II, approximately 70%; for stage IIIA, 41%; for stage IIIB, 25%; for stage III overall, 23%; and for stage IV, 11%.[45] Older age, more aggressive histologic grade, mucinous and clear cell carcinoma cell types, and a greater number of residual lesions after cytoreductive surgery (20 or more) all confer poorer prognosis.[46]

CONCLUSION

Ovarian cancer remains one of the most challenging and frustrating cancers to treat. It frequently affects women in the prime of their lives and is a silent and insidious tumor. Stage for stage, this tumor is no more deadly and no more dangerous than any of the other gynecologic tumors and, indeed, may be somewhat more responsive to therapy in advanced stages than other tumors from the gynecologic tract. Be that as it may, because it is usually diagnosed late in its course, it remains the number one killer of women from gynecologic cancer.

Significant advances have been made over the past several decades in the treatment and overall management of patients with ovarian cancer. Unfortunately, a significant change has not been seen in overall survival. New approaches to the detection, prevention, and treatment of this cancer are necessary and are being diligently worked on at this time. Until a definitive screening study or a highly effective treatment modality for advanced disease is found, a high index of suspicion, aggressive management, and aggressive appropriate referral is paramount in maximizing the potential for survival.

REFERENCES

1. Landis SH, Marie T, Boldin S, Wingo TA. Cancer statistics, 1999. CA Cancer J Clin 1999;49(1):8–31.

2. Smith LH, Oi RH. Detection of malignant ovarian neoplasms, the review of the literature, detection of the patient at risk, clinical, radiological, and cytological detection. Obstet Gynecol Surv 1984;39:313–28.

3. Cancer facts and figures. New York: American Cancer Society; 1991.

4. Ries LAG, Kosary CL, Hankey BF, et al, editors. SEER cancer statistics review: 1973–1994, National Cancer Institute. Bethesda (MD): National Institutes of Health; 1997.

5. Daly M, Obrams GI. Epidemiology and risk assessment for ovarian cancer. Semin Oncol 1998;25:255–64.

6. Rodriguez C, Patel AV, Calle EE, et al. Estrogen replacement therapy and ovarian cancer mortality in a large prospective study of US women. JAMA 2001;285:1460–5.

7. Kramer DW, Hutchinson GB, Welch WR, et al. Determinance of ovarian cancer risk: reproductive experience in family history. J Nat Cancer Inst 1983;71:711.

8. Franceschi S, Parazzini F, Negri E, et al. Pooled analysis of three european case-controlled studies of epithelial ovarian cancer: 3. Oral contraceptive use. Int J Cancer 1991;49:61–5.

9. Schildkraut JM, Thompson WD. Familial ovarian cancer: a population of greatest case control study. Am J Epidemiol 1988;128:456–66.

10. Ponder B. Genetic testing for cancer risk. Science 1997;278:1050–4.

11. Frank TS, Manley SA, Olopad OI, et al. Sequence analysis of *BRCA-1* and *BRCA-2*: correlations of mutations with family history and ovarian cancer risk. J Clin Oncol 1998;16:2417–25.

12. Bewtra C, Watson P, Conway, et al. Hereditary ovarian cancer: a clinical pathologic study. Int J Gynecol Pathol 1992;11:180–7.

13. Greene MH, Clark JW, Blayney DW. The epidemiology of ovarian cancer. Semin Oncol 1984;11:209–26.

14. Longo DO, Young RC. Cosmetic talc and ovarian cancer. Lancet 1979;2:349–51.

15. Zurawski VR, Broderick SF, Pickens P, et al. Serum CA 125 levels in a group of non-hospitalized women. Relevance for early detection of ovarian cancer. Obstet Gynecol 1987;69:606–11.

16. Olt GJ, Berchuck F, Bast RC. Gynecologic tumor markers. Semin Surg Oncol 1990;6:305–13.

17. Campbell S, Bahn V, Royston P, et al. Transabdominal ultrasound screening for ovarian cancer. BMJ 1989;299:1363.

18. DePriest PD, VanNagell JR, Gallion HH, et al. Ovarian cancer screening in asymptomatic postmenopausal women. Gynecol Oncol 1993;51:205–9.

19. Karlan BY, Platt LD. The current status of ultrasound in color doppler imaging in the screening of ovarian cancer. Gynecol Oncol 1994;55:S28–33.

20. National Institutes of Health consensus development conference statement. Ovarian cancer: screening, treatment, and follow-up. Gynecol Oncol 1994;55:S4–14.

21. Bourne TH, Campbell S, Reynolds K, et al. The potential role of CA 125 in an ultrasound based screening program, familial ovarian cancer. Gynecol Oncol 1994;52:379–85.

22. Olt GJ, Berchuck A, Bast RC. Gynecologic tumor markers. Semin Surg Oncol 1990;6:305–13.

23. Chen SS, Lee L. Incidence of periaortic and pelvic lymph nodes, metastasis in epithelial ovarian cancer. Gynecol Oncol 1983;16:95–100.

24. Young RC, Decker DG, Wharten JT, et al. Staging laparotomy in early ovarian cancer. [JAMA] 1983;250:3072–6.

25. Heintz AP, Van Oostrom AT, Baptist J, et al. The treatment of advanced ovarian cancer: clinical variables associated with prognosis. Gynecol Oncol 1988;30:347–58.

26. Heintz AP, Haker NF, Berek JS, et al. Cytoreductive surgery in ovarian cancer: feasibility and morbidity. Obstet Gynecol 1986;67:783–8.

27. Barnhill DR, Kurman RJ, Brady MF, et al. Preliminary analysis of the behavior of stage 1 ovarian serous tumors of low malignant potential: a gynecologic oncology group study. J Clin Oncol 1995;13:2752–6.

28. Sutton GP, Bundy GM, Omura GA, et al. Stage 3 ovarian tumors of low malignant potential, treated with cisplatin combination therapy: a gynecologic oncology group study. Gynecol Oncol 1991;41:230–33.

29. Smith JP, Day TD. Review of ovarian cancer at the University of Texas, System Cancer Center, M.D. Anderson Hospital and Tumor Institute. Am J Obstet Gynecol 1979;135:984–93.

30. McGuire WP, Rowensky EK, Rosenshine NE, et al. Taxol: a unique antineoplastic agent with significant

activity in advanced ovarian epithelial neoplasms. Ann Intern Med 1989;111:273–9.

31. McGuire WP, Hoskins WJ, Brady MF, et al. Cyclophosphamide and platinum compared with paclitaxel and cisplatin in patients with stage 3 and stage 4 ovarian cancer. N Engl J Med 1996;334:1–6.

32. Stuart G, Bertelsen K, Mangioni C, et al. Updated analysis shows a highly significant improved survival for cisplatin, paclitaxel as first line treatment of advanced stage epithelial ovarian cancer: mature results of the EORTC-GCC, NOCOVA, NCIC CTG, and Scottish Inter-group Trial. Proc Am Soc Clin Oncol 1989;34:1394.

33. Ozols RF, Ostchega Y, Kurt G, Young RC. High dose carboplatin and the effect to ovarian cancer patients. J Clin Oncol 1987;5:197–201.

34. Ozols RF, Bundy BN, Fowler J, et al. Randomized phase 3 study of cisplatin/paclitaxel vs. carboplatin/paclitaxel in optimal stage 3 epithelial ovarian cancer: a gynecologic oncology group trial (GOG 158). Proc Am Soc Clin Oncol 1999;35:1373.

35. Dembol AJ. Epithelial ovarian cancer. The role of radiotherapy. Int J Radiat Oncol Biol Phys 1992; 22:835–45.

36. Krebbs H, Goplerud ER, Kirkpatrick JS, et al. The role of CA 125 as a tumor marker in ovarian cancer. Obstet Gynecol 1986;155:56.

37. Patsner B, Orr JW, Mann JW, et al. The serum CA 125 level prior to second look laparotomy for invasive ovarian adenocancer to predict the size of residual disease. Gynecol Oncol 1990;37:319–22.

38. Bater JF, Barnes WA. Second look laparotomy. In: Wuben SC, Sutton GP, editors. Ovarian cancer. 1st ed. New York: McGraw-Hill; 1993. p. 269–300.

39. DeRosa V, Mangioni Di Stefano ML, Burnetti A, et al. Computed tomography and second look surgery in ovarian cancers: correlation. Actual role and limitations of CT scan. Eur J Gynecol Oncol 1995;16:123.

40. Cohen CJ, Jennings TS. Screening for ovarian cancer: the role of noninvasive imaging techniques. Am J Obstet Gynecol 1994;170:1088–94.

41. Podratz KC, Cliby WA. Second-look surgery in the management of epithelial ovarian cancer. Gynecol Oncol 1994;55:S128.

42. Gershinson DM, Coplin LJ, Warten JT, et al. Prognosis of surgically determined complete responders in advanced ovarian cancer. Cancer 1985;55:1129.

43. Eisenhauer EA, Vermorken JB, Van Glabbeke M. Predictors of response to subsequent chemotherapy in platinum pretreated ovarian cancer: a multi-varied analysis of 704 patients. Ann Oncol 1997;8:963–8.

44. Reuben SC, Benjamine I, Barrick JS. Secondary cytoreductive surgery. In: Colon N, Gershinson D, McGuire W, editors. Ovarian cancer: controversies in management. New York: Churchill Livingstone; 1998. p. 102.

45. Pecorelli S, Odicino F, Maisonneuve P, et al. Cancer of the ovary. Annual report on the results of treatment of gynecologic cancer. J Epidemiol Biostat 1998;3:75.

46. Hoskins WJ, Bundy BN, Thigpen JT, Gaomura GA. The influence of cytoreductive surgery on recurrence-free interval and survival in small volumes, stage 3 epithelial ovarian cancer: a Gynecologic Oncology Group study. Gynecol Oncol 1992;47:159–66.

84

URINARY TRACT INFECTIONS

Annapoorna Chirra, MD

Urinary tract infections (UTIs) are among the most commonly encountered infections in medical practice. According to surveys of ambulatory care practice in the United States, about 7 million episodes of acute cystitis and about 250,000 episodes of acute pyelonephritis occur yearly.[1] Due to several factors, UTIs affect primarily women. Forty to 50% of adult women report that they have had a UTI at some time during their life, and 20% of affected women note recurrent infections. The diagnosis and treatment of women with UTIs accounts for 7 million office visits and 1 million hospitalizations annually and is estimated to cost more than 1 billion dollars each year. According to one study, acute uncomplicated cystitis in young women was associated with 6.1 days of symptoms, 2.4 days of reduced activity at work, 1.2 days away from work, and 0.4 days at home in bed.[2]

"Urinary tract infection" is a term used to describe the microbial colonization and infection of the urine and/or structures of the urinary tract.[3] Traditionally, UTIs have been described in terms of asymptomatic bacteriuria, cystitis (an infection of the bladder), and pyelonephritis (an infection of the kidney). Such concrete divisions do not take into account a significant number of patients who have symptoms of cystitis and occult upper tract involvement (ie, subclinical pyelonephritis). This chapter reviews the types of UTI commonly encountered in clinical practice, including asymptomatic bacteriuria, uncomplicated cystitis and pyelonephritis, and complicated pyelonephritis.

PATHOPHYSIOLOGY

Anatomy

The structures of the urinary tract, including the urethra, bladder, ureters, and kidneys, are all sus-

ceptible to microbial invasion. Fortunately, the urinary tract is amazingly resistant to infection, considering the large microbial presence in close proximity in the vagina, perineum, and rectum. Most infections in adults are considered to be ascending infections, in which microorganisms enter the urinary tract from the distal portions of the urethra. Women are at particular risk because the female urethra is short and in close proximity to the vagina, which can become colonized with pathogenic bacteria. Sexual activity is often associated with UTIs. This is felt to be because sexual intercourse aids the ascension of periurethral and urethral bacteria into the urinary tract.[4]

Host Factors

The entry of microorganisms into the urinary tract is normally limited by various lines of defense. Normal perineal flora, the antibacterial properties of urine, regular micturition, complex immunologic processes, and the anatomic integrity of the urinary system all provide protection against microbial invasion. Normal perineal flora, such as lactobacilli, maintain an acidic vaginal environment that inhibits pathogenic bacteria. During and after menopause, decreasing estrogen levels are associated with a loss of lactobacilli, resulting in loss of the protective acidic milieu of the vagina. This partly explains the increased susceptibility of older women to recurrent infections. The use of spermicide in association with diaphragm use has also been shown to suppress the lactobacilli-producing flora, causing recurrent UTIs.[5]

Small quantities of urinary pathogens are inhibited in dilute urine by the acidic pH, by urea, and by high organic content. Micturation prevents attachment and colonization of the bladder,[6] which suggests that irregular urination habits may support colonization. Secreted inhibitors of adherence and a complex inflammatory response also work together to prevent microbial adhesion and invasion. Any defect in this system can potentially lead to UTIs.

The association of diabetes with UTI is multifactorial and depends on the degree of associated complications. The glucosuria associated with diabetes provides an excellent medium for bacterial replication. Autonomic dysfunction leading to delayed bladder emptying, leukocyte dysfunction, and renal abnormalities all predispose diabetic persons to UTIs.[4]

Obstruction from mechanical narrowing or neurologic dysfunction leads to incomplete bladder emptying and to bacterial proliferation within the bladder.[4] This partly explains the increased incidence of UTIs in pregnant patients, in whom there is a functional obstruction caused by an enlarging uterus. Elderly patients with obstructive uropathy also have an increased risk of UTI associated with decreased bladder emptying.

Bacterial Virulence

Bacterial virulence plays an important role in the pathogenesis of UTI. *Escherichia coli* serogroups (O1,O4, O6, O7, O16, O18, and O75) are a distinct subset of *E. coli* that cause most UTIs.[7] Several virulence factors, including fimbrial adhesins, hemolysin, and aerobactin, have been associated with uropathogenic *E. coli* strains.[8] Adherence and attachment mechanisms, through the use of virulence factors, are thought to encourage the formation and persistence of infection. It has been postulated that some patients with increased susceptibility and a history of recurrent infections have genetic factors that lead to increased adhesiveness of the uropathogenic *E. coli*.

P-fimbriated *E. coli* are a frequent cause of acute pyelonephritis in patients with the P blood group type. Patients with this blood type produce a glycolipid that is present in the bladder, ureter, and parts of the kidney. Under the influence of the P blood group antigen, this glycolipid encourages adhesion and subsequent infection by P-fimbriated *E. coli*. The Lewis blood group phenotype and the human leukocyte antigen (HLA)-A3 subtype are also more common in women with recurrent UTI and are postulated to facilitate the infection of the urinary tract through a similar mechanism.[9,10]

Virulence factors in organisms other than *E. coli* have not been extensively studied. *Staphylococcus saprophyticus* may cause UTIs by its remarkable adherence to uroepithelial cells.[11] Urease production and stone production by *Proteus mirabilis* and other organisms increase their ability to infect the urinary tract.

Microbiology

Gram-negative bacteria that originate from bowel flora cause most UTIs. *Escherichia coli* accounts for 90% of all community-acquired infections.[12] Most of the rest of community-acquired infections are due to *Staphylococcus saprophyticus*. *Staphylococcus saprophyticus* infections are especially prevalent in young sexually active females, and infection with this organism is more likely to be recurrent, relapsing, and persistent.[11] *Staphylococcus aureus* infections are less common and are usually from a hematogenous source. Endocarditis or other sources of bacteremia should be considered when a patient presents with a community-acquired *S. aureus* infection. *Proteus mirabilis*, *Klebsiella*, and *Enterococcus* are less common causes of community-acquired UTI but have an increased prevalence in the elderly population. Group B streptococci also can be found in community-acquired UTIs, and their presence has important implications during pregnancy.

Complicated UTIs (those associated with risk factors for infection, such as obstruction) and hospital-acquired UTIs are associated with a wider variety of pathogens. *Escherichia coli* remains the most common cause albeit at a lesser incidence. Instrumentation, as well as multiple courses of antibiotics, selects for pathogens such as *Pseudomonas*, *Serratia*, and *Citrobacter*.

In 15% of symptomatic patients, bacteriuria is not detected with routine culture. Fastidious organisms such as *Gardnerella vaginalis* and *Ureaplasma urealyticum* have been identified in bladder aspirates of symptomatic women and may be a cause of infection; however, routine culturing for fastidious organisms is not indicated.[13] Often cultured but rarely considered pathogenic are *Staphylococcus epidermidis*, diptheroids, α-hemolytic streptococci, and lactobacilli, which are usually considered to be contaminants. Nonbacterial organisms that may be responsible for dysuria include *Chlamydia*, gonococcus, *Candida*, *Trichomonas vaginalis*, and herpes simplex virus. Chlamydial infections are estimated to account for more than 30% of nonbacterial UTIs.[12]

ASYMPTOMATIC BACTERIURIA

Asymptomatic bacteriuria, by its very definition, is not associated with symptoms or pyuria and is discovered on urinanalysis or culture. Asymptomatic bacteriuria may or may not increase the likelihood of infection or morbidity, depending on the affected population.

The diagnosis of asymptomatic bacteriuria requires $\geq 10^5$ colony-forming units (CFU)/mL on two consecutive urine cultures in a patient without symptoms. By definition, pyuria should be absent.

As is discussed in the screening and prevention section of this chapter, treatment of asymptomatic bacteriuria has been shown to be beneficial only for pregnant patients, patients undergoing urologic procedures or other high-risk surgeries, and patients with renal transplants.[14] The treatment is the same as for uncomplicated acute cystitis, which is discussed below.

UNCOMPLICATED AND COMPLICATED URINARY TRACT INFECTIONS

Uncomplicated cystitis and pyelonephritis have predictable pathogens and courses of illness. Diagnosis is based on clinical findings, treatment is largely empiric, and significant laboratory or radiologic evaluations are not needed. By definition, complicated UTIs are associated with risk factors that increase the likelihood of acquiring infections, lead to recurrence and to failure of therapy, and promote resistant organisms. The risk factors can be structural (caused by anatomic abnormalities due to surgery or other causes) or functional (as in pregnancy or as associated with underlying diseases [such as diabetes and immunosuppression] that predispose to infection). Fifty percent of complicated UTIs recur if the underlying abnormality is not corrected. The distinction between uncomplicated and complicated UTIs is critical to diagnosis, treatment, follow up, and prognosis.

Acute Cystitis

SIGNS AND SYMPTOMS

Acute cystitis patients complain of acute dysuria, increased urgency and frequency of urination, and (often) suprapubic pain. Forty percent of women with cystitis have hematuria. Hematuria is not by itself a predictor of a more severe infection or complicated course.[15] If the patient uses a diaphragm and spermicide, has symptoms that are similar to prior episodes of cystitis, has a history of recent urinary catheter placement, or notes a temporal association of dysuria with sexual intercourse, acute cystitis should be considered. Naturally, if the patient has known structural or functional abnormalities, has a history of repeated infections, or is immunocompromised, the clinician should maintain a low threshold of suspicion for cystitis. The physical examination in a patient with acute cystitis is notable for suprapubic pain. Fever and flank pain should be absent.

DIAGNOSIS

Many UTIs are diagnosed simply from the constellation of presenting symptoms. As the pathogens of uncomplicated cystitis are predictable and the course of the illness is generally known, extensive diagnostic evaluations are not required. A urine dipstick analysis that suggests pyuria or bacteriuria is sufficient for diagnosis in the presence of a typical clinical picture. The urine dipstick can identify significant pyuria and bacteria by detecting leukocyte esterase and bacterial nitrates, respectively. Leukocyte esterase is found in neutrophil granules, and nitrate-reducing bacteria reduce nitrates to nitrites. Leukocyte esterase has a sensitivity of 75 to 90% and a 95% specificity for detecting pyuria. Nitrite dipstick analysis is 35 to 85% sensitive for the detection of bacteria because only some uropathogens convert nitrate to nitrites. The use of pyuria tests for the detection of UTI is associated with low specificity, mostly due to vaginal contaminants. Therefore, caution should be used in interpreting dipstick results in the absence of typical symptoms of UTI.

If the dipstick test is negative, then a culture should be obtained. When the number of bacteria in the urine is determined by quantitative bacterial counting, infected urine has been defined traditionally as containing $\geq 100,000$ (10^5) bacterial CFU/mL of a single bacterial species. Because up to a third of women with acute cystitis do not have culture counts $\geq 100,000$ CFU/mL, diagnostic criteria have since been modified.[16] It is now generally accepted that in *symptomatic* women, colony counts of 100 or more are significant for infection, yielding a sensitivity of 95% and a specificity of 85%.[17] Urine

TABLE 84–1. Summary of Diagnostic Tests for Urinary Tract Infection

Type of Infection	Culture (CFU/mL)	Wet Mount Urinalysis			Dipstick	
		Pyuria	Hematuria	Casts	Leukocyte Esterase	Nitrites
Asymptomatic bacteriuria	$\geq 10^5$	Ø	Ø	Ø	Ø	(+)/–
Acute cystitis	$\geq 10^2$	(+)	(+)	Ø	(+)	(+)/–
Urethritis	$< 10^2$	(+)	Ø	Ø	(+)	–
Vaginitis	$< 10^2$	Ø*	Ø	Ø	Ø	Ø
Acute pyelonephritis	$\geq 10^5$	(+)	(+)	(+)	(+)	(+)/–

*May be minimally positive in noncatheterized specimens.
+ = presence of; Ø = absence of; (+)/– = equivocal.

culture is not required for the diagnosis of uncomplicated cystitis but is recommended in complicated infections and for pregnant patients, to determine antibiotic sensitivities.

Urine wet mount analysis (microscopic urinalysis) can be used to detect bacteriuria and pyuria, but it is more costly than dipstick analysis. Most women with a UTI have ≥ 100 white blood cells (WBCs)/mm³. More than 10 WBCs/mm³ by counting chamber is considered abnormal and has a sensitivity of 91% for the diagnosis of UTI. Similarly, more than 10 WBC per high-power field (hpf) by wet mount is considered abnormal (Table 84–1).

DIFFERENTIAL DIAGNOSIS

Urethritis caused by *Chlamydia*, gonococci, and herpes simplex virus can cause dysuria. Dysuria caused by these organisms is generally of gradual onset and associated with vulvovaginal or cervical findings. Lower abdominal or pelvic pain and a concomitant history of a new sexual partner are also suggestive of a sexually transmitted disease.[15] Pyuria in the absence of bacteriuria is suggestive of urethritis. When urine culture for typical UTI organisms is performed in patients with urethritis, it generally demonstrates < 100 CFU/mL.

Vaginitis from *Trichomonas* or *Candida* can cause increased urinating frequency and dysuria. Generally this is associated with vaginal discharge and pruritus. Patients may also note external dysuria and dyspareunia. Urine culture colony counts for typical UTI organisms are ≤ 100 CFU/mL. *Trichomonas* may produce pyuria, but *Candida* typically does not.[18]

Noninfectious causes such as irritation or allergies from chemicals, soaps, or deodorants uncommonly cause urethral symptoms. Postmeno-

pausal women may develop dysuria due to a dry and irritated vaginal mucosa. Cultures will be unremarkable. Unrecognized interstitial cystitis may also present with symptoms of dysuria and frequency initially; however, patients will not respond to antibiotics, and repeated urine cultures will be negative.

An algorithm for the differential diagnosis of acute dysuria is presented in Figure 84–1.

TREATMENT

If untreated, acute uncomplicated cystitis resolves spontaneously in 26% of women. However, untreated patients may have symptoms for prolonged periods of time.[12] Based on clinical symptoms and either a urine or dipstick analysis, empiric therapy can be prescribed. Treatment for uncomplicated cystitis can be short because the superficial mucosa of the bladder is very responsive to therapy. Depending on the risk factors of the treated population, 3 to 7 days of therapy has been found to be optimal.[19] Three days of therapy is acceptable, except for patients who have had symptoms for more than 7 days, diabetic patients, diaphragm users, pregnant women, and patients with a history of recent antibiotic use. Because of its short half-life, treatment with nitrofurantoin should be for 7 days. Single-day therapies have lower success rates and a significant rate of recurrence, felt to be due to the failure to eradicate rectal and vaginal colonization.[20] Compared to the traditional 7- to 10-day therapies, 3- to 7-day therapies are associated with a lower side effect profile, increased compliance, less antibiotic resistance, and lower cost.[12,15]

Common oral antibiotic treatments for UTI have included amoxicillin, trimethoprim/sulfamethoxazole, ß-lactams, nitrofurantoin, and

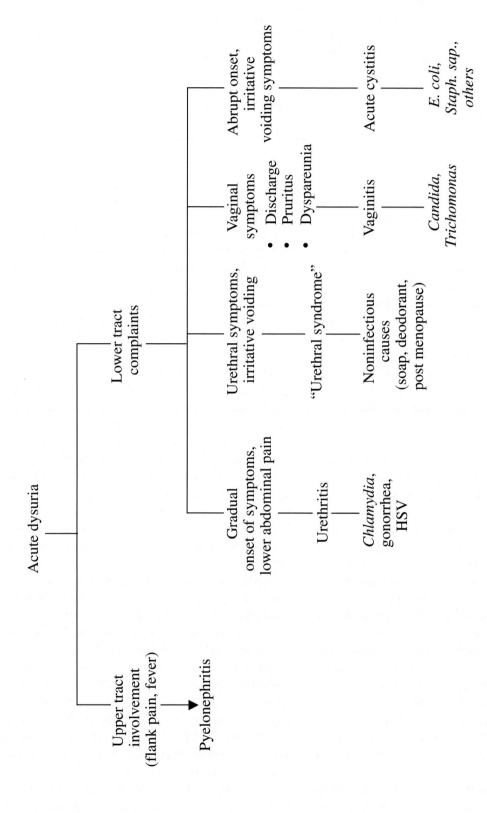

FIGURE 84-1. Differential diagnosis of acute dysuria. *E. coli = Escherichia coli;* HSV = herpes simplex virus; *Staph. sap. = Staphylococcus saprophyticus.*

TABLE 84–2. Antibiotic Regimens for Acute Cystitis

Type of Cystitis	Duration of Therapy	Antibiotics of Choice
Acute uncomplicated	3-d therapy routine 7-d therapy for diabetics, age > 65 yr, history of recent UTI, symptoms for > 7 d 7-d therapy for nitrofurantoin	Trimethoprim/sulfamethoxazole 160 mg/800 mg PO q12h Trimethoprim 100 mg PO q12h *Ciprofloxacin 100–250 mg PO q12h *Levofloxacin 250 mg PO qd *Ofloxacin 200 mg PO q12h *Norfloxacin 400 mg PO q12h *Lomefloxacin 400 mg PO qd *Enoxacin 400 mg PO q12h *Sparfloxacin 400 mg PO × 1 day, then 200 mg qd Cefpodoxime proxetil 100 mg PO q12h Cefixime 400 mg PO qd Augmentin 500 mg PO bid Nitrofurantoin (monohydrate crystals) 100 mg PO q12h Nitrofurantoin (macrocrystals) 50–100 mg PO qid
Acute complicated	7-d therapy	Quinolones only (ie, above antiobotics marked with asterisk)

*Quinolone used as therapy also for acute complicated cystitis.
UTI = urinary tract infection.
Adapted from Stamm WE, Hooton TM, Diagnosis and treatment of uncomplicated urinary tract infection. Infect Dis Clin North Am 1997;11(3):551–81.

quinolones. Although amoxicillin has been used historically and is less costly than other alternatives, 15 to 20% of UTI organisms in the United States are resistant to amoxicillin, so it should not be considered as first-line empiric therapy. Trimethoprim/sulfamethoxazole (TMP/SMZ) is the antibiotic of choice for empiric therapy for acute uncomplicated cystitis. This combination is superior in efficacy to ß-lactams and nitrofurantoin and is less costly.[19,20] It has been shown to maintain longer periods of high urinary concentration than the ß-lactams and has also been shown to eradicate *Escherichia coli* in vaginal secretions without altering vaginal flora.[14,21] However, up to 30% of the organisms that cause UTIs are resistant to TMP/SMZ in some patient populations.

Quinolones produce a higher cure rate when compared to TMP/SMZ but should not be used as first-line therapy because of their relatively high cost. Quinolone-resistant organisms are also increasingly found in community-based populations. Quinolones should be considered if the patient comes from an area with a high TMP/SMZ resistance, has TMP/SMZ intolerance, or has failed TMP/SMZ therapy. For patients with uncompli-

cated UTIs, routine post-treatment cultures are not required unless symptoms fail to resolve.

Patients with complicated acute cystitis should have a culture obtained on diagnosis and another culture 1 to 2 weeks after the completion of therapy. Until culture results (including antibiotic sensitivities) are available, the patient should be treated empirically with a quinolone. The use of the sensitivities is imperative in this population because of the high incidence of resistance.

Phenazopyridine (Pyridium), a urinary analgesic, can be used in conjunction with antibiotics but for no more than 1 or 2 days.

Approaches to treatment of acute cystitis are presented in Table 84–2 and Figure 84–2.

Acute Pyelonephritis

SIGNS AND SYMPTOMS
Flank pain, fever, and urinary symptoms should suggest pyelonephritis to the clinician. Most patients initially complain of several days of cystitis-like discomfort followed by the subsequent development of fever, shaking chills, flank pain, and (often) nausea, vomiting, and diarrhea. Patients can present with sepsis and life-threatening complications such

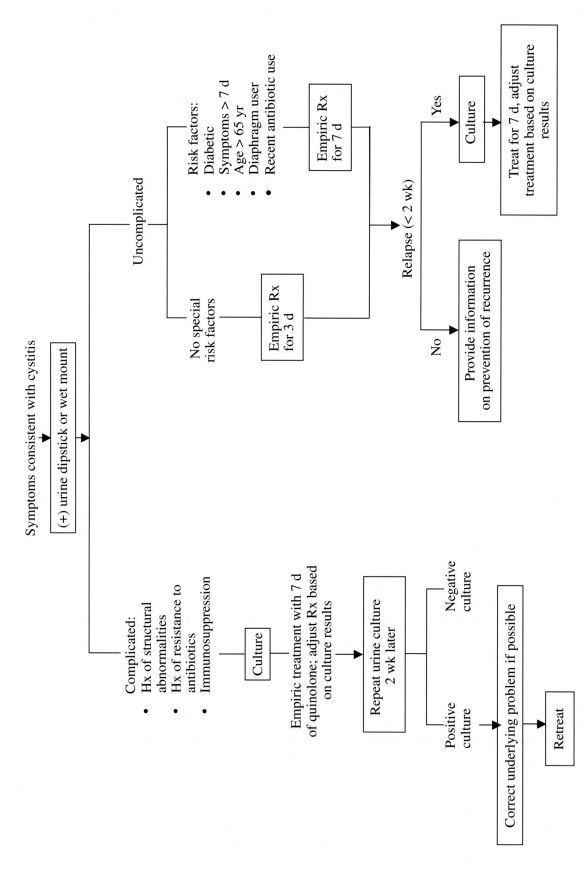

FIGURE 84–2. Approach to acute cystitis. Hx = history of; Rx = prescription. Adapted from Hooton TM. A simplified approach to urinary tract infection. Hosp Pract 1995;30(2):23–30.

as hypotension and respiratory distress. Physical examination findings are notable for exquisite costovertebral-angle tenderness, fever, and (often) suprapubic pain.

DIAGNOSIS

In patients with acute pyelonephritis, urinanalysis shows pyuria and bacteriuria. Hematuria and white cell casts often are seen. On urine culture, 80% of patients have $> 10^5$ CFU/mL.[14] Blood cultures may be positive in 12 to 20% of patients. However, positive blood cultures do not predict poorer outcomes.[15] Complete blood count may show leukocytosis with left shift. Renal function should not be significantly compromised in a patient with uncomplicated pyelonephritis, but, if present, it usually suggests dehydration. However, patients with complicated infections and known structural abnormalities often present with compromised renal function, compared to baseline function. Septic patients may present with hematologic and electrolyte abnormalities. Routine radiologic evaluation is not required for uncomplicated pyelonephritis. However, renal ultrasonography should be considered in patients with a poor response to therapy, a known history of structural abnormalities, or severe infectious complications.

DIFFERENTIAL DIAGNOSIS

Intra-abdominal processes such as pancreatitis, appendicitis, diverticulitis, and cholecystitis can mimic pyelonephritis. Liver function tests and measurements of serum amylase and lipase, if abnormal, may help to identify some of these disorders. Urinanalysis is normal with these disorders, except when inflammation of adjacent organs causes hematuria or pyuria. Lower-lobe pneumonia may present with flank pain and can present with symptoms similar to those of pyelonephritis.[22]

TREATMENT

In the absence of nausea or evidence of sepsis or other complicating factors, many patients with acute pyelonephritis can be treated as outpatients with 14 days of oral antibiotics. A urine culture should be obtained on diagnosis, and antibiotic therapy should be adjusted if appropriate, once sensitivities are known. The recommended empiric regimens are listed in Table 84–3. Trimethoprim/ sulfamethoxazole should be used only for patients from areas of low resistance and in general should not be used as empiric therapy for pyelonephritis. If the patient remains asymptomatic after treatment, a repeat culture is not required.

The indications for hospital admission and parenteral antibiotics include pregnancy, inability to take oral medications, signs of sepsis, temperature $> 40°C$, diabetes, immunosuppression, advanced age (over age 65 years), and potential noncompliance. Urine and blood cultures should be obtained on admission. A positive blood culture does not necessarily suggest a worse prognosis, and obtaining blood cultures does not change outcomes according to some studies. The traditional therapy for hospitalized patients includes an aminoglycoside for coverage of gram-negative organisms (ie, *E. coli*) and ampicillin for coverage of *Enterococcus*. Some authors suggest checking a urine Gram stain to evaluate the presence of gram-positive organisms (*Enterococcus*) and adjusting the antibiotics accordingly. Intravenous ceftriaxone has also been recommended for treatment. The quinolones have been widely studied and promoted for the treatment of complicated UTI and can be effective but are costly for uncomplicated pyelonephritis. Trimethoprim/ sulfamethoxazole is no longer considered first-line empiric therapy because of emerging resistance but can be used if sensitivities are known.

When patients are admitted for intravenous therapy, oral therapy is usually begun after the patient has been afebrile for 24 to 48 hours and has shown evidence of significant improvement. The oral therapy should be continued, to complete a total of 14 days of antibiotics, and should be based on urine culture and/or blood culture sensitivities. Quinolones are chosen as first-line empiric oral therapy, but TMP/SMZ or other antibiotics can be used, based on the culture sensitivities. In patients with complicated pyelonephritis, a repeat culture should be obtained 1 to 2 weeks after therapy, to document the eradication of infection.

Routine uroradiologic studies are not indicated for evaluation of adult women with uncomplicated pyelonephritis. However, if the patient remains febrile after 72 hours of parenteral therapy, a radiologic study should be pursued. Ultrasonography or computed tomography (CT) scan should be performed to evaluate for signs of obstruction, nephrolithiasis, or abscess. A urologic consultation for cystoscopy or excretory urography should be

TABLE 84–3. Antibiotic Regimens for Treatment of Pyelonephritis

Type of Pyelonephritis	Antibiotic and Dosage	Duration
Acute uncomplicated pyelonephritis	Ciprofloxacin 500 mg PO bid	14 d of therapy
	Levofloxacin 250 mg PO qd	
	Ofloxacin 200–300 mg PO q12h	
	Norfloxacin 400 mg PO q12h	
	Lomefloxacin 400 mg PO qd	
	Enoxacin 400 mg PO q12h	
	Sparfloxacin 400 mg PO day 1, then 200 mg PO qd	
	Trimethoprim/sulfamethoxazole 160/800 mg PO q12h[*]	
	Cefixime 400 mg PO qd	
	Cefpodoxime proxetil 200 mg PO q12h	
	Amoxicillin/clavulanate 875/125 mg PO bid or 500/125 mg PO bid	
Acute complicated pyelonephritis— IV regimens	Ceftriaxone 1–2 g qd	IV regimen until afebrile for 24–48h, then oral therapy (see above), based on sensitivities, to complete 14 d therapy
	Ciprofloxacin 200–400 mg q12h	
	Levofloxacin 250 mg qd	
	Ofloxacin 200–400 mg q12h	
	Gentamicin 3–5 mg/kg qd, or 1 mg/kg q8h with or without ampicillin 1 g q12h	
	Trimethoprim/sulfamethoxazole 160/800 mg q12h[*]	
	Ticarcillin-clavulanate 3.1 g q6h	
	Imipenem-cilastatin 250–500 mg q6h–q8h	
	Cefoxitin 2 g q8h	

[*]Use only when sensitivities are known.
Adapted from Stamm WE, Hooton TM. Diagnosis and treatment of uncomplicated urinary tract infection. Infect Dis Clin North Am 1997;11(3):551–81; Gilbert D, Moellering R, et al. The Sanford guide to antimicrobial therapy—2000. 30th ed. Hyde Park (VT): Antimicrobial Therapy Inc; and Hooton TM. A simplified approach to urinary tract infection. Hosp Pract 1995;273:41–5.

obtained if there is evidence of significant obstruction or hematuria after the infection has been eradicated.[15] Urodynamic studies may be indicated if the patient has a suspected neurogenic bladder or an abnormal voiding pattern. Preservation of renal function is excellent in patients with uncomplicated pyelonephritis but may be impaired in patients with structural abnormalities as a result of inflammatory changes.

An algorithm for the evaluation and treatment of acute pyelonephritis appears in Figure 84–3.

RECURRENCE AND PREVENTION

Nearly one-half of women whose uncomplicated UTIs resolve spontaneously (without antibiotic treatment) develop a recurrent UTI within the first year.[23] With antibiotic treatment the incidence of recurrence is significantly reduced but may still be

as high as 27% in young women[24] and up to 53% in women older than 55 years.[25] A major challenge in the treatment of UTI is to prevent recurrent infections due to relapse or re-infection.

Most recurrences appear to occur within 3 months of the initial infection. Recurrent infections that occur within 2 weeks are considered to be a relapse from the same causative organism. Relapses are managed with a pretreatment urine culture, antimicrobial susceptibility testing, and treatment for 2 to 6 weeks.

Eighty percent of recurrences are re-infections. Although originally thought to be caused by different organisms, re-infections appear to be due to the repeated contraction of infection from a reservoir of fecal flora. The re-infecting strain in such instances may be identical to the last infecting strain, presumably reflecting its persistence in the fecal flora.

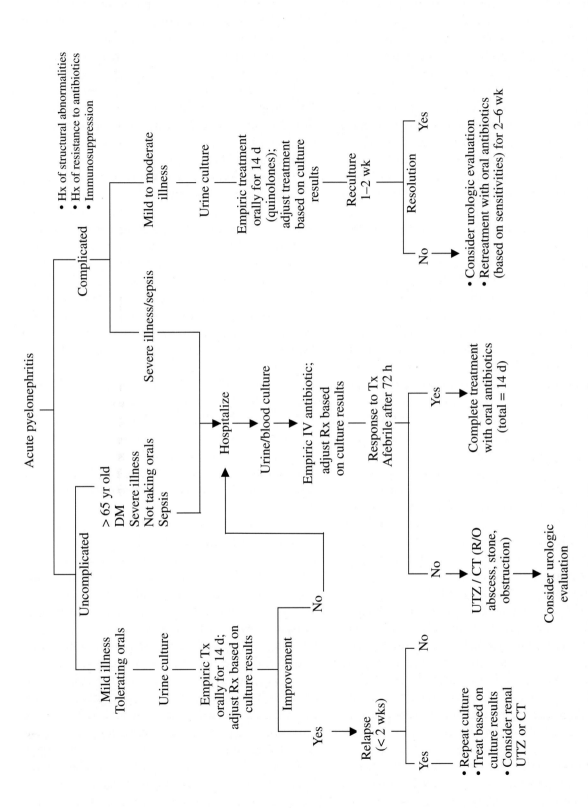

FIGURE 84-3. Evaluation and treatment of acute pyelonephritis. CT = computed tomography; DM = diabetes mellitus; Rx = prescription; UTZ = ultrasound; HX = history of; Tx = treatment; R/O = rule out. Adapted from Hooton TM. A simplified approach to urinary tract infection. Hosp Pract 1995;30(2):23–30.

Urinary tract infections can be prevented through behavioral and pharmacologic means. Behaviors that traditionally have been considered to increase the risk of infection include wiping from back to front after bowel movements, using tampons, using vaginal deodorant products, douching, wearing occlusive underclothing, and practicing poor perineal hygiene. Case-control studies have shown none of the above behaviors alter the likelihood of infection,[26] and relevant randomized prospective studies do not exist. However, basic behavioral modifications such as wiping from front to back, regular urination, and attention to perineal hygiene seem to be intuitive and are reasonable lifestyle changes.

Other behaviors that might be associated with an increased risk of UTI include decreased fluid intake, inconsistent voiding habits, and delayed micturation after intercourse. Small retrospective studies suggested that women who retained urine for more than 1 hour after urgency were noted to have a higher risk of UTI. Other studies suggested that women with a reduced fluid intake and a low frequency of urination had a higher incidence of UTI compared with controls.[27] However, this observation has not been confirmed in a case-control study. One retrospective case-control study showed that voiding soon after intercourse was protective;[4] however, this also has not been confirmed by another large prospective study.[28,29] The lifestyle modifications of regular and frequent urination, postcoital micturation, and the drinking of plenty of water are simple and innocuous and may be proved effective in further studies.

It has been estimated that diaphragm and spermicide use may contribute to one-third of acute UTIs.[5] Spermicidal creams alter the normal vaginal bacterial flora, reducing the number of lactobacilli, increasing the pH, and improving the milieu for colonization of the vagina by pathogenic bacteria. The use of a diaphragm that traps the spermicide in the vagina for long periods prolongs the effect. In addition, the diaphragm may partially obstruct the urethra and prevent the bladder from emptying completely, thus causing additional risk of UTI. In a prospective study by Hooton and Hillier,[30] the use of a diaphragm with spermicidal jelly or the use of spermicidal foam with a condom was shown to strongly predispose users to the development of vaginal colonization and bacteriuria by *Escherichia coli*.

On the other hand, epidemiologic studies have found weak associations or no association of oral contraceptive use with the incidence of UTIs.[5] Oral contraceptive users have an increased frequency of asymptomatic bacteriuria, but it is unclear whether this is secondary to sexual activity. This suggests that an alternative form of birth control, possibly the oral contraceptive pill, could be beneficial for diaphragm and/or spermicide users with recurrent UTI.

Another nonpharmacologic prevention measure commonly recommended is the ingestion of cranberry juice. In a double-blind placebo-controlled trial of postmenopausal women with asymptomatic bacteriuria, 300 mL of cranberry juice per day reduced the odds of bacteriuria and pyuria to 42% of the control group.[31] Cranberry juice has been shown to contain substances that inhibit the adherence of uropathogenic *E. coli* to uroepithelial cells. Extracts of cranberry contain lectins that bind type 1 fimbriae of *E. coli* bacteria. This approach has not been studied in premenopausal women.

Recent antibiotic use (ie, within 2 to 4 weeks) increases the risk of UTI and is particularly marked with the use of ß-lactams.[32] This is thought to be due to changes in vaginal and urogenital flora. Trimethoprim/sulfamethoxazole does not seem to change flora to as great a degree. Therefore, more selective use of antibiotics may reduce the risk of UTI.

Probably the most clearly identified risk factor for UTI is catheter use. The incidence of catheter-related UTIs is extremely high. Avoiding the placement of a catheter remains the best way to reduce the mortality, morbidity, and costs of catheter-associated infection. Because of the high morbidity associated with bacteriuria, catheterization should be done with great hesitancy and caution in certain populations. For instance, in pregnant patients the rate of catheter-induced UTIs is on the order of 4 to 6%. Prophylactic systemic antimicrobial agents may be useful in selected patients at high risk who are undergoing short-term catheterization (eg, patients undergoing urologic or gynecologic surgery, surgery involving a foreign body, or renal transplantation). However, the routine use of prophylactic antibiotics in patients with catheters is not indicated because of the cost and the potential for inducing resistant organisms.[14]

In a randomized placebo-controlled trial, intravaginal estriol in postmenopausal women significantly reduced the incidence of UTI and prevented its recurrence.[33] (The role of estrogen replacement therapy is discussed in Chapter 4)

Despite the use of the interventions just described, a minority of women continue to suffer from relatively frequent UTIs. Although some patients clearly have a structural abnormality that predisposes them to recurrent infections, the majority do not. Most patients with recurrent infections are presumed to have a yet-unidentified defect in some defense mechanism. Some authors recommend pursuing a urologic evaluation in patients with poorly identified risk factors for recurrence; however, the yield of such evaluations is low. Urologic evaluation may be indicated if a patient has more than three episodes of cystitis per year or two episodes of pyelonephritis per year. The evaluation might include ultrasonography, intravenous pyelography, or CT urography to evaluate anatomy; it also might include cystoscopy. Intravenous pyelography reveals a significant abnormality in less than 1% of women with re-infections. Cystoscopy has been reported to diagnose surgically amenable bladder diverticula in up to 4% of patients who have more than three UTIs per year.[18]

For patients who have up to two UTIs per year, patient-initiated self-treatment of a single dose or a 3-day course of standard therapy may be appropriate.[34] For patients who have at least three UTIs per year, the following management strategies have been proposed. Antimicrobial prophylaxis may be initiated with TMP/SMZ (40 mg/200 mg), nitrofurantoin (50 to 100 mg), norfloxacin (200 mg), or cephalexin (250 mg orally daily or three times per week). Continuous antimicrobial prophylaxis typically is continued for 6 months but has been found to be highly effective for up to 5 years without the development of resistance. Upon discontinuation of prophylaxis, 40 to 60% of women re-establish their pattern or frequency of recurrence.[29,35] Postcoital prophylaxis may be successful in patients who associate their recurrence with intercourse. Typically, TMP/SMZ (40 mg/200 mg) or trimethoprim (100 mg) have been used.

SCREENING OF THE GENERAL POPULATION FOR URINARY TRACT INFECTION

Screening for asymptomatic bacteriuria has little apparent value in adults, with three exceptions: pregnant women, patients who are about to undergo genitourinary tract procedures, and patients with renal transplants.[14] The screening of pregnant women is discussed in detail below.

Screening urinalysis might be appropriate for certain high-risk groups such as diabetic and non-institutionalized elderly women, but firm evidence of benefit is not available. Potential benefits must be weighed against the high likelihood of re-infection after treatment in these groups and against the adverse effects associated with antibiotic use and potential resistance. Screening is not justified in the general adult population because serious urinary tract disorders are uncommon and because the positive predictive value of screening is low. Furthermore, the effectiveness of early detection and treatment is unproven.[36]

At this time, the major authorities have established that the evidence is insufficient for making recommendations for or against screening diabetic or elderly ambulatory women for asymptomatic bacteriuria. The American College of Physicians and the US Preventive Services Task Force recommend against the routine screening of adults for asymptomatic bacteriuria by urinalysis or urine culture.

URINARY TRACT INFECTIONS IN PREGNANCY

The incidence (2 to 11%) of asymptomatic bacteriuria in pregnant women is similar to that seen in nonpregnant women. Pregnancy is not believed to be a predisposing factor in the development of asymptomatic bacteriuria (10^5CFU/mL). In most patients, asymptomatic bacteriuria reflects prior colonization rather than acquisition. Physiologic changes such as hydroureter, renal dilation and lengthening, decreased ureteral peristalsis, and bladder compression promote the persistence of bacteriuria and the development of symptomatic UTIs. Pregnancy-induced glucosuria and aminoaciduria also promote bacterial proliferation.[37]

If untreated, asymptomatic bacteriuria during pregnancy is associated with low birth weight and preterm delivery.[38] The mechanisms for premature labor developing in patients with infection are not completely clear but may be related to microorganism production of phospholipase A. Labor is thought to be initiated by amniotic and chorionic phospholipase, which may then lead to the production of prostaglandins E_2 and F_2 and to the induction of spontaneous labor. *Escherichia coli* and other gram-negative organisms have been shown to produce phospholipase A.[39] Pyelonephritis, which occurs in 2% of pregnancies, has severe clinical complications, including rates of prematurity in the range of 20 to 50% and increased fetal mortality.[40]

The microbiology of UTIs in pregnant women is similar to that seen in nonpregnant women. In order of frequency, *E. coli, Klebsiella pneumoniae, Proteus mirabilis,* and (less commonly) gram-positive organisms such as group B hemolytic *Streptococcus, Staphylococcus saprophyticus,* and coagulase-negative staphylococci cause UTIs in pregnancy.[41] Anaerobic organisms such as *Gardnerella vaginalis* and *Ureaplasma urealyticum* are often isolated in numbers less than 10^5 CFU/mL in patients with asymptomatic bacteriuria, but their pathogenic role is unclear.

Screening

The diagnosis and managementof asymptomatic bacteriuria are of paramount importance. All major authorities in the United States, including the American College of Obstetricians and Gynecologists, the US Preventive Services Task Force, and the American Academy of Family Physicians, recommend screening as a routine part of perinatal evaluation. Patients should be screened at 12 to 16 weeks of gestation to optimize the greatest number of bacteriuria-free weeks.[42] Although 1 to 2% of women acquire bacteriuria during pregnancy,[43] repeat screenings are not routinely recommended at this time. However, for patients with a history of recurrent UTIs and known structural abnormalities, a repeat culture at the beginning of the third trimester is reasonable.[44]

Screening in pregnant patients should be by urine culture or semiquantitative culture because urine dipstick analysis has been found to be insensitive.[45] If a positive semiquantitative culture is present, a quantitative culture should be obtained. In practice, only one culture is routinely obtained due to cost. A single "clean-catch" urine culture detects 80% of cases of asymptomatic bacteriuria.[46] When two or more consecutive specimens contain the same organism, the probability of true bacteriuria increases to over 95%, which is similar to catheterization results. Catheterization in pregnant women is associated with a significant risk for inducing infection (4 to 6%) and should be done with extreme caution and only if a clear indication is present.

Asymptomatic bacteriuria, defined by a urine culture count $\geq 10^5$ CFU/mL, mandates treatment. Treatment alternatives are summarized in Table 84–4. A follow-up culture should be obtained to document treatment efficacy. Once asymptomatic bacteriuria has been documented, repeated monthly screening cultures during the duration of the pregnancy are indicated to detect recurrence.

If fewer than 10^5 organisms are cultured, repeat cultures should be obtained; treatment should be considered if 25,000 to 100,000 organisms are found on repeat testing. The significance of 10^2 to 10^4 gram-positive or fastidious organisms is unclear in asymptomatic patients. However, fewer than 10^5 organisms in a symptomatic patient suggests infection, and the patient should be treated accordingly.

Acute Cystitis

The clinical presentation of UTIs in pregnant patients is similar to that in nonpregnant patients but may be more complicated and severe. Unfortunately, symptoms (such as frequency) consistent with cystitis occur frequently in pregnant women who are without infection. Patients with cystitis will have a positive urine culture.

Treatment options are presented in Table 84–4. The various regimens have roughly equal efficacy, and a 7-day course of antibiotics is usually sufficient. Repeat cultures should be obtained 7 to 10 days after the completion of therapy, and patients should have monthly screening cultures until the time of delivery. If a positive culture result persists, treatment should be lengthened, and long-term suppression should be considered. Because *Escherichia coli* is resistant to ampicillin/amoxicillin in up to one-third of isolates, ampicillin/amoxicillin should not be used empirically[47] but can be used on the return of sensitivities.

Acute Pyelonephritis

The incidence of acute pyelonephritis has decreased dramatically during the last 20 years, in large part due to the screening for asymptomatic bacteriuria. Patients with acute pyelonephritis usually present with fever, chills, nausea, and vomiting, but the clinical picture is usually more severe in pregnant patients. Acute pyelonephritis has been associated with adult respiratory distress syndrome, sepsis, renal insufficiency, hematologic abnormalities, and hypothalamic instability.[48]

TABLE 84–4. Antibiotic Treatment of Urinary Tract Infections during Pregnancy and Breast-Feeding

Drug	Dosage	Remarks, Safety in Pregnancy	Breast-Feeding Safety
Asymptomatic bacteriuria or acute cystitis			
Amoxicillin	250–500 mg q6h for 7 d	Use only if sensitivities are known (because of high resistance)	Safe
Cephalexin	250–500 mg PO q6h for 7 d		Safe
Nitrofurantoin			
Macrocrystals	50–100 mg PO q6h for 7 d	Glucose-6-phosphate dehydrogenase (G6PD) deficiency–associated hemolytic anemia.	Safe
Monohydrate/ macrocrystals	100 mg q12h for 7 d		
Sulfisoxazole	500 mg PO q6h for 7 d	G6PD-deficient patients can develop hemolytic anemia; avoid in third trimester (potential risk of fetal kernicterus); increasing resistance.	Safe
Trimethoprim	200 mg PO q12h for 7 d	Increasing resistance found.	Safe
Trimethoprim/ sulfamethoxazole	160/800 mg PO q12h for 7 d	Unclear teratogenicity; avoid in third trimester (potential risk of kernicterus); stop 2 wk before term; increasing resistance found.	Safe
Acute pylenonephritis			
Ampicillin and gentamicin	1–2 g q6h IV 1.5 mg/kg q8h IV	Caution in patients with renal insufficiency and in areas with high rates of ampicillin resistance.	Safe
Ceftriaxone	1–2 g IM q24h		Safe
Cefazolin	1g IV q8h		Safe
Trimethoprim/ sulfamethoxazole*	160/800 mg IV q8h	Unclear teratogenicity; avoid in third trimester (potential risk of kernicterus); stop 2 wk before term; increasing resistance found.	Safe
Suppression			
Nitrofurantoin	50–100 mg PO qhs	See above comments.	Safe
Sulfisoxazole	500 mg qhs	See above comments.	Safe
Cephalexin	250 mg po qhs	—	Safe

*Use only if sensitivities are known.

Adapted from Gilbert D, Moellering R, et al. The Sanford guide to antimicrobial therapy—2000. 30th ed. Hyde Park (VT): Antimicrobial Therapy Inc; Andriole VT, Patterson TF. Detection, significance, and therapy of bacteriuria in pregnancy. Infect Dis Clin North Am 1997;11:593–608; and Alger L. Antimicrobial therapy for obstetric patients. ACOG Educational Bulletin, Number 245, March 1998.

Laboratory diagnosis of pyelonephritis in the pregnant patient is similar to that in the nonpregnant patient. Significant pyuria and casts will be detected on urine microscopy, and culture will usually have $\geq 10^5$ CFU/mL. Blood cultures are positive in 10 to 20% of patients but do not change management.[49]

Most pregnant patients with acute pyelonephritis are treated as inpatients because of the high risk of maternal complications and the risk of preterm labor. Intravenous antibiotics are usually used for 24 to 48 hours after the patient becomes afebrile. Frequently used regimens are summarized in Table 84–4. In a recent study, regimens including intravenous ampicillin and gentamicin, intramuscular ceftriaxone, and intravenous cefazolin had similar clinical outcomes.[50] Patients should be treated to complete 2 weeks of antibiotics with oral antibiotics, based on sensitivities. Quinolones and tetracycline are contraindicated.

If the patient does not respond within 72 hours, renal ultrasonography should be performed to look for associated structural abnormalities or complications, such as nephrolithiasis or abscess, which may require surgical intervention. Respiratory insufficiency occurs in 2 to 8% of patients with pyelonephritis. Renal dysfunction occurs in 25% of pregnant patients, but renal function normalizes after treatment. Hemolysis and anemia may be present. These complications are treated supportively.

Recently, outpatient management of acute pyelonephritis in pregnant patients has been investigated. However, no long-term data regarding outcome is available, and the trials have been limited in size. It has been shown that in selected patients at less than 24 weeks' gestation, outpatient management may be feasible. Patients were excluded from outpatient treatment if they had obvious signs of sepsis, had abnormal serum laboratory values, or experienced nausea and vomiting.[51] One randomized controlled trial compared inpatient treatment with intravenous cefazolin to outpatient treatment with intramuscular ceftriaxone and found similar rates of persistence and recurrence.[52] In the outpatient management of acute pyelonephritis in pregnancy, close follow-up and patient education are mandatory, and monitoring by home health nurses should be strongly considered.

Up to 40% of pregnant patients with pyelonephritis have recurrent infection. Therefore, antibiotic suppression is strongly recommended in addition to monthly screening cultures. Daily oral antibiotic suppression is generally recommended until delivery. However, one randomized controlled trial did not show a significant advantage in suppression.[53] Common regimens include nitrofurantoin, sulfisoxazole, and cephalexin. Follow-up cultures should be performed in patients with recurrent infection after delivery and urologic evaluation should be considered at 3 to 6 months post partum.[54] Radiologic evaluation usually is not indicated during pregnancy, and few patients need urologic evaluation post partum.[55] Further evaluation should be considered if there is any evidence of obstruction, structural abnormality, or failure to respond to therapy.

An algorithm for screening and treatment of pregnant patients with urinary tract infections is presented in Figure 84–4.

BREAST-FEEDING

Postpartum and breast-feeding patients, although not at increased risk for UTI, are nonetheless susceptible to urinary infections. Interestingly, in a preliminary study, breast-feeding was shown to have a protective effect against UTIs in both mother and infant.[56] Certain oligosaccharides found in urine from babies and in breast milk and urine from nursing mothers inhibit bacterial adhesion.

Treatment of UTI during breast-feeding must take into account the risk of exposure to the baby. Penicillin analogues such as ampicillin, cephalosporins such as cefazolin and ceftriaxone, and TMP/SMZ are generally considered safe during breast-feeding. As in pregnancy, quinolones (such as ciprofloxacin) and tetracyclines should be avoided during breast-feeding. Aminoglycosides are generally considered safe.

MENOPAUSE AND AGING

The hormonal and physiologic changes of aging, in association with disease processes that occur more commonly with age, predispose older women to UTIs. Up to 20% of elderly women have UTIs,[57] and women more than 80 years of age have a 20 to 50% incidence of bacteriuria. Institutionalized elderly women and women with debilitating disease are more likely to have bacteriuria and UTIs than are women living at home.[58]

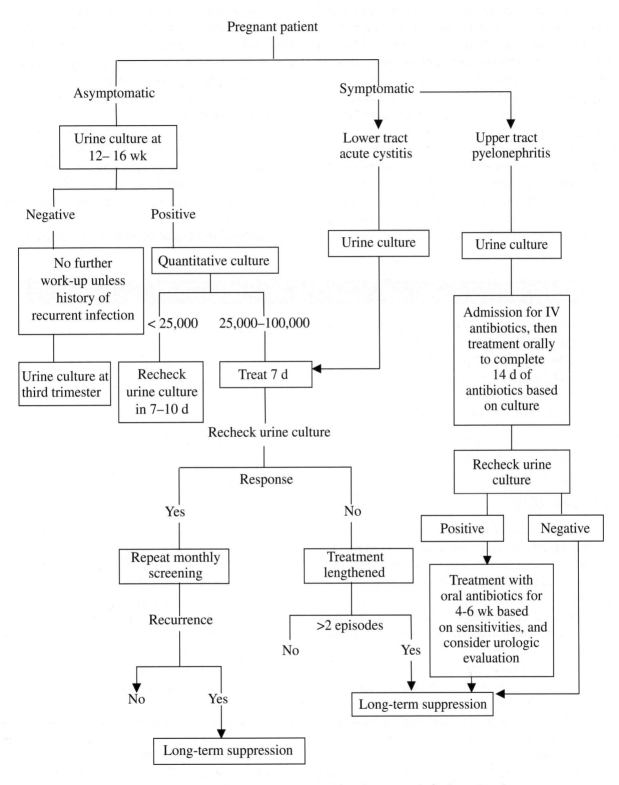

FIGURE 84–4. Screening and treatment of pregnant patients with urinary tract infections. IV = intravenous.

Decreasing estrogen levels are an important risk factor for UTI. In premenopausal women estrogen causes an accumulation of glycogen in vaginal epithelial cells. The conversion of glycogen to lactic acid by lactobacilli results in acidification of the vaginal fluid. An acidic vaginal environment has been shown to inhibit the growth of some urinary tract pathogens.[59]

In atrophic vaginitis there is an increase in vaginal pH and a high incidence of asymptomatic bacteriuria. Exogenous estrogen can decrease vaginal pH by increasing lactobacilli which in turn creates an acidic environment. In a randomized double-blind placebo-controlled trial, Raz and Stamm showed that intravaginal estriol cream used in postmenopausal women resulted in significantly fewer UTIs and recurrences, probably by modifying the vaginal flora.[33] Physiologic changes associated with menopause and age, such as bladder and uterine prolapse, lead to significant postvoid residual volumes and promote UTIs.

Because of added risk factors for complications and recurrences of UTI, postmenopausal women (especially those over the age of 65 years) should be treated conservatively. Seven days of therapy for acute cystitis is recommended. Inpatient treatment with intravenous antibiotics should be administered in the case of acute pyelonephritis.

RESOURCE

National Institute of Diabetes and Digestive and Kidney Diseases
3 Information Way
Bethesda, Maryland 20892-3580
Telephone: (301) 468-6345
E-mail: nkudic@infor.niddk.nih.gov.
Web site: www.niddk.nih.gov

The NIDDK provides information about urinary tract infection for patients and clinicians and provides links to clinical guidelines.

REFERENCES

1. Schappert SM. National ambulatory medical care survey: 1992 summary. Advanced data from vital and health statistics. Hyattsville (MD): National Center for Health Statistics; 1994. DHHS Publication No.: (PHS) 253. p. 94.

2. Foxman B. Epidemiology of urinary tract infection. I. Diaphragm use and sexual intercourse. Am J Public Health 1985;75:1308.

3. Kunin CM. Urinary tract infections: detection, prevention and management. Baltimore: Williams and Wilkins; 1997.

4. Sobel J. Pathogenesis of urinary tract infection—role of host defenses. Infect Dis Clin North Am 1997; 11:531–49.

5. Hooton TM, Scholes D. A prospective study of risk factors for symptomatic urinary tract infection. I. Young women. N Engl J Med 1996;335:468–74.

6. Korzeniowski O. Urinary tract infection in the impaired host. Med Clin North Am 1991;75:391–404.

7. Sobel JD. Bacterial etiologic agents in the pathogenesis. Med Clin North Am1991;75:253–73.

8. Hooton T. A simplified approach to urinary tract infection. Hosp Pract 1995;30(2):23–30.

9. Sheinfeld J, Schaeffer A, Cordon-Cardo C, et al. Association of the Lewis blood-group phenotype with recurrent urinary tract infections in women. N Engl J Med 1989;320:773–7.

10. Schaeffer AJ, Radvany RM, Chmiel JS. Human leukocyte antigens in women with recurrent urinary tract infection. J Infect Dis 1983;148:604.

11. Hovelius B, Mardh PA. *Staphylococcus saprophyticus* as a common cause of urinary tract infection. Rev Infect Dis 1984;6:328–37.

12. Faro S, Fenner DE. Urinary tract infections. Clin Obstet Gynecol 1998;41:744–54.

13. Fairley KF, Birth CF. Detection of bladder bacteriuria in patients with acute urinary symptoms. J Infect Dis 1989;159:226–31.

14. Stamm WE, Hooton TM. Management of urinary tract infections in adults. N Engl J Med 1993; 329:1328–34.

15. Hooton TM, Stamm WE. Diagnosis and treatment of uncomplicated urinary tract infection. Infect Dis Clin North Am 1997;11:551–81.

16. Kunin CM. A reassessment of the importance of "low count" bacteriuria in young women with acute urinary symptoms. Ann Intern Med 1993;119:445–60.

17. Stamm WE, Johnson JR. Urinary tract infections in women: diagnosis and treatment. Ann Intern Med 1989;111:906–17.

18. Komaroff A. Acute dysuria and urinary tract infections. In: Carlson KJ, et al, editors. Primary care of women. St. Louis (MO): Mosby; 1995. p. 126–32.

19. Hooton TM, Winter C, Tiu F, et al. Randomized comparative trial and cost analysis of 3 day antimicrobial regimens for treatment of acute cystitis in women. JAMA 1995;273:41–5.

20. Norrby SR. Short-term treatment of uncomplicated lower urinary tract infections in women. Rev Infect Dis 1990;12:458–67.

21. Hooton TM, Running K, Stamm WE. Single dose therapy for cystitis in women: a comparison of trimethoprim-sulfamethoxazole, amoxicillin and cyclacillin. JAMA 1985;253:387.

22. Presti JC, et al. Genitourinary tract infections. In: Tierney LM, et al, editors. Current medical diagnosis and treatment 1997. Stamford (CT): Appleton and Lange; 1997. p. 859–66.

23. Mabeck CE. Treatment of uncomplicated urinary tract infection in nonpregnant women. Postgrad Med J 1972;48:69.

24. Foxman B. Recurring urinary tract infection: incidence and risk factors. Am J Public Health 1990;80:331–3.

25. Ikaheimo R, Siitonen, Heiskanen T, et al. Recurrence of urinary tract infection in a primary care setting: analysis of a 1 year follow up of 179 women. Clin Infect Dis 1996;22:91.

26. Strom BL, Collins N, West SL, et al. Sexual activity, contraceptive use, and other risk factors for symptomatic and asymptomatic bacteriuria: a case-control study. Ann Intern Med 1987;107:816–23.

27. Ervin C. Behavioral factors and urinary tract infection. JAMA 1980;243:330–1.

28. Hooton TM, Scholes D. A prospective study of risk factors for urinary tract infection in young women, N Engl J Med 1996;335:468–74.

29. Stapleton A, Stamm W. Prevention of urinary tract infection. Infect Dis Clin North Am 1997; 11:719–33.

30. Hooton TM, Hillier S. Escherichia coli bacteriuria and contraceptive method. JAMA 1991;265:64–9.

31. Avorn J, Monane M. Reduction of bacteriuria and pyuria after ingestion of cranberry juice. JAMA 1994; 271:751–4.

32. Winberg J, Herthelius-Elman M, Mollby R, Nord CE. Pathogenesis of urinary tract infection: experimental studies of vaginal resistance to colonization. Pediatr Nephrol 1993;7:509–14.

33. Raz R, Stamm WE. A controlled trial of intravaginal estrogen in postmenopausal women with recurrent urinary tract infection. N Engl J Med 1993;329:753–6.

34. Wong ES, McKevitt, Running K, et al. Management of recurrent urinary tract infections with patient-administered single-dose therapy. Ann Intern Med 1985;102:302–7.

35. Nicolle LE. Prophylaxis: recurrent urinary tract infection in women. Infection 1992;20 Suppl 3:S203–5.

36. DiGuiseppi C, et al. Screening for asymptomatic bacteriuria. In: Guide to clinical preventive services. Baltimore (MD): Williams & Wilkins; 1996. p. 347–59.

37. Lindheimer MD, Katz AL. The kidney in pregnancy. N Engl J Med 1970;283:1095.

38. Romero R, Oyarzun E, Mazor M, et al. Meta-analysis of the relationship between asymptomatic bacteriuria and preterm delivery/low birth weight. Obstet Gynecol 1989;73:576–82.

39. Behar R, Curbelo V. Bacterial sources of phospholipase. Obstet Gynecol 1981;57:479.

40. McGrady GA, Daling JR, Peterson DR. Maternal urinary tract infection and adverse fetal outcomes. Am J Epidemiol 1985;121:377.

41. Millar L, Cox S. Urinary tract infections complicating pregnancy. Infect Dis Clin North Am 1997; 11(1):13–25.

42. Stenqvist K, Dahlen-Nilsson, Lidin-Janson G, et al. Bacteriuria in pregnancy. Am J Epidemiol 1989; 129:372–9.

43. Norden W. Bacteriuria of pregnancy: a critical appraisal. Ann Rev Med 1968;19:431.

44. Andriole VT, Patterson TF. Urinary tract infections in pregnancy. Med Clin North Am 1991;75:359–73.

45. Archbald FJ, Verma V. Screening for asymptomatic bacteriuria with microstix. J Reprod Med 1984;29:272.

46. Kass EH. Bacteriuria and pyelonephritis of pregnancy. Arch Intern Med 1960;105:194–8.

47. Alger L. Antimicrobial therapy for obstetric patients. ACOG Educational Bulletin, Number 245, March 1998.

48. Millar LK, Cox SM. Urinary tract infections complicating pregnancy. Infect Dis Clin North Am 1997; 11(1):13–25.

49. MacMillan MC, Grimes DA. The limited usefulness of urine and blood cultures in treating pyelonephritis in pregnancy. Obstet Gynecol 1995;173:597–602.

50. Wing D, Hendershott CM, Dubuque L, Millar LK. A randomized trial of three antibiotic regimens for the treatment of pyelonephritis in pregnancy. Obstet Gynecol 1998;92:249–53.

51. Millar LK, Wing DA, Paul RH, Grimes DA. Outpatient treatment of pyelonephritis in pregnancy: a randomized controlled trial. Obstet Gynecol 1995; 86:560–4.

52. Sanchez-Ramos L, McAlpine KJ, Adair CD, et al. Pyelonephritis in pregnancy: once a day cefriaxone versus multiple doses of cefazolin. Am J Obstet Gynecol 1995;172:129–33.

53. Lenke RR, Van Dorsten JP. Pyelonephritis in pregnancy: a prospective randomized trial to prevent recurrent disease evaluating suppressive therapy with nitrofurantoin and close surveillance. Am J Obstet Gynecol 1983;146:953–7.

54. Diokno AC, Compton A, Seski J, Vinson R. Urologic evaluation of urinary tract infection in pregnancy. J Reprod Med 1986;31:23.

55. Gillenwater JY. The role of the urologist in urinary tract infection. Med Clin North Am 1991;75:471–9.

56. Coppa G, Gabrielli O. Preliminary study of breastfeeding and bacterial adhesion to uroepithelial cells. Lancet 1990;335:569–71.

57. Boscia, JA, Kobasa WD, Knight RA, et al. Therapy vs. no therapy for bacteriuria in elderly ambulatory nonhospitalized women. JAMA 1987;257:1067–71.

58. Hatton J, Hughes M. Management of bacterial urinary tract infections in adults. Ann Pharmacother 1994:28:1264–72.

59. Griebling T, Nygaard I. The role of estrogen replacement in the management of urinary incontinence and urinary tract infection in postmenopausal women. Endocrinol Metab Clin North Am 1997; 26:347–60.

85

INTERSTITIAL CYSTITIS

Ann Davis, MD

Confusion in defining and understanding interstitial cystitis has resulted in the failure to diagnose and treat thousands of afflicted patients, committing them to a life of intractable pain.

—Vicki Ratner, MD, a physician with interstitial cystitis and founder of the Interstitial Cystitis Association[1]

Interstitial cystitis (IC) is a poorly understood condition that presents with symptoms of urinary frequency, urinary urgency, and bladder pain.[2] Ninety percent of patients diagnosed with IC are women.[3] Most are diagnosed between the ages of 30 and 50 years.[4] Interstitial cystitis is a condition that often is overlooked, although it is a relatively common problem. Patients with IC spend an average of 2 years seeing multiple clinicians before a diagnosis is made.[4]

Interstitial cystitis may be a frequently undiagnosed cause of pelvic pain. The standard evaluation of patients whose symptoms include pelvic pain varies tremendously. Gynecologists tend to evaluate patients for gynecologic diseases such as endometriosis, urologists for urinary symptomatology, and gastroenterologists for bowel-related diseases.[5] In a retrospective study of the natural history of IC, 44% of patients had undergone hysterectomy.[6] Other studies have documented rates of hysterectomy from 25%.[7,8] Although the majority of patients with IC suffer from associated pelvic pain, hysterectomy is not effective treatment.[2] In one study the frequency of symptoms in interstitial cystitis were as follows: urinary frequency 92%, urinary urgency 92%, and pelvic pain 70%.[2] It is important for clinicians to suspect and diagnose IC, not only so that appropriate treatment can be suggested but also so that unnecessary diagnostic and therapeutic procedures can be avoided.

PATHOPHYSIOLOGY

The etiology of IC remains obscure. Most experts have concluded that IC is multifactorial and that IC

is actually a syndrome rather than a disease.[9,10] An increase in mast cell infiltrates within the bladder is seen in approximately half of all IC patients. Mast cells release a variety of inflammatory factors such as prostaglandins and histamines that mediate the signs and symptoms of IC. Estradiol increases mast cell activity.[11,12] This is a possible explanation for the female predominance of patients with IC.

A variety of etiologies have been considered. Interstitial cystitis does not appear to be infectious in origin, although a urinary infection possibly could serve as an initial trigger of the disease. Other researchers have suggested that an altered glycosaminoglycan (GAG) layer might increase the permeability of the bladder epithelium, allowing toxins to diffuse into the bladder compartment, thus beginning a process of mast cell activation ultimately leading to neurogenic inflammation.[13] However, this alteration in the GAG layer also may be a result rather than a cause of IC.

Interstitial cystitis may have an autoimmune etiology. In epidemiologic studies, patients with IC have been found to have a high incidence of concomitant immunologically mediated disorders, including allergies, asthma, systemic lupus erythematosus, and inflammatory bowel disease.[14,15]

DIAGNOSIS

Bladder pain relieved by voiding and urinary urgency are characteristic symptoms of IC. Pain may be experienced in the suprapublic region but also is sometimes described as perineal, vaginal, upper or lower abdominal, or back pain.[12] Symptoms may become worse after sexual activity.[12] Symptoms typically exacerbate and remit.

Initial evaluation includes a history and physical examination, focusing on clues to alternative diagnoses, including urinary tract infection, genital herpes, vaginitis, endometriosis, tuberculosis, bladder stones, malignancy, and prior chemotherapy and radiation of the bladder. Suprapubic tenderness and bladder tenderness may be present. The rest of the physical examination is usually unrevealing.[14]

In 1987, the National Institutes of Health developed consensus criteria for the diagnosis of IC, which were modified 1 year later.[9] These are summarized in Table 85–1. These research criteria may exclude up to 60% of women with clinical IC.[16,17] In clinical practice, IC is often a diagnosis of exclusion.

All patients suspected of IC should undergo urinalysis and urinary culture, as well as antigen testing for *Chlamydia*. Patients should keep a voiding diary for several days, recording the time of all voids, measuring the amount voided, and describing associated symptoms. Patients with IC usually void frequently during the day and wake up at night to void. The typical IC patient voids 16 times per day and averages voids of approximately 100 mL.[18] Patients also should record intake of both food and beverages to identify dietary bladder irritants. An initial voiding diary also establishes a baseline from which to evaluate therapy.

Urodynamic evaluation can be useful, particularly when the differential diagnosis is focused mainly on alternative explanations for urinary urgency. Patients typically report first sensation of bladder filling at less than 100 mL and first desire to void at less than 150 mL. A decreased maximum bladder capacity (less than 350 mL) is often noted. Patients with advanced IC may have a small fibrotic bladder.[18]

TABLE 85–1. **National Institutes of Health Criteria for Diagnosis of Interstitial Cystitis for Purposes of Research**[23]

All of the following are required:
  1. Urinary urgency and/or bladder pain
  2. Glomerulations on cystoscopic examination and/or a classic Hunner's ulcer[*]

None of the following may be present:
  1. Less than 8 voids per day while awake
  2. Absence of nocturia
  3. Diagnosis of bacterial cystitis within prior 3 months
  4. Symptoms relieved by antimicrobial agents, urinary antiseptics, anticholinergics, or antispasmodics
  5. Cyclophosphamide or any type of chemical cystitis
  6. Tuberculous cystitis
  7. Radiation cystitis
  8. Active genital herpes
  9. Uterine, cervical, vaginal, or urethral cancer
 10. Vaginitis
 11. Benign or malignant bladder tumors
 12. Urethral diverticulum
 13. Bladder or ureteral calculi
 14. Bladder capacity > 350 mL
 15. Absence of intense urge to void when the bladder is filled to 150 mL of H_2O during cystometry[†]
 16. Presence of phasic involuntary bladder contraction on cystometry[†]
 17. Duration of symptoms of less than 9 months
 18. Age < 18 years

---

[*]At least 10 glomerulations per quadrant, present in at least three quadrants of the bladder, not along the path of the cystoscope (to eliminate artifact). Examination undertaken after distention of the bladder under anesthesia to 80–100 cm H_2O for 1–2 minutes, up to twice.
[†]Using fill rate of 30–100 mL/min.
Adapted from Hanno et al.[16,17]

Cystoscopy is essential for diagnosis and for ruling out other causes of bladder symptoms, particularly malignancy. Patients are evaluated for IC after hydrodistention. Hydrodistention consists of filling the bladder to 80 to 100 cm H_2O and maintaining pressure by urethral compression for 1 to 2 minutes. Anesthesia is often required. Terminal blood-tinged hematuria is present following bladder distention in the majority of patients with IC. Findings consistent with IC are a bladder capacity of less than 850 mL under anesthesia (normal is more than 1,000) and glomerulations and ulcerations. Hunner's ulcers, first described by a gynecologist in 1915, are areas of erythema with central pallor and radiating small vessels noted after bladder filling. These are seen in less than 10% of patients with IC.[18] Biopsies are taken to rule out carcinoma in situ and should include all suspicious areas.

Visual findings and biopsy cannot completely confirm or exclude IC. Glomerulations and ulcerations have been identified in normal women.[19] Prior biopsy sites and infections can mimic IC on cystoscopy. Many women with symptoms of IC and no alternative diagnosis have no visual findings on cystoscopy.[18]

TREATMENT

Since the etiology of IC is unknown, treatment is aimed at symptom relief. There are relatively few randomized controlled trials of most current treatments, making it difficult to define which are best. However, most patients obtain relief from available treatments.[9]

Up to half of patients report specific foods and/or beverages that exacerbate their symptoms; these should be avoided. Commonly implicated are alcohol, carbonated and other acidic beverages, spicy foods, caffeine, and chocolate.[2] Bladder retraining, during which patients gradually extend the time interval between voids, may result in symptom improvement.[14] Treatment with standard chronic pain therapies, such as antidepressants (eg, low-dose amitriptyline at 25–75 mg) and behavioral/pain modification programs, may be useful.[20]

Sodium pentosanpolysulfate was the first oral medication approved by the US Food and Drug Administration (FDA) for use in IC. A polysaccharide similar to heparin, it has no significant anticoagulant activity. Its mechanism of action is unknown. In one double-blind placebo-controlled crossover study of 148 patients, sodium pentosanpolysulfate improved pain, urgency, and frequency. Thirty-two percent of patients in the active treatment arm reported improvement, compared with 16% of patients who received placebo.[21] Significant clinical improvement occurred after 3 months. Although these results were initially promising, another double-blind trial did not show significant benefit.[21,22]

Intravesical therapy with dimethyl sulfoxide was the first therapy for IC approved by the FDA.[14] Dimethyl sulfoxide is an analgesic and muscle relaxant and inhibits mast cells. It is often instilled once to twice weekly for 1 to 2 months. Relief of symptoms is seen in 50 to 77% of patients. Approximately half relapse and require repetitive treatments.[9,23] The most frequent side effect is a persistent odor, described as similar to the odor of garlic or smoked oysters. Other intravesical therapies have included oxycholorosene sodium (chlorpactin) and heparin. Both have been reported effective in uncontrolled trials.[14]

As with many chronic pain syndromes, surgical intervention is problematic. Bladder augmentation, denervation, and removal have all been performed for IC. Uncontrolled series have shown some benefit but significant relapse rates.[14]

RESOURCE

Interstitial Cystitis Association
51 Monroe Street, Suite 1402
Rockville, Maryland 20850
Telephone: 1-800-HELP-ICA (1-800-435-7422)
Web site: www.ichelp.org

The ICA is a not-for-profit national organization that provides educational information for patients and clinicians. ICA also funds and advocates for research on interstitial cystitis. Information on its Web site includes details about bladder training and possible dietary triggers of IC, as well as explanations of pharmacologic treatments. The ICA Web site provides information for patients in both English and Spanish.

REFERENCES

1. Ratner V, Slade D, Greene G. Interstitial cystitis. A patient's perspective. Urol Clin North Am 1994;21(1): 1–5.

2. Koziol JA. Epidemiology of interstitial cystitis. Urol Clin North Am 1994;21(1):7–20.

3. Taylor PJ, Gomel V. Pelvic pain. Curr Probl Obstet Gynecol Fertil 1987;X:9.

4. Thoren H. Interstitial cystitis presents a diagnostic challenge. Quoted in OB/KozoilGYN News 1994; 29(11):2.

5. Baskin LS, Tanagho EA, Reida FS, et al. Case reports: pelvic pain without pelvic organs. J Urol 1992; 147:683–6.

6. Koziol JA, Clark DC, Gittes RF, et al. The natural history of interstitial cystitis: a survey of 374 patients. J Urol 1993;149:465–9.

7. Holm-Bentzen M, Jacobsen F, Nerstrom B, et al. Painful bladder disease: clinical and pathoanatomical differences in 115 patients. J Urol 1987;138:500–2.

8. DeJuana CP, Everett JC. Interstitial cystitis: experience and review of recent literature. Urology 1977;10:325–9.

9. Sant G. Interstitial cystitis. Curr Opin Obstet Gynecol 1997;9:332–6.

10. Fall M, Johansson SL, Aldenborg F. Chronic interstitial cystitis. A heterogenous syndrome. J Urol 1987;137: 35–8.

11. Vliagoftis H, Dimitriadou V, Boucher W, et al. Estradiol augments while tamoxifen inhibits rat mast cell secretion. Int Arch Allergy Immunol 1992;98:398–409.

12. Spanos C, el-Mansoury M, Letourneau R, et al. Carbachol-induced bladder mast cell activation: augmentation by estradiol and implications for interstitial cystitis. Urology 1996;48:809–16.

13. Elbadawi A. Interstitial cystitis: a critique of current concepts with a new proposal for pathologic diagnosis and pathogenesis. Urology 1997;49 Suppl 5A:14–40.

14. Rosamilia A, Dwyer PL. Interstitial cystic and the gynecologist. Obstet Gynecol Surv 1998;53:309–19.

15. Alagiri M, Chottiner S, Ratner V, et al. Interstitial cystitis: unexplained associations with other chronic disease and pain syndromes. Urology 1997;49 Suppl 5A:52–7.

16. Hanno PM, Landis JR, Matthews-Cook Y, et al. The diagnosis of interstitial cystitis revisited: lessons learned from the National Institutes of Health Interstitial Cystitis Database Study. J Urol 1999;161:553–7.

17. Hanno PM. Diagnosis of interstitial cystitis. Urol Clin North Am 1994;21(1):63–6.

18. Parsons CL. Interstitial cystitis: clinical manifestations and diagnostic criteria in over 200 cases. Neuroul Urodyn 1990;9:241–50.

19. Waxman JA, Sulak PJ, Kuehl TJ. Cystoscopic findings consistent with interstitial cystitis in normal women undergoing tubal ligation. J Urol 1998;160:1663–7.

20. Hanno PM, Buehler J, Wein AJ. Use of amitriptyline in the treatment of interstitial cystitis. J Urol 1989; 141:846–8.

21. Parsons CL, Mulholland SG. Successful therapy of interstitial cystitis with pentosanpolysulfate. J Urol 1987;138:513–6.

22. Holm-Bentzen M, Jacobsen F, Nerstrøm B, et al. A prospective double-blind clinically controlled multicenter trial of sodium pentosanpolysulfate in the treatment of interstitial cystitis and related painful bladder disease. J Urol 1987;138:503–7.

23. Perez-Marrero R, Emerson LE, Feltis JT. A controlled study of dimethyl sulfoxide in interstitial cystitis. J Urol 1988;140:36–9.

86

APPROACH TO THE PATIENT WITH URINARY INCONTINENCE

Michelle Eslami, MD

Urinary incontinence (UI) is a common problem affecting over 17 million Americans, most of whom are women and the elderly. At present the estimated yearly cost of managing incontinence in the United States is 16 billion dollars.[1] The prevalence of UI increases with age, but UI is not a part of normal aging. For women between 30 and 60 years of age, the prevalence of UI is 10 to 30%; in women over age 60 years, the prevalence ranges from 15 to 43%.[2] In contrast, the prevalence of UI in men at all ages ranges from 1.6 to 24.0%.[2] Several risk factors likely contribute to the higher prevalence in women; these include multiple pregnancies and vaginal deliveries, estrogen depletion (eg, menopause), and having had a hysterectomy.[1,3] Other risk factors for UI include increasing age, medications (especially diuretics), immobility, degenerative joint disease, morbid obesity, diabetes, stroke, dementia, and delirium. Unfortunately, only about 32% of primary care clinicians routinely ask all their patients about UI, and only about 25 to 50% of incontinent community-dwelling patients describe their symptoms to clinicians.[4]

Urinary incontinence has been defined as (1) any uncontrolled urine loss in the prior 12 months, (2) two or more incontinent episodes in a month, or (3) a condition in which involuntary loss of urine is a social or hygiene problem.[2] Despite the variety of definitions of UI, there is little disagreement about its basic types. These include "stress" incontinence, "urge" incontinence, "overflow" incontinence, and "functional" incontinence, which may not include any abnormalities of the lower urinary tract.

This chapter describes each type of incontinence as well as an office-based approach to the evaluation of UI and treatment options that are available for the patient who suffers from UI.

ANATOMY AND PHYSIOLOGY OF CONTINENCE

The physiology of continence is regulated by the autonomic and somatic nervous systems. These processes are under the control of the cerebral cortex (which has an inhibitory influence over urination), and the brain stem (which contains the pons micturition center and facilitates urination). In the lower urinary tract (Figure 86–1) the bladder (detrusor muscle) is largely under the control of the sacral plexus (S2–S4), which provides cholinergic innervation and contracts the bladder when stimulated, to cause bladder emptying. The dome of the bladder is under ß-adrenergic innervation; when stimulated, it relaxes and allows the filling of the bladder. The bladder neck and internal urethral sphincter are under the control of the hypogastric plexus (T11–L2), which provides α-adrenergic innervation and which (when stimulated) causes contractions of the internal urethral sphincter and leads to the storage of urine. The other component of the bladder outlet, the external urethral sphincter, is innervated by the somatic (voluntary) nervous system; the pudendal nerve, when stimulated, causes contraction or closure of the external sphincter and contraction of the pelvic floor musculature.

For micturation to occur, sympathetic and somatic tone diminishes, and parasympathetic impulses cause the bladder to contract and empty. During bladder filling, parasympathetic tone diminishes, and sympathetic and somatic impulses

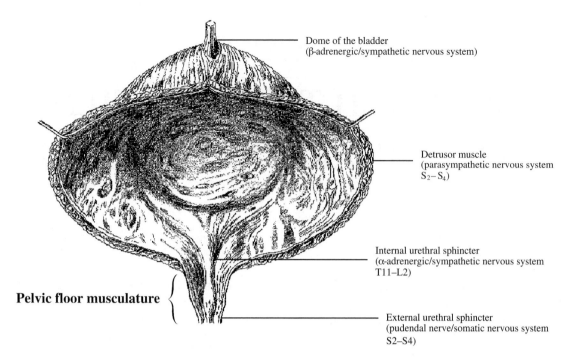

Dome of the bladder
(β-adrenergic/sympathetic nervous system)

Detrusor muscle
(parasympathetic nervous system
S_2–S_4)

Internal urethral sphincter
(α-adrenergic/sympathetic nervous system
T11–L2)

Pelvic floor musculature

External urethral sphincter
(pudendal nerve/somatic nervous system
S2–S4)

FIGURE 86–1. Innervation and functional anatomy of the bladder.

cause contraction and closure of the internal and external urethral sphincters. Normal bladder capacity is between 300 and 600 cc, with the first urge to void occurring between 150 and 300 cc.

The hormonal effects of estrogen also have an impact on continence. The urethra, trigone of the bladder, vagina, and pelvic floor musculature all have estrogen receptors. Therefore, estrogen deficiency can predispose women to urethritis, trigonitis, cystitis, and atrophic vaginitis, all of which may exacerbate urge UI.[5] Estrogen deficiency can also reduce the ability of the urethral sphincters and pelvic floor musculature to support the bladder, which may exacerbate stress UI.

Several urinary tract changes occur with normal aging. There is a decrease in total bladder capacity, urethral compliance, and the strength of pelvic support muscles. Increases in postvoid residual volume, involuntary bladder contractions (urgency), and nocturia (one to two times per night) are characteristic of normal aging.[6] These changes can predispose patients to UI, but again, UI is not a part of normal aging.

BASIC TYPES AND CAUSES OF URINARY INCONTINENCE

During the initial evaluation, it is important to distinguish between acute (or reversible) UI and persistent UI. Potentially reversible causes of UI usually have been present for less than 4 weeks and can be classified best by the DIAPPERS mnemonic (Table 86–1).[7] With the identification and management of these reversible factors, UI may be cured in some cases. Persistent types of UI (Table 86–2) can be classified as disorders of storage (urge and stress UI) or disorders of emptying (overflow incontinence).

Urge incontinence has also been referred to as detrusor instability, detrusor hyper-reflexia, overactive bladder, or irritable bladder. Urge incontinence

TABLE 86–1. Potentially Reversible Causes of Urinary Incontinence

D	Delirium
I	Infection
A	Atrophic vaginitis or urethritis
P	Pharmaceuticals: benzodiazepines, alcohol, diuretics, anticholinergic agents, α-adrenergic agents, calcium channel blockers
P	Psychological disorders
E	Endocrine disorders, excessive urine production
R	Restricted mobility
S	Stool impaction

Adapted from Resnick NM. Urinary incontinence in the elderly. Med Grand Rounds 1984;3:281–90.

TABLE 86–2. Types of Persistent Incontinence

Type of Incontinence	Symptoms	Urodynamic Features	Causes	Diagnostic Test Options
Urge	Involuntary loss of urine associated with a sudden and strong desire to void	Usually associated with involuntary detrusor contractions	Idiopathic; cystitis, bladder cancer, bladder stone, stroke, dementia, Parkinson's Disease	Simple cystometry or referral to a specialist for more specialized tests of bladder function, esp. if PVR volume > 200 cc
Stress	Involuntary loss of urine during coughing, sneezing, laughing, or other physical activities that increase abdominal pressure	Urine loss coincident with an increase in abdominal pressure, in the absence of a detrusor contraction or an overdistended bladder	Pelvic muscle laxity in women, radiation and multiple anti-incontinence procedures	Cough stress testing, cotton-swab test, or referral for more specialized tests of bladder function
Overflow	Involuntary loss of urine associated with overdistension of the bladder	May be due to an underactive or acontractile detrusor or bladder outlet urethral obstruction, leading to over-distension and overflow	Drugs, fecal impaction, autonomic neuropathy (diabetes and alcholism), grade III cystocele, low spinal cord injury; idiopathic	Tests for PVR volume or referral for more specialized tests of bladder function
Functional	Loss of urine associated with inability to toilet	Usually associated with normal bladder function	Impairment of cognitive and/or physical functioning; psychological unwillingness or environmental barriers	A diagnosis of exclusion: may want to measure PVR volume if possible, or treat the underlying impairment, or put the patient on a timed toileting schedule every 2–3 h, or refer for more specialized tests of bladder function
Mixed	Usually a combination of symptoms of urge and stress incontinence	Usually has features of urge and stress incontinence	See "Urge" and "Stress" incontinence, above	See "Urge" and "Stress" incontinence, above

PVR = postvoid residual.

is most common in women over the age of 75 years. Patients feel an abrupt desire to void (urgency) that cannot be suppressed, whether or not the bladder is full. They report losing their urine before being able to reach the bathroom. The urine loss can be of either small or large quantities. Patients also may complain of frequency and nocturia. Idiopathic detrusor instability is the most common form of urge incontinence and results from unsuppressed involuntary contractions of the bladder muscle. Other causes can include urinary tract infection, bladder cancer, or bladder stones. When unsuppressed spontaneous bladder contractions are associated with a neurologic disorder (such as dementia, stroke, Parkinson's disease, or spinal injuries), the condition is referred to as detrusor hyper-reflexia.

Stress incontinence is the most common type of UI in women, especially those under 75 years of age. Stress incontinence can result when an increase in abdominal pressure (eg, Valsalva's maneuver) places "stress" on the bladder and its support structures and leads to "hypermobility" of the bladder neck and the urethra. This type of stress UI is responsible for about 85% of cases and is associated with aging, hormonal changes, multiple childbirths, hysterectomy, and pelvic surgery.[8] The remaining 15% of stress UI cases are due to intrinsic sphincter deficiency;[8] this can be secondary to pelvic or anti-incontinence surgery, pelvic radiation, trauma, or neurogenic disorders.

Overflow incontinence, an involuntary loss of urine that occurs when overdistention of the bladder causes constant or frequent dribbling, is rare in women. This type of UI in women can occur from a bladder outlet obstruction due to a urethral stricture, a grade III cystocele, or a fecal impaction. It can also occur as a result of an acontractile bladder (also known as detrusor hypoactivity or an atonic bladder) due to diabetes, multiple sclerosis, spinal cord injury, or medication (eg, narcotics).

Functional incontinence is urine loss associated with the inability to reach the toilet. This form of incontinence may not involve any abnormalities of the lower urinary tract; it results instead from physical (arthritis, stroke, restraints, hip fractures) and/or cognitive (dementia, delirium, severe depression) impairment. The diagnosis is usually one of exclusion and may be reversible.

Mixed UI is a combination of different types of UI. In most patients it is usually a combination of urge and stress incontinence. It is common in women, especially older women. Usually one type of incontinence is predominant.

BASIC EVALUATION

The basic evaluation of the patient with UI includes a history, a physical examination, a postvoid residual urine measurement, and urinalysis and urine culture (in selected patients).[1] Other diagnostic tests can help the clinician distinguish among the types of incontinence.

History

The history should include questions about the onset and duration of symptoms and the type of incontinence (stress, urge, mixed, etc) as well as the presence of voiding difficulty (hesitancy, straining, incomplete emptying), irritative symptoms (dysuria, frequency, urgency, nocturia), or hematuria. A bladder record (Figure 86–2) can be a useful asset to the history. It can be given to the patient prior to the initial evaluation and allows the patient to record the frequency, timing, and amount of continent and incontinent episodes. A pattern of fluid intake (including beverages containing caffeine and alcohol) is also important to ascertain. The presence of active medical conditions such as diabetes mellitus, congestive heart failure, venous insufficiency, and neurologic disorders (eg, stroke, dementia, Parkinson's disease, and spinal cord lesions) are other key aspects of the history. A review of medications, (both prescription and over-the-counter [OTC] medications) is essential as these may exacerbate or cause UI (Table 86–3). Past genitourinary history that includes childbirth, surgery, urinary retention, radiation, or recurrent urinary tract infections may contribute to incontinence. Bowel problems such as constipation or fecal incontinence may contribute to UI or may be the result of pelvic floor laxity. Lastly, discussion should occur with the patient regarding her perceptions of the effect of her incontinence on her daily activities, sexual activity, and quality of life.

Physical Examination

A complete physical examination should be performed in the incontinent female patient, with the emphasis on mobility, mental status, and neurologic, abdominal, rectal, and pelvic examination.

DATE: _____   BEDTIME _____ □AM □PM
(MO/DAY/YR)

NUMBER OF INCONTINENCE PADS USED: _____

TIME	URINATED IN TOILET? (circle one)	STRONG URGE? (circle one)	AMOUNT (IF MEASURED) (ounces)	ACCIDENT? (circle one)	REASON FOR ACCIDENT (circle one)
□ AM ___ □ PM	Yes No	Yes No	_____	None Small Large	Urge Stress Both Other
□ AM ___ □ PM	Yes No	Yes No	_____	None Small Large	Urge Stress Both Other
□ AM ___ □ PM	Yes No	Yes No	_____	None Small Large	Urge Stress Both Other
□ AM ___ □ PM	Yes No	Yes No	_____	None Small Large	Urge Stress Both Other
□ AM ___ □ PM	Yes No	Yes No	_____	None Small Large	Urge Stress Both Other
□ AM ___ □ PM	Yes No	Yes No	_____	None Small Large	Urge Stress Both Other
□ AM ___ □ PM	Yes No	Yes No	_____	None Small Large	Urge Stress Both Other
□ AM ___ □ PM	Yes No	Yes No	_____	None Small Large	Urge Stress Both Other
□ AM ___ □ PM	Yes No	Yes No	_____	None Small Large	Urge Stress Both Other
□ AM ___ □ PM	Yes No	Yes No	_____	None Small Large	Urge Stress Both Other

PLEASE RECORD ANY UNUSUAL SYMPTOMS: _____

_____

FIGURE 86–2. Sample voiding diary.

The neurologic examination should include an assessment of cognitive function (eg, the Mini–Mental State Examination), including an assessment of motivation, mood and affect, and the ability to self-toilet. (The Mini–Mental State Examination is reproduced in Chapter 5.) Any extremity weakness or gait abnormalities (eg, suggestive of parkinsonism or normal-pressure hydrocephalus) should be noted. The S2–S4 nerve roots should be tested to establish the integrity of the lower urinary tract by checking the bulbocavernosus reflex (contraction of the external anal sphincter when the labia majora are brushed). Lower-extremity sensation should also be evaluated, and deep tendon reflexes should be checked. Evidence of sensory loss in a stocking distribution may suggest a peripheral neuropathy due to diabetes or alcoholism. Normal deep tendon reflexes of the quadriceps (L4) and Achilles tendon

TABLE 86–3. Medications That May Affect Continence

Type of Medication		Potential Effects on Continence
Sedatives/hypnotics	→	Sedation, delirium, immobility
Alcohol	→	Polyuria, frequency, urgency
Anticholinergics, antipsychotics, antidepressents, antihistamines	→	Urinary retention, overflow incontinence, fecal impaction, delirium
Narcotic analgesics	→	Urinary retention, sedation, fecal impaction
α-Adrenergic antagonist	→	Urinary relaxation → Stress UI
α-Adrenergic agonist	→	Urinary retention
Calcium channel blockers (dihydropyridines)	→	Urinary retention, nocturnal urination
Potent diuretics	→	Polyuria, frequency, urgency
ACE inhibitors	→	Drug-induced cough

ACE = angiotensin converting enzyme; UI = urinary incontinence.

(S1) indicate normal function of the anterior lumbosacral spinal cord, which innervates the lower urinary tract.

On abdominal examination, the clinician should palpate for suprapubic tenderness, bladder distention, or a lower abdominal mass (which can cause an increase in intra-abdominal pressure and affect urinary function). The rectal examination should include an assessment of resting and active sphincter tone (the sphincter shares similar innervation with the lower urinary tract via the sacral nerve roots) and a check for stool impaction or a rectal mass.

A pelvic examination should be performed in every female patient with UI. This involves inspecting the skin of the perineum for rashes or local infection. The vaginal epithelium is inspected for atrophy (loss of rugae; shiny, pale, thin, or friable vaginal wall). After the speculum examination, the physician can assess for pelvic organ prolapse (cystocele, uterine prolapse, or rectocele) with the posterior blade of the speculum. A bimanual examination is done, looking for pelvic masses and assessing paravaginal muscle tone by asking the patient to tighten the vagina around the examining fingers and to hold them as long as she can. (This is also a good time to instruct the patient on how to perform Kegel exercises.) The urethra is then inspected for mucosal prolapse, carbuncles (a sign of inadequate estrogen levels), and urethral deformity (diverticulum or fistula). If a urethral diverticulum is suspected, a massage of the area can cause urine and/or pus to come out of the urethral meatus, confirming

the diagnosis. A "Q-Tip" test for urethral hypermobility can be performed if stress UI is suspected.[8] With the patient still in the lithotomy position, a sterile cotton swab lubricated with betadine and 2% lidocaine jelly is placed in the urethra to the level of the bladder neck past the internal urethral sphincter. The patient is then asked to cough or strain. If the angle of the cotton swab deflects more than 30°, the urethrovesical junction can be considered hypermobile.

Stress-Test and Postvoid Residual Urine Measurement

Diagnostic tests that can be performed at the time of the physical examination include the cough stress test and measurement of the postvoid residual urine. The cough stress test is performed with the patient standing prior to voiding with a full bladder. A pad is placed between the patient's legs, and she is asked to cough forcefully three times. If immediate leakage occurs, the test is positive and the patient likely suffers from stress incontinence. If leakage occurs a few seconds later, the patient may have cough-induced detrusor overactivity, and further testing is usually warranted.[1] Within 5 to 10 minutes of voiding, a postvoid residual (PVR) urine volume can be measured by straight catherization or bladder ultrasonography.

In general, a PVR volume < 50 cc indicates adequate bladder emptying. A PVR volume of < 100 cc is normal in an elderly woman. A PVR between 100 and 199 cc is in the intermediate range; clinical judgment must be exercised in interpreting the significance of this volume. A volume ≥ 200 cc is considered inadequate emptying and is abnormal. The PVR volume may be affected by the readiness of the patient to void, the environment in which the patient is voiding, or the volume voided before the PVR volume measurement. Therefore, one measurement of PVR volume may not be accurate, and repeated measurements (especially for those patients with intermediate-range PVR volumes) should be made before referring the patient to a specialist for further testing.[1]

Urinalysis and Urine Culture

Urinalysis and urine culture is essential to the basic evaluation. The urinalysis is used to detect conditions associated with or contributing to urinary incontinence, such as hematuria (infection, cancer, or stone), pyuria, and glucosuria.[1] A urinary tract infection can be a cause of transient urge incontinence and also has been found to cause transient stress incontinence. Laboratory tests may be helpful in the initial evaluation of the incontinence patient and should include assessments of calcium and glucose levels (especially if polyuria is present) and serum creatinine level (especially if the PVR volume is > 200 cc, suggestive of obstruction and/or urinary retention).[1]

Sometimes the basic evaluation fails to reveal the cause of urinary incontinence, and further evaluation is necessary. Further tests (mainly urodynamic) are useful for determining the anatomic and functional status of the bladder and urethra. Simple cystometry, a test for urge incontinence, can be performed. In this procedure, the clinician instills sterile water through a nonballooned Foley catheter into the empty bladder until the patient feels a strong urge to void or until a bladder contraction occurs. A strong urge to void before 300 cc of sterile water is instilled into the bladder suggests a diagnosis of urge UI.[9] Likewise, the presence of involuntary bladder contractions as seen by a rise and fall in the meniscus of the syringe used to fill the bladder also suggests urge UI.[9] Simple cystometry also can be used to determine bladder capacity, to detect abnormal bladder compliance, and to measure PVR volume. Compared with multichannel cystometrics, simple cystometry has a reported positive predictive value of 74 to 91% for urge incontinence.[9]

Other Tests and Studies

Other urodynamic tests and endoscopy require referral to either a urogynecologist or a urologist. These tests include multichannel cystometry: a simultaneous measurement of intra-abdominal, total bladder, true detrusor pressure and urethral closure pressure that improves the sensitivity of the diagnosis of urge incontinence.[1] Cystourethroscopy, an examination of the urethra and bladder, may help identify urethral lesions such as diverticulae, fistulae, strictures, intrinsic sphincter deficiency, or a bladder stone or tumor. Although not part of the routine evaluation of incontinence, cystourethroscopy is indicated for sterile hematuria, recent onset of frequency and urgency symptoms in the absence of any reversible causes (see Table 86–1), recurrent cystitis, and when urodynamics fail to duplicate the symptoms of UI.[1]

Last, radiographic studies involving lower urinary tract imaging with and without voiding may be useful in examining the anatomy of the bladder and urethra. Nonvoiding cystourethrography allows the identification of hypermobility of the bladder neck and the degree of cystocele. The voiding component can identify vesicoureteral reflex, a urethral diverticulum, or an obstruction. Videourodynamics uses fluoroscopy and cystometry to further evaluate UI. This technique may be helpful in sorting out complex types of incontinence problems.[1]

TREATMENT

Several treatment options exist for the persistent causes of UI. The three major categories of treatment are behavioral, pharmacologic, and surgical. Behavioral interventions are the first choice;[1] however, a combination of behavioral and pharmacologic therapies may be appropriate for most patients. Behavioral and pharmacologic therapies for persistent UI are summarized in Table 86–4.

Behavioral Interventions

Behavioral interventions that may be beneficial regardless of the type of UI include reducing the amount of fluid intake and changing its timing (eg, no fluids from 3 hours before bedtime if possible), avoiding bladder stimulants such as caffeine or alcohol, using diuretics judiciously and not before bedtime, and elevating lower extremities (or wearing tight support stockings, for patients with pedal

TABLE 86–4. Treatment of Persistent Urinary Incontinence

Type of Incontinence	Behavioral Therapy	Pharmacologic Therapy	Indications for Referral
Urge	Bladder or habit training; pelvic muscle exercises with or without biofeedback scheduled toileting	Oxybutynin (Ditropan) 2.5–5 mg bid–tid; oxybutynin XL (Ditropan XL) 5–30 mg qd; Propantheline (Pro-Banthine) 15–30 mg tid–qid and 60 mg qhs; tolterodine (Detrol) 1–2 mg bid; tolterodine LA (Detrol LA) 4 mg qd; imipramine 10–25 mg qd–tid	Detrusor overactivity, PVR volume > 200 cc
Stress	Pelvic muscle exercises with or without biofeedback; bladder training	Pseudoephedrine hydrochloride (Sudafed) 30–60 mg qid; conjugated estrogen (Premarin)* 0.3–1.5 mg PO qd or 2 g vaginally 5× per week	Intrinsic sphincter deficiency, urethral hypermobility, or large cystocele
Overflow	—	Doxazosin (Cardura) or terazosin (Hytrin): start with 1 mg at bedtime and increase slowly†; tamsulosin (Flomax) 0.4 mg PO qd	Anatomic obstruction with contractile detrusor†, stricture, severe pelvic organ prolapse
Functional	Scheduled toileting, habit training‡	—	—

*Women who have an intact uterus should combine therapy with progestin (Provera, 2.5 mg qd) to reduce reduce risk of uterine cancer.
†Patients with a persistently underactive detrusor are best treated by intermittent catherization.
‡If this fails, and other causes of incontinence have been excluded, incontinence undergarments or external collection devices should be considered.
PVR = postvoid residual.

edema) to help reduce nocturia. A bedside commode can provide easy access to a toilet. Other behavioral interventions for urge and/or stress incontinence include bladder training, pelvic floor rehabilitation, biofeedback, and scheduled toileting.

Bladder training requires educating the patient about the physiology of urination and then implementing a voiding schedule with a systematic delay of voiding (initially at 2- to 3-hour intervals). This technique has a reported 20% "dry" rate, and 75% of patients have reduction of at least a 50% in the number of incontinent episodes.[1]

Pelvic floor rehabilitation is indicated for women with stress incontinence and can reduce urgency and prevent urge UI. These exercises (Kegel exercises) require the drawing in or lifting up of the perivaginal (levator ani) muscles and the anal sphincter for a 10-second contraction and then a 10-second relaxation. This needs to be done

in sets of 10 contractions between three to ten times a day. Both written and verbal instructions increase the success of these exercises, which, according to some studies, have resulted in up to a 95% reduction in incontinent episodes and 51% cure rates for stress UI.[10] These exercises should be done for a minimum of 6 weeks and may need to be continued indefinitely. Figure 86–3 presents a typical written set of instructions for pelvic muscle exercises.

Biofeedback therapy is useful for urge, stress, and mixed UI (ie, both urge and stress UI symptoms) and can be used in conjunction with pelvic muscle exercises and bladder training. This technique usually involves electromyography (EMG) or manometric methods with a vaginal or anal probe and simultaneous measurement of pelvic, abdominal, and detrusor muscle activity. Using this multi-measurement method, a 75.9 to 80% reduction in

WHAT ARE PELVIC MUSCLE EXERCISES?

They are exercises designed to strengthen the muscles that help to control the bladder and urination.

HOW DOES ONE LEARN TO DO THE EXERCISES?

The best way is to learn to stop the flow of urine in the middle of urinating in order to get a good idea of the muscles that are used to do so.

It is very important that only the pelvic muscles are used and not the muscles of the stomach. The stomach should stay relaxed when the exercises are done.

Breathing in and out while doing the exercise will help the stomach relax.

HOW ARE THE EXERCISES PRACTICED?

Once you get the feel of using the right muscles, you should do the exercises as follows:
- Squeeze the muscles and hold for 10 seconds.
- Relax for 10 seconds.
- Repeat, gradually building up 10 squeezes and 10 relaxations 3 times per day.

NOTE: You can practice anytime while you are sitting, standing, or lying down.

WHEN SHOULD THE EXERCISES BE DONE?

The purpose of the pelvic muscle exercises is to prevent urinary accidents. The exercises must be done at times that normally cause you to leak urine, such as while coughing, laughing, or straining, or when a very strong urge to urinate begins.

HOW LONG DO THE EXERCISES TAKE TO WORK?

If they are practiced properly, you should begin to notice a difference within a few weeks.

CAN THE EXERCISES BE HARMFUL?

NO! If you get any stomach or back pain with the exercises, you are not doing them correctly.

REMEMBER: Like any other exercise, pelvic muscle exercises must be continuously practiced to be effective.

FIGURE 86–3. Pelvic muscle exercise instructional handout for patients.

UI in various patient groups has been seen.[1] Another form of biofeedback uses weighted vaginal cones (Feminina Cone, Urohealth Systems, Inc., [800-879-3111], Innerflex, Inc., [877-445-3435], Kegel Exercise Kone, Milex Products, Inc. [312-631-6484]). These cones come in sets of five and range from 20 to 100 g in weight. They are placed in a graded fashion intravaginally for 15 minutes at a time twice a day, until the patient can retain the cone for up to 30 minutes. This method has been shown to have a 41% success rate after 12 to 24 months of use.[11]

Other behavioral interventions exist for urge and functional incontinence and are usually caregiver-dependent techniques for patients with physical or cognitive impairments. **Scheduled toileting** is toileting on a fixed schedule at regular intervals every 2 to 4 hours, including night-time. It leads to a 29 to 85% improvement in UI in uncontrolled studies.[1] **Habit training** is a toileting schedule that matches the patient's voiding habits. This intervention has been used primarily in the nursing home setting, where it was found to reduce UI in 86% of subjects during a 3-month intervention period.[1]

Pharmacologic Therapies

Pharmacologic therapies can be added to behavioral interventions to treat UI (see Table 86–4). For urge incontinence, anticholingeric and/or antispasmodic medications are used. These agents improve the symptoms of urinary frequency and urgency by increasing bladder capacity and decreasing detrusor tone. By doing this, however, these agents increase residual volumes to some degree. Therefore, the clinician needs to use caution with these medications if the patient has a pretreatment PVR volume of > 100 cc.

Anticholinergic agents are the first-line therapy for patients with urge incontinence. **Oxybutynin** is the anticholinergic agent of choice.[1] Used at a dosage of 2.5 to 5 mg three times a day, it reduces incontinence by 9 to 56% and has a cure rate of up to 44%. A controlled-release formulation of oxybutynin is also available (Ditropan XL). The efficacy of the once-a-day controlled-release oxybutynin is equivalent to that of 5 mg of oxybutynin three times a day with regard to the reduction of weekly episodes of urge incontinence.[12] The side effects of this medication include dry mouth, which is dose dependent and a common reason for discontinuation of therapy. Less dry mouth occurs with controlled-release oxybutynin. Other potential side effects include constipation, visual blurring, elevated intraocular pressure, sedation, confusion, and urinary retention. **Propantheline** is the second-line anticholinergic agent, as determined by a consensus panel.[1] Propantheline reduces urge incontinence episodes by up to 53% and has a cure rate of only up to 5%. The possible side effects include dry mouth, visual blurring, constipation, sedation, confusion, and urinary retention. Dosages range from 15 mg tid plus 60 mg at bedtime to 30 mg qid.

Tolterodine is a muscarinic receptor antagonist that is more selective for the bladder than for the salivary gland. It reduces urge incontinence episodes by up to 50% at a dosage of 2 mg bid. The side effects include dry mouth (with a lower incidence as compared to oxybutynin—40% versus 78%), visual blurring, constipation, sedation, confusion, and urinary retention.[13] A long-acting form, Detrol LA, is available for once-daily use.

Imipramine has both anticholinergic and α-adrenergic properties that make this agent ideal for the treatment of both urge and stress incontinence. It is used for childhood enuresis and has been shown to decrease nocturnal incontinence. The possible side effects include dry mouth, visual blurring, sedation, confusion, urinary retention, postural hypotension, and cardiac conduction disturbances. It should be used with extreme care in older women, particularly as it has been associated with an increased risk of falling and hip fracture. The dose is 10 to 25 mg one to three times a day.

Desmopressin is effective for nocturia associated with urge incontinence, and is available in an intranasal spray. The side effects include headache, nausea, rhinitis, change in blood pressure, and hyponatremia. Caution should be used in elderly patients and in patients with renal disease, in which fluid and electrolyte imbalances are more likely to occur. A periodic check of the serum sodium level should be done in patients using intranasal desmopressin. The dosage of the intranasal spray (10 μg per spray) is one to two sprays at bedtime. Phase III trials of the use of oral desmopressin were under way at the time of this publication.

Medications used for the treatment of stress incontinence include α-adrenergic agents, estrogen, and imipramine. **α-Adrenergic agents** increase the muscle tone of the bladder base, bladder neck, and internal urethral sphincter. Pseudoephedrine is a first-line therapy in women with stress incontinence who have no pre-existing cardiovascular disease (eg, hypertension or arrhythmias). Pseudoephedrine improves stress incontinence by up to 60%, with a cure rate of up to 14%.[1] The side effects include anxiety, insomnia, agitation, sweating, headache, hypertension, and cardiac arrthymias. The recommended dosage for pseudoephedrine is 15 to 30 mg three times a day.

Estrogen therapy is useful for stress incontinence in postmenopausal women and may help women with urgency and/or frequency incontinence related to atrophic vaginitis or urethritis. It works by strengthening vaginal tissues and increasing periurethral blood flow and can be used as an adjuvant therapy with α-adrenergic agents in women with stress UI or mixed incontinence. Estrogen has been found to improve stress incontinence by 66% over 6 to 12 weeks of continuous use.[14] Topical estrogen as well as the estradiol vaginal ring (Estring) may also reduce the risk of urinary tract infections.[15,16]

To improve urogenital symptoms, estrogen can be given orally or may be used topically. Because the use of estrogen alone greatly increases a woman's risk of endometrial cancer, a progestational agent must be used in conjunction with oral estrogen as well as with any dose of topical estrogen that results in significant systemic absorption. Patients who have had a hysterectomy do not need concomitant progestational therapy. The usual dosage of oral estrogen is 0.3 to 1.25 mg/d, accompanied by medroxyprogesterone acetate (2.5 to 5 mg daily) in women with a uterus.

Commonly used topical estrogen regimens include (1) estradiol cream (Estrace 0.1 mg/g), 2 to 4 g nightly for 1 to 2 weeks, followed by 1 g nightly three times weekly, and (2) conjugated equine estrogen cream (Premarin 0.625 mg/g), 2 to 4 g nightly three times weekly. However, both regimens result in significantly increased systemic estrogen levels. Therefore, progestins should be administered concurrently to women with an intact uterus, and these regimens are relatively contraindicated in women with hormone-dependent malignancies.[17]

Low-dose (0.3 mg of conjugated equine estrogen) vaginal estrogen cream administered three times weekly has been shown to relieve symptoms. When dosed at this level, only 1 of 20 subjects developed endometrial proliferation on uterine biopsy.[17] Estrogen is now also available as an impregnated ring (Estring) that can be worn in the vagina continuously for 3 months and that provides a very low dose of estrogen to the vagina and surrounding tissues. Because its effects are almost exclusively local, patients with an intact uterus can use the ring without the addition of progestins. The side effects of all forms of estrogen can include breast tenderness and vaginal bleeding.

Surgical and Other Interventions

Various surgical procedures exist for stress incontinence due to urethral hypermobility or intrinsic sphincter deficiency. Retropubic suspension, the Marshall-Marchetti-Krantz procedure, or Burch colosuspension is used in women with urethral hypermobility. These procedures are done abdominally or vaginally and involve elevating the lower urinary tract, in particular the urethrovesical junction, within the retropubic space. Cure rates with these techniques are between 79 to 92%, but success rates drop to about 50% after 10 years.[1] For those patients with intrinsic sphincter deficiency, a pubovaginal sling procedure can be done, with a cure rate of 84%.[1] Prior to any of these surgical interventions,

all patients should have diagnostic testing to make sure the bladder itself is functioning normally.

Other management strategies for stress incontinence include pessaries, various occlusive devices (patches, plugs), and periurethral bulking injections. Absorbent pads or diapers should be used as an adjunctive therapy. Urinary catheterization is not a treatment for UI, with the exception of overflow incontinence. The treatment for this type of UI may include intermittent catherization every 6 to 8 hours. Other indications for an indwelling catheter may include nonhealing pressure sores and a request by the patient or family for comfort care.

Pessaries can be used in women with stress incontinence related to urethral hypermobility, as a temporary measure before surgery or in those women who are unable (for medical reasons) or unwilling to undergo surgical correction.[18] These devices are individually fitted and are worn intravaginally. They support the bladder neck, correct the vesicourethral angle, and increase outflow resistance by compressing the urethra against the posterior-superior aspect of the pubic symphysis. The common types of pessaries for a cystocele are the ring (with or without a diaphragm support), the Gelhorn, the doughnut, or the cube pessary. The cube pessary is the only pessary that requires daily removal. All other pessaries can be worn continuously for up to 2 months before they need to be removed for cleaning by the clinician, with an inspection of the vaginal epithelium for erosions, infection, and the development of rectovaginal and/or vesicovaginal fistulae.

Occlusive devices work by either occluding the urethral meatus or mechanically blocking leakage by supporting the urethrovesical junction. The **Reliance Urinary Control Insert** is an intraurethral occlusive device that uses a 3 cc balloon plug. It has been found to have a cure rate of up to 80% for pure genuine stress UI.[19] The **Fem Assist** occludes the urethral meatus by creating suction over the urethra. The suction device is removed with each voiding episode and can be reused for up to 1 week at a time. **Introl** is a ring-shaped intrasurgical device with two fingerlike prongs on one side that support the urethrovesical junction. It works similarly to a pessary, must be individually fitted, and requires daily removal by the patient. It has been found to have an 84% cure rate in a selected group of patients.[20]

Treatment with periurethral bulking agents for an incompetent internal sphincter involves the injection of polytetrafluoroethylene (PTFE), collagen, or autologous fat under cystoscopic guidance into an incompetent periurethral area. The most common side effects include worsening UI and transient urethral irritation. Complications include urgency, UI, and urinary retention. This procedure has a 2-year 49% cure rate and a 67% improvement rate.[1]

CRITERIA FOR FURTHER EVALUATION

Most of the evaluation and treatment of UI can be effectively provided by the primary care clinician

TABLE 86–5. Criteria for Referral to Specialist

Previous anti-incontinence surgery
Radical pelvic surgery
Symptomatic pelvic prolapse
Incontinence associated with symptomatic UTIs
PVR volume > 200 cc
Hematuria in the absence of infection
Failure to respond to an adequate therapeutic trial

PVR = postvoid residual; UTI = urinary tract infection.

(Figure 86–4). However, further evaluation and/or management by a urologist or a urogynecologist is necessary for a minority of patients. Criteria for further evaluation by a specialist are included in Table 86–5.[1]

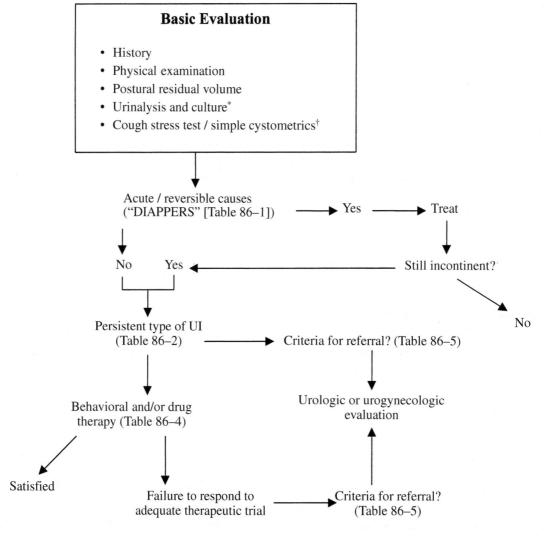

FIGURE 86–4. An approach to the patient with urinary incontinence. *If symptomatic urinary tract infection suspected; †selected patients, office-based primary care procedures. UI = urinary incontinence.

RESOURCES

The Agency for Health Care Research and Quality (formerly The Agency for Health Care Policy and Research)
Office of Health Care Information
Suite 501, Executive Office Center
2101 East Jefferson Street
Rockville, Maryland 20852
Telephone: (301) 594-1364
Web site: www.ahcpr.gov

The Agency for Health Care Research and Quality has developed clinical practice guidelines and a consumer booklet on the topic of urinary incompetence.

The Bladder Health Council
c/o American Foundation for Urologic Disease
300 West Pratt Street, Suite 401
Baltimore, Maryland 21201
Telephone: 1-800-242-2382 (Hotline)
Web site: www.incontinence.org

The Bladder Health Council provides a number of educational materials and has an overactive-bladder hotline.

The National Association for Continence
PO Box 8310
Spartanburg, South Carolina 29305-8310
Telephone: 1-800-252-3337
Web site: www.nafc.org

The National Association for Continence has materials for both the clinician and patient, including a newsletter, pelvic floor exercise tapes, and referrals to specialists around the nation.

The Simon Foundation for Continence
PO Box 835
Wilmette, Wisconsin 60091
Telephone: 1-800-237-4666
Web site: www.simonfoundation.org

The Simon Foundation for Continence offers an information packet, a quarterly newsletter, and books on the management of incontinence.

REFERENCES

1. Fantl JA, Newman DK, Coiling J, et al. Urinary incontinence in adults. Acute and chronic management. Clinical practice guidelines, No. 2, 1996 update. Rockville (MD): US Department of Health and Human Services, Public Health Service, Agency for Health Care Policy and Research; 1996. AHCPR Publication No.: 92-0682. p. 3–90.
2. Hampel C, Wienhold D, Benken N, et al. Definition of overactive bladder and epidemiology of urinary incontinence. Urology 1997;50 6A Suppl:4–14.

3. Brown J, Seely D, Fong J, et al. Urinary incontinence in older women. Who is at risk? Obstet Gynecol 1996;87:1–7.

4. Chutka DS, Fleming KC, Evans MP, et al. Urinary incontinence in the elderly population. Mayo Clin Proc 1996;71:93–101.

5. Batra SC, Iosif CS. The female urethra: target for estrogen action. J Urol 1983;129:418–21.

6. Kane RL, Ouslander JG, Abrams IB, editors. Essentials of clinical geriatrics. 3rd ed. San Francisco: McGraw-Hill, Inc.; 1994. p. 145–96.

7. Resnick NM. Urinary incontinence in the elderly. Med Grand Rounds 1984;3:281–9.

8. Rackely RR, Appell RA. Evaluation and medical management of female urinary incontinence. Cleve Clin J Med 1997;64(2):83–92.

9. Ouslander JG, Leach GE, Stasker DR. Simplified tests of lower urinary tract function in evaluation of geriatric urinary incontinence. J Am Geriatr Soc 1989; 37:706–14.

10. Burgio KL, Robinson JC, Engel BT. The role of biofeedback in Kegel exercise training for stress urinary incontinence. Am J Obstet Gynecol 1986; 154(1):58–64.

11. Wilson PD, Borland M. Vaginal cones for the treatment of genuine stress incontinence. Aust N Z J Obstet Gynaecol 1990;30:157–60.

12. Anderson RV, Mobley D, Blank B, et al. OROS Oxybutynin Study Group. Once daily controlled versus immediate release oxybutynin chloride for urge urinary incontinence. J Urol 1999;161:1809–12.

13. Appell RA. Clinical efficacy and safety of tolterodine in the treatment of overactive bladder: a pooled analysis. Urology 1997;50 Suppl 6A:90–6.

14. Fanti JA, Cardoro L, McClish D. Estrogen therapy in the management of urinary incontinence in post-menopausal women: a meta-analysis. Obstet Gynecol 1994;83:12–8.

15. Raz R, Stamm WE. A controlled trial of intravaginal estriol in postmenopausal women with recurrent urinary tract infections. N Engl J Med 1993;329: 753–7.

16. Eriksen B. A randomized, open, parallel-group study on the preventive effect of an estradiol-releasing vaginal ring (Estring) on recurrent urinary tract infections in postmenopausal women. Am J Obstet Gynecol 1999;180:1072–9.

17. Nathan L. Vulvovaginal disorders in the elderly woman. Clin Obstet Gynecol 1998;34:933–45.

18. Zeitlin MP, Lehherz TB. Pessaries in the geriatric patient. J Am Geriatr Soc 1992;140:635–63.

19. Staskin D, Bavendam T, Miller T, et al. Effectiveness of urinary control insert in the management of stress urinary incontinence: early results of a multicenter study. Urology 1996;47:629–36.

20. Davlia GW, Osterman KV. The bladderneck support prosthesis: a nonsurgical approach to stress incontinence in adult women. Am J Obstet Gynecol 1994; 71:206–11.

87

PRIMARY CARE OF THE WOMAN EXPOSED TO DIETHYLSTILBESTROL

Janet P. Pregler, MD

Diethylstilbestrol (DES), a nonsteroidal estrogen, was the first synthetic estrogen discovered.[1] Initially synthesized in 1938, it was prescribed until 1971 to pregnant women in the United States to prevent miscarriage and premature delivery.[2] Although a randomized placebo-controlled clinical trial demonstrated in 1953 that DES was ineffective in preventing pregnancy complications, it was still prescribed until it was discovered that women exposed to DES in utero had an increased risk of a rare gynecologic cancer, clear cell adenocarcinoma of the vagina and cervix.[3,4] In 1971 the US Food and Drug Administration issued a bulletin stating that the use of DES was contraindicated in pregnancy.[2] It is estimated that between 5 and 10 million people were exposed to DES, either while pregnant or in utero, between 1938 and 1971.[5]

Although DES has not been prescribed to pregnant women in the United States for over 30 years, complications from its use continue to affect women who were exposed to it decades ago. There is an association between the use of DES and an increased risk of breast cancer in women exposed to DES while pregnant.[6] Women exposed to DES in utero are at increased risk for cancer and anatomic abnormalities of the genital tract, infertility, ectopic pregnancy, miscarriage, and preterm labor.[5,7–9]

Studies of midlife and later health effects on persons exposed to DES in utero have not yet been completed.[10] Animal studies suggest that children of women exposed to DES in utero (grandchildren of women exposed to DES while pregnant) may be at risk for health effects as well.[11–13] Studies of the children and grandchildren of women who took DES are ongoing.

IDENTIFICATION OF WOMEN EXPOSED TO DES

A challenge to the primary care clinician is to identify persons exposed to DES, many of whom remain unaware of this aspect of their health history. No central registry exists of persons prescribed DES. When the risks were recognized in the 1970s, public education campaigns were undertaken. However, there was no method available to systematically inform all those at risk. Clinicians were encouraged to inform women who had taken DES, and many did so. However, a large number of women were never directly informed of their DES exposure.

Sometimes, identification of persons exposed to DES is relatively straightforward. Some women know they took DES during pregnancy. Some women know their mothers took DES. In these cases, it is necessary only to ask patients directly about exposure.

However, a group of patients exists who were likely to have been exposed to DES that cannot be identified simply by asking about DES. Women more likely to have been exposed while pregnant are those with a history of miscarriage who were pregnant in the 1940s, 1950s, and 1960s. To identify such women (and therefore their children who were exposed to DES in utero), it is important to include questions about miscarriage and pregnancy complications in historic screening of older women. Women who endorse a history of relevant pregnancy complications should then be asked if they took medication to prevent pregnancy complications. Never patented, DES and related cogeners were manufactured by over 200 companies and prescribed under many different brand names (Table 87–1). It is best to obtain obstetric records for patients who may have been exposed, but, of course, this is not always possible.

Women who may have been exposed in utero most often present with anatomic abnormalities of the genital tract and/or infertility. These are discussed further below. Women who present with clear cell adenocarcinoma of the vagina and cervix before the age of 40 years should be considered exposed unless proven otherwise. Mothers of such women also should be considered exposed.

WOMEN EXPOSED TO DES WHILE PREGNANT

In 1941 it was discovered that estrogen levels declined prior to miscarriage. Based on this observation, clinicians began to advocate for the use of DES to prevent miscarriage.[14] Advertising campaigns by pharmaceutical companies promoted DES not only for women with a known risk of pregnancy complications but also routinely to promote healthier pregnancies.[5]

It has been difficult to assess the health risks for women exposed to DES while pregnant. Women who have been identified as having been exposed to DES while pregnant differ in many ways from the general population as they are more likely to be Caucasian and middle or upper middle class and to have suffered complications of pregnancy. Long-term data from randomized trial of DES exist, but the number of women on whom follow-up data are available is not large enough to detect all possible significant health effects. Nevertheless, most experts believe that the only identified significant possible health effect for women exposed to DES while pregnant is a slightly increased risk of breast cancer.[5]

The National Cancer Institute has concluded that the weight of evidence supports the fact that women who took DES during pregnancy have a slightly increased risk of breast cancer.[15] A definite link will never be established because most data come from small and/or nonrandomized studies,

and the majority of women exposed while pregnant are now elderly. Data support a relative risk of 1.3, compared with a relative risk of 1.0 to 1.5 for women who take postmenopausal hormone replacement therapy and 2.6 for women with one first-degree relative with breast cancer.[16]

Like all older women, women exposed to DES while pregnant should be advised to have yearly clinical breast examinations and mammograms. In addition, the contribution of exposure to DES while pregnant should be taken into account in overall estimates of breast cancer risk when discussing issues such as hormone replacement therapy, as well as when considering the use of tamoxifen to prevent breast cancer in women at overall high risk.

WOMEN EXPOSED TO DES IN UTERO ("DES DAUGHTERS")

Clear Cell Carcinoma of the Vagina and Cervix

Women exposed to DES in utero ("DES daughters") were the first group identified to have suffered significant health effects from DES. In 1971 seven cases of clear cell carcinoma of the vagina and cervix were reported in young women exposed to DES in utero. Previously, this cancer had been reported rarely and in elderly women.[3] Subsequent case-control studies suggested a relative risk of 40.0 for clear cell carcinoma of the vagina and cervix among women exposed to DES in utero. This translates to approximately one case of clear cell adenocarcinoma of the vagina and cervix for each 1,000 DES daughters.[10]

The peak incidence of clear cell adenocarcinoma of the vagina and cervix in women exposed to DES in utero is in adolescence and the early twenties. However, cases of clear cell adenocarcinoma of the vagina and cervix have been reported in women in their thirties, forties, and fifties (Herbst AL, personal communication to the Centers for Disease Control and Prevention National DES Education Campaign, 2001).[10] In the absence of DES exposure, clear cell adenocarcinoma of the vagina and cervix occurs in elderly women. Most women enrolled in studies of women exposed to DES in utero are not yet elderly. Therefore, it is not certain that the risk of adenocarcinoma of the vagina and cervix will not continue to be present as DES daughters age.[10]

TABLE 87–1. Diethylstilbestrol Brand Names*

Nonsteroidal estrogens:

Benzestrol	Gynben	Restrol
Chlorotianisens	Gyneben	Stil-Rol
Comestrol	Hexestrol	Stilbal
Cyen A.	Hexoestrol	Stilbestrol
Cyen B.	H-Bestrol	Stilbestronate
Delvinal	Menocrin	Stilbetin
DES	Meprane	Stilbinol
DesPlex	Mestibol	Stilboestroform
Dibestil	Methallenestril	Stilboestrol
Dienestrol	Microest	Stilboestrol DP.
Dienoestrol	Mikarol	Stilestrate
Diestryl	Mikarol forti	Stilpalmitate
Diethylstilbestrol	Milestrol	Stilphostrol
Digestil	Monomenstrol	Stilronate
Dipalmitate	Neo-Oestranol I	Stilrone
Diphosphate	Neo-Oestranol II	Stils
Dipropionate	Nulabort	Synestrin
Domestrol	Oestrogenine	Synestrol
Estilen	Oesromenin	Synthoestrin
Estrobene	Oestromon	Tace
Estrobene DP.	Orestrol	Vallestril
Estrosyn	Pabestrol D.	Willestrol
Fonatol	Palestrol	

Nonsteroidal estrogen-androgen combinations:

Amperone	Estan	Tylandril
Di-Erone	Metylstil	Tylosterone
	Teserene	

Nonsterodial estrogen-progesterone combination:
    Progravidium

Vaginal cream-suppositories with nonsteroidal estrogens:

AVC Cream with Dienestrol	Dienestrol cream

*Names under which DES has been sold in the United States.
Reproduced from Kaufman RH, Adam E, Haynes SG, et al. Physician information: how to identify and managed DES exposed individuals. Bethesda (MD): National Cancer Institute; 1995.

National Cancer Institute recommendations for screening of women exposed to DES in utero are summarized in Table 87–2. It should be noted that no one has ever reported changes in the vulva associated with DES exposure. Also, there is no known increased risk of breast cancer in DES daughters; standard recommendations for breast cancer screening apply. Although much attention has been given to the use of screening vaginal cytology in DES daughters, its efficacy remains unknown. Cases of clear cell adenocarcinoma of the vagina and cervix have been diagnosed in the presence of negative cytologic smears.[3]

The most important part of the examination for detection of clear cell adenocarcinoma of the vagina and cervix is visual inspection and palpation. Any visible or palpable lesion of the vagina or cervix should be biopsied, regardless of cytology results. Clear cell adenocarcinoma of the vagina and cervix also may present with vaginal bleeding or discharge;

TABLE 87–2. National Cancer Institute Recommendations for Screening of Women Exposed to DES in Utero

Annual examination to include:
    Clinical breast examination
    Inspection of the vulva, vagina, and cervix
    Vaginal cytology
    Cervical cytology
    Digital vaginal examination
    Digital cervical palpation
    Bimanual examination, including rectal examination
    Mammography according to established guidelines
        for women at average risk*

*DES exposure in utero is not known to increase the risk of breast cancer.
Reproduced from Kaufman RH, Adam E, Haynes SG, et al. Physician information: how to identify and manage DES exposed individuals. Bethesda (MD): National Cancer Institute; 1995.

such symptoms should be evaluated thoroughly.[5] When abnormalities are found, the patient should be examined by a gynecologist experienced in evaluating DES daughters. Women diagnosed with clear cell adenocarcinoma of the vagina and cervix should be referred to a gynecologic oncologist for further evaluation and treatment. Stage I cancers have a 10-year survival of over 90%. Treatment of more advanced cancers is less successful.[5]

Reproductive Tract Abnormalities, Infertility, and Pregnancy

Anatomic abnormalities in DES daughters occur in tissues derived from the müllerian duct. Estimates of the percentage of DES daughters with identifiable reproductive tract abnormalities vary widely. This is likely because DES daughters with anatomic abnormalities or infertility are more likely to be identified as having in utero exposure to DES.

Benign vaginal adenosis appears to be the most common abnormality. It is defined as the presence of glandular epithelium in the vagina, and its presence may correlate with the dosage and timing of DES exposure during pregnancy. Adenosis appears to be converted by an active metaplastic process to squamous epithelium as DES daughters age. No treatment is necessary.[5,17]

Cervical abnormalities (collars, hoods, cockscombs, and septae) and uterine abnormalities are also commonly encountered. A "T"-shaped uterus

encountered on hysterosalpingography or ultrasonography is highly associated with prenatal exposure to DES.[7,8]

Up to one-third of women exposed to DES in utero may be infertile. Potential mechanisms include direct effects from structural abnormalities, hypothalamic-pituitary-ovarian dysfunction, and failure of implantation.[18,19] All women presenting for infertility treatment should be asked questions to determine whether they were exposed to DES in utero. All DES daughters undergoing infertility evaluation should have a hysterosalpingogram performed to assess for upper tract abnormalities.

Most women exposed to DES in utero who become pregnant carry a normal pregnancy to term. However, rates of ectopic pregnancy, miscarriage, and premature birth are higher than in the general population. In women with documented reproductive tract abnormalities, these rates are even higher. The relative risk of ectopic pregnancy has been estimated to be 8.6 overall and 13.5 for women with documented reproductive tract abnormalities.[5] The relative risk of miscarriage has been estimated at 1.3 for the first trimester and 4.2 for the second trimester.[20] The relative risk of premature birth has been estimated at 4.7 and 9.6 for women with documented reproductive tract abnormalities.[5]

DES daughters should be referred to an obstetrician-gynecologist for preconception counseling and pregnancy management. Care by a maternal-fetal medicine specialist should be considered, particularly for women with documented reproductive tract abnormalities and/or prior complications of pregnancy. Preconception counseling should stress that the majority of DES daughters are able to complete normal pregnancies. However, the risks of infertility, ectopic pregnancy, miscarriage, premature labor, and premature birth should be reviewed. Pelvic examination should be performed to assess reproductive tract abnormalities.

Early diagnosis of pregnancy is essential because of the heightened risk of ectopic pregnancy. All DES daughters should be counseled to report abdominal pain and vaginal bleeding immediately. Ultrasonography and frequent cervical examinations during pregnancy have been recommended to monitor for possible complications. Prophylactic cervical cerclage has been advocated for pregnant DES daughters but was not found to be superior to close monitoring, with obstetric intervention only when indicated by signs and symptoms.[5,15,20]

Other Health Issues

Animal studies have suggested a possible increased risk for autoimmune diseases in females exposed to DES. Human studies have not confirmed a statistically significant association between DES exposure and any autoimmune disease.[21] Some studies of DES-exposed women have suggested a slightly increased risk of cervical intraepithelial neoplasia, but this has not been demonstrated consistently.[5,10] Cohort studies of women exposed to DES have not demonstrated an increased risk of any cancer other than clear cell carcinoma of the vagina and cervix. The median age of women enrolled in studies currently reported is less than 50 years, raising the possibility that additional risks will be identified as DES daughters age.[10]

MEN EXPOSED TO DES IN UTERO AND THE "THIRD GENERATION"

Clinicians who actively identify women exposed to DES should be prepared to answer questions about the effects of DES on men exposed in utero ("DES sons") and on the children of DES daughters ("DES grandchildren"). Studies of men exposed to DES in utero have been hampered by small sample size and a bias toward identifying men as DES exposed who present with genitourinary abnormalities and/or infertility. Some studies have reported an increased risk of other genitourinary abnormalities, including hypoplastic testes and microphallus, although others have not confirmed this finding.[22–25] Infertility does not appear to be more common among DES sons, although abnormal semen analyses may be found more commonly in men exposed to DES in utero.[23,25]

Studies of the possible carcinogenic effects of DES on the male reproductive system have yielded contradictory results. Small sample size and lack of confirmation of DES exposure have hampered results. A prospective cohort study of over 3,600 men found a trend toward increased rates of testicular cancer compared with rates in the general population, but this finding did not reach statistical significance.[26] Animal studies suggest that in utero DES exposure may increase the risk of cancers of the rete testis and prostatic utricle in elderly mice; whether increased rates of these very rare cancers will be detected as cohorts of DES sons age is as yet unknown. The rete testis and prostatic utricle are derived embryologically from the müllerian duct, the same tissue affected by clear cell adenocarcinoma in DES daughters.[11] Cohort studies of DES sons are ongoing.

No health effects have yet been demonstrated in the children of DES daughters. However, animal studies have demonstrated an increased risk of reproductive tumors in elderly female and male mice born to female mice exposed to DES in utero.[11–13] Cohort studies of DES grandchildren also have been established.

SUMMARY

Millions of women currently living in the United States were exposed to DES either during pregnancy or in utero. Significant health risks have been identified for these women. DES daughters require specific ongoing surveillance for clear cell adenocarcinoma of the vagina and cervix, as well as specialized preconception counseling and pregnancy care. Studies of additional, possible risks for DES daughters, sons, and grandchildren are ongoing. Because women exposed to DES during pregnancy are now elderly, it is important to identify them and their children now, despite the fact that all possible

---

RESOURCE

DES Action USA
610 16th Street, Suite 301
Oakland, California 94612
Telephone: 1-800-DES-NEWS (1-800-337-6397)
Web site: www.desaction.org

DES Action is a nonprofit organization dedicated to informing the public about DES and assisting DES-exposed women and men.

health risks are not yet defined. Future research may yet identify new risks that require screening or treatment.

REFERENCES

1. Dodds EC, Goldberg L, Lawson W, Robinson R. Estrogenic activity of certain synthetic compounds. Nature 1938;141:247–8.

2. Noller KL, Fish CR. Diethylstilbestrol usage: its interesting past, important present, and questionable future. Med Clin North Am 1974;58:793–810.

3. Herbst AL, Ulferlder H, Poskanzer DC. Adenocarcinoma of the vagina. N Engl J Med 1971;284:878–81.

4. Dieckmann WJ, Davis ME, Rynkiewicz LM, Pottinger RE. Does the administration of diethylstilbestrol during pregnancy have therapeutic value? Am J Obstet Gynecol 1953;66:1062–81.

5. Giusti RM, Iwamoto K, Hatch E. Diethylstilbestrol revisited: a review of the long-term health effects. Ann Intern Med 1995;122:778–88.

6. Titus-Ernstoff L, Hatch EE, Hoover RN, et al. Long term cancer risk in women given diethylstilbestrol (DES) during pregnancy. Br J Cancer 2001;84:126–33.

7. Kaufman RH, Noller K, Adam E, et al. Upper gentital tract abnormalities and pregnancy outcome in diethylstibestrol-exposed progeny. Am J Obstet Gynecol 1984;148:973–84.

8. Kaufman RH, Binder GL, Gray PM, Adam E. Upper genital tract changes associated with exposure in utero to diethylstilbestrol. Am J Obstet Gynecol 1977;128:51–9.

9. Barnes AB, Colton T, Gundersen J, et al. Fertility and outcome of pregnancy in women exposed in utero to diethylstilbestrol. N Engl J Med 1980;302:609–13.

10. Hatch EE, Palmer JR, Titus-Ernstoff L, et al. Cancer risk in women exposed to diethylstilbestrol in utero. JAMA 1998;280:630–4.

11. Newbold RR, Hanson RB, Jefferson WN, et al. Proliferative lesions and reproductive tract tumors in male descendants of mice exposed developmentally to diethylstilbestrol. Carcinogenesis 2000;21:1355–63.

12. Walker BE, Kurth LA. Multi-generational carcinogenesis from diethylstilbestrol investigated by blastocyst transfers in mice. Int J Cancer 1995;61:249–52.

13. Walker BE, Haven MI. Intensity of multigenerational carcinogenesis from diethylstilbestrol in mice. Carcinogenesis 1997;18:791–3.

14. Smith OW, Smith GVS. The influence of diethylstilbestrol on the progress and outcome of pregnancy as based on a comparison of treated with untreated primigravidas. Am J Obstet and Gynecol 1949;58:994–1009.

15. Kaufman RH, Adam E, Haynes SG, et al. Physician information: how to identify and manage DES exposed individuals. Bethesda (MD): National Cancer Institute; 1995.

16. Armstrong K, Eisen A, Weber B. Assessing the risk of breast cancer. N Engl J Med 2000;342:564–71.

17. Stillman RJ. In utero exposure to diethylstilbesterol: adverse effects on the reproductive tract and reproductive performance in male and female offspring. Am J Obstet Gynecol 1982;142:905–21.

18. Karande VC, Lester RG, Muasher SJ, et al. Are implantation and pregnancy outcome impaired in diethylstilbestrol-exposed women after in vitro fertilization and embryo transfer? Fertil Steril 1990;54:287–91.

19. Peress MR, Tsai CC, Mathur RS, Williamson HO. Hirsutism and menstrual patterns in women exposed to diethylstilbesterol in utero. Am J Obstet Gynecol 1982;144:135–40.

20. Kaufman RH, Adam E, Hatch EE, et al. Continued follow-up of pregnancy outcomes in diethylstilbestrol-exposed offspring. Obstet Gynecol 2000;96:483–9.

21. Noller KL, Blair PB, O'Brien PC, et al. Increased occurrence of autoimmune disease among women exposed in utero to diethylstilbestrol. Fertil Steril 1988;49:1080–2.

22. Beard CM, Melton LJ, O'Fallon WM, et al. Cryptorchism and maternal estrogen exposure. Am J Epidemiol 1984;120:707–16.

23. Gill WB, Schumacher GFB, Bibbo M, et al. Association of diethylstilbestrol exposure in utero with cryptorchidism, testicular hypoplasia and semen abnormalities. J Urol 1979;122:36–9.

24. Leary FJ, Resseguire LJ, Kurland LT, et al. Males exposed in utero to diethylstilbestrol. JAMA 1984;252:2984–9.

25. Wilcox AJ, Baird DD, Weinberg CR, et al. Fertility in men exposed prenatally to diethylstilbestrol. N Engl J Med 1995;332:1411–6.

26. Strohsnitter WC, Noller KL, Hoover RN, et al. Cancer risk in men exposed in utero to diethlystilbesterol. J Natl Cancer Ins 2001;93:545–51.

88

DOMESTIC VIOLENCE

Carolyn Sachs, MD, MPH

The term "domestic violence" sounds like it applies to any violence that occurs in the home. However, over the last several decades the medical literature has used this term to describe abuse between intimate or formerly intimate partners. Hence the term "intimate partner violence" may be a more appropriate term to describe the subject of this chapter. To complicate issues further, much of the literature on domestic violence suffers from a lack of a clear-cut definition of "abuse." Many studies include emotional, verbal, and financial abuse as well as threats or acts of physical or sexual abuse. More recent studies have used improved and validated detection devices that lead to more uniform definitions of domestic violence.

Despite variations in definition and study methodology it is clear that domestic violence (DV) has a major impact on the health and well-being of many people. Although men in heterosexual and same-sex relationships are also victims of DV, 95% of the reported cases of DV involve a male perpetrator and a female victim,[1] and less than 0.5% of men seen as assault victims in the medical setting suffer the injury secondary to a female partner.[2] The remainder of this chapter focuses on the female victim of DV, both in heterosexual and homosexual relationships. Estimates of the yearly prevalence of DV alone range from 4% for severe physical abuse to 12% for all physical abuse.[3,4] Over a lifetime at least 1 of 3 American women is physically assaulted by a partner.[3,5] Population-based studies performed in other English-speaking countries have found similar 1-year and lifetime prevalence rates.[6,7] The potential lethality of DV in the United States is illustrated by the estimated 2,000 to 3,000 female DV homicides yearly.[8,9] These DV homicides account for the majority of women killed in the United States.[10] Acts of DV are rarely isolated events; DV is a pattern of abusive behavior marked by mental and physical domination of one person over another. Victims in these relationships report an average of six violent incidents per year.[11]

Due to the high prevalence of DV against women, primary care clinicians who see female patients will encounter many victims in their practices. The incidence and prevalence of DV cases in the primary care and emergency department (ED) settings has been well studied over the last two decades (Tables 88–1 and 88–2).[12–29] Due to variations in data collection and definitions of DV, the lifetime prevalence ranges from 12 to 55% in the primary care setting and reaches up to 54.2% in the ED setting. One-year prevalence rates range from 6 to 26% in the primary care setting and from 10 to 14.4% in the ED setting. Female victims of DV most often present for care that is not directly related to injuries at the hands of their partners. However, almost 30% of these women return for care related to a DV injury during the next 5 years.[30]

Approximately 2 to 3% of all women seen in the ED present for care of a DV injury.[21,29] Prevalence rates of abuse in pregnant patients generally exceed those in the general population and range from 8 to 17%. Pregnant adolescents are at even greater risk and were found to have a prevalence rate of 20.7% in one study.[31] Another study showed that women may be at even greater risk for DV during the postpartum period, with DV rates increasing from 19% during pregnancy to 25% during the postpartum period.[32] Clearly all clinicians who see female patients in the primary care setting are seeing victims of DV. In addition to the potential lethal outcome, these women suffer the enormous physical and mental health consequences of untreated DV.

TABLE 88–1. Studies of the Incidence and/or Prevalence of Domestic Violence Cases Seen in the Primary Care Setting

Author, Yr	Reference No.	Location	N	Sex	Type of Abuse	Rate (%)	I/P
Gin 1991	12	Internal medicine	453	B	Physical	28	P
Elliot 1995	13	Family practice clinic	42	F	Physical, social, emotional	45	P
					Physical	36	P
Freund 1996	14	Internal medicine	689	F	Physical	11.6	P
Hamberger 1992	15	Family practice clinic	394	F	Physical	23	I
					Physical with injuries	13	I
					Physical	39	P
Johnson 1997	16	Rural family practice	280	F	Physical	8	P1
					Physical, emotional	34	P
McCauley 1995	17	Internal medicine	1,932	F	Physical, sexual	5.5	P1
					Physical, sexual	21.4	P
McKenzie 1998	18	Nontrauma inpatients	101	F	Physical	26	P
					Physical	2	I
McFarlane 1992	19	Public prenatal clinic	691	F	Physical or sexual abuse during current pregnancy	17	P
Rath 1989	20	Primary care clinic	218	F	Verbal	48	P

I = incidence; P = prevalence; P1 = 1-year prevalence; B = both male and female; F = female; N = population size.

TABLE 88–2. Studies of the Incidence and/or Prevalence of Domestic Violence Cases Seen in the Emergency Department Setting

Author, Yr	Reference No.	N	Sex	Type of Abuse	Rate (%)	I/P
Abbott 1995	21	648	F	Threats, fear, physical injury	12	I
				Threats, fear, physical injury	54	P
Anglin 1996	22	1,891	B	Physical	5.5	I
				Physical	18	P
Bates 1995	23	401	F	Physical abuse	2	I
				Physical abuse	25	P
Dearwater 1998	24	3,455	F	Injury from partner	2.2	I
				Physical or sexual	14.4	P1
				Physical or sexual	36.9	P
Feldhaus 1997	25	491	F	Physical abuse or fear	30	P
Muelleman 1996	26	9,057	F	Injury from male partner	3	I
Olson 1996	27	4,073	F	Injury from male partner	3	I
Roberts 1996	28	1,223	B	Fear or actual physical injury	16	P
				Fear or actual physical injury	1	I
Sachs 1998	29	1,003	B	Injury from partner	2	I
				Physical abuse	10	P

I = incidence; P = prevalence; P1 = 1-year prevalence; B = both male and female; F = female; N = population size.

Although DV victims often seek medical attention for injuries due to battery alone, they also suffer from many other physical illnesses at rates much greater than those in the general population. Battered women suffer more from chronic headaches, sexually transmitted diseases, and irritable bowel syndrome, and they use health services six to eight times more often than nonbattered women.[20,33,34]

As expected, DV has a significant impact also on the mental health of victims. Most experts feel that the mental health consequences of DV can be attributed to living in a constantly traumatic environment. This environment of unpredictable violence and domination produces feelings of helplessness and depression. One representative study found female victims of DV 4.5 times as likely to suffer anxiety, 4.0 times as likely to suffer depression, 3.0 times to suffer from dysthymia, and 2.7 times as likely to have significant phobias, as compared with nonbattered women.[35] Pregnant women and their unborn children also suffer from the negative health consequences of DV. Battering during pregnancy correlates with delayed prenatal care, low birth weight, anemia, infections, and increased bleeding.[19,36–38]

After birth, exposure to parental DV can have lasting and damaging effects on children. The majority of children of battered mothers witness the violence. This group comprises an estimated 3.3 million children between the ages of 3 and 17 years annually in the United States.[39] Witnessing parental DV has been found to cause post-traumatic stress disorder in children, similar to that exhibited by children who are direct victims of physical abuse or sexual abuse.[40] Children of battered women may sustain developmental delays while growing up in an environment marked by physical and verbal abuse.[41] Additionally, witnessing parental DV is the greatest risk factor for becoming a perpetrator or victim of DV as an adult.[42] As the philosopher Jean Paul-Sartre put it so eloquently, "One is never finished with the family. It's like the smallpox—it catches you in childhood and marks you for life."

The remainder of this chapter illustrates how clinicians can intervene with their current adult patients to break this intergeneration transmission

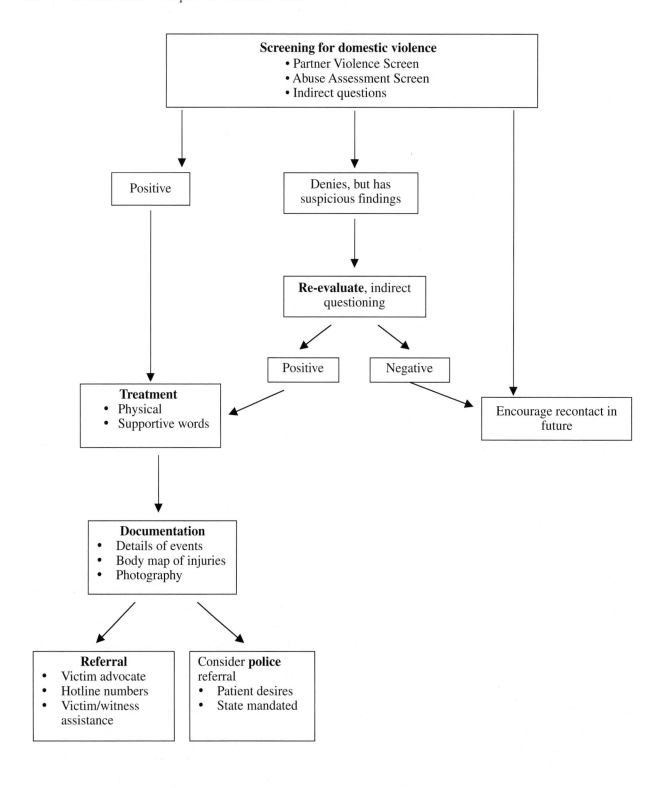

FIGURE 88–1. Domestic violence assessment, treatment, documentation, and referral.

TABLE 88–3. Screening Questions for Domestic Violence

Partner Violence Screen*

    Have you been hit, kicked, punched, or otherwise hurt by someone within the past year? If so, by whom?

    Do you feel safe in your current relationship?

    Is there a partner from a previous relationship who is making you feel unsafe now?

Abuse Assessment Screen†

    Has your partner or someone important to you ever emotionally or physically abused you?

    Within the last year, have you been hit, slapped, kicked, or otherwise physically hurt by someone?

    Since you've been pregnant, have you been hit, slapped, kicked, or otherwise physically hurt by someone?

    Within the last year, has anyone forced you to have sexual activities?

    Are you afraid of your partner or anyone listed above?

Indirect questioning

    Because relationship conflict and violence are problems in many of my patients' lives, I ask all my patients about this: Is violence at home occurring in your life?

    You seem bothered by something today. Often marital or relationship problems are a source of concern in my patients' lives. Do you have concerns about your relationship?

    All couples argue sometimes. What happens when you and your husband (partner) argue? Do the arguments ever become physical?

    Often when I have seen this type of injury it is due to a punch or a slap. Is this how your injury happened? (This is a possible approach to a patient with a suspicious injury.)

    Often when I have seen patients with these symptoms it is due to stress or fighting at home (or with a partner). Is this going on in your life? (This is an approach to a patient with suspicious psychosomatic complaints.)

*Data from Feldhaus et al.[25]
†Data from Soeken et al.[52]
More examples of indirect questions can be obtained from the Health Resource Center on Domestic Violence (see "Resources" section).

of DV. The general algorithm for clinician intervention includes identification, treatment, documentation, and referral (Figure 88–1) .

UNCOVERING DOMESTIC VIOLENCE: THE CLINICAL SETTING

History

Clinicians may be the only professionals in a woman's life to uncover DV. Patients are more likely to disclose DV to clinicians than to police or religious leaders. As many as 43% of battered women use medical services as their primary source of help with the abuse.[43] Many medical organizations, including the American Medical Association, the American College of Emergency Physicians, the American College of Obstetricians and Gynecologists, the American Academy of Family Practice, the American Academy of Nurse Practitioners, and the Emergency Nurses Association formally support the screening of all patients for DV.[44–49] Several written

and verbal screening tools have been tested in various clinical settings. The Index of Spousal Abuse and the Conflict Tactics Scale are lengthy research instruments that have demonstrated content validity and reliability.[50,51] However, they are too long to be of practical use in the clinical setting. Shorter screening tools such as the Abuse Assessment Screen (AAS)[52] and the Partner Violence Screen[25] (Table 88–3) are more practical and have been proven to be sensitive and valid in the clinical setting. Initially developed for the pregnant patient, the AAS can easily be adapted to all patients by modifying question number three. Alternative indirect methods (see Table 88–3) for asking about abuse may be just as effective or even more effective in uncovering DV but have not been formally studied. Clinicians should use whichever method seems appropriate for the individual patient.

Partners should be asked to leave in a routine manner before the patient is asked about DV. Patients will rarely admit to abuse unless they are guaranteed privacy, and initiation of the topic is potentially dangerous in the presence of an abusive partner. Usually a patient's companion will leave cooperatively before the physical examination when asked. If a companion is resistant to leaving, the patient may be taken to the rest room for a urine sample or taken to the radiology area and questioned about DV alone in those locations. Questioning about DV must be done in a nonthreatening manner devoid of blame and judgment. An atmosphere of support and understanding will facilitate patient disclosure of abuse.

Although not all are well proven in prospective studies, the following historic factors are considered by experts to be suggestive of abuse: frequent clinician visits for trauma, chronic pain syndromes, or gastrointestinal complaints;[53] delays in seeking medical treatment after an injury; an overprotective partner; injuries during pregnancy; a history of depression or suicide attempts; and a history of abuse as a child.[17] The presence of any one of these factors should heighten a clinician's suspicion of DV as a reason for the visit.

Physical Examination

Potential DV victims must be carefully and completely examined. Many injuries are not seen unless the examiner looks at all parts of the body. The DV medical literature lacks many prospective studies that document the predictive value of specific injuries. However, experts consider the following to be suggestive of DV:

1. Injuries incompatible with the given history. For example, a patient states that she fell, and she presents with an orbital blow-out fracture. Blow-out fractures require that an object small enough to fit into the orbit strike it. The increased intraocular pressure then forces the orbital contents through the path of least resistance, usually the inferior orbital wall. A fall on a flat surface would not be expected to cause an orbital blow-out fracture.
2. Multiple injuries in various stages of healing. Although bruises heal differently depending on how deep they are and where they are located, they generally pass though color stages, from red to blue to green and to yellow, over several days or weeks. The presence of several differently colored bruises in several areas should be a red flag for abuse.

3. Injuries that suggest a defensive posture. A classic example of this is a midshaft ulnar fracture, or a "night-stick" fracture (so-named because victims attempt to defend themselves from a clubbing with a nightstick by using their forearms to protect their faces). Other injuries to the ulnar aspect of the forearm should arouse similar suspicions.
4. Pattern injuries. Pattern injures include multiple linear streaks suggestive of a hand slap, multiple small round contusions suggestive of finger pressure marks, burns from cigarettes or lighters, any marks on the neck from choking, bite marks, and ligature marks on the wrists or ankles caused by the wrists or ankles being bound.

A central pattern of injury has also been described in the medical setting as being linked to DV. A central pattern of injury includes damage inflicted to the head, neck, chest, abdomen, and back. A large ED-based study by Muelleman et al found that battered women exhibited a central pattern of injury more often than women who sustained unintentional injuries. However, 20% of the battered women had different injury types, and the positive predictive value of one of the specific injury types identified was only 29.7%. The authors concluded that physicians should ask all patients about DV regardless of injury pattern.[26]

Asking about Domestic Violence

Thus, despite the absence of risk factors in the history or suggestive elements in the physical examination, patients universally must be asked about DV. Natural times to ask about DV include the social portion of an initial evaluation and subsequent annual examinations, ED visits, visits for psychiatric complaints, and prenatal visits. Routine prenatal screening for DV is especially important because battering during pregnancy is more common than (and just as dangerous as) other conditions routinely screened in the prenatal period, such as diabetes (a prevalence of 2 to 3%) and preeclampsia (a prevalence of 6 to 14%).[54]

Left to ask about DV without a formal protocol, clinicians traditionally do a poor job of detecting DV.[21] And many battered women view medical professionals as unhelpful compared with other sources of formal support.[55] Practical ways to increase inquiry and subsequent detection include a written or computerized pre-examination questionnaire, screening by the nurse during assessment of vital signs, and chart modification to include a DV reminder. Putting the last suggestion into effect increased detection by 1.8 times over baseline in one New Mexico ED-based study.[27] A study performed in the Midwest found that DV detection increased to 18% of a population screened by triage nurses, versus a prescreening detection rate of only 1%.[56]

It is also important to ask patients about forced sex by their partners as 40 to 45% of battered women are also raped by their partners.[57] If the sexual assault occurred within 72 hours of medical treatment, an evidentiary examination should be offered to the victim.

TREATMENT AND SUPPORT

Often the DV patient presents with traumatic injuries or medical conditions that require treatment. These conditions should be treated appropriately, and physical symptoms should not be minimized and ascribed solely to DV. However, psychological treatment and support is also essential. Brief supportive counseling by the clinician can effect a dramatic catharsis for a victim who has been suffering in silence. It is very important for the clinician to let a victim know that the battering is *not her fault*. Victims universally feel that they did something to deserve the abuse. Abusers reinforce this feeling with every beating. A few kind and supportive words from an authority figure such as a clinician can go a tremendous way in alleviating some of the guilt and shame a victim feels when her abuse has been revealed. Unfortunately, only 53% of battered women in one study received these important messages from their clinicians, and 24% of the victims actually reported that clinicians seemed to blame the victim for the abuse.[58] Samples of comforting phrases to use after abuse is uncovered are as follows:

- "No one deserves to be physically abused. It doesn't matter what you did or what he said you did, you do not deserve to be hit."
- "You are not the only one who has suffered this kind of abuse. Battering is a common problem."
- "You don't have to deal with this alone. We have people here (or in the community) that can help you."

Documentation

Documentation of DV in the medical chart may be the only written evidence of the abuse and may play a crucial role in the ability of a victim to separate herself from the perpetrator. Appropriate documentation by the clinician can be crucial in subsequent legal proceedings against the perpetrator or in child custody cases. Many district attorney's offices now file charges against perpetrators of DV solely on the basis of carefully documented medical and police records and do not require the victim to press charges or testify in court against her batterer. Clearly, the clinician's documentation can make or break a case in these circumstances. Guidelines for effective documentation include the following:

1. Record what the patient tells you, and use the patient's exact words (with quotes).
2. Note spontaneous utterances such as "He said he was going to beat me until he killed me," which can be used in court and for danger assessment.
3. Record prior incidents of abuse and the use or presence of a weapon.
4. Record specific threats made by the perpetrator as quotations.
5. Record any inconsistencies that lead you to suspect DV despite the patient's denial.
6. Record the name of the alleged perpetrator and his relationship to the victim, along with the time, date, and place of assault.
7. Record the details of any injuries, and label their location on a body map.
8. Record old injuries as well as new ones.
9. Document the services provided during the visit, either in the clinician's note or in the social worker's or victim advocate's note. This note should indicate the physical evidence given to police, photographs taken, referrals given, safety planning and assessment, and recommended subsequent medical care.

PHOTOGRAPHY

Carefully obtained photographs of DV injuries provide the victim with permanent evidence of the assault even after the injuries have completely healed. As with appropriate written documentation, these photographs can make all the difference in subsequent legal proceedings. Clinicians have several options for photographing injuries, and the best method depends on what is available in each given setting. Instant photography (ie, Polaroid) is convenient and is most often used in clinical practice. Photographs can be affixed to the chart and are extremely valuable in court. Additionally, most law enforcement personnel carry equipment for instant photography and will allow medical personnel to use it to document injuries for the medical record. Other types of photography (print film, digital, slide film, and video) can be used if the clinic or hospital has an established protocol to deal with this type of documentation and if a secure chain of evidence can be established. In this case the film must be accounted for and signed over on a written form through every step, from picture taking to film developing and return.

Most institutions that use colposcopy for sexual assault examinations have a formal chain-of-evidence protocol for dealing with slide or print film that often involves handing over the film to law enforcement personnel at the end of the examination. These protocols can be adapted easily to DV photography. Slide or print film in the 35-mm format generally provides greater resolution than instant photography provides and may document subtle injuries better. Although not mandated by all state laws, patient consent for photography is required by most institutions if the patient's face is included in the image. Clinicians must be aware of their own state and institutional policies regarding consent. Photographs should include a standard, such as a ruler, so that the size of the injury can be easily determined. With proper photographic documentation forensic experts can retrospectively comment on the likelihood that a given injury was caused by a particular weapon. Additionally, properly photographed and measured bite marks can be matched to potential perpetrators. At least one photograph that includes the patient's face along with the injury is recommended so that the identification of the injured person cannot be challenged. Photographs should be labeled with patient information, the date, and the photographer's name.

PHYSICAL EVIDENCE

Domestic violence victims who are also recent (< 72 hours) victims of sexual assault must be offered an evidentiary examination and a standard collecting of physical evidence per state protocol. In standard DV cases physical evidence (when applicable) should also be collected and turned over to police, using the completeness of sexual assault protocols. Appropriate specimens include torn or bloody clothes, saliva from bite marks, and bullet, glass, or weapon fragments. All evidence should be placed in a paper (not plastic) bag, to avoid bacterial overgrowth and decomposition of the specimen. As with regular photographs and sexual assault evidence, the transfer of this material must be documented through a written chain of evidence.

Referral

Next to identifying abuse, providing appropriate referral is perhaps the clinician's most crucial function in dealing with victims of DV. The identification, documentation, and treatment of injuries mean little unless a victim can obtain the resources needed to change her situation. However, clinicians generally have neither the time nor the expertise to counsel a victim adequately. Referral services fulfill this important obligation. The level of referral will naturally depend on the nature of the DV situation and the victim's desire for legal intervention. Many hospitals and clinics have a formal affiliation with a victim's advocate group or a local women's shelter. Under some circumstances these groups will dispatch a representative to the medical setting for immediate counseling, legal advocacy, and shelter placement (if necessary). A revelation of abuse in the medical setting often comes at a time of crisis. This is a window of opportunity for intervention, a time when a victim is more likely to make a change in her situation. Immediate contact with experienced advocates can make a tremendous difference. Medical personnel often are unaware of these services within their institutions or communities. Referrals to these local services must be included in a written protocol that pertains to any medical establishment. In fact, the Joint Commission on Accreditation of Healthcare Organizations and several state laws mandate a written protocol for the treatment and referral of DV victims.[59,60] Resources for medical personnel on protocol development and general DV information are listed at the end of this chapter. Web-based information often provides links to local resources in the user's area, and information on state laws pertaining to DV can be found through each state legislature's Web site. The national DV hotline (1-800-799-SAFE) can be used by victim and clinician alike and will be channeled to local shelter services automatically. Additional resources for victims, both on the Internet and through toll-free telephone numbers, can be found at the end of this chapter.

Safety Assessment

Almost every DV protocol includes a safety assessment of a victim's situation. Usually this assessment can be done in the course of counseling a victim by a victim advocate, a hospital social worker, or law enforcement personnel. In situations without these resources, a clinician or nurse may perform the safety assessment. Although experts feel that danger increases with increasing positives on the safety screen, a quantification of the increased danger in the presence of these risk factors cannot be found in the literature. Hence there is little support for telling a victim without many risk factors that she is safe or for informing a woman with many risk factors that she is at great risk of being killed by her partner. A large case-control study that hopes to predict and quantify exactly which risk factors place a woman in greater danger of homicide or attempted homicide at the hands of her partner is under way at the time of this publication.[61] Until the results of this study are published, clinicians may use the danger assessment screen developed by Campbell after decades of research on DV homicide (Figure 88–2). Assessment of safety should also include an assessment of the risk of the victim committing suicide or homicide. Suicide risk increases in the presence of DV,[62] and homicide on the part of the victim is a serious concern if the victim feels this is her only way out. Clearly, if the victim expresses suicidal or homicidal intentions, a psychiatric consultation must be obtained immediately, or the patient should be transferred to the closest ED for psychiatric evaluation and probable admission.

Safety assessment must also include dialogue about children in the home. Approximately half of all children of DV victims are also physically or sexually abused.[63] If uncovered during evaluation, child abuse must be reported to authorities.[64] Additionally, some jurisdictions consider just the presence of DV in the home as child abuse. By law in these jurisdictions, the DV must be reported to child abuse authorities at the time of discovery.

Safety Planning for Partner Separation

Crisis intervention in the medical setting may lead a victim to leave her partner. The period of attempted separation is the most dangerous time for a victim.[65]

Most DV homicides occur during or shortly after separation.[66] A safety plan for the period after discharge is critical. As with safety assessment, safety planning is best done by a victim advocate, a social worker, or a special law enforcement team. Safety planning often can be done over the phone by victim advocates if no resources are available to immediately counsel the victim in person. Depending on the level of injury and the victim's wishes at the time, safety planning can include (1) the relocation of the victim and/or the arrest of the perpetrator or (2) a safety plan for later relocation; this plan may involve the following:

- Teaching children about the "911" emergency telephone number and its use
- Establishing code words to secretly notify family and friends of impending danger in the presence of a perpetrator
- Establishing emergency referral numbers
- Storing legal and medical documents and extra money, clothes, keys, and medications in a safe location away from the batterer

SPECIAL CIRCUMSTANCES

Women Who Deny Abuse

Some victims may be reluctant to admit to DV upon initial questioning by medical personnel. These women often feel more comfortable revealing the abuse if the clinician uses indirect questions (see Table 88–3). A patient with suspicious injuries, vague medical complaints, or depression should be given several opportunities to discuss potential violence. One survey of battered women who had seen medical professionals found that 56% of them felt that clinicians too easily accepted false explanations of injuries, and 45% stated that clinicians treated injuries without asking about their cause.[58]

If the patient continues to deny abuse, she should not be badgered. A kind and reassuring manner will lead to the greatest success in helping a victim. Victims may purposely choose not to reveal abuse at a given point, and they can benefit most from a close clinician-patient relationship and an open invitation to discuss possible abuse in future appointments. Patients who deny abuse unconvincingly and leave the clinician still wondering should be given referral numbers and literature, "in case abuse becomes a problem" in the future. They

ID# _____

Danger Assessment

Several risk factors have been associated with homicide (murder) of both batterers and battered women in research conducted after the killings have taken place. We cannot predict what will happen in your case, but we would like you to be aware of the danger of homicide in situations of severe battering and for you to see how many of the risk factors apply to your situation. (The *he* in the questions refers to your husband, partner, ex-husband, or whoever currently is physically hurting you.)

A. On the calendar, please mark the approximate dates during the past year when you were beaten by your husband or partner. Write on that date how long each incident lasted in approximate hours and rate the incident according to the following scale:

1. Slapping, pushing; no injuries and/or lasting pain
2. Punching, kicking; bruises, cuts, and/or continuing pain
3. "Beating up"; severe contusions, burns, broken bones
4. Threat to use weapon; head injury, internal injury, permanent injury
5. Use of weapon; wounds from weapon

(If any of the descriptions for the higher number apply, use the higher number.)

B. Answer these questions yes or no.
_____ 1. Has the physical violence increased in frequency during the past year?
_____ 2. Has the physical violence increased in severity during the past year and/or has a weapon or threat with weapon been used?
_____ 3. Does he ever try to choke you?
_____ 4. Is there a gun in the house?
_____ 5. Has he ever forced you into sex when you did not wish to have sex?
_____ 6. Does he use drugs? (By drugs I mean "uppers" or amphetamines, speed, angel dust, cocaine, crack, street drugs, heroin, or mixtures.)
_____ 7. Does he threaten to kill you and/or do you believe he is capable of killing you?
_____ 8. Is he drunk every day or almost every day? (in terms of quantity of alcohol)
_____ 9. Does he control most or all of your daily activities? (For instance, does he tell you whom you can be friends with, how much money you can take with you shopping, or when you can take the car?) (If he tries, but you do not let him, check here. _____)
_____ 10. Have you ever been beaten by him while you were pregnant? (If never pregnant by him, check here. _____)
_____ 11. Is he violently and constantly jealous of you? (For instance, does he say, "If I can't have you, no one can.")
_____ 12. Have you ever threatened or tried to commit suicide?
_____ 13. Has he ever threatened or tried to commit suicide?
_____ 14. Is he violent toward your children?
_____ 15. Is he violent outside your home?
_____ TOTAL YES ANSWERS

THANK YOU. PLEASE TALK WITH YOUR NURSE, ADVOCATE, OR COUNSELOR ABOUT WHAT THE DANGER ASSESSMENT MEANS IN TERMS OF YOUR SITUATION.

FIGURE 88–2. Domestic violence danger assessment screen. Reproduced with permission from Campbell JC, editor. Assessing dangerousness. Thousand Oaks (CA): Sage Publications; 1995. p. 105.

should also be scheduled for a close follow-up appointment. In some cases of acute injury in which abuse seems irrefutable, state law may require medical personnel to contact police despite victim denial. Clinicians must be aware of their own state laws regarding this. More discussion of mandatory reporting to law enforcement agencies can be found in the section of this chapter entitled "Involvement of Law Enforcement Agencies."

Woman Who Stay with the Batterer

This discussion is perhaps out of place under "Special Circumstances," for the woman who stays with her batterer (at least for a while) is the norm, and the woman who leaves after the first episode of violence is the rare exception. A woman's refusal to leave often frustrates medical professionals who may have spent time and effort obtaining referrals and shelter services for her. However, clinicians must not become angry with the victim for not leaving immediately as this will only alienate the victim and push her further away from help-seeking behaviors. Battered women have real and often valid fears about leaving a relationship, fears that cannot always be resolved during the course of an office visit. Fear of partner revenge and further violence is a major and real danger in the minds of DV victims. The perpetrator threatens to harm or kill not only the victim but also the victim's family and friends. Additionally, victims fear losing their children since DV perpetrators often threaten to take or harm the children.

Familiarity with the Lenore Walker's concept of the "cycle of violence" may also help clinicians understand why victims have difficulty leaving their batterers. "Cycle of violence" refers to a three-stage sequence of events common in DV relationships.[67] During the tension-building first phase, verbal abuse, emotional abuse, and controlling behavior create an atmosphere of "walking on eggshells" for the victim. The tension escalates until a violent eruption marks the second phase of the cycle. During the third phase (often referred to as the "honeymoon" phase), the batterer expresses remorse and again becomes the loving attentive person with whom the victim fell in love. Clinicians who see victims during the honeymoon phase rarely encounter a woman who is ready to leave the relationship. At this point victims view the relationship through the loving eyes of a newlywed. The cycle of violence also

can be thought of as a type of "intermittent reinforcement."[68] The victim's decision to stay with the batterer is viewed as an intermittently reinforced behavior, which is classically the most difficult type of behavior to change. Other reasons victims cite for not leaving an abusive partner include a belief in commitment, a desire to shield their partner from legal harm, financial dependence on a partner, and religious convictions about divorce. (Further discussion of this complex topic can be found in the text by Barnett and La Violette's *It Could Happen to Anyone: Why Battered Women Stay.*[69])

Same-Sex Relationships

Little is known about the incidence and prevalence of homosexual female DV victims found in the medical setting. Most hospital- or clinic-based studies specifically ask women about aggression from a male partner and thus exclude women in same-sex relationships. Studies in other settings have found that lesbian women experience levels of DV equal to those of heterosexual women.[70] Unfortunately, professionals often receive inadequate or no coursework or practical experience helping lesbian women deal with DV.[71] Just as with heterosexual patients, practitioners must universally screen their lesbian patients for DV. Questions about DV should be framed in gender-neutral terms so that a lesbian woman can feel comfortable talking about abuse to a clinician who may be unaware of her orientation. Furthermore, local referral services should be tailored to helping those in same-sex relationships as much shelter-based counseling is limited to female victims of male violence.

Immigrant Women

Battered immigrant women may be less likely to reveal abuse, due to cultural norms that embrace husband-to-wife marital violence and control. Many cultures blame the woman for any type of marital discord, including violence directed only at her. A victim's own family may desert her if she leaves her husband for any reason, even fear of homicide. Additionally, undocumented immigrant women may fear deportation of themselves and their partners if the abuse draws the attention of law enforcement agencies. Although an immigrant victim may have legal residence after marriage to a citizen batterer, the batterer often uses his wife's immigration status to control her and to force her to remain in the violent relationship. If a battered immigrant woman decides to leave her abuser, the financial and legal services available to her may not match those available to a US citizen.

The language barrier may be a further impediment to an immigrant victim's obtaining help. In recent years federal and state governments have attempted to correct some of the legal problems that plague battered immigrant women. According to the federal 1994 Violence Against Women Act, battered women who depend on their perpetrator to legally stay in the United States may self-petition for legal permanent residence as they attempt to separate.[72] Clinicians who treat immigrant patients must be aware of these issues when asking about and uncovering DV. Information on local resources for ethnic minorities and for immigrants should be part of any protocol for treating DV victims in a medical setting.

Involvement of Law Enforcement Agencies

In general most patients should be given the choice of whether or not to involve law enforcement officers in their situation. Immediate consultation with law enforcement personnel may enhance victim safety by giving the victim immediate access to restraining orders (in some states). Additionally, acute injuries to the victim often lead to the immediate arrest of the perpetrator and to temporary victim safety. In the last several years many states, counties, and cities have begun DV training for law enforcement officers that provides them with the sensitivity and knowledge to appropriately interview and counsel victims. However, this training is not universal, and clinicians must be aware of the limitations of their local law enforcement agencies. In several special circumstances law enforcement must be contacted regardless of the victim's wishes. Almost all states have laws that require medical personnel to notify law enforcement agencies when a patient presents with injuries caused by a firearm or some other deadly weapon. Many states also require that clinicians report any victim of aggravated assault or a violent crime. Since DV is considered a crime in all areas of the country, clinicians again must be aware of their local reporting mandates.

Several states recently passed legislation specifically targeted at DV reporting. These laws may require medical personnel to report victims with injuries to state agencies[73–75] or, as in the cases of California[76] and Colorado,[77] to law enforcement agencies. Victim advocates and battered-women focus groups express ambivalence about these mandatory laws regarding DV reporting.[78,79] These groups fear that the involvement of law enforcement agencies against the will of a victim further strips power from her and may anger the perpetrator, leading to more aggressive violence. However, preliminary work in surveying battered women finds that the majority of them favor mandatory reporting legislation.[80] No outcome-based evidence exists to either support or refute the benefit of mandatory reporting. Clinicians should follow their patients' wishes when possible but should also adhere to their local legal reporting obligations.

CONCLUSION

"Battering happens because society somehow has given its consent."[69]

The ultimate solution to the problem of DV lies in a change in this societal attitude. All areas of the community, including law enforcement agencies, schools, the media, and welfare services, have a role to play in changing old attitudes that ignore DV and in helping those who are already battered improve their situations. As well, medical professionals must cease to be part of a society that sanctions domestic violence. The literature overwhelmingly supports the concept that DV victims want help from their doctors and that they are contacting the medical setting frequently for this help. Clearly, medical resources alone cannot solve this societal problem, but through collaborative community response and the four principles of identification, documentation, treatment, and referral, clinicians can give their patients and society's next generation a chance to live without the burden of domestic violence.

RESOURCES

Violence Against Women Office
Office for Victims of Crime
US Department of Justice
810 7th Street Northwest
Washington, DC 20531
Telephone: 1-800-799-SAFE (1-800-799-7233) (National Domestic Violence Hotline)
       1-800-787-3224 (TDD for hearing impaired)
       (202) 616-8894
Web site: www.usdoj.gov/vawo (Violence Against Women Office)
      www.ohp.usdoj.gov/ovc (Office for Victims of Crime)

The Violence Against Women Office of the US Department of Justice provides emergency and non-emergency referrals to local domestic violence (DV) resources throughout the United States. Information is available in over 140 languages through the use of interpreters. The Office for Victims of Crime provides information on state compensation for medical and legal expenses and lost wages due to DV.

American Bar Association
Commission on Domestic Violence
740 15th Street Northwest
9th Floor
Washington, DC 20005-1022
Telephone: (202) 662-1737
Web site: abanet.org

The American Bar Association offers information about domestic violence, including free educational information for patients, accessible through the ABA Web site.

The American College of Obstetricians and Gynecologists
409 12th Street Southwest
Washington, DC 20090-6920
Web site: acog.org

Information for victims of violence against women (including written materials, resources, and phone numbers) is available at the ACOG Web site.

National Center for Victims of Crime
2111 Wilson Boulevard, Suite 300
Arlington, Virginia 22201
Telephone: 1-800-394-2255
       1-800-211-7996 (TDD for hearing impaired)
Web site: www.nvc.org

The National Center for Victims of Crime provides information on the rights of crime victims.

Ayuda
1736 Columbia Road Northwest
Washington, DC 20009
Telephone: (202) 387-4848
Web site: incacorp.com/ayuda

Ayuda provides help and resources for Spanish-speaking patients.

RESOURCES (continued)

Advocates for Abused and Battered Lesbians
PO Box 85596
Seattle, Washington 98105-9998
Telephone: (206) 547-8191
Web site: www.aabl.org

Advocates for Abused and Battered Lesbians provides information and referrals for battered lesbian women.

Health Resource Center on Domestic Violence
383 Rhode Island Street, Suite 304
San Francisco, California 94103-5133
Telephone: (415) 252-8900
       1-800-313-1310
       1-888-Rx-ABUSE (1-888-792-2873)
Web site: fvpf.org/health

The Health Resource Center on Domestic Violence provides extensive information for clinicians on all aspects of caring for victims of domestic violence. Materials are also available by mail.

Family Peace Project
Family and Community Medicine
Medical College of Wisconsin
210 NW Barstow #201
Waukesha, Wisconsin 53188
Telephone: (414) 548-6903
Web site: www.family.mcw.edu

Run by the Medical College of Wisconsin, this site provides guidelines and protocols to the clinician for comprehensive treatment of victims of domestic violence.

Family Violence Prevention Fund
383 Rhode Island Street, Suite 304
San Francisco, California 94103-5133
Telephone: (415) 252-8900
Web site: www.fvpf.org

The Family Violence Prevention Fund provides survivor's stories and basic information on domestic violence (DV), health care and legal issues surrounding DV, and innovative DV programs.

American College of Emergency Physicians
Mailing address:
American College of Emergency Physicians
PO Box 619911
Dallas, Texas 75261-9911

RESOURCES (continued)

Street address:
American College of Emergency Physicians
1125 Executive Circle
Irving, Texas 75038-2522
Telephone: (979) 550-0911
            1-800-798-1822
Web site: www.acep.org

The American College of Emergency Physicians maintains a Web site on domestic violence (DV). The site contains updated DV facts, information about related publications, and copies of policies that relate to DV in the health care setting.

American Medical Association
515 North State Street
Chicago, Illinois 60610
Telephone: (312) 464-5000
Web site: www.ama-assn.org

The American Medical Association provides abstracts and some full texts of important domestic violence (DV) medical literature. Additionally, DV clinical treatment guidelines are available on request.

Physicians for a Violence-Free Society
San Francisco General Hospital
Building 1, Room 300
San Francisco, California 94110
Telephone: (415) 821-8209
Web site: www.pvs.org

Physicians for a Violence-Free Society provides educational materials for health care workers, including "The Physician's Guide to DV: How to Ask the Right Questions and Recognize Abuse" and a self-contained domestic violence documentation course.

National Resource Center on Domestic Violence
Telephone: 1-800-537-2238

The National Resource Center on Domestic Violence provides information and resources, policy development, and technical assistance to enhance community response and prevention of domestic violence.

Resource Center on Child Protection and Custody
Telephone: 1-800-527-3223

The Resource Center on Child Protection and Custody of the National Council of Juvenile and Family Court Judges provides information, consultation, technical assistance, and legal research for child protection and custody issues related to domestic violence.

REFERENCES

1. Bachman R. Violence against women: a National Crime Victimization Survey report. Bureau of Justice Statistics report. Washington (DC): US Department of Justice; 1994. Publication No.: NCJ-145325.

2. Muelleman RL, Burgess P. Male victims of domestic violence and their history of perpetrating violence. Acad Emerg Med 1998;5:866–70.

3. Straus MA, Gelles RJ, Steinmetz SK. Violence in the home. In: Straus MS, Gelles RJ, Steinmetz SK, editors. Behind closed doors: violence in the American family. Newbury Park (CA): Sage Publications Ltd.; 1981. p. 4–28.

4. Straus MA, Gelles RJ. Societal change and change in family violence from 1975 to 1985 as revealed by two national surveys. J Marriage Fam 1986;48:465–79.

5. Browne A. Violence against women by male partners. Am Psychol 1993;48:1077–87.

6. Rodgers K. Wife assault: the findings of a national survey. Stat Can Cat 1994;14:1–21.

7. McLennan W. Women's safety Australia. Canberra: Australian Bureau of Statistics. 1996.

8. Smith PH, Morroco KE, Butts J. Partner homicide in context: a population-based perspective. Homicide Studies 1998;2:400–21.

9. Morroco KE, Runyan C, Butts JD. Femicide in North Carolina, 1991-1993: a statewide study of patterns and precursors. Homicide Studies 1998;2:422–46.

10. Campbell JC. "If I can't have you, no one can." Power and control in homicide of female partners. In: Radford J, Russell D, editors. Femicide: the politics of women killing. Boston: Twayne; 1992. p. 99–113.

11. Straus MA, Gelles RJ. Physical violence in American families. New Brunswick (NJ): Transaction Publishers; 1990.

12. Gin NE, Rucker L, Frayne S, et al. Prevalence of domestic violence among patients in three ambulatory care internal medicine clinics. J Gen Intern Med 1991;6:317–22.

13. Elliott BA, Johnson MM. Domestic violence in a primary care setting. Arch Fam Med 1995;4:113–9.

14. Freund KM, Bak SM, Blackhall L. Identifying domestic violence in primary care practice. J Gen Intern Med 1996;11:44–6.

15. Hamberger KL, Saunders DG, Hovey M. Prevalence of domestic violence in community practice and rate of physician inquiry. Fam Med 1992;24:283–7.

16. Johnson D, Elliott B. Screening for domestic violence in a rural family practice. Minn Med 1997;80:43–5.

17. McCauley J, Kern DE, Kolodner K, et al. The "battering syndrome": prevalence and clinical characteristics of domestic violence in primary care internal medicine practices. Ann Intern Med 1995;123: 737–46.

18. McKenzie KC, Burns RB, Mcarthy EP, et al. Prevalence of domestic violence in an inpatient female population. J Gen Intern Med 1998;13:277–9.

19. McFarlane J, Parker B, Soeken K, et al. Assessing for abuse during pregnancy. JAMA 1992;267:3176–8.

20. Rath GD, Jaratt LG, Leonardson G. Rates of domestic violence against adult women by men partners. J Am Board Fam Pract 1989;227:227–33.

21. Abbott J, Johnson R, Koziol-McLain J, et al. Domestic violence against women: incidence and prevalence in an emergency department population. JAMA 1995; 273:1763–7.

22. Anglin D, Heger AH, Hutson HR, Chan L. Violence among intimates in an inner-city ED population. Acad Emerg Med 1996;3:444.

23. Bates L, Redman S, Brown W, Hancock L. Domestic violence experienced by women attending an accident and emergency department. Aust J Public Health 1995;19:293–9.

24. Dearwater SR, Coben JH, Campbell JC, et al. Prevalence of intimate partner abuse in women treated at community hospital emergency departments. JAMA 1998;280:433–8.

25. Feldhaus KM, Koziol-McLain J, Amsbury HL, et al. Accuracy of 3 brief screening questions for detecting partner abuse in the emergency department. JAMA 1997;277:1357–61.

26. Muelleman RL, Lenaghan PA, Pakieser RA. Battered women: injury locations and types. Ann Emerg Med 1996;28:486–92.

27. Olson L, Anctil C, Fullerton L, et al. Increasing emergency physician's recognition of domestic violence. Ann Emerg Med 1996;27:741–6.

28. Roberts GL, O'Toole BI, Raphael B, et al. Prevalence study of domestic violence victims in an emergency department. Ann Emerg Med 1996;27:747–53.

29. Sachs CJ, Baraff LJ, Peek C. Need for law enforcement in cases of intimate partner violence in a university ED. Am J Emerg Med 1998;16:60–3.

30. Muelleman RL, Liewer JD. How often do women in the emergency department without intimate violence injuries return with such injuries? Acad Emerg Med 1998;5:982–5.

31. Parker B, McFarlane J, Soeken K, et al. Physical and emotional abuse in pregnancy: a comparison of adult and teenage women. Nurs Res 1993;42:173–8.

32. Geilen AC, O'Campo PJ, Faden RR, et al. Interpersonal conflict and physical violence during the childbearing year. Soc Sci Med 1994;39:781–7.

33. Gelles RJ, Straus MA. The medical and psycological cost of family violence. In: Straus M, Gelles RJ, editors. Physical violence in American families: risk factors and adaptations to violence in 8,145 families. New Brunswick (NJ): Transaction Publishers; 1990.

34. Eby K, Campbell J, Sullivan C, Davidson WS. Health effects of experiences of sexual violence for women with abusive partners. Health Care Women Int 1995;16:563–76.

35. Roberts GL, Williams GM, Lawrence JM, Raphael B. How does domestic violence affect women's mental health? Aust Woman's Health 1998;28:117-29.

36. Taggart L, Mattson S. Delay in prenatal care as a result of battering in pregnancy. Health Care Women Int 1996;17:25–34.

37. Parker B, McFarlane J, Soeken K. Abuse during pregnancy: effects on maternal complications and infant birthweight in adult and teen women. Obstet Gynecol 1994;84:323–8.

38. McFarlane J, Parker B, Soeken K. Abuse during pregnancy: associations with maternal health and infant birthweight. Nurs Res 1996;45:37–42.

39. Jaffe PG, Wolfe DA, Wilson SK. Children of battered; women. Newbury Park (CA), Sage Publications Ltd., 1990.

40. Kilpatrick KL, Litt M, Williams LM. Post-traumatic stress disorder in child witnesses to domestic violence. Am J Orthopsychiatry 1997;67:693–44.

41. Widom CS. The cycle of violence. Washington (DC): US Department of Justice, National Institute of Justice; 1992.

42. Hotaling GT, Sugarman DB. An analysis of risk markers in husband to wife violence: the current state of knowledge. Violence Vict 1986;1:101–24.

43. Bowker LH, Maurer L. The medical treatment of battered wives. Womens Health 1987;12:25–45.

44. Council on Scientific Affairs, American Medical Association. Violence against women: relevance for medical practitioners. JAMA 1992;267:3184–95.

45. American College of Emergency Physicians. Emergency medicine and domestic violence. Ann Emerg Med 1995;25:442–3.

46. American College of Obstetricians and Gynecologists. ACOG technical bulletin no. 209: domestic violence. Int J Gynaecol Obstet 1995;51:161–70.

47. American Academy of Family Practice. Family violence. Am Fam Physician 1994;50:1636–46.

48. Quillian JP. Screening for spousal or partner abuse in a community health setting. J Am Acad Nurse Pract 1996;8:155–60.

49. Emergency Nurses Association. Position statement: domestic violence. Park Ridge (IL): Emergency Nurses Association; 1996.

50. Hudson WW, McIntosh SR. The assessment of spouse abuse. Two quantifiable dimensions. J Marriage Fam 1981;43:873–85.

51. Straus MA. Measuring intrafamily conflict and violence: the Conflict Tactics (CT) Scales. J Marriage Fam 1979;4:75–88.

52. Soeken KL, McFarlane J, Parker B, Lominack MC. The Abuse Assessment Screen; a clinical instrument to measure frequency, severity, and perpetrator of abuse against women. In: Campbell JC, editor. Empowering survivors of abuse. Sage Publications Ltd.; 1998. p. 195–202.

53. Drossman DA, Talley NJ, Leserman J, et al. Sexual and physical abuse and gastrointestinal illness. Ann Intern Med 1995;123:782–94.

54. Gabbe S, Neibyl J, Simpson J. Obstetrics: normal and problem pregnancies. 3rd ed. New York: Churchill Livingstone; 1996. p. 936, 1048.

55. Brendtro M, Bowker L. Battered women: how nurses can help. Issues Mental Health Nurs 1989;10:169–80.

56. Larkin GL, Hyman KB, Mathias SR, et al. Universal screening for intimate partner violence in the emergency department: importance of patient and provider factors. Ann Emerg Med 1999;33:669–75.

57. Campbell JC, Alford P. The dark consequences of marital rape. Am J Nurs 1989;89:946–9.

58. Hamberger LK, Ambuel B, Marbella A, Donze J. Physician interaction with battered women; the women's perspective. Arch Fam Med 1998;7:575–82.

59. Joint Commission on Accreditation of Healthcare Organizations. 1996 accreditation manual for hospitals. Oakbrook Terrace (IL): The Joint Commission; 1996. p. 39–50.

60. California Assembly Bill No. 890. California Health and Safety Code §1233.5 (2001).

61. Campbell J, Sharps P, Block CR, et al. Risk factors for homicide in violent intimate relationships. NIJ/NIH Grant No.: Ro1 DA/AA11156. Baltimore (MD); 1998.

62. Tompson MP, Kaslow NJ, Kingree JB, et al. Partner abuse and posttraumatic stress disorder as risk factors for suicide attempts in a sample of low-income, inner city women. J Trauma Stress 1999; 12:59–72.

63. McKibbon L, De Vos E, Newberger EK. Victimization of mothers of abused children: a controlled study. Pediatrics 1989;84:531–5.

64. Isaacs JL. The Law and the abused and neglected child. Pediatrics 1973;51 Suppl 4:783–92.

65. Hart B. Beyond the "duty to warn": a therapist's "duty to protect" battered woman and children. In: Yool K, Bograd M, editors. Feminist perspectives on wife abuse. Newbury Park (CA): Sage Publications Ltd.; 1988. p. 234–48.

66. Florida Governor's Task Force on Domestic and Sexual Violence. Florida mortality review project. 1997. p. 47.

67. Walker LE. The battered woman. New York: Harper and Row; 1979.

68. Wetzel L, Ross MA. Psychology and social ramifications of battering: observations leading to a counseling methodology for victims of domestic violence. Personnel Guidance J 1983;61:423–8.

69. Barnett OW, La Violette AD. It could happen to anyone: why battered women stay. Newbury Park (CA): Sage Publications, Inc.; 1993.

70. Waldner-Haugrud LK, Gratch LV, Magruder B. Victimization and perpetration rates of violence in gay and lesbian relationships: gender issues explored. Violence Vict 1997;12:173–84.

71. Wise AJ, Bowman SL. Comparison of beginning counselors' responses to lesbian vs. heterosexual partner abuse. Violence Vict 1997;12:127–35.

72. Self-Petitioning for LPR Status if Battered, 8 US Code Sect. 1154(a)(1) (1952).

73. Kentucky Rev. Stat. Ann. 209.010-.990 (Jan 2, 1978).

74. New Hampshire Rev. Stat. Ann. 631:6 (7/3/1969).

75. New Mexico Stat. Ann. 27-7-14 to 13 (1978).

76. California Penal Code §11160 (2001).

77. Colorado House Bill No. 95-1114 (1995).

78. Kaplan B. Should laws requiring doctors to report domestic violence be repealed? Physicians Wkly 1995;12:40.

79. Rodriguez MA, Craig AM, Mooney DR, et al. Patient attitudes about mandatory reporting of domestic violence: implications for health care professionals. West J Med 1998;169:337–41.

80. Sachs CJ, Campbell J, Chu L, Gomberg L. Intimate partner violence victims' attitude toward mandatory reporting [abstract]. Acad Emerg Med 1999;6:465.

89

OBESITY

Carolyn Crandall, MD, FACP

Obesity has reached epidemic proportions in the United States.[1] The prevalence of obesity is 18% among Caucasian women aged 25 to 34 years and 35% among those aged 55 to 64 years. The prevalence of obesity in African American women is twice that of Caucasian women.[2] The impact of obesity on the health status of American women continues to grow. Obesity is the second leading cause of preventable death in the United States, after smoking.[3] One hundred billion dollars a year of combined health (70 billion dollars) and diet food (33 billion dollars) spending are attributed to obesity.[4]

Despite the tremendous impact of obesity on the health of women and the difficulty patients have in achieving weight loss, most clinicians have little or no formal training in the treatment of obesity. This chapter summarizes current research and treatment recommendations.

DEFINITION

Because the "gold standard" for measuring body fat is densitometry (ie, the cumbersome process of weighing the subject in air and totally immersed in water),[5] more convenient tools have evolved for defining obesity more easily. Such tools have traditionally been derived from measures of height and weight, comparing individual measurements to standardized tables. Each of these tools has drawbacks. However, in clinical practice, all will accurately identify the vast majority of patients who are at increased health risk from obesity.

A table of average weights (eg, the National Health and Nutrition Examination Surveys) is a percentile ranking of weight for height and sex. Weight above the 85th percentile is called overweight. This measurement does not allow a risk to be associated with each weight level.[6] Ideal weight tables, such as the 1983 Metropolitan Life Insurance tables, categorize by height and body frame.[7] These tables tell at what weight levels people live the longest. However, the insured are not a randomly selected group from the population at large, and they are of above-average health.[8] The body mass index (BMI) is the weight in kilograms divided by the square of the height in meters and is expressed as kilograms per squared meter (kg/m^2) (Table 89–1). Patients with a BMI ≥ 25 are generally considered to be overweight. The use of BMI can lead to the overdiagnosis of obesity in muscular people because of excess lean body mass (Figure 89–1).

Bioelectric impedance, the use of which is growing in popularity, is based on the observation that fat-free mass has much greater electrical conductivity than has fat. It is safe, noninvasive, and portable.[9] With the use of bioelectric impedance, obesity for younger and older women is defined as $> 32\%$ and $> 35\%$ of body fat, respectively.[10] Obesity is defined at a higher level in older women because body fat increases with age.[11]

ETIOLOGY: ROLES OF GENES, ENVIRONMENT, AND GENDER

The heritability of obesity is at least as strong as that of hypertension, alcoholism, and schizophrenia.[12] Identical twins have similar body weights when brought up apart, and adopted children do not follow their adoptive parents' weight the way the natural children of their adoptive parents do.[13] Monozygotic twins have a higher correlation of obesity than do dizygotic twins.[14] It has been estimated that 25 to 35% of the variance in BMI in the general population can be attributed to genetic factors.[6]

There are several known genetic obesity syndromes, of which Prader-Willi syndrome is the

TABLE 89–1. Disease Risk by Body Mass Index and Waist Circumference*

Type of Overweight/Obesity	Waist Circumference (cm)	BMI	Disease Risk
Overweight	≤ 88	25.0–29.9	Increased
Class I obesity	≤ 88	30.0–34.9	High
	> 88	25.0–29.9	High
Class II obesity	≤ 88	35.0–39.9	Very high
	> 88	30.0–39.9	Very high
Class III obesity	Any	≥ 40	Extremely high

*As determined by the Expert Panel on the Identification, Evaluation, and Treatment of Overweight and Obesity in Adults.
BMI = body mass index.
Adapted from Executive summary of the clinical guidelines on the identification, evaluation, and treatment of overweight and obesity in adults. Arch Intern Med 1998;158:1855–67.

most common. However, these identified obesity syndromes account for a tiny minority of obese patients.[15,16] For the vast majority of obese patients, genetic factors leading to obesity are likely due to a large number of genetic loci.[17]

Leptin is an adipose tissue–derived signaling factor encoded by the *obese* gene. Its possible role in the etiology of obesity has received much attention

in the scientific and lay literature. It is hypothesized to be a satiety factor in animals. However, the biologic activity of leptin in humans has not yet been established.[18] Individual variations in plasma leptin levels are strongly correlated to BMI, systolic and diastolic blood pressures, triglycerides, uric acid, and fasting insulin and glucose.[19] Leptin levels, corrected for fat mass, are greater in premenopausal

	19	20	21	22	23	24	25	26	27	28	29	30	31	32	33	34	35
Height (inches)							**Body Weight (pounds)**										
58	91	96	100	105	110	115	119	124	129	134	138	143	148	153	158	162	167
59	94	99	104	109	114	119	124	128	133	138	143	148	153	158	163	168	173
60	97	102	107	112	118	123	128	133	138	143	148	153	158	163	168	174	179
61	100	106	111	116	122	127	132	137	143	148	153	158	164	169	174	180	185
62	104	109	115	120	126	131	136	142	147	153	158	164	169	175	180	186	191
63	107	113	118	124	130	135	141	146	152	158	163	169	175	180	186	191	197
64	110	116	122	128	134	140	145	151	157	163	169	174	180	186	192	197	204
65	114	120	126	132	138	144	150	156	162	168	174	180	186	192	198	204	210
66	118	124	130	136	142	148	155	161	167	173	179	186	192	198	204	210	216
67	121	127	134	140	146	153	159	166	172	178	185	191	198	204	211	217	223
68	125	131	138	144	151	158	164	171	177	184	190	197	203	210	216	223	230
69	128	135	142	149	155	162	169	176	182	189	196	203	209	216	223	230	236
70	132	139	146	153	160	167	174	181	188	195	202	209	216	222	229	236	243
71	136	143	150	157	165	172	179	186	193	200	208	215	222	229	236	243	250
72	140	147	154	162	169	177	184	191	199	206	213	221	228	235	242	250	258
73	144	151	159	166	174	182	189	197	204	212	219	227	235	242	250	257	265
74	148	155	163	171	179	186	194	202	210	218	225	233	241	249	256	264	272
75	152	160	168	176	184	192	200	208	216	224	232	240	248	256	264	272	279
76	156	164	172	180	189	197	205	213	221	230	238	246	254	263	271	279	287

FIGURE 89–1. Body mass index chart. (Data from the National Heart, Lung, and Blood Institute. Clinical guidelines on the identification, evaluation, and treatment of overweight and obesity in adults: executive summary, 1998.)

females than in postmenopausal females, whose levels in turn are greater than those in males.[20] Increases in leptin concentration with increasing BMI are greater in women than in men.[20]

Because leptin levels are relatively high in obese humans compared to lean humans, obesity may result from inadequate leptin signaling for a given leptin concentration.[21] This has practical implications: exogenous leptin may not be effective in the obese if leptin transporters are already saturated.[22] Most human obesity is probably not due to defective leptin production.[20] Additional genes will have to be found to explain all of the genetic contribution to obesity.[23]

Although there may be a genetic influence on the amount and distribution of fat in humans, obesity occurs within genetically diverse populations, suggesting an environmental component. Twin studies show a range of 30 to 80% heritability of obesity, suggesting a significant role left to environmental causes.[14] In some patients, an important environmental component of obesity is iatrogenic. Medications that potentially cause weight gain include phenothiazines, tricyclic antidepressants, antiepileptics, and steroids (megestrol acetate, glucocorticoids).

RISK ASSESSMENT: USE OF THE HIP-TO-WAIST RATIO

Weight distribution is described as either upper (android), which is more common in men, or lower (gynecoid), which is more common in women.[6] The distinction is important because compared to gynecoid obesity, android (abdominal) obesity (whether in men or women) is associated with greater risks of hypertension, cardiovascular disease, hyperinsulinemia, diabetes mellitus, and stroke. Obese men are more likely to have the android kind of obesity and hence are generally at higher risk of obesity complications than are women, but women with the android type of obesity are at higher risk for complications than are women with the gynecoid type of obesity.[6]

Determination of weight distribution is via the measurement of body circumference at the waist and hips. The waist is measured halfway between the rib cage and the top of the pelvis in the anterior axillary line; the hip is measured at the level of the greater trochanters.[24] The waist-to-hip ratio is a better correlate of abdominal visceral adipose tissue volume, insulin resistance, glucose intolerance, hypertriglyceridemia, hypertension, and hyperandrogenicity than is the BMI.[25]

An abnormal waist-to-hip ratio is defined as > 0.85 in women because a waist-to-hip ratio above this cutoff has the potential to change the risk of morbidity and mortality.[4,6] The Iowa Women's Health Study found that the waist-to-hip ratio also predicts the risk of death in older women better than the BMI.[25] The women at the highest risk of death in the Iowa Women's Health Study were those with a low BMI and a high waist-to-hip ratio. These results may be a reflection of the fact that excess abdominal fat is thought to be more hazardous than overall body size.

Some experts recently began recommending the use of waist circumference, as opposed to the waist-to-hip ratio, in the assessment of cardiovascular risk.[26] Waist circumference cutoffs are reported to identify not only those with a high BMI but also those with a lower BMI in the setting of a high waist-to-hip ratio, the latter group being at an increased health risk that is related to their fat distribution.[27] The report of the Expert Panel on the Identification, Evaluation, and Treatment of Overweight and Obesity in Adults (henceforth referred to as the Expert Panel) stratifies obesity risk based on waist circumference (see Table 89–1).[28]

Many women notice weight gain at the time of menopause. However, weight gain in women may be an aging-associated phenomenon and not a menopause-associated phenomenon.[29] The distribution of fat, on the other hand, may be affected by the hormonal changes of menopause. Premenopausal women have more gynecoid fat distribution, and postmenopausal women have more android fat distribution whereas the fat distribution in perimenopausal women is less gynecoid than in premenopausal women.[30] This android distribution may be partly responsible for the association of lipid worsening and glucose intolerance with the postmenopausal state.[31] The relationship of obesity to cardiovascular disease and stroke is mainly due to the specific association of these end points to android-type obesity.[32]

Combined hormone replacement therapy (HRT) may prevent abdominal fat increase after menopause and may maintain the premenopausal relation between fat mass and lean mass.[33] Since it is accepted that female fat deposition is generally femoral it makes intuitive sense that the female sex hormones would affect lipid accumulation in the femoral (but not the abdominal) region. Users of HRT have lower waist-to-hip ratios and waist circumferences and higher high-density lipoprotein levels than do nonusers.[34,35] However, there may be other (confounding) differences between users and nonusers, based on differences in cardiac risk factors. More data are needed.

COMPLICATIONS

Documented complications of obesity are summarized in Table 89–2. In addition to simply affecting overall weight, weight gain and the distribution of fat in adulthood may also affect risks for certain conditions. The Framingham Heart Study found that weight gain after young adulthood increased the risk of cardiovascular disease (CVD) in women.[36] The subsequent Nurses' Health Study confirmed that a weight gain of 10 kg or more during adulthood doubled the risk of coronary events.[37] Another Nurses' Health Study report found a direct relationship between weight gain from 18 years of age or BMI $\geq$ 27 kg/m^2 and the risk of ischemic stroke.[38] The Iowa Women's Health Study found an association of hip-to-waist ratio with breast cancer risk that was mostly limited to those women with a family history of breast cancer.[39]

The alarming rise in diabetes mellitus (DM) is probably due to the current rapid rise in the prevalence of obesity.[12] The Nurses' Health Study reported that the risk of DM rose with a BMI > 22 and that weight gain since age 18 years was strongly associated to risk.[40] Even women with a "normal" BMI of 23 to 25 had a fourfold increased risk. Weight gain at any age (up to 65 years in this study) is associated with increased risk for DM among women.

The Nurses' Health Study reports the lowest mortality among women that weigh at least 15% less than the US average for age-matched women.[41] Mortality was more than twice as high in women with a BMI > 29.0, compared with the leanest women. A 10-kg weight gain since age 18 years was associated with higher mortality from cardiovascular disease, cancer, and all causes. Based on multiple studies and for multiple medical reasons, it is not necessarily healthy to gain weight, even within the same weight range.[42]

TABLE 89–2. Complications of Obesity*

Diabetes
Hypertension
Lipid abnormalities
  Low HDL
  High LDL
  High triglycerides
Coronary artery disease
Cardiomyopathy
Ischemic stroke
Irregular menses
Birth defects (neural tube defects)
Sleep apnea
Pulmonary embolism
Osteoarthritis
Varicose veins
Gallstones
Cancer
  Endometrial
  Ovarian
  Cervical
  Colorectal
  Gallbladder and biliary system

*Conditions with a statistically significant increased relative risk for obese persons when compared to lean individuals. HDL = high-density lipoprotein; LDL = low-density lipoprotein. Adapted from Bray et al,[10] Barbieri,[29] Hubert et al,[36] Manson et al,[37] Rexrode et al,[38] Sellers et al,[39] Colditz et al,[40] and Stunkard,[87] Sjostrom L, Larsson B, Backman L, et al. Swedish obese subjects (SOS). Recruitment for an intervention study and a selected description of the obese state. Int J Obes Relat Metab Disord 1992;16:465–79; Pi-Sunyer FX. Medical hazards of obesity. Ann Intern Med 1993;119:655–60; and Maclure KM, Hayes KC, Colditz GA, et al. Weight, diet, and the risk of symptomatic gallstones in middle-aged women. N Engl J Med 1989;321:563–9.

Weight loss can beneficially affect obesity complications. Even a modest ($\leq$ 10%) weight loss in obese patients improves glycemic control, HTN, and cholesterol in the obese.[43–45] A weight loss of only 5 to 10 kg can noticeably improve sleep apnea.[46] The Framingham Knee Osteoarthritis Study reported that weight loss decreased the risk for symptomatic knee osteoarthritis in women.[47] Also, the pain and disability of low back pain and osteoarthritis of the knee can improve with weight loss.[44] Moderate weight loss brings about a marked clinical improvement in hirsutism and the ability to conceive, as well as normalization of menses, reduction in insulin

TABLE 89–3. An Approach to the Obese Patient

Assess

 Patient's present desire to lose weight

 Patient's current level of exercise

 Patient's current level of support at home and
   at work

 Patient's understanding of potential or established
   obesity-related comorbidity

 Patient's body mass index

Begin treatment

 Review appropriate daily caloric goal and food
   pyramid.

 If patient is not ready to change diet immediately,
   reassess at regular intervals.

 Start daily exercise (may be minimal, depending
   on pre-existing level of fitness).

 Review portion control and food substitution.

 After several months of compliance with diet and
   exercise modification, consider medication
   for those who meet criteria.

concentrations, and increases in sex hormone binding globulin in obese women with polycystic ovarian syndrome (PCOS).[29,48–51]

INITIAL TREATMENT

For most patients, the initial approach to weight loss should include a low-calorie diet, behavioral modification, and exercise. This approach is summarized in Table 89–3 and is described in more detail below.

Low-Calorie Diet

Weight loss necessitates a decrease of 500 kcal/d below calculated maintenance needs. The Expert Panel recommends an initial goal of a loss of 10% of the patient's baseline weight over approximately 6 months via a calorie deficit of 500 to 1,000 kcal/d.[28] Weight normalization need not (should not) be the ultimate goal of a weight reduction strategy.[52] Normalization of food intake is the first priority for patients with the tendency to fast. The importance of eating regular meals at least three times daily should be impressed upon patients.

The Expert Panel recommends a diet with an intake of 1,000 to 1,200 kcal/d for women, to result in 0.45 to 0.90 kg/week of weight loss in 6 months,

via reduction of both dietary fat and carbohydrate. Since the basal metabolic rate is higher at heavier weights, patients who weigh more lose weight faster at a given energy intake level.

The emphasis on reducing dietary fat as part of an overall weight loss plan comes from studies of the role of fat intake in obesity. Fat intake is poorly regulated (ie, excess intake at one meal does not cause a compensatory decreased intake at the next meal).[13] Since dietary fat is converted to body fat 25% more efficiently than is carbohydrate, weight gain is more likely after fat consumption than after calorically equivalent carbohydrate consumption over the long term.[29] In regard to the reduction of dietary fat intake, there is still debate about whether the proportion of calories derived from fat each day or the absolute amount of fat ingested each day is the most important aspect to emphasize.[53] The 1995 US Department of Agriculture/Department of Health and Human Services (DHHS) document "Dietary Guidelines for Americans" includes a review of the "food pyramid" for healthy eating, a section on what portions constitute a serving, and advice on reading labels.[42] Patient resources on dietary guidelines are summarized at the end of this chapter.

Behavior Modification

The behavior modification process optimally involves the supplying of weight maintenance tools that last forever. Besides being acutely useful for weight loss, behavior modification is of critical importance in the long-term maintenance of weight loss from other weight loss modalities.[46] The central behavioral concept in weight control is called "self-monitoring."

Teaching patients to use self-monitoring techniques involves asking them to maintain detailed food intake diaries (ie, recording what was eaten, with whom, and where). Diaries include measures of the degree of hunger, descriptions of how the food was eaten, and records of the feelings or emotions involved. People generally underestimate their food intake by one-third. Patients who self-monitor most consistently lose more weight than those who self-monitor least consistently. Regardless of the consistency of monitoring, patients lose more weight during the periods of their most consistent monitoring.[54]

Stimulus control is a process whereby cues causing inappropriate eating or exercise are reduced.[55]

Cognitive-behavioral strategy addresses the effects that thoughts, moods, diets, and social pressures have on eating control.[56] An individualized plan developed jointly with a patient that addresses how to avoid unhealthy eating in stressful situations is called **contingency management**. These behavioral strategies may be particularly important for women. Women may be more likely to regard depression, stress, low self-esteem, and the need to avoid situations as important reasons for their weight gain, as well as to feel terrible and to regain weight as a response to relapse.[57] Most female "maintainers" are conscious of their behaviors, use social support, and confront problems directly. In contrast, relapsers do not make use of social support, do not directly confront problems, and mostly eat in unconscious response to emotions.[58]

Exercise

The principal cause of obesity may be not diet but inactivity relative to diet. Physical activity is the single best predictor of long-term weight maintenance.[59] Low daily energy expenditure is strongly correlated with the rate of weight gain. This suggests that it is the activity-related energy expenditure part of daily energy expenditure that may predispose to obesity.[60] This is a reason why many feel that decreased physical activity is likely the primary determinant of the increasing prevalence of obesity.[60]

In women, however, the evidence is especially strong that although exercise may help maintain lean body mass, it is not a significantly useful isolated approach to weight loss.[61] Exercise with diet is more effective than either alone, and long-term low-intensity exercise is as effective as high-intensity activity.[12]

Lean tissue is metabolically more active than fat. However, this does not mean that lean patients have higher "metabolisms" than obese patients.[62] Obese persons have higher lean body masses and therefore have higher resting metabolic rates.[63] Therefore, 24-hour energy expenditure in the obese patient is typically greater than that of the sedentary lean patient.[64]

The 1995 Centers for Disease Control and Prevention (CDC)/American College of Sports Medicine (ACSM) recommendations, the Expert Panel, and the 1996 National Institutes of Health (NIH) Consensus Panel reports call for at least 30 minutes of moderate-intensity physical activity "on most, preferably all days of the week."[65,66] The CDC/ACSM recommendations are unique in allowing requirements to be met via the accumulation of intermittent short bouts of activity totaling ≥ 30 minutes on most days.

Exercise prescriptions must be individualized for each patient. Patients with knee pain may be wise to avoid stepping or long-distance running exercises and may be happiest swimming, as may those with low back pain. The creation of an exercise program necessitates creativity on the patient's part. It is best to emphasize consistency first, then duration, intensity, and frequency.[67] Some patients may have to start with 60 seconds of low-intensity aerobic work, then 60 seconds of moderate-intensity exercise, until continuous exercise is possible.[68] Severely obese or sedentary patients may only be able to start an exercise program by standing with support.[46]

WEIGHT MAINTENANCE: PREDICTORS AND BARRIERS TO SUCCESS

Program length is a good predictor of program success for behavioral weight loss strategies; longer programs are more effective. Without a post-treatment program, obese patients abandon behavior techniques and gradually regain weight whereas they experience greater weight maintenance with structured post-treatment maintenance strategies.[69] Regular contact with the patient in some form thus helps in the maintenance phase.[70] Included should be a plan for "high-risk" situations like holidays. Positive predictors of success in weight loss programs include high initial weight, perceived self-efficacy, frequent attendance, and early success.[52] A functioning social network, increased physical activity, and behavior modification improve the likelihood of success. Repeated previous failure and stress are negative predictors.

One of the frustrations regarding weight loss is the effect of weight loss itself on metabolism. Since total energy expenditure declines 15% more than the decline in body weight, metabolic compensations actually appear to confound efforts at weight loss.[29] A formerly obese person requires 15% fewer calories to maintain normal body weight than a person with the same body composition but

TABLE 89–4. Frequently Prescribed Medications for Obesity

Medication	Usual Dosage	Side Effects
Sibutramine	10 mg daily	Elevated blood pressure
Phentermine resin	15 mg twice daily (hydrochloride form also available)	Elevated blood pressure
Orlistat	120 mg capsule three times daily with meals, in conjunction with multivitamin at bedtime	Steatorrhea, flatulence, abdominal cramping

without a history of obesity.[16] With each kilogram of lost weight there is a decreased energy expenditure of 20 kcal/d.[16]

Unfortunately, exercise "costs" less energy as weight is lost.[71] After significant diet-induced weight loss, obese women expend less energy for the same activity, even after accounting for the decrease in body weight.[72]

PHARMACOTHERAPY

Obesity is a chronic disorder requiring long-term treatment.[70] The National Task Force on the Prevention and Treatment of Obesity states, "There is little justification for the short-term use of anorexient medications." However, it continues, "few studies have evaluated their safety and efficacy for more than one year."[73] The safety of long-term obesity medications has yet to be established. This is of great concern, because if pharmacotherapy were to be widely used in uncomplicated obesity (BMI ≥ 30), 34.7 million American adults between 20 and 74 years of age would qualify for medications. An additional 26.4 million would be potentially eligible on the basis of having a BMI ≥ 27 with comorbid conditions such as diabetes and hypertension.[74]

There are a variety of medications that have been used to aid in weight loss. Most have a similar effect in inducing a moderate improvement in the amount of weight lost, compared to placebo. (These are discussed in detail below.) The Expert Panel recommends a combination of behavior therapy, a low-calorie diet, and increased physical activity for at least 6 months prior to the consideration of pharmacotherapy.[28] Potential causes of secondary obesity, including hypothyroidism, Cushing's syndrome, hypogonadism, pituitary disorders, depression, and insulinoma, should be investigated prior to the use of pharmacotherapy.[5]

There are special concerns regarding the use of weight loss medications in elderly persons. Many complex age-related changes alter medication absorption, metabolism, and distribution.[2] Most studies of weight loss interventions have excluded the elderly population. It is unclear whether the link between excess weight and increased risk of death holds in elderly persons;[75] therefore, it is more difficult to justify the risks associated with the use of weight loss medication in older patients.

General Principles

The patient must be firmly established with a diet and exercise program before beginning medication for obesity. Referral to a clinician is crucial for most patients. The expected time-course of weight loss and a reasonable goal weight should be outlined. The clinician and patient should review the potential side effects of medication in advance. Commonly used medications are summarized in Table 89–4 and are described in more detail below.

There should be weekly visits until a stable dose, an acceptable side effect profile, and successful weight loss is achieved. If there is no weight loss after 4 weeks, medication should be stopped.[24] If weight loss is achieved, monthly maintenance visits should follow.

Medications used for medical illnesses other than obesity may themselves have a direct effect on obesity. For example, in contrast to sulfonylureas or insulin, metformin in the obese diabetic patient can help improve glycemic control, decrease insulin resistance, and improve lipids, without causing weight gain.[76,77] Metformin should probably be the first-line drug for treating both diabetes and obesity in the obese diabetic patient.[76]

Serotonergic and Serotonergic-Noradrenergic Drugs

Serotonin produces a central satiety signal.[74] Serotonergic drugs increase the release or prevent the reuptake of brain serotonin. Serotonergic agents have been used widely for weight loss.[78] Currently in the United States, serotonergic medications used to promote weight loss include fluoxetine and sibutramine. Fenfluramine (part of the combination known as "fen/phen") and dexfenfluramine were widely used in the early 1990s but are no longer used because of safety concerns. Patients who have taken fenfluramine or dexfenfluramine should be monitored for long-term cardiac complications.

Fluoxetine, a selective serotonin reuptake inhibitor (SSRI), has been used widely to treat depression. It is not approved for use in weight loss regimens per se.[79] However, because of some data suggesting efficacy, fluoxetine has been used to aid weight loss, at a dosage of 60 mg/d;[80] this is a much higher dosage than the usual dosages for depression therapy. Recent data challenge fluoxetine's benefit in weight loss.[81] It should not be used with monoamine oxidase inhibitors or within 14 days of their use because of a potentially fatal reaction consisting of hyperthermia, rigidity, myoclonus, autonomic instability, and mental-status changes progressing to coma.[79] It has no significant abuse potential.[82] Other SSRIs are being evaluated for efficacy in weight loss.

Sibutramine, which inhibits serotonin and norepinephrine uptake in a dose-dependent manner, was first clinically tested as an antidepressant in 1984[13] but was found to be devoid of antidepressant activity.[83] It was approved by the Food and Drug Administration (FDA) in 1997 for the management of obesity (including weight loss and the maintenance of weight loss), in conjunction with a reduced calorie diet, in those with a BMI ≥30 (or ≥27 when in the presence of other risk factors).

Sibutramine may increase systolic and diastolic blood pressure and heart rate.[84] The increase in heart rate and blood pressure are dose dependent and are related to the drug's mechanism of action.[85] These side effects theoretically may not allow the expected decrease in blood pressure resulting from weight loss.[83] Sleep problems, irritability, constipation, and dry mouth are also possible side effects.[86–89] The Expert Panel recommends against the drug's use in patients with a history of hypertension, coronary heart disease, congestive heart failure, arrhythmias, or stroke.[28] Data on its long-term safety and efficacy are lacking.

In 1997 the FDA asked the manufacturers to withdraw both dexfenfluramine and fenfluramine from the market voluntarily.[90] The basis for withdrawal was five surveys showing that 30% of patients who took either drug had cardiac valvular abnormalities even though most had no symptoms.[91] The DHHS then issued recommendations for the care of patients who had taken either drug. The four key elements were that (1) all patients exposed to dexfenfluramine or fenfluramine for any period should have a history and a physical examination; (2) echocardiography should be performed on all patients with suggestive symptoms and signs; (3) echocardiography should be strongly considered before any invasive procedure, regardless of signs and symptoms; and (4) the current case definition of drug-associated valvulopathy is aortic regurgitation of at least mild severity or mitral regurgitation of at least moderate severity. There were no recommendations included to guide repeat echocardiographic monitoring.

In recent reports, the association of dexfenfluramine and fenfluramine with valvular abnormalities is much lower than that in the original report, and the final extent and duration of clinical harm has yet to be clearly defined.[92–95] Still unknown are whether valve abnormalities reverse after drug cessation, the prevalence of valve disease at baseline in the comparison with non-drug-treated obese patients, and the mechanism of valve damage.

Serotonergic drugs and other weight loss medications may cause pulmonary complications as well. An international prospective case-control study reported an association between pulmonary hypertension and use of any anorectic agents in the preceding year for over 3 months' duration, with a 23.1 odds ratio for the development of pulmonary hypertension.[96] The initial symptom in 91% of patients was dyspnea. This complication seemed to be most closely related to dexfenfluramine or fenfluramine use as compared with the use of other medications.[97] Given that the mechanism of drug-induced pulmonary hypertension remains unknown, it may be that other obesity medications currently in use cause pulmonary hypertension as well.[98,99]

Catecholamine Agents and Thermogenic Agents

Catecholaminergic drugs (centrally acting adrenergic drugs) that have been commonly used for weight loss include amphetamines, phenmetrazine, phenylpropanolamine, and phentermine. All catecholaminergic drugs may produce central nervous system (CNS) excitation. None has a clear advantage over another, and all may cause weight loss for 3 to 6 months, after which a plateau of effect generally occurs.[2] Amphetamines and phenmetrazine are not used currently because of their excessive stimulant properties and addictive potential.[100] In some US states there may be limitations on the prescribing of some drugs in this class.

Phentermine was approved in 1959 for short-term single-drug treatment of obesity. It is indicated for short-term use (ie, a few weeks) as an adjunct to a calorie restriction program.[104] Along with fenfluramine, it constituted the other half of the popular fen/phen combination. Phentermine is available in both a resin and nonresin form. The resin is absorbed at a threefold slower rate and probably produces more consistent sustained blood levels.[74] Adverse effects reported with phentermine use include palpitations, tachycardia, elevation of blood pressure, overstimulation, restlessness, dizziness, insomnia, euphoria, dysphoria, tremor, headache, dryness of the mouth, unpleasant taste, diarrhea, and constipation.[104] Shorter-acting forms of phentermine may be preferable in the presence of new anxiety or sleep disturbance.

Contraindications to phentermine use include advanced arteriosclerosis, symptomatic cardiovascular disease, moderate to severe hypertension, known hypersensitivity, glaucoma, agitated states, a history of drug abuse, and use during or within 14 days of the use of monoamine oxidase inhibitors.[24,104] Phentermine and SSRIs have not been combined in large randomized studies, so this combination should not be used. Many obese patients may be on SSRI agents for depression and may not mention this when phentermine is prescribed. No heart valve disease meeting the FDA's case definition have been reported from the use of phentermine alone.[105] The safety and efficacy of phentermine in those with existing valve abnormalities is not established. Its long-term safety is also unknown.

Thermogenic drugs include phenylpropanolamine, caffeine and other xanthine derivatives, and ephedrine, all of which increase metabolic rate.[83] Apparent PPA-associated intracerebral hemorrhage and/or infarction have been reported.[102,103] The US FDA has asked for voluntary withdrawal of PPA-containing agents due to increased risk of cardiovascular complications.

Ephedrine's thermogenic activity can be potentiated by caffeine. Ephedrine increases energy expenditure and fat loss.[2] It should not be used in patients with concurrent angle-closure glaucoma.[2] Despite ephedrine's being an effective agent, the marked risks associated with it (such as hypertension, arrhythmias, seizures, myocardial infarction, strokes, and death) suggest that its use should be avoided.[45]

To date, chromium chelated as chromium picolinate has shown equivocal results in studies for weight loss although it has been purported to increase energy expenditure.[2]

Blockers of Fat Absorption

Orlistat is a lipase inhibitor; it inhibits gastric, carboxylester, and pancreatic lipase and decreases the absorption of dietary fat, due to the inhibition of triglyceride hydrolysis.[13] Regardless of the amount of dietary fat, fat absorption does not increase above 36% ingested fat.[106]

In 1999 orlistat was approved for obesity management (weight loss and weight maintenance) in conjunction with a reduced-calorie diet. Orlistat is indicated when BMI ≥ 30 (or ≥ 27 in the presence of obesity-associated risk factors). Orlistat therapy causes significant weight loss, lessens the weight regained, and improves low-density lipoprotein (LDL) cholesterol and fasting insulin levels.[107,108] Orlistat in type 2 diabetes additionally improves hemoglobin A_{1c} (HbA_{1c}) and fasting glucose, possibly allowing a reduction in oral sulfonylurea dosage.[109] Outcomes in major health end points have yet to be shown.[110]

Typically, 120-mg capsules are taken three times a day, during or up to 1 hour after each fat-containing meal. Higher doses are thought to be no more efficacious than the recommended dosing. Prescription information recommends that patients take a concurrent multivitamin once daily, at least 2 hours before or after taking orlistat so as to counteract possible orlistat-induced malabsorption of fat-soluble vitamins.

Most of the drug is excreted in the feces, decreasing the potential for systemic side effects.[2] Due to the mechanism of action, gastrointestinal symptoms are the most common side effects. Orlistat commonly causes steatorrhea, increased defecation, abdominal pain, and fecal urgency.[13]

These symptoms are much more prominent if patients do not adhere to dietary recommendations and consume a high-fat diet (>30% calories from fat). Orlistat is contraindicated chronic malabsorption or cholestasis. There are no data yet regarding the potential long-term adverse effects of increased fat in the colon with orlistat use.

Alternative and Complementary Treatments: Herbal Remedies

Herbal weight loss remedies are popular. "Herbal fen/phen" does not contain fenfluramine, dexfenfluramine, or phentermine but often contains ephedra and caffeine.[105] It has not been FDA-reviewed for safety and efficacy. Hydroxycitric acid, the active ingredient in the herbal compound *Garcinia cambogia*, did not produce weight loss when compared to placebo in a recent study.[111]

Other herbs prescribed for weight loss can have potentially serious side effects. Chinese herbal compounds containing *Stephania tetranda* and *Magnolia officinalis* were reported to be associated with rapidly progressive fibrosing interstitial nephritis.[112] The term "Aristolochia nephropathy" is used to describe a type of Chinese herb nephropathy. Aristolochia contains a known carcinogen.[113] Also, germander (*Teucrium chamaedrys*) has caused hepatitis.[114]

No herbal weight loss remedies yet have been shown to be safe and effective in large stringently designed trials. The purity of these remedies is not under FDA control, and studies have shown that herbal remedies often contain ingredients other than those listed on their packaging.[115]

OTHER FORMS OF WEIGHT TREATMENT

Very-Low-Calorie Diets

Medically supervised very-low-calorie diets (VLCDs) are generally recommended only for patients who are 30% or more overweight[70] and only when more traditional approaches have failed or when rapid weight loss is indicated for medical reasons (such as pending surgery). Very-low-calorie diets involve the use of liquid formulations in combination with a very restricted diet to achieve an intake of 800 kcal per day; fish or lean meat is the usual protein, contributing most of this intake.[116] No evidence exists supporting diets with an intake of < 800 kcal per day.[29]

Very-low-calorie diets result in two to three times greater weight loss than conventional diets at the same duration.[70] The expected weight loss during VLCDs is on the order of 4.5 to 7 kg in the first week and 1.5 to 2 kg/wk thereafter.[29] There are no good long-term data on the efficacy of VLCDs.

Side effects of VLCDs include fatigue, cold intolerance, dry skin, hair loss, menstrual abnormalities, cholelithiasis, cholecystitis, electrolyte abnormalities, and nephrolithiasis.[117–119] Constipation and muscle cramps may occur. Rapid weight loss may be associated with a substantial incidence of gallstones and can precipitate hyperuricemia and hyperkalemia. These diets are contraindicated for pregnant women, adolescents, growing children, and those with hepatic, renal, and cardiac disease. Modern VLCDs (whose liquid supplements contain high-quality protein, such as casein, egg, and soy, as well as vitamins, minerals, and electrolytes) cause less cardiac dysrhythmia and death than did the VLCDs of the late 1970s.[46,117] However, patients with a history of arrythmia or cardiac abnormality should not undertake in VLCDs.[44]

Liquid supplements are expensive and do not mimic the normal seeing, smelling, chewing, and cooking of food; they thus remove the opportunity to change cooking and eating behaviors. Liquid diets will not serve as a substitute for re-education regarding unhealthy eating habits.[120] Most weight loss early on is caused by water loss (diuresis) in the higher-protein diet programs. After the VLCD part of the program, the "refeeding period" is a critical transitional period, during which complex carbohydrates, fruits, and vegetables are re-introduced. Behavior modification, exercise, and special dietary maintenance therapy are required after the initial phase is over, even when that phase has been an apparent initial success.[29]

Surgery

Because patients with serious complications of obesity (eg, sleep apnea or heart failure) are at significantly increased risk for not meeting a normal life expectancy, and because other methods most likely will not result in a permanent solution to the weight problem, surgery is sometimes considered.[24] The Expert Panel recommends limiting obesity surgery to gastric resection or Roux-en-Y gastric bypass in those with a BMI ≥40 (BMI ≥35 with comorbid conditions).[28]

Gastroplasty partitions part of the stomach into a small "pouch" that communicates with the rest of the stomach through a "stoma." Currently a vertical banded gastroplasty is the usual procedure. The channel is wrapped with a nonexpandable prosthetic material to prevent stomal enlargement, thus preventing the ingestion of large amounts of food.[121] The procedure is technically easy and is safe, as severe metabolic side effects are not induced.[121] There may be a behavioral adaptation such that approximately 50% of patients learn that high-calorie soft foods and liquids can pass through the stoma; these patients consequently change their diet composition, resulting in an increased caloric intake.

A gastric (Roux-en-Y) bypass circumvents such a problem by separating the cardia from the rest of the stomach. The proximal gastric pouch (< 30 cc in volume) is drained directly into the jejunum.[121] It therefore acts in two ways: (1) by inducing a dumping syndrome triggered by high-carbohydrate meals and (2) by preventing the ingestion of large amounts at a meal.[121] It may cause gastrointestinal (GI) distress, vomiting, electrolyte abnormalities, compensatory overeating, and complications related to the surgery itself (gastric-pouch dilatation, stoma dilation, stoma obstruction, or staple dehiscence). Also, when patients eat highly sugared high-calorie foods like candy bars, a "dumping" syndrome can result, consisting of abdominal cramps, nausea, and light-headedness.[24] Patients must be monitored for long-term iron and vitamin B$_{12}$ malabsorption.[121]

Results from surgery depend mostly on motivation, not on metabolic or technical factors.[122] Active substance abuse and psychiatric disorders are absolute contraindications to obesity surgery.[121] If the mark of success is either loss of at least 50% of the excess weight or the resolution of weight-associated comorbidities, most patients are "successful" (ie, they lose > 50% of excess weight in the long term) and have a consequent resolution or lessening of adult-onset diabetes mellitus (AODM), HTN, high cholesterol, and sleep apnea.[121]

Long-term weight loss is best with a Roux-en-Y gastric bypass, which has a 0.1 to 0.5% operative mortality.[11] The somewhat greater weight loss with gastric bypass must be balanced against the higher risk of micronutrient deficiencies.[118] There is an overall 5 to 10% risk of significant surgery-related morbidity.[24] The long-term efficacy and safety of surgical treatment of obesity has yet to be documented.[118] Although there is evidence of surgery reducing comorbid conditions, there is insufficient evidence of benefit against end-organ damage.[118]

RESOURCES

United States Department of Agriculture
Center for Nutrition Policy and Promotion
14th and Independence Avenue Southwest
Washington, DC 20250
Telephone: (202) 720-2791
Web site: www.usda.gov/fcs

The US Department of Agriculture Center for Nutrition Policy and Promotion maintains on-line resources, including the revised food pyramid and detailed menu and recipe plans for low-cost healthful eating that have been tested by low-income families from diverse ethnic groups.

Centers for Disease Control and Prevention
1600 Clifton Road
Atlanta, Georgia 30333
Telephone: 1-888-CDC-4NRG (1-888-232-4674)
Web site: www.cdc.gov

The 1996 Surgeon General's Report on Physical Activity and Health is available on-line through the Centers for Disease Control and Prevention.

REFERENCES

1. Poston WS 2nd, Foreyt JP, Borrell L, Haddock CK. Challenges in obesity management. South Med J 1998;91:710–20.

2. Dvorak R, Starling RD, Calles-Escandon J, et al. Drug therapy for obesity in the elderly. Drugs Aging 1997;11:338–51.

3. Healy BP. Obesity and the diet pill dilemma [editorial]. J Womens Health 1997;6:391–2.

4. Summary: weighing the options—criteria for evaluating weight-management programs. Committee to Develop Criteria for Evaluating the Outcomes of Approaches to Prevent and Treat Obesity Food and Nutrition Board, Institute of Medicine, National Academy of Sciences. J Am Diet Assoc 1995; 95:96–105.

5. Cheah JS. Current management of obesity. Singapore Med J 1996;37:299–303.

6. Pi-Sunyer FX. Obesity. In: Bennett JC, Plum F, editors. Cecil textbook of medicine. Philadelphia: W.B. Saunders Company, 1996. p. 1161–8.

7. 1983 Metropolitan height and weight tables. Statistical bulletin. Vol. Jan–Jun. New York: Metropolitan Life Insurance Company; 1983. p. 2–9.

8. Pi-Sunyer FX. Obesity. In: Wyngaarden JB, Smith LH, Bennett JC, editors. Cecil textbook of medicine. Vol. 2. Philadelphia: W.B. Saunders Company; 1992. p. 1162–8.

9. Lukaski HC, Johnson PE, Bolonchuk WW, Lykken GI. Assessment of fat-free mass using bioelectrical impedance measurements of the human body. Am J Clin Nutr 1985;41:810–7.

10. Bray GA. Obesity. Curr Ther Endocrinol Metab 1994;5:465–74.

11. Bray GA. Obesity. In: Fauci AS, Braunwald E, Isselbacher KJ, et al, editors. Harrison's principles of internal medicine. New York: McGraw-Hill Co.; 1998. p. 454–62.

12. Bjorntorp P. Obesity. Lancet 1997;350:423–6.

13. Weiser M, Frishman WH, Michaelson MD, Abdeen MA. The pharmacologic approach to the treatment of obesity. J Clin Pharmacol 1997;37:453–73.

14. Sorensen TI. The genetics of obesity. Metabolism 1995;44:4–6.

15. Misra A, Garg A. Leptin, its receptor and obesity. J Investig Med 1996;44:540–8.

16. Rosenbaum M, Leibel RL, Hirsch J. Obesity. N Engl J Med 1997;337:396–407.

17. Comuzzie AG, Allison DB. The search for human obesity genes. Science 1998;280:1374–7.

18. Ostlund RE Jr, Yang JW, Klein S, Gingerich R. Relation between plasma leptin concentration and body fat, gender, diet, age, and metabolic covariates. J Clin Endocrinol Metab 1996;81:3909–13.

19. Leyva F, Godsland IF, Ghatei M, et al. Hyperleptinemia as a component of a metabolic syndrome of cardiovascular risk. Arterioscler Thromb Vasc Biol 1998;18:928–33.

20. Ma Z, Gingerich RL, Santiago JV, et al. Radioimmunoassay of leptin in human plasma. Clin Chem 1996; 42:942–6.

21. Auwerx J, Staels B. Leptin. Lancet 1998;351:737–42.

22. Caro JF, Kolaczynski JW, Nyce MR, et al. Decreased cerebrospinal-fluid/serum leptin ratio in obesity: a possible mechanism for leptin resistance. Lancet 1996;348:159–61.

23. Lindpaintner K. Finding an obesity gene—a tale of mice and man. N Engl J Med 1995;332:679–80.

24. Fujioka K. Medical management of obesity. Hosp Med 1996:28–35.

25. Folsom AR, Kaye SA, Sellers TA, et al. Body fat distribution and 5-year risk of death in older women [published erratum appears in JAMA 1993 Mar 10;269(10):1254]. JAMA 1993;269:483–7.

26. Pouliot MC, Despres JP, Lemieux S, et al. Waist circumference and abdominal sagittal diameter: best simple anthropometric indexes of abdominal visceral adipose tissue accumulation and related cardiovascular risk in men and women. Am J Cardiol 1994; 73:460–8.

27. Lean ME, Han TS, Morrison CE. Waist circumference as a measure for indicating need for weight management. BMJ 1995;311:158–61.

28. Executive summary of the clinical guidelines on the identification, evaluation, and treatment of overweight and obesity in adults. Arch Intern Med 1998; 158:1855–67.

29. Barbieri RL. Obesity in women: pathophysiology, diagnosis and treatment. In: Barbieri RL, editor. APGO educational series on women's health issues. Vol. 1. Crofton (MD): Association of Professors of Gynecology and Obstetrics, 1997. p. 30.

30. Kirchengast S, Gruber D, Sator M, et al. Menopause-associated differences in female fat patterning estimated by dual-energy X-ray absorptiometry. Ann Hum Biol 1997;24:45–54.

31. Gaspard UJ, Gottal JM, van den Brule FA. Postmenopausal changes of lipid and glucose metabolism: a review of their main aspects. Maturitas 1995;21:171–8.

32. Bjorntorp P. Neuroendocrine abnormalities in human obesity. Metabolism 1995;44:38–41.

33. Haarbo J, Marslew U, Gotfredsen A, Christiansen C. Postmenopausal hormone replacement therapy prevents central distribution of body fat after menopause. Metabolism 1991;40:1323–6.

34. Troisi RJ, Wolf AM, Mason JE, et al. Relation of body fat distribution to reproductive factors in pre- and postmenopausal women. Obes Res 1995;3:143–51.

35. Perry AC, Applegate EB, Allison MD, et al. Clinical predictability of the waist-to-hip ratio in assessment of cardiovascular disease risk factors in overweight, premenopausal women [published erratum appears in Am J Clin Nutr 1999;69:577]. Am J Clin Nutr 1998;68:1022–7.

36. Hubert HB, Feinleib M, McNamara PM, Castelli WP. Obesity as an independent risk factor for cardiovascular disease: a 26-year follow-up of participants in the Framingham Heart Study. Circulation 1983; 67:968–77.

37. Manson JE, Colditz GA, Stampfer MJ, et al. A prospective study of obesity and risk of coronary heart disease in women. N Engl J Med 1990;322:882–9.

38. Rexrode KM, Hennekens CH, Willett WC, et al. A prospective study of body mass index, weight change, and risk of stroke in women. JAMA 1997; 277:1539–45.

39. Sellers TA, Kushi LH, Potter JD, et al. Effect of family history, body-fat distribution, and reproductive factors on the risk of postmenopausal breast cancer [published erratum appears in N Engl J Med 1992; 327:1612]. N Engl J Med 1992;326:1323–9.

40. Colditz GA, Willett WC, Rotnitzky A, Manson JE. Weight gain as a risk factor for clinical diabetes mellitus in women. Ann Intern Med 1995;122:481–6.

41. Manson JE, Willett WC, Stampfer MJ, et al. Body weight and mortality among women. N Engl J Med 1995;333:677–85.

42. US Department of Agriculture. Nutrition and your health: dietary guidelines for Americans. Washington (DC): US Dept. of Agriculture, US Dept. of Health and Human Services; 1995.

43. Goldstein DJ. Beneficial health effects of modest weight loss. Int J Obes Relat Metab Disord 1992; 16:397–415.

44. Pi-Sunyer FX. Short-term medical benefits and adverse effects of weight loss. Ann Intern Med 1993; 119:722–6.

45. Obesity management: current challenges and future directions. In: Dialogues in obesity. Minneapolis: University of Minnesota; 1997.

46. Caterson ID. Management strategies for weight control. Eating, exercise and behaviour. Drugs 1990;39 Suppl 3:20–32.

47. Felson DT, Zhang Y, Anthony JM, et al. Weight loss reduces the risk for symptomatic knee osteoarthritis in women. The Framingham Study. Ann Intern Med 1992;116:535–9.

48. Kiddy DS, Hamilton-Fairley D, Bush A, et al. Improvement in endocrine and ovarian function during dietary treatment of obese women with polycystic ovary syndrome. Clin Endocrinol (Oxf) 1992;36:105–11.

49. Pasquali R, Casimirri F. The impact of obesity on hyperandrogenism and polycystic ovary syndrome in premenopausal women. Clin Endocrinol (Oxf) 1993;39:1–16.

50. Clark AM, Ledger W, Galletly C, et al. Weight loss results in significant improvement in pregnancy and ovulation rates in anovulatory obese women. Hum Reprod 1995;10:2705–12.

51. Galletly C, Clark A, Tomlinson L, Blaney F. Improved pregnancy rates for obese, infertile women following a group treatment program. An open pilot study. Gen Hosp Psychiatry 1996;18:192–5.

52. Rossner S. Defining success in obesity management. Int J Obes Relat Metab Disord 1997;21 Suppl 1:S2–4.

53. Glasziou P, Rowan S, Del Mar C. Managing the overweight and obese. A low fat approach. Aust Fam Physician 1997;26:1259–63, 1265.

54. Boutelle KN, Kirschenbaum DS. Further support for consistent self-monitoring as a vital component of successful weight control. Obes Res 1998;6:219–24.

55. Brownell KD, Kramer FM. Behavioral management of obesity. Med Clin North Am 1989;73:185–201.

56. Foreyt JP, Goodrick GK. Evidence for success of behavior modification in weight loss and control. Ann Intern Med 1993;119:698–701.

57. Cachelin FM, Striegel-Moore RH, Brownell KD. Beliefs about weight gain and attitudes toward relapse in a sample of women and men with obesity. Obes Res 1998;6:231–7.

58. Kayman S, Bruvold W, Stern JS. Maintenance and relapse after weight loss in women: behavioral aspects. Am J Clin Nutr 1990;52:800–7.

59. Obesity as a chronic disease: new implications for management. Clinical Management Conference summary statement. Proceedings of the Clinical Management Conference; 1996 Nov; Dallas (TX). Minneapolis: University of Minnesota.

60. Weinsier RL, Hunter GR, Heini AF, et al. The etiology of obesity: relative contribution of metabolic factors, diet, and physical activity. Am J Med 1998;105:145–50.

61. Gleim GW. Exercise is not an effective weight loss modality in women. J Am Coll Nutr 1993;12:363–7.

62. Wilding J. Science, medicine, and the future. Obesity treatment. BMJ 1997;315:997–1000.

63. Segal KR, Pi-Sunyer FX. Exercise and obesity. Med Clin North Am 1989;73:217–36.

64. Nair KS, Halliday D, Garrow JS. Thermic response to isoenergetic protein, carbohydrate or fat meals in lean and obese subjects. Clin Sci 1983;65:307–12.

65. Pate RR, Pratt M, Blair SN, et al. Physical activity and public health. A recommendation from the Centers for Disease Control and Prevention and the American College of Sports Medicine. JAMA 1995;273:402–7.

66. Physical activity and cardiovascular health. NIH Consensus Development Panel on Physical Activity and Cardiovascular Health. JAMA 1996;276:241–6.

67. Surgeon General's report on physical activity and health. From the Centers for Disease Control and Prevention. JAMA 1996;276:522.

68. Zelasko CJ. Exercise for weight loss: what are the facts? J Am Diet Assoc 1995;95:1414–7.

69. Perri MG, Sears SF Jr, Clark JE. Strategies for improving maintenance of weight loss. Toward a continuous care model of obesity management. Diabetes Care 1993;16:200–9.

70. Wadden TA. Treatment of obesity by moderate and severe caloric restriction. Results of clinical research trials. Ann Intern Med 1993;119:688–93.

71. Hill JO, Drougas H, Peters JC. Obesity treatment: can diet composition play a role? Ann Intern Med 1993;119:694–7.

72. Foster GD, Wadden TA, Kendrick ZV, et al. The energy cost of walking before and after significant weight loss. Med Sci Sports Exerc 1995;27:888–94.

73. Long-term pharmacotherapy in the management of obesity. National Task Force on the Prevention and Treatment of Obesity. JAMA 1996;276:1907–15.

74. Lerman RH. Obesity: an escalating problem. Contemp Intern Med 1997;9:9–19.

75. Wickelgren I. Obesity: how big a problem? Science 1998;280:1364–7.

76. Scheen AJ, Lefebvre PJ. Pharmacological treatment of the obese diabetic patient. Diabetes Metab 1993; 19:547–59.

77. Scheen AJ, Desaive C, Lefebvre PJ. Therapy for obesity—today and tomorrow. Baillieres Clin Endocrinol Metab 1994;8:705–27.

78. Guy-Grand B. INDEX (international dexfenfluramine study) as a model for long-term pharmacotherapy of obesity in the 1990s. Int J Obes Relat Metab Disord 1992;16 Suppl 3:S5–14.

79. Prozac. In: Physicians' drug reference. Vol. 96. Montvale (NJ): Medical Economics Co.; 1998. p. 1–26.

80. Connolly VM, Gallagher A, Kesson CM. A study of fluoxetine in obese elderly patients with type 2 diabetes. Diabetes Med 1995;12:416–8.

81. Fernandez-Soto ML, Gonzalez-Jimenez A, Barredo-Acedo F, et al. Comparison of fluoxetine and placebo in the treatment of obesity. Ann Nutr Metab 1995; 39:159–63.

82. Bray GA. A case for drug treatment of obesity. Hosp Pract (Off Ed) 1994;29:53,57–8, 60.

83. Finer N. Present and future pharmacological approaches. Br Med Bull 1997;53:409–32.

84. King DJ, Devaney N. Clinical pharmacology of sibutramine hydrochloride (BTS 54524), a new antidepressant, in healthy volunteers. Br J Clin Pharmacol 1988;26:607–11.

85. Lean ME. Sibutramine—a review of clinical efficacy. Int J Obes Relat Metab Disord 1997;21 Suppl 1:S30–9.

86. Weintraub M, Rubio A, Golik A, et al. Sibutramine in weight control: a dose-ranging efficacy study. Clin Pharmacol Ther 1991;50:330–7.

87. Stunkard AJ. Current views on obesity. Am J Med 1996;100:230–6.

88. Ryan DH, Kaiser P, Bray GA. Sibutramine: a novel new agent for obesity treatment. Obes Res 1995;3 Suppl 4:553–9S.

89. Sibutramine for obesity. Med Lett Drugs Ther 1998;40:32.

90. US Department of Health and Human Services. FDA announces withdrawal of fenfluramine and dexfenfluramine. Rockville (MD): US Dept of Health and Human Services; 1997.

91. From the Centers for Disease Control and Prevention. Cardiac valvulopathy associated with exposure to fenfluramine or dexfenfluramine: US Department of Health and Human Services interim public health recommendations, November 1997. JAMA 1997; 278:1729–31.

92. Baird IM. Risks of heart-valve abnormalities with appetite suppressants. Lancet 1998;352:1403–4.

93. Devereux RB. Appetite suppressants and valvular heart disease [editorial]. N Engl J Med 1998; 339:765–6.

94. Parisi AF. Diet-drug debacle [editorial]. Ann Intern Med 1998;129:903–5.

95. Wee CC, Phillips RS, Aurigemma G, et al. Risk for valvular heart disease among users of fenfluramine and dexfenfluramine who underwent echocardiography before use of medication. Ann Intern Med 1998;129:870–4.

96. Abenhaim L, Moride Y, Brenot F, et al. Appetite-suppressant drugs and the risk of primary pulmonary hypertension. International Primary Pulmonary Hypertension Study Group. N Engl J Med 1996;335:609–16.

97. Gonzalez AM, Smith A, Emery C, Higenbottam T. Pulmonary hypertension, family and environment. J Hum Hypertens 1997;11:559–61.

98. Thompson PD. Valvular heart disease associated with fenfluramine-phentermine. N Engl J Med 1997;337:1772, 1775.

99. Marshall EM. Valvular heart disease associated with fenfluramine-phentermine. N Engl J Med 1997; 337:1775–6.

100. Silverstone T. Appetite suppressants. A review. Drugs 1992;43:820–36.

101. Bradley MH, Raines J. The effects of phenylpropanolamine hydrochloride in overweight patients with controlled stable hypertension. Curr Ther Res 1989;46:74–84.

102. Kase CS, Foster TE, Reed JE, et al. Intracerebral hemorrhage and phenylpropanolamine use. Neurology 1987;37:399–404.

103. Johnson DA, Etter HS, Reeves DM. Stroke and phenylpropanolamine use. Lancet 1983;2:970.

104. Physicians' Desk Reference. Vol. 1. In: Wesley GJ, editor. Montvale (NJ): Medical Economics; 1999.

105. Center for Drug Evaluation and Research. Questions and answers about withdrawal of fenfluramine (pondimin) and dexfenfluramine (redux). Rockville (MD): US Food and Drug Administration, Center for Drug Evaluation and Research. 1997.

106. Hauptman JB, Jeunet FS, Hartmann D. Initial studies in humans with the novel gastrointestinal lipase inhibitor Ro 18-0647 (tetrahydrolipstatin). Am J Clin Nutr 1992;55:309–13S.

107. Davidson MH, Hauptman J, DiGirolamo M, et al. Weight control and risk factor reduction in obese subjects treated for 2 years with orlistat: a randomized controlled trial. JAMA 1999;281:235–42.

108. Sjostrom L, Rissanen A, Andersen T, et al. Randomised placebo-controlled trial of orlistat for weight loss and prevention of weight regain in obese patients. European Multicentre Orlistat Study Group. Lancet 1998;352:167–72.

109. Hollander PA, Elbein SC, Hirsch IB, et al. Role of orlistat in the treatment of obese patients with type 2 diabetes. A 1-year randomized double-blind study. Diabetes Care 1998;21:1288–94.

110. Williamson DF. Pharmacotherapy for obesity [editorial]. JAMA 1999;281:278–80.

111. Heymsfield SB, Allison DB, Vasselli JR, et al. Garcinia cambogia (hydroxycitric acid) as a potential anti-obesity agent: a randomized controlled trial. JAMA 1998;280:1596–600.

112. Vanherweghem JL, Depierreux M, Tielemans C, et al. Rapidly progressive interstitial renal fibrosis in young women: association with slimming regimen including Chinese herbs. Lancet 1993;341:387–91.

113. Van Ypersele de Strihou C. Valvular heart disease and Chinese-herb nephropathy. Lancet 1998;351:991–2.

114. Larrey D, Vial T, Pauwels A, et al. Hepatitis after germander (*Teucrium chamaedrys*) administration: another instance of herbal medicine hepatotoxicity. Ann Intern Med 1992;117:129–32.

115. Ko RJ. Adulterants in Asian patent medicines [letter]. N Engl J Med 1998;339:847.

116. Walters JK, Hoogwerf BJ, Reddy SSK. The protein-sparing modified fast for obesity-related medical problems. Cleve Clin J Med 1997;64:242–4.

117. National Institutes of Health Technology Assessment Conference statement: methods for voluntary weight loss and control, March 30–April 1, 1992. Nutr Rev 1992;50:340–5.

118. NIH conference. Gastrointestinal surgery for severe obesity. Consensus Development Conference Panel. Ann Intern Med 1991;115:956–61.

119. Kochar MS. Hypertension in obese patients. Postgrad Med 1993;93:193–5,199–200.

120. Munro JF, Cantley P. The management of obesity. One view. Int J Obes Relat Metab Disord 1992;16 Suppl 2:S53–7.

121. Balsiger BM, Luque de Leon E, Sarr MG. Surgical treatment of obesity: who is an appropriate candidate? Mayo Clin Proc 1997;72:551–7.

122. Kral JG. Overview of surgical techniques for treating obesity. Am J Clin Nutr 1992;55:552–5S.

90

ALTERNATIVE MEDICINE

Belinda J. Chan, MD

Patients are increasingly interested in alternative medicine. However, good scientific evidence supporting the claims of alternative medicine is in short supply. As a result, traditionally trained clinicians often must decide how to treat patients who prefer to use some form of alternative medicine or who either cannot tolerate or do not improve from conventional treatment. To help patients receive the best overall care it is important to become acquainted with the most common alternative medical systems and to gain an understanding of their associated risks and benefits. Only by understanding all medical treatments can we clinicians formulate an optimal treatment plan.

Before beginning, it is important to note that the term "alternative medicine" encompasses a wide range of medical practices that are considered to be outside conventional medicine. These practices include acupuncture, homeopathy, naturopathy, herbalism, holistic medicine, chiropractic, Ayurveda (traditional East Indian medicine that includes herbal medicine, massage, and yoga as popularized by Deepak Chopra), Chinese traditional medicine, massage, and nutritional medicine. In addition, even though "alternative medicine" is the term most widely used and understood by clinicians and their patients, "complementary medicine" and "integrated medicine" may be more appropriate because these practices should be viewed as additions to conventional medicine rather than substitutes for it. Indeed, given that some aspects of alternative medicine have been incorporated into medical school training and mainstream medical practices, defining what constitutes alternative medicine has become even more difficult.

USE OF ALTERNATIVE MEDICINE BY WOMEN

Recent studies suggest that Americans frequently make use of alternative medicine. A 1997 study estimated annual spending on alternative medicine is approximately 21.2 billion dollars.[1] The study, which compares a 1990 survey[2] with a 1997 follow-up, found that the percentage of Americans using some form of alternative medicine has increased from 33.8 to 42.1%. In addition, it noted an increase in the percentage of women seeking these therapies: in 1990 there was no difference in use of therapies based on gender, but by 1997 use among women was significantly higher than was use among men (48.9% versus 37.8%). A similar discrepancy was found in a study of Australians, in which 55% of participant women used some form of alternative medicine compared with 42% of men and 48.5% of Australians overall. That study found that women used vitamins, herbs, minerals, homeopathic medicines, and aromatherapy significantly more often than did men.[3] One British study found that women comprised a large majority of the patients who visited alternative clinicians.[4] Although these results are suggestive, other studies in the United States have indicated no difference in the use of alternative clinicians between men and women.[5]

Use of alternative medicine is also common in settings where medication and traditional care may be too expensive or perceived as too expensive or inaccessible for patients. However, although alternative medicine often is viewed as being cheaper than traditional medicine, it is not always inexpensive. Indeed, some therapies are quite labor intensive. Acupuncture, for example, often involves biweekly treatments.

REASONS FOR USE OF ALTERNATIVE MEDICINE

There are several theories that attempt to explain why patients seek alternative medical treatment. One of the most popular theories attributes its use to dissatisfaction with traditional medicine, but at least one study has found that patients who were highly dissatisfied with their clinician used alternative medicine at the same rate as did patients who were satisfied with their clinician.[3] Dissatisfaction with conventional medicine seems to be a significant factor in the use of alternative medicine only in the small percentage of patients that seek the exclusive advice of an alternative clinician. One survey reports that just 1.8% of Americans see only an unconventional clinician.[6] This study also found that patients who sought alternative medical clinicians were more likely to have had more visits to a clinician.

A study of alternative medicine use and breast cancer patients showed that use was not associated with the type of treatment chosen for stage I or II breast cancer. It did show that use of alternative medicine was more common among women who had higher levels of psychological distress and poorer quality of life.[7] Alternative medicine's perceived "beauty" as a more natural, spiritual, and holistic solution to problems seems to account for some of its popularity. One study indicates that people who seek alternative medicine think of it as being more compatible with their own beliefs of health and disease.[5] People often seek alternative medicine as a solution for their symptoms, especially when physicians have not been concerned about a particular symptom, or have failed to offer treatment to relieve the symptom.

APPROACH TO THE PATIENT WHO USES ALTERNATIVE MEDICINE

Determining which patients are using alternative medicine, assessing the treatments they employ, and understanding the implications for clinical care can be challenging for primary care clinicians. Obtaining an accurate history can be difficult, because patients are often reluctant to volunteer information about their use of alternative medicine because they feel the clinician would not support their use of it. In addition, patients often assume that alternative medical treatments are without side effects or potential interactions with traditional treatments. For this reason patients can decide it is unnecessary to discuss their alternative treatment plan with their health clinician.

To obtain necessary information from the patient it is important for the clinician to be open-minded about other forms of care a patient may seek. A clinician that instantly shuns any discussion of the potential benefits of alternative medicine may be viewed as hostile to the patient who is seeking both alternative and traditional care, especially when the patient feels she has benefited from alternative treatments. A clinician that expresses knowledge and interest in alternative medicine is more likely to gain the trust of the patient, especially when recommending that certain forms should or should not be used.

SYSTEMS OF ALTERNATIVE MEDICINE

There are many different systems of alternative medicine, and it can be difficult to find useful sources of information on all of them. The following is a brief summary of a few of the most common systems. In general, systems tend to be similar, emphasizing a holistic view of the body and health, a belief in the body's own healing powers to recover from disease, and a conviction that the natural is superior to the "unnatural."

Acupuncture and Traditional Chinese Medicine

Traditional Chinese medicine originally dates from 2500 BC. Records exist from 1500 BC relating specifically to the topics of gynecology and women's health.[8] Traditional Chinese medicine is based on the theory of yin and yang: a concept of the world as being comprised of two opposite but complementary forces.[9] In medicine five substances dominate the notion of health and illness: qi (vital energy in the body), blood, jing (life), shen (mind), and fluids. At the core of the theory are the organ systems—heart, lungs, spleen, liver, kidneys, pericardium, gall bladder, small intestine, large intestine, bladder, stomach, and triple burner. These organs have functions related to our concept of the organ, plus additional functions. For example, the heart has functions of the circulation and the mind. The emotions are thought to have an effect related to the menstrual cycle because of the heart's relation to the uterus. In general, illness and disease are thought to result from an imbalance in one, more than one, or all of the systems.

Acupuncture is based on the 12 meridians (channels that connect blood and qi to the organs). The meridians are mapped on the body as lines connecting the 361 main acupoints. Stimulation of the points with massage, a needle, or electrical current is thought to help regulate the imbalances that result in symptoms. Acupuncture has been shown to have beneficial effects in postoperative and chemotherapy-induced nausea and vomiting, and postoperative dental pain; further research is necessary to evaluate its potential benefits in treating other diseases, such as fibromylagia, menstrual cramps, headache, myofascial pain, and osteoarthritis.[10]

In traditional Chinese medicine it is thought that menstrual disorders arise from deficiencies or excesses in the uterus, kidney, liver, and blood. A diagnosis such as premenstrual syndrome can have many different diagnoses in traditional Chinese medicine, such as liver-qi stagnation, phlegm-fire harassing upward, liver-blood deficiency, liver-kidney yin deficiency, or spleen-kidney yang deficiency. The treatment would vary depending on the diagnosis, leading to a variety of prescriptions for what would be, according to Western medical thinking, the same diagnosis.[8]

Herbalism

Phytomedicinals are pharmaceutical preparations of herbs. These may be prepared as teas (steeping), decoctions (boiling), tinctures (alcohol extracts), and powders. The amount of active drug in herbal preparations can vary widely from product to product. Further, more than one component of an herbal preparation can be an active ingredient. These factors make it difficult to form standards on content and quality. In addition, some of the components of an otherwise beneficial preparation may be toxic. For example, comfrey has some beneficial components and some that are toxic. In the United States, there is minimal regulation of the herbal products industry, in contrast to Germany where herbs are regulated and can only be purchased via prescription. In 1994 the United States Food and Drug Administration (FDA) passed the Dietary and Supplement Health and Education Act, which stated that herbs can be labeled with information about their effects on the body's structure and

function. However, the FDA does not control which herbs may be sold for what indication in the way it controls the sale of prescription and over-the-counter drugs.

Quality can be a problem when purchasing herbs. This can be especially true for ginseng. Since its cost is expensive and since there are different plants used (American ginseng and Chinese ginseng), different preparations can vary greatly in the amount of ginseng they contain. In addition, some types of ginseng, such as Siberian ginseng, do not contain the ginsenosides that are thought to be the active component.[11]

A list of commonly used herbs and their uses and dosages is presented in Table 90–1.[12,13]

Manual Healing Techniques

Manual healing techniques can range from touch to thrust techniques. These include physical therapy, chiropractic, osteopathy, and massage. Doctors of Chiropractic, who believe that spinal abnormalities, or subluxations, are responsible for many medical problems, perform the majority of manipulative therapies in the United States. Although some chiropractors assert that a wide variety of medical illnesses can be treated with manipulation, most advocate the use of manipulation for musculoskeletal and pain disorders and may incorporate other techniques (such as massage and heat) to alleviate symptoms. There is currently no evidence that chiropractic manipulation benefits other illnesses or symptoms. Meta-analyses of studies of chiropractic manipulation for the relief of acute low back pain have demonstrated overall benefit, but experts feel that better randomized controlled trials are needed.[14] Research into the effectiveness of manipulation for neck pain and headache are less conclusive but promising.

The incorporation of chiropractic manipulation into mainstream medicine has benefited from the 1994 guidelines of the Agency for Health Care Policy and Research (AHCPR), which recommend the use of manipulation as an option for treating low back pain.[15] Studies indicate that 5 to 10% of Americans have visited a chiropractor, and surveys reveal that patients generally feel that they benefit from chiropractic therapy. Indeed, one study has shown that patients with back pain are more satisfied with their progress from chiropractic manipulation than from conventional medical treatment.[16]

TABLE 90–1. Commonly Used Herbs

Herb	Reasons for Use	Dosage[*]
Black cohosh	Menopausal symptoms	40 mg qd
Cranberry	Urinary tract infections	340–908 mL qd
Echinacea	Upper respiratory infections	Variable
Feverfew	Headache	Variable
Garlic	Hyperlipidemia	600–900 mg qd
Ginger	Nausea, vomiting	250–1000 mg tid–qid
Ginkgo	Dementia, claudication	40–80 mg bid–tid
Ginseng	Fatigue, weakness	Variable
Milk thistle	Hepatitis, liver disease	140 mg bid–tid
St. John's wort	Depression	300 mg tid
Valerian	Insomnia	400 mg qhs

[*]Many herbs are not standardized; therefore, dosages will vary depending on the preparation.
Data from O'hara et al[12] and Tyler.[13]

Homeopathy

Homeopathy is a system of medicine that is based upon the "law of similars"; it treats symptoms by employing dilutions of substances that, in high doses, produce the symptoms. These dilutions are referred to as "potencies." For example, premenstrual syndrome (PMS) is treated with a dilution of a drug that produces PMS symptoms in full doses.

Homeopathy has been used by many cultures including the Mayans, Chinese, Greeks, Native American, and Indians. Interestingly, a meta-analysis of homeopathy studies of many conditions including menopause, vaginal discharge, labor pains, premenstrual syndrome, and cystitis, showed that homeopathy's effects do not appear to be due completely to placebo effects. These studies concluded that more careful research is necessary before definitive conclusions about the effectiveness of homeopathy can be drawn.[17]

TREATMENT IN THE OUTPATIENT SETTING BY PRIMARY CARE CLINICIAN

Safe Use of Alternative Medicine

The situation in which alternative medicine use takes place is one of the most important factors in assessing its safety. It is critical that patients undergo an adequate medical evaluation before any alternative medical regimen is started. Patients must be made fully aware of conventional treatment options and how they compare to alternative remedies. Patients should be encouraged to use alternative medicines only for appropriate indications. As an example, a patient with treatable breast cancer should be discouraged from forgoing conventional treatment in favor of herbal remedies. On the other hand, it may be perfectly reasonable for the same patient to make use of acupuncture to alleviate chemotherapy-induced nausea and vomiting.

In addition to using alternative medicine to treat existing ailments, patients often employ it as preventive medicine. In one study, 58% of users of alternative medicine used the medicine to "prevent future illness from occurring or to maintain health and vitality."[1] In addition, as the population ages, patients seek methods for preventing effects of aging. It is important to stress that many alternative "antiaging" remedies are experimental and that their effectiveness is unproven. As a result, any use of these remedies should be followed up closely by the patient's clinician.

Patients have the perception that since alternative medicines are "natural" they are safe. Unfortunately, the danger of some alternative medicines can be all too similar to toxic side effects of prescription drugs, as in the case of a liver-toxic herb such as chaparral, whose possible side effects are rarely fully disclosed to patients by herbalists. Acupuncture, too, can have complications, including infection, pneumothorax, syncope, and broken

TABLE 90–2. Herbs to Avoid

Herb	Reasons for Use	Toxicity
Atropa belladonna	Abdominal pain, asthma, muscle pain	Contains atropine; neurotoxicity
Borage seed oil	Cough, menopause, diuretic, heart disease	Bradycardia; toxic alkaloids
Chaparral	Cancer	Hepatotoxicity
Comfrey	Cuts, bruises, ulcers	Poisonings, hepatotoxicity
Ephedra (ma huang)	Stimulant, asthma	Adrenergic agonist; cardiac toxicity and acute hepatitis
Germander	Weight loss, fever	Hepatotoxicity
Licorice	GI symptoms	Hypertension, pseudoaldosternism, tachycardia, hypokalemia
Pennyroyal	Menstrual symptoms	Hepatotoxicity, neurotoxicity
Sassafras	Stimulant, anti-inflammatory	Carcinogenicity

GI = gastrointestinal.
Data from O'hara et al,[12] Tyler,[13] and Physicians Desk Reference.[23]

needles. Manipulation has been associated with strokes that may be caused by vertebral artery dissection, intramural bleeding, or pseudoaneurysm with resultant thrombosis or emboli.[18] In addition, chiropractic manipulation should be limited to treating neck or back pain and discontinued if the patient develops any neurologic symptoms.[19]

Patients also must guard against indirect toxicity that can result from mislabeling and misinformation.[20] The World Wide Web provides patients with a wealth of information about potentially useful alternative medicines, but it is often difficult for patients to determine the reliability of this information. Thus, clinicians need to remind patients that if they are going to buy herbs or homeopathic remedies, they should purchase standardized amounts from reputable sources. Although homeopathic medicines are generally safe, cases of contamination with arsenic and cadmium have been reported.[21] One study found that 32% of a sample of Asian patent medicine contained pharmaceuticals not listed in the active ingredients.[22] Potentially toxic ingredients that were not disclosed included ephedrine, chlorpheniramine, methyltestosterone, and phenacetin.

Patients also should be warned that herbs and supplements should be used with caution because they may interfere with many conventional drugs, especially those with a low therapeutic index such as warfarin and digoxin.[11] Finally, intravenous or intramuscular injections must be used with extreme

caution. (Table 90–2 contains a list of herbs that generally should be avoided.[12,13,23]) The risks of contamination and toxicity must be reviewed with the patient.

Integrating Alternative Medicine with Primary Care

The following list of recommendations is useful as a guide for clinicians who serve patients who integrate alternative medicine and traditional medical care (adapted from Eisenberg, 1997[24]):

- Become acquainted with the commonly used systems.
- Ask all patients about alternative medicine use, including the use of alternative clinicians. Routinely ask about the use of vitamins and herbs when asking about a patient's medication list.
- When a patient is using or considering using alternative therapy, perform a complete history and physical examination, review health care maintenance, and perform the necessary work-up for all of the patient's problems. Review conventional treatment options.
- If the patient prefers to try an alternative medicine for a suitable reason (ie, for problems not well relieved by conventional medicine, or if all conventional approaches have been tried), review the alternative options she is considering. Some alternatives may be of more benefit than are others for certain problems. For example, acupuncture may

be better for pain, and herbs may help with insomnia.

- Review possible side effects of alternative medicine with the patient.
- Review the alternative plan.
- Assess the safety of the alternative plan. Herbal medicines may be the form of alternative medicine that is most likely to be associated with toxic side effects.
- Consider performing liver function tests and chemistries for patients who are using herbal medicines. Perform thyroid function tests in patients using alternative thyroid preparations. Recommend compliance with routine mammography to patients taking alternative estrogen preparations.
- Arrange follow-up visits so that the patient receives a proper medical work-up if the symptoms change or persist.

PREGNANCY AND BREAST-FEEDING

There is little research on the safety of herbs and other alternative medicine treatments in pregnancy and breast-feeding. For that reason, all herbs are labeled as being unsafe during pregnancy, even though there is little data to support the contention that any are teratogenic. Women should be cautioned against taking herbs during pregnancy, especially during the first trimester. In addition, as noted above, patients must be reminded that some herbal preparations can be contaminated with other medications (eg, steroids or aspirin) that are best avoided during pregnancy. One study has demonstrated that hamster oocytes exposed to St. John's wort, *Echinacea purpurea*, and *Ginkgo biloba* experienced reduced penetration by sperm.[25] This suggests that high concentrations of herbal medicine may affect fertility, although it is far from conclusive.

With respect to acupuncture, needling certain acupoints can induce labor and, as a result, acupuncture should be used with extreme caution during pregnancy. Acupressure, on the other hand, may be useful in treating nausea and vomiting in pregnancy.[26] In particular, the use of acupressure on point P6 on the wrist (located about 3 fingerbreaths proximal to the wrist on the volar side) has been reported as a promising treatment. Although the studies reaching this conclusion are of limited scale, involving between 16 and 350 patients and lasting only 2 to 7 days, use of acupressure at point P6 is considered safe.[26] Patients can now purchase in many drug stores a wrist band equipped with a plastic button to exert pressure on the point. Other alternative medicines reviewed for nausea in pregnancy include ginger and vitamin B_6. One study of 27 hospitalized patients showed a significant improvement in nausea and vomiting among those taking ginger 250 mg PO qid compared with those taking placebo.[26] Another randomized trial of 342 women showed a significant reduction in nausea and a nonsignificant trend in reduction in vomiting in women taking 25 mg of vitamin B_6.[26]

An interesting study of moxibustion (the burning of herbal medicine to stimulate acupuncture points) for breech presentation showed that moxibustion significantly increased the number of fetuses that were cephalic at 35 weeks' gestation, from 47.7% in the control group to 75.4% in the intervention group ($p < .001$). The safety and efficacy of moxibustion is in need of further evaluation.[27]

MENOPAUSE

Although hormone replacement therapy is successful in alleviating menopausal symptoms, many women do not initiate treatment or quickly stop using it. The reasons women avoid the use of hormonal therapy include side effects, such as vaginal bleeding, and fear of breast cancer. As a result, some women have turned to alternative therapies, in particular phytoestrogens, to control their menopausal symptoms. Scientific studies on phytoestrogens and other herbal therapies are few, but they do suggest that these therapies may be efficacious.

There are two main varieties of phytoestrogens or "naturally found" estrogens in plants. They include the isoflavones (soy and garbanzo beans, bluegrass, and clover), and lignans (flaxseed, cereal bran, whole cereals, and legumes). Isoflavones have been found to be weak binders to estrogen receptors. Studies in Asia have found that women there have fewer menopausal complaints and fewer incidents of breast cancer, potentially related to the relatively high concentration of isoflavones in their diet. A typical Asian diet, for example, consists of about 25 to 45 mg/d of isoflavones (the active phytoestrogen in soy) compared with the 1 to 3 mg/d of isoflavones in the average American diet.[28]

Soy protein also has been found in a small study to result in a significant reduction of hot flashes.[29] One hundred four postmenopausal patients were given 60 g of soy protein per day or

60 g of placebo per day. A 45% reduction in hot flushes was found in the treatment group versus only a 30% reduction in symptoms in the placebo group after 12 weeks of treatment. However, this amount of soy protein caused a significant degree of gastrointestinal side effects. Thus, although the optimal amount of soy protein to take to treat hot flushes is unclear, patients can safely try adding up to 60 mg per day of isoflavones to their diet. Note that although the isoflavone content of soy foods can vary significantly, about 125 mL of tofu or soybeans, or 250 mL cup of soy milk is equal to approximately 20 to 40 mg of isoflavones. In addition to their benefit in hot flashes, soy protein also may have benefits in osteoporosis, cardiovascular disease, and breast cancer. [28,30]

Other menopausal remedies that have been popularized included wild yam creams, dong quai, and black cohosh. Black cohosh may be the most efficacious. Black cohosh (*Cimicifuga racemosa*) has been used for premenstrual syndrome and for menopausal symptoms. It performed as well as estrogen for menopausal complaints in one study,[31] and a review concluded it to be a safe treatment for menopausal symptoms.[32] Side effects are generally few, but at high doses it can cause nausea, vomiting, and hypotension.

Wild yams have been advertised as a source of natural progesterone. However, they cannot be converted in the human body to active progesterone, so they are unlikely to be efficacious as a substitute for synthetic progesterone.[33]

Dong quai is a Chinese herbal medicine often used for relief of an assortment of symptoms in women from premenstrual syndrome to menopause. It has been reported to have estrogenic effects on the uterus and vagina, although at least one study of this herb for menopause found no significant difference in symptoms, endometrial thickness, or vaginal maturation when dong quai was used compared with symptoms during placebo use.[34] Other studies need to be done on the efficacy of Chinese herbal medicine preparations that include dong quai in addition to other herbs, as dong quai is rarely prescribed alone in traditional Chinese medicine.

DEPRESSION

St. John's wort (*Hypericum perforatum*) has become popular for use in depression. It has over 10 com-

ponents that contribute to its effects, some of which are monoamine oxidase (MAO) inhibitor–acting substances (however, no MAO inhibitor–type drug interactions have been described). A meta-analysis of studies done on St. John's wort by Linde et al concluded that it is as effective as tricyclic antidepressants and better than placebo in the treatment of depression.[35] Another meta-analysis that included only studies done on depression diagnosed on standard scales showed that St. John's wort also was more likely than placebo to improve depression but to a lesser extent than that reported by Linde.[36] The side effects appeared to be mild and significantly less than those with tricyclic antidepressants. Most studies used a dosage of 300 mg tid. Currently, a study is being done to compare St. John's wort with serotonin reuptake inhibitors. In addition, studies need to define whether St. John's wort is useful in both mild and severe depression.

CONCLUSION

Clinicians can perform an important service for patients by helping those who express interest to decide among the many alternative medicine options available. In particular, it is important to assist patients in distinguishing what may be helpful from what is likely to be useless or, even worse, toxic.

REFERENCES

1. Eisenberg DM, Davis RB, Ettner SL, et al. Trends in alternative medicine use in the United States, 1990–1997: results of a follow-up national survey. JAMA 1998;280:1569–75.
2. Eisenberg DM, Kessler RC, Foster C, et al. Unconventional medicine in the United States—prevalence, costs, and patterns of use. N Engl J Med 1993;328: 246–52.
3. MacLennon AH, Wilson DH, Taylor AW. Prevalence and cost of alternative medicine in Australia. Lancet 1996;347:569–73.
4. Zollman C, Vickers A. ABC of complementary medicine: users and practitioners of complementary medicine. BMJ 1999;319:836–8.
5. Astin JA. Why patients use alternative medicine: results of a national survey. JAMA 1998;279:1548–53.
6. Druss BG, Rosenheck RA. Association between use of unconventional therapies and conventional medical servies. JAMA 1999;282:651–6.

RESOURCES

National Center for Complementary and Alternative Medicine
NCCAM Clearinghouse
PO Box 8218
Silver Spring, Maryland 20907-8218
Telephone: 1-888-644-6226
Web site: nccam.nih.gov

The office of Alternative Medicine was established in the National Institutes of Health in 1992. The office is to facilitate the evaluation of alternative medicines and determine their effectiveness. Part of its goal is to provide public information at the NCCAM Clearinghouse. It also has funded research in several alternative fields.

Office of Special Nutritionals, US Food and Drug Administration
The Special Nutritionals Adverse Event Monitoring System
200 C Street Southwest
Washington, DC 20204
Telephone: (202) 205-4198
          1-800-332-1088 MedWatch
Web sites: www.fda.gov

The Special Nutritionals Adverse Event Monitoring System collects data on adverse effects of special nutritionals. On the site a database is maintained of all adverse effects that have been reported through the FDA's MedWatch program. It provides links to download information to file a report through the FDA.

The Herb Research Foundation
1007 Pearl Street, Suite 200
Boulder, Colorado 80302
Telephone: 1-800-748-2617
Web site: www.herbs.org

The HRF is a nonprofit research and educational organization focusing on herbs and medicinal plants.

National Acupuncture and Oriental Medicine Alliance
14637 Starr Road Southeast
Olalla, Washington 98359
Telephone: (253) 851-6896
Web site: www.acuall.org

The National Acupuncture and Oriental Medicine Alliance is a professional society of acupuncturists. It maintains a list of certified or licensed acupuncturists throughout the United States.

Federation of Chiropractic Licensing Board
901 54th Avenue, Suite 101
Greeley, Colorado 80634
Telephone: (970) 356-3500
Web site: www.fclb.org

The Federation of Chiropractic Licensing Board provides links to search for board action against any practitioner.

7. Burstein HJ, Gelber S, Guadagnoli E, Weeks JC. Use of alternative medicine by women with early-stage breast cancer. N Engl J Med 1999;34:1733–9.

8. Maciocia G. Obstetrics and gynecology in Chinese medicine. New York: Churchill Livingstone; 1998.

9. Kaptchuk T. The web that has no weaver. Chicago: Condon and Weed; 1983.

10. National Institutes of Health. Consensus development conference statement: acupuncture. Acupuncture NIH Consensus Statement 1997, Nov 3–5;15(5):1–34.

11. Miller LG. Herbal medicinals: selected clinical considerations focusing on known or potential drug-herb interactions. Arch Intern Med 1998;158:2200–11.

12. O'hara MA, Kiefer D, Farrell K, Kemper K. A review of 12 commonly used medicinal herbs. Arch Fam Med 1998;7:523–36.

13. Tyler V. Herbs of choice. Binghamton (NY): Haworth Herbal Press; 1999.

14. Kaptchuk TJ, Eisenberg DM. Chiropractic: origins, controversies, and contributions. Arch Intern Med 1998;158;2215–24.

15. Bigos S, Bowyer O, Braen G, et al. Acute low back problems in adults. Clinical practice guideline no. 14. Rockville (MD): Agency for Health Care Policy and Research, Public Health Service, U.S. Department of Health and Human Services. 1994, Dec. AHCPR Publication No.: 95-0642.

16. Cherkin DC, Deyo RA, Battie M, et al. A comparison of physical therapy, chiropractic manipulation and provision of an educational booklet for the treatment of patients with low back pain. N Engl J Med 1998;339:1021–9.

17. Linke K, Clausius N, Ramirez G, et al. Are the clinical effects of homeopathy placebo effects? A meta-anlysis of placebo-controlled trials. Lancet 1997;350:834–43.

18. Frisoni GB, Anzola GP. Vertebrobasilar ischemia after neck motion. Stroke 1991;22:1452–60.

19. Homola S. Finding a good chiropractor. Arch Fam Med 1998;7:20–23.

20. Ernst E. Harmless herbs? A review of the recent literature. Am J Med 1998:104;170–8.

21. Ernst E. Direct risks associated with complementary therapies. In: Ernst E, editor. Complementary medicine—an objective appraisal. Oxford: Butterworth-Heinemann; 1996. p. 112–25

22. Ko RJ. Adulterants in Asian patent medicines. [correspondence]. N Engl J Med 1998;339:847.

23. Physicians' desk reference. Herbal medicinals. Medical Economics Company. Montvale (NJ); 1999.

24. Eisenberg DM. Advising patients who seek alternative medical therapies. Ann Intern Med 1997;127:61–9.

25. Ondrizek RR, Chan PJ, Patton WC, King AK. An alternative medicine study of herbal effects on the pentration of zona-free hamster oocytes and the integrity of sperm deoxyribonucleic acid. Fertil Steril 1999;71:517–22.

26. Murphy PA. Alternative therapies for nausea and vomiting of pregnancy. Obstet Gynecol 1998;91: 149–55.

27. Cardini F, Weixin H. Moxibustion for correction of breech presentation. JAMA 1998;280:1580–4.

28. Hasler CM, Finn SC. Nutrition communique—soy: just a hill of beans? J Women's Health 1998;7:519–23.

29. Albertazzi P, Pansini F, Bonaccorsi G, et al. The effects of dietary soy supplementation on hot flushes. Obstet and Gynecol 1998;91:6–11.

30. Ingram D, Sanders K, Kolybab M, Lopez D. Case-control study of phyto-oestrogens and breast cancer. Lancet 1997;350:990–4.

31. Ducker EM, Kopanski HJ, Wuttke W. Effects of extracts from *Cimicifuga racemosa* on gonadotopin release in menopausal women and ovarietomized rats. Planta Med 1991:57;420.

32. Lieberman S. A review of the effectiveness of *Cimicifuga racemosa* (black cohosh) for the symptoms of menopause. J Women's Health 1998;7:525–9.

33. Taffe AM, Cauffield J. "Natural" hormone replacement therapy and dietary supplements used in the treatment of menopausal symptoms. Lippincott's Primary Care Practice 1998;2:292–302.

34. Hirata JD, Swiersz LM, Zell B, et al. Does dong quai have estrogenic effects in postmenopausal women? A double-blind, placebo-controlled trial. Fertil Steril 1997;68:981–6.

35. Linde K, Ramirez G, Mulrow CD, et al. St. John's wort for depression—an overview and meta-analysis of randomised clinical trials. BMJ 1996;313:253–8.

36. Kim HL, Streltzer J, Goebert D. St. John's wort for depression: a meta-analysis of well-defined clinical trials. J Nerv Ment Dis 1999;187:532–8.

91

QUALITY MANAGEMENT FOR WOMEN'S HEALTH CARE

Joseph C. Gambone, DO, MPH, and Mitzi Krockover, MD

Assessing and improving the quality of health care has become a major activity for health care providers and facilities. There are several reasons for this recent development. The Joint Commission on the Accreditation of Health Care Organizations (JCAHO), the National Committee on Quality Assurance (NCQA), and other surveying agencies have set standards that must be met for hospitals and health plans to receive accreditation. Failure to become accredited can result in loss of contracts, reduced consumer confidence, and loss of market share. These improvement efforts have been accelerated recently because of the need to reduce costs. Government and other large employers purchase over 80% of the health care services in the United States. These large-scale purchasers are asking for demonstrated value for the money they are spending.[1]

There is also a growing recognition that the major principles that guide the ethical practice of medicine—nonmaleficence ("first, do no harm"), autonomy (patient self-determination), and beneficence (acting in the best interest of an individual patient)—must also include the principle of *justice*, (ie, the need to be cost conscious and to establish a system that distributes health services in an equitable manner). Cost-effectiveness should therefore be considered an essential component of ethical practice.[2]

During these times of scarce resources, organizations are finding a direct connection between their quality management efforts and the cost reductions that they must attain. Many have invested substantially in programs for utilization review and continuous quality improvement (CQI).

Health care purchasers and health plans are requesting greater involvement in the day-to-day management of patients. There is reason to believe that this trend toward "third-party" management of care will continue for the foreseeable future although recently there has been a consumer "backlash" against the perceived micromanagement of patient care by health plan representatives. Some experts are predicting that a better-informed patient/consumer will begin to take on a greater role in health care decision making and in the evaluation of his or her own medical and surgical care.

Those who provide health care for women have a particular need to assess and improve the quality of the care that they provide. Women seek and receive more health services than do men. In fact, women receive about 60% more outpatient care and 35% more inpatient care even when obstetric services have been excluded.[3] There is reason to believe that not all of this care is appropriate, however. Surgical procedures such as cesarean delivery and hysterectomy have been studied, and a significant percentage have been judged to be inappropriate.[4,5] Significant regional variation in usage rates for both of these procedures have been demonstrated, and overall US usage rates are significantly higher than those of other industrialized nations.[6,7] Also, even though women receive more health services overall, there is reason to believe that they may receive less attention in some specific areas, such as screening for colon cancer, cardiovascular risk, and depression.

When an organization or clinic has decided that there is a need for ongoing assessment and improvement in clinical performance, a method must be chosen to initiate a comprehensive program. One model that has been proposed provides for the application of eight key elements or domains

---

TABLE 91–1. IMPROVED: A Mnemonic for Managing the Quality of Health Care

Key Element	Definition
Investment	Leadership providing the mandate and resources for improvement
Measurement	Being committed to ongoing measurement of processes and outcomes
Patient focus	Improving communication and meeting patient expectations
Risk adjustment	Accounting for severity of illness and comorbidities
Outcomes	Assessing quality of life, functional status, adverse events, satisfaction, and cost
Variation	Reducing wasteful variation, using clinical pathways and benchmarking
Efficiency	Providing value in terms of clinical and nonclinical resource use
Decision making	Making information from measurements available for on-site decision making

Adapted from Regents of the University of California, 1995 (JGAMBONE@UCLA.EDU).

---

that should be incorporated into a quality management program.[8] Table 91–1 lists these eight domains along with a brief description of each.

An organization or individual clinician must make an *investment* in resources and a commitment to apply these resources to continuous performance improvement. Without the enthusiastic support of top leadership in an organization, efforts to improve quality do usually not succeed. In the past, health care quality was assumed, and consumers had little information with which to evaluate the performance of a health care facility or practitioner, aside from word-of-mouth reputation. Consumers and those who purchase health care coverage for them are now asking for objective measures of performance, stated in terms that they can understand.

This investment of resources for quality improvement should include (but is not limited to) the following:

- Adequate staffing, including a clear identification of the individual responsible for developing, implementing, and evaluating performance, as well as adequate support staff to accomplish the goals; this may mean reassessing current job descriptions and modifying them to include such activities
- Information and technology support to track trends, productivity, and outcomes
- A process for internal and external communication of quality management plans and outcomes; this will better ensure continued internal support for the process, as well as help in gaining community recognition for quality efforts

A clinic, practice, or individual clinician must make a commitment to the *measurement* of both clinical and operational performance. The benefits

of quality management can be documented only through measurable improvement in performance over time. Interestingly, the process of measurement itself usually promotes continuous improvement. This measurement should be built into the process of care. Ideally, it should not add significant expense to the delivery of care. The elimination or reduction of unnecessary measurements of seldom-used or never-used data can allow for additional data collection at little or no extra cost.[9]

Some health plans provide information to contracted clinicians about individual and group resource use and practice patterns. These plans have a vested interest in meeting stated goals in order to receive favorable accreditation from oversight agencies, as well as to achieve a competitive advantage. This information may provide clinicians with additional knowledge about patient care that they may not have been able to access previously, including rates of compliance with prescriptions, hospitalization rates, and lengths of hospitalizations. Health plans may also provide feedback as to the number of patients who have had screening and preventive services such as mammography, Pap tests, and immunizations. All of this information may be an additional source of quality measurement for the clinician to incorporate into the overall quality process.

One of the better indications of the quality of goods or services is the extent to which the product meets customer expectations. The primary customer of health services is the patient, and it is now recognized that the delivery of health care should be based upon meeting patient expectations. *Patient-focused* health care should therefore be the goal of any organization that is attempting to improve the care that it delivers. This means improving communication between patients and clinicians and measuring the outcomes of health care, with end points that a patient can understand without explanation by health care clinicians whenever possible. The routine measurement of patient satisfaction should be incorporated into the quality process.

Whenever possible, the measurement of health care delivered should be compared and benchmarked with other facilities so that clinicians and health care organizations can know how well they are doing with respect to others. Health plans may provide information that compares individual practice patterns of clinicians with the practice patterns of the local clinician community. Organizations such as the Institute for Healthcare Improvement (IHI) in Boston and the University Healthsystems Consortium (UHC) in Chicago provide forums for such benchmarking. The IHI works with community- and university-based health systems, and the UHC works with the university-based members of its consortium to compare data.

Benchmarking and comparisons among diverse groups of patients cannot be done accurately without a method for *risk adjustment*. Although the science of risk adjustment in health services is still not perfect, recent improvements in methodology control for variation in the severity of illness and comorbidity among groups of patients so that outcomes can be compared in a valid way.

Although there are times when health services must be measured primarily by the process of care that is provided, actual health *outcomes* should be measured when possible. Improvements in the care that is delivered should be based on attaining the best possible outcomes. A "health outcome" is defined as a treatment end point that can be experienced and valued by a patient, without interpretation by a health care professional. Measurements of health-related quality of life and functional status are examples of this. Table 91–2 lists several intermediate or surrogate outcomes that generally need interpretation for a patient to understand their value, along with their corresponding health outcomes. In addition, the outcomes of the health services that are measured should include patient/consumer satisfaction and the costs of care.

Examples of health outcomes in women's health programs may include the number of pregnancies resulting in low–birth weight or premature

TABLE 91–2. Health Outcomes and Their Corresponding Intermediate End Points

Health Outcome	Intermediate End Point
Longevity	Dilated coronary arteries
Quality of life	5-year survival rate
Take home baby rate	Pregnancy
Pain relief	Fewer adhesions
No transfusion	Less blood loss

Reprinted with permission from Gambone JC, Reiter RC. Quality assessment and improvement. In: Berek JS, Adashi EY, Hilliard PA, editors. Novak's gynecology. 12th ed. Baltimore (MD): Williams & Wilkins; 1996. p. 33–49.

babies, changes in lifestyle behavior (including smoking cessation), and changes in diet or activity level. Process measures would include rates of Pap tests or mammography, or compliance with hormone therapy for menopause. Examples of measurements of health-related quality of life include self-image in breast cancer patients and sexual satisfaction in menopausal women.

One of the most reliable signs of reduced quality in goods and services is the presence of unnecessary *variation*. Wasteful variation robs products and services of the predictability and reliability they should have. Recently, tools such as clinical pathways and case management protocols have been designed, implemented, and monitored, to decrease unintended and wasteful variation in medical and surgical practice. Another kind of variation in health services that should be identified, investigated, and reduced is the clinically unexplained variation that may occur in the use of certain procedures. An example of this in women's health care is the previously mentioned regional and international variation that exists with respect to the use of such major operative procedures as hysterectomy and cesarean delivery.[6] The inappropriately lower or higher use of these procedures should be identified and corrected by a CQI process.

Health plans and hospitals routinely evaluate and review new technologies, procedures, and pharmaceuticals, comparing them to older technologies and medications and developing appropriate guidelines for use, based on principles of evidence-based medicine. Clinician groups may also decide to engage in such a process to reduce variation, improve patient outcomes, and use resources most effectively.

Certainly, part of quality is the *efficiency* with which products and services are produced and delivered. Patients and purchasers of health services are looking for value in the care that they receive and purchase. Value is defined as the attainment of optimal outcomes with the lowest use of operational and clinical resources. Value can be demonstrated by description of successful processes, health outcome measurements, and patient satisfaction measurements, and it should be communicated to internal and external constituencies on a regular basis.

Finally, all of these data from measurements (which should have been documented during a CQI program) will be of little use unless the measurements are fed back in an organized system of *decision support* so that data can be transformed into information that then can be used to improve care. Currently, health care organizations are working to upgrade significantly their information systems, which generally have lagged behind those used in other industries. The electronic medical record will eventually replace the paper-based system, which is inefficient and which contributes significantly to waste and dangerous medical error.[10] In several medical schools now, incoming students are required to have a computer rather than the more traditional microscope, so that they can learn the science of evidence-based medicine, much of which currently exists in the electronically stored medical literature. As the results of additional properly performed outcomes studies (off-line research) become available along with the measured experience in actual practice (on-line research), health care should become more evidence based.

SUMMARY

Women seek and receive more health care than men, and there are areas in which there is evidence of both overuse and underuse of health services for them. A model for improvement, which includes eight domains or activities, begins with *investment* by top leadership and all other stakeholders in the process. A commitment to *measurement* (in real time) that is *patient focused* should provide information on *risk-adjusted outcomes*. (Health outcomes are those that are experienced and valued by patients, such as health-related quality of life and functional status). Wasteful *variation* in processes and in the use of procedures should be corrected to appropriate levels by using tools such as clinical pathways and bench-

marking. *Efficiency* is important, and clinicians now are realizing that the ethical principle of justice should guide practice so that scarce resources are made available to as many people as possible. *Decision-support* systems that feed back performance information in real time should be made available to clinicians, patients, and other decision makers.

REFERENCES

1. Bodenheimer T, Sullivan K. How large employers are shaping the health care marketplace. N Engl J Med 1998;338:1003–7.
2. Lo B. Resolving ethical dilemmas: a guide for clinicians. Baltimore (MD): Williams and Wilkins; 1995. p. 17–23.
3. Gambone JC, Reiter RC. Quality assessment and improvement. In: Berek JS, Adashi EY, Hilliard PA, editors. Novak's gynecology. 12th ed. Baltimore (MD): Williams and Wilkins; 1996. p. 33–49.
4. Bernstein SJ, McGlynn EA, Siu AL, et al. The appropriateness of hysterectomy: a comparison of care in seven health plans. Health Maintenance Organization Quality of Care Consortium. JAMA 1993;18:2398–402.
5. Gleicher H. Cesarean section rates in the United States: the short-term failure of the National Consensus Development Conference in 1980. JAMA 1984;252:3273–6.
6. McPherson K, Wennberg JE, Hovind OB, Clifford P. Small-area variations in the use of common surgical procedures: an international comparison of New England, England, and Norway. N Engl J Med 1982;307:1310–4.
7. Overhulse PR. The cesarean section rate. JAMA 1990;264:971.
8. Gambone JC, Reiter RC, Moore JG. Assessing the quality of medical and surgical care. In: Hacker NF, Moore JG, editors. Essentials of obstetrics and gynecology. 3rd ed. Philadelphia (PA): W.B. Saunders; 1998. p. 41.
9. Blegen MA, Reiter RC, Goode CJ, Murphy RR. Outcomes of hospital-based managed care: a multivariate analysis of cost and quality. Obstet Gynecol 1995;86:809–14.
10. Kohn LT, Corrigan JM, Donaldson MS, editors. To err is human: building a safer health system. Committee on Quality of Health Care in America. Washington (DC): Institute of Medicine, National Academy of Sciences; 2000.

INDEX

In this index, page numbers in *italic* designate figures; page numbers followed by the letter "t" designate tables.
See also designates related topics or more detailed subtopic breakdowns.